Official

BASEBALL REGISTER

1984 EDITION

Editor/Baseball Register
BARRY SIEGEL

Contributing Editors/Baseball Register
DAVE SLOAN
JOHN DUXBURY
TOM SHIEBER
CRAIG CARTER

President-Chief Executive Officer
RICHARD WATERS

Editor
DICK KAEGEL

Director of Books and Periodicals
RON SMITH

Published by

The Sporting News

1212 North Lindbergh Boulevard
P.O. Box 56 — St. Louis, Mo. 63166

ISBN 0-89204-148-X   ISSN 0067-4281

Table
of
CONTENTS

⚔⊘⚔

Players included are those who played in at least one game in the major leagues in 1983, those who were part of a team's 40-man roster and selected invitees to spring training.

————◆————

ON THE COVER: Philadelphia righthander John Denny came back strong after a dismal 1982 season in Cleveland to post a 19-6 record and capture the National League Cy Young Award.

—**Photo by Richard Pilling.**

————◆————

EXPLANATION OF ABBREVIATIONS
G—Games played. Pos.—Position. AB—At Bats. R—Runs. H—Hits. 2B—Two-Base Hits. 3B—Three-Base Hits. HR—Home Runs. RBI—Runs Batted In. B.A.—Batting Average. PO—Putouts. A—Assists. E—Errors. F.A.—Fielding Average. IP—Innings Pitched. W—Won. L—Lost. Pct.—Percentage. R—Runs. ER—Earned Runs. SO—Strikeouts. BB—Bases on Balls. ERA—Earned-Run Average.

Players

*Denotes led league. ●Tied for lead. Mark before position (where more than one position is given) denotes where played as leader in department shown.

DONALD WILLIAM AASE

Name pronounced AH-see.

(Don)

Born September 8, 1954, at Orange, Calif.
Height, 6.03. Weight, 210.
Throws and bats righthanded.
Attended California State University, Fullerton, Calif.

Led International League pitchers in games started with 29 in 1975.
Led Carolina League pitchers in games started with 30, complete games with 18 and tied for lead in shutouts with 4 in 1974.
Named Carolina League Pitcher of the Year, 1974.

Year Club	League	G.	IP.	W.	L.	Pct.	H.	R.	ER.	SO.	BB.	ERA.
1972—Williamsport	NYP	12	62	0	*10	.000	60	48	40	40	34	5.81
1973—Winter Haven	Florida St.	29	170	12	●15	.444	153	82	68	127	73	3.60
1974—Winston-Salem	Carolina	32	*230	*17	8	.680	185	72	62	*176	84	*2.43
1975—Pawtucket	Int'national	29	186	8	13	.381	173	85	75	125	88	3.63
1976—Rhode Island†	Int'national	10	54	5	2	.714	42	23	20	40	34	3.33
1977—Pawtucket	Int'national	18	109	6	6	.500	118	67	61	64	60	5.04
1977—Boston‡	American	13	92	6	2	.750	85	36	32	49	19	3.13
1978—California	American	29	179	11	8	.579	185	88	80	93	80	4.02
1979—California	American	37	185	9	10	.474	200	104	99	96	77	4.82
1980—California	American	40	175	8	13	.381	193	83	79	74	66	4.06
1981—California	American	39	65	4	4	.500	56	17	17	38	24	2.35
1982—California§	American	24	52	3	3	.500	45	20	20	40	23	3.46
1983—California x	American					(Did not play)						
Major League Totals		182	748	41	40	.506	764	348	327	390	289	3.93

Selected by Boston Red Sox' organization in 6th round of free-agent draft, June 6, 1972.
†On disabled list, June 23, 1976 through remainder of season.
‡Traded with cash to California Angels for Second Baseman Jerry Remy, December 8, 1977.
§On disabled list, June 3 to June 27 and July 20 to September 7, 1982.
xOn emergency disabled list, March 30, 1983 through remainder of season.

CHAMPIONSHIP SERIES RECORD

Year Club	League	G.	IP.	W.	L.	Pct.	H.	R.	ER.	SO.	BB.	ERA.
1979—California	American	2	5	1	0	1.000	4	1	1	6	2	1.80

WILLIAM GLENN ABBOTT

(Known by middle name.)

Born February 16, 1951, at Little Rock, Ark.
Height, 6.06. Weight, 210.
Throws and bats righthanded.
Attended State College of Arkansas, Conway, Ark.

Tied for American Association lead in balks with 2 in 1972.

Year Club	League	G.	IP.	W.	L.	Pct.	H.	R.	ER.	SO.	BB.	ERA.
1970—Coos Bay-North Bend	Northwest	14	101	8	3	.727	106	55	43	92	40	3.83
1971—Burlington	Midwest	24	179	11	10	.524	166	67	54	195	52	2.72
1972—Birmingham	Southern	13	97	3	8	.273	84	38	27	78	31	2.51
1972—Iowa	Am. Assoc.	15	107	6	8	.429	90	42	40	62	35	3.36
1973—Tucson	P. Coast	29	206	*18	8	.692	219	97	80	120	67	3.50
1973—Oakland	American	5	19	1	0	1.000	16	8	8	6	7	3.79
1974—Tucson	P. Coast	11	85	6	2	.750	109	44	39	39	25	4.13
1974—Oakland	American	19	96	5	7	.417	89	38	32	38	34	3.00
1975—Tucson	P. Coast	4	30	2	2	.500	30	14	12	18	11	3.60
1975—Oakland	American	30	114	5	5	.500	109	61	54	51	50	4.26
1976—Oakland†	American	19	62	2	4	.333	87	41	38	27	16	5.52
1977—Seattle	American	36	204	12	13	.480	212	111	101	100	56	4.46
1978—Seattle‡	American	29	155	7	15	.318	191	99	91	67	44	5.28
1979—Seattle§	American	23	117	4	10	.286	138	78	67	25	38	5.15
1980—Seattle	American	31	215	12	12	.500	228	110	98	78	49	4.10
1981—Seattle x	American	22	130	4	9	.308	127	64	57	35	28	3.95
1982—Seattle y	American					(Did not play)						
1982—Salt Lake City	P. Coast	2	10	1	1	.500	15	10	9	3	3	8.10
1983—Seattle za-Detroit	American	21	129	7	4	.636	146	58	52	50	22	3.63
1983—Salt Lake City	P. Coast	4	23⅔	0	2	.000	33	21	16	12	6	6.08
Major League Totals		235	1241	59	79	.428	1343	668	598	477	344	4.34

Selected by Oakland A's organization in 15th round of free-agent draft, June 5, 1969.
†Selected by Seattle Mariners in American League expansion draft, November 5, 1976.
‡On disabled list, April 21 to May 11, 1978.

§On disabled list, August 18 to September 7, 1979.
xGranted free agency, November 13, 1981; re-signed by Mariners, January 15, 1982.
yOn disabled list, March 26, 1982; transferred to emergency disabled list, May 13, 1982 through remainder of season; included rehabilitation disability assignment to Salt Lake City, July 16 to August 5, 1982.
zOn Seattle disabled list, March 24 to June 9, 1983; included rehabilitation disability assignment to Salt Lake City, May 22 to June 9, 1983.
aSold on waivers to Detroit Tigers, August 23, 1983.

CHAMPIONSHIP SERIES RECORD

Year Club	League	G.	IP.	W.	L.	Pct.	H.	R.	ER.	SO.	BB.	ERA.
1975—Oakland	American	1	1	0	0	.000	0	0	0	0	0	0.00

JOHNNY RAY ABREGO

Born July 4, 1962, at Corpus Christi, Tex.
Height, 6.01. Weight, 185.
Throws and bats righthanded.

Led Northwest League in hit batsmen with 14 and tied for lead in games started by pitchers with 14 in 1983.

Year Club	League	G.	IP.	W.	L.	Pct.	H.	R.	ER.	SO.	BB.	ERA.
1981—Helena	Pioneer	12	67	3	4	.429	60	40	35	52	52	4.70
1982—Helena	Pioneer					(Did not play)						
1983—Bend†	Northwest	14	88⅓	7	5	.583	81	58	39	59	40	3.97

Selected by Philadelphia Phillies' organization in 1st round (20th player selected) of free-agent draft, June 11, 1981.
†Drafted by Chicago Cubs, December 5, 1983.

JAMES JUSTIN ACKER
(Jim)

Born September 24, 1958, at Freer, Tex.
Height, 6.02. Weight, 210.
Throws and bats righthanded.
Attended University of Texas, Austin, Tex.
Brother of Bill Acker, defensive lineman with Buffalo Bills.

Year Club	League	G.	IP.	W.	L.	Pct.	H.	R.	ER.	SO.	BB.	ERA.
1980—Bradenton Braves	Gulf Coast	1	5	1	0	1.000	1	0	0	5	0	0.00
1980—Savannah	Southern	13	95	5	5	.500	84	33	28	47	29	2.65
1981—Savannah	Southern	10	77	5	5	.500	57	34	23	37	34	2.69
1981—Richmond	Int'national	21	118	8	7	.533	112	63	55	72	74	4.19
1982—Savannah†‡	Southern	26	142	9	14	.391	120	96	70	96	86	4.44
1983—Toronto	American	38	97⅔	5	1	.833	103	52	47	44	38	4.33
Major League Totals		38	97⅔	5	1	.833	103	52	47	44	38	4.33

Selected by Atlanta Braves' organization in 1st round (21st player selected) of free-agent draft, June 3, 1980.
†On disabled list, April 9 to April 20, 1982.
‡Drafted by Toronto Blue Jays, December 6, 1982.

RICKY LEE ADAMS

Born January 21, 1959, at Upland, Calif.
Height, 6.02. Weight, 180.
Throws and bats righthanded.

Year Club	League	Pos.	G.	AB.	R.	H.	2B.	3B.	HR.	RBI.	B.A.	PO.	A.	E.	F.A.
1977—Sarasota Astros	Gulf C.	SS	39	151	15	34	3	0	1	9	.225	54	132	19	.907
1978—Daytona Beach	Fla. St.	SS-3B-2B	112	396	46	88	12	3	0	32	.222	161	378	45	.923
1979—Daytona Beach†	Fla. St.	2B	107	305	31	89	12	2	0	26	.292	189	279	24	.951
1980—Salinas	Calif.	SS	15	56	5	14	2	0	0	4	.250	33	44	2	.975
1980—El Paso	Texas	SS-3B	92	382	68	112	16	0	12	53	.293	183	288	24	.952
1981—Holyoke	East.	2-S-1-O	120	446	85	117	11	3	10	48	.262	222	333	11	.981
1982—Holyoke	East.	2-S-1-O	60	227	37	69	9	4	4	28	.304	119	187	6	.981
1982—Spokane	P. C.	2B-SS-OF	71	248	42	77	10	3	6	33	.310	155	181	9	.974
1982—California	Amer.	SS	8	14	1	2	0	0	0	0	.143	6	12	1	.947
1983—California	Amer.	SS-3B-2B	57	112	22	28	2	0	2	6	.250	58	141	8	.961
1983—Edmonton	P. C.	2-3-O-S	54	208	38	65	10	4	6	38	.313	69	90	5	.970
Major League Totals			65	126	23	30	2	0	2	6	.238	64	153	9	.960

Selected by Houston Astros' organization in 1st round (14th player selected) of free-agent draft, June 7, 1977.
†Released, April 4, 1980; signed by Salinas (California Angels' organization), May 2, 1980.

JAMES DAVID ADDUCI
(Jim)

Born August 9, 1959, at Chicago, Ill.
Height, 6.04. Weight, 200.
Throws and bats lefthanded.
Attended Southern Illinois University, Carbondale, Ill.

Led Texas League in game-winning RBIs with 14 and strikeouts with 103 in 1982.

Year Club	League	Pos.	G.	AB.	R.	H.	2B.	3B.	HR.	RBI.	B.A.	PO.	A.	E.	F.A.
1980—Johnson City	Appal.	OF	17	63	15	21	4	0	5	16	.333	27	2	1	.967
1980—St. Petersburg	Fla. St.	OF	37	118	29	32	4	0	2	13	.271	62	3	2	.970

Year — Club	League	Pos.	G.	AB.	R.	H.	2B.	3B.	HR.	RBI.	B.A.	PO.	A.	E.	F.A.
1981—St. Petersburg....... Fla. St.		OF	92	321	44	87	12	7	7	45	.271	185	4	7	.964
1981—Arkansas................ Texas		OF	40	131	16	36	8	3	5	14	.275	55	3	1	.983
1982—Arkansas................ Texas		OF	121	392	64	117	28	5	22	92	.298	178	6	3	.984
1983—Louisville .... A. A.		OF-1B	129	467	81	131	29	7	25	★101	.281	327	17	14	.961
1983—St. Louis .... Nat.		1B-OF	10	20	0	1	0	0	0	0	.050	47	4	0	1.000
Major League Totals....................			10	20	0	1	0	0	0	0	.050	47	4	0	1.000

Selected by Philadelphia Phillies' organization in 28th round of free-agent draft, June 7, 1977.
Selected by St. Louis Cardinals' organization in 7th round of free-agent draft, June 3, 1980.

JUAN ROBERTO AGOSTO

Born February 23, 1958, at Rio Piedras, P.R.
Height, 6.00. Weight, 175.
Throws and bats lefthanded.

Major League saves: 1983 (7).
Led Carolina League in balks with 4 in 1977 and 5 in 1978.

Year — Club	League	G.	IP.	W.	L.	Pct.	H.	R.	ER.	SO.	BB.	ERA.
1975—Winter Haven............... Florida St.		6	28	0	4	.000	35	23	18	19	24	5.79
1975—Elmira........................ NYP		9	23	1	4	.200	27	37	22	22	34	8.61
1976—Winter Haven............... Florida St.		28	107	5	11	.313	97	70	55	80	69	4.63
1977—Winston-Salem .... Carolina		30	119	4	9	.308	128	106	79	98	★111	5.97
1978—Winter Haven............... Florida St.		1	1	0	0	.000	5	2	2	0	0	27.00
1978—Winston-Salem† .... Carolina		23	120	5	11	.313	114	76	51	74	89	3.83
1979—Puerto Rico‡............... Int.-Amer.		10	31	3	2	.600	31	13	9	9	17	2.61
1980—Glens Falls................. Eastern		8	22	1	0	1.000	26	18	17	8	18	6.95
1980—Appleton.................... Midwest		23	144	11	6	.647	118	60	43	93	52	2.69
1981—Edmonton................... P. Coast		48	120	7	10	.412	128	61	52	57	49	3.90
1981—Chicago...................... American		2	6	0	0	.000	5	3	3	3	0	4.50
1982—Edmonton................... P. Coast		50	95⅓	3	4	.429	101	63	53	39	49	5.00
1982—Chicago...................... American		1	2	0	0	.000	7	4	4	1	0	18.00
1983—Denver....................... Am. Assoc.		19	26	4	1	.800	19	8	6	19	10	2.08
1983—Chicago...................... American		39	41⅔	2	2	.500	41	20	19	29	11	4.10
Major League Totals.....................		42	49⅔	2	2	.500	53	27	26	33	11	4.71

Signed as free agent by Boston Red Sox' organization, August 29, 1974.
†Released, September 21, 1978; signed by Puerto Rico of Inter-American League, March 10, 1979.
‡Declared free agent when Inter-American League folded, June 15, 1979; signed by Chicago White Sox' organization, January 18, 1980.

CHAMPIONSHIP SERIES RECORD

Year — Club	League	G.	IP.	W.	L.	Pct.	H.	R.	ER.	SO.	BB.	ERA.
1983—Chicago..................... American		1	⅓	0	0	.000	0	0	0	0	0	0.00

LUIS AGUAYO (MURIEL)

Name pronounced Ah-GWA-yo.

Born March 13, 1959, at Vega Baja, P.R.
Height, 5.09. Weight, 173.
Throws and bats righthanded

Led Carolina League second basemen in assists with 365, errors with 30 and fielding percentage with .953 in 1977.

Year — Club	League	Pos.	G.	AB.	R.	H.	2B.	3B.	HR.	RBI.	B.A.	PO.	A.	E.	F.A.
1976—Spartanburg......... W. Car.		2B	3	11	0	1	0	0	0	0	.091	5	2	1	.875
1976—Auburn .... NYP		2B-3B-SS	51	197	27	49	9	2	0	23	.249	79	99	10	.947
1977—Peninsula.............. Carol.		2B-SS	130	497	73	127	28	2	9	41	.256	271	409	34	.952
1978—Reading .... East.		SS-2B	115	378	49	74	19	5	4	33	.196	198	341	25	.956
1979—Oklahoma City ..... A. A.		SS-2B	113	370	54	101	21	1	8	46	.273	191	320	27	.950
1980—Philadelphia† .... Nat.		2B-SS	20	47	7	13	1	2	1	8	.277	44	44	3	.967
1980—Oklahoma City‡ ... A. A.		SS	84	291	37	71	19	2	9	40	.244	154	268	★28	.938
1981—Philadelphia .... Nat.		2B-SS-3B	45	84	11	18	4	0	1	7	.214	39	63	5	.953
1982—Philadelphia .... Nat.		2B-SS-3B	50	56	11	15	1	2	3	7	.268	27	49	4	.950
1983—Philadelphia§ .... Nat.		SS	2	4	1	1	0	0	0	0	.250	3	0	0	1.000
1983—Portland................ P.C.		SS-2B	71	229	38	65	14	3	5	33	.284	121	216	10	.971
Major League Totals....................			117	191	30	47	6	4	5	22	.246	113	156	12	.957

Signed as free agent by Philadelphia Phillies' organization, December 27, 1975.
†On supplemental disabled list, May 7 to May 22, 1980.
‡On disabled list, May 22 to August 30, 1980.
§On disabled list, March 23, 1983; transferred to emergency disabled list, April 4 to June 13, 1983.

DIVISION SERIES RECORD

Year — Club	League	Pos.	G.	AB.	R.	H.	2B.	3B.	HR.	RBI.	B.A.	PO.	A.	E.	F.A.
1981—Philadelphia .... Nat.		PR	2	0	1	0	0	0	0	0	.000	0	0	0	.000

WILLIE MAYS AIKENS

Born October 14, 1954, at Seneca, S. C.
Height, 6.02. Weight, 220.
Throws right and bats lefthanded.
Attended South Carolina State College, Orangeburg, S.C.

Tied major league record for most consecutive games, home runs, bases filled (2), June 13 and 14, 1979.

Led American League in intentional bases on balls received with 12 in 1981.
Led Texas League in total bases with 285 in 1976.
Led Midwest League in sacrifice flies with 9 in 1975.

Year—Club	League	Pos.	G.	AB.	R.	H.	2B.	3B.	HR.	RBI.	B.A.	PO.	A.	E.	F.A.
1975—Quad Cities	Midw.	1B	125	443	69	126	17	1	17	*91	.284	1038	53	*26	.977
1976—El Paso	Texas	1B	133	514	*99	163	24	4	*30	*117	.317	971	52	*20	.981
1977—Salt Lake City	P. C.	1B-C	77	295	62	99	23	2	14	73	.336	700	48	10	.987
1977—California	Amer.	1B	42	91	5	18	4	0	0	6	.198	94	8	3	.971
1978—Salt Lake City	P. C.	*1B-OF	133	470	82	153	19	0	*29	110	.326	1030	*83	*25	.978
1979—California†	Amer.	1B	116	379	59	106	18	0	21	81	.280	462	31	2	.996
1980—Kansas City	Amer.	1B	151	543	70	151	24	0	20	98	.278	1081	65	*12	.990
1981—Kansas City	Amer.	1B	101	349	45	93	16	0	17	53	.266	844	56	7	.992
1982—Kansas City‡	Amer.	1B	134	466	50	131	29	1	17	74	.281	1048	75	7	.994
1983—Kansas City §x	Amer.	1B	125	410	49	124	26	1	23	72	.302	884	64	11	.989
Major League Totals			669	2238	278	623	117	2	98	384	.278	4413	299	42	.991

Selected by California Angels' organization in 1st round (second player selected) of free-agent draft, January 9, 1975.

†Traded with Shortstop Rance Mulliniks to Kansas City Royals for Outfielder Al Cowens, Shortstop Todd Cruz and a player to be named later, December 6, 1979; California Angels acquired Pitcher Craig Eaton to complete deal, April 1, 1980.

‡On supplemental disabled list, April 23 to May 8, 1982.

§On suspended list, December 15, 1983.

xTraded to Toronto Blue Jays for Designated Hitter Jorge Orta, December 19, 1983.

DIVISION SERIES RECORD

Year—Club	League	Pos.	G.	AB.	R.	H.	2B.	3B.	HR.	RBI.	B.A.	PO.	A.	E.	F.A.
1981—Kansas City	Amer.	1B	3	9	0	3	0	0	0	0	.333	27	1	0	1.000

CHAMPIONSHIP SERIES RECORD

Year—Club	League	Pos.	G.	AB.	R.	H.	2B.	3B.	HR.	RBI.	B.A.	PO.	A.	E.	F.A.
1980—Kansas City	Amer.	1B	3	11	0	4	0	0	0	2	.364	22	1	0	1.000

WORLD SERIES RECORD

Tied World Series record for most home runs, two consecutive innings (2), October 18, 1980 (first and second inning).

Year—Club	League	Pos.	G.	AB.	R.	H.	2B.	3B.	HR.	RBI.	B.A.	PO.	A.	E.	F.A.
1980—Kansas City	Amer.	1B	6	20	5	8	0	1	4	8	.400	55	2	2	.966

DOYLE LAFAYETTE ALEXANDER

Born September 4, 1950, at Cordova, Ala.
Height, 6.03. Weight, 205.
Throws and bats righthanded.
Attended Jefferson State Junior College, Birmingham, Ala.

Year—Club	League	G.	IP.	W.	L.	Pct.	H.	R.	ER.	SO.	BB.	ERA.
1968—Tri-City	Northwest	13	70	3	*9	.250	66	47	32	58	47	4.11
1969—Daytona Beach	Florida St.	30	185	13	9	.591	154	75	56	140	100	2.72
1969—Albuquerque	Texas	3	15	0	3	.000	19	10	10	3	12	6.00
1970—Albuquerque	Texas	10	80	4	3	.571	72	29	28	60	20	3.15
1970—Spokane	P. Coast	19	137	9	7	.563	137	66	55	78	26	3.61
1971—Spokane	P. Coast	15	110	6	3	.667	114	49	42	65	31	3.44
1971—Los Angeles†	National	17	92	6	6	.500	105	45	39	30	18	3.82
1972—Baltimore	American	35	106	6	8	.429	78	36	29	49	30	2.46
1973—Baltimore‡	American	29	175	12	8	.600	169	85	75	63	52	3.86
1974—Baltimore	American	30	114	6	9	.400	127	65	51	40	43	4.03
1975—Baltimore	American	32	133	8	8	.500	127	47	45	46	47	3.05
1976—Balt.§-N.Y. x	American	30	201	13	9	.591	172	81	75	58	63	3.36
1977—Texas	American	34	237	17	11	.607	221	103	96	82	82	3.65
1978—Texas	American	31	191	9	10	.474	198	84	82	81	71	3.86
1979—Texas y	American	23	113	5	7	.417	114	65	56	50	69	4.46
1980—Atlanta z	National	35	232	14	11	.560	227	120	108	114	74	4.19
1981—San Francisco a	National	24	152	11	7	.611	156	51	49	77	44	2.90
1982—Ft. Lauderdale	Florida St.	2	11	0	1	.000	12	5	5	4	2	4.09
1982—New York bc	American	16	66⅔	1	7	.125	81	52	45	26	14	6.08
1982—Columbus	Int'national	1	3⅔	0	0	.000	5	4	4	1	2	9.82
1983—New York d-Toronto	American	25	145	7	8	.467	157	76	71	63	33	4.41
1983—Kinston	Carolina	1	6	0	0	.000	3	0	0	4	0	0.00
National League Totals		76	476	31	24	.564	488	216	196	216	136	3.71
American League Totals		285	1481⅔	84	85	.497	1444	694	625	558	504	3.80
Major League Totals		361	1957⅔	115	109	.513	1932	910	821	779	640	3.77

Selected by Los Angeles Dodgers' organization in 44th round of free-agent draft, June 7, 1968.

†Traded with Pitcher Bob O'Brien, Catcher Sergio Robles and First Baseman-Outfielder Royle Stillman to Baltimore Orioles for Pitcher Pete Richert and Outfielder Frank Robinson, December 2, 1971.

‡On disabled list, July 10 to August 6, 1973.

§Traded with Pitchers Ken Holtzman and Grant Jackson, Catcher Elrod Hendricks and Pitcher Jimmy Freeman to New York Yankees for Pitchers Rudy May, Tippy Martinez, Dave Pagan, Scott McGregor and Catcher Rick Dempsey, June 15, 1976.

xPlayed out option year and granted free agency, November 1, 1976; signed as free agent by Texas Rangers, November 23, 1976.

yTraded with Shortstop Larvell Blanks to Atlanta Braves for Pitcher Adrian Devine, Shortstop Pepe Frias and a player to be named later, December 7, 1979; Atlanta received $50,000 to complete deal when Outfielder Jeff Burroughs exercised no-trade clause.

zTraded to San Francisco Giants for Pitcher John Montefusco and Outfielder Craig Landis, December 12, 1980.

aTraded to New York Yankees for Pitcher Andy McGaffigan and Outfielder Ted Wilborn, March 30, 1982.

bOn disabled list, May 10 to July 8, 1982; included rehabilitation disability assignment to Columbus, June 22 to July 8, 1982.

cOn disabled list, August 11 to September 10, 1982.

dReleased, May 31, 1983; signed by Toronto Blue Jays' organization, June 21, 1983.

CHAMPIONSHIP SERIES RECORD

Year Club	League	G.	IP.	W.	L.	Pct.	H.	R.	ER.	SO.	BB.	ERA.
1973—Baltimore	American	1	3⅔	0	1	.000	5	3	2	1	0	4.91

WORLD SERIES RECORD

Year Club	League	G.	IP.	W.	L.	Pct.	H.	R.	ER.	SO.	BB.	ERA.
1976—New York	American	1	6	0	1	.000	9	5	5	1	2	7.50

BRIAN MARSHALL ALLARD

Name pronounced AL-ard.

Born January 3, 1958, at Spring Valley, Ill.
Height, 6.01. Weight, 185.
Throws and bats righthanded.
Attending Western Illinois University, Macomb, Ill.

Year Club	League	G.	IP.	W.	L.	Pct.	H.	R.	ER.	SO.	BB.	ERA.
1976—Sarasota Rangers	Gulf Coast	13	68	5	1	.833	46	25	18	35	33	2.38
1977—Asheville†	W. Carol.	26	166	8	9	.471	179	98	76	124	78	4.12
1978—Tulsa	Texas	26	155	7	10	.412	171	92	73	102	75	4.24
1979—Tucson	P. Coast	22	138	10	6	.625	159	81	69	70	54	4.50
1979—Texas	American	7	33	1	3	.250	36	17	16	14	13	4.36
1980—Charleston	Int'national	22	152	8	8	.500	146	62	53	68	43	3.14
1980—Texas‡	American	5	14	0	1	.000	13	13	9	10	10	5.79
1981—Spokane	P. Coast	2	14	1	1	.500	9	2	2	11	2	1.29
1981—Seattle§	American	7	48	3	2	.600	48	22	20	20	8	3.75
1982—Seattle x	American					(Did not play)						
1982—Salt Lake City	P. Coast	5	24⅔	1	2	.333	31	26	25	10	11	9.12
1983—Salt Lake City y	P. Coast	35	164⅔	10	10	.500	203	124	★111	75	85	6.07
Major League Totals		19	95	4	6	.400	97	52	45	44	31	4.26

Selected by Texas Rangers' organization in 4th round of free-agent draft, June 8, 1976.

†Played one game as an outfielder with 2 putouts.

‡Traded with Outfielder Richie Zisk, Pitchers Ken Clay, Steve Finch and Jerry Don Gleaton and Shortstop Rick Auerbach to Seattle Mariners for Catcher Larry Cox, Pitcher Rick Honeycutt, Outfielders Willie Horton and Leon Roberts and Shortstop Mario Mendoza, December 12, 1980.

§On disabled list, August 6, 1981 through remainder of season; included rehabilitation disability assignment to Spokane, August 9 to August 28, 1981.

xOn disabled list, March 26, 1982; transferred to emergency disabled list, June 28, 1982 through remainder of season; included rehabilitation disability assignment to Salt Lake City, May 7 to May 27, 1982.

yGranted free agency, October 20, 1983.

JAMES BRADLEY ALLEN

(Jamie)

Born May 29, 1958, at Yakima, Wash.
Height, 6.00. Weight, 205.
Throws and bats righthanded.
Attended Arizona State University, Tempe, Ariz.

Led Pacific Coast League in sacrifice hits with 11 and grounding into double plays with 24 in 1982.

Year Club	League	Pos.	G.	AB.	R.	H.	2B.	3B.	HR.	RBI.	B.A.	PO.	A.	E.	F.A.
1979—Bellingham	N'west	DH	21	85	11	14	3	0	1	13	.165	0	0	0	.000
1980—Lynn	East.	3B-SS	120	446	60	128	24	7	6	56	.287	95	214	27	.920
1981—Spokane†	P. C.	3B	22	61	3	12	3	0	0	8	.197	17	20	7	.868
1982—Salt Lake City	P. C.	★3B-SS	135	496	73	139	22	5	3	65	.280	106	271	★29	.929
1983—Salt Lake City	P. C.	3B	20	65	15	22	6	1	3	13	.338	12	38	4	.926
1983—Seattle	Amer.	3B	86	273	23	61	10	0	4	21	.223	55	155	9	.959
Major League Totals			86	273	23	61	10	0	4	21	.223	55	155	9	.959

Selected by Minnesota Twins' organization in 1st round (10th player selected) of free-agent draft, June 8, 1976.

Selected by Seattle Mariners' organization in 2nd round of free-agent draft, June 5, 1979.

†On disabled list, April 15 to May 18 and June 11, 1981 through remainder of season.

NEIL PATRICK ALLEN

Born January 24, 1958, at Kansas City, Kan.
Height, 6.02. Weight, 190.
Throws and bats righthanded.

Major League saves: 1979 (8), 1980 (22), 1981 (18), 1982 (19), 1983 (2). Total—69.
Tied for Carolina League lead in complete games with 11 in 1977.

Year Club	League	G.	IP.	W.	L.	Pct.	H.	R.	ER.	SO.	BB.	ERA.
1976—Marion	Ap'lachian	6	33	2	0	1.000	23	8	7	29	6	1.91
1976—Wausau	Midwest	6	48	4	2	.667	51	27	20	34	20	3.75
1977—Lynchburg†	Carolina	20	142	10	2	.833	136	55	44	*126	43	2.79
1978—Jackson	Texas	16	120	5	9	.357	88	38	28	111	38	*2.10
1978—Tidewater	Int'national	10	57	2	7	.222	65	35	28	30	12	4.42
1979—New York‡	National	50	99	6	10	.375	100	46	39	65	47	3.55
1980—New York	National	59	97	7	10	.412	87	43	40	79	40	3.71
1981—New York	National	43	67	7	6	.538	64	26	22	50	26	2.96
1982—New York	National	50	64⅔	3	7	.300	65	22	22	59	30	3.06
1983—New York§-St. Louis	National	46	175⅔	12	13	.480	179	84	77	106	84	3.94
Major League Totals		248	503⅓	35	46	.432	495	221	200	359	227	3.58

Selected by New York Mets' organization in 11th round of free-agent draft, June 8, 1976.
†On disabled list, July 26 to September 1, 1977.
‡On disabled list, June 1 to June 25, 1979.
§Traded with Pitcher Rick Ownbey to St. Louis Cardinals for First Baseman Keith Hernandez, June 15, 1983.

RODERICK BERNET ALLEN
(Rod)

Born October 5, 1959, at Los Angeles, Calif.
Height, 6.01. Weight, 185.
Throws and bats righthanded.

Year Club	League	Pos.	G.	AB.	R.	H.	2B.	3B.	HR.	RBI.	B.A.	PO.	A.	E.	F.A.
1977—Sarasota W. Sox	Gulf C.	OF	43	176	21	54	5	2	1	23	.307	60	2	2	.969
1978—Appleton	Midw.	OF	100	342	48	83	16	4	7	55	.243	134	7	8	.946
1979—Knoxville	South.	OF	86	281	32	75	12	2	6	45	.267	98	6	5	.954
1980—Glens Falls†	East.	OF	31	121	26	43	5	4	3	27	.355	29	1	0	1.000
1980—Iowa‡	A. A.	OF	38	131	23	34	4	0	6	24	.260	42	0	0	1.000
1981—Edmonton§	P. C.	OF	109	388	47	114	25	3	11	52	.294	144	12	4	.975
1982—Salt Lake City	P. C.	OF	117	436	82	141	25	2	15	75	.323	178	8	6	.969
1983—Seattle	Amer.	OF	11	12	1	2	0	0	0	0	.167	5	0	0	1.000
1983—Salt Lake City x	P. C.	OF	81	290	48	94	17	4	12	69	.324	55	1	1	.982
Major League Totals			11	12	1	2	0	0	0	0	.167	5	0	0	1.000

Selected by Chicago White Sox' organization in 6th round of free-agent draft, June 7, 1977.
†On disabled list, August 1 to August 31, 1980.
‡On disabled list, July 8 to July 30, 1980.
§Traded with Catcher Jim Essian and Shortstop Todd Cruz to Seattle Mariners for Outfielder Tom Paciorek, December 11, 1981.
xGranted free agency, October 20, 1983.

GARY MARTIN ALLENSON

Born February 4, 1955, at Culver City, Calif.
Height, 5.11. Weight, 185.
Throws and bats righthanded.
Attended Arizona State University, Tempe, Ariz.

Led International League catchers in putouts with 735 and assists with 86 in 1978.
Named International League Most Valuable Player, 1978.

Year Club	League	Pos.	G.	AB.	R.	H.	2B.	3B.	HR.	RBI.	B.A.	PO.	A.	E.	F.A.
1976—Bristol	East.	C	50	160	18	38	7	0	1	20	.238	190	36	6	.974
1977—Winter Haven	Fla. St.	C	105	312	42	83	18	4	5	43	.266	474	*80	6	*.989
1977—Pawtucket	Int.	C-1B	3	8	1	2	0	0	1	2	.250	4	1	0	1.000
1978—Pawtucket	Int.	C-1B	133	445	82	133	31	3	20	76	.299	763	90	7	.992
1979—Boston	Amer.	C-3B	108	241	27	49	10	2	3	22	.203	410	42	9	.980
1980—Boston	Amer.	C-3B	36	70	9	25	6	0	0	10	.357	100	8	2	.982
1981—Boston†	Amer.	C	47	139	23	31	8	0	5	25	.223	235	18	8	.969
1982—Boston	Amer.	C	92	264	25	54	11	0	6	33	.205	454	39	4	.992
1983—Boston	Amer.	C	84	230	19	53	11	0	3	30	.230	393	29	7	.984
Major League Totals			367	944	103	212	46	2	17	120	.225	1592	136	30	.983

Selected by Boston Red Sox' organization in 9th round of free-agent draft, June 8, 1976.
†On disabled list, May 12 to June 6, 1981.

WILLIAM FRANCIS ALMON
(Bill)

Born November 21, 1952, at Providence, R. I.
Height, 6.03. Weight, 170.
Throws and bats righthanded.
Received bachelor of arts degree from Brown University, Providence, R. I., in 1979.
Brother of John Almon, outfielder in San Diego Padres' organization, 1977 through 1979.

Led National League in sacrifice hits with 20 in 1977.
Led National League shortstops in total chances with 882 in 1977.
Led Pacific Coast League shortstops in total chances with 792 in 1975.
Tied for Pacific Coast League lead in stolen bases with 34 in 1975.
Named College Player of the Year by THE SPORTING NEWS, 1974.
Received reported $100,000 bonus to sign with San Diego Padres, 1974.

Year	Club	League	Pos.	G.	AB.	R.	H.	2B.	3B.	HR.	RBI.	B.A.	PO.	A.	E.	F.A.
1974—Hawaii	P. C.		SS	14	36	6	8	0	0	0	3	.222	16	33	7	.875
1974—Alexandria	Texas		SS	25	97	9	18	2	2	0	5	.186	48	70	8	.937
1974—San Diego	Nat.		SS	16	38	4	12	1	0	0	3	.316	13	30	4	.915
1975—Hawaii	P. C.		SS	●144	496	76	113	22	0	1	47	.228	★288	456	★48	.939
1975—San Diego	Nat.		SS	6	10	0	4	0	0	0	0	.400	6	5	0	1.000
1976—Hawaii	P. C.		SS	129	454	67	132	16	2	3	44	.291	★248	395	★36	.947
1976—San Diego	Nat.		SS	14	57	6	14	3	0	1	6	.246	23	52	3	.962
1977—San Diego	Nat.		SS	155	613	75	160	18	11	2	43	.261	★303	538	★41	.954
1978—San Diego†	Nat.		3B-SS-2B	138	405	39	102	19	2	0	21	.252	102	255	23	.939
1979—San Diego†	Nat.		2B-SS-OF	100	198	20	45	3	0	1	8	.227	142	193	7	.980
1980—Mtl.‡-N.Y.§	Nat.		SS-2B-3B	66	150	15	29	4	3	0	7	.193	79	134	12	.947
1981—Chicago	Amer.		SS	103	349	46	105	10	2	4	41	.301	190	340	17	.969
1982—Chicago x	Amer.		SS	111	308	40	79	10	4	4	26	.256	164	317	●26	.949
1983—Oakland	Amer.		S-3-1-O-2	143	451	45	120	29	1	4	63	.266	327	176	20	.962
	National League Totals			495	1471	159	366	48	16	4	88	.249	668	1207	90	.954
	American League Totals			357	1108	131	304	49	7	12	130	.274	681	833	63	.960
	Major League Totals			852	2579	290	670	97	23	16	218	.260	1349	2040	153	.957

Selected by San Diego Padres' organization in 10th round of free-agent draft, June 8, 1971.
Selected by San Diego Padres' organization in 1st round (first player selected) of free-agent draft, June 5, 1974.
†Traded with First Baseman-Outfielder Dan Briggs to Montreal Expos for Second Baseman Dave Cash, November 27, 1979.
‡Became free agent after refusing option to Denver, July 7, 1980; signed by New York Mets, July 11, 1980.
§Released, December 19, 1980; signed by Chicago White Sox' organization, February 4, 1981.
xGranted free agency, November 10, 1982; signed by Oakland A's, January 18, 1983.

PORFIRIO ALTAMIRANO (RAMIREZ)
(Porfie)
Born May 17, 1952, at Esteli, Nicaragua.
Height, 6.00. Weight, 175.
Throws and bats righthanded.

Year	Club	League	G.	IP.	W.	L.	Pct.	H.	R.	ER.	SO.	BB.	ERA.
1979—Miami†‡	Int.-Amer.	16	57	5	4	.556	51	27	13	31	18	2.05
1979—Oklahoma City	Am. Assoc.	21	51	2	5	.286	56	25	22	41	27	3.88
1980—Oklahoma City§	Am. Assoc.	38	89	7	2	.778	87	51	48	39	27	4.85
1981—Oklahoma City	Am. Assoc.	29	133	10	6	.625	163	86	70	88	42	4.74
1982—Oklahoma City	Am. Assoc.	6	14	1	0	1.000	12	3	1	17	3	0.64
1982—Philadelphia x	National	29	39	5	1	.833	41	19	18	26	14	4.15
1983—Philadelphia	National	31	41⅓	2	3	.400	38	18	17	24	15	3.70
1983—Portland	P. Coast	25	40⅔	5	4	.556	37	13	13	39	18	2.88
	Major League Totals		60	80⅓	7	4	.636	79	37	35	50	29	3.92

†Loaned to Oklahoma City (Philadelphia Phillies' organization), June 21, 1979; returned, October 26, 1979.
‡Sold to Oklahoma City (Philadelphia Phillies' organization), February 20, 1980.
§On disabled list, May 14 to June 15, 1980.
xOn disabled list, August 9 to September 1, 1982.

LARRY EUGENE ANDERSEN
Born May 6, 1953, at Portland, Ore.
Height, 6.03. Weight, 195.
Throws and bats righthanded.
Attended Bellevue Community College, Bellevue, Wash.

Pitched 6-0 no-hit victory against Victoria, June 1, 1974.
Led Pacific Coast League in saves with 25 in 1978 and 22 in 1983.
Led American Association in balks with 4 in 1975.

Year	Club	League	G.	IP.	W.	L.	Pct.	H.	R.	ER.	SO.	BB.	ERA.
1971—Reno	California	7	24	1	0	1.000	37	20	18	10	9	6.75
1971—Sarasota Indians	Gulf Coast	4	15	0	3	.000	15	7	5	10	7	3.00
1972—Reno	California	27	124	4	14	.222	166	102	90	79	57	6.53
1973—Reno	California	29	164	10	8	.556	173	91	72	115	67	3.95
1974—San Antonio	Texas	25	169	10	6	.625	176	84	72	64	51	3.83
1975—Oklahoma City	Am. Assoc.	25	156	10	11	.476	179	87	73	64	52	4.21
1975—Cleveland	American	3	6	0	0	.000	4	3	3	4	2	4.50
1976—Toledo	Int'national	6	23	0	2	.000	47	33	33	8	6	12.91
1976—Williamsport	Eastern	21	133	9	6	.600	117	47	40	74	34	2.71
1977—Toledo†	Int'national	45	65	5	6	.455	52	20	14	40	37	1.94
1977—Cleveland	American	11	14	0	1	.000	10	7	5	8	9	3.21
1978—Portland	P. Coast	57	99	10	7	.588	92	42	38	65	45	3.45
1979—Tacoma	P. Coast	27	112	10	6	.625	124	59	50	52	32	4.02
1979—Cleveland‡	American	8	17	0	0	.000	25	14	14	7	4	7.41
1980—Portland§	P. Coast	52	93	5	7	.417	78	24	18	65	16	1.74
1981—Seattle	American	41	68	3	3	.500	57	27	20	40	18	2.65
1982—Seattle x	American	40	79⅔	0	0	.000	100	56	53	32	23	5.99
1982—Salt Lake City y	P. Coast	5	6⅔	1	0	1.000	2	0	0	8	3	0.00
1983—Portland	P. Coast	52	70⅓	7	8	.467	63	35	16	64	30	2.05
1983—Philadelphia	National	17	26⅓	1	0	1.000	19	7	7	14	9	2.39
	American League Totals		103	184⅔	3	4	.429	196	107	95	91	56	4.63
	National League Totals		17	26⅓	1	0	1.000	19	7	7	14	9	2.39
	Major League Totals		120	211	4	4	.500	215	114	102	105	65	4.35

Selected by Cleveland Indians' organization in 7th round of free-agent draft, June 8, 1971.

†Appeared as first baseman with no chances.

‡Traded to Pittsburgh Pirates for Outfielder Larry Littleton and Pitcher John Burden, December 21, 1979.

§Traded to Seattle Mariners, October 29, 1980, completing deal in which Seattle traded Pitcher Odell Jones to Pittsburgh Pirates for a player to be named later, April 1, 1980.

xOn supplemental disabled list, August 11 to September 1, 1982; included rehabilitation disability assignment to Salt Lake City, August 11 to August 31, 1982.

yLoaned to Portland (Philadelphia Phillies' organization), April 1, 1983; sold to Philadelphia Phillies, July 29, 1983.

WORLD SERIES RECORD

Year	Club	League	G.	IP.	W.	L.	Pct.	H.	R.	ER.	SO.	BB.	ERA.
1983—Philadelphia		National	2	4	0	0	.000	4	1	1	1	0	2.25

DAVID CARTER ANDERSON
(Dave)

Born August 1, 1960, at Louisville, Ky.
Height, 6.02. Weight, 185.
Throws and bats righthanded.
Attended Memphis State University, Memphis, Tenn.

Led Pacific Coast League shortstops in double plays with 81 in 1982.

Year	Club	League	Pos.	G.	AB.	R.	H.	2B.	3B.	HR.	RBI.	B.A.	PO.	A.	E.	F.A.
1981—Vero Beach	Fla. St.	SS	65	200	44	54	8	1	0	18	.270	109	218	23	.934
1982—Albuquerque	P. C.	SS	132	507	100	174	19	7	5	76	.343	223	397	★34	.948
1983—Albuquerque	P. C.	SS	9	27	10	11	1	1	0	3	.407	17	26	1	.977
1983—Los Angeles	Nat.	SS-3B	61	115	12	19	4	2	1	2	.165	56	100	5	.969
Major League Totals			61	115	12	19	4	2	1	2	.165	56	100	5	.969

Selected by Los Angeles Dodgers' organization in 1st round (22nd player selected) of free-agent draft, June 8, 1981.

JAMES LEA ANDERSON
(Jim)

Born February 23, 1957, at Los Angeles, Calif.
Height, 6.00. Weight, 170.
Throws and bats righthanded.

Led Texas League shortstops in double plays with 93 in 1977.

Year	Club	League	Pos.	G.	AB.	R.	H.	2B.	3B.	HR.	RBI.	B.A.	PO.	A.	E.	F.A.
1975—Idaho Falls	Pion.	★SS-2B	71	253	42	73	3	6	0	27	.289	●94	★239	27	★.925
1976—Salinas	Calif.	SS	136	469	67	124	14	4	4	51	.264	188	★406	★40	.937
1977—El Paso	Texas	SS-2B	120	417	87	119	24	1	18	73	.285	243	381	27	.959
1978—Salt Lake City	P. C.	SS-2B	72	248	36	64	13	1	5	32	.258	124	244	22	.944
1978—California	Amer.	SS-2B	48	108	6	21	7	0	0	7	.194	72	99	8	.955
1979—California†	Amer.	SS-3-2-C	96	234	33	58	13	1	3	23	.248	141	205	17	.953
1980—Seattle	Amer.	SS-3-2-C	116	317	46	72	7	0	8	30	.227	120	255	22	.945
1981—Seattle‡	Amer.	SS-3B	70	162	12	33	7	0	2	19	.204	88	184	15	.948
1982—Denver§	A. A.	3B-SS	128	488	95	153	30	3	16	83	.314	130	296	28	.938
1983—Texas	Amer.	S-2-O-3-C	50	102	8	22	1	1	0	6	.216	46	102	5	.967
Major League Totals			380	923	105	206	35	2	13	85	.223	467	845	67	.951

Selected by California Angels' organization in 2nd round of free-agent draft, June 4, 1975.

†Traded to Seattle Mariners, December 2, 1979, completing deal in which Seattle traded Pitcher John Montague to California Angels for a player to be named later, August 29, 1979.

‡Released, March 29, 1982; signed by Denver (Texas Rangers' organization), April 13, 1982.

§Released, December 7, 1982; signed by Texas Rangers' organization, January 25, 1983.

CHAMPIONSHIP SERIES RECORD

Year	Club	League	Pos.	G.	AB.	R.	H.	2B.	3B.	HR.	RBI.	B.A.	PO.	A.	E.	F.A.
1979—California	Amer.	SS	4	11	0	1	0	0	0	0	.091	4	11	0	1.000

KARL ADAM ANDERSON
(Bud)

Born May 27, 1956, at Westbury, N.Y.
Height, 6.03. Weight, 210.
Throws and bats righthanded.
Attended Rutgers University, New Brunswick, N.J.

Led California League in complete games with 16 in 1978.
Led Northwest League in balks with 3 in 1977.

Year	Club	League	G.	IP.	W.	L.	Pct.	H.	R.	ER.	SO.	BB.	ERA.
1977—Bellingham	Northwest	10	75	5	3	.625	66	30	18	63	29	2.16
1978—Stockton	California	26	185	12	8	.600	167	79	62	157	83	3.02
1979—Spokane	P. Coast	19	105	2	13	.133	124	84	75	56	60	6.43
1979—San Jose†	California	9	49	5	3	.625	49	23	21	47	17	3.86
1980—Chattanooga‡	Southern	20	128	7	9	.438	116	68	59	98	50	4.15
1981—Chattanooga	Southern	25	55	2	3	.400	41	25	19	35	28	3.11
1981—Charleston	Int'national	16	93	9	3	.750	71	31	25	48	28	2.42
1982—Charleston	Int'national	11	73⅓	1	5	.167	81	40	30	60	39	3.68
1982—Cleveland	American	25	80⅔	3	4	.429	84	37	30	44	30	3.35

Year Club	League	G.	IP.	W.	L.	Pct.	H.	R.	ER.	SO.	BB.	ERA.
1983—Charleston	Int'national	13	20	1	0	1.000	21	11	8	15	9	3.60
1983—Cleveland	American	39	68⅓	1	6	.143	64	34	31	32	32	4.08
Major League Totals		64	149	4	10	.286	148	71	61	76	62	3.68

Selected by Seattle Mariners' organization in 3rd round of free-agent draft, June 7, 1977.

†Traded to Cleveland Indians' organization, March 29, 1980, completing deal in which Seattle Mariners traded Pitchers Rob Pietroburgo and Rafael Vasquez and a player to be named later to Cleveland for Third Baseman-Outfielder Ted Cox, December 6, 1979.

‡On disabled list, June 11 to July 7, 1980.

JOAQUIN ANDUJAR

Name pronounced Wah-KEEN AHN-doo-hahr.

Born December 21, 1952, at San Pedro de Macoris, Dominican Republic.
Height, 6.00. Weight, 180.
Throws right and bats left and righthanded.

Tied for National League lead in balks with 5 in 1976.

Year Club	League	G.	IP.	W.	L.	Pct.	H.	R.	ER.	SO.	BB.	ERA.
1970—Bradenton Reds	Gulf Coast	12	82	3	5	.375	★86	★58	★38	88	56	4.17
1971—Sioux Falls	Northern	19	75	4	7	.364	61	67	53	82	63	6.36
1972—Three Rivers	Eastern	22	112	7	6	.538	87	59	44	101	73	3.54
1973—Indianapolis	Am. Assoc.	11	40	2	5	.286	42	45	40	23	45	9.00
1973—Three Rivers†	Eastern	10	59	5	2	.714	38	29	13	39	38	1.98
1974—Indianapolis	Am. Assoc.	33	111	8	8	.500	85	62	44	92	93	3.57
1975—Three Rivers‡§	Eastern	18	62	4	8	.333	57	36	28	44	40	4.06
1976—Houston	National	28	172	9	10	.474	163	74	69	59	75	3.61
1977—Houston	National	26	159	11	8	.579	149	80	65	69	64	3.68
1978—Houston x	National	35	111	5	7	.417	88	45	42	55	58	3.41
1979—Houston	National	46	194	12	12	.500	168	86	74	77	88	3.43
1980—Houston	National	35	122	3	8	.273	132	59	53	75	43	3.91
1981—Houston y-St. Louis z	National	20	79	8	4	.667	85	41	36	37	23	4.10
1982—St. Louis	National	38	265⅔	15	10	.600	237	85	73	137	50	2.47
1983—St. Louis	National	39	225	6	16	.273	215	112	104	125	75	4.16
Major League Totals		267	1327⅔	69	75	.479	1237	582	516	634	476	3.50

Signed as free agent by Cincinnati Reds' organization, November 14, 1969.

†On disabled list, August 5 to August 15, 1973.

‡On disabled list, May 11 to July 4, 1975.

§Traded to Houston Astros for two minor league players to be named later, October 24, 1975; Cincinnati Reds' organization acquired Pitchers Carlos Alfonso and Luis Sanchez to complete deal, December 12, 1975.

xOn disabled list, July 8 to July 30, 1978.

yTraded to St. Louis Cardinals for Outfielder Tony Scott, June 7, 1981.

zGranted free agency, November 13, 1981; re-signed by Cardinals, December 29, 1981.

CHAMPIONSHIP SERIES RECORD

Year Club	League	G.	IP.	W.	L.	Pct.	H.	R.	ER.	SO.	BB.	ERA.
1980—Houston	National	1	1	0	0	.000	0	0	0	0	1	0.00
1982—St. Louis	National	1	6⅔	1	0	1.000	6	2	2	4	2	2.70
Championship Series Totals		2	7⅔	1	0	1.000	6	2	2	4	3	2.35

WORLD SERIES RECORD

Year Club	League	G.	IP.	W.	L.	Pct.	H.	R.	ER.	SO.	BB.	ERA.
1982—St. Louis	National	2	13⅓	2	0	1.000	10	3	2	4	1	1.35

ALL-STAR GAME RECORD

Year League		IP.	W.	L.	Pct.	H.	R.	ER.	SO.	BB.	ERA.
1979—National		2	0	0	.000	2	2	1	0	1	4.50

Member of National League All-Star Team in 1977; did not play.

LUIS E. APONTE (YURIPA)

Born July 14, 1954, at Lel Tigre, Venezuela.
Height, 6.00. Weight, 165.
Throws and bats righthanded.

Led Carolina League in intentional bases on balls issued with 10 in 1975.
Tied for New York-Pennsylvania League lead in balks with 2 in 1973.

Year Club	League	G.	IP.	W.	L.	Pct.	H.	R.	ER.	SO.	BB.	ERA.
1973—Winter Haven	Florida St.	4	9	0	0	.000	12	7	3	5	2	3.00
1973—Elmira	NYP	16	84	2	7	.222	★113	55	45	47	22	4.82
1974—Winston-Salem	Carolina	28	56	3	1	.750	49	32	24	36	25	3.86
1975—Winston-Salem	Carolina	40	62	3	0	1.000	52	20	19	38	37	2.76
1976—Winter Haven	Florida St.	48	78	3	4	.429	83	42	30	45	23	3.46
1977—Bristol†	Eastern					(Did not play)						
1978—Bristol‡	Eastern					(Did not play)						
1979—Maracaibo§	Inter.-Amer.	11	44	3	5	.375	70	30	26	19	16	5.32
1980—Bristol	Eastern	29	54	9	1	.900	46	17	15	43	23	2.50
1980—Pawtucket	Int'national	31	49	6	2	.750	27	15	12	42	21	2.20
1980—Boston	American	4	7	0	0	.000	6	1	1	1	2	1.29
1981—Pawtucket	Int'national	51	79	7	5	.583	58	26	17	67	31	1.94

Year Club	League	G.	IP.	W.	L.	Pct.	H.	R.	ER.	SO.	BB.	ERA.
1981—Boston..............	American	7	16	1	0	1.000	11	1	1	11	3	0.56
1982—Boston..............	American	40	85	2	2	.500	78	31	30	44	25	3.18
1983—Boston..............	American	34	62	5	4	.556	74	28	25	32	23	3.63
Major League Totals........................		85	170	8	6	.571	169	61	57	88	53	3.02

Signed as free agent by Boston Red Sox' organization, January 12, 1973.
†On suspended list, April 14, 1977; transferred to restricted list, May 3, 1977 through May 10, 1979.
‡Released, May 10, 1979; signed by Maracaibo of Inter-American League, June 1, 1979.
§Signed as free agent by Boston Red Sox' organization, February 28, 1980.

ANTONIO RAFAEL ARMAS (MACHADO)
(Tony)

Born July 12, 1953, at Anzoategui, Venezuela.
Height, 6.01. Weight, 192.
Throws and bats righthanded.

Established major league records for most putouts (11) and chances accepted by right fielder, game (12), June 12, 1982.
Tied major league record for fewest double plays by outfielder, season, for leader in most double plays (4), 1977.
Led American League batters in strikeouts with 115 in 1981.
Tied for American League lead in grounding into double plays with 31 in 1983.
Tied for American League lead in double plays by outfielders with 4 in 1977.
Named American League Player of the Year by THE SPORTING NEWS, 1981.
Named outfielder on THE SPORTING NEWS American League All-Star Team, 1981.

Year Club	League	Pos.	G.	AB.	R.	H.	2B.	3B.	HR.	RBI.	B.A.	PO.	A.	E.	F.A.
1971—Monroe............	W. Car.	OF	31	88	7	20	3	0	1	10	.227	37	3	6	.870
1971—Bradenton Pir.	Gulf C.	OF	43	169	12	39	3	3	0	17	.231	★98	5	3	.972
1972—Gastonia	W. Car.	OF	117	399	50	106	18	4	9	51	.266	165	7	8	.956
1973—Sherbrooke†........	East.	OF	84	302	46	91	15	5	11	45	.301	150	6	8	.951
1974—Thetford Mines...	East.	OF	★137	476	64	132	26	3	15	81	.277	★329	18	10	.972
1975—Charleston............	Int.	OF	128	450	65	135	28	4	12	72	.300	220	●14	3	.987
1976—Charleston............	Int.	OF-1B	114	409	62	96	24	1	21	67	.235	210	8	7	.969
1976—Pittsburgh‡	Nat.	OF	4	6	0	2	0	0	0	1	.333	3	0	0	1.000
1977—Oakland§............	Amer.	OF-SS	118	363	26	87	8	2	13	53	.240	294	9	6	.981
1978—Oakland x	Amer.	OF	91	239	17	51	6	1	2	13	.213	214	3	2	.991
1979—Oakland y	Amer.	OF	80	278	29	69	9	3	11	34	.248	194	7	5	.976
1980—Oakland.................	Amer.	OF	158	628	87	175	18	8	35	109	.279	374	17	10	.975
1981—Oakland.................	Amer.	OF	●109	440	51	115	24	3	●22	76	.261	259	8	2	.993
1982—Oakland za	Amer.	OF	138	536	58	125	19	2	28	89	.233	333	9	6	.983
1983—Boston..................	Amer.	OF	145	574	77	125	23	2	36	107	.218	326	5	5	.985
National League Totals...............			4	6	0	2	0	0	0	1	.333	3	0	0	1.000
American League Totals........................			839	3058	345	747	107	21	147	481	.244	1994	58	36	.983
Major League Totals........................			843	3064	345	749	107	21	147	482	.244	1997	58	36	.983

Signed as free agent by Pittsburgh Pirates' organization, January 18, 1971.
†On disabled list, May 27 to July 12, 1973.
‡Traded with Pitchers Dave Giusti, Doc Medich, Doug Bair and Rick Langford and Outfielder Mitchell Page to Oakland Athletics for Infielders Tommy Helms and Phil Garner and Pitcher Chris Batton, March 15, 1977.
§On supplemental disabled list, August 5 to September 1, 1977.
xOn supplemental disabled list, April 28 to June 2, 1978.
yOn disabled list, April 15 to June 5, 1979.
zOn supplemental disabled list, May 13 to May 28, 1982.
aTraded with Catcher Jeff Newman to Boston Red Sox for Third Baseman Carney Lansford, Outfielder Garry Hancock and a player to be named later, December 6, 1982; Oakland A's acquired Pitcher Jerry King to complete deal, December 20, 1982.

DIVISION SERIES RECORD
Year Club	League	Pos.	G.	AB.	R.	H.	2B.	3B.	HR.	RBI.	B.A.	PO.	A.	E.	F.A.
1981—Oakland.................	Amer.	OF	3	11	1	6	2	0	0	3	.545	6	0	1	.857

CHAMPIONSHIP SERIES RECORD
Year Club	League	Pos.	G.	AB.	R.	H.	2B.	3B.	HR.	RBI.	B.A.	PO.	A.	E.	F.A.
1981—Oakland.................	Amer.	OF	3	12	0	2	0	0	0	0	.167	5	2	0	1.000

ALL-STAR GAME RECORD
Year League		Pos.	AB.	R.	H.	2B.	3B.	HR.	RBI.	B.A.	PO.	A.	E.	F.A.
1981—American		OF	1	0	0	0	0	0	0	.000	0	0	0	.000

MICHAEL DENNIS ARMSTRONG
(Mike)

Born March 7, 1954, at Glen Cove, N.Y.
Height, 6.03. Weight, 206.
Throws and bats righthanded.
Attended University of Miami, Coral Gables, Fla.

Led Eastern League pitchers in games started with 29 in 1977.

Year Club	League	G.	IP.	W.	L.	Pct.	H.	R.	ER.	SO.	BB.	ERA.
1974—Tampa.................	Florida St.	6	16	0	2	.000	26	17	17	14	18	9.56
1974—Seattle.................	Northwest	15	102	6	7	.462	85	45	30	86	47	2.65

Year Club	League	G.	IP.	W.	L.	Pct.	H.	R.	ER.	SO.	BB.	ERA.
1975—Three Rivers	Eastern	25	150	5	10	.333	116	55	45	86	44	2.70
1976—Three Rivers	Eastern	24	146	10	10	.500	143	77	57	91	52	3.51
1977—Three Rivers	Eastern	30	184	*16	10	.615	185	91	77	107	83	3.77
1978—Chattanooga	Southern	31	74	9	6	.600	61	34	25	54	37	3.04
1978—Indianapolis	Am. Assoc.	16	23	1	2	.333	26	18	17	17	17	6.65
1979—Nashville†	Southern	32	64	5	1	.833	58	30	24	53	29	3.38
1979—Amarillo	Texas	7	31	2	3	.400	32	15	12	34	14	3.48
1979—Hawaii	P. Coast	3	7	0	0	.000	6	2	2	4	5	2.57
1980—Hawaii	P. Coast	42	74	4	4	.500	48	18	16	67	26	1.95
1980—San Diego	National	11	14	0	0	.000	16	10	9	14	13	5.79
1981—Hawaii	P. Coast	22	36	5	2	.714	21	7	6	39	12	1.50
1981—San Diego‡	National	10	12	0	2	.000	14	9	8	9	11	6.00
1982—Omaha	Am. Assoc.	15	28	4	2	.667	19	12	10	27	20	3.21
1982—Kansas City	American	52	112⅔	5	5	.500	88	45	40	75	43	3.20
1983—Kansas City§	American	58	102⅔	10	7	.588	86	53	44	52	45	3.86
National League Totals		21	26	0	2	.000	30	19	17	23	24	5.88
American League Totals		110	215⅓	15	12	.556	174	98	84	127	88	3.51
Major League Totals		131	241⅓	15	14	.517	204	117	101	150	112	3.77

Selected by Cleveland Indians' organization in 9th round of free-agent draft, June 6, 1972.
Selected by Cincinnati Reds' organization in 1st round (24th player selected) of free-agent draft, January 9, 1974.
†Traded to San Diego Padres' organization for Third Baseman Paul O'Neill, July 25, 1979.
‡Traded to Kansas City Royals' organization for a player to be named later, April 4, 1982; San Diego Padres' organization acquired Pitcher Walt Vanderbush to complete deal, December 8, 1982.
§Traded with Catcher Duane Dewey to New York Yankees for First Baseman Steve Balboni and Pitcher Roger Erickson, December 8, 1983.

ALAN DEAN ASHBY

Born July 8, 1951, at Long Beach, Calif.
Height, 6.02. Weight, 190.
Throws right and bats left and righthanded.
Attended Los Angeles Harbor Junior College, Wilmington, Calif.

Tied National League record for most games, switch-hit home runs, season (1), September 27, 1982.
Led National League in passed balls with 14 in 1980.
Led California League catchers in double plays with 12 in 1971.

Year Club	League	Pos.	G.	AB.	R.	H.	2B.	3B.	HR.	RBI.	B.A.	PO.	A.	E.	F.A.
1969—Sarasota Indians	Gulf C.	C	48	117	10	28	3	1	0	14	.239	219	20	2	*.992
1970—Reno†	Calif.	C	40	121	15	23	5	1	3	18	.190	321	27	7	.980
1971—Jacksonville	South.	C	13	35	4	7	2	0	0	8	.200	76	6	1	.988
1971—Reno‡	Calif.	C-3B	77	239	52	70	14	1	18	60	.293	492	59	10	.982
1972—Portland	P. C.	C	95	291	33	65	9	2	9	28	.223	601	50	8	.988
1973—Ok.C.§-Evan.	A. A.	C-OF	41	124	20	28	8	0	3	16	.226	253	26	2	.993
1973—Cleveland	Amer.	C	11	29	4	5	1	0	1	3	.172	45	0	1	.978
1974—Oklahoma City	A. A	C	66	211	26	60	19	1	2	24	.284	405	33	8	.982
1974—Cleveland	Amer.	C	10	7	1	1	0	0	0	0	.143	12	0	0	1.000
1975—Cleveland	Amer.	C-1B-3B	90	254	32	57	10	1	5	32	.224	450	43	6	.988
1976—Cleveland xy	Amer.	C-1B-3B	89	247	26	59	5	1	4	32	.239	476	52	7	.987
1977—Toronto	Amer.	C	124	396	25	83	16	3	2	29	.210	619	71	11	.984
1978—Toronto z	Amer.	C	81	264	27	69	15	0	9	29	.261	399	38	6	.986
1979—Houston a	Nat.	C	108	336	25	68	15	2	2	35	.202	548	57	8	.987
1980—Houston	Nat.	C	116	352	30	90	19	2	3	48	.256	608	60	6	.991
1981—Houston	Nat.	C	83	255	20	69	13	0	4	33	.271	434	58	9	.982
1982—Houston b	Nat.	C	100	339	40	87	14	2	12	49	.257	530	55	14	.977
1983—Houston c	Nat.	C	87	275	31	63	18	1	8	34	.229	435	56	13	.974
American League Totals			405	1197	115	274	47	5	21	125	.229	2001	204	31	.986
National League Totals			494	1557	146	377	79	7	29	199	.242	2555	286	50	.983
Major League Totals			899	2754	261	651	126	12	50	324	.236	4556	490	81	.984

Selected by Cleveland Indians' organization in 3rd round of free-agent draft, June 5, 1969.
†On military list, January 1 to May 23, 1970.
‡On temporary inactive list, August 27 to September 13, 1971.
§Loaned to Evansville (Milwaukee Brewers' organization), May 22, 1973; returned, July 2, 1973.
xOn supplemental disabled list, August 9, 1976 through remainder of season.
yTraded with Outfielder-First Baseman Doug Howard to Toronto Blue Jays for Pitcher Al Fitzmorris, November 5, 1976.
zTraded to Houston Astros for Pitcher Mark Lemongello, Outfielder Joe Cannon and Shortstop Pedro Hernandez, November 27, 1978.
aOn supplemental disabled list, August 30 to September 17, 1979.
bGranted free agency, November 10, 1982; re-signed by Astros, December 21, 1982.
cOn supplemental disabled list, June 27 to July 24, 1983.

DIVISION SERIES RECORD

Year Club	League	Pos.	G.	AB.	R.	H.	2B.	3B.	HR.	RBI.	B.A.	PO.	A.	E.	F.A.
1981—Houston	Nat.	C	3	9	1	1	0	0	1	2	.111	24	2	0	1.000

CHAMPIONSHIP SERIES RECORD

Year Club	League	Pos.	G.	AB.	R.	H.	2B.	3B.	HR.	RBI.	B.A.	PO.	A.	E.	F.A.
1980—Houston	Nat.	C-PH	2	8	0	1	0	0	0	1	.125	11	2	0	1.000

THOMAS STEVEN ASHFORD
(Tucker)

Born December 4, 1954, at Memphis, Tenn.
Height, 6.01. Weight, 185.
Throws and bats righthanded.
Attended University of Mississippi, University, Miss., and
Shelby State Community College, Memphis, Tenn.

Led International League third basemen in fielding percentage with .955 and putouts with 113 in 1982.
Led International League in total bases with 250 in 1981.
Led International League third basemen in putouts with 87, assists with 250 and double plays with 24 in 1980.
Led Pacific Coast League third basemen in putouts with 131, assists with 314 and double plays with 31 in 1979.
Led Texas League third basemen in putouts with 100, errors with 34 and double plays with 33 in 1976.
Led Northwest League shortstops in double plays with 40 in 1974.
Named International League Most Valuable Player, 1982.

Year	Club	League	Pos.	G.	AB.	R.	H.	2B.	3B.	HR.	RBI.	B.A.	PO.	A.	E.	F.A.
1974—Walla Walla	N'west	SS-OF-3B	77	263	56	64	7	2	4	30	.243	123	159	26	.916
1975—Alexandria	Texas	3B-SS-OF	120	376	33	89	12	1	3	38	.237	125	254	36	.913
1976—Amarillo	Texas	3B-SS	132	519	91	141	29	0	12	67	.272	112	288	38	.913
1976—San Diego	Nat.	3B	4	5	0	3	1	0	0	0	.600	1	2	0	1.000
1977—Hawaii	P. C.	3B	73	281	53	79	21	4	7	45	.281	67	142	14	.937
1977—San Diego	Nat.	3B-SS-2B	81	249	25	54	18	0	3	24	.217	49	159	15	.933
1978—Hawaii	P. C.	2B-3B	14	45	6	14	4	0	0	6	.311	20	36	3	.949
1978—San Diego	Nat.	3B-2B-1B	75	155	11	38	11	0	3	26	.245	108	53	6	.946
1979—Hawaii†	P. C.	3-S-1-2	146	509	70	130	25	6	13	62	.255	141	321	26	.947
1980—Charleston	Int.	3B-SS	107	366	50	102	18	3	8	38	.279	97	262	23	.940
1980—Texas‡	Amer.	3B-SS	15	32	2	4	0	0	0	3	.125	10	25	2	.946
1981—Columbus	Int.	3B-2B	132	504	81	151	32	8	17	86	.300	133	249	23	.943
1981—New York	Amer.	2B	3	0	0	0	0	0	0	0	.000	0	0	0	.000
1982—Columbus§x	Int.	3B-2B	137	540	98	179	★35	4	10	101	.331	140	211	14	.962
1983—Tidewater	Int.	3B	12	49	8	16	3	0	1	8	.327	14	20	1	.971
1983—New York	Nat.	3B-2B-C	35	56	3	10	0	1	0	2	.179	14	31	1	.978
National League Totals			195	465	39	105	30	1	6	52	.226	172	245	22	.950
American League Totals			18	32	2	4	0	0	0	3	.125	10	25	2	.946
Major League Totals			213	497	41	109	30	1	6	55	.219	182	270	24	.950

Selected by San Diego Padres' organization in 1st round (second player selected) of free-agent draft, January 9, 1974.

†Traded with Pitchers Gaylord Perry and Joe Carroll to Texas Rangers for First Baseman Willie Montanez and a player to be named later, February 15, 1980; Hawaii (San Diego Padres' organization) purchased Infielder Tony Phillips to complete deal, September 11, 1980.

‡Traded to New York Yankees' organization, December 8, 1980; completing deal in which Texas Rangers acquired Infielder Roger Holt, October 24, 1980.

§Sold on conditional basis to Toronto Blue Jays, October 27, 1982; returned, April 5, 1983.

xTraded to New York Mets' organization for Pitcher Steve Ray and a player to be named later, April 18, 1983; New York Yankees' organization acquired Infielder Felix Perdomo to complete deal, May 3, 1983.

KEITH ROWE ATHERTON

Born February 19, 1959, at Mathews, Va.
Height, 6.04. Weight, 200.
Throws and bats righthanded.

Led Eastern League in complete games with 13 in 1980.
Tied for Northwest League lead in shutouts with 2 in 1978.

Year	Club	League	G.	IP.	W.	L.	Pct.	H.	R.	ER.	SO.	BB.	ERA.
1978—Bend	Northwest	12	92	7	3	.700	86	44	35	81	40	3.42
1979—Waterbury	Eastern	4	21	0	3	.000	28	23	13	7	13	5.57
1979—Modesto	California	21	146	9	8	.529	190	107	97	103	51	5.98
1980—West Haven	Eastern	27	190	11	12	.478	185	101	87	117	58	4.12
1981—West Haven	Eastern	27	175	11	13	.458	174	83	70	116	64	3.60
1982—Tacoma	P. Coast	28	★200	12	9	.571	214	108	97	128	54	4.37
1983—Tacoma	P. Coast	26	120⅓	3	8	.273	117	60	53	93	44	3.96
1983—Oakland†	American	29	68⅓	2	5	.286	53	22	21	40	23	2.77
Major League Totals			29	68⅓	2	5	.286	53	22	21	40	23	2.77

Selected by Oakland A's organization in 2nd round of free-agent draft, June 6, 1978.

†Struck out in only at bat during season when designated hitter took the field.

GERALD LEE AUGUSTINE
(Jerry)

Born July 24, 1952, at Green Bay, Wis.
Height, 6.00. Weight, 185.
Throws and bats lefthanded.
Received bachelor of science degree in education from
University of Wisconsin at La Crosse, La Crosse, Wis.

Year	Club	League	G.	IP.	W.	L.	Pct.	H.	R.	ER.	SO.	BB.	ERA.
1974—Danville	Midwest	13	88	7	4	.636	81	34	25	52	34	2.56
1975—Sacramento†	P. Coast	15	79	4	3	.571	90	49	42	27	40	4.78
1975—Milwaukee	American	5	27	2	0	1.000	26	9	9	8	12	3.00

Year Club	League	G.	IP.	W.	L.	Pct.	H.	R.	ER.	SO.	BB.	ERA.
1976—Milwaukee	American	39	172	9	12	.429	167	69	63	59	56	3.30
1977—Milwaukee	American	33	209	12	18	.400	222	119	104	68	72	4.48
1978—Milwaukee	American	35	188	13	12	.520	204	100	95	59	61	4.55
1979—Milwaukee	American	43	86	9	6	.600	95	38	33	41	30	3.45
1980—Milwaukee	American	38	70	4	3	.571	83	37	35	22	36	4.50
1981—Milwaukee	American	27	61	2	2	.500	75	30	29	26	18	4.28
1982—Milwaukee	American	20	62	1	3	.250	63	43	35	22	26	5.08
1983—Milwaukee‡	American	34	64⅓	3	3	.500	89	45	41	40	25	5.74
Major League Totals		275	939⅓	55	59	.482	1024	490	444	345	336	4.25

Selected by Milwaukee Brewers' organization in 15th round of free-agent draft, June 5, 1974.
†On disabled list, April 18 to June 28, 1975.
‡On disabled list, April 28 to May 20, 1983.

BENIGNO FELIX AYALA

Name pronounced Eye-AL-uh.

(Benny)

Born February 7, 1951, at Yauco, Puerto Rico.
Height, 6.01. Weight, 195.
Throws and bats righthanded.
Attended Puerto Rico Junior College, Rio Piedras, P. R.

Hit home run in first major league at bat, August 27, 1974.

Year Club	League	Pos.	G.	AB.	R.	H.	2B.	3B.	HR.	RBI.	B.A.	PO.	A.	E.	F.A.
1971—Visalia	Calif.	3B	21	46	3	10	0	1	1	7	.217	8	16	7	.774
1971—Pompano Beach	Fla. St.	3B-OF	63	208	38	58	7	4	8	34	.279	57	59	17	.872
1972—Visalia	Calif.	1B-OF	113	348	68	79	15	2	19	66	.227	442	38	22	.956
1973—Memphis	Texas	OF	136	462	69	119	17	6	17	68	.258	44	5	3	.942
1974—Tidewater	Int.	OF	92	288	41	79	21	1	11	40	.274	125	4	★16	.890
1974—New York	Nat.	OF	23	68	9	16	1	0	2	8	.235	37	1	3	.927
1975—Tidewater†	Int.	OF	65	177	24	49	13	0	6	28	.277	66	1	4	.944
1976—New York‡	Nat.	OF	22	26	2	3	0	0	1	2	.115	7	1	1	.889
1976—Tidewater	Int.	OF-1B	87	293	41	66	9	2	12	48	.225	47	2	3	.942
1977—New Orleans	A. A.	OF	126	450	71	134	27	5	18	73	.298	199	8	5	.976
1977—St. Louis	Nat.	OF	1	3	0	1	0	0	0	0	.333	6	1	0	1.000
1978—Springfield§	A. A.	OF	47	165	16	41	2	0	5	21	.248	70	1	3	.959
1978—Columbus xy	Int.	OF	59	203	30	69	11	4	6	35	.340	62	3	4	.942
1979—Rochester	Int.	OF	17	62	10	22	1	3	1	7	.355	37	0	2	.949
1979—Baltimore	Amer.	OF	42	86	15	22	5	0	6	13	.256	38	0	1	.974
1980—Baltimore	Amer.	OF	76	170	28	45	8	1	10	33	.265	20	2	0	1.000
1981—Baltimore	Amer.	OF	44	86	12	24	2	0	3	13	.279	3	2	0	1.000
1982—Baltimore	Amer.	OF-1B	64	128	17	39	6	0	6	24	.305	59	0	1	.983
1983—Baltimore	Amer.	OF	47	104	12	23	7	0	4	13	.221	41	0	2	.953
American League Totals		273	574	84	153	28	1	29	96	.267	161	4	4	.976
National League Totals		46	97	11	20	1	0	3	10	.206	50	3	4	.930
Major League Totals		319	671	95	173	29	1	32	106	.258	211	7	8	.965

Signed as free agent by New York Mets' organization, January 28, 1971.
†On disabled list, April 22 to May 29, 1975.
‡Traded to St. Louis Cardinals' organization for Infielder Doug Clarey, March 30, 1977.
§Loaned to Columbus (Pittsburgh Pirates' organization), June 21, 1978; returned, September 5, 1978.
xOn suspended list, August 27 to September 5, 1978.
yTraded to Baltimore Orioles' organization for Outfielder Mike Dimmel, January 16, 1979.

CHAMPIONSHIP SERIES RECORD

Year Club	League	Pos.	G.	AB.	R.	H.	2B.	3B.	HR.	RBI.	B.A.	PO.	A.	E.	F.A.
1983—Baltimore	Amer.	PH	1	0	0	0	0	0	0	1	.000	0	0	0	.000

WORLD SERIES RECORD

Year Club	League	Pos.	G.	AB.	R.	H.	2B.	3B.	HR.	RBI.	B.A.	PO.	A.	E.	F.A.
1979—Baltimore	Amer.	OF-PH	4	6	1	2	0	0	1	2	.333	4	0	0	1.000
1983—Baltimore	Amer.	PH	1	1	1	1	0	0	0	1	1.000	0	0	0	.000
World Series Totals		5	7	2	3	0	0	1	3	.429	4	0	0	1.000

WALTER WAYNE BACKMAN

(Wally)

Born September 22, 1959, at Hillsboro, Ore.
Height, 5.09. Weight, 160.
Throws right and bats right and lefthanded.

Led International League in bases on balls received with 87 in 1980.
Led Carolina League in caught stealing with 17 in 1978.

Year Club	League	Pos.	G.	AB.	R.	H.	2B.	3B.	HR.	RBI.	B.A.	PO.	A.	E.	F.A.
1977—Little Falls	NYP	SS-3B	69	255	44	83	10	2	6	30	.325	96	185	19	.937
1978—Lynchburg	Carol.	SS	132	494	86	149	19	●9	3	38	.302	★202	★329	30	★.947
1979—Jackson	Texas	SS-2B	110	404	63	114	11	5	2	19	.282	184	259	31	.935
1980—Tidewater	Int.	2B-SS	125	400	53	117	15	5	1	51	.293	237	320	22	.962
1980—New York	Nat.	2B-SS	27	93	12	30	1	1	0	9	.323	62	55	1	.992

Year Club League	Pos.	G.	AB.	R.	H.	2B.	3B.	HR.	RBI.	B.A.	PO.	A.	E.	F.A.
1981—New York.............. Nat.	2B-3B	26	36	5	10	2	0	0	0	.278	14	21	2	.946
1981—Tidewater†‡.......... Int.	SS-3B-2B	21	59	6	9	3	1	0	6	.153	12	38	1	.980
1982—New York§........... Nat.	2B-3B-SS	96	261	37	71	13	2	3	22	.272	173	209	16	.960
1983—New York............. Nat.	2B-3B	26	42	6	7	0	1	0	3	.167	16	15	2	.939
1983—Tidewater............. Int.	2B-SS-3B	101	361	69	114	11	3	1	28	.316	175	278	13	.972
Major League Totals.................		175	432	60	118	16	4	3	34	.273	265	300	21	.964

Selected by New York Mets' organization in 1st round (16th player selected) of free-agent draft, June 7, 1977.
†On suspended list, June 18 to June 20, 1981.
‡On disabled list, July 9 to September 1, 1981.
§On disabled list, August 15 to September 8, 1982.

HOWARD L. BAILEY III

Born July 31, 1958, at Grand Haven, Mich.
Height, 6.03. Weight, 195.
Throws left and bats righthanded.
Attended Grand Valley State College, Allendale, Mich.

Led American Association in hit batsmen with 10, wild pitches with 13 and tied for lead in shutouts with 2 in 1982.
Led Southern League in hit batsmen with 22 in 1980.
Led Florida State League in home runs allowed with 11, hit batsmen with 12 and tied for lead in intentional bases on balls issued with 10 in 1979.

Year Club League	G.	IP.	W.	L.	Pct.	H.	R.	ER.	SO.	BB.	ERA.
1979—Lakeland......................... Florida St.	25	142	8	12	.400	147	83	★72	76	64	4.56
1980—Montgomery.................... Southern	27	186	12	12	.500	174	84	71	132	55	3.44
1981—Detroit............................ American	9	37	1	4	.200	45	31	30	17	13	7.30
1981—Evansville†..................... Am. Assoc.	17	86	2	7	.222	101	61	48	56	41	5.02
1982—Evansville .... Am. Assoc.	26	153⅔	11	10	.524	169	89	71	83	64	4.16
1982—Detroit............................ American	8	10	0	0	.000	6	0	0	3	2	0.00
1983—Detroit............................ American	33	72	5	5	.500	69	45	39	21	25	4.88
Major League Totals.................	50	119	6	9	.400	120	76	69	41	40	5.22

Signed as free agent by Detroit Tigers' organization, August 26, 1978.
†On disabled list, August 24 to September 1, 1981.

ROBERT MICHAEL BAILOR
(Bob)

Born July 10, 1951, at Connellsville, Pa.
Height, 5.10. Weight, 160.
Throws and bats righthanded.
Attended California State College, California, Pa.

Led American League outfielders in double plays with 7 in 1978.
Led California League in stolen bases with 63 in 1972.
Led Southern League shortstops in double plays with 85 in 1973 and tied for International League lead with 64 in 1975.
Led California League shortstops in putouts with 218 and errors with 53 in 1972.

Year Club League	Pos.	G.	AB.	R.	H.	2B.	3B.	HR.	RBI.	B.A.	PO.	A.	E.	F.A.
1970—Bluefield .... Appal.	2-O-3-S-P	46	121	18	33	3	0	0	8	.273	53	43	6	.941
1971—Aberdeen.............. North.	S-3-O-2	68	268	★71	★91	11	2	2	50	★.340	92	140	32	.879
1972—Lodi........................ Calif.	SS-OF-2B	129	528	95	153	16	3	2	34	.290	241	330	54	.914
1973—Asheville.............. South.	SS	115	468	77	137	23	3	0	29	.293	★222	386	22	★.965
1973—Rochester............. Int.	SS	17	47	5	13	1	0	1	4	.277	30	34	4	.941
1974—Rochester............. Int.	S-O-3-2	96	330	45	76	13	3	1	25	.230	174	160	13	.963
1975—Rochester............. Int.	SS	129	★501	68	147	19	6	5	39	.293	198	★386	★32	.948
1975—Baltimore.............. Amer.	SS-2B	5	7	0	1	0	0	0	0	.143	5	9	0	1.000
1976—Rochester†........... Int.	3B-SS-OF	36	103	21	32	10	1	1	12	.311	10	24	0	1.000
1976—Baltimore‡ .... Amer.	SS	9	6	2	2	0	1	0	0	.333	0	0	0	.000
1977—Toronto .... Amer.	OF-SS	122	496	62	154	21	5	5	32	.310	235	165	12	.971
1978—Toronto .... Amer.	OF-3B-SS	154	621	74	164	29	7	1	52	.264	329	82	15	.965
1979—Toronto .... Amer.	OF-3B	130	414	50	95	11	5	1	38	.229	217	32	3	.988
1980—Toronto§ x........... Amer.	O-S-3-2-P	117	347	44	82	14	2	1	16	.236	233	61	2	.933
1981—New York y .... Nat.	S-2-O-3	51	81	11	23	3	1	0	8	.284	43	60	4	.963
1982—New York............. Nat.	SS-2-3-O	110	376	44	104	14	1	0	31	.277	166	272	11	.976
1983—New York za......... Nat.	S-2-3-O	118	340	33	85	8	0	1	30	.250	171	296	16	.967
American League Totals.............		537	1891	232	498	75	20	8	138	.263	1019	349	32	.977
National League Totals.............		279	797	88	212	25	2	1	69	.266	380	628	31	.970
Major League Totals.................		816	2688	320	710	100	22	9	207	.264	1399	977	63	.974

Signed as free agent by Baltimore Orioles' organization, August 13, 1969.
†On Baltimore supplemental disabled list, April 14 to June 7; on Rochester disabled list, June 8 to June 18 and August 1 to August 16, 1976.
‡Selected by Toronto Blue Jays in American League expansion draft, November 5, 1976.
§On supplemental disabled list, June 12 to July 3, 1980.
xTraded to New York Mets for Pitcher Roy Lee Jackson, December 12, 1980.
yOn supplemental disabled list, March 31 to April 21, 1981.
zOn supplemental disabled list, May 1 to May 17, 1983.
aTraded to Los Angeles Dodgers, December 9, 1983, completing deal in which Los Angeles traded Pitcher Sid Fernandez and Infielder Ross Jones to New York Mets for Pitcher Carlos Diaz and a player to be named later, December 8, 1983.

PITCHING RECORD

Year—Club	League	G.	IP.	W.	L.	Pct.	H.	R.	ER.	SO.	BB.	ERA.
1970—Bluefield	Ap'lachian	1	1	0	0	.000	7	8	8	1	2	72.00
1980—Toronto	American	3	2	0	0	.000	4	2	2	0	1	9.00
Major League Totals		3	2	0	0	.000	4	2	2	0	1	9.00

HAROLD DOUGLASS BAINES

Born March 15, 1959, at St. Michaels, Md.
Height, 6.02. Weight, 175.
Throws and bats lefthanded.

Hit three home runs in a game, July 7, 1982.
Led American League in game-winning RBIs with 22 in 1983.
Tied for American Association lead in double plays by outfielders with 4 in 1979.

Year—Club	League	Pos.	G.	AB.	R.	H.	2B.	3B.	HR.	RBI.	B.A.	PO.	A.	E.	F.A.
1977—Appleton	Midw.	OF	69	222	37	58	11	2	5	29	.261	94	10	7	.937
1978—Knoxville	South.	OF-1B	137	502	70	138	16	6	13	72	.275	291	22	13	.960
1979—Iowa	A. A.	OF	125	466	87	139	25	8	22	87	.298	222	●16	11	.956
1980—Chicago	Amer.	OF	141	491	55	125	23	6	13	49	.255	229	6	9	.963
1981—Chicago	Amer.	OF	82	280	42	80	11	7	10	41	.286	120	10	2	.985
1982—Chicago	Amer.	OF	161	608	89	165	29	8	25	105	.271	326	10	7	.980
1983—Chicago	Amer.	OF	156	596	76	167	32	3	20	99	.280	312	10	9	.973
Major League Totals			540	1975	262	537	95	24	68	294	.272	987	36	27	.974

Selected by Chicago White Sox' organization in 1st round (first player selected) of free-agent draft, June 7, 1977.

CHAMPIONSHIP SERIES RECORD

Year—Club	League	Pos.	G.	AB.	R.	H.	2B.	3B.	HR.	RBI.	B.A.	PO.	A.	E.	F.A.
1983—Chicago	Amer.	OF	4	16	0	2	0	0	0	0	.125	5	1	0	1.000

CHARLES DOUGLAS BAIR
(Doug)

Born August 22, 1949, at Defiance, O.
Height, 6.00. Weight, 180.
Throws and bats righthanded.
Received bachelor of science degree in industrial education from
Bowling Green State University, Bowling Green, O.

Major League saves: 1977 (8), 1978 (28), 1979 (16), 1980 (6), 1981 (1), 1982 (8), 1983 (5). Total—72.
Led Carolina League in complete games with 15 in 1972.
Named Carolina League Pitcher of the Year, 1972.

Year—Club	League	G.	IP.	W.	L.	Pct.	H.	R.	ER.	SO.	BB.	ERA.
1971—Salem†	Carolina	6	29	2	3	.400	35	22	19	18	26	5.90
1971—Waterbury	Eastern	1	7	1	0	1.000	5	0	0	2	0	0.00
1972—Salem	Carolina	24	180	15	7	.682	170	●86	57	186	★95	2.85
1972—Charleston	Int'national	1	4	0	1	.000	5	3	3	5	0	6.75
1973—Charleston	Int'national	26	158	7	11	.389	173	103	77	94	87	4.39
1974—Charleston‡	Int'national	26	170	7	★16	.304	166	87	77	117	91	4.08
1975—Charleston	Int'national	26	167	9	12	.429	157	72	56	113	58	3.02
1976—Charleston	Int'national	45	122	7	10	.412	102	48	43	108	57	3.17
1976—Pittsburgh§	National	4	6	0	0	.000	4	4	4	4	5	6.00
1977—San Jose	P. Coast	20	33	5	2	.714	24	8	8	49	17	2.18
1977—Oakland x	American	45	83	4	6	.400	78	39	32	68	57	3.47
1978—Cincinnati	National	70	100	7	6	.538	87	23	22	91	38	1.98
1979—Cincinnati	National	65	94	11	7	.611	93	47	45	86	51	4.31
1980—Cincinnati	National	61	85	3	6	.333	91	42	40	62	39	4.24
1981—Cincinnati y-St. Louis	National	35	55	4	2	.667	55	34	31	30	19	5.07
1982—St. Louis	National	63	91⅔	5	3	.625	69	27	26	68	36	2.55
1983—St. Louis z	National	26	29⅔	1	1	.500	24	11	10	21	13	3.03
1983—Detroit a	American	27	55⅔	7	3	.700	51	27	24	39	19	3.88
National League Totals		324	461⅓	31	25	.554	423	188	178	362	201	3.47
American League Totals		72	138⅔	11	9	.550	129	66	56	107	76	3.63
Major League Totals		396	600	42	34	.553	552	254	234	469	277	3.51

Selected by Pittsburgh Pirates' organization in 2nd round of free-agent draft, June 8, 1971.
†On temporary inactive list, June 23 to July 22, 1971.
‡Conditionally released to Detroit Tigers' organization, December 17, 1974; returned, March 28, 1975.
§Traded with Pitchers Doc Medich, Dave Giusti and Rick Langford, Outfielders Mitchell Page and Tony Armas to Oakland A's for Infielders Phil Garner and Tommy Helms, and Pitcher Chris Batton, March 15, 1977.
xTraded to Cincinnati Reds for First Baseman Dave Revering and cash, February 25, 1978.
yTraded to St. Louis Cardinals for Pitcher Joe Edelen and Second Baseman Neil Fiala, September 10, 1981.
zTraded to Detroit Tigers for a player to be named later, June 21, 1983; St. Louis Cardinals acquired Pitcher Dave Rucker to complete deal, July 5, 1983.
aGranted free agency, November 7, 1983; re-signed by Tigers, December 24, 1983.

CHAMPIONSHIP SERIES RECORD

Year—Club	League	G.	IP.	W.	L.	Pct.	H.	R.	ER.	SO.	BB.	ERA.
1979—Cincinnati	National	1	1	0	1	.000	2	1	1	0	1	9.00
1982—St. Louis	National	1	1	0	0	.000	2	0	0	0	3	0.00
Championship Series Totals		2	2	0	1	.000	4	1	1	0	4	4.50

Year	Club	League	G.	IP.	W.	L.	Pct.	H.	R.	ER.	SO.	BB.	ERA.
1982—St. Louis		National	3	2	0	1	.000	2	2	2	3	2	9.00

DAVID GLENN BAKER
(Dave)

Born November 8, 1956, at Des Moines, Iowa.
Height, 6.00. Weight, 185.
Throws right and bats lefthanded.
Attended University of California at Los Angeles, Los Angeles, Calif.
Brother of Doug Baker, shortstop in Detroit Tigers' organization.
Led International League third basemen in total chances with 409 and double plays with 27 in 1983.

Year	Club	League	Pos.	G.	AB.	R.	H.	2B.	3B.	HR.	RBI.	B.A.	PO.	A.	E.	F.A.
1978—Dunedin	Fla. St.		3B	76	266	43	72	15	5	8	39	.271	45	145	4	.979
1979—Syracuse	Int.		3B-SS	116	396	42	88	17	5	7	43	.222	78	188	19	.933
1980—Syracuse	Int.		3B	34	101	9	18	2	2	1	11	.178	26	61	4	.956
1980—Knoxville	South.		3B	98	341	44	82	16	4	12	56	.240	54	197	29	.896
1981—Syracuse	Int.		3B	116	367	38	88	13	0	6	40	.240	66	203	15	.947
1982—Syracuse	Int.		3-2-1-O	116	369	52	103	19	2	16	63	.279	113	231	17	.953
1982—Toronto†	Amer.		3B	9	20	3	5	1	0	0	2	.250	5	16	5	.808
1983—Toledo	Int.		3B	∗140	518	71	144	22	1	14	88	.278	∗82	∗305	22	.946
Major League Totals				9	20	3	5	1	0	0	2	.250	5	16	5	.808

Selected by St. Louis Cardinals' organization in 23rd round of free-agent draft, June 5, 1974.
Selected by Toronto Blue Jays' organization in 11th round of free-agent draft, June 6, 1978.
†Traded to Toledo (Minnesota Twins' organization) for Pitcher Don Cooper, December 10, 1982.

JOHNNIE B. BAKER JR.
(Dusty)

Born June 15, 1949, at Riverside, Calif.
Height, 6.02. Weight, 200.
Throws and bats righthanded.
Attended American River Junior College, Sacramento, Calif.
Tied major league records for most plate appearances, most at bats and most times faced pitcher as batsman, inning (3), September 20, 1972 (second game of doubleheader).
Established National League record for fewest chances accepted by outfielder, season, 150 or more games (235), 1977.
Led National League outfielders in total chances with 407 in 1973.
Named outfielder on THE SPORTING NEWS National League All-Star Team, 1980.
Named outfielder on THE SPORTING NEWS National League All-Star fielding team, 1981.
Named outfielder on THE SPORTING NEWS National League Silver Slugger team, 1980 and 1981.

Year	Club	League	Pos.	G.	AB.	R.	H.	2B.	3B.	HR.	RBI.	B.A.	PO.	A.	E.	F.A.
1967—Austin	Texas		OF	9	39	6	9	1	0	0	1	.231	17	0	1	.944
1968—W. Palm B'ch†	Fla. St.		OF	6	21	2	4	0	0	0	2	.190	6	2	0	1.000
1968—Greenwood	W. Car.		OF	52	199	45	68	11	3	6	39	.342	82	1	3	.965
1968—Atlanta	Nat.		OF	6	5	0	2	0	0	0	0	.400	0	0	0	.000
1969—Shreveport	Texas		OF	73	265	40	68	5	1	9	31	.257	135	10	3	.980
1969—Richmond	Int.		OF-3B	25	89	7	22	4	0	0	8	.247	40	9	4	.925
1969—Atlanta	Nat.		OF	3	7	0	0	0	0	0	0	.000	2	0	0	1.000
1970—Richmond	Int.		OF	118	461	97	150	29	3	11	51	.325	236	10	7	.972
1970—Atlanta	Nat.		OF	13	24	3	7	0	0	0	4	.292	11	1	3	.800
1971—Richmond	Int.		OF-3B	80	341	62	106	23	2	11	41	.311	136	13	4	.974
1971—Atlanta	Nat.		OF	29	62	2	14	2	0	0	4	.226	29	1	0	1.000
1972—Atlanta‡	Nat.		OF	127	446	62	143	27	2	17	76	.321	344	8	4	.989
1973—Atlanta	Nat.		OF	159	604	101	174	29	4	21	99	.288	∗390	10	7	.983
1974—Atlanta	Nat.		OF	149	574	80	147	35	0	20	69	.256	359	10	7	.981
1975—Atlanta§	Nat.		OF	142	494	63	129	18	2	19	72	.261	287	10	3	.990
1976—Los Angeles	Nat.		OF	112	384	36	93	13	0	4	39	.242	254	3	1	.996
1977—Los Angeles	Nat.		OF	153	533	86	155	26	1	30	86	.291	227	8	3	.987
1978—Los Angeles	Nat.		OF	149	522	62	137	24	1	11	66	.262	250	13	4	.985
1979—Los Angeles	Nat.		OF	151	554	86	152	29	1	23	88	.274	289	14	3	.990
1980—Los Angeles	Nat.		OF	153	579	80	170	26	4	29	97	.294	308	5	3	.991
1981—Los Angeles	Nat.		OF	103	400	48	128	17	3	9	49	.320	181	8	2	.990
1982—Los Angeles	Nat.		OF	147	570	80	171	19	1	23	88	.300	226	7	6	.975
1983—Los Angeles	Nat.		OF	149	531	71	138	25	1	15	73	.260	249	4	5	.981
Major League Totals				1745	6289	860	1760	290	20	221	910	.280	3406	102	51	.986

Selected by Atlanta Braves' organization in 26th round of free-agent draft, June 6, 1967.
†On restricted list, April 5 to June 13, 1968.
‡On military list, June 17 to July 3, 1972.
§Traded with First Baseman-Third Baseman Ed Goodson to Los Angeles Dodgers for Outfielder Jimmy Wynn, Second Baseman Lee Lacy, First Baseman-Outfielder Tom Paciorek and Infielder Jerry Royster, November 17, 1975.

DIVISION SERIES RECORD

Year	Club	League	Pos.	G.	AB.	R.	H.	2B.	3B.	HR.	RBI.	B.A.	PO.	A.	E.	F.A.
1981—Los Angeles	Nat.		OF	5	18	2	3	1	0	0	1	.167	12	0	0	1.000

Tied Championship Series records for highest batting average, four-game Series (.467), 1978; most home runs with bases filled, game (1), October 5, 1977; most runs batted in, four-game Series (8), 1977; most runs batted in, inning (4), October 5, 1977 (fourth inning).

Tied National League Championship Series records for most consecutive hits, one Series (4), 1978; most hits, game (4), October 7, 1978.

Year	Club	League	Pos.	G.	AB.	R.	H.	2B.	3B.	HR.	RBI.	B.A.	PO.	A.	E.	F.A.
1977—Los Angeles		Nat.	OF	4	14	4	5	1	0	2	8	.357	3	0	0	1.000
1978—Los Angeles		Nat.	OF	4	15	1	7	2	0	0	1	.467	5	0	0	1.000
1981—Los Angeles		Nat.	OF	5	19	3	6	1	0	0	3	.316	10	0	1	.909
1983—Los Angeles		Nat.	OF	4	14	4	5	1	0	1	1	.357	9	0	0	1.000
Championship Series Totals				17	62	12	23	5	0	3	13	.371	27	0	1	.964

WORLD SERIES RECORD

Year	Club	League	Pos.	G.	AB.	R.	H.	2B.	3B.	HR.	RBI.	B.A.	PO.	A.	E.	F.A.
1977—Los Angeles		Nat.	OF	6	24	4	7	0	0	1	5	.292	11	0	1	.917
1978—Los Angeles		Nat.	OF	6	21	2	5	0	0	1	1	.238	12	0	0	1.000
1981—Los Angeles		Nat.	OF	6	24	3	4	0	0	0	1	.167	13	0	0	1.000
World Series Totals				18	69	9	16	0	0	2	7	.232	36	0	1	.973

ALL-STAR GAME RECORD

Year	League	Pos.	AB.	R.	H.	2B.	3B.	HR.	RBI.	B.A.	PO.	A.	E.	F.A.
1981—National		OF	2	0	1	0	0	0	0	.500	2	0	0	1.000
1982—National		OF	2	0	0	0	0	0	0	.000	0	0	0	.000
All-Star Game Totals			4	0	1	0	0	0	0	.250	2	0	0	1.000

STEVEN BYRNE BAKER
(Steve)

Born August 30, 1956, at Eugene, Ore.
Height, 6.00. Weight, 200.
Throws and bats righthanded.
Attended University of Oregon, Eugene, Ore. and
Grossmont Junior College, San Diego, Calif.
Brother of Richard Baker, pitcher in Milwaukee Brewers' organization, 1973 and 1974.

Tied for American Association lead in shutouts with 3 in 1978.

Year	Club	League	G.	IP.	W.	L.	Pct.	H.	R.	ER.	SO.	BB.	ERA.
1976—Lakeland		Florida St.	19	97	5	4	.556	83	38	27	60	61	2.51
1977—Montgomery†		Southern	15	69	4	5	.444	65	44	33	71	35	4.30
1978—Evansville		Am. Assoc.	16	101	8	1	.889	93	39	36	87	53	3.21
1978—Detroit		American	15	63	2	4	.333	66	37	32	39	42	4.57
1979—Detroit		American	21	84	1	7	.125	97	63	62	54	51	6.64
1979—Evansville		Am. Assoc.	5	14	0	2	.000	18	13	12	15	10	7.71
1980—Evansville‡		Am. Assoc.	9	34	1	3	.250	43	27	25	18	23	6.62
1980—Syracuse		Int'national	17	107	6	5	.545	93	47	38	54	68	3.20
1981—Syracuse§		Int'national	30	160	8	14	.364	170	94	81	79	77	4.56
1982—Tacoma x		P. Coast	23	163	13	5	.722	147	65	45	79	68	2.48
1982—Oakland		American	5	25⅔	1	1	.500	30	14	13	14	4	4.56
1983—Oakland		American	35	54	3	3	.500	59	32	26	23	26	4.33
1983—Tacoma y		P. Coast	13	85	4	9	.308	75	49	43	67	30	4.55
1983—St. Louis		National	8	10	0	1	.000	10	4	2	1	4	1.80
American League Totals			76	226⅔	7	15	.318	252	146	133	130	123	5.28
National League Totals			8	10	0	1	.000	10	4	2	1	4	1.80
Major League Totals			84	236⅔	7	16	.304	262	150	135	131	127	5.13

Selected by New York Mets' organization in 18th round of free-agent draft, June 5, 1974.
Signed as free agent by Detroit Tigers' organization, May 10, 1976.
†On disabled list, May 2 to July 24, 1977.
‡Sold to Syracuse (Toronto Blue Jays' organization), June 6, 1980.
§Released, January 28, 1982; signed by Tacoma (Oakland A's organization), March 9, 1982.
xOn disabled list, June 3 to July 6, 1982.
yTraded to St. Louis Cardinals for two players to be named later, September 2, 1983; Oakland A's organization acquired Pitchers Tom Dozier and Jim Strichek to complete deal, September 16, 1983.

STEPHEN CHARLES BALBONI
(Steve)

Born January 16, 1957, at Brockton, Mass.
Height, 6.03. Weight, 225.
Throws and bats righthanded.
Attended Eckerd College, St. Petersburg, Fla.

Led International League batters in strikeouts with 146 in 1981.
Led Southern League in total bases with 288 and intentional bases on balls received with 17 in 1980.
Led Florida State League batters in strikeouts with 154 in 1979.
Led Florida State League first basemen in double plays with 106 in 1979 and Southern League first basemen with 125 in 1980.
Named Southern League Most Valuable Player, 1980.
Named Florida State League Most Valuable Player, 1979.

Year Club League	Pos.	G.	AB.	R.	H.	2B.	3B.	HR.	RBI.	B.A.	PO.	A.	E.	F.A.
1978—West Haven .... East.	DH	2	2	0	0	0	0	0	0	.000	0	0	0	.000
1978—Ft. Lauderdale ..... Fla. St.	1B	60	176	19	36	5	0	1	19	.205	475	19	4	.992
1979—Ft. Lauderdale ..... Fla. St.	1B	*140	*504	69	127	19	2	*26	*91	.252	*1297	*97	11	*.992
1980—Nashville................ South.	1B	141	521	*101	157	25	2	*34	*122	.301	*1218	76	13	*.990
1981—Columbus............... Int.	1B	125	434	68	107	21	2	*33	*98	.247	631	55	*14	.980
1981—New York............. Amer.	1B	4	7	2	2	1	1	0	2	.286	14	1	0	1.000
1982—Columbus............... Int.	1B	83	313	57	89	17	1	*32	86	.284	426	38	8	.983
1982—New York............. Amer.	1B	33	107	8	20	2	1	2	4	.187	194	13	2	.990
1983—Columbus............... Int.	1B	84	317	72	87	14	0	27	81	.274	479	47	11	.980
1983—New York†........... Amer.	1B	32	86	8	20	2	0	5	17	.233	178	9	3	.984
Major League Totals.....................		69	200	18	42	5	2	7	23	.210	386	23	5	.988

Selected by New York Yankees' organization in 4th round of free-agent draft, June 6, 1978.

†Traded with Pitcher Roger Erickson to Kansas City Royals for Pitcher Mike Armstrong and Catcher Duane Dewey, December 8, 1983.

JAY SCOT BALLER

Born October 6, 1960, at Stayton, Ore.
Height, 6.06. Weight, 215.
Throws and bats righthanded.

Led International League in hit batsmen with 12 in 1983.
Led Eastern League in hit batsmen with 12 in 1982.
Led South Atlantic League in hit batsmen with 10 in 1980.
Led Pioneer League in home runs allowed with 9 in 1979.

Year Club League	G.	IP.	W.	L.	Pct.	H.	R.	ER.	SO.	BB.	ERA.
1979—Helena............................. Pioneer	13	67	5	6	.455	89	59	43	68	34	5.78
1980—Spartanburg.................... S. Atlantic	26	139	10	5	.667	132	69	55	95	72	3.56
1981—Peninsula........................ Carolina	27	147	9	14	.391	119	85	64	166	78	3.92
1982—Reading.......................... Eastern	50	151⅓	9	8	.529	110	64	45	155	85	*2.68
1982—Philadelphia† .... National	4	8	0	0	.000	7	4	3	7	2	3.38
1983—Charleston...................... Int'national	20	78⅔	4	12	.250	91	79	77	62	66	8.81
1983—Buffalo........................... Eastern	16	34⅔	1	2	.333	32	34	29	35	35	7.53
Major League Totals........................	4	8	0	0	.000	7	4	3	7	2	3.38

Selected by Philadelphia Phillies' organization in 3rd round of free-agent draft, June 5, 1979.

†Traded with Second Baseman Manny Trillo, Outfielder George Vukovich, Infielder Julio Franco and Catcher Gerry Willard to Cleveland Indians for Outfielder Von Hayes, December 9, 1982.

CHRISTOPHER MICHAEL BANDO
(Chris)

Born February 4, 1956, at Cleveland, O.
Height, 6.00. Weight, 195.
Throws right and bats left and righthanded
Attended Arizona State University, Tempe, Ariz.
Brother of Sal Bando, infielder with Kansas City Athletics, Oakland A's and
Milwaukee Brewers, 1966 through 1981; Milwaukee Brewers' Special Assistant
to the General Manager, 1982; and coach with Milwaukee Brewers, 1983.

Received reported $25,000 bonus to sign with Cleveland Indians, 1978.

Year Club League	Pos.	G.	AB.	R.	H.	2B.	3B.	HR.	RBI.	B.A.	PO.	A.	E.	F.A.
1978—Chattanooga .... South.	C	76	241	30	55	12	0	4	21	.228	285	51	10	.971
1979—Chattanooga† .... South.	C-3B	21	62	5	15	4	1	0	7	.242	61	13	0	1.000
1980—Chattanooga‡ ...... South.	C-3B	121	404	78	141	31	3	12	73	*.349	480	97	12	.980
1981—Charleston............ Int.	C-3B	96	320	47	98	16	2	11	45	.306	414	51	10	.979
1981—Cleveland.............. Amer.	C	21	47	3	10	3	0	0	6	.213	53	5	2	.967
1982—Cleveland§............ Amer.	C-3B	66	184	13	39	6	1	3	16	.212	268	23	3	.990
1983—Cleveland............. Amer.	C	48	121	15	31	3	0	4	15	.256	170	19	1	.995
Major League Totals.....................		135	352	31	80	12	1	7	37	.227	491	47	6	.989

Selected by Milwaukee Brewers' organization in 22nd round of free-agent draft, June 7, 1977.
Selected by Cleveland Indians' organization in 2nd round of free-agent draft, June 6, 1978.
†On disabled list, April 16 to August 9, 1979.
‡On disabled list, April 24 to May 6, 1980.
§On disabled list, May 2 to June 17, 1982.

DARRYL DWAYNE BANKS

Born June 12, 1960, at Reno, Nev.
Height, 6.02. Weight 205.
Throws and bats righthanded.
Attended College of Southern Idaho, Twin Falls, Ida.

Tied for Texas League lead in games started by pitchers with 27 in 1983.
Led New York-Pennsylvania League in hit batsmen with 7 in 1980 and tied for lead with 6 in 1981.

Year Club League	G.	IP.	W.	L.	Pct.	H.	R.	ER.	SO.	BB.	ERA.
1980—Geneva............... NYP	12	64	3	4	.429	49	44	36	37	16	5.06
1981—Geneva............... NYP	10	50	1	5	.167	46	38	34	28	42	6.12
1982—Quad City......................... Midwest	31	162⅔	13	6	.684	154	79	59	137	75	3.26
1983—Midland............................. Texas	27	163	12	11	.522	187	109	99	97	71	5.47

Selected by Pittsburgh Pirates' organization in 1st round (24th player selected) of free-agent draft, January 8, 1980.
Selected by Chicago Cubs' organization in secondary phase of free-agent draft, June 3, 1980.

ALAN BANNISTER

Born September 3, 1951, at Montebello, Calif.
Height, 5.11. Weight, 175.
Throws and bats righthanded.
Attended Arizona State University, Tempe, Ariz., and California State University
at Long Beach, Long Beach, Calif.

Tied for American League lead in sacrifice flies with 11 in 1977.
Led International League shortstops in errors with 24 in 1974.
Received reported $85,000 bonus to sign with Philadelphia Phillies, 1973.

Year Club	League	Pos.	G.	AB.	R.	H.	2B.	3B.	HR.	RBI.	B.A.	PO.	A.	E.	F.A.
1973—Eugene	P. C.	2-3-S-O	130	460	72	105	17	2	4	46	.228	207	342	27	.953
1974—Toledo	Int.	SS-OF	94	343	56	99	17	7	4	40	.289	164	173	27	.926
1974—Philadelphia	Nat.	OF-SS	26	25	4	3	0	0	0	1	.120	10	0	0	1.000
1975—Philadelphia†	Nat.	OF-SS-2B	24	61	10	16	3	1	0	0	.262	54	4	2	.967
1975—Toledo	Int.	OF	101	335	50	74	7	3	5	27	.221	209	3	6	.972
1976—Iowa	A. A.	SS	32	118	24	29	6	0	3	12	.246	64	106	9	.950
1976—Chicago	Amer.	O-S-2-3	73	145	19	36	6	2	0	8	.248	92	36	5	.962
1977—Chicago	Amer.	*S-2-O	139	560	87	154	20	3	3	57	.275	265	331	*40	.937
1978—Chicago‡	Amer.	OF-SS-2B	49	107	16	24	3	2	0	8	.224	34	16	2	.962
1979—Chicago	Amer.	2-O-3-1	136	506	71	144	28	8	2	55	.285	250	187	21	.954
1980—Chi.§-Clev.	Amer.	O-2-3-S	126	392	57	111	23	4	1	41	.283	189	153	14	.961
1981—Cleveland	Amer.	O-1-2-S	68	232	36	61	11	1	1	17	.263	129	76	3	.986
1982—Cleveland xy	Amer.	O-2-S-3	101	348	40	93	16	1	4	41	.267	207	124	10	.971
1983—Cleveland	Amer.	OF-2B-1B	117	377	51	100	25	4	5	45	.265	186	66	7	.973
American League Totals			809	2667	377	723	132	25	16	272	.271	1352	989	102	.958
National League Totals			50	86	14	19	3	1	0	1	.221	64	4	2	.971
Major League Totals			859	2753	391	742	135	26	16	273	.270	1416	993	104	.959

Selected by California Angels' organization in 1st round (fifth player selected) of free-agent draft, June 5, 1969.
Selected by Philadelphia Phillies' organization in 1st round (first player selected) of free-agent draft, January 10, 1973.

†Traded with Pitchers Dick Ruthven and Roy Thomas to Chicago White Sox for Pitcher Jim Kaat and Shortstop Mike Buskey, December 10, 1975.
‡On emergency disabled list, July 29, 1978 through remainder of season.
§Traded to Cleveland Indians for Catcher-Outfielder Ron Pruitt, June 14, 1980.
xOn supplemental disabled list, July 16 to August 16, 1982.
yGranted free agency, November 10, 1982; re-signed by Indians, January 27, 1983.

FLOYD FRANKLIN BANNISTER

Born June 10, 1955, at Pierre, S. Dakota.
Height, 6.01. Weight, 195.
Throws and bats lefthanded.
Attended Arizona State University, Tempe, Ariz.
Brother-in-law of Greg Cochran, pitcher in Oakland A's and New York Yankees'
organizations, 1975 through 1982.

Named College Player of the Year by THE SPORTING NEWS, 1976.

Year Club	League	G.	IP.	W.	L.	Pct.	H.	R.	ER.	SO.	BB.	ERA.
1976—Covington	Ap'lachian	3	13	0	0	.000	3	0	0	27	2	0.00
1976—Columbus	Southern	3	24	1	0	1.000	16	4	4	20	14	1.50
1976—Memphis	Int'national	1	6	1	0	1.000	7	1	1	6	3	1.50
1977—Houston†	National	24	143	8	9	.471	138	70	64	112	68	4.03
1978—Houston‡	National	28	110	3	9	.250	120	59	59	94	63	4.83
1979—Seattle	American	30	182	10	15	.400	185	92	82	115	68	4.05
1980—Seattle	American	32	218	9	13	.409	200	96	84	155	66	3.47
1981—Seattle§	American	21	121	9	9	.500	128	62	60	85	39	4.46
1982—Seattle x	American	35	247	12	13	.480	225	112	94	*209	77	3.43
1983—Chicago	American	34	217⅓	16	10	.615	191	88	81	193	71	3.35
National League Totals		52	253	11	18	.379	258	129	123	206	131	4.38
American League Totals		152	985⅓	56	60	.483	929	450	401	757	321	3.66
Major League Totals		204	1238⅓	67	78	.462	1187	579	524	963	452	3.81

Selected by Oakland A's organization in 3rd round of free-agent draft, June 5, 1973.
Selected by Houston Astros' organization in 1st round (first player selected) of free-agent draft, June 8, 1976.
†On disabled list, July 26 to August 22, 1977.
‡Traded to Seattle Mariners for Shortstop Craig Reynolds, December 8, 1978.
§On disabled list, August 8 to August 29, 1981.
xGranted free agency, November 10, 1982; signed by Chicago White Sox, December 13, 1982.

CHAMPIONSHIP SERIES RECORD

Year Club	League	G.	IP.	W.	L.	Pct.	H.	R.	ER.	SO.	BB.	ERA.
1983—Chicago	American	1	6	0	1	.000	5	4	3	5	1	4.50

ALL-STAR GAME RECORD

Year League		IP.	W.	L.	Pct.	H.	R.	ER.	SO.	BB.	ERA.
1982—American		1	0	0	.000	1	0	0	0	0	0.00

JESSE LEE BARFIELD

Born October 29, 1959, at Joliet, Ill.
Height, 6.01. Weight, 190.
Throws and bats righthanded.

Led Florida State League batters in strikeouts with 125 in 1978.

Year Club	League	Pos.	G.	AB.	R.	H.	2B.	3B.	HR.	RBI.	B.A.	PO.	A.	E.	F.A.
1977—Utica	NYP	OF	70	234	37	53	9	3	5	35	.226	122	6	●13	.908
1978—Dunedin	Fla. St.	OF	133	441	40	91	12	3	2	34	.206	229	★22	★15	.944
1979—Kinston	Carol.	OF	136	477	66	126	24	5	8	71	.264	284	19	17	.947
1980—Knoxville†	South.	OF	124	433	63	104	12	8	14	65	.240	309	14	12	.964
1981—Knoxville	South.	OF	141	524	83	137	24	13	16	70	.261	270	★23	6	.980
1981—Toronto	Amer.	OF	25	95	7	22	3	2	2	9	.232	71	2	0	1.000
1982—Toronto	Amer.	OF	139	394	54	97	13	2	18	58	.246	217	15	9	.963
1983—Toronto	Amer.	OF	128	388	58	98	13	3	27	68	.253	213	16	8	.966
Major League Totals			292	877	119	217	29	7	47	135	.247	501	33	17	.969

Selected by Toronto Blue Jays' organization in 9th round of free-agent draft, June 7, 1977.
†On disabled list, August 15 to August 29, 1980.

GREGORY ROBERT BARGAR
(Greg)

Born January 27, 1959, at Inglewood, Calif.
Height, 6.02. Weight, 185.
Throws and bats righthanded.
Attended El Camino College, Torrance, Calif.,
and University of Arizona, Tucson, Ariz.

Year Club	League	G.	IP.	W.	L.	Pct.	H.	R.	ER.	SO.	BB.	ERA.
1980—Memphis	Southern	14	86	5	5	.500	95	52	48	54	48	5.02
1981—Memphis	Southern	9	65	5	2	.714	58	29	26	52	27	3.60
1981—Denver	Am. Assoc.	23	91	5	6	.455	108	63	61	58	58	6.03
1982—Wichita	Am. Assoc.	9	31⅓	0	4	.000	53	45	39	18	22	11.20
1982—Memphis	Southern	16	118⅔	5	6	.455	100	61	54	124	63	4.10
1983—Memphis	Southern	8	59	4	4	.500	51	25	20	50	28	3.05
1983—Wichita	Am. Assoc.	12	73⅓	6	2	.750	78	41	38	53	32	4.66
1983—Montreal	National	8	20	2	0	1.000	23	15	15	9	8	6.75
Major League Totals		8	20	2	0	1.000	23	15	15	9	8	6.75

Selected by St. Louis Cardinals' organization in 10th round of free-agent draft, January 9, 1979.
Selected by Montreal Expos' organization in 3rd round of free-agent draft, June 3, 1980.

LEONARD HAROLD BARKER II
(Len)

Born July 7, 1955, at Ft. Knox, Ky.
Height, 6.04. Weight, 215.
Throws and bats righthanded.

Pitched 3-0 perfect game victory against Toronto Blue Jays, May 15, 1981.
Led American League in wild pitches with 14 in 1980.
Led Western Carolinas League in shutouts with 5 in 1974.

Year Club	League	G.	IP.	W.	L.	Pct.	H.	R.	ER.	SO.	BB.	ERA.
1973—Sarasota Rangers	Gulf Coast	11	59	★7	1	★.875	34	13	9	54	27	1.37
1974—Gastonia	W. Carol.	20	124	11	7	.611	101	57	46	140	53	3.34
1975—Pittsfield	Eastern	24	159	7	12	.368	117	72	51	133	109	2.89
1976—Sacramento	P. Coast	27	141	11	10	.524	140	103	87	92	96	5.55
1976—Texas	American	2	15	1	0	1.000	7	4	4	7	6	2.40
1977—Tucson	P. Coast	20	109	9	7	.563	114	77	69	93	77	5.70
1977—Texas	American	15	47	4	1	.800	36	15	14	51	24	2.68
1978—Tucson	P. Coast	8	26	4	0	1.000	22	8	3	16	16	1.04
1978—Texas†	American	29	52	1	5	.167	63	31	28	33	29	4.85
1979—Cleveland	American	29	137	6	6	.500	146	79	75	93	70	4.93
1980—Cleveland	American	36	246	19	12	.613	237	127	114	★187	92	4.17
1981—Cleveland	American	22	154	8	7	.533	150	72	67	★127	46	3.92
1982—Cleveland	American	33	244⅔	15	11	.577	211	117	106	187	88	3.90
1983—Cleveland‡	American	24	149⅔	8	13	.381	150	92	85	105	52	5.11
1983—Atlanta	National	6	33	1	3	.250	31	17	14	21	14	3.82
American League Totals		190	1045⅓	62	55	.530	1000	537	493	790	407	4.24
National League Totals		6	33	1	3	.250	31	17	14	21	14	3.82
Major League Totals		196	1078⅓	63	58	.521	1031	554	507	811	421	4.23

Selected by Texas Rangers' organization in 3rd round of free-agent draft, June 5, 1973.
†Traded with Outfielder Bobby Bonds to Cleveland Indians for Infielder Larvell Blanks and Pitcher Jim Kern, October 3, 1978.
‡Traded to Atlanta Braves for three players to be named later, August 28, 1983; Cleveland Indians acquired Pitcher Rick Behenna, September 2, 1983, and Outfielder Brett Butler and Infielder Brook Jacoby, October 21, 1983, to complete deal.

ALL-STAR GAME RECORD

Year League	IP.	W.	L.	Pct.	H.	R.	ER.	SO.	BB.	ERA.
1981—American	2	0	0	.000	0	0	0	1	0	0.00

RICHARD MONROE BARNES

Born July 21, 1959, at Palm Beach, Fla.
Height, 6.04. Weight, 186.
Throws left and bats righthanded.

Tied for Southern League lead in hit batsmen with 13 in 1979.
Tied for Gulf Coast League lead in games started by pitchers with 12 in 1977.
Named American Association Pitcher of the Year, 1983.

Year	Club	League	G.	IP.	W.	L.	Pct.	H.	R.	ER.	SO.	BB.	ERA.
1977—Sarasota White Sox	Gulf Coast	13	73	⋆8	1	.889	46	22	13	⋆61	37	1.60
1977—Knoxville	Southern	3	13	0	1	.000	11	5	3	9	7	2.08
1978—Knoxville	Southern	25	146	8	6	.571	144	72	53	69	75	3.27
1979—Knoxville	Southern	22	131	8	8	.500	136	79	61	91	86	4.19
1979—Iowa	Am. Assoc.	3	10	0	1	.000	12	6	5	5	7	4.50
1980—Iowa	Am. Assoc.	26	123	3	9	.250	131	73	63	59	93	4.61
1981—Edmonton	P. Coast	26	163	13	8	.619	181	100	86	80	82	4.75
1982—Edmonton	P. Coast	19	117⅓	10	6	.625	125	79	72	56	59	5.52
1982—Chicago	American	6	17	0	2	.000	21	15	9	6	4	4.76
1983—Denver†	Am. Assoc.	12	73⅓	6	2	.750	78	41	38	53	32	4.66
1983—Charleston	Int'national	2	12⅓	1	0	1.000	9	5	5	3	9	3.65
1983—Cleveland	American	4	11⅔	1	1	.500	18	10	9	2	10	6.94
Major League Totals		10	28⅔	1	3	.250	39	25	18	8	14	5.65

Selected by Chicago White Sox' organization in 2nd round of free-agent draft, June 7, 1977.

†Traded to Cleveland Indians' organization for a player to be named later, August 25, 1983; Chicago White Sox acquired Outfielder Miguel Dilone to complete deal, September 1, 1983.

WILLIAM HENRY BARNES III
(Skeeter)

Born March 7, 1957, at Cincinnati, O.
Height, 5.10. Weight, 170.
Throws and bats righthanded.
Attended University of Cincinnati, Cincinnati, O.

Tied for Pioneer League lead in sacrifice flies with 6 in 1978.
Led Eastern League third basemen in fielding percentage with .947 in 1982 and putouts with 104 in 1981.

Year	Club	League	Pos.	G.	AB.	R.	H.	2B.	3B.	HR.	RBI.	B.A.	PO.	A.	E.	F.A.
1978—Billings	Pion.	O-3-S-2-1	68	277	66	102	⋆22	5	3	⋆76	.368	56	50	16	.869
1979—Nashville	South.	3B	⋆145	500	54	133	19	4	12	77	.266	123	⋆291	⋆35	.922
1980—Waterbury	East.	OF	⋆138	533	62	156	27	6	4	64	.293	264	15	13	.955
1981—Indianapolis	A.A.	1B-OF-3B	36	118	10	31	6	1	1	11	.263	254	23	3	.989
1981—Waterbury	East.	3-O-1-2	96	363	45	93	17	0	6	49	.256	115	185	15	.952
1982—Waterbury	East.	3B-1B-SS	112	418	67	128	24	6	12	72	.306	252	192	19	.959
1982—Indianapolis	A.A.	3B-1B	18	59	8	18	5	1	1	3	.305	25	25	2	.962
1983—Indianapolis	A.A.	3-1-O-2	109	377	67	127	19	6	7	56	.337	203	140	16	.955
1983—Cincinnati	Nat.	1B-3B	15	34	5	7	0	0	1	4	.206	45	11	1	.982
Major League Totals			15	34	5	7	0	0	1	4	.206	45	11	1	.982

Selected by Cincinnati Reds' organization in 16th round of free-agent draft, June 6, 1978.

SALOME BAROJAS (ROMERO)

Name pronounced Sahl-low-may BAR-oh-hass.

Born June 16, 1957, at Cordoba, Veracruz, Mex.
Height, 5.09. Weight, 183.
Throws and bats righthanded.

Major League saves: 1982 (21), 1983 (12). Total—33.

Year	Club	League	G.	IP.	W.	L.	Pct.	H.	R.	ER.	SO.	BB.	ERA.
1976—Cordoba	Mexican	15	43	3	1	.750	32	12	9	17	14	1.88
1977—Cordoba	Mexican	41	126	5	4	.556	109	46	28	85	45	2.00
1978—Cordoba	Mexican	40	66	8	3	.727	54	22	18	27	34	2.45
1979—Cordoba	Mexican	41	148	7	6	.538	143	49	43	64	76	2.61
1980—Reynosa	Mexican	29	126	9	5	.643	105	40	33	82	49	2.36
1981—Mexico City Reds†	Mexican	50	98	12	3	.800	81	40	33	42	41	3.04
1982—Chicago	American	61	106⅔	6	6	.500	96	43	42	56	46	3.54
1983—Chicago	American	52	87⅓	3	3	.500	70	24	24	38	32	2.47
Major League Totals		113	194	9	9	.500	166	67	66	94	78	3.06

†Sold to Chicago White Sox, December 9, 1981.

CHAMPIONSHIP SERIES RECORD

Year	Club	League	G.	IP.	W.	L.	Pct.	H.	R.	ER.	SO.	BB.	ERA.
1983—Chicago	American	2	1	0	0	.000	4	2	2	0	0	18.00

—DID YOU KNOW—

That the Baltimore Orioles were the only major league team to have a .500-or-better record in each of the seven months of the 1983 season?

JAMES LELAND BARR
(Jim)

Born February 10, 1948, at Lynwood, Calif.
Height, 6.03. Weight, 215.
Throws and bats righthanded.
Received bachelor of arts degree in business administration
from University of Southern California, Los Angeles, Calif. in 1970.
Brother of Mark Barr, pitcher in Boston Red Sox' organization, 1974 through 1976.

Established major league record for most batters retired, consecutive, season, (41), August 23 through 29, 1972.

Year Club	League	G.	IP.	W.	L.	Pct.	H.	R.	ER.	SO.	BB.	ERA.
1970—Amarillo	Texas	14	98	6	5	.545	107	51	36	48	23	3.31
1971—Phoenix	P. Coast	47	79	6	3	.667	72	36	33	71	26	3.76
1971—San Francisco	National	17	35	1	1	.500	33	15	14	16	5	3.60
1972—San Francisco	National	44	179	8	10	.444	166	66	57	86	41	2.87
1973—San Francisco	National	41	231	11	17	.393	240	105	98	88	49	3.82
1974—San Francisco	National	44	240	13	9	.591	223	81	73	84	47	2.74
1975—San Francisco	National	35	244	13	14	.481	244	94	83	77	58	3.06
1976—San Francisco	National	37	252	15	12	.556	260	104	81	75	60	2.89
1977—San Francisco†	National	38	234	12	16	.429	286	130	124	97	56	4.77
1978—San Francisco‡	National	32	163	8	11	.421	180	69	64	44	35	3.53
1979—California	American	36	197	10	12	.455	217	100	92	69	55	4.20
1980—California§x	American	24	68	1	4	.200	90	43	42	22	23	5.56
1981—Edmonton y	P. Coast	10	61	4	5	.444	74	41	33	18	21	4.87
1982—San Francisco	National	53	128⅔	4	3	.571	125	54	47	36	20	3.29
1983—San Francisco	National	53	92⅔	5	3	.625	106	47	41	47	20	3.98
American League Totals		60	265	11	16	.407	307	143	134	91	78	4.55
National League Totals		394	1799⅓	90	96	.484	1863	765	682	650	391	3.41
Major League Totals		454	2064⅓	101	112	.474	2170	908	816	741	469	3.56

Selected by California Angels' organization in 13th round of free-agent draft, June 6, 1966.
Selected by Philadelphia Phillies' organization in 3rd round of free-agent draft, June 7, 1968.
Selected by New York Yankees' organization in secondary phase of free-agent draft, February 1, 1969.
Selected by Pittsburgh Pirates' organization in secondary phase of free-agent draft, June 5, 1969.
Selected by Minnesota Twins' organization in secondary phase of free-agent draft, January 17, 1970.
Selected by San Francisco Giants' organization in secondary phase of free-agent draft, June 4, 1970.
†On suspended list, June 1 to June 4, 1977.
‡Granted free agency, November 2, 1978; signed by California Angels, December 3, 1978.
§On disabled list, June 26 to August 5, 1980.
xReleased, April 1, 1981; signed by Edmonton (Chicago White Sox' organization), July 6, 1981.
yReleased, September 4, 1981; signed by San Francisco Giants, April 5, 1982.

CHAMPIONSHIP SERIES RECORD

Year Club	League	G.	IP.	W.	L.	Pct.	H.	R.	ER.	SO.	BB.	ERA.
1971—San Francisco	National	1	1	0	0	.000	3	1	1	2	0	9.00

MARTIN GLENN BARRETT
(Marty)

Born June 23, 1958, at Arcadia, Calif.
Height, 5.10. Weight, 170.
Throws and bats righthanded.
Attended Mesa Community College, Mesa, Ariz. and Arizona State University, Tempe, Ariz.
Brother of Charlie Barrett, pitcher in Los Angeles Dodgers' organization, 1973 through 1978.

Led Eastern League in sacrifice hits with 15 in 1980.
Led Florida State League in sacrifice flies with 9 in 1979.
Led International League second basemen in double plays with 99 in 1982.

Year Club	League	Pos.	G.	AB.	R.	H.	2B.	3B.	HR.	RBI.	B.A.	PO.	A.	E.	F.A.
1979—Winter Haven	Fla. St.	2B	57	178	25	53	7	0	1	28	.298	124	144	6	.978
1980—Bristol	East.	★2B-SS	128	475	72	130	17	2	1	41	.274	279	372	10	★.985
1981—Pawtucket†	Int.	2B	88	343	36	91	12	2	1	28	.265	186	254	10	.978
1982—Pawtucket	Int.	2B	131	477	72	143	27	1	5	57	.300	303	★415	11	★.985
1982—Boston	Amer.	2B	8	18	0	1	0	0	0	0	.056	11	21	0	1.000
1983—Boston	Amer.	2B	33	44	7	10	1	1	0	2	.227	32	28	1	.984
1983—Pawtucket	Int.	2B	36	119	24	41	4	2	1	18	.345	70	115	1	.995
Major League Totals			41	62	7	11	1	1	0	2	.177	43	49	1	.989

Selected by California Angels' organization in 11th round of free-agent draft, January 11, 1977.
Selected by New York Mets' organization in 3rd round of free-agent draft, January 10, 1978.
Selected by Boston Red Sox' organization in secondary phase of free-agent draft, June 5, 1979.
†On disabled list, June 25 to July 15 and July 17 to August 4, 1981.

ERIC WALTER BARRY

Born February 5, 1961, at Santa Maria, Calif.
Height, 6.03. Weight, 196.
Throws and bats lefthanded.
Attended California State University, Fullerton, Calif.

Led Northwest League in complete games with 9 and shutouts with 2 in 1982.

Year Club	League	G.	IP.	W.	L.	Pct.	H.	R.	ER.	SO.	BB.	ERA.
1982—Medford	Northwest	15	*124	*13	2	.867	*108	44	33	*106	43	2.40
1983—Modesto	California	26	174⅓	12	9	.571	208	102	83	104	57	4.28

Selected by California Angels' organization in 4th round of free-agent draft, June 5, 1979.
Selected by Oakland A's organization in 20th round of free-agent draft, June 7, 1982.

KEVIN CHARLES BASS

Born May 12, 1959, at Menlo Park, Calif.
Height, 6.00. Weight, 180.
Throws right and bats right and lefthanded.
Brother of Richard Bass, minor league outfielder, 1976 and 1977;
cousin of James Lofton, wide receiver with Green Bay Packers.

Led Midwest League in being hit by pitch with 10 in 1978.
Led Eastern League outfielders in double plays with 7 in 1980.

Year Club	League	Pos.	G.	AB.	R.	H.	2B.	3B.	HR.	RBI.	B.A.	PO.	A.	E.	F.A.
1977—Newark	NYP	OF	48	189	30	56	11	●7	1	33	.296	56	2	3	.951
1978—Burlington	Midw.	OF	129	499	81	132	27	5	18	69	.265	*281	14	11	.964
1979—Holyoke	East.	OF	135	490	69	129	15	4	8	54	.263	280	●16	*17	.946
1980—Holyoke	East.	OF	136	490	79	147	*31	7	4	51	.300	305	14	*18	.947
1981—Vancouver†	P. C.	OF	97	339	40	87	10	5	2	30	.257	175	14	7	.964
1982—Milwaukee	Amer.	OF	18	9	4	0	0	0	0	0	.000	7	0	0	1.000
1982—Vancouver‡	P. C.	OF	102	413	70	130	23	7	17	65	.315	199	15	10	.955
1982—Houston	Nat.	OF	12	24	2	1	0	0	0	1	.042	11	0	1	.917
1983—Houston	Nat.	OF	88	195	25	46	7	3	2	18	.236	68	1	4	.945
American League Totals			18	9	4	0	0	0	0	0	.000	7	0	0	1.000
National League Totals			100	219	27	47	7	3	2	19	.215	79	1	5	.941
Major League Totals			118	228	31	47	7	3	2	19	.206	86	1	5	.946

Selected by Milwaukee Brewers' organization in 2nd round of free-agent draft, June 7, 1977.
†On disabled list, July 29 to September 1, 1981.
‡Traded with Pitchers Mike Madden and Frank DiPino to Houston Astros, September 3, 1982, completing deal in which Houston traded Pitcher Don Sutton to Milwaukee Brewers for three players to be named later, August 30, 1982.

WILLIAM DAVID BATHE
(Bill)

Born October 14, 1960, at Downey, Calif.
Height, 6.02. Weight, 195.
Throws and bats righthanded.
Attended Pepperdine University, Malibu, Calif.

Led Pacific Coast League catchers in putouts with 632 and tied for lead in double plays with 9 in 1983.

Year Club	League	Pos.	G.	AB.	R.	H.	2B.	3B.	HR.	RBI.	B.A.	PO.	A.	E.	F.A.
1981—San Jose†	Calif.	C-OF	51	177	20	45	9	1	4	22	.254	234	42	8	.972
1982—West Haven	East.	C	128	370	57	104	22	0	17	57	.281	*763	55	9	*.989
1983—Tacoma	P.C.	C-1B	116	399	56	101	18	1	16	62	.253	633	55	15	.979

Selected by Pittsburgh Pirates' organization in 10th round of free-agent draft, January 8, 1980.
Selected by Oakland A's organization in 8th round of free-agent draft, June 8, 1981.
†Loaned to San Jose (Co-op), June 23, 1981; returned, October 22, 1981.

DONALD EDWARD BAYLOR
(Don)

Born June 28, 1949, at Austin, Tex.
Height, 6.01. Weight, 210.
Throws and bats righthanded.
Attended Miami-Dade Junior College, Miami, Fla., and
Blinn Junior College, Brenham, Tex.

Established major league record for most times caught stealing, inning, (2), June 15, 1974 (9th inning).
Tied major league records for most long hits, opening game of season (4), April 6, 1973 (2 doubles, 1 triple, 1 home run); most consecutive home runs, consecutive games (4), July 1 and 2, 1975 (bases on balls included).
Tied modern major league record for most at bats, game (7), August 25, 1979.
Tied American League record for most hits, two consecutive games (9), August 13 and 14, 1973.
Major League stolen bases: 1970 (1), 1972 (24), 1973 (32), 1974 (29), 1975 (32), 1976 (52), 1977 (26), 1978 (22), 1979 (22), 1980 (6), 1981 (3), 1982 (10), 1983 (17). Total—276.
Hit three home runs in a game, July 2, 1975.
Led American League in game-winning RBIs with 21 in 1982.
Led American League in sacrifice flies with 12 in 1978.
Led American League in being hit by pitch with 13 in 1973, 20 in 1976, 18 in 1978 and tied for lead with 13 in 1975.
Led International League in being hit by pitch with 19 in 1970 and 16 in 1971.
Led International League in total bases with 296 in 1970.
Led Texas League in being hit by pitch with 13 in 1969.
Led Appalachian League in stolen bases with 26, total bases with 135 and tied for lead in caught stealing with 6 in 1967.
Named American League Most Valuable Player by Baseball Writers' Association of America, 1979.
Named American League Player of the Year by The Sporting News, 1979.
Named designated hitter on The Sporting News American League Silver Slugger team, 1983.
Named designated hitter on The Sporting News American League All-Star Team, 1979.

Named Appalachian League Player of the Year, 1967.
Named Minor League Player of the Year by THE SPORTING NEWS, 1970.

Year	Club	League	Pos.	G.	AB.	R.	H.	2B.	3B.	HR.	RBI.	B.A.	PO.	A.	E.	F.A.
1967—Bluefield	Appal.	OF	●67	246	50	*85	10	*8	8	47	*.346	106	5	5	.957
1968—Stockton	Calif.	OF	68	244	52	90	6	3	7	40	.369	135	3	7	.952
1968—Elmira	East.	OF	6	24	4	8	1	1	1	3	.333	10	1	0	1.000
1968—Rochester	Int.	OF	15	46	4	10	2	0	0	4	.217	29	1	4	.882
1969—Miami	Fla. St.	OF	17	56	13	21	5	4	3	24	.375	30	2	3	.914
1969—Dal.-Ft. Worth	Texas	OF	109	406	71	122	17	●10	11	57	.300	241	7	*13	.950
1970—Rochester	Int.	OF	●140	508	*127	166	*34	*15	22	107	.327	286	5	7	.977
1970—Baltimore	Amer.	OF	8	17	4	4	0	0	0	4	.235	15	0	0	1.000
1971—Rochester	Int.	OF	136	492	104	154	●31	10	20	95	.313	210	4	9	.960
1971—Baltimore	Amer.	OF	1	2	0	0	0	0	0	1	.000	4	0	0	1.000
1972—Baltimore	Amer.	OF-1B	102	320	33	81	13	3	11	38	.253	206	4	5	.977
1973—Baltimore	Amer.	OF-1B	118	405	64	116	20	4	11	51	.286	228	10	6	.975
1974—Baltimore	Amer.	OF-1B	137	489	66	133	22	1	10	59	.272	260	2	5	.981
1975—Baltimore†	Amer.	OF-1B	145	524	79	148	21	6	25	76	.282	286	8	5	.983
1976—Oakland‡	Amer.	OF-1B	157	595	85	147	25	1	15	68	.247	781	45	12	.986
1977—California	Amer.	OF-1B	154	561	87	141	27	0	25	75	.251	280	16	7	.977
1978—California	Amer.	OF-1B	158	591	103	151	26	0	34	99	.255	194	9	6	.971
1979—California	Amer.	OF-1B	●162	628	*120	186	33	3	36	*139	.296	203	3	5	.976
1980—California§	Amer.	OF	90	340	39	85	12	2	5	51	.250	119	4	4	.969
1981—California	Amer.	1B-OF	103	377	52	90	18	1	17	66	.239	38	3	0	1.000
1982—California x	Amer.	DH	157	608	80	160	24	1	24	93	.263	0	0	0	.000
1983—New York	Amer.	OF-1B	144	534	82	162	33	3	21	85	.303	23	2	1	.962
Major League Totals			1636	5991	894	1604	274	25	234	905	.268	2637	106	56	.980

Selected by Baltimore Orioles' organization in 2nd round of free-agent draft, June 6, 1967.
†Traded with Pitchers Mike Torrez and Paul Mitchell to Oakland Athletics for Outfielder Reggie Jackson and Pitchers Ken Holtzman and Bill Van Bommel, April 2, 1976.
‡Played out option year and granted free agency, November 1, 1976; signed as free agent by California Angels, November 16, 1976.
§On disabled list, May 11 to June 26, 1980.
xGranted free agency, November 10, 1982; signed by New York Yankees, December 1, 1982.

CHAMPIONSHIP SERIES RECORD

Established Championship Series record for most runs batted in, five-game Series (10), 1982.
Tied Championship Series records for most home runs filled, game (1), October 9, 1982; most runs batted in, game (5), October 5, 1982; most runs batted in, inning (4), October 9, 1982 (eighth inning).
Tied American League Championship Series record for most times on losing club (4).

Year	Club	League	Pos.	G.	AB.	R.	H.	2B.	3B.	HR.	RBI.	B.A.	PO.	A.	E.	F.A.
1973—Baltimore	Amer.	OF-PH	4	11	3	3	0	0	0	1	.273	7	0	0	1.000
1974—Baltimore	Amer.	OF	4	15	0	4	0	0	0	0	.267	9	0	0	1.000
1979—California	Amer.	DH-OF	4	16	2	3	0	0	1	2	.188	4	0	0	1.000
1982—California	Amer.	DH	5	17	2	5	1	1	1	10	.294	0	0	0	.000
Championship Series Totals			17	59	7	15	1	1	2	13	.254	20	0	0	1.000

ALL-STAR GAME RECORD

Year	League	Pos.	AB.	R.	H.	2B.	3B.	HR.	RBI.	B.A.	PO.	A.	E.	F.A.
1979—American		OF	4	2	2	1	0	0	1	.500	1	0	0	1.000

WILLIAM LAMAR BEANE

Name pronounced Bean.

(Billy)

Born March 29, 1962, at Orlando, Fla.
Height, 6.04. Weight, 195.
Throws and bats righthanded.
Attending University of California at San Diego, La Jolla, Calif.

Led Texas League outfielders in fielding percentage with .994 in 1983.
Tied for Carolina League lead in sacrifice flies with 8 in 1981.

Year	Club	League	Pos.	G.	AB.	R.	H.	2B.	3B.	HR.	RBI.	B.A.	PO.	A.	E.	F.A.
1980—Little Falls	NYP	OF	43	138	10	29	3	2	1	14	.210	93	5	3	.970
1981—Lynchburg	Carol.	OF	114	403	47	108	13	●9	9	59	.268	233	8	11	.956
1982—Jackson	Texas	OF	126	418	39	88	13	4	5	36	.211	200	6	10	.954
1983—Jackson	Texas	OF-1B	121	423	53	104	14	1	11	75	.246	382	24	8	.981

Selected by New York Mets' organization in 1st round (23rd player selected) of free-agent draft, June 3, 1980.

DAVID CHARLES BEARD

(Dave)

Born October 2, 1959, at Chamblee, Ga.
Height, 6.05. Weight, 215.
Throws right and bats lefthanded.

Major League saves: 1980 (1), 1981 (3), 1982 (11), 1983 (10). Total—25.
Led Eastern League in complete games with 20 in 1979.
Tied for Pacific Coast League lead in balks with 3 in 1980.
Tied for Eastern League lead in intentional bases on balls issued with 9 in 1979.
Tied for California League lead in shutouts with 5 in 1978.

Year Club	League	G.	IP.	W.	L.	Pct.	H.	R.	ER.	SO.	BB.	ERA.
1977—Medicine Hat	Pioneer	11	71	4	5	.444	79	50	36	30	31	4.56
1978—Modesto	California	25	185	12	6	.667	161	94	60	142	64	2.42
1979—Waterbury	Eastern	25	*191	10	●14	.417	192	87	64	111	63	3.02
1980—Ogden†	P. Coast	16	97	7	8	.467	110	76	69	70	44	6.40
1980—Oakland	American	13	16	0	1	.000	12	6	6	12	7	3.38
1981—Tacoma	P. Coast	42	129	11	11	.500	132	67	61	114	51	4.26
1981—Oakland	American	8	13	1	1	.500	9	5	4	15	4	2.77
1982—Tacoma	P. Coast	1	1	0	0	.000	0	0	0	1	0	0.00
1982—Oakland	American	54	91⅔	10	9	.526	85	41	35	73	35	3.44
1983—Oakland‡	American	43	61	5	5	.500	55	39	38	40	36	5.61
1983—Modesto§	California	1	1	0	0	.000	0	0	0	0	0	0.00
Major League Totals		118	181⅔	16	16	.500	161	91	83	140	82	4.11

Selected by Oakland A's organization in 6th round of free-agent draft, June 7, 1977.

†On disabled list, April 20 to May 2, 1980.

‡On disabled list, June 9 to July 1, 1983; included rehabilitation disability assignment to Modesto, June 28 to July 1, 1983.

§Traded with Catcher Bob Kearney to Seattle Mariners for Pitcher Bill Caudill and a player to be named later, November 21, 1983; Oakland A's acquired Pitcher Darrel Akerfelds to complete deal, December 7, 1983.

DIVISION SERIES RECORD

Year Club	League	G.	IP.	W.	L.	Pct.	H.	R.	ER.	SO.	BB.	ERA.
1981—Oakland	American	1	1⅓	0	0	.000	0	0	0	2	0	0.00

CHAMPIONSHIP SERIES RECORD

Year Club	League	G.	IP.	W.	L.	Pct.	H.	R.	ER.	SO.	BB.	ERA.
1981—Oakland	American	1	⅔	0	0	.000	5	3	3	0	0	40.50

JAMES LOUIS BEATTIE

Name pronounced BEE-tee.

(Jim)

Born July 4, 1954, at Langeley AFB, Hampton, Va.
Height, 6.06. Weight, 220.
Throws and bats righthanded.
Received bachelor of arts degree in art from Dartmouth College, Hanover, N. H., in 1976.

Tied major league records for most putouts by pitcher, inning (3), September 13, 1978 (second inning); most putouts by pitcher, nine-inning game (5), September 13, 1978.

Pitched seven-inning, 2-0 no-hit victory against Spokane, July 9, 1978.

Year Club	League	G.	IP.	W.	L.	Pct.	H.	R.	ER.	SO.	BB.	ERA.
1975—Oneonta†	NYP	5	24	2	0	1.000	15	11	5	22	7	1.88
1975—Syracuse	Int'national	5	33	2	2	.500	25	14	12	30	21	3.27
1976—Syracuse	Int'national	17	100	5	5	.500	106	76	67	74	80	6.03
1976—West Haven	Eastern	8	60	5	2	.714	47	19	15	48	33	2.25
1977—West Haven‡	Eastern	3	27	2	0	1.000	14	5	1	22	8	0.33
1977—Ft. Lauderdale	Florida St.	9	38	1	3	.250	52	27	25	28	17	5.92
1977—Syracuse	Int'national	12	80	6	5	.545	70	41	37	53	43	4.16
1978—Tacoma	P. Coast	4	23	3	0	1.000	17	5	4	15	12	1.57
1978—New York	American	25	128	6	9	.400	123	60	53	65	51	3.73
1979—Columbus	Int'national	8	53	5	1	.833	31	9	8	47	25	1.36
1979—New York§x	American	15	76	3	6	.333	85	45	44	32	41	5.21
1980—Seattle	American	33	187	5	15	.250	205	115	101	67	98	4.86
1981—Seattle	American	13	67	3	2	.600	59	24	22	36	18	2.96
1981—Spokane	P. Coast	18	120	6	9	.400	115	60	42	70	48	3.15
1982—Seattle	American	28	172⅓	8	12	.400	149	73	64	140	65	3.34
1983—Seattle y	American	30	196⅔	10	15	.400	197	89	84	132	66	3.84
1983—Salt Lake City	P. Coast	3	16⅔	2	1	.667	19	12	11	13	8	5.94
Major League Totals		144	827	35	59	.372	818	406	368	472	339	4.00

Selected by New York Yankees' organization in 4th round of free-agent draft, June 4, 1975.

†On disabled list, July 13 to July 29, 1975.

‡On disabled list, April 15 to May 2, 1977.

§On disabled list, June 25 to July 22, 1979.

xTraded with Outfielder Juan Beniquez, Catcher Jerry Narron and Pitcher Rick Anderson to Seattle Mariners for Outfielder Ruppert Jones and Pitcher Jim Lewis, November 1, 1979.

yOn disabled list, March 24 to April 27, 1983; included rehabilitation disability assignment to Salt Lake City, April 12 to April 27, 1983.

CHAMPIONSHIP SERIES RECORD

Year Club	League	G.	IP.	W.	L.	Pct.	H.	R.	ER.	SO.	BB.	ERA.
1978—New York	American	1	5⅓	1	0	1.000	2	1	1	3	5	1.69

WORLD SERIES RECORD

Year Club	League	G.	IP.	W.	L.	Pct.	H.	R.	ER.	SO.	BB.	ERA.
1978—New York	American	1	9	1	0	1.000	9	2	2	8	4	2.00

THOMAS JOSEPH BECKWITH
(Joe)

Born January 28, 1955, at Auburn, Ala.
Height, 6.03. Weight, 200.
Throws right and bats lefthanded.
Attended Auburn University, Auburn, Ala.

Year	Club	League	G.	IP.	W.	L.	Pct.	H.	R.	ER.	SO.	BB.	ERA.
1977—San Antonio	Texas	12	78	5	5	.500	88	40	29	31	20	3.35
1978—Albuquerque	P. Coast	28	150	8	9	.471	186	118	97	59	80	5.82
1979—Albuquerque	P. Coast	27	113	8	8	.500	119	74	58	64	46	4.62
1979—Los Angeles	National	17	37	1	2	.333	42	18	18	28	15	4.38
1980—Albuquerque	P. Coast	7	14	2	1	.667	15	8	4	12	5	2.57
1980—Los Angeles	National	38	60	3	3	.500	60	17	13	40	23	1.95
1981—Los Angeles†	National					(Did not play)						
1982—Albuquerque	P. Coast	26	101⅓	5	6	.455	138	90	76	80	55	6.68
1982—Los Angeles	National	19	40	2	1	.667	38	14	12	33	14	2.70
1983—Los Angeles‡	National	42	71	3	4	.429	73	40	28	50	35	3.55
Major League Totals		116	208	9	10	.474	213	89	71	151	87	3.07

Selected by Cleveland Indians' organization in 12th round of free-agent draft, June 8, 1976.
Selected by Los Angeles Dodgers' organization in 2nd round of free-agent draft, June 7, 1977.
†On disabled list, April 8, 1981 through remainder of season.
‡Traded to Kansas City Royals for Catcher Joe Szekely and Pitchers Jose Torres and John Serritella, December 8, 1983.

CHAMPIONSHIP SERIES RECORD

Year	Club	League	G.	IP.	W.	L.	Pct.	H.	R.	ER.	SO.	BB.	ERA.
1983—Los Angeles	National	2	2⅓	0	0	.000	1	0	0	3	2	0.00

STEPHEN WAYNE BEDROSIAN

Name pronounced Bed-ROHZ-ee-un.

(Steve)

Born December 6, 1957, at Methuen, Mass.
Height, 6.03. Weight, 200.
Throws and bats righthanded.
Attended North Essex Community College, Haverhill, Mass., and
University of New Haven, New Haven, Conn.

Major League saves: 1982 (11), 1983 (19). Total—30.
Tied for Southern League lead in games started by pitchers with 29 in 1980.
Named National League Rookie Pitcher of the Year by THE SPORTING NEWS, 1982.

Year	Club	League	G.	IP.	W.	L.	Pct.	H.	R.	ER.	SO.	BB.	ERA.
1978—Kingsport	Ap'lachian	6	38	2	2	.500	38	18	13	29	25	3.08
1978—Greenwood	W. Carol.	8	55	5	1	.833	45	17	13	58	34	2.13
1979—Savannah†	Southern	13	89	5	5	.500	71	36	30	73	58	3.03
1980—Savannah	Southern	29	★203	14	10	.583	167	91	72	★161	96	3.19
1981—Richmond	Int'national	26	184	10	10	.500	143	76	55	144	99	2.69
1981—Atlanta	National	15	24	1	2	.333	15	14	12	9	15	4.50
1982—Atlanta	National	64	137⅔	8	6	.571	102	39	37	123	57	2.42
1983—Atlanta	National	70	120	9	10	.474	100	50	48	114	51	3.60
Major League Totals		149	281⅔	18	18	.500	217	103	97	246	123	3.10

Selected by Atlanta Braves' organization in 3rd round of free-agent draft, June 6, 1978.
†On disabled list, June 24 to September 18, 1979.

CHAMPIONSHIP SERIES RECORD

Year	Club	League	G.	IP.	W.	L.	Pct.	H.	R.	ER.	SO.	BB.	ERA.
1982—Atlanta	National	2	1	0	0	.000	3	2	2	2	1	18.00

RAMON ANDREW BEENE
(Andy)

Born October 13, 1956, at Freeport, Tex.
Height, 6.04. Weight, 205.
Throws and bats righthanded.
Attended Baylor University, Waco, Tex.
Nephew of Fred Beene, pitcher with Baltimore Orioles, New York Yankees
and Cleveland Indians, 1968 through 1970, and 1972 through 1975; minor
league coach, 1980; and scout with Milwaukee Brewers since 1982.

Year	Club	League	G.	IP.	W.	L.	Pct.	H.	R.	ER.	SO.	BB.	ERA.
1979—Butte†	Pioneer	5	12	0	2	.000	7	11	6	16	12	4.50
1980—Stockton	California	15	58	2	1	.667	46	34	28	53	43	4.34
1981—Stockton	California	19	63	3	5	.375	62	25	18	74	35	2.57
1982—El Paso‡	Texas	16	80⅓	8	2	.800	73	45	37	62	51	4.15
1983—Vancouver	P. Coast	26	154	13	6	.684	138	94	86	95	104	5.03
1983—Milwaukee	American	1	2	0	0	.000	3	3	1	0	1	4.50
Major League Totals		1	2	0	0	.000	3	3	1	0	1	4.50

Selected by New York Yankees' organization in 14th round of free-agent draft, June 6, 1978.
Selected by Milwaukee Brewers' organization in 5th round of free-agent draft, June 5, 1979.

RICHARD KIPP BEHENNA
(Rick)

Born March 6, 1960, at Miami, Fla.
Height, 6.02. Weight, 170.
Throws and bats righthanded.
Pitched 8-0 no-hit victory against Rocky Mount, August 29, 1980.

Year Club	League	G.	IP.	W.	L.	Pct.	H.	R.	ER.	SO.	BB.	ERA.
1978—Kingsport	Ap'lachian	12	74	6	4	.600	66	37	31	37	50	3.77
1979—Greenwood	W. Carol.	8	43	0	6	.000	38	30	25	22	32	5.23
1979—Kingsport	Ap'lachian	12	83	5	3	.625	76	52	42	36	42	4.55
1980—Durham	Carolina	27	180	8	●13	.381	181	97	★83	107	81	4.15
1981—Durham	Carolina	29	★196	13	12	.520	182	92	79	162	76	3.63
1982—Savannah	Southern	28	201⅓	13	10	.565	195	97	83	153	97	3.71
1983—Atlanta	National	14	37⅓	3	3	.500	37	20	19	17	12	4.58
1983—Richmond†	Int'national	17	94⅔	6	5	.545	91	55	47	50	61	4.47
1983—Cleveland	American	5	26	0	2	.000	22	13	12	9	14	4.15
National League Totals		14	37⅓	3	3	.500	37	20	19	17	12	4.58
American League Totals		5	26	0	2	.000	22	13	12	9	14	4.15
Major League Totals		19	63⅓	3	5	.375	59	33	31	26	26	4.41

Selected by Atlanta Braves' organization in 4th round of free-agent draft, June 6, 1978.
†Traded to Cleveland Indians, September 2, 1983, as partial completion of deal in which Cleveland traded Pitcher Len Barker to Atlanta Braves for three players to be named later, August 28, 1983; Cleveland acquired Outfielder Brett Butler and Infielder Brook Jacoby to complete deal, October 21, 1983.

DAVID GUS BELL
(Buddy)

Born August 27, 1951, at Pittsburgh, Pa.
Height, 6.02. Weight, 185.
Throws and bats righthanded.
Attended Xavier University, Cincinnati, O., and Miami University, Oxford, O.
Son of Gus Bell, outfielder with Pittsburgh Pirates, Cincinnati Reds, New York Mets and Milwaukee Braves, 1950 through 1964.

Tied major league record for most home runs, opening day of season (2), April 8, 1982.
Led American League in sacrifice flies with 10 in 1981.
Led American League third basemen in total chances with 495 in 1978, 361 in 1981, 540 in 1982 and 523 in 1983.
Led American League third basemen in assists with 364 in 1979 and 281 in 1981.
Led American League third basemen in putouts with 144 and double plays with 44 in 1973.
Tied for American League lead in game-winning RBIs with 16 in 1979.
Tied for American League lead in double plays by third basemen with 30 in 1978.
Led Gulf Coast League second basemen in double plays with 26 in 1969.
Named third baseman on THE SPORTING NEWS American League All-Star Team, 1981.
Named third baseman on THE SPORTING NEWS American League All-Star fielding team, 1979 through 1983.

Year Club	League	Pos.	G.	AB.	R.	H.	2B.	3B.	HR.	RBI.	B.A.	PO.	A.	E.	F.A.
1969—Sarasota Ind.	Gulf C.	2B	51	170	18	39	4	●3	3	24	.229	119	108	7	★.970
1970—Sumter	W. Car.	3B-2B-SS	121	442	81	117	19	3	12	75	.265	116	189	27	.919
1971—Wichita	A. A.	★3-2-S-O	129	470	65	136	23	1	11	59	.289	★139	203	16	.955
1972—Cleveland	Amer.	OF-3B	132	466	49	119	21	1	9	36	.255	284	23	3	.990
1973—Cleveland	Amer.	3B-OF	156	631	86	169	23	7	14	59	.268	146	363	22	.959
1974—Cleveland†	Amer.	3B	116	423	51	111	15	1	7	46	.262	112	274	15	.963
1975—Cleveland	Amer.	3B	153	553	66	150	20	4	10	59	.271	★146	330	25	.950
1976—Cleveland	Amer.	3B-1B	159	604	75	170	26	2	7	60	.281	109	331	20	.957
1977—Cleveland	Amer.	3B-OF	129	479	64	140	23	4	11	64	.292	134	253	16	.960
1978—Cleveland‡	Amer.	3B	142	556	71	157	27	8	6	62	.282	125	★355	15	.970
1979—Texas	Amer.	3B-SS	●162	★670	89	200	42	3	18	101	.299	147	429	17	.971
1980—Texas§	Amer.	★3B-SS	129	490	76	161	24	4	17	83	.329	125	282	8	★.981
1981—Texas	Amer.	3B-SS	97	360	44	106	16	1	10	64	.294	67	284	14	.962
1982—Texas	Amer.	★3B-SS	148	537	62	159	27	2	13	67	.296	★131	397	13	★.976
1983—Texas	Amer.	3B	156	618	75	171	35	3	14	66	.277	123	★383	17	.967
Major League Totals			1679	6387	808	1813	299	40	136	767	.284	1644	3703	185	.967

Selected by Cleveland Indians' organization in 16th round of free-agent draft, June 5, 1969.
†On disabled list, May 27 to June 17 and August 8 to September 1, 1974.
‡Traded to Texas Rangers for Third Baseman Toby Harrah, December 8, 1978.
§On supplemental disabled list, June 9 to June 24, 1980.

ALL-STAR GAME RECORD

Year League	Pos.	AB.	R.	H.	2B.	3B.	HR.	RBI.	B.A.	PO.	A.	E.	F.A.
1973—American	PH	1	0	1	0	1	0	0	1.000	0	0	0	.000
1980—American	3B	2	0	0	0	0	0	0	.000	0	2	0	1.000
1981—American	3B	1	0	0	0	0	0	1	.000	1	2	0	1.000
1982—American	PH-3B	3	0	0	0	0	0	0	.000	0	1	1	.500
All-Star Game Totals		7	0	1	0	1	0	1	.143	1	5	1	.857

GEORGE ANTONIO BELL (MATHY)

Born October 21, 1959, at San Pedro de Macoris, Dominican Republic
Height, 6.01. Weight, 185.
Throws and bats righthanded.

Tied for International League lead in double plays by outfielders with 4 in 1983.
Led Western Carolinas League in total bases with 270 in 1979.

Year	Club	League	Pos.	G.	AB.	R.	H.	2B.	3B.	HR.	RBI.	B.A.	PO.	A.	E.	F.A.
1978—Helena		Pion.	OF	33	106	20	33	6	1	0	14	.311	39	4	4	.915
1979—Spartanburg		W. Car.	OF	130	491	78	150	24	*15	22	*102	.305	206	14	8	.965
1980—Reading†‡		East.	OF	22	55	11	17	5	2	0	11	.309	24	0	1	.960
1981—Toronto		Amer.	OF	60	163	19	38	2	1	5	12	.233	92	3	3	.969
1982—Syracuse§		Int.	OF	37	125	11	25	5	4	3	19	.200	72	3	1	.987
1983—Syracuse		Int.	OF	85	317	37	86	11	4	15	59	.271	135	12	6	.961
1983—Toronto		Amer.	OF	39	112	5	30	5	4	2	17	.268	61	1	3	.954
Major League Totals				99	275	24	68	7	5	7	29	.247	153	4	6	.963

Signed as free agent by Philadelphia Phillies' organization, June 23, 1978.
†On disabled list, June 22, 1980 through remainder of season.
‡Drafted by Toronto Blue Jays, December 8, 1980.
§On disabled list, April 20 to May 1, June 14 to June 30 and July 8, 1982 through remainder of season.

RAFAEL LEONIDAS BELLIARD (MATIAS)

Name pronounced BELL-ee-ard.

Born October 24, 1961, at Pueblo Nuevo, Mao, D.R.
Height, 5.09. Weight, 139.
Throws and bats righthanded.

· Tied for Eastern League lead in double plays by outfielders with 69 in 1983.
Led Carolina League in sacrifice hits with 12 and tied for lead in caught stealing with 15 in 1981.

Year	Club	League	Pos.	G.	AB.	R.	H.	2B.	3B.	HR.	RBI.	B.A.	PO.	A.	E.	F.A.
1980—Bradenton Pir.		Gulf C.	SS-2B-3B	12	42	6	9	1	0	0	2	.214	24	39	1	.984
1980—Shelby		S. Atl.	SS	8	24	1	3	0	0	0	2	.125	10	27	5	.881
1981—Alexandria		Carol.	SS	127	472	58	102	6	5	0	33	.216	●205	330	29	.949
1982—Buffalo†		East.	SS	40	124	14	34	1	1	0	19	.274	56	87	5	.966
1982—Pittsburgh		Nat.	SS	9	2	3	1	0	0	0	0	.500	2	2	0	1.000
1983—Lynn		East.	SS-2B	127	431	63	113	13	2	2	37	.262	203	307	26	.951
1983—Pittsburgh		Nat.	SS	4	1	1	0	0	0	0	0	.000	1	3	0	1.000
Major League Totals				13	3	4	1	0	0	0	0	.333	3	5	0	1.000

Signed as free agent by Pittsburgh Pirates' organization, July 10, 1980.
†On disabled list, April 19 to July 24, 1982.

JOHNNY LEE BENCH

Born December 7, 1947, at Oklahoma City, Okla.
Height, 6.01. Weight, 210.
Throws and bats righthanded.

Established major league records for most games, catcher, rookie season (154), 1968; most home runs by catcher, lifetime (325).

Tied major league records for most consecutive seasons leading league in sacrifice flies (2); fewest passed balls, season, 100 or more games (0), 1975; most bases on balls, game (5), July 22, 1979; most years and most consecutive years by catcher, with 100 or more games (13).

Established National League records for most putouts by catcher, lifetime (9,260); most chances accepted by catcher, lifetime (10,110).

Tied National League records for most home runs, five consecutive games (7), May 30 through June 3, 1972; most home runs through July 31 (36), 1970; most seasons leading league in sacrifice flies (3); most home runs, bases filled, month (2), May, 1975; most two-base hits by catcher, season (40), 1968.

Hit three home runs in a game, July 26, 1970, May 9, 1973 and May 29, 1980.
Hit home runs in all 12 National League parks, 1972.
Led National League in total bases with 315 in 1974.
Led National League in sacrifice flies with 11 in 1970, 12 in 1972 and tied for lead with 10 in 1973.
Led National League in intentional bases on balls received with 23 in 1972.
Led National League catchers in putouts with 651, total chances with 713 and fielding percentage with .997 in 1976.
Led National League catchers in double plays with 16 in 1974.
Led National League in passed balls with 18 in 1968.
Led International League catchers in assists with 70 in 1967.
Named Major League Player of the Year by THE SPORTING NEWS, 1970.
Named National League Player of the Year by THE SPORTING NEWS, 1970.
Named National League Most Valuable Player by Baseball Writers' Association of America, 1970 and 1972.
Named catcher on THE SPORTING NEWS National League All-Star Team, 1968, 1969, 1970, 1972, 1973, 1974 and 1975.
Named catcher on THE SPORTING NEWS National League All-Star fielding team, 1968 through 1977.
Named National League Rookie Player of the Year by THE SPORTING NEWS, 1968.
Named National League Rookie of the Year by Baseball Writers' Association of America, 1968.
Named Minor League Player of the Year by THE SPORTING NEWS, 1967.
Named Carolina League Player of the Year, 1966.

Year	Club	League	Pos.	G.	AB.	R.	H.	2B.	3B.	HR.	RBI.	B.A.	PO.	A.	E.	F.A.
1965—Tampa		Fla. St.	C-OF	68	214	29	53	13	1	2	35	.248	415	40	6	.987
1966—Peninsula		Carol.	C	98	350	59	103	16	0	22	68	.294	692	●87	*17	.979
1966—Buffalo†‡		Int.	C	1	0	0	0	0	0	0	0	.000	2	0	0	1.000
1967—Buffalo§		Int.	C-3-O-1	98	344	39	89	17	2	23	68	.259	577	82	13	.981

Year Club	League	Pos.	G.	AB.	R.	H.	2B.	3B.	HR.	RBI.	B.A.	PO.	A.	E.	F.A.
1967—Cincinnati	Nat.	C	26	86	7	14	3	1	1	6	.163	175	16	1	.995
1968—Cincinnati	Nat.	C	154	564	67	155	40	2	15	82	.275	*942	*102	9	.991
1969—Cincinnati x	Nat.	C	148	532	83	156	23	1	26	90	.293	793	76	7	.992
1970—Cincinnati	Nat.	C-O-1-3	158	605	97	177	35	4	*45	*148	.293	854	78	15	.984
1971—Cincinnati y	Nat.	C-O-1-3	149	562	80	134	19	2	27	61	.238	735	67	10	.988
1972—Cincinnati	Nat.	C-O-1-3	147	538	87	145	22	2	*40	*125	.270	791	63	10	.988
1973—Cincinnati	Nat.	C-O-1-3	152	557	83	141	17	3	25	104	.253	757	63	6	.993
1974—Cincinnati	Nat.	C-3B-1B	160	621	108	174	38	2	33	*129	.280	794	123	9	.990
1975—Cincinnati	Nat.	C-OF-1B	142	530	83	150	39	1	28	110	.283	646	52	8	.989
1976—Cincinnati	Nat.	C-OF-1B	135	465	62	109	24	1	16	74	.234	655	60	4	.994
1977—Cincinnati	Nat.	C-O-1-3	142	494	67	136	34	2	31	109	.275	735	69	11	.987
1978—Cincinnati	Nat.	C-1B-OF	120	393	52	102	17	1	23	73	.260	680	53	9	.988
1979—Cincinnati	Nat.	C-1B	130	464	73	128	19	0	22	80	.276	632	69	10	.986
1980—Cincinnati	Nat.	C	114	360	52	90	12	0	24	68	.250	505	39	5	.991
1981—Cincinnati z	Nat.	1B-C	52	178	14	55	8	0	8	25	.309	375	28	7	.983
1982—Cincinnati	Nat.	3B-1B-C	119	399	44	103	16	0	13	38	.258	108	159	19	.934
1983—Cincinnati a	Nat.	3-1-C-O	110	310	32	79	15	2	12	54	.255	292	74	10	.973
Major League Totals			2158	7658	1091	2048	381	24	389	1376	.267	10469	1191	150	.987

Selected by Cincinnati Reds' organization in 2nd round of free-agent draft, June 21, 1965.
†On disabled list, July 31 to September 6, 1966.
‡On military list, November 7, 1966 through April 9, 1967.
§On temporary inactive list, July 29 to August 14, 1967.
xOn military list, July 11 to July 18, 1969.
yOn military list, June 13 to June 17, 1971.
zOn disabled list, May 29 to August 22, 1981.
aOn voluntarily retired list, October 19, 1983.

CHAMPIONSHIP SERIES RECORD

Established Championship Series record for most Series, one or more home runs (5).
Tied Championship Series record for most games, total Series, one club (22).
Established National League Championship Series record for most long hits, total Series (11).
Tied National League Championship Series records for most Series played, one club (6); most three-base hits, total Series (2).

Year Club	League	Pos.	G.	AB.	R.	H.	2B.	3B.	HR.	RBI.	B.A.	PO.	A.	E.	F.A.
1970—Cincinnati	Nat.	C	3	9	2	2	0	0	1	1	.222	20	3	0	1.000
1972—Cincinnati	Nat.	C	5	18	3	6	1	1	1	2	.333	28	3	1	.969
1973—Cincinnati	Nat.	C	5	19	1	5	2	0	1	1	.263	31	2	0	1.000
1975—Cincinnati	Nat.	C	3	13	1	1	0	0	0	0	.077	18	4	0	1.000
1976—Cincinnati	Nat.	C	3	12	3	4	1	0	1	1	.333	11	4	0	1.000
1979—Cincinnati	Nat.	C	3	12	1	3	0	1	1	1	.250	17	2	0	1.000
Championship Series Totals			22	83	11	21	4	2	5	6	.253	125	18	1	.993

WORLD SERIES RECORD

Tied World Series records for most double plays by catcher, total Series (6); most double plays by catcher, Series (3), 1975; one or more hits, each game, four-game Series, 1976.

Year Club	League	Pos.	G.	AB.	R.	H.	2B.	3B.	HR.	RBI.	B.A.	PO.	A.	E.	F.A.
1970—Cincinnati	Nat.	C	5	19	3	4	0	0	1	3	.211	36	3	0	1.000
1972—Cincinnati	Nat.	C	7	23	4	6	1	0	1	1	.261	41	7	1	.980
1975—Cincinnati	Nat.	C	7	29	5	6	2	0	1	4	.207	44	6	0	1.000
1976—Cincinnati	Nat.	C	4	15	4	8	1	1	2	6	.533	18	2	0	1.000
World Series Totals			23	86	16	24	4	1	5	14	.279	139	18	1	.994

ALL-STAR GAME RECORD

Tied All-Star Game records for most strikeouts, nine-inning game (3), July 14, 1970; most putouts by catcher, game (10), July 15, 1975; most chances accepted by catcher, game (11), July 15, 1975.

Year League	Pos.	AB.	R.	H.	2B.	3B.	HR.	RBI.	B.A.	PO.	A.	E.	F.A.
1968—National	C	0	0	0	0	0	0	0	.000	2	0	0	1.000
1969—National	C	3	2	2	0	0	1	2	.667	4	0	0	1.000
1970—National	C	3	0	0	0	0	0	0	.000	5	1	0	1.000
1971—National	C	4	1	2	0	0	1	2	.500	5	0	0	1.000
1972—National	C	2	0	1	0	0	0	0	.500	3	0	0	1.000
1973—National	C	3	1	1	0	0	1	1	.333	3	0	0	1.000
1974—National	C	3	1	2	0	0	0	0	.667	7	0	1	.875
1975—National	C	4	0	1	0	0	0	1	.250	10	1	0	1.000
1976—National	C	2	0	1	0	0	0	0	.500	1	0	0	1.000
1977—National	C	2	0	0	0	0	0	0	.000	4	0	0	1.000
1980—National	C	1	0	0	0	0	0	0	.000	5	0	0	1.000
1983—National	PH	1	0	0	0	0	0	0	.000	0	0	0	.000
All-Star Game Totals		28	5	10	0	0	3	6	.357	49	2	1	.981

Named to National League All-Star Team for 1978 game; replaced due to injury by Biff Pocoroba.
Named to National League All-Star Team for 1979 game; replaced due to injury by John Stearns.

—DID YOU KNOW—

That Johnny Bench's 10 Gold Gloves are the most for any catcher since the award was established in 1957?

BRUCE EDWIN BENEDICT

Born August 18, 1955, at Birmingham, Ala.
Height, 6.01. Weight, 185.
Throws and bats righthanded.
Attended University of Nebraska at Omaha.
Son of David Benedict, pitcher in New York Yankees', Washington Senators'
and St. Louis Cardinals' organizations, 1950 through 1958.

Year	Club	League	Pos.	G.	AB.	R.	H.	2B.	3B.	HR.	RBI.	B.A.	PO.	A.	E.	F.A.
1976—Kingsport	Appal.		C	17	63	10	18	1	0	0	4	.286	98	25	3	.976
1976—Greenwood	W. Car.		C	21	54	7	13	1	0	1	10	.241	93	12	5	.955
1976—Savannah	South.		C	24	73	10	21	1	0	0	7	.288	107	12	2	.983
1977—Savannah	South.		C	124	395	55	104	15	0	7	40	.263	★770	★112	13	.985
1978—Richmond	Int.		C	111	348	41	97	13	0	2	34	.279	592	56	4	★.994
1978—Atlanta	Nat.		C	22	52	3	13	2	0	0	1	.250	81	14	1	.990
1979—Atlanta	Nat.		C	76	204	14	46	11	0	0	15	.225	344	35	6	.984
1980—Richmond	Int.		C	3	10	0	3	0	0	0	0	.300	10	5	0	1.000
1980—Atlanta	Nat.		C	120	359	18	91	14	1	2	34	.253	502	76	7	.988
1981—Atlanta	Nat.		C	90	295	26	78	12	1	5	35	.264	404	★73	7	.986
1982—Atlanta	Nat.		C	118	386	34	95	11	1	3	44	.246	602	73	5	★.993
1983—Atlanta	Nat.		C	134	423	43	126	13	1	2	43	.298	738	91	7	.992
Major League Totals				560	1719	138	449	63	4	12	172	.261	2671	362	33	.989

Selected by Atlanta Braves' organization in 5th round of free-agent draft, June 8, 1976.

CHAMPIONSHIP SERIES RECORD

Year	Club	League	Pos.	G.	AB.	R.	H.	2B.	3B.	HR.	RBI.	B.A.	PO.	A.	E.	F.A.
1982—Atlanta	Nat.		C	3	8	1	2	1	0	0	0	.250	16	2	0	1.000

ALL-STAR GAME RECORD

Year	League	Pos.	AB.	R.	H.	2B.	3B.	HR.	RBI.	B.A.	PO.	A.	E.	F.A.
1981—National		C	1	0	0	0	0	0	0	.000	3	0	0	1.000
1983—National		C	1	0	1	0	0	0	0	1.000	5	0	0	1.000
All-Star Game Totals			2	0	1	0	0	0	0	.500	8	0	0	1.000

JUAN JOSE BENIQUEZ (TORRES)

Name pronounced Be-NEE-kez.

Born May 13, 1950, at San Sebastian, Puerto Rico.
Height, 5.11. Weight, 175.
Throws and bats righthanded.

Established modern major league record for most errors, shortstop, two consecutive games (6), July 13 and 14, 1972.
Led American League outfielders in putouts with 410 and total chances with 434 in 1976.
Led International League in sacrifice hits with 11 in 1971.
Led Florida State League shortstops in assists with 372 and double plays with 51 in 1969.
Named outfielder on THE SPORTING NEWS American League All-Star fielding team, 1977.

Year	Club	League	Pos.	G.	AB.	R.	H.	2B.	3B.	HR.	RBI.	B.A.	PO.	A.	E.	F.A.
1969—Winter Haven	Fla. St.		★SS-2B	120	426	59	111	15	★14	2	59	.261	175	373	★49	.918
1969—Winston-Salem	Carol.		SS	2	10	0	2	0	0	0	0	.200	2	6	0	1.000
1970—Winston-Salem	Carol.		SS	92	335	53	91	12	2	9	37	.272	144	275	35	.923
1970—Pawtucket	East.		SS	56	233	29	58	5	3	4	25	.249	105	167	29	.904
1971—Louisville	Int.		SS	132	534	82	149	12	★16	4	51	.279	205	364	★55	.912
1971—Boston	Amer.		SS	16	57	8	17	2	0	0	4	.298	24	27	6	.895
1972—Louisville	Int.		SS	66	277	40	82	10	7	5	32	.296	114	172	21	.932
1972—Boston	Amer.		SS	33	99	10	24	4	1	1	8	.242	38	88	14	.900
1973—Pawtucket	Int.		O-S-2-3	131	440	80	131	24	4	13	52	★.298	196	176	26	.934
1974—Boston†	Amer.		OF	106	389	60	104	14	3	5	33	.267	264	4	6	.978
1975—Boston‡§	Amer.		OF-3B	78	254	43	74	14	4	2	17	.291	110	17	1	.992
1976—Texas	Amer.		★OF-2B	145	478	49	122	14	4	0	33	.255	411	★18	7	.984
1977—Texas x	Amer.		OF	123	424	56	114	19	6	10	50	.269	311	10	4	.988
1978—Texas yz	Amer.		OF	127	473	61	123	17	3	11	50	.260	309	8	9	.972
1979—New York abc	Amer.		OF-3B	62	142	19	36	6	1	4	17	.254	100	15	2	.983
1980—Seattle defg	Amer.		OF	70	237	26	54	10	0	6	21	.228	176	3	8	.957
1981—California	Amer.		OF	58	166	18	30	5	0	3	13	.181	117	0	5	.959
1982—California	Amer.		OF	112	196	25	52	11	2	3	24	.265	113	4	2	.983
1983—California h	Amer.		OF	92	315	44	96	15	0	3	34	.305	174	8	6	.968
Major League Totals				1022	3230	419	846	131	24	48	304	.262	2147	202	71	.971

Signed as free agent by Boston Red Sox' organization, October 1, 1968.
†On disabled list, July 3 to July 28, 1974.
‡On supplemental disabled list, July 2 to July 18, 1975.
§Traded with Pitcher Steve Barr, a minor league player to be named later and an estimated $200,000 to Texas Rangers for Pitcher Ferguson Jenkins, November 17, 1975; Texas acquired Pitcher Craig Skok to complete deal, December 12, 1975.
xOn supplemental disabled list, July 31 to August 15, 1977.
yOn disabled list, June 13 to July 13, 1978.
zTraded with Pitchers Paul Mirabella, Mike Griffin and Dave Righetti and Outfielder Greg Jemison to New York Yankees for Pitchers Sparky Lyle, Larry McCall and Dave Rajsich, Catcher Mike Heath, Shortstop Domingo Ramos and cash, November 10, 1978.
aOn disabled list, July 9 to July 30, 1979.
bOn supplemental disabled list, July 31 to September 1, 1979.
cTraded with Catcher Jerry Narron and Pitchers Jim Beattie and Rick Anderson to Seattle Mariners for Outfield-

er Ruppert Jones and Pitcher Jim Lewis, November 1, 1979.
  dOn disabled list, April 9 to June 2, 1980.
  eOn supplemental disabled list, July 19 to August 8, 1980.
  fOn suspended list, September 2 to September 7, 1980.
  gGranted free agency, October 24, 1980; signed by California Angels, December 29, 1980.
  hOn disabled list, June 20 to August 9, 1983.

CHAMPIONSHIP SERIES RECORD

Tied American League Championship Series record for most stolen bases, three-game Series (2), 1975.

Year Club	League	Pos.	G.	AB.	R.	H.	2B.	3B.	HR.	RBI.	B.A.	PO.	A.	E.	F.A.
1975—Boston	Amer.	DH	3	12	2	3	0	0	0	1	.250	0	0	0	.000
1982—California	Amer.	OF	2	0	0	0	0	0	0	0	.000	1	0	0	1.000
Championship Series Totals			5	12	2	3	0	0	0	1	.250	1	0	0	1.000

WORLD SERIES RECORD

Year Club	League	Pos.	G.	AB.	R.	H.	2B.	3B.	HR.	RBI.	B.A.	PO.	A.	E.	F.A.
1975—Boston	Amer.	OF-PH	3	8	0	1	0	0	0	1	.125	6	1	0	1.000

JUAN BAUTISTA BERENGUER

Name pronounced Bare-en-GARE.

Born November 30, 1954, at Aguadulce, Panama.
Height, 5.11. Weight, 215.
Throws and bats righthanded.

Led Carolina League pitchers in games started with 28 and hit batsmen with 13 in 1976.
Tied for American Association lead in complete games with 9 in 1982.
Tied for Texas League pitchers lead in games started with 26 in 1977.
Tied for Midwest League lead in hit batsmen with 8 in 1975.
Named International League Pitcher of the Year, 1978.

Year Club	League	G.	IP.	W.	L.	Pct.	H.	R.	ER.	SO.	BB.	ERA.
1975—Wausau	Midwest	18	95	5	4	.556	83	41	31	58	50	2.94
1976—Lynchburg	Carolina	28	187	10	13	.435	*175	89	*75	114	*118	3.61
1977—Jackson	Texas	26	181	9	8	.529	143	89	69	*160	*126	3.43
1978—Tidewater	Int'national	24	147	10	7	.588	117	60	60	130	91	3.67
1978—New York†	National	5	13	0	2	.000	17	12	12	8	11	8.31
1979—Tacoma	P. Coast	26	166	8	8	.500	128	101	90	*220	129	4.88
1979—New York	National	5	31	1	1	.500	28	13	10	25	12	2.90
1980—Tidewater	Int'national	27	157	9	●15	.375	122	78	67	*178	76	3.84
1980—New York‡	National	6	9	0	1	.000	9	9	6	7	10	6.00
1981—Kansas City§-Toronto x	American	20	91	2	*13	.133	84	62	53	49	51	5.24
1982—Evansville	Am. Assoc.	25	156⅓	11	10	.524	152	85	80	127	80	4.61
1982—Detroit	American	2	6⅔	0	0	.000	5	5	5	8	9	6.75
1983—Detroit	American	37	157⅔	9	5	.643	110	58	55	129	71	3.14
National League Totals		16	53	1	4	.200	54	34	28	40	33	4.75
American League Totals		59	255⅓	11	18	.379	199	125	113	186	131	3.98
Major League Totals		75	308⅓	12	22	.353	253	159	141	226	164	4.12

Signed as free agent by New York Mets' organization, February 22, 1975.
†Loaned to Tacoma (Cleveland Indians' organization), March 24, 1979; returned August 29, 1979.
‡Traded to Kansas City for Outfielder Marvell Wynne and Pitcher John Skinner, March 31, 1981.
§Sold on waivers to Toronto Blue Jays, August 8, 1981.
xReleased, March 28, 1982; signed by Evansville (Detroit Tigers' organization), April 4, 1982.

BRUCE MICHAEL BERENYI

Name pronounced Ber-ENN-ee.

Born August 21, 1954, at Bryan, O.
Height, 6.03. Weight, 215.
Throws and bats righthanded.
Attended Glen Oaks Community College, Centerville, Mich. and
Northeast Missouri State University, Kirksville, Mo.
Nephew of Ned Garver, pitcher with St. Louis Browns, Detroit Tigers,
Kansas City A's and Los Angeles Angels, 1948 through 1961.

Led American Association in shutouts with 3 and wild pitches with 13 in 1979.
Named Southern League Pitcher of the Year, 1978.

Year Club	League	G.	IP.	W.	L.	Pct.	H.	R.	ER.	SO.	BB.	ERA.
1976—Eugene	Northwest	12	49	3	1	.750	50	37	26	39	55	4.78
1977—Shelby	W. Carol.	25	145	10	8	.556	102	55	37	120	75	*2.30
1978—Nashville†	Southern	23	135	10	5	.667	107	44	37	103	63	2.47
1979—Indianapolis	Am. Assoc.	25	166	9	9	.500	134	64	52	*136	98	*2.82
1980—Indianapolis	Am. Assoc.	20	123	5	8	.385	111	66	59	*121	●100	4.32
1980—Cincinnati	National	6	28	2	2	.500	34	26	24	19	23	7.71
1981—Cincinnati	National	21	126	9	6	.600	97	55	49	106	*77	3.50
1982—Cincinnati	National	34	222⅓	9	*18	.333	208	90	83	157	96	3.36
1983—Cincinnati	National	32	186⅓	9	14	.391	173	92	80	151	102	3.86
Major League Totals		93	562⅔	29	40	.420	512	263	236	433	298	3.77

Selected by Detroit Tigers' organization in 19th round of free-agent draft, June 4, 1975.
Selected by Cincinnati Reds' organization in secondary phase of free-agent draft, June 8, 1976.
†On disabled list, June 30 to July 27, 1978.

DAVID BRUCE BERGMAN
(Dave)

Born June 6, 1953, at Evanston, Ill.
Height, 6.02. Weight, 180.
Throws and bats lefthanded.
Received bachelor of arts degree in business administration
from Illinois State University, Normal, Ill., in 1974.

Led International League in bases on balls received with 95 in 1979.
Led International League first basemen in putouts with 1,199 in 1976.
Led Eastern League first basemen in assists with 58 in 1975.
Named Eastern League Player of the Year, 1975.

Year Club	League	Pos.	G.	AB.	R.	H.	2B.	3B.	HR.	RBI.	B.A.	PO.	A.	E.	F.A.
1974—Oneonta	NYP	1B	56	201	60	70	6	•7	10	48	*.348	494	*29	8	*.985
1975—West Haven	East.	1B-OF	124	399	76	124	15	6	11	60	*.311	610	61	5	.993
1975—New York.............	Amer.	OF	7	17	0	0	0	0	0	0	.000	10	1	1	.917
1976—Syracuse	Int.	*1B-OF	134	455	68	134	23	2	7	65	.295	1201	82	10	*.992
1977—Syracuse	Int.	OF-1B	132	468	88	146	29	4	16	59	.312	534	39	8	.986
1977—New York†...........	Amer.	OF-1B	5	4	1	1	0	0	0	1	.250	8	0	0	1.000
1978—Houston..................	Nat.	1B-OF	104	186	15	43	5	1	0	12	.231	328	16	4	.989
1979—Charleston.............	Int.	1B-OF	138	461	78	129	23	3	6	58	.280	910	61	11	.989
1979—Houston..................	Nat.	1B	13	15	4	6	0	0	1	2	.400	8	0	0	1.000
1980—Houston..................	Nat.	1B-OF	90	78	12	20	6	1	0	3	.256	187	16	1	.995
1981—Hou.‡-S.F............	Nat.	1B-OF	69	151	17	38	9	0	4	14	.252	255	25	3	.989
1982—San Francisco	Nat.	1B-OF	100	121	22	33	3	1	4	14	.273	321	20	4	.988
1983—San Francisco	Nat.	1B-OF	90	140	16	40	4	1	6	24	.286	299	27	2	.994
National League Totals............			466	691	86	180	27	4	15	69	.260	1398	104	14	.991
American League Totals............			12	21	1	1	0	0	0	1	.048	18	1	1	.950
Major League Totals....................			478	712	87	181	27	4	15	70	.254	1416	105	15	.990

Selected by Chicago Cubs' organization in 12th round of free-agent draft, June 8, 1971.
Selected by New York Yankees' organization in 2nd round of free-agent draft, June 5, 1974.
†Traded to Houston Astros, November 23, 1977, completing deal in which Houston traded First Baseman-Catcher Cliff Johnson to New York Yankees for Infielder Mike Fischlin, Pitcher Randy Niemann and a player to be named later, June 15, 1977.
‡Traded with Outfielder Jeff Leonard to San Francisco Giants for First Baseman Mike Ivie, April 20, 1981.

CHAMPIONSHIP SERIES RECORD

Year Club	League	Pos.	G.	AB.	R.	H.	2B.	3B.	HR.	RBI.	B.A.	PO.	A.	E.	F.A.
1980—Houston..................	Nat.	PR-1B	4	3	0	1	0	1	0	2	.333	8	2	1	.909

ANTONIO BERNAZARD (GARCIA)
(Tony)

Born August 24, 1956, at Caguas, P.R.
Height, 5.09. Weight, 160.
Throws right and bats right and lefthanded.
Attended Humacao College, Humacao, P.R.
Brother of Oscar Bernazard, outfielder in Pittsburgh Pirates'
and Montreal Expos' organizations, 1975 through 1978.

Led Eastern League in caught stealing with 20 in 1977.
Led American Association second basemen in putouts with 297, assists with 386 and double plays with 101 in 1978.
Led Eastern League second basemen in double plays with 70 in 1976.
Led Florida State League second basemen in assists with 386 in 1975.

Year Club	League	Pos.	G.	AB.	R.	H.	2B.	3B.	HR.	RBI.	B.A.	PO.	A.	E.	F.A.
1974—Kinston†................	Carol.	2B	56	225	22	45	3	1	0	16	.200	129	142	19	.934
1974—Sarasota Expos‡..	Gulf C.	2B	34	109	11	18	2	1	1	6	.165	95	71	7	.960
1975—W. Palm Beach....	Fla. St.	2B-SS	*134	*509	65	121	16	2	6	50	.238	282	389	28	.960
1976—Quebec City..........	East.	2B	106	334	35	72	8	3	1	26	.216	227	257	18	.964
1977—Quebec City..........	East.	2B	125	425	68	119	11	6	1	34	.280	273	379	25	.963
1978—Denver	A. A.	*2-3-O	128	479	*107	137	30	9	9	65	.286	302	390	*32	.956
1979—Denver	A. A.	2B	82	273	58	82	15	2	3	29	.300	178	275	•19	.960
1979—Montreal................	Nat.	2B	22	40	11	12	2	0	1	8	.300	22	34	1	.982
1980—Montreal§..............	Nat.	2B-SS	82	183	26	41	7	1	5	18	.224	82	151	9	.963
1981—Chicago.................	Amer.	2B-SS	106	384	53	106	14	4	6	34	.276	228	320	7	.987
1982—Chicago x..............	Amer.	2B	137	540	90	138	25	9	11	56	.256	353	443	12	.985
1983—Chi. y-Sea. z	Amer.	2B	139	533	65	141	34	3	8	56	.265	262	422	19	.973
National League Totals............			104	223	37	53	9	1	6	26	.238	104	185	10	.967
American League Totals............			382	1457	208	385	73	16	25	146	.264	843	1185	38	.982
Major League Totals....................			486	1680	245	438	82	17	31	172	.261	947	1370	48	.980

Signed as free agent by Montreal Expos' organization, November 13, 1973.
†On disabled list, June 10 to June 17, 1974.
‡On temporary inactive list, August 15 to September 25, 1974.
§Traded to Chicago White Sox for Pitcher Richard Wortham, December 12, 1980.
xOn supplemental disabled list, September 13, 1982 through remainder of season.
yTraded to Seattle Mariners for Second Baseman Julio Cruz, June 15, 1983.
zTraded to Cleveland Indians for Outfielder Gorman Thomas and Second Baseman Jack Perconte, December 7, 1983.

DALE ANTHONY BERRA

Born December 13, 1956, at Ridgewood, N. J.
Height, 6.00. Weight, 190.
Throws and bats righthanded.
Son of Yogi Berra, Hall of Fame catcher with New York Yankees and New·York Mets, 1946 through
1963 and 1965; manager, New York Yankees, 1964 and for 1984; manager, New York Mets,
1972 through 1975; coach, New York Yankees, 1976 through 1983; brother of
Larry Berra Jr., catcher in New York Mets' organization, 1971 and 1972; and
Tim Berra, wide receiver with Baltimore Colts, 1974.

Established major league record for most times awarded first base on catcher's interference, season (7), 1983.
Led National League in intentional bases on balls received with 19 in 1983.
Led New York-Pennsylvania League in sacrifice flies with 8 in 1975.
Led Western Carolinas League third basemen in double plays with 27 in 1976.
Tied for New York-Pennsylvania League lead in double plays by third basemen with 13 in 1975.

Year Club	League	Pos.	G.	AB.	R.	H.	2B.	3B.	HR.	RBI.	B.A.	PO.	A.	E.	F.A.
1975—Niagara Falls	NYP	3B	67	*269	36	69	6	4	3	*49	.257	67	*137	*24	.895
1976—Charleston	W. Car.	3B	*139	527	78	157	28	5	16	89	.298	129	*269	*41	.907
1977—Columbus	Int.	*3B-SS	125	438	68	127	18	7	18	54	.290	97	252	*29	.923
1977—Pittsburgh	Nat.	3B	17	40	0	7	1	0	0	3	.175	14	22	1	.973
1978—Columbus	Int.	SS-3B	99	361	58	101	18	5	18	63	.280	142	280	22	.950
1978—Pittsburgh	Nat.	3B-SS	56	135	16	28	2	0	6	14	.207	31	84	11	.913
1979—Portland	P. C.	SS-3B	56	210	37	68	13	2	6	32	.324	68	158	8	.966
1979—Pittsburgh	Nat.	SS-3B	44	123	11	26	5	0	3	15	.211	43	86	12	.915
1980—Pittsburgh	Nat.	3B-SS-2B	93	245	21	54	8	2	6	31	.220	88	171	11	.959
1981—Pittsburgh	Nat.	3B-SS-2B	81	232	21	56	12	0	2	27	.241	89	167	8	.970
1982—Pittsburgh	Nat.	SS-3B	156	529	64	139	25	5	10	61	.263	241	505	30	.961
1983—Pittsburgh	Nat.	SS	161	537	51	135	25	1	10	52	.251	286	505	30	.963
Major League Totals			608	1841	184	445	78	8	37	203	.242	792	1540	103	.958

Selected by Pittsburgh Pirates' organization in 1st round (20th player selected) of free-agent draft, June 4, 1975.

KARL JON BEST

Born March 6, 1959, at Aberdeen, Wash.
Height, 6.04. Weight, 205.
Throws and bats righthanded.

Year Club	League	G.	IP.	W.	L.	Pct.	H.	R.	ER.	SO.	BB.	ERA.
1978—Stockton	California	12	40	1	5	.167	42	37	21	32	33	4.73
1978—Bellingham	Northwest	10	54	3	3	.500	58	32	30	47	32	5.00
1979—Alexandria	Carolina	24	167	8	11	.421	150	74	60	108	85	3.23
1980—Lynn	Eastern	26	154	9	14	.391	144	116	95	92	*106	5.55
1981—Lynn†	Eastern	13	71	4	4	.500	73	37	30	50	31	3.80
1982—Lynn	Eastern	21	138⅓	9	4	.692	104	63	53	125	90	3.45
1983—Salt Lake City	P. Coast	51	84	7	4	.636	86	51	45	108	64	4.82
1983—Seattle	American	4	5⅓	0	1	.000	14	9	8	3	5	13.50
Major League Totals		4	5⅓	0	1	.000	14	9	8	3	5	13.50

Selected by Seattle Mariners' organization in 12th round of free-agent draft, June 7, 1977.
†On disabled list, May 9 to July 25, 1981.

JEFFREY ALLEN BETTENDORF
(Jeff)

Born December 10, 1961, at Lompoc, Calif.
Height, 6.03. Weight, 180.
Throws and bats righthanded.
Related to Matt Fitts, pitcher in New York Mets' organization.

Led Northwest League in wild pitches with 13 in 1979.

Year Club	League	G.	IP.	W.	L.	Pct.	H.	R.	ER.	SO.	BB.	ERA.
1979—Grays Harbor	Northwest	9	44	1	4	.200	50	33	20	36	33	4.09
1980—Little Falls	NYP	12	40	0	5	.000	47	49	43	29	41	9.68
1981—Lynchburg	Carolina	24	109	10	9	.526	129	86	76	68	68	6.28
1982—Lynchburg	Carolina	4	20⅔	0	1	.000	20	19	15	8	18	6.53
1982—Shelby	S. Atlantic	20	117⅔	9	5	.643	111	69	56	86	62	4.28
1983—Lynchburg	Carolina	21	148⅓	13	4	.765	142	74	48	138	62	2.91
1983—Jackson†	Texas	6	31⅓	3	0	1.000	31	15	11	24	17	3.16

Selected by New York Mets' organization in 2nd round of free-agent draft, June 5, 1979.
†Drafted by Oakland A's, December 5, 1983.

KURT ANTHONY BEVACQUA

Name pronounced Buh-VAHK-wuh.

Born January 23, 1947, at Miami Beach, Fla.
Height, 6.02. Weight, 195.
Throws and bats righthanded.
Attended Miami-Dade (North) Community College, Miami, Fla.

Led American Association third basemen in putouts with 73, assists with 168, total chances with 253, double plays
with 26 and fielding percentage with .953 in 1970.
Tied for Southern League lead in double plays by third basemen with 24 in 1969.

Year	Club	League	Pos.	G.	AB.	R.	H.	2B.	3B.	HR.	RBI.	B.A.	PO.	A.	E.	F.A.
1967—Tampa	Fla. St.	2B	65	217	13	48	2	1	0	11	.221	119	143	10	.963
1968—Tampa	Fla. St.	2B-1B	91	219	18	55	11	2	2	26	.251	264	74	7	.980
1969—Asheville	South.	3B	133	490	72	155	26	6	16	91	.316	★129	245	29	.928
1970—Indianapolis	A. A.	3-0-S-1-2	135	482	62	126	26	5	15	67	.261	157	216	21	.947
1971—Ind.†-Wichita	A. A.	3-S-2-0	60	235	36	71	16	1	9	38	.302	107	130	11	.956
1971—Cleveland	Amer.	2-0-3-S	55	137	9	28	3	1	3	13	.204	77	72	5	.968
1972—Portland	P. C.	3-2-0-S	145	537	57	168	27	7	9	72	.313	223	252	30	.941
1972—Cleveland‡	Amer.	OF-3B	19	35	2	4	0	0	1	1	.114	11	5	1	.941
1973—Kansas City§	Amer.	3-2-0-1	99	276	39	71	8	3	2	40	.257	120	90	9	.959
1974—Pittsburgh x	Nat.	3B-OF	18	35	1	4	1	0	0	0	.114	8	13	1	.955
1974—Kansas City y	Amer.	1-3-2-S	39	90	10	19	0	0	0	3	.211	90	29	5	.960
1975—Milwaukee	Amer.	3-2-S-1	104	258	30	59	14	0	2	24	.229	157	168	13	.962
1976—Milwaukee	Amer.	2B	12	7	3	1	0	0	0	0	.143	0	6	0	1.000
1976—Spokane z a	P. C.	3-S-2-0	95	356	70	120	24	0	12	49	.337	116	197	22	.934
1977—Tucson	P. C.	3B-SS	94	358	75	126	29	4	9	76	.352	74	231	23	.930
1977—Texas	Amer.	O-3-1-2	39	96	13	32	7	2	5	28	.333	42	31	1	.986
1978—Texas b	Amer.	3B-2B-1B	90	248	21	55	12	0	6	30	.222	62	116	18	.908
1979—San Diego	Nat.	3-2-1-0	114	297	23	75	12	4	1	34	.253	115	156	11	.961
1980—S.D.c-Pitt.	Nat.	3-0-1-2	84	114	5	26	7	1	0	16	.228	32	31	2	.969
1981—Pittsburgh	Nat.	2B-3B	29	27	2	7	1	0	1	4	.259	7	10	1	.944
1981—Portland d	P. C.	3B	14	52	6	13	1	0	0	5	.250	12	24	1	.973
1982—San Diego	Nat.	1B-OF-3B	64	123	15	31	9	0	0	24	.252	256	16	3	.989
1983—San Diego	Nat.	1B-3B-OF	74	156	17	38	7	0	2	24	.244	207	28	2	.992
National League Totals			383	752	63	181	37	5	4	102	.241	625	254	20	.978
American League Totals			457	1147	127	269	44	6	19	139	.235	559	517	52	.954
Major League Totals			840	1899	190	450	81	11	23	241	.237	1184	771	72	.964

Selected by New York Mets' organization in 36th round of free-agent draft, June 6, 1966.
Selected by Atlanta Braves' organization in 6th round of free-agent draft, January 28, 1967.
Selected by Cincinnati Reds' organization in secondary phase of free-agent draft, June 7, 1967.
†Traded to Cleveland Indians for Outfielder Charles Bradford, May 8, 1971.
‡Traded to Kansas City Royals for Pitcher Mike Hedlund, November 2, 1972.
§Traded with Catcher-Outfielder Ed Kirkpatrick and First Baseman Winston Cole to Pittsburgh Pirates for Pitcher Nelson Briles and Infielder Fernando Gonzalez, December 4, 1973.
xTraded to Kansas City Royals for cash and Infielder Cal Meier, July 8, 1974.
ySold to Milwaukee Brewers, March 6, 1975.
zSold to Seattle Mariners, October 22, 1976.
aReleased, March 28, 1977; signed by Texas Rangers' organization, April 8, 1977.
bTraded with Catcher Bill Fahey and First Baseman Mike Hargrove to San Diego Padres for Outfielder Oscar Gamble, Catcher Dave Roberts and cash estimated at $300,000, October 25, 1978.
cTraded with a player to be named later to Pittsburgh Pirates for Outfielders Rick Lancellotti and Luis Salazar, August 5, 1980; Pittsburgh acquired Pitcher Mark Lee to complete deal, August 12, 1980.
dReleased, October 26, 1981; signed by San Diego Padres, April 2, 1982.

ROLAND AMERICO BIANCALANA

Name pronounced Bee-AHN-ka-la-na.

(Buddy)

Born February 2, 1960, at Larkspur, Calif.
Height, 5.11. Weight, 160.
Throws right and bats right and lefthanded.
Attended College of Marin, Kentfield, Calif., and University of San Francisco, San Francisco, Calif.
Led American Association shortstops in double plays with 79 in 1982.

Year	Club	League	Pos.	G.	AB.	R.	H.	2B.	3B.	HR.	RBI.	B.A.	PO.	A.	E.	F.A.
1978—Sarasota Royals	Gulf C.	SS	32	76	12	13	1	1	0	2	.171	36	81	6	.951
1979—Ft. Myers	Fla. St.	SS	125	357	44	·71	7	4	2	32	.199	★236	342	36	.941
1980—Ft. Myers	Fla. St.	SS	92	258	30	44	5	2	0	28	.171	189	232	23	.948
1981—Jacksonville	South.	SS	132	385	47	81	7	2	2	27	.210	208	374	48	.924
1982—Omaha	A. A.	SS	130	415	56	104	16	9	2	36	.251	204	●357	18	★.969
1982—Kansas City	Amer.	SS	3	2	0	1	0	1	0	0	.500	2	8	0	1.000
1983—Omaha	A. A.	SS	113	367	41	82	13	3	5	39	.223	184	341	23	.958
1983—Kansas City	Amer.	SS	6	15	2	3	0	0	0	0	.200	11	21	3	.914
Major League Totals			9	17	2	4	0	1	0	0	.235	13	29	3	.933

Selected by Kansas City Royals' organization in 1st round (25th player selected) or free-agent draft, June 6, 1978.

JAMES BLAIR BIBBY

(Jim)

Born October 29, 1944, at Franklinton, N. C.
Height, 6.05. Weight, 250.
Throws and bats righthanded.
Attended Fayetteville State College, Fayetteville, N. C., and received bachelor of science degree in physical education from Lynchburg College, Lynchburg, Va. in 1976.
Brother of Henry Bibby, guard with New York Knicks, New Orleans Jazz, Philadelphia 76ers and San Diego Clippers, 1972-73 through 1980-81.

Pitched 6-0 no-hit victory against Oakland Athletics, July 30, 1973.
Led American League in balks with 4 in 1977.
Led American Association in hit batsmen with 12 in 1972.
Led International League in wild pitches with 20 in 1971.
Named righthanded pitcher on THE SPORTING NEWS National League All-Star Team, 1980.

Year Club	League	G.	IP.	W.	L.	Pct.	H.	R.	ER.	SO.	BB.	ERA.
1965—Marion	Ap'lachian	13	24	2	3	.400	30	35	30	24	27	11.25
1966—Greenville	Carolina					(In Military Service)						
1967—Jacksonville	Int'national					(In Military Service)						
1968—Raleigh-Durham	Carolina	23	131	7	7	.500	79	49	41	118	74	2.82
1969—Memphis	Texas	17	122	10	6	.625	94	58	45	115	57	3.32
1969—Tidewater	Int'national	11	75	4	4	.500	64	33	29	65	34	3.48
1970—Tidewater†	Int'national					(Did not play)						
1971—Tidewater‡	Int'national	27	76	●15	6	.174	145	87	79	150	109	4.04
1972—Tulsa	Am. Assoc.	27	195	13	9	.591	155	76	67	208	76	3.09
1972—St. Louis§	National	6	40	1	3	.250	29	18	15	28	19	3.38
1973—St. Louis§	National	6	16	0	2	.000	19	17	17	12	17	9.56
1973—Texas	American	26	180	9	10	.474	121	73	65	155	106	3.25
1974—Texas	American	41	264	19	19	.500	255	146	★139	149	113	4.74
1975—Texas x-Cleveland	American	36	181	7	15	.318	172	89	78	93	78	3.88
1976—Cleveland	American	34	163	13	7	.650	162	61	58	84	56	3.20
1977—Cleveland y	American	37	207	12	13	.480	197	100	82	141	73	3.57
1978—Pittsburgh	National	34	107	8	7	.533	100	52	42	72	39	3.53
1979—Pittsburgh	National	34	138	12	4	★.750	110	51	43	103	47	2.80
1980—Pittsburgh	National	35	238	19	6	★.760	210	95	88	144	88	3.33
1981—Pittsburgh	National	14	94	6	3	.667	79	30	26	48	26	2.49
1982—Pittsburgh z	National					(Did not play)						
1983—Pittsburgh a	National	29	78	5	12	.294	92	60	58	44	51	6.69
National League Totals		158	711	51	37	.580	639	323	289	451	287	3.66
American League Totals		174	995	60	64	.484	907	469	422	622	426	3.82
Major League Totals		332	1706	111	101	.524	1546	792	711	1073	713	3.75

Signed as free agent by New York Mets' organization, July 19, 1965.

†On disabled list, April 17, 1970 through remainder of season.

‡Traded with Pitchers Rich Folkers and Charlie Hudson and Outfielder-First Baseman Art Shamsky to St. Louis Cardinals for Pitchers Chuck Taylor and Harry Parker, Infielder Tom Coulter and Outfielder Jim Beauchamp, October 18, 1971.

§Traded to Texas Rangers for Pitcher Mike Nagy and Catcher John Wockenfuss, June 6, 1973.

xTraded with Pitchers Jackie Brown and Rick Waits and an estimated $100,000 to Cleveland Indians for Pitcher Gaylord Perry, June 12, 1975.

yDeclared free agent in arbitration, March 6, 1978; signed by Pittsburgh Pirates, March 15, 1978.

zOn disabled list, April 2, 1982 through remainder of season.

aGranted free agency, November 7, 1983.

CHAMPIONSHIP SERIES RECORD

Year Club	League	G.	IP.	W.	L.	Pct.	H.	R.	ER.	SO.	BB.	ERA.
1979—Pittsburgh	National	1	7	0	0	.000	4	1	1	5	4	1.29

WORLD SERIES RECORD

Year Club	League	G.	IP.	W.	L.	Pct.	H.	R.	ER.	SO.	BB.	ERA.
1979—Pittsburgh	National	2	10⅓	0	0	.000	10	4	3	10	2	2.61

ALL-STAR GAME RECORD

Year League		IP.	W.	L.	Pct.	H.	R.	ER.	SO.	BB.	ERA.
1980—National		1	0	0	.000	1	0	0	0	0	0.00

MICHAEL JOSEPH BIELECKI
(Mike)

Born July 31, 1959, at Baltimore, Md.
Height, 6.03. Weight, 180.
Throws and bats righthanded.
Attended Valencia Community College, Orlando, Fla.

Tied for Eastern League lead in home runs allowed with 24 in 1982.
Tied for South Atlantic League lead in games started with 28 in 1981.

Year Club	League	G.	IP.	W.	L.	Pct.	H.	R.	ER.	SO.	BB.	ERA.
1979—Bradenton Pirates	Gulf Coast	9	51	1	4	.200	48	21	13	35	21	2.29
1980—Shelby	S. Atlantic	29	99	3	5	.375	106	60	50	78	58	4.55
1981—Greenwood	S. Atlantic	28	192	12	11	.522	172	95	73	163	82	3.42
1982—Buffalo	Eastern	25	157⅓	7	12	.368	165	96	●85	135	75	4.86
1983—Lynn	Eastern	25	163⅔	●15	7	.682	126	73	58	★143	69	3.19

Selected by Kansas City Royals' organization in 6th round of free-agent draft, January 9, 1979.
Selected by Pittsburgh Pirates' organization in secondary phase of free-agent draft, June 5, 1979.

LAWRENCE DAVID BIITTNER

Name pronounced BITT-nur.

(Larry)

Born July 27, 1947, at Pocahontas, Ia.
Height, 6.02. Weight, 200.
Throws and bats lefthanded.
Attended Drake University, Des Moines, Iowa and received bachelor of arts degree
in physical education from Buena Vista College, Storm Lake, Ia.

Led International League in sacrifice flies with 9 in 1974.

Year Club	League	Pos.	G.	AB.	R.	H.	2B.	3B.	HR.	RBI.	B.A.	PO.	A.	E.	F.A.
1968—Savannah	South.	OF-1B	58	199	24	57	12	2	1	21	.286	160	6	3	.982
1969—Savannah†	South.	OF	14	44	4	9	2	0	0	2	.205	13	2	1	.938
1970—Pittsfield	East.	1B-OF	102	388	51	126	27	6	9	62	.325	658	46	6	.992
1970—Washington	Amer.	PH	2	2	0	0	0	0	0	0	.000	0	0	0	.000
1971—Denver	A. A.	1B	25	101	20	36	10	2	2	18	.356	223	28	3	.988
1971—Washington‡	Amer	OF-1B	66	171	12	44	4	1	0	16	.257	83	7	6	.938
1972—Texas	Amer.	1B-OF	137	382	34	99	18	1	3	31	.259	503	41	8	.986
1973—Texas§	Amer.	OF-1B	83	258	19	65	8	2	1	12	.252	234	20	2	.992
1974—Memphis	Int.	1B-OF	94	303	53	99	16	1	3	48	.327	413	36	6	.987
1974—Montreal	Nat.	OF	18	26	2	7	1	0	0	3	.269	7	1	0	1.000
1975—Montreal	Nat.	OF	121	346	34	109	13	5	3	28	.315	166	8	5	.972
1976—Mont.y-Chi.z	Nat.	1B-OF	89	224	23	53	14	1	0	18	.237	283	35	5	.984
1977—Chicago	Nat.	1B-OF-P	138	493	74	147	28	1	12	62	.298	792	65	11	.987
1978—Chicago	Nat.	1B-OF	120	343	32	88	15	1	4	50	.257	601	53	9	.986
1979—Chicago	Nat.	OF-1B	111	272	35	79	13	3	3	50	.290	282	23	6	.981
1980—Chicago a	Nat.	1B-OF	127	273	21	68	12	2	1	34	.249	305	23	2	.994
1981—Cincinnati	Nat.	1B-OF	42	61	1	13	4	0	0	8	.213	57	5	0	1.000
1982—Cincinnati b	Nat.	OF-1B	97	184	18	57	9	2	2	24	.310	170	14	2	.989
1983—Texas c	Amer.	1B-OF	66	116	5	32	5	1	0	18	.276	140	15	2	.987
American League Totals			354	929	70	240	35	5	4	77	.258	960	83	18	.983
National League Totals			863	2222	240	621	109	15	25	277	.279	2663	237	40	.986
Major League Totals			1217	3151	310	861	144	20	29	354	.273	3623	320	58	.986

Selected by Washington Senators' organization in 16th round of free-agent draft, June 7, 1968.
†On military list, February 2 to August 8, 1969.
‡On military list, August 3 to August 24, 1971.
§Traded to Montreal Expos for Pitcher Pat Jarvis, December 20, 1973.
yTraded with Pitcher Steve Renko to Chicago Cubs for First Baseman Andre Thornton, May 17, 1976.
zOn supplemental disabled list, July 26 to August 10, 1976.
aGranted free agency, October 23, 1980; signed by Cincinnati Reds, January 12, 1981.
bReleased, December 6, 1982; signed by Texas Rangers, December 29, 1982.
cReleased, October 31, 1983.

PITCHING RECORD

Year Club	League	G.	IP.	W.	L.	Pct.	H.	R.	ER.	SO.	BB.	ERA.
1977—Chicago	National	1	1	0	0	.000	5	6	6	3	1	54.00

DANN JAMES BILARDELLO

Born May 26, 1959, at Santa Cruz, Calif.
Height, 6.00. Weight, 185.
Throws and bats righthanded.
Attended Cabrillo College, Aptos, Calif.

Led Texas League catchers in double plays with 15 in 1982.
Led Pioneer League catchers in double plays with 5 in 1978.
Tied for Texas League lead in stealers caught with 42 in 1982.

Year Club	League	Pos.	G.	AB.	R.	H.	2B.	3B.	HR.	RBI.	B.A.	PO.	A.	E.	F.A.
1978—Lethbridge	Pion.	C	42	133	21	33	8	1	2	20	.248	210	36	7	.972
1979—Clinton†	Midw.	C	52	142	18	34	4	0	2	15	.239	283	31	3	.991
1980—Lodi‡	Calif.	C	41	117	22	36	4	0	6	15	.308	169	30	8	.961
1981—Lodi	Calif.	C	105	352	72	108	19	2	21	80	.307	203	39	9	.964
1981—San Antonio	Texas	C	6	19	0	1	0	0	0	1	.053	34	2	1	.973
1982—San Antonio§	Texas	C	103	347	49	99	14	2	17	48	.285	546	*80	15	.977
1983—Cincinnati	Nat.	C	109	298	27	71	18	0	9	38	.238	494	72	5	.991
Major League Totals			109	298	27	71	18	0	9	38	.238	494	72	5	.991

Selected by Seattle Mariners' organization in 3rd round of free-agent draft, January 10, 1978.
Selected by Los Angeles Dodgers' organization in secondary phase of free-agent draft, June 6, 1978.
†On disabled list, May 9 to June 14, 1979.
‡On disabled list, June 12 to August 13, 1980.
§Drafted by Cincinnati Reds, December 6, 1982.

JAMES DOUGLAS BIRD
(Doug)

Born March 5, 1950, at Corona, Calif.
Height, 6.04. Weight, 190.
Throws and bats righthanded.
Attended Mesa Community College, Mesa, Ariz., and Mount San Antonio Junior College, Walnut, Calif.

Major league saves: 1973 (20), 1974 (10), 1975 (11), 1976 (2), 1977 (14), 1978 (1), 1980 (1), 1983 (1). Total—60.
Tied for National League lead in home runs allowed with 26 in 1982.
Led Northern League in home runs allowed with 10 in 1969.
Tied for California League lead in games started by pitchers with 27 and shutouts with 3 in 1971.

Year Club	League	G.	IP.	W.	L.	Pct.	H.	R.	ER.	SO.	BB.	ERA.
1969—Winnipeg	Northern	16	99	6	2	.750	105	45	38	88	17	3.45
1970—San Jose	California	3	10	0	2	.000	10	10	7	14	3	6.30
1970—Waterloo	Midwest	22	147	11	9	.550	122	49	30	149	32	*1.84
1971—San Jose	California	29	*182	*15	9	.625	175	84	69	143	48	3.41
1972—Jacksonville	Southern	24	122	10	7	.588	117	43	33	72	32	2.43

Year Club	League	G.	IP.	W.	L.	Pct.	H.	R.	ER.	SO.	BB.	ERA.
1972—Omaha	Am. Assoc.	7	9	1	1	.500	9	4	3	13	5	3.00
1973—Omaha	Am. Assoc.	4	6	1	0	1.000	5	0	0	3	1	0.00
1973—Kansas City	American	54	102	4	4	.500	81	37	34	83	30	3.00
1974—Kansas City	American	55	92	7	6	.538	100	31	28	62	27	2.74
1975—Kansas City	American	51	105	9	6	.600	100	42	38	81	40	3.26
1976—Kansas City	American	39	198	12	10	.545	191	90	74	107	31	3.36
1977—Kansas City	American	53	118	11	4	.733	120	52	51	83	29	3.89
1978—Kansas City†	American	40	99	6	6	.500	110	63	58	48	31	5.27
1979—Philadelphia‡§	National	32	61	2	0	1.000	73	35	35	33	16	5.16
1980—Columbus	Int'national	15	48	6	0	1.000	33	15	12	36	13	2.25
1980—New York	American	22	51	3	0	1.000	47	16	15	17	14	2.65
1981—New York x	American	17	53	5	1	.833	58	19	16	28	16	2.72
1981—Chicago	National	12	75	4	5	.444	72	34	30	34	16	3.60
1982—Chicago y	National	35	191	9	14	.391	230	119	*109	71	30	5.14
1983—Boston z	American	22	67⅔	1	4	.200	91	52	50	33	16	6.65
American League Totals		353	885⅔	58	41	.586	898	402	364	542	234	3.70
National League Totals		79	327	15	19	.441	375	188	174	138	62	4.79
Major League Totals		432	1212⅔	73	60	.549	1273	590	538	680	296	3.99

Selected by Cleveland Indians' organization in 29th round of free-agent draft, June 7, 1968.
Selected by Seattle Pilots' organization in secondary phase of free-agent draft, February 1, 1969.
Selected by Kansas City Royals' organization in secondary phase of free-agent draft, June 5, 1969.
†Traded to Philadelphia Phillies for Shortstop Todd Cruz, April 3, 1979.
‡On disabled list, June 14 to July 5, 1979.
§Released, April 9, 1980; signed by New York Yankees' organization, April 29, 1980.
xTraded with $400,000 and a player to be named later to Chicago Cubs for Pitcher Rick Reuschel, June 12, 1981; Chicago acquired Pitcher Mike Griffin to complete deal, August 5, 1981.
yTraded to Boston Red Sox for Pitcher Chuck Rainey, December 10, 1982.
zGranted free agency, November 7, 1983.

CHAMPIONSHIP SERIES RECORD

Year Club	League	G.	IP.	W.	L.	Pct.	H.	R.	ER.	SO.	BB.	ERA.
1976—Kansas City	American	1	4⅔	1	0	1.000	4	1	1	1	0	1.93
1977—Kansas City	American	3	2	0	0	.000	4	0	0	1	0	0.00
1978—Kansas City	American	2	1	0	1	.000	2	1	1	1	0	9.00
Championship Series Totals		6	7⅔	1	1	.500	10	2	2	3	0	2.35

MICHAEL DAVID BISHOP
(Mike)

Born November 5, 1958, at Santa Maria, Calif.
Height, 6.02. Weight, 188.
Throws and bats righthanded.
Led Texas League in slugging percentage with .603 in 1980.

Year Club	League	Pos.	G.	AB.	R.	H.	2B.	3B.	HR.	RBI.	B.A.	PO.	A.	E.	F.A.
1976—Idaho Falls	Pion.	3-O-1-S	68	231	45	67	8	9	3	40	.290	107	62	20	.894
1977—Quad Cities	Midw.	3B-SS	137	474	57	112	23	4	7	61	.236	95	243	26	.929
1978—Salinas†	Calif.	3B	7	22	1	2	0	0	0	1	.091	1	9	2	.833
1978—Quad Cities	Midw.	3B	80	279	56	75	15	1	19	64	.269	49	164	20	.914
1979—Salinas	Calif.	1B-3B	62	218	47	67	11	1	13	45	.307	375	49	6	.986
1979—El Paso	Texas	1B	75	276	51	89	15	3	15	51	.322	653	44	11	.984
1980—El Paso	Texas	OF-1B	126	489	96	159	27	5	*33	*104	.325	402	25	16	.964
1980—Salt Lake City	P. C.	1B	9	32	8	11	1	3	1	7	.344	18	1	1	.950
1981—Salt Lake City	P. C.	3-1-O-C	133	470	73	130	21	3	15	91	.277	348	116	18	.963
1982—Spokane‡	P. C.	C-O-3-1	107	345	66	92	26	5	12	49	.267	422	51	12	.975
1983—New York	Nat.	C	3	8	2	1	1	0	0	0	.125	16	1	1	.944
1983—Tidewater	Int.	C-1-3-O	27	74	6	15	6	0	1	11	.203	144	20	4	.976
1983—Jackson	Texas	1B-3B	66	207	40	58	15	0	13	43	.280	485	49	1	.998
Major League Totals			3	8	2	1	1	0	0	0	.125	16	1	1	.944

Selected by California Angels' organization in 12th round of free-agent draft, June 8, 1976.
†On disabled list, April 19 to May 16, 1978.
‡Granted free agency, October 15, 1982; signed by New York Mets, January 10, 1983.

JEFFREY SCOTT BITTIGER
(Jeff)

Born April 10, 1962, at Jersey City, N. J.
Height, 5.10. Weight, 175.
Throws and bats righthanded.

Attended Montclair State College, Upper Montclair, N.J., and
attending Jersey City State College, Jersey City, N.J.
Tied for International League lead in games started by pitchers with 28 in 1983.
Named Texas League Pitcher of the Year, 1982.

Year Club	League	G.	IP.	W.	L.	Pct.	H.	R.	ER.	SO.	BB.	ERA.
1980—Little Falls	NYP	7	26	0	1	.000	10	6	3	33	20	1.04
1981—Lynchburg	Carolina	24	137	11	7	.611	121	72	60	*168	79	3.94
1981—Jackson	Texas	4	33	2	1	.667	24	4	4	27	8	1.09

Year Club	League	G.	IP.	W.	L.	Pct.	H.	R.	ER.	SO.	BB.	ERA.
1982—Jackson	Texas	25	164	12	5	.706	106	59	54	★190	94	2.96
1983—Tidewater.....................................	Int'national	28	163	12	10	.545	175	90	79	110	★111	4.36

Selected by New York Mets' organization in 7th round of free-agent draft, June 3, 1980.

RECORD AS THIRD BASEMAN

Year Club	League	Pos.	G.	AB.	R.	H.	2B.	3B.	HR.	RBI.	B.A.	PO.	A.	E.	F.A.
1980—Little Falls.............	NYP	3B-P	22	37	4	7	0	1	0	3	.189	11	24	8	.814

GEORGE ANTON BJORKMAN

Named pronounced Bee-YORK-mun.

Born August 26, 1956, at Ontario, Calif.
Height, 6.02. Weight, 190.
Throws and bats righthanded.
Attended Chaffey College, Alta Loma, Calif., and
Oral Roberts University, Tulsa, Okla.

Led American Association catchers in double plays with 10 in 1982.

Year Club	League	Pos.	G.	AB.	R.	H.	2B.	3B.	HR.	RBI.	B.A.	PO.	A.	E.	F.A.
1978—Johnson City	Appal.	C	12	41	8	11	0	1	4	8	.268	78	10	0	1.000
1978—Gastonia.................	W. Car.	C	46	152	20	39	11	0	6	22	.257	208	38	8	.969
1979—St. Petersburg......	Fla. St.	C-1B	118	384	56	95	21	2	9	53	.247	563	68	14	.978
1980—Arkansas†‡...........	Texas	C-OF	70	196	20	47	14	1	4	18	.240	298	30	10	.970
1981—Springfield............	A. A.	C-OF	107	323	69	82	14	1	★28	66	.254	538	61	14	.977
1982—Louisville§	A. A.	C	108	317	59	66	19	2	14	43	.208	530	60	12	.980
1983—Tucson..................	P. C.	C	17	57	7	13	5	0	0	4	.228	72	6	0	1.000
1983—Houston.................	Nat.	C	29	75	8	17	4	0	2	14	.227	136	16	1	.993
Major League Totals...................................			29	75	8	17	4	0	2	14	.227	136	16	1	.993

Selected by St. Louis Cardinals' organization in 4th round of free-agent draft, June 6, 1978.
†On disabled list, April 25 to June 12, 1980.
‡Drafted by San Francisco Giants, December 8, 1980; returned April 7, 1981.
§Traded to Houston Astros' organization for Pitcher Jeff Meadows, March 16, 1983.

HARRY RALSTON BLACK
(Bud)

Born June 30, 1957, at San Mateo, Calif.
Height, 6.01. Weight, 180.
Throws and bats lefthanded.
Attended Lower Columbia College, Longview, Wash. and received bachelor of science degree
in finance from San Diego State University, San Diego, Calif. in 1979.

Led American League in balks with 7 in 1982.

Year Club	League	G.	IP.	W.	L.	Pct.	H.	R.	ER.	SO.	BB.	ERA.
1979—Bellingham	Northwest	2	5	0	0	.000	3	0	0	8	5	0.00
1979—San Jose....................................	California	17	27	0	1	.000	17	11	9	24	16	3.00
1980—San Jose....................................	California	32	86	5	3	.625	67	34	33	73	49	3.45
1981—Lynn..	Eastern	22	87	2	6	.250	78	38	29	86	23	3.00
1981—Spokane.....................................	P. Coast	4	8	1	0	1.000	12	4	4	4	2	4.50
1981—Seattle†.....................................	American	2	1	0	0	.000	2	0	0	0	3	0.00
1982—Kansas City................................	American	22	88⅓	4	6	.400	92	48	45	40	34	4.58
1982—Omaha.......................................	Am. Assoc.	4	29	3	1	.750	23	9	8	20	10	2.48
1983—Omaha.......................................	Am. Assoc.	5	35	3	1	.750	31	13	13	32	13	3.34
1983—Kansas City................................	American	24	161⅓	10	7	.588	159	75	68	58	43	3.79
Major League Totals...........................		48	250⅔	14	13	.519	253	123	113	98	80	4.06

Selected by San Francisco Giants' organization in 3rd round of free-agent draft, January 11, 1977.
Selected by New York Mets' organization in secondary phase of free-agent draft, June 7, 1977.
Selected by Seattle Mariners' organization in 17th round of free-agent draft, June 5, 1979.
†Traded to Kansas City Royals, March 2, 1982, completing deal in which Kansas City traded Infielder Manny Castillo to Seattle Mariners for a player to be named later, October 23, 1981.

TIMOTHY P. BLACKWELL
(Tim)

Born August 19, 1952, at San Diego, Calif.
Height, 5.11. Weight, 185.
Throws right and bats left and righthanded.
Attended Grossmont College, El Cajon, Calif.

Led National League catchers in double plays with 16 in 1980.
Tied for Eastern League lead in double plays by catchers with 12 in 1973.

Year Club	League	Pos.	G.	AB.	R.	H.	2B.	3B.	HR.	RBI.	B.A.	PO.	A.	E.	F.A.
1970—Jamestown............	NYP	3B-C	28	81	8	19	3	2	0	10	.235	33	30	5	.926
1971—Greenville	W. Car.	C-OF-3B	55	140	18	25	6	0	0	10	.179	230	24	5	.981
1972—Winston-Salem† ....Carol.		C	60	177	25	44	14	3	3	26	.249	357	15	9	.976
1973—Bristol....................	East.	C-OF	102	318	39	90	15	0	5	38	.283	502	63	5	.991
1974—Pawtucket............	Int.	C	50	140	12	29	8	0	0	17	.207	302	24	6	.982
1974—Boston	Amer.	C	44	122	9	30	1	1	0	8	.246	182	21	6	.971
1975—Boston	Amer.	C	59	132	15	26	3	2	0	6	.197	230	23	4	.984

Year Club	League	Pos.	G.	AB.	R.	H.	2B.	3B.	HR.	RBI.	B.A.	PO.	A.	E.	F.A.
1976—Rhode Island‡	Int.	C	2	3	0	0	0	0	0	0	.000	3	1	0	1.000
1976—Philadelphia	Nat.	C	4	8	0	2	0	0	0	1	.250	17	0	0	1.000
1976—Reading	East.	*C-OF	91	299	29	74	10	2	2	25	.247	427	*64	10	.980
1977—Reading	East.	C	5	14	2	7	3	0	0	2	.500	27	3	0	1.000
1977—Phila.§-Mont. x	Nat.	C	17	22	4	2	1	0	0	0	.091	37	2	3	.929
1978—Wichita	A. A.	C	64	184	32	54	7	0	8	33	.293	351	24	8	.979
1978—Chicago	Nat.	C	49	103	8	23	3	0	0	7	.223	213	20	3	.987
1979—Chicago	Nat.	C	63	122	8	20	3	1	0	12	.164	245	28	7	.975
1980—Chicago	Nat.	C	103	320	24	87	16	4	5	30	.272	572	93	12	.982
1981—Chicago y	Nat.	C	58	158	21	37	10	2	1	11	.234	268	28	2	.993
1982—Montreal	Nat.	C	23	42	2	8	2	1	0	3	.190	58	9	1	.985
1983—Montreal z	Nat.	C	6	15	0	3	1	0	0	2	.200	28	1	2	.935
1983—Edmonton	P. C.	C	59	192	29	47	5	1	3	24	.245	272	31	11	.965
American League Totals			103	254	24	56	4	3	0	14	.220	412	44	10	.979
National League Totals			323	790	67	182	36	8	6	66	.230	1438	181	30	.982
Major League Totals			426	1044	91	238	40	11	6	80	.228	1850	225	40	.981

Selected by Boston Red Sox' organization in 13th round of free-agent draft, June 4, 1970.
†On disabled list, May 24 to June 16, 1972.
‡Sold to Philadelphia Phillies, April 19, 1976.
§Traded with Pitcher Wayne Twitchell to Montreal Expos for Catcher Barry Foote and Pitcher Dan Warthen, June 15, 1977.
xReleased, January 14, 1978; signed by Chicago Cubs' organization, February 10, 1978.
yGranted free agency, November 13, 1981; signed by Montreal Expos, January 14, 1982.
zReleased, May 31, 1983; signed by California Angels' organization, June 20, 1983.

TERRY FENNELL BLOCKER

Born August 18, 1959, at Columbia, S.C.
Height, 6.02. Weight, 195.
Throws and bats lefthanded.
Attended Tennessee State University, Nashville, Tenn.

Year Club	League	Pos.	G.	AB.	R.	H.	2B.	3B.	HR.	RBI.	B.A.	PO.	A.	E.	F.A.
1981—Little Falls	NYP	OF	36	135	28	46	8	1	7	16	.341	72	6	7	.918
1982—Jackson	Texas	OF	118	438	69	114	20	2	5	38	.260	248	7	3	*.988
1983—Jackson	Texas	OF	66	263	38	81	16	7	3	54	.308	92	5	5	.951
1983—Tidewater	Int.	OF	72	239	26	73	7	2	2	32	.305	133	4	6	.958

Selected by New York Mets' organization in 1st round (fourth player selected) of free-agent draft, June 8, 1981.

VIDA ROCHELLE BLUE JR.

Born July 28, 1949, at Mansfield, La.
Height, 6.00. Weight, 200.
Throws left and bats left and righthanded.
Attended Southern University, Baton Rouge, La.

Tied American League record for most strikeouts by lefthanded pitcher, extra-inning game (17), July 9, 1971 (pitched 11 of 20 innings).
Pitched 6-0 no-hit victory against Minnesota Twins, September 21, 1970.
Pitched seven-inning, 4-0 no-hit victory against Appleton, June 19, 1968.
Led American League in shutouts with 8 in 1971.
Named National League Pitcher of the Year by THE SPORTING NEWS, 1978.
Named American League Pitcher of the Year by THE SPORTING NEWS, 1971.
Named American League Most Valuable Player by Baseball Writers' Association of America, 1971.
Won American League Cy Young Memorial Award, 1971.
Named lefthanded pitcher on THE SPORTING NEWS National League All-Star Team, 1978.
Named lefthanded pitcher on THE SPORTING NEWS American League All-Star Team, 1971.

Year Club	League	G.	IP.	W.	L.	Pct.	H.	R.	ER.	SO.	BB.	ERA.
1968—Burlington	Midwest	24	152	8	●11	.421	102	67	42	*231	80	2.49
1969—Birmingham	Southern	15	104	10	3	.769	80	40	37	112	52	3.20
1969—Oakland	American	12	42	1	1	.500	49	34	31	24	18	6.64
1970—Iowa	Am. Assoc.	17	133	12	3	*.800	88	40	32	*165	55	2.17
1970—Oakland	American	6	39	2	0	1.000	20	12	9	35	12	2.08
1971—Oakland	American	39	312	24	8	.750	209	73	63	301	88	*1.82
1972—Oakland†	American	25	151	6	10	.375	117	55	47	111	48	2.80
1973—Oakland	American	37	264	20	9	.690	214	108	98	158	105	3.27
1974—Oakland	American	40	282	17	15	.531	246	118	102	174	98	3.26
1975—Oakland	American	39	278	22	11	.667	243	103	93	189	99	3.01
1976—Oakland	American	37	298	18	13	.581	268	90	78	166	63	2.36
1977—Oakland‡§	American	38	280	14	●19	.424	●284	138	●119	157	86	3.83
1978—San Francisco	National	35	258	18	10	.643	233	87	80	171	70	2.79
1979—San Francisco	National	34	237	14	14	.500	246	143	*132	138	111	5.01
1980—San Francisco x	National	31	224	14	10	.583	202	79	74	129	61	2.97
1981—San Francisco y	National	18	125	8	6	.571	97	40	34	63	54	2.45
1982—Kansas City	American	31	181	13	12	.520	163	80	76	103	80	3.78
1983—Kansas City z	American	19	85⅓	0	5	.000	96	62	57	53	35	6.01
National League Totals		118	844	54	40	.574	778	349	320	501	296	3.41
American League Totals		323	2212⅓	137	103	.571	1909	873	771	1471	732	3.14
Major League Totals		441	3056⅓	191	143	.572	2687	1222	1091	1972	1028	3.21

Selected by Kansas City A's organization in 2nd round of free-agent draft, June 6, 1967.

† On restricted list, March 30 to April 27, 1972.
‡ On disqualified list, April 5 to April 16, 1977.
§ Traded to San Francisco Giants for Outfielder Gary Thomasson, Catcher Gary Alexander, Pitchers Dave Heaverlo, Alan Wirth, John Johnson and Phillip Huffman, a player to be named later and cash estimated at $390,000, March 15, 1978; Oakland acquired Shortstop Mario Guerrero to to complete deal, April 7, 1978.
xOn disabled list, June 28 to August 2, 1980.
yTraded with Pitcher Bob Tufts to Kansas City Royals for Pitchers Atlee Hammaker, Craig Chamberlain and Renie Martin and a player to be named later, March 30, 1982; San Francisco Giants' organization acquired Second Baseman Brad Wellman to complete deal, April 19, 1982.
zReleased, August 5, 1983.

CHAMPIONSHIP SERIES RECORD

Tied Championship Series records for fewest hits allowed, game (2), October 8, 1974; most earned runs allowed, five-game Series (8), 1973.
Established American League Championship Series record for most games pitched, five game Series (4), 1972.

Year Club	League	G.	IP.	W.	L.	Pct.	H.	R.	ER.	SO.	BB.	ERA.
1971—Oakland	American	1	7	0	1	.000	7	5	5	8	2	6.43
1972—Oakland	American	4	5⅓	0	0	.000	4	0	0	5	1	0.00
1973—Oakland	American	2	7	0	1	.000	8	8	8	3	5	10.29
1974—Oakland	American	1	9	1	0	1.000	2	0	0	7	0	0.00
1975—Oakland	American	1	3	0	0	.000	6	3	3	2	0	9.00
Championship Series Totals		9	31⅓	1	2	.333	27	16	16	25	8	4.60

WORLD SERIES RECORD

Year Club	League	G.	IP.	W.	L.	Pct.	H.	R.	ER.	SO.	BB.	ERA.
1972—Oakland	American	4	8⅔	0	1	.000	8	4	4	5	5	4.15
1973—Oakland	American	2	11	0	1	.000	10	6	6	8	3	4.91
1974—Oakland	American	2	13⅔	0	1	.000	10	5	5	9	7	3.29
World Series Totals		8	33⅓	0	3	.000	28	15	15	22	15	4.05

ALL-STAR GAME RECORD

Only pitcher in All-Star Game history to start in each league: American League, 1971; National League, 1978.
Tied All-Star Game records for most home runs allowed, total games (4); most home runs allowed, inning (2), July 15, 1975 (second inning).

Year League	IP.	W.	L.	Pct.	H.	R.	ER.	SO.	BB.	ERA.
1971—American	3	1	0	1.000	2	3	3	3	0	9.00
1975—American	2	0	0	.000	5	2	2	1	0	9.00
1978—National	3	0	0	.000	5	3	3	2	1	9.00
1981—National	1	1	0	1.000	0	0	0	1	0	0.00
All-Star Game Totals	9	2	0	1.000	12	8	8	7	1	8.00

Named to American League All-Star Team in 1977; replaced due to injury.
Named to National League All-Star Team in 1980; replaced due to injury by Ed Whitson.

RIK AALBERT BLYLEVEN
(Bert)

Born April 6, 1951, at Zeist, The Netherlands.
Height, 6.03. Weight, 205.
Throws and bats righthanded.

Tied modern major league record for most consecutive strikeouts, start of game (6), September 16, 1970.
Tied American League record for longest one-hit complete game (10 innings), June 21, 1976.
Pitched 6-0 no-hit victory against California Angels, September 22, 1977.
Led American League in hit batsmen with 12 in 1976.
Led American League in shutouts with 9 in 1973.
Tied for American League lead in balks with 3 in 1970.
Named American League Rookie Pitcher of the Year by THE SPORTING NEWS, 1970.

Year Club	League	G.	IP.	W.	L.	Pct.	H.	R.	ER.	SO.	BB.	ERA.
1969—Sarasota Twins	Gulf Coast	7	32	2	2	.500	31	13	10	39	11	2.81
1969—Orlando	Florida St.	6	37	5	0	1.000	36	6	6	41	14	1.46
1970—Evansville	Am. Assoc.	8	54	4	2	.667	48	18	15	63	12	2.50
1970—Minnesota	American	27	164	10	9	.526	143	66	58	135	47	3.18
1971—Minnesota	American	38	278	16	15	.516	267	95	87	224	59	2.82
1972—Minnesota	American	39	287	17	17	.500	247	93	87	228	69	2.73
1973—Minnesota	American	40	325	20	17	.541	296	109	91	258	67	2.52
1974—Minnesota	American	37	281	17	17	.500	244	99	83	249	77	2.66
1975—Minnesota	American	35	276	15	10	.600	219	104	92	233	84	3.00
1976—Minnesota†-Texas	American	36	298	13	16	.448	283	106	95	219	81	2.87
1977—Texas‡	American	30	235	14	12	.538	181	81	71	182	69	2.72
1978—Pittsburgh	National	34	244	14	10	.583	217	94	82	182	66	3.02
1979—Pittsburgh	National	37	237	12	5	.706	238	102	95	172	92	3.61
1980—Pittsburgh§	National	34	217	8	13	.381	219	102	92	168	59	3.82
1981—Cleveland	American	20	159	11	7	.611	145	52	51	107	40	2.89
1982—Cleveland x	American	4	20⅓	2	2	.500	16	14	11	19	11	4.87
1983—Cleveland	American	24	156⅓	7	10	.412	160	74	68	123	44	3.91
National League Totals		105	698	34	28	.548	674	298	269	522	217	3.47
American League Totals		330	2479⅔	142	132	.518	2201	893	794	1977	648	2.88
Major League Totals		435	3177⅔	176	160	.524	2875	1191	1063	2499	865	3.01

Selected by Minnesota Twins' organization in 3rd round of free-agent draft, June 5, 1969.
†Traded with Shortstop Danny Thompson to Texas Rangers for Pitcher Bill Singer, Infielders Roy Smalley and

Mike Cubbage, Pitcher Jim Gideon and a reported $250,000 cash, June 1, 1976.

‡Traded with First Baseman-Outfielder John Milner to Pittsburgh Pirates for Outfielder-First Baseman Al Oliver and Infielder Nelson Norman, December 8, 1977.

§Traded with Catcher Manny Sanguillen to Cleveland Indians for Pitchers Bob Owchinko, Rafael Vasquez and Victor Cruz and Catcher Gary Alexander, December 9, 1980.

xOn emergency disabled list, May 2, 1982 through remainder of season.

CHAMPIONSHIP SERIES RECORD

Year Club	League	G.	IP.	W.	L.	Pct.	H.	R.	ER.	SO.	BB.	ERA.
1970—Minnesota	American	1	2	0	0	.000	2	1	0	2	0	0.00
1979—Pittsburgh	National	1	9	1	0	1.000	8	1	1	9	0	1.00
Championship Series Totals		2	11	1	0	1.000	10	2	1	11	0	0.82

WORLD SERIES RECORD

Year Club	League	G.	IP.	W.	L.	Pct.	H.	R.	ER.	SO.	BB.	ERA.
1979—Pittsburgh	National	2	10	1	0	1.000	8	2	2	4	3	1.80

ALL-STAR GAME RECORD

Year League	IP.	W.	L.	Pct.	H.	R.	ER.	SO.	BB.	ERA.
1973—American	1	0	1	.000	2	2	2	0	2	18.00

BRUCE ANTON BOCHTE

Name pronounced BOCK-tee.

Born November 12, 1950, at Pasadena, Calif.
Height, 6.03. Weight, 200.
Throws and bats lefthanded.
Received bachelor of science degree in commerce from
University of Santa Clara, Santa Clara, Calif.

Led American League in grounding into double plays with 27 in 1979.

Year Club	League	Pos.	G.	AB.	R.	H.	2B.	3B.	HR.	RBI.	B.A.	PO.	A.	E.	F.A.
1972—Stockton	Calif.	1B-OF	72	266	36	87	14	2	11	42	.327	470	27	9	.982
1973—El Paso	Texas	1B-OF	122	417	57	133	32	4	10	79	.319	775	41	11	.987
1974—Salt Lake City	P. C.	OF-1B	92	332	55	118	15	2	9	56	.355	218	12	6	.975
1974—California	Amer.	OF-1B	57	196	24	53	4	1	5	26	.270	248	9	5	.981
1975—California†	Amer.	1B	107	375	41	107	19	3	3	48	.285	850	51	12	.987
1976—California	Amer.	OF-1B	146	466	53	120	17	1	2	49	.258	651	42	7	.990
1977—Calif.‡-Cleve.§	Amer.	OF-1B	137	492	64	148	23	1	7	51	.301	486	33	9	.983
1978—Seattle	Amer.	OF-1B	140	486	58	128	25	3	11	51	.263	180	7	3	.984
1979—Seattle	Amer.	1B	150	554	81	175	38	6	16	100	.316	1361	114	★14	.991
1980—Seattle	Amer.	1B	148	520	62	156	34	4	13	78	.300	1273	98	6	.996
1981—Seattle	Amer.	1B-OF	99	335	39	87	16	0	6	30	.260	766	49	4	.995
1982—Seattle x	Amer.	OF-1B	144	509	58	151	21	0	12	70	.297	428	26	3	.993
1983—							(Did not play)								
Major League Totals			1128	3933	480	1125	197	19	75	503	.286	6243	429	63	.991

Selected by California Angels' organization in 2nd round of free-agent draft, June 6, 1972.

†On disabled list, June 24 to August 13, 1975.

‡Traded with Pitcher Sid Monge and cash estimated at $250,000 to Cleveland Indians for Pitchers Dave Schuler and Dave LaRoche, May 11, 1977.

§Granted free agency, November 2, 1977; signed by Seattle Mariners, December 20, 1977.

xGranted free agency, November 10, 1982; signed by Oakland A's, November 14, 1983.

ALL-STAR GAME RECORD

Year League	Pos.	AB.	R.	H.	2B.	3B.	HR.	RBI.	B.A.	PO.	A.	E.	F.A.
1979—American	PH-1B	1	0	1	0	0	0	1	1.000	2	0	0	1.000

BRUCE DOUGLAS BOCHY

Name pronounced BOW-chee.

Born April 16, 1955, At Landes de Bussac, France.
Height, 6.04. Weight, 215.
Throws and bats righthanded.
Attended Brevard Community College, Cocoa, Fla., and
Florida State University, Tallahassee, Fla.
Brother of Joe Bochy, catcher in Minnesota Twins' organization, 1969 through 1972.

Tied for Florida State League lead in passed balls with 12 in 1977.

Year Club	League	Pos.	G.	AB.	R.	H.	2B.	3B.	HR.	RBI.	B.A.	PO.	A.	E.	F.A.
1975—Covington	Appal.	C	37	145	31	49	9	0	4	34	.338	231	36	4	.985
1976—Columbus	South.	C	69	230	9	53	6	0	0	16	.230	266	45	6	.981
1976—Dubuque	Midw.	C-1B	30	103	9	25	4	0	1	8	.243	165	25	5	.974
1977—Cocoa	Fla. St.	C	128	430	40	109	18	2	3	35	.253	★492	67	12	.979
1978—Columbus	South.	C	79	261	25	70	10	2	7	34	.268	419	49	7	.985
1978—Houston	Nat.	C	54	154	8	41	8	0	3	15	.266	268	35	8	.974
1979—Houston	Nat.	C	56	129	11	28	4	0	1	6	.217	198	29	7	.970
1980—Houston†	Nat.	C-1B	22	22	0	4	1	0	0	0	.182	19	1	0	1.000
1981—Tidewater	Int.	C	85	269	23	61	11	2	8	38	.227	253	35	3	.990
1982—Tidewater	Int.	C	81	251	32	57	11	0	15	52	.227	427	57	5	★.990
1982—New York‡	Nat.	C-1B	17	49	4	15	4	0	2	8	.306	92	8	4	.962

Year Club	League	Pos.	G.	AB.	R.	H.	2B.	3B.	HR.	RBI.	B.A.	PO.	A.	E.	F.A.
1983—Las Vegas..............	P.C.	C	42	145	28	44	8	1	11	33	.303	157	21	3	.983
1983—San Diego	Nat.	C	23	42	2	9	1	1	0	3	.214	51	5	0	1.000
Major League Totals....................................			172	396	25	97	18	1	6	32	.245	628	78	19	.974

Selected by Chicago White Sox' organization in 8th round of free-agent draft, January 9, 1975.
Selected by Houston Astros' organization in secondary phase of free-agent draft, June 4, 1975.
†Traded to New York Mets' organization for two players to be named later, February 11, 1981; Houston Astros acquired Infielder Randy Rogers and Catcher Stan Hough to complete deal, April 3, 1981.
‡Released, January 21, 1983; signed by Las Vegas (San Diego Padres' organization), February 23, 1983.

CHAMPIONSHIP SERIES RECORD

Year Club	League	Pos.	G.	AB.	R.	H.	2B.	3B.	HR.	RBI.	B.A.	PO.	A.	E.	F.A.
1980—Houston..................	Nat.	C	1	1	0	0	0	0	0	0	.000	5	1	0	1.000

MICHAEL JAMES BODDICKER

Name pronounced BOD-dick-er

(Mike)

Born August 23, 1957, at Cedar Rapids, Iowa.
Height, 5.11. Weight, 172.
Throws and bats righthanded.
Attended University of Iowa, Iowa City, Iowa.

Led American League in shutouts with 5 in 1983.
Named American League Rookie Pitcher of the Year by THE SPORTING NEWS, 1983.

Year Club	League	G.	IP.	W.	L.	Pct.	H.	R.	ER.	SO.	BB.	ERA.
1978—Bluefield..	Ap'lachian	8	19	2	1	.667	9	2	1	28	10	0.47
1978—Charlotte	Southern	10	65	4	3	.571	42	15	14	48	17	1.94
1978—Rochester	Int'national	1	5	1	0	1.000	4	1	1	3	2	1.80
1979—Charlotte	Southern	14	102	9	3	.750	82	40	34	89	36	3.00
1979—Rochester	Int'national	15	72	4	6	.400	88	48	48	48	27	6.00
1980—Rochester	Int'national	25	190	12	9	.571	149	57	46	109	35	2.18
1980—Baltimore	American	1	7	0	1	.000	6	6	5	4	5	6.43
1981—Rochester	Int'national	30	182	10	10	.500	182	91	85	109	66	4.20
1981—Baltimore	American	2	6	0	0	.000	6	4	3	2	2	4.50
1982—Rochester	Int'national	20	133⅓	10	5	.667	121	59	53	82	36	3.58
1982—Baltimore	American	7	25⅔	1	0	1.000	25	10	10	20	12	3.51
1983—Rochester	Int'national	4	23⅔	3	1	.750	17	6	5	18	13	1.90
1983—Baltimore	American	27	179	16	8	.667	141	65	55	120	52	2.77
Major League Totals..........................		37	217⅔	17	9	.654	178	85	73	146	71	3.02

Selected by Montreal Expos' organization in 8th round of free-agent draft, June 4, 1975.
Selected by Baltimore Orioles' organization in 6th round of free-agent draft, June 6, 1978.

CHAMPIONSHIP SERIES RECORD

Established Championship Series record for most strikeouts, four-game Series (14), 1983.
Tied Championship Series record for most strikeouts, game (14), October 6, 1983.

Year Club	League	G.	IP.	W.	L.	Pct.	H.	R.	ER.	SO.	BB.	ERA.
1983—Baltimore	American	1	9	1	0	1.000	5	0	0	14	3	0.00

WORLD SERIES RECORD

Year Club	League	G.	IP.	W.	L.	Pct.	H.	R.	ER.	SO.	BB.	ERA.
1983—Baltimore	American	1	9	1	0	1.000	3	1	0	6	0	0.00

THOMAS WINTON BOGGS

(Tommy)

Born October 25, 1955, at Poughkeepsie, N.Y.
Height, 6.02. Weight, 200.
Throws and bats righthanded.

Led International League pitchers in games started with 33, complete games with 16 and wild pitches with 18 in 1979.
Tied for Gulf Coast League lead in shutouts with 2 in 1974.

Year Club	League	G.	IP.	W.	L.	Pct.	H.	R.	ER.	SO.	BB.	ERA.
1974—Sarasota Rangers........................	Gulf Coast	10	64	5	2	.714	50	21	18	55	35	2.53
1975—Pittsfield	Eastern	24	162	10	11	.476	153	84	63	100	73	3.50
1976—Sacramento	P. Coast	18	115	6	11	.353	153	101	88	77	60	6.89
1976—Texas..	American	13	90	1	7	.125	87	42	35	36	34	3.50
1977—Tucson	P. Coast	22	97	5	10	.333	131	107	92	70	83	8.54
1977—Texas†	American	6	27	0	3	.000	40	18	18	15	12	6.00
1978—Richmond	Int'national	8	54	5	1	.833	51	20	17	29	22	2.83
1978—Atlanta	National	16	59	2	8	.200	80	46	44	21	26	6.71
1979—Richmond	Int'national	33	★227	15	10	.600	★230	★108	91	★138	99	3.61
1979—Atlanta	National	3	13	0	2	.000	21	11	9	1	4	6.23
1980—Atlanta	National	32	192	12	9	.571	180	80	73	84	46	3.42
1981—Atlanta	National	25	143	3	13	.188	140	72	65	81	54	4.09
1982—Atlanta‡	National	10	46⅓	2	2	.500	43	22	17	29	22	3.30
1982—Richmond......................................	Int'national	3	12	1	1	.500	9	5	2	13	13	1.50

Year	Club	League	G.	IP.	W.	L.	Pct.	H.	R.	ER.	SO.	BB.	ERA.
1983—Atlanta§	National		5	6⅓	0	0	.000	8	4	4	5	1	5.68
1983—Richmond x	Int'national		4	12	0	4	.000	19	20	19	5	9	14.25
National League Totals			91	459⅔	19	34	.358	472	235	212	221	153	4.15
American League Totals			19	117	1	10	.091	127	60	53	51	46	4.08
Major League Totals			110	576⅔	20	44	.313	599	295	265	272	199	4.14

Selected by Texas Rangers' organization in 1st round (second player selected) of free-agent draft, June 5, 1974.

†Traded with Pitcher Adrian Devine and Outfielder Eddie Miller to Atlanta Braves for First Baseman Willie Montanez, December 8, 1977.

‡On disabled list, April 23 to August 30, 1982; included rehabilitation disability assignment to Richmond, July 28 to August 12, 1982.

§On disabled list, March 22, 1983; transferred to emergency disabled list, May 10 to September 2, 1983; included rehabilitation disability assignment to Richmond, July 7 to July 26, 1983.

xReleased, October 4, 1983.

WADE ANTHONY BOGGS

Born June 15, 1958, at Omaha, Nebraska.
Height, 6.02. Weight, 185.
Throws right and bats lefthanded.
Attended Hillsborough Community College, Tampa, Fla.

Established American League record for highest batting average, rookie season, 100 or more games (.349), 1982.
Named third baseman on THE SPORTING NEWS American League All-Star Team, 1983.
Named third baseman on THE SPORTING NEWS American League Silver Slugger team, 1983.

Year	Club	League	Pos.	G.	AB.	R.	H.	2B.	3B.	HR.	RBI.	B.A.	PO.	A.	E.	F.A.
1976—Elmira	NYP		3B	57	179	29	47	6	0	0	15	.263	36	75	16	.874
1977—Winston-Salem	Carol.		3B-2B-SS	117	422	67	140	13	1	2	55	.332	145	223	27	.932
1978—Bristol	East.		3-S-2-O	109	354	63	110	14	2	1	32	.311	62	107	7	.960
1979—Bristol†	East.		*3-S-2	113	406	56	132	17	2	0	41	.325	94	213	15	*.953
1980—Pawtucket	Int.		3B-1B	129	418	51	128	21	0	1	45	.306	108	156	12	.957
1981—Pawtucket	Int.		3B-1B	137	498	67	*167	*41	3	5	60	*.335	359	238	26	.958
1982—Boston	Amer.		1B-3B-OF	104	338	51	118	14	1	5	44	.349	489	168	8	.988
1983—Boston	Amer.		3B	153	582	100	210	44	7	5	74	*.361	118	368	*27	.947
Major League Totals				257	920	151	328	58	8	10	118	.357	607	536	35	.970

Selected by Boston Red Sox' organization in 7th round of free-agent draft, June 8, 1976.

†On disabled list, April 20 to May 2, 1979.

JUAN GUILLERMO BONILLA

Name pronounced Boh-NEE-yah.
Born February 12, 1956, at Santurce, Puerto Rico.
Height, 5.09. Weight, 170.
Throws and bats righthanded.
Attended Florida State University, Tallahassee. Fla.

Led Midwest League in sacrifice flies with 13 in 1978.
Led Midwest League second basemen in double plays with 84 in 1978, Southern League second basemen with 104 in 1979 and Pacific Coast League second basemen with 110 in 1980.

Year	Club	League	Pos.	G.	AB.	R.	H.	2B.	3B.	HR.	RBI.	B.A.	PO.	A.	E.	F.A.
1978—Waterloo	Midw.		2B	130	470	81	137	32	1	13	78	.291	*285	*381	21	*.969
1979—Chattanooga	South.		2B	138	550	80	150	26	0	5	59	.273	332	360	18	.975
1980—Tacoma†	P. C.		2B	139	502	66	152	27	2	4	55	.303	*366	*422	15	.981
1981—San Diego	Nat.		2B	99	369	30	107	13	2	1	25	.290	229	290	*13	.976
1982—San Diego‡	Nat.		2B	45	182	21	51	6	2	0	8	.280	99	134	6	.975
1983—San Diego	Nat.		2B	152	556	55	132	17	4	4	45	.237	335	414	11	.986
Major League Totals				296	1107	106	290	36	8	5	78	.262	663	838	30	.980

Selected by New York Yankees' organization in 24th round of free-agent draft, June 7, 1977.

Signed as free agent by Cleveland Indians' organization, January 6, 1978.

†Traded to San Diego Padres for Pitcher Bob Lacey, April 1, 1981.

‡On emergency disabled list, May 20 to September 21, 1982.

ROBERTO MARTIN ANTONIO BONILLA
(Bobby)

Born February 23, 1963, at New York, N.Y.
Height, 6.03. Weight, 210.
Throws and bats righthanded.

Year	Club	League	Pos.	G.	AB.	R.	H.	2B.	3B.	HR.	RBI.	B.A.	PO.	A.	E.	F.A.
1981—Bradenton Pir.	Gulf C.		1B-C-3B	22	69	6	15	5	0	0	7	.217	124	23	5	.967
1982—Bradenton Pir.	Gulf C.		1B	47	167	20	38	3	0	5	26	.228	318	36	*14	.962
1983—Alexandria	Carol.		OF-1B	●136	504	88	129	19	7	11	59	.256	259	12	15	.948

Signed as free agent by Pittsburgh Pirates' organization, July 11, 1981.

—DID YOU KNOW—

That Rusty Staub of the Mets has hit home runs in 32 parks during his regular-season career in the majors, tying him with Frank Robinson for the major league record?

ROBERT BARRY BONNELL

Name pronounced Buh-NELL.
(Known by middle name.)
Born October 27, 1953, at Cincinnati, O.
Height, 6.03. Weight, 205.
Throws and bats righthanded.
Attended Ohio State University, Columbus, O.
Brother of Glenn Bonnell, infielder in Cincinnati Reds' organization, 1976.

Year Club	League	Pos.	G.	AB.	R.	H.	2B.	3B.	HR.	RBI.	B.A.	PO.	A.	E.	F.A.
1975—Spart.†-Green.	W. Car.	OF	124	457	86	148	20	•6	12	80	★.324	276	19	12	.961
1976—Savannah...............	South.	OF	51	188	31	42	6	2	6	23	.223	117	6	5	.961
1976—Richmond.............	Int.	OF	66	227	36	64	13	2	5	31	.282	134	4	3	.979
1977—Richmond.............	Int.	OF	14	50	8	19	3	0	0	10	.380	42	2	1	.978
1977—Atlanta‡	Nat.	OF-3B	100	360	41	108	11	0	1	45	.300	203	65	8	.971
1978—Atlanta	Nat.	OF-3B	117	304	36	73	11	3	1	16	.240	187	35	6	.974
1979—Atlanta§	Nat.	OF-3B	127	375	47	97	20	3	12	45	.259	221	8	4	.983
1980—Toronto x..............	Amer.	OF	130	463	55	124	22	4	13	56	.268	271	15	8	.973
1981—Toronto	Amer.	OF	66	227	21	50	7	4	4	28	.220	148	5	4	.975
1982—Toronto	Amer.	OF-3B	140	437	59	128	26	3	6	49	.293	234	7	5	.980
1983—Toronto y..............	Amer.	OF-3B	121	377	49	120	21	3	10	54	.318	213	13	3	.987
National League Totals............................			344	1039	124	278	42	6	14	106	.268	611	108	18	.976
American League Totals........................			457	1504	184	422	76	14	33	187	.281	866	40	20	.978
Major League Totals..................................			801	2543	308	700	118	20	47	293	.275	1477	148	38	.977

Selected by Chicago White Sox' organization in 8th round of free-agent draft, June 8, 1971.
Selected by Philadelphia Phillies' organization in secondary phase of free-agent draft, January 9, 1975.
†Traded with Catcher Jim Essian and cash to Atlanta Braves for First Baseman Dick Allen and Catcher Johnny Oates, May 7, 1975.
‡On supplemental disabled list, June 29 to July 21, 1977.
§Traded with Pitcher Joey McLaughlin and Shortstop Pat Rockett to Toronto Blue Jays for First Baseman Chris Chambliss and Shortstop Luis Gomez, December 5, 1979.
xOn supplemental disabled list, August 13 to September 2, 1980.
yTraded to Seattle Mariners for Pitcher Bryan Clark, December 9, 1983.

ROBERT AVERILL BONNER
(Bob)

Born August 12, 1956, at Uvalde, Tex.
Height, 6.00. Weight, 185.
Throws and bats righthanded.
Attended Texas A&M University, College Station, Tex.

Led International League shortstops in assists with 454, double plays with 73 and fielding percentage with .956 in 1980.

Year Club	League	Pos.	G.	AB.	R.	H.	2B.	3B.	HR.	RBI.	B.A.	PO.	A.	E.	F.A.
1978—Charlotte...............	South.	SS	35	107	8	25	2	0	0	10	.234	60	91	11	.932
1979—Charlotte...............	South.	SS-2B-OF	119	460	55	134	29	3	7	67	.291	136	322	20	.947
1979—Rochester	Int.	2B-SS	4	11	1	3	0	0	0	0	.273	10	12	0	1.000
1980—Rochester	Int.	★SS-2B	133	469	46	113	8	2	2	41	.241	230	467	★31	.957
1980—Baltimore	Amer.	SS	4	4	1	0	0	0	0	1	.000	2	6	1	.889
1981—Rochester†	Int.	SS-2B	84	301	19	69	10	1	3	35	.229	164	292	25	.948
1981—Baltimore	Amer.	SS	10	27	6	8	2	0	0	2	.296	15	26	1	.976
1982—Baltimore	Amer.	SS-2B	41	77	8	13	3	1	0	5	.169	33	61	4	.959
1982—Rochester	Int.	2B-SS	48	155	12	32	1	0	2	18	.206	110	175	1	.997
1983—Rochester‡	Int.	2B-SS	61	198	36	44	6	2	1	15	.222	131	181	4	.987
1983—Baltimore	Amer.	2B	6	0	0	0	0	0	0	0	.000	1	0	0	1.000
Major League Totals..................................			61	108	15	21	5	1	0	8	.194	51	93	6	.960

Selected by Montreal Expos' organization in 10th round of free-agent draft, June 5, 1974.
Selected by Kansas City Royals' organization in 9th round of free-agent draft, June 7, 1977.
Selected by Baltimore Orioles' organization in 3rd round of free-agent draft, June 6, 1978.
†On disabled list, July 10 to July 20 and July 27 to August 21, 1981.
‡On disabled list, June 5 to August 13, 1983.

GREGORY SCOTT BOOKER
(Greg)

Born June 22, 1960, at Lynchburg, Va.
Height, 6.06. Weight, 230.
Throws and bats righthanded.
Attended Elon College, Elon College, N.C.

Led California League in wild pitches with 20 in 1982.

Year Club	League	G.	IP.	W.	L.	Pct.	H.	R.	ER.	SO.	BB.	ERA.
1981—Walla Walla	Northwest	11	53	2	3	.400	55	41	31	25	35	5.26
1982—Reno	California	27	161⅔	8	★13	.381	160	★133	★114	81	★157	6.35
1983—Las Vegas	P. Coast	46	102⅓	5	6	.455	120	77	63	58	68	5.54
1983—San Diego	National	6	11⅔	0	1	.000	18	10	10	5	9	7.71
Major League Totals...................		6	11⅔	0	1	.000	18	10	10	5	9	7.71

Selected by Oakland A's organization in 32nd round of free-agent draft, June 6, 1978.
Selected by San Diego Padres' organization in 10th round of free-agent draft, June 8, 1981.

Year Club	League	Pos.	G.	AB.	R.	H.	2B.	3B.	HR.	RBI.	B.A.	PO.	A.	E.	F.A.
1981—Walla Walla	N'west	*P-1B	31	64	8	12	0	0	4	15	.188	26	14	0	*1.000

ROBERT RAYMOND BOONE
(Bob)

Born November 19, 1947, at San Diego, Calif.
Height, 6.02. Weight, 202.
Throws and bats righthanded.
Received bachelor of arts degree in psychology from Stanford University, Palo Alto, Calif.
Son of Raymond Otis Boone, infielder with Cleveland, Detroit, Chicago A.L., Kansas City,
Milwaukee and Boston, 1948 through 1960; and scout with Boston Red Sox since 1961;
brother of Rodney Alan Boone, catcher-outfielder in Kansas City Royals' and
Houston Astros' organization, 1972 through 1975.

Led American League catchers in double plays with 12 in 1983.
Led American League catchers in total chances with 745 in 1982.
Led National League catchers in fielding percentage with .991 in 1978.
Led National League catchers in total chances with 924 in 1974.
Led Pacific Coast League catchers in passed balls with 18 and double plays with 13 in 1972.
Tied for Carolina League lead in double plays by third basemen with 18 in 1969.
Named catcher on THE SPORTING NEWS National League All-Star Team, 1976.
Named catcher on THE SPORTING NEWS American League All-Star fielding team, 1982.
Named catcher on THE SPORTING NEWS National League All-Star fielding team, 1978 and 1979.

Year Club	League	Pos.	G.	AB.	R.	H.	2B.	3B.	HR.	RBI.	B.A.	PO.	A.	E.	F.A.
1969—Raleigh-Dur.	Carol.	3B	80	300	45	90	13	1	5	46	.300	71	160	20	.920
1970—Reading†	East.	3B	20	80	12	23	2	0	2	10	.288	28	38	7	.904
1971—Reading‡	East.	3B-C-SS	92	328	41	87	14	3	4	37	.265	206	138	17	.953
1972—Eugene	P. C.	C	138	513	77	158	32	4	17	67	.308	*699	*77	*24	.970
1972—Philadelphia	Nat.	C	16	51	4	14	1	0	1	4	.275	66	7	5	.936
1973—Philadelphia	Nat.	C	145	521	42	136	20	2	10	61	.261	868	*89	10	.990
1974—Philadelphia	Nat.	C	146	488	41	118	24	3	3	52	.242	*825	77	*22	.976
1975—Philadelphia	Nat.	C-3B	97	289	28	71	14	2	2	20	.246	459	48	5	.990
1976—Philadelphia	Nat.	C-1B	121	361	40	98	18	2	4	54	.271	587	39	6	.990
1977—Philadelphia	Nat.	C-3B	132	440	55	125	26	4	11	66	.284	654	83	8	.989
1978—Philadelphia	Nat.	C-1B-OF	132	435	48	123	18	4	12	62	.283	650	55	8	.989
1979—Philadelphia	Nat.	C-3B	119	398	38	114	21	3	9	58	.286	527	66	8	.987
1980—Philadelphia	Nat.	C	141	480	34	110	23	1	9	55	.229	741	88	*18	.979
1981—Philadelphia§	Nat.	C	76	227	19	48	7	0	4	24	.211	365	32	6	.985
1982—California..............	Amer.	C	143	472	42	121	17	0	7	58	.256	*650	*87	8	.989
1983—California..............	Amer.	C	142	468	46	120	18	0	9	52	.256	606	*83	*14	.980
National League Totals............................			1125	3690	349	957	172	21	65	456	.259	5742	584	96	.958
American League Totals..........................			285	940	88	241	35	0	16	110	.256	1256	170	22	.985
Major League Totals.........................			1410	4630	437	1198	207	21	81	566	.259	6998	754	118	.985

Selected by Philadelphia Phillies' organization in 20th round of free-agent draft, June 5, 1969.
†On military list, May 26, 1970 through remainder of season.
‡On disabled list, April 10 to June 4, 1971.
§Sold to California Angels, December 6, 1981.

DIVISION SERIES RECORD

Year Club	League	Pos.	G.	AB.	R.	H.	2B.	3B.	HR.	RBI.	B.A.	PO.	A.	E.	F.A.
1981—Philadelphia	Nat.	C	3	5	0	0	0	0	0	0	.000	10	2	0	1.000

CHAMPIONSHIP SERIES RECORD

Year Club	League	Pos.	G.	AB.	R.	H.	2B.	3B.	HR.	RBI.	B.A.	PO.	A.	E.	F.A.
1976—Philadelphia	Nat.	C	3	7	0	2	0	0	0	1	.286	8	2	0	1.000
1977—Philadelphia	Nat.	C	4	10	1	4	0	0	0	0	.400	18	2	0	1.000
1978—Philadelphia	Nat.	C	3	11	0	2	0	0	0	0	.182	16	2	1	.947
1980—Philadelphia	Nat.	C	5	18	1	4	0	0	0	2	.222	22	3	0	1.000
1982—California..............	Amer.	C	5	16	3	4	0	0	1	4	.250	30	3	0	1.000
Championship Series Totals			20	62	5	16	0	0	1	7	.258	94	12	1	.991

WORLD SERIES RECORD

Year Club	League	Pos.	G.	AB.	R.	H.	2B.	3B.	HR.	RBI.	B.A.	PO.	A.	E.	F.A.
1980—Philadelphia	Nat.	C	6	17	3	7	2	0	0	4	.412	49	3	0	1.000

ALL-STAR GAME RECORD

Year League	Pos.	AB.	R.	H.	2B.	3B.	HR.	RBI.	B.A.	PO.	A.	E.	F.A.
1976—National	C	2	0	0	0	0	0	0	.000	5	0	0	1.000
1978—National	C	1	1	1	0	0	0	2	1.000	3	1	0	1.000
1979—National	C	2	1	1	0	0	0	0	.500	0	0	0	.000
1983—American	C	0	0	0	0	0	0	0	.000	1	0	0	1.000
All-Star Game Totals		5	2	2	0	0	0	2	.400	9	1	0	1.000

—DID YOU KNOW—

That of the 28 homers hit by the Twins' Tom Brunansky in 1983, only eight came at home?

RICHARD ALBERT BORDI
Name pronounced BORD-ee.
(Rich)

Born April 18, 1959, at South San Francisco, Calif.
Height, 6.07. Weight, 220.
Throws and bats righthanded.
Attended Fresno State University, Fresno, Calif.

Tied for Pacific Coast League lead in complete games with 15 in 1981.

Year Club	League	G.	IP.	W.	L.	Pct.	H.	R.	ER.	SO.	BB.	ERA.
1980—West Haven	Eastern	11	76	4	6	.400	75	42	35	49	30	4.14
1980—Oakland	American	1	2	0	0	.000	4	1	1	0	0	4.50
1981—Tacoma	P. Coast	27	191	9	11	.450	197	98	78	101	66	3.68
1981—Oakland†	American	2	2	0	0	.000	1	0	0	0	1	0.00
1982—Salt Lake City	P. Coast	25	168⅓	12	9	.571	212	105	84	118	31	4.49
1982—Seattle‡	American	7	13	0	2	.000	18	12	12	10	1	8.31
1983—Iowa§	Am. Assoc.	18	111⅓	7	2	.778	134	62	57	80	21	4.61
1983—Chicago	National	11	25⅓	0	2	.000	34	15	14	20	12	4.97
American League Totals		10	17	0	2	.000	23	13	13	10	2	6.88
National League Totals		11	25⅓	0	2	.000	34	15	14	20	12	4.97
Major League Totals		21	42⅓	0	4	.000	57	28	27	30	14	5.74

Selected by Minnesota Twins' organization in 5th round of free-agent draft, June 7, 1977.
Selected by Oakland A's organization in 3rd round of free-agent draft, June 3, 1980.
†Traded to Seattle Mariners for Third Baseman-Outfielder Dan Meyer, December 9, 1981.
‡Traded to Chicago Cubs for Outfielder Steve Henderson, December 9, 1982.
§On disabled list, April 25 to May 10, 1983.

THADDIS BOSLEY JR.
Name pronounced BAHZ-lee.
(Thad)

Born September 17, 1956, at Oceanside, Calif.
Height, 6.03. Weight, 175.
Throws and bats lefthanded.
Attended Mira Costa Community College, Oceanside, Calif.

Led California League in stolen bases with 90 and caught stealing with 17 in 1976.
Led Pioneer League in bases on balls received with 71 in 1974.
Named California League Most Valuable Player, 1976.

Year Club	League	Pos.	G.	AB.	R.	H.	2B.	3B.	HR.	RBI.	B.A.	PO.	A.	E.	F.A.
1974—Idaho Falls	Pion.	OF	68	223·	55	54	3	4	0	14	.242	101	4	★11	.905
1975—Quad Cities†	Midw.	OF	108	379	67	113	12	3	1	50	.298	206	2	4	★.981
1976—Salinas	Calif.	OF	134	527	105	171	26	4	2	72	★.324	285	13	7	★.977
1977—Salt Lake City	P. C.	OF	69	298	55	97	22	2	2	38	.326	169	6	5	.972
1977—California‡§	Amer.	OF	58	212	19	63	10	2	0	19	.297	130	1	5	.963
1978—Iowa	A. A.	OF	47	·179	27	52	3	0	3	15	.291	77	5	2	.976
1978—Chicago x	Amer.	OF	66	219	25	59	5	1	2	13	.269	155	3	4	.975
1979—Iowa y	A. A.	OF	95	382	62	101	14	5	1	24	.264	140	6	5	.967
1979—Chicago	Amer.	OF	36	77	13	24	1	1	1	8	.312	57	2	2	.967
1980—Chicago zab	Amer.	OF	70	147	12	33	2	0	2	14	.224	91	1	4	.958
1981—Vancouver	P. C.	OF	34	122	15	39	5	2	0	14	.320	75	0	5	.938
1981—Milwaukee c	Amer.	OF	42	105	11	24	2	0	0	3	.229	55	1	2	.966
1982—Seattle	Amer.	OF	22	46	3	8	1	0	0	2	.174	12	1	0	1.000
1982—Salt Lake C. defg	P. C.	OF	22	84	15	25	2	2	3	9	.298	24	2	0	1.000
1983—Mexico City	Mex.	OF	31	107	24	35	7	3	4	18	.327	24	1	0	1.000
1983—Iowa	A. A.	OF	39	124	22	36	11	0	7	24	.290	3	0	1	.750
1983—Chicago	Nat.	OF	43	72	12	21	4	1	2	12	.292	27	1	0	1.000
American League Totals			294	806	83	211	21	4	5	59	.262	500	9	17	.968
National League Totals			43	72	12	21	4	1	2	12	.292	27	1	0	1.000
Major League Totals			337	878	95	232	25	5	7	71	.264	527	10	17	.969

Selected by California Angels' organization in 4th round of free-agent draft, June 5, 1974.
†On disabled list, April 19 to May 6, 1975.
‡On disabled list, June 29 to July 10, 1977.
§Traded with Outfielder Bobby Bonds and Pitcher Dick Dotson to Chicago White Sox for Pitchers Chris Knapp and Dave Frost and Catcher Brian Downing, December 5, 1977.
xOn supplemental disabled list, June 29 to July 17, 1978.
yOn supplemental disabled list, July 15 to July 25, 1979.
zOn supplemental disabled list, August 12 to October 3, 1980.
aOn emergency disabled list, October 3 to October 6, 1980.
bTraded to Milwaukee Brewers' organization for First Baseman-Outfielder John Poff, April 1, 1981.
cTraded to Seattle Mariners for Pitcher Mike Parrott, March 5, 1982.
dOn disabled list, June 6 to July 1 and August 3 to September 2, 1982.
eGranted free agency, September 5, 1982; signed by Tacoma (Oakland A's organization), February 14, 1983.
fSold to Iowa (Chicago Cubs' organization), March 30, 1983.
gLoaned to Mexico City Tigers, April 3, 1983; returned, May 28, 1983.

DIVISION SERIES RECORD

Year Club	League	Pos.	G.	AB.	R.	H.	2B.	3B.	HR.	RBI.	B.A.	PO.	A.	E.	F.A.
1981—Milwaukee	Amer.	PR-DH	1	0	0	0	0	0	0	0	.000	0	0	0	.000

DARYL LAMONT BOSTON

Born January 4, 1963, at Cincinnati, O.
Height, 6.03. Weight, 185.
Throws and bats lefthanded.

Led Midwest League outfielders in total chances with 312 in 1982.

Year Club	League	Pos.	G.	AB.	R.	H.	2B.	3B.	HR.	RBI.	B.A.	PO.	A.	E.	F.A.
1981—Sarasota W. S........	Gulf C.	OF	56	189	30	55	6	3	1	30	.291	84	9	3	.969
1982—Appleton	Midw.	OF *139	512	86	143	19	9	15	77	.279	*293	9	10	.968
1983—Glens Falls...........	East.	OF	113	435	65	104	15	1	18	50	.239	271	8	13	.955
1983—Denver	A. A.	OF	14	51	11	13	4	1	2	7	.255	26	1	5	.844

Selected by Chicago White Sox' organization in 1st round (seventh player selected) of free-agent draft, June 8, 1981.

DEREK WAYNE BOTELHO

Name pronounced Boh-TELL-oh.

Born August 2, 1956, at Long Beach, Calif.
Height, 6.02. Weight, 180.
Throws and bats righthanded.
Attended Miami Dade (South) Community College, Miami, Fla.

Pitched seven-inning, 8-0 no-hit victory against Miami, June 17, 1981 (first game).
Tied for Eastern League lead in shutouts with 4 in 1978.

Year Club	League	G.	IP.	W.	L.	Pct.	H.	R.	ER.	SO.	BB.	ERA.
1976—Spartanburg.....................	W. Carol	20	134	9	9	.500	120	69	54	90	49	3.62
1977—Peninsula.....................	Carolina	26	173	13	5	*.722	167	86	72	107	67	3.75
1978—Reading†.....................	Eastern	27	178	15	7	.682	175	77	70	130	65	3.54
1979—Wichita‡§x	Am. Assoc.	4	19	1	2	.333	30	20	18	18	8	8.53
1980—						(Out of Organized Baseball)						
1981—Ft. Myers.....................	Florida St.	8	39	2	3	.400	25	10	7	32	9	1.62
1981—Jacksonville y	Southern	7	37	2	2	.500	27	9	8	15	4	1.95
1982—Jacksonville.....................	Southern	9	65	3	4	.429	54	35	33	35	25	4.57
1982—Omaha.....................	Am. Assoc.	15	105⅓	7	5	.583	86	51	49	74	37	4.19
1982—Kansas City.....................	American	8	24	2	1	.667	25	11	11	12	8	4.13
1983—Omaha.....................	Am. Assoc.	25	152⅔	10	*14	.417	155	105	92	101	73	5.42
Major League Totals.............................		8	24	2	1	.667	25	11	11	12	8	4.13

Selected by Philadelphia Phillies' organization in 26th round of free-agent draft, June 5, 1974.
Selected by California Angels' organization in secondary phase of free-agent draft, June 9, 1975.
Selected by Philadelphia Phillies' organization in 2nd round of free-agent draft, January 7, 1976.
†Traded with Outfielder Jerry Martin, Catcher Barry Foote, Second Baseman Ted Sizemore and Pitcher Henry Mack to Chicago Cubs for Second Baseman Manny Trillo, Outfielder Greg Gross and Catcher Dave Rader, February 23, 1979.
‡On temporary inactive list, April 11 to April 26, 1979.
§On disabled list, June 4 to August 31, 1979.
xReleased February 5,1980; signed by Jacksonville (Kansas City Royals' organization), January 6, 1981.
yOn disabled list, April 9 to May 17, 1981.

LAWRENCE ROBERT BOWA
(Larry)

Born December 6, 1945, at Sacramento, Calif.
Height, 5.10. Weight, 155.
Throws right and bats left and righthanded.
Attended Sacramento City College, Sacramento, Calif.
Son of Paul Bowa, infielder in St. Louis Cardinals' organization, 1944 and 1946; manager,
St. Louis Cardinals' organization, 1947; nephew of Frank Bowa, minor
league infielder, 1944 through 1949.

Established major league records for highest fielding percentage by shortstop, lifetime, 1,000 or more games (.981); highest fielding percentage by shortstop, season (.991), 1979; most years leading league in fielding average by shortstop, 100 or more games (6).
Tied modern major league record for most at bats, game (7), July 12, 1975.
Established National League record for fewest errors, season, 150 or more games, by shortstop (9), 1972; most seasons leading league in fielding percentage by shortstop, 100 or more games (6), 1971, 1972, 1974, 1978, 1979 and 1983.
Major League stolen bases: 1970 (24), 1971 (28), 1972 (17), 1973 (10), 1974 (39), 1975 (24), 1976 (30), 1977 (32), 1978 (27), 1979 (20), 1980 (21), 1981 (16), 1982 (8), 1983 (7). Total—303.
Led National League in sacrifice hits with 18 in 1972.
Led National League shortstops in total chances with 843 in 1971.
Tied for National League lead in double plays by shortstops with 97 in 1971.
Led Pacific Coast League in stolen bases with 48 in 1969.
Led Pacific Coast League shortstops in putouts with 468 in 1969.
Led Eastern League shortstops in double plays with 77 in 1968.
Named shortstop on THE SPORTING NEWS National League All-Star Team, 1975 and 1978.
Named shortstop on THE SPORTING NEWS National League All-Star fielding team, 1972 and 1978.

Year Club	League	Pos.	G.	AB.	R.	H.	2B.	3B.	HR.	RBI.	B.A.	PO.	A.	E.	F.A.
1966—Spartanburg..........	W. Car.	SS	97	429	70	134	14	4	2	36	.312	138	284	12	*.972
1966—San Diego	P. C.	SS	5	19	0	6	0	1	0	1	.316	13	20	2	.943
1967—Bakersfield†.........	Calif.	SS-2B	7	32	4	6	2	0	0	3	.188	15	12	1	.964
1967—Reading	East.	SS	22	89	11	25	4	0	0	9	.281	35	79	9	.927
1968—Reading	East.	SS	133	480	47	116	14	2	3	36	.242	192	●395	24	.961
1969—Eugene.................	P. C.	*SS-2B	135	568	80	163	11	6	1	26	.287	*215	469	18	*.974
1970—Philadelphia	Nat.	SS-2B	145	547	50	137	17	6	0	34	.250	202	418	13	.979

Year Club League	Pos.	G.	AB.	R.	H.	2B.	3B.	HR.	RBI.	B.A.	PO.	A.	E.	F.A.
1971—Philadelphia .... Nat.	SS	159	*650	74	162	18	5	0	25	.249	272	*560	11	*.987
1972—Philadelphia .... Nat.	SS	152	579	67	145	11	*13	1	31	.250	212	494	9	*.984
1973—Philadelphia‡ ...... Nat.	SS	122	446	42	94	11	3	0	23	.211	191	361	12	.979
1974—Philadelphia .... Nat.	SS	162	669	97	184	19	10	1	36	.275	256	462	12	*.984
1975—Philadelphia§ .... Nat.	SS	136	583	79	178	18	9	2	38	.305	227	403	25	.962
1976—Philadelphia .... Nat.	SS	156	624	71	155	15	9	0	49	.248	180	492	17	.975
1977—Philadelphia .... Nat.	SS	154	624	93	175	19	3	4	41	.280	222	518	13	.983
1978—Philadelphia .... Nat.	SS	156	654	78	192	31	5	3	43	.294	224	502	10	*.986
1979—Philadelphia x...... Nat.	SS	147	539	74	130	17	11	0	31	.241	229	448	6	*.991
1980—Philadelphia .... Nat.	SS	147	540	57	144	16	4	2	39	.267	225	449	17	.975
1981—Philadelphia y ...... Nat.	SS	103	360	34	102	14	3	0	31	.283	117	309	11	.975
1982—Chicago .... Nat.	SS	142	499	50	123	15	7	0	29	.246	210	396	17	.973
1983—Chicago .... Nat.	SS	147	499	73	133	20	5	2	43	.267	230	464	11	*.984
Major League Totals..................................		2028	7813	939	2054	241	93	15	493	.263	2997	6276	184	.981

Signed as free agent by Philadelphia Phillies' organization, October 12, 1965.
†On military list, March 7 to July 18, 1967.
‡On disabled list, July 26 to September 1, 1973.
§On supplemental disabled list, May 27 to June 23, 1975.
xOn supplemental disabled list, May 25 to June 9, 1979.
yTraded with Infielder Ryne Sandberg to Chicago Cubs for Shortstop Ivan DeJesus, January 27, 1982.

DIVISION SERIES RECORD

Year Club League	Pos.	G.	AB.	R.	H.	2B.	3B.	HR.	RBI.	B.A.	PO.	A.	E.	F.A.
1981—Philadelphia .... Nat.	SS	5	17	0	3	1	0	0	1	.176	12	9	1	.955

CHAMPIONSHIP SERIES RECORD

Year Club League	Pos.	G.	AB.	R.	H.	2B.	3B.	HR.	RBI.	B.A.	PO.	A.	E.	F.A.
1976—Philadelphia .... Nat.	SS	3	8	1	1	1	0	0	1	.125	2	11	0	1.000
1977—Philadelphia .... Nat.	SS	4	17	2	2	0	0	0	1	.118	0	17	0	1.000
1978—Philadelphia .... Nat.	SS	4	18	2	6	0	0	0	0	.333	5	16	0	1.000
1980—Philadelphia .... Nat.	SS	5	19	2	6	0	0	0	0	.316	4	11	1	.938
Championship Series Totals		16	62	7	15	1	0	0	2	.242	11	55	1	.985

WORLD SERIES RECORD

Established World Series record for most double plays started by shortstop, six-game Series (7), 1980.
Tied World Series record for most double plays started by shortstop, nine-inning game (3), October 15, 1980.

Year Club League	Pos.	G.	AB.	R.	H.	2B.	3B.	HR.	RBI.	B.A.	PO.	A.	E.	F.A.
1980—Philadelphia .... Nat.	SS	6	24	3	9	1	0	0	2	.375	5	18	0	1.000

ALL-STAR GAME RECORD

Year League	Pos.	AB.	R.	H.	2B.	3B.	HR.	RBI.	B.A.	PO.	A.	E.	F.A.
1974—National	SS	2	0	0	0	0	0	0	.000	2	0	0	1.000
1975—National	SS	0	1	0	0	0	0	0	.000	2	0	0	1.000
1976—National	SS	1	0	0	0	0	0	0	.000	2	1	0	1.000
1978—National	SS	3	1	2	0	0	0	0	.667	2	4	0	1.000
1979—National	SS	2	0	0	0	0	0	0	.000	1	3	0	1.000
All-Star Game Totals		8	2	2	0	0	0	0	.250	9	8	0	1.000

DENNIS RAY BOYD
(Oil Can)

(Given nickname from beer drinking friends in Meridian, Miss.
where beer is referred to as oil.)
Born October 6, 1959, at Meridian, Miss.
Height, 6.01. Weight, 155.
Throws and bats righthanded.
Attended Jackson State University, Jackson, Miss.
Son of Willie James Boyd, who played for Homestead Grays of Negro League;
brother of Don Boyd, outfielder in St. Louis Cardinals' organization, 1973.

Led Florida State League pitchers in games started with 28 and home runs allowed with 11 in 1981.
Tied for Eastern League lead in games started by pitchers with 27 and complete games with 13 in 1982.

Year Club	League	G.	IP.	W.	L.	Pct.	H.	R.	ER.	SO.	BB.	ERA.
1980—Elmira..............................	NYP	12	69	7	1	.875	54	20	19	79	30	2.48
1981—Winter Haven..............................	Florida St.	28	186	14	8	.636	*195	90	75	154	54	3.63
1982—Bristol..............................	Eastern	27	*205	14	8	.636	190	71	64	*191	49	2.81
1982—Boston..............................	American	3	8⅓	0	1	.000	11	5	5	2	2	5.40
1983—Pawtucket..............................	Int'national	20	122⅔	5	8	.385	119	69	55	129	41	4.04
1983—Boston..............................	American	15	98⅔	4	8	.333	103	46	36	43	23	3.28
Major League Totals..............................		18	107	4	9	.308	114	51	41	45	25	3.45

Selected by Boston Red Sox' organization in 16th round of free-agent draft, June 3, 1980.

MARK ALLEN BRADLEY

Born December 3, 1956, at Elizabethtown, Ky.
Height, 6.01. Weight, 185.
Throws and bats righthanded.
Led Texas League in bases on balls received with 97 and being hit by pitch with 12 in 1980.

Led Midwest League in being hit by pitch with 12 in 1976.
Tied for Pacific Coast League lead in sacrifice flies with 10 in 1982.
Received reported $50,000 bonus to sign with Los Angeles Dodgers, 1975.

Year Club	League	Pos.	G.	AB.	R.	H.	2B.	3B.	HR.	RBI.	B.A.	PO.	A.	E.	F.A.
1975—Bellingham .... N'west.	SS-OF-2B	76	239	27	61	7	2	2	33	.255	138	140	34	.891
1976—Danville .... Midw.	★SS-OF	119	381	73	117	19	3	6	47	.307	197	343	★62	.897
1977—Lodi .... Calif.	OF-3B	★140	486	104	160	35	6	16	87	.329	199	16	13	.943
1978—San Antonio.......... Texas	OF	92	277	49	56	14	1	3	30	.202	123	12	5	.964
1978—Lodi .... Calif.	OF	29	109	23	27	2	0	2	11	.248	51	1	1	.981
1979—Lodi .... Calif.	OF	31	101	24	28	5	1	1	14	.277	39	3	2	.955
1979—San Antonio.......... Texas	OF	98	328	46	95	18	4	8	55	.290	163	10	7	.961
1980—San Antonio.......... Texas	OF	●136	469	95	117	19	6	12	76	.249	241	17	8	.970
1981—San Antonio.......... Texas	OF	129	472	●98	149	26	4	20	89	.316	240	10	5	.980
1981—Los Angeles .... Nat.	OF	9	6	2	1	1	0	0	0	.167	3	1	0	1.000
1982—Albuquerque .... P. C.	OF	139	523	112	166	31	11	12	101	.317	255	13	7	.975
1982—Los Angeles† .... Nat.	OF	8	3	1	1	0	0	0	0	.333	1	0	0	1.000
1983—New York.............. Nat.	OF	73	104	10	21	4	0	3	5	.202	41	2	0	1.000
Major League Totals....................................		90	113	13	23	5	0	3	5	.204	45	3	0	1.000

Selected by Los Angeles Dodgers' organization in 1st round (24th player selected) of free-agent draft, June 4, 1975.
†Traded to New York Mets' organization for Pitchers Jody Johnston and Steve Walker, March 29, 1983.

PHILIP POOLE BRADLEY
(Phil)

Born March 11, 1959, at Bloomington, Ind.
Height, 6.00. Weight, 175.
Throws and bats righthanded.
Received bachelor of science degree in personnel management from
University of Missouri, Columbia, Mo., in 1982.

Year Club	League	Pos.	G.	AB.	R.	H.	2B.	3B.	HR.	RBI.	B.A.	PO.	A.	E.	F.A.
1981—Bellingham .... N'west	OF	53	193	38	58	12	5	1	20	.301	94	3	1	★.990
1982—Bakersfield............ Calif.	OF	109	405	98	134	17	10	0	37	.331	226	13	6	.976
1983—Salt Lake City....... P. Coast	OF	130	458	100	148	14	4	2	41	.323	284	13	1	★.997
1983—Seattle.................... Amer.	OF	23	67	8	18	2	0	0	5	.269	36	1	1	.974
Major League Totals....................................		23	67	8	18	2	0	0	5	.269	36	1	1	.974

Selected by Seattle Mariners' organization in 3rd round of free-agent draft, June 8, 1981.

STEVEN BERT BRADLEY

(Known by middle name.)

Born December 23, 1956, at Athens, Ga.
Height, 6.01. Weight, 185.
Throws and bats righthanded.
Attended Lake Land College, Mattoon, Ill., and
Brigham Young University, Provo, Utah.

Year Club	League	G.	IP.	W.	L.	Pct.	H.	R.	ER.	SO.	BB.	ERA.
1979—Modesto.. California	9	35	2	2	.500	28	19	15	24	10	3.86
1979—Waterbury...................................... Eastern	5	45	2	2	.500	36	11	10	8	13	2.00
1979—Ogden .... P. Coast	6	27	0	2	.000	27	16	14	12	14	4.67
1980—West Haven .... Eastern	24	146	3	★15	.167	190	★121	★105	56	51	6.47
1981—West Haven .... Eastern	30	54	4	5	.444	61	41	35	38	27	5.83
1981—Modesto.. California	27	52	7	4	.636	41	15	14	43	21	2.42
1982—West Haven† .... Eastern	39	59⅓	6	3	.667	47	23	16	48	32	2.43
1982—Tacoma... P. Coast	17	23⅔	1	1	.500	25	12	10	13	13	3.80
1983—Tacoma... P. Coast	★65	84⅔	6	5	.545	72	35	26	45	29	2.76
1983—Oakland.. American	6	8⅓	0	0	.000	14	7	6	3	4	6.48
Major League Totals...	6	8⅓	0	0	.000	14	7	6	3	4	6.48

Selected by Oakland A's organization in 27th round of free-agent draft, June 5, 1979.
†On disabled list, May 5 to May 16, 1982.

MARSHALL LEE BRANT

Born September 17, 1955, at Garberville, Calif.
Height, 6.04. Weight, 215.
Throws and bats righthanded.
Attended Santa Rosa Junior College, Santa Rosa, Calif.

Led International League in being hit by pitch with 14 in 1982.
Led International League in game-winning RBIs with 15 in 1981.
Led International League in sacrifice flies with 11 in 1980 and tied for lead with 6 in 1981.
Led International League batters in strikeouts with 119 in 1979.
Led Carolina League in total bases with 238 and in sacrifice flies with 11 in 1976.
Led Appalachian League in total bases with 144 in 1975.
Led International League first basemen in double plays with 124 in 1979.
Led Texas League first basemen in putouts with 1,192 and tied for lead in assists with 81 in 1977.
Led Carolina League first basemen in double plays with 101 in 1976.
Led Appalachian League first basemen in assists with 50, fielding percentage with .981 and tied for lead in double plays with 38 in 1975.
Named International League Most Valuable Player, 1980.
Named Carolina League Most Valuable Player, 1976.

Year Club League	Pos.	G.	AB.	R.	H.	2B.	3B.	HR.	RBI.	B.A.	PO.	A.	E.	F.A.
1975—Marion.................... Appal.	1B-C	64	245	49	80	15	5	*13	45	.327	529	51	12	.980
1976—Lynchburg............ Carol.	1B	135	476	75	123	*32	7	*23	*93	.258	*1208	69	*15	*.988
1977—Jackson .... Texas	1B-OF	*130	496	71	143	26	6	17	84	.288	1193	82	8	.994
1978—Tidewater............. Int.	1B	119	389	50	102	23	3	14	54	.262	736	51	10	.987
1979—Tidewater†........... Int.	1B	138	488	58	123	21	2	22	65	.252	*1231	74	11	.992
1980—Columbus.............. Int.	1B	126	409	69	118	22	5	*23	*92	.289	1086	64	8	*.993
1980—New York‡.......... Amer.	1B	3	6	0	0	0	0	0	0	.000	9	1	0	1.000
1981—Columbus.............. Int.	1B-3B	127	456	80	119	19	1	25	95	.261	626	47	2	.997
1982—Columbus.............. Int.	1B	132	482	86	135	21	1	31	96	.280	648	66	7	.990
1983—Columbus§............ Int.	1B	37	119	21	23	2	1	7	19	.193	81	6	1	.989
1983—Tacoma................. P.C.	1B	49	164	20	38	6	0	10	25	.232	306	26	5	.985
1983—Oakland x .... Amer.	1B	5	14	2	2	0	0	0	2	.143	19	0	2	.905
Major League Totals..................................		8	20	2	2	0	0	0	2	.100	28	1	2	.935

Selected by New York Mets' organization in 4th round of free-agent draft, January 9, 1975.
†Sold to New York Yankees' organization, April 1, 1980.
‡Released, November 4, 1980; re-signed by Yankees' organization, February 3, 1981.
§Traded with Pitcher Ben Callahan to Oakland A's for Pitcher Matt Keough, June 15, 1983.
xReleased, December 2, 1983.

STEPHEN RUSSELL BRAUN III
(Steve)

Born May 8, 1948, at Trenton, N. J.
Height, 5.10. Weight, 180.
Throws right and bats lefthanded.

Led Carolina League third basemen in fielding percentage with .925 in 1970.
Led Gulf Coast League second basemen in double plays with 47 in 1967.

Year Club League	Pos.	G.	AB.	R.	H.	2B.	3B.	HR.	RBI.	B.A.	PO.	A.	E.	F.A.
1966—Sarasota Twins .... Gulf C.	2B	45	152	23	35	5	*5	0	15	.230	70	85	*16	.906
1967—Wis. Rapids.......... Midw.	2B	10	9	1	2	1	0	0	2	.222	0	0	0	.000
1967—Sarasota Twins† ...Gulf C.	2B	54	184	37	45	6	*8	1	13	.245	*111	*153	*14	.950
1968-69—..............................						(In military service)								
1970—Lynchburg............. Carol.	3B-2B	118	387	52	108	24	1	4	43	.279	109	253	29	.926
1971—Minnesota.............. Amer.	3-2-S-O	128	343	51	87	12	2	5	35	.254	107	193	13	.958
1972—Minnesota.............. Amer.	3-2-S-O	121	402	40	116	21	0	2	50	.289	110	207	13	.961
1973—Minnesota.............. Amer.	3B-OF	115	361	46	102	28	5	6	42	.283	86	175	16	.942
1974—Minnesota.............. Amer.	OF-3B	129	453	53	127	12	1	8	40	.280	195	47	12	.953
1975—Minnesota.............. Amer.	O-1-3-2	136	453	70	137	18	3	11	45	.302	271	14	10	.966
1976—Minnesota‡............ Amer.	OF-3B	122	417	73	120	12	3	3	61	.288	71	32	6	.954
1977—Seattle................... Amer.	OF-3B	139	451	51	106	19	1	5	31	.235	186	11	5	.975
1978—Sea.§-Kan. City ..... Amer.	OF-3B	96	211	27	53	14	1	3	29	.251	68	9	4	.951
1979—Kansas City x .... Amer.	OF-3B	58	116	15	31	2	0	4	10	.267	26	4	0	1.000
1980—K.C. y-Tor............. Amer.	OF-3B	51	78	4	16	2	0	1	10	.205	2	1	0	1.000
1980—Syracuse z............. Int.	DH	19	61	11	20	3	1	2	11	.328	0	0	0	.000
1981—St. Louis................. Nat.	OF-3B	44	46	9	9	2	1	0	2	.196	15	2	0	1.000
1982—St. Louis a .... Nat.	OF-3B	58	62	6	17	4	0	0	4	.274	6	5	1	.917
1983—St. Louis................. Nat.	OF-3B	78	92	8	25	2	1	3	7	.272	26	4	0	1.000
American League Totals...........................		1095	3285	430	895	140	16	48	353	.272	1122	693	79	.958
National League Totals............................		180	200	23	51	8	2	3	13	.255	47	11	1	.983
Major League Totals................................		1275	3485	453	946	148	18	51	366	.271	1169	704	80	.959

Selected by Minnesota Twins' organization in 10th round of free-agent draft, June 22, 1966.
†On military list, September 6, 1967 through September 23, 1969.
‡Selected by Seattle Mariners in American League expansion draft, November 5, 1976.
§Traded to Kansas City Royals for Pitcher Jim Colborn, June 1, 1978.
xOn supplemental disabled list, July 29 to September 1, 1979.
yReleased, June 2, 1980; signed by Toronto Blue Jays' organization, July 10, 1980.
zGranted free agency, November 5, 1980; signed by St. Louis Cardinals' organization, March 3, 1981.
aOn supplemental disabled list, June 7 to June 22, 1982.

CHAMPIONSHIP SERIES RECORD

Year Club League	Pos.	G.	AB.	R.	H.	2B.	3B.	HR.	RBI.	B.A.	PO.	A.	E.	F.A.
1978—Kansas City........... Amer.	OF-PH	2	5	0	0	0	0	0	0	.000	5	0	0	1.000
1982—St. Louis................. Nat.	PH	1	1	0	0	0	0	0	0	.000	0	0	0	.000
Championship Series Totals		3	6	0	0	0	0	0	0	.000	5	0	0	1.000

WORLD SERIES RECORD

Year Club League	Pos.	G.	AB.	R.	H.	2B.	3B.	HR.	RBI.	B.A.	PO.	A.	E.	F.A.
1982—St. Louis................. Nat.	PH-DH	2	2	0	1	0	0	0	2	.500	0	0	0	.000

SIDNEY EUGENE BREAM
(Sid)

Born August 3, 1960, at Carlisle, Pa.
Height, 6.04. Weight, 220.
Throws and bats lefthanded.
Attended Liberty Baptist College, Lynchburg, Va.

Year Club League	Pos.	G.	AB.	R.	H.	2B.	3B.	HR.	RBI.	B.A.	PO.	A.	E.	F.A.
1981—Vero Beach........... Fla. St.	1B	70	260	35	85	12	5	1	47	.327	613	45	10	.985

Year Club League	Pos.	G.	AB.	R.	H.	2B.	3B.	HR.	RBI.	B.A.	PO.	A.	E.	F.A.
1982—Vero Beach........... Fla. St.	1B	63	226	41	70	13	5	4	43	.310	523	40	5	.991
1982—San Antonio........... Texas	1B	70	259	43	83	18	0	8	50	.320	621	40	12	.982
1982—Albuquerque........ P. C.	1B	3	8	3	3	1	0	1	2	.375	11	0	0	1.000
1983—Albuquerque........ P. C.	1B	138	485	115	149	23	4	●32	★118	.307	1264	★123	24	.983
1983—Los Angeles .... Nat.	1B	15	11	0	2	0	0	0	2	.182	8	0	0	1.000
Major League Totals....................		15	11	0	2	0	0	0	2	.182	8	0	0	1.000

Selected by Los Angeles Dodgers' organization in 2nd round of free-agent draft, June 8, 1981.

FRED LAWRENCE BREINING

Name pronounced BRYN-ing.
Born November 15, 1955, at San Francisco, Calif.
Height, 6.04. Weight, 185.
Throws and bats righthanded.
Attended College of San Mateo, San Mateo, Calif.

Led Carolina League in home runs allowed with 14 in 1976.

Year Club	League	G.	IP.	W.	L.	Pct.	H.	R.	ER.	SO.	BB.	ERA.
1974—Niagara Falls†-Auburn	NYP	11	38	3	2	.600	47	33	21	16	35	4.97
1975—Charleston	W. Carol.	35	92	3	8	.273	75	57	46	82	60	4.50
1976—Salem..	Carolina	31	127	9	4	.692	127	70	49	106	58	3.47
1977—Shreveport	Texas	36	92	3	4	.429	77	37	26	79	41	2.54
1978—Columbus...	Int'national	21	55	2	2	.500	54	45	39	34	33	6.38
1978—Shreveport	Texas	16	56	3	6	.333	53	35	23	50	21	3.70
1979—Buffalo‡..	Eastern	12	82	5	4	.556	77	39	24	73	41	2.63
1979—Shreveport	Texas	10	60	4	2	.667	50	12	8	50	17	1.20
1980—Phoenix..	P. Coast	54	100	6	★13	.316	106	57	46	84	56	4.14
1980—San Francisco	National	5	7	0	0	.000	8	4	4	3	4	5.14
1981—San Francisco	National	45	78	5	2	.714	66	28	22	37	38	2.54
1982—San Francisco	National	54	143⅓	11	6	.647	146	61	49	98	52	3.08
1983—San Francisco	National	32	202⅔	11	12	.478	202	97	86	117	60	3.82
Major League Totals....................		136	431	27	20	.574	422	190	161	255	154	3.36

Selected by Pittsburgh Pirates' organization in 3rd round of free-agent draft, January 9, 1974.
†Loaned to Auburn (Philadelphia Phillies' organization), July 25, 1974; returned, September 30, 1974.
‡Traded with Pitchers Eddie Whitson and Al Holland to San Francisco Giants for Third Basemen Bill Madlock and Lenny Randle and Pitcher Dave Roberts, June 28, 1979.

ROBERT EARL BRENLY
(Bob)

Born February 25, 1954, at Coshocton, Ohio.
Height, 6.02. Weight, 210.
Throws and bats righthanded.
Received bachelor of science degree in health education from
Ohio University, Athens, Ohio in 1976.

Led California League third basemen in double plays with 30 in 1978.
Led Midwest League third basemen in double plays with 21 in 1977.

Year Club	League	Pos.	G.	AB.	R.	H.	2B.	3B.	HR.	RBI.	B.A.	PO.	A.	E.	F.A.
1976—Great Falls........... Pion.	3B	25	86	16	27	5	1	1	17	.314	10	16	2	.929
1976—Fresno .... Calif.	3B	17	60	16	22	3	1	1	9	.367	2	6	1	.889
1977—Cedar Rapids........ Midw.	★3B-OF	136	499	85	135	16	1	22	73	.271	90	★263	●31	.919
1978—Fresno .... Calif.	3B	135	489	102	139	34	5	17	89	.284	★118	247	27	.931
1979—Fresno .... Calif.	3B	56	212	49	65	11	2	9	37	.307	39	133	17	.910
1979—Shreveport .... Texas	C-3-O-1	64	193	33	57	8	1	9	30	.295	199	55	7	.973
1980—Shreveport .... Texas	3B	2	10	2	3	0	0	1	3	.300	1	2	0	1.000
1980—Phoenix................. P. C.	3-C-S-O	84	287	34	74	9	6	7	45	.258	183	110	20	.936
1981—Phoenix................. P. C.	C-OF-3B	76	257	42	75	11	3	7	41	.292	177	41	9	.960
1981—San Francisco ...... Nat.	C-3B-OF	19	45	5	15	2	1	1	4	.333	52	6	4	.935
1982—San Francisco† .... Nat.	C-3B	65	180	26	51	4	1	4	15	.283	265	32	12	.961
1983—San Francisco ...... Nat.	C-1B-OF	104	281	36	63	12	2	7	34	.224	465	73	9	.984
Major League Totals....................		188	506	67	129	18	4	12	53	.255	782	111	25	.973

Signed as free agent by San Francisco Giants' organization, June 21, 1976.
†On disabled list, March 25 to May 13, 1982.

THOMAS MARTIN BRENNAN
(Tom)

Born October 30, 1952, at Chicago, Ill.
Height, 6.01. Weight, 180.
Throws and bats righthanded.
Received bachelor of arts degree in English from Lewis University, Lockport, Ill.

Led International League in shutouts with 6 and tied for lead in complete games with 11 in 1981.
Led Pacific Coast League in home runs allowed with 23 in 1978.

Year Club	League	G.	IP.	W.	L.	Pct.	H.	R.	ER.	SO.	BB.	ERA.
1974—Oklahoma City	Am. Assoc.	13	50	3	5	.375	46	42	38	44	56	6.79
1975—Oklahoma City	Am. Assoc.	25	122	5	14	.263	149	103	96	52	98	7.08
1976—Williamsport..................................	Eastern	11	61	3	4	.429	63	37	30	22	40	4.43

Year Club	League	G.	IP.	W.	L.	Pct.	H.	R.	ER.	SO.	BB.	ERA.
1976—San Jose	California	16	72	3	9	.250	95	64	46	28	37	5.75
1977—Waterloo	Midwest	9	58	4	3	.571	61	35	32	30	35	4.97
1977—Jersey City	Eastern	4	28	3	1	.750	33	10	8	13	13	2.57
1977—Toledo	Int'national	11	75	1	4	.200	79	36	29	17	31	3.48
1978—Portland	P. Coast	27	172	10	8	.556	202	108	87	82	32	4.55
1979—Tacoma	P. Coast	26	176	12	7	.632	176	70	62	102	38	3.17
1980—Tacoma	P. Coast	24	152	9	3	.750	167	48	42	77	29	2.49
1981—Charleston	Int'national	25	156	11	8	.579	163	77	68	64	24	3.92
1981—Cleveland	American	7	48	2	2	.500	49	20	17	15	14	3.19
1982—Cleveland	American	30	92⅔	4	2	.667	112	51	44	46	10	4.27
1983—Charleston	Int'national	21	114⅓	9	5	.643	105	44	42	72	29	*3.31
1983—Cleveland	American	11	39⅔	2	2	.500	45	22	17	21	8	3.86
Major League Totals		48	180⅓	8	6	.571	206	93	78	82	32	3.89

Selected by Cleveland Indians' organization in 1st round (fourth player selected) of free-agent draft, June 5, 1974.

GEORGE HOWARD BRETT

Born May 15, 1953, at Wheeling, W. Va.
Height, 6.00.   Weight, 200.
Throws right and bats lefthanded.
Attended Longview Community College, Lee's Summit, Mo. and
El Camino College, Torrance, Calif.
Brother of Ken Brett, pitcher with Boston, Milwaukee, Philadelphia, Pittsburgh, New York AL,
Chicago AL, California, Minnesota, Los Angeles and Kansas City, 1967 and 1969 through 1981;
John Brett, third baseman in Boston Red Sox' organization, 1968;
and Bob Brett, outfielder in Kansas City Royals' organization, 1972.

Established major league record for most consecutive games, three or more hits, season (6), May 8 through 13, 1976.
Tied major league record for most consecutive seasons leading major league in triples (2), 1975 and 1976.
Established American League record for fewest putouts by third baseman for leader in most putouts, season (140), 1976.
Became sixth major-league player to collect 20 or more doubles, triples and home runs in one season, 1979.
Hit three home runs in a game, July 22, 1979 and April 20, 1983.
Hit for the cycle, May 28, 1979.
Led American League in slugging percentage with .664 in 1980 and .563 in 1983.
Led American League in total bases with 298 in 1976.
Led American League third basemen in assists with 373, errors with 30 and total chances with 532 in 1979.
Led American League third baseman in putouts with 140 in 1976.
Led California League in sacrifice hits with 8 in 1972.
Led California League third basemen in assists with 172 in 1972.
Named Man of the Year by THE SPORTING NEWS, 1980.
Named Major League Player of the Year by THE SPORTING NEWS, 1980.
Named American League Player of the Year by THE SPORTING NEWS, 1980.
Named American League Most Valuable Player by Baseball Writers' Association of America, 1980.
Named third baseman on THE SPORTING NEWS American League All-Star Team, 1976, 1979 and 1980.
Named third baseman on THE SPORTING NEWS Silver Slugger team, 1980.

Year Club	League	Pos.	G.	AB.	R.	H.	2B.	3B.	HR.	RBI.	B.A.	PO.	A.	E.	F.A.
1971—Billings	Pion.	SS-3B	68	258	44	75	8	5	5	44	.291	87	140	28	.890
1972—San Jose†	Calif.	*3-S-2	117	431	66	118	13	5	10	68	.274	101	213	*30	.913
1973—Omaha	A. A.	3B-OF	117	405	66	115	16	4	8	64	.284	92	219	26	.923
1973—Kansas City	Amer.	3B	13	40	2	5	2	0	0	0	.125	9	28	1	.974
1974—Omaha	A. A.	3B	16	64	9	17	2	0	2	14	.266	8	31	4	.907
1974—Kansas City	Amer.	3B-SS	133	457	49	129	21	5	2	47	.282	102	279	21	.948
1975—Kansas City	Amer.	●3B-SS	159	*634	84	*195	35	●13	11	89	.308	132	356	●26	.949
1976—Kansas City	Amer.	3B-SS	159	*645	94	*215	34	*14	7	67	*.333	146	350	26	.950
1977—Kansas City	Amer.	3B-SS	139	564	105	176	32	13	22	88	.312	115	325	21	.954
1978—Kansas City‡	Amer.	3B-SS	128	510	79	150	*45	8	9	62	.294	104	289	16	.961
1979—Kansas City	Amer.	3B-1B	154	645	119	*212	42	*20	23	107	.329	176	378	31	.947
1980—Kansas City§	Amer.	3B-1B	117	449	87	175	33	9	24	118	*.390	107	256	17	.955
1981—Kansas City	Amer.	3B	89	347	42	109	27	7	6	43	.314	74	170	14	.946
1982—Kansas City	Amer.	3B-OF	144	552	101	166	32	9	21	82	.301	130	295	17	.962
1983—Kansas City x	Amer.	3B-1B-OF	123	464	90	144	38	2	25	93	.310	210	192	25	.941
Major League Totals			1358	5307	852	1676	341	100	150	796	.316	1305	2918	215	.952

Selected by Kansas City Royals' organization in 2nd round of free-agent draft, June 8, 1971.
†On disabled list, April 29 to May 11, 1972.
‡On supplemental disabled list, May 4 to May 19 and July 27 to August 14, 1978.
§On supplemental disabled list, June 11 to July 10, 1980.
xOn supplemental disabled list, June 8 to June 29, 1983.

DIVISION SERIES RECORD

Year Club	League	Pos.	G.	AB.	R.	H.	2B.	3B.	HR.	RBI.	B.A.	PO.	A.	E.	F.A.
1981—Kansas City	Amer.	3B	3	12	0	2	0	0	0	0	.167	1	6	1	.876

CHAMPIONSHIP SERIES RECORD

Established Championship Series records for highest slugging average, total Series, 10 or more games and 30 or more at-bats (.791); most three-base hits, total Series (4); most runs, four-game Series (7), 1978; most long hits, total Series (13).
Tied Championship Series records for most three-base hits, Series (2), 1977; most home runs, game (3), October 6,

1978; most times home run as leadoff batter, start of game (1), October 6, 1978; most Series, two or more home runs (2).

Established American League Championship Series records for most runs, total Series (16); most home runs, four-game Series (3), 1978; highest slugging average, four-game Series (1.056), 1978; most hits, four-game Series (7), 1978; most total bases, four-game Series (19), 1978; most long hits, four-game Series (5), 1978; most long hits, two consecutive games, one series (4), October 6 and 7, 1978; most total bases, game (12), October 6, 1978.

Tied American League Championship Series records for most at-bats, four-game Series (18), 1978; most home runs, total Series (6); most long hits, game (3), October 6, 1978; most consecutive games, one or more hits (9); most home runs, three-game Series (2), 1980.

Year	Club	League	Pos.	G.	AB.	R.	H.	2B.	3B.	HR.	RBI.	B.A.	PO.	A.	E.	F.A.
1976—Kansas City		Amer.	3B	5	18	4	8	1	1	1	5	.444	3	7	3	.769
1977—Kansas City		Amer.	3B	5	20	2	6	0	2	0	2	.300	5	12	2	.895
1978—Kansas City		Amer.	3B	4	18	7	7	1	1	3	3	.389	3	8	1	.917
1980—Kansas City		Amer.	3B	3	11	3	3	1	0	2	4	.273	2	7	0	1.000
Championship Series Totals				17	67	16	24	3	4	6	14	.358	13	34	6	.887

WORLD SERIES RECORD

Year	Club	League	Pos.	G.	AB.	R.	H.	2B.	3B.	HR.	RBI.	B.A.	PO.	A.	E.	F.A.
1980—Kansas City		Amer.	3B	6	24	3	9	2	1	1	3	.375	4	17	1	.955

ALL-STAR GAME RECORD

Year	League	Pos.	AB.	R.	H.	2B.	3B.	HR.	RBI.	B.A.	PO.	A.	E.	F.A.
1976—American		3B	2	0	0	0	0	0	0	.000	0	1	0	1.000
1977—American		3B	2	0	0	0	0	0	0	.000	2	1	0	1.000
1978—American		3B	3	1	2	1	0	0	2	.667	0	2	0	1.000
1979—American		3B	3	1	0	0	0	0	0	.000	1	2	0	1.000
1981—American		3B	3	0	0	0	0	0	0	.000	0	1	0	1.000
1982—American		3B	2	0	2	0	0	0	0	1.000	0	0	0	.000
1983—American		3B	4	2	2	1	1	0	1	.500	1	5	0	1.000
All-Star Game Totals			19	4	6	2	1	0	3	.316	4	12	0	1.000

Named to American League All-Star Team in 1980; replaced due to injury.

ANTHONY BRUCE BREWER
(Tony)

Born November 25, 1957, at Shreveport, La.
Height, 5.11. Weight, 175.
Throws and bats righthanded.
Attended University of Miami, Coral Gables, Fla.
Brother of Mike Brewer, outfielder in Kansas City Royals' organization.

Led Pacific Coast League in game-winning RBI's with 14 and sacrifice flies with 12 in 1983.

Year	Club	League	Pos.	G.	AB.	R.	H.	2B.	3B.	HR.	RBI.	B.A.	PO.	A.	E.	F.A.
1980—Vero Beach		Fla. St.	OF	137	470	79	134	17	●12	3	59	.285	242	9	1	★.996
1981—Lodi†		Calif.	OF	118	434	86	161	22	5	16˙	85	.371	88	8	3	.970
1982—San Antonio		Texas	OF-3B	135	496	88	145	35	5	22	88	.292	154	19	13	.930
1982—Albuquerque		P. C.	OF	2	6	2	2	0	0	0	3	.333	3	0	0	1.000
1983—Albuquerque		P. C.	OF	130	467	99	147	29	5	24	96	.315	158	16	4	.978

Signed as free agent by Los Angeles Dodgers' organization, October 14, 1979.
†On disabled list, June 13 to June 23, 1981.

MICHAEL QUINN BREWER
(Mike)

Born October 24, 1959, at Shreveport, La.
Height, 6.05. Weight, 190.
Throws and bats righthanded.
Attended Foothill Junior College, Los Altos Hills, Calif.
Brother of Tony Brewer, outfielder in Los Angeles Dodgers' organization.

Led Gulf Coast League in total bases with 105 and tied for lead in caught stealing with 7 in 1979.
Named Gulf Coast League Most Valuable Player, 1979.

Year	Club	League	Pos.	G.	AB.	R.	H.	2B.	3B.	HR.	RBI.	B.A.	PO.	A.	E.	F.A.
1979—Sarasota Gold		Gulf C.	OF	51	★205	38	★76	7	5	4	★47	★.371	72	5	●5	.939
1980—Ft. Myers		Fla. St.	OF	123	426	54	102	13	4	6	63	.239	199	8	★11	.950
1981—Ft. Myers		Fla. St.	OF	128	459	69	132	16	9	16	84	.288	209	12	9	.961
1982—Jacksonville		South.	OF	121	438	74	109	15	4	20	68	.249	269	13	11	.962
1982—Omaha		A. A.	OF	18	56	10	16	5	0	1	7	.286	37	3	1	.976
1983—Omaha		A. A.	OF	120	412	63	104	23	3	9	42	.252	233	10	11	.957

Selected by Kansas City Royals' organization in 1st round (22nd player selected) of free-agent draft, January 9, 1979.

JOSE OSCAR BRITO

Name pronounced BREET-oh.

Born October 28, 1959, at Salcedo, Dominican Republic.
Height, 6.02. Weight, 160.
Throws and bats righthanded.

Year	Club	League	G.	IP.	W.	L.	Pct.	H.	R.	ER.	SO.	BB.	ERA.
1977—Eugene		Northwest	15	90	6	6	.500	119	66	52	69	26	5.20

Year Club	League	G.	IP.	W.	L.	Pct.	H.	R.	ER.	SO.	BB.	ERA.
1978—Shelby	W. Carol.	30	155	10	8	.556	132	74	63	107	67	3.66
1979—Tampa	Florida St.	28	167	11	7	.611	126	57	45	154	82	2.43
1980—Waterbury	Eastern	25	172	12	6	.667	125	66	60	175	75	3.14
1981—Indianapolis†	Am. Assoc.	25	116	6	11	.353	114	77	63	91	77	4.89
1982—Louisville	Am. Assoc.	36	119⅔	5	8	.385	107	64	60	94	62	4.51
1983—Louisville‡§	Am. Assoc.	26	77	3	3	.500	82	50	47	56	45	5.49
1983—Vancouver	P. Coast					(Did not play)						
1983—Arkansas	Texas	3	18⅔	2	1	.667	11	7	6	19	17	2.89

Signed as free agent by Cincinnati Reds' organization, March 2, 1977.

†Traded with Pitcher Jeff Lahti to St. Louis Cardinals' organization for Pitcher Bob Shirley, April 1, 1982.

‡On disabled list, April 15 to May 3, 1983.

§Loaned to Vancouver (Milwaukee Brewers' organization), July 6, 1983; returned, July 15, 1983.

ANTHONY JOHN BRIZZOLARA

Name pronounced Briz-zuh-LAIR-uh.

(Tony)

Born January 14, 1957, at Santa Monica, Calif.
Height, 6.05. Weight, 210.
Throws and bats righthanded.
Attended University of Texas, Austin, Tex.

Led International League pitchers in games started with 30 in 1980 and 32 in 1982.

Year Club	League	G.	IP.	W.	L.	Pct.	H.	R.	ER.	SO.	BB.	ERA.
1977—Kingsport	Ap'lachian	6	27	3	2	.600	21	8	7	27	10	2.33
1978—Greenwood	W. Carol.	3	20	3	0	1.000	9	3	2	21	8	0.90
1978—Savannah†	Southern	10	70	4	4	.500	57	19	15	55	21	1.93
1978—Richmond	Int'national	9	50	3	4	.429	57	34	33	40	18	5.94
1979—Richmond	Int'national	9	66	4	2	.667	47	15	14	42	28	1.91
1979—Atlanta	National	20	107	6	9	.400	133	70	63	64	33	5.30
1980—Richmond	Int'national	30	★206	10	●15	.400	198	102	85	128	56	3.71
1981—Richmond	Int'national	25	141	10	3	.769	138	62	56	59	44	3.57
1982—Richmond	Int'national	32	193	15	11	.577	★231	★119	★108	102	75	5.04
1983—Richmond	Int'national	21	127⅔	9	7	.563	136	58	53	90	44	3.74
1983—Atlanta	National	14	20⅓	1	0	1.000	22	8	8	17	6	3.54
Major League Totals		34	127⅓	7	9	.438	155	78	71	81	39	5.02

Selected by Atlanta Braves' organization in 2nd round of free-agent draft, June 7, 1977.

†On disabled list, June 20 to June 29, 1978.

GREGORY ALLEN BROCK

(Greg)

Born June 14, 1957, at McMinnville, Ore.
Height, 6.03. Weight, 200.
Throws right and bats lefthanded.
Attended University of Wyoming, Laramie, Wyo.
Brother of Eric Brock, shortstop in Los Angeles Dodgers' organization.

Led Pacific Coast League in bases on balls received with 105 and intentional bases on balls received with 15 in 1982.

Led Pioneer League in bases on balls received with 54 in 1979.

Led Pacific Coast League first basemen in double plays with 106 in 1982.

Year Club	League	Pos.	G.	AB.	R.	H.	2B.	3B.	HR.	RBI.	B.A.	PO.	A.	E.	F.A.
1979—Lethbridge	Pion.	1B	66	247	61	88	18	2	16	77	.356	543	★36	8	★.986
1980—Lodi	Calif.	1B	121	418	72	125	19	3	★29	95	.299	906	★79	5	★.995
1981—San Antonio	Texas	1B	128	499	86	147	25	3	★32	106	.295	1071	★90	9	.992
1982—Albuquerque	P. C.	1B	135	480	118	149	21	8	44	138	.310	★1076	★106	★20	.983
1982—Los Angeles	Nat.	1B	18	17	1	2	1	0	0	1	.118	9	0	0	1.000
1983—Los Angeles	Nat.	1B	146	455	64	102	14	2	20	66	.224	1162	106	12	.991
Major League Totals			164	472	65	104	15	2	20	67	.220	1171	106	12	.991

Selected by Los Angeles Dodgers' organization in 13th round of free-agent draft, June 5, 1979.

CHAMPIONSHIP SERIES RECORD

Year Club	League	Pos.	G.	AB.	R.	H.	2B.	3B.	HR.	RBI.	B.A.	PO.	A.	E.	F.A.
1983—Los Angeles	Nat.	1B	3	9	1	0	0	0	0	0	.000	13	0	0	1.000

THOMAS DALE BROOKENS

(Tom)

Born August 10, 1953, at Chambersburg, Pa.
Height, 5.10. Weight, 170.
Throws and bats righthanded.
Attended Mansfield State College, Mansfield, Pa.

Twin brother of Tim Brookens, infielder-outfielder in Detroit Tigers' organization, 1975 through 1978; cousin of Ike Brookens, pitcher with Detroit Tigers, 1975.

Tied American League record for most errors by third baseman, game (4), September 6, 1980.

Year Club	League	Pos.	G.	AB.	R.	H.	2B.	3B.	HR.	RBI.	B.A.	PO.	A.	E.	F.A.
1975—Montgomery	South.	SS	100	329	37	73	11	2	7	36	.222	139	298	31	.934
1976—Montgomery	South.	2B	137	492	76	127	22	5	11	56	.258	310	★389	★25	.965

Year Club	League	Pos.	G.	AB.	R.	H.	2B.	3B.	HR.	RBI.	B.A.	PO.	A.	E.	F.A.
1977—Evansville	A. A.	3B-2B	118	440	70	127	22	5	8	52	.289	132	250	25	.939
1978—Evansville†	A. A.	3B-2B-1B	65	206	27	58	11	1	6	25	.282	76	100	20	.898
1979—Evansville	A. A.	3B-2B	77	265	51	81	23	2	14	46	.306	71	166	16	.937
1979—Detroit	Amer.	3B-2B	60	190	23	50	5	2	4	21	.263	76	141	11	.952
1980—Detroit	Amer.	*3-2-S	151	509	64	140	25	9	10	66	.275	127	307	*29	.937
1981—Detroit‡	Amer.	3B	71	239	19	58	10	1	4	25	.243	58	139	10	.952
1982—Detroit	Amer.	3-2-S-O	140	398	40	92	15	3	9	58	.231	119	276	20	.952
1983—Detroit	Amer.	3B-SS-2B	138	332	50	71	13	3	6	32	.214	97	254	22	.941
Major League Totals....................			560	1668	196	411	68	18	33	202	.246	477	1117	92	.945

Selected by Detroit Tigers' organization in 1st round (fourth player selected) of free-agent draft, January 9, 1975.
†On disabled list, April 14 to May 9 and June 4 to June 21, 1978.
‡On disabled list, March 30 to May 4, 1981.

HUBERT BROOKS JR.
(Hubie)

Born September 24, 1956, at Los Angeles, Calif.
Height, 6.00. Weight, 188.
Throws and bats righthanded.
Attended Mesa Community College, Mesa, Ariz., and received bachelor of science
degree in health science from Arizona State University, Tempe, Ariz.
Grandson of Leandrus Brooks, player with Philadelphia of Negro National League;
cousin of Donnie Moore, pitcher with Atlanta Braves.

Tied modern National League record for most errors in inning by third baseman (3), May 10, 1981 (fourth inning).
Led International League in game-winning RBIs with 12 in 1980.

Year Club	League	Pos.	G.	AB.	R.	H.	2B.	3B.	HR.	RBI.	B.A.	PO.	A.	E.	F.A.
1978—Jackson	Texas	SS-OF-3B	45	153	19	33	8	1	3	16	.216	49	84	14	.905
1979—Jackson	Texas	3B-SS	112	406	68	124	21	2	3	28	.305	92	218	29	.942
1979—Tidewater	Int.	SS-3B-OF	5	15	1	6	1	0	1	3	.400	4	8	1	.923
1980—Tidewater	Int.	OF-3B-SS	113	417	50	124	18	5	3	50	.297	152	90	18	.931
1980—New York..............	Nat.	3B	24	81	8	25	2	1	1	10	.309	16	40	2	.966
1981—New York..............	Nat.	*3-O-S	98	358	34	110	21	2	4	38	.307	67	193	*21	.925
1982—New York†.............	Nat.	3B	126	457	40	114	21	2	2	40	.249	89	237	24	.931
1983—New York..............	Nat.	3B-2B	150	586	53	147	18	4	5	58	.251	116	303	21	.952
Major League Totals....................			398	1482	135	396	62	9	12	146	.267	288	773	68	.940

Selected by Montreal Expos' organization in 19th round of free-agent draft, June 5, 1974.
Selected by Kansas City Royals' organization in secondary phase of free-agent draft, January 7, 1976.
Selected by Chicago White Sox' organization in secondary phase of free-agent draft, June 8, 1976.
Selected by Oakland A's organization in secondary phase of free-agent draft, January 11, 1977.
Selected by Chicago White Sox' organization in secondary phase of free-agent draft, June 7, 1977.
Selected by New York Mets' organization in 1st round (third player selected) of free-agent draft, June 6, 1978.
†On supplemental disabled list, June 28 to July 22, 1982.

MARK STEVEN BROUHARD

Name pronounced BRO-hard.
Born May 22, 1956, at Burbank, Calif.
Height, 6.01. Weight, 200.
Throws and bats righthanded.
Attended Pierce Junior College, Woodland Hills, Calif.

Led Texas League in total bases with 308 and slugging percentage with .596 in 1979.
Tied for California League lead in being hit by pitch with 11 in 1978.
Named Texas League Most Valuable Player, 1979.

Year Club	League	Pos.	G.	AB.	R.	H.	2B.	3B.	HR.	RBI.	B.A.	PO.	A.	E.	F.A.
1976—Idaho Falls...........	Pion.	OF-1B	69	255	43	80	5	8	7	57	.314	46	2	5	.906
1977—Salinas	Calif.	OF	136	507	85	141	27	3	16	87	.278	216	8	9	.961
1978—Salinas	Calif.	OF-3B	133	532	86	165	29	5	21	91	.310	230	10	7	.972
1979—El Paso†	Texas	OF	132	517	97	●181	29	7	*28	*107	.350	171	10	5	.973
1980—Milwaukee.............	Amer.	OF-1B	45	125	12	29	6	0	5	16	.232	77	4	1	.988
1981—Vancouver.............	P. C.	OF	16	59	10	17	2	2	1	5	.288	33	3	0	1.000
1981—Milwaukee.............	Amer.	OF	60	186	19	51	6	3	2	20	.274	92	7	1	.990
1982—Milwaukee.............	Amer.	OF	40	108	16	29	4	1	4	10	.269	69	2	1	.986
1982—Vancouver.............	P. C.	OF	17	71	12	20	1	2	2	8	.282	30	3	1	.971
1983—Vancouver.............	P.C.	OF	45	165	23	53	15	0	5	30	.321	57	2	2	.967
1983—Milwaukee‡.............	Amer.	OF	56	185	25	51	10	1	7	23	.276	112	1	1	.991
Major League Totals....................			201	604	77	160	26	5	18	69	.265	350	14	4	.989

Selected by California Angels' organization in 4th round of free-agent draft, January 7, 1976.
†Drafted by Milwaukee Brewers, December 3, 1979.
‡On supplemental disabled list, June 21 to July 11, 1983.

CHAMPIONSHIP SERIES RECORD

Tied Championship Series record for most runs, game (4), October 9, 1982.

Year Club	League	Pos.	G.	AB.	R.	H.	2B.	3B.	HR.	RBI.	B.A.	PO.	A.	E.	F.A.
1982—Milwaukee.............	Amer.	OF	1	4	4	3	1	0	1	3	.750	1	0	0	1.000

CURTIS STEVEN BROWN
(Curt)

Born January 15, 1960, at Ft. Lauderdale, Fla.
Height, 6.03. Weight, 170.
Throws and bats righthanded.
Attended Broward Community College Central, Ft. Lauderdale, Fla.

Led Pacific Coast League in saves with 15 in 1982.

Year Club	League	G.	IP.	W.	L.	Pct.	H.	R.	ER.	SO.	BB.	ERA.
1979—Idaho Falls	Pioneer	12	72	2	6	.250	86	49	37	47	13	4.63
1980—Salinas†	California	20	73	7	3	.700	80	32	24	28	19	2.96
1981—Redwood	California	5	9	1	0	1.000	10	6	6	2	2	6.00
1981—Holyoke	Eastern	32	67	5	3	.625	55	15	11	32	19	1.48
1982—Spokane	P. Coast	50	72⅔	3	4	.429	85	40	36	36	23	4.46
1983—Edmonton	P. Coast	40	57⅓	3	4	.429	66	37	26	32	16	4.08
1983—California‡	American	10	16	1	1	.500	25	13	13	7	4	7.31
Major League Totals		10	16	1	1	.500	25	13	13	7	4	7.31

Signed as free agent by California Angels' organization, April 19, 1979.
†On disabled list, July 25 to August 4 and August 13 to August 23, 1980.
‡Traded to New York Yankees for Pitcher Mike Browning, December 19, 1983.

DARRELL WAYNE BROWN

Born October 29, 1955, at Oklahoma City, Okla.
Height, 6.00. Weight, 180.
Throws and bats righthanded.
Attended East Los Angeles Junior College, Monterey Park, Calif., and
California State University at Los Angeles, Los Angeles, Calif.

Led American Association outfielders in fielding percentage with .988 in 1981.

Year Club	League	Pos.	G.	AB.	R.	H.	2B.	3B.	HR.	RBI.	B.A.	PO.	A.	E.	F.A.
1977—Lakeland	Fla. St.	OF	59	166	13	44	2	2	0	18	.265	84	4	3	.967
1978—Montgomery	South.	OF	54	212	23	56	1	5	1	12	.264	94	4	6	.942
1978—Lakeland	Fla. St.	OF-SS	70	224	31	56	3	1	0	13	.250	138	53	12	.941
1979—Evansville	A. A.	OF	23	43	8	11	0	0	1	4	.256	33	0	1	.971
1979—Montgomery	South.	OF	95	384	40	98	17	2	4	32	.255	232	7	6	.976
1980—Evansville	A. A.	OF	123	498	62	138	15	6	3	43	.277	288	5	8	.973
1981—Evansville	A. A.	OF-2B	101	430	53	116	17	3	1	30	.270	252	14	5	.982
1981—Birmingham	South.	OF	19	66	8	14	0	1	0	3	.212	29	0	0	1.000
1981—Detroit†	Amer.	OF	16	4	4	1	0	0	0	0	.250	2	0	0	1.000
1982—Tacoma	P. C.	OF	140	534	75	154	26	5	5	65	.288	261	*20	5	.983
1982—Oakland‡	Amer.	OF	8	18	2	6	0	1	0	3	.333	9	0	0	1.000
1983—Minnesota	Amer.	OF	91	309	40	84	6	2	0	22	.272	188	2	1	.995
Major League Totals			115	331	46	91	6	3	0	25	.275	199	2	1	.995

Selected by Houston Astros' organization in 1st round (13th player selected) of free-agent draft, January 9, 1975.
Selected by San Francisco Giants' organization in secondary phase of free-agent draft, June 4, 1975.
Selected by Milwaukee Brewers' organization in secondary phase of free-agent draft, June 8, 1976.
Selected by Detroit Tigers' organization in 3rd round of free-agent draft, June 7, 1977.
†Traded with Pitchers Jack Smith and Mark Fellows to Oakland A's organization for Infielder Jeff Cox and Catcher Scott Meyer, March 4, 1982.
‡Released, December 6, 1982; signed by Tacoma (Minnesota Twins' organization), December 14, 1982.

JOHN CHRISTOPHER BROWN
(Chris)

Born August 15, 1961, at Jackson, Miss.
Height, 6.00. Weight, 185.
Throws and bats righthanded.

Year Club	League	Pos.	G.	AB.	R.	H.	2B.	3B.	HR.	RBI.	B.A.	PO.	A.	E.	F.A.
1979—Great Falls	Pion.	3B	47	171	24	46	5	3	5	30	.269	31	77	11	.908
1980—Clinton	Midw.	3B-1B	103	337	38	80	5	3	7	35	.237	352	132	19	.962
1981—Fresno	Calif.	3B-OF-1B	85	291	37	84	11	2	8	44	.289	89	156	23	.914
1982—Shreveport	Texas	3B-2B	58	185	26	49	14	0	1	21	.265	51	82	9	.937
1982—Fresno	Calif.	3B-1B-SS	41	133	22	39	9	1	4	31	.293	41	71	6	.949
1983—Shreveport	Texas	3B	102	322	44	88	21	0	10	58	.273	63	182	17	.935

Selected by San Francisco Giants' organization in 2nd round of free-agent draft, June 5, 1979.

MARK ANTHONY BROWN

Born July 13, 1959, at Bellows Falls, Vt.
Height, 6.02. Weight, 190.
Throws right and bats left and righthanded.
Attended University of Massachusetts, Amherst, Mass.

Year Club	League	G.	IP.	W.	L.	Pct.	H.	R.	ER.	SO.	BB.	ERA.
1980—Bluefield	Ap'lachian	6	19	1	0	1.000	11	5	2	16	8	0.95
1980—Miami	Florida St.	10	59	3	5	.375	58	40	31	40	35	4.73
1981—Miami	Florida St.	17	53	3	3	.500	47	25	20	35	21	3.40
1981—Hagerstown	Carolina	10	21	1	0	1.000	19	7	5	16	8	2.14
1982—Hagerstown	Carolina	14	20⅓	0	0	.000	23	9	7	16	6	3.10
1982—Charlotte	Southern	19	73⅓	8	2	*.800	46	20	17	57	44	2.09

Year Club	League	G.	IP.	W.	L.	Pct.	H.	R.	ER.	SO.	BB.	ERA.
1982—Rochester	Int'national	3	6⅓	1	0	1.000	5	1	1	5	2	1.42
1983—Rochester‡	Int'national	19	53⅓	6	1	.857	41	23	21	44	20	3.54

Selected by Baltimore Orioles' organization in 6th round of free-agent draft, June 3, 1980.
†On disabled list, April 10 to April 22, 1981.
‡On disabled list, May 31 to August 4, 1983.

MICHAEL CHARLES BROWN
(Mike)

Born December 29, 1959, at San Francisco, Calif.
Height, 6.02. Weight, 195.
Throws and bats righthanded.
Attended San Jose State University, San Jose, Calif.

Year Club	League	Pos.	G.	AB.	R.	H.	2B.	3B.	HR.	RBI.	B.A.	PO.	A.	E.	F.A.
1980—Salinas	Calif.	OF-C	47	152	24	40	7	0	5	35	.263	72	4	5	.938
1981—Holyoke	East.	OF	135	499	64	160	25	8	6	83	.321	182	9	9	.955
1982—Spokane	P. C.	OF	134	476	74	135	30	7	11	73	.284	261	20	14	.957
1983—Edmonton	P.C.	OF	115	442	91	157	39	6	22	106	.355	190	11	2	.990
1983—California	Amer.	OF	31	104	12	24	5	1	3	9	.231	52	4	3	.949
Major League Totals			31	104	12	24	5	1	3	9	.231	52	4	3	.949

Selected by California Angels' organization in 7th round of free-agent draft, June 3, 1980.

MICHAEL GARY BROWN
(Mike)

Born March 4, 1959, at Haddon Township, N.J.
Height, 6.02. Weight, 205.
Throws and bats righthanded.
Attended Clemson University, Clemson, S.C.

Led Carolina League in complete games with 12 and shutouts with 6 in 1981.
Named Carolina League Pitcher of the Year, 1981.

Year Club	League	G.	IP.	W.	L.	Pct.	H.	R.	ER.	SO.	BB.	ERA.
1980—Winter Haven	Florida St.	17	71	3	4	.429	79	37	34	50	32	4.31
1981—Winston-Salem	Carolina	21	145	*14	4	.778	94	32	24	144	39	*1.49
1982—Bristol†	Eastern	16	110	9	6	.600	92	39	30	113	35	2.45
1982—Boston	American	3	6	1	0	1.000	7	0	0	4	1	0.00
1983—Boston‡	American	19	104	6	6	.500	110	62	54	35	43	4.67
Major League Totals		22	110	7	6	.538	117	62	54	39	44	4.42

Selected by Atlanta Braves' organization in 20th round of free-agent draft, June 7, 1977.
Selected by Boston Red Sox' organization in 2nd round of free-agent draft, June 3, 1980.
†On disabled list, April 27 to June 16, 1982.
‡On disabled list, July 28 to August 19, 1983.

ROGERS LEE BROWN
(Bobby)

Born May 24, 1954, at Norfolk, Va.
Height, 6.01. Weight, 205.
Throws right and bats right and lefthanded.

Led Carolina League in caught stealing with 12 in 1976.
Named International League co-Most Valuable Player, 1979.

Year Club	League	Pos.	G.	AB.	R.	H.	2B.	3B.	HR.	RBI.	B.A.	PO.	A.	E.	F.A.
1972—Bluefield	Appal.	OF	49	172	29	44	11	2	3	27	.256	53	4	8	.877
1973—Miami	Fla. St.	OF	100	279	35	79	8	3	3	17	.283	88	5	7	.930
1974—Miami	Fla. St.	OF	29	94	9	18	3	1	0	2	.191	50	1	4	.927
1974—Lodi	Calif.	OF-1B	95	359	44	108	7	6	8	58	.301	148	11	8	.952
1975—Lodi	Calif.	OF-1B-3B	133	491	77	146	15	8	6	64	.297	178	10	12	.940
1975—Asheville†	South.	OF	6	27	5	7	0	0	0	2	.259	13	2	0	1.000
1976—Peninsula	Carol.	OF-3B-1B	102	393	68	137	18	*10	8	41	*.349	299	89	21	.949
1977—Reading	East.	OF	56	238	38	69	12	5	5	28	.290	151	2	5	.968
1977—Oklahoma City	A. A.	OF	79	312	53	98	12	5	4	22	.314	78	184	6	.969
1978—Oklahoma City‡	A. A.	OF-3B	50	216	31	62	10	6	4	18	.287	105	20	7	.947
1978—Tacoma§x	P. C.	OF	66	261	51	81	11	4	10	39	.310	151	2	7	.956
1979—Tor.y-N.Y.z	Amer.	OF	34	78	8	17	3	1	0	3	.218	64	0	3	.955
1979—San Juan	Int.-Am.	PR	10	0	1	0	0	0	0	1	.000	0	0	0	.000
1979—Columbus	Int.	OF	70	258	53	90	14	3	8	41	.349	166	7	3	.983
1980—New York	Amer.	OF	137	412	65	107	12	5	14	47	.260	303	7	9	.972
1981—Columbus	Int.	OF	40	152	28	50	6	3	6	27	.329	78	3	3	.964
1981—New York a	Amer.	OF	31	62	5	14	1	0	0	6	.226	54	2	3	.949
1982—Salt Lake City	P. C.	OF	22	84	12	21	2	2	1	9	.250	44	2	1	.979
1982—Seattle bc	Amer.	OF	79	245	29	59	7	1	4	17	.241	148	5	5	.968
1983—Las Vegas	P.C.	OF	97	405	85	134	27	7	15	70	.331	166	4	5	.971
1983—San Diego	Nat.	OF	57	225	40	60	5	3	5	22	.267	103	1	4	.963
American League Totals			281	797	107	197	23	7	18	73	.247	569	14	20	.967
National League Totals			57	225	40	60	5	3	5	22	.267	103	1	4	.963
Major League Totals			338	1022	147	257	28	10	23	95	.251	672	15	24	.966

Selected by Baltimore Orioles' organization in 11th round of free-agent draft, June 6, 1972.
†Released, April 8, 1976; signed by Peninsula (Philadelphia Phillies' organization), May 14, 1976.
‡Traded with Outfielder Jay Johnstone to New York Yankees for Pitcher Rawly Eastwick, June 14, 1978.
§Drafted by New York Mets, December 4, 1978.
xSold on waivers to Toronto Blue Jays, March 25, 1979.
ySold to New York Yankees, April 19, 1979.
zLoaned to San Juan, April 20, 1979; returned, May 1, 1979.
aTraded to Seattle Mariners' organization, April 6, 1982, completing deal in which New York Yankees traded Pitchers Gene Nelson and Bill Caudill, a player to be named later and cash to Seattle for Pitcher Shane Rawley, April 1, 1982.
bOn disabled list, August 19 to September 9, 1982.
cReleased, March 28, 1983; signed by San Diego Padres' organization, April 19, 1983.

DIVISION SERIES RECORD

Year Club	League	Pos.	G.	AB.	R.	H.	2B.	3B.	HR.	RBI.	B.A.	PO.	A.	E.	F.A.
1981—New York.............	Amer.	PR	1	0	0	0	0	0	0	0	.000	0	0	0	.000

CHAMPIONSHIP SERIES RECORD

Year Club	League	Pos.	G.	AB.	R.	H.	2B.	3B.	HR.	RBI.	B.A.	PO.	A.	E.	F.A.
1980—New York.............	Amer.	OF	3	10	1	0	0	0	0	0	.000	7	0	0	1.000
1981—New York.............	Amer.	PR-OF	3	1	2	1	0	0	0	0	1.000	0	0	0	.000
Championship Series Totals			6	11	3	1	0	0	0	0	.091	7	0	0	1.000

WORLD SERIES RECORD

Year Club	League	Pos.	G.	AB.	R.	H.	2B.	3B.	HR.	RBI.	B.A.	PO.	A.	E.	F.A.
1981—New York.............	Amer.	PR-O-PH	4	1	1	0	0	0	0	0	.000	1	0	0	.000

STEVEN ELBERT BROWN
(Steve)

Born February 12, 1957, at San Francisco, Calif.
Height, 6.05. Weight, 200.
Throws and bats righthanded.
Attended University of California at Davis, Davis, Calif.
Tied for Pacific Coast League lead in complete games with 12 in 1982.
Tied for Texas League lead in complete games with 16 in 1980.

Year Club	League	G.	IP.	W.	L.	Pct.	H.	R.	ER.	SO.	BB.	ERA.
1978—Idaho Falls.....................	Pioneer	14	99	7	3	.700	90	40	31	*95	31	2.82
1979—Salinas..........................	California	17	123	10	5	.667	109	52	33	89	57	*2.41
1979—El Paso..........................	Texas	10	73	4	4	.500	80	45	43	51	26	5.30
1980—El Paso..........................	Texas	27	*209	14	●12	.538	215	103	85	103	81	3.66
1981—Salt Lake City.................	P. Coast	26	187	11	13	.458	239	123	113	76	48	5.44
1982—Spokane.........................	P. Coast	27	185⅔	14	11	.560	206	96	80	117	53	3.88
1983—Edmonton.......................	P. Coast	20	124⅓	10	4	.714	154	95	85	64	48	6.15
1983—California.......................	American	12	46	2	3	.400	45	19	18	23	16	3.52
Major League Totals...............................		12	46	2	3	.400	45	19	18	23	16	3.52

Signed as free agent by California Angels' organization, June 9, 1978.

GLENN EDWARD BRUMMER

Born November 23, 1954, at Olney, Ill.
Height, 6.00. Weight, 200.
Throws and bats righthanded.
Attended Lake Land College, Mattoon, Ill.
Brother of Tom Brummer, infielder in Boston Red Sox' organization, 1979 through 1981.
Led American Association in passed balls with 13 in 1980.

Year Club	League	Pos.	G.	AB.	R.	H.	2B.	3B.	HR.	RBI.	B.A.	PO.	A.	E.	F.A.
1974—Sarasota Cards.....	Gulf C.	C	24	69	7	20	4	1	0	7	.290	118	15	2	.985
1975—Johnson City	Appal.	C	50	183	27	47	7	1	5	23	.257	278	23	9	.971
1976—St. Petersburg.......	Fla. St.	C	113	367	41	96	14	1	0	41	.262	*644	*77	10	.986
1977—Arkansas...............	Texas	C	15	52	2	9	1	0	0	2	.173	97	6	6	.945
1977—St. Petersburg.......	Fla. St.	C	21	51	7	11	1	0	0	1	.216	113	5	1	.992
1977—Lynchburg.............	Carol.	C	40	137	16	45	3	2	0	16	.328	190	12	2	.990
1978—Arkansas...............	Texas	C-OF	44	92	11	25	2	0	0	11	.272	135	14	3	.980
1979—Springfield†..........	A. A.	C	44	104	19	22	2	0	1	11	.212	196	12	4	.981
1980—Springfield...........	A. A.	C	110	323	36	83	12	0	1	40	.257	*562	55	12	.981
1981—Springfield...........	A. A.	C	26	77	12	18	2	1	1	8	.234	153	13	4	.976
1981—St. Louis..................	Nat.	C	21	30	2	6	1	0	0	2	.200	43	3	0	1.000
1982—St. Louis..................	Nat.	C	35	64	4	15	4	0	0	8	.234	88	8	3	.970
1982—Louisville	A. A.	C	8	28	2	3	0	0	1	2	.107	34	6	0	1.000
1983—St. Louis..................	Nat.	C	45	87	7	24	7	0	0	9	.276	122	11	3	.978
Major League Totals.....................			101	181	13	45	12	0	0	19	.249	253	22	6	.979

Signed as free agent by St. Louis Cardinals' organization, May 20, 1974.
†On disabled list, July 17 to September 1, 1979.

WORLD SERIES RECORD

Year Club	League	Pos.	G.	AB.	R.	H.	2B.	3B.	HR.	RBI.	B.A.	PO.	A.	E.	F.A.
1982—St. Louis..................	Nat.	C	1	0	0	0	0	0	0	0	.000	0	0	0	.000

THOMAS ANDREW BRUNANSKY
(Tom)

Born August 20, 1960, at West Covina, Calif.
Height, 6.04. Weight, 210.
Throws and bats righthanded.

Led American League outfielders in double plays with 8 in 1983.
Tied for Texas League lead in double plays by outfielders with 4 in 1980.

Year	Club	League	Pos.	G.	AB.	R.	H.	2B.	3B.	HR.	RBI.	B.A.	PO.	A.	E.	F.A.
1978—Idaho Falls	Pioneer		OF	48	190	55	63	14	4	6	45	.332	85	1	8	.915
1979—Salinas	Calif.		OF	★140	485	85	131	23	1	23	76	.270	279	11	6	.980
1980—El Paso	Texas		OF	128	495	103	160	24	8	24	97	.323	306	17	★14	.958
1980—Salt Lake City	P. C.		OF	9	32	7	11	2	2	1	8	.344	28	1	0	1.000
1981—Salt Lake City†	P. C.		OF	96	343	61	114	17	10	22	81	.332	250	14	5	.981
1981—California	Amer.		OF	11	33	7	5	0	0	3	6	.152	27	3	2	.938
1982—Spokane‡	P. C.		OF	25	88	12	18	6	1	1	6	.205	44	7	1	.981
1982—Minnesota	Amer.		OF	127	463	77	126	30	1	20	46	.272	343	8	5	.986
1983—Minnesota	Amer.		OF	151	542	70	123	24	5	28	82	.227	375	16	6	.985
Major League Totals				289	1038	154	254	54	6	51	134	.245	745	27	13	.983

Selected by California Angels' organization in 1st round (14th player selected) of free-agent draft, June 6, 1978.
†On disabled list, August 8 to August 31, 1981.
‡Traded with Pitcher Mike Walters and cash to Minnesota Twins for Pitcher Doug Corbett and Second Baseman Rob Wilfong, May 12, 1982.

WARREN SCOTT BRUSSTAR

Name pronounced BROO-stur.
Born February 2, 1952, at Oakland, Calif.
Height, 6.03. Weight, 200.
Throws and bats righthanded.
Attended Napa Junior College, Napa, Calif., and
Fresno State University, Fresno, Calif.

Led Eastern League in complete games with 19 in 1976.
Led Carolina League in wild pitches with 23 in 1975.
Tied for Eastern League lead in games started by pitchers with 27, intentional bases on balls issued with 12 and wild pitches with 13 in 1976.

Year	Club	League	G.	IP.	W.	L.	Pct.	H.	R.	ER.	SO.	BB.	ERA.
1974—Spartanburg	W. Carol.		22	42	2	4	.333	39	23	9	34	24	1.93
1975—Rocky Mount†	Carolina		25	162	●14	8	.636	117	61	40	123	94	2.22
1976—Reading	Eastern		27	★199	10	★17	.370	167	83	60	119	★90	2.71
1977—Oklahoma City	Am. Assoc.		2	6	0	1	.000	3	3	1	5	5	1.50
1977—Philadelphia	National		46	71	7	2	.778	64	26	21	46	24	2.66
1978—Philadelphia	National		58	89	6	3	.667	74	25	23	60	30	2.33
1979—Philadelphia‡	National		13	14	1	0	1.000	23	12	11	3	2	7.07
1979—Reading	Eastern		1	2	0	0	.000	1	0	0	1	0	0.00
1980—Peninsula	Carolina		7	14	1	1	.500	16	7	7	8	2	4.61
1980—Philadelphia§	National		26	39	2	2	.500	42	16	16	21	13	3.69
1981—Oklahoma City	Am. Assoc.		46	93	3	2	.600	93	36	29	47	31	2.81
1981—Philadelphia	National		14	12	0	1	.000	12	6	6	8	10	4.50
1982—Philadelphia	National		22	22⅔	2	3	.400	31	12	12	11	5	4.76
1982—Oklahoma City x	Am. Assoc.		22	28	4	2	.667	25	11	8	13	14	2.57
1982—Chicago y	American		10	18⅓	2	0	1.000	19	7	7	8	3	3.44
1983—Chicago	National		59	80⅓	3	1	.750	67	21	21	46	37	2.35
National League Totals			238	328	21	12	.636	313	118	110	195	121	3.02
American League Totals			10	18⅓	2	0	1.000	19	7	7	8	3	3.44
Major League Totals			248	346⅓	23	12	.657	332	125	117	203	124	3.04

Selected by San Francisco Giants' organization in 27th round of free-agent draft, June 4, 1970.
Selected by San Francisco Giants' organization in secondary phase of free-agent draft, January 13, 1971.
Selected by New York Mets' organization in 33rd round of free-agent draft, June 5, 1973.
Selected by Philadelphia Phillies' organization in secondary phase of free-agent draft, January 9, 1974.
†On disabled list, May 29 to June 9, 1975.
‡On disabled list, March 29 to June 27, 1979.
§On disabled list, April 9 to July 12, 1980; included rehabilitation disability assignment to Peninsula, June 16 to July 5, 1980.
xSold to Chicago White Sox, August 30, 1982.
yTraded with Pitcher Steve Trout to Chicago Cubs for Pitchers Dick Tidrow and Randy Martz and Infielders Scott Fletcher and Pat Tabler, January 25, 1983.

DIVISION SERIES RECORD

Year	Club	League	G.	IP.	W.	L.	Pct.	H.	R.	ER.	SO.	BB.	ERA.
1981—Philadelphia	National		2	3⅔	0	0	.000	5	2	2	3	1	4.91

CHAMPIONSHIP SERIES RECORD

Year	Club	League	G.	IP.	W.	L.	Pct.	H.	R.	ER.	SO.	BB.	ERA.
1977—Philadelphia	National		2	2⅔	0	0	.000	2	1	1	2	1	3.38
1978—Philadelphia	National		3	2⅔	0	0	.000	2	0	0	0	1	0.00
1980—Philadelphia	National		2	2⅔	1	0	1.000	1	1	1	0	1	3.38
Championship Series Totals			7	8	1	0	1.000	5	2	2	2	3	2.25

Year Club	League	G.	IP.	W.	L.	Pct.	H.	R.	ER.	SO.	BB.	ERA.
1980—Philadelphia	National	1	2⅓	0	0	.000	0	0	0	0	1	0.00

KEVIN JOHN BUCKLEY

Born January 16, 1959, at Quincy, Mass.
Height, 6.01. Weight, 195.
Throws and bats righthanded.
Received degree from University of Maine, Orono, Me.
Tied for Gulf Coast League lead in double plays by outfielders with 2 in 1981.

Year Club	League	Pos.	G.	AB.	R.	H.	2B.	3B.	HR.	RBI.	B.A.	PO.	A.	E.	F.A.
1981—Sarasota Rangers	Gulf C.	OF	50	176	21	52	8	3	2	29	.295	52	●9	0	1.000
1982—Burlington	Midw.	OF-1B-3B	123	418	76	120	16	1	29	93	.287	232	22	16	.941
1983—Tulsa	Texas	1B-OF-P	134	512	73	150	30	2	32	104	.293	616	61	12	.983

Selected by Texas Rangers' organization in 17th round of free-agent draft, June 8, 1981.

PITCHING RECORD

Year Club	League	G.	IP.	W.	L.	Pct.	H.	R.	ER.	SO.	BB.	ERA.
1983—Tulsa	Texas	4	5	0	0	.000	7	4	3	5	1	5.40

WILLIAM JOSEPH BUCKNER
(Bill)

Born December 14, 1949, at Vallejo, Calif.
Height, 6.01. Weight, 185.
Throws and bats lefthanded.
Attended University of Southern California, Los Angeles, Calif., and
Arizona State University, Tempe, Ariz.
Brother of Jim Buckner, minor league outfielder, 1972 through 1981;
and Bob Buckner, minor league infielder, 1966 through 1970;
and part-time scout with Chicago Cubs, 1977 through 1979.

Established major league record for most assists, first baseman, season (161), 1983.
Established National League record for fewest double plays, first baseman, season, 150 or more games (89), 1982.
Tied National League record for fewest errors by first baseman for leader in errors, season (13), 1983.
Led Pioneer League first basemen in double plays with 37 in 1968.

Year Club	League	Pos.	G.	AB.	R.	H.	2B.	3B.	HR.	RBI.	B.A.	PO.	A.	E.	F.A.
1968—Ogden	Pion.	1B	★64	★256	54	★88	10	★8	4	41	★.344	468	28	4	★.992
1969—Albuquerque	Texas	OF-1B	70	257	44	79	7	3	7	50	.307	220	15	3	.987
1969—Spokane	P. C.	OF-1B	36	143	21	45	1	1	2	27	.315	128	12	5	.966
1969—Los Angeles	Nat.	PH	1	1	0	0	0	0	0	0	.000	0	0	0	.000
1970—Spokane	P. C.	1B-OF	111	465	78	156	33	2	3	74	.335	582	22	7	.989
1970—Los Angeles	Nat.	OF-1B	28	68	6	13	3	1	0	4	.191	37	1	0	1.000
1971—Los Angeles	Nat.	OF-1B	108	358	37	99	15	1	5	41	.277	235	11	1	.996
1972—Los Angeles	Nat.	OF-1B	105	383	47	122	14	3	5	37	.319	434	22	4	.991
1973—Los Angeles	Nat.	1B-OF	140	575	68	158	20	0	8	46	.275	981	50	3	.997
1974—Los Angeles	Nat.	OF-1B	145	580	83	182	30	3	7	58	.314	284	5	7	.976
1975—Los Angeles†	Nat.	OF	92	288	30	70	11	2	6	31	.243	138	4	2	.986
1976—Los Angeles‡	Nat.	OF-1B	154	642	76	193	28	4	7	60	.301	315	7	5	.985
1977—Chicago§	Nat.	1B	122	426	40	121	27	0	11	60	.284	966	58	10	.990
1978—Chicago x	Nat.	1B	117	446	47	144	26	1	5	74	.323	1075	83	6	.995
1979—Chicago	Nat.	1B	149	591	72	168	34	7	14	66	.284	1258	124	7	.995
1980—Chicago	Nat.	1B-OF	145	578	69	187	41	3	10	68	★.324	916	78	8	.992
1981—Chicago	Nat.	1B	106	421	45	131	★35	3	10	75	.311	996	81	★17	.984
1982—Chicago	Nat.	1B	161	★657	93	201	34	5	15	105	.306	1547	★159	12	.993
1983—Chicago	Nat.	★●1B-OF	153	626	79	175	●38	6	16	66	.280	1391	★161	●13	.992
Major League Totals			1726	6640	792	1964	356	39	119	791	.296	10573	844	95	.992

Selected by Los Angeles Dodgers' organization in 2nd round of free-agent draft, June 7, 1968.
†On supplemental disabled list, April 21 to May 12, 1975.
‡Traded with Infielder Ivan DeJesus and Pitcher Jeff Albert to Chicago Cubs for Outfielder Rick Monday and Pitcher Mike Garman, January 11, 1977.
§On disabled list, March 28 to April 19, 1977.
xOn supplemental disabled list, June 22 to July 7, 1978.

CHAMPIONSHIP SERIES RECORD

Year Club	League	Pos.	G.	AB.	R.	H.	2B.	3B.	HR.	RBI.	B.A.	PO.	A.	E.	F.A.
1974—Los Angeles	Nat.	OF	4	18	0	3	1	0	0	0	.167	6	0	0	1.000

WORLD SERIES RECORD

Year Club	League	Pos.	G.	AB.	R.	H.	2B.	3B.	HR.	RBI.	B.A.	PO.	A.	E.	F.A.
1974—Los Angeles	Nat.	OF	5	20	1	5	1	0	1	1	.250	11	0	0	1.000

ALL-STAR GAME RECORD

Year League	Pos.	AB.	R.	H.	2B.	3B.	HR.	RBI.	B.A.	PO.	A.	E.	F.A.
1981—National	PH	1	0	0	0	0	0	0	.000	0	0	0	.000

TERRY CHARLES BULLING
(Bud)

Born December 15, 1952, at Lynwood, Calif.
Height, 6.00. Weight, 200.
Throws and bats righthanded.
Attended Golden West Junior College, Huntington Beach, Calif., and received degree in
business administration from California State University, Los Angeles, Calif., in 1974.

Led Midwest League in bases on balls received with 102 in 1976.
Tied for Midwest League lead in double plays by catchers with 10 in 1975.

Year	Club	League	Pos.	G.	AB.	R.	H.	2B.	3B.	HR.	RBI.	B.A.	PO.	A.	E.	F.A.
1974—Wis. Rapids†	Midw.		C	4	12	1	3	0	0	0	3	.250	31	1	1	.970
1975—Wis. Rapids	Midw.		C	104	296	31	71	11	0	9	40	.240	*596	51	13	.980
1976—Wis. Rapids	Midw.		C	112	352	85	109	13	2	8	50	.310	*623	*105	17	.977
1977—Orlando	South.		C	67	253	36	72	13	2	5	36	.285	313	45	8	.978
1977—Minnesota	Amer.		C	15	32	2	5	1	0	0	5	.156	37	3	2	.952
1978—Orlando‡	South.		C	110	373	43	92	19	1	3	36	.247	471	63	9	.983
1979—Spokane	P. C.		C	52	160	23	54	14	2	2	18	.338	218	31	4	.984
1980—Spokane	P. C.		C	109	323	44	90	14	3	4	40	.279	450	59	19	.964
1981—Seattle	Amer.		C	62	154	15	38	3	0	2	15	.247	239	21	6	.977
1982—Seattle§	Amer.		C	56	154	17	34	7	0	1	8	.221	304	24	3	.991
1983—Seattle	Amer.		C	5	5	0	0	0	0	0	0	.000	17	0	0	1.000
1983—Salt Lake City	P. C.		C-1B	61	168	27	44	9	1	3	25	.262	332	38	10	.974
Major League Totals				138	345	34	77	11	0	3	28	.223	597	48	11	.983

Selected by Minnesota Twins' organization in 14th round of free-agent draft, June 5, 1974.
†On temporary inactive list, July 8 to August 30, 1974.
‡Sold to Seattle Mariners' organization, March 29, 1979.
§On supplemental disabled list, August 20 to September 4, 1982.

ERIC GERALD BULLOCK

Born February 16, 1960, at Los Angeles, Calif.
Height, 5.10. Weight, 185.
Throws and bats righthanded.
Attended Los Angeles Harbor Junior College, Woodland Hills, Calif.

Year	Club	League	Pos.	G.	AB.	R.	H.	2B.	3B.	HR.	RBI.	B.A.	PO.	A.	E.	F.A.
1981—Sarasota Orange	Gulf C.		OF	56	184	38	54	8	3	1	15	.293	67	6	3	.961
1981—Daytona Beach	Fla. St.		DH	1	2	1	1	0	0	0	1	.500	0	0	0	.000
1982—Daytona Beach	Fla. St.		OF	117	442	90	150	24	11	5	●85	.339	180	11	5	.974
1982—Columbus	South.		OF	18	66	6	20	1	0	2	13	.303	21	1	0	1.000
1983—Columbus	South.		OF	130	475	65	131	15	6	9	59	.276	196	9	3	.986

Selected by Los Angeles Dodgers' organization in 18th round of free-agent draft, June 6, 1978.
Selected by San Diego Padres' organization in 1st round (fifth player selected) of free-agent draft, January 13, 1981.
Selected by Houston Astros' organization in secondary phase of free-agent draft, June 8, 1981.

ALONZA BENJAMIN BUMBRY
(Al)

Born April 21, 1947, at Fredericksburg, Va.
Height, 5.08. Weight, 175.
Throws right and bats lefthanded.
Received bachelor of science degree in physical education from
Virginia State College, Petersburg, Va.

Tied modern major league record for most triples, game, (3), September 22, 1973.
Major League stolen bases: 1972 (1), 1973 (23), 1974 (12), 1975 (16), 1976 (42), 1977 (19), 1978 (5), 1979 (37), 1980 (44), 1981 (22), 1982 (10), 1983 (12). Total—243.
Named outfielder on THE SPORTING NEWS American League All-Star Team, 1980.
Named American League Rookie Player of the Year by THE SPORTING NEWS, 1973.
Named American League Rookie of the Year by Baseball Writers' Association of America, 1973.
Named Northern League Player of the Year, 1971.

Year	Club	League	Pos.	G.	AB.	R.	H.	2B.	3B.	HR.	RBI.	B.A.	PO.	A.	E.	F.A.
1969—Stockton†	Calif.		OF-1B	35	73	19	13	4	0	0	3	.178	31	3	2	.944
1970—							(In Military Service.)									
1971—Aberdeen	North.		OF	66	247	68	83	14	6	6	53	.336	85	5	5	.947
1972—Asheville	South.		OF	26	121	26	42	4	4	4	10	.347	60	4	3	.955
1972—Rochester	Int.		OF	108	435	83	150	29	*15	6	47	*.345	198	14	0	*1.000
1972—Baltimore	Amer.		OF	9	11	5	4	0	1	0	0	.364	4	0	0	1.000
1973—Baltimore	Amer.		OF	110	356	73	120	15	●11	7	34	.337	134	2	3	.978
1974—Baltimore	Amer.		OF	94	270	35	63	10	3	1	19	.233	115	7	6	.953
1975—Baltimore	Amer.		OF-3B	114	349	47	94	19	4	2	32	.269	70	2	0	1.000
1976—Baltimore	Amer.		OF	133	450	71	113	15	7	9	36	.251	251	9	3	.989
1977—Baltimore‡	Amer.		OF	133	518	74	164	31	3	4	41	.317	329	7	3	.991
1978—Baltimore§x	Amer.		OF	33	114	21	27	5	2	2	6	.237	62	2	1	.985
1979—Baltimore	Amer.		OF	148	569	80	162	29	1	7	49	.285	367	7	7	.982
1980—Baltimore	Amer.		OF	160	645	118	205	29	9	9	53	.318	488	7	5	.990
1981—Baltimore	Amer.		OF	101	392	61	107	18	2	1	27	.273	255	6	2	.992
1982—Baltimore	Amer.		OF	150	562	77	147	20	4	5	40	.262	404	9	6	.986
1983—Baltimore	Amer.		OF	124	378	63	104	14	4	3	31	.275	235	3	3	.988
Major League Totals				1309	4614	725	1310	205	51	50	368	.284	2714	61	39	.986

— 63 —

Selected by Baltimore Orioles' organization in 11th round of free-agent draft, June 7, 1968.
†On temporary inactive list, June 16, 1969; transferred to military list, July 22, 1969 through June 3, 1971.
‡On supplemental disabled list, July 28 to August 12, 1977.
§On emergency disabled list, May 12 to September 1, 1978.
xGranted free agency, November 2, 1978; re-signed by Orioles, January 30, 1979.

CHAMPIONSHIP SERIES RECORD

Year Club	League	Pos.	G.	AB.	R.	H.	2B.	3B.	HR.	RBI.	B.A.	PO.	A.	E.	F.A.
1973—Baltimore	Amer.	OF	2	7	1	0	0	0	0	0	.000	4	1	1	.833
1974—Baltimore	Amer.	PR-PH	2	1	0	0	0	0	0	0	.000	0	0	0	.000
1979—Baltimore	Amer.	OF	4	16	5	4	0	1	0	0	.250	10	0	1	.909
1983—Baltimore	Amer.	OF-PR	3	8	0	1	1	0	0	1	.125	3	0	0	1.000
Championship Series Totals			11	32	6	5	1	1	0	1	.156	17	1	2	.900

WORLD SERIES RECORD

Year Club	League	Pos.	G.	AB.	R.	H.	2B.	3B.	HR.	RBI.	B.A.	PO.	A.	E.	F.A.
1979—Baltimore	Amer.	OF-PH	7	21	3	3	0	0	0	1	.143	14	1	1	.938
1983—Baltimore	Amer.	OF	4	11	0	1	1	0	0	1	.091	12	0	0	1.000
World Series Totals			11	32	3	4	1	0	0	2	.125	26	1	1	.964

ALL-STAR GAME RECORD

Year League	Pos.	AB.	R.	H.	2B.	3B.	HR.	RBI.	B.A.	PO.	A.	E.	F.A.
1980—American	OF	1	0	0	0	0	0	0	.000	2	0	0	1.000

GUS EDWARD BURGESS

Born December 18, 1961, at Boynton Beach, Fla.
Height, 5.11. Weight, 185.
Throws and bats lefthanded.
Attended Palm Beach Junior College, Lake Worth, Fla.

Led International League in sacrifice flies with 12 in 1983.
Led Carolina League in stolen bases with 68 and tied for lead in sacrifice flies with 8 and caught stealing with 15 in 1981.

Year Club	League	Pos.	G.	AB.	R.	H.	2B.	3B.	HR.	RBI.	B.A.	PO.	A.	E.	F.A.
1980—Elmira	NYP	OF	58	130	23	27	6	1	2	18	.208	66	3	2	.972
1981—Winston-Salem	Carol.	OF	135	510	102	144	27	7	7	74	.282	250	8	★22	.921
1982—Bristol	East.	OF	133	477	71	138	25	5	11	62	.289	198	12	14	.938
1983—Pawtucket	Int.	OF	130	449	62	121	11	6	8	66	.269	195	★16	8	.963

Selected by Montreal Expos' organization in 15th round of free-agent draft, June 5, 1979.
Selected by Boston Red Sox' organization in secondary phase of free-agent draft, January 9, 1980.

THOMAS HENRY BURGMEIER
(Tom)

Born August 2, 1943, at St. Paul, Minn.
Height, 5.11. Weight, 180.
Throws and bats lefthanded.

Major League saves: 1970 (1), 1971 (17), 1972 (9), 1973 (1), 1974 (4), 1975 (11), 1976 (1), 1977 (7), 1978 (4), 1979 (4), 1980 (24), 1981 (6), 1982 (2), 1983 (4). Total—95.
Led Pacific Coast League in complete games with 15 in 1967.

Year Club	League	G.	IP.	W.	L.	Pct.	H.	R.	ER.	SO.	BB.	ERA.
1962—Modesto	California	34	197	12	11	.522	204	122	95	210	100	4.34
1963—San Antonio	Texas	6	34	1	4	.200	46	27	24	19	14	6.35
1963—Durham	Carolina	15	76	3	9	.250	98	55	40	43	30	4.74
1964—Modesto†-San Jose	California	22	122	8	7	.533	149	82	67	89	30	4.94
1965—Seattle	P. Coast	22	129	8	7	.533	114	57	46	94	32	3.21
1966—Seattle	P. Coast	12	41	2	5	.286	50	31	28	23	16	6.15
1966—El Paso	Texas	16	73	4	8	.333	87	52	40	40	28	4.93
1967—Seattle	P. Coast	32	230	11	14	.440	199	81	71	114	44	2.78
1968—California‡§	American	56	73	1	4	.200	65	41	35	33	24	4.32
1969—Kansas City‡	American	31	54	3	1	.750	67	31	25	23	21	4.17
1970—Omaha	Am. Assoc.	10	22	3	1	.750	10	3	3	9	7	1.23
1970—Kansas City	American	41	68	6	6	.500	59	31	24	43	23	3.18
1971—Kansas City	American	67	88	9	7	.563	71	23	17	44	30	1.74
1972—Kansas City	American	51	55	6	2	.750	67	32	26	18	33	4.25
1973—Kansas City	American	6	0	0	0	.000	13	6	6	4	4	5.40
1973—Omaha x	Am. Assoc.	24	61	2	4	.333	75	35	35	31	19	5.16
1974—Minnesota	American	50	92	5	3	.625	92	46	46	34	26	4.50
1975—Minnesota	American	46	76	5	8	.385	76	32	26	41	23	3.08
1976—Minnesota	American	57	115	8	1	.889	95	36	32	45	29	2.50
1977—Minnesota y	American	61	97	6	4	.600	113	56	55	35	33	5.10
1978—Boston	American	35	61	2	1	.667	74	33	30	24	23	4.43
1979—Boston	American	44	89	3	2	.600	89	32	27	60	16	2.73
1980—Boston‡	American	62	99	5	4	.556	87	30	22	54	20	2.00
1981—Boston z	American	32	60	4	5	.444	61	23	19	35	17	2.85
1982—Boston z	American	40	102⅓	7	0	1.000	98	30	26	44	22	2.29
1983—Oakland a	American	49	96	6	7	.462	89	33	28	39	32	2.63
Major League Totals		728	1235⅓	76	55	.580	1216	515	444	576	376	3.23

Signed as free agent by Houston Colt .45's organization, September 24, 1961.

†Released, June 10, 1964; signed by Los Angeles Angels' organization, July 22, 1964.
‡Appeared as outfielder with no chances.
§Selected by Kansas City Royals from California Angels in expansion draft, October 15, 1968.
xTraded to Minnesota Twins for Pitcher Ken Gill, October 24, 1973.
yGranted free agency, November 2, 1977; signed by Boston Red Sox, February 17, 1978.
zGranted free agency, November 10, 1982; signed by Oakland A's, November 16, 1982.
aAppeared in two games as a pinchrunner.

ALL-STAR GAME RECORD

Member of American League All-Star Team in 1980; did not play.

RICHARD PAUL BURLESON
(Rick)

Born April 29, 1951, at Lynwood, Calif.
Height, 5.10. Weight, 160.
Throws and bats righthanded.
Attended Cerritos Junior College, Norwalk, Calif.

Established major league records for most double plays by shortstop, season (147), 1980; most assists by shortstop, game (15), April 13, 1982 (20 innings).
Led American League shortstops in total chances with 851 in 1980 and 615 in 1981.
Led American League shortstops in double plays with 147 in 1980 and 88 in 1981.
Led International League shortstops in fielding percentage with .961 in 1973.
Led Eastern League shortstops in double plays with 80 in 1972.
Named shortstop on THE SPORTING NEWS American League All-Star Team, 1977 and 1981.
Named shortstop on THE SPORTING NEWS American League All-Star fielding team, 1979.
Named shortstop on THE SPORTING NEWS American League Silver Slugger team, 1981.

Year Club	League	Pos.	G.	AB.	R.	H.	2B.	3B.	HR.	RBI.	B.A.	PO.	A.	E.	F.A.
1970—Winter Haven	Fla. St.	SS	118	419	42	92	13	4	1	29	.220	188	*400	38	.939
1971—Greenville	W. Car.	SS	29	118	24	31	4	2	2	12	.263	32	68	11	.901
1971—Winston-Salem†	Carol.	SS	77	299	35	82	14	2	4	30	.274	118	262	23	.943
1972—Pawtucket	East.	SS	136	488	59	115	26	0	9	51	.236	*191	380	23	*.961
1973—Pawtucket	Int.	SS-2B	*146	477	58	120	20	1	6	45	.252	241	431	25	.964
1974—Pawtucket	Int.	SS	10	41	7	14	4	0	1	4	.341	10	36	3	.939
1974—Boston	Amer.	SS-2B-3B	114	384	36	109	22	0	4	44	.284	209	329	21	.962
1975—Boston	Amer.	SS	158	580	66	146	25	1	6	62	.252	267	498	29	.963
1976—Boston	Amer.	SS	152	540	75	157	27	1	7	42	.291	274	478	34	.957
1977—Boston	Amer.	SS	154	*663	80	194	36	7	3	52	.293	*285	482	24	.970
1978—Boston‡	Amer.	SS	145	626	75	155	32	5	5	49	.248	285	482	15	.981
1979—Boston	Amer.	SS	153	627	93	174	32	5	5	60	.278	272	523	16	*.980
1980—Boston§	Amer.	SS	155	644	89	179	29	2	8	51	.278	*301	*528	22	.974
1981—California	Amer.	SS	●109	430	53	126	17	1	5	33	.293	*208	*394	13	.979
1982—California x	Amer.	SS	11	45	4	7	1	0	0	2	.156	19	51	1	.986
1983—California yz	Amer.	SS	33	119	22	34	7	0	0	11	.286	54	102	5	.969
1983—Edmonton	P. C.	SS	14	51	3	10	3	0	0	4	.196	17	16	3	.917
Major League Totals			1184	4658	593	1281	228	22	43	406	.275	2174	3867	180	.971

Selected by Minnesota Twins' organization in 8th round of free-agent draft, June 5, 1969.
Selected by Boston Red Sox' organization in secondary phase of free-agent draft, January 17, 1970.
†On disabled list, June 1 to June 19, 1971.
‡On supplemental disabled list, July 14 to July 28, 1978.
§Traded with Third Baseman Butch Hobson to California Angels for Third Baseman Carney Lansford, Pitcher Mark Clear and Outfielder Rick Miller, December 10, 1980.
xOn disabled list, April 18, 1982; transferred to emergency disabled list, April 28, 1982 through remainder of season.
yOn disabled list, March 10, 1983; transferred to special disabled list, April 6 to June 30, 1983; included rehabilitation disability assignment to Edmonton, June 10 to June 27, 1983.
zOn supplemental disabled list, August 19 to September 3, 1983.

CHAMPIONSHIP SERIES RECORD

Year Club	League	Pos.	G.	AB.	R.	H.	2B.	3B.	HR.	RBI.	B.A.	PO.	A.	E.	F.A.
1975—Boston	Amer.	SS	3	9	2	4	2	0	0	1	.444	4	12	1	.941

WORLD SERIES RECORD

Year Club	League	Pos.	G.	AB.	R.	H.	2B.	3B.	HR.	RBI.	B.A.	PO.	A.	E.	F.A.
1975—Boston	Amer.	SS	7	24	1	7	1	0	0	2	.292	9	19	1	.966

ALL-STAR GAME RECORD

Year League	Pos.	AB.	R.	H.	2B.	3B.	HR.	RBI.	B.A.	PO.	A.	E.	F.A.
1977—American	SS	2	0	0	0	0	0	0	.000	0	0	0	.000
1979—American	PR-SS	2	1	0	0	0	0	0	.000	0	1	0	1.000
1981—American	SS	1	0	0	0	0	0	0	.000	1	3	0	1.000
All-Star Game Totals		5	1	0	0	0	0	0	.000	1	4	0	1.000

Named to American League All-Star Team for 1978 game; replaced due to injury by Jerry Remy.

ROBERT BRITT BURNS

(Known by middle name.)
Born June 8, 1959, at Houston, Tex.
Height, 6.05. Weight, 218.
Throws left and bats righthanded.

Tied for American League lead in balks with 4 in 1980.

Named American League Rookie Pitcher of the Year by THE SPORTING NEWS, 1980.

Year Club	League	G.	IP.	W.	L.	Pct.	H.	R.	ER.	SO.	BB.	ERA.
1978—Appleton	Midwest	6	30	3	2	.600	25	8	8	28	2	2.40
1978—Chicago	American	2	8	0	2	.000	14	12	11	3	3	12.38
1978—Knoxville	Southern	4	21	1	1	.500	24	16	10	17	4	4.29
1979—Knoxville	Southern	20	110	6	10	.375	126	68	59	92	37	4.83
1979—Iowa	Am. Assoc.	7	41	2	3	.400	41	17	15	34	15	3.29
1979—Chicago	American	6	5	0	0	.000	10	5	3	2	1	5.40
1980—Chicago	American	34	238	15	13	.536	213	83	75	133	63	2.84
1981—Chicago	American	24	157	10	6	.625	139	52	46	108	49	2.64
1982—Chicago	American	28	169⅓	13	5	.722	168	89	76	116	67	4.04
1983—Chicago†	American	29	173⅔	10	11	.476	165	79	69	115	55	3.58
Major League Totals		123	751	48	37	.565	709	320	280	477	238	3.36

Selected by Chicago White Sox' organization in 3rd round of free-agent draft, June 6, 1978.
†On disabled list, March 29 to May 9, 1983.

CHAMPIONSHIP SERIES RECORD

Year Club	League	G.	IP.	W.	L.	Pct.	H.	R.	ER.	SO.	BB.	ERA.
1983—Chicago	American	1	9⅓	0	1	.000	6	1	1	8	5	0.96

ALL-STAR GAME RECORD

Member of American League All-Star Team in 1981; did not play.

BERTRAM RAY BURRIS
(Known by middle name.)

Born August 22, 1950, at Idabel, Okla.
Height, 6.05. Weight, 210.
Throws and bats righthanded.
Received bachelor of arts degree in recreational leadership from Southwestern State, Weatherford, Okla.
Tied for National League lead in home runs allowed with 29 in 1977.

Year Club	League	G.	IP.	W.	L.	Pct.	H.	R.	ER.	SO.	BB.	ERA.
1972—Midland	Texas	14	95	7	5	.583	98	43	37	91	20	3.51
1973—Wichita	Am. Assoc.	8	59	4	3	.571	72	45	37	34	19	5.64
1973—Chicago	National	31	65	1	1	.500	65	22	21	57	27	2.91
1974—Wichita	Am. Assoc.	7	46	2	3	.400	52	33	26	34	23	5.09
1974—Chicago	National	40	75	3	5	.375	91	61	55	40	26	6.60
1975—Chicago	National	36	238	15	10	.600	259	121	109	108	73	4.12
1976—Chicago	National	37	249	15	13	.536	251	102	86	112	70	3.11
1977—Chicago	National	39	221	14	16	.467	270	132	116	105	67	4.72
1978—Chicago	National	40	199	7	13	.350	210	112	105	94	79	4.75
1979—Chicago†-New York§	National	18	43	0	2	.000	44	27	23	24	21	4.81
1979—New York‡	American	15	28	1	3	.250	40	22	19	19	10	6.11
1980—New York xy	National	29	170	7	13	.350	181	86	76	83	54	4.02
1981—Montreal	National	22	136	9	7	.563	117	56	46	52	41	3.04
1982—Montreal	National	37	123⅔	4	14	.222	143	77	65	55	53	4.73
1983—Montreal z	National	40	154	4	7	.364	139	68	63	100	56	3.68
American League Totals		15	28	1	3	.250	40	22	19	19	10	6.11
National League Totals		369	1673⅔	79	101	.439	1770	864	765	830	567	4.11
Major League Totals		384	1701⅔	80	104	.435	1810	886	784	849	577	4.15

Selected by Chicago Cubs' organization in 17th round of free-agent draft, June 6, 1972.
†Traded to New York Yankees for Pitcher Dick Tidrow, May 23, 1979.
‡Sold on waivers to New York Mets, August 20, 1979.
§On emergency disabled list, September 15 to October 3, 1979.
xOn disabled list, July 3 to August 4, 1980.
yGranted free agency, October 27, 1980; signed by Montreal Expos, February 18, 1981.
zTraded to Oakland A's for Outfielder Rusty McNealy and cash, December 8, 1983.

DIVISION SERIES RECORD

Year Club	League	G.	IP.	W.	L.	Pct.	H.	R.	ER.	SO.	BB.	ERA.
1981—Montreal	National	1	5⅓	0	1	.000	7	4	3	4	4	5.06

CHAMPIONSHIP SERIES RECORD

Established National League Championship Series record for most innings pitched, five-game Series (17), 1981.

Year Club	League	G.	IP.	W.	L.	Pct.	H.	R.	ER.	SO.	BB.	ERA.
1981—Montreal	National	2	17	1	0	1.000	10	1	1	4	3	0.53

JEFFREY ALAN BURROUGHS
(Jeff)

Born March 7, 1951, at Long Beach, Calif.
Height, 6.01. Weight, 200.
Throws and bats righthanded.
Attended Long Beach City College, Long Beach, Calif.

Tied major league record for fewest caught stealing, season, 150 or more games (0), 1976.
Hit three home runs in a game, August 14, 1981 (second game).
Led National League in bases on balls received with 117 in 1978.
Led American League batters in strikeouts with 155 in 1975.

Led American League in sacrifice flies with 11 in 1973.
Led American League outfielders in double plays with 5 in 1974.
Named American League Most Valuable Player by Baseball Writers' Association of America, 1974.
Named American League Player of the Year by THE SPORTING NEWS, 1974.
Named outfielder on THE SPORTING NEWS American League All-Star Team, 1974.
Received reported $88,000 bonus to sign with Washington Senators, 1969.

Year	Club	League	Pos.	G.	AB.	R.	H.	2B.	3B.	HR.	RBI.	B.A.	PO.	A.	E.	F.A.
1969—Wytheville	Appal.	1B-OF	52	183	41	65	16	4	6	48	.355	192	12	10	.953
1970—Denver	A. A.	OF-3B-1B	115	390	64	105	17	6	17	71	.269	250	52	16	.950
1970—Washington	Amer.	OF	6	12	1	2	0	0	0	1	.167	5	0	0	1.000
1971—Denver	A. A.	OF	81	298	51	87	13	3	12	58	.292	108	7	10	.920
1971—Washington	Amer.	OF	59	181	20	42	9	0	5	25	.232	82	3	3	.966
1972—Texas†	Amer.	OF-1B	22	65	4	12	1	0	1	3	.185	33	2	2	.946
1972—Denver	A. A.	OF	84	307	60	93	13	2	24	59	.303	118	5	5	.961
1973—Texas	Amer.	OF-1B	151	526	71	147	17	1	30	85	.279	320	14	8	.977
1974—Texas	Amer.	OF-1B	152	554	84	167	33	2	25	*118	.301	242	11	8	.969
1975—Texas	Amer.	OF	152	585	81	132	20	0	29	94	.226	249	10	9	.966
1976—Texas‡	Amer.	OF	158	604	71	143	22	2	18	86	.237	289	12	4	.987
1977—Atlanta	Nat.	OF	154	579	91	157	19	1	41	114	.271	249	9	7	.974
1978—Atlanta	Nat.	OF	153	488	72	147	30	6	23	77	.301	224	13	6	.975
1979—Atlanta	Nat.	OF	116	397	49	89	14	1	11	47	.224	175	8	7	.963
1980—Atlanta§	Nat.	OF	99	278	35	73	14	0	13	51	.263	129	0	3	.977
1981—Seattle x	Amer.	OF	89	319	32	81	13	1	10	41	.254	127	4	2	.985
1982—Oakland	Amer.	OF	113	285	42	79	13	2	16	48	.277	52	0	1	.981
1983—Oakland	Amer.	DH	121	401	43	108	15	1	10	56	.269	0	0	0	.000
American League Totals			1023	3532	449	913	143	9	144	557	.258	1399	56	37	.975
National League Totals			522	1742	247	466	77	8	88	289	.268	777	30	23	.972
Major League Totals			1545	5274	696	1379	220	17	232	846	.261	2176	86	60	.974

Selected by Washington Senators' organization in 1st round (first player selected) of free-agent draft, June 5, 1969.
†On supplemental disabled list, April 27 to May 16, 1972.
‡Traded to Atlanta Braves for Outfielders Ken Henderson and Dave May, Pitchers Carl Morton, Roger Moret and Adrian Devine, and cash estimated at $250,000, December 9, 1976.
§Traded to Seattle Mariners for Pitcher Carlos Diaz, March 6, 1981.
xGranted free agency, November 13, 1981; signed by Oakland A's, April 7, 1982.

ALL-STAR GAME RECORD

Year	League	Pos.	AB.	R.	H.	2B.	3B.	HR.	RBI.	B.A.	PO.	A.	E.	F.A.
1974—American		OF	0	0	0	0	0	0	0	.000	1	0	0	1.000

Member of National League All-Star Team for 1978 game; did not play.

DENNIS ALLEN BURTT

Born November 29, 1957, at San Diego, Calif.
Height, 6.00. Weight, 180.
Throws and bats righthanded.
Attended Santa Ana Junior College, Santa Ana, Calif.
Tied for International League lead in intentional bases on balls issued with 9 in 1982.

Year	Club	League	G.	IP.	W.	L.	Pct.	H.	R.	ER.	SO.	BB.	ERA.
1976—Elmira		NYP	8	44	5	0	1.000	22	7	6	34	20	1.23
1977—Winter Haven†		Florida St.	7	32	2	1	.667	20	13	3	12	18	0.84
1978—Winter Haven		Florida St.	29	100	8	4	.667	76	35	29	76	39	2.61
1979—Winter Haven		Florida St.	35	152	11	10	.524	113	53	40	109	74	2.37
1980—Bristol		Eastern	31	165	11	8	.579	141	74	65	102	93	3.55
1981—Bristol		Eastern	27	170	10	8	.556	134	77	53	108	80	2.81
1982—Pawtucket		Int'national	25	150⅓	13	7	.650	163	96	80	79	98	4.79
1983—Pawtucket‡		Int'national	23	110⅓	4	5	.444	109	72	65	66	75	5.30

Selected by Boston Red Sox' organization in 2nd round of free-agent draft, January 7, 1976.
†On disabled list, June 13 to August 8, 1977.
‡On disabled list, May 1 to May 31, 1983.

ROBERT RANDALL BUSH
(Randy)

Born October 5, 1958, at Dover, Delaware.
Height, 6.01. Weight, 184.
Throws and bats lefthanded.
Attended Miami-Dade North Community College, Miami, Fla.,
and University of New Orleans, New Orleans, La.
Led Southern League in being hit by pitch with 8 in 1979 and 12 in 1981.

Year	Club	League	Pos.	G.	AB.	R.	H.	2B.	3B.	HR.	RBI.	B.A.	PO.	A.	E.	F.A.
1979—Orlando	South.	1B	76	243	33	62	12	2	6	34	.255	653	38	13	.982
1980—Toledo†	Int.	OF-1B	40	108	11	21	1	0	1	7	.194	112	6	1	.992
1980—Orlando	South.	1B	51	175	32	41	2	1	7	26	.234	458	28	4	.992
1981—Orlando	South.	OF-1B	136	482	98	140	26	3	22	94	.290	174	7	5	.973
1982—Toledo	Int.	OF	49	160	21	52	14	0	8	27	.325	68	0	1	.986
1982—Minnesota	Amer.	OF	55	119	13	29	6	1	4	13	.244	7	0	0	1.000
1983—Minnesota	Amer.	1B	124	373	43	93	24	3	11	56	.249	21	3	0	1.000
Major League Totals				179	492	56	122	30	4	15	69	.248	28	3	0	1.000

Selected by Minnesota Twins' organization in 2nd round of free-agent draft, June 5, 1979.
†On disabled list, May 25 to June 27, 1980.

JUAN FRANCISCO BUSTABAD

Born August 16, 1961, at Havana, Cuba.
Height, 5.10. Weight, 150.
Throws right and bats lefthanded.
Attended Miami-Dade Community College-North, Miami, Fla.

Year	Club	League	Pos.	G.	AB.	R.	H.	2B.	3B.	HR.	RBI.	B.A.	PO.	A.	E.	F.A.
1980—Winter Haven	Fla. St.	SS		128	431	58	109	7	2	0	35	.253	●205	341	28	.951
1981—Winter Haven	Fla. St.	SS		44	175	30	50	5	1	0	10	.286	73	155	10	.958
1981—Bristol	East.	SS		79	306	46	81	3	4	2	38	.265	110	229	19	.947
1982—Pawtucket	Int.	SS		133	440	61	117	5	2	0	23	.266	211	384	★35	.944
1983—Pawtucket	Int	SS		71	215	26	46	8	2	1	24	.214	122	194	13	.960
1983—New Britain	East.	SS		67	215	26	57	4	1	0	19	.265	105	177	7	.976

Selected by Oakland A's organization in 1st round (fifth player selected) of free-agent draft, June 5, 1979.
Selected by Boston Red Sox' organization in secondary phase of free-agent draft, January 8, 1980.

JOHN DANIEL BUTCHER

Born March 8, 1957, at Glendale, Calif.
Height, 6.04. Weight, 190.
Throws and bats righthanded.
Attended Yavapai College, Prescott, Ariz.

Led International League in complete games with 14 in 1980.

Year	Club	League	G.	IP.	W.	L.	Pct.	H.	R.	ER.	SO.	BB.	ERA.
1977—Sarasota Rangers	Gulf Coast	6	42	3	2	.600	28	10	6	23	11	1.29
1977—Asheville	W. Carol.	2	16	1	0	1.000	13	4	2	13	6	1.13
1978—Asheville	W. Carol.	24	154	10	9	.526	150	81	57	103	77	3.33
1979—Tulsa†	Texas	26	155	9	12	.429	197	106	88	82	53	5.11
1980—Charleston	Int'national	22	152	10	7	.588	141	57	56	71	50	3.32
1980—Texas	American	6	35	3	3	.500	34	19	16	27	13	4.11
1981—Wichita	Am. Assoc.	24	136	8	10	.444	171	100	85	87	60	5.63
1981—Texas	American	5	28	1	2	.333	18	6	5	19	8	1.61
1982—Denver	Am. Assoc.	8	59	5	1	.833	54	20	18	31	14	2.75
1982—Texas	American	18	94⅓	1	5	.167	102	53	51	39	34	4.87
1983—Texas‡	American	38	123	6	6	.500	128	50	48	58	41	3.51
Major League Totals		67	280⅓	11	16	.407	282	128	120	143	96	3.85

Selected by St. Louis Cardinals' organization in 2nd round of free-agent draft, January 7, 1976.
Selected by Atlanta Braves' organization in secondary phase of free-agent draft, June 8, 1976.
Selected by Houston Astros' organization in secondary phase of free-agent draft, January 11, 1977.
Selected by Texas Rangers' organization in secondary phase of free-agent draft, June 7, 1977.
†On disabled list, July 30 to August 10, 1979.
‡Traded with Pitcher Mike Smithson and Catcher Sam Sorce to Minnesota Twins for Outfielder Gary Ward, December 7, 1983.

SALVATORE PHILIP BUTERA
(Sal)

Born September 25, 1952, at Richmond Hill, N.Y.
Height, 6.00. Weight, 189.
Throws and bats righthanded.
Attended Suffolk Community College, Selden, N.Y.

Led Carolina League in passed balls with 20 in 1974.
Tied for Carolina League lead in double plays by catchers with 9 in 1974.

Year	Club	League	Pos.	G.	AB.	R.	H.	2B.	3B.	HR.	RBI.	B.A.	PO.	A.	E.	F.A.
1972—Sarasota W. Sox†	Gulf C.	C	36	114	18	28	7	0	0	16	.246	253	20	10	.965
1973—Ft. Lauderdale	Fla. St.	C	99	319	21	76	12	1	1	32	.238	503	★86	10	.983
1974—Lynchburg	Carol.	C	124	417	35	90	16	2	3	55	.216	589	★102	7	★.990
1975—Orlando	South.	C	20	51	8	9	2	0	0	4	.176	61	14	0	1.000
1975—Tacoma	P. C.	C	73	215	21	52	9	0	2	26	.242	376	36	6	.986
1976—Orlando	South.	C	90	267	45	73	8	0	3	28	.273	326	41	6	.984
1977—Tacoma	P. C.	C	87	252	27	70	13	0	4	45	.278	257	49	9	.971
1978—Toledo	Int.	C	74	206	20	52	7	0	4	28	.252	334	32	5	.987
1979—Toledo	Int.	C	78	236	20	70	13	0	2	29	.297	392	33	11	.975
1980—Minnesota	Amer.	C	34	85	4	23	1	0	0	2	.271	106	9	6	.950
1981—Minnesota	Amer.	C-1B	62	167	13	40	7	1	0	18	.240	256	41	9	.971
1982—Minnesota‡	Amer.	C	54	126	9	32	2	0	0	8	.254	230	26	3	.988
1983—Detroit	Amer.	C	4	5	1	1	0	0	0	0	.200	12	1	1	.929
1983—Evansville§	A. A.	C	67	219	23	65	11	0	2	21	.297	300	26	11	.967
Major League Totals			154	383	27	96	10	1	0	28	.251	604	77	19	.973

Signed as free agent by Minnesota Twins' organization, May 15, 1972.
†Loaned to Sarasota White Sox (Chicago White Sox' organization), June 26, 1972; returned, September 14, 1972.
‡Traded to Detroit Tigers for Catcher Stine Poole, March 25, 1983.
§Released, October 21, 1983.

BRETT MORGAN BUTLER

Born June 15, 1957, at Los Angeles, Calif.
Height, 5.10. Weight, 160.
Throws and bats lefthanded.
Attended Arizona State University, Tempe, Ariz., and received bachelor of science degree in education from Southeastern Oklahoma State University, Durant, Okla., in 1979.

Tied major league record for fewest double plays by outfielder, season, for leader in most double plays (4), 1983.
Major league stolen bases: 1981 (9), 1982 (21), 1983 (39). Total—69.
Tied for National League lead in double plays by outfielders with 4 in 1983.
Led International League in bases on balls received with 103 in 1981.
Named International League Most Valuable Player, 1981.

Year	Club	League	Pos.	G.	AB.	R.	H.	2B.	3B.	HR.	RBI.	B.A.	PO.	A.	E.	F.A.
1979—Greenwood	W. Car.		OF	35	117	26	37	2	4	1	11	.316	45	2	0	1.000
1979—Bradenton	Gulf C.		OF	30	111	36	41	7	5	3	20	.369	66	5	0	1.000
1980—Anderson	S. Atl.		OF	70	255	73	76	12	6	1	26	.298	190	5	1	.995
1980—Durham	Carol.		OF	66	224	47	82	15	6	2	39	.366	156	4	3	.982
1981—Richmond	Int.		OF	125	466	★93	156	19	4	3	36	.335	286	15	3	.990
1981—Atlanta	Nat.		OF	40	126	17	32	2	3	0	4	.254	76	2	1	.987
1982—Atlanta	Nat.		OF	89	240	35	52	2	0	0	7	.217	129	2	0	1.000
1982—Richmond	Int.		OF	41	157	22	57	8	3	1	22	.363	101	2	1	.990
1983—Atlanta†	Nat.		OF	151	549	84	154	21	★13	5	37	.281	284	13	4	.987
Major League Totals				280	915	136	238	25	16	5	48	.260	489	17	5	.990

Selected by Atlanta Braves' organization in 23rd round of free-agent draft, June 5, 1979.
†Traded with Infielder Brook Jacoby to Cleveland Indians, October 21, 1983, completing deal in which Atlanta Braves acquired Pitcher Len Barker for three players to be named later, August 28, 1983. Cleveland acquired Pitcher Rick Behenna as partial completion of deal, September 2, 1983.

CHAMPIONSHIP SERIES RECORD

Year	Club	League	Pos.	G.	AB.	R.	H.	2B.	3B.	HR.	RBI.	B.A.	PO.	A.	E.	F.A.
1982—Atlanta	Nat.		OF-PH	2	1	0	0	0	0	0	0	.000	0	0	0	.000

MARTIN EUGENE BYSTROM
(Marty)

Born July 26, 1958, at Miami, Fla.
Height, 6.05. Weight, 200.
Throws and bats righthanded.
Attended Miami-Dade South Junior College, Miami, Fla.

Pitched 3-0 perfect game victory against Winston-Salem, August 12, 1978.
Led National League in hit batsmen with 7 in 1983.
Led American Association in balks with 5 and tied for lead in games started by pitchers with 26 in 1979.
Tied for Carolina League lead in complete games with 13 and shutouts with 5 in 1978.
Tied for Western Carolinas League lead in games started by pitchers with 27 in 1977.

Year	Club	League	G.	IP.	W.	L.	Pct.	H.	R.	ER.	SO.	BB.	ERA.
1977—Spartanburg	W. Carol.	27	184	13	11	.542	★199	83	69	99	49	3.38
1978—Peninsula	Carolina	26	★197	●15	7	.682	170	71	62	★159	46	2.83
1979—Oklahoma City	Am. Assoc.	26	172	9	5	.643	174	102	78	108	69	4.08
1980—Oklahoma City†	Am. Assoc.	14	91	6	5	.545	89	49	37	68	27	3.66
1980—Philadelphia	National	6	36	5	0	1.000	26	6	6	21	9	1.50
1981—Philadelphia	National	9	54	4	3	.571	55	21	20	24	16	3.33
1981—Reading	Eastern	2	4	0	0	.000	5	2	2	2	1	4.50
1982—Philadelphia‡	National	19	89	5	6	.455	93	53	48	50	35	4.85
1983—Philadelphia§x	National	24	119⅓	6	9	.400	136	75	61	87	44	4.60
1983—Peninsula	Carolina	1	6	1	0	1.000	5	1	0	9	1	0.00
Major League Totals		58	298⅓	20	18	.526	310	155	135	182	104	4.07

Signed as free agent by Philadelphia Phillies' organization, December 15, 1976.
†On disabled list, April 14 to May 16 and May 27 to June 12, 1980.
‡On disabled list, March 22 to June 8, 1982.
§On Philadelphia disabled list, March 27 to May 3, 1983; included rehabilitation disability assignment to Peninsula, April 28 to May 3, 1983.
xOn disabled list, August 21 to September 11, 1983.

CHAMPIONSHIP SERIES RECORD

Year	Club	League	G.	IP.	W.	L.	Pct.	H.	R.	ER.	SO.	BB.	ERA.
1980—Philadelphia	National	1	5⅓	0	0	.000	7	2	1	1	2	1.69

WORLD SERIES RECORD

Year	Club	League	G.	IP.	W.	L.	Pct.	H.	R.	ER.	SO.	BB.	ERA.
1980—Philadelphia	National	1	5	0	0	.000	10	3	3	4	1	5.40
1983—Philadelphia	National	1	1	0	0	.000	0	0	0	1	0	0.00
World Series Totals		2	6	0	0	.000	10	3	3	5	1	4.50

ENOS MILTON CABELL JR.

Name pronounced Kuh-BELL.

Born October 8, 1949, at Fort Riley, Kan.
Height, 6.05. Weight, 185.
Throws and bats righthanded.
Attended Harbor Junior College, San Pedro, Calif.

Cousin of Dick Davis, outfielder with Milwaukee Brewers, Philadelphia Phillies, Pittsburgh Pirates and Toronto Blue Jays, 1977 through 1982; and Ken Landreaux, outfielder with Los Angeles Dodgers.

Major league stolen bases: 1973 (1), 1974 (5), 1975 (12), 1976 (35), 1977 (42), 1978 (33), 1979 (37), 1980 (21), 1981 (6), 1982 (15), 1983 (3). Total—210.

Led National League third basemen in putouts with 140 and errors with 23 in 1977.
Led Appalachian League in total bases with 149 in 1969.
Led International League first basemen in assists with 90 and fielding percentage with .090 in 1972.
Led Texas League first basemen in assists with 121 in 1971.
Led California League first basemen in assists with 80 and errors with 26 in 1970.
Named Texas League Player of the Year, 1971.
Named Appalachian League Player of the Year, 1969.

Year Club League	Pos.	G.	AB.	R.	H.	2B.	3B.	HR.	RBI.	B.A.	PO.	A.	E.	F.A.
1969—Bluefield .... Appal.	1B ●69	★270	★62	★101	14	2	10	43	.374	★471	30	9	.982
1970—Stockton .... Calif.	1B-OF	138	517	78	147	25	6	10	67	.284	844	81	33	.966
1971—Dall-Ft. Worth ...... Texas	●1-3-O	140	521	65	★162	24	6	6	79	★.311	1135	122	●20	.984
1972—Rochester .... Int.	1-0-3-S	141	★540	82	145	26	9	8	66	.269	893	110	11	.989
1972—Baltimore .... Amer.	1B	3	5	0	0	0	0	0	1	.000	7	0	0	1.000
1973—Rochester .... Int.	1B-3B-2B	60	229	43	81	9	1	2	24	.354	510	47	10	.982
1973—Baltimore .... Amer.	1B-3B	32	47	12	10	2	0	1	3	.213	111	4	1	.991
1974—Baltimore† .... Amer.	1-0-3-2	80	174	24	42	4	2	3	17	.241	223	45	4	.985
1975—Houston .... Nat.	OF-1B-3B	117	348	43	92	17	6	2	43	.264	197	58	6	.977
1976—Houston .... Nat.	3B-1B	144	586	85	160	13	7	2	43	.273	131	263	17	.959
1977—Houston .... Nat.	3B-1B-SS	150	625	101	176	36	7	16	68	.282	176	288	24	.951
1978—Houston .... Nat.	3B-1B-SS ●162	★660	92	195	31	8	7	71	.295	211	277	18	.964
1979—Houston .... Nat.	3B-1B	155	603	60	164	30	5	6	67	.272	396	199	14	.977
1980—Houston‡ .... Nat.	★3B-1B	152	604	69	167	23	8	2	55	.276	118	250	★29	.927
1981—San Francisco§ .... Nat.	1B-3B	96	396	41	101	20	1	2	36	.255	634	90	16	.978
1982—Detroit .... Amer.	1B-3B-OF	125	464	45	121	17	3	2	37	.261	592	143	16	.979
1983—Detroit x .... Amer.	1B-3B-SS	121	392	62	122	23	5	5	46	.311	830	79	3	.997
American League Totals............................		361	1082	143	295	46	10	11	104	.273	1763	271	24	.988
National League Totals............................		976	3822	491	1055	170	42	37	383	.276	1863	1425	124	.964
Major League Totals................................		1337	4904	634	1350	216	52	48	487	.275	3626	1696	148	.973

Signed as free agent by Baltimore Orioles' organization, September 22, 1968.
†Traded with Second Baseman Rob Andrews to Houston Astros for First Baseman Lee May and Outfielder Jay Schlueter, December 3, 1974.
‡Traded to San Francisco Giants for Outfielder Chris Bourjos and Pitcher Bob Knepper, December 8, 1980.
§Traded with cash to Detroit Tigers for Outfielder Champ Summers, March 4, 1982.
xGranted free agency, November 7, 1983.

CHAMPIONSHIP SERIES RECORD

Year Club League	Pos.	G.	AB.	R.	H.	2B.	3B.	HR.	RBI.	B.A.	PO.	A.	E.	F.A.
1974—Baltimore .... Amer.	O-PH-PR	3	4	0	1	0	0	0	0	.250	2	0	0	1.000
1980—Houston .... Nat.	3B	5	21	1	5	1	0	0	0	.238	1	9	0	1.000
Championship Series Totals		8	25	1	6	1	0	0	0	.240	3	9	0	1.000

IVAN CALDERON (PEREZ)

Name pronounced Call-durh-OWN

Born March 19, 1962, at Fajardo, Puerto Rico.
Height, 5.11. Weight, 160.
Throws and bats righthanded.

Tied for Southern League lead in total bases with 267 in 1983.

Year Club League	Pos.	G.	AB.	R.	H.	2B.	3B.	HR.	RBI.	B.A.	PO.	A.	E.	F.A.
1980—Bellingham .... N'west	OF	57	195	44	62	7	★9	4	32	.318	56	4	7	.896
1981—Wausau.................. Midw.	OF-SS	117	402	79	123	19	1	20	62	.306	130	17	6	.961
1982—Wausau.................. Midw.	S-O-3-1	126	461	91	132	22	5	24	89	.286	215	202	45	.903
1983—Chattanooga .... South.	OF	139	546	92	●170	34	★15	11	80	★.311	251	10	13	.953

Signed as free agent by Seattle Mariners' organization, July 30, 1979.

RALPH MICHAEL CALDWELL
(Mike)

Born January 22, 1949, at Tarboro, N. C.
Height, 6.00. Weight, 185.
Throws left and bats righthanded.
Attended North Carolina State University, Raleigh, N. C.
Son of Ralph Franklin Caldwell, minor league catcher, 1946 through 1953.

Tied American League record for most home runs allowed, inning (4), May 31, 1980 (fourth inning).
Led American League in complete games with 23 in 1978.
Tied for American League lead in home runs allowed with 18 in 1981.
Named American League Comeback Player of the Year by THE SPORTING NEWS, 1978.

Year Club	League	G.	IP.	W.	L.	Pct.	H.	R.	ER.	SO.	BB.	ERA.
1971—Tri-City	Northwest	2	11	2	0	1.000	9	2	2	19	5	1.64
1971—Lodi	California	17	32	4	1	.800	31	14	13	38	12	3.66
1971—San Diego	National	6	7	1	0	1.000	4	0	0	5	3	0.00
1972—San Diego	National	42	164	7	11	.389	183	92	73	102	49	4.01
1973—San Diego†	National	55	149	5	14	.263	146	77	62	86	53	3.74
1974—San Francisco.......................	National	31	189	14	5	.737	176	80	62	83	63	2.95
1975—San Francisco.......................	National	38	163	7	13	.350	194	102	87	57	48	4.80
1976—San Francisco‡§....................	National	50	107	1	7	.125	145	74	58	55	20	4.88
1977—Cincinnati x..........................	National	14	25	0	0	.000	25	11	11	11	8	3.96
1977—Milwaukee............................	American	21	94	5	8	.385	101	58	48	38	36	4.60
1978—Milwaukee............................	American	37	293	22	9	.710	258	90	77	131	54	2.37

Year	Club	League	G.	IP.	W.	L.	Pct.	H.	R.	ER.	SO.	BB.	ERA.
1979—Milwaukee	American	30	235	16	6	.727	252	96	86	89	39	3.29
1980—Milwaukee	American	34	225	13	11	.542	248	112	101	74	56	4.04
1981—Milwaukee	American	24	144	11	9	.550	151	70	63	41	38	3.94
1982—Milwaukee	American	35	258	17	13	.567	269	119	112	75	58	3.91
1983—Milwaukee	American	32	228⅓	12	11	.522	269	125	115	58	51	4.53
National League Totals		236	804	35	50	.412	873	436	353	399	244	3.95
American League Totals		213	1477⅓	96	67	.589	1548	670	602	506	332	3.67
Major League Totals		449	2281⅓	131	117	.528	2421	1106	955	905	576	3.77

Selected by San Diego Padres' organization in 11th round of free-agent draft, June 8, 1971.

†Traded to San Francisco Giants for First Baseman Willie McCovey and Outfielder Bernie Williams, October 25, 1973.

‡Traded with Pitcher John D'Acquisto and Catcher Dave Rader to St. Louis Cardinals for Outfielder Willie Crawford, Pitcher John Curtis, and Infielder-Outfielder Vic Harris, October 26, 1976.

§Traded to Cincinnati Reds' organization for Pitcher Pat Darcy, March 29, 1977.

xTraded to Milwaukee Brewers for Pitcher Richard O'Keeffe and Infielder Garry Pyka, June 15, 1977.

DIVISION SERIES RECORD

Year	Club	League	G.	IP.	W.	L.	Pct.	H.	R.	ER.	SO.	BB.	ERA.
1981—Milwaukee	American	2	8⅓	0	1	.000	9	4	4	4	0	4.32

CHAMPIONSHIP SERIES RECORD

Year	Club	League	G.	IP.	W.	L.	Pct.	H.	R.	ER.	SO.	BB.	ERA.
1982—Milwaukee	American	1	3	0	1	.000	7	6	5	2	1	15.00

WORLD SERIES RECORD

Year	Club	League	G.	IP.	W.	L.	Pct.	H.	R.	ER.	SO.	BB.	ERA.
1982—Milwaukee	American	3	17⅔	2	0	1.000	19	4	4	6	3	2.04

BENJAMIN FRANKLIN CALLAHAN III
(Ben)

Born May 19, 1958, at Mt. Airy, N.C.
Height, 6.07. Weight, 230.
Throws and bats righthanded.
Attended Pembroke State University, Pembroke, N.C., and received bachelor of arts degree in physical education and health from Catawba College, Salisbury, N.C. in 1980.

Year	Club	League	G.	IP.	W.	L.	Pct.	H.	R.	ER.	SO.	BB.	ERA.
1980—Paintsville	Ap'lachian	13	68	6	1	.857	55	22	18	53	23	*2.38
1981—Ft. Lauderdale	Florida St.	25	180	*17	8	.680	144	69	50	121	66	2.50
1982—Nashville	Southern	29	180	13	13	.500	190	109	95	120	72	4.75
1983—Columbus	Int'national	9	53⅓	3	2	.600	57	42	37	22	37	6.24
1983—Nashville†	Southern	2	18	2	0	1.000	17	3	3	5	7	1.50
1983—Oakland	American	4	9⅓	1	2	.333	18	16	13	2	5	12.54
1983—Tacoma	P. Coast	15	31⅔	2	4	.333	37	32	27	15	31	7.67
Major League Totals		4	9⅓	1	2	.333	18	16	13	2	5	12.54

Selected by New York Yankees' organization in 31st round of free-agent draft, June 3, 1980.

†Traded with First Baseman Marshall Brant to Oakland A's for Pitcher Matt Keough, June 15, 1983.

MARK CALVERT

Born September 29, 1956, at Tulsa, Okla.
Height, 6.01. Weight, 200.
Throws and bats righthanded.
Attended Connors State College, Warner, Okla.
and University of Tulsa, Tulsa, Okla.

Year	Club	League	G.	IP.	W.	L.	Pct.	H.	R.	ER.	SO.	BB.	ERA.
1978—Fresno	California	16	96	7	3	.700	103	49	44	63	50	4.13
1979—Shreveport†	Texas	8	40	2	2	.500	56	36	28	17	32	6.30
1980—Shreveport	Texas	14	88	6	7	.462	79	38	29	56	40	2.97
1980—Phoenix	P. Coast	10	54	2	4	.333	63	43	38	26	34	6.33
1981—Phoenix‡	P. Coast	18	101	7	4	.636	100	59	50	31	53	4.46
1982—Phoenix§	P. Coast	6	7⅔	0	2	.000	9	7	6	1	8	7.04
1983—San Francisco	National	18	37⅓	1	4	.200	46	33	26	14	34	6.27
1983—Phoenix	P. Coast	14	85⅔	4	5	.444	115	69	56	33	31	5.88
Major League Totals		18	37⅓	1	4	.200	46	33	26	14	34	6.27

Selected by San Francisco Giants' organization in 21st round of free agent draft, June 6, 1978.

†On disabled list, June 5 to September 25, 1979.

‡On disabled list, July 31 to August 22, 1981.

§On disabled list, April 13 to August 13, 1982.

ERNIE CARLOS CAMACHO

Born February 1, 1956, at Salinas, Calif.
Height, 6.00. Weight, 185.
Throws and bats righthanded.
Attended Hartnell Junior College, Salinas, Calif.

Year	Club	League	G.	IP.	W.	L.	Pct.	H.	R.	ER.	SO.	BB.	ERA.
1976—Modesto	California	10	56	3	4	.429	69	47	35	29	39	5.63

Year Club	League	G.	IP.	W.	L.	Pct.	H.	R.	ER.	SO.	BB.	ERA.
1977—Modesto†	California	5	32	2	1	.667	30	19	14	21	23	3.94
1977—Chattanooga	Southern	11	60	3	8	.273	74	50	43	20	28	6.45
1978—Modesto‡	California	1	2	0	0	.000	0	0	0	2	2	0.00
1979—Ogden	P. Coast	21	97	7	9	.438	102	86	71	60	70	6.59
1980—Ogden	P. Coast	33	64	5	3	.625	60	29	28	58	26	3.94
1980—Oakland§	American	5	12	0	0	.000	20	9	9	9	5	6.75
1981—Portland x	P. Coast	18	38	2	3	.400	45	24	20	31	22	4.74
1981—Pittsburgh y	National	7	22	0	1	.000	23	13	12	11	15	4.91
1982—Edmonton zab	P. Coast	7	19⅔	0	0	.000	10	8	7	18	16	3.20
1982—Mexico City Reds	Mexican	15	20⅓	3	1	.750	21	12	12	15	6	5.31
1982—Rochester c	Int'national	8	17⅔	0	1	.000	16	7	4	11	10	2.04
1983—Vancouver d	P. Coast	11	23⅔	0	2	.000	31	21	18	16	12	6.85
1983—Charleston	Int'national	24	33⅓	4	0	1.000	19	5	5	27	17	1.35
1983—Cleveland	American	4	5⅓	0	1	.000	5	3	3	2	2	5.06
American League Totals		9	17⅓	0	1	.000	25	12	12	11	7	6.23
National League Totals		7	22	0	1	.000	23	13	12	11	15	4.91
Major League Totals		16	39⅓	0	2	.000	48	25	24	22	22	5.49

Selected by Pittsburgh Pirates' organization in 12th round of free-agent draft, June 4, 1975.

Selected by California Angels' organization in secondary phase of free-agent draft, January 7, 1976.

Selected by Oakland A's organization in secondary phase of free-agent draft, June 8, 1976.

†On disabled list, April 23 to June 14, 1977.

‡On Jersey City temporary inactive list, April 14 to July 18, 1978; on Modesto temporary inactive list, July 18 to August 30, 1978.

§Traded to Pittsburgh Pirates, April 10, 1981, completing deal in which Pittsburgh traded Pitcher Bob Owchinko to Oakland A's for cash and player to be named later, April 6, 1981.

xOn disabled list, June 23 to July 15, 1981.

yTraded with Infielder Vance Law to Chicago White Sox for Pitchers Ross Baumgarten and Butch Edge, March 21, 1982.

zOn suspended list, April 5 to April 25, 1982.

aLoaned to Mexico City Reds, May 16, 1982; returned, August 2, 1982.

bLoaned to Rochester (Baltimore Orioles' organization), August 5, 1982; returned, September 17, 1982.

cGranted free agency, October 22, 1982; signed by Vancouver (Milwaukee Brewers' organization), December 19, 1982.

dTraded with Outfielder Gorman Thomas and Pitcher Jamie Easterly to Cleveland Indians for Outfielder Rick Manning and Pitcher Rick Waits, June 6, 1983.

RICK LAMAR CAMP

Born June 10, 1953, at Trion, Ga.
Height, 6.01. Weight, 198.
Throws and bats righthanded.
Attended West Georgia College, Carrollton, Ga.

Major League saves: 1977 (10), 1980 (22), 1981 (17), 1982 (5). Total—54.

Led International League in balks with 5 in 1976.

Year Club	League	G.	IP.	W.	L.	Pct.	H.	R.	ER.	SO.	BB.	ERA.
1974—Kingsport	Ap'lachian	7	43	3	2	.600	44	23	15	52	16	3.14
1975—Savannah	Southern	25	176	12	10	.545	161	68	56	100	62	2.86
1976—Richmond	Int'national	49	164	10	11	.476	177	90	78	85	68	4.28
1976—Atlanta	National	5	11	0	1	.000	13	9	8	6	2	6.55
1977—Atlanta†	National	54	79	6	3	.667	89	47	35	51	47	3.99
1978—Atlanta	National	42	74	2	4	.333	99	42	31	23	32	3.77
1979—Richmond‡	Int'national	22	55	3	2	.600	59	31	26	33	12	4.25
1980—Atlanta	National	77	108	6	4	.600	92	26	23	33	29	1.92
1981—Atlanta	National	48	76	9	3	.750	68	17	15	47	12	1.78
1982—Atlanta	National	51	177⅓	11	13	.458	199	84	72	68	52	3.65
1983—Atlanta	National	40	140	10	9	.526	146	64	59	61	38	3.79
Major League Totals		317	665⅓	44	37	.543	706	289	243	289	212	3.29

Selected by Atlanta Braves' organization in 7th round of free-agent draft, June 5, 1974.

†On disabled list, July 28 to September 1, 1977.

‡On disabled list, April 13 to May 7 and August 7 to August 27, 1979.

CHAMPIONSHIP SERIES RECORD

Year Club	League	G.	IP.	W.	L.	Pct.	H.	R.	ER.	SO.	BB.	ERA.
1982—Atlanta	National	1	1	0	1	.000	4	4	4	0	1	36.00

DAGOBERTO BLANCO CAMPANERIS
(Bert or Campy)

Born March 9, 1942, at Pueblo Nuevo, Matanzas, Cuba.
Height, 5,10. Weight, 160.
Throws and bats righthanded.
Cousin of Jose Cardenal, outfielder with San Francisco, California, Cleveland,
St. Louis, Milwaukee, Chicago N.L., Philadelphia, New York N.L.
and Kansas City, 1963 through 1980.

Established major league record for most double plays, shortstop, extra-inning game (6), September 13, 1970, first game (11 innings).

Tied major league records for most home runs, first major league game (2), July 23, 1964; fewest caught stealing, season, 50 or more stolen bases (8), 1962; most stolen bases by pinch-runner, inning (2), October 4, 1972 (fourth inning);

most bases on balls, inning (2), June 18, 1975 (seventh inning); most positions played, season (9), 1965; most positions played, game (9), September 8, 1965.

Tied modern major league record for most triples, game (3), August 29, 1967.

Established American League records for fewest hits, for leader in hits, season (177), 1968; most times caught stealing, lifetime (199).

Tied American League records for most home runs as leadoff batter, season (6), 1970; most home runs, first two major league games (2), July 23 and 24, 1964.

On August 13, 1962, pitching in relief for Daytona Beach against Ft. Lauderdale, Campaneris pitched righthanded to the righthanded batters and lefthanded to the lefthanded batters. In two innings he gave up one run and one hit while walking two and striking out four.

Major League stolen bases: 1964 (10), 1965 (51), 1966 (52), 1967 (55), 1968 (62), 1969 (62), 1970 (42), 1971 (34), 1972 (52), 1973 (34), 1974 (34), 1975 (24), 1976 (54), 1977 (27), 1978 (22), 1979 (13), 1980 (10), 1981 (5), 1983 (6). Total—649.

Led American League in stolen bases with 51 in 1965, 52 in 1966, 55 in 1967, 62 in 1968, 42 in 1970 and 52 in 1972.

Led American League in sacrifice hits with 20 in 1972 and 40 in 1977.

Led American League shortstops in total chances with 795 in 1972.

Named shortstop on THE SPORTING NEWS American League All-Star Team, 1973 and 1974.

Year	Club	League	Pos.	G.	AB.	R.	H.	2B.	3B.	HR.	RBI.	B.A.	PO.	A.	E.	F.A.
1962—Daytona Beach	Fla. St.	O-1-C-S-P	100	334	59	97	15	2	1	33	.290	384	68	24	.950
1962—Binghamton	East.	I-OF-P	13	44	11	16	3	0	0	3	.364	12	4	2	.889
1963—Lewiston	N'west	PH	11	6	2	0	0	0	0	1	.000	0	0	0	.000
1963—Binghamton	East.	SS-C-1B	35	117	21	36	5	1	0	12	.308	99	49	12	.925
1964—Birmingham	South.	SS	86	354	69	115	18	★11	6	40	.325	163	229	23	.945
1964—Kansas City	Amer.	SS-OF-3B	67	269	27	69	14	3	4	22	.257	102	108	8	.963
1965—Kansas City	Amer.	S-O-P†	144	578	67	156	23	●12	6	42	.270	258	276	35	.938
1966—Kansas City	Amer.	SS	142	573	82	153	29	10	5	42	.267	283	350	19	.971
1967—Kansas City	Amer.	SS	147	601	85	149	29	6	3	32	.248	★259	365	●30	.954
1968—Oakland	Amer.	★SS-OF	159	★642	87	★177	25	9	4	38	.276	★283	458	★34	.956
1969—Oakland	Amer.	SS	135	547	71	142	15	2	2	25	.260	220	391	21	.967
1970—Oakland	Amer.	SS	147	603	97	168	28	4	22	64	.279	267	414	19	.973
1971—Oakland‡	Amer.	SS	134	569	80	143	18	4	5	47	.251	231	303	●26	.954
1972—Oakland	Amer.	SS	149	★625	85	150	25	2	8	32	.240	★283	494	18	.977
1973—Oakland	Amer.	SS	151	601	89	150	17	6	4	46	.250	228	496	23	.969
1974—Oakland§	Amer.	SS	134	527	77	153	18	8	2	41	.290	207	423	22	.966
1975—Oakland	Amer.	SS	137	509	69	135	15	3	4	46	.265	199	378	23	.962
1976—Oakland x	Amer.	SS	149	536	67	137	14	1	1	52	.256	231	490	23	.969
1977—Texas	Amer.	SS	150	552	77	140	19	7	5	46	.254	269	483	25	.968
1978—Texas y	Amer.	SS	98	269	30	50	5	3	1	17	.186	151	263	20	.954
1979—Tex. z-Calif.	Amer.	SS	93	248	29	57	4	4	0	15	.230	148	233	17	.957
1980—California	Amer.	SS-2B	77	210	32	53	8	1	2	18	.252	108	157	12	.957
1981—California a	Amer.	3B-SS-2B	55	82	11	21	2	1	1	10	.256	10	49	6	.908
1982—V'cruz-P. Rica b	Mex.	3B-SS	104	350	44	97	11	4	2	37	.277	122	248	24	.939
1983—Columbus	Int.	3B-2B	13	45	7	15	2	1	1	7	.333	7	19	2	.929
1983—New York cd	Amer.	2B-3B	59	143	19	46	5	0	0	11	.322	52	96	7	.955
Major League Totals			2327	8684	1181	2249	313	86	79	646	.259	3339	6227	388	.961

Signed as free agent by Kansas City A's organization, April 25, 1961.

†On September 8 against the California Angels, Campaneris played one inning at each of the nine positions.

‡On disabled list, July 3 to July 23, 1971.

§On supplemental disabled list, July 28 to August 12, 1974.

xPlayed out option year and granted free agency, November 1, 1976; signed as free agent by Texas Rangers, November 17, 1976.

yOn supplemental disabled list, May 19 to June 6, 1978.

zTraded to California Angels for Third Baseman Dave Chalk, May 4, 1979.

aGranted free agency, November 13, 1981; signed with Veracruz of Mexican League, March 19, 1982.

bSigned as free agent by New York Yankees' organization, February 24, 1983.

cOn supplemental disabled list, August 5 to August 20, 1983.

dGranted free agency, November 7, 1983.

PITCHING RECORD

Year	Club	League	G.	IP.	W.	L.	Pct.	H.	R.	ER.	SO.	BB.	ERA.
1962—Daytona Beach	Florida St.	3	6	0	0	.000	5	2	2	6	2	3.00
1962—Binghamton	Eastern	1	2	0	0	.000	2	5	1	0	4	4.50
1965—Kansas City	American	1	1	0	0	.000	1	1	1	1	2	9.00
Major League Totals		1	1	0	0	.000	1	1	1	1	2	9.00

CHAMPIONSHIP SERIES RECORD

Tied Championship Series record for most times home run as leadoff batter, start of game (1), October 7, 1973.

Established American League Championship Series records for most consecutive hitless times at bat, total Series (24), 1974 (last 13 times at bat), 1975 (all 11 times at bat); most stolen bases, five-game series (3), 1973.

Tied American League Championship Series record for most home runs, five-game Series (2), 1973.

Year	Club	League	Pos.	G.	AB.	R.	H.	2B.	3B.	HR.	RBI.	B.A.	PO.	A.	E.	F.A.
1971—Oakland	Amer.	SS	3	12	0	2	1	0	0	0	.167	3	6	0	1.000
1972—Oakland	Amer.	SS	2	7	3	3	0	0	0	0	.429	3	7	0	1.000
1973—Oakland	Amer.	SS	5	21	3	7	1	0	2	3	.333	6	15	1	.955
1974—Oakland	Amer.	SS	4	17	0	3	0	0	0	3	.176	3	17	0	1.000
1975—Oakland	Amer.	SS	3	11	1	0	0	0	0	0	.000	2	10	0	1.000
1979—California	Amer.	SS	1	0	0	0	0	0	0	0	.000	0	0	0	.000
Championship Series Totals			18	68	7	15	2	0	2	6	.221	17	55	1	.986

WORLD SERIES RECORD

Tied World Series records for most times hit by pitch, total Series (3); fewest chances accepted by shortstop, game (0), October 18, 1972.

Year Club	League	Pos.	G.	AB.	R.	H.	2B.	3B.	HR.	RBI.	B.A.	PO.	A.	E.	F.A.
1972—Oakland	Amer.	SS	7	28	1	5	0	0	0	0	.179	17	15	1	.970
1973—Oakland	Amer.	SS	7	31	6	9	0	1	1	3	.290	10	28	1	.974
1974—Oakland	Amer.	SS	5	17	1	6	2	0	0	2	.353	6	16	2	.917
World Series Totals			19	76	8	20	2	1	1	5	.263	33	59	4	.958

ALL-STAR GAME RECORD

Year League	Pos.	AB.	R.	H.	2B.	3B.	HR.	RBI.	B.A.	PO.	A.	E.	F.A.
1968—American	SS	1	0	0	0	0	0	0	.000	1	0	0	1.000
1973—American	SS	3	0	0	0	0	0	0	.000	1	2	0	1.000
1974—American	SS	4	0	0	0	0	0	0	.000	2	3	0	1.000
1975—American	SS	2	0	2	0	0	0	0	1.000	3	2	0	1.000
1977—American	SS	1	1	0	0	0	0	0	.000	0	1	0	1.000
All-Star Game Totals		11	1	2	0	0	0	0	.182	7	8	0	1.000

Member of American League All-Star Team for the 1972 game; did not play.

WILLIAM RICHARD CAMPBELL
(Bill)

Born August 9, 1948, at Highland Park, Mich.
Height, 6.04. Weight, 200.
Throws and bats righthanded.
Attended Mount San Antonio Junior College, Walnut, Calif.

Tied American League record for most games won, season, all as relief pitcher (17), 1976.
Major League saves: 1973 (7), 1974 (19), 1975 (5), 1976 (20), 1977 (31), 1978 (4), 1979 (9), 1981 (7), 1982 (8), 1983 (8). Total—118.
Led National League in intentional bases on balls issued with 18 in 1983.
Led American League in saves with 31 in 1977.
Led American League in games finished in relief with 68 in 1976 and tied for lead with 60 in 1977.
Led Southern League in complete games with 14 and tied for lead in games started by pitchers with 29 in 1972.
Named American League Fireman of the Year by THE SPORTING NEWS, 1976 and 1977.
Named Southern League Pitcher of the Year, 1972.

Year Club	League	G.	IP.	W.	L.	Pct.	H.	R.	ER.	SO.	BB.	ERA.
1971—Wisconsin Rapids†	Midwest	9	63	5	3	.625	42	43	8	91	19	1.14
1972—Charlotte	Southern	29	219	13	10	.565	181	74	59	★204	69	2.42
1973—Tacoma	P. Coast	18	133	10	5	.667	123	63	54	110	46	3.65
1973—Minnesota	American	28	52	3	3	.500	44	20	18	42	20	3.12
1974—Minnesota	American	63	120	8	7	.533	109	37	35	89	55	2.63
1975—Minnesota	American	47	121	4	6	.400	119	58	51	76	46	3.79
1976—Minnesota‡	American	★78	168	17	5	★.773	145	63	56	115	62	3.00
1977—Boston	American	69	140	13	9	.591	112	48	46	114	60	2.96
1978—Boston	American	29	51	7	5	.583	62	25	22	47	17	3.88
1979—Boston	American	41	55	3	4	.429	55	28	26	25	23	4.25
1980—Boston§	American	23	41	4	0	1.000	44	26	22	17	22	4.83
1981—Boston x	American	30	48	1	1	.500	45	23	17	37	20	3.19
1982—Chicago	National	62	100	3	6	.333	89	44	41	71	40	3.69
1983—Chicago	National	★82	121⅓	6	8	.429	128	65	61	97	49	4.49
American League Totals		408	796	60	40	.600	735	328	293	562	325	3.31
National League Totals		144	221⅓	9	14	.391	217	109	102	168	89	4.13
Major League Totals		552	1018⅓	69	54	.561	952	437	395	730	414	3.49

Signed as free agent by Minnesota Twins' organization, September 25, 1970.
†On disabled list, June 14, 1971 through remainder of season.
‡Granted free agency, November 1, 1976; signed by Boston Red Sox, November 6, 1976.
§On emergency disabled list, March 25 to June 20, 1980.
xGranted free agency, November 13, 1981; signed by Chicago Cubs, December 8, 1981.

ALL-STAR GAME RECORD

Year League	IP.	W.	L.	Pct.	H.	R.	ER.	SO.	BB.	ERA.
1977—American	1	0	0	.000	0	0	0	2	1	0.00

CHUCKIE RAY CANADY

Born August 12, 1959, at Onslow County, N.C.
Height, 5.10. Weight, 195.
Throws and bats righthanded.
Attended North Carolina State University, Raleigh, N.C.

Year Club	League	Pos.	G.	AB.	R.	H.	2B.	3B.	HR.	RBI.	B.A.	PO.	A.	E.	F.A.
1981—Sarasota Rangers	Gulf C.	OF	8	30	3	5	0	1	0	1	.167	16	1	0	1.000
1981—Asheville	S. Atl.	OF	35	120	20	36	6	0	2	26	.300	39	4	2	.956
1982—Burlington	Midw.	OF	138	473	90	126	25	5	20	75	.266	178	10	7	.964
1983—Tulsa	Texas	OF	132	486	100	144	21	4	25	80	.296	230	7	●13	.948

Selected by Milwaukee Brewers' organization in 22nd round of free-agent draft, June 6, 1978.
Selected by Texas Rangers' organization in 2nd round of free-agent draft, June 8, 1981.

JOHN ROBERT CANDELARIA

Born November 6, 1953, at Brooklyn, N.Y.
Height, 6.07. Weight, 232.
Throws left and bats right and lefthanded.

Pitched 2-0 no-hit victory against Los Angeles Dodgers, August 9, 1976.
Tied for National League lead in home runs allowed with 29 in 1977.
Led Carolina League in home runs allowed with 17 in 1974.
Received reported $40,000 bonus to sign with Pittsburgh Pirates, 1973.

Year Club	League	G.	IP.	W.	L.	Pct.	H.	R.	ER.	SO.	BB.	ERA.
1973—Charleston	W. Carol.	18	95	10	2	★.833	84	45	40	60	38	3.79
1974—Salem	Carolina	25	154	11	8	.579	146	80	63	147	63	3.68
1974—Charleston	Int'national	1	11	0	0	.000	7	2	2	10	1	1.64
1975—Charleston	Int'national	10	61	7	1	.875	53	15	12	48	17	1.77
1975—Pittsburgh	National	18	121	8	6	.571	95	47	37	95	36	2.75
1976—Pittsburgh	National	32	220	16	7	.696	173	87	77	138	60	3.15
1977—Pittsburgh	National	33	231	20	5	★.800	197	64	60	133	52	★2.34
1978—Pittsburgh	National	30	189	12	11	.522	191	73	68	94	49	3.24
1979—Pittsburgh	National	33	207	14	9	.609	201	83	74	101	41	3.22
1980—Pittsburgh	National	35	233	11	14	.440	246	114	104	97	50	4.02
1981—Pittsburgh†	National	6	41	2	2	.500	42	17	16	14	11	3.51
1982—Pittsburgh	National	31	174⅔	12	7	.632	166	62	57	133	37	2.94
1983—Pittsburgh	National	33	197⅔	15	8	.652	191	73	71	157	45	3.23
Major League Totals		251	1614⅓	110	69	.615	1502	620	564	962	379	3.14

Selected by Pittsburgh Pirates' organization in 2nd round of free-agent draft, June 6, 1972.
†On disabled list, May 11, 1981 through remainder of season.

CHAMPIONSHIP SERIES RECORD

Established Championship Series record for most strikeouts, three-game Series (14), 1975.
Tied Championship Series records for most strikeouts, game (14), October 7, 1975; most consecutive strikeouts, start of game (4), October 7, 1975.

Year Club	League	G.	IP.	W.	L.	Pct.	H.	R.	ER.	SO.	BB.	ERA.
1975—Pittsburgh	National	1	7⅔	0	0	.000	3	3	3	14	2	3.52
1979—Pittsburgh	National	1	7	0	0	.000	5	2	2	4	1	2.57
Championship Series Totals		2	14⅔	0	0	.000	8	5	5	18	3	3.07

WORLD SERIES RECORD

Year Club	League	G.	IP.	W.	L.	Pct.	H.	R.	ER.	SO.	BB.	ERA.
1979—Pittsburgh	National	2	9	1	1	.500	14	6	5	4	2	5.00

ALL-STAR GAME RECORD

Member of National League All-Star Team in 1977; did not play.

THOMAS CAESAR CANDIOTTI
(Tom)

Born August 31, 1957, at Walnut Creek, Calif.
Height, 6.03. Weight, 195.
Throws and bats righthanded.
Received bachelor of science degree in business administration
from St. Mary's College, Moraga, Calif., in 1979.

Year Club	League	G.	IP.	W.	L.	Pct.	H.	R.	ER.	SO.	BB.	ERA.
1979—Victoria†	Northwest	12	70	5	1	.833	63	23	19	66	16	2.44
1980—Ft. Myers	Florida St.	7	44	3	2	.600	32	16	11	31	9	2.25
1980—Jacksonville‡§	Southern	17	117	7	8	.467	98	45	36	93	40	2.77
1981—El Paso x	Texas	21	119	7	6	.538	137	51	37	68	27	2.80
1982—Vancouver y	P. Coast					(Did not play)						
1983—El Paso	Texas	7	24⅔	1	0	1.000	23	10	8	18	7	2.92
1983—Vancouver	P. Coast	15	99⅓	6	4	.600	87	35	31	61	16	2.81
1983—Milwaukee	American	10	55⅔	4	4	.500	62	21	20	21	16	3.23
Major League Totals		10	55⅔	4	4	.500	62	21	20	21	16	3.23

Signed as free-agent by Victoria (Independent), July 17, 1979.
†Released, January 4, 1980; signed by Ft. Myers (Kansas City Royals' organization), January 5, 1980.
‡On disabled list, June 7 to June 26, 1980.
§Drafted by Vancouver (Milwaukee Brewers' organization), December 9, 1980.
xOn disabled list, April 10 to May 12, 1981.
yOn disabled list, April 13, 1982 through remainder of season.

NICK LEE CAPRA

Born March 8, 1958, at Denver, Colo.
Height, 5.08. Weight, 165.
Throws and bats righthanded.
Attended Blinn College, Brenham, Tex., Lamar Community College, Lamar, Colo. and
University of Oklahoma, Norman, Okla.

Led Texas League in stolen bases with 55 and tied for lead in game-winning RBIs with 13 in 1980.
Led American Association outfielders in total chances with 330 in 1983.

Year	Club	League	Pos.	G.	AB.	R.	H.	2B.	3B.	HR.	RBI.	B.A.	PO.	A.	E.	F.A.
1979—Tulsa†	Texas		3B-2B-SS	66	212	29	59	7	0	3	26	.278	60	173	22	.914
1980—Tulsa	Texas		2B-OF-SS	117	440	90	127	25	9	6	53	.289	288	303	19	.969
1981—Wichita	A. A.		OF	123	398	74	104	16	4	4	38	.261	226	6	7	.971
1982—Denver	A. A.		OF	121	416	82	117	15	10	9	40	.281	275	11	3	.990
1982—Texas	Amer.		OF	13	15	2	4	0	0	1	1	.267	14	2	0	1.000
1983—Oklahoma City	A.A.		OF	124	441	84	113	17	4	13	41	.256	★307	12	11	.967
1983—Texas	Amer.		OF	8	2	2	0	0	0	0	0	.000	0	0	0	.000
Major League Totals				21	17	4	4	0	0	1	1	.235	14	2	0	1.000

Selected by Montreal Expos' organization in 12th round of free-agent draft, June 8, 1976.
Selected by Texas Rangers' organization in 3rd round of free-agent draft, June 5, 1979.
†On disabled list, July 4 to July 19, 1979.

RODNEY CLINE CAREW
(Rod)

Born October 1, 1945, at Gatun, Panama.
Height, 6.00. Weight, 182.
Throws right and bats lefthanded.

Tied major league records for most times stealing home, season (7), 1969; most stolen bases, inning (3), May 18, 1969 (3rd inning); most home runs with bases filled by pinch-hitter, game (1), September 9, 1976.

Established American League record for most games, one or more hits, season (131), 1977.

Tied American League records for most double plays, first baseman, extra-inning game (6), August 29, 1977 (1st game, 10 innings); most putouts by first baseman, game (32), April 13, 1982 (20 innings); most chances accepted by first baseman, game (34), April 13, 1982 (20 innings); most seasons leading league, intentional bases on balls (3).

Major league stolen bases: 1967 (5), 1968 (12), 1969 (19), 1970 (4), 1971 (6), 1972 (12), 1973 (41), 1974 (38), 1975 (35), 1976 (49), 1977 (23), 1978 (27), 1979 (18), 1980 (23), 1981 (16), 1982 (10), 1983 (6). Total—344.

Hit for the cycle, May 20, 1970.

Led American League in intentional bases on balls received with 18 in 1975, 15 in 1977 and 19 in 1978.

Led American League first basemen in double plays with 149 in 1976 and 161 in 1977.

Led American League first basemen in assists with 121 in 1977.

Led American League first basemen in total chances with 1,590 in 1977.

Named Major League Player of the Year by THE SPORTING NEWS, 1977.

Named American League Player of the Year by THE SPORTING NEWS, 1977.

Named American League Most Valuable Player by Baseball Writers' Association of America, 1977.

Named American League Rookie Player of the Year by THE SPORTING NEWS, 1967.

Named American League Rookie of the Year by Baseball Writers' Association of America, 1967.

Named first baseman on THE SPORTING NEWS American League All-Star Team, 1977 and 1978.

Named second baseman on THE SPORTING NEWS American League All-Star Team, 1967 through 1969 and 1972 through 1975.

Year	Club	League	Pos.	G.	AB.	R.	H.	2B.	3B.	HR.	RBI.	B.A.	PO.	A.	E.	F.A.
1964—Melbourne Twins	Coc. Rk.		2B	37	123	17	40	5	●3	0	21	.325	86	48	7	.950
1965—Orlando	Fla. St.		2B	125	439	57	133	20	8	1	52	.303	290	328	●28	.957
1966—Wilson	Carol.		2B	112	383	64	112	19	3	1	30	.292	248	275	21	.961
1967—Minnesota†	Amer.		2B	137	514	66	150	22	7	8	51	.292	289	314	15	.976
1968—Minnesota‡	Amer.		●2B-SS	127	461	46	126	27	2	1	42	.273	266	285	●18	.968
1969—Minnesota§	Amer.		2B	123	458	79	152	30	4	8	56	★.332	244	302	17	.970
1970—Minnesota x	Amer.		2B-1B	51	191	27	70	12	3	4	28	.366	79	122	8	.962
1971—Minnesota	Amer.		2B-3B	147	577	88	177	16	10	2	48	.307	324	331	16	.976
1972—Minnesota	Amer.		2B	142	535	61	170	21	6	0	51	★.318	331	378	16	.978
1973—Minnesota	Amer.		2B	149	580	98	★203	30	●11	6	62	★.350	383	413	13	.984
1974—Minnesota	Amer.		2B	153	599	86	★218	30	5	3	55	★.364	375	416	★33	.960
1975—Minnesota	Amer.		2B-1B	143	535	89	192	24	4	14	80	★.359	408	377	21	.974
1976—Minnesota	Amer.		1B-2B	156	605	97	200	29	12	9	90	.331	1398	110	16	.990
1977—Minnesota	Amer.		1B-2B	155	616	★128	★239	38	★16	14	100	★.388	1463	124	10	.994
1978—Minnesota y	Amer.		1B-2B-OF	152	564	85	188	26	10	5	70	★.333	1363	105	16	.989
1979—California z	Amer.		1B	110	409	78	130	15	3	3	44	.318	804	55	10	.988
1980—California	Amer.		1B	144	540	74	179	34	7	3	59	.331	897	57	6	.994
1981—California	Amer.		1B	93	364	57	111	17	1	2	21	.305	877	60	5	.995
1982—California	Amer.		1B	138	523	88	167	25	5	3	44	.319	1339	94	12	.992
1983—California a	Amer.		1B-2B	129	472	66	160	24	2	2	44	.339	891	42	6	.994
Major League Totals				2249	8543	1313	2832	420	108	87	945	.331	11731	3585	238	.985

Signed as free agent by Minnesota Twins' organization, June 25, 1964.

†On military list, August 5 to August 21, 1967.

‡On military list, June 8 to June 24, 1968.

§On military list, August 17 to September 1, 1969.

xOn disabled list, June 24 to September 1, 1970.

yTraded to California Angels for Outfielder Ken Landreaux, Pitchers Paul Hartzell and Brad Havens and Third Baseman Dave Engle, February 3, 1979.

zOn supplemental disabled list, June 5 to July 19, 1979.

aGranted free agency, November 7, 1983; re-signed by Angels, November 22, 1983.

CHAMPIONSHIP SERIES RECORD

Tied Championship Series record for most two-base hits, four-game Series (3), 1979.

Tied American League Championship Series records for most times on losing club (4); most hits, four-game Series (7), 1979.

Year	Club	League	Pos.	G.	AB.	R.	H.	2B.	3B.	HR.	RBI.	B.A.	PO.	A.	E.	F.A.
1969—Minnesota	Amer.		2B	3	14	0	1	0	0	0	0	.071	6	3	1	.900
1970—Minnesota	Amer.		PH	2	2	0	0	0	0	0	0	.000	0	0	0	.000

Year Club	League	Pos.	G.	AB.	R.	H.	2B.	3B.	HR.	RBI.	B.A.	PO.	A.	E.	F.A.
1979—California............. Amer.		1B	4	17	4	7	3	0	0	1	.412	34	1	0	1.000
1982—California............. Amer.		1B	5	17	2	3	1	0	0	0	.176	43	4	0	1.000
Championship Series Totals			14	50	6	11	4	0	0	1	.220	83	8	1	.989

ALL-STAR GAME RECORD

Established All-Star Game record for most three-base hits, game (2), July 11, 1978.
Tied All-Star Game record for most at bats, nine-inning game (5), July 15, 1975.

Year League	Pos.	AB.	R.	H.	2B.	3B.	HR.	RBI.	B.A.	PO.	A.	E.	F.A.
1967—American	2B	3	0	0	0	0	0	0	.000	2	3	0	1.000
1968—American	2B	3	0	0	0	0	0	0	.000	2	2	0	1.000
1969—American	2B	3	0	0	0	0	0	0	.000	0	2	0	1.000
1971—American	2B	1	1	0	0	0	0	0	.000	1	2	0	1.000
1972—American	2B	2	0	1	0	0	0	1	.500	2	3	0	1.000
1973—American	2B	3	0	0	0	0	0	0	.000	5	1	0	1.000
1974—American	2B	1	1	0	0	0	0	0	.000	0	1	0	1.000
1975—American	2B	5	0	1	0	0	0	0	.200	3	1	0	1.000
1976—American	1B	3	0	0	0	0	0	0	.000	9	2	0	1.000
1977—American	1B	3	1	1	0	0	0	0	.333	7	0	0	1.000
1978—American	1B	4	2	2	0	2	0	0	.500	6	1	0	1.000
1980—American	1B	2	1	2	1	0	0	0	1.000	4	0	0	1.000
1981—American	1B	3	0	1	0	0	0	0	.333	12	0	0	1.000
1983—American	1B	3	2	2	0	0	0	1	.667	3	0	1	.750
All-Star Game Totals		39	8	10	1	2	0	2	.256	56	18	1	.987

Named to American League All-Star Team for 1970, 1979 and 1982 games; replaced due to injury.

STEVEN NORMAN CARLTON
(Steve)

Born December 22, 1944, at Miami, Fla.
Height, 6.05. Weight, 219.
Throws and bats lefthanded.
Attended Miami-Dade Community College, Miami, Fla.

Established major league records for most strikeouts, game by lefthanded pitcher and losing pitcher (19), September 15, 1969; most balks, season (11), 1979; most strikeouts, lifetime (3,709).
Established modern major league record for most consecutive games, no relief appearances in between, lifetime (463).
Tied major league record for most strikeouts, game (19), September 15, 1969.
Established modern National League record for most bases on balls issued, lifetime (1,524).
Tied National League records for most years, 100 or more strikeouts (17); most consecutive years, 100 or more strikeouts (17).
Tied modern National League record for most games won, season, by lefthander (27), 1972.
Led National League pitchers in games started with 41 in 1972, 38 in 1982 and tied for lead with 40 in 1973 and 38 in 1980.
Led National League in shutouts with 6 in 1982.
Led National League in complete games with 30 in 1972, 19 in 1982 and tied for lead with 18 in 1973.
Led National League in balks with 7 in 1977, 11 in 1979, 7 in 1980 and 9 in 1982 and 1983 and tied for lead with 7 in 1975 and 1978.
Led National League in wild pitches with 17 in 1980.
Led National League in home runs allowed with 30 in 1978.
Won National League Cy Young Memorial Award, 1972, 1977, 1980 and 1982.
Named National League Pitcher of the Year by THE SPORTING NEWS, 1972, 1977, 1980 and 1982.
Named lefthanded pitcher on THE SPORTING NEWS National League All-Star Team, 1969, 1971, 1972, 1977, 1979, 1980 and 1982.
Named pitcher on THE SPORTING NEWS National League All-Star fielding team, 1981.

Year Club	League	G.	IP.	W.	L.	Pct.	H.	R.	ER.	SO.	BB.	ERA.
1964—Rock Hill	W. Carol.	11	79	10	1	.909	39	17	9	91	36	1.03
1964—Winnipeg	Northern	12	75	4	4	.500	63	40	28	79	48	3.36
1964—Tulsa	Texas	4	24	1	1	.500	16	13	7	21	18	2.63
1965—St. Louis.....................	National	15	25	0	0	.000	27	7	7	21	8	2.52
1966—Tulsa	P. Coast	19	128	9	5	.643	110	65	51	108	54	3.59
1966—St. Louis	National	9	52	3	3	.500	56	22	18	25	18	3.12
1967—St. Louis	National	30	193	14	9	.609	173	71	64	168	62	2.98
1968—St. Louis	National	34	232	13	11	.542	214	87	77	162	61	2.99
1969—St. Louis	National	31	236	17	11	.607	185	66	57	210	93	2.17
1970—St. Louis	National	34	254	10	★19	.345	239	123	105	193	109	3.72
1971—St. Louis†	National	37	273	20	9	.690	275	120	108	172	98	3.56
1972—Philadelphia	National	41	★346	★27	10	.730	★257	84	76	★310	87	★1.98
1973—Philadelphia	National	40	●293	13	★20	.394	★293	★146	★127	223	113	3.90
1974—Philadelphia	National	39	291	16	13	.552	249	118	104	★240	★136	3.22
1975—Philadelphia	National	37	255	15	14	.517	217	116	101	192	104	3.56
1976—Philadelphia	National	35	253	20	7	★.741	224	94	88	195	72	3.13
1977—Philadelphia	National	36	283	★23	10	.697	229	99	83	198	89	2.64
1978—Philadelphia	National	34	247	16	13	.552	228	91	78	161	63	2.84
1979—Philadelphia	National	35	251	18	11	.621	202	112	101	213	89	3.62
1980—Philadelphia	National	38	★304	★24	9	.727	243	87	79	★286	90	2.34
1981—Philadelphia	National	24	190	13	4	.765	152	59	51	179	62	2.42
1982—Philadelphia	National	38	★295⅔	★23	11	.676	★253	114	102	★286	86	3.10
1983—Philadelphia	National	37	★283⅔	15	16	.484	★277	117	98	★275	84	3.11
Major League Totals.....................		624	4557⅓	300	200	.600	3993	1733	1524	3709	1524	3.01

Signed as free agent by St. Louis Cardinals' organization, October 8, 1963.
†Traded to Philadelphia Phillies for Pitcher Rick Wise, February 25, 1972.

DIVISION SERIES RECORD

Year	Club	League	G.	IP.	W.	L.	Pct.	H.	R.	ER.	SO.	BB.	ERA.
1981—Philadelphia		National	2	14	0	2	.000	14	6	6	13	8	3.86

CHAMPIONSHIP SERIES RECORD

Established Championship Series record for most bases on balls, total Series (28).

Tied Championship Series records for most games won, total Series (4); most games won, Series (2); most home runs by pitcher, total Series (1); most bases on balls, four-game Series (8), 1977; most bases on balls, five-game series (8), 1980.

Established National League Championship Series records for most strikeouts, total Series (39); most games started, total Series (8); most innings pitched, total Series (53⅔); most hits allowed, total Series (53); most runs allowed, total Series (22); most earned runs allowed, total Series (21).

Tied National League Championship Series records for most strikeouts, four-game Series (13), 1983; most bases on balls, three-game Series (5), 1976.

Year	Club	League	G.	IP.	W.	L.	Pct.	H.	R.	ER.	SO.	BB.	ERA.
1976—Philadelphia		National	1	7	0	1	.000	8	5	4	6	5	5.14
1977—Philadelphia		National	2	11⅔	0	1	.000	13	9	9	6	8	6.94
1978—Philadelphia		National	1	9	1	0	1.000	8	4	4	8	2	4.00
1980—Philadelphia		National	2	12⅓	1	0	1.000	11	3	3	6	8	2.19
1983—Philadelphia		National	2	13⅔	2	0	1.000	13	1	1	13	5	0.66
Championship Series Totals			8	53⅔	4	2	.667	53	22	21	39	28	3.52

WORLD SERIES RECORD

Tied World Series record for most games won, losing none, six-game Series (2), 1980.

Year	Club	League	G.	IP.	W.	L.	Pct.	H.	R.	ER.	SO.	BB.	ERA.
1967—St. Louis		National	1	6	0	1	.000	3	1	0	5	2	0.00
1968—St. Louis		National	2	4	0	0	.000	7	3	3	3	1	6.75
1980—Philadelphia		National	2	15	2	0	1.000	14	5	4	17	9	2.40
1983—Philadelphia		National	1	6⅔	0	1	.000	5	3	2	7	3	2.70
World Series Totals			6	31⅔	2	2	.500	29	12	9	32	15	2.56

ALL-STAR GAME RECORD

Year League	IP.	W.	L.	Pct.	H.	R.	ER.	SO.	BB.	ERA.
1968—National	1	0	0	.000	0	0	0	1	0	0.00
1969—National	3	1	0	1.000	2	2	2	2	1	6.00
1972—National	1	0	0	.000	0	0	0	1	0	0.00
1979—National	1	0	0	.000	2	3	3	0	1	27.00
1982—National	2	0	0	.000	1	0	0	4	2	0.00
All-Star Game Totals	8	1	0	1.000	5	5	5	7	5	5.63

Member of National League All-Star Team in 1971, 1974, 1977, 1980 and 1981; did not play.

DONALD WAYNE CARMAN
(Don)

Born August 14, 1959, at Oklahoma City, Okla.
Height, 6.03. Weight, 190.
Throws and bats lefthanded.
Attended Seminole Junior College, Seminole, Okla.,
and University of Oklahoma, Norman, Okla.

Year	Club	League	G.	IP.	W.	L.	Pct.	H.	R.	ER.	SO.	BB.	ERA.
1979—Spartanburg		W. Carol.	37	78	6	3	.667	72	36	34	70	28	3.92
1980—Peninsula		Carolina	27	150	14	5	.737	149	73	57	★141	53	3.42
1981—Reading		Eastern	28	176	12	13	.480	167	93	79	105	75	4.04
1982—Oklahoma City		Am. Assoc.	10	33	0	1	.000	37	29	25	29	23	6.82
1982—Reading		Eastern	20	97⅓	6	7	.462	99	58	45	81	62	4.16
1983—Reading		Eastern	★56	124⅓	8	5	.615	85	51	41	93	71	2.97
1983—Philadelphia		National	1	1	0	0	.000	0	0	0	0	0	0.00
Major League Totals			1	1	0	0	.000	0	0	0	0	0	0.00

Signed as free agent by Philadelphia Phillies' organization, August 25, 1978.

DON KEITH CARTER

Born December 11, 1961, at Kansas City, Kan.
Height, 5.10. Weight, 160.
Throws right and bats lefthanded.
Attended Kansas City Community College, Kansas City, Kan.,
and University of Arkansas, Fayetteville, Ark.

Tied for California League lead in caught stealing with 20 in 1982.

Year	Club	League	Pos.	G.	AB.	R.	H.	2B.	3B.	HR.	RBI.	B.A.	PO.	A.	E.	F.A.
1981—Calgary		Pion.	OF-2B	50	159	31	44	3	3	0	11	.277	54	8	4	.939
1982—San Jose		Calif.	OF	105	434	73	131	5	1	1	43	.302	231	2	1	★.996
1982—Memphis		South.	OF	12	29	2	5	0	0	0	0	.172	18	1	0	1.000
1982—Wichita		A. A.		4	8	0	0	0	0	0	0	.000	figures unavailable			

Year Club League	Pos.	G.	AB.	R.	H.	2B.	3B.	HR.	RBI.	B.A.	PO.	A.	E.	F.A.
1983—Memphis† .... South.	OF	112	423	61	128	7	2	0	30	.303	269	13	4	.986
1983—Buffalo.................... East.	OF	16	60	10	16	1	2	0	10	.267	29	0	1	.967

Selected by Montreal Expos' organization in 12th round of free-agent draft, June 8, 1981.

†Traded with cash to Cleveland Indians' organization for Second Baseman Manny Trillo, August 17, 1983.

GARY EDMUND CARTER

Born April 8, 1954, at Culver City, Calif.
Height, 6.02. Weight, 215.
Throws and bats righthanded.
Brother of Gordon Carter, outfielder in San Francisco Giants'
organization, 1972 and 1973.

Established major league record for fewest passed balls, season, 150 or more games (1), 1978.
Established National League record for most seasons leading league in games by catcher (6).
Tied National League records for most years leading league in putouts by catcher (6); most years leading league in chances accepted by catcher (6).
Hit three home runs in a game, April 20, 1977.
Led National League catchers in assists with 107 in 1983.
Led National League catchers in total chances with 921 in 1977, 874 in 1978, 848 in 1979, 937 in 1980, 571 in 1981 and 1,068 in 1982.
Led National League in passed balls with 12 in 1979.
Led National League catchers in putouts with 811 in 1977, 781 in 1978, and 509 in 1981.
Led National League catchers in double plays with 14 in 1977, 9 in 1978, 12 in 1979 and 14 in 1983.
Led International League catchers in putouts with 794, assists with 65, double plays with 15 and fielding percentage with .990 in 1974.
Named National League Rookie Player of the Year by THE SPORTING NEWS, 1975.
Named catcher on THE SPORTING NEWS National League All-Star Team, 1980 through 1982.
Named catcher on THE SPORTING NEWS National League All-Star fielding team, 1980 through 1982.
Named catcher on THE SPORTING NEWS National League Silver Slugger team, 1981 and 1982.

Year Club League	Pos.	G.	AB.	R.	H.	2B.	3B.	HR.	RBI.	B.A.	PO.	A.	E.	F.A.
1972—Cocoa Expos......... Fla.E.C.	C-1B-3B	18	71	6	17	3	0	2	9	.239	111	12	10	.925
1972—W. Palm Beach.... Fla. St.	C	20	50	9	16	2	2	0	5	.320	84	12	2	.980
1973—Quebec City .... East.	C-1B-OF	130	439	65	111	16	1	15	68	.253	823	75	20	.978
1973—Peninsula............... Int.	C	8	25	2	7	2	0	0	1	.280	5	1	0	1.000
1974—Memphis............... Int.	C-1B-3B	135	441	62	118	14	7	23	83	.268	908	76	12	.988
1974—Montreal .... Nat.	C-OF	9	27	5	11	0	1	1	6	.407	28	4	0	1.000
1975—Montreal .... Nat.	OF-C-3B	144	503	58	136	20	1	17	68	.270	430	38	9	.981
1976—Montreal† .... Nat.	C-OF	91	311	31	68	8	1	6	38	.219	364	42	2	.995
1977—Montreal .... Nat.	★C-OF	154	522	86	148	29	2	31	84	.284	813	★101	9	.990
1978—Montreal .... Nat.	C-1B	157	533	76	136	27	1	20	72	.255	787	83	10	.989
1979—Montreal .... Nat.	C	141	505	74	143	26	5	22	75	.283	★751	★88	9	.989
1980—Montreal .... Nat.	C	154	549	76	145	25	5	29	101	.264	★822	★108	7	★.993
1981—Montreal .... Nat.	C-1B	100	374	48	94	20	2	16	68	.251	515	58	4	.993
1982—Montreal .... Nat.	C	154	557	91	163	32	1	29	97	.293	★954	★104	10	.991
1983—Montreal .... Nat.	★C-1B	145	541	63	146	37	3	17	79	.270	855	108	5	★.995
Major League Totals.....................		1249	4422	608	1190	224	22	188	688	.269	6319	734	65	.991

Selected by Montreal Expos' organization in 3rd round of free-agent draft, June 6, 1972.

†On disabled list, June 6 to July 22, 1976.

DIVISION SERIES RECORD

Year Club League	Pos.	G.	AB.	R.	H.	2B.	3B.	HR.	RBI.	B.A.	PO.	A.	E.	F.A.
1981—Montreal .... Nat.	C	5	19	3	8	3	0	2	6	.421	21	5	0	1.000

CHAMPIONSHIP SERIES RECORD

Year Club League	Pos.	G.	AB.	R.	H.	2B.	3B.	HR.	RBI.	B.A.	PO.	A.	E.	F.A.
1981—Montreal .... Nat.	C	5	16	3	7	1	0	0	0	.438	27	3	0	1.000

ALL-STAR GAME RECORD

Tied All-Star Game record for most home runs, game (2), August 9, 1981.

Year League	Pos.	AB.	R.	H.	2B.	3B.	HR.	RBI.	B.A.	PO.	A.	E.	F.A.
1975—National	OF	0	0	0	0	0	0	0	.000	1	0	0	1.000
1979—National	C	2	0	1	0	0	0	0	.500	6	1	0	1.000
1980—National	C	1	0	0	0	0	0	0	.000	1	0	0	1.000
1981—National	C	3	2	2	0	0	2	2	.667	5	1	0	1.000
1982—National	C	3	0	1	0	0	0	1	.333	7	0	0	1.000
1983—National	C	2	0	0	0	0	0	0	.000	3	0	0	1.000
All-Star Game Totals		11	2	4	0	0	2	4	.364	23	2	0	1.000

JOSEPH CARTER

(Joe)

Born March 7, 1960, at Oklahoma City, Okla.
Height, 6.03. Weight, 215.
Throws and bats righthanded.
Attended Wichita State University, Wichita, Kan.

Led American Association in total bases with 265 and tied for lead in strikeouts by batters with 103 in 1983.
Named College Player of the Year by THE SPORTING NEWS, 1981.
Received reported $150,000 bonus to sign with Chicago Cubs, 1981.

Year Club	League	Pos.	G.	AB.	R.	H.	2B.	3B.	HR.	RBI.	B.A.	PO.	A.	E.	F.A.
1981—Midland.................	Texas	OF	67	249	42	67	15	3	5	35	.269	100	10	4	.965
1982—Midland†..............	Texas	OF	110	427	84	136	22	8	25	98	.319	182	6	5	.974
1983—Iowa....................	A. A.	OF	124	*522	82	160	27	6	22	83	.307	204	9	12	.947
1983—Chicago.................	Nat.	OF	23	51	6	9	1	1	0	1	.176	26	0	0	1.000
Major League Totals..................			23	51	6	9	1	1	0	1	.176	26	0	0	1.000

Selected by Chicago Cubs' organization in 1st round (second player selected) of free-agent draft, June 8, 1981.

†On disabled list, April 9 to April 19, 1982.

ESTEBAN MANUEL ANTONIO CASTILLO (CABRERA)

Name pronounced Cas-TEE-yo.

(Manny)

Born April 1, 1957, at Santo Domingo, Dominican Republic.
Height, 5.09. Weight, 180.
Throws right and bats right and lefthanded.

Led American Association third basemen in fielding percentage with .959, assists with 286, total chances with 419 and double plays with 31 in 1981.

Led American Association third basemen in double plays with 27 in 1980.

Led Texas League second basemen in double plays with 83 in 1977.

Named American Association Most Valuable Player, 1981.

Year Club	League	Pos.	G.	AB.	R.	H.	2B.	3B.	HR.	RBI.	B.A.	PO.	A.	E.	F.A.
1973—Marion...................	Appal.	3B-2B	10	19	1	2	0	0	0	1	.105	8	10	2	.900
1974—Marion...................	Appal.	3B-2B	42	144	19	42	6	1	1	21	.292	41	55	9	.914
1975—Wausau†...............	Midw.	3B-OF	68	212	28	69	9	4	1	34	.325	39	110	19	.887
1976—Arkansas...............	Texas	3B-2B-1B	116	355	36	99	11	2	0	35	.279	130	194	15	.956
1977—Arkansas...............	Texas	SS	115	430	39	128	20	5	0	43	.298	239	*357	21	.966
1977—New Orleans.........	A. A.	2B-SS	13	48	3	8	1	0	0	6	.167	28	49	2	.975
1978—Springfield.............	A. A.	2B-3B-OF	108	382	39	96	21	1	2	39	.251	145	220	16	.958
1979—Springfield‡..........	A. A.	3-2-S-O	127	*524	75	*169	29	4	2	57	.323	120	231	20	.946
1980—Omaha...................	A. A.	*3-O-P	*137	*599	86	*173	20	●11	6	70	.289	*139	*272	20	*.954
1980—Kansas City..........	Amer.	3B-2B	7	10	1	2	0	0	0	0	.200	2	8	0	1.000
1981—Omaha§.................	A. A.	*3B-2B	*136	*543	79	*182	31	4	10	91	.335	*116	288	17	.960
1982—Seattle..................	Amer.	3B-2B	138	506	49	130	29	1	3	49	.257	109	220	21	.940
1983—Seattle..................	Amer.	3-1-2-P	91	203	13	42	6	3	0	24	.207	78	118	6	.970
Major League Totals..................			236	719	63	174	35	4	3	73	.242	189	346	27	.952

Signed as free agent by New York Mets' organization, March 3, 1973.

†Drafted by St. Louis Cardinals' organization, December 9, 1975.

‡Drafted by Kansas City Royals, December 3, 1979.

§Traded to Seattle Mariners for a player to be named later, October 23, 1981; Kansas City Royals acquired Pitcher Bud Black to complete deal, March 2, 1982.

PITCHING RECORD

Year Club	League	G.	IP.	W.	L.	Pct.	H.	R.	ER.	SO.	BB.	ERA.
1980—Omaha..............................	Am. Assoc.	1	1	0	0	.000	0	3	3	1	6	27.00
1983—Seattle................................	American	1	2⅔	0	0	.000	8	7	7	2	3	23.63
Major League Totals.........................		1	2⅔	0	0	.000	8	7	7	2	3	23.63

JUAN CASTILLO

Name pronounced Cas-TEE-yo.

Born January 25, 1962, at San Pedro de Macoris, Dominican Republic.
Height, 5.11. Weight, 155.
Throws and bats righthanded.

Led Texas League in caught stealing with 17 in 1983.

Led Texas League second basemen in putouts with 247, assists with 360, errors with 27, double plays with 79 and total chances with 634 in 1983.

Led California League second basemen in double plays with 88 in 1982.

Year Club	League	Pos.	G.	AB.	R.	H.	2B.	3B.	HR.	RBI.	B.A.	PO.	A.	E.	F.A.
1980—Burlington	Midw.	2B	30	103	12	22	0	0	0	6	.214	60	72	3	.978
1980—Butte	Pion.	2B	59	183	28	53	9	3	0	20	.290	87	99	18	.912
1981—Burlington	Midw.	2B	110	365	36	90	8	4	4	34	.247	244	284	18	*.967
1982—Stockton	Calif.	2B	134	483	60	130	9	8	0	42	.269	273	*428	23	.968
1983—El Paso.................	Texas	2B-SS-OF	123	461	79	125	24	2	8	62	.271	250	363	28	.956

Signed as free agent by Milwaukee Brewers' organization, October 11, 1979.

MARTIN HORACE CASTILLO

Name pronounced Cas-TEE-yo.

(Marty)

Born January 16, 1957, at Long Beach, Calif.
Height, 6.01. Weight, 190.
Throws and bats righthanded.
Attended Chapman College, Orange, Calif.
Brother of Art Castillo, outfielder in Minnesota Twins' organization, 1973 through 1975.

Led American Association catchers in assists with 78, passed balls with 14 and stealers caught with 50 in 1982.

Led American Association in passed balls with 21 in 1981.

Year Club League	Pos.	G.	AB.	R.	H.	2B.	3B.	HR.	RBI.	B.A.	PO.	A.	E.	F.A.
1978—Lakeland................ Fla. St.	3B	67	205	24	53	4	2	5	25	.259	73	95	9	.949
1979—Montgomery†...... South.	3B	74	274	47	84	17	1	9	47	.307	70	174	22	.917
1979—Evansville‡ .... A. A.	3B	31	103	11	24	4	1	1	6	.233	27	66	3	.969
1980—Evansville .... A. A.	★3-C-1	132	455	59	114	28	4	12	62	.251	137	268	★26	.940
1981—Evansville .... A. A.	C-3B-1B	120	396	63	105	23	2	17	68	.265	393	149	21	.945
1981—Detroit.................. Amer.	3B-OF	6	8	1	1	0	0	0	0	.125	4	8	0	1.000
1982—Evansville .... A. A.	C-3-O-1	116	388	52	94	20	3	12	56	.242	525	117	13	.980
1982—Detroit.................. Amer.	C	1	0	0	0	0	0	0	0	.000	1	0	0	.000
1983—Evansville .... A. A.	3B-SS	54	186	29	50	2	0	12	29	.269	33	71	7	.937
1983—Detroit.................. Amer.	3B-C	67	119	10	23	4	0	2	10	.193	73	69	1	.993
Major League Totals......................		74	127	11	24	4	0	2	10	.189	78	77	1	.994

Selected by Minnesota Twins' organization in 21st round of free-agent draft, June 4, 1975.
Selected by California Angels' organization in 8th round of free-agent draft, January 11, 1977.
Selected by Detroit Tigers' organization in 5th round of free-agent draft, June 6, 1978.
†On disabled list, April 21 to May 1, 1979.
‡On disabled list, July 30 to August 11, 1979.

MONTE CARMELO CASTILLO

Name pronounced Cas-TEE-yo.

(Carmen)

Born June 8, 1958, at San Francisco de Macoris, Dominican Republic.
Height, 6.01. Weight, 185.
Throws and bats righthanded.

Year Club League	Pos.	G.	AB.	R.	H.	2B.	3B.	HR.	RBI.	B.A.	PO.	A.	E.	F.A.
1978—Auburn† .... NYP	OF	53	174	37	41	10	2	4	21	.236	109	6	11	.913
1978—Helena.................. Pion.	OF	5	15	1	6	2	0	0	2	.400	2	0	1	.667
1979—Waterloo.............. Midw.	OF	49	138	25	28	5	1	3	12	.203	54	1	7	.887
1979—Batavia................. NYP	OF	36	128	29	43	8	1	8	28	.336	56	4	5	.923
1980—Waterloo.............. Midw.	OF	117	390	69	103	14	1	11	64	.264	173	10	14	.929
1981—Chattanooga .... South.	OF	119	441	63	124	17	6	11	58	.281	236	13	15	.943
1982—Charleston........... Int.	OF	71	281	46	78	12	1	9	39	.278	159	10	11	.939
1982—Cleveland............. Amer.	OF	47	120	11	25	4	0	2	11	.208	91	0	2	.978
1983—Charleston‡.......... Int.	OF	36	148	29	40	5	2	4	22	.270	85	6	6	.938
1983—Cleveland............. Amer.	OF	23	36	9	10	2	1	1	3	.278	23	3	2	.929
Major League Totals......................		70	156	20	35	6	1	3	14	.224	114	3	4	.967

Signed as free agent by Philadelphia Phillies' organization, June 30, 1978.
†Drafted by Chattanooga (Cleveland Indians' organization), December 5, 1978.
‡On disabled list, May 5 to July 4, 1983.

ROBERT ERNIE CASTILLO JR.

Name pronounced Cas-TEE-yo.

(Bobby)

Born April 18, 1955, at Los Angeles, Calif.
Height, 5.10. Weight, 175.
Throws and bats righthanded.
Attended Los Angeles Valley Junior College, Van Nuys, Calif.

Year Club League	G.	IP.	W.	L.	Pct.	H.	R.	ER.	SO.	BB.	ERA.
1976—Reynosa.................................... Mexican	13	72	5	5	.500	52	16	14	56	36	1.75
1977—Monterrey†.............................. Mexican	34	255	19	11	.633	216	72	63	199	110	2.22
1977—Los Angeles.................................... National	6	11	1	0	1.000	12	5	5	7	2	4.09
1978—Albuquerque .... P. Coast	15	82	5	3	.625	81	54	49	65	51	5.38
1978—Los Angeles.................................... National	18	34	0	4	.000	28	19	15	30	33	3.97
1979—Albuquerque‡............................ P. Coast	16	45	4	3	.571	49	34	28	42	31	5.60
1979—Los Angeles.................................... National	19	24	2	0	1.000	26	5	3	25	13	1.13
1980—Los Angeles§.................................. National	61	98	8	6	.571	70	31	30	60	45	2.76
1981—Los Angeles x................................ National	34	51	2	4	.333	50	31	30	35	24	5.29
1982—Minnesota................................ American	40	218⅔	13	11	.542	194	96	89	123	85	3.66
1983—Minnesota................................ American	27	158⅓	8	12	.400	170	91	84	90	65	4.77
National League Totals..	138	218	13	14	.481	186	91	83	157	117	3.43
American League Totals..	67	377	21	23	.477	364	187	173	213	150	4.13
Major League Totals..	205	595	34	37	.479	550	278	256	370	267	3.87

Selected by Kansas City Royals' organization in 6th round of free-agent draft, January 9, 1974.
†Sold to Los Angeles Dodgers, June 16, 1977.
‡On disabled list, May 22 to July 21, 1979.
§Appeared in one game as an outfielder with no chances.
xTraded with Outfielder Bobby Mitchell to Minnesota Twins for Pitcher Paul Voigt and Catcher Scotti Madison, January 7, 1982.

CHAMPIONSHIP SERIES RECORD

Year Club League	G.	IP.	W.	L.	Pct.	H.	R.	ER.	SO.	BB.	ERA.
1981—Los Angeles .... National	1	1	0	0	.000	0	0	0	1	0	0.00

WORLD SERIES RECORD

Year Club League	G.	IP.	W.	L.	Pct.	H.	R.	ER.	SO.	BB.	ERA.
1981—Los Angeles .... National	1	1	0	0	.000	0	1	1	0	5	9.00

Year	Club	League	Pos.	G.	AB.	R.	H.	2B.	3B.	HR.	RBI.	B.A.	PO.	A.	E.	F.A.
1974—Sarasota Royals†	..Gulf C.	●3B-OF	47	150	15	38	7	4	3	21	.253	31	70	●13	.886
1975—	....					(Out of Organized Baseball)									
1976—Reynosa	.... Mex.		3B	1	2	0	0	0	0	0	0	.000	0	2	2	.500

†Released, April 7, 1975; signed by Reynosa of Mexican League, May 1, 1976.

JOHN ANTHONY CASTINO

Name pronounced Cass-TEE-no.

Born October 23, 1954, at Evanston, Ill.
Height, 5.11. Weight, 177.
Throws and bats righthanded.
Attended Rollins College, Winter Park, Fla.

Led American League third basemen in fielding percentage with .975 in 1981.
Led American League third basemen in double plays with 31 in 1979.
Tied for American League lead in putouts by third basemen with 86 in 1981.
Tied for American League lead in assists by third basemen with 340 in 1980.
Named American League Co-Rookie of the Year by Baseball Writers' Association of America, 1979.

Year	Club	League	Pos.	G.	AB.	R.	H.	2B.	3B.	HR.	RBI.	B.A.	PO.	A.	E.	F.A.
1976—Wis. Rapids	.... Midw.	3B	65	252	42	72	15	2	6	41	.286	60	155	16	.931
1977—Orlando	.... South.	3B	36	111	8	21	2	1	2	7	.189	28	89	11	.914
1977—Visalia	.... Calif.	3B	72	275	54	90	14	5	16	54	.327	68	152	13	.944
1978—Orlando	.... South.	3B	137	494	59	136	21	7	11	63	.275	★122	312	15	★.967
1979—Minnesota	.... Amer.	3B-SS	148	393	49	112	13	8	5	52	.285	91	286	15	.962
1980—Minnesota	.... Amer.	3B-SS	150	546	67	165	17	7	13	64	.302	128	395	22	.960
1981—Minnesota	.... Amer.	3B-2B	101	381	41	102	13	★9	6	36	.268	96	236	9	.974
1982—Minnesota†	.... Amer.	2B-3B-OF	117	410	48	99	12	6	6	37	.241	230	278	4	.992
1983—Minnesota	.... Amer.	2B-3B	142	563	83	156	30	4	11	57	.277	316	430	8	.989
Major League Totals	....		658	2293	288	634	85	34	41	246	.276	861	1625	58	.977

Selected by Minnesota Twins' organization in 3rd round of free-agent draft, June 8, 1976.
†On supplemental disabled list, April 4 to April 19, 1982.

WILLIAM RADHAMES CASTRO (CHECO)
(Bill)

Born December 13, 1953, at Barrero, Santiago, Dominican Republic.
Height, 6.00. Weight, 180.
Throws and bats righthanded.

Led Midwest League in saves with 17 in 1972.

Year	Club	League	G.	IP.	W.	L.	Pct.	H.	R.	ER.	SO.	BB.	ERA.
1971—Newark	.... NYP	9	13	0	1	.000	20	7	6	10	6	4.15
1972—Danville	.... Midwest	45	74	10	9	.526	59	31	25	66	26	3.04
1973—Danville	.... Midwest	46	114	11	4	●.733	96	33	23	104	24	1.82
1974—Sacramento	.... P. Coast	50	105	9	5	.643	133	68	55	52	35	4.71
1974—Milwaukee	.... American	8	18	0	0	.000	19	10	9	10	5	4.50
1975—Milwaukee†	.... American	18	75	3	2	.600	78	28	21	25	17	2.52
1976—Milwaukee‡	.... American	39	70	4	6	.400	70	29	27	23	19	3.47
1977—Milwaukee	.... American	51	69	8	6	.571	76	34	32	28	23	4.17
1978—Milwaukee	.... American	42	50	5	4	.556	43	14	10	17	14	1.80
1979—Milwaukee	.... American	39	44	3	1	.750	40	14	10	10	13	2.05
1980—Milwaukee§	.... American	56	84	2	4	.333	89	35	26	32	17	2.79
1981—Columbus	.... Int'national	17	73	8	1	.889	92	41	37	40	20	4.56
1981—New York xy	.... American	11	19	1	1	.500	26	13	8	4	5	3.79
1982—Tacoma z	.... P. Coast	12	30	2	0	1.000	34	11	10	15	5	3.00
1982—Kansas City	.... American	21	75⅔	3	2	.600	72	34	29	37	20	3.45
1983—Kansas City a	.... American	18	40⅔	2	0	1.000	51	34	30	17	12	6.64
1983—Vancouver	.... P. Coast	18	41⅓	1	2	.333	42	17	17	20	6	3.70
Major League Totals	....	303	545⅓	31	26	.544	564	245	202	203	145	3.33

Signed as free agent by Milwaukee Brewers' organization, October 24, 1970.
†On disabled list, July 23 to September 1, 1975.
‡On disabled list, May 19 to June 9, 1976.
§Granted free agency, October 22, 1980; signed by New York Yankees, February 17, 1981.
xTraded to California Angels for Third Baseman Butch Hobson, March 24, 1982.
yReleased, April 6, 1982; signed by Oakland A's organization, May 2, 1982.
zReleased, June 25, 1982; signed by Kansas City Royals, July 6, 1982.
aReleased, July 8, 1983; signed by Milwaukee Brewers' organization, July 15, 1983.

JOHN KEEFE CATO

(Known by middle name.)

Born May 6, 1958, at Yonkers, N.Y.
Height, 6.01. Weight, 185.
Throws and bats righthanded.
Attended Fairfield University, Fairfield, Conn.

Year	Club	League	G.	IP.	W.	L.	Pct.	H.	R.	ER.	SO.	BB.	ERA.
1979—Billings	.... Pioneer	11	88	9	1	.900	55	14	13	101	8	1.33
1980—Tampa	.... Florida St.	11	74	6	3	.667	59	21	14	42	14	1.70
1980—Waterbury	.... Eastern	12	73	3	7	.300	75	36	31	25	28	3.82

Year	Club	League	G.	IP.	W.	L.	Pct.	H.	R.	ER.	SO.	BB.	ERA.
1981—Waterbury†		Eastern	8	34	2	3	.400	34	22	20	25	18	5.29
1982—Waterbury		Eastern	18	43	2	0	1.000	43	15	14	42	15	2.50
1982—Indianapolis		Am. Assoc.	16	88	6	4	.600	83	46	35	49	25	3.58
1983—Waterbury		Eastern	7	51	3	1	.750	37	18	18	40	9	3.18
1983—Indianapolis		Am. Assoc.	18	69	3	3	.500	78	31	28	38	21	3.65
1983—Cincinnati		National	4	3⅔	1	0	1.000	2	1	1	3	1	2.45
Major League Totals			4	3⅔	1	0	1.000	2	1	1	3	1	2.45

Selected by Cincinnati Reds' organization in 2nd round of free-agent draft, June 5, 1979.

†On disabled list, April 27 to May 18 and June 18, 1981 through remainder of season.

WILLIAM HOLLAND CAUDILL

Name pronounced KAH-dull.

(Bill)

Born July 13, 1956, at Santa Monica, Calif.
Height, 6.01. Weight, 210.
Throws and bats righthanded.

Pitched six-inning, 4-0 no-hit victory against Winter Haven, May 14, 1975.
Major League saves: 1980 (1), 1982 (26), 1983 (26). Total—53.
Led Florida State League in complete games with 12 in 1975.

Year	Club	League	G.	IP.	W.	L.	Pct.	H.	R.	ER.	SO.	BB.	ERA.
1974—Sarasota Cardinals		Gulf Coast	8	30	1	0	1.000	18	9	6	35	13	1.80
1975—St. Petersburg		Florida St.	25	163	●14	8	.636	123	63	57	★153	87	3.15
1976—Arkansas†		Texas	27	140	6	15	.286	128	79	69	★140	84	4.44
1977—Three Rivers‡		Eastern	19	114	13	4	★.765	97	56	53	93	72	4.18
1977—Indianapolis		Am. Assoc.	8	44	2	2	.500	31	20	18	25	31	3.68
1978—Wichita		Am. Assoc.	29	158	8	9	.471	151	103	97	124	105	5.53
1979—Wichita		Am. Assoc.	6	36	3	1	.750	27	11	11	36	17	2.75
1979—Chicago		National	29	90	1	7	.125	89	57	48	104	41	4.80
1980—Chicago		National	72	128	4	6	.400	100	37	31	112	59	2.18
1981—Chicago§x		National	30	71	1	5	.167	87	50	46	45	31	5.83
1982—Seattle		American	70	95⅔	12	9	.571	65	25	25	111	35	2.35
1983—Seattle yz		American	63	72⅔	2	8	.200	70	39	38	73	38	4.71
National League Totals			131	289	6	18	.250	276	144	125	261	131	3.89
American League Totals			133	168⅓	14	17	.452	135	64	63	184	73	3.37
Major League Totals			264	457⅓	20	35	.364	411	208	188	445	204	3.70

Selected by St. Louis Cardinals' organization in 8th round of free-agent draft, June 5, 1974.

†Traded to Cincinnati Reds' organization for Infielder-Outfielder Joel Youngblood, March 28, 1977.

‡Traded with Pitcher Woodie Fryman to Chicago Cubs for Pitcher Bill Bonham, October 31, 1977.

§Traded to New York Yankees, April 1, 1982, as partial completion of deal in which Chicago Cubs acquired Second Baseman Pat Tabler from New York on waivers for two players to be named later, August 19, 1981; New York organization acquired Pitcher Jay Howell to complete deal, August 2, 1982.

xTraded with Pitcher Gene Nelson, a player to be named later and cash by New York Yankees to Seattle Mariners for Pitcher Shane Rawley, April 1, 1982; Seattle organization acquired Outfielder Bobby Brown to complete deal, April 6, 1982.

yOn disabled list, August 17 to September 4, 1983.

zTraded with a player to be named later to Oakland A's for Pitcher Dave Beard and Catcher Bob Kearney, November 21, 1983; Oakland acquired Pitcher Darrel Akerfelds to complete deal, December 7, 1983.

CESAR CEDENO

Name pronounced Suh-DAYN-yo.

Born February 25, 1951, at Santo Domingo, Dominican Republic.
Height, 6.02. Weight, 195.
Throw and bats righthanded.

Tied major league record for most doubles, inning (2), April 9, 1973 (1st game, 6th inning).
Hit for the cycle, August 2, 1972 and August 9, 1976.
Major League stolen bases: 1970 (17), 1971 (20), 1972 (55), 1973 (56), 1974 (57), 1975 (50), 1976 (58), 1977 (61), 1978 (23), 1979 (30), 1980 (48), 1981 (12), 1982 (16), 1983 (13). Total—516.
Led National League in caught stealing with 21 in 1972 and 17 in 1975.
Led National League outfielders in double plays with 5 in 1976.
Led National League outfielders in total chances with 460 in 1974.
Tied for National League lead in sacrifice flies with 9 in 1979.
Tied for Carolina League lead in being hit by pitch with 14 in 1969.
Named outfielder on THE SPORTING NEWS National League All-Star Team, 1972, 1973, 1976 and 1980.
Named outfielder on THE SPORTING NEWS National League All-Star fielding team, 1972 through 1976.

Year	Club	League	Pos.	G.	AB.	R.	H.	2B.	3B.	HR.	RBI.	B.A.	PO.	A.	E.	F.A.
1968—Covington		Appal.	OF	36	131	23	49	5	6	0	21	.374	49	●8	7	.891
1968—Cocoa		Fla. St.	OF	69	180	19	46	8	2	0	16	.256	70	4	7	.914
1969—Peninsula		Carol.	1B-OF	142	497	62	136	★32	3	5	39	.274	761	52	17	.980
1970—Okla. City		A. A.	OF	54	233	47	87	14	9	14	61	.373	113	6	4	.967
1970—Houston		Nat.	OF	90	355	46	110	21	4	7	42	.310	211	1	7	.968
1971—Houston		Nat.	OF-1B	161	611	85	161	★40	6	10	81	.264	348	6	4	.989
1972—Houston		Nat.	OF	139	559	103	179	●39	8	22	82	.320	345	9	7	.981
1973—Houston		Nat.	OF	139	525	86	168	35	2	25	70	.320	357	10	7	.981
1974—Houston		Nat.	OF	160	610	95	164	29	5	26	102	.269	★446	11	3	.993
1975—Houston†		Nat.	OF	131	500	93	144	31	3	13	63	.288	322	8	6	.982
1976—Houston		Nat.	OF	150	575	89	171	26	5	18	83	.297	377	11	8	.980

Year Club League	Pos.	G.	AB.	R.	H.	2B.	3B.	HR.	RBI.	B.A.	PO.	A.	E.	F.A.
1977—Houston‡ .... Nat.	OF	141	530	92	148	36	8	14	71	.279	335	14	1	★.997
1978—Houston§ .... Nat.	OF	50	192	31	54	8	2	7	23	.281	149	2	2	.987
1979—Houston .... Nat.	★1B-OF	132	470	57	123	27	4	6	54	.262	948	35	★17	.983
1980—Houston .... Nat.	OF	137	499	71	154	32	8	10	73	.309	338	9	8	.977
1981—Houston x .... Nat.	1B-OF	82	306	42	83	19	0	5	34	.271	510	28	5	.991
1982—Cincinnati .... Nat.	OF-1B	138	492	52	142	35	1	8	57	.289	301	5	3	.990
1983—Cincinnati .... Nat.	OF-1B	98	332	40	77	16	0	9	39	.232	258	10	1	.996
Major League Totals..................................		1748	6556	982	1878	394	56	180	874	.286	5245	159	79	.986

Signed as free agent by Houston Astros' organization, October 25, 1967.
†On supplemental disabled list, July 20 to August 8, 1975.
‡On disabled list, March 23 to April 13, 1977.
§On disabled list, June 17 to September 29, 1978.
xTraded to Cincinnati Reds for Third Baseman Ray Knight, December 18, 1981.

DIVISION SERIES RECORD

Year Club League	Pos.	G.	AB.	R.	H.	2B.	3B.	HR.	RBI.	B.A.	PO.	A.	E.	F.A.
1981—Houston .... Nat.	1B	4	13	0	3	1	0	0	0	.231	36	2	1	.974

CHAMPIONSHIP SERIES RECORD

Year Club League	Pos.	G.	AB.	R.	H.	2B.	3B.	HR.	RBI.	B.A.	PO.	A.	E.	F.A.
1980—Houston .... Nat.	OF	3	11	1	2	0	0	0	1	.182	5	0	0	1.000

ALL-STAR GAME RECORD

Year League	Pos.	AB.	R.	H.	2B.	3B.	HR.	RBI.	B.A.	PO.	A.	E.	F.A.
1972—National	OF	2	1	1	0	0	0	0	.500	0	0	0	.000
1973—National	OF	3	0	1	0	0	0	1	.333	3	0	0	1.000
1974—National	OF	2	0	0	0	0	0	0	.000	2	0	0	1.000
1976—National	OF	2	1	1	0	0	1	2	.500	1	0	0	1.000
All-Star Game Totals		9	2	3	0	0	1	3	.333	6	0	0	1.000

RICHARD ALDO CERONE

(Rick)

Born May 19, 1954, at Newark, N. J.
Height, 5.11. Weight, 185.
Throws and bats righthanded.
Received bachelor of science degree in physical education from
Seton Hall University, South Orange, N. J.

Named catcher on THE SPORTING NEWS American League All-Star Team, 1980.
Received reported $60,000 bonus to sign with Cleveland Indians, 1975.

Year Club League	Pos.	G.	AB.	R.	H.	2B.	3B.	HR.	RBI.	B.A.	PO.	A.	E.	F.A.
1975—Okla. City .... A. A.	C-OF	46	140	22	35	6	1	2	13	.250	178	30	3	.986
1975—Cleveland .... Amer.	C	7	12	1	3	1	0	0	0	.250	18	1	0	1.000
1976—Toledo† .... Int.	C	96	339	38	86	19	0	11	49	.254	351	50	★18	.957
1976—Cleveland‡ .... Amer.	C	7	16	1	2	0	0	0	1	.125	25	1	1	.963
1977—Charleston .... Int.	C-OF	70	231	30	54	10	1	6	40	.234	254	32	5	.983
1977—Toronto .... Amer.	C	31	100	7	20	4	0	1	10	.200	146	15	1	.944
1978—Toronto .... Amer.	C	88	282	25	63	8	2	3	20	.223	426	44	4	.992
1979—Toronto§ .... Amer.	C	136	469	47	112	27	4	7	61	.239	560	68	13	.980
1980—New York .... Amer.	C	147	519	70	144	30	4	14	85	.277	800	73	9	.990
1981—New York x .... Amer.	C	71	234	23	57	13	2	2	21	.244	353	26	3	.992
1982—New York y .... Amer.	C	89	300	29	68	10	0	5	28	.227	509	25	6	.989
1983—New York .... Amer.	C-3B	80	246	18	54	7	0	2	22	.220	412	18	4	.991
Major League Totals..................................		656	2178	221	523	100	12	34	248	.240	3249	271	41	.988

Selected by Cleveland Indians' organization in 1st round (seventh player selected) of free-agent draft, June 4, 1975.
†On disabled list, May 13 to May 24, 1976.
‡Traded with Infielder-Outfielder John Lowenstein to Toronto Blue Jays for Outfielder Rico Carty, December 6, 1976.
§Traded with Pitcher Tom Underwood and Outfielder Ted Wilborn to New York Yankees for First Baseman Chris Chambliss, Infielder Damaso Garcia and Pitcher Paul Mirabella, November 1, 1979.
xOn disabled list, April 19 to May 24, 1981.
yOn disabled list, May 12 to July 15, 1982.

DIVISION SERIES RECORD

Year Club League	Pos.	G.	AB.	R.	H.	2B.	3B.	HR.	RBI.	B.A.	PO.	A.	E.	F.A.
1981—New York .... Amer.	C	5	18	1	6	2	0	1	5	.333	42	1	1	.977

CHAMPIONSHIP SERIES RECORD

Tied Championsip Series record for hitting home run in first Series at-bat, October 8, 1980.

Year Club League	Pos.	G.	AB.	R.	H.	2B.	3B.	HR.	RBI.	B.A.	PO.	A.	E.	F.A.
1980—New York .... Amer.	C	3	12	1	4	0	0	1	2	.333	14	4	0	1.000
1981—New York .... Amer.	C	3	10	1	1	0	0	0	0	.100	23	2	0	1.000
Championship Series Totals		6	22	2	5	0	0	1	2	.227	37	6	0	1.000

WORLD SERIES RECORD

Year Club League	Pos.	G.	AB.	R.	H.	2B.	3B.	HR.	RBI.	B.A.	PO.	A.	E.	F.A.
1981—New York .... Amer.	C	6	21	2	4	1	0	1	3	.190	42	4	0	1.000

JOHN JOSEPH CERUTTI

Born April 28, 1960, at Albany, N. Y.
Height, 6.02. Weight, 180.
Throws and bats lefthanded.
Attended Amherst College, Amherst, Mass.

Tied for Southern League lead in shutouts with 3 in 1983.
Tied for Pioneer League lead in home runs allowed with 8 and games started by pitchers with 14 in 1981.

Year Club	League	G.	IP.	W.	L.	Pct.	H.	R.	ER.	SO.	BB.	ERA.
1981—Medicine Hat	Pioneer	14	*107	8	4	.667	87	45	36	120	43	3.03
1982—Kinston	Carolina	16	113	10	5	.667	88	47	40	136	49	3.19
1982—Knoxville	Southern	4	32⅓	4	0	1.000	18	4	4	17	10	1.11
1982—Syracuse	Int'national	6	30	0	3	.000	42	25	22	20	16	6.60
1983—Knoxville	Southern	29	188⅔	9	13	.409	182	89	72	131	65	3.43

Selected by Toronto Blue Jays' organization in 1st round (21st player selected) of free-agent draft, June 8, 1981.

RONALD CHARLES CEY

Name pronounced Say.

(Ron)

Born February 15, 1948, at Tacoma, Wash.
Height, 5.09. Weight, 185.
Throws and bats righthanded.
Attended Washington State University, Pullman, Wash., and Western
Washington State College, Bellingham, Wash.

Led National League third basemen in double plays with 39 in 1973.
Led Pacific Coast League in bases on balls received with 117 in 1972.
Led Northwest League in sacrifice flies with 7 in 1968.
Led Pacific Coast League third baseman in putouts with 106, assists with 274 and tied for lead in double plays with 24 in 1972.
Led California League third basemen in double plays with 22 in 1969.
Tied for Pacific Coast League lead in being hit by pitch with 9 in 1971.

Year Club	League	Pos.	G.	AB.	R.	H.	2B.	3B.	HR.	RBI.	B.A.	PO.	A.	E.	F.A.
1968—Tri-City	N'west	3B	74	254	50	76	11	4	9	*62	.299	46	*175	10	*.957
1969—Albuquerque	Texas	3B	13	32	8	5	1	0	0	2	.156	13	19	1	.970
1969—Bakersfield	Calif.	3B	98	353	68	117	16	1	22	56	.331	82	197	22	.927
1970—Albuquerque	Texas	3B	71	239	31	79	22	1	4	56	.331	44	132	10	.946
1971—Spokane	P. C.	3B	137	500	85	164	26	4	32	*123	.328	95	283	24	*.940
1971—Los Angeles	Nat.	PH	2	2	0	0	0	0	0	0	.000	0	0	0	.000
1972—Albuquerque	P. C.	3B-2B	142	496	99	163	25	7	23	103	.329	108	279	21	.949
1972—Los Angeles	Nat.	3B	11	37	3	10	1	0	1	3	.270	7	20	3	.900
1973—Los Angeles	Nat.	3B	152	507	60	124	18	4	15	80	.245	111	*328	18	.961
1974—Los Angeles	Nat.	3B	159	577	88	151	20	2	18	97	.262	155	365	22	.959
1975—Los Angeles	Nat.	3B	158	566	72	160	29	2	25	101	.283	144	309	19	.960
1976—Los Angeles	Nat.	3B	145	502	69	139	18	3	23	80	.277	111	334	16	.965
1977—Los Angeles	Nat.	3B	153	564	77	136	22	3	30	110	.241	138	346	18	.964
1978—Los Angeles	Nat.	3B	159	555	84	150	32	0	23	84	.270	116	336	16	.966
1979—Los Angeles	Nat.	3B	150	487	77	137	20	1	28	81	.281	123	265	9	*.977
1980—Los Angeles	Nat.	3B	157	551	81	140	25	0	28	77	.254	*127	317	13	.972
1981—Los Angeles	Nat.	3B	85	312	42	90	15	2	13	50	.288	71	184	16	.941
1982—Los Angeles†	Nat.	3B	150	556	62	141	23	1	24	79	.254	93	320	16	.963
1983—Chicago	Nat.	3B	159	581	73	160	33	1	24	90	.275	90	270	17	.955
Major League Totals			1640	5797	788	1538	256	19	252	932	.265	1286	3394	183	.962

Selected by New York Mets' organization in 24th round of free-agent draft, June 6, 1966.
Selected by Los Angeles Dodgers' organization in 3rd round of free-agent draft, June 7, 1968.
†Traded to Chicago Cubs for Outfielder Dan Cataline and Pitcher Vance Lovelace, January 19, 1983.

CHAMPIONSHIP SERIES RECORD

Tied Championship Series records for most home runs with bases filled, game (1), October 4, 1977; most runs batted in, inning (4), October 4, 1977 (seventh inning); most two-base hits, four-game Series (3), 1974.
Tied National League Championship records for most consecutive hits, one Series (4); most hits, game (4), October 6, 1974.

Year Club	League	Pos.	G.	AB.	R.	H.	2B.	3B.	HR.	RBI.	B.A.	PO.	A.	E.	F.A.
1974—Los Angeles	Nat.	3B	4	16	2	5	3	0	1	1	.313	2	4	2	.750
1977—Los Angeles	Nat.	3B	4	13	4	4	1	0	1	4	.308	7	14	1	.955
1978—Los Angeles	Nat.	3B	4	16	4	5	1	0	1	3	.313	2	13	0	1.000
1981—Los Angeles	Nat.	3B	5	18	1	5	1	0	0	3	.278	5	16	1	.955
Championship Series Totals			17	63	11	19	6	0	3	11	.302	16	47	4	.940

WORLD SERIES RECORD

Tied World Series record for batting in all club's runs, game, most (4), October 11, 1978.

Year Club	League	Pos.	G.	AB.	R.	H.	2B.	3B.	HR.	RBI.	B.A.	PO.	A.	E.	F.A.
1974—Los Angeles	Nat.	3B	5	17	1	3	0	0	0	0	.176	5	9	1	.933
1977—Los Angeles	Nat.	3B	6	21	2	4	1	0	1	3	.190	5	7	0	1.000
1978—Los Angeles	Nat.	3B	6	21	2	6	0	0	1	4	.286	2	12	0	1.000
1981—Los Angeles	Nat.	3B	6	20	3	7	0	0	1	6	.350	4	11	0	1.000
World Series Totals			23	79	8	20	1	0	3	13	.253	16	39	1	.982

Year League	Pos.	AB.	R.	H.	2B.	3B.	HR.	RBI.	B.A.	PO.	A.	E.	F.A.
1974—National	3B	2	0	1	1	0	0	2	.500	0	0	0	.000
1975—National	3B	3	0	1	0	0	0	0	.333	0	1	0	1.000
1976—National	3B	0	0	0	0	0	0	0	.000	0	0	0	.000
1977—National	3B	2	0	0	0	0	0	0	.000	0	0	0	.000
1978—National	3B	1	0	0	0	0	0	0	.000	1	0	0	1.000
1979—National	3B	1	0	0	0	0	0	0	.000	2	1	0	1.000
All-Star Game Totals		9	0	2	1	0	0	2	.222	3	2	0	1.000

ALBERT EUGENE CHAMBERS JR.
(Al)

Born March 24, 1961, at Harrisburg, Pa.
Height, 6.04. Weight, 217.
Throws and bats lefthanded.

Led Eastern League in bases on balls received with 91 in 1981.

Year Club League	Pos.	G.	AB.	R.	H.	2B.	3B.	HR.	RBI.	B.A.	PO.	A.	E.	F.A.
1979—Bellingham .... N'west	OF	55	166	26	41	4	1	2	22	.247	63	1	3	.955
1980—San Jose .... Calif.	OF	115	426	76	128	18	*12	9	85	.300	122	3	5	.962
1981—Lynn .... East.	OF	134	446	71	120	20	4	20	77	.269	178	5	9	.953
1982—Salt Lake City† ..... P. C.	OF	97	343	57	96	28	5	8	50	.280	165	3	5	.971
1983—Salt Lake City .... P. C.	OF	99	347	77	115	26	6	12	75	.331	71	0	6	.922
1983—Seattle.................... Amer.	OF	31	67	11	14	3	0	1	7	.209	3	0	0	1.000
Major League Totals.....................		31	67	11	14	3	0	1	7	.209	3	0	0	1.000

Selected by Seattle Mariners' organization in 1st round (first player selected) of free-agent draft, June 5, 1979.
†On disabled list, August 4 to August 14, 1983.

CARROLL CHRISTOPHER CHAMBLISS
(Chris)

Born December 26, 1948, at Dayton, O.
Height, 6.01. Weight, 220.
Throws right and bats lefthanded.
Attended Mira Costa Junior College, Oceanside, Calif., and University of California
at Los Angeles, Los Angeles, Calif.; and received degree in physical education and recreation from
Montclair State College, Upper Montclair, N.J.
Cousin of Jo Jo White, guard with Boston Celtics, Golden State Warriors
and Kansas City Kings, 1969-70 through 1980-81.

Tied major league record for fewest caught stealing, season, 150 or more games (0), 1976 and 1977.
Led National League first basemen in double plays with 144 in 1982.
Led National League first basemen in total chances with 1,739 in 1980 and 1,144 in 1981.
Led American League first basemen in total chances with 1,565 in 1973.
Named American League Rookie Player of the Year by THE SPORTING NEWS, 1971.
Named American League Rookie of the Year by Baseball Writers' Association of America, 1971.
Named first baseman on THE SPORTING NEWS American League All-Star Team, 1976.
Named first baseman on THE SPORTING NEWS American League All-Star fielding team, 1978.

Year Club League	Pos.	G.	AB.	R.	H.	2B.	3B.	HR.	RBI.	B.A.	PO.	A.	E.	F.A.
1970—Wichita† .... A. A.	OF-1B	105	383	60	131	17	8	7	52	*.342	413	21	13	.971
1971—Wichita .... A. A.	OF-1B	13	42	8	12	3	0	2	6	.286	42	3	0	1.000
1971—Cleveland.............. Amer.	1B	111	415	49	114	20	4	9	48	.275	943	55	8	.992
1972—Cleveland‡.............. Amer.	1B	121	466	51	136	27	2	6	44	.292	1109	56	8	.993
1973—Cleveland............... Amer.	1B	155	572	70	156	30	2	11	53	.273	1437	114	*14	.991
1974—Cleve.§-N.Y. .... Amer.	1B	127	467	46	119	20	3	6	50	.255	1035	84	11	.990
1975—New York.............. Amer.	1B	150	562	66	171	38	4	9	72	.304	1222	106	12	.991
1976—New York.............. Amer.	1B	156	641	79	188	32	6	17	96	.293	1440	109	9	.994
1977—New York.............. Amer.	1B	157	600	90	172	32	6	17	90	.287	1368	98	16	.989
1978—New York.............. Amer.	1B	158	625	81	171	26	3	12	90	.274	1366	111	4	*.997
1979—New York xy .... Amer.	1B	149	554	61	155	27	3	18	63	.280	1299	95	7	.995
1980—Atlanta .... Nat.	1B	158	602	83	170	37	2	18	72	.282	*1626	101	12	.993
1981—Atlanta .... Nat.	1B	107	404	44	110	25	2	8	51	.272	1046	*94	4	.997
1982—Atlanta .... Nat.	1B	157	534	57	144	25	2	20	86	.270	1352	138	10	.993
1983—Atlanta z .... Nat.	1B	131	447	59	125	24	3	20	78	.280	1092	89	5	.996
American League Totals........................		1288	4902	593	1382	252	33	105	606	.282	11219	828	89	.993
National League Totals...........................		553	1987	243	549	111	9	66	287	.276	5116	422	31	.994
Major League Totals..................................		1841	6889	836	1931	363	42	171	893	.280	16335	1250	120	.993

Selected by Cincinnati Reds' organization in 31st round of free-agent draft, June 6, 1967.
Selected by Cincinnati Reds' organization in secondary phase of free-agent draft, January 27, 1968.
Selected by Cleveland Indians' organization in 1st round (first player selected) of free-agent draft, January 17, 1970.

†On disabled list, May 25 to June 16, 1970.
‡On military list, June 23 to June 30, 1972.
§Traded with Pitchers Dick Tidrow and Cecil Upshaw to New York Yankees for Fritz Peterson, Steve Kline, Fred Beene and Tom Buskey, April 26, 1974.
xTraded with Infielder Damaso Garcia and Pitcher Paul Mirabella to Toronto Blue Jays for Catcher Rick Cerone, Pitcher Tom Underwood and Outfielder Ted Wilborn, November 1, 1979.
yTraded with Shortstop Luis Gomez to Atlanta Braves for Outfielder Barry Bonnell and Pitcher Joey McLaughlin, December 5, 1979.
zOn supplemental disabled list, August 8 to August 23, 1983.

Established Championship Series records for highest slugging average, five-game Series (.952), 1976; most total bases, five-game Series (20), 1976.

Tied Championship Series records for most hits, five-game Series (11), 1976; most hits, two consecutive games, one Series (6), October 3 and 4, 1978; most consecutive hits, one Series (5), 1978.

Tied American League Championship Series records for most consecutive hits, total Series (5); most one-base hits, four-game Series (6), 1978; most home runs, five-game Series (2), 1976.

Year	Club	League	Pos.	G.	AB.	R.	H.	2B.	3B.	HR.	RBI.	B.A.	PO.	A.	E.	F.A.
1976—New York		Amer.	1B	5	21	5	11	1	1	2	8	.524	50	3	1	.981
1977—New York		Amer.	1B	5	17	0	1	0	0	0	0	.059	35	7	0	1.000
1978—New York		Amer.	1B	4	15	1	6	0	0	0	2	.400	28	1	0	1.000
1982—Atlanta		Nat.	1B	3	10	0	0	0	0	0	0	.000	30	5	0	1.000
Championship Series Totals				17	63	6	18	1	1	2	10	.286	143	16	1	.994

WORLD SERIES RECORD

Tied World Series records for most errors by first baseman, four-game Series (1), 1976; one or more hits, each game, four-game Series, 1976.

Year	Club	League	Pos.	G.	AB.	R.	H.	2B.	3B.	HR.	RBI.	B.A.	PO.	A.	E.	F.A.
1976—New York		Amer.	1B	4	16	1	5	1	0	0	1	.313	26	3	1	.967
1977—New York		Amer.	1B	6	24	4	7	2	0	1	4	.292	55	5	0	1.000
1978—New York		Amer.	1B	3	11	1	2	0	0	0	0	.182	17	1	0	1.000
World Series Totals				13	51	6	14	3	0	1	5	.275	98	9	1	.991

ALL-STAR GAME RECORD

Year	League	Pos.	AB.	R.	H.	2B.	3B.	HR.	RBI.	B.A.	PO.	A.	E.	F.A.
1976—American		PH	1	0	0	0	0	0	0	.000	0	0	0	.000

PEDRO JOSE CHAVEZ

Born February 23, 1962, at Los Teques, Venezuela.
Height, 5.11. Weight, 160.
Throws and bats righthanded.

Year	Club	League	Pos.	G.	AB.	R.	H.	2B.	3B.	HR.	RBI.	B.A.	PO.	A.	E.	F.A.
1981—Macon		S. Atl.	SS	99	324	42	80	10	2	2	24	.247	147	303	36	.926
1982—Lakeland†		Fla. St.	SS-3B	83	254	27	68	11	1	2	29	.268	71	174	22	.918
1983—Birmingham‡		South.	3-2-S-1	20	49	7	11	1	0	0	3	.224	23	37	7	.896
1983—San Jose		Calif.	SS	107	401	56	111	12	3	6	42	.277	159	303	41	.918

Signed as free agent by Detroit Tigers' organization, August 20, 1980.
†On disabled list, April 9 to May 7, 1982.
‡Loaned to San Jose (Co-op), May 9, 1983; returned, September 8, 1983.

FLOYD JOHN CHIFFER

Born April 20, 1956, at Glen Cove, N.Y.
Height, 6.02. Weight, 180.
Throws and bats righthanded.
Received bachelor of arts degree in history from University of California,
Los Angeles, Calif., in 1978.

Year	Club	League	G.	IP.	W.	L.	Pct.	H.	R.	ER.	SO.	BB.	ERA.
1978—Reno		California	15	103	6	5	.545	127	76	61	80	38	5.33
1979—Amarillo		Texas	43	82	3	2	.600	121	72	64	62	38	7.02
1980—Amarillo†		Texas	39	62	4	5	.444	41	17	15	61	28	2.18
1981—Hawaii		P. Coast	42	68	4	5	.444	63	33	26	51	22	3.44
1982—San Diego		National	51	79⅓	4	3	.571	73	33	26	48	34	2.95
1983—San Diego		National	15	22⅔	0	2	.000	17	10	8	15	10	3.18
1983—Las Vegas		P. Coast	42	78⅓	10	4	.714	74	38	28	62	33	3.22
Major League Totals			66	102	4	5	.444	90	43	34	63	44	3.00

Selected by California Angels' organization in 8th round of free-agent draft, June 5, 1974.
Selected by St. Louis Cardinals' organization in 23rd round of free-agent draft, June 7, 1977.
Selected by San Diego Padres' organization in 5th round of free-agent draft, June 6, 1978.
†On disabled list, June 26 to July 6, 1980.

MICHAEL CHRIS
(Mike)

Born October 8, 1957, at Santa Monica, Calif.
Height, 6.02. Weight, 175.
Throws and bats lefthanded.
Attended Pierce Junior College, Woodland Hills, Calif. and
West Los Angeles Junior College, Culver City, Calif.

Pitched 1-0 no-hit victory against St. Petersburg, May 6, 1977.

Year	Club	League	G.	IP.	W.	L.	Pct.	H.	R.	ER.	SO.	BB.	ERA.
1977—Lakeland		Florida St.	26	188	●18	5	*.783	150	53	42	99	67	*2.01
1978—Montgomery		Southern	16	105	9	6	.600	80	44	34	85	48	2.91
1978—Evansville		Am. Assoc.	8	41	3	3	.500	38	23	14	21	23	3.07
1979—Evansville		Am. Assoc.	19	105	7	8	.467	113	78	65	71	67	5.57
1979—Detroit		American	13	39	3	3	.500	46	30	30	31	21	6.92
1980—Evansville		Am. Assoc.	28	140	7	*14	.333	148	82	71	85	90	4.56

Year Club	League	G.	IP.	W.	L.	Pct.	H.	R.	ER.	SO.	BB.	ERA.
1981—Evansville	Am. Assoc.	16	39	2	2	.500	52	34	28	21	38	6.46
1981—Birmingham†	Southern	14	89	5	5	.500	82	46	41	77	69	4.15
1982—Phoenix	P. Coast	17	109⅔	11	4	.733	107	54	48	62	71	3.94
1982—San Francisco	National	9	26	0	2	.000	23	16	14	10	26	4.85
1983—San Francisco	National	7	13⅓	0	0	.000	16	14	12	5	16	8.10
1983—Phoenix‡	P. Coast	24	145	3	12	.200	171	115	93	94	82	5.77
American League Totals		13	39	3	3	.500	46	30	30	31	21	6.92
National League Totals		16	39⅓	0	2	.000	39	30	26	15	42	5.95
Major League Totals		29	78⅓	3	5	.375	85	60	56	46	63	6.43

Selected by Oakland A's organization in 24th round of free-agent draft, June 4, 1975.
Selected by California Angels' organization in secondary phase of free-agent draft, January 7, 1976.
Selected by Oakland A's organization in secondary phase of free-agent draft, June 8, 1976.
Selected by Detroit Tigers' organization in secondary phase of free-agent draft, January 11, 1977.
†Traded with Pitcher Dan Schatzeder to San Francisco Giants for Outfielder Larry Herndon, December 9, 1981.
‡Sold on waivers to Chicago Cubs, September 30, 1983.

JOHN LAWRENCE CHRISTENSEN

Born September 5, 1960, at Downey, Calif.
Height, 6.03. Weight, 205.
Throws and bats righthanded.
Attended California State University, Fullerton, Calif.

Year Club	League	Pos.	G.	AB.	R.	H.	2B.	3B.	HR.	RBI.	B.A.	PO.	A.	E.	F.A.
1982—Shelby	S. Atl.	OF	125	440	100	147	24	2	22	•97	.334	156	9	2	.988
1982—Lynchburg	Carol.	OF	8	31	7	10	1	1	0	4	.323	11	1	1	.923
1983—Jackson	Texas	OF-1B-3B	109	405	76	135	26	2	12	72	.333	417	49	11	.977

Selected by California Angels' organization in 16th round of free-agent draft, June 6, 1978.
Selected by New York Mets' organization in 2nd round of free-agent draft, June 8, 1981.

LARRY RICHARD CHRISTENSON

Born November 10, 1953, at Everett, Wash.
Height, 6.04. Weight, 213.
Throws and bats righthanded.
Tied for National League lead in balks with 7 in 1978.

Year Club	League	G.	IP.	W.	L.	Pct.	H.	R.	ER.	SO.	BB.	ERA.
1972—Pulaski	Ap'lachian	8	38	4	2	.667	27	26	12	42	14	2.84
1973—Philadelphia	National	10	34	1	4	.200	53	25	25	11	20	6.62
1973—Eugene	P. Coast	16	100	7	6	.538	109	65	57	64	54	5.13
1974—Toledo	Int'national	27	172	11	9	.550	131	77	63	137	82	3.30
1974—Philadelphia	National	10	23	1	1	.500	20	11	11	18	15	4.30
1975—Toledo†	Int'national	2	12	2	0	1.000	5	0	0	10	3	0.00
1975—Philadelphia	National	29	172	11	6	.647	149	73	70	88	45	3.66
1976—Philadelphia	National	32	169	13	8	.619	199	77	69	54	42	3.67
1977—Philadelphia	National	34	219	19	6	.760	229	113	99	118	69	4.07
1978—Philadelphia‡	National	33	228	13	14	.481	209	90	82	131	47	3.24
1979—Philadelphia‡	National	19	106	5	10	.333	118	56	53	53	30	4.50
1980—Philadelphia§	National	14	74	5	1	.833	62	35	33	49	27	4.01
1981—Philadelphia xy	National	20	107	4	7	.364	108	48	42	70	30	3.53
1982—Philadelphia	National	33	223	9	10	.474	212	95	86	145	53	3.47
1983—Philadelphia za	National	9	48⅓	2	4	.333	42	25	21	44	17	3.91
Major League Totals		243	1403⅓	83	71	.539	1401	648	591	781	395	3.79

Selected by Philadelphia Phillies' organization in 1st round (third player selected) of free-agent draft, June 6, 1972.
†On disabled list, April 11 to April 30, 1975.
‡On disabled list, March 29 to May 11 and July 4 to August 3, 1979.
§On emergency disabled list, May 26 to August 11, 1980.
xOn disabled list, September 29, 1981; re-signed by Phillies, January 25, 1982.
yGranted free agency, November 13, 1981; re-signed by Phillies, January 25, 1982.
zOn disabled list, June 7, 1983; transferred to emergency disabled list, June 21, 1983 through remainder of season.
aReleased, November 3, 1983.

DIVISION SERIES RECORD

Year Club	League	G.	IP.	W.	L.	Pct.	H.	R.	ER.	SO.	BB.	ERA.
1981—Philadelphia	National	1	6	1	0	1.000	4	1	1	8	1	1.50

CHAMPIONSHIP SERIES RECORD

Year Club	League	G.	IP.	W.	L.	Pct.	H.	R.	ER.	SO.	BB.	ERA.
1977—Philadelphia	National	1	3⅓	0	0	.000	7	3	3	2	0	8.10
1978—Philadelphia	National	1	4⅓	0	1	.000	7	7	6	3	1	12.46
1980—Philadelphia	National	2	6⅔	0	0	.000	5	3	3	2	5	3.05
Championship Series Totals		4	14⅓	0	1	.000	19	13	12	7	6	7.53

WORLD SERIES RECORD

Year Club	League	G.	IP.	W.	L.	Pct.	H.	R.	ER.	SO.	BB.	ERA.
1980—Philadelphia	National	1	⅓	0	1	.000	5	4	4	0	0	108.00

CLAY C. CHRISTIANSEN

Born June 28, 1958, at Wichita, Kan.
Height, 6.04. Weight, 215.
Throws and bats righthanded.
Attended University of Kansas, Lawrence, Kan.

Led International League in wild pitches with 16 in 1983.

Year	Club	League	G.	IP.	W.	L.	Pct.	H.	R.	ER.	SO.	BB.	ERA.
1980—Oneonta	NYP	15	92	4	3	.571	89	43	26	62	24	2.54
1981—Ft. Lauderdale	Florida St.	26	178	16	7	.696	158	59	45	98	46	2.28
1982—Nashville	Southern	29	214⅓	●16	8	.667	214	102	73	157	80	3.07
1983—Columbus	Int'national	32	160⅓	8	9	.471	★196	118	97	92	81	5.44

Selected by New York Mets' organization in 29th round of free-agent draft, June 5, 1979.
Selected by New York Yankees' organization in 15th round of free-agent draft, June 8, 1980.

STEPHEN RANDALL CHRISTMAS
(Steve)

Born December 9, 1957, at Orlando, Fla.
Height, 6.00. Weight, 190.
Throws right and bats lefthanded.
Attended Oklahoma City Southwestern Junior College, Oklahoma City, Okla.

Led Eastern League catchers in total chances with 702 in 1981.
Led Eastern League catchers in fielding percentage with .984 in 1980.
Led Florida State League catchers in putouts with 646 and assists with 113 in 1979.
Led Western Carolinas League catchers in total chances with 627 in 1978.
Tied for Eastern League lead in passed balls with 15 in 1981.
Tied for Florida State League lead in passed balls with 17 in 1979.

Year	Club	League	Pos.	G.	AB.	R.	H.	2B.	3B.	HR.	RBI.	B.A.	PO.	A.	E.	F.A.
1977—Eugene	N'west	C-3B-1B	46	173	30	53	13	1	6	30	.306	214	24	7	.971
1978—Shelby	W. Car.	C	106	352	53	88	10	0	9	40	.250	★532	★77	18	.971
1979—Tampa	Fla. St.	●C-1B	122	377	50	99	18	2	6	39	.263	684	119	●17	.979
1980—Waterbury	East.	C-1B	115	347	44	84	15	2	7	44	.242	621	81	11	.985
1981—Waterbury	East.	C	126	395	40	104	21	0	7	63	.263	594	★95	13	.982
1982—Indianapolis†	A. A.	C-1B	85	252	31	77	14	1	7	37	.306	409	39	12	.974
1983—Tucson	P. C.	C-1B	48	164	18	47	6	0	2	18	.287	159	21	6	.968
1983—Indianapolis	A. A.	C-1B	31	98	14	24	6	1	4	20	.245	187	16	3	.985
1983—Cincinnati‡	Nat.	C	9	17	0	1	0	0	1	.059	28	3	0	1.000
Major League Totals			9	17	0	1	0	0	0	1	.059	28	3	0	1.000

Selected by Minnesota Twins' organization in 33rd round of free-agent draft, June 4, 1975.
Signed as free agent by Cincinnati Reds' organization, February 13, 1977.
†Loaned to Tucson (Houston Astros' organization), April 2, 1983; returned, June 27, 1983.
‡Traded to Chicago White Sox for Infielder Fran Mullins, November 21, 1983.

DARRYL RICHARD CIAS

Born April 23, 1957, at New York, N.Y.
Height, 5.11. Weight, 190.
Throws and bats righthanded.

Year	Club	League	Pos.	G.	AB.	R.	H.	2B.	3B.	HR.	RBI.	B.A.	PO.	A.	E.	F.A.
1975—Bluefield	Appal.	3-1-O-C	48	164	15	37	6	1	0	17	.226	137	49	10	.949
1976—Miami	Fla. St.	OF-3B-1B	52	156	16	25	3	1	0	14	.160	69	7	2	.974
1976—Bluefield†‡	Appal.	3B	38	131	8	24	4	1	0	10	.183	22	65	15	.853
1977—					(Out of Organized Baseball)										
1978—Salem§	N'west	C	59	230	36	67	18	3	6	43	.291	298	★69	8	.979
1979—Medford	N'west	1B-C	16	56	11	20	5	2	1	11	.357	58	7	1	.985
1979—Modesto	Calif.	C	56	180	26	51	8	2	1	33	.283	237	29	3	.989
1980—West Haven	East.	C-OF	91	310	36	74	13	1	8	33	.239	287	53	7	.980
1981—West Haven	East.	C-OF	66	153	23	48	6	1	7	29	.314	342	36	4	.990
1981—Tacoma	P.C.	C	20	57	5	11	3	0	0	6	.193	83	3	1	.989
1982—Tacoma	P.C.	C	47	117	20	37	4	0	2	13	.316	163	13	5	.972
1983—Tacoma x	P.C.	C	34	88	8	12	0	0	1	5	.136	144	11	3	.981
1983—Oakland	Amer.	C	19	18	1	6	1	0	0	1	.333	27	2	1	.967
Major League Totals			19	18	1	6	1	0	0	1	.333	27	2	1	.967

Selected by Baltimore Orioles' organization in 6th round of free-agent draft, June 4, 1975.
†Released, November 1, 1976; signed by Bristol (Boston Red Sox' organization), November 22, 1976.
‡Released, April 5, 1977; signed by Salem (Independent) June 18, 1978.
§Sold to Modesto (Oakland A's organization), February 26, 1979.
xOn disabled list, July 10 to August 13, 1983.

JOSEPH JOHN CIPOLLONI
(Joe)

Born August 12, 1960, at Philadelphia, Pa.
Height, 5.08. Weight, 180.
Throws and bats righthanded.
Attended Phoenix College, Phoenix, Ariz., and
University of Arizona, Tucson, Ariz.

Led Carolina League catchers in double plays with 10 in 1983.

Year	Club	League	Pos.	G.	AB.	R.	H.	2B.	3B.	HR.	RBI.	B.A.	PO.	A.	E.	F.A.
1981—Helena		Pion.	C	15	46	5	10	2	0	1	4	.217	85	14	2	.980
1982—Spartanburg		S. Atl.	C-3B	73	230	33	59	16	0	2	29	.257	422	64	12	.976
1983—Peninsula		Carol.	C	98	347	41	80	14	1	5	39	.231	625	76	14	.980

Selected by Pittsburgh Pirates' organization in 25th round of free-agent draft, June 3, 1980.
Signed as free agent by Philadelphia Phillies' organization, August 8, 1981.

RALPH ALEXANDER CITARELLA

Born February 7, 1958, at East Orange, N.J.
Height, 6.00. Weight, 180.
Throws and bats righthanded.
Attended Florida Southern College, Lakeland, Fla., and Brevard Community College, Cocoa, Fla.

Year	Club	League	G.	IP.	W.	L.	Pct.	H.	R.	ER.	SO.	BB.	ERA.
1979—Johnson City		Ap'lachian	4	21	0	2	.000	23	15	13	16	12	5.57
1979—St. Petersburg		Florida St.	7	26	0	0	.000	31	8	5	10	11	1.73
1980—Gastonia		S. Atlantic	★51	126	11	4	.733	87	35	23	113	49	★1.64
1981—Arkansas		Texas	31	125	8	9	.491	120	57	53	81	37	3.82
1981—Springfield		Am. Assoc.	1	7	0	0	.000	7	3	3	2	2	3.86
1982—Louisville		Am. Assoc.	28	153	★15	6	.714	171	95	83	82	62	4.88
1983—Louisville		Am. Assoc.	37	109⅔	7	6	.538	122	67	58	64	41	4.76
1983—St. Louis		National	6	11	0	0	.000	8	2	2	4	3	1.64
Major League Totals			6	11	0	0	.000	8	2	2	4	3	1.64

Selected by Minnesota Twins' organization in 1st round (15th player selected) of free-agent draft, January 10, 1978.
Selected by Cincinnati Reds' organization in secondary phase of free-agent draft, June 6, 1978.
Selected by St. Louis Cardinals' organization in secondary phase of free-agent draft, June 5, 1979.

JAMES CLANCY
(Jim)

Born December 18, 1955, at Chicago, Ill.
Height, 6.04. Weight, 207.
Throws and bats righthanded.
Led American League pitchers in games started with 40 in 1982.
Tied for Gulf Coast League lead in shutouts with 2 in 1974.

Year	Club	League	G.	IP.	W.	L.	Pct.	H.	R.	ER.	SO.	BB.	ERA.
1974—Sarasota Rangers		Gulf Coast	9	53	3	3	.500	40	21	16	58	28	2.72
1975—Anderson		W. Carol.	23	148	6	13	.316	139	85	63	109	91	3.83
1976—San Antonio†‡		Texas	23	125	6	8	.429	133	94	★89	77	98	6.41
1977—Jersey City		Eastern	20	118	5	13	.278	116	87	64	99	75	4.88
1977—Toronto		American	13	77	4	9	.308	80	47	43	44	47	5.03
1978—Toronto		American	31	194	10	12	.455	199	96	88	106	91	4.08
1979—Toronto§		American	12	64	2	7	.222	65	44	39	33	31	5.48
1980—Toronto		American	34	251	13	16	.448	217	108	92	152	★128	3.30
1981—Toronto		American	22	125	6	12	.333	126	77	68	56	64	4.90
1982—Toronto		American	40	266⅔	16	14	.533	251	122	110	139	77	3.71
1983—Toronto		American	34	223	15	11	.577	238	115	97	99	61	3.91
Major League Totals			186	1200⅔	66	81	.449	1176	609	537	629	499	4.03

Selected by Texas Rangers' organization in 4th round of free-agent draft, June 5, 1974.
†On disabled list, June 15 to June 26, 1976.
‡Selected by Toronto Blue Jays from Texas Rangers in American League expansion draft, November 5, 1976.
§On disabled list, May 12 to July 4 and August 5 to October 3, 1979.

ALL-STAR GAME RECORD

Year	League	IP.	W.	L.	Pct.	H.	R.	ER.	SO.	BB.	ERA.
1982—American		1	0	0	.000	0	0	0	0	0	0.00

BRYAN DONALD CLARK

Born July 12, 1956, at Madera, Calif.
Height, 6.02. Weight, 200.
Throws and bats lefthanded.
Attended Fresno City College, Fresno, Calif.
Led Carolina League in wild pitches with 24 in 1977 and 27 in 1979.
Led Western Carolinas League in wild pitches with 31 in 1976.
Led New York-Pennsylvania League in wild pitches with 24 in 1975.
Tied for Carolina League lead in shutouts with 3 in 1979.
Tied for Gulf Coast League lead in shutouts with 2 in 1974.

Year	Club	League	G.	IP.	W.	L.	Pct.	H.	R.	ER.	SO.	BB.	ERA.
1974—Bradenton Pirates		Gulf Coast	11	62	4	6	.400	49	35	23	47	★40	3.34
1975—Charleston		W. Carol.	12	57	4	7	.364	56	48	34	38	67	5.37
1975—Niagara Falls		NYP	13	74	3	★10	.231	47	49	37	59	★71	4.50
1976—Charleston		W. Carol.	22	103	1	13	.071	97	87	70	79	104	6.12
1977—Salem		Carolina	26	125	5	★13	.278	135	105	66	108	105	4.75
1978—Charleston†		W. Carol.	12	56	1	6	.143	55	53	38	44	55	6.11
1978—Bellingham		Northwest	2	4	0	0	.000	4	1	1	6	3	2.25
1978—Stockton		California	11	27	0	4	.000	30	32	22	18	39	7.33
1979—Alexandria		Carolina	23	167	●14	5	.737	124	57	49	116	★112	2.64

— 90 —

Year Club	League	G.	IP.	W.	L.	Pct.	H.	R.	ER.	SO.	BB.	ERA.
1980—Spokane	P. Coast	8	41	2	5	.286	43	35	24	19	37	5.27
1980—Lynn	Eastern	16	116	9	5	.643	102	49	40	93	50	3.10
1981—Seattle	American	29	93	2	5	.286	92	54	45	52	55	4.35
1982—Salt Lake City	P. Coast	4	5⅓	1	1	.500	5	6	6	2	5	10.13
1982—Seattle	American	37	114⅔	5	2	.714	104	44	35	70	58	2.75
1983—Seattle‡	American	41	162⅓	7	10	.412	160	82	71	76	72	3.94
Major League Totals		107	370	14	17	.452	356	180	151	198	185	3.67

Selected by Pittsburgh Pirates' organization in 10th round of free-agent draft, June 5, 1974.
†Sold to Seattle Mariners' organization, June 12, 1978.
‡Traded to Toronto Blue Jays for Outfielder Barry Bonnell, December 9, 1983.

JACK ANTHONY CLARK

Born November 10, 1955, at New Brighton, Pa.
Height, 6.03. Weight, 205.
Throws and bats righthanded.

Led National League in game-winning RBIs with 18 in 1980 and tied for lead with 21 in 1982.
Tied for National League lead in double plays by outfielders with 5 in 1978, 7 in 1979 and 4 in 1981.
Led California League in total bases with 254 in 1974 and Texas League with 239 in 1975.
Led Texas League third basemen in putouts with 102, assists with 278, double plays with 29 and fielding percentage with .872 in 1975.
Named outfielder on THE SPORTING NEWS National League All-Star Team, 1978.

Year Club	League	Pos.	G.	AB.	R.	H.	2B.	3B.	HR.	RBI.	B.A.	PO.	A.	E.	F.A.
1973—Great Falls	Pion.	OF-P-3B	65	234	46	75	20	1	9	54	.321	73	9	1	.988
1974—Fresno	Calif.	3B	131	495	88	156	23	9	19	★117	.315	100	204	★53	.852
1975—Lafayette	Texas	★3B-OF	126	466	94	141	25	2	●23	77	.303	107	279	★56	.873
1975—San Francisco	Nat.	OF-3B	8	17	3	4	0	0	0	2	.235	8	1	0	1.000
1976—Phoenix	P. C.	OF-3B	131	470	111	152	29	★16	17	86	.323	188	23	9	.959
1976—San Francisco	Nat.	OF	26	102	14	23	6	2	2	10	.225	71	3	1	.987
1977—San Francisco	Nat.	OF	136	413	64	104	17	4	13	51	.252	226	11	6	.975
1978—San Francisco	Nat.	OF	156	592	90	181	46	8	25	98	.306	320	16	6	.982
1979—San Francisco	Nat.	OF-3B	143	527	84	144	25	2	26	86	.273	262	13	5	.971
1980—San Francisco†	Nat.	OF	127	437	77	124	20	8	22	82	.284	229	7	8	.967
1981—San Francisco	Nat.	OF	99	385	60	103	19	2	17	53	.268	193	●14	4	.981
1982—San Francisco	Nat.	OF	157	563	90	154	30	3	27	103	.274	281	10	6	.980
1983—San Francisco	Nat.	OF-1B	135	492	82	132	25	0	20	66	.268	262	20	9	.969
Major League Totals			987	3528	564	969	188	29	152	551	.275	1852	95	45	.977

Selected by San Francisco Giants' organization in 13th round of free-agent draft, June 5, 1973.
†On supplemental disabled list, August 23 to September 8, 1980.

All-STAR GAME RECORD

Year League	Pos.	AB.	R.	H.	2B.	3B.	HR.	RBI.	B.A.	PO.	A.	E.	F.A.
1978—National	OF	1	0	0	0	0	0	0	.000	0	0	0	.000
1979—National	PH	1	0	0	0	0	0	0	.000	0	0	0	.000
All-Star Game Totals		2	0	0	0	0	0	0	.000	0	0	0	.000

PITCHING RECORD

Year Club	League	G.	IP.	W.	L.	Pct.	H.	R.	ER.	SO.	BB.	ERA.
1973—Great Falls	Pioneer	5	15	0	2	.000	24	24	10	17	19	6.00

ROBERT CALE CLARK
(Bobby)

Born June 13, 1955, at Sacramento, Calif.
Height, 6.00. Weight, 190.
Throws and bats righthanded.
Attended Riverside City Junior College, Riverside, Calif. and University of California, Riverside, Calif.

Led Texas League in total bases with 297 in 1978.
Led Midwest League outfielders in double plays with 9 in 1977.
Led Pioneer League outfielders in fielding percentage with .978 in 1975.
Named Texas League Most Valuable Player, 1978.

Year Club	League	Pos.	G.	AB.	R.	H.	2B.	3B.	HR.	RBI.	B.A.	PO.	A.	E.	F.A.
1975—Idaho Falls	Pion.	OF-1B-3B	●72	253	43	64	7	★9	4	38	.253	154	10	6	.965
1976—Quad Cities	Midw.	★OF-1B	●129	477	82	139	19	8	10	77	.291	365	★28	10	.975
1977—Salinas	Calif.	★O-C-1B	137	524	107	149	19	10	23	88	.284	311	11	7	★.979
1978—El Paso	Texas	OF	129	491	108	155	35	7	★31	★111	.316	261	★23	9	.969
1979—Salt Lake City	P. C.	OF	129	474	85	144	30	9	15	91	.304	★328	12	7	.980
1979—California	Amer.	OF	19	54	8	16	2	2	1	5	.296	41	4	1	.978
1980—Salt Lake City	P. C.	OF	33	113	18	39	6	4	4	21	.345	57	2	1	.983
1980—California	Amer.	OF	78	261	26	60	10	1	5	23	.230	213	6	4	.982
1981—California	Amer.	OF	34	88	12	22	2	1	4	19	.250	66	5	0	1.000
1982—California	Amer.	OF	102	90	11	19	1	0	2	8	.211	88	2	0	1.000
1983—California†	Amer.	OF-3B	76	212	17	49	9	1	5	21	.231	122	0	0	1.000
1983—Edmonton‡	P.C.	OF	7	31	3	8	2	0	2	7	.258	7	0	0	1.000
Major League Totals			309	705	74	166	24	5	17	76	.235	530	17	5	.991

Selected by Houston Astros' organization in 14th round of free-agent draft, June 5, 1973.
Selected by California Angels' organization in secondary phase of free-agent draft, January 9, 1975.

†On disabled list, July 20 to September 3, 1983; included rehabilitation disability assignment to Edmonton, August 16 to August 26, 1983.
‡Traded to Milwaukee Brewers for Pitcher Jim Slaton, December 20, 1983.

CHAMPIONSHIP SERIES RECORD

Year Club	League	Pos.	G.	AB.	R.	H.	2B.	3B.	HR.	RBI.	B.A.	PO.	A.	E.	F.A.
1979—California	Amer.	OF	1	3	0	0	0	0	0	0	.000	3	0	0	1.000
1982—California	Amer.	OF	2	0	0	0	0	0	0	0	.000	1	0	0	1.000
Championship Series Totals			3	3	0	0	0	0	0	0	.000	4	0	0	1.000

TERRY LEE CLARK

Born October 18, 1960, at Los Angeles, Calif.
Height, 6.02. Weight, 195.
Throws and bats righthanded.
Attended Mount San Antonio College, Walnut, Calif.

Led Florida State League in games finished in relief with 51 in 1982.
Led South Atlantic League in games finished in relief with 51 in 1981.
Led Appalachian League in saves with 8 in 1979.

Year Club	League	G.	IP.	W.	L.	Pct.	H.	R.	ER.	SO.	BB.	ERA.
1979—Johnson City	Ap'lachian	•23	32	4	2	.667	31	10	7	22	11	1.97
1980—Gastonia	S. Atlantic	49	88	4	7	.364	82	34	31	50	22	3.17
1981—Gastonia	S. Atlantic	*53	75	4	5	.444	56	23	18	66	25	2.16
1982—St. Petersburg	Florida St.	*58	88⅓	10	7	.588	81	32	25	61	34	2.55
1983—Arkansas	Texas	52	81⅓	6	6	.500	68	31	29	63	19	3.21

Selected by St. Louis Cardinals' organization in 22nd round of free-agent draft, June 5, 1979.

STANLEY MARTIN CLARKE
(Stan)

Born August 9, 1960, at Toledo, O.
Height, 5.11. Weight, 160.
Throws and bats lefthanded.
Attended University of Toledo, Toledo, O.

Led Pioneer League in balks with 6 and tied for lead in complete games with 6 in 1981.

Year Club	League	G.	IP.	W.	L.	Pct.	H.	R.	ER.	SO.	BB.	ERA.
1981—Medicine Hat	Pioneer	17	94	8	4	.667	96	54	42	112	35	4.02
1982—Florence	S. Atlantic	50	95	6	4	.600	60	26	20	136	52	1.89
1982—Knoxville	Southern	11	16	0	1	.000	11	3	3	12	3	1.69
1983—Knoxville	Southern	26	43⅓	2	4	.333	30	18	12	51	20	2.49
1983—Toronto	American	10	11	1	1	.500	10	4	4	7	5	3.27
1983—Syracuse	Int'national	33	53	0	3	.000	39	26	17	58	34	2.89
Major League Totals		10	11	1	1	.500	10	4	4	7	5	3.27

Selected by Toronto Blue Jays' organization in 6th round of free-agent draft, June 8, 1981.

MARK ALAN CLEAR

Born May 27, 1956, at Los Angeles, Calif.
Height, 6.04. Weight, 200.
Throws and bats righthanded.
Attended Mount San Antonio College, Walnut, Calif.
Nephew of Bob Clear, minor league pitcher, 1945 through 1955; minor league player-manager, 1956 through 1961; minor league manager, 1962 through 1973; scout with California Angels, 1974 and 1975; and coach with California Angels since 1976.

Major League saves: 1979 (14), 1980 (9), 1981 (9), 1982 (14), 1983 (4). Total—50.
Led Appalachian League in hit batsmen with 11 in 1974.
Named American League Rookie Pitcher of the Year by THE SPORTING NEWS, 1979.

Year Club	League	G.	IP.	W.	L.	Pct.	H.	R.	ER.	SO.	BB.	ERA.
1974—Pulaski†	Ap'lachian	14	51	0	1	.000	73	*69	49	38	43	8.65
1975—Idaho Falls	Pioneer	13	28	1	2	.333	24	14	6	29	30	1.93
1976—Quad Cities	Midwest	30	144	8	10	.444	135	84	63	109	111	3.94
1977—Quad Cities	Midwest	13	74	6	3	.667	64	47	40	48	50	4.86
1977—Salinas	California	13	44	1	4	.200	49	36	32	26	45	6.55
1978—Salinas	California	10	53	3	5	.375	51	38	32	55	40	5.43
1978—El Paso	Texas	31	52	4	2	.667	28	14	14	80	32	2.42
1979—California	American	52	109	11	5	.688	87	48	44	98	68	3.63
1980—California‡	American	58	106	11	11	.500	82	51	39	105	65	3.31
1981—Boston	American	34	77	8	3	.727	69	36	35	82	51	4.09
1982—Boston	American	55	105	14	9	.609	92	39	35	109	61	3.00
1983—Boston	American	48	96	4	5	.444	101	71	67	81	68	6.28
Major League Totals		247	493	48	33	.593	431	245	220	475	313	4.02

Selected by Philadelphia Phillies' organization in 8th round of free-agent draft, June 5, 1974.
†Released, April 2, 1975; signed by California Angels' organization, June 16, 1975.
‡Traded with Third Baseman Carney Lansford and Outfielder Rick Miller to Boston Red Sox for Shortstop Rick Burleson and Third Baseman Butch Hobson, December 10, 1980.

CHAMPIONSHIP SERIES RECORD

Year Club	League	G.	IP.	W.	L.	Pct.	H.	R.	ER.	SO.	BB.	ERA.
1979—California	American	1	5⅔	0	0	.000	4	3	3	3	2	4.76

Year	League	IP.	W.	L.	Pct.	H.	R.	ER.	SO.	BB.	ERA.
1979—American		2	0	0	.000	2	1	1	0	1	4.50

Member of American League All-Star Team in 1982; did not play.

WILLIAM ROGER CLEMENS

(Known by middle name.)

Born August 4, 1962, at Dayton, O.

Height, 6.04. Weight, 205.

Throws and bats righthanded.

Attended San Jacinto College (North), Houston, Tex.,

and University of Texas, Austin, Tex.

Year	Club	League	G.	IP.	W.	L.	Pct.	H.	R.	ER.	SO.	BB.	ERA.
1983—Winter Haven		Florida St.	4	29	3	1	.750	22	4	4	36	0	1.24
1983—New Britain		Eastern	7	52	4	1	.800	31	8	8	59	12	1.38

Selected by New York Mets' organization in 12th round of free-agent draft, June 8, 1981.

Selected by Boston Red Sox' organization in 1st round (19th player selected) of free-agent draft, June 6, 1983.

WESLEY WAYNE CLEMENTS

(Wes)

Born May 28, 1958, at Inglewood, Calif.

Height, 6.04. Weight, 195.

Throws and bats righthanded.

Attended El Camino College, Torrance, Calif., and University of Arizona, Tucson, Ariz.

Led Pacific Coast League in strikeouts with 155 in 1983.

Led Florida State League in game-winning RBIs with 14 in 1981.

Year	Club	League	Pos.	G.	AB.	R.	H.	2B.	3B.	HR.	RBI.	B.A.	PO.	A.	E.	F.A.
1980—Sarasota Astros		Gulf C.	1B	54	193	37	58	15	0	6	34	.301	516	28	12	.978
1980—Daytona Beach		Fla. St.	1B	4	13	2	4	0	0	1	1	.308	29	0	1	.967
1981—Daytona Beach		Fla. St.	1B-3B	129	415	72	123	20	2	*19	83	.296	1048	68	21	.982
1982—Columbus†		South.	1B	67	252	46	79	18	1	14	52	.313	586	41	12	.981
1982—Tucson†		P. C.	1B	48	176	29	50	10	2	6	25	.284	333	35	6	.984
1983—Tucson		P. C.	1B	132	480	83	123	38	5	20	89	.256	1061	100	*25	.979

Selected by Houston Astros' organization in 6th round of free-agent draft, June 3, 1980.

†On disabled list, August 17 to August 28, 1982.

JAMES STANLEY COCANOWER

(Jaime)

Nickname pronounced HI-me.

Born February 14, 1957, at Balboa Heights, Canal Zone

Height, 6.04. Weight, 200.

Throws and bats righthanded.

Received Bachelor of Business Administration degree in accounting

from Baylor University, Waco, Tex., in 1980.

Led California League in balks with 6 in 1980.

Named California League co-Most Valuable Player, 1980.

Year	Club	League	G.	IP.	W.	L.	Pct.	H.	R.	ER.	SO.	BB.	ERA.
1978—Burlington†		Midwest						(Did not play)					
1979—Stockton‡		California	20	78	2	4	.333	73	42	36	36	45	4.15
1980—Stockton		California	27	●198	17	5	.773	143	74	48	132	105	2.18
1981—Vancouver		P. Coast	26	137	6	12	.333	144	95	86	78	102	5.65
1982—Vancouver		P. Coast	14	74	4	3	.571	81	49	40	32	59	4.86
1982—El Paso§		Texas	9	62⅓	3	1	.750	73	36	23	29	30	3.32
1983—Vancouver x		P. Coast	23	153⅓	10	10	.500	177	100	82	79	59	4.81
1983—Milwaukee		American	5	30	2	0	1.000	21	8	6	8	12	1.80
Major League Totals			5	30	2	0	1.000	21	8	6	8	12	1.80

Signed as free agent by Milwaukee Brewers' organization, June 7, 1978.

†On disabled list, June 17 to September 27, 1978.

‡On temporary inactive list, August 16 to September 8, 1979.

§On temporary inactive list, June 30 to July 15, 1982.

xOn disabled list, July 15 to July 24, 1983.

DAVID CARTER COCHRANE

(Dave)

Born January 31, 1963, at Riverside, Calif.

Height, 6.01. Weight, 175.

Throws right and bats left and righthanded.

Led Carolina League in game-winning RBIs with 18 in 1983.

Led New York-Pennsylvania League batters in strikeouts with 117 and intentional bases on balls received with 7 in 1982.

Year	Club	League	Pos.	G.	AB.	R.	H.	2B.	3B.	HR.	RBI.	B.A.	PO.	A.	E.	F.A.
1982—Little Falls		NYP	3B	70	269	51	81	16	2	22	62	.301	49	110	*29	.846
1983—Lynchburg		Carol.	3B	120	445	73	117	16	1	25	*102	.263	66	167	26	.900

Selected by New York Mets' organization in 4th round of free-agent draft, June 8, 1981.

CHRISTOPHER ALLEN CODIROLI
Name pronounced Coda-RO-lee.
(Chris)

Born March 26, 1958, at Oxnard, Calif.
Height, 6.01. Weight, 160.
Throws and bats righthanded.
Attended San Jose City College, San Jose, Calif.,
and San Jose State University, San Jose, Calif.

Year Club	League	G.	IP.	W.	L.	Pct.	H.	R.	ER.	SO.	BB.	ERA.
1978—Lakeland	Florida St.	16	102	4	6	.400	93	44	37	72	40	3.26
1978—Montgomery	Southern	10	78	5	2	.714	60	20	17	57	24	1.96
1979—Montgomery†	Southern	8	49	2	3	.400	41	24	18	34	27	3.31
1980—Lakeland‡	Florida St.	9	50	1	1	.500	33	13	10	26	19	1.80
1980—Montgomery§	Southern	2	4	0	1	.000	6	7	6	1	4	13.50
1981—San Jose	California	14	35	3	2	.600	23	8	6	26	24	1.54
1981—West Haven	Eastern	21	50	3	2	.600	35	25	15	47	25	2.70
1982—West Haven x	Eastern	12	45	6	1	.857	37	14	12	45	19	2.40
1982—Tacoma	P. Coast	16	121½	10	3	*.769	100	36	26	85	21	*1.90
1982—Oakland	American	3	16⅔	1	2	.333	16	8	8	5	4	4.32
1983—Oakland	American	37	205⅔	12	12	.500	208	115	102	85	72	4.46
Major League Totals		40	222⅓	13	14	.481	224	123	110	90	76	4.45

Selected by Detroit Tigers' organization in 1st round (11th player selected) of free-agent draft, January 10, 1978.
†On disabled list, May 25, 1979 through remainder of season.
‡On disabled list, April 11 to June 10, 1980.
§Released, April 3, 1981; signed by Oakland A's organization, April 14, 1981.
xOn disabled list, April 19 to April 29, 1982.

WILLIAM RODGERS COLE
(Roger)

Born March 21, 1961, at Ann Arbor, Mich.
Height, 5.09. Weight, 160.
Throws and bats righthanded.
Attended Wiley College, Marshall, Texas.

Year Club	League	G.	IP.	W.	L.	Pct.	H.	R.	ER.	SO.	BB.	ERA.
1982—Helena	Pioneer	13	86⅔	7	3	.700	76	43	31	69	27	3.22
1983—Peninsula	Carolina	25	167⅓	9	13	.409	173	91	72	105	73	3.87

Selected by Philadelphia Phillies' organization in 27th round of free-agent draft, June 7, 1982.

VINCENT MAURICE COLEMAN
(Vince)

Born September 22, 1960, at Jacksonville, Fla.
Height, 6.00. Weight, 170.
Throws and bats righthanded.
Received degree in physical education from Florida A&M University, Tallahassee, Fla.
Cousin of Greg Coleman, punter with Minnesota Vikings.

Led South Atlantic League in stolen bases with 145 and caught stealing with 31 in 1983.
Tied for Appalachian League lead in stolen bases with 43 in 1982.
Named South Atlantic League Most Valuable Player, 1983.

Year Club	League	Pos.	G.	AB.	R.	H.	2B.	3B.	HR.	RBI.	B.A.	PO.	A.	E.	F.A.
1982—Johnson City	Appal.	OF	58	212	40	53	2	1	0	16	.250	123	7	8	.942
1983—Macon	S. Atl.	OF	113	446	99	156	8	7	0	53	*.350	225	18	8	.968

Selected by Philadelphia Phillies' organization in 20th round of free-agent draft, June 8, 1981.
Selected by St. Louis Cardinals' organization in 10th round of free-agent draft, June 7, 1982.

DARNELL COLES
First name pronounced Darr-NELL.

Born June 2, 1962, at San Bernardino, Calif.
Height, 6.01. Weight, 180.
Throws and bats righthanded.
Attended Orange Coast College, Costa Mesa, Calif.

Led Midwest League shortstops in double plays with 66 in 1981.

Year Club	League	Pos.	G.	AB.	R.	H.	2B.	3B.	HR.	RBI.	B.A.	PO.	A.	E.	F.A.
1980—Bellingham	N'west	SS	35	117	23	25	3	1	2	12	.214	37	80	*28	.807
1981—Wausau	Midw.	SS	111	354	53	97	20	3	9	48	.274	154	335	52	.904
1982—Bakersfield	Calif.	SS	136	482	91	146	24	4	11	55	.303	200	419	*73	.895
1983—Chattanooga	South.	SS	72	261	49	75	10	4	5	24	.287	131	232	30	.924
1983—Salt Lake City	P. C.	SS	61	234	43	74	12	5	10	41	.316	100	178	25	.917
1983—Seattle	Amer.	3B	27	92	9	26	7	0	1	6	.283	17	47	4	.941
Major League Totals			27	92	9	26	7	0	1	6	.283	17	47	4	.941

Selected by Seattle Mariners' organization in 1st round (sixth player selected) of free-agent draft, June 3, 1980.

DAVID S. COLLINS
(Dave)

Born October 20, 1952, at Rapid City, S. D.
Height, 5.10. Weight, 175.
Throws left and bats left and righthanded.
Attended Mesa Community College, Mesa, Ariz.

Major league stolen bases: 1975 (24), 1976 (32), 1977 (25), 1978 (7), 1979 (16), 1980 (79), 1981 (26), 1982 (13), 1983 (31). Total—253.
Led Pioneer League outfielders in double plays with 3 in 1972.
Named Pioneer League Most Valuable Player, 1972.

Year	Club	League	Pos.	G.	AB.	R.	H.	2B.	3B.	HR.	RBI.	B.A.	PO.	A.	E.	F.A.
1972—Idaho Falls	Pion.	★OF-1B	68	252	40	69	8	★8	1	27	.274	101	★11	3	.974
1973—Quad Cities†	Midw.	OF	110	387	61	100	15	7	4	49	.258	229	10	11	.956
1974—Salinas	Calif.	OF-1B	39	143	30	49	3	5	1	21	.343	109	0	5	.956
1974—El Paso	Texas	1B-OF	82	324	64	114	15	4	4	49	★.352	381	14	12	.971
1975—Salt Lake City	P. C.	OF	51	193	41	60	7	6	0	24	.311	58	2	1	.984
1975—California	Amer.	OF	93	319	41	85	13	4	3	29	.266	159	3	2	.988
1976—Salt Lake City	P. C.	OF	35	136	28	49	13	4	0	12	.360	50	3	2	.964
1976—California‡	Amer.	OF	99	365	45	96	12	1	4	28	263	160	3	1	.994
1977—Seattle§	Amer.	OF	120	402	46	96	9	3	5	28	.239	124	6	2	.985
1978—Cincinnati	Nat.	OF	102	102	13	22	1	0	0	7	.216	30	1	1	.969
1979—Cincinnati	Nat.	OF-1B	122	396	59	126	16	4	3	35	.318	223	3	4	.983
1980—Cincinnati	Nat.	OF	144	551	94	167	20	4	3	35	.303	337	5	5	.986
1981—Cincinnati x	Nat.	OF	95	360	63	98	18	6	3	23	.272	167	4	4	.977
1982—New York y	Amer.	OF-1B	111	348	41	88	12	3	3	25	.253	498	28	7	.987
1983—Toronto z	Amer.	OF-1B	118	402	55	109	12	4	1	34	.271	270	9	3	.989
National League Totals			463	1409	229	413	55	14	9	100	.293	757	13	14	.982
American League Totals			541	1836	228	474	58	15	16	144	.258	1211	49	15	.988
Major League Totals			1004	3245	457	887	113	29	25	244	.273	1968	62	29	.986

Selected by Cincinnati Reds' organization in 23rd round of free-agent draft, June 8, 1971.
Selected by Kansas City Royals' organization in secondary phase of free-agent draft, January 12, 1972.
Selected by California Angels' organization in secondary phase of free-agent draft, June 6, 1972.
†On disabled list, May 21 to May 31, 1973.
‡Selected by Seattle Mariners in special American League expansion draft, November 5, 1976.
§Traded to Cincinnati Reds for Pitcher Shane Rawley, December 9, 1977.
xGranted free agency, November 13, 1981; signed by New York Yankees, December 23, 1981.
yTraded with Pitcher Mike Morgan, First Baseman Fred McGriff and a reported $400,000 to Toronto Blue Jays for Pitcher Dale Murray and Outfielder-Catcher Tom Dodd, December 9, 1982.
zOn supplemental disabled list, June 4 to June 22, 1983.

CHAMPIONSHIP SERIES RECORD

Year	Club	League	Pos.	G.	AB.	R.	H.	2B.	3B.	HR.	RBI.	B.A.	PO.	A.	E.	F.A.
1979—Cincinnati	Nat.	OF	3	14	0	5	1	0	0	1	.357	5	0	0	1.000

STEVEN MICHAEL COMER
(Steve)

Born January 13, 1954, at Minneapolis, Minn.
Height, 6.03. Weight, 205.
Throws right and bats right and lefthanded.
Attended University of Minnesota, Minneapolis, Minn.

Tied for Gulf Coast League lead in shutouts with 2 in 1976.

Year	Club	League	G.	IP.	W.	L.	Pct.	H.	R.	ER.	SO.	BB.	ERA.
1976—Sarasota Rangers	Gulf Coast	9	60	7	2	.778	35	9	6	40	18	★0.90
1977—Tulsa	Texas	14	105	7	6	.538	102	50	37	53	28	3.17
1977—Tucson	P. Coast	14	84	6	4	.600	101	45	39	32	33	4.18
1978—Texas	American	30	117	11	5	.688	107	36	30	65	37	2.31
1979—Texas	American	36	242	17	12	.586	230	114	99	86	84	3.68
1980—Texas†	American	12	42	2	4	.333	65	41	37	9	22	7.93
1980—Tulsa	Texas	3	14	1	2	.333	22	10	10	8	2	6.43
1981—Texas	American	36	77	8	2	.800	70	25	22	2	31	2.57
1982—Texas‡§ x	American	37	97	1	6	.143	133	64	55	23	36	5.10
1983—Salt Lake City y-Portland	P. Coast	29	122	8	4	.667	137	65	51	59	38	3.76
1983—Philadelphia	National	3	8⅔	1	0	1.000	11	6	5	1	3	5.19
American League Totals		151	575	39	29	.574	605	280	243	205	210	3.80
National League Totals		3	8⅔	1	0	1.000	11	6	5	1	3	5.19
Major League Totals		154	583⅔	40	29	.580	616	286	248	206	213	3.82

Signed as free agent by Texas Rangers' organization, July 10, 1976.
†On disabled list, May 25 to June 28 and August 15 to September 11, 1980.
‡On disabled list, July 7 to August 3, 1982.
§Released, December 13, 1982; signed by New York Yankees, January 21, 1983.
xReleased, March 28, 1983; signed by Seattle Mariners' organization, April 11, 1983.
yReleased, June 16, 1983; signed by Philadelphia Phillies' organization, June 22, 1983.

—DID YOU KNOW—

That in the five games in which a player had a three-homer performance in 1983, his team won by an 8-7 score three times?

KEITH MARTIN COMSTOCK

Born December 23, 1955, at San Francisco, Calif.
Height, 6.00. Weight, 160.
Throws and bats lefthanded.
Attended Canada College, Redwood City, Calif.

Tied for Southern League lead in shutouts with 3 in 1983.

Year—Club	League	G.	IP.	W.	L.	Pct.	H.	R.	ER.	SO.	BB.	ERA.
1976—Idaho Falls†	Pioneer	15	37	1	4	.200	33	18	16	45	32	3.89
1977—Quad Cities	Midwest	18	32	1	0	1.000	22	18	18	39	18	5.06
1977—Salinas	California	23	33	1	1	.500	35	26	17	41	18	4.64
1978—Salinas	California	27	82	6	4	.600	70	31	26	71	46	2.85
1979—El Paso‡	Texas	16	63	2	5	.286	95	64	50	18	35	7.14
1980—West Haven	Eastern	29	73	2	4	.333	64	40	34	52	37	4.19
1981—West Haven	Eastern	35	145	8	7	.533	123	76	66	133	80	4.10
1982—West Haven	Eastern	24	125	9	5	.643	99	48	42	132	69	3.02
1982—Tacoma§	P. Coast	5	27⅔	1	2	.333	34	24	22	22	12	7.16
1983—Birmingham x	Southern	37	145⅔	12	3	●.800	130	58	52	136	63	3.21

Selected by California Angels' organization in 5th round of free-agent draft, January 7, 1976.
†On disabled list, July 29, 1976 through remainder of season.
‡Released, July 6, 1979; signed by West Haven (Oakland A's organization), February 29, 1980.
§Sold to Detroit Tigers' organization, March 28, 1983.
xGranted free agency, October 23, 1983.

DAVID ISMAEL CONCEPCION (BONITEZ)

Name pronounced Con-sep-see-OHN.

(Dave)

Born June 17, 1948, at Ocumare de la Costa, Aragua, Venezuela.
Height, 6.01. Weight, 180.
Throws and bats righthanded.
Attended College Augustin Codazzi, Aragua, Venezuela.

Tied major league records for most stolen bases by pinch-runner, inning, (2), July 7, 1974 (1st game, 7th inning); most double plays by shortstop, game, (5), June 25, 1975.
Major league stolen bases: 1970 (10), 1971 (9), 1972 (13), 1973 (22), 1974 (41), 1975 (33), 1976 (21), 1977 (29), 1978 (23), 1979 (19), 1980 (12), 1981 (4), 1982 (13), 1983 (14). Total—263.
Led National League in game-winning RBIs with 14 in 1981.
Tied for National League lead in grounding into double plays with 21 in 1983.
Led National League shortstops in total chances with 805 in 1974 and 837 in 1976.
Tied for National League lead in double plays by shortstops with 102 in 1979.
Led Southern League shortstops in double plays with 64 in 1969.
Led Florida State League shortstops in fielding percentage with .953 in 1968.
Named shortstop on THE SPORTING NEWS National League All-Star Team, 1974, 1976, 1977 and 1981.
Named shortstop on THE SPORTING NEWS National League All-Star fielding team, 1974 through 1977 and 1979.
Named shortstop on THE SPORTING NEWS National League Silver Slugger team, 1981 and 1982.

Year—Club	League	Pos.	G.	AB.	R.	H.	2B.	3B.	HR.	RBI.	B.A.	PO.	A.	E.	F.A.
1968—Tampa	Fla. St.	SS-2B	120	329	47	77	11	1	0	22	.234	151	239	20	.951
1969—Asheville	South.	SS	96	340	47	100	11	5	1	37	.294	★157	★292	★29	★.939
1969—Indianapolis	A. A.	S-2-3-O	42	167	29	57	7	1	0	17	.341	76	128	9	.958
1970—Cincinnati	Nat.	SS-2B	101	265	38	69	6	3	1	19	.260	144	247	22	.947
1971—Cincinnati†	Nat.	S-2-3-O	130	327	24	67	4	4	1	20	.205	182	310	13	.974
1972—Cincinnati	Nat.	SS-3B-2B	119	378	40	79	13	2	2	29	.209	197	372	19	.968
1973—Cincinnati‡	Nat.	SS-OF	89	328	39	94	18	3	8	46	.287	167	292	12	.975
1974—Cincinnati	Nat.	★SS-OF	160	594	70	167	25	1	14	82	.281	239	★536	30	.963
1975—Cincinnati	Nat.	SS-3B	140	507	62	139	23	1	5	49	.274	241	446	16	.977
1976—Cincinnati	Nat.	SS	152	576	74	162	28	7	9	69	.281	★304	★506	27	.968
1977—Cincinnati	Nat.	SS	156	572	59	155	26	3	8	64	.271	280	490	11	★.986
1978—Cincinnati	Nat.	SS	153	565	75	170	33	4	6	67	.301	255	459	23	.969
1979—Cincinnati	Nat.	SS	149	590	91	166	25	3	16	84	.281	284	495	27	.967
1980—Cincinnati	Nat.	SS-2B	156	622	72	162	31	8	5	77	.260	265	451	16	.978
1981—Cincinnati	Nat.	SS	106	421	57	129	28	0	5	67	.306	208	322	22	.960
1982—Cincinnati	Nat.	SS-1B-3B	147	572	48	164	25	4	5	53	.287	271	459	17	.977
1983—Cincinnati	Nat.	SS-3B-1B	143	528	54	123	22	0	1	47	.233	227	387	13	.979
Major League Totals			1901	6845	803	1846	307	43	86	773	.270	3264	5772	268	.971

Signed as free agent by Cincinnati Reds' organization, September 12, 1967.
†On disabled list March 21 to April 20, 1971.
‡On disabled list July 22, 1973 through remainder of season.

CHAMPIONSHIP SERIES RECORD

Tied World Series records for most sacrifice flies, total Series (3); fewest chances accepted by shortstop, game (0), October 16, 1975; one or more hits, each game, four-game Series, 1976

Year—Club	League	Pos.	G.	AB.	R.	H.	2B.	3B.	HR.	RBI.	B.A.	PO.	A.	E.	F.A.
1970—Cincinnati	Nat.	PR-SS	3	0	0	0	0	0	0	0	.000	1	1	0	1.000
1972—Cincinnati	Nat.	PH-S-PR	3	2	0	0	0	0	0	0	.000	0	0	0	.000
1975—Cincinnati	Nat.	SS	3	11	2	5	0	0	1	1	.455	6	8	1	.933
1976—Cincinnati	Nat.	SS	3	10	4	2	1	0	0	0	.200	2	12	0	1.000
1979—Cincinnati	Nat.	SS	3	14	1	6	1	0	0	0	.429	3	14	0	1.000
Championship Series Totals			15	37	7	13	2	0	1	1	.351	12	35	1	.979

WORLD SERIES RECORD

Tied World Series records for most sacrifice flies, total Series (3); fewest chances accepted by shortstop, game (0), October 16, 1975; one or more hits, each game, four-game Series, 1976.

Year Club	League	Pos.	G.	AB.	R.	H.	2B.	3B.	HR.	RBI.	B.A.	PO.	A.	E.	F.A.
1970—Cincinnati............	Nat.	SS	3	9	0	3	0	1	0	3	.333	2	2	0	1.000
1972—Cincinnati............	Nat.	S-PR-PH	6	13	2	4	0	1	0	2	.308	4	11	1	.938
1975—Cincinnati............	Nat.	SS	7	28	3	5	1	0	1	4	.179	12	22	1	.971
1976—Cincinnati............	Nat.	SS	4	14	1	5	1	1	0	3	.357	6	11	1	.944
World Series Totals.....................................			20	64	6	17	2	3	1	12	.266	24	46	3	.959

ALL STAR GAME RECORD

Year League	Pos.	AB.	R.	H.	2B.	3B.	HR.	RBI.	B.A.	PO.	A.	E.	F.A.
1975—National	SS	2	0	1	0	0	0	0	.500	1	1	1	.667
1976—National	SS	2	0	1	0	0	0	0	.500	2	3	0	1.000
1977—National	SS	1	0	0	0	0	0	0	.000	1	1	0	1.000
1978—National	SS	0	1	0	0	0	0	0	.000	2	0	0	1.000
1980—National	SS	1	1	0	0	0	0	0	.000	0	2	0	1.000
1981—National	SS	3	0	0	0	0	0	0	.000	0	0	0	.000
1982—National	SS	3	1	1	0	0	1	2	.333	1	1	0	1.000
All-Star Game Totals		12	3	3	0	0	1	2	.250	7	8	1	.938

Named to National League All-Star Team for 1973 game; replaced due to injury.
Named to National League All-Star Team for 1979 game; replaced due to injury by Larry Parrish.

ONIX CONCEPCION (CARDONA)

Name pronounced Con-CEP-see-own.
Born October 5, 1958, at Dorado, Puerto Rico.
Height, 5.06. Weight, 160.
Throws and bats righthanded.

Led California League shortstops in double plays with 85 in 1979.

Year Club	League	Pos.	G.	AB.	R.	H.	2B.	3B.	HR.	RBI.	B.A.	PO.	A.	E.	F.A.
1976—Jacksonville.........	South.	2B-SS	5	13	1	4	0	0	0	4	.308	10	18	2	.933
1976—Sarasota Royals...	Gulf C.	SS	18	47	13	11	3	0	0	4	.234	16	40	8	.875
1977—Sarasota Royals...	Gulf C.	2B-SS-1B	28	59	7	11	1	0	0	0	.186	45	37	5	.943
1978—Ft. Myers..............	Fla. St.	SS-2B	79	213	29	50	·7	0	0	13	.235	120	223	24	.935
1979—Bakersfield...........	Calif.	SS	127	504	88	151	25	3	14	75	.300	*227	*454	*55	.925
1980—Jacksonville.........	South.	SS	74	273	48	88	13	3	12	44	.322	117	249	16	.958
1980—Omaha...................	A. A.	SS	58·	210	22	59	9	3	4	34	.281	74	135	11	.950
1980—Kansas City..........	Amer.	SS	12	15	1	2	0	0	0	2	.133	5	10	3	.833
1981—Omaha...................	A. A.	SS	118	438	62	112	15	2	6	57	.256	126	211	23	.936
1981—Kansas City..........	Amer.	SS	2	0	0	0	0	0	0	0	.000	0	0	0	.000
1982—Kansas City†........	Amer.	SS-2B	74	205	17	48	9	1	0	15	.234	92	168	11	.959
1983—Kansas City..........	Amer.	3B-2B-SS	80	219	22	53	11	3	0	20	.242	92	175	15	.947
Major League Totals.....................................			168	439	40	103	20	4	0	37	.235	189	353	29	.949

Signed as free agent by Kansas City Royals' organization, March 10, 1976.
†On supplemental disabled list, April 2 to April 23, 1982.

WORLD SERIES RECORD

Year Club	League	Pos.	G.	AB.	R.	H.	2B.	3B.	HR.	RBI.	B.A.	PO.	A.	E.	F.A.
1980—Kansas City..........	Amer.	PR	3	0	0	0	0	0	0	0	.000	0	0	0	.000

DAVID BRIAN CONE

Born January 2, 1963, at Kansas City, Mo.
Height, 6.01. Weight, 180.
Throws right and bats lefthanded.

Year Club	League	G.	IP.	W.	L.	Pct.	H.	R.	ER.	SO.	BB.	ERA.
1981—Sarasota Royals-Blue	Gulf Coast	14	67	6	4	.600	52	24	19	45	33	2.55
1982—Charleston..	S. Atlantic	16	104⅔	9	2	.818	84	38	24	87	47	2.06
1982—Ft. Myers..	Florida St.	10	72⅓	7	1	.875	56	21	17	57	25	2.12
1983—Jacksonville†.................................	Southern					(Did not play)						

Selected by Kansas City Royals' organization in 3rd round of free-agent draft, June 8, 1981.
†On disabled list, April 8, 1983 through remainder of season.

FRITZIE LEE CONNALLY
(Fritz)

Born May 19, 1958, at Bryan, Tex.
Height, 6.03. Weight, 210.
Throws and bats righthanded.
Received bachelor of business administration degree in marketing
from Baylor University, Waco, Tex.

Led American Association third basemen in putouts with 104, double plays with 16, total chances with 357 and fielding percentage with .947 in 1983.
Led Texas League third basemen in fielding percentage with .948 in 1982.

Year Club	League	Pos.	G.	AB.	R.	H.	2B.	3B.	HR.	RBI.	B.A.	PO.	A.	E.	F.A.
1980—Geneva..................	NYP	1B	67	229	46	70	*18	0	14	43	.306	*674	*46	1	*.999
1981—Quad Cities...........	Midw.	1B-3B	32	105	23	33	10	0	4	23	.314	240	39	3	.989

Year	Club	League	Pos.	G.	AB.	R.	H.	2B.	3B.	HR.	RBI.	B.A.	PO.	A.	E.	F.A.
1981—Midland	Texas		3B-1B	94	344	61	106	21	0	12	57	.308	129	182	11	.966
1982—Midland	Texas		3B-1B-SS	123	428	75	124	23	3	24	91	.290	162	244	19	.955
1983—Iowa	A. A.		*3B-1B	128	451	74	130	25	2	22	85	.288	110	*234	19	.948
1983—Chicago†	Nat.		3B	8	10	0	1	0	0	0	0	.100	1	3	0	1.000
Major League Totals				8	10	0	1	0	0	0	0	.100	1	3	0	1.000

Selected by Chicago Cubs' organization in 7th round of free-agent draft, June 3, 1980.

†Traded with First Baseman Carmelo Martinez and Pitcher Craig Lefferts to San Diego Padres for Pitcher Scott Sanderson, December 7, 1983.

TIMOTHY JAMES CONROY
(Tim)

Born April 3, 1960, at Monroeville, Pa.
Height, 6.00. Weight, 180.
Throws and bats lefthanded.

Led Eastern League in wild pitches with 22 in 1979 and tied for lead with 16 in 1980.

Year	Club	League	G.	IP.	W.	L.	Pct.	H.	R.	ER.	SO.	BB.	ERA.
1978—Oakland	American	2	5	0	0	.000	3	6	4	0	9	7.20
1978—Vancouver†	P. Coast	3	9	0	1	.000	13	16	16	3	10	16.00
1979—Waterbury	Eastern	25	138	7	●14	.333	115	95	80	106	*119	5.22
1980—West Haven	Eastern	25	147	8	14	.364	160	119	101	72	93	6.18
1981—West Haven	Eastern	14	57	2	6	.250	59	50	38	51	43	6.00
1981—Modesto	California	8	39	1	3	.250	50	37	34	46	23	7.85
1982—Modesto	California	27	171⅔	15	4	.789	139	59	43	*184	62	2.25
1982—Oakland	American	5	25⅓	2	2	.500	20	13	10	17	18	3.55
1983—Oakland	American	39	162⅓	7	10	.412	141	89	71	112	98	3.94
Major League Totals		46	192⅔	9	12	.429	164	108	85	129	125	3.97

Selected by Oakland A's organization in 1st round (20th player selected) of free-agent draft, June 6, 1978.

†On disabled list, July 16 to September 1, 1978.

DOUGLAS BRICE COOK
(Doug)

Born August 2, 1962, at West Palm Beach, Fla.
Height, 6.02. Weight, 175.
Throws and bats righthanded.

Year	Club	League	G.	IP.	W.	L.	Pct.	H.	R.	ER.	SO.	BB.	ERA.
1980—Sarasota Royals Gold	Gulf Coast	8	34	0	4	.000	36	16	12	27	28	3.18
1981—Charleston	S. Atlantic	17	87	3	7	.300	98	65	56	71	64	5.79
1981—Sarasota Royals Blue	Gulf Coast	7	43	4	2	.667	28	12	11	41	24	2.30
1982—Charleston	S. Atlantic	12	75⅓	7	7	.222	58	35	29	53	36	3.46
1983—Charleston	S. Atlantic	9	52⅓	2	2	.500	50	27	20	55	29	3.44
1983—Ft. Myers	Florida St.	12	71	6	4	.600	55	25	23	66	41	2.92

Selected by Kansas City Royals' organization in 3rd round of free-agent draft, June 3, 1980.

GLEN PATRICK COOK

Born September 8, 1959, at Buffalo, N.Y.
Height, 5.10. Weight, 180.
Throws and bats righthanded.
Attended Ithaca College, Ithaca, N.Y.

Year	Club	League	G.	IP.	W.	L.	Pct.	H.	R.	ER.	SO.	BB.	ERA.
1981—Sarasota Rangers	Gulf Coast	14	43	2	2	.500	40	26	23	43	20	4.81
1982—Burlington†	Midwest	18	42⅔	3	4	.400	47	30	20	37	15	4.22
1983—Burlington	Midwest	9	52⅔	4	2	.667	50	28	24	59	24	4.10
1983—Tulsa	Texas	11	72	4	6	.400	60	33	25	70	26	3.13
1983—Oklahoma City	Am. Assoc.	3	20	0	1	.000	16	10	10	16	7	4.50

Selected by San Diego Padres' organization in 17th round of free-agent draft, June 3, 1980.
Selected by Texas Rangers' organization in 24th round of free-agent draft, June 8, 1981.
†On disabled list, June 22, 1982 through remainder of season.

CECIL CELESTER COOPER

Born December 20, 1949, at Brenham, Tex.
Height, 6.02. Weight, 190.
Throws and bats lefthanded.
Attended Prairie View A&M College, Prairie View, Tex.

Tied major league record for most strikeouts, extra-inning game (6), June 14, 1974 (15 innings).
Tied American League record for most years leading league in double plays, first baseman (4).
Hit three home runs in a game, July 27, 1979.
Led American League in total bases with 335 in 1980.
Led American League first basemen in total chances with 1,068 in 1981 and 1,550 in 1983.
Led American League first basemen in double plays with 160 in 1980, 111 in 1981, 156 in 1982 and 144 in 1983.
Tied for American League lead in game-winning RBIs with 16 in 1979.
Named first baseman on THE SPORTING NEWS American League All-Star Team, 1979 through 1982.
Named first baseman on THE SPORTING NEWS American League All-Star fielding team, 1979 and 1980.
Named first baseman on THE SPORTING NEWS American League Silver Slugger team, 1980 through 1982.
Named Midwest League Player of the Year, 1970.

Year Club	League	Pos.	G.	AB.	R.	H.	2B.	3B.	HR.	RBI.	B.A.	PO.	A.	E.	F.A.
1968—Jamestown	NYP	1B	26	84	16	38	6	0	0	6	.452	130	0	1	.992
1969—Greenville†	W. Car.	1B-OF	62	212	27	63	12	2	1	18	.297	434	32	8	.983
1970—Danville‡	Midw.	1B-OF	114	420	86	141	16	8	3	39	★.336	535	33	12	.979
1971—Winston-Salem	Carol.	1B	42	153	31	58	6	3	6	26	.379	359	21	5	.987
1971—Pawtucket	East.	1B-OF	98	367	55	126	21	2	10	60	.343	740	35	12	.985
1971—Boston	Amer.	1B	14	42	9	13	4	1	0	3	.310	82	3	1	.988
1972—Louisville	Int.	1B	134	515	86	★162	★31	9	10	78	.315	1102	78	★17	.986
1972—Boston	Amer.	1B	12	17	0	4	1	0	0	2	.235	19	0	0	1.000
1973—Pawtucket	Int.	1B	128	450	68	132	27	1	15	77	.293	1082	84	12	.990
1973—Boston	Amer.	1B	30	101	12	24	2	0	3	11	.238	227	17	4	.984
1974—Boston	Amer.	1B	121	414	55	114	24	1	8	43	.275	637	40	12	.983
1975—Boston	Amer.	1B	106	305	49	95	17	6	14	44	.311	197	20	1	.995
1976—Boston§	Amer.	1B	123	451	66	127	22	6	15	78	.282	600	42	4	.994
1977—Milwaukee	Amer.	1B	160	643	86	193	31	7	20	78	.300	1386	118	12	.992
1978—Milwaukee x	Amer.	1B	107	407	60	127	23	2	13	54	.312	842	66	11	.988
1979—Milwaukee	Amer.	1B	150	590	83	182	●44	1	24	106	.308	1323	78	10	.993
1980—Milwaukee	Amer.	1B	153	622	96	219	33	4	25	★122	.352	1336	★106	5	★.997
1981—Milwaukee	Amer.	1B	106	416	70	133	★35	1	12	60	.320	★987	72	●9	.992
1982—Milwaukee	Amer.	1B	155	654	104	205	38	3	32	121	.313	1428	98	5	.997
1983—Milwaukee	Amer.	1B	160	661	106	203	37	3	30	●126	.307	★1452	87	11	.993
Major League Totals			1397	5323	796	1639	311	35	196	848	.308	10516	747	85	.993

Selected by Boston Red Sox' organization in 27th round of free-agent draft, June 7, 1968.
†On temporary inactive list, April 13 to June 4, 1969.
‡Drafted by St. Louis Cardinals, November 30, 1970; returned, April 5, 1971.
§Traded to Milwaukee Brewers for First Baseman George Scott and Outfielder Bernie Carbo, December 6, 1976.
xOn supplemental disabled list, June 9 to July 21, 1978.

DIVISION SERIES RECORD

Year Club	League	Pos.	G.	AB.	R.	H.	2B.	3B.	HR.	RBI.	B.A.	PO.	A.	E.	F.A.
1981—Milwaukee	Amer.	1B	5	18	1	4	0	0	0	3	.222	47	4	1	.981

CHAMPIONSHIP SERIES RECORD

Year Club	League	Pos.	G.	AB.	R.	H.	2B.	3B.	HR.	RBI.	B.A.	PO.	A.	E.	F.A.
1975—Boston	Amer.	1B	3	10	0	4	2	0	0	1	.400	24	1	1	.962
1982—Milwaukee	Amer.	1B	5	20	1	3	2	0	0	4	.150	37	3	2	.952
Championship Series Totals			8	30	1	7	4	0	0	5	.233	61	4	3	.956

WORLD SERIES RECORD

Established World Series records for most assists by first baseman, seven-game Series (10), 1982; most chances accepted by first baseman, seven-game Series (81), 1982.

Year Club	League	Pos.	G.	AB.	R.	H.	2B.	3B.	HR.	RBI.	B.A.	PO.	A.	E.	F.A.
1975—Boston	Amer.	1B-PH	5	19	0	1	1	0	0	1	.053	40	1	0	1.000
1982—Milwaukee	Amer.	1B	7	28	3	8	1	0	1	6	.286	71	10	1	.988
World Series Totals			12	47	3	9	2	0	1	7	.191	111	11	1	.992

ALL-STAR GAME RECORD

Year League		Pos.	AB.	R.	H.	2B.	3B.	HR.	RBI.	B.A.	PO.	A.	E.	F.A.
1979—American		PH	0	0	0	0	0	0	0	.000	0	0	0	.000
1980—American		1B	1	0	0	0	0	0	0	.000	6	0	0	1.000
1982—American		1B	2	0	1	0	0	0	0	.500	5	0	0	1.000
1983—American		PH	1	1	1	0	0	0	0	1.000	0	0	0	.000
All-Star Game Totals			4	1	2	0	0	0	0	.500	11	0	0	1.000

DONALD JAMES COOPER
(Don)

Born January 15, 1957, at New York, N.Y.
Height, 6.00. Weight, 180.
Throws and bats righthanded.
Attended New York Institute of Technology, Old Westbury, N.Y.
Nephew of Robert Beier, minor league shortstop, 1952 through 1956.

Pitched 5-0, no-hit victory against Fort Myers, August 7, 1978.
Tied for International League lead in games finished in relief with 41 in 1983.
Tied for Eastern League lead in intentional bases on balls issued with 9 in 1979.

Year Club	League	G.	IP.	W.	L.	Pct.	H.	R.	ER.	SO.	BB.	ERA.
1978—Oneonta	NYP	5	20	1	2	.333	18	12	8	22	10	3.60
1978—Ft. Lauderdale	Florida St.	10	52	2	3	.400	41	22	13	34	20	2.25
1979—West Haven	Eastern	28	54	6	4	.600	49	31	26	44	30	4.33
1979—Columbus	Int'national	8	18	0	0	.000	19	11	11	14	11	5.50
1980—Nashville	Southern	32	60	9	5	.643	43	18	12	62	29	1.80
1980—Columbus†	Int'national	12	38	3	2	.600	30	11	9	29	16	2.13
1981—Minnesota	American	27	59	1	5	.167	61	33	28	33	32	4.27
1982—Toledo	Int'national	28	176⅔	12	10	.545	196	105	91	★125	69	4.64
1982—Minnesota‡	American	6	11⅓	0	1	.000	14	12	12	5	11	9.53
1983—Syracuse	Int'national	46	87	10	5	.667	69	33	31	73	33	3.21
1983—Toronto	American	4	5⅓	0	0	.000	8	4	4	5	0	6.75
Major League Totals		37	75⅔	1	6	.143	83	49	44	43	43	5.23

Selected by New York Yankees' organization in 17th round of free-agent draft, June 6, 1978.
†Drafted by Minnesota Twins, December 8, 1980.
‡Traded to Syracuse (Toronto Blue Jays' organization) for third baseman Dave Baker, December 10, 1982.

DOUGLAS MITCHELL CORBETT
(Doug)

Born November 4, 1952, at Sarasota, Fla.
Height, 6.01. Weight, 192.
Throws and bats righthanded.
Received bachelor of science degree in physical education from University of Florida, Gainesville, Fla.
Major League saves: 1980 (23), 1981 (17), 1982 (11). Total—51.
Led American League in games finished in relief with 45 and intentional bases on balls issued with 13 in 1981.
Led American Association in saves with 12 in 1978.
Led Gulf Coast League in intentional bases on balls issued with 3 in 1974.

Year Club	League	G.	IP.	W.	L.	Pct.	H.	R.	ER.	SO.	BB.	ERA.
1974—Sarasota Royals†	Gulf Coast	11	42	4	2	.667	36	22	14	32	18	3.00
1975—Tampa	Florida St.	27	61	2	3	.400	42	11	10	48	21	1.48
1976—Tampa	Florida St.	45	85	10	5	.667	86	25	21	37	22	2.22
1977—Three Rivers	Eastern	39	88	4	5	.444	72	35	27	65	40	2.76
1978—Nashville	Southern	15	25	2	1	.667	18	11	7	33	7	2.52
1978—Indianapolis	Am. Assoc.	38	68	4	4	.500	54	22	15	46	17	1.99
1979—Indianapolis‡	Am. Assoc.	∗69	110	3	6	.333	94	38	36	77	39	2.95
1980—Minnesota	American	73	136	8	6	.571	102	31	30	89	42	1.99
1981—Minnesota	American	∗54	88	2	6	.250	80	29	25	60	34	2.56
1982—Minnesota§-California	American	43	79	1	9	.100	73	45	45	52	35	5.13
1982—Spokane	P. Coast	8	19	1	0	1.000	16	11	8	19	4	3.79
1983—California	American	11	17⅓	1	1	.500	26	10	7	18	4	3.63
1983—Edmonton	P. Coast	32	83	6	6	.500	95	55	43	61	29	4.66
Major League Totals		181	320⅓	12	22	.353	281	115	107	219	115	3.01

Signed as free agent by Kansas City Royals' organization, June 11, 1974.
†Released, April 10, 1975; signed by Cincinnati Reds' organization, May 6, 1975.
‡Drafted by Minnesota Twins, December 3, 1979.
§Traded with Second Baseman Rob Wilfong to California Angels for Outfielder Tom Brunansky, Pitcher Mike Walters and cash, May 12, 1982.

ALL-STAR GAME RECORD

Member of American League All-Star team in 1981; did not play.

TIMOTHY MICHAEL CORCORAN
(Tim)

Born March 19, 1953, at Glendale, Calif.
Height, 5.11. Weight, 175.
Throws and bats lefthanded.
Attended Mount San Antonio Junior College, Walnut, Calif. and California
State University at Los Angeles, Calif.
Brother of Pat Corcoran, infielder in Oakland A's organization, 1976 through 1978.

Year Club	League	Pos.	G.	AB.	R.	H.	2B.	3B.	HR.	RBI.	B.A.	PO.	A.	E.	F.A.
1974—Bristol	Appal.	OF	27	92	20	34	6	0	3	25	.370	32	0	0	1.000
1974—Lakeland	Fla. St.	OF	36	126	15	34	1	3	1	16	.270	71	3	1	.987
1975—Montgomery	South.	OF-1B	122	388	42	95	20	3	3	36	.245	283	21	4	.987
1976—Montgomery	South.	OF-1B	129	437	66	135	25	5	5	60	.309	607	49	5	.992
1977—Evansville	A. A.	1B-OF	39	136	27	47	11	3	7	33	.346	303	21	8	.976
1977—Detroit	Amer.	OF	55	103	13	29	3	0	3	15	.282	38	0	0	1.000
1978—Detroit	Amer.	OF	116	324	37	86	13	1	1	27	.265	186	6	3	.985
1979—Evansville	A. A.	OF-1B	87	287	40	97	15	0	4	50	.338	292	23	2	.994
1979—Detroit	Amer.	OF-1B	18	22	4	5	1	0	0	6	.227	45	2	0	1.000
1980—Detroit	Amer.	1B-OF	84	153	20	44	7	1	3	18	.288	274	19	5	.983
1981—Evansville†‡	A. A.	1B-OF	106	336	48	100	17	1	8	63	.298	644	41	12	.983
1981—Minnesota§	Amer.	1B	22	51	4	9	3	0	0	4	.176	108	9	0	1.000
1982—Oklahoma City	A. A.	OF-1B	120	433	60	125	28	5	7	69	.289	330	11	9	.974
1983—Portland	P. C.	OF-1B	128	454	75	141	30	7	9	93	.311	437	32	6	.987
1983—Philadelphia	Nat.	1B	3	0	0	0	0	0	0	0	.000	4	0	0	1.000
American League Totals			295	653	78	173	27	2	7	70	.265	651	36	8	.988
National League Totals			3	0	0	0	0	0	0	0	.000	4	0	0	1.000
Major League Totals			298	653	78	173	27	2	7	70	.265	655	36	8	.989

Signed as free agent by Detroit Tigers' organization, June 10, 1974.
†On disabled list, July 14 to July 24 and July 27 to August 10, 1981.
‡Traded to Minnesota Twins, September 4, 1981, completing deal in which Minnesota traded First Baseman-Outfielder Ron Jackson to Detroit Tigers for a player to be named later, August 23, 1981.
§Released, March 26, 1982; signed by Oklahoma City (Philadelphia Phillies' organization), April 13, 1982.

PITCHING RECORD

Year Club	League	G.	IP.	W.	L.	Pct.	H.	R.	ER.	SO.	BB.	ERA.
1977—Evansville	Am. Assoc.	1	3	0	0	.000	2	2	2	2	1	6.00

TERRY JEFFREY CORMACK

Born October 13, 1962, at Long Beach, Calif.
Height, 6.00. Weight, 180.
Throws right and bats lefthanded.
Attended Long Beach City College, Long Beach, Calif.

Year Club	League	Pos.	G.	AB.	R.	H.	2B.	3B.	HR.	RBI.	B.A.	PO.	A.	E.	F.A.
1981—Bradenton Brav...	Gulf C.	C	22	75	12	27	8	1	2	16	.360	67	8	4	.949
1981—Anderson	S. Atl.	C	27	68	2	17	3	1	0	8	.250	140	12	0	1.000
1982—Anderson	S. Atl.	C	67	213	25	53	11	0	1	33	.249	306	42	16	.956
1983—Durham†	Carol.	C	87	302	35	70	14	1	11	31	.232	553	62	12	.981

Selected by Atlanta Braves' organization in 1st round (11th player selected) in free-agent draft, January 13, 1981.
†Drafted by Toronto Blue Jays, December 5, 1983.

HENRY COTTO

Name pronounced KOTT-oh.

Born January 5, 1961, at New York, N. Y.
Height, 6.02. Weight, 180.
Throws and bats righthanded.

Led Texas League in stolen bases with 52 in 1982.
Tied for American Association lead in caught stealing with 17 in 1983.
Led Texas League outfielders in total chances with 333 in 1982.

Year Club	League	Pos.	G.	AB.	R.	H.	2B.	3B.	HR.	RBI.	B.A.	PO.	A.	E.	F.A.
1980—Sarasota Cubs	Gulf C.	OF	43	166	24	47	7	5	0	30	.283	93	6	3	.971
1980—Quad Cities	Midw.	OF	19	78	9	22	1	1	0	5	.282	27	2	4	.879
1981—Quad Cities	Midw.	OF	128	493	80	144	15	6	1	46	.292	249	★23	13	.954
1982—Midland	Texas	OF	130	524	103	161	12	5	1	36	.307	★310	16	7	.979
1983—Iowa†	A. A.	OF	104	426	52	111	7	10	0	35	.261	253	8	7	.974

Signed as free agent by Chicago Cubs' organization, June 7, 1980.
†On disabled list, May 10 to May 30, 1983.

MICHAEL EUGENE COUCHEE

Name pronounced Cu-CHAY.

(Mike)

Born December 4, 1957, at San Jose, Calif.
Height, 6.00. Weight, 190.
Throws and bats righthanded.
Attended San Diego State University, San Diego, Calif.;
San Jose City College, San Jose, Calif., and
University of Southern California, Los Angeles, Calif.

Led Texas League in saves with 19, games finished in relief with 49 and intentional bases on balls issued with 13 in 1982.
Led California League in saves with 16 in 1981.
Tied for Northwest League lead in intentional bases on balls issued with 5 in 1980.

Year Club	League	G.	IP.	W.	L.	Pct.	H.	R.	ER.	SO.	BB.	ERA.
1980—Grays Harbor†	Northwest	24	51	4	4	.500	43	22	16	41	25	2.82
1980—Reno	California	2	2	0	0	.000	2	3	2	3	1	9.00
1981—Reno	California	53	68	7	5	.583	73	41	35	44	23	4.63
1982—Amarillo	Texas	51	87	7	5	.583	87	35	24	52	29	2.48
1982—Hawaii	P. Coast	11	17	3	1	.750	11	4	4	11	3	2.12
1983—San Diego‡	National	8	14	0	1	.000	12	8	8	5	6	5.14
1983—Las Vegas	P. Coast	19	26⅔	2	0	1.000	39	13	12	25	6	4.05
Major League Totals		8	14	0	1	.000	12	8	8	5	6	5.14

Selected by San Francisco Giants' organization in 23rd round of free-agent draft, June 8, 1976.
Selected by Minnesota Twins' organization in secondary phase of free-agent draft, January 10, 1978.
Selected by San Diego Padres' organization in 19th round of free-agent draft, June 3, 1980.
†Loaned to Grays Harbor (Co-op), June 16, 1980; returned, August 29, 1980.
‡On disabled list, May 28 to July 3, 1983; included rehabilitation disability assignement to Las Vegas, June 19 to July 2, 1983.

ALFRED EDWARD COWENS JR.

(Al)

Born October 25, 1951, at Los Angeles, Calif.
Height, 6.02. Weight, 200.
Throws and bats righthanded.

Named outfielder on THE SPORTING NEWS American League All-Star fielding team, 1977.
Named Southern League Player of the Year, 1973.

Year Club	League	Pos.	G.	AB.	R.	H.	2B.	3B.	HR.	RBI.	B.A.	PO.	A.	E.	F.A.
1969—Kingsport	Appal.	3B-SS-OF	51	180	30	53	6	1	2	30	.294	48	85	16	.893
1970—Billings	Pion.	OF-SS	62	237	45	67	9	5	7	47	.283	82	20	5	.953
1971—Waterloo	Midw.	3B-1B-OF	16	48	5	14	5	0	0	5	.292	37	12	3	.942
1971—San Jose	Calif.	OF	99	380	60	108	14	5	8	66	.284	138	14	3	★.981
1972—Waterloo	Midw.	3B	8	31	5	7	1	0	0	3	.226	5	17	2	.917
1972—San Jose	Calif.	OF-3B-1B	83	307	36	86	17	2	5	53	.280	134	53	10	.949

Year—Club	League	Pos.	G.	AB.	R.	H.	2B.	3B.	HR.	RBI.	B.A.	PO.	A.	E.	F.A.
1972—Jacksonville	South.	OF	35	120	17	24	2	1	4	9	.200	48	5	2	.964
1973—Jacksonville	South.	OF-1B-3B	135	491	91	142	25	7	16	81	.289	444	52	18	.965
1974—Kansas City	Amer.	OF-3B	110	269	28	65	7	1	1	25	.242	151	14	3	.982
1975—Kansas City	Amer.	OF	120	328	44	91	13	8	4	42	.277	214	4	5	.978
1976—Kansas City	Amer.	OF	152	581	71	154	23	6	3	59	.265	329	13	5	.986
1977—Kansas City†	Amer.	OF	●162	606	98	189	32	14	23	112	.312	307	14	6	.982
1978—Kansas City†	Amer.	OF-3B	132	485	63	133	24	8	5	63	.274	280	20	4	.987
1979—Kansas City‡§	Amer.	OF	136	516	69	152	18	7	9	73	.295	288	3	4	.986
1980—Calif.x-Det.	Amer.	OF	142	522	69	140	20	3	6	59	.268	263	11	3	.989
1981—Detroit y	Amer.	OF	85	253	27	66	11	4	1	18	.261	166	3	1	.994
1982—Seattle z	Amer.	OF	146	560	72	151	39	8	20	78	.270	280	14	4	.987
1983—Seattle a	Amer.	OF	110	356	39	73	19	2	7	35	.205	124	7	2	.985
Major League Totals			1295	4476	580	1214	206	61	79	564	.271	2402	103	37	.985

Selected by Kansas City Royals' organization in 84th round of free agent draft, June 5, 1969.

†On supplemental disabled list, June 29 to July 24, 1978.

‡On disabled list, May 9 to May 30, 1979.

§Traded to Shortstop Todd Cruz and a player to be named later to California Angels for First Baseman Willie Aikens and Shortstop Rance Mulliniks, December 6, 1979; California organization acquired Pitcher Craig Eaton to complete deal, April 1, 1980.

xTraded to Detroit Tigers for First Baseman Jason Thompson, May 27, 1980.

ySold to Seattle Mariners, March 28, 1982.

zGranted free agency, November 10, 1982; re-signed by Mariners, January 14, 1983.

aOn supplemental disabled list, July 23 to August 21, 1983.

CHAMPIONSHIP SERIES RECORD

Year—Club	League	Pos.	G.	AB.	R.	H.	2B.	3B.	HR.	RBI.	B.A.	PO.	A.	E.	F.A.
1976—Kansas City	Amer.	OF	5	21	3	4	0	1	0	0	.190	15	0	0	1.000
1977—Kansas City	Amer.	OF	5	19	2	5	0	0	1	5	.263	14	0	0	1.000
1978—Kansas City	Amer.	OF	4	15	2	2	0	0	0	1	.133	5	0	0	1.000
Championship Series Totals			14	55	7	11	0	1	1	6	.200	34	0	0	1.000

JOSEPH ALAN COWLEY

(Joe)

Born August 15, 1958, at Lexington, Ky.
Height, 6.05. Weight, 205.
Throws and bats righthanded.

Led International League in shutouts with 4 in 1983.
Led Western Carolinas League in hit batsmen with 19 and tied for lead in balks with 3 in 1978.
Tied for Southern League lead in hit batsmen with 13 in 1979.

Year—Club	League	G.	IP.	W.	L.	Pct.	H.	R.	ER.	SO.	BB.	ERA.
1976—Bradenton Braves	Gulf Coast	5	13	0	4	.000	17	16	13	12	19	9.00
1977—Greenwood	W. Carol.	10	32	1	0	1.000	31	29	29	25	43	8.16
1977—Kingsport	Ap'lachian	14	70	6	5	.545	73	59	48	59	50	6.17
1978—Greenwood	W. Carol.	25	161	11	7	.611	133	85	★71	141	★113	3.97
1979—Savannah	Southern	25	144	7	9	.438	115	74	60	103	81	3.75
1980—Savannah†	Southern	4	12	1	3	.250	24	18	17	13	9	12.75
1980—Durham	Carolina	10	64	6	0	1.000	57	26	20	44	25	2.81
1981—Savannah	Southern	11	69	6	0	1.000	47	22	21	56	16	2.74
1981—Richmond	Int'national	18	45	3	2	.600	33	15	14	39	16	2.80
1982—Atlanta‡	National	17	52⅓	1	2	.333	53	27	26	27	16	4.47
1982—Richmond	Int'national	9	51⅓	4	2	.667	46	24	23	33	30	4.03
1983—Richmond§	Int'national	28	124⅔	9	7	.563	106	69	61	108	72	4.40
Major League Totals		17	52⅓	1	2	.333	53	27	26	27	16	4.47

Signed as free agent by Atlanta Braves' organization, July 22, 1976.

†On disabled list, April 26 to July 3, 1980.

‡On disabled list, May 10 to June 12, 1982.

§Granted free agency, October 20, 1983; signed by New York Yankees, November 22, 1983.

DANNY BRADFORD COX

Born September 21, 1959, at Northhampton, England.
Height, 6.04. Weight, 225.
Throws and bats righthanded.
Attended Chattahoochee Valley Community College, Phenix, Ala.,
and Troy State University, Troy, Ala.

Pitched 11-0 no-hit victory against Bristol, August 9, 1981.
Led Appalachian League in complete games with 10 and shutouts with 4 in 1981.
Named Appalachian League Player of the Year, 1981.

Year—Club	League	G.	IP.	W.	L.	Pct.	H.	R.	ER.	SO.	BB.	ERA.
1981—Johnson City	Ap'lachian	13	★109	9	4	.692	80	27	25	★87	36	★2.06
1982—Springfield	Midwest	15	84⅓	5	3	.625	82	46	24	68	29	2.56
1983—Arkansas†	Texas	11	86⅓	8	3	.727	60	31	22	73	24	2.29
1983—St. Petersburg	Florida St.	5	32	2	2	.500	26	10	9	22	14	2.53
1983—Louisville	Am. Assoc.	2	11	0	0	.000	10	3	3	8	0	2.45
1983—St. Louis	National	12	83	3	6	.333	92	38	30	36	23	3.25
Major League Totals		12	83	3	6	.333	92	38	30	36	23	3.25

Selected by St. Louis Cardinals' organization in 13th round of free-agent draft, June 8, 1981.

†On disabled list, April 8 to April 21, 1983.

STEVEN RAY CRAWFORD
(Steve)

Born April 29, 1958, at Pryor, Okla.
Height, 6.05. Weight, 225.
Throws and bats righthanded.
Attended Claremore Junior College, Claremore, Okla. and attending
Northeastern Oklahoma State University, Tahlequah, Okla.

Led Carolina League pitchers in games started with 28 and complete games with 15 in 1979.
Tied for Carolina League lead in shutouts with 3 in 1979.

Year—Club	League	G.	IP.	W.	L.	Pct.	H.	R.	ER.	SO.	BB.	ERA.
1978—Winston-Salem	Carolina	19	110	9	5	.643	109	53	42	60	48	3.44
1979—Winston-Salem	Carolina	29	★211	11	11	.500	★208	88	●69	127	67	2.94
1980—Bristol†	Eastern	24	177	9	7	.563	170	68	52	97	64	2.64
1980—Boston	American	6	32	2	0	1.000	41	14	13	10	8	3.66
1981—Boston	American	14	58	0	5	.000	69	38	32	29	18	4.97
1982—Boston‡	American	5	9	1	0	1.000	14	3	2	2	0	2.00
1982—Pawtucket	Int'national	10	46	1	4	.200	55	25	21	20	15	4.11
1983—Pawtucket	Int'national	27	154⅔	8	11	.421	181	98	89	104	80	5.18
Major League Totals		25	99	3	5	.375	124	55	47	41	26	4.27

Signed as free agent by Boston Red Sox' organization, May 6, 1978.
†On disabled list, April 14 to May 2, 1980.
‡On disabled list, April 1 to August 12, 1982; included rehabilitation disability assignment to Pawtucket, July 21 to August 9, 1982.

STEVEN KEITH CREEL
(Known by middle name.)

Born February 4, 1959, at Dallas, Tex.
Height, 6.02. Weight, 180.
Throws and bats righthanded.
Attended University of Texas, Austin, Tex.

Year—Club	League	G.	IP.	W.	L.	Pct.	H.	R.	ER.	SO.	BB.	ERA.
1980—Ft. Myers	Florida St.	6	26	2	2	.500	48	29	24	5	16	8.31
1980—Sarasota Royals-Blue	Gulf Coast	9	54	6	2	.750	46	21	13	39	9	2.17
1981—Jacksonville	Southern	20	149	12	7	.632	106	52	45	105	44	2.72
1981—Omaha	Am. Assoc.	6	38	4	1	.800	35	19	18	29	13	4.26
1982—Omaha	Am. Assoc.	18	114⅔	6	8	.429	120	69	56	56	67	4.40
1982—Kansas City	American	9	41⅔	1	4	.200	43	28	25	13	25	5.40
1983—Omaha	Am. Assoc.	7	53⅓	4	2	.667	44	18	18	41	24	3.04
1983—Kansas City	American	25	89⅓	2	5	.286	116	66	63	31	35	6.35
Major League Totals		34	131	3	9	.250	159	94	88	44	60	6.05

Selected by Oakland A's organization in 2nd round of free-agent draft, June 7, 1977.
Selected by Pittsburgh Pirates' organization in secondary phase of free-agent draft, January 8, 1980.
Selected by Kansas City Royals' organization in secondary phase of free-agent draft, June 3, 1980.

WARREN LIVINGSTON CROMARTIE
Name pronounced Kroh-MART-ee.

Born September 29, 1953, at Miami, Fla.
Height, 6.00. Weight, 200.
Throws and bats lefthanded.
Attended Miami-Dade (North) Community College, Miami, Fla.

Led National League in intentional bases on balls received with 24 in 1980.
Tied for National League lead in grounding into double plays with 24 in 1980.
Tied for National League lead in double plays by outfielders with 5 in 1978.
Led Eastern League in total bases with 235 in 1974.

Year—Club	League	Pos.	G.	AB.	R.	H.	2B.	3B.	HR.	RBI.	B.A.	PO.	A.	E.	F.A.
1974—Quebec City	East.	OF-1B	129	482	94	★162	20	7	13	61	.336	389	22	9	.979
1974—Montreal	Nat.	OF	8	17	2	3	0	0	0	0	.176	8	0	0	1.000
1975—Memphis	Int.	OF-1B	119	400	42	107	16	6	3	38	.268	478	35	15	.972
1976—Denver†	A. A.	OF-1B	107	415	69	140	12	5	8	60	.337	274	13	6	.980
1976—Montreal	Nat.	OF	33	81	8	17	1	0	0	2	.210	61	1	2	.969
1977—Montreal	Nat.	OF	155	620	64	175	41	7	5	50	.282	319	10	8	.976
1978—Montreal	Nat.	●OF-1B	159	607	77	180	32	6	10	56	.297	351	●24	8	.979
1979—Montreal	Nat.	OF	158	659	84	181	46	5	8	46	.275	343	16	9	.976
1980—Montreal	Nat.	★1B-OF	162	597	74	172	33	5	14	70	.288	1459	93	★14	.991
1981—Montreal	Nat.	1B-OF	99	358	41	109	19	2	6	42	.304	570	33	4	.993
1982—Montreal	Nat.	OF-1B	144	497	59	126	24	3	14	62	.254	308	13	6	.982
1983—Montreal‡	Nat.	OF-1B	120	360	37	100	26	2	3	43	.278	209	12	6	.974
Major League Totals			1038	3796	446	1063	222	30	60	371	.280	3628	202	57	.985

Selected by Chicago White Sox' organization in 7th round of free-agent draft, June 8, 1971.
Selected by Minnesota Twins' organization in secondary phase of free-agent draft, January 12, 1972.
Selected by San Diego Padres' organization in secondary phase of free-agent draft, June 6, 1972.
Selected by Oakland A's organization in secondary phase of free-agent draft, January 10, 1973.
Selected by Montreal Expos' organization in secondary phase of free-agent draft, June 5, 1973.
†On suspended list, May 19 to May 21, 1976.
‡Granted free agency, November 7, 1983; signed by Tokyo Giants of Japanese baseball.

Year Club League	Pos.	G.	AB.	R.	H.	2B.	3B.	HR.	RBI.	B.A.	PO.	A.	E.	F.A.
1981—Montreal .... Nat.	1B	5	22	1	5	2	0	0	1	.227	37	3	1	.976

CHAMPIONSHIP SERIES RECORD

Year Club League	Pos.	G.	AB.	R.	H.	2B.	3B.	HR.	RBI.	B.A.	PO.	A.	E.	F.A.
1981—Montreal .... Nat.	1B	5	18	0	3	1	0	0	2	.167	48	2	0	1.000

TERRENCE MICHAEL CROWLEY
(Terry)

Born February 16, 1947, at Staten Island, N. Y.
Height, 6.00. Weight, 182.
Throws and bats lefthanded.
Attended Long Island University, Brooklyn, N. Y.

Led International League in slugging percentage with .600 in 1977.
Led International League in total bases with 246 in 1969.

Year Club	League	Pos.	G.	AB.	R.	H.	2B.	3B.	HR.	RBI.	B.A.	PO.	A.	E.	F.A.
1966—Miami	Fla. St.	OF	19	51	5	13	1	0	0	3	.255	15	0	1	.938
1967—Miami	Fla. St.	1B-OF	135	497	50	130	★24	10	3	49	.262	1057	56	23	.980
1968—Elmira	East.	OF-1B	55	181	19	49	8	1	0	22	.271	132	5	3	.979
1968—Rochester	Int.	OF-1B	75	271	37	71	13	3	8	34	.262	274	18	6	.980
1969—Rochester	Int.	OF-1B	132	475	78	134	24	2	28	83	.282	247	4	6	.977
1969—Baltimore	Amer.	1B-OF	7	18	2	6	0	0	0	3	.333	23	2	0	1.000
1970—Baltimore	Amer.	OF-1B	83	152	25	39	5	0	5	20	.257	138	6	2	.986
1971—Rochester	Int.	1B-OF	78	259	56	73	9	4	19	63	.282	591	47	5	.992
1971—Baltimore	Amer.	OF-1B	18	23	2	4	0	0	0	1	.174	7	0	0	1.000
1972—Baltimore	Amer.	OF-1B	97	247	30	57	10	0	11	29	.231	170	8	1	.994
1973—Baltimore†‡	Amer.	OF-1B	54	131	16	27	4	0	3	15	.206	33	5	3	.927
1974—Cincinnati	Nat.	OF-1B	84	125	11	30	12	0	1	20	.240	58	5	2	.969
1975—Cincinnati§	Nat.	1B-OF	66	71	8	19	6	0	1	11	.268	43	4	0	1.000
1976—Atlanta x	Nat.	PH	7	6	0	0	0	0	0	1	.000	0	0	0	.000
1976—Rochester	Int.	1B	20	69	4	18	7	0	2	7	.261	14	1	0	1.000
1976—Baltimore y	Amer.	1B	33	61	5	15	1	0	0	5	.246	13	2	0	1.000
1977—Rochester	Int.	1B-OF	108	403	69	124	24	2	★30	80	.308	407	28	7	.984
1977—Baltimore	Amer.	1B	18	22	3	8	1	0	1	9	.364	3	0	0	1.000
1978—Baltimore	Amer.	OF-1B	62	95	9	24	2	0	0	12	.253	1	1	0	1.000
1979—Baltimore	Amer.	1B	61	63	8	20	5	1	1	8	.317	5	0	0	1.000
1980—Baltimore	Amer.	1B	92	233	33	67	8	0	12	50	.288	19	5	0	1.000
1981—Baltimore	Amer.	1B	68	134	12	33	6	0	4	25	.246	30	2	0	1.000
1982—Baltimore z	Amer.	1B	65	93	8	22	2	0	3	17	.237	74	6	1	.988
1983—Montreal a	Nat.	1B	50	44	2	8	0	0	0	3	.182	19	0	0	1.000
American League Totals..........................			658	1272	156	322	44	1	40	194	.253	516	37	7	.988
National League Totals...............................			207	246	21	57	18	0	2	35	.232	120	9	2	.985
Major League Totals.....................................			865	1518	174	379	62	1	42	229	.250	636	46	9	.987

Selected by Baltimore Orioles' organization in 11th round of free-agent draft, June 10, 1966.
†Sold to Texas Rangers for an estimated $100,000, December 6, 1973.
‡Sold to Cincinnati Reds, March 19, 1974.
§Traded to Atlanta Braves for Pitcher Mike Thompson, April 6, 1976.
xReleased, May 6, 1976; signed by Baltimore Orioles' organization, May 26, 1976.
yReleased, March 26, 1977; re-signed by Baltimore Orioles' organization, April 12, 1977.
zReleased, April 4, 1983; signed by Montreal Expos, May 25, 1983.
aReleased, October 7, 1983.

CHAMPIONSHIP SERIES RECORD

Year Club	League	Pos.	G.	AB.	R.	H.	2B.	3B.	HR.	RBI.	B.A.	PO.	A.	E.	F.A.
1973—Baltimore	Amer.	PH-OF	2	2	0	0	0	0	0	0	.000	1	0	0	1.000
1975—Cincinnati	Nat.	PH	1	0	0	0	0	0	0	0	.000	0	0	0	.000
1979—Baltimore	Amer.	PH	2	2	0	1	0	0	0	1	.500	0	0	0	.000
Championship Series Totals			5	4	0	1	0	0	0	1	.250	1	0	0	1.000

WORLD SERIES RECORD

Tied World Series record for most games as pinch-hitter, series (5), 1979.

Year Club	League	Pos.	G.	AB.	R.	H.	2B.	3B.	HR.	RBI.	B.A.	PO.	A.	E.	F.A.
1970—Baltimore	Amer.	PH	1	1	0	0	0	0	0	0	.000	0	0	0	.000
1975—Cincinnati	Nat.	PH	2	2	0	1	0	0	0	0	.500	0	0	0	.000
1979—Baltimore	Amer.	PH	5	4	0	1	1	0	0	2	.250	0	0	0	.000
World Series Totals.................................			8	7	0	2	1	0	0	2	.286	0	0	0	.000

JOSE CRUZ (DILAN)

Born August 8, 1947, at Arroyo, Puerto Rico.
Height, 6.00. Weight, 175.
Throws and bats lefthanded.
Brother of Hector Cruz, third baseman-outfielder with St. Louis, Chicago N.L., San Francisco
and Cincinnati, 1973 and 1975 through 1982, and currently with Yomiuri Giants of
Japanese baseball; and Cirilo (Tommy) Cruz,
outfielder with St. Louis Cardinals and Chicago White Sox, 1973 and 1977,
and currently with Nippon Ham Fighters in Japanese baseball.

Tied major league record for fewest double plays by outfielder, season, 150 or more games (0), 1978.
Major league stolen bases: 1971 (6), 1972 (9), 1973 (10), 1974 (4), 1975 (6), 1976 (28), 1977 (44), 1978 (37), 1979 (36), 1980 (36), 1981 (5), 1982 (21), 1983 (30). Total—272.
Led National League outfielders in double plays with 5 in 1972.
Tied for National League lead in sacrifice flies with 10 in 1977.
Named outfielder on THE SPORTING NEWS National League Silver Slugger Team, 1983.
Led Texas League in total bases with 254 in 1970.

Year	Club	League	Pos.	G.	AB.	R.	H.	2B.	3B.	HR.	RBI.	B.A.	PO.	A.	E.	F.A.
1967—St. Petersburg	Fla. St.	OF-1B	78	205	33	57	8	9	1	20	.278	113	5	7	.944
1968—Modesto	Calif.	OF-SS	133	504	101	144	24	10	13	53	.286	219	10	11	.954
1969—Arkansas†	Texas	OF	102	400	56	109	18	9	6	49	.273	235	16	9	.965
1970—Arkansas	Texas	OF	133	493	89	148	★29	7	21	90	.300	★276	10	12	.960
1970—St. Louis	Nat.	OF	6	17	2	6	1	0	0	1	.353	16	0	0	1.000
1971—Tulsa	A. A.	OF	67	254	56	83	15	7	15	49	.327	146	1	7	.955
1971—St. Louis	Nat.	OF	83	292	46	80	13	2	9	27	.274	197	2	5	.975
1972—St. Louis	Nat.	OF	117	332	33	78	14	4	2	23	.235	220	9	5	.979
1973—St. Louis	Nat.	OF	132	406	51	92	22	5	10	57	.227	276	2	6	.979
1974—St. Louis‡	Nat.	OF-1B	107	161	24	42	4	3	5	20	.261	81	2	2	.976
1975—Houston	Nat.	OF	120	315	44	81	15	2	9	49	.257	187	6	4	.980
1976—Houston	Nat.	OF	133	439	49	133	21	5	4	61	.303	265	10	8	.972
1977—Houston	Nat.	OF	157	579	87	173	31	10	17	87	.299	311	11	9	.973
1978—Houston	Nat.	OF-1B	153	565	79	178	34	9	10	83	.315	328	5	8	.977
1979—Houston	Nat.	OF	157	558	73	161	33	7	9	72	.289	320	7	14	.959
1980—Houston	Nat.	OF	160	612	79	185	29	7	11	91	.302	323	16	●11	.969
1981—Houston	Nat.	OF	107	409	53	109	16	5	13	55	.267	237	5	4	.984
1982—Houston	Nat.	OF	155	570	62	157	27	2	9	68	.275	340	9	★13	.964
1983—Houston	Nat.	OF	160	594	85	●189	28	8	14	92	.318	322	9	7	.979
Major League Totals			1747	5849	767	1664	288	69	122	786	.284	3423	93	96	.973

Signed as free agent by St. Louis Cardinals' organization, October 27, 1966.
†On disabled list, April 8 to May 12, 1969.
‡Sold to Houston Astros, October 24, 1974.

DIVISION SERIES RECORD

Year	Club	League	Pos.	G.	AB.	R.	H.	2B.	3B.	HR.	RBI.	B.A.	PO.	A.	E.	F.A.
1981—Houston	Nat.	OF	5	20	0	6	1	0	0	0	.300	15	0	1	.938

CHAMPIONSHIP SERIES RECORD

Established Championship Series record for most walks, five-game series (8), 1980.

Year	Club	League	Pos.	G.	AB.	R.	H.	2B.	3B.	HR.	RBI.	B.A.	PO.	A.	E.	F.A.
1980—Houston	Nat.	OF	5	15	3	6	1	1	0	4	.400	19	0	0	1.000

ALL-STAR GAME RECORD

Member of National League All-Star Team in 1980; did not play.

JULIO LUIS CRUZ

Born December 2, 1954, at Brooklyn, N. Y.
Height, 5.09. Weight, 160.
Throws right and bats right and lefthanded.
Attended San Bernardino Valley College, San Bernardino, Calif.

Tied major league record for most chances accepted by second baseman, nine-inning game (18), June 7, 1981.
Established American League record for most games played with two clubs, season (160), Seattle (61), Chicago (99), 1983.
Tied American League record for most consecutive stolen bases without caught stealing (32).
Major League stolen bases: 1977 (15), 1978 (59), 1979 (49), 1980 (45), 1981 (43), 1982 (46), 1983 (57). Total—314.
Led American League second basemen in fielding percentage with .987 in 1978.
Led Pioneer League in stolen bases with 34, in being hit by pitch with 7 and tied for lead in caught stealing with 11 in 1974.
Tied for Pacific Coast League lead in sacrifice hits with 9 in 1977.
Tied for Midwest League lead in sacrifice hits with 11 in 1975.

Year	Club	League	Pos.	G.	AB.	R.	H.	2B.	3B.	HR.	RBI.	B.A.	PO.	A.	E.	F.A.
1974—Idaho Falls	Pioneer	2B-SS-3B	72	237	44	57	4	1	0	27	.241	137	185	22	.936
1975—Quad Cities	Midw.	2B	108	368	79	96	6	6	0	35	.261	228	259	14	.972
1976—Salinas	Calif.	2B	96	348	92	107	12	3	1	45	.307	234	314	10	★.982
1976—El Paso	Texas	2B	13	49	9	16	4	1	0	9	.327	23	21	0	1.000
1976—Salt Lake C.†	P. C.	2B-3B-OF	20	69	11	17	2	2	0	6	.246	30	47	1	.987
1977—Hawaii	P. C.	2B	75	303	71	111	9	9	0	33	.366	189	237	7	.984
1977—Seattle	Amer.	2B	60	199	25	51	3	1	1	7	.256	114	171	5	.983
1978—Seattle	Amer.	2B-SS	147	550	77	129	14	1	1	25	.235	295	482	11	.986
1979—Seattle‡	Amer.	2B	107	414	70	112	16	2	1	29	.271	258	361	13	.979
1980—Seattle§	Amer.	2B	119	422	66	88	9	3	2	16	.209	269	355	11	.983
1981—Seattle	Amer.	2B-SS	94	352	57	90	12	3	2	24	.256	240	297	11	.980
1982—Seattle	Amer.	2B-SS-3B	154	549	83	133	22	5	8	49	.242	322	438	10	.987
1983—Sea. x-Chi. y	Amer.	2B	160	515	71	130	19	5	3	52	.252	344	471	14	.983
Major League Totals			841	3001	449	733	95	20	18	202	.244	1842	2575	75	.983

Signed as free agent by California Angels' organization, May 7, 1974.
†Selected by Seattle Mariners from California Angels in American League expansion draft, November 5, 1976.
‡On disabled list, June 5 to August 3, 1979.
§On supplemental disabled list, April 24 to May 9, 1980.

CHAMPIONSHIP SERIES RECORD

Year	Club	League	Pos.	G.	AB.	R.	H.	2B.	3B.	HR.	RBI.	B.A.	PO.	A.	E.	F.A.
1983—Chicago		Amer.	2B	4	12	0	4	0	0	0	0	.333	10	14	0	1.000

TODD RUBEN CRUZ

Born November 23, 1955, at Highland Park, Mich.
Height, 6.00. Weight, 175.
Throws and bats righthanded.
Son of Robert Cruz, former minor league player in Detroit Tigers' organization.

Led American League shortstops in double plays with 98 in 1982.
Led Carolina League batters in strikeouts with 127 and sacrifice flies with 10 in 1974.
Led Eastern League shortstops in total chances with 714 in 1977.
Led Carolina League shortstops in double plays with 69 in 1974 and 74 in 1975.
Tied for Appalachian League lead in strikeouts by batters with 76 in 1973.
Tied for Eastern League lead in double plays by shortstops with 77 in 1977.

Year	Club	League	Pos.	G.	AB.	R.	H.	2B.	3B.	HR.	RBI.	B.A.	PO.	A.	E.	F.A.
1973—Pulaski		Appal.	SS	69	208	29	38	10	1	4	18	.183	95	174	★49	.846
1974—Rocky Mount		Carol.	SS	126	445	35	87	13	6	1	43	.196	★219	324	★50	.916
1974—Toledo		Int.	SS	4	10	1	1	1	0	0	1	.100	3	8	2	.846
1975—Rocky Mount		Carol.	SS	134	453	57	92	23	1	11	67	.203	★218	★457	41	★.943
1976—Reading		East.	SS	123	424	34	98	126	11	1	5	.231	203	388	★53	.918
1977—Reading		East.	SS	131	464	42	100	23	3	2	51	.216	★228	★436	★50	.930
1978—Oklahoma City		A. A.	SS	121	459	58	120	22	2	11	69	.261	209	379	★40	.936
1978—Philadelphia†		Nat.	SS	3	4	0	2	0	0	0	2	.500	1	6	0	1.000
1979—Omaha		A. A.	SS	23	91	14	24	4	2	7	21	.264	47	86	5	.964
1979—Kansas City‡		Amer.	SS-3B	55	118	9	24	7	0	2	15	.203	54	118	7	.961
1980—Calif.§-Chi.		Amer.	S-3-2-O	108	333	28	79	14	1	3	23	.237	156	323	28	.956
1981—Edmonton		P. C.	SS	8	27	2	7	0	1	1	3	.259	15	34	1	.980
1981—Chicago xyz		Amer.							(Did not play)								
1982—Seattle a		Amer.	SS	136	492	44	113	20	2	16	57	.230	215	439	25	.963
1983—Sea. b-Balt.		Amer.	3B-SS-2B	146	437	37	87	13	3	10	48	.199	146	386	25	.955
National League Totals				3	4	0	2	0	0	0	2	.500	1	6	0	1.000
American League Totals				445	1380	118	303	54	6	31	143	.220	571	1266	85	.956
Major League Totals				448	1384	118	305	54	6	31	145	.220	572	1272	85	.956

Selected by Philadelphia Phillies' organization in 2nd round of free agent draft, June 5, 1973.
†Traded to Kansas City Royals' organization for Pitcher Doug Bird, April 3, 1979.
‡Traded with Outfielder Al Cowens and a player to be named later to California Angels for First Baseman Willie Aikens and Shortstop Rance Mulliniks, December 6, 1979; California organization acquired Pitcher Craig Eaton to complete deal, April 1, 1980.
§Traded to Chicago White Sox for Pitcher Randy Scarbery, June 12, 1980.
xOn Chicago supplemental disabled list, April 5 to June 2, 1981; included rehabilitation disability assignment to Edmonton, May 6 to May 24, 1981; transferred to restricted list, June 2 to August 2, 1981.
yOn supplemental disabled list, August 10, 1981 through remainder of season.
zTraded with Catcher Jim Essian and Outfielder Rod Allen to Seattle Mariners for Outfielder Tom Paciorek, December 11, 1981.
aOn supplemental disabled list, June 21 to July 6, 1982.
bSold to Baltimore Orioles, June 30, 1983.

CHAMPIONSHIP SERIES RECORD

Tied American League Championship Series record for most strikeouts, four-game Series (5), 1983.

Year	Club	League	Pos.	G.	AB.	R.	H.	2B.	3B.	HR.	RBI.	B.A.	PO.	A.	E.	F.A.
1983—Baltimore		Amer.	3B	4	15	0	2	0	0	0	1	.133	6	13	0	1.000

WORLD SERIES RECORD

Year	Club	League	Pos.	G.	AB.	R.	H.	2B.	3B.	HR.	RBI.	B.A.	PO.	A.	E.	F.A.
1983—Baltimore		Amer.	3B	5	16	1	2	0	0	0	0	.125	0	17	2	.895

VICTOR MANUEL CRUZ

Born December 24, 1957, at Rancho Viejo La Vega, Dominican Republic.
Height, 5.09. Weight, 215.
Throws and bats righthanded.

Led American Association in saves with 14 in 1983 and tied for lead in saves with 14 in 1982.
Led Appalachian League in shutouts with 3 in 1976.

Year	Club	League	G.	IP.	W.	L.	Pct.	H.	R.	ER.	SO.	BB.	ERA.
1976—Johnson City		Ap'lachian	12	80	6	3	.667	57	23	18	100	23	2.03
1977—Arkansas		Texas	18	83	3	8	.273	79	57	46	83	40	4.99
1977—St. Petersburg†		Florida St.	13	30	2	3	.400	14	12	11	48	13	3.30
1978—Syracuse		Int'national	25	42	3	2	.600	31	23	21	56	35	4.50
1978—Toronto‡		American	32	47	7	3	.700	28	10	9	51	35	1.72
1979—Cleveland		American	61	79	3	9	.250	70	41	37	63	44	4.22
1980—Cleveland§		American	55	86	6	7	.462	71	36	33	88	27	3.45
1981—Portland		P. Coast	9	24	2	1	.667	25	11	11	19	5	4.13
1981—Pittsburgh x		National	22	34	1	1	.500	33	10	10	28	15	2.65
1982—Denver		Am. Assoc.	44	56	3	3	.500	48	28	24	62	25	3.86

Year Club	League	G.	IP.	W.	L.	Pct.	H.	R.	ER.	SO.	BB.	ERA.
1983—Oklahoma City	Am. Assoc.	30	33⅓	4	3	.571	22	8	8	35	9	2.16
1983—Texas	American	17	25	1	3	.250	16	7	4	18	10	1.44
American League Totals		165	237	17	22	.436	185	94	83	220	116	3.15
National League Totals		22	34	1	1	.500	33	10	10	28	15	2.65
Major League Totals		187	271	18	23	.439	218	104	93	248	131	3.09

Signed as free agent by St. Louis Cardinals' organization, January 9, 1976.

†Traded with Pitcher Tom Underwood to Toronto Blue Jays for Pitcher Pete Vuckovich and a player to be named later, December 6, 1977; St. Louis Cardinals' organization acquired Outfielder John Scott to complete deal, December 16, 1977.

‡Traded to Cleveland Indians for Shortstop Alfredo Griffin and Third Baseman Phil Lansford, December 6, 1978.

§Traded with Pitchers Bob Owchinko and Rafael Vasquez and Catcher Gary Alexander to Pittsburgh Pirates for Pitcher Bert Blyleven and Catcher Manny Sanguillen, December 9, 1980.

xTraded to Texas Rangers' organization for Shortstop Nelson Norman, April 1, 1982.

WILFRED HILLARD CULMER
(Wil)

Born November 11, 1958, at Nassau, Bahamas.
Height, 6.04. Weight, 210.
Throws and bats righthanded.
Attended Chipola Junior College, Marianna, Fla.

Led Carolina League in total bases with 276 in 1980.

Year Club	League	Pos.	G.	AB.	R.	H.	2B.	3B.	HR.	RBI.	B.A.	PO.	A.	E.	F.A.
1978—Helena	Pion.	OF-1B	55	187	44	67	5	3	10	44	.358	50	4	4	.931
1979—Peninsula	Carol.	OF	33	107	10	16	1	0	0	7	.150	45	4	7	.875
1979—Spartanbrug	W. Car.	OF	68	228	35	70	17	3	6	46	.307	40	2	8	.840
1980—Peninsula	Carol.	OF-3B	139	498	★112	★184	28	5	18	93	★.369	140	65	27	.884
1981—Reading	East.	OF	120	411	58	116	16	5	10	53	.282	127	12	13	.915
1982—Oklahoma City†	A. A.	OF-1B	119	403	58	116	16	5	14	58	.288	178	13	12	.941
1983—Cleveland	Amer.	OF	7	19	0	2	0	0	0	1	.105	2	0	0	1.000
1983—Charleston	Int.	OF	87	286	39	70	14	2	7	29	.245	102	7	5	.956
Major League Totals			7	19	0	2	0	0	0	1	.105	2	0	0	1.000

Signed as free agent by Philadelphia Phillies' organization, October 25, 1977.

†Traded with Pitchers Jerry Reed and Roy Smith to Cleveland Indians for Pitcher John Denny, September 12, 1982.

JOHN DUFFIELD CURTIS II

Born March 9, 1948, at Newton, Mass.
Height, 6.02. Weight, 185.
Throws and bats lefthanded.
Received bachelor of arts degree in English from Clemson University, Clemson, S. C.

Year Club	League	G.	IP.	W.	L.	Pct.	H.	R.	ER.	SO.	BB.	ERA.
1968—Winston-Salem	Carolina	16	103	6	8	.429	82	49	39	101	41	3.41
1969—Greenville	W. Carol.	25	149	6	★12	.333	141	★91	★74	★158	★97	4.47
1970—Pawtucket	Eastern	21	138	9	8	.529	113	65	57	114	75	3.72
1970—Boston	American	1	2	0	0	.000	4	4	3	1	1	13.50
1971—Louisville	Int'national	27	187	10	12	.455	167	99	71	165	★111	3.42
1971—Boston	American	5	26	2	2	.500	30	9	9	19	6	3.12
1972—Louisville	Int'national	8	67	4	3	.571	55	19	15	64	27	2.01
1972—Boston	American	26	154	11	8	.579	161	69	64	106	50	3.74
1973—Boston†	American	35	221	13	13	.500	225	103	88	101	83	3.58
1974—St. Louis	National	33	195	10	14	.417	199	91	82	89	83	3.78
1975—St. Louis	National	39	147	8	9	.471	151	70	56	67	65	3.43
1976—St. Louis‡	National	37	134	6	11	.353	139	68	67	52	65	4.50
1977—San Francisco	National	43	77	3	3	.500	95	48	47	47	48	5.49
1978—San Francisco	National	46	63	4	3	.571	60	31	26	38	29	3.71
1979—San Francisco§	National	27	121	10	9	.526	121	62	56	85	42	4.17
1980—San Diego	National	30	187	10	8	.556	184	84	73	71	67	3.51
1981—San Diego	National	28	67	2	6	.250	70	41	38	31	30	5.10
1982—San Diego x	National	26	116⅓	8	6	.571	121	62	53	54	46	4.10
1982—California	American	8	12	0	1	.000	16	8	8	10	3	6.00
1983—California	American	37	90	1	2	.333	89	44	38	36	40	3.80
American League Totals		112	505	27	26	.509	525	237	210	273	183	3.74
National League Totals		309	1107⅓	61	69	.469	1140	557	498	534	475	4.05
Major League Totals		421	1612⅓	88	95	.481	1665	794	708	807	658	3.95

Selected by Cleveland Indians' organization in 1st round (12th player selected) of free-agent draft, June 6, 1966.

Selected by Boston Red Sox' organization in secondary phase of free-agent draft, June 7, 1968.

†Traded with Pitchers Mike Garman and Lynn McGlothen to St. Louis Cardinals for Infielder Terry Hughes and Pitchers Reggie Cleveland and Diego Segui, December 7, 1973.

‡Traded with Outfielder Willie Crawford and Infielder-Outfielder Vic Harris to San Francisco Giants for Pitchers John D'Acquisto and Mike Caldwell and Catcher Dave Rader, October 20, 1976.

§Granted free agency, November 1, 1979; signed by San Diego Padres, November 26, 1979.

xSold to California Angels, August 31, 1982.

MARK DACKO

Name pronounced DACK-oh.

Born August 26, 1958, at Monessen, Pa.
Height, 6.05. Weight, 190.
Throws right and bats lefthanded.
Attended James Madison University, Harrisonburg, Va.

Led American Association in complete games with 9 and tied for lead in shutouts with 2 in 1983.
Tied for Appalachian League lead in shutouts with 6 in 1980.

Year Club	League	G.	IP.	W.	L.	Pct.	H.	R.	ER.	SO.	BB.	ERA.
1980—Bristol	Ap'lachian	9	46	3	2	.600	33	12	6	35	7	1.17
1980—Lakeland	Florida St.	5	31	2	3	.400	33	17	15	11	14	4.35
1981—Birmingham	Southern	27	168	13	7	.653	177	96	83	115	56	4.45
1982—Evansville	Am. Assoc.	26	173	12	10	.545	173	94	80	86	54	4.16
1983—Evansville	Am. Assoc.	24	143	6	12	.333	167	97	84	74	50	5.29

Selected by San Francisco Giants' organization in 23rd round of free-agent draft, June 5, 1979.
Selected by Detroit Tigers' organization in 31st round of free-agent draft, June 3, 1980.

RONALD MAURICE DARLING JR.
(Ron)

Born August 19, 1960, at Honolulu, Hawaii.
Height, 6.03. Weight, 205.
Throws and bats righthanded.
Attended Yale University, New Haven, Conn.
Brother of Eddie Darling, first baseman in New York Yankees' organization, 1981 and 1982.

Year Club	League	G.	IP.	W.	L.	Pct.	H.	R.	ER.	SO.	BB.	ERA.
1981—Tulsa†	Texas	13	71	4	2	.667	72	43	35	53	33	4.44
1982—Tidewater	Int'national	26	152	7	9	.438	143	76	63	114	95	3.73
1983—Tidewater	Int'national	27	159	10	9	.526	137	83	71	107	102	4.02
1983—New York	National	5	35⅓	1	3	.250	31	11	11	23	17	2.80
Major League Totals		5	35⅓	1	3	.250	31	11	11	23	17	2.80

Selected by Texas Rangers' organization in 1st round (ninth player selected) of free-agent draft, June 8, 1981.
†Traded with Pitcher Walt Terrell to New York Mets' organization for Outfielder Lee Mazzilli, April 1, 1982.

DANNY WAYNE DARWIN

Born October 25, 1955, at Bonham, Tex.
Height, 6.03. Weight, 195.
Throws and bats righthanded.
Attended Grayson County College, Denison, Tex.

Tied for Texas League lead in shutouts with 4 and hit batsmen with 8 in 1977.
Tied for Western Carolinas League lead in balks with 5 in 1976.

Year Club	League	G.	IP.	W.	L.	Pct.	H.	R.	ER.	SO.	BB.	ERA.
1976—Asheville	W. Carol.	16	102	6	3	.667	96	54	41	76	48	3.62
1977—Tulsa†	Texas	23	154	13	4	.765	130	53	43	129	72	2.51
1978—Tucson	P. Coast	23	125	8	9	.471	147	100	87	126	83	6.26
1978—Texas	American	3	9	1	0	1.000	11	4	4	8	1	4.00
1979—Tucson	P. Coast	13	95	6	6	.500	89	43	38	65	42	3.60
1979—Texas	American	20	78	4	4	.500	50	36	35	58	30	4.04
1980—Texas‡	American	53	110	13	4	.765	98	37	32	104	50	2.62
1981—Texas	American	22	146	9	9	.500	115	67	59	98	57	3.64
1982—Texas	American	56	89	10	8	.556	95	38	34	61	37	3.44
1983—Texas§	American	28	183	8	13	.381	175	86	71	92	62	3.49
Major League Totals		182	615	45	38	.542	544	268	235	421	237	3.44

Signed as free agent by Texas Rangers' organization, May 18, 1976.
†On disabled list, April 25 to May 4 and May 22 to June 11, 1977.
‡On disabled list, June 5 to June 26, 1980.
§On disabled list, March 25 to April 10 and August 9 to September 1, 1983.

RICHARD FREMONT DAUER

Name pronounced DOW-er.

(Rich)

Born July 27, 1952, at San Bernardino, Calif.
Height, 6.00. Weight, 180.
Throws and bats righthanded.
Attended San Bernardino Valley College, San Bernardino, Calif., and
University of Southern California, Los Angeles, Calif.

Established American League records for most consecutive errorless games by second baseman, season (86), 1978; most consecutive errorless chances accepted by second baseman, season (425), 1978.
Led International League in fielding percentage with .975 in 1976.
Led Southern League third basemen in double plays with 28 in 1975.
Named International League co-Most Valuable Player, 1976.

Year Club	League	Pos.	G.	AB.	R.	H.	2B.	3B.	HR.	RBI.	B.A.	PO.	A.	E.	F.A.
1974—Asheville	South.	2B-3B	53	180	30	59	7	0	11	35	.328	72	104	3	.983
1975—Rochester	Int.	2B-3B	18	47	2	8	1	0	0	0	.170	17	30	2	.959

Year Club	League	Pos.	G.	AB.	R.	H.	2B.	3B.	HR.	RBI.	B.A.	PO.	A.	E.	F.A.
1975—Asheville	South.	*3B-2B	106	374	51	94	13	0	6	44	.251	98	195	6	*.980
1976—Rochester	Int.	2B-SS-1B	132	524	84	*176	26	3	11	78	*.336	276	402	18	.974
1976—Baltimore	Amer.	2B	11	39	0	4	0	0	0	3	.103	22	22	0	1.000
1977—Baltimore	Amer.	2B-3B	96	304	38	74	15	1	5	25	.243	182	233	7	.983
1978—Baltimore	Amer.	2B-3B	133	459	57	121	23	0	6	46	.264	222	321	7	.987
1979—Baltimore	Amer.	2B-3B	142	479	63	123	20	0	9	61	.257	234	355	17	.972
1980—Baltimore	Amer.	2B-3B	152	557	71	158	32	0	2	63	.284	334	418	8	.989
1981—Baltimore	Amer.	*2B-3B	96	369	41	97	27	0	4	38	.263	201	256	5	*.989
1982—Baltimore	Amer.	2B-3B	158	558	75	156	24	2	8	57	.280	289	354	8	.988
1983—Baltimore	Amer.	2B-3B	140	459	49	108	19	0	5	41	.235	280	333	8	.987
Major League Totals			928	3224	394	841	160	3	39	334	.261	1764	2292	60	.985

Selected by Oakland A's organization in 5th round of free agent draft, January 13, 1971.
Selected by Oakland A's organization in 9th round of free agent draft, January 12, 1972.
Selected by Cleveland Indians' organization in secondary phase of free agent draft, June 6, 1972.
Selected by Baltimore Orioles' organization in 1st round (24th player selected) of free agent draft, June 5, 1974.

CHAMPIONSHIP SERIES RECORD

Year Club	League	Pos.	G.	AB.	R.	H.	2B.	3B.	HR.	RBI.	B.A.	PO.	A.	E.	F.A.
1979—Baltimore	Amer.	2B	4	11	0	2	0	0	0	0	.182	10	12	0	1.000
1983—Baltimore	Amer.	2B	4	14	0	0	0	0	0	1	.000	8	12	0	1.000
Championship Series Totals			8	25	0	2	0	0	0	1	.080	18	24	0	1.000

WORLD SERIES RECORD

Year Club	League	Pos.	G.	AB.	R.	H.	2B.	3B.	HR.	RBI.	B.A.	PO.	A.	E.	F.A.
1979—Baltimore	Amer.	PH-2B	6	17	2	5	1	0	1	1	.294	10	10	0	1.000
1983—Baltimore	Amer.	2B-3B	5	19	2	4	1	0	0	3	.211	14	8	0	1.000
World Series Totals			11	36	4	9	2	0	1	4	.250	24	18	0	1.000

DARREN ARTHUR DAULTON

Born January 3, 1962, at Arkansas City, Kan.
Height, 6.02. Weight, 190.
Throws right and bats lefthanded.
Attends Cowley County Community College, Arkansas City, Kan.

Tied for Eastern League lead in sacrifice flies with 10 in 1983.

Year Club	League	Pos.	G.	AB.	R.	H.	2B.	3B.	HR.	RBI.	B.A.	PO.	A.	E.	F.A.
1980—Helena	Pioneer	C	37	100	13	20	2	1	1	10	.200	224	17	4	.984
1981—Spartanburg	S. Atl.	C-OF-3B	98	270	44	62	11	1	3	29	.230	378	34	4	.990
1982—Peninsula	Carol.	C-1B	110	417	65	78	21	2	11	44	.241	654	63	9	.990
1983—Reading	East.	C-1B-OF	113	362	77	95	16	4	19	83	.262	557	57	14	.978
1983—Philadelphia	Nat.	C	2	3	1	1	0	0	0	0	.333	8	0	0	1.000
Major League Totals			2	3	1	1	0	0	0	0	.333	8	0	0	1.000

Selected by Philadelphia Phillies' organization in 25th round of free-agent draft, June 3, 1980.

ALVIN GLENN DAVIS

Born September 9, 1960, at Riverside, Calif.
Height, 6.01. Weight, 190.
Throws right and bats lefthanded.
Attended Arizona State University, Tempe, Ariz.

Led Southern League in bases on balls received with 120 and sacrifice flies with 12 in 1983.
Led Southern League first basemen in total chances with 1,348 and double plays with 118 in 1983.

Year Club	League	Pos.	G.	AB.	R.	H.	2B.	3B.	HR.	RBI.	B.A.	PO.	A.	E.	F.A.
1982—Lynn	East	1B	74	225	37	64	10	1	12	56	.284	579	51	6	.991
1983—Chattanooga	South.	*●1B-OF	131	422	87	125	24	3	18	83	.296	*1233	*99	●16	.988

Selected by San Francisco Giants' organization in 8th round of free-agent draft, June 6, 1978.
Selected by Oakland A's organization in 6th round of free-agent draft, June 8, 1981.
Selected by Seattle Mariners' organization in 6th round of free-agent draft, June 7, 1982.

CHARLES THEODORE DAVIS
(Chili)

Born January 17, 1960, at Kingston, Jamaica.
Height, 6.03. Weight, 195.
Throws right and bats left and righthanded.

Tied National League record for most games, switch-hit home runs, season (1), June 5, 1983.

Year Club	League	Pos.	G.	AB.	R.	H.	2B.	3B.	HR.	RBI.	B.A.	PO.	A.	E.	F.A.
1978—Cedar Rapids	Midw.	C-OF	124	424	63	119	18	5	16	73	.281	365	45	25	.943
1979—Fresno	Calif.	OF-C	134	490	91	132	24	5	21	95	.269	339	43	20	.950
1980—Shreveport	Texas	OF-C	129	442	50	130	30	4	12	67	.294	184	20	12	.944
1981—San Francisco	Nat.	OF	8	15	1	2	0	0	0	0	.133	7	0	0	1.000
1981—Phoenix†	P. C.	OF	88	334	76	117	16	6	19	75	.350	175	7	6	.968
1982—San Francisco	Nat.	OF	154	641	86	167	27	6	19	76	.261	404	●16	12	.972
1983—San Francisco	Nat.	OF	137	486	54	113	21	2	11	59	.233	357	7	9	.976
1983—Phoenix	P. C.	OF	10	44	12	13	2	0	2	9	.295	15	0	2	.882
Major League Totals			299	1142	141	282	48	8	30	135	.247	768	23	21	.974

Selected by San Francisco Giants' organization in 11th round of free-agent draft, June 7, 1977.
†On disabled list, August 19 to August 28, 1982.

ERIC KEITH DAVIS

Born May 29, 1962, at Los Angeles, Calif.
Height, 6.03. Weight, 175.
Throws and bats righthanded.

Led Northwest League in stolen bases with 40 in 1981.

Year Club	League	Pos.	G.	AB.	R.	H.	2B.	3B.	HR.	RBI.	B.A.	PO.	A.	E.	F.A.
1980—Eugene	N'west	SS-2B	33	73	12	16	1	0	1	11	.219	24	35	11	.843
1981—Eugene	N'west	OF	62	214	*67	69	10	4	11	39	.322	94	11	4	.963
1982—Cedar Rapids	Midw.	OF	111	434	80	120	20	5	15	56	.276	239	9	9	.965
1983—Waterbury	East.	OF	89	293	56	85	13	1	15	43	.290	214	8	2	.991
1983—Indianapolis	A. A.	OF	19	77	18	23	4	0	7	19	.299	61	1	1	.984

Selected by Cincinnati Reds' organization in 8th round of free-agent draft, June 3, 1980.

GEORGE EARL DAVIS
(Storm)

Born December 26, 1961, at Dallas, Tex.
Height, 6.04. Weight, 210.
Throws and bats righthanded.

Year Club	League	G.	IP.	W.	L.	Pct.	H.	R.	ER.	SO.	BB.	ERA.
1979—Bluefield	Ap'lachian.	10	58	4	4	.500	44	34	25	54	30	3.88
1980—Miami	Florida St.	25	151	9	12	.429	157	85	59	90	55	3.52
1981—Charlotte	Southern	28	187	14	10	.583	*215	86	72	119	65	3.47
1982—Rochester	Int'national	4	26⅔	2	1	.667	25	13	11	27	7	3.71
1982—Baltimore	American	29	100⅔	8	4	.667	96	40	39	67	28	3.49
1983—Baltimore	American	34	200⅓	13	7	.650	180	90	80	125	64	3.59
Major League Totals		63	301	21	11	.656	276	130	119	192	92	3.56

Selected by Baltimore Orioles' organization in 7th round of free-agent draft, June 5, 1979.

CHAMPIONSHIP SERIES RECORD

Year Club	League	G.	IP.	W.	L.	Pct.	H.	R.	ER.	SO.	BB.	ERA.
1983—Baltimore	American	1	6	0	0	.000	5	0	0	2	2	0.00

WORLD SERIES RECORD

Year Club	League	G.	IP.	W.	L.	Pct.	H.	R.	ER.	SO.	BB.	ERA.
1983—Baltimore	American	1	5	1	0	1.000	6	3	3	3	1	5.40

GERALD EDWARD DAVIS
(Jerry)

Born December 25, 1958, at Trenton, N.J.
Height, 6.01. Weight, 185.
Throws and bats righthanded.
Attended Howard University, Washington, D.C.

Led Carolina League in bases on balls received with 161 and being hit by pitch with 14 in 1981.

Year Club	League	Pos.	G.	AB.	R.	H.	2B.	3B.	HR.	RBI.	B.A.	PO.	A.	E.	F.A.
1980—Walla Walla	N'west	3B	54	197	39	60	4	1	8	50	.305	42	104	24	.859
1981—Salem	Carol.	OF-3B	*138	431	*114	132	24	3	*34	103	.306	140	49	30	.863
1982—Amarillo	Texas	OF	95	365	78	129	18	1	14	67	.353	158	4	10	.942
1982—Hawaii	P. C.	OF	41	145	26	39	8	0	3	19	.269	68	11	7	.919
1983—Las Vegas	P. C.	OF	139	503	113	150	29	8	23	100	.298	296	17	9	.972
1983—San Diego	Nat.	OF	5	15	3	5	2	0	0	1	.333	8	1	0	1.000
Major League Totals		5	15	3	5	2	0	0	1	.333	8	1	0	1.000

Selected by Boston Red Sox' organization in 22nd round of free-agent draft, June 7, 1977.
Selected by San Diego Padres' organization in 6th round of free-agent draft, June 3, 1980.

GLENN EARL DAVIS

Born March 28, 1961, at Jacksonville, Fla.
Height, 6.03. Weight, 210.
Throws and bats righthanded.
Attended Manatee Junior College, Bradenton, Fla.,
and University of Georgia, Athens, Ga.

Led Gulf Coast League first basemen in total chances with 520 and tied for lead in double plays with 35 in 1981.

Year Club	League	Pos.	G.	AB.	R.	H.	2B.	3B.	HR.	RBI.	B.A.	PO.	A.	E.	F.A.
1981—Sara. Astros-Or.	Gulf C.	*1B-OF	54	188	27	49	7	1	6	35	.261	*469	*37	*14	.973
1982—Daytona Beach	Fla. St.	1B-3B	103	378	70	119	28	3	●19	79	.315	759	70	16	.981
1982—Columbus	South.	1B	26	97	14	24	6	1	4	8	.247	257	11	2	.993
1983—Columbus	South.	OF	118	445	68	133	19	3	*25	85	.299	186	17	9	.958

Selected by Baltimore Orioles' organization in 32nd round of free-agent draft, June 5, 1979.
Selected by Houston Astros' organization in secondary phase of free-agent draft, January 13, 1981.

JODY RICHARD DAVIS

Born November 12, 1956, at Gainesville, Ga.
Height, 6.04. Weight, 192.
Throws and bats righthanded.
Attended Middle Georgia College, Cochran, Ga.

Led National League in passed balls with 21 in 1983.
Tied for National League lead in double plays by catchers with 11 in 1982.
Led Carolina League in sacrifice flies with 13 in 1978.
Led Carolina League catchers in double plays with 8 in 1978.

Year	Club	League	Pos.	G.	AB.	R.	H.	2B.	3B.	HR.	RBI.	B.A.	PO.	A.	E.	F.A.
1976—Marion	Appal.		C	50	164	20	38	5	1	5	19	.232	290	30	*13	.961
1977—Little Falls	NYP		C-1B	64	214	37	62	11	2	11	46	.290	369	50	12	.972
1978—Lynchburg	Carol.		C-1B-3B	120	408	57	107	24	2	16	94	.262	595	79	15	.978
1979—Jackson†	Texas		C-1B	132	433	57	128	23	4	21	91	.296	661	81	15	.980
1980—St. Petersburg	Fla. St.		C-1B	45	155	27	43	4	0	6	27	.277	171	20	5	.974
1980—Springfield‡§	A. A.		C-1B	13	36	3	6	1	0	0	2	.167	59	7	1	.985
1981—Chicago	Nat.		C	56	180	14	46	5	1	4	21	.256	274	44	9	.972
1982—Chicago	Nat.		C	130	418	41	109	20	2	12	52	.261	598	89	11	.984
1983—Chicago	Nat.		C	151	510	56	138	31	2	24	84	.271	730	75	13	.984
Major League Totals				337	1108	111	293	56	5	40	157	.264	1602	208	33	.982

Selected by New York Mets' organization in 3rd round of free-agent draft, January 7, 1976.
†Traded to St. Louis Cardinals' organization for Pitcher Ray Searage, December 10, 1979.
‡On disabled list, April 14 to June 20, 1980.
§Drafted by Chicago Cubs, December 8, 1980.

MARK WILLIAM DAVIS

Born October 19, 1960, at Livermore, Calif.
Height, 6.03. Weight, 180.
Throws and bats lefthanded.
Attended Chabot College, Hayward, Calif.

Led Western Carolinas League in shutouts with 5, home runs allowed with 18 and tied for lead in balks with 5 in 1979.
Tied for Eastern League lead in shutouts with 4 and in games started by pitchers with 28 in 1980.
Named Eastern League Player of the Year, 1980.

Year	Club	League	G.	IP.	W.	L.	Pct.	H.	R.	ER.	SO.	BB.	ERA.
1979—Spartanburg	W. Carol.		26	166	11	9	.550	147	76	59	135	49	3.20
1980—Reading	Eastern		28	*193	*19	6	*.760	140	63	53	*185	75	*2.47
1980—Philadelphia	National		2	7	0	0	.000	4	2	2	5	5	2.57
1981—Oklahoma City†	Am. Assoc.		13	65	5	2	.714	66	34	28	56	47	3.88
1981—Philadelphia	National		9	43	1	4	.200	49	37	37	29	24	7.74
1982—Oklahoma City‡§	Am. Assoc.		21	96⅔	5	12	.294	111	75	67	95	50	6.24
1983—Phoenix	P. Coast		13	72⅔	6	3	.667	89	57	51	64	33	6.32
1983—San Francisco	National		20	111	6	4	.600	93	51	43	83	50	3.49
Major League Totals			31	161	7	8	.467	146	90	82	117	79	4.58

Selected by New York Mets' organization in 21st round of free-agent draft, June 6, 1978.
Selected by Philadelphia Phillies' organization in secondary phase of free-agent draft, January 9, 1979.
†On disabled list, April 14 to June 11, 1981.
‡On disabled list, August 3 to August 30, 1982.
§Traded with Pitcher Mike Krukow and Outfielder Charles Penigar to San Francisco Giants for Second Baseman Joe Morgan and Pitcher Al Holland, December 14, 1982.

MICHAEL DWAYNE DAVIS
(Mike)

Born June 11, 1959, at San Diego, Calif.
Height, 6.03. Weight, 190.
Throws and bats lefthanded.
Attended Mesa College, Mesa, Ariz.
Cousin of Dave Grayson, defensive back with Dallas Texans,
Kansas City Chiefs and Oakland Raiders, 1961 through 1970.

Major League stolen bases: 1980 (2), 1982 (3), 1983 (32). Total—37.

Year	Club	League	Pos.	G.	AB.	R.	H.	2B.	3B.	HR.	RBI.	B.A.	PO.	A.	E.	F.A.
1977—Medicine Hat	Pion.		*OF-1-2	59	213	53	67	5	3	2	18	.315	82	6	*15	.854
1978—Modesto	Calif.		OF-1B	106	406	74	136	12	4	2	35	.335	201	10	13	.942
1979—Modesto	Calif.		OF	41	161	48	63	10	4	0	19	.391	76	3	7	.919
1979—Waterbury	East.		OF	97	351	51	77	9	5	6	39	.219	208	7	15	.935
1980—Ogden	P. C.		OF	19	69	14	21	7	2	1	14	.304	34	2	1	.973
1980—Oakland	Amer.		OF-1B	51	95	11	20	2	1	1	8	.211	76	7	1	.988
1981—Tacoma	P. C.		OF-1B	133	515	84	148	28	6	6	71	.287	286	7	7	.977
1981—Oakland	Amer.		OF-1B	17	20	0	1	1	0	0	0	.050	3	0	0	1.000
1982—Tacoma†	P. C.		OF-1B	100	374	71	118	23	3	12	68	.316	197	13	9	.959
1982—Oakland	Amer.		OF-1B	23	75	12	30	4	0	1	10	.400	65	4	5	.932
1983—Oakland‡	Amer.		OF	128	443	61	122	24	4	8	62	.275	278	16	8	.974
Major League Totals				219	633	84	173	31	5	10	80	.273	422	27	14	.970

Selected by Minnesota Twins' organization in 31st round of free agent draft, June 8, 1976.
Selected by Oakland A's organization in 3rd round of free agent draft, June 7, 1977.
†On disabled list, April 13 to May 24, 1982.
‡On supplemental disabled list, July 13 to July 31, 1983.

CHAMPIONSHIP SERIES RECORD

Year	Club	League	Pos.	G.	AB.	R.	H.	2B.	3B.	HR.	RBI.	B.A.	PO.	A.	E.	F.A.
1981—Oakland	Amer.		PH	1	1	0	1	0	0	0	0	1.000	0	0	0	.000

RONALD GENE DAVIS
(Ron)

Born August 6, 1955, at Houston Tex.
Height, 6.04. Weight, 198.
Throws and bats righthanded.
Attended Blinn Junior College, Brenham, Tex.

Established major league record for most consecutive strikeouts by relief pitcher, game (8), May 4, 1981.
Established American League record for most wins by rookie relief pitcher, season (14), 1979.
Tied American League record for most consecutive strikeouts, game (8), May 4, 1981.
Major League saves: 1979 (9), 1980 (7), 1981 (6), 1982 (22), 1983 (30). Total—74.
Led American League in intentional bases on balls issued with 12 in 1982.

Year Club	League	G.	IP.	W.	L.	Pct.	H.	R.	ER.	SO.	BB.	ERA.
1976—Pompano Beach	Florida St.	18	115	8	8	.500	110	62	48	78	51	3.76
1977—Midland†	Texas					(Did not play)						
1977—Pompano Beach	Florida St.	21	111	8	7	.533	119	63	51	58	59	4.14
1978—Midland‡	Texas	12	68	3	3	.500	80	51	48	45	38	6.35
1978—West Haven	Eastern	21	60	9	2	.818	41	14	10	39	27	1.50
1978—New York	American	4	2	0	0	.000	3	4	3	0	3	13.50
1979—Columbus	Int'national	11	19	0	1	.000	13	9	9	10	15	4.26
1979—New York	American	44	85	14	2	★.875	84	29	27	43	28	2.86
1980—New York	American	53	131	9	3	.750	121	50	43	65	32	2.95
1981—New York§	American	43	73	4	5	.444	47	22	22	83	25	2.71
1982—Minnesota	American	63	106	3	9	.250	106	53	52	89	47	4.42
1983—Minnesota	American	66	89	5	8	.385	89	34	33	84	33	3.34
Major League Totals		273	486	35	27	.565	450	192	180	364	168	3.33

Selected by Chicago Cubs' organization in 3rd round of free-agent draft, January 7, 1976.

†On disabled list, April 9 to May 6, 1977.

‡Traded to New York Yankees' organization, June 12, 1978; completing deal in which New York traded Pitcher Ken Holtzman to Chicago Cubs for a player to be named later, June 10, 1978.

§Traded with Pitcher Paul Boris and Shortstop Greg Gagne and a reported $400,000 to Minnesota Twins for Shortstop Roy Smalley, April 10, 1982.

DIVISION SERIES RECORD

Year Club	League	G.	IP.	W.	L.	Pct.	H.	R.	ER.	SO.	BB.	ERA.
1981—New York	American	3	6	1	0	1.000	1	0	0	6	2	0.00

CHAMPIONSHIP SERIES RECORD

Year Club	League	G.	IP.	W.	L.	Pct.	H.	R.	ER.	SO.	BB.	ERA.
1980—New York	American	1	4	0	0	.000	3	1	1	3	1	2.25
1981—New York	American	2	3⅓	0	0	.000	0	0	0	4	2	0.00
Championship Series Totals		3	7⅓	0	0	.000	3	1	1	7	3	1.23

WORLD SERIES RECORD

Year Club	League	G.	IP.	W.	L.	Pct.	H.	R.	ER.	SO.	BB.	ERA.
1981—New York	American	4	2⅓	0	0	.000	4	8	6	4	5	23.14

ALL-STAR GAME RECORD

Year League		IP.	W.	L.	Pct.	H.	R.	ER.	SO.	BB.	ERA.
1981—American		1	0	0	.000	1	1	1	1	0	9.00

TRENCH NEAL DAVIS

Born September 12, 1960, at Baltimore, Md.
Height, 6.01. Weight, 185.
Throws and bats lefthanded.

Led Pacific Coast League in caught stealing with 22 in 1982.

Year Club	League	Pos.	G.	AB.	R.	H.	2B.	3B.	HR.	RBI.	B.A.	PO.	A.	E.	F.A.
1980—Bradenton Pir.	Gulf C.	1B	43	142	16	39	3	3	1	12	.275	184	15	10	.952
1981—Greenwood	S. Atl.	1B-OF	●141	●530	70	★158	24	9	4	73	.298	917	31	31	.968
1982—Portland	P. C.	OF	141	★571	80	153	16	5	2	46	.268	333	16	★14	.961
1983—Hawaii	P.C.	OF-1B	79	277	41	71	6	9	0	23	.256	147	9	3	.981
1983—Lynn	East.	OF-1B	59	219	37	61	7	4	2	16	.279	110	7	5	.959

Signed as free agent by Pittsburgh Pirates' organization, June 23, 1980.

WALLACE McARTHUR DAVIS
(Butch)

Born June 19, 1958, at Martin County, N.C.
Height, 6.00. Weight, 185.
Throws and bats righthanded.
Attended East Carolina University, Greenville, N.C.

Led Gulf Coast League in total bases with 105 and stolen bases with 31 in 1980.

Year Club	League	Pos.	G.	AB.	R.	H.	2B.	3B.	HR.	RBI.	B.A.	PO.	A.	E.	F.A.
1980—Sarasota Royals	Gulf C.	OF	61	235	46	★74	★17	4	2	35	.315	117	5	3	.976
1981—Ft. Myers	Fla. St.	OF	126	464	★89	139	17	10	13	70	.300	239	5	12	.953
1982—Jacksonville	South.	OF	122	450	˙64	115	18	4	10	57	.256	231	7	2	.992
1983—Jacksonville	South.	OF-1B	90	331	51	105	15	7	14	63	.317	117	4	4	.968

Year Club League	Pos.	G.	AB.	R.	H.	2B.	3B.	HR.	RBI.	B.A.	PO.	A.	E.	F.A.
1983—Omaha.................A.A.	OF	46	171	27	54	10	3	5	21	.316	10	0	1	.909
1983—Kansas City...........Amer.	OF	33	122	13	42	2	6	2	18	.344	83	1	2	.977
Major League Totals..................................		33	122	13	42	2	6	2	18	.344	83	1	2	.977

Selected by Kansas City Royals' organization in 12th round of free-agent draft, June 3, 1980.

WILLIAM CHESTER DAWLEY
(Bill)

Born February 6, 1958, at Norwich, Conn.
Height, 6.05. Weight, 230.
Throws and bats righthanded.

Major League saves: 1983 (14).
Led American Association pitchers in games started with 28 in 1982.

Year Club	League	G.	IP.	W.	L.	Pct.	H.	R.	ER.	SO.	BB.	ERA.
1976—Billings..............................	Pioneer	13	78	6	4	.600	62	42	24	80	37	2.77
1977—Tampa...............................	Florida St.	24	181	10	8	.556	151	69	57	110	69	2.83
1978—Nashville..........................	Southern	27	141	7	13	.350	135	78	63	86	55	4.02
1979—Nashville†........................	Southern	25	140	9	9	.500	144	72	62	84	41	3.99
1980—Indianapolis.....................	Am. Assoc.	25	77	4	6	.400	90	46	39	28	31	4.56
1980—Waterbury........................	Eastern	7	49	2	2	.500	43	18	16	33	25	2.94
1981—Indianapolis.....................	Am. Assoc.	26	133	6	8	.429	141	77	73	109	69	4.94
1982—Indianapolis‡§..................	Am. Assoc.	29	★179	11	7	.611	196	86	76	106	48	3.82
1983—Houston ....:.......	National	48	79⅔	6	6	.500	51	26	25	60	22	2.82
Major League Totals..................................		48	79⅔	6	6	.500	51	26	25	60	22	2.82

Selected by Cincinnati Reds' organization in 7th round of free-agent draft, June 8, 1976.
†On temporary inactive list, May 21 to May 31, 1979.
‡Appeared in one game as an outfielder with no chances.
§Traded with Outfielder Anthony Walker to Houston Astros' organization for Catcher Alan Knicely, March 31, 1983.

ALL-STAR GAME RECORD

Year League	IP.	W.	L.	Pct.	H.	R.	ER.	SO.	BB.	ERA.
1983—National..	1⅓	0	0	.000	1	0	0	1	0	0.00

ANDRE FERNANDO DAWSON

Born July 10, 1954, at Miami, Fla.
Height, 6.03. Weight, 192.
Throws and bats righthanded.
Attended Florida A&M University, Tallahassee, Fla.
Nephew of Theodore Taylor, third baseman-outfielder in Pittsburgh Pirates'
organization, 1967 through 1969.

Tied major league records for most total bases, inning (8) and most home runs, inning (2), July 30, 1978 (third inning).
Major league stolen bases: 1976 (1), 1977 (21), 1978 (28), 1979 (35), 1980 (34), 1981 (26), 1982 (39), 1983 (25). Total—209.
Led National League in being hit by pitch with 12 in 1978 and 7 in 1981.
Led National League in total bases with 341 and sacrifice flies with 18 in 1983.
Led National League outfielders in total chances with 344 in 1981, 435 in 1982 and 450 in 1983.
Tied for National League lead in being hit by pitch with 6 in 1980 and 9 in 1983.
Led Pioneer League in total bases with 166, in being hit by pitch with 6 and tied for lead in sacrifice flies with 5 in 1975.
Named National League Player of the Year by THE SPORTING NEWS, 1981.
Named National League Rookie Player of the Year by THE SPORTING NEWS, 1977.
Named National League Rookie of the Year by Baseball Writers' Association of America, 1977.
Named outfielder on THE SPORTING NEWS National League All-Star Team, 1981 and 1983.
Named outfielder on THE SPORTING NEWS National League All-Star fielding team, 1980 through 1983.
Named outfielder on THE SPORTING NEWS National League Silver Slugger team, 1980, 1981 and 1983.

Year Club League	Pos.	G.	AB.	R.	H.	2B.	3B.	HR.	RBI.	B.A.	PO.	A.	E.	F.A.
1975—Lethbridge ....Pion.	OF	●72	★300	52	★99	14	7	★13	50	.330	★142	7	★10	.937
1976—Quebec City ....East.	OF	40	143	27	51	6	0	8	27	.357	89	3	6	.939
1976—Denver ....A. A.	OF	74	240	51	84	19	4	20	46	.350	97	2	2	.980
1976—Montreal..............Nat.	OF	24	85	9	20	4	1	0	7	.235	61	1	2	.969
1977—Montreal..............Nat.	OF	139	525	64	148	26	9	19	65	.282	352	9	4	.989
1978—Montreal..............Nat.	OF	157	609	84	154	24	8	25	72	.253	411	17	5	.988
1979—Montreal..............Nat.	OF	155	639	90	176	24	12	25	92	.275	394	7	5	.988
1980—Montreal..............Nat.	OF	151	577	96	178	41	7	17	87	.308	410	14	6	.986
1981—Montreal..............Nat.	OF	103	394	71	119	21	3	24	64	.302	★327	10	7	.980
1982—Montreal..............Nat.	OF	148	608	107	183	37	7	23	83	.301	★419	8	8	.982
1983—Montreal..............Nat.	OF	159	633	104	●189	36	10	32	113	.299	★435	6	9	.980
Major League Totals....................		1036	4070	625	1167	213	57	165	583	.287	2809	72	46	.984

Selected by Montreal Expos' organization in 11th round of free-agent draft, June 4, 1975.

DIVISION SERIES RECORD

Year Club League	Pos.	G.	AB.	R.	H.	2B.	3B.	HR.	RBI.	B.A.	PO.	A.	E.	F.A.
1981—Montreal...............Nat.	OF	5	20	1	6	0	1	0	0	.300	12	1	1	.929

Year Club League	Pos.	G.	AB.	R.	H.	2B.	3B.	HR.	RBI.	B.A.	PO.	A.	E.	F.A.
1981—Montreal .... Nat.	OF	5	20	2	3	0	0	0	0	.150	12	0	0	1.000

ALL-STAR GAME RECORD

Year League	Pos.	AB.	R.	H.	2B.	3B.	HR.	RBI.	B.A.	PO.	A.	E.	F.A.
1981—National	OF	4	0	1	0	0	0	0	.250	4	0	0	1.000
1982—National	OF	4	0	1	0	0	0	0	.250	4	0	0	1.000
1983—National	OF	3	0	0	0	0	0	0	.000	3	0	0	1.000
All-Star Game Totals		11	0	2	0	0	0	0	.182	11	0	0	1.000

BRIAN KELLY DAYETT

Born January 22, 1957, at New London, Conn.
Height, 5.10. Weight, 185.
Throws and bats righthanded.
Attended St. Leo College, St. Leo, Fla.

Led International League in total bases with 281 in 1983.
Led Southern League in total bases with 285 and game-winning RBIs with 15 in 1982.
Tied for New York-Pennsylvania League lead in double plays by third basemen with 20 in 1978.
Named Southern League Most Valuable Player, 1982.

Year Club League	Pos.	G.	AB.	R.	H.	2B.	3B.	HR.	RBI.	B.A.	PO.	A.	E.	F.A.
1978—Oneonta .... NYP	3B-C-1B	68	256	53	79	●20	4	11	63	.309	207	106	14	.957
1979—West Haven .... East.	3B	135	465	58	119	21	4	11	74	.256	86	226	24	.929
1980—Nashville............... South.	3B	35	100	15	21	8	0	0	9	.210	16	60	6	.927
1980—Alexandria .... Carol.	3B-2B	13	48	12	21	5	1	3	17	.438	7	17	3	.889
1980—Ft. Lauderdale ..... Fla. St.	3B	52	174	31	43	8	2	4	21	.247	51	103	11	.933
1981—Nashville............... South.	3B-OF	112	338	53	91	15	3	18	62	.269	55	125	15	.923
1982—Nashville............... South.	OF-3B	●144	536	89	150	29	2	34	96	.280	201	9	12	.946
1983—Columbus............... Int.	OF-1B-3B	128	479	105	138	28	5	★35	★108	.288	224	10	6	.975
1983—New York............. Amer.	OF	11	29	3	6	0	1	0	5	.207	22	1	0	1.000
Major League Totals..................................		11	29	3	6	0	1	0	5	.207	22	1	0	1.000

Selected by New York Yankees' organization in 16th round of free-agent draft, June 6, 1978.

KENNETH GRANT DAYLEY
(Ken)

Born February 25, 1959, at Jerome, Idaho.
Height, 6.00. Weight, 178.
Throws and bats lefthanded.
Attended University of Portland, Portland, Ore.

Led International League pitchers in games started with 31 in 1981.

Year Club League	G.	IP.	W.	L.	Pct.	H.	R.	ER.	SO.	BB.	ERA.
1980—Savannah.. Southern	16	105	8	3	.727	86	38	30	104	54	2.57
1981—Richmond.. Int'national	31	★200	●13	8	.619	180	82	74	★162	★117	3.33
1982—Richmond.. Int'national	13	98⅓	8	3	.727	89	43	34	79	47	3.11
1982—Atlanta .... National	20	71⅓	5	6	.455	79	39	36	34	25	4.54
1983—Richmond.. Int'national	14	90⅔	9	3	.750	79	39	33	74	49	3.28
1983—Atlanta .... National	24	104⅔	5	8	.385	100	59	50	70	39	4.30
Major League Totals...	44	176	10	14	.417	179	98	86	104	64	4.40

Selected by Atlanta Braves' organization in 1st round (third player selected) of free-agent draft, June 3, 1980.

DOUGLAS VERNON DeCINCES

Name pronounced Duh-SIN-say.

(Doug)

Born August 29, 1950, at Burbank, Calif.
Height, 6.02. Weight, 195.
Throws and bats righthanded.
Attended Pierce Junior College, Woodland Hills, Calif., and University of
California at Los Angeles, Los Angeles, Calif.

Tied major league record for most times, three or more home runs, game, season (2), August 3 and August 8, 1982.
Tied American League record for most assists, third baseman, game (11), May 7, 1983, 12 innings.
Hit three home runs in a game, August 3 and August 8, 1982.
Led American League third basemen in assists with 330 in 1977 and 399 in 1982.
Led American League third basemen in total chances with 474 in 1977 and 479 in 1980.
Led American League third basemen in double plays with 34 in 1977, 41 in 1980 and 31 in 1981.
Tied for American League lead in putouts by third basemen with 86 in 1981.
Led Southern League second basemen in errors with 26 in 1972.
Named third baseman on THE SPORTING NEWS American League All-Star Team, 1982.
Named third baseman on THE SPORTING NEWS American League Silver Slugger team, 1982.

Year Club League	Pos.	G.	AB.	R.	H.	2B.	3B.	HR.	RBI.	B.A.	PO.	A.	E.	F.A.
1970—Bluefield .... Appal.	S-1-2-3-P	54	164	28	48	10	0	4	27	.293	105	98	18	.919
1970—Dallas-Ft. W........... Texas	SS	11	35	3	6	1	0	0	2	.171	25	19	3	.936
1971—Dallas-Ft. W.†....... Texas	2B-SS	78	235	29	61	10	1	5	29	.260	154	164	12	.964
1972—Asheville............... South.	2B-SS	123	396	71	104	23	7	10	60	.263	254	314	28	.953
1973—Rochester............. Int.	★3B-S-2	131	438	79	117	25	3	19	79	.267	150	264	17	★.961
1973—Baltimore............. Amer.	3B-2B-SS	10	18	2	2	0	0	0	3	.111	4	19	2	.920

Year Club	League	Pos.	G.	AB.	R.	H.	2B.	3B.	HR.	RBI.	B.A.	PO.	A.	E.	F.A.
1974—Rochester	Int.	3B	132	444	70	125	17	4	11	66	.282	98	255	★32	.917
1974—Baltimore	Amer.	3B	1	1	0	0	0	0	0	0	.000	0	2	0	1.000
1975—Baltimore	Amer.	3-S-2-1	61	167	20	42	6	3	4	23	.251	92	115	7	.967
1976—Baltimore	Amer.	3-2-1-S	129	440	36	103	17	2	11	42	.234	191	257	20	.957
1977—Baltimore	Amer.	3B-1B-2B	150	522	63	135	28	3	19	69	.259	125	331	20	.958
1978—Baltimore	Amer.	3B-2B	142	511	72	146	37	1	28	80	.286	138	308	14	.970
1979—Baltimore‡	Amer.	3B	120	422	67	97	27	1	16	61	.230	99	247	13	.964
1980—Baltimore	Amer.	●3B-1B	145	489	64	122	23	2	16	64	.249	122	●340	19	.960
1981—Baltimore§	Amer.	●3-1-O	100	346	49	91	23	2	13	55	.263	91	191	●17	.943
1982—California	Amer.	3B-SS	153	575	94	173	42	5	30	97	.301	113	400	22	.959
1983—California x	Amer.	3B	95	370	49	104	19	3	18	65	.281	79	216	14	.955
Major League Totals			1106	3861	516	1015	222	22	155	559	.263	1054	2426	148	.959

Selected by San Diego Padres' organization in 3rd round of free-agent draft, June 5, 1969.
Selected by Baltimore Orioles' organization in secondary phase of free-agent draft, January 17, 1970.
†On disabled list, June 25 to July 27, 1971.
‡On supplemental disabled list, April 27, 1979; transferred to disabled list, May 14 to June 5, 1979.
§Traded with Pitcher Jeff Schneider to California Angels for Outfielder Dan Ford, January 28, 1982.
xOn supplemental disabled list, July 14 to August 19, 1983.

CHAMPIONSHIP SERIES RECORD

Year Club	League	Pos.	G.	AB.	R.	H.	2B.	3B.	HR.	RBI.	B.A.	PO.	A.	E.	F.A.
1979—Baltimore	Amer.	3B	4	13	4	4	1	0	0	3	.308	5	8	0	1.000
1982—California	Amer.	3B	5	19	5	6	2	0	0	0	.316	9	12	3	.875
Championship Series Totals			9	32	9	10	3	0	0	3	.313	14	20	3	.919

WORLD SERIES RECORD

Tied World Series records for hitting home run in first series at bat, October 10, 1979; most errors by third baseman, inning (2), October 10, 1979 (sixth inning); most bases on balls, game (4), October 13, 1979.

Year Club	League	Pos.	G.	AB.	R.	H.	2B.	3B.	HR.	RBI.	B.A.	PO.	A.	E.	F.A.
1979—Baltimore	Amer.	3B	7	25	2	5	0	0	1	3	.200	7	21	3	.903

ALL-STAR GAME RECORD

Year League	Pos.	AB.	R.	H.	2B.	3B.	HR.	RBI.	B.A.	PO.	A.	E.	F.A.
1983—American	PH	1	0	0	0	0	0	0	.000	0	0	0	.000

PITCHING RECORD

Year Club	League	G.	IP.	W.	L.	Pct.	H.	R.	ER.	SO.	BB.	ERA.
1970—Bluefield	Ap'lachian	1	2	0	1	.000	3	2	1	1	1	4.50

DEE MARTIN DECKER
(Marty)

Born June 7, 1957, at Upland, Calif.
Height, 5.11. Weight, 170.
Throws and bats righthanded.
Received bachelor of arts degree in physical education from
Point Loma College, San Diego, Calif.

Led Carolina League in saves with 18 in 1981.
Led Pioneer League in saves with 9 in 1980.

Year Club	League	G.	IP.	W.	L.	Pct.	H.	R.	ER.	SO.	BB.	ERA.
1980—Helena	Pioneer	25	42	4	1	.800	23	10	10	68	12	2.14
1981—Peninsula	Carolina	55	50	3	5	.375	50	24	19	108	36	2.09
1982—Oklahoma City†	Am. Assoc.	10	14⅔	0	3	.000	72	15	13	19	11	7.98
1983—Portland‡	P. Coast	58	96	8	3	.727	105	77	71	102	65	6.66
1983—San Diego	National	4	8⅔	0	0	.000	5	2	2	9	3	2.08
Major League Totals		4	8⅔	0	· 0	.000	5	2	2	9	3	2.08

Selected by Philadelphia Phillies' organization in 23rd round of free-agent draft, June 3, 1980.
†On disabled list, May 25, 1982 through remainder of season.
‡Traded with Pitchers Ed Wojna, Darren Burroughs and Lance McCullers to San Diego Padres, September 20, 1983, as partial completion of deal in which San Diego traded Outfielder Sixto Lezcano and a player to be named later to Philadelphia Phillies for four players to be named later, August 31, 1983; Philadelphia organization acquired Pitcher Steve Fireovid to complete deal, October 11, 1983.

JEFFREY LINDEN DEDMON
(Jeff)

Born March 4, 1960, at Torrance, Calif.
Height, 6.02. Weight, 185.
Throws right and bats lefthanded.
Attended West Los Angeles College, Culver City, Calif.

Year Club	League	G.	IP.	W.	L.	Pct.	H.	R.	ER.	SO.	BB.	ERA.
1980—Bradenton Braves	Gulf Coast	10	64	3	4	.429	55	26	21	28	11	2.95
1980—Anderson	S. Atlantic	2	11	1	0	1.000	10	3	1	8	3	0.82
1981—Durham	Carolina	28	165	7	8	.467	178	97	79	115	50	4.31
1982—Durham	Carolina	31	121⅓	5	6	.455	113	57	37	102	54	2.74
1983—Savannah	Southern	21	50	4	1	.800	46	18	16	26	16	2.88

Year	Club	League	G.	IP.	W.	L.	Pct.	H.	R.	ER.	SO.	BB.	ERA.
1983—Richmond		Int'national	21	36	2	2	.500	28	9	7	33	14	1.75
1983—Atlanta		National	5	4	0	0	.000	10	6	6	3	0	13.50
Major League Totals			5	4	0	0	.000	10	6	6	3	0	13.50

Selected by Houston Astros' organization in 1st round (seventh player selected), of free-agent draft, January 9, 1979.

Selected by Oakland A's organization in secondary phase of free-agent draft, June 5, 1979.

Selected by San Francisco Giants' organization in secondary phase of free-agent draft, January 8, 1980.

Selected by Atlanta Braves' organization in secondary phase of free-agent draft, June 3, 1980.

ROBERT GEORGE DEER
(Rob)

Born September 29, 1960, at Orange, Calif.
Height, 6.03. Weight, 215.
Throws and bats righthanded.
Attended Fresno City College, Fresno, Calif.

Led Texas League batters in strikeouts with 177 in 1982 and 185 in 1983.
Tied for Texas League lead in game-winning RBIs with 13 in 1983.
Led California League batters in strikeouts with 146 in 1981.

Year	Club	League	Pos.	G.	AB.	R.	H.	2B.	3B.	HR.	RBI.	B.A.	PO.	A.	E.	F.A.
1978—Great Falls		Pion.	OF	48	137	20	34	6	5	0	18	.248	83	3	4	.956
1979—Cedar Rapids		Midw.	OF	29	86	7	18	0	1	1	16	.209	35	1	4	.900
1979—Great Falls		Pion.	OF	63	218	49	69	18	7	7	44	.317	95	10	5	.955
1980—Clinton		Midw.	OF	127	434	60	114	31	5	13	58	.263	184	●17	11	.948
1981—Fresno		Calif.	OF	135	479	86	137	24	4	★33	107	.286	211	14	6	.974
1982—Shreveport		Texas	OF-1B	128	410	58	85	26	0	27	73	.207	184	10	11	.946
1983—Shreveport		Texas	OF	132	448	89	97	15	1	★35	99	.217	252	13	7	.974

Selected by San Francisco Giants' organization in 4th round of free-agent draft, June 6, 1978.

IVAN DeJESUS (ALVAREZ)
Name pronounced Day-HAY-soos.

Born January 9, 1953, at Santurce, Puerto Rico.
Height, 5.11. Weight, 175.
Throws and bats righthanded.
Attended University of Puerto Rico, Rio Piedras, Puerto Rico.

Tied Major League record for fewest double plays by shortstop, season, 150 or more games (64), 1983.
Major League stolen bases: 1975 (1), 1977 (24), 1978 (41), 1979 (24), 1980 (44), 1981 (21), 1982 (14), 1983 (11). Total—180.
Hit for the cycle, April 22, 1980.
Led National League shortstops in double plays with 81 in 1981.
Led Pacific Coast League shortstops in double plays with 114 in 1974.
Led California League shortstops in double plays with 87 in 1973.
Led California League shortstops in assists with 311, errors with 48 and double plays with 53 in 1971.
Led Florida State League shortstops in double plays with 56 in 1970.

Year	Club	League	Pos.	G.	AB.	R.	H.	2B.	3B.	HR.	RBI.	B.A.	PO.	A.	E.	F.A.
1970—Daytona Beach		Fla. St.	SS	123	396	51	92	12	7	2	38	.232	164	361	38	.933
1971—Bakersfield		Calif.	SS-2B	126	462	77	108	16	2	6	30	.234	159	323	49	.908
1972—Daytona Beach		Fla. St.	SS	131	442	56	108	15	4	7	39	.244	187	★452	37	.945
1973—Bakersfield		Calif.	SS	132	519	77	125	17	1	7	57	.241	221	★403	★47	.930
1974—Albuquerque		P. C.	SS	140	510	81	152	17	5	7	55	.298	★268	★479	38	.952
1974—Los Angeles		Nat.	SS	3	3	1	1	0	0	0	0	.333	1	0	0	1.000
1975—Albuquerque		P. C.	SS	62	221	24	60	10	2	1	21	.271	97	265	24	.938
1975—Los Angeles		Nat.	SS	63	87	10	16	2	1	0	2	.184	45	107	4	.974
1976—Albuquerque		P. C.	SS-3B	108	405	69	123	27	7	7	64	.304	161	341	35	.935
1976—Los Angeles†		Nat.	SS-3B	22	41	4	7	2	1	0	2	.171	20	47	3	.957
1977—Chicago		Nat.	SS	155	624	91	166	31	7	3	40	.266	234	★595	33	.962
1978—Chicago		Nat.	SS	160	619	★104	172	24	7	3	35	.278	234	★558	27	.967
1979—Chicago		Nat.	SS	160	636	92	180	26	10	5	52	.283	235	507	32	.959
1980—Chicago		Nat.	SS	157	618	78	160	26	3	3	33	.259	229	529	24	.969
1981—Chicago‡		Nat.	SS	106	403	49	78	8	4	0	13	.194	★221	343	24	.959
1982—Philadelphia		Nat.	SS-3B	161	536	53	128	21	5	3	59	.239	222	488	21	.971
1983—Philadelphia		Nat.	SS	158	497	60	126	15	7	4	45	.254	214	438	23	.966
Major League Totals			1145	4064	542	1034	155	45	21	281	.254	1653	3612	191	.965

Signed as free agent by Los Angeles Dodgers' organization, May 23, 1969.

†Traded with First Baseman Bill Buckner and Pitcher Jeff Albert to Chicago Cubs for Outfielder Rick Monday and Pitcher Mike Garman, January 11, 1977.

‡Traded to Philadelphia Phillies for Shortstop Larry Bowa and Infielder Ryne Sandberg, January 27, 1982.

CHAMPIONSHIP SERIES RECORD

Year	Club	League	Pos.	G.	AB.	R.	H.	2B.	3B.	HR.	RBI.	B.A.	PO.	A.	E.	F.A.
1983—Philadelphia		Nat.	SS	4	12	0	3	0	0	0	1	.250	4	11	2	.882

WORLD SERIES RECORD

Year	Club	League	Pos.	G.	AB.	R.	H.	2B.	3B.	HR.	RBI.	B.A.	PO.	A.	E.	F.A.
1983—Philadelphia		Nat.	SS	5	16	0	2	0	0	0	0	.125	5	14	1	.950

JOSE DeLEON (CHESTARO)

Born December 20, 1960, at LaVega, D.R.
Height, 6.03. Weight, 195.
Throws and bats righthanded.

Led Gulf Coast League in home runs allowed with 7 in 1979.
Tied for South Atlantic League lead in home runs allowed with 19 in 1980.
Tied for Gulf Coast League lead in wild pitches with 9 in 1979.

Year Club	League	G.	IP.	W.	L.	Pct.	H.	R.	ER.	SO.	BB.	ERA.
1979—Bradenton Pirates	Gulf Coast	11	59	2	4	.333	76	47	42	33	38	6.41
1980—Shelby	S. Atlantic	26	168	10	15	.400	160	108	*90	118	69	4.82
1981—Buffalo	Eastern	25	159	12	6	.667	136	72	55	158	94	3.11
1982—Portland†	P. Coast	24	119	10	7	.588	138	81	79	94	65	5.97
1983—Hawaii	P. Coast	20	127⅓	11	6	.647	90	50	43	128	68	*3.04
1983—Pittsburgh	National	15	108	7	3	.700	75	36	34	118	47	2.83
Major League Totals		15	108	7	3	.700	75	36	34	118	47	2.83

Selected by Pittsburgh Pirates' organization in 3rd round of free-agent draft June 5, 1979.
†On disabled list, July 5 to July 29, 1982.

LUIS ANTONIO DeLEON (TRICOCHE)

Born August 19, 1958, at Ponce, Puerto Rico.
Height, 6.01. Weight, 165.
Throws and bats righthanded.
Son of Luis A. DeLeon, minor league pitcher, 1957, 1958 and 1960; brother of Luis A. DeLeon, shortstop in
Cleveland Indians' organization; and Desiderio DeLeon, minor league pitcher, 1977.

Major League saves: 1982 (15), 1983 (13). Total—28.
Tied for Florida State League lead in saves with 14 and intentional bases on balls issued with 10 in 1979.
Tied for Appalachian League lead in shutouts with 2 in 1978.

Year Club	League	G.	IP.	W.	L.	Pct.	H.	R.	ER.	SO.	BB.	ERA.
1978—Johnson City	Ap'lachian	13	84	7	6	.538	84	37	31	74	26	3.32
1979—St. Petersburg	Florida St.	*59	92	8	3	.727	63	20	15	100	28	1.47
1979—Arkansas	Texas	2	3	0	0	.000	1	2	2	4	2	6.00
1980—Arkansas	Texas	*76	107	7	6	.538	85	46	39	92	49	3.28
1981—Springfield	Am. Assoc.	52	99	8	7	.533	73	34	28	96	35	2.55
1981—St. Louis†	National	10	15	0	1	.000	11	4	4	8	3	2.40
1982—San Diego	National	61	102	9	5	.643	77	25	23	60	16	2.03
1983—San Diego	National	63	111	6	6	.500	89	34	33	90	27	2.68
Major League Totals		134	228	15	12	.556	177	63	60	158	46	2.37

Signed as free agent by St. Louis Cardinals' organization, November 21, 1977.
†Traded to San Diego Padres for Pitcher Al Olmsted, February 19, 1982, completing deal in which San Diego
traded Pitcher Steve Mura and a player to be named later to St. Louis Cardinals for Outfielder Sixto Lezcano and a
player to be named later, December 10, 1981.

JOHN RIKARD DEMPSEY
(Rick)

Born September 13, 1949, at Fayetteville, Tenn.
Height, 6.00. Weight, 184.
Throws and bats righthanded.
Attended Pierce Junior College, Woodland Hills, Calif.
Brother of Pat Dempsey, catcher in Baltimore Orioles' organization.

Tied major league record for most double plays by catcher, game (3), June 1, 1977.
Tied for American League lead in double plays by catchers with 14 in 1978.
Led International League in passed balls with 14 in 1973.
Led New York-Pennsylvania League catchers in putouts with 468, assists with 35, fielding percentage with .990 and
tied for lead in double plays with 4 in 1968.

Year Club	League	Pos.	G.	AB.	R.	H.	2B.	3B.	HR.	RBI.	B.A.	PO.	A.	E.	F.A.
1967—Sarasota Twins	Gulf C.	C-OF-1B	40	102	9	21	4	3	0	9	.206	133	16	2	.987
1968—Wis. Rapids	Midw.	C	11	35	12	8	2	0	1	6	.229	68	2	1	.986
1968—Auburn	NYP	C-1B-OF	73	270	48	79	10	7	7	61	.293	505	38	7	.987
1969—Wis. Rapids	Midw.	C	50	151	35	55	11	2	6	31	.364	341	30	●13	.966
1969—Minnesota	Amer.	C	5	6	1	3	1	0	0	0	.500	5	0	1	.833
1970—Charlotte	South	C-OF-2B	105	351	28	86	20	6	4	42	.245	506	76	18	.970
1970—Minnesota	Amer.	C	5	7	1	0	0	0	0	0	.000	12	0	1	.923
1971—Charlotte	South	C-OF	105	338	39	82	16	2	8	47	.243	599	65	8	.988
1971—Minnesota	Amer.	C	6	13	2	4	1	0	0	0	.308	30	4	2	.944
1972—Minnesota†	Amer.	C	25	40	0	8	1	0	0	0	.200	67	5	1	.986
1972—Tacoma	P. C.	C-OF	48	161	13	38	6	2	3	18	.236	284	33	5	.984
1973—Syracuse	Int.	C-OF-3B	122	387	53	96	14	4	6	47	.248	585	69	9	.986
1973—New York	Amer.	C	6	11	0	2	0	0	0	0	.182	9	0	2	.818
1974—New York	Amer.	C-OF	43	109	12	26	3	0	2	12	.239	152	22	4	.978
1975—New York	Amer.	C-OF-3B	71	145	18	38	8	0	1	11	.262	92	9	3	.971
1976—N.Y.‡-Balt.	Amer.	C-OF	80	216	12	42	2	0	0	12	.194	302	39	4	.988
1977—Baltimore§	Amer.	C	91	270	27	61	7	4	3	34	.226	416	52	11	.977
1978—Baltimore	Amer.	C	136	441	41	114	25	0	6	32	.259	636	79	11	.985
1979—Baltimore	Amer.	C	124	368	48	88	23	0	6	41	.239	615	*81	7	.990
1980—Baltimore	Amer.	C-OF-1B	119	362	51	95	26	3	9	40	.262	544	55	8	.987
1981—Baltimore	Amer.	C	92	251	24	54	10	1	6	15	.215	384	35	1	*.998

Year Club	League	Pos.	G.	AB.	R.	H.	2B.	3B.	HR.	RBI.	B.A.	PO.	A.	E.	F.A.
1982—Baltimore	Amer.	C	125	344	35	88	15	1	5	36	.256	491	46	5	.991
1983—Baltimore	Amer.	C	128	347	33	80	16	2	4	32	.231	591	65	2	★.997
Major League Totals...................			1056	2930	305	703	138	11	42	265	.240	4346	492	63	.987

Selected by Minnesota Twins' organization in 12th round of free-agent draft, June 6, 1967.
†Traded to New York Yankees' organization for Outfielder Danny Walton, October 27, 1972.
‡Traded with Pitchers Rudy May, Tippy Martinez, Dave Pagan and Scott McGregor to Baltimore Orioles for Pitchers Ken Holtzman, Doyle Alexander and Grant Jackson, Catcher Ellie Hendricks and Pitcher Jimmy Freeman, June 15, 1976.
§On supplemental disabled list, July 9, 1977; transferred to disabled list, July 28 to August 21, 1977.

CHAMPIONSHIP SERIES RECORD

Year Club	League	Pos.	G.	AB.	R.	H.	2B.	3B.	HR.	RBI.	B.A.	PO.	A.	E.	F.A.
1979—Baltimore	Amer.	C	3	10	3	4	2	0	0	2	.400	10	1	0	1.000
1983—Baltimore	Amer.	C	4	12	1	2	0	0	0	0	.167	29	5	1	.971
Championship Series Totals			7	22	4	6	2	0	0	2	.273	39	6	1	.978

WORLD SERIES RECORD

Established World Series record for most long hits, five-game Series (5), 1983.
Tied World Series record for most two-base hits, five-game Series (4), 1983.

Year Club	League	Pos.	G.	AB.	R.	H.	2B.	3B.	HR.	RBI.	B.A.	PO.	A.	E.	F.A.
1979—Baltimore	Amer.	C-PR	7	21	3	6	2	0	0	0	.286	38	2	0	1.000
1983—Baltimore	Amer.	C	5	13	3	5	4	0	1	2	.385	27	4	0	1.000
World Series Totals..................			12	34	6	11	6	0	1	2	.324	65	6	0	1.000

MARK STEVEN DEMPSEY

Born December 17, 1957, at Dayton, Ohio.
Height, 6.06. Weight, 225.
Throws and bats righthanded.
Received bachelor of science degree from
Ohio State University, Columbus, Ohio, in 1980.

Led Pacific Coast League in complete games with 9 and home runs allowed with 35 in 1983.
Led Pioneer League in complete games with 9 and tied for lead in games started by pitchers with 14 in 1980.

Year Club	League	G.	IP.	W.	L.	Pct.	H.	R.	ER.	SO.	BB.	ERA.
1980—Great Falls......................................	Pioneer	15	★114	★14	1	.933	96	33	20	109	27	★1.58
1981—Shreveport	Texas	26	165	●15	7	.682	178	83	69	136	58	3.76
1982—Phoenix..................................	P. Coast	27	156⅓	10	10	.500	167	95	87	118	72	5.01
1982—San Francisco	National	3	5⅔	0	0	.000	11	5	5	4	2	7.94
1983—Phoenix..................................	P. Coast	24	148	9	9	.500	162	105	95	105	50	5.78
Major League Totals.................................		3	5⅔	0	0	.000	11	5	5	4	2	7.94

Selected by Houston Astros' organization in 9th round of free-agent draft, June 5, 1979.
Selected by San Francisco Giants' organization in 24th round of free-agent draft, June 3, 1980.

BRIAN JOHN DENMAN

Born February 12, 1956, at Minneapolis, Minn.
Height, 6.04. Weight, 205.
Throws and bats righthanded.
Attended University of Minnesota, Minneapolis, Minn.

Pitched 4-1 no-hit victory against West Haven, July 6, 1981.
Led Eastern League in shutouts with 3 in 1979 and complete games with 13 in 1981.

Year Club	League	G.	IP.	W.	L.	Pct.	H.	R.	ER.	SO.	BB.	ERA.
1978—Winter Haven...............................	Florida St.	27	189	★16	5	.762	147	51	43	122	34	2.05
1979—Bristol	Eastern	28	188	●14	10	.583	★194	88	77	97	54	3.69
1980—Bristol†......................................	Eastern	10	58	6	0	1.000	71	26	20	35	12	3.10
1981—Pawtucket	Int'national	1	2	0	0	.000	1	1	1	3	0	4.50
1981—Bristol	Eastern	25	★188	●15	3	.833	172	65	51	109	51	★2.44
1982—Pawtucket	Int'national	20	92⅔	7	4	.636	120	56	52	41	30	5.05
1982—Bristol	Eastern	5	38⅓	3	0	1.000	26	11	9	21	15	2.11
1982—Boston......................................	American	9	49	3	4	.429	55	32	26	9	9	4.78
1983—Pawtucket‡	Int'national	26	154⅓	8	11	.421	182	99	86	76	66	5.02
Major League Totals.................................		9	49	3	4	.429	55	32	26	9	9	4.78

Selected by California Angels' organization in 14th round of free-agent draft, June 7, 1977.
Selected by Boston Red Sox' organization in secondary phase of free-agent draft, January 10, 1978.
†On disabled list, April 14 to July 14, 1980.
‡On disabled list, June 9 to June 29, 1983.

JOHN ALLEN DENNY

Born November 8, 1952, at Prescott, Ariz.
Height, 6.03. Weight, 190.
Throws and bats righthanded.
Attended Yavapai College, Prescott, Ariz., and Southern Illinois University, Edwardsville, Ill.

Tied National League record for fewest games won, season, for leader in games won (19), 1983.
Pitched 8-1 no-hit victory against Midland, May 17, 1973.
Named National League Pitcher of the Year by THE SPORTING NEWS, 1983.
Won National League Cy Young Memorial Award, 1983.

Named National League Comeback Player of the Year by THE SPORTING NEWS, 1983.
Named righthanded pitcher on THE SPORTING NEWS National League All-Star Team, 1983.

Year	Club	League	G.	IP.	W.	L.	Pct.	H.	R.	ER.	SO.	BB.	ERA.
1970—Sarasota Cardinals	Gulf Coast	11	42	2	2	.500	32	14	6	43	9	1.29
1971—St. Petersburg	Florida St.	26	139	8	13	.381	123	58	47	77	62	3.04
1972—Modesto†	California	14	92	7	5	.583	95	54	45	65	39	4.40
1973—Arkansas‡	Texas	20	147	10	6	.625	128	57	51	81	52	3.11
1974—Tulsa	Am. Assoc.	21	132	9	8	.529	127	66	55	79	57	3.74
1974—St. Louis	National	2	2	0	0	.000	3	2	0	1	0	0.00
1975—Tulsa	Am. Assoc.	7	60	3	1	.750	47	12	12	44	32	1.80
1975—St. Louis	National	25	136	10	7	.588	149	73	60	72	51	3.97
1976—St. Louis	National	30	207	11	9	.550	189	71	58	74	74	★2.52
1977—St. Louis§	National	26	150	8	8	.500	165	85	75	60	62	4.50
1978—St. Louis	National	33	234	14	11	.560	200	81	77	103	74	2.96
1979—St. Louis x	National	31	206	8	11	.421	206	116	111	99	100	4.85
1980—Cleveland y	American	16	109	8	6	.571	116	54	53	59	47	4.38
1981—Cleveland z	American	19	146	10	6	.625	139	62	51	94	66	3.14
1982—Cleveland a	American	21	138⅓	6	11	.353	126	80	77	94	73	5.01
1982—Philadelphia	National	4	22⅓	0	2	.000	18	12	10	19	10	4.03
1983—Philadelphia	National	36	242⅔	★19	6	★.760	229	77	64	139	53	2.37
National League Totals		187	1200	70	54	.565	1159	517	455	567	424	3.41
American League Totals		56	393⅓	24	23	.511	381	196	181	247	186	4.14
Major League Totals		243	1593⅓	94	77	.550	1540	713	636	814	610	3.59

Selected by St. Louis Cardinals' organization in 29th round of free-agent draft, June 4, 1970.
†On disabled list, July 17, 1972 through remainder of season.
‡On disabled list, August 11, 1973 through remainder of season.
§On disabled list, June 22 to July 29, 1977.
xTraded with Outfielder Jerry Mumphrey to Cleveland Indians for Outfielder Bobby Bonds, December 7, 1979.
yOn disabled list, July 15 to September 8, 1980.
zGranted free agency, November 13, 1981; re-signed by Indians, February 13, 1982.
aTraded to Philadelphia Phillies for Pitchers Jerry Reed and Roy Smith and Outfielder Wil Culmer, September 11, 1982.

CHAMPIONSHIP SERIES RECORD

Year	Club	League	G.	IP.	W.	L.	Pct.	H.	R.	ER.	SO.	BB.	ERA.
1983—Philadelphia	National	1	6	0	1	.000	5	3	0	3	3	0.00

WORLD SERIES RECORD

Tied World Series record for most putouts, pitcher, inning (2), October 15, 1983 (fifth inning).

Year	Club	League	G.	IP.	W.	L.	Pct.	H.	R.	ER.	SO.	BB.	ERA.
1983—Philadelphia	National	2	13	1	1	.500	12	5	5	9	3	3.46

RUSSELL EARL DENT
(Bucky)

(Nicknamed by grandmother; word means "small Indian boy.")

Born November 25, 1951, at Savannah, Ga.
Height, 5.11. Weight, 184.
Throws and bats righthanded.
Attended Miami-Dade (North) Community College, Miami, Fla.

Led Amercian League in sacrifice hits with 23 in 1974.
Led American League shortstops in total chances with 838 in 1975.
Tied for American League lead in double plays by shortstops with 108 in 1974 and 105 in 1975.
Led American Association in sacrifice hits with 12 in 1973.
Led Midwest League in sacrifice hits with 12 in 1971.
Led Midwest League shortstops in double plays with 51 in 1971.
Tied for Gulf Coast League lead in sacrifice flies with 5 in 1970.

Year	Club	League	Pos.	G.	AB.	R.	H.	2B.	3B.	HR.	RBI.	B.A.	PO.	A.	E.	F.A.
1970—Sarasota W. S.	Gulf C.	3B-SS-2B	22	77	18	27	2	1	0	13	.351	30	55	11	.885
1970—Appleton	Midw.	SS-2B	39	163	23	42	4	2	3	12	.258	53	116	17	.909
1971—Appleton†	Midw.	SS-3B	83	294	34	68	16	0	1	29	.231	109	230	24	.934
1972—Knoxville	South.	SS	125	453	58	134	10	6	6	56	.296	167	437	31	.951
1973—Iowa	A. A.	★SS-3B	95	356	58	105	10	3	3	38	.295	137	308	★33	.931
1973—Chicago	Amer.	SS-2B-3B	40	117	17	29	2	0	0	10	.248	55	134	7	.964
1974—Chicago	Amer.	SS	154	496	55	136	15	3	5	45	.274	251	499	22	.972
1975—Chicago	Amer.	SS	157	602	52	159	29	4	3	58	.264	★279	★543	16	★.981
1976—Chicago‡	Amer.	SS	158	562	44	138	18	4	2	52	.246	279	468	18	.976
1977—New York	Amer.	SS	158	477	54	118	18	4	8	49	.247	250	434	18	.974
1978—New York§	Amer.	SS	123	379	40	92	11	1	5	40	.243	178	341	10	.981
1979—New York	Amer.	SS	141	431	47	99	14	2	2	32	.230	219	512	17	.977
1980—New York x	Amer.	SS	141	489	57	128	26	2	5	52	.262	224	489	13	★.982
1981—New York y	Amer.	SS	73	227	20	54	11	0	7	27	.238	104	217	10	.970
1982—N.Y. z-Tex.	Amer.	SS	105	306	27	59	10	1	1	23	.193	129	323	14	.970
1983—Texas	Amer.	SS	131	417	36	99	15	2	2	34	.237	150	369	11	★.979
Major League Totals			1381	4503	449	1111	169	23	40	422	.247	2118	4329	156	.976

Selected by St. Louis Cardinals' organization in 5th round of free-agent draft, June 5, 1969.
Selected by St. Louis Cardinals' organization in secondary phase of free-agent draft, January 17, 1970.

Selected by Chicago White Sox' organization in secondary phase of free-agent draft, June 4, 1970.
†On military list, December 31, 1970 through May 14, 1971.
‡Traded to New York Yankees for Outfielder Oscar Gamble, Pitchers Bob Polinsky and LaMarr Hoyt and cash estimated at $200,000, April 5, 1977.
§On supplemental disabled list, July 9 to July 31, 1978.
xOn supplemental disabled list, June 15 to June 30, 1980.
yOn disabled list, August 31, 1981 through remainder of season.
zTraded to Texas Rangers for Outfielder Lee Mazzilli, August 8, 1982.

CHAMPIONSHIP SERIES RECORD

Year—Club	League	Pos.	G.	AB.	R.	H.	2B.	3B.	HR.	RBI.	B.A.	PO.	A.	E.	F.A.
1977—New York	Amer.	SS	5	14	1	3	1	0	0	2	.214	10	14	1	.960
1978—New York	Amer.	SS	4	15	0	3	0	0	0	4	.200	2	8	1	.909
1980—New York	Amer.	SS	3	11	0	2	0	0	0	0	.182	8	12	0	1.000
Championship Series Totals			12	40	1	8	1	0	0	6	.200	20	34	2	.964

WORLD SERIES RECORD

Tied World Series record for one or more hits, each game, six-game Series, 1978.

Year—Club	League	Pos.	G.	AB.	R.	H.	2B.	3B.	HR.	RBI.	B.A.	PO.	A.	E.	F.A.
1977—New York	Amer.	SS	6	19	0	5	0	0	0	2	.263	2	15	1	.944
1978—New York	Amer.	SS	6	24	3	10	1	0	0	7	.417	8	16	2	.923
World Series Totals			12	43	3	15	1	0	0	9	.349	10	31	3	.932

ALL-STAR GAME RECORD

Year—League	Pos.	AB.	R.	H.	2B.	3B.	HR.	RBI.	B.A.	PO.	A.	E.	F.A.
1975—American	SS	1	0	0	0	0	0	0	.000	0	1	0	1.000
1980—American	SS	2	0	1	0	0	0	0	.500	0	1	0	1.000
1981—American	SS	2	0	2	1	0	0	0	1.000	0	2	0	1.000
All-Star Game Totals		5	0	3	1	0	0	0	.600	0	4	0	1.000

ROBERT EUGENE DERNIER

Name pronounced Dur-NEER.

(Bob)

Born January 5, 1957, at Kansas City, Mo.
Height, 6.00. Weight, 160.
Throws and bats righthanded.
Attended Longview Community College, Lee's Summit, Mo.

Major League stolen bases: 1980 (3), 1981 (2), 1982 (42), 1983 (35). Total—82.
Led Carolina League in stolen bases with 77 in 1979, Eastern League with 71 in 1980 and American Association with 72 in 1981.
Led Carolina League outfielders in putouts with 315 in 1979.
Tied for Carolina League lead in sacrifice hits with 12 in 1979.
Tied for Pioneer League lead in double plays by third basemen with 9 in 1978.
Named Carolina League Most Valuable Player, 1979.

Year—Club	League	Pos.	G.	AB.	R.	H.	2B.	3B.	HR.	RBI.	B.A.	PO.	A.	E.	F.A.
1978—Spartanburg	W. Car.	SS	22	57	9	8	1	0	0	5	.140	23	61	16	.840
1978—Helena	Pion.	3B	53	186	49	56	6	2	4	27	.301	38	104	22	.866
1979—Peninsula	Carol.	OF-3B	135	491	102	143	19	2	4	42	.291	331	23	10	.973
1980—Reading	East.	OF	136	*536	*111	160	29	4	10	57	.299	*325	9	9	.974
1980—Philadelphia	Nat.	OF	10	7	5	4	0	0	0	1	.571	9	0	0	1.000
1981—Oklahoma City	A. A.	OF	127	497	*105	150	26	7	5	35	.302	*317	7	5	.985
1981—Philadelphia	Nat.	OF	10	4	0	3	0	0	0	0	.750	2	0	0	1.000
1982—Philadelphia	Nat.	OF	122	370	56	92	10	2	4	21	.249	255	5	5	.981
1983—Philadelphia	Nat.	OF	122	221	41	51	10	0	1	15	.231	164	3	2	.988
1983—Reading	East.	OF	14	56	8	13	1	1	1	4	.232	36	0	0	1.000
Major League Totals			264	602	102	150	20	2	5	37	.249	430	8	7	.984

Selected by Cincinnati Reds' organization in 12th round of free-agent draft, January 11, 1977.
Signed as free agent by Philadelphia Phillies' organization, August 5, 1977.

CHAMPIONSHIP SERIES RECORD

Year—Club	League	Pos.	G.	AB.	R.	H.	2B.	3B.	HR.	RBI.	B.A.	PO.	A.	E.	F.A.
1983—Philadelphia	Nat.	OF	1	0	0	0	0	0	0	0	.000	0	0	0	.000

WORLD SERIES RECORD

Year—Club	League	Pos.	G.	AB.	R.	H.	2B.	3B.	HR.	RBI.	B.A.	PO.	A.	E.	F.A.
1983—Philadelphia	Nat.	PR	1	0	1	0	0	0	0	0	.000	0	0	0	.000

ORESTES DESTRADE

Name pronounced Des-TRAD-a.

Born May 8, 1962, at Santiago, Cuba.
Height, 6.02. Weight, 220.
Throws right and bats lefthanded.

Tied for Florida State League lead in bases on balls received with 82 and game-winning RBIs with 15 in 1983.
Tied for Appalachian League lead in double plays by first basemen with 42 in 1981.

Year	Club	League	Pos.	G.	AB.	R.	H.	2B.	3B.	HR.	RBI.	B.A.	PO.	A.	E.	F.A.
1981—Paintsville	Appal.		1B	63	208	51	57	12	1	*14	46	:274	461	22	11	.978
1982—Greensboro	S. Atl.		1B	43	122	9	22	4	1	1	14	.180	359	15	4	.989
1982—Oneonta	NYP		1B	64	194	44	45	12	1	4	30	.232	298	33	10	.971
1983—Ft. Lauderdale	Fla. St.		OF-1B	127	425	61	124	24	5	18	74	.292	425	24	9	.980

Selected by California Angels' organization in 23rd round of free-agent draft, June 3, 1980.
Signed as free agent by New York Yankees' organization, May 17, 1981.

BAUDILIO JOSE DIAZ (SEIJAS)
Name pronounced DEE-az.
(Bo)

Born March 23, 1953, at Cua, Miranda, Venezuela.
Height, 5.11. Weight, 190.
Throws and bats righthanded.
Tied for International League lead in double plays by catchers with 7 in 1977.

Year	Club	League	Pos.	G.	AB.	R.	H.	2B.	3B.	HR.	RBI.	B.A.	PO.	A.	E.	F.A.
1971—Winter Haven	Fla. St.		C	4	10	1	0	0	0	0	0	.000	25	1	0	1.000
1971—Williamsport	NYP		PH	1	1	0	0	0	0	0	0	.000	0	0	0	.000
1971—Pawtucket	East.		C	1	2	0	0	0	0	0	0	.000	4	0	0	1.000
1971—Greenville	W. Car.		C	10	25	2	5	1	0	0	0	.200	35	2	2	.949
1972—Winter Haven	Fla. St.		C	14	44	3	7	1	0	0	0	.159	72	7	0	1.000
1973—Elmira	NYP		C	25	69	3	17	3	0	0	9	.246	107	16	1	.992
1974—Winter Haven	Fla. St.		C-3B	97	327	31	79	20	1	1	38	.242	476	75	14	.975
1975—Winston-Salem	Carol.		C	59	179	22	47	8	1	6	29	.263	271	45	9	.972
1976—Rhode Island	Int.		C-OF	62	117	10	29	1	0	4	18	.248	222	28	3	.988
1977—Pawtucket	Int.		*C-3B	105	308	37	81	14	1	7	54	.263	459	67	6	*.989
1977—Boston†	Amer.		C	2	1	0	0	0	0	0	0	.000	5	0	0	1.000
1978—Cleveland‡	Amer.		C	44	127	12	30	4	0	2	11	.236	183	18	6	.971
1979—Tacoma	P. C.		C	34	115	5	28	7	0	2	11	.243	223	24	5	.980
1979—Cleveland§	Amer.		C	15	32	0	5	2	0	0	1	.156	63	6	3	.958
1980—Cleveland	Amer.		C	76	207	15	47	11	2	3	32	.227	317	35	4	.989
1981—Cleveland x	Amer.		C	63	182	25	57	19	0	7	38	.313	247	27	7	.975
1982—Philadelphia	Nat.		C	144	525	69	151	29	1	18	85	.288	850	80	10	.989
1983—Philadelphia	Nat.		C	136	471	49	111	17	0	15	64	.236	903	97	*14	.986
American League Totals				200	549	52	139	36	2	12	82	.253	815	86	20	.978
National League Totals				280	996	118	262	46	1	33	149	.263	1753	177	24	.988
Major League Totals				480	1545	170	401	82	3	45	231	.260	2568	263	44	.985

Signed as free agent by Boston Red Sox' organization, November 25, 1970.
†Traded with Pitchers Rick Wise and Mike Paxton and Third Baseman Ted Cox to Cleveland Indians for Pitcher Dennis Eckersley and Catcher Fred Kendall, March 30, 1978.
‡On emergency disabled list, April 16 to June 16, 1978.
§On supplemental disabled list, March 31 to April 17 and June 8 to July 20, 1979.
xTraded to Philadelphia Phillies for Outfielder Lonnie Smith and a player to be named later, November 20, 1981; Cleveland organization acquired Pitcher Scott Munninghoff to complete deal, December 9, 1981.

CHAMPIONSHIP SERIES RECORD

Year	Club	League	Pos.	G.	AB.	R.	H.	2B.	3B.	HR.	RBI.	B.A.	PO.	A.	E.	F.A.
1983—Philadelphia	Nat.		C	4	13	0	2	1	0	0	0	.154	32	2	0	1.000

WORLD SERIES RECORD

Year	Club	League	Pos.	G.	AB.	R.	H.	2B.	3B.	HR.	RBI.	B.A.	PO.	A.	E.	F.A.
1983—Philadelphia	Nat.		C	5	15	1	5	1	0	0	0	.333	37	1	1	.974

ALL-STAR GAME RECORD

Year	League	Pos.	AB.	R.	H.	2B.	3B.	HR.	RBI.	B.A.	PO.	A.	E.	F.A.
1981—American		C	1	0	0	0	0	0	0	.000	2	0	0	1.000

CARLOS ANTONIO DIAZ JR.

Name pronounced DEE-az.

Born January 7, 1958, at Kaneohe, Hawaii.
Height, 6.00. Weight, 170.
Throws left and bats righthanded.
Attended Allan Hancock Junior College, Santa Maria, Calif.

Year	Club	League	G.	IP.	W.	L.	Pct.	H.	R.	ER.	SO.	BB.	ERA.
1979—Bellingham	Northwest		2	8	0	0	.000	5	0	0	8	2	0.00
1979—San Jose	California		26	24	4	1	.800	26	18	17	36	13	6.38
1980—Spokane†	P. Coast		*58	64	3	5	.375	72	31	28	51	27	3.94
1981—Richmond	Int'national		35	49	3	3	.500	32	17	15	29	20	2.81
1982—Richmond	Int'national		31	53⅓	3	4	.429	52	21	16	52	17	2.70
1982—Atlanta‡-New York	National		23	29	3	2	.600	37	17	13	16	13	4.03
1983—New York§	National		54	83⅓	3	1	.750	62	22	19	64	35	2.05
Major League Totals			77	112⅓	6	3	.667	99	39	32	80	48	2.56

Selected by Seattle Mariners' organization in 3rd round of free-agent draft, January 9, 1979.
Selected by Seattle Mariners' organization in secondary phase of free-agent draft, June 5, 1979.
†Traded to Atlanta Braves' organization for Outfielder Jeff Burroughs, March 6, 1981.
‡Traded to New York Mets for Pitcher Tom Hausman, September 10, 1982.

§Traded with a player to be named later to Los Angeles Dodgers for Pitcher Sid Fernandez and Infielder Ross Jones, December 8, 1983; Los Angeles acquired Infielder Bob Bailor to complete deal, December 9, 1983.

MICHAEL ANTHONY DIAZ

Name pronounced DEE-az.

(Mike)

Born April 15, 1960, at San Francisco, Calif.
Height, 6.02. Weight, 205.
Throws and bats righthanded.
Led Texas League catchers in total chances with 684 in 1981.

Year Club	League	Pos.	G.	AB.	R.	H.	2B.	3B.	HR.	RBI.	B.A.	PO.	A.	E.	F.A.
1978—Bradenton Cubs ...	Gulf C.	C-OF	26	68	10	19	3	0	1	7	.279	54	8	3	.954
1979—Geneva	NYP	C	63	237	45	74	*19	1	7	36	.312	*423	35	7	.985
1980—Davenport	Midw.	C	105	386	51	113	17	1	8	47	.293	*627	63	*16	.977
1981—Midland	Texas	C	110	390	56	103	19	2	10	60	.264	*593	*75	16	.977
1982—Midland	Texas	C	121	443	54	128	23	4	22	75	.289	417	42	15	.968
1983—Iowa	A. A.	C-1B-OF	74	238	43	77	13	3	15	47	.324	223	14	12	.952
1983—Chicago	National	C	6	7	2	2	1	0	0	1	.286	5	0	0	1.000
Major League Totals			6	7	2	2	1	0	0	1	.286	5	0	0	1.000

Selected by Chicago Cubs' organization in 30th round of free-agent draft, June 6, 1978.

DARREN JOSEPH DILKS

Born June 30, 1960, at Ontario, Calif.
Height, 6.03. Weight, 190.
Throws and bats lefthanded.
Attended Chaffey College, Alta Loma, Calif., and
Oklahoma State University, Stillwater, Okla.

Year Club	League	G.	IP.	W.	L.	Pct.	H.	R.	ER.	SO.	BB.	ERA.
1981—Memphis	Southern	12	75	1	7	.125	65	42	34	63	49	4.08
1982—Memphis	Southern	27	158⅓	9	9	.500	153	98	86	99	79	4.89
1983—Wichita	Am. Assoc.	32	99	4	6	.400	110	71	69	64	58	6.27

Selected by Baltimore Orioles' organization in 1st round (20th player selected) of free-agent draft, January 9, 1979.
Selected by Toronto Blue Jays' organization in secondary phase of free-agent draft, June 5, 1979.
Selected by Montreal Expos' organization in 1st round (18th player selected) of free-agent draft, June 8, 1981.

MIGUEL ANGEL DILONE (REYES)

Name pronounced Me-GUELL Dee-loh-NAY.

Born November 1, 1954, at Santiago, Dominican Republic.
Height, 6.00. Weight, 160.
Throws right and bats left and righthanded.
Established National League record for most stolen bases with no caught stealing, season (12), 1977.
Major League stolen bases: 1974 (2), 1975 (2), 1976 (5), 1977 (12), 1978 (50), 1979 (21), 1980 (61), 1981 (29), 1982 (33), 1983 (8). Total—223.
Led American League in caught stealing with 23 in 1978.
Led Western Carolinas League in stolen bases with 95 in 1973, Carolina League with 84 in 1974 and International League with 48 in 1975 and 61 in 1976.
Led Western Carolinas League in caught stealing with 18 in 1973, Carolina League with 23 in 1974 and International League with 21 in 1976.
Led New York-Pennsylvania League in caught stealing with 10 in 1972.
Named Carolina League Most Valuable Player, 1974.

Year Club	League	Pos.	G.	AB.	R.	H.	2B.	3B.	HR.	RBI.	B.A.	PO.	A.	E.	F.A.
1972—Niagara Falls	NYP	OF	61	223	50	50	6	0	0	16	.224	83	4	5	.946
1973—Charleston	W. Car.	OF	115	438	*94	119	8	5	1	24	.272	228	11	7	.972
1974—Salem	Carol.	OF	132	532	106	*176	28	9	1	47	.331	271	8	13	.955
1974—Pittsburgh	Nat.	PR-OF	12	2	3	0	0	0	0	0	.000	1	0	0	1.000
1975—Charleston	Int.	OF	125	471	61	102	12	5	1	26	.217	275	11	6	.978
1975—Pittsburgh	Nat.	OF	18	6	8	0	0	0	0	0	.000	3	0	0	1.000
1976—Charleston	Int.	OF-3B	100	408	63	137	7	6	1	17	.336	202	26	9	.962
1976—Pittsburgh	Nat.	OF	16	17	7	4	0	0	0	0	.235	11	0	0	1.000
1977—Pittsburgh†	Nat.	OF	29	44	5	6	0	0	0	0	.136	21	1	0	1.000
1977—Columbus‡	Int.	OF	38	144	28	31	5	1	0	7	.215	101	2	1	.990
1978—Oakland§	Amer.	OF-3B	135	258	34	59	8	0	1	14	.229	196	4	5	.976
1979—Oakland§	Amer.	OF	30	91	15	17	1	2	1	6	.187	47	0	2	.959
1979—Ogden	P.C.	OF	6	29	5	8	1	1	0	6	.276	14	0	0	1.000
1979—Chicago	Nat.	OF	43	36	14	11	0	0	0	1	.306	27	0	0	1.000
1980—Wichita x	A. A.	OF-2B	20	84	12	20	5	0	0	2	.238	48	0	1	.980
1980—Cleveland	Amer.	OF	132	528	82	180	30	9	0	40	.341	249	7	7	.973
1981—Cleveland	Amer.	OF	72	269	33	78	5	5	0	19	.290	126	7	4	.971
1982—Cleveland y	Amer.	OF	104	379	50	89	12	3	3	25	.235	187	3	7	.964
1983—Clev. z-Chi. ab	Amer.	OF	35	71	16	13	3	1	0	7	.183	47	0	0	1.000
1983—Charleston	Int.	OF	34	141	39	48	4	1	0	14	.340	69	1	1	.986
1983—Pittsburgh	Nat.	PR-PH	7	0	1	0	0	0	0	0	.000	0	0	0	.000
American League Totals			508	1596	230	436	59	20	5	111	.273	852	21	25	.972
National League Totals			125	105	38	21	0	0	0	1	.200	63	1	0	1.000
Major League Totals			633	1701	268	457	59	20	5	112	.269	915	22	25	.974

Originally signed as a free agent by Pittsburgh Pirates but on a later date the St. Louis Cardinals also signed him not realizing that the Pittsburgh club had a valid contract. The National Association ruled in favor of the Pirates, April 20, 1972.

†On supplemental disabled list, May 16 to June 25, 1977.

‡Traded with Pitcher Elias Sosa and a player to be named later to Oakland A's for Catcher Manny Sanguillen, April 4, 1978; Oakland acquired Infielder Mike Edwards to complete deal, April 10, 1978.

§Sold to Chicago Cubs, July 4, 1979.

xSold to Cleveland Indians, May 7, 1980.

yGranted free agency, November 10, 1982; re-signed by Indians, February 9, 1983.

zTraded to Chicago White Sox, September 1, 1983, completing deal in which Chicago traded Pitcher Richard Barnes to Cleveland Indians' organization for a player to be named later, August 25, 1983.

aTraded with Pitcher Mike Maitland to Pittsburgh Pirates for Pitcher Randy Niemann, September 7, 1983.

bGranted free agency, November 7, 1983.

FRANK MICHAEL DiPINO

Born October 22, 1956, at Syracuse, N.Y.
Height, 5.10. Weight, 175.
Throws and bats lefthanded.
Attended St. Leo College, St. Leo, Fla.

Pitched seven-inning, 6-0 no-hit victory against Reading, June 8, 1980 (second game).
Major League saves: 1983 (20).

Year Club	League	G.	IP.	W.	L.	Pct.	H.	R.	ER.	SO.	BB.	ERA.
1977—Newark	NYP	14	29	1	3	.250	14	12	8	41	22	2.48
1978—Burlington	Midwest	15	88	5	4	.556	98	58	46	68	36	4.70
1979—Stockton†	California	16	99	5	3	.625	92	45	38	67	46	3.45
1980—Holyoke	Eastern	16	76	7	0	1.000	46	13	11	58	27	1.30
1980—Vancouver	P. Coast	24	28	3	1	.750	24	10	7	32	14	2.25
1981—Vancouver‡	P. Coast	27	81	3	5	.375	83	45	39	81	39	4.33
1981—Milwaukee	American	2	2	0	0	.000	0	0	0	3	3	0.00
1982—Vancouver§	P. Coast	26	189⅔	13	9	.591	187	102	85	115	86	4.03
1982—Houston	National	6	28⅓	2	2	.500	32	20	19	25	11	6.04
1983—Houston	National	53	71½	3	4	.429	52	21	21	67	20	2.65
American League Totals		2	2	0	0	.000	0	0	0	3	3	0.00
National League Totals		59	99⅔	5	6	.455	84	41	40	92	31	3.61
Major League Totals		61	101⅔	5	6	.455	84	41	40	95	34	3.54

Signed as free agent by Milwaukee Brewers' organization, July 11, 1977.

†On disabled list, May 19 to June 11, 1979.

‡On disabled list, May 9 to June 10, 1981.

§Traded with Outfielder Kevin Bass and Pitcher Mike Madden to Houston Astros, September 3, 1982, completing deal in which Houston traded Pitcher Don Sutton to Milwaukee Brewers for three players to be named later, August 30, 1982.

BENITO JAMES DISTEFANO
(Benny)

Born January 23, 1962, at Brooklyn, N.Y.
Height, 6.01. Weight, 195.
Throws and bats lefthanded.
Attended Alvin Community College, Alvin, Tex.

Year Club	League	Pos.	G.	AB.	R.	H.	2B.	3B.	HR.	RBI.	B.A.	PO.	A.	E.	F.A.
1982—Greenwood	S. Atl.	1B	136	477	74	138	23	•8	15	89	.289	*1184	*104	19	.985
1983—Lynn	East.	OF-1B	*137	480	71	130	19	7	25	92	.271	271	13	13	.956

Selected by Los Angeles Dodgers' organization in 16th round of free-agent draft, January 13, 1981.

Selected by Toronto Blue Jays' organization in secondary phase of free-agent draft, June 8, 1981.

Selected by Pittsburgh Pirates' organization in secondary phase of free-agent draft, January 12, 1982.

KENNETH JOHN DIXON
(Ken)

Born October 17, 1960, at Monroe, Va.
Height, 5.10. Weight, 175.
Throws right and bats left and righthanded.

Tied for Appalachian League lead in hit batsmen with 5 in 1980.

Year Club	League	G.	IP.	W.	L.	Pct.	H.	R.	ER.	SO.	BB.	ERA.
1980—Bluefield	Ap'lachian	13	78	4	5	.444	69	46	40	62	*48	4.62
1981—Miami	Florida St.	11	60	1	8	.111	57	41	29	40	42	4.35
1981—Bluefield	Ap'lachian	3	18	2	1	.667	23	12	12	22	11	6.00
1981—Hagerstown	Carolina	9	65	3	5	.375	44	25	21	73	30	2.91
1982—Hagerstown	Carolina	15	97⅔	7	8	.467	97	59	50	71	50	4.61
1982—Charlotte	Southern	13	76⅔	3	8	.273	72	44	39	61	42	4.58
1983—Charlotte	Southern	20	130	8	7	.533	123	64	57	73	70	3.95
1983—Rochester	Int'national	11	64⅓	3	6	.333	65	41	32	34	26	4.48

Selected by Baltimore Orioles' organization in 3rd round of free-agent draft, June 3, 1980.

THOMAS EARL DIXON
(Tom)

Born April 23, 1955, at Orlando, Fla.
Height, 5.11. Weight, 175.
Throws and bats righthanded.

Led International League in shutouts with 6 in 1977.
Tied for International League lead in complete games with 11 in 1981.
Tied for American Association lead in shutouts with 2 and home runs allowed with 23 in 1983.

Year Club	League	G.	IP.	W.	L.	Pct.	H.	R.	ER.	SO.	BB.	ERA.
1974—Sarasota Cardinals	Gulf Coast	7	34	2	0	1.000	23	5	5	23	2	1.32
1974—St. Petersburg†	Florida St.	1	0	0	0	.000	3	3	3	0	0	......
1975—Dubuque‡	Midwest	32	80	2	4	.333	66	35	26	63	44	2.93
1976—Columbus	Southern	27	167	11	10	.524	145	58	45	98	49	2.43
1977—Charleston	Int'national	21	140	13	4	.765	122	43	35	44	42	∗2.25
1977—Houston	National	9	30	1	0	1.000	40	12	11	15	7	3.30
1978—Houston	National	30	140	7	11	.389	140	70	62	66	40	3.99
1979—Houston§x	National	19	26	1	2	.333	39	23	19	9	15	6.58
1980—Tidewater	Int'national	32	138	8	12	.400	149	62	53	88	38	3.46
1981—Tidewater yz	Int'national	27	177	9	11	.450	149	93	80	113	93	4.07
1982—Syracuse-Tidewater a	Int'national	22	118⅔	8	9	.471	108	63	50	92	47	3.79
1982—Wichita	Am. Assoc.	3	18	1	1	.500	15	8	8	13	6	4.00
1983—Wichita	Am. Assoc.	28	174	12	9	.571	187	114	∗103	105	72	5.33
1983—Montreal	National	4	3⅔	0	1	.000	6	4	4	4	1	9.82
Major League Totals		62	199⅔	9	14	.391	225	109	96	94	63	4.33

Selected by Los Angeles Dodgers' organization in 18th round of free-agent draft, June 5, 1973.
Signed as free agent by St. Louis Cardinals' organization, January 16, 1974.
†Sold to Dubuque (Houston Astros' organization), April 8, 1975.
‡On disabled list, July 22 to August 4, 1975.
§On disabled list, April 21 to May 12 and July 13 to September 1, 1979.
xReleased, February 8, 1980; signed by Tidewater (New York Mets' organization), March 15, 1980.
yOn disabled list, August 3 to August 14, 1981.
zLoaned to Syracuse (Toronto Blue Jays' organization), April 6, 1982; returned, July 6, 1982.
aLoaned to Wichita (Montreal Expos' organization), August 16, 1982; returned, August 31, 1982.
bTraded to Wichita (Montreal Expos' organization) for Pitcher Bob Baldrick, January 31, 1983.

WILLIAM DONALD DORAN

Name pronounced DOOR-un.

(Bill)

Born May 28, 1958, at Cincinnati, Ohio.
Height, 6.00. Weight, 175.
Throws right and bats right and lefthanded.
Attended Miami University, Oxford, Ohio.

Led Pacific Coast League second basemen in double plays with 123 in 1982.
Led Gulf Coast League second basemen in double plays with 33 in 1979.

Year Club	League	Pos.	G.	AB.	R.	H.	2B.	3B.	HR.	RBI.	B.A.	PO.	A.	E.	F.A.
1979—Sarasota Astros	Gulf C.	2B	44	164	21	42	6	0	1	16	.256	107	∗144	11	.958
1980—Daytona Beach	Fla. St.	2B-SS	102	369	62	90	11	3	2	45	.244	232	259	21	.959
1981—Columbus	South.	2B-SS	124	427	83	120	17	7	5	56	.281	263	355	17	.973
1982—Tucson	P. C.	2B	∗142	559	100	169	32	7	1	65	.302	∗361	∗424	∗23	.972
1982—Houston	Nat.	2B	26	97	11	27	3	0	0	6	.278	41	78	3	.975
1983—Houston	Nat.	2B	154	535	70	145	12	7	8	39	.271	∗347	461	17	.979
Major League Totals			180	632	81	172	15	7	8	45	.272	388	539	20	.979

Selected by Houston Astros' organization in 6th round of free-agent draft, June 5, 1979.

RICHARD ELLIOTT DOTSON

Born January 10, 1959, at Cincinnati, O.
Height, 6.00. Weight, 196.
Throws and bats righthanded.

Tied for American League lead in shutouts with 4 in 1981.

Year Club	League	G.	IP.	W.	L.	Pct.	H.	R.	ER.	SO.	BB.	ERA.
1977—Idaho Falls†	Pioneer	13	66	4	5	.444	65	61	42	83	63	5.73
1978—Knoxville	Southern	26	145	11	10	.524	128	85	69	152	∗105	4.28
1979—Knoxville	Southern	25	163	9	9	.500	133	81	67	133	88	3.70
1979—Chicago	American	5	24	2	0	1.000	28	13	10	13	6	3.75
1980—Chicago	American	33	198	12	10	.545	185	105	94	109	87	4.27
1981—Chicago	American	24	141	9	8	.529	145	67	59	73	49	3.77
1982—Chicago	American	34	196⅔	11	15	.423	219	97	84	109	73	3.84
1983—Chicago	American	35	240	22	7	∗.759	209	92	86	138	∗106	3.23
Major League Totals		131	799⅔	56	40	.583	786	374	333	442	321	3.75

Selected by California Angels' organization in 1st round (seventh player selected) of free-agent draft, June 7, 1977.
†Traded with Outfielders Bobby Bonds and Thad Bosley to Chicago White Sox for Catcher Brian Downing and Pitchers Chris Knapp and Dave Frost, December 5, 1977.

CHAMPIONSHIP SERIES RECORD

Year Club	League	G.	IP.	W.	L.	Pct.	H.	R.	ER.	SO.	BB.	ERA.
1983—Chicago	American	1	5	0	1	.000	6	6	6	3	3	10.80

KENNETH ALLEN DOWELL
(Ken)

Born January 19, 1960, at Sacramento, Calif.
Height, 5.09. Weight, 160.
Throws and bats righthanded.
Attended Sacramento City College, Sacramento, Calif.

Led South Atlantic League in bases on balls received with 114 in 1981.
Tied for Carolina League lead in sacrifice flies with 9 in 1982.
Led Eastern League shortstops in fielding percentage with .957 in 1983.
Tied for Pioneer League lead in double plays by shortstops with 32 in 1980.

Year	Club	League	Pos.	G.	AB.	R.	H.	2B.	3B.	HR.	RBI.	B.A.	PO.	A.	E.	F.A.
1980—Helena	Pion.		SS	47	154	17	35	1	0	1	24	.227	74	163	17	.933
1981—Spartanburg	S. Atl.		3-S-2-O	137	451	70	102	19	5	2	51	.226	136	357	36	.932
1982—Peninsula	Carol.		SS-3B-2B	114	381	55	84	14	2	0	35	.220	126	305	32	.931
1983—Reading	East.		SS-2B-3B	126	367	64	108	13	1	2	42	.294	199	377	24	.960

Selected by San Diego Padres' organization in 1st round (sixth player selected) of free-agent draft, January 8, 1980.
Selected by Philadelphia Phillies' organization in secondary phase of free-agent draft, June 3, 1980.

BRIAN JAY DOWNING

Born October 9, 1950, at Los Angeles, Calif.
Height, 5.10. Weight, 200.
Throws and bats righthanded.
Attended Cypress Junior College, Cypress, Calif.

Tied major league records for highest fielding percentage by outfielder, season, 150 or more games (1.000), 1982; fewest errors by outfielder, season, 150 or more games (0), 1982; fewest double plays by outfielder, season, 150 or more games (0), 1982.
Established American League record for most consecutive errorless games by an outfielder (244), May 25, 1981 through July 21, second game, 1983.
Tied American League record for most home runs as leadoff batter, season (6), 1982.

Year	Club	League	Pos.	G.	AB.	R.	H.	2B.	3B.	HR.	RBI.	B.A.	PO.	A.	E.	F.A.
1970—Sarasota W. S.	Gulf C.		C-OF	34	96	16	21	1	1	0	14	.219	167	11	1	.994
1971—Appleton	Midw.		3B-C-OF	99	333	51	82	6	3	3	22	.246	353	98	13	.972
1972—Knoxville	South.		OF-3B-C	135	442	75	123	24	7	15	67	.278	250	123	21	.947
1973—Iowa	A. A.		3B-OF-C	68	228	34	56	6	1	7	27	.246	84	90	8	.956
1973—Chicago†	Amer.		OF-C-3B	34	73	5	13	1	0	2	4	.178	72	17	5	.947
1974—Chicago	Amer.		C-OF	108	293	41	66	12	1	10	39	.225	337	30	2	.995
1975—Chicago	Amer.		C	138	420	58	101	12	1	7	41	.240	730	84	8	.990
1976—Chicago‡	Amer.		C	104	317	38	81	14	0	3	30	.256	450	38	6	.988
1977—Chicago§	Amer.		C-OF	69	169	28	48	4	2	4	25	.284	325	28	6	.983
1978—California	Amer.		C	133	412	42	105	15	0	7	46	.255	681	82	5	.993
1979—California	Amer.		C	148	509	87	166	27	3	12	75	.326	669	35	11	.985
1980—California x	Amer.		C	30	93	5	27	6	0	2	25	.290	69	6	0	1.000
1981—California	Amer.		OF-C	93	317	47	79	14	0	9	41	.249	237	18	2	.992
1982—California	Amer.		OF	158	623	109	175	37	2	28	84	.281	321	9	0	●1.000
1983—California y	Amer.		OF	113	403	68	99	15	1	19	53	.246	160	9	1	.994
Major League Totals				1128	3629	528	960	157	10	103	463	.265	4051	374	46	.990

Signed as free-agent by Chicago White Sox' organization, August 19, 1969.
†On disabled list, June 1 to July 9, 1973.
‡On disabled list, July 30 to August 15, 1976.
§Traded with Pitchers Chris Knapp and Dave Frost to California Angels for Outfielders Bobby Bonds and Thad Bosley and Pitcher Dick Dotson, December 5, 1977.
xOn supplemental disabled list, April 20, 1980; transferred to emergency disabled list, May 14 to September 1, 1980.
yOn supplemental disabled list, May 10, 1983; transferred to regular disabled list, June 18 to June 20, 1983.

CHAMPIONSHIP SERIES RECORD

Year	Club	League	Pos.	G.	AB.	R.	H.	2B.	3B.	HR.	RBI.	B.A.	PO.	A.	E.	F.A.
1979—California	Amer.		C	4	15	1	3	0	0	0	1	.200	27	0	0	1.000
1982—California	Amer.		C	5	19	3	3	1	0	0	0	.158	5	0	0	1.000
Championship Series Totals				9	34	4	6	1	0	0	1	.176	32	0	0	1.000

ALL-STAR GAME RECORD

Year	League	Pos.	AB.	R.	H.	2B.	3B.	HR.	RBI.	B.A.	PO.	A.	E.	F.A.
1979—American		C	1	0	1	0	0	0	0	1.000	3	0	0	1.000

KELLY ROBERT DOWNS

Born October 25, 1960, at Ogden, Utah.
Height, 6.04. Weight, 195.
Throws and bats righthanded.
Brother of Dave Downs, pitcher with Philadelphia Phillies, 1972.

Tied for Pacific Coast League lead in games started by pitchers with 29 in 1983.

Year	Club	League	G.	IP.	W.	L.	Pct.	H.	R.	ER.	SO.	BB.	ERA.
1980—Spartanburg	W. Carol.		14	90	5	7	.417	85	41	26	40	17	2.60
1981—Peninsula	Carolina		25	175	13	7	.650	176	79	58	124	35	2.98
1982—Oklahoma City	Am. Assoc.		32	156⅔	2	★15	.118	182	★116	93	70	72	5.34
1983—Portland	P. Coast		29	159⅓	9	●13	.409	186	98	79	71	61	4.46

Selected by Philadelphia Phillies' organization in 26th round of free-agent draft, June 5, 1979.

JEFFREY DONALD DOYLE
(Jeff)

Born October 2, 1956, at Havre, Mont.
Height, 5.09. Weight, 160.
Throws right and bats left and righthanded.
Attended Oregon State University, Corvallis, Ore.

Led Western Carolinas League in sacrifice hits with 14 in 1979.
Led American Association second basemen in double plays with 97 in 1983.
Led Texas League second basemen in assists with 403, double plays with 88 and fielding percentage with .979 in 1981.
Led Western Carolinas League second basemen in total chances with 713 and double plays with 69 in 1979.

Year Club	League	Pos.	G.	AB.	R.	H.	2B.	3B.	HR.	RBI.	B.A.	PO.	A.	E.	F.A.
1977—Calgary	Pion.	2B	36	131	37	41	7	4	4	28	.313	69	81	7	.955
1978—Johnson City†........	Appal.					(Did not play)									
1979—Gastonia................	W. Car.	2B ●138	531	★90	★168	28	5	7	70	.316	★295	★400	18	★.975
1980—St. Petersburg.......	Fla. St.	2B-3B	130	484	65	142	20	6	0	52	.293	190	243	14	.969
1981—Arkansas	Texas	2B-3B	132	479	73	127	24	8	7	71	.265	256	433	15	.979
1982—Louisville	A.A.	2B-3B	119	415	53	102	17	4	8	49	.246	208	295	14	.973
1983—Louisville	A.A.	2B	127	474	87	142	25	6	5	65	.300	279	344	17	.973
1983—St. Louis‡..............	Nat.	2B	13	37	4	11	1	2	0	2	.297	29	28	2	.966
Major League Totals....................			13	37	4	11	1	2	0	2	.297	29	28 ·	2	.966

Selected by St. Louis Cardinals' organization in 6th round of free-agent draft, June 7, 1977.
†On disabled list, June 22, 1978 through remainder of season.
‡Released, December 15, 1983.

RICHARD MICHAEL DOYLE
(Rich)

Born February 4, 1963, at LaMirada, Calif.
Height, 6.05. Weight, 205.
Throws and bats righthanded.

Pitched 6-1 no-hit victory against Albany, June 7, 1983 (first game).

Year Club	League	G.	IP.	W.	L.	Pct.	H.	R.	ER.	SO.	BB.	ERA.
1981—Batavia	NYP	15	58	2	6	.250	68	49	32	36	38	4.97
1982—Waterloo†	Midwest	21	121	7	6	.538	113	61	53	124	55	3.94
1983—Buffalo‡.........................	Eastern	18	98⅔	5	7	.417	95	55	51	80	50	4.65

Selected by Cleveland Indians' organization in 5th round of free-agent draft, June 8, 1981.
†On disabled list, April 9 to April 22, 1982.
‡On disabled list, June 14 to July 7, 1983.

DAVID FRANCIS DRAVECKY
(Dave)

Born February 14, 1956, at Youngstown, Ohio.
Height, 6.00. Weight, 190.
Throws left and bats righthanded.
Attended Youngstown State University, Youngstown, Ohio.

Led Texas League in shutouts with 4 in 1981.

Year Club	League	G.	IP.	W.	L.	Pct.	H.	R.	ER.	SO.	BB.	ERA.
1978—Charleston......................	W. Carol.	20	52	4	2	.667	54	30	24	31	32	4.15
1979—Buffalo..........................	Eastern	35	114	6	7	.462	125	71	54	81	59	4.26
1980—Buffalo†........................	Eastern	27	161	13	7	.650	165	76	60	64	60	3.35
1981—Amarillo........................	Texas	30	172	●15	5	.750	157	69	51	141	45	2.67
1982—Hawaii	P. Coast	16	36⅓	4	1	.800	28	15	10	26	14	2.48
1982—San Diego	National	31	105	5	3	.625	86	37	30	59	33	2.57
1983—San Diego	National	28	183⅔	14	10	.583	181	78	73	74	44	3.58
Major League Totals.....................		59	288⅔	19	13	.594	267	115	103	133	77	3.21

Selected by Pittsburgh Pirates' organization in 21st round of free-agent draft, June 6, 1978.
†Traded to San Diego Padres' organization for Outfielder Robert D. (Bobby) Mitchell, April 5, 1981.

ALL-STAR GAME RECORD

Year League		IP.	W.	L.	Pct.	H.	R.	ER.	SO.	BB.	ERA.
1983—National		2	0	0	.000	1	0	0	2	0	0.00

DANIEL DRIESSEN
(Dan)

Born July 29, 1951, at Hilton Head, S. C.
Height, 5.11. Weight, 190.
Throws right and bats lefthanded.
Uncle of Gerald Perry, infielder in Atlanta Braves' organization;
cousin of Reggie Kinlaw, noseguard with Los Angeles Raiders.

Tied for National League lead in bases on balls received with 93 and in being hit by pitch with 6 in 1980.
Led Eastern League first basemen in fielding percentage with .994 in 1972.

Year Club	League	Pos.	G.	AB.	R.	H.	2B.	3B.	HR.	RBI.	B.A.	PO.	A.	E.	F.A.
1970—Tampa...................	Fla. St.	1B	93	242	28	54	2	1	0	20	.223	473	37	5	.990
1971—Tampa...................	Fla. St.	1B	136	468	72	153	27	9	4	62	.327	1064	86	15	.987

Year Club League	Pos.	G.	AB.	R.	H.	2B.	3B.	HR.	RBI.	B.A.	PO.	A.	E.	F.A.
1972—Three Rivers .... East.	1B-3B	136	481	62	155	37	4	4	65	.322	805	138	9	.991
1973—Indianapolis .... A. A.	3B-1B	47	181	42	74	14	4	6	46	.409	50	97	6	.961
1973—Cincinnati .... Nat.	3B-1B-OF	102	366	49	110	15	2	4	47	.301	160	157	12	.964
1974—Cincinnati .... Nat.	3B-1B-OF	150	470	63	132	23	6	7	56	.281	186	206	26	.938
1975—Cincinnati† .... Nat.	1B-OF	88	210	38	59	8	1	7	38	.281	309	20	5	.985
1976—Cincinnati .... Nat.	1B-OF	98	219	32	54	11	1	7	44	.247	314	23	2	.994
1977—Cincinnati .... Nat.	1B	151	536	75	161	31	4	17	91	.300	1182	75	7	.994
1978—Cincinnati .... Nat.	1B	153	524	68	131	23	3	16	70	.250	1264	93	6	★.996
1979—Cincinnati .... Nat.	1B	150	515	72	129	24	3	18	75	.250	1289	79	9	.993
1980—Cincinnati .... Nat.	1B	154	524	81	139	36	1	14	74	.265	1349	85	7	.995
1981—Cincinnati .... Nat.	1B	82	233	35	55	14	0	7	33	.236	558	30	3	.995
1982—Cincinnati .... Nat.	1B	149	516	64	139	25	1	17	57	.269	1239	78	3	★.998
1983—Cincinnati‡ .... Nat.	1B	122	386	57	107	17	1	12	57	.277	917	71	4	★.996
Major League Totals....................................		1399	4499	634	1216	227	23	126	642	.270	8770	917	84	.991

Signed as free agent by Cincinnati Reds' organization, August 28, 1969.
†On disabled list, March 23 to April 15, 1975.
‡On supplemental disabled list, June 11 to July 1, 1983.

CHAMPIONSHIP SERIES RECORD

Year Club League	Pos.	G.	AB.	R.	H.	2B.	3B.	HR.	RBI.	B.A.	PO.	A.	E.	F.A.
1973—Cincinnati .... Nat.	3B-PR	4	12	0	2	1	0	0	1	.167	3	2	1	.833
1976—Cincinnati .... Nat.	PH	1	1	0	0	0	0	0	0	.000	0	0	0	.000
1979—Cincinnati .... Nat.	1B	3	12	1	1	0	0	0	0	.083	32	0	0	1.000
Championship Series Totals		8	25	1	3	1	0	0	1	.120	35	2	1	.974

WORLD SERIES RECORD

Year Club League	Pos.	G.	AB.	R.	H.	2B.	3B.	HR.	RBI.	B.A.	PO.	A.	E.	F.A.
1975—Cincinnati .... Nat.	PH	2	2	0	0	0	0	0	0	.000	0	0	0	.000
1976—Cincinnati .... Nat.	DH	4	14	4	5	2	0	1	1	.357	0	0	0	.000
World Series Totals...................................		6	16	4	5	2	0	1	1	.313	0	0	0	.000

THOMAS JEROME DUNBAR
(Tommy)

Born November 24, 1959, at Graniteville, S. C.
Height, 6.02. Weight, 185.
Throws and bats lefthanded.
Attended Middle Georgia College, Cochran, Ga.

Year Club League	Pos.	G.	AB.	R.	H.	2B.	3B.	HR.	RBI.	B.A.	PO.	A.	E.	F.A.
1980—Asheville................ S. Atl.	OF	75	262	39	79	9	6	1	39	.302	101	9	11	.909
1981—Asheville................ S. Atl.	OF	138	●530	101	157	★33	7	15	76	.296	184	15	13	.939
1982—Tulsa .... Texas	OF	131	461	93	149	★44	4	16	85	.323	201	5	7	.967
1983—Oklahoma City ..... A. A.	OF	★135	498	73	140	34	5	4	65	.281	244	13	5	.981
1983—Texas .... Amer.	OF	12	24	3	6	0	0	0	3	.250	7	0	1	.875
Major League Totals....................................		12	24	3	6	0	0	0	3	.250	7	0	1	.875

Selected by Boston Red Sox' organization in 11th round of free-agent draft, June 5, 1979.
Selected by Texas Rangers' organization in secondary phase of free-agent draft, January 8, 1980.

SHAWON DONNELL DUNSTON

Born March 21, 1963, at Brooklyn, N.Y.
Height, 6.01. Weight, 175.
Throws and bats righthanded.

Received reported $150,000 bonus to sign with Chicago Cubs, 1982.

Year Club League	Pos.	G.	AB.	R.	H.	2B.	3B.	HR.	RBI.	B.A.	PO.	A.	E.	F.A.
1982—Sarasota Cubs....... Gulf C.	SS-3B	53	190	27	61	11	0	2	28	.321	61	129	24	.888
1983—Quad Cities† .... Midw.	SS	117	455	65	141	17	8	4	62	.310	172	326	47	.914

Selected by Chicago Cubs' organization in 1st round (first player selected) of free-agent draft, June 7, 1982.
†On disabled list, May 31 to June 10, 1983.

LEON DURHAM

Born July 31, 1957, at Cincinnati, O.
Height, 6.01. Weight, 185.
Throws and bats lefthanded.

Major League stolen bases: 1980 (8), 1981 (25), 1982 (28), 1983 (12). Total—73.
Led Texas League first basemen in double plays with 96 in 1978.
Led Gulf Coast League first basemen in errors with 10 in 1976.
Named outfielder on THE SPORTING NEWS National League Silver Slugger team, 1982.

Year Club League	Pos.	G.	AB.	R.	H.	2B.	3B.	HR.	RBI.	B.A.	PO.	A.	E.	F.A.
1976—Sarasota Cards..... Gulf C.	1B-OF	44	156	25	35	3	5	2	18	.224	296	5	12	.962
1977—Gastonia................ W. Car.	1B	63	239	45	88	18	3	4	44	.368	492	28	8	.985
1977—St. Petersburg....... Fla. St.	1B	63	209	26	60	3	6	0	25	.287	533	27	9	.984
1978—Arkansas† .... Texas	1B	102	367	72	116	21	5	12	70	.316	931	42	8	★.992
1979—Springfield............. A. A.	OF-1B	127	449	84	139	33	4	23	88	.310	304	19	6	.982
1980—Springfield............. A. A.	OF-1B	32	128	20	33	5	5	5	23	.258	96	8	4	.963
1980—St. Louis‡................ Nat.	OF-1B	96	303	42	82	15	4	8	42	.271	180	22	3	.985

Year Club League	Pos.	G.	AB.	R.	H.	2B.	3B.	HR.	RBI.	B.A.	PO.	A.	E.	F.A.
1981—Chicago§ .... Nat.	OF-1B	87	328	42	95	14	6	10	35	.290	175	4	5	.973
1982—Chicago .... Nat.	OF-1B	148	539	84	168	33	7	22	90	.312	311	12	12	.964
1983—Chicago x .... Nat.	OF-1B	100	337	58	87	18	8	12	55	.258	203	4	6	.972
Major League Totals....................................		431	1507	226	432	80	25	52	222	.287	869	42	26	.972

Selected by St. Louis Cardinals' organization in 1st round (15th player selected) of free-agent draft, June 8, 1976.

†On disabled list, April 23 to May 25, 1978.

‡Traded with Third Baseman Ken Reitz and a player to be named later to Chicago Cubs for Pitcher Bruce Sutter, December 9, 1980; Chicago acquired Third Baseman Tye Waller to complete deal, December 22, 1980.

§On supplemental disabled list, June 2 to August 9, 1981.

xOn supplemental disabled list, June 9 to June 24, 1983.

ALL-STAR GAME RECORD

Year League	Pos.	AB.	R.	H.	2B.	3B.	HR.	RBI.	B.A.	PO.	A.	E.	F.A.
1983—National	OF	2	0	0	0	0	0	0	.000	0	0	0	.000

Member of National League All-Star Team in 1982; did not play.

JAMES EDWARD DWYER
(Jimmy)

Born January 3, 1950, at Evergreen Park, Ill.
Height, 5.10. Weight, 175.
Throws and bats lefthanded.
Received bachelor of arts degree in accounting from Southern Illinois University, Carbondale, Ill., in 1973.
Nephew of Don Dwyer, second baseman in New York Giants' organization, 1947.

Tied for American Association lead in caught stealing with 13 in 1978.

Year Club League	Pos.	G.	AB.	R.	H.	2B.	3B.	HR.	RBI.	B.A.	PO.	A.	E.	F.A.
1971—Cedar Rapids........ Midw.	OF	58	201	30	63	6	6	2	15	.313	73	3	3	.962
1972—Modesto .... Calif.	OF	92	354	87	115	15	★13	9	45	.325	149	8	4	.975
1972—Arkansas............... Texas	OF	44	162	16	41	1	0	2	14	.253	101	6	2	.982
1973—Tulsa .... A.A.	OF	87	349	63	135	22	8	1	40	★.387	127	8	5	.964
1973—St. Louis................. Nat.	OF	28	57	7	11	1	1	0	0	.193	32	0	0	1.000
1974—Tulsa .... A.A.	OF-1B	36	119	20	40	7	2	1	15	.336	120	13	3	.978
1974—St. Louis................. Nat.	OF-1B	74	86	13	24	1	0	2	11	.279	31	3	0	1.000
1975—Tulsa .... A.A.	OF	33	109	17	44	8	2	1	17	.404	49	2	2	.962
1975—St.L.†-Mont. .... Nat.	OF	81	206	26	56	8	1	3	21	.272	104	8	4	.966
1976—Mont.‡-N.Y.§ .... Nat.	OF-PH	61	105	9	19	3	1	0	5	.181	35	0	1	.972
1976—Tidewater .... Int.	OF	8	26	0	5	1	0	0	1	.192	14	0	1	.933
1977—Wichita x .... A.A.	OF	130	464	★113	★154	★38	12	18	70	★.332	245	6	8	.969
1977—St. Louis................. Nat.	OF	13	31	3	7	1	0	0	2	.226	16	0	0	1.000
1978—St.L. y-S.F. z.......... Nat.	OF-1B	107	238	30	53	12	2	6	26	.223	216	15	3	.987
1979—Boston.................... Amer.	1B-OF	76	113	19	30	7	0	2	14	.265	167	16	4	.979
1980—Boston a .... Amer.	OF-1B	93	260	41	74	11	1	9	38	.285	143	15	4	.975
1981—Baltimore .... Amer.	OF-1B	68	134	16	30	0	1	3	10	.224	97	2	2	.980
1982—Baltimore .... Amer.	OF-1B	71	148	28	45	4	3	6	15	.304	87	0	2	.978
1983—Baltimore .... Amer.	OF-1B	100	196	37	56	17	1	8	38	.286	123	2	4	.969
National League Totals.............................		364	723	88	170	26	5	11	65	.235	434	26	8	.983
American League Totals		408	851	141	235	39	6	28	115	.276	617	35	16	.976
Major League Totals..................................		772	1574	229	405	65	11	39	180	.257	1051	61	24	.979

Selected by St. Louis Cardinals' organization in 11th round of free-agent draft, June 8, 1971.

†Traded to Montreal Expos for Infielder Larry Lintz, July 25, 1975.

‡Traded with Outfielder Jose (Pepe) Mangual to New York Mets for Outfielder Del Unser and Infielder Wayne Garrett, July 21, 1976.

§In three-club deal, Chicago Cubs traded Outfielder-First Baseman Pete LaCock to Kansas City Royals, the New York Mets traded Outfielder Jim Dwyer to Chicago Cubs' organization, and New York received a player to be named later, December 8, 1976; New York acquired Outfielder Sheldon Mallory from Kansas City to complete deal, December 13, 1976.

xReleased, September 7, 1977, signed by St. Louis Cardinals, September 13, 1977.

yTraded to San Francisco Giants, June 15, 1978, completing deal in which San Francisco traded Pitcher Frank Riccelli to St. Louis Cardinals for a player to be named later, October 25, 1977.

zSold to Boston Red Sox, March 15, 1979.

aGranted free agency, October 22, 1980; signed by Baltimore Orioles, December 23, 1980.

CHAMPIONSHIP SERIES RECORD

Year Club League	Pos.	G.	AB.	R.	H.	2B.	3B.	HR.	RBI.	B.A.	PO.	A.	E.	F.A.
1983—Baltimore .... Amer.	PH-OF	2	4	1	1	1	0	0	0	.250	4	0	0	1.000

WORLD SERIES RECORD

Tied World Series record for hitting home run in first Series at-bat, October 11, 1983 (first inning).

Year Club League	Pos.	G.	AB.	R.	H.	2B.	3B.	HR.	RBI.	B.A.	PO.	A.	E.	F.A.
1983—Baltimore .... Amer.	OF	2	8	3	3	1	0	1	1	.375	2	0	0	1.000

—DID YOU KNOW—

That Seattle was the only major league team which failed to win half of its games in any month of the 1983 season?

JEROME MATTHEW DYBZINSKI

Name pronounced DIB-zin-ski.

(Jerry)

Born July 7, 1955, at Cleveland, O.
Height, 6.02. Weight, 180.
Throws and bats righthanded.
Received bachelor of arts degree in physical education and health
from Cleveland State University, Cleveland, O., in 1977.

Led New York-Pennsylvania League shortstops in double plays with 51 in 1977.
Tied for Pacific Coast League lead in being hit by pitch with 7 in 1979.

Year	Club	League	Pos.	G.	AB.	R.	H.	2B.	3B.	HR.	RBI.	B.A.	PO.	A.	E.	F.A.
1977—Batavia	NYP	SS	58	169	39	37	7	0	0	16	.219	★117	★198	19	★.943
1978—Waterloo	Midw.	SS	134	508	96	144	15	2	12	63	.283	★191	412	★47	.928
1979—Tacoma	P. C.	SS	132	469	58	119	16	3	1	25	.254	★269	409	30	.958
1980—Cleveland	Amer.	SS-2B-3B	114	248	32	57	11	1	1	23	.230	140	263	13	.969
1981—Cleveland	Amer.	SS-2B-3B	48	57	10	17	0	0	0	6	.298	35	70	5	.955
1982—Cleveland	Amer.	SS-3B	80	212	19	49	6	2	0	22	.231	120	244	17	.955
1982—Charleston†‡	Int.	SS	30	107	14	32	6	1	2	12	.299	71	107	8	.957
1983—Chicago	Amer.	SS-3B	127	256	30	59	10	1	1	32	.230	141	258	14	.966
Major League Totals			369	773	91	182	27	4	2	83	.235	436	835	49	.963

Selected by Cleveland Indians' organization in 15th round of free-agent draft, June 7, 1977.
†On suspended list, July 7 to July 31, 1982.
‡Traded to Chicago White Sox for Infielder Pat Tabler, April 1, 1983.

CHAMPIONSHIP SERIES RECORD

Year	Club	League	Pos.	G.	AB.	R.	H.	2B.	3B.	HR.	RBI.	B.A.	PO.	A.	E.	F.A.
1983—Chicago	Amer.	SS	2	4	0	1	0	0	0	0	.250	3	8	0	1.000

SCOTT ANTHONY DYE

Born January 9, 1957, at Biloxi, Miss.
Height, 6.01. Weight, 200.
Throws and bats righthanded.
Attended Bakersfield College, Bakersfield, Calif.

Led Northwest League in intentional bases on balls issued with 6 in 1977.

Year	Club	League	G.	IP.	W.	L.	Pct.	H.	R.	ER.	SO.	BB.	ERA.
1977—Eugene	Northwest	22	34	3	4	.429	27	16	10	33	24	2.65
1978—Tampa	Florida St.	46	71	3	5	.375	63	26	16	65	31	2.03
1979—Tampa	Florida St.	51	100	12	3	.800	81	24	20	74	24	1.80
1980—Waterbury†	Eastern	48	102	9	7	.563	96	48	47	75	37	4.15
1981—Tidewater‡	Int'national	19	75	4	4	.500	91	45	40	42	30	4.80
1982—Jackson	Texas	16	105	7	5	.583	105	41	37	53	30	3.17
1982—Tidewater	Int'national	20	38⅓	3	2	.600	29	8	7	27	16	1.64
1983—Tidewater§	Int'national	27	37	1	3	.250	47	26	25	23	20	6.08
1983—Tacoma	P. Coast	16	34	1	0	1.000	34	17	15	20	9	3.97

Signed as free agent by Cincinnati Reds' organization, December 14, 1976.
†Traded to Tidewater (New York Mets' organization) for Outfielder Dave Howard, March 28, 1981.
‡On disabled list, July 19 to August 11, 1981.
§Traded to Oakland A's organization for First Baseman Kelvin Moore, July 22, 1983.

LENNY KYLE DYKSTRA

Born February 10, 1963, at Santa Ana, Calif.
Height, 5.10. Weight, 160.
Throws and bats lefthanded.
Grandson of Pete Leswick, forward with New York Americans and Boston Bruins
of NHL, 1936-37 and 1944-45; nephew of Tony Leswick, forward with
New York Rangers, Detroit Red Wings and Chicago Black
Hawks of NHL, 1945-46 through 1955-56 and 1957-58.

Led Carolina League in bases on balls received with 107, stolen bases with 105 and caught stealing with 23 in 1983.
Named Carolina League Player of the Year, 1983.

Year	Club	League	Pos.	G.	AB.	R.	H.	2B.	3B.	HR.	RBI.	B.A.	PO.	A.	E.	F.A.
1981—Shelby	S. Atl.	OF-SS	48	157	34	41	7	2	0	18	.261	86	3	4	.957
1982—Shelby	S. Atl.	OF	120	413	95	120	13	7	3	38	.291	239	11	14	.947
1983—Lynchburg	Carol.	OF	●136	★525	★132	★188	24	★14	8	81	★.358	268	9	7	.975

Selected by New York Mets' organization in 12th round of free-agent draft, June 8, 1981.

WILLIAM SCOTT EARL

(Scottie)

Born September 18, 1960, at Seymour, Ind.
Height, 5.11. Weight, 165.
Throws and bats righthanded.
Attended Glen Oaks Community College, Centerville, Mich., and received
degree in liberal arts from Eastern Kentucky University, Richmond, Ky.

Led Southern League second basemen in putouts with 318, errors with 31, total chances with 765 and tied for lead
in assists with 416 in 1983.

Led Florida State League second basemen in double plays with 96 and total chances with 742 in 1982.

Year Club	League	Pos.	G.	AB.	R.	H.	2B.	3B.	HR.	RBI.	B.A.	PO.	A.	E.	F.A.
1981—Bristol	Appal.	2B	52	181	38	47	6	0	3	18	.260	89	169	13	.952
1982—Lakeland	Fla. St.	2B	★136	464	86	133	17	5	12	47	.287	★298	419	25	.966
1983—Birmingham	South.	2B-SS	144	529	96	138	22	10	10	60	.261	325	424	32	.959

Selected by Detroit Tigers' organization in 14th round of free-agent draft, June 8, 1981.

MICHAEL ANTHONY EASLER
(Mike)

Born November 29, 1950, at Cleveland, O.
Height, 6.01. Weight, 196.
Throws right and bats lefthanded.
Attended Cleveland State University, Cleveland, O.
Brother-in-law of Cliff Johnson, catcher-first baseman with Toronto Blue Jays.

Hit for the cycle, June 12, 1980.
Tied for Southern League lead in being hit by pitch with 8 in 1972.
Tied for American Association lead in double plays by outfielders with 4 in 1976.

Year Club	League	Pos.	G.	AB.	R.	H.	2B.	3B.	HR.	RBI.	B.A.	PO.	A.	E.	F.A.
1969—Covington	Appal.	OF-3B	33	113	21	36	7	2	0	11	.319	25	10	4	.897
1970—Cocoa†	Fla. St.	OF	96	314	30	79	11	4	1	24	.252	142	5	7	.955
1971—Cocoa‡	Fla. St.	OF	109	392	61	115	15	5	11	68	.293	153	14	8	.954
1972—Columbus	South.	OF	106	372	52	100	11	4	13	46	.269	149	7	8	.951
1973—Columbus	South.	OF	48	168	27	52	11	1	6	32	.310	81	2	1	.988
1973—Denver	A. A.	OF	48	176	24	50	11	2	7	26	.284	74	2	6	.927
1973—Houston	Nat.	OF	6	7	1	0	0	0	0	0	.000	1	0	1	.500
1974—Denver	A. A.	OF	100	367	75	104	18	8	19	63	.283	172	7	5	.973
1974—Houston	Nat.	PH	15	15	0	1	0	0	0	0	.067	0	0	0	.000
1975—Iowa§-Tulsa	A. A.	OF	113	415	69	130	31	6	15	69	.313	161	6	8	.954
1975—Houston x	Nat.	PH	5	5	0	0	0	0	0	0	.000	0	0	0	.000
1976—Tulsa y	A. A.	OF	118	378	75	133	31	2	26	77	★.352	172	★16	8	.959
1976—California z	Amer.	DH	21	54	6	13	1	1	0	4	.241	0	0	0	.000
1977—Columbus	Int.	OF	127	451	83	136	29	5	18	75	.302	171	7	3	.983
1977—Pittsburgh	Nat.	OF	10	18	3	8	2	0	1	5	.444	7	0	0	1.000
1978—Columbus ab	Int.	OF-1B	126	448	84	148	26	3	18	84	★.330	378	31	5	.988
1979—Pittsburgh	Nat.	OF	55	54	8	15	1	1	2	11	.278	0	0	0	.000
1980—Pittsburgh	Nat.	OF	132	393	66	133	27	3	21	74	.338	201	6	3	.986
1981—Pittsburgh	Nat.	OF	95	339	43	97	18	5	7	42	.286	188	13	4	.980
1982—Pittsburgh	Nat.	OF	142	475	52	131	27	2	15	58	.276	243	8	7	.973
1983—Pittsburgh cd	Nat.	OF	115	381	44	117	17	2	10	54	.307	158	6	6	.965
National League Totals			575	1687	217	502	92	13	56	244	.298	798	33	21	.975
American League Totals			21	54	6	13	1	1	0	4	.241	0	0	0	.000
Major League Totals			596	1741	223	515	93	14	56	248	.296	798	33	21	.975

Selected by Houston Astros' organization in 6th round of free-agent draft, June 5, 1969.
†On temporary inactive list, May 13 to May 25, 1970.
‡On temporary inactive list, May 25 to June 14, 1971.
§Loaned to St. Louis Cardinals' organization, June 25, 1975.
xTraded to St. Louis Cardinals for Pitcher Mike Barlow, September 30, 1975.
yTraded to California Angels for a player to be named later, September 3, 1976; St. Louis Cardinals acquired Infielder Ron Farkas to complete deal, September 7, 1976.
zTraded to Pittsburgh Pirates for Pitcher Randy Sealy, April 4, 1977.
aSold to Boston Red Sox, October 27, 1978.
bTraded to Pittsburgh Pirates for Outfielder George Hill and Pitcher Martin Rivas, March 15, 1979.
cOn disabled list, August 11 to September 2, 1983.
dTraded to Boston Red Sox for Pitcher John Tudor, December 6, 1983.

CHAMPIONSHIP SERIES RECORD

Year Club	League	Pos.	G.	AB.	R.	H.	2B.	3B.	HR.	RBI.	B.A.	PO.	A.	E.	F.A.
1979—Pittsburgh	Nat.	PH	1	1	0	0	0	0	0	0	.000	0	0	0	.000

WORLD SERIES RECORD

Year Club	League	Pos.	G.	AB.	R.	H.	2B.	3B.	HR.	RBI.	B.A.	PO.	A.	E.	F.A.
1979—Pittsburgh	Nat.	PH	2	1	0	0	0	0	0	0	.000	0	0	0	.000

ALL-STAR GAME RECORD

Year League	Pos.	AB.	R.	H.	2B.	3B.	HR.	RBI.	B.A.	PO.	A.	E.	F.A.
1981—National	OF	1	1	0	0	0	0	0	.000	0	0	0	.000

JAMES MORRIS EASTERLY
(Jamie)

Born February 17, 1953, at Houston, Tex.
Height, 5.10. Weight, 180.
Throws left and bats left and righthanded.
Attended Sam Houston State University, Huntsville, Tex.

Pitched seven-inning, 10-0 perfect game victory against Iowa, July 14, 1979.

Year Club	League	G.	IP.	W.	L.	Pct.	H.	R.	ER.	SO.	BB.	ERA.
1971—Greenwood	W. Carol.	8	29	3	0	1.000	14	3	2	33	9	0.62
1972—Greenwood	W. Carol.	7	24	1	0	1.000	11	0	0	29	13	0.00

Year Club	League	G.	IP.	W.	L.	Pct.	H.	R.	ER.	SO.	BB.	ERA.
1972—Savannah†	Southern	2	4	0	1	.000	7	2	2	4	4	4.50
1973—Savannah‡	Southern	15	67	5	3	.625	62	40	28	53	41	3.76
1974—Richmond	Int'national	26	138	9	6	.600	115	48	39	84	75	2.54
1974—Atlanta	National	3	3	0	0	.000	6	7	5	0	4	15.00
1975—Richmond	Int'national	2	10	1	1	.500	11	3	2	4	6	1.80
1975—Atlanta	National	21	69	2	9	.182	73	47	38	34	42	4.96
1976—Richmond	Int'national	33	137	7	6	.583	133	56	45	91	88	2.96
1976—Atlanta§	National	4	22	1	1	.500	23	12	12	11	13	4.91
1977—Atlanta§	National	22	59	2	4	.333	72	46	40	37	30	6.10
1978—Atlanta	National	37	78	3	6	.333	91	52	49	42	45	5.67
1979—Richmond	Int'national	10	13	0	0	.000	5	0	0	12	7	0.00
1979—Atlanta xy	National	4	3	0	0	.000	7	6	4	3	3	12.00
1979—Denver	Am. Assoc.	20	88	5	6	.455	100	40	32	55	39	3.27
1980—Denver z	Am. Assoc.	56	134	9	8	.529	118	64	54	105	56	3.63
1981—Milwaukee	American	44	62	3	3	.500	46	23	22	31	34	3.19
1982—Milwaukee a	American	28	30⅔	0	2	.000	39	19	16	16	15	4.70
1983—Milwaukee bc-Cleveland d	American	53	68⅔	4	3	.571	83	32	28	45	32	3.67
National League Totals		91	234	8	20	.286	272	170	148	127	137	5.69
American League Totals		125	161⅓	7	8	.467	168	74	66	92	81	3.68
Major League Totals		216	395⅓	15	28	.349	440	244	214	219	218	4.87

Selected by Atlanta Braves' organization in 2nd round of free-agent draft, June 8, 1971.

†On disabled list, April 11 to April 27, July 7 to July 28 and August 5, 1972 through remainder of season.

‡On disabled list, April 24 to May 12 and May 24 to July 9, 1973.

§On disabled list, June 6 to July 4 and July 21 to September 19, 1977.

xLoaned to Denver (Montreal Expos' organization), June 6, 1979; returned, August 31, 1979.

ySold to Montreal Expos, October 17, 1979.

zSold to Milwaukee Brewers, September 22, 1980.

aOn disabled list, July 12 to September 1, 1982.

bHad a sacrifice bunt and a ground out in only plate appearances during season when designated hitter took the field.

cTraded with Outfielder Gorman Thomas and Pitcher Ernie Camacho to Cleveland Indians for Outfielder Rick Manning and Pitcher Rick Waits, June 6, 1983.

dGranted free agency, November 7, 1983.

DIVISION SERIES RECORD

Year Club	League	G.	IP.	W.	L.	Pct.	H.	R.	ER.	SO.	BB.	ERA.
1981—Milwaukee	American	2	1⅓	0	0	.000	2	1	1	1	0	6.75

DENNIS LEE ECKERSLEY

Born October 3, 1954, at Oakland, Calif.
Height, 6.02. Weight, 190.
Throws and bats righthanded.
Son-in-law of Al Jacinto, second baseman in Chicago White Sox' organization, 1947 through 1954.

Tied American League record for most low-hit (no-hit and one-hit) games, season (3), 1977.
Pitched 1-0 no-hit victory against California Angels, May 30, 1977.
Led American League in home runs allowed with 30 in 1978.
Tied for American League lead in intentional bases on balls issued with 11 in 1977.
Led Texas League in hit batsmen with 10 in 1974.
Led California League pitchers in games started with 31 and tied for lead in shutouts with 5 in 1973.
Named American League Rookie Pitcher of the Year by THE SPORTING NEWS, 1975.
Received reported $32,000 bonus to sign with Cleveland Indians, 1972.

Year Club	League	G.	IP.	W.	L.	Pct.	H.	R.	ER.	SO.	BB.	ERA.
1972—Reno	California	12	75	5	5	.500	87	46	40	56	33	4.80
1973—Reno	California	31	202	12	8	.600	182	97	82	218	91	3.65
1974—San Antonio	Texas	23	167	●14	3	*.824	141	66	63	*163	60	3.40
1975—Cleveland	American	34	187	13	7	.650	147	61	54	152	90	2.60
1976—Cleveland	American	36	199	13	12	.520	155	82	76	200	78	3.44
1977—Cleveland†	American	33	247	14	13	.519	214	100	97	191	54	3.53
1978—Boston	American	35	268	20	8	.714	258	99	89	162	71	2.99
1979—Boston	American	33	247	17	10	.630	234	89	82	150	59	2.99
1980—Boston	American	30	198	12	14	.462	188	101	94	121	44	4.27
1981—Boston	American	23	154	9	8	.529	160	82	73	79	35	4.27
1982—Boston	American	33	224⅓	13	13	.500	228	101	93	127	43	3.73
1983—Boston	American	28	176⅓	9	13	.409	223	119	110	77	39	5.61
Major League Totals		285	1900⅔	120	98	.550	1807	834	768	1259	513	3.64

Selected by Cleveland Indians' organization in 3rd round of free-agent draft, June 6, 1972.

†Traded with Catcher Fred Kendall to Boston Red Sox for Pitchers Rick Wise and Mike Paxton, Third Baseman Ted Cox and Catcher Bo Diaz, March 30, 1978.

ALL-STAR GAME RECORD

Year League		IP.	W.	L.	Pct.	H.	R.	ER.	SO.	BB.	ERA.
1977—American		2	0	0	.000	0	0	0	1	0	0.00
1982—American		3	0	1	.000	2	3	3	1	2	9.00
All-Star Game Totals		5	0	1	.000	2	3	3	2	2	5.40

DAVID DELMAR EDLER
(Dave)

Born August 5, 1956, at Sioux City, Iowa.
Height, 6.00. Weight, 185.
Throws and bats righthanded.
Attended Washington State University, Pullman, Wash.

Led California League in sacrifice flies with 12 in 1979.
Led California League third basemen in double plays with 26 in 1979.

Year	Club	League	Pos.	G.	AB.	R.	H.	2B.	3B.	HR.	RBI.	B.A.	PO.	A.	E.	F.A.
1978—Bellingham	N'west.		3B	69	248	42	67	12	4	6	46	.270	46	132	21	.894
1979—San Jose	Calif.		3B	138	508	101	152	28	7	14	104	.299	★111	★309	29	.935
1980—Spokane	P. C.		3B-SS-1B	140	458	79	132	25	6	10	72	.288	101	220	25	.928
1980—Seattle	Amer.		3B	28	89	11	20	1	0	3	9	.225	18	64	3	.965
1981—Seattle	Amer.		3B-SS	29	78	7	11	3	0	0	5	.141	18	43	8	.884
1981—Spokane†‡	P. C.		3B-OF-1B	66	224	31	57	9	0	6	30	.254	65	85	13	.920
1982—Omaha	A. A.		3B	71	262	40	80	11	6	9	51	.305	53	113	17	.907
1982—Seattle	Amer.		3B-OF	40	104	14	29	2	2	2	18	.279	24	53	6	.928
1983—Seattle	Amer.		3B-1B-OF	29	63	2	12	1	1	1	4	.190	29	22	4	.927
1983—Salt Lake City	P.C.		3-C-O-1	64	245	49	75	14	5	7	53	.306	76	101	12	.937
Major League Totals				126	334	34	72	7	3	6	36	.216	89	182	21	.928

Selected by Seattle Mariners' organization in 22nd round of free-agent draft, June 6, 1978.
†On disabled list, June 12 to July 6, 1981.
‡Loaned to Omaha (Kansas City Royals' organization), April 6, 1982; returned, June 28, 1982.

MARSHALL LYNN EDWARDS

Born August 27, 1952, at Fort Lewis, Wash.
Height, 5.09. Weight, 157.
Throws and bats lefthanded.
Attended Los Angeles City College, Los Angeles, Calif., and University
of California at Los Angeles, Los Angeles, Calif.
Brother of Dave Edwards, outfielder with Minnesota Twins and San Diego Padres, 1978 through 1982; twin brother of
Mike Edwards, infielder with Pittsburgh Pirates and Oakland A's, 1977 through 1980; infielder with Poza
Rica and Mexico City in Mexican League, 1982; and currently with Kintetsu Buffaloes of Japanese baseball.

Led Pacific Coast League in sacrifice hits with 15 in 1980.
Led Florida State League in stolen bases with 57 in 1977.
Led Florida State League in caught stealing with 19 in 1975.
Tied for Pioneer League lead in sacrifice hits with 14 and caught stealing with 11 in 1974.

Year	Club	League	Pos.	G.	AB.	R.	H.	2B.	3B.	HR.	RBI.	B.A.	PO.	A.	E.	F.A.
1974—Ogden	Pion.		OF	72	234	37	68	6	5	0	15	.291	★124	●8	8	.943
1975—Miami	Fla. St.		OF	124	459	62	128	8	3	0	31	.279	234	12	6	.976
1976—Miami	Fla. St.		OF	123	449	69	133	7	1	0	34	.296	240	14	5	.981
1977—Charlotte	South.		OF	36	129	15	22	3	1	0	9	.171	66	4	1	.986
1977—Miami†	Fla. St.		OF	94	344	62	115	12	4	0	27	★.334	137	7	3	.980
1978—Holyoke	East.		OF	136	★515	63	147	20	●11	1	56	.285	★354	5	★16	.957
1979—Vancouver	P. C.		OF	111	385	39	105	10	1	2	44	.273	200	11	6	.972
1980—Vancouver	P. C.		OF	134	478	70	139	14	★17	2	68	.291	234	13	7	.972
1981—Milwaukee	Amer.		OF	40	58	10	14	1	1	0	4	.241	46	1	1	.979
1981—Vancouver	P. C.		OF	12	51	6	19	3	2	0	3	.373	18	1	1	.950
1982—Vancouver	P. C.		OF	18	75	16	26	3	2	0	11	.347	21	1	2	.917
1982—Milwaukee	Amer.		OF	69	178	24	44	4	1	2	14	.247	119	2	2	.984
1983—Milwaukee	Amer.		OF	51	74	14	22	1	1	0	5	.297	57	4	0	1.000
Major League Totals				160	310	48	80	6	3	2	23	.258	222	7	3	.987

Signed as free agent by Baltimore Orioles' organization, June 24, 1974.
†Drafted by Milwaukee Brewers' organization, December 6, 1977.

DIVISION SERIES RECORD

Year	Club	League	Pos.	G.	AB.	R.	H.	2B.	3B.	HR.	RBI.	B.A.	PO.	A.	E.	F.A.
1981—Milwaukee	Amer.		PR-OF	3	1	0	0	0	0	0	0	.000	0	0	0	.000

CHAMPIONSHIP SERIES RECORDS

Year	Club	League	Pos.	G.	AB.	R.	H.	2B.	3B.	HR.	RBI.	B.A.	PO.	A.	E.	F.A.
1982—Milwaukee	Amer.		PR-DH-O	3	0	2	0	0	0	0	0	.000	2	0	0	1.000

WORLD SERIES RECORD

Year	Club	League	Pos.	G.	AB.	R.	H.	2B.	3B.	HR.	RBI.	B.A.	PO.	A.	E.	F.A.
1982—Milwaukee	Amer.		PR-OF	1	0	0	0	0	0	0	0	.000	0	0	0	.000

JUAN TYRONE EICHELBERGER
Name pronounced EYE-kul-burg-ur.

Born October 21, 1953, at St. Louis, Mo.
Height, 6.02. Weight, 195.
Throws and bats righthanded.
Attended University of California, Berkeley, Calif.

Tied major league record for most consecutive strikeouts as batter, season (14), 1980.
Tied for National League lead in balks with 5 in 1981.

Year Club	League	G.	IP.	W.	L.	Pct.	H.	R.	ER.	SO.	BB.	ERA.
1975—Reno	California	16	117	10	4	.714	105	52	36	92	54	2.77
1975—Alexandria	Texas	8	50	3	4	.429	52	31	24	31	21	4.32
1976—Amarillo	Texas	11	66	2	6	.250	77	50	41	41	45	5.59
1976—Reno	California	13	89	6	1	.857	71	48	35	77	63	3.54
1977—Amarillo†	Texas	25	162	12	7	.632	177	90	74	92	77	4.11
1978—Hawaii	P. Coast	26	156	8	13	.381	143	95	78	106	★113	4.50
1978—San Diego	National	3	3	0	0	.000	4	4	4	2	2	12.00
1979—Hawaii	P. Coast	28	195	13	9	.591	151	79	73	159	★137	3.37
1979—San Diego	National	3	21	1	1	.500	15	10	8	12	11	3.43
1980—Hawaii	P. Coast	11	77	7	3	.700	56	35	30	62	49	3.51
1980—San Diego‡	National	15	89	4	2	.667	73	41	36	43	55	3.64
1981—San Diego	National	25	141	8	8	.500	136	60	55	81	74	3.51
1982—San Diego§x	National	31	177⅔	7	14	.333	171	98	83	74	72	4.20
1983—Cleveland	American	28	134	4	11	.267	132	80	73	56	59	4.90
National League Totals		77	431⅓	20	25	.444	399	213	186	212	214	3.88
American League Totals		28	134	4	11	.267	132	80	73	56	59	4.90
Major League Totals		105	565⅔	24	36	.400	531	293	259	268	273	4.12

Selected by San Francisco Giants' organization in 36th round of free-agent draft, June 8, 1971.
Selected by San Diego Padres' organization in secondary phase of free-agent draft, January 9, 1975.
†Appeared as outfielder in two games with 3 putouts.
‡On disabled list, July 18 to August 8, 1980.
§On disabled list, July 16 to August 6, 1982.
xTraded with First Baseman-Outfielder Broderick Perkins to Cleveland Indians for Pitcher Ed Whitson, November 18, 1982.

MARK ANTHONY EICHHORN

Name pronounced IKE-horn

Born November 21, 1960, at San Jose, Calif.
Height, 6.03. Weight, 180.
Throws and bats righthanded.
Attended Cabrillo Junior College, Aptos, Calif.

Year Club	League	G.	IP.	W.	L.	Pct.	H.	R.	ER.	SO.	BB.	ERA.
1979—Medicine Hat	Pioneer	16	93	7	6	.538	101	62	35	66	26	3.39
1980—Kinston	Carolina	26	183	14	10	.583	158	72	59	119	56	2.90
1981—Knoxville	Southern	30	192	10	14	.417	202	112	85	99	57	3.98
1982—Syracuse	Int'national	27	156⅔	10	11	.476	158	92	79	71	83	4.54
1982—Toronto	American	7	38	0	3	.000	40	28	23	16	14	5.45
1983—Syracuse	Int'national	7	30⅔	0	5	.000	36	32	27	12	21	7.92
1983—Knoxville	Southern	21	120⅔	6	12	.333	124	65	58	54	47	4.33
Major League Totals		7	38	0	3	.000	40	28	23	16	14	5.45

Selected by Toronto Blue Jays' organization in 2nd round of free-agent draft, January 9, 1979.

JAMES MICHAEL EISENREICH

Name pronounced EYES-en-rike.

(Jim)

Born April 18, 1959, at St. Cloud, Minn.
Height, 5.11. Weight, 180.
Throws and bats lefthanded.
Attending St. Cloud State University, St. Cloud, Minn.

Named Appalachian League Co-Player of the Year, 1980.

Year Club	League	Pos.	G.	AB.	R.	H.	2B.	3B.	HR.	RBI.	B.A.	PO.	A.	E.	F.A.
1980—Elizabethton	Appal.	OF	67	258	47	77	12	●4	3	41	.298	151	7	3	.981
1980—Wis. Rapids	Midw.	DH	5	16	4	7	0	0	0	5	.438	0	0	0	.000
1981—Wis. Rapids	Midw.	OF	★134	489	101	●152	★27	0	23	99	.311	★295	17	9	.972
1982—Minnesota†	Amer.	OF	34	99	10	30	6	0	2	9	.303	72	0	2	.973
1983—Minnesota‡	Amer.	OF	2	7	1	2	1	0	0	0	.286	6	1	0	1.000
Major League Totals			36	106	11	32	7	0	2	9	.302	78	1	2	.975

Selected by Minnesota Twins' organization in 16th round of free-agent draft, June 3, 1980.
†On supplemental disabled list, May 6 to May 28 and June 18 to September 1, 1982.
‡On supplemental disabled list, April 7, 1983; transferred to voluntarily retired list, May 27, 1983 through remainder of season.

GUY KENNETH ELSTON

Born June 10, 1960, at Hudson, Mich.
Height, 6.04. Weight, 193.
Throws and bats righthanded.
Attended Jackson Community College, Jackson, Mich., and University of Toledo, Toledo, Ohio.

Led Appalachian League in saves with 11 and games finished in relief with 27 in 1981.

Year Club	League	G.	IP.	W.	L.	Pct.	H.	R.	ER.	SO.	BB.	ERA.
1981—Paintsville	Ap'lachian	27	45	9	0	●1.000	25	4	3	67	7	0.60
1981—Nashville	Southern	1	2	0	0	.000	5	2	2	1	2	9.00
1982—Greensboro	S. Atlantic	18	26⅔	3	0	1.000	13	2	2	44	10	0.68
1982—Nashville	Southern	31	45	4	1	.800	24	7	7	51	25	1.40
1983—Columbus†	Int'national	40	64	4	2	.667	60	34	32	53	29	4.50

Signed as free agent by New York Yankees' organization, June 22, 1981.
†On disabled list, July 6 to July 25, 1983.

RALPH DAVID ENGLE
(Dave)

Born November 30, 1956, at San Diego, Calif.
Height, 6.03. Weight, 210.
Throws and bats righthanded.
Attended University of Southern California, Los Angeles, Calif.

Year Club	League	Pos.	G.	AB.	R.	H.	2B.	3B.	HR.	RBI.	B.A.	PO.	A.	E.	F.A.
1978—Salinas†	Calif.	3B	53	203	34	62	11	0	6	40	.305	20	65	10	.895
1979—Toledo	Int.	3B	106	363	46	104	17	1	7	51	.287	72	197	23	.921
1980—Toledo	Int.	OF	133	489	74	150	27	3	7	73	★.307	225	16	5	.980
1981—Minnesota	Amer.	OF-3B	82	248	29	64	14	4	5	32	.258	144	4	3	.980
1982—Minnesota	Amer.	OF	58	186	20	42	7	2	4	16	.226	63	3	1	.985
1982—Toledo	Int.	OF	9	34	14	15	1	1	5	12	.441	15	4	0	1.000
1983—Minnesota	Amer.	C-OF	120	374	46	114	22	4	8	43	.305	306	26	9	.974
Major League Totals			260	808	95	220	43	10	17	91	.272	513	33	13	.977

Selected by California Angels' organization in 2nd round of free-agent draft, June 6, 1978.
†Traded with Outfielder Ken Landreaux and Pitchers Paul Hartzell and Brad Havens to Minnesota Twins for First Baseman Rod Carew, February 3, 1979.

JAMES GERHARD EPPARD
(Jim)

Born April 27, 1961, at South Bend, Ind.
Height, 6.02. Weight, 180.
Throws and bats lefthanded.
Attended University of California, Berkeley, Calif.

Year Club	League	Pos.	G.	AB.	R.	H.	2B.	3B.	HR.	RBI.	B.A.	PO.	A.	E.	F.A.
1982—Medford	N'west	★1B-OF	64	242	58	★91	13	2	1	41	★.376	459	★38	10	.980
1983—Modesto	Calif.	1B	134	488	68	138	18	4	4	45	.283	1086	74	10	★.991

Selected by Chicago Cubs' organization in 11th round of free-agent draft, January 8, 1980.
Selected by Oakland A's organization in 13th round of free-agent draft, June 7, 1980.

ROGER FARRELL ERICKSON

Born August 30, 1956, at Springfield, Ill.
Height, 6.03. Weight, 199.
Throws and bats righthanded.
Attended Springfield College of Illinois, Springfield, Ill.; and
University of New Orleans, New Orleans, La.

Led American League in balks with 4 in 1979.
Tied for American League lead in balks with 5 in 1981.

Year Club	League	G.	IP.	W.	L.	Pct.	H.	R.	ER.	SO.	BB.	ERA.
1977—Orlando	Southern	16	109	8	4	.667	99	34	24	72	27	1.98
1978—Minnesota	American	37	266	14	13	.519	268	★129	117	121	79	3.96
1979—Toledo†	Int'national	5	33	3	1	.750	30	8	6	19	10	1.59
1979—Minnesota	American	24	123	3	10	.231	154	86	77	47	48	5.63
1980—Minnesota	American	32	191	7	13	.350	198	83	69	97	56	3.25
1981—Minnesota‡	American	14	91	3	8	.273	93	48	39	44	31	3.86
1982—Minnesota§-New York x	American	23	111⅓	8	8	.500	142	65	57	49	29	4.61
1983—Columbus y	Int'national	24	134	9	7	.563	175	99	90	59	59	6.04
1983—New York z	American	5	16⅔	0	1	.000	13	8	8	7	8	4.32
Major League Totals		135	799	35	53	.398	868	419	367	365	251	4.13

Selected by Minnesota Twins' organization in 3rd round of free-agent draft, June 7, 1977.
†On disabled list, July 4 to July 24, 1979.
‡On disabled list, August 19, 1981 through remainder of season.
§Traded with Catcher Butch Wynegar to New York Yankees for Infielder Larry Milbourne and Pitchers John Pacella and Pete Filson, May 12, 1982.
xOn disabled list, August 4 to September 1, 1982.
yOn suspended list, April 18 to May 4, 1983.
zTraded with First Baseman Steve Balboni to Kansas City Royals for Pitcher Mike Armstrong and Catcher Duane Dewey, December 8, 1983.

NICHOLAS ANDREW ESASKY

Name pronounced Ee-SAH-skee.
(Nick)

Born February 24, 1960, at Hialeah, Fla.
Height, 6.03. Weight, 190.
Throws and bats righthanded.

Led Eastern League batters in strikeouts with 131 and game-winning RBIs with 14 in 1980.

Year Club	League	Pos.	G.	AB.	R.	H.	2B.	3B.	HR.	RBI.	B.A.	PO.	A.	E.	F.A.
1978—Billings	Pion.	3B	64	213	38	65	10	5	4	48	.305	★62	88	22	.872
1979—Tampa	Fla. St.	3B	124	439	52	118	16	3	10	66	.269	91	234	27	.923
1980—Waterbury	East.	3B	135	425	79	115	18	4	★30	79	.271	98	241	23	.936
1981—Indianapolis	A. A.	3B	121	423	55	112	22	4	17	62	.265	99	220	★37	.896
1982—Indianapolis	A. A.	3B	105	341	59	90	15	3	27	62	.264	77	150	21	★.915

Year Club	League	Pos.	G.	AB.	R.	H.	2B.	3B.	HR.	RBI.	B.A.	PO.	A.	E.	F.A.
1983—Indianapolis	A. A.	3B	49	158	33	44	5	0	14	37	.278	27	71	14	.875
1983—Cincinnati	Nat.	3B	85	302	41	80	10	5	12	46	.265	53	133	13	.935
Major League Totals			85	302	41	80	10	5	12	46	.265	53	133	13	.935

Selected by Cincinnati Reds' organization in 1st round (17th player selected) of free-agent draft, June 6, 1978.

JUAN ESPINO (REYES)

Born March 16, 1956, at Bonao, Dominican Republic.
Height, 6.00. Weight, 185.
Throws and bats righthanded.
Led New York-Pennsylvania League batters in strikeouts with 61 in 1975.

Year Club	League	Pos.	G.	AB.	R.	H.	2B.	3B.	HR.	RBI.	B.A.	PO.	A.	E.	F.A.
1975—Oneonta	NYP	C-OF	48	157	24	36	5	5	2	23	.229	26	3	2	.935
1976—Ft. Lauderdale†	Fla. St.	C	39	118	18	30	5	3	4	20	.254	170	20	3	.984
1977—Ft. Lauderdale	Fla. St.	C	52	141	8	28	8	0	0	16	.199	266	40	9	.971
1978—West Haven	East.	C	82	261	32	73	14	0	6	37	.280	426	44	6	*.987
1979—West Haven	East.	C	95	296	40	70	11	1	8	44	.236	509	57	13	.978
1980—Nashville	South.	C	17	56	3	9	1	0	0	9	.161	115	6	2	.984
1980—Columbus	Int.	C	48	129	11	27	7	1	1	16	.209	238	29	5	.982
1981—Columbus	Int.	C	80	253	22	59	8	2	7	32	.233	434	53	8	.984
1982—Columbus‡	Int.	C	54	163	30	46	10	1	3	27	.282	264	34	5	.983
1982—New York	Amer.	C	3	2	0	0	0	0	0	0	.000	4	0	0	1.000
1983—Columbus	Int.	C	77	211	35	59	10	1	10	42	.280	326	42	7	.981
1983—New York	Amer.	C	10	23	1	6	0	0	1	3	.261	38	1	0	1.000
Major League Totals			13	25	1	6	0	0	1	3	.240	42	1	0	1.000

Signed as free agent by New York Yankees' organization, December 26, 1974.
†On disabled list, May 26 to June 9, 1976.
‡On disabled list, August 3 to August 23, 1982.

ALVARO ALBERTO ESPINOZA (RAMIREZ)

Born February 19, 1962, at Valencia, Venezuela.
Height, 6.00. Weight, 160.
Throws and bats righthanded.
Led Gulf Coast League shortstops in assists with 217, double plays with 33 and total chances with 356 in 1980.

Year Club	League	Pos.	G.	AB.	R.	H.	2B.	3B.	HR.	RBI.	B.A.	PO.	A.	E.	F.A.
1979—Sarasota Astros	Gulf C.	SS-2B-3B	11	32	3	7	0	0	0	5	.219	18	27	1	.978
1980—Sara. Astros-O.†	Gulf C.	*SS-3B	59	200	24	43	5	0	0	14	.215	*114	219	*25	.930
1981—						(Out of Organized Baseball)									
1982—Wis. Rapids	Midw.	SS-3B-1B	112	379	41	101	9	0	5	29	.266	237	241	33	.935
1983—Visalia	Calif.	SS	130	486	57	155	20	1	4	57	.319	*256	364	40	.939

Signed as free agent by Houston Astros' organization, October 30, 1978.
†Released, September 30, 1980; signed by Wisconsin Rapids (Minnesota Twins' organization), March 18, 1982.

CECIL EDWARD ESPY

Born January 20, 1963, at San Diego, Calif.
Height, 6.03. Weight, 190.
Throws right and bats left and righthanded.
Led Florida State League in stolen bases with 74 in 1982.

Year Club	League	Pos.	G.	AB.	R.	H.	2B.	3B.	HR.	RBI.	B.A.	PO.	A.	E.	F.A.
1980—Sarasota W. Sox	Gulf C.	OF	58	212	33	58	7	3	0	26	.274	138	4	7	.953
1981—Appleton	Midw.	OF	72	273	37	55	2	2	1	19	.201	143	5	5	.967
1981—Sarasota W. Sox†	Gulf C.	OF	43	142	24	40	3	1	0	16	.282	54	1	4	.932
1982—Vero Beach	Fla. St.	OF	131	*523	*100	*166	14	7	1	34	.317	275	9	10	.966
1983—San Antonio	Texas	OF	133	*564	88	151	16	11	4	38	.268	258	12	10	.964
1983—Los Angeles	Nat.	OF	20	11	4	3	1	0	0	1	.273	11	0	0	1.000
Major League Totals			20	11	4	3	1	0	0	1	.273	11	0	0	1.000

Selected by Chicago White Sox' organization in 1st round (eighth player selected) of free-agent draft, June 3, 1980.
†Traded with Pitcher Burt Geiger to Los Angeles Dodgers' organization for Outfielder Rudy Law, March 30, 1982.

JAMES SARKIS ESSIAN JR.

Name pronounced ES-ee-en.

(Jim)

Born January 2, 1951, at Detroit, Mich.
Height, 6.01. Weight, 187.
Throws and bats righthanded.
Attended Arizona State University, Tempe, Ariz.
Led Eastern League catchers in errors with 20 in 1973.
Led Carolina League catchers in double plays with 13 in 1971.

Year Club	League	Pos.	G.	AB.	R.	H.	2B.	3B.	HR.	RBI.	B.A.	PO.	A.	E.	F.A.
1970—Pulaski	Appal.	*C-3B	36	119	17	36	9	0	5	30	.303	243	21	2	*.992
1970—Spartanburg	W. Car.	C	35	119	19	35	8	2	6	20	.294	204	21	5	.978
1971—Peninsula	Carol.	C	131	429	54	107	20	0	12	46	.249	*856	68	*22	.977
1972—Reading	East.	C	96	312	45	79	14	1	4	33	.253	512	60	20	.966

Year	Club	League	Pos.	G.	AB.	R.	H.	2B.	3B.	HR.	RBI.	B.A.	PO.	A.	E.	F.A.
1973—Reading	East.	C-1-3-O	105	315	58	92	15	5	10	55	.292	609	57	22	.968
1973—Philadelphia	Nat.	C	2	3	0	0	0	0	0	0	.000	0	0	0	.000
1974—Toledo	Int.	1B-C-3B	58	181	24	51	4	0	5	24	.282	372	50	11	.975
1974—Philadelphia	Nat.	C-1B-3B	17	20	1	2	0	0	0	0	.100	38	4	1	.977
1975—Reading	East.	C-3B	12	36	5	7	2	0	1	2	.194	61	12	1	.986
1975—Philadelphia†‡§	Nat.	C	2	1	1	1	0	0	0	1	1.000	1	1	0	1.000
1975—Hawaii	P. C.	C	40	129	14	27	2	0	2	9	.209	228	22	2	.992
1976—Chicago	Amer.	C-1B-3B	78	199	20	49	7	0	0	21	.246	320	53	10	.974
1977—Chicago x	Amer.	C-3B	114	322	50	88	18	2	10	44	.273	593	62	9	.986
1978—Oakland	Amer.	C-1B-2B	126	278	21	62	9	1	3	26	.223	452	79	10	.982
1979—Oakland y	Amer.	C-3-1-O	98	313	34	76	16	0	8	40	.243	400	79	9	.982
1980—Oakland z	Amer.	C-1B	87	285	19	66	11	0	5	29	.232	339	46	5	.987
1981—Chicago a	Amer.	C-3B	27	52	6	16	3	0	0	5	.308	92	9	2	.981
1982—Seattle b	Amer.	C	48	153	14	42	8	0	3	20	.275	282	26	2	.994
1982—Salt Lake City c	P. C.	C	10	31	1	7	1	0	0	1	.226	53	8	2	.968
1983—Cleveland d	Amer.	C-3B	48	93	11	19	4	0	2	11	.204	170	14	2	.989
National League Totals			21	24	2	3	0	0	0	1	.125	39	5	1	.978
American League Totals			626	1695	175	418	76	3	31	196	.247	2648	368	49	.984
Major League Totals			647	1719	177	421	76	3	31	197	.245	2687	373	50	.984

Signed as free agent by Philadelphia Phillies' organization, August 29, 1969.

†Traded with Outfielder Barry Bonnell and cash to Atlanta Braves for First Baseman Dick Allen and Catcher Johnny Oates, May 7, 1975.

‡Traded by Atlanta Braves to Chicago White Sox, May 15, 1975, to complete deal in which Atlanta acquired First Baseman Dick Allen from Chicago for $5,000 and a player to be named later, December 3, 1974.

§Loaned to Hawaii (San Diego Padres' organization), July 18, 1975; returned, September 8, 1975.

xTraded with Pitcher Steve Renko to Oakland A's for Pitcher Pablo Torrealba, March 30, 1978.

yOn supplemental disabled list, June 13 to June 28, 1979.

zGranted free agency, October 31, 1980; signed by Chicago White Sox, November 20, 1980.

aTraded with Shortstop Todd Cruz and Outfielder Rod Allen to Seattle Mariners for Outfielder Tom Paciorek, December 11, 1981.

bOn emergency disabled list, May 12 to August 21, 1982; included rehabilitation disability assignment to Salt Lake City, August 9 to August 21, 1982.

cTraded to Cleveland Indians for a player to be named later, January 21, 1983; Cleveland organization acquired Pitcher Tom Owens to complete deal, May 18, 1983.

dTraded to Oakland A's for a player to be named later, December 5, 1983; Cleveland Indians acquired Infielder Luis Quinones to complete deal, December 8, 1983.

FRANK ANTHONY EUFEMIA

Born December 23, 1959, at Bronx, N.Y.
Height, 5.10. Weight, 170.
Throws and bats righthanded.
Attended Ramapo College of New Jersey, Mahwah, N. J.

Led California League in games finished in relief with 53 in 1983.

Year	Club	League	G.	IP.	W.	L.	Pct.	H.	R.	ER.	SO.	BB.	ERA.
1982—Wisconsin Rapids	Midwest	27	58	2	1	.667	47	18	11	36	17	1.71
1983—Visalia	California	64	95⅔	10	4	.714	79	27	26	78	29	2.45

Selected by Minnesota Twins' organization in 18th round of free-agent draft, June 7, 1982.

BARRY STEVEN EVANS

Born November 30, 1956, at Atlanta, Ga.
Height, 6.01. Weight, 180.
Throws and bats righthanded.
Attended West Georgia College, Carrollton, Ga.

Led Northwest League in total bases with 146 in 1977.
Led Texas League third basemen in fielding percentage with .957 in 1978.

Year	Club	League	Pos.	G.	AB.	R.	H.	2B.	3B.	HR.	RBI.	B.A.	PO.	A.	E.	F.A.
1977—Walla Walla	N'west	2B-3B-SS	67	271	47	★97	12	2	11	★64	.358	92	165	13	.952
1978—Amarillo	Texas	3-SS-O	128	514	69	157	24	2	10	67	.305	138	350	23	.955
1978—San Diego	Nat.	3B	24	90	7	24	1	1	0	4	.267	13	59	4	.947
1979—San Diego†	Nat.	3B-SS-2B	56	162	9	35	5	0	1	14	.216	30	110	7	.952
1980—Hawaii	P. C.	2B	20	104	13	26	8	1	2	15	.250	57	95	3	.981
1980—San Diego	Nat.	3-2-S-1	73	125	11	29	3	2	1	14	.232	52	87	2	.986
1981—San Diego‡§	Nat.	1-3-2-S	54	93	11	30	5	0	0	7	.323	98	33	2	.985
1982—Columbus xy	Int.	SS-2B-3B	69	239	27	66	14	3	6	39	.276	109	184	6	.980
1982—New York	Amer.	2B-3B-SS	17	31	2	8	3	0	0	2	.258	14	26	0	1.000
1983—Columbus zab	Int.	3B-2B-SS	62	218	41	58	9	1	6	39	.266	54	109	6	.964
National League Totals			207	470	38	118	14	3	2	39	.251	193	289	15	.970
American League Totals.			17	31	2	8	3	0	0	2	.258	14	26	0	1.000
Major League Totals			224	501	40	126	17	3	2	41	.251	207	315	15	.972

Selected by New York Mets' organization in 8th round of free-agent draft, June 8, 1976.

Selected by San Diego Padres' organization in 2nd round of free-agent draft, June 7, 1977.

†Placed on suspended list, June 26 to September 4, 1979, when he did not report to Amarillo (Texas), June 22, 1979.

‡On supplemental disabled list, August 14 to September 1, 1981.

§Sold to New York Yankees' organization, February 22, 1982.

xOn temporary inactive list, April 16 to May 18, 1982.

yOn disabled list, May 28 to June 8, 1982.

zOn disabled list, April 12 to May 4, 1983.
aOn temporary inactive list, July 5 to July 15 and July 25 to August 5, 1983.
bDrafted by Toledo (Minnesota Twins' organization), December 6, 1983.

DARRELL WAYNE EVANS

Born May 26, 1947, at Pasadena, Calif.
Height, 6.02. Weight, 205.
Throws right and bats lefthanded.
Attended Pasadena City College, Pasadena, Calif. and
California State Univeristy at Los Angeles.
Grandson of David Salazar, former minor league player.

Established National League records for most double plays, third baseman, (45), 1974; most games, consecutive, one or more bases on balls (15), April 9 through 27, 1976.
Tied modern National League record for most errors in inning by third baseman (3), April 11, 1980 (7th inning).
Hit three home runs in a game, June 15, 1983.
Led National League in bases on balls received with 124 in 1973 and 126 in 1974.
Led National League third basemen in putouts with 161 and assists with 381 in 1975.
Led National League third basemen in double plays with 45 in 1974 and 41 in 1975.
Led National League third basemen in total chances with 471 in 1973, 578 in 1974, 578 in 1975, 520 in 1978 and 528 in 1979.
Led International League third basemen in fielding percentage with .951 in 1970.
Named third baseman on THE SPORTING NEWS National League All-Star Team, 1973.
Named Player of the Year in Gulf Coast League, 1967.

Year	Club	League	Pos.	G.	AB.	R.	H.	2B.	3B.	HR.	RBI.	B.A.	PO.	A.	E.	F.A.
1967—Peninsula	Carol.	3B	8	28	4	11	1	1	0	6	.393	6	13	2	.905
1967—Bradenton A's	Gulf C.	3B-SS	14	45	13	22	3	3	2	11	.489	25	30	2	.965
1967—Leesburg	Fla. St.	3B-SS	39	142	18	37	4	2	0	12	.261	49	81	11	.922
1968—Birmingham†	South.	3B-1B-2B	56	187	18	45	6	3	3	25	.241	103	101	10	.953
1969—Richmond	Int.	3B	59	211	43	76	12	4	7	45	.360	51	103	19	.890
1969—Shreveport	Texas	3B-SS-OF	24	79	14	22	5	4	2	14	.278	25	40	3	.956
1969—Atlanta	Nat.	3B	12	26	3	6	0	0	0	1	.231	4	7	1	.917
1970—Richmond	Int.	3B-1B-OF	120	447	92	134	20	7	20	83	.300	99	220	16	.952
1970—Atlanta	Nat.	3B	12	44	4	14	1	1	0	9	.318	6	26	2	.941
1971—Richmond	Int.	OF-3B	31	101	20	31	2	2	6	30	.307	59	11	1	.986
1971—Atlanta	Nat.	3B-OF	89	260	42	63	11	1	12	38	.242	77	138	14	.939
1972—Atlanta‡	Nat.	3B	125	418	67	106	12	0	19	71	.254	126	273	25	.941
1973—Atlanta	Nat.	3B-1B	161	595	114	167	25	8	41	104	.281	266	335	24	.962
1974—Atlanta	Nat.	3B	160	571	99	137	21	3	25	79	.240	★185	367	26	.955
1975—Atlanta	Nat.	★3B-1B	156	567	82	138	22	2	22	73	.243	164	382	★36	.938
1976—Atl.§-S.F.	Nat.	1B-3B	136	396	53	81	9	1	11	46	.205	978	110	10	.991
1977—San Francisco	Nat.	OF-1B-3B	144	461	64	117	18	3	17	72	.254	324	83	13	.969
1978—San Francisco x	Nat.	3B	159	547	82	133	24	2	20	78	.243	★147	★348	★25	.952
1979—San Francisco	Nat.	3B	160	562	68	142	23	2	17	70	.253	★129	★369	★30	.943
1980—San Francisco	Nat.	3B-1B	154	556	69	147	23	0	20	78	.264	232	340	27	.955
1981—San Francisco	Nat.	3B-1B	102	357	51	92	13	4	12	48	.258	188	202	14	.965
1982—San Francisco	Nat.	3B-1B-SS	141	465	64	119	20	4	16	61	.256	471	233	21	.971
1983—San Francisco y	Nat.	1B-3B-SS	142	523	94	145	29	3	30	82	.277	1001	164	19	.984
Major League Totals			1853	6348	956	1607	251	34	262	910	.253	4298	3377	287	.964

Selected by Chicago Cubs' organization in 8th round of free-agent draft, June 22, 1965.
Selected by New York Yankees' organization in secondary phase of free-agent draft, January 29, 1966.
Selected by Detroit Tigers' organization in 5th round of free-agent draft, June 6, 1966.
Selected by Philadelphia Phillies' organization in 3rd round of free-agent draft, January 28, 1967.
Selected by Kansas City A's organization in secondary phase of free-agent draft, June 7, 1967.
†Drafted by Atlanta Braves, December 2, 1968.
‡On military list, June 17 to July 3, 1972.
§Traded with Shortstop Marty Perez to San Francisco Giants for First Baseman-Outfielder Willie Montanez, Shortstop Craig Robinson, Infielder Mike Eden and Outfielder Jake Brown, June 13, 1976.
xGranted free agency, November 2, 1978; re-signed by Giants, December 5, 1978.
yGranted free agency, November 7, 1983; signed by Detroit Tigers, December 17, 1983.

ALL-STAR GAME RECORD

Year	League	Pos.	AB.	R.	H.	2B.	3B.	HR.	RBI.	B.A.	PO.	A.	E.	F.A.
1973—National		PH	0	0	0	0	0	0	0	.000	0	0	0	.000
1983—National		1B	1	0	0	0	0	0	0	.000	2	1	0	1.000
All-Star Game Totals			1	0	0	0	0	0	0	.000	2	1	0	1.000

DWIGHT MICHAEL EVANS

Born November 3, 1951, at Santa Monica, Calif.
Height, 6.03. Weight, 205.
Throws and bats righthanded.

Led American League in total bases with 215 and bases on balls received with 85 in 1981.
Led American League outfielders in double plays with 8 in 1975.
Led Western Carolinas League in sacrifice flies with 8 in 1970.
Tied for Carolina League lead in double plays by outfielders with 3 in 1971.
Named outfielder on THE SPORTING NEWS American League All-Star Team, 1982.
Named outfielder on THE SPORTING NEWS American League All-Star fielding team, 1976, 1978, 1979 and 1981 through 1983.
Named outfielder on THE SPORTING NEWS American League Silver Slugger team, 1981.

Named International League Most Valuable Player, 1972.

Year	Club	League	Pos.	G.	AB.	R.	H.	2B.	3B.	HR.	RBI.	B.A.	PO.	A.	E.	F.A.
1969—Jamestown		NYP	OF-3B	34	100	13	28	3	2	1	12	.280	44	10	3	.947
1970—Greenville		W. Car.	OF-3B	108	355	69	98	14	★11	7	68	.276	130	11	7	.953
1971—Winston-Salem		Carol.	OF-1B	118	402	63	115	20	4	12	63	.286	219	17	10	.959
1972—Louisville		Int.	OF	●144	496	90	149	23	8	17	★95	.300	270	12	6	.979
1972—Boston		Amer.	OF	18	57	2	15	3	1	1	6	.263	25	3	0	1.000
1973—Boston		Amer.	OF	119	282	46	63	13	1	10	32	.223	178	4	1	.995
1974—Boston		Amer.	OF	133	463	60	130	19	8	10	70	.281	294	8	3	.990
1975—Boston		Amer.	OF	128	412	61	113	24	6	13	56	.274	281	15	4	.987
1976—Boston		Amer.	OF	146	501	61	121	34	5	17	62	.242	324	15	2	★.994
1977—Boston†		Amer.	OF	73	230	39	66	9	2	14	36	.287	126	2	1	.992
1978—Boston		Amer.	OF	147	497	75	123	24	2	24	63	.247	305	14	6	.982
1979—Boston		Amer.	OF	152	489	69	134	24	1	21	58	.274	307	15	4	.988
1980—Boston		Amer.	OF	148	463	72	123	37	5	18	60	.266	268	11	5	.982
1981—Boston		Amer.	OF	108	412	84	122	19	4	●22	71	.296	259	9	2	.993
1982—Boston		Amer.	OF	●162	609	122	178	37	7	32	98	.292	346	9	10	.973
1983—Boston‡		Amer.	OF	126	470	74	112	19	4	22	58	.238	222	6	3	.987
Major League Totals				1460	4885	765	1300	262	46	204	670	.266	2935	111	41	.987

Selected by Boston Red Sox' organization in 5th round of free-agent draft, June 5, 1969.
†On supplemental disabled list, June 21 to July 8 and August 25 to September 21, 1977.
‡On supplemental disabled list, August 13 to September 1, 1983.

CHAMPIONSHIP SERIES RECORD

Year	Club	League	Pos.	G.	AB.	R.	H.	2B.	3B.	HR.	RBI.	B.A.	PO.	A.	E.	F.A.
1975—Boston		Amer.	OF	3	10	1	1	0	0	0	0	.100	7	0	0	1.000

WORLD SERIES RECORD

Tied World Series record for highest fielding average by outfielder, seven-game Series (1.000 with 24 chances), 1975.

Year	Club	League	Pos.	G.	AB.	R.	H.	2B.	3B.	HR.	RBI.	B.A.	PO.	A.	E.	F.A.
1975—Boston		Amer.	OF	7	24	3	7	1	1	1	5	.292	23	1	0	1.000

ALL-STAR GAME RECORD

Year	League	Pos.	AB.	R.	H.	2B.	3B.	HR.	RBI.	B.A.	PO.	A.	E.	F.A.
1978—American		OF	1	0	0	0	0	0	0	.000	3	0	0	1.000
1981—American		PH-OF	2	1	1	0	0	0	0	.500	2	0	0	1.000
All-Star Game Totals			3	1	1	0	0	0	0	.333	5	0	0	1.000

LEONARDO LAGO FAEDO

Name pronounced Fah-A-doh.

(Lenny)

Born May 13, 1960, at Tampa, Fla.
Height, 6.00. Weight, 170.
Throws and bats righthanded.

Led Appalachian League in sacrifice flies with 6 in 1978.
Received reported $60,000 bonus to sign with Minnesota Twins, 1978.

Year	Club	League	Pos.	G.	AB.	R.	H.	2B.	3B.	HR.	RBI.	B.A.	PO.	A.	E.	F.A.
1978—Elizabethton		Appal.	SS	55	232	29	65	8	1	2	35	.280	77	166	22	.917
1979—Orlando†		South.	SS	103	336	35	91	13	3	3	34	.271	153	352	30	.944
1980—Orlando‡		South.	SS-3B	114	437	47	105	13	1	6	26	.240	187	365	21	.963
1980—Minnesota§		Amer.	SS	5	8	1	2	1	0	0	0	.250	4	5	2	.818
1981—Charl.-Tol.		Int.	SS-2B-OF	107	348	41	87	15	3	7	44	.250	185	321	21	.960
1981—Minnesota		Amer.	SS	12	41	3	8	0	1	0	6	.195	24	42	2	.971
1982—Minnesota		Amer.	SS	90	255	16	62	8	0	3	22	.243	129	218	12	.967
1983—Minnesota x		Amer.	SS	51	173	16	48	7	0	1	18	.277	53	133	9	.954
1983—Orlando		South.	SS	15	52	2	11	1	0	0	4	.212	19	42	2	.968
Major League Totals				158	477	36	120	16	1	4	46	.252	210	398	25	.961

Selected by Minnesota Twins' organization in 1st round (16th player selected) of free-agent draft, June 6, 1978.
†On disabled list, April 27 to May 24, 1979.
‡On disabled list, April 11 to May 3, 1980.
§Loaned to Charleston (Cleveland Indians' organization), April 6, 1981; returned, July 4, 1981.
xOn supplemental disabled list, June 4, 1983; transferred to regular disabled list, June 21 to September 1, 1983; included rehabilitation disability assignment to Orlando, August 12 to September 1, 1983.

WILLIAM ROGER FAHEY

(Bill)

Born June 14, 1950, at Detroit, Mich.
Height, 6.00. Weight, 200.
Throws right and bats lefthanded.
Attended University of Detroit, Detroit, Mich., St. Clair County Community College,
Port Huron, Mich., and University of Tampa, Tampa, Fla.

Led Pacific Coast League in passed balls with 15 in 1973.

Year	Club	League	Pos.	G.	AB.	R.	H.	2B.	3B.	HR.	RBI.	B.A.	PO.	A.	E.	F.A.
1970—Burlington		Carol.	C	118	377	49	92	10	2	3	36	.244	★724	76	10	.988
1971—Pittsfield		East.	C	99	325	44	93	13	4	6	38	.286	536	54	6	★.990

Year Club League	Pos.	G.	AB.	R.	H.	2B.	3B.	HR.	RBI.	B.A.	PO.	A.	E.	F.A.
1971—Denver.................. A. A.	C	4	15	1	4	0	0	1	2	.267	19	2	0	1.000
1971—Washington........... Amer.	C	2	8	0	0	0	0	0	0	.000	8	2	1	.909
1972—Denver.................. A. A.	C	75	226	28	61	5	4	1	25	.270	421	43	6	.987
1972—Texas..................... Amer.	C	39	119	8	20	2	0	1	10	.168	236	26	2	.992
1973—Spokane .... P. C.	C	104	370	45	103	15	2	1	44	.278	535	52	8	★.987
1974—Spokane .... P. C.	C	92	317	39	82	9	2	3	39	.259	553	43	3	★.995
1974—Texas..................... Amer.	C	6	16	1	4	0	0	0	0	.250	21	2	0	1.000
1975—Texas†.................... Amer.	C	21	37	3	11	1	1	0	3	.297	54	5	1	.983
1976—Texas..................... Amer.	C	38	80	12	20	2	0	1	9	.250	126	19	1	.993
1977—Texas..................... Amer.	C	37	68	3	15	4	0	0	5	.221	104	5	0	1.000
1978—Tucson................... P. C.	C-OF	66	212	35	53	7	0	2	19	.250	333	44	5	.987
1978—Texas‡§.................. Amer.						(Did not play)								
1979—San Diego .... Nat.	C	73	209	14	60	8	1	3	19	.287	277	33	2	.994
1980—San Diego x........... Nat.	C	93	241	18	62	4	0	1	22	.257	309	34	8	.977
1981—Detroit y................ Amer.	C	27	67	5	17	2	0	1	9	.254	96	9	2	.981
1982—Detroit z................ Amer.	C	28	67	7	10	2	0	0	4	.149	85	16	0	1.000
1983—Detroit a................ Amer.	C	19	22	4	6	1	0	0	2	.273	39	2	0	1.000
1983—Evansville b .... A. A.	C	8	23	4	7	2	0	1	6	.304	42	3	0	1.000
American League Totals...........................		217	484	43	103	14	1	3	42	.213	769	86	7	.992
National League Totals............................		166	450	32	122	12	1	4	41	.271	586	67	10	.985
Major League Totals..................................		383	934	75	225	26	2	7	83	.241	1355	153	17	.989

Selected by Baltimore Orioles' organization in 13th round of free-agent draft, June 7, 1968.
Selected by Washington Senators' organization in secondary phase of free-agent draft, January 17, 1970.
†On disabled list, June 22 to August 14, 1975.
‡On emergency disabled list, August 22 to October 23, 1978.
§Traded with Third Baseman Kurt Bevacqua and First Baseman Mike Hargrove to San Diego Padres for Outfielder Oscar Gamble, Catcher Dave Roberts and cash estimated at $300,000, October 25, 1978.
xSold to Detroit Tigers for cash estimated at $90,000, March 24, 1981.
yOn supplemental disabled list, April 4 to May 8, 1981.
zOn supplemental disabled list, May 3 to June 1, 1982.
aOn disabled list, March 21 to May 16, 1983; included rehabilitation disability assignment to Evansville, April 25 to May 15, 1983.
bReleased, August 5, 1983; signed by Detroit Tigers as a coach, August 11, 1983.

PETER FALCONE

Name pronounced Fowl-KOHN.

(Pete)

Born October 1, 1953, at Brooklyn, N. Y.
Height, 6.02. Weight, 185.
Throws and bats lefthanded.
Attended Kingsborough Community College, Brooklyn, N. Y.
Cousin of Joe Pignatano, catcher with Brooklyn Dodgers, Los Angeles Dodgers, Kansas City A's, San Francisco Giants and New York Mets, 1957 through 1962; coach, Washington Senators, 1965 through 1967; coach New York Mets, 1968 through 1981; and coach with Atlanta Braves since 1982.

Led Pioneer League in balks with 2 in 1973.

Year Club	League	G.	IP.	W.	L.	Pct.	H.	R.	ER.	SO.	BB.	ERA.
1973—Great Falls.....................................	Pioneer	12	72	8	1	★.889	49	19	12	102	53	★1.50
1974—Fresno..	California	17	137	10	4	.714	116	61	46	172	61	3.02
1974—Amarillo...	Texas	7	37	2	4	.333	41	14	11	35	18	2.68
1975—San Francisco†	National	34	190	12	11	.522	171	97	88	131	111	4.17
1976—St. Louis..	National	32	212	12	16	.429	173	87	76	138	93	3.23
1977—St. Louis..	National	27	124	4	8	.333	130	79	75	75	61	5.44
1977—New Orleans..................................	Am. Assoc.	7	44	2	5	.286	45	107	99	32	22	4.91
1978—St. Louis‡......................................	National	19	75	2	7	.222	94	52	48	28	48	5.76
1979—New York......................................	National	33	184	6	14	.300	194	91	85	113	76	4.16
1980—New York......................................	National	37	157	7	10	.412	163	89	79	109	58	4.53
1981—New York......................................	National	35	95	5	3	.625	84	32	27	56	36	2.56
1982—New York§....................................	National	40	171	8	10	.444	159	82	73	101	71	3.84
1983—Atlanta	National	33	106⅔	9	4	.692	102	47	43	59	60	3.63
Major League Totals...................................		290	1314⅔	65	83	.439	1270	656	594	710	614	4.07

Selected by Minnesota Twins' organization in 13th round of free-agent draft, June 6, 1972.
Selected by Atlanta Braves' organization in secondary phase of free-agent draft, January 10, 1973.
Selected by San Francisco Giants' organization in secondary phase of free-agent draft, June 5, 1973.
†Traded to St. Louis Cardinals for Third Baseman Ken Reitz, December 8, 1975.
‡Traded to New York Mets for Outfielder Tom Grieve and Pitcher Kim Seaman, December 5, 1978.
§Granted free agency, November 10, 1982; signed by Atlanta Braves, January 27, 1983.

ROBERT JOSEPH FALLON

(Bob)

Born February 18, 1960, at New York, N.Y.
Height, 6.03. Weight, 200.
Throws and bats lefthanded.
Attended Miami-Dade Community College-North, Miami, Fla.

Tied for Eastern League lead in games started by pitchers with 27 in 1982.

Year Club	League	G.	IP.	W.	L.	Pct.	H.	R.	ER.	SO.	BB.	ERA.
1979—Niagara Falls	NYP	15	83	3	7	.300	70	48	32	52	66	3.47
1980—Appleton	Midwest	22	122	11	5	.688	103	62	48	103	82	3.54
1981—Glens Falls	Eastern	26	135	11	9	.550	155	*112	81	81	78	5.40
1982—Glens Falls	Eastern	28	147⅔	9	9	.500	142	90	78	119	87	4.75
1983—Denver†	Am. Assoc.	24	138⅓	10	5	.667	119	74	66	105	73	4.29

Selected by Oakland A's organization in 2nd round of free-agent draft, January 9, 1979.
Selected by Chicago White Sox' organization in secondary phase of free-agent draft, June 5, 1979.
†On disabled list, July 13 to July 24, 1983.

EDWARD JOSEPH FARMER
(Ed)

Born October 18, 1949, at Evergreen Park, Ill.
Height, 6.05. Weight, 212.
Throws and bats righthanded.
Attended Chicago State College, Chicago, Ill.

Major League saves: 1971 (4), 1972 (7), 1973 (3), 1978 (1), 1979 (14), 1980 (30), 1981 (10), 1982 (6). Total—75.
Led International League in wild pitches with 13 in 1977.

Year Club	League	G.	IP.	W.	L.	Pct.	H.	R.	ER.	SO.	BB.	ERA.
1967—Sarasota Indians	Gulf Coast	7	32	3	0	1.000	12	13	7	29	30	1.97
1968—Waterbury	Eastern	4	14	0	3	.000	12	15	11	9	13	7.07
1968—Reno	California	23	125	8	5	.615	132	74	65	122	69	4.68
1969—Waterbury	Eastern	7	26	0	4	.000	36	26	20	12	19	6.92
1969—Monroe	W. Carol.	10	46	3	5	.375	44	39	30	30	43	5.87
1970—Wichita†	Am. Assoc.	23	121	5	7	.417	114	64	54	69	70	4.02
1971—Wichita	Am. Assoc.	7	40	2	2	.500	35	22	20	19	15	4.50
1971—Cleveland	American	43	79	5	4	.556	77	42	38	48	41	4.33
1972—Cleveland	American	46	61	2	5	.286	51	32	30	33	27	4.43
1973—Cleveland‡-Detroit§x	American	40	62	3	2	.600	77	38	34	38	32	4.94
1974—Toledo	Int'national	7	47	2	3	.400	33	18	14	34	23	2.68
1974—Philadelphia y	National	14	31	2	1	.667	41	32	29	20	27	8.42
1975—Sacramento	P. Coast	14	61	2	8	.200	69	59	53	53	67	7.82
1975—Union Laguna	Mexican	2	1	0	1	.000	1	4	3	0	4	27.00
1976—Salt Lake City z	P. Coast					(Did not play)						
1977—Rochester	Int'national	24	131	11	5	.688	127	72	65	96	*89	4.47
1977—Baltimore a	American	1	0	0	0	.000	1	1	1	0	1	.....
1978—Spokane	P.Coast	55	90	9	7	.563	103	73	60	50	53	6.00
1978—Milwaukee b	American	3	11	1	0	1.000	7	1	1	6	4	0.82
1979—Texas c-Chicago	American	53	114	5	7	.417	96	57	38	73	53	3.00
1980—Chicago	American	64	100	7	9	.438	92	37	37	54	56	3.33
1981—Chicago d	American	42	53	3	3	.500	53	33	27	42	34	4.58
1982—Philadelphia	National	47	76	2	6	.250	66	44	41	58	50	4.86
1983—Philadelphia e	National	12	26⅔	0	6	.000	35	22	18	16	20	6.08
1983—Portland f-Tacoma	P. Coast	15	23⅔	1	1	.500	29	18	13	16	8	4.94
1983—Oakland	American	5	10⅓	0	0	.000	15	4	4	7	0	3.48
American League Totals		297	490⅓	26	30	.464	469	245	210	301	248	3.85
National League Totals		73	133⅔	4	13	.235	142	98	88	94	97	5.93
Major League Totals		370	624	30	43	.411	611	343	298	395	345	4.30

Selected by Cleveland Indians' organization in 5th round of free-agent draft, June 6, 1967.
†On disabled list, July 23 to August 21, 1970.
‡Traded to Detroit Tigers for Pitcher Tom Timmerman and Infielder Kevin Collins, June 15, 1973.
§Traded to New York Yankees for Catcher Jerry Moses in three-team deal in which Cleveland Indians acquired Pitcher Jim Perry from Detroit Tigers and Cleveland sent Outfielder Walt Williams and Pitcher Rick Sawyer to New York, March 19, 1974.
xSold to Philadelphia Phillies, March 21, 1974.
yTraded to Milwaukee Brewers for Infielder-Outfielder Steve McCartney, December 3, 1974.
zReleased, April 4, 1976; signed by Baltimore Orioles' organization, March 2, 1977.
aReleased, March 28, 1978; signed by Milwaukee Brewers' organization, April 1, 1978.
bTraded with First Baseman Gary Holle and cash to Texas Rangers for Pitcher Reggie Cleveland, December 15, 1978.
cTraded with First Baseman Gary Holle to Chicago White Sox for Third Baseman Eric Soderholm, June 15, 1979.
dGranted free agency, November 13, 1981; signed by Philadelphia Phillies as Type A player, January 28, 1982. (Catcher Joel Skinner selected from player compensation pool by Chicago White Sox, February 2, 1982.)
eOn disabled list, July 3 to August 13, 1983; included rehabilitation disability assignment to Portland, July 27 to August 13, 1983.
fReleased, August 13, 1983; signed by Tacoma (Oakland A's organization), August 23, 1983.

ALL-STAR GAME RECORD

Year League	IP.	W.	L.	Pct.	H.	R.	ER.	SO.	BB.	ERA.
1980—American	⅔	0	0	.000	1	0	0	0	0	0.00

STEVEN MICHAEL FARR
(Steve)

Born December 12, 1956, at LaPlata, Md.
Height, 5.10. Weight, 190.
Throws and bats righthanded.

Year Club	League	G.	IP.	W.	L.	Pct.	H.	R.	ER.	SO.	BB.	ERA.
1977—Niagara Falls	NYP	10	52	1	5	.167	53	30	23	43	30	3.98
1978—Charleston	W. Carol.	21	77	5	3	.625	72	45	36	54	63	4.21
1978—Salem	Ap'lacian	2	16	2	0	1.000	13	2	1	12	1	0.56
1979—Salem†	Carolina	26	119	3	10	.231	138	81	66	105	47	4.99
1980—Buffalo	Eastern	23	161	11	6	.647	158	84	71	71	64	3.97
1980—Portland	P. Coast	2	7	0	1	.000	11	9	8	0	2	10.29
1981—Buffalo	Eastern	29	106	8	3	.727	102	50	44	82	48	3.74
1981—Portland	P. Coast	4	23	0	3	.000	39	28	20	19	12	7.83
1982—Buffalo‡§	Eastern	25	76⅓	5	8	.385	72	40	34	84	38	4.01
1983—Buffalo	Eastern	18	112	13	1	*.929	88	28	20	108	50	*1.61

Signed as a free agent by Pittsburgh Pirates' organization, December 13, 1976.
†On disabled list, June 6 to June 22, 1979.
‡On Lynn suspended list, April 16, 1983; transferred to restricted list, April 27 to June 8, 1983.
§Traded to Buffalo (Cleveland Indians' organization) for Catcher John Malkin, June 8, 1983.

MICHAEL OTIS FELDER
(Mike)

Born November 18, 1961, at Vallejo, Calif.
Height, 5.08. Weight, 160.
Throws right and bats left and righthanded.
Attended Contra Costa College, San Pablo, Calif.

Led Texas League in stolen bases with 71 in 1983.
Led California League in stolen bases with 92 in 1982.
Led Texas League outfielders in putouts with 332, total chances with 363 and tied for lead in assists with 18 in 1983.

Year Club	League	Pos.	G.	AB.	R.	H.	2B.	3B.	HR.	RBI.	B.A.	PO.	A.	E.	F.A.
1981—Stockton	Calif.	2B-OF	91	338	66	91	8	1	3	30	.269	172	162	13	.963
1982—Stockton	Calif.	OF	137	524	102	138	18	11	7	47	.263	314	9	10	.970
1983—El Paso	Texas	●OF-2B	133	554	108	156	23	10	9	78	.282	334	24	●13	.965

Selected by Milwaukee Brewers' organization in 3rd round of free-agent draft, January 13, 1981.

JOSEPH VANCE FERGUSON
(Joe)

Born September 19, 1946, at San Francisco, Calif.
Height, 6.02. Weight, 215.
Throws and bats righthanded.
Attended University of the Pacific, Stockton, Calif.

Established major league record for fewest errors, season, catcher (700 or more chances), 3, 1973.
Led National League in passed balls with 16 in 1977.
Led National League catchers in fielding percentage with .996 and double plays with 17 in 1973.
Tied for National League lead in sacrifice flies with 10 in 1973.
Led Texas League catchers in fielding percentage with .988 in 1970.
Led Northwest League batters in bases on balls received with 54 and strikeouts with 77 in 1968.
Led Florida State League catchers in putouts with 706, assists with 87, errors with 25 and passed balls with 44 in 1969.

Year Club	League	Pos.	G.	AB.	R.	H.	2B.	3B.	HR.	RBI.	B.A.	PO.	A.	E.	F.A.
1968—Tri-City	N'west	OF	70	226	44	65	9	4	*12	52	.288	101	6	2	.982
1969—Daytona Beach	Fla. St.	C-OF-1B	123	391	66	112	21	4	9	58	.286	728	90	26	.969
1970—Albuquerque	Texas	C-OF-3B	109	364	72	111	20	4	16	65	.305	606	83	8	.989
1970—Los Angeles	Nat.	C	5	4	0	1	0	0	0	1	.250	9	0	0	1.000
1971—Spokane	P. C.	C-OF	60	213	27	54	10	1	10	43	.254	345	31	7	.982
1971—Los Angeles	Nat.	C	36	102	13	22	3	0	2	7	.216	167	9	3	.983
1972—Albuquerque	P. C.	C-OF	123	380	68	99	21	4	10	67	.261	516	40	10	.982
1972—Los Angeles	Nat.	C-OF	8	24	2	7	3	0	1	5	.292	42	1	0	1.000
1973—Los Angeles†	Nat.	C-OF	136	487	84	128	26	0	25	88	.263	786	57	5	.994
1974—Los Angeles	Nat.	C-OF	111	349	54	88	14	1	16	57	.252	486	40	7	.987
1975—Los Angeles‡	Nat.	C-OF	66	202	15	42	2	1	5	23	.208	215	20	2	.992
1976—L.A.§ St. L. x	Nat.	C-OF	125	374	46	79	15	4	10	39	.211	409	46	14	.970
1977—Houston	Nat.	C-1B	132	421	59	108	21	3	16	61	.257	644	80	11	.985
1978—Hous. y-L.A.	Nat.	C-OF	118	348	40	78	16	0	14	50	.224	573	52	7	.989
1979—Los Angeles	Nat.	C-OF	122	363	54	95	14	0	20	69	.262	414	37	9	.980
1980—Los Angeles z	Nat.	C-OF	77	172	20	41	3	2	9	29	.238	297	23	7	.979
1981—Los Angeles a	Nat.	OF	17	14	2	2	1	0	0	1	.143	0	0	0	.000
1981—California	Amer.	C-OF	12	30	5	7	1	0	1	5	.233	41	5	1	.979
1982—California	Amer.	C-OF	36	84	10	19	2	0	3	8	.226	139	13	1	.993
1983—California bc	Amer.	C-OF	12	27	3	2	0	0	0	2	.074	31	3	1	.971
National League Totals			953	2860	389	691	118	11	118	430	.241	4069	365	65	.986
American League Totals			60	141	18	28	3	0	4	15	.199	211	21	3	.987
Major League Totals			1013	3001	407	719	121	11	122	445	.240	4280	386	68	.986

Selected by Los Angeles Dodgers' organization in 13th round of free-agent draft, June 7, 1968.
†On supplemental disabled list, June 21 to July 10, 1973.
‡On disabled list, July 2 to September 29, 1975.
§Traded with Outfielder Bobby Detherage and Infielder Freddie Tisdale to St. Louis Cardinals for Outfielder Reggie Smith, June 15, 1976.
xTraded with Outfielder Bobby Detherage to Houston Astros for Pitcher Larry Dierker and Infielder Jerry DaVanon, November 23, 1976.
yTraded to Los Angeles Dodgers for two players to be named later, July 1, 1978; Houston Astros acquired Infielder Rafael Landestoy, July 7, 1978, and Outfielder Jeff Leonard, September 11, 1978, to complete deal.

zOn disabled list, April 16 to May 9, 1980.
aReleased, August 13, 1981; signed by California Angels, September 1, 1981.
bOn supplemental disabled list, June 18 to July 3, 1983.
cReleased, July 6, 1983.

CHAMPIONSHIP SERIES RECORD

Year	Club	League	Pos.	G.	AB.	R.	H.	2B.	3B.	HR.	RBI.	B.A.	PO.	A.	E.	F.A.
1974—Los Angeles		Nat.	OF-C	4	13	3	3	0	0	0	2	.231	9	0	1	.900
1978—Los Angeles		Nat.	PH	2	2	0	0	0	0	0	0	.000	0	0	0	.000
Championship Series Totals				6	15	3	3	0	0	0	2	.200	9	0	1	.900

WORLD SERIES RECORD

Tied World Series records for most errors, catcher, 5-game series, 2, in 1974, and most errors, catcher, game, 2, October 15, 1974.

Year	Club	League	Pos.	G.	AB.	R.	H.	2B.	3B.	HR.	RBI.	B.A.	PO.	A.	E.	F.A.
1974—Los Angeles		Nat.	OF-C	5	16	2	2	0	0	1	2	.125	14	1	2	.882
1978—Los Angeles		Nat.	C	2	4	1	2	2	0	0	0	.500	11	0	1	.917
World Series Totals				7	20	3	4	2	0	1	2	.200	25	1	3	.897

MARK WILLIAM FERGUSON

Born February 5, 1961, at Salem, O.
Height, 6.02. Weight, 195.
Throws and bats righthanded.
Attended Ohio State University, Columbus, O.

Pitched 9-0 no-hit victory against Nashua, June 5, 1983 (first game).
Led California League in complete games with 20 and shutouts with 8 in 1982.

Year	Club	League	G.	IP.	W.	L.	Pct.	H.	R.	ER.	SO.	BB.	ERA.
1979—Medford		Northwest	12	57	1	8	.111	63	54	36	46	36	5.68
1980—Modesto		California	24	162	10	10	.500	149	85	67	120	104	3.72
1981—Modesto		California	24	68	3	5	.375	91	60	52	28	36	6.88
1982—Modesto†		California	26	198	17	6	.739	154	48	39	124	52	*1.77
1983—Albany		Eastern	22	118	8	8	.500	116	79	67	75	64	5.11

Selected by Oakland A's organization in 2nd round of free-agent draft, June 5, 1979.
†On disabled list, April 9 to April 22, 1982.

CHARLES SID FERNANDEZ

(Known by middle name.)

Born October 12, 1962, at Honolulu, Hawaii.
Height, 6.01. Weight, 220.
Throws and bats lefthanded.

Pitched 1-0 no-hit victory against Fort Lauderdale, June 8, 1982.
Pitched 5-0 no-hit victory against Winter Haven, April 24, 1982.
Named Texas League Pitcher of the Year, 1983.

Year	Club	League	G.	IP.	W.	L.	Pct.	H.	R.	ER.	SO.	BB.	ERA.
1981—Lethbridge		Pioneer	11	76	5	1	.833	43	21	13	*128	31	*1.54
1982—Vero Beach		Florida St.	12	84⅔	8	1	.889	38	19	18	*137	38	1.91
1982—Albuquerque		P. Coast	13	88	6	5	.545	76	54	53	86	52	5.42
1983—San Antonio		Texas	24	153	●13	4	.765	111	61	48	*209	96	*2.82
1983—Los Angeles†		National	2	6	0	1	.000	7	4	4	9	7	6.00
Major League Totals			2	6	0	1	.000	7	4	4	9	7	6.00

Selected by Los Angeles Dodgers' organization in 3rd round of free-agent draft, June 8, 1981.
†Traded with Infielder Ross Jones to New York Mets for Pitcher Carlos Diaz and a player to be named later, December 8, 1983; Los Angeles Dodgers acquired Infielder Bob Bailor to complete deal, December 9, 1983.

OCTAVIO ANTONIO FERNANDEZ (CASTRO)

(Tony)

Born August 6, 1962, at San Pedro de Macoris, Dominican Republic.
Height, 6.01. Weight, 160.
Throws right and bats right and lefthanded.

Led International League shortstops in double plays with 87 in 1983.

Year	Club	League	Pos.	G.	AB.	R.	H.	2B.	3B.	HR.	RBI.	B.A.	PO.	A.	E.	F.A.
1980—Kingston		Carol.	SS	62	187	28	52	6	2	0	12	.278	93	205	28	.914
1981—Kingston		Carol.	SS	75	280	57	89	10	6	1	13	.318	121	227	19	.948
1981—Syracuse†		Int.	SS	31	115	13	32	6	2	1	9	.278	69	80	3	.980
1982—Syracuse		Int.	SS	134	523	78	158	21	6	4	56	.302	*246	364	23	*.964
1983—Syracuse		Int.	SS	117	437	65	131	18	6	5	38	.300	*211	361	26	.957
1983—Toronto		Amer.	SS	15	34	5	9	1	1	0	2	.265	16	17	0	1.000
Major League Totals				15	34	5	9	1	1	0	2	.265	16	17	0	1.000

Signed as free agent by Toronto Blue Jays' organization, April 24, 1979.
†On disabled list, August 10 to August 27, 1981.

ANTHONY ROSS FERREIRA
(Tony)

Born October 4, 1962, at Riverside, Calif.
Height, 6.02. Weight, 160.
Throws and bats lefthanded.
Cousin of Derek Diaz, pitcher in Milwaukee Brewers' organization.

Pitched 6-0 no-hit victory against Knoxville, July 9, 1983.

Year Club	League	G.	IP.	W.	L.	Pct.	H.	R.	ER.	SO.	BB.	ERA.
1981—Sarasota Royals-Gold	Gulf Coast	12	48	4	0	1.000	40	19	12	45	22	2.25
1982—Ft. Myers	Florida St.	22	150⅓	12	7	.632	144	64	48	120	66	2.87
1982—Jacksonville	Southern	6	37⅓	2	4	.333	38	20	17	30	14	4.10
1983—Jacksonville	Southern	35	136⅓	7	11	.389	122	77	64	85	68	4.22

Selected by Kansas City Royals' organization in 2nd round of free-agent draft, June 8, 1981.

GREGORY GERARD FIELD
(Greg)

Born January 6, 1957, at West Palm Beach, Fla.
Height, 6.04. Weight, 175.
Throws and bats righthanded.

Tied for Southern League lead in shutouts with 4 in 1977.
Tied for Midwest League lead in complete games with 13 in 1976.
Named Southern League Pitcher of the Year, 1977.

Year Club	League	G.	IP.	W.	L.	Pct.	H.	R.	ER.	SO.	BB.	ERA.
1975—Elizabethton	Ap'lachian	13	69	5	5	.500	86	48	37	53	15	4.83
1976—Wisconsin Rapids	Midwest	25	163	10	7	.588	168	79	55	123	49	3.04
1977—Orlando	Southern	24	162	14	7	.667	156	62	50	103	33	2.78
1978—Toledo	Int'national	21	113	6	6	.500	145	69	62	68	37	4.94
1978—Orlando†‡	Southern	5	32	2	2	.500	31	13	13	20	7	3.66
1979—Portland§	P. Coast	23	117	4	13	.235	153	75	63	58	33	4.85
1980—Buffalo x	Eastern	2	12	1	1	.500	13	11	3	6	6	2.25
1980—Richmond	Int'national	13	65	4	6	.400	79	38	33	28	29	4.57
1980—Savannah	Southern	10	72	6	2	.750	76	31	28	37	27	3.50
1981—Savannah	Southern	27	172	11	10	.524	198	98	80	101	64	4.19
1982—Savannah	Southern	29	102⅔	8	3	.727	86	35	31	73	37	2.72
1983—Richmond yz	Int'national	20	47	2	1	.667	56	30	23	26	17	4.40

Selected by Minnesota Twins' organization in 4th round of free-agent draft, June 4, 1975.

†Traded with a player to be named later to New York Mets for Pitcher Jerry Koosman, December 8, 1978; New York acquired Pitcher Jesse Orosco to complete deal, February 7, 1979.

‡Traded with Shortstop Tim Foli to Pittsburgh Pirates for Shortstop Frank Taveras, April 19, 1979.

§On disabled list, July 1 to July 23, 1979.

xTraded to Atlanta Braves' organization, April 25, 1980, completing deal in which Atlanta traded Pitcher Eddie Solomon to Pittsburgh Pirates for a player to be named later, March 28, 1980.

yOn disabled list, June 21 to August 17, 1983.

zGranted free agency, October 20, 1983; signed by Minnesota Twins' organization, November 14, 1983.

WILLIAM PETER FILSON
(Pete)

Born September 28, 1958, at Darby, Pa.
Height, 6.02. Weight, 190.
Throws left and bats left and righthanded.
Attended Temple University, Philadelphia, Pa.

Pitched seven-inning, 4-0 no-hit victory against Gastonia, April 25, 1980 (first game).
Pitched seven-inning, 10-0 no-hit victory against Kingsport, August 7, 1979 (second game).
Led International League in complete games with 11 and balks with 8 in 1982.
Led Appalachian League in complete games with 9, shutouts with 3 and balks with 4 in 1979.

Year Club	League	G.	IP.	W.	L.	Pct.	H.	R.	ER.	SO.	BB.	ERA.
1979—Paintsville	Ap'lachian	13	*91	*9	0	*1.000	51	19	17	*118	39	*1.68
1979—Oneonta	NYP	1	1	0	0	.000	0	0	0	1	0	0.00
1980—Greensboro	S. Atlantic	4	27	3	0	1.000	13	5	5	34	14	1.67
1980—Ft. Lauderdale	Florida St.	23	144	10	9	.526	105	56	48	86	69	3.00
1981—Ft. Lauderdale	Florida St.	11	68	7	1	.875	56	20	15	68	20	1.99
1981—Nashville	Southern	14	99	10	2	●.833	73	30	20	77	28	1.82
1982—Columbus†-Toledo	Int'national	23	150⅔	8	10	.444	168	87	77	84	53	4.60
1982—Minnesota	American	5	12⅓	0	2	.000	17	12	12	10	8	8.76
1983—Minnesota‡	American	26	90	4	1	.800	87	34	34	49	29	3.40
1983—Toledo	Int'national	2	7	0	1	.000	8	6	6	6	3	7.71
Major League Totals		31	102⅓	4	3	.571	104	46	46	59	37	4.05

Selected by New York Yankees' organization in 8th round of free-agent draft, June 5, 1979.

†Traded with Infielder Larry Milbourne and Pitcher John Pacella to Minnesota Twins for Catcher Butch Wynegar and Pitcher Roger Erickson, May 12, 1982.

‡On disabled list, July 13 to August 3, 1983.

—DID YOU KNOW—

That Montreal pitcher Chris Welsh had a game-winning RBI in 1983 but failed to post a victory?

JOHN JOSEPH FIMPLE
(Jack)

Born February 10, 1959, at Darby, Pa.
Height, 6.02. Weight, 185.
Throws and bats righthanded.
Attended Humboldt State University, Arcata, Calif.

Led Midwest League in sacrifice flies with 8 in 1981.
Led Pacific Coast League catchers in stealers caught with 44 in 1983.
Led Florida State League catchers in putouts with 542 and assists with 54 in 1982.
Led Midwest League in passed balls with 36 in 1981.

Year	Club	League	Pos.	G.	AB.	R.	H.	2B.	3B.	HR.	RBI.	B.A.	PO.	A.	E.	F.A.
1980—Bat.†-Auburn.........	NYP		2B-3B	61	215	27	52	7	0	5	24	.242	113	121	14	.944
1981—Waterloo‡............	Midw.		C-1B	108	371	53	107	21	2	10	76	.288	676	92	10	.987
1982—Vero Beach..........	Fla. St.		C-1B	111	359	53	101	14	5	9	54	.281	610	58	11	.984
1983—Albuquerque	P. C.		C	80	235	44	58	12	3	10	51	.247	397	★73	14	.971
1983—Los Angeles	Nat.		C	54	148	16	37	8	1	2	22	.250	336	32	4	.989
Major League Totals.................................				54	148	16	37	8	1	2	22	.250	336	32	4	.989

Selected by Cleveland Indians' organization in 29th round of free-agent draft, June 3, 1980.
†Loaned to Auburn (Co-op), July 27, 1980; returned, September 5, 1980.
‡Traded with Pitcher Larry White and Outfielder Jorge Orta to Los Angeles Dodgers for Pitcher Rick Sutcliffe and Second Baseman Jack Perconte, December 9, 1981.

CHAMPIONSHIP SERIES RECORD

Year	Club	League	Pos.	G.	AB.	R.	H.	2B.	3B.	HR.	RBI.	B.A.	PO.	A.	E.	F.A.
1983—Los Angeles	Nat.		C	3	7	0	1	0	0	0	1	.143	14	2	0	1.000

ROLAND GLEN FINGERS
(Rollie)

Born August 25, 1946, at Steubenville, O.
Height, 6.04. Weight, 195.
Throws and bats righthanded.
Attended Chaffey Junior College, Alta Loma, Calif.
Son of George M. Fingers, former minor league player in St. Louis Cardinals' organization; brother of
Gordon Fingers, pitcher in Oakland Athletics' organization, 1970; uncle of
Bob Fingers, pitcher in Milwaukee Brewers' organization.

Established major league record for most saves, lifetime (301).
Tied National League record for most saves, season (37), 1978.
Major League saves: 1969 (12), 1970 (2), 1971 (17), 1972 (21), 1973 (22), 1974 (18), 1975 (24), 1976 (20), 1977 (35), 1978 (37), 1979 (13), 1980 (23), 1981 (28), 1982 (29). Total—301.
Led American League in saves with 28 in 1981.
Led National League in saves with 35 in 1977 and 37 in 1978.
Led National League in games finished in relief with 69 in 1977.
Led American League in games finished in relief with 59 in 1975.
Tied for Southern League lead in shutouts with 3 in 1968.
Named American League Most Valuable Player by Baseball Writers' Association of America, 1981.
Won American League Cy Young Memorial Award, 1981.
Named American League Fireman of the Year by THE SPORTING NEWS, 1981.
Named National League Fireman of the Year by THE SPORTING NEWS, 1977 and 1978.
Named National League co-Fireman of the Year by THE SPORTING NEWS, 1980.

Year	Club	League	G.	IP.	W.	L.	Pct.	H.	R.	ER.	SO.	BB.	ERA.
1965—Leesburg..................	Florida St.		25	175	8	15	.348	148	83	58	108	69	2.98
1966—Modesto..................	California		22	159	11	6	.647	120	61	49	152	43	2.77
1967—Birmingham††‡..........	Southern		18	102	6	5	.545	75	34	25	61	36	2.21
1968—Birmingham..............	Southern		18	108	10	4	.714	94	38	36	93	28	3.00
1968—Oakland..................	American		1	1	0	0	.000	4	4	4	0	1	36.00
1969—Oakland..................	American		60	119	6	7	.462	116	60	49	61	41	3.71
1970—Oakland..................	American		45	148	7	9	.438	137	65	60	79	48	3.65
1971—Oakland..................	American		45	129	4	6	.400	94	46	43	98	30	3.00
1972—Oakland..................	American		65	111	11	9	.550	85	35	31	113	32	2.51
1973—Oakland..................	American		62	127	7	8	.467	107	41	27	110	39	1.91
1974—Oakland..................	American		★76	119	9	5	.643	104	41	35	95	29	2.65
1975—Oakland..................	American		★75	127	10	6	.625	95	43	42	115	33	2.98
1976—Oakland§................	American		70	135	13	11	.542	118	40	37	113	40	2.47
1977—San Diego	National		★78	132	8	9	.471	123	47	44	113	36	3.00
1978—San Diego	National		67	107	6	13	.316	84	33	30	72	29	2.52
1979—San Diego	National		54	84	9	9	.500	91	47	42	65	37	4.50
1980—San Diego xy	National		66	103	11	9	.550	101	35	32	69	32	2.80
1981—Milwaukee...............	American		47	78	6	3	.667	55	9	9	61	13	1.04
1982—Milwaukee...............	American		50	79⅔	5	6	.455	63	23	23	71	20	2.60
1983—Milwaukee z	American		(Did not play)										
National League Totals..........................			265	426	34	40	.459	399	162	148	319	134	3.13
American League Totals			599	1173⅔	78	70	.527	978	407	360	916	326	2.76
Major League Totals..............................			864	1599⅔	112	110	.505	1377	569	508	1235	460	2.86

Signed as free agent by Kansas City A's organization, December 24, 1964.
†On disabled list, April 18 to June 1, 1967.
‡On military list, December 29, 1967 through May 12, 1968.
§Played out option year and granted free agency, November 1, 1976; signed as free agent with San Diego Padres, December 14, 1976.

xTraded with Pitcher Bob Shirley, Catcher-First Baseman Gene Tenace and a player to be named later to St. Louis Cardinals for Catchers Terry Kennedy and Steve Swisher, Pitchers John Littlefield, Al Olmsted, Kim Seaman and John Urrea and Infielder Mike Phillips, December 8, 1980; St. Louis organization acquired Catcher Bob Geren to complete deal, December 10, 1980.

yTraded with Catcher Ted Simmons and Pitcher Pete Vuckovich to Milwaukee Brewers for Outfielders Sixto Lezcano and David Green and Pitchers Lary Sorensen and Dave LaPoint, December 12, 1980.

zOn disabled list, March 26, 1983; transferred to emergency disabled list, July 13, 1983 through remainder of season.

DIVISION SERIES RECORD

Year	Club	League	G.	IP.	W.	L.	Pct.	H.	R.	ER.	SO.	BB.	ERA.
1981—Milwaukee	American	3	4⅔	1	0	1.000	7	3	2	5	1	3.86

CHAMPIONSHIP SERIES RECORD

Established American League Championship Series record for most games pitched, total Series (11).
Tied American League Championship Series record for most saves, total Series (2).

Year	Club	League	G.	IP.	W.	L.	Pct.	H.	R.	ER.	SO.	BB.	ERA.
1971—Oakland	American	2	2⅓	0	0	.000	2	2	2	2	1	7.71
1972—Oakland	American	3	5⅓	1	0	1.000	4	1	1	3	1	1.69
1973—Oakland	American	3	4⅔	0	1	.000	4	1	1	4	2	1.93
1974—Oakland	American	2	3	0	0	.000	3	1	1	3	1	3.00
1975—Oakland	American	1	4	0	1	.000	5	3	3	3	1	6.75
Championship Series Totals			11	19⅓	1	2	.333	18	8	8	15	6	3.72

WORLD SERIES RECORD

Established World Series record for most saves, total Series (6); most games as relief pitcher, total Series (16).
Tied World Series record for most saves, five-game Series (2), 1974.

Year	Club	League	G.	IP.	W.	L.	Pct.	H.	R.	ER.	SO.	BB.	ERA.
1972—Oakland	American	6	10⅓	1	1	.500	4	2	2	11	4	1.74
1973—Oakland	American	6	13⅔	0	1	.000	13	5	1	8	4	0.66
1974—Oakland	American	4	9⅓	1	0	1.000	8	2	2	6	2	1.93
World Series Totals			16	33⅓	2	2	.500	25	9	5	25	10	1.35

ALL-STAR GAME RECORD

Year	League	IP.	W.	L.	Pct.	H.	R.	ER.	SO.	BB.	ERA.
1973—American		1	0	0	.000	0	0	0	0	0	0.00
1974—American		1	0	0	.000	1	2	2	0	1	18.00
1978—National		2	0	0	.000	1	0	0	1	0	0.00
1981—American		⅓	0	1	.000	2	2	2	0	2	54.00
1982—American		1	0	0	.000	2	0	0	0	0	0.00
All-Star Game Totals		5⅓	0	1	.000	6	4	4	1	3	6.75

Member of American League All-Star Team in 1975 and 1976; did not play.

STEPHEN JOHN FIREOVID

Name pronounced FYR-oh-vid.

(Steve)

Born June 6, 1957, at Bryan, O.
Height, 6.02. Weight, 195.
Throws right and bats left and righthanded.
Attended Miami University, Oxford, O.

Year	Club	League	G.	IP.	W.	L.	Pct.	H.	R.	ER.	SO.	BB.	ERA.
1978—Walla Walla	Northwest	14	106	9	2	.818	82	45	29	99	52	2.46
1979—Reno	California	26	168	13	9	.591	182	92	76	135	65	4.07
1980—Amarillo	Texas	27	164	12	6	.667	196	100	86	106	52	4.72
1981—Hawaii	P. Coast	25	162	11	7	.611	173	77	57	57	55	3.17
1981—San Diego	National	5	26	0	1	.000	30	8	8	11	7	2.77
1982—Hawaii	P. Coast	25	135⅔	10	8	.556	171	87	81	56	39	5.37
1983—Las Vegas	P. Coast	28	184⅔	14	10	.583	*212	124	98	80	63	4.78
1983—San Diego†	National	3	5	0	0	.000	4	2	1	1	2	1.80
Major League Totals		8	31	0	1	.000	34	10	9	12	9	2.61

Selected by San Diego Padres' organization in 7th round of free-agent draft, June 6, 1978.

†Traded to Philadelphia Phillies' organization, October 11, 1983, completing deal in which San Diego Padres traded Outfielder Sixto Lezcano and a player to be named later to Philadelphia for four players to be named later, August 31, 1983; San Diego acquired Pitchers Marty Decker, Ed Wojna, Darren Burroughs and Lance McCullers as partial completion of deal, September 20, 1983.

MICHAEL THOMAS FISCHLIN

(Mike)

Born September 13, 1955, at Sacramento, Calif.
Height, 6.01. Weight, 165.
Throws and bats righthanded.
Attended Cosumnes River Junior College, Sacramento, Calif.,
and Sacramento State University, Sacramento, Calif.

Tied National League record for fewest chances offered by shortstop, two consecutive games (1), June 18 and 20, 1978.

Led International League in sacrifice hits with 15 in 1981.
Led Pacific Coast league shortstops in putouts with 200 and double plays with 88 in 1980.

Year	Club	League	Pos.	G.	AB.	R.	H.	2B.	3B.	HR.	RBI.	B.A.	PO.	A.	E.	F.A.
1975—Oneonta	NYP		SS	35	135	22	31	4	3	0	6	.230	34	128	15	.915
1975—Ft. Lauderdale	Fla. St.		SS	29	104	7	19	4	0	0	7	.183	54	90	10	.935
1976—West Haven	East.		SS-3B-2B	91	248	16	38	7	1	2	20	.153	149	243	27	.936
1976—Oneonta	NYP		SS	14	55	13	14	3	0	0	5	.255	36	48	7	.923
1977—Ft. Lauderdale†	Fla. St.		SS-2B	53	201	28	59	6	4	0	20	.294	84	188	16	.944
1977—Columbus	South.		SS	66	223	23	54	5	0	1	16	.242	104	204	16	.951
1977—Houston	Nat.		SS	13	15	0	3	0	0	0	0	.200	3	17	0	1.000
1978—Charleston†	Int.		SS	82	280	38	59	10	2	0	19	.211	141	279	13	.970
1978—Houston	Nat.		SS	44	86	3	10	1	0	0	0	.116	49	67	9	.928
1979—Charleston‡	Int.		SS	44	138	13	31	4	1	0	8	.225	73	134	8	.963
1980—Tucson	P. C.		★SS-OF	131	417	65	117	24	7	3	49	.281	201	★437	★40	★.941
1980—Houston§	Nat.		SS	1	0	0	0	0	0	0	0	.000	0	0	0	.000
1981—Charleston	Int.		SS-2B	136	463	83	110	14	7	5	43	.238	224	433	31	.955
1981—Cleveland	Amer.		SS-2B	22	43	3	10	1	0	0	5	.233	33	39	4	.947
1982—Cleveland	Amer.		S-3-2-C	112	276	34	74	12	1	0	21	.268	142	257	13	.968
1983—Cleveland	Amer.		2B-SS-3B	95	225	31	47	5	2	2	23	.209	169	226	14	.966
National League Totals				58	102	3	13	1	0	0	0	.127	52	84	9	.938
American League Totals				229	544	68	131	18	3	2	49	.241	344	522	31	.965
Major League Totals				287	646	71	144	19	3	2	49	.223	396	606	40	.962

Selected by New York Yankees' organization in 7th round of free-agent draft, June 4, 1975.

†Traded with Pitcher Randy Niemann and a player to be named later to Houston Astros' organization for Catcher-First Baseman Cliff Johnson, June 15, 1977; Houston acquired First Baseman-Outfielder Dave Bergman to complete deal, November 23, 1977.

‡On disabled list, June 18 to August 28, 1979.

§Traded to Cleveland Indians' organization for cash and a player to be named later, April 3, 1981; Houston Astros' organization acquired Outfielder Jim Lentine to complete deal, September 28, 1981.

BRIAN KEVIN FISHER

Born March 18, 1962, at Honolulu, Hawaii.
Height, 6.04. Weight, 210.
Throws and bats righthanded.
Attended Columbia College, Aurora, Col.

Tied for South Atlantic League lead in balks with 4 in 1981.

Year	Club	League	G.	IP.	W.	L.	Pct.	H.	R.	ER.	SO.	BB.	ERA.
1980—Bradenton Braves	Gulf Coast		12	61	5	3	.625	55	34	26	48	★53	3.84
1981—Anderson	S. Atlantic		25	152	6	8	.429	139	96	72	152	94	4.26
1982—Durham†	Carolina		18	104	6	6	.500	72	43	32	129	43	2.77
1983—Savannah	Southern		27	150	8	11	.421	172	101	87	103	56	5.22

Selected by Atlanta Braves' organization in 2nd round of free-agent draft, June 3, 1980.

†On disabled list, May 18 to July 1, 1982.

CARLTON ERNEST FISK

Born December 26, 1947, at Bellows Falls, Vt.
Height, 6.02. Weight, 220.
Throws and bats righthanded.
Attended University of New Hampshire, Durham, N. H.
Brother of Calvin Fisk, former catcher in Baltimore Orioles' organization,
brother-in-law of Rick Miller, outfielder with Boston Red Sox; cousin of
Dave Jennings, punter with New York Giants.

Tied major league record for most home runs, opening game of season (2), April 6, 1973.
Tied modern major league record for most long hits, inning (2), May 15, 1975 (eighth inning) and June 30, 1977 (eighth inning).
Tied American League record for fewest passed balls, season, 150 or more games (4), 1977.
Led American League in being hit by pitch with 13 in 1980.
Led American League catchers in passed balls with 11 in 1983.
Led American League catches in putouts with 470 and double plays with 10 in 1981.
Led American League catchers in errors with 10 in 1980.
Led American League catchers in total chances with 933 in 1972, 803 in 1973 and 519 in 1981.
Led International League catchers in double plays with 12 in 1971.
Named THE SPORTING NEWS American League Rookie Player of the Year, 1972.
Named American League Rookie of the Year by Baseball Writers' Association of America, 1972.
Named catcher on THE SPORTING NEWS American League All-Star Team, 1972, 1977 and 1983.
Named catcher on THE SPORTING NEWS American League All-Star fielding team, 1972.
Named catcher on THE SPORTING NEWS American League Silver Slugger team, 1981.

Year	Club	League	Pos.	G.	AB.	R.	H.	2B.	3B.	HR.	RBI.	B.A.	PO.	A.	E.	F.A.
1967—Greenville†	W. Car.					(In Military Service)										
1968—Waterloo‡	Midw.		C	62	195	31	66	11	2	12	34	.338	385	42	8	.982
1969—Pittsfield	East.		C	97	309	38	75	18	3	10	41	.243	551	65	★22	.966
1969—Boston	Amer.		C	2	5	0	0	0	0	0	0	.000	2	0	0	1.000
1970—Pawtucket	East.		C-O-1	93	284	43	65	18	1	12	44	.229	482	50	7	.987
1971—Louisville	Int.		C-O-3	94	308	45	81	10	4	10	43	.263	588	51	13	.980
1971—Boston	Amer.		C	14	48	7	15	2	1	2	6	.313	72	6	2	.975
1972—Boston	Amer.		C	131	457	74	134	28	●9	22	61	.293	★846	★72	●15	.984
1973—Boston	Amer.		C	135	508	65	125	21	0	26	71	.246	★739	50	★14	.983
1974—Boston§x	Amer.		C	52	187	36	56	12	1	11	26	.299	267	26	6	.980
1975—Boston y	Amer.		C	79	263	47	87	14	4	10	52	.331	347	30	8	.979

Year Club	League	Pos.	G.	AB.	R.	H.	2B.	3B.	HR.	RBI.	B.A.	PO.	A.	E.	F.A.
1976—Boston	Amer.	C	134	487	76	124	17	5	17	58	.255	649	73	12	.984
1977—Boston	Amer.	C	152	536	106	169	26	3	26	102	.315	779	69	11	.987
1978—Boston....................	Amer.	*C-OF	157	571	94	162	39	5	20	88	.284	734	90	*17	.980
1979—Boston z	Amer.	C-OF	91	320	49	87	23	2	10	42	.272	155	8	3	.982
1980—Boston a	Amer.	C-1-O-3	131	478	73	138	25	3	18	62	.289	543	56	11	.982
1981—Chicago	Amer.	C-1-3-O	96	338	44	89	12	0	7	46	.263	479	46	6	.989
1982—Chicago	Amer.	C-1B	135	476	66	127	17	3	14	65	.267	648	63	5	.993
1983—Chicago	Amer.	C	138	488	85	141	26	4	26	86	.289	*709	46	7	.991
Major League Totals....................			1447	5162	822	1454	262	40	209	765	.282	6969	635	117	.985

Selected by Baltimore Orioles' organization in 36th round of free-agent draft, June, 1965.
Selected by Boston Red Sox' organization in 1st round (fourth player selected) of free-agent draft, January, 1967.
†On temporary inactive list, April 17, 1967; transferred to military list, May 18, 1967 through April 9, 1968.
‡On temporary inactive list, August 5 to August 20, 1968.
§On disabled list, March 21 to April 26, 1974.
xOn emergency disabled list, June 28, 1974 through remainder of season.
yOn disabled list, March 24 to June 23, 1975.
zOn supplemental disabled list, April 14 to May 21, 1979.
aGranted free agency by arbitrator's ruling, February 12, 1981; signed by Chicago White Sox, March 18, 1981.

CHAMPIONSHIP SERIES RECORD

Year Club	League	Pos.	G.	AB.	R.	H.	2B.	3B.	HR.	RBI.	B.A.	PO.	A.	E.	F.A.
1975—Boston	Amer.	C	3	12	4	5	1	0	0	2	.417	15	0	0	1.000
1983—Chicago	Amer.	C	4	17	0	3	1	0	0	0	.176	27	3	0	1.000
Championship Series Totals			7	29	4	8	2	0	0	2	.276	42	3	0	1.000

WORLD SERIES RECORD

Tied World Series records for most at bats inning and most times faced pitcher inning (2), October 15, 1975 (fourth inning); most errors by catcher, game (2), October 14, 1975.

Year Club	League	Pos.	G.	AB.	R.	H.	2B.	3B.	HR.	RBI.	B.A.	PO.	A.	E.	F.A.
1975—Boston	Amer.	C	7	25	5	6	0	0	2	4	.240	37	3	2	.952

ALL-STAR GAME RECORD

Year League	Pos.	AB.	R.	H.	2B.	3B.	HR.	RBI.	B.A.	PO.	A.	E.	F.A.
1972—American................................	C	2	1	1	0	0	0	0	.500	2	0	0	1.000
1973—American................................	C	2	0	0	0	0	0	0	.000	3	0	0	1.000
1976—American................................	C	1	0	0	0	0	0	0	.000	1	0	0	1.000
1977—American................................	C	2	0	0	0	0	0	0	.000	6	1	0	1.000
1978—American	C	2	0	0	0	0	0	1	.000	4	0	0	1.000
1980—American	C	2	0	0	0	0	0	0	.000	5	0	0	1.000
1981—American	C	3	1	1	0	0	0	0	.333	4	0	0	1.000
1982—American	C	2	0	0	0	0	0	0	.000	2	0	0	1.000
All-Star Game Totals		16	2	2	0	0	0	1	.125	27	1	0	1.000

Named to American League All-Star Team for 1974 game; replaced due to injury.

MICHAEL ROY FITZGERALD
(Mike)

Born July 13, 1960, at Long Beach, Calif.
Height, 6.00. Weight, 185.
Throws and bats righthanded.
Nephew of Dan Gausepohl, outfielder in San Diego
Padres' organization, 1979 through 1982.

Tied major league record by hitting home run in first major league at-bat, September 13, 1983.
Led Carolina League in sacrifice flies with 11 in 1979.

Year Club	League	Pos.	G.	AB.	R.	H.	2B.	3B.	HR.	RBI.	B.A.	PO.	A.	E.	F.A.
1978—Little Falls............	NYP.	C	48	140	25	36	10	0	5	21	.257	230	37	1	.996
1979—Lynchburg............	Carol.	C	117	368	55	93	16	4	13	*75	.253	424	60	10	.980
1980—Alex.†-Lynch........	Carol.	C-1B-OF	105	338	36	71	10	2	10	44	.210	438	45	7	.986
1981—Jackson	Texas	C-1-O-3	66	218	28	68	14	2	4	29	.312	344	52	3	.992
1981—Tidewater.............	Int.	C-OF	24	58	9	9	2	0	1	3	.155	124	9	2	.985
1982—Tidewater.............	Int.	C-1-O-3	94	302	33	74	9	2	4	36	.245	451	34	7	986
1983—Tidewater.............	Int.	C-1-3-O	111	370	64	105	17	1	14	65	.284	588	62	8	.988
1983—New York	Nat.	C	8	20	1	2	0	0	1	2	.100	37	8	2	.957
Major League Totals....................			8	20	1	2	0	0	1	2	.100	37	8	2	.957

Selected by New York Mets' organization in 6th round of free-agent draft, June 6, 1978.
†Loaned to Alexandria (Co-op), April 8, 1980; returned, May 31, 1980.

MICHAEL KENDALL FLANAGAN
(Mike)

Born December 16, 1951, at Manchester, N. H.
Height, 6.00. Weight, 195.
Throws and bats lefthanded.
Attended University of Massachusetts, Amherst, Mass.
Son of Ed Flanagan, Jr., minor league pitcher, 1947 through 1952.

Tied for American League lead in shutouts with 5 in 1979.

Tied for American League lead in games started by pitchers with 40 in 1978.
Tied for International League lead in shutouts with 4 in 1975.
Tied for Southern League lead in shutouts with 3 in 1974.
Named American League Pitcher of the Year by THE SPORTING NEWS, 1979.
Won American League Cy Young Memorial Award, 1979.
Named lefthanded pitcher on THE SPORTING NEWS American League All-Star Team, 1979.

Year Club	League	G.	IP.	W.	L.	Pct.	H.	R.	ER.	SO.	BB.	ERA.
1973—Miami	Florida St.	11	61	4	1	.800	39	21	15	61	25	2.21
1974—Miami	Florida St.	14	103	6	6	.500	67	32	24	119	48	2.10
1974—Asheville	Southern	11	84	6	4	.600	61	19	17	62	18	1.82
1975—Rochester	Int'national	27	173	13	4	*.765	155	58	48	135	56	2.50
1975—Baltimore	American	2	10	0	1	.000	9	4	3	7	6	2.70
1976—Baltimore	American	20	85	3	5	.375	83	41	39	56	33	4.13
1976—Rochester	Int'national	7	51	6	1	.857	40	16	12	24	14	2.12
1977—Baltimore	American	36	235	15	10	.600	235	100	95	149	70	3.64
1978—Baltimore	American	40	281	19	15	.559	271	128	*126	167	87	4.04
1979—Baltimore	American	39	266	*23	9	.719	245	107	91	190	70	3.08
1980—Baltimore	American	37	251	16	13	.552	*278	121	115	128	71	4.12
1981—Baltimore	American	20	116	9	6	.600	108	55	54	72	37	4.19
1982—Baltimore	American	36	236	15	11	.577	233	110	104	103	76	3.97
1983—Baltimore†	American	20	125⅓	12	4	.750	135	53	46	50	31	3.30
Major League Totals		250	1605⅓	112	74	.602	1597	719	673	922	481	3.77

Selected by Houston Astros' organization in 15th round of free-agent draft, June 8, 1971.
Selected by Baltimore Orioles' organization in 7th round of free-agent draft, June 5, 1973.
†On disabled list, May 18, 1983; transferred to emergency disabled list, July 9 to August 7, 1983.

CHAMPIONSHIP SERIES RECORD

Year Club	League	G.	IP.	W.	L.	Pct.	H.	R.	ER.	SO.	BB.	ERA.
1979—Baltimore	American	1	7	1	0	1.000	6	6	4	2	1	5.14
1983—Baltimore	American	1	5	1	0	1.000	5	1	1	1	0	1.80
Championship Series Total		2	12	2	0	1.000	11	7	5	3	1	3.75

WORLD SERIES RECORD

Year Club	League	G.	IP.	W.	L.	Pct.	H.	R.	ER.	SO.	BB.	ERA.
1979—Baltimore	American	3	15	1	1	.500	18	7	5	13	2	3.00
1983—Baltimore	American	1	4	0	0	.000	6	2	2	1	1	4.50
World Series Totals		4	19	1	1	.500	24	9	7	14	3	3.32

ALL-STAR GAME RECORD
Named to American League All-Star Team for 1978 game; did not play.

KEVIN THOMAS FLANNERY

Born November 30, 1957, at Detroit, Mich.
Height, 6.03. Weight, 195.
Throws right and bats lefthanded.
Attended Central Michigan University, Mt. Pleasant, Mich.

Year Club	League	G.	IP.	W.	L.	Pct.	H.	R.	ER.	SO.	BB.	ERA.
1979—Billings	Pioneer	5	16	0	0	.000	17	11	9	13	3	5.06
1979—Eugene†	Northwest	1	6	0	1	.000	5	5	4	2	1	6.00
1980—Sarasota White Sox	Gulf Coast	8	12	1	1	.500	10	5	5	13	5	3.75
1980—Glens Falls	Eastern	8	16	0	0	.000	27	15	9	7	6	5.06
1981—Appleton	Midwest	38	89	5	6	.455	30	35	28	74	28	2.83
1982—Appleton	Midwest	16	19	2	0	.000	20	3	3	17	3	1.42
1982—Glens Falls‡	Eastern	26	72⅔	5	2	.714	68	27	26	36	16	3.22
1983—Toledo	Int'national	30	97⅔	6	4	.600	117	66	58	57	49	5.34

Selected by Cincinnati Reds' organization in 19th round of free-agent draft, June 5, 1979.
†Released, April 7, 1980; signed by Sarasota White Sox (Chicago White Sox' organization), June 17, 1980.
‡Traded to Minnesota Twins' organization, October 22, 1982, as replacement for Third Baseman Ron Perry in trade of Pitcher Jerry Koosman from Minnesota to Chicago White Sox for Perry, Shortstop Ivan Mesa, a player to be named later and cash, August 30, 1981. Minnesota organization acquired Outfielder Randy Johnson to complete deal, September 2, 1981.

TIMOTHY EARL FLANNERY
(Tim)

Born September 29, 1957, at Tulsa, Okla.
Height, 5.11. Weight, 170.
Throws right and bats lefthanded.
Attended Chapman College, Orange, Calif.
Nephew of Hal Smith, catcher with St. Louis Cardinals and Pittsburgh Pirates,
1956 through 1961 and 1965; minor league manager, 1966; coach, Pittsburgh Pirates, 1967;
coach, Cincinnati Reds, 1968 and 1969; and scout with
St. Louis Cardinals, 1970 through 1975 and 1978 through 1983.

Year Club	League	Pos.	G.	AB.	R.	H.	2B.	3B.	HR.	RBI.	B.A.	PO.	A.	E.	F.A.
1978—Reno	Calif.	2B-P	84	340	65	119	11	5	2	49	.350	213	269	19	.962
1979—Amarillo	Texas	2B-SS	125	524	88	●181	23	6	6	71	.345	287	374	28	.959
1979—San Diego	Nat.	2B	22	65	2	10	0	1	0	4	.154	45	60	1	.991
1980—Hawaii	P. C.	2B	47	182	27	63	10	3	1	16	.346	102	146	5	.980

Year Club	League	Pos.	G.	AB.	R.	H.	2B.	3B.	HR.	RBI.	B.A.	PO.	A.	E.	F.A.
1980—San Diego	Nat.	2B-3B	95	292	15	70	12	0	0	25	.240	140	204	8	.977
1981—Hawaii	P. C.	2B	21	78	16	22	3	1	0	10	.282	47	62	2	.982
1981—San Diego	Nat.	3B-2B	37	67	4	17	4	1	0	6	.254	16	32	2	.960
1982—San Diego	Nat.	2B-3B-SS	122	379	40	100	11	7	0	30	.264	226	278	14	.973
1983—San Diego	Nat.	3B-2B-SS	92	214	24	50	7	3	3	19	.234	63	156	4	.982
Major League Totals			368	1017	85	247	34	12	3	84	.243	490	730	29	.977

Selected by San Diego Padres' organization in 6th round of free-agent draft, June 6, 1978.

PITCHING RECORD

Year Club	League	G.	IP.	W.	L.	Pct.	H.	R.	ER.	SO.	BB.	ERA.
1978—Reno	California	1	1/3	0	1	.000	3	6	5	0	1	135.00

SCOTT BRIAN FLETCHER

Born July 30, 1958, at Fort Walton Beach, Fla.
Height, 5.11. Weight, 170.
Throws and bats righthanded.
Attended University of Toledo, Toledo, Ohio; Valencia Community College,
Orlando, Fla., and Georgia Southern College, Statesboro, Ga.
Son of Richard W. Fletcher, minor league pitcher, 1952 through 1959.

Led American Association in being hit by pitch with 9 and grounding into double plays with 20 in 1981.
Led American Association shortstops in total chances with 607 in 1982.
Led Texas League second basemen in double plays with 112 in 1980.

Year Club	League	Pos.	G.	AB.	R.	H.	2B.	3B.	HR.	RBI.	B.A.	PO.	A.	E.	F.A.
1979—Geneva	NYP	SS	67	261	59	81	12	3	4	43	.310	99	195	18	★.942
1980—Midland	Texas	★2B-SS	130	501	★111	164	16	★11	6	65	.327	★354	★390	★29	.962
1981—Iowa	A. A.	SS	119	458	66	117	26	4	4	33	.255	★222	337	28	.952
1981—Chicago	Nat.	2B-SS-3B	19	46	6	10	4	0	0	1	.217	34	44	3	.963
1982—Iowa	A. A.	SS	129	502	90	157	26	3	4	60	.313	224	●357	26	.957
1982—Chicago†	Nat.	SS	11	24	4	4	0	0	0	1	.167	11	23	0	1.000
1983—Chicago	Amer.	SS-2B-3B	114	262	42	62	16	5	3	31	.237	126	308	16	.964
National League Totals			30	70	10	14	4	0	0	2	.200	45	67	3	.974
American League Totals			114	262	42	62	16	5	3	31	.237	126	308	16	.964
Major League Totals			144	332	52	76	20	5	3	33	.229	171	375	19	.966

Selected by Los Angeles Dodgers' organization in 33rd round of free-agent draft, June 8, 1976.
Selected by Oakland A's organization in secondary phase of free-agent draft, January 10, 1978.
Selected by Houston Astros' organization in secondary phase of free-agent draft, June 6, 1978.
Selected by Chicago Cubs' organization in secondary phase of free-agent draft, June 5, 1979.

†Traded with Pitchers Dick Tidrow and Randy Martz and Infielder Pat Tabler to Chicago White Sox for Pitchers Steve Trout and Warren Brusstar, January 25, 1983.

CHAMPIONSHIP SERIES RECORD

Year Club	League	Pos.	G.	AB.	R.	H.	2B.	3B.	HR.	RBI.	B.A.	PO.	A.	E.	F.A.
1983—Chicago	Amer.	SS	3	7	0	0	0	0	0	0	.000	3	8	0	1.000

JOHN RICHARD FLINN

Born September 2, 1954, at Merced, Calif.
Height, 6.01. Weight, 180.
Throws and bats righthanded.
Attended Los Angeles Valley Junior College, Van Nuys, Calif.

Led International League in hit batsmen with 11 in 1977.
Led Florida State League in shutouts with 6 and hit batsmen with 14 in 1974.

Year Club	League	G.	IP.	W.	L.	Pct.	H.	R.	ER.	SO.	BB.	ERA.
1973—Bluefield	Ap'lachian	23	42	4	2	.667	29	15	10	51	22	2.14
1974—Miami	Florida St.	33	181	12	10	.545	137	46	35	151	63	1.74
1974—Asheville	Southern	4	4	2	1	.667	8	4	4	2	3	9.00
1975—Asheville	Southern	20	85	0	9	.000	99	58	50	53	37	5.29
1975—Miami	Florida St.	4	13	1	2	.333	15	8	8	14	9	5.54
1976—Charlotte	Southern	24	148	9	8	.529	151	62	47	76	28	2.86
1977—Rochester	Int'national	48	119	10	7	.588	110	63	47	80	54	3.55
1978—Rochester†	Int'national	24	38	1	0	1.000	42	25	22	36	14	5.21
1978—Baltimore	American	13	16	1	1	.500	24	18	14	8	13	7.88
1979—Rochester	Int'national	26	100	6	6	.500	92	36	30	71	22	2.70
1979—Baltimore‡	American	4	3	0	0	.000	2	0	0	0	1	0.00
1980—Vancouver	P. Coast	17	43	2	3	.400	24	24	21	28	15	4.40
1980—Milwaukee	American	20	37	2	1	.667	31	20	16	15	20	3.89
1981—Vancouver§	P. Coast	31	85	7	6	.538	82	44	38	55	27	4.02
1982—Rochester x	Int'national	39	87⅓	9	3	★.750	92	45	35	59	34	3.61
1982—Baltimore	American	5	13⅔	2	0	1.000	13	3	2	13	3	1.32
1983—Rochester	Int'national	49	88⅓	5	7	.417	93	55	48	60	45	4.89
Major League Totals		42	69⅔	5	2	.714	70	41	32	36	37	4.13

Selected by Baltimore Orioles' organization in 28th round of free-agent draft, June 6, 1972.
Selected by Baltimore Orioles' organization in secondary phase of free-agent draft, January 10, 1973.
†On disabled list, August 3 to September 1, 1978.
‡Traded to Milwaukee Brewers for Second Baseman Lenn Sakata, December 6, 1979.
§Released, February 26, 1982; signed by Rochester (Baltimore Orioles' organization), March 4, 1982.
xOn disabled list, April 8 to April 27, 1982.

ROBERT DOUGLAS FLYNN JR.
(Doug)

Born April 18, 1951, at Lexington, Ky.
Height, 5.11. Weight, 160.
Throws and bats righthanded.
Attended University of Kentucky, Lexington, Ky., and Somerset
Community College, Somerset, Ky.
Son of Robert Douglas Flynn, Sr., player in Brooklyn Dodgers' organization, 1949.

Tied modern major league record for most three-base hits, game (3), August 5, 1980.
Led National League second basemen in putouts with 369, total chances with 762 and double plays with 98 in 1979.
Led American Association shortstops in double plays with 91 in 1974.
Led Eastern League shortstops in double plays with 97 in 1973.
Tied for Eastern League lead in sacrifice flies with 9 in 1973.
Named second baseman on THE SPORTING NEWS National League All-Star fielding team, 1980.

Year—Club	League	Pos.	G.	AB.	R.	H.	2B.	3B.	HR.	RBI.	B.A.	PO.	A.	E.	F.A.
1972—Tampa	Fla. St.	3-S-2-P	98	313	32	66	12	2	1	37	.211	109	240	18	.951
1973—Three Rivers	East.	SS	*139	*500	52	129	11	0	3	42	.258	*231	*453	34	.953
1974—Indianapolis	A. A.	SS	134	458	57	116	13	6	2	34	.253	213	*392	33	.948
1975—Cincinnati	Nat.	3B-2B-SS	89	127	17	34	7	0	1	20	.268	57	118	2	.989
1976—Cincinnati	Nat.	2B-3B-SS	93	219	20	62	5	2	1	20	.283	107	152	4	.985
1977—Cinc.†-N.Y.	Nat.	SS-2B-3B	126	314	14	62	7	2	0	19	.197	171	235	14	.967
1978—New York	Nat.	2B-SS	156	532	37	126	12	8	0	36	.237	332	426	15	.981
1979—New York	Nat.	2B-SS	157	555	35	135	19	5	4	61	.243	402	421	16	.981
1980—New York‡	Nat.	*2B-SS	128	443	46	113	9	8	0	24	.255	284	374	6	*.991
1981—New York§	Nat.	2B-SS	105	325	24	72	12	4	1	20	.222	229	319	7	.987
1982—Texas x	Amer.	2B-SS	88	270	13	57	6	2	0	19	.211	161	254	9	.979
1982—Montreal	Nat.	2B	58	193	13	47	6	2	0	20	.244	135	157	5	.983
1983—Montreal	Nat.	2B-SS	143	452	44	107	18	4	0	26	.237	249	375	11	.983
National League Totals			1055	3160	250	758	95	35	7	246	.240	1966	2577	80	.983
American League Totals			88	270	13	57	6	2	0	19	.211	161	254	9	.979
Major League Totals			1143	3430	263	815	101	37	7	265	.238	2127	2831	89	.982

Signed as free agent by Cincinnati Reds' organization, August 25, 1971.
†Traded with Outfielders Dan Norman and Steve Henderson and Pitcher Pat Zachry to New York Mets for Pitcher Tom Seaver, June 15, 1977.
‡On supplemental disabled list, August 20 to September 6, 1980.
§Traded with Pitcher Dan Boitano to Texas Rangers for Pitcher Jim Kern, December 11, 1981.
xSold to Montreal Expos for an estimated $40,000, August 2, 1982.

CHAMPIONSHIP SERIES RECORD

Year—Club	League	Pos.	G.	AB.	R.	H.	2B.	3B.	HR.	RBI.	B.A.	PO.	A.	E.	F.A.
1976—Cincinnati	Nat.	2B	1	0	0	0	0	0	0	0	.000	0	0	0	.000

PITCHING RECORD

Year—Club	League	G.	IP.	W.	L.	Pct.	H.	R.	ER.	SO.	BB.	ERA.
1972—Tampa	Florida St.	1	3	0	0	.000	3	1	1	3	1	3.00

MARVIS EDWIN FOLEY
(Marv)

Born August 29, 1953, at Stanford, Ky.
Height, 6.00. Weight, 195.
Throws right and bats lefthanded.
Received bachelor of general studies degree from University of Kentucky, Lexington, Ky.

Led Southern League catchers in double plays with 12 in 1978.

Year—Club	League	Pos.	G.	AB.	R.	H.	2B.	3B.	HR.	RBI.	B.A.	PO.	A.	E.	F.A.
1975—Appleton	Midw.	1B-OF	6	13	1	4	0	0	0	1	.308	16	1	0	1.000
1975—Knoxville	South.	C-1B	51	150	22	44	9	0	1	27	.293	74	6	4	.952
1976—Knoxville	South.	1B-C-3B	126	414	44	104	12	2	2	36	.251	755	86	13	.985
1977—Appleton	Midw.	1B-C-3B	48	162	24	44	6	2	3	21	.272	404	48	6	.987
1977—Iowa	A. A.	1B-C-3B	10	27	1	5	3	0	1	4	.185	66	5	2	.973
1977—Knoxville	South.	1B-C	66	226	33	68	13	3	6	42	.301	410	39	2	.996
1978—Knoxville†	South.	C-1B	103	338	52	93	20	5	1	44	.275	584	69	7	.989
1978—Chicago	Amer.	C	11	34	3	12	0	0	0	6	.353	41	4	3	.938
1979—Iowa	A. A.	C-1B	77	250	32	70	15	1	2	25	.280	387	40	8	.982
1979—Chicago	Amer.	C	34	97	6	24	3	0	2	10	.247	128	11	1	.993
1980—Glens Falls	East.	C	21	68	10	22	5	0	1	9	.324	59	10	1	.986
1980—Iowa	A. A.	C-OF	25	76	20	16	4	0	3	9	.211	112	9	1	.984
1980—Chicago	Amer.	C-1B	68	137	14	29	5	0	4	15	.212	220	17	2	.992
1981—Edmonton	P. C.	C-3B	99	294	48	87	14	2	11	43	.296	401	81	12	.976
1982—Chicago‡	Amer.	C-3B-1B	27	36	1	4	0	0	0	1	.111	47	4	1	.981
1983—Denver§x	A. A.	C-1B	78	257	44	82	11	2	10	43	.319	210	20	0	1.000
Major League Totals			140	304	24	69	8	0	6	32	.227	436	36	7	.985

Selected by Chicago White Sox' organization in 17th round of free-agent draft, June 4, 1975.
†On disabled list, June 4 to June 29, 1978.
‡On supplemental disabled list, August 19 to September 3, 1982.
§On disabled list, July 16 to July 27, 1983.
xGranted free agency, October 20, 1983; signed by Texas Rangers, November 21, 1983.

THOMAS MICHAEL FOLEY
(Tom)

Born September 9, 1959, at Columbus, Ga.
Height, 6.01. Weight, 160.
Throws right and bats lefthanded.
Attended Miami-Dade Community College South, Miami, Fla.

Led Pioneer League in caught stealing with 10 in 1977.
Led Florida State League shortstops in double plays with 71 in 1979.
Led Western Carolinas League shortstops in double plays with 98 in 1978.

Year Club	League	Pos.	G.	AB.	R.	H.	2B.	3B.	HR.	RBI.	B.A.	PO.	A.	E.	F.A.
1977—Billings	Pion.	3B-SS	59	209	37	53	7	1	2	21	.254	53	109	24	.871
1978—Shelby	W. Car.	SS	124	424	55	98	19	1	2	41	.231	★217	●352	30	★.950
1979—Tampa	Fla. St.	SS	125	414	38	95	12	6	0	37	.229	223	★394	35	.946
1980—Waterbury	East.	2B	131	477	49	119	16	4	4	41	.249	★222	329	31	.947
1981—Indianapolis	A. A.	SS	103	347	47	81	12	2	6	27	.233	175	267	27	.942
1982—Indianapolis	A. A.	SS	129	427	65	115	20	9	8	63	.269	★227	343	27	.955
1983—Cincinnati	Nat.	SS-2B	68	98	7	20	4	1	0	9	.204	54	76	2	.985
Major League Totals..................................			68	98	7	20	4	1	0	9	.204	54	76	2	.985

Selected by Cincinnati Reds' organization in 7th round of free-agent draft, June 7, 1977.

TIMOTHY JOHN FOLI
(Tim)

Born December 8, 1950, at Culver City, Calif.
Height, 6.00. Weight, 175.
Throws and bats righthanded.
Brother of Ernie Foli, minor league infielder-outfielder, 1962 through 1968.

Established American League record for fewest bases on balls received, 150 or more games, season (14), 1982.
Hit for the cycle, April 21, 1976.
Led American League in sacrifice hits with 26 in 1982.
Led American League shortstops in fielding percentage with .985 in 1982.
Led National League shortstops in putouts with 260 in 1975.
Led National League shortstops in total chances with 795 in 1972 and 778 in 1975.
Led National League shortstops in double plays with 104 in 1975 and 102 in 1976.
Tied for National League lead in being hit by pitch with 6 in 1980.
Led California League shortstops in double plays with 72 in 1969.
Led Appalachian League shortstops in putouts with 97, fielding percentage with .920 and double plays with 29 in 1968.

Received reported $75,000 bonus to sign with New York Mets, 1968.

Year Club	League	Pos.	G.	AB.	R.	H.	2B.	3B.	HR.	RBI.	B.A.	PO.	A.	E.	F.A.
1968—Marion...................	Appal.	★SS-1B	63	235	38	66	10	3	4	36	.281	105	★167	23	.922
1968—Memphis†	Texas	SS	5	20	4	5	0	0	0	1	.250	8	10	2	.900
1969—Visalia	Calif.	SS	95	383	60	116	10	0	15	62	.303	154	280	36	.923
1970—Tidewater	Int.	SS-2B	103	375	63	98	10	4	6	30	.261	181	289	20	.959
1970—New York.............	Nat.	SS-3B	5	11	0	4	0	0	0	1	.364	4	10	0	1.000
1971—New York‡§	Nat.	2-3-S-O	97	288	32	65	12	2	0	24	.226	150	199	12	.967
1972—Montreal...............	Nat.	★SS-2B	149	540	45	130	12	2	2	35	.241	★281	487	27	.966
1973—Montreal x	Nat.	SS-2B-O	126	458	37	110	11	0	2	36	.240	248	399	27	.960
1974—Montreal y	Nat.	SS-3B	121	441	41	112	10	3	0	39	.254	220	412	19	.971
1975—Montreal...............	Nat.	★SS-2B	152	572	64	136	25	2	1	29	.238	261	★497	21	.973
1976—Montreal...............	Nat.	SS-3B	149	546	41	144	36	1	6	54	.264	249	470	18	.976
1977—Mont. z-S.F. ab	Nat.	S-2-3-O	117	425	32	94	22	4	4	30	.221	217	345	13	.977
1978—New York c...........	Nat.	SS	113	413	37	106	21	1	1	27	.257	190	314	18	.966
1979—N.Y. d-Pitts...........	Nat.	SS	136	532	70	153	23	1	1	65	.288	259	410	15	.978
1980—Pittsburgh e	Nat.	SS	127	495	61	131	22	0	3	38	.265	212	402	12	★.981
1981—Pittsburgh f	Nat.	SS	86	316	32	78	12	2	0	20	.247	140	247	14	.965
1982—California..............	Amer.	SS-2B-3B	150	480	46	121	14	2	3	56	.252	247	462	12	.983
1983—California gh.........	Amer.	SS-3B	88	330	29	83	10	0	2	29	.252	131	298	13	.971
National League Totals............................			1378	5037	492	1263	206	18	20	398	.251	2431	4192	196	.971
American League Totals...........................			238	810	75	204	24	2	5	85	.252	378	760	25	.979
Major League Totals..................................			1616	5847	567	1467	230	20	25	483	.251	2809	4952	221	.972

Selected by New York Mets' organization in 1st round (first player selected) of free-agent draft, June 7, 1968.
†On military list, January 13 to May 24, 1969.
‡On military list, August 16 to September 1, 1971.
§Traded with Outfielder Ken Singleton and First Baseman Mike Jorgensen to Montreal Expos for Outfielder Rusty Staub, April 5, 1972.
xOn supplemental disabled list, July 9 to August 7, 1973.
yOn supplemental disabled list, May 13 to May 29, 1974
zTraded to San Francisco Giants for Shortstop Chris Speier, April 27, 1977.
aOn supplemental disabled list, June 21 to July 21, 1977.
bSold to New York Mets, December 7, 1977.
cOn disabled list, April 26 to May 22, 1978.
dTraded with Pitcher Greg Field to Pittsburgh Pirates for Shortstop Frank Taveras, April 19, 1979.
eOn supplemental disabled list, May 29 to June 13, 1980.
fTraded to California Angels for Catcher Brian Harper, December 11, 1981.
gOn suspended list, September 1 to September 13, 1983.
hTraded to New York Yankees for Pitcher Curt Kaufman and cash, December 8, 1983.

CHAMPIONSHIP SERIES RECORD

Year Club League	Pos.	G.	AB.	R.	H.	2B.	3B.	HR.	RBI.	B.A.	PO.	A.	E.	F.A.
1979—Pittsburgh.............. Nat.	SS	3	12	1	4	1	0	0	3	.333	3	9	0	1.000
1982—California.............. Amer.	SS	5	16	0	2	0	0	0	1	.125	6	7	0	1.000
Championship Series Totals		8	28	1	6	1	0	0	4	.214	9	16	0	1.000

WORLD SERIES RECORD

Established World Series records for fewest strikeouts, most at bats, Series (0 and 30), 1979; most assists by shortstop, seven-game Series (32), 1979.

Tied World Series records for most double plays by shortstop, seven-game Series (7), 1979; most double plays started by shortstop, seven-game Series (4), 1979; most assists by shortstop, inning (3), October 12, 1979 (second inning).

Year Club League	Pos.	G.	AB.	R.	H.	2B.	3B.	HR.	RBI.	B.A.	PO.	A.	E.	F.A.
1979—Pittsburgh.............. Nat.	SS	7	30	6	10	1	1	0	3	.333	8	32	3	.930

SILTON RAY FONTENOT

Name pronounced FON-ten-oh.

(Known by middle name.)

Born August 8, 1957, at Lake Charles, La.
Height, 6.00. Weight, 175.
Throws and bats lefthanded.
Received degree from McNeese State University, Lake Charles, La., in 1979.

Year Club	League	G.	IP.	W.	L.	Pct.	H.	R.	ER.	SO.	BB.	ERA.
1979—Sarasota Rangers†	Gulf Coast	8	31	3	1	.750	28	20	14	42	12	4.06
1980—Greensboro‡§	S. Atlantic	11	49	2	2	.500	41	27	20	50	19	3.67
1981—Greensboro x	S. Atlantic	9	59	4	2	.667	53	22	18	62	23	2.75
1981—Ft. Lauderdale y	Florida St.	8	45	1	4	.200	50	34	28	37	31	5.60
1982—Ft. Lauderdale	Florida St.	12	74	6	5	.545	57	29	24	72	31	2.92
1982—Nashville....................................	Southern	14	91⅓	5	6	.455	85	34	22	69	17	2.17
1983—Columbus....................................	Int'national	26	35	3	2	.600	25	16	11	36	17	2.83
1983—New York....................................	American	15	97⅓	8	2	.800	101	41	36	27	25	3.33
Major League Totals................................		15	97⅓	8	2	.800	101	41	36	27	25	3.33

Selected by Texas Rangers' organization in 34th round of free-agent draft, June 5, 1979.

†Traded with Pitcher Gene Nelson to New York Yankees' organization for Pitchers Bob Polinsky, Neal Mersch and Mark Softy, October 8, 1979; completing deal in which New York traded Outfielder Mickey Rivers and three players to be named later to Texas Rangers for Third Baseman Amos Lewis and two players to be named later, August 1, 1979.

‡On disabled list, April 22 to May 12, 1980.
§On disabled list, July 14, 1980 through remainder of season.
xOn disabled list, April 9 to May 5, 1981.
yOn disabled list, August 27, 1981 through remainder of season.

DARNELL GLENN FORD SR.
(Dan)

Born May 19, 1952, at Los Angeles, Calif.
Height, 6.01. Weight, 185.
Throws and bats righthanded.
Attended Southwestern College, Chula Vista, Calif., and Mesa Community College, Mesa, Ariz.

Hit three home runs in a game, July 20, 1983.
Hit for the cycle, August 10, 1979.
Tied for American League lead in sacrifice flies with 13 in 1979.
Led Midwest League in being hit by pitch with 12 in 1971.
Led Pacific Coast League outfielders in double plays with 7 in 1973.

Year Club	League	Pos.	G.	AB.	R.	H.	2B.	3B.	HR.	RBI.	B.A.	PO.	A.	E.	F.A.
1971—Burlington .... Midw.	OF	107	397	75	106	21	4	14	80	.267	186	11	10	.952
1972—Burlington† .... Midw.	OF	72	246	55	87	15	4	18	61	.354	137	4	8	.946
1973—Tucson‡................. P. C.	OF	128	465	80	136	21	12	14	70	.292	310	●16	11	.967
1974—Tucson§x .... P. C.	OF	115	428	62	117	11	9	12	65	.273	263	11	14	.951
1975—Minnesota.............. Amer.	OF	130	440	72	123	21	1	15	59	.280	246	3	3	.988
1976—Minnesota.............. Amer.	OF	145	514	87	137	24	7	20	86	.267	267	6	9	.968
1977—Minnesota.............. Amer.	OF	144	453	66	121	25	7	11	60	.267	205	9	8	.964
1978—Minnesota y .... Amer.	OF	151	592	78	162	36	10	11	82	.274	376	6	9	.977
1979—California.............. Amer.	OF	142	569	100	165	26	5	21	101	.290	332	10	8	.977
1980—California z........... Amer.	OF	65	226	22	63	11	0	7	26	.279	75	3	5	.940
1981—California a .... Amer.	OF	97	375	53	104	14	1	15	48	.277	188	3	●8	.960
1982—Baltimore .... Amer.	OF	123	421	46	99	21	3	10	43	.235	263	6	7	.975
1983—Baltimore bc......... Amer.	OF	103	407	63	114	30	4	9	55	.280	218	2	3	.987
Major League Totals		1100	3997	587	1088	208	38	119	560	.272	2170	48	60	.974

Selected by Oakland A's organization in 1st round (16th player selected) of free-agent draft, June 4, 1970.

†On temporary inactive list, April 15 to May 20, 1972.
‡On temporary inactive list, April 13 to April 16, 1973.
§On temporary inactive list, July 12 to August 2, 1974.
xTraded with Pitcher Dennis Myers to Minnesota Twins for First Baseman Pat Bourque, October 23, 1974.
yTraded to California Angels for Third Baseman Ron Jackson and Catcher Danny Goodwin, December 4, 1978.
zOn supplemental disabled list, June 3 to August 5, 1980.
aTraded to Baltimore Orioles for Third Baseman Doug DeCinces and Pitcher Jeff Schneider, January 28, 1982.

CHAMPIONSHIP SERIES RECORD

Tied Championship Series record by hitting home run in first Series at-bat, October 3, 1979.

Year	Club	League	Pos.	G.	AB.	R.	H.	2B.	3B.	HR.	RBI.	B.A.	PO.	A.	E.	F.A.
1979—California		Amer.	OF	4	17	2	5	1	0	2	4	.294	6	0	1	.857
1983—Baltimore		Amer.	OF-PH	2	5	0	1	1	0	0	0	.200	1	0	0	1.000
Championship Series Totals				6	22	2	6	2	0	2	4	.273	7	0	1	.875

WORLD SERIES RECORD

Year	Club	League	Pos.	G.	AB.	R.	H.	2B.	3B.	HR.	RBI.	B.A.	PO.	A.	E.	F.A.
1983—Baltimore		Amer.	PH-OF	5	12	1	2	0	0	1	1	.167	5	1	0	1.000

KENNETH ROTH FORSCH
(Ken)

Born September 8, 1946, at Sacramento, Calif.
Height, 6.04. Weight, 205.
Throws and bats righthanded.
Attended Sacramento City College, Sacramento, Calif., and Oregon
State University, Corvallis, Ore.
Brother of Bob Forsch, pitcher with St. Louis Cardinals.

Pitched 6-0 no-hit victory against Atlanta Braves, April 7, 1979.
Major League saves: 1973 (4), 1974 (10), 1975 (2), 1976 (19), 1977 (8), 1978 (7). Total—50.
Led American League in hit batsmen with 11 in 1982.
Tied for American League lead in shutouts with 4 in 1981.
Led Southern League in shutouts with 5 in 1970.

Year	Club	League	G.	IP.	W.	L.	Pct.	H.	R.	ER.	SO.	BB.	ERA.
1968—Greensboro		Carolina	3	6	0	0	.000	6	2	2	6	3	3.00
1968—Williamsport		NYP	4	26	1	2	.333	14	6	4	40	9	1.38
1969—Peninsula†		Carolina	17	94	6	5	.545	67	40	33	100	53	3.16
1970—Columbus		Southern	22	167	●13	8	.619	135	48	38	152	39	2.05
1970—Oklahoma City		Am. Assoc.	5	40	4	0	1.000	25	7	7	37	10	1.58
1970—Houston		National	4	24	1	2	.333	28	15	15	13	5	5.63
1971—Houston		National	33	188	8	8	.500	162	60	53	131	53	2.54
1972—Houston		National	30	156	6	8	.429	163	75	68	113	62	3.92
1973—Houston		National	46	201	9	12	.429	197	101	94	149	74	4.21
1974—Houston		National	70	103	8	7	.533	98	38	32	48	37	2.80
1975—Houston‡		National	34	109	4	8	.333	114	42	39	54	30	3.22
1976—Houston		National	52	92	4	3	.571	76	23	22	49	26	2.15
1977—Houston		National	42	86	5	8	.385	80	32	26	45	28	2.72
1978—Houston		National	52	133	10	6	.625	136	44	40	71	37	2.71
1979—Houston x		National	26	178	11	6	.647	155	67	60	58	35	3.03
1980—Houston x		National	32	222	12	13	.480	230	90	79	84	41	3.20
1981—California		American	20	153	11	7	.611	143	54	50	55	27	2.94
1982—California		American	37	228	13	11	.542	225	108	98	73	57	3.87
1983—California		American	31	219⅓	11	12	.478	226	107	99	81	61	4.60
American League Totals			88	600⅓	35	30	.538	594	269	247	209	145	3.70
National League Totals			421	1492	78	81	.491	1439	587	528	815	428	3.18
Major League Totals			509	2092⅓	113	111	.504	2033	856	775	1024	573	3.33

Selected by California Angels' organization in 13th round of free-agent draft, June, 1966.
Selected by Chicago Cubs' organization in secondary phase of free-agent draft, June 7, 1967.
Selected by Houston Astros' organization in 18th round of free-agent draft, June, 1968.
†On disabled list, June 11 to July 11, 1969.
‡On disabled list, July 31 to September 22, 1975.
§On disabled list, May 23 to June 26, 1979.
xTraded to California Angels for Second Baseman Dickie Thon, April 1, 1981.

CHAMPIONSHIP SERIES RECORD

Year	Club	League	G.	IP.	W.	L.	Pct.	H.	R.	ER.	SO.	BB.	ERA.
1980—Houston		National	2	8⅔	0	1	.000	10	4	4	6	1	4.15

ALL-STAR GAME RECORD

Year	League	IP.	W.	L.	Pct.	H.	R.	ER.	SO.	BB.	ERA.
1976—National		1	0	0	.000	0	0	0	1	0	0.00
1981—American		1	0	0	.000	1	1	1	0	0	0.00
All-Star Game Totals		2	0	0	.000	1	1	1	1	0	0.00

ROBERT HERBERT FORSCH
(Bob)

Born January 13, 1950, at Sacramento, Calif.
Height, 6.04. Weight, 200.
Throws and bats righthanded.
Attended Sacramento City College, Sacramento, Calif.
Brother of Ken Forsch, pitcher with California Angels.

Pitched 3-0 no-hit victory against Montreal Expos, September 26, 1983.
Pitched 5-0 no-hit victory against Philadelphia Phillies, April 16, 1978.

Pitched 5-0 no-hit victory against Denver, May 25, 1973.
Pitched seven-inning, 4-0 no-hit victory against Memphis, May 13, 1972.
Led Midwest League in hit batsmen with 11 in 1971.
Tied for Texas League lead in hit batsmen with 10 in 1972.
Named pitcher on THE SPORTING NEWS National League Silver Slugger team, 1980.
Received reported $25,000 bonus to sign with St. Louis Cardinals, 1968.

Year	Club	League	G.	IP.	W.	L.	Pct.	H.	R.	ER.	SO.	BB.	ERA.
1970—Cedar Rapids	Midwest	1	3	0	0	.000	6	4	4	1	2	12.00
1970—Lewiston	Northwest	7	28	2	3	.400	32	22	13	15	17	4.18
1971—Cedar Rapids	Midwest	23	158	11	7	.611	140	74	55	134	41	3.13
1972—Arkansas	Texas	24	153	8	10	.444	158	85	★74	109	47	4.35
1973—Tulsa	Am. Assoc.	27	166	12	12	.500	169	91	81	124	66	4.36
1974—Tulsa	Am. Assoc.	15	103	8	5	.615	95	49	42	71	33	3.67
1974—St. Louis	National	19	100	7	4	.636	84	38	33	39	34	2.97
1975—St. Louis	National	34	230	15	10	.600	213	89	73	108	70	2.86
1976—St. Louis	National	33	194	8	10	.444	209	112	85	76	71	3.94
1977—St. Louis	National	35	217	20	7	.741	210	97	84	95	69	3.48
1978—St. Louis	National	34	234	11	17	.393	205	110	96	114	97	3.69
1979—St. Louis	National	33	219	11	11	.500	215	102	93	92	52	3.82
1980—St. Louis	National	31	215	11	10	.524	225	102	90	87	33	3.77
1981—St. Louis	National	20	124	10	5	.667	106	47	44	41	29	3.19
1982—St. Louis	National	36	233	15	9	.625	238	95	90	69	54	3.48
1983—St. Louis	National	34	187	10	12	.455	190	104	89	56	54	4.28
Major League Totals		309	1953	118	95	.554	1895	896	777	777	563	3.58

Selected by St. Louis Cardinals' organization in 38th round of free-agent draft, June 7, 1968.

CHAMPIONSHIP SERIES RECORD

Year	Club	League	G.	IP.	W.	L.	Pct.	H.	R.	ER.	SO.	BB.	ERA.
1982—St. Louis	National	1	9	1	0	1.000	3	0	0	6	0	0.00

WORLD SERIES RECORD

Tied World Series record for most games lost, seven-game Series (2), 1982.

Year	Club	League	G.	IP.	W.	L.	Pct.	H.	R.	ER.	SO.	BB.	ERA.
1982—St. Louis	National	2	12⅔	0	2	.000	18	10	7	4	3	4.97

RECORD AS INFIELDER

Year	Club	League	Pos.	G.	AB.	R.	H.	2B.	3B.	HR.	RBI.	B.A.	PO.	A.	E.	F.A.
1968—Sarasota Cards	Gulf C.	3B	44	143	17	32	5	0	0	16	.224	29	80	12	★.901
1969—Lewiston	N'west	3B-OF-2B	26	74	11	15	3	0	3	10	.203	12	45	13	.814
1969—Modesto	Calif.	3B-OF	33	119	8	28	2	0	1	7	.235	33	58	6	.938
1970—Modesto	Calif.	3B-OF	20	47	4	7	3	0	1	1	.149	19	20	3	.929
1970—Cedar Rapids	Midw.	3B-1B-P	19	34	2	3	2	0	0	1	.088	9	19	3	.903
1970—Lewiston	N'west	P-S-2-3	18	30	5	4	0	1	0	3	.133	9	13	6	.786

TERRY JAY FORSTER

Born January 14, 1952, at Sioux Falls, S. D.
Height, 6.03. Weight, 210.
Throws and bats lefthanded.
Attended Grossmont College, El Cajon, Calif.

Major League saves: 1971 (1), 1972 (29), 1973 (16), 1974 (24), 1975 (4), 1976 (1), 1977 (1), 1978 (22), 1979 (2), 1982 (3), 1983 (13). Total—116.
Led American League in saves with 24 in 1974.
Named American League Fireman of the Year by THE SPORTING NEWS, 1974.

Year	Club	League	G.	IP.	W.	L.	Pct.	H.	R.	ER.	SO.	BB.	ERA.
1970—Appleton	Midwest	10	54	6	1	.857	30	11	8	42	29	1.33
1971—Chicago	American	45	50	2	3	.400	46	23	22	48	23	3.96
1972—Chicago	American	62	100	6	5	.545	75	31	25	104	44	2.25
1973—Chicago	American	51	173	6	11	.353	174	69	62	120	78	3.23
1974—Chicago	American	59	134	7	8	.467	120	57	54	105	48	3.63
1975—Chicago†	American	17	37	3	3	.500	30	12	9	32	24	2.19
1976—Chicago‡	American	29	111	2	12	.143	126	61	54	70	41	4.38
1977—Pittsburgh§	National	33	87	6	4	.600	90	47	43	58	32	4.45
1978—Los Angeles	National	47	65	5	4	.556	56	19	14	46	23	1.94
1979—Los Angeles xy	National	17	16	1	2	.333	18	11	10	8	11	5.63
1980—Los Angeles z	National	9	12	0	0	.000	10	4	4	2	4	3.00
1981—Los Angeles	National	21	31	0	1	.000	37	14	14	17	15	4.06
1982—Los Angeles a	National	56	83	5	6	.455	66	38	28	52	31	3.04
1983—Atlanta	National	56	79⅓	3	2	.600	60	19	19	54	31	2.16
American League Totals		263	605	26	42	.382	571	253	226	479	258	3.36
National League Totals		239	373⅓	20	19	.513	337	152	132	237	147	3.18
Major League Totals		502	978⅓	46	61	.430	908	405	358	716	405	3.29

Selected by Chicago White Sox' organization in 2nd round of free-agent draft, June 4, 1970.
†On disabled list, May 25 to July 1, July 26 to August 17 and August 18 to September 29, 1975.
‡Traded with Pitcher Rich Gossage to Pittsburgh Pirates for Outfielder Richie Zisk and Pitcher Silvio Martinez, December 10, 1976.
§Granted free agency, October 20, 1977; signed by Los Angeles Dodgers, November 22, 1977.
xOn disabled list, March 21 to May 25, 1979.
yOn emergency disabled list, August 13, 1979 through remainder of season.

zOn disabled list, April 2 to July 14 and August 5 to September 15, 1980.
aGranted free agency, November 10, 1982; signed by Atlanta Braves, December 1, 1982.

DIVISION SERIES RECORD

Year Club	League	G.	IP.	W.	L.	Pct.	H.	R.	ER.	SO.	BB.	ERA.
1981—Los Angeles	National	1	⅓	0	0	.000	0	0	0	0	0	0.00

CHAMPIONSHIP SERIES RECORD

Year Club	League	G.	IP.	W.	L.	Pct.	H.	R.	ER.	SO.	BB.	ERA.
1978—Los Angeles	National	1	1	1	0	1.000	1	0	0	2	0	0.00
1981—Los Angeles	National	1	⅓	0	0	.000	0	0	0	1	0	0.00
Championship Series Totals		2	1⅓	1	0	1.000	1	0	0	3	0	0.00

WORLD SERIES RECORD

Year Club	League	G.	IP.	W.	L.	Pct.	H.	R.	ER.	SO.	BB.	ERA.
1978—Los Angeles	National	3	4	0	0	.000	5	0	0	6	1	0.00
1981—Los Angeles	National	2	2	0	0	.000	1	0	0	3	—	0.00
World Series Totals		5	6	0	0	.000	6	0	0	6	4	0.00

GEORGE ARTHUR FOSTER

Born December 1, 1948, at Tuscaloosa, Ala.
Height, 6.01. Weight, 195.
Throws and bats righthanded.
Attended El Camino College, Torrance, Calif.

Established major league record for most home runs, righthanded batter on road (31), 1977.
Tied major league record for most consecutive seasons leading league in runs batted in (3), 1976, 1977 and 1978.
Tied National League record for most home runs, bases filled, month (2), August, 1983.
Hit three home runs in a game, July 14, 1977.
Led National League in total bases with 388 and slugging percentage with .631 in 1977.
Led California League outfielders in total chances with 285 in 1969.
Led Northwest League outfielders in double plays with 4 in 1968.
Named National League Player of the Year by THE SPORTING NEWS, 1976 and 1977.
Named National League Most Valuable Player by Baseball Writers' Association of America, 1977.
Named outfielder on THE SPORTING NEWS National League All-Star Team, 1976 through 1978 and 1981.
Named outfielder on THE SPORTING NEWS National League Silver Slugger team, 1981.

Year Club	League	Pos.	G.	AB.	R.	H.	2B.	3B.	HR.	RBI.	B.A.	PO.	A.	E.	F.A.
1968—Medford	N'west	OF	72	253	47	70	9	5	3	30	.277	★142	6	5	.967
1969—Fresno	Calif.	OF	121	449	68	144	5	8	14	85	.321	★267	14	4	★.986
1969—San Francisco	Nat.	OF	9	5	1	2	0	0	0	1	.400	3	0	0	1.000
1970—Phoenix†	P. C.	OF	114	403	54	124	18	6	8	66	.308	202	5	9	.958
1970—San Francisco	Nat.	OF	9	19	2	6	1	1	4	4	.316	10	0	0	1.000
1971—S.F.‡-Cin.	Nat.	OF	140	473	50	114	23	4	13	58	.241	315	9	5	.985
1972—Cincinnati	Nat.	OF	59	145	15	29	4	1	2	12	.200	71	1	2	.973
1973—Indianapolis	A. A.	OF	134	496	77	130	26	1	15	60	.262	★332	7	10	.971
1973—Cincinnati	Nat.	OF	17	39	6	11	3	0	4	9	.282	19	1	0	1.000
1974—Cincinnati	Nat.	OF	106	276	31	73	18	0	7	41	.264	172	2	2	.989
1975—Cincinnati	Nat.	OF-1B	134	463	71	139	24	4	23	78	.300	299	11	3	.990
1976—Cincinnati	Nat.	★OF-1B	144	562	86	172	21	9	29	★121	.306	322	9	2	★.994
1977—Cincinnati	Nat.	OF	158	615	★124	197	31	2	★52	★149	.320	352	12	3	.992
1978—Cincinnati	Nat.	OF	158	604	97	170	26	7	★40	★120	.281	319	10	10	.971
1979—Cincinnati§	Nat.	OF	121	440	68	133	18	3	30	98	.302	214	7	4	.982
1980—Cincinnati	Nat.	OF	144	528	79	144	21	5	25	93	.273	295	6	1	.997
1981—Cincinnati x	Nat.	OF	108	414	64	122	23	2	22	90	.295	224	8	2	.991
1982—New York	Nat.	OF	151	550	64	136	23	2	13	70	.247	289	12	8	.974
1983—New York	Nat.	OF	157	601	74	145	19	2	28	90	.241	314	12	4	.988
Major League Totals			1615	5734	832	1593	255	42	289	1034	.278	3218	100	46	.986

Selected by San Francisco Giants' organization in 3rd round of free-agent draft, January 27, 1968.
†On disabled list, June 10 to June 30, 1970.
‡Traded to Cincinnati Reds for Shortstop Frank Duffy and Pitcher Vern Geishert, May 29, 1971.
§On supplemental disabled list, July 22 to August 12, 1979.
xTraded to New York Mets for Catcher Alex Trevino and Pitchers Jim Kern and Greg Harris, February 10, 1982.

CHAMPIONSHIP SERIES RECORD

Tied Championship Series record for most consecutive games, one or more runs batted in (4).

Year Club	League	Pos.	G.	AB.	R.	H.	2B.	3B.	HR.	RBI.	B.A.	PO.	A.	E.	F.A.
1972—Cincinnati	Nat.	PR	1	0	1	0	0	0	0	0	.000	0	0	0	.000
1975—Cincinnati	Nat.	OF	3	11	3	4	0	0	0	0	.364	7	0	0	1.000
1976—Cincinnati	Nat.	OF	3	12	2	2	0	0	2	4	.167	7	0	0	1.000
1979—Cincinnati	Nat.	OF	3	10	1	2	0	0	1	2	.200	6	2	0	1.000
Championships Series Totals			10	33	7	8	0	0	3	6	.242	20	2	0	1.000

WORLD SERIES RECORD

Established World Series records for most putouts by left fielder, game (8), October 21, 1976; most chances accepted by left fielder, game (8), October 21, 1976.
Tied World Series record for most times caught stealing, four-game Series (2), 1976; one or more hits, each game, four-game Series, 1976; most putouts by outfielder, game (8), October 21, 1976.

Year Club	League	Pos.	G.	AB.	R.	H.	2B.	3B.	HR.	RBI.	B.A.	PO.	A.	E.	F.A.
1972—Cincinnati	Nat.	PR-OF	2	0	0	0	0	0	0	0	.000	0	0	0	.000
1975—Cincinnati	Nat.	OF	7	29	1	8	1	0	0	2	.276	13	1	0	1.000
1976—Cincinnati	Nat.	OF	4	14	3	6	1	0	0	4	.429	14	0	0	1.000
World Series Totals			13	43	4	14	2	0	0	6	.326	27	1	0	1.000

ALL-STAR GAME RECORD

Year League	Pos.	AB.	R.	H.	2B.	3B.	HR.	RBI.	B.A.	PO.	A.	E.	F.A.
1976—National	OF	3	1	1	0	0	1	3	.333	0	0	0	.000
1977—National	OF	3	1	1	1	0	0	1	.333	2	0	0	1.000
1978—National	OF	2	1	0	0	0	0	0	.000	2	0	0	1.000
1979—National	OF	1	0	1	1	0	0	1	1.000	0	0	0	.000
1981—National	OF	2	0	0	0	0	0	0	.000	0	0	0	.000
All-Star Game Totals		11	3	3	2	0	1	5	.273	4	0	0	1.000

ALAN KIM FOWLKES

Name pronounced Folks.

Born August 8, 1958, at Brawley, Calif.

Height, 6.02. Weight, 190.

Throws and bats righthanded.

Attended California State Poly University, Pomona, Calif.

Brother of George Fowlkes, pitcher in Philadelphia

Phillies' organization, 1965 through 1967.

Named Texas League Pitcher of the Year, 1981.

Year Club	League	G.	IP.	W.	L.	Pct.	H.	R.	ER.	SO.	BB.	ERA.
1980—Great Falls	Pioneer	4	19	2	0	1.000	18	5	5	22	5	2.37
1980—Fresno	California	18	88	5	5	.500	69	26	20	90	16	2.05
1981—Shreveport	Texas	32	★203	14	10	.583	186	81	63	★152	51	2.79
1982—San Francisco	National	21	85	4	2	.667	111	55	49	50	24	5.19
1982—Phoenix	P. Coast	13	73⅓	6	3	.667	78	26	22	31	14	2.70
1983—Phoenix†	P. Coast	27	134	9	11	.450	181	118	97	78	58	6.51
Major League Totals		21	85	4	2	.667	111	55	49	50	24	5.19

Selected by San Francisco Giants' organization in 8th round of free-agent draft, June 3, 1980.

†On San Francisco disabled list, March 27 to April 21, 1983.

JOHN ANTHONY FRANCO

(Johnny)

Born September 17, 1960, at Brooklyn, N.Y.

Height, 5.10. Weight, 175.

Throws and bats lefthanded.

Attended St. John's University, Jamaica, N.Y.

Year Club	League	G.	IP.	W.	L.	Pct.	H.	R.	ER.	SO.	BB.	ERA.
1981—Vero Beach	Florida St.	13	78	7	4	.636	78	41	31	60	41	3.53
1982—Albuquerque	P. Coast	5	27⅓	1	2	.333	41	22	22	24	15	7.24
1982—San Antonio	Texas	17	105⅓	10	5	.667	137	70	58	76	46	4.96
1983—Albuquerque†	P. Coast	11	15	0	0	.000	10	11	9	8	11	5.40
1983—Indianapolis	Am. Assoc.	23	115	6	10	.375	148	69	62	54	42	4.85

Selected by Los Angeles Dodgers' organization in 5th round of free-agent draft, June 8, 1981.

†Traded with Pitcher Brett Wise to Cincinnati Reds' organization for Infielder Rafael Landestoy, May 9, 1983.

JULIO CESAR FRANCO

Name pronounced FRANHK-oh.

Born August 23, 1961, at San Pedro de Macoris, Dominican Republic.

Height, 6.01. Weight, 180.

Throws and bats righthanded.

Major League stolen bases: 1983 (32).

Led Northwest League in total bases with 153 in 1979.

Led Carolina League shortstops in double plays with 73 in 1980.

Led Northwest League shortstops in double plays with 45 in 1979.

Named Carolina League Most Valuable Player, 1980.

Year Club	League	Pos.	G.	AB.	R.	H.	2B.	3B.	HR.	RBI.	B.A.	PO.	A.	E.	F.A.
1978—Butte	Appal.	SS	47	141	34	43	5	2	3	28	.305	37	52	25	.781
1979—Central Ore.	N'west	SS	●71	299	57	★98	15	5	●10	45	.328	103	★256	31	.921
1980—Peninsula	Carol.	SS	●140	★555	105	178	25	6	11	★99	.321	179	★412	42	.934
1981—Reading	East.	SS	★139	★532	70	160	17	3	8	74	.301	246	437	30	.958
1982—Oklahoma City	A. A.	★SS-3B	120	463	80	139	19	5	21	66	.300	211	350	★42	.930
1982—Philadelphia†	Nat.	SS-3B	16	29	3	8	1	0	0	3	.276	8	25	0	1.000
1983—Cleveland	Amer.	SS	149	560	68	153	24	8	8	80	.273	247	438	28	.961
National League Totals			16	29	3	8	1	0	0	3	.276	8	25	0	1.000
American League Totals			149	560	68	153	24	8	8	80	.273	247	438	28	.961
Major League Totals			165	589	71	161	25	8	8	83	.273	255	463	28	.962

Signed as free agent by Philadelphia Phillies' organization, June 23, 1978.

†Traded with Second Baseman Manny Trillo, Outfielder George Vukovich, Pitcher Jay Baller and Catcher Gerry Willard to Cleveland Indians for Outfielder Von Hayes, December 9, 1982.

TERRY JON FRANCONA

Born April 22, 1959, at New Brighton, Pa.
Height, 6.01. Weight, 190.
Throws and bats lefthanded.
Attended University of Arizona, Tucson, Ariz.
Son of John (Tito) Francona, outfielder-first baseman with Baltimore, Chicago A.L., Detroit,
Cleveland, St. Louis, Philadelphia, Atlanta, Oakland and Milwaukee, 1956 through 1970.
Named College Player of the Year by THE SPORTING NEWS, 1980.

Year	Club	League	Pos.	G.	AB.	R.	H.	2B.	3B.	HR.	RBI.	B.A.	PO.	A.	E.	F.A.
1980—Memphis	South.		OF	60	210	20	63	13	2	1	23	.300	59	4	4	.940
1981—Memphis	South.		OF-1B	41	161	20	56	8	1	0	18	.348	102	7	5	.956
1981—Denver	A. A.		OF	93	355	53	125	17	*9	1	58	.352	158	7	3	.982
1981—Montreal	Nat.		OF-1B	34	95	11	26	0	1	1	8	.274	41	5	0	1.000
1982—Montreal†	Nat.		OF-1B	46	131	14	42	3	0	0	9	.321	65	0	3	.956
1983—Montreal	Nat.		OF-1B	120	230	21	59	11	1	3	22	.257	172	10	3	.984
Major League Totals				200	456	46	127	14	2	4	39	.279	278	15	6	.980

Selected by Chicago Cubs' organization in 2nd round of free-agent draft, June 7, 1977.
Selected by Montreal Expos' organization in 1st round (22nd player selected) of free-agent draft, June 3, 1980.
†On disabled list, June 17, 1982; transferred to emergency disabled list, June 21 to September 27, 1982.

DIVISION SERIES RECORD

Year	Club	League	Pos.	G.	AB.	R.	H.	2B.	3B.	HR.	RBI.	B.A.	PO.	A.	E.	F.A.
1981—Montreal	Nat.		OF	5	12	0	4	0	0	0	0	.333	8	0	0	1.000

CHAMPIONSHIP SERIES RECORD

Year	Club	League	Pos.	G.	AB.	R.	H.	2B.	3B.	HR.	RBI.	B.A.	PO.	A.	E.	F.A.
1981—Montreal	Nat.		PH-OF	2	1	0	0	0	0	0	0	.000	0	0	0	.000

GEORGE ALLEN FRAZIER

Born October 13, 1954, at Oklahoma City, Okla.
Height, 6.05. Weight, 205.
Throws and bats righthanded.
Attended University of Oklahoma, Norman, Okla.
Major League saves: 1980 (3), 1981 (3), 1982 (1), 1983 (8). Total—15.

Year	Club	League	G.	IP.	W.	L.	Pct.	H.	R.	ER.	SO.	BB.	ERA.
1976—Newark	NYP	6	15	2	1	.667	11	3	3	17	4	1.80
1976—Burlington	Midwest	20	36	7	2	.778	30	9	7	28	14	1.75
1977—Spokane	P. Coast	7	11	2	2	.500	9	5	5	9	5	4.09
1977—Holyoke†	Eastern	45	98	12	7	.632	94	44	36	71	29	3.31
1978—Springfield	Am. Assoc.	32	69	6	5	.545	59	33	26	52	25	3.39
1978—St. Louis	National	14	22	0	3	.000	22	14	10	8	6	4.09
1979—Springfield	Am. Assoc.	24	56	1	2	.333	40	17	15	56	23	2.41
1979—St. Louis	National	25	32	2	4	.333	35	19	16	14	12	4.50
1980—Springfield	Am. Assoc.	35	60	1	3	.250	44	22	20	55	23	3.00
1980—St. Louis	National	22	23	1	4	.200	24	10	7	11	7	2.74
1981—Springfield‡	Am. Assoc.	21	31	1	2	.333	35	14	11	28	11	3.19
1981—Columbus	Int'national	27	59	4	1	.800	58	23	21	50	12	3.20
1981—New York	American	16	28	0	1	.000	26	7	5	17	11	1.61
1982—New York	American	63	111⅔	4	4	.500	103	51	43	69	39	3.47
1983—New York	American	61	115⅓	4	4	.500	94	44	44	78	45	3.43
National League Totals		61	77	3	11	.214	81	43	33	33	25	3.86
American League Totals		140	255	8	9	.471	223	102	92	164	95	3.25
Major League Totals		201	332	11	20	.355	304	145	125	197	120	3.39

Selected by Texas Rangers' organization in 13th round of free-agent draft, June 6, 1976.
Selected by Milwaukee Brewers' organization in 9th round of free-agent draft, June 8, 1976.
†Traded to St. Louis Cardinals' organization for Catcher Buck Martinez, December 9, 1977.
‡Traded to New York Yankees' organization, June 7, 1981, completing deal in which New York organization
traded Shortstop Rafael Santana to St. Louis Cardinals for a player to be named later, February 16, 1981.

CHAMPIONSHIP SERIES RECORD

Established American League Championship Series record for most strikeouts by a relief pitcher, game (5),
October 14, 1981.

Year	Club	League	G.	IP.	W.	L.	Pct.	H.	R.	ER.	SO.	BB.	ERA.
1981—New York	American	1	5⅔	1	0	1.000	5	0	0	5	1	0.00

WORLD SERIES RECORD

Established World Series record for most games lost, six-game Series (3), 1981.

Year	Club	League	G.	IP.	W.	L.	Pct.	H.	R.	ER.	SO.	BB.	ERA.
1981—New York	American	3	3⅔	0	3	.000	9	7	7	2	3	17.18

—DID YOU KNOW—

That the Brewers' Ted Simmons is the only major league player to have collected at
least a dozen game-winning RBIs in each of the last four seasons? He had exactly 12 in
1980, 1981 and 1982 and totaled 17 in 1983.

DOUGLAS STEVEN FROBEL
Name pronounced Froh-bul.
(Doug)

Born June 6, 1959, at Ottawa, Ont.
Height, 6.03. Weight, 190.
Throws right and bats lefthanded.

Year	Club	League	Pos.	G.	AB.	R.	H.	2B.	3B.	HR.	RBI.	B.A.	PO.	A.	E.	F.A.
1978—Charleston	W. Car.	OF-1B	93	287	30	68	15	1	2	33	.237	80	12	9	.911
1979—Shelby	W. Car.	OF-1B-3B	48	130	11	24	3	0	3	13	.185	153	33	3	.984
1979—Auburn	NYP	3B-1B	35	118	16	34	4	2	4	31	.288	18	30	11	.814
1980—Shelby†	S. Atl.	1B-3B-2B	67	246	42	80	14	1	13	41	.325	220	56	13	.955
1980—Salem	Carol.	1B-3B-OF	40	144	21	34	8	1	7	18	.236	294	29	8	.976
1981—Buffalo	East.	OF-1B	135	479	72	120	17	3	28	78	.251	624	57	19	.973
1982—Portland	P. C.	OF	135	472	76	123	38	3	23	75	.261	229	11	11	.956
1982—Pittsburgh	Nat.	OF	16	34	5	7	2	0	2	3	.206	18	0	0	1.000
1983—Hawaii	P. C.	OF	101	378	66	115	18	6	24	80	.304	169	11	9	.952
1983—Pittsburgh	Nat.	OF	32	60·	10	17	4	1	3	11	.283	27	0	1	.964
Major League Totals			48	94	15	24	6	1	5	14	.255	45	0	1	.978

Signed as free agent by Pittsburgh Pirates' organization, August 18, 1977.
†On disabled list, May 19 to June 4, 1980.

WOODROW THOMPSON FRYMAN
(Woodie)

Born April 12, 1940, at Ewing, Ky.
Height, 6.02. Weight, 215.
Throws left and bats righthanded.

Major League saves: 1971 (2), 1972 (1), 1975 (3), 1976 (2), 1977 (1), 1978 (1), 1979 (10), 1980 (17), 1981 (7), 1982 (12).
Total—56.
Led National League in hit batsmen with 9 in 1976.
Tied for National League lead in balks with 3 in 1970.

Year	Club	League	G.	IP.	W.	L.	Pct.	H.	R.	ER.	SO.	BB.	ERA.
1965—Batavia	NYP	6	30	3	1	.750	13	5	5	45	14	1.50
1965—Columbus	Int'national	6	34	0	3	.000	32	15	14	29	15	3.71
1966—Pittsburgh	National	36	182	12	9	.571	182	86	77	105	47	3.81
1967—Pittsburgh†	National	28	113	3	8	.273	121	67	51	74	44	4.06
1968—Philadelphia	National	34	214	12	14	.462	198	78	66	151	64	2.78
1969—Philadelphia	National	36	228	12	15	.444	243	123	112	150	89	4.42
1970—Philadelphia‡	National	27	128	8	6	.571	122	61	58	97	43	4.08
1971—Philadelphia	National	37	149	10	7	.588	133	61	56	104	46	3.38
1972—Philadelphia§	National	23	120	4	10	.286	131	64	58	69	39	4.35
1972—Detroit	American	16	114	10	3	.769	93	31	26	72	31	2.05
1973—Detroit	American	34	170	6	13	.316	200	106	101	119	64	5.35
1974—Detroit x	American	27	142	6	9	.400	120	73	68	92	67	4.31
1975—Montreal	National	38	157	9	12	.429	141	69	58	118	68	3.32
1976—Montreal y	National	34	216	13	13	.500	218	89	81	123	76	3.38
1977—Cincinnati za	National	17	75	5	5	.500	83	45	45	57	45	5.40
1978—Chicago b-Montreal	National	32	150	7	11	.389	157	76	70	81	74	4.20
1979—Montreal	National	44	58	3	6	.333	52	25	18	44	22	2.79
1980—Montreal	National	61	80	7	4	.636	61	23	20	59	30	2.25
1981—Montreal	National	35	43	5	3	.625	38	16	9	25	14	1.88
1982—Montreal c	National	60	69⅔	9	4	.692	66	36	29	46	26	3.75
1983—Montreal de	National	6	3	0	3	.000	8	7	7	1	1	21.00
National League Totals		548	1985⅔	119	130	.478	1954	926	815	1304	728	3.69
American League Totals		77	426	22	25	.468	413	210	195	283	162	4.12
Major League Totals		625	2411⅔	141	155	.476	2367	1136	1010	1587	890	3.77

Signed as free agent by Pittsburgh Pirates' organization, July 6, 1965.
†Traded with Pitchers Harold Clem and Bill Laxton and Infielder Don Money to Philadelphia Phillies for Pitcher Jim Bunning, December 15, 1967.
‡On disabled list, July 29 to August 31, 1970.
§Released on waivers to Detroit Tigers, August 2, 1972.
xTraded to Montreal Expos for Pitcher Tom Walker and Catcher Terry Humphrey, December 4, 1974.
yTraded with Pitcher Dale Murray to Cincinnati Reds for First Baseman Tony Perez and Pitcher Will McEnaney, December 16, 1976.
zPlaced on suspended list, July 12, 1977; transferred to disqualified list, July 13, 1977 through remainder of season.
aTraded with Pitcher Bill Caudill to Chicago Cubs for pitcher Bill Bonham, October 31, 1977.
bTraded to Montreal Expos for a player to be named later, June 9, 1978; Chicago Cubs acquired Outfielder Jerry White to complete deal, June 23, 1978.
cGranted free agency, November 10, 1982; re-signed by Expos, December 23, 1982.
dOn disabled list, April 11 to July 11 and July 29 to September 20, 1983.
eReleased, October 7, 1983.

DIVISION SERIES RECORD

Year	Club	League	G.	IP.	W.	L.	Pct.	H.	R.	ER.	SO.	BB.	ERA.
1981—Montreal	National	1	1⅓	0	0	.000	3	1	1	0	1	6.75

CHAMPIONSHIP SERIES RECORD
Tied Championship Series record for most games lost, Series (2), 1972.

Year Club	League	G.	IP.	W.	L.	Pct.	H.	R.	ER.	SO.	BB.	ERA.
1972—Detroit	American	2	12⅓	0	2	.000	11	6	5	8	2	3.65
1981—Montreal	National	1	1	0	0	.000	3	4	4	1	1	36.00
Championship Series Total		3	13⅓	0	2	.000	14	10	9	9	3	6.08

ALL-STAR GAME RECORD
Member of National League All-Star Team in 1968 and 1976; did not play.

MICHAEL JAY FUENTES
(Mike)

Born July 11, 1958, at Miami, Fla.
Height, 6.03. Weight, 185.
Throws and bats righthanded.
Attended Florida State University, Tallahassee, Fla.

Tied for American Association lead in strikeouts by batters with 103 in 1983.

Year Club	League	Pos.	G.	AB.	R.	H.	2B.	3B.	HR.	RBI.	B.A.	PO.	A.	E.	F.A.
1981—W. Palm Beach....	Fla. St.	OF	67	223	43	65	6	1	15	45	.291	127	5	2	.985
1981—Memphis	South.	OF	3	13	0	3	1	0	0	0	.231	0	0	0	.000
1982—Memphis	South.	OF	142	*539	*104	144	24	2	*37	*115	.267	284	*22	5	.984
1982—Wichita	A. A.	OF	1	2	0	0	0	0	0	0	.000	6	0	0	1.000
1983—Wichita	A. A.	OF	132	448	*96	134	23	3	30	91	.299	244	13	6	.977
1983—Montreal	Nat.	PH-PR	6	4	1	1	0	0	0	0	.250	0	0	0	.000
Major League Totals			6	4	1	1	0	0	0	0	.250	0	0	0	.000

Selected by Minnesota Twins' organization in 5th round of free-agent draft, June 3, 1980.
Selected by Montreal Expos' organization in 2nd round of free-agent draft, June 8, 1981.

GARY JOSEPH GAETTI

Name pronounced Guy-ETT-ee.

Born August 19, 1958, at Centralia, Ill.
Height, 6.00. Weight, 192.
Throws and bats righthanded.
Attended Lake Land College, Mattoon, Ill., and Northwest
Missouri State University, Maryville, Mo.

Tied major league records by hitting home run in first major league at-bat, September 20, 1981; most home runs, opening day of season (2), April 6, 1982; most sacrifice flies, rookie season (13), 1982.
Led American League in sacrifice flies with 13 in 1982.
Led American League third basemen in double plays with 46 in 1983.
Led Southern League third basemen in putouts with 122 and assists with 281 in 1981.
Led Midwest League third basemen in double plays with 35 in 1980.
Tied for Appalachian League lead in errors by third basemen with 18 in 1979.

Year Club	League	Pos.	G.	AB.	R.	H.	2B.	3B.	HR.	RBI.	B.A.	PO.	A.	E.	F.A.
1979—Elizabethton	Appal.	3B-SS	66	230	50	59	15	2	14	42	.257	70	134	21	.907
1980—Wis. Rapids	Midw.	3B	138	503	77	134	27	3	*22	82	.266	*94	*363	●35	.929
1981—Orlando	South.	*3B-1B	137	561	92	137	19	2	30	93	.277	143	283	*32	.930
1981—Minnesota	Amer.	3B	9	26	4	5	0	0	2	3	.192	5	17	0	1.000
1982—Minnesota	Amer.	3B-SS	145	508	59	117	25	4	25	84	.230	106	291	17	.959
1983—Minnesota	Amer.	3B-SS	157	584	81	143	30	3	21	78	.245	*131	361	17	.967
Major League Totals			311	1118	144	265	55	7	48	165	.237	242	669	34	.964

Selected by St. Louis Cardinals' organization in 4th round of free-agent draft, January 10, 1978.
Selected by Chicago White Sox' organization in secondary phase of free-agent draft, June 6, 1978.
Selected by Minnesota Twins' organization in secondary phase of free-agent draft, June 5, 1979.

BRENT ALLEN GAFF

Born October 5, 1958, at Fort Wayne, Ind.
Height, 6.02. Weight, 200.
Throws and bats righthanded.
Attended Central Arizona College, Coolidge, Ariz.

Tied for Texas League lead in balks with 4 in 1980.

Year Club	League	G.	IP.	W.	L.	Pct.	H.	R.	ER.	SO.	BB.	ERA.
1978—Wausau	Midwest	25	128	1	13	.071	159	106	●82	71	68	5.77
1979—Wausau	Midwest	20	145	10	5	.667	147	71	48	99	48	2.98
1980—Jackson	Texas	25	158	8	10	.444	184	95	76	83	55	4.33
1981—Jackson	Texas	7	57	5	1	.833	48	18	16	27	13	2.53
1981—Tidewater	Int'national	23	147	9	5	.643	150	54	48	59	64	2.94
1982—Tidewater	Int'national	23	132	9	8	.529	142	63	59	83	41	4.02
1982—New York	National	7	31⅔	0	3	.000	41	22	16	14	10	4.55
1983—Tidewater	Int'national	37	111⅔	6	7	.462	132	87	75	60	43	6.04
1983—New York	National	4	10⅓	1	0	1.000	18	9	7	4	1	6.10
Major League Totals		11	42	1	3	.250	59	31	23	18	11	4.93

Selected by New York Mets' organization in 6th round of free-agent draft, June 7, 1977.

GREGORY CARPENTER GAGNE

Name pronounced GAHN-ya.

(Greg)

Born November 12, 1961, at Fall River, Mass.
Height, 5.11. Weight, 165.
Throws and bats righthanded.

Led International League shortstops in total chances with 599 in 1983.

Year Club	League	Pos.	G.	AB.	R.	H.	2B.	3B.	HR.	RBI.	B.A.	PO.	A.	E.	F.A.
1979—Paintsville .... Appal.		SS	41	106	10	19	2	3	0	7	.179	28	62	14	.865
1980—Greensboro† .... S. Atl.		SS-3B-2B	98	337	39	91	20	5	3	32	.270	133	233	35	.913
1981—Greensboro .... S. Atl.		2B-SS-3B	104	364	71	108	21	3	9	48	.297	172	280	25	.948
1982—Ft. Lauderdale‡ ... Fla. St.		SS	1	3	0	1	0	0	0	0	.333	3	5	0	1.000
1982—Orlando .... South.		SS-2B	136	504	73	117	23	5	11	57	.232	185	403	39	.938
1983—Toledo .... Int.		SS	119	392	61	100	22	4	17	66	.255	201	★364	★34	.943
1983—Minnesota............. Amer.		SS	10	27	2	3	1	0	0	3	.111	10	14	2	.923
Major League Totals....................			10	27	2	3	1	0	0	3	.111	10	14	2	.923

Selected by New York Yankees' organization in 5th round of free-agent draft, June 5, 1979.
†On disabled list, September 4 to September 22, 1980.
‡Traded with Pitchers Ron Davis and Paul Boris and a reported $400,000 to Minnesota Twins for Shortstop Roy Smalley, April 10, 1982.

TELMANCH GAINEY

(Ty)

Born December 25, 1960, at Cheraw, S. C.
Height, 6.01. Weight, 190.
Throws right and bats lefthanded.

Year Club	League	Pos.	G.	AB.	R.	H.	2B.	3B.	HR.	RBI.	B.A.	PO.	A.	E.	F.A.
1979—Sarasota Astros .... Gulf C.		OF	21	61	5	14	1	1	0	7	.230	13	1	1	.933
1980—Sarasota Astros .... Gulf C.		OF	47	167	41	47	4	2	2	26	.281	48	2	3	.943
1980—Daytona Beach .... Fla. St.		OF	5	12	3	1	0	0	0	0	.083	4	0	0	1.000
1981—Daytona Beach .... Fla. St.		OF	114	347	40	86	11	8	6	38	.248	127	7	3	.978
1982—Daytona Beach .... Fla. St.		OF	106	425	92	145	20	11	10	58	★.341	161	6	9	.949
1982—Columbus............... South.		OF	16	58	9	17	5	0	1	5	.293	19	1	0	1.000
1983—Columbus............... South.		OF	110	397	65	107	15	1	9	43	.270	56	1	0	1.000

Selected by Houston Astros' organization in 2nd round of free-agent draft, June 5, 1979.

RICHARD BLACKWELL GALE

(Rich)

Born January 19, 1954, at Littleton, N. H.
Height, 6.07. Weight, 225.
Throws and bats righthanded.
Attended University of New Hampshire, Durham, N. H.

Named American League Rookie Pitcher of the Year by THE SPORTING NEWS, 1978.

Year Club	League	G.	IP.	W.	L.	Pct.	H.	R.	ER.	SO.	BB.	ERA.
1975—Sarasota Royals .... Gulf Coast		9	33	3	1	.750	23	11	10	18	16	2.73
1976—Waterloo .... Midwest		23	148	11	6	.647	118	64	57	88	76	3.47
1977—Jacksonville .... Southern		12	80	6	5	.545	64	32	32	68	24	3.60
1977—Omaha.. Am. Assoc.		12	71	6	2	.750	60	31	29	62	31	3.68
1978—Omaha.. Am. Assoc.		3	21	1	1	.500	17	13	10	24	8	4.29
1978—Kansas City................................... American		31	192	14	8	.636	171	78	66	88	100	3.09
1979—Kansas City................................... American		34	182	9	10	.474	197	131	114	103	99	5.64
1980—Kansas City................................... American		32	191	13	9	.591	169	90	83	97	78	3.91
1981—Kansas City†................................. American		19	102	6	6	.500	107	63	61	47	38	5.38
1982—San Francisco‡ .... National		33	170⅓	7	14	.333	193	91	80	102	81	4.23
1983—Cincinnati§................................... National		33	89⅔	4	6	.400	103	64	58	53	43	5.82
American League Totals.........................		116	667	42	33	.560	644	362	324	335	315	4.37
National League Totals..........................		66	260	11	20	.355	296	155	138	155	124	4.78
Major League Totals..............................		182	927	53	53	.500	940	517	462	490	439	4.49

Selected by Kansas City Royals' organization in 5th round of free-agent draft, June 4, 1975.
†Traded with Pitcher Bill Laskey to San Francisco Giants for Outfielder Jerry Martin, December 10, 1981.
‡Traded to Cincinnati Reds for Outfielder Mike Vail, January 5, 1983.
§Released, November 9, 1983.

WORLD SERIES RECORD

Year Club	League	G.	IP.	W.	L.	Pct.	H.	R.	ER.	SO.	BB.	ERA.
1980—Kansas City.................................... American		2	6⅓	0	1	.000	11	4	3	4	4	4.26

DAVID THOMAS GALLAGHER

(Dave)

Born September 20, 1960, at Trenton, N.J.
Height, 6.00. Weight, 180.
Throws and bats righthanded.
Attended Mercer County Community College, Trenton, N.J.

Led Midwest League in sacrifice hits with 21 in 1982.

Tied for Eastern League lead in double plays by outfielders with 4 in 1983.

Year	Club	League	Pos.	G.	AB.	R.	H.	2B.	3B.	HR.	RBI.	B.A.	PO.	A.	E.	F.A.
1980—Batavia	NYP	OF	69	241	33	66	6	3	5	36	.274	114	4	2	.983
1981—Waterloo	Midw.	OF-3B	127	435	55	102	22	1	3	34	.234	224	22	7	.972
1982—Chattanooga	South.	OF	15	54	10	12	2	1	0	4	.222	32	1	0	1.000
1982—Waterloo	Midw.	OF	110	409	61	118	25	7	6	47	.289	232	15	4	*.984
1983—Buffalo†	East.	OF-3B	107	376	64	127	21	3	2	47	*.338	223	13	5	.979

Selected by Oakland A's organization in 1st round (third player selected) of free-agent draft, January 8, 1980.
Selected by Cleveland Indians' organization in secondary phase of free-agent draft, June 3, 1980.
†On disabled list, May 2 to June 6, 1983.

OSCAR CHARLES GAMBLE

Born December 20, 1949, at Ramer, Ala.
Height, 5.11. Weight, 177.
Throws right and bats lefthanded.

Year	Club	League	Pos.	G.	AB.	R.	H.	2B.	3B.	HR.	RBI.	B.A.	PO.	A.	E.	F.A.
1968—Caldwell	Pion.	OF	34	94	18	25	2	0	2	12	.266	42	4	4	.920
1969—San Antonio	Texas	OF	119	477	62	142	*32	3	7	32	.298	247	10	8	.970
1969—Chicago†	Nat.	OF	24	71	6	16	1	1	1	5	.225	41	1	4	.913
1970—Eugene	P. C.	OF	28	108	26	32	7	2	1	8	.296	54	3	0	1.000
1970—Philadelphia	Nat.	OF	88	275	31	72	12	4	1	19	.262	148	4	7	.956
1971—Eugene	P. C.	OF	39	138	30	40	5	2	4	20	.290	65	4	3	.958
1971—Philadelphia	Nat.	OF	92	280	24	62	11	1	6	23	.221	125	4	4	.970
1972—Eugene	P. C.	OF	42	144	30	42	8	1	8	20	.292	67	8	1	.987
1972—Philadelphia‡	Nat.	OF-1B	74	135	17	32	5	2	1	13	.237	54	2	0	1.000
1973—Cleveland	Amer.	OF	113	390	56	104	11	3	20	44	.267	67	1	2	.971
1974—Cleveland	Amer.	OF	135	454	74	132	16	4	19	59	.291	19	1	0	1.000
1975—Cleveland§	Amer.	OF	121	348	60	91	16	3	15	45	.261	146	8	2	.987
1976—New York x	Amer.	OF	110	340	43	79	13	1	17	57	.232	199	10	4	.981
1977—Chicago y	Amer.	OF	137	408	75	121	22	2	31	83	.297	73	1	1	.987
1978—San Diego z	Nat.	OF	126	375	46	103	15	3	7	47	.275	172	12	4	.979
1979—Tex. a-N.Y.	Amer.	OF	100	274	48	98	10	1	19	64	.358	88	5	3	.969
1980—New York b	Amer.	OF	78	194	40	54	10	2	14	50	.278	65	2	0	1.000
1981—New York	Amer.	OF	80	189	24	45	8	0	10	27	.238	77	0	0	1.000
1982—New York	Amer.	OF	108	316	49	86	21	2	18	57	.272	59	6	0	1.000
1983—New York c	Amer.	OF	74	180	26	47	10	2	7	26	.261	64	1	4	.942
National League Totals			404	1136	124	285	44	11	16	107	.251	540	23	19	.967
American League Totals			1056	3093	495	857	137	20	170	512	.277	857	35	16	.982
Major League Totals			1460	4229	619	1142	181	31	186	619	.270	1397	58	35	.977

Selected by Chicago Cubs' organization in 16th round of free-agent draft, June 7, 1968.
†Traded with Pitcher Dick Selma to Philadelphia Phillies for Outfielder Johnny Callison, November 17, 1969.
‡Traded with Outfielder Roger Freed to Cleveland Indians for Outfielder Del Unser and Infielder Terry Wedgewood, November 30, 1972.
§Traded to New York Yankees for Pitcher Pat Dobson, November 22, 1975.
xTraded with Pitchers Bob Polinsky and LaMarr Hoyt, and cash estimated at $250,000 to Chicago White Sox for Shortstop Bucky Dent, April 5, 1977.
yGranted free agency, October 28, 1977; signed by San Diego Padres, November 29, 1977.
zTraded with Catcher Dave Roberts to Texas Rangers for Third Baseman Kurt Bevacqua, Catcher Bill Fahey, First Baseman Mike Hargrove and cash estimated at $300,000, October 25, 1978.
aTraded with Third Baseman Amos Lewis and two players to be named later to New York Yankees for Outfielder Mickey Rivers and three players to be named later, August 1, 1979; New York sent Pitchers Bob Polinsky, Neal Mersch and Mark Softy and Texas sent Pitchers Gene Nelson and Ray Fontenot to complete deal, October 8, 1979.
bOn supplemental disabled list, May 14, 1980; transferred to disabled list, June 15 to June 23, 1980.
cGranted free agency, November 7, 1983.

DIVISION SERIES RECORD

Year	Club	League	Pos.	G.	AB.	R.	H.	2B.	3B.	HR.	RBI.	B.A.	PO.	A.	E.	F.A.
1981—New York	Amer.	DH	4	9	2	5	1	0	2	3	.555	0	0	0	.000

CHAMPIONSHIP SERIES RECORD

Year	Club	League	Pos.	G.	AB.	R.	H.	2B.	3B.	HR.	RBI.	B.A.	PO.	A.	E.	F.A.
1976—New York	Amer.	OF-PH	3	8	1	2	1	0	0	1	.250	4	0	2	.667
1980—New York	Amer.	O-DH-PH	2	5	1	1	0	0	0	0	.200	1	0	0	1.000
1981—New York	Amer.	DH-OF	3	6	2	1	0	0	0	1	.167	4	0	0	1.000
Championship Series Totals			8	19	4	4	1	0	0	2	.211	9	0	2	.818

WORLD SERIES RECORD

Year	Club	League	Pos.	G.	AB.	R.	H.	2B.	3B.	HR.	RBI.	B.A.	PO.	A.	E.	F.A.
1976—New York	Amer.	PH-OF	3	8	0	1	0	0	0	1	.125	3	0	0	1.000
1981—New York	Amer.	OF-PH	3	6	1	2	0	0	0	1	.333	4	0	0	1.000
World Series Totals			6	14	1	3	0	0	0	2	.214	7	0	0	1.000

JAMES ELMER GANTNER

(Jim)

Born January 5, 1954, at Fond du Lac, Wis.
Height, 5.11. Weight, 175.
Throws right and bats lefthanded.
Attended University of Wisconsin (Oshkosh), Oshkosh, Wis.

Led American League second basemen in total chances with 613 in 1981 and 900 in 1983.
Led American League second basemen in double plays with 95 in 1981 and 128 in 1983.
Led Pacific Coast League third basemen in putouts with 136 and in fielding percentage with .936 in 1977.
Led Eastern League third basemen in fielding percentage with .953 in 1976.
Led Eastern League third basemen in putouts with 118 and assists with 310 in 1975.

Year	Club	League	Pos.	G.	AB.	R.	H.	2B.	3B.	HR.	RBI.	B.A.	PO.	A.	E.	F.A.
1974—Newark	NYP	SS-3B	62	177	35	54	6	2	5	21	.305	64	134	14	.934
1975—Thetford Mines	East.	3B-SS	●138	456	61	117	17	0	12	48	.257	129	317	33	.931
1976—Berkshire	East.	3B-SS	126	403	56	118	21	1	6	53	.293	120	294	20	.954
1976—Milwaukee	Amer.	3B	26	69	6	17	1	0	0	7	.246	17	37	1	.982
1977—Spokane	P. C.	★3B-OF	●143	541	98	152	35	5	15	80	.281	137	★321	31	.937
1977—Milwaukee	Amer.	3B	14	47	4	14	1	0	1	2	.298	8	29	4	.902
1978—Milwaukee	Amer.	2-3-S-1	43	97	14	21	1	0	1	8	.216	46	82	5	.962
1979—Milwaukee	Amer.	3-2-S-P	70	208	29	59	10	3	2	22	.284	80	161	7	.972
1980—Milwaukee	Amer.	3B-2B-SS	132	415	47	117	21	3	4	40	.282	159	335	15	.971
1981—Milwaukee	Amer.	2B	107	352	35	94	14	1	2	33	.267	251	352	10	.984
1982—Milwaukee	Amer.	2B	132	447	48	132	17	2	4	43	.295	307	398	13	.982
1983—Milwaukee	Amer.	2B	161	603	85	170	23	8	11	74	.282	374	★512	14	.984
Major League Totals				685	2238	268	624	88	17	25	229	.279	1242	1906	69	.979

Selected by Milwaukee Brewers' organization in 12th round of free-agent draft, June 5, 1974.

DIVISION SERIES RECORD

Year	Club	League	Pos.	G.	AB.	R.	H.	2B.	3B.	HR.	RBI.	B.A.	PO.	A.	E.	F.A.
1981—Milwaukee	Amer.	2B	4	14	1	2	1	0	0	0	.143	3	15	2	.900

CHAMPIONSHIP SERIES RECORD

Year	Club	League	Pos.	G.	AB.	R.	H.	2B.	3B.	HR.	RBI.	B.A.	PO.	A.	E.	F.A.
1982—Milwaukee	Amer.	2B	5	16	1	3	0	0	0	2	.188	12	8	0	1.000

WORLD SERIES RECORD

Established World Series records for most assists by second baseman, seven-game Series (33), 1982; most errors by second baseman, seven-game Series (5), 1982.

Year	Club	League	Pos.	G.	AB.	R.	H.	2B.	3B.	HR.	RBI.	B.A.	PO.	A.	E.	F.A.
1982—Milwaukee	Amer.	2B	7	24	5	8	4	1	0	4	.333	9	33	5	.894

PITCHING RECORD

Year	Club	League	G.	IP.	W.	L.	Pct.	H.	R.	ER.	SO.	BB.	ERA.
1979—Milwaukee	American	1	1	0	0	.000	2	0	0	0	0	0.00

HENRY EUGENE GARBER
(Gene)

Born November 13, 1947, at Lancaster, Pa.
Height, 5.10. Weight, 175.
Throws and bats righthanded.
Received bachelor of arts degree in history and political science from
Elizabethtown College, Elizabethtown, Pa.

Established major league record for most games lost by relief pitcher, season (16), 1979.
Tied major league record for most consecutive games won by relief pitcher, three consecutive games (3), May 15 through 17, 1975.
Major League Saves: 1973 (11), 1974 (5), 1975 (14), 1976 (11), 1977 (19), 1978 (25), 1979 (25), 1980 (7), 1981 (2), 1982 (30), 1983 (9). Total—158.
Led National League in games finished in relief with 47 in 1975.
Tied for International League lead in complete games with 13 in 1972.
Named International League Pitcher of the Year, 1972.

Year	Club	League	G.	IP.	W.	L.	Pct.	H.	R.	ER.	SO.	BB.	ERA.
1965—Salem	Ap'lachian	1	⅔	0	0	.000	0	0	0	2	2	0.00
1965—Batavia	NYP	11	72	4	3	.571	71	42	28	40	31	3.50
1966—Raleigh	Carolina	16	94	4	4	.500	106	53	48	76	28	4.60
1967—Raleigh	Carolina	18	138	8	6	.571	103	41	29	68	47	1.89
1968—York	Eastern	16	118	7	2	.778	79	33	21	86	30	1.60
1968—Columbus	Int'national	23	59	5	1	.833	62	21	16	32	17	2.44
1969—York	Eastern	11	73	5	3	.625	61	40	25	57	40	3.08
1969—Pittsburgh	National	2	5	0	0	.000	6	3	3	1	1	5.40
1969—Columbus†	Int'national	17	123	7	6	.538	116	51	42	74	37	3.07
1970—Columbus	Int'national	30	95	5	2	.714	96	57	50	75	38	4.74
1970—Pittsburgh	National	14	22	0	3	.000	22	13	13	7	10	5.32
1971—Charleston‡	Int'national	24	170	14	6	.700	★184	85	79	105	54	4.18
1972—Charleston	Int'national	20	163	14	3	★.824	131	49	41	103	45	★2.26
1972—Pittsburgh§	National	4	6	0	0	.000	7	5	5	3	3	7.50
1973—Kansas City	American	48	153	9	9	.500	164	78	72	60	49	4.24
1974—Kansas City x	American	17	28	1	2	.333	35	21	15	14	13	4.82
1974—Toledo	Int'national	3	22	2	1	.667	19	7	1	17	3	0.41
1974—Philadelphia	National	34	48	4	0	1.000	39	15	11	27	31	2.06
1975—Philadelphia	National	★71	110	10	12	.455	104	48	44	69	27	3.60
1976—Philadelphia	National	59	93	9	3	.750	78	33	29	92	30	2.81
1977—Philadelphia	National	64	103	8	6	.571	82	30	27	78	23	2.36
1978—Philadelphia y-Atlanta	National	65	117	6	5	.545	84	32	28	85	24	2.15
1979—Atlanta	National	68	106	6	16	.273	121	66	51	56	24	4.33
1980—Atlanta	National	68	82	5	5	.500	95	42	35	51	24	3.84

Year Club	League	G.	IP.	W.	L.	Pct.	H.	R.	ER.	SO.	BB.	ERA.
1981—Atlanta z	National	35	59	4	6	.400	49	23	17	34	20	2.59
1982—Atlanta	National	69	119⅓	8	10	.444	100	40	31	68	32	2.34
1983—Atlanta a	National	43	60⅔	4	5	.444	72	37	31	45	23	4.60
American League Totals		65	181	10	11	.476	199	99	87	74	62	4.33
National League Totals		596	931	64	71	.474	859	387	325	618	272	3.14
Major League Totals		661	1112	74	82	.474	1058	486	412	692	334	3.33

Selected by Pittsburgh Pirates' organization in 13th round of free-agent draft, June 14, 1965.
†On military list, September 2, 1969, through February 18, 1970.
‡On temporary inactive list, June 24 to July 12, 1971.
§Traded to Kansas City Royals for Pitcher Jim Rooker, October 25, 1972.
xSold to Philadelphia Phillies, July 12, 1974.
yTraded to Atlanta Braves for Pitcher Dick Ruthven, June 15, 1978.
zOn disabled list, May 4 to August 9, 1981.
aOn disabled list, June 25 to July 27, 1983.

CHAMPIONSHIP SERIES RECORD

Year Club	League	G.	IP.	W.	L.	Pct.	H.	R.	ER.	SO.	BB.	ERA.
1976—Philadelphia	National	2	⅔	0	1	.000	2	2	1	0	1	13.50
1977—Philadelphia	National	3	5⅓	1	1	.500	4	3	2	3	0	3.38
1982—Atlanta	National	2	3⅓	0	1	.000	4	3	3	3	1	8.10
Championship Series Totals		7	9⅓	1	3	.250	10	8	6	6	2	5.79

BARBARO GARBEY GARBEY

Name pronounced BAR-bar-o Gar-BAY.

Born December 4, 1956, at Santiago, Cuba.

Height, 5.09. Weight, 165.

Throws and bats righthanded.

Tied for Southern League lead in double plays by outfielders with 5 in 1982.

Year Club	League	Pos.	G.	AB.	R.	H.	2B.	3B.	HR.	RBI.	B.A.	PO.	A.	E.	F.A.
1980—Lakeland	Fla. St.	OF	26	88	15	32	4	0	1	16	.364	60	4	3	.955
1981—Birmingham†	South.	OF	107	391	56	112	17	4	6	55	.286	106	3	5	.956
1981—Evansville	A. A.	OF	4	12	4	1	0	0	0	0	.083	7	0	0	1.000
1982—Birmingham‡	South.	OF-1B	120	480	69	143	32	4	17	99	.298	206	22	11	.956
1983—Evansville	A. A.	OF-3B-1B	101	377	60	121	21	6	14	59	.321	147	55	12	.944

Signed as free agent by Detroit Tigers' organization, June 6, 1980.
†On disabled list, April 16 to May 4, 1981.
‡On disabled list, August 22, 1982 through remainder of season.

ALFONSO RAFAEL GARCIA
(Kiko)

(Nicknamed by grandparents.)

Born October 14, 1953, at Martinez, Calif.

Height, 5.11. Weight, 178.

Throws and bats righthanded.

Led International League shortstops in double plays with 112 in 1976.
Led International League second basemen in double plays with 71 in 1975.
Led Southern League shortstops in double plays with 105 in 1974.

Year Club	League	Pos.	G.	AB.	R.	H.	2B.	3B.	HR.	RBI.	B.A.	PO.	A.	E.	F.A.
1971—Bluefield	Appal.	SS	56	203	35	51	3	★5	2	23	.251	95	128	24	.503
1971—Stockton	Calif.	SS	4	14	1	4	0	1	0	2	.286	8	13	2	.913
1972—Miami	Fla. St.	SS-3B	126	445	51	112	15	6	2	39	.252	176	416	40	.937
1973—Lodi	Calif.	SS	129	494	89	128	15	10	3	36	.259	★237	361	43	.933
1974—Asheville	South.	SS	135	511	68	140	18	5	7	53	.274	★250	★510	48	.941
1975—Rochester	Int.	2B-SS	122	405	34	99	11	1	3	32	.244	260	255	25	.953
1976—Rochester	Int.	SS	130	450	75	124	11	★10	3	44	.276	★241	★473	★38	.949
1976—Baltimore	Amer.	SS	11	32	2	7	1	1	1	4	.219	15	27	0	1.000
1977—Baltimore	Amer.	SS-2B	65	131	20	29	6	0	2	10	.221	78	152	8	.966
1978—Baltimore	Amer.	SS-2B	79	186	17	49	6	4	0	13	.263	87	175	16	.942
1979—Baltimore	Amer.	S-2-O-3	126	417	54	103	15	9	5	24	.247	209	321	27	.952
1980—Baltimore†‡	Amer.	3B-2B-OF	111	311	27	62	8	0	1	27	.199	177	292	11	.977
1981—Houston§	Nat.	SS-2B-3B	48	136	9	37	6	1	0	15	.272	58	119	11	.941
1982—Houston xy	Nat.	SS-3B-2B	34	76	5	16	5	0	1	5	.211	29	62	5	.948
1983—Portland	P. C.	SS-3B-1B	35	113	19	39	7	1	1	16	.345	47	76	3	.976
1983—Philadelphia	Nat.	2B-SS-3B	84	118	22	34	7	1	2	9	.288	94	115	6	.972
American League Totals		392	1077	120	250	36	14	9	78	.232	566	967	62	.961
National League Totals		166	330	36	87	18	2	3	29	.264	181	296	22	.956
Major League Totals		558	1407	156	337	54	16	12	107	.240	747	1263	84	.960

Selected by Baltimore Orioles' organization in 3rd round of free-agent draft, June 8, 1971.
†On supplemental disabled list, May 23 to June 7, 1980.
‡Traded to Houston Astros for Outfielder Chris Bourjos and cash, April 1, 1981.
§On supplemental disabled list, April 4 to April 19, 1981.
xOn supplemental disabled list, August 21 to September 5, 1982.
yGranted free agency, November 10, 1982; signed by Philadelphia Phillies' organization, March 1, 1983.

DIVISION SERIES RECORD

Year — Club	League	Pos.	G.	AB.	R.	H.	2B.	3B.	HR.	RBI.	B.A.	PO.	A.	E.	F.A.
1981—Houston	Nat.	SS	2	4	0	0	0	0	0	0	.000	2	4	0	1.000

CHAMPIONSHIP SERIES RECORD

Year — Club	League	Pos.	G.	AB.	R.	H.	2B.	3B.	HR.	RBI.	B.A.	PO.	A.	E.	F.A.
1979—Baltimore	Amer.	SS	3	11	1	3	0	0	0	2	.273	6	16	2	.917

WORLD SERIES RECORD

Tied World Series records for most times reached first base safely, game (5), October 12, 1979; most at bats and most times faced pitcher, inning (2), October 13, 1979 (eighth inning); most three-base hits, game, batting in three runs (1), October 12, 1979.

Year — Club	League	Pos.	G.	AB.	R.	H.	2B.	3B.	HR.	RBI.	B.A.	PO.	A.	E.	F.A.
1979—Baltimore	Amer.	SS	6	20	4	8	2	1	0	6	.400	10	17	1	.964

DAMASO DOMINGO GARCIA

First name pronounced Da-MAH-so.

Born February 7, 1957, at Moca, Dominican Republic.
Height, 6.00. Weight, 170.
Throws and bats righthanded.
Attended Madre y Maestra University, Santiago, Dominican Republic.

Major League stolen bases: 1978 (1), 1979 (2), 1980 (13), 1981 (13), 1982 (54), 1983 (31). Total—114.
Led Florida State League second baseman in double plays with 83 in 1976.
Tied for New York-Pennsylvania League lead in double plays by second basemen with 33 in 1975.
Named second baseman on THE SPORTING NEWS American League All-Star Team, 1982.
Named second baseman on THE SPORTING NEWS American League Silver Slugger team, 1982.

Year — Club	League	Pos.	G.	AB.	R.	H.	2B.	3B.	HR.	RBI.	B.A.	PO.	A.	E.	F.A.
1975—Oneonta	NYP	2B	50	157	28	42	4	2	0	17	.268	103	118	⋆17	.929
1976—Ft. Lauderdale†	Fla.St.	2B	124	412	55	109	●22	4	1	41	.265	⋆273	353	21	⋆.968
1977—West Haven	East.	2B	129	445	62	118	13	9	0	53	.265	263	382	19	.971
1978—Tacoma	P. C.	2B-SS	102	385	51	103	18	6	1	53	.268	217	345	25	.957
1978—New York	Amer.	2B-SS	18	41	5	8	0	0	0	1	.195	36	35	4	.947
1979—Columbus ‡	Int.	SS-1B	39	118	18	32	1	0	1	3	.271	53	85	6	.958
1979—New York §	Amer.	SS-3B	11	38	3	10	1	0	0	4	.263	9	28	4	.902
1980—Toronto	Amer.	2B	140	543	50	151	30	7	4	46	.278	316	471	16	.980
1981—Toronto x	Amer.	2B	64	250	24	63	8	1	1	13	.252	132	181	9	.972
1982—Toronto	Amer.	2B	147	597	89	185	32	3	5	42	.310	273	461	15	.980
1983—Toronto	Amer.	2B	131	525	84	161	23	6	3	38	.307	266	360	12	.981
Major League Totals			511	1994	255	578	94	17	13	144	.290	1032	1536	60	.977

Signed as free agent by New York Yankees' organization, March 10, 1975.
†On suspended list, June 4 to June 7, 1976.
‡On disabled list, May 14 to July 24 and July 31 to August 13, 1979.
§Traded with First Baseman Chris Chambliss and Pitcher Paul Mirabella to Toronto Blue Jays for Catcher Rick Cerone, Pitcher Tom Underwood and Outfielder Ted Wilborn, November 1, 1979.
xOn supplemental disabled list, August 22, 1981 through remainder of season.

RONALD CLYDE GARDENHIRE
(Ron)

Born October 24, 1957, at Butzbach, Germany.
Height, 6.01. Weight, 170.
Throws and bats righthanded.
Attended Paris Junior College, Paris, Tex., and University of Texas, Austin, Tex.

Led Texas League shortstops in assists with 406 and errors with 40 in 1980.

Year — Club	League	Pos.	G.	AB.	R.	H.	2B.	3B.	HR.	RBI.	B.A.	PO.	A.	E.	F.A.
1979—Lynchburg	Carol.	SS	70	277	36	82	13	3	4	27	.296	120	252	21	.947
1980—Jackson	Texas	SS-2B	127	458	58	118	16	6	6	64	.258	168	411	41	.934
1981—Tidewater	Int.	SS-2B-3B	125	414	52	105	17	8	2	40	.254	206	373	33	.946
1981—New York	Nat.	SS-2B-3B	27	48	2	13	1	0	0	3	.271	28	50	2	.975
1982—New York	Nat.	SS-2B-3B	141	384	29	92	17	1	3	33	.240	235	399	29	.956
1983—New York	Nat.	SS	17	32	1	2	0	0	0	1	.063	13	30	0	1.000
1983—Tidewater	Int.	SS	102	387	63	111	20	6	4	39	.287	202	321	27	.951
Major League Totals			185	464	32	107	18	1	3	37	.231	276	479	31	.961

Selected by New York Mets' organization in 6th round of free-agent draft, June 5, 1979.

PHILIP MASON GARNER
(Phil)

Born April 30, 1949, at Jefferson City, Tenn.
Height, 5.10. Weight, 177.
Throws and bats righthanded.
Received bachelor of science degree in general business from
University of Tennessee, Knoxville, Tenn., in 1973.

Tied major league record for most home runs, bases filled, two consecutive games (2), September 14 and 15, 1978.
Tied National League record for most home runs, bases filled, month (2), September, 1978.

Major League stolen bases: 1974 (1), 1975 (4), 1976 (35), 1977 (32), 1978 (27), 1979 (17), 1980 (32), 1981 (10), 1982 (24), 1983 (18). Total—200.
Led American League second basemen in total chances with 865 in 1976.
Led National League second basemen in assists with 499, total chances with 869 and double plays with 116 in 1980.
Led Pacific Coast League third basemen in putouts with 104, assists with 261 and double plays with 23 in 1973.

Year	Club	League	Pos.	G.	AB.	R.	H.	2B.	3B.	HR.	RBI.	B.A.	PO.	A.	E.	F.A.
1971—Burlington	Midw.		3B	116	439	73	122	22	4	11	70	.278	*122	203	29	.918
1972—Birmingham	South.		3B	71	264	45	74	10	6	12	40	.280	74	116	13	.936
1972—Iowa	A. A.		3B	70	247	33	60	18	4	9	22	.243	50	140	10	.950
1973—Tucson	P. C.		*3B-2B	138	516	87	149	23	12	14	73	.289	107	270	*35	.915
1973—Oakland	Amer.		3B	9	5	0	0	0	0	0	0	.000	2	3	0	1.000
1974—Tucson	P. C.		3B-SS	96	388	78	128	29	10	11	51	.330	92	182	15	.948
1974—Oakland	Amer.		3B-SS-2B	30	28	4	5	1	0	0	1	.179	11	24	1	.972
1975—Oakland	Amer.		*2B-SS	●160	488	46	120	21	5	6	54	.246	355	427	*26	.968
1976—Oakland†	Amer.		2B	159	555	54	145	29	12	8	74	.261	378	*465	22	.975
1977—Pittsburgh	Nat.		3B-2B-SS	153	585	99	152	35	10	17	77	.260	223	351	17	.971
1978—Pittsburgh	Nat.		3B-2B-SS	154	528	66	138	25	9	10	66	.261	258	389	28	.959
1979—Pittsburgh	Nat.		3B-2B-SS	150	549	76	161	32	8	11	59	.293	234	396	22	.966
1980—Pittsburgh	Nat.		*2B-SS	151	548	62	142	27	6	5	58	.259	349	500	*21	.976
1981—Pitt‡§-Hou.	Nat.		2B	87	294	35	73	9	3	1	26	.248	183	250	12	.973
1982—Houston	Nat.		2B-3B	155	588	65	161	33	8	13	83	.274	285	464	17	.978
1983—Houston	Nat.		3B	154	567	76	135	24	2	14	79	.238	100	311	24	.945
American League Totals				358	1076	104	270	51	17	14	129	.251	746	919	49	.971
National League Totals				1004	3659	479	962	185	46	71	448	.263	1632	2661	141	.968
Major League Totals				1362	4735	583	1232	236	63	85	577	.260	2378	3580	190	.969

Selected by Montreal Expos' organization in 8th round of free-agent draft, June 4, 1970.
Selected by Oakland A's organization in secondary phase of free-agent draft, January 13, 1971.
†Traded with Infielder Tommy Helms and Pitcher Chris Batton to Pittsburgh Pirates for Pitchers Doc Medich, Dave Giusti, Rick Langford and Doug Bair and Outfielders Mitchell Page and Tony Armas, March 15, 1977.
‡On disabled list, April 2 to April 23, 1981.
§Traded to Houston Astros for Second Baseman Johnny Ray and two players to be named later, August 31, 1981; Pittsburgh Pirates' organization acquired Outfielder Kevin Houston and Pitcher Randy Niemann to complete deal, September 9, 1981.

DIVISION SERIES RECORD

Year	Club	League	Pos.	G.	AB.	R.	H.	2B.	3B.	HR.	RBI.	B.A.	PO.	A.	E.	F.A.
1981—Houston	Nat.		2B	5	18	1	2	0	0	0	0	.111	6	8	1	.933

CHAMPIONSHIP SERIES RECORD

Year	Club	League	Pos.	G.	AB.	R.	H.	2B.	3B.	HR.	RBI.	B.A.	PO.	A.	E.	F.A.
1975—Oakland	Amer.		2B	3	5	0	0	0	0	0	0	.000	7	4	1	.917
1979—Pittsburgh	Nat.		2B-SS	3	12	4	5	0	1	1	1	.417	8	9	0	1.000
Championship Series Totals				6	17	4	5	0	1	1	1	.294	15	13	1	.966

WORLD SERIES RECORD

Established World Series record for most double plays by second baseman, seven-game Series (9), 1979.
Tied World Series records for highest batting average, seven-game Series (.500), 1979; one or more hits, each game, seven-game Series, 1979; most assists by second baseman, inning (3), October 13, 1979 (ninth inning).

Year	Club	League	Pos.	G.	AB.	R.	H.	2B.	3B.	HR.	RBI.	B.A.	PO.	A.	E.	F.A.
1979—Pittsburgh†	Nat.		2B	7	24	4	12	4	0	0	5	.500	21	23	2	.957

ALL-STAR GAME RECORD

Year	League		Pos.	AB.	R.	H.	2B.	3B.	HR.	RBI.	B.A.	PO.	A.	E.	F.A.
1976—American			2B	1	0	0	0	0	0	0	.000	1	1	0	1.000
1980—National			2B	2	1	1	0	0	0	0	.500	1	3	0	1.000
1981—National			2B	0	0	0	0	0	0	0	.000	0	0	0	.000
All-Star Game Totals				3	1	1	0	0	0	0	.333	2	4	0	1.000

SCOTT WILLIAM GARRELTS
Name pronounced Guh-RELTZ.

Born October 30, 1961, at Urbana, Ill.
Height, 6.04. Weight, 210.
Throws and bats righthanded.

Pitched seven-inning, 1-0 no-hit victory against Tacoma, August 20, 1983.
Tied for Midwest League lead in games started by pitchers with 27 in 1980.

Year	Club	League	G.	IP.	W.	L.	Pct.	H.	R.	ER.	SO.	BB.	ERA.
1979—Great Falls	Pioneer		8	43	1	4	.200	45	37	28	26	40	5.86
1980—Clinton	Midwest		27	176	11	11	.500	155	98	76	*159	*149	3.89
1981—Shreveport†	Texas		14	71	3	8	.273	56	43	35	73	43	4.44
1982—Shreveport	Texas		27	151⅓	9	10	.474	131	76	64	159	90	3.81
1982—San Francisco	National		1	2	0	0	.000	3	3	3	4	2	13.50
1983—Phoenix‡	P. Coast		21	97⅔	5	5	.500	86	64	50	89	81	4.61
1983—San Francisco	National		5	35⅔	2	2	.500	33	11	10	16	19	2.52
Major League Totals			6	37⅔	2	2	.500	36	14	13	20	21	3.11

Selected by San Francisco Giants' organization in 1st round (15th player selected) of free-agent draft, June 5, 1979.
†On disabled list, July 15 to August 16, 1981.
‡On disabled list, May 12 to June 6 and July 8 to July 24, 1983.

STEVEN PATRICK GARVEY
(Steve)

Born December 22, 1948, at Tampa, Fla.
Height, 5.10. Weight, 190.
Throws and bats righthanded.
Received bachelor of science degree in education from
Michigan State University, East Lansing, Mich. in 1971.

Tied major league records for most seasons leading league in games by first baseman (7); most games, first baseman, season (162), 1976, 1978 and 1979; most unassisted double plays, first baseman, game (2), August 31, 1976; highest fielding percentage by first baseman, season, 100 or more games (.999); most long hits, consecutive, game (5), August 28, 1977; most long hits, game (5), August 28, 1977.

Established National League records for most consecutive years playing in all clubs' games (7); most consecutive games played (1,207); fewest errors, first baseman, season, 1,500 or more total chances (3), 1976; highest fielding average by first baseman, season, 150 or more games (.998), 1976.

Tied National League record for most long hits, consecutive, season (5), August 28, 1977.

Led National League in grounding into double plays with 25 in 1979.

Led National League first basemen in total chances with 1,606 in 1974, 1,585 in 1975, 1,669 in 1977 and 1,629 in 1978.

Led Pacific Coast League third basemen in errors with 24 in 1970.

Led Pioneer League in total bases with 151 and tied for league lead in sacrifice flies with 4 in 1968.

Led Pioneer League third basemen in double plays with 10 in 1968.

Named Most Valuable Player in National League, 1974.

Named first baseman on THE SPORTING NEWS National League All-Star Team, 1974, 1975, 1977 and 1978.

Named first baseman on THE SPORTING NEWS National League All-Star fielding team, 1974, 1975, 1976 and 1977.

Year Club	League	Pos.	G.	AB.	R.	H.	2B.	3B.	HR.	RBI.	B.A.	PO.	A.	E.	F.A.
1968—Ogden	Pion.	3B	62	216	49	73	12	3	★20	★59	.338	★51	★109	★23	.874
1969—Albuquerque	Texas	3B-1B	83	316	51	118	18	2	14	85	.373	348	86	20	.956
1969—Los Angeles	Nat.	PH	3	3	0	1	0	0	0	0	.333	0	0	0	.000
1970—Spokane	P. C.	3B-2B-OF	95	376	71	120	26	5	15	87	.319	103	178	26	.915
1970—Los Angeles	Nat.	3B-2B	34	93	8	25	5	0	1	6	.269	23	59	5	.943
1971—Los Angeles†	Nat.	3B	81	225	27	51	12	1	7	26	.227	53	161	14	.939
1972—Los Angeles	Nat.	★3B-1B	96	294	36	79	14	2	9	30	.269	104	189	★28	.913
1973—Los Angeles	Nat.	1B-OF	114	349	37	106	17	3	8	50	.304	731	27	7	.991
1974—Los Angeles	Nat.	1B	156	642	95	200	32	3	21	111	.312	★1536	62	8	.995
1975—Los Angeles	Nat.	1B	160	659	85	210	38	6	18	95	.319	★1500	77	8	★.995
1976—Los Angeles	Nat.	1B	162	631	85	200	37	4	13	80	.317	★1583	67	3	★.998
1977—Los Angeles	Nat.	1B ●162		646	91	192	25	3	33	115	.297	★1606	55	8	★.995
1978—Los Angeles	Nat.	1B ●162		639	89	★202	36	9	21	113	.316	★1546	74	9	.994
1979—Los Angeles	Nat.	1B	162	648	92	204	32	1	28	110	.315	1402	93	7	.995
1980—Los Angeles	Nat.	1B ★163		658	78	★200	27	1	26	106	.304	1502	112	6	.996
1981—Los Angeles‡	Nat.	1B ●110		431	63	122	23	1	10	64	.283	1019	55	1	★.999
1982—Los Angeles‡	Nat.	1B ●162		625	66	176	35	1	16	86	.282	1539	111	8	.995
1983—San Diego§	Nat.	1B	100	388	76	114	22	0	14	59	.294	888	49	6	.994
Major League Totals			1827	6931	928	2082	355	35	225	1051	.300	15032	1191	118	.993

Selected by Minnesota Twins' organization in 3rd round of free-agent draft, June, 1966.

Selected by Los Angeles Dodgers' organization in secondary phase of free-agent draft, June 7, 1968.

†On disabled list, June 23 to July 26, 1971.

‡Granted free agency, November 10, 1982; signed by San Diego Padres, December 21, 1982.

§On disabled list, July 30, 1983 through remainder of season.

DIVISION SERIES RECORD

Year Club	League	Pos.	G.	AB.	R.	H.	2B.	3B.	HR.	RBI.	B.A.	PO.	A.	E.	F.A.
1981—Los Angeles	Nat.	1B	5	19	4	7	0	1	2	4	.368	49	5	0	1.000

CHAMPIONSHIP SERIES RECORD

Established Championship Series records for most consecutive hits, total Series (6), 1978; most long hits, Series (6), 1978; most home runs, total Series (7); most total bases, four-game Series (22), 1978.

Tied Championship Series records for most home runs, four-game Series (4), 1978; most runs, game (4), October 9, 1974.

Established National League Championship Series records for most runs, four-game Series (6), 1978; most runs batted in, total Series (14); highest slugging average, total Series, 10 or more games and 30 or more at bats (.700).

Tied National League Championship Series records for most consecutive hits, one Series (4); most hits, game (4), October 9, 1974.

Year Club	League	Pos.	G.	AB.	R.	H.	2B.	3B.	HR.	RBI.	B.A.	PO.	A.	E.	F.A.
1974—Los Angeles	Nat.	1B	4	18	4	7	1	0	2	5	.389	40	2	1	.977
1977—Los Angeles	Nat.	1B	4	13	2	4	0	0	0	0	.308	40	1	0	1.000
1978—Los Angeles	Nat.	1B	4	18	6	7	1	1	4	7	.389	44	5	0	1.000
1981—Los Angeles	Nat.	1B	5	21	2	6	0	0	1	2	.286	49	2	0	1.000
Championship Series Totals			17	70	14	24	2	1	7	14	.343	173	10	1	.995

WORLD SERIES RECORD

Tied World Series record for most singles, five-game Series, (8), 1974; one or more hits, each game, five-game Series, 1974.

Year Club	League	Pos.	G.	AB.	R.	H.	2B.	3B.	HR.	RBI.	B.A.	PO.	A.	E.	F.A.
1974—Los Angeles	Nat.	1B	5	21	2	8	0	0	0	1	.381	34	3	0	1.000
1977—Los Angeles	Nat.	1B	6	24	5	9	1	1	1	3	.375	59	6	0	1.000
1978—Los Angeles	Nat.	1B	6	24	1	5	1	0	0	0	.208	58	3	1	.984
1981—Los Angeles	Nat.	1B	6	24	3	10	1	0	0	0	.417	44	3	0	1.000
World Series Totals			23	93	11	32	3	1	1	4	.344	195	15	1	.995

Tied All-Star game record for most games played at first base (8).

Year League	Pos.	AB.	R.	H.	2B.	3B.	HR.	RBI.	B.A.	PO.	A.	E.	F.A.
1974—National	1B	4	1	2	1	0	0	1	.500	6	2	0	1.000
1975—National	1B	3	1	2	0	0	1	1	.667	4	1	0	1.000
1976—National	1B	3	1	1	0	1	0	1	.333	6	0	0	1.000
1977—National	1B	3	1	1	0	0	1	1	.333	1	0	0	1.000
1978—National	1B	3	1	2	0	1	0	2	.667	7	1	0	1.000
1979—National	1B	2	1	0	0	0	0	0	.000	5	0	0	1.000
1980—National	1B	2	0	0	0	0	0	0	.000	7	0	0	1.000
1981—National	1B	2	0	1	1	0	0	0	.500	3	1	0	1.000
All-Star Game Totals		22	6	9	2	2	2	6	.409	39	5	0	1.000

MICHAEL GRANT GATES
(Mike)

Born September 20, 1956, at Culver City, Calif.
Height, 6.01. Weight, 165.
Throws right and bats lefthanded.
Attended Pierce Junior College, Woodland Hills, Calif.,
and Pepperdine University, Malibu, Calif.
Cousin of Jerry Lane, minor league infielder, 1979 through 1981.

Tied for Southern League lead in sacrifice flies with 9 in 1980.

Year Club	League	Pos.	G.	AB.	R.	H.	2B.	3B.	HR.	RBI.	B.A.	PO.	A.	E.	F.A.
1979—W. P. Beach	Fla. St.	2B-SS	78	289	44	82	9	3	0	27	.284	131	228	20	.947
1980—Memphis	South.	2B-3B-SS	143	538	87	137	18	6	5	67	.255	338	402	20	.974
1981—Denver	A. A.	2B-3B	127	498	91	154	★36	4	3	57	.309	222	259	12	.976
1981—Montreal	Nat.	2B	1	2	1	1	0	1	0	1	.500	0	1	0	1.000
1982—Wichita†	A. A.	2B-3B	64	248	52	82	8	5	6	35	.331	129	156	8	.973
1982—Montreal	Nat.	2B	36	121	16	28	2	3	0	8	.231	53	91	0	1.000
1983—Wichita	A. A.	2B-3B-SS	126	431	69	118	24	2	4	43	.274	165	264	12	.973
Major League Totals			37	123	17	29	2	4	0	9	.236	53	92	0	1.000

Selected by Montreal Expos' organization in 7th round of free-agent draft, June 5, 1979.
†On disabled list, August 21, 1982 through remainder of season.

RICHARD LEO GEDMAN
(Rich)

Born September 26, 1959, at Worcester, Mass.
Height, 6.00. Weight, 210.
Throws right and bats lefthanded.

Led International League catchers in double plays with 13 in 1980.
Named American League Rookie Player of the Year by THE SPORTING NEWS, 1981.

Year Club	League	Pos.	G.	AB.	R.	H.	2B.	3B.	HR.	RBI.	B.A.	PO.	A.	E.	F.A.
1978—Winter Haven	Fla. St.	C	98	297	35	89	17	3	3	32	.300	377	39	2	★.995
1979—Bristol	East.	C	130	470	48	129	25	1	12	63	.274	497	58	11	★.981
1980—Pawtucket	Int.	C	111	347	43	82	18	2	11	29	.236	367	★65	7	.984
1980—Boston	Amer.	C	9	24	2	5	0	0	0	1	.208	13	0	2	.867
1981—Pawtucket	Int.	C	25	81	8	24	3	0	2	11	.296	176	20	6	.969
1981—Boston	Amer.	C	62	205	22	59	15	0	5	26	.288	275	30	3	.990
1982—Boston	Amer.	C	92	289	30	72	17	2	4	26	.249	397	29	10	.977
1983—Boston	Amer.	C	81	204	21	60	16	1	2	18	.294	274	26	6	.980
Major League Totals			244	722	75	196	48	3	11	71	.271	959	85	21	.980

Signed as free agent by Boston Red Sox' organization, August 5, 1977.

JOHN DAVID GEISEL

Name pronounced GUY-sul.

(Dave)

Born January 18, 1955, at Windber, Pa.
Height, 6.03. Weight, 210.
Throws and bats lefthanded.

Year Club	League	G.	IP.	W.	L.	Pct.	H.	R.	ER.	SO.	BB.	ERA.
1974—Midland	Texas	24	150	12	7	.632	170	72	63	92	37	3.78
1975—Midland	Texas	35	132	8	5	.615	149	67	59	75	44	4.02
1976—Midland	Texas	20	107	5	8	.385	114	59	44	59	45	3.70
1976—Wichita	Am. Assoc.	9	50	2	4	.333	50	33	28	27	25	5.04
1977—Wichita†	Am. Assoc.	28	94	4	6	.400	95	49	46	57	62	4.40
1978—Wichita	Am. Assoc.	19	107	6	9	.400	102	68	59	62	65	4.96
1978—Chicago	National	18	23	1	0	1.000	27	12	11	15	11	4.30
1979—Wichita‡	Am. Assoc.	45	79	5	5	.500	76	29	22	49	47	2.51
1979—Chicago	National	7	15	0	0	.000	10	1	1	5	4	0.60
1980—Wichita§	Am. Assoc.	9	15	1	0	1.000	14	12	11	17	13	6.60
1981—Iowa x	Am. Assoc.	28	38	1	2	.333	38	24	19	43	31	4.50
1981—Chicago y	National	11	16	2	0	1.000	11	3	1	7	10	0.56
1982—Syracuse	Int'national	21	80⅔	4	2	.667	74	38	35	43	38	3.90

Year Club	League	G.	IP.	W.	L.	Pct.	H.	R.	ER.	SO.	BB.	ERA.
1982—Toronto	American	16	31⅔	1	1	.500	32	15	14	22	17	3.98
1983—Toronto z	American	47	52⅓	0	3	.000	47	28	27	50	31	4.64
National League Totals		36	54	3	0	1.000	48	16	13	27	25	2.17
American League Totals		63	84	1	4	.200	79	43	41	72	48	4.39
Major League Totals		99	138	4	4	.500	127	59	54	99	73	3.52

Selected by Chicago Cubs' organization in 5th round of free-agent draft, June 5, 1973.

†On disabled list, April 15 to May 6, 1977.

‡On disabled list, June 17 to June 28, 1979.

§On disabled list, April 14 to July 29, 1980.

xOn temporarily inactive list, April 14 to May 28, 1981.

yTraded to Toronto Blue Jays' organization, March 25, 1982, completing deal in which Toronto traded Pitcher Paul Mirabella to Chicago Cubs' organization for a player to be named later, December 28, 1981.

zDrafted by Seattle Mariners, December 5, 1983.

ROBERT P. GEREN III
(Bob)

Born September 22, 1961, at San Diego, Calif.

Height, 6.03. Weight, 205.

Throws and bats righthanded.

Led Midwest League catchers in putouts with 826, assists with 102 and total chances with 939 in 1983.

Year Club	League	Pos.	G.	AB.	R.	H.	2B.	3B.	HR.	RBI.	B.A.	PO.	A.	E.	F.A.
1979—Walla Walla	N'west	C	54	151	19	26	5	0	0	16	.172	183	23	9	.958
1980—Reno	Calif.	C	48	157	24	45	7	1	4	23	.287	89	17	4	.964
1980—Walla Walla†	N'west	C	51	177	19	45	8	1	2	28	.254	306	40	10	.972
1981—St. Petersburg	Fla. St.	C	64	167	15	37	9	1	0	13	.222	204	24	3	.987
1982—St. Petersburg	Fla.St.	*C-OF-1B	110	352	38	86	24	1	1	45	.244	500	*72	10	.983
1983—Springfield	Midw.	C-1B	124	434	67	115	21	3	24	73	.265	829	104	11	.988

Selected by San Diego Padres' organization in 1st round (24th player selected) of free-agent draft, June 5, 1979.

†Traded to St. Louis Cardinals' organization, December 10, 1980, completing deal in which San Diego Padres traded Pitchers Rollie Fingers and Bob Shirley, Catcher-First Baseman Gene Tenace and a player to be named later to St. Louis Cardinals for Catchers Terry Kennedy and Steve Swisher, Pitchers John Littlefield, Al Olmsted, Kim Seaman and John Urrea and Infielder Mike Phillips, December 8, 1980.

CESAR FRANCISCO GERONIMO

Name pronounced Juh-RON-uh-moh.

Born March 11, 1948, at El Seibo, Dominican Republic.

Height, 6.02. Weight, 175.

Throws and bats lefthanded.

Led National League outfielders in total chances with 423 and double plays with 5 in 1975.

Named as outfielder on THE SPORTING NEWS National League All-Star fielding team, 1974, 1975, 1976 and 1977.

Year Club	League	Pos.	G.	AB.	R.	H.	2B.	3B.	HR.	RBI.	B.A.	PO.	A.	E.	F.A.
1967—Oneonta†	NYP	OF	4	10	1	1	0	0	0	1	.100	2	0	1	.667
1967—Johnson City	Appal.	OF-P	18	14	1	1	0	0	0	0	.071	5	1	0	1.000
1968—Ft. Lauderdale‡	Fla. St.	OF	109	324	35	63	11	5	1	27	.194	186	17	4	.981
1969—Houston	Nat.	OF	28	8	8	2	1	0	0	0	.250	1	0	0	1.000
1970—Columbus	South.	OF	74	264	26	71	9	4	0	21	.269	113	8	2	.984
1970—Houston	Nat.	OF	47	37	5	9	0	0	0	2	.243	23	0	2	.920
1971—Houston§	Nat.	OF	94	82	13	18	2	2	1	6	.220	42	1	1	.977
1972—Cincinnati	Nat.	OF	120	255	32	70	9	7	4	29	.275	150	10	3	.982
1973—Cincinnati	Nat.	OF	139	324	35	68	14	3	4	33	.210	243	9	2	.992
1974—Cincinnati	Nat.	OF	150	474	73	133	17	8	7	54	.281	355	13	5	.987
1975—Cincinnati	Nat.	OF	148	501	69	129	25	5	6	53	.257	*408	12	3	.993
1976—Cincinnati	Nat.	OF	149	486	59	149	24	11	2	49	.307	386	4	6	.985
1977—Cincinnati	Nat.	OF	149	492	54	131	22	4	10	52	.266	375	9	3	.992
1978—Cincinnati	Nat.	OF	122	296	28	67	15	1	5	27	.226	259	4	5	.981
1979—Cincinnati	Nat.	OF	123	356	38	85	17	4	4	38	.239	291	11	2	.993
1980—Cincinnati x	Nat.	OF	103	145	16	37	5	0	2	9	.255	110	2	0	1.000
1981—Kansas City y	Amer.	OF	59	118	14	29	0	2	2	13	.246	96	1	2	.980
1982—Kansas City z	Amer.	OF	53	119	14	32	6	3	4	23	.269	93	3	0	1.000
1983—Kansas City ab	Amer.	OF	38	87	2	18	4	0	0	4	.207	69	2	1	.986
National League Totals			1372	3456	430	898	151	45	45	352	.260	2643	75	32	.988
American League Totals			150	324	30	79	10	5	6	40	.244	258	6	3	.989
Major League Totals			1522	3780	460	977	161	50	51	392	.258	2901	81	35	.988

Signed as free agent by New York Yankees' organization, February 23, 1967.

†On disabled list, April 17 to June 20, 1967.

‡Drafted by Houston Astros, December 2, 1968.

§Traded with Second Baseman Joe Morgan, Infielder Denis Menke, Pitcher Jack Billingham and Outfielder Ed Armbrister to Cincinnati Reds for First Baseman Lee May, Second Baseman Tommy Helms and Infielder Jim Stewart, November 29, 1971.

xTraded to Kansas City Royals for Infielder German Barranca, January 21, 1981.

yGranted free agency, November 13, 1981; re-signed by Royals, December 11, 1981.

zOn supplemental disabled list, June 27 to July 21, 1982.

aOn supplemental disabled list, July 28 to August 15, 1983.

bReleased, October 11, 1983.

Year	Club	League	Pos.	G.	AB.	R.	H.	2B.	3B.	HR.	RBI.	B.A.	PO.	A.	E.	F.A.
1981—Kansas City		Amer.	PR	1	0	0	0	0	0	0	0	.000	0	0	0	.000

CHAMPIONSHIP SERIES RECORD

Established Championship Series records for most consecutive strikeouts, one Series, consecutive at-bats (7), 1975; most consecutive strikeouts, one Series, consecutive plate appearances (5), 1975.

Tied Championship Series records for most strikeouts, three-game Series (7), 1975; most strikeouts, five-game Series (7), 1973.

Established National League Championship Series records for most consecutive hitless times at-bat, total Series (30); most strikeouts, total Series (24).

Year	Club	League	Pos.	G.	AB.	R.	H.	2B.	3B.	HR.	RBI.	B.A.	PO.	A.	E.	F.A.
1972—Cincinnati		Nat.	OF	5	20	2	2	0	0	1	1	.100	11	1	0	1.000
1973—Cincinnati		Nat.	OF	4	15	0	1	0	0	0	0	.067	11	1	0	1.000
1975—Cincinnati		Nat.	OF	3	10	0	0	0	0	0	1	.000	13	0	0	1.000
1976—Cincinnati		Nat.	OF	3	11	0	2	0	1	0	2	.182	10	0	0	1.000
1979—Cincinnati		Nat.	OF	2	7	0	1	0	0	0	0	.143	8	0	1	.889
Championship Series Totals				17	63	2	6	0	1	1	4	.095	53	2	1	.982

WORLD SERIES RECORD

Tied World Series record for highest fielding average by outfielder, seven-game Series (1.000, with 24 chances), 1975; most stolen bases, four-game Series (2), 1976.

Year	Club	League	Pos.	G.	AB.	R.	H.	2B.	3B.	HR.	RBI.	B.A.	PO.	A.	E.	F.A.
1972—Cincinnati		Nat.	OF	7	19	1	3	0	0	0	3	.158	9	0	0	1.000
1975—Cincinnati		Nat.	OF	7	25	3	7	0	1	2	3	.280	23	1	0	1.000
1976—Cincinnati		Nat.	OF	4	13	3	4	2	0	0	1	.308	12	0	1	.923
World Series Totals				18	57	7	14	2	1	2	7	.246	44	1	1	.978

PITCHING RECORD

Year	Club	League	G.	IP.	W.	L.	Pct.	H.	R.	ER.	SO.	BB.	ERA.
1967—Johnson City		Ap'lachian	1	2	0	0	.000	3	4	2	1	2	9.00

ANTHONY PAUL GHELFI

Named pronounced GEL-fee.

(Tony)

Born August 23, 1961, at La Crosse, Wis.
Height, 6.02. Weight, 185.
Throws and bats righthanded.
Attended Iowa Western Community College, Clarinda, Ia.
Son of Dick Ghelfi, minor league pitcher, 1952 through 1956.

Year	Club	League	G.	IP.	W.	L.	Pct.	H.	R.	ER.	SO.	BB.	ERA.
1980—Helena		Pioneer	12	61	3	2	.600	74	41	31	43	17	4.57
1981—Spartanburg		S. Atlantic	27	164	10	11	.476	165	85	56	108	55	3.07
1982—Peninsula		Carolina	25	160⅓	12	6	.667	147	70	47	★162	60	2.64
1983—Portland		P. Coast	8	32	1	2	.333	45	25	22	28	21	6.19
1983—Reading		Eastern	16	110	10	3	.769	99	48	45	96	42	3.68
1983—Philadelphia		National	3	14⅓	1	1	.500	15	5	5	14	6	3.14
Major League Totals			3	14⅓	1	1	.500	15	5	5	14	6	3.14

Selected by Philadelphia Phillies' organization in 1st round (14th player selected) of free-agent draft, January 8, 1980.

JOHN MICHAEL GIBBONS

Born June 8, 1962, at Great Falls, Mont.
Height, 5.11. Weight, 185.
Throws and bats righthanded.

Tied for Appalachian League lead in being hit by pitch with 7 in 1980.
Led South Atlantic League catchers in double plays with 8 in 1982.
Tied for Appalachian League lead in passed balls with 11 in 1980.

Year	Club	League	Pos.	G.	AB.	R.	H.	2B.	3B.	HR.	RBI.	B.A.	PO.	A.	E.	F.A.
1980—Kingsport		Appal.	C	53	181	28	50	7	1	7	34	.276	177	11	7	.964
1981—Shelby		S. Atl.	C	109	360	33	68	11	4	8	57	.189	629	65	18	.975
1982—Shelby		S. Atl.	C-1B	99	321	60	85	13	2	12	67	.265	559	72	17	.974
1982—Jackson		Texas	C	6	18	1	5	0	1	0	3	.278	21	1	0	1.000
1983—Jackson		Texas	C	110	373	63	111	25	1	18	67	.298	575	62	12	.982

Selected by New York Mets' organization in 1st round (24th player selected) of free-agent draft, June 3, 1980.

KIRK HAROLD GIBSON

Born May 28, 1957, at Pontiac, Mich.
Height, 6.03. Weight, 210.
Throws and bats lefthanded.
Attended Michigan State University, East Lansing, Mich.

Named as wide receiver on THE SPORTING NEWS College Football All-America Team, 1978.
Selected by St. Louis Cardinals in 7th round of 1979 NFL draft.
Received reported $200,000 bonus to sign with Detroit Tigers, 1978.

Year	Club	League	Pos.	G.	AB.	R.	H.	2B.	3B.	HR.	RBI.	B.A.	PO.	A.	E.	F.A.
1978—Lakeland†	....	Fla. St.	OF	54	175	27	42	5	4	8	40	.240	115	2	6	.951
1979—Evansville‡	....	A. A.	OF	89	327	50	80	13	5	9	42	.245	100	5	9	.921
1979—Detroit	....	Amer.	OF	12	38	3	9	3	0	1	4	.237	15	0	0	1.000
1980—Detroit§	....	Amer.	OF	51	175	23	46	2	1	9	16	.263	122	1	1	.992
1981—Detroit	....	Amer.	OF	83	290	41	95	11	3	9	40	.328	142	1	4	.973
1982—Detroit x	....	Amer.	OF	69	266	34	74	16	2	8	35	.278	167	4	1	.994
1983—Detroit	....	Amer.	OF	128	401	60	91	12	9	15	51	.227	116	2	3	.975
Major League Totals	....			343	1170	161	315	44	15	42	146	.269	562	8	9	.984

Selected by Detroit Tigers' organization in 1st round (12th player selected) of free-agent draft, June 6, 1978.
†On restricted list, August 15, 1978, to March 1, 1979.
‡On disabled list, April 13 to May 21, 1979.
§On supplemental disabled list, June 18 to October 6, 1980.
xOn supplemental disabled list, July 11, 1982 through remainder of season.

ROBERT LOUIS GIBSON
(Bob)

Born June 19, 1957, at Philadelphia, Pa.
Height, 6.00. Weight, 195.
Throws and bats righthanded.

Year	Club	League	G.	IP.	W.	L.	Pct.	H.	R.	ER.	SO.	BB.	ERA.
1979—Burlington	....	Midwest	25	137	5	12	.294	152	99	84	111	81	5.52
1980—Stockton	....	California	33	67	6	3	.667	45	32	29	59	58	3.90
1981—Stockton	....	California	49	66	6	8	.429	61	31	22	67	38	3.00
1982—El Paso	....	Texas	47	66⅓	6	2	.750	55	23	16	66	39	2.17
1982—Vancouver	....	P. Coast	6	8	1	1	.500	3	2	1	6	10	1.13
1983—Milwaukee	....	American	27	80⅔	3	4	.429	71	40	35	46	46	3.90
Major League Totals	....		27	80⅔	3	4	.429	71	40	35	46	46	3.90

Signed as free agent by Milwaukee Brewers' organization, March 7, 1979.

BRIAN JEFFREY GILES

Born April 27, 1960, at Manhattan, Kan.
Height, 6.01. Weight, 165.
Throws and bats righthanded.
Grandson of George F. Giles, first baseman in Negro National and American Leagues,
1927 through 1938; son of George F. Giles, Jr., minor league infielder, 1953 through 1955.

Year	Club	League	Pos.	G.	AB.	R.	H.	2B.	3B.	HR.	RBI.	B.A.	PO.	A.	E.	F.A.
1978—Little Falls	....	NYP	2B	61	195	36	44	5	5	4	21	.226	★135	144	16	.946
1979—Lynchburg†	....	Carol.	2B	86	278	40	83	16	2	2	33	.299	180	271	13	.972
1980—Jackson	....	Texas	2B	132	448	76	128	30	8	10	57	.286	291	325	26	.960
1981—Tidewater	....	Int.	2B-SS	121	400	60	107	17	3	7	40	.268	267	384	24	.964
1981—New York	....	Nat.	SS-2B	9	7	0	0	0	0	0	0	.000	5	8	0	1.000
1982—Tidewater	....	Int.	2B-SS	108	352	48	98	32	4	11	54	.278	240	354	17	.972
1982—New York	....	Nat.	2B-SS	45	138	14	29	5	0	3	10	.210	122	133	2	.992
1983—New York	....	Nat.	2B-SS	145	400	39	98	15	0	2	27	.245	309	390	14	.980
Major League Totals	....			199	545	53	127	20	0	5	37	.233	436	531	16	.984

Selected by New York Mets' organization in 2nd round of free-agent draft, June 6, 1978.
†On disabled list, July 10 to August 11, 1979.

MICHAEL DANA GIORDANO
(Mike)

Born August 12, 1959, at Neubruke, West Germany.
Height, 6.00. Weight, 180.
Throws and bats righthanded.
Received degree in communications from University of New Haven, New Haven, Conn., in 1981.

Year	Club	League	G.	IP.	W.	L.	Pct.	H.	R.	ER.	SO.	BB.	ERA.
1981—Wisconsin Rapids	....	Midwest	15	70	4	3	.571	78	28	24	56	14	3.09
1982—Visalia	....	California	50	92⅓	6	6	.500	52	22	17	57	26	1.66
1983—Orlando	....	Southern	31	43	3	2	.600	33	6	5	29	13	1.05
1983—Toledo	....	Int'national	16	19	1	2	.333	20	13	11	10	14	5.21

Selected by Minnesota Twins' organization in 20th round of free-agent draft, June 8, 1981.

CLINTON DANIEL GLADDEN III
(Dan)

Born July 7, 1957, at San Jose, Calif.
Height, 5.11. Weight, 180.
Throws right and bats left and righthanded.
Attended DeAnza College, Cupertino, Calif., and
Fresno State University, Fresno, Calif.
Brother of Jeff Gladden, pitcher in San Francisco Giants' organization.

Led Texas League in stolen bases with 52 and caught stealing with 26 in 1981.

Year	Club	League	Pos.	G.	AB.	R.	H.	2B.	3B.	HR.	RBI.	B.A.	PO.	A.	E.	F.A.
1979—Fresno	....	Calif.	OF-2B-SS	60	228	41	70	9	1	3	31	.307	56	16	3	.960
1980—Fresno	....	Calif.	OF	62	237	46	72	10	2	9	41	.304	68	3	1	.986

Year	Club	League	Pos.	G.	AB.	R.	H.	2B.	3B.	HR.	RBI.	B.A.	PO.	A.	E.	F.A.
1980—Shreveport	Texas	OF-SS	74	292	51	86	11	2	9	35	.295	169	14	5	.973
1981—Shreveport	Texas	OF-SS-2B	124	472	81	148	23	9	8	44	.314	211	12	3	.987
1982—Phoenix	P. C.	OF	130	503	93	155	40	5	10	74	.308	264	16	7	.976
1983—Phoenix	P. C.	OF	127	505	113	153	30	9	12	80	.303	319	6	7	.979
1983—San Francisco	Nat.	OF	18	63	6	14	2	0	1	9	.222	53	0	0	1.000
Major League Totals			18	63	6	14	2	0	1	9	.222	53	0	0	1.000

Signed as free agent by San Francisco Giants' organization, June 17, 1979.

TIMOTHY JAMES GLASS
(Tim)

Born April 23, 1958, at Springfield, O.
Height, 6.02. Weight, 215.
Throws and bats righthanded.
Nephew of Don Glass, former member of Baltimore Orioles' organization, 1955.

Led new York-Pennsylvania League batters in strikeouts with 84 in 1977.
Tied for Eastern League lead in passed balls with 14 in 1983.
Received reported $40,000 bonus to sign with Cleveland Indians, 1976.

Year	Club	League	Pos.	G.	AB.	R.	H.	2B.	3B.	HR.	RBI.	B.A.	PO.	A.	E.	F.A.
1976—Batavia	NYP	C	41	103	15	17	5	0	1	7	.165	146	4	6	.962
1977—Waterloo	Midw.	C	1	0	0	0	0	0	0	0	.000	2	0	0	1.000
1977—Batavia	NYP	C	66	209	43	53	7	2	*21	55	.254	324	26	3	.992
1978—Waterloo†	Midw.	C	53	158	23	27	5	0	5	17	.171	263	19	5	.983
1979—Waterloo	Midw.	C	98	314	50	77	9	0	14	52	.245	491	28	14	.974
1980—Waterloo	Midw.	C-1B	96	236	43	59	15	1	16	33	.250	294	17	9	.972
1981—Chattanooga‡	South.	1B-C	62	189	28	41	6	1	10	25	.217	27	2	2	.935
1982—Chattanooga	South	C-1B	137	480	68	127	21	5	20	88	.265	262	7	9	.968
1983—Buffalo	East.	C-1B	118	395	58	101	18	0	16	61	.256	437	25	6	.987

Selected by Cleveland Indians' organization in 1st round (14th player selected) of free-agent draft, June 8, 1976
†On disabled list, May 18 to July 12, 1978.
‡On disabled list, July 4, 1981 through remainder of season.

JERRY DON GLEATON

Born September 14, 1957, at Brownwood, Tex.
Height, 6.03. Weight, 210.
Throws and bats lefthanded.
Attended University of Texas, Austin, Tex.

Tied for Eastern League lead in complete games with 13 in 1982.
Tied for Texas League lead in home runs allowed with 17 in 1980.

Year	Club	League	G.	IP.	W.	L.	Pct.	H.	R.	ER.	SO.	BB.	ERA.
1979—Tulsa	Texas	5	35	3	2	.600	37	19	19	21	15	4.89
1979—Texas	American	5	10	0	1	.000	15	7	7	2	2	6.30
1980—Tulsa	Texas	25	178	13	7	.650	179	83	72	138	68	3.64
1980—Texas†	American	5	7	0	0	.000	5	2	2	2	4	2.57
1981—Seattle	American	20	85	4	7	.364	88	50	45	31	38	4.76
1981—Spokane	P. Coast	13	91	5	7	.417	104	53	42	57	39	4.15
1982—Lynn	Eastern	24	182	15	7	.682	175	71	55	132	54	2.72
1982—Seattle	American	3	4⅔	0	0	.000	7	7	7	1	2	13.50
1983—Salt Lake City	P. Coast	24	137⅓	9	9	.500	189	112	102	73	81	6.68
Major League Totals		33	106⅔	4	8	.333	115	66	61	36	46	5.15

Selected by Baltimore Orioles' organization in 2nd round of free-agent draft, June 8, 1976.
Selected by Texas Rangers' organization in 1st round (17th player selected) of free-agent draft, June 5, 1979.
†Traded with Pitchers Brian Allard, Ken Clay and Steve Finch, Shortstop Rick Auerbach and Outfielder Richie Zisk to Seattle Mariners for Catcher Larry Cox, Pitcher Rick Honeycutt, Outfielders Willie Horton and Leon Roberts and Shortstop Mario Mendoza, December 12, 1980.

EDWARD PAUL GLYNN
(Ed)

Born June 3, 1953, at Flushing, N. Y.
Height, 6.02. Weight, 180.
Throws left and bats righthanded.
Attended York College, Jamaica, N. Y.

Pitched seven-inning, 3-0 no-hit victory against Iowa, July 15, 1976.
Led American Association in intentional bases on balls issued with 11 in 1978.
Tied for American Association lead in balks with 4 in 1977.

Year	Club	League	G.	IP.	W.	L.	Pct.	H.	R.	ER.	SO.	BB.	ERA.
1972—Lakeland	Florida St.	15	57	1	4	.200	52	30	28	54	50	4.42
1972—Bristol	Ap'alachian	11	57	4	2	.667	38	35	30	67	46	4.74
1973—Clinton	Midwest	24	135	9	6	.600	109	71	68	130	84	4.53
1974—Clinton	Midwest	15	114	8	4	.667	104	46	38	104	46	3.00
1974—Montgomery	Southern	9	49	1	4	.200	60	44	30	31	29	5.51
1975—Montgomery	Southern	19	127	10	5	.667	116	50	44	66	72	3.12
1975—Evansville	Am. Assoc.	7	40	1	2	.333	40	18	11	23	19	2.48
1975—Detroit	American	3	15	0	2	.000	11	8	7	8	8	4.20
1976—Evansville	Am. Assoc.	24	148	9	7	.563	146	76	59	92	82	3.59

Year Club	League	G.	IP.	W.	L.	Pct.	H.	R.	ER.	SO.	BB.	ERA.
1976—Detroit	American	5	24	1	3	.250	22	18	16	17	20	6.00
1977—Evansville	Am. Assoc.	28	156	6	8	.429	163	97	86	125	71	4.96
1977—Detroit	American	8	27	2	1	.667	36	17	16	13	12	5.33
1978—Evansville	Am. Assoc.	27	38	3	2	.600	32	14	14	28	32	3.32
1978—Detroit†	American	10	15	0	0	.000	11	5	5	9	4	3.00
1979—Tidewater	Int'national	17	29	0	1	.000	22	10	7	16	9	2.17
1979—New York	National	46	60	1	4	.200	57	22	20	32	40	3.00
1980—New York‡§	National	38	52	3	3	.500	49	26	24	32	23	4.15
1981—Charleston	Int'national	42	71	4	6	.400	50	34	28	70	42	3.55
1981—Cleveland	American	4	8	0	0	.000	5	1	1	4	4	1.13
1982—Charleston	Int'national	7	9⅔	3	1	.750	7	5	5	17	2	4.66
1982—Cleveland	American	47	49⅔	5	2	.714	43	27	23	54	30	4.17
1983—Cleveland	American	11	12⅓	0	2	.000	22	11	8	13	6	5.84
1983—Charleston	Int'national	37	47	3	5	.375	43	30	26	51	28	4.98
American League Totals		88	151	8	10	.444	150	87	76	118	84	4.53
National League Totals		84	112	4	7	.364	106	48	44	64	63	3.54
Major League Totals		172	263	12	17	.414	256	135	120	182	147	4.11

Signed as free agent by Detroit Tigers' organization, September 25, 1971.
†Traded to New York Mets for Pitcher Mardie Cornejo, March 13, 1979.
‡On disabled list, August 16 to September 6, 1980.
§Traded to Cleveland Indians' organization for a player to be named later, April 6, 1981; New York Mets' organization acquired Pitcher Dominick Bullinger to complete deal, December 14, 1981.

DAVID ALLAN GOLTZ
(Dave)

Born June 23, 1949, at Pelican Rapids, Minn.
Height, 6.04. Weight, 215.
Throws and bats righthanded.
Attended Moorhead State College, Moorhead, Minn.

Pitched seven-inning, 5-0 no-hit victory against Burlington, August 26, 1971.
Led American League in wild pitches with 15 in 1976.
Tied for American League lead in games started by pitchers with 39 in 1977.
Led Northern League in complete games with 12 and tied for lead in games started by pitchers with 16 and balks with 1 in 1968.

Year Club	League	G.	IP.	W.	L.	Pct.	H.	R.	ER.	SO.	BB.	ERA.
1967—Sarasota Twins	Gulf Coast	12	72	●6	2	●.750	63	23	16	51	14	★2.00
1968—St. Cloud	Northern	16	★123	10	3	.769	103	39	22	★122	29	1.61
1969—Minnesota	American					(In Military Service)						
1970—Charlotte†	Southern	1	2	0	1	.000	1	1	0	2	1	0.00
1970—Orlando	Florida St.	1	6	0	1	.000	3	4	4	2	6	6.00
1971—Orlando	Florida St.	7	53	7	0	1.000	49	16	13	34	16	2.21
1971—Lynchburg	Carolina	13	87	7	3	.700	76	37	32	64	32	3.31
1972—Tacoma	P. Coast	19	118	8	8	.500	131	65	51	99	42	3.89
1972—Minnesota	American	15	91	3	3	.500	75	30	27	38	26	2.67
1973—Minnesota	American	32	106	6	4	.600	138	68	62	65	32	5.26
1974—Tacoma	P. Coast	4	30	3	1	.750	25	13	11	26	15	3.30
1974—Minnesota	American	28	174	10	10	.500	192	81	63	89	45	3.26
1975—Minnesota	American	32	243	14	14	.500	235	112	99	128	72	3.67
1976—Minnesota	American	36	249	14	14	.500	239	113	93	133	91	3.36
1977—Minnesota	American	39	303	●20	11	.645	●284	129	113	186	91	3.36
1978—Minnesota	American	29	220	15	10	.600	209	72	61	116	67	2.50
1979—Minnesota‡	American	36	251	14	13	.519	★282	124	116	132	69	4.16
1980—Los Angeles	National	35	171	7	11	.389	198	91	82	91	59	4.32
1981—Los Angeles §	National	26	77	2	7	.222	83	35	35	48	25	4.09
1982—Los Angeles§	National	2	3⅔	0	1	.000	6	4	2	3	0	4.91
1982—California x	American	28	86	8	5	.615	82	43	39	49	32	4.08
1983—California y	American	15	63⅔	0	6	.000	81	48	44	27	37	6.22
American League Totals		290	1786⅔	104	90	.536	1817	820	717	963	562	3.61
National League Totals		63	251⅔	9	19	.321	287	130	119	142	84	4.26
Major League Totals		353	2038⅓	113	109	.509	2104	950	836	1105	646	3.69

Selected by Minnesota Twins' organization in 17th round of free-agent draft, June 6, 1967.
†On disabled list, May 26 to June 6 and June 15 to July 13, 1970.
‡Granted free agency, November 1, 1979; signed by Los Angeles Dodgers, November 14, 1979.
§Released, April 27, 1982; signed by California Angels, May 24, 1982.
xOn disabled list, August 26 to September 16, 1982.
yReleased, July 6, 1983.

CHAMPIONSHIP SERIES RECORD

Year Club	League	G.	IP.	W.	L.	Pct.	H.	R.	ER.	SO.	BB.	ERA.
1982—California	American	1	3⅔	0	0	.000	4	3	3	2	2	7.36

WORLD SERIES RECORD

Year Club	League	G.	IP.	W.	L.	Pct.	H.	R.	ER.	SO.	BB.	ERA.
1981—Los Angeles	National	2	3⅓	0	0	.000	4	2	2	2	1	5.40

JOSE SIMON GOMEZ

Born December 19, 1962, at Santiago, Dominican Republic.
Height, 6.03. Weight, 195.
Throws and bats lefthanded.
Brother of Nelson Gomez, outfielder in California Angels' organization.
Led Northwest League first basemen in double plays with 48 in 1982.

Year Club	League	Pos.	G.	AB.	R.	H.	2B.	3B.	HR.	RBI.	B.A.	PO.	A.	E.	F.A.
1980—Grays Harbor†	N'west	OF	28	55	9	13	1	1	0	7	.236	10	2	2	.857
1981—Salem	Carol.	1B	17	32	4	4	1	0	2	5	.125	41	2	3	.935
1981—Brad'ton Padres ..	Gulf C.	1B	61	200	34	58	●14	2	4	35	.290	450	16	10	.979
1982—Reno	Calif.	1B	49	171	23	42	7	3	3	26	.246	363	14	8	.979
1982—Walla Walla	N'west	1B	64	196	42	69	16	1	8	39	.352	511	31	11	.980
1983—Miami	Fla. St.	1B	51	167	26	49	15	2	3	27	.293	437	11	9	.980
1983—Salem	Carol.	1B	71	231	40	60	7	1	8	38	.260	535	37	★13	.978

Signed as free agent by San Diego Padres' organization, March 14, 1980.
†Loaned to Grays Harbor (New York Mets' organization), June 16, 1980; returned, September 30, 1980.

RANDALL SCOTT GOMEZ
(Randy)

Born February 4, 1958, at San Mateo, Calif.
Height, 5.09. Weight, 180.
Throws and bats righthanded.
Attended College of San Mateo, San Mateo, Calif., and
University of Utah, Salt Lake City, Utah.
Led Texas League in grounding into double plays with 23 in 1983.
Led Texas League catchers in total chances with 812 and stealers caught with 62 in 1983.
Led Pioneer League catchers in total chances with 497 in 1980.

Year Club	League	Pos.	G.	AB.	R.	H.	2B.	3B.	HR.	RBI.	B.A.	PO.	A.	E.	F.A.
1980—Great Falls...........	Pion.	C	66	241	63	87	14	4	8	53	.361	★447	★42	8	.984
1981—Fresno†	Calif.	C-3B	105	399	59	122	14	4	3	43	.306	518	82	23	.963
1982—Shreveport	Texas	C-3B	84	274	33	72	15	1	2	25	.263	380	58	10	.978
1983—Shreveport	Texas	C	119	418	57	116	18	1	5	48	.278	★699	★98	15	.982

Selected by Cincinnati Reds' organization in 13th round of free-agent draft, June 5, 1979.
Selected by San Francisco Giants' organization in 24th round of free-agent draft, June 3, 1980.
†On disabled list, July 17 to August 7, 1981.

DENIO MARIANO GONZALEZ (MANZUETA)
(Denny)

Born July 22, 1963, at Sabana Grande Boya, D.R.
Height 5.11. Weight, 165.
Throws and bats righthanded.

Year Club	League	Pos.	G.	AB.	R.	H.	2B.	3B.	HR.	RBI.	B.A.	PO.	A.	E.	F.A.
1981—Bradenton Pir.	Gulf C.	2B-3B	50	179	32	62	5	3	2	24	.346	102	113	14	.939
1982—Portland................	P. C.	2B-3B	51	164	23	37	4	6	0	9	.226	106	133	20	.923
1982—Buffalo..................	East.	2B	68	252	28	70	5	4	3	21	.278	137	176	11	.966
1983—Hawaii...................	P. C.	SS-2B	125	449	76	121	18	8	9	48	.269	193	319	34	.938

Signed as free agent by Pittsburgh Pirates' organization, June 25, 1981.

JOSE ALTA GONZALEZ (URIBE)

Born January 21, 1959, at San Cristobal, D.R.
Height, 5.10. Weight, 156.
Throws right and bats left and righthanded.
Led American Association shortstops in total chances with 664 and double plays with 90 in 1983.
Led Texas League shortstops in double plays with 88 in 1982.

Year Club	League	Pos.	G.	AB.	R.	H.	2B.	3B.	HR.	RBI.	B.A.	PO.	A.	E.	F.A.
1981—St. Petersburg†	Fla. St.	SS	128	463	54	124	15	2	0	40	.268	171	★387	32	.946
1982—Arkansas...............	Texas	SS	123	465	73	115	17	7	0	41	.247	185	385	36	.941
1982—Louisville	A. A.	SS	8	28	5	10	2	0	0	4	.357	15	18	1	.971
1983—Louisville	A. A.	SS	122	423	64	120	19	6	3	44	.284	206	425	★33	.950

Signed as free agent by New York Yankees' organization, February 18, 1977.
†Released, July 5, 1977; signed by St. Louis Cardinals' organization, August 18, 1980.

JOSE RAFAEL GONZALEZ

Born November 23, 1964, at Puerto Plata, Dominican Republic.
Height, 6.03. Weight, 197.
Throws and bats righthanded.

Year Club	League	Pos.	G.	AB.	R.	H.	2B.	3B.	HR.	RBI.	B.A.	PO.	A.	E.	F.A.
1981—Lethbridge	Pion.	OF	34	103	11	14	1	1	0	7	.136	65	6	5	.934
1982—Lethbridge	Pion.	OF	55	209	35	63	14	1	4	47	.301	112	7	1	.992
1983—Lodi†	Calif.	OF	76	310	48	91	17	4	6	36	.294	182	7	4	.979

Signed as free agent by Los Angeles Dodgers' organization, August 12, 1980.
†On disabled list, July 7, 1983 through remainder of season.

JULIAN JOSE GONZALEZ

Born May 13, 1960, at Tampa, Fla.
Height, 5.11. Weight, 190.
Throws and bats lefthanded.

Led Southern League in balks with 9 in 1983 and tied for lead with 4 in 1980.

Year Club	League	G.	IP.	W.	L.	Pct.	H.	R.	ER.	SO.	BB.	ERA.
1979—Miami	Florida St.	13	78	8	3	.727	75	28	25	77	21	2.88
1980—Charlotte	Southern	16	92	5	5	.500	100	61	54	80	49	5.28
1980—Miami	Florida St.	8	46	3	3	.500	40	24	19	48	29	3.72
1981—Hagerstown	Carolina	12	77	5	5	.500	63	38	33	94	50	3.86
1981—Charlotte	Southern	16	45	2	2	.500	45	24	21	38	27	4.20
1982—Hagerstown	Carolina	30	102⅔	7	6	.538	82	48	39	117	70	3.42
1983—Charlotte	Southern	17	105⅔	10	6	.625	88	49	39	105	71	3.32
1983—Rochester	Int'national	12	67	5	3	.625	55	39	33	61	42	4.43

Selected by Baltimore Orioles' organization in 6th round of free-agent draft, June 5, 1979.

JULIO CESAR GONZALEZ (HERNANDEZ)

Born December 25, 1953, at Caguas, Puerto Rico.
Height, 5.11. Weight, 165.
Throws and bats righthanded.

Led Midwest League shortstops in double plays with 63 in 1973.

Year Club	League	Pos.	G.	AB.	R.	H.	2B.	3B.	HR.	RBI.	B.A.	PO.	A.	E.	F.A.
1972—Quincy	Midw.	SS	96	346	39	82	14	7	7	37	.237	111	248	45	.889
1973—Quincy	Midw.	SS	•125	★492	81	146	16	8	5	39	.297	★190	★342	★61	.897
1974—Key West†	Fla. St.	SS-2B	87	333	26	74	12	2	1	20	.222	145	222	29	.926
1975—Midland	Texas	3B-SS-2B	81	324	37	88	13	2	2	27	.272	95	174	24	.918
1975—Wichita	A. A.	2B-3B	56	171	13	35	5	0	0	11	.205	90	128	10	.956
1976—Wichita‡	A. A.	2B-SS-3B	128	484	49	136	12	5	3	41	.281	264	372	38	.943
1977—Houston	Nat.	SS-2B	110	383	34	94	18	3	1	27	.245	154	293	27	.943
1978—Charleston	Int.	SS-3B-2B	8	30	3	11	1	0	0	2	.367	6	28	2	.944
1978—Houston	Nat.	2B-SS-3B	78	223	24	52	3	1	1	16	.233	83	139	7	.969
1979—Houston	Nat.	2B-SS-3B	68	181	16	45	5	2	0	10	.249	92	146	12	.952
1980—Tucson	P. C.	3B	38	149	21	44	9	2	2	25	.295	22	105	9	.934
1980—Houston§	Nat.	SS-2B-3B	40	52	5	6	1	0	0	1	.115	22	31	1	.981
1981—St. Louis	Nat.	SS-2B-3B	20	22	2	7	1	0	1	3	.318	7	13	1	.952
1982—St. Louis x	Nat.	3B-2B-SS	42	87	9	21	3	2	1	7	.241	21	44	4	.942
1983—Evansville	A. A.	SS-3B-2B	59	199	17	47	8	1	0	27	.236	69	136	14	.936
1983—Detroit	Amer.	SS-2B-3B	12	21	0	3	1	0	0	2	.143	10	26	4	.900
National League Totals			358	948	90	225	31	8	4	64	.237	379	666	52	.953
American League Totals			12	21	0	3	1	0	0	2	.143	10	26	4	.900
Major League Totals			370	969	90	228	32	8	4	66	.235	389	692	56	.951

Signed as free agent by Chicago Cubs' organization, February 14, 1972.
†On Midland disabled list, April 10 to May 16, 1974.
‡Traded to Houston Astros for Outfielder Greg Gross, December 8, 1976.
§Released, March 27, 1981; signed by St. Louis Cardinals, April 3, 1981.
xReleased, December 2, 1982; signed by Detroit Tigers' organization, March 15, 1983.

OTTO LUIS GONZALEZ (CINTRON)

Born October 15, 1963, at Caguas, Puerto Rico.
Height, 6.02. Weight, 195.
Throws and bats righthanded.

Year Club	League	Pos.	G.	AB.	R.	H.	2B.	3B.	HR.	RBI.	B.A.	PO.	A.	E.	F.A.
1981—Sarasota Rangers	Gulf. C.	C-OF	33	120	17	26	3	0	1	11	.217	195	30	4	.983
1982—Burlington	Midw.	C-1B	82	268	26	71	14	2	7	43	.265	441	64	12	.977
1983—Burlington	Midw.	C-1B	108	389	49	104	28	0	12	58	.267	425	63	8	.984

Signed as free agent by Texas Rangers' organization, January 12, 1981.

DWIGHT EUGENE GOODEN

Born November 16, 1964, at Tampa, Fla.
Height, 6.02. Weight, 190.
Throws and bats righthanded

Led Carolina League in shutouts with 6 in 1983.
Named Carolina League Pitcher of the Year, 1983.

Year Club	League	G.	IP.	W.	L.	Pct.	H.	R.	ER.	SO.	BB.	ERA.
1982—Kingsport	Ap'lachian	9	65⅔	5	4	.556	53	34	18	66	25	2.47
1982—Little Falls	NYP	2	13	0	1	.000	11	6	6	18	3	4.15
1983—Lynchburg	Carolina	27	191	★19	4	.826	121	58	53	★300	★112	★2.50

Selected by New York Mets' organization in 1st round (fifth player selected) of free-agent draft, June 7, 1982.

—DID YOU KNOW—

That in 1983, the Pirates' Bill Madlock became the first player since Ernie Lombardi of the Braves in 1942 to win a major league batting crown without hitting a triple?

THOMAS PATRICK GORMAN
(Tom)

Born December 16, 1957, at Woodburn, Ore.
Height, 6.03. Weight, 195.
Throws and bats lefthanded.
Attended Gonzaga University, Spokane, Wash.

Tied for Southern League lead in saves with 22 in 1981.

Year—Club	League	G.	IP.	W.	L.	Pct.	H.	R.	ER.	SO.	BB.	ERA.
1980—Memphis	Southern	25	69	6	4	.600	64	34	21	45	22	2.74
1981—Memphis	Southern	52	91	12	9	.571	82	39	31	91	30	3.07
1981—Montreal	National	9	15	0	0	.000	12	7	7	13	6	4.20
1982—Wichita	Am. Assoc.	23	119⅓	8	7	.533	131	77	69	69	35	5.20
1982—Montreal†-New York	National	8	16⅓	1	1	.500	16	5	5	13	4	2.76
1982—Tidewater	Int'national	4	11⅓	1	1	.500	12	8	8	6	4	6.35
1983—Tidewater	Int'national	10	61⅔	6	1	.857	54	25	20	58	18	2.92
1983—New York	National	25	49⅓	1	4	.200	45	29	27	30	15	4.93
Major League Totals		42	80⅔	2	5	.286	73	41	39	56	25	4.35

Selected by Montreal Expos' organization in 4th round of free-agent draft, June 3, 1980.

†Traded to New York Mets' organization, August 14, 1982, completing deal in which New York traded Outfielder Joel Youngblood to Montreal Expos for a player to be named later, August 4, 1982.

RICHARD MICHAEL GOSSAGE
(Rich or Goose)

Born July 5, 1951, at Colorado Springs, Colo.
Height, 6.03. Weight, 217.
Throws and bats righthanded.
Attended Southern Colorado State College, Pueblo, Colo.

Established National League record for most strikeouts by relief pitcher, season (151), 1977.

Major League saves: 1972 (2), 1974 (1), 1975 (26), 1976 (1), 1977 (26), 1978 (27), 1979 (18), 1980 (33), 1981 (20), 1982 (30), 1983 (22). Total—206.

Led American League in saves with 26 in 1975 and 27 in 1978.

Led American League in games finished in relief with 55 in 1978.

Tied for American League lead in saves with 33 in 1980.

Tied for American League lead in intentional bases on balls issued with 15 in 1975.

Led Midwest League in complete games with 15 and shutouts with 7 in 1971.

Named American League Fireman of the Year by THE SPORTING NEWS, 1975 and 1978.

Named Midwest League Player of the Year, 1971.

Year—Club	League	G.	IP.	W.	L.	Pct.	H.	R.	ER.	SO.	BB.	ERA.
1970—Sarasota White Sox	Gulf Coast	3	16	0	0	.000	11	6	5	21	4	2.81
1970—Appleton	Midwest	10	35	0	3	.000	41	27	23	21	19	5.91
1971—Appleton	Midwest	25	187	*18	2	*.900	141	48	38	149	50	*1.83
1972—Chicago	American	36	80	7	1	.875	72	44	38	57	44	4.28
1973—Iowa	Am. Assoc.	12	71	5	4	.556	59	32	29	66	28	3.68
1973—Chicago	American	20	50	0	4	.000	57	44	41	33	37	7.38
1974—Appleton	Midwest	2	8	0	2	.000	8	6	3	5	4	3.38
1974—Chicago	American	39	89	4	6	.400	92	45	41	64	47	4.15
1975—Chicago	American	61	142	9	8	.529	99	32	29	130	70	1.84
1976—Chicago†	American	31	224	9	17	.346	214	104	98	135	90	3.94
1977—Pittsburgh‡	National	72	133	11	9	.550	78	27	24	151	49	1.62
1978—New York	American	63	134	10	11	.476	87	41	30	122	59	2.01
1979—New York§	American	36	58	5	3	.625	48	18	17	41	19	2.64
1980—New York	American	64	99	6	2	.750	74	29	25	103	37	2.27
1981—New York	American	32	47	3	2	.600	22	6	4	48	14	0.77
1982—New York x	American	56	93	4	5	.444	63	23	23	102	28	2.23
1983—New York x	American	57	87⅓	13	5	.722	82	27	22	90	25	2.27
National League Totals		72	133	11	9	.550	78	27	24	151	49	1.62
American League Totals		496	1103⅓	70	64	.522	910	413	368	925	470	3.00
Major League Totals		568	1236⅓	81	73	.526	988	440	392	1076	519	2.85

Selected by Chicago White Sox' organization in 9th round of free-agent draft, June 4, 1970.

†Traded with Pitcher Terry Forster to Pittsburgh Pirates for Outfielder Richie Zisk and Pitcher Silvio Martinez, December 10, 1976.

‡Granted free agency, October 28, 1977; signed by New York Yankees, November 23, 1977.

§On disabled list, April 21 to July 9, 1979.

xGranted free agency, November 7, 1983.

DIVISION SERIES RECORD

Year—Club	League	G.	IP.	W.	L.	Pct.	H.	R.	ER.	SO.	BB.	ERA.
1981—New York	American	3	6⅔	0	0	.000	3	0	0	8	2	0.00

CHAMPIONSHIP SERIES RECORD

Tied American League Championship Series record for most saves, total Series (2).

Year—Club	League	G.	IP.	W.	L.	Pct.	H.	R.	ER.	SO.	BB.	ERA.
1978—New York	American	2	4	1	0	1.000	3	2	2	3	0	4.50
1980—New York	American	1	⅓	0	1	.000	3	2	2	0	0	54.00
1981—New York	American	2	2⅔	0	0	.000	1	0	0	2	0	0.00
Championship Series Totals		5	7	1	1	.500	7	4	4	5	0	5.14

WORLD SERIES RECORD

Tied World Series record for most saves, six-game Series (2), 1981.

Year Club	League	G.	IP.	W.	L.	Pct.	H.	R.	ER.	SO.	BB.	ERA.
1978—New York	American	3	6	1	0	1.000	1	0	0	4	1	0.00
1981—New York	American	3	5	0	0	.000	2	0	0	5	2	0.00
World Series Totals		6	11	1	0	1.000	3	0	0	9	3	0.00

ALL-STAR GAME RECORD

Tied All-Star game record for most games finished (4).

Year League	IP.	W.	L.	Pct.	H.	R.	ER.	SO.	BB.	ERA.
1975—American	1	0	0	.000	1	1	1	0	0	9.00
1977—National	1	0	0	.000	1	2	2	2	1	18.00
1978—American	1	0	1	.000	4	4	4	1	1	36.00
1980—American	1	0	0	.000	0	0	0	0	0	0.00
All-Star Game Totals	4	0	0	.000	6	7	7	3	2	15.75

Named to American League All-Star Team for 1981 game; replaced due to injury.
Member of American League All-Star Team in 1976 and 1982; did not play.

JAMES WILLIAM GOTT
(Jim)

Born August 3, 1959, at Hollywood, Calif.
Height, 6.03. Weight, 215.
Throws and bats righthanded.

Led Western Carolinas League in wild pitches with 21 in 1979.
Tied for Pioneer League lead in games started by pitchers with 14 in 1978.

Year Club	League	G.	IP.	W.	L.	Pct.	H.	R.	ER.	SO.	BB.	ERA.
1977—Calgary	Pioneer	14	65	3	4	.429	71	*82	*69	60	*83	9.55
1978—Gastonia	W. Carol.	22	145	9	6	.600	100	67	64	130	●113	3.97
1978—St. Petersburg	Flordia St.	5	28	1	3	.250	23	9	4	15	12	1.29
1979—St. Petersburg	Florida St.	4	18	0	3	.000	18	13	13	9	13	6.50
1979—Gastonia	W. Carol.	19	77	5	5	.500	63	57	48	102	88	5.61
1979—Arkansas†	Texas	2	5	0	1	.000	3	6	3	7	13	5.40
1980—St. Petersburg	Florida St.	25	137	5	11	.313	138	96	70	103	113	4.60
1981—Arkansas‡	Texas	28	131	5	9	.357	133	68	50	93	65	3.44
1982—Toronto	American	30	136	5	10	.333	134	76	67	82	66	4.43
1983—Toronto	American	34	176⅔	9	14	.391	195	103	93	121	68	4.74
Major League Totals		64	312⅔	14	24	.368	329	179	160	203	134	4.61

Selected by St. Louis Cardinals' organization in 4th round of free-agent draft, June 7, 1977.
†On disabled list, August 16 to September 1, 1979.
‡Drafted by Toronto Blue Jays, December 7, 1981.

LEE WILLARD GRAHAM

Born September 22, 1959, at Summerfield, Fla.
Height, 5.10. Weight, 170.
Throws and bats lefthanded.

Year Club	League	Pos.	G.	AB.	R.	H.	2B.	3B.	HR.	RBI.	B.A.	PO.	A.	E.	F.A.
1977—Elmira	NYP	OF	53	187	36	51	11	4	2	15	.273	91	8	7	.934
1978—Winston-Salem	Carol.	OF	124	477	62	124	10	1	0	30	.260	270	*18	6	.980
1979—Winter Haven	Fla. St.	OF	117	404	65	103	9	2	1	31	.255	176	4	4	.978
1980—Bristol	East.	OF	132	463	70	128	11	0	1	37	.276	253	14	13	.954
1981—Pawtucket	Int.	OF	133	472	50	103	22	1	0	30	.218	255	9	5	.981
1982—Pawtucket	Int.	OF	125	472	76	137	16	1	5	43	.290	284	5	10	.967
1983—Pawtucket	Int.	OF	136	507	78	140	23	3	11	59	.276	242	15	6	.977
1983—Boston	Amer.	OF	5	6	2	0	0	0	0	1	.000	6	1	0	1.000
Major League Totals			5	6	2	0	0	0	0	1	.000	6	1	0	1.000

Selected by Boston Red Sox' organization in 26th round of free-agent draft, June 7, 1977.

MARK ANDREW GRANT

Born October 24, 1963, at Aurora, Ill.
Height, 6.02. Weight, 205.
Throws and bats righthanded.

Cousin of Rick Ramos, pitcher in Montreal Expos' organization, and nephew
of Richard Ramos, pitcher in Chicago White Sox' organization, 1953 through 1958.

Pitched 9-0 no-hit victory against Danville, August 12, 1982.
Tied for Midwest League lead in shutouts with 4 in 1982.

Year Club	League	G.	IP.	W.	L.	Pct.	H.	R.	ER.	SO.	BB.	ERA.
1981—Great Falls	Pioneer	10	64	2	6	.250	63	36	31	50	35	4.36
1982—Clinton	Midwest	27	*198⅔	*16	5	*.762	139	63	52	*243	60	2.36
1983—Shreveport	Texas	26	*186⅔	10	8	.556	182	83	76	159	71	3.66

Selected by San Francisco Giants' organization in 1st round (10th player selected) of free-agent draft, June 8, 1981.

THOMAS RAYMOND GRANT
(Tom)

Born May 28, 1957, at Worcester, Mass.
Height, 6.02. Weight, 190.
Throws right and bats lefthanded.
Received bachelor of arts degree in psychology from University of New Haven, New Haven, Conn., in 1979.
Led American Association in intentional bases on balls received with 16 in 1983.
Tied for American Association lead in double plays by outfielders with 5 in 1982.

Year Club	League	Pos.	G.	AB.	R.	H.	2B.	3B.	HR.	RBI.	B.A.	PO.	A.	E.	F.A.
1979—Geneva	NYP	OF	48	148	35	45	5	1	●10	32	.304	18	1	0	1.000
1980—Midland	Texas	OF	135	523	99	161	38	6	10	92	.308	239	13	3	★.988
1981—Midland	Texas	OF	48	189	34	66	13	5	10	39	.349	77	12	2	.978
1981—Iowa	A. A.	OF	91	298	37	81	12	1	6	39	.272	187	10	4	.980
1982—Iowa	A. A.	OF	122	389	53	103	25	5	11	59	.265	147	13	7	.958
1983—Iowa	A. A.	OF	112	394	68	123	24	1	17	59	.312	177	6	4	.979
1983—Chicago	Nat.	OF	16	20	2	3	1	0	0	2	.150	6	1	0	1.000
Major League Totals			16	20	2	3	1	0	0	2	.150	6	1	0	1.000

Selected by Chicago Cubs' organization in 16th round of free-agent draft, June 5, 1979.

RICHARD RAY GRAPENTHIN
Name pronounced Grapp-un-thin.
(Rick)

Born April 16, 1958, at Linn Grove, Iowa.
Height, 6.03. Weight, 205.
Throws and bats righthanded.
Attended Mesa Community College, Mesa, Ariz., and received bachelor of science degree in physical education from Indiana State University, Terre Haute, Ind., in 1980.

Year Club	League	G.	IP.	W.	L.	Pct.	H.	R.	ER.	SO.	BB.	ERA.
1980—Jamestown	NYP	7	27	2	2	.500	30	17	17	24	14	5.67
1981—West Palm Beach	Fla. St.	31	80	5	4	.556	96	47	40	44	22	4.50
1982—San Jose	California	27	45	2	1	.667	41	7	4	39	19	0.80
1982—Wichita	Am. Assoc.	20	32⅓	2	2	.500	36	21	17	23	16	4.73
1983—Montreal	National	1	4	0	1	.000	4	4	4	3	1	9.00
1983—Wichita	Am. Assoc.	40	70⅓	5	5	.500	72	35	30	33	26	3.84
Major League Totals		1	4	0	1	.000	4	4	4	3	1	9.00

Signed as free agent by Montreal Expos' organization, July 9, 1980.

LORENZO GRAY

Born March 4, 1958, at Mound Bayou, Miss.
Height, 6.01. Weight, 190.
Throws and bats righthanded.
Attended California State University, Carson, Calif.
Led Eastern League in being hit by pitch with 15 in 1980.
Led Eastern League third basemen in putouts with 101, assists with 287, errors with 31 and double plays with 26 in 1980.

Year Club	League	Pos.	G.	AB.	R.	H.	2B.	3B.	HR.	RBI.	B.A.	PO.	A.	E.	F.A.
1976—Sarasota W. Sox	Gulf C.	3B-SS-OF	42	151	19	35	3	0	0	7	.232	22	53	13	.852
1977—Appleton	Midw.	3B-1B	55	186	25	44	5	3	2	15	.237	146	67	9	.959
1977—Sarasota W. Sox	Gulf C.	3B	51	170	37	47	3	4	0	26	.276	★51	88	11	★.927
1978—Appleton	Midw.	1-O-3-2-S	100	317	49	93	13	3	2	35	.293	339	42	8	.979
1979—Appleton	Midw.	1-3-O-2	17	67	24	21	4	0	2	8	.313	104	12	2	.983
1979—Knoxville	South.	O-S-1-3-2	116	402	68	101	12	2	5	32	.251	294	121	14	.967
1980—Glens Falls	East.	3B-2B	135	503	94	145	24	2	6	68	.288	110	302	32	.928
1981—Edmonton	P. C.	3B-SS	35	101	17	21	3	2	0	5	.208	33	72	8	.929
1981—Glens Falls	East.	3B-SS	58	218	47	59	9	2	4	26	.271	38	120	12	.929
1982—Edmonton	P. C.	O-3-2-1	124	481	97	172	33	5	16	79	.358	207	126	16	.954
1982—Chicago	Amer.	3B	17	28	4	8	1	0	0	0	.286	9	10	3	.864
1983—Chicago	Amer.	3B	41	78	18	14	3	0	1	4	.179	17	46	4	.940
1983—Denver	A. A.	3B-OF	42	169	26	56	8	4	4	31	.331	16	37	3	.946
Major League Totals			58	106	22	22	4	0	1	4	.208	26	56	7	.921

Selected by Chicago White Sox' organization in 8th round of free-agent draft, June 8, 1976.

CHRISTOPHER DeWAYNE GREEN
(Chris)

Born September 5, 1961, at Los Angeles, Calif.
Height, 6.02. Weight, 180.
Throws and bats lefthanded.
Led Carolina League in balks with 4 in 1982.

Year Club	League	G.	IP.	W.	L.	Pct.	H.	R.	ER.	SO.	BB.	ERA.
1979—Bradenton Pirates	Gulf Coast	9	32	1	2	.333	28	28	22	31	40	6.19
1980—Shelby†‡	W. Carol.	19	95	6	7	.462	103	57	45	57	28	4.26
1981—Greenwood	S. Atlantic	27	184	15	7	.682	148	87	63	128	86	3.08
1982—Alexandria	Carolina	14	86⅓	9	1	★.900	76	29	24	84	33	2.50
1982—Buffalo	Eastern	13	99⅓	7	5	.583	71	41	36	82	52	3.26

Year Club	League	G.	IP.	W.	L.	Pct.	H.	R.	ER.	SO.	BB.	ERA.
1983—Hawaii	P. Coast	13	77⅓	0	9	.000	94	53	45	49	36	5.24
1983—Lynn	Eastern	23	74⅔	5	6	.455	76	38	33	73	31	3.98

Selected by Pittsburgh Pirates' organization in 3rd round of free-agent draft, June 5, 1979.
†On disabled list, April 21 to May 9, 1980.
‡On suspended list, May 9 to May 13, 1980.

DAVID ALEJANDRO GREEN (CASAYA)

Born December 4, 1960, at Managua, Nicaragua.
Height, 6.03. Weight, 185.
Throws and bats righthanded.

Major League stolen bases: 1982 (11), 1983 (34). Total—45.

Year Club	League	Pos.	G.	AB.	R.	H.	2B.	3B.	HR.	RBI.	B.A.	PO.	A.	E.	F.A.
1979—Stockton	Calif.	OF	136	500	68	131	16	9	8	70	.262	282	8	6	.980
1980—Holyoke†	East.	OF	129	446	71	130	13	★19	8	67	.291	261	18	13	.955
1981—Springfield‡	A. A.	OF	106	430	66	116	26	3	10	67	.270	251	12	4	.985
1981—St. Louis	Nat.	OF	21	34	6	5	1	0	0	2	.147	31	1	1	.970
1982—St. Louis§	Nat.	OF	76	166	21	47	7	1	2	23	.283	111	4	1	.991
1982—Louisville	A. A.	OF	46	174	45	60	5	4	9	40	.345	111	17	1	.992
1983—St. Louis	Nat.	OF	146	422	52	120	14	10	8	69	.284	214	10	7	.970
Major League Totals			243	622	79	172	22	11	10	94	.277	356	15	9	.976

Signed as free agent by Milwaukee Brewers' organization, September 24, 1978.
†Traded with Outfielder Sixto Lezcano and Pitchers Lary Sorensen and Dave LaPoint to St. Louis Cardinals for Catcher Ted Simmons and Pitchers Pete Vuckovich and Rollie Fingers, December 12, 1180.
‡On disabled list, June 20 to July 2, 1981.
§On supplemental disabled list, May 8 to May 23, 1982.

CHAMPIONSHIP SERIES RECORD

Year Club	League	Pos.	G.	AB.	R.	H.	2B.	3B.	HR.	RBI.	B.A.	PO.	A.	E.	F.A.
1982—St. Louis	Nat.	OF	2	1	1	1	0	0	0	0	1.000	0	0	0	.000

WORLD SERIES RECORD

Year Club	League	Pos.	G.	AB.	R.	H.	2B.	3B.	HR.	RBI.	B.A.	PO.	A.	E.	F.A.
1982—St. Louis	Nat.	O-PH-DH	7	10	3	2	1	1	0	0	.200	4	0	0	1.000

BRIAN KEITH GREER

Born May 13, 1959, at Lynwood, Calif.
Height, 6.03. Weight, 210.
Throws and bats righthanded.

Led Carolina League batters in strikeouts with 183 in 1981.
Led Northwest League batters in strikeouts with 87 and tied for lead in sacrifice flies with 5 in 1977.
Led Texas League in strikeouts with 160 in 1978 and 153 in 1979.
Tied for Carolina League lead in double plays by outfielders with 5 in 1981.

Year Club	League	Pos.	G.	AB.	R.	H.	2B.	3B.	HR.	RBI.	B.A.	PO.	A.	E.	F.A.
1977—Walla Walla	N'west	OF	50	170	28	32	9	1	7	27	.188	83	9	7	.929
1977—San Diego	Nat.	PH	1	1	0	0	0	0	0	0	.000	0	0	0	.000
1978—Amarillo	Texas	OF	98	309	30	54	8	3	6	19	.175	196	12	10	.954
1979—Amarillo	Texas	OF	●136	489	66	112	21	1	18	79	.229	335	13	★21	.943
1979—San Diego	Nat.	OF	4	3	0	0	0	0	0	0	.000	4	0	0	1.000
1980—Amarillo†	Texas	OF	101	317	42	58	11	2	8	35	.183	213	9	7	.969
1981—Salem	Carol.	★OF-P	136	456	79	91	11	4	25	89	.200	★278	15	5	★.983
1982—Amarillo	Texas	OF	94	334	69	92	17	2	27	80	.275	185	6	10	.950
1982—Hawaii	P. C.	OF	37	118	17	22	8	3	4	19	.186	54	2	0	1.000
1983—Reno‡§	Calif.	OF-1B	73	244	32	50	10	2	4	31	.205	198	16	9	.960
Major League Totals			5	4	0	0	0	0	0	0	.000	4	0	0	.000

Selected by San Diego Padres' organization in 1st round (eighth player selected) of free-agent draft, June 7, 1977.
†On disabled list, April 25 to May 27, 1980.
‡On Las Vegas disabled list, April 10 to May 30, 1983.
§Granted free agency, October 20, 1983.

PITCHING RECORD

Year Club	League	G.	IP.	W.	L.	Pct.	H.	R.	ER.	SO.	BB.	ERA.
1981—Salem	Carolina	1	1	0	0	.000	1	2	0	1	3	0.00

ROBERT ANTHONY GRICH
(Bobby)

Born January 15, 1949, at Muskegon, Mich.
Height, 6.02. Weight, 190.
Throws and bats righthanded.
Attended University of California at Los Angeles, Los Angeles, Calif., and
Fresno State University, Fresno, Calif.

Established major league record for most putouts, second baseman, season (484), 1974.
Tied major league record for fewest errors by second baseman (800 or more chances), season (5), 1973.
Tied American League record for most games, second baseman, season (162), 1973.
Hit three home runs in a game, June 18, 1974.

Led American League in slugging percentage with .543 in 1981.
Led American League in being hit by pitch with 20 in 1974.
Led American League second basemen in double plays with 130 in 1973, 132 in 1974 and 122 in 1975.
Led American League second basemen in total chances with 945 in 1973, 957 in 1974 and 928 in 1975.
Led International League in total bases with 299 in 1971.
Led International League shortstops in double plays with 81 in 1971.
Named Minor League Player of the Year by THE SPORTING NEWS, 1971.
Named International League Most Valuable Player, 1971.
Named Texas League co-Most Valuable Player, 1969.
Named second baseman on THE SPORTING NEWS American League All-Star Team, 1976, 1979 and 1981.
Named second baseman on THE SPORTING NEWS American League All-Star fielding team, 1973 through 1976.
Named second baseman on THE SPORTING NEWS American League Silver Slugger team, 1981.
Received reported $40,000 bonus to sign with Baltimore Orioles, 1967.

Year	Club	League	Pos.	G.	AB.	R.	H.	2B.	3B.	HR.	RBI.	B.A.	PO.	A.	E.	F.A.
1967—Bluefield	Appal.		SS	58	213	43	54	10	4	3	26	.254	74	126	24	.893
1968—Stockton	Calif.		SS	113	426	63	97	18	2	8	44	.228	205	★379	35	.943
1969—Dal.-Ft. Worth†	Texas		SS	121	413	60	128	16	8	2	50	.310	★199	368	29	.951
1970—Rochester	Int.		2B-SS	63	235	67	90	11	3	9	42	.383	144	199	9	.974
1970—Baltimore	Amer.		SS-2-3	30	95	11	20	1	3	0	8	.211	56	79	7	.951
1971—Rochester	Int.		SS	130	473	★124	159	26	9	★32	83	★.336	★238	★394	17	★.974
1971—Baltimore	Amer.		SS-2	7	30	7	9	0	0	1	6	.300	11	31	0	1.000
1972—Baltimore	Amer.		S-2-1-3	133	460	66	128	21	3	12	50	.278	299	338	20	.970
1973—Baltimore	Amer.		2B	●162	581	82	146	29	7	12	50	.251	★431	★509	5	★.995
1974—Baltimore	Amer.		2B	160	582	92	153	29	6	19	82	.263	★484	★453	20	.979
1975—Baltimore	Amer.		2B	150	524	81	136	26	4	13	57	.260	★423	★484	21	.977
1976—Baltimore‡	Amer.		★2B-3B	144	518	93	138	31	4	13	54	.266	★389	400	12	.985
1977—California§	Amer.		SS	52	181	24	44	6	0	7	23	.243	88	141	4	.983
1978—California	Amer.		2B	144	487	68	122	16	2	6	42	.251	325	419	13	.983
1979—California	Amer.		2B	153	534	78	157	30	5	30	101	.294	340	438	13	.984
1980—California	Amer.		2B-1B	150	498	60	135	22	2	14	62	.271	353	464	9	.989
1981—California x	Amer.		2B	100	352	56	107	14	2	●22	61	.304	230	349	10	.983
1982—California	Amer.		2B	145	506	74	132	28	5	19	65	.261	338	450	11	.986
1983—California y	Amer.		★2B-SS	120	387	65	113	17	0	16	62	.292	271	415	★22	.969
Major League Totals				1650	5735	857	1540	270	43	184	723	.269	4038	4970	167	.982

Selected by Baltimore Orioles' organization in 1st round (18th player selected) of free-agent draft, June 6, 1967.
†On military list, September 2, 1969 through April 1, 1970.
‡Granted free agency, November 1, 1976; signed by California Angels, November 24, 1976.
§On supplemental disabled list, June 9, 1977; transferred to disabled list, June 26, 1977; transferred to emergency disabled list, July 5, 1977 through remainder of season.
xOn supplemental disabled list, June 10 to August 8, 1981.
yOn disabled list, August 30, 1983 through remainder of season.

CHAMPIONSHIP SERIES RECORD

Tied American League Championship Series records for most times on losing club (4); most strikeouts, five-game Series (7), 1982; most consecutive strikeouts, one Series, consecutive at-bats and plate appearances (4), 1982.

Year	Club	League	Pos.	G.	AB.	R.	H.	2B.	3B.	HR.	RBI.	B.A.	PO.	A.	E.	F.A.
1973—Baltimore	Amer.		2B	5	20	1	2	0	0	1	1	.100	16	9	0	1.000
1974—Baltimore	Amer.		2B	4	16	2	4	1	0	1	2	.250	13	12	1	.962
1979—California	Amer.		2B	4	13	0	2	1	0	0	2	.154	4	12	1	.941
1982—California	Amer.		2B	5	15	1	3	1	0	0	1	.200	10	17	0	1.000
Championship Series Totals				18	64	4	11	3	0	2	6	.172	43	50	2	.979

ALL-STAR GAME RECORD

Year	League	Pos.	AB.	R.	H.	2B.	3B.	HR.	RBI.	B.A.	PO.	A.	E.	F.A.
1972—American		SS	4	0	0	0	0	0	0	.000	0	3	0	1.000
1974—American		2B	3	0	1	0	0	0	0	.333	0	2	0	1.000
1976—American		2B	2	0	0	0	0	0	0	.000	1	1	0	1.000
1979—American		2B	1	0	0	0	0	0	0	.000	2	0	0	1.000
1980—American		2B	0	0	0	0	0	0	0	.000	0	1	0	1.000
1982—American		2B	1	0	0	0	0	0	0	.000	2	2	0	1.000
All-Star Game Totals			11	0	1	0	0	0	0	.091	5	9	0	1.000

GEORGE KENNETH GRIFFEY
(Ken)

Born April 10, 1950, at Donora, Pa.
Height, 6.00. Weight, 200.
Throws and bats lefthanded.

Tied major league record for most at bats, game, since 1900 (7), June 13, 1975.
Major league stolen bases: 1973 (4), 1974 (9), 1975 (16), 1976 (34), 1977 (17), 1978 (23), 1979 (12), 1980 (23), 1981 (12), 1982 (10), 1983 (5). Total—165.
Led American Association in stolen bases with 43 in 1973.
Tied for Eastern League lead in double plays by outfielders with 6 in 1972.
Named as outfielder on THE SPORTING NEWS National League All-Star Team, 1976.

Year	Club	League	Pos.	G.	AB.	R.	H.	2B.	3B.	HR.	RBI.	B.A.	PO.	A.	E.	F.A.
1969—Bradenton Reds	Gulf C.		★OF-1B	49	153	22	43	★11	1	1	12	.281	57	4	★10	.859
1970—Sioux Falls	North.		OF	51	164	20	40	2	1	2	24	.244	76	2	7	.918
1971—Tampa	Fla. St.		OF	88	281	60	96	7	11	3	33	.342	137	13	8	.949
1971—Three Rivers	East.		OF	9	32	1	13	1	2	0	4	.406	17	0	1	.944

Year Club League	Pos.	G.	AB.	R.	H.	2B.	3B.	HR.	RBI.	B.A.	PO.	A.	E.	F.A.
1972—Three Rivers .... East.	●OF-SS	128	472	★96	150	21	3	14	52	.318	212	10	●15	.937
1973—Indianapolis .... A. A.	OF	107	397	88	130	18	5	10	58	.327	171	11	6	.968
1973—Cincinnati .... Nat.	OF	25	86	19	33	5	1	3	14	.384	25	1	0	1.000
1974—Indianapolis .... A. A.	OF	43	162	34	54	6	4	5	18	.333	70	4	1	.987
1974—Cincinnati .... Nat.	OF	88	227	24	57	9	5	2	19	.251	115	5	0	1.000
1975—Cincinnati .... Nat.	OF	132	463	95	141	15	9	4	46	.305	202	6	7	.967
1976—Cincinnati .... Nat.	OF	148	562	111	189	28	9	6	74	.336	270	10	6	.976
1977—Cincinnati .... Nat.	OF	154	585	117	186	35	8	12	57	.318	298	10	3	.990
1978—Cincinnati .... Nat.	OF	158	614	90	177	33	8	10	63	.288	296	13	10	.969
1979—Cincinnati† .... Nat.	OF	95	380	62	120	27	4	8	32	.316	175	8	3	.984
1980—Cincinnati .... Nat.	OF	146	544	89	160	28	10	13	85	.294	266	5	6	.978
1981—Cincinnati‡ .... Nat.	OF	101	396	65	123	21	6	2	34	.311	268	8	3	.989
1982—New York .... Amer.	OF	127	484	70	134	23	2	12	54	.277	282	8	5	.983
1983—New York§ .... Amer.	1B-OF	118	458	60	140	21	3	11	46	.306	870	57	8	.991
National League Totals............................		1047	3857	672	1186	201	60	60	424	.307	1915	66	38	.981
American League Totals		245	942	130	274	44	5	23	100	.291	1152	65	13	.989
Major League Totals..................................		1292	4799	802	1460	245	65	83	524	.304	3067	131	51	.984

Selected by Cincinnati Reds' organization in 29th round of free-agent draft, June 5, 1969.

†On disabled list, August 14 to September 7, 1979.

‡Traded to New York Yankees for Pitcher Brian Ryder and a player to be named later, November 4, 1981; Cincinnati Reds' organization acquired Pitcher Freddie Toliver to complete deal, December 10, 1981.

§On disabled list, July 2 to August 2, 1983.

CHAMPIONSHIP SERIES RECORD

Tied Championship Series record for most stolen bases, game (3), October 5, 1975.

Year Club League	Pos.	G.	AB.	R.	H.	2B.	3B.	HR.	RBI.	B.A.	PO.	A.	E.	F.A.
1973—Cincinnati .... Nat.	OF-PH	3	7	0	1	1	0	0	0	.143	2	0	0	1.000
1975—Cincinnati .... Nat.	OF	3	12	3	4	1	0	0	4	.333	4	1	0	1.000
1976—Cincinnati .... Nat.	OF	3	13	2	5	0	1	0	2	.385	11	0	0	1.000
Championship Series Totals		9	32	5	10	2	1	0	6	.312	17	1	0	1.000

WORLD SERIES RECORD

Tied World Series record for fewest chances accepted by outfielder, extra-inning game (0), October 21, 1975 (12 innings); most at-bats, game, no hits (5), October 21, 1976.

Year Club League	Pos.	G.	AB.	R.	H.	2B.	3B.	HR.	RBI.	B.A.	PO.	A.	E.	F.A.
1975—Cincinnati .... Nat.	OF	7	26	4	7	3	1	0	4	.269	10	1	0	1.000
1976—Cincinnati .... Nat.	OF	4	17	2	1	0	0	0	1	.059	5	0	0	1.000
World Series Totals		11	43	6	8	3	1	0	5	.186	15	1	0	1.000

ALL-STAR GAME RECORD

Year League	Pos.	AB.	R.	H.	2B.	3B.	HR.	RBI.	B.A.	PO.	A.	E.	F.A.
1976—National	OF	1	1	1	0	0	0	1	1.000	1	0	0	1.000
1980—National	OF	3	1	2	0	0	1	1	.667	0	0	0	.000
All-Star Game Totals		4	2	3	0	0	1	2	.750	1	0	0	1.000

Member of National League All-Star Team in 1977; did not play.

ALFREDO CLAUDINO GRIFFIN

Born March 6, 1957, at Dominican Republic City, Dominican Republic.
Height, 5.11. Weight, 165.
Throws right and bats left and righthanded.

Tied American League records for most three-base hits by switch-hitter, season (15), 1980; most games by shortstop, season (162), 1982.

Led American League shortstops in putouts with 280 in 1983.

Led American League shortstops in total chances with 824 in 1982.

Named American League Co-Rookie of the Year by the Baseball Writers' Association of America, 1979.

Year Club League	Pos.	G.	AB.	R.	H.	2B.	3B.	HR.	RBI.	B.A.	PO.	A.	E.	F.A.
1974—Reno .... Calif.	SS	11	35	4	9	0	0	0	1	.257	10	22	9	.780
1974—Sarasota Ind......... Gulf C.	SS	49	158	17	41	1	0	0	11	.259	67	133	★25	.889
1975—San Jose .... Calif.	SS	124	358	42	82	4	3	0	25	.229	189	281	47	.909
1976—San Jose .... Calif.	SS	64	224	40	58	3	1	0	17	.259	91	145	24	.908
1976—Williamsport........ East.	SS	58	200	22	55	3	0	0	17	.275	86	172	17	.938
1976—Toledo .... Int.	SS	22	88	5	19	7	1	0	6	.216	44	71	7	.943
1976—Cleveland.............. Amer.	SS	12	4	0	1	0	0	0	0	.250	1	2	1	.750
1977—Toledo .... Int.	SS	125	457	60	114	14	5	1	32	.249	★223	398	★49	.927
1977—Cleveland.............. Amer.	SS	14	41	5	6	1	0	0	3	.146	17	30	3	.940
1978—Portland .... P. C.	★SS-OF	133	474	82	138	22	10	5	48	.291	201	395	★40	.937
1978—Cleveland† .... Amer.	SS	5	4	1	2	1	0	0	0	.500	4	7	1	.917
1979—Toronto .... Amer.	SS	153	624	81	179	22	10	2	31	.287	272	501	★36	.956
1980—Toronto .... Amer.	SS	155	653	63	166	26	●15	2	41	.254	295	489	★37	.955
1981—Toronto .... Amer.	★SS-3B-2B	101	388	30	81	19	6	0	21	.209	191	279	★31	.938
1982—Toronto .... Amer.	SS	●162	539	57	130	20	8	1	48	.241	★319	479	●26	.968
1983—Toronto .... Amer.	SS-2B	●162	528	62	132	22	9	4	47	.250	287	422	25	.966
Major League Totals		764	2781	299	697	111	48	9	191	.251	1386	2209	160	.957

Signed as free agent by Cleveland Indians' organization, August 22, 1973.

†Traded with Third Baseman Phil Lansford to Toronto Blue Jays for Pitcher Victor Cruz, December 6, 1978.

GREGORY EUGENE GROSS
(Greg)

Born August 1, 1952, at York, Pa.
Height, 5.11. Weight, 175.
Throws and bats lefthanded.

Established major league record for most times caught stealing, rookie season (20), 1974.
Tied for Appalachian League lead in double plays by outfielders with 3 in 1970.
Named National League Rookie Player of the Year by THE SPORTING NEWS, 1974.
Named Appalachian League Player of the Year, 1970.

Year Club	League	Pos.	G.	AB.	R.	H.	2B.	3B.	HR.	RBI.	B.A.	PO.	A.	E.	F.A.
1970—Covington	Appal.	OF	54	211	40	*74	8	3	2	27	.351	93	*10	3	.972
1971—Columbus	South.	OF-1B	132	494	57	144	14	4	2	33	.291	244	13	9	.966
1972—Columbus	South.	OF	101	367	55	111	14	2	0	25	.302	172	9	3	.984
1972—Okla. City	A. A.	OF	28	109	15	27	4	0	0	8	.248	64	4	1	.986
1973—Denver	A. A.	OF	131	528	98	*174	25	6	0	55	.330	226	11	10	.960
1973—Houston	Nat.	OF	14	39	5	9	2	1	0	1	.231	13	2	0	1.000
1974—Houston	Nat.	OF	156	589	78	185	21	8	0	36	.314	296	15	2	.994
1975—Houston†	Nat.	OF	132	483	67	142	14	10	0	41	.294	216	14	10	.958
1976—Houston‡	Nat.	OF	128	426	52	122	12	3	0	27	.286	208	13	5	.978
1977—Chicago	Nat.	OF	115	239	43	77	10	4	5	32	.322	109	3	1	.991
1978—Chicago§	Nat.	OF	124	347	34	92	12	7	1	39	.265	182	6	4	.979
1979—Philadelphia x	Nat.	OF	111	174	21	58	6	3	0	15	.333	82	5	2	.978
1980—Philadelphia	Nat.	OF-1B	127	154	19	37	7	2	0	12	.240	69	5	2	.974
1981—Philadelphia	Nat.	OF	83	102	14	23	6	1	0	7	.225	48	7	1	.982
1982—Philadelphia	Nat.	OF	119	134	14	40	4	0	0	10	.299	55	3	1	.983
1983—Philadelphia	Nat.	OF-1B	136	245	25	74	12	3	0	29	.302	105	1	1	.991
Major League Totals			1245	2932	372	859	106	42	6	249	.293	1383	74	29	.980

Selected by Houston Astros' organization in 4th round of free-agent draft, June 4, 1970.
†On supplemental disabled list, April 2 to April 24, 1975.
‡Traded to Chicago Cubs for Infielder Julio Gonzalez, December 8, 1976.
§Traded with Second Baseman Manny Trillo and Catcher Dave Rader to Philadelphia Phillies for Outfielder Jerry Martin, Catcher Barry Foote, Second Baseman Ted Sizemore and Pitchers Derek Botelho and Henry Mack, February 23, 1979.
xGranted free agency, November 1, 1979; re-signed by Phillies, December 13, 1979.

DIVISION SERIES RECORD

Year Club	League	Pos.	G.	AB.	R.	H.	2B.	3B.	HR.	RBI.	B.A.	PO.	A.	E.	F.A.
1981—Philadelphia	Nat.	PH-OF	4	4	0	0	0	0	0	0	.000	0	0	0	.000

CHAMPIONSHIP SERIES RECORD

Year Club	League	Pos.	G.	AB.	R.	H.	2B.	3B.	HR.	RBI.	B.A.	PO.	A.	E.	F.A.
1980—Philadelphia	Nat.	PH-OF	4	4	2	3	0	0	0	1	.750	1	0	0	1.000
1983—Philadelphia	Nat.	OF-PH	4	5	1	0	0	0	0	0	.000	4	0	0	1.000
Championship Series Totals			8	9	3	3	0	0	0	1	.333	5	0	0	1.000

WORLD SERIES RECORD

Year Club	League	Pos.	G.	AB.	R.	H.	2B.	3B.	HR.	RBI.	B.A.	PO.	A.	E.	F.A.
1980—Philadelphia	Nat.	PH-OF	4	2	0	0	0	0	0	0	.000	1	0	0	1.000
1983—Philadelphia	Nat.	OF	2	6	0	0	0	0	0	0	.000	8	0	0	1.000
World Series Totals			6	8	0	0	0	0	0	0	.000	9	0	0	1.000

KEVIN FRANK GROSS

Born June 8, 1961, at Downey, Calif.
Height, 6.04. Weight, 203.
Throws and bats righthanded.
Attended Oxnard College, Oxnard, Calif.,
and California Lutheran College, Thousand Oaks, Calif.

Tied for South Atlantic League lead in games started by pitchers with 28 in 1981.

Year Club	League	G.	IP.	W.	L.	Pct.	H.	R.	ER.	SO.	BB.	ERA.
1981—Spartanburg	S. Atlantic	28	192	13	12	.520	173	94	76	123	62	3.56
1982—Reading	Eastern	26	151	10	15	.400	138	81	71	136	89	4.23
1983—Portland	P. Coast	15	80	3	5	.375	82	60	60	61	45	6.75
1983—Philadelphia	National	17	96	4	6	.400	100	46	38	66	35	3.56
Major League Totals		17	96	4	6	.400	100	46	38	66	35	3.56

Selected by Baltimore Orioles' organization in 32nd round of free-agent draft, June 5, 1979.
Selected by Philadelphia Phillies' organization in secondary phase of free-agent draft, January 13, 1981.

WAYNE DALE GROSS

Born January 14, 1952, at Riverside, Calif.
Height, 6.02. Weight, 205.
Throws right and bats lefthanded.
Attended California Poly State University, Pomona, Calif.

Year Club	League	Pos.	G.	AB.	R.	H.	2B.	3B.	HR.	RBI.	B.A.	PO.	A.	E.	F.A.
1973—Lewiston	N'west.	1B	8	29	4	7	2	0	1	1	.241	58	4	0	1.000
1973—Burlington	Midw.	1B-OF	56	187	27	44	8	3	4	36	.235	426	19	4	.991
1974—Birmingham	South.	1B-OF-3B	105	316	36	77	12	2	14	54	.244	503	42	15	.973

Year Club	League	Pos.	G.	AB.	R.	H.	2B.	3B.	HR.	RBI.	B.A.	PO.	A.	E.	F.A.
1975—Birmingham	South.	OF-1B	130	435	69	121	23	2	19	71	.278	193	16	13	.941
1976—Tucson	P. C.	3B-1B-OF	115	395	77	128	30	7	19	75	.324	273	164	16	.965
1976—Oakland	Amer.	1B-OF	10	18	0	4	0	0	0	1	.222	30	1	1	.969
1977—Oakland	Amer.	★3B-1B	146	485	66	113	21	1	22	63	.233	127	242	★27	.932
1978—Vancouver	P. C.	3B-1B-OF	17	56	20	23	5	0	3	10	.411	32	33	5	.929
1978—Oakland	Amer.	3B-1B	118	285	18	57	10	2	7	23	.200	120	150	22	.925
1979—Oakland	Amer.	3B-1B-OF	138	442	54	99	19	1	14	50	.224	252	225	21	.958
1980—Oakland	Amer.	3B-1B	113	366	45	103	20	3	14	61	.281	125	136	11	.960
1981—Oakland	Amer.	3B-1B	82	243	29	50	7	1	10	31	.206	68	127	12	.942
1982—Oakland	Amer.	3B-1B	129	386	43	97	14	0	9	41	.251	203	189	11	.973
1983—Oakland†	Amer.	1B-3B-P	136	339	34	79	18	0	12	44	.233	473	113	9	.985
Major League Totals			872	2564	289	602	109	8	88	314	.235	1398	1183	114	.958

Selected by Oakland A's organization in 9th round of free-agent draft, June 5, 1973.
†Traded to Baltimore Orioles for Pitcher Tim Stoddard, December 9, 1983.

DIVISION SERIES RECORD

Year Club	League	Pos.	G.	AB.	R.	H.	2B.	3B.	HR.	RBI.	B.A.	PO.	A.	E.	F.A.
1981—Oakland	Amer.	3B-PH	2	5	1	2	0	0	1	3	.400	1	4	0	1.000

CHAMPIONSHIP SERIES RECORD

Year Club	League	Pos.	G.	AB.	R.	H.	2B.	3B.	HR.	RBI.	B.A.	PO.	A.	E.	F.A.
1981—Oakland	Amer.	PH-3B	3	5	0	0	0	0	0	0	.000	2	0	0	1.000

ALL-STAR GAME RECORD

Member of American League All-Star Team in 1977; did not play.

PITCHING RECORD

Year Club	League	G.	IP.	W.	L.	Pct.	H.	R.	ER.	SO.	BB.	ERA.
1983—Oakland	American	1	2⅓	0	0	.000	2	0	0	0	1	0.00

JOHN MAYWOOD GRUBB JR.

Born August 4, 1948, at Richmond, Va.
Height, 6.03. Weight, 188.
Throws right and bats lefthanded.
Attended Manatee Junior College, West Bradenton, Fla., and received degree from
Florida State University, Tallahassee, Fla.

Tied for Texas League lead in double plays by outfielders with 4 in 1972.

Year Club	League	Pos.	G.	AB.	R.	H.	2B.	3B.	HR.	RBI.	B.A.	PO.	A.	E.	F.A.
1971—Lodi	Calif.	OF-3B-2B	116	409	69	126	23	5	12	56	.308	158	84	14	.945
1972—Alexandria	Texas	★OF-1B	126	446	66	132	25	2	10	61	.296	205	12	2	★.991
1972—San Diego	Nat.	OF	7	21	4	7	1	1	0	1	.333	16	0	0	1.000
1973—San Diego	Nat.	OF-3B	113	389	52	121	22	3	8	37	.311	229	11	3	.988
1974—San Diego	Nat.	OF-3B	140	444	53	127	20	4	8	42	.286	321	8	8	.976
1975—San Diego	Nat.	OF	144	553	72	149	36	2	4	38	.269	334	3	3	.991
1976—San Diego†‡	Nat.	OF-1B-2B	109	384	54	109	22	1	5	27	.284	248	7	6	.977
1977—Cleveland§x	Amer.	OF	34	93	8	28	3	3	2	14	.301	47	2	0	1.000
1978—Cleve. y-Tex.	Amer.	OF	134	411	62	113	19	6	15	67	.275	213	16	6	.974
1979—Texas z	Amer.	OF	102	289	42	79	14	0	10	37	.273	135	8	2	.986
1980—Texas	Amer.	OF	110	274	40	76	12	1	9	32	.277	112	6	6	.952
1981—Texas	Amer.	OF	67	199	26	46	9	1	3	26	.231	95	2	1	.990
1982—Texas ab	Amer.	OF	103	308	35	86	13	3	3	26	.279	135	4	5	.965
1983—Detroit c	Amer.	OF	57	134	20	34	5	2	4	22	.254	34	1	0	1.000
National League Totals			513	1791	235	513	101	11	25	145	.286	1148	29	20	.983
American League Totals			607	1708	233	462	75	16	46	224	.270	771	39	20	.976
Major League Totals			1120	3499	468	975	176	27	71	369	.279	1919	68	40	.980

Selected by Boston Red Sox' organization in 3rd round of free-agent draft, February 1, 1969.
Selected by Cincinnati Reds' organization in secondary phase of free-agent draft, June 5, 1969.
Selected by Atlanta Braves' organization in secondary phase of free-agent draft, June 4, 1970.
Selected by San Diego Padres' organization in secondary phase of free-agent draft, January 13, 1971.
†On disabled list, April 26 to May 28, 1976.
‡Traded with Catcher Fred Kendall and Shortstop Hector Torres to Cleveland Indians for Outfielder George Hendrick, December 8, 1976.
§On disabled list, April 1 to April 23, 1977.
xOn supplemental disabled list, July 8, 1977 through remainder of season.
yTraded to Texas Rangers for a player to be named later, August 31, 1978; Cleveland Indians acquired Pitcher Bobby Cuellar and Outfielder David Rivera to complete deal, October 3, 1978.
zOn disabled list, August 6 to September 1, 1979.
aOn disabled list, March 27 to April 26, 1982.
bTraded to Detroit Tigers for Pitcher Dave Tobik, March 24, 1983.
cOn supplemental disabled list, July 27 to September 13, 1983.

ALL-STAR GAME RECORD

Year League	Pos.	AB.	R.	H.	2B.	3B.	HR.	RBI.	B.A.	PO.	A.	E.	F.A.
1974—National	OF	1	0	0	0	0	0	0	.000	0	20	0	.000

KELLY WAYNE GRUBER

Born February 26, 1962, at Bellaire, Tex.
Height, 6.00. Weight, 175.
Throws and bats righthanded.
Attended University of Texas, Austin, Tex.

Led Southern League shortstops in errors with 43 in 1982.

Year—Club	League	Pos.	G.	AB.	R.	H.	2B.	3B.	HR.	RBI.	B.A.	PO.	A.	E.	F.A.
1980—Batavia	NYP	SS	61	212	27	46	3	2	2	19	.217	87	155	21	.920
1981—Waterloo	Midw.	SS	127	458	64	133	25	4	14	59	.290	★180	★389	★56	.910
1982—Chattanooga	South.	SS-3B	128	441	53	107	18	4	13	54	.243	161	333	44	.918
1983—Buffalo†	East.	3B-SS-OF	111	403	60	106	20	4	15	54	.263	98	170	27	.908

Selected by Cleveland Indians' organization in 1st round (10th player selected) of free-agent draft, June 3, 1980.
†Drafted by Toronto Blue Jays, December 5, 1983.

CECILIO GUANTE (MAGALLANES)

Name pronounced Goo-AHN-tay.

Born February 1, 1961, at Villa Mella, D.R.
Height, 6.03. Weight, 185.
Throws and bats righthanded.

Major League saves: 1983 (9).
Led South Atlantic League in saves with 19 in 1980.

Year—Club	League	G.	IP.	W.	L.	Pct.	H.	R.	ER.	SO.	BB.	ERA.
1980—Shelby	S. Atlantic	39	90	6	6	.500	58	32	29	114	25	2.90
1980—Salem	Carolina	6	14	0	0	.000	7	2	2	18	8	1.29
1981—Buffalo	Eastern	10	14	1	1	.500	8	3	1	17	9	0.64
1981—Portland†	P. Coast	19	104	6	6	.500	110	64	62	70	58	5.37
1982—Portland	P. Coast	21	35	3	2	.600	34	17	15	29	26	3.86
1982—Pittsburgh	National	10	27	0	0	.000	28	16	10	26	5	3.33
1983—Hawaii	P. Coast	15	25⅔	2	1	.667	22	12	10	24	12	3.51
1983—Pittsburgh	National	49	100⅓	2	6	.250	90	45	37	82	46	3.32
Major League Totals		59	127⅓	2	6	.250	118	61	47	108	51	3.32

Signed as free agent by Pittsburgh Pirates' organization, November 24, 1979.
†On disabled list, July 25 to August 5, 1981.

MARK STEVEN GUBICZA

Name pronounced Gu-BAH-za.

Born August 14, 1962, at Philadelphia, Pa.
Height, 6.05. Weight, 215.
Throws and bats righthanded.
Son of Anthony F. Gubicza, minor league pitcher, 1950 and 1951.

Year—Club	League	G.	IP.	W.	L.	Pct.	H.	R.	ER.	SO.	BB.	ERA.
1981—Sarasota Royals-Gold	Gulf Coast	11	56	●8	1	★.889	39	18	14	40	23	2.25
1982—Ft. Myers†	Florida St.	11	48	2	5	.286	49	33	22	36	25	4.13
1983—Jacksonville	Southern	28	196	14	12	.538	146	81	67	★146	93	3.08

Selected by Kansas City Royals' organization in 2nd round of free-agent draft, June 8, 1981.
†On disabled list, June 29, 1982 through remainder of season.

PEDRO GUERRERO

Name pronounced Guh-RAIR-oh.

Born June 29, 1956, at San Pedro de Macoris, Dominican Republic.
Height, 5.11. Weight, 176.
Throws and bats righthanded.

Led National League third basemen in errors with 30 and tied for lead in total chances with 458 in 1983.
Led Pacific Coast League in sacrifice flies with 15 in 1978.
Tied for Northwest League lead in double plays by third basemen with 13 in 1974.
Named outfielder on THE SPORTING NEWS National League All-Star Team, 1981 and 1982.
Named outfielder on THE SPORTING NEWS National League Silver Slugger team, 1982.

Year—Club	League	Pos.	G.	AB.	R.	H.	2B.	3B.	HR.	RBI.	B.A.	PO.	A.	E.	F.A.
1973—Sarasota Ind.†	Gulf C.	3B-SS	44	153	13	39	2	3	2	22	.255	32	82	11	.912
1974—Orangeburg	W. Car.	3B	19	55	3	8	1	0	0	1	.145	11	22	5	.868
1974—Bellingham	N'west	3B	82	297	49	94	●23	2	3	55	.316	★69	124	23	.894
1975—Danville	Midw.	3B-OF	104	351	81	121	25	5	10	76	★.345	111	168	31	.900
1976—Waterbury	East.	1B	132	495	73	151	★30	10	5	66	.305	1129	★96	★19	.985
1977—Albuquerque‡	P. C.	1B	32	129	30	52	11	4	4	39	.403	329	17	10	.972
1978—Albuquerque	P. C.	1B-3B	134	492	92	166	28	4	14	★116	.337	982	80	10	.991
1978—Los Angeles	Nat.	1B	5	8	3	5	0	1	0	1	.625	25	1	0	1.000
1979—Albuquerque	P. C.	OF-3B-1B	113	453	94	151	33	9	22	★103	.333	188	9	5	.975
1979—Los Angeles	Nat.	OF-1B-3B	25	62	7	15	2	0	2	9	.242	53	4	1	.983
1980—Los Angeles§	Nat.	O-2-3-1	75	183	27	59	9	1	7	31	.322	103	110	3	.986
1981—Los Angeles	Nat.	OF-3B-1B	98	347	46	104	17	2	12	48	.300	165	55	11	.952
1982—Los Angeles	Nat.	OF-3B	150	575	87	175	27	5	32	100	.304	282	53	12	.965
1983—Los Angeles	Nat.	3B-1B	160	584	87	174	28	6	32	103	.298	130	308	31	.934
Major League Totals			513	1759	257	532	83	15	85	292	.302	758	531	58	.957

Signed as free agent by Cleveland Indians' organization, January 15, 1973.

†Traded to Los Angeles Dodgers for Pitcher Bruce Ellingsen, April 4, 1974.
‡On disabled list, May 19 to August 30, 1977.
§On disabled list, August 23 to September 15, 1980.

DIVISION SERIES RECORD

Year Club	League	Pos.	G.	AB.	R.	H.	2B.	3B.	HR.	RBI.	B.A.	PO.	A.	E.	F.A.
1981—Los Angeles	Nat.	3B	5	17	1	3	1	0	1	1	.176	3	15	0	1.000

CHAMPIONSHIP SERIES RECORD

Year Club	League	Pos.	G.	AB.	R.	H.	2B.	3B.	HR.	RBI.	B.A.	PO.	A.	E.	F.A.
1981—Los Angeles	Nat.	OF	5	19	1	2	0	0	1	2	.105	9	2	0	1.000
1983—Los Angeles	Nat.	3B	4	12	1	3	1	1	0	2	.250	0	9	0	1.000
Championship Series Totals			9	31	2	5	1	1	1	4	.161	9	11	0	1.000

WORLD SERIES RECORD

Year Club	League	Pos.	G.	AB.	R.	H.	2B.	3B.	HR.	RBI.	B.A.	PO.	A.	E.	F.A.
1981—Los Angeles	Nat.	OF	6	21	2	7	1	1	2	7	.333	17	1	0	1.000

ALL-STAR GAME RECORD

Year League	Pos.	AB.	R.	H.	2B.	3B.	HR.	RBI.	B.A.	PO.	A.	E.	F.A.
1981—National	PH	1	0	0	0	0	0	0	.000	0	0	0	.000
1983—National	3B-OF	1	0	0	0	0	0	0	.000	0	0	1	.000
All-Star Game Totals		2	0	0	0	0	0	0	.000	0	0	1	.000

RONALD AMES GUIDRY

Name pronounced GID-ree.

(Ron)

Born August 28, 1950, at Lafayette, La.
Height, 5.11. Weight, 160.
Throws and bats lefthanded.
Attended University of Southwestern Louisiana, Lafayette, La.

Established major league record for highest winning percentage, season, 20 or more wins (.893), 1978.
Established American League record for most strikeouts by lefthanded pitcher, game (18), June 17, 1978.
Tied American League record for most shutouts by lefthanded pitcher, season (9), 1978.
Led American League in complete games with 21 in 1983.
Led American League in shutouts with 9 in 1978.
Named Man of the Year by THE SPORTING NEWS, 1978.
Named Major League Player of the Year by THE SPORTING NEWS, 1978.
Named American League Pitcher of the Year by THE SPORTING NEWS, 1978.
Won American League Cy Young Memorial Award, 1978.
Named lefthanded pitcher on THE SPORTING NEWS American League All-Star Team, 1978, 1981 and 1983.
Named pitcher on THE SPORTING NEWS American League All-Star fielding team, 1982 and 1983.

Year Club	League	G.	IP.	W.	L.	Pct.	H.	R.	ER.	SO.	BB.	ERA.
1971—Johnson City	Ap'lachian	7	47	2	2	.500	34	13	11	61	27	2.11
1972—Ft. Lauderdale†	Florida St.	15	66	2	4	.333	53	35	28	61	50	3.82
1973—Kinston‡	Carolina	20	101	7	6	.538	85	53	36	97	70	3.21
1974—West Haven	Eastern	37	77	2	4	.333	80	48	45	79	53	5.26
1975—Syracuse	Int'national	42	62	6	5	.545	46	24	20	76	37	2.90
1975—New York	American	10	16	0	1	.000	15	6	6	15	9	3.38
1976—New York	American	7	16	0	0	.000	20	12	10	12	4	5.63
1976—Syracuse	Int'national	22	40	5	1	.833	16	5	3	50	13	0.68
1977—New York	American	31	211	16	7	.696	174	72	66	176	65	2.82
1978—New York	American	35	274	★25	3	★.893	187	61	53	248	72	★1.74
1979—New York§	American	33	236	18	8	.692	203	83	73	201	71	★2.78
1980—New York	American	37	220	17	10	.630	215	97	87	166	80	3.56
1981—New York x	American	23	127	11	5	.688	100	41	39	104	26	2.76
1982—New York	American	34	222	14	8	.636	216	104	94	162	69	3.81
1983—New York§	American	31	250⅓	21	9	.700	232	99	95	156	60	3.42
Major League Totals		241	1572⅓	122	51	.705	1362	575	523	1240	456	2.99

Selected by New York Yankees' organization in 3rd round of free-agent draft, June 8, 1971.
†Appeared as outfielder in one game with one putout.
‡On temporary inactive list, July 13 to August 3, 1973.
§Appeared as outfielder in one game with no chances.
xGranted free agency, November 13, 1981; re-signed by Yankees, December 15, 1981.

DIVISION SERIES RECORD

Year Club	League	G.	IP.	W.	L.	Pct.	H.	R.	ER.	SO.	BB.	ERA.
1981—New York	American	2	8⅓	0	0	.000	11	5	5	8	3	5.40

CHAMPIONSHIP SERIES RECORD

Year Club	League	G.	IP.	W.	L.	Pct.	H.	R.	ER.	SO.	BB.	ERA.
1977—New York	American	2	11⅓	1	0	1.000	9	5	5	8	3	3.97
1978—New York	American	1	8	1	0	1.000	7	1	1	7	1	1.13
1980—New York	American	1	3	0	1	.000	5	4	4	2	4	12.00
Championship Series Totals		4	22⅓	2	1	.667	21	10	10	17	8	4.03

Appeared as pinch-runner for New York Yankees in one game of 1976 Championship Series.

Tied World Series record for most consecutive home runs allowed, inning (2), October 25, 1981 (seventh inning).

Year	Club	League	G.	IP.	W.	L.	Pct.	H.	R.	ER.	SO.	BB.	ERA.
1977—New York		American	1	9	1	0	1.000	4	2	2	7	3	2.00
1978—New York		American	1	9	1	0	1.000	8	1	1	4	7	1.00
1981—New York		American	2	14	1	1	.500	8	3	3	15	4	1.93
World Series Totals			4	32	3	1	.750	20	6	6	26	14	1.69

ALL-STAR GAME RECORD

Year	League	IP.	W.	L.	Pct.	H.	R.	ER.	SO.	BB.	ERA.
1978—American		⅓	0	0	.000	0	0	0	0	0	0.00
1979—American		⅓	0	0	.000	0	0	0	0	1	0.00
All-Star Game Totals		⅔	0	0	.000	0	0	0	0	1	0.00

Member of American League All-Star Team in 1982; did not play.
Named to American League All-Star Team for 1983 game; replaced due to injury by Tippy Martinez.

OSWALDO JOSE GUILLEN (BARRIOS)
Name pronounced Gee-IN.
(Ozzie)

Born January 20, 1964, at Ocumare del Tuy, Miranda, Venezuela.
Height, 5.10. Weight, 160.
Throws right and bats left and righthanded.
Tied for California League lead in sacrifice hits with 14 in 1982.

Year	Club	League	Pos.	G.	AB.	R.	H.	2B.	3B.	HR.	RBI.	B.A.	PO.	A.	E.	F.A.
1981—Bradenton Padr...	Gulf C.		SS-2B	55	189	26	49	4	1	0	16	.259	105	135	15	.941
1982—Reno	Calif.		SS	130	528	★103	★183	33	1	2	54	.347	★240	399	41	.940
1983—Beaumont	Texas		SS	114	427	62	126	20	4	2	48	.295	185	327	★38	.931

Signed as free agent by San Diego Padres' organization, December 17, 1980.

BRADLEY LEE GULDEN
(Brad)

Born June 10, 1956, at New Ulm, Minn.
Height, 5.11. Weight, 182.
Throws right and bats lefthanded.
Led Pacific Coast League in passed balls with 22 and tied for lead in double plays by catchers with 11 in 1978.
Led California League in passed balls with 18 in 1977.
Led Northwest League catchers in double plays with 9 and passed balls with 23 in 1975.

Year	Club	League	Pos.	G.	AB.	R.	H.	2B.	3B.	HR.	RBI.	B.A.	PO.	A.	E.	F.A.
1975—Bellingham	N'west		C	66	203	25	33	4	0	2	15	.163	★319	★70	★33	.922
1976—Danville	Midw.		★C-OF	103	334	42	95	20	2	3	51	.284	521	90	★39	.939
1977—Lodi	Calif.		C	118	423	76	127	23	2	15	86	.300	★704	★66	★24	.970
1978—Albuquerque	P. C.		C	125	436	69	128	21	4	8	72	.294	★610	★88	★23	.968
1978—Los Angeles†	Nat.		C	3	4	0	0	0	0	0	0	.000	8	1	0	1.000
1979—Columbus	Int.		C	80	230	28	57	10	0	6	34	.248	326	22	3	.991
1979—New York	Amer.		C	40	92	10	15	4	0	0	6	.163	178	24	1	.995
1980—Columbus	Int.		C	14	51	6	8	2	0	2	10	.157	54	13	4	.944
1980—Nashville‡	South.		C-OF	85	295	34	70	13	6	6	46	.237	543	80	12	.981
1980—New York§	Amer.		C	2	3	1	1	0	0	1	2	.333	3	0	0	1.000
1981—Seattle	Amer.		C	8	16	0	3	2	0	0	1	.188	24	3	0	1.000
1981—Spokane x	P. C		C	15	51	9	14	5	0	2	9	.275	37	3	5	.889
1981—Columbus y	Int.		C-OF	73	237	37	70	13	4	17	42	.295	362	39	7	.983
1982—Wichita	A. A.		C-OF	64	212	37	61	16	2	7	35	.288	219	20	6	.976
1982—Montreal z	Nat.		C	5	6	1	0	0	0	0	0	.000	6	2	0	1.000
1983—Columbus a	Int.		C	94	275	45	87	16	1	9	47	.316	512	45	●13	.977
National League Totals				8	10	1	0	0	0	0	0	.000	14	3	0	1.000
American League Totals				50	111	11	19	6	0	1	9	.171	205	27	1	.996
Major League Totals				58	121	12	19	6	0	1	9	.157	219	30	1	.996

Selected by Los Angeles Dodgers' organization in 17th round of free-agent draft, June 4, 1975.
†Traded to New York Yankees for Outfielder Gary Thomasson, February 15, 1979.
‡On disabled list, August 7 to August 17, 1980.
§Traded to Seattle Mariners for Infielder Larry Milbourne, November 18, 1980.
xSold to New York Yankees, May 18, 1981.
yTraded to Montreal Expos' organization for Catcher Bobby Ramos, April 5, 1982.
zSold to New York Yankees, October 26, 1982.
aGranted free agency, October 20, 1983; signed by Cincinnati Reds, November 4, 1983.

WILLIAM LEE GULLICKSON
(Bill)

Born February 20, 1959, at Marshall, Minn.
Height, 6.03. Weight, 210.
Throws and bats righthanded.
Tied modern major league record for most wild pitches, game (6), April 10, 1982.
Named National League Rookie Pitcher of the Year by THE SPORTING NEWS, 1980.

Year Club	League	G.	IP.	W.	L.	Pct.	H.	R.	ER.	SO.	BB.	ERA.
1977—West Palm Beach	Florida St.	10	56	3	3	.500	67	30	25	35	17	4.02
1978—West Palm Beach	Florida St.	20	148	9	9	.500	121	45	30	127	52	1.82
1978—Memphis	Southern	8	50	1	4	.200	44	19	17	43	19	3.06
1979—Denver	Am. Assoc.	11	54	3	3	.500	65	44	40	31	26	6.67
1979—Memphis	Southern	16	116	10	3	.769	110	52	47	115	42	3.65
1979—Montreal	National	1	1	0	0	.000	2	0	0	0	0	0.00
1980—Denver	Am. Assoc.	9	66	6	2	.750	47	14	14	64	29	1.91
1980—Montreal	National	24	141	10	5	.667	127	53	47	120	50	3.00
1981—Montreal	National	22	157	7	9	.438	142	54	49	115	34	2.81
1982—Montreal	National	34	236⅔	12	14	.462	231	101	94	155	61	3.57
1983—Montreal	National	34	242⅓	17	12	.586	230	108	101	120	59	3.75
Major League Totals		115	778	46	40	.535	732	316	291	510	204	3.37

Selected by Montreal Expos' organization in 1st round (second player selected) of free-agent draft, June 7, 1977.

DIVISION SERIES RECORD

Year Club	League	G.	IP.	W.	L.	Pct.	H.	R.	ER.	SO.	BB.	ERA.
1981—Montreal	National	1	7⅔	1	0	1.000	6	1	1	3	1	1.17

CHAMPIONSHIP SERIES RECORD

Tied Championship Series record for most games lost, Series (2), 1981.

Year Club	League	G.	IP.	W.	L.	Pct.	H.	R.	ER.	SO.	BB.	ERA.
1981—Montreal	National	2	14⅓	0	2	.000	12	5	4	12	6	2.51

GLENN JAMES GULLIVER

Born October 15, 1954, at Detroit, Mich.
Height, 5.11. Weight, 180.
Throws right and bats lefthanded.
Attended Eastern Michigan University, Ypsilanti, Mich.

Led International League in bases on balls received with 117 in 1983.
Led American Association in bases on balls received with 87 in 1981.

Year Club	League	Pos.	G.	AB.	R.	H.	2B.	3B.	HR.	RBI.	B.A.	PO.	A.	E.	F.A.
1976—Montgomery	South.	SS	51	130	26	36	10	1	2	22	.277	75	124	16	.926
1977—Evansville	A. A.	SS-3B-2B	83	228	26	55	7	2	3	30	.241	71	167	16	.937
1977—Montgomery	South.	3B-SS	27	89	12	22	3	1	3	9	.247	16	30	4	.920
1978—Montgomery	South.	3B-SS	82	247	34	62	13	0	4	23	.251	56	196	15	.944
1978—Evansville	A. A.	3B-SS	28	83	12	23	4	0	4	12	.277	20	43	5	.926
1979—Evansville	A. A.	3B-SS	43	123	15	19	7	0	4	12	.154	33	69	6	.944
1979—Montgomery	South.	SS-3B-1B	75	226	45	59	15	2	8	30	.261	99	191	14	.954
1980—Evansville	A. A.	2-S-O-3	117	348	47	89	29	2	4	43	.256	158	241	17	.959
1981—Evansville†	A. A.	3-O-2-S	121	366	67	97	15	3	7	41	.265	106	216	19	.944
1982—Rochester	Int.	3B-2B-SS	85	268	48	79	9	2	12	35	.295	84	168	14	.947
1982—Baltimore	Amer.	3B	50	145	24	29	7	0	1	5	.200	34	97	4	.970
1983—Rochester	Int.	3B-2B	123	411	86	127	28	3	11	63	.309	124	277	23	.946
1983—Baltimore	Amer.	3B	23	47	5	10	3	0	0	2	.213	14	31	0	1.000
Major League Totals			73	192	29	39	10	0	1	7	.203	48	128	4	.978

Selected by Detroit Tigers' organization in 8th round of free-agent draft, June 8, 1976.
†Sold to Rochester (Baltimore Orioles' organization), March 26, 1982.

DAVID LAWRENCE GUMPERT
(Dave)

Born May 5, 1958, at South Haven, Mich.
Height, 6.03. Weight, 190.
Throws and bats righthanded.

Year Club	League	G.	IP.	W.	L.	Pct.	H.	R.	ER.	SO.	BB.	ERA.
1981—Lakeland	Florida St.	14	108	8	5	.615	97	33	30	75	26	2.50
1981—Birmingham	Southern	11	74	6	3	.667	78	39	34	25	16	4.14
1981—Evansville	Am. Assoc.	1	4	0	0	.000	5	2	2	3	2	4.50
1982—Birmingham	Southern	42	70⅔	9	6	.600	56	20	17	52	23	2.17
1982—Evansville	Am. Assoc.	2	5⅔	1	0	1.000	0	0	0	2	3	0.00
1982—Detroit	American	5	2	0	0	.000	7	6	6	0	2	27.00
1983—Evansville	Am. Assoc.	14	27⅔	5	1	.833	23	8	7	17	9	2.28
1983—Detroit	American	26	44⅓	0	2	.000	43	16	13	14	7	2.64
Major League Totals		31	46⅓	0	2	.000	50	22	19	14	9	3.69

Signed as free agent by Detroit Tigers' organization, November 4, 1980.

LAWRENCE CYRIL GURA
(Larry)

Born November 26, 1947, at Joliet, Ill.
Height, 6.01. Weight, 185.
Throws and bats lefthanded.
Received bachelor of arts degree in physical education from
Arizona State University, Tempe, Ariz., in 1969.

Established major league record for most sacrifice flies allowed, season (17), 1983.
Tied for International League lead in shutouts with 4 in 1974.

Received reported $50,000 bonus to sign with Chicago Cubs, 1969.

Year	Club	League	G.	IP.	W.	L.	Pct.	H.	R.	ER.	SO.	BB.	ERA.
1969—Tacoma		P. Coast	16	88	4	8	.333	79	39	31	47	24	3.17
1970—Tacoma		P. Coast	10	61	3	4	.429	55	32	27	32	17	3.98
1970—Chicago		National	20	38	1	3	.250	35	18	16	21	23	3.79
1971—Tacoma		P. Coast	30	190	11	8	.579	199	93	75	140	50	3.55
1971—Chicago		National	6	3	0	0	.000	6	3	2	2	1	6.00
1972—Wichita		Am. Assoc.	26	130	11	4	*.733	127	60	53	109	38	3.65
1972—Chicago		National	7	12	0	0	.000	11	5	5	13	3	3.75
1973—Wichita		Am. Assoc.	5	31	1	2	.333	38	18	16	29	11	4.65
1973—Chicago†		National	21	65	2	4	.333	79	39	35	43	11	4.85
1974—Spokane‡		P. Coast	7	29	1	1	.500	34	14	10	25	9	3.10
1974—Syracuse		Int'national	17	118	7	7	.500	89	32	28	97	19	*2.14
1974—New York		American	8	56	5	1	.833	54	17	15	17	12	2.41
1975—New York§		American	26	151	7	8	.467	173	65	59	65	41	3.52
1976—Kansas City x		American	20	63	4	0	1.000	47	20	16	22	20	2.29
1977—Kansas City		American	52	106	8	5	.615	108	43	37	46	28	3.14
1978—Kansas City y		American	26	222	16	4	.800	183	73	67	81	60	2.72
1979—Kansas City		American	39	234	13	12	.520	226	137	116	85	73	4.46
1980—Kansas City		American	36	283	18	10	.643	272	107	93	113	76	2.96
1981—Kansas City		American	23	172	11	8	.579	139	61	52	61	35	2.72
1982—Kansas City		American	37	248	18	12	.600	251	124	111	98	64	4.03
1983—Kansas City z		American	34	200⅓	11	*18	.379	220	119	109	57	76	4.90
National League Totals			54	118	3	7	.300	131	65	58	79	38	4.42
American League Totals			301	1735⅓	111	78	.587	1673	766	675	645	485	3.50
Major League Totals			355	1853⅓	114	85	.573	1804	831	733	724	523	3.56

Selected by Chicago Cubs' organization in 2nd round of free-agent draft, June 5, 1969.

†Traded to Texas Rangers, November 14, 1973, completing deal in which Texas traded Pitcher Mike Paul to Chicago Cubs for a player to be named later, August 31, 1973.

‡Traded to New York Yankees for Catcher Duke Sims, May 8, 1974.

§Traded to Kansas City Royals for Catcher Fran Healy, May 15, 1976.

xOn disabled list, June 1 to June 23, 1976.

yGranted free agency, November 2, 1978; re-signed by Royals, November 13, 1978.

zAppeared in one game as a pinch-runner.

DIVISION SERIES RECORD

Year	Club	League	G.	IP.	W.	L.	Pct.	H.	R.	ER.	SO.	BB.	ERA.
1981—Kansas City		American	1	3⅔	0	1	.000	7	4	3	3	3	7.36

CHAMPIONSHIP SERIES RECORD

Established Championship Series record for most hits allowed, game (12), October 9, 1976.

Established American League Championship Series record for most hits allowed, five-game Series (18), 1976.

Year	Club	League	G.	IP.	W.	L.	Pct.	H.	R.	ER.	SO.	BB.	ERA.
1976—Kansas City		American	2	10⅔	0	1	.000	18	6	5	4	1	4.22
1977—Kansas City		American	2	2	0	1	.000	7	5	4	2	1	18.00
1978—Kansas City		American	1	6⅓	1	0	1.000	8	2	2	2	2	2.84
1980—Kansas City		American	1	9	1	0	1.000	10	2	2	4	1	2.00
Championship Series Totals			6	28	2	2	.500	43	15	13	12	5	4.18

WORLD SERIES RECORD

Tied World Series record for most double plays by pitcher, six-game Series (2), 1980.

Year	Club	League	G.	IP.	W.	L.	Pct.	H.	R.	ER.	SO.	BB.	ERA.
1980—Kansas City		American	2	12⅓	0	0	.000	8	4	3	4	3	2.19

ALL-STAR GAME RECORD

Named to American League All-Star Team in 1980; did not play.

JOAQUIN FERNANDO GUTIERREZ

Name pronounced Wah-KEEN GOO-Tee-erz.

(Jackie)

Born June 27, 1960, at Cartagena, Colombia.
Height, 5.11. Weight, 168.
Throws and bats righthanded.

Led Carolina League shortstops in assists with 423 and tied for lead in putouts with 205 and errors with 53 in 1981.

Year	Club	League	Pos.	G.	AB.	R.	H.	2B.	3B.	HR.	RBI.	B.A.	PO.	A.	E.	F.A.
1978—Elmira	NYP		SS	63	216	23	42	8	0	0	18	.194	*131	197	20	*.943
1979—Elmira	NYP		SS-2B	63	183	29	46	4	2	0	14	.251	97	157	12	.955
1980—Winter Haven	Fla. St.		3B-SS-2B	111	368	46	94	4	1	1	40	.255	103	179	19	.937
1981—Winston-Salem	Carol.		SS-3B	137	507	56	126	14	5	1	45	.249	207	428	55	.920
1982—Bristol	East.		SS	138	468	64	130	20	2	1	44	.278	*199	368	37	*.939
1983—New Britain	East.		SS	67	248	36	69	7	2	4	25	.278	116	194	13	.960
1983—Pawtucket	Int.		SS	66	233	30	62	11	1	1	17	.266	109	211	20	.941
1983—Boston	Amer.		SS	5	10	2	3	0	0	0	0	.300	9	6	1	.938
Major League Totals				5	10	2	3	0	0	0	0	.300	9	6	1	.938

Signed as free agent by Boston Red Sox' organization, January 14, 1978.

JOSE A. GUZMAN (MIRABEL)

Born April 9, 1963, at Santa Isable, Puerto Rico.
Height, 6.02. Weight, 160.
Throws and bats righthanded.

Year Club	League	G.	IP.	W.	L.	Pct.	H.	R.	ER.	SO.	BB.	ERA.
1981—Sarasota Rangers	Gulf Coast	14	39	3	3	.500	44	30	23	13	14	5.31
1982—Sarasota Rangers	Gulf Coast	12	66	5	4	.556	51	21	16	42	13	2.18
1983—Burlington	Midwest	25	154⅔	12	8	.600	135	68	51	146	52	2.97

Signed as free agent by Texas Rangers' organization, February 10, 1981.

DOUGLAS WAYNE GWOSDZ

Name pronounced Goosh.

(Doug)

Born June 20, 1960, at Houston, Tex.
Height, 5.11. Weight, 180.
Throws and bats righthanded.

Year Club	League	Pos.	G.	AB.	R.	H.	2B.	3B.	HR.	RBI.	B.A.	PO.	A.	E.	F.A.
1978—Walla Walla	N'west	C	48	170	25	42	6	0	5	26	.247	256	51	5	*.984
1979—Reno	Calif.	C-OF	85	258	37	67	7	3	6	40	.260	583	51	8	.988
1980—Amarillo	Texas	C	97	286	40	70	18	2	7	43	.245	597	66	14	.979
1981—Hawaii	P. C.	C-1B	66	201	36	53	12	1	8	28	.264	322	42	8	.978
1981—San Diego	Nat.	C	16	24	1	4	2	0	0	3	.167	40	5	0	1.000
1982—San Diego	Nat.	C	7	17	1	3	0	0	0	0	.176	34	2	0	1.000
1982—Hawaii†	P. C.	C-OF	29	86	11	16	5	0	2	12	.186	133	16	4	.974
1983—San Diego	Nat.	C	39	55	7	6	1	0	1	4	.109	95	5	3	.971
Major League Totals			62	96	9	13	3	0	1	7	.135	169	12	3	.984

Selected by San Diego Padres' organization in 2nd round of free-agent draft, June 6, 1978.
†On disabled list, July 15 to September 3, 1982.

ANTHONY KEITH GWYNN

(Tony)

Born May 9, 1960, at Los Angeles, Calif.
Height, 5.11. Weight, 195.
Throws and bats lefthanded.
Attended San Diego State University, San Diego, Calif.

Named Northwest League Most Valuable Player, 1981.

Year Club	League	Pos.	G.	AB.	R.	H.	2B.	3B.	HR.	RBI.	B.A.	PO.	A.	E.	F.A.
1981—Walla Walla	N'west	OF	42	178	46	59	12	1	12	37	*.331	76	2	3	.963
1981—Amarillo	Texas	OF	23	91	22	42	8	2	4	19	.462	41	1	0	1.000
1982—Hawaii	P. C.	OF	93	366	65	120	23	2	5	46	.328	208	11	4	.982
1982—San Diego†	Nat.	OF	54	190	33	55	12	2	1	17	.289	110	1	1	.991
1983—San Diego‡	Nat.	OF	86	304	34	94	12	2	1	37	.309	163	9	1	.994
1983—Las Vegas	P. C.	OF	17	73	15	25	6	0	0	7	.342	23	2	3	.893
Major League Totals			140	494	67	149	24	4	2	54	.302	273	10	2	.993

Selected by San Diego Padres' organization in 3rd round of free-agent draft, June 8, 1981.
†On supplemental disabled list, August 26 to September 10, 1982.
‡On disabled list, March 26 to June 21, 1983; included rehabilitation assignment to Las Vegas, May 31 to June 20, 1983.

BRYAN EDMUND HAAS

(Moose)

Born April 22, 1956, at Baltimore, Md.
Height, 6.00. Weight, 170.
Throws and bats righthanded.
Attended Catonsville Junior College, Catonsville, Md.

Year Club	League	G.	IP.	W.	L.	Pct.	H.	R.	ER.	SO.	BB.	ERA.
1974—Newark	NYP	13	96	5	5	.500	91	43	34	89	41	3.19
1975—Burlington	Midwest	25	171	11	8	.579	149	66	39	146	49	2.05
1976—Spokane	P. Coast	30	172	13	9	.591	208	116	*106	130	86	5.55
1976—Milwaukee	American	5	16	0	1	.000	12	8	7	9	12	3.94
1977—Milwaukee	American	32	198	10	12	.455	195	104	95	113	84	4.32
1978—Milwaukee†	American	7	31	2	3	.400	33	22	21	32	8	6.10
1979—Milwaukee	American	29	185	11	11	.500	198	112	98	59	59	4.77
1980—Milwaukee	American	33	252	16	15	.516	246	96	87	146	56	3.11
1981—Milwaukee	American	24	137	11	7	.611	146	69	68	64	40	4.47
1982—Milwaukee	American	32	193⅓	11	8	.517	232	101	96	104	39	4.47
1983—Milwaukee‡	American	25	179	13	3	.813	170	66	65	75	42	3.27
Major League Totals		187	1191⅓	74	60	.552	1232	578	537	638	340	4.06

Selected by Milwaukee Brewers' organization in 2nd round of free-agent draft, June 5, 1974.
†On disabled list, April 20 to June 21 and June 27 to September 15, 1978.
‡Appeared in one game as a pinch-runner.

Year Club	League	G.	IP.	W.	L.	Pct.	H.	R.	ER.	SO.	BB.	ERA.
1981—Milwaukee	American	2	6⅔	0	2	.000	13	7	7	1	1	9.45

CHAMPIONSHIP SERIES RECORD

Year Club	League	G.	IP.	W.	L.	Pct.	H.	R.	ER.	SO.	BB.	ERA.
1982—Milwaukee	American	1	7⅓	1	0	1.000	5	5	4	7	5	4.91

WORLD SERIES RECORD

Year Club	League	G.	IP.	W.	L.	Pct.	H.	R.	ER.	SO.	BB.	ERA.
1982—Milwaukee	American	2	7⅓	0	0	.000	8	7	6	4	3	7.36

KEVIN EUGENE HAGEN

Born March 8, 1960, at Renton, Wash.
Height, 6.03. Weight, 195.
Throws and bats righthanded.
Attended Bellevue Community College, Bellevue, Wash.

Led Texas League in hit batsmen with 9 and tied for lead in balks with 4 in 1981.
Tied for American Association lead in shutouts with 2 in 1983.
Tied for Texas League lead in balks with 4 in 1982.

Year Club	League	G.	IP.	W.	L.	Pct.	H.	R.	ER.	SO.	BB.	ERA.
1980—Gastonia	S. Atlantic	29	177	14	8	.636	171	91	78	104	71	3.97
1981—Arkansas	Texas	27	165	8	11	.421	179	95	73	66	69	3.98
1982—Arkansas	Texas	27	189⅔	11	10	.524	176	88	76	102	75	3.61
1983—Louisville	Am. Assoc.	21	131⅓	6	9	.400	122	72	63	60	46	4.32
1983—St. Louis	National	9	22⅓	2	2	.500	34	15	12	7	7	4.84
Major League Totals		9	22⅓	2	2	.500	34	15	12	7	7	4.84

Selected by St. Louis Cardinals' organization in 4th round of free-agent draft, January 8, 1980.

JERRY WAYNE HAIRSTON

Born February 16, 1952, at Birmingham, Ala.
Height, 5.10. Weight, 185.
Throws right and bats left and righthanded.
Attended Lawson State Junior College, Birmingham, Ala.
Son of Sam Hairston, Sr., catcher with Chicago White Sox, 1951; and scout and minor league instructor with
Chicago White Sox since 1978; brother of John Hairston, catcher-outfielder
with Chicago Cubs, 1969; and Sam Hairston, Jr., second baseman
in Chicago White Sox' organization, 1966.

Led Mexican League in bases on balls received with 122 in 1978, 77 in 1980 and 122 in 1981.
Led Midwest League second baseman in double plays with 77 in 1971.
Tied for Mexican League lead in double plays by outfielders with 4 in 1981.

Year Club	League	Pos.	G.	AB.	R.	H.	2B.	3B.	HR.	RBI.	B.A.	PO.	A.	E.	F.A.
1970—Sarasota W. Sox	Gulf C.	2B	56	183	37	61	8	2	1	36	.333	129	130	*19	.932
1971—Appleton	Midw.	2B	121	448	86	120	15	4	0	39	.268	*260	*333	*31	.950
1972—Knoxville	South.	2-1-O-3	132	459	82	134	19	●9	10	64	.292	591	225	27	.968
1973—Iowa	A. A.	O-2-3-1	84	274	51	95	18	6	9	65	.347	70	36	7	.938
1973—Chicago	Amer.	OF-1B	60	210	25	57	11	1	0	23	.271	194	13	5	.976
1974—Iowa	A. A.	OF	42	140	31	53	10	2	5	42	.379	48	1	2	.961
1974—Chicago†	Amer.	OF	45	109	8	25	7	0	0	8	.229	24	1	2	.926
1975—Denver	A. A.	DH	40	139	28	51	9	0	3	31	.367	0	0	0	.000
1975—Chicago	Amer.	OF	69	219	26	62	8	0	0	23	.283	111	6	6	.951
1976—Iowa	A. A.	OF-INF	94	325	53	94	24	3	5	64	.289	199	13	5	.977
1976—Chicago	Amer.	OF	44	119	20	27	2	2	0	10	.227	71	1	2	.973
1977—Chicago‡	Amer.	OF	13	26	3	8	2	0	0	4	.308	15	1	0	1.000
1977—Chicago§	Nat.	OF-2B	51	52	5	10	2	0	2	6	.192	13	0	1	.929
1978—Durango	Mex.	OF	144	488	97	177	21	7	9	77	.363	297	19	11	.966
1979—Durango	Mex.	OF	128	427	87	151	22	5	12	56	.354	295	8	6	.981
1980—Campeche	Mex.	OF-1B	77	235	50	74	15	2	7	28	.315	189	11	3	.985
1981—Mex. C. Reds x	Mex.	OF	123	536	74	118	14	8	7	73	.296	*334	11	6	.983
1981—Chicago	Amer.	OF	9	25	5	7	1	0	1	6	.280	14	0	1	.933
1982—Chicago	Amer.	OF	85	90	11	21	5	0	5	18	.233	34	2	0	1.000
1983—Chicago	Amer.	OF	101	126	17	37	9	1	5	22	.294	29	1	1	.968
American League Totals			426	924	115	244	45	4	11	114	.264	492	25	17	.968
National League Totals			51	52	5	10	2	0	2	6	.192	13	0	1	.929
Major League Totals			477	976	120	254	47	4	13	120	.260	505	25	18	.967

Selected by Chicago White Sox' organization in 3rd round of free-agent draft, June 4, 1970.
†On supplemental disabled list, June 27 to July 12, 1974.
‡Sold to Pittsburgh Pirates, June 13, 1977.
§Sold to Durango of Mexican League, March 2, 1978.
xSold to Chicago White Sox, September 10, 1981.

CHAMPIONSHIP SERIES RECORD

Year Club	League	Pos.	G.	AB.	R.	H.	2B.	3B.	HR.	RBI.	B.A.	PO.	A.	E.	F.A.
1983—Chicago	Amer.	PH-OF	2	3	0	0	0	0	0	0	.000	0	0	1	.000

ALBERT HALL

Born March 7, 1959, at Birmingham, Ala.
Height, 5.11. Weight, 155.
Throws right and bats left and righthanded.

Led International League in stolen bases with 62 in 1982.
Led Carolina League in being hit by pitch with 9, stolen bases with 100 and caught stealing with 27 in 1980.
Led Western Carolinas League in stolen bases with 66 in 1979.
Led Gulf Coast League shortstops in double plays with 23 in 1978.
Tied for Southern League lead in caught stealing with 17 in 1981.

Year	Club	League	Pos.	G.	AB.	R.	H.	2B.	3B.	HR.	RBI.	B.A.	PO.	A.	E.	F.A.
1977—Kingsport	Appal.	SS	35	68	11	11	0	0	0	3	.162	10	28	10	.792
1978—Bradenton Brav...	Gulf C.	SS	34	123	15	36	4	2	0	14	.293	55	100	●15	.912
1979—Greenwood	W. Car.	SS	105	368	84	106	10	3	0	38	.288	120	288	★72	.850
1980—Durham	Carol.	OF-SS	125	491	95	139	16	7	4	41	.283	166	32	16	.925
1981—Savannah	South.	OF	133	487	83	150	28	10	5	27	.308	263	16	10	.965
1981—Atlanta	Nat.	OF	6	2	1	0	0	0	0	0	.000	0	0	0	.000
1982—Richmond	Int.	OF	129	528	97	139	18	★15	3	42	.263	297	6	7	.977
1982—Atlanta	Nat.	PR	5	0	1	0	0	0	0	0	.000	0	0	0	.000
1983—Richmond	Int.	★OF-SS	130	521	120	153	28	★11	1	42	.294	280	10	★12	.960
1983—Atlanta	Nat.	OF	10	8	2	0	0	0	0	0	.000	3	0	1	.750
Major League Totals			21	10	4	0	0	0	0	0	.000	3	0	1	.750

Selected by Atlanta Braves' organization in 6th round of free-agent draft, June 7, 1977.

MELVIN HALL JR.
(Mel)

Born September 16, 1960, at Lyons, N.Y.
Height, 6.00. Weight, 185.
Throws and bats lefthanded.
Son of Melvin Hall, minor league player in Cincinnati Reds' organization, 1949.

Led American Association in game-winning RBIs with 17 in 1982.
Led Texas League in total bases with 286 in 1981.
Led American Association outfielders in total chances with 339 in 1982.
Led Texas League outfielders in total chances with 324 and double plays with 5 in 1981.

Year	Club	League	Pos.	G.	AB.	R.	H.	2B.	3B.	HR.	RBI.	B.A.	PO.	A.	E.	F.A.
1978—Bradenton Cubs...	Gulf C.	OF	43	145	30	42	7	3	2	17	.290	★97	5	4	.962
1979—Geneva	NYP	OF	66	251	49	79	18	5	3	53	.315	113	5	7	.944
1980—Midland	Texas	OF	37	128	17	34	7	3	1	14	.266	58	3	3	.953
1980—Quad Cities	Midw.	OF	97	347	54	102	14	4	6	42	.294	171	9	5	.973
1981—Midland	Texas	OF	131	533	●98	★170	34	5	24	95	.319	★302	14	8	.975
1981—Chicago	Nat.	OF	10	11	1	1	0	0	1	2	.091	0	0	0	.000
1982—Iowa	A. A.	OF	133	502	★116	165	★34	6	32	125	.329	★317	13	●9	.973
1982—Chicago	Nat.	OF	24	80	6	21	3	2	0	4	.263	42	4	3	.939
1983—Chicago†	Nat.	OF	112	410	60	116	23	5	17	56	.283	239	8	3	.988
1983—Midland	Texas	OF	6	19	9	9	2	1	3	7	.474	8	0	0	1.000
Major League Totals			146	501	67	138	26	7	18	62	.275	281	12	6	.980

Selected by Chicago Cubs' organization in 2nd round of free-agent draft, June 6, 1978.

†On disabled list, April 15 to May 31, 1983; included rehabilitation disability assignment to Midland, May 25 to May 31, 1983.

CHARLTON ATLEE HAMMAKER
(Known by middle name.)

Born January 24, 1958, at Carmel, Calif.
Height, 6.02. Weight, 195.
Throws and bats lefthanded.
Attended East Tennessee State University, Johnson City, Tenn.

Year	Club	League	G.	IP.	W.	L.	Pct.	H.	R.	ER.	SO.	BB.	ERA.
1979—Sarasota Royals-Gold	Gulf Coast	1	5	1	0	1.000	3	1	1	6	1	1.80
1979—Ft. Myers†	Florida St.	1	5	0	1	.000	9	5	1	5	0	1.80
1980—Jacksonville‡	Southern	20	137	8	9	.471	131	64	51	88	37	3.35
1981—Omaha	Am. Assoc.	21	146	11	5	.688	147	70	59	63	40	3.64
1981—Kansas City§	American	10	39	1	3	.250	44	24	24	11	12	5.54
1982—Phoenix	P. Coast	1	5⅔	0	1	.000	13	5	4	6	2	6.35
1982—San Francisco	National	29	175	12	8	.600	189	86	80	102	28	4.11
1983—San Francisco x	National	23	172⅓	10	9	.526	147	57	43	127	32	★2.25
American League Totals		10	39	1	3	.250	44	24	24	11	12	5.54
National League Totals		52	347⅓	22	17	.564	336	143	123	229	60	3.19
Major League Totals		62	386⅓	23	20	.535	380	167	147	240	72	3.42

Selected by Kansas City Royals' organization in 1st round (21st player selected) of free-agent draft, June 5, 1979.
†On disabled list, July 6 to October 26, 1979.
‡On disabled list, August 3 to August 22, 1980.
§Traded with Pitchers Craig Chamberlain and Renie Martin and a player to be named later to San Francisco Giants for Pitchers Vida Blue and Bob Tufts, March 30, 1982; San Francisco organization acquired Second Baseman Brad Wellman to complete deal, April 19, 1982.
xOn disabled list, July 26 to August 21, 1983.

Established All-Star Game and inning records for most runs and earned runs allowed (7), July 6, 1983 (third inning).

Tied All-Star Game record for most home runs allowed, inning (2), July 6, 1983 (third inning).

Year	League	IP.	W.	L.	Pct.	H.	R.	ER.	SO.	BB.	ERA.
1983—National		⅔	0	0	.000	6	7	7	0	1	94.50

RONALD GARRY HANCOCK

(Known by middle name.)

Born January 23, 1954, at Tampa, Fla.
Height, 6.00. Weight, 175.
Throws and bats lefthanded.
Attended University of South Carolina, Columbia, S. C.

Led International League in sacrifice flies with 8 in 1982.
Led California League outfielders in double plays with 4 in 1976.

Year	Club	League	Pos.	G.	AB.	R.	H.	2B.	3B.	HR.	RBI.	B.A.	PO.	A.	E.	F.A.
1976—San Jose	Calif.	★OF-1B	135	526	56	162	22	5	5	77	.308	215	★20	9	.963
1977—Jersey City†	East.	OF	63	240	22	77	9	9	1	34	.321	117	6	5	.961
1977—Toledo‡	Int.	OF	53	189	17	50	6	1	3	16	.265	103	7	4	.965
1978—Pawtucket	Int.	OF	84	310	41	94	15	4	8	44	.303	146	11	6	.963
1978—Boston	Amer.	OF	38	80	10	18	3	0	0	4	.225	29	3	0	1.000
1979—Pawtucket§	Int.	OF-1B	111	406	51	132	22	3	15	58	★.325	166	15	3	.983
1980—Pawtucket	Int.	OF-1B	60	216	24	52	6	2	6	19	.241	144	11	4	.975
1980—Boston	Amer.	OF	46	115	9	33	6	0	4	19	.287	49	3	2	.963
1981—Boston	Amer.	OF	26	45	4	7	3	0	0	3	.156	11	2	0	1.000
1982—Pawtucket	Int.	OF-1B	123	449	53	132	18	3	21	71	.294	441	27	5	.989
1982—Boston x	Amer.	OF	11	14	3	0	0	0	0	0	.000	4	0	0	1.000
1983—Oakland	Amer.	OF-1B	100	256	29	70	7	3	8	30	.273	249	10	4	.985
Major League Totals			221	510	55	128	19	3	12	56	.251	342	18	6	.984

Selected by Baltimore Orioles' organization in 25th round of free-agent draft, June 4, 1970.
Selected by Texas Rangers' organization in 22nd round of free-agent draft, June 6, 1972.
Selected by Cleveland Indians' organization in 10th round of free-agent draft, January 9, 1974.
Selected by Texas Rangers' organization in secondary phase of free-agent draft, June 5, 1974.
Selected by California Angels' organization in secondary phase of free-agent draft, June 4, 1975.
Selected by Cleveland Indians' organization in secondary phase of free-agent draft, January 7, 1976.
†On disabled list, May 15 to May 29, 1977.
‡Traded to Boston Red Sox' organization for First Baseman Jack Baker, December 7, 1977.
§On disabled list, June 3 to June 17, 1979.
xTraded with Third Baseman Carney Lansford and a player to be named later to Oakland A's for Outfielder Tony Armas and Catcher Jeff Newman, December 6, 1982; Oakland acquired Pitcher Jerry King to complete deal, December 20, 1982.

ROGER CHRISTIAN HANSEN

Born August 28, 1961, at Johnstown, Pa.
Height, 6.00. Weight, 200.
Throws and bats righthanded.
Son of Jim Hansen, minor league pitcher, 1958 through 1964.

Led South Atlantic League in sacrifice flies with 12 in 1982.
Tied for Florida State League lead in sacrifice flies with 9 in 1983.
Led South Atlantic League first basemen in double plays with 93 in 1981.

Year	Club	League	Pos.	G.	AB.	R.	H.	2B.	3B.	HR.	RBI.	B.A.	PO.	A.	E.	F.A.
1980—Sarasota Blue	Gulf C.	3B	55	167	28	38	3	2	0	15	.228	25	55	13	.860
1981—Charleston	S. Atl.	1B-3B	●141	516	55	125	28	6	6	71	.242	1197	80	19	.985
1982—Charleston	S. Atl.	C-1B	137	505	78	148	34	0	15	94	.293	677	62	16	.979
1983—Ft. Myers	Fla. St.	★C-1B	107	387	51	109	13	1	2	62	.282	524	33	4	★.993
1983—Jacksonville	South.	C	1	3	0	1	0	0	0	0	.333	6	0	0	1.000

Selected by Kansas City Royals' organization in 2nd round of free-agent draft, June 3, 1980.

ALAN ROBERT HARGESHEIMER

Name pronounced HAHR-guh-shy-mer.

(Al)

Born November 21, 1956, at Chicago, Ill.
Height, 6.03. Weight, 200.
Throws and bats righthanded.
Attended Mayfair Junior College, Chicago, Ill. and received bachelor of science degree
in physical education from Northeastern Illinois University, Chicago, Ill.

Tied for California League lead in games started by pitchers with 28 in 1978.

Year	Club	League	G.	IP.	W.	L.	Pct.	H.	R.	ER.	SO.	BB.	ERA.
1978—Fresno	California	29	176	7	11	.389	★216	117	96	109	82	4.91
1979—Shreveport	Texas	24	141	6	10	.375	165	96	71	80	60	4.53
1980—Shreveport	Texas	12	81	2	6	.250	67	28	16	40	30	1.78
1980—Phoenix	P. Coast	2	17	1	1	.500	18	8	8	13	13	4.24
1980—San Francisco	National	15	75	4	6	.400	82	38	36	40	32	4.32
1981—Phoenix†	P. Coast	20	118	6	8	.429	127	58	48	64	41	3.66
1981—San Francisco	National	6	19	1	2	.333	20	9	9	6	9	4.26
1982—Phoenix‡	P. Coast	29	152⅔	6	12	.333	214	★136	111	89	95	6.54

Year Club	League	G.	IP.	W.	L.	Pct.	H.	R.	ER.	SO.	BB.	ERA.
1983—Iowa	Am. Assoc.	49	78⅓	7	4	.636	78	35	30	50	48	3.45
1983—Chicago	National	5	4	0	0	.000	6	4	4	5	2	9.00
Major League Totals		26	98	5	8	.385	108	51	49	51	43	4.50

Signed as free agent by San Francisco Giants' organization, March 21, 1978.
†On disabled list, June 13 to July 12, 1981.
‡Traded to Chicago Cubs' organization for Pitcher Herman Segelke, October 15, 1982.

DUDLEY MICHAEL HARGROVE
(Mike)

Born October 26, 1949, at Perryton, Tex.
Height, 6.00. Weight, 195.
Throws and bats lefthanded.
Received bachelor of science degree in physical education and social sciences
from Northwestern State University, Alva, Okla.

Led American League in bases on balls received with 97 in 1976 and 107 in 1978.
Led American League first basemen in total chances with 1,489 in 1980.
Led Western Carolinas League in total bases with 247 in 1973.
Led Western Carolinas League first basemen in double plays with 118 in 1973 and led New York-Pennsylvania League first basemen with 58 in 1972.
Named American League Rookie Player of the Year by THE SPORTING NEWS, 1974.
Named American League Rookie of the Year by Baseball Writers' Association of America, 1974.
Named Western Carolinas League Player of the Year, 1973.

Year Club	League	Pos.	G.	AB.	R.	H.	2B.	3B.	HR.	RBI.	B.A.	PO.	A.	E.	F.A.
1972—Geneva	NYP	1B	●70	243	38	65	8	0	4	37	.267	★537	●40	10	★.983
1973—Gastonia	W. Car.	1B	●130	456	88	★160	★35	8	12	82	★.351	★1121	★77	14	★.988
1974—Texas	Amer.	1B-OF	131	415	57	134	18	6	4	66	.323	638	72	9	.987
1975—Texas	Amer.	OF-1B	145	519	82	157	22	2	11	62	.303	513	45	13	.977
1976—Texas	Amer.	1B	151	541	80	155	30	1	7	58	.287	1222	110	★21	.984
1977—Texas	Amer.	1B	153	525	98	160	28	4	18	69	.305	1393	100	11	.993
1978—Texas†	Amer.	1B	146	494	63	124	24	1	7	40	.251	1221	★116	★17	.987
1979—San Diego‡	Nat.	1B	52	125	15	24	5	0	0	8	.192	323	17	5	.986
1979—Cleveland	Amer.	OF-1B	100	338	60	110	21	4	10	56	.325	356	16	2	.995
1980—Cleveland	Amer.	1B	160	589	86	179	22	2	11	85	.304	★1391	88	10	.993
1981—Cleveland	Amer.	1B	94	322	43	102	21	0	2	49	.317	766	76	●9	.989
1982—Cleveland	Amer.	1B	160	591	67	160	26	1	4	65	.271	1293	★123	5	.996
1983—Cleveland	Amer.	1B	134	469	57	134	21	4	3	57	.286	1098	115	7	.994
American League Totals			1374	4803	693	1415	233	25	77	607	.295	9891	861	104	.990
National League Totals			52	125	15	24	5	0	0	8	.192	323	17	5	.986
Major League Totals			1426	4928	708	1439	238	25	77	615	.292	10214	878	109	.990

Selected by Texas Rangers' organization in 25th round of free-agent draft, June 6, 1972.

†Traded with Third Baseman Kurt Bevacqua and Catcher Bill Fahey to San Diego Padres for Outfielder Oscar Gamble, Catcher Dave Roberts and cash estimated at $300,000, October 25, 1978.

‡Traded to Cleveland Indians for Outfielder Paul Dade, June 14, 1979.

ALL-STAR GAME RECORD

Year League	Pos.	AB.	R.	H.	2B.	3B.	HR.	RBI.	B.A.	PO.	A.	E.	F.A.
1975—American	PH	1	0	0	0	0	0	0	.000	0	0	0	.000

BRIAN DAVID HARPER

Born October 16, 1959, at Los Angeles, Calif.
Height, 6.02. Weight, 195.
Throws and bats righthanded.

Led Pacific Coast League in total bases with 339 in 1981.
Led Pacific Coast League catchers in errors with 19 in 1981.
Led Texas League in passed balls with 19 in 1979.

Year Club	League	Pos.	G.	AB.	R.	H.	2B.	3B.	HR.	RBI.	B.A.	PO.	A.	E.	F.A.
1977—Idaho Falls	Pion.	C	52	186	28	60	9	3	1	33	.323	352	36	13	.968
1978—Quad Cities	Midw.	C	129	508	80	149	31	2	24	★101	.293	430	46	16	.967
1979—El Paso	Texas	C	132	531	85	167	★37	3	14	90	.315	443	66	★29	.946
1979—California	Amer.	DH	1	2	0	0	0	0	0	0	.000	0	0	0	.000
1980—El Paso†	Texas	C	105	400	61	114	23	3	12	66	.285	214	30	7	.972
1981—Salt Lake City	P. C.	C-OF-1B	134	549	99	★192	45	9	28	122	.350	421	30	24	.949
1981—California‡	Amer.	OF	4	11	1	3	0	0	0	1	.273	5	0	1	.833
1982—Pittsburgh	Nat.	OF	20	29	4	8	1	0	2	4	.276	10	0	0	1.000
1982—Portland	P. C.	OF-3B-C	101	395	71	112	29	8	17	73	.284	164	36	8	.962
1983—Pittsburgh	Nat.	OF-1B	61	131	16	29	4	1	7	20	.221	40	0	0	1.000
American League Totals			5	13	1	3	0	0	0	1	.231	5	0	1	.833
National League Totals			81	160	20	37	5	1	9	24	.231	50	0	0	1.000
Major League Totals			86	173	21	40	5	1	9	25	.231	55	0	1	.982

Selected by California Angels' organization in 4th round of free-agent draft, June 7, 1977.
†On disabled list, July 1 to July 17, 1980.
‡Traded to Pittsburgh Pirates for Shortstop Tim Foli, December 11, 1981.

TERRY JOE HARPER

Born August 19, 1955, at Douglasville, Ga.
Height, 6.01. Weight, 195.
Throws and bats righthanded.

Led International League in caught stealing with 18 in 1980.
Led International League outfielders in double plays with 5 in 1980.

Year	Club	League	Pos.	G.	AB.	R.	H.	2B.	3B.	HR.	RBI.	B.A.	PO.	A.	E.	F.A.
1973—Wytheville	Appal.	P	13	17	3	4	0	0	0	2	.235	3	7	4	.714
1974—Greenwood†	W. Car.	P	15	15	0	4	0	1	0	1	.267	1	11	2	.857
1975—Greenwood‡	W. Car.	P	14	0	0	0	0	0	0	0	.000	6	17	0	1.000
1976—Greenwood§	W. Car.	P	2	0	0	0	0	0	0	0	.000	1	0	0	1.000
1976—Brad. Braves	Gulf C.	OF-3B-1B	51	185	21	48	6	6	1	37	.259	87	8	6	.941
1977—Greenwood	W. Car.	OF-3B-1B	70	251	45	74	12	3	4	43	.295	200	10	4	.981
1977—Savannah	South.	OF	54	149	14	36	3	5	1	18	.242	94	8	2	.981
1978—Savannah	South.	OF	47	174	17	46	9	1	4	21	.264	85	10	2	.979
1978—Richmond	Int.	OF	73	205	21	52	5	3	0	24	.254	137	5	2	.896
1979—Richmond x	Int.	OF	108	327	49	99	18	3	10	58	.303	164	9	9	.951
1980—Richmond	Int.	OF	*140	512	66	143	19	8	13	72	.279	315	19	6	.982
1980—Atlanta	Nat.	OF	21	54	3	10	2	1	0	3	.185	30	0	1	.968
1981—Atlanta	Nat.	OF	40	73	9	19	1	0	2	8	.260	38	2	1	.976
1981—Richmond	Int.	OF	10	44	3	10	3	0	2	4	.227	22	0	0	1.000
1982—Richmond	Int.	OF	37	146	25	56	12	2	9	42	.384	77	8	1	.988
1982—Atlanta yz	Nat.	OF	48	150	16	43	3	0	2	16	.287	74	4	1	.987
1983—Atlanta	Nat.	OF	80	201	19	53	13	1	3	26	.264	95	5	5	.952
Major League Totals			189	478	47	125	19	2	7	53	.262	237	11	8	.969

Selected by Atlanta Braves' organization in 16th round of free-agent draft, June 5, 1973.
†On disabled list, May 5 to May 31 and June 24 to July 9, 1974.
‡On disabled list, June 18 to July 7 and August 2 to August 16, 1975.
§On disabled list, April 27 to June 25, 1976.
xOn disabled list, August 20 to September 26, 1979.
yOn disabled list, June 1 to July 1 and July 23 to July 31, 1982.
zOn supplemental disabled list, July 8 to July 23, 1982.

CHAMPIONSHIP SERIES RECORD

Year	Club	League	Pos.	G.	AB.	R.	H.	2B.	3B.	HR.	RBI.	B.A.	PO.	A.	E.	F.A.
1982—Atlanta	Nat.	PR-OF	1	1	1	0	0	0	0	0	.000	0	0	0	.000

PITCHING RECORD

Year	Club	League	G.	IP.	W.	L.	Pct.	H.	R.	ER.	SO.	BB.	ERA.
1973—Wytheville	Ap'lachian	12	58	3	3	.500	60	36	25	42	36	3.88
1974—Greenwood	W. Carol.	15	43	4	2	.667	44	23	19	37	25	3.98
1975—Greenwood	W. Carol.	14	69	1	5	.167	95	48	40	27	39	5.22
1976—Greenwood	W. Carol.	2	8	1	1	.500	9	10	10	4	7	11.25

COLBERT DALE HARRAH

Name pronounced HAIR-uh.

(Toby)

Born October 26, 1948, at Sissonville, W. Va.
Height, 6.00. Weight, 180.
Throws and bats righthanded.
Attended Ohio Northern University, Ada, O.

Established major league records for most innings by third baseman, no assists, game (17), September 17, 1977; fewest chances offered by shortstop, doubleheader (0), June 25, 1976.
Tied major league record for fewest chances offered by shortstop, two consecutive games (0), June 25, 1976 (doubleheader).
Major League stolen bases: 1971 (10), 1972 (16), 1973 (10), 1974 (15), 1975 (23), 1976 (8), 1977 (27), 1978 (31), 1979 (20), 1980 (17), 1981 (12), 1982 (17), 1983 (16). Total—222.
Led American League in bases on balls received with 109 in 1977.
Led American League shortstops in putouts with 281 in 1974 and tied for lead with 290 in 1976.
Led American League shortstops in errors with 36 in 1976.
Named shortstop on THE SPORTING NEWS American League All-Star Team, 1975.

Year	Club	League	Pos.	G.	AB.	R.	H.	2B.	3B.	HR.	RBI.	B.A.	PO.	A.	E.	F.A.
1967—Huron†	North.	2B-SS	63	207	34	53	6	0	3	22	.256	136	163	23	.929
1968—Burlington	Carol.	SS	135	468	73	112	16	3	6	39	.239	217	356	*50	.920
1969—Burlington‡	Carol.	SS-2B	46	147	27	45	4	2	4	12	.306	76	152	10	.958
1969—Savannah	South.	SS	28	80	8	19	2	0	2	7	.238	36	78	11	.912
1969—Washington	Amer.	SS	8	1	4	0	0	0	0	0	.000	0	0	0	.000
1970—Pittsfield§	East.	SS-3B	95	359	57	99	18	1	3	37	.276	159	293	27	.944
1971—Washington	Amer.	SS-3B	127	383	45	88	11	3	2	22	.230	187	321	24	.955
1972—Texas x	Amer.	SS	116	374	47	97	14	3	1	31	.259	166	308	20	.960
1973—Texas y	Amer.	SS-3B	118	461	64	120	16	1	10	50	.260	155	332	27	.947
1974—Texas	Amer.	●SS-3B	161	573	79	149	23	2	21	74	.260	283	474	●29	.963
1975—Texas	Amer.	SS-3B-2B	151	522	81	153	24	1	20	93	.293	253	481	29	.962
1976—Texas	Amer.	SS-3B	155	584	64	152	21	1	15	67	.260	294	481	37	.954
1977—Texas z	Amer.	3B-SS	159	539	90	142	25	5	27	87	.263	108	278	15	.963
1978—Texas z	Amer.	3B-SS	139	450	56	103	17	3	12	59	.229	129	330	11	.977
1979—Cleveland	Amer.	3B-SS	149	527	99	147	25	1	20	77	.279	113	215	19	.947
1980—Cleveland	Amer.	3B-SS	160	561	100	150	22	4	11	72	.267	121	319	13	.971

Year—Club	League	Pos.	G.	AB.	R.	H.	2B.	3B.	HR.	RBI.	B.A.	PO.	A.	E.	F.A.
1981—Cleveland..............	Amer.	3B-SS	103	361	64	105	12	4	5	44	.291	64	180	13	.949
1982—Cleveland..............	Amer.	3B-2B-SS	●162	602	100	183	29	4	25	78	.304	126	279	12	.971
1983—Cleveland a..........	Amer.	★3B-2B	138	526	81	140	23	1	9	53	.266	101	273	11	★.971
Major League Totals................................			1846	6464	974	1729	262	33	178	807	.267	2100	4271	260	.961

Signed as free agent by Philadelphia Phillies' organization, December 27, 1966.
†Drafted by Washington Senators' organization, November 28, 1967.
‡On military list, January 28 to June 2, 1969.
§On temporary inactive list, July 24 to August 11, 1970.
xOn disabled list, August 14 to September 6, 1972.
yOn supplemental disabled list, July 2 to August 7, 1973.
zTraded to Cleveland Indians for Third Baseman Buddy Bell, December 8, 1978.
aOn supplemental disabled list, April 17 to May 14, 1983.

ALL-STAR GAME RECORD

Year—League	Pos.	AB.	R.	H.	2B.	3B.	HR.	RBI.	B.A.	PO.	A.	E.	F.A.
1976—American......................................	SS	2	0	0	0	0	0	0	.000	0	0	0	.000

Named to American League All-Star Team for the 1972 game; replaced due to an injury.
Member of American League All-Star Team in 1975 and 1982; did not play.

GREG ALLEN HARRIS

Born November 2, 1955, at Lynwood, Calif.
Height, 6.00. Weight, 165.
Throws right and bats left and righthanded.
Attended Long Beach City College, Long Beach, Calif.

Year—Club	League	G.	IP.	W.	L.	Pct.	H.	R.	ER.	SO.	BB.	ERA.
1977—Jackson	Texas	30	83	3	6	.333	96	63	50	56	36	5.42
1978—Lynchburg	Carolina	21	154	8	9	.471	114	52	37	102	74	2.16
1978—Jackson	Texas	6	33	2	3	.400	24	13	11	18	10	3.00
1979—Jackson	Texas	25	163	9	11	.450	125	58	41	89	81	★2.26
1980—Tidewater..................	Int'national	39	110	2	9	.182	99	45	33	92	40	2.70
1981—Tidewater..................	Int'national	7	48	4	0	1.000	37	14	11	26	16	2.06
1981—New York†	National	16	69	3	5	.375	65	36	34	54	28	4.43
1982—Indianapolis	Am. Assoc.	8	48	4	1	.800	27	18	16	44	24	3.00
1982—Cincinnati	National	34	91⅓	2	6	.250	96	56	49	67	37	4.83
1983—Indianapolis	Am. Assoc.	28	152⅓	9	12	.429	155	83	70	★146	66	4.14
1983—Cincinnati‡	National	1	1	0	0	.000	2	3	3	1	3	27.00
Major League Totals...............................		51	161⅓	5	11	.313	163	95	86	122	68	4.80

Selected by California Angels' organization in 10th round of free-agent draft, June 5, 1974.
Selected by New York Mets' organization in secondary phase of free-agent draft, January 9, 1975.
Selected by New York Mets' organization in 7th round of free-agent draft, January 7, 1976.
Signed as free agent by New York Mets' organization, September 17, 1976.
†Traded with Catcher Alex Trevino and Pitcher Jim Kern to Cincinnati Reds for Outfielder George Foster, February 10, 1982.
‡Claimed on waivers by Montreal Expos, September 27, 1983.

RONALD DWAYNE HARRISON
(Ron)

Born October 15, 1960, at Sacramento, Calif.
Height, 6.00. Weight, 170.
Throws right and bats lefthanded.
Tied for Eastern League lead in sacrifice hits with 12 in 1983.
Led Midwest League outfielders in double plays with 6 in 1982.

Year—Club	League	Pos.	G.	AB.	R.	H.	2B.	3B.	HR.	RBI.	B.A.	PO.	A.	E.	F.A.
1981—Medford	N'west	OF	32	90	10	16	5	1	1	7	.178	32	3	5	.875
1982—Madison	Midw.	OF	127	447	59	125	20	4	8	64	.280	238	15	12	.955
1983—Albany	Eastern	OF	106	398	65	116	17	3	11	50	.291	215	12	11	.954

Signed as free agent by Oakland A's organization, May 19, 1981.

MICHAEL LAWRENCE HART
(Mike)

Born February 17, 1958, at Milwaukee, Wis.
Height, 5.11. Weight, 185.
Throws and bats lefthanded.
Attended University of Wisconsin, Madison, Wis.
Nephew of Bill Mosser, minor league pitcher, 1946 through 1952.

Year—Club	League	Pos.	G.	AB.	R.	H.	2B.	3B.	HR.	RBI.	B.A.	PO.	A.	E.	F.A.
1979—Bellingham	N'west	OF	4	8	0	1	0	0	0	0	.125	8	1	1	.900
1979—Wausau.................	Midw.	OF	52	177	34	46	9	1	1	21	.260	79	3	0	1.000
1980—Lynn......................	East.	OF	117	399	69	119	15	6	10	61	.298	204	5	6	.972
1981—Spokane†	P. C.	OF	105	357	51	99	19	4	6	48	.277	237	7	3	.988
1982—Salt Lake City‡.....	P. C.	OF	134	472	86	127	15	6	10	74	.269	268	10	5	.982
1983—Toledo	Int.	OF	137	487	95	141	18	.7	17	66	.290	311	12	10	.970

Selected by Seattle Mariners' organization in 13th round of free-agent draft, June 5, 1979.
†On disabled list, April 8 to May 14, 1981.
‡Released, January 28, 1983; signed by Toledo (Minnesota Twins' organization), January 31, 1983.

RONALD WILLIAM HASSEY
(Ron)

Born February 27, 1953, at Tucson, Ariz.
Height, 6.02. Weight, 195.
Throws right and bats lefthanded.
Attended University of Arizona, Tucson, Ariz.
Son of Bill Hassey, minor league outfielder, 1949 through 1952.

Year Club	League	Pos.	G.	AB.	R.	H.	2B.	3B.	HR.	RBI.	B.A.	PO.	A.	E.	F.A.
1976—San Jose	Calif.	C-3B	22	62	7	19	4	0	1	7	.306	55	2	2	.966
1976—Williamsport	East.	C	21	68	6	19	3	0	0	8	.279	63	10	4	.948
1977—Toledo	Int.	C-3-1-O	129	446	50	132	21	1	10	57	.296	484	82	21	.964
1978—Portland	P. C.	C-3B	72	235	42	76	12	1	12	52	.323	312	32	7	.980
1978—Cleveland	Amer.	C	25	74	5	15	0	0	2	9	.203	130	15	1	.993
1979—Tacoma	P. C.	C-3B	44	157	25	53	10	0	3	27	.338	282	44	2	.994
1979—Cleveland	Amer.	C-1B	75	223	20	64	14	0	4	32	.287	368	29	3	.993
1980—Cleveland	Amer.	C-1B	130	390	43	124	18	4	8	65	.318	564	52	4	.994
1981—Cleveland	Amer.	C-1B	61	190	8	44	4	0	1	25	.232	327	44	3	.992
1982—Cleveland	Amer.	C-1B	113	323	33	81	18	0	5	34	.251	566	38	4	.993
1983—Cleveland	Amer.	C	117	341	48	92	21	0	6	42	.270	514	43	3	.995
Major League Totals			521	1541	157	420	75	4	26	207	.273	2469	221	18	.993

Selected by Cincinnati Reds' organization in 23rd round of free-agent draft, June 6, 1972.
Selected by Kansas City Royals' organization in 22nd round of free-agent draft, June 4, 1975.
Selected by Cleveland Indians' organization in 18th round of free-agent draft, June 8, 1976.

ANDREW EARL HASSLER
(Andy)

Born October 18, 1951, at Texas City, Tex.
Height, 6.05. Weight, 215.
Throws and bats lefthanded.

Tied for Pacific Coast League lead in games started by pitchers with 31 and wild pitches with 14 in 1972.

Year Club	League	G.	IP.	W.	L.	Pct.	H.	R.	ER.	SO.	BB.	ERA.
1970—El Paso†	Texas	22	144	10	7	.588	138	80	62	122	87	3.88
1971—Salt Lake City‡	P. Coast	9	51	5	1	.833	50	34	26	42	39	4.59
1971—California	American	6	19	0	3	.000	25	10	8	13	15	3.79
1972—Salt Lake City	P. Coast	32	174	9	10	.474	163	106	85	150	★114	4.40
1973—Salt Lake City	P. Coast	24	163	13	8	.619	166	93	76	127	81	4.20
1973—California	American	7	32	0	4	.000	33	23	13	19	19	3.66
1974—Salt Lake City	P. Coast	12	79	5	7	.417	98	61	52	52	48	5.92
1974—California	American	23	162	7	11	.389	132	64	47	76	79	2.61
1975—California	American	30	133	3	12	.200	158	94	88	82	53	5.95
1976—Calif.§-K. C.	American	33	147	5	12	.294	139	68	59	61	56	3.61
1977—Kansas City x	American	29	156	9	6	.600	166	88	73	83	75	4.21
1978—Kan. City y-Boston	American	24	88	3	5	.375	114	49	38	49	37	3.89
1979—Boston z	American	8	15	1	2	.333	23	17	15	7	7	9.00
1979—New York a	National	29	80	4	5	.444	74	35	33	53	42	3.71
1980—Pittsburgh b	National	6	12	0	0	.000	9	6	5	4	4	3.75
1980—California	American	41	83	5	1	.833	67	25	23	75	37	2.49
1981—California	American	42	76	4	3	.571	72	29	27	44	33	3.20
1982—California	American	54	71⅓	2	1	.667	58	24	22	38	40	2.78
1983—California	American	42	36⅓	0	5	.000	42	22	22	20	17	5.45
National League Totals		35	92	4	5	.444	83	41	38	57	46	3.72
American League Totals		339	1018⅔	39	65	.375	1029	513	435	567	468	3.84
Major League Totals		374	1110⅔	43	70	.381	1112	554	473	624	514	3.83

Selected by California Angels' organization in 25th round of free-agent draft, June 5, 1969.
†On disabled list, August 10 to September 6, 1970.
‡On disabled list April 27 to May 12 and June 28 to August 31, 1971.
§Sold to Kansas City Royals, July 5, 1976.
xOn disabled list, April 27 to May 25, 1977.
ySold to Boston Red Sox, July 24, 1978.
zSold to New York Mets, June 15, 1979.
aGranted free agency, November 1, 1979; signed by Pittsburgh Pirates, November 21, 1979.
bSold to California Angels, June 10, 1980.

CHAMPIONSHIP SERIES RECORD

Year Club	League	G.	IP.	W.	L.	Pct.	H.	R.	ER.	SO.	BB.	ERA.
1976—Kansas City	American	2	7⅓	0	1	.000	8	6	5	4	6	6.14
1977—Kansas City	American	1	5⅔	0	1	.000	5	3	3	3	0	4.76
1982—California	American	2	2⅔	0	0	.000	0	0	0	2	0	0.00
Championship Series Totals		5	15⅔	0	2	.000	13	9	8	9	6	4.60

MICHAEL VAUGHN HATCHER JR.
(Mickey)

Born March 15, 1955, at Cleveland, O.
Height, 6.02. Weight, 195.
Throws and bats righthanded.
Attended Mesa Community College, Mesa, Ariz., and
University of Oklahoma, Norman, Okla.
Brother of Hal Hatcher, catcher in Kansas City Royals' organization.

Year Club	League	Pos.	G.	AB.	R.	H.	2B.	3B.	HR.	RBI.	B.A.	PO.	A.	E.	F.A.
1977—Clinton	Midw.	OF	78	288	47	89	12	4	11	53	.309	126	9	4	.971
1978—San Antonio†	Texas	3B	83	334	60	111	12	6	8	62	.332	55	124	22	.891
1978—Albuquerque	P. C.	3B-OF	41	155	25	51	11	5	7	39	.329	24	63	8	.916
1979—Albuquerque	P. C.	3B-OF	103	420	88	156	29	12	10	93	*.371	127	156	12	.959
1979—Los Angeles	Nat.	OF-3B	33	93	9	25	4	1	1	5	.269	47	24	5	.934
1980—Albuquerque	P. C.	OF-3B	43	181	28	65	7	2	7	40	.359	52	32	9	.903
1980—Los Angeles‡	Nat.	3B-OF	57	84	4	19	2	0	1	5	.226	31	23	3	.947
1981—Minnesota	Amer.	OF-1B-3B	99	377	36	96	23	2	3	37	.255	296	11	3	.990
1982—Minnesota	Amer.	OF-3B	84	277	23	69	13	2	3	26	.249	81	17	1	.990
1983—Minnesota§	Amer.	OF-1B-3B	106	375	50	119	15	3	9	47	.317	199	11	3	.986
National League Totals			90	177	13	44	6	1	2	10	.249	78	47	8	.940
American League Totals			289	1029	109	284	51	7	15	110	.276	576	39	7	.989
Major League Totals			379	1206	122	328	57	8	17	120	.272	654	86	15	.980

Selected by Houston Astros' organization in 14th round of free-agent draft, June 5, 1974.
Selected by New York Mets' organization in 2nd round of free-agent draft, January 7, 1976.
Selected by Los Angeles Dodgers' organization in 5th round of free-agent draft, June 7, 1977.
†On disabled list, July 13 to July 23, 1978.
‡Traded with First Baseman Kelly Snider and Pitcher Matt Reeves to Minnesota Twins for Outfielder Ken Landreaux, March 30, 1981.
§On supplemental disabled list, June 21 to July 8 and August 1 to August 23, 1983.

WILLIAM AUGUSTUS HATCHER
(Billy)

Born October 4, 1960, at Williams, Ariz.
Height, 5.09. Weight, 175.
Throws and bats righthanded.
Attended Yavapai Community College, Prescott, Ariz.

Led New York-Pennsylvania League in being hit by pitch with 8 in 1981.

Year Club	League	Pos.	G.	AB.	R.	H.	2B.	3B.	HR.	RBI.	B.A.	PO.	A.	E.	F.A.
1981—Geneva	NYP	OF	●75	289	57	81	15	3	4	40	.280	138	7	11	.930
1982—Salinas	Calif.	OF	138	549	92	171	18	8	8	59	.311	235	10	12	.953
1983—Midland	Texas	OF	135	545	*132	163	33	11	10	80	.299	286	17	●13	.959

Signed as free agent by Chicago Cubs' organization, May 22, 1981.

BRADLEY DAVID HAVENS
(Brad)

Born November 17, 1959, at Highland Park, Mich.
Height, 6.01. Weight, 180.
Throws and bats lefthanded.

Led California League in complete games with 12 in 1980.
Led Midwest League in complete games with 17 in 1978.
Tied for California League lead in games started by pitchers with 28 in 1980.

Year Club	League	G.	IP.	W.	L.	Pct.	H.	R.	ER.	SO.	BB.	ERA.
1978—Quad Cities†	Midwest	26	*200	13	10	.565	171	80	59	*197	74	2.66
1979—Orlando	Southern	19	94	4	10	.286	128	85	76	63	50	7.28
1979—Wisconsin Rapids	Midwest	10	73	6	1	.857	62	35	34	80	18	4.19
1980—Visalia	California	28	195	14	9	.609	186	90	72	*179	82	3.32
1981—Orlando	Southern	11	74	6	2	.750	81	38	29	58	20	3.53
1981—Minnesota	American	14	78	3	6	.333	76	33	31	43	24	3.58
1982—Minnesota	American	33	208⅔	10	14	.417	201	112	100	129	80	4.31
1983—Minnesota	American	16	80⅓	5	8	.385	110	75	73	40	38	8.18
1983—Toledo	Int'national	11	69⅔	6	3	.667	60	34	30	64	37	3.88
Major League Totals		63	367	18	28	.391	387	220	204	212	142	5.00

Selected by California Angels' organization in 8th round of free-agent draft, June 7, 1977.
†Traded with Outfielder Ken Landreaux, Pitcher Paul Hartzell and Third Baseman Dave Engle to Minnesota Twins for First Baseman Rod Carew, February 3, 1979.

MELTON ANDREW HAWKINS
(Andy)

Born January 21, 1960, at Waco, Tex.
Height, 6.03. Weight, 200.
Throws and bats righthanded.

Led Pacific Coast League in shutouts with 6 in 1982.
Led Texas League in complete games with 14 and tied for lead in games started by pitchers with 27 in 1981.
Led Northwest League in balks with 4 in 1978.

Year Club	League	G.	IP.	W.	L.	Pct.	H.	R.	ER.	SO.	BB.	ERA.
1978—Walla Walla	Northwest	14	102	8	3	.727	95	52	24	73	45	2.12
1979—Reno	California	27	188	8	13	.381	*232	143	*117	130	97	5.60
1980—Reno	California	26	171	13	10	.565	183	108	81	124	79	4.26
1981—Amarillo	Texas	27	200	11	10	.524	*209	100	*93	144	48	4.19
1982—Hawaii	P. Coast	18	132⅔	9	7	.563	108	49	32	91	47	2.17
1982—San Diego	National	15	63⅔	2	5	.286	66	33	29	25	27	4.10

Year Club	League	G.	IP.	W.	L.	Pct.	H.	R.	ER.	SO.	BB.	ERA.
1983—Las Vegas	P. Coast	14	85⅓	6	4	.600	110	67	61	50	27	6.43
1983—San Diego	National	21	119⅔	5	7	.417	106	50	39	59	48	2.93
Major League Totals		36	183⅓	7	12	.368	172	83	68	84	75	3.34

Selected by San Diego Padres' organization in 1st round (fifth player selected) of free-agent draft, June 6, 1978.

BEN JOSEPH HAYES

Born August 4, 1957, at Niagara Falls, N. Y.
Height, 6.01. Weight, 170.
Throws and bats righthanded.
Attended St. Petersburg Junior College, St. Petersburg, Fla.,
University of Florida, Gainesville, Fla., and University of
South Florida, Tampa, Fla.

Major League saves: 1982 (2), 1983 (7). Total—9.

Year Club	League	G.	IP.	W.	L.	Pct.	H.	R.	ER.	SO.	BB.	ERA.
1978—Billings	Pioneer	16	38	2	0	1.000	31	16	15	49	23	3.55
1979—Greensboro†	W. Carol.	11	13	1	0	1.000	11	11	8	8	7	5.54
1980—Tampa	Florida St.	41	61	1	4	.200	49	33	26	59	42	3.84
1981—Tampa	Florida St.	32	54	5	2	.714	36	13	11	53	25	1.83
1981—Waterbury	Eastern	30	50	2	5	.286	40	21	18	50	20	3.24
1982—Indianapolis	Am. Assoc.	41	69⅓	5	5	.500	57	24	21	61	40	2.73
1982—Cincinnati	National	26	45⅔	2	0	1.000	37	12	10	38	22	1.97
1983—Cincinnati	National	60	69⅓	4	6	.400	82	53	50	44	37	6.49
1983—Indianapolis	Am. Assoc.	6	7⅔	2	0	1.000	4	5	4	4	4	4.70
Major League Totals		86	115	6	6	.500	119	65	60	82	59	4.70

Signed as free agent by Cincinnati Reds' organization, May 17, 1978.
†On disabled list, May 31 to September 18, 1979.

VON FRANCIS HAYES

Born August 31, 1958, at Stockton, Calif.
Height, 6.05. Weight, 185.
Throws right and bats lefthanded.
Attended St. Mary's College, Moraga, Calif.

Major League stolen bases: 1981 (8), 1982 (32), 1983 (20). Total—60.
Led Midwest League third basemen in fielding percentage with .930 in 1980.
Named Midwest League Most Valuable Player, 1980.

Year Club	League	Pos.	G.	AB.	R.	H.	2B.	3B.	HR.	RBI.	B.A.	PO.	A.	E.	F.A.
1980—Waterloo	Midw.	3B-SS	134	492	105	*162	*33	3	15	90	*.329	94	291	30	.928
1981—Cleveland	Amer.	OF-3B	43	109	21	28	8	2	1	17	.257	30	4	3	.919
1981—Charleston	Int.	3B-1B	105	382	58	120	19	6	10	73	.314	96	222	19	.944
1982—Cleveland†	Amer.	OF-3B-1B	150	527	65	132	25	3	14	82	.250	323	17	6	.983
1983—Philadelphia‡	Nat.	OF	124	351	45	93	9	5	6	32	.265	165	7	5	.972
American League Totals			193	636	86	160	33	5	15	99	.252	353	21	9	.977
National League Totals			124	351	45	93	9	5	6	32	.265	165	7	5	.972
Major League Totals			317	987	131	253	42	10	21	131	.256	518	28	14	.975

Selected by Cleveland Indians' organization in 7th round of free-agent draft, June 5, 1979.
†Traded to Philadelphia Phillies for Second Baseman Manny Trillo, Outfielder George Vukovich, Infielder Julio Franco, Pitcher Jay Baller and Catcher Gerry Willard, December 9, 1982.
‡On supplemental disabled list, March 27 to April 12, 1983.

CHAMPIONSHIP SERIES RECORD

Year Club	League	Pos.	G.	AB.	R.	H.	2B.	3B.	HR.	RBI.	B.A.	PO.	A.	E.	F.A.
1983—Philadelphia	Nat.	PH-OF	2	2	0	0	0	0	0	0	.000	0	0	0	.000

WORLD SERIES RECORD

Year Club	League	Pos.	G.	AB.	R.	H.	2B.	3B.	HR.	RBI.	B.A.	PO.	A.	E.	F.A.
1983—Philadelphia	Nat.	PH-OF	4	3	0	0	0	0	0	0	.000	1	0	0	1.000

RAYMOND ALTON HAYWARD
(Ray)

Born April 27, 1961, at Oklahoma City, Okla.
Height, 6.01. Weight, 185.
Throws and bats lefthanded.
Attended University of Oklahoma, Norman, Okla.

Year Club	League	G.	IP.	W.	L.	Pct.	H.	R.	ER.	SO.	BB.	ERA.
1983—Beaumont	Texas	10	66⅓	5	1	.833	45	16	13	71	30	1.76

Selected by Pittsburgh Pirates' organization in 12th round of free-agent draft, June 7, 1982.
Selected by San Diego Padres' organization in 1st round (10th player selected) of free-agent draft, June 6, 1983.

—DID YOU KNOW—

That Orioles lefthander Scott McGregor was a 2-1 loser in both the opening game of the 1983 American League Championship Series and Game 1 of the '83 World Series.

MICHAEL THOMAS HEATH
(Mike)

Born February 5, 1955, at Tampa, Fla.
Height, 5.11. Weight, 176.
Throws and bats righthanded.
Uncle of Kent Reber, cornerback at University of Arkansas.

Led New York-Pennsylvania League shortstops in double plays with 42 in 1974.
Tied for Appalachian League lead in sacrifice hits with 7 in 1973.

Year Club	League	Pos.	G.	AB.	R.	H.	2B.	3B.	HR.	RBI.	B.A.	PO.	A.	E.	F.A.
1973—Johnson City	Appal.	SS-2B-3B	48	166	17	29	5	2	0	10	.175	83	137	24	.902
1974—Oneonta	NYP	SS	65	234	51	66	6	3	3	34	.282	114	170	★27	.913
1975—Ft. Lauderdale†	Fla. St.	SS	98	376	43	87	7	3	1	23	.231	184	256	31	.934
1976—Ft. Lauderdale‡	Fla. St.	SS-3B-C-P	80	267	28	71	16	3	2	30	.266	143	121	16	.943
1977—West Haven	East.	C-3B	98	352	58	94	13	5	8	42	.267	492	72	16	.972
1978—West Haven	East.	C-SS	66	217	43	64	16	1	8	27	.295	335	53	10	.975
1978—New York§	Amer.	C	33	92	6	21	3	1	0	8	.228	151	11	5	.970
1979—Tucson x	P. C.	C	54	196	21	53	8	2	1	28	.270	183	24	7	.967
1979—Oakland	Amer.	OF-C-3B	74	258	19	66	8	0	3	27	.256	167	32	5	.975
1980—Oakland	Amer.	C-OF	92	305	27	74	10	2	1	33	.243	292	20	4	.987
1981—Oakland	Amer.	★C-OF	84	301	26	71	7	1	8	30	.236	399	45	★10	.978
1982—Oakland y	Amer.	C-OF-3B	101	318	43	77	18	4	3	39	.242	368	54	12	.972
1983—Oakland z	Amer.	C-OF-3B	96	345	45	97	17	0	6	33	.281	362	47	11	.974
Major League Totals			480	1619	166	406	63	8	21	170	.251	1739	209	47	.976

Selected by New York Yankees' organization in 2nd round of free-agent draft, June 5, 1973.
†On Syracuse disabled list, August 2 to September 16, 1975.
‡On disabled list, June 29 to July 13, 1976.
§Traded with Pitchers Sparky Lyle, Larry McCall and Dave Rajsich, Shortstop Domingo Ramos and cash to Texas Rangers for Outfielders Juan Beniquez and Greg Jemison and Pitchers Mike Griffin, Paul Mirabella and Dave Righetti, November 10, 1978.
xTraded with Third Baseman Dave Chalk and cash to Oakland A's for Pitcher John Henry Johnson, June 15, 1979.
yOn supplemental disabled list, March 28 to April 20, 1982.
zOn supplemental disabled list, April 25, 1983; transferred to disabled list, May 19 to May 25, 1983.

DIVISION SERIES RECORD

Year Club	League	Pos.	G.	AB.	R.	H.	2B.	3B.	HR.	RBI.	B.A.	PO.	A.	E.	F.A.
1981—Oakland	Amer.	C	2	8	0	0	0	0	0	0	.000	9	1	0	1.000

CHAMPIONSHIP SERIES RECORD

Year Club	League	Pos.	G.	AB.	R.	H.	2B.	3B.	HR.	RBI.	B.A.	PO.	A.	E.	F.A.
1981—Oakland	Amer.	C-OF	3	6	1	2	0	0	0	0	.333	3	1	0	1.000

WORLD SERIES RECORD

Year Club	League	Pos.	G.	AB.	R.	H.	2B.	3B.	HR.	RBI.	B.A.	PO.	A.	E.	F.A.
1978—New York	Amer.	C	1	0	0	0	0	0	0	0	.000	0	0	0	.000

PITCHING RECORD

Year Club	League	G.	IP.	W.	L.	Pct.	H.	R.	ER.	SO.	BB.	ERA.
1976—Ft. Lauderdale	Florida St.	1	1	0	0	.000	1	0	0	1	0	0.00

RONALD JEFFREY HEATHCOCK
(Jeff)

Born November 18, 1959, at West Covina, Calif.
Height, 6.04. Weight, 205.
Throws and bats righthanded.
Attended Golden West College, Huntington Beach, Calif.,
and Oral Roberts University, Tulsa, Okla.

Led Southern League in home runs allowed with 26 in 1982.
Tied for Southern League lead in shutouts with 3 in 1983.

Year Club	League	G.	IP.	W.	L.	Pct.	H.	R.	ER.	SO.	BB.	ERA.
1981—Daytona Beach	Florida St.	11	85	9	0	1.000	67	20	12	77	21	1.27
1981—Columbus	Southern	16	101	4	7	.364	104	57	52	59	35	4.63
1982—Columbus	Southern	29	191	13	13	.500	216	★119	★101	108	56	4.76
1983—Columbus	Southern	14	91⅓	4	4	.500	82	32	23	69	22	2.27
1983—Tucson	P. Coast	15	110⅓	10	3	.769	104	45	34	65	26	2.77
1983—Houston	National	6	28	2	1	.667	19	14	10	12	4	3.21
Major League Totals		6	28	2	1	.667	19	14	10	12	4	3.21

Selected by Milwaukee Brewers' organization in 2nd round of free-agent draft, January 9, 1979.
Selected by San Diego Padres' organization in secondary phase of free-agent draft, June 5, 1979.
Selected by Houston Astros' organization in secondary phase of free-agent draft, June 3, 1980.

NEAL HEATON

Born March 3, 1960, at Jamaica, N.Y.
Height, 6.01. Weight, 200.
Throws and bats lefthanded.
Attended University of Miami, Coral Gables, Fla.

Major League saves: 1983 (7).

Year	Club	League	G.	IP.	W.	L.	Pct.	H.	R.	ER.	SO.	BB.	ERA.
1981—Chattanooga		Southern	11	77	4	4	.500	61	42	34	50	27	3.97
1982—Charleston		Int'national	29	172⅔	10	5	.667	194	97	77	105	66	4.01
1982—Cleveland		American	8	31	0	2	.000	32	21	18	14	16	5.23
1983—Cleveland		American	39	149⅓	11	7	.611	157	79	69	75	44	4.16
Major League Totals			47	180⅓	11	9	.550	189	100	87	89	60	4.34

Selected by New York Mets' organization in 1st round (first player selected) of free-agent draft, January 9, 1979.
Selected by Cleveland Indians' organization in 2nd round of free-agent draft, June 8, 1981.

RICHARD JOSEPH HEBNER
(Richie)

Born November 26, 1947, at Norwood, Mass.
Height, 6.01. Weight, 195.
Throws right and bats lefthanded.
Brother of William Hebner, former International League umpire.

Tied major league record for most bases on balls, inning (2), August 27, 1974 (third inning).
Tied modern major league record for most at bats, game (7), September 16, 1975.
Led International League third basemen in errors with 19 in 1968.
Received reported $40,000 bonus to sign with Pittsburgh Pirates, 1966.

Year	Club	League	Pos.	G.	AB.	R.	H.	2B.	3B.	HR.	RBI.	B.A.	PO.	A.	E.	F.A.
1966—Salem†‡	Appal.	1B	26	92	17	33	9	3	4	20	.359	167	10	2	.989
1967—Raleigh§	Carol.	3B	78	274	45	92	15	6	2	33	.336	69	135	17	.923
1968—Columbus x	Int.	3B-SS	104	381	50	105	20	5	6	51	.276	77	224	23	.929
1968—Pittsburgh	Nat.	PH	2	1	0	0	0	0	0	0	.000	0	0	0	.000
1969—Pittsburgh	Nat.	3B-1B	129	459	72	138	23	4	8	47	.301	81	240	19	.944
1970—Pittsburgh y	Nat.	3B	120	420	60	122	24	8	11	46	.290	64	235	19	.940
1971—Pittsburgh z	Nat.	3B	112	388	50	105	17	8	17	67	.271	89	172	14	.949
1972—Pittsburgh	Nat.	3B	124	427	63	128	24	4	19	72	.300	76	210	9	.969
1973—Pittsburgh	Nat.	3B	144	509	73	138	28	1	25	74	.271	92	260	23	.939
1974—Pittsburgh	Nat.	3B	146	550	97	160	21	6	18	68	.291	115	304	★28	.937
1975—Pittsburgh	Nat.	3B	128	472	65	116	16	4	15	57	.246	86	244	19	.946
1976—Pittsburgh a	Nat.	3B	132	434	60	108	21	3	8	51	.249	87	236	16	.953
1977—Philadelphia b	Nat.	1B-3B-2B	118	397	67	113	17	4	18	62	.285	933	85	11	.989
1978—Philadelphia c	Nat.	1B-3B-2B	137	435	61	123	22	3	17	71	.283	994	94	8	.993
1979—New York d	Nat.	3B-1B	136	473	54	127	25	2	10	79	.268	125	248	23	.942
1980—Detroit	Amer.	1B-3B	104	341	48	99	10	7	12	82	.290	485	84	4	.993
1981—Detroit	Amer.	1B	78	226	19	51	8	2	5	28	.226	531	29	3	.995
1982—Detroit e	Amer.	1B	68	179	25	49	6	0	8	18	.274	286	25	3	.990
1982—Pittsburgh	Nat.	OF-1B-3B	25	70	6	21	2	0	2	12	.300	52	3	1	.982
1983—Pittsburgh f	Nat.	3B-1B-OF	78	162	23	43	4	1	5	26	.265	63	45	2	.982
National League Totals			1531	5197	751	1442	244	48	173	732	.277	2857	2376	192	.965
American League Totals			250	746	92	199	24	9	25	128	.267	1302	138	10	.993
Major League Totals			1781	5943	843	1641	268	57	198	860	.276	4159	2514	202	.971

Selected by Pittsburgh Pirates' organization in 1st round (15th player selected) of free-agent draft, June 28, 1966.
†On temporary inactive list, August 9 to August 18, 1966.
‡On military list, August 18, 1966 through April 6, 1967.
§On temporary inactive list, May 13 to May 15, June 10 to June 24 and July 20 to August 16, 1967.
xOn temporary inactive list, July 13 to July 29, 1968.
yOn military list, August 8 to August 24, 1970.
zOn military list, July 25 to August 9, 1971.
aPlayed out option year and granted free agency, November 1, 1976; signed as free agent by Philadelphia Phillies, December 15, 1976.
bOn disabled list, March 27 to April 29, 1977.
cTraded with Second Baseman Jose Moreno to New York Mets for Pitcher Nino Espinosa, March 27, 1979.
dTraded to Detroit Tigers for Third Baseman Phil Mankowski and Outfielder Jerry Morales, October 31, 1979.
eSold to Pittsburgh Pirates, August 16, 1982.
fGranted free agency, November 7, 1983.

CHAMPIONSHIP SERIES RECORD

Established Championship Series record for most times on losing club (6).
Tied Championship Series record for most two-base hits, total Series (7).
Tied National League Championship Series records for most Series played (7); most Series, one or more hits (7).

Year	Club	League	Pos.	G.	AB.	R.	H.	2B.	3B.	HR.	RBI.	B.A.	PO.	A.	E.	F.A.
1970—Pittsburgh	Nat.	3B	2	6	0	4	2	0	0	0	.667	0	4	0	1.000
1971—Pittsburgh	Nat.	PH-3B	4	17	3	5	1	0	2	4	.294	4	3	1	.875
1972—Pittsburgh	Nat.	3B	5	16	2	3	1	0	0	1	.188	5	11	0	1.000
1974—Pittsburgh	Nat.	3B	4	13	1	3	0	0	1	4	.231	5	7	0	1.000
1975—Pittsburgh	Nat.	3B	3	12	2	4	1	0	0	2	.333	0	2	0	1.000
1977—Philadelphia	Nat.	1B-PH	4	14	2	5	2	0	0	0	.357	32	0	0	1.000
1978—Philadelphia	Nat.	1B-PH	3	9	0	1	0	0	0	1	.111	21	0	0	1.000
Championship Series Totals			25	87	10	25	7	0	3	12	.287	67	27	1	.989

WORLD SERIES RECORD

Year	Club	League	Pos.	G.	AB.	R.	H.	2B.	3B.	HR.	RBI.	B.A.	PO.	A.	E.	F.A.
1971—Pittsburgh	Nat.	3B	3	12	2	2	0	0	1	3	.167	1	3	1	.800

DANIEL WILLIAM HEEP
(Danny)

Born July 3, 1957, at San Antonio, Tex.
Height, 5.11. Weight, 185.
Throws and bats lefthanded.
Attended St. Mary's University, San Antonio, Tex.

Led Southern League in total bases with 274 in 1979.
Named Southern League co-Most Valuable Player, 1979.

Year	Club	League	Pos.	G.	AB.	R.	H.	2B.	3B.	HR.	RBI.	B.A.	PO.	A.	E.	F.A.
1978—Daytona Beach	Fla. St.	OF	66	212	29	72	18	2	2	24	.340	89	9	2	.980
1979—Columbus	South.	OF	138	523	103	*171	30	5	21	84	.327	211	12	6	.974
1979—Houston	Nat.	OF	14	14	0	2	0	0	0	2	.143	7	0	0	1.000
1980—Tucson	P. C.	1B-OF	96	376	63	129	28	5	17	69	*.343	810	53	8	.991
1980—Houston	Nat.	1B	33	87	6	24	8	0	0	6	.276	188	8	2	.990
1981—Houston†	Nat.	1B-OF	33	96	6	24	3	0	0	11	.250	198	9	2	.990
1981—Tuscon	P. C.	1B-OF	78	285	55	96	23	5	11	60	.337	635	44	12	.983
1982—Houston‡	Nat.	OF-1B	85	198	16	47	14	1	4	22	.237	192	6	1	.995
1983—New York	Nat.	OF-1B	115	253	30	64	12	0	8	21	.253	159	11	0	1.000
Major League Totals				280	648	58	161	37	1	12	62	.248	744	34	5	.994

Selected by Houston Astros' organization in 2nd round of free-agent draft, June 6, 1978.
†On supplemental disabled list, April 19 to May 4, 1981.
‡Traded to New York Mets for Pitcher Mike Scott, December 10, 1982.

CHAMPIONSHIP SERIES RECORD

Year	Club	League	Pos.	G.	AB.	R.	H.	2B.	3B.	HR.	RBI.	B.A.	PO.	A.	E.	F.A.
1980—Houston	Nat.	PH	1	1	0	0	0	0	0	0	.000	0	0	0	.000

CURTIS JAY HEIDENREICH
(Curt)

Born July 14, 1959, at Woodstock, Ill.
Height, 6.06. Weight, 225.
Throws and bats righthanded.
Attended Illinois State University, Normal, Ill.

Led Eastern League in shutouts with 4 in 1983.
Led Northwest League in shutouts with 2 and hit batsmen with 7 in 1981.

Year	Club	League	G.	IP.	W.	L.	Pct.	H.	R.	ER.	SO.	BB.	ERA.
1981—Eugene	Northwest	16	98	5	7	.417	74	39	26	96	50	*2.39
1982—Cedar Rapids	Midwest	25	166⅔	11	9	.550	143	77	61	168	65	3.29
1983—Waterbury	Eastern	17	119⅓	11	4	.733	84	29	23	98	56	1.73
1983—Indianapolis	Am. Assoc.	7	41⅓	3	3	.500	45	27	21	23	16	4.57

Selected by Cincinnati Reds' organization in 32nd round of free-agent draft, June 3, 1980.

GORMAN JOHN HEIMUELLER JR.

Born September 24, 1955, at Los Angeles, Calif.
Height, 6.04. Weight, 195.
Throws and bats lefthanded.
Attended California Poly State U., San Luis Obispo, Calif.

Year	Club	League	G.	IP.	W.	L.	Pct.	H.	R.	ER.	SO.	BB.	ERA.
1977—Cedar Rapids	Midwest	9	15	0	1	.000	13	7	3	15	9	1.80
1978—Waterbury	Eastern	41	73	8	7	.533	67	49	39	63	48	4.81
1979—Shreveport	Texas	27	58	3	2	.600	58	29	25	29	31	3.88
1980—Shreveport†	Texas	32	127	7	8	.467	122	67	48	90	62	3.40
1981—West Haven	Eastern	28	108	9	4	.692	94	40	28	73	50	2.33
1981—Tacoma	P. Coast	6	37	3	3	.500	36	16	16	16	22	3.89
1982—Tacoma‡	P. Coast	5	17⅓	1	1	.500	16	16	14	9	9	7.27
1982—West Haven	Eastern	23	118⅔	7	9	.438	124	75	67	99	54	5.08
1983—Tacoma	P. Coast	20	117	8	4	.667	126	61	46	61	55	3.54
1983—Oakland	American	16	83⅔	3	5	.375	93	43	41	31	29	4.41
Major League Totals		16	83⅔	3	5	.375	93	43	41	31	29	4.41

Signed as free agent by San Francisco Giants' organization, August 11, 1977.
†Released, March 31, 1981; signed by West Haven (Oakland A's organization), April 10, 1981.
‡On disabled list, April 26 to May 6, 1982.

DAVID LEE HENDERSON
(Dave)

Born July 21, 1958, at Dos Palos, Calif.
Height, 6.02. Weight, 210.
Throws and bats righthanded.
Nephew of Joe Henderson, pitcher with Chicago
White Sox and Cincinnati Reds, 1974, 1976 and 1977.

Year	Club	League	Pos.	G.	AB.	R.	H.	2B.	3B.	HR.	RBI.	B.A.	PO.	A.	E.	F.A.
1977—Bellingham	N'west	OF	65	251	47	79	14	2	●16	63	.315	136	5	*11	.928
1978—Stockton	Calif.	OF	117	409	48	95	16	4	7	63	.232	204	12	14	.939
1979—San Jose	Calif.	OF	136	507	103	152	23	3	27	99	.300	264	18	4	.986

Year—Club	League	Pos.	G.	AB.	R.	H.	2B.	3B.	HR.	RBI.	B.A.	PO.	A.	E.	F.A.
1980—Spokane†	P. C.	OF	109	341	48	95	26	1	7	50	.279	258	9	7	.974
1981—Seattle	Amer.	OF	59	126	17	21	3	0	6	13	.167	105	4	0	1.000
1981—Spokane	P. C.	OF	80	272	47	76	23	1	12	50	.279	146	7	3	.981
1982—Seattle‡	Amer.	OF	104	324	47	82	17	1	14	48	.253	249	11	4	.985
1983—Seattle	Amer.	OF	137	484	50	130	24	5	17	55	.269	304	17	6	.982
Major League Totals			300	934	114	233	44	6	37	116	.249	658	32	10	.986

Selected by Seattle Mariners' organization in 1st round (26th player selected) of free-agent draft, June 7, 1977.
†On disabled list, June 26 to July 22, 1980.
‡On supplemental disabled list, May 3 to May 18, 1982.

RICKEY HENLEY HENDERSON

Born December 25, 1958, at Chicago, Ill.
Height, 5.10. Weight, 180.
Throws left and bats righthanded.

Established modern major league record for most stolen bases, season (130), 1982.
Established major league record for most times caught stealing, season (42), 1982.
Tied American League record for most stolen bases, two consecutive games (7), July 3, 4, 1983.
Major League stolen bases: 1979 (33), 1980 (100), 1981 (56), 1982 (130), 1983 (108). Total—427.
Led American League in bases on balls received with 116 in 1982 and 103 in 1983.
Led American League in stolen bases with 100 in 1980, 56 in 1981, 130 in 1982 and 108 in 1983.
Led American League in caught stealing with 26 in 1980, 22 in 1981, 42 in 1982 and 19 in 1983.
Led American League outfielders in total chances with 341 in 1981.
Led Eastern League with 81 and caught stealing with 28 in 1978.
Led California League in stolen bases with 95 and caught stealing with 22 in 1977.
Led Eastern League outfielders in double plays with 4 in 1978.
Won THE SPORTING NEWS Golden Shoe Award, 1983.
Won THE SPORTING NEWS Silver Shoe Award, 1982.
Named outfielder on THE SPORTING NEWS American League All-Star Team, 1981.
Named outfielder on THE SPORTING NEWS American League All-Star fielding team, 1981.
Named outfielder on THE SPORTING NEWS American League Silver Slugger team, 1981.

Year—Club	League	Pos.	G.	AB.	R.	H.	2B.	3B.	HR.	RBI.	B.A.	PO.	A.	E.	F.A.
1976—Boise	N'west.	OF	46	140	34	47	13	2	3	23	.336	99	3	*12	.895
1977—Modesto	Calif.	OF	134	481	120	166	18	4	11	69	.345	278	15	*20	.936
1978—Jersey City	East.	OF	133	455	81	141	14	4	0	34	.310	305	●15	7	.979
1979—Ogden	P. C.	OF	71	259	66	80	11	8	3	26	.309	149	6	6	.963
1979—Oakland	Amer.	OF	89	351	49	96	13	3	1	26	.274	215	5	6	.973
1980—Oakland	Amer.	OF	158	591	111	179	22	4	9	53	.303	407	15	7	.984
1981—Oakland	Amer.	OF	108	423	*89	*135	18	7	6	35	.319	*327	7	7	.979
1982—Oakland	Amer.	OF	149	536	119	143	24	4	10	51	.267	379	2	9	.977
1983—Oakland	Amer.	OF	145	513	105	150	25	7	9	48	.292	349	9	3	.992
Major League Totals			649	2414	473	703	102	25	35	213	.291	1677	38	32	.982

Selected by Oakland A's organization in 4th round of free-agent draft, June 8, 1976.

DIVISION SERIES RECORD

Year—Club	League	Pos.	G.	AB.	R.	H.	2B.	3B.	HR.	RBI.	B.A.	PO.	A.	E.	F.A.
1981—Oakland	Amer.	OF	3	11	3	2	0	0	0	0	.182	8	0	0	1.000

CHAMPIONSHIP SERIES RECORD

Tied American League Championship Series record for most stolen bases, three-game Series (2), 1981.

Year—Club	League	Pos.	G.	AB.	R.	H.	2B.	3B.	HR.	RBI.	B.A.	PO.	A.	E.	F.A.
1981—Oakland	Amer.	OF	3	11	0	4	2	1	0	1	.364	6	0	1	.857

ALL-STAR GAME RECORD

Tied All-Star Game record for most one-base hits, game (3), July 13, 1982.

Year—League	Pos.	AB.	R.	H.	2B.	3B.	HR.	RBI.	B.A.	PO.	A.	E.	F.A.
1980—American	OF	1	0	0	0	0	0	0	.000	0	0	0	.000
1982—American	OF	4	1	3	0	0	0	0	.750	3	0	1	.750
1983—American	OF	1	0	0	0	0	0	1	.000	0	0	0	.000
All-Star Game Totals		6	1	3	0	0	0	1	.500	3	0	1	.750

STEPHEN CURTIS HENDERSON
(Steve)

Born November 18, 1952, at Houston, Tex.
Height, 6.01. Weight, 185.
Throws and bats righthanded.
Attended Prairie View A & M University, Prairie View, Tex.

Led National League in grounding into double plays with 24 in 1978.
Led Eastern League in total bases with 255 and caught stealing with 17 in 1976.

Year—Club	League	Pos.	G.	AB.	R.	H.	2B.	3B.	HR.	RBI.	B.A.	PO.	A.	E.	F.A.
1974—Billings	Pion.	OF	72	249	*60	72	19	5	●8	●44	.289	114	6	6	*.952
1975—Tampa	Fla. St.	OF-SS	123	413	59	115	9	*16	0	54	.278	263	7	8	.971
1976—Three Rivers	East.	OF	134	506	90	●158	24	*11	17	61	.312	260	12	8	.971
1977—Indianapolis†	A. A.	OF	60	233	35	76	12	6	7	25	.326	107	3	3	.973
1977—New York	Nat.	OF	99	350	67	104	16	6	12	65	.297	189	4	4	.980
1978—New York	Nat.	OF	157	587	83	156	30	9	10	65	.266	315	18	11	.968

Year Club League	Pos.	G.	AB.	R.	H.	2B.	3B.	HR.	RBI.	B.A.	PO.	A.	E.	F.A.
1979—New York‡........... Nat.	OF	98	350	42	107	16	8	5	39	.306	201	6	2	.990
1980—New York§........... Nat.	OF	143	513	75	149	17	8	8	58	.290	299	7	6	.981
1981—Chicago x.............. Nat.	OF	82	287	32	84	9	5	5	35	.293	152	4	∗8	.951
1982—Chicago y.............. Nat.	OF	92	257	23	60	12	4	2	29	.233	126	5	6	.956
1983—Seattle z............... Amer.	OF	121	436	50	128	32	3	10	54	.294	182	15	6	.970
National League Totals.............................		671	2344	322	660	100	40	42	291	.282	1282	44	37	.973
American League Totals..........................		121	436	50	128	32	3	10	54	.294	182	15	6	.970
Major League Totals..................................		792	2780	372	788	132	43	52	345	.283	1464	59	43	.973

Selected by Cincinnati Reds' organization in 5th round of free-agent draft, June 5, 1974.

†Traded with Infielder Doug Flynn, Outfielder Dan Norman and Pitcher Pat Zachry to New York Mets for Pitcher Tom Seaver, June 15, 1977.

‡On disabled list, July 31 to September 17, 1979.

§Traded with cash to Chicago Cubs for Outfielder Dave Kingman, February 28, 1981.

xOn supplemental disabled list, May 29, 1981; transferred to disabled list, June 2 to August 11, 1981.

yTraded to Seattle Mariners for Pitcher Rich Bordi, December 9, 1982.

zGranted free agency, November 7, 1983.

GEORGE ANDREW HENDRICK JR.

Born October 18, 1949, at Los Angeles, Calif.
Height, 6.03. Weight, 195.
Throws and bats righthanded.
Attended East Los Angeles Junior College, Los Angeles, Calif.

Hit three home runs in a game, June 19, 1973.
Led National League in sacrifice flies with 14 in 1982.
Led American League outfielders in double plays with 6 in 1976.
Tied for National League lead in double plays by outfielders with 7 in 1979.
Named first baseman on THE SPORTING NEWS National League All-Star Team, 1983.
Named outfielder on THE SPORTING NEWS National League All-Star Team, 1980.
Named first baseman on THE SPORTING NEWS National League Silver Slugger team, 1983.
Named outfielder on THE SPORTING NEWS National League Silver Slugger team, 1980.

Year Club League	Pos.	G.	AB.	R.	H.	2B.	3B.	HR.	RBI.	B.A.	PO.	A.	E.	F.A.
1968—Burlington .... Midw.	OF	103	364	58	119	●25	4	5	60	∗.327∗	134	8	8	.947
1969—Lodi........................ Calif.	OF	86	316	47	97	13	2	4	28	.307	121	5	4	.969
1970—Burlington .... Midw.	OF	54	198	37	61	9	3	12	43	.308	80	1	5	.942
1970—Birmingham .... South.	OF	54	199	30	57	12	0	6	20	.286	115	4	5	.960
1971—Iowa .... A. A.	OF	63	249	57	83	9	2	21	63	.333	113	5	3	.975
1971—Oakland................. Amer.	OF	42	114	8	27	4	1	0	8	.237	52	1	1	.981
1972—Iowa .... A. A.	OF	8	33	0	9	0	0	0	4	.273	14	2	0	1.000
1972—Oakland†.............. Amer.	OF	58	121	10	22	1	1	4	15	.182	68	0	0	1.000
1973—Cleveland‡........... Amer.	OF	113	440	64	118	18	0	21	61	.268	242	7	3	.988
1974—Cleveland............. Amer.	OF	139	495	65	138	23	1	19	67	.279	355	9	4	.989
1975—Cleveland............. Amer.	OF	145	561	82	145	21	2	24	86	.258	338	4	6	.983
1976—Cleveland§........... Amer.	OF	149	551	72	146	20	3	25	81	.265	288	13	4	.987
1977—San Diego .... Nat.	OF	152	541	75	168	25	2	23	81	.311	386	11	7	.983
1978—S.D. x-St.L. .... Nat.	OF	138	493	64	137	31	1	20	75	.278	313	6	2	.994
1979—St. Louis................ Nat.	OF	140	493	67	148	27	1	16	75	.300	254	∗20	2	.993
1980—St. Louis................ Nat.	OF	150	572	73	173	33	2	25	109	.302	322	10	2	.994
1981—St. Louis................ Nat.	OF	101	394	67	112	19	3	18	61	.284	227	6	4	.983
1982—St. Louis................ Nat.	OF	136	515	65	145	20	5	19	104	.282	238	6	5	.980
1983—St. Louis................ Nat.	1B-OF	144	529	73	168	33	3	18	97	.318	904	79	8	.992
American League Totals..........................		646	2282	301	596	87	8	93	318	.261	1343	34	18	.987
National League Totals.............................		961	3537	484	1051	188	17	139	602	.297	2644	138	30	.989
Major League Totals..................................		1607	5819	785	1647	275	25	232	920	.283	3987	172	48	.989

Selected by Oakland A's organization in 1st round (first player selected) of free-agent draft, January 27, 1968.

†Traded with Catcher Dave Duncan to Cleveland Indians for Catcher Ray Fosse and Infielder Jack Heidemann, March 24, 1973.

‡On supplemental disabled list, August 14 to September 29, 1973.

§Traded to San Diego Padres for Outfielder John Grubb, Catcher Fred Kendall and Shortstop Hector Torres, December 8, 1976.

xTraded to St. Louis Cardinals for Pitcher Eric Rasmussen, May 26, 1978.

CHAMPIONSHIP SERIES RECORD

Year Club League	Pos.	G.	AB.	R.	H.	2B.	3B.	HR.	RBI.	B.A.	PO.	A.	E.	F.A.
1972—Oakland................. Amer.	PH-OF	5	7	2	1	0	0	0	0	.143	1	0	0	1.000
1982—St. Louis................. Nat.	OF	3	13	2	4	0	0	0	2	.308	5	0	0	1.000
Championship Series Totals		8	20	4	5	0	0	0	2	.250	6	0	0	1.000

WORLD SERIES RECORD

Tied World Series record for most times awarded first base on catcher's interference, game (1), October 15, 1982.

Year Club League	Pos.	G.	AB.	R.	H.	2B.	3B.	HR.	RBI.	B.A.	PO.	A.	E.	F.A.
1972—Oakland................. Amer.	OF	5	15	3	2	0	0	0	0	.133	12	0	0	1.000
1982—St. Louis................. Nat.	OF	7	28	5	9	0	0	0	5	.321	10	1	0	1.000
World Series Totals.......................................		12	43	8	11	0	0	0	5	.256	22	1	0	1.000

Year League	Pos.	AB.	R.	H.	2B.	3B.	HR.	RBI.	B.A.	PO.	A.	E.	F.A.
1974—American	OF	2	0	1	0	0	0	0	.500	3	0	0	1.000
1975—American	PR-OF	1	1	1	0	0	0	0	1.000	0	0	0	.000
1980—National	OF	2	0	1	0	0	0	1	.500	0	0	0	.000
All-Star Game Totals		5	1	3	0	0	0	1	.600	3	0	0	1.000

Member of National League All-Star Team in 1983; did not play.

THOMAS ANTHONY HENKE
Name pronounced HEN-key.
(Tom)

Born December 21, 1957, at Kansas City, Mo.
Height, 6.05. Weight, 210.
Throws and bats righthanded.
Attended East Central College, Union, Mo.

Year Club	League	G.	IP.	W.	L.	Pct.	H.	R.	ER.	SO.	BB.	ERA.
1980—Sarasota Rangers	Gulf Coast	8	38	3	3	.500	33	11	4	34	12	0.95
1980—Asheville	S. Atlantic	5	23	0	2	.000	25	21	20	19	20	7.83
1981—Asheville	S. Atlantic	28	92	8	6	.571	77	36	30	67	35	2.93
1981—Tulsa	Texas	15	32	4	3	.571	31	16	14	37	14	3.94
1982—Tulsa	Texas	*52	87⅔	3	6	.333	69	35	26	100	40	2.67
1982—Texas	American	8	15⅔	1	0	1.000	14	2	2	9	8	1.15
1983—Oklahoma City	Am. Assoc.	47	77⅔	9	6	.600	71	33	26	90	33	3.01
1983—Texas	American	8	16	1	0	1.000	16	6	6	17	4	3.38
Major League Totals		16	31⅔	2	0	1.000	30	8	8	26	12	2.27

Selected by Seattle Mariners' organization in 20th round of free-agent draft, June 5, 1979.
Selected by Chicago Cubs' organization in secondary phase of free-agent draft, January 8, 1980.
Selected by Texas Rangers' organization in secondary phase of free-agent draft, June 3, 1980.

DWAYNE ALLEN HENRY

Born February 16, 1962, at Elkton, Md.
Height, 6.03. Weight, 210.
Throws and bats righthanded.

Year Club	League	G.	IP.	W.	L.	Pct.	H.	R.	ER.	SO.	BB.	ERA.
1980—Sarasota Rangers	Gulf Coast	11	54	5	1	.833	36	23	16	47	28	2.67
1981—Asheville	S. Atlantic	25	134	8	7	.533	120	81	66	86	58	4.43
1982—Burlington†	Midwest	4	18⅔	2	0	1.000	6	0	0	25	6	0.00
1983—Tulsa‡	Texas	9	14	0	0	.000	16	14	9	14	19	5.79
1983—Sarasota Rangers	Gulf Coast	3	9	0	0	.000	10	6	4	11	1	4.00

Selected by Texas Rangers' organization in 2nd round of free-agent draft, June 3, 1980.
†On disabled list, May 4, 1982 through remainder of season.
‡On disabled list, April 8 to July 9, 1983.

GUILLERMO HERNANDEZ (VILLANUEVA)
(Willie)

Born November 14, 1955, at Aguada, Puerto Rico.
Height, 6.02. Weight, 180.
Throws and bats lefthanded.

Tied National League record for most consecutive strikeouts by relief pitcher, game (6), July 3, 1983.
Major League saves: 1977 (4), 1978 (3), 1981 (2), 1982 (10), 1983 (8). Total—27.
Led Western Carolinas League pitchers in games started with 26 and complete games with 13 in 1977.

Year Club	League	G.	IP.	W.	L.	Pct.	H.	R.	ER.	SO.	BB.	ERA.
1974—Spartanburg	W. Carol.	26	*190	11	11	.500	169	82	58	*179	49	2.75
1975—Reading	Eastern	13	91	8	2	.800	79	32	30	46	25	2.97
1975—Toledo	Int'national	13	80	6	4	.600	86	43	29	46	26	3.26
1976—Oklahoma City†	Am. Assoc.	25	135	8	9	.471	154	82	68	88	30	4.53
1977—Chicago	National	67	110	8	7	.533	94	42	37	78	28	3.03
1978—Chicago	National	54	60	8	2	.800	57	26	25	38	35	3.75
1979—Chicago	National	51	79	4	4	.500	85	50	44	53	39	5.01
1980—Chicago	National	53	108	1	9	.100	115	58	53	75	45	4.42
1981—Iowa	Am. Assoc.	18	74	4	5	.444	84	39	32	41	27	3.89
1981—Chicago	National	12	14	0	0	.000	14	7	6	13	8	3.86
1982—Chicago	National	75	75	4	6	.400	74	26	25	54	24	3.00
1983—Chicago‡-Philadelphia	National	74	115⅓	9	4	.692	109	47	42	93	32	3.28
Major League Totals		386	561⅓	34	32	.515	548	256	232	404	211	3.72

Signed as free agent by Philadelphia Phillies' organization, September 11, 1973.
†Drafted by Chicago Cubs, December 6, 1976.
‡Traded to Philadelphia Phillies for Pitchers Dick Ruthven and Bill Johnson, May 22, 1983.

WORLD SERIES RECORD

Year Club	League	G.	IP.	W.	L.	Pct.	H.	R.	ER.	SO.	BB.	ERA.
1983—Philadelphia	National	3	4	0	0	.000	0	0	0	4	1	0.00

KEITH HERNANDEZ

Born October 20, 1953, at San Francisco, Calif.
Height, 6.00. Weight, 185.
Throws and bats lefthanded.
Attended College of San Mateo, San Mateo, Calif.
Son of John Hernandez, minor league infielder, 1941 through 1950, brother of Gary Hernandez,
first baseman-outfielder in St. Louis Cardinals' organization, 1972 through 1975.

Tied National League records for most home runs with bases filled, month (2), September, 1977; fewest errors by first baseman for leader in errors, season (13), 1983.
Led National League in intentional bases on balls received with 19 in 1982.
Led National League first basemen in putouts with 1,054 in 1981 and 1,586 in 1982.
Led National League first basemen in double plays with 146 in 1977, 145 in 1979, 146 in 1980, 99 in 1981 and 147 in 1983.
Led National League first basemen in total chances with 1,643 in 1979, 1,732 in 1982 and 1,578 in 1983.
Tied for National League lead in game-winning RBIs with 21 in 1982.
Led Texas League first basemen in double plays with 101 in 1973.
Named National League Player of the Year by THE SPORTING NEWS, 1979.
Named National League co-Most Valuable Player by Baseball Writers' Association of America, 1979.
Named first baseman on THE SPORTING NEWS National League All-Star Team, 1979 and 1980.
Named first baseman on THE SPORTING NEWS National League All-Star fielding team, 1978 through 1983.
Named first baseman on THE SPORTING NEWS National League Silver Slugger team, 1980.

Year	Club	League	Pos.	G.	AB.	R.	H.	2B.	3B.	HR.	RBI.	B.A.	PO.	A.	E.	F.A.
1972—St. Petersburg†	Fla. St.	1B	84	309	38	79	16	5	5	41	.256	682	52	7	.991
1972—Tulsa	A. A.	1B	11	29	5	7	1	0	0	1	.241	54	2	0	1.000
1973—Arkansas	Texas	1B	105	388	62	101	20	2	3	52	.260	960	61	9	★.991
1973—Tulsa	A. A.	1B	31	120	20	40	6	1	5	25	.333	289	15	1	.997
1974—Tulsa‡	A. A.	1B-OF	102	353	67	124	18	6	14	63	★.351	690	50	12	.984
1974—St. Louis	Nat.	1B	14	34	3	10	1	2	0	2	.294	70	1	2	.973
1975—Tulsa	A. A.	●1B-OF	85	324	70	107	29	3	10	48	.330	597	53	●13	.980
1975—St. Louis	Nat.	1B	64	188	20	47	8	2	3	20	.250	469	36	2	.996
1976—St. Louis	Nat.	1B	129	374	54	108	21	5	7	46	.289	862	●107	10	.990
1977—St. Louis	Nat.	1B	161	560	90	163	41	4	15	91	.291	1453	106	12	.992
1978—St. Louis	Nat.	1B	159	542	90	138	32	4	11	64	.255	1436	96	10	.994
1979—St. Louis	Nat.	1B	161	610	★116	210	★48	11	11	105	★.344	★1489	★146	8	.995
1980—St. Louis	Nat.	1B	159	595	★111	191	39	8	16	99	.321	1572	115	9	.995
1981—St. Louis	Nat.	1B-OF	103	376	65	115	27	4	8	48	.306	1056	86	3	.997
1982—St. Louis	Nat.	1B-OF	160	579	79	173	33	6	7	94	.299	1591	135	11	.994
1983—St.L.§-N.Y.	Nat.	1B	150	538	77	160	23	7	12	63	.297	★1418	147	●13	.992
Major League Totals			1260	4396	705	1315	273	53	90	632	.299	11416	975	80	.994

Selected by St. Louis Cardinals' organization in 42nd round of free-agent draft, June 8, 1971.
†On disabled list, April 10 to May 30, 1972.
‡On disabled list, April 16 to May 20, 1974.
§Traded to New York Mets for Pitchers Neil Allen and Rick Ownbey, June 15, 1983.

CHAMPIONSHIP SERIES RECORD

Year	Club	League	Pos.	G.	AB.	R.	H.	2B.	3B.	HR.	RBI.	B.A.	PO.	A.	E.	F.A.
1982—St. Louis	Nat.	1B	3	12	3	4	0	0	0	1	.333	35	1	0	1.000

WORLD SERIES RECORD

Year	Club	League	Pos.	G.	AB.	R.	H.	2B.	3B.	HR.	RBI.	B.A.	PO.	A.	E.	F.A.
1982—St. Louis	Nat.	1B	7	27	4	7	2	0	1	8	.259	62	7	2	.972

ALL-STAR GAME RECORD

Year	League	Pos.	AB.	R.	H.	2B.	3B.	HR.	RBI.	B.A.	PO.	A.	E.	F.A.
1979—National		PH	1	0	0	0	0	0	0	.000	0	0	0	.000
1980—National		PH-1B	2	0	2	0	0	0	0	1.000	5	0	0	1.000
All-Star Game Totals			3	0	2	0	0	0	0	.667	5	0	0	1.000

LEONARDO JESUS HERNANDEZ
(Leo)

Born November 6, 1959, at Santa Lucia, Estado Miranda, Venezuela.
Height, 5.11. Weight, 170.
Throws and bats righthanded.

Tied for Texas League lead in game-winning RBIs with 12 in 1981.

Year	Club	League	Pos.	G.	AB.	R.	H.	2B.	3B.	HR.	RBI.	B.A.	PO.	A.	E.	F.A.
1978—Clinton	Midw.	3B	112	444	65	123	21	4	17	73	.277	86	222	20	★.939
1979—Clinton	Midw.	3B	29	113	24	38	8	1	2	23	.336	22	66	6	.936
1979—Lodi	Calif.	3B	61	257	48	82	12	2	8	52	.319	52	143	29	.871
1979—San Antonio	Texas	3B	36	128	19	32	7	0	2	11	.250	19	51	8	.897
1980—San Antonio	Texas	3B	41	136	27	33	9	2	2	26	.243	23	77	14	.877
1980—Vero Beach	Fla. St.	3B-OF-1B	82	307	53	95	13	3	10	46	.309	99	102	9	.957
1981—San Antonio	Texas	3B	131	497	90	148	34	3	25	91	.298	★107	271	★25	.938
1982—San Antonio†	Texas	3B-1B	19	75	8	24	4	1	3	14	.320	39	35	6	.925
1982—Charlotte	South.	3-1-O-2	68	270	46	78	18	2	20	62	.289	159	104	11	.960
1982—Rochester	Int.	3B-OF-2B	53	202	29	64	10	3	11	43	.317	41	98	6	.959
1982—Baltimore	Amer.	PH	2	2	0	0	0	0	0	0	.000	0	0	0	.000
1983—Baltimore	Amer.	3B	64	203	21	50	6	1	6	26	.246	44	109	13	.922
1983—Rochester	Int.	3B-OF-2B	57	201	24	69	13	2	8	25	.343	57	66	10	.925
Major League Totals			66	205	21	50	6	1	6	26	.244	44	109	13	.922

Signed as free agent by Los Angeles Dodgers' organization, January 18, 1978.
†Traded to Baltimore Orioles' organization for Catcher-First Baseman Jose Morales, April 28, 1982.

LARRY DARNELL HERNDON

Born November 3, 1953, at Sunflower, Miss.
Height, 6.03. Weight, 195.
Throws and bats righthanded.
Attended Tennessee State University, Nashville, Tenn. and Skyline College, San Bruno, Calif.

Tied major league record for most consecutive home runs, two consecutive games (4), May 16 and 18, 1982.
Hit three home runs in a game, May 18, 1982.
Led Texas League in stolen bases with 50 and caught stealing with 16 in 1974.
Tied for Texas League lead in double plays by outfielders with 4 in 1974.
Named National League Rookie Player of the Year by THE SPORTING NEWS, 1976.

Year Club	League	Pos.	G.	AB.	R.	H.	2B.	3B.	HR.	RBI.	B.A.	PO.	A.	E.	F.A.
1971—Sarasota Cards.....	Gulf C.	OF	40	138	13	33	2	0	0	8	.239	68	4	3	.960
1972—St. Petersburg	Fla. St.	OF	7	28	2	4	0	0	0	0	.143	12	1	2	.867
1972—Sarasota R. B.......	Gulf C.	OF	31	113	16	29	5	3	0	9	.257	50	5	3	.948
1972—Cedar Rapids†......	Midw.	OF	7	21	1	6	0	0	0	1	.286	10	0	0	1.000
1973—St. Petersburg	Fla. St.	OF	141	485	83	139	9	5	3	41	.287	233	10	8	.968
1974—Arkansas...............	Texas	OF	132	498	74	142	16	●10	2	41	.285	325	★24	16	.956
1974—St. Louis.................	Nat.	OF	12	1	3	1	0	0	0	0	1.000	1	0	0	1.000
1975—Tulsa‡...................	A. A.	OF	22	96	13	23	5	0	1	5	.240	35	2	3	.925
1975—Phoenix.................	P. C.	OF	115	427	49	115	6	4	2	44	.269	287	10	10	.967
1976—Phoenix.................	P. C.	OF	14	57	8	14	2	1	1	5	.246	38	3	0	1.000
1976—San Francisco	Nat.	OF	115	337	42	97	11	3	2	23	.288	226	8	8	.967
1977—San Francisco§x...	Nat.	OF	49	109	13	26	4	3	1	5	.239	87	2	4	.957
1978—San Francisco	Nat.	OF	151	471	52	122	15	9	1	32	.259	369	3	10	.974
1979—San Francisco	Nat.	OF	132	354	35	91	14	5	7	36	.257	196	10	8	.963
1980—San Francisco	Nat.	OF	139	493	54	127	17	11	8	49	.258	247	8	●11	.959
1981—San Francisco y ...	Nat.	OF	96	364	48	105	15	8	5	41	.288	207	8	5	.977
1982—Detroit.................	Amer.	OF	157	614	92	179	21	13	23	88	.292	328	11	6	.983
1983—Detroit.................	Amer.	OF	153	603	88	182	28	9	20	92	.302	283	6	★15	.951
National League Totals............................			694	2129	247	569	76	39	24	186	.267	1333	39	46	.968
American League Totals............................			310	1217	180	361	49	22	43	180	.297	611	17	21	.968
Major League Totals..................................			1004	3346	427	930	125	61	67	366	.278	1944	56	67	.968

Selected by St. Louis Cardinals' organization in 3rd round of free-agent draft, June 8, 1971.
†On disabled list, August 11, 1972 through remainder of season.
‡Traded with Pitcher Tony Gonzalez to San Francisco Giants for Pitcher Ron Bryant, May 9, 1975.
§On disabled list, June 19 to August 26, 1977.
xOn disqualified list, August 26, 1977 through remainder of season.
yTraded to Detroit Tigers for Pitchers Dan Schatzeder and Mike Chris, December 9, 1981.

THOMAS MITCHELL HERR
(Tom)

Born April 4, 1956, at Lancaster, Pa.
Height, 6.00. Weight, 175.
Throws right and bats left and righthanded.
Attended University of Delaware, Newark, Del.

Major League stolen bases: 1979 (1), 1980 (9), 1981 (23), 1982 (25), 1983 (6). Total—64.
Led National League second basemen in total chances with 590 and double plays with 74 in 1981.
Led Florida State League in stolen bases with 50 in 1977.
Led Florida State League second basemen in double plays with 91 in 1977.

Year Club	League	Pos.	G.	AB.	R.	H.	2B.	3B.	HR.	RBI.	B.A.	PO.	A.	E.	F.A.
1975—Johnson City	Appal.	2B-SS	42	133	29	41	8	1	0	15	.308	74	125	5	.975
1976—St. Petersburg	Fla. St.	SS-2B	82	275	47	74	6	1	0	21	.269	133	211	18	.950
1977—St. Petersburg	Fla. St.	2B	136	★515	★80	★156	13	7	1	53	.303	★348	★430	21	★.974
1978—Arkansas...............	Texas	2B	89	335	70	98	23	4	3	45	.293	207	280	13	.974
1978—Springfield.............	A. A.	2B	33	86	16	24	6	1	0	8	.279	45	63	7	.939
1979—Springfield.............	A. A.	2B	109	423	74	124	20	6	6	48	.293	225	324	10	★.982
1979—St. Louis.................	Nat.	2B	14	10	4	2	0	0	0	1	.200	12	11	0	1.000
1980—Springfield.............	A. A.	2B-3B	37	141	29	44	6	2	5	16	.312	29	52	1	.988
1980—St. Louis.................	Nat.	2B-SS	76	222	29	55	2	5	0	15	.248	124	184	7	.978
1981—St. Louis.................	Nat.	2B	103	411	50	110	14	9	0	46	.268	211	★374	5	★.992
1982—St. Louis.................	Nat.	2B	135	493	83	131	19	4	0	36	.266	263	427	9	.987
1983—St. Louis†...............	Nat.	2B	89	313	43	101	14	4	2	31	.323	178	245	6	.986
1983—Arkansas...............	Texas	2B	3	9	0	4	3	0	0	1	.444	4	9	0	1.000
Major League Totals..................................			417	1449	209	399	49	22	2	129	.275	788	1241	27	.987

Signed as free agent by St. Louis Cardinals' organization, August 22, 1974.
†On disabled list, March 25 to April 29 and August 9, 1983 through remainder of season; included rehabilitation disability assignment to Arkansas, April 18 to April 29, 1983.

CHAMPIONSHIP SERIES RECORD

Year Club	League	Pos.	G.	AB.	R.	H.	2B.	3B.	HR.	RBI.	B.A.	PO.	A.	E.	F.A.
1982—St. Louis.................	Nat.	2B	3	13	1	3	1	0	0	0	.231	6	10	0	1.000

WORLD SERIES RECORD

Established World Series record for most runs batted in on sacrifice fly (2), October 16, 1982 (second inning).

Year Club	League	Pos.	G.	AB.	R.	H.	2B.	3B.	HR.	RBI.	B.A.	PO.	A.	E.	F.A.
1982—St. Louis.................	Nat.	2B	7	25	2	4	2	0	0	5	.160	11	19	1	.968

OREL LEONARD HERSHISER

Name pronounced Hersh-HYZ-ur.
Born September 16, 1958, at Buffalo, N.Y.
Height, 6.03. Weight, 190.
Throws and bats righthanded.
Attended Bowling Green State University, Bowling Green, O.
Led Pacific Coast League in intentional bases on balls issued with 8 in 1983.

Year Club	League	G.	IP.	W.	L.	Pct.	H.	R.	ER.	SO.	BB.	ERA.
1979—Clinton	Midwest	15	43	4	0	1.000	33	15	10	33	17	2.09
1980—San Antonio	Texas	49	109	5	9	.357	120	59	43	75	59	3.55
1981—San Antonio	Texas	42	102	7	6	.538	94	54	53	95	50	4.68
1982—Albuquerque	P. Coast	47	123⅔	9	6	.600	121	73	51	93	63	3.71
1983—Albuquerque	P. Coast	49	134⅓	10	8	.556	132	73	61	95	57	4.09
1983—Los Angeles	National	8	8	0	0	.000	7	6	3	5	6	3.38
Major League Totals		8	8	0	0	.000	7	6	3	5	6	3.38

Selected by Los Angeles Dodgers' organization in 16th round of free-agent draft, June 5, 1979.

JOSEPH THOMAS HESKETH
(Joe)

Born February 15, 1959, at Lackawanna, N.Y.
Height, 6.02. Weight, 165.
Throws left and bats righthanded.
Attended State University of New York at Buffalo, Buffalo, N.Y.
Tied for American Association lead in shutouts with 2 in 1983.

Year Club	League	G.	IP.	W.	L.	Pct.	H.	R.	ER.	SO.	BB.	ERA.
1980—West Palm Beach	Florida St.	11	75	8	2	.800	71	30	16	43	32	1.92
1980—Memphis	Southern	3	20	1	0	1.000	20	13	9	20	7	4.05
1981—Memphis†	Southern					(Did Not Play)						
1982—Memphis‡	Southern					(Did Not Play)						
1982—West Palm Beach	Florida St.	8	45⅔	3	2	.600	41	16	14	24	16	2.76
1983—Memphis	Southern	11	74	6	4	.600	82	38	25	22	25	3.04
1983—Wichita	Am. Assoc.	15	88⅓	5	5	.500	98	53	50	41	46	5.09

Selected by Montreal Expos' organization in 2nd round of free-agent draft, June 3, 1980.
†On disabled list, April 9, 1981, through remainder of season.
‡On disabled list, April 8 to July 8, 1982.

KEVIN JOHN HICKEY

Born February 25, 1957, at Chicago, Ill.
Height, 6.01. Weight, 170.
Throws and bats lefthanded.
Led Eastern League in home runs allowed with 20 and balks with 6 in 1980.
Led Midwest League in balks with 5 in 1979.

Year Club	League	G.	IP.	W.	L.	Pct.	H.	R.	ER.	SO.	BB.	ERA.
1978—Paintsville	Ap'lachian	9	36	2	4	.333	37	19	16	24	23	4.00
1979—Appleton	Midwest	29	121	5	10	.333	122	64	48	100	71	3.57
1980—Glens Falls	Eastern	26	169	9	7	.563	184	92	81	80	73	4.31
1981—Chicago	American	41	44	0	2	.000	38	22	18	17	18	3.68
1982—Chicago	American	60	78	4	4	.500	73	32	26	38	30	3.00
1983—Chicago†	American	23	20⅔	1	2	.333	23	14	12	8	11	5.23
Major League Totals		124	142⅔	5	8	.385	134	68	56	63	59	3.53

Signed as free agent by Chicago White Sox' organization, August 18, 1977.
†On disabled list, August 1 to September 5, 1983.

TEODORO HIGUERAS (VALENZUELA)

Born November 9, 1958, at Las Mochis, Mexico.
Height, 5.10. Weight, 180.
Throws and bats righthanded.

Year Club	League	G.	IP.	W.	L.	Pct.	H.	R.	ER.	SO.	BB.	ERA.
1979—Ciudad Juarez	Mexican	2	1	0	1	.000	4	5	5	1	4	45.00
1980—Ciudad Juarez†	Mexican	19	117	8	3	.727	111	30	24	76	59	1.85
1980—Ciudad Juarez‡	Mexican	8	49	2	5	.286	44	22	20	29	17	3.67
1981—Ciudad Juarez	Mexican	16	36	1	2	.333	45	29	28	19	24	7.00
1982—Ciudad Juarez	Mexican	24	142⅓	9	12	.429	163	77	64	74	53	4.05
1983—Ciudad Juarez§	Mexican	27	222	17	8	.680	177	61	50	165	68	2.03

†20-team season.
‡6-team season.
§Sold to Vancouver (Milwaukee Brewers' organization), September 13, 1983.

DONALD EARL HILL
(Donnie)

Born November 20, 1960, at Pomona, Calif.
Height, 5.10. Weight, 165.
Throws right and bats left and righthanded.
Attended Arizona State University, Tempe, Ariz.

Tied for Eastern League lead in sacrifice flies with 8 in 1982.

Year	Club	League	Pos.	G.	AB.	R.	H.	2B.	3B.	HR.	RBI.	B.A.	PO.	A.	E.	F.A.
1981—Modesto	Calif.	SS-2B	46	149	21	29	3	0	6	22	.195	44	84	22	.853
1982—West Haven†	East.	SS-3B	132	405	66	103	21	3	10	59	.254	141	301	29	.938
1983—Tacoma‡	P. C.	SS	93	322	45	101	19	2	14	63	.314	148	256	18	.957
1983—Oakland	Amer.	SS	53	158	20	42	7	0	2	15	.266	87	136	9	.961
Major League Totals			53	158	20	42	7	0	2	15	.266	87	136	9	.961

Selected by Houston Astros' organization in 5th round of free-agent draft, January 8, 1980.
Selected by San Francisco Giants' organization in secondary phase of free-agent draft, June 3, 1980.
Selected by Oakland A's organization in secondary phase of free-agent draft, June 8, 1981.
†On temporary inactive list, April 13 to April 23, 1982.
‡On disabled list, April 30 to May 10, 1983.

MARC KEVIN HILL

Born February 18, 1952, at Louisiana, Mo.
Height, 6.03. Weight, 210.
Throws and bats righthanded.

Led American Association catchers in double plays with 18 in 1974.
Led Florida State League catchers in total chances with 983 and double plays with 14 in 1972.
Led Gulf Coast League catchers in double plays with 5 in 1970.

Year	Club	League	Pos.	G.	AB.	R.	H.	2B.	3B.	HR.	RBI.	B.A.	PO.	A.	E.	F.A.
1970—Sarasota Cards	Gulf C.	C	28	78	6	15	3	0	0	6	.192	176	24	2	.990
1971—Cedar Rapids	Midw.	C	87	272	21	63	9	1	1	27	.232	572	57	8	.987
1972—St. Petersburg	Fla. St.	C	124	421	34	104	12	1	8	65	.247	★876	★92	15	.985
1972—Modesto	Calif.	C-1B	7	24	2	8	2	0	0	4	.333	39	3	0	1.000
1973—Arkansas	Texas	C	122	403	41	97	19	2	9	49	.241	★670	64	8	.989
1973—Tulsa	A. A.	C	9	29	4	12	1	0	3	8	.414	61	5	0	1.000
1973—St. Louis	Nat.	C	1	3	0	0	0	0	0	0	.000	5	0	0	1.000
1974—Tulsa	A. A.	C-1B	96	327	46	91	16	1	14	58	.278	553	61	9	.986
1974—St. Louis†	Nat.	C	10	21	2	5	1	0	0	2	.238	41	5	0	1.000
1975—San Francisco	Nat.	C-3B	72	182	14	39	4	0	5	23	.214	282	27	2	.994
1976—San Francisco‡	Nat.	C-1B	54	131	11	24	5	0	3	15	.183	186	24	1	.995
1977—San Francisco	Nat.	C	108	320	28	80	10	0	9	50	.250	505	57	6	.989
1978—San Francisco	Nat.	C-1B	117	358	20	87	15	1	3	36	.243	592	56	9	.986
1979—San Francisco§	Nat.	C-1B	63	169	20	35	3	0	3	15	.207	285	31	3	.991
1980—San Francisco x	Nat.	C	17	41	1	7	2	0	0	0	.171	61	8	2	.972
1980—Seattle y	Amer.	C	29	70	8	16	2	1	2	9	.229	101	10	1	.991
1981—Chicago	Amer.	C-1B-3B	16	6	0	0	0	0	0	0	.000	11	1	0	1.000
1981—Glens Falls	East.	C	2	7	1	3	0	0	0	3	.429	6	1	0	1.000
1982—Chicago	Amer.	C-1B-3B	53	88	9	23	2	0	3	13	.261	136	16	1	.993
1983—Chicago	Amer.	C-1B	58	133	11	30	6	0	1	11	.226	215	12	2	.991
National League Totals			442	1225	96	277	40	1	23	141	.226	1957	208	23	.989
American League Totals			156	297	28	69	10	1	6	33	.232	463	39	4	.992
Major League Totals			598	1522	124	346	50	2	29	174	.227	2420	247	27	.990

Selected by St. Louis Cardinals' organization in 10th round of free-agent draft, June 4, 1970.
†Traded to San Francisco Giants for Pitcher Elias Sosa and Catcher Ken Rudolph, October 14, 1974.
‡On disabled list, August 4, 1976 through remainder of season.
§On disabled list, July 25, 1979 through remainder of season.
xSold on waivers to Seattle Mariners, June 20, 1980.
yGranted free agency, October 28, 1980; signed by Chicago White Sox, February 12, 1981.

GEORGE ADDISON HINSHAW

Born October 23, 1959, at Los Angeles, Calif.
Height, 6.00. Weight, 180.
Throws and bats righthanded.
Attended LaVerne College, LaVerne, Calif.

Led California League in total bases with 298 in 1981.

Year	Club	League	Pos.	G.	AB.	R.	H.	2B.	3B.	HR.	RBI.	B.A.	PO.	A.	E.	F.A.
1980—Walla Walla	N'west	OF-SS	63	230	46	66	10	4	3	29	.287	115	66	22	.892
1981—Reno	Calif.	OF-SS	128	510	113	★189	20	7	25	★131	.371	202	18	15	.936
1982—Amarillo	Texas	●OF-3B	129	519	90	154	24	3	18	89	.297	246	17	●17	.939
1982—San Diego	Nat.	OF	6	15	1	4	0	0	0	1	.267	9	1	0	1.000
1983—Las Vegas	P. C.	★3B-OF	133	480	92	136	19	5	16	67	.283	86	249	★41	.891
1983—San Diego	Nat.	3B-2B	7	16	1	7	1	0	0	4	.438	6	5	0	1.000
Major League Totals			13	31	2	11	1	0	0	5	.355	15	6	0	1.000

Selected by San Diego Padres' organization in 10th round of free-agent draft, June 3, 1980.

CLELL LAVERN HOBSON JR.
(Butch)

Born August 17, 1951, at Tuscaloosa, Ala.
Height, 6.01. Weight, 190.
Throws and bats righthanded.
Attended University of Alabama, University, Ala.
Son of Clell Hobson, minor league infielder, 1953 through 1957.

Led American League batters in strikeouts with 162 in 1977.
Led Eastern League in total bases with 201 in 1975.
Led International League third basemen in putouts with 89 and assists with 200 in 1976.

Year	Club	League	Pos.	G.	AB.	R.	H.	2B.	3B.	HR.	RBI.	B.A.	PO.	A.	E.	F.A.
1973—Winston-Salem	Carol.	3B-OF	17	39	8	7	2	1	0	5	.179	10	10	1	.952
1974—Winston-Salem	Carol.	OF-3B-1B	119	423	66	120	18	8	14	74	.284	211	79	12	.960
1975—Bristol	East.	3B	●138	471	68	125	25	3	15	73	.265	102	309	28	.936
1975—Boston	Amer.	3B	2	4	0	1	0	0	0	0	.250	1	3	0	1.000
1976—Rhode Island	Int.	3B-SS	90	360	56	103	21	1	25	72	.286	91	204	15	.952
1976—Boston	Amer.	3B	76	269	34	63	7	5	8	34	.234	60	146	14	.936
1977—Boston	Amer.	3B	159	593	77	157	33	5	30	112	.265	128	272	23	.946
1978—Boston	Amer.	3B	147	512	65	128	26	2	17	80	.250	122	261	★43	.899
1979—Boston	Amer.	3B-2B	146	528	74	138	26	7	28	93	.261	110	251	25	.935
1980—Boston†‡	Amer.	3B	93	324	35	74	6	0	11	39	.228	52	109	16	.910
1981—California§	Amer.	3B	85	268	27	63	7	4	4	36	.235	85	139	●17	.929
1982—New York x	Amer.	1B	30	58	2	10	2	0	0	3	.172	37	2	2	.951
1982—Columbus	Int.	1B-3B	27	83	17	27	5	1	4	20	.325	44	14	4	.935
1983—Columbus	Int.	3B-1B	112	379	68	93	17	4	19	63	.245	91	149	11	.956
Major League Totals				738	2556	314	634	107	23	98	397	.248	595	1183	140	.927

Selected by Boston Red Sox' organization in 8th round of free-agent draft, June 5, 1973.
†On supplemental disabled list, July 27 to August 11 and August 23 to September 7, 1980.
‡Traded with Shortstop Rick Burleson to California Angels for Third Baseman Carney Lansford, Pitcher Mark Clear and Outfielder Rick Miller, December 10, 1980.
§Traded to New York Yankees for Pitcher Bill Castro, March 24, 1982.
xOn supplemental disabled list, April 1 to April 24, 1982.

ED OLIVER HODGE
(Eddie)

Born April 19, 1958, at Bellflower, Calif.
Height, 6.02. Weight, 185.
Throws and bats lefthanded.
Attended Cerritos College, Norwalk, Calif.

Year	Club	League	G.	IP.	W.	L.	Pct.	H.	R.	ER.	SO.	BB.	ERA.
1979—Elizabethton	Ap'lachian	14	81	8	4	.667	82	46	39	56	21	4.33
1980—Orlando	Southern	27	186	14	9	.609	188	95	77	90	62	3.73
1981—Toledo	Int'national	29	163	8	★17	.320	173	92	82	84	60	4.53
1982—Toledo	Int'national	5	18	1	3	.250	23	17	17	20	13	8.50
1982—Orlando	Southern	39	79	6	9	.400	91	49	43	77	39	4.90
1983—Toledo	Int'national	28	143	11	6	.647	137	72	63	72	64	3.97

Selected by Minnesota Twins' organization in 5th round of free-agent draft, January 9, 1979.

RONALD WRAY HODGES
(Ron)

Born June 22, 1949, at Rocky Mount, Va.
Height, 6.01. Weight, 185.
Throws right and bats lefthanded.
Attended Appalachian State University, Boone, N. C.

Tied major league record for most double plays by catcher, extra-inning game (3), April 23, 1978.

Year	Club	League	Pos.	G.	AB.	R.	H.	2B.	3B.	HR.	RBI.	B.A.	PO.	A.	E.	F.A.
1972—Pompano Beach	Fla. St.	●C-3B-OF	112	359	59	92	15	4	15	48	.256	684	71	●18	.977
1973—Memphis	Texas	C	47	139	12	24	4	0	1	11	.173	275	3	6	.980
1973—New York	Nat.	C	45	127	5	33	2	0	1	18	.260	241	13	2	.992
1974—New York	Nat.	C	59	136	16	30	4	0	4	14	.221	227	14	12	.953
1975—Tidewater	Int.	C-OF-1B	95	278	27	74	8	0	2	33	.266	431	45	7	.986
1975—New York	Nat.	C	9	34	3	7	1	0	2	4	.206	69	1	0	1.000
1976—New York†	Nat.	C	56	155	21	35	6	0	4	24	.226	262	18	7	.976
1977—New York	Nat.	C	66	117	6	31	4	0	1	5	.265	112	19	1	.992
1978—New York	Nat.	C	47	102	4	26	4	1	0	7	.255	145	20	3	.982
1979—New York	Nat.	C	59	86	4	14	4	0	0	5	.163	82	16	2	.980
1980—New York‡	Nat.	C	36	42	4	10	2	0	0	5	.238	47	9	1	.982
1981—New York	Nat.	C	35	43	5	13	2	0	1	6	.302	23	1	0	1.000
1982—New York§	Nat.	C	80	228	26	56	12	1	5	27	.246	362	35	8	.980
1983—New York	Nat.	C	110	250	20	65	12	0	0	21	.260	360	45	12	.971
Major League Totals				602	1320	114	320	53	2	18	136	.242	1930	191	48	.978

Selected by Baltimore Orioles' organization in 6th round of free-agent draft, June 4, 1970.
Selected by Kansas City Royals' organization in secondary phase of free-agent draft, January 13, 1971.
Selected by Atlanta Braves' organization in secondary phase of free-agent draft, June 8, 1971.
Selected by New York Mets' organization in secondary phase of free-agent draft, January 12, 1972.
†On disabled list, June 13 to June 28, 1976.
‡On disabled list, July 5, 1980 through remainder of season.
§Granted free agency, November 10, 1982; re-signed by Mets, February 6, 1983.

WORLD SERIES RECORD

Year	Club	League	Pos.	G.	AB.	R.	H.	2B.	3B.	HR.	RBI.	B.A.	PO.	A.	E.	F.A.
1973—New York	Nat.	PH	1	0	0	0	0	0	0	0	.000	0	0	0	.000

GLENN EDWARD HOFFMAN

Born July 7, 1958, at Orange, Calif.
Height, 6.02. Weight, 170.
Throws and bats righthanded.

Led International League shortstops in double plays with 87 in 1978.
Tied for Florida State League lead in putouts by shortstops with 220 in 1977.

Year—Club	League	Pos.	G.	AB.	R.	H.	2B.	3B.	HR.	RBI.	B.A.	PO.	A.	E.	F.A.
1976—Elmira	NYP	SS	60	191	29	52	7	2	3	34	.272	★83	139	17	.925
1977—Winter Haven	Fla. St.	SS-3B-1B	126	425	51	123	17	2	3	61	.289	225	377	36	.944
1977—Pawtucket	Int.	SS	4	9	2	4	1	0	0	2	.444	4	10	1	.933
1978—Pawtucket	Int.	★SS-P	131	411	27	116	17	1	2	48	.282	★211	★391	45	.930
1979—Pawtucket	Int.	3B-SS-P	139	520	70	148	13	3	11	54	.285	172	286	19	.960
1980—Boston	Amer.	3B-SS-2B	114	312	37	89	15	4	4	42	.285	78	202	17	.943
1981—Boston	Amer.	SS-3B	78	242	28	56	10	0	1	20	.231	132	234	15	.961
1982—Boston	Amer.	SS	150	469	53	98	23	2	7	49	.209	246	439	20	.972
1983—Boston	Amer.	SS	143	473	56	123	24	1	4	41	.260	240	417	26	.962
Major League Totals			485	1496	174	366	72	7	16	152	.245	696	1292	78	.962

Selected by Boston Red Sox' organization in 2nd round of free-agent draft, June 8, 1976.

RECORD AS PITCHER

Year—Club	League	G.	IP.	W.	L.	Pct.	H.	R.	ER.	SO.	BB.	ERA.
1978—Pawtucket	Int'national	1	⅓	0	0	.000	0	0	0	0	0	0.00
1979—Pawtucket	Int'national	1	1	0	0	.000	1	1	1	0	1	9.00

GUY ALAN HOFFMAN

Born July 9, 1956, at Ottawa, Ill.
Height, 5.09, Weight, 175.
Throws and bats lefthanded.
Attended Bradley University, Peoria, Ill.

Year—Club	League	G.	IP.	W.	L.	Pct.	H.	R.	ER.	SO.	BB.	ERA.
1978—Appleton	Midwest	7	34	2	0	1.000	22	10	9	31	15	2.38
1979—Appleton	Midwest	2	5	0	0	.000	2	0	0	4	1	0.00
1979—Iowa	Am. Assoc.	13	70	6	0	1.000	62	30	26	34	40	3.34
1979—Chicago	American	24	30	0	5	.000	30	18	18	23	5	5.40
1980—Iowa	Am. Assoc.	15	75	6	3	.667	59	31	30	56	34	3.60
1980—Chicago	American	23	38	1	0	1.000	38	12	11	24	17	2.61
1981—Edmonton	P. Coast	20	111	4	6	.400	117	70	53	71	60	4.30
1982—Edmonton	P. Coast	28	138⅓	8	●14	.364	186	129	106	72	67	6.90
1983—Denver	Am. Assoc.	32	52⅔	5	3	.625	49	23	22	50	23	3.76
1983—Chicago	American	11	6	1	0	1.000	14	5	5	2	2	7.50
Major League Totals		58	74	2	5	.286	82	35	34	44	42	4.14

Signed as free agent by Chicago White Sox' organization, July 17, 1978.

ALFRED WILLIS HOLLAND
(Al)

Born August 16, 1952, at Roanoke, Va.
Height, 5.11. Weight, 210.
Throws left and bats righthanded.
Received bachelor of science degree in recreation from
North Carolina A&T University, Greensboro, N. C. in 1975.

Major League saves: 1980 (7), 1981 (7), 1982 (5), 1983 (25). Total—44.
Led New York-Pennsylvania League in balks with 5 and tied for lead in shutouts with 2 in 1975.
Named National League co-Fireman of the Year by THE SPORTING NEWS, 1983.

Year—Club	League	G.	IP.	W.	L.	Pct.	H.	R.	ER.	SO.	BB.	ERA.
1975—Bradenton Pirates	Gulf Coast	5	40	2	2	.500	24	6	5	39	20	1.13
1975—Niagara Falls	NYP	6	49	4	2	.667	44	20	14	50	14	2.57
1976—Salem	Carolina	39	76	4	2	.667	59	32	25	72	45	2.96
1977—Shreveport	Texas	21	36	4	1	.800	23	7	5	25	17	1.25
1977—Columbus	Int'national	27	86	6	4	.600	83	44	34	73	36	3.56
1977—Pittsburgh	National	2	2	0	0	.000	4	2	2	1	0	9.00
1978—Columbus†	Int'national	20	91	8	5	.615	102	59	54	65	34	5.34
1979—Portland‡-Phoenix	P. Coast	29	174	10	10	.500	173	99	87	140	87	4.50
1979—San Francisco	National	3	7	0	0	.000	3	0	0	7	5	0.00
1980—San Francisco	National	54	82	5	3	.625	71	21	16	65	34	1.76
1981—San Francisco	National	47	101	7	5	.583	87	31	27	78	44	2.41
1982—San Francisco§x	National	58	129⅔	7	3	.700	115	56	48	97	40	3.33
1983—Philadelphia y	National	68	91⅔	8	4	.667	63	26	23	100	30	2.26
Major League Totals		232	413⅓	27	15	.643	343	136	116	348	153	2.53

Selected by Texas Rangers' organization in 30th round of free-agent draft, June 5, 1974.
Selected by San Diego Padres' organization in secondary phase of free-agent draft, January 9, 1975.
Signed as free agent by Pittsburgh Pirates' organization, June 28, 1975.
†On disabled list, April 14 to May 28 and July 20 to July 31, 1978.
‡Traded with Pitchers Ed Whitson and Fred Breining to San Francisco Giants for Third Basemen Bill Madlock and Lenny Randle and Pitcher Dave Roberts, June 28, 1979.
§On disabled list, May 11 to June 4, 1982.

xTraded with Second Baseman Joe Morgan to Philadelphia Phillies for Pitchers Mike Krukow and Mark Davis and Outfielder Charles Penigar, December 14, 1982.

yOn disabled list, March 31 to April 29, 1983.

CHAMPIONSHIP SERIES RECORD

Year Club	League	G.	IP.	W.	L.	Pct.	H.	R.	ER.	SO.	BB.	ERA.
1983—Philadelphia	National	2	3	0	0	.000	1	0	0	3	0	0.00

WORLD SERIES RECORD

Year Club	League	G.	IP.	W.	L.	Pct.	H.	R.	ER.	SO.	BB.	ERA.
1983—Philadelphia	National	2	3⅔	0	0	.000	1	0	0	5	0	0.00

RANDY SCOTT HOLMAN
(Known by middle name.)

Born September 18, 1958, at Santa Paula, Calif.
Height, 6.00. Weight, 190.
Throws and bats righthanded.
Attended Ventura College, Ventura, Calif.

Led International League in shutouts with 4 in 1979.

Year Club	League	G.	IP.	W.	L.	Pct.	H.	R.	ER.	SO.	BB.	ERA.
1977—Wausau	Midwest	48	100	3	11	.214	96	51	39	83	37	3.51
1978—Jackson†	Texas	23	138	11	5	.688	128	57	50	68	66	3.26
1979—Tidewater	Int'national	24	149	13	7	.650	125	45	33	62	51	*1.99
1980—Tidewater‡	Int'national	11	48	3	3	.500	54	35	26	16	18	4.88
1980—New York	National	4	7	0	0	.000	6	2	1	3	1	1.29
1981—Jackson§	Texas	20	110	4	9	.308	106	57	47	43	71	3.85
1982—Tidewater	Int'national	24	141⅔	10	8	.556	125	61	54	67	95	3.43
1982—New York	National	4	26⅔	2	1	.667	23	10	7	11	7	2.36
1983—New York	National	35	101	1	7	.125	90	48	42	44	52	3.74
Major League Totals		43	134⅔	3	8	.273	119	60	50	58	60	3.34

Signed as free agent by New York Mets' organization, December 26, 1979.
†On disabled list, June 26 to July 6, 1978.
‡On disabled list, May 29 to July 31, 1980.
§On Tidewater disabled list, April 10 to May 15, 1981.

BRIAN JOHN HOLTON

Born November 29, 1959, at McKeesport, Pa.
Height, 6.02. Weight, 190.
Throws and bats righthanded.
Attended Louisburg College, Louisburg, N. C.

Tied for Texas League lead in complete games with 16 in 1980.
Tied for California League lead in shutouts with 3 in 1979.

Year Club	League	G.	IP.	W.	L.	Pct.	H.	R.	ER.	SO.	BB.	ERA.
1978—Clinton†	Midwest	14	79	6	4	.600	94	51	38	54	23	4.33
1979—Lodi	California	10	72	7	0	1.000	47	26	21	72	32	2.63
1979—San Antonio	Texas	13	51	3	5	.375	50	24	21	40	25	3.71
1980—San Antonio	Texas	27	207	●15	10	.600	204	93	79	139	65	3.43
1981—Albuquerque	P. Coast	26	191	16	6	.727	215	94	73	73	51	3.44
1982—Albuquerque	P. Coast	32	161⅓	12	8	.600	191	102	92	76	60	5.13
1983—Albuquerque‡	P. Coast	20	97⅔	7	5	.583	113	76	69	70	50	6.36

Selected by Los Angeles Dodgers' organization in 1st round (22nd player selected) of free-agent draft, January 10, 1978.
†On temporary inactive list, June 12 to July 7, 1978.
‡On disabled list, June 28 to July 15, 1983.

FREDERICK WAYNE HONEYCUTT
(Rick)

Born June 29, 1954, at Chattanooga, Tenn.
Height, 6.02. Weight, 190.
Throws and bats lefthanded.
Received bachelor of science degree in health education from
University of Tennessee, Knoxville, Tenn.

Tied for New York-Pennsylvania League lead in complete games with 7 in 1976.

Year Club	League	G.	IP.	W.	L.	Pct.	H.	R.	ER.	SO.	BB.	ERA.
1976—Niagara Falls†	NYP	13	*97	5	3	.625	91	36	28	*98	20	2.60
1977—Shreveport‡§	Texas	21	135	10	6	.625	144	53	37	82	42	*2.47
1977—Seattle	American	10	29	0	1	.000	26	16	14	17	11	4.34
1978—Seattle x	American	26	134	5	11	.313	150	81	73	50	49	4.90
1979—Seattle	American	33	194	11	12	.478	201	103	87	83	67	4.04
1980—Seattle y	American	30	203	10	17	.370	221	99	89	79	60	3.95
1981—Texas	American	20	128	11	6	.647	120	49	47	40	17	3.30
1982—Texas	American	30	164	5	17	.227	201	103	96	64	54	5.27

Year Club	League	G.	IP.	W.	L.	Pct.	H.	R.	ER.	SO.	BB.	ERA.
1983—Texas z	American	25	174⅔	14	8	.636	168	59	47	56	37	*2.42
1983—Los Angeles	National	9	39	2	3	.400	46	26	25	18	13	5.77
American League Totals		174	1026⅔	56	72	.438	1087	510	453	389	295	3.97
National League Totals		9	39	2	3	.400	46	26	25	18	13	5.77
Major League Totals		183	1065⅔	58	75	.436	1133	536	478	407	308	4.04

Selected by Baltimore Orioles' organization in 14th round of free-agent draft, June 6, 1972.
Selected by Pittsburgh Pirates' organization in 17th round of free-agent draft, June 8, 1976.
†Played two games as first baseman and one game as shortstop.
‡Traded to Seattle Mariners, August 22, 1977, completing deal in which Seattle traded Pitcher Dave Pagan to Pittsburgh Pirates for a player to be named later, July 27, 1977.
§Appeared as shortstop with no chances.
xOn disabled list, May 20 to June 26, 1978.
yTraded with Catcher Larry Cox, Outfielders Willie Horton and Leon Roberts and Shortstop Mario Mendoza to Texas Rangers for Pitchers Brian Allard, Ken Clay, Steve Finch and Jerry Don Gleaton, Shortstop Rick Auerbach and Outfielder Richie Zisk, December 12, 1980.
zTraded to Los Angeles Dodgers for Pitcher Dave Stewart and a player to be named later, August 19, 1983; Texas Rangers acquired Pitcher Ricky Wright to complete deal, September 16, 1983.

CHAMPIONSHIP SERIES RECORD

Year Club	League	G.	IP.	W.	L.	Pct.	H.	R.	ER.	SO.	BB.	ERA.
1983—Los Angeles	National	2	1⅔	0	0	.000	4	4	4	2	0	21.60

ALL-STAR GAME RECORD

Year League	IP.	W.	L.	Pct.	H.	R.	ER.	SO.	BB.	ERA.
1983—American	2	0	0	.000	5	2	2	0	0	9.00

Member of American League All-Star Team in 1980; did not play.

DONALD HARRIS HOOD
(Don)

Born October 16, 1949, at Florence, S. C.
Height, 6.03.   Weight, 188.
Throws and bats lefthanded.
Attended St. Petersburg Junior College, St. Petersburg, Fla.

Led American League in balks with 5 in 1975.
Led Texas League in balks with 4 in 1971.
Tied for American Association lead in wild pitches with 11 in 1981.
Tied for California League lead in shutouts with 5 in 1970.

Year Club	League	G.	IP.	W.	L.	Pct.	H.	R.	ER.	SO.	BB.	ERA.
1969—Bluefield	Ap'lachian	9	48	5	1	.833	53	29	24	54	24	4.50
1970—Stockton	California	28	178	10	10	.500	165	78	57	196	66	2.88
1971—Dallas-Ft. Worth	Texas	26	167	11	9	.550	146	68	50	96	60	2.69
1972—Rochester	Int'national	27	150	9	10	.474	160	66	58	84	58	3.48
1973—Rochester	Int'national	15	91	4	7	.364	75	40	32	62	33	3.16
1973—Baltimore	American	8	32	3	2	.600	31	17	14	18	6	3.94
1974—Baltimore†‡	American	20	57	1	1	.500	47	26	22	26	20	3.47
1975—Cleveland	American	29	135	6	10	.375	136	76	66	51	57	4.40
1976—Cleveland	American	33	78	3	5	.375	89	46	42	32	41	4.85
1977—Cleveland	American	41	105	2	1	.667	87	42	35	62	49	3.00
1978—Cleveland	American	36	155	5	6	.455	166	82	77	73	77	4.47
1979—Cleveland§-New York x	American	40	89	4	1	.800	75	33	32	29	44	3.24
1980—St. Louis y	National	33	82	4	6	.400	90	39	31	35	34	3.40
1981—Omaha	Am. Assoc.	30	95	4	3	.571	80	50	39	48	53	3.69
1982—Omaha	Am. Assoc.	8	37⅓	2	2	.500	34	19	18	21	19	4.34
1982—Kansas City z	American	30	66⅔	4	0	1.000	71	31	26	31	22	3.51
1983—Omaha	Am. Assoc.	5	9⅓	0	1	.000	7	7	4	5	2	3.86
1983—Kansas City ab	American	27	47⅔	2	3	.400	48	20	12	17	14	2.27
National League Totals		33	82	4	6	.400	90	39	31	35	34	3.40
American League Totals		264	765⅓	30	29	.508	750	373	326	339	330	3.83
Major League Totals		297	847⅓	34	35	.493	840	412	357	374	364	3.79

Selected by Baltimore Orioles' organization in 1st round (17th player selected) of free-agent draft, June 5, 1969.
†On restricted list, May 26 to June 4, 1974.
‡Traded with First Baseman Boog Powell to Cleveland Indians for Catcher Dave Duncan and Outfielder Alvin McGrew, February 25, 1974.
§Traded to New York Yankees for Catcher Cliff Johnson, June 15, 1979.
xGranted free agency, November 1, 1979; signed by St. Louis Cardinals, March 21, 1980.
yReleased, October 20, 1980; signed by Kansas City Royals' organization, February 28, 1981.
zGranted free agency, November 10, 1982; re-signed by Kansas City Royals' organization, April 5, 1983.
aOn disabled list, August 16 to September 6, 1983.
bGranted free agency, November 7, 1983.

CHAMPIONSHIP SERIES RECORD

Year Club	League	Pos.	G.	AB.	R.	H.	2B.	3B.	HR.	RBI.	B.A.	PO.	A.	E.	F.A.
1973—Baltimore	Amer.	PR	1	0	0	0	0	0	0	0	.000	0	0	0	.000

BURT CARLTON HOOTON

Born February 7, 1950, at Greenville, Tex.
Height, 6.01. Weight, 200.
Throws and bats righthanded.
Attended University of Texas, Austin, Tex.

Pitched 4-0 no-hit victory against Philadelphia Phillies, April 16, 1972.

Year Club	League	G.	IP.	W.	L.	Pct.	H.	R.	ER.	SO.	BB.	ERA.
1971—Tacoma	P. Coast	12	102	7	4	.636	73	26	19	135	19	1.68
1971—Chicago	National	3	21	2	0	1.000	8	5	5	22	10	2.14
1972—Chicago	National	33	218	11	14	.440	201	78	68	132	81	2.81
1973—Chicago	National	42	240	14	17	.452	248	107	98	134	73	3.68
1974—Chicago	National	48	176	7	11	.389	214	112	94	94	51	4.81
1975—Chicago†-Los Angeles	National	34	235	18	9	.667	190	88	80	153	68	3.06
1976—Los Angeles	National	33	227	11	15	.423	203	93	82	116	60	3.25
1977—Los Angeles	National	32	223	12	7	.632	184	74	65	153	60	2.62
1978—Los Angeles	National	32	236	19	10	.655	196	74	71	104	61	2.71
1979—Los Angeles	National	29	212	11	10	.524	191	85	70	129	63	2.97
1980—Los Angeles	National	34	207	14	8	.636	194	90	84	118	64	3.65
1981—Los Angeles	National	23	142	11	6	.647	124	42	36	74	33	2.28
1982—Los Angeles‡	National	21	120⅔	4	7	.364	130	57	54	51	33	4.03
1983—Los Angeles	National	33	160	9	8	.529	156	86	75	87	59	4.22
Major League Totals		397	2417⅔	143	122	.540	2239	991	882	1367	716	3.28

Selected by New York Mets' organization in 5th round of free-agent draft, June 7, 1968.
Selected by Chicago Cubs' organization in secondary phase of free-agent draft, June 8, 1971.
†Traded to Los Angeles Dodgers for Pitchers Geoff Zahn and Eddie Solomon, May 2, 1975.
‡On disabled list, May 18 to June 8 and June 21 to August 8, 1982.

DIVISION SERIES RECORD

Year Club	League	G.	IP.	W.	L.	Pct.	H.	R.	ER.	SO.	BB.	ERA.
1981—Los Angeles	National	1	7	1	0	1.000	3	1	1	2	3	1.29

CHAMPIONSHIP SERIES RECORD

Tied Championship Series record for most games won, Series (2), 1981; most bases on balls, inning (4), October 7, 1977 (second inning).
Tied National League Championship Series records for most hits allowed, game (10), October 4, 1978; most hits allowed, inning (5), October 4, 1978 (fifth inning).

Year Club	League	G.	IP.	W.	L.	Pct.	H.	R.	ER.	SO.	BB.	ERA.
1977—Los Angeles	National	1	1⅔	0	0	.000	2	3	3	1	4	16.20
1978—Los Angeles	National	1	4⅔	0	0	.000	10	4	4	5	0	7.71
1981—Los Angeles	National	2	14⅔	2	0	1.000	11	1	0	7	6	0.00
Championship Series Totals		4	21	2	0	1.000	23	8	7	13	10	3.00

WORLD SERIES RECORD

Year Club	League	G.	IP.	W.	L.	Pct.	H.	R.	ER.	SO.	BB.	ERA.
1977—Los Angeles	National	2	12	1	1	.500	8	5	5	9	2	3.75
1978—Los Angeles	National	2	8⅓	1	1	.500	13	7	6	6	3	6.48
1981—Los Angeles	National	2	11⅓	1	1	.500	8	3	2	3	9	1.59
World Series Totals		6	31⅔	3	3	.500	29	15	13	18	14	3.69

ALL-STAR GAME RECORD

Year League	IP.	W.	L.	Pct.	H.	R.	ER.	SO.	BB.	ERA.
1981—National	1⅔	0	0	.000	5	3	3	1	0	16.20

SAMUEL LEE HORN
(Sam)

Born November 2, 1963, at Fort Thomas, Ky.
Height, 6.05. Weight, 215.
Throws and bats lefthanded.

Year Club	League	Pos.	G.	AB.	R.	H.	2B.	3B.	HR.	RBI.	B.A.	PO.	A.	E.	F.A.
1982—Elmira	NYP	1B	61	213	47	64	13	1	11	48	.300	368	29	11	.973
1983—Winston-Salem†	Midw.	1B	68	217	33	52	9	0	9	29	.240	363	24	10	.975

Selected by Boston Red Sox' organization in 1st round (16th player selected) of free-agent draft, June 7, 1982.
†On disabled list, April 28 to June 23, 1983.

JAMES ROBERT HORNER
(Bob)

Born August 6, 1957, at Junction City, Kan.
Height, 6.01. Weight, 210.
Throws and bats righthanded.
Attended Arizona State University, Tempe, Ariz.

Named National League Rookie Player of the Year by THE SPORTING NEWS, 1978.
Named National League Rookie of the Year by Baseball Writers' Association of America, 1978.
Named College Player of the Year by THE SPORTING NEWS, 1978.
Received reported $175,000 bonus to sign with Atlanta Braves, 1978.

Year Club	League	Pos.	G.	AB.	R.	H.	2B.	3B.	HR.	RBI.	B.A.	PO.	A.	E.	F.A.
1978—Atlanta	Nat.	3B	89	323	50	86	17	1	23	63	.266	81	199	13	.956
1979—Atlanta†	Nat.	3B-1B	121	487	66	153	15	1	33	98	.314	470	167	22	.967
1980—Atlanta‡	Nat.	3B-1B	124	463	81	124	14	1	35	89	.268	80	253	23	.935
1981—Atlanta	Nat.	3B	79	300	42	83	10	0	15	42	.277	51	129	12	.938
1982—Atlanta	Nat.	3B	140	499	85	130	24	0	32	97	.261	102	217	10	.970
1983—Atlanta§	Nat.	3B-1B	104	386	75	117	25	1	20	68	.303	78	153	10	.959
Major League Totals....................			657	2458	399	693	105	4	158	457	.282	862	1118	90	.957

Selected by Oakland A's organization in 15th round of free-agent draft, June 4, 1975.
Selected by Atlanta Braves' organization in 1st round (first player selected) of free-agent draft, June 6, 1978.
†On supplemental disabled list, April 11 to April 26, 1979.
‡On disqualified list when refused option to Richmond (International), April 28, 1980; reinstated May 10, 1980.
§On disabled list, August 16, 1983 through remainder of season.

CHAMPIONSHIP SERIES RECORD

Year Club	League	Pos.	G.	AB.	R.	H.	2B.	3B.	HR.	RBI.	B.A.	PO.	A.	E.	F.A.
1982—Atlanta	Nat.	3B	3	11	0	1	0	0	0	0	.091	2	5	0	1.000

ALL-STAR GAME RECORD

Year League	Pos.	AB.	R.	H.	2B.	3B.	HR.	RBI.	B.A.	PO.	A.	E.	F.A.
1982—National	PH	1	0	0	0	0	0	0	.000	0	0	0	.000

RICKY NEAL HORTON

Born July 30, 1959, at Poughkeepsie, N.Y.
Height, 6.02. Weight, 197.
Throws and bats lefthanded.
Received bachelor of science degree in engineering from
University of Virginia, Charlottesville, Va. in 1982.
Led American Association in balks with 7 in 1983.

Year Club	League	G.	IP.	W.	L.	Pct.	H.	R.	ER.	SO.	BB.	ERA.
1980—St. Petersburg.............................	Florida St.	6	25	0	2	.000	29	18	17	13	17	6.12
1980—Gastonia.................................	S. Atlantic	14	42	2	4	.333	30	21	17	30	25	3.64
1981—St. Petersburg.............................	Florida St.	28	100	7	3	.700	101	52	49	66	49	4.41
1982—Arkansas.................................	Texas	16	108⅔	9	6	.600	83	45	38	90	52	3.15
1982—Louisville	Am. Assoc.	8	36⅓	2	3	.400	47	31	27	37	11	6.69
1983—Louisville	Am. Assoc.	30	157	10	6	.625	177	99	84	92	58	4.82

Selected by San Francisco Giants' organization in 20th round of free-agent draft, June 7, 1977.
Selected by St. Louis Cardinals' organization in 4th round of free-agent draft, June 3, 1980.

DAVID ALAN HOSTETLER
(Dave)

Born March 27, 1956, at Pasadena, Calif.
Height, 6.04. Weight, 215.
Throws and bats righthanded.
Attended Citrus College, Azusa, Calif., and University
of Southern California, Los Angeles, Calif.
Led Southern League in intentional bases on balls received with 13 in 1979.

Year Club	League	Pos.	G.	AB.	R.	H.	2B.	3B.	HR.	RBI.	B.A.	PO.	A.	E.	F.A.
1978—West Palm B'ch...	Fla. St.	1B	75	249	27	67	12	0	5	29	.269	541	36	11	.981
1979—Memphis...............	South.	1B	●145	548	77	148	28	4	20	★114	.270	959	55	9	.991
1980—Denver	A. A.	1B	126	453	62	122	17	1	9	58	.269	1039	63	★16	.986
1981—Denver	A. A.	1B	125	440	91	140	14	7	27	103	.318	1104	66	★13	.989
1981—Montreal†	Nat.	1B	5	6	1	3	0	0	1	1	.500	4	0	0	1.000
1982—Denver	A. A.	1B	36	128	24	34	8	0	12	36	.266	123	8	3	.978
1982—Texas....................	Amer.	1B	113	418	53	97	12	3	22	67	.232	1099	48	12	.990
1983—Texas....................	Amer.	1B	94	304	31	67	9	2	11	46	.220	11	0	0	1.000
National League Totals...........................			5	6	1	3	0	0	1	1	.500	4	0	0	1.000
American League Totals...........................			207	722	84	164	21	5	33	113	.227	1110	48	12	.990
Major League Totals....................			212	728	85	167	21	5	34	114	.229	1114	48	12	.990

Selected by San Francisco Giants' organization in 4th round of free-agent draft, January 9, 1975.
Selected by San Francisco Giants' organization in 4th round of free-agent draft, January 7, 1976.
Selected by Cleveland Indians' organization in secondary phase of free-agent draft, June 8, 1976.
Selected by San Francisco Giants' organization in secondary phase of free-agent draft, June 7, 1977.
Selected by Montreal Expos' organization in 3rd round of free-agent draft, June 6, 1978.
†Traded with Third Baseman Larry Parrish to Texas Rangers for First Baseman-Outfielder Al Oliver, March 31, 1982.

CHARLES OLIVER HOUGH
Name pronounced Huff.
(Charlie)

Born January 5, 1948, at Honolulu, Hawaii.
Height, 6.02. Weight, 190.
Throws and bats righthanded.
Major League saves: 1970 (2), 1973 (5), 1974 (1), 1975 (4), 1976 (18), 1977 (22), 1978 (7), 1980 (1), 1981 (1). Total—61.
Led Pacific Coast League in intentional bases on balls issued with 13 in 1972.

Led Pacific Coast League in saves with 18 in 1970.
Led Texas League in home runs allowed with 17 in 1969.
Named Pacific Coast League Pitcher of the Year, 1972.

Year Club	League	G.	IP.	W.	L.	Pct.	H.	R.	ER.	SO.	BB.	ERA.
1966—Ogden	Pioneer	21	68	5	●7	.417	82	56	36	68	29	4.76
1967—Santa Barbara	California	20	165	14	4	*.778	129	50	41	138	43	2.24
1967—Albuquerque	Texas	7	36	2	1	.667	57	31	28	25	10	7.00
1968—Albuquerque†	Texas	27	121	6	10	.375	145	72	53	74	26	3.94
1969—Albuquerque	Texas	27	163	10	9	.526	190	87	74	113	42	4.09
1970—Spokane	P. Coast	49	134	12	8	.600	98	43	29	90	44	1.95
1970—Los Angeles	National	8	17	0	0	.000	18	11	10	8	11	5.29
1971—Spokane‡	P. Coast	47	117	10	8	.556	95	56	51	104	52	3.92
1971—Los Angeles	National	4	4	0	0	.000	3	3	2	4	3	4.50
1972—Albuquerque§	P. Coast	58	125	14	5	.737	109	47	33	95	60	2.38
1972—Los Angeles	National	2	3	0	0	.000	2	1	1	4	2	3.00
1973—Los Angeles	National	37	72	4	2	.667	52	24	22	70	45	2.75
1974—Los Angeles	National	49	96	9	4	.692	65	45	40	63	40	3.75
1975—Los Angeles	National	38	61	3	7	.300	43	25	20	34	34	2.95
1976—Los Angeles	National	77	143	12	8	.600	102	43	35	81	77	2.20
1977—Los Angeles	National	70	127	6	12	.333	98	53	47	105	70	3.33
1978—Los Angeles	National	55	93	5	5	.500	69	38	34	66	48	3.29
1979—Los Angeles	National	42	151	7	5	.583	152	88	80	76	66	4.77
1980—Los Angeles x	National	19	32	1	3	.250	37	21	20	55	21	5.63
1980—Texas	American	16	61	2	2	.500	54	30	27	47	37	3.98
1981—Texas	American	21	82	4	1	.800	61	30	27	69	31	2.96
1982—Texas	American	34	228	16	13	.552	217	111	100	128	72	3.95
1983—Texas	American	34	252	15	13	.536	219	96	89	152	95	3.18
National League Totals		401	799	47	46	.505	641	352	311	566	417	3.50
American League Totals		105	623	37	29	.561	551	267	243	396	235	3.51
Major League Totals		506	1422	84	75	.528	1192	619	554	962	652	3.51

Selected by Los Angeles Dodgers' organization in 8th round of free-agent draft, June 9, 1966.
†On temporary inactive list, June 19 to July 1, 1968.
‡On temporary inactive list, July 10 to July 24, 1971.
§On temporary inactive list June 12 to June 15, July 22 to July 24 and August 7 to August 12, 1972.
xSold to Texas Rangers, July 11, 1980.

CHAMPIONSHIP SERIES RECORD

Year Club	League	G.	IP.	W.	L.	Pct.	H.	R.	ER.	SO.	BB.	ERA.
1974—Los Angeles	National	1	2⅓	0	0	.000	4	2	2	2	0	7.71
1977—Los Angeles	National	1	2	0	0	.000	2	1	1	3	0	4.50
1978—Los Angeles	National	1	2	0	0	.000	1	1	1	1	0	4.50
Championship Series Totals		3	6⅓	0	0	.000	7	4	4	6	0	5.68

WORLD SERIES RECORD

Tied World Series record for most wild pitches, inning and game (2), October 15, 1978 (seventh inning).

Year Club	League	G.	IP.	W.	L.	Pct.	H.	R.	ER.	SO.	BB.	ERA.
1974—Los Angeles	National	1	2	0	0	.000	0	0	0	4	1	0.00
1977—Los Angeles	National	2	5	0	0	.000	3	1	1	5	0	1.80
1978—Los Angeles	National	2	5⅓	0	0	.000	10	5	5	5	2	8.44
World Series Totals		5	12⅓	0	0	.000	13	6	6	14	3	4.38

BATTING RECORD

Year Club	League	Pos.	G.	AB.	R.	H.	2B.	3B.	HR.	RBI.	B.A.	PO.	A.	E.	F.A.
1967—Santa Barbara	Calif.	P-1B	28	72	8	14	2	0	0	4	.194	15	25	2	.953
1968—Albuquerque	Tex.	P-1-3	56	83	10	21	4	0	0	6	.253	43	25	4	.944
1969—Albuquerque	Tex.	P-3B	31	57	10	12	0	0	1	9	.211	10	19	2	.935
1970—Spokane	P. C.	P-O-1	49	33	1	6	0	0	1	3	.182	7	28	3	.921
1971—Spokane	P. C.	P-OF	48	36	2	10	0	0	0	3	.278	6	20	1	.963
1972—Albuquerque	P. C.	P-OF	58	34	4	9	1	0	0	5	.265	3	27	0	1.000

PAUL WESLEY HOUSEHOLDER

Born September 4, 1958, at Columbus, O.
Height, 6.00. Weight, 180.
Throws right and bats right and lefthanded.

Led Western Carolinas League batters in strikeouts with 130 in 1977.
Led American Association outfielders in total chances with 332 in 1981.
Led Southern League outfielders in fielding percentage with .989 and double plays with 5 in 1979.
Tied for American Association lead in game-winning RBIs with 11 in 1981.

Year Club	League	Pos.	G.	AB.	R.	H.	2B.	3B.	HR.	RBI.	B.A.	PO.	A.	E.	F.A.
1976—Billings	Pion.	OF-3B	50	149	23	38	3	2	2	19	.255	74	8	6	.932
1977—Shelby	W. Car.	OF	137	500	72	116	15	●9	10	63	.232	278	10	8	.973
1978—Tampa	Fla. St.	OF	123	415	59	103	8	10	10	42	.248	213	8	11	.953
1979—Nashville	South.	OF-3B	142	488	93	138	24	7	20	95	.283	247	18	4	.985
1980—Indianapolis	A. A.	OF-3B	125	464	74	137	26	5	9	50	.295	249	10	8	.970
1980—Cincinnati	Nat.	OF	20	45	3	11	1	1	0	7	.244	16	2	0	1.000
1981—Indianapolis	A. A.	OF	124	453	72	136	19	6	19	77	.300	315	10	7	.979
1981—Cincinnati	Nat.	OF	23	69	12	19	4	0	2	9	.275	32	1	0	1.000

Year Club	League	Pos.	G.	AB.	R.	H.	2B.	3B.	HR.	RBI.	B.A.	PO.	A.	E.	F.A.
1982—Cincinnati..............	Nat.	OF	138	417	40	88	11	5	9	34	.211	220	14	2	.992
1983—Cincinnati†............	Nat.	OF	123	380	40	97	24	4	6	43	.255	221	5	2	*.991
Major League Totals..................................			304	911	95	215	40	10	17	93	.236	489	22	4	.992

Selected by Cincinnati Reds' organization in 2nd round of free-agent draft, June 8, 1976.
†On disabled list, March 23 to April 26, 1983.

DENNIS RUSSELL HOWARD

Born April 24, 1959, at Buffalo, N.Y.
Height, 5.10. Weight, 180.
Throws and bats righthanded.
Attended State University of New York at Buffalo, Buffalo, N.Y.

Tied for New York-Pennsylvania League lead in games started by pitchers with 14 in 1980.

Year Club	League	G.	IP.	W.	L.	Pct.	H.	R.	ER.	SO.	BB.	ERA.
1980—Utica...............................	NYP	16	89	4	8	.333	*106	*63	*51	76	44	5.16
1981—Kinston...........................	Carolina	26	139	4	9	.308	122	68	54	107	72	3.50
1982—Knoxville.......................	Southern	30	194⅔	13	13	.500	181	96	88	150	85	4.07
1983—Syracuse	Int'national	22	114⅔	9	7	.563	114	72	47	64	63	3.69

Selected by Toronto Blue Jays' organization in 5th round of free-agent draft, June 3, 1980.

MICHAEL FREDRICK HOWARD
(Mike)

Born April 2, 1958, at Seattle, Wash.
Height, 6.02. Weight, 185.
Throws right and bats left and righthanded.

Led Texas League in caught stealing with 19 in 1980.
Led Pioneer League shortstops in double plays with 31 in 1977.

Year Club	League	Pos.	G.	AB.	R.	H.	2B.	3B.	HR.	RBI.	B.A.	PO.	A.	E.	F.A.
1976—Bellingham	N'west	OF	50	119	17	23	3	2	0	17	.193	58	4	1	.984
1977—Clinton†..................	Midw.					(Did not play)									
1977—Lodi	Calif.	SS-3B	5	6	0	0	0	0	0	0	.000	2	4	1	.857
1977—Lethbridge	Pioneer	SS	51	170	35	44	8	3	0	15	.259	86	139	24	.904
1978—Clinton‡..................	Midw.	S-2-O-3	95	294	53	85	15	2	2	29	.289	167	159	25	.929
1979—Jackson	Texas	O-1-S-2	131	447	43	102	13	3	2	42	.228	586	55	9	.986
1980—Jackson	Texas	O-S-1-2	135	508	91	148	30	8	9	56	.291	260	43	9	.971
1981—Tidewater §..........	Int.	OF-3B-SS	120	418	56	116	22	5	6	33	.278	260	13	3	.989
1981—New York..............	Nat.	OF	14	24	4	4	1	0	0	3	.167	18	2	1	.952
1982—Tidewater	Int.	O-S-3-1	99	332	62	95	12	10	5	33	.286	169	15	3	.984
1982—New York.............	Nat.	OF-2B	33	39	5	7	0	0	1	3	.179	32	6	0	1.000
1983—Tidewater x........	Int.	O-C-S-2-1	65	216	26	42	10	1	4	30	.194	109	6	3	.975
1983—Sarasota Mets.......	Gulf C.	C	15	38	3	12	3	0	0	4	.316	67	13	2	.976
1983—Jackson	Texas	INF-O-P	3	15	2	4	0	0	0	2	.267	9	3	0	1.000
1983—New York.............	Nat.	OF	1	3	0	1	0	0	0	1	.333	0	0	0	.000
Major League Totals..................................			48	66	9	12	1	0	1	7	.182	50	8	1	.983

Selected by Los Angeles Dodgers' organization in 6th round of free-agent draft, June 8, 1976.
†On temporary inactive list, April 16 to May 12, 1977.
‡Drafted by New York Mets' organization, December 5, 1978.
§On disabled list, April 16 to April 26, 1981.
xOn disabled list, July 9 to July 21, 1983.

PITCHING RECORD

Year Club	League	G.	IP.	W.	L.	Pct.	H.	R.	ER.	SO.	BB.	ERA.
1983—Jackson	Texas	1	1	0	1	.000	3	6	6	2	2	54.00

ARTHUR HENRY HOWE JR.
(Art)

Born December 15, 1946, at Pittsburgh, Pa.
Height, 6.01. Weight, 185.
Throws and bats righthanded.
Received bachelor of science degree in business administration
from University of Wyoming, Laramie, Wyo.

Led International League third basemen in errors with 22 and double plays with 24 in 1972.
Tied for Carolina League lead in putouts by third basemen with 95 in 1971.

Year Club	League	Pos.	G.	AB.	R.	H.	2B.	3B.	HR.	RBI.	B.A.	PO.	A.	E.	F.A.
1971—Salem......................	Carol.	3B-SS	114	382	77	133	27	7	12	79	*.348	110	221	21	.940
1972—Charleston†..........	Int.	3B-2B-SS	109	365	68	99	21	3	14	53	.271	105	248	24	.936
1973—Charleston‡..........	Int.	3B-2B-SS	119	372	50	85	20	1	8	44	.228	141	229	21	.946
1974—Charleston............	Int.	3B	60	207	26	70	17	4	8	36	.338	35	90	9	.933
1974—Pittsburgh	Nat.	3B-SS	29	74	10	18	4	1	1	5	.243	11	49	4	.938
1975—Charleston............	Int.	3B-2B	11	42	4	15	1	3	0	3	.357	15	23	1	.974
1975—Pittsburgh§..........	Nat.	3B-SS	63	146	13	25	9	0	1	10	.171	19	89	7	.939
1976—Memphis................	Int.	3B-1B	74	259	50	92	21	3	12	59	.355	93	120	14	.934
1976—Houston.................	Nat.	3B-2B	21	29	0	4	1	0	0	0	.138	17	16	1	.970
1977—Houston.................	Nat.	2B-3B-SS	125	413	44	109	23	7	8	58	.264	213	333	8	.986
1978—Houston.................	Nat.	2B-3B-1B	119	420	46	123	33	3	7	55	.293	240	302	13	.977

Year Club	League	Pos.	G.	AB.	R.	H.	2B.	3B.	HR.	RBI.	B.A.	PO.	A.	E.	F.A.
1979—Houston	Nat.	2B-3B-1B	118	355	32	88	15	2	6	33	.248	188	261	7	.985
1980—Houston	Nat.	1-3-2-S	110	321	34	91	12	5	10	46	.283	598	86	10	.986
1981—Houston	Nat.	3B-1B	103	361	43	107	22	4	3	36	.296	67	206	9	.968
1982—Houston x	Nat.	3B-1B	110	365	29	87	15	1	5	38	.238	344	174	7	.987
1983—Houston yz	Nat.						(Did not play)								
Major League Totals			798	2484	251	652	134	23	41	281	.262	1697	1516	66	.980

Signed as free agent by Pittsburgh Pirates' organization, June, 1971.

†On disabled list, August 17 to September 2, 1972.

‡On disabled list, April 13 to May 6, 1973.

§Traded to Houston Astros, January 6, 1976, completing deal in which Houston traded Second Baseman Tommy Helms to Pittsburgh Pirates for a player to be named later, December 12, 1975.

xOn supplemental disabled list, May 12 to June 19, 1982.

yOn disabled list, March 27, 1983; transferred to emergency disabled list, May 23, 1983 through remainder of season.

zGranted free agency, November 7, 1983.

DIVISION SERIES RECORD

Year Club	League	Pos.	G.	AB.	R.	H.	2B.	3B.	HR.	RBI.	B.A.	PO.	A.	E.	F.A.
1981—Houston	Nat.	3B	5	17	1	4	0	0	1	1	.235	6	9	0	1.000

CHAMPIONSHIP SERIES RECORD

Year Club	League	Pos.	G.	AB.	R.	H.	2B.	3B.	HR.	RBI.	B.A.	PO.	A.	E.	F.A.
1974—Pittsburgh	Nat.	PH	1	1	0	0	0	0	0	0	.000	0	0	0	.000
1980—Houston	Nat.	1B-PH	5	15	0	3	1	1	0	2	.200	29	3	0	1.000
Champion Series Totals			6	16	0	3	1	1	0	2	.188	29	3	0	1.000

STEVEN ROY HOWE
(Steve)

Born March 10, 1958, at Pontiac, Mich.
Height, 6.01. Weight, 180.
Throws and bats lefthanded.
Attended University of Michigan, Ann Arbor, Mich.

Major League saves: 1980 (17), 1981 (8), 1982 (13), 1983 (18). Total—56.

Named National League Rookie of the Year by Baseball Writers' Association of America, 1980.

Year Club	League	G.	IP.	W.	L.	Pct.	H.	R.	ER.	SO.	BB.	ERA.
1979—San Antonio	Texas	13	95	6	2	.750	78	36	33	57	22	3.13
1980—Los Angeles	National	59	85	7	9	.438	83	33	25	39	22	2.65
1981—Los Angeles	National	41	54	5	3	.625	51	17	15	32	18	2.50
1982—Los Angeles	National	66	99⅓	7	5	.583	87	27	23	49	17	2.08
1983—Los Angeles†‡§	National	46	68⅔	4	7	.364	55	15	11	52	12	1.44
Major League Totals		212	307	23	24	.489	276	92	74	172	69	2.17

Selected by Los Angeles Dodgers' organization in 1st round (16th player selected) of free-agent draft, June 5, 1979.

†On disabled list, May 28 to June 29, 1983.

‡On suspended list, July 16 to July 17 and September 23, 1983 through remainder of season.

§On suspended list, December 15, 1983.

DIVISION SERIES RECORD

Year Club	League	G.	IP.	W.	L.	Pct.	H.	R.	ER.	SO.	BB.	ERA.
1981—Los Angeles	National	2	2	0	0	.000	1	0	0	2	0	0.00

CHAMPIONSHIP SERIES RECORD

Year Club	League	G.	IP.	W.	L.	Pct.	H.	R.	ER.	SO.	BB.	ERA.
1981—Los Angeles	National	2	2	0	0	.000	1	0	0	2	0	0.00

WORLD SERIES RECORD

Year Club	League	G.	IP.	W.	L.	Pct.	H.	R.	ER.	SO.	BB.	ERA.
1981—Los Angeles	National	3	7	1	0	1.000	7	3	3	4	1	3.86

ALL-STAR GAME RECORD

Year League		IP.	W.	L.	Pct.	H.	R.	ER.	SO.	BB.	ERA.
1982—National		⅓	0	0	.000	0	0	0	0	0	0.00

JAY CANFIELD HOWELL

Born November 26, 1955, at Miami, Fla.
Height, 6.03. Weight, 200.
Throws and bats righthanded.
Attended University of Colorado, Boulder, Colo.

Tied for American Association lead in shutouts with 2 in 1982.

Tied for American Association lead in balks with 6 in 1981.

Named American Association Pitcher of the Year, 1982.

Year Club	League	G.	IP.	W.	L.	Pct.	H.	R.	ER.	SO.	BB.	ERA.
1976—Eugene	Northwest	13	73	5	4	.556	65	30	24	79	34	2.96
1977—Tampa	Florida St.	23	158	7	13	.350	141	60	52	99	52	2.96
1978—Nashville	Southern	28	166	9	14	.391	134	70	57	⋆173	55	3.09

Year Club	League	G.	IP.	W.	L.	Pct.	H.	R.	ER.	SO.	BB.	ERA.
1979—Indianapolis	Am. Assoc.	24	128	10	10	.500	121	82	73	79	84	5.13
1980—Indianapolis	Am. Assoc.	25	98	5	11	.313	95	70	55	73	71	5.05
1980—Cincinnati†	National	5	3	0	0	.000	8	5	5	1	0	15.00
1981—Iowa	Am. Assoc.	23	144	5	10	.333	141	74	60	90	62	3.75
1981—Chicago	National	10	22	2	0	1.000	23	13	12	10	10	4.91
1982—Iowa‡	Am. Assoc.	20	141⅓	13	4	∗.765	102	45	37	139	48	∗2.36
1982—Columbus	Int'national	5	37⅓	2	1	.667	18	13	10	33	19	2.41
1982—New York	American	6	28	2	3	.400	42	25	24	21	13	7.71
1983—New York§	American	19	82	1	5	.167	89	53	49	61	35	5.38
National League Totals		15	25	2	0	1.000	31	18	17	11	10	6.12
American League Totals		25	110	3	8	.273	131	78	73	82	48	5.97
Major League Totals		40	135	5	8	.385	162	96	90	93	58	6.00

Selected by Cincinnati Reds' organization in 12th round of free-agent draft, June 5, 1973.
Selected by Cincinnati Reds' organization in 31st round of free-agent draft, June 8, 1976.
†Traded to Chicago Cubs for Catcher Mike O'Berry, October 17, 1980.
‡Traded to New York Yankees' organization, August 2, 1982, completing deal in which Chicago Cubs acquired Second Baseman Pat Tabler from New York on waivers for two players to be named later, August 19, 1981; New York acquired Pitcher Bill Caudill as partial completion of deal, April 1, 1982.
§On disabled list, August 3, 1983 through remainder of season.

KENNETH HOWELL JR.
(Ken)

Born November 28, 1960, at Detroit, Mich.
Height, 6.03. Weight, 195.
Throws and bats righthanded.
Attended Tuskegee Institute, Tuskegee Institute, Ala.

Tied for Texas League lead in games started by pitchers with 27 in 1983.

Year Club	League	G.	IP.	W.	L.	Pct.	H.	R.	ER.	SO.	BB.	ERA.
1982—Vero Beach	Florida St.	11	59⅔	5	4	.556	58	40	28	37	36	4.22
1983—San Antonio	Texas	27	169⅓	8	11	.421	171	98	83	116	101	4.41

Selected by Los Angeles Dodgers' organization in 3rd round of free-agent draft, June 7, 1982.

ROY LEE HOWELL

Born December 18, 1953, at Lompoc, Calif.
Height, 6.01. Weight, 190.
Throws right and bats lefthanded.

Year Club	League	Pos.	G.	AB.	R.	H.	2B.	3B.	HR.	RBI.	B.A.	PO.	A.	E.	F.A.
1972—Pittsfield	East.	3B	48	116	12	29	3	0	2	9	.250	21	64	9	.904
1973—Pittsfield†	East.	3B-SS-OF	96	277	44	67	12	2	15	47	.242	51	156	23	.900
1974—Spokane	P. C.	3B	136	513	101	144	23	5	22	80	.281	98	247	25	.932
1974—Texas	Amer.	3B	13	44	2	11	1	0	1	3	.250	5	24	3	.906
1975—Texas	Amer.	3B	125	383	43	96	15	2	10	51	.251	80	214	21	.933
1976—Texas‡	Amer.	3B	140	491	55	124	28	2	8	53	.253	103	245	∗28	.926
1977—Tex.‡-Tor.	Amer.	3B-OF-1B	103	381	41	115	17	1	10	44	.302	94	165	13	.952
1978—Toronto	Amer.	3B-OF	140	551	67	149	28	3	8	61	.270	116	306	22	.950
1979—Toronto§	Amer.	3B	138	511	60	126	28	4	15	72	.247	108	290	20	.952
1980—Toronto x	Amer.	3B	142	528	51	142	28	9	10	57	.269	105	257	16	.958
1981—Milwaukee	Amer.	3B-1B-OF	76	244	37	58	13	1	6	33	.238	58	100	6	.963
1982—Milwaukee	Amer.	1B-OF	98	300	31	78	11	2	4	38	.260	28	2	2	.938
1983—Milwaukee	Amer.	1B	69	194	23	54	9	6	4	25	.278	20	4	1	.960
Major League Totals			1044	3627	410	953	178	30	76	437	.263	717	1607	132	.946

Selected by Texas Rangers' organization in 1st round (fourth player selected) of free-agent draft, June 6, 1972.
†On disabled list, July 29 to August 14, 1973.
‡Traded to Toronto Blue Jays for Infielder Jim Mason, Pitcher Steve Hargan, and cash estimated at $200,000, May 9, 1977.
§On supplemental disabled list, June 14 to June 30, 1979.
xGranted free agency, October 23, 1980; signed by Milwaukee Brewers, December 20, 1980.

DIVISION SERIES RECORD

Year Club	League	Pos.	G.	AB.	R.	H.	2B.	3B.	HR.	RBI.	B.A.	PO.	A.	E.	F.A.
1981—Milwaukee	Amer.	PH-DH	4	5	0	2	0	0	0	0	.400	0	0	0	.000

CHAMPIONSHIP SERIES RECORD

Year Club	League	Pos.	G.	AB.	R.	H.	2B.	3B.	HR.	RBI.	B.A.	PO.	A.	E.	F.A.
1982—Milwaukee	Amer.	DH	1	3	0	0	0	0	0	0	.000	0	0	0	.000

WORLD SERIES RECORD

Year Club	League	Pos.	G.	AB.	R.	H.	2B.	3B.	HR.	RBI.	B.A.	PO.	A.	E.	F.A.
1982—Milwaukee	Amer.	DH	4	11	1	0	0	0	0	0	.000	0	0	0	.000

ALL-STAR GAME RECORD

Year League	Pos.	AB.	R.	H.	2B.	3B.	HR.	RBI.	B.A.	PO.	A.	E.	F.A.
1978—American	PH	1	0	0	0	0	0	0	.000	0	0	0	.000

DEWEY LaMARR HOYT

(Known by middle name.)

Born January 1, 1955, at Columbia, S. C.
Height, 6.01. Weight, 222.
Throws and bats righthanded.
Son of Dewey Hoyt, minor league pitcher, 1947 and 1948.

Led Midwest League pitchers in games started with 27 and tied for lead in shutouts with 3 in 1978.
Tied for Florida State League lead in balks with 3 in 1974.
Named American League Pitcher of the Year by THE SPORTING NEWS, 1983.
Won American League Cy Young Memorial Award, 1983.
Named righthanded pitcher on THE SPORTING NEWS American League All-Star Team, 1983.

Year Club	League	G.	IP.	W.	L.	Pct.	H.	R.	ER.	SO.	BB.	ERA.
1973—Johnson City	Ap'lachian	12	76	6	6	.500	73	44	33	58	40	3.91
1974—Ft. Lauderdale	Florida St.	23	161	13	4	.765	143	66	43	77	60	2.40
1975—Ft. Lauderdale†	Florida St.	7	26	2	1	.667	24	14	13	12	8	4.50
1975—West Haven	Eastern	8	44	2	4	.333	45	25	15	22	13	3.07
1976—West Haven‡	Eastern	25	180	15	8	.652	169	66	50	103	46	2.50
1977—Knoxville	Southern	25	132	4	●13	.235	160	70	62	67	35	4.23
1977—Iowa	Am. Assoc.	6	25	1	2	.333	30	20	20	14	9	7.20
1978—Appleton	Midwest	28	189	*18	4	*.818	*187	74	61	115	60	2.90
1979—Iowa	Am. Assoc.	9	43	1	4	.200	50	29	22	27	24	4.60
1979—Knoxville	Southern	37	82	9	5	.643	80	29	27	60	35	2.96
1979—Chicago	American	2	3	0	0	.000	2	0	0	0	0	0.00
1980—Iowa	Am. Assoc.	18	62	5	2	.714	61	22	20	36	22	2.90
1980—Chicago	American	24	112	9	3	.750	123	66	57	55	41	4.58
1981—Chicago	American	43	91	9	3	.750	80	40	36	60	28	3.56
1982—Chicago	American	39	239⅔	*19	15	.559	248	104	94	124	48	3.53
1983—Chicago	American	36	260⅔	*24	10	.706	236	115	106	148	31	3.66
Major League Totals		144	706⅓	61	31	.663	689	325	293	387	148	3.73

Selected by New York Yankees' organization in 5th round of free-agent draft, June 5, 1973.
†On disabled list, April 16 to June 6, 1975.
‡Traded with Outfielder Oscar Gamble, Pitcher Bob Polinsky and cash estimated at $250,000 to Chicago White Sox for Shortstop Bucky Dent, April 5, 1977.

CHAMPIONSHIP SERIES RECORD

Year Club	League	G.	IP.	W.	L.	Pct.	H.	R.	ER.	SO.	BB.	ERA.
1983—Chicago	American	1	9	1	0	1.000	5	1	1	4	0	1.00

KENT ALAN HRBEK

Name pronounced HER-beck.

Born May 21, 1960, at Bloomington, Minn.
Height, 6.04. Weight, 215.
Throws right and bats lefthanded.

Led California League in slugging percentage with .630 and tied for lead in sacrifice flies with 9 in 1981.
Named California League Most Valuable Player, 1981.

Year Club	League	Pos.	G.	AB.	R.	H.	2B.	3B.	HR.	RBI.	B.A.	PO.	A.	E.	F.A.
1979—Elizabethton†‡	Appal.	1B	17	59	5	12	2	0	1	11	.203	126	11	2	.986
1980—Wisc. Rapids§	Midw.	1B	115	419	74	112	16	0	19	76	.267	1005	81	*20	.982
1981—Visalia	Calif.	1B	121	462	119	175	25	5	27	111	*.379	1034	53	11	*.989
1981—Minnesota	Amer.	1B	24	67	5	16	5	0	1	7	.239	124	4	0	1.000
1982—Minnesota	Amer.	1B	140	532	82	160	21	4	23	92	.301	1174	88	9	.993
1983—Minnesota	Amer.	1B	141	515	75	153	41	5	16	84	.297	1151	89	13	.990
Major League Totals			305	1114	162	329	67	9	40	183	.295	2449	181	22	.992

Selected by Minnesota Twins' organization in 17th round of free-agent draft, June 6, 1978.
†On Wisconsin Rapids disabled list, April 13 to June 21, 1979.
‡On Elizabethton disabled list, July 22 to September 6, 1979.
§On disabled list, May 27 to June 6, 1980.

ALL-STAR GAME RECORD

Year League	Pos.	AB.	R.	H.	2B.	3B.	HR.	RBI.	B.A.	PO.	A.	E.	F.A.
1982—American	PH	1	0	0	0	0	0	0	.000	0	0	0	.000

GLENN DEE HUBBARD

Born September 25, 1957, at Hann Air Force Base, Germany.
Height, 5.08, Weight, 165.
Throws and bats righthanded.

Led National League in sacrifice hits with 20 in 1982.
Led National League second basemen in double plays with 111 in 1982.
Led Appalachian League third basemen in fielding percentage with .932 in 1975.
Named second baseman on THE SPORTING NEWS National League All-Star Team, 1983.

Year Club	League	Pos.	G.	AB.	R.	H.	2B.	3B.	HR.	RBI.	B.A.	PO.	A.	E.	F.A.
1975—Kingsport	Appal.	3B-SS-2B	53	136	31	39	6	4	2	21	.287	44	88	9	.936
1976—Kingsport	Appal.	2B	37	136	29	40	8	0	2	15	.294	96	122	1	.995
1976—Greenwood†	W. Car.	2B	33	126	26	40	8	1	4	21	.317	62	83	6	.960
1977—Greenwood	W. Car.	2B	45	182	39	70	10	1	5	44	.385	114	133	4	.984
1977—Savannah	South.	2B	87	298	49	67	15	2	6	32	.225	209	239	10	.978

Year—Club	League	Pos.	G.	AB.	R.	H.	2B.	3B.	HR.	RBI.	B.A.	PO.	A.	E.	F.A.
1978—Richmond..............	Int.	2B	80	301	58	101	12	3	14	36	.336	208	243	11	.976
1978—Atlanta‡	Nat.	2B	44	163	15	42	4	0	2	13	.258	102	130	5	.979
1979—Richmond..............	Int.	3B-2B	34	125	21	42	5	1	2	17	.336	83	109	7	.965
1979—Atlanta	Nat.	2B	97	325	34	75	12	0	3	29	.231	193	268	●15	.968
1980—Richmond..............	Int.	2B	38	143	23	45	11	2	2	25	.315	89	127	4	.982
1980—Atlanta	Nat.	2B	117	431	55	107	21	3	9	43	.248	268	405	15	.978
1981—Atlanta	Nat.	2B	99	361	39	85	13	5	6	33	.235	188	344	5	.991
1982—Atlanta	Nat.	2B	145	532	75	132	25	1	9	59	.248	312	505	14	.983
1983—Atlanta	Nat.	2B	148	517	65	136	24	6	12	70	.263	313	484	12	.985
Major League Totals...................................			650	2329	283	577	99	15	41	247	.248	1376	2136	66	.982

Selected by Atlanta Braves' organization in 20th round of free-agent draft, June 4, 1975.
†On temporary inactive list, May 17 to June 22, 1976.
‡On supplemental disabled list, July 22 to August 23, 1978.

CHAMPIONSHIP SERIES RECORD

Year—Club	League	Pos.	G.	AB.	R.	H.	2B.	3B.	HR.	RBI.	B.A.	PO.	A.	E.	F.A.
1982—Atlanta	Nat.	2B	3	9	1	2	0	0	0	1	.222	4	11	0	1.000

ALL-STAR GAME RECORD

Year—League	Pos.	AB.	R.	H.	2B.	3B.	HR.	RBI.	B.A.	PO.	A.	E.	F.A.
1983—National..............	2B	1	0	1	0	0	0	0	1.000	0	0	0	.000

DAVID MARK HUDGENS
(Dave)

Born December 5, 1956, at Oroville, Calif.
Height, 6.02. Weight, 210.
Throws and bats lefthanded.
Attended Arizona State University, Tempe, Ariz.

Year—Club	League	Pos.	G.	AB.	R.	H.	2B.	3B.	HR.	RBI.	B.A.	PO.	A.	E.	F.A.
1979—Waterloo...............	Midw.	1B-OF	127	422	87	123	★34	2	26	85	.291	244	15	7	.974
1980—Chattanooga†	South.	OF-1B	113	376	31	79	9	4	8	49	.210	124	7	0	1.000
1981—West Haven	East.	OF	42	114	10	21	6	1	4	12	.184	34	0	2	.944
1981—San Jose	Calif.	1B-OF	59	208	28	54	6	2	5	28	.260	319	22	9	.974
1982—Modesto................	Calif.	OF-1B	132	435	75	131	27	5	24	82	.301	168	11	1	.994
1983—Tacoma.................	P. C.	OF-1B	125	416	59	116	23	2	21	72	.279	194	12	4	.981
1983—Oakland................	Amer.	1B	6	7	0	1	0	0	0	0	.143	4	0	0	1.000
Major League Totals..................			6	7	0	1	0	0	0	0	.143	4	0	0	1.000

Selected by New York Mets' organization in 1st round (fifth player selected) of free-agent draft, January 9, 1975.
Selected by Milwaukee Brewers' organization in 18th round of free-agent draft, June 7, 1977.
Signed as free agent by Cleveland Indians' organization, January 19, 1979.
†Released, January 8, 1981; signed by West Haven (Oakland A's organization), February 18, 1981.

REX ALLEN HUDLER

Born September 2, 1960, at Tempe, Ariz.
Height, 6.01. Weight, 180.
Throws and bats righthanded.

Year—Club	League	Pos.	G.	AB.	R.	H.	2B.	3B.	HR.	RBI.	B.A.	PO.	A.	E.	F.A.
1978—Oneonta.................	NYP	SS	58	221	33	62	5	5	0	24	.281	123	21	22	.906
1979—Ft. Lauderdale† ...	Fla. St.	S-3-2-O	116	414	37	104	14	1	1	25	.251	164	314	45	.914
1980—Ft. Lauderdale‡ ...	Fla. St.	3-2-O-1	37	125	14	26	4	0	0	6	.208	55	71	5	.962
1980—Greensboro	S. Atl.	2B	20	75	7	17	3	1	2	9	.227	51	52	5	.954
1981—Ft. Lauderdale§ ...	Fla. St.	2-S-3-O	79	259	35	77	11	1	2	26	.297	104	238	19	.947
1982—Nashville...............	South.	2B-SS-OF	89	299	27	71	14	1	0	24	.237	136	219	20	.947
1982—Ft. Lauderdale	Fla. St.	2B	9	32	2	8	1	0	1	6	.250	23	25	2	.960
1983—Ft. Lauderdale	Fla. St.	2B-SS	91	345	55	93	15	2	2	50	.270	195	245	15	.967
1983—Columbus...............	Int.	2B-3B-SS	40	118	17	36	5	0	1	11	.305	55	95	4	.974

Selected by New York Yankees' organization in 1st round (18th player selected) of free-agent draft, June 6, 1978.
†On disabled list, May 18 to May 31, 1979.
‡On disabled list, May 10 to June 15, 1980.
§On disabled list, May 11 to June 11, 1981.

CHARLES LYNN HUDSON

Born March 16, 1959, at Ennis, Tex.
Height, 6.03. Weight, 185.
Throws and bats righthanded.
Received bachelor of business administration degree in management from
Prairie View A&M University, Prairie View, Tex., in 1981.

Tied for Carolina League lead in shutouts with 3 in 1982.
Tied for Carolina League lead in games started by pitchers with 14 in 1981.
Named Carolina League Pitcher of the Year, 1982.

Year—Club	League	G.	IP.	W.	L.	Pct.	H.	R.	ER.	SO.	BB.	ERA.
1981—Helena.........................	Pioneer	14	87	5	5	.500	92	53	37	67	27	3.83
1982—Peninsula....................	Carolina	27	185	●15	5	.750	143	56	38	147	64	★1.85
1983—Portland......................	P. Coast	10	64	6	3	.667	48	19	19	51	16	2.67
1983—Philadelphia	National	26	169⅓	8	8	.500	158	73	63	101	53	3.35
Major League Totals...................		26	169⅓	8	8	.500	158	73	63	101	53	3.35

Selected by Philadelphia Phillies' organization in 12th round of free-agent draft, June 8, 1981.

Year Club	League	G.	IP.	W.	L.	Pct.	H.	R.	ER.	SO.	BB.	ERA.
1983—Philadelphia	National	1	9	1	0	1.000	4	2	2	9	2	2.00

WORLD SERIES RECORD

Tied World Series records for most games lost, five-game Series (2), 1983; most home runs allowed, five-game Series (4), 1983.

Year Club	League	G.	IP.	W.	L.	Pct.	H.	R.	ER.	SO.	BB.	ERA.
1983—Philadelphia	National	2	8⅓	0	2	.000	9	8	8	6	1	8.64

MARK LAWRENCE HUISMANN

Born May 11, 1958, at Lincoln, Neb.
Height, 6.02. Weight, 190.
Throws and bats righthanded.
Received bachelor of science degree in business and finance from
Colorado State University, Fort Collins, Colo., in 1980.

Year Club	League	G.	IP.	W.	L.	Pct.	H.	R.	ER.	SO.	BB.	ERA.
1980—Sarasota Royals Blue	Gulf Coast	28	59	1	2	.333	50	20	16	46	14	2.44
1981—Charleston	S. Atlantic	28	44	3	2	.600	36	16	8	42	17	1.64
1981—Ft. Myers	Florida St.	14	21	3	1	.750	15	9	8	19	16	3.43
1982—Ft. Myers	Florida St.	14	23	3	1	.750	16	1	1	21	4	0.39
1982—Jacksonville	Southern	36	54⅔	4	4	.500	52	18	13	60	15	2.14
1983—Jacksonville	Southern	37	61⅓	6	3	.667	60	25	22	46	25	3.23
1983—Omaha	Am. Assoc.	17	24⅓	0	2	.000	16	7	5	25	9	1.85
1983—Kansas City	American	13	30⅔	2	1	.667	29	20	19	20	17	5.58
Major League Totals..................................		13	30⅔	2	1	.667	29	20	19	20	17	5.58

Selected by Chicago Cubs' organization in 23rd round of free-agent draft, June 5, 1979.
Signed as free agent by Kansas City Royals' organization, June 16, 1980.

TIMOTHY CRAIG HULETT

Name pronounced HUGH-lit.

(Tim)

Born January 12, 1960, at Springfield, Ill.
Height, 6.00. Weight, 185.
Throws and bats righthanded.
Attended Miami-Dade Community College North, Miami, Fla.,
and University of South Florida, Tampa, Fla.

Led American Association in sacrifice flies with 9 in 1983.
Led American Association second basemen in total chances with 730 in 1983.
Led Eastern League second basemen in putouts with 343, assists with 386, double plays with 95, fielding percentage with .975 and total chances with 748 in 1982.
Led Eastern League second basemen in putouts with 332, assists with 415, double plays with 112 and total chances with 763 in 1981.

Year Club	League	Pos.	G.	AB.	R.	H.	2B.	3B.	HR.	RBI.	B.A.	PO.	A.	E.	F.A.
1980—Glens Falls	East.	SS	6	23	2	4	0	0	0	0	.174	14	13	2	.931
1980—Iowa	A. A.	3B	3	8	1	2	0	0	0	0	.250	0	6	3	.667
1980—Appleton	Midw.	2B-3B-SS	79	278	49	72	11	1	13	47	.259	162	258	17	.961
1981—Glens Falls	East.	2B-3B	134	437	59	99	27	1	10	55	.227	332	422	16	.979
1982—Glens Falls	East.	2B-SS	●140	★536	★113	145	28	5	22	87	.271	352	398	21	.973
1983—Denver	A. A.	2B	133	477	77	130	19	4	21	88	.273	★286	★424	★20	.973
1983—Chicago	Amer.	2B	6	5	0	1	0	0	0	0	.200	8	6	2	.875
Major League Totals..................................			6	5	0	1	0	0	0	0	.200	8	6	2	.875

Selected by Texas Rangers' organization in 39th round of free-agent draft, June 6, 1978.
Selected by Chicago White Sox' organization in secondary phase of free-agent draft, January 8, 1980.

THOMAS HUBERT HUME JR.

Name pronounced Yoom.

(Tom)

Born March 29, 1953, at Cincinnati, O.
Height, 6.01. Weight, 185.
Throws and bats righthanded.
Attended Manatee Junior College, West Bradenton, Fla.

Major League saves: 1978 (1), 1979 (17), 1980 (25), 1981 (13), 1982 (17), 1983 (9). Total—82.
Led National League in games finished in relief with 62 in 1980.
Tied for Eastern League lead in games started by pitchers with 27 in 1973.
Named National League co-Fireman of the Year by THE SPORTING NEWS, 1980.

Year Club	League	G.	IP.	W.	L.	Pct.	H.	R.	ER.	SO.	BB.	ERA.
1972—Tampa†	Florida St.	23	141	7	11	.389	135	69	54	112	68	3.45
1973—Three Rivers	Eastern	27	170	7	8	.467	186	97	81	103	99	4.29
1974—Three Rivers	Eastern	26	157	7	12	.368	★167	91	77	109	90	4.41
1975—Three Rivers	Eastern	7	45	3	2	.600	43	20	15	19	15	3.00
1975—Indianapolis	Am. Assoc.	17	100	6	6	.500	106	49	45	56	36	4.05
1976—Indianapolis	Am. Assoc.	27	182	9	12	.429	178	91	83	111	62	4.10
1977—Indianapolis	Am. Assoc.	28	106	5	6	.455	99	40	30	76	37	2.55
1977—Cincinnati	National	14	43	3	3	.500	54	36	34	22	17	7.12

Year Club	League	G.	IP.	W.	L.	Pct.	H.	R.	ER.	SO.	BB.	ERA.
1978—Cincinnati	National	42	174	8	11	.421	198	89	80	90	50	4.41
1979—Cincinnati	National	57	163	10	9	.526	162	54	50	80	33	2.76
1980—Cincinnati	National	78	137	9	10	.474	121	44	39	68	38	2.56
1981—Cincinnati	National	51	68	9	4	.692	63	27	26	27	31	3.44
1982—Cincinnati‡	National	46	63⅔	2	6	.250	57	24	22	22	21	3.11
1983—Cincinnati§	National	48	66	3	5	.375	66	40	35	34	41	4.77
Major League Totals		336	714⅔	44	48	.478	721	314	286	343	231	3.60

Selected by Los Angeles Dodgers' organzation in 35th round of free-agent draft, June 8, 1971.
Selected by Cincinnati Reds' organization in secondary phase of free-agent draft, January 12, 1972.
†Appeared in one game as a second basemen with three putouts and two assists and in one game as a third basemen with one assist.
‡On disabled list, July 27, 1982 through remainder of season.
§On disabled list, May 25 to June 19, 1983.

CHAMPIONSHIP SERIES RECORD

Year Club	League	G.	IP.	W.	L.	Pct.	H.	R.	ER.	SO.	BB.	ERA.
1979—Cincinnati	National	3	4	0	1	.000	6	3	3	2	0	6.75

ALL-STAR GAME RECORD

Year League	IP.	W.	L.	Pct.	H.	R.	ER.	SO.	BB.	ERA.
1982—National	⅓	0	0	.000	0	0	0	0	0	0.00

DAVID BLAIN HUPPERT
(Dave)

Born April 1, 1957, at Southgate, Calif.
Height, 6.01. Weight, 190.
Throws and bats righthanded.

Tied for Florida State League lead in double plays by catchers with 7 in 1978.

Year Club	League	Pos.	G.	AB.	R.	H.	2B.	3B.	HR.	RBI.	B.A.	PO.	A.	E.	F.A.
1977—Bluefield	Appal.	C	51	125	21	29	4	0	6	12	.232	★292	★46	6	.983
1978—Miami	Fla. St.	C	47	184	28	42	5	2	2	15	.228	375	56	7	.984
1978—Charlotte†	South.	C	24	63	9	15	1	0	0	4	.238	104	21	4	.969
1979—Charlotte	South.	C	102	300	37	67	12	2	5	37	.223	543	73	10	.984
1980—Charlotte	South.	C	107	319	43	70	15	2	3	23	.219	521	61	★20	.967
1981—Roch.-Toledo	Int.	C	68	176	22	32	6	1	2	12	.182	374	46	★13	.970
1981—Hagerstown‡	Carol.	C	1	2	0	1	0	0	0	0	.500	5	2	0	1.000
1982—Charlotte	South.	C-1B	83	220	28	49	9	0	4	24	.223	400	70	7	.986
1983—Rochester	Int.	C	67	151	21	30	7	2	0	11	.199	362	58	9	.979
1983—Baltimore§	Amer.	C	2	0	0	0	0	0	0	0	.000	3	0	0	1.000
Major League Totals			2	0	0	0	0	0	0	0	.000	3	0	0	1.000

Signed as free agent by Baltimore Orioles' organization, May 22, 1977.
†On disabled list, August 2 to October 11, 1978.
‡Loaned to Toledo (Minnesota Twins' organization), July 26, 1981; returned, August 28, 1981.
§Released, October 28, 1983.

CLINTON MERRICK HURDLE
(Clint)

Born July 30, 1957, at Big Rapids, Mich.
Height, 6.03. Weight, 195.
Throws right and bats lefthanded.

Led International League in intentional bases on balls received with 12 and tied for lead in game-winning hits with 14 in 1983.
Led American Association outfielders in double plays with 4 in 1977.
Tied for Gulf Coast League lead in being hit by pitch with 6 in 1975.
Tied for American Association lead in double plays by outfielders with 4 in 1979.
Received reported $50,000 bonus to sign with Kansas City Royals, 1975.

Year Club	League	Pos.	G.	AB.	R.	H.	2B.	3B.	HR.	RBI.	B.A.	PO.	A.	E.	F.A.
1975—Sarasota Royals	Gulf C.	OF	49	175	34	48	4	4	1	★31	.274	94	5	2	.980
1976—Waterloo	Midw.	OF	127	429	89	101	22	5	19	89	.235	179	12	7	.965
1977—Omaha	A. A.	OF	129	442	85	145	35	3	16	66	.328	198	★17	6	.973
1977—Kansas City	Amer.	OF	9	26	5	8	0	0	2	7	.308	17	0	0	1.000
1978—Kansas City	Amer.	OF-1B-3B	133	417	48	110	25	5	7	56	.264	544	30	12	.980
1979—Omaha	A. A.	OF	68	220	30	52	13	0	6	29	.236	124	14	4	.972
1979—Kansas City	Amer.	OF-3B	59	171	16	41	10	3	3	30	.240	89	2	3	.968
1980—Kansas City	Amer.	OF	130	395	50	116	31	2	10	60	.294	233	8	10	.960
1981—Kansas City‡	Amer.	OF	28	76	12	25	3	1	4	15	.329	59	1	0	1.000
1982—Cincinnati	Nat.	OF	19	34	2	7	1	0	0	1	.206	17	2	1	.950
1982—Indianapolis§x	A. A.	OF-1B	88	261	38	64	18	0	12	58	.245	113	7	4	.968
1983—Tidewater	Int.	3B-1B-OF	139	477	82	136	★33	4	22	105	.285	130	149	22	.927
1983—New York	Nat.	3B-OF	13	33	3	6	2	0	0	2	.182	1	15	4	.800
American League Totals			359	1085	131	300	69	11	26	168	.276	942	41	25	.975
National League Totals			32	67	5	13	3	0	0	3	.194	18	17	5	.875
Major League Totals			391	1152	136	313	72	11	26	171	.272	960	58	30	.971

Selected by Kansas City Royals' organization in 1st round (ninth player selected) of free-agent draft, June 4, 1975.
†On supplemental disabled list, April 20 to May 30 and August 9 to September 13, 1981.

‡Traded to Cincinnati Reds for Pitcher Scott Brown, December 11, 1981.
§Released, November 15, 1982; invited to Seattle Mariners' spring training, February, 1983.
xReleased, April 4, 1983; signed by New York Mets' organization, April 7, 1983.

DIVISION SERIES RECORD

Year Club	League	Pos.	G.	AB.	R.	H.	2B.	3B.	HR.	RBI.	B.A.	PO.	A.	E.	F.A.
1981—Kansas City	Amer.	OF	3	11	0	3	0	0	0	0	.273	6	0	0	1.000

CHAMPIONSHIP SERIES RECORD

Year Club	League	Pos.	G.	AB.	R.	H.	2B.	3B.	HR.	RBI.	B.A.	PO.	A.	E.	F.A.
1978—Kansas City	Amer.	PH-OF	4	8	1	3	0	1	0	1	.375	6	1	0	1.000
1980—Kansas City	Amer.	OF	3	2	0	0	0	0	0	0	.000	1	0	0	1.000
Championship Series Totals			7	10	1	3	0	1	0	1	.300	7	1	0	1.000

WORLD SERIES RECORD

Year Club	League	Pos.	G.	AB.	R.	H.	2B.	3B.	HR.	RBI.	B.A.	PO.	A.	E.	F.A.
1980—Kansas City	Amer.	OF	4	12	1	5	1	0	0	0	.417	8	0	0	1.000

BRUCE VEE HURST

Born March 24, 1958, at St. George, Utah.
Height, 6.03. Weight, 185.
Throws and bats lefthanded.
Attended Dixie College, St. George, Utah.

Year Club	League	G.	IP.	W.	L.	Pct.	H.	R.	ER.	SO.	BB.	ERA.
1976—Elmira	NYP	9	42	3	2	.600	25	18	14	40	38	3.00
1977—Winter Haven†	Florida St.	13	91	5	4	.556	77	28	21	69	25	2.08
1978—Bristol‡	Eastern	6	33	1	3	.250	32	15	10	35	17	2.73
1979—Winter Haven	Florida St.	12	84	8	2	.800	57	22	18	64	20	1.93
1979—Bristol	Eastern	16	113	9	4	.692	108	56	45	91	49	3.58
1980—Pawtucket	Int'national	17	105	8	6	.571	101	52	46	54	50	3.94
1980—Boston	American	12	31	2	2	.500	39	33	31	16	16	9.00
1981—Pawtucket	Int'national	32	157	12	7	.632	143	68	50	99	71	2.87
1981—Boston	American	5	23	2	0	1.000	23	11	11	11	12	4.30
1982—Boston	American	28	117	3	7	.300	161	87	75	53	40	5.77
1983—Boston	American	33	211⅓	12	12	.500	241	102	96	115	62	4.09
Major League Totals		78	382⅓	19	21	.475	464	233	213	195	130	5.01

Selected by Boston Red Sox' organization in 1st round (22nd player selected) of free-agent draft, June 8, 1976.
†On disabled list, August 8 to September 14, 1977.
‡On disabled list, May 23 to September 21, 1978.

DANE CHARLES IORG

Name pronounced Orj.

Born May 11, 1950, at Eureka, Calif.
Height, 6.00. Weight, 180.
Throws right and bats lefthanded.
Attended Brigham Young University, Provo, Utah.
Brother of Garth Iorg, second baseman with Toronto Blue Jays; and
Lee Iorg, outfielder in New York Mets' organization, 1974 through 1977.

Tied for Northwest League lead in sacrifice flies with 6 in 1971.
Led Eastern League first basemen in double plays with 78 in 1975.
Tied for Northwest League lead in double plays by outfielders with 2 in 1971.
Named Northwest League Most Valuable Player, 1971.

Year Club	League	Pos.	G.	AB.	R.	H.	2B.	3B.	HR.	RBI.	B.A.	PO.	A.	E.	F.A.
1971—Walla Walla	N'west	OF	77	275	64	101	●15	6	7	65	★.367	135	10	6	.960
1972—Reading	East.	OF	15	43	2	6	2	0	0	1	.140	18	0	1	.947
1972—Burlington	Carol.	OF-P	92	324	61	104	20	3	8	37	.321	119	5	5	.961
1973—Reading	East.	OF	116	386	64	119	21	6	7	49	.308	149	8	5	.969
1974—Toledo	Int.	★1B-OF	133	444	53	110	19	3	10	59	.248	947	★91	9	.991
1975—Toledo	Int.	1B-3B	13	36	7	7	2	0	0	2	.194	76	2	0	1.000
1975—Reading	East.	1B	97	319	47	88	19	5	6	59	.276	★827	44	9	★.990
1976—Oklahoma City	A. A.	1B-OF-C	120	396	65	129	25	11	11	68	.326	741	68	11	.987
1977—Okla. City-N.O.	A. A.	OF-1B-3B	75	273	47	90	14	4	9	48	.330	246	20	6	.978
1977—Phil.†-St.L.	Nat.	1B-OF	42	62	5	15	2	0	0	6	.242	71	4	2	.974
1978—Springfield	A. A.	1B-OF-3B	89	345	73	128	20	0	24	87	★.371	643	64	12	.983
1978—St. Louis	Nat.	OF	35	85	6	23	4	1	0	4	.271	33	5	0	1.000
1979—St. Louis	Nat.	OF-1B	79	179	12	52	11	1	1	21	.291	121	7	2	.985
1980—St. Louis	Nat.	OF-1B	105	251	33	76	23	1	3	36	.303	133	2	1	.993
1981—St. Louis	Nat.	OF-1B-3B	75	217	23	71	11	2	2	39	.327	125	7	3	.978
1982—St. Louis	Nat.	OF-1B-3B	102	238	17	70	14	1	0	34	.294	177	10	3	.984
1983—St. Louis‡	Nat.	OF-1B	58	116	6	31	9	1	0	11	.267	127	5	3	.978
1983—Louisville	A. A.	1B	3	10	2	2	0	0	0	0	.200	21	0	0	1.000
Major League Totals			496	1148	102	338	74	7	6	151	.294	787	40	14	.983

Selected by Kansas City Royals' organization in 13th round of free-agent draft, June 7, 1968.
Selected by Philadelphia Phillies' organization in secondary phase of free-agent draft, June 8, 1971.
†Traded with Outfielder Rick Bosetti and Pitcher Tom Underwood to St. Louis Cardinals for Outfielder Bake McBride and Pitcher Steve Waterbury, June 15, 1977.
‡On disabled list, July 17 to August 15, 1983; included rehabilitation disability assignment to Louisville, August 11 to August 15, 1983.

Tied World Series record for most at-bats, inning (2), October 19, 1982 (sixth inning).

Year	Club	League	Pos.	G.	AB.	R.	H.	2B.	3B.	HR.	RBI.	B.A.	PO.	A.	E.	F.A.
1982—St. Louis		Nat.	DH	5	17	4	9	4	1	0	1	.529	0	0	0	.000

PITCHING RECORD

Year	Club	League	G.	IP.	W.	L.	Pct.	H.	R.	ER.	SO.	BB.	ERA.
1972—Burlington		Carolina	1	1	0	0	.000	3	3	3	0	1	27.00

GARTH RAY IORG

Name pronounced Orj.

Born October 12, 1954, at Arcata, Calif.
Height, 5.11. Weight, 165.
Throws and bats righthanded.
Attended College of the Redwoods, Eureka, Calif.
Brother of Dane Iorg, first baseman-outfielder with St. Louis Cardinals; and Lee Iorg,
outfielder in New York Mets' organization, 1974 through 1977.

Led Florida State League in sacrifice hits with 20 in 1974.

Year	Club	League	Pos.	G.	AB.	R.	H.	2B.	3B.	HR.	RBI.	B.A.	PO.	A.	E.	F.A.
1973—Johnson City	Appal.	SS-2B	51	169	20	40	3	0	3	13	.237	88	120	20	.912
1974—Ft. Lauderdale	Fla. St.	SS-2B-3B	102	325	30	70	11	4	0	38	.215	134	245	28	.931
1975—Ft. Lauderdale	Fla. St.	3-2-O-S	50	186	10	47	4	2	0	16	.253	67	78	11	.929
1975—West Haven	East.	3B-SS-2B	76	236	19	59	6	2	0	21	.250	79	202	26	.915
1976—West Haven†	East.	2B	78	273	31	75	17	1	1	24	.275	172	236	18	.958
1977—Charleston‡	Int.	2B-SS	70	262	35	77	8	3	1	34	.294	158	234	18	.956
1978—Syracuse§	Int.	3B-2B-SS	89	324	29	70	16	2	6	25	.216	141	204	11	.969
1978—Toronto	Amer.	2B	19	49	3	8	0	0	0	3	.163	34	51	3	.966
1979—Syracuse	Int.	2-3-S-O	121	430	65	121	23	4	5	39	.281	150	250	20	.952
1980—Syracuse	Int.	2B-3B	32	134	17	40	6	3	1	14	.299	60	99	4	.975
1980—Toronto	Amer.	2-3-O-1-S	80	222	24	55	10	1	2	14	.248	122	155	3	.989
1981—Toronto	Amer.	2-3-S-1	70	215	17	52	11	0	0	10	.242	99	182	12	.959
1982—Toronto	Amer.	3B-2B	129	417	45	119	20	5	1	36	.285	114	236	14	.962
1983—Toronto	Amer.	3B-2B-SS	122	375	40	103	22	5	2	39	.275	106	223	9	.973
Major League Totals			420	1278	129	337	63	11	5	102	.264	475	847	41	.970

Selected by New York Yankees' organization in 8th round of free-agent draft, June 5, 1973.
†Selected by Toronto Blue Jays in American League expansion draft, November 5, 1976.
‡On disabled list, June 29 to September 1, 1977.
§On disabled list, June 18 to June 28, 1978.

MICHAEL WILSON IVIE

(Mike)

Born August 8, 1952, at Atlanta, Ga.
Height, 6.04. Weight, 215.
Throws and bats righthanded.

Tied major league records for most home runs with bases filled, season, pinch-hitter (2), 1978; most two-base hits, inning (2), May 30, 1977 (seventh inning).
Tied National League record for most two-base hits, doubleheader (5), May 30, 1977.
Led California League catchers in assists with 79 in 1971.
Led Northwest League catchers in putouts with 417 and passed balls with 18 in 1970.
Tied for Texas League lead in being hit by pitch with 12 in 1972.
Received reported $80,000 bonus to sign with San Diego Padres, 1970.

Year	Club	League	Pos.	G.	AB.	R.	H.	2B.	3B.	HR.	RBI.	B.A.	PO.	A.	E.	F.A.
1970—Tri-City	N'west	*C-OF	56	198	29	51	10	0	3	25	.258	419	4	*15	.968
1971—Lodi	Calif.	C-3B-1B	102	367	69	112	22	2	15	62	.305	685	83	22	.972
1971—San Diego	Nat.	C	6	17	0	8	0	0	0	3	.471	22	2	0	1.000
1972—Alexandria	Texas	*1B-3B	133	461	81	134	23	1	24	77	.291	404	*86	*18	.984
1973—Hawaii†	P. Coast	1B	59	226	33	61	8	3	5	21	.270	446	19	7	.985
1974—Alexandria	Texas	1B-OF-3B	108	397	57	116	16	1	18	68	.292	586	45	18	.972
1974—San Diego	Nat.	1B	12	34	1	3	0	0	1	3	.088	67	5	1	.986
1975—San Diego‡	Nat.	1B-3B-C	111	377	36	94	16	2	8	46	.249	540	138	23	.967
1976—San Diego	Nat.	1B-C-3B	140	405	51	118	19	5	7	70	.291	1032	71	7	.994
1977—San Diego§x	Nat.	1B-3B	134	489	66	133	29	2	9	66	.272	886	93	11	.989
1978—San Francisco	Nat.	1B-OF	117	318	34	98	14	3	11	55	.308	579	18	15	.975
1979—San Francisco	Nat.	1-O-3-2	133	402	58	115	18	3	27	89	.286	752	47	4	.995
1980—San Fran. yz	Nat.	1B	79	286	21	69	16	1	4	25	.241	669	32	5	.993
1981—S. F. a-Hou. b	Nat.	1B	26	59	3	15	5	0	0	9	.254	113	15	1	.992
1982—Houston c	Nat.	PH	7	6	0	2	0	0	0	0	.333	0	0	0	.000
1982—Detroit	Amer.	DH	80	259	35	60	12	1	14	38	.232	0	0	0	.000
1983—Detroit d	Amer.	1B	12	42	4	9	4	0	0	7	.214	86	6	0	1.000
National League Totals			765	2393	270	655	117	16	67	366	.274	4660	421	67	.987
American League Totals			92	301	39	69	16	1	14	45	.229	86	6	0	1.000
Major League Totals			857	2694	309	724	133	17	81	411	.269	4746	427	67	.987

Selected by San Diego Padres' organization in 1st round (first player selected) of free-agent draft, June 4, 1970.
†On suspended list, June 14, 1973 through remainder of season.
‡On supplemental disabled list, August 17 to September 1, 1975.
§On suspended list, May 2 to May 3, 1977.

xTraded to San Francisco Giants for Infielder Derrel Thomas, February 28, 1978.

yOn supplemental disabled list, June 3 to June 20, 1980.

zOn suspended list, June 25, 1980; transferred to disqualified list, June 27 to July 14, 1980.

aTraded to Houston Astros for First Baseman-Outfielder Dave Bergman and Outfielder Jeff Leonard, April 20, 1981.

bOn supplemental disabled list, May 13, 1981; transferred to disabled list, May 27 to September 1, 1981.

cReleased, April 30, 1982; signed by Detroit Tigers, May 6, 1982.

dReleased, May 16, 1983.

DANNY LYNN JACKSON

Born January 5, 1962, at San Antonio, Tex.
Height, 6.00. Weight, 190.
Throws left and bats righthanded.
Attended University of Oklahoma, Norman, Okla., and
Trinidad State Junior College, Trinidad, Colo.
Brother of Mike Jackson, fourth-round selection of Kansas City Kings in 1983 NBA draft.

Tied for American Association lead in shutouts with 2 in 1983.

Year Club	League	G.	IP.	W.	L.	Pct.	H.	R.	ER.	SO.	BB.	ERA.
1982—Charleston	S. Atlantic	13	96⅓	10	1	.909	80	37	28	62	39	2.62
1982—Jacksonville†	Southern	14	98	7	2	.778	78	30	26	74	42	2.39
1983—Omaha	Am. Assoc.	23	136	7	8	.467	126	74	60	93	73	3.97
1983—Kansas City	American	4	19	1	1	.500	26	12	11	9	6	5.21
Major League Totals		4	19	1	1	.500	26	12	11	9	6	5.21

Selected by Oakland A's organization in 24th round of free-agent draft, June 3, 1980.

Selected by Kansas City Royals' organization in secondary phase of free-agent draft, January 17, 1982.

†On disabled list, September 8, 1982 through remainder of season.

REGINALD MARTINEZ JACKSON
(Reggie)

Born May 18, 1946, at Wyncote, Pa.
Height, 6.00. Weight, 206.
Throws and bats lefthanded.
Attended Arizona State University, Tempe, Ariz.

Established major league records for most strikeouts, lifetime (2,106); most strikeouts by lefthanded batter, season (171), 1968; most years, 100 or more strikeouts (15); most consecutive years, 100 or more strikeouts (13).

Tied major league records for most consecutive years leading league in strikeouts (4), 1968 through 1971; most strikeouts, nine-inning game (5), September 27, 1968.

Tied American League records for most times, four or more strikeouts, game, season (5), April 7 (second game)—April 21—May 18—June 4—September 21 (first game), 1971; most consecutive games, one or more home runs (6), July 18 through 23, 1976; most seasons leading league, errors, outfielder (5), 1968, 1970, 1972, 1975 and 1976; fewest errors, season, for leader in most errors (9), 1972.

Hit three home runs in a game, July 2, 1969.

Hit home runs in all 12 parks, 1975.

Led American League batters in strikeouts with 171 in 1968, 142 in 1969, 135 in 1970, 161 in 1971 and 156 in 1982.

Led American League in slugging percentage with .608 in 1969, .531 in 1973 and .502 in 1976.

Led American League in intentional bases on balls received with 20 in 1974 and tied for lead with 20 in 1969.

Led American League in caught stealing with 17 in 1970.

Tied for American League lead in double plays by outfielders with 5 in 1972.

Led Southern League in total bases with 232 in 1967.

Named Major League Player of the Year by THE SPORTING NEWS, 1973.

Named American League Player of the Year by THE SPORTING NEWS, 1973.

Named American League Most Valuable Player by Baseball Writers' Association of America, 1973.

Named outfielder on THE SPORTING NEWS American League All-Star Team, 1969, 1973, 1975, 1976 and 1980.

Named outfielder on THE SPORTING NEWS American League Silver Slugger team, 1982.

Named designated hitter on THE SPORTING NEWS American League Silver Slugger team, 1980.

Named Southern League Player of the Year, 1967.

Named College Player of the Year by THE SPORTING NEWS, 1966.

Received reported $90,000 bonus to sign with Kansas City Athletics, 1966.

Year Club	League	Pos.	G.	AB.	R.	H.	2B.	3B.	HR.	RBI.	B.A.	PO.	A.	E.	F.A.
1966—Lewiston	N'west	OF	12	48	14	14	3	2	2	11	.292	23	0	1	.958
1966—Modesto	Calif.	OF	56	221	50	66	6	0	21	60	.299	108	3	9	.925
1967—Birmingham	South.	OF	114	413	*84	121	26	*17	17	58	.293	228	3	*18	.928
1967—Kansas City	Amer.	OF	35	118	13	21	4	4	1	6	.178	55	1	4	.933
1968—Oakland	Amer.	OF	154	553	82	138	13	6	29	74	.250	269	14	*12	.959
1969—Oakland	Amer.	OF	152	549	*123	151	36	3	47	118	.275	278	14	11	.964
1970—Oakland	Amer.	OF	149	426	57	101	21	2	23	66	.237	251	8	●12	.956
1971—Oakland	Amer.	OF	150	567	87	157	29	3	32	80	.277	285	15	7	.977
1972—Oakland†	Amer.	OF	135	499	72	132	25	2	25	75	.265	301	5	*9	.971
1973—Oakland	Amer.	OF	151	539	*99	158	28	2	*32	*117	.293	302	4	9	.971
1974—Oakland	Amer.	OF	148	506	90	146	25	1	29	93	.289	296	8	10	.968
1975—Oakland‡	Amer.	OF	157	593	91	150	39	3	●36	104	.253	315	13	*12	.965
1976—Baltimore§x	Amer.	OF	134	498	84	138	27	2	27	91	.277	284	8	*11	.964
1977—New York	Amer.	OF	146	525	93	150	39	2	32	110	.286	236	7	13	.949
1978—New York	Amer.	OF	139	511	82	140	13	5	27	97	.274	212	6	3	.986
1979—New York y	Amer.	OF	131	465	78	138	24	2	29	89	.297	274	7	4	.986
1980—New York	Amer.	OF	143	514	94	154	22	4	●41	111	.300	174	3	7	.962
1981—New York za	Amer.	OF	94	334	33	79	17	1	15	54	.237	111	3	3	.974

Year	Club	League	Pos.	G.	AB.	R.	H.	2B.	3B.	HR.	RBI.	B.A.	PO.	A.	E.	F.A.
1982—California		Amer.	OF	153	530	92	146	17	1	●39	101	.275	200	6	6	.972
1983—California		Amer.	OF	116	397	43	77	14	1	14	49	.194	66	4	1	.986
Major League Totals				2287	8124	1313	2176	393	44	478	1435	.268	3909	126	134	.968

Selected by Kansas City A's organization in 1st round (second player selected) of free-agent draft, June 13, 1966.

†On supplemental disabled list, August 10 to August 25, 1972.

‡Traded with Pitchers Ken Holtzman and Bill Van Bommel to Baltimore Orioles for Outfielder Don Baylor and Pitchers Mike Torrez and Paul Mitchell, April 2, 1976.

§On disqualified list, April 9 to May 2, 1976.

xPlayed out option year and granted free agency, November 1, 1976; signed as free agent with New York Yankees, November 29, 1976.

yOn supplemental disabled list, June 3 to June 27, 1979.

zOn supplemental disabled list, April 2 to April 17, 1981.

aGranted free agency, November 13, 1981; signed by California Angels, January 22, 1982.

DIVISION SERIES RECORD

Year	Club	League	Pos.	G.	AB.	R.	H.	2B.	3B.	HR.	RBI.	B.A.	PO.	A.	E.	F.A.
1981—New York		Amer.	OF	5	20	4	6	0	0	2	4	.300	7	0	0	1.000

CHAMPIONSHIP SERIES RECORD

Established Championship Series records for most Series played (10); most Series, one or more hits (9); most Series played all games (9); most games, total Series (39); most at-bats, total Series (137); most runs batted in, total Series (18); most times stealing home, game (1), October 12, 1972; most strikeouts, total Series (34).

Tied Championship Series records for most clubs, total Series (3); most times on winning club (6); most times reached first base safely, game (5), October 3, 1978.

Established American League Championship Series records for most hits, total Series (32); most one-base hits, total Series (21); highest batting average, four-game Series (.462), 1978; most total bases, total Series (55); most runs batted in, four-game Series (6), 1978; most bases on balls, total Series (15).

Tied American League Championship Series records for most times on losing club (4); most home runs, total Series (6); most home runs, three-game Series (2), 1971; most Series, one or more home runs (4); most total bases, three-game Series (11), 1971; highest slugging average, three-game Series (.917), 1971; most strikeouts, five-game Series (7), 1982; most bases on balls, four-game Series (5), 1974.

Year	Club	League	Pos.	G.	AB.	R.	H.	2B.	3B.	HR.	RBI.	B.A.	PO.	A.	E.	F.A.
1971—Oakland		Amer.	OF	3	12	2	4	1	0	2	2	.333	9	1	0	1.000
1972—Oakland		Amer.	OF	5	18	1	5	1	0	2	2	.278	14	0	1	.933
1973—Oakland		Amer.	OF	5	21	0	3	0	0	0	0	.143	19	0	1	1.000
1974—Oakland		Amer.	DH-OF	4	12	0	2	1	0	0	1	.167	0	0	0	.000
1975—Oakland		Amer.	OF	3	12	1	5	0	0	1	3	.417	5	1	0	1.000
1977—New York		Amer.	O-D-PH	5	16	1	2	0	0	0	1	.125	10	1	0	1.000
1978—New York		Amer.	DH-OF	4	13	5	6	1	0	2	6	.462	4	0	0	1.000
1980—New York		Amer.	OF	3	11	1	3	1	0	0	0	.273	5	0	0	1.000
1981—New York		Amer.	OF	2	4	1	0	0	0	0	1	.000	1	0	0	1.000
1982—California		Amer.	OF	5	18	2	2	0	0	1	2	.111	2	0	0	1.000
Championship Series Totals				39	137	14	32	5	0	6	18	.234	69	3	1	.986

WORLD SERIES RECORD

Established World Series records for most home runs, two consecutive Series, two consecutive years (7), 1977 and 1978; highest slugging percentage, six-game Series (1.250), 1977; most home runs, Series (5), 1977; most total bases, Series (25), 1977; most runs, Series (10), 1977; most long hits, six-game Series (6), 1977 (tied record for any length Series); most extra bases on long hits, Series (16), 1977; most home runs, three consecutive games, one Series (5), 1977; most home runs, two consecutive games, Series (4), October 16 and 18, 1977; most consecutive home runs, two consecutive games (4), October 16 and 18, 1977; most home runs, four consecutive games, one in each game (6); highest slugging average, total Series, 20 or more games (.755).

Tied World Series records for most times reached first base safely, game (batting 1.000) (5), October 24, 1981; most home runs, game (3), October 18, 1977 (consecutive, each on first pitch); most home runs, two consecutive innings (2), October 18, 1977 (fourth and fifth inning); most total bases, game (12), October 18, 1977; most runs, game (4), October 18, 1977; most consecutive games, one or more runs batted in (6); one or more hits, each game, six-game Series, 1978; most times hit by pitch, total Series (3).

Year	Club	League	Pos.	G.	AB.	R.	H.	2B.	3B.	HR.	RBI.	B.A.	PO.	A.	E.	F.A.
1973—Oakland		Amer.	OF	7	29	3	9	3	1	1	6	.310	17	0	0	1.000
1974—Oakland		Amer.	OF	5	14	3	4	1	0	1	1	.286	6	1	1	.875
1977—New York		Amer.	OF	6	20	10	9	1	0	5	8	.450	9	0	0	1.000
1978—New York		Amer.	DH	6	23	2	9	1	0	2	8	.391	0	0	0	.000
1981—New York		Amer.	OF	3	12	3	4	1	0	1	1	.333	5	0	1	.832
World Series Totals				27	98	21	35	7	1	10	24	.357	37	1	2	.950

ALL-STAR GAME RECORD

Tied All-Star Game record for most home runs by pinch-hitter, game (1), July 13, 1971.

Year	League	Pos.	AB.	R.	H.	2B.	3B.	HR.	RBI.	B.A.	PO.	A.	E.	F.A.
1969—American		OF	2	0	0	0	0	0	0	.000	2	0	0	1.000
1971—American		PH	1	1	1	0	0	1	2	1.000	0	0	0	1.000
1972—American		OF	4	0	2	1	0	0	0	.500	5	0	0	1.000
1973—American		OF	4	1	1	1	0	0	0	.250	0	0	0	.000
1974—American		OF	3	0	0	0	0	0	0	.000	3	0	0	1.000
1975—American		OF	3	0	1	0	0	0	0	.333	2	0	0	1.000
1977—American		OF	2	0	1	0	0	0	0	.500	0	0	0	.000
1979—American		PH-OF	1	0	0	0	0	0	0	.000	0	0	0	.000
1980—American		OF	2	0	1	0	0	0	0	.500	0	0	0	.000

Year	League	Pos.	AB.	R.	H.	2B.	3B.	HR.	RBI.	B.A.	PO.	A.	E.	F.A.
1981—American		OF	1	0	0	0	0	0	0	.000	0	0	0	.000
1982—American		OF	1	0	0	0	0	0	1	.000	3	0	0	1.000
All-Star Game Totals			24	2	7	2	0	1	3	.292	15	0	0	1.000

Named to American League All-Star Team for 1978 game; replaced due to injury by Graig Nettles.
Named to American League All-Star Team for 1983 game; replaced due to injury by Ben Oglivie.

RONNIE DAMIEN JACKSON
(Ron)

Born May 9, 1953, at Birmingham, Ala.
Height, 6.00. Weight, 217.
Throws and bats righthanded.
Attended Lawson State Junior College, Birmingham, Ala.
Brother of Lawrence Jackson, outfielder in Chicago White Sox'
organization, 1968 and 1969.

Led American League first basemen in assists with 137, total chances with 1,593 and in double plays with 175 in 1979.
Led Pacific Coast League third basemen in putouts with 89, assists with 260, errors with 25, fielding percentage with .933 and double plays with 31 in 1975.
Led Pioneer League third basemen in double plays with 8 in 1971.
Led Texas League third basemen in putouts with 118 and tied for lead in double plays with 26 in 1973.
Led Midwest League third basemen in putouts with 101 in 1972.

Year	Club	League	Pos.	G.	AB.	R.	H.	2B.	3B.	HR.	RBI.	B.A.	PO.	A.	E.	F.A.
1971—Idaho Falls	Pion.	3B	●70	260	36	54	8	0	1	22	.208	★60	★111	★32	.842
1972—Quad Cities	Midw.	3B-SS	★126	★489	62	134	★29	7	12	73	.274	116	243	30	.923
1973—El Paso	Texas	★3B-SS	136	481	75	128	31	4	7	68	.266	120	252	★36	.912
1974—El Paso	Texas	3B	133	519	84	170	36	8	11	74	.328	82	257	★33	.911
1975—Salt Lake City	P. C.	3B-OF-1B	●144	513	82	144	24	5	9	85	.281	189	269	26	.946
1975—California	Amer.	OF-3B	13	39	2	9	2	0	0	2	.231	19	4	2	.920
1976—Salt Lake City	P. C.	3B	10	33	9	12	2	0	2	10	.364	14	18	2	.941
1976—California	Amer.	3B-2B-OF	127	410	44	93	18	3	8	40	.227	91	225	16	.952
1977—California	Amer.	1-3-O-S	106	292	38	71	15	2	8	28	.243	314	75	6	.985
1978—California†‡	Amer.	1B-3B-OF	105	387	49	115	18	6	6	57	.297	606	88	8	.989
1979—Minnesota	Amer.	1-3-S-O	159	583	85	158	40	5	14	68	.271	1448	140	9	.994
1980—Minnesota	Amer.	1B-OF-3B	131	396	48	105	29	3	5	42	.265	1000	74	10	.991
1981—Minn.§-Det.x	Amer.	1B-OF-3B	85	270	29	73	17	1	5	40	.270	547	45	5	.992
1982—Spokane	P. C.	1B	7	30	5	9	1	1	0	2	.300	67	8	1	.987
1982—California	Amer.	1B-3B	53	142	15	47	6	0	2	19	.331	317	31	2	.994
1983—California	Amer.	3B-1B-OF	102	348	41	80	16	1	8	39	.230	402	114	13	.975
Major League Totals			881	2867	351	751	161	21	56	335	.262	4744	796	71	.987

Selected by California Angels' organization in 2nd round of free-agent draft, June 8, 1971.
†On supplemental disabled list, July 31 to September 1, 1978.
‡Traded with Catcher Danny Goodwin to Minnesota Twins for Outfielder Dan Ford, December 4, 1978.
§Traded to Detroit Tigers for a player to be named later, August 23, 1981; Minnesota Twins acquired First Baseman-Outfielder Tim Corcoran to complete deal, September 4, 1981.
xGranted free agency, November 13, 1981; signed by Spokane (California Angels' organization), April 11, 1982.

CHAMPIONSHIP SERIES RECORD

Year	Club	League	Pos.	G.	AB.	R.	H.	2B.	3B.	HR.	RBI.	B.A.	PO.	A.	E.	F.A.
1982—California	Amer.	PH	1	1	0	1	0	0	0	0	1.000	0	0	0	.000

ROY LEE JACKSON

Born May 1, 1954, at Opelika, Ala.
Height, 6.02. Weight, 195.
Throws and bats righthanded.
Attended Tuskegee Institute, Tuskegee, Ala.

Major league saves: 1980 (1), 1981 (7), 1982 (6), 1983 (7). Total—21.

Year	Club	League	G.	IP.	W.	L.	Pct.	H.	R.	ER.	SO.	BB.	ERA.
1975—Marion	Ap'lachian	8	50	4	2	.667	35	10	8	35	14	1.44
1975—Wausau	Midwest	5	38	1	3	.250	29	12	10	35	7	2.37
1976—Lynchburg	Carolina	7	55	2	3	.400	51	26	21	19	15	3.44
1976—Jackson	Texas	20	132	8	6	.571	136	51	44	82	39	3.00
1977—Tidewater	Int'national	28	168	13	7	.650	174	78	69	110	73	3.70
1977—New York	National	4	24	0	2	.000	25	16	16	13	15	6.00

—DID YOU KNOW—

That Reggie Jackson has tied for the American League homer championship three times for three different teams—and each time shared the title with a Milwaukee player? Jackson, playing for the Oakland A's in 1975, the New York Yankees in 1980 and the California Angels in 1982, finished in deadlocks with the Brewers' George Scott (36 homers), Ben Oglivie (41) and Gorman Thomas (39). Jackson was the A.L.'s outright champion in 1973, hitting 32 homers for the A's.

Year Club	League	G.	IP.	W.	L.	Pct.	H.	R.	ER.	SO.	BB.	ERA.
1978—Tidewater	Int'national	27	176	11	10	.524	176	91	73	132	51	3.73
1978—New York	National	4	13	0	0	.000	21	13	13	6	6	9.00
1979—Tidewater	Int'national	33	137	12	7	.632	143	63	57	89	33	3.74
1979—New York	National	8	16	1	0	1.000	11	4	4	10	5	2.25
1980—Tidewater	Int'national	22	78	3	5	.375	63	33	20	56	51	2.31
1980—New York†	National	24	71	1	7	.125	78	37	33	58	20	4.18
1981—Toronto	American	39	62	1	2	.333	65	23	18	27	25	2.61
1982—Toronto	American	48	97	8	8	.500	77	37	33	71	31	3.06
1983—Toronto	American	49	92	8	3	.727	92	48	46	48	41	4.50
National League Totals		40	124	2	9	.182	135	70	66	87	46	4.79
American League Totals		136	251	17	13	.567	234	108	97	146	97	3.48
Major League Totals		176	375	19	22	.463	369	178	163	233	143	3.91

Selected by Houston Astros' organization in 12th round of free-agent draft, June 6, 1972.
Signed as free agent by New York Mets' organization, June 27, 1975.
†Traded to Toronto Blue Jays for Outfielder Bob Bailor, December 12, 1980.

BROOK WALLACE JACOBY

Born November 23, 1959, at Philadelphia, Pa.
Height, 5.11. Weight, 175.
Throws and bats righthanded.
Attended Ventura College, Ventura, Calif.
Son of Brook Jacoby, minor league pitcher, 1956 through 1958.
Led International League third basemen in total chances with 331 and double plays with 22 in 1982.

Year Club	League	Pos.	G.	AB.	R.	H.	2B.	3B.	HR.	RBI.	B.A.	PO.	A.	E.	F.A.
1979—Kingsport	Appal.	OF	8	28	3	7	2	0	0	1	.250	9	0	0	1.000
1979—Bradenton	Gulf C.	OF	42	160	24	43	11	1	3	35	.269	65	7	4	.947
1980—Anderson	S. Atl.	OF-3B	132	496	82	147	★40	4	19	★108	.296	219	30	10	.961
1980—Savannah	South.	3B	3	8	0	1	0	0	0	0	.125	0	2	0	1.000
1981—Savannah	South.	3B-OF	140	507	59	148	28	3	24	82	.292	103	232	31	.915
1981—Atlanta	Nat.	3B	11	10	0	2	0	0	0	1	.200	3	4	0	1.000
1982—Richmond	Int.	3B	134	501	74	150	21	3	18	58	.299	83	★229	★19	★.943
1983—Richmond	Int.	3B	133	489	88	154	32	2	25	100	.315	62	247	18	.945
1983—Atlanta†	Nat.	3B	4	8	0	0	0	0	0	0	.000	0	2	0	1.000
Major League Totals			15	18	0	2	0	0	0	1	.111	3	6	0	1.000

Selected by Atlanta Braves' organization in 7th round of free-agent draft, January 9, 1979.
†Traded with Outfielder Brett Butler to Cleveland Indians, October 21, 1983, completing deal in which Atlanta Braves acquired Pitcher Len Barker for three players to be named later, August 28, 1983. Cleveland acquired Pitcher Rick Behenna as partial completion of deal, September 2, 1983.

DION JAMES

Born November 9, 1962, at Philadelphia, Pa.
Height, 6.01. Weight, 170.
Throws and bats lefthanded.
Led California League outfielders in fielding percentage with .988 in 1981.

Year Club	League	Pos.	G.	AB.	R.	H.	2B.	3B.	HR.	RBI.	B.A.	PO.	A.	E.	F.A.
1980—Butte	Pion.	OF-1B	59	224	57	71	14	1	0	27	.317	80	4	7	.923
1980—Burlington	Midw.	OF	3	10	0	1	0	0	1	.100	8	4	7	.923
1981—Stockton	Calif.	OF-1B	124	451	70	137	17	3	2	49	.304	250	10	3	.989
1982—El Paso†	Texas	OF	106	422	103	136	25	3	9	72	.322	237	9	7	.972
1983—Vancouver	P. C.	OF	129	467	84	157	29	5	8	68	.336	289	6	2	.993
1983—Milwaukee	Amer.	OF	11	20	1	2	0	0	0	1	.100	12	1	0	1.000
Major League Totals			11	20	1	2	0	0	0	1	.100	12	1	0	1.000

Selected by Milwaukee Brewers' organization in 1st round (25th player selected) of free-agent draft, June 3, 1980.
†On disabled list, July 1 to August 1, 1982.

ROBERT HARVEY JAMES
(Bob)

Born August 15, 1958, at Glendale, Calif.
Height, 6.04. Weight, 215.
Throws and bats righthanded.
Major League saves: 1983 (7).
Led American Association in balks with 7 in 1980.
Led Florida State League in wild pitches with 19 in 1978.
Tied for American Association lead in games started by pitchers with 26 in 1979.

Year Club	League	G.	IP.	W.	L.	Pct.	H.	R.	ER.	SO.	BB.	ERA.
1976—Lethbridge	Pioneer	3	8	0	1	.000	7	8	4	11	9	4.50
1977—West Palm Beach†	Florida St.	21	100	5	5	.500	99	51	37	83	76	3.33
1978—West Palm Beach‡	Florida St.	21	127	10	7	.588	99	53	44	139	86	3.11
1978—Memphis	Southern	3	20	2	1	.667	14	5	1	25	11	0.45
1978—Montreal	National	4	4	0	1	.000	4	4	4	3	4	9.00
1979—Denver	Am. Assoc.	26	132	8	13	.381	139	★112	★98	122	★123	6.68
1979—Montreal	National	2	2	0	0	.000	2	3	3	1	3	13.50
1980—Denver§	Am. Assoc.	17	87	9	2	.818	66	42	37	79	74	3.83
1981—Denver	Am. Assoc.	20	57	1	2	.333	43	43	36	46	69	5.68
1982—Montreal x	National	7	9	0	0	.000	10	6	6	11	8	6.00

Year Club	League	G.	IP.	W.	L.	Pct.	H.	R.	ER.	SO.	BB.	ERA.
1982—Evansville	Am. Assoc.	9	21⅔	1	1	.500	9	6	5	30	14	2.08
1982—Detroit	American	12	19⅔	0	2	.000	22	13	11	20	8	5.03
1983—Detroit y	American	4	4	0	0	.000	5	5	5	4	3	11.25
1983—Wichita	Am. Assoc.	22	31	4	2	.667	27	17	16	40	25	4.65
1983—Montreal	National	27	50	1	0	1.000	37	17	16	56	23	2.88
National League Totals		40	65	1	1	.500	53	30	29	71	38	4.02
American League Totals		16	23⅔	0	2	.000	27	18	16	24	11	6.08
Major League Totals		56	88⅔	1	3	.250	80	48	45	95	49	4.57

Selected by Montreal Expos' organization in 1st round (ninth player selected) of free-agent draft, June 8, 1976.
†On temporary inactive list, April 13 to May 6, 1977.
‡On disabled list, April 10 to April 21, 1978.
§On disabled list, July 13 to September 1, 1980.
xSold to Evansville (Detroit Tigers' organization), June 10, 1982.
ySold to Wichita (Montreal Expos' organization), May 3, 1983.

STANLEY JULIAN JAVIER
(Stan)

Born September 1, 1965, at San Francisco Macoris, Dominican Republic.
Height, 6.00. Weight, 180.
Throws right and bats left and righthanded.
Son of Julian Javier, infielder with St. Louis Cardinals,
1960 through 1971, and Cincinnati Reds, 1972.

Year Club	League	Pos.	G.	AB.	R.	H.	2B.	3B.	HR.	RBI.	B.A.	PO.	A.	E.	F.A.
1981—Johnson City	Appal.	OF	53	144	30	36	5	4	3	19	.250	53	2	3	.948
1982—Johnson City†	Appal.	OF	57	185	45	51	3	•4	8	36	.276	94	8	4	.962
1983—Greensboro	S. Atl.	OF	129	489	109	152	★34	6	12	77	.311	250	10	15	.945

Signed as free agent by St. Louis Cardinals' organization, March 26, 1981.
†Traded with shortstop Bob Meacham to New York Yankees' organization for Outfielder Bob Helsom and Pitchers Marty Mason and Steve Fincher, December 14, 1982.

JAMES MICHAEL JEFFCOAT
(Mike)

Born August 3, 1959, at Pine Bluff, Ark.
Height, 6.02. Weight, 189.
Throws and bats lefthanded.
Attended Louisiana Tech University, Ruston, La.

Year Club	League	G.	IP.	W.	L.	Pct.	H.	R.	ER.	SO.	BB.	ERA.
1980—Waterloo	Midwest	4	6	0	0	.000	12	12	4	7	3	6.00
1980—Batavia	NYP	12	68	4	3	.571	65	40	30	71	45	3.97
1981—Waterloo	Midwest	25	147	10	8	.556	151	71	63	109	78	3.86
1982—Waterloo	Midwest	9	62	5	4	.556	58	29	28	68	15	4.06
1982—Chattanooga	Southern	18	128⅓	8	8	.500	122	49	41	107	51	2.88
1983—Charleston	Int'natonal	26	167	12	8	.600	187	95	84	96	46	4.53
1983—Cleveland	American	11	32⅔	1	3	.250	32	13	12	9	13	3.31
Major League Totals		11	32⅔	1	3	.250	32	13	12	9	13	3.31

Selected by St. Louis Cardinals' organization in 30th round of free-agent draft, June 7, 1977.
Selected by Cleveland Indians' organization in 13th round of free-agent draft, June 3, 1980.

LARRY STEVEN JELTZ
(Steve)

Born May 28, 1959, at Paris, France.
Height, 5.11. Weight, 175.
Throws right and bats left and righthanded.
Attended University of Kansas, Lawrence, Kan.

Led Carolina League second basemen in double plays with 84 in 1981.
Tied for Carolina League lead in caught stealing with 15 in 1981.

Year Club	League	Pos.	G.	AB.	R.	H.	2B.	3B.	HR.	RBI.	B.A.	PO.	A.	E.	F.A.
1980—Spartanburg†	S. Atl.	2B	31	107	19	31	2	1	0	8	.290	51	61	4	.966
1981—Peninsula	Carol.	2B	133	482	81	112	18	0	2	32	.232	★293	★369	25	.964
1982—Reading	East.	2B-SS-3B	126	380	61	92	10	3	7	28	.242	251	297	22	.961
1983—Portland	P. C.	3-2-S-O	71	181	34	48	6	1	0	16	.265	106	113	11	.952
1983—Philadelphia	Nat.	2B-SS-3B	13	8	0	1	0	1	0	1	.125	4	5	0	1.000
Major League Totals			13	8	0	1	0	1	0	1	.125	4	5	0	1.000

Selected by Philadelphia Phillies' organization in 9th round of free-agent draft, June 3, 1980.
†On disabled list, July 27, 1980 through remainder of season.

FERGUSON ARTHUR JENKINS
(Fergie)

Born December 13, 1943, at Chatham, Ontario, Canada.
Height, 6.05. Weight, 210.
Throws and bats righthanded.
Established modern major league record for most putouts by pitcher, lifetime (363).

Tied major league record for most 1-0 games lost, season (5), 1968; most years leading league in home runs allowed (5).

Led American League in home runs allowed with 37 in 1975 and 40 in 1979.

Led National League in home runs allowed with 30 in 1967, 29 in 1971, 32 in 1972, 35 in 1973 and tied for lead with 26 in 1968.

Led American League in complete games with 29 in 1974.

Led National League in complete games with 20 in 1967, 24 in 1970 and 30 in 1971.

Led National League pitchers in games started with 40 in 1968, 42 in 1969 and tied for lead with 39 in 1971.

Led National League in balks with 4 in 1971.

Won National League Cy Young Memorial Award, 1971.

Named National League Pitcher of the Year by THE SPORTING NEWS, 1971.

Named American League Comeback Player of the Year by THE SPORTING NEWS, 1974.

Named righthanded pitcher on THE SPORTING NEWS National League All-Star Team, 1971, 1972.

Named pitcher on THE SPORTING NEWS National League All-Star Team, 1967.

Year Club	League	G.	IP.	W.	L.	Pct.	H.	R.	ER.	SO.	BB.	ERA.
1962—Miami	Florida St.	11	65	7	2	.778	34	10	7	69	19	0.97
1962—Buffalo	Int'national	3	13	1	1	.500	18	9	8	6	5	5.54
1963—Arkansas	Int'national	4	10	0	1	.000	13	7	7	13	3	6.30
1963—Miami	Florida St.	20	140	12	5	.706	110	66	53	135	59	3.41
1964—Chattanooga	Southern	21	139	10	6	.625	124	61	48	149	42	3.11
1964—Arkansas	P. Coast	11	57	5	5	.500	40	27	20	49	34	3.16
1965—Arkansas	P. Coast	32	122	8	6	.571	104	48	40	112	42	2.95
1965—Philadelphia	National	7	12	2	1	.667	7	3	3	10	2	2.25
1966—Philadelphia†-Chicago	National	61	184	,6	8	.429	150	77	68	150	52	3.33
1967—Chicago	National	38	289	20	13	.606	230	101	90	236	83	2.80
1968—Chicago	National	40	308	20	15	.571	255	96	90	260	65	2.63
1969—Chicago	National	43	311	21	15	.583	284	122	111	*273	71	3.21
1970—Chicago	National	40	313	22	16	.579	265	128	●118	274	60	3.39
1971—Chicago	National	39	*325	*24	13	.649	*304	114	100	263	37	2.77
1972—Chicago	National	36	289	20	12	.625	253	111	*103	184	62	3.21
1973—Chicago‡	National	38	271	14	16	.467	267	133	117	170	57	3.89
1974—Texas	American	41	328	●25	12	.676	286	117	103	225	45	2.83
1975—Texas§	American	37	270	17	18	.486	261	130	118	157	56	3.93
1976—Boston	American	30	209	12	11	.522	201	85	76	142	43	3.27
1977—Boston x	American	28	193	10	10	.500	190	91	79	105	36	3.68
1978—Texas	American	34	249	18	8	.692	228	92	84	157	41	3.04
1979—Texas	American	37	259	16	14	.533	252	127	117	164	81	4.07
1980—Texas	American	29	198	12	12	.500	190	90	83	129	52	3.77
1981—Texas y	American	19	106	5	8	.385	122	55	53	63	40	4.50
1982—Chicago	National	34	217⅓	14	15	.483	221	92	76	134	68	3.15
1983—Chicago	National	33	167⅓	6	9	.400	176	89	80	96	46	4.30
American League Totals		255	1812	115	93	.553	1730	787	713	1142	394	3.54
National League Totals		409	2686⅔	169	133	.560	2412	1066	956	2050	603	3.20
Major League Totals		664	4498⅔	284	226	.557	4142	1853	1669	3192	997	3.34

Signed as free agent by Philadelphia Phillies' organization, June 15, 1962.

†Traded with Outfielder Adolfo Phillips and Outfielder-First Baseman John Herrnstein to Chicago Cubs for Pitchers Bob Buhl and Larry Jackson, April 21, 1966.

‡Traded to Texas Rangers for Infielders Bill Madlock and Vic Harris, October 25, 1973.

§Traded to Boston Red Sox for Outfielder Juan Beniquez, Pitcher Steve Barr, a player to be named later and an estimated $200,000, November 17, 1975; Texas Rangers acquired Pitcher Craig Skok to complete deal, December 12, 1975.

xTraded to Texas Rangers for Pitcher John Poloni and cash estimated at $20,000, December 14, 1977.

yGranted free agency, November 13, 1981; signed by Chicago Cubs, December 8, 1981.

ALL-STAR GAME RECORD

Tied All-Star Game record for most strikeouts, game (6), July 11, 1967.

Year League	IP.	W.	L.	Pct.	H.	R.	ER.	SO.	BB.	ERA.
1967—National	3	0	0	.000	3	1	1	6	0	3.00
1971—National	1	0	0	.000	3	2	2	0	0	18.00
All-Star Game Totals	4	0	0	.000	6	3	3	6	0	6.75

Named to National League All-Star Team for 1972 game; did not play.

ALFONSO JIMENEZ (GONZALEZ)

Name pronounced Him-EN-ez.

(Houston)

Born October 30, 1957, at Navojoa, Sonora, Mex.

Height, 5.07. Weight, 140.

Throws and bats righthanded.

Led Mexican League in sacrifice hits with 25 in 1978 and tied for lead with 19 in 1979.

Led Florida State League in bases on balls received with 105 in 1975.

Led Mexican League shortstops in double plays with 105 in 1979.

Led Mexican League shortstops in double plays with 108 and total chances with 856 in 1978.

Led Florida State League shortstops in putouts with 232, assists with 444, fielding percentage with .951, total chances with 711 and tied for lead in double plays with 73 in 1975.

Year Club	League	Pos.	G.	AB.	R.	H.	2B.	3B.	HR.	RBI.	B.A.	PO.	A.	E.	F.A.
1974—Puebla	Mex.	SS	20	33	4	7	1	0	1	3	.212	15	34	8	.860
1975—Key West	Fla. St.	SS-2B-OF	132	446	63	96	17	5	2	34	.215	242	452	35	.952
1976—Puebla	Mex.	SS	131	427	51	98	12	2	6	42	.230	250	476	28	.963

Year Club League	Pos.	G.	AB.	R.	H.	2B.	3B.	HR.	RBI.	B.A.	PO.	A.	E.	F.A.
1977—Puebla .... Mex.	SS	145	482	66	146	22	7	0	56	.303	*293	*527	32	.962
1978—Puebla .... Mex.	SS-2B	142	538	74	144	14	10	1	35	.268	*286	*544	26	.970
1978—Iowa .... A. A.	SS	13	41	7	9	2	0	0	6	.220	18	40	2	.967
1979—Puebla .... Mex.	SS	132	442	62	135	23	5	1	42	.305	243	513	27	.966
1980—Puebla†‡ .... Mex.	SS	75	254	29	62	8	1	1	24	.244	139	263	20	.953
1981—Reynosa .... Mex.					(Did not play)									
1982—Reynosa§ .... Mex.					(Did not play)									
1982—Toledo .... Int.	SS	37	115	7	26	3	0	0	12	.226	54	122	5	.972
1983—Toledo .... Int.	SS	22	64	13	16	3	0	3	6	.250	31	56	3	.967
1983—Minnesota .... Amer.	SS	36	86	5	15	5	1	0	9	.174	43	83	4	.969
Major League Totals...........		36	86	5	15	5	1	0	9	.174	43	83	4	.969

Signed as free agent by Puebla of Mexican League, September 13, 1973.
†Released, July 2, 1980; signed as free agent by Minnesota Twins' organization, October 28, 1980.
‡Sold by Minnesota Twins' organization to Reynosa of Mexican League, April 1, 1981.
§Sold to Toledo (Minnesota Twins' organization), July 21, 1982.

THOMAS EDWARD JOHN
(Tommy)

Born May 22, 1943, at Terre Haute, Ind.
Height, 6.03. Weight, 203.
Throws left and bats righthanded.
Attended Indiana State College, Terre Haute, Ind.

Tied American League record for most hit batsmen, game, nine-innings (4), June 15, 1968.
Led American League in shutouts with 6 in 1980.
Tied for American League lead in shutouts with 5 in 1966 and 6 in 1967.
Tied for American League lead in wild pitches with 17 and in intentional bases on balls issued with 16 in 1970.
Named National League Comeback Player of the Year by THE SPORTING NEWS, 1976.
Named lefthanded pitcher on THE SPORTING NEWS American League All-Star Team, 1980.
Received reported $40,000 bonus to sign with Cleveland Indians, 1961.

Year Club	League	G.	IP.	W.	L.	Pct.	H.	R.	ER.	SO.	BB.	ERA.
1961—Dubuque..	Midwest	14	88	10	4	.714	74	47	31	99	59	3.17
1962—Charleston	Eastern	21	128	6	8	.429	129	67	55	114	71	3.87
1962—Jacksonville	Int'national	8	34	2	2	.500	29	20	18	27	16	4.76
1963—Charleston	Eastern	12	95	9	2	.818	85	25	17	45	12	1.61
1963—Jacksonville	Int'national	18	102	6	8	.429	115	53	40	63	39	3.53
1963—Cleveland	American	6	20	0	2	.000	23	10	5	9	6	2.25
1964—Cleveland	American	25	94	2	9	.182	97	53	41	65	35	3.93
1964—Portland†	P. Coast	13	74	6	6	.500	75	38	35	72	24	4.26
1965—Chicago	American	39	184	14	7	.667	162	67	63	126	58	3.08
1966—Chicago	American	34	223	14	11	.560	195	76	65	138	57	2.62
1967—Chicago	American	31	178	10	13	.435	143	62	49	110	47	2.48
1968—Chicago‡	American	25	177	10	5	.667	135	45	39	117	49	1.98
1969—Chicago	American	33	232	9	11	.450	230	91	84	128	90	3.26
1970—Chicago	American	37	269	12	17	.414	253	117	98	138	101	3.28
1971—Chicago§	American	38	229	13	16	.448	244	115	92	131	58	3.62
1972—Los Angeles	National	29	187	11	5	.688	172	68	60	117	40	2.89
1973—Los Angeles	National	36	218	16	7	*.696	202	88	75	116	50	3.10
1974—Los Angeles x	National	22	153	13	3	.813	133	51	44	78	42	2.59
1975—Los Angeles y	National					(Did not play)						
1976—Los Angeles	National	31	207	10	10	.500	207	76	71	91	61	3.09
1977—Los Angeles	National	31	220	20	7	.741	225	82	68	123	50	2.78
1978—Los Angeles z	National	33	213	17	10	.630	230	95	78	124	53	3.30
1979—New York	American	37	276	21	9	.700	268	109	91	111	65	2.97
1980—New York	American	36	265	22	9	.710	270	115	101	78	56	3.43
1981—New York a	American	20	140	9	8	.529	135	50	41	50	39	2.64
1982—New York b-California.................	American	37	221⅔	14	12	.538	239	102	91	68	39	3.69
1983—California	American	34	234⅔	11	13	.458	*287	126	113	65	49	4.33
American League Totals.........................		432	2743⅓	161	142	.531	2681	1138	973	1334	749	3.19
National League Totals..........................		182	1198	87	42	.674	1169	460	396	649	296	2.97
Major League Totals..............................		614	3941⅓	248	184	.574	3850	1598	1369	1983	1045	3.13

Signed as free agent by Cleveland Indians' organization, June 12, 1961.
†Traded to Chicago White Sox with Catcher John Romano and Outfielder Tommie Agee for Catcher Camilo Carreon and Outfielder Rocky Colavito, January 20, 1965, as part of three-way deal which saw Chicago obtain Colavito from Kansas City Athletics earlier same day for Outfielders Jim Landis and Mike Hershberger and a pitcher to be named later; Kansas City acquired Pitcher Fred Talbot to complete deal, February 10, 1965.
‡On disabled list, August 22 through remainder of season.
§Traded with Infielder Steve Huntz to Los Angeles Dodgers for Infielder-Outfielder Richie Allen, December 2, 1971.
xOn disabled list, July 17, 1974 through remainder of season.
yOn emergency disabled list, April 6, 1975 through remainder of season.
zGranted free agency, November 2, 1978; signed by New York Yankees, November 21, 1978.
aOn disabled list, June 1 to August 5, 1981.
bTraded to California Angels for a player to be named later, August 31, 1982; New York Yankees acquired Pitcher Dennis Rasmussen to complete deal, November 24 1982.

DIVISION SERIES RECORD

Year Club	League	G.	IP.	W.	L.	Pct.	H.	R.	ER.	SO.	BB.	ERA.
1981—New York.......................................	American	1	7	0	1	.000	8	5	5	0	2	6.43

Established Championship Series record for most runs allowed, five-game Series (9), 1982.
Tied Championship Series record for most games won, total Series (4).
Tied National League Championship Series record for most complete games, total Series (2).

Year Club	League	G.	IP.	W.	L.	Pct.	H.	R.	ER.	SO.	BB.	ERA.
1977—Los Angeles	National	2	13⅔	1	0	1.000	11	5	1	11	5	0.66
1978—Los Angeles	National	1	9	1	0	1.000	4	0	0	4	2	0.00
1980—New York	American	1	6⅔	0	0	.000	8	2	2	3	1	2.70
1981—New York	American	1	6	1	0	1.000	6	1	1	3	1	1.50
1982—California	American	2	12⅓	1	1	.500	11	9	7	6	6	5.11
Championship Series Totals		7	47⅔	4	1	.800	40	17	11	27	15	2.08

WORLD SERIES RECORD

Year Club	League	G.	IP.	W.	L.	Pct.	H.	R.	ER.	SO.	BB.	ERA.
1977—Los Angeles	National	1	6	0	1	.000	9	5	4	7	3	6.00
1978—Los Angeles	National	2	14⅔	1	0	1.000	14	8	5	6	4	3.07
1981—New York	American	3	13	1	0	1.000	11	1	1	8	0	0.69
World Series Totals		6	33⅔	2	1	.667	34	14	10	21	7	2.67

ALL-STAR GAME RECORD

Year League	IP.	W.	L.	Pct.	H.	R.	ER.	SO.	BB.	ERA.
1968—American	⅔	0	0	.000	1	0	0	0	0	0.00
1980—American	2⅓	0	1	.000	4	3	3	1	0	11.57
All-Star Game Totals	3	0	1	.000	5	3	3	1	0	9.00

Member of National League All-Star Team for 1978 game; did not play.
Member of American League All-Star Team for 1979 game; did not play.

BOBBY EARL JOHNSON
(Bob)

Born July 31, 1959, at Dallas, Tex.
Height, 6.03. Weight, 195.
Throws and bats righthanded.
Nephew of Ernie Banks, Hall of Fame shortstop-first baseman with Chicago Cubs, 1953 through 1971;
coach, Chicago Cubs, 1972 through 1974; and public relations representative for Chicago Cubs, 1982 and 1983.

Led Texas League batters in strikeouts with 106 in 1980.
Led American Association catchers in fielding percentage with .992 in 1982.
Tied for Midwest League lead in double plays by catchers with 9 in 1979.

Year Club	League	Pos.	G.	AB.	R.	H.	2B.	3B.	HR.	RBI.	B.A.	PO.	A.	E.	F.A.
1977—Sarasota Rang.	Gulf C.	C	36	115	10	28	7	3	0	9	.243	165	30	9	.956
1978—Asheville	W. Car.	C	76	203	23	45	12	0	4	33	.222	427	48	15	.969
1979—Wausau	Midw.	C	124	433	89	131	20	0	24	79	.303	*666	*86	*18	.977
1980—Tulsa	Texas	C	115	382	64	93	25	3	13	70	.243	520	70	16	.974
1980—Charleston	Int.	C	12	34	5	5	2	0	0	3	.147	36	1	1	.974
1981—Wichita	A. A.	C-1B	109	354	46	93	18	1	20	57	.263	458	54	11	.979
1981—Texas	Amer.	C-1B	6	18	2	5	0	0	2	4	.278	31	0	0	1.000
1982—Texas	Amer.	C-1B	20	56	4	7	2	0	2	7	.125	92	5	0	1.000
1982—Denver	A.A.	C-1B	93	305	57	76	10	5	22	76	.249	511	54	4	.993
1983—Texas	Amer.	C-1B	72	175	18	37	6	1	5	16	.211	346	19	2	.995
Major League Totals			98	249	24	49	8	1	9	27	.197	469	24	2	.996

Selected by Texas Rangers' organization in 9th round of free-agent draft, June 7, 1977.

CLIFFORD JOHNSON JR.
(Cliff)

Born July 22, 1947, at San Antonio, Tex.
Height, 6.04. Weight, 225.
Throws and bats righthanded.
Brother-in-law of Mike Easler, outfielder with Boston Red Sox;
Cousin of Elijah Johnson, infielder-outfielder in Houston Astros' and Baltimore Orioles'
organizations, 1961 through 1970 and 1972.

Tied major league records for most home runs, inning (2) and most total bases, inning (8), June 30, 1977 (eighth inning); most home runs by pinch-hitter, lifetime (18).
Tied modern major league record for most long hits, inning (2), May 31, 1975 (eighth inning) and June 30, 1977 (eighth inning).
Hit three home runs in a game, June 30, 1977.
Led National League in passed balls with 12 in 1976.
Led American Association in total bases with 285 and being hit by pitch with 16 in 1973.
Led American Association in passed balls with 17 and tied for lead in errors with 13 in 1972.
Tied for Southern League lead in being hit by pitch with 8 in 1972.
Tied for Southern League lead in passed balls with 15 in 1971.
Tied for Appalachian League lead in double plays by catchers with 3 in 1967.
Named American Association Most Valuable Player, 1973.
Named Carolina League Most Valuable Player, 1970.

Year Club	League	Pos.	G.	AB.	R.	H.	2B.	3B.	HR.	RBI.	B.A.	PO.	A.	E.	F.A.
1967—Cocoa	Fla. St.	C-OF	53	156	13	41	5	1	4	20	.263	168	13	10	.948
1967—Covington	Appal.	OF-C-1B	36	110	21	34	7	2	5	24	.309	103	10	6	.950

Year Club	League	Pos.	G.	AB.	R.	H.	2B.	3B.	HR.	RBI.	B.A.	PO.	A.	E.	F.A.
1968—Cocoa	Fla. St.	★C-OF-1B	117	353	60	102	17	3	10	61	.289	641	55	★26	.964
1969—Peninsula	Carol.	C	103	327	37	75	16	1	11	54	.229	615	68	21	.970
1970—Raleigh-Durham	Carol.	C-OF	102	343	74	114	24	0	★27	★91	.332	474	40	9	.983
1970—Oklahoma City	A. A.	C-OF-1B	22	55	12	21	4	1	1	5	.382	63	9	2	.973
1971—Oklahoma City	A. A.	C-1B	31	105	16	26	5	2	5	15	.248	219	20	2	.992
1971—Columbus	South.	C-1B	58	164	16	30	10	0	4	21	.183	350	35	5	.987
1972—Columbus	South.	C-3B-1B	42	160	28	46	11	2	10	38	.288	235	36	8	.971
1972—Oklahoma City	A. A.	C-1B	89	313	55	88	12	5	17	59	.281	600	59	15	.978
1972—Houston	Nat.	C	5	4	0	1	0	0	0	0	.250	6	0	0	1.000
1973—Denver	A. A.	1B	133	490	★105	148	30	4	★33	★117	.302	132	15	4	.974
1973—Houston	Nat.	1B	7	20	6	6	2	0	2	6	.300	47	2	0	1.000
1974—Houston	Nat.	C-1B	83	171	26	39	4	1	10	29	.228	270	18	4	.986
1975—Houston	Nat.	1B-C-OF	122	340	52	94	16	1	20	65	.276	604	38	12	.982
1976—Houston	Nat.	C-OF-1B	108	318	36	72	21	2	10	49	.226	468	35	9	.982
1977—Houston†	Nat.	OF-1B	51	144	22	43	8	0	10	23	.299	113	11	3	.976
1977—New York	Amer.	C-1B	56	142	24	42	8	0	12	31	.296	145	14	1	.994
1978—New York	Amer.	C-1B	76	174	20	32	9	1	6	19	.184	71	10	2	.976
1979—N.Y.‡-Cleve.	Amer.	C	100	304	48	82	16	0	20	67	.270	10	1	0	1.000
1980—Cleveland§	Amer.	DH	54	174	25	40	3	1	6	28	.230	0	0	0	.000
1980—Chicago x	Nat.	1B-C	68	196	28	46	8	0	10	34	.235	469	16	4	.992
1981—Oakland	Amer.	1B	84	273	40	71	8	0	17	59	.260	42	1	0	1.000
1982—Oakland yz	Amer.	1B	73	214	19	51	10	0	7	31	.238	66	8	1	.987
1983—Toronto	Amer.	1B	142	407	59	108	23	1	22	76	.265	47	4	0	1.000
National League Totals			444	1193	170	301	59	4	62	206	.252	1977	120	32	.985
American League Totals			585	1688	235	426	77	3	90	311	.252	381	38	4	.991
Major League Totals			1029	2881	405	727	136	7	152	517	.252	2358	158	36	.986

Selected by Houston Astros' organization in 5th round of free-agent draft, June 7, 1966.

†Traded to New York Yankees for Infielder Mike Fischlin, Pitcher Randy Niemann and a player to be named later, June 15, 1977; Houston Astros acquired First Baseman-Outfielder Dave Bergman to complete deal, November 23, 1977.

‡Traded to Cleveland Indians for Pitcher Don Hood, June 15, 1979.

§Traded to Chicago Cubs for two players to be named later, June 23, 1980; Cleveland Indians acquired Outfielder-First Baseman Karl Pagel and cash to complete deal, June 30, 1980.

xTraded with Infielder Keith Drumright to Oakland A's for Pitcher Mike King, December 11, 1980.

yOn supplemental disabled list, August 5 to September 1, 1982.

zTraded to Toronto Blue Jays for Outfielder Al Woods, November 5, 1982.

DIVISION SERIES RECORD

Year Club	League	Pos.	G.	AB.	R.	H.	2B.	3B.	HR.	RBI.	B.A.	PO.	A.	E.	F.A.
1981—Oakland	Amer.	DH	2	7	0	2	1	0	0	0	.286	0	0	0	.000

CHAMPIONSHIP SERIES RECORD

Year Club	League	Pos.	G.	AB.	R.	H.	2B.	3B.	HR.	RBI.	B.A.	PO.	A.	E.	F.A.
1977—New York	Amer.	DH-PH	5	15	2	6	2	0	1	2	.400	0	0	0	.000
1978—New York	Amer.	PH	1	1	0	0	0	0	0	0	.000	0	0	0	.000
1981—Oakland	Amer.	DH	2	6	0	0	0	0	0	0	.000	0	0	0	.000
Championship Series Totals			8	22	2	6	2	0	1	2	.273	0	0	0	.000

WORLD SERIES RECORD

Year Club	League	Pos.	G.	AB.	R.	H.	2B.	3B.	HR.	RBI.	B.A.	PO.	A.	E.	F.A.
1977—New York	Amer.	PH-C	2	1	0	0	0	0	0	0	.000	0	0	0	.000
1978—New York	Amer.	PH	2	2	0	0	0	0	0	0	.000	0	0	0	.000
World Series Totals			4	3	0	0	0	0	0	0	.000	0	0	0	.000

HOWARD MICHAEL JOHNSON

Born November 29, 1960, at Clearwater, Fla.
Height, 5.11. Weight, 175.
Throws right and bats right and lefthanded.
Attended St. Petersburg Junior College, St. Petersburg, Fla.

Led Florida State League in sacrifice hits with 16 in 1980.
Led American Association third basemen in double plays with 19 in 1982.
Led Florida State League third basemen in double plays with 21 in 1980.

Year Club	League	Pos.	G.	AB.	R.	H.	2B.	3B.	HR.	RBI.	B.A.	PO.	A.	E.	F.A.
1979—Lakeland	Fla. St.	3B-SS-OF	132	456	49	107	9	6	3	49	.235	130	240	36	.911
1980—Lakeland	Fla. St.	3B	130	474	83	135	★28	1	10	69	.285	★110	★264	13	★.966
1981—Birmingham	South.	3B	138	488	84	130	28	7	22	83	.266	103	218	26	.925
1982—Evansville	A. A.	3B-OF	98	366	70	116	16	4	23	67	.317	69	139	23	.900
1982—Detroit	Amer.	3B-OF	54	155	23	49	5	0	4	14	.316	36	40	7	.916
1983—Detroit	Amer.	3B	27	66	11	14	0	0	3	5	.212	10	30	7	.851
1983—Evansville†	A. A.	3B	3	9	1	2	1	0	0	0	.222	1	11	2	.857
Major League Totals			81	221	34	63	5	0	7	19	.285	46	70	14	.892

Selected by New York Yankees' organization in 23rd round of free-agent draft, June 6, 1978.
Selected by Detroit Tigers' organization in secondary phase of free-agent draft, January 9, 1979.
†On disabled list, June 2 to August 8, 1983.

JOHN HENRY JOHNSON

Born August 21, 1956, at Houston, Tex.
Height, 6.02. Weight, 185.
Throws and bats lefthanded.

Year Club	League	G.	IP.	W.	L.	Pct.	H.	R.	ER.	SO.	BB.	ERA.
1974—Great Falls	Pioneer	14	33	2	1	.667	25	12	10	33	25	2.73
1975—Cedar Rapids	Midwest	22	127	4	12	.250	127	72	53	89	49	3.76
1976—Cedar Rapids	Midwest	20	131	13	2	.867	93	42	28	94	50	1.92
1977—Fresno†	California	23	149	14	2	*.875	142	79	56	155	64	*3.38
1978—Oakland	American	33	186	11	10	.524	164	81	70	91	82	3.39
1979—Oakland‡-Texas	American	31	167	4	14	.222	168	95	86	96	72	4.63
1980—Charleston	Int'national	16	77	3	9	.250	84	49	33	55	35	3.86
1980—Texas	American	33	39	2	2	.500	27	12	10	44	15	2.31
1981—Texas	American	24	24	3	1	.750	19	7	7	8	6	2.63
1982—Pawtucket§ x	Int'national	29	42⅓	3	1	.750	37	21	19	45	23	4.04
1983—Boston	American	34	53⅓	3	2	.600	58	28	22	51	20	3.71
Major League Totals		155	469⅓	23	29	.442	436	223	195	290	195	3.74

Selected by San Francisco Giants' organization in 15th round of free-agent draft, June 5, 1974.
†Traded with Outfielder Gary Thomasson, Catcher Gary Alexander, Pitchers Dave Heaverlo, Alan Wirth and Phillip Huffman, a player to be named later and cash estimated at $390,000 to Oakland A's for Pitcher Vida Blue, March 15, 1978; Oakland acquired Shortstop Mario Guerrero to complete deal, April 7, 1978.
‡Traded to Texas Rangers for Third Baseman Dave Chalk and Catcher Mike Heath, June 15, 1979.
§Traded to Pawtucket (Boston Red Sox' organization) for Pitcher Mike Smithson, April 9, 1982.
xOn disabled list, May 30 to June 28 and August 11 to August 21, 1982.

MICHAEL LEE JOHNSON
(Mike)

Born December 30, 1960, at Minneapolis, Minn.
Height, 6.00. Weight, 190.
Throws and bats righthanded.

Year Club	League	G.	IP.	W.	L.	Pct.	H.	R.	ER.	SO.	BB.	ERA.
1979—Bradenton Pirates	Gulf Coast	9	53	2	2	.500	45	26	24	23	28	4.08
1980—Shelby†	W. Carolina	24	125	6	10	.375	139	89	79	67	69	5.69
1981—Alexandria‡	Carolina	24	143	8	9	.471	139	83	70	83	77	4.41
1982—Wausau	Midwest	30	106	9	7	.563	97	77	59	103	76	5.01
1983—Bakersfield	Calif.	49	67⅓	2	7	.222	49	26	19	97	52	2.54

Selected by Pittsburgh Pirates' organization in 11th round of free-agent draft, June 5, 1979.
†On disabled list, May 2 to May 14, 1980.
‡Traded to Seattle Mariners' organization for Outfielder Reggie Walton, March 25, 1982.

MITCHELL DREW JOHNSON
(Mitch)

Born August 2, 1962, at Columbia, Pa.
Height, 6.05. Weight, 210.
Throws and bats righthanded.

Led Carolina League in complete games with 14 in 1983.
Tied for Florida State League lead in wild pitches with 18 in 1981.
Tied for New York-Pennsylvania League lead in games started by pitchers with 14 in 1980.

Year Club	League	G.	IP.	W.	L.	Pct.	H.	R.	ER.	SO.	BB.	ERA.
1980—Elmira	NYP	15	69	5	3	.625	69	32	20	28	35	2.61
1981—Winter Haven	Florida St.	32	118	4	8	.333	130	73	52	79	58	3.97
1982—Winter Haven	Florida St.	34	118⅓	6	9	.400	122	70	62	65	65	4.72
1983—Winston-Salem	Carolina	31	*214	15	8	.652	197	97	74	146	59	3.11

Selected by Boston Red Sox' organization in 3rd round of free-agent draft, June 3, 1980.

RANDALL GLENN JOHNSON
(Randy)

Born June 10, 1956, at Escondido, Calif.
Height, 6.01. Weight, 190.
Throws and bats righthanded.
Attended Palomar College, San Marcos, Calif., and San Jose State University, San Jose, Calif.
Brother of Don Johnson, pitcher in California Angels' organization, 1974.

Year Club	League	Pos.	G.	AB.	R.	H.	2B.	3B.	HR.	RBI.	B.A.	PO.	A.	E.	F.A.
1978—Little Falls	NYP	3B-1B	5	23	5	8	2	0	0	2	.348	17	7	0	1.000
1978—Wausau†	Midw.	SS-3B-1B	62	230	34	54	8	2	6	30	.235	162	136	23	.928
1979—Jackson	Texas	3-1-O-2	86	228	23	67	7	0	2	20	.294	144	53	7	.966
1980—Jackson‡§	Texas	3-O-1-2	28	72	9	22	0	0	0	5	.306	20	22	0	1.000
1980—Savannah x	South.	3B	54	167	18	53	10	0	2	11	.317	46	111	12	.929
1981—Richmond	Int.	3B	126	470	78	132	20	4	12	72	.281	110	225	19	.946
1982—Atlanta	Nat.	2B-3B	27	46	5	11	5	0	0	6	.239	21	47	3	.958
1982—Richmond	Int.	3B-SS-2B	7	22	5	8	1	0	3	7	.364	16	10	1	.963
1983—Atlanta	Nat.	3B-2B	86	144	22	36	3	0	1	17	.250	44	72	1	.991
Major League Totals			113	190	27	47	8	0	1	23	.247	65	119	4	.979

Selected by New York Mets' organization in 10th round of free-agent draft, June 6, 1978.
†On Lynchburg disabled list, April 13 to May 22, 1979.

‡On disabled list, May 8 to June 17, 1980.
§Traded to Atlanta Braves' organization for Pitcher Terry Leach, July 1, 1980.
xOn disabled list, August 30 to September 26, 1980.

RONALD DAVID JOHNSON
(Ron)

Born March 23, 1956, at Long Beach, Calif.
Height, 6.03. Weight, 215.
Throws and bats righthanded.
Attended Fullerton College, Fullerton, Calif., and Fresno State University, Fresno, Calif.

Year—Club	League	Pos.	G.	AB.	R.	H.	2B.	3B.	HR.	RBI.	B.A.	PO.	A.	E.	F.A.
1978—Sarasota Royals...	Gulf C.	1B	14	49	10	16	1	0	0	13	.327	60	4	0	1.000
1978—Ft. Myers..............	Fla. St.	1B	29	78	9	18	2	1	1	10	.231	7	0	1	.875
1979—Ft. Myers..............	Fla. St.	1B	116	381	47	117	19	2	8	58	.307	104	6	1	.991
1979—Jacksonville........	South.	1B-OF	17	61	8	15	6	0	2	10	.246	11	0	0	1.000
1980—Jacksonville........	South.	1B	142	514	81	139	★40	0	23	104	.270	626	34	6	.991
1981—Omaha†................	A. A.	1B	88	297	36	73	20	1	7	41	.246	723	52	12	.985
1982—Omaha.................	A. A.	1B	★137	494	65	★166	27	3	11	73	.336	1044	74	★23	.980
1982—Kansas City..........	Amer.	1B	8	14	2	4	2	0	0	0	.286	39	2	1	.976
1983—Omaha..................	A. A.	1B-C	104	356	47	113	21	1	10	49	.317	716	49	8	.990
1983—Kansas City..........	Amer.	1B-C	9	27	2	7	0	0	0	1	.259	66	3	2	.972
Major League Totals....................			17	41	4	11	2	0	0	1	.268	105	5	3	.973

Selected by California Angels' organization in 13th round of free-agent draft, January 7, 1976.
Selected by Kansas City Royals' organization in 24th round of free-agent draft, June 6, 1978.
†On disabled list, July 17 to September 1, 1981.

ROY EDWARD JOHNSON

Born June 27, 1959, at Parkin, Ark.
Height, 6.04. Weight, 224.
Throws and bats lefthanded.
Attended Tennessee State University, Nashville, Tenn.

Tied for New York-Pennsylvania League lead in caught stealing with 6 in 1980.

Year—Club	League	Pos.	G.	AB.	R.	H.	2B.	3B.	HR.	RBI.	B.A.	PO.	A.	E.	F.A.
1980—Jamestown............	NYP	OF	36	126	29	41	6	3	6	19	.325	63	1	3	.955
1980—W. Palm Beach....	Fla. St.	OF	24	85	11	19	4	1	1	12	.224	44	1	1	.978
1981—Memphis................	South.	OF	130	477	83	126	19	10	18	90	.264	★340	8	11	.969
1982—Wichita.................	A. A.	OF	102	376	73	138	19	6	14	76	★.367	238	4	8	.968
1982—Montreal...............	Nat.	OF	17	32	2	7	2	0	0	2	.219	18	0	0	1.000
1983—Wichita†................	A. A.	OF	79	248	39	72	13	1	5	43	.290	89	1	3	.968
Major League Totals....................			17	32	2	7	2	0	0	2	.219	18	0	0	1.000

Selected by Montreal Expos' organization in 5th round of free-agent draft, June 3, 1980.
†On temporary inactive list, April 19 to May 21, 1983.

WALLACE DARNELL JOHNSON

Born December 25, 1956, at Gary, Ind.
Height, 5.11. Weight, 173.
Throws right and bats right and lefthanded.
Attended Indiana State University, Terre Haute, Ind.

Led Florida State League in stolen bases with 58 and caught stealing with 22 in 1980.

Year—Club	League	Pos.	G.	AB.	R.	H.	2B.	3B.	HR.	RBI.	B.A.	PO.	A.	E.	F.A.
1979—Jamestown............	NYP	2B	70	★284	60	96	11	6	6	42	.338	157	155	17	.948
1980—W. Palm Beach....	Fla. St.	2B-OF	126	488	86	★163	17	5	3	49	★.334	294	350	31	.954
1980—Memphis................	South.	2B	4	13	1	1	0	0	0	0	.077	5	12	0	1.000
1981—Memphis†..............	South.	2B-OF	28	102	15	37	9	0	1	18	.363	44	52	10	.906
1981—Denver	A. A.	2B-OF	59	215	39	64	13	4	0	16	.298	72	116	7	.964
1981—Montreal...............	Nat.	PH	11	9	1	2	0	1	0	3	.222	1	2	0	1.000
1982—Montreal...............	Nat.	2B	36	57	5	11	0	2	0	2	.193	22	18	2	.952
1982—Wichita.................	A. A.	2B-OF	76	298	62	105	12	4	6	36	.352	128	79	12	.945
1983—Wichita.................	A. A.	OF	16	53	7	14	3	1	0	6	.264	26	0	2	.929
1983—Mont.‡-S. F.	Nat.	2B	10	10	1	2	0	0	0	1	.200	3	2	0	1.000
1983—Phoenix.................	P. C.	2B	63	229	42	66	8	2	2	26	.288	105	150	15	.944
Major League Totals....................			57	76	7	15	0	3	0	6	.197	26	22	2	.960

Selected by Montreal Expos' organization in 6th round of free-agent draft, June 5, 1979.
†On disabled list, April 29 to May 15, 1981.
‡Traded to San Francisco Giants for Outfielder Mike Vail, May 25, 1983.

DIVISION SERIES RECORD

Year—Club	League	Pos.	G.	AB.	R.	H.	2B.	3B.	HR.	RBI.	B.A.	PO.	A.	E.	F.A.
1981—Montreal................	Nat.	PH	2	2	0	1	0	0	0	1	.500	0	0	0	.000

WILLIAM C. JOHNSON
(Bill)

Born October 6, 1960, at Wilmington, Del.
Height, 6.04. Weight, 204.
Throws and bats righthanded.

Led Northwest League in saves with 8 in 1980.

Year	Club	League	G.	IP.	W.	L.	Pct.	H.	R.	ER.	SO.	BB.	ERA.
1980—Central Oregon		Northwest	27	42	4	4	.500	37	28	23	30	29	4.93
1981—Spartanburg		S. Atlantic	52	57	8	3	.727	45	26	18	40	40	2.84
1982—Peninsula		Carolina	50	89⅔	8	3	.727	69	26	18	54	39	1.81
1983—Reading†		Eastern	11	15	1	1	.500	14	11	7	11	10	4.20
1983—Midland		Texas	45	63⅔	6	6	.500	76	39	34	22	31	4.81
1983—Chicago		National	10	12⅓	1	0	1.000	17	6	6	4	3	4.38
Major League Totals			10	12⅓	1	0	1.000	17	6	6	4	3	4.38

Signed as free agent by Philadelphia Phillies' organization, March 5, 1980.

†Traded with Pitcher Dick Ruthven to Chicago Cubs for Pitcher Willie Hernandez, May 22, 1983.

JOHN WILLIAM JOHNSTONE JR.
(Jay)

Born November 20, 1945, at Manchester, Conn.
Height, 6.01. Weight, 190.
Throws right and bats lefthanded.
Attended Mount San Antonio Junior College, Walnut, Calif.

Year	Club	League	Pos.	G.	AB.	R.	H.	2B.	3B.	HR.	RBI.	B.A.	PO.	A.	E.	F.A.
1963—San Jose	Calif.	OF-SS-3B	48	155	21	39	5	3	1	18	.252	51	31	9	.901	
1964—San Jose	Calif.	OF	126	454	66	132	27	●11	4	48	.291	250	14	12	.957	
1965—El Paso	Texas	OF	35	137	21	39	9	2	1	21	.285	82	4	4	.956	
1965—San Jose	Calif.	OF	97	356	53	107	17	6	6	60	.301	198	11	10	.954	
1966—El Paso	Texas	OF	7	25	5	9	2	0	1	1	.360	19	0	0	1.000	
1966—Seattle	P. C.	OF	81	318	60	108	14	7	7	42	.340	170	7	4	.978	
1966—California	Amer.	OF	61	254	35	67	12	4	3	17	.264	114	2	3	.975	
1967—California	Amer.	OF	79	230	18	48	7	1	2	10	.209	141	3	4	.973	
1967—Seattle	P. C.	OF	49	184	21	58	11	1	4	21	.315	117	3	4	.968	
1968—California	Amer.	OF	41	115	11	30	4	1	0	3	.261	58	4	1	.984	
1968—Seattle	P. C.	OF	84	314	45	87	15	4	13	56	.277	203	11	9	.960	
1969—California	Amer.	OF	148	540	64	146	20	5	10	59	.270	331	12	6	.983	
1970—California†	Amer.	OF	119	320	34	76	10	5	11	39	.238	200	7	4	.981	
1971—Chicago	Amer.	OF	124	388	53	101	14	1	16	40	.260	232	9	8	.968	
1972—Chicago‡	Amer.	OF	113	261	27	49	9	0	4	17	.188	154	5	2	.988	
1973—Tucson	P. C.	OF	69	242	58	84	15	5	9	44	.347	125	2	6	.955	
1973—Oakland§	Amer.	OF-2B	23	28	1	3	1	0	0	3	.107	7	0	0	1.000	
1974—Toledo	Int.	OF-1B	57	155	31	49	15	1	8	25	.316	77	6	3	.965	
1974—Philadelphia	Nat.	OF	64	200	30	59	10	4	6	30	.295	88	4	3	.968	
1975—Philadelphia	Nat.	OF	122	350	50	115	19	2	7	54	.329	152	10	4	.976	
1976—Philadelphia	Nat.	OF-1B	129	440	62	140	38	4	5	53	.318	293	10	8	.974	
1977—Philadelphia	Nat.	OF-1B	112	363	46	103	18	4	15	59	.284	294	15	1	.997	
1978—Philadelphia x	Nat.	1B-OF	35	56	3	10	2	0	0	4	.179	77	7	1	.988	
1978—New York y	Amer.	OF	36	65	6	17	0	0	1	6	.262	31	0	0	1.000	
1979—New York y	Amer.	OF	23	48	7	10	1	0	1	7	.208	32	0	0	1.000	
1979—San Diego z	Nat.	OF-1B	75	201	10	59	8	2	0	32	.294	185	18	4	.981	
1980—Los Angeles	Nat.	OF	109	251	31	77	15	2	2	20	.307	100	9	4	.965	
1981—Los Angeles	Nat.	OF-1B	61	83	8	17	3	0	3	6	.205	33	4	1	.974	
1982—L.A. a-Chi.	Nat.	OF	119	282	40	68	14	1	10	45	.241	154	8	3	.982	
1983—Chicago	Nat.	OF	86	140	16	36	7	0	6	22	.257	55	3	4	.935	
National League Totals			912	2366	314	684	134	19	54	325	.289	1431	88	33	.979	
American League Totals			767	2249	256	547	78	17	48	201	.243	1300	42	28	.980	
Major League Totals			1679	4615	570	1231	212	36	102	526	.267	2731	130	61	.979	

Signed as free agent by California Angels' organization, June 30, 1963.

†Traded with Pitcher Tom Bradley and Catcher Tom Egan to Chicago White Sox for Outfielder Ken Berry, Second Baseman Syd O'Brien and Pitcher Billy Wynne, November 30, 1970.

‡Released, March 7, 1973; signed by Oakland Athletics, March 31, 1973.

§Conditionally released to St. Louis Cardinals, January 9, 1974; released by St. Louis, March 26, 1974; signed by Philadelphia Phillies, April 3, 1974.

xTraded with Outfielder Bobby Brown to New York Yankees for Pitcher Rawly Eastwick, June 14, 1978.

yTraded to San Diego Padres for Pitcher Dave Wehrmeister, June 15, 1979.

zGranted free agency, November 1, 1979; signed by Los Angeles Dodgers, December 4, 1979.

aReleased, May 25, 1982; signed by Chicago Cubs, June 1, 1982.

DIVISION SERIES RECORD

Year	Club	League	Pos.	G.	AB.	R.	H.	2B.	3B.	HR.	RBI.	B.A.	PO.	A.	E.	F.A.
1981—Los Angeles	Nat.	PH	1	1	0	0	0	0	0	0	.000	0	0	0	.000	

CHAMPIONSHIP SERIES RECORD

Established Championship Series record for highest batting average, three-game Series (.778), 1976.

Tied Championship Series records for most hits, three-game Series (7), 1976; most hits, two consecutive games, one Series (6), October 10 and 12, 1976.

Year	Club	League	Pos.	G.	AB.	R.	H.	2B.	3B.	HR.	RBI.	B.A.	PO.	A.	E.	F.A.
1976—Philadelphia	Nat.	PH-OF	3	9	1	7	1	1	0	2	.778	3	0	0	1.000	
1977—Philadelphia	Nat.	OF-PH	2	5	0	1	0	0	0	0	.200	4	0	0	1.000	
1981—Los Angeles	Nat.	PH	2	2	0	0	0	0	0	0	.000	0	0	0	.000	
Championship Series Totals			7	16	1	8	1	1	0	2	.500	7	0	0	1.000	

Tied World Series record for most home runs as pinch-hitter, game (1), October 24, 1981.

Year	Club	League	Pos.	G.	AB.	R.	H.	2B.	3B.	HR.	RBI.	B.A.	PO.	A.	E.	F.A.
1978—New York		Amer.	OF	2	0	0	0	0	0	0	0	.000	1	0	0	1.000
1981—Los Angeles		Nat.	PH	3	3	1	2	0	0	1	3	.667	0	0	0	1.000
World Series Totals				5	3	1	2	0	0	1	3	.667	1	0	0	1.000

ALFORNIA JONES
(Al)

Born February 10, 1959, at Charleston, Miss.
Height, 5.11. Weight, 165.
Throws and bats righthanded.
Attended Alcorn State University, Lorman, Miss.

Led Midwest League in games finished in relief with 50 in 1983.

Year	Club	League	G.	IP.	W.	L.	Pct.	H.	R.	ER.	SO.	BB.	ERA.
1981—Sarasota White Sox		Gulf Coast	11	58	3	5	.375	50	19	9	41	20	1.40
1982—Appleton		Midwest	26	57	2	4	.333	53	27	21	64	34	3.32
1983—Appleton		Midwest	★55	102	11	1	★.917	54	13	11	124	39	0.97
1983—Chicago		American	2	2⅓	0	0	.000	3	1	1	2	2	3.86
Major League Totals			2	2⅓	0	0	.000	3	1	1	2	2	3.86

Selected by Chicago White Sox' organization in 13th round of free-agent draft, June 8, 1981.

CRAIG STEVEN JONES

Born August 19, 1958, at Natrona Heights, Pa.
Height, 6.02. Weight, 195.
Throws and bats righthanded.
Attended United States Military Academy, West Point, N.Y.

Year	Club	League	G.	IP.	W.	L.	Pct.	H.	R.	ER.	SO.	BB.	ERA.
1980—Durham		Carolina	13	86	6	5	.545	69	34	27	77	34	2.83
1981—Savannah		Southern	24	141	6	8	.429	133	79	65	94	75	4.15
1982—Savannah		Southern	22	151	8	13	.381	156	84	66	110	51	3.93
1982—Richmond		Int'national	2	8⅓	0	1	.000	12	11	8	1	4	8.64
1983—Savannah		Southern	27	137⅓	11	7	.611	144	79	70	106	46	4.59
1983—Richmond		Int'national	1	3	0	1	.000	2	1	1	1	0	3.00

Selected by New York Mets' organization in 3rd round of free-agent draft, June 5, 1979.
Selected by Atlanta Braves' organization in 4th round of free-agent draft, June 3, 1980.

JAMES CONDIA JONES
(Jim)

Born April 20, 1964, at Dallas, Tex.
Height, 6.02. Weight, 185.
Throws and bats righthanded.

Year	Club	League	G.	IP.	W.	L.	Pct.	H.	R.	ER.	SO.	BB.	ERA.
1982—Walla Walla		Northwest	14	78⅓	4	6	.400	64	49	28	78	71	3.22
1983—Reno		California	17	116⅔	7	5	.583	96	50	35	79	49	2.70

Selected by San Diego Padres' organization in 1st round (third player selected) of free-agent draft, June 7, 1982.

JEFFREY ALLEN JONES
(Jeff)

Born July 29, 1956, at Detroit, Mich.
Height, 6.03. Weight, 210.
Throws and bats righthanded.
Attended St. Clair College, Port Huron, Mich., and
Bowling Green State University, Bowling Green, O.

Led Pacific Coast League in balks with 5 in 1979.
Led Eastern League pitchers in games started with 29 and tied for lead in balks with 2 in 1978.

Year	Club	League	G.	IP.	W.	L.	Pct.	H.	R.	ER.	SO.	BB.	ERA.
1977—Modesto		California	11	46	4	3	.571	35	28	26	41	32	5.09
1977—Chattanooga		Southern	7	9	0	0	.000	9	0	0	5	3	0.00
1978—Jersey City		Eastern	29	191	10	13	.435	187	102	79	121	84	3.72
1979—Ogden		P. Coast	28	175	13	7	.650	152	79	68	126	89	3.50
1980—Oakland		American	35	44	1	3	.250	32	21	14	34	26	2.86
1981—Oakland		American	33	61	4	1	.800	51	27	23	43	40	3.39
1982—Oakland		American	18	37	3	1	.750	44	29	21	18	26	5.11
1982—Tacoma†		P. Coast	8	10⅓	1	1	.500	17	10	10	6	7	8.71
1983—Tacoma		P. Coast	26	121⅓	6	9	.400	123	69	48	80	38	3.56
1983—Oakland		American	13	29⅔	1	1	.500	43	19	19	14	8	5.76
Major League Totals			99	171⅔	9	6	.600	170	96	77	109	100	4.04

Selected by Oakland A's organization in 13th round of free-agent draft, June 7, 1977.
†On disabled list, June 5 to July 27, 1982.

CHAMPIONSHIP SERIES RECORD

Year	Club	League	G.	IP.	W.	L.	Pct.	H.	R.	ER.	SO.	BB.	ERA.
1981—Oakland		American	1	2	0	0	.000	2	1	1	0	1	4.50

JEFFRY RAYMOND JONES
(Jeff)

Born October 22, 1957, at Philadelphia, Pa.
Height, 6.02. Weight, 200.
Throws and bats righthanded.
Attended University of Iowa, Iowa City, Ia.

Led Midwest League batters in strikeouts with 151, total bases with 286 and slugging percentage with .662 in 1982.
Led Midwest League outfielders in double plays with 7 in 1980.
Tied for Pioneer League lead in being hit by pitch with 8 in 1979.

Year Club	League	Pos.	G.	AB.	R.	H.	2B.	3B.	HR.	RBI.	B.A.	PO.	A.	E.	F.A.
1979—Billings	Pion.	OF-1B	66	232	49	69	9	1	11	49	.297	124	10	10	.931
1980—Cedar Rapids†	Midw.	OF	100	332	48	66	13	3	11	33	.199	192	16	8	.963
1981—Cedar Rapids	Midw.	OF	79	246	52	57	6	2	17	50	.232	113	8	7	.945
1981—Waterbury	East.	OF	48	127	19	23	5	1	3	16	.181	75	3	3	.963
1982—Cedar Rapids	Midw.	OF-1B	135	432	111	130	26	2	*42	101	.301	453	18	10	.979
1983—Cincinnati	Nat.	OF-1B	16	44	6	10	3	0	0	5	.227	33	1	0	1.000
1983—Indianapolis	A. A.	OF-1B	31	75	12	14	1	0	3	12	.187	49	3	5	.912
1983—Waterbury	East.	1B-OF	91	298	52	70	7	0	17	50	.235	461	38	8	.984
Major League Totals			16	44	6	10	3	0	0	5	.227	33	1	0	1.000

Selected by Cincinnati Reds' organization in 20th round of free-agent draft, June 5, 1979.
†On disabled list, June 27 to July 21 1980.

LYNN MORRIS JONES

Born January 1, 1953, at Meadville, Pa.
Height, 5.09. Weight, 175.
Throws and bats righthanded.
Received bachelor of arts degree in sociology
from Thiel College, Greenville, Pa.
Brother of Darryl Jones, outfielder with New York Yankees, 1979.

Tied for Eastern League lead in sacrifice flies with 8 in 1976.

Year Club	League	Pos.	G.	AB.	R.	H.	2B.	3B.	HR.	RBI.	B.A.	PO.	A.	E.	F.A.
1974—Seattle	N'west.	OF	76	282	53	74	15	2	2	37	.262	166	*13	4	.978
1975—Three Rivers	East.	OF-SS	53	141	12	29	3	1	1	14	.206	89	25	6	.950
1975—Eugene	N'west.	OF-3B	62	211	53	71	13	3	13	63	.336	90	9	6	.943
1976—Three Rivers	East.	OF	131	418	41	105	17	0	2	36	.251	196	5	8	.962
1977—Three Rivers†	East.	OF	94	324	49	87	14	2	5	32	.269	229	14	1	*.996
1978—Indianapolis‡	A. A.	OF-2B	126	482	81	158	28	4	9	62	.328	246	14	3	.989
1979—Detroit	Amer.	OF	95	213	33	63	8	0	4	26	.296	142	3	3	.980
1980—Evansville	A. A.	OF	34	121	10	33	4	0	0	11	.273	29	1	1	.968
1980—Detroit§	Amer.	OF	30	55	9	14	2	2	0	6	.255	31	0	0	1.000
1981—Detroit	Amer.	OF	71	174	19	45	5	0	2	19	.259	85	5	1	.989
1982—Detroit	Amer.	OF	58	139	15	31	3	1	0	14	.223	86	3	0	1.000
1983—Detroit x	Amer.	OF	49	64	9	17	1	2	0	6	.266	28	2	1	.968
Major League Totals			303	645	85	170	19	5	6	71	.264	372	13	5	.987

Selected by Cincinnati Reds' organization in 10th round of free-agent draft, June 5, 1974.
†On disabled list, July 8 to August 8, 1977.
‡Drafted by Detroit Tigers, December 4, 1978.
§On disabled list, April 30 to July 25, 1980.
xGranted free agency when he refused option to minors, December 1, 1983; signed by Kansas City Royals, December 7, 1983.

ODELL JONES JR.

Born January 13, 1953, at Tulare, Calif.
Height, 6.03. Weight, 175.
Throws and bats righthanded.
Attended Compton College, Compton, Calif.

Pitched 7-0 no-hit victory against Pittsfield, April 29, 1974.
Major league saves: 1983 (10).
Led Eastern League in balks with 3 in 1974.

Year Club	League	G.	IP.	W.	L.	Pct.	H.	R.	ER.	SO.	BB.	ERA.
1972—Niagara Falls	NYP	11	79	7	3	.700	78	34	27	53	20	3.08
1973—Charleston	W. Carol.	10	62	2	3	.400	42	22	10	62	29	1.45
1973—Salem	Carolina	11	67	5	4	.556	64	40	36	55	38	4.84
1974—Thetford Mines	Eastern	24	161	11	8	.579	103	63	58	153	*120	3.24
1975—Charleston	Int'national	26	*188	●14	9	.609	133	67	56	*157	88	2.68
1975—Pittsburgh	National	2	3	0	0	.000	1	0	0	2	0	0.00
1976—Charleston†	Int'national	16	84	2	7	.222	81	49	46	47	43	4.93
1977—Pittsburgh	National	34	108	3	7	.300	118	63	61	66	31	5.08
1978—Columbus	Int'national	28	181	12	9	.571	174	100	*92	*169	69	4.57
1978—Pittsburgh‡	National	3	9	2	0	1.000	7	3	2	10	4	2.00
1979—Seattle§	American	25	119	3	11	.214	151	90	80	72	58	6.05
1980—Portland x	P. Coast	19	98	6	7	.462	96	49	45	89	46	4.13
1981—Portland	P. Coast	23	153	12	6	.667	138	73	60	*135	68	3.53
1981—Pittsburgh	National	13	54	4	5	.444	51	23	20	30	23	3.33

— 237 —

Year Club	League	G.	IP.	W.	L.	Pct.	H.	R.	ER.	SO.	BB.	ERA.
1982—Portland y	P. Coast	28	190⅓	★16	9	.640	162	103	90	★172	94	4.26
1983—Texas z	American	42	67	3	6	.333	56	28	23	50	22	3.09
National League Totals		52	174	9	12	.429	177	89	83	108	58	4.29
American League Totals		67	186	6	17	.261	207	118	103	122	80	4.98
Major League Totals		119	360	15	29	.341	384	207	186	230	138	4.65

Signed as free agent by Pittsburgh Pirates' organization, November 25, 1971.

†On disabled list, July 13 to August 24, 1976.

‡Traded with Shortstop Mario Mendoza and Pitcher Rafael Vasquez to Seattle Mariners for Pitchers Enrique Romo and Rick Jones and Shortstop Tom McMillan, December 5, 1978.

§Traded to Pittsburgh Pirates' organization for a player to be named later, April 1, 1980; Seattle Mariners acquired Pitcher Larry Andersen to complete deal, October 29, 1980.

xOn disabled list, June 16 to July 6 and July 13 to August 3, 1980.

yDrafted by Texas Rangers, December 6, 1982.

zOn disabled list, August 19 to September 9, 1983.

ROBERT OLIVER JONES JR.
(Bob)

Born October 11, 1949, at Elkton, Md.
Height, 6.03. Weight, 200.
Throws and bats lefthanded.

Tied major league record for most two-base hits, inning (2), July 3, 1983 (fifteenth inning).
Tied for American Association lead in game-winning RBIs with 11 in 1981.

Year Club	League	Pos.	G.	AB.	R.	H.	2B.	3B.	HR.	RBI.	B.A.	PO.	A.	E.	F.A.
1967—Geneva	NYP	1B	19	60	5	13	2	1	0	2	.217	115	5	0	1.000
1968—Salisbury	W. Car.	OF-1B	102	354	33	87	11	5	5	39	.246	327	24	17	.954
1969—Burlington	Carol.	OF-1B	39	111	7	22	1	0	1	6	.198	73	3	3	.962
1969—Shelby†	W. Car.	OF-1B	20	74	9	20	3	0	1	7	.270	50	2	1	.981
1970—						(In Military Service)									
1971—Anderson	W. Car.	1B-OF	116	424	82	136	19	5	23	77	.321	721	27	10	.987
1972—Denver	A. A.	OF	118	345	46	99	15	6	5	46	.287	159	6	4	.976
1973—Spokane	P. C.	OF	121	437	57	121	25	7	9	71	.277	186	6	1	★.995
1974—Spokane	P. C.	OF	131	466	87	140	18	5	16	91	.300	221	9	5	.979
1974—Texas	Amer.	OF	2	5	0	0	0	0	0	0	.000	5	0	0	1.000
1975—Spokane	P. C.	OF-1B	109	404	69	112	12	6	17	67	.277	210	4	3	.986
1975—Texas	Amer.	OF	9	11	2	1	0	0	0	0	.091	6	0	0	1.000
1976—Sacramento‡	P. C.	OF	26	93	16	33	5	2	10	29	.355	51	4	1	.982
1976—California	Amer.	OF-DH	78	166	22	35	6	0	6	17	.211	98	6	1	.990
1977—California	Amer.	DH	14	17	3	3	0	0	1	3	.176	0	0	0	.000
1977—Salt Lake City	P. C.	OF-1B	94	353	71	120	28	10	18	85	.340	224	4	5	.979
1978—Salt Lake City§x	P. C.	OF-1B	122	460	79	141	31	6	14	102	.307	344	13	5	.986
1979-80—						(Did not play)									
1981—Wichita	A. A.	OF-1B	117	352	53	111	15	3	20	72	.315	332	19	2	.994
1981—Texas	Amer.	OF	10	34	4	9	1	0	3	7	.265	20	4	0	1.000
1982—Denver	A. A.	OF	82	261	44	83	19	5	12	51	.318	120	5	2	.984
1983—Oklahoma City	A. A.	1B	46	171	25	61	14	3	4	29	.357	268	22	2	.993
1983—Texas	Amer.	OF-1B	41	72	5	16	4	0	1	11	.222	24	0	0	1.000
Major League Totals			154	305	36	64	11	0	11	38	.210	153	10	1	.994

Selected by Washington Senators' organization in 36th round of free-agent draft, June 6, 1967.

†On military list, August 18, 1969 through February 15, 1971.

‡Sold on waivers to California Angels, May 17, 1976.

§On disabled list, July 11 to July 21, 1978.

xReleased, January 29, 1979; signed by Wichita (Texas Rangers' organization), December 18, 1980.

RICHARD MIRON JONES
(Ricky)

Born June 4, 1959, at Tupelo, Miss.
Height, 6.03. Weight, 190.
Throws and bats righthanded.
Attended Chipola Junior College, Marianna, Fla., and West
Georgia College, Carrollton, Ga.

Led International League shortstops in double plays with 101 and total chances with 689 in 1982.
Led Southern League shortstops in double plays with 75 in 1981.

Year Club	League	Pos.	G.	AB.	R.	H.	2B.	3B.	HR.	RBI.	B.A.	PO.	A.	E.	F.A.
1980—Bluefield	Appal.	OF-SS	59	199	27	55	9	3	6	33	.276	78	68	12	.924
1981—Charlotte	South.	SS	134	479	66	125	17	2	11	56	.261	175	402	38	.938
1982—Rochester	Int.	SS	★139	457	66	105	15	2	13	51	.230	221	★440	28	.959
1983—Rochester†	Int.	SS	95	339	28	78	16	1	7	38	.230	151	265	22	.950

Selected by Atlanta Braves' organization in 18th round of free-agent draft, June 8, 1976.

Selected by Baltimore Orioles' organization in 15th round of free-agent draft, June 3, 1980.

†On disabled list, May 18 to June 5, July 17 to July 27 and August 3 to August 13, 1983.

—DID YOU KNOW—

That Jesse Orosco of the Mets won both games of a July 31, 1983, doubleheader against Pittsburgh?

ROSS A. JONES

Born January 14, 1960, at Miami, Fla.
Height, 6.02. Weight, 185.
Throws and bats righthanded.
Attended Miami-Dade Community College-New World Center, Miami, Fla.,
and University of Miami, Coral Gables, Fla.

Year	Club	League	Pos.	G.	AB.	R.	H.	2B.	3B.	HR.	RBI.	B.A.	PO.	A.	E.	F.A.
1980—Vero Beach	Fla. St.		SS	70	223	35	59	14	3	4	37	.253	122	215	16	.955
1981—San Antonio	Texas		SS	129	444	75	118	17	2	5	43	.266	185	328	39	.929
1982—Albuquerque	P. C.		2B-SS	128	459	84	132	19	3	9	74	.288	273	350	24	.963
1983—Albuquerque†	P. C.		SS-2B	131	469	67	128	18	8	3	56	.273	217	434	36	.948

Selected by Los Angeles Dodgers' organization in 1st round (ninth player selected) of free-agent draft, June 3, 1980.
†Traded with Pitcher Sid Fernandez to New York Mets for Pitcher Carlos Diaz and a player to be named later, December 8, 1983; Los Angeles Dodgers acquired Infielder Bob Bailor to complete deal, December 9, 1983.

RUPPERT SANDERSON JONES

Born March 12, 1955, at Dallas, Tex.
Height, 5.10. Weight, 171.
Throws and bats lefthanded.

Tied major league records for most strikeouts, two consecutive games (8), July 16 and 17, 1982; most putouts by outfielder, game (12), May 16, 1978, 16 innings.
Tied American League record for most chances accepted by outfielder, game (12), May 16, 1978, 16 innings.
Tied for Pioneer League lead in double plays by outfielders with 1 in 1973.

Year	Club	League	Pos.	G.	AB.	R.	H.	2B.	3B.	HR.	RBI.	B.A.	PO.	A.	E.	F.A.
1973—Billings	Pion.		OF	61	193	45	58	10	4	4	31	.301	55	5	5	.923
1974—Waterloo	Midw.		OF	68	249	44	88	15	0	13	43	.353	94	7	3	.971
1974—San Jose	Calif.		OF	53	191	29	53	7	3	8	45	.277	101	2	4	.963
1975—Omaha	A. A.		OF	119	403	62	98	25	5	13	54	.243	171	15	*13	.935
1976—Omaha	A. A.		OF	102	359	65	94	15	9	19	73	.262	243	2	8	.968
1976—Kansas City†	Amer.		OF	28	51	9	11	1	1	1	7	.216	21	0	0	1.000
1977—Seattle	Amer.		OF	160	597	85	157	26	8	24	76	.263	465	11	9	.981
1978—Seattle‡	Amer.		OF	129	472	48	111	24	3	6	46	.235	393	10	6	.985
1979—Seattle§	Amer.		OF	●162	622	109	166	29	9	21	78	.267	453	13	5	.989
1980—New York xy	Amer.		OF	83	328	38	73	11	3	9	42	.223	246	4	3	.988
1981—San Diego	Nat.		OF	105	397	53	99	34	1	4	39	.249	295	9	2	.993
1982—San Diego z	Nat.		OF	116	424	69	120	20	2	12	61	.283	314	3	5	.984
1983—San Diego a	Nat.		OF-1B	133	335	42	78	12	3	12	49	.233	268	6	6	.979
American League Totals				562	2070	289	518	91	24	61	249	.250	1578	38	23	.986
National League Totals				354	1156	164	297	66	6	28	149	.257	877	18	13	.986
Major League Totals				916	3226	453	815	157	30	89	398	.253	2455	56	36	.986

Selected by Kansas City Royals' organization in 3rd round of free-agent draft, June 5, 1973.
†Selected by Seattle Mariners in American League expansion draft, November 5, 1976.
‡On disabled list, June 16 to July 20, 1978.
§Traded with Pitcher Jim Lewis to New York Yankees for Outfielder Juan Beniquez, Pitchers Jim Beattie and Rick Anderson and Catcher Jerry Narron, November 1, 1979.
xOn disabled list, May 27 to July 10 and August 26, 1980 through remainder of season.
yTraded with Outfielder Joe Lefebvre and Pitchers Tim Lollar and Chris Welsh to San Diego Padres for Outfielder Jerry Mumphrey and Pitcher John Pacella, April 1, 1981.
zOn supplemental disabled list, August 6 to August 21, 1982.
aGranted free agency, November 7, 1983.

ALL-STAR GAME RECORD

Year	League	Pos.	AB.	R.	H.	2B.	3B.	HR.	RBI.	B.A.	PO.	A.	E.	F.A.
1977—American		PH	1	0	0	0	0	0	0	.000	0	0	0	.000
1982—National		PH	1	1	1	0	1	0	0	1.000	0	0	0	.000
All-Star Game Totals			2	1	1	0	1	0	0	.500	0	0	0	.000

MICHAEL JORGENSEN
(Mike)

Born August 16, 1948, at Passaic, N. J.
Height, 6.00. Weight, 192.
Throws and bats lefthanded.
Attended St. John's University, Jamaica, N. Y.

Tied for International League lead in sacrifice flies with 8 in 1969.
Named first baseman on THE SPORTING NEWS National League All-Star fielding team, 1973.

Year	Club	League	Pos.	G.	AB.	R.	H.	2B.	3B.	HR.	RBI.	B.A.	PO.	A.	E.	F.A.
1966—Marion	Appal.		1B	46	150	30	47	0	0	8	37	.313	298	16	4	.987
1967—Winter Haven	Fla. St.		1B-OF	84	302	56	89	11	4	5	41	.295	639	29	7	.990
1968—New York	Nat.		1B	8	14	0	2	1	0	0	0	.143	32	1	0	1.000
1968—Memphis	Texas		1B	28	100	7	16	1	2	0	10	.160	211	11	0	1.000
1968—Raleigh-Dur.	Carol.		1B-OF	57	213	34	67	13	4	3	21	.315	311	25	3	.991
1969—Tidewater	Int.		1B	105	359	75	104	15	5	21	69	.290	882	50	5	*.995
1970—New York	Nat.		1B-OF	76	87	15	17	3	1	3	4	.195	145	12	3	.981
1971—Tidewater	Int.		1B-OF	65	228	50	78	12	1	15	41	.342	157	7	3	.982
1971—New York†	Nat.		OF-1B	45	118	16	26	1	1	5	11	.220	64	2	3	.957
1972—Montreal‡	Nat.		1B-OF	113	372	48	86	12	3	13	47	.231	801	57	6	.993
1973—Montreal	Nat.		*1B-OF	138	413	49	95	16	2	9	47	.230	1002	80	5	*.995

Year Club	League	Pos.	G.	AB.	R.	H.	2B.	3B.	HR.	RBI.	B.A.	PO.	A.	E.	F.A.
1974—Montreal	Nat.	1B-OF	131	287	45	89	16	1	11	59	.310	653	54	1	.999
1975—Montreal	Nat.	1B-OF	144	445	58	116	18	0	18	67	.261	1153	91	7	.994
1976—Montreal	Nat.	1B-OF	125	343	36	87	13	0	6	23	.254	651	58	8	.989
1977—Montreal§	Nat.	1B	19	20	3	4	1	0	0	0	.200	23	4	0	1.000
1977—Oakland xy	Amer.	1B-OF	66	203	18	50	4	1	8	32	.246	365	32	4	.990
1978—Texas	Amer.	1B-OF	96	97	20	19	3	0	1	9	.196	317	31	2	.994
1979—Texas za	Amer.	1B-OF	90	157	21	35	7	0	6	16	.223	320	31	4	.989
1980—New York	Nat.	1B-OF	119	321	43	82	11	0	7	43	.255	562	37	4	.993
1981—New York	Nat.	1B-OF	86	122	8	25	5	2	3	15	.205	143	9	1	.993
1982—New York	Nat.	1B-OF	120	114	16	29	6	0	2	14	.254	131	5	2	.986
1983—N.Y.b-Atl.	Nat.	1B-OF	95	72	10	18	4	0	2	11	.250	81	6	0	1.000
National League Totals			1219	2728	347	676	107	10	79	341	.248	5441	396	40	.993
American League Totals			252	457	59	104	14	1	15	57	.228	1002	94	10	.991
Major League Totals			1471	3185	406	780	121	11	94	398	.245	6443	490	50	.993

Selected by New York Mets' organization in free-agent draft, June 30, 1966.

†Traded with Infielder Tim Foli and Outfielder Ken Singleton to Montreal Expos for Outfielder Rusty Staub, April 6, 1972.

‡On military list, July 7 to July 10 and July 20 to August 6, 1972.

§Traded to Oakland Athletics for Pitcher Stan Bahnsen, May 22, 1977.

xOn disabled list, July 11 to August 31, 1977.

yGranted free agency, October 20, 1977; signed by Texas Rangers, January 21, 1978.

zOn supplemental disabled list, June 1 to July 1, 1979.

aTraded to New York Mets, October 23, 1979; completing deal in which the Texas Rangers acquired First Baseman Willie Montanez for two players to be named later, August 12, 1979; New York organization acquired Pitcher Ed Lynch as partial completion of deal, September 18, 1979.

bSold to Atlanta Braves, June 15, 1983.

EDWARD JAMES JURAK

Name pronounced YOU-rack.

(Ed)

Born October 24, 1957, at Los Angeles, Calif.
Height, 6.02. Weight, 180.
Throws and bats righthanded.

Led Eastern League shortstops in double plays with 76 in 1979.

Year Club	League	Pos.	G.	AB.	R.	H.	2B.	3B.	HR.	RBI.	B.A.	PO.	A.	E.	F.A.
1975—Elmira	NYP	SS	68	250	41	63	9	3	0	25	.252	104	192	*43	.873
1976—Winston-Salem	Carol.	SS	113	401	49	88	6	2	4	35	.219	168	346	*55	.903
1977—Bristol	East.	SS	123	441	74	116	12	8	1	36	.263	173	345	26	.952
1978—Pawtucket	Int.	SS-3B	23	46	9	12	1	1	0	6	.261	11	34	8	.849
1978—Winter Haven†	Fla. St.	SS-3B-1B	38	139	14	37	0	1	0	11	.266	49	99	16	.902
1979—Bristol	East.	SS	135	435	50	96	17	2	0	41	.221	*208	*374	*40	.936
1980—Pawtucket‡	Int.	SS-3B	83	221	16	58	8	1	3	31	.262	72	130	19	.914
1981—Bristol§	East.	SS-3B-2B	87	297	63	101	19	3	1	25	*.340	114	194	29	.914
1981—Pawtucket	Int.	SS	23	90	13	27	3	2	1	9	.300	39	81	10	.923
1982—Pawtucket	Int.	3B-SS	81	284	39	84	14	1	9	43	.296	53	177	17	.931
1982—Boston	Amer.	3B-OF	12	21	3	7	0	0	0	7	.333	7	17	2	.923
1983—Boston	Amer.	S-1-3-2	75	159	19	44	8	4	0	18	.277	197	117	11	.966
Major League Totals			87	180	22	51	8	4	0	25	.283	204	134	13	.963

Selected by Boston Red Sox' organization in 3rd round of free-agent draft, June 4, 1975.

†On disabled list, May 4 to June 16, 1978.

‡On disabled list, April 16 to April 28 and May 28 to June 7, 1980.

§On disabled list, June 10 to July 4, 1981.

JAMES LEE KAAT

Name pronounced Cott.

(Jim)

Born November 7, 1938, at Zeeland, Mich.
Height, 6.05. Weight, 195.
Throws and bats lefthanded.
Attended Hope College, Holland, Mich.

Established major league records for most sacrifice flies allowed, lifetime (141); most games taken out as starting pitcher, season (35), 1965; most years pitched (25); most consecutive years pitched (25).

Tied major league record for most home runs allowed, bases filled, lifetime (9).

Established American League records for most games lost by lefthanded pitcher, career (191); most sacrifice flies allowed, career (108); most years leading league in hits allowed (4), 1965, 1966, 1967 and 1975.

Led American League in complete games with 19 in 1966.

Led American League pitchers in games started with 42 in 1965 and 41 in 1966.

Led American League in hit batsmen with 11 in 1961 and 18 in 1966.

Led American League in wild pitches with 13 in 1962 and tied for lead with 10 in 1961.

Tied for American League lead in shutouts with 5 in 1962.

Led Pioneer League pitchers in games started with 30, shutouts with 5, and tied for lead in complete games with 15 in 1958.

Named American League Pitcher of the Year by THE SPORTING NEWS, 1966.
Named lefthanded pitcher on THE SPORTING NEWS American League All-Star Team, 1975.
Named pitcher on THE SPORTING NEWS American League All-Star Team, 1966.
Named pitcher on THE SPORTING NEWS National League All-Star fielding team, 1976 and 1977.
Named pitcher on THE SPORTING NEWS American League All-Star fielding team, 1962 through 1975.

Year	Club	League	G.	IP.	W.	L.	Pct.	H.	R.	ER.	SO.	BB.	ERA.
1957—Superior	Neb. St.	14	73	5	6	.455	65	45	30	95	35	3.70
1958—Missoula	Pioneer	39	★223	16	9	.640	189	108	74	★245	118	★2.99
1959—Chattanooga	Southern	24	134	8	8	.500	126	71	61	132	73	4.10
1959—Washington	American	3	5	0	2	.000	7	9	7	2	4	12.60
1960—Washington	American	13	50	1	5	.167	48	39	31	25	31	5.58
1960—Charleston	Am. Assoc.	30	146	7	10	.412	154	80	62	106	51	3.82
1961—Minnesota	American	36	201	9	17	.346	188	105	87	122	82	3.90
1962—Minnesota	American	39	269	18	14	.563	243	106	94	173	75	3.14
1963—Minnesota	American	31	178	10	10	.500	195	96	83	105	38	4.20
1964—Minnesota	American	36	243	17	11	.607	231	100	87	171	60	3.22
1965—Minnesota	American	45	264	18	11	.621	★267	★121	83	154	63	2.83
1966—Minnesota	American	41	★305	★25	13	.658	★271	114	93	205	55	2.74
1967—Minnesota	American	42	263	16	13	.552	★269	110	89	211	42	3.05
1968—Minnesota	American	30	208	14	12	.538	192	78	68	130	40	2.94
1969—Minnesota	American	40	242	14	13	.519	252	114	94	139	75	3.50
1970—Minnesota	American	45	230	14	10	.583	244	110	91	120	58	3.56
1971—Minnesota	American	39	260	13	14	.481	275	104	96	137	47	3.32
1972—Minnesota†	American	15	113	10	2	.833	94	36	26	64	20	2.07
1973—Minnesota‡-Chicago	American	36	224	15	13	.536	250	124	109	109	43	4.38
1974—Chicago	American	42	277	21	13	.618	263	106	90	142	63	2.92
1975—Chicago§	American	43	304	20	14	.588	★321	121	105	142	77	3.11
1976—Philadelphia	National	38	228	12	14	.462	241	95	88	83	32	3.47
1977—Philadelphia	National	35	160	6	11	.353	211	100	96	55	40	5.40
1978—Philadelphia	National	26	140	8	5	.615	150	67	64	48	32	4.11
1979—Philadelphia x	National	3	8	1	0	1.000	9	4	4	2	5	4.50
1979—New York y	American	40	58	2	3	.400	64	29	25	23	14	3.88
1980—New York z	American	4	5	0	1	.000	8	5	4	1	4	7.20
1980—St. Louis	National	49	130	8	7	.533	140	61	55	36	33	3.81
1981—St. Louis	National	41	53	6	6	.500	60	25	20	8	17	3.40
1982—St. Louis	National	62	75	5	3	.625	79	40	34	35	23	4.08
1983—St. Louis a	National	24	34⅔	0	0	.000	48	19	15	19	10	3.89
American League Totals		620	3699	237	191	.554	3682	1627	1362	2175	891	3.31
National League Totals		278	828⅔	46	46	.500	938	411	376	286	192	4.08
Major League Totals		898	4527⅔	283	237	.544	4620	2038	1738	2461	1083	3.45

Signed as free agent by Washington Senators' organization, June 17, 1957.
†On disabled list, July 6 to September 27, 1972.
‡Sold on waivers to Chicago White Sox, August 15, 1973.
§Traded with Shortstop Mike Buskey to Philadelphia Phillies for Outfielder-Infielder Alan Bannister and Pitchers Dick Ruthven and Roy Thomas, December 10, 1975.
xSold to New York Yankees, May 11, 1979.
yGranted free agency, November 1, 1979; re-signed by Yankees, April 1, 1980.
zSold to St. Louis Cardinals, April 30, 1980.
aReleased, July 6, 1983.

CHAMPIONSHIP SERIES RECORD

Year	Club	League	G.	IP.	W.	L.	Pct.	H.	R.	ER.	SO.	BB.	ERA.
1970—Minnesota	American	1	2	0	1	.000	6	4	2	1	2	9.00
1976—Philadelphia	National	1	6	0	0	.000	2	2	2	1	2	3.00
Championship Series Totals		2	8	0	1	.000	8	6	4	2	4	4.50

WORLD SERIES RECORD

Established World Series records for most putouts, pitcher, seven-game Series (5), 1965 and most putouts, game, nine innings, pitcher (5), October 7, 1965.

Year	Club	League	G.	IP.	W.	L.	Pct.	H.	R.	ER.	SO.	BB.	ERA.
1965—Minnesota	American	3	14⅓	1	2	.333	18	7	6	6	2	3.77
1982—St. Louis	National	4	2⅓	0	0	.000	4	1	1	2	2	3.86
World Series Totals		7	16⅔	1	2	.333	22	8	7	8	4	3.78

ALL-STAR GAME RECORD

Year	League	IP.	W.	L.	Pct.	H.	R.	ER.	SO.	BB.	ERA.
1966—American		2	0	0	.000	3	1	1	1	0	4.50
1975—American		2	0	0	.000	0	0	0	0	0	0.00
All-Star Game Totals		4	0	0	.000	3	1	1	1	0	2.25

Member of American League All-Star Team in 1962 (second game); did not play.

—DID YOU KNOW—

That pitcher Jim Kaat is one of only 17 men to have played major league baseball in four decades?

CURT GERRARD KAUFMAN

Born July 19, 1957, at Omaha, Neb.
Height, 6.02. Weight, 175.
Throws and bats righthanded.
Attended Iowa State University, Ames, Iowa.

Led International League in saves with 25 and tied for lead in games finished in relief with 41 in 1983.
Tied for New York-Pennsylvania League lead in saves with 9 in 1979.

Year Club	League	G.	IP.	W.	L.	Pct.	H.	R.	ER.	SO.	BB.	ERA.
1979—Oneonta	NYP	17	30	4	1	.800	10	3	3	50	16	0.90
1980—Ft. Lauderdale	Florida St.	27	65	5	1	.833	41	10	7	63	18	0.97
1980—Nashville	Southern	11	46	6	2	.750	43	24	23	35	29	4.50
1981—Nashville	Southern	44	78	9	5	.643	62	28	25	77	33	2.88
1982—Columbus	Int'national	55	91	6	3	.667	76	40	35	103	47	3.46
1982—New York	American	7	8⅔	1	0	1.000	9	5	5	1	6	5.19
1983—Columbus	Int'national	50	78⅔	6	3	.667	60	24	24	93	33	2.75
1983—New York†	American	4	8⅔	0	0	.000	10	3	3	8	4	3.12
Major League Totals		11	17⅓	1	0	1.000	19	8	8	9	10	4.15

Signed as free agent by New York Yankees' organization, July 10, 1979.
†Traded with cash to California Angels for Shortstop Tim Foli, December 8, 1983.

ROBERT HENRY KEARNEY
(Bob)

Born October 3, 1956, at San Antonio, Tex.
Height, 6.00. Weight, 190.
Throws and bats righthanded.
Attended University of Texas, Austin, Tex.

Tied for Pioneer League lead in double plays by catchers with 4 in 1977.

Year Club	League	Pos.	G.	AB.	R.	H.	2B.	3B.	HR.	RBI.	B.A.	PO.	A.	E.	F.A.
1977—Great Falls	Pion.	C	58	211	49	50	7	0	7	34	.237	★417	★56	10	.979
1978—Cedar Rapids	Midw.	C	28	89	8	24	3	0	1	15	.270	182	23	2	.990
1978—Waterbury	East.	C	38	125	10	21	3	0	1	8	.168	195	33	9	.962
1979—Shreveport	Texas	C	63	224	27	60	9	1	4	24	.268	312	49	7	.981
1979—Phoenix	P. C.	C	38	124	11	17	2	1	2	10	.137	183	27	7	.968
1979—San Francisco	Nat.	C	2	0	0	0	0	0	0	0	.000	0	0	0	.000
1980—Phoenix†	P. C.	C	92	298	42	68	8	3	2	24	.228	358	68	11	.975
1981—Tacoma	P. C.	C	86	278	38	70	13	2	3	29	.252	487	73	9	.984
1981—Oakland	Amer.	C	1	0	0	0	0	0	0	0	.000	0	0	0	.000
1982—Oakland	Amer.	C	22	71	7	12	3	0	0	5	.169	114	14	4	.970
1982—Tacoma	P.C.	C	115	388	41	98	13	3	7	55	.253	589	93	9	.987
1983—Oakland‡	Amer.	C	108	298	33	76	11	0	8	32	.255	437	41	9	.982
National League Totals			2	0	0	0	0	0	0	0	.000	0	0	0	.000
American League Totals			131	369	40	88	14	0	8	37	.238	551	55	13	.979
Major League Totals			133	369	40	88	14	0	8	37	.238	551	55	13	.979

Selected by San Francisco Giants' organization in 14th round of free-agent draft, June 7, 1977.
†Drafted by Tacoma (Oakland A's organization), December 9, 1980.
‡Traded with Pitcher Dave Beard to Seattle Mariners for Pitcher Bill Caudill and a player to be named later, November 21, 1983; Oakland A's acquired Pitcher Darrel Akerfelds to complete deal, December 7, 1983.

CHARLES PATRICK KEEDY
(Pat)

Born January 10, 1959, at Birmingham, Ala.
Height, 6.04. Weight, 205.
Throws and bats righthanded.
Attended Auburn University, Auburn, Ala.

Led Eastern League third basemen in double plays with 25 in 1981.

Year Club	League	Pos.	G.	AB.	R.	H.	2B.	3B.	HR.	RBI.	B.A.	PO.	A.	E.	F.A.
1979—Salinas	Calif.	3B-SS	52	125	22	26	3	0	4	15	.208	47	109	9	.945
1980—El Paso	Texas	SS-3B	26	98	11	14	3	0	1	10	.143	29	87	14	.892
1980—Salinas†	Calif.	SS-3B	42	118	16	26	4	0	4	17	.220	32	89	11	.917
1981—Holyoke	East.	3B-2B-1B	107	367	45	90	14	2	6	34	.245	63	239	23	.929
1982—Holyoke	East.	3B-SS	125	437	68	108	19	6	19	73	.247	91	279	30	.925
1983—Edmonton‡	P. C.	3-O-1-2-S	66	210	38	47	13	1	14	40	.224	46	123	17	.909

Selected by Chicago White Sox' organization in 13th round of free-agent draft, June 8, 1976.
Selected by California Angels' organization in 5th round of free-agent draft, June 5, 1979.
†On disabled list, August 13, 1980 through remainder of season.
‡On disabled list, May 17 to June 17 and July 5 to July 20, 1983.

JEFFREY BRUCE KEENER
(Jeff)

Born January 14, 1959, at Pana, Ill.
Height, 6.00. Weight, 170.
Throws right and bats lefthanded.
Attended Southeastern Illinois Junior College, Harrisburg, Ill.,
and University of Kentucky, Lexington, Ky.

Led International League in intentional bases on balls issued with 15 in 1983.

Year Club	League	G.	IP.	W.	L.	Pct.	H.	R.	ER.	SO.	BB.	ERA.
1981—Arkansas	Texas	30	42	0	3	.000	29	16	9	42	15	1.93
1982—Arkansas	Texas	24	38	4	3	.571	29	11	10	39	14	2.37
1982—St. Louis	National	19	22⅓	1	1	.500	19	8	4	25	19	1.61
1982—Louisville	Am. Assoc.	9	10⅔	1	0	1.000	15	8	7	6	5	5.91
1983—Louisville	Am. Assoc.	*60	96⅓	11	5	.688	84	43	42	69	70	3.92
1983—St. Louis	National	4	4⅓	0	0	.000	6	4	4	4	1	8.31
Major League Totals		23	26⅔	1	1	.500	25	12	8	29	20	2.70

Selected by St. Louis Cardinals' organization in 6th round of free-agent draft, June 8, 1981.

BRYAN KEITH KELLY

Born February 24, 1959, at Silver Springs, Md.
Height, 6.03. Weight, 195.
Throws and bats righthanded.
Attended Valencia Community College, Orlando, Fla., and
University of Alabama, Tuscaloosa, Ala.

Year Club	League	G.	IP.	W.	L.	Pct.	H.	R.	ER.	SO.	BB.	ERA.
1981—Macon	S. Atlantic	11	53	4	3	.571	50	30	27	46	45	4.58
1981—Lakeland	Florida St.	2	11	1	1	.500	10	3	3	8	7	2.45
1982—Lakeland	Florida St.	11	64	5	6	.455	55	36	30	39	51	4.22
1982—Birmingham	Southern	16	95⅓	8	3	.727	78	44	38	91	74	3.59
1983—Evansville†	Am. Assoc.	14	57	2	4	.333	64	50	39	41	60	6.16

Selected by Montreal Expos' organization in 8th round of free-agent draft, January 8, 1980.
Selected by Detroit Tigers' organization in 6th round of free-agent draft, June 8, 1981.
†On disabled list, April 15 to May 31, 1983.

STEVEN F. KEMP
(Steve)

Born August 7, 1954, at San Angelo, Tex.
Height, 6.00. Weight, 190.
Throws and bats lefthanded.
Attended University of Southern California, Los Angeles, Calif.
Received reported $50,000 bonus to sign with Detroit Tigers, 1976.

Year Club	League	Pos.	G.	AB.	R.	H.	2B.	3B.	HR.	RBI.	B.A.	PO.	A.	E.	F.A.
1976—Montgomery	South.	OF-1B	73	256	41	74	17	2	8	43	.289	91	4	2	.979
1976—Evansville	A. A.	OF	52	171	37	66	14	3	11	38	.386	91	2	5	.945
1977—Detroit	Amer.	OF	151	552	75	142	29	4	18	88	.257	252	10	5	.981
1978—Detroit	Amer.	OF	159	582	75	161	18	4	15	79	.277	325	11	8	.977
1979—Detroit	Amer.	OF	134	490	88	156	26	3	26	105	.318	229	12	6	.976
1980—Detroit	Amer.	OF	135	508	88	149	23	3	21	101	.293	197	4	1	.995
1981—Detroit†	Amer.	OF	105	372	52	103	18	4	9	49	.277	207	4	3	.986
1982—Chicago‡	Amer.	OF	160	580	91	166	23	1	19	98	.286	280	6	7	.976
1983—New York§	Amer.	OF	109	373	53	90	17	3	12	49	.241	215	5	3	.987
Major League Totals			953	3457	522	967	154	22	120	569	.280	1705	52	33	.982

Selected by Detroit Tigers' organization in 1st round (first player selected) of free-agent draft, January 7, 1976.
†Traded to Chicago White Sox for Outfielder Chet Lemon, November 27, 1981.
‡Granted free agency, November 10, 1982; signed by New York Yankees as Type A player, December 8, 1982.
(Pitcher Steve Mura was selected from player compensation pool by Chicago White Sox, January 26, 1983.)
§On emergency disabled list, September 15, 1983 through remainder of season.

ALL-STAR GAME RECORD

Year League	Pos.	AB.	R.	H.	2B.	3B.	HR.	RBI.	B.A.	PO.	A.	E.	F.A.
1979—American	PH	1	0	0	0	0	0	0	.000	0	0	0	.000

JEFFREY LEE KENAGA
Name pronounced Ken-AY-ga.
(Jeff)

Born July 12, 1957, at Detroit, Mich.
Height, 6.00. Weight, 170.
Throws right and bats lefthanded.
Attended Western Michigan University, Kalamazoo, Mich.

Year Club	League	Pos.	G.	AB.	R.	H.	2B.	3B.	HR.	RBI.	B.A.	PO.	A.	E.	F.A.
1979—Lakeland	Fla. St.	OF	60	187	17	44	8	1	1	21	.235	77	2	0	1.000
1980—Montgomery	South.	OF-1B	124	450	58	118	27	0	11	56	.262	143	6	9	.943
1981—Birmingham	South.	OF	99	376	57	113	20	3	16	64	.301	40	4	1	.978
1981—Evansville	A. A.	OF	22	61	4	16	2	0	0	3	.262	28	1	2	.935
1982—Evansville	A. A.	OF	116	410	60	107	29	5	18	68	.261	149	5	3	.981
1983—Evansville	A. A.	OF	112	365	43	103	21	5	14	36	.282	107	3	7	.940

Selected by Milwaukee Brewers' organization in 17th round of free-agent draft, June 4, 1975.
Selected by Detroit Tigers' organization in 15th round of free-agent draft, June 5, 1979.

JUNIOR RAYMOND KENNEDY

Born August 9, 1950, at Fort Gibson, Okla.
Height, 6.00. Weight, 185.
Throws and bats righthanded.
Attended Bakersfield College, Bakersfield, Calif.
Brother of James Kennedy, infielder with St. Louis Cardinals, 1970.

Led American Association second basemen in fielding percentage with .976 in 1976.
Led International League shortstops in double plays with 80 in 1972.
Tied for Northern League lead in caught stealing with 6 in 1968.
Received reported $50,000 bonus to sign with Baltimore Orioles, 1968.

Year Club	League	Pos.	G.	AB.	R.	H.	2B.	3B.	HR.	RBI.	B.A.	PO.	A.	E.	F.A.
1968—Aberdeen	North.	SS	65	225	32	59	5	0	0	22	.262	68	186	*33	.885
1969—Stockton	Calif.	SS	115	375	38	99	16	1	2	34	.264	159	332	*47	.913
1970—Dallas-Ft. Wth.†	Texas	2B	3	9	1	3	0	0	0	2	.333	7	14	0	1.000
1971—Dallas-Ft. Wth.	Texas	SS	118	420	58	95	12	1	2	29	.226	198	310	34	.937
1972—Rochester	Int.	SS	123	388	41	93	14	5	3	33	.240	178	343	33	.940
1973—Rochester‡	Int.	SS	58	196	40	43	7	1	1	15	.219	100	159	21	.925
1973—Indianapolis§x	A. A.	SS	46	142	21	40	3	3	0	5	.282	64	140	4	.981
1974—Indianapolis	A. A.	2B-3B	84	271	50	77	9	4	1	22	.284	159	232	15	.963
1974—Cincinnati	Nat.	2B-3B	22	19	2	3	0	0	0	0	.158	15	13	2	.933
1975—Indianapolis y	A. A.	SS-2B	116	405	49	112	13	5	3	46	.277	234	278	18	.966
1976—Indianapolis	A. A.	2B-SS	122	348	53	87	15	4	2	44	.250	226	320	16	.975
1977—Phoenix	P. C.	SS-2B-3B	135	481	88	152	16	9	0	76	.316	282	529	29	.965
1978—Cincinnati	Nat.	2B-3B	89	157	22	40	2	2	0	11	.255	94	142	5	.979
1979—Cincinnati	Nat.	2B-SS-3B	83	220	29	60	7	0	1	17	.273	105	162	5	.982
1980—Cincinnati	Nat.	2B	104	337	31	88	16	3	1	34	.261	200	303	6	.988
1981—Cincinnati z	Nat.	2B-3B	27	44	5	11	1	0	0	5	.250	22	32	1	.982
1982—Chicago	Nat.	2B-SS-3B	105	242	22	53	3	1	2	25	.219	138	228	12	.968
1983—Chicago a	Nat.	2B-3B-SS	17	22	3	3	0	0	0	3	.136	12	17	0	1.000
Major League Totals			447	1041	114	258	29	6	4	95	.248	586	897	31	.980

Selected by Baltimore Orioles' organization in 1st round (10th player selected) of free-agent draft, June 7, 1968.
†On disabled list, May 19 to September 7, 1970.
‡Option transferred to Indianapolis in exchange for Infielder Tim Nordbrook, June 14, 1973.
§On disabled list, July 5 to August 3, 1973.
xTraded with Outfielder Merv Rettenmund and Catcher Bill Wood to Cincinnati Reds for Pitcher Ross Grimsley and Catcher Wally Williams, December 4, 1973.
yOn disabled list, June 8 to June 26, 1975.
zSold to Chicago Cubs for an estimated $50,000, October 23, 1981.
aReleased, August 1, 1983.

TERRENCE EDWARD KENNEDY
(Terry)

Born June 4, 1956, at Euclid, O.
Height, 6.04. Weight, 220.
Throws right and bats lefthanded.
Attended Florida State University, Tallahassee, Fla.
Son of Bob Kennedy, third baseman-outfielder with Chicago AL, Cleveland, Baltimore, Detroit and Brooklyn, 1939 through 1957; scout, Cleveland, 1958 through 1961; minor league manager, Chicago Cubs' organization, 1962; coach, Chicago Cubs, 1963 and 1964; Chicago Cubs executive, 1965; minor league manager, Los Angeles Dodgers' organization, 1966; coach, Atlanta Braves, 1967; manager, Oakland A's, 1968; Director of Player Development, St. Louis Cardinals, 1969 through 1976; Executive Vice President, Chicago Cubs, 1977 through 1981, and Houston Astros Vice-President-Baseball Operations since 1982; brother of Bob Kennedy Jr., pitcher in St. Louis Cardinals' organization, 1971 through 1975; scout, Seattle Mariners, 1976; scout, Chicago Cubs, 1977 through 1981, and scout with Houston Astros since 1982.

Tied National League record for most two-base hits by catcher, season (40), 1982.
Led National League catchers in double plays with 12 in 1981 and tied for lead with 11 in 1982.
Named catcher on THE SPORTING NEWS National League Silver Slugger team, 1983.
Named College Player of the Year by THE SPORTING NEWS, 1977.
Received reported $100,000 bonus to sign with St. Louis Cardinals, 1977.

Year Club	League	Pos.	G.	AB.	R.	H.	2B.	3B.	HR.	RBI.	B.A.	PO.	A.	E.	F.A.
1977—Johnson City	Appal.	C-1B	12	39	14	23	7	2	3	15	.590	66	3	1	.986
1977—St. Petersburg	Fla. St.	C	45	166	22	41	8	0	4	22	.247	168	22	6	.969
1978—Arkansas	Texas	C-OF	69	239	55	69	14	0	10	54	.289	365	30	7	.983
1978—Springfield	A. A.	C-1B	64	230	35	76	13	0	10	46	.330	331	26	7	.981
1978—St. Louis	Nat.	C	10	29	0	5	0	0	0	2	.172	46	4	1	.980
1979—Springfield	A. A.	C	84	294	35	86	18	1	13	64	.293	434	38	13	.973
1979—St. Louis	Nat.	C	33	109	11	31	7	0	2	17	.284	135	7	1	.993
1980—St. Louis†	Nat.	C-OF	84	248	28	63	12	3	4	34	.254	231	22	7	.973
1981—San Diego	Nat.	C	101	382	32	115	24	1	2	41	.301	465	63	*20	.964
1982—San Diego	Nat.	C-1B	153	562	75	166	42	1	21	97	.295	777	66	9	.989
1983—San Diego	Nat.	C-1B	149	549	47	156	27	2	17	98	.284	807	82	12	.987
Major League Totals			530	1879	193	536	112	7	46	289	.285	2461	244	50	.982

Selected by St. Louis Cardinals' organization in 1st round (sixth player selected) of free-agent draft, June 7, 1977.
†Traded with Catcher Steve Swisher, Pitchers John Littlefield, Al Olmsted, Kim Seaman and John Urrea and Infielder Mike Phillips to San Diego Padres for Pitchers Rollie Fingers and Bob Shirley, Catcher-First Baseman Gene Tenace and a player to be named later, December 8, 1980; St. Louis Cardinals' organization acquired catcher Bob Geren to complete deal, December 10, 1980.

Year League	Pos.	AB.	R.	H.	2B.	3B.	HR.	RBI.	B.A.	PO.	A.	E.	F.A.
1981—National..	PH	1	0	0	0	0	0	0	.000	0	0	0	.000

Member of National League All-Star Team in 1983; did not play.

MATTHEW LON KEOUGH

Name pronounced KEE-oh.

(Matt)

Born July 3, 1955, at Pomona, Calif.
Height, 6.02. Weight, 175.
Throws and bats righthanded.
Attended University of California-Los Angeles, Los Angeles, Calif.
Son of Marty Keough, outfielder-first baseman with Boston, Cleveland, Washington, Cincinnati,
Atlanta and Chicago N.L., 1956 through 1966; minor league manager, San Diego Padres' organization,
1970; scout, San Diego Padres, 1969 through 1976; scout, Los Angeles Dodgers,
1977 through 1979; and scout with St. Louis Cardinals since 1980; nephew of Joe Keough, outfielder with
Oakland A's, Kansas City Royals and Chicago White Sox, 1968 through 1973.

Tied major league record for most consecutive games lost, start of season (14), 1979.
Led American League in home runs allowed with 38 in 1982.
Tied for California League lead in sacrifice flies with 9 in 1975.
Named American League Comeback Player of the Year by The Sporting News, 1980.

Year Club	League	G.	IP.	W.	L.	Pct.	H.	R.	ER.	SO.	BB.	ERA.
1976—Chattanooga...................	Southern	2	2	0	0	.000	1	0	0	2	0	0.00
1977—Chattanooga...................	Southern	26	175	9	12	.429	162	87	74	★153	67	3.81
1977—Oakland...........................	American	7	43	1	3	.250	39	25	23	23	22	4.81
1978—Oakland...........................	American	32	197	8	15	.348	178	90	71	108	85	3.24
1979—Oakland...........................	American	30	177	2	17	.105	220	115	99	95	78	5.03
1980—Oakland...........................	American	34	250	16	13	.552	218	94	81	121	94	2.92
1981—Oakland...........................	American	19	140	10	6	.625	125	56	53	60	45	3.41
1982—Oakland...........................	American	34	209⅓	11	●18	.379	233	★144	★133	75	101	5.72
1983—Oakland†-New York...................	American	26	99⅔	5	7	.417	109	71	59	54	51	5.33
Major League Totals...............................		182	1116	53	79	.402	1122	595	519	536	476	4.19

Selected by Oakland A's organization in 7th round of free-agent draft, June 5, 1973.
†Traded to New York Yankees for First Baseman Marshall Brant and Pitcher Ben Callahan, June 15, 1983.

CHAMPIONSHIP SERIES RECORD

Year Club	League	G.	IP.	W.	L.	Pct.	H.	R.	ER.	SO.	BB.	ERA.
1981—Oakland................	American	1	8⅓	0	1	.000	7	2	1	4	6	1.08

ALL-STAR GAME RECORD

Year League	IP.	W.	L.	Pct.	H.	R.	ER.	SO.	BB.	ERA.
1978—American	⅓	0	0	.000	1	0	0	0	0	0.00

RECORD AS INFIELDER

Led Southern League third basemen in putouts with 110 and assists with 252 in 1976.
Led California League shortstops in errors with 56 in 1975.

Year Club	League	Pos.	G.	AB.	R.	H.	2B.	3B.	HR.	RBI.	B.A.	PO.	A.	E.	F.A.
1974—Burlington.............	Midw.	SS-1B	98	323	31	64	14	2	4	24	.198	143	207	34	.911
1975—Modesto	Calif.	SS-3B	123	445	73	135	★34	2	13	81	.303	191	312	57	.898
1976—Chattanooga	South.	3-S-O-1-P	124	420	43	88	13	3	6	52	.210	125	274	25	.941

KURT DAVID KEPSHIRE

Born July 3, 1959, at Bridgeport, Conn.
Height, 6.02. Weight, 195.
Throws right and bats lefthanded.
Attended University of New Haven, New Haven, Conn.

Tied for Pioneer League lead in intentional bases on balls issued with 4 in 1979.

Year Club	League	G.	IP.	W.	L.	Pct.	H.	R.	ER.	SO.	BB.	ERA.
1979—Billings...............................	Pioneer	24	50	4	0	1.000	30	16	14	57	27	2.52
1980—Tampa................................	Florida St.	29	54	5	4	.556	48	20	12	26	19	2.00
1980—Eugene..............................	Northwest	8	42	3	3	.500	54	36	29	18	15	6.21
1981—Cedar Rapids...................	Midwest	39	98	7	5	.583	98	63	47	94	32	4.32
1982—Cedar Rapids...................	Midwest	21	33	3	1	.750	23	11	8	29	10	2.18
1982—Waterbury.........................	Eastern	30	46⅓	1	4	.200	35	22	21	31	22	4.08
1982—Indianapolis†....................	Am. Assoc.	5	9	0	0	.000	7	5	5	5	2	5.00
1983—Arkansas...........................	Texas	19	35⅔	3	2	.600	35	17	14	23	5	3.53
1983—Louisville..........................	Am. Assoc.	21	83⅓	6	2	.750	88	44	34	52	24	3.67

Selected by Cincinnati Reds' organization in 24th round of free-agent draft, June 5, 1979.
†Drafted by St. Louis Cardinals, December 6, 1982.

—DID YOU KNOW—

That each of the starting outfielders for the Boston Red Sox has won or shared a home run title? Jim Rice (39 homers in 1977 and 1983, plus 46 in 1978), Tony Armas and Dwight Evans (both with 22 in 1981) have led the American League in homers.

JAMES LESTER KERN
(Jim)

Born March 15, 1949, at Gladwin, Mich.
Height, 6.05. Weight, 205.
Throws and bats righthanded.
Attended Delta Junior College, University Center, Mich., and
Michigan State University, East Lansing, Mich.

Pitched seven-inning, 2-0 no-hit victory against San Jose, May 29, 1971.
Major League saves: 1976 (15), 1977 (18), 1978 (13), 1979 (29), 1980 (2), 1981 (6), 1982 (5). Total—88.
Led Western Carolinas League in wild pitches with 25 in 1970.
Tied for American Association lead in wild pitches with 17 and balks with 2 in 1974.
Tied for California League lead in balks with 2 in 1971.
Named American League co-Fireman of the Year by THE SPORTING NEWS, 1979.
Named righthanded pitcher on THE SPORTING NEWS American League All-Star Team, 1979.
Named American Association Pitcher of the Year, 1974.

Year	Club	League	G.	IP.	W.	L.	Pct.	H.	R.	ER.	SO.	BB.	ERA.
1968—Rock Hill	W. Carol.	12	28	0	3	.000	29	30	21	25	26	6.75
1968—Sarasota Indians	Gulf Coast	12	45	4	4	.500	44	32	19	48	32	3.80
1969—†						(In Military Service)						
1970—Reno	California	4	15	0	0	.000	9	12	10	20	20	6.00
1970—Sumter	W. Carol.	14	72	5	6	.455	57	47	39	71	70	4.88
1971—Reno	California	24	100	7	9	.438	99	91	73	109	100	6.57
1972—Elmira	Eastern	22	104	3	11	.214	87	55	50	90	73	4.33
1973—San Antonio	Texas	25	166	11	7	.611	130	76	55	182	★129	2.98
1974—Oklahoma City	Am. Assoc.	25	189	★17	7	.708	139	63	53	★220	104	2.52
1974—Cleveland	American	4	15	0	1	.000	16	9	8	11	14	4.80
1975—Oklahoma City	Am. Assoc.	3	14	1	1	.500	12	10	10	11	11	6.43
1975—Cleveland	American	13	72	1	2	.333	60	31	30	55	45	3.75
1976—Cleveland	American	50	118	10	7	.588	91	38	31	111	50	2.36
1977—Cleveland	American	60	92	8	10	.444	85	39	35	91	47	3.42
1978—Cleveland‡	American	58	99	10	10	.500	77	36	34	95	58	3.09
1979—Texas	American	71	143	13	5	.722	99	35	25	136	62	1.57
1980—Texas§	American	38	63	3	11	.214	65	38	34	40	45	4.86
1981—Texas xyz	American	23	30	1	2	.333	21	10	9	20	22	2.70
1981—Wichita	Am. Assoc.	2	6	0	0	.000	2	0	0	6	5	0.00
1982—Cincinnati a	National	50	76	3	5	.375	67	27	24	43	48	2.84
1982—Chicago	American	13	28	2	1	.667	20	16	16	23	12	5.14
1983—Chicago b	American	1	⅔	0	0	.000	1	1	0	0	0	0.00
American League Totals		331	660⅔	48	49	.495	535	253	222	582	355	3.02
National League Totals		50	76	3	5	.375	67	27	24	43	48	2.84
Major League Totals		381	736⅔	51	54	.486	596	280	246	625	403	3.01

Signed as free agent by Cleveland Indians' organization, September 4, 1967.
†On military list, May 11, 1969 through January 7, 1970.
‡Traded with Infielder Larvell Blanks to Texas Rangers for Outfielder Bobby Bonds and Pitcher Len Barker, October 3, 1978.
§On disabled list, August 19 to September 15, 1980.
xOn disabled list, April 30 to June 2, 1981; included rehabilitation disability assignment to Wichita, May 26 to June 2, 1981.
yTraded to New York Mets for Second Baseman Doug Flynn and Pitcher Dan Boitano, December 11, 1981.
zTraded with Catcher Alex Trevino and Pitcher Greg Harris by New York Mets to Cincinnati Reds for Outfielder George Foster, February 10, 1982.
aTraded to Chicago White Sox for two players to be named later, August 23, 1982; Cincinnati Reds' organization acquired Third Baseman Wade Rowdon and Outfielder Leo Garcia to complete deal, September 7, 1982.
bOn disabled list, April 6, 1983; transferred to emergency disabled list, April 18, 1983 through remainder of season.

ALL-STAR GAME RECORD

Year	League	IP.	W.	L.	Pct.	H.	R.	ER.	SO.	BB.	ERA.
1977—American		1	0	0	.000	0	0	0	2	0	0.00
1978—American		⅔	0	0	.000	1	0	0	1	1	0.00
1979—American		2⅔	0	1	.000	2	2	2	3	3	6.75
All-Star Game Totals		4⅓	0	1	.000	3	2	2	6	4	4.15

JAMES EDWARD KEY
(Jimmy)

Born April 22, 1961, at Huntsville, Ala.
Height, 6.01. Weight, 180.
Throws left and bats righthanded.
Attended Clemson University, Clemson, S.C.

Year	Club	League	G.	IP.	W.	L.	Pct.	H.	R.	ER.	SO.	BB.	ERA.
1982—Medicine Hat	Pioneer	5	31⅓	2	1	.667	27	12	8	25	10	2.30
1982—Florence	S. Atlantic	9	58	5	2	.714	59	33	24	49	18	3.72
1983—Knoxville	Southern	14	101	6	5	.545	86	35	32	57	40	2.85
1983—Syracuse	Int'national	17	97⅔	5	8	.385	93	59	42	77	33	3.87

Selected by Chicago White Sox' organization in 10th round of free-agent draft, June 5, 1979.
Selected by Toronto Blue Jays' organization in 3rd round of free-agent draft, June 7, 1982.

SAM KHALIFA

Born December 5, 1963, at Fontana, Calif.
Height, 5.10. Weight, 160.
Throws and bats righthanded.

Year	Club	League	Pos.	G.	AB.	R.	H.	2B.	3B.	HR.	RBI.	B.A.	PO.	A.	E.	F.A.
1982—Bradenton Pir.		Gulf. C.	55	6	25	1	2	0	0	0	0	.080	12	26	4	.905
1982—Greenwood		S. Atl.	SS	48	177	29	54	6	1	0	19	.305	69	136	19	.915
1983—Alexandria†		Carol.	*SS-2B	103	356	42	96	19	6	1	49	.270	156	279	*33	.929

Selected by Pittsburgh Pirates' organization in 1st round (seventh player selected) of free-agent draft, June 7, 1982.
†On disabled list, May 6 to May 21, 1983.

JAY LYNN KIBBE

Born April 12, 1958, at Alton, Ill.
Height, 6.03. Weight, 200.
Throws and bats righthanded.
Attended Louisiana Tech University, Ruston, La.

Led California League in intentional bases on balls issued with 10 in 1981.

Year	Club	League	G.	IP.	W.	L.	Pct.	H.	R.	ER.	SO.	BB.	ERA.
1979—Idaho Falls	Pioneer	13	46	3	2	.600	58	45	32	41	24	6.26
1980—Redwood	California	28	138	5	9	.357	161	88	69	86	79	4.50
1981—Redwood	California	31	170	10	14	.417	185	127	107	115	92	5.66
1982—Redwood	California	8	49⅓	4	2	.667	44	25	21	28	16	3.83
1982—Holyoke	Eastern	23	143⅔	12	6	.667	127	74	64	115	62	4.01
1983—Edmonton	P. Coast	27	174⅓	10	11	.476	194	*127	103	73	79	5.32

Selected by California Angels' organization in 26th round of free-agent draft, June 5, 1979.

STEVEN GEORGE KIEFER

Born October 18, 1960, at Chicago, Ill.
Height, 6.00. Weight, 165.
Throws and bats righthanded.
Attended Fullerton College, Fullerton, Calif.

Tied for Eastern League lead in sacrifice hits with 12 in 1983.

Year	Club	League	Pos.	G.	AB.	R.	H.	2B.	3B.	HR.	RBI.	B.A.	PO.	A.	E.	F.A.
1981—Medford	N'west	SS-3B	55	192	38	47	7	5	4	22	.245	68	175	17	.935
1982—Madison	Midw.	SS	124	415	72	97	24	1	15	58	.234	173	395	44	.928
1983—Albany	East.	SS-3B-OF	123	415	68	102	18	1	19	81	.246	186	306	38	.928

Selected by Oakland A's organization in 1st round (16th player selected) of free-agent draft, January 13, 1981.

BRIAN PAUL KINGMAN

Born July 27, 1954, at Los Angeles, Calif.
Height, 6.01. Weight, 190.
Throws and bats righthanded.
Attended Santa Monica City College, Santa Monica, Calif. and received bachelor of
arts degree in sociology from University of California at Santa Barbara, Santa Barbara, Calif.

Year	Club	League	G.	IP.	W.	L.	Pct.	H.	R.	ER.	SO.	BB.	ERA.
1975—Boise	Northwest	16	74	4	6	.400	73	46	32	70	32	3.89
1976—Chattanooga	Southern	26	184	14	11	.560	167	69	54	101	47	2.64
1977—San José†	P. Coast	16	60	3	6	.333	76	52	49	47	32	7.35
1978—Modesto	California	10	38	2	2	.500	27	13	10	43	29	2.37
1979—Ogden	P. Coast	13	83	7	2	.778	90	47	43	62	38	4.66
1979—Oakland	American	18	113	8	7	.533	113	59	54	59	33	4.30
1980—Oakland	American	32	211	8	*20	.286	209	105	90	116	82	3.84
1981—Oakland	American	18	100	3	6	.333	112	48	44	52	32	3.96
1982—Tacoma‡	P. Coast	8	53⅓	5	1	.833	59	28	21	27	20	3.54
1982—Oakland§x	American	23	122⅔	4	12	.250	131	64	61	46	57	4.48
1983—Phoenix	P. Coast	25	94⅓	6	6	.500	106	65	58	56	42	5.53
1983—San Francisco	National	3	4⅔	0	0	.000	10	6	4	1	1	7.71
American League Totals		91	546⅔	23	45	.338	565	276	249	272	204	4.10
National League Totals		3	4⅔	0	0	.000	10	6	4	1	1	7.71
Major League Totals		94	551⅓	23	45	.338	575	282	253	273	205	4.13

Selected by California Angels' organization in 12th round of free-agent draft, June 5, 1973.
Signed as free agent by Oakland A's organization, June 18, 1975.
†On disabled list, May 6 to June 20 and August 27 to September 16, 1977.
‡On suspended list, April 13 to April 26, 1982.
§Traded to Boston Red Sox for a player to be named later, January 17, 1983.
xReleased, March 25, 1983; signed by San Francisco Giants' organization, May 1, 1983.

CHAMPIONSHIP SERIES RECORD

Year	Club	League	G.	IP.	W.	L.	Pct.	H.	R.	ER.	SO.	BB.	ERA.
1981—Oakland	American	1	⅓	0	0	.000	3	3	3	0	0	81.00

DAVID ARTHUR KINGMAN
(Dave)

Born December 21, 1948, at Pendleton, Ore.
Height, 6.06. Weight, 210.
Throws and bats righthanded.
Attended Harper College, Palatine, Ill., and University of Southern
California, Los Angeles, Calif.

Tied major league records for most home runs, two consecutive games (5), July 27 and 28, 1979; most times, three or more home runs, game, season (2), May 17 and July 28, 1979.
Tied modern major league record for most clubs played on, season, major leagues (4), 1977.
Tied National League record for fewest errors by first baseman for leader in errors, season (13), 1974.
Hit three home runs in a game June 4, 1976, May 14, 1978 and May 17 and July 28, 1979.
Hit for the cycle, April 16, 1972.
Led National League batters in strikeouts with 131 in 1979, 105 in 1981 and 156 in 1982.
Led National League in slugging percentage with .613 in 1979.
Led National League first basemen in errors with 13 in 1974.
Named outfielder on THE SPORTING NEWS National League All-Star Team, 1979.

Year	Club	League	Pos.	G.	AB.	R.	H.	2B.	3B.	HR.	RBI.	B.A.	PO.	A.	E.	F.A.
1970—Amarillo	Texas		1B-OF	60	210	41	62	9	1	15	41	.295	226	9	9	.963
1971—Phoenix	P. C.		OF-1B	105	392	89	109	29	5	26	99	.278	785	40	8	.990
1971—San Francisco	Nat.		1B-OF	41	115	17	32	10	2	6	24	.278	168	9	4	.978
1972—San Francisco	Nat.		3B-1B-OF	135	472	65	106	17	4	29	83	.225	496	159	22	.968
1973—San Francisco	Nat.		3B-1B-P	112	305	54	62	10	1	24	55	.203	313	146	22	.954
1974—San Francisco†	Nat.		1B-3B-OF	121	350	41	78	18	2	18	55	.223	696	98	25	.969
1975—New York	Nat.		OF-1B-3B	134	502	65	116	22	1	36	88	.231	526	69	14	.977
1976—New York‡	Nat.		OF-1B	123	474	70	113	14	1	37	86	.238	293	18	9	.972
1977—N.Y.§-S.D. x	Nat.		OF-1B-3B	114	379	38	84	16	0	20	67	.222	333	24	7	.981
1977—Cal. y-N.Y. z	Amer.		1B-OF	18	60	9	13	4	0	6	11	.217	73	5	2	.975
1978—Chicago a	Nat.		OF-1B	119	395	65	105	17	4	28	79	.266	226	10	6	.975
1979—Chicago	Nat.		OF	145	532	97	153	19	5	★48	115	.288	240	11	12	.954
1980—Chicago bcd	Nat.		OF-1B	81	255	31	71	8	0	18	57	.278	119	10	8	.942
1981—New York	Nat.		1B-OF	100	353	40	78	11	3	22	59	.221	548	34	20	.967
1982—New York	Nat.		1B	149	535	80	109	9	1	★37	99	.204	1232	69	18	.986
1983—New York	Nat.		1B-OF	100	248	25	49	7	0	13	29	.198	450	28	3	.994
National League Totals				1474	4915	688	1156	178	24	336	896	.235	5640	685	170	.974
American League Totals				18	60	9	13	4	0	6	11	.217	73	5	2	.975
Major League Totals				1492	4975	697	1169	182	24	342	907	.235	5713	690	172	.974

Selected by California Angels' organization in 2nd round of free-agent draft, June 6, 1967.
Selected by Baltimore Orioles' organization in secondary phase of free-agent draft, January 27, 1968.
Selected by San Francisco Giants' organization in secondary phase of free-agent draft, June 4, 1970.
†Sold to New York Mets for an estimated $125,000, February 28, 1975.
‡On disabled list, July 20 to August 27, 1976.
§Traded to San Diego Padres for Third Baseman-Outfielder Bobby Valentine and Pitcher Paul Siebert, June 15, 1977.
xSold on waivers to California Angels, September 6, 1977.
ySold to New York Yankees, September 15, 1977.
zGranted free agency, November 2, 1977; signed by Chicago Cubs, November 30, 1977.
aOn disabled list, July 1 to July 26, 1978.
bOn supplemental disabled list, June 13 to June 28 and July 10 to August 6, 1980.
cOn disabled list, August 6 to August 12, 1980.
dTraded to New York Mets for Outfielder Steve Henderson and cash, February 28, 1981.

CHAMPIONSHIP SERIES RECORD

Year	Club	League	Pos.	G.	AB.	R.	H.	2B.	3B.	HR.	RBI.	B.A.	PO.	A.	E.	F.A.
1971—San Francisco	Nat.		PH-OF	4	9	0	1	0	0	0	0	.111	5	0	0	1.000

ALL-STAR GAME RECORD

Year	League	Pos.	AB.	R.	H.	2B.	3B.	HR.	RBI.	B.A.	PO.	A.	E.	F.A.
1976—National		OF	2	0	0	0	0	0	0	.000	1	0	0	1.000
1980—National		OF	1	0	0	0	0	0	0	.000	0	0	0	.000
All-Star Game Totals			3	0	0	0	0	0	0	.000	1	0	0	1.000

Named to National League All-Star Team for 1979 game; replaced due to injury by Keith Hernandez.

PITCHING RECORD

Year	Club	League	G.	IP.	W.	L.	Pct.	H.	R.	ER.	SO.	BB.	ERA.
1973—San Francisco	National		2	4	0	0	.000	3	4	4	4	6	9.00

—DID YOU KNOW—

That when Neil Allen, first as a Met and later as a Cardinal, threw shutouts against the Dodgers in 1983, it marked the first time since 1976 that a major league pitcher had tossed shutouts against the same team while pitching for two different clubs in one season? In '76, Rudy May and Doyle Alexander—as members of both the Yankees and the Orioles—tossed shutouts against the Tigers, and Bill Singer shut out the Angels twice—first as a Ranger and then in a Twins uniform.

BRUCE EUGENE KISON

Name pronounced KEE-son.

Born February 18, 1950, at Pasco, Wash.
Height, 6.04. Weight, 173.
Throws and bats righthanded.
Attended Columbia Basin Junior College, Pasco, Wash., Manatee Junior College,
West Bradenton, Fla., and Central Washington State
College, Ellensburgh, Wash.

Led International League in hit batsmen with 14 in 1973.
Led Eastern League in hit batsmen with 21 in 1970.

Year	Club	League	G.	IP.	W.	L.	Pct.	H.	R.	ER.	SO.	BB.	ERA.
1968—Bradenton Pirates	Gulf Coast	10	24	2	1	.667	24	9	6	9	6	2.25
1969—Geneva†	NYP	13	94	5	2	.714	84	48	33	77	39	3.16
1970—Salem	Carolina	5	33	3	1	.750	17	5	3	26	7	0.82
1970—Waterbury	Eastern	19	130	10	4	.714	93	42	33	82	54	2.28
1971—Charleston	Int'national	12	85	10	1	.909	53	29	27	57	38	2.86
1971—Pittsburgh	National	18	95	6	5	.545	93	40	36	60	36	3.41
1972—Pittsburgh‡	National	32	152	9	7	.563	123	61	55	102	69	3.26
1973—Pittsburgh§	National	7	44	3	0	1.000	36	17	15	26	24	3.07
1973—Charleston x	Int'national	20	114	8	6	.571	94	59	50	70	82	3.95
1974—Pittsburgh	National	40	129	9	8	.529	123	64	50	71	57	3.49
1975—Pittsburgh	National	33	192	12	11	.522	160	89	69	89	92	3.23
1976—Pittsburgh	National	31	193	14	9	.609	180	83	66	98	52	3.08
1977—Pittsburgh	National	33	193	9	10	.474	209	113	105	122	55	4.90
1978—Pittsburgh y	National	28	96	6	6	.500	81	40	34	62	39	3.19
1979—Pittsburgh z	National	33	172	13	7	.650	157	70	61	105	45	3.19
1980—California ab	American	13	73	3	6	.333	73	46	40	28	32	4.93
1981—California c	American	11	44	1	1	.500	40	18	17	19	14	3.48
1982—California	American	33	142	10	5	.667	120	54	50	86	44	3.17
1983—California d	American	26	126⅔	11	5	.688	128	59	57	83	43	4.05
National League Totals		255	1266	81	63	.563	1162	577	491	735	469	3.49
American League Totals		83	385⅔	25	17	.595	361	177	164	216	133	3.83
Major League Totals		338	1651⅔	106	80	.570	1523	754	655	951	602	3.57

Selected by Pittsburgh Pirates' organization in 6th round of free-agent draft, June 7, 1968.
†On restricted list, March 13 to June 18, 1969.
‡On disabled list, March 29 to April 20, 1972.
§On disabled list, March 23 to April 21, 1973.
xOn disabled list, June 14 to July 5, 1973.
yOn disabled list, May 28 to July 6, 1978.
zGranted free agency, November 1, 1979; signed by California Angels, November 16, 1979.
aOn disabled list, June 11 to July 14, 1980.
bOn emergency disabled list, July 15, 1980 through remainder of season.
cOn disabled list, April 7 to August 8, 1981.
dOn disabled list, May 30 to June 27, 1983.

CHAMPIONSHIP SERIES RECORD

Tied Championship Series record for most games won, total series (4).
Established National League Championship Series record for most bases on balls, game (6), October 8, 1974.
Tied National League Championship Series record for most games won, total Series (3).

Year	Club	League	G.	IP.	W.	L.	Pct.	H.	R.	ER.	SO.	BB.	ERA.
1971—Pittsburgh	National	1	4⅔	1	0	1.000	2	0	0	3	2	0.00
1972—Pittsburgh	National	2	2⅓	1	0	1.000	1	0	0	3	0	0.00
1974—Pittsburgh	National	1	6⅔	1	0	1.000	2	0	0	5	6	0.00
1975—Pittsburgh	National	1	2	0	0	.000	2	1	1	1	1	4.50
1982—California	American	2	14	1	0	1.000	8	4	3	12	3	1.93
Championship Series Totals		7	29⅔	4	0	1.000	15	5	4	24	12	1.21

WORLD SERIES RECORD

Established World Series record for most hit batsmen, game (3), October 13, 1971.
Tied World Series record for most hit batsmen, Series (3), 1971.

Year	Club	League	G.	IP.	W.	L.	Pct.	H.	R.	ER.	SO.	BB.	ERA.
1971—Pittsburgh	National	2	6⅓	1	0	1.000	1	0	0	3	3	0.00
1979—Pittsburgh	National	1	⅓	0	1	.000	3	5	4	0	2	108.00
World Series Totals		3	6⅔	1	1	.500	4	5	4	3	5	5.40

RONALD DALE KITTLE
(Ron)

Born January 5, 1958, at Gary, Indiana.
Height, 6.03. Weight, 195.
Throws and bats righthanded.

Led American League batters in strikeouts with 150 in 1983.
Led Pacific Coast League in total bases with 355, slugging percentage with .752 and tied for lead in being hit by pitch with 10 in 1982.
Led Eastern League in total bases with 270 and slugging percentage with .694 in 1981.
Named Minor League Player of the Year by THE SPORTING NEWS, 1982.
Named Pacific Coast League Most Valuable Player, 1982.
Named American League Rookie Player of the Year by THE SPORTING NEWS, 1983.

Named American League Rookie of the Year by Baseball Writers' Association of America, 1983.
Named Eastern League Player of the Year, 1981.

Year	Club	League	Pos.	G.	AB.	R.	H.	2B.	3B.	HR.	RBI.	B.A.	PO.	A.	E.	F.A.
1977—Clinton†	Midw.		OF	22	53	9	10	4	0	0	3	.189	16	0	0	1.000
1977—Lethbridge	Pion.		OF	34	100	22	25	3	0	7	21	.250	29	2	6	.838
1978—Clinton‡	Midw.		OF	13	35	2	5	2	1	0	4	.143	4	1	1	.833
1979—Knoxville	South.		OF-C	53	157	28	43	9	1	6	26	.274	44	1	6	.980
1979—Appleton	Midw.		OF-C	35	120	18	31	3	1	2	12	.258	33	1	2	.972
1980—Appleton	Midw.		C-OF	61	209	31	66	15	3	12	56	.316	56	9	1	.985
1980—Glens Falls§	East.		OF	17	65	11	20	3	1	4	9	.308	24	4	3	.903
1981—Glens Falls x	East.		OF	109	389	97	127	17	3	★40	★103	.326	28	0	3	.903
1982—Edmonton	P. C.		OF-C	127	472	★121	163	22	10	★50	★144	.345	149	15	8	.953
1982—Chicago	Amer.		OF	20	29	3	7	2	0	1	7	.241	3	0	0	1.000
1983—Chicago	Amer.		OF	145	520	75	132	19	3	35	100	.254	234	7	9	.964
Major League Totals				165	549	78	139	21	3	36	107	.253	237	7	9	.964

Signed as free agent by Los Angeles Dodgers' organization, July 5, 1977.
†On disabled list, April 30 to May 14, 1977.
‡Released, July 7, 1978; signed by Knoxville (Chicago White Sox' organization), September 4, 1978.
§On disabled list, July 27 to August 31, 1980.
xOn disabled list, April 21 to May 10, 1981.

CHAMPIONSHIP SERIES RECORD

Year	Club	League	Pos.	G.	AB.	R.	H.	2B.	3B.	HR.	RBI.	B.A.	PO.	A.	E.	F.A.
1983—Chicago	Amer.		OF	3	7	1	2	1	0	0	0	.286	3	0	0	1.000

ALL-STAR GAME RECORD

Year	League	Pos.	AB.	R.	H.	2B.	3B.	HR.	RBI.	B.A.	PO.	A.	E.	F.A.
1983—American		OF	2	1	1	0	0	0	0	.500	1	0	0	1.000

GENE ELLIS KLUTTS
(Mickey)

Born September 30, 1954, at Montebello, Calif.
Height, 5.11. Weight, 189.
Throws and bats righthanded.

Named International League co-Most Valuable Player, 1976.

Year	Club	League	Pos.	G.	AB.	R.	H.	2B.	3B.	HR.	RBI.	B.A.	PO.	A.	E.	F.A.
1972—Johnson City	Appal.		SS-3B	54	182	25	46	7	3	3	22	.253	54	114	19	.898
1973—Ft. Lauderdale	Fla. St.		SS-3B	34	94	4	12	1	0	1	9	.128	31	57	7	.926
1973—Oneonta	NYP		SS-2B	37	135	28	43	7	5	2	22	.319	57	107	8	.953
1974—Ft. Lauderdale†	Fla. St.		3B-SS	85	268	24	61	9	2	5	30	.228	101	237	20	.944
1975—West Haven‡	East.		3B-SS-1B	69	221	26	48	10	1	2	23	.217	53	180	19	.875
1976—Syracuse	Int.		SS-3B	119	430	75	137	22	3	24	80	.319	191	293	28	.945
1976—New York	Amer.		SS	2	3	0	0	0	0	0	0	.000	4	3	1	.875
1977—Syracuse	Int.		3B-SS-2B	85	320	52	92	19	7	14	66	.288	72	171	17	.935
1977—New York§	Amer.		3B-SS	5	15	3	4	1	0	1	4	.267	5	15	0	1.000
1978—New York xy	Amer.		3B	1	2	1	2	1	0	0	0	1.000	1	2	1	.750
1978—Vancouver za	P. C.		3B-OF-SS	11	41	7	12	2	0	4	14	.293	6	6	0	1.000
1979—Oakland b	Amer.		SS-2B-3B	24	73	3	14	2	1	1	4	.192	35	50	7	.924
1980—Oakland c	Amer.		3B-SS-2B	75	197	20	53	14	0	4	21	.269	63	104	9	.949
1981—Tacoma	P. C.		3B	9	28	3	11	2	1	1	4	.393	1	4	0	1.000
1981—Oakland d	Amer.		3B	15	46	9	17	0	0	5	11	.370	7	15	1	.957
1982—Oakland ef	Amer.		3B	55	157	10	28	8	0	0	14	.178	41	82	7	.946
1983—Toronto	Amer.		3B	22	43	3	11	0	0	3	5	.256	4	11	0	1.000
1983—Syracuse	Int.		3B-2B	12	32	3	12	2	0	0	6	.375	0	6	0	1.000
Major League Totals				199	536	49	129	26	1	14	59	.241	160	282	26	.944

Selected by New York Yankees' organization in 4th round of free-agent draft, June 6, 1972.
†On disabled list, May 23 to June 6, 1974.
‡On disabled list, August 2 to September 16, 1975.
§On disabled list, March 23 to April 30, 1977.
xOn supplemental disabled list, April 22 to May 19, 1978.
yTraded with Outfielder Dell Alston and $50,000 to Oakland A's for Outfielder Gary Thomasson, June 15, 1978.
zOn Oakland supplemental disabled list, June 16 to July 7, 1978.
aOn disabled list, July 30 to September 1, 1978.
bOn disabled list, May 24, 1979; transferred to emergency disabled list, July 12, 1979 through remainder of season.
cOn supplemental disabled list, June 29 to September 1, 1980.
dOn disabled list, April 3 to August 27, 1981; included rehabilitation disability assignment to Tacoma, August 8 to August 27, 1981.
eOn supplemental disabled list, May 10, 1982; transferred to disabled list, May 13 to May 31, 1982.
fReleased, November 4, 1982; signed by Toronto Blue Jays, February 11, 1983.

DIVISION SERIES RECORD

Year	Club	League	Pos.	G.	AB.	R.	H.	2B.	3B.	HR.	RBI.	B.A.	PO.	A.	E.	F.A.
1981—Oakland	Amer.		3B	2	7	0	1	0	0	0	0	.143	0	2	0	1.000

CHAMPIONSHIP SERIES RECORD

Year	Club	League	Pos.	G.	AB.	R.	H.	2B.	3B.	HR.	RBI.	B.A.	PO.	A.	E.	F.A.
1981—Oakland	Amer.		3B	3	7	1	3	0	0	0	0	.429	3	5	1	.889

ROBERT WESLEY KNEPPER

Name pronounced NEPP-ur.

(Bob)

Born May 25, 1954, at Akron, O.
Height, 6.02. Weight, 200.
Throws and bats lefthanded.

Led National League in shutouts with 6 in 1978.
Tied for National League lead in hit batsmen with 8 in 1980.
Led California League pitchers in games started with 30 and tied for lead in complete games with 16 in 1974.
Tied for Pacific Coast League lead in shutouts with 3 in 1976.
Named National League Comeback Player of the Year by THE SPORTING NEWS, 1981.

Year Club	League	G.	IP.	W.	L.	Pct.	H.	R.	ER.	SO.	BB.	ERA.
1972—Great Falls	Pioneer	12	68	7	1	.875	53	20	11	75	19	1.46
1973—Decatur	Midwest	11	79	7	2	.778	65	28	17	68	23	1.94
1973—Fresno	California	13	71	2	8	.200	78	54	32	66	35	4.06
1974—Fresno	California	30	★238	★20	5	●.800	★239	103	84	★247	80	3.18
1975—Phoenix	P. Coast	26	155	11	11	.500	169	101	79	94	78	4.59
1976—Phoenix	P. Coast	29	205	14	10	.583	209	105	98	130	64	4.30
1976—San Francisco	National	4	25	1	2	.333	26	9	9	11	7	3.24
1977—Phoenix	P. Coast	10	51	3	6	.333	68	51	42	24	25	7.41
1977—San Francisco	National	27	166	11	9	.550	151	73	62	100	72	3.36
1978—San Francisco	National	36	260	17	11	.607	218	85	76	147	85	2.63
1979—San Francisco	National	34	207	9	12	.429	241	117	107	123	77	4.65
1980—San Francisco†	National	35	215	9	16	.360	242	114	98	103	61	4.10
1981—Houston	National	22	157	9	5	.643	128	41	38	75	38	2.18
1982—Houston	National	33	180	5	15	.250	193	100	89	108	60	4.45
1983—Houston	National	35	203	6	13	.316	202	93	72	125	71	3.19
Major League Totals		226	1413	67	83	.447	1401	632	551	792	471	3.51

Selected by San Francisco Giants' organization in 2nd round of free-agent draft, June 6, 1972.
†Traded with Outfielder Chris Bourjos to Houston Astros for Third Baseman Enos Cabell, December 8, 1980.

DIVISION SERIES RECORD

Year Club	League	G.	IP.	W.	L.	Pct.	H.	R.	ER.	SO.	BB.	ERA.
1981—Houston	National	1	5	0	1	.000	6	3	3	4	2	5.40

ALL-STAR GAME RECORD

Year League	IP.	W.	L.	Pct.	H.	R.	ER.	SO.	BB.	ERA.
1981—National	2	0	0	.000	1	0	0	3	2	0.00

ALAN LEE KNICELY

Name pronounced NYSS-lee.

Born May 19, 1955, at Harrisonburg, Va.
Height, 6.00. Weight, 194.
Throws and bats righthanded.
Brother of Harold Knicely, catcher in Houston Astros' organization, 1974.

Led Pacific Coast League in passed balls with 16 in 1980.
Tied for Southern League lead in strikeouts by batters with 112 in 1978.
Tied for Pacific Coast League lead in double plays by catchers with 8 in 1980.
Named Southern League co-Most Valuable Player, 1979.

Year Club	League	Pos.	G.	AB.	R.	H.	2B.	3B.	HR.	RBI.	B.A.	PO.	A.	E.	F.A.
1974—Covington	Appal.	P	15	41	5	9	2	1	0	6	.220	3	★19	3	.880
1975—Dubuque	Midw.	P	27	35	5	11	1	0	1	9	.314	11	15	1	.963
1976—Dubuque	Midw.	P-1B	77	156	23	45	9	1	4	20	.288	84	23	3	.973
1977—Columbus	South.	3B-P	99	277	28	73	10	3	6	35	.264	84	140	24	.903
1978—Columbus	South.	OF	140	427	97	159	13	2	15	50	.227	262	22	10	.966
1979—Columbus	South.	C	120	422	77	122	12	3	★33	76	.289	446	51	15	.971
1979—Houston	Nat.	C-3B	7	6	0	0	0	0	0	0	.000	2	0	0	1.000
1980—Tucson	P. C.	C	133	468	69	149	18	4	22	★105	.318	511	★93	●23	.963
1980—Houston	Nat.	PH	1	1	0	0	0	0	0	0	.000	0	0	0	.000
1981—Tucson	P. C.	C-OF	138	490	81	150	32	5	18	96	.306	549	81	15	.977
1981—Houston	Nat.	C-OF	3	7	2	4	0	0	2	2	.571	11	2	0	1.000
1982—Houston†	Nat.	C-OF-3B	59	133	10	25	2	0	2	12	.188	128	15	4	.973
1983—Cincinnati	Nat.	C-OF-1B	59	98	11	22	3	0	2	10	.224	124	13	0	1.000
Major League Totals			129	245	23	51	5	0	6	24	.208	265	30	4	.987

Selected by Houston Astros' organization in 3rd round of free-agent draft, June 5, 1974.
†Traded to Cincinnati Reds for Pitcher Bill Dawley and Outfielder Anthony Walker, March 31, 1983.

PITCHING RECORD

Year Club	League	G.	IP.	W.	L.	Pct.	H.	R.	ER.	SO.	BB.	ERA.
1974—Covington	Ap'lachian	12	81	7	3	.700	78	35	31	53	42	3.44
1975—Dubuque	Midwest	26	122	4	10	.286	113	59	49	87	62	3.61
1976—Dubuque	Midwest	24	107	7	3	.700	100	58	47	87	62	3.95
1977—Columbus	Southern	14	42	1	5	.167	40	32	24	25	25	5.14

CHARLES RAY KNIGHT
(Known by middle name.)

Born December 28, 1952, at Albany, Ga.
Height, 6.02. Weight, 190.
Throws and bats righthanded.
Attended Albany Junior College, Albany, Ga.

Tied major league records for most home runs, inning (2) and most total bases, inning (8), May 13, 1980 (fifth inning); most seasons, consecutive, leading league, grounded into double plays (2), 1980 and 1981.
Led National League in grounding into double plays with 18 in 1981 and tied for lead with 24 in 1980.
Led American Association third basemen in putouts with 102 in 1976.
Tied for American Association lead in double plays by third basemen with 24 in 1974.

Year—Club	League	Pos.	G.	AB.	R.	H.	2B.	3B.	HR.	RBI.	B.A.	PO.	A.	E.	F.A.
1971—Sioux Falls	North.	O-INF-P	64	239	34	68	5	2	6	31	.285	69	79	17	.897
1972—Three Rivers	East.	O-INF-P	97	302	25	64	8	1	2	35	.212	102	142	20	.924
1973—Three Rivers	East.	3-O-1-P	78	253	20	55	10	4	1	16	.217	72	126	11	.947
1974—Indianapolis	A. A.	★3B-OF	107	352	36	80	13	4	5	37	.227	94	177	11	★.961
1974—Cincinnati	Nat.	3B	14	11	1	2	1	0	0	2	.182	2	8	0	1.000
1975—Indianapolis	A. A.	★3B-1B	123	434	58	118	16	5	4	48	.272	★116	227	17	.953
1976—Indianapolis†	A. A.	3B-1B	110	396	47	106	24	3	10	41	.268	136	181	13	.961
1977—Cincinnati	Nat.	3-2-O-S	80	92	8	24	5	1	1	13	.261	45	45	4	.957
1978—Cincinnati‡	Nat.	3-2-O-S-1	83	65	7	13	3	0	1	4	.200	13	41	7	.885
1979—Cincinnati	Nat.	3B	150	551	64	175	37	4	10	79	.318	120	262	15	.962
1980—Cincinnati	Nat.	3B	162	618	71	163	39	7	14	78	.264	120	291	13	.969
1981—Cincinnati§	Nat.	3B	106	386	43	100	23	1	6	34	.259	69	176	11	.957
1982—Houston	Nat.	1B-3B	158	609	72	179	36	6	6	70	.294	1002	186	17	.986
1983—Houston	Nat.	1B	145	507	43	154	36	4	9	70	.304	1285	73	9	.993
Major League Totals			898	2839	309	810	180	23	47	350	.285	2656	1082	76	.980

Selected by Cincinnati Reds' organization in 10th round of free-agent draft, June 4, 1970.
†On disabled list, June 21 to July 2, 1976.
‡On disabled list, April 17 to May 8, 1978.
§Traded to Houston Astros for First Baseman-Outfielder Cesar Cedeno, December 18, 1981.

CHAMPIONSHIP SERIES RECORD

Year—Club	League	Pos.	G.	AB.	R.	H.	2B.	3B.	HR.	RBI.	B.A.	PO.	A.	E.	F.A.
1979—Cincinnati	Nat.	3B	3	14	0	4	1	0	0	0	.286	0	5	0	1.000

ALL-STAR GAME RECORD

Year	League	Pos.	AB.	R.	H.	2B.	3B.	HR.	RBI.	B.A.	PO.	A.	E.	F.A.
1980—National		3B	1	1	1	0	0	0	0	1.000	0	1	0	1.000
1982—National		3B	3	0	0	0	0	0	0	.000	1	4	0	1.000
All-Star Game Totals			4	1	1	0	0	0	0	.250	1	5	0	1.000

PITCHING RECORD

Year—Club	League	G.	IP.	W.	L.	Pct.	H.	R.	ER.	SO.	BB.	ERA.
1971—Sioux Falls	Northern	3	4	1	1	.500	5	6	5	4	5	11.25
1972—Three Rivers	Eastern	2	4	0	0	.000	3	1	1	2	4	2.25
1973—Indianapolis	Am. Assoc.	1	2	0	0	.000	2	1	1	0	4	4.50

BRAD LYNN KOMMINSK

Name pronounced Kuh-MINSK.

Born April 4, 1961, at Lima, Ohio.
Height, 6.03. Weight, 187.
Throws and bats righthanded.

Led International League in slugging percentage with .596 and tied for lead in game-winning RBIs with 14 in 1983.
Led Carolina League in total bases with 278 and grounding into double plays with 24 in 1981.
Led Appalachian League batters in strikeouts with 74 and stolen bases with 20 in 1979.
Named Carolina League Most Valuable Player, 1981.
Received reported $72,000 bonus to sign with Atlanta Braves, 1979.

Year—Club	League	Pos.	G.	AB.	R.	H.	2B.	3B.	HR.	RBI.	B.A.	PO.	A.	E.	F.A.
1979—Kingsport	Appal.	OF	59	185	37	41	9	1	7	34	.222	112	1	2	.983
1980—Anderson	S. Atl.	OF	121	425	86	111	17	5	20	67	.261	217	5	12	.949
1981—Durham	Carol.	OF	132	459	108	●148	27	2	33	★104	★.322	154	7	10	.942
1982—Savannah	South.	OF	133	454	88	124	18	7	26	78	.273	158	6	10	.943
1982—Richmond	Int.	OF	5	17	4	6	1	0	2	5	.353	10	0	0	1.000
1983—Richmond	Int.	OF	117	413	94	139	24	6	24	103	.334	179	4	3	.984
1983—Atlanta	Nat.	OF	19	36	2	8	2	0	0	4	.222	16	1	1	.944
Major League Totals			19	36	2	8	2	0	0	4	.222	16	1	1	.944

Selected by Atlanta Braves' organization in 1st round (fourth player selected) of free-agent draft, June 5, 1979.

JERRY MARTIN KOOSMAN

Born December 23, 1942, at Appleton, Minn.
Height, 6.02. Weight, 225.
Throws left and bats righthanded.
Attended University of Minnesota, Morris, Minn., and
State School of Science, Wahpeton, N.D.

Established National League record for most strikeouts, season, by pitcher as batter (62), 1968.

Tied modern National League record for most shutout games won or tied, rookie season (7), 1968.
Tied for National League lead in balks with 3 in 1970 and 7 in 1975.
Named National League Rookie Pitcher of the Year by THE SPORTING NEWS, 1968.

Year Club	League	G.	IP.	W.	L.	Pct.	H.	R.	ER.	SO.	BB.	ERA.
1965—Greenville	W. Carol.	27	107	5	11	.313	101	70	56	128	56	4.71
1965—Williamsport	Eastern	2	12	0	2	.000	11	7	5	11	11	3.75
1966—Auburn	NYP	24	170	12	7	.632	109	43	26	174	43	*1.38
1967—New York	National	9	22	0	2	.000	22	17	15	11	19	6.14
1967—Jacksonville	Int'national	25	178	11	10	.524	137	60	48	*183	46	2.43
1968—New York	National	35	264	19	12	.613	221	72	61	178	69	2.08
1969—New York	National	32	241	17	9	.684	187	66	61	180	68	2.28
1970—New York	National	30	212	12	7	.632	189	87	74	118	71	3.14
1971—New York†	National	26	166	6	11	.353	160	66	56	96	51	3.04
1972—New York	National	34	163	11	12	.478	155	81	75	147	52	4.14
1973—New York	National	35	263	14	15	.483	234	93	83	156	76	2.84
1974—New York	National	35	265	15	11	.577	258	113	99	188	85	3.36
1975—New York	National	36	240	14	13	.519	234	106	91	173	98	3.41
1976—New York	National	34	247	21	10	.677	205	81	74	200	66	2.70
1977—New York	National	32	227	8	●20	.286	195	102	88	192	81	3.49
1978—New York‡	National	38	235	3	15	.167	221	110	98	160	84	3.75
1979—Minnesota	American	37	264	20	13	.606	268	108	99	157	83	3.38
1980—Minnesota	American	38	243	16	13	.552	252	119	109	149	69	4.04
1981—Minnesota§-Chicago	American	27	121	4	●13	.235	125	59	54	76	41	4.02
1982—Chicago	American	42	173⅓	11	7	.611	194	81	74	88	38	3.84
1983—Chicago x	American	37	169⅔	11	7	.611	176	96	90	90	53	4.77
National League Totals		376	2545	140	137	.505	2281	994	875	1799	820	3.09
American League Totals		181	971	62	53	.539	1015	463	426	560	284	3.95
Major League Totals		557	3516	202	190	.515	3296	1457	1301	2359	1104	3.33

Signed as free agent by New York Mets' organization, August 27, 1964.
†On disabled list, July 7 to August 9, 1971.
‡Traded to Minnesota Twins for Pitcher Greg Field and a player to be named later, December 8, 1978; New York Mets acquired Pitcher Jesse Orosco to complete deal, February 7, 1979.
§Traded to Chicago White Sox for Shortstop Ivan Mesa, Third Baseman Ron Perry, a player to be named later and cash, August 30, 1981; Minnesota Twins' organization acquired Outfielder Randy Johnson to complete deal, September 2, 1981. (Pitcher Kevin Flannery replaced Perry due to injuries, October 18, 1982.)
xGranted free agency, November 7, 1983; re-signed by White Sox, December 2, 1983.

CHAMPIONSHIP SERIES RECORD

Established National League Championship Series record for most earned runs allowed, inning (5), October 5, 1969 (fifth inning).
Tied National League Championship Series record for most runs allowed, inning (5), October 5, 1969 (fifth inning).

Year Club	League	G.	IP.	W.	L.	Pct.	H.	R.	ER.	SO.	BB.	ERA.
1969—New York	National	1	4⅔	0	0	.000	7	6	6	5	4	11.57
1973—New York	National	1	9	1	0	1.000	8	2	2	9	0	2.00
1983—Chicago	American	1	⅓	0	0	.000	1	3	2	0	2	54.00
Championship Series Totals		3	14	1	0	1.000	16	11	10	14	6	6.43

WORLD SERIES RECORD

Year Club	League	G.	IP.	W.	L.	Pct.	H.	R.	ER.	SO.	BB.	ERA.
1969—New York	National	2	17⅔	2	0	1.000	7	4	4	9	4	2.04
1973—New York	National	2	8⅔	1	0	1.000	9	3	3	8	7	3.12
World Series Totals		4	26⅓	3	0	1.000	16	7	7	17	11	2.39

ALL-STAR GAME RECORD

Year League	IP.	W.	L.	Pct.	H.	R.	ER.	SO.	BB.	ERA.
1968—National	⅓	0	0	.000	0	0	0	1	0	0.00
1969—National	1⅔	0	0	.000	1	0	0	1	0	0.00
All-Star Game Totals	2	0	0	.000	1	0	0	2	0	0.00

RAYMOND ALLEN KRAWCZYK
(Ray)

Born October 9, 1959, at Pittsburgh, Pa.
Height, 6.02. Weight, 190.
Throws and bats righthanded.
Attended Golden West College, Huntington Beach, Calif.,
and Oral Roberts University, Tulsa, Okla.

Year Club	League	G.	IP.	W.	L.	Pct.	H.	R.	ER.	SO.	BB.	ERA.
1981—Bradenton Pirates	Gulf Coast	4	18	0	1	.000	11	5	3	14	7	1.50
1981—Alexandria	Carolina	8	46	2	4	.333	48	32	25	41	14	4.89
1982—Alexandria	Carolina	6	18⅔	1	0	1.000	10	1	1	25	13	0.48
1982—Buffalo	Eastern	38	101⅓	3	5	.375	93	59	53	102	59	4.71
1983—Hawaii	P. Coast	41	88⅔	5	7	.417	80	46	37	88	33	3.76

Selected by Boston Red Sox' organization in 1st round (23rd player selected) of free-agent draft, January 8, 1980.
Selected by St. Louis Cardinals' organization in secondary phase of free-agent draft, June 3, 1980.
Selected by Pittsburgh Pirates' organization in secondary phase of free-agent draft, June 8, 1981.

WAYNE RICHARD KRENCHICKI

Name pronounced Kren-CHIK-ee.
Born September 17, 1954, at Trenton, N.J.
Height, 6.01. Weight, 175.
Throws right and bats lefthanded
Attended University of Miami, Miami, Fla.
Brother of Tom Krenchicki, shortstop in Los Angeles Dodgers' organization, 1968.

Led Southern League second basemen in double plays with 114 in 1977.
Led Florida State League shortstops in assists with 378, double plays with 60 and fielding percentage with .968 in 1976.

Year Club	League	Pos.	G.	AB.	R.	H.	2B.	3B.	HR.	RBI.	B.A.	PO.	A.	E.	F.A.
1976—Miami	Fla. St.	SS-3B	133	459	38	109	14	1	0	35	.237	190	439	19	.971
1977—Charlotte	South.	2B	131	510	69	140	17	9	3	42	.275	★325	★455	25	.969
1978—Rochester	Int.	3B-2B-SS	★140	520	★93	154	26	1	12	71	.296	204	389	32	.949
1979—Rochester†	Int.	2B-SS-3B	66	249	21	65	7	2	0	22	.261	129	173	9	.971
1979—Baltimore	Amer.	3B-2B	16	21	1	4	1	0	0	0	.190	12	12	2	.923
1980—Rochester‡	Int.	2B-3B-SS	87	311	42	82	13	3	2	39	.264	137	230	10	.973
1980—Baltimore	Amer.	SS-2B	9	14	1	2	0	0	0	0	.143	9	9	0	1.000
1981—Baltimore	Amer.	2B-3B-SS	33	56	7	12	4	0	0	6	.214	23	56	3	.963
1981—Rochester§	Int.	2B-3B-SS	16	56	5	10	0	0	0	4	.179	28	58	1	.988
1982—Cincinnati	Nat.	3B-2B	94	187	19	53	6	1	2	21	.283	40	103	6	.960
1983—Cincinnati x	Nat.	3B-2B	51	77	6	21	2	0	0	11	.273	7	41	1	.980
1983—Detroit y	Amer.	3-2-S-1	59	133	18	37	7	0	1	16	.278	43	75	8	.937
American League Totals			117	224	27	55	12	0	1	22	.246	87	152	13	.948
National League Totals			145	264	25	74	8	1	2	32	.280	47	144	7	.965
Major League Totals			262	488	52	129	20	1	3	54	.264	134	296	20	.956

Selected by Philadelphia Phillies' organization in 8th round of free-agent draft, June 6, 1972.
Selected by Baltimore Orioles' organization in secondary phase of free-agent draft, January 7, 1976.
†On disabled list, May 10 to June 1 and August 5 to August 15, 1979.
‡On disabled list, July 12 to August 1, 1980.
§Traded to Cincinnati Reds, February 16, 1982, completing deal in which Cincinnati traded Pitcher Paul Moskau to Baltimore Orioles for a player to be named later, February 9, 1982.
xTraded to Detroit Tigers for Pitcher Pat Underwood, June 30, 1983.
ySold to Cincinnati Reds, November 18, 1983.

WILLIAM CULP KRUEGER

Name pronounced KREW-ger.

(Bill)

Born April 24, 1958, at Waukegan, Ill.
Height, 6.05. Weight, 210.
Throws and bats lefthanded.
Received bachelor of arts degree in business administration from
University of Portland, Portland, Ore. in 1979.

Tied for Eastern League lead in games started by pitchers with 27 and shutouts with 3 in 1982.

Year Club	League	G.	IP.	W.	L.	Pct.	H.	R.	ER.	SO.	BB.	ERA.
1980—Medford	Northwest	9	44	0	4	.000	54	38	25	48	29	5.11
1981—Modesto	California	16	98	3	5	.375	87	49	40	76	52	3.67
1981—West Haven	Eastern	11	68	3	6	.333	74	36	27	36	31	3.57
1982—West Haven	Eastern	28	181	15	9	.625	160	69	57	163	81	2.83
1983—Oakland†	American	17	109⅔	7	6	.538	104	54	44	58	53	3.61
Major League Totals		17	109⅔	7	6	.538	104	54	44	58	53	3.61

Signed as free agent by Oakland A's organization, July 12, 1980.
†On disabled list, August 5, 1983 through remainder of season.

MICHAEL EDWARD KRUKOW

Name pronounced KROO-koh.

(Mike)

Born January 21, 1952, at Long Beach, Calif.
Height, 6.04. Weight, 195.
Throws and bats righthanded.
Attended California Poly State University, San Luis Obispo, Calif.

Tied for National League lead in games started by pitchers with 25 in 1981.
Tied for National League lead in hit batsmen with 8 in 1980.
Led Gulf Coast League in intentional bases on balls issued with 4 and tied for lead in complete games with 4 in 1973.

Year Club	League	G.	IP.	W.	L.	Pct.	H.	R.	ER.	SO.	BB.	ERA.
1973—Bradenton Cubs	Gulf Coast	13	77	4	3	.571	76	32	27	★80	28	3.16
1974—Midland	Texas	6	30	1	1	.500	42	24	17	21	19	5.10
1974—Key West	Florida St.	20	130	5	10	.333	121	66	46	94	47	3.18
1975—Midland†	Texas	24	153	13	6	.684	143	65	58	100	66	3.41
1976—Wichita	Am. Assoc.	26	144	7	9	.438	142	61	53	108	47	3.31
1976—Chicago	National	2	4	0	0	.000	6	4	4	1	2	9.00
1977—Chicago	National	34	172	8	14	.364	195	96	84	106	61	4.40
1978—Wichita	Am. Assoc.	7	53	2	3	.400	51	27	23	29	21	3.91
1978—Chicago	National	27	138	9	3	.750	125	62	60	81	53	3.91

Year Club	League	G.	IP.	W.	L.	Pct.	H.	R.	ER.	SO.	BB.	ERA.
1979—Chicago	National	28	165	9	9	.500	172	84	77	119	81	4.20
1980—Chicago	National	34	205	10	15	.400	200	117	100	130	80	4.39
1981—Chicago‡	National	25	144	9	9	.500	146	68	59	101	55	3.69
1982—Philadelphia§	National	33	208	13	11	.542	211	87	72	138	82	3.12
1983—San Francisco x	National	31	184⅓	11	11	.500	189	95	81	136	76	3.95
Major League Totals		214	1220⅓	69	72	.489	1244	613	537	812	490	3.96

Selected by California Angels' organization in 32nd round of free-agent draft, June 4, 1970.
Selected by Chicago Cubs' organization in 8th round of free-agent draft, June 5, 1973.
†On disabled list, May 19 to June 7, 1975.
‡Traded with cash to Philadelphia Phillies for Catcher Keith Moreland and Pitchers Dan Larson and Dickie Noles, December 8, 1981.
§Traded with Pitcher Mark Davis and Outfielder Charles Penigar to San Francisco Giants for Second Baseman Joe Morgan and Pitcher Al Holland, December 14, 1982.
xOn disabled list, April 11 to May 8, 1983.

JOSEPH NEAL KUCHARSKI

Name pronounced Koo-CHAR-ski.

(Joe)

Born February 3, 1961, at Houston, Tex.
Height, 6.03. Weight, 230.
Throws and bats righthanded.
Attended University of South Carolina, Columbia, S. C.

Year Club	League	G.	IP.	W.	L.	Pct.	H.	R.	ER.	SO.	BB.	ERA.
1982—Hagerstown	Carolina	7	37⅔	3	2	.600	43	17	14	27	20	3.35
1982—Charlotte	Southern	4	30	2	2	.500	20	10	9	21	6	2.70
1983—Charlotte	Southern	27	185⅔	9	13	.409	181	97	81	86	73	3.93

Selected by Texas Rangers' organization in 18th round of free-agent draft, June 5, 1979.
Selected by Baltimore Orioles' organization in 1st round (24th player selected) of free-agent draft, June 7, 1982.

DUANE EUGENE KUIPER

Name pronounced KIPE-er.

Born June 19, 1950, at Racine, Wis.
Height, 6.00. Weight, 175.
Throws right and bats lefthanded.
Attended Indian Hills Community College, Centerville, Ia., and received
bachelor of arts degree from Southern Illinois University, Carbondale, Ill.
Second cousin of Dick Bosman, pitcher with Washington Senators, Texas Rangers,
Cleveland Indians and Oakland Athletics, 1966 through 1976.

Tied major league record for most triples, bases filled, game (2), July 27, 1978.
Led American League second basemen in fielding percentage with .987 in 1976.
Led American Association in stolen bases with 28 in 1974.

Year Club	League	Pos.	G.	AB.	R.	H.	2B.	3B.	HR.	RBI.	B.A.	PO.	A.	E.	F.A.
1972—Reno	Calif.	2B-SS-3B	124	496	89	149	20	3	2	53	.300	264	283	18	.968
1973—Okla. City	A. A.	2B	18	56	6	9	1	1	0	6	.161	42	34	3	.962
1973—San Antonio	Texas	2B	107	395	46	113	11	2	1	42	.286	220	317	19	.966
1974—Okla. City	A. A.	2B	●135	⋆554	83	172	27	5	3	53	.310	291	⋆365	11	⋆.984
1974—Cleveland	Amer.	2B	10	22	7	11	2	0	0	4	.500	16	19	0	1.000
1975—Okla. City	A. A.	2B	40	164	18	40	5	0	1	12	.244	110	94	3	.986
1975—Cleveland†	Amer.	2B	90	346	42	101	11	1	0	25	.292	192	230	12	.972
1976—Cleveland	Amer.	2B-1B	135	506	47	133	13	6	0	37	.263	321	367	11	.984
1977—Cleveland	Amer.	2B	148	610	62	169	15	8	1	50	.277	334	449	12	.985
1978—Cleveland	Amer.	2B	149	547	52	155	18	6	0	43	.283	341	408	16	.979
1979—Cleveland	Amer.	2B	140	479	46	122	9	5	0	39	.255	345	380	9	⋆.988
1980—Cleveland‡	Amer.	2B	42	149	10	42	5	0	0	9	.282	87	111	1	.995
1981—Cleveland§x	Amer.	2B	72	206	15	53	6	0	0	14	.257	118	174	5	.983
1982—San Francisco	Nat.	2B	107	218	26	61	9	1	0	17	.280	101	124	5	.978
1983—San Francisco y	Nat.	2B	72	176	14	44	2	2	0	14	.250	107	140	3	.988
American League Totals			786	2865	281	786	79	26	1	221	.274	1754	2138	66	.983
National League Totals			179	394	40	105	11	3	0	31	.266	208	264	8	.983
Major League Totals			965	3259	321	891	90	29	1	252	.273	1962	2402	74	.983

Selected by New York Yankees' organization in 12th round of free-agent draft, June 7, 1968.
Selected by Seattle Pilots' organization in secondary phase of free-agent draft, February 1, 1969.
Selected by Chicago White Sox' organization in 1st round (fifth player selected) of free-agent draft, January 17, 1970.
Selected by Cincinnati Reds' organization in secondary phase of free-agent draft, June 4, 1970.
Selected by Boston Red Sox' organization in secondary phase of free-agent draft, June 8, 1971.
Selected by Cleveland Indians' organization in secondary phase of free-agent draft, January 12, 1972.
†On supplemental disabled list, July 22 to August 11, 1975.
‡On emergency disabled list, June 2, 1980 through remainder of season.
§On disabled list, March 31 to April 30, 1981.
xTraded to San Francisco Giants for Pitcher Ed Whitson, November 16, 1981.
yOn supplemental disabled list, May 28 to July 8, 1983.

JEFFREY WILLIAM KUNKEL
(Jeff)

Born March 25, 1962, at Leonardo, N.J.
Height, 6.02. Weight, 175.
Throws and bats righthanded.
Attended Rider College, Lawrenceville, N.J.
Son of American League umpire Bill Kunkel, former pitcher with
Kansas City A's and New York Yankees, 1961 through 1963.

Year Club	League	Pos.	G.	AB.	R.	H.	2B.	3B.	HR.	RBI.	B.A.	PO.	A.	E.	F.A.
1983—Burlington	Midw.	SS	31	122	22	35	7	1	6	18	.287	38	88	13	.906
1983—Tulsa	Texas	SS-2B	37	130	21	37	14	0	5	25	.285	68	106	9	.951

Selected by Texas Rangers' organization in 1st round (3rd player selected) of free-agent draft, June 6, 1983.

RUSSELL JAY KUNTZ

Name pronounced COON-ts.

(Rusty)

Born February 4, 1955, at Orange, Calif.
Height, 6.03. Weight, 190.
Throws and bats righthanded.
Attended Cuesta College, San Luis Obispo, Calif.,
and California State University.

Led American Association batters in strikeouts with 111 in 1979.
Led Gulf Coast League in sacrifice flies with 6 and bases on balls received with 40 in 1977.

Year Club	League	Pos.	G.	AB.	R.	H.	2B.	3B.	HR.	RBI.	B.A.	PO.	A.	E.	F.A.
1977—Sara. W. Sox	Gulf C.	OF	51	174	●49	50	9	5	3	33	.287	87	●9	3	.970
1978—Knoxville	South.	OF	113	395	68	104	25	7	10	57	.263	244	9	3	.988
1979—Iowa	A. A.	OF	122	394	67	116	27	5	15	57	.294	287	12	5	.984
1979—Chicago	Amer.	OF	5	11	0	1	0	0	0	0	.091	12	1	0	1.000
1980—Iowa†	A. A.	OF	91	339	47	99	20	2	11	54	.292	198	9	7	.967
1980—Chicago	Amer.	OF	36	62	5	14	4	0	0	3	.226	45	2	1	.979
1981—Chicago	Amer.	OF	67	55	15	14	2	0	0	4	.255	54	0	0	1.000
1982—Edmonton‡	P. C.	OF	69	193	35	52	11	2	7	34	.269	134	3	5	.965
1982—Chicago	Amer.	OF	21	26	4	5	1	0	0	3	.192	21	0	0	1.000
1983—Chi.§-Minn.	Amer.	OF	59	142	19	30	4	0	3	6	.211	106	3	2	.982
1983—Denver x	A. A.	OF	13	43	6	15	2	1	1	8	.349	25	0	1	.962
Major League Totals...................................			188	296	43	64	11	0	3	16	.216	238	6	3	.988

Selected by Chicago White Sox' organization in 11th round of free-agent draft, June 7, 1977.
†On disabled list, May 24 to June 17, 1980.
‡On disabled list, April 30 to May 31, 1982.
§Traded to Minnesota Twins for Third Baseman Mike Sodders, June 21, 1983.
xTraded to Detroit Tigers for Pitcher Larry Pashnick, December 5, 1983.

STANLEY KYLES
(Stan)

Born February 26, 1961, at Chicago, Ill.
Height, 6.01. Weight, 160.
Throws and bats righthanded.

Brother of Mack Payne, pitcher in Kansas City Royals' organization, 1970 through 1972.

Year Club	League	G.	IP.	W.	L.	Pct.	H.	R.	ER.	SO.	BB.	ERA.
1979—Sarasota Cubs...............................	Gulf Coast	7	16	1	4	.200	23	18	15	10	21	8.44
1980—Geneva.......................................	NYP	9	47	2	5	.286	46	34	28	29	40	5.36
1981—Quad Cities................................	Midwest	8	18	0	2	.000	29	29	24	12	16	12.00
1981—Geneva.......................................	NYP	12	61	1	8	.111	66	46	31	24	38	4.57
1982—Salinas.......................................	California	26	172	11	5	.688	160	71	48	118	66	2.51
1983—Midland......................................	Texas	23	155⅓	7	11	.389	164	79	66	74	67	3.82
1983—Iowa	Am. Assoc.	4	25	2	1	.667	16	9	9	9	10	3.24

Selected by Chicago Cubs' organization in 4th round of free-agent draft, June 5, 1979.

ROBERT JOSEPH LACEY JR.
(Bob)

Born August 25, 1953, at Fredericksburg, Va.
Height, 6.04. Weight, 190.
Throws left and bats righthanded.
Attended Central Arizona College, Coolidge, Ariz.

Year Club	League	G.	IP.	W.	L.	Pct.	H.	R.	ER.	SO.	BB.	ERA.
1972—Coos Bay-North Bend†................	Northwest	8	39	0	3	.000	43	34	30	25	22	30	5.77
1973—Key West	Florida St.	13	90	6	1	.857	85	23	13	57	17	1.30
1973—Burlington	Midwest	15	83	7	1	.875	86	35	30	63	25	3.25
1974—Birmingham	Southern	32	155	6	13	.316	203	★111	79	72	35	4.59
1975—Birmingham	Southern	33	68	3	6	.333	81	34	28	47	39	3.71
1975—Tucson......................................	*P. Coast	10	35	3	1	.750	35	14	12	17	9	3.09
1976—Tucson‡.....................................	P. Coast	29	105	3	9	.250	139	73	69	35	26	5.91
1977—San Jose	P. Coast	11	16	2	0	1.000	10	0	0	9	6	0.00

Year Club	League	G.	IP.	W.	L.	Pct.	H.	R.	ER.	SO.	BB.	ERA.
1977—Oakland	American	64	122	6	8	.429	100	46	41	69	43	3.02
1978—Oakland	American	•74	120	8	9	.471	126	52	40	60	35	3.00
1979—Oakland§	American	42	48	1	5	.167	66	34	31	33	24	5.81
1980—Oakland xy	American	47	80	3	2	.600	68	29	26	45	21	2.93
1981—Cleveland z-Texas	American	15	22	0	0	.000	37	21	19	11	3	7.77
1981—Charleston a	Int'national	2	8	1	0	1.000	8	1	1	5	2	1.13
1982—Saltillo b	Mexican	14	92⅓	8	4	.667	94	32	28	43	28	2.73
1983—Edmonton	P. Coast	54	101	7	3	.700	117	60	53	71	30	4.72
1983—California c	American	8	8⅔	1	2	.333	12	5	5	7	0	5.19
Major League Totals		250	400⅔	19	26	.422	409	187	162	225	126	3.64

Selected by Oakland A's organization in 10th round of free-agent draft, January 12, 1972.
†On suspended list, July 31, 1972 through remainder of season.
‡On disabled list, June 5 to June 16 and August 4 to September 8, 1976.
§On disabled list, July 14 to September 18, 1979.
xTraded with Pitcher Roy Moretti to San Diego Padres for Pitcher Eric Mustad and Infielders Kevin Bell and Tony Phillips, March 27, 1981.
yTraded by San Diego to Cleveland Indians for Second Baseman Juan Bonilla, April 1, 1981.
zSold to Texas Rangers, September 8, 1981.
aReleased, March 26, 1982; signed by Saltillo of Mexican League, May 17, 1982.
bSigned as free agent by California Angels' organization, March 19, 1983.
cGranted free agency when refused option to minors, November 12,˙1983.

ALLEN ROBERT LACHOWICZ
(Al)

Born September 6, 1960,˙ at Pittsburgh, Pa.
Height, 6.03. Weight, 195.
Throws and bats righthanded.
Attended University of Pittsburgh, Pittsburgh, Pa.

Year Club	League	G.	IP.	W.	L.	Pct.	H.	R.	ER.	SO.	BB.	ERA.
1981—Sarasota Rangers	Gulf Coast	6	24	2	3	.400	19	9	5	14	15	1.88
1982—Tulsa	Texas	25	146	12	8	.600	137	69	63	109	53	3.88
1983—Oklahoma City†	Am. Assoc.	17	115⅓	5	3	.625	101	48	38	96	52	2.97
1983—Texas	American	2	8	0	1	.000	9	2	2	8	2	2.25
Major League Totals		2	8	0	1	.000	9	2	2	8	2	2.25

Selected by New York Mets' organization in 26th round of free-agent draft, June 6, 1978.
Selected by Texas Rangers' organization in 1st round (24th player selected) of free-agent draft, June 8, 1981.
†On disabled list, May 3 to June 23, 1983.

FRANK JOSEPH LaCORTE JR.

Name pronounced Luh-KORT-ee.

Born October 13, 1952, at San Jose, Calif.
Height, 6.01.   Weight, 180.
Throws and bats righthanded.
Attended Gavilan College, Gilroy, Calif.

Year Club	League	G.	IP.	W.	L.	Pct.	H.	R.	ER.	SO.	BB.	ERA.
1973—Greenwood	W. Carol.	18	105	7	8	.467	70	44	30	109	51	2.57
1973—Savannah	Southern	7	30	2	1	.667	19	14	12	34	22	3.60
1974—Savannah	Southern	23	120	7	8	.467	106	76	63	106	89	4.73
1975—Richmond	Int'national	24	128	9	7	.563	121	65	61	108	71	4.29
1975—Atlanta	National	3	14	0	3	.000	13	10	8	10	6	5.14
1976—Richmond	Int'national	14	78	3	3	.500	91	55	46	77	47	5.31
1976—Atlanta	National	19	105	3	12	.200	97	58	55	79	53	4.71
1977—Richmond†	Int'national	8	37	2	3	.400	38	25	25	40	29	6.08
1977—Atlanta	National	14	37	1	8	.111	67	51	48	28	29	11.68
1978—Richmond‡	Int'national	23	130	6	7	.462	125	67	61	99	66	4.22
1978—Atlanta	National	2	15	0	1	.000	9	6	6	7	4	3.60
1979—Atlanta§-Houston	National	18	35	1	2	.333	30	23	22	30	15	5.66
1979—Charleston	Int'national	12	79	4	7	.364	68	32	24	57	31	2.73
1980—Houston	National	55	83	8	5	.615	61	29	26	66	43	2.82
1981—Houston	National	37	42	4	2	.667	41	18	17	40	21	3.64
1982—Houston	National	55	76⅓	1	5	.167	71	44	38	51	46	4.48
1983—Houston xy	National	37	53⅓	4	4	.500	35	32	30	48	28	5.06
Major League Totals		240	460⅔	22	42	.344	424	271	250	359	245	4.88

Signed as free agent by Atlanta Braves' organization, September 5, 1972.
†On disabled list, July 31 to August 11, 1977.
‡On disabled list, August 2 to August 16, 1978.
§Traded to Houston Astros for Pitcher Bo McLaughlin, May 25, 1979.
xOn disabled list, July 25 to September 1, 1983.
yGranted free agency, November 7, 1983; signed by California Angels, December 8, 1983.

DIVISION SERIES RECORD

Year Club	League	G.	IP.	W.	L.	Pct.	H.	R.	ER.	SO.	BB.	ERA.
1981—Houston	National	2	3⅔	0	0	.000	2	0	0	5	1	0.00

CHAMPIONSHIP SERIES RECORD

Year Club	League	G.	IP.	W.	L.	Pct.	H.	R.	ER.	SO.	BB.	ERA.
1980—Houston	National	2	3	1	1	.500	7	2	1	2	2	3.00

MICHAEL JAMES LaCOSS
(Mike)

Born May 30, 1956, at Glendale, Calif.
Height, 6.04. Weight, 190.
Throws and bats righthanded.

Tied for American Association lead in shutouts with 3 in 1978.

Year Club	League	G.	IP.	W.	L.	Pct.	H.	R.	ER.	SO.	BB.	ERA.
1974—Billings	Pioneer	13	87	6	5	.545	81	40	27	58	38	2.79
1975—Tampa	Florida St.	23	151	4	7	.412	131	61	48	72	41	2.86
1976—Three Rivers	Eastern	25	162	12	10	.545	148	66	53	80	53	2.94
1977—Indianapolis	Am. Assoc.	27	186	11	*13	.458	181	93	80	104	65	3.87
1978—Indianapolis	Am. Assoc.	19	130	11	5	.688	129	62	50	67	49	3.46
1978—Cincinnati	National	16	96	4	8	.333	104	56	48	31	46	4.50
1979—Cincinnati	National	35	206	14	8	.636	202	92	80	73	79	3.50
1980—Cincinnati	National	34	169	10	12	.455	207	101	87	59	68	4.63
1981—Cincinnati†	National	20	78	4	7	.364	102	55	53	22	30	6.12
1982—Houston	National	41	115	6	6	.500	107	41	37	51	54	2.90
1983—Houston‡	National	38	138	5	7	.417	142	81	68	53	56	4.43
Major League Totals		184	802	43	48	.473	864	426	373	289	333	4.19

Selected by Cincinnati Reds' organization in 3rd round of free-agent draft, June 5, 1974.
†Sold on waivers to Houston Astros, April 4, 1982.
‡On disabled list, June 17 to July 8, 1983.

CHAMPIONSHIP SERIES RECORD

Year Club	League	G.	IP.	W.	L.	Pct.	H.	R.	ER.	SO.	BB.	ERA.
1979—Cincinnati	National	1	1⅔	0	1	.000	1	2	2	0	4	10.80

ALL-STAR GAME RECORD

Year League		IP.	W.	L.	Pct.	H.	R.	ER.	SO.	BB.	ERA.
1979—National		1⅓	0	0	.000	1	0	0	0	0	0.00

LEONDAUS LACY
(Lee)

Born April 10, 1949, at Longview, Tex.
Height, 6.01. Weight, 175.
Throws and bats righthanded.
Attended Laney Junior College, Oakland, Calif.

Tied major league record for most home runs by pinch-hitter, consecutive at-bats (3), May 2, 6 and 17, 1978 (includes one base on balls during streak).
Led California League shortstops in errors with 63 in 1970.
Led Pioneer League third basemen in putouts with 50, assists with 116, errors with 26 and double plays with 9 in 1969.

Year Club	League	Pos.	G.	AB.	R.	H.	2B.	3B.	HR.	RBI.	B.A.	PO.	A.	E.	F.A.
1969—Ogden	Pion	3B-SS-2B	71	239	43	70	6	7	1	38	.293	54	121	127	.866
1970—Bakersfield	Calif.	SS-3B	124	502	96	151	19	5	4	49	.301	189	291	66	.879
1971—Albuquerque	Texas	2-3-S-O	132	488	54	150	17	7	0	57	.307	263	358	31	.952
1972—El Paso	Texas	2B-SS	68	258	39	96	22	4	1	35	.372	123	191	7	.978
1972—Los Angeles	Nat.	2B	60	243	34	63	7	3	0	12	.259	125	161	8	.973
1973—Los Angeles	Nat.	2B	57	135	14	28	2	0	0	8	.207	80	85	6	.965
1974—Los Angeles	Nat.	2B-3B	48	78	13	22	6	0	0	8	.282	38	53	3	.968
1975—Los Angeles†	Nat.	2B-OF-SS	101	306	44	96	11	5	7	40	.314	152	75	13	.946
1976—Atl.-L.A.	Nat.	2B-OF-3B	103	338	42	91	11	3	3	34	.269	193	111	9	.971
1977—Los Angeles§	Nat.	OF-2B-3B	75	169	28	45	7	0	6	21	.266	56	69	4	.969
1978—Los Angeles x	Nat.	O-2-3-S	103	245	29	64	16	4	13	40	.261	114	64	9	.952
1979—Pittsburgh	Nat.	OF-2B	84	182	17	45	9	3	5	15	.247	77	8	3	.966
1980—Pittsburgh	Nat.	OF-3B	109	278	45	93	20	4	7	33	.335	175	11	3	.984
1981—Pittsburgh	Nat.	OF-3B	78	213	31	57	11	4	2	10	.268	121	8	3	.977
1982—Pittsburgh	Nat.	OF-3B	121	359	66	112	16	3	5	31	.312	186	9	7	.965
1983—Pittsburgh	Nat.	OF	108	288	40	87	12	3	4	13	.302	167	2	0	1.000
Major League Totals			1047	2834	403	803	128	32	52	265	.283	1484	656	68	.969

Selected by Los Angeles Dodgers' organization in 2nd round of free-agent draft, February 1, 1969.
†Traded with Outfielder Jimmy Wynn, First Baseman-Outfielder Tom Paciorek and Infielder Jerry Royster to Atlanta Braves for Outfielder Dusty Baker and First Baseman-Third Baseman Ed Goodson, November 17, 1975.
‡Traded with Pitcher Elias Sosa to Los Angeles Dodgers for Pitcher Mike Marshall, June 23, 1976.
§On supplemental disabled list, June 20 to July 15, 1977.
xGranted free agency, November 2, 1978; signed by Pittsburgh Pirates, January 19, 1979.

CHAMPIONSHIP SERIES RECORD

Year Club	League	Pos.	G.	AB.	R.	H.	2B.	3B.	HR.	RBI.	B.A.	PO.	A.	E.	F.A.
1974—Los Angeles	Nat.	PR	1	0	0	0	0	0	0	0	.000	0	0	0	.000
1977—Los Angeles	Nat.	PH	1	1	1	1	0	0	0	0	1.000	0	0	0	.000
1978—Los Angeles	Nat.	PH	2	2	0	0	0	0	0	0	.000	0	0	0	.000
Championship Series Totals			4	3	1	1	0	0	0	0	.333	0	0	0	.000

Year Club League	Pos.	G.	AB.	R.	H.	2B.	3B.	HR.	RBI.	B.A.	PO.	A.	E.	F.A.
1974—Los Angeles .... Nat.	PH	1	1	0	0	0	0	0	0	.000	0	0	0	.000
1977—Los Angeles .... Nat.	PH-OF	4	7	1	3	0	0	0	2	.429	2	0	0	1.000
1978—Los Angeles .... Nat.	DH	4	14	0	2	0	0	0	1	.143	0	0	0	.000
1979—Pittsburgh.............. Nat.	PH	4	4	0	1	0	0	0	0	.250	0	0	0	.000
World Series Totals		13	26	1	6	0	0	0	3	.231	2	0	0	1.000

PETER LINWOOD LADD
(Pete)

Born July 17, 1956, at Portland, Me.
Height, 6.03. Weight, 240.
Throws and bats righthanded.
Attended University of Massachusetts, Amherst, Mass.

Major League saves: 1982 (3), 1983 (25). Total—28.
Led Florida State League in saves with 18 in 1978.

Year Club	League	G.	IP.	W.	L.	Pct.	H.	R.	ER.	SO.	BB.	ERA.
1977—Winter Haven............................ Florida St.		19	27	4	1	.800	19	8	5	27	7	1.67
1978—Winter Haven............................ Florida St.		44	85	8	2	.800	69	36	30	66	30	3.18
1979—Bristol†.. Eastern		18	29	3	1	.750	11	2	2	26	8	0.62
1979—Columbus‡............................ Southern		13	41	6	1	.857	24	13	12	31	23	2.63
1979—Houston............................ National		10	12	1	1	.500	8	5	4	6	8	3.00
1980—Columbus............................ Southern		33	55	6	5	.545	47	27	21	38	29	3.44
1980—Tucson............................ P. Coast		18	21	1	2	.333	18	7	6	24	4	2.57
1981—Tucson§............................ P. Coast		47	96	5	4	.556	90	43	36	68	44	3.38
1982—Vancouver............................ P. Coast		34	55⅔	10	2	.833	42	19	18	63	18	2.91
1982—Milwaukee............................ American		16	18	1	3	.250	16	8	8	12	6	4.00
1983—Milwaukee............................ American		44	49⅓	3	4	.429	30	17	14	41	16	2.55
1983—Vancouver............................ P. Coast		12	13⅓	0	0	.000	10	2	2	16	4	1.35
National League Totals..............................		10	12	1	1	.500	8	5	4	6	8	3.00
American League Totals..		60	67⅓	4	7	.364	46	25	22	53	22	2.94
Major League Totals................................		70	79⅓	5	8	.385	54	30	26	59	30	2.95

Selected by Boston Red Sox' organization in 25th round of free-agent draft, June 7, 1977.
†Traded with cash and a player to be named later to Houston Astros' organization for First Baseman Bob Watson, June 13, 1979; Houston acquired Pitcher Bob Sprowl to complete deal, June 19, 1979.
‡On disabled list, July 4 to July 18, 1979.
§Traded to Milwaukee Brewers' organization for Pitcher Buster Keeton, October 23, 1981.

CHAMPIONSHIP SERIES RECORD

Tied Championship Series record for most saves, five-game Series (2), 1982.
Tied American League Championship Series record for most saves, total Series (2), 1982.

Year Club	League	G.	IP.	W.	L.	Pct.	H.	R.	ER.	SO.	BB.	ERA.
1982—Milwaukee.. American		3	3⅓	0	0	.000	0	0	0	5	0	0.00

WORLD SERIES RECORD

Year Club	League	G.	IP.	W.	L.	Pct.	H.	R.	ER.	SO.	BB.	ERA.
1982—Milwaukee.. American		1	⅔	0	0	.000	1	0	0	0	2	0.00

ROGER VICTOR LaFRANCOIS

Name pronounced La-fran-swa.

Born August 2, 1956, at Norwich, Conn.
Height, 6.02. Weight, 215.
Throws right and bats lefthanded.
Attended University of Oklahoma, Norman, Okla.
and University of Connecticut, Storrs, Conn.
Son of Roger LaFrancois, minor league catcher, 1944 through 1952.

Led Carolina League catchers in assists with 75 in 1978.
Tied for International League lead in errors by catchers with 13 and double plays with 13 in 1983.

Year Club	League	Pos.	G.	AB.	R.	H.	2B.	3B.	HR.	RBI.	B.A.	PO.	A.	E.	F.A.
1977—Elmira.................... NYP	PH	1	1	0	0	0	0	0	0	.000	0	0	0	.000
1978—Winston-Salem ..... Carol.	C-1B	112	395	50	123	14	4	8	72	.311	599	97	14	.980
1979—Pawtucket............ Int.	C	106	305	19	70	10	2	5	24	.230	489	●73	8	.986
1980—Bristol.................... East.	1B-C	59	197	34	52	9	0	9	41	.264	425	41	9	.981
1980—Pawtucket............ Int.	C-1B	62	158	14	39	7	2	3	16	.247	161	22	3	.984
1981—Pawtucket............ Int.	★C-1B-OF	95	309	26	71	13	1	6	16	.230	500	66	7	★.988
1982—Boston.................... Amer.	C	8	10	1	4	1	0	0	1	.400	15	0	0	1.000
1983—Pawtucket†.......... Int.	C-1B	75	235	25	53	10	1	7	39	.226	396	65	14	.971
Major League Totals................................			8	10	1	4	1	0	0	1	.400	15	0	0	1.000

Selected by Boston Red Sox' organization in 8th round of free-agent draft, June 7, 1977.
†Granted free agency, October 20, 1983; signed by Atlanta Braves, December 9, 1983.

—DID YOU KNOW—

That two brothers broke into the majors in 1983? Seattle's Spike Owen made his debut on June 25, and brother Dave appeared for the first time with the Cubs on September 6.

MICHAEL RUSSELL LAGA
(Mike)

Born June 14, 1960, at Ridgewood, N. J.
Height, 6.03. Weight, 190.
Throws and bats lefthanded.
Attended Bergen Community College, Paramus, N. J.,
and Fairleigh Dickinson University, Teaneck, N. J.

Led American Association in being hit by pitch with 13 in 1982.
Led American Association first basemen in total chances with 1,221 in 1982.

Year Club	League	Pos.	G.	AB.	R.	H.	2B.	3B.	HR.	RBI.	B.A.	PO.	A.	E.	F.A.
1980—Lakeland	Fla. St.	1B	122	407	60	111	14	6	12	74	.273	1025	84	★18	.984
1981—Birmingham	South.	1B	142	547	89	158	28	7	31	86	.289	1193	★105	★23	.983
1982—Evansville	A. A.	1B	126	444	77	111	15	3	34	90	.250	★1135	68	18	.985
1982—Detroit	Amer.	1B	27	88	6	23	9	0	3	11	.261	163	4	1	.994
1983—Evansville	A. A.	1B	105	355	46	82	24	1	16	58	.231	835	62	★11	.988
1983—Detroit	Amer.	1B	12	21	2	4	0	0	0	2	.190	9	1	0	1.000
Major League Totals			39	109	8	27	9	0	3	13	.248	172	5	1	.994

Selected by Detroit Tigers' organization in 1st round (17th player selected) of free-agent draft, January 8, 1980.

JEFFREY ALLEN LAHTI
Name pronounced LOT-ee.
(Jeff)

Born October 8, 1956, at Oregon City, Ore.
Height, 6.00. Weight, 180.
Throws and bats righthanded.
Attended Treasure Valley Community College, Ontario, Ore. and
Portland State University, Portland, Ore.

Tied for Western Carolinas League lead in saves with 13 in 1979.

Year Club	League	G.	IP.	W.	L.	Pct.	H.	R.	ER.	SO.	BB.	ERA.
1978—Eugene	Northwest	16	53	1	5	.167	58	34	26	32	21	4.42
1979—Greensboro	W. Carol.	53	92	7	2	.778	83	43	29	89	33	2.84
1979—Nashville	Southern	6	16	2	0	1.000	10	4	3	12	5	1.69
1980—Waterbury	Eastern	55	91	7	8	.467	75	34	28	78	40	2.77
1981—Indianapolis†	Am. Assoc.	50	100	6	6	.500	78	38	33	70	31	2.97
1982—Louisville	Am. Assoc.	21	30⅓	3	2	.600	27	15	15	17	7	4.45
1982—St. Louis	National	33	56⅔	5	4	.556	53	27	24	22	21	3.81
1983—St. Louis‡	National	53	74	3	3	.500	64	31	26	26	29	3.16
1983—Louisville‡	Am. Assoc.	1	2	0	0	.000	2	1	1	0	0	4.50
Major League Totals		86	130⅔	8	7	.533	117	58	50	48	50	3.44

Selected by Philadelphia Phillies' organization in 12th round of free-agent draft, January 7, 1976.
Selected by San Francisco Giants' organization in 7th round of free-agent draft, January 11, 1977.
Selected by Cincinnati Reds' organization in 5th round of free-agent draft, June 6, 1978.
†Traded with Pitcher Jose Brito to St. Louis Cardinals' organization for Pitcher Bob Shirley, April 1, 1982.
‡On disabled list, June 1 to June 22, 1983; included rehabilitation disability assignment to Louisville, June 19 to June 22, 1983.

WORLD SERIES RECORD

Year Club	League	G.	IP.	W.	L.	Pct.	H.	R.	ER.	SO.	BB.	ERA.
1982—St. Louis	National	2	1⅔	0	0	.000	4	2	2	1	1	10.80

STEVEN MICHAEL LAKE
(Steve)

Born March 14, 1957, at Inglewood, Calif.
Height, 6.01. Weight, 180.
Throws and bats righthanded.
Cousin of Mike Lake, minor league pitcher, 1941 through 1946.

Led Appalachian League in passed balls with 15 in 1975.

Year Club	League	Pos.	G.	AB.	R.	H.	2B.	3B.	HR.	RBI.	B.A.	PO.	A.	E.	F.A.
1975—Bluefield	Appal.	C	49	162	17	45	12	0	3	24	.278	254	★39	9	.970
1976—Miami	Fla. St.	PH	1	1	0	1	0	0	0	1	1.000	0	0	0	.000
1977—Miami	Fla. St.	C	79	232	25	55	10	1	2	24	.237	357	47	6	.985
1978—Miami†‡	Fla. St.	C	69	223	19	57	10	0	2	26	.256	300	49	6	.983
1979—Stockton§	Calif.	C	94	329	36	93	12	3	6	40	.283	504	73	8	.986
1980—Holyoke	East.	C-OF	102	325	26	84	9	2	2	44	.258	445	107	10	.982
1981—Vancouver x	P. C.	C	109	348	27	80	14	1	2	38	.230	502	102	7	.989
1982—Tucson y	P. C.	C	112	378	42	100	15	4	3	45	.265	504	91	12	.980
1983—Chicago	Nat.	C	38	85	9	22	4	1	1	7	.259	115	22	0	1.000
Major League Totals			38	85	9	22	4	1	1	7	.259	115	22	0	1.000

Selected by Baltimore Orioles' organization in 3rd round of free-agent draft, June 4, 1975.
†On disabled list, April 17 to May 16, 1978.
‡Sold to Milwaukee Brewers' organization, December 21, 1978.
§On disabled list, June 20 to July 6, 1979.
xLoaned to Tucson (Houston Astros' organization), April 5, 1982; returned, September 7, 1982.
yTraded to Chicago Cubs for a player to be named later, April 1, 1983; Milwaukee Brewers' organization acquired Pitcher Rich Buonantony to complete deal, October 25, 1983.

DENNIS PATRICK LAMP

Born September 23, 1952, at Los Angeles, Calif.
Height, 6.03. Weight, 190.
Throws and bats righthanded.
Established National League record for most games taken out as starting pitcher, season (35), 1980.
Major League saves: 1982 (5), 1983 (15). Total—20.

Year Club	League	G.	IP.	W.	L.	Pct.	H.	R.	ER.	SO.	BB.	ERA.
1971—Caldwell	Pioneer	14	46	1	2	.333	51	39	33	43	32	6.46
1972—Bradenton Cubs	Gulf Coast	14	70	7	2	.778	56	20	15	56	21	1.93
1973—Quincy	Midwest	13	89	6	4	.600	67	32	26	71	29	2.63
1973—Midland	Texas	9	48	2	4	.333	54	29	25	23	11	4.69
1974—Key West	Florida St.	8	49	1	5	.167	39	15	8	20	14	1.47
1974—Midland	Texas	24	60	1	1	.500	70	38	31	42	22	4.65
1975—Midland	Texas	37	127	7	5	.583	112	52	47	71	54	3.33
1976—Wichita	Am. Assoc.	30	153	8	★14	.364	182	94	69	98	52	4.06
1977—Wichita	Am. Assoc.	20	129	11	4	★.733	116	54	42	52	23	2.93
1977—Chicago	National	11	30	0	2	.000	43	21	21	12	8	6.30
1978—Chicago	National	37	224	7	15	.318	221	96	82	73	56	3.29
1979—Chicago	National	38	200	11	10	.524	223	96	78	86	46	3.51
1980—Chicago†	National	41	203	10	14	.417	259	★123	★117	83	82	5.19
1981—Chicago	American	27	127	7	6	.538	103	41	34	71	43	2.41
1982—Chicago	American	44	189⅔	11	8	.579	206	96	84	78	59	3.99
1983—Chicago‡	American	49	116⅓	7	7	.500	123	52	48	44	29	3.71
National League Totals		127	657	28	41	.406	746	336	298	254	192	4.08
American League Totals		120	433	25	21	.543	432	189	166	193	131	3.45
Major League Totals		247	1090	53	62	.461	1178	525	464	447	323	3.83

Selected by Chicago Cubs' organization in 3rd round of free-agent draft, June 8, 1971.
†Traded to Chicago White Sox for Pitcher Ken Kravec, March 28, 1981.
‡Granted free agency, November 7, 1983.

CHAMPIONSHIP SERIES RECORD

Tied American League Championship Series record for most games pitched, four-game Series (3), 1983.

Year Club	League	G.	IP.	W.	L.	Pct.	H.	R.	ER.	SO.	BB.	ERA.
1983—Chicago	American	3	2	0	0	.000	0	1	0	1	2	0.00

RAFAEL SILVIALDO CAMILO LANDESTOY (SANTANA)

Born May 28, 1953, at Bani, Dominican Republic.
Height, 5.09. Weight, 163.
Throws right and bats left and righthanded.
Led Pacific Coast League in stolen bases with 56 in 1977.
Led Eastern League shortstops in putouts with 199, assists with 387 and double plays with 73 in 1975.

Year Club	League	Pos.	G.	AB.	R.	H.	2B.	3B.	HR.	RBI.	B.A.	PO.	A.	E.	F.A.
1972—Ogden	Pion.	OF	49	119	13	29	4	2	0	14	.244	50	2	4	.929
1973—Daytona Beach	Fla. St.	OF	96	288	31	84	11	0	0	24	.292	145	11	3	.981
1974—Orangeburg	W. Car.	SS-OF-2B	●134	492	71	135	13	5	2	49	.274	264	218	47	.911
1975—Waterbury	East.	★SS-OF	130	439	61	123	10	7	0	31	.280	203	388	★60	.908
1976—Albuquerque	P. C.	S-2-3-O	140	463	68	128	14	7	0	54	.276	226	399	38	.943
1977—Albuquerque	P. C.	2B-OF	130	558	113	154	21	10	0	41	.276	270	391	21	.969
1977—Los Angeles	Nat.	2B-SS	15	18	6	5	0	0	0	0	.278	8	18	0	1.000
1978—Albuquerque†	P. C.	2B	66	277	46	76	12	6	1	35	.274	148	198	18	.951
1978—Houston	Nat.	SS-OF-2B	59	218	18	58	5	1	0	9	.266	70	132	4	.981
1979—Houston	Nat.	2B-3B	129	282	33	76	9	6	0	30	.270	168	237	12	.971
1980—Houston	Nat.	2B-SS-3B	149	393	42	97	13	8	1	27	.247	185	295	9	.982
1981—Hou.‡-Cin.	Nat.	2B	47	85	8	13	1	1	0	5	.153	55	64	4	.967
1982—Cincinnati	Nat.	3-2-O-S	73	111	11	21	3	0	1	9	.189	41	54	0	1.000
1983—Cin.§-L.A.	Nat.	2-3-O-1-S	71	69	6	11	1	1	1	1	.159	34	28	3	.954
Major League Totals			543	1176	124	281	32	17	3	81	.239	561	828	32	.977

Signed as free agent by Los Angeles Dodgers' organization, May 29, 1972.
†Traded to Houston Astros, July 7, 1978, as partial completion of deal in which Los Angeles Dodgers acquired Catcher Joe Ferguson for two players to be named later, July 1, 1978; Houston acquired Outfielder Jeff Leonard complete deal, September 11, 1978.
‡Traded to Cincinnati Reds for First Baseman Harry Spilman, June 8, 1981.
§Traded to Los Angeles Dodgers for Pitchers Brett Wise and John Franco, May 9, 1983.

CHAMPIONSHIP SERIES RECORD

Year Club	League	Pos.	G.	AB.	R.	H.	2B.	3B.	HR.	RBI.	B.A.	PO.	A.	E.	F.A.
1980—Houston	Nat.	2-PR-S	5	9	3	2	0	0	0	2	.222	5	8	1	.929
1983—Los Angeles	Nat.	PH	2	2	0	0	0	0	0	0	.000	0	0	0	.000
Championship Series Totals			7	11	3	2	0	0	0	2	.182	5	8	1	.929

WORLD SERIES RECORD

Year Club	League	Pos.	G.	AB.	R.	H.	2B.	3B.	HR.	RBI.	B.A.	PO.	A.	E.	F.A.
1977—Los Angeles	Nat.	PR	1	0	0	0	0	0	0	0	.000	0	0	0	.000

KENNETH FRANCIS LANDREAUX

Name pronounced LAN-droh.

(Ken)

Born December 22, 1954, at Los Angeles, Calif.
Height, 5.11. Weight, 164.
Throws right and bats lefthanded.
Attended Arizona State University, Tempe, Ariz.
Cousin of Enos Cabell, infielder with Detroit Tigers.

Tied major league record for most two-base hits, inning (2), July 3, 1979 (seventh inning).
Tied modern major league record for most three-base hits, game (3), July 3, 1980.
Major League stolen bases: 1977 (1), 1978 (7), 1979 (10), 1980 (8), 1981 (18), 1982 (31), 1983 (30). Total—105.
Named Minor League Player of the Year by THE SPORTING NEWS, 1977.

Year Club	League	Pos.	G.	AB.	R.	H.	2B.	3B.	HR.	RBI.	B.A.	PO.	A.	E.	F.A.
1976—El Paso†	Texas	OF	21	59	15	13	3	1	2	11	.220	32	4	0	1.000
1977—El Paso	Texas	OF	57	209	57	74	17	4	16	59	.354	117	6	6	.953
1977—Salt Lake City	P. C.	OF	62	256	67	92	16	4	11	57	.359	164	3	4	.977
1977—California	Amer.	OF	23	76	6	19	5	1	0	5	.250	59	5	2	.970
1978—California‡	Amer.	OF	93	260	37	58	7	5	5	23	.223	138	6	2	.986
1979—Minnesota	Amer.	OF	151	564	81	172	27	5	15	83	.305	292	10	6	.981
1980—Minnesota§	Amer.	OF	129	484	56	136	23	11	7	62	.281	231	8	6	.976
1981—Los Angeles	Nat.	OF	99	390	48	98	16	4	7	41	.251	210	4	0	●1.000
1982—Los Angeles	Nat.	OF	129	461	71	131	23	7	7	50	.284	281	3	4	.986
1983—Los Angeles	Nat.	OF	141	481	63	135	25	3	17	66	.281	299	4	3	.990
American League Totals			396	1384	180	385	62	22	27	173	.278	720	29	16	.979
National League Totals			369	1332	182	364	64	14	31	157	.273	790	11	7	.991
Major League Totals			765	2716	362	749	126	36	58	330	.276	1510	40	23	.985

Selected by Houston Astros' organization in 8th round of free-agent draft, June 5, 1973.
Selected by California Angels' organization in 1st round (sixth player selected) of free-agent draft, June 8, 1976.
†On disabled list, July 17 to August 4, 1976.
‡Traded with Pitchers Paul Hartzell and Brad Havens and Third Baseman Dave Engle to Minnesota Twins for First Baseman Rod Carew, February 3, 1979.
§Traded to Los Angeles Dodgers for Third Baseman-Outfielder Mickey Hatcher, First Baseman Kelly Snider and Pitcher Matt Reeves, March 30, 1981.

DIVISION SERIES RECORD

Year Club	League	Pos.	G.	AB.	R.	H.	2B.	3B.	HR.	RBI.	B.A.	PO.	A.	E.	F.A.
1981—Los Angeles	Nat.	OF	5	20	1	4	1	0	0	1	.200	16	0	0	1.000

CHAMPIONSHIP SERIES RECORD

Year Club	League	Pos.	G.	AB.	R.	H.	2B.	3B.	HR.	RBI.	B.A.	PO.	A.	E.	F.A.
1981—Los Angeles	Nat.	OF	5	10	1	1	1	0	0	0	.100	4	0	0	1.000
1983—Los Angeles	Nat.	OF	4	14	0	2	0	0	0	1	.143	12	0	0	1.000
Championship Series Totals			9	24	0	3	1	0	0	1	.125	16	0	0	1.000

WORLD SERIES RECORD

Year Club	League	Pos.	G.	AB.	R.	H.	2B.	3B.	HR.	RBI.	B.A.	PO.	A.	E.	F.A.
1981—Los Angeles	Nat.	PH-O-PR	5	6	1	1	1	0	0	0	.167	6	0	0	1.000

ALL-STAR GAME RECORD

Year League	Pos.	AB.	R.	H.	2B.	3B.	HR.	RBI.	B.A.	PO.	A.	E.	F.A.
1980—American	PH-OF	1	0	0	0	0	0	0	.000	1	0	0	1.000

TERRY LEE LANDRUM

(Tito)

Born October 25, 1954, at Joplin, Mo.
Height, 5.11. Weight, 175.
Throws and bats righthanded.

Led Florida State League in stolen bases with 68 in 1978.

Year Club	League	Pos.	G.	AB.	R.	H.	2B.	3B.	HR.	RBI.	B.A.	PO.	A.	E.	F.A.
1973—Orangeburg	W. Car.	OF	70	262	30	73	7	3	1	27	.279	168	7	1	.994
1974—St. Petersburg†	Fla. St.	OF	87	309	38	73	5	9	3	39	.236	214	7	8	.965
1975—St. Petersburg	Fla. St.	OF	132	435	76	96	21	4	11	45	.221	★313	5	7	.978
1976—Arkansas‡	Texas	OF	99	359	49	99	13	3	7	45	.276	201	12	7	.968
1976—Tulsa	A. A.	OF	9	24	1	6	1	0	0	1	.250	17	0	0	1.000
1977—Arkansas	Texas	OF	26	84	11	18	3	1	0	13	.214	50	5	1	.982
1977—St. Petersburg	Fla. St.	OF	67	249	40	61	15	3	4	40	.245	157	7	1	.994
1978—St. Petersburg	Fla. St.	OF	117	434	66	129	★25	1	4	45	.297	★305	8	3	.991
1979—Arkansas	Texas	OF	71	265	44	71	20	5	3	33	.268	134	7	4	.972
1979—Springfield	A. A.	OF	61	193	28	50	8	2	6	34	.259	126	5	2	.985
1980—Springfield	A. A.	OF	93	350	55	106	23	6	12	46	.303	193	6	4	.980
1980—St. Louis	Nat.	OF	35	77	6	19	2	2	0	7	.247	40	1	1	.976
1981—St. Louis	Nat.	OF	81	119	13	31	5	4	0	10	.261	72	6	0	1.000
1982—St. Louis	Nat.	OF	79	72	12	20	3	0	2	14	.278	50	2	0	1.000
1982—Louisville	A. A.	OF	25	94	10	19	2	1	0	6	.202	46	0	2	.958
1983—St. Louis	Nat.	OF	6	5	0	1	0	1	0	0	.200	1	0	0	1.000

Year Club	League	Pos.	G.	AB.	R.	H.	2B.	3B.	HR.	RBI.	B.A.	PO.	A.	E.	F.A
1983—Louisville§ .... A. A.		OF	111	431	79	126	23	★12	18	77	.292	286	8	8	.974
1983—Baltimore .... Amer.		OF	26	41	8	13	2	0	1	4	.317	39	0	0	1.000
National League Totals............................			201	273	31	71	10	7	2	31	.260	163	9	1	.994
American League Totals...........................			26	41	8	13	2	0	1	4	.317	39	0	0	1.000
Major League Totals...............................			227	314	39	84	12	7	3	35	.268	202	9	1	.995

Signed as free agent by St. Louis Cardinals' organization, October 10, 1972.
†On disabled list, July 19 to September 20, 1974.
‡On disabled list, April 24 to May 10, 1976.
§Sold to Baltimore Orioles, August 31, 1983, completing deal in which Baltimore traded Infielder-Catcher Floyd Rayford to St. Louis Cardinals for a player to be named later, June 14, 1983.

CHAMPIONSHIP SERIES RECORD

Year Club	League	Pos.	G.	AB.	R.	H.	2B.	3B.	HR.	RBI.	B.A.	PO.	A.	E.	F.A.
1983—Baltimore .... Amer.		PR-O-PH	4	10	2	2	0	0	1	1	.200	5	0	0	1.000

WORLD SERIES RECORD

Year Club	League	Pos.	G.	AB.	R.	H.	2B.	3B.	HR.	RBI.	B.A.	PO.	A.	E.	F.A.
1983—Baltimore .... Amer.		PR-OF	3	0	0	0	0	0	0	0	.000	1	0	0	1.000

JAMES RICK LANGFORD
(Known by middle name.)

Born March 20, 1952, at Farmville, Va.
Height, 6.00. Weight, 180.
Throws and bats righthanded.
Attended Manatee Junior College, Bradenton, Fla., and
Florida State University, Tallahassee, Fla.

Pitched 11-0 no-hit victory against Memphis, May 30, 1976.
Led American League in wild pitches with 16 in 1979.
Led American League in complete games with 28 in 1980 and 18 in 1981.

Year Club	League	G.	IP.	W.	L.	Pct.	H.	R.	ER.	SO.	BB.	ERA.
1973—Bradenton Pirates†......................	Gulf Coast	3	10	1	0	1.000	5	3	0	10	7	0.00
1974—Salem..................................	Carolina	26	174	11	7	.611	143	63	52	125	74	2.69
1975—Shreveport............................	Texas	16	42	5	2	.714	40	25	17	39	22	3.64
1975—Charleston	Int'national	13	65	7	2	.778	55	26	24	41	20	3.32
1976—Charleston	Int'national	16	121	9	5	.643	106	51	43	95	48	3.20
1976—Pittsburgh‡..........................	National	12	23	0	1	.000	27	17	16	17	14	6.26
1977—Oakland..............................	American	37	208	8	●19	.296	223	107	93	141	73	4.02
1978—Oakland..............................	American	37	176	7	13	.350	169	77	67	92	56	3.43
1979—Oakland..............................	American	34	219	12	16	.429	233	114	104	101	57	4.27
1980—Oakland..............................	American	35	★290	19	12	.613	276	119	105	102	64	3.26
1981—Oakland..............................	American	24	195	12	10	.545	190	81	65	84	58	3.00
1982—Oakland§.............................	American	32	237⅓	11	16	.407	265	121	111	79	49	4.21
1983—Oakland xy...........................	American	7	20	0	4	.000	43	28	27	2	10	12.15
1983—Modesto..............................	California	1	6	0	0	.000	4	2	2	2	2	3.00
National League Totals....................		12	23	0	1	.000	27	17	16	17	14	6.26
American League Totals...................		206	1345⅓	69	90	.434	1399	647	572	601	367	3.83
Major League Totals.....................		218	1368⅓	69	91	.431	1426	664	588	618	381	3.87

Selected by St. Louis Cardinals' organization in 11th round of free-agent draft, January 13, 1971.
Selected by Cleveland Indians' organization in 36th round of free-agent draft, June 6, 1972.
Signed as free agent by Pittsburgh Pirates' organization, June 17, 1973.
†On suspended list, July 17, 1973 through remainder of season.
‡Traded with Pitchers Doc Medich, Dave Giusti and Doug Bair, and Outfielders Mitchell Page and Tony Armas to Oakland A's for Infielders Phil Garner and Tommy Helms, and Pitcher Chris Batton, March 15, 1977.
§Appeared in one game as outfielder with one putout and had one at-bat with no hits.
xOn disabled list, April 5 to May 2 and May 20 to July 17, 1983; included rehabilitation disability assignment to Modesto, July 12 to July 17, 1983.
yOn disabled list, July 31, 1983; transferred to emergency disabled list, August 11, 1983 through remainder of season.

DIVISION SERIES RECORD

Year Club	League	G.	IP.	W.	L.	Pct.	H.	R.	ER.	SO.	BB.	ERA.
1981—Oakland................................	American	1	7⅓	1	0	1.000	10	1	1	3	0	1.23

MARK EDWARD LANGSTON

Born August 20, 1960, at San Diego, Calif.
Height, 6.01. Weight, 175.
Throws left and bats righthanded.
Attended San Jose State University, San Jose, Calif.

Year Club	League	G.	IP.	W.	L.	Pct.	H.	R.	ER.	SO.	BB.	ERA.
1981—Bellingham	Northwest	13	85	7	3	.700	81	37	32	97	46	3.39
1982—Bakersfield	California	26	177⅓	12	7	.632	143	71	50	161	102	2.54
1983—Chattanooga	Southern	28	198	14	9	.609	187	104	79	142	102	3.59

Selected by Chicago Cubs' organization in 15th round of free-agent draft, June 6, 1978.
Selected by Seattle Mariners' organization in 3rd round of free-agent draft, June 8, 1981.

CARNEY RAY LANSFORD

Born February 7, 1957, at San Jose, Calif.
Height, 6.02. Weight, 195.
Throws and bats righthanded.
Brother of Phil Lansford, infielder in Cleveland Indians' and Toronto Blue Jays' organizations,
1978 through 1981; and Jody Lansford, first baseman with San Diego Padres.

Hit three home runs in a game, September 1, 1979.
Led American League in sacrifice flies with 11 in 1980.
Led Texas League third basemen in double plays with 16 in 1977.
Named third baseman on THE SPORTING NEWS American League Silver Slugger team, 1981.

Year—Club	League	Pos.	G.	AB.	R.	H.	2B.	3B.	HR.	RBI.	B.A.	PO.	A.	E.	F.A.
1975—Idaho Falls†	Pion.	3B-SS	8	27	5	6	2	0	1	1	.222	8	14	9	.710
1976—Quad Cities	Midw.	3B-OF-SS	121	418	87	120	19	5	14	86	.287	130	215	36	.906
1977—El Paso	Texas	3B	120	443	98	147	17	3	18	94	.332	★110	★210	15	★.955
1978—California‡	Amer.	3B-SS	121	453	63	133	23	2	8	52	.294	94	186	18	.940
1979—California	Amer.	3B	157	654	114	188	30	5	19	79	.287	★135	263	7	★.983
1980—California§	Amer.	3B	151	602	87	157	27	3	15	80	.261	★151	250	19	.955
1981—Boston	Amer.	3B	102	399	61	134	23	3	4	52	★.336	70	180	13	.951
1982—Boston xy	Amer.	3B	128	482	65	145	28	4	11	63	.301	83	216	10	.968
1983—Oakland z	Amer.	3B-SS	80	299	43	92	16	2	10	45	.308	60	163	10	.957
Major League Totals			739	2889	433	849	147	19	67	371	.295	593	1258	77	.960

Selected by California Angels' organization in 3rd round of free-agent draft, June 4, 1975.
†On disabled list, July 21 to September 30, 1975.
‡On supplemental disabled list, June 11 to July 7, 1978.
§Traded with Pitcher Mark Clear and Outfielder Rick Miller to Boston Red Sox for Shortstop Rick Burleson and Third Baseman Butch Hobson, December 10, 1980.
xOn supplemental disabled list, June 24 to July 21, 1982.
yTraded with Outfielder Garry Hancock and a player to be named later to Oakland A's for Outfielder Tony Armas and Catcher Jeff Newman, December 6, 1982; Oakland acquired Pitcher Jerry King to complete deal, December 20, 1982.
zOn supplemental disabled list, May 19 to June 7, 1983.

CHAMPIONSHIP SERIES RECORD

Year—Club	League	Pos.	G.	AB.	R.	H.	2B.	3B.	HR.	RBI.	B.A.	PO.	A.	E.	F.A.
1979—California	Amer.	3B	4	17	2	5	0	0	0	3	.294	4	8	0	1.000

JOSEPH DALE LANSFORD
(Joe)

Born January 15, 1961, at San Jose, Calif.
Height, 6.05. Weight, 225.
Throws and bats righthanded.
Brother of Carney Lansford, third baseman with Oakland A's; and Phil Lansford,
infielder in Cleveland Indians' and Toronto Blue Jays' organizations, 1978 through 1981.

Led Texas League batters in strikeouts with 142 in 1981.
Led Pacific Coast League first basemen in putouts with 1,272 and double plays with 142 in 1983.
Led Texas League first basemen in total chances with 1,357 and double plays with 137 in 1981.
Led California League first basemen in double plays with 101 in 1980.
Received reported $100,000 bonus to sign with San Diego Padres, 1979.

Year—Club	League	Pos.	G.	AB.	R.	H.	2B.	3B.	HR.	RBI.	B.A.	PO.	A.	E.	F.A.
1979—Walla Walla	N'west	1B	44	146	17	21	2	0	6	31	.144	204	21	6	.974
1980—Reno†	Calif.	1B	112	410	80	108	21	2	24	95	.263	★1067	73	10	.991
1981—Amarillo	Texas	1B	●133	464	67	110	20	2	25	86	.237	★1283	61	★13	.990
1982—Hawaii	P. C.	1B	116	417	54	99	18	2	13	75	.237	1057	66	15	.987
1982—San Diego	Nat.	1B	13	22	6	4	0	0	0	3	.182	69	3	1	.986
1983—Las Vegas	P. C.	★1B-OF	140	528	111	134	23	4	27	116	.254	1280	104	9	★.994
1983—San Diego	Nat.	1B	12	8	1	2	0	0	1	2	.250	11	1	0	1.000
Major League Totals			25	30	7	6	0	0	1	5	.200	80	4	1	.988

Selected by San Diego Padres' organization in 1st round (14th player selected) of free-agent draft, June 5, 1979.
†On disabled list, April 10 to May 8, 1980.

DAVID JEFFREY LaPOINT
(Dave)

Born July 29, 1959, at Glens Falls, N. Y.
Height, 6.03. Weight, 205.
Throws and bats lefthanded.
Pitched 4-0 no-hit victory against Reno, July 25, 1979.
Tied for American Association lead in complete games with 9 in 1981.
Tied for California League lead in shutouts with 3 and complete games with 11 in 1979.
Tied for Midwest League lead in home runs allowed with 20 in 1978.

Year—Club	League	G.	IP.	W.	L.	Pct.	H.	R.	ER.	SO.	BB.	ERA.
1977—Newark	NYP	13	69	5	2	.714	73	40	36	60	22	4.70
1978—Burlington	Midwest	25	161	12	12	.500	177	98	72	134	41	4.02
1979—Stockton	California	27	180	12	10	.545	144	74	63	★208	85	3.15
1980—Vancouver†	P. Coast	17	93	7	4	.636	71	48	29	64	45	2.81
1980—Milwaukee‡	American	5	15	1	0	1.000	17	14	10	5	13	6.00

Year Club	League	G.	IP.	W.	L.	Pct.	H.	R.	ER.	SO.	BB.	ERA.
1981—Springfield	Am. Assoc.	25	172	13	9	.591	160	83	61	*129	66	3.19
1981—St. Louis	National	3	11	1	0	1.000	12	5	5	4	2	4.09
1982—St. Louis	National	42	152⅔	9	3	.750	170	63	58	81	52	3.42
1983—St. Louis	National	37	191⅓	12	9	.571	191	92	84	113	84	3.95
American League Totals		5	15	1	0	1.000	17	14	10	5	13	6.00
National League Totals		82	355	22	12	.647	373	160	147	198	138	3.73
Major League Totals		87	370	23	12	.657	390	174	157	203	151	3.82

Selected by Milwaukee Brewers' organization in 10th round of free-agent draft, June 7, 1977.

†On disabled list, May 6 to May 17 and June 6 to July 15, 1980.

‡Traded with Pitcher Lary Sorensen and Outfielders Sixto Lezcano and David Green to St. Louis Cardinals for Pitchers Pete Vuckovich and Rollie Fingers and Catcher Ted Simmons, December 12, 1980.

WORLD SERIES RECORD

Year Club	League	G.	IP.	W.	L.	Pct.	H.	R.	ER.	SO.	BB.	ERA.
1982—St. Louis	National	2	8⅓	0	0	.000	10	6	3	3	2	3.24

PATRICK CLIBBORN LARKIN
(Pat)

Born June 14, 1960, at Arcadia, Calif.
Height, 6.00. Weight, 180.
Throws and bats lefthanded.
Received degree in management from
University of Santa Clara, Santa Clara, Calif.
Brother of Mike Larkin, pitcher in Kansas City Royals' organization, 1973 through 1975.

Led Pioneer League in saves with 11 in 1982.

Year Club	League	G.	IP.	W.	L.	Pct.	H.	R.	ER.	SO.	BB.	ERA.
1982—Great Falls	Pioneer	27	46⅓	7	4	.636	37	14	11	58	21	2.14
1983—Shreveport	Texas	41	54	3	4	.429	51	19	11	39	23	1.83
1983—San Francisco	National	5	10⅓	0	0	.000	13	6	5	6	3	4.35
1983—Phoenix	P. Coast	4	9⅓	1	0	1.000	12	5	3	8	8	2.89
Major League Totals		5	10⅓	0	0	.000	13	6	5	6	3	4.35

Signed as free agent by San Francisco Giants' organization, June 14, 1982.

DAVID EUGENE LaROCHE
(Dave)

Born May 14, 1948, at Colorado Springs, Colo.
Height, 6.02. Weight, 195.
Throws and bats lefthanded.
Attended University of Nevada at Las Vegas, Las Vegas, Nev.

Major league saves: 1970 (4), 1971 (9), 1972 (10), 1973 (4), 1974 (5), 1975 (17), 1976 (21), 1977 (17), 1978 (25), 1979 (10), 1980 (4). Total—126.

Year Club	League	G.	IP.	W.	L.	Pct.	H.	R.	ER.	SO.	BB.	ERA.
1968—Quad Cities	Midwest	33	84	5	7	.417	76	33	22	80	29	2.36
1969—San Jose	California	11	21	2	1	.667	21	11	9	19	8	3.68
1969—El Paso	Texas	33	49	6	3	.667	43	16	16	46	25	2.94
1970—Hawaii	P. Coast	22	58	6	0	1.000	31	11	8	67	19	1.24
1970—California	American	38	50	4	1	.800	41	20	19	44	21	3.42
1971—California†	American	56	72	5	1	.833	55	21	20	63	27	2.50
1972—Minnesota‡	American	62	95	5	7	.417	72	33	30	79	39	2.84
1973—Chicago§	National	45	54	4	1	.800	55	37	35	34	29	5.83
1974—Wichita	Am. Assoc.	6	32	1	3	.250	37	19	18	17	7	5.06
1974—Chicago x	National	49	92	5	6	.455	103	54	49	49	47	4.79
1975—Cleveland	American	61	82	5	3	.625	61	26	20	94	57	2.20
1976—Cleveland	American	61	96	1	4	.200	57	25	24	104	49	2.25
1977—Cleveland y-California	American	59	100	8	7	.533	79	44	39	79	44	3.51
1978—California	American	59	96	10	9	.526	73	35	30	70	48	2.81
1979—California	American	53	86	7	11	.389	107	54	53	59	32	5.55
1980—California z	American	52	128	3	5	.375	122	62	58	89	39	4.08
1981—New York a	American	26	47	4	1	.800	38	16	13	24	16	2.49
1982—Columbus	Int'national	17	31	3	1	.750	27	17	13	20	14	3.77
1982—New York b	American	25	50	4	2	.667	54	19	19	31	11	3.42
1983—Columbus	Int'national	7	8⅓	1	1	.500	11	5	5	8	7	5.40
1983—New York	American	1	1	0	0	.000	2	2	2	0	0	18.00
American League Totals		553	903	56	51	.523	761	357	327	736	383	3.26
National League Totals		94	146	9	7	.563	158	91	84	83	76	5.18
Major League Totals		647	1049	65	58	.528	919	448	411	819	459	3.53

Signed as free agent by California Angels' organization, March 9, 1967.

†Traded to Minnesota Twins for Shortstop Leo Cardenas, November 30, 1971.

‡Traded to Chicago Cubs for Pitchers Bill Hands, George (Joe) Decker and Bob Maneely, November 30, 1972.

§On disabled list, March 25 to April 17, 1973.

xTraded with Outfielder Brock Davis to Cleveland Indians for Pitcher Milt Wilcox, February 28, 1975.

yTraded with Pitcher Dave Schuler to California Angels for First Baseman-Outfielder Bruce Bochte, Pitcher Sid Monge, and cash estimated at $250,000, May 11, 1977.

zReleased, April 1, 1981; signed by 222 York Yankees, April 17, 1981.

aGranted free agency, November 13, 1981; signed by Columbus (New York Yankees' organization), April 9, 1982.

bReleased, October 20, 1982; signed by Columbus (New York Yankees' organization), July 25, 1983.

Year Club	League	G.	IP.	W.	L.	Pct.	H.	R.	ER.	SO.	BB.	ERA.
1979—California	American	1	1⅓	0	0	.000	2	1	1	1	1	6.75

WORLD SERIES RECORD

Year Club	League	G.	IP.	W.	L.	Pct.	H.	R.	ER.	SO.	BB.	ERA.
1981—New York	American	1	1	0	0	.000	0	0	0	2	0	0.00

ALL-STAR GAME RECORD

Year League		IP.	W.	L.	Pct.	H.	R.	ER.	SO.	BB.	ERA.
1977—American		1	0	0	.000	1	0	0	0	1	0.00

Member of American League All-Star Team in 1976; did not play.

RECORD AS OUTFIELDER

Year Club	League	Pos.	G.	AB.	R.	H.	2B.	3B.	HR.	RBI.	B.A.	PO.	A.	E.	F.A.
1967—San Jose	Calif.	OF	16	55	4	10	2	0	0	6	.182	18	1	0	1.000
1967—Quad Cities	Midw.	OF	95	342	39	80	17	0	6	40	.234	189	8	8	.961
1968—Quad Cities	Midw.	P-O-1	58	98	15	21	3	0	2	9	.214	51	18	3	.958

WILLIAM ALAN LASKEY
(Bill)

Born December 20, 1957, at Toledo, O.
Height, 6.05. Weight, 190.
Throws and bats righthanded.
Attended Monroe County Community College, Monroe, Mich., and
Kent State University, Kent, O.

Year Club	League	G.	IP.	W.	L.	Pct.	H.	R.	ER.	SO.	BB.	ERA.
1978—Sarasota Royals	Gulf Coast	4	23	1	2	.333	13	7	5	9	11	1.96
1978—Jacksonville	Southern	7	27	3	2	.600	23	14	13	13	15	4.33
1979—Ft. Myers	Florida St.	13	93	7	4	.636	71	24	23	72	35	2.23
1979—Jacksonville	Southern	15	97	4	3	.571	78	44	38	53	46	3.53
1980—Omaha	Am. Assoc.	27	145	5	8	.385	155	81	67	77	72	4.16
1981—Omaha†	Am. Assoc.	23	138	10	8	.556	136	67	60	87	52	3.91
1982—Phoenix	P. Coast	2	14	1	0	1.000	12	5	2	10	2	1.29
1982—San Francisco	National	32	189⅓	13	12	.520	186	74	66	88	43	3.14
1983—San Francisco	National	25	148⅓	13	10	.565	151	75	69	81	45	4.19
Major League Totals		57	337⅔	26	22	.542	337	149	135	169	88	3.60

Selected by Detroit Tigers' organization in 8th round of free-agent draft, January 11, 1977.
Selected by Detroit Tigers' organization in secondary phase of free-agent draft, June 7, 1977.
Selected by Kansas City Royals' organization in secondary phase of free-agent draft, June 6, 1978.
†Traded with Pitcher Rich Gale to San Francisco Giants for Outfielder Jerry Martin, December 10, 1981.

TIMOTHY JON LAUDNER

Name pronounced LAWD-ner.

(Tim)

Born June 7, 1958, at Mason City, Ia.
Height, 6.03. Weight, 195.
Throws and bats righthanded.
Attended University of Missouri, Columbia, Mo.

Tied American League record for most home runs, first two major league games (2), August 28 and 29, 1981.
Led Southern League in slugging percentage with .628 and game-winning RBIs with 14 in 1981.
Named Southern League Most Valuable Player, 1981.

Year Club	League	Pos.	G.	AB.	R.	H.	2B.	3B.	HR.	RBI.	B.A.	PO.	A.	E.	F.A.
1979—Orlando	South.	C	45	141	17	34	7	0	3	20	.241	224	29	6	.977
1980—Orlando†	South.	C	17	61	7	14	5	0	2	5	.230	81	10	1	.989
1980—Visalia	Calif.	C	56	186	23	42	13	0	10	29	.226	251	36	5	.983
1981—Orlando	South.	C-1B	130	433	87	123	21	1	★42	104	.284	631	66	15	.979
1981—Minnesota	Amer.	C	14	43	4	7	2	0	2	5	.163	49	5	0	1.000
1982—Toledo	Int.	C	20	71	4	12	2	0	2	12	.169	121	9	0	1.000
1982—Minnesota	Amer.	C	93	306	37	78	19	1	7	33	.255	454	41	★12	.976
1983—Minnesota	Amer.	C	62	168	20	31	9	0	6	18	.185	259	22	4	.986
Major League Totals			169	517	61	116	30	1	15	56	.224	762	68	16	.981

Selected by Cincinnati Reds' organization in 33rd round of free-agent draft, June 8, 1976.
Selected by Minnesota Twins' organization in 3rd round of free-agent draft, June 5, 1979.
†On disabled list, April 11 to April 21, 1980.

GARY ROBERT LAVELLE

Born January 3, 1949, at Scranton, Pa.
Height, 6.02. Weight, 205.
Throws left and bats right and lefthanded.

Pitched seven-inning, 4-0 no-hit game against Clinton, August 15, 1969.
Major league saves: 1975 (8), 1976 (12), 1977 (20), 1978 (14), 1979 (20), 1980 (9), 1981 (4), 1982 (8), 1983 (20).
Total—115.

Led National League in intentional bases on balls issued with 18 in 1977.
Tied for Pacific Coast League lead in shutouts with 3 in 1974.

Year Club	League	G.	IP.	W.	L.	Pct.	H.	R.	ER.	SO.	BB.	ERA.
1967—Salt Lake City	Pioneer	17	37	3	2	.600	37	18	12	32	23	2.92
1968—Medford	Northwest	13	60	3	3	.500	53	33	23	67	42	3.45
1969—Decatur†	Midwest	7	48	4	2	.667	41	17	9	30	24	1.69
1970—Amarillo	Texas	21	100	6	12	.333	99	75	60	64	72	5.40
1971—Amarillo	Texas	23	136	11	8	.579	132	65	53	77	56	3.50
1972—Phoenix	P. Coast	37	147	11	14	.440	161	91	69	107	55	4.22
1973—Phoenix‡	P. Coast	36	101	5	7	.417	112	56	51	61	43	4.54
1974—Phoenix	P. Coast	35	182	8	●16	.333	228	119	106	105	76	5.24
1974—San Francisco	National	10	17	0	3	.000	14	7	4	12	10	2.12
1975—San Francisco	National	65	82	6	3	.667	80	30	27	51	48	2.96
1976—San Francisco	National	65	110	10	6	.625	102	37	33	71	52	2.70
1977—San Francisco	National	73	118	7	7	.500	106	35	27	93	37	2.06
1978—San Francisco	National	67	98	13	10	.565	96	41	36	63	44	3.31
1979—San Francisco	National	70	97	7	9	.438	86	31	27	80	42	2.51
1980—San Francisco	National	62	100	6	8	.429	106	43	38	66	36	3.42
1981—San Francisco	National	34	66	2	6	.250	58	33	28	45	23	3.82
1982—San Francisco	National	68	104⅔	10	7	.588	97	35	31	76	29	2.67
1983—San Francisco§	National	56	87	7	4	.636	73	33	25	68	19	2.59
Major League Totals		570	879⅔	68	63	.519	818	325	276	625	340	2.82

Selected by San Francisco Giants' organization in 34th round of free-agent draft, June 6, 1967.
†On suspended list, April 11, 1969; transferred to military list through July 5, 1969.
‡On temporary inactive list, June 2 to June 20, 1973.
§On disabled list, July 15 to August 5, 1983.

ALL-STAR GAME RECORD

Year League	IP.	W.	L.	Pct.	H.	R.	ER.	SO.	BB.	ERA.
1977—National	2	0	0	.000	1	0	0	2	0	0.00

Member of National League All-Star Team in 1983; did not play.

RUDY KARL LAW

Born October 7, 1956, at Waco, Tex.
Height, 6.01. Weight, 165.
Throws and bats lefthanded.

Major League stolen bases: 1978 (3), 1980 (40), 1982 (36), 1983 (77). Total—156.
Led Pacific Coast League in stolen bases with 79 and caught stealing with 20 in 1978.

Year Club	League	Pos.	G.	AB.	R.	H.	2B.	3B.	HR.	RBI.	B.A.	PO.	A.	E.	F.A.
1976—Bellingham	N'west.	OF-1B	54	161	40	54	7	1	1	16	.335	58	2	4	.938
1977—Lodi	Calif.	OF	122	451	124	174	22	5	9	88	★.386	124	2	6	.948
1978—Albuquerque	P. C.	OF	138	★573	118	179	21	9	4	72	.312	236	10	10	.961
1978—Los Angeles	Nat.	OF	11	12	2	3	0	0	0	1	.250	3	0	0	1.000
1979—Albuquerque†	P. C.	OF	72	270	46	80	4	2	0	28	.296	142	2	3	.980
1980—Los Angeles	Nat.	OF	128	388	55	101	5	4	1	23	.260	233	6	3	.988
1981—Albuquerque‡	P. C.	OF	107	397	75	133	16	9	0	39	.335	158	5	5	.970
1982—Chicago	Amer.	OF	121	336	55	107	15	8	3	32	.318	215	2	6	.973
1983—Chicago	Amer.	OF	141	501	95	142	20	7	3	33	.283	302	5	2	★.994
National League Totals			139	400	57	104	5	4	1	24	.260	236	6	3	.988
American League Totals			262	837	150	249	35	15	6	65	.297	517	7	8	.985
Major League Totals			401	1237	207	353	40	19	7	89	.285	753	13	11	.986

Signed as free agent by Los Angeles Dodgers' organization, September 1, 1975.
†On disabled list, June 22 to August 31, 1979.
‡Traded to Chicago White Sox for Outfielder Cecil Espy and Pitcher Bert Geiger, March 30, 1982.

CHAMPIONSHIP SERIES RECORD

Tied American League Championship Series records for most at-bats, four-game Series (18), 1983; most hits, four-game Series (7), 1983; most one-base hits, four-game Series (6), 1983.

Year Club	League	Pos.	G.	AB.	R.	H.	2B.	3B.	HR.	RBI.	B.A.	PO.	A.	E.	F.A.
1983—Chicago	Amer.	OF	4	18	1	7	1	0	0	0	.389	10	0	0	1.000

VANCE AARON LAW

Born October 1, 1956, at Boise, Ida.
Height, 6.02. Weight, 185.
Throws and bats righthanded.
Attended Brigham Young University, Provo, Utah.
Son of Vern Law, pitcher with Pittsburgh Pirates, 1950, 1951 and 1954 through 1967.

Led Pacific Coast League in sacrifice hits with 14 in 1979.

Year Club	League	Pos.	G.	AB.	R.	H.	2B.	3B.	HR.	RBI.	B.A.	PO.	A.	E.	F.A.
1978—Bradenton Pir.	Gulf C.	SS	1	3	0	1	0	0	0	0	.333	2	5	0	1.000
1978—Salem	Carol.	SS	60	213	48	68	13	7	2	30	.319	96	180	22	.926
1979—Portland	P. C.	SS-3B-2B	131	448	62	139	16	8	2	52	.310	201	308	22	.959
1980—Portland	P. C.	SS	96	339	59	100	23	5	5	54	.295	169	295	14	.971
1980—Pittsburgh	Nat.	2B-SS-3B	25	74	11	17	2	2	0	3	.230	31	54	3	.966
1981—Pittsburgh	Nat.	2B-SS-3B	30	67	1	9	0	1	0	3	.134	50	58	0	1.000
1981—Portland†‡	P. C.	2B-SS-3B	88	310	55	86	14	9	5	43	.277	168	218	9	.977

Year Club	League	Pos.	G.	AB.	R.	H.	2B.	3B.	HR.	RBI.	B.A.	PO.	A.	E.	F.A.
1982—Chicago	Amer.	S-3-2-O	114	359	40	101	20	1	5	54	.281	156	313	26	.947
1983—Chicago	Amer.	3-2-S-O	145	408	55	99	21	5	4	42	.243	94	311	14	.967
National League Totals			55	141	12	26	2	3	0	6	.184	81	112	3	.985
American League Totals			259	767	95	200	41	6	9	96	.261	250	624	40	.956
Major League Totals			314	908	107	226	43	9	9	102	.249	331	736	43	.961

Selected by Pittsburgh Pirates' organization in 38th round of free-agent draft, June 6, 1978.

†On disabled list, July 5 to July 15, 1981.

‡Traded with Pitcher Ernie Camacho to Chicago White Sox for Pitchers Ross Baumgarten and Butch Edge, March 21, 1982.

CHAMPIONSHIP SERIES RECORD

Year Club	League	Pos.	G.	AB.	R.	H.	2B.	3B.	HR.	RBI.	B.A.	PO.	A.	E.	F.A.
1983—Chicago	Amer.	3B	4	11	0	2	0	0	0	1	.182	1	9	1	.909

THOMAS JAMES LAWLESS
(Tom)

Born December 19, 1956, at Erie, Pa.
Height, 5.09. Weight, 165.
Throws and bats righthanded.
Received bachelor of arts degree in political science from
Pennsylvania State University-Behrend, Erie, Pa.

Led American Association in stolen bases with 46 in 1983.
Led Florida State League in sacrifice hits with 13 and stolen bases with 60 in 1979.
Led Pioneer League shortstops in putouts with 116 in 1978.

Year Club	League	Pos.	G.	AB.	R.	H.	2B.	3B.	HR.	RBI.	B.A.	PO.	A.	E.	F.A.
1978—Billings	Pioneer	SS-2B	63	254	64	70	5	●7	5	35	.276	117	186	24	.927
1979—Tampa	Fla. St.	2B	131	469	66	126	9	5	1	39	.269	★296	376	17	★.975
1980—Waterbury	East.	2B	130	498	83	137	20	7	2	29	.275	★316	333	14	.979
1981—Waterbury	East.	2B	136	522	77	152	20	10	8	50	.291	323	379	15	.979
1982—Indianapolis	A. A.	2B-SS	86	351	76	108	18	6	2	28	.308	185	251	13	.971
1982—Cincinnati	Nat.	2B	49	165	19	35	6	0	0	4	.212	87	136	5	.978
1983—Indianapolis	A. A.	2B	115	423	93	118	23	3	13	35	.279	255	303	17	.970
Major League Totals			49	165	19	35	6	0	0	4	.212	87	136	5	.978

Selected by Cincinnati Reds' organization in 17th round of free-agent draft, June 6, 1978.

CHARLES WILLIAM LEA

Name pronounced Lee.

(Charlie)

Born December 25, 1956, at Orleans, France.
Height, 6.04. Weight, 194.
Throws and bats righthanded.
Attended University of Mississippi, Oxford, Miss., Shelby State Community College,
Memphis, Tenn., and Memphis State University, Memphis, Tenn.

Pitched 4-0 no-hit victory against San Francisco Giants, May 10, 1981 (second game).

Year Club	League	G.	IP.	W.	L.	Pct.	H.	R.	ER.	SO.	BB.	ERA.
1978—Memphis	Southern	12	68	3	3	.500	57	34	27	37	32	3.57
1979—Memphis	Southern	24	162	8	8	.500	161	88	79	81	71	4.39
1980—Memphis	Southern	9	75	9	0	1.000	34	10	7	54	21	0.84
1980—Denver	Am. Assoc.	2	12	0	0	.000	8	2	2	9	5	1.50
1980—Montreal	National	21	104	7	5	.583	103	51	43	56	55	3.72
1981—Montreal	National	16	64	5	4	.556	63	34	33	31	26	4.64
1982—Montreal	National	27	177⅔	12	10	.545	145	70	64	115	56	3.24
1983—Montreal	National	33	222	16	11	.593	195	87	77	137	84	3.12
Major League Totals		97	567⅔	40	30	.571	506	242	217	339	221	3.44

Selected by New York Mets' organization in 15th round of free-agent draft, June 4, 1975.
Selected by St. Louis Cardinals' organization in secondary phase of free-agent draft, June 8, 1976.
Selected by Chicago White Sox' organization in secondary phase of free-agent draft, January 11, 1977.
Selected by Montreal Expos' organization in 8th round of free-agent draft, June 6, 1978.

RICHARD MAX LEACH
(Rick)

Born May 4, 1957, at Ann Arbor, Mich.
Height, 6.01. Weight, 180.
Throws and bats lefthanded.
Attended University of Michigan, Ann Arbor, Mich.

Selected by Denver Broncos in 5th round of 1979 NFL draft.
Received reported $200,000 bonus to sign with Detroit Tigers, 1979.

Year Club	League	Pos.	G.	AB.	R.	H.	2B.	3B.	HR.	RBI.	B.A.	PO.	A.	E.	F.A.
1979—Lakeland†	Fla. St.	OF	48	168	21	51	10	1	2	23	.304	104	8	3	.974
1980—Evansville	A. A.	1B-OF	126	430	69	117	14	1	5	58	.272	767	62	9	.989
1981—Evansville	A. A.	1B	13	44	8	18	5	0	2	16	.409	129	16	2	.986
1981—Detroit	Amer.	1B-OF	54	83	9	16	3	1	1	11	.193	149	14	0	1.000
1982—Detroit‡	Amer.	1B-OF	82	218	23	52	7	2	3	12	.239	430	29	2	.996

Year Club League	Pos.	G.	AB.	R.	H.	2B.	3B.	HR.	RBI.	B.A.	PO.	A.	E.	F.A.
1982—Evansville .... A. A.	DH	11	38	6	11	2	0	0	2	.289	0	0	0	.000
1983—Detroit................... Amer.	1B-OF	99	242	22	60	17	0	3	26	.248	465	45	4	.992
Major League Totals..................		235	543	54	128	27	3	7	49	.236	1044	88	6	.995

Selected by Philadelphia Phillies' organization in 11th round of free-agent draft, June 4, 1975.
Selected by Philadelphia Phillies' organization in 24th round of free-agent draft, June 6, 1978.
Selected by Detroit Tigers' organization in 1st round (13th player selected) of free-agent draft, June 5, 1979.
†On disabled list, June 18 to June 29, 1979.
‡On disabled list, April 12 to May 17, 1982; included rehabilitation disability assignment to Evansville, May 6 to May 17, 1982.

TERRY HESTER LEACH

Born March 13, 1954, at Selma, Ala.
Height, 6.00. Weight, 205.
Throws and bats righthanded.
Received business administration degree in personnel management-industrial relations
from Auburn University, Auburn University, Ala.
Led Gulf States League in home runs allowed with 12 in 1976.

Year Club League	G.	IP.	W.	L.	Pct.	H.	R.	ER.	SO.	BB.	ERA.
1976—Baton Rouge†‡............................ Gulf States	5	19	2	0	1.000	43	21	13	15	14	6.16
1977—Greenwood................................. W. Carol.	20	67	3	2	.600	47	25	19	67	24	2.55
1978—Savannah§................................. Southern	9	25	1	0	1.000	24	17	14	21	13	5.04
1978—Kinston.................................... Carolina	34	66	5	4	.556	57	29	24	46	25	3.27
1979—Savannah................................. Southern	40	92	2	9	.182	77	33	20	68	26	1.96
1979—Richmond................................. Int'national	7	14	3	1	.750	14	3	3	12	4	1.93
1980—Savannah xy............................. Southern	22	87	5	1	.833	83	36	31	58	17	3.21
1980—Jackson.................................... Texas	8	54	5	1	.833	50	16	9	30	15	1.50
1981—Tidewater................................. Int'national	15	76	5	2	.714	63	27	23	42	19	2.72
1981—Jackson.................................... Texas	8	58	5	1	.833	47	14	11	43	12	1.71
1981—New York................................. National	21	35	1	1	.500	26	11	10	16	12	2.57
1982—Tidewater................................. Int'national	30	48⅔	4	1	.800	48	20	16	34	19	2.96
1982—New York................................. National	21	45⅓	2	1	.667	46	22	21	30	18	4.17
1983—Tidewater z............................. Int'national	37	113	5	7	.417	120	66	56	66	42	4.46
Major League Totals..............................	42	80⅓	3	2	.600	72	33	31	46	30	3.47

Selected by Boston Red Sox' organization in 7th round of free-agent draft, January 7, 1976.
†Signed as free agent by Baton Rouge (Independent), June 29, 1976; released when Baton Rouge withdrew from league, August 13, 1976.
‡Signed by Greenwood (Atlanta Braves' organization) as free agent, May 28, 1977.
§Loaned to Kinston (Independent), June 3, 1978; returned, October 25, 1978.
xOn disabled list, June 12 to July 23, 1980.
yReleased, July 23, 1980; signed by Jackson (New York Mets' organization), July 27, 1980.
zTraded to Chicago Cubs' organization for Pitchers Jim Adamczak and Mitch Cook, September 26, 1983.

LUIS ENRIQUE LEAL

Born March 21, 1957, at Barquisimento, Venezuela.
Height, 6.03. Weight, 205.
Throws and bats righthanded.
Brother of Carlos Leal, outfielder in Toronto Blue Jays' organization, 1979 through 1982.
Tied American League record for most consecutive hits allowed, start of game (5), June 2, 1980.
Pitched 2-0 no-hit victory against Tampa, May 11, 1979.

Year Club League	G.	IP.	W.	L.	Pct.	H.	R.	ER.	SO.	BB.	ERA.
1979—Dunedin .... Florida St.	21	150	12	2	.857	137	51	44	90	45	2.64
1979—Syracuse .... Int'national	1	6	1	0	1.000	4	3	3	2	2	4.50
1980—Syracuse .... Int'national	16	110	6	5	.545	102	44	40	76	31	3.27
1980—Toronto .... American	13	60	3	4	.429	72	35	30	26	31	4.50
1981—Toronto .... American	29	130	7	●13	.350	127	63	53	71	44	3.67
1982—Toronto .... American	38	249⅔	12	15	.444	250	113	109	111	79	3.93
1983—Toronto .... American	35	217⅓	13	12	.520	216	113	104	116	65	4.31
Major League Totals................................	115	657	35	44	.443	665	324	296	324	219	4.05

Signed as free agent by Toronto Blue Jays' organization, 1979.

TIMOTHY JAMES LEARY
(Tim)

Born December 23, 1958, at Santa Monica, Calif.
Height, 6.03. Weight, 195.
Throws and bats righthanded.
Attended University of California at Los Angeles, Los Angeles, Calif.
Led Texas League in shutouts with 6 in 1980.
Named Texas League Most Valuable Player, 1980.

Year Club League	G.	IP.	W.	L.	Pct.	H.	R.	ER.	SO.	BB.	ERA.
1979—Jackson†.................................... Texas					(Did not play)						
1980—Jackson .... Texas	26	173	●15	8	.652	150	67	53	138	62	2.76
1981—New York‡................................ National	1	2	0	0	.000	0	0	0	3	1	0.00
1981—Tidewater.................................... Int'national	6	34	1	3	.250	27	16	14	15	27	3.71
1982—Tidewater§.................................Int'national					(Did not play)						

Year	Club	League	G.	IP.	W.	L.	Pct.	H.	R.	ER.	SO.	BB.	ERA.
1983—Tidewater		Int'national	27	160⅓	8	*16	.333	170	100	78	106	73	4.38
1983—New York		National	2	10⅔	1	1	.500	15	10	4	9	4	3.38
Major League Totals			3	12⅔	1	1	.500	15	10	4	12	5	2.84

Selected by New York Mets' organization in 1st round (second player selected) of free-agent draft, June 5, 1979.
†On disabled list, July 19 to October 1, 1979.
‡On disabled list, April 16 to August 1, 1981.
§On disabled list, April 13, 1982 through remainder of season.

JOSEPH HENRY LEFEBVRE
Name pronounced Luh-FAY.

(Joe)

Born Feburary 22, 1956, at Penacook, N.H.
Height, 5.10. Weight, 170.
Throws right and bats lefthanded.
Attended Eckerd College, St. Petersburg, Fla.

Tied American League record for most home runs, first two major league games (2), May 22 and 23, 1980.
Collected six hits in one game, September 13, 1982 (16 innings).
Tied for Eastern League lead in assists by outfielders with 16 in 1979.

Year	Club	League	Pos.	G.	AB.	R.	H.	2B.	3B.	HR.	RBI.	B.A.	PO.	A.	E.	F.A.
1977—Ft. Lauderdale		Fla. St.	OF-P	48	172	20	53	6	9	2	29	.308	76	4	2	.976
1977—West Haven		East.	OF	6	22	8	8	2	0	0	3	.364	7	2	0	1.000
1978—West Haven		East.	OF-3B-C	134	459	*102	122	21	●11	19	70	.266	240	48	14	.954
1979—West Haven		East.	O-I-P-C	138	487	85	142	28	10	21	●107	.292	248	31	10	.965
1980—Columbus		Int.	OF-3B	56	198	37	55	11	3	10	26	.278	89	3	5	.948
1980—New York†		Amer.	OF	74	150	26	34	1	1	8	21	.227	75	3	2	.975
1981—San Diego		Nat.	OF	86	246	31	63	13	4	8	31	.256	167	6	1	.994
1982—San Diego		Nat.	3B-OF-C	102	239	25	57	9	0	4	21	.238	72	74	3	.980
1982—Hawaii		P. C.	OF-3B	8	32	7	11	3	1	0	5	.344	14	6	1	.952
1983—S. D.‡-Phila.		Nat.	OF-3B-C	119	278	35	85	20	8	8	39	.306	105	22	5	.962
American League Totals				74	150	26	34	1	1	8	21	.227	75	3	2	.975
National League Totals				307	763	91	205	42	12	20	91	.269	344	102	9	.980
Major League Totals				381	913	117	239	43	13	28	112	.262	419	105	11	.979

Selected by New York Yankees' organization in 3rd round of free-agent draft, June 7, 1977.
†Traded with Outfielder Ruppert Jones and Pitchers Tim Lollar and Chris Welsh to San Diego Padres for Outfielder Jerry Mumphrey and Pitcher John Pacella, April 1, 1981.
‡Traded to Philadelphia Phillies for Pitcher Sid Monge, May 22, 1983.

CHAMPIONSHIP SERIES RECORD

Year	Club	League	Pos.	G.	AB.	R.	H.	2B.	3B.	HR.	RBI.	B.A.	PO.	A.	E.	F.A.
1980—New York		Amer.	OF	1	0	0	0	0	0	0	0	.000	0	0	0	.000
1983—Philadelphia		Nat.	PH-OF	2	2	0	0	0	0	0	1	.000	2	0	0	1.000
Championship Series Totals				3	2	0	0	0	0	0	1	.000	2	0	0	1.000

WORLD SERIES RECORD

Year	Club	League	Pos.	G.	AB.	R.	H.	2B.	3B.	HR.	RBI.	B.A.	PO.	A.	E.	F.A.
1983—Philadelphia		Nat.	PH-OF	3	5	0	1	1	0	0	2	.200	3	0	0	1.000

PITCHING RECORD

Year	Club	League	G.	IP.	W.	L.	Pct.	H.	R.	ER.	SO.	BB.	ERA.
1977—Ft. Lauderdale		Florida St.	1	1	0	0	.000	1	1	1	1	2	9.00
1979—West Haven		Eastern	2	5	0	0	.000	5	2	2	4	1	3.60

CRAIG LINDSEY LEFFERTS

Born September 29, 1957, in Munich, West Germany.
Height, 6.01. Weight, 180.
Throws and bats lefthanded.
Attended University of Arizona, Tucson, Ariz.

Year	Club	League	G.	IP.	W.	L.	Pct.	H.	R.	ER.	SO.	BB.	ERA.
1980—Geneva		NYP	12	94	9	1	*.900	74	35	29	*99	24	2.78
1981—Midland		Texas	26	185	12	●12	.500	203	95	85	135	36	4.14
1982—Iowa†		Am. Assoc.	18	97⅓	8	5	.615	97	50	33	71	25	3.05
1983—Chicago‡		National	56	89	3	4	.429	80	35	31	60	29	3.13
Major League Totals			56	89	3	4	.429	80	35	31	60	29	3.13

Selected by Kansas City Royals' organization in 6th round of free-agent draft, June 5, 1979.
Selected by Chicago Cubs' organization in 9th round of free-agent draft, June 3, 1980.
†On disabled list, April 24 to June 4, 1982.
‡Traded with First Baseman Carmelo Martinez and Third Baseman Fritz Connally to San Diego Padres for Pitcher Scott Sanderson, December 7, 1983.

—DID YOU KNOW—
That the last time a pitcher got a hit in the All-Star Game was in 1969 when Steve Carlton doubled for the National League off Blue Moon Odom?

RONALD LeFLORE
(Ron)

Born June 16, 1948, at Detroit, Mich.
Height, 6.00. Weight, 200.
Throws and bats righthanded.

Tied major league records for fewest double plays by outfielder, season, 150 or more games (0), 1977; most stolen bases by pinch-runner, inning (2), October 5, 1980 (eighth inning).
Major league stolen bases: 1974 (23), 1975 (28), 1976 (58), 1977 (39), 1978 (68), 1979 (78), 1980 (97), 1981 (36), 1982 (28). Total—455.
Led National League in stolen bases with 97 in 1980.
Led American League in stolen bases with 68 in 1978.
Led American League outfielders in total chances with 460 in 1978.
Named Florida State League Most Valuable Player, 1974.

Year—Club	League	Pos.	G.	AB.	R.	H.	2B.	3B.	HR.	RBI.	B.A.	PO.	A.	E.	F.A.
1973—Clinton	Midw.	OF	32	65	10	18	1	0	1	8	.277	17	0	1	.944
1974—Lakeland	Fla. St.	OF	93	386	*79	131	11	7	6	38	*.339	202	9	*12	.946
1974—Evansville	A. A.	OF	9	34	5	8	1	0	1	3	.235	11	0	1	.917
1974—Detroit	Amer.	OF	59	254	37	66	8	1	2	13	.260	151	8	*11	.935
1975—Detroit	Amer.	OF	136	550	66	142	13	6	8	37	.258	317	13	9	.973
1976—Detroit†	Amer.	OF	135	544	93	172	23	8	4	39	.316	381	14	*11	.973
1977—Detroit	Amer.	OF	154	652	100	212	30	10	16	57	.325	365	12	11	.972
1978—Detroit	Amer.	OF	155	666	*126	198	30	3	12	62	.297	*440	9	11	.976
1979—Detroit‡	Amer.	OF	148	600	110	180	22	10	9	57	.300	293	6	3	.990
1980—Montreal§	Nat.	OF	139	521	95	134	21	11	4	39	.257	233	14	●11	.957
1981—Chicago	Amer.	OF	82	337	46	83	10	4	0	24	.246	162	6	7	.960
1982—Chicago xy	Amer.	OF	91	334	58	96	15	4	4	25	.287	179	7	*12	.939
1983						(Out of Organized Baseball)									
American League Totals			960	3937	636	1149	151	46	55	314	.292	2288	75	75	.969
National League Totals			139	521	95	134	21	11	4	39	.257	233	14	11	.957
Major League Totals			1099	4458	731	1283	172	57	59	353	.288	2521	89	86	.968

Signed as free agent by Detroit Tigers' organization, July 2, 1973.
†On disabled list, September 15 to October 4, 1976.
‡Traded to Montreal Expos for Pitcher Dan Schatzeder, December 7, 1979.
§Granted free agency, October 28, 1980; signed by Chicago White Sox, December 5, 1980.
xOn suspended list, July 19 to July 22 and October 1, 1982 through remainder of season.
yReleased, April 2, 1983.

ALL-STAR GAME RECORD

Year—League	Pos.	AB.	R.	H.	2B.	3B.	HR.	RBI.	B.A.	PO.	A.	E.	F.A.
1976—American	OF	2	0	1	0	0	0	0	.500	2	0	0	1.000

CHARLES LOUIS LEIBRANDT JR.
(Charlie)

Born October 4, 1956, at Chicago, Ill.
Height, 6.04. Weight, 200.
Throws left and bats righthanded.
Received bachelor of science degree in management from
Miami University, Oxford, O.

Tied for American Association lead in games started by pitchers with 26 in 1979.

Year—Club	League	G.	IP.	W.	L.	Pct.	H.	R.	ER.	SO.	BB.	ERA.
1978—Eugene	Northwest	3	20	2	0	1.000	24	13	9	18	5	4.05
1978—Tampa	Florida St.	6	47	4	1	.800	26	4	4	40	17	0.77
1978—Indianapolis	Am. Assoc.	4	29	2	1	.667	20	9	9	12	12	2.79
1979—Indianapolis	Am. Assoc.	27	162	8	*14	.364	146	67	53	100	65	2.94
1979—Cincinnati	National	3	4	0	0	.000	2	0	0	1	2	0.00
1980—Cincinnati	National	36	174	10	9	.526	200	84	82	62	54	4.24
1981—Indianapolis	Am. Assoc.	25	169	9	7	.563	149	76	55	101	75	2.93
1981—Cincinnati	National	7	30	1	1	.500	28	12	12	9	15	3.60
1982—Cincinnati	National	36	107⅔	5	7	.417	130	68	61	34	48	5.10
1983—Indianapolis†-Omaha	Am. Assoc.	27	185⅓	9	10	.474	181	113	88	128	77	4.27
Major League Totals		82	315⅔	16	17	.485	360	164	155	106	119	4.42

Selected by Cincinnati Reds' organization in 9th round of free-agent draft, June 6, 1978.
†Traded to Kansas City Royals for Pitcher Bob Tufts, June 7, 1983.

CHAMPIONSHIP SERIES RECORD

Year—Club	League	G.	IP.	W.	L.	Pct.	H.	R.	ER.	SO.	BB.	ERA.
1979—Cincinnati	National	1	⅓	0	0	.000	0	0	0	0	0	0.00

JOHNNIE LEE LeMASTER

Born June 19, 1954, at Portsmouth, O.
Height, 6.02. Weight, 165.
Throws and bats righthanded.
Cousin of Ron Salyer, minor league pitcher, 1970 through 1977;
cousin of Frank LeMaster, linebacker with Philadelphia Eagles.

Tied major league record by hitting home run in first major league at-bat, September 2, 1975 (inside the park).
Led Pioneer League batters in strikeouts with 71 in 1973.

Led Pacific Coast League shortstops in double plays with 107 in 1975.
Led Pioneer League shortstops in double plays with 32 in 1973.

Year Club	League	Pos.	G.	AB.	R.	H.	2B.	3B.	HR.	RBI.	B.A.	PO.	A.	E.	F.A.
1973—Great Falls	Pion.	SS	70	250	34	61	8	2	2	33	.244	★106	★178	★38	.882
1974—Decatur	Midw.	SS	104	399	51	103	14	4	3	28	.258	145	280	★48	.899
1974—Fresno	Calif.	SS	21	84	15	24	3	0	1	4	.286	30	68	8	.925
1975—Phoenix	P. C.	SS	143	520	75	152	26	8	4	58	.292	207	★489	33	.955
1975—San Francisco	Nat.	SS	22	74	4	14	4	0	2	9	.189	26	62	3	.967
1976—Phoenix	P. C.	SS	105	380	60	94	14	5	4	35	.247	151	349	26	.951
1976—San Francisco	Nat.	SS	33	100	9	21	3	2	0	9	.210	54	109	11	.937
1977—Phoenix	P. C.	SS-2B	22	70	12	22	7	2	0	13	.314	37	71	6	.947
1977—San Francisco	Nat.	SS-3B	68	134	13	20	5	1	0	8	.149	66	134	14	.935
1978—San Francisco	Nat.	SS-2B	101	272	23	64	18	3	1	14	.235	135	261	14	.966
1979—San Francisco	Nat.	SS	108	343	42	87	11	2	3	29	.254	160	303	20	.959
1980—San Francisco	Nat.	SS	135	405	33	87	16	6	3	31	.215	200	372	26	.957
1981—San Francisco	Nat.	SS	104	324	27	82	9	1	0	28	.253	166	294	17	.964
1982—San Francisco†	Nat.	SS	130	436	34	94	14	1	2	30	.216	223	382	23	.963
1983—San Francisco	Nat.	SS	141	534	81	128	16	1	6	30	.240	215	402	23	.964
Major League Totals			842	2622	266	597	96	17	17	188	.228	1245	2319	151	.959

Selected by San Francisco Giants' organization in 1st round (sixth player selected) of free-agent draft, June 5, 1973.
†On supplemental disabled list, August 15 to September 1, 1982.

CHESTER EARL LEMON
(Chet)

Born February 12, 1955, at Jackson, Miss.
Height, 6.00. Weight, 190.
Throws and bats righthanded.
Attended Pepperdine University, Malibu, Calif., and Cerritos College, Norwalk, Calif.

Established American League records for most chances accepted by outfielder, season (524), 1977; most putouts by outfielder, season (512), 1977.
Tied American League record for most years by outfielder, 500 or more putouts (1), 1977.
Led American League in being hit by pitch with 13 in 1979, 13 in 1981, 15 in 1982 and 20 in 1983.
Led American League outfielders in total chances with 536 in 1977.

Year Club	League	Pos.	G.	AB.	R.	H.	2B.	3B.	HR.	RBI.	B.A.	PO.	A.	E.	F.A.
1972—Coos Bay-N. B.	N'west	SS-3B	38	140	33	40	8	1	2	16	.286	56	94	16	.904
1972—Burlington	Midw.	3B-SS	33	129	18	33	5	0	1	8	.256	24	62	13	.869
1973—Burlington	Midw.	3B-SS	113	392	73	121	21	1	19	★88	.309	102	215	36	.898
1974—Birmingham†	South.	3B-SS	79	272	52	79	22	2	10	61	.290	84	135	23	.905
1975—Tucson‡	P. C.	3B-OF	65	243	43	68	7	2	5	33	.280	60	70	19	.872
1975—Denver	A. A.	3B-OF	70	254	40	78	15	6	8	49	.307	39	76	19	.858
1975—Chicago	Amer.	3B-OF	9	35	2	9	2	0	0	1	.257	5	7	1	.923
1976—Chicago	Amer.	OF	132	451	46	111	15	5	4	38	.246	353	12	3	.992
1977—Chicago	Amer.	OF	150	553	99	151	38	4	19	67	.273	★512	12	12	.978
1978—Chicago§	Amer.	OF	105	357	51	107	24	6	13	55	.300	284	8	5	.983
1979—Chicago	Amer.	OF	148	556	79	177	●44	2	17	86	.318	411	10	10	.977
1980—Chicago	Amer.	OF-2B	147	514	76	150	32	6	11	51	.292	347	11	7	.981
1981—Chicago x	Amer.	OF	94	328	50	99	23	6	9	50	.302	240	2	4	.984
1982—Detroit	Amer.	OF	125	436	75	116	20	1	19	52	.266	242	11	4	.984
1983—Detroit	Amer.	OF	145	491	78	125	21	5	24	69	.255	406	6	5	.988
Major League Totals			1055	3721	556	1045	219	35	116	469	.281	2800	79	51	.983

Selected by Oakland A's organization in 1st round (20th player selected) of free-agent draft, June 6, 1972.
†On disabled list, July 16 to September 16, 1974.
‡Traded with Pitcher Dave Hamilton to Chicago White Sox for Pitchers Stan Bahnsen and Lee (Skip) Pitlock, June 15, 1975.
§On supplemental disabled list, August 12 to August 27, 1978.
xTraded to Detroit Tigers for Outfielder Steve Kemp, November 27, 1981.

ALL-STAR GAME RECORD

Year League	Pos.	AB.	R.	H.	2B.	3B.	HR.	RBI.	B.A.	PO.	A.	E.	F.A.
1978—American	OF	0	0	0	0	0	0	0	.000	0	0	1	.000
1979—American	OF	2	1	0	0	0	0	0	.000	2	0	0	1.000
All-Star Game Totals		2	1	0	0	0	0	0	.000	2	0	1	.667

DENNIS PATRICK LEONARD

Born May 8, 1951, at Brooklyn, N. Y.
Height, 6.01. Weight, 190.
Throws and bats righthanded.
Attended Iona College, New Rochelle, N. Y.

Pitched 2-0 no-hit victory against Visalia, April 26, 1973.
Pitched seven-inning, 3-0 no-hit victory against Quincy, July 15, 1972.
Led American League in home runs allowed with 30 in 1980.
Led American League pitchers in games started with 38 in 1980, 26 in 1981 and tied for lead with 40 in 1978.
Tied for American League lead in shutouts with 5 in 1979.
Led American Association in complete games with 18, shutouts with 4 and tied for lead in games started by pitchers with 29 in 1974.
Tied for California League lead in complete games with 16 and shutouts with 5 in 1973.

Year Club	League	G.	IP.	W.	L.	Pct.	H.	R.	ER.	SO.	BB.	ERA.
1972—Kingsport	Ap'lachian	4	22	2	1	.667	19	9	8	31	6	3.27
1972—Waterloo	Midwest	10	67	4	3	.571	58	28	23	63	26	3.09
1973—San Jose	California	29	206	★15	9	.625	152	70	59	212	81	2.58
1974—Omaha	Am. Assoc.	29	★223	12	13	.480	178	96	86	193	91	3.47
1974—Kansas City	American	5	22	0	4	.000	28	15	13	8	12	5.32
1975—Omaha	Am. Assoc.	3	19	0	2	.000	19	11	9	14	10	4.26
1975—Kansas City	American	32	212	15	7	.682	212	98	89	146	90	3.78
1976—Kansas City	American	35	259	17	10	.630	247	113	101	150	70	3.51
1977—Kansas City	American	38	293	●20	12	.625	246	117	99	244	79	3.04
1978—Kansas City	American	40	295	21	17	.553	★283	125	109	183	78	3.33
1979—Kansas City	American	32	236	14	12	.538	226	117	107	126	56	4.08
1980—Kansas City	American	38	280	20	11	.645	271	127	★118	155	80	3.79
1981—Kansas City	American	26	★202	13	11	.542	★202	79	67	107	41	2.99
1982—Kansas City†	American	21	130⅔	10	6	.625	145	82	74	58	46	5.10
1982—Ft. Myers	Florida St.	1	5	0	0	.000	4	0	0	3	2	0.00
1982—Sarasota Royals	Gulf Coast	1	5	0	1	.000	5	3	3	2	1	5.40
1982—Omaha	Am. Assoc.	3	20⅔	1	2	.333	19	17	17	13	9	7.40
1983—Kansas City‡	American	10	63	6	3	.667	69	29	26	31	19	3.71
Major League Totals		277	1992⅔	136	93	.594	1929	902	803	1208	571	3.63

Selected by Kansas City Royals' organization in 2nd round of free-agent draft, June 6, 1972.

†On disabled list, May 22 to August 8, 1982; included rehabilitation disability assignment to Ft. Myers, July 8 to July 12, 1982; Sarasota, July 13 to July 14, 1982, and Omaha, July 23 to August 4, 1982.

‡On disabled list, May 29, 1983; transferred to emergency disabled list, May 31, 1983 through remainder of season.

DIVISION SERIES RECORD

Year Club	League	G.	IP.	W.	L.	Pct.	H.	R.	ER.	SO.	BB.	ERA.
1981—Kansas City	American	1	8	0	1	.000	7	4	1	3	1	1.13

CHAMPIONSHIP SERIES RECORD

Tied Championship Series record for most games lost, Series (2), 1978.
Established American League Championship Series record for most hits allowed, four-game Series (13), 1978.
Tied American League Championship Series record for most games lost, total Series (3).

Year Club	League	G.	IP.	W.	L.	Pct.	H.	R.	ER.	SO.	BB.	ERA.
1976—Kansas City	American	2	2⅓	0	0	.000	9	5	5	0	2	19.29
1977—Kansas City	American	2	9	1	1	.500	5	4	3	4	2	3.00
1978—Kansas City	American	2	12	0	2	.000	13	5	5	11	2	3.75
1980—Kansas City	American	1	8	1	0	1.000	7	2	2	8	1	2.25
Championship Series Totals		7	31⅓	2	3	.400	34	16	15	23	7	4.31

WORLD SERIES RECORD

Year Club	League	G.	IP.	W.	L.	Pct.	H.	R.	ER.	SO.	BB.	ERA.
1980—Kansas City	American	2	10⅔	1	1	.500	15	9	8	5	2	6.75

JEFFREY N. LEONARD
(Jeff)

Born September 22, 1955, at Philadelphia, Pa.
Height, 6.04. Weight, 200.
Throws and bats righthanded.
Named National League Rookie Player of the Year by THE SPORTING NEWS, 1979.

Year Club	League	Pos.	G.	AB.	R.	H.	2B.	3B.	HR.	RBI.	B.A.	PO.	A.	E.	F.A.
1973—Bellingham	N'west	OF	55	187	30	52	4	3	2	20	.278	46	2	5	.906
1974—Orangeburg	W. Car.	OF	8	15	0	1	0	0	0	1	.067	5	1	1	.857
1974—Bellingham	N'west	OF	78	278	47	90	12	4	3	43	.324	115	7	6	.953
1975—Bakersfield	Calif.	OF	106	320	44	89	11	3	4	37	.278	137	5	7	.953
1976—Lodi	Calif.	OF	133	509	93	168	29	9	8	85	.330	214	13	★15	.938
1976—Albuquerque	P. C.	OF	7	27	2	8	2	1	1	6	.296	14	0	0	1.000
1977—San Antonio	Texas	OF	122	468	75	147	17	10	12	70	.314	241	12	8	.969
1977—Los Angeles	Nat.	OF	11	10	1	3	0	1	0	2	.300	7	0	0	1.000
1978—Albuquerque†	P. C.	OF	133	502	111	★183	23	14	11	93	★.365	216	8	6	.974
1978—Houston	Nat.	OF	8	26	2	10	2	0	0	4	.385	16	1	0	1.000
1979—Houston	Nat.	OF	134	411	47	119	15	5	0	47	.290	227	6	10	.959
1980—Houston	Nat.	OF	88	216	29	46	7	5	3	20	.213	161	9	3	.983
1981—Hou.‡-S.F.	Nat.	OF-1B	44	145	21	42	12	4	4	29	.290	152	5	1	.994
1981—Phoenix	P. C.	OF	47	187	38	75	17	3	7	45	.401	90	2	2	.979
1982—San Francisco§	Nat.	OF-1B	80	278	32	72	16	1	9	49	.259	137	2	9	.939
1982—Phoenix	P. C.	OF	17	59	14	21	5	0	4	12	.356	5	0	0	1.000
1983—San Francisco	Nat.	OF	139	516	74	144	17	7	21	87	.279	253	17	7	.975
Major League Totals			504	1602	206	436	69	23	37	238	.272	953	40	30	.971

Signed as free agent by Los Angeles Dodgers' organization, June 7, 1973.

†Traded to Houston Astros, September 11, 1978, completing deal in which Los Angeles Dodgers acquired Catcher Joe Ferguson for two players to be named later, July 1, 1978; Houston acquired Shortstop Rafael Landestoy as partial completion of deal, July 7, 1978.

‡Traded with First Baseman-Outfielder Dave Bergman to San Francisco Giants for First Baseman Mike Ivie, April 20, 1981.

§On supplemental disabled list, May 23 to July 19, 1982; included rehabilitation disability assignment to Phoenix, July 1 to July 19, 1982.

CHAMPIONSHIP SERIES RECORD

Year Club	League	Pos.	G.	AB.	R.	H.	2B.	3B.	HR.	RBI.	B.A.	PO.	A.	E.	F.A.
1980—Houston	Nat.	PH-OF	3	3	0	0	0	0	0	0	.000	2	1	0	1.000

RANDY LOUIS LERCH

Born October 9, 1954, at Sacramento, Calif.
Height, 6.03. Weight, 195.
Throws and bats lefthanded.

Tied major league record for most sacrifice flies allowed, season (15), 1979.
Led American Association pitchers in games started with 29 and tied for lead in complete games with 11 in 1976.

Year Club	League	G.	IP.	W.	L.	Pct.	H.	R.	ER.	SO.	BB.	ERA.
1973—Auburn	NYP	16	96	9	2	.818	88	41	31	75	29	2.91
1974—Rocky Mount	Carolina	22	143	7	7	.500	150	73	58	114	54	3.65
1975—Reading	Eastern	25	177	*16	6	*.727	173	66	53	108	45	2.69
1975—Philadelphia	National	3	7	0	0	.000	6	5	5	8	1	6.43
1976—Oklahoma City	Am. Assoc.	29	*207	13	11	.542	*203	91	77	*152	47	3.35
1976—Philadelphia	National	1	3	0	0	.000	3	1	1	0	0	3.00
1977—Philadelphia	National	32	169	10	6	.625	207	102	95	81	75	5.06
1978—Philadelphia	National	33	184	11	8	.579	183	89	81	96	70	3.96
1979—Philadelphia	National	37	214	10	13	.435	228	98	89	92	60	3.74
1980—Philadelphia†	National	30	150	4	14	.222	178	98	86	57	55	5.16
1981—Milwaukee	American	23	111	7	9	.438	134	63	53	53	43	4.30
1982—Milwaukee‡	American	21	108⅔	8	7	.533	123	68	60	33	51	4.97
1982—Montreal	National	6	23⅔	2	0	1.000	26	11	9	4	8	3.42
1983—Montreal§-San Francisco	National	26	49⅓	2	3	.400	54	33	33	30	26	6.02
1983—Phoenix	P. Coast	5	8⅓	0	0	.000	8	5	3	7	3	3.24
National League Totals		168	800	39	44	.470	885	437	399	368	295	4.49
American League Totals		44	219⅔	15	16	.484	257	131	113	86	94	4.63
Major League Totals		212	1019⅔	54	60	.474	1142	568	512	454	389	4.52

Selected by Philadelphia Phillies' organization in 8th round of free-agent draft, June 5, 1973.
†Traded to Milwaukee Brewers for Outfielder Dick Davis, March 1, 1981.
‡Sold to Montreal Expos, August 14, 1982.
§Released, July 28, 1983; signed by Phoenix (San Francisco Giants' organization), August 9, 1983.

DIVISION SERIES RECORD

Year Club	League	G.	IP.	W.	L.	Pct.	H.	R.	ER.	SO.	BB.	ERA.
1981—Milwaukee	American	1	6	0	0	.000	3	1	1	3	4	1.50

CHAMPIONSHIP SERIES RECORD

Year Club	League	G.	IP.	W.	L.	Pct.	H.	R.	ER.	SO.	BB.	ERA.
1978—Philadelphia	National	1	5⅓	0	0	.000	7	3	3	0	0	5.06

BRADLEY JAY LESLEY
(Brad)

Born September 11, 1958, at Turlock, Calif.
Height, 6.06. Weight, 225.
Throws and bats righthanded.
Attended Merced Junior College, Merced, Calif.

Tied for American Association lead in saves with 14 and intentional bases on balls issued with 8 in 1982.

Year Club	League	G.	IP.	W.	L.	Pct.	H.	R.	ER.	SO.	BB.	ERA.
1978—Eugene	Northwest	13	79	5	4	.556	97	47	44	60	26	5.01
1979—Greensboro†	W. Carol.	19	101	3	7	.300	112	67	52	62	34	4.63
1980—Tampa	Florida St.	37	76	4	2	.667	67	23	17	44	40	2.01
1981—Cedar Rapids	Midwest	22	34	4	1	.800	14	4	3	51	21	0.79
1981—Waterbury	Eastern	26	45	4	1	.800	45	17	13	37	15	2.60
1982—Indianapolis	Am. Assoc.	40	59⅔	6	4	.600	55	27	24	47	25	3.62
1982—Cincinnati	National	28	38⅓	0	2	.000	27	13	11	29	13	2.58
1983—Indianapolis‡	Am. Assoc.	13	17⅔	3	1	.750	11	5	5	19	5	2.55
1983—Cincinnati	National	5	8⅓	0	0	.000	9	2	2	5	0	2.16
Major League Totals		33	46⅔	0	2	.000	36	15	13	34	13	2.51

Selected by Minnesota Twins' organization in 7th round of free-agent draft, January 11, 1977.
Selected by Cincinnati Reds' organization in 1st round (18th player selected) of free-agent draft, January 10, 1978.
Selected by Cincinnati Reds' organization in secondary phase of free-agent draft, June 6, 1978.
†On disabled list, May 5 to May 19, 1979.
‡On disabled list, July 4 to July 29, 1983.

JAMES MARTIN LEWIS
(Jim)

Born October 12, 1955, at Miami, Fla.
Height, 6.03. Weight, 195.
Throws and bats righthanded.
Attended Miami-Dade Community College, Miami, Fla.,
and University of South Carolina, Columbia, S. C.

Tied for California League lead in shutouts with 5 in 1978.
Tied for International League lead in intentional bases on balls issued with 13 in 1980.

Year Club	League	G.	IP.	W.	L.	Pct.	H.	R.	ER.	SO.	BB.	ERA.
1977—Bellingham	Northwest	12	27	3	2	.600	33	23	17	31	14	5.67
1978—Stockton	California	26	212	12	11	.522	166	70	50	*189	61	*2.12
1979—Spokane	P. Coast	28	183	13	11	.542	206	95	75	98	56	3.69
1979—Seattle†	American	2	2	0	0	.000	10	7	4	0	1	18.00

Year Club	League	G.	IP.	W.	L.	Pct.	H.	R.	ER.	SO.	BB.	ERA.
1980—Columbus	Int'national	47	93	10	7	.588	73	34	24	76	45	2.32
1981—Columbus	Int'national	54	150	8	7	.533	147	89	83	100	65	4.98
1982—Columbus	Int'national	32	166	12	6	.667	139	61	48	107	64	★2.60
1982—New York‡	American	1	⅔	0	0	.000	3	7	4	0	3	54.00
1983—Toledo	Int'national	38	123	11	9	.550	128	81	69	76	86	5.05
1983—Minnesota§	American	6	18	0	0	.000	24	13	13	8	7	6.50
Major League Totals		9	20⅔	0	0	.000	37	27	21	8	11	9.15

Signed as free agent by Seattle Mariners' organization, June 22, 1977.

†Traded with Outfielder Ruppert Jones to New York Yankees for Pitchers Rick Anderson and Jim Beattie, Outfielder Juan Beniquez and Catcher Jerry Narron, November 1, 1979.

‡Drafted by Toledo (Minnesota Twins' organization), December 7, 1982.

§Granted free agency, October 20, 1983.

SIXTO LEZCANO

Name pronounced Lezz-KAHN-oh.

Born November 28, 1953, at Arecibo, Puerto Rico.
Height, 5.10. Weight, 175.
Throws and bats righthanded.
Cousin of Carlos Lezcano, outfielder in Chicago Cubs' organization.

Tied major league record for most home runs, opening day of season (2), April 10, 1980.
Tied modern major league record for most chances accepted by right fielder, game (10), May 20, 1977.
Led National League outfielders in double plays with 8 in 1982.
Named outfielder on THE SPORTING NEWS American League All-Star fielding team, 1979.

Year Club	League	Pos.	G.	AB.	R.	H.	2B.	3B.	HR.	RBI.	B.A.	PO.	A.	E.	F.A.
1971—Newark	NYP	OF-3B	53	152	24	44	5	1	7	23	.289	55	11	5	.930
1972—Danville	Midw.	OF	114	423	67	114	20	5	10	56	.270	147	13	10	.941
1973—Shreveport	Texas	OF	134	458	69	134	★35	★7	18	90	.293	264	★17	13	.956
1974—Sacramento	P. C.	OF	131	508	100	165	23	8	34	99	.325	245	24	3	.989
1974—Milwaukee	Amer.	OF	15	54	5	13	2	0	2	9	.241	32	3	1	.972
1975—Milwaukee	Amer.	OF	134	429	55	106	19	3	11	43	.247	240	10	6	.977
1976—Milwaukee	Amer.	OF	145	513	53	146	19	5	7	56	.285	345	10	10	.973
1977—Milwaukee†	Amer.	OF	109	400	50	109	21	4	21	49	.273	238	11	3	.988
1978—Milwaukee	Amer.	OF	132	442	62	129	21	4	15	61	.292	262	★18	6	.979
1979—Milwaukee	Amer.	OF	138	473	84	152	29	3	28	101	.321	281	10	4	.986
1980—Milwaukee‡	Amer.	OF	112	411	51	94	19	3	18	55	.229	228	8	4	.983
1981—St. Louis§	Nat.	OF	72	214	26	57	8	2	5	28	.266	103	5	3	.973
1982—San Diego	Nat.	OF	138	470	73	136	26	6	16	84	.289	275	●16	3	.990
1983—S.D. x-Phila.	Nat.	OF	115	356	49	85	12	2	8	56	.239	189	10	6	.971
American League Totals			785	2722	360	749	130	22	102	374	.275	1626	70	34	.980
National League Totals			325	1040	148	278	46	10	29	168	.267	567	31	12	.980
Major League Totals			1110	3762	508	1027	176	32	131	542	.273	2193	101	46	.980

Signed as free agent by Milwaukee Brewers' organization, October 1, 1970.

†On disabled list, July 23 to August 16, 1977.

‡Traded with Pitchers Lary Sorensen and Dave LaPoint and Outfielder David Green to St. Louis Cardinals for Catcher Ted Simmons and Pitchers Pete Vuckovich and Rollie Fingers, December 12, 1980.

§Traded with a player to be named later to San Diego Padres for Pitcher Steve Mura and a player to be named later, December 10, 1981; San Diego acquired Pitcher Luis DeLeon and St. Louis Cardinals' organization acquired Pitcher Al Olmsted to complete deal, February 19, 1982.

xTraded with a player to be named later to Philadelphia Phillies for four players to be named later, August 31, 1983; San Diego Padres acquired Pitchers Marty Decker, Ed Wojna, Darren Burroughs and Lance McCullers, September 20, 1983, and Philadelphia organization acquired Pitcher Steve Fireovid to complete deal, October 11, 1983.

CHAMPIONSHIP SERIES RECORD

Year Club	League	Pos.	G.	AB.	R.	H.	2B.	3B.	HR.	RBI.	B.A.	PO.	A.	E.	F.A.
1983—Philadelphia	Nat.	OF-PH	4	13	2	4	0	0	1	2	.308	5	1	1	.857

WORLD SERIES RECORD

Year Club	League	Pos.	G.	AB.	R.	H.	2B.	3B.	HR.	RBI.	B.A.	PO.	A.	E.	F.A.
1983—Philadelphia	Nat.	PH-OF	4	8	0	1	0	0	0	0	.125	2	0	0	1.000

RUFINO LINARES

Name pronounced Luh-NAHR-ess.

Born February 28, 1955, at San Pedro de Macoris, Dominican Republic.
Height 6.00. Weight, 170.
Throws and bats righthanded.

Year Club	League	Pos.	G.	AB.	R.	H.	2B.	3B.	HR.	RBI.	B.A.	PO.	A.	E.	F.A.
1974—Kingsport	Appal.	OF	56	220	32	64	7	1	6	41	.291	106	5	6	.949
1975—Greenwood	W. Car.	OF	106	302	36	77	12	2	2	35	.255	178	6	10	.948
1976—Greenwood	W. Car.	OF-1B	109	389	57	127	20	4	3	54	.326	52	4	1	.982
1977—Savannah	South.	OF	85	262	32	76	12	5	2	29	.290	93	9	5	.953
1978—Savannah	South.	OF	116	400	49	121	15	5	8	51	.303	158	12	3	.983
1978—Richmond	Int.	DH	4	9	1	1	0	1	0	3	.111	0	0	0	.000
1979—Savannah	South.	OF	53	198	35	65	11	1	8	37	.328	40	1	2	.953
1979—Richmond†	Int.	OF	36	104	9	31	4	1	1	13	.298	22	1	5	.821
1980—Richmond	Int.	OF	63	234	31	77	12	4	3	41	.329	56	5	0	1.000
1980—Savannah	South.	OF	51	200	37	85	18	6	2	38	.425	100	4	5	.954

Year	Club	League	Pos.	G.	AB.	R.	H.	2B.	3B.	HR.	RBI.	B.A.	PO.	A.	E.	F.A.
1981—Atlanta		Nat.	OF	78	253	27	67	9	2	5	25	.265	124	6	5	.963
1982—Atlanta		Nat.	OF	77	191	28	57	7	1	2	17	.298	92	4	0	1.000
1983—Richmond‡		Int.	OF	29	107	10	24	6	2	1	24	.224	20	1	1	.955
Major League Totals				155	444	55	124	16	3	7	42	.279	216	10	5	.978

Signed as free agent by Atlanta Braves' organization, December 30, 1973.
†On disabled list, August 3 to August 13, 1979.
‡On Atlanta disabled list, March 24 to August 15, 1983; included rehabilitation disability assignment to Richmond, July 26 to August 15, 1983.

RICCARDO PATRICK EMILIE LISI
(Rick)

Born March 17, 1956, at Halifax, Nova Scotia.
Height 6.00. Weight, 175.
Throws and bats righthanded.
Tied for International League lead in being hit by pitch with 9 in 1983.
Led Gulf Coast League third basemen in putouts with 39 in 1974.
Led Western Carolinas League third basemen in double plays with 26 in 1975.
Tied for International League lead in double plays by outfielders with 4 in 1983.

Year	Club	League	Pos.	G.	AB.	R.	H.	2B.	3B.	HR.	RBI.	B.A.	PO.	A.	E.	F.A.
1974—Sara. Rangers		Gulf C.	3B-C	51	170	16	37	8	1	2	29	.218	48	96	12	.923
1975—Anderson		W. Car.	3B	135	436	74	102	21	3	12	67	.234	★123	★274	★42	★.904
1976—Asheville		W. Car.	3B-1B	126	473	73	127	24	4	16	75	.268	88	127	26	.912
1977—Tulsa		Texas	O-C-3-1	112	375	55	95	23	3	6	50	.253	264	62	18	.948
1978—Tulsa		Texas	C-1-O-3	101	342	44	78	16	5	9	46	.228	429	49	16	.968
1979—Tulsa		Texas	OF-1B	120	435	86	133	32	5	22	84	.306	453	28	8	.984
1979—Tucson		P. C.	OF	6	13	1	2	1	0	0	0	.154	2	0	0	1.000
1980—Charleston		Int.	OF	132	461	51	113	20	5	14	65	.245	278	16	8	.974
1981—Wichita		A. A.	OF	103	326	49	84	11	0	11	47	.258	203	6	7	.968
1981—Texas†		Amer.	OF	9	16	6	5	0	0	0	1	.313	9	0	0	1.000
1982—Rochester		Int.	OF-3B-1B	93	294	34	68	9	1	6	40	.231	117	41	6	.963
1983—Rochester‡		Int.	OF-2B	126	476	81	120	20	10	3	37	.252	252	25	11	.962
Major League Totals				9	16	6	5	0	0	0	1	.313	9	0	0	1.000

Selected by Texas Rangers' organization in 13th round of free-agent draft, June 5, 1974.
†Traded to Baltimore Orioles for pitcher Steve Leubber, February 19, 1982.
‡Granted free agency, October 20, 1983; signed by Atlanta Braves, November 18, 1983.

DONALD JEFFERY LITTLE
(Jeff)

Born December 25, 1954, at Woodville, O.
Height, 6.06. Weight, 220.
Throws left and bats righthanded.
Son of Donald Little, minor league pitcher, 1953 and 1957.
Pitched seven-inning, 1-0 no-hit victory against Dubuque, June 12, 1974.
Tied for Pacific Coast League lead in games started by pitchers with 28 in 1978.

Year	Club	League	G.	IP.	W.	L.	Pct.	H.	R.	ER.	SO.	BB.	ERA.
1973—Great Falls		Pioneer	14	69	4	7	.364	81	39	29	62	42	3.78
1974—Decatur		Midwest	23	153	7	★14	.333	153	85	58	129	59	3.41
1975—Lafayette		Texas	26	115	5	12	.294	143	84	69	59	53	5.40
1976—Lafayette		Texas	29	110	4	9	.308	107	67	60	66	59	4.91
1977—Waterbury		Eastern	26	162	14	10	.583	146	86	78	111	96	4.33
1978—Phoenix		P. Coast	29	175	11	7	.611	189	96	80	74	77	4.11
1979—Phoenix†‡		P. Coast	28	140	7	13	.350	179	110	92	72	76	5.91
1980—Arkansas§		Texas	9	11	3	1	.750	13	7	6	9	7	4.91
1980—Springfield		Am. Assoc.	22	62	3	4	.429	60	32	31	46	28	4.50
1980—St. Louis		National	7	19	1	1	.500	18	9	8	17	9	3.79
1981—Springfield x		Am. Assoc.	47	114	6	7	.462	98	57	49	99	65	3.87
1982—Toledo		Int'national	25	41	2	2	.500	21	12	8	40	21	1.76
1982—Orlando		Southern	9	20⅓	1	2	.333	15	6	3	29	7	1.33
1982—Minnesota		American	33	36⅓	2	0	1.000	33	20	17	26	27	4.21
1983—Toledo		Int'national	23	33	2	4	.333	40	33	29	34	39	7.91
1983—Orlando yz		Southern	10	9⅓	0	0	.000	5	3	3	11	8	2.89
National League Totals			7	19	1	1	.500	18	9	8	17	9	3.79
American League Totals			33	36⅓	2	0	1.000	33	20	17	26	27	4.21
Major League Totals			40	55⅓	3	1	.750	51	29	25	43	36	4.07

Selected by San Francisco Giants' organization in 3rd round of free-agent draft, June 5, 1973.
†On disabled list, July 27 to August 7, 1979.
‡Released, April 2, 1980; signed by St. Louis Cardinals' organization, April 7, 1980.
§On disabled list, April 10 to May 5, 1980.
xTraded to Minnesota Twins' organization for Pitcher Mike Kinnunen, October 23, 1981.
yOn disabled list, July 8 to August 8, 1983.
zGranted free agency, October 20, 1983; signed by Pittsburgh Pirates' organization, November 29, 1983.

RICHARD BRYAN LITTLE

(Known by middle name.)
Born October 8, 1959, at Houston, Texas.
Height, 5.11. Weight, 155.
Throws right and bats right and lefthanded.
Attended Texas A & M University, College Station, Texas.

Year Club	League	Pos.	G.	AB.	R.	H.	2B.	3B.	HR.	RBI.	B.A.	PO.	A.	E.	F.A.
1980—Jamestown............	NYP	2B-SS	7	27	6	8	0	0	0	3	.296	11	21	2	.941
1980—W. Palm Beach....	Fla. St.	SS	64	195	23	43	2	0	0	11	.221	95	212	12	.962
1981—Memphis...............	South.	SS	●143	553	98	162	15	3	1	46	.293	★237	399	24	★.964
1982—Wichita.................	A. A.	SS-2B	99	388	67	111	13	3	1	35	.286	165	305	17	.965
1982—Montreal...............	Nat.	2B-3B	29	42	6	9	0	0	0	3	.214	21	32	1	.981
1983—Montreal...............	Nat.	SS-2B	106	350	48	91	15	3	1	36	.260	181	248	9	.979
Major League Totals...................		·	135	392	54	100	15	3	1	39	.255	202	280	10	.980

Selected by Montreal Expos' organization in 9th round of free-agent draft, June 3, 1980.

WILLIAM TIMOTHY LOLLAR
(Tim)

Born March 17, 1956, at Poplar Bluff, Mo.
Height, 6.03. Weight, 200.
Throws and bats lefthanded.
Attended Mineral Area Community College, Flat River, Mo., and University of Arkansas, Fayetteville, Ark.

Year Club	League	G.	IP.	W.	L.	Pct.	H.	R.	ER.	SO.	BB.	ERA.
1978—West Haven†	Eastern	8	31	1	1	.500	40	24	20	20	14	5.81
1979—West Haven	Eastern	22	119	8	5	.615	122	55	42	60	36	3.18
1980—Columbus..........................	Int'national	21	49	2	1	.667	29	15	14	50	27	2.57
1980—New York‡..........................	American	14	32	1	0	1.000	33	14	12	13	20	3.38
1981—San Diego	National	24	77	2	8	.200	87	56	52	38	51	6.08
1982—San Diego	National	34	232⅔	16	9	.640	192	82	81	150	87	3.13
1983—San Diego	National	30	175⅔	7	12	.368	170	98	90	135	85	4.61
American League Totals..		14	32	1	0	1.000	33	14	12	13	20	3.38
National League Totals..		88	485⅓	25	29	.463	449	236	223	323	223	4.14
Major League Totals..........................		102	517⅓	26	29	.473	482	250	235	336	243	4.09

Selected by Cleveland Indians' organization in 5th round of free-agent draft, June 6, 1977.
Selected by New York Yankees' organization in 4th round of free-agent draft, June 6, 1978.
†On disabled list, August 2 to August 14, 1978.
‡Traded with Outfielder Ruppert Jones and Joe Lefebvre and Pitcher Chris Welsh to San Diego Padres for Outfielder Jerry Mumphrey and Pitcher John Pacella, April 1, 1981.

RECORD AS INFIELDER

Year Club	League	Pos.	G.	AB.	R.	H.	2B.	3B.	HR.	RBI.	B.A.	PO.	A.	E.	F.A.
1978—West Haven	East.	P-1B	28	55	11	14	2	1	2	7	.255	16	3	0	1.000
1979—West Haven	East.	P-1B	65	122	16	28	3	0	5	15	.230	137	9	1	.993

GERARDO LOMASTRO
(Jerry)

Born August 9, 1958, at Miami, Fla.
Height, 5.11. Weight, 190.
Throws and bats righthanded.
Attended Miami-Dade Community College (North), Miami, Fla.,
and Louisiana Tech University, Ruston, La.

Tied for Southern League lead in total bases with 267 in 1983.

Year Club	League	Pos.	G.	AB.	R.	H.	2B.	3B.	HR.	RBI.	B.A.	PO.	A.	E.	F.A.
1981—Wis. Rapids...........	Midw.	OF	69	229	42	63	8	0	13	39	.275	66	2	3	.958
1982—Visalia	Calif.	OF	133	501	84	151	31	2	19	91	.301	188	7	6	.970
1983—Orlando	South.	OF	142	528	89	158	36	5	21	92	.299	174	9	6	.968

Selected by Minnesota Twins' organization in 20th round of free-agent draft, June 8, 1981.

STEPHEN PAUL LOMBARDOZZI
(Steve)

Born April 26, 1960, at Malden, Mass.
Height, 6.00. Weight, 175.
Throws and bats righthanded.
Attended Gulf Coast Community College, Panama City, Fla.,
and University of Florida, Gainesville, Fla.

Led California League shortstops in fielding percentage with .947 in 1982.

Year Club	League	Pos.	G.	AB.	R.	H.	2B.	3B.	HR.	RBI.	B.A.	PO.	A.	E.	F.A.
1981—Elizabethton	Appal.	SS	65	246	48	79	13	2	6	38	.321	89	192	14	★.953
1982—Visalia	Calif.	SS-OF-P	122	441	81	131	24	1	6	67	.297	185	393	33	.946
1983—Orlando	South.	SS-2B	137	492	76	143	23	6	3	52	.291	203	364	33	.945

Selected by Minnesota Twins' organization in 9th round of free-agent draft, June 8, 1981.

Year Club	League	G.	IP.	W.	L.	Pct.	H.	R.	ER.	SO.	BB.	ERA.
1982—Visalia	California	1	1	0	1	.000	5	4	4	2	0	36.00

DAVID EARL LOPES
Name rhymes with Ropes.
(Davey)
Born May 3, 1946, at East Providence, R. I.
Height, 5.09. Weight, 170.
Throws and bats righthanded.
Attended Iowa Wesleyan College, Mt. Pleasant, Iowa, and received bachelor of science degree in education from Washburn University, Topeka, Kan. in 1969.

Established major league record for most consecutive stolen bases, season (38), June 10 through August 24, 1975.
Tied major league record for most errors, inning, second baseman, (3), June 2, 1973 (1st inning).
Established National League record for highest stolen base percentage, lifetime, 300 or more attempts (.831).
Tied National League records for most stolen bases, game, since 1900 (5), August 24, 1974; most double plays, second baseman, game (5), May 18, 1975.
Hit three home runs in a game, August 20, 1974.
Major league stolen bases: 1972 (4), 1973 (36), 1974 (59), 1975 (77), 1976 (63), 1977 (47), 1978 (45), 1979 (44), 1980 (23), 1981 (20), 1982 (28), 1983 (22). Total—468.
Led National League in stolen bases with 77 in 1975 and 63 in 1976.
Led Pacific Coast League in stolen bases with 48 in 1972.
Led Pacific Coast League second basemen in errors with 18 in 1972.
Tied for Pacific Coast League lead in errors by outfielders with 10 in 1970.
Named second baseman on THE SPORTING NEWS National League All-Star Team, 1978 and 1979.
Named second baseman on THE SPORTING NEWS National League All-Star fielding team, 1978.

Year Club	League	Pos.	G.	AB.	R.	H.	2B.	3B.	HR.	RBI.	B.A.	PO.	A.	E.	F.A.
1968—Daytona Beach†...Fla. St.		OF	82	271	39	67	6	6	5	33	.247	109	7	4	.967
1969—Daytona Bea.‡§.... Fla. St.		OF	72	264	53	74	7	4	9	33	.280	138	16	7	.957
1970—Spokane x	P. C.	OF-2B	100	343	48	90	15	4	6	35	.262	202	19	12	.948
1971—Spokane y	P. C.	OF-2B	94	353	78	108	9	9	6	36	.306	157	103	11	.959
1972—Albuquerque z	P. C.	2B-OF-SS	104	397	94	126	18	6	11	53	.317	213	270	21	.958
1972—Los Angeles	Nat.	2B	11	42	6	9	4	0	0	1	.214	27	27	2	.964
1973—Los Angeles	Nat.	2-O-S-3	142	535	77	147	13	5	6	37	.275	323	380	11	.985
1974—Los Angeles	Nat.	2B	145	530	95	141	26	3	10	35	.266	309	360	★24	.965
1975—Los Angeles	Nat.	2B-OF-SS	155	618	108	162	24	6	8	41	.262	360	386	16	.979
1976—Los Angeles a	Nat.	2B-OF	117	427	72	103	17	7	4	20	.241	254	268	19	.965
1977—Los Angeles	Nat.	2B	134	502	85	142	19	5	11	53	.283	287	380	14	.979
1978—Los Angeles	Nat.	★2B-OF	151	587	93	163	25	4	17	58	.278	340	424	★20	.974
1979—Los Angeles	Nat.	2B	153	582	109	154	20	6	28	73	.265	341	★384	14	.981
1980—Los Angeles	Nat.	2B	141	553	79	139	15	3	10	49	.251	304	416	15	.980
1981—Los Angeles bc	Nat.	2B	58	214	35	44	2	0	5	17	.206	129	161	2	.993
1982—Oakland	Amer.	2B-OF	128	450	58	109	19	3	11	42	.242	295	338	15	.977
1983—Oakland	Amer.	2B-OF-3B	147	494	64	137	13	4	17	67	.277	267	287	9	.984
National League Totals			1207	4590	759	1204	165	39	99	384	.262	2674	3186	137	.977
American League Totals			275	944	122	246	32	7	28	109	.261	562	625	24	.980
Major League Totals			1482	5534	881	1450	197	46	127	493	.262	3236	3811	161	.978

Selected by San Francisco Giants' organization in 28th round of free-agent draft, June 6, 1967.
Selected by Los Angeles Dodgers' organization in secondary phase of free-agent draft, January 27, 1968.
†On restricted list, April 11 to June 13, 1968.
‡On temporary inactive list, April 11 to April 27, 1969.
§On military list, July 22, 1969 to April 8, 1970.
xOn temporary inactive list, June 9 to June 30, 1970.
yOn temporary inactive list, April 26 to April 29 and June 8 to July 2, 1971.
zOn temporary inactive list, June 16 to June 30 and August 28 to September 1, 1972.
aOn supplemental disabled list, March 31 to May 3, 1976.
bOn supplemental disabled list, August 18 to September 2, 1981.
cTraded to Oakland A's for Second Baseman Lance Hudson, February 8, 1982.

DIVISION SERIES RECORD

Year Club	League	Pos.	G.	AB.	R.	H.	2B.	3B.	HR.	RBI.	B.A.	PO.	A.	E.	F.A.
1981—Los Angeles	Nat.	2B	5	20	1	4	1	0	0	0	.200	7	12	0	1.000

CHAMPIONSHIP SERIES RECORD

Established Championship Series records for most stolen bases, total Series (9); most stolen bases, five-game Series (5), 1981.
Tied Championship Series records for most consecutive games, one or more runs batted in, total Series (4); most hits, two consecutive games, one Series (6), October 4 and 5, 1978.
Tied National League Championship Series record for most three-base hits, total Series (2).

Year Club	League	Pos.	G.	AB.	R.	H.	2B.	3B.	HR.	RBI.	B.A.	PO.	A.	E.	F.A.
1974—Los Angeles	Nat.	2B	4	15	4	4	0	1	0	3	.267	9	18	1	.964
1977—Los Angeles	Nat.	2B	4	17	2	4	0	0	0	3	.235	9	10	1	.950
1978—Los Angeles	Nat.	2B	4	18	3	7	1	1	2	5	.389	10	10	2	.909
1981—Los Angeles	Nat.	2B	5	18	0	5	0	0	0	0	.278	13	13	0	1.000
Championship Series Totals			17	68	9	20	1	2	2	11	.294	41	51	4	.958

Established World Series records for most stolen bases, six-game Series (4), 1981; most putouts by second baseman, six-game Series (26), 1981; most chances accepted by second baseman, six-game Series (40), 1981; most errors by second baseman, six-game Series (6), 1981.

Tied World Series records for most stolen bases, inning (2), October 15, 1974 (first inning); most putouts by second baseman, game (8), October 16, 1974; most chances accepted by second baseman, game (13), October 16, 1974; most putouts by second baseman, inning (3), October 16, 1974 (sixth inning) and October 21 1981 (fourth inning); most times home run as leadoff batter, start of game (1), October 17, 1978; most errors by second baseman, game (3), October 25, 1981; most errors by second baseman, inning (2), October 25, 1981 (fourth inning).

Year	Club	League	Pos.	G.	AB.	R.	H.	2B.	3B.	HR.	RBI.	B.A.	PO.	A.	E.	F.A.
1974—Los Angeles		Nat.	2B	5	18	2	2	0	0	0	0	.111	19	9	0	1.000
1977—Los Angeles		Nat.	2B	6	24	3	4	0	1	1	2	.167	12	22	0	1.000
1978—Los Angeles		Nat.	2B	6	26	7	8	0	0	3	7	.308	10	19	1	.967
1981—Los Angeles		Nat.	2B	6	22	6	5	1	0	0	2	.227	26	14	6	.870
World Series Totals				23	90	18	19	1	1	4	11	.211	67	64	7	.949

ALL-STAR GAME RECORD

Year	League	Pos.	AB.	R.	H.	2B.	3B.	HR.	RBI.	B.A.	PO.	A.	E.	F.A.
1978—National		PH-2B	1	0	1	0	0	0	1	1.000	0	1	0	1.000
1979—National		2B	3	0	1	0	0	0	0	.333	4	1	0	1.000
1980—National		2B	1	0	0	0	0	0	0	.000	0	2	0	1.000
1981—National		2B	0	0	0	0	0	0	0	.000	1	0	0	.000
All-Star Game Totals			5	0	2	0	0	0	1	.400	5	4	0	1.000

AURELIO ALEJANDRO LOPEZ (RIOS)

Born October 5, 1948, at Tecamachalco, Puebla, Mexico.
Height, 6.00. Weight, 230.
Throws and bats righthanded.

Pitched 1-0 no-hit victory against Carmen, May 24, 1969.
Major League saves: 1979 (21), 1980 (21), 1981 (3), 1982 (3), 1983 (18). Total—66.
Led Mexican League in wild pitches with 18 in 1975.
Led Mexican League in saves with 20 in 1974, 23 in 1975 and 16 in 1976.
Named Mexican League Most Valuable Player, 1977.

Year	Club	League	G.	IP.	W.	L.	Pct.	H.	R.	ER.	SO.	BB.	ERA.
1967—Las Choapas		Mex. SE.	27	96	5	3	.625	93	62	46	80	66	4.31
1968—Mexico City Reds		Mexican	31	162	10	10	.500	154	73	47	99	64	2.61
1969—Minatitlan		Mex. SE.	16	83	7	4	.636	56	29	18	64	40	1.95
1969—Mexico City Reds		Mexican	21	105	10	4	.714	131	53	45	76	49	3.86
1970—Mexico City Reds		Mexican	37	172	16	11	.593	153	64	57	127	100	2.98
1971—Mexico City Reds†		Mexican	21	83	4	7	.364	86	49	45	36	59	4.88
1972—Mexico City Reds		Mexican	46	121	5	7	.417	109	57	49	89	58	3.64
1973—Mexico City Reds		Mexican	53	127	12	10	.545	115	58	47	117	82	3.33
1974—Mexico City Reds‡		Mexican	*60	113	7	7	.500	94	50	32	134	70	2.55
1974—Kansas City§		American	8	16	0	0	.000	21	12	10	5	10	5.63
1975—Mexico City Reds		Mexican	*71	114	10	8	.556	97	46	36	114	68	2.84
1976—Mexico City Reds		Mexican	*59	98	4	11	.267	111	61	49	65	49	4.50
1977—Mexico City Reds x		Mexican	*73	157	19	8	.704	132	39	35	165	49	2.01
1978—Springfield		Am. Assoc.	34	76	6	6	.500	72	37	30	81	39	3.55
1978—St. Louis y		National	25	65	4	2	.667	52	35	31	46	32	4.29
1979—Detroit		American	61	127	10	5	.667	95	37	34	106	51	2.41
1980—Detroit		American	67	124	13	6	.684	125	56	52	97	45	3.77
1981—Detroit		American	29	82	5	2	.714	70	34	33	53	31	3.62
1982—Detroit z		American	19	41	3	1	.750	41	27	24	26	19	5.27
1982—Evansville		Am. Assoc.	12	30⅔	4	0	1.000	23	6	6	30	10	1.76
1983—Detroit		American	57	115⅓	9	8	.529	87	36	36	90	49	2.81
American League Totals			241	505⅓	40	22	.645	439	202	189	377	205	3.37
National League Totals			25	65	4	2	.667	52	35	31	46	32	4.29
Major League Totals			266	570⅓	44	24	.647	491	237	220	423	237	3.47

Signed as free agent by Las Choapas, March 28, 1967.
†On disabled list, April 30 to May 27 and June 28 to July 12, 1971.
‡Sold to Kansas City Royals, August 29, 1974.
§Sold to Mexico City Reds, March 27, 1975.
xSold to St. Louis Cardinals, October 26, 1977.
yTraded with Outfielder Jerry Morales to Detroit Tigers for Pitchers Bob Sykes and Jack Murphy, December 4, 1978.
zOn disabled list, March 23 to May 13, 1982; included rehabilitation disability assignment to Evansville, April 19 to May 11, 1982.

ALL-STAR GAME RECORD

Member of American League All-Star Team in 1983; did not play.

—DID YOU KNOW—

That the Orioles' Mike Boddicker, who did not hit a batter during his 179 innings pitched during the 1983 regular season, hit two batters in his only appearance during the American League Championship Series?

SCOTT GREGORY LOUCKS

Born November 11, 1956, at Anchorage, Alaska.
Height, 6.00. Weight, 178.
Throws and bats righthanded.
Attended Southeastern Oklahoma State University, Durant, Okla.

Led Pacific Coast League in stolen bases with 71 in 1983.
Led Florida State League in bases on balls received with 77 in 1979.

Year Club	League	Pos.	G.	AB.	R.	H.	2B.	3B.	HR.	RBI.	B.A.	PO.	A.	E.	F.A.
1977—Sara. Astros	Gulf C.	OF	46	142	41	38	2	7	1	20	.268	46	5	●4	.927
1978—Daytona Beach	Fla. St.	OF	43	128	21	26	3	2	0	9	.203	71	4	7	.915
1978—Columbus	South.	OF	76	232	38	45	4	4	3	17	.194	131	1	5	.964
1979—Daytona Beach	Fla. St.	OF	108	338	80	83	6	3	2	18	.246	164	13	3	.983
1979—Columbus	South.	OF	9	8	3	1	0	0	0	1	.125	6	0	1	.857
1980—Columbus	South.	OF	137	515	90	125	13	6	10	45	.243	264	12	6	.979
1980—Houston	Nat.	OF	8	3	4	1	0	0	0	0	.333	1	0	0	1.000
1981—Tucson†	P. C.	OF-3B	88	339	60	92	11	5	3	22	.271	158	7	5	.971
1981—Houston	Nat.	OF	10	7	2	4	0	0	0	0	.571	5	0	0	1.000
1982—Tucson	P. C.	OF	74	310	48	82	12	5	1	21	.265	173	6	6	.968
1982—Houston	Nat.	OF	44	49	6	11	2	0	0	3	.224	41	3	1	.978
1983—Tucson	P. C.	OF	138	541	107	155	33	●13	8	58	.287	338	12	9	.975
1983—Houston	Nat.	OF	7	14	2	3	0	0	0	0	.214	12	1	0	1.000
Major League Totals			69	73	14	19	2	0	0	3	.260	59	4	1	.984

Selected by Houston Astros' organization in 5th round of free-agent draft, June 7, 1977.
†On disabled list, April 24 to May 20, 1981.

VANCE ODELL LOVELACE

Born August 9, 1963, at Tampa, Fla.
Height, 6.05. Weight, 190.
Throws and bats lefthanded.

Led Florida State League in hit batsmen with 25, wild pitches with 25 and tied for lead in balks with 6 in 1983.

Year Club	League	G.	IP.	W.	L.	Pct.	H.	R.	ER.	SO.	BB.	ERA.
1981—Sarasota Cubs	Gulf Coast	7	30	0	5	.000	27	22	11	31	26	3.30
1982—Quad Cities†‡	Midwest	21	94	4	6	.400	62	67	52	107	94	4.98
1983—Vero Beach	Florida State	24	115	8	10	.444	104	80	61	95	93	4.77

Selected by Chicago Cubs' organization in 1st round (16th player selected) of free-agent draft, June 8, 1981.
†On disabled list, April 20 to May 6, 1982.
‡Traded with Outfielder Dan Cataline to Los Angeles Dodgers' organization for Third Baseman Ron Cey, January 20, 1983.

JOHN PAUL LOVIGLIO

Name pronounced Loh-VIG-lee-oh.

(Jay)

Born May 30, 1956, at Freeport, N.Y.
Height, 5.09. Weight, 160.
Throws and bats righthanded.
Attended Suffolk County Community College, Selden, N. Y.

Led Eastern League in stolen bases with 55 in 1979.

Year Club	League	Pos.	G.	AB.	R.	H.	2B.	3B.	HR.	RBI.	B.A.	PO.	A.	E.	F.A.
1977—Auburn	NYP	2B	29	84	9	18	1	0	2	11	.214	71	71	9	.940
1977—Spartanburg	W. Car.	2B	28	101	12	19	2	1	0	3	.188	65	86	6	.962
1978—Peninsula	Carol.	2B	130	★495	89	133	14	4	4	46	.269	270	325	20	.967
1979—Reading	East.	2B	131	504	92	148	21	4	4	52	.294	211	★451	15	★.978
1980—Oklahoma City	A. A.	2B	123	498	98	138	13	6	6	39	.277	262	413	8	.988
1980—Philadelphia†	Nat.	2B	16	5	7	0	0	0	0	0	.000	3	2	0	1.000
1981—Edmonton‡	P. C.	2B-SS	113	461	71	138	23	5	11	57	.299	231	340	15	.974
1981—Chicago	Amer.	3B-2B	14	15	5	4	0	0	0	2	.267	9	10	3	.864
1982—Edmonton	P. C.	2B	111	451	72	116	16	3	3	38	.257	244	291	11	★.980
1982—Chicago§	Amer.	2B	15	31	5	6	0	0	0	2	.194	24	30	2	.964
1983—Iowa x	A. A.	2B	24	66	6	15	2	1	0	8	.227	24	51	1	.987
1983—Midland	Texas	2B-3B	35	144	22	45	2	2	2	13	.313	38	118	7	.957
1983—Chicago y	Nat.	PH	1	1	0	0	0	0	0	0	.000	0	0	0	.000
National League Totals			17	6	7	0	0	0	0	0	.000	3	2	0	1.000
American League Totals			29	46	10	10	0	0	0	4	.217	33	40	5	.936
Major League Totals			46	52	17	10	0	0	0	4	.192	36	42	5	.940

Signed as free agent by Philadelphia Phillies' organization, May 16, 1977.
†Traded to Chicago White Sox for Pitcher Mike Proly, April 1, 1981.
‡On disabled list, May 29 to June 9, 1981.
§Sold to Chicago Cubs, November 29, 1982.
xOn disabled list, April 15 to April 25, 1983.
yGranted free agency, October 20, 1983.

JOHN LEE LOWENSTEIN

Name pronounced LOW-in-stine.

Born January 27, 1947, at Wolf Point, Mont.
Height, 6.01. Weight, 180.
Throws right and bats lefthanded.
Received bachelor of arts degree in anthropology from
University of California, Riverside, Calif.

Year	Club	League	Pos.	G.	AB.	R.	H.	2B.	3B.	HR.	RBI.	B.A.	PO.	A.	E.	F.A.
1968—Waterbury	East.		PH	3	2	0	0	0	0	0	0	.000	0	0	0	.000
1968—Reno	Calif.		2B-3B	48	164	22	53	8	2	7	38	.323	71	106	8	.957
1969—Reno†	Calif.		1B-OF	26	67	7	19	4	2	1	11	.284	93	5	2	.980
1970—Wichita	A. A.		3-S-O-2	108	369	69	109	15	6	18	52	.295	130	218	13	.964
1970—Cleveland	Amer.		2-3-O-S	17	43	5	11	3	1	1	6	.256	15	37	2	.963
1971—Wichita	A. A.		OF-3B	37	125	27	40	8	0	8	24	.320	55	4	2	.967
1971—Cleveland	Amer.		2B-OF-SS	58	140	15	26	5	0	4	9	.186	103	66	4	.977
1972—Cleveland	Amer.		OF-1B	68	151	16	32	8	1	6	21	.212	82	7	0	1.000
1973—Cleveland	Amer.		O-2-3-1	98	305	42	89	16	1	6	40	.292	124	85	7	.968
1974—Cleveland	Amer.		O-3-1-2	140	508	65	123	14	2	8	48	.242	314	84	6	.985
1975—Cleveland	Amer.		OF-3B-2B	91	265	37	64	5	1	12	33	.242	61	16	2	.975
1976—Cleveland‡§	Amer.		OF-1B	93	229	33	47	8	2	2	14	.205	178	10	7	.964
1977—Cleveland x	Amer.		OF-1B	81	149	24	36	6	1	4	12	.242	63	1	0	1.000
1978—Texas y	Amer.		3B-OF	77	176	28	39	8	3	5	21	.222	34	42	6	.927
1979—Baltimore z	Amer.		OF-1B-3B	97	197	33	50	8	2	11	34	.254	124	7	1	.992
1980—Baltimore a	Amer.		OF	104	196	38	61	8	0	4	27	.311	128	3	1	.992
1981—Baltimore	Amer.		OF	83	189	19	47	7	0	6	20	.249	100	3	1	.990
1982—Baltimore b	Amer.		OF	122	322	69	103	15	2	24	66	.320	202	2	0	●1.000
1983—Baltimore	Amer.		OF-2B	122	311	52	87	13	2	15	60	.280	155	8	3	.982
Major League Totals				1251	3181	476	815	124	18	108	411	.256	1683	371	40	.981

Selected by Cleveland Indians' organization in 18th round of free-agent draft, June 7, 1968.
†On military list, January 31 to August 2, 1969.
‡Traded with Catcher Rick Cerone to Toronto Blue Jays for Outfielder Rico Carty, December 6, 1976.
§Traded to Cleveland Indians for Infielder Hector Torres, March 29, 1977.
xTraded with Pitcher Tom Buskey to Texas Rangers for Outfielder-Designated Hitter Willie Horton and Pitcher David Clyde, February 28, 1978.
ySold on waivers to Baltimore Orioles, November 27, 1978.
zOn supplemental disabled list, August 9 to August 24, 1979.
aOn disabled list, May 19 to June 11, 1980.
bGranted free agency, November 10, 1982; re-signed by Orioles, February 24, 1983.

CHAMPIONSHIP SERIES RECORD

Tied Championship Series records for hitting home run in first Series at-bat, October 3, 1979; most home runs by pinch-hitter, game (1), October 3, 1979.

Year	Club	League	Pos.	G.	AB.	R.	H.	2B.	3B.	HR.	RBI.	B.A.	PO.	A.	E.	F.A.
1979—Baltimore	Amer.		PH-OF	4	6	2	1	0	0	1	3	.167	6	0	0	1.000
1983—Baltimore	Amer.		OF-PH	3	6	0	1	1	0	0	2	.167	4	0	0	1.000
Championship Series Totals				7	12	2	2	1	0	1	5	.167	10	0	0	1.000

WORLD SERIES RECORD

Year	Club	League	Pos.	G.	AB.	R.	H.	2B.	3B.	HR.	RBI.	B.A.	PO.	A.	E.	F.A.
1979—Baltimore	Amer.		OF-PH	6	13	2	3	1	0	0	3	.231	6	0	1	.857
1983—Baltimore	Amer.		OF	4	13	2	5	1	0	1	1	.385	4	0	1	.800
World Series Totals				10	26	4	8	2	0	1	4	.308	10	0	2	.833

DWIGHT LOWRY

Born October 23, 1957, in Robeson County, N. C.
Height, 6.03. Weight, 210.
Throws right and bats lefthanded.
Attended University of North Carolina, Chapel Hill, N. C.

Led Florida State League catchers in double plays with 8 in 1982.

Year	Club	League	Pos.	G.	AB.	R.	H.	2B.	3B.	HR.	RBI.	B.A.	PO.	A.	E.	F.A.
1980—Lakeland	Fla. St.		C	45	142	18	28	5	0	0	16	.197	171	25	4	.980
1981—Birmingham	South.		C	19	52	3	8	2	0	0	4	.154	108	11	3	.975
1981—Macon	S. Atl.		C	67	231	30	58	6	0	2	32	.251	225	22	5	.980
1982—Lakeland	Fla. St.		C	93	278	33	77	11	2	7	28	.277	350	53	3	*.993
1983—Birmingham	South.		C-OF	90	288	42	77	9	2	9	44	.267	424	51	6	.988

Selected by Detroit Tigers' organization in 11th round of free-agent draft, June 3, 1980.

STEVEN GEORGE LUBRATICH

Name pronounced Lu-BRAT-ich.

(Steve)

Born May 1, 1955, at Oakland, Calif.
Height, 6.00. Weight, 170.
Throws and bats righthanded.
Attended Chabot College, Hayward, Calif., and University of California
at Riverside, Riverside, Calif.

Led Pacific Coast League second basemen in putouts with 325 in 1981.

Tied for Pacific Coast League lead in being hit by pitch with 10 in 1982.

Year Club	League	Pos.	G.	AB.	R.	H.	2B.	3B.	HR.	RBI.	B.A.	PO.	A.	E.	F.A.
1977—Idaho Falls	Pion.	SS-2B	18	75	20	29	4	2	1	16	.387	32	58	6	.938
1977—Salinas	Calif.	SS	52	184	28	44	7	1	0	16	.239	79	138	9	.960
1978—Salinas	Calif.	SS-3B	78	251	25	63	6	1	1	28	.251	96	191	11	.963
1979—El Paso	Texas	2B-3B	101	388	66	125	20	3	8	69	.322	143	199	8	.977
1979—Salt Lake City	P. C	3B	4	12	3	4	2	0	0	2	.333	0	10	0	1.000
1980—Salt Lake City	P. C.	3B-SS-2B	139	542	83	146	32	4	4	60	.269	140	300	17	.963
1981—Salt Lake City	P. C.	*2B-3B	132	*551	100	164	30	0	13	68	.298	327	*407	12	*.984
1981—California	Amer.	3B	7	21	2	3	1	0	0	1	.143	2	17	0	1.000
1982—Spokane†	P. C.	2B-3B	132	535	92	*181	*43	6	9	88	.338	226	342	18	.969
1983—Edmonton	P. C.	3B-2B-1B	90	380	69	122	23	1	10	78	.321	106	207	4	.987
1983—California	Amer.	SS-3B-2B	57	156	12	34	9	0	0	7	.218	91	149	7	.972
Major League Totals			64	177	14	37	10	0	0	8	.209	93	166	7	.974

Signed as free agent by California Angels' organization, June 20, 1977.
†On disabled list, August 25, 1982 through remainder of season.

GARY PAUL LUCAS

Born November 8, 1954, at Riverside, Calif.
Height, 6.05. Weight, 200.
Throws and bats lefthanded.
Attended Chapman College, Orange, Calif.

Major League saves: 1980 (3), 1981 (13), 1982 (16), 1983 (17). Total—49.
Tied for National League lead in intentional bases on balls issued with 15 in 1981.

Year Club	League	G.	IP.	W.	L.	Pct.	H.	R.	ER.	SO.	BB.	ERA.
1976—Walla Walla	Northwest	14	93	7	3	.700	91	40	32	49	30	3.10
1977—Reno	California	28	176	13	7	.650	205	114	90	98	48	4.60
1978—Amarillo	Texas	25	159	8	17	.320	182	104	86	115	26	4.87
1979—Hawaii†	P. Coast	24	178	10	7	.588	151	64	55	98	58	2.78
1980—San Diego	National	46	150	5	8	.385	138	59	54	85	43	3.24
1981—San Diego	National	*57	90	7	7	.500	78	26	20	53	36	2.00
1982—San Diego	National	65	97⅓	1	10	.091	89	42	35	64	29	3.24
1983—San Diego‡	National	62	91	5	8	.385	85 ·	38	29	60	34	2.87
Major League Totals		230	428⅓	18	33	.353	390	165	138	262	142	2.90

Selected by Cincinnati Reds' organization in 1st round (21st player selected) of free-agent draft, January 10, 1973.
Selected by Cincinnati Reds' organization in secondary phase of free-agent draft, June 5, 1973.
Selected by San Diego Padres' organization in 19th round of free-agent draft, June 8, 1976.
†On disabled list, August 5 to August 30, 1979.
‡Traded to Montreal Expos for Pitcher Scott Sanderson, December 7, 1983.

GREGORY MICHAEL LUZINSKI
(Greg)

Born November 22, 1950, at Chicago, Ill.
Height, 6.01. Weight, 217.
Throws and bats righthanded.
Brother of Richard Luzinski, outfielder in Philadelphia Phillies' organization, 1974;
and William Luzinski, outfielder in Chicago White Sox' organization, 1980 and 1981.

Tied major league record for fewest double plays by outfielder, season, 150 or more games (0), 1975.
Tied modern National League record for most home runs, October (3), 1972.
Led National League in being hit by pitch with 10 in 1979 and tied for lead with 11 in 1976 and 6 in 1980.
Led National League batters in strikeouts with 140 in 1977.
Led National League in total bases with 322 in 1975.
Tied for National League lead in intentional bases on balls received with 17 in 1975.
Led Carolina League batters in strikeouts with 148 in 1969, Eastern League with 148 in 1970 and Pacific Coast League with 167 in 1971.
Led Carolina League in total bases with 255 in 1969, Eastern League with 287 in 1970 and Pacific Coast League with 319 in 1971.
Led Eastern League in being hit by pitch with 12 in 1970.
Led Eastern League first basemen in double plays with 119 in 1970 and Pacific Coast League first basemen with 129 in 1971.
Led Northern League first basemen in fielding percentage with .984 in 1968.
Named designated hitter on THE SPORTING NEWS American League All-Star Team, 1983.
Named outfielder on THE SPORTING NEWS National League All-Star Team, 1975 and 1977.
Named Eastern League Player of the Year, 1970.

Year Club	League	Pos.	G.	AB.	R.	H.	2B.	3B.	HR.	RBI.	B.A.	PO.	A.	E.	F.A.
1968—Huron	North.	1B-3B	57	212	22	55	5	0	*13	●43	.250	417	26	13	.971
1969—Raleigh-Durham	Carol.	1B	129	464	75	134	22	3	*31	*92	.289	1067	67	*21	.985
1970—Reading	East.	1B	*141	471	*94	153	25	5	33	*120	*.325	1122	65	*21	.983
1970—Philadelphia	Nat.	1B	8	12	0	2	0	0	0	0	.167	20	3	0	1.000
1971—Eugene	P. C.	1B	142	548	104	171	30	5	36	114	.312	1071	76	●19	.984
1971—Philadelphia	Nat.	1B	28	100	13	30	8	0	3	15	.300	247	34	1	.996
1972—Philadelphia	Nat.	OF-1B	150	563	66	158	33	5	18	68	.281	257	9	12	.957
1973—Philadelphia	Nat.	OF	161	610	76	174	26	4	29	97	.285	262	7	2	*.993
1974—Philadelphia†	Nat.	OF	85	302	29	82	14	1	7	48	.272	146	10	3	.981
1975—Philadelphia	Nat.	OF	161	596	85	179	35	3	34	*120	.300	248	10	9	.966
1976—Philadelphia	Nat.	OF	149	533	74	162	28	1	21	95	.304	204	8	8	.964
1977—Philadelphia	Nat.	OF	149	554	99	171	35	3	39	130	.309	205	11	8	.964
1978—Philadelphia	Nat.	OF	155	540	85	143	32	2	35	101	.265	232	7	4	.984

Year Club League	Pos.	G.	AB.	R.	H.	2B.	3B.	HR.	RBI.	B.A.	PO.	A.	E.	F.A.
1979—Philadelphia .... Nat.	OF	137	452	47	114	23	1	18	81	.252	156	3	9	.946
1980—Philadelphia‡§ ..... Nat.	OF	106	368	44	84	19	1	19	56	.228	137	2	1	.993
1981—Chicago .... Amer.	DH	104	378	55	100	15	1	21	62	.265	0	0	0	.000
1982—Chicago .... Amer.	DH	159	583	87	170	37	1	18	102	.292	0	0	0	.000
1983—Chicago .... Amer.	1B	144	502	73	128	26	1	32	95	.255	6	1	0	1.000
National League Totals...............		1289	4630	618	1299	253	21	223	811	.281	2114	104	57	.975
American League Totals..............		407	1463	215	398	78	3	71	259	.272	6	1	0	1.000
Major League Totals....................		1696	6093	833	1697	331	24	294	1070	.279	2120	105	57	.975

Selected by Philadelphia Phillies' organization in 1st round (11th player selected) of free-agent draft, June 7, 1968.
†On disabled list, June 6 to August 26, 1974.
‡On supplemental disabled list, July 8 to August 24, 1980.
§Sold to Chicago White Sox, March 30, 1981.

CHAMPIONSHIP SERIES RECORD

Tied Championship Series record for most consecutive games, one or more runs batted in, total Series (4).
Tied National League Championship Series record for most long hits, total Series (11).
Tied American League Championship Series record for most strikeouts, four-game Series (5), 1983.

Year Club League	Pos.	G.	AB.	R.	H.	2B.	3B.	HR.	RBI.	B.A.	PO.	A.	E.	F.A.
1976—Philadelphia .... Nat.	OF	3	11	2	3	2	0	1	3	.273	6	0	0	1.000
1977—Philadelphia .... Nat.	OF	4	14	2	4	1	0	1	2	.286	4	1	0	1.000
1978—Philadelphia .... Nat.	OF	4	16	3	6	0	1	2	3	.375	5	1	0	1.000
1980—Philadelphia .... Nat.	OF-PH	5	17	3	5	2	0	1	4	.294	5	0	1	.833
1983—Chicago .... Amer.	DH	4	15	0	2	1	0	0	0	.133	0	0	0	.000
Championship Series Totals		20	73	10	20	6	1	5	12	.274	20	2	1	.957

WORLD SERIES RECORD

Year Club League	Pos.	G.	AB.	R.	H.	2B.	3B.	HR.	RBI.	B.A.	PO.	A.	E.	F.A.
1980—Philadelphia .... Nat.	DH-OF	3	9	0	0	0	0	0	0	.000	1	0	0	1.000

ALL-STAR GAME RECORD

Year League	Pos.	AB.	R.	H.	2B.	3B.	HR.	RBI.	B.A.	PO.	A.	E.	F.A.
1975—National	PH	1	0	0	0	0	0	0	.000	0	0	0	.000
1976—National	OF	3	0	0	0	0	0	0	.000	0	0	0	.000
1977—National	OF	2	1	1	0	0	1	2	.500	0	0	0	.000
1978—National	OF	2	0	1	0	0	0	1	.500	0	0	0	.000
All-Star Game Totals...........		8	1	2	0	0	1	3	.250	0	0	0	.000

EDWARD FRANCIS LYNCH
(Ed)

Born February 25, 1956, at Brooklyn, N.Y.
Height, 6.05. Weight, 210.
Throws and bats righthanded.
Received bachelor of science degree in finance from University of South Carolina, Columbia, S.C.,
and master's degree in business administration from University of Miami, Coral Gables, Fla.

Year Club	League	G.	IP.	W.	L.	Pct.	H.	R.	ER.	SO.	BB.	ERA.
1977—Sarasota Rangers........................	Gulf Coast	13	56	1	4	.200	61	31	23	36	15	3.70
1978—Asheville..............................	W. Carol.	18	123	7	9	.438	122	55	45	79	33	3.29
1978—Tulsa.................................	Texas	7	54	4	3	.571	61	25	16	44	14	2.67
1979—Tucson†..............................	P. Coast	27	156	10	11	.476	184	96	84	65	37	4.85
1980—Tidewater.............................	Int'national	24	163	13	6	.684	151	69	57	91	42	3.15
1980—New York.............................	National	5	19	1	1	.500	24	12	11	9	5	5.21
1981—Tidewater.............................	Int'national	15	99	7	6	.538	93	46	43	54	29	3.91
1981—New York.............................	National	17	80	4	5	.444	79	32	26	27	21	2.93
1982—New York.............................	National	43	139⅓	4	8	.333	145	57	55	51	40	3.55
1983—New York.............................	National	30	174⅔	10	10	.500	208	94	83	44	41	4.28
Major League Totals.............................		95	413	19	24	.442	456	195	175	131	107	3.81

Selected by Texas Rangers' organization in 22nd round of free-agent draft, June 7, 1977.
†Traded to New York Mets' organization, September 18, 1979, as partial completion of deal in which Texas Rangers acquired First Baseman Willie Montanez for two players to be named later, August 12, 1979; New York acquired First Baseman Mike Jorgensen to complete deal, October 23, 1979.

FREDRIC MICHAEL LYNN
(Fred)

Born February 3, 1952, at Chicago, Ill.
Height, 6.01. Weight, 190.
Throws and bats lefthanded.
Attended University of Southern California, Los Angeles, Calif.

Established American League record for most doubles, rookie season (47), 1975.
Tied American League record for most total bases, game (16), June 18, 1975.
Hit three home runs in a game, June 18, 1975.
Hit for the cycle, May 13, 1980.
Led American League in slugging percentage with .566 in 1975 and .637 in 1979.
Named American League Player of the Year by THE SPORTING NEWS, 1975.
Named American League Most Valuable Player by Baseball Writers' Association of America, 1975.
Named American League Rookie of the Year by Baseball Writers' Association of America, 1975.
Named American League Rookie Player of the Year by THE SPORTING NEWS, 1975.

Year Club	League	Pos.	G.	AB.	R.	H.	2B.	3B.	HR.	RBI.	B.A.	PO.	A.	E.	F.A.
1973—Bristol	East.	OF	53	162	26	42	9	4	6	36	.259	79	3	5	.943
1974—Pawtucket	Int.	OF	124	415	65	117	19	2	21	68	.282	247	12	7	.974
1974—Boston	Amer.	OF	15	43	5	18	2	2	2	10	.419	18	2	0	1.000
1975—Boston	Amer.	OF	145	528	*103	175	*47	7	21	105	.331	404	11	7	.983
1976—Boston	Amer.	OF	132	507	76	159	32	8	10	65	.314	367	13	6	.984
1977—Boston†	Amer.	OF	129	497	81	129	29	5	18	76	.260	333	7	2	.994
1978—Boston	Amer.	OF	150	541	75	161	33	3	22	82	.298	408	11	7	.984
1979—Boston	Amer.	OF	147	531	116	177	42	1	39	122	*.333	381	10	5	.987
1980—Boston‡	Amer.	OF	110	415	67	125	32	3	12	61	.301	302	11	2	.994
1981—California	Amer.	OF	76	256	28	56	8	1	5	31	.219	176	4	4	.978
1982—California	Amer.	OF	138	472	89	141	38	1	21	86	.299	317	6	3	.991
1983—California	Amer.	OF	117	437	56	119	20	3	22	74	.272	274	8	2	.993
Major League Totals			1159	4227	696	1260	283	34	172	712	.298	2980	83	38	.988

Selected by New York Yankees' organization in 3rd round of free-agent draft, June 4, 1970.
Selected by Boston Red Sox' organization in 2nd round of free-agent draft, June 5, 1973.
†On disabled list, March 24 to May 6, 1977.
‡Traded with Pitcher Steve Renko to California Angels for Pitchers Frank Tanana and Jim Dorsey and Outfielder Joe Rudi, January 23, 1981.

CHAMPIONSHIP SERIES RECORD

Established Championship Series record for highest batting average, five-game Series (.611), 1982.
Tied Championship Series records for most hits, five-game Series (11), 1982; most one-base hits, five-game Series (8), 1982.
Established American League Championship Series record for most hits, two consecutive Series (15), 1975 and 1982.

Year Club	League	Pos.	G.	AB.	R.	H.	2B.	3B.	HR.	RBI.	B.A.	PO.	A.	E.	F.A.
1975—Boston	Amer.	OF	3	11	1	4	1	0	0	3	.364	12	1	1	.929
1982—California	Amer.	OF	5	18	5	11	2	0	1	5	.611	16	0	1	.941
Championship Series Totals			8	29	6	15	3	0	1	8	.517	28	1	2	.935

WORLD SERIES RECORD

Tied World Series record for highest fielding average by outfielder, seven-game Series (1.000 with 24 chances), 1975.

Year Club	League	Pos.	G.	AB.	R.	H.	2B.	3B.	HR.	RBI.	B.A.	PO.	A.	E.	F.A.
1975—Boston	Amer.	OF	7	25	3	7	1	0	1	5	.280	23	1	0	1.000

ALL-STAR GAME RECORD

Hit only All-Star Game home run with bases loaded, July 6, 1983.
Established All-Star Game record for most runs batted in, inning (4), July 6, 1983.

Year League	Pos.	AB.	R.	H.	2B.	3B.	HR.	RBI.	B.A.	PO.	A.	E.	F.A.
1975—American	PH-OF	2	0	0	0	0	0	0	.000	1	0	0	1.000
1976—American	OF	3	1	1	0	0	1	1	.333	0	0	0	1.000
1977—American	OF	1	1	0	0	0	0	0	.000	2	0	0	1.000
1978—American	OF	4	0	1	0	0	0	0	.250	3	0	0	1.000
1979—American	OF	1	1	1	0	0	1	2	1.000	0	0	0	.000
1980—American	PH	3	1	1	0	0	1	2	.333	2	0	0	1.000
1981—American	PH	1	0	1	0	0	0	1	1.000	0	0	0	.000
1982—American	OF	2	0	0	0	0	0	0	.000	0	0	0	.000
1983—American	OF	3	1	1	0	0	1	4	.333	1	0	0	1.000
All-Star Game Totals		20	5	6	0	0	4	10	.300	9	0	0	1.000

STEPHEN JOHN LYONS
(Steve)

Born June 3, 1960, at Tacoma, Wash.
Height, 6.03. Weight, 190.
Throws right and bats lefthanded.
Attended Oregon State University, Corvallis, Ore.

Year Club	League	Pos.	G.	AB.	R.	H.	2B.	3B.	HR.	RBI.	B.A.	PO.	A.	E.	F.A.
1981—Winston-Salem	Carol.	OF-SS	64	252	43	61	9	3	6	40	.242	137	23	8	.952
1982—Bristol	East.	OF-SS	135	460	86	112	23	3	13	58	.243	275	11	9	.969
1983—New Britain	East.	3-O-S-P	132	456	83	112	24	7	7	62	.246	145	207	17	.954

Selected by Boston Red Sox' organization in 1st round (19th player selected) of free-agent draft, June 8, 1981.

PITCHING RECORD

Year Club	League	G.	IP.	W.	L.	Pct.	H.	R.	ER.	SO.	BB.	ERA.
1983—New Britain	Eastern	3	3⅔	1	0	1.000	3	1	1	2	1	2.45

—DID YOU KNOW—

That Bert Campaneris has played in a record 11 no-hitters in the majors? The latest was on July 4, 1983, when he was the Yanks' third baseman in Dave Righetti's no-hit game against the Boston Red Sox. Campaneris has been on the winning side five times.

WILLIAM ALLEN LYONS
(Bill)

Born April 26, 1958, at Alton, Ill.
Height, 6.01. Weight, 175.
Throws and bats righthanded.
Received bachelor of science degree in marketing from
Southern Illinois University, Carbondale, Ill. in 1980.
Led New York-Pennsylvania League in game-winning RBIs with 12 in 1981.

Year Club	League	Pos.	G.	AB.	R.	H.	2B.	3B.	HR.	RBI.	B.A.	PO.	A.	E.	F.A.
1980—Butte†	Pion.	SS-3B	36	92	22	29	6	5	0	15	.315	38	99	9	.938
1981—Erie	NYP	2B-3B-SS	73	269	63	88	19	2	6	*65	.327	101	213	12	.963
1982—Springfield	Midw.	3B-2B-SS	55	205	56	68	5	2	9	31	.332	78	129	8	.963
1982—Louisville	A. A.	3B	29	82	8	22	4	1	2	9	.268	15	33	0	1.000
1982—Arkansas	Texas	SS-3B	26	79	18	24	3	1	2	10	.304	29	45	7	.914
1983—Louisville	A. A.	3-S-2-O-1	77	266	60	72	14	1	5	25	.271	113	139	10	.962
1983—St. Louis	Nat.	2B-3B-SS	42	60	3	10	1	1	0	3	.167	30	44	1	.987
Major League Totals			42	60	3	10	1	1	0	3	.167	30	44	1	.987

Signed as free-agent by Milwaukee Brewers' organization, July 24, 1980.
†Released, April 4, 1981; signed by Johnson City (St. Louis Cardinals' organization), April 29, 1981.

RICHARD EUGENE LYSANDER
(Rick)

Born February 21, 1953, at Huntington Park, Calif.
Height, 6.02. Weight, 190.
Throws and bats righthanded.
Attended Citrus Junior College, Azusa, Calif., San Jose State University, San Jose, Calif.,
and attending California State University at Los Angeles, Los Angeles, Calif.
Led Pacific Coast League in intentional bases on balls issued with 13 in 1980.

Year Club	League	G.	IP.	W.	L.	Pct.	H.	R.	ER.	SO.	BB.	ERA.
1974—Lewiston	Northwest	11	58	5	3	.625	54	28	17	25	18	2.64
1975—Modesto	California	21	131	8	8	.500	152	92	70	82	38	4.81
1975—Birmingham	Southern	8	57	5	2	.714	58	24	21	25	20	3.32
1976—Tucson	P. Coast	17	28	2	2	.500	41	21	20	21	15	6.43
1976—Chattanooga	Southern	18	118	7	6	.538	108	47	46	31	34	3.20
1977—Chattanooga	Southern	14	84	4	5	.444	104	55	46	41	31	4.93
1977—San Jose	P. Coast	29	61	3	3	.500	68	38	29	38	26	4.28
1978—Vancouver	P. Coast	14	29	0	0	.000	42	26	26	12	12	8.07
1978—Jersey City	Eastern	17	127	9	6	.600	128	58	36	58	40	2.55
1979—Ogden	P. Coast	50	84	10	3	.769	94	54	41	60	46	4.39
1980—Ogden	P. Coast	35	81	4	5	.444	103	55	46	46	43	5.11
1980—Oakland	American	5	14	0	0	.000	24	13	12	5	4	7.71
1981—Tacoma†	P. Coast	25	161	9	3	.750	159	80	71	91	53	3.97
1982—Tucson‡	P. Coast	42	161⅓	10	7	.588	203	95	73	99	49	4.05
1983—Minnesota	American	61	125	5	12	.294	132	63	47	58	43	3.38
Major League Totals		66	139	5	12	.294	156	76	59	63	47	3.82

Selected by Oakland A's organization in 19th round of free-agent draft, June 5, 1974.
†Traded to Houston Astros, September 17, 1981, completing deal in which Houston traded Infielder Jimmy Sexton to Oakland A's for a player to be named later, February 12, 1981.
‡Traded to Minnesota Twins' organization for Pitcher Bob Veselic, January 12, 1983.

MICHAEL ANTHONY MADDEN
(Mike)

Born January 13, 1958, at Denver, Colo.
Height, 6.01. Weight, 185.
Throws and bats lefthanded.
Attended University of Northern Colorado, Greeley, Colo.

Year Club	League	G.	IP.	W.	L.	Pct.	H.	R.	ER.	SO.	BB.	ERA.
1979—Burlington	Midwest	5	32	2	1	.667	21	11	7	23	15	1.97
1980—Stockton	California	29	134	12	4	.750	88	46	29	92	63	*1.95
1981—El Paso†	Texas	22	125	6	8	.429	154	94	79	140	40	5.69
1982—Vancouver‡	P. Coast	18	80⅔	3	8	.273	92	69	63	41	60	7.03
1983—Houston§	National	28	94⅔	9	5	.643	76	37	33	44	45	3.14
1983—Tucson	P. Coast	4	22	1	1	.500	25	9	9	15	8	3.68
Major League Totals		28	94⅔	9	5	.643	76	37	33	44	45	3.14

Selected by Pittsburgh Pirates' organization in 3rd round of free-agent draft, June 8, 1976.
Signed as free agent by Milwaukee Brewers' organization, July 18, 1979.
†On disabled list, July 9 to August 5, 1981.
‡Traded with Outfielder Kevin Bass and Pitcher Frank DiPino to Houston Astros, September 3, 1982, completing deal in which Houston traded Pitcher Don Sutton to Milwaukee Brewers for three players to be named later, August 30, 1982.
§On disabled list, June 1 to June 22, 1983.

GARRY LEE MADDOX

Born September 1, 1949, at Cincinnati, O.
Height, 6.03. Weight, 185.
Throws and bats righthanded.
Attended Harbor College, Wilmington, Calif.

Major League stolen bases: 1972 (13), 1973 (24), 1974 (21), 1975 (25), 1976 (29), 1977 (22), 1978 (33), 1979 (26), 1980 (25), 1981 (9), 1982 (7), 1983 (7). Total—241.
Led National League in sacrifice flies with 8 in 1981.
Led National League outfielders in total chances with 456 in 1976 and 459 in 1978.
Tied for National League lead in double plays by outfielders with 4 in 1981.
Led Pioneer League batters in strikeouts with 68 in 1968.
Led Pioneer League outfielders in double plays with 2 in 1968.
Named outfielder on THE SPORTING NEWS National League All-Star fielding team, 1975 through 1982.

Year Club	League	Pos.	G.	AB.	R.	H.	2B.	3B.	HR.	RBI.	B.A.	PO.	A.	E.	F.A.
1968—Salt Lake City	Pion.	OF	58	206	34	52	11	2	5	29	.252	98	6	★10	.912
1968—Fresno	Calif.	OF	5	19	2	6	0	0	0	5	.316	7	0	0	1.000
1969-70—†						(In Military Service)									
1971—Fresno	Calif.	OF	120	475	105	142	25	5	30	106	.299	215	13	0	.962
1972—Phoenix	P. C.	OF	11	48	16	21	3	2	9	22	.438	22	1	2	.920
1972—San Francisco	Nat.	OF	125	458	62	122	26	7	12	58	.266	279	7	6	.979
1973—San Francisco	Nat.	OF	144	587	81	187	30	10	11	76	.319	370	4	●12	.969
1974—San Francisco	Nat.	OF	135	538	74	153	31	3	8	50	.284	345	3	5	.986
1975—S.F.‡-Phil.§	Nat.	OF	116	426	54	116	26	8	5	50	.272	325	13	5	.985
1976—Philadelphia	Nat.	OF	146	531	75	175	37	6	6	68	.330	★441	10	5	.989
1977—Philadelphia x	Nat.	OF	139	571	85	167	27	10	14	74	.292	383	7	9	.977
1978—Philadelphia	Nat.	OF	155	598	62	172	34	3	11	68	.288	★444	7	8	.983
1979—Philadelphia	Nat.	OF	148	548	70	154	28	6	13	61	.281	433	13	2	.996
1980—Philadelphia	Nat.	OF	143	549	59	142	31	3	11	73	.259	405	7	10	.976
1981—Philadelphia	Nat.	OF	94	323	37	85	7	1	5	40	.263	249	8	6	.977
1982—Philadelphia y	Nat.	OF	119	412	39	117	27	2	8	61	.284	253	8	2	★.992
1983—Philadelphia z	Nat.	OF	97	324	27	89	14	2	4	32	.275	216	1	5	.977
Major League Totals			1561	5865	725	1679	318	61	108	711	.286	4143	88	75	.983

Selected by San Francisco Giants' organization in 2nd round of free-agent draft, January 27, 1968.
†On military list, October 31, 1968 through February 21, 1971.
‡Traded to Philadelphia Phillies for First Baseman Willie Montanez, May 4, 1975.
§On disabled list, May 25 to June 30, 1975.
xOn supplemental disabled list, August 13 to August 28, 1977.
yOn supplemental disabled list, June 20 to July 5 and July 18 to August 5, 1982.
zOn supplemental disabled list, June 23 to July 8, 1983.

DIVISION SERIES RECORD

Year Club	League	Pos.	G.	AB.	R.	H.	2B.	3B.	HR.	RBI.	B.A.	PO.	A.	E.	F.A.
1981—Philadelphia	Nat.	OF	2	3	0	1	1	0	0	0	.333	3	0	0	1.000

CHAMPIONSHIP SERIES RECORD

Tied Championship Series records for most consecutive games, one or more runs batted in, total Series (4); most at bats, four-game Series (19), 1978.

Year Club	League	Pos.	G.	AB.	R.	H.	2B.	3B.	HR.	RBI.	B.A.	PO.	A.	E.	F.A.
1976—Philadelphia	Nat.	OF	3	13	2	3	1	0	0	1	.231	9	0	0	1.000
1977—Philadelphia	Nat.	OF	2	7	1	3	0	0	0	2	.429	6	0	0	1.000
1978—Philadelphia	Nat.	OF	4	19	1	5	0	0	0	2	.263	16	0	1	.941
1980—Philadelphia	Nat.	OF	5	20	2	6	2	0	0	3	.300	23	0	0	1.000
1983—Philadelphia	Nat.	OF	3	11	0	3	1	0	0	1	.273	8	0	1	.889
Championship Series Totals			17	70	6	20	4	0	0	9	.286	62	0	2	.969

WORLD SERIES RECORD

Year Club	League	Pos.	G.	AB.	R.	H.	2B.	3B.	HR.	RBI.	B.A.	PO.	A.	E.	F.A.
1980—Philadelphia	Nat.	OF	6	22	1	5	2	0	0	1	.227	11	1	0	1.000
1983—Philadelphia	Nat.	PH-OF	4	12	1	3	1	0	1	1	.250	7	0	0	1.000
World Series Totals			10	34	2	8	3	0	1	2	.235	18	1	0	1.000

BILL MADLOCK JR.

Born January 12, 1951, at Memphis, Tenn.
Height, 5.11. Weight, 185.
Throws and bats righthanded.
Attended Southeastern Community College, Keokuk, Ia.

Collected six hits in one game, July 26, 1975 (10 innings).
Tied for National League lead in grounding into double plays with 25 in 1977.
Tied for National League lead in being hit by pitch with 11 in 1976.
Led Pacific Coast League in total bases with 268 in 1973.
Led Eastern League third basemen in errors with 33 in 1971.
Led New York-Pennsylvania League shortstops in putouts with 107 in 1970.
Named third baseman on THE SPORTING NEWS National League All-Star Team, 1975.

Year Club	League	Pos.	G.	AB.	R.	H.	2B.	3B.	HR.	RBI.	B.A.	PO.	A.	E.	F.A.
1970—Geneva	NYP	SS-3B	66	234	44	63	5	1	6	29	.269	123	132	25	.911
1971—Pittsfield	East.	3-2-S-O	112	376	62	88	14	2	10	37	.234	100	214	34	.902

Year Club	League	Pos.	G.	AB.	R.	H.	2B.	3B.	HR.	RBI.	B.A.	PO.	A.	E.	F.A.
1972—Pittsfield	East.	2B-3B	42	131	29	43	13	3	4	26	.328	81	88	7	.960
1972—Denver	A. A.	3B-2B	26	61	7	13	3	0	1	9	.213	10	30	2	.952
1973—Spokane	P. C.	2-3-O	123	491	★119	166	22	7	22	90	.338	172	245	25	.943
1973—Texas†	Amer.	3B	21	77	16	27	5	3	1	5	.351	13	32	4	.918
1974—Chicago‡	Nat.	3B	128	453	65	142	21	5	9	54	.313	84	229	18	.946
1975—Chicago	Nat.	3B	130	514	77	182	29	7	7	64	★.354	79	250	20	.943
1976—Chicago§	Nat.	3B	142	514	68	174	36	1	15	84	★.339	107	234	14	.961
1977—San Francisco	Nat.	3B-2B	140	533	70	161	28	1	12	46	.302	101	234	18	.949
1978—San Francisco	Nat.	2B-1B	122	447	76	138	26	3	15	44	.309	234	300	14	.974
1979—S. F.x-Pitts.	Nat.	3B-2B-1B	154	560	85	167	26	5	14	85	.298	209	297	14	.973
1980—Pittsburgh y	Nat.	3B-1B	137	494	62	137	22	4	10	53	.277	159	217	7	.982
1981—Pittsburgh	Nat.	3B	82	279	35	95	23	1	6	45	★.341	50	147	9	.956
1982—Pittsburgh	Nat.	3B-1B	154	568	92	181	33	3	19	95	.319	114	267	18	.955
1983—Pittsburgh	Nat.	3B	130	473	68	153	21	0	12	68	★.323	59	193	11	.958
American League Totals			21	77	16	27	5	3	1	5	.351	13	32	4	.918
National League Totals			1319	4835	698	1530	265	30	119	638	.316	1196	2368	143	.961
Major League Totals			1340	4912	714	1557	270	33	120	643	.317	1209	2400	147	.961

Selected by St. Louis Cardinals' organization in 14th round of free-agent draft, June 5, 1969.
Selected by Washington Senators' organization in secondary phase of free-agent draft, January 17, 1970.
†Traded with Infielder-Outfielder Vic Harris to Chicago Cubs for Pitcher Ferguson Jenkins, October 25, 1973.
‡On supplemental disabled list, May 4 to June 4, 1974.
§Traded with Infielder Rob Sperring to San Francisco Giants for Outfielder Bobby Murcer, Infielder Steve Ontiveros and Pitcher Andrew Muhlstock, February 11, 1977.
xTraded with Third Baseman Lenny Randle and Pitcher Dave Roberts to Pittsburgh Pirates for Pitchers Ed Whitson, Fred Breining and Al Holland, June 28, 1979.
yOn suspended list, June 5 to June 20, 1980.

CHAMPIONSHIP SERIES RECORD

Year Club	League	Pos.	G.	AB.	R.	H.	2B.	3B.	HR.	RBI.	B.A.	PO.	A.	E.	F.A.
1979—Pittsburgh	Nat.	3B	3	12	1	3	0	0	1	2	.250	1	7	0	1.000

WORLD SERIES RECORD

u Tied World Series records for most double plays by third baseman, seven-game Series (4), 1979; fewest chances offered by third baseman, game (0), October 12, 1979.

Year Club	League	Pos.	G.	AB.	R.	H.	2B.	3B.	HR.	RBI.	B.A.	PO.	A.	E.	F.A.
1979—Pittsburgh	Nat.	3B	7	24	2	9	1	0	0	3	.375	3	10	1	.929

ALL-STAR GAME RECORD

Year League	Pos.	AB.	R.	H.	2B.	3B.	HR.	RBI.	B.A.	PO.	A.	E.	F.A.
1975—National	3B	2	0	1	0	0	0	2	.500	0	0	0	.000
1981—National	3B	1	0	0	0	0	0	0	.000	0	1	0	.000
1983—National	PH-3B	1	0	0	0	0	0	0	.000	0	0	0	.000
All-Star Game Totals		4	0	1	0	0	0	2	.250	0	1	0	1.000

RICHARD KEITH MAHLER

Name pronounced MAY-ler.

(Rick)

Born August 5, 1953, at Austin, Tex.
Height, 6.01. Weight, 195.
Throws and bats righthanded.
Attended Trinity University, San Antonio, Tex.
Brother of Mickey Mahler, pitcher with Atlanta Braves, Pittsburgh Pirates,
and California Angels, 1977 through 1982.

Year Club	League	G.	IP.	W.	L.	Pct.	H.	R.	ER.	SO.	BB.	ERA.
1975—Kingsport	Ap'lachian	26	64	2	2	.500	52	23	21	58	26	2.95
1976—Greenwood	W. Carol.	31	105	6	6	.500	96	49	34	68	49	2.91
1977—Savannah	Southern	17	86	6	2	.750	71	31	22	53	38	2.30
1977—Richmond	Int'national	14	40	0	2	.000	45	29	27	25	23	6.08
1978—Richmond	Int'national	32	126	9	5	.643	130	65	55	66	53	3.93
1979—Richmond	Int'national	24	54	4	6	.400	46	26	20	40	18	3.33
1979—Atlanta	National	15	22	0	0	.000	28	16	15	12	11	6.14
1980—Richmond	Int'national	29	188	12	6	.667	172	68	54	101	80	2.59
1980—Atlanta	National	2	4	0	0	.000	2	1	1	1	0	2.25
1981—Atlanta	National	34	112	8	6	.571	109	41	35	54	43	2.81
1982—Atlanta	National	39	205⅓	9	10	.474	213	105	96	105	62	4.21
1983—Atlanta	National	10	14⅓	0	0	.000	16	8	8	7	9	5.02
1983—Richmond	In'national	24	162⅔	12	7	.632	165	102	89	103	85	4.92
Major League Totals		100	357⅔	17	16	.515	368	171	155	179	125	3.90

Signed as free agent by Atlanta Braves' organization, June 16, 1975.

CHAMPIONSHIP SERIES RECORD

Year Club	League	G.	IP.	W.	L.	Pct.	H.	R.	ER.	SO.	BB.	ERA.
1982—Atlanta	National	1	1⅔	0	0	.000	3	0	0	0	2	0.00

CANDIDO MALDONADO (GUADARRAMA)
(Candy)

Born September 5, 1960, at Humacao, Puerto Rico.
Height, 6.00. Weight, 185.
Throws and bats righthanded.

Led California League in total bases with 247 in 1980.
Tied for Pioneer League lead in sacrifice flies with 6 in 1978.
Named California League co-Most Valuable Player, 1980.

Year	Club	League	Pos.	G.	AB.	R.	H.	2B.	3B.	HR.	RBI.	B.A.	PO.	A.	E.	F.A.
1978—Lethbridge		Pion.	OF	57	210	45	61	15	5	12	48	.290	112	6	8	.937
1979—Clinton		Midw.	OF	50	158	25	37	13	1	2	26	.234	81	5	2	.977
1979—Lethbridge		Pion.	OF	59	234	42	70	★20	3	5	33	.299	81	5	4	.956
1980—Lodi†		Calif.	OF	121	456	75	139	27	3	25	★102	.305	211	13	11	.953
1981—Albuquerque		P. C.	OF	126	460	96	154	40	9	21	104	.335	221	21	8	.968
1981—Los Angeles		Nat.	OF	11	12	0	1	0	0	0	0	.083	8	0	0	1.000
1982—Albuquerque		P. C.	OF	138	541	91	163	28	6	24	96	.301	303	15	10	.970
1982—Los Angeles		Nat.	OF	6	4	0	0	0	0	0	0	.000	5	0	0	1.000
1983—Los Angeles		Nat.	OF	42	62	5	12	1	1	1	6	.194	26	0	0	1.000
1983—Albuquerque		P. C.	OF-3B	38	144	23	46	6	1	4	20	.319	66	11	4	.951
Major League Totals				59	78	5	13	1	1	1	6	.167	39	0	0	1.000

Signed as free agent by Los Angeles Dodgers' organization, June 6, 1978.
†On disabled list, August 16 to September 16, 1980.

CHAMPIONSHIP SERIES RECORD

Year	Club	League	Pos.	G.	AB.	R.	H.	2B.	3B.	HR.	RBI.	B.A.	PO.	A.	E.	F.A.
1983—Los Angeles		Nat.	PH	2	2	0	0	0	0	0	0	.000	0	0	0	.000

JAMES MICHAEL MALER

Name pronounced MAY-ler.

(Jim)

Born August 16, 1958, at New York, N.Y.
Height, 6.04. Weight, 230.
Throws and bats righthanded.
Attended University of Eiami, Coral Gables, Fla., and
Miami-Dade Community College South, Miami, Fla.

Tied major league record for most assists by first baseman, inning (3), April 29, 1982, (third inning).
Led Pacific Coast League first basemen in double plays with 117 in 1980.
Led California League first basemen in double plays with 111 in 1979.
Received reported $50,000 bonus to sign with Seattle Mariners, 1978.

Year	Club	League	Pos.	G.	AB.	R.	H.	2B.	3B.	HR.	RBI.	B.A.	PO.	A.	E.	F.A.
1978—Stockton†		Calif.	1B	32	121	20	37	6	3	3	26	.306	294	18	5	.984
1979—San Jose		Calif.	1B	139	523	89	162	30	5	24	100	.310	★1260	75	17	.987
1980—Spokane		P. C.	1B	130	455	60	122	26	3	9	59	.268	1056	★122	★16	.985
1981—Spokane		P. C.	1B	139	518	84	158	29	8	19	99	.305	1123	93	17	.986
1981—Seattle		Amer.	1B	12	23	1	8	1	0	0	2	.348	36	2	0	1.000
1982—Seattle		Amer.	1B	64	221	18	50	8	3	4	26	.226	529	41	5	.991
1982—Salt Lake City		P. C.	1B	63	253	51	85	18	4	6	53	.336	557	58	6	.990
1983—Salt Lake City		P. C.	1B-3B	68	247	52	82	21	0	6	51	.332	432	47	2	.996
1983—Seattle		Amer.	1B	26	66	5	12	1	0	1	3	.182	152	9	0	1.000
Major League Totals				102	310	24	70	10	3	5	31	.226	717	52	5	.994

Selected by Seattle Mariners' organization in 1st round (fifth player selected) of free-agent draft, January 10, 1978.
†On disabled list, May 21 to September 6, 1978.

JOHN HAROLD MALKIN

Born November 28, 1960, at New York, N. Y.
Height, 6.03. Weight, 195.
Throws and bats righthanded.

Led Midwest League catchers in double plays with 10 and tied for lead in passed balls with 23 in 1982.
Tied for Eastern League lead in passed balls with 14 in 1983.
Tied for New York-Pennsylvania League lead in errors by catchers with 12 in 1980.

Year	Club	League	Pos.	G.	AB.	R.	H.	2B.	3B.	HR.	RBI.	B.A.	PO.	A.	E.	F.A.
1978—Lethbridge		Pion.	C	28	73	12	27	5	0	3	15	.370	93	12	4	.963
1979—Lodi		Calif.	C	21	68	10	10	1	0	0	3	.147	131	9	1	.993
1979—Clinton		Midw.	C	16	38	2	3	0	0	0	0	.079	75	9	1	.988
1979—Lethbridge		Pion.	C	24	83	11	19	2	0	2	18	.229	151	26	6	.967
1980—Vero Beach		Fla. St.	C	20	54	5	10	1	0	0	6	.185	34	1	3	.921
1980—Auburn†		NYP	C-1B	63	209	27	52	9	1	8	28	.249	361	39	12	.971
1981—Waterloo‡		Midw.	1B-C-3B	56	194	30	47	8	1	12	34	.242	318	36	6	.983
1981—Chattanooga		South.	C	31	76	4	18	6	0	3	13	.237	140	19	4	.976
1982—Waterloo§		Midw.	C-1B-3B	112	392	63	104	22	1	20	72	.265	737	100	16	.981
1983—Buff. x-Lynn		East.	C	104	339	43	104	20	1	11	61	.307	353	36	6	.985

Selected by Los Angeles Dodgers' organization in 11th round of free-agent draft, June 6, 1978.
†Released, April 4, 1981; signed by Waterloo (Cleveland Indians' organization), April 13, 1981.
‡On disabled list, May 27 to June 9, 1981.
§On suspended list, July 7 to July 13, 1982.
xTraded to Lynn (Pittsburgh Pirates' organization) for Pitcher Steve Farr, June 8, 1983.

DAVID BLAIR MALPESO

Born December 18, 1960, at Franklin, Va.
Height, 6.00. Weight, 200.
Throws and bats righthanded.
Attended Miami-Dade Community College (North), Miami, Fla.

Year Club	League	Pos.	G.	AB.	R.	H.	2B.	3B.	HR.	RBI.	B.A.	PO.	A.	E.	F.A.
1981—Elmira	NYP	C-1B-OF	67	250	53	73	14	1	12	50	.292	124	17	14	.910
1982—Winston-Salem	Carol.	C-OF -1B	116	441	68	140	24	1	★29	91	.317	609	81	14	.980
1983—New Britain	East	C-1-O-3	120	430	54	111	19	3	9	72	.258	555	79	18	.972

Selected by Chicago White Sox' organization in 2nd round of free-agent draft, January 8, 1980.
Selected by Minnesota Twins' organization in secondary phase of free-agent draft, June 3, 1980.
Selected by Boston Red Sox' organization in secondary phase of free-agent draft, January 13, 1981.

RICHARD EUGENE MANNING
(Rick)

Born September 2, 1954, at Niagara Falls, N. Y.
Height, 6.01. Weight, 180.
Throws right and bats lefthanded.

Tied major league records for most strikeouts, game (5), May 15, 1977; most putouts by outfielder, game (12), July 11, 1983, 15 innings; fewest double plays by outfielder, season, 150 or more games (0), 1983.
Tied American League record for most chances accepted by outfielder, game (12), July 11, 1983, 15 innings.
Major League stolen bases: 1975 (19), 1976 (16), 1977 (9), 1978 (12), 1979 (30), 1980 (12), 1981 (25), 1982 (12), 1983 (18). Total—153.
Led American League outfielders in total chances with 478 in 1983.
Named outfielder on THE SPORTING NEWS American League All-Star fielding team, 1976.
Received reported $65,000 bonus to sign with Cleveland Indians, 1972.

Year Club	League	Pos.	G.	AB.	R.	H.	2B.	3B.	HR.	RBI.	B.A.	PO.	A.	E.	F.A.
1972—Reno	Calif.	OF-SS	57	216	45	52	4	4	3	23	.241	71	45	19	.859
1973—Reno	Calif.	OF-SS	137	486	★101	136	40	★14	6	67	.280	184	8	7	.965
1974—Oklahoma City	A. A.	OF	122	402	58	108	16	5	5	39	.269	207	12	8	.965
1975—Oklahoma City	A. A.	OF	30	117	18	37	5	2	0	15	.316	62	4	0	1.000
1975—Cleveland	Amer.	OF	120	480	69	137	16	5	3	35	.285	331	12	9	.974
1976—Cleveland	Amer.	OF	138	552	73	161	24	7	6	43	.292	359	8	5	.987
1977—Cleveland†	Amer.	OF	68	252	33	57	7	3	5	18	.226	191	2	2	.990
1978—Cleveland	Amer.	OF	148	566	65	149	27	3	3	50	.263	377	7	2	.995
1979—Cleveland	Amer.	OF	144	560	67	145	12	2	3	51	.259	417	9	6	.986
1980—Cleveland	Amer.	OF	140	471	55	110	17	4	3	52	.234	379	7	4	.990
1981—Cleveland	Amer.	OF	103	360	47	88	15	3	4	33	.244	305	6	4	.987
1982—Cleveland‡	Amer.	OF	152	562	71	152	18	2	8	44	.270	387	10	9	.978
1983—Clev.§-Milw	Amer.	OF	158	569	60	140	20	4	4	43	.246	★471	2	5	.990
Major League Totals			1171	4372	540	1139	156	33	39	369	.261	3217	63	46	.986

Selected by Cleveland Indians' organization in 1st round (second player selected) of free-agent draft, June 6, 1972.
†On supplemental disabled list, June 21 to July 8, 1977; transferred to disabled list, July 8 to September 1, 1977.
‡Granted free agency, November 10, 1982; re-signed with Indians, December 15, 1982.
§Traded with Pitcher Rick Waits to Milwaukee Brewers for Outfielder Gorman Thomas and Pitchers Jamie Easterly and Ernie Camacho, June 6, 1983.

FRED ELOY MANRIQUE

Name pronounced Man-ree-KEE.
Born November 5, 1961, at Bolivar, Venezuela.
Height, 6.01. Weight, 175.
Throws and bats righthanded.

Led International League second basemen in errors with 22 in 1983.

Year Club	League	Pos.	G.	AB.	R.	H.	2B.	3B.	HR.	RBI.	B.A.	PO.	A.	E.	F.A.
1979—Dunedin	Fla. St.	SS	5	15	0	2	0	0	0	0	.133	4	7	3	.786
1979—Medicine Hat	Pion.	SS	66	270	47	81	8	●10	2	30	.300	103	208	★37	.894
1980—Kinston	Carol.	SS-OF	111	390	49	108	9	5	7	50	.277	120	192	37	.894
1981—Knoxville†	South.	SS	115	469	62	131	15	6	5	42	.279	161	330	45	.916
1981—Toronto	Amer.	SS-3B	14	28	1	4	0	0	0	1	.143	10	27	3	.925
1982—Syracuse‡	Int.	2B-3B-SS	103	362	41	91	9	2	4	37	.251	186	255	24	.948
1983—Syracuse	Int.	2-S-3-O	128	485	55	130	22	8	10	50	.268	211	351	36	.940
Major League Totals			14	28	1	4	0	0	0	1	.143	10	27	3	.925

Signed as free agent by Toronto Blue Jays' organization, November 24, 1978.
†On disabled list, April 9 to April 19, 1981.
‡On disabled list, June 27 to July 12, 1982.

RAVELO MANZANILLO

Born October 17, 1963, at San Pedro de Macoris, D. R.
Height, 5.09. Weight, 165.
Throws and bats lefthanded.

Year Club	League	G.	IP.	W.	L.	Pct.	H.	R.	ER.	SO.	BB.	ERA.
1981—Bradenton Pirates	Gulf Coast	9	48	3	1	.750	35	11	6	34	10	1.13
1982—Greenwood	S. Atlantic	27	157⅔	9	9	.500	156	108	87	93	109	4.97
1983—Alexandria	Carolina	22	105⅓	7	7	.500	107	68	52	66	79	4.44

Signed as free agent by Pittsburgh Pirates' organization, August 21, 1980.

MICHAEL ALLEN MARSHALL
(Mike)

Born January 12, 1960, at Libertyville, Ill.
Height, 6.05. Weight, 215.
Throws and bats righthanded.

Led California League in total bases with 301 in 1979.
Led Pacific Coast League first basemen in double plays with 136 in 1981.
Led Texas League first basemen in double plays with 120 in 1980.
Named Minor League Player of the Year by THE SPORTING NEWS, 1981.
Named Pacific Coast League Most Valuable Player, 1981.
Named California League co-Most Valuable Player, 1979.

Year	Club	League	Pos.	G.	AB.	R.	H.	2B.	3B.	HR.	RBI.	B.A.	PO.	A.	E.	F.A.
1978—Lethbridge	Pion.	1B-OF	65	256	48	83	15	2	12	70	.324	308	16	7	.979
1979—Lodi	Calif.	1B	137	525	101	★186	★37	3	24	116	★.354	1173	71	20	.984
1980—San Antonio	Texas	1B	134	470	95	151	21	6	16	82	.321	★1157	64	●16	.987
1981—Albuquerque	P. C.	1B	128	467	★114	174	25	7	★34	★137	.373	1127	54	9	.992
1981—Los Angeles	Nat.	1-3-OF	14	25	2	5	3	0	0	1	.200	14	2	0	1.000
1982—Albuquerque	P. C.	O-1-3	66	255	74	99	20	1	14	58	.388	113	3	4	.966
1982—Los Angeles	Nat.	OF-1B	49	95	10	23	3	0	5	9	.242	122	5	2	.984
1983—Los Angeles	Nat.	OF-1B	140	465	47	132	17	1	17	65	.284	395	21	6	.986
Major League Totals			203	585	59	160	23	1	22	75	.274	531	28	8	.986

Selected by Los Angeles Dodgers' organization in 5th round of free-agent draft, June 6, 1978.

DIVISION SERIES RECORD

Year	Club	League	Pos.	G.	AB.	R.	H.	2B.	3B.	HR.	RBI.	B.A.	PO.	A.	E.	F.A.
1981—Los Angeles	Nat.	PH	1	1	0	0	0	0	0	0	.000	0	0	0	.000

CHAMPIONSHIP SERIES RECORD

Year	Club	League	Pos.	G.	AB.	R.	H.	2B.	3B.	HR.	RBI.	B.A.	PO.	A.	E.	F.A.
1983—Los Angeles	Nat.	1B-OF	4	15	1	2	1	0	1	2	.133	22	2	0	1.000

DONALD RENIE MARTIN
(Known by middle name.)

Born August 30, 1955, at Dover, Del.
Height, 6.04. Weight, 185.
Throws and bats righthanded.
Received bachelor of science degree in finance from
University of Richmond, Richmond, Va. in 1977.

Tied for Gulf Coast League lead in shutouts with 1 in 1977.

Year	Club	League	G.	IP.	W.	L.	Pct.	H.	R.	ER.	SO.	BB.	ERA.
1977—Sarasota Royals	Gulf Coast	4	31	3	1	.750	35	13	12	19	12	3.48
1977—Daytona Beach	Florida St.	10	20	2	2	.500	16	6	6	12	7	2.70
1978—Ft. Myers	Florida St.	26	44	4	7	.429	27	19	10	29	18	2.05
1978—Omaha	Am. Assoc.	13	19	2	2	.500	16	9	7	10	9	3.32
1979—Jacksonville	Southern	8	18	3	1	.750	10	3	2	14	4	1.00
1979—Kansas City	American	25	35	0	3	.000	32	20	20	25	14	5.14
1979—Omaha	Am. Assoc.	33	63	6	2	.750	56	27	22	47	38	3.14
1980—Kansas City	American	32	137	10	10	.500	133	84	67	68	70	4.40
1981—Kansas City†	American	29	62	4	5	.444	55	25	19	25	29	2.76
1982—San Francisco	National	29	141⅓	7	10	.412	148	91	73	63	64	4.65
1982—Phoenix	P. Coast	3	19	1	2	.333	25	12	10	12	2	4.74
1983—San Francisco	National	37	94⅓	2	4	.333	95	50	44	43	51	4.20
American League Totals		86	234	14	18	.438	220	129	106	118	113	4.08
National League Totals		66	235⅔	9	14	.391	243	141	117	106	115	4.47
Major League Totals		152	469⅔	23	32	.418	463	270	223	224	228	4.27

Selected by Kansas City Royals' organization in 19th round of free-agent draft, June 7, 1977.

‡Traded with Pitchers Atlee Hammaker and Craig Chamberlain and a player to be named later to San Francisco Giants for Pitchers Vida Blue and Bob Tufts, March 30, 1982; San Francisco organization acquired Second Baseman Brad Wellman to complete deal, April 19, 1982.

DIVISION SERIES RECORD

Year	Club	League	G.	IP.	W.	L.	Pct.	H.	R.	ER.	SO.	BB.	ERA.
1981—Kansas City	American	2	5⅓	0	0	.000	1	0	0	2	2	0.00

WORLD SERIES RECORD

Year	Club	League	G.	IP.	W.	L.	Pct.	H.	R.	ER.	SO.	BB.	ERA.
1980—Kansas City	American	3	9⅔	0	0	.000	11	3	3	2	3	2.79

JERRY LINDSEY MARTIN

Born May 11, 1949, at Columbia, S. C.
Height, 6.01. Weight, 195.
Throws and bats righthanded.
Attended Spartanburg Junior College, Spartanburg, S. C., and
Furman University, Greenville, S. C.
Son of Barney Martin, Sr., pitcher in New York Giants' and Cincinnati Reds' organizations, 1946 through 1948 and 1950 through 1956; brother of Mike Martin, minor league pitcher, 1970 through 1978; pitcher in Inter-American League, 1979.

Led Western Carolinas League in total bases with 240 and tied for lead in sacrifice flies with 7 in 1972.
Tied for Eastern League lead in sacrifice flies with 9 in 1973.
Named Western Carolinas League Most Valuable Player, 1972.

Year	Club	League	Pos.	G.	AB.	R.	H.	2B.	3B.	HR.	RBI.	B.A.	PO.	A.	E.	F.A.
1971—Pulaski	Appal.		OF	40	156	35	49	8	1	6	28	.314	54	1	6	.902
1972—Spartanburg	W. Car.		OF	*132	*513	86	*162	*30	6	12	*112	.316	186	*15	8	.962
1973—Reading	East.		OF-3B	135	460	73	138	23	5	17	86	.300	214	11	7	.970
1974—Toledo	Int.		OF	139	497	67	144	23	4	8	64	.290	285	6	3	.990
1974—Philadelphia	Nat.		OF	13	14	2	3	1	0	0	1	.214	5	0	0	1.000
1975—Toledo	Int.		OF	94	342	64	89	12	4	14	40	.260	205	7	3	.986
1975—Philadelphia	Nat.		OF	57	113	15	24	7	1	2	11	.212	90	3	2	.979
1976—Philadelphia	Nat.		OF-1B	130	121	30	30	7	0	2	15	.248	85	0	2	.977
1977—Philadelphia	Nat.		OF-1B	116	215	34	56	16	3	6	28	.260	117	4	2	.984
1978—Philadelphia†	Nat.		OF	128	266	40	72	13	4	9	36	.271	148	8	2	.987
1979—Chicago	Nat.		OF	150	534	74	145	34	3	19	73	.272	297	11	6	.981
1980—Chicago‡	Nat.		OF	141	494	57	112	22	2	23	73	.227	262	8	6	.978
1981—San Francisco§	Nat.		OF	72	241	23	58	5	3	4	25	.241	138	4	1	.993
1982—Kansas City	Amer.		OF	147	519	52	138	22	1	15	65	.266	333	4	7	.980
1983—Kansas City xyz	Amer.		OF	13	44	4	14	2	0	2	13	.318	22	0	1	.957
National League Totals				807	1998	275	500	105	16	65	262	.250	1142	38	21	.983
American League Totals				160	563	56	152	24	1	17	78	.270	355	4	8	.978
Major League Totals				967	2561	331	652	129	17	82	340	.255	1497	42	29	.982

Signed as free agent by Philadelphia Phillies' organization, July 17, 1971.

†Traded with Catcher Barry Foote, Second Baseman Ted Sizemore and Pitchers Derek Botelho and Henry Mack to Chicago Cubs for Second Baseman Manny Trillo, Outfielder Greg Gross and Catcher Dave Rader, February 23, 1979.

‡Traded with Outfielder Jesus Figueroa and a player to be named later to San Francisco Giants for Pitcher Phil Nastu and Second Baseman Joe Strain, December 12, 1980; San Francisco organization acquired Infielder-Outfielder Mike Turgeon to complete deal, August 11, 1981.

§Traded to Kansas City Royals for Pitchers Rich Gale and Bill Laskey, December 10, 1981.

xOn supplemental disabled list, April 30, 1983; transferred to disabled list, May 16, 1983; transferred to emergency disabled list, July 1, 1983 through remainder of season.

yGranted free agency, November 7, 1983.

zOn suspended list, December 15, 1983.

CHAMPIONSHIP SERIES RECORD

Tied Championship Series records for most home runs by pinch hitter, game, Series and total Series (1), October 4, 1978.

Year	Club	League	Pos.	G.	AB.	R.	H.	2B.	3B.	HR.	RBI.	B.A.	PO.	A.	E.	F.A.
1976—Philadelphia	Nat.		OF	1	1	1	0	0	0	0	0	.000	1	0	0	1.000
1977—Philadelphia	Nat.		O-PR-PH	3	4	0	0	0	0	0	0	.000	1	0	0	1.000
1978—Philadelphia	Nat.		PH-OF	4	9	1	2	1	0	1	2	.222	7	0	0	1.000
Championship Series Totals				8	14	2	2	1	0	1	2	.143	9	0	0	1.000

JOHN ROBERT MARTIN

Born April 11, 1956, at Wyandotte, Mich.
Height, 6.00. Weight, 190.
Throws left and bats left and righthanded.
Attended Eastern Michigan University, Ypsilanti, Mich.

Year	Club	League	G.	IP.	W.	L.	Pct.	H.	R.	ER.	SO.	BB.	ERA.
1978—Bristol	Ap'lachian	2	5	0	1	.000	2	3	3	5	4	5.40
1978—Lakeland	Florida St.	12	50	4	1	.800	54	11	10	22	9	1.80
1979—Montgomery	Southern	11	27	2	0	1.000	15	8	6	18	9	2.00
1979—Evansville	Am. Assoc.	37	59	7	1	.875	49	12	9	53	25	1.37
1980—Evansville†-Springfield‡	Am. Assoc.	20	38	2	2	.500	39	25	25	31	22	5.92
1980—Arkansas	Texas	5	27	1	1	.500	23	7	5	19	7	1.67
1980—St. Louis	National	9	42	2	3	.400	39	20	20	23	9	4.29
1981—Springfield	Am. Assoc.	5	37	2	2	.500	26	8	6	25	9	1.46
1981—St. Louis	National	17	103	8	5	.615	85	43	39	36	26	3.41
1982—St. Louis	National	24	66	4	5	.444	56	33	31	21	30	4.23
1982—Louisville	Am. Assoc.	11	83	5	3	.625	62	37	32	41	38	3.47
1983—St. Louis§	National	26	66⅓	3	1	.750	60	31	26	29	26	3.53
1983—Detroit	American	15	13⅓	0	0	.000	15	11	11	11	4	7.43
National League Totals		76	277⅓	17	14	.548	240	127	116	109	91	3.76
American League Totals		15	13⅓	0	0	.000	15	11	11	11	4	7.43
Major League Totals		91	290⅔	17	14	.548	255	138	127	120	95	3.93

Selected by Detroit Tigers' organization in 27th round of free-agent draft, June 6, 1978.

†Traded with a player to be named later to St. Louis Cardinals' organization for Outfielder Jim Lentine, June 2, 1980; St. Louis organization acquired Outfielder Al Greene to complete deal, June 9, 1980.

‡On disabled list, June 23 to July 31, 1980.

§Sold to Detroit Tigers, August 4, 1983.

CARMELO MARTINEZ (SALGADO)
(Bitu)

Born July 28, 1960, at Dorado, Puerto Rico.
Height, 6.02. Weight, 185.
Throws and bats righthanded.
Attended Central College of Bayamon, Bayamon, Puerto Rico.

Tied major league record by hitting home run in first major league at-bat, August 22, 1983.

Led American Association first basemen in total chances with 1,283 and tied for lead in double plays with 99 in 1983.

Led Texas League first basemen in putouts with 1,087, total chances with 1,180 and double plays with 102 in 1982.

Year	Club	League	Pos.	G.	AB.	R.	H.	2B.	3B.	HR.	RBI.	B.A.	PO.	A.	E.	F.A.
1979—Sarasota Cubs	Gulf C.	OF-1B	40	143	18	29	4	0	1	23	.203	139	9	6	.961
1980—Quad Cities	Midw.	O-1-3-2-S	128	460	65	118	23	0	12	64	.257	433	99	13	.976
1981—Midland	Texas	3-O-2-1	116	392	65	116	22	1	21	84	.296	61	80	24	.855
1982—Midland	Texas	1B-OF	131	467	100	156	35	4	27	93	.334	1098	78	17	.986
1983—Iowa	A. A.	★1B-2B	123	458	76	115	25	1	★31	94	.251	★1191	★83	9	.993
1983—Chicago†	Nat.	1B-3B-OF	29	89	8	23	3	0	6	16	.258	233	17	2	.992
Major League Totals			29	89	8	23	3	0	6	16	.258	233	17	2	.992

Signed as free agent by Chicago Cubs' organization, December 9, 1978.

†Traded with Pitcher Craig Lefferts and Third Baseman Fritz Connally to San Diego Padres for Pitcher Scott Sanderson, December 7, 1983.

FELIX ANTHONY MARTINEZ
(Tippy)

Born May 31, 1950, at La Junta, Colo.
Height, 5.10. Weight, 175.
Throws and bats lefthanded.
Attended Colorado State University, Fort Collins, Colo.

Major League saves: 1975 (8), 1976 (10), 1977 (9), 1978 (5), 1979 (3), 1980 (10), 1981 (11), 1982 (16), 1983 (21). Total—93.

Tied for Carolina League lead in saves with 15 and wild pitches with 17 in 1973.

Year	Club	League	G.	IP.	W.	L.	Pct.	H.	R.	ER.	SO.	BB.	ERA.
1972—Oneonta	NYP	2	9	1	0	1.000	3	2	2	9	10	2.00
1972—Kinston	Carolina	5	20	0	0	.000	22	10	10	18	13	4.50
1973—Kinston	Carolina	54	105	13	8	.619	74	38	31	160	61	2.66
1974—Syracuse	Int'national	36	64	7	5	.583	49	29	27	70	32	3.80
1974—New York	American	10	13	0	0	.000	14	7	6	10	9	4.15
1975—Syracuse	Int'national	14	110	8	2	.800	91	39	25	105	35	2.05
1975—New York	American	23	37	1	2	.333	27	15	11	20	32	2.68
1976—New York†	American	11	28	2	0	1.000	18	6	6	14	14	1.93
1976—Baltimore	American	28	42	3	1	.750	32	13	12	31	28	2.57
1977—Baltimore	American	41	50	5	1	.833	47	17	15	29	27	2.70
1978—Baltimore	American	42	69	3	3	.500	77	41	37	57	40	4.83
1979—Baltimore	American	39	78	10	3	.769	59	29	25	61	31	2.88
1980—Baltimore	American	53	81	4	4	.500	69	30	27	68	34	3.00
1981—Baltimore	American	37	59	3	3	.500	48	21	19	50	32	2.90
1982—Baltimore	American	76	95	8	8	.500	81	39	36	78	37	3.41
1983—Baltimore‡	American	65	101⅓	9	3	.750	76	30	27	81	37	2.35
Major League Totals		425	655⅓	48	28	.632	548	248	221	499	321	3.04

Selected by Washington Senators' organization in 35th round of free-agent draft, June 5, 1969.

Signed as free agent by New York Yankees' organization, July 22, 1972.

†Traded with Pitchers Rudy May, Dave Pagan and Scott McGregor and Catcher Rick Dempsey to Baltimore Orioles for Pitchers Ken Holtzman, Doyle Alexander and Grant Jackson, Catcher Ellie Hendricks and Pitcher Jimmy Freeman, June 15, 1976.

‡On disabled list, July 9 to July 31, 1983.

CHAMPIONSHIP SERIES RECORD

Year	Club	League	G.	IP.	W.	L.	Pct.	H.	R.	ER.	SO.	BB.	ERA.
1983—Baltimore	American	2	6	1	0	1.000	5	0	0	5	3	0.00

WORLD SERIES RECORD

Tied World Series record for most saves, five-game Series (2), 1983.

Year	Club	League	G.	IP.	W.	L.	Pct.	H.	R.	ER.	SO.	BB.	ERA.
1979—Baltimore	American	3	1⅓	0	0	.000	3	1	1	1	0	6.75
1983—Baltimore	American	3	3	0	0	.000	3	1	1	0	0	3.00
World Series Totals		6	4⅓	0	0	.000	6	2	2	1	0	4.15

ALL-STAR GAME RECORD

Member of American League All-Star Team in 1983; did not play.

JOHN ALBERT MARTINEZ
(Buck)

Born November 7, 1948, at Redding, Calif.
Height, 5.11. Weight, 190.
Throws and bats righthanded.
Attended Sacramento City College, Sacramento, Calif., and
Sacramento State College, Sacramento, Calif.

Led American Association catchers in fielding percentage with .994 in 1973.

Year	Club	League	Pos.	G.	AB.	R.	H.	2B.	3B.	HR.	RBI.	B.A.	PO.	A.	E.	F.A.
1967—Eugene	N'west	●C-OF-3B	77	269	53	96	16	4	2	46	.357	294	●48	8	.977
1968—Spartanburg	W. Car.	C	8	28	6	11	4	0	0	11	.393	51	2	0	1.000
1968—Tidewater†‡	Carol.	C	36	110	10	31	12	1	1	14	.282	272	16	1	.997

Year Club League	Pos.	G.	AB.	R.	H.	2B.	3B.	HR.	RBI.	B.A.	PO.	A.	E.	F.A.
1969—Kansas City§......... Amer.	C-OF	72	205	14	47	6	1	4	23	.229	292	26	9	.972
1970—Kansas City x .... Amer.	C	6	9	1	1	0	0	0	0	.111	20	3	1	.958
1971—Omaha.................. A. A.	C	75	269	34	77	23	1	5	39	.286	502	37	8	.985
1971—Kansas City.......... Amer.	C	22	46	3	7	2	0	0	1	.152	84	6	3	.968
1972—Omaha y .... A. A.	C	67	195	23	34	9	0	4	12	.174	493	47	6	.989
1973—Omaha.................. A. A.	C-1B	82	254	24	69	13	0	5	38	.272	522	47	3	.995
1973—Kansas City.......... Amer.	C	14	32	2	8	1	0	1	6	.250	52	4	2	.966
1974—Kansas City.......... Amer.	C	43	107	10	23	3	1	1	8	.215	151	16	4	.977
1975—Kansas City.......... Amer.	C	80	226	15	51	9	2	3	23	.226	361	39	8	.980
1976—Kansas City z....... Amer.	C	95	267	24	61	13	3	5	34	.228	420	40	4	.991
1977—Kansas City a .... Amer.	C	29	80	3	18	4	0	1	9	.225	133	8	1	.993
1978—Milwaukee............ Amer.	C	89	256	26	56	10	1	1	20	.219	327	32	8	.978
1979—Milwaukee............ Amer.	C-P	69	196	17	53	8	0	4	26	.270	198	39	8	.967
1980—Milwaukee b........ Amer.	C	76	219	16	49	9	0	3	17	.224	293	33	5	.985
1981—Toronto c.............. Amer.	C	45	128	13	29	8	1	4	21	.227	192	22	2	.991
1982—Toronto .... Amer.	C	96	260	26	63	17	0	10	37	.242	382	35	5	.988
1983—Toronto .... Amer.	C	88	221	27	56	14	0	10	33	.253	331	25	4	.989
Major League Totals....................................		824	2252	197	522	104	9	47	258	.232	3236	328	64	.982

Selected by Philadelphia Phillies' organization in 7th round of free-agent draft, January 28, 1967.

†Drafted by Houston Astros, December 2, 1968.

‡Traded with Infielder Mickey Sinnerud and Catcher Tommie Smith by Houston Astros to Kansas City Royals for Catcher John Jones, December 16, 1968.

§On restricted list, April 7 to June 17, 1969.

xOn military list, April 2 to August 10, 1970.

yOn disabled list, July 9 to August 25, 1972.

zOn supplemental disabled list, May 20 to June 5, 1976.

aTraded with Pitcher Mark Littell to St. Louis Cardinals for Pitcher Al Hrabosky, December 8, 1977; traded by St. Louis to Milwaukee Brewers for Pitcher George Frazier, December 8, 1977.

bTraded to Toronto Blue Jays for Outfielder Gil Kubski, May 10, 1981 (appeared in no games with Milwaukee).

cGranted free agency, November 13, 1981; re-signed by Blue Jays, December 6, 1981.

CHAMPIONSHIP SERIES RECORD

Year Club League	Pos.	G.	AB.	R.	H.	2B.	3B.	HR.	RBI.	B.A.	PO.	A.	E.	F.A.
1976—Kansas City........... Amer.	C	5	15	0	5	0	0	0	4	.333	15	4	0	1.000

PITCHING RECORD

Year Club League	G.	IP.	W.	L.	Pct.	H.	R.	ER.	SO.	BB.	ERA.
1979—Milwaukee...................... American	1	1	0	0	.000	1	1	1	0	1	9.00

JOSE DENNIS MARTINEZ

(Known by middle name.)

Born May 14, 1955, at Granada, Nicaragua.
Height, 6.01. Weight, 183.
Throws and bats righthanded.

Led American League pitchers in games started with 39 and complete games with 18 in 1979.
Led International League in complete games with 16 in 1976.
Named International League Pitcher of the Year, 1976.

Year Club	League	G.	IP.	W.	L.	Pct.	H.	R.	ER.	SO.	BB.	ERA.
1974—Miami	Florida St.	25	179	15	6	.714	124	48	41	162	53	2.06
1975—Miami	Florida St.	20	145	12	4	.750	125	54	42	114	35	2.61
1975—Asheville	Southern	6	45	4	1	.800	45	16	13	18	12	2.60
1975—Rochester	Int'national	2	5	0	0	.000	7	4	3	4	2	5.40
1976—Rochester	Int'national	25	180	★14	8	.636	148	64	50	★140	50	★2.50
1976—Baltimore	American	4	28	1	2	.333	23	8	8	18	8	2.57
1977—Baltimore	American	42	167	14	7	.667	157	86	76	107	64	4.10
1978—Baltimore	American	40	276	16	11	.593	257	121	108	142	93	3.25
1979—Baltimore	American	40	★292	15	16	.484	279	129	119	132	78	3.67
1980—Baltimore†	American	25	100	6	4	.600	103	44	44	42	44	3.96
1980—Miami	Florida St.	2	12	0	0	.000	3	1	0	7	5	0.00
1981—Baltimore	American	25	179	●14	5	.737	173	84	66	88	62	3.32
1982—Baltimore	American	40	252	16	12	.571	262	123	118	111	87	4.21
1983—Baltimore	American	32	153	7	16	.304	209	108	94	71	45	5.53
Major League Totals		248	1447	89	73	.549	1463	703	633	711	481	3.94

Signed as free agent by Baltimore Orioles' organization, December 10, 1973.

†On disabled list, March 28 to April 20 and June 3 to July 10, 1980; included rehabilitation disability assignment to Miami, July 1 to July 10, 1980.

CHAMPIONSHIP SERIES RECORD

Year Club	League	G.	IP.	W.	L.	Pct.	H.	R.	ER.	SO.	BB.	ERA.
1979—Baltimore .... American		1	8⅓	0	0	.000	8	3	3	4	0	3.24

WORLD SERIES RECORD

Year Club	League	G.	IP.	W.	L.	Pct.	H.	R.	ER.	SO.	BB.	ERA.
1979—Baltimore .... American		2	2	0	0	.000	6	4	4	0	0	18.00

RANDY CARL MARTZ

Born May 28, 1956, at Harrisburg, Pa.
Height, 6.04. Weight, 210.
Throws right and bats lefthanded.
Attended University of South Carolina, Columbia, S. C.

Tied for American Association lead in games started by pitchers with 26 in 1979.

Year—Club	League	G.	IP.	W.	L.	Pct.	H.	R.	ER.	SO.	BB.	ERA.
1977—Bradenton Cubs	Gulf Coast	2	9	0	1	.000	4	1	0	8	2	0.00
1977—Midland	Texas	12	85	5	3	.625	96	45	39	42	14	4.13
1978—Midland	Texas	18	127	8	6	.571	126	53	44	74	44	3.12
1978—Wichita	Am. Assoc.	11	59	3	7	.300	82	51	47	24	27	7.17
1979—Wichita	Am. Assoc.	30	178	8	13	.381	196	96	81	66	47	4.10
1980—Wichita†	Am. Assoc.	16	107	8	6	.571	98	41	37	53	29	3.11
1980—Chicago	National	6	30	1	2	.333	28	14	7	5	11	2.10
1981—Chicago	National	33	108	5	7	.417	103	49	44	32	49	3.67
1982—Chicago‡§	National	28	147⅔	11	10	.524	157	80	69	40	36	4.21
1983—Denver	Am. Assoc.	21	128⅓	8	7	.533	158	79	73	60	44	5.12
1983—Chicago	American	1	5	0	0	.000	4	2	2	1	4	3.60
National League Totals		67	285⅔	17	19	.472	288	143	120	77	96	3.78
American League Totals		1	5	0	0	.000	4	2	2	1	4	3.60
Major League Totals		68	290⅔	17	19	.472	292	145	122	78	100	3.78

Selected by Chicago Cubs' organization in 1st round (12th player selected) of free-agent draft, June 7, 1977.
†On disabled list, May 12 to July 16, 1980.
‡On disabled list, June 27 to July 22, 1982.
§Traded with Pitcher Dick Tidrow and Infielders Scott Fletcher and Pat Tabler to Chicago White Sox for Pitchers Steve Trout and Warren Brusstar, January 25, 1983.

MICHAEL PAUL MASON
(Mike)

Born November 21, 1958, at Fairbault, Minn.
Height, 6.02. Weight, 200.
Throws and bats lefthanded.
Attended Normandale Community College, Bloomington, Minn., and
Oral Roberts University, Tulsa, Okla.

Tied for Texas League lead in balks with 4 in 1982.

Year—Club	League	G.	IP.	W.	L.	Pct.	H.	R.	ER.	SO.	BB.	ERA.
1980—Sarasota Rangers	Gulf Coast	12	61	6	1	.857	40	17	14	*55	46	2.07
1981—Asheville†	S. Atlantic	12	85	8	3	.727	58	28	20	39	35	2.12
1982—Tulsa	Texas	26	155	10	9	.526	153	84	67	111	46	3.89
1982—Texas	American	4	23	1	2	.333	21	13	13	8	9	5.09
1983—Texas	American	5	10⅔	0	2	.000	10	7	7	9	6	5.91
1983—Oklahoma City	Am. Assoc.	16	88⅔	5	5	.500	100	50	41	50	26	4.16
Major League Totals		9	33⅓	1	4	.200	31	20	20	17	15	5.35

Selected by Detroit Tigers' organization in 14th round of free-agent draft, June 6, 1978.
Selected by Minnesota Twins' organization in secondary phase of free-agent draft, January 9, 1979.
Selected by St. Louis Cardinals' organization in secondary phase of free-agent draft, June 5, 1979.
Selected by Texas Rangers' organization in secondary phase of free-agent draft, June 3, 1980.
†On disabled list, July 26, 1981 through remainder of season.

ROGER LeROY MASON

Born September 18, 1958, at Bellaire, Mich.
Height, 6.06. Weight, 215.
Throws and bats righthanded.
Attended Saginaw Valley State College, University Center, Mich.

Year—Club	League	G.	IP.	W.	L.	Pct.	H.	R.	ER.	SO.	BB.	ERA.
1981—Macon	S. Atlantic	26	148	10	10	.500	153	77	64	105	50	3.89
1982—Lakeland	Florida St.	22	132⅔	7	7	.500	124	60	51	72	52	3.46
1983—Birmingham	Southern	17	126⅔	7	4	.636	116	45	29	83	43	*2.06
1983—Evansville	Am. Assoc.	11	78⅔	5	5	.500	84	39	37	43	21	4.23

Signed as free agent by Detroit Tigers' organization, September 21, 1980.

RONALD VANCE MATHIS
(Ron)

Born September 25, 1958, at Kansas City, Mo.
Height, 6.00. Weight, 175.
Throws and bats righthanded.
Received bachelor of arts degree in computer science from
University of Missouri, Columbia, Mo., in 1980.

Led Pacific Coast League in shutouts with 3 in 1983.

Year—Club	League	G.	IP.	W.	L.	Pct.	H.	R.	ER.	SO.	BB.	ERA.
1980—Bristol	Ap'lachian	3	16	1	2	.333	19	11	11	18	5	6.19
1980—Macon	S. Atlantic	12	86	9	2	.818	60	25	20	78	38	2.09
1980—Montgomery	Southern	1	3	0	1	.000	4	4	4	3	4	12.00
1981—Birmingham†	Southern	23	134	8	8	.500	129	79	68	125	53	4.57
1982—Birmingham‡-Columbus	Southern	12	71⅓	6	2	.750	59	26	26	69	29	3.28

Year Club	League	G.	IP.	W.	L.	Pct.	H.	R.	ER.	SO.	BB.	ERA.
1982—Tucson	P. Coast	14	84⅓	4	8	.333	90	50	42	79	42	4.48
1983—Tucson	P. Coast	28	182⅔	11	●13	.458	179	101	88	137	73	4.34

Selected by Detroit Tigers' organization in 30th round of free-agent draft, June 7, 1980.
†On disabled list, August 3 to August 18, 1981.
‡Released April 19, 1982; signed by Columbus (Houston Astros' organization), May 5, 1982.

JONATHAN TRUMPBOUR MATLACK
(Jon)

Born January 19, 1950, at West Chester, Pa.
Height, 6.03. Weight, 200.
Throws and bats lefthanded.
Attended University of Pittsburgh, Pittsburgh, Pa., and West
Chester State College, West Chester, Pa.

Led National League in shutouts with 7 in 1974.
Tied for National League lead in shutouts with 6 in 1976.
Named National League Rookie Pitcher of the Year by THE SPORTING NEWS, 1972.
Named National League Rookie of the Year by Baseball Writers' Association of America, 1972.
Received reported $55,000 bonus to sign with New York Mets, 1967.

Year Club	League	G.	IP.	W.	L.	Pct.	H.	R.	ER.	SO.	BB.	ERA.
1967—Williamsport	Eastern	2	5	0	1	.000	10	8	8	4	4	14.40
1968—Raleigh-Dur.	Carolina	24	173	13	6	.684	133	59	53	188	66	2.76
1969—Tidewater	Int'national	26	176	14	7	.667	176	83	81	99	66	4.14
1970—Tidewater	Int'national	26	183	12	11	.522	168	94	84	146	90	4.13
1971—Tidewater	Int'national	22	152	11	7	.611	141	82	67	145	55	3.97
1971—New York	National	7	37	0	3	.000	31	18	17	24	15	4.14
1972—New York	National	34	244	15	10	.600	215	79	63	169	71	2.32
1973—New York	National	34	242	14	16	.467	210	93	86	205	99	3.20
1974—New York	National	34	265	13	15	.464	221	82	71	195	76	2.41
1975—New York	National	33	229	16	12	.571	224	105	86	154	58	3.38
1976—New York	National	35	262	17	10	.630	236	94	86	153	57	2.95
1977—New York†	National	26	169	7	15	.318	175	86	79	123	43	4.21
1978—Texas‡	American	35	270	15	13	.536	252	93	68	157	51	2.27
1979—Texas‡	American	13	85	5	4	.556	98	43	39	35	15	4.13
1980—Texas	American	35	235	10	10	.500	265	111	96	142	48	3.68
1981—Texas	American	17	104	4	7	.364	101	59	48	43	41	4.15
1982—Texas	American	33	147⅔	7	7	.500	158	64	58	78	37	3.53
1983—Texas§	American	25	73⅓	2	4	.333	90	43	38	38	27	4.66
National League Totals		203	1448	82	81	.503	1312	557	488	1023	419	3.03
American League Totals		158	915	43	45	.489	964	413	347	493	219	3.41
Major League Totals		361	2363	125	126	.498	2276	970	835	1516	638	3.18

Selected by New York Mets' organization in 1st round (fourth player selected) of free-agent draft, June 6, 1967.
†Traded with First Baseman-Outfielder John Milner to Texas Rangers for First Baseman Willie Montanez, Outfielder Tom Grieve, and a player to be named later, December 8, 1977; New York Mets acquired Outfielder Ken Henderson to complete deal, March 15, 1978.
‡On disabled list, April 8 to May 1 and July 10 to September 12, 1979.
§Released, October 31, 1983.

CHAMPIONSHIP SERIES RECORD
Tied Championship Series record for fewest hits allowed, game (2), October 7, 1973.

Year Club	League	G.	IP.	W.	L.	Pct.	H.	R.	ER.	SO.	BB.	ERA.
1973—New York	National	1	9	1	0	1.000	2	0	0	9	3	0.00

WORLD SERIES RECORD

Year Club	League	G.	IP.	W.	L.	Pct.	H.	R.	ER.	SO.	BB.	ERA.
1973—New York	National	3	16⅔	1	2	.333	10	7	4	11	5	2.16

ALL-STAR GAME RECORD

Year League		IP.	W.	L.	Pct.	H.	R.	ER.	SO.	BB.	ERA.
1974—National		1	0	0	.000	1	0	0	0	1	0.00
1975—National		2	1	0	1.000	2	0	0	4	0	0.00
All-Star Game Totals		3	1	0	1.000	3	0	0	4	1	0.00

Member of National League All-Star Team in 1976; did not play.

GARY NATHANIEL MATTHEWS

Born July 5, 1950, at San Fernando, Calif.
Height, 6.03. Weight, 190.
Throws and bats righthanded.

Hit three home runs in a game, September 25, 1976.
Led National League in grounding into double plays with 23 in 1982.
Led Texas League in total bases with 232 and tied for lead in sacrifice flies with 10 in 1971.
Tied for California League lead in double plays by outfielders with 3 in 1970.
Named National League Rookie Player of the Year by THE SPORTING NEWS , 1973.
Named National League Rookie of the Year by Baseball Writers' Association of America, 1973.

Year Club	League	Pos.	G.	AB.	R.	H.	2B.	3B.	HR.	RBI.	B.A.	PO.	A.	E.	F.A.
1969—Decatur	Midw.	OF	53	174	31	56	11	2	8	30	.322	63	7	8	.897
1970—Fresno	Calif.	OF	117	380	77	106	11	5	23	74	.279	133	15	★15	.908

Year	Club	League	Pos.	G.	AB.	R.	H.	2B.	3B.	HR.	RBI.	B.A.	PO.	A.	E.	F.A.
1971—Amarillo	Texas		OF	●142	493	82	138	★37	6	15	★86	.280	290	10	5	★.984
1972—Phoenix	P. C.		OF	136	480	101	150	27	8	21	108	.313	218	●16	★13	.947
1972—San Francisco	Nat.		OF	20	62	11	18	1	1	4	14	.290	34	0	1	.971
1973—San Francisco	Nat.		OF	148	540	74	162	22	10	12	58	.300	277	11	5	.983
1974—San Francisco	Nat.		OF	154	561	87	161	27	6	16	82	.287	281	9	9	.970
1975—San Francisco†	Nat.		OF	116	425	67	119	22	3	12	58	.280	225	11	8	.967
1976—San Francisco‡	Nat.		OF	156	587	79	164	28	4	20	84	.279	265	8	7	.975
1977—Atlanta	Nat.		OF	148	555	89	157	25	5	17	64	.283	262	11	10	.965
1978—Atlanta§	Nat.		OF	129	474	75	135	20	5	18	62	.285	238	10	8	.969
1979—Atlanta	Nat.		OF	156	631	97	192	34	5	27	90	.304	292	12	8	.974
1980—Atlanta x	Nat.		OF	155	571	79	159	17	3	19	75	.278	258	8	●11	.960
1981—Philadelphia	Nat.		OF	101	359	62	108	21	3	9	67	.301	170	11	7	.963
1982—Philadelphia	Nat.		OF	●162	616	89	173	31	1	19	83	.281	268	14	10	.966
1983—Philadelphia	Nat.		OF	132	446	66	115	18	2	10	50	.258	174	11	5	.974
Major League Totals				1577	5827	875	1663	266	48	183	787	.285	2744	116	89	.970

Selected by San Francisco Giants' organization in 1st round (17th player selected) of free-agent draft, June 7, 1968.
†On disabled list, June 5 to July 18, 1975.
‡Granted free agency, November 1, 1976; signed by Atlanta Braves, November 17, 1976.
§On disabled list, April 15 to May 2, 1978.
xTraded to Philadelphia Phillies for Pitcher Bob Walk, March 25, 1981.

DIVISION SERIES RECORD

Year	Club	League	Pos.	G.	AB.	R.	H.	2B.	3B.	HR.	RBI.	B.A.	PO.	A.	E.	F.A.
1981—Philadelphia	Nat.		OF	5	20	3	8	0	1	1	1	.400	6	0	0	1.000

CHAMPIONSHIP SERIES RECORD
Tied Championship Series record for most runs batted in, four-game Series (8), 1983.

Year	Club	League	Pos.	G.	AB.	R.	H.	2B.	3B.	HR.	RBI.	B.A.	PO.	A.	E.	F.A.
1983—Philadelphia	Nat.		OF	4	14	4	6	0	0	3	8	.429	6	0	0	1.000

WORLD SERIES RECORD

Year	Club	League	Pos.	G.	AB.	R.	H.	2B.	3B.	HR.	RBI.	B.A.	PO.	A.	E.	F.A.
1983—Philadelphia	Nat.		OF	5	16	1	4	0	0	1	1	.250	15	0	0	1.000

ALL-STAR GAME RECORD

Year	League	Pos.	AB.	R.	H.	2B.	3B.	HR.	RBI.	B.A.	PO.	A.	E.	F.A.
1979—National		OF	2	0	0	0	0	0	0	.000	2	0	0	1.000

DONALD ARTHUR MATTINGLY
(Don)

Born April 20, 1961, at Evansville, Ind.
Height, 5.11. Weight, 185.
Throws and bats lefthanded.

Led South Atlantic League in sacrifice flies with 12 in 1980.
Named South Atlantic League Most Valuable Player, 1980.

Year	Club	League	Pos.	G.	AB.	R.	H.	2B.	3B.	HR.	RBI.	B.A.	PO.	A.	E.	F.A.
1979—Oneonta	NYP		OF-1B	53	166	20	58	10	2	3	31	.349	29	2	2	.939
1980—Greensboro	S. Atl.		OF-1B	133	494	92	★177	32	5	9	105	★.358	205	16	8	.976
1981—Nashville	South.		OF-1B	141	547	74	173	35	4	7	98	.316	846	69	12	.987
1982—Columbus	Int.		OF-1B	130	476	67	150	24	2	10	75	.315	271	17	5	.983
1982—New York	Amer.		OF-1B	7	12	0	2	0	0	0	1	.167	15	1	0	1.000
1983—New York	Amer.		OF-1B-2B	91	279	34	79	15	4	4	32	.283	350	15	3	.992
1983—Columbus	Int.		1B-OF	43	159	35	54	11	3	8	37	.340	325	29	1	.997
Major League Totals				98	291	34	81	15	4	4	33	.278	365	16	3	.992

Selected by New York Yankees' organization in 19th round of free-agent draft, June 5, 1979.

LEONARD JAMES MATUSZEK
Named pronounced Mu-TU-zek.
(Len)

Born September 27, 1954, at Toledo, O.
Height, 6.02. Weight, 190.
Throws right and bats lefthanded.
Attended University of Toledo, Toledo, O.

Led American Association in intentional bases on balls received with 22 in 1981.

Year	Club	League	Pos.	G.	AB.	R.	H.	2B.	3B.	HR.	RBI.	B.A.	PO.	A.	E.	F.A.
1976—Peninsula	Carol.		1B	47	166	23	46	9	1	3	21	.277	426	34	1	.998
1977—Peninsula	Carol.		1B	122	410	56	94	18	4	10	56	.229	1051	74	12	★.989
1978—Reading†	East.		1B-3B	92	294	41	80	16	4	5	36	.272	556	85	13	.980
1979—Reading	East.		1B-3B	32	108	19	31	9	4	3	16	.287	145	42	5	.974
1979—Oklahoma City	A. A.		1B-3B	72	228	31	60	9	3	4	31	.263	421	55	10	.979
1980—Oklahoma City‡	A. A.		1B-3B	67	256	38	78	16	5	7	35	.305	580	55	6	.991
1981—Oklahoma City	A. A.		★1B-3B	129	463	87	146	27	2	21	91	.315	1146	101	6	★.995
1981—Philadelphia	Nat.		1B-3B	13	11	1	3	1	0	0	1	.273	5	4	0	1.000
1982—Philadelphia§	Nat.		3B-1B	25	39	1	3	1	0	0	3	.077	12	8	3	.870
1982—Oklahoma City	A. A.		1B	67	231	41	67	16	4	7	46	.290	560	59	8	.987

Year Club	League	Pos.	G.	AB.	R.	H.	2B.	3B.	HR.	RBI.	B.A.	PO.	A.	E.	F.A.
1983—Philadelphia	Nat.	1B	28	80	12	22	6	1	4	16	.275	144	9	0	1.000
1983—Portland.................	P. C.	1B-OF	113	412	82	136	28	6	24	92	.330	811	67	10	.989
Major League Totals....................................			66	130	14	28	8	1	4	20	.215	161	21	3	.984

Selected by Philadelphia Phillies' organization in 5th round of free-agent draft, June 8, 1976.
†On disabled list, June 23 to July 26, 1978.
‡On disabled list, April 14 to May 16 and May 17 to June 21, 1980.
§On supplemental disabled list, April 29 to May 15, 1982

MILTON SCOTT MAY
(Milt)

Born August 1, 1950, at Gary, Ind.
Height, 6.00.   Weight, 192.
Throws right and bats lefthanded.
Attended Manatee Junior College, West Bradenton, Fla.
Son of Merrill (Pinky) May, third baseman with Philadelphia Phillies, 1939 through
1943; minor league manager, 1947 through 1972.
Tied for American League lead in double plays by catchers with 12 in 1977.
Led Western Carolinas League catchers in assists with 62 and double plays with 10 in 1969.
Tied for Western Carolinas League lead in sacrifice flies with 7 in 1969.
Tied for International League lead in passed balls with 10 in 1970.

Year Club	League	Pos.	G.	AB.	R.	H.	2B.	3B.	HR.	RBI.	B.A.	PO.	A.	E.	F.A.
1968—Bradenton Pir.	Gulf C.	C	52	166	21	40	4	0	0	23	.241	★337	31	★13	.966
1969—Gastonia†	W. Caro.	C-1B	86	301	58	87	17	2	11	57	.289	485	63	11	.980
1970—Columbus..............	Int.	C	111	397	49	111	14	3	21	86	.280	688	★68	15	.981
1970—Pittsburgh	Nat.	PH	5	4	1	2	1	0	0	2	.500	0	0	0	.000
1971—Pittsburgh‡	Nat.	C	49	126	15	35	1	0	6	25	.278	168	12	0	1.000
1972—Pittsburgh§	Nat.	C	57	139	12	39	10	0	0	14	.281	179	21	3	.985
1973—Pittsburgh x	Nat.	C	101	283	29	76	8	1	7	31	.269	402	36	12	.973
1974—Houston	Nat.	C	127	405	47	117	17	4	7	54	.289	568	★70	9	★.993
1975—Houston y..............	Nat.	C	111	386	29	93	15	1	4	52	.241	568	★70	9	.986
1976—Detroit z................	Amer.	C	6	25	2	7	1	0	0	1	.280	33	5	0	1.000
1977—Detroit.................	Amer.	C	115	397	32	99	9	3	12	46	.249	551	78	9	.986
1978—Detroit...................	Amer.	C	105	352	24	88	9	0	10	37	.250	406	58	10	.979
1979—Det. a-Chi. b	Amer.	C	71	213	24	54	15	0	7	31	.254	296	28	6	.982
1980—San Fran. c..........	Nat.	C	111	358	27	93	16	2	6	50	.260	500	59	8	.986
1981—San Francisco	Nat.	C	97	316	20	98	17	0	2	33	.310	468	48	6	.989
1982—San Francisco	Nat.	C	114	395	29	104	19	0	9	39	.263	552	61	8	.987
1983—S.F. de - Pitt.	Nat.	C	73	198	18	49	6	0	6	20	.247	308	35	6	.983
National League Totals..............................			845	2610	227	706	110	8	47	320	.270	3670	405	56	.986
American League Totals............................			297	987	82	248	34	3	29	115	.251	1286	169	25	.983
Major League Totals..................................			1142	3597	309	954	144	11	76	435	.265	4956	574	81	.986

Selected by Pittsburgh Pirates' organization in 17th round of free-agent draft, June 7, 1968.
†On temporary inactive list, April 13 to April 25 and August 16 to September 30, 1969.
‡On military list, July 25 to August 8, 1971.
§On military list, July 15 to July 29, 1972.
xTraded to Houston Astros for Pitcher Jerry Reuss, October 31, 1973.
yTraded with Pitchers Dave Roberts and Jim Crawford to Detroit Tigers for Outfielder Leon Roberts, Catcher Terry Humphrey and Pitchers Gene Pentz and Mark Lemongello, December 6, 1975.
zOn disabled list, April 21 to September 3, 1976.
aSold to Chicago White Sox, May 27, 1979.
bGranted free agency, November 1, 1979; signed by San Francisco Giants, December 12, 1979.
cOn supplemental disabled list, July 31 to August 16, 1980.
dOn supplemental disabled list, March 27 to April 11, 1983.
eTraded with cash to Pittsburgh Pirates for Catcher Steve Nicosia, August 19, 1983.

CHAMPIONSHIP SERIES RECORD

Year Club	League	Pos.	G.	AB.	R.	H.	2B.	3B.	HR.	RBI.	B.A.	PO.	A.	E.	F.A.
1971—Pittsburgh	Nat.	PH	1	1	0	0	0	0	0	0	.000	0	0	0	.000
1972—Pittsburgh	Nat.	C	1	2	0	1	0	0	0	1	.500	8	1	0	1.000
Championship Series Totals			2	3	0	1	0	0	0	1	.333	8	1	0	1.000

WORLD SERIES RECORD

Year Club	League	Pos.	G.	AB.	R.	H.	2B.	3B.	HR.	RBI.	B.A.	PO.	A.	E.	F.A.
1971—Pittsburgh	Nat.	PH	2	2	0	1	0	0	0	1	.500	0	0	0	.000

RUDOLPH MAY JR.
(Rudy)

Born July 18, 1944, at Coffeyville, Kan.
Height, 6.02.   Weight, 195.
Throws and bats lefthanded.
Attended San Francisco State College, San Francisco, Calif.
Led American League in balks with 3 in 1973.
Led Northern League in wild pitches with 25 in 1963.
Tied for Carolina League lead in shutouts with 4 in 1964.

Year—Club	League	G.	IP.	W.	L.	Pct.	H.	R.	ER.	SO.	BB.	ERA.
1963—Bismarck-Mandan†	Northern	24	168	11	11	.500	142	100	●80	173	⋆120	4.29
1964—Tidewater	Carolina	20	155	13	6	.684	107	52	44	187	98	2.55
1964—Indianapolis‡§	P. Coast	10	52	4	2	.667	39	20	16	48	38	2.77
1965—California	American	30	124	4	9	.308	111	59	54	76	78	3.92
1966—Seattle	P. Coast	7	30	3	1	.750	36	18	17	12	15	5.10
1966—El Paso x	Texas	2	5	0	0	.000	4	2	2	4	7	3.60
1967—San Jose	California	14	84	7	2	.778	62	33	29	51	40	3.11
1968—El Paso	Texas	22	129	8	7	.533	133	71	64	112	39	4.47
1969—California	American	43	180	10	13	.435	142	81	69	133	66	3.45
1970—California y	American	38	209	7	13	.350	190	102	93	164	81	4.00
1971—California z	American	32	208	11	12	.478	160	74	70	156	87	3.03
1972—California	American	35	205	12	11	.522	162	79	67	169	82	2.94
1973—California	American	34	185	7	17	.292	177	101	90	134	80	4.38
1974—Calif. a-N.Y. b	American	35	141	8	5	.615	104	60	50	102	58	3.19
1975—New York	American	32	212	14	12	.538	179	87	72	145	99	3.06
1976—New York c-Baltimore	American	35	220	15	10	.600	205	105	91	109	70	3.72
1977—Baltimore d	American	37	252	18	14	.563	243	114	101	105	78	3.61
1978—Montreal e	National	27	144	8	10	.444	141	73	62	87	42	3.88
1979—Montreal f	National	33	94	10	3	.769	88	30	24	67	31	2.30
1980—New York g	American	41	175	15	5	.750	144	56	48	133	39	⋆2.47
1981—New York	American	27	148	6	11	.353	137	71	68	79	41	4.14
1982—New York h	American	41	106	6	6	.500	109	43	34	85	14	2.89
1982—Columbus	Int'national	1	3⅔	0	0	.000	1	2	2	5	4	4.91
1983—New York i	American	15	18⅓	1	5	.167	22	15	14	16	12	6.87
1983—Columbus	Int'national	4	7⅓	0	0	.000	5	2	2	6	3	2.45
American League Totals		475	2383⅓	134	143	.484	2085	1047	921	1606	885	3.48
National League Totals		60	238	18	13	.581	229	103	86	154	73	3.25
Major League Totals		535	2621⅓	152	156	.494	2314	1150	1007	1760	958	3.46

Signed as free agent by Minnesota Twins' organization, November 5, 1962.

†Drafted by Chicago White Sox, December 2, 1963.

‡Traded to Philadelphia Phillies for Catcher Bill Heath and a player to be named later, October 15, 1964; Chicago White Sox acquired Pitcher Joel Gibson to complete deal, November 23, 1964.

§Traded by Philadelphia Phillies to Los Angeles Angels with First Baseman Costen Shockley for Pitcher Robert (Bo) Belinsky, December 3, 1964.

xOn disabled list, June 4, 1966 through remainder of season.

yOn military list, July 10 to July 27, 1970.

zOn disabled list, May 25 to June 17, 1971.

aSold to New York Yankees, June 15, 1974.

bOn disabled list, July 11 to August 1, 1974.

cTraded with Pitchers Felix Martinez, Dave Pagan and Scott McGregor and Catcher Rick Dempsey to Baltimore Orioles for Pitchers Ken Holtzman, Doyle Alexander and Grant Jackson, Catcher Ellie Hendricks, and Pitcher Jimmy Freeman, June 15, 1976.

dTraded with Pitchers Randy Miller and Bryn Smith to Montreal Expos for Pitchers Don Stanhouse and Joe Kerrigan and Outfielder Gary Roenicke, December 7, 1977.

eOn disabled list, July 20 to September 1, 1978.

fGranted free agency, November 1, 1979; signed by New York Yankees, November 8, 1979.

gOn disabled list, April 1 to April 22, 1980.

hOn disabled list, June 4 to June 27, 1982; included rehabilitation disability assignment to Columbus, June 22 to June 27, 1982.

iOn disabled list, June 19 to September 3, 1983; included rehabilitation disability assignment to Columbus, August 25 to September 3, 1983.

DIVISION SERIES RECORD

Year—Club	League	G.	IP.	W.	L.	Pct.	H.	R.	ER.	SO.	BB.	ERA.
1981—New York	American	1	2	0	0	.000	1	0	0	1	0	0.00

CHAMPIONSHIP SERIES RECORD

Year—Club	League	G.	IP.	W.	L.	Pct.	H.	R.	ER.	SO.	BB.	ERA.
1980—New York	American	1	8	0	1	.000	6	3	3	4	3	3.38
1981—New York	American	1	3⅓	0	0	.000	6	3	3	5	0	8.10
Championship Series Totals		2	11⅓	0	1	.000	12	6	6	9	3	4.76

WORLD SERIES RECORD

Year—Club	League	G.	IP.	W.	L.	Pct.	H.	R.	ER.	SO.	BB.	ERA.
1981—New York	American	3	6⅓	0	0	.000	5	2	2	5	1	2.84

LEE LOUIS MAZZILLI

Born March 25, 1955, at Brooklyn, N.Y.

Height, 6.01. Weight, 180.

Throws right and bats left and righthanded.

Son of Libero Mazzilli, former professional welterweight boxer.

Major League stolen bases: 1976 (5), 1977 (22), 1978 (20), 1979 (34), 1980 (41), 1981 (17), 1982 (13), 1983 (15). Total—167.

Led Texas League in bases on balls received with 111, caught stealing with 15 and tied for lead in being hit by pitch with 7 in 1976.

Led California League in caught stealing with 16 in 1975.

Received reported $50,000 bonus to sign with New York Mets, 1973.

Year—Club	League	Pos.	G.	AB.	R.	H.	2B.	3B.	HR.	RBI.	B.A.	PO.	A.	E.	F.A.
1974—Anderson	W. Car.	OF	132	472	82	127	24	3	11	48	.269	227	9	9	.963
1975—Visalia	Calif.	OF-1B	125	430	103	121	10	4	13	52	.281	185	9	9	.956
1976—Jackson	Texas	OF	131	439	91	128	21	6	13	43	.292	262	8	8	.971
1976—New York	Nat.	OF	24	77	9	15	2	0	2	7	.195	55	2	1	.983
1977—New York	Nat.	OF	159	537	66	134	24	3	6	46	.250	386	9	3	.992
1978—New York	Nat.	OF	148	542	78	148	28	5	16	61	.273	386	8	5	.987
1979—New York	Nat.	OF-1B	158	597	78	181	34	4	15	79	.303	480	24	5	.990
1980—New York	Nat.	1B-OF	152	578	82	162	31	4	16	76	.280	874	53	14	.985
1981—New York†	Nat.	OF	95	324	36	74	14	5	6	34	.228	192	5	6	.970
1982—Tex.‡§-N.Y. x	Amer.	OF-1B	95	323	43	81	10	0	10	34	.251	234	8	4	.984
1983—Pittsburgh	Nat.	OF-1B	109	246	37	59	9	0	5	24	.240	173	3	4	.978
National League Totals			845	2901	386	773	142	21	66	327	.266	2546	104	38	.986
American League Totals			95	323	43	81	10	0	10	34	.251	234	8	4	.984
Major League Totals			940	3224	429	854	152	21	76	361	.265	2780	112	42	.986

Selected by New York Mets' organization in 1st round (14th player selected) of free-agent draft, June 5, 1973.

†Traded to Texas Rangers for Pitchers Ron Darling and Walt Terrell, April 1, 1982.

‡On disabled list, May 20 to June 29, 1982.

§Traded to New York Yankees for Shortstop Bucky Dent, August 8, 1982.

xTraded to Pittsburgh Pirates for Outfielder Don Aubin, Pitcher Tim Burke, Catcher John Holland and Infielder Jose Rivera, December 22, 1982.

ALL-STAR GAME RECORD

Tied All-Star Game record for most home runs by pinch-hitter, game (1), July 17, 1979.

Year—League		Pos.	AB.	R.	H.	2B.	3B.	HR.	RBI.	B.A.	PO.	A.	E.	F.A.
1979—National		PH-OF	1	1	1	0	0	1	2	1.000	0	0	0	.000

ARNOLD RAY McBRIDE
(Bake)

Born February 3, 1949, at Fulton, Mo.
Height, 6.02. Weight, 184.
Throws right and bats lefthanded.
Received bachelor of arts degree in physical education from
Westminster College, Fulton, Mo.

Tied modern National League record for most chances accepted by right fielder, game (10), September 8, 1978.

Major League stolen bases: 1974 (30), 1975 (26), 1976 (10), 1977 (36), 1978 (28), 1979 (25), 1980 (13), 1981 (5), 1982 (2), 1983 (8). Total—183.

Named National League Rookie of the Year by Baseball Writers' Association of America, 1974.

Year—Club	League	Pos.	G.	AB.	R.	H.	2B.	3B.	HR.	RBI.	B.A.	PO.	A.	E.	F.A.
1970—Sarasota Cards	Gulf C.	OF	17	71	15	30	2	4	2	13	.423	27	1	0	1.000
1970—Modesto	Calif.	OF	26	85	17	25	4	2	0	7	.294	26	1	4	.871
1971—Modesto	Calif.	OF	118	468	85	142	19	5	8	54	.303	181	9	6	.969
1972—Arkansas	Texas	OF	67	286	51	94	10	4	12	34	.329	130	3	3	.978
1972—Tulsa	A. A.	OF	60	232	41	73	14	5	5	24	.315	108	5	1	.991
1973—Tulsa	A. A.	OF	58	225	45	65	15	2	6	34	.289	111	7	3	.975
1973—St. Louis	Nat.	OF	40	63	8	19	3	0	0	5	.302	39	1	1	.976
1974—St. Louis	Nat.	OF	150	559	81	173	19	5	6	56	.309	395	9	4	.990
1975—St. Louis†	Nat.	OF	116	413	70	124	10	9	5	36	.300	289	4	3	.990
1976—St. Louis‡	Nat.	OF	72	272	40	91	13	4	3	24	.335	201	5	4	.981
1977—St.L.§-Phil.	Nat.	OF	128	402	76	127	25	6	15	61	.316	188	8	2	.990
1978—Philadelphia	Nat.	OF	122	472	68	127	20	4	10	49	.269	234	8	1	*.996
1979—Philadelphia	Nat.	OF	151	582	82	163	16	12	12	60	.280	341	12	4	.989
1980—Philadelphia	Nat.	OF	137	554	68	171	33	10	9	87	.309	282	6	3	.990
1981—Philadelphia xy	Nat.	OF	58	221	26	60	17	1	2	21	.271	76	2	1	.987
1982—Cleveland z	Amer.	OF	27	85	8	31	3	3	0	13	.365	37	0	0	1.000
1983—Cleveland ab	Amer.	OF	70	230	21	67	8	1	1	18	.291	81	4	2	.977
National League Totals			974	3538	519	1055	156	51	62	399	.298	2045	55	23	.989
American League Totals			97	315	29	98	11	4	1	31	.311	118	4	2	.984
Major League Totals			1071	3853	548	1153	167	55	63	430	.299	2163	59	25	.989

Selected by St. Louis Cardinals' organization in 37th round of free-agent draft, June 4, 1970.

†On supplemental disabled list, May 13 to June 4, 1975.

‡On disabled list, May 9 to May 24 and August 7, 1976, through remainder of season.

§Traded to Philadelphia Phillies with Pitcher Steve Waterbury for Pitcher Tom Underwood, First Baseman Dane Iorg, and Outfielder Rick Bosetti, June 15, 1977.

xOn disabled list, May 24 to August 7, 1981.

yTraded to Cleveland Indians for Pitcher Sid Monge, February 16, 1982.

zOn supplemental disabled list, June 12, 1982; transferred to disabled list, July 16, 1982 through remainder of season.

aOn supplemental disabled list, June 17 to July 24 and August 16 to August 31, 1983.

bGranted free agency, November 7, 1983.

DIVISION SERIES RECORD

Year—Club	League	Pos.	G.	AB.	R.	H.	2B.	3B.	HR.	RBI.	B.A.	PO.	A.	E.	F.A.
1981—Philadelphia	Nat.	OF	4	15	1	3	1	0	0	0	.200	6	0	0	1.000

CHAMPIONSHIP SERIES RECORD

Tied Championship Series records for most home runs by pinch hitter, game, Series and total Series (1), October 7, 1978.

Year	Club	League	Pos.	G.	AB.	R.	H.	2B.	3B.	HR.	RBI.	B.A.	PO.	A.	E.	F.A.
1977—Philadelphia	....	Nat.	OF	4	18	2	4	0	0	1	2	.222	6	2	0	1.000
1978—Philadelphia	....	Nat.	OF-PH	3	9	2	2	0	0	1	1	.222	1	0	0	1.000
1980—Philadelphia	....	Nat.	OF	5	21	0	5	0	0	0	0	.238	11	3	1	.933
Championship Series Totals	....			12	48	4	11	0	0	2	3	.229	18	5	1	.958

WORLD SERIES RECORD

Year	Club	League	Pos.	G.	AB.	R.	H.	2B.	3B.	HR.	RBI.	B.A.	PO.	A.	E.	F.A.
1980—Philadelphia	....	Nat.	OF	6	23	3	7	1	0	1	5	.304	13	1	0	1.000

ALL-STAR GAME RECORD

Member of National League All-Star Team in 1976; did not play.

KIRK EDWARD McCASKILL

Born April 9, 1961, at Burlington, Vt.
Height, 6.01. Weight, 195.
Throws and bats righthanded.
Attended University of Vermont, Burlington, Vt.
Drafted by Winnipeg Jets in 1981 NHL entry draft (fourth Jets pick, 64th overall, fourth round).

Year	Club	League	G.	IP.	W.	L.	Pct.	H.	R.	ER.	SO.	BB.	ERA.
1982—Salem	....	Northwest	11	71⅓	5	5	.500	63	43	34	87	51	4.29
1983—Redwood	....	California	16	108⅓	6	5	.545	78	39	28	100	60	2.33
1983—Nashua	....	Eastern	13	87	4	8	.333	90	47	43	63	43	4.45

Selected by California Angels' organization in 4th round of free-agent draft, June 7, 1982.

STEVEN EARL McCATTY
(Steve)

Born March 20, 1954, at Detroit, Mich.
Height, 6.03. Weight, 205.
Throws and bats righthanded.
Attended Macomb Community College, Warren, Mich.
Tied for American League lead in shutouts with 4 in 1981.

Year	Club	League	G.	IP.	W.	L.	Pct.	H.	R.	ER.	SO.	BB.	ERA.
1973—Lewiston	....	Northwest	19	70	2	2	.500	83	48	37	49	31	4.76
1974—Lewiston	....	Northwest	15	96	8	3	.727	99	58	35	62	42	3.28
1975—Modesto	....	California	37	126	4	8	.333	138	80	64	75	54	4.57
1976—Chattanooga	....	Southern	36	77	5	4	.556	73	44	27	40	31	3.16
1976—Tucson	....	P. Coast	5	10	1	1	.500	13	8	7	5	7	6.30
1977—Chattanooga	....	Southern	14	56	4	2	.667	46	14	12	39	10	1.93
1977—San Jose	....	P. Coast	23	146	7	8	.467	175	105	93	78	69	5.73
1977—Oakland	....	American	4	14	0	0	.000	16	9	8	9	7	5.14
1978—Vancouver†	....	P. Coast	39	55	7	4	.636	53	23	19	51	23	3.11
1978—Oakland	....	American	9	20	0	0	.000	26	14	10	10	9	4.50
1979—Ogden	....	P. Coast	8	20	1	1	.500	12	7	7	16	18	3.15
1979—Oakland	....	American	31	186	11	12	.478	207	106	87	87	80	4.21
1980—Oakland	....	American	33	222	14	14	.500	202	104	95	114	99	3.85
1981—Oakland	....	American	22	186	●14	7	.667	140	50	48	91	61	★2.32
1982—Oakland‡	....	American	21	128⅔	6	3	.667	124	62	57	66	70	3.99
1983—Oakland§	....	American	38	167	6	9	.400	156	79	74	65	82	3.99
Major League Totals	....		158	923⅔	51	45	.531	871	424	379	442	408	3.69

Signed as free agent by Oakland A's organization, June 24, 1973.
†Appeared as outfielder with no chances.
‡On disabled list, June 4 to June 25, 1982.
§Appeared in one game as a pinch-runner.

DIVISION SERIES RECORD

Year	Club	League	G.	IP.	W.	L.	Pct.	H.	R.	ER.	SO.	BB.	ERA.
1981—Oakland	....	American	1	9	1	0	1.000	6	1	1	3	4	1.00

CHAMPIONSHIP SERIES RECORD

Year	Club	League	G.	IP.	W.	L.	Pct.	H.	R.	ER.	SO.	BB.	ERA.
1981—Oakland	....	American	1	3⅓	0	1	.000	6	5	5	2	2	13.50

ROBERT CRAIG McCLURE
(Bob)

Born April 29, 1952, at Oakland, Calif.
Height, 5.11. Weight, 170.
Throws left and bats righthanded.
Attended College of San Mateo, San Mateo, Calif.
Led American League in balks with 6 in 1983.
Tied for Pioneer League lead in shutouts with 3 in 1973.

Year Club	League	G.	IP.	W.	L.	Pct.	H.	R.	ER.	SO.	BB.	ERA.
1973—Billings	Pioneer	14	94	*10	2	.833	64	41	22	110	67	2.11
1974—Omaha	Am. Assoc.	21	136	5	8	.385	140	71	58	88	65	3.84
1975—Jacksonville†	Southern	9	42	3	2	.600	31	18	11	39	23	2.36
1975—Kansas City	American	12	15	1	0	1.000	4	0	0	15	14	0.00
1976—Omaha	Am. Assoc.	21	133	9	8	.529	133	61	44	91	41	2.98
1976—Kansas City‡	American	8	4	0	0	.000	3	4	4	3	8	9.00
1977—Milwaukee	American	68	71	2	1	.667	64	25	20	57	34	2.54
1978—Milwaukee	American	44	65	2	6	.250	53	30	27	47	30	3.74
1979—Milwaukee	American	36	51	5	2	.714	53	29	22	37	24	3.88
1980—Milwaukee	American	52	91	5	8	.385	83	34	31	47	37	3.07
1981—Burlington	Midwest	4	14	0	2	.000	19	15	15	11	11	9.64
1981—Milwaukee§	American	4	8	0	0	.000	7	3	3	6	4	3.38
1982—Milwaukee x	American	34	172⅔	12	7	.632	160	90	81	99	74	4.22
1983—Milwaukee y	American	24	142	9	9	.500	152	75	71	68	68	4.50
Major League Totals		282	619⅔	36	33	.522	579	290	259	379	293	3.76

Selected by Los Angeles Dodgers' organization in 3rd round of free-agent draft, January 10, 1973.

Selected by Kansas City Royals' organization in secondary phase of free-agent draft, June 5, 1973.

†On disabled list, April 15 to May 13 and June 5 to July 25, 1975.

‡Traded to Milwaukee Brewers, March 15, 1977; completing deal in which Kansas City Royals traded Infielder Jamie Quirk, Outfielder Jim Wohlford and a player to be named later to Milwaukee for Pitcher Jim Colborn and Catcher Darrell Porter, December 6, 1976.

§On disabled list, March 28 to September 1, 1981; included rehabilitation disability assignment to Burlington, August 7 to August 24, 1981.

xGranted free agency, November 10, 1982; re-signed by Brewers, December 6, 1982.

yOn disabled list, August 22 to September 12, 1983.

DIVISION SERIES RECORD

Year Club	League	G.	IP.	W.	L.	Pct.	H.	R.	ER.	SO.	BB.	ERA.
1981—Milwaukee	American	3	3⅓	0	0	.000	4	0	0	2	0	0.00

CHAMPIONSHIP SERIES RECORD

Year Club	League	G.	IP.	W.	L.	Pct.	H.	R.	ER.	SO.	BB.	ERA.
1982—Milwaukee	American	1	1⅔	1	0	1.000	2	0	0	0	0	0.00

WORLD SERIES RECORD

Tied World Series record for most games lost, seven-game Series (2), 1982.

Year Club	League	G.	IP.	W.	L.	Pct.	H.	R.	ER.	SO.	BB.	ERA.
1982—Milwaukee	American	5	4⅓	0	2	.000	5	2	2	5	3	4.15

ANDREW JOSEPH McGAFFIGAN
(Andy)

Born October 25, 1956, at West Palm Beach, Fla.
Height, 6.03. Weight, 185.
Throws and bats righthanded.
Attended Palm Beach Junior College, Lake Worth, Fla., and
Florida Southern College, Lakeland, Fla.

Named Southern League Pitcher of the Year, 1980.

Year Club	League	G.	IP.	W.	L.	Pct.	H.	R.	ER.	SO.	BB.	ERA.
1978—Oneonta	NYP	2	12	0	1	.000	14	8	6	13	9	4.50
1978—Ft. Lauderdale	Florida St.	11	66	4	5	.444	45	28	21	36	20	2.86
1979—West Haven	Eastern	23	144	10	6	.625	136	75	61	113	54	3.81
1980—Nashville†	Southern	31	170	15	5	.750	139	62	45	125	62	*2.38
1981—Columbus‡	Int'national	17	103	8	6	.571	85	45	37	57	37	3.23
1981—New York§	American	2	7	0	0	.000	5	3	2	2	3	2.57
1982—Phoenix x	P. Coast	18	96	1	6	.143	115	72	64	64	51	6.00
1982—San Francisco	National	4	8	1	0	1.000	5	1	0	4	1	0.00
1983—San Francisco	National	43	134⅓	3	9	.250	131	67	64	93	39	4.29
American League Totals		2	7	0	0	.000	5	3	2	2	3	2.57
National League Totals		47	142⅓	4	9	.308	136	68	64	97	40	4.05
Major League Totals		49	149⅓	4	9	.308	141	71	66	99	43	3.98

Selected by Cincinnati Reds' organization in 36th round of free-agent draft, June 5, 1974.

Selected by Chicago White Sox' organization in 5th round of free-agent draft, January 7, 1976.

Selected by New York Yankees' organization in 6th round of free-agent draft, June 6, 1978.

†On disabled list, September 1 to September 22, 1980.

‡On disabled list, April 10 to June 14, 1981.

§Traded with Outfielder Ted Wilborn to San Francisco Giants' organization for Pitcher Doyle Alexander, March 30, 1982.

xOn disabled list, June 20 to August 13, 1982.

WILLIE DEAN McGEE

Born November 2, 1958, at San Francisco, Calif.
Height, 6.01. Weight, 176.
Throws right and bats right and lefthanded.
Attended Diablo Valley College, Pleasant Hill, Calif.

Major League stolen bases: 1982 (24), 1983 (39). Total—63.

Named outfielder on THE SPORTING NEWS National League All-Star fielding team, 1983.

Year Club	League	Pos.	G.	AB.	R.	H.	2B.	3B.	HR.	RBI.	B.A.	PO.	A.	E.	F.A.
1977—Oneonta	NYP	OF	65	225	31	53	4	3	2	22	.236	103	5	10	.915
1978—Ft. Lauderdale	Fla. St.	OF	124	423	62	106	6	6	0	37	.251	243	12	9	.966
1979—West Haven	East.	OF	49	115	21	28	3	1	1	8	.243	88	3	3	.968
1979—Ft. Lauderdale	Fla. St.	OF	46	176	25	56	8	3	1	18	.318	103	3	2	.981
1980—Nashville†	South.	OF	78	223	35	63	4	5	1	22	.283	127	6	6	.957
1981—Nashville‡§	South.	OF	100	388	77	125	20	5	7	63	.322	203	10	6	.973
1982—Louisville x	A. A.	OF	13	55	11	16	2	2	1	3	.291	40	0	1	.976
1982—St. Louis	Nat.	OF	123	422	43	125	12	8	4	56	.296	245	3	11	.958
1983—St. Louis y	Nat.	OF	147	601	75	172	22	8	5	75	.286	385	7	5	.987
1983—Arkansas	Texas	OF	7	29	5	8	1	1	0	2	.276	7	0	0	1.000
Major League Totals			270	1023	118	297	34	16	9	131	.290	630	10	16	.976

Selected by Chicago White Sox' organization in 7th round of free-agent draft, June 8, 1976.
Selected by New York Yankees' organization in secondary phase of free-agent draft, January 11, 1977.
†On disabled list, May 22 to June 7 and July 14 to August 7, 1980.
‡On disabled list, April 24 to June 4, 1981.
§Traded to St. Louis Cardinals' organization for Pitcher Bob Sykes, October 21, 1981.
xOn disabled list, April 13 to April 23, 1982.
yOn supplemental disabled list, March 30 to April 29, 1983; included rehabilitation disability assignment to Arkansas, April 18 to April 29, 1983.

CHAMPIONSHIP SERIES RECORD

Tied Championship Series record for most three-base hits, Series (2), 1982.
Tied National League Championship Series record for most three-base hits, total Series (2).

Year Club	League	Pos.	G.	AB.	R.	H.	2B.	3B.	HR.	RBI.	B.A.	PO.	A.	E.	F.A.
1982—St. Louis	Nat.	OF	3	13	4	4	0	2	1	5	.308	12	0	1	.923

WORLD SERIES RECORD

Tied World Series records for most home runs, game, by rookie (2), October 15, 1982; highest fielding average by outfielder, seven-game Series (1,000 with 24 chances), 1982; most putouts by outfielder, seven-game Series (24), 1982.

Year Club	League	Pos.	G.	AB.	R.	H.	2B.	3B.	HR.	RBI.	B.A.	PO.	A.	E.	F.A.
1982—St. Louis	Nat.	OF	6	25	6	6	0	0	2	5	.240	24	0	0	1.000

ALL-STAR GAME RECORD

Year League	Pos.	AB.	R.	H.	2B.	3B.	HR.	RBI.	B.A.	PO.	A.	E.	F.A.
1983—National	OF	2	0	1	0	0	0	0	.500	2	0	0	1.000

FRANK EDWIN McGRAW, JR.
(Tug)
(Named by parents because he tugged on so many things as a baby.)

Born August 30, 1944, at Martinez, Calif.
Height, 6.00. Weight, 180.
Throws left and bats righthanded.
Attended Vallejo Junior College, Vallejo, Calif.
Brother of Hank McGraw, minor league outfielder-catcher, 1961 through 1972.

Tied major league record for most home runs allowed, bases filled, season (4), 1979.
Pitched seven-inning 4-0 no-hit victory against Cocoa, July 3, 1964.
Established National League record for most innings pitched by relief pitcher, lifetime (1,264⅔).
Major League saves: 1969 (12), 1970 (10), 1971 (8), 1972 (27), 1973 (25), 1974 (3), 1975 (14), 1976 (11), 1977 (9), 1978 (9), 1979 (16), 1980 (20), 1981 (10), 1982 (5). Total—179.
Led International League in balks with 4 in 1967.

Year Club	League	G.	IP.	W.	L.	Pct.	H.	R.	ER.	SO.	BB.	ERA.
1964—Florida Mets	Cocoa Rook.	8	47	5	2	.714	12	11	8	37	52	1.53
1964—Auburn	NYP	3	19	1	2	.333	17	12	4	14	15	1.89
1965—New York	National	37	98	2	7	.222	88	47	36	57	48	3.31
1966—New York	National	15	62	2	9	.182	72	38	37	34	25	5.37
1966—Jacksonville†	Int'national	11	32	2	2	.500	34	16	15	38	9	4.22
1967—Jacksonville	Int'national	22	167	10	9	.526	111	39	37	161	55	⋆1.99
1967—New York	National	4	17	0	3	.000	13	16	15	18	13	7.94
1968—Jacksonville‡§	Int'national	24	166	9	9	.500	149	70	63	132	61	3.42
1969—New York	National	42	100	9	3	.750	89	31	25	92	47	2.25
1970—New York	National	57	91	4	6	.400	77	40	33	81	49	3.26
1971—New York†	National	51	111	11	4	.733	73	22	21	109	41	1.70
1972—New York	National	54	106	8	6	.571	71	26	20	92	40	1.70
1973—New York	National	60	119	5	6	.455	106	53	51	81	55	3.86
1974—New York xy	National	41	89	6	11	.353	96	43	41	54	32	4.15
1975—Philadelphia z	National	56	103	9	6	.600	84	38	34	55	36	2.97
1976—Philadelphia	National	58	97	7	6	.538	81	34	27	76	42	2.51
1977—Philadelphia a	National	45	79	7	3	.700	62	25	23	58	24	2.62
1978—Philadelphia	National	55	90	8	7	.533	82	39	32	63	23	3.20
1979—Philadelphia	National	65	84	4	3	.571	83	56	48	57	29	5.14
1980—Philadelphia bc	National	57	92	5	4	.556	62	16	15	75	23	1.47
1981—Philadelphia	National	34	44	2	4	.333	35	13	13	26	14	2.66
1982—Philadelphia d	National	34	39⅔	3	3	.500	50	19	19	25	12	4.31
1983—Philadelphia	National	34	55⅔	2	1	.667	58	24	22	30	19	3.56
Major League Totals		799	1477⅓	94	92	.505	1282	580	512	1083	572	3.12

Signed as free agent by New York Mets' organization, June 12, 1964.
†On disabled list, May 18 to June 11 and June 28 to July 8, 1966.

‡On disabled list, April 20 to April 30, 1968.
§On temporary inactive list, May 17 to May 20 and July 10 to July 20, 1968.
xOn disabled list, May 16 to June 10, 1974.
yTraded with Outfielders Don Hahn and Dave Schneck to Philadelphia Phillies for Outfielder Del Unser, Pitcher Mac Scarce and Catcher John Stearns, December 3, 1974.
zOn disabled list, March 23 to April 25, 1975.
aOn disabled list, April 20 to June 18, 1977.
bOn disabled list, June 26 to July 17, 1980.
cGranted free agency, November 5, 1980; re-signed by Phillies, December 6, 1980.
dOn disabled list, April 2 to June 21, 1982.

DIVISION SERIES RECORD

Year Club	League	G.	IP.	W.	L.	Pct.	H.	R.	ER.	SO.	BB.	ERA.
1981—Philadelphia	National	2	4	1	0	1.000	2	0	0	2	0	0.00

CHAMPIONSHIP SERIES RECORD

Established Championship Series records for most games pitched, total Series (15); most games as relief pitcher, total Series (15); most saves, total Series (5); most games pitched, five-game Series (5), 1980.
Tied Championship Series records for most Series pitched (6); most saves, five-game Series (2), 1980; most games finished, total Series (9).

Year Club	League	G.	IP.	W.	L.	Pct.	H.	R.	ER.	SO.	BB.	ERA.
1969—New York	National	1	3	0	0	.000	1	0	0	1	1	0.00
1973—New York	National	2	5	0	0	.000	4	0	0	3	3	0.00
1976—Philadelphia	National	2	2⅓	0	0	.000	4	3	3	5	1	11.57
1977—Philadelphia	National	2	3	0	0	.000	1	0	0	3	2	0.00
1978—Philadelphia	National	3	5⅔	0	1	.000	3	2	1	5	5	1.59
1980—Philadelphia	National	5	8	0	1	.000	8	4	4	5	4	4.50
Championship Series Totals		15	27	0	2	.000	21	9	8	22	16	2.67

WORLD SERIES RECORD

Tied World Series record for most saves, six-game Series (2), 1980.

Year Club	League	G.	IP.	W.	L.	Pct.	H.	R.	ER.	SO.	BB.	ERA.
1973—New York	National	5	13⅔	1	0	1.000	8	5	4	14	9	2.63
1980—Philadelphia	National	4	7⅔	1	1	.500	7	1	1	10	8	1.17
World Series Totals		9	21⅓	2	1	.667	15	6	5	24	17	2.11

ALL-STAR GAME RECORD

Year League	IP.	W.	L.	Pct.	H.	R.	ER.	SO.	BB.	ERA.
1972—National	2	1	0	1.000	1	0	0	4	0	0.00

Member of National League All-Star Team for 1975 game; did not play.

SCOTT HOUSTON McGREGOR

Born January 18, 1954, at Inglewood, Calif.
Height, 6.01.   Weight, 190.
Throws left and bats right and lefthanded.
Attended El Camino Junior College, Torrance, Calif. and Loyola Marymount University, Los Angeles, Calif.

Led International League in complete games with 12 and tied for lead in balks with 3 in 1974.
Led Eastern League pitchers in complete games with 14 and tied for lead in games started with 27 in 1973.
Led International League in shutouts with 6 in 1976.
Named International League Pitcher of the Year, 1974.
Received reported $80,000 bonus to sign with New York Yankees, 1972.

Year Club	League	G.	IP.	W.	L.	Pct.	H.	R.	ER.	SO.	BB.	ERA.
1972—Ft. Lauderdale	Florida St.	11	79	7	3	.700	66	30	24	54	25	2.73
1973—West Haven	Eastern	27	★197	●12	●13	.480	★197	95	72	126	63	3.29
1974—Syracuse	Int'national	27	★199	13	10	.565	204	88	76	124	75	3.44
1975—Syracuse†	Int'national	21	124	6	9	.400	134	73	55	72	60	3.99
1976—Syracuse‡-Rochester	Int'national	24	162	12	6	.667	159	59	55	83	40	3.06
1976—Baltimore	American	3	15	0	1	.000	17	7	6	6	5	3.60
1977—Baltimore	American	29	114	3	5	.375	119	57	56	55	30	4.42
1978—Baltimore	American	35	233	15	13	.536	217	98	86	94	47	3.32
1979—Baltimore	American	27	175	13	6	.684	165	70	65	81	23	3.34
1980—Baltimore	American	36	252	20	8	.714	254	101	93	119	58	3.32
1981—Baltimore	American	24	160	13	5	.722	167	63	58	82	40	3.26
1982—Baltimore	American	37	226⅓	14	12	.538	238	126	116	84	52	4.61
1983—Baltimore	American	36	260	18	7	.720	271	101	92	86	45	3.18
Major League Totals		227	1435⅓	96	57	.627	1448	623	572	607	300	3.59

Selected by New York Yankees' organization in 1st round (14th player selected) of free-agent draft, June 6, 1972.
†On disabled list, August 1 to August 29, 1975.
‡Traded with Pitchers Rudy May, Felix Martinez and Dave Pagan, and Catcher Rich Dempsey to Baltimore Orioles for Pitchers Ken Holtzman, Doyle Alexander and Grant Jackson, Catcher Ellie Hendricks and Pitcher Jimmy Freeman, June 15, 1976.

CHAMPIONSHIP SERIES RECORD

Year Club	League	G.	IP.	W.	L.	Pct.	H.	R.	ER.	SO.	BB.	ERA.
1979—Baltimore	American	1	9	1	0	1.000	6	0	0	4	1	0.00
1983—Baltimore	American	1	6⅔	0	1	.000	6	2	1	2	3	1.35
Championship Series Totals		2	15⅔	1	1	.500	12	2	1	6	4	0.57

Year Club	League	G.	IP.	W.	L.	Pct.	H.	R.	ER.	SO.	BB.	ERA.
1979—Baltimore	American	2	17	1	1	.500	16	6	6	8	2	3.18
1983—Baltimore	American	2	17	1	1	.500	9	2	2	12	2	1.06
World Series Totals		4	34	2	2	.500	25	8	8	20	4	2.12

ALL-STAR GAME RECORD

Member of American League All-Star Team in 1981; did not play.

FREDERICK STANLEY McGRIFF
(Fred)

Born October 31, 1963, at Tampa, Fla.
Height, 6.03. Weight, 190.
Throws and bats lefthanded.

Led Gulf Coast League in bases on balls received with 48 and tied for league lead in game-winning RBIs with 6 in 1982.

Year Club	League	Pos.	G.	AB.	R.	H.	2B.	3B.	HR.	RBI.	B.A.	PO.	A.	E.	F.A.
1981—Bradenton Yanks	Gulf C.	1B	29	81	6	12	2	0	0	9	.148	176	8	7	.963
1982—Braden. Yanks†	Gulf C.	1B	62	217	38	59	11	1	★9	●41	.272	514	★56	8	.986
1983—Kinston	Carol.	1B	94	350	53	85	14	1	21	57	.243	784	57	10	.988

Selected by New York Yankees' organization in 9th round of free-agent draft, June 8, 1981.
†Traded with Outfielder Dave Collins, Pitcher Mike Morgan and a reported $400,000 to Toronto Blue Jays for Outfielder-Catcher Tom Dodd and Pitcher Dale Murray, December 9, 1982.

JONATHAN ANDREW McKNIGHT
(Jack)

Born June 7, 1961, at Alvin, Tex.
Height, 6.02. Weight, 180.
Throws and bats righthanded.

Year Club	League	G.	IP.	W.	L.	Pct.	H.	R.	ER.	SO.	BB.	ERA.
1981—Florence	S. Atlantic	27	172	9	8	.529	139	73	62	119	77	3.24
1982—Kinston	Carolina	26	167⅔	★15	6	.714	149	78	64	124	●87	3.44
1983—Knoxville	Southern	30	172	8	12	.400	162	97	79	96	107	4.13

Signed as free agent by Toronto Blue Jays' organization, October 12, 1980.

BYRON SCOTT McLAUGHLIN

Born September 29, 1955, at Van Nuys, Calif.
Height, 6.01. Weight, 175.
Throws and bats righthanded.
Attended Los Angeles Valley College, Van Nuys, Calif.

Tied for Gulf States League lead in hit batsmen with 5 in 1976.

Year Club	League	G.	IP.	W.	L.	Pct.	H.	R.	ER.	SO.	BB.	ERA.
1975—Lodi	California	12	27	0	1	.000	29	17	14	12	17	4.67
1975—Bluefield†	Ap'lachian	14	35	1	2	.333	45	31	29	32	15	7.46
1976—Victoria‡§	Gulf States	15	115	★10	4	.714	104	48	39	74	46	3.05
1977—Nuevo Laredo	Mexican	33	244	18	13	.581	186	76	50	★221	63	1.84
1977—Seattle	American	1	1	0	0	.000	5	4	4	1	0	36.00
1978—San Jose	P. Coast	8	54	5	2	.714	45	23	21	52	32	3.50
1978—Seattle	American	20	107	4	8	.333	97	58	52	87	39	4.37
1979—Seattle	American	47	124	7	7	.500	114	58	58	74	60	4.21
1980—Seattle xy	American	45	91	3	6	.333	124	74	69	41	50	6.82
1981—Nuevo Laredo	Mexican	21	142	12	5	.706	116	32	25	108	44	1.58
1982—Nuevo Laredo z	Mexican	28	161⅓	12	6	.667	135	69	58	123	51	3.22
1982—Spokane	P. Coast	6	14⅓	1	0	1.000	10	6	2	9	5	1.26
1983—Edmonton	P. Coast	14	46⅓	1	2	.333	51	33	30	42	15	5.83
1983—California ab	American	16	55⅔	2	4	.333	63	32	32	45	22	5.17
Major League Totals		129	378⅔	16	25	.390	403	226	215	248	171	5.11

Signed as free agent by Montreal Expos' organization, December 24, 1973.
†Released, March 31, 1976; signed by Victoria, May 28, 1976.
‡Released, December 21, 1976; signed by Seattle Mariners' organization, January 8, 1977.
§Loaned to Nuevo Laredo, April 1, 1977; returned, September 11, 1977.
xTraded to Minnesota Twins for Outfielder Willie Norwood, December 12, 1980.
yReleased, March 31, 1981; signed by Nuevo Laredo of Mexican League, April 8, 1981.
zSold to Spokane (California Angels' organization), August 9, 1982.
aOn disabled list, July 23 to August 17, 1983.
bReleased, December 5, 1983.

RECORD AS HITTER

Year Club	League	Pos.	G.	AB.	R.	H.	2B.	3B.	HR.	RBI.	B.A.	PO.	A.	E.	F.A.
1974—W. Palm Beach†	Fla. St.	DH-PH	7	16	1	5	0	0	1	1	.313	0	0	0	.000

†Released, June 6, 1974; signed by Baltimore Orioles' organization, March 4, 1975.

JOEY RICHARD McLAUGHLIN

Born July 11, 1956, at Tulsa, Okla.
Height, 6.02. Weight, 205.
Throws and bats righthanded.

Major League saves: 1979 (5), 1980 (4), 1981 (10), 1982 (8), 1983 (9). Total—36.
Led International League in home runs allowed with 22 in 1978.
Led International League in balks with 4 in 1977.

Year Club	League	G.	IP.	W.	L.	Pct.	H.	R.	ER.	SO.	BB.	ERA.
1974—Kingsport	Ap'lachian	8	34	2	5	.286	41	27	20	32	15	5.29
1975—Greenwood	W. Carol.	20	122	12	5	.706	112	47	35	59	49	★2.58
1975—Savannah	Southern	8	53	4	3	.571	41	21	20	29	16	3.40
1976—Savannah	Southern	24	169	12	8	.600	165	69	52	70	44	2.77
1976—Richmond	Int'national	1	1	0	0	.000	1	1	1	1	1	9.00
1977—Richmond†	Int'national	26	179	9	10	.474	188	96	76	70	74	3.82
1977—Atlanta	National	3	6	0	0	.000	10	10	10	0	3	15.00
1978—Richmond‡	Int'national	26	179	9	13	.409	199	86	79	84	51	3.97
1979—Richmond	Int'national	18	42	2	2	.500	31	16	10	33	18	2.14
1979—Atlanta§	National	37	69	5	3	.625	54	23	19	40	34	2.48
1980—Toronto	American	55	136	6	9	.400	159	79	68	70	53	4.50
1981—Toronto	American	40	60	1	5	.167	55	24	19	38	21	2.85
1982—Toronto	American	44	70	8	6	.571	54	27	25	49	30	3.21
1983—Toronto	American	50	64⅔	7	4	.636	63	33	32	47	37	4.45
National League Totals		40	75	5	3	.625	64	33	29	40	37	3.48
American League Totals		189	330⅔	22	24	.478	331	163	144	204	141	3.92
Major League Totals		229	405⅔	27	27	.500	395	196	173	244	178	3.84

Selected by Atlanta Braves' organization in 2nd round of free-agent draft, June 5, 1974.
†On disabled list, April 15 to April 28, 1977.
‡On disabled list, April 14 to May 1, 1978.
§Traded with Outfielder Barry Bonnell to Toronto Blue Jays for First Baseman Chris Chambliss and Shortstop Luis Gomez, December 5, 1979.

JOE CRAIG McMURTRY

(Known by middle name.)
Born November 5, 1959, at Troy, Tex.
Height, 6.05. Weight, 195.
Throws and bats righthanded.
Attended McLennan Community College, Waco, Tex.

Tied for International League lead in games started by pitchers with 32 in 1982.
Named National League Rookie Pitcher of the Year by THE SPORTING NEWS, 1983.
Named International League Pitcher of the Year, 1982.

Year Club	League	G.	IP.	W.	L.	Pct.	H.	R.	ER.	SO.	BB.	ERA.
1980—Savannah	Southern	14	86	7	4	.636	82	40	34	37	35	3.56
1981—Savannah	Southern	28	202	★15	11	.577	168	87	62	111	95	2.76
1982—Richmond	Int'national	32	★210	★17	9	.654	198	98	89	96	107	3.81
1983—Atlanta	National	36	224⅔	15	9	.625	204	86	77	105	88	3.08
Major League Totals		36	224⅔	15	9	.625	204	86	77	105	88	3.08

Selected by Atlanta Braves' organization in 1st round (fourth player selected) of free-agent draft, January 8, 1980.

ROBERT LEE McNEALY
(Rusty)

Born August 12, 1958, at Sacramento, Calif.
Height, 5.08. Weight, 165.
Throws and bats lefthanded.
Attended College of Southern Idaho, Twin Falls, Ida.,
and received bachelor of science degree from Florida International University, Miami, Fla.

Led California League in stolen bases with 63 in 1981.

Year Club	League	Pos.	G.	AB.	R.	H.	2B.	3B.	HR.	RBI.	B.A.	PO.	A.	E.	F.A.
1980—Bellingham	N'west	OF	18	65	12	20	2	0	0	7	.308	32	3	1	.972
1980—San Jose	Calif.	OF	15	53	12	9	0	1	0	5	.170	29	1	4	.882
1981—San Jose†	Calif.	OF	128	450	100	145	22	8	3	48	.322	228	14	14	.945
1982—West Haven	East.	OF	130	390	80	121	11	4	5	41	.310	232	10	8	.968
1983—Tacoma	P. C.	OF	134	425	89	113	20	2	0	42	.266	271	12	9	.969
1983—Oakland‡	Amer.	OF	15	4	5	0	0	0	0	0	.000	6	0	0	1.000
Major League Totals			15	4	5	0	0	0	0	0	.000	6	0	0	1.000

Selected by New York Yankees' organization in fourth round of free-agent draft, January 10, 1978.
Selected by Seattle Mariners' organization in 17th round of free-agent draft, June 3, 1980.
†Traded with Pitcher Tim Hallgren to Oakland A's organization for Pitcher Roy Thomas, December 9, 1981.
‡Traded with cash to Montreal Expos for Pitcher Ray Burris, December 8, 1983.

HAROLD ABRAHAM McRAE
(Hal)

Born July 10, 1946, at Avon Park, Fla.
Height, 5.11. Weight, 180.
Throws and bats righthanded.
Attended Florida A&M University, Tallahassee, Fla.

Tied major league record for most long hits, doubleheader, 6, August 27, 1974, 5 doubles, 1 home run.
Led American League in being hit by pitch with 13 in 1977.

Named designated hitter on THE SPORTING NEWS American League All-Star Team, 1976, 1977 and 1982.
Named designated hitter on THE SPORTING NEWS American League Silver Slugger team, 1982.

Year—Club	League	Pos.	G.	AB.	R.	H.	2B.	3B.	HR.	RBI.	B.A.	PO.	A.	E.	F.A.
1965—Tampa	Fla. St.	OF	22	65	3	10	3	0	0	4	.154	19	0	0	1.000
1966—Peninsula†	Carol.	2B	109	394	65	113	19	4	11	56	.287	252	226	★28	.945
1967—Buffalo‡	Int.	2B	73	259	30	65	14	3	10	34	.251	133	208	23	.937
1967—Knoxville	South.	2B	51	186	26	54	10	3	6	25	.290	140	136	12	.958
1968—Indianapolis	P. C.	2B-OF	119	444	64	131	31	11	16	65	.295	222	307	14	.974
1968—Cincinnati	Nat.	2B	17	51	1	10	1	0	0	2	.196	33	30	5	.926
1969—Indianapolis§	A. A.	OF	17	41	2	9	1	0	0	4	.220	0	0	0	.000
1970—Cincinnati	Nat.	OF-3B-2B	70	165	18	41	6	1	8	23	.248	53	7	1	.984
1971—Cincinnati	Nat.	OF	99	337	39	89	24	2	9	34	.264	167	6	6	.966
1972—Cincinnati x	Nat.	OF-3B	61	97	9	27	4	0	5	26	.278	16	14	6	.833
1973—Kansas City	Amer.	OF-3B	106	338	36	79	18	3	9	50	.234	101	6	5	.955
1974—Kansas City	Amer.	OF-3B	148	539	71	167	36	4	15	88	.310	132	3	7	.951
1975—Kansas City	Amer.	OF-3B	126	480	57	147	38	6	5	71	.306	207	7	3	.986
1976—Kansas City	Amer.	OF	149	527	75	175	34	5	8	73	.332	63	2	2	.970
1977—Kansas City	Amer.	OF	●162	641	104	191	★54	11	21	92	.298	81	8	4	.957
1978—Kansas City	Amer.	OF	156	623	90	170	39	5	16	72	.273	3	1	0	1.000
1979—Kansas City y	Amer.	DH	101	393	55	113	32	4	10	74	.288	0	0	0	.000
1980—Kansas City z	Amer.	OF	124	489	73	145	39	5	14	83	.297	17	0	0	1.000
1981—Kansas City	Amer.	OF	101	389	38	106	23	2	7	36	.272	10	0	1	.909
1982—Kansas City a	Amer.	OF	159	613	91	189	●46	8	27	★133	.308	1	0	1	.500
1983—Kansas City	Amer.	DH	157	589	84	183	41	6	12	82	.311	0	0	0	.000
National League Totals			247	650	67	167	35	3	22	85	.257	269	57	18	.948
American League Totals			1489	5621	775	1665	400	59	144	854	.296	615	27	23	.965
Major League Totals			1736	6271	842	1832	435	62	166	939	.292	884	84	41	.959

Selected by Cincinnati Reds' organization in 6th round of free-agent draft, June, 1965.
†On disabled list, June 23 to July 6, 1966.
‡On disabled list, April 26 to May 7, 1967.
§On disabled list, April 18 to May 28 and July 4 to August 5, 1969.
xTraded with Pitcher Wayne Simpson to Kansas City Royals for Pitcher Roger Nelson and Outfielder Richie Scheinblum, November 30, 1972.
yOn supplemental disabled list, June 11, 1979; transferred to disabled list, July 6 to August 2, 1979.
zOn supplemental disabled list, May 13 to June 2, 1980.
aGranted free agency, November 10, 1982; re-signed by Royals, November 15, 1982.

DIVISION SERIES RECORD

Year—Club	League	Pos.	G.	AB.	R.	H.	2B.	3B.	HR.	RBI.	B.A.	PO.	A.	E.	F.A.
1981—Kansas City	Amer.	DH	3	11	0	1	1	0	0	0	.091	0	0	0	.000

CHAMPIONSHIP SERIES RECORD

Established Championship Series record for most runs, five-game Series (6), 1977.

Year—Club	League	Pos.	G.	AB.	R.	H.	2B.	3B.	HR.	RBI.	B.A.	PO.	A.	E.	F.A.
1970—Cincinnati	Nat.	PH-OF	2	4	0	0	0	0	0	0	.000	2	0	0	1.000
1972—Cincinnati	Nat.	PH	1	0	0	0	0	0	0	0	.000	0	0	0	.000
1976—Kansas City	Amer.	DH	5	17	2	2	1	1	0	1	.118	5	1	0	1.000
1977—Kansas City	Amer.	OF-DH	5	18	6	8	3	0	1	2	.444	2	1	0	1.000
1978—Kansas City	Amer.	DH	4	14	0	3	0	0	0	2	.214	0	0	0	.000
1980—Kansas City	Amer.	DH	3	10	0	2	0	0	0	0	.200	0	0	0	.000
Championship Series Totals			20	63	8	15	4	1	1	5	.238	9	2	1	1.000

WORLD SERIES RECORD

Year—Club	League	Pos.	G.	AB.	R.	H.	2B.	3B.	HR.	RBI.	B.A.	PO.	A.	E.	F.A.
1970—Cincinnati	Nat.	OF	3	11	1	5	2	0	0	3	.455	2	1	0	1.000
1972—Cincinnati	Nat.	PH-OF	5	9	1	4	1	0	0	2	.444	4	0	0	1.000
1980—Kansas City	Amer.	DH	6	24	3	9	3	0	0	1	.375	0	0	0	.000
World Series Totals			14	44	5	18	6	0	0	6	.409	6	1	0	1.000

ALL-STAR GAME RECORD

Year—League	Pos.	AB.	R.	H.	2B.	3B.	HR.	RBI.	B.A.	PO.	A.	E.	F.A.
1975—American	PH	1	0	0	0	0	0	0	.000	0	0	0	.000
1976—American	PH	1	0	0	0	0	0	0	.000	0	0	0	.000
1982—American	PH	0	0	0	0	0	0	0	.000	0	0	0	.000
All-Star Game Totals		2	0	0	0	0	0	0	.000	0	0	0	.000

WALTER KEVIN McREYNOLDS

(Known by middle name.)

Born October 16, 1959, at Little Rock, Ark.
Height, 6.01. Weight, 205.
Throws and bats righthanded.
Attended University of Arkansas, Fayetteville, Ark.

Led Pacific Coast League in total bases with 328 in 1983.
Named Minor League Player of the Year by THE SPORTING NEWS, 1983.
Named Pacific Coast League Player of the Year, 1983.
Named California League Most Valuable Player, 1982.
Received reported $125,000 bonus to sign with San Diego Padres, 1982.

Year Club	League	Pos.	G.	AB.	R.	H.	2B.	3B.	HR.	RBI.	B.A.	PO.	A.	E.	F.A.
1982—Reno	Calif.	OF	90	338	83	127	17	5	*28	98	*.376	52	7	3	.952
1982—Amarillo	Texas	OF	40	162	30	57	8	3	5	39	.352	76	3	2	.975
1983—Las Vegas..............	P. C.	OF	113	446	98	168	*46	9	●32	116	.377	257	3	9	.967
1983—San Diego	Nat.	OF	39	140	15	31	3	1	4	14	.221	87	4	1	.989
Major League Totals....................................			39	140	15	31	3	1	4	14	.221	87	4	1	.989

Selected by Milwaukee Brewers' organization in 18th round of free-agent draft, June 6, 1978.
Selected by San Diego Padres' organization in 1st round (sixth player selected) of free-agent draft, June 8, 1981.

LARRY DEAN McWILLIAMS

Born February 10, 1954, at Wichita, Kan.
Height, 6.05. Weight, 175.
Throws and bats lefthanded.
Attended Paris Junior College, Paris, Tex.

Tied major league record for most strikeouts by batter, inning (2), April 22, 1979 (fourth inning).
Named lefthanded pitcher on THE SPORTING NEWS National League All-Star Team, 1983.

Year Club	League	G.	IP.	W.	L.	Pct.	H.	R.	ER.	SO.	BB.	ERA.
1974—Greenwood†................................	W. Carol.	11	64	4	3	.571	64	26	20	61	23	2.81
1975—Greenwood‡................................	W. Carol.	17	93	8	4	.667	83	36	29	71	18	2.81
1976—Greenwood................................	W. Carol.	8	48	2	2	.500	40	19	14	44	13	2.63
1976—Savannah	Southern	16	74	3	8	.273	82	41	38	37	33	4.62
1977—Savannah	Southern	26	158	8	9	.471	153	70	59	139	64	3.36
1978—Richmond................................	Int'national	15	108	6	5	.545	87	36	34	78	41	2.83
1978—Atlanta	National	15	99	9	3	.750	84	38	31	42	35	2.82
1979—Atlanta§	National	13	66	3	2	.600	69	41	41	32	22	5.59
1980—Atlanta	National	30	164	9	14	.391	188	97	90	77	39	4.94
1981—Richmond................................	Int'national	29	178	●13	10	.565	174	98	●86	157	79	4.35
1981—Atlanta	National	6	38	2	1	.667	31	13	13	23	8	3.08
1982—Atlanta x-Pittsburgh	National	46	159⅓	8	8	.500	158	79	68	118	44	3.84
1983—Pittsburgh................................	National	35	238	15	8	.652	205	99	86	199	87	3.25
Major League Totals....................		145	764⅓	46	36	.561	735	367	329	491	235	3.87

Selected by Atlanta Braves' organization in 1st round (sixth player selected) of free-agent draft, January 9, 1974.
†On disabled list, July 22 to September 25, 1974.
‡On disabled list, April 11 to June 3, 1975.
§On disabled list, May 18 to June 15 and July 7 to September 1, 1979.
xTraded to Pittsburgh Pirates for Pitcher Pascual Perez and a player to be named later, June 30, 1982; Atlanta Braves' organization acquired Shortstop Carlos Rios to complete deal, September 8, 1982.

ROBERT ANDREW MEACHAM
(Bobby)

Born August 25, 1960, at Los Angeles, Calif.
Height, 6.01. Weight, 180.
Throws right and bats left and righthanded.
Attended San Diego State University, San Diego, Calif.

Year Club	League	Pos.	G.	AB.	R.	H.	2B.	3B.	HR.	RBI.	B.A.	PO.	A.	E.	F.A.
1981—Gastonia.................	S. Atl.	SS	74	274	24	50	8	2	1	18	.182	107	235	25	.932
1982—St. Petersburg†.....	Fla. St.	SS	120	421	57	109	15	4	0	37	.259	201	306	*47	.915
1983—Columbus	Int.	SS	120	423	58	111	18	3	9	60	.262	206	348	30	.949
1983—New York..............	Amer.	SS-3B	22	51	5	12	2	0	0	4	.235	16	64	6	.930
Major League Totals....................................			22	51	5	12	2	0	0	4	.235	16	64	6	.930

Selected by Chicago White Sox' organization in 14th round of free agent draft, June 6, 1978.
Selected by St. Louis Cardinals' organization in 1st round (eighth player selected) of free-agent draft, June 8, 1981.
†Traded with Outfielder Stan Javier to New York Yankees' organization for Pitchers Marty Mason and Steve Fincher and Outfielder Bob Helsom, December 14, 1982.

DAVID KEITH MEIER
(Dave)

Born August 8, 1959, at Helena, Mont.
Height, 6.00. Weight, 185.
Throws and bats righthanded.
Attended Fresno City College, Fresno, Calif.,
and Stanford University, Stanford, Calif.

Tied for Southern League lead in double plays by outfielders with 5 in 1982.

Year Club	League	Pos.	G.	AB.	R.	H.	2B.	3B.	HR.	RBI.	B.A.	PO.	A.	E.	F.A.
1981—Visalia	Calif.	SS-OF-3B	71	273	53	92	12	0	9	50	.337	65	85	13	.920
1982—Orlando	South.	O-3-2-S	134	474	71	136	19	7	8	63	.287	254	27	6	.979
1983—Toledo	Int.	OF-P	126	426	63	143	21	6	8	68	.336	224	6	7	.970

Selected by California Angels' organization in 31st round of free-agent draft, June 7, 1977.
Selected by St. Louis Cardinals' organization in secondary phase of free-agent draft, January 10, 1978.
Selected by Minnesota Twins' organization in 5th round of free-agent draft, June 8, 1981.

PITCHING RECORD

Year Club	League	G.	IP.	W.	L.	Pct.	H.	R.	ER.	SO.	BB.	ERA.
1983—Toledo	Int'national	1	1	0	0	.000	2	1	1	0	0	9.00

FRANCISCO MELENDEZ (VILLEGAS)

Born January 25, 1964, at Rio Piedras, Puerto Rico.
Height, 6.00. Weight, 160.
Throws and bats lefthanded.

Led Eastern League first basemen in putouts with 1,080, total chances with 1,166 and double plays with 99 in 1983.

Year	Club	League	Pos.	G.	AB.	R.	H.	2B.	3B.	HR.	RBI.	B.A.	PO.	A.	E.	F.A.
1981—Peninsula	Carol.	1B-OF	32	74	6	10	3	0	0	6	.135	154	13	6	.965
1981—Spartanburg	S. Atl.	1B-OF	85	306	44	82	13	1	3	36	.268	760	57	17	.980
1982—Peninsula	Carol.	1B	118	424	54	124	★33	3	4	69	.292	739	75	11	.987
1983—Reading	East.	1B-OF	126	450	81	134	17	4	5	75	.298	1082	73	12	.990

Signed as free agent by Philadelphia Phillies' organization, October 4, 1980.

ROBERT PAUL MELVIN
(Bob)

Born October 28, 1961, at Palo Alto, Calif.
Height, 6.04. Weight, 205.
Throws and bats righthanded.
Attended University of California, Berkeley, Calif.,
and Canada College, Redwood City, Calif.

Year	Club	League	Pos.	G.	AB.	R.	H.	2B.	3B.	HR.	RBI.	B.A.	PO.	A.	E.	F.A.
1981—Macon	S. Atl.	C	114	412	56	112	19	1	14	64	.272	456	67	2	★.996
1982—Birmingham†	South.	★C-1B-3B	98	364	33	86	12	1	13	52	.236	638	54	9	★.987
1983—Birmingham	South.	C-1B-2B	78	285	43	82	14	2	10	56	.288	404	30	2	.995
1983—Evansville	A. A.	C-1B	45	142	10	27·	6	0	2	11	.190	213	16	1	.996

Selected by Baltimore Orioles' organization in 3rd round of free-agent draft, June 5, 1979.
Selected by Detroit Tigers' organization in secondary phase of free-agent draft, January 13, 1981.
†On disabled list, May 1 to May 25, 1982.

ORLANDO MERCADO

Born November 7, 1961, at Arecibo, Puerto Rico.
Height, 6.00. Weight, 180.
Throws and bats righthanded.

Led Eastern League in passed balls with 23 in 1980.
Led California League in passed balls with 24 in 1979.

Year	Club	League	Pos.	G.	AB.	R.	H.	2B.	3B.	HR.	RBI.	B.A.	PO.	A.	E.	F.A.
1978—Bellingham	N'west	C	38	49	7	6	2	0	0	5	.122	184	20	4	.981
1979—San Jose	Calif.	C-1B	110	335	53	86	18	2	10	54	.257	629	71	17	.976
1980—Lynn	East.	C-1B	117	396	55	101	25	6	11	71	.255	607	78	11	.984
1981—Spokane	P. C.	C-OF	95	312	32	67	21	2	4	31	.215	446	60	13	.975
1982—Salt Lake City	P. C.	C-O-1-3	90	321	43	90	19	2	16	66	.280	497	43	13	.976
1982—Seattle	Amer.	C	9	17	1	2	0	0	1	6	.118	31	1	0	1.000
1983—Seattle	Amer.	C	66	178	10	35	11	2	1	16	.197	342	27	2	.995
1983—Salt Lake City	P. C.	C-3B	26	88	12	20	2	1	2	12	.227	131	13	2	.986
Major League Totals			75	195	11	37	11	2	2	22	.190	373	28	2	.995

Signed as free agent by Seattle Mariners' organization, January 6, 1978.

DANIEL THOMAS MEYER
(Dan)

Born August 3, 1952, at Hamilton, O.
Height, 5.11. Weight, 180.
Throws right and bats lefthanded.
Attended Santa Ana College, Santa Ana, Calif., and University
of Arizona, Tucson, Ariz.

Tied major league record for most times awarded first base on catcher's interference, game (2), May 3, 1977.
Led Appalachian League in total bases with 158 in 1972.
Led Appalachian League third basemen in assists with 97 in 1972.
Tied for American Association lead in sacrifice flies with 9 in 1974.
Named Appalachian League Player of the Year, 1972.

Year	Club	League	Pos.	G.	AB.	R.	H.	2B.	3B.	HR.	RBI.	B.A.	PO.	A.	E.	F.A.
1972—Bristol	Appal.	3B-2B-OF	65	235	54	★93	11	6	14	46	★.396	69	124	13	.937
1973—Lakeland	Fla. St.	2B	133	473	63	114	17	6	10	59	.241	295	297	21	.966
1974—Evansville	A. A.	3B-OF-1B	129	484	75	146	26	7	9	57	.302	238	153	22	.947
1974—Detroit	Amer.	OF	13	50	5	10	1	1	3	7	.200	29	0	1	.967
1975—Detroit†	Amer.	OF-1B	122	470	56	111	17	3	8	47	.236	571	41	12	.981
1976—Detroit‡	Amer.	OF-1B	105	294	37	74	8	4	2	16	.252	244	14	2	.992
1977—Seattle	Amer.	1B	159	582	75	159	24	4	22	90	.273	1407	109	12	.992
1978—Seattle§	Amer.	1B-OF	123	444	38	101	18	1	8	56	.227	1107	79	13	.989
1979—Seattle	Amer.	3B-OF-1B	144	525	72	146	21	7	20	74	.278	198	205	22	.948
1980—Seattle	Amer.	OF-3B-1B	146	531	56	146	25	6	11	71	.275	219	22	10	.960
1981—Seattle xy	Amer.	3B-OF-1B	83	252	26	66	10	1	3	22	.262	79	88	7	.960
1982—Oakland	Amer.	OF	120	383	28	92	17	3	8	50	.240	387	32	5	.988
1983—Oakland z	Amer.	1B-OF-3B	69	169	15	32	9	0	1	13	.189	305	16	4	.988
Major League Totals			1084	3700	408	937	150	30	86	455	.253	4546	606	88	.983

Selected by Detroit Tigers' organization in 4th round of free-agent draft, June 6, 1972.

LAWRENCE WILLIAM MILBOURNE

Name pronounced MILL-born.

(Larry)

Born February 14, 1951, at Port Norris, N.J.
Height, 6.00. Weight, 165.
Throws right and bats left and righthanded.
Attended Glassboro State College, Glassboro, N.J., and Cumberland
County Junior College, Vineland, N.J.

Year Club	League	Pos.	G.	AB.	R.	H.	2B.	3B.	HR.	RBI.	B.A.	PO.	A.	E.	F.A.
1969—Bluefield†	Appal.	SS	●69	246	49	75	10	5	4	35	.305	94	171	★28	.904
1970—						(Did not play)									
1971—Decatur‡	Midw.	★2-S-3	★123	★518	69	★156	23	5	5	38	.301	267	256	27	★.951
1972—Shreveport§	Texas	2B	122	416	50	110	14	5	2	36	.264	273	314	25	.959
1973—Tulsa x	A. A.	2-3-O-S	111	367	55	104	13	6	5	43	.283	158	197	16	.957
1974—Houston	Nat.	2B-SS-OF	112	136	31	38	2	1	0	9	.279	102	148	7	.973
1975—Iowa	A. A.	2B	24	77	9	17	3	1	1	6	.221	33	47	8	.909
1975—Houston	Nat.	2B-SS	73	151	17	32	1	2	1	9	.212	95	136	10	.959
1976—Houston	Nat.	2B	59	145	22	36	4	0	0	7	.248	67	100	6	.965
1976—Memphis y	Int.	2B-SS	71	292	45	95	12	2	5	31	.325	132	245	13	.967
1977—Seattle	Amer.	2B-SS-3B	86	242	24	53	10	0	2	21	.219	120	209	12	.965
1978—Seattle	Amer.	3B-SS-2B	93	234	31	53	6	2	2	20	.226	92	169	9	.967
1979—Seattle	Amer.	SS-2B-3B	123	356	40	99	13	4	2	26	.278	144	265	12	.971
1980—Seattle z	Amer.	SS-3B-2B	106	258	31	68	6	6	0	26	.264	103	195	8	.987
1981—New York	Amer.	SS-2B-3B	61	163	24	51	7	2	1	12	.313	74	121	8	.961
1982—N.Y.a-Min.b-Cle.c.	Amer.	2B-SS-3B	125	416	40	107	13	5	2	26	.257	210	297	18	.966
1983—Philadelphia d	Nat.	2B-SS-3B	41	66	3	16	0	1	0	4	.242	40	48	3	.967
1983—New York	Amer.	2B-SS-3B	31	70	5	14	4	0	0	2	.200	46	57	1	.990
National League Totals			285	498	73	122	7	4	1	29	.245	304	432	26	.966
American League Totals			625	1739	195	445	59	19	9	133	.256	789	1313	68	.969
Major League Totals			910	2237	268	567	66	23	10	162	.253	1093	1745	94	.968

Signed as free agent by Baltimore Orioles' organization, June 18, 1969.
†Released, April 7, 1970; signed by Decatur (San Francisco Giants' organization), April 2, 1971.
‡Drafted by Salt Lake City (California Angels' organization), November 29, 1971.
§Drafted by Tulsa (St. Louis Cardinals' organization), November 27, 1972.
xDrafted by Houston Astros, December 3, 1973.
yTraded to Seattle Mariners for Pitcher Roy Thomas, March 30, 1977.
zTraded to New York Yankees for Catcher Brad Gulden, November 18, 1980.
aTraded with Pitchers John Pacella and Pete Filson to Minnesota Twins for Catcher Butch Wynegar and Pitcher Roger Erickson, May 12, 1982.
bTraded to Cleveland Indians for Outfielder Larry Littleton, July 3, 1982.
cTraded to Philadelphia Phillies for a player to be named later, December 9, 1982; deal settled with cash.
dSold to New York Yankees, July 16, 1983.

DIVISION SERIES RECORD

Year Club	League	Pos.	G.	AB.	R.	H.	2B.	3B.	HR.	RBI.	B.A.	PO.	A.	E.	F.A.
1981—New York	Amer.	SS	5	19	4	6	1	0	0	0	.316	5	14	0	1.000

CHAMPIONSHIP SERIES RECORD

Year Club	League	Pos.	G.	AB.	R.	H.	2B.	3B.	HR.	RBI.	B.A.	PO.	A.	E.	F.A.
1981—New York	Amer.	SS	3	13	4	6	0	0	0	1	.462	2	7	0	1.000

WORLD SERIES RECORD

Year Club	League	Pos.	G.	AB.	R.	H.	2B.	3B.	HR.	RBI.	B.A.	PO.	A.	E.	F.A.
1981—New York	Amer.	SS	6	20	2	5	2	0	0	3	.250	5	16	2	.913

LEMMIE EARL MILLER

Born June 2, 1960, at Dallas, Tex.
Height, 6.01. Weight, 190.
Throws and bats righthanded.
Attended Santa Barbara City Junior College,
Santa Barbara, Calif., and Arizona State University, Tempe, Ariz.

Year Club	League	Pos.	G.	AB.	R.	H.	2B.	3B.	HR.	RBI.	B.A.	PO.	A.	E.	F.A.
1981—Vero Beach	Fla. St.	OF	68	270	52	88	10	3	3	35	.326	104	10	6	.950
1981—San Antonio	Texas	OF	2	6	4	2	0	1	0	0	.333	3	0	0	1.000
1982—San Antonio	Texas	OF	★138	★570	88	159	21	3	8	51	.279	228	13	9	.964
1983—Albuquerque	P. C.	OF	136	545	122	★180	31	5	10	66	.330	180	13	6	.960

Selected by Oakland A's organization in 1st round (sixth player selected) of free-agent draft, January 9, 1979.
Selected by Houston Astros' organization in secondary phase of free-agent draft, June 5, 1979.
Selected by Los Angeles Dodgers' organization in 2nd round of free-agent draft, June 8, 1981.

RICHARD ALAN MILLER
(Rick)

Born April 19, 1948, at Grand Rapids, Mich.
Height, 6.00. Weight, 185.
Throws and bats lefthanded.
Attended Michigan State University, East Lansing, Mich.
Brother-in-law of Carlton Fisk, catcher with Chicago White Sox.

Led International League in bases on balls received with 106 in 1971.
Named outfielder on THE SPORTING NEWS American League All-Star fielding team, 1978.

Year Club	League	Pos.	G.	AB.	R.	H.	2B.	3B.	HR.	RBI.	B.A.	PO.	A.	E.	F.A.
1969—Pittsfield	East.	OF	77	221	25	58	7	1	6	32	.262	150	8	3	.981
1970—Pawtucket	East.	OF	113	381	69	94	16	4	12	56	.247	227	5	5	.979
1971—Louisville	Int.	OF	133	461	79	114	24	2	15	58	.247	267	21	6	.980
1971—Boston	Amer.	OF	15	33	9	11	5	0	1	7	.333	30	1	1	.969
1972—Boston	Amer.	OF	89	98	13	21	4	1	3	15	.214	80	7	3	.967
1973—Boston	Amer.	OF	143	441	65	115	17	7	6	43	.261	301	4	7	.978
1974—Boston	Amer.	OF	114	280	41	73	8	1	5	22	.261	253	7	3	.989
1975—Boston	Amer.	OF	77	108	21	21	2	1	0	15	.194	101	2	2	.981
1976—Boston	Amer.	OF	105	269	40	76	15	3	0	27	.283	220	4	2	.991
1977—Boston†‡	Amer.	OF	86	189	34	48	9	3	0	24	.254	118	5	1	.992
1978—California	Amer.	OF	132	475	66	125	25	4	1	37	.263	353	9	4	.989
1979—California§	Amer.	OF	120	427	60	125	15	5	2	28	.293	349	3	4	.989
1980—California x	Amer.	OF	129	412	52	113	14	3	2	38	.274	299	11	5	.984
1981—Boston	Amer.	OF	97	316	38	92	17	2	2	33	.291	219	5	3	.987
1982—Boston	Amer.	OF	135	409	50	104	13	2	4	38	.254	277	6	5	.983
1983—Boston	Amer.	OF	104	262	41	75	10	2	2	21	.286	151	5	1	.994
Major League Totals			1346	3719	530	999	154	34	28	348	.269	2751	69	41	.986

Selected by Boston Red Sox' organization in 2nd round of free-agent draft, June 5, 1969.
†On disabled list, May 3 to May 30, 1977.
‡Granted free agency, November 2, 1977; signed by California Angels, December 21, 1977.
§On disabled list, June 2 to July 9, 1979.
xTraded with Pitcher Mark Clear and Third Baseman Carney Lansford to Boston Red Sox for Shortstop Rick Burleson and Third Baseman Butch Hobson, December 10, 1980.

CHAMPIONSHIP SERIES RECORD

Year Club	League	Pos.	G.	AB.	R.	H.	2B.	3B.	HR.	RBI.	B.A.	PO.	A.	E.	F.A.
1979—California	Amer.	OF	4	16	2	4	0	0	0	0	.250	14	2	0	1.000

WORLD SERIES RECORD

Year Club	League	Pos.	G.	AB.	R.	H.	2B.	3B.	HR.	RBI.	B.A.	PO.	A.	E.	F.A.
1975—Boston	Amer.	OF-PH	3	2	0	0	0	0	0	0	.000	1	0	0	1.000

JAMES BRADLEY MILLS
(Brad)

Born January 19, 1957, at Exeter, Calif.
Height, 6.00. Weight, 195.
Throws right and bats lefthanded.
Attended College of the Sequoias, Visalia, Calif., and
University of Arizona, Tucson, Ariz.

Year Club	League	Pos.	G.	AB.	R.	H.	2B.	3B.	HR.	RBI.	B.A.	PO.	A.	E.	F.A.
1979—W. Palm Beach	Fla. St.	3B	78	258	43	70	12	1	5	30	.271	66	110	9	.951
1980—Memphis	South.	3B	55	190	32	56	18	2	6	44	.295	39	135	9	.951
1980—Montreal	Nat.	3B	21	60	1	18	1	0	0	8	.300	19	24	1	.977
1980—Denver	A. A.	3B-2B	52	201	43	58	10	3	2	27	.289	42	113	9	.945
1981—Denver	A. A.	3B-2B	118	427	65	134	34	1	12	66	.314	85	236	16	.952
1981—Montreal	Nat.	3B-2B	17	21	3	5	1	0	0	1	.238	6	6	0	1.000
1982—Montreal	Nat.	3B	54	67	6	15	3	0	1	2	.224	4	9	2	.867
1982—Wichita	A. A.	3B	4	17	3	8	0	0	0	6	.471	4	8	3	.800
1983—Montreal†	Nat.	3B-1B	14	20	1	5	0	0	0	1	.250	1	4	1	.833
1983—Wichita	A. A.	3B-1B	81	271	47	86	21	0	8	46	.317	140	115	4	.985
Major League Totals			106	168	11	43	5	0	1	12	.256	30	43	4	.948

Selected by Minnesota Twins' organization in 16th round of free-agent draft, January 11, 1977.
Selected by Montreal Expos' organization in 16th round of free-agent draft, June 5, 1979.
†On supplemental disabled list, May 4 to May 20, 1983.

EDDIE JAMES MILNER

Born May 21, 1955, at Columbus, O.
Height, 5.11. Weight, 170.
Throws and bats lefthanded.
Attended Muskingum College, New Concord, O., and received bachelor of science degree
in business from Central State University, Wilberforce, O. in 1978.
Brother of Hobson Milner, 12th round selection of Minnesota Vikings in 1982 NFL draft;
cousin of John Milner, first baseman-outfielder with New York Mets,
Pittsburgh Pirates and Montreal Expos, 1971 through 1982.

Major League stolen bases: 1982 (18), 1983 (41). Total—59.

Tied for Pioneer League lead in double plays by outfielders with 1 in 1976.
Named Florida State League Most Valuable Player, 1978.

Year Club	League	Pos.	G.	AB.	R.	H.	2B.	3B.	HR.	RBI.	B.A.	PO.	A.	E.	F.A.
1976—Billings	Pion.	OF	67	231	51	59	14	3	2	27	.255	★149	★12	7	.958
1977—Shelby....................	W. Car.	OF	110	414	62	111	15	8	3	30	.268	254	10	10	.964
1978—Tampa...................	Fla. St.	OF	133	497	79	141	16	★16	8	44	.284	283	7	6	.980
1979—Indianapolis.........	A. A.	OF	30	98	9	18	0	2	0	5	.184	49	2	2	.962
1979—Nashville...............	South.	OF	104	369	70	97	12	12	11	51	.263	259	9	5	.982
1980—Indianapolis.........	A. A.	OF	130	468	63	118	11	7	5	37	.252	★363	6	7	.981
1980—Cincinnati.............	Nat.	PH-PR	6	3	1	0	0	0	0	0	.000	0	0	0	.000
1981—Indianapolis.........	A. A.	OF	127	453	69	130	14	6	3	42	.287	228	12	4	.984
1981—Cincinnati.............	Nat.	OF	8	5	0	1	1	0	0	1	.200	2	0	0	1.000
1982—Cincinnati†...........	Nat.	OF	113	407	61	109	23	5	4	31	.268	215	8	3	.987
1983—Cincinnati.............	Nat.	OF	146	502	77	131	23	6	9	33	.261	392	9	4	.990
Major League Totals..................................			273	917	139	241	47	11	13	65	.263	609	17	7	.989

Selected by Cincinnati Reds' organization in 21st round of free-agent draft, June 8, 1976.
†On supplemental disabled list, August 11 to September 7, 1982.

GREGORY BRIAN MINTON
(Greg)

Born July 29, 1951, at Lubbock, Tex.
Height, 6.02. Weight, 191.
Throws right and bats left and righthanded.
Attended San Diego Mesa College, San Diego, Calif.

Major League saves: 1979 (4), 1980 (19), 1981 (21), 1982 (30), 1983 (22). Total—96.
Led National League in games finished in relief with 44 in 1981 and 66 in 1982.
Led Pacific Coast League in wild pitches with 18 in 1977.
Led Pacific Coast League in balks with 6 in 1975.

Year Club	League	G.	IP.	W.	L.	Pct.	H.	R.	ER.	SO.	BB.	ERA.
1970—Billings†	Pioneer	16	40	1	4	.200	37	23	14	36	16	3.15
1971—Waterloo	Midwest	27	124	11	6	.647	118	52	42	117	55	3.05
1972—San Jose‡	California	28	178	12	12	.500	182	117	78	153	77	3.94
1973—Phoenix..	P. Coast	5	13	0	0	.000	11	6	6	4	8	4.15
1973—Amarillo..	Texas	38	122	5	11	.313	138	87	61	77	48	4.50
1974—Fresno...	California	13	96	10	1	.909	85	32	24	81	18	2.25
1974—Amarillo..	Texas	6	29	1	4	.200	42	26	19	21	10	5.90
1975—Phoenix..	P. Coast	42	177	10	6	.625	178	73	51	76	76	2.59
1975—San Francisco	National	4	17	1	1	.500	19	14	13	6	11	6.88
1976—San Francisco	National	10	26	0	3	.000	32	18	14	7	12	4.85
1976—Phoenix§......................................	P. Coast	13	74	4	5	.444	91	57	46	31	32	5.59
1977—Phoenix..	P. Coast	29	161	14	6	★.700	188	93	87	77	70	4.86
1977—San Francisco	National	2	14	1	1	.500	14	8	7	5	4	4.50
1978—Phoenix..	P. Coast	14	92	7	4	.636	97	54	46	32	38	4.50
1978—San Francisco	National	11	16	0	1	.000	22	14	14	6	8	7.88
1979—San Francisco x	National	46	80	4	3	.571	59	25	16	33	27	1.80
1980—San Francisco	National	68	91	4	6	.400	81	28	25	42	34	2.47
1981—San Francisco	National	55	84	4	5	.444	84	28	27	29	36	2.89
1982—San Francisco	National	78	123	10	4	.714	108	29	25	58	42	1.83
1983—San Francisco	National	73	106⅔	7	11	.389	117	51	42	38	47	3.54
Major League Totals......................		347	557⅔	31	35	.470	536	215	183	224	221	2.95

Selected by Kansas City Royals' organization in 3rd round of free-agent draft, January 17, 1970.
†Appeared in two games as an outfielder with one putout.
‡Traded to San Francisco Giants for Catcher Fran Healy, April 2, 1973.
§On disabled list, July 24 to August 5, 1976.
xOn disabled list, March 26 to May 31, 1979.

ALL-STAR GAME RECORD

Year League	IP.	W.	L.	Pct.	H.	R.	ER.	SO.	BB.	ERA.
1982—National...	⅔	0	0	.000	0	0	0	0	1	0.00

PAUL THOMAS MIRABELLA

Born March 20, 1954, at Bellville, N. J.
Height, 6.02. Weight, 196.
Throws and bats lefthanded.
Attended Montclair State University, Upper Montclair, N. J.

Tied for Pacific Coast League lead in balks with 4 in 1978.
Tied for Texas League lead in shutouts with 4 and games started by pitchers with 26 in 1977.
Tied for Western Carolinas League lead in balks with 5 in 1976.

Year Club	League	G.	IP.	W.	L.	Pct.	H.	R.	ER.	SO.	BB.	ERA.
1976—Asheville	W. Carol.	22	149	10	7	.588	149	77	66	★136	69	3.99
1977—Tulsa	Texas	26	176	12	7	.632	167	90	75	112	70	3.83
1978—Tucson	P. Coast	22	143	9	6	.600	158	77	63	85	68	3.97
1978—Texas†	American	10	28	3	2	.600	30	18	18	23	17	5.79
1979—Columbus..........................	Int'national	22	144	11	7	.611	129	75	62	98	50	3.88
1979—New York‡.........................	American	10	14	0	4	.000	16	15	14	4	10	9.00
1980—Syracuse	Int'national	4	31	1	2	.333	28	13	9	23	8	2.61

Year Club	League	G.	IP.	W.	L.	Pct.	H.	R.	ER.	SO.	BB.	ERA
1980—Toronto	American	33	131	5	12	.294	151	73	63	53	66	4.33
1981—Syracuse	Int'national	22	153	11	7	.611	150	63	52	79	53	3.06
1981—Toronto§x	American	8	15	0	0	.000	20	16	12	9	7	7.20
1982—Texas y	American	40	50⅔	1	1	.500	46	28	27	29	22	4.80
1983—Rochester	Int'national	19	76⅓	3	5	.375	87	44	31	32	29	3.66
1983—Baltimore z	American	3	9⅔	0	0	.000	9	6	6	4	7	5.59
Major League Totals		104	248⅓	9	19	.321	272	156	140	122	129	5.07

Selected by Minnsota Twins' organization in 16th round of free-agent draft, June 4, 1975.

Selected by Texas Rangers' organization in secondary phase of free-agent draft, January 7, 1976.

†Traded with Pitchers Mike Griffin and Dave Righetti and Outfielders Juan Beniquez and Greg Jemison to New York Yankees for Pitchers Sparky Lyle, Larry McCall and Dave Rajsich, Catcher Mike Heath, Shortstop Domingo Ramos and cash, November 10, 1978.

‡Traded with First Baseman Chris Chambliss and Infielder Damaso Garcia to Toronto Blue Jays for Catcher Rick Cerone, Pitcher Tom Underwood and Outfielder Ted Wilborn, November 1, 1979.

§Traded to Chicago Cubs' organization for a player to be named later, December 28, 1981; Toronto Blue Jays' organization acquired Pitcher Dave Geisel to complete deal, March 25, 1982.

xTraded with a player to be named later and cash to Texas Rangers for Second Baseman Bump Wills, March 26, 1982; Texas organization acquired Pitcher Paul Semall to complete deal, April 21, 1982.

yReleased, March 26, 1983; signed by Rochester (Baltimore Orioles' organization), April 16, 1983.

zGranted free agency, October 20, 1983.

KEVIN DARRNELL MITCHELL

Born January 13, 1962, at San Diego, Calif.
Height, 5.10. Weight, 185.
Throws and bats righthanded.

Year Club	League	Pos.	G.	AB.	R.	H.	2B.	3B.	HR.	RBI.	B.A.	PO.	A.	E.	F.A.
1981—Kingsport	Appal.	3B-OF	62	221	39	74	9	2	7	45	.335	44	102	18	.890
1982—Lynchburg†	Carol.	3B	29	85	19	27	5	1	1	16	.318	11	33	10	.815
1983—Jackson	Texas	★3B-OF	120	441	75	132	25	2	15	85	.299	81	★224	21	.936

Signed as free agent by New York Mets' organization, November 16, 1980.

†On disabled list, July 21, 1982 through remainder of season.

ROBERT VAN MITCHELL
(Bobby)

Born April 7, 1955, at Salt Lake City, Utah.
Height, 5.10. Weight, 170.
Throws and bats lefthanded.
Attended University of Southern California,
Los Angeles, Calif.

Year Club	League	Pos.	G.	AB.	R.	H.	2B.	3B.	HR.	RBI.	B.A.	PO.	A.	E.	F.A.
1977—Clinton	Midw.	OF	74	221	37	72	19	1	3	28	.326	145	9	3	.981
1978—San Antonio	Texas	OF	131	480	76	140	17	5	1	42	.292	★302	10	4	.987
1979—Albuquerque	P. C.	OF	123	453	104	148	24	8	2	59	.327	279	21	7	.977
1980—Albuquerque	P. C.	OF	109	347	62	111	20	6	3	53	.320	292	11	2	.993
1980—Los Angeles	Nat.	OF	9	3	1	1	0	0	0	0	.333	5	0	0	1.000
1981—Albuquerque	P. C.	OF	104	341	68	106	17	5	1	63	.311	250	8	0	1.000
1981—Los Angeles†	Nat.	OF	10	8	0	1	0	0	0	0	.125	6	0	0	1.000
1982—Minnesota	Amer.	OF	124	454	48	113	11	6	2	28	.249	350	8	1	.997
1982—Toledo	Int.	OF	12	43	10	15	7	0	1	5	.349	44	1	2	.957
1983—Minnesota	Amer.	OF	59	152	26	35	4	2	1	15	.230	94	2	1	.990
National League Totals			19	11	1	2	0	0	0	0	.182	11	0	0	1.000
American League Totals			183	606	74	148	15	8	3	43	.244	444	10	2	.996
Major League Totals			202	617	75	150	15	8	3	43	.243	455	10	2	.996

Selected by San Francisco Giants' organization in 5th round of free-agent draft, June 5, 1973.

Selected by Los Angeles Dodgers' organization in 7th round of free-agent draft, June 7, 1977.

†Traded with Pitcher Bobby Castillo to Minnesota Twins for Catcher Scotti Madison and Pitcher Paul Voigt, January 7, 1982.

JOHN JOSEPH MIZEROCK

Name pronounced MIZZ-rock.

Born December 8, 1960, at Punxsutawney, Pa.
Height, 6.00. Weight, 180.
Throws right and bats lefthanded.

Led Southern League in intentional bases on balls received with 12 in 1982.

Led Southern League catchers in putouts with 762 and total chances with 865 in 1982.

Led Florida State League catchers in fielding percentage with .993 and passed balls with 13 in 1981.

Tied for Florida State League lead in double plays by catchers with 8 in 1980.

Year Club	League	Pos.	G.	AB.	R.	H.	2B.	3B.	HR.	RBI.	B.A.	PO.	A.	E.	F.A.
1979—Daytona Beach	Fla. St.	C	53	152	13	39	6	1	3	12	.257	255	25	5	.982
1980—Daytona Beach	Fla. St.	C	99	299	37	66	11	1	2	39	.221	532	52	9	.985
1981—Daytona Beach	Fla. St.	C-1B-OF	92	304	36	67	11	0	1	42	.220	515	50	4	.993
1981—Columbus	South.	C	11	35	6	8	2	0	0	2	.229	80	11	2	.979
1982—Columbus	South.	★C-1B	128	420	46	96	14	1	12	48	.229	785	★87	17	.981

Year Club League	Pos.	G.	AB.	R.	H.	2B.	3B.	HR.	RBI.	B.A.	PO.	A.	E.	F.A.
1983—Houston† .... Nat.	C	33	85	8	13	4	1	1	10	.153	154	24	6	.967
1983—Tucson .... P. C.	C-1B	53	176	18	46	12	2	5	31	.261	298	29	5	.985
Major League Totals....................................		33	85	8	13	4	1	1	10	.153	154	24	6	.967

Selected by Houston Astros' organization in 1st round (eighth player selected) of free-agent draft, June 5, 1979.
†On disabled list, July 3 to July 26, 1983.

RANDALL JAMES MOFFITT
(Randy)

Born October 13, 1948, at Long Beach, Calif.
Height, 6.03. Weight, 195.
Throws and bats righthanded.
Attended California State College, Long Beach, Calif.
Son of Bill Moffitt, scout with Milwaukee Brewers; brother of tennis star Billie Jean King.

Major League saves: 1972 (4), 1973 (14), 1974 (15), 1975 (11), 1976 (14), 1977 (11), 1978 (12), 1979 (2), 1982 (3), 1983 (10). Total—96.
Led Pacific Coast League in hit batsmen with 9 in 1971.

Year Club	League	G.	IP.	W.	L.	Pct.	H.	R.	ER.	SO.	BB.	ERA.
1970—Fresno†	California	18	135	9	6	.600	91	35	24	149	23	1.60
1971—Phoenix‡	P. Coast	42	121	6	7	.462	147	78	69	94	48	5.13
1972—Phoenix	P. Coast	19	24	1	3	.250	22	9	6	24	15	2.25
1972—San Francisco	National	40	71	1	5	.167	72	31	29	37	30	3.68
1973—San Francisco	National	60	100	4	4	.500	86	30	27	65	31	2.43
1974—San Francisco	National	61	102	5	7	.417	99	52	51	49	29	4.50
1975—San Francisco	National	55	74	4	5	.444	73	35	32	39	32	3.89
1976—San Francisco	National	58	103	6	6	.500	92	36	26	50	35	2.27
1977—San Francisco	National	64	88	4	9	.308	91	41	35	68	39	3.58
1978—San Francisco	National	70	82	8	4	.667	79	35	30	52	33	3.29
1979—San Francisco§	National	28	35	2	5	.286	53	33	30	16	14	7.71
1980—San Francisco x	National	13	17	1	1	.500	18	10	9	10	4	4.76
1981—San Francisco y	National	10	11	0	0	.000	15	10	10	11	2	8.18
1982—Tucson	P. Coast	7	8⅓	0	1	.000	11	6	4	7	0	4.32
1982—Houston z	National	30	41⅔	2	4	.333	36	15	14	20	13	3.02
1983—Toronto a	American	45	57⅓	6	2	.750	52	27	24	38	24	3.77
National League Totals............................		489	724⅔	37	50	.425	714	328	293	417	262	3.64
American League Totals		45	57⅓	6	2	.750	52	27	24	38	24	3.77
Major League Totals.................................		534	782	43	52	.453	766	355	317	455	286	3.65

Selected by San Francisco Giants' organization in 1st round (18th player selected) of free-agent draft, January 17, 1970.
†On military list, February 16 to June 5, 1970.
‡On disabled list, August 22 to September 2, 1971.
§On disabled list, February 20 to April 20 and June 22 to August 12, 1979.
xOn disabled list, May 12 to August 14, 1980.
yReleased, August 4, 1981; signed by Tucson (Houston Astros' organization), February 5, 1982.
zGranted free agency, November 10, 1982; signed by Toronto Blue Jays, February 15, 1983.
aGranted free agency, November 7, 1983.

ROBERT JOSEPH MOLINARO

Name pronounced Moh-luh-NAHR-oh.

(Bobby)

Born May 21, 1950, at Newark, N. J.
Height, 6.00. Weight, 180.
Throws right and bats lefthanded.

Led American Association in sacrifice flies with 9 in 1977.
Tied for American Association lead in double plays by outfielders with 4 in 1976.

Year Club	League	Pos.	G.	AB.	R.	H.	2B.	3B.	HR.	RBI.	B.A.	PO.	A.	E.	F.A.
1968—Sarasota Tigers....	Gulf C.	OF	55	176	32	57	5	4	0	13	.324	68	5	2	.973
1969—Rocky Mount........	Carol.	OF	111	415	66	107	9	4	4	28	.258	194	9	5	.976
1970—Montgomery........	South.	OF	96	335	30	82	15	4	1	35	.245	150	8	6	.963
1971—Montgomery†	South.	OF	45	166	26	50	11	2	4	25	.301	71	7	6	.929
1972—Toledo	Int.	OF	106	349	41	92	15	1	4	39	.264	138	8	5	.967
1973—Montgomery........	South.	OF	69	248	33	78	5	2	5	45	.315	73	8	2	.976
1973—Toledo	Int.	OF	49	183	19	44	14	0	4	30	.240	86	0	2	.977
1974—Evansville	A. A.	OF	118	393	56	106	14	2	11	51	.270	92	8	3	.971
1975—Evansville	A. A.	OF	126	471	69	135	20	4	13	75	.287	174	2	5	.972
1975—Detroit...................	Amer.	OF	6	19	2	5	0	1	0	1	.263	8	1	0	1.000
1976—Evansville	A. A.	OF	135	491	72	142	27	9	6	67	.289	211	12	12	.949
1977—Evansville	A. A.	OF	125	455	85	138	25	2	17	91	.303	196	12	7	.967
1977—Det.‡-Chi.	Amer.	OF	5	6	0	2	1	0	0	0	.333	1	0	0	1.000
1978—Chicago	Amer.	OF	105	286	39	75	5	5	6	27	.262	88	2	0	1.000
1979—Iowa§	A. A.	OF	133	475	90	156	23	5	13	93	.328	65	10	2	.974
1979—Baltimore x..........	Amer.	OF	8	6	0	0	0	0	0	0	.000	7	0	0	1.000
1980—Chicago	Amer.	OF	119	344	48	100	16	4	5	36	.291	85	3	4	.957
1981—Chicago y.............	Amer.	OF	47	42	7	11	1	1	1	9	.262	3	0	0	1.000
1982—Chi. z-Phil.	Nat.	OF	84	80	6	17	1	0	1	14	.213	2	0	0	1.000

Year Club League	Pos.	G.	AB.	R.	H.	2B.	3B.	HR.	RBI.	B.A.	PO.	A.	E.	F.A.
1983—Philadelphia a...... Nat.	PH	19	18	1	2	1	0	1	3	.111	0	0	0	.000
1983—Detroit b .... Amer.	PR-PH	8	2	3	0	0	0	0	0	.000	0	0	0	.000
American League Totals...........................		298	705	99	193	23	11	12	73	.274	192	6	4	.980
National League Totals.............................		103	98	7	19	2	0	2	17	.194	2	0	0	1.000
Major League Totals.................................		401	803	106	212	25	11	14	90	.264	194	6	4	.980

Selected by Detroit Tigers' organization in 2nd round of free-agent draft, June 7, 1968.

†On disabled list, June 12 to August 29, 1971.

‡Sold on waivers to Chicago White Sox, September 22, 1977.

§Sold on waivers to Baltimore Orioles, August 31, 1979.

xSold on waivers to Chicago White Sox, October 3, 1979.

yTraded to Chicago Cubs, March 29, 1982, completing deal in which Chicago Cubs traded Pitcher Lynn McGlothen to Chicago White Sox for a player to be named later, August 15, 1981.

zSold to Philadelphia Phillies, September 1, 1982.

aReleased, June 6, 1983; signed by Detroit Tigers, September 1, 1983.

bReleased, October 21, 1983.

PAUL LEO MOLITOR

Born August 22, 1956, at St. Paul, Minn.
Height, 6.00. Weight, 175.
Throws and bats righthanded.
Attending University of Minnesota, Minneapolis, Minn.

Hit three home runs in a game, May 12, 1982.

Major league stolen bases: 1978 (30), 1979 (33), 1980 (34), 1981 (10), 1982 (41), 1983 (41). Total—189.

Led American League third basemen in errors with 29 and double plays with 48 in 1982.

Named American League Rookie Player of the Year by THE SPORTING NEWS, 1978.

Named Midwest League Most Valuable Player, 1977.

Received reported $100,000 bonus to sign with Milwaukee Brewers, 1977.

Year Club League	Pos.	G.	AB.	R.	H.	2B.	3B.	HR.	RBI.	B.A.	PO.	A.	E.	F.A.
1977—Burlington .... Midw.	SS	64	228	52	79	12	0	8	50	.346	83	207	28	.912
1978—Milwaukee............. Amer.	2B-SS-3B	125	521	73	142	26	4	6	45	.273	253	401	22	.967
1979—Milwaukee............. Amer.	2B-SS	140	584	88	188	27	16	9	62	.322	309	440	16	.979
1980—Milwaukee†.......... Amer.	2B-SS-3B	111	450	81	137	29	2	9	37	.304	260	336	20	.968
1981—Milwaukee‡.......... Amer.	OF	64	251	45	67	11	0	2	19	.267	119	4	3	.976
1982—Milwaukee............. Amer.	3B-SS	160	*666	*136	201	26	8	19	71	.302	134	350	32	.938
1983—Milwaukee............. Amer.	3B	153	613	96	167	29	6	15	47	.272	105	343	16	.966
Major League Totals..................................		753	3085	519	902	148	36	60	281	.292	1180	1874	109	.966

Selected by St. Louis Cardinals' organization in 28th round of free-agent draft, June 5, 1974.

Selected by Milwaukee Brewers' organization in 1st round (third player selected) of free-agent draft, June 7, 1977.

†On supplemental disabled list, June 24 to July 18, 1980.

‡On supplemental disabled list, May 3, 1981; transferred to emergency disabled list, May 6 to August 12, 1981.

DIVISION SERIES RECORD

Year Club League	Pos.	G.	AB.	R.	H.	2B.	3B.	HR.	RBI.	B.A.	PO.	A.	E.	F.A.
1981—Milwaukee............. Amer.	OF	5	20	2	5	0	0	1	1	.250	12	7	0	1.000

CHAMPIONSHIP SERIES RECORD

Tied American League Championship Series record for most home runs, five-game Series (2), 1982.

Year Club League	Pos.	G.	AB.	R.	H.	2B.	3B.	HR.	RBI.	B.A.	PO.	A.	E.	F.A.
1982—Milwaukee............. Amer.	3B	5	19	4	6	1	0	2	5	.316	4	11	2	.882

WORLD SERIES RECORD

Established World Series records for most hits, game (5), October 12, 1982; most one-base hits, game (5), October 12, 1982.

Tied World Series records for most at-bats, nine-inning game (6), October 12, 1982; most hits, two consecutive games, one Series (7), October 12, 13, 1982.

Year Club League	Pos.	G.	AB.	R.	H.	2B.	3B.	HR.	RBI.	B.A.	PO.	A.	E.	F.A.
1982—Milwaukee............. Amer.	3B	7	31	5	11	0	0	0	3	.355	4	9	0	1.000

ALL-STAR GAME RECORD

Named to American League All-Star Team in 1980; replaced due to injury.

ROBERT JAMES MONDAY JR.
(Rick)

Born November 20, 1945, at Batesville, Ark.
Height, 6.03. Weight, 200.
Throws and bats lefthanded.
Attended Arizona State University, Tempe, Ariz.

Tied major league records for most strikeouts, game (5), April 29, 1970; most at bats, doubleheader, more than 18 innings (14), June 17, 1967 (28 innings); most strikeouts, two consecutive games (8), April 28 and 29, 1970.

Hit three home runs in a game, May 16, 1972.

Tied for National League lead in double plays by outfielders with 5 in 1974.

Tied for American League lead in double plays by outfielders with 6 in 1967.

Led Southern League batters in strikeouts with 143 in 1966.

Named College Player of the Year by THE SPORTING NEWS, 1965.

Received reported $104,000 bonus to sign with Kansas City Athletics, 1965.

Year—Club	League	Pos.	G.	AB.	R.	H.	2B.	3B.	HR.	RBI.	B.A.	PO.	A.	E.	F.A.
1965—Lewiston	N'west	OF-1B	72	247	45	67	12	2	13	44	.271	205	6	8	.963
1966—Mobile	South.	OF	127	469	86	125	16	10	23	72	.267	★287	10	13	.958
1966—Kansas City	Amer.	OF	17	41	4	4	1	1	0	2	.098	26	1	1	.964
1967—Kansas City	Amer.	OF	124	406	52	102	14	6	14	58	.251	260	14	8	.972
1968—Oakland	Amer.	OF	148	482	56	132	24	7	8	49	.274	299	11	7	.978
1969—Oakland	Amer.	OF	122	399	57	108	17	4	12	54	.271	262	3	10	.964
1970—Oakland†	Amer.	OF	112	376	63	109	19	7	10	37	.290	257	3	5	.981
1971—Oakland‡	Amer.	OF	116	355	53	87	9	3	18	56	.245	238	6	4	.984
1972—Chicago	Nat.	OF	138	434	68	108	22	5	11	42	.249	268	6	1	★.996
1973—Chicago	Nat.	OF	149	554	93	148	24	5	26	56	.267	317	9	9	.973
1974—Chicago	Nat.	OF	142	538	84	158	19	7	20	58	.294	302	10	5	.984
1975—Chicago§	Nat.	OF	136	491	89	131	29	4	17	60	.267	315	6	9	.973
1976—Chicago§	Nat.	OF-1B	137	534	107	145	20	5	32	77	.272	587	26	5	.992
1977—Los Angeles	Nat.	OF-1B	118	392	47	90	13	1	15	48	.230	221	5	2	.991
1978—Los Angeles	Nat.	OF-1B	119	342	54	87	14	1	19	57	.254	217	3	1	.995
1979—Los Angeles x	Nat.	OF	12	33	2	10	0	0	0	2	.303	27	0	1	.964
1980—Los Angeles	Nat.	OF	96	194	35	52	7	1	10	25	.268	92	1	3	.969
1981—Los Angeles y	Nat.	OF	66	130	24	41	1	2	11	25	.315	50	1	2	.962
1982—Los Angeles	Nat.	OF-1B	104	210	37	54	6	4	11	42	.257	86	7	4	.959
1983—Los Angeles	Nat.	OF-1B	99	178	21	44	7	1	6	20	.247	80	2	3	.965
American League Totals			639	2059	285	542	84	28	62	256	.263	1342	38	35	.975
National League Totals			1316	4030	661	1068	162	36	178	512	.265	2562	76	45	.983
Major League Totals			1955	6089	946	1610	246	64	240	768	.264	3904	114	80	.980

Selected by Kansas City A's organization in 1st round (first player selected) of free-agent draft, June 15, 1965.
†On military list June 18 to July 8, 1970.
‡Traded to Chicago Cubs for Pitcher Ken Holtzman, November 29, 1971.
§Traded with Pitcher Mike Garman to Los Angeles Dodgers for First Baseman-Outfielder Bill Buckner, Shortstop Ivan DeJesus and Pitcher Jeff Albert, January 11, 1977.
xOn disabled list, May 8, 1979; transferred to emergency disabled list, July 26, 1979 through remainder of season.
yGranted free agency, November 13, 1981; re-signed by Dodgers, December 2, 1981.

DIVISION SERIES RECORD

Year—Club	League	Pos.	G.	AB.	R.	H.	2B.	3B.	HR.	RBI.	B.A.	PO.	A.	E.	F.A.
1981—Los Angeles	Nat.	OF	5	14	1	3	0	0	0	1	.214	12	0	0	1.000

CHAMPIONSHIP SERIES RECORD

Year—Club	League	Pos.	G.	AB.	R.	H.	2B.	3B.	HR.	RBI.	B.A.	PO.	A.	E.	F.A.
1971—Oakland	Amer.	OF	1	3	0	0	0	0	0	0	.000	4	0	0	1.000
1977—Los Angeles	Nat.	OF-PH	3	7	1	2	1	0	0	0	.286	6	0	0	1.000
1978—Los Angeles	Nat.	OF-PH	3	10	2	2	0	1	0	0	.200	6	0	0	1.000
1981—Los Angeles	Nat.	PH-OF	3	9	2	3	0	0	1	1	.333	2	0	0	1.000
1983—Los Angeles	Nat.	PH	1	0	0	0	0	0	0	0	.000	0	0	0	.000
Championship Series Totals			11	29	5	7	1	1	1	1	.241	18	0	0	1.000

WORLD SERIES RECORD

Year—Club	League	Pos.	G.	AB.	R.	H.	2B.	3B.	HR.	RBI.	B.A.	PO.	A.	E.	F.A.
1977—Los Angeles	Nat.	OF	4	12	0	2	0	0	0	0	.167	5	0	0	1.000
1978—Los Angeles	Nat.	OF-DH	5	13	2	2	1	0	0	0	.154	5	0	0	1.000
1981—Los Angeles	Nat.	OF-PH	5	13	1	3	1	0	0	0	.231	9	0	0	1.000
World Series Totals			14	38	3	7	2	0	0	0	.184	19	0	0	1.000

ALL-STAR GAME RECORD

Year—League		Pos.	AB.	R.	H.	2B.	3B.	HR.	RBI.	B.A.	PO.	A.	E.	F.A.
1968—American		OF	2	0	0	0	0	0	0	.000	0	0	0	.000
1978—National		OF	2	0	0	0	0	0	0	.000	1	0	0	1.000
All-Star Game Totals			4	0	0	0	0	0	0	.000	1	0	0	1.000

PITCHING RECORD

Year—Club	League	G.	IP.	W.	L.	Pct.	H.	R.	ER.	SO.	BB.	ERA.
1965—Lewiston	Northwest	1	1	0	0	.000	0	0	0	2	2	0.00

DONALD WAYNE MONEY
(Don)

Born June 7, 1947, at Washington, D. C.
Height, 6.01. Weight, 190.
Throws and bats righthanded.

Established major league records for highest fielding average by third baseman, season (.9894), 1974; fewest errors by third baseman, season (150 or more games) (5), 1974; most consecutive errorless games by third baseman, season (86), April 5 to July 16, 1974; most consecutive errorless chances accepted by third baseman, lifetime (261), September 28, 1973 (1st game) to July 16, 1974; most consecutive errorless chances accepted by third baseman, season (257), April 5 to July 16, 1974.

Tied major league record for most assists by second baseman, game (12), June 24, 1977.

Established American League record for most consecutive errorless games, third baseman, lifetime (88), September 28, 1973 (2nd game) to July 16, 1974.

Established National League record for most consecutive errorless chances accepted by third baseman, season (163), July 23-September 11, 1972.

Led American League third basemen in fielding percentage with .971 in 1973.
Led National League third basemen in putouts with 139 in 1972.
Tied for National League lead in double plays by third basemen with 31 in 1972.
Led Appalachian League shortstops in double plays with 34 in 1965 and Carolina League shortstops with 87 in 1967.
Named Carolina League Most Valuable Player, 1967.

Year	Club	League	Pos.	G.	AB.	R.	H.	2B.	3B.	HR.	RBI.	B.A.	PO.	A.	E.	F.A.
1965—Salem	Appal.		SS	66	216	46	52	7	0	6	24	.241	★88	★171	24	.915
1966—Clinton	Midw.		SS-2B	●125	458	40	108	17	5	7	61	.236	186	345	33	.941
1967—Raleigh†	Carol.		SS	136	480	66	149	★37	5	16	86	.310	★250	★418	33	.953
1968—Philadelphia	Nat.		SS	4	13	1	3	2	0	0	2	.231	6	8	0	1.000
1968—San Diego	P. C.		SS	127	482	63	146	26	4	9	59	.303	226	441	26	.962
1969—Philadelphia	Nat.		SS	127	450	41	103	22	2	6	42	.229	212	443	21	.969
1970—Philadelphia	Nat.		3B-SS	120	447	66	132	25	4	14	66	.295	133	236	15	.961
1971—Philadelphia‡	Nat.		3B-OF-2B	121	439	40	98	22	8	7	38	.223	167	197	11	.970
1972—Philadelphia§	Nat.		★3B-SS	152	536	54	119	16	2	15	52	.222	140	316	10	★.978
1973—Milwaukee	Amer.		3B-SS	145	556	75	158	28	2	11	61	.284	146	276	13	.970
1974—Milwaukee	Amer.		★3B-2B	159	★629	85	178	32	3	15	86	.283	131	336	5	★.989
1975—Milwaukee x	Amer.		3B-SS	109	405	58	112	16	1	15	43	.277	109	194	15	.953
1976—Milwaukee	Amer.		3B-SS	117	439	51	117	18	4	12	62	.267	96	202	13	.958
1977—Milwaukee	Amer.		2B-OF-3B	152	570	86	159	28	3	25	83	.279	306	390	16	.978
1978—Milwaukee	Amer.		1-2-3-S	137	518	88	152	30	2	14	54	.293	705	216	9	.990
1979—Milwaukee y	Amer.		3B-1B-2B	92	350	52	83	20	1	6	38	.237	240	117	2	.994
1980—Milwaukee	Amer.		3B-2B-1B	86	289	39	74	17	1	17	46	.256	176	129	12	.962
1981—Milwaukee	Amer.		3B-1B	60	185	17	40	7	0	2	14	.216	33	100	3	.978
1982—Milwaukee	Amer.		3B-1B-2B	96	275	40	78	14	3	16	55	.284	72	49	4	.968
1983—Milwaukee z	Amer.		3B	43	114	5	17	5	0	1	8	.149	25	33	1	.983
National League Totals				524	1885	202	455	87	16	42	200	.241	658	1200	57	.70
American League Totals				1196	4330	596	1168	215	20	134	529	.270	2039	2042	93	.978
Major League Totals				1720	6215	798	1623	302	36	176	729	.261	2697	3242	150	.975

Signed as free agent by Pittsburgh Pirates' organization, June 20, 1965.
†Traded with Pitchers Woodie Fryman, Bill Laxton and Harold Clem to Philadelphia Phillies for Pitcher Jim Bunning, December 15, 1967.
‡On military list June 12 to June 30, 1972.
§Traded with Infielder John Vukovich and Pitcher Billy Champion to Milwaukee Brewers for Pitchers Ken Brett, Ken Sanders, Jim Lonborg and Earl Stephenson, October 31, 1972.
xOn disabled list, May 28 to June 24, 1975.
yOn disabled list, May 2 to June 16, 1979.
zOn supplemental disabled list, August 5 to September 1, 1983.

DIVISION SERIES RECORD

Year	Club	League	Pos.	G.	AB.	R.	H.	2B.	3B.	HR.	RBI.	B.A.	PO.	A.	E.	F.A.
1981—Milwaukee	Amer.		PH-DH	2	3	0	0	0	0	0	0	.000	1	1	0	1.000

CHAMPIONSHIP SERIES RECORD

Year	Club	League	Pos.	G.	AB.	R.	H.	2B.	3B.	HR.	RBI.	B.A.	PO.	A.	E.	F.A.
1982—Milwaukee	Amer.		DH	4	11	2	2	0	0	0	1	.182	0	0	0	.000

WORLD SERIES RECORD

Tied World Series record for most at-bats, inning (2), October 16, 1982 (seventh inning).

Year	Club	League	Pos.	G.	AB.	R.	H.	2B.	3B.	HR.	RBI.	B.A.	PO.	A.	E.	F.A.
1982—Milwaukee	Amer.		PH-DH	5	13	4	3	1	0	0	1	.231	0	0	0	.000

ALL-STAR GAME RECORD

Year	League	Pos.	AB.	R.	H.	2B.	3B.	HR.	RBI.	B.A.	PO.	A.	E.	F.A.
1976—American		3B	1	0	0	0	0	0	0	.000	0	1	0	1.000
1978—American		2B	2	0	0	0	0	0	0	.000	1	1	0	1.000
All-Star Game Totals			3	0	0	0	0	0	0	.000	1	2	0	1.000

Member of American League All-Star Team in 1974 game; did not play.
Named to American League All-Star Team in 1977; replaced due to injury.

ISIDRO PEDROZA MONGE

Name pronounced MON-jee.

(Sid)

Born April 11, 1951, at Agua Prieta, Sonora, Mexico.
Height, 6.02. Weight, 195.
Throws left and bats left and righthanded.

Pitched 6-0 no-hit victory against Cedar Rapids, May 4, 1971.
Major League saves: 1977 (4), 1978 (6), 1979 (19), 1980 (14), 1981 (4), 1982 (2), 1983 (7). Total—56.
Tied for Texas League lead in home runs allowed with 16 in 1973.

Year	Club	League	G.	IP.	W.	L.	Pct.	H.	R.	ER.	SO.	BB.	ERA.
1970—Idaho Falls	Pioneer		17	62	5	1	.833	60	35	29	54	42	4.21
1971—Quad Cities	Midwest		25	169	12	11	.522	120	62	45	158	83	2.40
1972—Shreveport†	Texas		24	135	5	10	.333	116	62	52	106	73	3.47
1973—El Paso	Texas		25	147	7	11	.389	173	100	75	90	72	4.59
1974—El Paso	Texas		25	163	●14	5	.737	182	99	84	111	67	4.64
1975—Salt Lake City	P. Coast		27	167	14	9	.609	175	98	86	106	93	4.63
1975—California	American		4	20	0	2	.000	22	12	11	17	10	4.13

Year Club	League	G.	IP.	W.	L.	Pct.	H.	R.	ER.	SO.	BB.	ERA.
1976—California	American	32	118	6	7	.462	108	50	44	53	49	3.36
1977—Calif.‡-Cleve.	American	37	51	1	3	.250	61	37	31	29	33	5.47
1978—Cleveland	American	48	85	4	3	.571	71	36	26	54	51	2.75
1979—Cleveland	American	76	131	12	10	.545	96	37	35	108	64	2.40
1980—Cleveland	American	67	94	3	5	.375	80	39	37	61	40	3.54
1981—Cleveland§ x	American	31	58	3	5	.375	58	31	28	41	21	4.34
1982—Philadelphia	National	47	72	7	1	.875	70	35	30	43	22	3.75
1983—Philadelphia y-San Diego	National	61	80⅓	10	3	.769	85	34	33	39	37	3.70
American League Totals		295	561	29	35	.453	496	242	212	363	268	3.40
National League Totals		108	152⅓	17	4	.810	155	69	63	82	59	3.72
Major League Totals		403	713⅓	46	39	.541	651	311	275	445	327	3.47

Selected by California Angels' organization in 24th round of free-agent draft, June 4, 1970.

†On temporary inactive list, August 10, 1972 through remainder of season.

‡Traded with First Baseman-Outfielder Bruce Bochte and cash estimated at $250,000 to Cleveland Indians for Pitchers Dave LaRoche and Dave Schuler, May 11, 1977.

§Granted free agency, November 13, 1981; re-signed by Indians, January 21, 1982.

xTraded to Philadelphia Phillies for Outfielder Bake McBride, February 16, 1982.

yTraded to San Diego Padres for Outfielder Joe Lefebvre, May 22, 1983.

ALL-STAR GAME RECORD
Member of American League All-Star Team for 1979 game; did not play.

JOHN JOSEPH MONTEFUSCO JR.

Name pronounced Mon-tuh-FYOOS-koh.
Born May 25, 1950, at Long Branch, N. J.
Height, 6.01. Weight, 192.
Throws and bats righthanded.
Attended Brookdale Community College, Lincroft, N. J.

Pitched 9-0 no-hit victory against Atlanta Braves, September 29, 1976.
Hit home run on first official major league time at bat, September 3, 1974.
Struck out eight consecutive batters against Salt Lake City, August 11, 1974.
Tied for National League lead in shutouts by pitchers with 6 in 1976.
Led Texas League in shutouts with 4 in 1974.
Tied for Pacific Coast League lead in shutouts with 3 in 1974.
Named National League Rookie of the Year by Baseball Writers' Association of America, 1975.
Named National League Rookie Pitcher of the Year by THE SPORTING NEWS, 1975.

Year Club	League	G.	IP.	W.	L.	Pct.	H.	R.	ER.	SO.	BB.	ERA.
1973—Decatur	Midwest	24	120	9	2	.818	94	40	29	126	44	2.18
1974—Amarillo	Texas	19	144	8	9	.471	143	61	50	107	37	3.13
1974—Phoenix	P. Coast	11	77	7	3	.700	60	35	28	90	26	3.27
1974—San Francisco	National	7	39	3	2	.600	41	22	21	34	19	4.85
1975—San Francisco	National	35	244	15	9	.625	210	85	78	215	86	2.88
1976—San Francisco	National	37	253	16	14	.533	224	90	80	172	74	2.85
1977—San Francisco†	National	26	157	7	12	.368	170	82	61	110	46	3.50
1978—San Francisco	National	36	239	11	9	.550	233	110	101	177	68	3.80
1979—San Francisco‡	National	22	137	3	8	.273	145	64	60	76	51	3.94
1980—San Francisco§x	National	22	113	4	8	.333	120	61	55	85	39	4.38
1981—Atlanta y	National	26	77	2	3	.400	75	32	30	34	27	3.51
1982—San Diego	National	32	184⅓	10	11	.476	177	93	82	83	41	4.00
1983—San Diego z	National	31	95⅓	9	4	.692	94	38	35	52	32	3.30
1983—New York	American	6	38	5	0	1.000	39	14	14	15	10	3.32
National League Totals		274	1538⅔	80	80	.500	1489	677	603	1038	483	3.53
American League Totals		6	38	5	0	1.000	39	14	14	15	10	3.32
Major League Totals		280	1576⅔	85	80	.515	1528	691	617	1053	493	3.52

Signed as free agent by San Francisco Giants' organization, October 6, 1972.

†On disabled list, May 27 to July 6, 1977.

‡On disabled list, April 26 to June 13, 1979.

§On disabled list, July 17 to August 24, 1980.

xTraded with Outfielder Craig Landis to Atlanta Braves for Pitcher Doyle Alexander, December 12, 1980.

yGranted free agency, November 13, 1981; signed by San Diego Padres, March 6, 1982.

zTraded to New York Yankees for two players to be named later, August 26, 1983; San Diego Padres acquired Pitcher Dennis Rasmussen and Second Baseman Edwin Rodriguez to complete deal, September 12, 1983.

ALL-STAR GAME RECORD
Year League	IP.	W.	L.	Pct.	H.	R.	ER.	SO.	BB.	ERA.
1976—National	2	0	0	.000	0	0	0	2	2	0.00

WILLIAM CRAIG MOONEYHAM
(Bill)

Born August 16, 1960, at Livermore, Calif.
Height, 6.00. Weight, 175.
Throws and bats righthanded.
Attended Merced Community College, Merced, Calif.

Year Club	League	G.	IP.	W.	L.	Pct.	H.	R.	ER.	SO.	BB.	ERA.
1980—Salinas	California	12	74	4	7	.364	66	44	31	88	64	3.77
1981—Holyoke	Eastern	25	135	9	11	.450	124	90	68	155	★131	4.53

Year—Club	League	G.	IP.	W.	L.	Pct.	H.	R.	ER.	SO.	BB.	ERA.
1982—Holyoke†	Eastern	8	49	2	3	.400	44	26	23	46	24	4.22
1983—Nashua	Eastern	19	110	8	6	.571	99	67	56	76	83	4.58
1983—Edmonton	P. Coast	7	35⅔	2	0	1.000	51	39	39	26	22	9.84

Selected by Montreal Expos' organization in 6th round of free-agent draft, June 6, 1978.
Selected by St. Louis Cardinals' organization in secondary phase of free-agent draft, January 9, 1979.
Selected by New York Mets' organization in secondary phase of free-agent draft, June 5, 1979.
Selected by Seattle Mariners' organization in secondary phase of free-agent draft, January 8, 1980.
Selected by California Angels' organization in secondary phase of free-agent draft, June 3, 1980.
†On disabled list, March 26 to July 22, 1982.

CHARLES WILLIAM MOORE JR.
(Charlie)

Born June 21, 1953, at Birmingham, Ala.
Height, 5.11. Weight, 180.
Throws and bats righthanded.
Attended Mesa Junior College, Mesa, Ariz., and University of Alabama, Birmingham, Ala.
Son of Charles William Moore, Sr., minor league pitcher, 1948 through 1952.

Hit for the cycle, October 1, 1980.
Led American League outfielders in double plays with 6 in 1982.
Led American League in passed balls with 14 in 1977.
Led Midwest League catchers in putouts with 721, assists with 91, double plays with 12 and tied for lead in passed balls with 30 in 1972.
Led New York-Pennsylvania League in passed balls with 16 in 1971.

Year—Club	League	Pos.	G.	AB.	R.	H.	2B.	3B.	HR.	RBI.	B.A.	PO.	A.	E.	F.A.
1971—Newark	NYP	C	60	209	36	62	12	3	6	27	.297	★439	★34	5	.990
1972—Danville	Midw.	★C-1B	106	348	56	90	14	4	12	44	.259	723	92	★25	.970
1973—Shreveport	Texas	C	76	271	47	69	14	2	8	45	.255	402	46	14	.970
1973—Evansville	A. A.	C	50	178	27	52	9	1	7	25	.292	274	30	2	.993
1973—Milwaukee	Amer.	C	8	27	0	5	0	1	0	3	.185	48	5	1	.981
1974—Milwaukee	Amer.	C	72	204	17	50	10	4	0	19	.245	229	28	4	.985
1975—Milwaukee	Amer.	C-OF	73	241	26	70	20	1	1	29	.290	234	23	10	.963
1976—Milwaukee	Amer.	C-O-3	87	241	33	46	7	4	3	16	.191	249	45	9	.970
1977—Milwaukee	Amer.	C	138	375	42	93	15	6	5	45	.248	566	78	●13	.980
1978—Milwaukee	Amer.	C	96	268	30	72	7	1	5	31	.269	314	41	6	.983
1979—Milwaukee	Amer.	C	111	337	45	101	16	2	5	38	.300	414	58	10	.979
1980—Milwaukee	Amer.	C	111	320	42	93	13	2	2	30	.291	319	28	4	.989
1981—Milwaukee	Amer.	C-OF	48	156	16	47	8	3	1	9	.301	160	7	5	.973
1982—Milwaukee	Amer.	OF-C-2B	133	456	53	116	22	4	6	45	.254	317	23	7	.980
1983—Milwaukee	Amer.	OF-C	151	529	65	150	27	6	2	49	.284	309	10	7	.979
Major League Totals			1028	3154	369	843	145	34	30	314	.267	3159	356	76	.979

Selected by Milwaukee Brewers' organization in 4th round of free-agent draft, June 8, 1971.

DIVISION SERIES RECORD

Year—Club	League	Pos.	G.	AB.	R.	H.	2B.	3B.	HR.	RBI.	B.A.	PO.	A.	E.	F.A.
1981—Milwaukee	Amer.	DH-OF	4	9	0	2	0	0	0	1	.222	7	0	0	1.000

CHAMPIONSHIP SERIES RECORD

Year—Club	League	Pos.	G.	AB.	R.	H.	2B.	3B.	HR.	RBI.	B.A.	PO.	A.	E.	F.A.
1982—Milwaukee	Amer.	OF	5	13	3	6	0	0	0	0	.462	7	1	0	1.000

WORLD SERIES RECORD

Tied World Series record for most putouts by right fielder, inning (3), October 12, 1982 (eighth inning).

Year—Club	League	Pos.	G.	AB.	R.	H.	2B.	3B.	HR.	RBI.	B.A.	PO.	A.	E.	F.A.
1982—Milwaukee	Amer.	OF	7	26	3	9	3	0	0	2	.346	13	0	0	1.000

DONNIE RAY MOORE

Born February 13, 1954, at Lubbock, Tex.
Height, 6.00. Weight, 175.
Throws right and bats lefthanded.
Attended Ranger Junior College, Ranger, Tex.
Cousin of Hubie Brooks, third baseman with New York Mets.

Led American Association in home runs allowed with 25 in 1976.
Led Texas League pitchers in games started with 27 and tied for lead in shutouts with 3 and home runs allowed with 16 in 1975.
Received reported $50,000 bonus to sign with Chicago Cubs, 1973.

Year—Club	League	G.	IP.	W.	L.	Pct.	H.	R.	ER.	SO.	BB.	ERA.
1973—Bradenton Cubs	Gulf Coast	4	10	0	1	.000	9	5	4	6	6	3.60
1974—Key West†	Florida St.	26	174	11	12	.478	167	73	54	97	69	2.79
1974—Midland	Texas	5	22	0	4	.000	32	18	17	9	5	6.95
1975—Midland	Texas	28	●185	14	8	.636	191	79	61	123	67	2.97
1975—Chicago	National	4	9	0	0	.000	12	4	4	8	4	4.00
1976—Wichita	Am. Assoc.	24	152	7	11	.389	170	96	80	92	61	4.74
1977—Wichita	Am. Assoc.	11	66	4	4	.500	68	38	36	34	22	4.91
1977—Chicago	National	27	49	4	2	.667	51	27	22	34	18	4.04
1978—Chicago	National	71	103	9	7	.563	117	55	47	50	31	4.11
1979—Wichita	Am. Assoc.	5	29	1	3	.250	29	26	26	16	20	8.07

Year Club	League	G.	IP.	W.	L.	Pct.	H.	R.	ER.	SO.	BB.	ERA.
1979—Chicago‡	National	39	73	1	4	.200	95	46	42	43	25	5.18
1980—St. Louis	National	11	22	1	1	.500	25	15	15	10	5	6.14
1980—Springfield	Am. Assoc.	14	85	6	5	.545	74	32	29	49	32	3.07
1981—Springfield§xy	Am. Assoc.	21	108	8	6	.571	115	49	41	47	31	3.42
1981—Milwaukee	American	3	4	0	0	.000	4	3	3	2	4	6.75
1982—Richmond	Int'national	36	55	5	3	.625	51	17	14	45	18	2.29
1982—Atlanta	National	16	27⅔	3	1	.750	32	13	13	17	7	4.23
1983—Richmond	Int'national	12	16⅔	0	2	.000	12	6	6	9	7	3.24
1983—Atlanta z	National	43	68⅔	2	3	.400	72	30	28	41	10	3.67
National League Totals		211	352⅓	20	18	.526	404	190	171	203	100	4.37
American League Totals		3	4	0	0	.000	4	3	3	2	4	6.75
Major League Totals		214	356⅓	20	18	.526	408	193	174	205	104	4.39

Selected by Boston Red Sox' organization in 12th round of free-agent draft, June 6, 1972.
Signed as free agent by Chicago Cubs' organization, June 3, 1973.
†Appeared in two games as an outfielder with two putouts.
‡Traded to St. Louis Cardinals for Second Baseman Mike Tyson, October 17, 1979.
§On temporary inactive list, April 14 to May 11, 1981.
xSold conditionally to Milwaukee Brewers, September 3, 1981; returned, October 23, 1981.
yTraded to Atlanta Braves' organization for Pitcher Dan Morogiello, February 1, 1982.
zOn disabled list, August 3 to August 24, 1983.

CHAMPIONSHIP SERIES RECORD

Year Club	League	G.	IP.	W.	L.	Pct.	H.	R.	ER.	SO.	BB.	ERA.
1982—Atlanta	National	2	2⅔	0	0	.000	2	0	0	1	0	0.00

KELVIN ORLANDO MOORE

Born September 26, 1957, at LeRoy, Ala.
Height, 6.01. Weight, 195.
Throws left and bats righthanded.
Attended Jackson State University, Jackson, Miss.
Led Pacific Coast League batters in strikeouts with 132 in 1980 and 140 in 1981.

Year Club	League	Pos.	G.	AB.	R.	H.	2B.	3B.	HR.	RBI.	B.A.	PO.	A.	E.	F.A.
1978—Jersey City	East.	1B	59	214	23	58	5	6	2	28	.271	517	58	11	.981
1979—Modesto	Calif.	OF-1B	51	199	45	64	5	1	16	55	.322	116	3	14	.895
1979—Waterbury	East.	1B	83	317	46	106	19	3	14	56	.334	700	35	★13	.983
1980—Ogden	P. C.	1B	126	461	75	130	21	8	25	100	.282	1045	76	12	.989
1981—Tacoma	P. C.	1B	134	508	93	166	24	4	31	109	.327	★1203	85	★19	.985
1981—Oakland	Amer.	1B	14	47	5	12	0	1	1	3	.255	99	7	0	1.000
1982—Tacoma	P. C.	1B	113	421	77	111	19	4	21	82	.264	889	73	9	.991
1982—Oakland	Amer.	1B	21	67	6	15	1	1	2	6	.224	123	9	4	.971
1983—Oakland	Amer.	1B	41	124	12	26	4	0	5	16	.210	293	16	2	.994
1983—Tacoma†‡	P. C.	1B	35	122	17	34	3	3	5	22	.279	191	17	6	.972
1983—Tidewater	Int.	1B	30	101	11	21	3	1	2	14	.208	42	2	1	.978
Major League Totals			76	238	23	53	5	2	8	25	.223	515	32	6	.989

Selected by Oakland A's organization in 6th round of free-agent draft, June 6, 1978.
†On suspended list, June 9 to June 13, 1983.
‡Traded to New York Mets' organization for Pitcher Scott Dye, July 22, 1983.

DIVISION SERIES RECORD

Year Club	League	Pos.	G.	AB.	R.	H.	2B.	3B.	HR.	RBI.	B.A.	PO.	A.	E.	F.A.
1981—Oakland	Amer.	1B	2	8	0	0	0	0	0	0	.000	7	1	0	1.000

CHAMPIONSHIP SERIES RECORD

Year Club	League	Pos.	G.	AB.	R.	H.	2B.	3B.	HR.	RBI.	B.A.	PO.	A.	E.	F.A.
1981—Oakland	Amer.	1B	3	8	0	2	0	0	0	0	.250	13	3	0	1.000

MICHAEL WAYNE MOORE
(Mike)

Born November 26, 1959, at Eakly, Okla.
Height, 6.04. Weight, 210.
Throws and bats righthanded.
Attended Oral Roberts University, Tulsa, Okla.
Received reported $100,000 bonus to sign with Seattle Mariners, 1981.

Year Club	League	G.	IP.	W.	L.	Pct.	H.	R.	ER.	SO.	BB.	ERA.
1981—Lynn	Eastern	13	94	6	5	.545	83	42	38	81	34	3.64
1982—Seattle	American	28	144⅓	7	14	.333	159	91	86	73	79	5.36
1982—Salt Lake City	P. Coast	1	8	0	0	.000	9	4	4	6	5	4.50
1983—Seattle	American	22	128	6	8	.429	130	75	67	108	60	4.71
1983—Salt Lake City	P. Coast	11	82⅓	4	4	.500	78	48	33	80	54	3.61
Major League Totals		50	272⅓	13	22	.371	289	166	153	181	139	5.06

Selected by St. Louis Cardinals' organization in 3rd round of free-agent draft, June 6, 1978.
Selected by Seattle Mariners' organization in 1st round (first player selected) of free-agent draft, June 8, 1981.

JOSE MANUEL MORALES

Name pronounced Mor-AHL-ess.

Born December 30, 1944, at Frederiksted, St. Croix, Virgin Islands.
Height, 6.00. Weight, 195.
Throws and bats righthanded.

Established major league record for most hits as pinch-hitter, season (25), 1976.
Led California League in passed balls with 29 in 1965 and American Association with 21 in 1969.

Year	Club	League	Pos.	G.	AB.	R.	H.	2B.	3B.	HR.	RBI.	B.A.	PO.	A.	E.	F.A.
1964—Lexington†	W. Car.	C	73	233	29	56	11	1	3	34	.240	640	40	13	.981
1965—Fresno	Calif.	C	95	321	39	91	13	1	4	48	.283	602	61	★26	.962
1966—Waterbury‡	East.	C	64	215	18	54	9	1	7	26	.251	319	33	10	.972
1967—Waterbury	East.	C-OF	94	246	19	61	7	4	4	31	.248	421	36	14	.970
1968—Amarillo§	Texas	C	105	307	35	88	22	4	8	41	.287	566	70	★19	.971
1969—Iowa	A. A.	★C-OF	98	363	54	102	11	3	16	61	.281	350	60	★18	.958
1970—Iowa	A. A.	C	93	229	36	70	14	0	12	31	.306	327	31	9	.975
1971—Iowa x	A. A.	C-OF	71	153	15	38	7	0	9	22	.248	212	18	7	.970
1972—Tidewater y	Int.	●C-OF-1B	86	256	28	75	18	2	7	48	.293	380	15	●14	.966
1973—Tucson	P. C.	C-1B-3B	76	248	37	88	17	2	4	50	.355	20	4	5	.828
1973—Oakland z	Amer.	DH-PH	6	14	0	4	1	0	0	1	.286	0	0	0	.000
1973—Montreal	Nat.	PH	5	5	0	2	0	0	0	0	.400	0	0	0	.000
1974—Memphis	Int.	1B-C	66	216	20	60	13	0	6	32	.278	442	29	6	.987
1974—Montreal	Nat.	C	25	26	3	7	4	0	1	5	.269	3	1	1	.800
1975—Montreal	Nat.	1-OF-3	93	163	18	49	6	1	2	24	.301	234	28	4	.985
1976—Montreal	Nat.	1B-C	104	158	12	50	11	0	4	37	.316	137	21	3	.981
1977—Montreal a	Nat.	1B-C	65	74	3	15	4	1	1	9	.203	52	3	0	1.000
1978—Minnesota	Amer.	1B-OF-C	101	242	22	76	13	1	2	38	.314	1	2	0	1.000
1979—Minnesota	Amer.	1B	92	191	21	51	5	1	2	27	.267	2	0	0	1.000
1980—Minnesota bc	Amer.	1B-C	97	241	36	73	17	2	8	36	.303	19	0	0	1.000
1981—Baltimore	Amer.	1B	38	86	6	21	3	0	2	14	.244	13	0	0	1.000
1982—Baltimore d	Amer.	PH	3	3	0	0	0	0	0	0	.000	0	0	0	.000
1982—Los Angeles	Nat.	PH	35	30	1	9	1	0	1	8	.300	0	0	0	.000
1983—Los Angeles	Nat.	PH	47	53	4	15	3	0	3	8	.283	37	2	2	.951
American League Totals			337	777	85	225	39	4	14	116	.290	35	2	0	1.000
National League Totals			374	509	41	147	29	2	12	91	.289	463	55	10	.981
Major League Totals			711	1286	126	372	68	6	26	207	.289	498	57	10	.982

Signed as free agent by San Francisco Giants' organization, September 13, 1963.
†On disabled list, July 25, 1964 through remainder of season.
‡On disabled list, May 28 to June 18 and July 21, 1966 through remainder of season.
§Drafted by Vancouver (Oakland Athletics' organization), December 2, 1968.
xLoaned to Tidewater (New York Mets' organization), April 14, 1972; returned, September 29, 1972.
yOn disabled list, July 12 to July 28, 1972.
zSold to Montreal Expos, September 18, 1973.
aSold to Minnesota Twins, March 28, 1978.
bOn supplemental disabled list, May 10 to May 16, 1980.
cGranted free agency, October 24, 1980; signed by Baltimore Orioles, December 17, 1980.
dTraded to Los Angeles Dodgers for Third Baseman Leo Hernandez, April 28, 1982.

CHAMPIONSHIP SERIES RECORD

Year	Club	League	Pos.	G.	AB.	R.	H.	2B.	3B.	HR.	RBI.	B.A.	PO.	A.	E.	F.A.
1983—Los Angeles	Nat.	PH	2	2	0	0	0	0	0	0	.000	0	0	0	.000

JULIO RUBEN MORALES

Name pronounced Mor-AHL-ess.

(Jerry)

Born February 18, 1949, at Yabucoa, Puerto Rico.
Height, 5.10. Weight, 165.
Throws and bats righthanded.

Led National League outfielders in double plays with 6 in 1976.
Led Eastern League outfielders in putouts with 348 in 1969.
Tied for Pacific Coast League lead in double plays by outfielders with 3 in 1971.
Tied for California League lead in double plays by outfielders with 4 in 1968.
Led Appalachian League outfielders in double plays with 2 in 1966.
Named Appalachian League Player of the Year, 1966.

Year	Club	League	Pos.	G.	AB.	R.	H.	2B.	3B.	HR.	RBI.	B.A.	PO.	A.	E.	F.A.
1966—Marion	Appal.	OF	38	119	33	41	8	2	1	25	.345	78	6	3	.966
1967—Winter Haven	Fla. St.	OF-2B-3B	139	501	82	124	11	14	8	48	.248	308	56	16	.958
1968—Raleigh-Durham	Carol.	OF	43	129	18	29	9	1	1	15	.225	83	2	3	.966
1968—Visalia†	Calif.	OF	70	250	44	66	7	2	6	33	.264	143	9	4	.974
1969—Elmira	East.	OF-SS	127	459	62	125	11	★12	15	63	.272	349	8	7	.981
1969—San Diego	Nat.	OF	19	41	5	8	2	0	1	6	.195	27	2	0	1.000
1970—Salt Lake City	P. C.	OF	109	433	50	107	20	7	6	35	.247	237	7	4	★.984
1970—San Diego	Nat.	OF	28	58	6	9	0	1	1	4	.155	25	0	2	.926
1971—Hawaii	P. C.	OF	137	470	81	128	12	11	11	52	.272	285	14	2	★.993
1971—San Diego	Nat.	OF	12	17	1	2	0	0	0	1	.118	8	0	0	1.000
1972—San Diego	Nat.	OF-3B	115	347	38	83	15	7	4	18	.239	214	8	4	.982
1973—San Diego‡	Nat.	OF	122	388	47	109	23	2	9	34	.281	214	5	2	.991

Year Club League	Pos.	G.	AB.	R.	H.	2B.	3B.	HR.	RBI.	B.A.	PO.	A.	E.	F.A.
1974—Chicago .... Nat.	OF	151	534	70	146	21	7	15	82	.273	266	5	7	.975
1975—Chicago .... Nat.	OF	153	578	62	156	21	0	12	91	.270	273	11	6	.979
1976—Chicago .... Nat.	OF	140	537	66	147	17	0	16	67	.274	273	12	5	.983
1977—Chicago§ .... Nat.	OF	136	490	56	142	34	5	11	69	.290	247	8	4	.985
1978—St. Louis x .... Nat.	OF	130	457	44	109	19	8	4	46	.239	254	5	6	.977
1979—Detroit y .... Amer.	OF	129	440	50	93	23	1	14	56	.211	206	6	3	.986
1980—New York z .... Nat.	OF	94	193	19	49	7	1	3	30	.254	107	3	3	.973
1981—Chicago .... Nat.	OF	84	245	27	70	6	2	1	25	.286	142	2	2	.986
1982—Chicago a .... Nat.	OF	65	116	14	33	2	2	4	30	.284	72	5	0	1.000
1982—Midland .... Texas	OF	7	25	3	10	3	0	0	7	.400	8	0	0	1.000
1983—Chicago bc .... Nat.	OF	63	87	11	17	9	0	0	11	.195	29	1	0	1.000
American League Totals		129	440	50	93	23	1	14	56	.211	206	6	3	.986
National League Totals		1312	4088	466	1080	176	35	81	514	.264	2151	67	41	.982
Major League Totals		1441	4528	516	1173	199	36	95	570	.259	2357	73	44	.982

Signed as free agent by New York Mets' organization, June 23, 1966.

†Selected by San Diego Padres in expansion draft, October 14, 1968.

‡Traded to Chicago Cubs for Second Baseman Glenn Beckert and Infielder Bob Fenwick, November 12, 1973.

§Traded with Catcher Steve Swisher to St. Louis Cardinals for Catcher Dave Rader and Outfielder-Third Baseman Hector Cruz, December 8, 1977.

xTraded with Pitcher Aurelio Lopez to Detroit Tigers for Pitchers Jack Murphy and Bob Sykes, December 4, 1978.

yTraded with Third Baseman Phil Mankowski to New York Mets for Third Baseman-First Baseman Richie Hebner, October 31, 1979.

zGranted free agency, October 31, 1980; signed by Chicago Cubs' organization, February 17, 1981.

aOn supplemental disabled list, May 16, 1982; transferred to disabled list, June 18 to June 26, 1982; included rehabilitation disability assignment to Midland, June 16 to June 26, 1982.

bOn supplemental disabled list, August 22 to September 6, 1983.

cReleased, September 30, 1983.

ALL-STAR GAME RECORD

Year League	Pos.	AB.	R.	H.	2B.	3B.	HR.	RBI.	B.A.	PO.	A.	E.	F.A.
1977—National	OF	0	1	0	0	0	0	0	.000	1	0	0	1.000

BOBBY KEITH MORELAND

(Known by middle name.)

Born May 2, 1954, at Dallas, Tex.
Height, 6.00. Weight, 200.
Throws and bats righthanded.
Attended University of Texas, Austin, Texas.

Led American Association in sacrifice flies with 10 in 1978 and with 13 in 1979.
Led American Association catchers in double plays with 10 in 1978.
Led American Association in passed balls with 11 in 1979 and tied for lead with 10 in 1978.
Led Eastern League in passed balls with 18 in 1977.
Tied for Carolina League lead in double plays by third basemen with 19 in 1976.

Year Club League	Pos.	G.	AB.	R.	H.	2B.	3B.	HR.	RBI.	B.A.	PO.	A.	E.	F.A.
1975—Spartanburg .... W. Car.	3B	69	246	28	68	13	1	1	41	.276	52	128	17	.914
1976—Peninsula .... Carol.	●3B-SS	78	294	38	83	12	2	4	47	.282	50	221	●26	.912
1976—Reading .... East.	3B-2B	61	199	7	52	5	0	0	7	.261	62	99	13	.925
1977—Reading .... East.	C-3B	104	401	61	131	19	1	8	55	.327	339	60	8	.980
1977—Oklahoma City ..... A. A.	C	7	13	3	1	0	0	0	1	.077	17	1	0	1.000
1978—Oklahoma City ..... A. A.	C-1-3-O	130	501	73	145	25	4	16	98	.289	641	75	13	.982
1978—Philadelphia .... Nat.	C	1	2	0	0	0	0	0	0	.000	4	0	0	1.000
1979—Oklahoma City ..... A. A.	C-3B-OF	130	494	86	149	●34	3	20	109	.302	397	44	13	.971
1979—Philadelphia .... Nat.	C	14	48	3	18	3	2	0	8	.375	71	3	0	1.000
1980—Philadelphia .... Nat.	C-OF	62	159	13	50	8	0	4	29	.314	186	22	7	.967
1981—Philadelphia† .... Nat.	C-3-1-O	61	196	16	50	7	0	6	37	.255	267	31	9	.971
1982—Chicago .... Nat.	OF-C-3B	138	476	50	124	17	2	15	68	.261	384	38	8	.981
1983—Chicago .... Nat.	OF-C	154	533	76	161	30	3	16	70	.302	244	7	6	.977
Major League Totals		430	1414	158	403	65	7	41	212	.285	1156	101	30	.977

Selected by Philadelphia Phillies' organization in 7th round of free-agent draft, June 4, 1975.

†Traded with Pitchers Dan Larson and Dickie Noles to Chicago Cubs for Pitcher Mike Krukow and cash, December 8, 1981.

DIVISION SERIES RECORD

Year Club League	Pos.	G.	AB.	R.	H.	2B.	3B.	HR.	RBI.	B.A.	PO.	A.	E.	F.A.
1981—Philadelphia .... Nat.	C	4	13	2	6	0	0	1	3	.462	30	2	1	.970

CHAMPIONSHIP SERIES RECORD

Year Club League	Pos.	G.	AB.	R.	H.	2B.	3B.	HR.	RBI.	B.A.	PO.	A.	E.	F.A.
1980—Philadelphia .... Nat.	C-PH	2	1	0	0	0	0	0	1	.000	0	0	0	.000

WORLD SERIES RECORD

Year Club League	Pos.	G.	AB.	R.	H.	2B.	3B.	HR.	RBI.	B.A.	PO.	A.	E.	F.A.
1980—Philadelphia .... Nat.	DH	3	12	1	4	0	0	0	1	.333	0	0	0	.000

ANGEL MORENO (VERNEROS)

Born May 6, 1955, at Vera Cruz, Mexico.
Height, 5.09. Weight, 165.
Throws and bats lefthanded.

Year Club	League	G.	IP.	W.	L.	Pct.	H.	R.	ER.	SO.	BB.	ERA.
1975—Aguascalientes	Mexican	3	3	0	1	.000	2	4	4	0	5	12.00
1976—Aguascalientes	Mexican	24	103	5	5	.500	128	64	48	51	53	4.19
1977—Aguascalientes	Mexican	41	165	12	5	.706	161	74	53	86	68	2.89
1978—Aguascalientes	Mexican	37	216	15	8	.652	223	91	68	131	84	2.83
1979—Aguascalientes	Mexican	32	226	12	17	.414	197	92	84	124	90	3.35
1980—Aguascalientes†	Mexican	5	23	2	0	1.000	20	6	4	8	9	1.57
1981—Salt Lake City	P. Coast	3	17	1	0	1.000	11	9	9	14	13	4.76
1981—California	American	8	31	1	3	.250	27	10	10	12	14	2.90
1982—California	American	13	49⅓	3	7	.300	55	31	26	22	23	4.74
1982—Spokane	P. Coast	22	44	5	0	1.000	54	28	28	35	30	5.73
1983—Edmonton	P. Coast	27	163⅓	8	●13	.381	182	113	104	102	76	5.73
Major League Totals		21	80⅓	4	10	.286	82	41	36	34	37	4.03

Signed as free agent by Aguascalientes of Mexican League, February 22, 1975.
†Sold to California Angels' organization, July 16, 1981.

OMAR RENAN MORENO (QUINTERO)

Born October 24, 1953, at Puerto Armuelles, Panama.
Height, 6.03. Weight, 170.
Throws and bats lefthanded.

Major League stolen bases: 1975 (1), 1976 (15), 1977 (53), 1978 (71), 1979 (77), 1980 (96), 1981 (39), 1982 (60), 1983 (37). Total—449.
Led National League in caught stealing with 33 in 1980 and 14 in 1981.
Led National League in stolen bases with 71 in 1978 and 77 in 1979.
Led National League outfielders in total chances with 514 in 1979 and 499 in 1980.
Tied for National League lead in caught stealing with 26 in 1982.
Led Carolina League in stolen bases with 77 in 1973.
Led Eastern League in stolen bases with 67 in 1974.
Named outfielder on THE SPORTING NEWS National League All-Star Team, 1979.

Year Club	League	Pos.	G.	AB.	R.	H.	2B.	3B.	HR.	RBI.	B.A.	PO.	A.	E.	F.A.
1969—Bradenton Pir.	Gulf C.	OF	25	62	7	18	1	0	0	4	.290	22	0	3	.880
1970—Bradenton Pir.	Gulf C.	OF-1B	51	219	32	51	7	4	1	19	.233	129	9	8	.945
1970—Niagara Falls	NYP	OF	10	23	1	4	0	0	0	3	.174	10	0	0	1.000
1971—Bradenton Pir.	Gulf C.	OF	38	101	11	33	5	2	0	9	.327	35	4	2	.951
1972—Gastonia	W. Car.	OF	51	144	18	31	5	2	1	17	.215	95	3	3	.970
1972—Niagara Falls	NYP	OF	68	259	52	75	11	6	2	34	.290	87	4	5	.948
1973—Salem	Carol.	OF	136	529	★112	150	22	8	9	56	.284	242	14	13	.952
1973—Charleston	Int.	OF	3	12	1	4	0	1	1	3	.333	4	0	0	1.000
1974—Thetford Mines	East.	OF	112	407	88	122	15	6	7	39	.300	193	13	9	.958
1974—Charleston	Int.	OF	23	82	16	18	3	0	0	4	.220	40	2	1	.977
1975—Charleston	Int.	OF	130	447	73	127	20	2	9	51	.284	★328	10	6	.983
1975—Pittsburgh	Nat.	OF	6	6	1	1	0	0	0	0	.167	0	0	1	1.000
1976—Charleston	Int.	OF	94	330	70	104	11	7	3	36	.315	200	★17	1	★.955
1976—Pittsburgh	Nat.	OF	48	122	24	33	4	1	2	12	.270	93	3	4	.960
1977—Pittsburgh	Nat.	OF	150	492	69	118	19	9	7	34	.240	366	10	9	.977
1978—Pittsburgh	Nat.	OF	155	515	95	121	15	7	2	33	.235	409	9	7	.984
1979—Pittsburgh	Nat.	OF	162	★695	110	196	21	12	8	69	.282	★490	11	13	.975
1980—Pittsburgh	Nat.	OF	162	★676	87	168	20	●13	2	36	.249	★479	15	5	.990
1981—Pittsburgh	Nat.	OF	103	434	62	120	18	8	1	35	.276	302	6	1	.997
1982—Pittsburgh†	Nat.	OF	158	645	82	158	18	9	3	44	.245	396	10	7	.983
1983—Houston‡	Nat.	OF	97	405	48	98	12	11	0	25	.242	251	8	6	.977
1983—New York	Amer.	OF	48	152	17	38	9	1	1	17	.250	120	1	1	.992
National League Totals			1041	3990	578	1013	127	70	25	288	.254	2786	72	53	.982
American League Totals			48	152	17	38	9	1	1	17	.250	120	1	1	.992
Major League Totals			1089	4142	595	1051	136	71	26	305	.254	2906	73	54	.982

Signed as free agent by Pittsburgh Pirates' organization, March 30, 1969.
†Granted free agency, November 10, 1982; signed by Houston Astros, December 10, 1982.
‡Traded to New York Yankees for Outfielder Jerry Mumphrey, August 10, 1983.

CHAMPIONSHIP SERIES RECORD

Year Club	League	Pos.	G.	AB.	R.	H.	2B.	3B.	HR.	RBI.	B.A.	PO.	A.	E.	F.A.
1979—Pittsburgh	Nat.	OF	3	12	3	3	0	1	0	0	.250	7	0	0	1.000

WORLD SERIES RECORD

Tied World Series record for most at bats, seven-game Series (33), 1979.

Year Club	League	Pos.	G.	AB.	R.	H.	2B.	3B.	HR.	RBI.	B.A.	PO.	A.	E.	F.A.
1979—Pittsburgh	Nat.	OF	7	33	4	11	2	0	0	3	.333	20	1	0	1.000

—DID YOU KNOW—

That Rick Manning had a 17-game hitting streak with Cleveland when he was traded to the Brewers on June 6? In his first game with Milwaukee, Manning went hitless.

JOE LEONARD MORGAN

Born September 19, 1943, at Bonham, Tex.
Height, 5.07. Weight, 155.
Throws right and bats lefthanded.
Attended Oakland City College, Oakland, Calif., and California State University
at Hayward, Hayward, Calif.
Cousin of Marsh White, running back with New York Giants, 1975 through 1977.

Established major league record for most consecutive errorless games by second baseman, lifetime (91).
Tied major league records for most seasons by second baseman (21); fewest errors by second baseman, season, 150 or more games (5), 1977.
Established National League records for most bases on balls received, lifetime (1,799); most games by second baseman, lifetime (2,427); most putouts by second baseman, lifetime (5,541); most assists by second baseman, lifetime (6,738); most chances accepted by second baseman, lifetime (12,279).
Tied National League records for most runs batted in, two consecutive innings (7), August 19, 1974 (second and third innings).
Tied modern National League record for most bases on balls, game (5), June 2, 1966.
First player to steal 60 or more bases and hit 25 or more home runs in the same season, 1973 and 1976; and one of two players in major league history to steal 50 or more bases and hit 20 or more home runs in same season (67 stolen bases and 26 home runs in 1974, 58 stolen bases and 22 home runs in 1974, and 60 stolen bases and 27 home runs in 1976).
Collected six hits in one game, July 8, 1965, (12 innings).
Major league stolen bases: 1963 (1), 1965 (20), 1966 (11), 1967 (29), 1968 (3), 1969 (49), 1970 (42), 1971 (40), 1972 (58), 1973 (67), 1974 (58), 1975 (67), 1976 (60), 1977 (49), 1978 (19), 1979 (28), 1980 (24), 1981 (14), 1982 (24), 1983 (18). Total—681.
Led National League in slugging percentage with .576 in 1976.
Led National League in sacrifice flies with 12 in 1976.
Led National League in bases on balls received with 97 in 1965, 115 in 1972 and 132 in 1975.
Led National League second basemen in total chances with 814 in 1972.
Tied for National League lead in bases on balls received with 93 in 1980.
Tied for National League lead in double plays by second basemen with 106 in 1973.
Led Texas League second basemen in double plays with 106 in 1964.
Named Major League Player of the Year by THE SPORTING NEWS, 1975 and 1976.
Named National League Player of the Year by THE SPORTING NEWS, 1975.
Named National League Most Valuable Player by Baseball Writers' Association of America, 1975 and 1976.
Named National League Comeback Player of the Year by THE SPORTING NEWS, 1982.
Named National League Rookie Player of the Year by THE SPORTING NEWS, 1965.
Named second baseman on THE SPORTING NEWS National League All-Star Team, 1972 and 1974 through 1977.
Named second baseman on THE SPORTING NEWS National League All-Star fielding team, 1973 through 1977.
Named second baseman on THE SPORTING NEWS National League Silver Slugger team, 1982.
Named Texas League Most Valuable Player, 1964.

Year	Club	League	Pos.	G.	AB.	R.	H.	2B.	3B.	HR.	RBI.	B.A.	PO.	A.	E.	F.A.
1963—Modesto	Calif.		2B	45	152	42	40	5	3	5	27	.263	81	104	15	.925
1963—Durham	Carol.		2B	95	322	74	107	20	2	13	43	.332	217	273	24	.953
1963—Houston	Nat.		2B	8	25	5	6	0	1	0	3	.240	15	15	3	.909
1964—San Antonio	Texas		2B	●140	496	113	160	★42	8	12	90	.323	319	405	25	★.967
1964—Houston	Nat.		2B	10	37	4	7	0	0	0	0	.189	31	25	3	.949
1965—Houston	Nat.		2B	157	601	100	163	22	12	14	40	.271	348	492	★27	.969
1966—Houston†	Nat.		2B	122	425	60	121	14	8	5	42	.285	256	316	21	.965
1967—Houston	Nat.		2B-OF	133	494	73	136	27	11	6	42	.275	299	344	14	.979
1968—Houston‡§	Nat.		2B-OF	10	20	6	5	0	1	0	0	.250	10	6	2	.889
1969—Houston	Nat.		2B-OF	147	535	94	126	18	5	15	43	.236	315	328	18	.973
1970—Houston x	Nat.		2B	144	548	102	147	28	9	8	52	.268	349	430	17	.979
1971—Houston y	Nat.		2B	160	583	87	149	27	●11	13	56	.256	336	★482	12	.986
1972—Cincinnati	Nat.		2B	149	552	★122	161	23	4	16	73	.292	★370	436	8	★.990
1973—Cincinnati	Nat.		2B	157	576	116	167	35	2	26	82	.290	★417	440	9	.990
1974—Cincinnati	Nat.		2B	149	512	107	150	31	3	22	67	.293	344	385	13	.982
1975—Cincinnati	Nat.		2B	146	498	107	163	27	6	17	94	.327	356	425	11	★.986
1976—Cincinnati	Nat.		2B	141	472	113	151	30	5	27	111	.320	342	335	13	.981
1977—Cincinnati	Nat.		2B	153	521	113	150	21	6	22	78	.288	★351	359	5	★.993
1978—Cincinnati	Nat.		2B	132	441	68	104	27	0	13	75	.236	252	290	11	.980
1979—Cincinnati z	Nat.		2B	127	436	70	109	26	1	9	32	.250	259	329	12	.980
1980—Houston a	Nat.		2B	141	461	66	112	17	5	11	49	.243	244	348	7	.988
1981—San Francisco	Nat.		2B	90	308	47	74	16	1	8	31	.240	177	258	4	.991
1982—San Francisco b	Nat.		2B-3B	134	463	68	134	19	4	14	61	.289	255	366	8	.987
1983—Philadelphia cd	Nat.		2B	123	404	72	93	20	1	16	59	.230	231	331	17	.971
Major League Totals				2533	8912	1600	2428	428	96	262	1090	.272	5557	6740	235	.981

Signed as free agent by Houston Colt .45s' organization, November 1, 1962.
†On disabled list, June 26 to August 5, 1966.
‡On military list, April 27 to April 29, 1968.
§On disabled list, May 18 to September 14, 1968.
xOn military list, June 6 to June 20, 1970.
yTraded with Pitcher Jack Billingham, Infielder Denis Menke and Outfielders Cesar Geronimo and Ed Armbrister to Cincinnati Reds for First Baseman Lee May, Second Baseman Tommy Helms and Outfielder Jim Stewart, November 29, 1971.
zGranted free agency, November 1, 1979; signed by Houston Astros, January 31, 1980.
aReleased, December 8, 1980; signed by San Francisco Giants, February 9, 1981.
bTraded with Pitcher Al Holland to Philadelphia Phillies for Pitchers Mike Krukow and Mark Davis and Outfielder Charles Penigar, December 14, 1982.
cOn supplemental disabled list, May 13 to May 28, 1983.
dReleased, October 31, 1983; signed by Oakland A's, December 13, 1983.

CHAMPIONSHIP SERIES RECORD

Established Championship Series records for most bases on balls, total Series (23).

Tied Championship Series records for hitting home run in first Series at bat, October 7, 1972; most clubs, total Series (3); most bases on balls, three-game Series (6), 1976; most two-base hits, three-game Series (3), 1975; most stolen bases, game (3), October 4, 1975; most stolen bases, Series (4), 1975.

Tied National League Championship Series records for most Series played (7); most runs, five-game Series (5), 1972.

Year Club	League	Pos.	G.	AB.	R.	H.	2B.	3B.	HR.	RBI.	B.A.	PO.	A.	E.	F.A.
1972—Cincinnati..............	Nat.	2B	5	19	5	5	0	0	2	3	.263	11	18	0	1.000
1973—Cincinnati..............	Nat.	2B	5	20	1	2	1	0	0	1	.100	12	27	0	1.000
1975—Cincinnati..............	Nat.	2B	3	11	2	3	3	0	0	1	.273	2	9	0	1.000
1976—Cincinnati..............	Nat.	2B	3	7	2	0	0	0	0	0	.000	9	5	0	1.000
1979—Cincinnati..............	Nat.	2B	3	11	0	0	0	0	0	0	.000	12	11	0	1.000
1980—Houston..................	Nat.	2B	4	13	1	2	1	1	0	0	.154	9	8	0	1.000
1983—Philadelphia	Nat.	2B	4	15	1	1	0	0	0	0	.067	8	7	0	1.000
Championship Series Totals			27	96	12	13	5	1	2	5	.135	63	85	0	1.000

WORLD SERIES RECORD

Tied World Series record for most stolen bases, four-game Series (2), 1976; most putouts by second baseman, four-game Series (13), 1976; most errors by second baseman, four-game Series (2), 1976; one or more hits, each game, four-game Series, 1976.

Year Club	League	Pos.	G.	AB.	R.	H.	2B.	3B.	HR.	RBI.	B.A.	PO.	A.	E.	F.A.
1972—Cincinnati..............	Nat.	2B	7	24	4	3	2	0	0	1	.125	18	18	1	.973
1975—Cincinnati..............	Nat.	2B	7	27	4	7	1	0	0	3	.259	17	28	0	1.000
1976—Cincinnati..............	Nat.	2B	4	15	3	5	1	1	1	2	.333	13	10	2	.920
1983—Philadelphia	Nat.	2B	5	19	3	5	0	1	2	2	.263	8	10	0	1.000
World Series Totals...................			23	85	14	20	4	2	3	8	.235	56	66	3	.976

ALL-STAR GAME RECORD

Tied All-Star Game records for most consecutive games batted safely (7); most times home run as leadoff batter, start of game (1), July 19, 1977.

Year League	Pos.	AB.	R.	H.	2B.	3B.	HR.	RBI.	B.A.	PO.	A.	E.	F.A.
1970—National...............................	2B	2	1	1	0	0	0	0	.500	1	2	0	1.000
1972—National...............................	2B	4	0	1	0	0	0	1	.250	3	5	0	1.000
1973—National...............................	2B	3	2	1	1	0	0	0	.333	2	2	0	1.000
1974—National...............................	2B	2	0	1	1	0	0	1	.500	3	4	0	1.000
1975—National...............................	2B	4	0	1	0	0	0	0	.250	0	1	0	1.000
1976—National...............................	2B	3	1	1	0	0	0	0	.333	2	3	0	1.000
1977—National...............................	2B	4	1	1	0	0	1	1	.250	1	0	0	1.000
1978—National...............................	2B	3	1	0	0	0	0	0	.000	2	1	0	1.000
1979—National...............................	PH-2B	1	1	0	0	0	0	0	.000	1	1	0	1.000
All-Star Game Totals....................................		26	7	7	2	0	1	3	.269	15	19	0	1.000

Named to National League All-Star Team for the 1966 game; replaced due to injury.

MICHAEL THOMAS MORGAN
(Mike)

Born October 8, 1959, at Tulare, Calif.
Height, 6.03. Weight, 195.
Throws and bats righthanded.

Received reported $50,000 bonus to sign with Oakland A's, 1978.

Year Club	League	G.	IP.	W.	L.	Pct.	H.	R.	ER.	SO.	BB.	ERA.
1978—Oakland..............................	American	3	12	0	3	.000	19	12	10	0	8	7.50
1978—Vancouver.....................................	P. Coast	14	92	5	6	.455	109	67	57	31	54	5.58
1979—Ogden.................................	P. Coast	13	101	5	5	.500	93	48	39	42	49	3.48
1979—Oakland..............................	American	13	77	2	10	.167	102	57	51	17	50	5.96
1980—Ogden†‡.............................	P. Coast	20	115	6	9	.400	135	79	69	46	77	5.40
1981—Nashville§........................	Southern	26	169	8	7	.533	164	97	83	100	83	4.42
1982—New York x	American	30	150⅓	7	11	.389	167	77	73	71	67	4.37
1983—Toronto y.........................	American	16	45⅓	0	3	.000	48	26	26	22	21	5.16
1983—Syracuse...........................	Int'national	5	19⅓	0	3	.000	20	12	12	17	13	5.59
Major League Totals........................		62	284⅔	9	27	.250	336	172	160	110	146	5.06

Selected by Oakland A's organizaton in 1st round (fourth player selected) of free-agent draft, June 6, 1978.

†On disabled list, May 14 to June 27, 1980.

‡Traded to New York Yankees for Shortstop Fred Stanley and a player to be named later, November 3, 1980; Oakland A's acquired Second Baseman Brian Doyle to complete deal, November 17, 1980.

§On disabled list, April 9 to April 22, 1981.

xTraded with Outfielder-First Baseman Dave Collins, First Baseman Fred McGriff and a reported $400,000 to Toronto Blue Jays for Pitcher Dale Murray and Outfielder-Catcher Tom Dodd, December 9, 1982.

yOn disabled list, July 2 to August 23, 1983; included rehabilitation disability assignment to Syracuse, August 1 to August 18, 1983.

DANIEL JOSEPH MOROGIELLO
(Dan)

Born March 26, 1955, at Brooklyn, N.Y.
Height, 6.01. Weight, 200.
Throws and bats lefthanded.
Attended Seton Hall University, South Orange, N.J.

Year Club	League	G.	IP.	W.	L.	Pct.	H.	R.	ER.	SO.	BB.	ERA.
1976—Kingsport	Ap'lachian	5	25	1	2	.333	28	11	9	26	5	3.24
1976—Greenwood	W. Carol.	8	41	4	1	.800	41	18	15	24	23	3.29
1977—Savannah	Southern	26	169	13	12	.520	164	87	75	109	*99	3.99
1978—Savannah	Southern	27	180	8	14	.364	184	81	62	96	81	3.10
1979—Richmond	Int'national	31	200	12	13	.480	186	90	79	116	76	3.56
1980—Richmond	Int'national	29	196	11	12	.478	*206	102	*88	71	50	4.04
1981—Savannah†	Southern	43	66	5	4	.556	78	39	31	50	35	4.23
1982—Louisville‡	Am. Assoc.	57	80	5	4	.556	102	44	40	43	22	4.50
1983—Rochester	Int'national	17	33	1	1	.500	41	24	21	16	12	5.73
1983—Baltimore	American	22	37⅔	0	1	.000	39	10	10	15	10	2.39
Major League Totals		22	37⅔	0	1	.000	39	10	10	15	10	2.39

Selected by Detroit Tigers' organization in 8th round of free-agent draft, June 5, 1974.
Selected by Atlanta Braves' organization in 3rd round of free-agent draft, June 8, 1976.
†Traded to St. Louis Cardinals' organization for Pitcher Donnie Moore, February 1, 1982.
‡Granted free agency, October 22, 1982; signed by Baltimore Orioles, November 29, 1982.

JOHN DANIEL MORRIS

Born February 23, 1961, at Freeport, N.Y.
Height, 6.01. Weight, 190.
Throws and bats lefthanded.
Attended Seton Hall University, South Orange, N.J.
Named Southern League Most Valuable Player, 1983.

Year Club	League	Pos.	G.	AB.	R.	H.	2B.	3B.	HR.	RBI.	B.A.	PO.	A.	E.	F.A.
1982—Ft. Myers	Fla. St.	OF	45	137	21	39	7	2	2	17	.285	64	2	2	.971
1983—Jacksonville	South.	OF	140	490	96	141	27	8	23	92	.288	260	8	3	*.989

Selected by Kansas City Royals' organization in 1st round (10th player selected) of free-agent draft, June 7, 1982.

JOHN SCOTT MORRIS
(Jack)

Born May 16, 1956, at St. Paul, Minn.
Height, 6.03. Weight, 190.
Throws and bats righthanded.
Attended Brigham Young University, Provo, Utah.
Led American League in wild pitches with 18 in 1983.
Named American League Pitcher of the Year by THE SPORTING NEWS, 1981.
Named righthanded pitcher on THE SPORTING NEWS American League All-Star Team, 1981.

Year Club	League	G.	IP.	W.	L.	Pct.	H.	R.	ER.	SO.	BB.	ERA.
1976—Montgomery	Southern	12	36	2	3	.400	37	31	25	18	36	6.25
1977—Evansville	Am. Assoc.	20	135	6	7	.462	141	68	54	95	42	3.60
1977—Detroit	American	7	46	1	1	.500	38	20	19	28	23	3.72
1978—Detroit	American	28	106	3	5	.375	107	57	51	48	49	4.33
1979—Evansville	Am. Assoc.	5	34	2	2	.500	22	13	9	28	18	2.38
1979—Detroit	American	27	198	17	7	.708	179	76	72	113	59	3.27
1980—Detroit	American	36	250	16	15	.516	252	125	*116	112	87	4.18
1981—Detroit	American	25	198	●14	7	.667	153	69	67	97	*78	3.05
1982—Detroit	American	37	266⅓	17	16	.515	247	131	120	135	96	4.06
1983—Detroit†	American	37	*293⅔	20	13	.606	257	117	109	*232	83	3.34
Major League Totals		197	1358	88	64	.579	1233	592	554	765	475	3.67

Selected by Detroit Tigers' organization in 5th round of free-agent draft, June 8, 1976.
†Appeared in seven games as a pinch-runner.

ALL-STAR GAME RECORD

Year League	IP.	W.	L.	Pct.	H.	R.	ER.	SO.	BB.	ERA.
1981—American	2	0	0	.000	2	0	0	2	1	0.00

JAMES FORREST MORRISON
(Jim)

Born September 23, 1952, at Pensacola, Fla.
Height, 5.11. Weight, 178.
Throws and bats righthanded.
Attended Georgia Southern College, Statesboro, Ga.
Tied major league record for fewest three-base hits, most at-bats, season (0 and 604), 1980.
Led American League second basemen in assists with 481, total chances with 932 and double plays with 117 in 1980.
Led Carolina League in total bases with 239 in 1975.
Led American Association third basemen in assists with 236 in 1977.
Led American Association third basemen in double plays with 22 in 1976.
Led Carolina League third basemen in assists with 311, errors with 32 and double plays with 35 in 1975.

Year Club	League	Pos.	G.	AB.	R.	H.	2B.	3B.	HR.	RBI.	B.A.	PO.	A.	E.	F.A.
1974—Spartanburg	W. Car.	3B	3	8	1	3	1	0	1	3	.375	4	5	1	.900
1974—Rocky Mount	Carol.	3B	72	265	30	67	9	1	4	24	.253	54	157	19	.917
1975—Rocky Mount	Carol.	3B-SS	140	497	*98	143	24	6	*20	88	.288	135	331	35	.930
1976—Oklahoma City	A. A.	*3B-SS	126	422	79	122	17	6	18	71	.289	100	*239	24	.934
1977—Oklahoma City	A. A.	3B-2B-OF	127	452	72	133	23	4	12	71	.294	99	272	25	.937

Year—Club	League	Pos.	G.	AB.	R.	H.	2B.	3B.	HR.	RBI.	B.A.	PO.	A.	E.	F.A.
1977—Philadelphia	Nat.	3B	5	7	3	3	0	0	0	1	.429	0	7	1	.875
1978—Oklahoma City	A. A.	2B-3B-1B	54	189	37	52	6	1	10	28	.275	111	134	10	.961
1978—Philadelphia	Nat.	2B-3B-OF	53	108	12	17	1	1	3	10	.157	88	97	6	.969
1979—Oklahoma City† ...	A. A.	2B-3B-OF	79	281	59	90	15	0	22	61	.320	129	226	17	.954
1979—Chicago	Amer.	2B-3B	67	240	38	66	14	0	14	35	.275	121	185	9	.971
1980—Chicago	Amer.	★2B-SS	162	604	66	171	40	0	15	57	.283	★422	482	★29	.969
1981—Chicago	Amer.	3B-2B	90	290	27	68	8	1	10	34	.234	64	200	12	.957
1982—Chicago‡	Amer.	3B	51	166	17	37	7	3	7	19	.223	19	87	10	.914
1982—Pittsburgh.............	Nat.	3-2-O-S	44	86	10	24	4	1	4	15	.279	17	43	2	.968
1983—Pittsburgh.............	Nat.	2B-3B-SS	66	158	16	48	7	2	6	25	.304	56	99	7	.957
National League Totals.............................			168	359	41	92	12	4	13	51	.256	161	246	16	.962
American League Totals...........................			370	1300	148	342	69	4	46	145	.263	626	954	60	.963
Major League Totals...................................			538	1659	189	434	81	8	59	196	.262	787	1200	76	.963

Selected by Pittsburgh Pirates' organization in 5th round of free-agent draft, January 12, 1972.
Selected by Pittsburgh Pirates' organization in secondary phase of free-agent draft, June 6, 1972.
Selected by Philadelphia Phillies' organization in 5th round of free-agent draft, June 5, 1974.
†Traded to Chicago White Sox, July 10, 1979, completing deal in which Chicago traded Pitcher Jack Kucek to Philadelphia Phillies for a player to be named later, April 13, 1979.
‡Traded to Pittsburgh Pirates for Pitcher Eddie Solomon, June 14, 1982.

CHAMPIONSHIP SERIES RECORD

Year Club	League	Pos.	G.	AB.	R.	H.	2B.	3B.	HR.	RBI.	B.A.	PO.	A.	E.	F.A.
1978—Philadelphia	Nat.	PH	1	1	0	0	0	0	0	0	.000	0	0	0	.000

MICHAEL LEE MORSE
(Mike)

Born March 28, 1962, at Miami, Fla.
Height, 5.11. Weight, 155.
Throws and bats righthanded.

Year Club	League	Pos.	G.	AB.	R.	H.	2B.	3B.	HR.	RBI.	B.A.	PO.	A.	E.	F.A.
1980—Sarasota W. Sox ...	Gulf C.	SS	37	122	23	31	9	0	0	11	.254	40	74	18	.864
1980—Glens Falls............	East.	SS	8	32	5	6	2	0	1	4	.188	8	35	4	.915
1981—Appleton	Midw.	SS	126	458	67	120	16	5	6	48	.262	179	354	52	.911
1982—Glens Falls†	East.	SS	62	256	40	63	9	0	7	19	.246	79	193	26	.913
1983—Glens Falls............	East.	3B-SS-2B	130	468	96	103	19	1	14	45	.220	174	319	34	.935

Selected by Chicago White Sox' organization in 6th round of free-agent draft, June 3, 1980.
†On disabled list, May 11 to July 7, 1982.

LLOYD ANTHONY MOSEBY

Born November 5, 1959, at Portland, Ark.
Height, 6.03. Weight, 200.
Throws right and bats lefthanded.

Major League stolen bases: 1980 (4), 1981 (11), 1982 (11), 1983 (26). Total—52.
Led Florida State League in total bases with 237 and tied for lead in being hit by pitch with 10 in 1979.
Led Pioneer League in being hit by pitch with 11 and tied for lead in caught stealing with 7 in 1978.
Named outfielder on THE SPORTING NEWS American League All-Star team, 1983.
Named outfielder on THE SPORTING NEWS American League Silver Slugger team, 1983.

Year Club	League	Pos.	G.	AB.	R.	H.	2B.	3B.	HR.	RBI.	B.A.	PO.	A.	E.	F.A.
1978—Medicine Hat........	Pion.	OF	67	253	65	77	12	4	10	38	.304	76	3	6	.929
1979—Dunedin	Fla. St.	OF	129	446	★89	★148	23	6	18	84	.332	190	11	9	.957
1980—Syracuse	Int.	OF	37	146	28	47	8	6	3	19	.322	83	1	3	.966
1980—Toronto	Amer.	OF	114	389	44	89	24	1	9	46	.229	208	12	4	.982
1981—Toronto	Amer.	OF	100	378	36	88	16	2	9	43	.233	259	4	3	.989
1982—Toronto	Amer.	OF	147	487	51	115	20	9	9	52	.236	361	4	3	.992
1983—Toronto	Amer.	OF	151	539	104	170	31	7	18	81	.315	399	10	7	.983
Major League Totals...................................			512	1793	235	462	91	19	45	222	.258	1227	30	17	.987

Selected by Toronto Blue Jays' organization in 1st round (second player selected) of free-agent draft, June 6, 1978.

JOHN WILLIAM MOSES

Born August 9, 1957, at Los Angeles, Calif.
Height, 5.09. Weight, 165.
Throws left and bats left and righthanded.
Attended Golden West College, Huntington Beach, Calif., and
University of Arizona, Tucson, Ariz.

Led Midwest League in caught stealing with 21 and bases on balls received with 103 in 1981.
Led Eastern League outfielders in double plays with 6 in 1982.
Tied for Midwest League lead in sacrifice hits with 13 in 1981.

Year Club	League	Pos.	G.	AB.	R.	H.	2B.	3B.	HR.	RBI.	B.A.	PO.	A.	E.	F.A.
1980—Bellingham	N'west	OF	60	227	55	60	5	2	2	32	.264	92	6	3	.970
1981—Wausau...................	Midw.	OF	123	429	★102	120	24	3	3	48	.280	204	10	5	.977
1982—Lynn.......................	East.	OF	128	466	87	133	25	6	6	52	.285	259	★20	0	★1.000
1982—Seattle....................	Amer.	OF	22	44	7	14	5	1	1	3	.318	16	2	1	.947
1983—Seattle....................	Amer.	OF	93	130	19	27	4	1	0	6	.208	87	8	2	.979
1983—Salt Lake City.......	P. C.	OF	16	65	14	17	4	0	0	10	.262	26	0	0	1.000
Major League Totals...................................			115	174	26	41	9	2	1	9	.236	103	10	3	.974

Selected by Seattle Mariners' organization in 16th round of free-agent draft, June 3, 1980.

PAUL RICHARD MOSKAU

Name pronounced MOSS-koh.

Born December 20, 1953, at St. Joseph, Mo.
Height, 6.02. Weight, 205.
Throws and bats righthanded.
Attended Arizona State University, Tempe, Ariz., and Azusa Pacific College, Azusa, Calif.

Tied for National League lead in balks with 7 in 1978.
Led Eastern League pitchers in shutouts with 6 in 1976.

Year—Club	League	G.	IP.	W.	L.	Pct.	H.	R.	ER.	SO.	BB.	ERA.
1975—Billings	Pioneer	1	4	0	1	.000	3	5	1	6	3	2.25
1975—Eugene	Northwest	13	84	*10	1	*.909	52	22	14	*92	41	*1.50
1976—Three Rivers	Eastern	26	180	13	6	.684	134	42	31	124	58	*1.55
1977—Indianapolis	Am. Assoc.	12	81	7	1	.875	69	35	32	55	26	3.56
1977—Cincinnati	National	20	108	6	6	.500	116	51	48	71	40	4.00
1978—Indianapolis	Am. Assoc.	4	26	1	1	.500	21	14	9	27	15	3.12
1978—Cincinnati	National	26	145	6	4	.600	139	65	64	88	57	3.97
1979—Indianapolis	Am. Assoc.	2	5	0	0	.000	2	0	0	5	1	0.00
1979—Cincinnati	National	21	106	5	4	.556	107	53	46	58	51	3.91
1980—Cincinnati	National	33	153	9	7	.563	147	69	68	94	41	4.00
1981—Cincinnati†‡	National	27	55	2	1	.667	54	31	30	32	32	4.91
1982—Pittsburgh§	National	13	35	1	3	.250	43	21	17	15	8	4.37
1982—Portland x	P. Coast	4	11⅓	0	4	.000	17	13	13	10	11	10.32
1983—Chicago	National	8	32	3	2	.600	44	25	24	16	14	6.75
1983—Iowa y	Am. Assoc.	11	54⅔	2	2	.500	57	36	36	26	27	5.93
Major League Totals		148	634	32	27	.542	650	315	297	374	243	4.22

Selected by Cleveland Indians' organization in 5th round of free-agent draft, January 9, 1974.
Selected by Cincinnati Reds' organization in 3rd round of free-agent draft, June 4, 1975.
†Traded to Baltimore Orioles for a player to be named later, February 9, 1982; Cincinnati Reds acquired Infielder Wayne Krenchicki to complete deal, February 16, 1982.
‡Sold on waivers to Pittsburgh Pirates, April 3, 1982.
§On disabled list, June 27 to September 1, 1982; included rehabilitation disability assignment to Portland, August 12 to August 31, 1982.
xReleased, October 4, 1982; signed by Chicago Cubs, January 14, 1983.
yReleased, August 8, 1983.

DARRYL DeWAYNE MOTLEY

Born January 21, 1960, at Muskogee, Okla.
Height, 5.09. Weight, 196.
Throws and bats righthanded.

Year—Club	League	Pos.	G.	AB.	R.	H.	2B.	3B.	HR.	RBI.	B.A.	PO.	A.	E.	F.A.
1978—Sarasota Royals	Gulf C.	OF	10	41	10	20	1	0	2	9	.488	23	1	1	.960
1978—Ft. Myers	Fla. St.	OF	49	151	13	36	3	2	0	12	.238	100	1	4	.962
1979—Ft. Myers	Fla. St.	3B	123	447	47	106	20	2	8	45	.237	*109	183	●29	.910
1980—Ft. Myers†	Fla. St.	3B-OF-SS	32	119	20	36	7	0	4	24	.303	33	56	9	.908
1980—Jacksonville‡	South.	3B	51	182	30	58	15	1	5	31	.319	43	100	10	.935
1981—Omaha	A. A.	OF	109	410	63	118	18	5	18	64	.288	201	7	3	.986
1981—Kansas City	Amer.	OF	42	125	15	29	4	0	2	8	.232	88	3	3	.968
1982—Omaha§	A. A.	OF	114	409	51	104	12	6	8	52	.254	216	4	3	.987
1983—Evansville	A. A.	OF	130	506	89	142	32	5	16	60	.281	282	14	5	.983
1983—Kansas City	Amer.	OF	19	68	9	16	1	2	3	11	.235	42	2	1	.978
Major League Totals			61	193	24	45	5	2	5	19	.233	130	5	4	.971

Selected by Kansas City Royals' organization in 2nd round of free-agent draft, June 6, 1978.
†On disabled list, April 11 to May 18, 1980.
‡On disabled list, August 9, 1980 through remainder of season.
§Loaned to Evansville (Detroit Tigers' organization), April 2, 1983; returned, September 1, 1983.

STEVEN RANCE MULLINIKS

Name pronounced MUL-in-iks.

(Known by middle name.)

Born January 15, 1956, at Tulare, Calif.
Height, 6.00. Weight, 170.
Throws right and bats lefthanded.
Son of Harvey Mulliniks, pitcher in New York Yankees' organization, 1956 and 1957.

Led Pacific Coast League shortstops in fielding percentage with .968 in 1979.

Year—Club	League	Pos.	G.	AB.	R.	H.	2B.	3B.	HR.	RBI.	B.A.	PO.	A.	E.	F.A.
1974—Idaho Falls	Pion.	SS	66	202	28	44	8	3	0	24	.218	*110	*170	*33	.895
1975—Quad Cities	Midw.	SS	52	186	34	50	6	2	1	21	.269	82	136	17	.928
1975—Salinas	Calif.	SS-2B	59	209	38	54	8	0	0	10	.258	88	146	14	.944
1976—El Paso†	Texas	SS-2B	90	333	81	105	22	4	7	51	.315	140	247	20	.951
1977—Salt Lake City	P. C.	SS	58	220	48	68	17	3	11	51	.309	116	207	15	.956
1977—California	Amer.	SS	78	271	36	73	13	2	3	21	.269	112	229	13	.963
1978—Salt Lake City	P. C.	SS	34	127	34	39	6	2	3	21	.307	65	109	12	.935
1978—California	Amer.	SS	50	119	6	22	3	1	1	6	.185	68	93	8	.953
1979—Salt Lake City	P. C.	SS-2B	116	402	94	138	21	7	3	59	.343	204	331	17	.969
1979—California‡	Amer.	SS	22	68	7	10	0	0	1	8	.147	46	43	4	.957
1980—Kansas City	Amer.	SS-2B	36	54	8	14	3	0	0	6	.259	30	53	1	.988

Year Club	League	Pos.	G.	AB.	R.	H.	2B.	3B.	HR.	RBI.	B.A.	PO.	A.	E.	F.A.
1981—Kansas City§	Amer.	2B-SS-3B	24	44	6	10	3	0	0	5	.227	25	39	5	.928
1982—Toronto	Amer.	3B-SS	112	311	32	76	25	0	4	35	.244	69	154	14	.941
1983—Toronto	Amer.	3B-SS-2B	129	364	54	100	35	3	10	48	.275	77	185	7	.974
Major League Totals			451	1231	149	305	82	6	19	129	.248	427	796	52	.959

Selected by California Angels' organization in 3rd round of free-agent draft, June 5, 1974.

†On disabled list, May 4 to June 9 and September 2 to September 24, 1976.

‡Traded with First Baseman Willie Aikens to Kansas City Royals for Outfielder Al Cowens, Shortstop Todd Cruz and a player to be named later, December 6, 1979; California Angels acquired Pitcher Craig Eaton to complete deal, April 1, 1980.

§Traded to Toronto Blue Jays for Pitcher Phil Huffman, March 25, 1982.

FRANCIS JOSEPH MULLINS
(Fran)

Born May 14, 1957, at Oakland, Calif.
Height, 6.00. Weight, 180.
Throws and bats righthanded.
Received bachelor of science degree in accounting from
University of Santa Clara, Santa Clara, Calif.

Tied for American Association lead in being hit by pitch with 8 in 1983.

Year Club	League	Pos.	G.	AB.	R.	H.	2B.	3B.	HR.	RBI.	B.A.	PO.	A.	E.	F.A.
1979—Knoxville	South.	SS	53	164	21	44	5	1	4	22	.268	57	150	17	.924
1980—Glens Falls	East.	SS-2B	59	212	46	64	7	2	12	39	.302	109	197	20	.939
1980—Iowa	A. A.	3B-2B-SS	53	201	25	51	12	1	6	35	.254	41	88	8	.942
1980—Chicago	Amer.	3B	21	62	9	12	4	0	0	3	.194	15	36	1	.981
1981—Edmonton†	P. C.	SS-2B-3B	77	238	46	58	8	1	8	27	.244	125	257	11	.972
1982—Edmonton	P. C.	SS	98	309	55	87	15	2	14	57	.282	135	305	29	.938
1983—Denver‡§	A. A	3B-SS-2B	100	355	65	96	18	2	18	55	.270	98	198	18	.943
Major League Totals			21	62	9	12	4	0	0	3	.194	15	36	1	.981

Selected by Detroit Tigers' organization in 3rd round of free-agent draft, June 6, 1978.

Selected by Chicago White Sox' organization in 3rd round of free-agent draft, June 5, 1979.

†On disabled list, April 15 to May 29 and August 1 to August 11, 1981.

‡Traded to Cincinnati Reds for Catcher Steve Christmas, November 21, 1983.

§Drafted by San Francisco Giants, December 5, 1983.

JERRY WAYNE MUMPHREY

Born September 9, 1952, at Tyler, Tex.
Height, 6.02. Weight, 185.
Throws right and bats left and righthanded.

Major League stolen bases: 1976 (22), 1977 (22), 1978 (14), 1979 (8), 1980 (52), 1981 (13), 1982 (11), 1983 (7). Total—149.

Led American Association in stolen bases with 44 and caught stealing with 21 in 1975.

Led Gulf Coast League batters in strikeouts with 45 in 1971.

Year Club	League	Pos.	G.	AB.	R.	H.	2B.	3B.	HR.	RBI.	B.A.	PO.	A.	E.	F.A.
1971—Sarasota Cards	Gulf C.	OF	38	141	20	36	3	2	0	6	.255	52	1	3	.946
1972—Sarasota Cards	Gulf C.	OF	26	111	21	38	5	2	0	12	.342	63	2	0	1.000
1972—Cedar Rapids	Midw.	OF	11	33	6	6	2	0	0	1	.182	15	0	0	1.000
1972—St. Petersburg	Fla. St.	OF	17	44	7	15	2	1	0	1	.341	11	1	1	.923
1973—St. Petersburg	Fla. St.	OF	142	*556	*93	*159	20	●9	5	52	.286	210	6	4	982
1974—Arkansas	Tex.	OF	130	507	87	147	21	6	10	54	.290	209	11	9	.961
1974—St. Louis	Nat.	OF	5	2	2	0	0	0	0	0	.000	0	0	0	.000
1975—Tulsa	A. A.	OF	127	495	87	141	19	6	8	59	.285	248	7	6	.977
1975—St. Louis	Nat.	OF	11	16	2	6	2	0	0	1	.375	9	0	0	1.000
1976—Tulsa	A. A.	OF	19	68	14	23	9	1	1	8	.338	42	4	0	1.000
1976—St. Louis	Nat.	OF	112	384	51	99	15	5	1	26	.258	261	6	2	.993
1977—St. Louis	Nat.	OF	145	463	73	133	20	10	2	38	.287	291	8	9	.971
1978—St. Louis	Nat.	OF	125	367	41	96	13	4	2	37	.262	178	10	1	.995
1979—St. Louis †‡§	Nat.	OF	124	339	53	100	10	3	3	32	.295	180	3	3	.984
1980—San Diego x	Nat.	OF	160	564	61	168	24	3	4	59	.298	398	10	●11	.974
1981—New York	Amer.	OF	80	319	44	98	11	5	6	32	.307	219	5	●8	.966
1982—New York y	Amer.	OF	123	477	76	143	24	10	9	68	.300	336	5	5	.986
1983—New York z	Amer.	OF	83	267	41	70	11	4	7	36	.262	227	7	4	.983
1983—Houston	Nat.	OF	44	143	17	48	10	2	1	17	.336	103	1	1	.990
National League Totals			726	2278	300	650	94	27	13	210	.285	1420	38	27	.982
American League Totals			286	1063	161	311	46	19	22	136	.293	782	17	17	.979
Major League Totals			1012	3341	461	961	140	46	35	346	.288	2202	55	44	.981

Selected by St. Louis Cardinals' organization in 4th round of free-agent draft, June 8, 1971.

†On disabled list, March 29 to April 20, 1979.

‡Traded with Pitcher John Denny to Cleveland Indians for Outfielder Bobby Bonds, December 7, 1979.

§Traded by Cleveland Indians to San Diego Padres for Pitcher Bob Owchinko and Outfielder Jim Wilhelm, February 15, 1980.

xTraded with Pitcher John Pacella to New York Yankees for Outfielders Ruppert Jones and Joe Lefebvre and Pitchers Tim Lollar and Chris Welsh, April 1, 1981.

yOn supplemental disabled list, May 10, 1982; transferred to disabled list, May 20 to June 21, 1982.

zTraded to Houston Astros for Outfielder Omar Moreno, August 10, 1983.

DIVISION SERIES RECORD

Year Club League	Pos.	G.	AB.	R.	H.	2B.	3B.	HR.	RBI.	B.A.	PO.	A.	E.	F.A.
1981—New York............. Amer.	OF	5	21	2	2	0	0	0	0	.095	15	1	0	1.000

CHAMPIONSHIP SERIES RECORD

Year Club League	Pos.	G.	AB.	R.	H.	2B.	3B.	HR.	RBI.	B.A.	PO.	A.	E.	F.A.
1981—New York............. Amer.	OF	3	12	2	6	1	0	0	0	.500	4	0	0	1.000

WORLD SERIES RECORD

Year Club League	Pos.	G.	AB.	R.	H.	2B.	3B.	HR.	RBI.	B.A.	PO.	A.	E.	F.A.
1981—New York............. Amer.	OF	5	15	2	3	0	0	0	0	.200	6	0	0	1.000

STEPHEN ANDREW MURA

Name pronounced MYUR-uh.

(Steve)

Born February 12, 1955, at New Orleans, La.
Height, 6.02. Weight, 188.
Throws and bats righthanded.
Attended Tulane University, New Orleans, La.

Led Pacific Coast League in complete games with 16 in 1978.
Tied for Pacific Coast League lead in shutouts with 3 in 1977.

Year Club	League	G.	IP.	W.	L.	Pct.	H.	R.	ER.	SO.	BB.	ERA.
1976—Walla Walla	Northwest	8	59	7	0	★1.000	41	14	9	68	18	★1.37
1976—Amarillo....................................	Texas	7	59	4	2	.667	48	22	17	50	27	2.59
1977—Hawaii.....................................	P. Coast	28	165	12	10	.545	164	106	87	123	122	4.75
1978—Hawaii.....................................	P. Coast	26	177	10	★16	.385	177	94	82	★158	90	4.17
1978—San Diego	National	5	8	0	2	.000	15	10	10	5	5	11.25
1979—San Diego†	National	38	73	4	4	.500	57	30	25	59	37	3.08
1980—San Diego	National	37	169	8	7	.533	149	74	69	109	86	3.67
1981—San Diego‡	National	23	139	5	●14	.263	156	72	66	70	50	4.27
1982—St. Louis§	National	35	184⅓	12	11	.522	196	89	83	84	80	4.05
1983—Chicago....................................	American	6	12⅓	0	0	.000	13	11	6	4	6	4.38
1983—Denver x...................................	Am. Assoc.	19	121⅓	3	11	.214	121	73	65	85	49	4.82
American League Totals........................		6	12⅓	0	0	.000	13	11	6	4	6	4.38
National League Totals.........................		138	573⅓	29	38	.433	573	275	253	327	258	3.97
Major League Totals............................		144	585⅔	29	38	.433	586	286	259	331	264	3.98

Selected by San Diego Padres' organization in 2nd round of free-agent draft, June 8, 1976.

†On disabled list, May 23 to June 28, 1979.

‡Traded with a player to be named later to St. Louis Cardinals for Outfielder Sixto Lezcano and a player to be named later, December 10, 1981; St. Louis organization acquired Pitcher Al Olmsted and San Diego Padres acquired Pitcher Luis DeLeon to complete deal, February 19, 1982.

§Selected by Chicago White Sox' organization in player compensation pool draft, January 26, 1983. (Chicago received compensation for New York Yankees' signing of free-agent Outfielder Steve Kemp, December 9, 1982.)

xOn disabled list, June 29 to July 10, 1983.

BOBBY RAY MURCER

Born May 20, 1946, at Oklahoma City, Okla.
Height, 5.11. Weight, 185.
Throws right and bats lefthanded.
Attended University of Oklahoma, Norman, Okla.

Tied major league records for most consecutive home runs, two games (4), June 24, 1970; most home runs, consecutive appearances (4), June 24, 1970, doubleheader, 1972.

Tied American League record for most home runs, doubleheader (4), June 24, 1970.

Hit three home runs in a game, June 24, 1970 (second game) and July 13, 1973.

Hit for the cycle, August 29, 1972 (first game).

Led National League in sacrifice flies with 12 in 1975.

Led American League in total bases with 314 in 1972.

Led American League outfielders in total chances with 396 in 1972.

Tied for National League lead in sacrifice flies with 10 in 1977.

Led International League shortstops in double plays with 91 in 1966.

Named outfielder on THE SPORTING NEWS American League All-Star Team, 1971 through 1973.

Named outfielder on THE SPORTING NEWS American League All-Star fielding team, 1972.

Named Carolina League Most Valuable Player, 1965.

Received reported $20,000 bonus to sign with New York Yankees, 1964.

Year Club	League	Pos.	G.	AB.	R.	H.	2B.	3B.	HR.	RBI.	B.A.	PO.	A.	E.	F.A.
1964—Johnson City	Appal.	SS-2B	32	126	34	46	7	4	2	29	.365	39	78	34	.775
1965—Greensboro†	Carol.	SS	126	478	95	154	30	5	16	90	.322	166	320	★55	.898
1965—New York.............	Amer.	SS	11	37	2	9	0	1	1	4	.243	28	41	5	.932
1966—New York.............	Amer.	SS	21	69	3	12	1	1	0	5	.174	31	50	6	.931
1966—Toledo	Int.	SS	133	492	69	131	19	9	15	62	.266	207	349	★36	.939
1967-68—New York‡........	Amer.					(In Military Service)									
1969—New York.............	Amer.	OF-3B	152	564	82	146	24	4	26	82	.259	235	81	22	.935
1970—New York.............	Amer.	OF	159	581	95	146	23	3	23	78	.251	375	●15	3	.992
1971—New York.............	Amer.	OF	146	529	94	175	25	6	25	94	.331	317	10	5	.985
1972—New York.............	Amer.	OF	153	585	★102	171	30	7	33	96	.292	★382	11	3	.992
1973—New York.............	Amer.	OF	160	616	83	187	29	2	22	95	.304	380	●14	6	.985
1974—New York§...........	Amer.	OF	156	606	69	166	25	4	10	88	.274	297	★21	7	.978

Year Club League	Pos.	G.	AB.	R.	H.	2B.	3B.	HR.	RBI.	B.A.	PO.	A.	E.	F.A.
1975—San Francisco ...... Nat.	OF	147	526	80	157	29	4	11	91	.298	201	10	4	.981
1976—San Francisco x....Nat.	OF	147	533	73	138	20	2	23	90	.259	282	11	12	.961
1977—Chicago .... Nat.	OF-2B-SS	154	554	90	147	18	3	27	89	.265	238	11	5	.980
1978—Chicago .... Nat.	OF	146	499	66	140	22	6	9	64	.281	225	8	5	.979
1979—Chicago y.............. Nat.	OF	58	190	22	49	4	1	7	22	.258	110	4	0	1.000
1979—New York .... Amer.	OF	74	264	42	72	12	0	8	33	.273	169	4	3	.983
1980—New York.............. Amer.	OF	100	297	41	80	9	1	13	57	.269	82	2	4	.955
1981—New York z.......... Amer.	DH	50	117	14	31	6	0	6	24	.265	0	0	0	.000
1982—New York............. Amer.	DH	65	141	12	32	6	0	7	30	.227	0	0	0	.000
1983—New York a .... Amer.	DH	9	22	2	4	2	0	1	1	.182	0	0	0	.000
American League Totals........................		1256	4428	641	1231	192	29	175	687	.278	2296	249	64	.975
National League Totals..............................		652	2302	331	631	93	16	77	356	.274	1056	44	26	.977
Major League Totals...................................		1908	6730	972	1862	285	45	252	1043	.277	3352	293	90	.976

Signed as free agent by New York Yankees' organization, June 2, 1964.
†On disabled list, May 3 to May 15, 1965.
‡On military list, March 6, 1967 through December 6, 1968.
§Traded to San Francisco Giants for Outfielder Bobby Bonds, October 21, 1974.
xTraded with Infielder Steve Ontiveros and Pitcher Andrew Muhlstock to Chicago Cubs for Third Baseman Bill Madlock and Infielder Rob Sperring, February 11, 1977.
yTraded to New York Yankees for Pitcher Paul Semall and cash, June 26, 1979.
zGranted free agency, November 13, 1981; re-signed by Yankees, April 5, 1982.
aReleased, June 20, 1983.

DIVISION SERIES RECORD

Year Club League	Pos.	G.	AB.	R.	H.	2B.	3B.	HR.	RBI.	B.A.	PO.	A.	E.	F.A.
1981—New York.............. Amer.	PH	2	1	0	0	0	0	0	0	.000	0	0	0	.000

CHAMPIONSHIP SERIES RECORD

Year Club League	Pos.	G.	AB.	R.	H.	2B.	3B.	HR.	RBI.	B.A.	PO.	A.	E.	F.A.
1980—New York.............. Amer.	DH	1	4	0	0	0	0	0	0	.000	0	0	0	.000
1981—New York.............. Amer.	DH	1	3	0	1	0	0	0	0	.333	0	0	0	.000
Championship Series Totals		2	7	0	1	0	0	0	0	.143	0	0	0	.000

WORLD SERIES RECORD

Year Club League	Pos.	G.	AB.	R.	H.	2B.	3B.	HR.	RBI.	B.A.	PO.	A.	E.	F.A.
1981—New York............. Amer.	PH	4	3	0	0	0	0	0	0	.000	0	0	0	.000

ALL-STAR GAME RECORD

Year League	Pos.	AB.	R.	H.	2B.	3B.	HR.	RBI.	B.A.	PO.	A.	E.	F.A.
1971—American.................................	OF	3	0	1	0	0	0	0	.333	1	0	0	1.000
1972—American.................................	OF	3	0	0	0	0	0	0	.000	1	0	0	1.000
1973—American.................................	OF	3	0	0	0	0	0	0	.000	0	1	0	1.000
1974—American.................................	OF	2	0	0	0	0	0	0	.000	0	0	0	.000
1975—National	OF	2	0	0	0	0	0	0	.000	1	0	0	1.000
All-Star Game Totals..		13	0	1	0	0	0	0	.077	3	1	0	1.000

DALE BRYAN MURPHY

Born March 12, 1956, at Portland, Ore.
Height, 6.05. Weight, 215.
Throws and bats righthanded.
Attended Portland Community College, Portland, Ore.

Major League stolen bases: 1978 (11), 1979 (6), 1980 (9), 1981 (14), 1982 (23), 1983 (30). Total—93.
Tied major league record for fewest double plays by outfielder, season, 150 or more games (0), 1983.
Hit three home runs in a game, May 18, 1979.
Led National League in slugging percentage with .540 in 1983.
Led National League batters in strikeouts with 145 in 1978 and 133 in 1980.
Led National League first basemen in errors with 20 in 1978.
Tied for National League lead in double plays by outfielders with 4 in 1981.
Led International League catchers in putouts with 510, passed balls with 14 and tied for lead in double plays with 7 in 1977.
Tied for International League lead in total bases with 249 in 1977.
Named National League Player of the Year by THE SPORTING NEWS, 1982 and 1983.
Named National League Most Valuable Player by Baseball Writers' Association of America, 1982 and 1983.
Named outfielder on THE SPORTING NEWS National League All-Star Team, 1982 and 1983.
Named outfielder on THE SPORTING NEWS National League All-Star fielding team, 1982 and 1983.
Named outfielder on THE SPORTING NEWS National League Silver Slugger team, 1982 and 1983.

Year Club League	Pos.	G.	AB.	R.	H.	2B.	3B.	HR.	RBI.	B.A.	PO.	A.	E.	F.A.
1974—Kingsport .... Appal.	C	54	181	28	46	7	0	5	31	.254	389	28	7	.983
1975—Greenwood .... W. Car.	C-1B	131	443	48	101	20	1	5	48	.228	723	81	18	.978
1976—Savannah .... South.	C	104	352	37	94	13	5	12	55	.267	444	40	10	.980
1976—Richmond.............. Int.	C-OF	18	50	10	13	1	1	4	8	.260	60	9	4	.945
1976—Atlanta .... Nat.	C	19	65	3	17	6	0	0	9	.262	100	13	3	.974
1977—Richmond.............. Int.	C-1B	127	466	71	142	●33	4	22	★90	.305	600	50	15	.977
1977—Atlanta .... Nat.	C	18	76	5	24	8	1	2	14	.316	114	11	6	.954
1978—Atlanta .... Nat.	1B-C	151	530	66	120	14	3	23	79	.226	1220	105	23	.983
1979—Atlanta† .... Nat.	1B-C	104	384	53	106	7	2	21	57	.276	812	57	20	.978
1980—Atlanta .... Nat.	OF-1B	156	569	98	160	27	2	33	89	.281	384	15	6	.985
1981—Atlanta .... Nat.	OF-1B	104	369	43	91	12	1	13	50	.247	264	11	5	.982

Year Club League	Pos.	G.	AB.	R.	H.	2B.	3B.	HR.	RBI.	B.A.	PO.	A.	E.	F.A.
1982—Atlanta .... Nat.	OF	●162	598	113	168	23	2	36	●109	.281	407	6	9	.979
1983—Atlanta .... Nat.	OF	★162	589	131	178	24	4	36	★121	.302	373	10	6	.985
Major League Totals..................................		876	3180	512	864	121	15	164	528	.272	3674	228	78	.980

Selected by Atlanta Braves' organization in 1st round (fifth player selected) of free-agent draft, June 5, 1974.
†On disabled list, May 25 to July 19, 1979.

CHAMPIONSHIP SERIES RECORD

Year Club League	Pos.	G.	AB.	R.	H.	2B.	3B.	HR.	RBI.	B.A.	PO.	A.	E.	F.A.
1982—Atlanta .... Nat.	OF	3	11	1	3	0	0	0	0	.273	8	0	0	1.000

ALL-STAR GAME RECORD

Year League	Pos.	AB.	R.	H.	2B.	3B.	HR.	RBI.	B.A.	PO.	A.	E.	F.A.
1980—National	OF	0	0	0	0	0	0	0	.000	0	0	0	.000
1982—National	OF	2	1	0	0	0	0	0	.000	2	0	0	1.000
1983—National	OF	3	0	1	0	0	0	1	.333	0	0	0	.000
All-Star Game Totals		6	1	1	0	0	0	1	.167	2	0	0	1.000

DWAYNE KEITH MURPHY

Born March 18, 1955, at Merced, Calif.
Height, 6.01. Weight, 180.
Throws right and bats lefthanded.

Tied major league record for fewest double plays by outfielder, season, 150 or more games (0), 1980.
Major League stolen bases: 1979 (15), 1980 (26), 1981 (10), 1982 (26), 1983 (7). Total—84.
Led American League in sacrifice hits with 22 in 1980 and game-winning RBIs with 15 in 1981.
Led American League outfielders in total chances with 525 in 1980 and 474 in 1982.
Led Southern League in bases on balls received with 97 in 1977.
Tied for Southern League lead in double plays by outfielders with 4 in 1977.
Named outfielder on THE SPORTING NEWS American League All-Star Team, 1981.
Named outfielder on THE SPORTING NEWS American League All-Star fielding team, 1980 through 1983.

Year Club League	Pos.	G.	AB.	R.	H.	2B.	3B.	HR.	RBI.	B.A.	PO.	A.	E.	F.A.
1973—Lewiston .... N'west	OF	68	215	25	50	7	2	3	19	.233	102	★13	6	.950
1974—Burlington† .... Midw.	OF	53	150	16	33	6	2	2	10	.220	55	2	3	.959
1975—Modesto .... Calif.	OF	126	429	81	125	20	7	8	71	.291	250	7	9	.966
1976—Chattanooga .... South.	OF	68	200	32	52	6	0	1	23	.260	138	6	1	.993
1976—Tucson .... P. C.	OF	52	179	32	42	7	2	3	11	.235	125	6	4	.970
1977—Chattanooga .... South.	OF	132	406	53	104	11	9	5	53	.256	320	14	5	★.985
1978—Vancouver............. P. C.	OF-SS	42	148	35	39	4	1	7	17	.264	125	9	3	.978
1978—Oakland .... Amer.	OF	60	52	15	10	2	0	0	5	.192	49	1	0	1.000
1979—Oakland‡ .... Amer.	OF	121	388	57	99	10	4	11	40	.255	322	10	4	.988
1980—Oakland .... Amer.	OF	159	573	86	157	18	2	13	68	.274	★507	13	5	.990
1981—Oakland .... Amer.	OF	107	390	58	98	10	3	15	60	.251	326	6	5	.985
1982—Oakland§ .... Amer.	★OF-SS	151	543	84	129	15	1	27	94	.238	★452	18	8	.983
1983—Oakland .... Amer.	OF	130	471	55	107	17	2	17	75	.227	365	7	8	.979
Major League Totals....................................		728	2417	355	600	72	12	83	342	.248	2021	55	30	.986

Selected by Oakland A's organization in 15th round of free-agent draft, June 5, 1973.
†On disabled list, July 16 to September 16, 1974.
‡On disabled list, June 21 to July 14, 1979.
§On supplemental disabled list, June 24 to July 11, 1983.

DIVISION SERIES RECORD

Year Club League	Pos.	G.	AB.	R.	H.	2B.	3B.	HR.	RBI.	B.A.	PO.	A.	E.	F.A.
1981—Oakland................. Amer.	OF	3	11	4	6	1	0	1	2	.545	13	0	0	1.000

CHAMPIONSHIP SERIES RECORD

Year Club League	Pos.	G.	AB.	R.	H.	2B.	3B.	HR.	RBI.	B.A.	PO.	A.	E.	F.A.
1981—Oakland................. Amer.	OF	3	8	0	2	1	0	0	1	.250	9	0	0	1.000

DALE ALBERT MURRAY

Born February 2, 1950, at Cuero, Tex.
Height, 6.03. Weight, 205.
Throws and bats righthanded.
Attended Blinn Junior College, Brenham, Tex., and Victoria College, Victoria, Tex.

Tied major league record for most intentional bases on balls allowed, season (23), 1978.
Major League saves: 1974 (10), 1975 (9), 1976 (13), 1977 (4), 1978 (7), 1979 (5), 1982 (11), 1983 (1). Total—60.
Led National League in intentional bases on balls issued with 23 in 1978.
Led International League in saves with 16 in 1981.
Led Northern League in intentional bases on balls issued with 6 in 1970.

Year Club	League	G.	IP.	W.	L.	Pct.	H.	R.	ER.	SO.	BB.	ERA.
1970—Watertown	Northern	22	51	4	6	.400	50	41	32	48	39	5.65
1971—West Palm Beach†	Florida St.	1	1	0	1	.000	4	4	4	2	2	36.00
1972—West Palm Beach	Florida St.	7	10	3	1	.750	10	6	6	8	7	5.40
1972—Quebec City	Eastern	39	108	11	5	.688	85	41	29	64	53	2.42
1973—Peninsula	Int'national	28	150	8	●13	.381	145	77	71	89	75	4.26
1974—Memphis	Int'national	30	43	4	2	.667	34	11	7	36	19	1.47
1974—Montreal	National	32	70	1	1	.500	46	12	8	31	23	1.03
1975—Montreal‡	National	63	111	15	8	.652	134	59	49	43	39	3.97

Year Club	League	G.	IP.	W.	L.	Pct.	H.	R.	ER.	SO.	BB.	ERA.
1976—Montreal§	National	★81	113	4	9	.308	117	47	41	35	37	3.27
1977—Cincinnati	National	61	102	7	2	.778	125	60	56	42	46	4.94
1978—Cincinnati x-New York	National	68	119	9	6	.600	119	59	50	62	53	3.78
1979—New York y-Montreal	National	67	110	5	10	.333	119	62	56	41	55	4.58
1980—Denver	Am. Assoc.	16	44	4	1	.800	31	13	8	25	17	1.64
1980—Montreal z	National	16	29	0	1	.000	39	23	20	16	12	6.21
1981—Syracuse	Int'national	52	78	5	4	.556	57	23	16	57	28	1.85
1981—Toronto	American	11	15	1	0	1.000	12	2	2	12	5	1.20
1982—Toronto a	American	56	111	8	7	.533	115	48	39	60	32	3.16
1983—New York b	American	40	94⅓	2	4	.333	113	56	47	45	22	4.48
National League Totals...............		388	654	41	37	.526	699	322	280	270	265	3.85
American League Totals...............		107	220⅓	11	11	.500	240	106	88	117	59	3.59
Major League Totals...............		495	874⅓	52	48	.520	939	428	368	387	324	3.79

Selected by Montreal Expos' organization in 18th round of free-agent draft, June 4, 1970.
†On disabled list, April 16 to September 30, 1971.
‡On disabled list, May 12 to June 17, 1975.
§Traded with Pitcher Woodie Fryman to Cincinnati Reds for First Baseman Tony Perez and Pitcher Will McEnaney, December 16, 1976.
xTraded to New York Mets for Outfielder Ken Henderson, May 19, 1978.
ySold to Montreal Expos, August 30, 1979.
zReleased, August 28, 1980; signed by Toronto Blue Jays' organization, January 20, 1981.
aTraded with Outfielder-Catcher Tom Dodd to New York Yankees for Outfielder-First Baseman Dave Collins, Pitcher Mike Morgan, First Baseman Fred McGriff and a reported $400,000, December 9, 1982.
bGranted free agency, November 7, 1983; re-signed by Yankees, November 21, 1983.

RECORD AS OUTFIELDER

Year Club	League	Pos.	G.	AB.	R.	H.	2B.	3B.	HR.	RBI.	B.A.	PO.	A.	E.	F.A.
1970—W. Palm Beach....	Fla. St.	OF	4	3	0	1	0	0	0	0	.333	0	0	0	.000

EDDIE CLARENCE MURRAY

Born February 24, 1956, at Los Angeles, Calif.
Height, 6.02.   Weight, 200.
Throws right and bats left and righthanded.
Attended California State University at Los Angeles, Los Angeles, Calif.
Brother of Richard Murray, first baseman with San Francisco Giants, 1980 and 1983;
Leon Murray, first baseman in San Franciso Giants' organization, 1970;
Charles Murray, minor league outfielder, 1962 through 1966
and 1969; and Venice Murray, first baseman in
San Francisco Giants' organization, 1978.

Tied major league record for most games, switch-hit home runs, season (2), 1982.
Hit three home runs in a game, August 29, 1979 (second game) and September 14, 1980 (13 innings).
Switch-hit home runs in one game five times: August 3, 1977, August 29, 1979 (two righthanded and one lefthanded); August 16, 1981, April 24, 1982 and August 26, 1982.
Led American League first basemen in putouts with 1,504 and total chances with 1,615 in 1978.
Tied for American League lead in intentional bases on balls received with 18 in 1982.
Led Florida State League in total bases with 212 in 1974.
Led Florida State League first basemen in double plays with 113 in 1974.
Named American League Rookie of the Year by Baseball Writers' Association of America, 1977.
Named first baseman on THE SPORTING NEWS American League All-Star Team, 1983.
Named first baseman on THE SPORTING NEWS American League All-Star fielding team, 1982 and 1983.
Named first baseman on THE SPORTING NEWS American League Silver Slugger team, 1983.
Named Appalachian League Player of the Year, 1973.

Year Club	League	Pos.	G.	AB.	R.	H.	2B.	3B.	HR.	RBI.	B.A.	PO.	A.	E.	F.A.
1973—Bluefield	Appal.	1B	50	188	34	54	6	0	11	32	.287	421	14	13	.971
1974—Miami	Fla. St.	1B	131	460	64	133	★29	7	12	63	.289	★1114	★51	★25	.979
1974—Asheville...............	South.	1B	2	7	1	2	2	0	0	2	.286	17	0	0	1.000
1975—Asheville...............	South.	1B-3B	124	436	66	115	13	5	17	68	.264	637	58	15	.979
1976—Charlotte...............	South.	1B	88	299	46	89	15	2	12	46	.298	746	45	9	.989
1976—Rochester.............	Int.	1B-OF-3B	54	168	35	46	6	2	11	40	.274	291	13	5	.984
1977—Baltimore	Amer.	OF-1B	160	611	81	173	29	2	27	88	.283	482	20	4	.992
1978—Baltimore	Amer.	1B-3B	161	610	85	174	32	3	27	95	.285	1507	112	6	.996
1979—Baltimore	Amer.	1B	159	606	90	179	30	2	25	99	.295	★1456	107	10	.994
1980—Baltimore	Amer.	1B	158	621	100	186	36	2	32	116	.300	1369	77	9	.994
1981—Baltimore	Amer.	1B	99	378	57	111	21	2	●22	★78	.294	899	★91	1	★.999
1982—Baltimore	Amer.	1B	151	550	87	174	30	1	32	110	.316	1269	97	4	★.997
1983—Baltimore	Amer.	1B	156	582	115	178	30	3	33	111	.306	1393	114	10	.993
Major League Totals...................			1044	3958	615	1175	208	15	198	697	.297	8375	618	44	.995

Selected by Baltimore Orioles' organization in 3rd round of free-agent draft, June 5, 1973.

CHAMPIONSHIP SERIES RECORD

Tied Championship Series record for most runs, game (4), October 7, 1983.
Tied American League Championship Series record for most bases on balls, four-game Series (5), 1979.

Year Club	League	Pos.	G.	AB.	R.	H.	2B.	3B.	HR.	RBI.	B.A.	PO.	A.	E.	F.A.
1979—Baltimore	Amer.	1B	4	12	3	5	0	0	1	5	.417	44	3	2	.959
1983—Baltimore	Amer.	1B	4	15	5	4	0	0	1	3	.267	34	3	1	.974
Championship Series Totals			8	27	8	9	0	0	2	8	.333	78	6	3	.966

Established World Series record for most double plays started by first baseman, game (2), October 11, 1979.

Year	Club	League	Pos.	G.	AB.	R.	H.	2B.	3B.	HR.	RBI.	B.A.	PO.	A.	E.	F.A.
1979—Baltimore		Amer.	1B	7	26	3	4	1	0	1	2	.154	60	7	0	1.000
1983—Baltimore		Amer.	1B	5	20	2	5	0	0	2	3	.250	46	1	1	.979
World Series Totals				12	46	5	9	1	0	3	5	.196	106	8	1	.991

ALL-STAR GAME RECORD

Year	League	Pos.	AB.	R.	H.	2B.	3B.	HR.	RBI.	B.A.	PO.	A.	E.	F.A.
1981—American		PH-1B	2	0	0	0	0	0	0	.000	2	1	0	1.000
1982—American		PH-1B	1	0	0	0	0	0	0	.000	4	0	0	1.000
1983—American		1B	2	0	0	0	0	0	0	.000	4	0	0	1.000
All-Star Game Totals			5	0	0	0	0	0	0	.000	10	1	0	1.000

Named to American League All-Star Team for 1978 game; did not play.

RICHARD DALE MURRAY
(Rich)

Born July 6, 1957, at Los Angeles, Calif.
Height, 6.04. Weight, 205.
Throws and bats righthanded.
Brother of Eddie Murray, first basemen with Baltimore Orioles;
Leon Murray, first baseman in San Francisco Giants' organization, 1970;
Charles Murray, minor league outfielder, 1962 through 1966 and 1969;
and Venice Murray, first baseman in San Francisco Giants' organization, 1978.

Led Pacific Coast League first basemen in double plays with 155 in 1978.
Tied for Midwest League lead in double plays by first basemen with 105 in 1977.

Year	Club	League	Pos.	G.	AB.	R.	H.	2B.	3B.	HR.	RBI.	B.A.	PO.	A.	E.	F.A.
1975—Great Falls		Pion.	1B-OF	25	85	8	23	2	1	1	14	.271	128	3	7	.949
1976—Cedar Rapids†		Midw.	1B-OF	66	178	24	47	7	4	6	30	.264	213	11	8	.966
1977—Cedar Rapids		Midw.	1B	129	494	72	136	27	0	21	94	.275	1149	54	16	.987
1978—Phoenix‡		P. C.	1B	117	442	66	124	23	6	5	58	.281	*1109	64	13	.989
1979—Phoenix		P. C.	*1B-OF	125	441	63	116	13	8	5	67	.263	1043	86	*26	.977
1980—Phoenix		P. C.	3B-1B	49	168	22	44	6	1	7	31	.262	53	87	19	.881
1980—San Francisco§		Nat.	1B	53	194	19	42	8	2	4	24	.216	508	35	7	.987
1981—Phoenix x		P. C.	1B	94	359	52	117	15	4	12	69	.326	821	52	12	.986
1982—Charleston y		Int.	1B-3B	40	153	21	37	2	0	4	22	.242	239	29	4	.985
1982—Wichita z		A. A.	3B-1B-OF	80	285	48	82	18	1	13	54	.288	179	71	16	.940
1983—Phoenix		P. C.	1B-3B-OF	120	431	68	129	23	2	19	82	.299	418	101	22	.959
1983—San Francisco a		Nat.	1B	4	10	0	2	0	0	0	1	.200	20	1	0	1.000
Major League Totals				57	204	19	44	8	2	4	25	.216	528	36	7	.988

Selected by San Francisco Giants' organization in 6th round of free-agent, draft, June 4, 1975.
†On disabled list, June 21 to July 29, 1976.
‡On disabled list, June 9 to June 28, 1978.
§On emergency disabled list, July 11 to September 9, 1980.
xDrafted by Cleveland Indians, December 7, 1981.
ySold to Wichita (Montreal Expos' organization), June 7, 1982.
zReleased, February 19, 1983; signed by Phoenix (San Francisco Giants' organization), April 4, 1983.
aGranted free agency, October 20, 1983.

RALPH RONALD MUSSELMAN
(Ron)

Born November 11, 1954, at Wilmington, N.C.
Height, 6.01. Weight, 190.
Throws and bats righthanded.
Attended Louisburg Junior College, Louisburg, N.C., and
Clemson University, Clemson, S.C.

Led Pacific Coast League in games finished in relief with 44 in 1982.

Year	Club	League	G.	IP.	W.	L.	Pct.	H.	R.	ER.	SO.	BB.	ERA.
1977—Bellingham		Northwest	12	70	4	4	.500	75	44	36	67	26	4.63
1978—Alexandria		Carolina	25	161	6	12	.333	182	96	76	111	69	4.25
1979—Alexandria		Carolina	27	90	3	4	.429	87	44	31	60	30	3.10
1980—Lynn		Eastern	53	86	6	6	.500	75	49	37	47	34	3.87
1981—Spokane†		P. Coast	43	67	1	8	.111	69	31	28	25	27	3.76
1982—Salt Lake City		P. Coast	●51	68⅔	5	4	.556	68	25	25	40	19	3.28
1982—Seattle‡		American	12	15⅔	1	0	1.000	18	7	6	9	6	3.45
1983—Oklahoma City		Am. Assoc.	28	137⅔	9	12	.429	166	99	84	85	50	5.49
Major League Totals			12	15⅔	1	0	1.000	18	7	6	9	6	3.45

Selected by California Angels' organization in 22nd round of free-agent draft, June 4, 1975.
Selected by Houston Astros' organization in secondary phase of free-agent draft, June 8, 1976.
Selected by Seattle Mariners' organization in 5th round of free-agent draft, June 7, 1977.
†On disabled list, April 23 to May 7, 1981.
‡Traded to Texas Rangers for First Baseman Pat Putnam, December 21, 1982.

WILLIAM GERARD NAHORODNY

Name pronounced Na-ha-ROD-knee.

(Bill)

Born August 31, 1953, at Hamtramck, Mich.
Height, 6.02. Weight, 195.
Throws and bats righthanded.
Attended St. Clair County Community College, Port Huron, Mich.

Led American Association catchers in putouts with 598 and tied for lead in double plays with 8 in 1976.
Led International League catchers in fielding percentage with .994 in 1975.
Led New York-Pennsylvania League catchers in putouts with 531, passed balls with 13 and tied for lead in assists with 39 and double plays with 6 in 1972.
Tied for New York-Pennsylvania League lead in sacrifice flies with 6 in 1972.

Year Club	League	Pos.	G.	AB.	R.	H.	2B.	3B.	HR.	RBI.	B.A.	PO.	A.	E.	F.A.
1972—Auburn	NYP	*C-3B	69	217	36	57	14	2	6	33	.263	532	40	13	*.978
1973—Rocky Mount	Carol.	*C-1B-3B	118	389	40	102	23	1	14	76	.262	798	64	10	*.989
1974—Reading	East.	C-1B-3B	110	388	58	93	17	2	19	77	.240	642	70	13	.982
1975—Toledo	Int.	C-1B	125	411	51	105	17	4	*19	64	.255	691	71	7	.991
1976—Oklahoma City	A. A.	C-1B	114	391	74	114	22	3	23	78	.292	606	50	7	.989
1976—Philadelphia	Nat.	C	3	5	0	1	1	0	0	0	.200	7	0	0	1.000
1977—Oklahoma City†	A. A.	1B-C	115	386	52	101	16	4	17	69	.262	878	57	6	.994
1977—Chicago	Amer.	C	7	23	3	6	1	0	1	4	.261	29	6	0	1.000
1978—Chicago	Amer.	C-1B	107	347	29	82	11	2	8	35	.236	509	55	11	.981
1979—Chicago‡§	Amer.	C	65	179	20	46	10	0	6	29	.257	223	25	7	.973
1980—Atlanta x	Nat.	C-1B	59	157	14	38	12	0	5	18	.242	178	24	2	.990
1981—Atlanta yz	Nat.	C-1B	14	13	0	3	1	0	0	2	.231	7	0	0	1.000
1982—Charleston	Int.	C-1B	15	55	9	16	2	0	6	18	.291	91	15	2	.981
1982—Cleveland a	Amer.	C	39	94	6	21	5	1	4	18	.223	111	11	0	1.000
1983—Evansville	A. A.	1B-C	127	463	70	155	●37	1	21	94	.335	338	24	2	.995
1983—Detroit b	Amer.	PH	2	1	0	0	0	0	0	0	.000	0	0	0	.000
National League Totals			76	175	14	42	14	0	5	20	.240	192	24	3	.986
American League Totals			220	644	58	155	27	3	19	86	.241	872	97	18	.982
Major League Totals			296	819	72	197	41	3	24	106	.241	1064	121	21	.983

Selected by Philadelphia Phillies' organization in 6th round of free-agent draft, June 6, 1972.
†Sold on waivers to Chicago White Sox, September 8, 1977.
‡On supplemental disabled list, June 30 to July 23, 1979.
§Traded to Atlanta Braves for Pitcher Rick Wieters, December 3, 1979.
xOn disabled list, March 29 to April 23, 1980.
yOn disabled list from beginning of season until May 12, 1981.
zReleased, August 8, 1981; signed by Cleveland Indians' organization, January 20, 1982.
aReleased, November 2, 1982; signed by Detroit Tigers' organization, March 1, 1983.
bReleased, October 21, 1983.

CHARLES EVERETT NAIL

(Charlie)

Born November 22, 1961, at Jackson, Miss.
Height, 6.04. Weight, 210.
Throws and bats righthanded.

Year Club	League	G.	IP.	W.	L.	Pct.	H.	R.	ER.	SO.	BB.	ERA.
1979—Bristol	Ap'lachian	11	30	0	3	.000	46	50	39	15	44	11.70
1980—Lakeland	Florida St.	13	53	4	6	.400	66	52	43	30	37	7.30
1980—Bristol†	Ap'lachian					(Did not play)						
1981—Macon	S. Atlantic	13	90	6	5	.545	68	38	27	73	34	2.70
1981—Lakeland‡	Florida St.	6	22	1	4	.200	32	20	17	15	16	6.95
1982—Birmingham	Southern	24	143	9	6	.600	139	64	53	109	46	3.34
1983—Evansville	Am. Assoc.	25	145	8	10	.444	167	85	79	79	54	4.90

Selected by Detroit Tigers' organization in 7th round of free-agent draft, June 5, 1979.
†On temporarily inactive list, June 16, 1980 through remainder of season.
‡On disabled list, August 18, 1981 through remainder of season.

TITO ANGELO NANNI JR.

Name pronounced NAN-ee.

Born December 3, 1959, at Philadelphia, Pa.
Height, 6.04. Weight, 220.
Throws and bats lefthanded.

Led Eastern League in intentional bases on balls received with 11 in 1982.
Led Carolina League batters in strikeouts with 132 in 1979.

Year Club	League	Pos.	G.	AB.	R.	H.	2B.	3B.	HR.	RBI.	B.A.	PO.	A.	E.	F.A.
1979—Alexandria	Carol.	OF	113	402	49	91	19	1	6	48	.226	150	5	11	.934
1980—San Jose	Calif.	OF	57	191	25	38	6	2	3	23	.199	98	3	3	.971
1980—Wausau	Midw.	OF	64	237	33	60	8	0	12	40	.253	129	11	6	.959
1981—Lynn	East.	OF	116	361	46	90	14	1	7	40	.249	203	6	9	.959
1982—Lynn	East.	OF	134	475	71	139	25	5	16	77	.293	165	6	*17	.910
1983—Salt Lake City	P. C.	OF-1B	122	416	64	100	18	5	11	57	.240	347	24	9	.976

Selected by Seattle Mariners' organization in 1st round (sixth player selected) of free-agent draft, June 6, 1978.

JERRY AUSTIN NARRON

Born January 15, 1956, at Goldsboro, N. C.
Height, 6.03. Weight, 205.
Throws right and bats lefthanded.
Attends East Carolina University, Greenville, N. C.
Brother of John Narron, Jr., first baseman in New York Yankees' and Chicago White
Sox' organizations, 1974 and 1975; nephew of Sam Narron, catcher with St. Louis Cardinals,
1935, 1942 and 1943; and coach, Pittsburgh Pirates, 1951 through 1964; nephew of
Milton Narron, former minor league catcher-outfielder.

Led Pacific Coast League in intentional bases on balls received with 15 in 1983.
Tied for Florida State League lead in being hit by pitch with 10 in 1975.
Led Florida State League catchers in fielding percentage with .986 and double plays with 7 in 1976.
Tied for Pacific Coast League lead in double plays by catchers with 11 in 1978.

Year	Club	League	Pos.	G.	AB.	R.	H.	2B.	3B.	HR.	RBI.	B.A.	PO.	A.	E.	F.A.
1974—Johnson City	Appal.	C-OF	66	226	43	68	15	3	7	49	.301	249	19	8	.971
1975—Ft. Lauderdale	Fla. St.	1B-C-OF	113	360	39	76	12	0	2	34	.211	425	33	2	.996
1976—Ft. Lauderdale	Fla. St.	C-1B	119	412	35	101	17	0	6	56	.245	563	56	8	.987
1977—West Haven	East.	C-1B	121	438	80	131	16	0	28	93	.299	625	40	7	.990
1978—Tacoma	P. C.	C-1B	120	435	67	121	25	1	15	84	.278	552	78	18	.972
1979—New York†	Amer.	C	61	123	17	21	3	1	4	18	.171	167	15	5	.973
1980—Spokane	P. C.	C-1B	67	233	40	66	14	2	9	39	.283	223	19	6	.976
1980—Seattle	Amer.	C	48	107	7	21	3	0	4	18	.196	115	11	1	.992
1981—Seattle‡	Amer.	C	76	203	13	45	5	0	3	17	.222	248	11	1	.996
1982—Spokane	P. C.	C	110	408	60	127	24	2	12	61	.311	446	46	12	.976
1983—Edmonton	P. C.	1B-C	139	532	93	160	30	5	27	102	.301	1298	70	13	.991
1983—California	Amer.	C	10	22	1	3	0	0	1	4	.136	14	3	2	.895
Major League Totals				195	455	38	90	11	1	12	57	.198	544	40	9	.985

Selected by New York Yankees' organization in 6th round of free-agent draft, June 5, 1974.
†Traded with Outfielder Juan Beniquez and Pitchers Jim Beattie and Rick Anderson to Seattle Mariners for
Outfielder Ruppert Jones and Pitcher Jim Lewis, November 1, 1979.
‡Released, March 30, 1982; signed by California Angels' organization, April 1, 1982.

JAMES VICTOR NELSON
(Jamie)

Born September 5, 1959, at Clinton, Okla.
Height, 5.11. Weight, 185.
Throws and bats righthanded.
Attended Orange Coast College, Costa Mesa, Calif.

Led Pacific Coast League catchers in errors with 18 in 1983.

Year	Club	League	Pos.	G.	AB.	R.	H.	2B.	3B.	HR.	RBI.	B.A.	PO.	A.	E.	F.A.
1978—Wausau	Midw.	C-3B	64	202	32	54	13	3	4	26	.267	176	53	9	.962
1979—Bakersfield	Calif.	C-3B-1B	116	378	58	106	20	2	12	65	.280	514	98	24	.962
1980—Lynchburg†	Carol.	C	25	65	10	15	3	0	1	8	.231	76	10	3	.966
1981—Lynn	East.	C-1-3-O	90	246	33	67	8	1	7	32	.272	333	43	6	.984
1982—Lynn	East.	C-1-O-3	111	316	48	90	15	4	8	42	.285	663	60	13	.982
1983—Salt Lake City	P. C.	C-3B-1B	80	231	41	57	7	1	6	36	.247	375	77	21	.956
1983—Seattle‡	Amer.	C	40	96	9	21	3	0	1	5	.219	202	16	5	.978
Major League Totals				40	96	9	21	3	0	1	5	.219	202	16	5	.978

Selected by New York Mets' organization in 8th round of free-agent draft, January 10, 1978.
†Released, April 3, 1981; signed by Lynn (Seattle Mariners' organization), April 8, 1981.
‡Drafted by Milwaukee Brewers, December 5, 1983.

RICKY LEE NELSON

Born May 8, 1959, at Eloy, Ariz.
Height, 6.00. Weight, 195.
Throws right and bats lefthanded.
Attended Arizona State University, Tempe, Ariz.

Tied for California League lead in total bases with 245 and game-winning RBIs with 15 in 1982.

Year	Club	League	Pos.	G.	AB.	R.	H.	2B.	3B.	HR.	RBI.	B.A.	PO.	A.	E.	F.A.
1981—Bellingham	N'west	OF	56	197	35	56	5	0	6	37	.284	49	7	3	.949
1982—Bakersfield	Calif.	OF	*140	*566	65	174	*36	1	11	*101	.307	197	13	9	.959
1983—Salt Lake City	P. C.	OF-3B	29	102	20	34	6	3	5	27	.333	55	4	1	.983
1983—Seattle	Amer.	OF	98	291	32	74	13	3	5	36	.254	122	10	4	.971
Major League Totals				98	291	32	74	13	3	5	36	.254	122	10	4	.971

Selected by California Angels' organization in 24th round of free-agent draft, June 3, 1980.
Selected by Seattle Mariners' organization in 4th round of free-agent draft, June 8, 1981.

WAYLAND EUGENE NELSON II
(Gene)

Born December 3, 1960, at Tampa, Fla.
Height, 6.00. Weight, 172.
Throws and bats righthanded.

Led Florida State League in shutouts with 5 and complete games with 16 in 1980.

Year Club	League	G.	IP.	W.	L.	Pct.	H.	R.	ER.	SO.	BB.	ERA.
1978—Sarasota Rangers	Gulf Coast	14	52	5	0	●1.000	41	18	13	28	20	2.25
1979—Asheville†	W. Carol.	33	155	13	5	★.722	149	77	62	96	44	3.60
1980—Ft. Lauderdale	Florida St.	27	196	★20	3	★.870	146	51	43	130	70	1.97
1981—New York‡	American	8	39	3	1	.750	40	24	21	16	23	4.85
1981—Ft. Lauderdale	Florida St.	2	10	0	0	.000	9	6	6	8	5	5.40
1981—Columbus§	Int'national	5	32	4	0	1.000	25	9	9	37	14	2.53
1982—Seattle	American	22	122⅔	6	9	.400	133	70	63	71	60	4.62
1982—Salt Lake City	P. Coast	5	37⅔	1	3	.250	36	18	14	22	28	3.35
1983—Salt Lake City	P. Coast	16	99	9	4	.692	115	65	57	74	28	5.18
1983—Seattle	American	10	32	0	3	.000	38	29	28	11	21	7.88
Major League Totals		40	193⅔	9	13	.409	211	123	112	98	104	5.20

Selected by Texas Rangers' organization in 29th round of free-agent draft, June 6, 1978.

†Traded with Pitcher Ray Fontenot to New York Yankees' organization for Pitchers Bob Polinsky, Neal Mersch and Mark Softy, October 8, 1979; completing deal in which New York traded Outfielder Mickey Rivers and three players to be named later to Texas Rangers for Third Baseman Amos Lewis and two players to be named later, August 1, 1979.

‡On disabled list, April 10 to May 4, 1981; included rehabilitation disability assignment to Ft. Lauderdale, April 17 to May 4, 1981.

§Traded with Pitcher Bill Caudill, a player to be named later and cash to Seattle Mariners for Pitcher Shane Rawley, April 1, 1982; Seattle organization acquired Outfielder Bobby Brown to complete deal, April 6, 1982.

GRAIG NETTLES

Born August 20, 1944, at San Diego, Calif.
Height, 6.00. Weight, 187.
Throws right and bats lefthanded.
Attended San Diego State College, San Diego, Calif.
Brother of Jim Nettles, player-coach in Oakland A's organization.

Established major league records for most assists by third baseman, season (412), and most double plays by third baseman, season (54), 1971.

Tied major league records for most home runs month of April (11), 1974; fewest three-base hits, season, 150 or more games (0), 1972 and 1973.

Established American League record for most home runs by third baseman, lifetime (319).

Tied American League record for most home runs, doubleheader (4), April 14, 1974.

Led American League in sacrifice flies with 11 in 1975.

Led American League third basemen in total chances with 587 in 1971, 553 in 1973, 545 in 1974 and 539 in 1976.

Led American League third basemen in double plays with 54 in 1971, 30 in 1976 and tied for lead with 30 in 1978.

Led American League third basemen in assists with 383 in 1976.

Led Southern League third basemen in double plays with 34 in 1967 and led Pacific Coast League third basemen with 20 in 1968.

Named third baseman on The Sporting News American League All-Star Team, 1975, 1977 and 1978.

Named third baseman on The Sporting News American League All-Star fielding team, 1977 and 1978.

Year Club	League	Pos.	G.	AB.	R.	H.	2B.	3B.	HR.	RBI.	B.A.	PO.	A.	E.	F.A.
1966—Wis. Rapids	Midw.	2B-3B	117	413	84	111	19	6	★28	75	.269	240	245	28	.945
1967—Charlotte	South.	3B	140	499	69	116	18	4	●19	86	.232	107	★318	24	.947
1967—Minnesota	Amer.	PH	3	3	0	1	1	0	0	0	.333	0	0	0	.000
1968—Denver	P. C.	3B-OF-1B	130	451	84	134	17	●12	22	83	.297	125	266	17	.958
1968—Minnesota	Amer.	OF-3B-1B	22	76	13	17	2	1	5	8	.224	50	9	2	.967
1969—Minnesota†	Amer.	OF-3B	96	225	27	50	9	2	7	26	.222	88	44	2	.985
1970—Cleveland	Amer.	★3B-OF	157	549	81	129	13	1	26	62	.235	135	358	17	★.967
1971—Cleveland	Amer.	3B	158	598	78	156	18	1	28	86	.261	★159	★412	16	.973
1972—Cleveland‡	Amer.	3B	150	557	65	141	28	0	17	70	.253	114	★358	★21	.957
1973—New York	Amer.	3B	160	552	65	129	18	0	22	81	.234	117	★410	26	.953
1974—New York	Amer.	★3B-SS	155	566	74	139	21	1	22	75	.246	★147	377	21	.961
1975—New York	Amer.	3B	157	581	71	155	24	4	21	91	.267	135	★379	19	.964
1976—New York	Amer.	3B-SS	158	583	88	148	29	2	★32	93	.254	137	384	19	.965
1977—New York	Amer.	3B	158	589	99	150	23	4	37	107	.255	132	321	12	.974
1978—New York	Amer.	3B-SS	159	587	81	162	23	2	27	93	.276	110	326	11	.975
1979—New York	Amer.	3B	145	521	71	132	15	1	20	73	.253	110	339	16	.966
1980—New York§	Amer.	3B-SS	89	324	52	79	14	0	16	45	.244	59	183	10	.960
1981—New York	Amer.	3B	103	349	46	85	7	1	15	46	.244	63	214	8	.972
1982—New York x	Amer.	3B	122	405	47	94	11	2	18	55	.232	73	255	23	.934
1983—New York	Amer.	3B	129	462	56	123	17	3	20	75	.266	78	273	16	.956
Major League Totals			2121	7527	1014	1890	273	25	333	1086	.251	1707	4642	239	.964

Selected by Minnesota Twins' organization in 4th round of free-agent draft, June 9, 1965.

†Traded with Pitchers Dean Chance and Robert L. Miller and Outfielder Ted Uhlaender to Cleveland Indians for Pitchers Luis Tiant and Stan Williams, December 12, 1969.

‡Traded with Catcher Jerry Moses to New York Yankees for Catcher-First Baseman John Ellis, Infielder Jerry Kenney and Outfielders Charlie Spikes and Rosendo Torres, November 27, 1972.

§On supplemental disabled list, July 27, 1980; transferred to disabled list, August 21 to October 2, 1980.

xOn disabled list, April 26 to May 17, 1982.

DIVISION SERIES RECORD

Year Club	League	Pos.	G.	AB.	R.	H.	2B.	3B.	HR.	RBI.	B.A.	PO.	A.	E.	F.A.
1981—New York	Amer.	3B	5	17	1	1	0	0	0	1	.059	7	7	0	1.000

CHAMPIONSHIP SERIES RECORD

Established Championship Series records for most hits, inning (2), October 14, 1981; most runs batted in, three-game Series (9), 1981.

Tied Championship Series record for most times reached first base safely, game (5), October 14, 1981.

Tied American League Championship Series records for most home runs, five-game Series (2), 1976; highest slugging average, three-game Series (.917), 1981; most Series, one or more home runs (4).

Year Club	League	Pos.	G.	AB.	R.	H.	2B.	3B.	HR.	RBI.	B.A.	PO.	A.	E.	F.A.
1969—Minnesota.............	Amer.	PH	1	1	0	1	0	0	0	0	1.000	0	0	0	.000
1976—New York.............	Amer.	3B	5	17	2	4	1	0	2	4	.235	5	14	0	1.000
1977—New York.............	Amer.	3B	5	20	1	3	0	0	0	1	.150	2	12	0	1.000
1978—New York.............	Amer.	3B	4	15	3	5	0	1	1	2	.333	6	7	0	1.000
1980—New York.............	Amer.	3B-PH	2	6	1	1	0	0	1	1	.167	0	2	0	1.000
1981—New York.............	Amer.	3B	3	12	2	6	2	0	1	9	.500	4	4	1	.889
Championship Series Totals			20	71	9	20	3	1	5	17	.282	17	39	1	.982

WORLD SERIES RECORD

Established World Series records for most double plays by third baseman, four-game Series (3), 1976; most assists by third baseman, six-game Series (20), 1977; highest fielding average by third baseman, six-game Series, most chances accepted (1.000 and 26), 1978; most double plays by third baseman, total Series (6); most double plays and double plays started by third baseman, six-game Series (3), 1978.

Tied World Series records for most double plays started by third baseman, four-game Series (2), 1976; most double plays started, game (2), October 19, 1976; fewest chances accepted by third baseman, game (0), October 18, 1977.

Year Club	League	Pos.	G.	AB.	R.	H.	2B.	3B.	HR.	RBI.	B.A.	PO.	A.	E.	F.A.
1976—New York.............	Amer.	3B	4	12	0	3	0	0	0	2	.250	8	8	0	1.000
1977—New York.............	Amer.	3B	6	21	1	4	1	0	0	2	.190	2	20	1	.957
1978—New York.............	Amer.	3B	6	25	2	4	0	0	1	1	.160	8	18	0	1.000
1981—New York.............	Amer.	3B	3	10	1	4	1	0	0	0	.400	3	10	1	.929
World Series Totals			19	68	4	15	2	0	0	5	.221	21	56	2	.975

ALL-STAR GAME RECORD

Year League	Pos.	AB.	R.	H.	2B.	3B.	HR.	RBI.	B.A.	PO.	A.	E.	F.A.
1975—American.................................	3B	4	0	1	0	0	0	0	.250	2	2	0	1.000
1977—American.................................	3B	2	0	0	0	0	0	0	.000	0	1	0	1.000
1978—American.................................	3B	0	0	0	0	0	0	0	.000	0	1	0	1.000
1979—American.................................	3B	1	0	1	0	0	0	0	1.000	1	2	0	1.000
1980—American.................................	3B	2	0	0	0	0	0	0	.000	0	1	0	1.000
All-Star Game Totals		9	0	2	0	0	0	0	.222	3	7	0	1.000

Originally replaced due to injury by Larry Hisle, then re-named to replace Reggie Jackson in 1978.

JEFFREY LYNN NEWMAN
(Jeff)

Born September 11, 1948, at Fort Worth, Tex.
Height, 6.02. Weight, 215.
Throws and bats righthanded.
Received bachelor of science degree in education from
Texas Christian University, Fort Worth, Tex.

Led Texas League catchers in double plays with 10 and passed balls with 29 in 1973.
Led California League catchers in errors with 24 and passed balls with 51 in 1972.

Year Club	League	Pos.	G.	AB.	R.	H.	2B.	3B.	HR.	RBI.	B.A.	PO.	A.	E.	F.A.
1970—Sara. Indians.........	Gulf C.	1B-3B-OF	55	195	27	61	9	0	●6	★53	.313	302	33	15	.957
1971—Reno†.....................	Calif.	O-1-3-C	67	234	35	63	11	3	16	53	.269	173	19	9	.955
1972—Reno	Calif.	C-1B-3B	107	410	59	106	20	6	20	84	.259	718	81	29	.965
1973—San Antonio‡.........	Texas	C	112	394	50	97	29	0	13	63	.246	668	★72	10	.987
1974—Oklahoma City.....	A. A.	C-1B	57	188	19	46	3	1	7	28	.245	292	17	6	.981
1974—Salt Lake City......	P. C.	C	28	109	15	33	8	0	4	21	.303	30	1	0	1.000
1975—Toledo§	Int.	C	32	64	7	12	4	0	2	5	.188	87	6	2	.976
1975—Salt Lake City......	P. C.	C-1B	58	176	24	40	10	0	5	25	.227	267	22	12	.960
1976—Tucson..................	P. C.	C	68	231	23	62	11	1	5	38	.268	311	26	13	.963
1976—Oakland................	Amer.	C	43	77	5	15	4	0	0	4	.195	140	18	3	.981
1977—Oakland................	Amer.	C-P	94	162	17	36	9	0	4	15	.222	251	36	9	.970
1978—Oakland x	Amer.	C-1B	105	268	25	64	7	1	9	32	.239	399	41	12	.973
1979—Oakland................	Amer.	C-1B-3B	143	516	53	119	17	2	22	71	.231	730	95	18	.979
1980—Oakland................	Amer.	1-C-3-2	127	438	37	102	19	1	15	56	.233	675	54	15	.980
1981—Oakland................	Amer.	C-1B	68	216	17	50	12	0	3	15	.231	367	28	2	.995
1982—Oakland y	Amer.	C-1B-3B	72	251	19	50	11	0	6	30	.199	347	28	5	.987
1983—Boston...................	Amer.	C	59	132	11	25	4	0	3	7	.189	171	19	2	.990
Major League Totals....................................			711	2060	184	461	83	4	62	230	.224	3080	319	66	.981

Selected by Cleveland Indians' organization in 26th round of free-agent draft, June 4, 1970.
†On military list, December 24, 1970 through June 13, 1971.
‡On temporary inactive list, May 31 to June 17, 1973.
§Sold to Oakland A's, October 24, 1975.
xOn supplemental disabled list, August 17 to September 1, 1978.
yTraded with Outfielder Tony Armas to Boston Red Sox for Third Baseman Carney Lansford, Outfielder Garry Hancock and a player to be named later, December 6, 1982; Oakland A's acquired Pitcher Jerry King to complete deal, December 20, 1982.

DIVISION SERIES RECORD

Year Club	League	Pos.	G.	AB.	R.	H.	2B.	3B.	HR.	RBI.	B.A.	PO.	A.	E.	F.A.
1981—Oakland.................	Amer.	C	1	3	0	0	0	0	0	0	.000	4	0	0	1.000

CHAMPIONSHIP SERIES RECORD

Year Club	League	Pos.	G.	AB.	R.	H.	2B.	3B.	HR.	RBI.	B.A.	PO.	A.	E.	F.A.
1981—Oakland.................	Amer.	C	2	5	0	0	0	0	0	0	.000	9	1	0	1.000

Member of American League All-Star Team for 1979 game; did not play.

RECORD AS PITCHER

Year Club	League	G.	IP.	W.	L.	Pct.	H.	R.	ER.	SO.	BB.	ERA.
1977—Oakland...............................	American	1	1	0	0	.000	1	0	0	0	0	0.00

THOMAS REID NICHOLS

(Known by middle name.)

Born August 5, 1958, at Ocala, Fla.
Height, 5.11. Weight, 165.
Throws and bats righthanded.

Led Carolina League in total bases with 227 and being hit by pitch with 12 in 1979.
Led Carolina League outfielders in assists with 23 in 1979.

Year Club	League	Pos.	G.	AB.	R.	H.	2B.	3B.	HR.	RBI.	B.A.	PO.	A.	E.	F.A.
1976—Elmira...................	NYP	2B-3B-OF	23	53	8	18	1	0	0	9	.340	11	12	2	.920
1977—Winter Haven.......	Fla. St.	OF-2B	116	387	41	102	15	7	2	34	.264	166	41	7	.967
1978—Winter Haven.......	Fla. St.	OF-3B	125	413	52	102	20	1	5	34	.247	200	24	9	.961
1979—Winston-Salem	Carol.	OF-3B	134	★532	★107	★156	25	5	12	59	.293	240	23	10	.963
1980—Pawtucket.............	Int.	OF	134	511	68	141	27	5	4	42	.276	250	12	6	.978
1980—Boston....................	Amer.	OF	12	36	5	8	0	1	0	3	.222	24	1	1	.961
1981—Boston....................	Amer.	OF-3B	39	48	13	9	0	1	0	3	.188	35	4	0	1.000
1982—Boston†.................	Amer.	OF	92	245	35	74	16	1	7	33	.302	169	9	2	.989
1983—Boston....................	Amer.	OF-SS	100	274	35	78	22	1	6	22	.285	168	5	1	.994
Major League Totals..................................			243	603	88	169	38	4	13	61	.280	396	19	4	.990

Selected by Boston Red Sox' organization in 12th round of free-agent draft, June 8, 1976.
†On supplemental disabled list, July 21 to August 6, 1982.

STEVEN RICHARD NICOSIA

Name pronounced Nuh-KOH-see-uh.

(Steve)

Born August 6, 1955, at Paterson, N. J.
Height, 5.10. Weight, 185.
Throws and bats righthanded.

Led Texas League catchers in putouts with 525 in 1975.
Led Carolina League catchers in putouts with 833 and errors with 12 in 1974.

Year Club	League	Pos.	G.	AB.	R.	H.	2B.	3B.	HR.	RBI.	B.A.	PO.	A.	E.	F.A.
1973—Charleston............	W. Car.	C-OF	54	165	22	38	8	2	2	21	.230	389	25	7	.983
1973—Sherbrooke...........	East.	C	3	9	1	1	0	0	0	0	.111	29	1	0	1.000
1974—Salem...................	Carol.	C-1B-OF	118	413	63	126	16	9	15	92	.305	860	89	13	.986
1975—Shreveport	Tex.	★C-OF	110	370	52	99	15	6	6	39	.268	527	45	8	★.986
1976—Charleston............	Int.	★C-1B	117	378	29	99	20	0	8	49	.262	★616	57	8	.988
1977—Columbus†............	Int.	C	25	85	12	18	5	0	4	12	.212	132	16	2	.987
1978—Columbus.............	Int.	C-O-1-3	111	366	66	118	20	5	12	74	.322	486	38	9	.983
1978—Pittsburgh.............	Nat.	C	3	5	0	0	0	0	0	0	.000	8	1	0	1.000
1979—Pittsburgh.............	Nat.	C	70	191	22	55	16	0	4	13	.288	320	25	3	.991
1980—Pittsburgh.............	Nat.	C	60	176	16	38	8	0	1	22	.216	284	25	5	.984
1981—Pittsburgh.............	Nat.	C	54	169	21	39	10	1	2	18	.231	257	23	5	.982
1982—Pittsburgh.............	Nat.	C-OF	39	100	6	28	3	0	1	7	.280	183	22	2	.990
1983—Pitt.‡§-S.F..............	Nat.	C	36	79	8	17	2	0	1	7	.215	131	9	2	.986
Major League Totals..................................			262	720	73	177	39	1	9	67	.246	1183	105	17	.987

Selected by Pittsburgh Pirates' organization in 1st round (24th player selected) of free-agent draft, June 5, 1973.
†On disabled list, May 17 to August 23, 1977.
‡On supplemental disabled list, July 13 to August 8, 1983.
§Traded to San Francisco Giants for Catcher Milt May and cash, August 19, 1983.

WORLD SERIES RECORD

Year Club	League	Pos.	G.	AB.	R.	H.	2B.	3B.	HR.	RBI.	B.A.	PO.	A.	E.	F.A.
1979—Pittsburgh.............	Nat.	C	4	16	1	1	0	0	0	0	.063	23	2	0	1.000

THOMAS EDWARD NIEDENFUER

Name pronounced NEED-un-fyoor.

(Tom)

Born August 13, 1959, at St. Louis Park, Minn.
Height, 6.04. Weight, 220.
Throws and bats righthanded.
Attended Washington State University, Pullman, Wash.

Major League saves: 1981 (2), 1982 (9), 1983 (11). Total—22.

Year Club	League	G.	IP.	W.	L.	Pct.	H.	R.	ER.	SO.	BB.	ERA.
1981—San Antonio....................	Texas	36	90	13	3	★.813	61	19	18	95	34	1.80
1981—Los Angeles	National	17	26	3	1	.750	25	11	11	12	6	3.81
1982—Albuquerque	P. Coast	4	10⅔	2	0	1.000	6	0	0	15	2	0.00
1982—Los Angeles	National	55	69⅔	3	4	.429	71	22	21	60	25	2.71
1983—Los Angeles	National	66	94⅔	8	3	.727	55	22	20	66	29	1.90
Major League Totals................................		138	190⅓	14	8	.636	151	55	52	138	60	2.46

Selected by Los Angeles Dodgers' organization in 36th round of free-agent draft, June 7, 1977.
Signed as free agent by Los Angeles Dodgers' organization, August 14, 1980.

DIVISION SERIES RECORD

Year Club	League	G.	IP.	W.	L.	Pct.	H.	R.	ER.	SO.	BB.	ERA.
1981—Los Angeles	National	1	⅓	0	0	.000	1	0	0	1	1	0.00

CHAMPIONSHIP SERIES RECORD

Year Club	League	G.	IP.	W.	L.	Pct.	H.	R.	ER.	SO.	BB.	ERA.
1981—Los Angeles	National	1	⅓	0	0	.000	2	0	0	0	0	0.00
1983—Los Angeles	National	2	2	0	0	.000	0	0	0	3	1	0.00
Championship Series Totals		3	2⅓	0	0	.000	2	0	0	3	1	0.00

WORLD SERIES RECORD

Year Club	League	G.	IP.	W.	L.	Pct.	H.	R.	ER.	SO.	BB.	ERA.
1981—Los Angeles	National	2	5	0	0	.000	3	2	0	0	1	0.00

JOSEPH FRANKLIN NIEKRO

Name pronounced NEE-krow.

(Joe)

Born November 7, 1944, at Martins Ferry, O.
Height, 6.01. Weight, 190.
Throws and bats righthanded.
Attended West Liberty State College, West Liberty, W. Va.
Brother of Phil Niekro, pitcher with Milwaukee Braves and Atlanta Braves, 1964 through 1983.

Pitched seven-inning, 2-0 perfect game against Tidewater, July 16, 1972 (second game).
Led National League pitchers in games started with 38 in 1983.
Led National League in wild pitches with 19 in 1982, 14 in 1983 and tied for lead with 19 in 1979.
Tied for National League lead in shutouts with 5 in 1979.
Named National League Pitcher of the Year by THE SPORTING NEWS, 1979.
Named righthanded pitcher on THE SPORTING NEWS National League All-Star Team, 1979.

Year Club	League	G.	IP.	W.	L.	Pct.	H.	R.	ER.	SO.	BB.	ERA.
1966—Treasure Valley	Pioneer	1	4	0	0	.000	4	0	0	7	1	0.00
1966—Quincy	Midwest	4	25	1	2	.333	17	7	3	14	6	1.08
1966—Dallas-Fort Worth	Texas	12	79	5	4	.556	71	28	22	50	15	2.51
1967—Chicago	National	36	170	10	7	.588	171	68	63	77	32	3.34
1968—Chicago	National	34	177	14	10	.583	204	93	85	65	59	4.32
1969—Chicago†-San Diego‡	National	41	221	8	18	.308	237	100	91	62	51	3.71
1970—Detroit	American	38	213	12	13	.480	221	107	96	101	72	4.06
1971—Detroit	American	31	122	6	7	.462	136	62	61	43	49	4.28
1972—Toledo§	Int'national	2	14	2	0	1.000	6	1	1	11	3	0.64
1972—Detroit x	American	18	47	3	2	.600	62	20	20	24	8	3.83
1973—Toledo x	Int'national	26	143	7	10	.412	148	74	59	77	47	3.71
1973—Atlanta	National	20	24	2	4	.333	23	11	11	12	11	4.13
1974—Richmond	Int'national	30	52	8	1	.889	44	14	12	50	18	2.08
1974—Atlanta y	National	27	43	3	2	.600	36	19	17	31	18	3.56
1975—Iowa	Am. Assoc.	7	9	1	0	1.000	7	6	5	9	7	5.00
1975—Houston	National	40	88	6	4	.600	79	32	30	54	39	3.07
1976—Houston	National	36	118	4	8	.333	107	60	44	77	56	3.36
1977—Houston	National	44	181	13	8	.619	155	66	61	101	64	3.03
1978—Houston	National	35	203	14	14	.500	190	97	87	97	73	3.86
1979—Houston	National	38	264	●21	11	.656	221	102	88	119	107	3.00
1980—Houston	National	37	256	20	12	.625	268	119	101	127	79	3.55
1981—Houston	National	24	166	9	9	.500	150	60	52	77	47	2.82
1982—Houston	National	35	270	17	12	.586	224	79	74	130	64	2.47
1983—Houston	National	38	263⅔	15	14	.517	238	115	102	152	101	3.48
National League Totals		485	2444⅔	156	133	.540	2303	1021	906	1181	801	3.34
American League Totals		87	382	21	22	.488	419	189	177	168	129	4.17
Major League Totals		572	2826⅔	177	155	.533	2722	1210	1083	1349	930	3.45

Selected by Cleveland Indians' organization in 7th round of free-agent draft, January, 1966.
Selected by Chicago Cubs' organization in 3rd round of free-agent draft, June, 1966.
†Traded with Pitcher Gary Ross and Infielder Francisco Libran to San Diego Padres for Pitcher Dick Selma, April 24, 1969. Libran remained on Cubs' San Antonio farm team but became San Diego property.
‡Traded to Detroit Tigers for Pitcher Pat Dobson and Shortstop-Outfielder Dave Campbell, December 4, 1969.
§On disabled list, August 7 to September 1, 1972.
xSold on waivers to Atlanta Braves, August 7, 1973.
ySold to Houston Astros, April 5, 1975.

DIVISION SERIES RECORD

Year Club	League	G.	IP.	W.	L.	Pct.	H.	R.	ER.	SO.	BB.	ERA.
1981—Houston	National	1	8	0	0	.000	7	0	0	4	3	0.00

CHAMPIONSHIP SERIES RECORD

Established National League Championship Series record for most innings pitched, game (10), October 10, 1980.

Year Club	League	G.	IP.	W.	L.	Pct.	H.	R.	ER.	SO.	BB.	ERA.
1980—Houston	National	1	10	0	0	.000	6	0	0	2	1	0.00

ALL-STAR GAME RECORD

Member of National League All-Star Team for 1979 game; did not play.

PHILIP HENRY NIEKRO

Name pronounced NEE-krow.

(Phil)

Born April 1, 1939, at Blaine, O.
Height, 6.02. Weight, 195.
Throws and bats righthanded.
Brother of Joe Niekro, pitcher with Houston Astros.

Established major league records for fewest sacrifice flies allowed, season, most innings (0 and 284), 1969; most seasons and most consecutive seasons leading major leagues, runs allowed (3); most wild pitches, lifetime (200).

Tied major league records for most strikeouts, inning (4), July 29, 1977 (sixth inning); most seasons and most consecutive seasons leading league, runs allowed (3), 1977 through 1979; most wild pitches, inning (4), August 4, 1979, second game (fifth inning); most seasons and most consecutive seasons leading league, games lost (4), 1977 through 1980.

Tied modern major league record for most wild pitches, game (6), August 4, 1979, second game.

Established National League records for most putouts by pitcher, lifetime (340); most games started, no relief appearances, season (44), 1979.

Pitched 9-0 no-hit victory against San Diego Padres, August 5, 1973.

Led National League in home runs allowed with 40 in 1970, 29 in 1975, 41 in 1979 and 30 in 1980.

Led National League in hit batsmen with 11 in 1975, 13 in 1978 and 11 in 1979.

Led National League in complete games with 18 in 1974, 20 in 1977, 22 in 1978 and 23 in 1979.

Led National League in wild pitches with 19 in 1967, 14 in 1976 and 17 in 1977.

Led National League pitchers in games started with 43 in 1977, 42 in 1978, 44 in 1979, and tied for lead with 38 in 1980.

Led National League batters in sacrifice hits with 18 in 1968.

Tied for National League lead in balks with 3 in 1968 and 3 in 1972.

Named pitcher on THE SPORTING NEWS National League All-Star fielding team, 1978 through 1980, 1982 and 1983.

Year Club	League	G.	IP.	W.	L.	Pct.	H.	R.	ER.	SO.	BB.	ERA.
1959—Wellsville	NYP	10	35	2	1	.667	47	38	29	16	24	7.46
1959—McCook	Neb. State	*23	52	7	1	.875	35	20	18	48	29	3.12
1960—Jacksonville	Sally	38	84	6	4	.600	66	36	26	52	52	2.79
1960—Louisville	Am. Assoc.	6	10	1	0	1.000	11	5	4	2	9	3.60
1961—Austin	Texas	*51	110	4	4	.500	100	45	36	84	53	2.95
1962—Louisville	Am. Assoc.	49	98	9	6	.600	111	50	42	48	41	3.86
1963—Denver	P. Coast					(In Military Service)						
1964—Milwaukee	National	10	15	0	0	.000	15	10	8	8	7	4.80
1964—Denver	P. Coast	29	172	11	5	.688	172	79	66	119	45	3.45
1965—Milwaukee	National	41	75	2	3	.400	73	32	24	49	26	2.88
1966—Atlanta	National	28	50	4	3	.571	48	32	23	17	23	4.14
1966—Richmond	Int'national	17	54	3	4	.429	43	27	22	36	16	3.67
1967—Atlanta	National	46	207	11	9	.550	164	64	43	129	55	*1.87
1968—Atlanta	National	37	257	14	12	.538	228	83	74	140	45	2.59
1969—Atlanta	National	40	284	23	13	.639	235	93	81	193	57	2.57
1970—Atlanta	National	34	230	12	18	.400	222	124	109	168	68	4.27
1971—Atlanta	National	42	269	15	14	.517	248	112	89	173	70	2.98
1972—Atlanta	National	38	282	16	12	.571	254	112	96	164	53	3.06
1973—Atlanta	National	42	245	13	10	.565	214	103	90	131	89	3.31
1974—Atlanta	National	41	*302	●20	13	.606	249	91	80	195	88	2.38
1975—Atlanta	National	39	276	15	15	.500	285	115	98	144	72	3.20
1976—Atlanta	National	38	271	17	11	.607	249	116	99	173	101	3.29
1977—Atlanta	National	44	*330	16	●20	.444	*315	*166	*148	*262	*164	4.04
1978—Atlanta	National	44	*334	19	*18	.514	*295	*129	●107	248	102	2.88
1979—Atlanta	National	44	*342	●21	*20	.512	*311	*160	129	208	*113	3.39
1980—Atlanta	National	40	275	15	*18	.455	256	119	111	176	85	3.63
1981—Atlanta	National	22	139	7	7	.500	120	56	48	62	56	3.11
1982—Atlanta†	National	35	234⅓	17	4	*.810	225	106	94	144	73	3.61
1983—Atlanta‡	National	34	201⅔	11	10	.524	212	94	89	128	105	3.97
Major League Totals		739	4619	268	230	.538	4218	1917	1640	2912	1452	3.20

Signed as free agent by Atlanta Braves' organization, July 19, 1958.
†On disabled list, March 31 to April 21, 1982.
‡Released, October 7, 1983.

CHAMPIONSHIP SERIES RECORD

Established Championship Series record for most runs allowed, game (9), October 4, 1969.
Tied Championship Series record for most runs allowed, three-game Series (9), 1969.
Tied National League Championship Series record for most runs allowed, inning (5), October 4, 1969 (fifth inning).

Year Club	League	G.	IP.	W.	L.	Pct.	H.	R.	ER.	SO.	BB.	ERA.
1969—Atlanta	National	1	8	0	1	.000	9	9	4	4	4	4.50
1982—Atlanta	National	1	6	0	0	.000	6	2	2	5	4	3.00
Championship Series Totals		2	14	0	1	.000	15	11	6	9	8	3.86

ALL-STAR GAME RECORD

Year League	IP.	W.	L.	Pct.	H.	R.	ER.	SO.	BB.	ERA.
1969—National	1	0	0	.000	0	0	0	2	0	0.00
1978—National	⅓	0	0	.000	0	0	0	0	0	0.00
All-Star Game Totals	1⅓	0	0	.000	0	0	0	2	0	0.00

Member of National League All-Star Team in 1975 and 1982; did not play.

RANDY HAROLD NIEMANN

Born November 15, 1955, at Fortuna, Calif.
Height, 6.04. Weight, 200.
Throws and bats lefthanded.
Attended College of the Redwoods, Eureka, Calif.

Tied for Florida State League lead in hit batsmen with 14 in 1976.

Year—Club	League	G.	IP.	W.	L.	Pct.	H.	R.	ER.	SO.	BB.	ERA.
1975—Oneonta	NYP	8	55	3	3	.500	53	26	15	23	20	2.45
1976—Fort Lauderdale	Florida St.	25	190	9	10	.474	173	74	60	79	73	2.84
1977—West Haven†	Eastern	13	62	4	4	.500	73	44	38	18	26	5.52
1977—Columbus	Southern	15	34	0	3	.000	36	22	18	15	19	4.76
1978—Columbus	Southern	29	123	9	5	.643	125	44	28	53	39	2.05
1979—Charleston	Int'national	8	47	3	2	.600	49	25	21	17	10	4.02
1979—Houston	National	26	67	3	2	.600	68	32	28	24	22	3.76
1980—Tucson	P. Coast	9	52	4	1	.800	64	36	28	26	26	4.85
1980—Houston	National	22	33	0	1	.000	40	21	20	18	12	5.45
1981—Tucson‡§x-Portland	P. Coast	10	57	4	2	.667	68	40	31	39	38	4.89
1982—Portland	P. Coast	8	44⅔	3	2	.600	41	22	19	28	26	3.83
1982—Pittsburgh	National	20	35⅓	1	1	.500	34	22	20	26	17	5.09
1983—Pittsburgh	National	8	13⅔	0	1	.000	20	14	14	8	7	9.22
1983—Hawaii y	P. Coast	16	82	2	3	.400	95	49	41	52	45	4.50
Major League Totals		76	149	4	5	.444	162	89	82	76	58	4.95

Selected by Montreal Expos' organization in 5th round of free-agent draft, January 9, 1974.
Selected by Minnesota Twins' organization in 3rd round of free-agent draft, January 9, 1975.
Selected by New York Yankees' organization in secondary phase of free-agent draft, June 4, 1975.
†Traded with Infielder Mike Fischlin and a player to be named later to Houston Astros for Catcher Cliff Johnson, June 15, 1977; Houston Astros acquired First Baseman-Outfielder Dave Bergman to complete deal, November 23, 1977.
‡On Houston disabled list, March 28 to May 11, 1981.
§On disabled list, July 1 to September 1, 1981.
xTraded with Outfielder Kevin Houston to Pittsburgh Pirates' organization, September 9, 1981, completing deal in which Houston Astros traded Second Baseman Johnny Ray and two players to be named later to Pittsburgh for Second Baseman Phil Garner, August 31, 1981.
yTraded to Chicago White Sox for Outfielder Miguel Dilone and Pitcher Mike Maitland, September 7, 1983.

THOMAS ANDREW NIETO
(Tom)

Born October 27, 1960, at Downey, Calif.
Height, 6.01. Weight, 205.
Throws and bats righthanded.
Attended Cerritos College, Norwalk, Calif., and Oral
Roberts University, Tulsa, Okla.

Tied for American Association lead in being hit by pitch with 8 in 1983.

Year—Club	League	Pos.	G.	AB.	R.	H.	2B.	3B.	HR.	RBI.	B.A.	PO.	A.	E.	F.A.
1981—Arkansas	Texas	C	62	184	12	33	2	0	2	19	.179	270	37	8	.975
1982—Arkansas†	Texas	C	96	298	33	72	11	3	5	31	.242	466	58	3	*.994
1983—Louisville	A. A.	C	115	383	44	104	17	1	5	52	.272	605	71	15	.978

Selected by Minnesota Twins' organization in 31st round of free-agent draft, June 5, 1979.
Selected by Pittsburgh Pirates' organization in secondary phase of free-agent draft, January 8, 1980.
Selected by St. Louis Cardinals' organization in 3rd round of free-agent draft, June 8, 1981.
†On disabled list, June 19 to June 30, 1982.

JUAN MANUEL NIEVES

Born January 5, 1965, at Santurce, Puerto Rico.
Height, 6.03. Weight, 175.
Throws and bats lefthanded.

Year—Club	League	G.	IP.	W.	L.	Pct.	H.	R.	ER.	SO.	BB.	ERA.
1983—Beloit	Midwest	12	69⅓	7	1	.875	43	11	10	89	15	1.30

Signed as free agent by Milwaukee Brewers' organization, July 1, 1983.

ALBERT SAMUEL NIPPER
(Al)

Born April 2, 1959, at San Diego, Calif.
Height, 6.01. Weight, 190.
Throws and bats righthanded.
Attended Northeast Missouri State University, Kirksville, Mo.

Led Florida State League in complete games with 15 in 1981.

Year—Club	League	G.	IP.	W.	L.	Pct.	H.	R.	ER.	SO.	BB.	ERA.
1980—Winter Haven	Florida St.	16	85	6	4	.600	82	29	24	48	49	2.54
1981—Winter Haven	Florida St.	29	*212	14	8	.636	191	59	40	139	60	*1.70
1982—Bristol†	Eastern	19	115	6	7	.462	108	50	47	66	45	3.68
1983—New Britain	Eastern	10	67	4	3	.571	46	26	21	42	25	2.82
1983—Pawtucket	Int'national	18	109⅓	9	4	.692	108	62	54	58	54	4.45
1983—Boston	American	3	16	1	1	.500	17	4	4	5	7	2.25
Major League Totals		3	16	1	1	.500	17	4	4	5	7	2.25

Selected by Boston Red Sox' organization in 8th round of free-agent draft, June 3, 1980.
†On disabled list, June 26 to July 25, 1982.

OTIS JUNIOR NIXON

Born January 9, 1959, at Columbus County, N.C.
Height, 6.02. Weight, 175.
Throws right and bats right and lefthanded.
Attended Louisburg College, Louisburg, N.C.
Brother of Donell Nixon, infielder in Seattle Mariners' organization.

Led International League in stolen bases with 94 and caught stealing with 29 in 1983.
Led Southern League in bases on balls received with 110 in 1981.
Led South Atlantic League in bases on balls received with 113 and stolen bases with 67 in 1980.
Led Appalachian League in bases on balls received with 57 in 1979.
Led International League outfielders in fielding percentage with .992, putouts with 363 and total chances with 371 in 1983.
Led Appalachian League third basemen in fielding percentage with .945, putouts with 52, assists with 120, and double plays with 12 in 1979.

Year Club	League	Pos.	G.	AB.	R.	H.	2B.	3B.	HR.	RBI.	B.A.	PO.	A.	E.	F.A.
1979—Paintsville	Appal.	3B-SS	63	203	58	58	10	3	1	25	.286	54	122	11	.941
1980—Greensboro	S. Atl.	3B-SS	136	493	*124	137	12	5	3	48	.278	164	308	36	.929
1981—Nashville	South.	SS	127	407	89	102	9	2	0	20	.251	198	348	*56	.907
1982—Nashville	South.	SS-2B	72	283	47	80	3	2	0	20	.283	126	211	23	.936
1982—Columbus	Int.	2B-SS	59	207	43	58	4	0	0	14	.280	104	169	14	.951
1983—Columbus	Int.	OF-2B	138	*557	*129	*162	11	6	0	41	.291	385	24	4	.990
1983—New York	Amer.	OF	13	14	2	2	0	0	0	0	.143	14	1	1	.938
Major League Totals			13	14	2	2	0	0	0	0	.143	14	1	1	.938

Selected by Cincinnati Reds' organization in 21st round of free-agent draft, June 6, 1978.
Selected by California Angels' organization in secondary phase of free-agent draft, January 9, 1979.
Selected by New York Yankees' organization in secondary phase of free-agent draft, June 5, 1979.

ROBERT DONELL NIXON

(Known by middle name.)

Born December 31, 1961, at Evergreen, N. C.
Height, 6.01. Weight, 185.
Throws and bats righthanded.
Attended Louisburg College, Louisburg, N. C.
Brother of Otis Nixon, infielder in New York Yankees' organization.

Led California League in stolen bases with 144 and caught stealing with 24 in 1983.
Led Midwest League in stolen bases with 85 in 1982.

Year Club	League	Pos.	G.	AB.	R.	H.	2B.	3B.	HR.	RBI.	B.A.	PO.	A.	E.	F.A.
1981—Wausau†	Midw.	1B-2B-OF	59	204	35	58	7	2	5	26	.284	252	9	3	.989
1982—Wausau	Midw.	*3B-1B	116	461	102	156	18	7	11	56	.338	*87	187	*49	.848
1982—Lynn	Midw.	3B	6	24	5	7	2	1	0	1	.292	0	2	0	1.000
1983—Bakersfield	Calif.	*3B-OF	135	542	*116	174	27	4	4	51	.321	98	249	*51	.872

Selected by Seattle Mariners' organization in 10th round of free-agent draft, June 3, 1980.
†On disabled list, July 7, 1981 through remainder of season.

MILICIADES A. NOBOA JR.
(Junior)

Born November 10, 1964, at Santo Domingo, Dominican Republic.
Height, 5.09. Weight, 150.
Throws and bats righthanded.

Led Midwest League in sacrifice hits with 18 in 1983.
Led Midwest League second basemen in putouts with 257 and double plays with 81 in 1983.

Year Club	League	Pos.	G.	AB.	R.	H.	2B.	3B.	HR.	RBI.	B.A.	PO.	A.	E.	F.A.
1981—Batavia	NYP	2B	50	162	15	49	8	0	0	14	.302	82	100	*18	.910
1982—Waterloo	Midw.	SS	121	385	69	96	12	5	0	23	.249	*207	306	46	.918
1983—Waterloo	Midw.	2B-SS	132	449	64	115	22	3	1	29	.256	260	355	24	.962

Signed as free agent by Cleveland Indians' organization, May 26, 1981.

MATTHEW DODGE NOKES
(Matt)

Born October 31, 1963, at San Diego, Calif.
Height, 6.01. Weight, 180.
Throws right and bats lefthanded.

Led California League catchers in double plays with 9 in 1983.
Led Pioneer League in passed balls with 19 in 1981.

Year Club	League	Pos.	G.	AB.	R.	H.	2B.	3B.	HR.	RBI.	B.A.	PO.	A.	E.	F.A.
1981—Great Falls	Pion.	C	44	146	14	33	6	2	0	13	.226	288	35	*13	.961
1982—Clinton	Midw.	C	82	247	19	53	12	0	3	23	.215	363	41	13	.969
1983—Fresno	Calif.	C	125	429	62	138	26	6	14	82	.322	595	62	16	.976

Selected by San Francisco Giants' organization in 20th round of free-agent draft, June 8, 1981.

JOSEPH WILLIAM NOLAN JR.
(Joe)

Born May 12, 1951, at St. Louis, Mo.
Height, 6.00. Weight, 190.
Throws right and bats lefthanded.

Led National League in passed balls with 14 in 1978.
Led Texas League catchers in double plays with 10 in 1972.
Led California League catchers in putouts with 728 in 1971.
Tied for Appalachian League lead in double plays by catchers with 3 in 1969.

Year—Club	League	Pos.	G.	AB.	R.	H.	2B.	3B.	HR.	RBI.	B.A.	PO.	A.	E.	F.A.
1969—Marion	Appal.	C	52	160	33	40	5	0	2	19	.250	312	30	6	.983
1970—Pompano Beach	Fla. St.	*C-OF-3B	95	281	38	65	6	4	0	30	.231	438	59	*18	.965
1971—Visalia	Calif.	C-3B-OF	120	393	76	109	17	3	13	75	.277	746	95	17	.980
1972—Memphis	Texas	C	130	418	51	90	13	3	4	41	.215	*868	67	12	.987
1972—New York	Nat.	C	4	10	0	0	0	0	0	0	.000	12	3	1	.938
1973—Tidewater	Int.	C	97	287	34	69	9	1	4	29	.240	526	43	10	.983
1974—Tidewater†	Int.	C	57	145	18	39	8	0	5	20	.269	274	24	8	.974
1975—Richmond	Int.	C-3-O-2	111	342	41	92	13	0	6	53	.269	572	51	7	.989
1975—Atlanta	Nat.	C	4	4	0	1	0	0	0	0	.250	2	0	0	1.000
1976—Richmond‡	Int.	C	32	87	9	25	6	1	0	9	.287	134	14	0	1.000
1977—Atlanta§	Nat.	C	62	82	13	23	3	0	3	9	.280	80	7	0	1.000
1978—Atlanta	Nat.	C	95	213	22	49	7	3	4	22	.230	295	24	7	.979
1979—Atlanta	Nat.	C	89	230	28	57	9	3	4	21	.248	328	27	6	.983
1980—Atl.x-Cin.	Nat.	C	70	176	16	54	8	0	3	26	.307	271	26	5	.983
1981—Cincinnati y	Nat.	C	81	236	25	73	18	1	1	26	.309	393	18	2	*.995
1982—Baltimore z	Amer.	C	77	219	24	51	7	1	6	35	.233	292	22	7	.978
1983—Baltimore a	Amer.	C	73	184	25	51	11	1	5	24	.277	223	16	5	.980
National League Totals			405	951	104	257	45	7	15	104	.270	1381	105	21	.986
American League Totals			150	403	49	102	18	2	11	59	.253	515	38	12	.979
Major League Totals			555	1354	153	359	63	9	26	163	.265	1896	143	33	.984

Selected by New York Mets' organization in 2nd round of free-agent draft, June 5, 1969.
†Traded to Atlanta Braves for Infielder Leo Foster, April 4, 1975.
‡On disabled list, April 21 to July 14, 1976.
§On disabled list, May 4 to May 19, 1977.
xGranted free agency when refused option to minors, June 12, 1980; signed by Cincinnati Reds, June 13, 1980.
yTraded to Baltimore Orioles for Pitcher Brooks Carey and Outfielder Dallas Williams, March 26, 1982.
zGranted free agency, November 10, 1982; re-signed by Orioles, January 15, 1983.
aOn supplemental disabled list, June 22 to July 14, 1983.

CHAMPIONSHIP SERIES RECORD

Year—Club	League	Pos.	G.	AB.	R.	H.	2B.	3B.	HR.	RBI.	B.A.	PO.	A.	E.	F.A.
1983—Baltimore	Amer.	PH	1	0	0	0	0	0	0	1	.000	0	0	0	.000

WORLD SERIES RECORD

Year—Club	League	Pos.	G.	AB.	R.	H.	2B.	3B.	HR.	RBI.	B.A.	PO.	A.	E.	F.A.
1983—Baltimore	Amer.	PH-C	2	2	0	0	0	0	0	0	.000	3	0	0	1.000

DICKIE RAY NOLES

Born November 19, 1956, at Charlotte, N. C.
Height, 6.02. Weight, 178.
Throws and bats righthanded.

Led Eastern League in hit batsmen with 15 in 1978.
Led Carolina League in games started by pitchers with 27 in 1977.
Led Western Carolinas League in hit batsmen with 13 in 1976.
Tied for Carolina League lead in hit batsmen with 11 in 1977.
Tied for Western Carolinas League lead in home runs allowed with 13 in 1976.

Year—Club	League	G.	IP.	W.	L.	Pct.	H.	R.	ER.	SO.	BB.	ERA.
1975—Auburn	NYP	9	50	2	2	.500	49	30	20	31	27	3.60
1976—Spartanburg	W. Carol.	24	137	4	*16	.200	166	*110	*90	95	65	5.91
1977—Peninsula	Carolina	27	*199	10	11	.476	188	103	81	114	78	3.66
1978—Reading	Eastern	27	159	12	8	.600	177	100	75	78	72	4.25
1979—Oklahoma City†	Am. Assoc.	12	76	6	4	.600	69	38	33	48	28	3.91
1979—Philadelphia	National	14	90	3	4	.429	80	40	38	42	38	3.80
1979—Reading	Eastern	1	9	0	1	.000	7	5	4	2	4	4.00
1980—Philadelphia	National	48	81	1	4	.200	80	42	35	57	42	3.89
1981—Oklahoma City‡	Am. Assoc.	22	104	6	6	.500	85	45	38	82	46	3.29
1981—Philadelphia§	National	13	58	2	2	.500	30	27	34	23	4	4.19
1982—Chicago x	National	31	171	10	13	.435	180	99	84	85	61	4.42
1983—Chicago y	National	24	116⅓	5	10	.333	133	69	61	59	37	4.72
1983—Quad Cities	Midwest	3	12	0	1	.000	19	11	7	12	5	5.25
Major League Totals		130	516⅓	21	33	.389	530	280	245	277	201	4.27

Selected by Philadelphia Phillies' organization in 4th round of free-agent draft, June 4, 1975.
†On disabled list, April 13 to April 24, 1979.
‡Appeared as outfielder with no chances.
§Traded with Catcher Keith Moreland and Pitcher Dan Larson to Chicago Cubs for Pitcher Mike Krukow and cash, December 8, 1981.

xOn disabled list, June 13 to July 4, 1982.

yOn disabled list, April 12 to June 4, 1983; included rehabilitation disability assignment to Quad Cities, May 21 to June 4, 1983.

DIVISION SERIES RECORD

Year Club	League	G.	IP.	W.	L.	Pct.	H.	R.	ER.	SO.	BB.	ERA.
1981—Philadelphia	National	1	4	0	0	.000	4	2	2	5	2	4.50

CHAMPIONSHIP SERIES RECORD

Year Club	League	G.	IP.	W.	L.	Pct.	H.	R.	ER.	SO.	BB.	ERA.
1980—Philadelphia	National	2	2⅔	0	0	.000	1	0	0	0	3	0.00

WORLD SERIES RECORD

Year Club	League	G.	IP.	W.	L.	Pct.	H.	R.	ER.	SO.	BB.	ERA.
1980—Philadelphia	National	1	4⅔	0	0	.000	5	1	1	6	2	1.93

WAYNE OREN NORDHAGEN

Born July 4, 1948, at Thief River Falls, Minn.
Height, 6.02. Weight, 195.
Throws and bats righthanded.
Attended Treasure Valley Community College, Ontario, Ore., and
Portland State University, Portland, Ore.

Led American Association in sacrifice flies with 10 in 1976.

Year Club	League	Pos.	G.	AB.	R.	H.	2B.	3B.	HR.	RBI.	B.A.	PO.	A.	E.	F.A.
1968—Johnson City	Appal.	OF	63	213	35	62	9	1	7	34	.291	★107	●8	4	.966
1969—Kinston†................	Carol.	OF	25	90	17	21	1	0	4	9	.233	62	3	5	.929
1970—Kinston.................	Carol.	OF-1B	88	283	31	65	10	3	2	30	.230	175	9	10	.948
1971—Kinston.................	Carol.	OF	114	412	65	121	25	3	14	76	.294	224	10	7	.971
1972—West Haven	East.	OF	117	414	50	109	21	4	14	73	.263	204	14	●15	.936
1973—Syra.‡-Rich.........	Int.	OF	130	438	46	115	15	0	13	70	.263	222	9	8	.967
1974—Richmond.............	Int.	OF	112	374	53	108	18	6	16	77	.289	192	6	7	.966
1975—Richmond§...........	Int.	OF-1B-3B	34	90	8	23	3	0	2	8	.256	50	2	0	1.000
1975—Tulsa xy..........	A. A.	OF	74	268	40	94	19	2	13	60	.351	102	7	5	.956
1976—Ok. City z-Iowa.....	A. A.	OF-C	99	350	56	106	30	6	11	78	.303	182	12	7	.965
1976—Chicago	Amer.	OF-C	22	53	6	10	2	0	0	5	.189	35	3	1	.974
1977—Chicago	Amer.	OF-C	52	124	16	39	7	3	4	22	.315	52	1	5	.914
1978—Chicago a..............	Amer.	OF-C	68	206	28	62	16	0	5	35	.301	87	12	6	.943
1979—Chicago	Amer.	OF-C	78	193	20	54	15	0	7	25	.280	28	4	3	.914
1980—Chicago	Amer.	OF	123	415	45	115	22	4	15	59	.277	120	6	4	.969
1981—Chicago b..............	Amer.	OF	65	208	19	64	8	1	6	33	.308	85	4	5	.947
1982—Toronto cef..........	Amer.	OF	72	185	12	50	6	0	1	20	.270	15	1	0	1.000
1982—Pittsburgh d.........	Nat.	OF	1	4	0	2	0	0	0	2	.500	2	0	0	1.000
1983—Chicago g..............	Nat.	OF	21	35	1	5	1	0	1	4	.143	7	0	0	1.000
American League Totals...........................			480	1384	146	394	76	8	38	199	.285	422	31	24	.950
National League Totals...................			22	39	1	7	1	0	1	6	.179	9	0	0	1.000
Major League Totals..................................			502	1423	147	401	77	8	39	205	.282	431	31	24	.951

Selected by New York Yankees' organization in 7th round of free-agent draft, June 7, 1968.

†On temporary inactive list, May 10, 1969; transferred to military list, May 23, 1969 through remainder of season.

‡Traded with First Baseman Frank Tepedino and two players to be named later to Atlanta Braves for Pitcher Pat Dobson, June 7, 1973; Atlanta acquired Pitcher Alan Closter, September 5, 1973, and Pitcher Dave Cheadle, September 10, 1973, to complete deal.

§Traded to St. Louis Cardinals, June 2, 1975, completing deal in which St. Louis traded Pitchers Elias Sosa and Ray Sadecki to Atlanta Braves for Pitcher Ron Reed and a player to be named later, May 28, 1975.

xOn disabled list, June 22 to July 2, 1975.

ySold to Philadelphia Phillies, April 9, 1976.

zTraded to Chicago White Sox for Outfielder Rich Coggins, July 14, 1976.

aOn supplemental disabled list, July 19, 1978; transferred to disabled list, August 12 to December 1, 1978.

bTraded to Toronto Blue Jays for Third Baseman Aurelio Rodriguez, April 2, 1982.

cTraded to Philadelphia Phillies for Outfielder Dick Davis, June 15, 1982; Traded by Philadelphia to Pittsburgh Pirates for Outfielder-First Baseman Bill Robinson, June 15, 1982.

dSold on waivers to Toronto Blue Jays, June 25, 1982, completing deal in which Toronto sold Outfielder Dick Davis on waivers to Pittsburgh Pirates for a player to be named later, June 22, 1982.

eOn disabled list, June 30 to August 20, 1982.

fGranted free agency, November 10, 1982; signed by Chicago Cubs, December 10, 1982.

gReleased, June 9, 1983.

PITCHING RECORD

Year Club	League	G.	IP.	W.	L.	Pct.	H.	R.	ER.	SO.	BB.	ERA.
1979—Chicago.............................	American	2	2	0	0	.000	2	2	2	2	1	9.00

—DID YOU KNOW—

That when the Texas Rangers scored 12 runs in the 15th inning of their July 3, 1983, game against Oakland the outburst broke two major league records? One was for the most runs scored in the 15th inning, topping the mark of seven set by the 1928 St. Louis Cardinals. The other was for the most runs scored in any extra inning; the 1928 Yankees and 1969 Twins shared that mark with 11. The Rangers crushed the A's, 16-4.

MICHAEL KELVIN NORRIS
(Mike)

Born March 19, 1955, at San Francisco, Calif.
Height, 6.02. Weight, 172.
Throws and bats righthanded.
Attended City College of San Francisco, San Francisco, Calif.

Pitched shutout in first major league game, April 10, 1975.
Led American League in wild pitches with 14 in 1981.
Tied for American League lead in balks with 4 in 1980 and 5 in 1981.
Named pitcher on The Sporting News American League All-Star fielding team, 1980 and 1981.
Received reported $25,000 bonus to sign with Oakland Athletics, 1973.

Year—Club	League	G.	IP.	W.	L.	Pct.	H.	R.	ER.	SO.	BB.	ERA.
1973—Burlington	Midwest	20	110	8	4	.667	81	38	27	130	40	2.21
1974—Birmingham†	Southern	21	109	7	8	.467	107	64	49	103	65	4.05
1975—Oakland‡	American	4	17	1	0	1.000	6	2	0	5	8	0.00
1976—Tucson	P. Coast	5	33	2	1	.667	28	15	14	19	23	3.82
1976—Oakland	American	24	96	4	5	.444	91	53	51	44	56	4.78
1977—San Jose§	P. Coast	6	46	3	2	.600	42	18	18	35	18	3.52
1977—Oakland	American	16	77	2	7	.222	77	45	41	35	31	4.79
1978—Vancouver	P. Coast	7	42	3	3	.500	42	28	27	32	27	5.79
1978—Jersey City x	Eastern	9	66	2	6	.250	58	35	25	51	36	3.41
1978—Oakland	American	14	49	0	5	.000	46	34	30	36	35	5.51
1979—Oakland y	American	29	146	5	8	.385	146	87	78	96	94	4.81
1980—Oakland	American	33	284	22	9	.710	215	88	80	180	83	2.54
1981—Oakland z	American	23	173	12	9	.571	145	77	72	78	63	3.75
1982—Oakland z	American	28	166⅓	7	11	.389	154	103	88	83	84	4.76
1983—Oakland a	American	16	88⅔	4	5	.444	68	42	37	63	36	3.76
1983—Tacoma	P. Coast	1	4	0	0	.000	6	6	4	3	1	9.00
Major League Totals		187	1097	57	59	.491	948	531	477	620	490	3.91

Selected by Oakland A's organization in 1st round (24th player selected) of free-agent draft, January 10, 1973.
†On disabled list, June 14 to June 24, 1974.
‡On emergency disabled list, April 28 to September 19, 1975.
§On disabled list, August 27 to September 6, 1977.
xOn suspended list, May 19 to May 28, 1978.
yOn disabled list, July 12 to August 7, 1969.
zOn disabled list, June 17 to July 8, 1982.
aOn disabled list, June 18 to July 26 and August 11, 1983 through remainder of season; included rehabilitation disability assignment to Tacoma, July 6 to July 26, 1983.

DIVISION SERIES RECORD

Year—Club	League	G.	IP.	W.	L.	Pct.	H.	R.	ER.	SO.	BB.	ERA.
1981—Oakland	American	1	9	1	0	1.000	4	0	0	2	3	0.00

CHAMPIONSHIP SERIES RECORD

Year—Club	League	G.	IP.	W.	L.	Pct.	H.	R.	ER.	SO.	BB.	ERA.
1981—Oakland	American	1	7⅓	0	1	.000	6	3	3	4	2	3.68

ALL-STAR GAME RECORD

Year—League		IP.	W.	L.	Pct.	H.	R.	ER.	SO.	BB.	ERA.
1981—American		1	0	0	.000	2	1	1	1	0	9.00

EDWIN NUNEZ (MARTINEZ)

Name pronounced NOON-yez.

Born May 27, 1963, at Humacao, Puerto Rico.
Height, 6.05. Weight, 235.
Throws and bats righthanded.

Led Midwest League in complete games with 13 in 1981.

Year—Club	League	G.	IP.	W.	L.	Pct.	H.	R.	ER.	SO.	BB.	ERA.
1979—Bellingham	Northwest	6	39	4	1	.800	39	14	9	30	5	2.08
1980—Wausau	Midwest	22	138	9	7	.563	145	71	57	91	58	3.72
1981—Wausau	Midwest	25	*186	*16	3	.842	143	61	51	*205	58	2.47
1982—Seattle†	American	8	35⅓	1	2	.333	36	18	18	27	16	4.58
1982—Salt Lake City‡	P. Coast	11	55⅓	4	3	.571	40	26	21	42	23	3.42
1983—Seattle	American	14	37	0	4	.000	40	21	18	35	22	4.38
1983—Salt Lake City	P. Coast	14	77⅓	4	4	.500	99	70	61	52	36	7.10
Major League Totals		22	72⅓	1	6	.143	76	39	36	62	38	4.48

Signed as free agent by Seattle Mariners' organization, March 17, 1979.
†On disabled list, April 23 to May 15, 1982.
‡On disabled list, June 4 to June 29, 1982.

CHRISTOPHER CURTIS NYMAN
(Chris)

Born June 6, 1955, at Pomona, Calif.
Height, 6.04. Weight, 200.
Throws and bats righthanded.
Attended Arizona State University, Tempe, Ariz.
Brother of Nyls Nyman, outfielder with Chicago White Sox, 1974 through 1977.

Tied for American Association lead in double plays by first basemen with 99 in 1983.
Led Pacific Coast League first basemen in fielding percentage with .994 in 1982.

Year Club	League	Pos.	G.	AB.	R.	H.	2B.	3B.	HR.	RBI.	B.A.	PO.	A.	E.	F.A.
1977—Appleton	Midw.	1B	59	213	30	64	11	1	5	17	.300	474	30	4	.992
1978—Knoxville	South.	1B	59	192	15	35	6	0	3	19	.182	418	28	10	.978
1978—Appleton	Midw.	1B	22	72	14	21	2	0	5	20	.292	102	8	5	.957
1979—Iowa	A. A.	1B	39	98	15	18	5	0	3	13	.184	255	18	3	.989
1979—Knoxville	South.	1B	86	302	59	93	20	2	18	67	.308	695	52	5	.993
1980—Iowa	A. A.	1B-3B	126	421	75	108	21	1	11	45	.257	960	82	14	.987
1981—Edmonton	P. C.	1-O-3-C	128	461	79	137	24	4	16	90	.297	1112	71	12	.990
1982—Edmonton	P. C.	1B-3B	118	465	96	156	28	5	14	92	.335	1037	110	12	.990
1982—Chicago	Amer.	1B-OF	28	65	6	16	1	0	0	2	.246	161	12	1	.994
1983—Denver	A. A.	1B	107	398	69	127	18	7	23	90	.319	1041	81	7	.994
1983—Chicago†	Amer.	1B	21	28	12	8	0	0	2	4	.286	87	5	0	1.000
Major League Totals			49	93	18	24	1	0	2	6	.258	248	17	1	.996

Selected by Chicago White Sox' organization in 21st round of free agent draft, June 5, 1973.
Signed as free agent by Chicago White Sox' organization, June 25, 1977.
†Sold to Nankia Hawks of Japanese baseball, October 31, 1983.

KENNETH RAY OBERKFELL

Name pronounced OH-burk-fell.

(Ken)

Born May 4, 1956, at Maryville, Illinois.
Height, 6.01. Weight, 185.
Throws right and bats lefthanded.
Attended Belleville Area Junior College, Belleville, Ill.

Led National League third basemen in double plays with 23 and tied for lead in total chances with 338 in 1981.
Led National League second basemen in fielding percentage with .985 in 1979.

Year Club	League	Pos.	G.	AB.	R.	H.	2B.	3B.	HR.	RBI.	B.A.	PO.	A.	E.	F.A.
1975—Johnson City	Appal.	SS	17	54	15	19	3	0	1	8	.352	21	58	4	.952
1975—St. Petersburg	Fla. St.	SS	41	134	14	47	6	1	0	22	.351	71	107	6	.967
1976—Arkansas	Texas	2B-SS	128	456	64	131	19	2	3	47	.287	259	321	18	.970
1977—New Orleans	A. A.	2B-SS	120	418	67	105	18	5	4	32	.251	205	325	17	.969
1977—St. Louis	Nat.	2B	9	9	0	1	0	0	0	1	.111	3	4	0	1.000
1978—Springfield	A. A.	3B-2B-SS	64	242	41	69	13	4	6	38	.285	77	113	6	.969
1978—St. Louis	Nat.	2B-3B	24	50	7	6	1	0	0	0	.120	30	48	1	.987
1979—St. Louis	Nat.	2B-3B-SS	135	369	53	111	19	5	1	35	.301	223	343	9	.984
1980—St. Louis†	Nat.	2B-3B	116	422	58	128	27	6	3	46	.303	227	340	7	.988
1981—St. Louis	Nat.	3B-SS	102	376	43	110	12	6	2	45	.293	77	247	15	.956
1982—St. Louis‡	Nat.	★3B-2B	137	470	55	136	22	5	2	34	.289	80	305	11	★.972
1983—St. Louis	Nat.	★3B-2B-SS	151	488	62	143	26	5	3	38	.293	132	303	18	★.960
Major League Totals			674	2184	278	635	107	27	11	199	.291	772	1590	61	.975

Signed as free agent by St. Louis Cardinals' organization, May 4, 1975.
†On supplemental disabled list, May 11 to June 20, 1980.
‡On supplemental disabled list, March 31 to April 23, 1982.

CHAMPIONSHIP SERIES RECORD

Tied Championship Series record for most at-bats, three-game Series (15).

Year Club	League	Pos.	G.	AB.	R.	H.	2B.	3B.	HR.	RBI.	B.A.	PO.	A.	E.	F.A.
1982—St. Louis	Nat.	3B	3	15	1	3	0	0	0	2	.200	2	4	1	.857

WORLD SERIES RECORD

Year Club	League	Pos.	G.	AB.	R.	H.	2B.	3B.	HR.	RBI.	B.A.	PO.	A.	E.	F.A.
1982—St. Louis	Nat.	3B	7	24	4	7	1	0	0	1	.292	3	21	1	.960

PRESTON MICHAEL O'BERRY

(Mike)

Born April 20, 1954, at Birmingham, Ala.
Height, 6.02. Weight, 190.
Throws and bats righthanded.
Received bachelor of science degree in education from
University of South Alabama, Mobile, Ala., and attends University of Alabama
at Birmingham, Birmingham, Ala.

Led Eastern League catchers in double plays with 10 in 1977.
Led Carolina League catchers in double plays with 10 in 1976.
Tied for Pacific Coast League lead in passed balls with 13 in 1983.

Year Club	League	Pos.	G.	AB.	R.	H.	2B.	3B.	HR.	RBI.	B.A.	PO.	A.	E.	F.A.
1975—Winter Haven	Fla. St.	C	39	96	5	8	2	1	0	5	.083	120	24	11	.929
1976—Winston-Salem	Carol.	C	111	330	51	66	12	4	4	32	.200	★608	★69	★13	.981
1977—Bristol	East.	C	125	352	46	72	10	2	2	25	.205	682	★89	★16	.980
1978—Bristol	East.	C	114	339	41	80	12	1	6	41	.236	★648	★76	13	.982
1979—Pawtucket	Int.	C-1B	34	78	6	13	1	0	1	5	.167	168	16	8	.958
1979—Boston†	Amer.	C	43	59	8	10	1	0	1	4	.169	103	7	5	.957
1980—Midland	Texas	C	57	173	31	42	9	3	1	23	.243	337	39	11	.972
1980—Wichita	A. A.	C-OF	9	23	4	6	2	0	0	6	.261	26	5	2	.939

Year Club League	Pos.	G.	AB.	R.	H.	2B.	3B.	HR.	RBI.	B.A.	PO.	A.	E.	F.A.
1980—Chicago‡ .... Nat.	C	19	48	7	10	1	0	0	5	.208	94	16	2	.982
1981—Cincinnati .... Nat.	C	55	111	6	20	3	1	1	5	.180	208	22	4	.983
1982—Cincinnati .... Nat.	C	21	45	5	10	2	0	0	3	.222	84	12	1	.990
1982—Indianapolis§x...... A. A.	C-1B-OF	45	105	11	20	3	1	0	5	.190	172	18	4	.979
1983—Edmonton.......... P. C.	C-3B	57	179	43	55	8	1	4	24	.307	289	19	8	.975
1983—California y .... Amer.	C	26	60	7	10	1	0	1	5	.167	77	8	0	1.000
American League Totals...........................		69	119	15	20	2	0	2	9	.168	180	15	5	.975
National League Totals...........................		95	204	18	40	6	1	1	13	.196	386	50	7	.984
Major League Totals...............................		164	323	33	60	8	1	3	22	.186	566	65	12	.981

Selected by Boston Red Sox' organization in 22nd round of free-agent draft, June 4, 1975.

†Traded to Chicago Cubs, October 23, 1979, completing deal in which Chicago traded Second Baseman Ted Sizemore to Boston Red Sox for a player to be named later, August 17, 1979.

‡Traded to Cincinnati Reds for Pitcher Jay Howell, October 17, 1980.

§On suspended list, June 14 to June 19, 1982.

xTraded to California Angels' organization for First Baseman John Harris, January 7, 1983.

yGranted free agency when refused option to minors, November 15, 1983; signed by New York Yankees, December 7, 1983.

PETER MICHAEL O'BRIEN
(Pete)

Born February 9, 1958, at Santa Monica, Calif.
Height, 6.01. Weight, 190.
Throws and bats lefthanded.
Attended University of Nebraska, Lincoln, Neb.

Led American League first basemen in assists with 120 in 1983.

Year Club League	Pos.	G.	AB.	R.	H.	2B.	3B.	HR.	RBI.	B.A.	PO.	A.	E.	F.A.
1979—Sarasota Rangers Gulf C.	1B	50	189	39	46	10	2	0	31	.243	★465	★44	7	.986
1980—Asheville................ S. Atl.	1B	134	505	98	149	34	2	17	94	.295	★1227	★96	14	.990
1981—Tulsa .... Texas	1B	110	382	57	109	19	3	17	78	.285	973	95	11	.990
1982—Denver .... A. A.	OF-1B	128	477	92	148	21	1	25	102	.310	418	37	8	.983
1982—Texas.................... Amer.	OF-1B	20	67	13	16	4	1	4	13	.239	39	3	0	1.000
1983—Texas.................... Amer.	1B-OF	154	524	53	124	24	5	8	53	.237	1191	121	11	.992
Major League Totals...............................		174	591	66	140	28	6	12	66	.237	1230	124	11	.992

Selected by Texas Rangers' organization in 15th round of free-agent draft, June 5, 1979.

JACK WILLIAM O'CONNOR

Born June 2, 1958, at Yucca Valley, Calif.
Height, 6.03. Weight, 215.
Throws and bats lefthanded.

Pitched 1-0 no-hit victory against Fort Myers, June 28, 1979.

Year Club	League	G.	IP.	W.	L.	Pct.	H.	R.	ER.	SO.	BB.	ERA.
1976—Lethbridge	Pioneer	5	21	2	3	.400	22	16	15	17	20	6.43
1977—Jamestown.....................................	NYP	13	77	6	6	.500	72	36	30	56	30	3.51
1978—West Palm Beach	Florida St.	29	76	4	6	.400	78	42	34	53	46	4.03
1979—West Palm Beach	Florida St.	24	146	9	7	.563	125	60	46	87	63	2.84
1980—Memphis..	Southern	7	29	1	2	.333	30	27	25	17	20	7.76
1980—West Palm Beach	Florida St.	17	139	9	6	.600	105	46	37	93	70	2.40
1980—Denver†	Am. Assoc.	2	5	0	0	.000	3	1	1	7	6	1.80
1981—Minnesota......................................	American	28	35	3	2	.600	46	27	23	16	30	5.91
1982—Toledo	Int'national	12	42⅓	3	3	.500	42	22	16	42	17	3.40
1982—Minnesota......................................	American	23	126	8	9	.471	122	63	60	56	57	4.29
1983—Minnesota......................................	American	27	83	2	3	.400	107	59	54	56	36	5.86
1983—Toledo	Int'national	14	43⅓	2	1	.667	52	30	24	39	23	4.98
Major League Totals................................		78	244	13	14	.481	275	149	137	128	123	5.05

Selected by Montreal Expos' organization in 9th round of free-agent draft, June 8, 1976.

†Drafted by Minnesota Twins, December 8, 1980.

BRYAN ALOIS OELKERS

Name pronounced ELK-ers.
Born March 1, 1961, at Zaragoza, Spain.
Height, 6.02. Weight, 190.
Throws and bats lefthanded.
Attending Wichita State University, Wichita, Kan.

Received reported $69,500 bonus to sign with Minnesota Twins, 1982.

Year Club	League	G.	IP.	W.	L.	Pct.	H.	R.	ER.	SO.	BB.	ERA.
1982—Visalia	California	5	33	2	2	.500	27	15	13	17	17	3.55
1982—Orlando	Southern	3	25	1	0	1.000	16	6	4	14	9	1.44
1983—Minnesota......................................	American	10	34⅓	0	5	.000	56	34	33	13	17	8.65
1983—Toledo	Int'national	17	104⅓	5	7	.417	121	68	60	60	49	5.18
Major League Totals................................		10	34⅓	0	5	.000	56	34	33	13	17	8.65

Selected by Chicago Cubs' organization in 20th round of free-agent draft, June 5, 1979.

Selected by Minnesota Twins' organization in 1st round (fourth player selected) of free-agent draft, June 7, 1982.

RONALD JOHN OESTER

Name pronounced O-ster.

(Ron)

Born May 5, 1956, at Cincinnati, O.
Height, 6.02. Weight, 185.
Throws right and bats left and righthanded.

Led American Association shortstops in double plays with 102 in 1978.
Led Eastern League shortstops in double plays with 84 in 1976.
Led Pioneer League shortstops in double plays with 27 in 1974.

Year—Club	League	Pos.	G.	AB.	R.	H.	2B.	3B.	HR.	RBI.	B.A.	PO.	A.	E.	F.A.
1974—Billings	Pion.	SS	53	167	23	52	11	1	0	21	.311	87	141	27	.894
1975—Tampa	Fla. St.	SS	117	375	40	82	3	4	0	25	.219	174	358	34	.940
1976—Three Rivers	East.	SS	138	447	57	110	14	4	0	44	.246	★233	★408	38	.944
1977—Indianapolis	A. A.	SS	134	455	60	116	16	5	3	33	.255	203	★386	39	.938
1978—Indianapolis	A. A.	SS	●135	514	78	133	21	4	7	49	.259	★300	★428	32	.958
1978—Cincinnati	Nat.	SS	6	8	1	3	0	0	0	1	.375	3	9	0	1.000
1979—Indianapolis	A. A.	SS	●136	509	62	143	19	6	2	33	.281	★244	397	31	.954
1979—Cincinnati	Nat.	SS	6	3	0	0	0	0	0	0	.000	1	2	0	1.000
1980—Cincinnati	Nat.	2B-SS-3B	100	303	40	84	16	2	2	20	.277	161	224	10	.975
1981—Cincinnati	Nat.	2B-SS	105	354	45	96	16	7	5	42	.271	213	341	11	.981
1982—Cincinnati	Nat.	2B-SS-3B	151	549	63	143	19	4	9	47	.260	304	403	22	.970
1983—Cincinnati	Nat.	2B	157	549	63	145	23	5	11	58	.264	315	413	17	.977
Major League Totals			525	1766	212	471	74	18	27	168	.267	997	1392	60	.976

Selected by Cincinnati Reds' organization in 9th round of free-agent draft, June 5, 1974.

ROWLAND JOHNIE OFFICE

Born October 25, 1952, at Sacramento, Calif.
Height, 6.00. Weight, 170.
Throws and bats lefthanded.
Attended Sacramento City College, Sacramento, Calif.

Led Western Carolinas League in caught stealing with 16 in 1971.

Year—Club	League	Pos.	G.	AB.	R.	H.	2B.	3B.	HR.	RBI.	B.A.	PO.	A.	E.	F.A.
1971—Greenwood	W. Car.	OF	117	394	68	119	23	3	12	68	.302	194	3	9	.956
1972—Savannah	South.	OF	128	416	71	112	19	6	8	52	.269	245	9	5	.981
1972—Atlanta	Nat.	OF	2	5	1	2	0	0	0	0	.400	3	0	0	1.000
1973—Richmond	Int.	OF-1B	139	461	53	109	17	4	10	43	.286	275	7	6	.979
1974—Atlanta	Nat.	OF	131	248	20	61	16	1	3	31	.246	171	0	1	.994
1975—Atlanta	Nat.	OF	126	355	30	103	14	1	3	30	.290	229	6	8	.967
1976—Atlanta	Nat.	OF	99	359	51	101	17	1	4	34	.281	204	3	3	.986
1977—Atlanta†	Nat.	OF-1B	124	428	42	103	13	1	5	39	.241	250	8	3	.989
1978—Atlanta	Nat.	OF	146	404	40	101	13	1	9	40	.250	291	4	3	.990
1979—Atlanta‡	Nat.	OF	124	277	35	69	14	2	2	37	.249	164	4	2	.988
1980—Montreal	Nat.	OF	116	292	36	78	13	4	6	30	.267	150	2	2	.987
1981—Montreal§	Nat.	OF	26	40	4	7	0	0	0	0	.175	15	0	1	.938
1982—Montreal x	Nat.	OF	3	3	0	1	1	0	0	0	.333	2	0	0	1.000
1982—Okla. City yz	A. A.	OF	26	93	12	17	3	0	0	5	.183	60	0	2	.968
1983—New York	Amer.	OF	2	2	0	0	0	0	0	1	.000	2	0	0	1.000
1983—Columbus a	Int.	OF	87	212	37	63	14	4	8	45	.297	75	3	2	.975
National League Totals			897	2411	259	626	101	11	32	241	.260	1479	27	23	.985
American League Totals			2	2	0	0	0	0	0	1	.000	2	0	0	1.000
Major League Totals			899	2413	259	626	101	11	32	242	.259	1481	27	23	.985

Selected by Atlanta Braves' organization in 4th round of free-agent draft, June 4, 1970.
†On supplemental disabled list, May 19 to June 6, 1977.
‡Granted free agency, November 1, 1979; signed by Montreal Expos, December 11, 1979.
§On disabled list, May 13 to September 1, 1981.
xReleased, May 5, 1982; signed by Philadelphia Phillies' organization, May 14, 1982.
yOn suspended list, June 17, 1982 through remainder of season.
zReleased, January 13, 1983; signed by New York Yankees' organization, February 28, 1983.
aReleased, November 9, 1983.

BENJAMIN A. OGLIVIE

(Ben)

Born February 11, 1949, at Colon, Panama.
Height, 6.02. Weight, 170.
Throws and bats lefthanded.
Attended Bronx Community College, Bronx, N. Y., Northeastern University, Boston, Mass.,
and Wayne State University, Detroit, Mich.

Hit three home runs in a game, July 8, 1979 (first game), June 20, 1982 and May 14, 1983.
Led American League in intentional bases on balls received with 19 in 1980.
Led Eastern League outfielders in double plays with 5 in 1970.
Named outfielder on THE SPORTING NEWS American League All-Star Team, 1980.
Named outfielder on THE SPORTING NEWS American League Silver Slugger team, 1980.

Year—Club	League	Pos.	G.	AB.	R.	H.	2B.	3B.	HR.	RBI.	B.A.	PO.	A.	E.	F.A.
1968—Jamestown	NYP	1B-OF	16	45	7	13	1	0	1	5	.289	66	2	2	.971
1969—Greenville	W. Car.	OF	106	363	48	115	15	●7	8	62	.317	128	6	12	.918

Year Club	League	Pos.	G.	AB.	R.	H.	2B.	3B.	HR.	RBI.	B.A.	PO.	A.	E.	F.A.
1969—Winter Haven	Fla. St.	OF	11	32	4	8	1	0	0	5	.250	13	1	1	.933
1970—Pawtucket	East.	OF	115	391	62	91	15	0	10	51	.233	172	14	5	.974
1971—Louisville	Int.	OF	134	474	82	144	27	7	17	86	.304	215	★26	12	.953
1971—Boston	Amer.	OF	14	38	2	10	3	0	0	4	.263	22	1	1	.958
1972—Boston	Amer.	OF	94	253	27	61	10	2	8	30	.241	98	5	2	.981
1973—Boston†	Amer.	OF	58	147	16	32	9	1	2	9	.218	56	2	1	.983
1974—Detroit	Amer.	OF-1B	92	252	28	68	11	3	4	29	.270	162	11	5	.972
1975—Detroit	Amer.	OF-1B	100	332	45	95	14	1	9	36	.286	232	8	5	.980
1976—Detroit	Amer.	OF-1B	115	305	36	87	12	3	15	47	.285	234	8	3	.988
1977—Detroit‡	Amer.	OF	132	450	63	118	24	2	21	61	.262	236	10	6	.976
1978—Milwaukee	Amer.	OF-1B	128	469	71	142	29	4	18	72	.303	275	8	6	.979
1979—Milwaukee	Amer.	OF-1B	139	514	88	145	30	4	29	81	.282	320	10	5	.985
1980—Milwaukee	Amer.	OF	156	592	94	180	26	2	●41	118	.304	384	18	9	.978
1981—Milwaukee	Amer.	OF	107	400	53	97	15	2	14	72	.243	211	3	4	.982
1982—Milwaukee	Amer.	OF	159	602	92	147	22	1	34	102	.244	359	15	7	.982
1983—Milwaukee	Amer.	OF	125	411	49	115	19	3	13	66	.280	259	8	4	.985
Major League Totals			1419	4765	664	1297	224	28	208	727	.272	2848	107	58	.981

Selected by Boston Red Sox' organization in 7th round of free-agent draft, June 7, 1968.
†Traded to Detroit Tigers for Second Baseman Dick McAuliffe, October 23, 1973.
‡Traded to Milwaukee Brewers for Pitchers Jim Slaton and Rich Folkers, December 9, 1977.

DIVISION SERIES RECORD

Year Club	League	Pos.	G.	AB.	R.	H.	2B.	3B.	HR.	RBI.	B.A.	PO.	A.	E.	F.A.
1981—Milwaukee	Amer.	OF	5	18	0	3	1	0	0	1	.166	13	1	0	1.000

CHAMPIONSHIP SERIES RECORD

Year Club	League	Pos.	G.	AB.	R.	H.	2B.	3B.	HR.	RBI.	B.A.	PO.	A.	E.	F.A.
1982—Milwaukee	Amer.	OF	4	15	1	2	0	0	1	1	.133	5	0	2	.714

WORLD SERIES RECORD

Tied World Series records for most putouts by left fielder, inning (3), October 19, 1982 (seventh inning); most consecutive putouts by outfielder (4), October 19, 1982.

Year Club	League	Pos.	G.	AB.	R.	H.	2B.	3B.	HR.	RBI.	B.A.	PO.	A.	E.	F.A.
1982—Milwaukee	Amer.	OF	7	27	4	6	0	1	1	1	.222	13	0	1	.929

ALL-STAR GAME RECORD

Year League	Pos.	AB.	R.	H.	2B.	3B.	HR.	RBI.	B.A.	PO.	A.	E.	F.A.
1980—American	OF	2	0	0	0	0	0	0	.000	1	0	0	1.000
1982—American	PH	1	0	0	0	0	0	0	.000	0	0	0	.000
1983—American	OF	1	0	0	0	0	0	0	.000	0	0	0	.000
All-Star Game Totals		4	0	0	0	0	0	0	.000	1	0	0	1.000

ROBERT MICHAEL OJEDA

Name pronounced Oh-HEED-a.

(Bob)

Born December 17, 1957, at Los Angeles, Calif.
Height, 6.01. Weight, 185.
Throws and bats lefthanded.
Attended College of the Sequoias, Visalia, Calif.

Tied for International League lead in balks with 3 in 1980.
Tied for Florida State League lead in games started by pitchers with 29 in 1979.
Named International League Pitcher of the Year, 1981.

Year Club	League	G.	IP.	W.	L.	Pct.	H.	R.	ER.	SO.	BB.	ERA.
1978—Elmira	NYP	18	43	1	6	.143	45	32	23	35	43	4.81
1979—Winter Haven	Florida St.	29	200	15	7	.682	163	66	54	150	84	2.43
1980—Pawtucket	Int'national	19	123	6	7	.462	107	54	44	78	56	3.22
1980—Boston	American	7	26	1	1	.500	39	20	20	12	14	6.92
1981—Pawtucket	Int'national	25	173	12	9	.571	136	52	41	113	73	★2.13
1981—Boston	American	10	66	6	2	.750	50	25	23	28	25	3.14
1982—Boston†	American	22	78⅓	4	6	.400	95	53	49	52	29	5.63
1983—Boston	American	29	173⅔	12	7	.632	173	85	78	94	73	4.04
Major League Totals		68	344	23	16	.590	357	183	170	186	141	4.45

Signed as free agent by Boston Red Sox' organization, May 20, 1978.
†On disabled list, August 20 to September 10, 1982.

ALBERT OLIVER JR.

(Al)

Born October 14, 1946, at Portsmouth, O.
Height, 6.01. Weight, 203.
Throws and bats lefthanded.
Attended Kent State University, Kent, O.

Tied major league records for most home runs, opening day of season (2), April 6, 1983; most errors by first baseman, inning (3), May 23, 1969 (fourth inning); most long hits, doubleheader (6), August 17, 1980; most extra bases on long hits, doubleheader (15), August 17, 1980.

Tied modern major league record for most at bats, game (7), September 16, 1975.
Established American League record for most total bases, doubleheader (21), August 17, 1980.
Tied American League record for most home runs, doubleheader, home run in each game (4), August 17, 1980.
Tied National League record for fewest errors by first baseman for leader in errors, season (13), 1983.
Hit three home runs in a game, May 23, 1979 and August 17, 1980 (second game).
Led National League in total bases with 317 in 1982.
Tied for National League lead in grounding into double plays with 21 in 1983.
Led Western Carolinas League first basemen in double plays with 93 in 1965.
Named first baseman on THE SPORTING NEWS National League All-Star Team, 1982.
Named outfielder on THE SPORTING NEWS National League All-Star Team, 1975.
Named first baseman on THE SPORTING NEWS National League Silver Slugger team, 1982.
Named outfielder on THE SPORTING NEWS American League Silver Slugger team, 1980.
Named designated hitter on THE SPORTING NEWS American League Silver Slugger team, 1981.

Year—Club	League	Pos.	G.	AB.	R.	H.	2B.	3B.	HR.	RBI.	B.A.	PO.	A.	E.	F.A.
1964—Salem†	Appal.						(Did not play)								
1965—Gastonia	W. Car.	1B	123	★515	77	★159	19	5	10	71	.309	★1031	★64	21	.981
1966—Raleigh‡	Carol.	1B	117	458	66	137	25	4	10	57	.299	1035	★75	16	.986
1967—Macon§	South.	1B-OF	38	126	18	28	1	2	1	4	.222	267	21	6	.980
1967—Raleigh x	Carol.	1B	40	145	20	43	4	4	2	15	.297	365	17	0	1.000
1968—Columbus	Int.	1B-OF	132	473	61	149	22	13	14	74	.315	968	28	16	.984
1968—Pittsburgh	Nat.	OF	4	8	1	1	0	0	0	0	.125	3	0	0	1.000
1969—Pittsburgh	Nat.	1B-OF	129	463	55	132	19	2	17	70	.285	911	50	9	.991
1970—Pittsburgh	Nat.	OF-1B	151	551	63	149	33	5	12	83	.270	718	52	9	.988
1971—Pittsburgh	Nat.	OF-1B	143	529	69	149	31	7	14	64	.282	497	15	6	.988
1972—Pittsburgh	Nat.	OF-1B	140	565	88	176	27	4	12	89	.312	353	4	5	.986
1973—Pittsburgh	Nat.	OF-1B	158	654	90	191	38	7	20	99	.292	692	36	13	.982
1974—Pittsburgh	Nat.	OF-1B	147	617	96	198	38	12	11	85	.321	702	26	7	.990
1975—Pittsburgh	Nat.	OF-1B	155	628	90	176	39	8	18	84	.280	409	6	5	.988
1976—Pittsburgh	Nat.	OF-1B	121	443	62	143	22	5	12	61	.323	327	4	5	.985
1977—Pittsburgh y	Nat.	OF	154	568	75	175	29	6	19	82	.308	305	6	6	.981
1978—Texas z	Amer.	OF	133	525	65	170	35	5	14	89	.324	219	8	3	.987
1979—Texas	Amer.	OF	136	492	69	159	28	4	12	76	.323	260	9	7	.975
1980—Texas	Amer.	OF-1B	★163	656	96	209	43	3	19	117	.319	315	9	9	.973
1981—Texas a	Amer.	1B	102	421	53	130	29	1	4	55	.309	2	0	0	1.000
1982—Montreal	Nat.	1B	160	617	90	★204	43	2	22	●109	★.331	1286	92	★19	.986
1983—Montreal	Nat.	●1B-OF	157	614	70	184	●38	3	8	84	.300	1207	118	●13	.990
National League Totals			1619	6257	849	1878	357	61	165	910	.300	7410	409	97	.988
American League Totals			534	2094	283	668	135	13	49	337	.319	796	26	19	.977
Major League Totals			2153	8351	1132	2546	492	74	214	1247	.305	8206	435	116	.987

Signed as free agent by Pittsburgh Pirates' organization, June 13, 1964.
†On disabled list, June 23 to July 1 and July 16 to September 22, 1964.
‡On temporary inactive list, May 26 to June 15, 1966.
§On military list, January 7 to May 7, 1967.
xOn temporary inactive list, June 21 to July 15, 1967.
yTraded with infielder Nelson Norman to Texas Rangers for Pitcher Bert Blyleven and First Baseman-Outfielder John Milner, December 8, 1977.
zOn supplemental disabled list, June 15 to July 13, 1978.
aTraded to Montreal Expos for Third Baseman Larry Parrish and First Baseman Dave Hostetler, March 31, 1982.

CHAMPIONSHIP SERIES RECORD

Year—Club	League	Pos.	G.	AB.	R.	H.	2B.	3B.	HR.	RBI.	B.A.	PO.	A.	E.	F.A.
1970—Pittsburgh	Nat.	1B	2	8	0	2	0	0	0	1	.250	22	1	0	1.000
1971—Pittsburgh	Nat.	PH-OF	4	12	2	3	0	0	1	5	.250	5	0	0	1.000
1972—Pittsburgh	Nat.	OF	5	20	3	5	2	1	1	3	.250	17	1	0	1.000
1974—Pittsburgh	Nat.	OF	4	14	1	2	0	0	1	1	.143	9	0	0	1.000
1975—Pittsburgh	Nat.	OF	3	11	1	2	0	0	1	2	.182	5	0	0	1.000
Championship Series Totals			18	65	7	14	2	1	3	12	.215	58	2	0	1.000

WORLD SERIES RECORD

Year—Club	League	Pos.	G.	AB.	R.	H.	2B.	3B.	HR.	RBI.	B.A.	PO.	A.	E.	F.A.
1971—Pittsburgh	Nat.	PH-OF	5	19	1	4	2	0	0	2	.211	11	0	1	.917

ALL-STAR GAME RECORD

Year—League	Pos.	AB.	R.	H.	2B.	3B.	HR.	RBI.	B.A.	PO.	A.	E.	F.A.
1972—National	OF	1	0	0	0	0	0	0	.000	0	0	0	.000
1975—National	PH-OF	1	1	1	1	0	0	0	1.000	0	0	0	.000
1976—National	OF	1	0	0	0	0	0	0	.000	1	0	0	1.000
1980—American	OF	1	0	0	0	0	0	0	.000	0	0	0	.000
1981—American	PH	1	0	0	0	0	0	0	.000	0	0	0	.000
1982—National	1B	2	1	2	1	0	0	0	1.000	2	0	0	1.000
1983—National	1B	2	1	1	1	0	0	0	.500	2	1	0	1.000
All-Star Game Totals		9	3	4	3	0	0	0	.444	5	1	0	1.000

THOMAS PATRICK O'MALLEY
(Tom)

Born December 25, 1960, at Orange, N. J.
Height, 6.00. Weight, 185.
Throws right and bats lefthanded.

Year	Club	League	Pos.	G.	AB.	R.	H.	2B.	3B.	HR.	RBI.	B.A.	PO.	A.	E.	F.A.
1979—Great Falls	Pion.	2-S-O-3	42	119	13	29	6	1	1	20	.244	41	34	9	.893
1980—Fresno	Calif.	3B	122	435	67	125	20	9	3	74	.287	69	253	22	★.936
1981—Shreveport	Texas	3B	123	467	50	135	23	6	6	53	.289	94	237	15	.957
1982—Phoenix	P. C.	3B	26	96	23	43	11	1	3	15	.448	12	44	6	.903
1982—San Francisco†	Nat.	3B-SS-2B	92	291	26	80	12	4	2	27	.275	60	161	8	.965
1983—San Francisco	Nat.	3B	135	410	40	106	16	1	5	45	.259	70	213	18	.940
Major League Totals			227	701	66	186	28	5	7	72	.265	130	374	26	.951

Selected by San Francisco Giants' organization in 16th round of free-agent draft, June 5, 1979.
†On disabled list, August 16 to September 6, 1982.

RANDALL JEFFREY O'NEAL
(Randy)

Born August 30, 1960, at West Palm Beach, Fla.
Height, 6.02. Weight, 195.
Throws and bats righthanded.
Attended Palm Beach Junior College, Lake Worth, Fla.,
and University of Florida, Gainesville, Fla.

Pitched seven-inning, 4-0 no-hit victory against Winter Haven, August 23, 1981 (first game).

Year	Club	League	G.	IP.	W.	L.	Pct.	H.	R.	ER.	SO.	BB.	ERA.
1981—Lakeland	Florida St.	13	69	4	5	.444	59	27	22	31	18	2.87
1982—Birmingham	Southern	27	185	11	7	.611	169	83	70	105	71	3.41
1983—Evansville	Am. Assoc.	23	140⅓	8	10	.444	159	80	66	70	45	4.23

Selected by Montreal Expos' organization in 4th round of free-agent draft, January 9, 1979.
Selected by Minnesota Twins' organization in secondary phase of free-agent draft, June 5, 1979.
Selected by Milwaukee Brewers' organization in secondary phase of free-agent draft, January 8, 1980.
Selected by Cincinnati Reds' organization in secondary phase of free-agent draft, June 3, 1980.
Selected by Detroit Tigers' organization in secondary phase of free-agent draft, June 8, 1981.

PAUL ANDREW O'NEILL

Born February 25, 1963, at Columbus, O.
Height, 6.04. Weight, 200.
Throws and bats lefthanded.
Attended Otterbein College, Westerville, O.
Son of Charles W. O'Neill, minor league pitcher, 1945 through 1948.

Year	Club	League	Pos.	G.	AB.	R.	H.	2B.	3B.	HR.	RBI.	B.A.	PO.	A.	E.	F.A.
1981—Billings	Pion.	OF	66	241	37	76	7	2	3	29	.315	87	4	5	.948
1982—Cedar Rapids	Midw.	OF	116	386	50	105	19	2	8	71	.272	137	7	8	.947
1983—Tampa	Fla. St.	OF-1B	121	413	62	115	23	7	8	51	.278	218	14	10	.959
1983—Waterbury	East.	OF	14	43	6	12	0	0	0	6	.279	26	0	0	1.000

Selected by Cincinnati Reds' organization in 4th round of free-agent draft, June 8, 1981.

JOSE MANUEL OQUENDO

Name pronounced Oh-KEN-doh.

Born July 4, 1963, at Rio Piedras, Puerto Rico.
Height, 5.10. Weight, 156.
Throws right and bats left and righthanded.

Led International League in sacrifice hits with 14 in 1982.
Led Carolina League in sacrifice hits with 13 in 1980.
Led Northwest League shortstops in errors with 40 in 1979.

Year	Club	League	Pos.	G.	AB.	R.	H.	2B.	3B.	HR.	RBI.	B.A.	PO.	A.	E.	F.A.
1979—Grays Harbor	N'west	★SS-2B	64	220	24	50	8	0	1	14	.227	90	177	★40	.870
1980—Lynchburg	Carol.	SS	109	301	38	51	10	3	0	26	.169	126	358	31	★.940
1981—Lynchburg	Carol.	SS	124	393	59	98	8	6	0	38	.249	169	390	23	★.961
1982—Tidewater	Int.	SS	114	337	40	72	8	3	0	22	.214	186	337	25	.954
1983—Tidewater	Int.	SS	13	34	3	4	0	0	0	3	.118	20	23	4	.915
1983—New York	Nat.	SS	120	328	29	70	7	0	1	17	.213	182	326	21	.960
Major League Totals			120	328	29	70	7	0	1	17	.213	182	326	21	.960

Signed as free agent by New York Mets' organization, April 15, 1979.

JESSE OROSCO

Name pronounced Oh-ROSS-koh.

Born April 21, 1957, at Santa Barbara, Calif.
Height, 6.02. Weight, 174.
Throws left and bats righthanded.
Attended Santa Barbara City College, Santa Barbara, Calif.

Major League saves: 1981 (1), 1982 (4), 1983 (17). Total—22.
Led Appalachian League in intentional bases on balls issued with 5 in 1978.

Year	Club	League	G.	IP.	W.	L.	Pct.	H.	R.	ER.	SO.	BB.	ERA.
1978—Elizabethton†	Ap'lachian	20	40	4	4	.500	29	7	5	48	20	1.13
1979—Tidewater	Int'national	16	81	4	4	.500	82	45	35	55	43	3.89
1979—New York	National	18	35	1	2	.333	33	20	19	22	22	4.89
1980—Jackson	Texas	37	71	4	4	.500	52	36	29	85	62	3.68
1981—Tidewater	Int'national	46	87	9	5	.643	80	39	32	81	32	3.31

Year	Club	League	G.	IP.	W.	L.	Pct.	H.	R.	ER.	SO.	BB.	ERA.
1981—New York		National	8	17	0	1	.000	13	4	3	18	6	1.59
1982—New York		National	54	109⅓	4	10	.286	92	37	33	89	40	2.72
1983—New York		National	62	110	13	7	.650	76	27	18	84	38	1.47
Major League Totals			142	271⅓	18	20	.474	214	88	73	213	106	2.42

Selected by St. Louis Cardinals' organization in 7th round of free-agent draft, January 11, 1977.
Selected by Minnesota Twins' organization in 2nd round of free-agent draft, January 10, 1978.
†Traded to New York Mets, February 7, 1979, completing deal in which Minnesota Twins traded Pitcher Greg Field and a player to be named later to New York for Pitcher Jerry Koosman, December 8, 1978.

ALL-STAR GAME RECORD

Year	League	IP.	W.	L.	Pct.	H.	R.	ER.	SO.	BB.	ERA.
1983—National		⅓	0	0	.000	0	0	0	1	0	0.00

JOSEPH MICHAEL ORSULAK
(Joe)

Born May 31, 1962, at Parsippany, N.J.
Height, 6.01. Weight, 175.
Throws and bats lefthanded.

Led Pacific Coast League outfielders in double plays with 8 in 1983.
Tied for South Atlantic League lead in double plays by outfielders with 4 in 1981.

Year	Club	League	Pos.	G.	AB.	R.	H.	2B.	3B.	HR.	RBI.	B.A.	PO.	A.	E.	F.A.
1981—Greenwood†	S. Atl.		OF	118	460	80	145	18	8	6	70	.315	249	16	4	★.985
1982—Alexandria	Carol.		OF-1B	129	463	92	134	18	4	14	65	.289	286	7	10	.967
1983—Hawaii	P. C.		OF	139	538	87	154	12	●13	10	58	.286	★341	18	8	.978
1983—Pittsburgh	Nat.		OF	7	11	0	2	0	0	0	1	.182	2	2	0	1.000
Major League Totals				7	11	0	2	0	0	0	1	.182	2	2	0	1.000

Selected by Pittsburgh Pirates' organization in 6th round of free-agent draft, June 3, 1980.
†On temporarily inactive list, July 10 to July 27, 1981.

JORGE ORTA (NUNEZ)
Named pronounced OR-ta.

Born November 26, 1950, at Mazatlan, Mexico.
Height, 5.10. Weight, 175.
Throws right and bats lefthanded.

Collected six hits in one game, June 15, 1980.

Year	Club	League	Pos.	G.	AB.	R.	H.	2B.	3B.	HR.	RBI.	B.A.	PO.	A.	E.	F.A.
1968—Fresnillo	Mex. Cen.		2B-SS	20	68	8	18	6	0	0	1	.265	29	39	4	.944
1969—S. Luis Potosi	Mex. C.						(Did not play)									
1970—Puerto Mex.	Mex. S.E.		2B-SS	18	43	6	13	1	0	0	3	.302	29	28	1	.983
1971—S. Luis Potosi	Mex. Cen.		2B	59	182	55	77	17	★7	7	53	★.423	115	108	15	.937
1971—Mexicali†	Mex. No.			58	207	45	75	14	2	16	48	.362	figures unavailable			
1972—Knoxville	South.		2B	53	196	41	62	6	7	7	34	.316	113	142	9	.966
1972—Chicago	Amer.		SS-2B-3B	51	124	20	25	3	1	3	11	.202	50	85	8	.944
1973—Chicago	Amer.		2B-SS	128	425	46	113	9	10	6	40	.266	255	301	18	.969
1974—Chicago	Amer.		2B-SS	139	525	73	166	31	2	10	67	.316	297	313	18	.971
1975—Chicago	Amer.		2B	140	542	64	165	26	10	11	83	.304	354	354	16	.978
1976—Chicago	Amer.		OF-3B	158	636	74	174	29	8	14	72	.274	187	111	15	.952
1977—Chicago	Amer.		2B	144	564	71	159	27	8	11	84	.282	287	335	19	.970
1978—Chicago	Amer.		2B	117	420	45	115	19	2	13	53	.274	275	290	9	.984
1979—Chicago‡	Amer.		2B	113	325	49	85	18	3	11	46	.262	57	75	3	.978
1980—Cleveland	Amer.		OF	129	481	78	140	18	3	10	64	.291	269	10	5	.982
1981—Cleveland§	Amer.		OF	88	338	50	92	14	3	5	34	.272	150	11	1	.994
1982—Los Angeles xy	Nat.		OF	86	115	13	25	5	0	2	8	.217	35	1	2	.947
1983—Toronto z	Amer.		OF	101	245	30	58	6	3	10	38	.237	16	1	0	1.000
American League Totals				1308	4625	600	1292	200	53	104	592	.279	2299	1886	112	.974
National League Totals				86	115	13	25	5	0	2	8	.217	35	1	2	.947
Major League Totals				1394	4740	613	1317	205	53	106	600	.278	2334	1887	114	.974

Signed as free agent by Fresnillo, June 13, 1968.
†Sold to Appleton (Chicago White Sox' organization), November 30, 1971.
‡Granted free agency, November 1, 1979; signed by Cleveland Indians, December 19, 1979.
§Traded with Catcher Jack Fimple and Pitcher Larry White to Los Angeles Dodgers for Pitcher Rick Sutcliffe and Second Baseman Jack Perconte, December 9, 1981.
xTraded to New York Mets for Pitcher Pat Zachry, December 28, 1982.
yTraded to Toronto Blue Jays for Pitcher Steve Senteney, February 4, 1983.
zTraded to Kansas City Royals for First Baseman Willie Aikens, December 19, 1983.

ALL-STAR GAME RECORD
Named to American League All-Star Team for 1975 game; replaced due to injury.
Member of American League All-Star Team in 1980; did not play.

—DID YOU KNOW—

That the Cincinnati Reds have never selected a college player in the first round of the amateur draft?

ADALBERTO ORTIZ JR. (COLON)

Name pronounced Orr-TEEZ.

(Junior)

Born October 24, 1959, at Humacao, Puerto Rico.
Height, 5.10. Weight, 170.
Throws and bats righthanded.
Brother of Alexander Ortiz, minor league outfielder, 1978 and 1979.

Led Pacific Coast League catchers in putouts with 744, double plays with 17 and stealers caught with 75 in 1982.
Led Carolina League catchers in double plays with 12 in 1979.
Tied for Western Carolinas League lead in passed balls with 22 in 1978.

Year	Club	League	Pos.	G.	AB.	R.	H.	2B.	3B.	HR.	RBI.	B.A.	PO.	A.	E.	F.A.
1977—Charleston†	W. Car.	C	21	53	2	14	3	0	0	10	.264	93	13	4	.964
1977—Bradenton Pir.	Gulf C.	C	34	118	11	24	5	1	1	12	.203	76	14	4	.957
1978—Charleston‡	W. Car.	C	41	122	12	26	4	0	1	16	.268	213	198	44	7	.972
1979—Salem	Carol.	*C-1B	108	396	35	112	21	2	5	66	.283	632	*84	*17	.977
1980—Buffalo	East.	C	126	515	79	*178	25	1	12	78	*.346	497	91	16	.974
1980—Portland	P. C.	C	8	27	1	3	0	1	0	3	.111	42	10	0	1.000
1981—Portland	P. C.	C	105	346	49	93	14	7	2	46	.269	606	76	15	.978
1982—Portland	P. C.	C-OF-1B	124	449	46	131	22	0	6	57	.292	751	*110	*19	.978
1982—Pittsburgh	Nat.	C	7	15	1	3	1	0	0	0	.200	27	3	0	1.000
1983—Pitt.§-N.Y.	Nat.	C	73	193	11	48	6	0	0	12	.249	293	31	11	.967
Major League Totals			80	208	12	51	7	0	0	12	.245	320	34	11	.970

Signed as free agent by Pittsburgh Pirates' organization, January 18, 1977.
†On temporary inactive list, June 18 to June 22, 1977.
‡On disabled list, June 16 to September 5, 1978.
§Traded with Pitcher Arthur Ray to New York Mets for Outfielder Marvell Wynne and Pitcher Steve Senteney, June 14, 1983.

AMOS JOSEPH OTIS

Born April 26, 1947, at Mobile, Ala.
Height, 5.11. Weight, 166.
Throws and bats righthanded.

Tied major league records for fewest times caught stealing, season, 50 or more stolen bases (8), 1971; fewest double plays by outfielder, season, for leader in most double plays (4), 1971.
Tied American League record for most stolen bases, two consecutive games (7), April 30 and May 4, 1975.
Major league stolen bases: 1969 (1), 1970 (33), 1971 (52), 1972 (28), 1973 (13), 1974 (18), 1975 (39), 1976 (26), 1977 (23), 1978 (32), 1979 (30), 1980 (16), 1981 (16), 1982 (9), 1983 (5). Total—341.
Led American League in stolen bases with 52 in 1971.
Led American League outfielders in total chances with 407 in 1970 and 418 in 1971.
Led American League outfielders in double plays with 6 in 1970 and tied for lead with 4 in 1971 and 5 in 1979.
Led Appalachian League third basemen in double plays with 13 in 1965.
Named outfielder on THE SPORTING NEWS American League All-Star Team, 1973.
Named outfielder on THE SPORTING NEWS American League All-Star fielding team, 1971, 1972 and 1974.

Year	Club	League	Pos.	G.	AB.	R.	H.	2B.	3B.	HR.	RBI.	B.A.	PO.	A.	E.	F.A.
1965—Harlan	Appal.	3B	67	252	55	83	11	5	9	39	.329	46	76	12	*.910
1966—Oneonta†	NYP	*1-O-3	116	419	54	113	17	7	3	46	.270	484	*74	22	.962
1967—Jacksonville	Int.	O-3-1-2	126	407	62	109	11	7	3	39	.268	251	65	8	.975
1967—New York	Nat.	OF-3B	19	59	6	13	2	0	0	1	.220	23	2	0	1.000
1968—Jacksonville‡	Int.	OF-1B	139	500	76	143	29	4	15	70	.286	428	23	9	.980
1969—Tidewater	Int.	OF	71	248	55	81	14	2	10	43	.327	157	9	1	.994
1969—New York§	Nat.	OF-3B	48	93	6	14	3	1	0	4	.151	49	6	1	.982
1970—Kansas City	Amer.	OF	159	620	91	176	•36	9	11	58	.284	*388	•15	4	.990
1971—Kansas City	Amer.	OF	147	555	80	167	26	4	15	79	.301	*404	10	4	.990
1972—Kansas City	Amer.	OF	143	540	75	158	28	2	11	54	.293	351	6	3	.992
1973—Kansas City	Amer.	OF	148	583	89	175	21	4	26	93	.300	330	10	5	.986
1974—Kansas City	Amer.	OF	146	552	87	157	31	9	12	73	.284	425	8	6	.986
1975—Kansas City x	Amer.	OF	132	470	87	116	26	6	9	46	.247	310	9	4	.988
1976—Kansas City	Amer.	OF	153	592	93	165	*40	2	18	86	.279	373	5	3	.992
1977—Kansas City	Amer.	OF	142	478	85	120	20	8	17	78	.251	326	10	3	.991
1978—Kansas City	Amer.	OF	141	486	74	145	30	7	22	96	.298	382	9	2	*.995
1979—Kansas City	Amer.	OF	151	577	100	170	28	2	18	90	.295	385	11	3	*.992
1980—Kansas City y	Amer.	OF	107	394	56	99	16	3	10	53	.251	310	6	4	.988
1981—Kansas City	Amer.	OF	99	372	49	100	22	3	9	57	.269	294	6	2	.993
1982—Kansas City	Amer.	OF	125	475	73	136	25	3	11	88	.286	308	5	1	.997
1983—Kansas City z	Amer.	OF	98	356	35	93	16	3	4	41	.261	233	6	1	.996
American League Totals			1891	7050	1074	1977	365	65	193	992	.280	4819	116	45	.991
National League Totals			67	152	12	27	5	1	0	5	.178	72	8	1	.988
Major League Totals			1958	7202	1086	2004	370	66	193	997	.278	4891	124	46	.991

Selected by Boston Red Sox' organization in 5th round of free-agent draft, June 13, 1965.
†Drafted by Jacksonville (New York Mets' organization), November 28, 1966.
‡On suspended list, May 31 to June 3, 1968.
§Traded with Pitcher Robert D. Johnson to Kansas City Royals for Third Baseman Joe Foy, December 3, 1969.
xOn supplemental disabled list, June 25 to July 14, 1975.
yOn disabled list, April 9 to May 22, 1980.
zGranted free agency, November 7, 1983; signed by Pittsburgh Pirates, December 19, 1983.

DIVISION SERIES RECORD

Year Club	League	Pos.	G.	AB.	R.	H.	2B.	3B.	HR.	RBI.	B.A.	PO.	A.	E.	F.A.
1981—Kansas City	Amer.	OF	3	12	0	0	0	0	0	1	.000	12	0	0	1.000

CHAMPIONSHIP SERIES RECORD

Established American League Championship Series records for most strikeouts, four-game Series (5), 1978; most stolen bases, total Series (8); most stolen bases, four-game Series (4), 1978.

Tied American League Championship Series record for most stolen bases, three-game Series (2), 1980.

Year Club	League	Pos.	G.	AB.	R.	H.	2B.	3B.	HR.	RBI.	B.A.	PO.	A.	E.	F.A.
1976—Kansas City	Amer.	OF	1	1	0	0	0	0	0	0	.000	0	0	0	.000
1977—Kansas City	Amer.	OF-PH	5	16	1	2	1	0	0	2	.125	11	1	0	1.000
1978—Kansas City	Amer.	OF	4	14	2	6	2	0	0	1	.429	8	0	1	.889
1980—Kansas City	Amer.	OF	3	12	2	4	1	0	0	0	.333	11	0	0	1.000
Championship Series Totals			13	43	5	12	4	0	0	3	.279	30	1	1	.969

WORLD SERIES RECORD

Established World Series record for most putouts by outfielder, extra-inning game (9), October 17, 1980 (10 innings).

Tied World Series records for hitting home run in first Series at bat, October 14, 1980 (second inning); most chances accepted by center fielder, 10-inning game (9), October 17, 1980.

Year Club	League	Pos.	G.	AB.	R.	H.	2B.	3B.	HR.	RBI.	B.A.	PO.	A.	E.	F.A.
1980—Kansas City	Amer.	OF	6	23	4	11	2	0	3	7	.478	21	0	0	1.000

ALL-STAR GAME RECORD

Year League	Pos.	AB.	R.	H.	2B.	3B.	HR.	RBI.	B.A.	PO.	A.	E.	F.A.
1970—American	OF	3	0	0	0	0	0	0	.000	2	0	0	1.000
1971—American	OF	1	0	0	0	0	0	0	.000	0	0	0	.000
1973—American	OF	2	0	2	0	0	0	1	1.000	0	0	0	.000
1976—American	OF	1	0	0	0	0	0	0	.000	0	0	0	.000
All-Star Game Totals		7	0	2	0	0	0	1	.286	2	0	0	1.000

Named to American League All-Star Team for the 1972 game; replaced due to injury.

NATHAN EDWARD OTT
(Ed)

Born July 11, 1951, at Muncy, Pa.
Height, 5.10. Weight, 190.
Throws right and bats lefthanded.

Led National League catchers in errors with 15 in 1978.
Led International League catchers in putouts with 688, errors with 20 and passed balls with 23 in 1975.
Led International League outfielders in assists with 21 and tied for lead in double plays with 4 in 1974.
Led Carolina League outfielders in double plays with 9 in 1972.

Year Club	League	Pos.	G.	AB.	R.	H.	2B.	3B.	HR.	RBI.	B.A.	PO.	A.	E.	F.A.
1970—Niagara Falls	NYP	OF	61	206	38	60	9	5	0	24	.291	84	8	2	.979
1971—Monroe	W. Car.	OF	105	356	58	104	12	6	10	48	.292	146	*16	5	.970
1972—Salem	Carol.	OF	133	450	84	137	18	*10	7	63	.304	211	19	8	.966
1973—Charleston	Int.	OF-C	126	440	56	115	18	3	6	52	.261	203	7	7	.968
1974—Charleston	Int.	OF-3B	121	423	57	112	13	7	14	49	.265	207	31	10	.960
1974—Pittsburgh	Nat.	OF	7	5	1	0	0	0	0	0	.000	1	0	0	1.000
1975—Charleston	Int.	C-OF	121	425	66	121	21	5	10	5	.285	697	59	21	.973
1975—Pittsburgh	Nat.	C	5	5	0	1	0	0	0	0	.200	2	0	0	1.000
1976—Pittsburgh†	Nat.	C	27	39	2	12	2	0	0	5	.308	20	6	0	1.000
1977—Pittsburgh	Nat.	C	104	311	40	82	14	3	7	38	.264	455	49	9	.982
1978—Pittsburgh	Nat.	C-OF	112	379	49	102	18	4	9	38	.269	547	43	16	.974
1979—Pittsburgh	Nat.	C	117	403	49	110	20	2	7	51	.273	612	53	4	.994
1980—Pittsburgh‡	Nat.	C-OF	120	392	35	102	14	0	8	41	.260	571	73	11	.983
1981—California§	Amer.	C	75	258	20	56	8	1	2	22	.217	287	36	7	.979
1982—California x	Amer.						(Did not play)								
1983—Redwood y	Calif.	C	2	3	1	1	0	0	0	0	.333	10	0	1	.909
National League Totals			492	1534	176	409	68	9	31	173	.267	2208	224	40	.984
American League Totals			75	258	20	56	8	1.	2	22	.217	287	36	7	.979
Major League Totals			567	1792	196	465	76	10	33	195	.259	2495	260	47	.983

Selected by Pittsburgh Pirates' organization in 23rd round of free-agent draft, June 4, 1970.
†On supplemental disabled list, August 10 to September 1, 1976.
‡Traded with Pitcher Mickey Mahler to California Angels for First Baseman Jason Thompson, April 1, 1981.
§Granted free agency, November 13, 1981; re-signed by Angels, January 29, 1982.
xOn disabled list, April 2, 1982; transferred to emergency disabled list, April 15, 1982 through remainder of season.
yOn California supplemental disabled list, March 30, 1983; transferred to disabled list, May 10, 1983; transferred to emergency disabled list, June 10, 1983 through remainder of season; included rehabilitation disability assignment to Redwood, April 29 to May 12, 1983.

CHAMPIONSHIP SERIES RECORD

Year Club	League	Pos.	G.	AB.	R.	H.	2B.	3B.	HR.	RBI.	B.A.	PO.	A.	E.	F.A.
1979—Pittsburgh	Nat.	C	3	13	0	3	0	0	0	0	.231	25	3	0	1.000

WORLD SERIES RECORD

Year Club	League	Pos.	G.	AB.	R.	H.	2B.	3B.	HR.	RBI.	B.A.	PO.	A.	E.	F.A.
1979—Pittsburgh	Nat.	C	3	12	2	4	1	0	0	3	.333	20	0	0	1.000

ROBERT DENNIS OWCHINKO
Name pronounced Oh-CHINK-oh.
(Bob)
Born January 1, 1955, at Detroit, Mich.
Height, 6.02. Weight, 195.
Throws and bats lefthanded.
Attended Eastern Michigan University, Ypsilanti, Mich.
Named National League Rookie Pitcher of the Year by THE SPORTING NEWS, 1977.

Year Club	League	G.	IP.	W.	L.	Pct.	H.	R.	ER.	SO.	BB.	ERA.
1976—Amarillo	Texas	13	91	6	2	.750	86	36	33	69	38	3.26
1976—San Diego	National	2	4	0	2	.000	11	8	8	4	3	18.00
1977—Hawaii	P. Coast	6	44	5	1	.833	36	7	7	30	20	1.43
1977—San Diego	National	30	170	9	12	.429	191	93	84	101	67	4.45
1978—San Diego	National	36	202	10	13	.435	198	87	80	94	78	3.56
1979—San Diego†	National	42	149	6	12	.333	144	73	62	66	55	3.74
1980—Cleveland‡§	American	29	114	2	9	.182	138	71	67	66	47	5.29
1981—Oakland x	American	29	39	4	3	.571	34	15	14	26	19	3.23
1982—Oakland x	American	54	102	2	4	.333	111	60	59	67	52	5.21
1983—Hawaii	P. Coast	22	137⅔	10	6	.625	150	86	65	124	56	4.25
1983—Pittsburgh y	National	1	0	0	0	.000	2	1	1	0	0	.....
National League Totals		111	525	25	39	.391	546	262	235	265	203	4.10
American League Totals		112	255	8	16	.333	283	146	140	159	118	4.94
Major League Totals		223	780	33	55	.375	829	408	375	424	321	4.37

Selected by San Diego Padres' organization in 1st round (fifth player selected) of free-agent draft, June 8, 1976.
†Traded with Outfielder Jim Wilhelm to Cleveland Indians for Outfielder Jerry Mumphrey, February 15, 1980.
‡Traded with Pitchers Victor Cruz and Rafael Vasquez and Catcher Gary Alexander to Pittsburgh Pirates for Pitcher Bert Blyleven and Catcher Manny Sanguillen, December 9, 1980.
§Traded to Oakland A's for cash and a player to be named later, April 6, 1981; Pittsburgh Pirates acquired Pitcher Ernie Camacho to complete deal, April 10, 1981.
xReleased, March 28, 1983; signed by Hawaii (Pittsburgh Pirates' organization), May 2, 1983.
yAcquired on waivers by Cincinnati Reds, November 11, 1983.

CHAMPIONSHIP SERIES RECORD

Year Club	League	G.	IP.	W.	L.	Pct.	H.	R.	ER.	SO.	BB.	ERA.
1981—Oakland	American	1	1⅔	0	0	.000	3	1	1	0	0	5.40

DAVE OWEN

Born April 25, 1958, at Cleburne, Tex.
Height, 6.01. Weight, 175.
Throws right and bats left and righthanded.
Attended University of Texas, Arlington, Tex.
Brother of Spike Owen, shortstop with Seattle Mariners.

Year Club	League	Pos.	G.	AB.	R.	H.	2B.	3B.	HR.	RBI.	B.A.	PO.	A.	E.	F.A.
1979—Sarasota Cubs	Gulf C.	SS	10	23	8	7	0	0	0	4	.304	17	26	7	.860
1979—Quad Cities	Midw.	SS	45	129	23	18	3	0	0	4	.140	56	139	11	.947
1980—Midland	Texas	SS	78	257	45	74	8	0	3	31	.288	96	213	32	.906
1980—Quad Cities	Midw.	SS	56	188	43	49	5	1	0	17	.261	88	155	17	.935
1981—Midland	Texas	SS-2B-3B	80	247	40	53	8	1	0	23	.215	109	205	26	.924
1982—Midland	Texas	SS-3B	125	427	59	135	12	9	4	40	.316	183	309	29	.944
1983—Iowa	A. A.	SS	126	425	67	110	21	3	6	39	.259	203	★431	25	★.962
1983—Chicago	Nat.	SS-3B	16	22	1	2	0	1	0	2	.091	10	29	0	1.000
Major League Totals			16	22	1	2	0	1	0	2	.091	10	29	0	1.000

Selected by Chicago Cubs' organization in 10th round of free-agent draft, June 5, 1979.

LAWRENCE THOMAS OWEN
(Larry)

Born May 31, 1955, at Cleveland, O.
Height, 5.11. Weight, 185.
Throws and bats righthanded.
Attended Bowling Green State University, Bowling Green, O.
Tied for International League lead in passed balls with 15 in 1979.

Year Club	League	Pos.	G.	AB.	R.	H.	2B.	3B.	HR.	RBI.	B.A.	PO.	A.	E.	F.A.
1977—Greenwood	W. Car.	C	61	170	26	48	9	2	3	24	.282	295	47	11	.969
1978—Savannah	South.	C	112	364	35	78	9	1	11	45	.214	★545	★89	★25	.962
1978—Richmond	Int.	C	14	40	2	10	1	0	0	3	.250	59	9	6	.919
1979—Richmond	Int.	C	110	358	32	70	7	3	7	31	.196	★615	●73	★13	.981
1980—Savannah	South.	C-3B	76	228	27	48	8	1	6	20	.211	304	44	7	.980
1981—Savannah	South.	C	90	279	30	64	8	3	5	23	.229	450	77	★23	.958
1981—Atlanta	Nat.	C	13	16	0	0	0	0	0	0	.000	23	4	1	.964
1982—Richmond	Int.	C	58	178	21	37	5	0	5	26	.208	265	37	6	.981
1982—Atlanta	Nat.	C	2	3	1	1	1	0	0	0	.333	2	1	0	1.000
1983—Atlanta	Nat.	C	17	17	0	2	0	0	0	1	.118	30	2	1	.970
1983—Richmond	Int.	C	5	12	4	5	0	1	1	2	.417	20	0	0	1.000
Major League Totals			32	36	1	3	1	0	0	1	.083	55	7	2	.970

Selected by California Angels' organization in 18th round of free-agent draft, June 8, 1976.
Selected by Atlanta Braves' organization in 17th round of free-agent draft, June 7, 1977.

SPIKE DEE OWEN

Born April 19, 1961, at Cleburne, Tex.
Height, 5.10. Weight, 165.
Throws right and bats left and righthanded.
Attended University of Texas, Austin, Tex.
Brother of Dave Owen, infielder in Chicago Cubs' organization.

Year Club	League	Pos.	G.	AB.	R.	H.	2B.	3B.	HR.	RBI.	B.A.	PO.	A.	E.	F.A.
1982—Lynn	East.	SS	78	241	32	64	9	2	1	27	.266	106	207	9	.972
1983—Salt Lake City	P. C.	SS	72	256	58	68	8	9	1	32	.266	111	212	14	.958
1983—Seattle	Amer.	SS	80	306	36	60	11	3	2	21	.196	122	233	11	.970
Major League Totals			80	306	36	60	11	3	2	21	.196	122	233	11	.970

Selected by Seattle Mariners' organization in 1st round (sixth player selected) of free-agent draft, June 7, 1982.

RICHARD WAYNE OWNBEY
(Rick)

Born October 20, 1957, at Corona, Calif.
Height, 6.03. Weight, 185.
Throws and bats righthanded.
Attended Santa Ana College, Santa Ana, Calif.

Year Club	League	G.	IP.	W.	L.	Pct.	H.	R.	ER.	SO.	BB.	ERA.
1980—Lynchburg	Carolina	12	92	8	1	.889	66	24	19	93	35	1.86
1980—Jackson	Texas	2	13	1	0	1.000	7	3	2	12	7	1.38
1981—Jackson†	Texas	20	133	10	7	.588	110	49	41	125	62	2.77
1982—Tidewater	Int'national	23	150⅓	8	7	.533	107	64	56	122	112	3.35
1982—New York	National	8	50⅓	1	2	.333	44	23	21	28	43	3.75
1983—New York‡	National	10	34⅔	1	3	.250	31	19	18	19	21	4.67
1983—Louisville	Am. Assoc.	16	104	7	5	.583	100	47	42	77	51	3.63
Major League Totals		18	85	2	5	.286	75	42	39	47	64	4.13

Selected by Pittsburgh Pirates' organization in 4th round of free-agent draft, January 9, 1979.
Selected by New York Mets' organization in 13th round of free-agent draft, June 3, 1980.
†On disabled list, May 24 to June 9, 1981.
‡Traded with Pitcher Neil Allen to St. Louis Cardinals for First Baseman Keith Hernandez, June 15, 1983.

THOMAS MARIAN PACIOREK

Name pronounced Pah-CHOR-eck.

(Tom)

Born November 2, 1946, at Detroit, Mich.
Height, 6.04. Weight, 210.
Throws and bats righthanded.
Received bachelor of science degree in education from University of Houston, Houston, Tex.
Brother of Jim Paciorek, outfielder in Milwaukee Brewers' organization;
Mike Paciorek, first baseman in Los Angeles Dodgers'
and Atlanta Braves' organizations, 1973 through 1977;
and John Paciorek, outfielder with Houston Astros, 1963.

Led Pacific Coast League in total bases with 310 and tied for lead in sacrifice flies with 12 in 1972.
Named Minor League Player of the Year by THE SPORTING NEWS, 1972.
Named Pacific Coast League Most Valuable Player, 1972.
Selected by Miami Dolphins in 9th round of 1968 NFL draft.

Year Club	League	Pos.	G.	AB.	R.	H.	2B.	3B.	HR.	RBI.	B.A.	PO.	A.	E.	F.A.
1968—Ogden	Pion.	OF-1B	29	101	25	39	6	3	5	23	.386	45	3	2	.960
1968—Bakersfield	Calif.	OF-1B	38	116	16	32	1	1	0	10	.276	44	1	0	1.000
1969—Bakersfield†	Calif.	OF-3B	91	359	59	114	20	3	15	53	.318	111	44	16	.906
1970—Spokane	P. C.	OF	●146	549	88	179	36	12	17	101	.326	262	5	6	.978
1970—Los Angeles	Nat.	OF	8	9	2	2	1	0	0	0	.222	1	0	0	1.000
1971—Spokane	P. C.	OF-3B	144	564	89	172	31	★14	15	105	.305	240	9	8	.969
1971—Los Angeles	Nat.	OF	2	2	0	1	0	0	0	1	.500	1	0	0	1.000
1972—Albuquerque	P. C.	1B	147	★605	★125	★186	★33	5	★27	107	.307	★1239	80	●13	.990
1972—Los Angeles	Nat.	1B-OF	11	47	4	12	4	0	1	6	.255	53	3	1	.982
1973—Los Angeles	Nat.	OF-1B	96	195	26	51	8	0	5	18	.262	117	3	2	.984
1974—Los Angeles	Nat.	OF-1B	85	175	23	42	8	6	1	24	.240	85	1	5	.945
1975—Los Angeles‡	Nat.	OF	62	145	14	28	8	0	1	5	.193	69	0	2	.972
1976—Atlanta	Nat.	OF-1B-3B	111	324	39	94	10	4	4	36	.290	216	10	3	.987
1977—Atlanta§	Nat.	1B-OF-3B	72	155	20	37	8	0	3	15	.239	248	16	5	.981
1978—Atlanta x	Nat.	1B	5	9	2	3	0	0	0	0	.333	21	0	0	1.000
1978—San Jose	P. C.	OF	16	57	7	16	1	2	3	17	.281	32	1	1	.971
1978—Seattle y	Amer.	OF-1B	70	251	32	75	20	3	4	30	.299	115	5	2	.984
1979—Seattle	Amer.	OF-1B	103	310	38	89	23	4	6	42	.287	237	12	1	.996
1980—Seattle	Amer.	OF-1B	126	418	44	114	19	1	15	59	.273	360	22	5	.987
1981—Seattle z	Amer.	OF	104	405	50	132	28	2	14	66	.326	253	10	7	.974
1982—Chicago ab	Amer.	1B-OF	104	382	49	119	27	4	11	55	.312	835	66	6	.993
1983—Chicago	Amer.	1B-OF	115	420	65	129	32	3	9	63	.307	629	38	1	.999
American League Totals			622	2186	278	658	149	17	59	315	.301	2429	153	22	.992
National League Totals			452	1061	130	270	47	10	15	105	.254	811	33	18	.979
Major League Totals			1074	3247	408	928	196	27	74	420	.286	3240	186	40	.988

Selected by Los Angeles Dodgers' organization in 42nd round of free-agent draft, June 7, 1968.
†On restricted list, April 3 to June 3, 1969.

— 356 —

‡Traded with Outfielder Jimmy Wynn, Second Baseman Lee Lacy and Infielder Jerry Royster to Atlanta Braves for Outfielder Dusty Baker and First Baseman-Third Baseman Ed Goodson, November 17, 1975.

§Released March 30, 1978; re-signed by Atlanta Braves, April 7, 1978.

xReleased, May 23, 1978; signed by Seattle Mariners' organization, May 31, 1978.

yGranted free agency, November 2, 1978; re-signed by Mariners, January 6, 1979.

zTraded to Chicago White Sox for Catcher Jim Essian, Shortstop Todd Cruz and Outfielder Rod Allen, December 11, 1981.

aOn supplemental disabled list, July 27 to August 11, 1982.

bOn disabled list, August 28 to September 17, 1982.

CHAMPIONSHIP SERIES RECORD

Year Club	League	Pos.	G.	AB.	R.	H.	2B.	3B.	HR.	RBI.	B.A.	PO.	A.	E.	F.A.
1974—Los Angeles	Nat.	PH-OF	1	1	0	1	0	0	0	0	1.000	0	0	0	.000
1983—Chicago	Amer.	1B-OF	4	16	1	4	0	0	0	1	.250	30	3	0	1.000
Championship Series Totals			5	17	1	5	0	0	0	1	.294	30	3	0	1.000

WORLD SERIES RECORD

Year Club	League	Pos.	G.	AB.	R.	H.	2B.	3B.	HR.	RBI.	B.A.	PO.	A.	E.	F.A.
1974—Los Angeles	Nat.	PH-PR	3	2	1	1	1	0	0	0	.500	0	0	0	.000

ALL-STAR GAME RECORD

Year League	Pos.	AB.	R.	H.	2B.	3B.	HR.	RBI.	B.A.	PO.	A.	E.	F.A.
1981—American	PH	1	0	1	0	0	0	0	1.000	0	0	0	.000

MITCHELL OTIS PAGE

Born October 15, 1951, at Los Angeles, Calif.
Height, 6.02. Weight, 205.
Throws right and bats lefthanded.
Attended California Poly State University, Pomona, Calif.

Major League stolen bases: 1977 (42), 1978 (23), 1979 (17), 1980 (14), 1981 (2), 1982 (3), 1983 (3). Total—104.

Named American League Rookie Player of the Year by THE SPORTING NEWS, 1977.

Year Club	League	Pos.	G.	AB.	R.	H.	2B.	3B.	HR.	RBI.	B.A.	PO.	A.	E.	F.A.
1973—Charleston............	W. Car.	OF	18	65	11	18	4	2	2	15	.277	31	1	5	.865
1973—Salem†.................	Carol.	OF	6	16	1	2	0	0	0	0	.125	9	0	1	1.000
1974—Salem..................	Carol.	OF	122	422	80	125	15	9	17	75	.296	165	15	12	.938
1975—Shreveport	Texas	OF	122	413	73	120	24	3	●23	★90	.291	191	8	●14	.934
1976—Charleston‡..........	Int.	★1B-OF	126	456	76	134	21	1	22	83	.294	1046	66	★20	.982
1977—Oakland...............	Amer.	OF	145	501	85	154	28	8	21	75	.307	279	11	★14	.954
1978—Oakland§..............	Amer.	OF	147	516	62	147	25	7	17	70	.285	211	4	6	.973
1979—Oakland...............	Amer.	OF	133	478	51	118	11	2	9	42	.247	6	0	0	1.000
1980—Oakland...............	Amer.	DH	110	348	58	85	10	4	17	51	.244	0	0	0	.000
1981—Oakland...............	Amer.	DH	34	92	9	13	1	0	4	13	.141	0	0	0	.000
1981—Tacoma................	P. C.	OF	71	250	46	82	12	2	17	68	.328	11	0	0	1.000
1982—Tacoma................	P. C.	OF	85	295	62	90	18	2	14	59	.305	5	0	0	1.000
1982—Oakland...............	Amer.	DH	31	78	14	20	5	0	4	7	.256	0	0	0	.000
1983—Oakland...............	Amer.	OF	57	80	16	19	3	0	0	1	.238	12	0	0	1.000
Major League Totals....................................			657	2093	295	556	83	21	72	259	.266	508	15	20	.963

Selected by Pittsburgh Pirates' organization in 3rd round of free-agent draft, June 5, 1973.

†On disabled list, July 16 to September 6, 1973.

‡Traded with Pitchers Doc Medich, Dave Giusti, Rick Langford and Doug Bair and Outfielder Tony Armas to Oakland A's for Infielders Tommy Helms and Phil Garner and Pitcher Chris Batton, March 15, 1977.

§On supplemental disabled list, March 25 to April 21, 1978.

KARL DOUGLAS PAGEL

Name pronounced PAY-gul.

Born March 29, 1955, at Madison, Wis.
Height, 6.02. Weight, 185.
Throws and bats lefthanded.
Attended Glendale College, Glendale, Ariz. and University of Texas, Austin, Tex.
Brother of Mike Pagel, quarterback with Baltimore Colts.

Led American Association in total bases with 291 and bases on balls received with 100 in 1979.

Led Texas League in bases on balls received with 88 and batters in strikeouts with 117 in 1977.

Named American Association Most Valuable Player, 1979.

Named Texas League Most Valuable Player, 1977.

Year Club	League	Pos.	G.	AB.	R.	H.	2B.	3B.	HR.	RBI.	B.A.	PO.	A.	E.	F.A.
1976—Midland..................	Texas	OF	15	43	3	8	0	0	1	2	.186	22	5	1	.964
1976—Pompano Beach ..	Fla. St.	OF	41	134	21	34	6	2	2	12	.254	68	4	2	.973
1977—Midland..................	Texas	OF	118	410	88	137	28	6	★28	104	.334	190	9	3	.985
1978—Wichita.................	A. A.	OF-1B	134	462	81	124	27	5	23	86	.268	466	16	14	.972
1978—Chicago	Nat.	PH	2	2	0	0	0	0	0	0	.000	0	0	0	.000
1979—Wichita.................	A. A.	OF-1B	●136	472	96	149	25	0	★39	★123	.316	270	14	4	.986
1979—Chicago†...............	Nat.	PH	1	1	0	0	0	0	0	0	.000	0	0	0	.000
1980—Wichita†§.............	A. A.	1B	56	187	34	50	10	2	11	32	.267	448	37	4	.992
1980—Tacoma................	P. C.	OF-1B	48	163	26	43	9	2	4	26	.264	138	18	3	.981
1981—Charleston............	Int.	1B-OF	114	323	62	88	13	1	20	67	.272	470	38	7	.986
1981—Cleveland..............	Amer.	1B	14	15	3	4	0	2	1	4	.267	28	6	0	1.000
1982—Charleston............	Int.	OF-1B	50	157	39	52	12	1	9	33	.331	211	16	3	.987
1982—Cleveland x	Amer.	1B	23	18	3	3	0	0	0	2	.167	30	2	1	.970

Year	Club	League	Pos.	G.	AB.	R.	H.	2B.	3B.	HR.	RBI.	B.A.	PO.	A.	E.	F.A.
1983—Charleston	Int.		OF-1B	124	381	78	124	12	3	20	82	.325	123	5	5	.962
1983—Cleveland y	Amer.		OF	8	20	1	6	0	0	0	1	.300	0	0	1	.000
National League Totals				3	3	0	0	0	0	0	0	.000	0	0	0	.000
American League Totals				45	53	7	13	0	2	1	7	.245	58	8	2	.971
Major League Totals				48	56	7	13	0	2	1	7	.232	58	8	2	.971

Selected by New York Mets' organization in 6th round of free-agent draft, January 9, 1975.
Selected by St. Louis Cardinals' organization in secondary phase of free-agent draft, June 4, 1975.
Selected by Chicago Cubs' organization in secondary phase of free-agent draft, June 8, 1976.
†On disabled list, September 12 to October 4, 1979.
‡On disabled list, April 24 to May 7, 1980.
§Traded to Cleveland Indians' organization with cash, June 30, 1980; completing deal in which Cleveland Indians traded Catcher-First Baseman Cliff Johnson to Chicago Cubs for two players to be named later, June 17, 1980.
xGranted free agency, October 20, 1982; re-signed by Indians' organization, December 15, 1982.
yReleased, November 21, 1983.

MICHAEL TIMOTHY PAGLIARULO
(Mike)

Born March 15, 1960, at Medford, Mass.
Height, 6.02. Weight, 195.
Throws right and bats left and righthanded.
Attended University of Miami, Coral Gables, Fla.
Son of Charles Pagliarulo, infielder in Chicago Cubs' organization, 1958.

Led Southern League third basemen in total chances with 433 in 1983.
Led New York-Pennsylvania League in intentional bases on balls received with 8 in 1981.
Led New York-Pennsylvania League third basemen in total chances with 214 in 1981.

Year	Club	League	Pos.	G.	AB.	R.	H.	2B.	3B.	HR.	RBI.	B.A.	PO.	A.	E.	F.A.
1981—Oneonta	NYP		3B	72	245	32	53	9	4	2	28	.216	40	★159	15	.930
1982—Greensboro	S. Atl.		3B	123	403	79	113	22	0	22	79	.280	73	★278	27	.929
1983—Nashville	South.		3B	135	450	82	117	19	4	19	80	.260	★98	★315	20	★.954

Selected by New York Yankees' organization in 6th round of free-agent draft, June 8, 1981.

DAVID WILLIAM PALMER JR.

Born October 19, 1957, at Glens Falls, N.Y.
Height, 6.01. Weight, 205.
Throws and bats righthanded.

Tied for Pioneer League lead in home runs allowed with 6 in 1976.

Year	Club	League	G.	IP.	W.	L.	Pct.	H.	R.	ER.	SO.	BB.	ERA.
1976—Lethbridge	Pioneer		13	45	0	5	.000	58	49	36	44	28	7.20
1977—West Palm Beach	Florida St.		25	119	6	8	.429	120	49	38	88	44	2.87
1978—West Palm Beach	Florida St.		7	51	4	2	.667	44	23	11	58	4	1.94
1978—Memphis	Southern		19	130	8	10	.444	107	57	44	78	44	3.05
1978—Montreal	National		5	10	0	1	.000	9	4	3	7	2	2.70
1979—Montreal	National		36	123	10	2	.833	110	41	36	72	30	2.63
1980—Montreal†	National		24	130	8	6	.571	124	53	43	73	30	2.98
1981—West Palm Beach‡	Florida St.		3	11	0	0	.000	9	1	1	7	5	0.82
1981—Memphis	Southern		1	0	0	0	.000	0	1	1	0	1	0.00
1982—Memphis	Southern		9	51⅓	3	2	.600	38	21	20	44	33	3.51
1982—Montreal §	National		13	73⅔	6	4	.600	60	34	26	46	36	3.18
1983—West Palm Beach x	Florida St.						(Did not play)						
Major League Totals			78	336⅔	24	13	.649	303	132	108	198	98	2.89

Selected by Montreal Expos' organization in 21st round of free-agent draft, June 8, 1976.
†On disabled list, July 21 to August 27, 1980.
‡On Montreal disabled list, March 25 to August 9, 1981; included rehabilitation disability assignment to West Palm Beach, May 6 to May 25, 1981.
§On disabled list, August 14 to September 27, 1982.
xOn Montreal disabled list, March 28, 1983; transferred to emergency disabled list, April 25 to September 20, 1983; included rehabilitation disability assignment to West Palm Beach, August 6 to August 26, 1983.

JAMES ALVIN PALMER
(Jim)

Born October 15, 1945, at New York City, N.Y.
Height, 6.03. Weight, 194.
Throws and bats righthanded.
Attended Arizona State University, Tempe, Ariz., and
Towson State College, Towson, Md.

Established American League record for most putouts by pitcher, lifetime (291).
Pitched 8-0 no-hit victory against Oakland A's, August 13, 1969.
Pitched 8-0 no-hit victory against Duluth-Superior, June 19, 1964.
Led American League in shutouts with 10 in 1975 and tied for lead with 5 in 1970.
Led American League pitchers in games started with 40 in 1976 and tied for lead with 39 in 1977.
Tied for American League lead in complete games with 22 in 1977.
Tied for American League lead in balks with 3 in 1970.
Led Northern League in wild pitches with 23 in 1964.
Named American League Pitcher of the Year by THE SPORTING NEWS, 1973, 1975 and 1976.
Won American League Cy Young Memorial Award, 1973, 1975 and 1976.

Named righthanded pitcher on THE SPORTING NEWS American League All-Star Team, 1971, 1973, 1975, 1976 and 1978.

Named pitcher on THE SPORTING NEWS American League All-Star fielding team, 1976 through 1979.

Received reported $60,000 bonus to sign with Baltimore Orioles, 1963.

Year—Club	League	G.	IP.	W.	L.	Pct.	H.	R.	ER.	SO.	BB.	ERA.
1964—Aberdeen	Northern	19	129	11	3	.786	75	42	36	107	★130	2.51
1965—Baltimore	American	27	92	5	4	.556	75	49	38	75	56	3.72
1966—Baltimore	American	30	208	15	10	.600	176	83	80	147	91	3.46
1967—Baltimore	American	9	49	3	1	.750	34	18	16	23	20	2.94
1967—Rochester†	Int'national	2	7	0	0	.000	12	9	9	6	5	11.57
1967—Miami	Florida St.	5	27	1	1	.500	20	6	6	16	10	2.00
1968—Miami	Florida St.	2	8	0	0	.000	4	2	0	5	9	0.00
1968—Rochester	Int'national	2	4	0	0	.000	4	6	6	6	8	13.50
1968—Elmira‡	Eastern	6	25	0	2	.000	18	13	12	26	19	4.32
1969—Baltimore§	American	26	181	16	4	★.800	131	48	47	123	64	2.34
1970—Baltimore	American	39	●305	20	10	.667	263	98	92	199	100	2.71
1971—Baltimore	American	37	282	20	9	.690	231	94	84	184	106	2.68
1972—Baltimore	American	36	274	21	10	.677	219	73	63	184	70	2.07
1973—Baltimore	American	38	296	22	9	.710	225	86	79	153	113	★2.40
1974—Baltimore x	American	26	179	7	12	.368	176	78	65	84	69	3.27
1975—Baltimore	American	39	323	●23	11	.676	253	87	75	193	80	★2.09
1976—Baltimore	American	40	★315	★22	13	.629	255	101	88	159	84	2.51
1977—Baltimore	American	39	★319	●20	11	.645	263	106	103	193	99	2.91
1978—Baltimore	American	38	★296	21	12	.636	246	94	81	138	97	2.46
1979—Baltimore y	American	23	156	10	6	.625	144	66	57	67	43	3.29
1980—Baltimore	American	34	224	16	10	.615	238	108	99	109	74	3.98
1981—Baltimore	American	22	127	7	8	.467	117	60	53	35	46	3.76
1982—Baltimore	American	36	227	15	5	●.750	195	85	79	103	63	3.13
1983—Baltimore z	American	14	76⅔	5	4	.556	86	42	36	34	19	4.23
1983—Hagerstown	Carolina	2	13	2	0	1.000	13	6	5	11	2	3.46
Major League Totals		553	3929⅔	268	149	.643	3327	1376	1235	2208	1294	2.83

Signed as free agent by Baltimore Orioles' organization, August 16, 1963.

†On disabled list, from July 3 to August 8, 1967.

‡On Baltimore disabled list, August 28, 1968 through remainder of season.

§On disabled list, June 29 to August 9, 1969.

xOn disabled list, June 20 to August 13, 1974.

yOn disabled list, July 16 to August 11, 1979.

zOn disabled list, April 29 to June 14 and June 30 to August 21, 1983; included rehabilitation disability assignment to Hagerstown, August 6 to August 21, 1983.

CHAMPIONSHIP SERIES RECORD

Established Championship Series records for most Series played, one club (7); most strikeouts, total Series (46); most complete games, total Series (5).

Tied Championship Series records for most series pitched (6); most games won, total Series (4); most bases on balls, five-game Series (8), 1973.

Established American League Championship Series records for most strikeouts, five-game Series (15), 1973; most strikeouts, three-game Series (12), 1970; most bases on balls, total Series (19).

Year—Club	League	G.	IP.	W.	L.	Pct.	H.	R.	ER.	SO.	BB.	ERA.
1969—Baltimore	American	1	9	1	0	1.000	10	2	2	4	2	2.00
1970—Baltimore	American	1	9	1	0	1.000	7	1	1	12	3	1.00
1971—Baltimore	American	1	9	1	0	1.000	7	3	3	8	3	3.00
1973—Baltimore	American	3	14⅔	1	0	1.000	11	3	3	15	8	1.84
1974—Baltimore	American	1	9	0	1	.000	4	1	1	4	1	1.00
1979—Baltimore	American	1	9	0	0	.000	7	3	3	3	2	3.00
Championship Series Totals		8	59⅔	4	1	.800	46	13	13	46	19	1.96

WORLD SERIES RECORD

Established World Series record for most bases on balls with bases loaded, game (2), October 11, 1971.

Youngest pitcher to win complete World Series shutout game (20 years, 11 months), October 6, 1966.

Year—Club	League	G.	IP.	W.	L.	Pct.	H.	R.	ER.	SO.	BB.	ERA.
1966—Baltimore	American	1	9	1	0	1.000	4	0	0	6	3	0.00
1969—Baltimore	American	1	6	0	1	.000	5	4	4	5	4	6.00
1970—Baltimore	American	2	15⅔	1	0	1.000	11	8	8	9	9	4.60
1971—Baltimore	American	2	17	1	0	1.000	15	5	5	15	9	2.65
1979—Baltimore	American	2	15	0	1	.000	18	6	6	8	5	3.60
1983—Baltimore	American	1	2	1	0	1.000	2	0	0	1	1	0.00
World Series Totals		9	64⅔	4	2	.667	55	23	23	44	31	3.20

ALL-STAR GAME RECORD

Established All-Star Game records for most bases on balls, total games (7); most home runs allowed, game (3), July 19, 1977.

Tied All-Star Game record for most home runs allowed, inning (2), July 19, 1977 (first inning).

Year—League	IP.	W.	L.	Pct.	H.	R.	ER.	SO.	BB.	ERA.
1970—American	3	0	0	.000	1	0	0	3	1	0.00
1971—American	2	0	0	.000	1	0	0	2	0	0.00
1972—American	3	0	0	.000	1	0	0	2	1	0.00
1977—American	2	0	1	.000	5	5	5	3	1	22.50
1978—American	2⅔	0	0	.000	3	3	3	4	4	10.11
All-Star Game Totals	12⅔	0	1	.000	11	8	8	14	7	5.68

Member of American League All-Star Team for 1975 game; did not play.

ALBERTO JUDAS PARDO
(Al)

Born September 8, 1962, at Oviedo, Spain.
Height, 6.02. Weight, 187.
Throws right and bats left and righthanded.

Year	Club	League	Pos.	G.	AB.	R.	H.	2B.	3B.	HR.	RBI.	B.A.	PO.	A.	E.	F.A.
1980—Bluefield	Appal.	C-1B	48	151	26	52	6	2	3	23	.344	66	8	0	1.000
1981—Miami	Fla. St.	C	91	291	25	63	9	3	3	32	.216	396	41	6	.987
1981—Hagerstown	Carol.	C	21	76	11	24	3	1	1	7	.316	37	7	2	.957
1982—Hagerstown	Carol.	C-1B-OF	130	492	76	142	24	4	17	86	.289	685	74	11	.986
1983—Rochester	Int.	C	69	220	25	56	11	2	1	31	.255	223	18	9	.964
1983—Charlotte	South.	C	37	141	20	44	11	3	4	19	.312	129	18	4	.974

Selected by Baltimore Orioles' organization in 2nd round of free-agent draft, June 3, 1980.

KELLY JAY PARIS

Born October 17, 1957, at Encino, Calif.
Height, 6.00. Weight, 175.
Throws and bats righthanded.
Brother of Brett Paris, infielder in San Francisco Giants' and
St. Louis Cardinals' organizations, 1975 and 1976.

Led Appalachian League in sacrifice flies with 7 in 1977.
Led Florida State League third basemen in double plays with 24 and tied for lead in errors with 29 in 1979.

Year	Club	League	Pos.	G.	AB.	R.	H.	2B.	3B.	HR.	RBI.	B.A.	PO.	A.	E.	F.A.
1975—Sarasota Cards	Gulf C.	SS	34	123	14	29	2	0	2	13	.236	59	92	14	.915
1976—Johnson City†	Appal.	1B	●70	247	40	68	7	3	5	30	.275	621	43	7	.990
1977—St. Petersburg‡	Fla. St.	1B-3B	44	124	14	22	3	0	0	9	.177	269	22	3	.990
1977—Johnson City‡	Appal.	1B-3B	51	169	32	53	8	1	2	28	.314	355	37	5	.987
1978—St. Petersburg	Fla. St.	1B	42	155	14	32	6	0	1	12	.206	319	23	5	.986
1978—Gastonia	W. Car.	1B-3B	79	297	48	75	9	3	2	20	.253	593	49	12	.982
1979—St. Petersburg	Fla. St.	3B-1B	118	388	52	110	15	3	2	53	.284	291	229	30	.945
1980—Arkansas	Texas	SS	116	399	63	120	28	3	4	49	.301	181	349	38	.933
1981—Springfield§	A. A.	SS-3B	90	292	38	78	10	1	6	31	.267	119	237	36	.908
1982—Louisville	A. A.	SS-3B-2B	129	482	71	158	32	5	11	83	.328	208	364	29	.952
1982—St. Louis x	Nat.	3B-2B	12	29	1	3	0	0	0	1	.103	9	25	4	.895
1983—Cincinnati	Nat.	3-2-S-1	56	120	13	30	6	0	0	7	.250	60	62	6	.953
1983—Indianapolis y	A. A.	SS-2B-3B	8	35	9	11	1	0	2	9	.314	10	26	0	1.000
Major League Totals			68	149	14	33	6	0	0	8	.221	69	87	10	.940

Selected by St. Louis Cardinals' organization in 2nd round of free-agent draft, June 4, 1975.
†On temporarily inactive list, April 16 to May 7, 1976.
‡Batted as switchhitter.
§On disabled list, July 25, 1981 through remainder of season.
xTraded to Cincinnati Reds' organization for Pitcher James Strichek, March 31, 1983.
ySold to Chicago White Sox, November 28, 1983.

ZACARIAS PORFIRIO PARIS

Name pronounced Puh-REES.

(Zac)

Born September 9, 1957, at San Pedro de Macoris, D.R.
Height, 6.02. Weight, 185.
Throws and bats righthanded.
Attended Universidad Central del Este, San Pedro de Macoris, D.R.

Led Gulf Coast League in shutouts with 2 in 1979.
Tied for Southern League lead in games started by pitchers with 29 in 1981.
Tied for Florida State League lead in hit batsmen with 10 in 1980.

Year	Club	League	G.	IP.	W.	L.	Pct.	H.	R.	ER.	SO.	BB.	ERA.
1978—Sarasota Astros	Gulf Coast	1	1	0	0	.000	0	0	0	0	0	0.00
1979—Sarasota Astros	Gulf Coast	10	65	6	2	.750	51	27	19	38	24	2.63
1980—Daytona Beach	Florida St.	23	154	14	4	.778	119	57	44	119	66	2.57
1981—Columbus	Southern	29	190	11	9	.550	184	105	★92	166	76	4.36
1982—Tucson	P. Coast	28	165⅔	6	8	.429	209	131	★114	85	104	6.19
1983—Columbus	Southern	23	107⅓	7	6	.538	106	78	69	63	72	5.79
1983—Daytona Beach	Florida St.	8	44⅔	5	3	.625	46	29	20	29	18	4.03

Signed as free agent by Houston Astros' organization, December 30, 1977.

DAVID GENE PARKER
(Dave)

Born June 9, 1951, at Jackson, Miss.
Height, 6.05. Weight, 230.
Throws right and bats lefthanded.

Led National League in total bases with 340 in 1978.
Led National League in slugging percentage with .541 in 1975 and .585 in 1978.
Led National League in intentional bases on balls received with 23 in 1978.
Led National League outfielders in total chances with 430 and double plays with 9 in 1977.
Tied for National League lead in sacrifice flies with 9 in 1979.

Led Carolina League in total bases with 270 and stolen bases with 38 in 1972.
Tied for Gulf Coast League lead in total bases with 107 in 1970.
Named National League Player of the Year by THE SPORTING NEWS, 1978.
Named National League Most Valuable Player by Baseball Writers' Association of America, 1978.
Named outfielder on THE SPORTING NEWS National League All-Star Team, 1975, 1977 and 1978.
Named outfielder on THE SPORTING NEWS National League All-Star fielding team, 1977 through 1979.
Named Carolina League Most Valuable Player, 1972.

Year	Club	League	Pos.	G.	AB.	R.	H.	2B.	3B.	HR.	RBI.	B.A.	PO.	A.	E.	F.A.
1970—Bradenton Pir.	Gulf C.	●OF-P	61	239	34	75	8	3	●6	41	.314	92	11	●8	.928
1971—Waterbury	East.	OF	30	114	10	26	4	1	0	7	.228	43	5	6	.889
1971—Monroe	W. Car.	OF	71	268	49	96	16	4	11	48	.358	104	8	10	.918
1972—Salem	Carol.	OF	135	*523	*91	*162	*30	6	22	*101	*.310	*250	*20	*20	.931
1973—Charleston	Int.	OF	84	309	44	98	20	7	9	57	.317	144	11	7	.957
1973—Pittsburgh†	Nat.	OF	54	139	17	40	9	1	4	14	.288	77	3	3	.964
1974—Pittsburgh†	Nat.	OF-1B	73	220	27	62	10	3	4	29	.282	154	8	4	.976
1975—Pittsburgh	Nat.	OF	148	558	75	172	35	10	25	101	.308	311	7	9	.972
1976—Pittsburgh	Nat.	OF	138	537	82	168	28	10	13	90	.313	294	13	*14	.956
1977—Pittsburgh	Nat.	*OF-2B	159	637	107	*215	*44	8	21	88	*.338	*389	*26	*15	.965
1978—Pittsburgh‡	Nat.	OF	148	581	102	194	32	12	30	117	*.334	302	12	*13	.960
1979—Pittsburgh	Nat.	OF	158	622	109	193	45	7	25	94	.310	34	15	*15	.960
1980—Pittsburgh	Nat.	OF	139	518	71	153	31	1	17	79	.295	235	14	9	.965
1981—Pittsburgh§	Nat.	OF	67	240	29	62	14	3	9	48	.258	110	1	7	.941
1982—Pittsburgh x	Nat.	OF	73	244	41	66	19	3	6	29	.270	108	2	5	.957
1983—Pittsburgh y	Nat.	OF	144	552	68	154	29	4	12	69	.279	282	3	8	.973
Major League Totals				1301	4848	728	1479	296	62	166	.758	.305	2603	103	102	.964

Selected by Pittsburgh Pirates' organization in 14th round of free-agent draft, June 4, 1970.
†On disabled list, June 7 to June 28 and July 5 to July 31, 1974.
‡On supplemental disabled list, July 1 to July 16, 1978.
§On supplemental disabled list, May 14 to May 29, 1981.
xOn supplemental disabled list, May 12 to June 7 and July 29 to September 7, 1982.
yGranted free agency, November 7, 1983; signed by Cincinnati Reds, December 7, 1983.

CHAMPIONSHIP SERIES RECORD

Year	Club	League	Pos.	G.	AB.	R.	H.	2B.	3B.	HR.	RBI.	B.A.	PO.	A.	E.	F.A.
1974—Pittsburgh	Nat.	OF-PH	3	8	0	1	0	0	0	0	.125	4	1	0	1.000
1975—Pittsburgh	Nat.	OF	3	10	2	0	0	0	0	0	.000	13	1	0	1.000
1979—Pittsburgh	Nat.	OF	3	12	2	4	0	0	0	2	.333	9	0	0	1.000
Championship Series Totals				9	30	4	5	0	0	0	2	.167	26	2	0	1.000

WORLD SERIES RECORD

Year	Club	League	Pos.	G.	AB.	R.	H.	2B.	3B.	HR.	RBI.	B.A.	PO.	A.	E.	F.A.
1979—Pittsburgh	Nat.	OF	7	29	2	10	3	0	0	4	.345	13	1	1	.933

ALL-STAR GAME RECORD

Established All-Star Game record for most assists by outfielder, game (2), July 17, 1979.

Year	League	Pos.	AB.	R.	H.	2B.	3B.	HR.	RBI.	B.A.	PO.	A.	E.	F.A.
1977—National		OF	3	1	1	0	0	0	0	.333	2	0	0	1.000
1979—National		OF	3	0	1	0	0	0	1	.333	0	2	0	1.000
1980—National		OF	2	0	0	0	0	0	0	.000	0	0	0	.000
1981—National		OF	3	1	1	0	0	1	1	.333	1	0	0	1.000
All-Star Game Totals			11	2	3	0	0	1	2	.273	3	2	0	1.000

PITCHING RECORD

Year	Club	League	G.	IP.	W.	L.	Pct.	H.	R.	ER.	SO.	BB.	ERA.
1970—Bradenton Pirates		Gulf Coast	1	4	0	0	.000	7	2	2	2	1	4.50

LANCE MICHAEL PARRISH

Born June 15, 1956, at McKeesport, Pa.
Height, 6.03. Weight, 210.
Throws and bats righthanded.

Established American League record for most home runs by catcher, season (32), 1982.
Led American League in sacrifice flies with 13 in 1983.
Led American League catchers in total chances with 772 in 1983.
Led American League in passed balls with 21 in 1979.
Tied for American League lead in passed balls with 17 in 1980.
Led Appalachian League in strikeouts with 92 in 1974.
Led American Association in double plays with 10 and passed balls with 21 in 1977.
Led Southern League in passed balls with 22 in 1976.
Led Florida State League catchers in double plays with 8 and passed balls with 31 in 1975.
Named catcher on THE SPORTING NEWS American League All-Star Team, 1982.
Named catcher on THE SPORTING NEWS American League Silver Slugger team, 1980, 1982, and 1983.
Named catcher on THE SPORTING NEWS American League All-Star fielding team, 1983.

Year	Club	League	Pos.	G.	AB.	R.	H.	2B.	3B.	HR.	RBI.	B.A.	PO.	A.	E.	F.A.
1974—Bristol	Appal.	3B-OF	68	253	45	54	11	1	11	46	.213	36	83	22	.844
1975—Lakeland	Fla. St.	C	100	341	30	75	15	2	5	37	.220	460	50	7	.986
1976—Montgomery	South.	C	107	340	46	75	9	2	14	55	.221	*600	*79	11	*.984
1977—Evansville	A. A.	C	115	416	74	116	21	2	25	90	.279	*722	*82	11	.987
1977—Detroit	Amer.	C	12	46	10	9	2	0	3	7	.196	76	6	0	1.000
1978—Detroit	Amer.	C	85	288	37	63	11	3	14	41	.219	353	39	5	.987

Year Club	League	Pos.	G.	AB.	R.	H.	2B.	3B.	HR.	RBI.	B.A.	PO.	A.	E.	F.A.
1979—Detroit	Amer.	C	143	493	65	136	26	3	19	65	.276	707	★79	9	.989
1980—Detroit	Amer.	C-1B-OF	144	553	79	158	34	6	24	82	.286	607	67	7	.990
1981—Detroit	Amer.	C	96	348	39	85	18	2	10	46	.244	407	40	3	.993
1982—Detroit	Amer.	C-OF	133	486	75	138	19	2	32	87	.284	627	76	8	.989
1983—Detroit	Amer.	C	155	605	80	163	42	3	27	114	.269	695	73	4	.995
Major League Totals			768	2819	385	752	152	19	129	442	.267	3472	380	36	.991

Selected by Detroit Tigers' organization in 1st round (16th player selected) of free-agent draft, June 5, 1974.

ALL-STAR GAME RECORD

Established All-Star Game record for most assists by catcher, game (3), July 13, 1982.

Year League	Pos.	AB.	R.	H.	2B.	3B.	HR.	RBI.	B.A.	PO.	A.	E.	F.A.
1980—American	C	1	0	0	0	0	0	0	.000	0	0	0	.000
1982—American	C	2	0	1	1	0	0	0	.500	2	3	0	1.000
1983—American	C	2	0	0	0	0	0	0	.000	1	0	0	1.000
All-Star Game Totals		5	0	1	1	0	0	0	.200	3	3	0	1.000

LARRY ALTON PARRISH

Born November 10, 1953, at Winter Haven, Fla.
Height, 6.03. Weight, 215.
Throws and bats righthanded.
Attended Seminole Community College, Sanford, Fla.

Tied major league records for most home runs, bases filled, month (3), July, 1982; most home runs, bases filled, week (3), July 4 through 10 (first game), 1982.
Hit three home runs in a game, May 29, 1977, July 30, 1978 and April 25, 1980.
Tied for National League lead in double plays by third basemen with 35 in 1976.
Led Florida State League in sacrifice flies with 9 in 1973.
Led Eastern League third basemen in double plays with 32 in 1974.
Led Florida State League third basemen in putouts with 95 and assists with 285 in 1973.
Named Florida State League Most Valuable Player, 1973.

Year Club	League	Pos.	G.	AB.	R.	H.	2B.	3B.	HR.	RBI.	B.A.	PO.	A.	E.	F.A.
1972—W. Palm B'ch	Fla. St.	OF	2	4	0	1	0	0	0	0	.250	2	0	0	1.000
1972—Jamestown	NYP	OF	62	223	32	58	4	3	4	28	.260	69	3	3	.960
1973—W. Palm B'ch	Fla. St.	★3B-SS	138	481	82	141	14	6	16	33	.293	100	★292	32	★.925
1974—Quebec City	East.	3B	119	437	61	124	14	2	13	77	.284	★108	●277	●31	.925
1974—Montreal	Nat.	3B	25	69	9	14	5	0	4	.203	20	51	1	.986
1975—Montreal	Nat.	3B-SS-2B	145	532	50	146	32	5	10	65	.274	105	291	35	.919
1976—Montreal	Nat.	3B	154	543	65	126	28	5	11	61	.232	122	310	25	.945
1977—Montreal	Nat.	3B	123	402	50	99	19	2	11	46	.246	81	225	21	.936
1978—Montreal	Nat.	3B	144	520	68	144	39	4	15	70	.277	122	288	23	.947
1979—Montreal	Nat.	3B	153	544	83	167	39	2	30	82	.307	119	290	23	.947
1980—Montreal†	Nat.	3B	126	452	55	115	27	3	15	72	.254	106	231	18	.949
1981—Montreal‡	Nat.	3B	97	349	41	85	19	3	8	44	.244	★91	141	16	.935
1982—Texas	Amer.	OF-3B	128	440	59	116	15	0	17	62	.264	190	12	8	.962
1983—Texas	Amer.	OF	145	555	76	151	27	4	26	88	.272	215	11	9	.962
National League Totals			967	3411	421	896	208	24	100	444	.263	866	1827	162	.943
American League Totals			273	995	135	267	42	4	43	150	.268	405	23	17	.962
Major League Totals			1240	4406	556	1163	250	28	143	594	.264	1271	1850	179	.946

Signed as free agent by Montreal Expos' organization, May 21, 1972.
†On supplemental disabled list, June 2 to June 30, 1980.
‡Traded with First Baseman Dave Hostetler to Texas Rangers for First Baseman-Outfielder Al Oliver, March 31, 1982.

DIVISION SERIES RECORD

Year Club	League	Pos.	G.	AB.	R.	H.	2B.	3B.	HR.	RBI.	B.A.	PO.	A.	E.	F.A.
1981—Montreal	Nat.	3B	5	20	3	3	1	0	0	1	.150	7	6	0	1.000

CHAMPIONSHIP SERIES RECORD

Year Club	League	Pos.	G.	AB.	R.	H.	2B.	3B.	HR.	RBI.	B.A.	PO.	A.	E.	F.A.
1981—Montreal	Nat.	3B	5	19	2	5	2	0	0	2	.263	3	13	1	.941

ALL-STAR GAME RECORD

Year League	Pos.	AB.	R.	H.	2B.	3B.	HR.	RBI.	B.A.	PO.	A.	E.	F.A.
1979—National	3B	0	0	0	0	0	0	0	.000	0	0	0	.000

CASEY ROBERT PARSONS

Born April 14, 1954, at Wenatchee, Wash.
Height, 6.00. Weight, 185.
Throws right and bats lefthanded.
Received bachelor of arts degree in marketing from Gonzaga University, Spokane, Wash. in 1976.
Relative of Charlie Gehringer, Hall of Fame second baseman with Detroit Tigers, 1924 through 1942.

Year Club	League	Pos.	G.	AB.	R.	H.	2B.	3B.	HR.	RBI.	B.A.	PO.	A.	E.	F.A.
1976—Great Falls	Pion.	OF	19	77	23	26	5	0	0	14	.338	50	3	1	.981
1976—Fresno	Calif.	OF	42	167	30	54	6	2	0	10	.323	56	4	2	.968
1977—Waterbury	East.	OF	●140	544	80	162	22	★12	5	75	.298	232	12	10	.961
1978—Phoenix	P. C.	OF	135	489	83	124	15	8	1	34	.254	225	7	●12	.951

Year Club	League	Pos.	G.	AB.	R.	H.	2B.	3B.	HR.	RBI.	B.A.	PO.	A.	E.	F.A.
1979—Phoenix	P. C.	OF	142	●566	99	175	35	★16	5	63	.309	232	12	3	.988
1980—Phoe.†-Spokane	P. C.	OF-1B	131	476	62	134	19	11	4	61	.282	186	15	3	.985
1981—Spokane	P. C.	OF	41	149	23	44	11	1	2	13	.295	76	2	0	1.000
1981—Seattle	Amer.	OF-1B	36	22	6	5	1	0	1	5	.227	22	2	0	1.000
1982—Salt Lake City‡§	P. C.	OF-1B	96	323	47	92	11	3	5	35	.285	250	18	9	.968
1983—Denver	A. A.	OF	134	520	89	156	27	7	20	95	.300	248	12	8	.970
1983—Chicago	Amer.	OF	8	5	1	1	0	0	0	0	.200	3	0	0	1.000
Major League Totals			44	27	7	6	1	0	1	5	.222	25	2	0	1.000

Signed as free agent by San Francisco Giants' organization, June 21,1976.
†Sold to Seattle Mariners' organization, June 16, 1980.
‡On disabled list, June 7 to June 29, 1982.
§Granted free agency, October 22, 1982; signed by Chicago White Sox, November 10, 1982.

PITCHING RECORD

Year Club	League	G.	IP.	W.	L.	Pct.	H.	R.	ER.	SO.	BB.	ERA.
1982—Salt Lake City	P. Coast	1	1⅔	0	0	.000	3	2	2	1	1	10.80

LARRY JOHN PASHNICK

Born April 25, 1956, at Lincoln Park, Mich.
Height, 6.03. Weight, 205.
Throws and bats righthanded.
Received bachelor of science degree in medical technology
from Michigan State University, East Lansing, Mich. in 1979.

Pitched 1-0 no-hit victory against Iowa, August 19, 1981.
Tied for American Association lead in shutouts with 4 in 1981.
Tied for Southern League lead in complete games with 12 in 1980.
Tied for Florida State League lead in balks with 5 in 1979.

Year Club	League	G.	IP.	W.	L.	Pct.	H.	R.	ER.	SO.	BB.	ERA.
1979—Lakeland	Florida St.	28	149	8	9	.471	146	72	58	70	67	3.50
1980—Montgomery	Southern	21	161	13	4	★.765	143	63	53	79	51	2.96
1980—Evansville	Am. Assoc.	6	38	2	2	.500	44	24	21	13	12	4.97
1981—Evansville	Am. Assoc.	25	165	9	10	.474	154	66	53	64	49	★2.89
1982—Detroit	American	28	94⅓	4	4	.500	110	46	42	19	25	4.01
1982—Evansville	Am. Assoc.	3	21½	1	1	.500	21	13	9	9	9	3.80
1983—Evansville	Am. Assoc.	23	50⅔	4	1	.800	42	19	16	36	16	2.84
1983—Detroit†	American	12	37⅔	1	3	.250	48	27	22	17	18	5.26
Major League Totals		40	132	5	7	.417	158	73	64	36	43	4.36

Signed as free agent by Detroit Tigers' organization, January 21, 1979.
†Traded to Minnesota Twins for Outfielder Rusty Kuntz, December 5, 1983.

DANIEL ANTHONY PASQUA

(Dan)

Born October 17, 1961, at Harrington Park, N.J.
Height, 6.00. Weight, 205.
Throws and bats lefthanded.
Attended William Paterson College, Wayne, N.J.

Named Appalachian League Player of the Year, 1983.

Year Club	League	Pos.	G.	AB.	R.	H.	2B.	3B.	HR.	RBI.	B.A.	PO.	A.	E.	F.A.
1982—Paintsville	Appal.	OF	60	239	43	72	10	2	16	●63	.301	114	4	4	.967
1982—Oneonta	NYP	OF	4	17	3	5	1	0	2	4	.294	2	1	1	.750
1983—Ft. Lauderdale	Fla. St.	OF	131	451	83	123	25	10	19	84	.273	213	8	5	.978

Selected by New York Yankees' organization in 3rd round of free-agent draft, June 7, 1982.

FRANK ENRICO PASTORE

Name pronounced Pass-TORR-ee.

Born August 21, 1957, at Alhambra, Calif.
Height, 6.03. Weight, 210.
Throws and bats righthanded.
Attended Cal Poly Pomona State University, Pomona, Calif.; and Stanford University, Palo Alto, Calif.

Year Club	League	G.	IP.	W.	L.	Pct.	H.	R.	ER.	SO.	BB.	ERA.
1975—Billings	Pioneer	15	88	5	●7	.417	89	47	25	69	27	2.56
1976—Tampa	Florida St.	21	107	5	7	.417	101	50	37	54	34	3.11
1977—Tampa	Florida St.	14	95	4	5	.444	78	31	24	36	22	2.27
1977—Three Rivers	Eastern	15	94	6	6	.500	98	43	38	51	32	3.64
1978—Indianapolis	Am. Assoc.	4	12	0	2	.000	24	15	9	8	5	6.75
1978—Nashville†	Southern	22	129	6	8	.429	106	58	50	120	46	3.49
1979—Cincinnati	National	30	95	6	7	.462	102	47	45	63	23	4.26
1979—Indianapolis	Am. Assoc.	10	68	7	2	.778	51	21	21	69	17	2.78
1980—Cincinnati‡	National	27	185	13	7	.650	161	72	67	110	42	3.26
1981—Cincinnati	National	22	132	4	9	.308	125	73	59	81	35	4.02
1982—Cincinnati§	National	31	188⅓	8	13	.381	210	86	83	94	57	3.97
1983—Cincinnati	National	36	184⅓	9	12	.429	207	104	100	93	64	4.88
Major League Totals		146	784⅔	40	48	.455	805	382	354	441	221	4.06

Selected by Cincinnati Reds' organization in 2nd round of free-agent draft, June 4, 1975.
†On disabled list, August 24 to August 31, 1978.
‡On disabled list, July 27 to August 22, 1980.
§On disabled list, June 24 to July 19, 1982.

CHAMPIONSHIP SERIES RECORD

Year Club	League	G.	IP.	W.	L.	Pct.	H.	R.	ER.	SO.	BB.	ERA.
1979—Cincinnati	National	1	7	0	0	.000	7	2	2	1	3	2.57

CLIFFORD SCOTT PASTORNICKY
(Cliff)

Born November 18, 1958, at Seattle, Wash.
Height, 5.10. Weight, 170.
Throws and bats righthanded.
Attended Brigham Young University, Provo, Utah.
Led South Atlantic League in total bases with 269 in 1982.

Year Club	League	Pos.	G.	AB.	R.	H.	2B.	3B.	HR.	RBI.	B.A.	PO.	A.	E.	F.A.
1980—Sarasota Blue	Gulf C.	SS	62	206	28	57	5	6	0	32	.277	83	183	24	.917
1981—Charleston†	S. Atl.	SS-3B-2B	80	296	36	64	15	2	5	36	.216	145	234	14	.964
1982—Charleston	S. Atl.	3B	135	*530	98	*182	*36	6	13	92	*.343	*133	258	27	*.935
1983—Omaha	A. A.	*3B-SS	108	404	51	109	23	2	11	52	.270	62	198	*27	.906
1983—Kansas City	Amer.	3B	9	32	4	4	0	0	2	5	.125	5	21	2	.929
Major League Totals			9	32	4	4	0	0	2	5	.125	5	21	2	.929

Selected by Kansas City Royals' organization in 8th round of free-agent draft, June 3, 1980.
†On disabled list, May 1 to June 3, 1981.

REGINALD ALLEN PATTERSON
(Reggie)

Born November 7, 1958, at Birmingham, Ala.
Height, 6.04. Weight, 180.
Throws right and bats lefthanded.
Led American Association in games started by pitchers with 28 and tied for lead in shutouts with 2 in 1983.
Led Pacific Coast League pitchers in games started with 29 in 1982.

Year Club	League	G.	IP.	W.	L.	Pct.	H.	R.	ER.	SO.	BB.	ERA.
1979—Niagara Falls	NYP	10	55	5	1	.833	43	17	14	44	21	2.29
1979—Knoxville	Southern	4	25	2	1	.667	22	12	9	7	15	3.24
1980—Glens Falls	Eastern	13	89	6	3	.667	80	46	37	52	45	3.74
1980—Iowa	Am. Assoc.	13	71	4	8	.333	84	54	50	56	28	6.34
1981—Edmonton	P. Coast	20	136	10	8	.556	111	63	50	80	71	3.31
1981—Chicago	American	6	7	0	1	.000	14	11	11	2	6	14.14
1981—Appleton	Midwest	1	5	0	0	.000	2	1	1	2	0	1.80
1982—Edmonton†	P. Coast	29	186⅔	14	10	.583	212	125	101	109	89	4.87
1983—Iowa	Am. Assoc.	28	172	10	10	.500	201	*116	100	114	84	5.23
1983—Chicago	National	5	18⅔	1	2	.333	17	12	10	10	6	4.82
American League Totals		6	7	0	1	.000	14	11	11	2	6	14.14
National League Totals		5	18⅔	1	2	.333	17	12	10	10	6	4.82
Major League Totals		11	25⅔	1	3	.250	31	23	21	12	12	7.36

Signed as free agent by Chicago White Sox' organization, June 20, 1979.
†Traded to Chicago Cubs' organization for Infielder-Outfielder Tye Waller, December 10, 1982.

MICHAEL EARL PAYNE
(Mike)

Born November 15, 1961, at Woodsocket, R.I.
Height, 5.11. Weight, 165.
Throws and bats righthanded.

Year Club	League	G.	IP.	W.	L.	Pct.	H.	R.	ER.	SO.	BB.	ERA.
1979—Kingsport	Ap'lachian	7	30	2	3	.400	30	23	13	14	17	3.90
1980—Anderson†	S. Atlantic	21	126	12	6	.667	129	76	61	70	73	4.36
1981—Durham	Carolina	29	105	6	6	.500	107	76	61	84	65	5.23
1982—Durham	Carolina	21	126	8	7	.533	127	66	57	88	55	4.07
1983—Savannah	Southern	25	145	10	7	.588	144	71	63	97	80	3.91

Selected by Atlanta Braves' organization in 6th round of free-agent draft, June 5, 1979.
†On disabled list, August 21, 1980 through remainder of season.

ADALBERTO PENA (RIVERA)
(Bert)

Born July 11, 1959, at Santurce, Puerto Rico.
Height, 5.11. Weight, 165.
Throws right and bats left and righthanded.
Led Southern League shortstops in double plays with 78 in 1980.
Led Florida State League shortstops in double plays with 66 in 1977.

Year Club	League	Pos.	G.	AB.	R.	H.	2B.	3B.	HR.	RBI.	B.A.	PO.	A.	E.	F.A.
1977—Cocoa	Fla. St.	SS	93	285	28	65	9	2	1	21	.228	161	279	29	.938
1978—Columbus	South.	SS	141	410	24	66	10	0	2	24	.161	★229	352	39	.937
1979—Daytona Beach	Fla. St.	SS	113	341	26	66	11	1	1	23	.194	152	290	★45	.908
1980—Columbus	South.	SS	124	386	47	97	20	0	9	49	.251	193	363	26	.955
1981—Tucson	P. C.	SS	135	468	69	122	24	12	7	66	.261	224	464	39	.946
1981—Houston	Nat.	SS	4	2	0	1	0	0	0	0	.500	1	1	0	1.000
1982—Tucson†	P. C.	SS-OF	97	362	53	78	17	5	5	33	.215	182	299	32	.938
1983—Tucson	P. C.	SS	112	382	45	94	21	3	5	63	.246	166	290	19	★.960
1983—Houston	Nat.	SS	4	8	0	1	0	0	0	0	.125	1	7	0	1.000
Major League Totals			8	10	0	2	0	0	0	0	.200	2	8	0	1.000

Signed as free agent by Houston Astros' organization, May 2, 1977.
†On disabled list, August 13 to September 1, 1982.

ALEJANDRO PENA (VASQUEZ)

Born June 25, 1959, at Cambiaso, Dominican Republic.
Height, 6.02. Weight, 200.
Throws and bats righthanded.

Led Pacific Coast League in saves with 22 in 1981.

Year Club	League	G.	IP.	W.	L.	Pct.	H.	R.	ER.	SO.	BB.	ERA.
1979—Clinton	Midwest	21	71	3	3	.500	53	39	33	57	44	4.18
1980—Vero Beach	Florida St.	35	73	10	3	.769	57	32	26	46	41	3.21
1981—Albuquerque	P. Coast	38	56	2	5	.286	36	12	10	40	21	1.61
1981—Los Angeles	National	14	25	1	1	.500	18	8	8	14	11	2.88
1982—Los Angeles	National	29	35⅔	0	2	.000	37	24	19	20	21	4.79
1982—Albuquerque	P. Coast	16	28⅔	1	1	.500	37	18	17	27	10	5.34
1983—Los Angeles	National	34	177	12	9	.571	152	67	54	120	51	2.75
Major League Totals		77	237⅔	13	12	.520	207	99	81	154	83	3.07

Signed as free agent by Los Angeles Dodgers' organization, September 10, 1978.

CHAMPIONSHIP SERIES RECORD

Year Club	League	G.	IP.	W.	L.	Pct.	H.	R.	ER.	SO.	BB.	ERA.
1981—Los Angeles	National	2	2⅓	0	0	.000	1	0	0	0	0	0.00
1983—Los Angeles	National	1	2⅔	0	0	.000	4	2	2	3	1	6.75
Championship Series Totals		3	5	0	0	.000	5	2	2	3	1	3.60

ANTONIO FRANCISCO PENA (PADILLA)
(Tony)

Born June 4, 1957, at Monte Cristy, Dominican Republic.
Height, 6.00. Weight, 175.
Throws and bats righthanded.

Led National League catchers in total chances with 1,075 in 1983.
Led Eastern League catchers in double plays with 14 in 1979.
Led Carolina League catchers in double plays with 9 in 1977.
Tied for Carolina League lead in passed balls with 16 in 1977.
Named catcher on THE SPORTING NEWS National League All-Star Team, 1983.
Named catcher on THE SPORTING NEWS National League All-Star fielding team, 1983.

Year Club	League	Pos.	G.	AB.	R.	H.	2B.	3B.	HR.	RBI.	B.A.	PO.	A.	E.	F.A.
1976—Bradenton Pir.	Gulf C.	O-1-C-3	33	110	10	23	2	2	1	11	.209	108	14	4	.968
1976—Charleston	W. Car.	C	14	49	4	11	2	0	1	8	.224	64	7	2	.973
1977—Charleston	W. Car.	C	29	101	10	24	4	0	3	16	.238	172	19	6	.970
1977—Salem	Carol.	C	84	319	36	88	15	3	7	46	.276	★470	★66	★17	.969
1978—Shreveport	Texas	C	104	348	34	80	14	0	8	42	.230	637	54	★25	.965
1979—Buffalo	East.	C	134	515	89	161	16	4	34	97	.313	★768	★120	★26	.972
1980—Portland	P. C.	C	124	452	57	148	24	13	9	77	.327	★639	85	●23	.969
1980—Pittsburgh	Nat.	C	8	21	1	9	1	1	0	1	.429	38	2	2	.952
1981—Pittsburgh	Nat.	C	66	210	16	63	9	1	2	17	.300	286	41	5	.985
1982—Pittsburgh	Nat.	C	138	497	53	147	28	4	11	63	.296	763	89	16	.982
1983—Pittsburgh	Nat.	C	151	542	51	163	22	3	15	70	.301	★976	90	9	.992
Major League Totals			363	1270	121	382	60	9	28	151	.301	2063	222	32	.986

Signed as free agent by Pittsburgh Pirates' organization, July 22, 1975.

ALL-STAR GAME RECORD

Year League		Pos.	AB.	R.	H.	2B.	3B.	HR.	RBI.	B.A.	PO.	A.	E.	F.A.
1982—National		PR-C	1	0	0	0	0	0	0	.000	3	0	0	1.000

CHARLES LEE PENIGAR JR.
(C.L.)

Born July 31, 1963, at Kansas City, Kan.
Height, 6.03. Weight, 177.
Throws right and bats left and righthanded.
Attended Chaffey College, Alta Loma, Calif.

Led California League batters in strikeouts with 136 in 1983.
Led South Atlantic League batters in strikeouts with 142 in 1982.

Year	Club	League	Pos.	G.	AB.	R.	H.	2B.	3B.	HR.	RBI.	B.A.	PO.	A.	E.	F.A.
1981—Helena		Pion.	OF	46	165	25	35	8	2	1	16	.212	45	4	2	.961
1982—Spartanburg†		S. Atl.	OF	133	455	95	118	17	7	5	53	.259	202	15	*21	.912
1983—Fresno		Calif.	OF	118	439	76	113	14	4	3	37	.257	201	11	8	.964

Selected by Philadelphia Phillies' organization in 2nd round of free agent draft, June 8, 1981.

†Traded with Pitchers Mike Krukow and Mark Davis to San Francisco Giants for Pitcher Al Holland and Second Baseman Joe Morgan, December 14, 1982.

JOHN PATRICK PERCONTE

Name pronounced PURR-con-tee.

(Jack)

Born August 31, 1954, at Joliet, Ill.
Height, 5.10. Weight, 160.
Throws right and bats lefthanded.
Received bachelor of science degree in sociology from
Murray State University, Murray, Ky. in 1976.

Year	Club	League	Pos.	G.	AB.	R.	H.	2B.	3B.	HR.	RBI.	B.A.	PO.	A.	E.	F.A.
1976—Lodi		Calif.	2B	68	252	58	72	7	1	1	19	.286	141	223	12	.968
1977—Lodi		Calif.	2B	131	515	*132	172	21	12	6	58	.334	292	390	22	.969
1978—San Antonio		Texas	2B	134	538	90	148	20	8	2	52	.275	286	357	21	.968
1979—Albuquerque		P. C.	2B	143	521	104	168	25	7	2	68	.322	278	403	*35	.951
1980—Albuquerque†		P. C.	2B	120	439	84	143	16	7	2	46	.326	291	320	15	.976
1980—Los Angeles		Nat.	2B	14	17	2	4	0	0	0	2	.235	13	18	0	1.000
1981—Albuquerque		P. C.	2B	127	448	107	155	26	6	1	58	.346	286	321	23	.963
1981—Los Angeles‡		Nat.	OF	8	9	2	2	0	1	0	1	.222	4	13	0	1.000
1982—Cleveland		Amer.	2B	93	219	27	52	4	4	0	15	.237	131	199	8	.976
1983—Charleston		Int.	*2B-3B	94	341	76	118	17	2	4	45	*.346	177	323	6	*.988
1983—Cleveland§		Amer.	2B	14	26	1	7	1	0	0	0	.269	20	37	3	.950
National League Totals				22	26	4	6	0	1	0	3	.231	17	31	0	1.000
American League Totals				107	245	28	59	5	4	0	15	.241	151	236	11	.972
Major League Totals				129	271	32	65	5	5	0	18	.240	168	267	11	.975

Selected by Los Angeles Dodgers' organization in 16th round of free-agent draft, June 8, 1976.

†On disabled list, May 18 to June 9, 1980.

‡Traded with Pitcher Rick Sutcliffe to Cleveland Indians for Outfielder Jorge Orta, Catcher Jack Fimple and Pitcher Larry White, December 9, 1981.

§Traded with Outfielder Gorman Thomas to Seattle Mariners for Second Baseman Tony Bernazard, December 7, 1983.

ATANASIO RIGAL PEREZ

Name pronounced PER-ez.

(Tony)

Born May 14, 1942, at Ciego de Avila, Camaguey, Cuba.
Height, 6.02. Weight, 205.
Throws and bats righthanded.

Tied modern major league record for most at bats, game (7), June 13, 1975.

Tied National League records for most home runs through May 31 (18), 1970; fewest errors by first baseman for leader in errors, season (13), 1973.

Led American League in grounding into double plays with 25 in 1980.

Led National League first basemen in double plays with 131 and total chances with 1,416 in 1973.

Led National League third basemen in assists with 304 and total chances with 435 in 1971.

Led National League third basemen in double plays with 35 in 1969 and tied for lead with 33 in 1968.

Led Carolina League third basemen in double plays with 23 in 1962.

Named first baseman on THE SPORTING NEWS National League All-Star Team, 1973.

Named third baseman on THE SPORTING NEWS National League All-Star Team, 1970.

Named Pacific Coast League Most Valuable Player, 1964.

Year	Club	League	Pos.	G.	AB.	R.	H.	2B.	3B.	HR.	RBI.	B.A.	PO.	A.	E.	F.A.
1960—Geneva†		NYP	INF-OF	104	384	82	107	21	4	6	43	.279	199	197	31	.927
1961—Geneva		NYP	3B	121	460	110	*160	32	7	27	*132	*.348	107	*232	*42	.890
1962—Rocky Mount‡§		Carol.	3B	100	384	72	112	20	8	18	74	.292	88	178	30	.899
1963—San Diego		P. C.	3B	8	29	4	11	3	1	1	5	.379	6	8	1	.933
1963—Macon x		Sally	3B	69	256	44	79	19	3	11	48	.309	57	100	18	.897
1964—San Diego		P. C.	1B-3B-OF	124	479	96	148	20	8	34	107	.309	816	104	19	.980
1964—Cincinnati		Nat.	1B	12	25	1	2	1	0	0	1	.080	51	0	1	.981
1965—Cincinnati		Nat.	1B	104	281	40	73	14	4	12	47	.260	525	40	6	.989
1966—Cincinnati		Nat.	1B	99	257	25	68	10	4	4	39	.265	530	23	6	.989
1967—Cincinnati		Nat.	3B-1B-2B	156	600	78	174	28	7	26	102	.290	249	234	13	.974
1968—Cincinnati		Nat.	3B	160	625	93	176	25	7	18	92	.282	*151	343	*25	.952
1969—Cincinnati		Nat.	3B	160	629	103	185	31	2	37	122	.294	136	*342	*32	.937
1970—Cincinnati		Nat.	*3B-1B	158	587	107	186	28	6	40	129	.317	167	292	*35	.929
1971—Cincinnati		Nat.	3B-1B	158	609	72	164	22	3	25	91	.269	281	308	20	.967
1972—Cincinnati		Nat.	1B	136	515	64	146	33	7	21	90	.283	1207	68	9	.993
1973—Cincinnati		Nat.	1B	151	564	73	177	33	3	27	101	.314	*1318	85	*13	.991
1974—Cincinnati		Nat.	1B	158	596	81	158	28	2	28	101	.265	1292	75	6	*.996
1975—Cincinnati		Nat.	1B	137	511	74	144	28	3	20	109	.282	1192	72	9	.993
1976—Cincinnati y		Nat.	1B	139	527	77	137	32	6	19	91	.260	1158	73	5	.996
1977—Montreal		Nat.	1B	154	559	71	158	32	6	19	91	.283	1312	110	11	.992
1978—Montreal		Nat.	1B	148	544	63	158	38	3	14	78	.290	1181	82	11	.991

Year Club	League	Pos.	G.	AB.	R.	H.	2B.	3B.	HR.	RBI.	B.A.	PO.	A.	E.	F.A.
1979—Montreal z	Nat.	1B	132	489	58	132	29	4	13	73	.270	1114	65	11	.991
1980—Boston	Amer.	1B	151	585	73	161	31	3	25	105	.275	1301	87	10	.993
1981—Boston	Amer.	1B	84	306	35	77	11	3	9	39	.252	519	37	4	.993
1982—Boston a	Amer.	1B	69	196	18	51	14	2	6	31	.260	5	1	1	.857
1983—Philadelphia b	Nat.	1B	91	253	18	61	11	2	6	43	.241	514	40	1	.998
National League Totals			2253	8171	1098	2299	423	69	329	1400	.281	12378	2252	214	.986
American League Totals			304	1087	126	289	56	8	40	175	.266	1825	125	15	.992
Major League Totals			2557	9258	1224	2588	479	77	369	1575	.280	14203	2377	229	.986

Signed as free agent by Cincinnati Reds' organization, March 12, 1960.
†On disabled list, June 25 to July 5, 1960.
‡On suspended list, April 13 to April 16, 1962.
§On disabled list, July 30 to September 4, 1962.
xOn suspended list, April 11, 1963; transferred to restricted list, April 23 to June 25, 1963.
yTraded with Pitcher Will McEnaney to Montreal Expos for Pitchers Woodie Fryman and Dale Murray, December 16, 1976.
zGranted free agency, November 1, 1979; signed by Boston Red Sox, November 16, 1979.
aReleased, November 1, 1982; signed by Philadelphia Phillies, January 31, 1983.
bTraded to Cincinnati Reds for a player to be named later, December 5, 1983.

CHAMPIONSHIP SERIES RECORD

Tied Championship Series records for most consecutive games, one or more runs batted in, total Series (4); most at bats, extra-inning game (6), October 9, 1973 (12 innings); most strikeouts, five-game Series (7), 1972.

Year Club	League	Pos.	G.	AB.	R.	H.	2B.	3B.	HR.	RBI.	B.A.	PO.	A.	E.	F.A.
1970—Cincinnati	Nat.	3B-1B	3	12	1	4	2	0	1	2	.333	6	6	1	.923
1972—Cincinnati	Nat.	1B	5	20	0	4	1	0	0	2	.200	45	3	0	1.000
1973—Cincinnati	Nat.	1B	5	22	1	2	0	0	1	2	.091	47	4	0	1.000
1975—Cincinnati	Nat.	1B	3	12	3	5	0	0	1	4	.417	27	5	0	1.000
1976—Cincinnati	Nat.	1B	3	10	1	2	0	0	0	3	.200	27	2	1	.967
1983—Philadelphia	Nat.	PH	1	1	0	1	0	0	0	0	1.000	0	0	0	.000
Championship Series Totals			20	77	6	18	3	0	3	13	.234	152	20	2	.989

WORLD SERIES RECORD

Tied World Series record for one or more hits, each game, seven-game Series, 1972; most unassisted double plays by first baseman, game (1), October 11, 1975.

Year Club	League	Pos.	G.	AB.	R.	H.	2B.	3B.	HR.	RBI.	B.A.	PO.	A.	E.	F.A.
1970—Cincinnati	Nat.	3B	5	18	2	1	0	0	0	0	.056	3	13	1	.941
1972—Cincinnati	Nat.	1B	7	23	3	10	2	0	0	2	.435	73	3	1	.987
1975—Cincinnati	Nat.	1B	7	28	4	5	0	0	3	7	.179	66	5	1	.986
1976—Cincinnati	Nat.	1B	4	16	1	5	1	0	0	2	.313	32	4	0	1.000
1983—Philadelphia	Nat.	PH-1B	4	10	0	2	0	0	0	0	.200	13	1	0	1.000
World Series Totals			27	95	10	23	3	0	3	11	.242	187	26	3	.986

ALL-STAR GAME RECORD

Year League	Pos.	AB.	R.	H.	2B.	3B.	HR.	RBI.	B.A.	PO.	A.	E.	F.A.
1967—National	3B	2	1	1	0	0	1	1	.500	0	3	0	1.000
1968—National	3B	0	0	0	0	0	0	0	.000	0	1	0	1.000
1969—National	3B	1	0	0	0	0	0	0	.000	1	1	0	1.000
1970—National	3B	3	0	0	0	0	0	0	.000	1	1	0	1.000
1974—National	PH	1	0	0	0	0	0	0	.000	0	0	0	.000
1975—National	1B	1	0	0	0	0	0	0	.000	1	1	0	1.000
1976—National	1B	0	0	0	0	0	0	0	.000	2	0	0	1.000
All-Star Game Totals		8	1	1	0	0	1	1	.125	5	7	0	1.000

PASCUAL PEREZ

Born May 17, 1957, at San Cristobal, Dominican Republic.
Height, 6.02. Weight, 162.
Throws and bats righthanded.
Brother of Valerio Perez, pitcher in Kansas City Royals' organization.

Led Western Carolinas League in balks with 6 in 1977.
Tied for Carolina League lead in shutouts with 5 in 1978.

Year Club	League	G.	IP.	W.	L.	Pct.	H.	R.	ER.	SO.	BB.	ERA.
1976—Bradenton Pirates†	Gulf Coast	10	56	2	5	.286	51	41	29	34	35	4.66
1977—Charleston	W. Carol.	25	156	10	5	.667	153	80	69	96	60	3.98
1978—Salem	Carolina	24	152	11	7	.611	133	70	44	126	51	2.61
1978—Columbus	Int'national	1	5	0	0	.000	4	0	0	4	1	0.00
1979—Portland‡	P. Coast	20	103	9	7	.563	121	70	63	51	47	5.50
1980—Portland	P. Coast	24	160	12	10	.545	172	76	72	105	48	4.05
1980—Pittsburgh	National	2	12	0	1	.000	15	6	5	7	2	3.75
1981—Portland	P. Coast	5	31	1	2	.333	40	19	17	11	14	4.94
1981—Pittsburgh	National	17	86	2	7	.222	92	50	38	46	34	3.98
1982—Portland§	P. Coast	19	106⅓	4	9	.308	111	59	57	59	37	4.82
1982—Richmond	Int'national	5	43	5	0	1.000	32	7	6	27	8	1.26
1982—Atlanta	National	16	79⅓	4	4	.500	85	35	27	29	17	3.06
1983—Atlanta	National	33	215⅓	15	8	.652	213	88	82	144	51	3.43
Major League Totals		68	392⅔	21	20	.512	405	179	152	226	104	3.48

Signed as free agent by Pittsburgh Pirates' organization, January 27, 1976.
†On suspended list, August 26 to August 28, 1976.
‡On disabled list, July 16 to August 14, 1979.
§Traded with a player to be named later to Atlanta Braves' organization for Pitcher Larry McWilliams, June 30, 1982; Atlanta organization acquired Shortstop Carlos Rios to complete deal, September 8, 1982.

CHAMPIONSHIP SERIES RECORD

Year Club	League	G.	IP.	W.	L.	Pct.	H.	R.	ER.	SO.	BB.	ERA.
1982—Atlanta	National	2	8⅔	0	1	.000	10	5	5	4	2	5.19

ALL-STAR GAME RECORD

Year League		IP.	W.	L.	Pct.	H.	R.	ER.	SO.	BB.	ERA.
1983—National		⅔	0	0	.000	3	2	2	1	1	27.00

BRODERICK PHILLIP PERKINS

Born November 23, 1954, at Pittsburg, Calif.
Height, 5.10. Weight, 180.
Throws and bats lefthanded.
Attended Diablo Valley College, Pleasant Hill, Calif., and
St. Mary's College, Moraga, Calif.

Led Northwest League in total bases with 128 in 1976.
Led Northwest League first basemen in double plays with 65 in 1976.

Year Club	League	Pos.	G.	AB.	R.	H.	2B.	3B.	HR.	RBI.	B.A.	PO.	A.	E.	F.A.
1976—Walla Walla	N'west.	1B	60	228	47	81	13	2	10	★63	.355	585	23	11	.982
1977—Amarillo†	Texas	1B-OF	116	438	71	151	30	1	4	66	.345	899	66	14	.986
1978—Hawaii	P. C.	1B	78	282	37	82	16	4	3	42	.291	641	35	6	.991
1978—San Diego	Nat.	1B	62	217	14	52	14	1	2	33	.240	538	41	4	.993
1979—San Diego‡	Nat.	1B	57	87	8	23	0	0	0	8	.264	155	10	3	.982
1979—Hawaii	P. C.	1B	43	159	19	52	9	2	2	17	.327	385	33	5	.988
1980—Hawaii	P. C.	1B	118	436	53	136	29	7	6	65	.312	1168	79	8	.994
1980—San Diego	Nat.	1B-OF	43	100	18	37	9	0	2	14	.370	159	9	3	.994
1981—San Diego	Nat.	1B-OF	92	254	27	71	18	3	2	40	.280	602	38	3	.995
1982—San Diego§	Nat.	1B-OF	125	347	32	94	10	4	2	34	.271	831	64	6	.993
1983—Cleveland	Amer.	1B-OF	79	184	23	50	10	0	0	24	.272	148	6	2	.987
National League Totals.............................			379	1005	99	277	51	8	8	129	.276	2285	162	19	.992
American League Totals............................			79	184	23	50	10	0	0	24	.272	148	6	2	.987
Major League Totals..................................			458	1189	122	327	61	8	8	153	.275	2433	168	21	.992

Selected by San Diego Padres' organization in 15th round of free-agent draft, June 8, 1976.
†On disabled list, July 16 to July 29, 1977.
‡On disabled list, July 2 to July 19, 1979.
§Traded with Pitcher Juan Eichelberger to Cleveland Indians for Pitcher Ed Whitson, November 18, 1982.

GAYLORD JACKSON PERRY

Born September 15, 1938, at Williamston, N.C.
Height, 6.04. Weight, 215.
Throws and bats righthanded.
Attended Campbell College, Buies Creek, N.C.
Brother of Jim Perry, pitcher with Cleveland Indians, Minnesota Twins,
Detroit Tigers and Oakland Athletics, 1959 through 1975.

Established major league record by winning Cy Young Memorial Award in both leagues.
Tied major league record for most years with 100 or more strikeouts (18).
Tied National League record for most putouts by pitcher, game (5), July 18, 1970.
Pitched 1-0 no-hit victory against St. Louis Cardinals, September 17, 1968.
Led American League in wild pitches with 17 in 1973 and 13 in 1982.
Led American League in complete games with 29 in 1972 and 29 in 1973.
Led American League in intentional bases on balls issued with 16 in 1972.
Led National League in shutouts with 5 in 1970.
Led National League pitchers in games started with 41 in 1970.
Won National League Cy Young Memorial Award, 1978.
Won American League Cy Young Memorial Award, 1972.
Named righthanded pitcher on THE SPORTING NEWS National League All-Star Team, 1978.
Named righthanded pitcher on THE SPORTING NEWS American League All-Star Team, 1972.
Named Pacific Coast League Pitcher of the Year, 1961.
Received reported $90,000 bonus to sign with San Francisco Giants, 1958.

Year Club	League	G.	IP.	W.	L.	Pct.	H.	R.	ER.	SO.	BB.	ERA.
1958—St. Cloud	Northern	17	128	9	5	.643	97	40	34	111	48	2.39
1959—Corpus Christi..............................	Texas	41	191	10	11	.476	★218	★120	86	119	69	4.05
1960—Tacoma..............................	P. Coast	1	1	0	0	.000	1	1	1	0	0	9.00
1960—Rio Grande Valley........................	Texas	31	188	9	13	.409	164	68	59	120	77	★2.82
1961—Tacoma..............................	P. Coast	33	★219	●16	10	.615	208	79	62	95	61	2.55
1962—San Francisco..............................	National	13	43	3	1	.750	54	29	25	20	14	5.23
1962—Tacoma..............................	P. Coast	22	156	10	7	.588	128	56	43	136	56	★2.48
1963—San Francisco..............................	National	31	76	1	6	.143	84	41	34	52	29	4.03
1963—Tacoma..............................	P. Coast	1	9	1	0	1.000	3	1	1	7	1	1.00
1964—San Francisco..............................	National	44	206	12	11	.522	179	65	63	155	43	2.75
1965—San Francisco..............................	National	47	196	8	12	.400	194	105	91	170	70	4.18
1966—San Francisco..............................	National	36	256	21	8	.724	242	92	85	201	40	2.99
1967—San Francisco..............................	National	39	293	15	17	.469	231	98	85	230	84	2.61

Year Club	League	G.	IP.	W.	L.	Pct.	H.	R.	ER.	SO.	BB.	ERA.
1968—San Francisco	National	39	291	16	15	.516	240	93	79	173	59	2.44
1969—San Francisco	National	40	★325	19	14	.576	290	115	90	233	91	2.49
1970—San Francisco	National	41	★329	●23	13	.639	★292	★138	117	214	84	3.20
1971—San Francisco†	National	37	280	16	12	.571	255	116	86	158	67	2.76
1972—Cleveland	American	41	343	●24	16	.600	253	79	73	234	82	1.92
1973—Cleveland	American	41	344	19	19	.500	315	143	129	238	115	3.38
1974—Cleveland	American	37	322	21	13	.618	230	98	90	216	99	2.52
1975—Cleveland‡-Texas	American	37	306	18	17	.514	277	127	110	233	70	3.24
1976—Texas	American	32	250	15	14	.517	232	93	90	143	52	3.24
1977—Texas§	American	34	238	15	12	.556	239	108	89	177	56	3.37
1978—San Diego	National	37	261	★21	6	★.778	241	96	79	154	66	2.72
1979—San Diego xy	National	32	233	12	11	.522	225	90	79	140	67	3.05
1980—Texas z-New York a	American	34	206	10	13	.435	224	107	84	135	64	3.67
1981—Atlanta b	National	23	151	8	9	.471	★182	70	66	60	24	3.93
1982—Seattle c	American	32	216⅔	10	12	.455	245	117	106	116	54	4.40
1983—Seattle d-Kansas City e	American	30	186⅓	7	14	.333	214	108	96	82	49	4.64
National League Totals		459	2940	175	135	.565	2709	1148	979	1960	738	3.00
American League Totals		318	2412	139	130	.517	2229	980	867	1574	641	3.24
Major League Totals		777	5352	314	265	.542	4938	2128	1846	3534	1379	3.10

Signed as free agent for reported $90,000 by San Francisco Giants' organization, June 3, 1958.

†Traded with Shortstop Frank Duffy to Cleveland Indians for Pitcher Sam McDowell, November 29, 1971.

‡Traded to Texas Rangers for Pitchers Jim Bibby, Jackie Brown and Rick Waits and estimated cash of $100,000, June 12, 1975.

§Traded to San Diego Padres for Pitcher Dave Tomlin and $125,000, February 15, 1978.

xOn suspended list, September 5 to October 3, 1979.

yTraded with Third Baseman Tucker Ashford and Pitcher Joe Carroll to Texas Rangers for First Baseman Willie Montanez and a player to be named later, February 15, 1980; Hawaii (San Diego Padres' organization) purchased Infielder Tony Phillips to complete deal, September 11, 1980.

zTraded to New York Yankees for Pitcher Ken Clay and a player to be named later, August 14, 1980; Texas Rangers' organization acquired Outfielder Marvin Thompson to complete deal, October 1, 1980.

aGranted free agency, October 23, 1980; signed by Atlanta Braves, January 12, 1981.

bReleased, October 5, 1981; signed by Seattle Mariners, March 5, 1982.

c On suspended list, September 17 to September 26, 1982.

dReleased, June 27, 1983; signed by Kansas City Royals, July 6, 1983.

eOn voluntarily retired list, September 24, 1983.

CHAMPIONSHIP SERIES RECORD

Established Championship Series records for most runs allowed, four-game Series (11), 1971; most hits allowed, four-game Series (19), 1971.

Tied Championship Series record for most earned runs allowed, game (7), October 6, 1971.

Tied National League Championship Series record for most hits allowed, game (10), October 6, 1971.

Year Club	League	G.	IP.	W.	L.	Pct.	H.	R.	ER.	SO.	BB.	ERA.
1971—San Francisco	National	2	14⅔	1	1	.500	19	11	10	11	3	6.14

ALL-STAR GAME RECORD

Year League	IP.	W.	L.	Pct.	H.	R.	ER.	SO.	BB.	ERA.
1966—National	2	1	0	1.000	1	0	0	1	1	0.00
1970—National	2	0	0	.000	4	2	2	0	1	9.00
1972—American	2	0	0	.000	3	2	2	1	0	9.00
1974—American	3	0	0	.000	3	1	1	4	0	3.00
1979—National	0	0	0	.000	3	1	1	0	0	......
All-Star Game Totals	9	1	0	1.000	14	6	6	6	2	6.00

GERALD JUNE PERRY

Born October 30, 1960, at Savannah, Ga.
Height, 5.11. Weight, 172.
Throws right and bats lefthanded.
Nephew of Dan Driessen, first baseman with Cincinnati Reds.

Led Carolina League first basemen in double plays with 109 in 1980.
Led Gulf Coast League first basemen in double plays with 46 in 1978.

Year Club	League	Pos.	G.	AB.	R.	H.	2B.	3B.	HR.	RBI.	B.A.	PO.	A.	E.	F.A.
1978—Bradenton Brav...	Gulf C.	1B	★55	191	32	51	★12	3	1	26	.267	★479	★37	6	★.989
1979—Greenwood	W. Car.	1B	109	400	69	133	17	4	9	71	★.333	881	59	19	.980
1980—Durham	Carol.	1B	138	497	102	124	19	5	15	92	.249	★1296	93	16	.989
1981—Savannah	South.	1B	137	476	71	132	18	3	19	84	.277	1221	86	18	.986
1982—Richmond	Int.	1B	133	492	94	146	22	4	15	92	.297	1110	94	●17	.986
1983—Richmond	Int.	1B	113	423	81	133	21	8	13	71	.314	943	88	11	.989
1983—Atlanta	Nat.	1B-OF	27	39	5	14	2	0	1	6	.359	55	0	1	.982
Major League Totals			27	39	5	14	2	0	1	6	.359	55	0	1	.982

Selected by Atlanta Braves' organization in 11th round of free-agent draft, June 6, 1978.

RICHARD DEVIN PETERS
(Rick)

Born November 21, 1955, at Lynwood, Calif.
Height, 5.10. Weight, 160.
Throws right and bats left and righthanded.
Attended Arizona State University, Tempe, Ariz.

Year	Club	League	Pos.	G.	AB.	R.	H.	2B.	3B.	HR.	RBI.	B.A.	PO.	A.	E.	F.A.
1977—Montgomery	South.		OF	38	108	9	33	2	1	0	8	.306	70	3	1	.986
1978—Evansville	A. A.		OF-3B	●135	463	92	128	28	8	2	48	.276	199	5	8	.962
1979—Evansville	A. A.		OF-3B-2B	107	387	88	124	17	10	3	42	.320	125	17	5	.966
1979—Detroit	Amer.		3B-OF	12	19	3	5	0	0	0	2	.263	3	0	2	.600
1980—Detroit	Amer.		OF	133	477	79	139	19	7	2	42	.291	296	1	7	.977
1981—Detroit	Amer.		OF	63	207	26	53	7	3	0	15	.256	103	3	1	.991
1982—Detroit†‡	Amer.						(Did not play)									
1983—Tacoma	P. C.		OF	66	232	50	69	9	3	1	19	.297	166	1	3	.982
1983—Oakland	Amer.		OF	55	178	20	51	7	0	0	20	.287	141	3	2	.986
Major League Totals				263	881	128	248	33	10	2	79	.281	543	7	12	.979

Selected by Minnesota Twins' organization in 18th round of free-agent draft, June 5, 1973.
Selected by Atlanta Braves' organization in 12th round of free-agent draft, June 8, 1976.
Selected by Detroit Tigers' organization in 7th round of free-agent draft, June 7, 1977.
†On emergency disabled list, April 6, 1982 through remainder of season.
‡Released, October 8, 1982; signed by Tacoma (Oakland A's organization), February 2, 1983.

EUGENE JAMES PETRALLI JR.
(Geno)

Born September 25, 1959, at Sacramento, Calif.
Height, 6.01. Weight, 180.
Throws right and bats left and righthanded.
Attended Sacramento City College, Sacramento, Calif.
Son of Gene Petralli, minor league first baseman, 1948 through 1951 and 1953.

Led International League catchers in putouts with 633, assists with 86, errors with 19, double plays with 10 and total chances with 738 in 1982.
Tied for Pioneer League lead in passed balls with 27 in 1978.

Year	Club	League	Pos.	G.	AB.	R.	H.	2B.	3B.	HR.	RBI.	B.A.	PO.	A.	E.	F.A.
1978—Medicine Hat	Pion.		C-3B	65	242	42	68	14	5	2	40	.281	238	68	19	.942
1979—Dunedin†	Fla. St.		C-3B-OF	52	184	18	53	13	0	1	24	.288	206	42	5	.980
1979—Syracuse	Int.		C	18	56	6	13	0	1	0	7	.232	67	12	1	.988
1980—Knoxville	South.		C-1B-OF	116	382	42	109	20	2	3	38	.285	569	82	18	.973
1981—Syracuse‡	Int.		C	45	151	17	40	11	0	0	16	.265	188	30	6	.973
1982—Syracuse	Int.		C-1B-3B	126	395	57	114	19	3	9	58	.289	674	89	20	.974
1982—Toronto	Amer.		C-3B	16	44	3	16	2	0	0	1	.364	51	4	1	.982
1983—Syracuse	Int.		C-1B	104	327	39	80	9	2	3	40	.245	541	68	7	.989
1983—Toronto	Amer.		C	6	4	0	0	0	0	0	0	.000	7	0	0	1.000
Major League Totals				22	48	3	16	2	0	0	1	.333	58	4	1	.984

Selected by Toronto Blue Jays' organization in 3rd round of free-agent draft, January 10, 1978.
†On suspended list, April 13 to April 27, 1979.
‡On disabled list, May 6 to June 1 and June 28 to August 18, 1981.

DANIEL JOSEPH PETRY
(Dan)

Born November 13, 1958, at Palo Alto, Calif.
Height, 6.04. Weight, 200.
Throws and bats righthanded.

Led American League pitchers in games started with 38 and home runs allowed with 37 in 1983.

Year	Club	League	G.	IP.	W.	L.	Pct.	H.	R.	ER.	SO.	BB.	ERA.
1976—Bristol	Ap'lachian	14	79	2	3	.400	54	42	33	51	★56	3.76
1977—Lakeland	Florida St.	25	145	10	11	.476	139	68	55	68	68	3.41
1978—Montgomery	Southern	14	92	6	7	.462	70	38	25	69	41	2.45
1978—Evansville	Am. Assoc.	13	71	4	3	.571	59	38	36	50	33	4.56
1979—Evansville	Am. Assoc.	15	91	4	3	.571	92	60	49	55	37	4.85
1979—Detroit	American	15	98	6	5	.545	90	46	43	43	33	3.95
1980—Evansville	Am. Assoc.	4	30	2	0	1.000	21	11	9	16	12	2.70
1980—Detroit	American	27	165	10	9	.526	156	82	72	88	83	3.93
1981—Detroit	American	23	141	10	9	.526	115	53	47	79	57	3.00
1982—Detroit	American	35	246	15	9	.625	220	98	88	132	100	3.22
1983—Detroit	American	38	266⅓	19	11	.633	256	126	116	122	99	3.92
Major League Totals		138	916⅓	60	43	.583	837	405	366	464	372	3.59

Selected by Detroit Tigers' organization in 4th round of free-agent draft, June 8, 1976.

HARRY JONATHAN PETTIBONE
(Jay)

Born June 21, 1957, at Mt. Clemens, Mich.
Height, 6.04. Weight, 185.
Throws and bats righthanded.
Attended Fullerton College, Fullerton, Calif., and received bachelor of arts degree
in physical education from Chapman College, Orange, Calif.

Year	Club	League	G.	IP.	W.	L.	Pct.	H.	R.	ER.	SO.	BB.	ERA.
1979—Sarasota Rangers	Gulf Coast	13	47	3	1	.750	57	29	19	26	15	3.64
1980—Asheville	S. Atlantic	36	73	1	5	.167	75	54	45	61	29	5.55
1980—Wausau†	Midwest	9	11	0	1	.000	16	8	8	9	6	6.55
1981—Visalia	California	27	187	14	8	.636	211	105	90	139	61	4.33

Year Club	League	G.	IP.	W.	L.	Pct.	H.	R.	ER.	SO.	BB.	ERA.
1982—Orlando‡	Southern	5	15⅓	0	3	.000	26	19	18	11	10	10.57
1982—Visalia	California	11	66⅓	8	1	.889	61	23	18	51	20	2.44
1983—Orlando	Southern	25	161	13	7	.650	157	78	71	105	61	3.97
1983—Toledo	Int'national	4	21⅔	0	0	.000	21	9	8	16	3	3.32
1983—Minnesota	American	4	27	0	4	.000	28	16	16	10	8	5.33
Major League Totals		4	27	0	4	.000	28	16	16	10	8	5.33

Selected by San Francisco Giants' organization in 8th round of free-agent draft, January 11, 1977.
Selected by Texas Rangers' organization in 30th round of free-agent draft, June 5, 1979.
†Released, December 15, 1980; signed by Visalia (Minnesota Twins' organization), February 23, 1981.
‡On disabled list, April 13 to June 7, 1982.

JOSEPH PAUL PETTINI
(Joe)

Born January 26, 1955, at Wheeling, W. Va.
Height, 5.09. Weight, 165.
Throws and bats righthanded.
Attended Mercer University, Macon, Ga.

Led American Association shortstops in assists with 413, errors with 33 and double plays with 87 in 1979.

Year Club	League	Pos.	G.	AB.	R.	H.	2B.	3B.	HR.	RBI.	B.A.	PO.	A.	E.	F.A.
1977—Sarasota Expos	Gulf C.	SS-3B	4	14	3	5	0	0	0	1	.357	4	9	4	.765
1977—Jamestown	NYP	3B-SS-2B	56	210	47	64	6	1	3	26	.305	57	96	11	.933
1977—W. Palm Beach	Fla. St.	SS	1	3	0	0	0	0	0	0	.000	3	4	1	.875
1978—Memphis†	South.	2B-3B-SS	113	355	52	87	14	3	0	25	.245	178	307	21	.958
1979—Denver‡	A. A.	SS-3B	132	446	70	131	21	6	4	46	.294	199	415	34	.948
1980—Phoenix	P. C.	SS	85	344	52	97	16	4	2	32	.282	157	284	29	.938
1980—San Francisco	Nat.	SS-3B-2B	63	190	19	44	3	1	1	9	.232	66	147	8	.964
1981—Phoenix	P. C.	SS-OF	21	86	13	21	5	0	0	5	.244	28	70	3	.970
1981—San Francisco	Nat.	2B-SS-3B	35	29	3	2	1	0	0	2	.069	13	37	5	.909
1982—San Francisco	Nat.	SS-3B	29	39	5	8	1	0	0	2	.205	24	33	4	.934
1982—Phoenix§	P. C.	SS-2B-3B	80	305	51	99	21	3	9	46	.325	137	243	17	.957
1983—San Francisco	Nat.	SS-2B-3B	61	86	11	16	0	1	0	7	.186	44	82	6	.955
Major League Totals			188	344	38	70	5	2	1	20	.203	147	299	23	.951

Signed as free agent by Montreal Expos' organization, June 22, 1977.
†On disabled list, May 23 to June 13, 1978.
‡Traded to San Francisco Giants' organization, March 14, 1980; completing deal in which San Francisco traded Catcher John Tamargo to Montreal Expos' organization for a player to be named later, June 13, 1979.
§On disabled list, June 2 to June 12, 1982.

GARY GEORGE PETTIS

Born April 3, 1958, at Oakland, Calif.
Height, 6.01. Weight, 165.
Throws right and bats left and righthanded.
Attended Laney College, Oakland, Calif.

Led Pacific Coast League in stolen bases with 53 in 1982.

Year Club	League	Pos.	G.	AB.	R.	H.	2B.	3B.	HR.	RBI.	B.A.	PO.	A.	E.	F.A.
1979—Idaho Falls	Pion.	3B-SS-2B	50	198	39	63	10	●10	3	26	.318	59	94	24	.864
1980—Salinas	Calif.	OF-SS-3B	118	393	71	94	15	3	2	31	.239	206	36	13	.949
1981—Holyoke	East.	OF	120	421	77	112	8	9	3	36	.266	237	5	4	.984
1982—Spokane	P. C.	OF	133	528	108	152	22	★14	5	59	.288	★345	9	6	★.983
1982—California	Amer.	OF	10	5	5	1	0	0	1	1	.200	5	1	0	1.000
1983—Edmonton	P. C.	OF	132	529	138	151	27	8	11	52	.285	325	10	5	.985
1983—California	Amer.	OF	22	85	19	25	2	3	3	6	.294	49	5	1	.982
Major League Totals			32	90	24	26	2	3	4	7	.289	54	6	1	.984

Selected by California Angels' organization in 6th round of free-agent draft, January 9, 1979.

ERIC MELVIN PEYTON

Born November 22, 1959, at Jacksonville, Fla.
Height, 5.10. Weight, 170.
Throws and bats lefthanded.
Attended California State Poly University,
San Luis Obispo, Calif.

Led Pioneer League in total bases with 174 and game-winning RBIs with 9 in 1981.
Led Pioneer League outfielders in assists with 19 in 1981.
Named Pioneer League Player of the Year, 1981.

Year Club	League	Pos.	G.	AB.	R.	H.	2B.	3B.	HR.	RBI.	B.A.	PO.	A.	E.	F.A.
1981—Butte	Pion.	OF-2B-SS	67	273	★64	★110	★24	★8	8	★65	★.403	104	22	8	.940
1982—El Paso	Texas	OF	129	524	104	149	34	6	17	91	.284	228	★26	●17	.937
1983—Vancouver	P. C.	OF	72	271	36	56	11	1	10	29	.207	126	12	3	.979
1983—El Paso	Texas	OF	54	210	38	72	8	4	8	40	.343	101	10	4	.965

Selected by Milwaukee Brewers' organization in 23rd round of free-agent draft, June 8, 1981.

KENNETH ALLEN PHELPS
(Ken)

Born August 6, 1954, at Seattle, Wash.
Height, 6.01. Weight, 209.
Throws and bats lefthanded.
Attended Washington State University, Pullman, Wash.; Mesa Community College,
Mesa, Ariz., and received bachelor of science degree in physical education from
Arizona State University, Tempe, Ariz.

Led American Association in total bases with 320 in 1982.
Led American Association in bases on balls received with 128 in 1980 and 108 in 1982.
Led Southern League in bases on balls received with 99 in 1978.
Led American Association first basemen in double plays with 111 in 1979, 103 in 1980 and 108 in 1982..
Tied for American Association lead in intentional bases on balls received with 12 in 1982.
Named American Association Most Valuable Player, 1982.

Year	Club	League	Pos.	G.	AB.	R.	H.	2B.	3B.	HR.	RBI.	B.A.	PO.	A.	E.	F.A.
1976—Sarasota Royals...	Gulf C.	1B	28	98	20	29	6	3	3	28	.296	166	16	2	.989
1976—Waterloo	Midw.	1B	25	72	12	19	8	0	1	10	.264	205	12	3	.986
1977—Daytona Beach	Fla. St.	1B	40	145	22	50	7	0	5	32	.345	341	31	8	.979
1977—Jacksonville	South.	1B	81	262	30	51	6	3	5	40	.195	691	38	10	.986
1978—Jacksonville	South.	1B	124	381	65	94	20	0	16	61	.247	1028	66	16	.986
1979—Omaha	A. A.	1B	130	430	71	114	26	3	20	77	.265	★1129	80	★13	.989
1980—Omaha	A. A.	1B	133	442	80	130	30	3	23	72	.294	★1154	51	12	.990
1980—Kansas City	Amer.	1B	3	4	0	0	0	0	0	0	.000	14	0	0	1.000
1981—Kansas City	Amer.	1B	21	22	1	3	0	1	0	1	.136	4	1	0	1.000
1981—Omaha†	A. A.	1B	19	66	9	22	8	1	5	21	.333	169	15	2	.989
1982—Wichita	A. A.	1B	132	453	112	151	23	4	★46	★141	.333	1047	74	14	.988
1982—Montreal‡	Nat.	PH	10	8	0	2	0	0	0	0	.250	0	0	0	.000
1983—Seattle	Amer.	1B	50	127	10	30	4	1	7	16	.236	164	16	0	1.000
1983—Salt Lake City	P. C.	1B	74	270	81	92	29	6	24	82	.341	535	37	7	.988
American League Totals				74	153	11	33	4	2	7	17	.216	182	17	0	1.000
National League Totals				10	8	0	2	0	0	0	0	.250	0	0	0	.000
Major League Totals				84	161	11	35	4	2	7	17	.217	182	17	0	1.000

Selected by Atlanta Braves' organization in 8th round of free-agent draft, June 6, 1972.
Selected by New York Yankees' organization in 1st round (11th player selected) of free-agent draft, January 9, 1974.
Selected by Philadelphia Phillies' organization in secondary phase of free-agent draft, June 5, 1974.
Selected by Kansas City Royals' organization in 15th round of free-agent draft, June 8, 1976.
†Traded to Montreal Expos' organization for Pitcher Grant Jackson, January 19, 1982.
‡Sold to Seattle Mariners, March 31, 1983.

KEITH ANTHONY PHILLIPS
(Tony)

Born April 25, 1959, at Atlanta, Ga.
Height, 5.10. Weight, 160.
Throws right and bats right and lefthanded.
Attended New Mexico Military Institute, Roswell, N.M.

Led Eastern League in being hit by pitch with 10 in 1981.
Led Southern League in bases on balls received with 98 in 1980.

Year	Club	League	Pos.	G.	AB.	R.	H.	2B.	3B.	HR.	RBI.	B.A.	PO.	A.	E.	F.A.
1978—W. Palm Beach†	Fla. St.	3B-SS-2B	32	54	8	9	0	0	0	3	.167	13	33	5	.902
1978—Jamestown	NYP	SS-2B-3B	52	152	24	29	5	2	1	17	.191	73	146	16	.932
1979—W. Palm Beach	Fla. St.	2B-SS	60	203	30	47	5	1	0	18	.232	120	156	21	.929
1979—Memphis	South.	SS-2B	52	156	31	44	4	2	3	11	.282	68	134	18	.914
1980—Memphis‡§	South.	★SS-2B	136	502	100	125	18	4	5	41	.249	226	408	★42	.938
1981—West Haven	East.	SS	131	461	79	114	25	3	9	64	.247	200	391	★33	.947
1981—Tacoma	P. C.	2B-SS	4	11	1	4	1	0	0	2	.364	8	10	0	1.000
1982—Tacoma	P. C.	SS	86	300	76	89	18	5	4	47	.297	138	236	30	.926
1982—Oakland	Amer.	SS	40	81	11	17	2	2	0	8	.210	46	95	7	.953
1983—Oakland	Amer.	SS-2B-3B	148	412	54	102	12	3	4	35	.248	218	383	30	.952
Major League Totals				188	493	65	119	14	5	4	43	.241	264	478	37	.953

Selected by Seattle Mariners' organization in 16th round of free-agent draft, June 7, 1977.
Selected by Montreal Expos' organization in secondary phase of free-agent draft, January 10, 1978.
†On temporary inactive list, April 11 to May 4, 1978.
‡Sold to Hawaii (San Diego Padres' organization), September 11, 1980, completing deal in which Texas Rangers traded First Baseman Willie Montanez and a player to be named later to San Diego Padres for Pitchers Gaylord Perry and Joe Carroll and Third Baseman Tucker Ashford, February 15, 1980.
§Traded with Pitcher Eric Mustad and Infielder Kevin Bell to Oakland A's organization for Pitcher Bob Lacey and Pitcher Roy Moretti, March 27, 1981.

MICHAEL DWAINE PHILLIPS
(Mike)

Born August 19, 1950, at Beaumont, Tex.
Height, 6.01. Weight, 185.
Throws right and bats right and lefthanded.
Attended Phoenix College, Phoenix, Ariz.

Hit for the cycle, June 25, 1976.

Led National League shortstops in errors with 31 in 1975.
Led Pioneer League shortstops in fielding percentage with .933 in 1969.

Year	Club	League	Pos.	G.	AB.	R.	H.	2B.	3B.	HR.	RBI.	B.A.	PO.	A.	E.	F.A.
1969—Great Falls	Pion.		SS-2B	55	167	23	36	9	1	0	18	.216	58	125	13	.934
1970—Fresno	Calif.		SS-2B	94	318	26	79	7	3	3	21	.248	133	264	34	.921
1971—Amarillo	Texas		SS	89	347	45	81	15	6	2	22	.233	116	290	30	.931
1972—Phoenix	P. C.		SS-2B-3B	114	375	57	93	17	7	0	32	.248	148	342	41	.932
1973—Phoenix	P. C.		SS	1	4	1	1	0	0	0	1	.250	1	2	0	1.000
1973—San Francisco	Nat.		3B-SS-2B	63	104	18	25	3	4	1	9	.240	42	69	6	.949
1974—San Francisco	Nat.		3B-2B-SS	100	283	19	62	6	1	2	20	.219	125	195	19	.944
1975—S. F.†-N. Y.	Nat.		SS-2B-3B	126	414	34	104	10	7	1	29	.251	203	364	32	.947
1976—New York	Nat.		SS-3B-2B	87	262	30	67	4	6	4	29	.256	115	191	11	.965
1977—N.Y.‡St.L.	Nat.		2B-SS-3B	86	173	22	39	5	3	1	12	.225	90	126	7	.969
1978—St. Louis	Nat.		2B-SS-3B	76	164	14	44	8	1	1	28	.268	107	135	7	.972
1979—St. Louis	Nat.		SS-2B-3B	44	97	10	22	3	1	1	6	.227	53	107	4	.976
1980—St. Louis§	Nat.		SS-2B-3B	63	128	13	30	5	0	0	7	.234	63	130	9	.955
1981—S.D. x-Mont.	Nat.		SS-2B	48	84	6	18	2	1	0	4	.214	57	74	3	.978
1982—Montreal y	Nat.		2B-SS	14	8	0	1	0	0	0	1	.125	8	10	0	1.000
1982—Wichita z	A. A.		SS-2B-3B	46	137	15	38	2	1	1	9	.277	74	117	12	.941
1983—Montreal a	Nat.		SS-3B	5	2	0	0	0	0	0	0	.000	0	0	1	.000
1983—Wichita b	A. A.		SS	14	47	7	16	2	0	1	12	.340	22	33	11	.833
Major League Totals				722	1719	166	412	46	24	11	145	.240	863	1401	99	.958

Selected by San Francisco Giants' organization in 1st round (18th player selected) of free-agent draft, June 5, 1969.
†Sold on waivers to New York Mets, May 3, 1975.
‡Traded to St. Louis Cardinals for Infielder-Outfielder Joel Youngblood, June 15, 1977.
§Traded with Catchers Terry Kennedy and Steve Swisher and Pitchers John Littlefield, Kim Seaman, Al Olmsted and John Urrea to San Diego Padres for Pitchers Rollie Fingers and Bob Shirley, Catcher-First Baseman Gene Tenace and a player to be named later, December 8, 1980; St. Louis Cardinals' organization acquired Catcher Bob Geren to complete deal, December 10, 1980.
xSold to Montreal Expos, May 10, 1981.
yReleased, May 30, 1982; signed by Wichita (Montreal Expos' organization), June 20, 1982.
zGranted free agency, November 10, 1982; re-signed by Expos, June 2, 1983.
aReleased, June 20, 1983; signed by Wichita (Montreal Expos' organization), August 23, 1983.
bReleased, September 16, 1983.

DIVISION SERIES RECORD

Year	Club	League	Pos.	G.	AB.	R.	H.	2B.	3B.	HR.	RBI.	B.A.	PO.	A.	E.	F.A.
1981—Montreal	Nat.		PR-2B	1	1	0	0	0	0	0	0	.000	1	1	0	1.000

ROBERT MICHAEL PICCIOLO

Name pronounced PEACH-alo.

(Rob)

Born February 4, 1953, at Santa Monica, Calif.
Height, 6.02. Weight, 185.
Throws and bats righthanded.
Attended Santa Monica City College, Santa Monica, Calif. and received
bachelor of arts degree in journalism from Pepperdine University, Malibu, Calif.

Led Southern League shortstops in double plays with 91 in 1975.

Year	Club	League	Pos.	G.	AB.	R.	H.	2B.	3B.	HR.	RBI.	B.A.	PO.	A.	E.	F.A.
1975—Birmingham	South.		SS	133	488	55	135	23	6	3	62	.277	★278	★404	18	★.974
1976—Tucson	P. C.		SS	139	★570	78	170	19	4	5	54	.298	220	★429	22	★.967
1977—San Jose	P. C.		SS	10	38	5	8	1	0	1	4	.211	23	25	0	1.000
1977—Oakland	Amer.		SS	148	419	35	84	12	3	2	22	.200	213	381	21	.966
1978—Vancouver	P. C.		SS	26	90	14	23	3	3	2	17	.256	53	87	3	.979
1978—Oakland	Amer.		SS-2B-3B	78	93	16	21	1	0	0	7	.226	74	90	7	.959
1979—Oakland	Amer.		S-2-3-O	115	348	37	88	16	2	2	27	.253	203	288	17	.967
1980—Oakland	Amer.		SS-2B-OF	95	271	32	65	9	2	5	18	.240	164	208	6	.984
1981—Oakland	Amer.		SS	82	179	23	48	5	3	4	13	.268	99	157	5	.981
1982—Oak.†-Milw.	Amer.		SS-2B	40	70	10	17	2	0	0	4	.243	47	72	3	.975
1983—Milwaukee‡	Amer.		S-2-3-1	14	27	2	6	3	0	0	1	.222	27	20	1	.979
Major League Totals				572	1407	155	329	48	10	15	92	.234	827	1216	60	.971

Selected by San Francisco Giants' organization in 2nd round of free-agent draft, January 10, 1973.
Selected by Kansas City Royals' organization in secondary phase of free-agent draft, June 5, 1973.
Selected by Detroit Tigers' organization in secondary phase of free-agent draft, June 5, 1974.
Selected by Oakland A's organization in secondary phase of free-agent draft, January 9, 1975.
†Traded to Milwaukee Brewers for Pitcher Mike Warren and First Baseman John Evans, May 14, 1982.
‡Granted free agency, November 7, 1983.

DIVISION SERIES RECORD

Year	Club	League	Pos.	G.	AB.	R.	H.	2B.	3B.	HR.	RBI.	B.A.	PO.	A.	E.	F.A.
1981—Oakland	Amer.		SS	1	3	0	1	0	0	0	0	.333	1	2	0	1.000

CHAMPIONSHIP SERIES RECORD

Year	Club	League	Pos.	G.	AB.	R.	H.	2B.	3B.	HR.	RBI.	B.A.	PO.	A.	E.	F.A.
1981—Oakland	Amer.		SS	2	5	1	1	0	0	0	0	.200	5	5	1	.909

RICHARD HENRY PICKETT
(Rich)

Born July 11, 1959, at Crystal Springs, Miss.
Height, 6.01. Weight, 195.
Throws and bats lefthanded.
Attended Alcorn State University, Lorman, Miss.

Year—Club	League	G.	IP.	W.	L.	Pct.	H.	R.	ER.	SO.	BB.	ERA.
1981—Little Falls	NYP	8	30	2	1	.667	31	15	11	24	13	3.30
1982—Shelby	S. Atlantic	50	93⅔	6	3	.667	81	39	31	78	34	2.98
1983—Lynchburg	Carolina	17	19	1	0	1.000	12	5	3	21	9	1.42
1983—Tidewater	Int'national	26	31⅔	1	0	1.000	31	16	14	27	18	3.98

Signed as free agent by New York Mets' organization, July 20, 1981.

LOUIS VICTOR PINIELLA
Name pronounced Pin-ELLA.
(Lou)

Born August 28, 1943, at Tampa, Fla.
Height, 6.02. Weight, 199.
Throws and bats righthanded.
Attended University of Tampa, Tampa, Fla.

Tied major league record for most assists by outfielder, inning (2), May 27, 1974 (third inning).
Led American League in grounding into double plays with 25 in 1972.
Named American League Rookie of the Year by Baseball Writers' Association of America, 1969.

Year—Club	League	Pos.	G.	AB.	R.	H.	2B.	3B.	HR.	RBI.	B.A.	PO.	A.	E.	F.A.
1962—Selma†	Ala.-Fl.	OF	70	278	40	75	10	5	8	44	.270	94	6	9	.917
1963—Peninsula	Carol.	OF	143	548	71	170	29	4	16	77	.310	271	★23	8	.974
1964—Aberdeen‡§	North.	OF	20	74	8	20	8	3	0	12	.270	37	1	1	.974
1964—Baltimore	Amer.	PH	4	1	0	0	0	0	0	0	.000	0	0	0	.000
1965—Elmira x	East.	OF	126	490	64	122	29	6	11	64	.249	176	5	7	.963
1966—Portland	P. C.	OF	133	457	47	132	22	3	7	52	.289	177	11	11	.945
1967—Portland	P. C.	OF	113	396	49	122	20	1	8	56	.308	199	7	6	.972
1968—Portland	P. C.	OF	88	331	49	105	15	3	13	62	.317	167	6	7	.961
1968—Cleveland yz	Amer.	OF	6	5	1	0	0	0	0	1	.000	1	0	0	1.000
1969—Kansas City	Amer.	OF	135	493	43	139	21	6	11	68	.282	278	13	7	.977
1970—Kansas City	Amer.	OF-1B	144	542	54	163	24	5	11	88	.301	250	6	4	.985
1971—Kansas City a	Amer.	OF	126	448	43	125	21	5	3	51	.279	201	6	3	.986
1972—Kansas City	Amer.	OF	151	574	65	179	★33	4	11	72	.312	275	8	7	.976
1973—Kansas City b	Amer.	OF	144	513	53	128	28	1	9	69	.250	196	9	3	.986
1974—New York c	Amer.	OF-1B	140	518	71	158	26	0	9	70	.305	270	16	3	.990
1975—New York	Amer.	OF	74	199	7	39	4	1	0	22	.196	65	5	1	.986
1976—New York	Amer.	OF	100	327	36	92	16	6	3	38	.281	199	10	4	.981
1977—New York	Amer.	OF-1B	103	339	47	112	19	3	12	45	.330	86	3	2	.978
1978—New York	Amer.	OF	130	472	67	148	34	5	6	69	.314	213	4	7	.969
1979—New York	Amer.	OF	130	461	49	137	22	2	11	69	.297	204	13	4	.982
1980—New York	Amer.	OF	116	321	39	92	18	0	2	27	.287	157	8	5	.971
1981—New York d	Amer.	OF	60	159	16	44	9	0	5	18	.277	69	2	1	.986
1982—New York	Amer.	OF	102	261	33	80	17	1	6	37	.307	68	2	0	1.000
1983—New York e	Amer.	OF	53	148	19	43	9	1	2	16	.291	67	4	3	.959
Major League Totals			1718	5781	643	1679	301	40	101	760	.290	2599	109	54	.980

Signed as free agent by Cleveland Indians' organization, June 9, 1962.
†Drafted by Washington Senators, November 26, 1962.
‡On military list, March 9 to July 20, 1964.
§Traded to Baltimore Orioles' organization, August 4, 1964, completing deal in which Baltimore traded Pitcher Lester (Buster) Narum to Washington Senators for cash and a player to be named later, March 31, 1964.
xTraded to Cleveland Indians' organization for Catcher Cam Carreon, March 10, 1966.
ySelected by Seattle Pilots in expansion draft, October 15, 1968.
zTraded by Seattle Pilots to Kansas City Royals for Outfielder Steve Whitaker and Pitcher John Gelnar, April 1, 1969.
aOn disabled list, May 5 to June 8, 1971.
bTraded with Pitcher Ken Wright to New York Yankees for Pitcher Lindy McDaniel, December 7, 1973.
cOn supplemental disabled list, June 17 to July 6, 1975.
dOn supplemental disabled list, August 23 to September 7, 1981.
eOn supplemental disabled list, March 30 to April 22, 1983.

DIVISION SERIES RECORD

Year—Club	League	Pos.	G.	AB.	R.	H.	2B.	3B.	HR.	RBI.	B.A.	PO.	A.	E.	F.A.
1981—New York	Amer.	DH-PH	4	10	1	2	1	0	1	3	.200	0	0	0	.000

CHAMPIONSHIP SERIES RECORD

Year—Club	League	Pos.	G.	AB.	R.	H.	2B.	3B.	HR.	RBI.	B.A.	PO.	A.	E.	F.A.
1976—New York	Amer.	DH-PH	4	11	1	3	1	0	0	0	.273	0	0	0	.000
1977—New York	Amer.	OF-DH	5	21	1	7	3	0	0	2	.333	9	1	0	1.000
1978—New York	Amer.	OF	4	17	2	4	0	0	0	0	.235	13	0	0	1.000
1980—New York	Amer.	OF	2	5	1	1	0	0	1	1	.200	5	0	0	1.000
1981—New York	Amer.	PH-D-O	3	5	2	3	0	0	1	3	.600	0	0	0	.000
Championship Series Totals			18	59	7	18	4	0	2	6	.305	27	1	0	1.000

WORLD SERIES RECORD

Tied World Series record for one or more hits, each game, six-game Series, 1978.

Year	Club	League	Pos.	G.	AB.	R.	H.	2B.	3B.	HR.	RBI.	B.A.	PO.	A.	E.	F.A.
1976—New York	Amer.	D-O-PH	4	9	1	3	1	0	0	0	.333	1	0	0	1.000
1977—New York	Amer.	OF	6	22	1	6	0	0	0	3	.273	16	1	1	.944
1978—New York	Amer.	OF	6	25	3	7	0	0	0	4	.280	14	1	0	1.000
1981—New York	Amer.	OF-PH	6	16	2	7	1	0	0	3	.438	7	0	0	1.000
World Series Totals				22	72	7	23	2	0	0	10	.319	38	2	1	.976

ALL-STAR GAME RECORD

Year	League	Pos.	AB.	R.	H.	2B.	3B.	HR.	RBI.	B.A.	PO.	A.	E.	F.A.
1972—American		PH	1	0	0	0	0	0	0	.000	0	0	0	.000

WILLIAM JAMES PINKHAM
(Bill)

Born August 25, 1959, at Worcester, Mass.
Height, 6.05. Weight, 215.
Throws and bats righthanded.
Attended University of San Diego, San Diego, Calif.

Led Carolina League catchers in total chances with 897, putouts with 783 and assists with 98 and tied for lead in double plays with 11 in 1982.

Year	Club	League	Pos.	G.	AB.	R.	H.	2B.	3B.	HR.	RBI.	B.A.	PO.	A.	E.	F.A.
1981—Medicine Hat	Pion.	C	69	283	39	85	17	2	9	59	.300	366	33	9	.978
1982—Kinston	Carol.	C-1B	133	471	55	124	28	1	10	59	.263	788	99	16	.982
1983—Knoxville†	South.	C-1B	72	250	23	63	14	0	10	41	.252	284	38	5	.985

Selected by Toronto Blue Jays' organization in 2nd round of free-agent draft, June 8, 1981.
†On disabled list, May 8 to June 28, 1983.

JOSEPH WAYNE PITTMAN
(Joe)

Born January 1, 1954, at Houston, Tex.
Height, 6.01. Weight, 180.
Throws and bats righthanded.
Attended Southern University, Baton Rouge, La.

Led Pacific Coast League second basemen in double plays with 96 in 1983.

Year	Club	League	Pos.	G.	AB.	R.	H.	2B.	3B.	HR.	RBI.	B.A.	PO.	A.	E.	F.A.
1975—Columbus	South.	2B-SS	21	71	8	19	2	0	0	1	.268	20	29	6	.891
1976—Dubuque	Midw.	2B-3B	109	442	68	123	19	6	2	34	.278	237	259	31	.941
1977—Columbus†	South.	2B-3B-SS	48	134	17	33	2	0	0	8	.246	102	132	6	.975
1977—Cocoa	Fla. St.	2B-3B	36	95	7	18	4	0	0	3	.189	35	47	5	.943
1978—Columbus	South.	OF-2B	92	306	44	78	6	1	1	17	.255	73	33	5	.955
1979—Charleston	Int.	2B	5	1	1	0	0	0	0	0	.000	1	1	0	1.000
1979—Columbus	South.	2B-3B	100	382	56	108	13	2	5	27	.283	157	226	14	.965
1980—Tucson	P. C.	3B-2B-1B	126	490	93	154	23	10	1	61	.314	82	191	21	.929
1981—Tucson	P. C.	3B-OF	6	23	4	8	0	1	1	5	.348	5	11	1	.941
1981—Houston	Nat.	2B-3B	52	135	11	38	4	2	0	7	.281	59	92	3	.981
1982—Hou.‡-S.D.	Nat.	2-S-3-O	70	128	16	32	3	0	0	7	.250	52	97	6	.961
1982—Tucson	P. C.	3B-OF	8	30	6	12	2	0	0	4	.400	7	10	2	.895
1983—Las Vegas§	P. C.	2B	129	*550	92	155	27	7	3	52	.282	234	371	23	.963
Major League Totals			122	263	27	70	7	2	0	14	.266	111	189	9	.971

Selected by Houston Astros' organization in 5th round of free-agent draft, June 4, 1975.
†On temporary inactive list, June 11 to June 23, 1977.
‡Traded to San Diego Padres for Pitcher Dan Boone, June 8, 1982.
§Traded with a player to be named later to San Francisco Giants for Outfielder Champ Summers, December 5, 1983; San Francisco acquired Outfielder Tommy Francis to complete deal, December 7, 1983.

DIVISION SERIES RECORD

Year	Club	League	Pos.	G.	AB.	R.	H.	2B.	3B.	HR.	RBI.	B.A.	PO.	A.	E.	F.A.
1981—Houston	Nat.	PH	2	2	0	0	0	0	0	0	.000	0	0	0	.000

BIFF POCOROBA

Name pronounced Poh-kuh-ROH-buh.

Born July 25, 1953, at Burbank, Calif.
Height, 5.10. Weight, 170.
Throws right and bats lefthanded.
Brother of Joseph Pocoroba, infielder in Los Angeles Dodgers' and Atlanta Braves' organizations, 1978 and 1979.

Year	Club	League	Pos.	G.	AB.	R.	H.	2B.	3B.	HR.	RBI.	B.A.	PO.	A.	E.	F.A.
1971—Wytheville	Appal.	C	42	124	17	37	7	0	3	19	.298	262	13	3	.989
1972—Greenwood	W. Car.	C	75	212	25	55	5	0	7	29	.259	446	25	10	*.979
1972—Richmond	Int.	PH	1	1	0	0	0	0	0	0	.000	0	0	0	.000
1973—Savannah†	South.	C	114	368	46	86	13	0	12	46	.234	417	38	7	.985
1974—Savannah‡	South.	*C-1B	79	241	48	75	10	2	9	45	.311	435	25	2	*.996
1975—Atlanta	Nat.	C	67	188	15	48	7	1	1	22	.255	237	25	8	.970
1976—Atlanta§	Nat.	C	54	174	16	42	7	0	0	14	.241	273	39	7	.978

Year	Club	League	Pos.	G.	AB.	R.	H.	2B.	3B.	HR.	RBI.	B.A.	PO.	A.	E.	F.A.
1977—Atlanta		Nat.	C	113	321	46	93	24	1	8	44	.290	542	78	7	.989
1978—Atlanta x		Nat.	C	92	289	21	70	8	0	6	34	.242	454	43	5	.990
1979—Atlanta y		Nat.	C	28	38	6	12	4	0	0	4	.316	7	39	3	.933
1980—Atlanta z		Nat.	C	70	83	7	22	4	0	2	8	.265	56	1	4	.934
1981—Atlanta a		Nat.	3B-C	57	122	4	22	4	0	0	8	.180	43	34	3	.963
1982—Atlanta b		Nat.	C-3B	56	120	5	33	7	0	2	22	.275	144	16	2	.988
1983—Atlanta		Nat.	C	55	120	11	32	6	0	2	16	.267	166	12	3	.983
Major League Totals				592	1455	131	374	71	2	21	172	.257	1922	287	42	.981

Selected by Atlanta Braves' organization in 17th round of free-agent draft, June 8, 1971.
†On disabled list, July 12 to July 22, 1973.
‡On disabled list, April 26 to June 7, 1974.
§On disabled list, June 2 to July 6 and August 9 to October 4, 1976.
xOn disabled list, August 15 to October 1, 1978.
yOn disabled list, April 4 to June 5 and July 19 to September 1, 1979.
zOn supplemental disabled list, April 20 to June 10, 1980.
aOn supplemental disabled list, August 9 to September 1, 1981.
bOn supplemental disabled list, August 22 to September 6, 1982.

CHAMPIONSHIP SERIES RECORD

Year	Club	League	Pos.	G.	AB.	R.	H.	2B.	3B.	HR.	RBI.	B.A.	PO.	A.	E.	F.A.
1982—Atlanta		Nat.	PH	1	1	0	0	0	0	0	0	.000	0	0	0	.000

ALL-STAR GAME RECORD

Year	League	Pos.	AB.	R.	H.	2B.	3B.	HR.	RBI.	B.A.	PO.	A.	E.	F.A.
1978—National		C	0	0	0	0	0	0	0	.000	0	0	0	.000

CARLOS DIAZ PONCE

Name pronounced PON-say.
Born February 7, 1959, at Rio Piedras, P.R.
Height, 5.10. Weight, 170.
Throws and bats righthanded.

Led Texas League in total bases with 299 in 1983.
Led Pioneer League in total bases with 143 in 1980.
Tied for California League lead in game-winning RBIs with 15 and sacrifice flies with 12 in 1982.
Led Texas League first basemen in double plays with 99 in 1983.
Led California League first basemen in double plays with 112 in 1982.

Year	Club	League	Pos.	G.	AB.	R.	H.	2B.	3B.	HR.	RBI.	B.A.	PO.	A.	E.	F.A.
1980—Butte		Pion.	1B-OF	69	259	48	90	18	7	7	55	.347	360	24	12	.970
1981—Burlington		Midw.	1B	130	487	70	131	25	7	15	62	.269	1111	58	★25	.979
1982—Stockton		Calif.	1B	132	489	59	140	31	★13	6	79	.286	★1225	78	19	.986
1983—El Paso		Texas	1B	129	506	114	★176	★50	5	21	111	.348	1133	69	●22	.982

Signed as free-agent by Milwaukee Brewers' organization, January 15, 1982.

STINE WALTER POOLE

Born November 6, 1958, at Lake Arrowhead, Calif.
Height, 6.01. Weight, 205.
Throws and bats righthanded.
Received bachelor of science degree in business administration
from University of Pacific, Stockton, Calif.

Year	Club	League	Pos.	G.	AB.	R.	H.	2B.	3B.	HR.	RBI.	B.A.	PO.	A.	E.	F.A.
1980—Montgomery		South.	C-OF	66	223	27	49	10	0	6	37	.220	349	47	8	.980
1981—Birmingham		South.	C-OF-3B	100	316	42	80	19	1	12	49	.253	510	54	16	.972
1982—Evansville		A. A.	C	16	35	5	8	2	0	1	7	.229	72	6	4	.951
1982—Birmingham†		South.	1B-C	95	351	46	90	17	2	18	60	.256	770	74	6	.993
1983—Toledo		Int.	C	93	267	35	54	10	0	8	27	.202	450	64	5	.990

Selected by Detroit Tigers' organization in 8th round of free-agent draft, June 3, 1980.
†Traded to Minnesota Twins' organization for Catcher Sal Butera, March 25, 1983.

CHARLES WILLIAM PORTER III
(Chuck)

Born January 12, 1956, at Baltimore, Md.
Height, 6.03. Weight, 187.
Throws and bats righthanded.
Attending Clemson University, Clemson, S.C.

Tied for Pacific Coast League lead in complete games with 12 in 1982.
Tied for Pacific Coast League lead in hit batsmen with 7 in 1979.

Year	Club	League	G.	IP.	W.	L.	Pct.	H.	R.	ER.	SO.	BB.	ERA.
1976—Quad Cities		Midwest	13	101	5	4	.556	90	42	36	65	27	3.21
1977—Salinas		California	13	96	11	1	.917	84	37	35	66	24	3.28
1977—El Paso		Texas	14	93	9	1	.900	106	45	40	45	16	3.87
1978—Salt Lake City		P. Coast	8	24	0	5	.000	34	29	26	7	12	9.75
1978—El Paso		Texas	18	124	10	5	.667	131	56	50	51	36	3.63
1979—Salt Lake City†		P. Coast	31	137	5	9	.357	164	100	87	41	44	5.72
1980—Burlington		Midwest	7	38	0	4	.000	40	25	14	22	5	3.32

Year Club	League	G	IP	W	L	Pct.	H	R	ER.	SO.	BB.	ERA.
1980—Holyoke	Eastern	14	90	8	2	.800	84	32	29	30	16	2.90
1981—Vancouver	P. Coast	27	140	7	10	.412	142	67	59	54	40	3.79
1981—Milwaukee	American	3	4	0	0	.000	6	2	2	1	1	4.50
1982—Vancouver‡	P. Coast	25	181⅓	8	12	.400	196	98	81	102	59	3.98
1982—Milwaukee	American	3	3⅔	0	0	.000	3	2	2	3	1	4.91
1983—Vancouver	P. Coast	7	19	0	1	.000	30	15	10	10	12	4.74
1983—Milwaukee	American	25	134	7	9	.438	162	72	67	76	38	4.50
Major League Totals		31	141⅔	7	9	.438	171	76	71	80	40	4.51

Selected by California Angels' organization in 7th round of free-agent draft, June 8, 1976.

†Released, March 31, 1980; signed by Burlington (Milwaukee Brewers' organization), May 16, 1980.

‡On temporary inactive list, April 25 to May 9, 1982.

DARRELL RAY PORTER

Born January 17, 1952, at Joplin, Mo.
Height, 6.01. Weight, 195.
Throws right and bats lefthanded.

Led American League in bases on balls received with 121 in 1979.
Led American League catchers in double plays with 15 in 1979.
Led American League in passed balls with 15 in 1975, 9 in 1978 and tied for lead with 12 in 1976.
Tied for American League lead in sacrifice flies with 13 in 1979.
Led Midwest League in passed balls with 19 in 1971.
Named catcher on THE SPORTING NEWS American League All-Star Team, 1979.
Received bonus reported in excess of $70,000 to sign with Milwaukee Brewers, 1970.

Year Club	League	Pos.	G.	AB.	R.	H.	2B.	3B.	HR.	RBI.	B.A.	PO.	A.	E.	F.A.
1970—Clinton	Midw.	C	62	185	24	37	11	0	4	21	.200	380	42	10	.977
1971—Danville	Midw.	C	101	332	75	90	9	7	24	70	.271	674	★69	★19	.975
1971—Milwaukee	Amer.	C	22	70	4	15	2	0	2	9	.214	108	18	3	.977
1972—Evansville	A. A.	C	88	255	37	55	7	2	13	45	.216	541	★56	7	.988
1972—Milwaukee	Amer.	C	18	56	2	7	1	0	1	2	.125	113	8	3	.976
1973—Milwaukee	Amer.	C	117	350	50	89	19	2	16	67	.254	372	47	10	.977
1974—Milwaukee	Amer.	C	131	432	59	104	15	4	12	56	.241	484	60	12	.978
1975—Milwaukee	Amer.	C	130	409	66	95	12	5	18	60	.232	532	82	13	.979
1976—Milwaukee†	Amer.	C	119	389	43	81	14	1	5	32	.208	491	52	4	.975
1977—Kansas City	Amer.	C	130	425	61	117	21	3	16	60	.275	663	61	●13	.982
1978—Kansas City	Amer.	C	150	520	77	138	27	6	18	78	.265	608	62	8	.988
1979—Kansas City	Amer.	C	157	533	101	155	23	10	20	112	.291	628	68	13	.982
1980—Kansas City‡§	Amer.	C	118	418	51	104	14	2	7	51	.249	322	37	8	.978
1981—St. Louis x	Nat.	C	61	174	22	39	10	2	6	31	.224	206	31	5	.979
1982—St. Louis y	Nat.	C	120	373	46	86	18	5	12	48	.231	469	64	9	.983
1983—St. Louis	Nat.	C	145	443	57	116	24	3	15	66	.262	578	70	7	.989
American League Totals			1092	3602	514	905	148	33	115	527	.251	4321	495	97	.980
National League Totals			326	990	125	241	52	10	33	145	.243	1253	165	21	.985
Major League Totals			1418	4592	639	1146	200	43	148	672	.250	5574	660	118	.981

Selected by Milwaukee Brewers' organization in 1st round (fourth player selected) of free-agent draft, June 4, 1970.

†Traded with Pitcher Jim Colborn to Kansas City Royals for Outfielder Jim Wohlford, Infielder Jamie Quirk and a player to be named later, December 6, 1976; Milwaukee Brewers acquired Pitcher Bob McClure to complete deal, March 15, 1977.

‡On supplemental disabled list, April 4 to May 2, 1980.

§Granted free agency, October 24, 1980; signed by St. Louis Cardinals, December 13, 1980.

xOn supplemental disabled list, May 18, 1981; transferred to disabled list, June 5 to August 19, 1981.

yOn disabled list, May 15 to June 5, 1982.

CHAMPIONSHIP SERIES RECORD

Tied Championship Series record for most two-base hits, three-game Series (3), 1982.

Year Club	League	Pos.	G.	AB.	R.	H.	2B.	3B.	HR.	RBI.	B.A.	PO.	A.	E.	F.A.
1977—Kansas City	Amer.	C	5	15	3	5	0	0	0	0	.333	18	0	0	1.000
1978—Kansas City	Amer.	C	4	14	1	5	1	0	0	3	.357	21	1	0	1.000
1980—Kansas City	Amer.	C	3	10	2	1	0	0	0	0	.100	17	1	0	1.000
1982—St. Louis	Nat.	C	3	9	3	5	3	0	0	1	.556	15	3	0	1.000
Championship Series Totals			15	48	9	16	4	0	0	4	.333	71	5	0	1.000

WORLD SERIES RECORD

Year Club	League	Pos.	G.	AB.	R.	H.	2B.	3B.	HR.	RBI.	B.A.	PO.	A.	E.	F.A.
1980—Kansas City	Amer.	PH-C	5	14	1	2	0	0	0	0	.143	13	2	0	1.000
1982—St. Louis	Nat.	C	7	28	1	8	2	0	1	5	.286	33	2	0	1.000
World Series Totals			12	42	2	10	2	0	1	5	.238	46	4	0	1.000

ALL-STAR GAME RECORD

Year League	Pos.	AB.	R.	H.	2B.	3B.	HR.	RBI.	B.A.	PO.	A.	E.	F.A.
1978—American	PH	1	0	0	0	0	0	0	.000	0	0	0	.000
1979—American	C	3	0	1	1	0	0	0	.333	2	0	0	1.000
1980—American	C	1	0	0	0	0	0	0	.000	0	1	0	.000
All-Star Game Totals		5	0	1	1	0	0	0	.200	2	1	0	1.000

Member of American League All-Star Team in 1974; did not play.

HOSKEN POWELL

Born May 14, 1955, at Salem, Ala.
Height, 6.01. Weight, 185.
Throws and bats lefthanded.
Attended Chipola Junior College, Marianna, Fla.

Year	Club	League	Pos.	G.	AB.	R.	H.	2B.	3B.	HR.	RBI.	B.A.	PO.	A.	E.	F.A.
1975—Elizabethton	....	Appal.	OF	64	249	45	82	★23	6	3	★58	.329	98	9	8	.930
1976—Reno	....	Calif.	OF	126	484	★118	167	22	9	7	73	.345	171	8	7	.962
1977—Tacoma	....	P. C.	OF	133	473	107	154	20	7	5	51	.326	190	8	9	.957
1978—Minnesota	....	Amer.	OF	121	381	55	94	20	2	3	31	.247	219	9	4	.983
1979—Minnesota†	....	Amer.	OF	104	338	49	99	17	3	2	36	.293	165	6	4	.977
1979—Toledo	....	Int.	OF	10	44	14	11	3	0	0	6	.250	15	1	1	.941
1980—Minnesota	....	Amer.	OF	137	485	58	127	17	5	6	35	.262	265	11	9	.968
1981—Minnesota‡	....	Amer.	OF	80	264	30	63	11	3	2	25	.239	122	6	4	.970
1982—Toronto	....	Amer.	OF	112	265	43	73	13	4	3	26	.275	111	2	3	.974
1983—Toronto§	....	Amer.	OF-1B	40	83	6	14	0	0	1	8	.169	52	1	1	.981
Major League Totals				594	1816	241	470	78	17	17	161	.259	944	35	25	.975

Selected by Pittsburgh Pirates' organization in 1st round (19th player selected) of free-agent draft, January 9, 1975.
Selected by Minnesota Twins' organization in secondary phase of free-agent draft, June 4, 1975.
†On disabled list, April 2 to May 7, 1979.
‡Traded to Toronto Blue Jays for a player to be named later, December 28, 1981; Minnesota Twins' organization acquired First Baseman Greg Wells to complete deal, January 18, 1982.
§Released, July 10, 1983.

TED HENRY POWER

Born January 31, 1955, at Guthrie, Okla.
Height, 6.04. Weight, 220.
Throws and bats righthanded.
Attended Kansas State University, Manhattan, Kan.

Year	Club	League	G.	IP.	W.	L.	Pct.	H.	R.	ER.	SO.	BB.	ERA.
1976—Lodi	....	California	13	51	1	3	.250	46	34	26	58	44	4.59
1977—San Antonio†	....	Texas	12	72	5	3	.625	51	35	31	60	55	3.88
1978—San Antonio‡	....	Texas	25	101	6	5	.545	92	57	45	97	75	4.01
1979—San Antonio	....	Texas	10	64	5	1	.833	69	44	37	52	43	5.20
1979—Albuquerque	....	P. Coast	18	101	5	5	.500	95	59	52	69	82	4.63
1980—Albuquerque	....	P. Coast	26	155	13	7	.650	160	93	78	113	95	4.53
1981—Albuquerque	....	P. Coast	27	187	★18	3	★.857	165	84	74	111	★103	3.56
1981—Los Angeles	....	National	5	14	1	3	.250	16	6	5	7	7	3.21
1982—Los Angeles	....	National	12	33⅔	1	1	.500	38	27	25	15	23	6.68
1982—Albuquerque§	....	P. Coast	14	73	5	4	.556	77	51	42	54	49	5.18
1983—Cincinnati	....	National	49	111	5	6	.455	120	62	56	57	49	4.54
Major League Totals			66	158⅔	7	10	.412	174	95	86	79	79	4.88

Selected by Los Angeles Dodgers' organization in 5th round of free-agent draft, June 8, 1976.
†On disabled list, July 18 to July 29 and August 20 to September 4, 1977.
‡On disabled list, July 5 to July 21, 1978.
§Sold to Cincinnati Reds, October 15, 1982.

JAMES ARTHUR PRESLEY
(Jim)

Born October 23, 1961, at Pensacola, Fla.
Height, 6.01. Weight, 176.
Throws and bats righthanded.

Led Eastern League in game-winning RBIs with 16 in 1982.
Led Eastern League third basemen in assists with 247 and total chances with 365 in 1982.
Led Midwest League in being hit by pitch with 12 in 1980.

Year	Club	League	Pos.	G.	AB.	R.	H.	2B.	3B.	HR.	RBI.	B.A.	PO.	A.	E.	F.A.
1979—Bellingham	....	N'west	SS	48	138	20	27	4	1	1	12	.196	42	127	27	.862
1980—Wausau	....	Midw.	3-S-2-1	126	429	45	105	21	1	12	52	.245	161	235	22	.947
1981—Wausau	....	Midw.	3B	57	208	48	58	10	0	12	53	.279	32	105	9	.938
1981—Lynn	....	East.	3B-2B	64	210	32	54	7	1	8	36	.257	49	110	11	.935
1982—Lynn	....	East.	★3B-OF	133	462	65	123	24	0	22	79	.266	84	250	★35	.905
1983—Chattanooga	....	South.	3B-SS	131	461	70	122	31	5	14	90	.265	122	329	27	.944

Selected by Seattle Mariners' organization in 4th round of free-agent draft, June 5, 1979.

JOSEPH WALTER PRICE
(Joe)

Born November 29, 1956, at Inglewood, Calif.
Height, 6.04. Weight, 220.
Throws left and bats righthanded.
Attended Oklahoma State University, Stillwater, Okla., and
University of Oklahoma, Norman, Okla.

Year	Club	League	G.	IP.	W.	L.	Pct.	H.	R.	ER.	SO.	BB.	ERA.
1977—Billings	....	Pioneer	15	94	6	5	.545	83	50	39	97	42	3.73
1978—Tampa	....	Florida St.	23	165	10	4	.714	123	40	27	128	51	1.47
1978—Nashville	....	Southern	2	10	0	0	.000	7	3	3	10	3	2.70

Year Club	League	G.	IP.	W.	L.	Pct.	H.	R.	ER.	SO.	BB.	ERA.
1979—Nashville	Southern	22	109	6	6	.500	101	58	48	69	41	3.96
1980—Indianapolis	Am. Assoc.	11	79	4	4	.500	64	36	34	83	30	3.87
1980—Cincinnati	National	24	111	7	3	.700	95	45	44	44	37	3.57
1981—Cincinnati	National	41	54	6	1	.857	42	19	15	41	18	2.50
1982—Cincinnati	National	59	72⅔	3	4	.429	73	26	23	71	32	2.85
1983—Cincinnati†	National	21	144	10	6	.625	118	46	46	83	46	2.88
Major League Totals		145	381⅔	26	14	.650	328	136	128	239	133	3.02

Selected by Cincinnati Reds' organization in 4th round of free-agent draft, June 7, 1977.
†On disabled list, August 7 to September 1, 1983.

MICHAEL JAMES PROLY
(Mike)

Born December 15, 1950, at Jamaica, N. Y.
Height, 5.10. Weight, 185.
Throws and bats righthanded.
Received bachelor of science degree in marketing from
St. John's University, Jamaica, N.Y. in 1973.

Year Club	League	G.	IP.	W.	L.	Pct.	H.	R.	ER.	SO.	BB.	ERA
1972—St. Petersburg	Florida St.	12	46	3	1	.750	28	9	4	41	10	0.78
1972—Modesto	California	6	29	1	3	.250	41	29	23	16	15	7.14
1973—St. Petersburg	Florida St.	37	164	14	5	*.737	129	44	32	112	28	*1.76
1974—Arkansas	Texas	39	101	8	2	.800	101	37	31	51	34	2.76
1975—Tulsa	Am. Assoc.	55	86	7	10	.412	101	42	37	51	43	3.87
1976—St. Louis	National	14	17	1	0	1.000	21	9	7	4	6	3.71
1976—Tulsa†	Am. Assoc.	50	67	6	4	.600	71	28	20	28	13	2.69
1977—Tacoma‡	P. Coast	55	130	9	12	.429	159	82	66	61	43	4.57
1978—Iowa	Am. Assoc.	22	66	6	2	.750	52	22	19	41	13	2.59
1978—Chicago§	American	14	66	5	2	.714	63	24	20	19	12	2.73
1979—Chicago x	American	38	88	3	8	.273	89	43	38	32	40	3.89
1980—Chicago y	American	62	147	5	10	.333	136	67	50	56	58	3.06
1981—Philadelphia z	National	35	63	2	1	.667	66	29	27	19	19	3.86
1982—Iowa a	Am. Assoc.	17	23⅓	2	1	.667	23	18	13	7	5	5.01
1982—Chicago	National	44	82	5	3	.625	77	22	21	24	22	2.30
1983—Chicago b	National	60	83	1	5	.167	79	35	33	31	38	3.58
National League Totals		153	245	9	9	.500	243	95	88	78	85	3.23
American League Totals		114	301	13	20	.394	288	134	108	107	110	3.23
Major League Totals		267	546	22	29	.431	531	229	196	185	195	3.23

Selected by St. Louis Cardinals' organization in 9th round of free-agent draft, June 6, 1972.
†Drafted by Tacoma (Minnesota Twins' organization), November 29, 1976.
‡Granted free agency November 2, 1977; signed by Chicago White Sox' organization, November 22, 1977.
§On disabled list, August 30, 1978 through remainder of season.
xOn disabled list, June 14 to July 28, 1979.
yTraded to Philadelphia Phillies for Second Baseman Jay Loviglio, April 1, 1981.
zReleased, March 29, 1982; signed by Iowa (Chicago Cubs' organization), April 9, 1982.
aOn disabled list, April 13 to April 23, 1982.
bOn disabled list, April 2 to April 23, 1983.

RONALD RALPH PRUITT
(Ron)

Born October 21, 1951, at Flint, Mich.
Height, 6.00. Weight, 185.
Throws and bats righthanded.
Attended Michigan State University, East Lansing, Mich.

Led Eastern League catchers in putouts with 577, assists with 80, double plays with 13 and tied for lead in errors with 14 in 1974.

Year Club	League	Pos.	G.	AB.	R.	H.	2B.	3B.	HR.	RBI.	B.A.	PO.	A.	E.	F.A.
1972—Denver	A. A.	OF-C-2B	60	167	22	36	5	0	5	24	.216	117	10	4	.969
1973—Spokane	P. C.	O-C-3-1	112	372	68	103	22	7	8	55	.277	319	68	11	.972
1974—Pittsfield	East.	C-O-1-3	129	415	74	111	28	2	15	77	.267	693	91	17	.979
1975—Spokane	P. C.	C-3B-OF	77	271	51	75	10	3	9	42	.277	183	62	14	.946
1975—Texas†	Amer.	C-OF	14	17	2	3	0	0	0	0	.176	21	5	0	1.000
1976—Cleveland	Amer.	O-C-2-1	47	86	7	23	1	1	0	5	.267	73	16	1	.989
1977—Toledo	Int.	OF-1-B-C	15	48	5	12	2	0	1	3	.250	32	1	0	1.000
1977—Cleveland	Amer.	OF-C-3B	78	219	29	63	10	2	2	32	.288	113	6	3	.975
1978—Cleveland	Amer.	C-OF-3B	71	187	17	44	6	1	6	17	.235	199	15	4	.982
1979—Cleveland	Amer.	OF-C-3B	64	166	23	47	7	0	2	21	.283	66	5	2	.973
1980—Clev.‡-Chi.§	Amer.	O-C-3-1	56	106	9	32	3	0	2	15	.302	34	2	1	.971
1981—Charleston xy	Int.	C-1B-OF	40	105	17	31	5	1	3	13	.295	157	22	10	.947
1981—Cleveland z	Amer.	OF-C	5	9	0	0	0	0	0	0	.000	3	0	0	1.000
1982—Phoenix	P. C.	C-OF	73	225	38	72	16	2	10	37	.320	221	31	5	.981
1982—San Francisco	Nat.	C-OF	5	4	1	2	1	0	0	2	.500	5	0	0	1.000
1983—San Francisco a	Nat.	PH	1	1	0	0	0	0	0	0	.000	0	0	0	.000
1983—Portland	P. C.	3-C-S-1	101	352	50	99	19	4	11	47	.281	148	124	24	.919
American League Totals			335	790	87	212	27	4	12	90	.268	509	49	11	.981
National League Totals			6	5	1	2	1	0	0	2	.400	5	0	0	1.000
Major League Totals			341	795	88	214	28	4	12	92	.269	514	49	11	.981

Selected by Texas Rangers' organization in 2nd round of free-agent draft, June 6, 1972.
†Traded with Pitcher Stan Thomas to Cleveland Indians for Catcher John Ellis, December 9, 1975.
‡Traded to Chicago White Sox for Infielder Alan Bannister, June 14, 1980.
§Released, April 7, 1981; signed by Cleveland Indians' organization, April 19, 1981.
xOn temporary inactive list, May 5 to June 20, 1981.
yOn disabled list, July 19 to August 13, 1981.
zReleased, January 19, 1982; signed by San Francisco Giants' organization, February 16, 1982.
aReleased, April 14, 1983; signed by Portland (Philadelphia Phillies' organization), April 26, 1983.

GREGORY RUSSELL PRYOR
(Greg)

Born October 2, 1949, at Marietta, O.
Height, 6.00. Weight, 175.
Throws and bats righthanded.
Received bachelor of science degree in industrial management from
Florida Southern College, Lakeland, Fla.
Brother of Jeff Pryor, pitcher in California Angels' organization, 1968 through 1972.

Led International League shortstops in assists with 417 and double plays with 87 in 1977.
Tied for Pacific Coast League lead in double plays by shortstop with 90 in 1976.

Year Club	League	Pos.	G.	AB.	R.	H.	2B.	3B.	HR.	RBI.	B.A.	PO.	A.	E.	F.A.
1971—Geneva	NYP	3-2-S-O	60	226	40	64	10	4	4	28	.283	76	138	21	.911
1972—Pittsfield	East.	SS	65	208	23	43	10	2	1	16	.207	89	155	29	.894
1972—Burlington	Carol.	SS-OF	39	119	16	28	2	1	1	15	.235	49	110	11	.935
1973—Rocky Mount	Carol.	SS-2B	126	443	53	130	20	9	2	44	.293	203	349	50	.917
1974—Pittsfield	East.	3B-SS-2B	122	441	61	104	20	1	5	37	.236	113	255	26	.934
1975—Spokane	P. C.	SS-3B-2B	135	481	59	117	21	2	5	53	.243	184	411	33	.947
1976—Sacramento	P. C.	SS	122	495	71	136	21	3	9	51	.275	158	409	32	.947
1976—Texas†	Amer.	2B-3B-SS	5	8	2	3	0	0	0	1	.375	4	8	0	1.000
1977—Syracuse‡	Int.	*S-3-2	124	461	60	125	18	6	7	52	.271	213	420	21	*.968
1978—Chicago	Amer.	2B-3B-SS	82	222	27	58	11	0	2	15	.261	100	202	11	.965
1979—Chicago	Amer.	SS-2B-3B	143	476	60	131	23	3	3	34	.275	218	447	26	.962
1980—Chicago	Amer.	SS-3B-2B	122	338	32	81	18	4	1	29	.240	130	344	16	.967
1981—Chicago§	Amer.	3B-SS-2B	47	76	4	17	1	0	0	6	.224	27	65	6	.939
1982—Kansas City	Amer.	3-2-1-S	73	152	23	41	10	1	2	12	.270	78	112	5	.974
1983—Kansas City	Amer.	3B-1B-2B	68	115	9	25	4	0	1	14	.217	38	100	5	.965
Major League Totals			540	1387	157	356	67	8	9	111	.257	595	1278	69	.964

Selected by Washington Senators' organization in 6th round of free-agent draft, June 8, 1971.
†Traded with Infielder Brian Doyle and cash estimated at $25,000 to New York Yankees for Infielder Sandy Alomar, February 17, 1977.
‡Granted free agency, November 5, 1977; signed by Chicago White Sox, November 28, 1977.
§Traded to Kansas City Royals for Pitcher Jeff Schattinger, March 24, 1982.

KIRBY PUCKETT

Born March 14, 1961, at Chicago, Ill.
Height, 5.08. Weight, 178.
Throws and bats righthanded.
Attended Bradley University, Peoria, Ill., and Triton College, River Grove, Ill.

Led Appalachian League in total bases with 135 and tied for lead in stolen bases with 43 in 1982.
Led California League outfielders in double plays with 5 in 1983.
Named California League Player of the Year, 1983.

Year Club	League	Pos.	G.	AB.	R.	H.	2B.	3B.	HR.	RBI.	B.A.	PO.	A.	E.	F.A.
1982—Elizabethton	Appal.	OF	65	*275	*65	*105	15	3	3	35	*.382	133	*11	5	.966
1983—Visalia	Calif.	OF	138	*548	105	172	29	7	9	97	.314	253	*22	5	.982

Selected by Minnesota Twins' organization in 1st round (third player selected) of free-agent draft, January 12, 1982.

TERRY STEPHEN PUHL

Name pronounced Pool.

Born July 8, 1956, at Melville, Saskatchewan, Canada.
Height, 6.02. Weight, 197.
Throws right and bats lefthanded.

Tied major league records for highest fielding percentage by outfielder, season, 150 or more games (1.000), 1979; fewest errors by outfielder, season, 150 or more games (0), 1979.
Major League stolen bases: 1977 (10), 1978 (32), 1979 (30), 1980 (27), 1981 (22), 1982 (17), 1983 (24). Total—162.

Year Club	League	Pos.	G.	AB.	R.	H.	2B.	3B.	HR.	RBI.	B.A.	PO.	A.	E.	F.A.
1974—Covington	Appal.	OF	59	211	42	60	11	0	0	21	.284	89	2	2	.978
1975—Dubuque	Midw.	OF-1B	104	346	57	115	10	2	0	28	.332	230	11	7	.971
1976—Columbus	South.	OF	28	98	13	28	5	0	1	14	.286	76	1	2	.975
1976—Memphis	Int.	OF	105	372	50	99	17	3	1	39	.266	191	5	3	.985
1977—Charleston	Int.	OF	78	285	53	87	12	6	4	33	.305	189	4	3	.985
1977—Houston	Nat.	OF	60	229	40	69	13	5	0	10	.301	119	3	1	.992
1978—Houston	Nat.	OF	149	585	87	169	25	6	3	35	.289	386	6	3	.992
1979—Houston	Nat.	OF	157	600	87	172	22	4	8	49	.287	352	7	0	*1.000
1980—Houston	Nat.	OF	141	535	75	151	24	5	13	55	.282	311	14	3	.991
1981—Houston	Nat.	OF	96	350	43	88	19	4	3	28	.251	185	5	0	●1.000

Year Club	League	Pos.	G.	AB.	R.	H.	2B.	3B.	HR.	RBI.	B.A.	PO.	A.	E.	F.A.
1982—Houston	Nat.	OF	145	507	64	133	17	9	8	50	.262	257	4	3	.989
1983—Houston	Nat.	OF	137	465	66	136	25	7	8	44	.292	220	4	2	.991
Major League Totals			885	3271	462	918	145	40	43	271	.281	1830	43	12	.994

Signed as free agent by Houston Astros' organization, September 19, 1973.

DIVISION SERIES RECORD

Year Club	League	Pos.	G.	AB.	R.	H.	2B.	3B.	HR.	RBI.	B.A.	PO.	A.	E.	F.A.
1981—Houston	Nat.	OF	5	21	2	4	1	0	0	0	.190	7	1	0	1.000

CHAMPIONSHIP SERIES RECORD

Tied Championship Series records for most at bats, extra-inning game (6), October 8, 1980; most one-base hits, five-game Series (8), 1980.

Established National League Championship Series records for highest batting average, five-game Series (.526), 1980; most hits, five-game Series (10), 1980.

Tied National League Championship Series record for most hits, game (4), October 12, 1980.

Year Club	League	Pos.	G.	AB.	R.	H.	2B.	3B.	HR.	RBI.	B.A.	PO.	A.	E.	F.A.
1980—Houston	Nat.	PH-OF	5	19	4	10	2	0	0	3	.526	13	0	0	1.000

ALL-STAR GAME RECORD

Member of National League All-Star Team for 1978 game; did not play.

LUIS BIENVENIDO PUJOLS (TORIBIA)

Name pronounced POO-hols.

Born November 18, 1955, at Santiago Rodriguez, Dominican Republic
Height, 6.01. Weight, 195.
Throws and bats righthanded.

Led National League in passed balls with 20 in 1982.
Led Appalachian League in sacrifice flies with 9 in 1974.
Tied for Appalachian League lead in double plays by catchers with 3 and passed balls with 24 in 1973.

Year Club	League	Pos.	G.	AB.	R.	H.	2B.	3B.	HR.	RBI.	B.A.	PO.	A.	E.	F.A.
1973—Covington	Appal.	C	26	86	8	23	2	0	1	4	.267	187	21	6	.972
1974—Cedar Rapids	Midw.	C	26	86	4	17	0	1	0	10	.198	186	19	2	.990
1974—Covington	Appal.	C	60	218	26	58	7	1	1	27	.266	★408	★49	★11	.976
1975—Dubuque	Midw.	C-OF-1B	102	341	23	75	13	1	0	31	.220	598	62	9	.987
1976—Columbus†	South.	C-3B-OF	53	142	12	28	2	0	2	16	.197	186	21	1	.995
1977—Charleston‡	Int.	C	58	180	15	41	4	0	1	19	.228	239	26	4	.985
1977—Houston	Nat.	C	6	15	0	1	0	0	0	0	.067	18	4	0	1.000
1978—Charleston	Int.	C	61	196	22	43	6	1	2	24	.219	277	19	3	.990
1978—Houston	Nat.	C-1B	56	153	11	20	8	1	1	11	.131	272	33	6	.981
1979—Charleston	Int.	C	105	345	29	86	18	2	6	41	.249	487	41	6	.989
1979—Houston	Nat.	C	26	75	7	17	2	1	0	8	.227	136	6	1	.993
1980—Houston	Nat.	C-3B	78	221	15	44	6	1	0	20	.199	349	35	4	.990
1981—Houston	Nat.	C	40	117	5	28	3	1	1	14	.239	192	14	1	.995
1982—Houston	Nat.	C	65	176	8	35	2	4	4	15	.199	295	39	3	.991
1983—Houston	Nat.	C	40	87	4	17	2	0	0	12	.195	180	20	6	.971
1983—Tucson	P. C.	C	33	112	18	28	7	0	1	9	.250	189	14	2	.990
Major League Totals			311	844	50	162	27	6	6	80	.192	1442	151	21	.987

Signed as free agent by Houston Astros' organization, January 9, 1973.
†On disabled list, June 11 to June 25, July 28 to August 14 and August 22 to September 15, 1976.
‡On disabled list, April 15 to April 25, 1977.

DIVISION SERIES RECORD

Year Club	League	Pos.	G.	AB.	R.	H.	2B.	3B.	HR.	RBI.	B.A.	PO.	A.	E.	F.A.
1981—Houston	Nat.	C	2	6	0	0	0	0	0	0	.000	12	1	0	1.000

CHAMPIONSHIP SERIES RECORD

Year Club	League	Pos.	G.	AB.	R.	H.	2B.	3B.	HR.	RBI.	B.A.	PO.	A.	E.	F.A.
1980—Houston	Nat.	C	4	10	1	1	0	1	0	0	.100	21	2	0	1.000

CHARLES MICHAEL PULEO

Name pronounced Puh-LAY-oh.

(Charlie)

Born February 7, 1955, at Glen Ridge, N. J.
Height, 6.03. Weight, 190.
Throws and bats righthanded.
Received bachelor of science degree in physical education and science from
Seton Hall University, South Orange, N. J. in 1977.

Pitched seven-inning, 3-0 no-hit victory against St. Petersburg, August 13, 1979 (second game).

Year Club	League	G.	IP.	W.	L.	Pct.	H.	R.	ER.	SO.	BB.	ERA.
1978—Utica	NYP	16	104	10	3	.769	81	46	31	★125	48	2.68
1979—Dunedin	Florida St.	22	123	10	10	.500	126	72	61	77	61	4.46
1980—Knoxville†‡	Southern	19	108	8	7	.533	87	51	34	97	66	2.83
1981—Tidewater	Int'national	26	169	12	9	.571	132	74	65	133	73	3.46

Year Club	League	G.	IP.	W.	L.	Pct.	H.	R.	ER.	SO.	BB.	ERA.
1981—New York	National	4	13	0	0	.000	8	1	0	8	8	0.00
1982—New York§	National	36	171	9	9	.500	179	99	85	98	90	4.47
1983—Cincinnati x	National	27	143⅔	6	12	.333	145	86	78	71	91	4.89
Major League Totals		67	327⅔	15	21	.417	332	186	163	177	189	4.48

Selected by Detroit Tigers' organization in 13th round of free-agent draft, June 5, 1973.

Signed as free agent by Toronto Blue Jays' organization, March 14, 1978.

†On disabled list, April 24 to June 14, 1980.

‡Traded to New York Mets' organization, April 14, 1981; completing deal in which New York traded Pitcher Mark Bomback to Toronto Blue Jays for a player to be named later, April 6, 1981.

§Traded with Catcher Lloyd McClendon and Outfielder Jason Felice to Cincinnati Reds for Pitcher Tom Seaver, December 16, 1982.

xOn disabled list, March 20 to May 2, 1983.

ALFONSO PULIDO (MANZO)

Born January 23, 1959, at Vera Cruz, Mexico.
Height, 5.11. Weight, 175.
Throws and bats lefthanded.

Led Mexican Center League in games started by pitchers with 16 in 1978 and tied for lead with 14 in 1977.

Tied for Mexican Center League lead in shutouts with 3 in 1978.

Year Club	League	G.	IP.	W.	L.	Pct.	H.	R.	ER.	SO.	BB.	ERA.
1977—Arandas	Mex. Cent.	14	99	6	6	.500	124	61	48	46	18	4.36
1978—Matamoras	Mex. Cent.	18	111	10	3	.769	103	39	26	81	16	2.11
1978—Cordoba	Mexican	5	12	2	0	1.000	5	1	1	10	2	0.75
1979—Cordoba	Mexican	20	47	3	2	.600	50	22	22	23	19	4.21
1980—Reynosa†	Mexican	26	132	9	6	.600	142	58	52	69	39	3.55
1980—Reynosa‡	Mexican	7	47	3	4	.429	59	18	12	19	13	2.30
1981—Mexico City Reds	Mexican	31	126	5	6	.455	121	46	43	46	25	3.07
1982—Mexico City Reds	Mexican	43	93⅓	8	8	.500	94	34	25	50	31	2.41
1983—Mexico City Reds§	Mexican	29	187⅓	●17	3	.850	170	46	42	83	31	2.02
1983—Pittsburgh	National	1	2	0	0	.000	4	3	2	1	1	9.00
Major League Totals		1	2	0	0	.000	4	3	2	1	1	9.00

†20-team season.

‡6-team season.

§Sold to Pittsburgh Pirates, July 22, 1983; remained with Mexico City Reds on loan until September 1, 1983.

PATRICK EDWARD PUTNAM
(Pat)

Born December 3, 1953, at Bethel, Vt.
Height, 6.01. Weight, 214.
Throws right and bats lefthanded.
Attended Miami-Dade Community College North, Miami, Fla. and
University of South Alabama, Mobile, Ala.

Led Western Carolinas League in total bases with 305, sacrifice flies with 12, and intentional bases on balls received with 15 in 1976.

Led Western Carolinas League first basemen in fielding percentage with .993 in 1976.

Named American League Rookie Player of the Year by THE SPORTING NEWS, 1979.

Named Minor League Player of the Year by THE SPORTING NEWS, 1976.

Year Club	League	Pos.	G.	AB.	R.	H.	2B.	3B.	HR.	RBI.	B.A.	PO.	A.	E.	F.A.
1975—Sara. Rangers	Gulf C.	1B-OF	18	73	13	21	4	1	2	17	.288	144	9	2	.981
1975—Lynchburg	Carol.	1B-C-OF	44	158	15	35	7	0	5	22	.222	366	23	3	.992
1976—Asheville	W. Car.	1B-C	138	538	100	★194	●33	3	★24	★142	★.361	1156	97	11	.991
1977—Tucson	P. C.	1B-OF	130	495	71	149	31	4	15	102	.301	759	53	11	.987
1977—Texas	Amer.	1B	11	26	3	8	4	0	0	3	.308	35	1	0	1.000
1978—Tucson	P. C.	1B-OF	114	447	81	138	25	2	21	96	.309	433	28	9	.981
1978—Texas	Amer.	1B	20	46	4	7	1	0	1	2	.152	15	1	0	1.000
1979—Texas	Amer.	1B	139	426	57	118	19	2	18	64	.277	832	62	5	.994
1980—Texas	Amer.	1B-3B	147	410	42	108	16	2	13	55	.263	979	80	9	.992
1981—Texas	Amer.	1B-OF	95	297	33	79	17	2	8	35	.266	771	64	7	.992
1982—Texas	Amer.	1B-OF-3B	43	122	14	28	8	0	2	9	.230	287	24	3	.990
1982—Denver†	A. A.	1B-OF	80	281	47	87	20	3	13	60	.310	627	48	8	.988
1983—Seattle	Amer.	1B	144	469	58	126	23	2	19	67	.269	1067	85	7	.994
Major League Totals			599	1796	211	474	88	8	61	235	.264	3986	316	31	.993

Selected by New York Mets' organization in 12th round of free-agent draft, June 5, 1974.

Selected by Texas Rangers' organization in secondary phase of free-agent draft, June 4, 1975.

†Traded to Seattle Mariners for Pitcher Ron Musselman, December 21, 1982.

TIMOTHY MATTHEW PYZNARSKI
(Tim)

Born February 4, 1960, at Chicago, Ill.
Height, 6.02. Weight, 190.
Throws and bats righthanded.
Attended Eastern Illinois University, Charleston, Ill.

Led Eastern League third basemen in putouts with 90, errors with 36, total chances with 336 and double plays with 24 in 1983.

Year Club	League	Pos.	G.	AB.	R.	H.	2B.	3B.	HR.	RBI.	B.A.	PO.	A.	E.	F.A.
1981—Modesto	Calif.	OF-3B	53	160	32	36	4	0	5	18	.225	71	29	10	.909
1982—West Haven†	East.	3B-1B	108	294	54	77	18	4	7	34	.262	66	168	31	.883
1983—Albany	East.	★3B-OF	124	416	84	116	15	4	29	79	.279	95	★210	37	.892

Selected by Oakland A's organization in 1st round (15th player selected) of free-agent draft, June 8, 1981.
†On disabled list, June 10 to June 25, 1982.

LUIS RAUL QUINONES

Name pronounced QUEEN-yo-nes.
Born April 28, 1962, at Ponce, Puerto Rico.
Height, 5.11. Weight, 165.
Throws right and bats left and righthanded.

Led Carolina League shortstops in double plays with 77 in 1981.
Tied for Northwest League lead in double plays by shortstops with 33 in 1980.

Year Club	League	Pos.	G.	AB.	R.	H.	2B.	3B.	HR.	RBI.	B.A.	PO.	A.	E.	F.A.
1980—Grays Harbor	N'west	SS	56	156	33	35	2	2	0	11	.224	70	157	24	.904
1981—Salem	Carol.	●SS-2B	123	455	64	102	10	4	7	37	.224	208	341	●53	.912
1982—Salem	Carol.	SS	41	173	32	48	1	4	5	28	.277	41	99	15	.903
1982—Amarillo†	Texas	SS	95	411	69	120	19	7	11	60	.292	164	288	31	.936
1983—Albany	East.	2B-OF-SS	56	213	35	51	5	0	6	23	.239	101	138	13	.948
1983—Oakland	Amer.	2-O-3-S	19	42	5	8	2	1	0	4	.190	22	24	1	.979
1983—Tacoma‡	P. C.	SS-OF-2B	45	133	14	35	3	1	2	14	.263	62	97	9	.946
Major League Totals			19	42	5	8	2	1	0	4	.190	22	24	1	.979

Signed as free agent by San Diego Padres' organization, April 28, 1980.
†Drafted by Oakland A's, December 6, 1982.
‡Traded to Cleveland Indians, December 8, 1983, completing deal in which Cleveland traded Catcher Jim Essian to Oakland A's for a player to be named later, December 5, 1983.

JAMES PATRICK QUIRK
(Jamie)

Born October 22, 1954, at Whittier, Calif.
Height, 6.04. Weight, 200.
Throws right and bats lefthanded.
Attended Whittier College, Whittier, Calif.

Led American Association third basemen in double plays with 31 in 1975.
Led Pioneer League shortstops in double plays with 16 in 1972.

Year Club	League	Pos.	G.	AB.	R.	H.	2B.	3B.	HR.	RBI.	B.A.	PO.	A.	E.	F.A.
1972—Billings	Pion.	SS	55	208	29	53	9	4	5	37	.255	★63	★162	★28	★.889
1973—San Jose	Calif.	SS	132	429	58	99	12	7	8	45	.231	160	330	39	.926
1974—Jacksonville	South.	SS	46	163	16	37	7	2	3	21	.227	75	133	20	.912
1974—Omaha	A. A.	SS-3B-2B	53	203	27	57	10	2	10	31	.281	64	141	14	.936
1975—Omaha	A. A.	3B	127	445	62	122	23	4	13	64	.274	109	★254	16	★.958
1975—Kansas City	Amer.	OF-3B	14	39	2	10	0	0	1	5	.256	19	3	2	.917
1976—Kansas City†	Amer.	SS-3B-1B	64	114	11	28	6	0	1	15	.246	9	14	2	.920
1977—Milwaukee	Amer.	OF-3B	93	221	16	48	14	1	3	13	.217	19	4	2	.920
1978—Spokane‡	P. C.	3B-1B	97	343	58	100	20	2	12	63	.292	235	142	20	.950
1978—Kansas City§	Amer.	3B-SS	17	29	3	6	2	0	0	2	.207	11	16	2	.931
1979—Kansas City	Amer.	C-SS-3B	51	79	8	24	6	1	1	11	.304	16	9	1	.960
1980—Kansas City	Amer.	C-3-O-1	62	163	13	45	5	0	5	21	.276	78	66	8	.947
1981—Kansas City	Amer.	C-3-2-O	46	100	8	25	7	0	0	10	.250	63	23	4	.956
1982—Kansas City xy	Amer.	C-1-3-O	36	78	8	18	3	0	1	5	.231	110	12	0	1.000
1983—St. Louis	Nat.	C-3B-SS	48	86	3	18	2	1	2	11	.209	68	13	6	.931
American League Totals			383	823	69	204	43	2	12	82	.248	325	147	21	.957
National League Totals			48	86	3	18	2	1	2	11	.209	68	13	6	.931
Major League Totals			431	909	72	222	45	3	14	93	.244	393	160	27	.953

Selected by Kansas City Royals' organization in 1st round (18th player selected) of free-agent draft, June 6, 1972.
†Traded with Outfielder Jim Wohlford and a player to be named later to Milwaukee Brewers for Pitcher Jim Colborn and Catcher Darrell Porter, December 6, 1976; Milwaukee acquired Pitcher Bob McClure to complete deal, March 15, 1977.
‡Traded to Kansas City Royals for Pitcher Gerry Ako and cash, August 3, 1978.
§On supplemental disabled list, August 14 to September 5, 1978.
xOn supplemental disabled list, August 10 to September 1, 1982.
yGranted free agency, November 10, 1982; signed by St. Louis Cardinals, February 16, 1983.

CHAMPIONSHIP SERIES RECORD

Year Club	League	Pos.	G.	AB.	R.	H.	2B.	3B.	HR.	RBI.	B.A.	PO.	A.	E.	F.A.
1976—Kansas City	Amer.	PH-DH	4	7	1	1	0	1	0	2	.143	0	0	0	.000

DANIEL RAYMOND QUISENBERRY
(Dan)

Born February 7, 1953, at Santa Monica, Calif.
Height, 6.02. Weight, 180.
Throws and bats righthanded.
Attended Orange Coast College, Costa Mesa, Calif., LaVerne College, LaVerne, Calif.,
and Pacific College, Fresno, Calif.

Established major league record for most saves, season (45), 1983.
Major League saves: 1979 (5), 1980 (33), 1981 (18), 1982 (35), 1983 (45). Total—136.
Led American League in games finished in relief with 68 in both 1980 and 1982 and 62 in 1983.
Led American League in saves with 35 in 1982, 45 in 1983 and tied for lead with 33 in 1980.
Tied for Southern League lead in saves with 15 in 1978.
Named American League Fireman of the Year by THE SPORTING NEWS, 1980, 1982 and 1983.

Year Club	League	G.	IP.	W.	L.	Pct.	H.	R.	ER.	SO.	BB.	ERA.
1975—Waterloo	Midwest	20	44	3	2	.600	40	16	12	31	6	2.45
1975—Jacksonville	Southern	6	8	0	1	.000	5	3	2	2	4	2.25
1976—Jacksonville	Southern	9	12	0	1	.000	8	6	3	6	2	2.25
1976—Waterloo	Midwest	34	42	2	1	.667	28	4	3	19	9	0.64
1977—Jacksonville	Southern	33	74	3	1	.750	61	18	11	33	11	1.34
1978—Jacksonville	Southern	48	64	4	2	.667	62	22	17	29	12	2.39
1979—Omaha	Am. Assoc.	26	35	2	1	.667	29	15	14	16	10	3.60
1979—Kansas City	American	32	40	3	2	.600	42	16	14	13	7	3.15
1980—Kansas City	American	*75	128	12	7	.632	129	47	44	37	27	3.09
1981—Kansas City	American	40	62	1	4	.200	59	16	12	20	15	1.74
1982—Kansas City	American	72	136⅔	9	7	.563	126	43	39	46	12	2.57
1983—Kansas City	American	*69	139	5	3	.625	118	35	30	48	11	1.94
Major League Totals		288	505⅔	30	23	.566	474	157	139	164	72	2.47

Signed as free agent by Kansas City Royals' organization, June 7, 1975.

DIVISION SERIES RECORD

Year Club	League	G.	IP.	W.	L.	Pct.	H.	R.	ER.	SO.	BB.	ERA.
1981—Kansas City	American	1	1	0	0	.000	1	0	0	0	0	0.00

CHAMPIONSHIP SERIES RECORD

Year Club	League	G.	IP.	W.	L.	Pct.	H.	R.	ER.	SO.	BB.	ERA.
1980—Kansas City	American	2	4⅔	1	0	1.000	4	1	0	1	2	0.00

WORLD SERIES RECORD

Established World Series records for most games pitched in relief, six-game Series (6), 1980; most games finished, six-game Series (6), 1980.

Year Club	League	G.	IP.	W.	L.	Pct.	H.	R.	ER.	SO.	BB.	ERA.
1980—Kansas City	American	6	10⅓	1	2	.333	10	6	6	0	3	5.23

ALL-STAR GAME RECORD

Year League	IP.	W.	L.	Pct.	H.	R.	ER.	SO.	BB.	ERA.
1982—American	2	0	0	.000	3	1	1	1	0	4.50
1983—American	1	0	0	.000	1	0	0	1	0	0.00
All-Star Game Totals	3	0	0	.000	4	1	1	2	0	3.00

JOHN ANDREW RABB

Born June 23, 1960, at Los Angeles, Calif.
Height, 6.01. Weight, 179.
Throws and bats righthanded.
Attended El Camino Junior College, Torrance, Calif.

Led California League catchers in putouts with 661 and tied for lead in passed balls with 17 in 1980.
Tied for Texas League lead in double plays by catchers with 6 in 1981.

Year Club	League	Pos.	G.	AB.	R.	H.	2B.	3B.	HR.	RBI.	B.A.	PO.	A.	E.	F.A.
1978—Great Falls	Pion.	C-O-3-1	54	184	32	52	5	3	8	32	.283	185	22	6	.972
1979—Cedar Rapids	Midw.	C-OF	125	447	63	118	19	1	19	90	.264	384	50	15	.967
1980—Fresno	Calif.	*C-OF-3B	128	395	69	96	21	2	19	80	.243	*661	70	11	.985
1981—Shreveport	Texas	*C-OF	102	355	51	98	16	2	16	58	.276	533	42	*18	.970
1982—Phoenix	P. C.	C-OF	119	413	66	115	27	2	22	73	.278	552	55	16	.974
1982—San Francisco	Nat.	OF	2	2	0	1	0	1	0	0	.500	1	0	0	1.000
1983—Phoenix	P. C.	C-OF	62	216	50	74	11	1	10	51	.343	291	17	5	.984
1983—San Francisco	Nat.	C-OF	40	104	10	24	9	0	1	14	.231	176	13	5	.974
Major League Totals			42	106	10	25	9	1	1	14	.236	177	13	5	.974

Selected by San Francisco Giants' organization in 11th round of free-agent draft, June 6, 1978.

TIMOTHY RAINES
(Tim)

Born September 16, 1959, at Sanford, Fla.
Height, 5.08. Weight, 170.
Throws right and bats left and righthanded.
Brother of Ned Raines, minor league outfielder, 1978 through 1980.

Established modern major league record for most stolen bases, rookie season (71), 1981.
Major League stolen bases: 1979 (2), 1980 (5), 1981 (71), 1982 (78), 1983 (90). Total—246.
Led National League in stolen bases with 71 in 1981, 78 in 1982 and 90 in 1983.
Led National League outfielders in assists with 21 in 1983.
Led American Association in stolen bases with 77 in 1980.
Named outfielder on THE SPORTING NEWS National League All-Star Team, 1983.
Named National League Rookie Player of the Year by THE SPORTING NEWS, 1981.
Named Minor League Player of the Year by THE SPORTING NEWS, 1980.

Year Club	League	Pos.	G.	AB.	R.	H.	2B.	3B.	HR.	RBI.	B.A.	PO.	A.	E.	F.A.
1977—Sarasota Expos	Gulf C.	2B-3B-OF	49	161	28	45	6	2	0	21	.280	79	72	13	.921
1978—W. Palm Beach†..	Fla. St.	2B-SS	100	359	67	103	10	0	0	23	.287	219	273	24	.953
1979—Memphis................	South.	2B	●145	552	★104	160	25	10	5	50	.290	★341	★413	★23	.970
1979—Montreal	Nat.	PR	6	0	3	0	0	0	0	0	.000	0	0	0	.000
1980—Denver	A. A.	2B	108	429	105	152	23	●11	6	64	★.354	226	338	16	.972
1980—Montreal	Nat.	2B-OF	15	20	5	1	0	0	0	0	.050	15	16	0	1.000
1981—Montreal	Nat.	OF-2B	88	313	61	95	13	7	5	37	.304	162	8	4	.977
1982—Montreal	Nat.	OF-2B	156	647	90	179	32	8	4	43	.277	293	126	8	.981
1983—Montreal	Nat.	OF-2B	156	615	★133	183	32	8	11	71	.298	314	23	4	.988
Major League Totals................			421	1595	292	458	77	23	20	151	.287	784	173	16	.984

Selected by Montreal Expos' organization in 5th round of free-agent draft, June 7, 1977.
†On disabled list, May 23 to June 5, 1978.

CHAMPIONSHIP SERIES RECORD

Year Club	League	Pos.	G.	AB.	R.	H.	2B.	3B.	HR.	RBI.	B.A.	PO.	A.	E.	F.A.
1981—Montreal	Nat.	OF	5	21	1	5	2	0	0	1	.238	9	0	0	1.000

ALL-STAR GAME RECORD

Year League	Pos.	AB.	R.	H.	2B.	3B.	HR.	RBI.	B.A.	PO.	A.	E.	F.A.
1981—National................	PR-OF	0	0	0	0	0	0	0	.000	1	0	0	1.000
1982—National................	OF	1	0	0	0	0	0	0	.000	0	0	0	.000
1983—National................	OF	3	0	0	0	0	0	0	.000	2	0	0	1.000
All-Star Game Totals		4	0	0	0	0	0	0	.000	3	0	0	1.000

CHARLES DAVID RAINEY
(Chuck)

Born July 14, 1954, at San Diego, Calif.
Height, 5.11. Weight, 195.
Throws and bats righthanded.
Attended San Diego Mesa Junior College, San Diego, Calif.

Year Club	League	G.	IP.	W.	L.	Pct.	H.	R.	ER.	SO.	BB.	ERA.
1974—Elmira........................	NYP	16	77	4	5	.444	89	59	48	63	51	5.61
1975—Winston-Salem	Carolina	20	109	4	9	.308	110	75	53	77	66	4.38
1976—Bristol	Eastern	22	101	7	4	.636	109	67	49	31	63	4.37
1977—Bristol	Eastern	7	59	4	3	.571	55	19	15	40	21	2.29
1977—Pawtucket	Int'national	19	123	5	9	.357	114	65	42	60	58	3.07
1978—Pawtucket	Int'national	24	170	13	7	.650	169	71	55	104	75	2.91
1979—Boston†	American	20	104	8	5	.615	97	47	44	41	41	3.81
1979—Pawtucket	Int'national	3	17	1	0	1.000	8	0	0	9	3	0.00
1980—Boston‡	American	16	87	8	3	.727	92	49	47	43	41	4.86
1981—Boston	American	11	40	0	1	.000	39	21	12	20	13	2.70
1981—Pawtucket	Int'national	4	20	1	1	.500	23	8	7	16	6	3.15
1982—Boston§	American	27	129	7	5	.583	146	75	72	57	63	5.02
1983—Chicago	National	34	191	14	13	.519	219	109	95	84	74	4.48
American League Totals..		74	360	23	14	.622	374	192	180	161	158	4.50
National League Totals..		34	191	14	13	.519	219	109	95	84	74	4.48
Major League Totals................		108	551	37	27	.578	593	301	275	245	232	4.49

Selected by Boston Red Sox' organization in 1st round (19th player selected) of free-agent draft, January 9, 1974.
†On disabled list, July 20 to August 11, 1979.
‡On disabled list, July 4 to October 21, 1980.
§Traded to Chicago Cubs for Pitcher Doug Bird, December 10, 1982.

GARY LOUIS RAJSICH

Name pronounced RAY-sich.

Born October 28, 1954, at Youngstown, O.
Height, 6.02. Weight, 190.
Throws and bats lefthanded.
Attended Arizona State University, Tempe, Ariz.
Brother of Dave Rajsich, pitcher in Texas Rangers' organization; and
Tim Rajsich, minor league shortstop, 1971 and 1972.

Tied for International League lead in being hit by pitch with 9 in 1983.
Led Florida State League first basemen in double plays with 115 in 1977.
Led Appalachian League first basemen in double plays with 58 in 1976.

Year Club	League	Pos.	G.	AB.	R.	H.	2B.	3B.	HR.	RBI.	B.A.	PO.	A.	E.	F.A.
1976—Covington	Appal.	1B	66	244	33	54	8	3	6	27	.221	★649	★75	★14	.981
1977—Cocoa....................	Fla. St.	★1B-OF	136	486	50	119	19	5	8	53	.245	1153	★119	25	.981
1978—Columbus...............	South.	OF-1B	80	286	37	69	12	5	7	34	.241	359	28	2	.995
1978—Charleston	Int.	OF	46	126	19	29	4	1	2	13	.230	74	3	1	.987
1979—Columbus...............	South.	OF-2B	66	232	43	68	25	4	14	53	.293	105	7	4	.966
1979—Charleston	Int.	OF	65	218	27	45	8	2	6	28	.206	114	1	4	.966
1980—Tucson†	P. C.	OF	134	445	94	143	22	14	21	99	.321	205	10	1	.995
1981—Tidewater‡............	Int.	OF-1B	74	253	47	70	11	1	24	56	.277	188	13	4	.980
1982—New York...............	Nat.	OF-1B	80	162	17	42	8	3	2	12	.259	70	1	0	1.000
1983—Tidewater	Int.	★1B-OF	129	430	68	116	15	2	28	83	.270	927	★120	10	.991
1983—New York...............	Nat.	1B	11	36	5	12	3	0	1	3	.333	94	6	0	1.000
Major League Totals................			91	198	22	54	11	3	3	15	.273	164	7	0	1.000

Selected by Houston Astros' organization in 11th round of free-agent draft, June 8, 1976.
†Traded to New York Mets' organization for Outfielder John Csefalvay, April 3, 1981.
‡On disabled list, July 16, 1981 through remainder of season.

DANIEL ALLAN RAMIREZ

(Known by middle name.)
Born May 1, 1957, at Victoria, Tex.
Height, 5.10. Weight, 190.
Throws and bats righthanded.
Attended Rice University, Houston, Tex.

Tied for Southern League lead in games started by pitchers with 29 in 1980.

Year Club	League	G.	IP.	W.	L.	Pct.	H.	R.	ER.	SO.	BB.	ERA.
1979—Miami	Florida St.	14	93	3	9	.250	97	40	27	54	35	2.61
1980—Charlotte	Southern	29	196	16	8	.667	151	73	65	160	92	2.98
1981—Miami	Florida St.	3	13	0	1	.000	10	8	4	10	8	2.77
1981—Rochester†	Int'national	8	41	1	3	.250	32	19	19	26	19	4.17
1982—Rochester‡	Int'national	24	124	6	10	.375	111	77	67	85	★117	4.86
1983—Rochester	Int'national	15	90	4	5	.444	76	42	38	78	55	3.80
1983—Baltimore	American	11	57	4	4	.500	46	22	22	20	30	3.47
Major League Totals		11	57	4	4	.500	46	22	22	20	30	3.47

Selected by Philadelphia Phillies' organization in 23rd round of free-agent draft, June 4, 1975.
Selected by Texas Rangers' organization in 9th round of free-agent draft, June 6, 1978.
Selected by Baltimore Orioles' organization in 4th round of free-agent draft, June 5, 1979.
†On disabled list, May 22 to July 6, 1981.
‡On disabled list, July 31 to August 15, 1982.

MARIO RAMIREZ (TORRES)

Born September 12, 1957, at Yauco, Puerto Rico.
Height, 5.09. Weight, 155.
Throws and bats righthanded.

Led International League shortstops in fielding percentage with .983 in 1979.

Year Club	League	Pos.	G.	AB.	R.	H.	2B.	3B.	HR.	RBI.	B.A.	PO.	A.	E.	F.A.
1976—Wausau	Midw.	SS	89	287	48	66	16	1	2	28	.230	145	253	46	.896
1977—Lynchburg	Carol.	SS	72	272	41	62	11	3	8	36	.228	123	186	19	.942
1977—Jackson	Texas	SS	60	206	23	52	5	1	6	21	.252	110	170	14	.952
1978—Tidewater	Int.	SS	126	389	43	81	14	4	5	41	.208	176	382	★46	.924
1979—Tidewater	Int.	SS-2B	132	376	42	82	10	2	6	31	.218	190	432	9	.986
1980—New York†	Nat.	SS-2B-3B	18	24	2	5	0	0	0	0	.208	13	21	0	1.000
1980—Tidewater†	Int.	SS-2B-OF	71	208	17	42	7	2	0	15	.202	129	173	17	.947
1981—Hawaii	P. C.	SS	118	411	51	103	13	7	5	49	.251	192	390	18	.970
1981—San Diego	Nat.	SS-2B	13	13	1	1	0	0	0	1	.077	5	11	0	1.000
1982—San Diego	Nat.	SS-3B-2B	13	23	1	4	1	0	0	1	.174	10	21	1	.969
1982—Hawaii	P. C.	SS	22	70	14	18	6	0	1	9	.257	29	64	5	.949
1983—Las Vegas	P. C.	SS	16	54	7	12	2	2	1	8	.222	25	46	1	.986
1983—San Diego	Nat.	SS-3B	55	107	11	21	6	3	0	12	.196	50	86	2	.986
Major League Totals			99	167	15	31	7	3	0	14	.186	78	139	3	.986

Signed as free agent by New York Mets' organization, March 5, 1976.
†Drafted by San Diego Padres, December 8, 1980.

RAFAEL EMILIO RAMIREZ (PEGUERO)

Born February 18, 1959, at San Pedro de Macoris, Dominican Republic.
Height, 6.00. Weight, 170.
Throws and bats righthanded.

Major League stolen bases: 1980 (2), 1981 (7), 1982 (27), 1983 (16). Total—52.
Led National League shortstops in double plays with 130 in 1982 and 116 in 1983.
Led National League shortstops in total chances with 866 in 1982.

Year Club	League	Pos.	G.	AB.	R.	H.	2B.	3B.	HR.	RBI.	B.A.	PO.	A.	E.	F.A.
1977—Brad. Braves	Gulf C.	SS-OF	49	175	20	31	2	1	4	19	.177	52	94	32	.820
1978—Greenwood	W. Car.	SS	81	282	54	77	15	3	6	46	.273	119	229	★43	.890
1978—Savannah	South.	SS	38	131	14	27	4	0	2	13	.206	61	123	15	.925
1979—Savannah†	South.	SS	113	386	47	80	17	3	10	39	.207	134	282	★38	.916
1980—Richmond‡	Int.	SS	80	281	33	79	15	3	5	38	.281	117	294	23	.947
1980—Atlanta	Nat.	SS	50	165	17	44	6	1	2	11	.267	63	140	11	.949
1981—Atlanta	Nat.	SS	95	307	30	67	16	2	2	20	.218	181	306	★30	.942
1982—Atlanta	Nat.	SS	157	609	74	169	24	4	10	52	.278	★300	528	★38	.956
1983—Atlanta	Nat.	SS	152	622	82	185	13	5	7	58	.297	232	490	★39	.949
Major League Totals			454	1703	203	465	59	12	21	141	.273	776	1464	118	.950

Signed as free agent by Atlanta Braves' organization, September 28, 1976.
†On disabled list, April 16 to April 27, 1979.
‡On disabled list, June 23 to July 17, 1980.

CHAMPIONSHIP SERIES RECORD

Year Club	League	Pos.	G.	AB.	R.	H.	2B.	3B.	HR.	RBI.	B.A.	PO.	A.	E.	F.A.
1982—Atlanta	Nat.	SS	3	11	1	2	0	0	0	1	.182	5	11	1	.941

DOMINGO ANTONIO RAMOS

Born March 29, 1958, at Santiago, Dominican Republic.
Height, 5.10. Weight, 154.
Throws and bats righthanded.

Tied for International League lead in sacrifice flies with 6 in 1981.

Year Club	League	Pos.	G.	AB.	R.	H.	2B.	3B.	HR.	RBI.	B.A.	PO.	A.	E.	F.A.
1975—Oneonta	NYP	SS-3B	49	166	29	39	4	1	0	21	.235	60	143	14	.935
1976—Ft. Lauderdale	Fla. St.	SS	103	328	34	79	11	3	0	29	.241	150	343	35	.934
1976—Syracuse	Int.	SS	11	39	7	10	2	1	0	8	.256	13	20	2	.943
1977—West Haven	East.	SS	129	431	55	106	18	6	2	50	.246	222	433	23	★.966
1978—Tacoma................	P. C.	SS	91	314	43	74	13	3	0	30	.236	155	290	28	.941
1978—West Haven	East.	SS	40	134	16	34	2	2	1	13	.254	40	128	6	.966
1978—New York†‡.........	Amer.	SS	1	0	0	0	0	0	0	0	.000	0	0	0	.000
1979—Syr.§-Colum. x.....	Int.	SS	115	376	38	92	11	4	1	28	.245	211	323	26	.954
1980—Syracuse	Int.	SS	84	319	45	80	8	4	4	27	.251	160	240	28	.935
1980—Toronto	Amer.	SS-2B	5	16	0	2	0	0	0	0	.125	5	10	0	1.000
1981—Syracuse y	Int.	SS-3B-2B	96	320	42	82	4	5	0	31	.256	158	248	19	.955
1982—Salt Lake City.....	P. C.	SS	112	427	75	134	19	8	6	56	.314	174	288	19	.960
1982—Seattle..................	Amer.	SS	8	26	3	4	2	0	0	1	.154	9	14	2	.920
1983—Seattle..................	Amer.	2B-SS-3B	52	127	14	36	4	0	2	10	.283	51	109	8	.952
Major League Totals....................			66	169	17	42	6	0	2	11	.249	65	133	10	.952

Signed as free agent by New York Yankees' organization, May 27, 1975.

†Traded with Pitchers Sparky Lyle, Larry McCall and Dave Rajsich, Catcher Mike Heath and cash to Texas Rangers for Outfielders Juan Beniquez and Greg Jemison and Pitchers Mike Griffin, Paul Mirabella and Dave Righetti, November 10, 1978.

‡Loaned to Toronto Blue Jays' organization, April 5, 1979.

§Loaned to New York Yankees' organization, July 30, 1979; returned to Texas Rangers, September 28, 1979.

xSold to Toronto Blue Jays, November 5, 1979.

yDrafted by Seattle Mariners, December 7, 1981.

ROBERTO RAMOS
(Bobby)

Born November 5, 1955, at Havana, Cuba.
Height, 5.11. Weight, 208.
Throws and bats righthanded.

Led Southern League in passed balls with 12 in 1978.
Tied for Eastern League lead in double plays by shortstops with 77 in 1977.
Led Florida State League in being hit by pitch with 10 in 1977.

Year Club	League	Pos.	G.	AB.	R.	H.	2B.	3B.	HR.	RBI.	B.A.	PO.	A.	E.	F.A.
1974—Sarasota Expos....	Gulf C.	★C-OF	48	144	16	36	3	4	2	16	.250	245	48	★14	.954
1975—W. Palm Beach....	Fla. St.	C	73	204	16	39	7	2	1	12	.191	374	49	13	.970
1976—W. Palm B'ch†	Fla. St.	C	101	297	29	81	9	2	3	39	.273	417	60	★15	.970
1977—W. Palm Beach....	Fla. St.	C	104	320	45	99	18	4	5	58	.309	430	47	8	.984
1978—Denver	A. A.	C	12	39	4	7	0	0	0	2	.179	56	15	1	.986
1978—Memphis...............	South.	C	109	343	36	91	16	2	9	51	.265	457	60	9	.983
1978—Montreal	Nat.	C	2	4	0	0	0	0	0	0	.000	3	1	0	1.000
1979—Denver‡§	A. A.	C	8	11	0	2	0	0	0	2	.182	14	3	1	.944
1979—Salt Lake City.....	P. C.	C-1B	58	179	27	51	9	1	3	21	.285	112	14	7	.947
1980—Denver	A. A.	C	74	244	36	72	6	1	4	30	.295	399	51	4	.991
1980—Montreal	Nat.	C	13	32	5	5	2	0	0	2	.156	47	7	2	.964
1981—Montreal x	Nat.	C	26	41	4	8	1	0	1	3	.195	70	5	2	.974
1982—Columbus y...........	Int.	C-3B	63	198	22	46	9	0	2	14	.232	313	31	6	.983
1982—New York z..........	Amer.	C	4	11	1	1	0	0	1	2	.091	21	1	0	1.000
1983—Montreal	Nat.	C	27	61	2	14	3	1	0	5	.230	111	14	2	.984
National League Totals.............................			68	138	11	27	6	1	1	10	.196	231	27	6	.977
American League Totals			4	11	1	1	0	0	1	2	.091	21	1	0	1.000
Major League Totals..................................			72	149	12	28	6	1	2	12	.188	252	28	6	.979

Selected by Montreal Expos' organization in 7th round of free-agent draft, June 5, 1974.

†On suspended list, July 6 to July 12, 1976.

‡On suspended list, May 4 to May 17, 1979.

§Loaned to California Angels' organization, May 25, 1979; returned, August 29, 1979.

xTraded to New York Yankees' organization for Catcher Brad Gulden, April 5, 1982.

yOn disabled list, May 26 to June 17 and July 20 to July 30, 1982.

zSold to Montreal Expos, November 1, 1982.

MICHAEL JEFFREY RAMSEY
(Mike)

Born March 29, 1954, at Roanoke, Va.
Height, 6.01. Weight, 170.
Throws right and bats left and righthanded.
Attended Appalachian State University, Boone, N.C.

Led Appalachian League in sacrifice hits with 12 in 1975.
Led Appalachian League shortstops in fielding percentage with .937 in 1975.

Year Club	League	Pos.	G.	AB.	R.	H.	2B.	3B.	HR.	RBI.	B.A.	PO.	A.	E.	F.A.
1975—Johnson City	Appal.	SS-2B	65	★277	43	79	14	1	0	25	.285	98	183	17	.943
1976—Arkansas†..............	Texas	SS	84	288	26	79	6	1	0	24	.274	109	231	32	.914

Year Club League	Pos.	G.	AB.	R.	H.	2B.	3B.	HR.	RBI.	B.A.	PO.	A.	E.	F.A.
1977—Arkansas................ Texas	SS	121	484	51	121	21	4	1	28	.250	166	317	★44	.917
1978—Springfield‡.......... A. A.	SS	99	382	53	92	8	4	2	30	.241	172	223	★41	.906
1978—St. Louis............... Nat.	SS	12	5	4	1	0	0	0	0	.200	4	6	1	.909
1979—Springfield............ A. A.	SS	97	281	28	62	9	3	1	27	.221	134	198	24	.933
1980—Springfield........... A. A.	SS-OF	21	69	7	18	1	0	0	6	.261	34	47	6	.931
1980—St. Louis.............. Nat.	2B-3B-SS	59	126	11	33	8	1	0	8	.262	62	94	9	.945
1981—St. Louis§............. Nat.	S-3-2-O	47	124	19	32	3	0	0	9	.258	56	126	6	.968
1982—St. Louis.............. Nat.	2-3-S-O	112	256	18	59	8	2	1	21	.230	135	219	10	.973
1983—St. Louis x............ Nat.	2-S-3-O	97	175	25	46	4	3	1	16	.263	94	149	8	.968
Major League Totals....................................		327	686	77	171	23	6	2	54	.249	351	594	34	.965

Selected by Chicago Cubs' organization in 26th round of free-agent draft, June 6, 1972.
Selected by St. Louis Cardinals' organization in 3rd round of free-agent draft, June 4, 1975.
†On disabled list, July 17 to September 7, 1976.
‡On disabled list, May 13 to May 25, 1978.
§On supplemental disabled list, June 5 to August 5, 1981.
xOn supplemental disabled list, June 14 to June 29, 1983.

WORLD SERIES RECORD

Year Club League	Pos.	G.	AB.	R.	H.	2B.	3B.	HR.	RBI.	B.A.	PO.	A.	E.	F.A.
1982—St. Louis.................. Nat.	3B-PR	3	1	1	0	0	0	0	0	.000	0	0	0	.000

WILLIAM LARRY RANDOLPH JR.
(Willie)

Born July 6, 1954, at Holly Hill, S. C.
Height, 5.11. Weight, 163.
Throws and bats righthanded.
Brother of Terry Randolph, defensive back with Green Bay Packers, 1977.

Tied major league record for most assists by second baseman in extra-inning game since 1900 (13), August 25, 1976 (19 innings).
Established American League record for most chances accepted by second baseman in extra-inning game (20), August 25, 1976 (19 innings).
Major League stolen bases: 1975 (1), 1976 (37), 1977 (13), 1978 (36), 1979 (33), 1980 (30), 1981 (14), 1982 (16), 1983 (12). Total—192.
Led American League in bases on balls received with 119 in 1980.
Led American League second basemen in total chances with 846 and double plays with 128 in 1979.
Led Eastern League in bases on balls received with 110 in 1974.
Led Western Carolinas League in bases on balls received with 90 and tied for lead in sacrifice flies with 8 in 1973.
Named second baseman on THE SPORTING NEWS American League All-Star Team, 1977 and 1980.
Named second baseman on THE SPORTING NEWS American League Silver Slugger team, 1980.

Year Club League	Pos.	G.	AB.	R.	H.	2B.	3B.	HR.	RBI.	B.A.	PO.	A.	E.	F.A.
1972—Bradenton Pir...... Gulf C.	SS-OF	44	167	21	53	6	5	0	10	.317	85	116	24	.893
1973—Charleston.......... W. Car.	2B	121	428	93	120	25	6	8	51	.280	★285	308	★24	.961
1974—Thetford Mines... East.	2B	135	461	★103	117	28	6	12	53	.254	269	319	21	.966
1975—Charleston............ Int.	2B	91	313	41	106	13	5	7	42	.339	189	250	16	.965
1975—Pittsburgh†.......... Nat.	2B-3B	30	61	9	10	1	0	0	3	.164	34	45	6	.929
1976—New York............ Amer.	2B	125	430	59	115	15	4	1	40	.267	307	415	19	.974
1977—New York............ Amer.	2B	147	551	91	151	28	11	4	40	.274	350	454	16	.980
1978—New York‡........... Amer.	2B	134	499	87	139	18	6	3	42	.279	296	400	16	.978
1979—New York............ Amer.	2B	153	574	98	155	15	13	5	61	.270	★355	★478	13	.985
1980—New York............ Amer.	2B	138	513	99	151	23	7	7	46	.294	361	401	19	.976
1981—New York............ Amer.	2B	93	357	59	83	14	3	2	24	.232	205	268	★11	.977
1982—New York............ Amer.	2B	144	553	85	155	21	4	3	36	.280	352	380	14	.981
1983—New York§........... Amer.	2B	104	420	73	117	21	1	2	38	.279	265	298	12	.979
National League Totals.............................		30	61	9	10	1	0	0	3	.164	34	45	6	.929
American League Totals............................		1038	3897	651	1066	155	49	27	327	.274	2491	3094	120	.979
Major League Totals.............................		1068	3958	660	1076	156	49	27	330	.272	2525	3139	126	.978

Selected by Pittsburgh Pirates' organization in 7th round of free-agent draft, June 6, 1972.
†Traded with Pitchers Ken Brett and Dock Ellis to New York Yankees for Pitcher Doc Medich, December 11, 1975.
‡On disabled list, June 23 to July 14, 1978.
§On supplemental disabled list, June 27 to July 12 and July 13 to August 5, 1983.

DIVISION SERIES RECORD

Year Club League	Pos.	G.	AB.	R.	H.	2B.	3B.	HR.	RBI.	B.A.	PO.	A.	E.	F.A.
1981—New York............. Amer.	2B	5	20	0	4	0	0	0	1	.200	7	10	0	1.000

CHAMPIONSHIP SERIES RECORD

Year Club League	Pos.	G.	AB.	R.	H.	2B.	3B.	HR.	RBI.	B.A.	PO.	A.	E.	F.A.
1975—Pittsburgh .... Nat.	PH-PR-2	2	2	1	0	0	0	0	0	.000	0	1	0	1.000
1976—New York............. Amer.	2B	5	17	0	2	0	0	0	1	.118	8	14	0	1.000
1977—New York............. Amer.	2B	5	18	4	5	1	0	0	2	.278	13	9	0	1.000
1980—New York............. Amer.	2B	3	13	0	5	2	0	0	1	.385	2	9	0	1.000
1981—New York............. Amer.	2B	3	12	2	4	0	0	1	2	.333	12	12	0	1.000
Championship Series Totals		18	62	7	16	3	0	1	6	.258	35	45	0	1.000

WORLD SERIES RECORD

Established World Series record for most bases on balls, six-game Series (9), 1981.
Tied World Series record for fewest chances accepted by second baseman, game (0), October 25, 1981.

Year	Club	League	Pos.	G.	AB.	R.	H.	2B.	3B.	HR.	RBI.	B.A.	PO.	A.	E.	F.A.
1976—New York	Amer.		2B	4	14	1	1	0	0	0	0	.071	13	8	0	1.000
1977—New York	Amer.		2B	6	25	5	4	2	0	1	1	.160	13	14	0	1.000
1981—New York	Amer.		2B	6	18	5	4	1	1	2	3	.222	13	11	0	1.000
World Series Totals				16	57	11	9	3	1	3	4	.158	39	33	0	1.000

ALL-STAR GAME RECORD

Established All-Star Game record for most assists by second baseman, nine-inning game (6), July 19, 1977.
Tied All-Star Game records for most at bats, nine-inning game (5), July 19, 1977; most errors, game (2), July 8, 1980.

Year	League	Pos.	AB.	R.	H.	2B.	3B.	HR.	RBI.	B.A.	PO.	A.	E.	F.A.
1977—American		2B	5	0	1	0	0	0	1	.200	2	6	0	1.000
1980—American		2B	4	0	2	0	0	0	0	.500	0	3	2	.600
1981—American		2B	3	0	1	0	0	0	0	.333	0	5	0	1.000
All-Star Game Totals			12	0	4	0	0	0	1	.333	2	14	2	.888

Named to American League All-Star Team for 1976 game; replaced due to injury.

JEFFREY DEAN RANSOM
(Jeff)

Born November 11, 1960, at Fresno, Calif.
Height, 5.11. Weight, 185.
Throws right and bats left and righthanded.

Led Texas League catchers in double plays with 13 in 1980.

Year	Club	League	Pos.	G.	AB.	R.	H.	2B.	3B.	HR.	RBI.	B.A.	PO.	A.	E.	F.A.
1978—Fresno	Calif.		OF-C	26	72	13	18	3	1	2	13	.250	64	10	4	.949
1979—Fresno	Calif.		C-OF	62	216	29	55	7	1	4	22	.255	374	41	14	.967
1979—Shreveport†	Texas		C	43	145	10	40	6	1	0	14	.276	140	16	3	.981
1980—Shreveport	Texas		C	124	394	38	104	14	2	0	39	.264	★618	90	★18	.975
1981—Phoenix	P. C.		C-OF-SS	108	358	45	83	12	4	3	39	.232	398	73	12	.975
1981—San Francisco	Nat.		C	5	15	2	4	1	0	0	0	.267	28	5	0	1.000
1982—San Francisco	Nat.		C	15	44	5	7	0	0	0	3	.159	71	8	1	.988
1982—Shreveport	Texas		C-OF-3B	76	238	33	56	7	2	10	36	.235	291	45	5	.985
1983—Phoenix	P. C.		C-OF-3B	102	289	43	65	13	1	7	37	.225	440	45	20	.960
1983—San Francisco	Nat.		C	6	20	3	4	0	0	1	3	.200	32	3	2	.946
Major League Totals				26	79	10	15	1	0	1	6	.190	131	16	3	.980

Selected by San Francisco Giants' organization in 5th round of free-agent draft, June 6, 1978.
†On disabled list, July 4 to July 26, 1979.

DENNIS LEE RASMUSSEN

Born April 18, 1959, at Los Angeles, Calif.
Height, 6.07. Weight, 225.
Throws and bats lefthanded.
Attended Creighton University, Omaha, Neb.
Grandson of Wilbur Lee (Bill) Brubaker, infielder with Pittsburgh
Pirates and Boston Braves, 1932 through 1940 and 1943.

Led Eastern League in wild pitches with 18 in 1981.
Tied for International League lead in games started by pitchers with 28 in 1983.

Year	Club	League	G.	IP.	W.	L.	Pct.	H.	R.	ER.	SO.	BB.	ERA.
1980—Salinas	California		11	76	4	6	.400	69	51	46	63	52	5.45
1981—Holyoke	Eastern		24	156	8	12	.400	134	95	69	125	99	3.98
1982—Spokane‡	P. Coast		27	171⅔	11	8	.579	166	110	96	162	★113	5.03
1983—Columbus‡	Int'national		28	181	●13	10	.565	161	106	92	★187	108	4.57
1983—San Diego	National		4	13⅔	0	0	.000	10	5	3	13	8	1.98
Major League Totals			4	13⅔	0	0	.000	10	5	3	13	8	1.98

Selected by Pittsburgh Pirates' organization in 18th round of free-agent draft, June 7, 1977.
Selected by California Angels' organization in 1st round (17th player selected) of free-agent draft, June 3, 1980.
†Traded to New York Yankees, November 24, 1982, completing deal in which New York traded Pitcher Tommy John to California Angels for a player to be named later, August 31, 1982.
‡Traded with Second Baseman Edwin Rodriguez to San Diego Padres, September 12, 1983, completing deal in which San Diego traded Pitcher John Montefusco to New York Yankees for two players to be named later, August 26, 1983.

ERIC RALPH RASMUSSEN

Name pronounced Ras-MUSS-un.

(Formerly known as Harry)

Born March 22, 1952, at Racine, Wis.
Height, 6.03. Weight, 205.
Throws and bats righthanded.
Attended Indian Hills Community College, Centerville, Ia., and
University of New Orleans, New Orleans, La.

Pitched shutout in first major league game, July 21, 1975.
Tied for Texas League lead in complete games with 13 in 1974.

Year Club	League	G.	IP.	W.	L.	Pct.	H.	R.	ER.	SO.	BB.	ERA.
1973—Sarasota Cardinals	Gulf Coast	3	23	2	0	1.000	16	4	3	27	4	1.17
1973—St. Petersburg	Florida St.	8	52	3	3	.500	47	17	13	33	6	2.25
1974—Arkansas	Texas	22	159	●14	5	.737	154	65	55	121	32	3.11
1975—Tulsa	Am. Assoc.	18	129	10	5	.667	133	56	53	89	36	3.70
1975—St. Louis	National	14	81	5	5	.500	86	44	34	59	20	3.78
1976—St. Louis	National	43	150	6	12	.333	139	67	59	76	54	3.54
1977—St. Louis†	National	34	233	11	17	.393	223	103	90	120	63	3.48
1978—St. Louis†-San Diego	National	37	207	14	15	.483	215	104	94	91	63	4.09
1979—San Diego	National	45	157	6	9	.400	142	59	57	54	42	3.27
1980—San Diego‡	National	40	111	4	11	.267	130	60	54	50	33	4.38
1981—Yucatan§x	Mexican	19	145	12	6	.667	130	47	37	70	36	2.30
1982—Yucatan y	Mexican	22	163⅓	10	8	.556	131	44	41	92	35	2.26
1982—Louisville	Am. Assoc.	4	28⅓	2	2	.500	27	13	13	20	9	4.13
1982—St. Louis	National	8	18⅓	1	2	.333	21	13	9	15	8	4.42
1983—St. Louis	National	6	7⅔	0	0	.000	16	11	10	6	4	11.74
1983—Louisville za-Omaha	Am. Assoc.	11	71	8	1	.889	60	21	18	46	18	2.28
1983—Kansas City b	American	11	52⅔	3	6	.333	61	28	28	18	22	4.78
National League Totals		227	965	47	71	.398	972	461	407	471	287	3.80
American League Totals		11	52⅔	3	6	.333	61	28	28	18	22	4.78
Major League Totals		238	1017⅔	50	77	.394	1033	489	435	489	309	3.85

Selected by Boston Red Sox' organization in 4th round of free-agent draft, January 13, 1971.
Selected by St. Louis Cardinals' organization in 32nd round of free-agent draft, June 5, 1973.
†Traded to San Diego Padres for Outfielder George Hendrick, May 26, 1978.
‡Released, March 27, 1981; signed by Yucatan of Mexican League, May 12, 1981.
§Sold to St. Louis Cardinals' organization, December 8, 1981.
xSold to Yucatan of Mexican League, April 6, 1982.
ySold to Louisville (St. Louis Cardinals' organization), August 11, 1982.
zOn disabled list, May 22 to June 17, 1983.
aSold to Kansas City Royals, August 2, 1983.
bReleased, October 24, 1983.

SHANE WILLIAM RAWLEY

Born July 27, 1955, at Racine, Wis.
Height, 6.00. Weight, 155.
Throws and bats lefthanded.
Attended Indian Hills Community College, Centerville, Ia.

Led American League in intentional bases on balls issued with 16 in 1980.

Year Club	League	G.	IP.	W.	L.	Pct.	H.	R.	ER.	SO.	BB.	ERA.
1974—Sarasota Expos	Gulf Coast	2	12	0	1	.000	12	9	3	16	4	2.25
1974—Kinston	Carolina	5	19	0	2	.000	22	15	13	11	12	6.16
1975—West Palm Beach	Florida St.	24	165	8	12	.400	148	80	56	113	73	3.05
1976—Quebec City	Eastern	25	164	11	7	.611	143	55	49	113	79	2.69
1977—Denver†	Am. Assoc.	7	47	1	4	.200	54	31	27	30	19	5.21
1977—Indianapolis‡§	Am. Assoc.	19	105	5	6	.455	96	58	53	62	49	4.54
1978—Seattle	American	52	111	4	9	.308	114	57	51	66	51	4.14
1979—Seattle x	American	48	84	5	9	.357	88	40	36	48	40	3.86
1980—Seattle	American	59	114	7	7	.500	103	44	42	68	63	3.32
1981—Spokane	P. Coast	3	6	0	0	.000	3	0	0	3	3	0.00
1981—Seattle yz	American	46	68	4	6	.400	64	31	30	35	38	3.97
1982—New York	American	47	164	11	10	.524	165	79	74	111	54	4.06
1983—New York	American	34	238⅓	14	14	.500	246	111	100	124	79	3.78
Major League Totals		286	779⅓	45	55	.450	780	362	333	452	325	3.85

Selected by Los Angeles Dodgers' organization in 4th round of free-agent draft, January 9, 1974.
Selected by Montreal Expos' organization in secondary phase of free-agent draft, June 5, 1974.
†Traded with Pitcher Angel Torres to Cincinnati Reds' organization, May 27, 1977, completing deal in which Cincinnati traded Pitcher Santo Alcala to Montreal Expos for two players to be named later, May 21, 1977.
‡Appeared in one game as an outfielder with no chances.
§Traded to Seattle Mariners for Outfielder Dave Collins, December 9, 1977.
xOn disabled list, June 30 to August 21, 1979.
yOn disabled list, April 1 to April 24, 1981; included rehabilitation disability assignment to Spokane, April 16 to April 24, 1981.
zTraded to New York Yankees for Pitchers Gene Nelson and Bill Caudill, a player to be named later and cash, April 1, 1982; Seattle Mariners' organization acquired Outfielder Bobby Brown to complete deal, April 6, 1982.

JOHNNY CORNELIUS RAY

Born March 1, 1957, at Chouteau, Okla.
Height, 5.11. Weight, 175.
Throws right and bats right and lefthanded.
Attended University of Arkansas, Fayetteville, Ark.

Led National League second basemen in total chances with 914 in 1982.
Named National League Rookie Player of the Year by THE SPORTING NEWS, 1982.
Named second baseman on THE SPORTING NEWS National League Silver Slugger team, 1983.

Year Club	League	Pos.	G.	AB.	R.	H.	2B.	3B.	HR.	RBI.	B.A.	PO.	A.	E.	F.A.
1979—Sarasota Astros	Gulf C.	3B-2B	37	132	25	41	8	1	3	25	.311	25	51	11	.874
1979—Daytona Beach	Fla. St.	3B-SS-2B	24	68	6	15	1	2	1	10	.221	21	38	8	.881
1980—Columbus	South.	2B-3B-OF	138	497	86	161	32	6	10	72	.324	203	331	24	.957
1981—Tucson†	P. C.	2B	131	525	111	183	★50	10	5	83	.349	309	369	19	.973

Year Club	League	Pos.	G.	AB.	R.	H.	2B.	3B.	HR.	RBI.	B.A.	PO.	A.	E.	F.A.
1981—Pittsburgh	Nat.	2B	31	102	10	25	11	0	0	6	.245	52	96	2	.987
1982—Pittsburgh	Nat.	2B	●162	647	79	182	30	7	7	63	.281	*381	*512	*21	.977
1983—Pittsburgh	Nat.	2B	151	576	68	163	●38	7	5	53	.283	319	452	13	.983
Major League Totals			344	1325	157	370	79	14	12	122	.279	752	1060	36	.981

Selected by Houston Astros' organization in 12th round of free-agent draft, June 5, 1979.

†Traded with two minor league players to be named later to Pittsburgh Pirates for Second Baseman Phil Garner, August 31, 1981; Pittsburgh organization acquired Pitcher Randy Niemann and Outfielder Kevin Houston to complete deal, September 9, 1981.

FLOYD KINNARD RAYFORD

Born July 27, 1957, at Memphis, Tenn.
Height, 5.10. Weight, 195.
Throws and bats righthanded.

Led International League third basemen in fielding percentage with .942 in 1980.
Led Texas League third basemen in putouts with 95 and in assists with 216 in 1978.
Led California League third basemen in assists with 202, double plays with 21 and fielding percentage with .944 in 1976.
Tied for California League lead in double plays by third basemen with 21 in 1977.

Year Club	League	Pos.	G.	AB.	R.	H.	2B.	3B.	HR.	RBI.	B.A.	PO.	A.	E.	F.A.
1975—Idaho Falls	Pion.	3-C-1-O-S	●72	272	43	77	12	5	2	43	.283	244	100	21	.942
1976—Salinas	Calif.	3B-C-2B	125	462	73	126	19	6	5	67	.273	162	216	16	.959
1977—Salinas	Calif.	3B	51	205	37	53	7	3	6	39	.259	40	117	7	.957
1977—El Paso	Texas	1-2-3-S-O	79	320	65	95	17	3	11	60	.297	427	133	12	.979
1978—El Paso	Texas	3-2-1-S	126	483	78	151	36	2	17	87	.313	113	230	14	.961
1979—Salt Lake City†	P. C.	*3-S-1-2	135	551	98	162	28	6	13	80	.294	134	316	20	*.957
1980—Rochester	Int.	3B-2B-SS	107	387	51	89	22	0	9	46	.230	86	213	19	.940
1980—Baltimore	Amer.	3B-2B	8	18	1	4	0	0	0	1	.222	3	11	2	.875
1981—Rochester	Int.	3B-C-SS	96	311	50	77	18	2	11	45	.248	208	106	11	.966
1982—Baltimore	Amer.	3B-C	34	53	7	7	0	0	3	5	.132	11	43	6	.900
1982—Rochester	Int.	2B	3	12	1	3	0	0	1	2	.250	2	6	0	1.000
1983—Rochester‡	Int.	2B-C-3B	43	144	24	52	16	1	2	38	.361	59	44	5	.954
1983—St. Louis	Nat.	3B	56	104	5	22	4	0	3	14	.212	13	40	7	.883
American League Totals			42	71	8	11	0	0	3	6	.155	14	54	8	.895
National League Totals			56	104	5	22	4	0	3	14	.212	13	40	7	.883
Major League Totals			98	175	13	33	4	0	6	20	.189	27	94	15	.890

Selected by California Angels' organization in 4th round of free-agent draft, June 4, 1975.

†Traded with cash to Baltimore Orioles' organization for Outfielder Larry Harlow, June 5, 1979. (Remained on option to Salt Lake City.)

‡Traded to St. Louis Cardinals for a player to be named later, June 14, 1983; Baltimore Orioles purchased Outfielder Tito Landrum to complete deal, August 31, 1983.

RANDY MAX READY

Born January 8, 1960, at Fremont, Calif.
Height, 5.11. Weight, 175.
Throws and bats righthanded.
Attended California State University, Hayward,
Calif., and Mesa College, Grand Junction, Colo.

Led Texas League in total bases with 281 in 1982.
Led Texas League third basemen in double plays with 27 and total chances with 456 in 1982.
Led Midwest League third basemen in double plays with 22 in 1981.

Year Club	League	Pos.	G.	AB.	R.	H.	2B.	3B.	HR.	RBI.	B.A.	PO.	A.	E.	F.A.
1980—Butte	Pion.	SS-2B-3B	61	226	*65	85	*23	4	8	50	.376	86	174	22	.922
1981—Burlington	Midw.	3B	110	367	74	113	17	0	17	56	.308	72	216	21	*.932
1982—El Paso	Texas	3B	132	475	*122	*178	33	5	20	99	*.375	*115	*312	●29	.936
1983—Vancouver	P. C.	3B	116	407	82	134	28	1	13	59	.329	136	231	24	.939
1983—Milwaukee	Amer.	3B	11	32	7	12	2	2	1	6	.375	5	8	0	1.000
Major League Totals			11	32	7	12	2	2	1	6	.375	5	8	0	1.000

Selected by Milwaukee Brewers' organization in 5th round of free-agent draft, June 3, 1980.

JEFFREY JAMES REARDON
(Jeff)

Born October 1, 1955, at Pittsfield, Mass.
Height, 6.01. Weight, 190.
Throws and bats righthanded.
Attended University of Massachusetts, Amherst, Mass.

Major League saves: 1979 (2), 1980 (6), 1981 (8), 1982 (26), 1983 (21). Total—63.
Led Carolina League in shutouts with 3 in 1977.

Year Club	League	G.	IP.	W.	L.	Pct.	H.	R.	ER.	SO.	BB.	ERA.
1977—Lynchburg	Carolina	16	101	8	3	.727	89	42	37	60	30	3.30
1978—Jackson	Texas	28	163	*17	4	*.810	128	56	46	115	65	2.53
1979—Tidewater†	Int'national	30	69	5	2	.714	46	18	16	64	21	2.09
1979—New York	National	18	21	1	2	.333	12	7	4	10	9	1.71
1980—New York	National	61	110	8	7	.533	96	36	32	101	47	2.62
1981—New York‡-Montreal	National	43	70	3	0	1.000	48	17	17	49	21	2.19

Year Club	League	G.	IP.	W.	L.	Pct.	H.	R.	ER.	SO.	BB.	ERA.
1982—Montreal	National	75	109	7	4	.636	87	28	25	86	36	2.06
1983—Montreal	National	66	92	7	9	.438	87	34	31	78	44	3.03
Major League Totals		263	402	26	22	.542	330	122	109	324	157	2.44

Selected by Montreal Expos' organization in 23rd round of free-agent draft, June 5, 1973.
Signed as free agent by New York Mets' organization, June 14, 1977.
†On disabled list, June 13 to June 24 and June 29 to July 26, 1979.
‡Traded with Outfielder Dan Norman to Montreal Expos for Outfielder Ellis Valentine, May 29, 1981.

DIVISION SERIES RECORD

Year Club	League	G.	IP.	W.	L.	Pct.	H.	R.	ER.	SO.	BB.	ERA.
1981—Montreal	National	3	4⅓	0	1	.000	1	1	1	2	1	2.08

CHAMPIONSHIP SERIES RECORD

Year Club	League	G.	IP.	W.	L.	Pct.	H.	R.	ER.	SO.	BB.	ERA.
1981—Montreal	National	1	1	0	0	.000	3	3	3	0	0	27.00

GARY EUGENE REDUS

Name pronounced REE-dus.

Born November 1, 1956, at Athens, Ala.
Height, 6.01. Weight, 180.
Throws and bats righthanded.
Attended Calhoun Junior College, Decatur, Ala., and Athens State College, Athens, Ala.

Major League stolen bases: 1982 (11), 1983 (39). Total—50.
Led American Association in stolen bases with 54 and tied for lead in sacrifice flies with 9 in 1982.
Led Florida State League in total bases with 220 in 1980.
Led Pioneer League in total bases with 199, stolen bases with 42 and tied for lead in sacrifice flies with 6 in 1978.
Tied for Western Carolinas League lead in errors by second basemen with 20 in 1979.
Named Pioneer League Player of the Year, 1978.

Year Club	League	Pos.	G.	AB.	R.	H.	2B.	3B.	HR.	RBI.	B.A.	PO.	A.	E.	F.A.
1978—Billings	Pion.	2B	68	253	*100	*117	19	6	17	62	*.462	124	*185	*28	.917
1979—Nashville	South.	OF	36	109	7	19	2	1	0	7	.174	74	3	3	.963
1979—Greensboro	W. Car.	2B-OF	83	309	79	86	17	1	16	52	.278	172	193	21	.946
1980—Tampa	Fla. St.	OF-3B-1B	128	452	78	136	18	9	16	68	.301	213	84	27	.917
1981—Waterbury	East.	OF-1B	138	477	71	119	26	4	20	75	.249	667	34	14	.980
1982—Indianapolis	A. A.	OF	122	439	112	146	29	9	24	93	.333	223	10	7	.971
1982—Cincinnati	Nat.	OF	20	83	12	18	3	2	1	7	.217	29	3	1	.970
1983—Cincinnati	Nat.	OF	125	453	90	112	20	9	17	51	.247	235	11	7	.972
Major League Totals			145	536	102	130	23	11	18	58	.243	264	14	8	.972

Selected by Boston Red Sox' organization in 17th round of free-agent draft, June 7, 1977.
Selected by Cincinnati Reds' organization in 15th round of free-agent draft, June 6, 1978.

JEFFREY SCOTT REED
(Jeff)

Born November 12, 1962, at Joliet, Ill.
Height, 6.02. Weight, 185.
Throws right and bats lefthanded.
Brother of Curtis Reed, outfielder in Chicago White Sox' organization.

Led Southern League catchers in total chances with 714 and double plays with 12 in 1983.
Led California League catchers in total chances with 758 and tied for lead in double plays with 9 in 1982.

Year Club	League	Pos.	G.	AB.	R.	H.	2B.	3B.	HR.	RBI.	B.A.	PO.	A.	E.	F.A.
1980—Elizabethton	Appal.	C	65	225	39	64	15	1	1	20	.284	269	*41	9	.972
1981—Wisconsin Rapids	Midw.	C	106	312	63	73	12	1	4	34	.234	547	*93	7	.989
1981—Orlando	South.	C	3	4	0	1	0	0	0	0	.250	4	1	0	1.000
1982—Visalia	Calif.	C	125	395	69	130	19	2	5	54	.329	*642	●106	10	.987
1983—Orlando	South.	C	118	379	52	100	16	5	6	45	.264	*618	*88	8	*.989
1983—Toledo	Int.	C	14	41	5	7	1	1	0	3	.171	77	6	1	.988

Selected by Minnesota Twins' organization in 1st round (12th player selected) of free-agent draft, June 3, 1980.

JERRY MAXWELL REED

Born October 8, 1955, at Bryson City, N.C.
Height, 6.01. Weight, 190.
Throws and bats righthanded.
Received bachelor of science degree in education from
Western Carolina University, Cullowhee, N.C. in 1977.

Tied for Eastern League lead in intentional bases on balls issued with 9 in 1979.

Year Club	League	G.	IP.	W.	L.	Pct.	H.	R.	ER.	SO.	BB.	ERA.
1977—Auburn	NYP	*32	56	3	5	.375	63	35	30	36	24	4.82
1978—Spartanburg	W. Carol.	39	66	7	2	.778	36	22	10	31	34	1.36
1978—Peninsula	Carolina	15	24	1	0	1.000	9	3	2	11	5	0.75
1979—Reading	Eastern	45	80	11	4	.733	67	25	17	37	28	1.91
1980—Oklahoma City	Am. Assoc.	33	97	6	5	.545	128	62	53	36	42	4.92
1980—Reading	Eastern	8	17	1	1	.500	17	6	6	10	10	3.18
1981—Reading	Eastern	56	80	5	4	.556	80	34	29	62	29	3.26
1981—Philadelphia	National	4	5	0	1	.000	7	4	4	5	6	7.20

Year Club	League	G.	IP.	W.	L.	Pct.	H.	R.	ER.	SO.	BB.	ERA.
1982—Oklahoma City	Am. Assoc.	25	131⅔	6	7	.462	135	78	64	73	59	4.37
1982—Philadelphia†	National	7	8⅔	1	0	1.000	11	6	5	1	3	5.19
1982—Cleveland	American	6	15⅔	1	1	.500	15	6	6	10	3	3.45
1983—Charleston	Int'national	21	145⅓	10	6	.625	141	70	58	57	67	3.59
1983—Cleveland	American	7	21⅓	0	0	.000	26	19	17	11	9	7.17
National League Totals		11	13⅔	1	1	.500	18	10	9	6	9	5.93
American League Totals		13	37	1	1	.500	41	25	23	21	12	5.59
Major League Totals		24	50⅔	2	2	.500	59	35	32	27	21	5.68

Selected by Minnesota Twins' organization in 11th round of free-agent draft, June 5, 1973.
Selected by Philadelphia Phillies' organization in 22nd round of free-agent draft, June 7, 1977.
†Traded with Pitcher Roy Smith and Outfielder Wil Culmer to Cleveland Indians for Pitcher John Denny, September 12, 1982.

RONALD LEE REED
(Ron)

Born November 2, 1942, at La Porte, Ind.
Height, 6.06. Weight, 225.
Throws and bats righthanded.
Attended University of Notre Dame, Notre Dame, Ind.

Tied National League record for fewest home runs allowed, season, 250 or more innings (5), 1975.
Major League saves: 1973 (1), 1976 (14), 1977 (15), 1978 (17), 1979 (5), 1980 (9), 1981 (8), 1982 (14), 1983 (8). Total—91.
Led International League in complete games with 17 and tied for lead in shutouts with 5 in 1967.

Year Club	League	G.	IP.	W.	L.	Pct.	H.	R.	ER.	SO.	BB.	ERA.
1965—West Palm Beach	Florida St.	7	43	3	2	.600	27	7	7	35	9	1.47
1966—Kinston	Carolina	8	51	5	2	.714	43	16	10	39	12	1.76
1966—Austin	Texas	4	30	3	1	.750	19	4	4	22	7	1.20
1966—Richmond	Int'national	14	87	5	2	.714	74	36	34	68	26	3.52
1966—Atlanta	National	2	8	1	1	.500	7	2	2	6	4	2.25
1967—Richmond	Int'national	28	*222	14	10	.583	179	68	62	172	53	2.51
1967—Atlanta	National	3	21	1	1	.500	21	8	7	11	3	3.00
1968—Atlanta	National	35	202	11	10	.524	189	87	75	111	49	3.34
1969—Atlanta	National	36	241	18	10	.643	227	103	93	160	56	3.47
1970—Shreveport	Texas	2	7	0	0	.000	5	2	2	6	2	2.57
1970—Atlanta†	National	21	135	7	10	.412	140	69	66	68	39	4.40
1971—Atlanta	National	32	222	13	14	.481	221	105	92	129	54	3.73
1972—Atlanta	National	31	213	11	15	.423	222	109	93	111	60	3.93
1973—Atlanta‡	National	20	116	4	11	.267	133	71	57	64	31	4.42
1974—Atlanta§	National	28	186	10	11	.476	171	76	70	78	41	3.39
1975—Atlanta x-St. Louis y	National	34	250	13	13	.500	274	118	98	139	53	3.53
1976—Philadelphia	National	59	128	8	7	.533	88	39	35	96	32	2.46
1977—Philadelphia	National	60	124	7	5	.583	101	41	38	84	37	2.76
1978—Philadelphia	National	66	109	3	4	.429	87	32	27	85	23	2.23
1979—Philadelphia	National	61	102	13	8	.619	110	52	47	58	32	4.15
1980—Philadelphia	National	55	91	7	5	.583	88	45	41	54	30	4.05
1981—Philadelphia z	National	39	61	5	3	.625	54	26	21	40	17	3.10
1982—Philadelphia	National	57	98	5	5	.500	85	30	29	57	24	2.66
1983—Philadelphia a	National	61	95⅔	9	1	.900	89	42	37	73	34	3.48
Major League Totals		700	2402⅔	146	134	.521	2307	1055	928	1424	619	3.48

Signed as free agent by Atlanta Braves' organization, July 17, 1965.
†On disabled list, March 24 to June 3, 1970.
‡On disabled list, July 10 to September 11, 1973.
§On disabled list, May 16 to June 25, 1974.
xTraded with a player to be named later to St. Louis Cardinals for Pitchers Elias Sosa and Ray Sadecki, May 28, 1975; St. Louis acquired Outfielder Wayne Nordhagen to complete deal, June 2, 1975.
yTraded to Philadelphia Phillies for Outfielder Mike Anderson, December 9, 1975.
zGranted free agency, November 13, 1981; re-signed by Phillies, January 20, 1982.
aTraded to Chicago White Sox for cash or a player to be named later, December 5, 1983.

DIVISION SERIES RECORD

Year Club	League	G.	IP.	W.	L.	Pct.	H.	R.	ER.	SO.	BB.	ERA.
1981—Philadelphia	National	4	6	0	0	.000	5	2	2	4	3	3.00

CHAMPIONSHIP SERIES RECORD

Tied Championship Series record for most Series pitched (6).

Year Club	League	G.	IP.	W.	L.	Pct.	H.	R.	ER.	SO.	BB.	ERA.
1969—Atlanta	National	1	1⅔	0	1	.000	5	4	4	3	3	21.60
1976—Philadelphia	National	2	4⅔	0	0	.000	6	4	4	2	2	7.71
1977—Philadelphia	National	3	5	0	0	.000	3	1	1	5	2	1.80
1978—Philadelphia	National	2	4	0	0	.000	6	1	1	2	0	2.25
1980—Philadelphia	National	3	2	0	1	.000	3	4	4	1	1	18.00
1983—Philadelphia	National	2	3⅓	0	0	.000	4	2	1	3	1	2.70
Championship Series Totals		13	20⅔	0	2	.000	27	16	15	16	9	6.53

WORLD SERIES RECORD

Year Club	League	G.	IP.	W.	L.	Pct.	H.	R.	ER.	SO.	BB.	ERA.
1980—Philadelphia	National	2	2	0	0	.000	2	0	0	2	0	0.00
1983—Philadelphia	National	3	3⅓	0	0	.000	4	1	1	4	2	2.70
World Series Totals		5	5⅓	0	0	.000	6	1	1	6	2	1.69

Year League	IP.	W.	L.	Pct.	H.	R.	ER.	SO.	BB.	ERA.
1968—National	⅓	0	0	.000	0	0	0	1	0	0.00

RECORD AS BASKETBALL PLAYER

Drafted by Detroit on third round, 1965.

NBA REGULAR SEASON RECORD

Sea.—Team	G.	Min.	FGA	FGM	Pct.	FTA	FTM	Pct.	Reb.	Ast.	PF	Disq.	Pts.	Avg.
65-66—Detroit	57	997	524	186	.355	100	54	.540	339	92	133	1	426	7.5
66-67—Detroit	61	1248	600	223	.372	133	79	.594	423	81	145	2	525	8.6
Totals	118	2245	1124	409	.364	233	133	.571	762	173	278	3	951	8.1

GERALD PETER REMY
(Jerry)

Born November 8, 1952, at Fall Rivers, Mass.
Height, 5.09. Weight, 165.
Throws right and bats lefthanded.
Attended Roger Williams College, Bristol, R. I.

Collected six hits in one game, September 3, 1981 (20 innings).
Major League stolen bases: 1975 (34), 1976 (35), 1977 (41), 1978 (30), 1979 (14), 1980 (14), 1981 (9), 1982 (16), 1983 (11).
Total—204.
Led American League second basemen in double plays with 114 in 1978.
Led California League in caught stealing with 18 in 1972.
Led Midwest League second basemen in double plays with 73 in 1973.
Led California League second basemen in assists with 402 and double plays with 86 in 1972.
Named Most Valuable Player in Midwest League, 1973.

Year Club	League	Pos.	G.	AB.	R.	H.	2B.	3B.	HR.	RBI.	B.A.	PO.	A.	E.	F.A.
1971—Magic Valley†	Pion.	2B-OF	32	104	25	32	5	3	0	6	.308	61	54	5	.958
1972—Stockton	Calif.	2B-SS	133	532	59	141	18	3	4	43	.265	275	404	28	.960
1973—Quad Cities...........	Midw.	2B	117	478	66	★160	23	10	4	36	★.335	★277	★330	24	.962
1974—El Paso.................	Texas	2B	91	394	74	133	34	5	4	46	.338	233	267	18	.965
1974—Salt Lake City.......	P. C.	2B	48	195	33	57	6	5	0	21	.292	108	135	7	.972
1975—California..............	Amer.	2B	147	569	82	147	17	5	1	46	.258	336	427	14	.982
1976—California..............	Amer.	2B	143	502	64	132	14	3	0	28	.263	279	406	16	.977
1977—California‡............	Amer.	2B-3B	154	575	74	145	19	10	4	44	.252	307	420	19	.975
1978—Boston..................	Amer.	2B-SS	148	583	87	162	24	6	2	44	.278	328	446	13	.983
1979—Boston§................	Amer.	2B	80	306	49	91	11	2	0	29	.297	147	205	11	.970
1980—Boston x...............	Amer.	2B-OF	63	230	24	72	7	2	0	9	.313	109	189	7	.977
1981—Boston y...............	Amer.	2B	88	358	55	110	9	1	0	31	.307	162	272	7	.984
1982—Boston..................	Amer.	2B	155	636	89	178	22	3	0	47	.280	290	432	13	.982
1983—Boston z...............	Amer.	2B	146	592	73	163	16	5	0	43	.275	295	376	7	.990
Major League Totals..................................			1124	4351	597	1200	139	37	7	321	.276	2253	3173	107	.981

Selected by Washington Senators' organization in 19th round of free-agent draft, June 4, 1970.
Selected by California Angels' organization in secondary phase of free-agent draft, January 13, 1971.
†On disabled list, August 12, 1971 through remainder of season.
‡Traded to Boston Red Sox for Pitcher Don Aase and cash, December 8, 1977.
§On disabled list, July 2 to August 8 and August 17 to September 1, 1979.
xOn emergency disabled list, July 15, 1980 through remainder of season.
yGranted free agency, November 13, 1981; re-signed by Red Sox, December 8, 1981.
zOn supplemental disabled list, March 27 to April 15, 1983.

ALL-STAR GAME RECORD

Named to American League All-Star Team for 1978 game to replace injured Rick Burleson; did not play.

STEVEN RENKO JR.
(Steve)

Born December 10, 1944, at Kansas City, Kan.
Height, 6.06. Weight, 225.
Throws and bats righthanded.
Attended University of Kansas, Lawrence, Kan.

Pitched seven-inning, 1-0 no-hit victory against Albuquerque, July 21, 1968.
Led National League in wild pitches with 19 in 1974.

Year Club	League	G.	IP.	W.	L.	Pct.	H.	R.	ER.	SO.	BB.	ERA.
1966—Williamsport..................	Eastern	1	2	0	0	.000	0	0	0	2	1	0.00
1967—Winter Haven†	Florida St.	11	84	8	1	.889	44	17	15	109	39	1.61
1968—Memphis	Texas	22	145	7	11	.389	116	63	53	106	73	3.29
1968—Jacksonville	Int'national	7	51	4	1	.800	35	20	17	41	17	3.00
1969—Tidewater‡....................	Int'national	12	66	3	6	.333	56	43	40	57	43	5.45
1969—Montreal	National	18	103	6	7	.462	94	54	46	68	50	4.02
1970—Montreal	National	41	223	13	11	.542	203	121	107	142	104	4.32
1971—Montreal	National	40	276	15	14	.517	256	128	★115	129	135	3.75
1972—Montreal	National	30	97	1	10	.091	96	60	56	66	67	5.20
1973—Montreal	National	36	250	15	11	.577	201	94	78	164	108	2.81
1974—Montreal	National	37	228	12	16	.429	222	115	102	138	81	4.03
1975—Montreal	National	31	170	6	12	.333	175	89	77	99	76	4.08
1976—Mont.§-Chi.	National	33	176	8	12	.400	179	87	78	116	46	3.99

Year Club	League	G.	IP.	W.	L.	Pct.	H.	R.	ER.	SO.	BB.	ERA.
1977—Chicago xy	National	13	51	2	2	.500	51	32	26	34	21	4.59
1977—Chicago z	American	8	53	5	0	1.000	55	23	21	36	17	3.57
1978—Oakland a	American	27	151	6	12	.333	152	77	72	89	67	4.29
1979—Boston	American	27	171	11	9	.550	174	86	78	99	53	4.11
1980—Boston b	American	32	165	9	9	.500	180	86	77	90	56	4.20
1981—California	American	22	102	8	4	.667	93	40	39	50	42	3.44
1982—California c	American	31	156	11	6	.647	163	78	77	81	51	4.44
1983—Kansas City d	American	25	121⅓	6	11	.353	144	63	58	54	36	4.30
National League Totals		279	1574	78	95	.451	1477	780	685	956	688	3.92
American League Totals		172	919⅓	56	51	.523	961	453	422	499	322	4.13
Major League Totals		451	2493⅓	134	146	.479	2438	1233	1107	1455	1010	4.00

Selected by New York Mets' organization in 14th round of free-agent draft, June, 1965.

†On disabled list, July 30, 1967 through remainder of season.

‡Traded with Pitchers Jay Carden and Dave Colon and Infielder Kevin Collins to Montreal Expos for First Baseman Donn Clendenon, June 15, 1969.

§Traded with Outfielder-First Baseman Larry Biittner to Chicago Cubs for First Baseman Andy Thornton, May 17, 1976.

xOn disabled list, April 28 to June 21, 1977.

yTraded to Chicago White Sox for cash and Pitcher Larry Anderson, August 18, 1977.

zTraded with Catcher Jim Essian to Oakland A's for Pitcher Pablo Torrealba, March 30, 1978.

aGranted free agency, November 2, 1978; signed by Boston Red Sox, January 23, 1979.

bTraded with Outfielder Fred Lynn to California Angels for Pitchers Frank Tanana and Jim Dorsey and Outfielder Joe Rudi, January 23, 1981.

cReleased, February 2, 1983; signed by Kansas City Royals, February 9, 1983.

dReleased, October 3, 1983.

RECORD AS FIRST BASEMAN

Year Club	League	Pos.	G.	AB.	R.	H.	2B.	3B.	HR.	RBI.	B.A.	PO.	A.	E.	F.A.
1965—Marion	Appal.	1B-OF	50	169	39	49	3	3	7	32	.290	199	11	11	.950
1966—Auburn	NYP	1B-OF	69	246	38	57	10	2	10	42	.232	516	33	12	.979
1966—Williamsport	East.	●1B-P	59	195	20	33	3	0	7	18	.169	450	24	●11	.977
1967—Winter Haven	Fla. St.	1B-P-OF	71	197	27	43	3	1	8	24	.218	355	36	8	.980
1969—Tidewater	Int.	P-1B	18	16	3	5	1	0	1	5	.313	15	4	1	.950
1972—Montreal	Nat.	P-1B	32	24	0	7	0	0	0	0	.292	9	17	1	.963

RICKY EUGENE REUSCHEL

Name pronounced RUSH-ul.

(Rick)

Born May 16, 1949, at Quincy, Ill.
Height, 6.03. Weight, 230.
Throws and bats righthanded.
Attended Western Illinois University, Macomb, Ill.
Brother of Paul Reuschel, pitcher with Chicago Cubs and Cleveland Indians, 1975 through 1978.

Tied major league record for most putouts, pitcher, inning (3), April 25, 1975 (third inning).
Tied for National League lead in games started by pitchers with 38 in 1980.
Led Northern League pitchers in complete games with 7 and tied for lead in games started with 14 in 1970.
Named righthanded pitcher on THE SPORTING NEWS National League All-Star Team, 1977.

Year Club	League	G.	IP.	W.	L.	Pct.	H.	R.	ER.	SO.	BB.	ERA.
1970—Huron	Northern	14	102	9	2	.818	96	52	40	88	22	3.52
1971—San Antonio†	Texas	16	121	8	4	.667	105	40	31	81	· 15	2.31
1972—Wichita	Am. Assoc.	12	102	9	2	.818	78	30	15	72	30	1.32
1972—Chicago	National	21	129	10	8	.556	127	46	42	87	29	2.93
1973—Chicago	National	36	237	14	15	.483	244	95	79	168	62	3.00
1974—Chicago	National	41	241	13	12	.520	262	130	115	160	83	4.29
1975—Chicago	National	38	234	11	★17	.393	244	116	97	155	67	3.73
1976—Chicago	National	38	260	14	12	.538	260	★117	100	146	64	3.46
1977—Chicago	National	39	252	20	10	.667	233	84	78	166	74	2.79
1978—Chicago	National	35	243	14	15	.483	235	98	92	115	54	3.41
1979—Chicago	National	36	239	18	12	.600	251	104	96	125	75	3.62
1980—Chicago	National	38	257	11	13	.458	★281	111	97	140	76	3.40
1981—Chicago‡	National	13	86	4	7	.364	87	40	33	53	23	3.45
1981—New York	American	12	71	4	4	.500	75	24	21	22	10	2.66
1982—New York§	American					(Did not play)						
1983—Columbus xy	Int'national	4	16	0	1	.000	21	9	9	7	6	5.06
1983—Quad Cities	Midwest	13	70⅔	3	4	.429	73	29	19	56	9	2.42
1983—Chicago	National	4	20⅔	1	1	.500	18	9	9	9	10	3.92
National League Totals		339	2198⅔	130	122	.516	2242	950	838	1324	617	3.43
American League Totals		12	71	4	4	.500	75	24	21	22	10	2.66
Major League Totals		351	2269⅔	134	126	.515	2317	974	859	1346	627	3.41

Selected by Chicago Cubs' organization in 3rd round of free-agent draft, June 4, 1970.

†On temporary inactive list, July 2, 1971; transferred to military list, July 8, 1971 through April 10, 1972.

‡Traded to New York Yankees for Pitcher Doug Bird, $400,000 and a player to be named later, June 12, 1981; Chicago Cubs acquired Pitcher Mike Griffin to complete deal, August 5, 1981.

§On disabled list, March 23, 1982; transferred to emergency disabled list, May 12, 1982 through remainder of season.

xOn New York emergency disabled list, April 4 to June 9, 1983; included rehabilitation disability assignment to Columbus, May 23 to June 9, 1983.

yReleased, June 9, 1983; signed by Quad Cities (Chicago Cubs' organization), June 28, 1983.

DIVISION SERIES RECORD

Year Club	League	G.	IP.	W.	L.	Pct.	H.	R.	ER.	SO.	BB.	ERA.
1981—New York	American	1	6	0	1	.000	4	2	2	3	1	3.00

WORLD SERIES RECORD

Year Club	League	G.	IP.	W.	L.	Pct.	H.	R.	ER.	SO.	BB.	ERA.
1981—New York	American	2	3⅔	0	0	.000	7	3	2	2	3	4.91

ALL-STAR GAME RECORD

Year League	IP.	W.	L.	Pct.	H.	R.	ER.	SO.	BB.	ERA.
1977—National	1	0	0	.000	1	0	0	0	0	0.00

JERRY REUSS
Name pronounced Royce.

Born June 19, 1949, at St. Louis, Mo.
Height, 6.05. Weight, 217.
Throws and bats lefthanded.
Attended Southern Illinois University, Carbondale, Ill., Central Missouri State College,
Warrensburg, Mo., and University of California at Santa Barbara, Santa Barbara, Calif.

Tied major league record for most home runs allowed, bases filled, lifetime (9).
Pitched 8-0 no-hit victory against San Francisco Giants, June 27, 1980.
Led National League in shutouts with 6 in 1980.
Led National League in hit batsmen with 10 in 1972.
Tied for National League lead in games started by pitchers with 40 in 1973.
Led American Association pitchers in games started with 29 in 1969.
Led Texas League in wild pitches with 16 in 1968.
Named National League Comeback Player of the Year by THE SPORTING NEWS, 1980.
Received reported $30,000 bonus to sign with St. Louis Cardinals, 1967.

Year Club	League	G.	IP.	W.	L.	Pct.	H.	R.	ER.	SO.	BB.	ERA.
1967—Sarasota Cards	Gulf Coast	2	7	0	0	.000	7	6	4	6	3	5.14
1967—Cedar Rapids	Midwest	9	58	2	5	.286	44	20	12	63	19	1.86
1967—Tulsa	P. Coast	1	1	0	0	.000	2	6	6	1	4	54.00
1968—Arkansas	Texas	17	112	7	8	.467	75	43	27	86	45	2.17
1969—Tulsa	Am. Assoc.	30	★186	●13	11	.542	188	●112	84	★151	116	4.06
1969—St. Louis	National	1	7	1	0	1.000	2	0	0	3	3	0.00
1970—Tulsa	Am. Assoc.	11	85	7	2	.778	69	26	20	69	28	2.12
1970—St. Louis	National	20	127	7	8	.467	132	62	58	74	49	4.11
1971—St. Louis†	National	36	211	14	14	.500	228	125	112	131	109	4.78
1972—Houston	National	33	192	9	13	.409	177	101	89	174	83	4.17
1973—Houston‡	National	41	279	16	13	.552	271	123	116	177	★117	3.74
1974—Pittsburgh	National	35	260	16	11	.593	259	115	101	105	101	3.50
1975—Pittsburgh	National	32	237	18	11	.621	224	73	67	131	78	2.54
1976—Pittsburgh	National	31	209	14	9	.609	209	98	82	108	51	3.53
1977—Pittsburgh	National	33	208	10	13	.435	225	109	95	116	71	4.11
1978—Pittsburgh§	National	23	83	3	2	.600	97	48	45	42	23	4.88
1979—Los Angeles	National	39	160	7	14	.333	178	88	63	83	60	3.54
1980—Los Angeles	National	37	229	18	6	.750	193	74	64	111	40	2.52
1981—Los Angeles	National	22	153	10	4	.714	138	44	39	51	27	2.29
1982—Los Angeles	National	39	254⅔	18	11	.621	232	98	88	138	50	3.11
1983—Los Angeles	National	32	223⅓	12	11	.522	233	94	73	143	50	2.94
Major League Totals		454	2833	173	140	.553	2798	1252	1092	1587	912	3.47

Selected by St. Louis Cardinals' organization in 2nd round of free-agent draft, June 6, 1967.
†Traded to Houston Astros for Pitchers Scipio Spinks and Lance Clemons, April 15, 1972.
‡Traded to Pittsburgh Pirates for Catcher Milt May, October 31, 1972.
§Traded to Los Angeles Dodgers for Pitcher Rick Rhoden, April 9, 1979.

DIVISION SERIES RECORD

Year Club	League	G.	IP.	W.	L.	Pct.	H.	R.	ER.	SO.	BB.	ERA.
1981—Los Angeles	National	2	18	1	0	1.000	10	0	0	7	5	0.00

CHAMPIONSHIP SERIES RECORD

Established Championship Series record for most games lost, total Series (6).
Tied Championship Series records for most games lost, Series (2), 1974, 1983; most bases on balls, four-game Series (8), 1974.

Year Club	League	G.	IP.	W.	L.	Pct.	H.	R.	ER.	SO.	BB.	ERA.
1974—Pittsburgh	National	2	9⅔	0	2	.000	7	4	4	3	8	3.72
1975—Pittsburgh	National	1	2⅔	0	1	.000	4	4	4	1	4	13.50
1981—Los Angeles	National	1	7	0	1	.000	7	4	4	2	1	5.14
1983—Los Angeles	National	2	12	0	2	.000	14	6	6	4	3	4.50
Championship Series Totals		6	31⅓	0	6	.000	32	18	18	10	16	5.17

WORLD SERIES RECORD

Year Club	League	G.	IP.	W.	L.	Pct.	H.	R.	ER.	SO.	BB.	ERA.
1981—Los Angeles	National	2	11⅔	1	1	.500	10	5	5	8	3	3.86

ALL-STAR GAME RECORD

Year League	IP.	W.	L.	Pct.	H.	R.	ER.	SO.	BB.	ERA.
1975—National	3	0	0	.000	3	0	0	2	0	0.00
1980—National	1	1	0	1.000	0	0	0	3	0	0.00
All-Star Game Totals	4	1	0	1.000	3	0	0	5	0	0.00

GILBERTO R. REYES (POLANCO)

Name pronounced Ray-us.

(Gil)

Born December 10, 1963, at Santo Domingo, Dominican Republic.
Height, 6.03. Weight, 195.
Throws and bats righthanded.

Tied for California League lead in assists by catchers with 106 and double plays with 9 in 1982.

Year	Club	League	Pos.	G.	AB.	R.	H.	2B.	3B.	HR.	RBI.	B.A.	PO.	A.	E.	F.A.
1980—Lethbridge	Pion.		1B	6	11	0	2	0	0	0	1	.182	16	0	2	.889
1981—Vero Beach	Fla. St.		1B-C	21	58	3	12	3	0	1	6	.207	71	6	2	.975
1981—Lethbridge	Pion.		C-1B	44	155	28	40	9	0	6	24	.258	240	24	4	.985
1982—Lodi	Calif.		C-3B	127	424	65	119	18	1	15	55	.281	493	106	20	.968
1983—San Antonio†	Texas		C	33	124	10	35	7	0	1	16	.282	167	30	5	.975
1983—Los Angeles	Nat.		C	19	31	1	5	2	0	0	0	.161	59	9	4	.944
1983—Albuquerque	P. C.		C	20	62	8	19	1	2	2	15	.306	103	17	8	.938
Major League Totals				19	31	1	5	2	0	0	0	.161	59	9	4	.944

Signed as free agent by Los Angeles Dodgers' organization, January 15, 1980.
†On disabled list, May 11 to June 1, 1983.

GORDON CRAIG REYNOLDS

(Known by middle name.)

Born December 27, 1952, at Houston, Tex.
Height, 6.01. Weight, 175.
Throws right and bats lefthanded.
Attended Houston Baptist College, Houston, Tex.

Tied modern major league record for most three-base hits, game (3), May 16, 1981.
Led National League in sacrifice hits with 34 in 1979 and 18 in 1981.
Led Carolina League shortstops in double plays with 81 in 1973 and tied for International League lead with 64 in 1975.
Tied for Gulf Coast League lead in sacrifice flies with 4 in 1971.

Year	Club	League	Pos.	G.	AB.	R.	H.	2B.	3B.	HR.	RBI.	B.A.	PO.	A.	E.	F.A.
1971—Bradenton Pir.	Gulf C.		SS	48	192	26	61	8	0	0	16	.318	★87	112	★25	.888
1972—Gastonia†	W. Car.		SS	41	146	18	35	4	1	0	9	.240	55	94	12	.925
1973—Salem	Carol.		SS-2B	138	★558	75	★160	18	5	13	86	.287	200	395	50	.922
1973—Charleston	Int.		SS-3B	4	14	2	3	0	0	0	0	.214	4	11	1	.938
1974—Thetford Mines	East.		SS	64	234	31	66	7	0	6	29	.282	76	170	13	.950
1974—Charleston‡	Int.		SS-2B	36	107	12	36	5	0	0	5	.336	40	71	3	.974
1975—Charleston	Int.		SS	108	425	51	131	22	3	6	42	.308	151	287	26	.944
1975—Pittsburgh	Nat.		SS	31	76	8	17	3	0	0	4	.224	43	82	4	.969
1976—Charleston	Int.		SS-2B	126	497	57	144	18	1	2	47	.290	198	262	31	.937
1976—Pittsburgh§	Nat.		SS-2B	7	4	1	1	0	0	1	1	.250	2	6	1	.889
1977—Seattle	Amer.		SS	135	420	41	104	12	3	4	28	.248	197	397	28	.955
1978—Seattle x	Amer.		SS	148	548	57	160	16	7	5	44	.292	243	461	29	.960
1979—Houston	Nat.		SS	146	555	63	147	20	9	0	39	.265	208	428	23	.965
1980—Houston	Nat.		SS	137	381	34	86	9	6	3	28	.226	162	362	17	.969
1981—Houston	Nat.		SS	87	323	43	84	10	●12	4	31	.260	139	261	11	.973
1982—Houston y	Nat.		SS-3B	54	118	16	30	2	3	1	7	.254	45	98	6	.960
1983—Houston	Nat.		2-3-S-O	65	98	10	21	3	0	1	6	.214	37	57	3	.969
American League Totals				283	968	98	264	28	10	9	72	.273	440	858	57	.958
National League Totals				527	1555	175	386	47	30	10	116	.248	636	1294	65	.967
Major League Totals				810	2523	273	650	75	40	19	188	.258	1076	2152	122	.964

Selected by Pittsburgh Pirates' organization in 1st round (22nd player selected) of free-agent draft, June 8, 1971.
†On disabled list, June 6 to August 30, 1972.
‡On disabled list, July 31 to August 21, 1974.
§Traded with Infielder Jim Sexton to Seattle Mariners for Pitcher Grant Jackson, December 7, 1976.
xTraded to Houston Astros for Pitcher Floyd Bannister, December 8, 1978.
yOn supplemental disabled list, April 11 to May 5, 1982.

DIVISION SERIES RECORD

Year	Club	League	Pos.	G.	AB.	R.	H.	2B.	3B.	HR.	RBI.	B.A.	PO.	A.	E.	F.A.
1981—Houston	Nat.		PH	2	3	1	1	0	0	0	0	.333	1	0	0	1.000

CHAMPIONSHIP SERIES RECORD

Year	Club	League	Pos.	G.	AB.	R.	H.	2B.	3B.	HR.	RBI.	B.A.	PO.	A.	E.	F.A.
1975—Pittsburgh	Nat.		SS	2	1	0	0	0	0	0	0	.000	0	0	1	.000
1980—Houston	Nat.		SS	4	13	2	2	1	0	0	0	.154	8	12	1	.952
Championship Series Totals				6	14	2	2	1	0	0	0	.143	8	12	2	.909

ALL-STAR GAME RECORD

Year	League	Pos.	AB.	R.	H.	2B.	3B.	HR.	RBI.	B.A.	PO.	A.	E.	F.A.
1979—National		SS	2	0	0	0	0	0	0	.000	0	1	0	1.000

Named to American League All-Star Team for 1978 game; did not play.

HAROLD CRAIG REYNOLDS

Born November 26, 1960, at Eugene, Ore.
Height, 5.11. Weight, 165.
Throws right and bats left and righthanded.
Attended San Diego State University, San Diego, Calif.;
Canada College, Redwood City, Calif., and attending
California State University, Long Beach, Calif.
Brother of Larry Reynolds, shortstop-outfielder in St. Louis Cardinals' organization;
and Don Reynolds, outfielder with San Diego Padres, 1978 and 1979.

Led Pacific Coast League in sacrifice hits with 14 in 1983.
Led Eastern League in caught stealing with 20 in 1982.
Led Midwest League in stolen bases with 69 in 1981.
Led Pacific Coast League second basemen in putouts with 286 in 1983.
Led Midwest League second basemen in double plays with 82 in 1981.

Year	Club	League	Pos.	G.	AB.	R.	H.	2B.	3B.	HR.	RBI.	B.A.	PO.	A.	E.	F.A.
1981—Wausau	Midw.	2B-OF-3B	127	493	98	146	23	3	11	59	.296	259	386	27	.960
1982—Lynn	East.	2B	102	375	58	102	14	4	2	48	.272	202	232	19	.958
1983—Salt Lake City	P. C.	*2B-SS	136	534	84	165	20	9	1	72	.309	287	*410	*27	.963
1983—Seattle	Amer.	2B	20	59	8	12	4	1	0	1	.203	30	48	2	.975
Major League Totals			20	59	8	12	4	1	0	1	.203	30	48	2	.975

Selected by San Diego Padres' organization in 5th round of free-agent draft, June 5, 1979.
Selected by Seattle Mariners' organization in secondary phase of free-agent draft, June 3, 1980.

JEFFREY ALAN REYNOLDS
(Jeff)

Born January 27, 1960, at Charleston, W. Va.
Height, 6.01. Weight, 190.
Throws and bats righthanded.
Attended Potomac State College, Keyser, W. Va.

Led International League batters in strikeouts with 123 in 1983.
Led South Atlantic League in total bases with 257 and game-winning RBIs with 16 in 1981.
Led International League third basemen in errors with 26 in 1983.
Led South Atlantic League third basemen in double plays with 27 in 1981.
Named South Atlantic League co-Most Valuable Player, 1981.

Year	Club	League	Pos.	G.	AB.	R.	H.	2B.	3B.	HR.	RBI.	B.A.	PO.	A.	E.	F.A.
1980—Ft. Lauderdale	Fla. St.	3B	21	63	4	15	2	2	0	7	.238	2	19	2	.913
1980—Oneonta	NYP	3B	70	265	39	75	14	3	7	*56	.283	41	*174	24	.900
1981—Greensboro	S. Atl.	3B	125	474	83	145	28	3	26	*103	.306	●88	*277	25	.936
1982—Nash.†-Knox.	South.	3B	132	471	71	114	30	3	20	63	.242	91	294	35	.917
1983—Syracuse	Int.	3B-1B-SS	128	434	46	95	15	1	13	50	.219	147	211	27	.930

Selected by New York Yankees' organization in 4th round of free-agent draft, January 8, 1980.
†Traded with First Baseman Dave Revering to Toronto Blue Jays for First Baseman John Mayberry, May 5, 1982.

ROBERT JAMES REYNOLDS
(R. J.)

Born April 19, 1959, at Sacramento, Calif.
Height, 6.00. Weight, 180.
Throws right and bats left and righthanded.
Attended Sacramento City College, Sacramento, Calif.

Led Texas League outfielders in double plays with 8 in 1983.
Led Florida State League outfielders in double plays with 6 and total chances with 395 in 1981.
Led California League outfielders in double plays with 6 in 1980.

Year	Club	League	Pos.	G.	AB.	R.	H.	2B.	3B.	HR.	RBI.	B.A.	PO.	A.	E.	F.A.
1980—Lodi	Calif.	OF	86	299	33	84	6	3	4	31	.281	188	10	12	.943
1981—Vero Beach	Fla. St.	OF	132	502	62	139	9	11	2	49	.277	*368	20	7	.982
1982—Lodi	Calif.	OF	108	403	67	126	19	3	6	35	.313	212	12	6	.974
1982—San Antonio	Texas	OF	3	12	3	2	0	0	1	2	.167	10	1	0	1.000
1983—San Antonio	Texas	OF	133	504	103	170	25	3	18	89	.337	255	●18	12	.958
1983—Los Angeles	Nat.	OF	24	55	5	13	0	0	2	11	.236	25	2	2	.931
Major League Totals			24	55	5	13	0	0	2	11	.236	25	2	2	.931

Selected by Los Angeles Dodgers' organization in 2nd round of free-agent draft, January 8, 1980.

RONN DWAYNE REYNOLDS

Born September 28, 1958, at Wichita, Kan.
Height, 6.00. Weight, 200.
Throws and bats righthanded.
Attended Garden City Community College, Garden City, Kan.,
and University of Arkansas, Fayetteville, Ark.

Led Texas League catchers in putouts with 583 and total chances with 651 in 1982.
Tied for Texas League lead in being hit by pitch with 10 in 1982.

Year	Club	League	Pos.	G.	AB.	R.	H.	2B.	3B.	HR.	RBI.	B.A.	PO.	A.	E.	F.A.
1980—Little Falls	NYP	C	15	44	6	8	1	1	1	8	.182	85	3	2	.978
1980—Lynchburg	Carol.	C	36	105	14	21	3	0	2	17	.200	206	23	3	.987
1981—Jackson	Texas	C	88	272	16	64	12	1	2	30	.235	493	67	12	.979

Year Club	League	Pos.	G.	AB.	R.	H.	2B.	3B.	HR.	RBI.	B.A.	PO.	A.	E.	F.A.
1982—Jackson	Texas	C-3B-OF	123	431	50	110	13	1	10	43	.255	585	57	14	.979
1982—New York	Nat.	C	2	4	0	0	0	0	0	0	.000	3	0	0	1.000
1983—Tidewater	Int.	C	40	128	8	27	8	0	0	9	.211	209	27	1	.996
1983—New York	Nat.	C	24	66	4	13	1	0	0	2	.197	99	14	7	.942
Major League Totals			26	70	4	13	1	0	0	2	.186	102	14	7	.943

Selected by Oakland A's organization in 5th round of free-agent draft, June 5, 1979.
Selected by New York Mets' organization in 5th round of free-agent draft, June 3, 1980.

RICHARD ALAN RHODEN

Name pronounced ROH-dun.

(Rick)

Born May 16, 1953, at Boynton Beach, Fla.
Height, 6.03. Weight, 195.
Throws and bats righthanded.

Pitched seven-inning, 1-0 no-hit victory against Phoenix, April 23, 1980 (first game).

Year Club	League	G.	IP.	W.	L.	Pct.	H.	R.	ER.	SO.	BB.	ERA.
1971—Daytona Beach	Florida St.	11	61	4	6	.400	59	32	27	67	29	3.98
1972—El Paso	Texas	13	87	6	4	.600	70	36	32	89	30	3.31
1972—Albuquerque	P. Coast	13	80	7	1	.875	83	41	34	55	34	3.83
1973—Albuquerque†	P. Coast	20	116	4	9	.308	117	66	58	68	70	4.50
1974—Albuquerque	P. Coast	26	178	9	10	.474	197	103	87	106	65	4.40
1974—Los Angeles	National	4	9	1	0	1.000	5	2	2	7	4	2.00
1975—Los Angeles	National	26	99	3	3	.500	94	40	34	40	32	3.09
1976—Los Angeles	National	27	181	12	3	.800	165	66	60	77	53	2.98
1977—Los Angeles	National	31	216	16	10	.615	223	98	90	122	63	3.75
1978—Los Angeles‡	National	30	165	10	8	.556	160	77	67	79	51	3.65
1979—Pittsburgh§	National	1	5	0	1	.000	5	4	4	2	2	7.20
1980—Portland	P. Coast	10	52	6	3	.667	47	22	17	24	21	2.94
1980—Pittsburgh	National	20	127	7	5	.583	133	58	54	70	40	3.83
1981—Pittsburgh	National	21	136	9	4	.692	147	66	59	76	53	3.90
1982—Pittsburgh	National	35	230⅓	11	14	.440	239	115	106	128	70	4.14
1983—Pittsburgh	National	36	244⅓	13	13	.500	256	95	84	153	68	3.09
Major League Totals		231	1412⅔	82	61	.573	1427	621	560	754	436	3.57

Selected by Los Angeles Dodgers' organization in 1st round (20th player selected) of free-agent draft, June 8, 1971.
†On disabled list, July 20 to August 15, 1973.
‡Traded to Pittsburgh Pirates for Pitcher Jerry Reuss, April 9, 1979.
§On disabled list, May 12 to October 4, 1979.

CHAMPIONSHIP SERIES RECORD

Year Club	League	G.	IP.	W.	L.	Pct.	H.	R.	ER.	SO.	BB.	ERA.
1977—Los Angeles	National	1	4⅓	0	0	.000	2	0	0	0	2	0.00
1978—Los Angeles	National	1	4	0	0	.000	2	1	1	3	1	2.25
Championship Series Totals		2	8⅓	0	0	.000	4	1	1	3	3	1.08

WORLD SERIES RECORD

Year Club	League	G.	IP.	W.	L.	Pct.	H.	R.	ER.	SO.	BB.	ERA.
1977—Los Angeles	National	2	7	0	1	.000	4	2	2	5	1	2.57

ALL-STAR GAME RECORD

Year League	IP.	W.	L.	Pct.	H.	R.	ER.	SO.	BB.	ERA.
1976—National	1	0	0	.000	1	0	0	0	0	0.00

KEVIN JAY RHOMBERG

Name pronounced ROM-burg.

Born November 22, 1955, at Dubuque, Ia.
Height, 6.00. Weight, 175.
Throws and bats righthanded.
Attended Lewis University, Romeoville, Ill., and College of St. Francis, Joliet, Ill.

Led International League in caught stealing with 23 in 1982.
Led Southern League in stolen bases with 74 and tied for lead in caught stealing with 17 in 1981.

Year Club	League	Pos.	G.	AB.	R.	H.	2B.	3B.	HR.	RBI.	B.A.	PO.	A.	E.	F.A.
1977—Batavia	NYP	3B	5	17	3	5	0	1	0	2	.294	2	4	2	.750
1977—Waterloo	Midw.	3B	50	150	26	43	6	3	1	23	.287	33	113	15	.907
1978—Waterloo	Midw.	OF	42	123	38	38	7	0	5	21	.309	36	3	5	.886
1978—Chattanooga	South.	OF-3B	58	199	35	61	9	2	0	16	.307	96	9	5	.955
1979—Chattanooga	South.	O-3-S-2	132	440	84	118	21	6	9	53	.268	238	96	13	.963
1980—Tacoma	P. C.	OF	142	447	80	137	20	14	1	51	.287	242	14	5	.981
1981—Chattanooga	South.	2B	141	511	104	★187	24	★14	1	55	★.366	281	335	21	.967
1982—Charleston†	Int.	2B-OF-3B	100	382	64	116	16	5	0	26	.304	228	238	14	.971
1982—Cleveland	Amer.	OF-3B	16	18	3	6	0	0	1	1	.333	9	2	1	.917
1983—Charleston	Int.	OF-3B-2B	133	508	102	158	17	7	1	60	.311	290	119	16	.962
1983—Cleveland	Amer.	OF	12	21	2	10	0	0	0	2	.476	10	0	0	1.000
Major League Totals			28	39	5	16	0	0	1	3	.410	19	2	1	.955

Selected by Cleveland Indians' organization in 14th round of free-agent draft, June 7, 1977.
†On disabled list, May 5 to June 8, 1982.

JAMES EDWARD RICE
(Jim)

Born March 8, 1953, at Anderson, S. C.
Height, 6.02. Weight, 205.
Throws and bats righthanded.

Tied major league record for most consecutive seasons leading major leagues, total bases (2).
Tied American League record for most consecutive seasons leading league, total bases (3).
Hit three home runs in a game, August 29, 1977 and August 29, 1983 (second game).
Led American League in grounding into double plays with 29 in 1982 and tied for lead with 31 in 1983.
Led American League in total bases with 382 in 1977, 406 in 1978, 369 in 1979 and 344 in 1983.
Led American League in slugging percentage with .593 in 1977 and .600 in 1978.
Led American League batters in strikeouts with 123 in 1976.
Led International League in total bases with 249 in 1974.
Led Florida State League in total bases with 240 in 1972.
Named American League Player of the Year by THE SPORTING NEWS, 1978.
Named American League Most Valuable Player by Baseball Writers' Association of America, 1978.
Named outfielder on THE SPORTING NEWS American League All-Star Team, 1975, 1977 through 1979 and 1983.
Named outfielder on THE SPORTING NEWS American League Silver Slugger team, 1983.
Named Minor League Player of the Year by THE SPORTING NEWS, 1974.
Named International League Most Valuable Player, 1974.
Received reported $45,000 bonus to sign with Boston Red Sox, 1971.

Year	Club	League	Pos.	G.	AB.	R.	H.	2B.	3B.	HR.	RBI.	B.A.	PO.	A.	E.	F.A.
1971—Williamsport	NYP		OF	60	223	34	57	9	5	5	27	.256	86	2	6	.936
1972—Winter Haven	Fla. St.		OF	130	*491	*80	*143	20	13	17	87	.291	190	10	9	.957
1973—Bristol	East.		OF	119	423	66	134	25	4	27	93	*.317	169	13	12	.938
1973—Pawtucket	Int.		OF	10	37	7	14	2	0	4	10	.378	21	0	0	1.000
1974—Pawtucket	Int.		OF	117	430	69	145	21	4	*25	*93	*.337	181	10	11	.946
1974—Boston	Amer.		OF	24	67	6	18	2	1	1	13	.269	4	0	1	.800
1975—Boston	Amer.		OF	144	564	92	174	29	4	22	102	.309	162	6	0	1.000
1976—Boston	Amer.		OF	153	581	75	164	25	8	25	85	.282	199	8	7	.967
1977—Boston	Amer.		OF	160	644	104	206	29	15	*39	114	.320	83	4	4	.956
1978—Boston	Amer.		OF	*163	*677	121	*213	25	*15	*46	*139	.315	245	13	3	.989
1979—Boston	Amer.		OF	158	619	117	201	39	6	39	130	.325	241	8	4	.984
1980—Boston†	Amer.		OF	124	504	81	148	22	6	24	86	.294	233	10	3	.988
1981—Boston	Amer.		OF	108	*451	51	128	18	1	17	62	.284	237	9	3	.988
1982—Boston	Amer.		OF	145	573	86	177	24	5	24	97	.309	273	10	9	.969
1983—Boston	Amer.		OF	155	626	90	191	34	1	*39	●126	.305	339	21	6	.984
	Major League Totals			1334	5306	823	1620	247	62	276	954	.305	2016	89	40	.981

Selected by Boston Red Sox' organization in 1st round (15th player selected) of free-agent draft, June 8, 1971.
†On supplemental disabled list, June 22 to July 27, 1980.

ALL-STAR GAME RECORD

Tied All-Star Game record for most at bats, game (5), July 17, 1979.

Year	League	Pos.	AB.	R.	H.	2B.	3B.	HR.	RBI.	B.A.	PO.	A.	E.	F.A.
1977—American		OF	2	0	1	0	0	0	0	.500	1	0	0	1.000
1978—American		OF	4	0	0	0	0	0	0	.000	2	0	0	1.000
1979—American		OF	5	0	1	1	0	0	0	.200	3	0	0	1.000
1983—American		OF	4	1	2	0	0	1	1	.500	1	0	0	1.000
	All-Star Game Totals		15	1	4	1	0	1	1	.267	7	0	0	1.000

Named to American League All-Star Team in 1980; replaced due to injury.

JAMES RODNEY RICHARD
(J. R.)

Born March 7, 1950, at Vienna, La.
Height, 6.08. Weight, 237.
Throws and bats righthanded.
Attended Arizona State University, Tempe, Ariz.

Tied major league record for most base on balls, shutout game through nine innings (10), July 6, 1976.
Tied modern major league records for most strikeouts, first major league game (15), September 5, 1971 (second game of doubleheader); most wild pitches, game (6), April 10, 1979.
Established modern National League record for most strikeouts by righthanded pitcher, season (313), 1979.
Tied modern National League record for most consecutive seasons, 300 or more strikeouts (2), 1978 and 1979.
Pitched seven-inning, 2-0 no-hit victory against Daytona Beach, August 28, 1970.
Led National League in wild pitches with 16 in 1978 and tied for lead with 19 in 1979.
Led American Association in wild pitches with 18 and tied for lead in shutouts with 3 in 1971.
Tied for American Association lead in balks with 2 in 1972.
Received reported $75,000 bonus to sign with Houston Astros, 1969.

Year	Club	League	G.	IP.	W.	L.	Pct.	H.	R.	ER.	SO.	BB.	ERA.
1969—Covington	Ap'alchian		12	56	5	4	.556	51	50	41	71	*52	6.59
1970—Cocoa	Florida St.		19	109	4	11	.267	67	53	29	138	68	2.39
1971—Houston	National		4	21	2	1	.667	17	9	8	29	16	3.43
1971—Oklahoma City	Am. Assoc.		24	173	12	7	.632	116	55	47	*202	*105	*2.45
1972—Oklahoma City	Am. Assoc.		19	128	10	8	.556	94	57	43	169	79	3.02
1972—Houston	National		4	6	1	0	1.000	10	9	9	8	8	13.50
1973—Denver	Am. Assoc.		8	52	2	4	.333	54	39	33	66	26	5.71
1973—Houston	National		16	72	6	2	.750	54	37	32	75	38	4.00
1974—Columbus	Southern		13	87	5	8	.385	103	65	52	77	61	5.38

Year Club	League	G.	IP.	W.	L.	Pct.	H.	R.	ER.	SO.	BB.	ERA.
1974—Denver	Am. Assoc.	4	33	4	0	1.000	15	2	0	26	12	0.00
1974—Houston	National	15	65	2	3	.400	58	31	30	42	36	4.15
1975—Houston	National	33	203	12	10	.545	178	107	99	176	★138	4.39
1976—Houston	National	39	291	20	15	.571	221	105	89	214	★151	2.75
1977—Houston	National	36	267	18	12	.600	212	94	88	214	104	2.97
1978—Houston	National	36	275	18	11	.621	192	104	95	★303	★141	3.11
1979—Houston	National	38	292	18	13	.581	220	98	88	★313	98	★2.71
1980—Houston†	National	17	114	10	4	.714	65	31	24	119	40	1.89
1981—Houston‡	National					(Did not play)						
1982—Houston§	National					(Did not play)						
1982—Daytona Beach	Florida St.	6	42	3	1	.750	36	14	13	28	15	2.79
1982—Tucson	P. Coast	6	24⅓	0	2	.000	35	45	37	13	27	13.68
1983—Sarasota Astros xy	Gulf Coast	9	51	2	3	.400	44	23	18	46	31	3.18
Major League Totals...................		238	1606	107	71	.601	1227	625	562	1493	770	3.15

Selected by Houston Astros' organization in 1st round (second player selected) of free-agent draft, June 5, 1969.

†On disabled list, July 16, 1980; transferred to emergency disabled list, August 25, 1980 through remainder of season.

‡On emergency disabled list, April 1 to September 1, 1981.

§On emergency disabled list, April 5 to September 6, 1982; included rehabilitation disability assignment to Daytona Beach, June 25 to August 5, 1982, and Tucson, August 6 to September 2, 1982.

xOn Houston emergency disabled list, March 30, 1983 through remainder of season; included rehabilitation disability assignment to Sarasota, June 23 to September 20, 1983.

yGranted free agency, November 7, 1983.

ALL-STAR GAME RECORD

Year League		IP.	W.	L.	Pct.	H.	R.	ER.	SO.	BB.	ERA.
1980—National		2	0	0	.000	1	0	0	3	2	0.00

EUGENE RICHARDS JR.
(Gene)

Born September 29, 1953, at Monticello, S. C.
Height, 6.00. Weight, 175.
Throws and bats lefthanded.
Attended South Carolina State College, Orangeburg, S. C.

Collected six hits in one game, July 26, 1977 (second game, 15 innings).
Major League stolen bases: 1977 (56), 1978 (37), 1979 (24), 1980 (61), 1981 (20), 1982 (30), 1983 (14). Total—242.
Led California League in total bases with 276 and stolen bases with 85 in 1975.
Named California League Most Valuable Player, 1975.

Year Club	League	Pos.	G.	AB.	R.	H.	2B.	3B.	HR.	RBI.	B.A.	PO.	A.	E.	F.A.
1975—Reno	Calif.	OF	134	501	★148	★191	29	10	12	58	★.381	203	6	8	.963
1976—Hawaii	P. C.	OF	137	522	102	★173	24	9	8	59	.331	231	13	12	.953
1977—San Diego	Nat.	OF-1B	146	525	79	152	16	11	5	32	.290	416	35	13	.972
1978—San Diego	Nat.	OF-1B	154	555	90	171	26	12	4	45	.308	421	20	17	.963
1979—San Diego	Nat.	OF	150	545	77	152	17	9	4	41	.279	320	7	9	.973
1980—San Diego	Nat.	OF	158	642	91	193	26	8	4	41	.301	307	★21	7	.979
1981—San Diego	Nat.	OF	104	393	47	113	14	●12	3	42	.288	178	●14	5	.975
1982—San Diego†	Nat.	OF-1B	132	521	63	149	13	8	3	28	.286	423	20	11	.976
1983—San Diego‡	Nat.	OF	95	233	37	64	11	3	3	22	.275	96	2	2	.980
Major League Totals..................			939	3414	484	994	123	63	26	251	.291	2161	119	64	.973

Selected by San Diego Padres' organization in 1st round (first player selected) of free-agent draft, January 9, 1975.
†On disabled list, May 1 to May 28, 1982.
‡Granted free agency, November 7, 1983.

MICHAEL ANTHONY RICHARDT
Name pronounced Richard.
(Mike)

Born May 24, 1958, at Los Angeles, Calif.
Height, 6.00. Weight, 170.
Throws and bats righthanded.
Attended Fresno City College, Fresno, Calif.

Led Gulf Coast League second basemen in fielding percentage with .982 and tied for lead in double plays with 24 in 1978.
Tied for Gulf Coast League lead in sacrifice hits with 6 in 1978.
Tied for International League lead in double plays by second basemen with 74 in 1980.

Year Club	League	Pos.	G.	AB.	R.	H.	2B.	3B.	HR.	RBI.	B.A.	PO.	A.	E.	F.A.
1978—Sara. Rangers.......	Gulf C.	2B-3B	45	160	30	45	9	2	0	14	.281	90	94	7	.963
1979—Asheville...............	W. Car.	2B	75	283	61	88	15	3	4	41	.311	173	212	16	.960
1979—Tulsa	Texas	2B	68	272	50	89	17	5	5	24	.327	162	218	6	.984
1980—Charleston.............	Int.	2B	124	487	74	136	21	13	12	46	.279	★262	385	10	★.985
1980—Texas.....................	Amer.	2B	22	71	2	16	2	0	0	8	.225	32	55	2	.978
1981—Wichita..................	A. A.	2B-3B-OF	90	350	53	124	17	2	8	60	★.354	86	151	8	.967
1982—Texas†	Amer.	2B-OF	119	402	34	97	10	0	3	43	.241	253	279	6	.989

Year Club League	Pos.	G.	AB.	R.	H.	2B.	3B.	HR.	RBI.	B.A.	PO.	A.	E.	F.A.
1983—Texas‡.................. Amer.	2B	22	83	9	13	2	1	1	7	.157	56	61	1	.992
1983—Okla. City.............. A. A.	2B-OF	30	116	7	31	5	0	2	13	.267	42	60	2	.981
Major League Totals...................................		163	556	45	126	14	1	4	58	.227	341	395	9	.988

Selected by Toronto Blue Jays' organization in 2nd round of free-agent draft, January 10, 1978.
Selected by Texas Rangers' organization in secondary phase of free-agent draft, June 6, 1978.
†On supplemental disabled list, May 6 to May 21, 1982.
‡On disabled list, April 22 to July 14, 1983; included rehabilitation disability assignment to Oklahoma City, July 8 to July 14, 1983.

JAMES RAY RIGGS
(Jim)

Born November 4, 1960, at Monroe, Mich.
Height, 6.01. Weight, 185.
Throws right and bats lefthanded.
Attended Eastern Michigan University, Ypsilanti, Mich.

Led South Atlantic League third basemen in putouts with 103 in 1983.

Year Club League	Pos.	G.	AB.	R.	H.	2B.	3B.	HR.	RBI.	B.A.	PO.	A.	E.	F.A.
1982—Oneonta................ NYP	3B	72	272	45	84	16	2	6	44	.309	45	113	17	.903
1983—Greensboro .... S. Atl.	3B-1B-2B	133	481	77	126	23	4	13	95	.262	104	228	32	.912

Selected by New York Yankees' organization in 4th round of free-agent draft, June 7, 1982.

DAVID ALLAN RIGHETTI
Name pronounced Ri-GET-tee.
(Dave)

Born November 28, 1958, at San Jose, Calif.
Height, 6.03. Weight, 195.
Throws and bats lefthanded.
Attended San Jose City College, San Jose, Calif.
Son of Leo Righetti, minor league infielder, 1944 through 1949 and 1951 through 1957;
Brother of Steven Righetti, third baseman in Texas Rangers' organization, 1977 through 1979.

Pitched 4-0 no-hit victory against Boston Red Sox, July 4, 1983.
Named American League Rookie Pitcher of the Year by THE SPORTING NEWS, 1981.
Named American League Rookie of the Year by Baseball Writers' Association of America, 1981.

Year Club League	G.	IP.	W.	L.	Pct.	H.	R.	ER.	SO.	BB.	ERA.
1977—Asheville.............. W. Carol.	17	109	11	3	★.786	98	47	38	101	53	3.14
1978—Tulsa†‡................. Texas	13	91	5	5	.500	66	40	32	127	49	3.16
1979—West Haven§ .... Eastern	11	69	4	3	.571	45	23	15	78	45	1.96
1979—Columbus x .... Int'national	8	40	3	2	.600	22	13	13	44	19	2.93
1979—New York .... American	3	17	0	1	.000	10	7	7	13	10	3.71
1980—Columbus.................... Int'national	24	142	6	10	.375	124	79	73	139	★101	4.63
1981—Columbus .... Int'national	7	45	5	0	1.000	30	8	5	50	26	1.00
1981—New York .... American	15	105	8	4	.667	75	25	24	89	38	2.06
1982—New York .... American	33	183	11	10	.524	155	88	77	163	★108	3.79
1982—Columbus .... Int'national	4	25⅔	1	0	1.000	22	11	8	33	12	2.81
1983—New York .... American	31	217	14	8	.636	194	96	83	169	67	3.44
Major League Totals...................................	82	522	33	23	.589	434	216	191	434	223	3.29

Selected by Texas Rangers' organization in 1st round (ninth player selected) of free-agent draft, January 11, 1977.
†On disabled list, July 31 to September 2, 1978.
‡Traded with Pitchers Mike Griffin and Paul Mirabella and Outfielders Juan Beniquez and Greg Jemison to New York Yankees for Pitchers Sparky Lyle, Larry McCall and Dave Rajsich, Catcher Mike Heath, Shortstop Domingo Ramos and cash, November 10, 1978.
§On disabled list, May 21 to June 28, 1979.
xOn disabled list, June 28 to July 20 and August 2 to August 23, 1979.

DIVISION SERIES RECORD

Year Club	League	G.	IP.	W.	L.	Pct.	H.	R.	ER.	SO.	BB.	ERA.
1981—New York....................... American		2	9	2	0	1.000	8	1	1	10	3	1.00

CHAMPIONSHIP SERIES RECORD

Year Club	League	G.	IP.	W.	L.	Pct.	H.	R.	ER.	SO.	BB.	ERA.
1981—New York....................... American		1	6	1	0	1.000	4	0	0	4	2	0.00

WORLD SERIES RECORD

Year Club	League	G.	IP.	W.	L.	Pct.	H.	R.	ER.	SO.	BB.	ERA.
1981—New York....................... American		1	2	0	0	.000	5	3	3	1	2	13.50

JOSE ANTONIO RIJO (ABREU)

Born May 13, 1965, at San Cristobal, Dominican Republic.
Height, 6.01. Weight, 160.
Throws and bats righthanded.

Led Florida State League in complete games with 15 and tied for lead in shutouts with 4 in 1983.
Named Florida State League Most Valuable Player, 1983.

Year Club	League	G.	IP.	W.	L.	Pct.	H.	R.	ER.	SO.	BB.	ERA.
1981—Bradenton Yankees	Gulf Coast	11	22	3	3	.500	37	16	11	22	7	4.50
1982—Paintsville	Ap'lachian	13	79⅓	8	4	.667	76	33	22	66	22	2.50
1983—Ft. Lauderdale	Florida St.	21	160⅓	*15	5	.750	129	38	30	152	43	*1.68
1983—Nashville	Southern	5	40⅓	3	2	.600	31	12	12	32	22	2.68

Signed as free agent by New York Yankees' organization, August 1, 1980.

EARNEST RILES
(Ernie)

Born October 2, 1960, at Cairo, Ga.
Height, 6.00. Weight, 180.
Throws right and bats lefthanded.
Attended Middle Georgia College, Cochran, Ga.

Led California League in bases on balls received with 84 in 1982.
Led Texas League shortstops in total chances with 670 and double plays with 77 in 1983.
Led California League shortstops in double plays with 95 and tied for lead in total chances with 692 in 1982.

Year Club	League	Pos.	G.	AB.	R.	H.	2B.	3B.	HR.	RBI.	B.A.	PO.	A.	E.	F.A.
1981—Butte	Pion.	SS-3B-2B	67	256	63	89	11	2	4	43	.348	97	217	27	.921
1982—Stockton	Calif.	SS	138	447	60	128	23	6	2	56	.286	204	*451	37	.947
1983—El Paso	Texas	SS	130	476	109	166	31	3	13	91	*.349	*193	*445	32	*.952

Selected by Seattle Mariners' organization in 21st round of free-agent draft, June 3, 1980.
Selected by Milwaukee Brewers' organization in secondary phase of free-agent draft, January 13, 1981.

GEORGE MICHAEL RILEY

Born October 6, 1956, at Philadelphia, Pa.
Height, 6.02. Weight, 200.
Throws and bats lefthanded.

Pitched 10-0, seven-inning no-hit victory against Fort Lauderdale, July 11, 1976.
Led Florida State League in games started with 26 in 1975.

Year Club	League	G.	IP.	W.	L.	Pct.	H.	R.	ER.	SO.	BB.	ERA.
1974—Bradenton Cubs	Gulf Coast	5	21	0	3	.000	18	14	8	16	8	3.43
1975—Key West	Florida St.	28	155	10	10	.500	141	75	62	84	81	3.60
1976—Pompano Beach	Florida St.	20	114	7	10	.412	122	73	49	76	47	3.87
1976—Midland	Texas	8	47	1	5	.167	61	37	34	29	36	6.51
1977—Midland	Texas	30	75	3	1	.750	79	41	36	57	36	4.32
1977—Wichita	Am. Assoc.	9	13	0	0	.000	15	7	7	11	8	4.85
1978—Wichita	Am. Assoc.	24	36	3	5	.375	47	31	29	17	23	7.25
1978—Midland	Texas	10	69	5	3	.625	77	37	34	50	39	4.43
1979—Wichita†	Am. Assoc.	38	74	3	8	.273	75	53	50	53	53	6.08
1979—Chicago	National	4	13	0	1	.000	16	9	8	5	6	5.54
1980—Wichita	Am. Assoc.	28	47	3	3	.500	60	23	23	32	19	4.40
1980—Chicago‡	National	22	36	0	4	.000	41	29	23	18	20	5.75
1981—Appleton§	Midwest	7	30	0	3	.000	30	13	12	27	13	3.60
1982—Reading	Eastern	37	58⅔	2	3	.400	56	27	23	46	25	3.53
1983—Reading	Eastern	27	81⅔	8	3	.727	69	27	22	58	44	2.42
1983—Portland	P. Coast	9	47	5	2	.714	48	36	33	27	32	6.32
Major League Totals		26	49	0	5	.000	57	38	31	23	26	5.69

Selected by Chicago Cubs' organization in 4th round of free-agent draft, June 5, 1974.
†On disabled list, April 17 to April 27, 1979.
‡Released, February 26, 1981; signed by Appleton (Chicago White Sox' organization), July 18, 1981.
§Released, March 29, 1982; signed by Reading (Philadelphia Phillies' organization), June 5, 1982.

ANDREW JOHN RINCON
(Andy)

Born March 5, 1959, at Pico Rivera, Calif.
Height, 6.03. Weight, 195.
Throws and bats righthanded.

Year Club	League	G.	IP.	W.	L.	Pct.	H.	R.	ER.	SO.	BB.	ERA.
1977—Calgary	Pioneer	7	40	3	1	.750	36	17	13	23	20	2.93
1978—Gastonia	W. Carol.	24	150	8	10	.444	132	85	69	67	86	4.14
1979—St. Petersburg	Florida St.	25	158	10	9	.526	153	74	59	89	66	3.36
1979—Arkansas	Texas	3	16	1	2	.333	18	8	8	7	5	4.50
1980—Arkansas	Texas	26	172	10	7	.588	165	80	65	138	51	3.40
1980—St. Louis	National	4	31	3	1	.750	23	9	9	22	7	2.61
1981—St. Louis†	National	5	36	3	1	.750	27	8	7	13	5	1.75
1981—Springfield	Am. Assoc.	8	22	1	3	.250	32	16	16	17	14	6.55
1981—Arkansas	Texas	2	8	0	2	.000	11	6	6	6	1	6.75
1982—St. Louis	National	11	40	2	3	.400	35	22	21	11	25	4.73
1982—Louisville	Am. Assoc.	18	116⅔	5	8	.385	115	80	66	75	61	5.09
1983—Louisville‡§	Am. Assoc.	6	31	1	2	.333	26	18	16	14	17	4.65
Major League Totals		20	107	8	5	.615	85	39	37	46	37	3.11

Selected by St. Louis Cardinals' organization in 5th round of free-agent draft, June 7, 1977.
†On disabled list, May 10 to June 10, 1981.
‡On disabled list, May 13 to July 8 and July 16, 1983 through remainder of season.
§Granted free agency, October 20, 1983; signed by Pittsburgh Pirates' organization, November 18, 1983.

CALVIN EDWIN RIPKEN JR.
(Cal)

Born August 24, 1960, at Havre de Grace, Md.
Height, 6.04. Weight, 200.
Throws and bats righthanded.
Son of Cal Ripken, minor league catcher-outfielder, 1957 through 1964; minor league player-manager, Baltimore Orioles' organization, 1961, 1962 and 1964; minor league manager, Baltimore Orioles' organization, 1963 and 1965 through 1974; scout, Baltimore Orioles, 1975; and coach with Baltimore Orioles since 1976; brother of Billy Ripken, infielder in Baltimore Orioles' organization; nephew of Bill Ripken, minor league outfielder, 1947 through 1949.

Established major league record for fewest stolen bases, season, most at-bats (0 and 663), 1983.
Tied American League record for most games by shortstop, season (162), 1983.
Led American League shortstops in total chances with 831 and double plays with 113 in 1983.
Led Southern League third basemen in fielding percentage with .933, putouts with 119, assists with 268, and double plays with 34 in 1980.
Tied for Southern League lead in sacrifice flies with 9 in 1980.
Tied for Appalachian League lead in double plays by shortstops with 31 in 1978.
Named Major League Player of the Year by THE SPORTING NEWS, 1983.
Named American League Player of the Year by THE SPORTING NEWS, 1983.
Named American League Most Valuable Player by Baseball Writers' Association of America, 1983.
Named shortstop on THE SPORTING NEWS American League All-Star Team, 1983.
Named shortstop on THE SPORTING NEWS Silver Slugger Team, 1983.
Named American League Rookie Player of the Year by THE SPORTING NEWS, 1982.
Named American League Rookie of the Year by Baseball Writers' Association of America, 1982.

Year—Club	League	Pos.	G.	AB.	R.	H.	2B.	3B.	HR.	RBI.	B.A.	PO.	A.	E.	F.A.
1978—Bluefield	Appal.	SS	63	239	27	63	7	1	0	24	.264	*92	204	*33	.900
1979—Miami	Fla. St.	3B-SS-2B	105	393	51	119	*28	1	5	54	.303	149	260	30	.932
1979—Charlotte	South.	3B	17	61	6	11	0	1	3	8	.180	13	26	3	.929
1980—Charlotte	South.	2B-SS	●144	522	91	144	28	5	25	78	.276	151	341	35	.934
1981—Rochester	Int.	3B-SS	114	437	74	126	31	4	23	75	.288	128	320	21	.955
1981—Baltimore	Amer.	SS-3B	23	39	1	5	0	0	0	0	.128	13	30	3	.935
1982—Baltimore	Amer.	SS-3B	160	598	90	158	32	5	28	93	.264	221	440	19	.972
1983—Baltimore	Amer.	SS	●162	*663	*121	*211	*47	2	27	102	.318	272	*534	25	.970
Major League Totals			345	1300	212	374	79	7	55	195	.288	506	1004	47	.970

Selected by Baltimore Orioles' organization in 2nd round of free-agent draft, June 6, 1978.

CHAMPIONSHIP SERIES RECORD

Year—Club	League	Pos.	G.	AB.	R.	H.	2B.	3B.	HR.	RBI.	B.A.	PO.	A.	E.	F.A.
1983—Baltimore	Amer.	SS	4	15	5	6	2	0	0	1	.400	7	11	0	1.000

WORLD SERIES RECORD

Year—Club	League	Pos.	G.	AB.	R.	H.	2B.	3B.	HR.	RBI.	B.A.	PO.	A.	E.	F.A.
1983—Baltimore	Amer.	SS	5	18	2	3	0	0	0	1	.167	6	14	0	1.000

ALL-STAR GAME RECORD

Year—League	Pos.	AB.	R.	H.	2B.	3B.	HR.	RBI.	B.A.	PO.	A.	E.	F.A.
1983—American	SS	0	0	0	0	0	0	0	.000	1	0	0	1.000

GERMAN RIVERA (DIAZ)

Born July 6, 1960, at Santurce, Puerto Rico.
Height, 6.02. Weight, 170.
Throws and bats righthanded.
Led Florida State League in sacrifice flies with 10 in 1980.
Led Pacific Coast League third basemen in assists with 333 and double plays with 31 in 1983.
Led Texas League third basemen in errors with 29 in 1982.
Tied for Pioneer League lead in double plays by third basemen with 9 in 1978.

Year—Club	League	Pos.	G.	AB.	R.	H.	2B.	3B.	HR.	RBI.	B.A.	PO.	A.	E.	F.A.
1978—Clinton	Midw.	3B-OF	36	108	11	22	3	1	3	13	.204	27	31	5	.921
1978—Lethbridge	Pion.	3B	66	252	61	79	15	2	7	47	.313	50	*120	12	*.934
1979—Lodi	Calif.	3B	36	139	26	26	6	1	1	17	.187	24	84	19	.850
1979—Clinton	Midw.	3B	100	338	43	82	18	5	4	42	.243	74	199	17	.941
1980—Vero Beach	Fla. St.	3B	137	530	77	137	19	10	4	*80	.258	81	203	●29	.907
1981—Lodi	Calif.	3B-SS	128	478	78	127	31	2	13	71	.266	157	419	40	.935
1982—San Antonio†	Texas	SS-3B	136	474	63	137	17	4	15	60	.289	171	342	61	.894
1983—Albuquerque	P. Coast	3B-SS	138	515	109	169	27	5	24	103	.328	116	343	34	.931
1983—Los Angeles	Nat.	3B	13	17	1	6	1	0	0	0	.353	2	11	1	.929
Major League Totals			13	17	1	6	1	0	0	0	.353	2	11	1	.929

Signed as free agent by Los Angeles Dodgers' organization, December 20, 1977.
†Drafted by Oakland A's, December 6, 1982; returned, March 25, 1983.

—DID YOU KNOW—

That Montreal lost on consecutive days to pitching brothers in 1983? Houston's Joe Niekro beat the Expos, 3-0, on July 14 and Atlanta's Phil Niekro defeated Montreal, 9-3, the next night.

JOHN MILTON RIVERS
(Mickey)

Born October 31, 1948, at Miami, Fla.
Height, 5.10. Weight, 162.
Throws and bats lefthanded.
Attended Miami-Dade (North) Community College, Miami, Fla.

Tied major league record for most seasons, consecutive, leading major leagues, fewest grounded into double plays (minimum 500 at bats) (2), 1977.

Major League stolen bases: 1970 (1), 1971 (13), 1972 (4), 1973 (8), 1974 (30), 1975 (70), 1976 (43), 1977 (22), 1978 (25), 1979 (10), 1980 (18), 1981 (9), 1983 (9). Total—262.

Led American League in stolen bases with 70 in 1975.
Led Pacific Coast League in stolen bases with 47 in 1973.
Led Pioneer League in bases on balls received with 66 and tied for lead in caught stealing with 6 in 1969.
Tied for Pacific Coast League lead in double plays by outfielders with 3 in 1971.
Named outfielder on THE SPORTING NEWS American League All-Star Team, 1976.
Named Texas League Most Valuable Player, 1970.

Year	Club	League	Pos.	G.	AB.	R.	H.	2B.	3B.	HR.	RBI.	B.A.	PO.	A.	E.	F.A.
1969—Magic Valley†		Pion.	OF	67	225	75	69	13	6	7	41	.307	67	8	*11	.872
1970—El Paso		Texas	OF	114	449	*99	●154	25	10	14	56	*.343	235	13	12	.954
1970—California		Amer.	OF	17	25	6	8	2	0	0	3	.320	10	0	0	1.000
1971—Salt Lake City		P. C.	OF	72	292	54	94	13	11	10	47	.322	153	11	8	.953
1971—California		Amer.	OF	78	268	31	71	12	2	1	12	.265	159	5	4	.976
1972—Salt Lake City		P. C.	OF	59	241	50	81	14	3	3	16	.336	129	3	5	.964
1972—California		Amer.	OF	58	159	18	34	6	2	0	7	.214	105	0	2	.981
1973—Salt Lake City		P. C.	OF	141	556	113	*187	18	14	9	71	.336	*327	12	7	.980
1973—California		Amer.	OF	30	129	26	45	6	4	0	16	.349	60	0	6	.909
1974—California‡		Amer.	OF	118	466	69	133	19	*11	3	31	.285	309	9	2	.994
1975—California§		Amer.	OF	155	616	70	175	17	●13	1	53	.284	371	13	9	.977
1976—New York		Amer.	OF	137	590	95	184	31	8	8	67	.312	407	6	6	.986
1977—New York		Amer.	OF	138	565	79	184	18	5	12	69	.326	380	11	7	.982
1978—New York x		Amer.	OF	141	559	78	148	25	8	11	48	.265	384	8	8	.980
1979—N. Y. yz-Tex.		Amer.	OF	132	533	72	156	27	8	9	50	.293	300	8	7	.978
1980—Texas		Amer.	OF	147	630	96	210	32	6	7	60	.333	342	*19	8	.978
1981—Texas		Amer.	OF	99	399	62	114	21	2	3	26	.286	225	12	1	.996
1982—Texas ab		Amer.	DH	19	68	6	16	1	1	1	4	.235	0	0	0	.000
1983—Texas		Amer.	OF	96	309	37	88	17	0	1	20	.285	48	1	1	.980
Major League Totals				1365	5316	745	1566	234	70	57	466	.295	3100	92	61	.981

Selected by Chicago White Sox' organization in 1st round (13th player selected) of free-agent draft, January 27, 1968.

Selected by New York Mets' organization in secondary phase of free-agent draft, June 7, 1968.

Selected by Washington Senators' organization in secondary phase of free-agent draft, February 1, 1969.

Selected by Atlanta Braves' organization in secondary phase of free-agent draft, June 5, 1969.

†Traded with Pitcher Clint Compton by Atlanta Braves to California Angels for Pitchers Hoyt Wilhelm and Bob Priddy, September 8, 1969.

‡On disabled list, August 21, 1974 through remainder of season.

§Traded with Pitcher Ed Figueroa to New York Yankees for Outfielder Bobby Bonds, December 11, 1975.

xOn supplemental disabled list, June 17 to July 2, 1978.

yOn disabled list, June 30 to July 20, 1978.

zTraded with three players to be named later to Texas Rangers for Outfielder Oscar Gamble, Infielder Amos Lewis and two players to be named later, August 1, 1979; New York Yankees' organization traded Pitchers Bob Polinsky, Neal Mersch and Mark Softy to Texas Rangers' organization for Pitchers Gene Nelson and Ray Fontenot to complete deal, October 8, 1979.

aOn supplemental disabled list, March 28 to May 6, 1982.

bOn disabled list, May 10 to July 15 and August 5 to September 23, 1982.

CHAMPIONSHIP SERIES RECORD

Established Championship Series record for highest batting average, total Series, 10 or more games and 30 or more at-bats (.386).

Tied Championship Series records for most consecutive hits, one Series (5), 1976; most hits, two consecutive games, one Series (6), October 8 and 9, 1977.

Tied American League Championship Series records for most consecutive hits, total Series (5); most at-bats, five-game Series (23), 1976 and 1977.

Year	Club	League	Pos.	G.	AB.	R.	H.	2B.	3B.	HR.	RBI.	B.A.	PO.	A.	E.	F.A.
1976—New York		Amer.	OF	5	23	5	8	0	1	0	0	.348	11	0	0	1.000
1977—New York		Amer.	OF	5	23	5	9	2	0	2	2	.391	19	0	0	1.000
1978—New York		Amer.	OF	4	11	0	5	0	0	0	0	.455	8	1	0	1.000
Championship Series Totals				14	57	10	22	2	1	0	2	.386	38	1	0	1.000

WORLD SERIES RECORD

Established World Series records for highest fielding percentage by outfielder, six-game Series (1.000 with 25 chances), 1977 (most chances accepted for any length Series); most putouts by outfielder, six-game Series (24), 1977; most chances accepted by outfielder, six-game Series (25), 1977.

Tied World Series record for most at bats, extra-inning game, no hits (6), October 11, 1977 (12 innings).

Year	Club	League	Pos.	G.	AB.	R.	H.	2B.	3B.	HR.	RBI.	B.A.	PO.	A.	E.	F.A.
1976—New York		Amer.	OF	4	18	1	3	0	0	0	0	.167	14	0	0	1.000
1977—New York		Amer.	OF	6	27	1	6	2	0	0	1	.222	24	1	0	1.000
1978—New York		Amer.	OF-PH	5	18	2	6	0	0	0	1	.333	7	0	0	1.000
World Series Totals				15	63	4	15	2	0	0	2	.238	45	1	0	1.000

Year League	Pos.	AB.	R.	H.	2B.	3B.	HR.	RBI.	B.A.	PO.	A.	E.	F.A.
1976—American	OF	2	0	1	0	0	0	0	.500	2	0	0	1.000

LEON KAUFFMAN ROBERTS

Born January 22, 1951, at Vicksburg, Mich.
Height, 6.03. Weight, 200.
Throws and bats righthanded.
Attended University of Michigan, Ann Arbor, Mich.
Brother of Bill Roberts, outfielder in Houston Astros' organization, 1976.

Year Club	League	Pos.	G.	AB.	R.	H.	2B.	3B.	HR.	RBI.	B.A.	PO.	A.	E.	F.A.
1972—Lakeland	Fla. St.	OF	74	254	36	78	14	3	5	52	.307	162	8	5	.971
1972—Rocky Mount	Carol.	OF	6	22	4	6	1	0	0	2	.273	15	0	0	1.000
1973—Montgomery	South.	OF	133	489	87	144	●30	1	14	70	.294	276	10	6	.979
1974—Evansville	A. A.	OF	132	481	74	137	31	4	12	79	.285	264	9	9	.968
1974—Detroit	Amer.	OF	17	63	5	17	3	2	0	7	.270	25	0	2	.926
1975—Detroit†	Amer.	OF	129	447	51	115	17	5	10	38	.257	268	10	5	.982
1976—Houston	Nat.	OF	87	235	31	68	11	2	7	33	.289	99	1	2	.980
1977—Charleston	Int.	OF-1B	73	264	39	79	20	2	2	34	.299	266	14	2	.993
1977—Houston‡	Nat.	OF	19	27	1	2	0	0	0	2	.074	3	2	0	1.000
1978—Seattle	Amer.	OF	134	472	78	142	21	7	22	92	.301	296	10	8	.975
1979—Seattle	Amer.	OF	140	450	61	122	24	6	15	54	.271	286	6	5	.983
1980—Seattle§	Amer.	OF	119	374	48	94	18	3	10	33	.251	238	6	4	.984
1981—Texas	Amer.	OF	72	233	26	65	17	2	4	31	.279	130	2	1	.992
1982—Tex. x-Tor. y	Amer.	OF	71	178	13	41	7	0	2	11	.230	66	0	0	1.000
1983—Kansas City	Amer.	OF	84	213	24	55	7	0	8	24	.258	139	3	3	.979
American League Totals			766	2430	306	651	114	25	71	290	.268	1448	37	28	.981
National League Totals			106	262	32	70	11	2	7	35	.267	102	3	2	.981
Major League Totals			872	2692	338	721	125	27	78	325	.268	1550	40	30	.981

Selected by Detroit Tigers' organization in 10th round of free-agent draft, June 6, 1972.
†Traded with Catcher Terry Humphrey and Pitchers Gene Pentz and Mark Lemongello to Houston Astros for Catcher Milt May and Pitchers Jim Crawford and Dave Roberts, December 6, 1975.
‡Traded to Seattle Mariners for Infielder Jimmy Sexton, December 5, 1977.
§Traded with Catcher Larry Cox, Pitcher Rick Honeycutt, Outfielder Willie Horton and Shortstop Mario Mendoza to Texas Rangers for Pitchers Brian Allard, Ken Clay, Steve Finch and Jerry Don Gleaton, Outfielder Richie Zisk and Shortstop Rick Auerbach, December 12, 1980.
xSold to Toronto Blue Jays, July 15, 1982.
yTraded to Kansas City Royals for First Baseman Cecil Fielder, February 4, 1983.

SCOTT ANTHONY ROBERTS

Born October 7, 1959, at Seattle, Wash.
Height, 6.04. Weight, 200.
Throws and bats righthanded.
Attended University of Hawaii, Honolulu, Haw.
Led Pioneer League in hit batsmen with 12 in 1981.

Year Club	League	G.	IP.	W.	L.	Pct.	H.	R.	ER.	SO.	BB.	ERA.
1981—Butte	Pioneer	12	78	6	1	★.857	51	23	16	74	28	1.85
1982—Stockton	California	24	174⅓	14	6	.700	151	65	49	137	41	2.53
1983—Vancouver†	P. Coast	21	109	6	10	.375	135	90	77	69	63	6.36

Selected by Pittsburgh Pirates' organization in 7th round of free-agent draft, June 6, 1978.
Selected by Milwaukee Brewers' organization in 2nd round of free-agent draft, June 8, 1981.
†On disabled list, May 20 to May 30, 1983.

ANDRE LEVETT ROBERTSON

Born October 2, 1957, at Orange, Tex.
Height, 5.10. Weight, 160.
Throws and bats righthanded.
Attending University of Texas, Austin, Tex.

Year Club	League	Pos.	G.	AB.	R.	H.	2B.	3B.	HR.	RBI.	B.A.	PO.	A.	E.	F.A.
1979—Dunedin	Fla. St.	SS-2B	70	264	35	57	14	2	2	18	.216	132	245	22	.945
1979—Syracuse†	Int.	SS	1	4	0	0	0	0	0	0	.000	1	4	0	1.000
1980—Ft. Lauderdale	Fla. St.	SS	63	233	30	58	7	4	0	22	.249	109	184	10	.967
1980—Columbus	Int.	SS	68	215	22	54	7	3	3	19	.251	88	222	13	.960
1980—Nashville	South.	SS	13	46	7	12	2	1	1	11	.261	23	43	5	.930
1981—Columbus‡	Int.	SS	123	402	55	104	13	6	9	49	.259	★210	★362	17	★.971
1981—New York	Amer.	SS-2B	10	19	1	5	1	0	0	0	.263	9	24	0	1.000
1982—Columbus	Int.	SS-2B	57	202	28	41	7	3	3	26	.203	115	144	12	.956
1982—New York	Amer.	SS-2B-3B	44	118	16	26	5	0	2	9	.220	84	98	6	.968
1983—New York§	Amer.	SS-2B	98	322	37	80	16	3	1	22	.248	163	302	15	.969
Major League Totals			152	459	54	111	22	3	3	31	.242	256	424	21	.970

Selected by Texas Rangers' organization in 12th round of free-agent draft, June 8, 1976.
Selected by Toronto Blue Jays' organization in 4th round of free-agent draft, June 5, 1979.
†Sold to New York Yankees' organization, December 10, 1979.
‡On disabled list, April 18 to May 3, 1981.
§On disabled list, August 18, 1983; transferred to emergency disabled list, August 26, 1983 through remainder of season.

Year Club	League	Pos.	G.	AB.	R.	H.	2B.	3B.	HR.	RBI.	B.A.	PO.	A.	E.	F.A.
1981—New York.............	Amer.	PH-SS	1	1	0	0	0	0	0	0	.000	2	1	0	1.000

WORLD SERIES RECORD

Year Club	League	Pos.	G.	AB.	R.	H.	2B.	3B.	HR.	RBI.	B.A.	PO.	A.	E.	F.A.
1981—New York.............	Amer.	PR	1	0	0	0	0	0	0	0	.000	0	0	0	.000

DON ALLEN ROBINSON

Born June 8, 1957, at Ashland, Ky.
Height, 6.04. Weight, 231.
Throws and bats righthanded.

Tied for National League lead in home runs allowed with 26 in 1982.
Led Western Carolinas League in complete games with 11 in 1976.
Tied for Gulf Coast League lead in hit batsmen with 6 in 1975.
Named National League Rookie Pitcher of the Year by THE SPORTING NEWS, 1978.
Named pitcher on THE SPORTING NEWS National League Silver Slugger team, 1982.

Year Club	League	G.	IP.	W.	L.	Pct.	H.	R.	ER.	SO.	BB.	ERA.
1975—Bradenton Pirates........................	Gulf Coast	10	66	2	3	.400	51	23	18	★70	31	2.45
1976—Charleston	W. Carol.	25	★172	12	9	.571	146	79	62	132	64	3.24
1977—Shreveport....................................	Texas	18	112	7	6	.538	113	58	51	103	41	4.06
1977—Columbus†....................................	Int'national	1	5	1	0	1.000	7	0	0	3	1	0.00
1978—Pittsburgh.....................................	National	35	228	14	6	.700	203	98	88	135	57	3.47
1979—Pittsburgh.....................................	National	29	161	8	8	.500	171	74	69	96	52	3.86
1980—Pittsburgh‡...................................	National	29	160	7	10	.412	157	74	71	103	45	3.99
1981—Pittsburgh§...................................	National	16	38	0	3	.000	47	27	25	17	23	5.92
1982—Pittsburgh.....................................	National	38	227	15	13	.536	213	★123	108	165	103	4.28
1983—Pittsburgh x	National	9	36⅓	2	2	.500	43	21	18	28	21	4.46
1983—Lynn..	Eastern	2	6⅔	0	1	.000	9	6	6	5	2	8.10
Major League Totals........................		156	850⅓	46	42	.523	834	417	379	544	301	4.01

Selected by Pittsburgh Pirates' organization in 3rd round of free-agent draft, June 4, 1975.
†On disabled list, July 28 to September 6, 1977.
‡On disabled list, March 31 to May 1, 1980.
§On disabled list, May 2 to June 6 and August 2 to August 26, 1981.
xOn disabled list, March 29 to June 10 and July 29 to September 2, 1983; included rehabilitation disability assignment to Lynn, April 29 to May 18, 1983.

CHAMPIONSHIP SERIES RECORD

Year Club	League	G.	IP.	W.	L.	Pct.	H.	R.	ER.	SO.	BB.	ERA.
1979—Pittsburgh.......................	National	2	2	1	0	1.000	0	0	0	3	1	0.00

WORLD SERIES RECORD

Year Club	League	G.	IP.	W.	L.	Pct.	H.	R.	ER.	SO.	BB.	ERA.
1979—Pittsburgh.......................	National	4	5	1	0	1.000	4	3	3	3	6	5.40

JEFFREY DANIEL ROBINSON
(Jeff)

Born December 13, 1960, at Santa Ana, Calif.
Height, 6.04. Weight, 195.
Throws and bats righthanded.
Attended California State University, Fullerton, Calif.

Year Club	League	G.	IP.	W.	L.	Pct.	H.	R.	ER.	SO.	BB.	ERA.
1983—Fresno...............................	California	14	94⅔	7	6	.538	88	35	24	78	21	2.28

Selected by Toronto Blue Jays' organization in 17th round of free-agent draft, June 5, 1979.
Selected by Detroit Tigers' organization in 14th round of free-agent draft, June 7, 1982.
Selected by San Francisco Giants' organization in 2nd round of free-agent draft, June 6, 1983.

WILLIAM HENRY ROBINSON JR.
(Bill)

Born June 26, 1943, at McKeesport, Pa.
Height, 6.03. Weight, 197.
Throws and bats righthanded.

Tied National League record for most home runs with bases filled, week (2), July 28 and 30, 1977.
Hit three home runs in a game, June 5, 1976 (15 innings).

Year Club	League	Pos.	G.	AB.	R.	H.	2B.	3B.	HR.	RBI.	B.A.	PO.	A.	E.	F.A.
1961—Wellsville..............	NYP	OF	67	251	37	60	15	4	2	25	.239	107	7	8	.934
1962—Eau Claire............	North.	OF	23	63	3	9	1	1	0	3	.143	27	2	0	1.000
1962—Dublin....................	Ga.-Fla.	OF	62	207	46	63	9	4	8	37	.304	71	1	5	.935
1963—Waycross................	Ga.-Fla.	OF	113	418	69	★132	18	★10	10	62	.316	★225	10	8	★.967
1964—Yakima	N'west.	OF	104	400	81	139	24	5	18	81	★.348	★247	21	10	.964
1965—Atlanta...................	Int.	OF	133	407	41	109	17	2	10	37	.268	228	8	12	.952
1966—Richmond...............	Int.	OF-2B-3B	139	509	86	159	30	4	20	79	.312	283	14	2	.993
1966—Atlanta†	Nat.	OF	6	11	1	3	0	1	0	3	.273	4	0	1	.800
1967—New York..............	Amer.	OF	116	342	31	67	6	1	7	29	.196	169	10	6	.968
1968—New York..............	Amer.	OF	107	342	34	82	16	7	6	40	.240	195	3	3	.985
1969—New York..............	Amer.	OF-1B	87	222	23	38	11	2	3	21	.171	103	5	4	.964

Year Club League	Pos.	G.	AB.	R.	H.	2B.	3B.	HR.	RBI.	B.A.	PO.	A.	E.	F.A.
1970—Syracuse‡ .... Int.	OF-3B	115	372	68	96	20	0	13	43	.258	166	6	2	.989
1971—Tucson§................. P. C.	OF-3B-1B	133	495	75	136	33	6	14	81	.275	328	26	6	.983
1972—Eugene................. P. C.	OF	65	240	47	73	9	2	20	66	.304	140	3	3	.979
1972—Philadelphia .... Nat.	OF	82	188	19	45	9	1	8	21	.239	109	2	2	.982
1973—Philadelphia x...... Nat.	OF-3B	124	452	62	130	32	1	25	65	.288	234	18	8	.969
1974—Philadelphia y...... Nat.	OF	100	280	32	66	14	1	5	29	.236	162	8	5	.971
1975—Pittsburgh .... Nat.	OF	92	200	26	56	12	2	6	33	.280	107	3	1	.991
1976—Pittsburgh .... Nat.	OF-3B-1B	122	393	55	119	22	3	21	64	.303	185	53	8	.967
1977—Pittsburgh .... Nat.	1B-OF-3B	137	507	74	154	32	1	26	104	.304	758	59	13	.984
1978—Pittsburgh z .... Nat.	OF-3B-1B	136	499	70	123	36	2	14	80	.246	268	51	8	.976
1979—Pittsburgh .... Nat.	OF-1B-3B	148	421	59	111	17	6	24	75	.264	394	29	3	.993
1980—Pittsburgh a .... Nat.	1B-OF	100	272	28	78	10	1	12	36	.287	427	22	7	.985
1981—Pittsburgh b .... Nat.	1B-OF-3B	39	88	8	19	3	0	2	8	.216	148	10	2	.988
1982—Pitt.c-Phil.d .... Nat.	OF-1B	66	140	14	35	9	0	7	31	.250	69	4	1	.986
1983—Philadelphia e...... Nat.	1B-3B-OF	10	7	0	1	0	0	0	2	.143	3	0	1	.750
American League Totals......................		310	906	88	187	33	10	16	90	.206	467	18	13	.974
National League Totals.............................		1162	3458	448	940	196	19	150	551	.272	2868	259	60	.981
Major League Totals................................		1472	4364	536	1127	229	29	166	641	.258	3335	277	73	.980

Signed as free agent by Atlanta Braves' organization, June 14, 1961.

†Traded with Pitcher Chi-Chi Olivo to New York Yankees for Third Baseman Clete Boyer and a player to be named later, November 29, 1966.

‡Traded to Chicago White Sox for Pitcher Barry Moore, December 3, 1970.

§Traded to Philadelphia Phillies for Catcher Jerry Rodriguez, December 13, 1971.

xOn disabled list, June 2 to June 25, 1973.

yTraded to Pittsburgh Pirates for Pitcher Wayne Simpson, April 5, 1975.

zOn supplemental disabled list, May 14 to May 29, 1978.

aOn supplemental disabled list, July 29, 1980; transferred to disabled list, August 18 to August 21, 1980.

bOn disabled list, April 22 to August 8, 1981.

cTraded to Philadelphia Phillies for Outfielder Wayne Nordhagen, June 15, 1982.

dGranted free agency, November 10, 1982; re-signed by Phillies, January 31, 1983.

eReleased, June 9, 1983; named coach with New York Mets for 1984 season.

CHAMPIONSHIP SERIES RECORD

Year Club League	Pos.	G.	AB.	R.	H.	2B.	3B.	HR.	RBI.	B.A.	PO.	A.	E.	F.A.
1975—Pittsburgh .... Nat.	PH	2	2	0	0	0	0	0	0	.000	0	0	0	.000
1979—Pittsburgh.............. Nat.	OF	3	3	0	0	0	0	0	0	.000	3	0	0	1.000
Championship Series Totals		5	5	0	0	0	0	0	0	.000	3	0	0	1.000

WORLD SERIES RECORD

Year Club League	Pos.	G.	AB.	R.	H.	2B.	3B.	HR.	RBI.	B.A.	PO.	A.	E.	F.A.
1979—Pittsburgh.............. Nat.	OF-PH	7	19	2	5	1	0	0	2	.263	11	1	0	1.000

PITCHING RECORD

Year Club	League	G.	IP.	W.	L.	Pct.	H.	R.	ER.	SO.	BB.	ERA.
1962—Dublin...	Ga.-Fla.	1	3	0	0	.000	5	6	5	0	1	15.00

RUBEN ROBLES

Name pronounced ROW-blez.

Born August 13, 1959, at Santo Domingo, D.R.

Height, 6.02. Weight, 196.

Throws and bats righthanded.

Led Florida State League in being hit by pitch with 13 in 1981.

Year Club League	Pos.	G.	AB.	R.	H.	2B.	3B.	HR.	RBI.	B.A.	PO.	A.	E.	F.A.
1979—Sarasota Astros.... Gulf C.	OF	2	4	0	0	0	0	0	0	.000	0	0	0	.000
1980—Sarasota Astros.... Gulf C.	OF	57	219	27	48	9	6	1	34	.219	118	9	1	*.992
1981—Daytona Beach.... Fla. St.	OF	109	339	60	96	12	2	5	39	.283	197	14	9	.959
1982—Columbus............... South.	OF-3B	125	445	70	132	13	3	11	55	.297	265	14	8	.972
1983—Tucson†................. P. C.	OF	50	172	30	48	10	5	5	33	.279	94	5	2	.980

Signed as free agent by Houston Astros' organization, March 11, 1979.

†On disabled list, April 11 to May 31 and June 8 to July 15, 1983.

RICHARD MARTIN RODAS
(Rich)

Born November 7, 1959, at Roseville, Calif.

Height, 6.02. Weight, 180.

Throws and bats lefthanded.

Attended Sacramento City College, Sacramento, Calif., and Sierra College, Rockin, Calif.

Led Pioneer League in complete games with 11 and tied for lead in shutouts with 2 in 1979.

Year Club	League	G.	IP.	W.	L.	Pct.	H.	R.	ER.	SO.	BB.	ERA.
1979—Lethbridge	Pioneer	13	*113	*12	0	*1.000	81	22	14	*148	18	*1.12
1980—Lodi†..	California					(Did not play)						
1981—San Antonio...................................	Texas	26	185	14	6	.700	193	100	85	148	60	4.14
1982—Albuquerque	P. Coast	29	187⅔	14	8	.636	*223	125	110	103	78	5.28

Year Club	League	G.	IP.	W.	L.	Pct.	H.	R.	ER.	SO.	BB.	ERA.
1983—Albuquerque	P. Coast	27	*186	*16	4	*.800	202	99	86	*157	69	4.16
1983—Los Angeles	National	7	4⅔	0	0	.000	4	1	1	5	3	1.93
Major League Totals		7	4⅔	0	0	.000	4	1	1	5	3	1.93

Signed as free agent by Los Angeles Dodgers' organization, June 15, 1979.
†On disabled list, April 10 to September 16, 1980.

AURELIO RODRIGUEZ (ITUARTE)

Born December 28, 1947, at Cananea, Sonora, Mexico.
Height, 5.11. Weight, 180.
Throws and bats righthanded.
Attended University of Guadalajara, Guadalajara, Mex.
Brother of Francisco Rodriguez, former shortstop in St. Louis Cardinals' organization;
presently playing in Mexican League with Aquascalientes.

Tied American League record for most long hits, inning (2), August 20, 1972 (sixth inning).
Led American League third basemen in double plays with 42 in 1969 and 41 in 1970.
Led American League third basemen in assists with 377 in 1970.
Led American League third basemen in total chances with 513 in 1970, 514 in 1972 and 536 in 1975.
Led Mexican League third basemen in double plays with 35 in 1966.
Named third baseman on THE SPORTING NEWS American League All-Star fielding team, 1976.

Year Club	League	Pos.	G.	AB.	R.	H.	2B.	3B.	HR.	RBI.	B.A.	PO.	A.	E.	F.A.
1965—Fresnillo	Mex. C.	3B-OF-2B	138	552	103	162	26	9	25	104	.293	197	263	31	.937
1965—Jalisco	Mex.	3B	15	50	5	13	1	1	0	3	.260	7	23	5	.857
1966—Jalisco†	Mex.	*3B-SS	135	480	64	140	17	*16	3	53	.292	*115	*316	*30	.935
1966—Seattle	P. C.	SS-3B	17	59	6	15	0	2	0	6	.254	23	34	5	.919
1967—El Paso	Texas	3B	79	309	49	101	20	9	11	47	.327	*69	148	6	.973
1967—Seattle	P. C.	3B	51	185	18	57	12	0	2	17	.308	36	79	3	.975
1967—California	Amer.	3B	29	130	14	31	3	1	1	8	.238	19	75	1	.989
1968—California	Amer.	3B-2B	76	223	14	54	10	1	1	16	.242	65	116	15	.923
1968—Seattle	P. C.	SS-3B-2B	46	181	21	45	8	0	3	15	.249	65	99	9	.948
1969—California	Amer.	3B	159	561	47	130	17	2	7	49	.232	145	352	●24	.954
1970—Cal.‡-Wash.§	Amer.	3B-SS	159	610	70	152	33	7	19	83	.249	127	398	18	.967
1971—Detroit	Amer.	3B-SS	154	604	68	153	30	7	15	39	.253	128	344	23	.954
1972—Detroit	Amer.	*3B-SS	153	601	65	142	23	5	13	56	.236	*150	350	17	.967
1973—Detroit	Amer.	3B-SS	160	555	46	123	27	3	9	58	.222	137	338	14	.971
1974—Detroit	Amer.	3B	159	571	54	127	23	5	5	49	.222	132	389	21	.961
1975—Detroit	Amer.	3B	151	507	47	124	20	6	13	60	.245	136	375	25	.953
1976—Detroit x	Amer.	3B	128	480	40	115	13	2	8	50	.240	120	280	9	*.978
1977—Detroit y	Amer.	3B-SS	96	306	30	67	14	1	10	32	.219	60	222	8	.972
1978—Detroit	Amer.	3B	134	385	40	102	25	2	7	43	.265	79	228	4	*.987
1979—Detroit z	Amer.	3B-1B	106	343	27	87	18	0	5	36	.254	72	211	13	.956
1980—San Diego a	Nat.	3B-SS	89	175	7	35	7	2	2	13	.200	38	130	6	.966
1980—New York	Amer.	3B-2B	52	164	14	36	6	1	3	14	.220	33	89	7	.946
1981—New York bc	Amer.	3B-2B-1B	27	52	4	18	2	0	2	8	.346	20	34	2	.964
1982—Chicago d	Amer.	3B-2B-SS	118	257	24	62	15	1	3	31	.241	79	209	9	.970
1983—Balt. e-Chi. f	Amer.	3B	67	87	1	12	1	0	1	3	.138	22	67	2	.978
National League Totals			89	175	7	35	7	2	2	13	.200	38	130	6	.966
American League Totals			1928	6436	605	1535	280	44	122	635	.239	1524	4077	212	.964
Major League Totals			2017	6611	612	1570	287	46	124	648	.237	1562	4207	218	.964

Signed as free agent by Fresnillo, January 25, 1965.
†Sold to Seattle (California Angels' organization), August 12, 1966.
‡Traded with Outfielder Rick Reichardt to Washington Senators for Third Baseman Ken McMullen, April 26, 1970.
§Traded with Shortstop Ed Brinkman and Pitchers Joe Coleman and Jim Hannan to Detroit Tigers for Pitcher Denny McLain, Third Baseman Don Wert, Pitcher Norm McRae and Infielder-Outfielder Elliott Maddox, October 9, 1970.

xOn disabled list, August 30 to October 4, 1976.
yOn supplemental disabled list, April 27 to May 31, 1977.
zSold to San Diego Padres for reported $200,000, December 7, 1979.
aSold to New York Yankees, August 4, 1980.
bTraded to Toronto Blue Jays for a player to be named later, November 18, 1981; New York Yankees' organization acquired Catcher Mike Lebo to complete deal, December 9, 1981.
cTraded to Chicago White Sox for Outfielder Wayne Nordhagen, April 2, 1982.
dGranted free agency, November 10, 1982; signed by Baltimore Orioles, February 3, 1983.
eReleased, August 13, 1983; signed by Chicago White Sox, August 31, 1983.
fGranted free agency, November 7, 1983.

CHAMPIONSHIP SERIES RECORD

Tied Championship Series record for most clubs, total Series (3).

Year Club	League	Pos.	G.	AB.	R.	H.	2B.	3B.	HR.	RBI.	B.A.	PO.	A.	E.	F.A.
1972—Detroit	Amer.	3B	5	16	0	0	0	0	0	0	.000	2	14	1	.941
1980—New York	Amer.	3B	2	6	0	2	1	0	0	0	.333	2	2	0	1.000
1981—New York	Amer.	3B	1	0	0	0	0	0	0	0	.000	0	0	0	.000
1983—Chicago	Amer.	3B	2	0	0	0	0	0	0	0	.000	0	0	1	.000
Championship Series Totals			10	22	0	2	1	0	0	0	.091	4	16	2	.909

WORLD SERIES RECORD

Year Club	League	Pos.	G.	AB.	R.	H.	2B.	3B.	HR.	RBI.	B.A.	PO.	A.	E.	F.A.
1981—New York	Amer.	3B-PR	4	12	1	5	0	0	0	0	.417	3	9	0	1.000

EDWIN RODRIGUEZ (MORALES)
(Ed)

Born August 14, 1960, at Ponce, Puerto Rico.
Height, 5.10. Weight, 175.
Throws and bats righthanded.

Year Club League	Pos.	G.	AB.	R.	H.	2B.	3B.	HR.	RBI.	B.A.	PO.	A.	E.	F.A.
1980—Bradenton Yanks Gulf C.	1B-2B	47	157	22	39	4	2	1	16	.248	179	9	6	.969
1981—Oneonta................ NYP	2B-3B-SS	50	146	27	45	5	3	0	19	.308	81	120	4	.980
1982—Greensboro.......... S. Atl.	2B	115	425	88	126	23	3	4	62	.296	227	320	25	.956
1982—Nashville.............. South.	SS	10	34	4	7	0	1	0	3	.206	19	38	4	.934
1982—New York.............. Amer.	2B	3	9	2	3	0	0	0	1	.333	2	12	2	.875
1983—Columbus†............ Int.	2B-SS-3B	112	393	73	98	7	8	2	54	.249	207	329	25	.955
1983—San Diego .... Nat.	2B-SS-3B	7	12	1	2	1	0	0	0	.167	8	8	0	1.000
American League Totals........................		3	9	2	3	0	0	0	1	.333	2	12	2	.875
National League Totals........................		7	12	1	2	1	0	0	0	.167	8	8	0	1.000
Major League Totals................		10	21	3	5	1	0	0	1	.238	10	20	2	.938

Signed as free agent by New York Yankees' organization, June 3, 1980.

†Traded with Pitcher Dennis Rasmussen to San Diego Padres, September 12, 1983, completing deal in which San Diego traded Pitcher John Montefusco to New York Yankees for two players to be named later, August 26, 1983.

VICTOR M. RODRIGUEZ (RIVERA)
(Vic)

Born July 14, 1961, at New York, N.Y.
Height, 5.11. Weight, 160.
Throws and bats righthanded.

Year Club League	Pos.	G.	AB.	R.	H.	2B.	3B.	HR.	RBI.	B.A.	PO.	A.	E.	F.A.
1977—Bluefield................ Appal.	3B-SS	53	188	28	55	10	4	3	23	.293	1	6	1	.875
1978—Bluefield................ Appal.	O-3B-SS	59	209	26	67	4	2	2	28	.321	39	14	5	.914
1979—Miami.................... Fla. St.	2B-3B-OF	67	228	23	70	10	2	1	31	.307	71	105	11	.941
1980—Alexandria† .... Carol.	2B	33	130	20	39	4	2	2	15	.300	62	94	6	.963
1980—Charlotte.............. South.	3B	19	65	4	15	0	0	0	4	.231	14	37	2	.962
1980—Miami.................... Fla. St.	2B	50	184	21	60	10	2	2	21	.326	103	144	14	.946
1981—Charlotte.............. South.	2B	138	553	68	169	22	1	9	65	.306	337	357	18	.975
1982—Rochester............. Int.	2B	87	300	26	74	10	2	0	18	.247	189	273	17	.965
1982—Charlotte.............. South.	2B	47	165	17	48	13	0	3	18	.291	95	116	10	.955
1983—Charlotte.............. South.	2B-3B	140	★571	80	●170	26	1	14	77	.298	291	386	19	.973

Signed as free agent by Baltimore Orioles' organization, February 11, 1977.

†Loaned to Alexandria (Co-op), April 6, 1980; returned, May 23, 1980.

GARY STEVEN ROENICKE

Name pronounced RENN-uh-kee.

Born December 5, 1954, at Covina, Calif.
Height, 6.03. Weight, 200.
Throws and bats righthanded.
Attended California Poly State University, Pomona, Calif., Whittier College,
Whittier, Calif., and University of California at Los Angeles, Los Angeles, Calif.
Brother of Ron Roenicke, outfielder with Seattle Mariners.

Led American Association in being hit by pitch with 13 in 1977.
Led Florida State League in being hit by pitch with 11 in 1974.
Tied for Eastern League lead in being hit by pitch with 12 in 1975.
Tied for Florida State League lead in double plays by third basemen with 32 in 1974.
Named Eastern League Most Valuable Player, 1975.

Year Club League	Pos.	G.	AB.	R.	H.	2B.	3B.	HR.	RBI.	B.A.	PO.	A.	E.	F.A.
1973—Jamestown............ NYP	3B	68	255	48	76	17	6	3	40	.298	★71	92	11	★.937
1974—W. Palm Beach.... Fla. St.	3B-OF-1B	131	470	68	130	24	0	14	★82	.277	152	216	31	.922
1974—Quebec City .... East.	3B	1	3	0	1	0	0	0	0	.333	1	2	0	1.000
1975—Quebec City .... East.	OF	131	466	67	133	23	0	14	★74	.285	223	★22	10	.961
1976—Denver .... A. A.	OF	77	252	56	73	11	5	12	44	.290	110	9	5	.960
1976—Montreal............... Nat.	OF	29	90	9	20	3	1	2	5	.222	39	3	2	.955
1977—Denver† .... A. A.	OF-3B-1B	124	448	87	144	31	4	11	72	.321	174	113	17	.944
1978—Rochester............. Int.	OF-1B-3B	98	329	49	101	15	1	13	64	.307	219	25	2	.992
1978—Baltimore .... Amer.	OF	27	58	5	15	3	0	3	15	.259	22	1	0	1.000
1979—Baltimore .... Amer.	OF	133	376	60	98	16	1	25	64	.261	246	10	5	.981
1980—Baltimore‡ .... Amer.	OF	118	297	40	71	13	0	10	28	.239	197	8	0	★1.000
1981—Baltimore .... Amer.	OF	85	219	31	59	16	0	3	20	.269	175	2	3	.983
1982—Baltimore .... Amer.	OF-1B	137	393	58	106	25	1	21	74	.270	363	13	3	.992
1983—Baltimore .... Amer.	OF-1B-3B	115	323	45	84	13	0	19	64	.260	219	9	3	.987
American League Totals........................		615	1666	239	433	86	2	81	265	.260	1222	43	14	.989
National League Totals........................		29	90	9	20	3	1	2	5	.222	39	3	2	.955
Major League Totals................		644	1756	248	453	89	3	83	270	.258	1261	46	16	.988

Selected by Montreal Expos' organization in 1st round (eighth player selected) of free-agent draft, June 5, 1973.

†Traded with Pitchers Joe Kerrigan and Don Stanhouse to Baltimore Orioles for Pitchers Rudy May, Randy Miller and Bryn Smith, December 7, 1977.

‡On disabled list, June 10 to July 15, 1980.

Tied Championship Series record for most consecutive games, one or more runs batted in, total Series (4).
Tied American League Championship Series record for most bases on balls, four-game Series (5), 1983.

Year Club	League	Pos.	G.	AB.	R.	H.	2B.	3B.	HR.	RBI.	B.A.	PO.	A.	E.	F.A.
1979—Baltimore	Amer.	OF-PH	2	5	1	1	0	0	0	1	.200	3	1	0	1.000
1983—Baltimore	Amer.	OF-PH	3	4	4	3	1	0	1	4	.750	4	1	0	1.000
Championship Series Totals			5	9	5	4	1	0	1	5	.444	7	2	0	1.000

WORLD SERIES RECORD

Year Club	League	Pos.	G.	AB.	R.	H.	2B.	3B.	HR.	RBI.	B.A.	PO.	A.	E.	F.A.
1979—Baltimore	Amer.	OF-PH	6	16	1	2	1	0	0	0	.125	14	1	0	1.000
1983—Baltimore	Amer.	PH-OF	3	7	0	0	0	0	0	0	.000	2	1	0	1.000
World Series Totals.................................			9	23	1	2	1	0	0	0	.087	16	2	0	1.000

RONALD JON ROENICKE

Name pronounced RENN-uh-kee.

(Ron)

Born August 19, 1956, at Covina, Calif.
Height, 6.00. Weight, 180.
Throws left and bats left and righthanded.
Attended Mount San Antonio College, Walnut, Calif., and
University of California at Los Angeles, Los Angeles, Calif.
Brother of Gary Roenicke, outfielder with Baltimore Orioles.

Led Pacific Coast League in on-base percentage with .464, bases on balls received with 110, and sacrifice flies with 16 in 1981.
Led Texas League outfielders in fielding percentage with .993 in 1979.

Year Club	League	Pos.	G.	AB.	R.	H.	2B.	3B.	HR.	RBI.	B.A.	PO.	A.	E.	F.A.
1977—Clinton....................	Midw.	OF-1B	76	250	35	64	12	0	5	25	.256	253	7	4	.985
1978—Lodi†	Calif.	OF	61	215	61	78	13	5	9	51	.363	100	8	6	.947
1978—San Antonio..........	Texas	OF	30	109	16	26	2	2	1	11	.239	51	4	2	.965
1979—San Antonio..........	Texas	OF-1B	130	464	82	140	24	6	13	69	.302	426	18	4	.991
1980—Albuquerque‡......	P. C.	OF-1B	77	270	60	80	18	3	7	47	.296	167	9	8	.957
1981—Albuquerque.........	P. C.	OF-1B	126	411	100	130	23	9	15	94	.316	217	14	4	.983
1981—Los Angeles	Nat.	OF	22	47	6	11	0	0	0	0	.234	38	1	0	1.000
1982—Albuquerque	P. C.	OF	23	78	18	24	5	1	4	15	.308	14	1	0	1.000
1982—Los Angeles	Nat.	OF	109	143	18	37	8	0	1	12	.259	59	1	1	.984
1983—Los Angeles§........	Nat.	OF	81	145	12	32	4	0	2	12	.221	75	1	1	.987
1983—Seattle....................	Amer.	OF-1B	59	198	23	50	12	0	4	23	.253	168	13	2	.989
National League Totals............................			212	335	36	80	12	0	3	24	.239	172	3	2	.989
American League Totals			59	198	23	50	12	0	4	23	.253	168	13	2	.989
Major League Totals..................................			271	533	59	130	24	0	7	47	.244	340	16	4	.989

Selected by Oakland A's organization in 7th round of free-agent draft, June 5, 1974.
Selected by Detroit Tigers' organization in secondary phase of free-agent draft, January 7, 1976.
Selected by Atlanta Braves' organization in secondary phase of free-agent draft, June 8, 1976.
Selected by Los Angeles Dodgers' organization in secondary phase of free agent draft, June 7, 1977.
†On disabled list, June 11 to July 17, 1978.
‡On disabled list, July 1 to August 27, 1980.
§Released, July 18, 1983; signed by Seattle Mariners, July 26, 1983.

STEPHEN DOUGLAS ROGERS

(Steve)

Born October 26, 1949, at Jefferson City, Mo.
Height, 6.01. Weight, 175.
Throws and bats righthanded.
Received bachelor of science degree in petroleum engineering from Tulsa University, Tulsa, Okla.

Established major league record for fewest complete games for leader in complete games (14), 1980.
Led National League in shutouts with 5 in 1983 and tied for lead with 5 in 1979.
Led National League in complete games with 14 in 1980.
Led National League in sacrifice hits with 20 in 1983.
Named National League Rookie Pitcher of the Year by THE SPORTING NEWS, 1973.
Named righthanded pitcher on THE SPORTING NEWS National League All-Star Team, 1982.

Year Club	League	G.	IP.	W.	L.	Pct.	H.	R.	ER.	SO.	BB.	ERA.
1971—Winnipeg	Int'national	15	102	3	10	.231	109	51	45	67	40	3.97
1972—Peninsula†......................................	Int'national	13	64	2	6	.250	75	32	29	39	25	4.08
1973—Quebec City....................................	Eastern	11	77	4	5	.444	61	29	23	64	33	2.69
1973—Peninsula	Int'national	4	29	3	1	.750	18	6	6	22	8	1.86
1973—Montreal	National	17	134	10	5	.667	93	28	23	64	49	1.54
1974—Montreal	National	38	254	15	●22	.405	255	★139	★126	154	80	4.46
1975—Montreal	National	35	252	11	12	.478	248	104	92	137	88	3.29
1976—Montreal‡	National	33	230	7	●17	.292	212	93	82	150	69	3.21
1977—Montreal	National	40	302	17	16	.515	272	122	104	206	81	3.10
1978—Montreal	National	30	219	13	10	.565	186	64	60	126	64	2.47
1979—Montreal	National	37	249	13	12	.520	232	97	83	143	78	3.00
1980—Montreal	National	37	281	16	11	.593	247	101	93	147	85	2.98
1981—Montreal	National	22	161	12	8	.600	149	64	61	87	41	3.41

Year Club	League	G.	IP.	W.	L.	Pct.	H.	R.	ER.	SO.	BB.	ERA.
1982—Montreal	National	35	277	19	8	.704	245	84	74	179	65	*2.40
1983—Montreal	National	36	273	17	12	.586	258	108	98	146	78	3.23
Major League Totals		360	2632	150	133	.530	2397	1004	896	1539	778	3.06

Selected by New York Yankees' organization in 60th round of free-agent draft, June 6, 1967.
Selected by Montreal Expos' organization in secondary phase of free-agent draft, June 8, 1971.
†On temporary inactive list, April 14 to June 9, 1972.
‡On disabled list, May 26 to June 28, 1976.

DIVISION SERIES RECORD

Year Club	League	G.	IP.	W.	L.	Pct.	H.	R.	ER.	SO.	BB.	ERA.
1981—Montreal	National	2	17⅔	2	0	1.000	16	1	1	5	3	0.51

CHAMPIONSHIP SERIES RECORD

Year Club	League	G.	IP.	W.	L.	Pct.	H.	R.	ER.	SO.	BB.	ERA.
1981—Montreal	National	2	10	1	1	.500	8	2	2	6	1	1.80

ALL-STAR GAME RECORD

Year League	IP.	W.	L.	Pct.	H.	R.	ER.	SO.	BB.	ERA.
1978—National	2	0	0	.000	2	0	0	2	0	0.00
1979—National	2	0	0	.000	0	0	0	2	0	0.00
1982—National	3	1	0	1.000	4	1	1	2	0	3.00
All-Star Game Totals	7	1	0	1.000	6	1	1	6	0	1.29

Member of National League All-Star Team in 1974 and 1983; did not play.

DANIEL JAY ROHN
(Dan)

Born January 10, 1956, at Alpena, Mich.
Height, 5.09. Weight, 165.
Throws right and bats lefthanded.
Attended Central Michigan University, Mt. Pleasant, Mich.
Led Texas League in bases on balls received with 105 in 1979.
Led Florida State League in bases on balls received with 117 in 1978.
Tied for American Association lead in caught stealing with 17 in 1983.
Led American Association second basemen in fielding percentage with .990 in 1983.
Led American Association second basemen in double plays with 104 in 1980.
Led Texas League second basemen in double plays with 120 in 1979.
Led Florida State League second basemen in double plays with 83 in 1978.

Year Club	League	Pos.	G.	AB.	R.	H.	2B.	3B.	HR.	RBI.	B.A.	PO.	A.	E.	F.A.
1977—Geneva	NYP	2B	21	72	8	15	0	0	1	5	.208	66	63	5	.963
1977—Pompano Beach	Fla. St.	2B-SS	54	173	23	48	6	3	0	22	.277	103	160	9	.967
1978—Pompano Beach	Fla. St.	2B	132	421	*95	116	17	2	2	48	.276	*302	400	26	.964
1979—Midland	Texas	2B	128	489	*122	150	26	6	5	52	.307	*315	*429	19	975
1980—Wichita	A. A.	2B	130	480	81	117	18	1	4	22	.244	*295	*434	●19	.975
1981—Iowa	A. A.	2B-3B	131	488	73	130	23	4	7	43	.266	194	278	10	.979
1982—Iowa	A. A.	2B-3B-SS	107	364	85	100	20	4	8	32	.275	178	241	9	.979
1983—Iowa	A. A.	2-3-S-O	117	413	84	130	29	5	8	56	.315	189	315	6	.988
1983—Chicago	Nat.	2B-SS	23	31	3	12	3	2	0	6	.387	12	12	2	.923
Major League Totals			23	31	3	12	3	2	0	6	.387	12	12	2	.923

Selected by Chicago Cubs' organization in 4th round of free-agent draft, June 7, 1977.

JOSE ROMAN

Born May 21, 1963, at Santo Domingo, Dominican Republic.
Height, 6.00. Weight, 160.
Throws and bats righthanded.
Led New York-Pennsylvania League in home runs allowed with 15 in 1981.

Year Club	League	G.	IP.	W.	L.	Pct.	H.	R.	ER.	SO.	BB.	ERA.
1981—Batavia	NYP	20	55	0	3	.000	63	45	39	46	27	6.38
1982—Waterloo	Midwest	24	57⅔	2	5	.286	64	42	33	56	37	5.15
1983—Waterloo	Midwest	34	126⅓	6	7	.462	103	49	36	132	56	2.56

Signed as free agent by Cleveland Indians' organization, May 23, 1981.

RONALD JAMES ROMANICK

Name pronounced Ro-MAN-ick.

(Ron)

Born November 6, 1960, at Burley, Ida.
Height, 6.04. Weight, 200.
Throws and bats righthanded.
Attended Arizona State University, Tempe, Ariz.
Pitched 1-0 no-hit victory against Buffalo, April 27, 1982.
Tied for Eastern League lead in games started by pitchers with 27 in 1983.

Year—Club	League	G.	IP.	W.	L.	Pct.	H.	R.	ER.	SO.	BB.	ERA.
1981—Redwood	California	28	★207	15	10	.600	173	88	67	178	76	★2.91
1982—Holyoke†	Eastern	16	86⅔	6	3	.667	104	52	41	62	26	4.26
1983—Nashua	Eastern	27	174	9	12	.429	★200	105	94	112	80	4.86

Selected by Toronto Blue Jays' organization in 3rd round of free-agent draft, June 5, 1979.
Selected by San Diego Padres' organization in secondary phase of free-agent draft, June 3, 1980.
Selected by California Angels' organization in secondary phase of free-agent draft, January 13, 1981.
†On disabled list, May 31 to July 29, 1982.

THOMAS MICHAEL ROMANO
(Tom)

Born October 25, 1958, at Syracuse, N.Y.
Height, 5.10. Weight, 170.
Throws and bats righthanded.
Attended Coastal Carolina College, Conway, S.C.

Led Eastern League in total bases with 278 in 1983.
Led Midwest League in caught stealing with 23 in 1982.
Led New York-Pennsylvania League in total bases with 155 in 1981.
Named Midwest League Most Valuable Player, 1982.

Year—Club	League	Pos.	G.	AB.	R.	H.	2B.	3B.	HR.	RBI.	B.A.	PO.	A.	E.	F.A.
1980—Sarasota Blue†	Gulf C.	OF	58	186	32	48	10	4	4	37	.258	104	8	5	.957
1981—Utica‡	NYP	OF	66	243	49	82	14	4	17	53	.377	113	5	11	.915
1982—Madison	Midw.	OF	128	485	102	165	32	4	26	98	.340	179	13	●15	.928
1983—Albany	East.	OF	134	★512	90	★164	28	7	24	89	.320	287	8	12	.961

Selected by Kansas City Royals' organization in 17th round of free-agent draft, June 3, 1980.
†Released, April 2, 1981; signed by Utica (Independent), June 19, 1981.
‡Sold to West Haven (Oakland A's organization), December 9, 1981.

EDGARDO ROMERO
(Ed)

Born December 9, 1957, at Santurce, Puerto Rico.
Height, 5.11. Weight, 150.
Throws and bats righthanded.

Led Pacific Coast League shortstops in double plays with 97 in 1979.
Led Midwest League shortstops in total chances with 647 and double plays with 64 in 1976.

Year—Club	League	Pos.	G.	AB.	R.	H.	2B.	3B.	HR.	RBI.	B.A.	PO.	A.	E.	F.A.
1976—Burlington	Midwest	SS	●129	462	58	101	23	1	1	32	.219	187	★419	41	.937
1977—Holyoke	East.	SS	121	457	63	118	19	6	1	38	.258	203	372	41	.933
1977—Milwaukee	Amer.	SS	10	25	4	7	1	0	0	2	.280	9	24	1	.971
1978—Spokane	P. C.	SS-3B	129	440	73	123	27	2	4	52	.280	221	349	32	.947
1979—Vancouver	P. C.	SS	139	515	65	134	26	6	0	39	.260	215	★414	26	.960
1980—Vancouver	P. C.	SS-2B	50	172	19	47	7	1	0	16	.273	72	153	6	.974
1980—Milwaukee	Amer.	SS-2B-3B	42	104	20	27	7	0	1	10	.260	60	102	12	.931
1981—Milwaukee	Amer.	SS-3B-2B	44	91	6	18	3	0	1	10	.198	61	102	6	.964
1982—Milwaukee	Amer.	2-S-3-O	52	144	18	36	8	0	1	7	.250	103	113	7	.969
1983—Milwaukee	Amer.	S-O-3-2	59	145	17	46	7	0	1	18	.317	59	58	5	.959
Major League Totals			207	509	65	134	26	0	4	47	.263	292	399	31	.957

Signed as free agent by Milwaukee Brewers' organization, November 14, 1975.

DIVISION SERIES RECORD

Year—Club	League	Pos.	G.	AB.	R.	H.	2B.	3B.	HR.	RBI.	B.A.	PO.	A.	E.	F.A.
1981—Milwaukee	Amer.	2B	1	2	1	1	0	0	0	0	.500	2	2	0	1.000

RAMON ROMERO (De Los SANTOS)

Born January 22, 1959, at San Pedro de Macoris, D.R.
Height, 6.04. Weight, 170.
Throws and bats lefthanded.

Year—Club	League	G.	IP.	W.	L.	Pct.	H.	R.	ER.	SO.	BB.	ERA.
1977—Batavia	NYP	1	1	0	0	.000	0	0	0	0	1	0.00
1977—Pulaski	Ap'lachian	16	48	0	0	.000	52	41	37	28	25	6.94
1978—Batavia	NYP	12	31	1	2	.333	33	24	18	30	32	5.23
1978—Waterloo	Midwest	1	3	0	0	.000	3	0	0	2	4	0.00
1979—Wausau	Midwest	17	66	4	1	.800	77	53	48	53	53	6.55
1980—Waterloo	Midwest	31	98	5	5	.500	78	53	40	87	62	3.67
1981—Waterloo	Midwest	8	19	0	2	.000	19	12	11	14	13	5.21
1981—Hagerstown	Carolina	17	29	1	3	.250	18	9	8	22	15	2.48
1981—Chattanooga	Southern	19	19	2	2	.500	23	11	11	16	11	5.21
1982—Waterloo	Midwest	7	31	3	1	.750	22	11	7	30	21	2.03
1982—Chattanooga	Southern	20	89	5	5	.500	87	49	39	55	39	3.94
1983—Buffalo	Eastern	44	98	10	4	.714	85	50	43	92	77	3.95

Signed as free agent by Cleveland Indians' organization, October 1, 1976.

EUGENE LAWRENCE ROOF
(Gene)

Born January 13, 1958, at Mayfield, Ky.
Height, 6.02. Weight, 180.
Throws right and bats left and righthanded.
Brother of Phil, Adrian, Paul and David Roof, former players in Organized Baseball. Phil was a
catcher for Milwaukee NL and AL, California, Cleveland, Kansas City, Oakland,
Minnesota, Chicago AL and Toronto in majors, 1961, 1964 through 1977.

Led American Association in being hit by pitch with 11 in 1980.
Led Appalachian League in being hit by pitch with 7 in 1977.

Year	Club	League	Pos.	G.	AB.	R.	H.	2B.	3B.	HR.	RBI.	B.A.	PO.	A.	E.	F.A.
1976—Sarasota Cards	Gulf C.	SS-2B-3B	5	21	0	5	0	0	0	2	.238	6	15	2	.913
1976—Johnson City	Appal.	3B-OF	53	174	21	39	4	0	2	28	.224	35	103	13	.914
1977—Johnson City	Appal.	1-O-3-S	59	219	43	79	11	2	5	33	★.361	243	25	8	.971
1977—Gastonia	W. Car.	3B-OF	42	138	19	28	3	1	1	11	.203	41	62	5	.954
1978—St. Petersburg†	Fla. St.	OF	101	360	50	93	7	6	2	31	.258	181	6	5	.974
1979—Arkansas	Texas	OF	128	478	86	145	22	3	11	53	.303	217	12	7	.970
1980—Springfield	A. A.	★O-3-2	133	481	68	124	23	0	10	57	.258	226	8	1	★.996
1981—Springfield‡	A. A.	OF	96	322	64	112	19	3	11	44	.348	126	3	4	.970
1981—St. Louis	Nat.	OF	23	60	11	18	6	0	0	3	.300	38	0	2	.950
1982—Louisville§	A. A.	★OF-1B	119	458	78	140	27	5	3	49	.306	223	7	2	★.991
1982—St. Louis	Nat.	OF	11	15	3	4	0	0	0	2	.267	5	0	0	1.000
1983—St. L. x-Mont.	Nat.	OF	14	15	3	2	2	0	0	1	.133	3	0	0	1.000
1983—Louisville	A. A.	OF	114	450	74	139	23	5	3	60	.309	221	3	2	★.991
Major League Totals				48	90	17	24	8	0	0	6	.267	46	0	2	.958

Selected by St. Louis Cardinals' organization in 12th round of free-agent draft, June 8, 1976.
†On disabled list, May 12 to June 23, 1978.
‡On disabled list, July 18 to August 9, 1981.
§On disabled list, April 22 to May 2, 1982.
xSold on waivers to Montreal Expos, September 16, 1983.

PETER EDWARD ROSE
(Pete)

Born April 14, 1941, at Cincinnati, O.
Height, 5.11. Weight, 203.
Throws right and bats right and lefthanded.
Brother of David Rose, pitcher in Cincinnati Reds' organization, 1967 and 1968.

Established major league records for most seasons, 200 or more hits (10); most seasons, 150 or more games (17);
most at-bats, lifetime (13,037); most plate appearances, lifetime (14,696); most consecutive seasons, 600 or more at bats
(13); highest fielding percentage by outfielder, lifetime, 1,000 or more games (.992); most seasons, 600 or more at bats
(17); most plate appearances, season (771), 1974.
Tied major league records for most 20-game hitting streaks, lifetime (7); most consecutive seasons leading major
leagues in runs scored (3), 1974 through 1976; most consecutive seasons leading major leagues in hits (2), 1972 and 1973;
most consecutive seasons leading major leagues in games (2), 1974 and 1975; fewest sacrifice flies, season, most at-bats
(0 and 680), 1973; most doubles by switch-hitter, season (51), 1978; most hits by switch-hitter, season (230), 1973; most
games, first basemen, season (162), 1980 and 1983; most stolen bases, inning (3), May 11, 1980, seventh inning.
Established National League records for most games, lifetime (3,250); most years playing in all clubs' games (10);
most base hits, lifetime (3,990); most seasons leading league, hits (7); most singles, lifetime (2,992); fewest chances
accepted by third baseman, season, 150 or more games (366), 1977; most one-base hits by switch-hitter, season (181),
1973; fewest stolen bases, season, most at-bats (0 and 662), 1975.
Established modern National League record for most seasons leading league, at-bats (4).
Tied National League records for most times five or more hits in one game, lifetime (9); most consecutive games,
one or more hits, season (44), 1978; most games, switch hit home runs, lifetime (2), August 30, 1966 and August 2, 1967.
Tied modern National League records for highest batting average, switch hitter, season, 100 or more games (.348),
1969; most seasons leading league in fielding percentage by outfielder, 100 or more games (3); most consecutive years
leading league in fielding percentage by outfielder, 100 or more games (2), 1970 and 1971 (tied).
Hit three home runs in a game, April 29, 1978.
Tied for National League lead in being hit by pitch with 6 in 1980.
Led Florida State League in total bases with 246 in 1961.
Named Player of the Decade for 1970-79 by THE SPORTING NEWS.
Named National League Player of the Year by THE SPORTING NEWS, 1968.
Named National League Most Valuable Player by Baseball Writers' Association of America, 1973.
Named National League Rookie Player of the Year by THE SPORTING NEWS, 1963.
Named National League Rookie of the Year by Baseball Writers' Association of America, 1963.
Named first baseman on THE SPORTING NEWS National League All-Star Team, 1981.
Named third baseman on THE SPORTING NEWS National League All-Star Team, 1978.
Named outfielder on THE SPORTING NEWS National League All-Star Team, 1968 and 1973.
Named second baseman on THE SPORTING NEWS National League All-Star Team, 1965 and 1966.
Named outfielder on THE SPORTING NEWS National League All-Star fielding team, 1969 and 1970.
Named first baseman on THE SPORTING NEWS National League Silver Slugger team, 1981.

Year	Club	League	Pos.	G.	AB.	R.	H.	2B.	3B.	HR.	RBI.	B.A.	PO.	A.	E.	F.A.
1960—Geneva	NYP	2B	85	321	60	89	8	5	1	43	.277	198	193	★36	.916
1961—Tampa	Fla. St.	2B	130	484	105	★160	20	★30	2	77	.331	256	294	21	.963
1962—Macon	Sally	2B	139	540	★136	178	31	★17	9	71	.330	317	368	24	.966
1963—Cincinnati†	Nat.	2B-OF	157	623	101	170	25	9	6	41	.273	360	366	22	.971
1964—Cincinnati	Nat.	2B	136	516	64	139	13	2	4	34	.269	301	301	12	.979
1965—Cincinnati	Nat.	2B	162	★670	117	★209	35	11	11	81	.312	★382	403	20	.975
1966—Cincinnati	Nat.	2B-3B	156	654	97	205	38	5	16	70	.313	409	374	18	.978

Year—Club	League	Pos.	G.	AB.	R.	H.	2B.	3B.	HR.	RBI.	B.A.	PO.	A.	E.	F.A.
1967—Cincinnati	Nat.	OF-2B	148	585	86	176	32	8	12	76	.301	287	93	11	.972
1968—Cincinnati‡	Nat.	●O-2-1	149	626	94	●210	42	6	10	49	★.335	270	●20	3	.990
1969—Cincinnati	Nat.	OF-2B	156	627	●120	218	33	11	16	82	★.348	317	10	4	.988
1970—Cincinnati	Nat.	OF	159	649	120	●205	37	9	15	52	.316	309	8	1	★.997
1971—Cincinnati	Nat.	OF	160	632	86	192	27	4	13	44	.304	306	13	2	●.994
1972—Cincinnati	Nat.	OF	★154	★645	107	★198	31	11	6	57	.307	330	●15	2	.994
1973—Cincinnati	Nat.	OF	160	★680	115	★230	36	8	5	64	★.338	343	15	3	.992
1974—Cincinnati	Nat.	OF	★163	652	★110	185	★45	7	3	51	.284	346	11	1	★.997
1975—Cincinnati	Nat.	3B-OF	●162	662	★112	210	★47	4	7	74	.317	161	230	14	.965
1976—Cincinnati	Nat.	★3B-OF	162	665	★130	★215	★42	6	10	63	.323	115	293	13	★.969
1977—Cincinnati	Nat.	3B	●162	★655	95	204	38	7	9	64	.311	98	268	16	.958
1978—Cincinnati§	Nat.	3B-OF-1B	159	655	103	198	★51	3	7	52	.302	135	256	15	.963
1979—Philadelphia	Nat.	1B-3B-2B	163	628	90	208	40	5	4	59	.331	1429	93	10	.993
1980—Philadelphia	Nat.	1B	162	655	95	185	★42	1	1	64	.282	1427	★123	5	★.997
1981—Philadelphia	Nat.	1B	107	431	73	★140	18	5	0	33	.325	929	91	4	.996
1982—Philadelphia	Nat.	1B	●162	634	80	172	25	4	3	54	.271	1428	123	8	.995
1983—Philadelphia x	Nat.	1B-OF	151	493	52	121	14	3	0	45	.245	827	74	10	.989
Major League Totals			3250	13037	2047	3990	711	129	158	1209	.306	10471	3180	194	.986

Signed as free agent by Cincinnati Reds' organization, July 8, 1960.
†On military list, October 1, 1963 through March 14, 1964.
‡On disabled list, July 6 to July 27, 1968.
§Granted free agency, November 2, 1978; signed by Philadelphia Phillies, December 5, 1978.
xReleased, October 19, 1983.

DIVISION SERIES RECORD

Year—Club	League	Pos.	G.	AB.	R.	H.	2B.	3B.	HR.	RBI.	B.A.	PO.	A.	E.	F.A.
1981—Philadelphia	Nat.	1B	5	20	1	6	1	0	0	2	.300	29	8	0	1.000

CHAMPIONSHIP SERIES RECORD

Established Championship Series records for most positions played, total Series (4); most runs, total Series (17); most consecutive games, one or more hits (15); most hits, total Series (45); most total bases, total Series (63); most one-base hits, total Series (34); most hits, two consecutive Series (17), 1972 and 1973.

Tied Championship Series records for most times on winning club (6); most one-base hits, five-game Series (8), 1980; most two-base hits, total Series (7); most two-base hits, five-game Series (4), 1972.

Established National League Championship Series records for most games, total Series (28); most Series, played all games (7); highest batting average, total Series, 10 or more games and 30 or more at-bats (.381); most at-bats, total Series (118); most long hits, total Series (11); most total bases, five-game Series (15), 1973.

Tied National League Championship Series records for most Series played (7); most Series, one or more hits (7).

Year—Club	League	Pos.	G.	AB.	R.	H.	2B.	3B.	HR.	RBI.	B.A.	PO.	A.	E.	F.A.
1970—Cincinnati	Nat.	OF	3	13	1	3	0	0	0	1	.231	3	0	0	1.000
1972—Cincinnati	Nat.	OF	5	20	1	9	4	0	0	2	.450	10	0	0	1.000
1973—Cincinnati	Nat.	OF	5	21	3	8	1	0	2	2	.381	10	1	0	1.000
1975—Cincinnati	Nat.	3B	3	14	3	5	0	0	1	2	.357	2	1	0	1.000
1976—Cincinnati	Nat.	3B	3	14	3	6	2	1	0	2	.429	2	5	1	.875
1980—Philadelphia	Nat.	1B	5	20	3	8	0	0	0	2	.400	53	7	0	1.000
1983—Philadelphia	Nat.	1B	4	16	3	6	0	0	0	0	.375	29	2	0	1.000
Championship Series Totals			28	118	17	45	7	1	3	11	.381	109	16	1	.992

WORLD SERIES RECORD

Tied World Series records for most positions played, total Series (4); most double plays by first baseman, six-game Series (8), 1980; most double plays by first baseman, nine-inning game (4), October 15, 1980; most times awarded first base on catcher's interference, game (1), October 10, 1970; most times home run as leadoff batter in game (1), October 20, 1972.

Year—Club	League	Pos.	G.	AB.	R.	H.	2B.	3B.	HR.	RBI.	B.A.	PO.	A.	E.	F.A.
1970—Cincinnati	Nat.	OF	5	20	2	5	1	0	1	2	.250	14	1	1	.938
1972—Cincinnati	Nat.	OF	7	28	3	6	0	0	1	2	.214	14	1	0	1.000
1975—Cincinnati	Nat.	3B	7	27	3	10	1	1	0	2	.370	7	9	0	1.000
1976—Cincinnati	Nat.	3B	4	16	1	3	1	0	0	1	.188	6	3	0	1.000
1980—Philadelphia	Nat.	1B	6	23	2	6	1	0	0	1	.261	49	6	0	1.000
1983—Philadelphia	Nat.	PH-1B-OF	5	16	1	5	1	0	0	1	.313	26	4	0	1.000
World Series Totals			34	130	12	35	5	1	2	9	.269	116	24	1	.993

ALL-STAR GAME RECORD

Established All-Star Game record for most positions played, total games (5).

Year—League	Pos.	AB.	R.	H.	2B.	3B.	HR.	RBI.	B.A.	PO.	A.	E.	F.A.
1965—National	2B	2	0	0	0	0	0	0	.000	2	4	0	1.000
1967—National	2B	1	0	0	0	0	0	0	.000	1	0	0	1.000
1969—National	OF	1	0	0	0	0	0	0	.000	2	0	0	1.000
1970—National	OF	3	1	1	0	0	0	0	.333	3	0	0	1.000
1971—National	OF	0	0	0	0	0	0	0	.000	0	0	0	.000
1973—National	OF	3	1	0	0	0	0	0	.000	1	0	0	1.000
1974—National	OF	2	0	0	0	0	0	0	.000	1	0	0	1.000
1975—National	OF	4	0	2	0	0	0	1	.500	4	0	0	1.000
1976—National	3B	3	1	2	0	1	0	0	.667	0	1	0	1.000
1977—National	PH-3B	2	0	0	0	0	0	0	.000	0	1	0	1.000
1978—National	3B	4	0	1	1	0	0	0	.250	1	0	0	1.000
1979—National	PH-1B	2	0	0	0	0	0	0	.000	2	0	0	1.000
1980—National	PH	1	0	0	0	0	0	0	.000	0	0	0	.000

Year League	Pos.	AB.	R.	H.	2B.	3B.	HR.	RBI.	B.A.	PO.	A.	E.	F.A.
1981—National	1B	3	0	1	0	0	0	0	.333	5	0	0	1.000
1982—National	1B	1	0	0	0	0	0	1	.000	4	0	0	1.000
All-Star Game Totals		32	3	7	1	1	0	2	.219	26	6	0	1.000

Named to National League All-Star Team for 1968 game; replaced due to injury.

WADE LEE ROWDON

Born September 7, 1960, at Riverhead, N.Y.
Height, 6.02. Weight, 170.
Throws and bats righthanded.
Attended Stetson University, Deland, Fla.
Led Eastern League third basemen in fielding percentage with .940 in 1983.
Led Midwest League third basemen in total chances with 362 and double plays with 24 in 1982.

Year Club League	Pos.	G.	AB.	R.	H.	2B.	3B.	HR.	RBI.	B.A.	PO.	A.	E.	F.A.
1981—Sarasota W. Sox... Gulf C.	SS	3	6	2	3	0	0	0	1	.500	1	3	0	1.000
1982—Appleton†	Midw.	3B	126	433	75	123	19	8	12	79	.284	81	*264	17	*.953
1983—Waterbury	East.	3B-2B-1B	135	480	62	112	29	1	21	76	.233	173	231	22	.948

Selected by Chicago White Sox' organization in 8th round of free-agent draft, June 8, 1981.
†Traded with Outfielder Leo Garcia to Cincinnati Reds' organization, September 7, 1982, completing deal in which Cincinnati traded Pitcher Jim Kern to Chicago White Sox for two players to be named later, August 23, 1982.

JERON KENNIS ROYSTER
(Jerry)

Born October 18, 1952, at Sacramento, Calif.
Height, 6.00. Weight, 165.
Throws and bats righthanded.
Attended Healds Business College, Sacramento, Calif.
Major league stolen bases: 1973 (1), 1975 (1), 1976 (24), 1977 (28), 1978 (27), 1979 (35), 1980 (22), 1981 (7), 1982 (14), 1983 (11). Total—170.
Led National League third basemen in putouts with 156 in 1976.
Tied for National League lead in double plays by third basemen with 35 in 1976.
Led Pacific Coast League third basemen in fielding percentage with .962 in 1974.
Led Texas League third basemen in double plays with 26 in 1972.
Tied for Pacific Coast League lead in stolen bases with 33 in 1975.
Named Pacific Coast League Player of the Year in 1975.

Year Club League	Pos.	G.	AB.	R.	H.	2B.	3B.	HR.	RBI.	B.A.	PO.	A.	E.	F.A.
1971—Bakersfield	Calif.	3B	7	20	2	2	1	0	0	2	.100	1	5	1	.857
1971—Daytona Beach	Fla. St.	3B-SS-2B	111	371	68	100	13	7	8	42	.270	90	265	29	.925
1972—El Paso	Texas	*3-S-O	127	479	*89	123	28	3	18	59	.257	103	209	*35	.899
1973—Albuquerque	P. C.	3B-SS-OF	122	463	78	140	24	11	6	68	.302	167	222	24	.942
1973—Los Angeles	Nat.	3B-2B	10	19	1	4	0	0	0	2	.211	3	14	3	.850
1974—Albuquerque	P. C.	3B-2B-SS	125	458	69	126	19	1	10	65	.275	121	257	14	.964
1974—Los Angeles	Nat.	2B-OF-3B	6	0	2	0	0	0	0	0	.000	0	3	0	1.000
1975—Albuquerque	P. C.	SS-3B	133	487	*91	162	31	7	10	65	*.333	183	349	38	.933
1975—Los Angeles†	Nat.	O-2-3-S	13	36	2	9	2	1	0	1	.250	12	15	2	.931
1976—Atlanta	Nat.	3B-SS	149	533	65	132	13	1	5	45	.248	158	310	19	.961
1977—Atlanta	Nat.	3-S-2-O	140	445	64	96	10	2	6	28	.216	182	267	28	.941
1978—Atlanta	Nat.	SS-2B-3B	140	529	67	137	17	8	2	35	.259	284	376	23	.966
1979—Atlanta	Nat.	3B-2B	154	601	103	164	25	6	3	51	.273	261	405	22	.968
1980—Atlanta	Nat.	2B-3B-OF	123	392	42	95	17	5	1	20	.242	195	166	18	.953
1981—Atlanta	Nat.	3B-2B	64	93	13	19	4	1	0	9	.204	35	48	4	.954
1982—Atlanta	Nat.	3-O-2-S	108	261	43	77	13	2	2	25	.295	105	112	11	.952
1983—Atlanta‡	Nat.	3-2-O-S	91	268	32	63	10	3	3	30	.235	112	156	10	.964
Major League Totals		998	3177	434	796	111	29	22	246	.251	1347	1872	140	.958

Signed as free agent by Los Angeles Dodgers' organization, August 21, 1970.
†Traded with Outfielder Jimmy Wynn, Second Baseman Lee Lacy and First Baseman-Outfielder Tom Paciorek to Atlanta Braves for Outfielder Dusty Baker and First Baseman-Third Baseman Ed Goodson, November 17, 1975.
‡On disabled list, August 19 to September 9, 1983.

CHAMPIONSHIP SERIES RECORD

Year Club League	Pos.	G.	AB.	R.	H.	2B.	3B.	HR.	RBI.	B.A.	PO.	A.	E.	F.A.
1982—Atlanta	Nat.	OF-3B	3	11	0	2	0	0	0	0	.182	4	0	0	1.000

DAVID SCOTT ROZEMA

Name pronounced ROZE-mah.

(Dave)

Born August 5, 1956, at Grand Rapids, Mich.
Height, 6.04 Weight, 200.
Throws and bats righthanded.
Attended Grand Rapids Junior College, Grand Rapids, Mich.
Tied for Southern League lead in shutouts with 4 in 1976.
Tied for Midwest League lead in shutouts with 5 in 1975.
Named American League Rookie Pitcher of the Year by THE SPORTING NEWS, 1977.

Year Club	League	G.	IP.	W.	L.	Pct.	H.	R.	ER.	SO.	BB.	ERA.
1975—Clinton	Midwest	27	164	14	5	.737	128	50	38	123	32	2.09
1976—Montgomery†	Southern	19	126	12	4	.750	98	29	22	96	15	★1.57
1977—Detroit	American	28	218	15	7	.682	222	87	75	92	34	3.10
1978—Detroit	American	28	209	9	12	.429	205	83	73	57	41	3.14
1979—Detroit‡	American	16	97	4	4	.500	101	52	38	33	30	3.53
1980—Detroit	American	42	145	6	9	.400	152	68	63	49	49	3.91
1981—Detroit	American	28	104	5	5	.500	99	42	42	46	25	3.63
1982—Detroit§	American	8	27⅔	3	0	1.000	17	5	5	15	7	1.63
1983—Detroit	American	29	105	8	3	.727	100	50	40	63	29	3.43
Major League Totals		179	905⅔	50	40	.556	896	387	336	355	215	3.34

Selected by San Francisco Giants' organization in 22nd round of free-agent draft, June 5, 1974.
Selected by Detroit Tigers' organization in secondary phase of free-agent draft, January 9, 1975.
†On disabled list, May 9 to June 21, 1976.
‡On disabled list, June 16 to August 27, 1979.
§On emergency disabled list, May 15, 1982 through remainder of season.

MICHAEL GERARD RUBEL
(Mike)

Born January 9, 1960, at Oakland, Calif.
Height, 6.04. Weight, 215.
Throws and bats righthanded.
Attended California State University, Fullerton, Calif.

Year Club	League	Pos.	G.	AB.	R.	H.	2B.	3B.	HR.	RBI.	B.A.	PO.	A.	E.	F.A.
1982—Tulsa	Texas	1B	63	221	43	60	11	2	13	43	.271	567	40	6	.990
1983—Tulsa	Texas	1B-3B	72	245	58	74	19	0	23	61	.302	505	43	9	.984
1983—Oklahoma City	A. A.	1B	50	180	26	45	11	0	4	18	.250	402	29	3	.993

Selected by Chicago White Sox' organization in 4th round of free-agent draft, June 6, 1978.
Selected by Houston Astros' organization in 6th round of free-agent draft, June 8, 1981.
Selected by Texas Rangers' organization in 2nd round of free-agent draft, June 7, 1982.

DAVID MICHAEL RUCKER
(Dave)

Born September 1, 1957, at San Bernardino, Calif.
Height, 6.01. Weight, 185.
Throws and bats lefthanded.
Attended University of California at Los Angeles, Los Angeles, Calif., and
LaVerne College, LaVerne, Calif.

Year Club	League	G.	IP.	W.	L.	Pct.	H.	R.	ER.	SO.	BB.	ERA.
1978—Bristol	Ap'lachian	3	7	1	0	1.000	10	5	4	7	2	5.14
1978—Lakeland	Florida St.	18	31	6	3	.667	26	13	11	18	13	3.19
1979—Montgomery	Southern	28	96	4	7	.364	97	56	49	64	66	4.59
1979—Evansville	Am. Assoc.	2	13	1	1	.500	11	4	4	8	1	2.77
1980—Evansville	Am. Assoc.	52	92	7	8	.467	94	53	35	53	52	3.42
1981—Detroit	American	2	4	0	0	.000	3	4	3	2	1	6.75
1981—Evansville	Am. Assoc.	35	67	7	4	.636	60	30	28	36	42	3.76
1982—Evansville	Am. Assoc.	30	58⅓	4	1	.800	53	27	22	42	29	3.39
1982—Detroit	American	27	64	5	6	.455	62	26	24	31	23	3.38
1983—Detroit	American	4	9	1	2	.333	18	17	17	6	8	17.00
1983—Evansville†	Am. Assoc.	18	29⅔	2	4	.333	25	12	11	30	21	3.34
1983—St. Louis	National	34	37	5	3	.625	36	14	10	22	18	2.43
American League Totals		33	77	6	8	.429	83	47	44	39	32	5.14
National League Totals		34	37	5	3	.625	36	14	10	22	18	2.43
Major League Totals		67	114	11	11	.500	119	61	54	61	50	4.26

Selected by Philadelphia Phillies' organization in 19th round of free-agent draft, June 4, 1975.
Selected by Detroit Tigers' organization in 16th round of free-agent draft, June 6, 1978.
†Traded to St. Louis Cardinals, July 5, 1983, completing deal in which St. Louis traded Pitcher Doug Bair to Detroit Tigers for a player to be named later, June 21, 1983.

VERNON GERALD RUHLE

Name pronounced Rule.

(Vern)

Born January 25, 1951, at Coleman, Mich.
Height, 6.01.   Weight, 187.
Throws and bats righthanded.
Attended Olivet College, Olivet, Mich.

Year Club	League	G.	IP.	W.	L.	Pct.	H.	R.	ER.	SO.	BB.	ERA.
1972—Bristol	Ap'lachian	4	28	0	2	.000	24	6	4	30	5	1.29
1972—Rocky Mount	Carolina	13	72	5	8	.385	87	53	38	53	28	4.75
1973—Lakeland	Florida St.	15	96	6	5	.545	81	27	22	67	24	2.06
1973—Montgomery	Southern	10	81	6	2	.750	72	33	26	34	17	2.89
1974—Montgomery	Southern	5	45	5	0	1.000	29	6	3	32	12	0.60
1974—Evansville	Am. Assoc.	22	156	13	5	.722	178	80	70	94	42	4.04
1974—Detroit	American	5	33	2	0	1.000	35	13	10	10	6	2.73
1975—Detroit	American	32	190	11	12	.478	199	104	85	67	65	4.03

Year Club	League	G.	IP.	W.	L.	Pct.	H.	R.	ER.	SO.	BB.	ERA.
1976—Detroit	American	32	200	9	12	.429	227	99	87	88	59	3.92
1977—Evansville†	Am. Assoc.	10	21	1	4	.200	31	19	16	15	9	6.86
1977—Detroit‡§	American	14	66	3	5	.375	83	44	42	27	15	5.73
1978—Columbus	Southern	5	39	4	1	.800	32	9	8	25	8	1.85
1978—Charleston	Int'national	13	94	4	4	.500	89	36	29	48	16	2.78
1978—Houston	National	13	68	3	3	.500	57	17	16	27	20	2.12
1979—Houston x	National	13	66	2	6	.250	64	33	30	33	8	4.09
1980—Houston	National	28	159	12	4	.750	148	51	42	55	29	2.38
1981—Houston y	National	20	102	4	6	.400	97	36	33	39	20	2.91
1982—Houston	National	31	149	9	13	.409	169	81	65	56	24	3.93
1983—Houston	National	41	114⅔	8	5	.615	107	49	47	43	36	3.69
American League Totals		83	489	25	29	.463	544	260	224	192	145	4.12
National League Totals		146	658⅔	38	37	.507	642	267	233	253	137	3.18
Major League Totals		229	1147⅔	63	66	.488	1186	527	457	445	282	3.58

Selected by Detroit Tigers' organization in 17th round of free-agent draft, June 6, 1972.
†On disabled list, July 24 to August 5, 1977.
‡On disabled list, May 21 to June 16, 1977.
§Released, March 27, 1978; signed by Houston Astros' organization, March 29, 1978.
xOn disabled list, May 14 to September 1, 1979.
yOn disabled list, April 30 to May 21, 1981.

DIVISION SERIES RECORD

Year Club	League	G.	IP.	W.	L.	Pct.	H.	R.	ER.	SO.	BB.	ERA.
1981—Houston	National	1	8	0	1	.000	4	2	2	1	2	2.25

CHAMPIONSHIP SERIES RECORD

Year Club	League	G.	IP.	W.	L.	Pct.	H.	R.	ER.	SO.	BB.	ERA.
1980—Houston	National	1	7	0	0	.000	8	3	3	3	1	3.86

CECILIO RUIZ (FERRER)

Born January 21, 1959, at Saragosa, Mexico.
Height, 5.10. Weight, 190.
Throws and bats lefthanded.

Year Club	League	G.	IP.	W.	L.	Pct.	H.	R.	ER.	SO.	BB.	ERA.
1982—Reno†	California	3	16⅔	0	1	.000	14	7	6	10	12	3.24
1983—Las Vegas	P. Coast	32	108	3	4	.429	142	87	81	62	37	6.75

Sold to San Diego Padres' organization, January 8, 1982.
†On suspended list, May 4, 1982 through remainder of season.

PAUL WILLIAM RUNGE

Born May 21, 1958, at Kingston, N.Y.
Height, 6.00. Weight, 165.
Throws and bats righthanded.
Attended Jacksonville University, Jacksonville, Fla.

Led International League in bases on balls received with 95 in 1982.
Led International League second basemen in total chances with 747 in 1982.
Led International League shortstops in double plays with 67 in 1981.
Led Appalachian League shortstops in double plays with 38 in 1979.

Year Club	League	Pos.	G.	AB.	R.	H.	2B.	3B.	HR.	RBI.	B.A.	PO.	A.	E.	F.A.
1979—Kingsport	Appal.	SS	66	229	57	67	11	0	6	45	.293	★104	★194	★24	.925
1980—Durham	Carol.	SS	74	245	37	64	8	4	8	37	.261	105	280	25	.939
1980—Savannah	South.	SS	75	248	32	68	11	3	9	34	.274	115	196	17	.948
1981—Richmond	Int.	SS	134	426	49	98	20	5	9	41	.230	191	450	★35	.948
1981—Atlanta	Nat.	SS	10	27	2	7	1	0	0	2	.259	14	27	4	.911
1982—Richmond	Int.	2B	134	507	★106	142	25	6	15	71	.280	★318	412	●17	.977
1982—Atlanta	Nat.	PH-PR	4	2	0	0	0	0	0	0	.000	0	0	0	.000
1983—Richmond	Int.	2B	137	472	76	129	17	4	15	72	.273	269	392	14	.979
1983—Atlanta	Nat.	2B	5	8	0	2	0	0	0	1	.250	4	3	0	1.000
Major League Totals			19	37	2	9	1	0	0	3	.243	18	30	4	.923

Selected by Atlanta Braves' organization in 8th round of free-agent draft, June 5, 1979.

JEFFREY LEE RUSSELL
(Jeff)

Born September 2, 1961, at Cincinnati, O.
Height, 6.04. Weight, 200.
Throws and bats righthanded.
Attended Gulf Coast Community College, Panama City, Fla.

Year Club	League	G.	IP.	W.	L.	Pct.	H.	R.	ER.	SO.	BB.	ERA.
1980—Eugene	Northwest	13	90	6	5	.545	80	47	30	75	50	3.00
1981—Tampa	Florida St.	22	143	10	4	.714	109	51	32	92	48	2.01
1982—Waterbury†	Eastern	14	79⅔	6	4	.600	67	27	21	88	23	2.37
1983—Indianapolis	Am. Assoc.	18	119	5	5	.500	106	51	47	98	44	3.55
1983—Cincinnati	National	10	68⅓	4	5	.444	58	30	23	40	22	3.03
Major League Totals		10	68⅓	4	5	.444	58	30	23	40	22	3.03

Selected by Cincinnati Reds' organization in 5th round of free-agent draft, June 5, 1979.
†On disabled list, May 5 to June 10 and July 28, 1982 through remainder of season.

WILLIAM ELLIS RUSSELL
(Bill)

Born October 21, 1948, at Pittsburg, Kan.
Height, 6.00. Weight, 175.
Throws and bats righthanded.
Attended Kansas State College, Pittsburg, Kan.

Established major league records for fewest putouts by shortstop, season, 150 or more games (194), 1974.
Tied major league record for most strikeouts, game (5), June 9, 1971; fewest double plays by shortstop, season, 150 or more games (64), 1982.
Led National League in intentional bases on balls received with 25 in 1974.
Led National League shortstops in double plays with 102 in 1977.
Led National League shortstops in total chances with 834 in 1973.
Tied for California League lead in double plays by outfielders with 4 in 1968.
Named shortstop on THE SPORTING NEWS National League All-Star Team, 1973.

Year Club	League	Pos.	G.	AB.	R.	H.	2B.	3B.	HR.	RBI.	B.A.	PO.	A.	E.	F.A.
1966—Ogden	Pion.	OF	39	87	19	31	5	1	3	21	.356	25	3	2	.933
1967—Dubuque	Midw.	OF	67	263	29	58	11	1	5	21	.221	98	11	10	.916
1968—Bakersfield	Calif.	OF	115	439	76	123	16	3	17	55	.280	255	★22	7	.975
1969—Los Angeles†	Nat.	OF	98	212	35	48	6	2	5	15	.226	132	4	3	.978
1970—Spokane	P. C.	OF-3B-SS	55	237	48	86	13	5	3	30	.363	112	39	6	.962
1970—Los Angeles‡	Nat.	OF-SS	81	278	30	72	11	9	0	28	.259	167	10	3	.983
1971—Los Angeles§	Nat.	2B-OF-SS	91	211	29	48	7	4	2	15	.227	131	124	8	.970
1972—Los Angeles x	Nat.	★SS-OF	129	434	47	118	19	5	4	34	.272	202	439	★34	.950
1973—Los Angeles	Nat.	SS	●162	615	55	163	26	3	4	56	.265	243	★560	31	.963
1974—Los Angeles	Nat.	★SS-OF	160	553	61	149	17	6	5	65	.269	194	491	★39	.946
1975—Los Angeles y	Nat.	SS	84	252	24	52	9	2	0	14	.206	94	230	11	.967
1976—Los Angeles	Nat.	SS	149	554	53	152	17	3	5	65	.274	251	476	28	.963
1977—Los Angeles	Nat.	SS	153	634	84	176	28	6	4	51	.278	234	523	29	.963
1978—Los Angeles	Nat.	SS	155	625	72	179	32	4	3	46	.286	245	533	31	.962
1979—Los Angeles	Nat.	SS	153	627	72	170	26	4	7	56	.271	218	452	30	.957
1980—Los Angeles	Nat.	SS	130	466	38	123	23	2	3	34	.264	179	387	19	.968
1981—Los Angeles	Nat.	SS	82	262	20	61	9	2	0	22	.233	128	261	14	.965
1982—Los Angeles	Nat.	SS	153	497	64	136	20	2	3	46	.274	216	502	29	.961
1983—Los Angeles	Nat.	SS	131	451	47	111	13	1	1	30	.246	192	392	22	.964
Major League Totals			1911	6671	731	1758	264	55	46	577	.264	2826	5384	331	.961

Selected by Los Angeles Dodgers' organization in 37th round of free-agent draft, June 12, 1966.
†On military list, August 1 to August 19, 1969.
‡On military list, July 3 to July 19, 1970.
§On military list, June 19 to July 3, 1971.
xOn military list, July 7 to July 22, 1972.
yOn disabled list, April 13 to May 6 and May 11 to June 30, 1975.

DIVISION SERIES RECORD

Year Club	League	Pos.	G.	AB.	R.	H.	2B.	3B.	HR.	RBI.	B.A.	PO.	A.	E.	F.A.
1981—Los Angeles	Nat.	SS	5	16	1	4	1	0	0	2	.250	10	15	2	.926

CHAMPIONSHIP SERIES RECORD

Established Championship Series record for most one-base hits, four-game Series (7), 1974.

Year Club	League	Pos.	G.	AB.	R.	H.	2B.	3B.	HR.	RBI.	B.A.	PO.	A.	E.	F.A.
1974—Los Angeles	Nat.	SS	4	18	1	7	0	0	0	3	.389	13	16	0	1.000
1977—Los Angeles	Nat.	SS	4	18	3	5	1	0	0	2	.278	11	12	2	.920
1978—Los Angeles	Nat.	SS	4	17	1	7	1	0	0	2	.412	4	14	0	1.000
1981—Los Angeles	Nat.	SS	5	16	2	5	0	1	0	1	.313	10	13	0	1.000
1983—Los Angeles	Nat.	SS	4	14	1	4	0	0	0	0	.286	4	10	1	.933
Championship Series Totals			21	83	8	28	2	1	0	8	.337	42	65	3	.973

WORLD SERIES RECORD

Established World Series record for most assists by shortstop, six-game Series (26), 1981.
Tied World Series record for one or more hits, each game, six-game Series, 1978.

Year Club	League	Pos.	G.	AB.	R.	H.	2B.	3B.	HR.	RBI.	B.A.	PO.	A.	E.	F.A.
1974—Los Angeles	Nat.	SS	5	18	0	4	0	1	0	2	.222	4	11	1	.938
1977—Los Angeles	Nat.	SS	6	26	3	4	0	1	0	2	.154	9	21	0	1.000
1978—Los Angeles	Nat.	SS	6	26	1	11	2	0	0	2	.423	11	20	3	.912
1981—Los Angeles	Nat.	SS	6	25	1	6	0	0	0	2	.240	4	26	1	.968
World Series Totals			23	95	5	25	2	2	0	8	.263	28	78	5	.955

ALL-STAR GAME RECORD

Year League	Pos.	AB.	R.	H.	2B.	3B.	HR.	RBI.	B.A.	PO.	A.	E.	F.A.
1973—National	SS	2	0	0	0	0	0	0	.000	0	2	0	1.000
1976—National	SS	1	0	0	0	0	0	0	.000	1	2	0	1.000
1980—National	SS	2	0	0	0	0	0	0	.000	0	2	0	1.000
All-Star Game Totals		5	0	0	0	0	0	0	.000	1	6	0	1.000

—DID YOU KNOW—

That in 17 of the last 22 years, the American League batting champion has come from either the Minnesota Twins or Boston Red Sox?

RICHARD DAVID RUTHVEN
(Dick)

Born March 27, 1951, at Sacramento, Calif.
Height, 6.03. Weight, 190.
Throws and bats righthanded.
Attended Fresno State University, Fresno, Calif.
Brother-in-law of Tommy Hutton, first baseman-outfielder with Los Angeles, Philadelphia,
Toronto and Montreal, 1966, 1969 and 1972 through 1981.

Tied major league record for most putouts by pitcher, nine-inning game (5), April 19, 1978.
Tied for National League lead in balks with 5 in 1976.

Year Club	League	G.	IP.	W.	L.	Pct.	H.	R.	ER.	SO.	BB.	ERA.
1973—Philadelphia†	National	25	128	6	9	.400	125	69	60	98	75	4.22
1974—Philadelphia	National	35	213	9	13	.409	182	106	95	153	116	4.01
1975—Toledo	Int'national	23	153	10	12	.455	148	72	54	114	69	3.18
1975—Philadelphia‡	National	11	41	2	2	.500	37	22	19	26	22	4.17
1976—Atlanta	National	36	240	14	●17	.452	255	★112	112	142	90	4.20
1977—Atlanta§	National	25	151	7	13	.350	158	86	71	84	62	4.23
1978—Atlanta x-Philadelphia	National	33	232	15	11	.577	214	95	87	120	56	3.38
1979—Philadelphia y	National	20	122	7	5	.583	121	59	58	58	37	4.28
1980—Philadelphia	National	33	223	17	10	.630	241	99	88	86	74	3.55
1981—Philadelphia	National	23	147	12	7	.632	162	★94	★84	80	54	5.14
1982—Philadelphia	National	33	204⅓	11	11	.500	189	99	86	115	59	3.79
1983—Philadelphia z-Chicago	National	32	183	13	12	.520	202	101	89	99	38	4.38
Major League Totals		306	1884⅓	113	110	.507	1886	942	849	1071	683	4.06

Selected by Baltimore Orioles' organization in 20th round of free-agent draft, June 5, 1969.
Selected by Minnesota Twins' organization in 1st round (eighth player selected) of free-agent draft, June 6, 1972.
Selected by Philadelphia Phillies' organization in secondary phase of free-agent draft, January 10, 1973.
†On disabled list, August 3 to September 1, 1973.
‡Traded with Pitcher Roy Thomas and Infielder-Outfielder Alan Bannister to Chicago White Sox for Pitcher Jim Kaat and Shortstop Mike Buskey, December 10, 1975. Traded with Outfielder Ken Henderson and Pitcher Danny Osborn by Chicago White Sox to Atlanta Braves for Outfielder Ralph Garr and Infielder Larvell Blanks, December 12, 1975.
§On disabled list, May 2, 1977; transferred to emergency disabled list, May 3 to July 4, 1977.
xTraded to Philadelphia Phillies for Pitcher Gene Garber, June 15, 1978.
yOn disabled list, July 2 to July 25 and August 16 to October 4, 1979.
zTraded with Pitcher Bill Johnson to Chicago Cubs for Pitcher Willie Hernandez, May 22, 1983.

DIVISION SERIES RECORD

Year Club	League	G.	IP.	W.	L.	Pct.	H.	R.	ER.	SO.	BB.	ERA.
1981—Philadelphia	National	1	4	0	1	.000	3	3	2	0	1	4.50

CHAMPIONSHIP SERIES RECORD

Year Club	League	G.	IP.	W.	L.	Pct.	H.	R.	ER.	SO.	BB.	ERA.
1978—Philadelphia	National	1	4⅔	0	1	.000	6	3	3	3	0	5.79
1980—Philadelphia	National	2	9	1	0	1.000	3	2	2	4	5	2.00
Championship Series Totals		3	13⅔	1	1	.500	9	5	5	7	5	3.29

WORLD SERIES RECORD

Year Club	League	G.	IP.	W.	L.	Pct.	H.	R.	ER.	SO.	BB.	ERA.
1980—Philadelphia	National	1	9	0	0	.000	9	3	3	7	0	3.00

ALL-STAR GAME RECORD

Year League		IP.	W.	L.	Pct.	H.	R.	ER.	SO.	BB.	ERA.
1981—National		⅓	0	0	.000	0	0	0	0	0	0.00

Member of National League All-Star Team in 1976; did not play.

MARK DWAYNE RYAL

Name pronounced Rile.
Born April 28, 1960, at Henryetta, Okla.
Height, 6.00. Weight, 190.
Throws and bats lefthanded.

Led American Association in grounding into double plays with 21 in 1983.
Tied for American Association lead in intentional bases on balls received with 12 in 1982.

Year Club	League	Pos.	G.	AB.	R.	H.	2B.	3B.	HR.	RBI.	B.A.	PO.	A.	E.	F.A.
1978—Sarasota Royals	Gulf C.	OF	27	83	11	20	0	1	0	10	.241	37	4	0	1.000
1979—Ft. Myers	Fla. St.	OF	107	360	27	79	12	1	4	34	.219	199	15	3	.986
1980—Ft. Myers	Fla. St.	OF	123	440	60	117	21	3	5	51	.266	174	8	2	.989
1981—Jacksonville	South.	OF	123	457	50	122	15	2	14	69	.267	237	8	11	.957
1981—Omaha	A. A.	OF	6	19	2	4	0	0	0	1	.211	9	1	0	1.000
1982—Omaha	A. A.	★OF-1B	129	473	69	135	27	2	20	77	.285	242	★18	6	.977
1982—Kansas City	Amer.	OF	6	13	0	1	0	0	0	0	.077	9	0	1	.900
1983—Omaha	A. A.	OF-1B	132	454	61	118	28	5	9	57	.260	203	11	8	.964
Major League Totals			6	13	0	1	0	0	0	0	.077	9	0	1	.900

Selected by Kansas City Royals' organization in 3rd round of free-agent draft, June 6, 1978.

LYNN NOLAN RYAN JR.
(Known by middle name.)

Born January 31, 1947, at Refugio, Tex.
Height, 6.02. Weight, 195.
Throws and bats righthanded.
Attended Alvin Junior College, Alvin, Tex.

Established major league records for most games, 15 or more strikeouts, lifetime (19); most games, 10 or more strikeouts, lifetime (151); most seasons, 300 or more strikeouts (5); most games, 10 or more strikeouts, season (23), 1973; most strikeouts, three consecutive games (including extra innings—27⅓) (47), August 12, 16 and 20, 1974; most strikeouts by losing pitcher, extra-inning game (19), August 20, 1974 (11 innings); most seasons leading league, bases on balls allowed (8); most bases on balls, lifetime (2,022); most no-hit games, lifetime (5).

Established modern major league records for most consecutive seasons, 300 or more strikeouts (3); most strikeouts, season (383), 1973.

Tied major league records for striking out side on nine pitches, April 19, 1968 (third inning) and July 9, 1972 (second inning); most no-hit games, season (2), 1973; most strikeouts game (19), August 12, 1974; most clubs shut out, season (8), 1972; most consecutive seasons leading major leagues, bases on balls allowed (3); most strikeouts, three consecutive nine-inning games (41), August 7, 12 and 16, 1974.

Established American League record for most games, 10 or more strikeouts, lifetime (114); most games, 15 or more strikeouts, lifetime (19).

Tied American League records for most seasons, 200 or more strikeouts (7); most consecutive strikeouts, game (8), July 9, 1972 and July 15, 1973; most low-hit (no-hit and one-hit) games, season (3), 1973; most wild pitches, season (21), 1977; most seasons leading league, errors by pitcher (4); most seasons leading league, wild pitches (3); most consecutive seasons leading league, wild pitches (2).

Pitched 5-0 no-hit victory against Los Angeles Dodgers, September 26, 1981.
Pitched 1-0 no-hit victory against Baltimore Orioles, June 1, 1975.
Pitched 4-0 no-hit victory against Minnesota Twins, September 28, 1974.
Pitched 6-0 no-hit victory against Detroit Tigers, July 15, 1973.
Pitched 3-0 no-hit victory against Kansas City Royals, May 15, 1973.
Led National League in hit batsmen with 8 in 1982.
Led National League in wild pitches with 16 in 1981.
Led American League in shutouts with 9 in 1972, 7 in 1976, and tied for lead with 5 in 1979.
Led American League in wild pitches with 18 in 1972, 21 in 1977 and 13 in 1978.
Tied for American League lead in complete games with 22 in 1977.
Led Western Carolinas League pitchers in games started with 28 in 1966.
Tied for Appalachian League lead in hit batsmen with 8 in 1965.
Named American League Pitcher of the Year by THE SPORTING NEWS, 1977.
Named righthanded pitcher on THE SPORTING NEWS American League All-Star Team, 1977.
Named Western Carolinas Pitcher of the Year, 1966.

Year Club	League	G.	IP.	W.	L.	Pct.	H.	R.	ER.	SO.	BB.	ERA.
1965—Marion	Ap'lachian	13	78	3	6	.333	61	47	38	115	56	4.38
1966—Greenville	W. Carol.	29	183	★17	2	.895	109	59	51	★272	★127	2.51
1966—Williamsport	Eastern	3	19	0	2	.000	9	6	2	35	12	0.95
1966—New York	National	2	3	0	1	.000	5	5	5	6	3	15.00
1967—Winter Haven†	Florida St.	1	4	0	0	.000	1	1	1	5	2	2.25
1967—Jacksonville‡	Int'national	3	7	1	0	1.000	3	1	0	18	3	0.00
1968—New York§	National	21	134	6	9	.400	93	50	46	133	75	3.09
1969—New York	National	25	89	6	3	.667	60	38	35	92	53	3.54
1970—New York	National	27	132	7	11	.389	86	59	50	125	97	3.41
1971—New York x	National	30	152	10	14	.417	125	78	67	137	116	3.97
1972—California	American	39	284	19	16	.543	166	80	72	★329	★157	2.28
1973—California	American	41	326	21	16	.568	238	113	104	★383	★162	2.87
1974—California	American	42	★333	22	16	.579	221	127	107	★367	★202	2.89
1975—California	American	28	198	14	12	.538	152	90	76	186	132	3.45
1976—California	American	39	284	17	★18	.486	193	117	106	★327	★183	3.36
1977—California	American	37	299	19	16	.543	198	110	92	★341	★204	2.77
1978—California y	American	31	235	10	13	.435	183	106	97	★260	★148	3.71
1979—California z	American	34	223	16	14	.533	169	104	89	★223	114	3.59
1980—Houston	National	35	234	11	10	.524	205	100	87	200	★98	3.35
1981—Houston	National	21	149	11	5	.688	99	34	28	140	68	★1.69
1982—Houston	National	35	250⅓	16	12	.571	196	100	88	245	★109	3.16
1983—Houston a	National	29	196⅓	14	9	.609	134	74	65	183	101	2.98
National League Totals		225	1339⅔	81	74	.523	1003	538	471	1261	720	3.16
American League Totals		291	2182	138	121	.533	1520	847	743	2416	1302	3.06
Major League Totals		516	3521⅔	219	195	.529	2523	1385	1214	3677	2022	3.10

Selected by New York Mets' organization in 8th round of free-agent draft, June, 1965.
†On military list, January 3 to May 13, 1967.
‡On disabled list, July 16 to August 30, 1967.
§On disabled list, July 30 to August 30, 1968.
xTraded with Pitcher Don Rose, Outfielder Leroy Stanton and Catcher Francisco Estrada to California Angels for Infielder Jim Fregosi, December 10, 1971.
yOn disabled list, June 14 to July 5, 1978.
zGranted free agency, November 1, 1979; signed by Houston Astros, November 19, 1979.
aOn disabled list, March 25 to April 17 and May 3 to June 6, 1983.

DIVISION SERIES RECORD

Year Club	League	G.	IP.	W.	L.	Pct.	H.	R.	ER.	SO.	BB.	ERA.
1981—Houston	National	2	15	1	1	.500	6	4	3	14	3	1.80

CHAMPIONSHIP SERIES RECORD

Established Championship Series record for most strikeouts by relief pitcher, game (7), October 6, 1969.

Tied Championship Series records for most clubs, total Series (3); most earned runs allowed, five-game Series (8), 1980; most strikeouts, start of game (4), October 3, 1979.
Established National League Championship Series records for most runs allowed, five-game Series (8), 1980; most hits allowed, five-game Series (16), 1980.

Year Club	League	G.	IP.	W.	L.	Pct.	H.	R.	ER.	SO.	BB.	ERA.
1969—New York	National	1	7	1	0	1.000	3	2	2	7	2	2.57
1979—California	American	1	7	0	0	.000	4	3	1	8	3	1.29
1980—Houston	National	2	13⅓	0	0	.000	16	8	8	14	3	5.40
Championship Series Totals		4	27⅓	1	0	1.000	23	13	11	29	8	3.62

WORLD SERIES RECORD

Year Club	League	G.	IP.	W.	L.	Pct.	H.	R.	ER.	SO.	BB.	ERA.
1969—New York	National	1	2⅓	0	0	.000	1	0	0	3	2	0.00

ALL-STAR GAME RECORD

Year League	IP.	W.	L.	Pct.	H.	R.	ER.	SO.	BB.	ERA.
1973—American	2	0	0	.000	2	2	2	2	2	9.00
1979—American	2	0	0	.000	5	3	3	2	1	13.50
1981—National	1	0	0	.000	0	0	0	1	0	0.00
All-Star Game Totals	5	0	0	.000	7	5	5	5	3	9.00

Member of American League All-Star Team for the 1972 and 1975 games; did not play.
Named to American League All-Star Team to replace Frank Tanana for 1977 game; declined.

RANDY ANTHONY ST. CLAIRE

Born August 23, 1960, at Glens Falls, N.Y.
Height, 6.03. Weight, 180.
Throws and bats righthanded.
Son of Ebba St. Claire, catcher with Boston Braves,
Milwaukee Braves and New York Giants, 1951 through 1954.

Year Club	League	G.	IP.	W.	L.	Pct.	H.	R.	ER.	SO.	BB.	ERA.
1979—Calgary	Pioneer	6	33	1	2	.333	30	22	16	17	15	4.36
1980—Calgary	Pioneer	21	57	5	7	.417	65	36	27	51	23	4.26
1981—Jamestown	NYP	13	51	4	1	.800	53	22	11	36	17	1.94
1982—San Jose	California	9	61	2	5	.286	58	32	28	44	20	4.13
1982—W. Palm Beach	Florida St.	19	65	3	8	.273	74	41	38	38	17	5.26
1983—W. Palm Beach	Florida St.	42	98	5	7	.417	72	33	23	77	31	2.11

Signed as free agent by Montreal Expos' organization, September 9, 1978.

LENN HARUKI SAKATA

Name pronounced Sa-COT-a.
Born June 8, 1953, at Honolulu, Hawaii
Height, 5.09. Weight, 160.
Throws and bats righthanded.
Attended Treasure Valley Community College, Ontario, Ore. and
Gonzaga University, Spokane, Wash.

Year Club	League	Pos.	G.	AB.	R.	H.	2B.	3B.	HR.	RBI.	B.A.	PO.	A.	E.	F.A.
1975—Thetford Mines†	East.	2B	121	421	63	108	9	3	9	43	.257	243	304	16	.972
1976—Spokane	P. C.	2B	141	510	64	143	23	5	10	70	.280	*327	428	●22	.972
1977—Spokane	P. C.	2B	94	345	52	105	19	4	4	73	.304	221	352	13	*.978
1977—Milwaukee	Amer.	2B	53	154	13	25	2	0	2	12	.162	102	159	4	.985
1978—Spokane	P. C.	2B	45	156	24	42	14	3	0	20	.269	73	160	5	.979
1978—Milwaukee	Amer.	2B	30	78	8	15	4	0	0	3	.192	50	66	3	.975
1979—Vancouver‡	P. C.	2B-3B	118	454	59	136	21	3	6	64	.300	266	409	14	.980
1979—Milwaukee§	Amer.	2B	4	14	1	7	2	0	0	1	.500	10	13	0	1.000
1980—Rochester x	Int.	2B	26	93	19	32	6	1	3	8	.344	45	87	4	.971
1980—Baltimore	Amer.	2B-SS	43	83	12	16	3	2	1	9	.193	55	73	2	.985
1981—Baltimore y	Amer.	SS-2B	61	150	19	34	4	0	5	15	.227	82	148	7	.970
1982—Baltimore	Amer.	2B-SS	136	343	40	89	18	1	6	31	.259	182	299	16	.968
1983—Baltimore	Amer.	2B-C	66	134	23	34	7	0	3	12	.254	84	117	2	.990
Major League Totals			393	956	116	220	40	3	17	83	.230	565	875	34	.977

Selected by San Francisco Giants' organization in 14th round of free-agent draft, June 6, 1972.
Selected by San Diego Padres' organization in 5th round of free-agent draft, June 5, 1974.
Selected by Milwaukee Brewers' organization in secondary phase of free-agent draft, January 9, 1975.
†On disabled list, August 26 to September 5, 1975.
‡On disabled list, April 30 to May 18, 1979.
§Traded to Baltimore Orioles for Pitcher John Flinn, December 6, 1979.
xOn suspended list, April 16 to April 21, 1980.
yOn supplemental disabled list, November 9, 1980 through May 28, 1981.

WORLD SERIES RECORD

Year Club	League	Pos.	G.	AB.	R.	H.	2B.	3B.	HR.	RBI.	B.A.	PO.	A.	E.	F.A.
1983—Baltimore	Amer.	PR-2B	1	1	0	0	0	0	0	0	.000	2	2	0	1.000

ARGENIS ANTONIO SALAZAR
(Angel)

Born November 4, 1961, at El Tigre, Venezuela.
Height, 6.00. Weight, 173.
Throws and bats righthanded.

Tied for Pioneer League lead in double plays by shortstops with 45 in 1981.

Year	Club	League	Pos.	G.	AB.	R.	H.	2B.	3B.	HR.	RBI.	B.A.	PO.	A.	E.	F.A.
1980—W. Palm Beach†...Fla. St.							(Did not play)									
1980—Calgary	Pion.	S-2-1-C	51	169	29	41	2	0	0	11	.243	60	126	17	.916
1981—Calgary	Pion.	SS	63	259	37	64	5	3	2	25	.247	89	★228	13	★.961
1982—W. Palm Beach....	Fla. St.	SS	112	408	63	109	15	2	2	36	.267	176	★364	35	.939
1983—Wichita..............	A. A.	SS	98	341	47	103	23	7	1	54	.302	152	256	24	.944
1983—Montreal...............	Nat.	SS	36	37	5	8	1	1	0	1	.216	28	28	2	.966
Major League Totals..................................			36	37	5	8	1	1	0	1	.216	28	28	2	.966

Signed as free agent by Montreal Expos' organization, January 20, 1980.
†On temporarily inactive list, April 10 to June 1, 1980.

LUIS ERNESTO SALAZAR

Born May 19, 1956, at Barcelona, Venezuela.
Height, 6.00. Weight, 185.
Throws and bats righthanded.

Major League stolen bases: 1980 (11), 1981 (11), 1982 (32), 1983 (24). Total—78.
Led National League third basemen in errors with 26 and tied for lead in double plays with 28 in 1982.
Led Eastern League outfielders in putouts with 312 and tied for lead in double plays with 3 in 1979.

Year	Club	League	Pos.	G.	AB.	R.	H.	2B.	3B.	HR.	RBI.	B.A.	PO.	A.	E.	F.A.
1974—Sarasota Royals† .	Gulf C.	SS	2	4	0	1	0	0	0	1	.250	0	2	0	1.000
1976—Niagara Falls	NYP	SS-OF	42	151	18	36	3	4	1	17	.238	71	49	17	.876
1977—Salem....................	Carol.	SS-3B-2B	116	433	72	117	17	5	11	48	.270	157	294	45	.909
1978—Salem....................	Carol.	OF-3B-SS	126	472	55	138	20	4	3	49	.292	160	77	19	.926
1979—Buffalo..................	East.	OF-3B	★139	★561	★108	★181	17	5	27	86	.323	321	42	13	.965
1980—Port.‡-Hawaii........	P. C.	OF	127	497	91	157	23	15	9	64	.316	304	11	8	.975
1980—San Diego	Nat.	3B-OF	44	169	28	57	4	7	1	25	.337	39	88	7	.948
1981—San Diego	Nat.	3B-OF	109	400	37	121	19	6	3	38	.303	108	191	14	.955
1982—San Diego	Nat.	3B-SS-OF	145	524	55	127	15	5	8	62	.242	133	326	29	.941
1983—San Diego	Nat.	3B-SS	134	481	52	124	16	2	14	45	.258	122	274	21	.950
Major League Totals....................			432	1574	172	429	54	20	26	170	.273	402	879	71	.947

Signed as free agent by Kansas City Royals' organization, November 29, 1973.
†Released, July 8, 1974; signed by Pittsburgh Pirates' organization, November 23, 1975.
‡Traded with Outfielder Rick Lancellotti to San Diego Padres' organization for Infielder Kurt Bevacqua and a player to be named later, August 4, 1980; Pittsburgh Pirates' organization acquired Pitcher Mark Lee to complete deal, August 12, 1980.

JOSEPH CHARLES SAMBITO

Name pronounced Sam-BEET-oh.

(Joe)

Born June 28, 1952, at Brooklyn, N.Y.
Height, 6.01. Weight, 190.
Throws and bats lefthanded.
Attended Adelphi University, Garden City, N.Y.

Major League saves: 1976 (1), 1977 (7), 1978 (11), 1979 (22), 1980 (17), 1981 (10), 1982 (4). Total—72.
Led Southern League in wild pitches with 14 and tied for lead in games started by pitchers with 28 in 1975.
Tied for Appalachian League lead in shutouts with 2 in 1973.

Year	Club	League	G.	IP.	W.	L.	Pct.	H.	R.	ER.	SO.	BB.	ERA.
1973—Columbus...............................	Southern	1	2	0	0	.000	4	4	4	2	1	18.00
1973—Covington........................	Ap'lachian	11	55	4	2	.667	32	18	9	57	13	1.47
1974—Cedar Rapids................................	Midwest	23	156	11	8	.579	133	59	52	182	49	3.00
1975—Columbus...........................	Southern	30	★209	12	9	.571	★200	85	70	★140	85	3.01
1976—Memphis...........................	Int'national	5	27	3	0	1.000	37	19	19	17	13	6.33
1976—Columbus...........................	Southern	12	100	8	2	.800	77	27	20	61	23	1.80
1976—Houston...........................	National	20	53	3	2	.600	45	21	21	26	14	3.57
1977—Houston...........................	National	54	89	5	5	.500	77	34	23	67	24	2.33
1978—Houston...........................	National	62	88	4	9	.308	85	32	30	96	32	3.07
1979—Houston...........................	National	63	91	8	7	.533	80	20	18	83	23	1.78
1980—Houston...........................	National	64	90	8	4	.667	65	26	22	75	22	2.20
1981—Houston...........................	National	49	64	5	5	.500	43	17	13	41	22	1.83
1982—Houston†...........................	National	9	12⅔	0	0	.000	7	2	1	7	2	0.71
1983—Houston‡...........................	National						(Did not play)						
Major League Totals........................		321	487⅔	33	32	.508	402	152	128	395	139	2.36

Selected by Houston Astros' organization in 17th round of free-agent draft, June 5, 1973.
†On disabled list, May 20, 1982; transferred to emergency disabled list, June 9, 1982 through remainder of season.
‡On emergency disabled list, March 30, 1983 through remainder of season.

DIVISION SERIES RECORD

Year	Club	League	G.	IP.	W.	L.	Pct.	H.	R.	ER.	SO.	BB.	ERA.
1981—Houston...............................	National	2	1⅔	1	0	1.000	5	3	3	2	2	16.20

Year	Club	League	G.	IP.	W.	L.	Pct.	H.	R.	ER.	SO.	BB.	ERA.
1980—Houston		National	3	3⅔	0	1	.000	4	2	2	6	2	4.91

ALL-STAR GAME RECORD

Year	League	IP.	W.	L.	Pct.	H.	R.	ER.	SO.	BB.	ERA.
1979—National		⅔	0	0	.000	0	0	0	0	1	0.00

WILLIAM AMOS SAMPLE
(Billy)

Born April 2, 1955, at Roanoke, Va.
Height, 5.09. Weight, 175.
Throws and bats righthanded.
Received bachelor of science degree in psychology from
James Madison University, Harrisonburg, Va.

Tied major league records for highest fielding percentage by outfielder, season, 100 or more games (1.000), 1979; most assists by outfielder, inning (2), April 28, 1979 (fourth inning).
Major League stolen bases: 1979 (8), 1980 (8), 1981 (4), 1982 (10), 1983 (44). Total—74.
Led Pacific Coast League in bases on balls received with 109 in 1978.
Led Gulf Coast League in total bases with 86 in 1976.
Led Texas League second basemen in errors with 23 in 1977.

Year	Club	League	Pos.	G.	AB.	R.	H.	2B.	3B.	HR.	RBI.	B.A.	PO.	A.	E.	F.A.
1976—Sarasota Rang.		Gulf C.	2B	45	152	35	58	7	*9	1	33	*.382	81	113	8	.960
1977—Tulsa		Texas	2B-OF-3B	113	408	86	142	26	*13	7	72	.348	169	122	26	.918
1978—Tucson		P. C.	OF-2B	131	483	*141	170	27	13	18	99	.352	234	11	6	.976
1978—Texas		Amer.	OF	8	15	2	7	2	0	0	3	.467	0	0	0	.000
1979—Texas		Amer.	OF	128	325	60	95	21	2	5	35	.292	173	7	0	1.000
1980—Texas		Amer.	OF	99	204	29	53	10	0	4	19	.260	105	2	3	.973
1981—Texas†		Amer.	OF	66	230	36	65	16	0	3	25	.283	132	4	1	.993
1981—Wichita		A. A.	OF	3	14	2	5	1	0	0	2	.357	9	0	0	1.000
1982—Texas		Amer.	OF	97	360	56	94	14	2	10	29	.261	196	6	4	.981
1983—Texas		Amer.	OF	147	554	80	152	28	3	12	57	.274	329	8	4	.988
Major League Totals				545	1688	263	466	91	7	34	168	.276	935	27	12	.988

Selected by Texas Rangers' organization in 28th round of free-agent draft, June 5, 1973.
Selected by Texas Rangers' organization in 10th round of free-agent draft, June 8, 1976.
†On supplemental disabled list, May 6 to June 2, 1981; included rehabilitation disability assignment to Wichita, May 28 to June 2, 1981.

JUAN MILTON SAMUEL

Name pronounced SAHM-well.

Born December 9, 1960, at San Pedro de Macoris, D.R.
Height, 5.11. Weight, 170.
Throws and bats righthanded.

Led Carolina League in total bases with 283 and tied for lead in being hit by pitch with 15 in 1982.
Led Northwest League batters in strikeouts with 87 and caught stealing with 10 in 1980.
Led Carolina League second basemen in double plays with 82 and total chances with 721 in 1982.
Led South Atlantic League second basemen in double plays with 82 and total chances with 737 in 1981.
Named Carolina League Most Valuable Player, 1982.

Year	Club	League	Pos.	G.	AB.	R.	H.	2B.	3B.	HR.	RBI.	B.A.	PO.	A.	E.	F.A.
1980—Cen. Oregon		N'west	2B	69	*298	66	84	11	2	17	44	.282	162	188	*30	.921
1981—Spartanburg		S. Atl.	2B	135	512	88	127	22	8	11	74	.248	*280	*409	*50	.932
1982—Peninsula		Carol.	2B	135	494	*111	158	29	6	28	94	.320	*244	*442	*35	.951
1983—Reading		East.	2B	47	184	36	43	10	0	11	39	.234	121	127	14	.947
1983—Portland		P. C.	2B	65	261	59	86	14	8	15	52	.330	110	168	15	.949
1983—Philadelphia		Nat.	2B	18	65	14	18	1	2	2	5	.277	44	54	9	.916
Major League Totals				18	65	14	18	1	2	2	5	.277	44	54	9	.916

Signed as free agent by Philadelphia Phillies' organization, April 29, 1980.

CHAMPIONSHIP SERIES RECORD

Year	Club	League	Pos.	G.	AB.	R.	H.	2B.	3B.	HR.	RBI.	B.A.	PO.	A.	E.	F.A.
1983—Philadelphia		Nat.	PR	1	0	0	0	0	0	0	0	.000	0	0	0	.000

WORLD SERIES RECORD

Year	Club	League	Pos.	G.	AB.	R.	H.	2B.	3B.	HR.	RBI.	B.A.	PO.	A.	E.	F.A.
1983—Philadelphia		Nat.	PR-PH	3	1	0	0	0	0	0	0	.000	0	0	0	.000

ALEJANDRO SANCHEZ (PIMENTEL)
(Al)

Born February 26, 1959, at San Pedro, Dominican Republic.
Height, 6.00. Weight, 175.
Throws and bats righthanded.

Year	Club	League	Pos.	G.	AB.	R.	H.	2B.	3B.	HR.	RBI.	B.A.	PO.	A.	E.	F.A.
1978—Helena		Pion.	OF	6	24	4	5	0	1	0	5	.208	2	1	0	1.000
1978—Auburn		NYP	OF	58	242	30	58	9	5	4	28	.240	120	6	*14	.900
1979—Cen. Oregon		N'west	OF	54	204	31	55	10	2	3	38	.270	97	6	5	.954

Year—Club	League	Pos.	G.	AB.	R.	H.	2B.	3B.	HR.	RBI.	B.A.	PO.	A.	E.	F.A.
1980—Spartanburg	S. Atl.	OF	127	490	84	140	26	8	15	76	.286	223	15	●16	.937
1981—Reading	East.	OF	138	495	77	136	19	★17	13	76	.275	216	13	15	.939
1982—Oklahoma City†	A. A.	OF	88	320	57	98	24	7	13	46	.306	155	10	●9	.948
1982—Philadelphia	Nat.	OF	7	14	3	4	1	0	2	4	.286	7	0	0	1.000
1983—Portland	P. C.	OF	125	458	75	113	21	5	17	74	.247	219	●18	★12	.952
1983—Philadelphia	Nat.	OF	8	7	2	2	0	0	0	2	.286	1	0	1	.500
Major League Totals			15	21	5	6	1	0	2	6	.286	8	0	1	.889

Signed as free agent by Philadelphia Phillies' organization, April 10, 1978.

†On disabled list, July 1 to August 5, 1982.

LUIS MERCEDES SANCHEZ

Born August 24, 1953, at Cariaco, Sucre, Venezuela.
Height, 6.02. Weight, 170.
Throws and bats righthanded.

Major League saves: 1981 (2), 1982 (5), 1983 (7). Total—14.
Led American League in intentional bases on balls issued with 14 in 1983.
Led Florida East Coast League in complete games with 6 in 1972.
Tied for Mexican League lead in complete games with 16 in 1980.

Year—Club	League	G.	IP.	W.	L.	Pct.	H.	R.	ER.	SO.	BB.	ERA.
1972—Cocoa Astros	Fla. E. C.	11	71	6	3	.667	55	29	20	49	31	2.54
1973—Cedar Rapids	Midwest	26	130	5	9	.357	140	75	61	93	43	4.22
1974—Cedar Rapids	Midwest	25	147	9	4	.692	122	39	26	130	44	★1.59
1975—Columbus	Southern	21	132	6	12	.333	137	76	59	60	64	4.02
1975—Dubuque†	Midwest	6	31	2	3	.400	25	19	12	19	10	3.48
1976—Tampa‡§x	Florida St.	2	8	0	2	.000	11	4	4	5	5	4.50
1977-78						(Did not play)						
1979—Caracas y	Int.-Amer.	13	35	2	4	.333	39	25	19	25	19	4.89
1980—Aguila z	Mexican	24	177	14	9	.609	149	47	40	●155	35	2.03
1980—Albuquerque a	P. Coast	5	22	2	1	.667	27	14	13	15	10	5.32
1981—California	American	17	34	0	2	.000	39	16	11	13	11	2.91
1981—Salt Lake City	P. Coast	6	8	0	0	.000	12	7	7	7	7	7.88
1982—California	American	46	92⅔	7	4	.636	89	36	33	58	34	3.21
1982—Spokane	P. Coast	2	9⅔	0	1	.000	13	13	10	5	8	9.31
1983—California	American	56	98⅓	10	8	.556	92	42	40	49	40	3.66
Major League Totals		119	225	17	14	.548	220	94	84	120	85	3.36

Signed as free agent by Houston Astros' organization, September 1, 1971.

†Traded with Pitcher Carlos Alfonso to Cincinnati Reds' organization, December 12, 1975, completing deal in which Cincinnati Reds traded Pitcher Joaquin Andujar to Houston Astros for two players to be named later, October 24, 1975.

‡On disabled list, April 17 to May 18, 1976.

§On temporary inactive list, May 28 to July 28, 1976.

xOn disqualified list, July 28, 1976 through March 30, 1979; signed by Caracas of Inter-American League, March 30, 1979.

ySigned by Aguila, December 29, 1979.

zLoaned to Los Angeles Dodgers' organization, July 31, 1980; returned, October 15, 1980.

aSold to California Angels, February 10, 1981.

CHAMPIONSHIP SERIES RECORD

Year—Club	League	G.	IP.	W.	L.	Pct.	H.	R.	ER.	SO.	BB.	ERA.
1982—California	American	2	2⅔	0	1	.000	4	2	2	1	1	6.75

ORLANDO SANCHEZ

Born September 7, 1956, at Canovanas, Puerto Rico.
Height, 6.00. Weight, 185.
Throws right and bats lefthanded.

Tied for Carolina League lead in double plays by outfielders with 3 in 1977.

Year—Club	League	Pos.	G.	AB.	R.	H.	2B.	3B.	HR.	RBI.	B.A.	PO.	A.	E.	F.A.
1974—Marion	Appal.	C	23	63	11	13	3	0	0	8	.206	131	15	1	.993
1975—Pulaski†	Appal.	1B-OF-P	52	167	34	44	11	0	7	46	.263	188	4	11	.946
1976—Spartanburg	W. Car.	1B-C	122	445	61	118	18	5	13	81	.265	803	34	22	.974
1977—Peninsula	Carol.	OF-1B-C	109	390	61	108	18	3	6	48	.277	232	19	19	.930
1978—Reading‡	East.	OF	80	288	50	84	12	3	14	48	.292	121	2	10	.925
1979—Reading	East.	OF-1B	70	219	23	71	11	1	6	30	.324	65	2	4	.944
1979—Oklahoma City	A. A.	OF	31	92	14	27	5	2	1	9	.293	27	0	1	.964
1980—Okla. City§ x	A. A.	OF	68	218	21	67	9	2	1	21	.307	35	3	3	.927
1981—St. Louis	Nat.	C	27	49	5	14	2	1	0	6	.286	50	0	4	.926
1982—St. Louis	Nat.	C	26	37	6	7	0	1	0	3	.189	34	4	0	1.000
1982—Louisville	A. A.	C-OF	41	132	14	31	9	0	3	14	.235	143	17	6	.964
1983—Louisville	A. A.	C-OF	116	424	70	125	27	2	16	89	.295	154	11	7	.959
1983—St. Louis y	Nat.	C	6	6	0	0	0	0	0	0	.000	1	0	0	1.000
Major League Totals			59	92	11	21	2	2	0	9	.228	85	4	4	.957

Signed as free agent by New York Mets' organization, February 18, 1974.

†Released, December 30, 1975; signed by Philadelphia Phillies' organization, April 16, 1976.

‡On disabled list, April 25 to May 4 and June 10 to July 7, 1978.

§On disabled list, May 3 to May 27 and July 5 to July 24, 1980.

xDrafted by St. Louis Cardinals, December 8, 1980.

RECORD AS PITCHER

Year Club	League	G.	IP.	W.	L.	Pct.	H.	R.	ER.	SO.	BB.	ERA.
1975—Pulaski	Ap'lachian	1	2	0	0	.000	3	6	5	0	4	22.50

RYNE DEE SANDBERG

Born September 18, 1959, at Spokane, Wash.
Height, 6.01. Weight, 175.
Throws and bats righthanded.

Major League stolen bases: 1982 (32), 1983 (37). Total—69.
Led National League second basemen in assists with 571, total chances with 914 and double plays with 126 in 1983.
Led Eastern League shortstops in fielding percentage with .964, assists with 386 and double plays with 81 in 1980.
Led Western Carolinas League shortstops in double plays with 80 in 1979.
Led Pioneer League shortstops in double plays with 39 in 1978.
Named second baseman on THE SPORTING NEWS National League All-Star fielding team, 1983.

Year Club	League	Pos.	G.	AB.	R.	H.	2B.	3B.	HR.	RBI.	B.A.	PO.	A.	E.	F.A.
1978—Helena	Pion.	SS	56	190	34	59	6	6	1	23	.311	92	★200	24	.924
1979—Spartanburg	W. Car.	SS	★138	★539	83	133	21	7	4	47	.247	134	★467	35	★.945
1980—Reading	East.	SS-3B	129	490	95	152	21	12	11	79	.310	156	388	20	.965
1981—Oklahoma City	A. A.	SS-2B	133	519	78	152	17	5	9	62	.293	229	396	21	.967
1981—Philadelphia†	Nat.	SS-2B	13	6	2	1	0	0	0	0	.167	7	7	0	1.000
1982—Chicago	Nat.	3B-2B	156	635	103	172	33	5	7	54	.271	136	373	12	.977
1983—Chicago	Nat.	★2B-SS	158	633	94	165	25	4	8	48	.261	330	572	13	★.986
Major League Totals			327	1274	199	338	58	9	15	102	.265	473	952	25	.983

Selected by Philadelphia Phillies' organization in 21st round of free-agent draft, June 6, 1978.
†Traded with Shortstop Larry Bowa to Chicago Cubs for Shortstop Ivan DeJesus, January 27, 1982.

SCOTT DOUGLAS SANDERSON

Born July 22, 1956, at Dearborn, Mich.
Height, 6.05. Weight, 198.
Throws and bats righthanded.
Attended Vanderbilt University, Nashville, Tenn.

Year Club	League	G.	IP.	W.	L.	Pct.	H.	R.	ER.	SO.	BB.	ERA.
1977—West Palm Beach	Florida St.	10	57	5	2	.714	58	22	17	37	23	2.68
1978—Memphis	Southern	9	58	5	3	.625	32	26	44	19	4.03	
1978—Denver	Am. Assoc.	9	49	4	2	.667	47	35	33	36	30	6.06
1978—Montreal	National	10	61	4	2	.667	52	20	17	50	21	2.51
1979—Montreal	National	34	168	9	8	.529	148	69	64	138	54	3.43
1980—Montreal	National	33	211	16	11	.593	206	76	73	125	56	3.11
1981—Montreal	National	22	137	9	7	.563	122	50	45	77	31	2.96
1982—Montreal	National	32	224	12	12	.500	212	98	86	158	58	3.46
1983—Montreal†‡	National	18	81⅓	6	7	.462	98	50	42	55	20	4.65
Major League Totals		149	882⅓	56	47	.544	838	363	327	603	240	3.34

Selected by Kansas City Royals' organization in 11th round of free-agent draft, June 5, 1974.
Selected by Montreal Expos' organization in 3rd round of free-agent draft, June 7, 1977.
†On disabled list, July 5 to September 1, 1983.
‡Traded to San Diego Padres for Pitcher Gary Lucas, December 7, 1983; Traded by San Diego to Chicago Cubs for First Baseman Carmelo Martinez, Pitcher Craig Lefferts and Third Baseman Fritz Connally, December 7, 1983.

DIVISION SERIES RECORD

Year Club	League	G.	IP.	W.	L.	Pct.	H.	R.	ER.	SO.	BB.	ERA.
1981—Montreal	National	1	2⅔	0	0	.000	4	4	2	2	2	6.75

RAFAEL FRANCISCO SANTANA (DeLaCRUZ)

Born January 31, 1958, at La Romana, Dominican Republic.
Height, 6.01. Weight, 156.
Throws and bats righthanded.

Led New York-Pennsylvania League in sacrifice hits with 8 in 1977.
Led Texas League shortstops in fielding percentage with .955 and tied for lead in double plays with 79 in 1981.

Year Club	League	Pos.	G.	AB.	R.	H.	2B.	3B.	HR.	RBI.	B.A.	PO.	A.	E.	F.A.
1977—Oneonta	NYP	SS	60	157	26	41	5	0	0	23	.261	62	162	★27	.892
1978—Ft. Lauderdale	Fla. St.	SS	131	431	37	111	8	5	0	35	.258	166	372	★48	.918
1979—Ft. Lauderdale	Fla. St.	SS-3B-2B	133	472	62	124	9	6	0	41	.263	160	351	16	.970
1980—Nashville	South.	SS	86	275	33	64	4	3	0	20	.233	125	247	25	.937
1980—Ft. Lauderdale†	Fla. St.	SS	51	168	20	38	2	0	1	17	.226	81	158	9	.964
1981—Arkansas	Texas	SS-3B-2B	110	326	34	76	14	3	0	19	.233	154	350	23	.956
1981—Springfield	A. A.	SS-3B	2	8	3	4	1	0	1	2	.500	1	8	3	.750
1982—Louisville	A. A.	3B-2B-SS	121	430	65	123	15	3	3	53	.286	163	275	11	.976
1983—St. Louis	Nat.	2B-SS-3B	30	14	1	3	0	0	0	2	.214	3	8	4	.733
1983—Louisville	A. A.	3-2-S-1	45	167	19	47	9	1	0	20	.281	60	117	10	.947
Major League Totals			30	14	1	3	0	0	0	2	.214	3	8	4	.733

Signed as free agent by New York Yankees' organization, August 31, 1976.
†Traded to St. Louis Cardinals for a player to be named later, February 16, 1981; New York Yankees' organization acquired Pitcher George Frazier to complete deal, June 7, 1981.

MANUEL EDUARDO SARMIENTO (APONTE)

Name pronounced Sar-mee-EN-toh.

(Manny)

Born February 2, 1956, at Cagua, Aragua, Venezuela.
Height, 5.11. Weight, 170.
Throws and bats righthanded.

Led Northwest League in saves with 14 in 1973 and Eastern League with 15 in 1975.

Year Club	League	G.	IP.	W.	L.	Pct.	H.	R.	ER.	SO.	BB.	ERA.
1972—Bradenton Reds	Gulf Coast	18	40	2	6	.250	40	22	13	34	15	2.93
1973—Seattle	Northwest	★36	67	2	6	.250	53	22	16	60	24	2.15
1974—Tampa	Florida St.	39	126	10	9	.526	112	42	40	80	47	2.86
1975—Three Rivers	Eastern	★64	129	6	8	.429	104	41	37	114	51	2.58
1976—Indianapolis	Am. Assoc.	43	65	11	5	.688	49	21	20	51	24	2.77
1976—Cincinnati	National	22	44	5	1	.833	36	14	10	20	12	2.05
1977—Indianapolis†	Am. Assoc.	25	35	3	4	.429	45	26	26	35	12	6.69
1977—Cincinnati	National	24	40	0	0	.000	28	13	11	23	11	2.48
1978—Cincinnati	National	63	127	9	7	.563	109	65	62	72	54	4.39
1979—Indianapolis	Am. Assoc.	19	38	1	0	1.000	41	14	10	34	11	2.37
1979—Cincinnati‡	National	23	39	0	4	.000	47	21	20	23	7	4.62
1980—Spokane	P. Coast	51	63	8	7	.533	57	27	21	66	20	3.00
1980—Seattle§	American	9	15	0	1	.000	14	7	6	15	6	3.60
1981—Pawtucket x	Int'national	47	96	7	5	.583	71	27	25	99	27	2.34
1982—Portland	P. Coast	6	9	1	0	1.000	10	2	1	8	4	1.00
1982—Pittsburgh	National	35	164⅔	9	4	.692	153	69	62	81	46	3.39
1983—Pittsburgh	National	52	84⅓	3	5	.375	74	35	28	49	36	2.99
National League Totals		219	499	26	21	.553	447	217	193	268	166	3.48
American League Totals		9	15	0	1	.000	14	7	6	15	6	3.60
Major League Totals		228	514	26	22	.542	461	224	199	283	172	3.48

Signed as free agent by Cincinnati Reds' organization, March 25, 1972.
†On disabled list, April 13 to May 4 and May 28 to June 17, 1977.
‡Released, April 2, 1980; signed by Seattle Mariners' organization, April 14, 1980.
§Traded to Boston Red Sox' organization for Pitcher Dick Drago, April 8, 1981.
xSold to Pittsburgh Pirates, October 23, 1981.

CHAMPIONSHIP SERIES RECORD

Year Club	League	G.	IP.	W.	L.	Pct.	H.	R.	ER.	SO.	BB.	ERA.
1976—Cincinnati	National	1	1	0	0	.000	2	2	2	0	1	18.00

WILLIAM JAMES SATTLER

(Bill)

Born August 19, 1957, at Youngstown, O.
Height, 6.00. Weight, 170.
Throws and bats righthanded.
Received bachelor of science degree in criminal justice from Youngstown State, Youngstown, Ohio in 1981.

Led American Association in home runs allowed with 28 in 1982 and tied for lead with 23 in 1983.
Led New York-Pennsylvania League in complete games with 9 in 1979.

Year Club	League	G.	IP.	W.	L.	Pct.	H.	R.	ER.	SO.	BB.	ERA.
1979—Jamestown	NYP	13	96	8	2	.800	83	42	33	●82	50	3.09
1980—West Palm Beach	Florida St.	16	113	7	5	.583	93	46	34	67	45	2.71
1981—Memphis	Southern	28	163	11	6	.647	136	67	50	94	45	2.76
1982—Wichita	Am. Assoc.	26	145⅓	10	6	.625	171	99	87	90	49	5.39
1983—Wichita	Am. Assoc.	41	120	5	10	.333	131	86	79	91	44	5.93

Selected by Montreal Expos' organization in 29th round of free-agent draft, June 5, 1979.

DAVID JOHN SAX

(Dave)

Born September 22, 1958, at Sacramento, Calif.
Height, 6.00. Weight, 175.
Throws and bats righthanded.
Brother of Steve Sax, second baseman with Los Angeles Dodgers.

Year Club	League	Pos.	G.	AB.	R.	H.	2B.	3B.	HR.	RBI.	B.A.	PO.	A.	E.	F.A.
1978—Lethbridge	Pion.	2-3-S-O	44	145	31	39	10	2	4	31	.269	79	80	13	.924
1979—Clinton	Midw.	C-3-O-1	97	282	37	76	18	1	6	49	.270	226	32	7	.974
1980—Lodi	Calif.	C-1-O-3	43	123	9	21	3	0	1	11	.171	159	25	8	.958
1980—Vero Beach	Fla. St.	OF-C-1B	58	193	33	68	8	5	2	33	.352	156	18	2	.989
1981—San Antonio†	Texas	C-OF	62	221	43	68	13	2	4	31	.308	231	17	5	.980
1982—Albuquerque	P. C.	C-3-1-O	117	417	71	132	29	1	12	75	.317	403	57	12	.975
1982—Los Angeles	Nat.	OF	2	2	0	0	0	0	0	0	.000	1	0	0	1.000
1983—Albuquerque	P. C.	C-1B	75	280	59	96	22	3	8	59	.343	159	18	3	.983
1983—Los Angeles	Nat.	C	7	8	0	0	0	0	0	1	.000	11	0	1	.917
Major League Totals			9	10	0	0	0	0	0	1	.000	12	0	1	.923

Signed as free agent by Los Angeles Dodgers' organization, June 16, 1978.
†On disabled list, July 3 to September 15, 1981.

STEPHEN LOUIS SAX
(Steve)

Born January 29, 1960, at Sacramento, Calif.
Height, 5.11. Weight, 185.
Throws and bats righthanded.
Brother of David Sax, catcher in Los Angeles Dodgers' organization.

Major League stolen bases: 1981 (5), 1982 (49), 1983 (56). Total—110.
Led National League in caught stealing with 30 in 1983.
Led Florida State League second basemen in double plays with 91 in 1980.
Named National League Rookie of the Year by Baseball Writers' Association of America, 1982.
Named Texas League Most Valuable Player, 1981.

Year Club	League	Pos.	G.	AB.	R.	H.	2B.	3B.	HR.	RBI.	B.A.	PO.	A.	E.	F.A.
1978—Lethbridge	Pion.	SS	39	131	24	43	6	3	0	21	.328	21	40	9	.871
1979—Clinton	Midw.	OF-2B-3B	115	386	64	112	15	2	2	52	.290	111	75	18	.912
1980—Vero Beach	Fla. St.	★2B-OF	●139	●530	78	150	18	8	3	61	.283	★360	★438	20	★.976
1981—San Antonio	Texas	2B	115	485	94	168	23	3	8	52	★.346	255	298	17	.970
1981—Los Angeles	Nat.	2B	31	119	15	33	2	0	2	9	.277	64	93	4	.975
1982—Los Angeles	Nat.	2B	150	638	88	180	23	7	4	47	.282	347	452	19	.977
1983—Los Angeles	Nat.	2B	155	623	94	175	18	5	5	41	.281	331	399	★30	.961
Major League Totals			336	1380	197	388	43	12	11	97	.281	742	944	53	.970

Selected by Los Angeles Dodgers' organization in 9th round of free-agent draft, June 6, 1978.

DIVISION SERIES RECORD

Year Club	League	Pos.	G.	AB.	R.	H.	2B.	3B.	HR.	RBI.	B.A.	PO.	A.	E.	F.A.
1981—Los Angeles	Nat.	2B	1	0	0	0	0	0	0	0	.000	0	0	0	.000

CHAMPIONSHIP SERIES RECORD

Year Club	League	Pos.	G.	AB.	R.	H.	2B.	3B.	HR.	RBI.	B.A.	PO.	A.	E.	F.A.
1981—Los Angeles	Nat.	2B	1	0	0	0	0	0	0	0	.000	0	1	0	1.000
1983—Los Angeles	Nat.	2B	4	16	0	4	0	0	0	0	.250	11	12	0	1.000
Championship Series Totals			5	16	0	4	0	0	0	0	.250	11	13	0	1.000

WORLD SERIES RECORD

Year Club	League	Pos.	G.	AB.	R.	H.	2B.	3B.	HR.	RBI.	B.A.	PO.	A.	E.	F.A.
1981—Los Angeles	Nat.	PH-PR-2	2	1	0	0	0	0	0	0	.000	0	0	0	.000

ALL-STAR GAME RECORD

Year League	Pos.	AB.	R.	H.	2B.	3B.	HR.	RBI.	B.A.	PO.	A.	E.	F.A.
1982—National	PR-2B	1	0	1	0	0	0	0	1.000	2	0	1	.667
1983—National	2B	3	1	1	0	0	0	1	.333	2	0	1	.667
All-Star Game Totals		4	1	2	0	0	0	1	.500	4	0	2	.667

DANIEL ERNEST SCHATZEDER
Name pronounced SCHATZ-uh-dur.
(Dan)

Born December 1, 1954, at Elmhurst, Ill.
Height, 6.00. Weight, 195.
Throws and bats lefthanded.
Received degree in business administration from University of Denver, Denver, Colo., in 1976.

Year Club	League	G.	IP.	W.	L.	Pct.	H.	R.	ER.	SO.	BB.	ERA.
1976—West Palm Beach	Florida St.	10	64	5	3	.625	49	22	19	49	20	2.67
1976—Quebec City	Eastern	5	28	2	3	.400	38	16	14	19	10	4.50
1977—Quebec City	Eastern	8	62	5	3	.625	39	20	19	59	15	2.76
1977—Denver†	Am. Assoc.	9	36	2	2	.500	45	25	24	28	14	6.00
1977—Montreal	National	6	22	2	1	.667	16	6	6	14	13	2.45
1978—Denver	Am. Assoc.	4	28	3	0	1.000	24	11	9	19	11	2.89
1978—Montreal	National	29	144	7	7	.500	108	54	49	69	68	3.06
1979—Montreal‡	National	32	162	10	5	.667	136	57	51	106	59	2.83
1980—Detroit§	American	32	193	11	13	.458	178	88	86	94	58	4.01
1981—Detroit x	American	17	71	6	8	.429	74	49	48	20	29	6.08
1982—San Francisco y-Montreal	National	39	69⅓	1	6	.143	84	46	41	33	24	5.23
1982—Phoenix	P. Coast	1	3⅔	0	0	.000	10	6	5	1	3	12.27
1983—Montreal z	National	58	87	5	2	.714	88	34	31	48	25	3.21
National League Totals		164	484⅓	25	21	.543	432	197	178	270	189	3.31
American League Totals		49	264	17	21	.447	252	137	134	114	87	4.57
Major League Totals		213	748⅓	42	42	.500	684	334	312	384	276	3.75

Selected by Montreal Expos' organization in 3rd round of free-agent draft, June 8, 1976.
†On disabled list, July 5 to August 30, 1977.
‡Traded to Detroit Tigers for Outfielder Ron LeFlore, December 7, 1979.
§On disabled list, May 27 to June 17, 1980.
xTraded with Pitcher Mike Chris to San Francisco Giants for Outfielder Larry Herndon, December 9, 1981.
ySold to Montreal Expos, June 15, 1982.
zGranted free agency, November 7, 1983; re-signed by Expos, December 19, 1983.

WILLIAM JOSEPH SCHERRER
Named pronounced SHURR-ur.
(Bill)

Born January 20, 1958, at Tonawanda, N. Y.
Height, 6.04. Weight, 180.
Throws and bats lefthanded.
Attended University of Nevada, Las Vegas, Nev.

Major League saves: 1983 (10).
Tied for American Association lead in shutouts with 2 in 1982.
Tied for Northwest League lead in shutouts with 2 in 1978.

Year Club	League	G.	IP.	W.	L.	Pct.	H.	R.	ER.	SO.	BB.	ERA.
1977—Shelby	W. Carol.	27	158	9	9	.500	132	87	62	122	105	3.53
1978—Shelby	W. Carol.	10	31	0	2	.000	27	19	14	18	26	4.06
1978—Eugene	Northwest	13	84	6	4	.600	61	43	33	87	42	3.54
1979—Tampa	Florida St.	25	159	12	3	.800	126	43	32	140	65	1.81
1980—Waterbury	Eastern	25	151	7	8	.467	139	58	56	84	58	3.34
1981—Waterbury	Eastern	50	119	5	9	.357	121	70	57	89	62	4.31
1982—Tampa	Florida St.	7	47⅓	3	2	.600	37	13	12	45	18	2.28
1982—Waterbury	Eastern	5	31	1	3	.250	30	15	13	18	15	3.77
1982—Indianapolis	Am. Assoc.	19	88⅔	6	4	.600	68	43	40	81	32	4.06
1982—Cincinnati	National	5	17⅓	0	1	.000	17	7	5	7	0	2.60
1983—Cincinnati	National	73	92	2	3	.400	73	31	28	57	33	2.74
Major League Totals		78	109⅓	2	4	.333	90	38	33	64	33	2.72

Selected by Cleveland Indians' organization in 6th round of free-agent draft, June 8, 1976.
Selected by Cincinnati Reds' organization in secondary phase of free-agent draft, January 11, 1977.

AUGUST ROBERT SCHMIDT
(Augie)

Born June 23, 1961, at Carthage, Ill.
Height, 6.02. Weight, 175.
Throws and bats righthanded.
Attended University of New Orleans, New Orleans, La.

Year Club	League	Pos.	G.	AB.	R.	H.	2B.	3B.	HR.	RBI.	B.A.	PO.	A.	E.	F.A.
1982—Kinston	Carol.	SS	50	182	31	54	10	1	3	22	.297	70	142	12	.946
1983—Knoxville	South.	SS	135	482	65	128	28	2	4	54	.266	143	282	29	.936

Selected by Cincinnati Reds' organization in 9th round of free-agent draft, June 5, 1979.
Selected by Toronto Blue Jays' organization in 1st round (second player selected) of free-agent draft, June 7, 1982.

DAVID JOSEPH SCHMIDT
(Dave)

Born April 22, 1957, at Niles, Mich.
Height, 6.01. Weight, 185.
Throws and bats righthanded.
Attended Los Angeles Valley College, Van Nuys, Calif., and University of California
at Los Angeles, Los Angeles, Calif.

Year Club	League	G.	IP.	W.	L.	Pct.	H.	R.	ER.	SO.	BB.	ERA.
1979—Sarasota Rangers	Gulf Coast	7	30	2	2	.500	30	19	14	27	8	4.20
1980—Asheville	S. Atlantic	12	91	8	1	.889	76	32	20	67	13	1.98
1980—Tulsa	Texas	12	73	4	6	.400	90	42	36	46	28	4.44
1981—Tulsa	Texas	3	24	1	1	.500	17	5	5	17	6	1.88
1981—Texas	American	14	32	0	1	.000	31	11	11	13	11	3.09
1981—Wichita	Am. Assoc.	12	87	2	5	.286	90	47	47	49	26	4.86
1982—Texas	American	33	109⅔	4	6	.400	118	45	39	69	25	3.20
1983—Texas†	American	31	46⅓	3	3	.500	42	20	20	29	14	3.88
Major League Totals		78	188	7	10	.412	191	76	70	111	50	3.35

Selected by Texas Rangers' organization in 26th round of free-agent draft, June 5, 1979.
†On disabled list, March 25 to May 1, 1983.

MICHAEL JACK SCHMIDT
(Mike)

Born September 27, 1949, at Dayton, O.
Height, 6.02. Weight, 203.
Throws and bats righthanded.
Received bachelor of arts degree in business administration from Ohio University, Athens, O. in 1971.

Established major league records for most total bases, extra-inning game (17), April 17, 1976 (10 innings); most home runs by third baseman, season (48), 1980.

Tied major league records for most home runs, extra-inning game (4), April 17, 1976 (10 innings); most consecutive home runs, extra-inning game (4), April 17, 1976 (10 innings); most home runs, consecutive plate appearances (4), April 17, 1976 and July 6 and 7, 1979; most extra bases on long hits, game (12), April 17, 1976 (10 innings); most home runs, two consecutive games (5), April 17 and 18, 1976; most home runs, three consecutive games (6), April 17-20, 1976; most home runs, April (11), 1976; most consecutive seasons leading major leagues in strikeouts (3), 1974 through 1976; most home runs, October (4), 1980.

Established National League record for most assists, third baseman, season (404), 1974; fewest singles, season, 150 or more games (65), 1975.

Tied National League records for most home runs, bases full, one month, 2, June, 1973; most home runs, June (14), 1977; most home runs through July 31 (36), 1979; most home runs, five consecutive games, one or more homer each game (7), July 6 through 10, 1979; most years leading league in extra bases on long hits (6); most consecutive years leading league in extra bases on long hits (3, performed twice); most consecutive years leading league in bases on balls (3); most years leading league in assists by third baseman (7).

Hit three home runs in a game, July 7, 1979.

Hit home runs in all 12 National League parks, 1979.

Led National League in intentional bases on balls received with 18 in 1981.

Led National League in total bases with 306 in 1976, 342 in 1980 and 228 in 1981.

Led National League in slugging percentage with .546 in 1974, .624 in 1980, .644 in 1981 and .547 in 1982.

Led National League batters in strikeouts with 138 in 1974, 180 in 1975, 149 in 1976 and 148 in 1983.

Led National League in bases on balls received with 120 in 1979, 73 in 1981, 107 in 1982 and 128 in 1983.

Led National League in sacrifice flies with 13 in 1980 and tied for lead with 9 in 1979.

Tied for National League lead in being hit by pitch with 11 in 1976.

Led National League third basemen in total chances with 537 in 1976, 521 in 1977, 497 in 1980, 457 in 1982 and tied for lead with 338 in 1981 and 458 in 1983.

Led National League third basemen in double plays with 34 in 1978, 36 in 1979, 31 in 1980, 29 in 1983 and tied for lead with 28 in 1982.

Led National League third basemen in assists with 396 in 1977 and 332 in 1983.

Led Pacific Coast League batters in strikeouts with 145 in 1972.

Named National League Player of the Year by THE SPORTING NEWS, 1980.

Named National League Most Valuable Player by Baseball Writers' Association of America, 1980 and 1981.

Named third baseman on THE SPORTING NEWS National League All-Star Team, 1974, 1976, 1977 and 1979 through 1983.

Named third baseman on THE SPORTING NEWS National League All-Star fielding team, 1976 through 1983.

Named third baseman on THE SPORTING NEWS National League Silver Slugger team, 1980 through 1983.

Year	Club	League	Pos.	G	AB	R	H	2B	3B	HR	RBI	B.A.	PO	A	E	F.A.
1971—Reading	East.		SS-3B	74	237	27	50	7	1	8	31	.211	100	224	23	.934
1972—Eugene	P. C.		2B-3B-SS	131	436	80	127	23	6	26	91	.291	271	324	25	.960
1972—Philadelphia†	Nat.		3B-2B	13	34	2	7	0	0	1	3	.206	10	25	2	.946
1973—Philadelphia‡	Nat.		3-2-1-S	132	367	43	72	11	0	18	52	.196	119	256	18	.954
1974—Philadelphia	Nat.		3B	162	568	108	160	28	7	*36	116	.282	134	*404	26	.954
1975—Philadelphia	Nat.		3B-SS	158	562	93	140	34	3	*38	95	.249	139	390	26	.953
1976—Philadelphia	Nat.		3B	160	584	112	153	31	4	*38	107	.262	139	*377	21	.961
1977—Philadelphia	Nat.		3B-SS-2B	154	544	114	149	27	11	38	101	.274	109	401	20	.962
1978—Philadelphia	Nat.		3B-SS	145	513	93	129	27	2	21	78	.251	98	325	16	.964
1979—Philadelphia	Nat.		3B-SS	160	541	109	137	25	4	45	114	.253	115	363	23	.954
1980—Philadelphia	Nat.		3B	150	548	104	157	25	8	*48	*121	.286	98	*372	27	.946
1981—Philadelphia	Nat.		3B	102	354	*78	112	19	2	*31	*91	.316	74	*249	15	.956
1982—Philadelphia§	Nat.		3B	148	514	108	144	26	3	35	87	.280	110	*324	23	.950
1983—Philadelphia	Nat.		3B-SS	154	534	104	136	16	4	*40	109	.255	108	333	19	.959
Major League Totals				1638	5663	1068	1496	269	48	389	1074	.264	1253	3819	236	.956

Selected by Philadelphia Phillies' organization in 2nd round of free-agent draft, June 8, 1971.

†On disabled list, August 21 to September 2, 1972.

‡On disabled list, March 28 to April 21, 1973.

§On supplemental disabled list, April 14 to April 29, 1982.

DIVISION SERIES RECORD

Year	Club	League	Pos.	G	AB	R	H	2B	3B	HR	RBI	B.A.	PO	A	E	F.A.
1981—Philadelphia	Nat.		3B	5	16	3	4	1	0	1	2	.250	6	10	1	.941

CHAMPIONSHIP SERIES RECORD

Established Championship Series record for most at-bats, five-game Series (24), 1980.

Tied Championship Series records for highest batting average, four-game Series (.467), 1983; most at-bats, extra-inning game (6), October 8, 1980.

Year	Club	League	Pos.	G	AB	R	H	2B	3B	HR	RBI	B.A.	PO	A	E	F.A.
1976—Philadelphia	Nat.		3B	3	13	1	4	2	0	0	2	.308	4	9	1	.929
1977—Philadelphia	Nat.		3B	4	16	2	1	0	0	0	1	.063	4	15	0	1.000
1978—Philadelphia	Nat.		3B	4	15	1	3	2	0	0	1	.200	3	18	2	.913
1980—Philadelphia	Nat.		3B	5	24	1	5	1	0	0	1	.208	3	17	1	.952
1983—Philadelphia	Nat.		3B	4	15	5	7	2	0	1	2	.467	6	7	1	.929
Championship Series Totals				20	83	10	20	7	0	1	7	.241	20	66	5	.945

WORLD SERIES RECORD

Tied World Series record for fewest chances accepted by third baseman, game (0), October 21, 1980.

Year	Club	League	Pos.	G	AB	R	H	2B	3B	HR	RBI	B.A.	PO	A	E	F.A.
1980—Philadelphia	Nat.		3B	6	21	6	8	1	0	2	7	.381	9	8	0	1.000
1983—Philadelphia	Nat.		3B	5	20	0	1	0	0	0	0	.050	1	10	1	.917
World Series Totals				11	41	6	9	1	0	2	7	.220	10	18	1	.966

ALL-STAR GAME RECORD

Year	League	Pos.	AB	R	H	2B	3B	HR	RBI	B.A.	PO	A	E	F.A.
1974—National		PH-3B	0	1	0	0	0	0	0	.000	0	1	0	1.000
1976—National		3B	1	0	0	0	0	0	0	.000	0	0	0	.000
1977—National		PR	0	0	0	0	0	0	0	.000	0	0	0	.000
1979—National		3B	3	2	2	1	1	0	1	.667	1	1	1	.667
1981—National		3B	4	1	2	1	0	1	2	.500	0	2	1	.667
1982—National		3B	1	0	0	0	0	0	0	.000	0	0	0	.000
1983—National		3B	3	0	0	0	0	0	0	.000	0	0	1	.000
All-Star Game Totals			12	4	4	2	1	1	3	.333	1	4	3	.625

Named to National League All-Star Team in 1980; replaced due to injury by Ray Knight.

RICHARD CRAIG SCHOFIELD
(Dick)

Born November 21, 1962, at Springfield, Ill.
Height, 5.10. Weight, 175.
Throws and bats righthanded.
Son of John Richard (Dick) Schofield, infielder with St. Louis Cardinals, Pittsburgh, San Francisco, New York Yankees, Los Angeles Dodgers, Boston and Milwaukee Brewers, 1953 through 1971.
Led Pioneer League in bases on balls received with 68 in 1981.
Received reported $100,000 bonus to sign with California Angels, 1981.

Year	Club	League	Pos.	G.	AB.	R.	H.	2B.	3B.	HR.	RBI.	B.A.	PO.	A.	E.	F.A.
1981—Idaho Falls		Pion.	★SS-2B	66	226	59	63	10	1	6	31	.279	★102	201	22	.932
1982—Danville		Midw.	SS	92	308	80	111	21	★10	12	53	★.360	129	249	23	.943
1982—Redwood		Calif.	SS	33	102	15	25	3	3	1	8	.245	35	103	3	.979
1982—Spokane		P. C.	SS-3B	7	30	4	9	4	1	1	12	.300	7	20	0	1.000
1983—Edmonton		P. C.	SS-3B	139	521	91	148	30	7	16	94	.284	220	402	30	.954
1983—California		Amer.	SS	21	54	4	11	2	0	3	4	.204	24	67	7	.929
Major League Totals				21	54	4	11	2	0	3	4	.204	24	67	7	.929

Selected by California Angels' organization in 1st round (third player selected) of free-agent draft, June 8, 1981.

DAVID LAWRENCE SCHOPPEE
Name pronounced Show-pay.
(Dave)

Born April 24, 1957, at Bangor, Me.
Height, 6.03. Weight, 205.
Throws and bats righthanded.
Led International League in intentional bases on balls issued with 9 in 1983 and tied for lead with 9 in 1982.
Led International League in games finished in relief with 38 and saves with 15 in 1982.
Led Eastern League in saves with 19 in 1980 and 22 in 1981.
Led Eastern League in games finished in relief with 48 in 1981.

Year	Club	League	G.	IP.	W.	L.	Pct.	H.	R.	ER.	SO.	BB.	ERA.
1975—Elmira		NYP	14	46	1	7	.125	59	39	23	28	32	4.50
1976—Elmira		NYP	12	51	4	2	.667	44	28	19	33	33	3.35
1977—Winter Haven		Florida St.	27	96	5	11	.313	108	75	51	40	55	4.78
1978—Kinston†		Carolina	24	87	4	8	.333	81	47	33	42	42	3.41
1979—Winston-Salem		Carolina	37	62	3	4	.429	50	23	17	47	14	2.47
1980—Bristol		Eastern	55	92	8	2	.800	85	33	27	50	41	2.64
1981—Bristol		Eastern	56	92	8	3	.727	71	21	18	70	42	1.76
1982—Pawtucket‡		Int'national	54	66⅓	4	6	.400	68	28	24	34	27	3.26
1983—Pawtucket§		Int'national	41	65⅔	3	2	.600	77	60	48	32	57	6.58

Selected by Boston Red Sox' organization in 16th round of free-agent draft, June 4, 1975.
†On disabled list, August 15 to September 29, 1978.
‡Appeared in one game as first baseman with no chances.
§On disabled list, May 6 to May 20, 1983.

ALFRED WILLIAM SCHROEDER III
Name pronounced SHRO-der.
(Bill)

Born September 7, 1958, at Baltimore, Md.
Height, 6.02. Weight, 210.
Throws and bats righthanded.
Attended Clemson University, Clemson, S. C.
Led Pacific Coast League in passed balls with 13 in 1983.
Led Pacific Coast League batters in strikeouts with 136 and game-winning RBIs with 15 in 1982.
Led California League batters in strikeouts with 141 in 1980.
Led Pioneer League in total bases with 170 in 1979.
Led California League catchers in total chances with 759 in 1980.

Year	Club	League	Pos.	G.	AB.	R.	H.	2B.	3B.	HR.	RBI.	B.A.	PO.	A.	E.	F.A.
1979—Butte		Pion.	C-1B	65	242	73	86	16	7	18	77	.355	474	50	9	.983
1980—Stockton		Calif.	★C-1B	123	437	68	117	20	3	18	97	.268	669	96	7	★.991
1981—El Paso		Texas	C-OF	95	335	41	87	20	2	15	61	.260	511	49	10	.982
1982—Vancouver		P. C.	C	116	425	66	113	16	3	22	77	.266	569	77	7	★.989
1983—Vancouver		P. C.	C	82	304	51	87	13	3	20	70	.286	399	68	6	★.987
1983—Milwaukee		Amer.	C	23	73	7	13	2	1	3	7	.178	92	5	2	.980
Major League Totals				23	73	7	13	2	1	3	7	.178	92	5	2	.980

Selected by Milwaukee Brewers' organization in 8th round of free-agent draft, June 5, 1979.

KENNETH MARVIN SCHROM
(Ken)

Born November 23, 1954, at Grangeville, Ida.
Height, 6.02. Weight, 195.
Throws and bats righthanded.
Attended University of Idaho, Moscow, Ida.
Tied for Texas League lead in home runs allowed with 24 in 1978.

Year—Club	League	G.	IP.	W.	L.	Pct.	H.	R.	ER.	SO.	BB.	ERA.
1976—Idaho Falls	Pioneer	16	48	1	5	.167	42	31	20	46	32	3.75
1977—Quad Cities	Midwest	16	44	3	1	.750	22	10	7	40	20	1.43
1977—Salinas	California	15	21	1	1	.500	22	8	8	22	11	3.43
1977—El Paso	Texas	10	18	1	0	1.000	14	4	4	7	8	2.00
1978—El Paso	Texas	33	165	9	6	.600	180	93	86	126	52	4.69
1979—El Paso	Texas	25	168	7	8	.467	204	111	97	107	75	5.20
1979—Salt Lake City	P. Coast	3	4	0	0	.000	3	0	0	3	3	0.00
1980—Salt Lake City†	P. Coast	14	23	0	1	.000	32	25	20	11	17	7.83
1980—Syracuse	Int'national	26	46	0	2	.000	41	19	17	32	20	3.33
1980—Toronto	American	17	31	1	0	1.000	32	18	18	13	19	5.23
1981—Syracuse	Int'national	42	104	4	6	.400	86	44	43	72	41	3.72
1982—Syracuse	Int'national	27	98	4	5	.444	102	61	56	49	41	5.14
1982—Toronto‡	American	6	15⅓	1	0	1.000	13	11	10	8	15	5.87
1983—Toledo	Int'national	5	31⅔	3	1	.750	30	19	16	20	14	4.55
1983—Minnesota§	American	33	196⅓	15	8	.652	196	92	81	80	80	3.71
Major League Totals		56	242⅔	17	8	.680	241	121	109	101	114	4.04

Selected by Minnesota Twins' organization in 10th round of free-agent draft, June 5, 1973.

Selected by California Angels' organization in 17th round of free-agent draft, June 8, 1976.

†Traded to Toronto Blue Jays' organization, June 10, 1980, completing deal in which Toronto traded Pitcher Dave Lemanczyk to California Angels for a player to be named later, June 3, 1980.

‡Released, August 30, 1982; signed by Minnesota Twins' organization, December 1, 1982.

§Appeared in one game as a pinch-runner.

RICK SPENCER SCHU
(Rich)

Born January 26, 1962, at Philadelphia, Pa.
Height, 6.00. Weight, 170.
Throws and bats righthanded.
Attended Sacramento City College, Sacramento, Calif.

Year—Club	League	Pos.	G.	AB.	R.	H.	2B.	3B.	HR.	RBI.	B.A.	PO.	A.	E.	F.A.
1981—Bend	N'west	3B-2B-SS	68	258	41	69	10	0	2	42	.267	55	137	24	.889
1982—Spartanburg	S. Atl.	3B-2B-SS	125	429	78	117	28	1	12	60	.273	157	257	45	.902
1983—Peninsula	Carol.	3B-SS-2B	122	444	69	119	22	3	14	63	.268	82	252	30	.918
1983—Portland	P. C.	3B-SS	9	29	7	11	2	1	1	3	.379	6	12	2	.900

Signed as free agent by Philadelphia Phillies' organization, November 25, 1980.

DONALD ARTHUR SCHULZE
Name pronounced SHULL-zee.
(Don)

Born September 27, 1962, at Roselle, Ill.
Height, 6.04. Weight, 230.
Throws and bats righthanded.

Led Gulf Coast League in complete games with 3 in 1980.
Tied for American Association lead in shutouts with 2 in 1983.

Year—Club	League	G.	IP.	W.	L.	Pct.	H.	R.	ER.	SO.	BB.	ERA.
1980—Sarasota Cubs	Gulf Coast	12	66	2	7	.222	58	38	30	30	36	4.09
1981—Quad Cities†	Midwest	17	105	8	5	.615	89	33	27	61	51	2.31
1982—Salinas	California	24	165	13	7	.650	150	61	52	122	59	2.84
1983—Iowa	Am. Assoc.	25	168⅔	11	9	.550	170	88	80	103	63	4.27
1983—Chicago	National	4	14	0	1	.000	19	11	11	8	7	7.07
Major League Totals		4	14	0	1	.000	19	11	11	8	7	7.07

Selected by Chicago Cubs' organization in 1st round (11th player selected) of free-agent draft, June 3, 1980.

†On disabled list, June 22 to July 16, 1981.

MICHAEL LORRI SCIOSCIA
Name pronounced SO-sha.
(Mike)

Born November 27, 1958, at Upper Darby, Pa.
Height, 6.02. Weight, 200.
Throws right and bats lefthanded.
Attends Pennsylvania State University, University Park, Pa.

Led National League in passed balls with 11 in 1981.
Led Pacific Coast League catchers in double plays with 19 and passed balls with 22 in 1979.
Led Midwest League catchers in errors with 20 and double plays with 12 in 1978.
Tied for Pacific Coast League lead in being hit by pitch with 7 in 1979.

Year—Club	League	Pos.	G.	AB.	R.	H.	2B.	3B.	HR.	RBI.	B.A.	PO.	A.	E.	F.A.
1976—Bellingham	N'west.	C	46	151	25	42	6	0	7	26	.278	202	35	14	.944
1977—Clinton	Midw.	C-1B	121	364	58	92	20	1	7	44	.253	764	95	22	.975
1978—San Antonio†	Texas	C	58	204	29	61	16	0	2	34	.299	214	17	4	.983
1979—Albuquerque	P. C.	C	143	461	80	155	34	0	3	68	.336	★690	★86	★15	.981
1980—Albuquerque	P. C.	C	52	160	33	53	11	1	3	33	.331	207	19	5	.978
1980—Los Angeles‡	Nat.	C-3B	54	134	8	34	5	1	1	8	.254	226	26	2	.992
1981—Los Angeles	Nat.	C	93	290	27	80	10	0	2	29	.276	493	48	7	.987

Year	Club	League	Pos.	G.	AB.	R.	H.	2B.	3B.	HR.	RBI.	B.A.	PO.	A.	E.	F.A.
1982—Los Angeles	....	Nat.	C	129	365	31	80	11	1	5	38	.219	631	57	10	.986
1983—Los Angeles§	....	Nat.	C	12	35	3	11	3	0	1	7	.314	55	4	0	1.000
Major League Totals	....			288	824	69	205	29	2	9	82	.249	1405	135	19	.988

Selected by Los Angeles Dodgers' organization in 1st round (19th player selected) of free-agent draft, June 8, 1976.
†On disabled list, May 19 to August 4, 1978.
‡On disabled list, April 10 to April 20, 1980.
§On supplemental disabled list, May 15, 1983; transferred to emergency disabled list, August 8, 1983 through remainder of season.

DIVISION SERIES RECORD

Year	Club	League	Pos.	G.	AB.	R.	H.	2B.	3B.	HR.	RBI.	B.A.	PO.	A.	E.	F.A.
1981—Los Angeles	....	Nat.	C	4	13	0	2	0	0	0	1	.154	21	3	0	1.000

CHAMPIONSHIP SERIES RECORD

Year	Club	League	Pos.	G.	AB.	R.	H.	2B.	3B.	HR.	RBI.	B.A.	PO.	A.	E.	F.A.
1981—Los Angeles	....	Nat.	C	5	15	1	2	0	0	1	1	.133	27	1	0	1.000

WORLD SERIES RECORD

Year	Club	League	Pos.	G.	AB.	R.	H.	2B.	3B.	HR.	RBI.	B.A.	PO.	A.	E.	F.A.
1981—Los Angeles	....	Nat.	C-PH	3	4	1	1	0	0	0	0	.250	7	1	0	1.000

DARYL ANTHONY SCONIERS
Name pronounced SCON-yers.

Born October 3, 1958, at San Bernardino, Calif.
Height, 6.02. Weight, 185.
Throws and bats lefthanded.
Attended Orange Coast College, Costa Mesa, Calif.

Tied American League record for most home runs by pinch-hitter, consecutive at-bats (2), April 30, May 7, 1983.
Led Texas League in total bases with 296 in 1980.
Led Midwest League first basemen in double plays with 106 in 1978.

Year	Club	League	Pos.	G.	AB.	R.	H.	2B.	3B.	HR.	RBI.	B.A.	PO.	A.	E.	F.A.
1977—Idaho Falls	....	Pion.	1B	49	158	34	49	10	1	0	24	.310	343	19	7	.961
1978—Quad Cities	....	Midw.	1B	126	466	88	133	★35	7	19	86	.285	★1194	52	16	.987
1979—Salinas†	....	Calif.	1B	108	365	60	105	17	6	11	50	.288	804	42	7	★.992
1980—El Paso	....	Texas	1B	●136	506	95	★187	★48	8	15	87	★.370	887	46	●16	.983
1981—Salt Lake City	....	P. C.	1B	108	410	91	145	24	8	13	74	.354	866	36	6	.993
1981—California	....	Amer.	1B	15	52	6	14	1	1	1	7	.269	95	8	0	1.000
1982—California	....	Amer.	1B	12	13	0	2	0	0	0	2	.154	23	1	0	1.000
1982—Spokane‡	....	P. C.	1B	98	383	64	126	33	10	5	73	.329	842	32	11	.988
1983—California	....	Amer.	1B-OF	106	314	49	86	19	3	8	46	.274	473	23	8	.984
Major League Totals	....			133	379	55	102	20	4	9	55	.269	591	32	8	.987

Selected by California Angels' organization in 3rd round of free-agent draft, January 11, 1977.
†On temporary inactive list, April 6 to May 9, 1979.
‡On suspended list, April 27 to May 12, 1982.

ANTHONY SCOTT
(Tony)

Born September 18, 1951, at Cincinnati, O.
Height, 6.00. Weight, 175.
Throws right and bats right and lefthanded.

Tied for Eastern League lead in caught stealing with 11 in 1972.
Tied for New York-Pennsylvania League lead in caught stealing with 6 in 1971.

Year	Club	League	Pos.	G.	AB.	R.	H.	2B.	3B.	HR.	RBI.	B.A.	PO.	A.	E.	F.A.
1969—Bradenton Expos	.Gulf C.		OF	38	95	13	17	1	2	0	7	.179	53	6	5	.922
1970—W. Palm Beach	....	Fla. St.	OF	3	2	0	1	0	0	0	0	.500	1	0	0	1.000
1970—Watertown	....	North.	OF	63	243	41	61	9	2	10	46	.251	108	★12	9	.930
1971—W. Palm Beach	....	Fla. St.	OF	47	84	21	19	3	2	1	9	.226	28	2	1	.968
1971—Jamestown	....	NYP	OF	69	258	41	68	13	3	2	22	.264	★173	8	6	.968
1972—Quebec City	....	East.	OF	135	412	47	88	9	0	2	39	.214	296	15	14	.957
1973—Quebec City	....	East.	OF	128	379	48	97	14	4	5	38	.256	231	21	4	.984
1973—Montreal	....	Nat.	OF	11	1	2	0	0	0	0	0	.000	0	0	1	.000
1974—Quebec City	....	East.	OF	109	359	76	102	8	4	10	38	.284	193	5	4	★.980
1974—Memphis	....	Int.	OF	11	6	2	0	0	0	0	0	.000	0	0	0	.000
1974—Montreal	....	Nat.	OF	19	7	2	2	0	0	0	1	.286	7	0	0	1.000
1975—Montreal	....	Nat.	OF	92	143	19	26	4	2	0	11	.182	94	6	4	.962
1976—Denver†	....	A. A.	OF	106	328	63	102	21	9	8	45	.311	162	7	0	1.000
1977—St. Louis‡	....	Nat.	OF	95	292	38	85	16	3	3	41	.291	223	5	1	.996
1978—St. Louis	....	Nat.	OF	96	219	28	50	5	2	1	14	.228	100	6	6	.946
1979—St. Louis	....	Nat.	OF	153	587	69	152	22	10	6	68	.259	427	14	7	.984
1980—St. Louis	....	Nat.	OF	143	415	51	104	19	3	0	28	.251	324	5	1	★.997
1981—St. Louis§-Hou.x	...	Nat.	OF	100	401	49	106	18	4	4	39	.264	247	7	2	.992
1982—Houston	....	Nat.	OF	132	460	43	110	16	3	1	29	.239	262	7	5	.982
1983—Houston	....	Nat.	OF	80	186	20	42	6	1	2	17	.226	89	2	0	1.000
Major League Totals	....			921	2711	321	677	106	28	17	248	.250	1773	52	27	.985

Selected by Montreal Expos' organization in 48th round of free-agent draft, June 5, 1969.

†Traded with Pitcher Steve Dunning and Infielder Pat Scanlon by Montreal Expos to St. Louis Cardinals for Pitchers Bill Greif and Angel Torres and Outfielder Sam Mejias, November 6, 1976.
‡On disabled list, August 19 to October 4, 1977.
§Traded to Houston Astros for Pitcher Joaquin Andujar, June 7, 1981.
xGranted free agency, November 13, 1981; re-signed by Astros, January 21, 1982.

DIVISION SERIES RECORD

Year Club	League	Pos.	G.	AB.	R.	H.	2B.	3B.	HR.	RBI.	B.A.	PO.	A.	E.	F.A.
1981—Houston	Nat.	OF	5	20	0	3	0	0	0	2	.150	9	0	0	1.000

DONALD MALCOLM SCOTT
(Donnie)

Born August 16, 1961, at Dunedin, Fla.
Height, 5.11. Weight, 185.
Throws right and bats left and righthanded.

Led American Association in passed balls with 22 in 1983.
Led Texas League in passed balls with 21 in 1982.
Led South Atlantic League in passed balls with 41 and tied for lead in double plays by catchers with 7 in 1980.

Year Club	League	Pos.	G.	AB.	R.	H.	2B.	3B.	HR.	RBI.	B.A.	PO.	A.	E.	F.A.
1979—Sarasota Rang.	Gulf C.	★C-OF	45	146	18	45	7	1	1	29	.308	190	19	4	★.981
1980—Asheville	S. Atl.	C	115	421	57	124	22	1	13	78	.295	593	★81	17	.975
1981—Tulsa	Texas	C-3B-OF	114	385	44	91	16	2	5	41	.236	509	103	19	.970
1982—Tulsa	Texas	★C-3B	108	367	55	104	19	3	12	61	.283	537	75	★21	.967
1983—Oklahoma City	A. A.	C	112	371	44	94	14	3	4	54	.253	596	★74	12	.982
1983—Texas	Amer.	C	2	4	0	0	0	0	0	0	.000	8	2	0	1.000
Major League Totals			2	4	0	0	0	0	0	0	.000	8	2	0	1.000

Selected by Texas Rangers' organization in 2nd round of free-agent draft, June 5, 1979.

MICHAEL WARREN SCOTT
(Mike)

Born April 26, 1955, at Santa Monica, Calif.
Height, 6.03. Weight, 215.
Throws and bats righthanded.
Attended Pepperdine University, Malibu, Calif.

Led Texas League in complete games with 14 and tied for lead in balks with 3 in 1977.
Tied for International League lead in games started by pitchers with 29 in 1978 and balks with 3 in 1980.

Year Club	League	G.	IP.	W.	L.	Pct.	H.	R.	ER.	SO.	BB.	ERA.
1976—Jackson	Texas	7	44	3	3	.500	34	20	14	19	14	2.86
1977—Jackson	Texas	25	★187	★14	10	.583	132	77	61	97	55	2.94
1977—Tidewater	Int'national	2	2	0	1	.000	4	5	4	0	3	18.00
1978—Tidewater	Int'national	29	192	10	10	.500	196	105	84	93	83	3.94
1979—Tidewater	Int'national	18	99	8	4	.667	103	37	35	40	27	3.18
1979—New York	National	18	52	1	3	.250	59	35	31	21	20	5.37
1980—Tidewater	Int'national	27	170	13	7	.650	165	69	56	88	64	2.96
1980—New York	National	6	29	1	1	.500	40	14	14	13	8	4.34
1981—New York	National	23	136	5	10	.333	130	65	59	54	34	3.90
1982—New York†	National	37	147	7	13	.350	185	100	84	63	60	5.14
1983—Houston‡	National	24	145	10	6	.625	143	67	60	73	46	3.72
Major League Totals		108	509	24	33	.421	557	281	248	224	168	4.39

Selected by New York Mets' organization in 2nd round of free-agent draft, June 8, 1976.
†Traded to Houston Astros for Outfielder-First Baseman Danny Heep, December 10, 1982.
‡On disabled list, April 5 to May 4, 1983.

JAMES DEAN SCRANTON
(Jim)

Born April 5, 1960, at Torrance, Calif.
Height, 6.00. Weight, 185.
Throws and bats righthanded.
Attended Palomar College, San Marcos, Calif., and
University of Arizona, Tucson, Ariz.

Led Southern League shortstops in double plays with 76 in 1982.
Led Florida State League second basemen in double plays with 65 in 1981.
Led South Atlantic League shortstops in fielding percentage with .952 in 1980.

Year Club	League	Pos.	G.	AB.	R.	H.	2B.	3B.	HR.	RBI.	B.A.	PO.	A.	E.	F.A.
1980—Charleston	S. Atl.	SS-2B-OF	121	450	69	114	16	3	2	33	.253	227	341	28	.953
1981—Ft. Myers	Fla. St.	SS	107	355	37	76	6	1	2	32	.214	★206	★346	30	.949
1982—Jacksonville	South.	SS	128	413	44	97	7	4	0	41	.235	★210	364	26	★.957
1983—Jacksonville	South.	SS	141	450	43	98	10	1	2	31	.218	211	469	★40	.944

Selected by Oakland A's organization in 14th round of free-agent draft, June 6, 1978.
Signed as free agent by Kansas City Royals' organization, February 27, 1980.

RODNEY GRANT SCURRY

Name pronounced SKUR-ee.

(Rod)

Born March 17, 1956, at Sacramento, Calif.
Height, 6.02. Weight, 180.
Throws and bats lefthanded.

Pitched seven-inning, 2-0 no-hit victory against Richmond, July 25, 1977.
Major League saves: 1981 (7), 1982 (14), 1983 (7). Total—28.
Led Carolina League pitchers in games started with 26 in 1975.
Led New York-Pennsylvania League in hit batsmen with 7 in 1974.

Year Club	League	G.	IP.	W.	L.	Pct.	H.	R.	ER.	SO.	BB.	ERA.
1974—Niagara Falls	NYP	14	89	5	6	.455	55	36	34	102	*74	3.44
1975—Salem	Carolina	26	150	9	12	.429	128	79	61	143	118	3.66
1976—Shreveport	Texas	24	123	8	8	.500	120	71	53	83	83	3.88
1977—Shreveport	Texas	18	113	3	11	.214	97	54	36	111	48	2.87
1977—Columbus	Int'national	8	37	3	2	.600	30	31	19	39	32	4.62
1978—Columbus†	Int'national	16	63	3	3	.500	69	44	40	57	43	5.71
1978—Shreveport	Texas	5	29	1	4	.200	27	19	15	38	24	4.66
1979—Portland‡	P. Coast	35	122	5	5	.500	121	64	56	94	72	4.13
1980—Pittsburgh	National	20	38	0	2	.000	23	12	9	28	17	2.13
1981—Pittsburgh	National	27	74	4	5	.444	74	33	31	65	40	3.77
1982—Pittsburgh	National	76	103⅔	4	5	.444	79	26	20	94	64	1.74
1983—Pittsburgh	National	61	68	4	9	.308	63	45	42	67	53	5.56
Major League Totals		184	283⅔	12	21	.364	239	116	102	254	174	3.24

Selected by Pittsburgh Pirates' organization in 1st round (11th player selected) of free-agent draft, June 5, 1974.
†On disabled list, June 12 to July 11, 1978.
‡On disabled list, August 4 to August 14, 1979.

GEORGE THOMAS SEAVER

(Tom)

Born November 17, 1944, at Fresno, Calif.
Height, 6.01. Weight, 210.
Throws and bats righthanded.
Attended Fresno City College, Fresno, Calif., and received bachelor of science degree in public relations from
University of Southern California, Los Angeles, Calif. in 1974.
Son of Charles Seaver, former U.S. Walker Cup golfer.

Established major league records for most seasons, 200 or more strikeouts (10); most consecutive seasons, 200 or more strikeouts (9), 1968 through 1976; most consecutive strikeouts, game (10), April 22, 1970.
Tied major league records for most strikeouts game (19), April 22, 1970; most times pitched opening game of season (14).
Established National League records for lowest earned run average, 200 or more games won, lifetime (2.73); most strikeouts, by righthanded pitcher, lifetime (3,272).
Tied National League record for most season opening games won, lifetime (6).
Pitched 4-0 no-hit victory against St. Louis Cardinals, June 16, 1978.
Led National League in shutouts with 7 in 1977.
Tied for National League lead in shutouts with 5 in 1979.
Tied for National League lead in complete games with 18 in 1973.
Led International League pitchers in games started with 32 in 1966.
Named National League Pitcher of the Year by The Sporting News, 1969 and 1975.
Won National League Cy Young Memorial Award, 1969, 1973 and 1975.
Named National League Rookie of the Year by Baseball Writers' Association of America, 1967.
Named righthanded pitcher on The Sporting News National League All-Star Team, 1969, 1973, 1975 and 1981.

Year Club	League	G.	IP.	W.	L.	Pct.	H.	R.	ER.	SO.	BB.	ERA.
1966—Jacksonville	Int'national	34	210	12	12	.500	184	87	73	188	66	3.13
1967—New York	National	35	251	16	13	.552	224	85	77	170	78	2.76
1968—New York	National	36	278	16	12	.571	224	73	68	205	48	2.20
1969—New York	National	36	273	*25	7	*.781	202	75	67	208	82	2.21
1970—New York	National	37	291	18	12	.600	230	103	91	*283	83	*2.81
1971—New York	National	36	286	20	10	.667	210	61	56	*289	61	*1.76
1972—New York	National	35	262	21	12	.636	215	92	85	249	77	2.92
1973—New York	National	36	290	19	10	.655	219	74	67	*251	64	*2.08
1974—New York	National	32	236	11	11	.500	199	89	84	201	75	3.20
1975—New York	National	36	280	*22	9	.710	217	81	74	*243	88	2.38
1976—New York	National	35	271	14	11	.560	211	83	78	*235	77	2.59
1977—New York†-Cincinnati	National	33	261	21	6	.778	199	78	75	196	66	2.59
1978—Cincinnati	National	36	260	16	14	.533	218	97	83	226	89	2.87
1979—Cincinnati	National	32	215	16	6	*.727	187	85	75	131	61	3.14
1980—Cincinnati‡	National	26	168	10	8	.556	140	74	68	101	59	3.64
1981—Cincinnati	National	23	166	*14	2	*.875	120	51	47	87	66	2.55
1982—Cincinnati§	National	21	111⅓	5	13	.278	136	75	68	62	44	5.50
1983—New York	National	34	231	9	14	.391	201	104	91	135	86	3.55
Major League Totals		559	4130⅓	273	170	.616	3352	1380	1254	3272	1204	2.73

Selected by Los Angeles Dodgers' organization in 22nd round of free-agent draft, June, 1965.
Signed by Atlanta Braves to Richmond contract for reported $40,000 bonus, February, 1966; subsequently, Commissioner William Eckert nullified the contract because the signing violated the college rule. However, since the University of Southern California then declared Seaver ineligible, Eckert decreed that any club other than the Braves which was willing to match terms of his Richmond contract would be eligible to draw for negotiation rights. Cleveland

Indians, Philadelphia Phillies and New York Mets expressed that willingness, and Eckert drew the name of the Mets in a special drawing, April 3, 1966; Mets then signed Seaver to Jacksonville contract for reported $50,000 bonus.

†Traded to Cincinnati Reds for Infielder Doug Flynn, Pitcher Pat Zachry and Outfielders Dan Norman and Steve Henderson, June 15, 1977.

‡On disabled list, July 1 to August 4, 1980.

§Traded to New York Mets for Pitcher Charlie Puleo, Catcher Lloyd McClendon and Outfielder Jason Felice, December 16, 1982.

CHAMPIONSHIP SERIES RECORD

Established Championship Series record for most strikeouts, five-game Series (17), 1973.

Year	Club	League	G.	IP.	W.	L.	Pct.	H.	R.	ER.	SO.	BB.	ERA.
1969	New York	National	1	7	1	0	1.000	8	5	5	2	3	6.43
1973	New York	National	2	16⅔	1	1	.500	13	4	3	17	5	1.62
1979	Cincinnati	National	1	8	0	0	.000	5	2	2	5	2	2.25
	Championship Series Totals		4	31⅔	2	1	.667	26	11	10	24	10	2.84

WORLD SERIES RECORD

Year	Club	League	G.	IP.	W.	L.	Pct.	H.	R.	ER.	SO.	BB.	ERA.
1969	New York	National	2	15	1	1	.500	12	5	5	9	3	3.00
1973	New York	National	2	15	0	1	.000	13	4	4	18	3	2.40
	World Series Totals		4	30	1	2	.333	25	9	9	27	6	2.70

ALL-STAR GAME RECORD

Year	League	IP.	W.	L.	Pct.	H.	R.	ER.	SO.	BB.	ERA.
1967	National	1	0	0	.000	0	0	0	1	1	0.00
1968	National	2	0	0	.000	2	0	0	5	0	0.00
1970	National	3	0	0	.000	1	0	0	4	0	0.00
1973	National	1	0	0	.000	0	0	0	1	0	0.00
1975	National	1	0	0	.000	2	3	3	2	1	27.00
1976	National	2	0	0	.000	2	1	1	1	0	4.50
1977	National	2	0	0	.000	4	3	2	2	1	9.00
1981	National	1	0	0	.000	3	1	1	1	0	9.00
	All-Star Game Totals	13	0	0	.000	14	8	7	16	4	4.85

Member of National League All-Star Team for 1969, 1971, 1972 and 1978 games; did not play.

HERMAN NEILS SEGELKE

Name pronounced Suh-GELL-kee.

Born April 24, 1958, at San Mateo, Calif.
Height, 6.04. Weight, 215.
Throws and bats righthanded.
Led Pacific Coast League in wild pitches with 20 in 1983.

Year	Club	League	G.	IP.	W.	L.	Pct.	H.	R.	ER.	SO.	BB.	ERA.
1976	Bradenton Cubs	Gulf Coast	8	45	3	2	.600	33	16	11	31	26	2.20
1977	Pompano Beach†	Florida St.	24	117	13	8	.619	128	69	58	60	48	4.46
1978	Midland	Texas	24	143	8	8	.500	159	92	73	58	95	4.59
1979	Midland	Texas	29	*184	13	8	.619	227	116	107	81	83	5.23
1980	Midland	Texas	47	129	7	10	.412	155	92	68	88	63	4.74
1981	Iowa	Am. Assoc.	38	107	5	7	.417	141	81	71	65	47	5.97
1982	Chicago	National	3	4⅓	0	0	.000	6	4	4	4	6	8.31
1982	Iowa‡	Am. Assoc.	27	117	7	9	.438	131	88	77	64	76	5.92
1983	Phoenix	P. Coast	34	114	6	9	.400	155	125	91	51	70	7.18
	Major League Totals		3	4⅓	0	0	.000	6	4	4	4	6	8.31

Selected by Chicago Cubs' organization in 1st round (seventh player selected) of free-agent draft, June 8, 1976.

†On disabled list, April 14 to April 24, 1977.

‡Traded to San Francisco Giants for Pitcher Al Hargesheimer, October 15, 1982.

STEVE LEONARD SENTENEY

Born August 7, 1957, at Indianapolis, Ind.
Height, 6.02. Weight, 205.
Throws and bats righthanded.
Attended St. Mary's College, Moraga, Calif.

Year	Club	League	G.	IP.	W.	L.	Pct.	H.	R.	ER.	SO.	BB.	ERA.
1979	Medicine Hat	Pioneer	26	64	2	5	.286	51	29	22	79	29	3.09
1980	Kinston	Carolina	54	85	4	4	.500	71	31	20	66	48	2.12
1981	Knoxville	Southern	46	106	10	5	.667	87	50	37	93	43	3.14
1982	Syracuse	Int'national	44	96	4	8	.333	73	32	26	98	42	2.44
1982	Toronto†	American	11	22	0	0	.000	23	16	12	20	6	4.91
1983	Tidewater‡	Int'national	20	34⅓	0	3	.000	25	12	11	39	20	2.88
1983	Hawaii	P. Coast	25	51⅔	4	4	.500	54	30	27	55	19	4.70
	Major League Totals		11	22	0	0	.000	23	16	12	20	6	4.91

Signed as free agent by Toronto Blue Jays' organization, June 22, 1979.

†Traded to New York Mets for Outfielder Jorge Orta, February 4, 1983.

‡Traded with Outfielder Marvell Wynne to Pittsburgh Pirates for Catcher Junior Ortiz and Pitcher Arthur Ray, June 14, 1983.

JIMMY DALE SEXTON

Born December 15, 1951, at Mobile, Ala.
Height, 5.10. Weight, 175.
Throws and bats righthanded.

Established major league record for most stolen bases with no caught stealing, season (16), 1982.
Led Texas League in stolen bases with 48 and being hit by pitch with 11 in 1975.
Led Pacific Coast League second basemen in errors with 20 in 1980.
Led Eastern League third basemen in fielding percentage with .943 in 1974.
Led Carolina League second basemen in errors with 32 in 1973.

Year Club	League	Pos.	G.	AB.	R.	H.	2B.	3B.	HR.	RBI.	B.A.	PO.	A.	E.	F.A.
1970—Bradenton Pir.....	Gulf C.	SS-2B-3B	33	113	17	32	2	0	0	7	.283	40	68	12	.900
1971—Bradenton Pir.....	Gulf C.	3B-2B-SS	35	119	23	29	2	1	0	11	.244	45	54	1	.990
1972—Niagara Falls.......	NYP	SS	69	212	41	61	2	3	0	23	.288	86	178	13	*.953
1973—Salem................	Carol.	2B-SS	124	446	86	120	17	3	3	39	.269	240	323	33	.945
1974—Thetford Mines....	East.	3B-SS-2B	115	350	53	87	14	1	3	32	.249	97	197	18	.942
1975—Shreveport...........	Tex.	SS	103	383	82	105	23	5	3	28	.274	148	279	34	.926
1976—Shreveport...........	Tex.	SS	59	207	43	67	14	2	4	30	.324	76	159	21	.918
1976—Charleston†..........	Int.	2B-SS	49	154	21	42	8	1	3	12	.273	85	109	6	.970
1977—San Jose‡§............	P. C.	SS-2B	89	305	63	78	13	5	2	23	.256	152	271	13	.970
1977—Seattle x................	Amer.	SS	14	37	5	8	1	1	1	3	.216	12	40	4	.929
1978—Houston.................	Nat.	SS-3B-2B	88	141	17	29	3	2	2	6	.206	62	104	5	.971
1979—Houston.................	Nat.	SS-3B-2B	52	43	8	9	0	0	0	1	.209	11	24	2	.946
1980—Tucson y	P. C.	2B-SS	113	446	81	132	18	6	1	33	.296	237	390	24	.963
1981—Tacoma.................	P. C.	SS-2B	103	385	75	123	16	8	4	35	.319	138	291	21	.953
1981—Oakland.................	Amer.	3B	7	3	3	0	0	0	0	0	.000	0	3	0	1.000
1982—Oakland.................	Amer.	SS-3B	69	139	19	34	4	0	2	14	.245	63	118	9	.953
1982—Tacoma.................	P. C.	SS-2B	24	100	20	31	4	0	2	6	.310	47	70	6	.951
1983—Oakland za............	Amer.						(Did not play)								
1983—Den. b-Lou...........	A. A.	3B-SS-1B	36	130	19	39	4	1	5	17	.300	23	40	5	.926
1983—St. Louis..............	Nat.	SS-3B	6	9	1	1	1	0	0	0	.111	4	8	0	1.000
American League Totals...........................			90	179	27	42	5	1	3	17	.235	75	161	13	.948
National League Totals.............................			146	193	26	39	4	2	2	7	.202	77	136	7	.968
Major League Totals....................................			236	372	53	81	9	3	5	24	.218	152	297	20	.957

Signed as free agent by Pittsburgh Pirates' organization, July 25, 1970.
†Traded with Infielder Craig Reynolds to Seattle Mariners for Pitcher Grant Jackson, December 7, 1976.
‡On temporary inactive list, May 10 to May 29, 1977.
§On disabled list, June 8 to June 22, 1977.
xTraded to Houston Astros for Outfielder Leon Roberts, December 5, 1977.
yTraded to Oakland A's organization for a player to be named later, February 12, 1981; Houston Astros acquired Pitcher Rick Lysander to complete deal, September 17, 1981.
zOn supplemental disabled list, April 3, 1983; transferred to disabled list, April 18 to May 20, 1983.
aReleased, June 15, 1983; signed by Denver (Chicago White Sox' organization), June 23, 1983.
bReleased, August 10, 1983; signed by Louisville (St. Louis Cardinals' organization), August 15, 1983.

THEODORE SHAW JR.
(Theo)

Born May 30, 1962, at Cook County, Ill.
Height, 6.00. Weight, 185.
Throws and bats righthanded.

Year Club	League	G.	IP.	W.	L.	Pct.	H.	R.	ER.	SO.	BB.	ERA.
1980—Sarasota Royals Gold.....................Gulf Coast		13	61	5	7	.417	61	34	23	29	24	3.39
1981—Charleston...S. Atlantic		6	30	1	2	.333	27	15	13	24	25	3.90
1981—Ft. Myers .... Florida St.		14	86	7	1	.875	66	29	20	60	49	2.09
1982—Jacksonville†................................. Southern		20	128⅔	7	5	.583	80	53	40	114	79	2.80
1983—Jacksonville..................................... Southern		16	105⅔	5	7	.417	102	60	52	68	69	4.43
1983—Omaha‡.. Am. Assoc.						(Did not play)						

Selected by Kansas City Royals' organization in 16th round of free-agent draft, June 3, 1980.
†On disabled list, July 2 to August 12, 1982.
‡On disabled list, July 3, 1983 through remainder of season.

LARRY KENT SHEETS

Born December 6, 1959, at Staunton, Va.
Height, 6.04. Weight, 210.
Throws right and bats lefthanded.

Year Club	League	Pos.	G.	AB.	R.	H.	2B.	3B.	HR.	RBI.	B.A.	PO.	A.	E.	F.A.
1978—Bluefield................	Appal.	OF-1B	67	225	32	60	9	2	11	*48	.267	121	8	4	.970
1979—Miami†....................	Fla. St.						(Did not play)								
1979—Bluefield................	Appal.	OF	3	12	2	4	2	0	0	2	.333	1	0	0	1.000
1980—Bluefield‡..............	Appal.	OF	37	124	29	47	9	1	*14	47	.379	40	3	2	.956
1980—Charlotte...............	South.	OF	13	48	1	9	4	0	0	5	.188	4	1	0	1.000
1981—Rochester§............	Int.						(Did not play)								
1982—Rochester x..........	Int.						(Did not play)								
1982—Hagerstown y	Carol.	OF	88	324	46	96	21	0	18	59	.296	123	5	6	.955
1983—Charlotte...............	South.	OF-1B	138	503	72	145	*37	3	●25	87	.288	256	15	7	.975
1983—Rochester............	Int.	OF	3	13	1	2	1	0	0	2	.154	5	0	1	.833

Selected by Baltimore Orioles' organization in 2nd round of free-agent draft, June 6, 1978.
†On suspended list, May 1 to August 29, 1979.

‡On restricted list, June 18 to June 23, 1980.
§On restricted list, April 14 to May 28 and June 18, 1981 through remainder of season.
xOn suspended list, April 13, 1982, then transferred to restricted list, April 23 to May 13, 1982.
yOn disabled list, August 23, 1982 through remainder of season.

JOHN T. SHELBY

Born February 23, 1958, at Lexington, Ky.
Height, 6.01. Weight, 175.
Throws right and bats right and lefthanded.
Attended Columbia State Community College, Columbia, Tenn.

Led Florida State League outfielders in double plays with 7 in 1979.
Led Appalachian League outfielders in double plays with 3 in 1978.

Year Club	League	Pos.	G.	AB.	R.	H.	2B.	3B.	HR.	RBI.	B.A.	PO.	A.	E.	F.A.
1977—Bluefield	Appal.	OF	60	211	28	54	9	1	0	1	.256	90	●12	7	.936
1978—Miami	Fla. St.	OF	13	26	4	6	1	0	0	3	.231	14	2	2	.889
1978—Bluefield	Appal.	OF	64	248	49	70	9	1	6	25	.282	128	★11	6	.959
1979—Miami	Fla. St.	OF	132	478	50	96	11	6	3	38	.201	★252	●22	8	.972
1980—Charlotte	South.	OF	134	★560	66	135	27	11	6	51	.241	★361	21	★16	.960
1981—Charlotte	South.	OF	62	251	40	59	11	4	2	21	.235	120	3	10	.925
1981—Rochester	Int.	OF	76	326	42	86	21	8	3	32	.264	189	8	6	.970
1981—Baltimore	Amer.	OF	7	2	2	0	0	0	0	0	.000	1	0	0	1.000
1982—Rochester	Int.	OF	133	★548	92	153	26	6	16	52	.279	331	13	8	.977
1982—Baltimore	Amer.	OF	26	35	8	11	3	0	1	2	.314	20	1	0	1.000
1983—Baltimore	Amer.	OF	126	325	52	84	15	2	5	27	.258	200	9	4	.981
Major League Totals			159	362	62	95	18	2	6	29	.262	221	10	4	.983

Selected by Baltimore Orioles' organization in 1st round (19th player selected) of free-agent draft, January 11, 1977.

CHAMPIONSHIP SERIES RECORD

Year Club	League	Pos.	G.	AB.	R.	H.	2B.	3B.	HR.	RBI.	B.A.	PO.	A.	E.	F.A.
1983—Baltimore	Amer.	OF-PH	3	9	1	2	0	0	0	0	.222	3	0	0	1.000

WORLD SERIES RECORD

Year Club	League	Pos.	G.	AB.	R.	H.	2B.	3B.	HR.	RBI.	B.A.	PO.	A.	E.	F.A.
1983—Baltimore	Amer.	PH-OF	5	9	1	4	0	0	0	1	.444	10	0	0	1.000

RONALD WAYNE SHEPHERD
(Ron)

Born October 27, 1960, at Longview, Tex.
Height, 6.04. Weight, 180.
Throws and bats righthanded.
Brother of Larry Shepherd, wide receiver at University of Houston.

Year Club	League	Pos.	G.	AB.	R.	H.	2B.	3B.	HR.	RBI.	B.A.	PO.	A.	E.	F.A.
1979—Medicine Hat	Pion.	OF	49	178	21	37	6	2	3	20	.208	92	5	8	.924
1980—Kinston	Carol.	OF	110	384	53	80	16	4	11	61	.208	239	7	●13	.950
1981—Kinston	Carol.	OF	135	486	71	114	15	3	16	66	.235	★280	9	12	.960
1982—Knoxville	South.	OF	136	482	62	119	19	8	15	65	.247	260	4	9	.967
1983—Syracuse	Int.	OF	119	404	60	110	20	3	13	62	.272	254	6	4	.985

Selected by Toronto Blue Jays' organization in 2nd round of free-agent draft, June 5, 1979.

PATRICK ARTHUR SHERIDAN
(Pat)

Born December 4, 1957, at Ann Arbor, Mich.
Height, 6.03. Weight, 180.
Throws right and bats lefthanded.
Attended Eastern Michigan University, Ypsilanti, Mich.
Son of Arthur Sheridan, minor league pitcher, 1952 through 1956.

Year Club	League	Pos.	G.	AB.	R.	H.	2B.	3B.	HR.	RBI.	B.A.	PO.	A.	E.	F.A.
1979—Ft. Myers	Fla. St.	OF	67	235	25	66	4	3	0	16	.281	142	8	1	.993
1980—Ft. Myers	Fla. St.	OF-C	20	79	17	32	1	0	1	13	.405	37	4	1	.976
1980—Jacksonville†	South.	OF	97	367	63	112	17	7	5	42	.305	201	7	9	.959
1981—Omaha‡	A. A.	OF	86	315	49	94	15	8	5	31	.298	193	2	3	.985
1981—Kansas City	Amer.	OF	3	1	0	0	0	0	0	0	.000	2	0	0	1.000
1982—Omaha§	A. A.	OF	41	135	8	34	8	1	0	13	.252	92	3	0	1.000
1983—Omaha	A. A.	OF	20	75	16	23	4	5	4	14	.307	53	2	0	1.000
1983—Kansas City	Amer.	OF	109	333	43	90	12	2	7	36	.270	237	6	3	.988
Major League Totals			112	334	43	90	12	2	7	36	.269	239	6	3	.988

Selected by Cincinnati Reds' organization in 36th round of free-agent draft, June 8, 1976.
Selected by Kansas City Royals' organization in 3rd round of free-agent draft, June 5, 1979.
†On disabled list, May 16 to June 2, 1980.
‡On disabled list, May 25 to June 25, 1981.
§On disabled list, April 27 to June 25 and June 27 to July 19, 1982.

ANTHONY RAYMOND SHINES
(Razor)

Born July 18, 1956, at Durham, N.C.
Height, 6.01. Weight, 210.
Throws right and bats left and righthanded.
Attended St. Augustine's College, Raleigh, N.C.

Year Club League	Pos.	G.	AB.	R.	H.	2B.	3B.	HR.	RBI.	B.A.	PO.	A.	E.	F.A.
1978—Jamestown............ NYP	1B	63	224	39	66	12	0	9	39	.295	514	26	14	.975
1979—W. Palm Beach†.. Fla. St.	1B	122	406	44	104	13	0	4	53	.256	860	53	16	.983
1980—W. Palm Beach‡.. Fla. St.	C-1B	73	267	27	64	15	1	6	40	.240	506	64	13	.978
1981—Memphis............... South.	1-3-C-O	119	359	50	79	7	4	10	42	.220	673	108	20	.975
1981—W. Palm Beach.... Fla. St.	3B-1B-C	8	26	4	6	0	0	3	6	.231	24	7	6	.838
1982—Memphis............... South.	1B-C-3B	122	432	67	121	18	2	16	66	.280	573	63	14	.979
1983—Memphis............... South.	1B-C-3B	109	388	72	111	27	2	20	63	.286	611	83	20	.972
1983—Montreal.............. Nat.	OF	3	2	0	1	0	0	0	0	.500	0	0	0	.000
Major League Totals...................		3	2	0	1	0	0	0	0	.500	0	0	0	.000

Selected by Montreal Expos' organization in 18th round of free-agent draft, June 6, 1978.
†On disabled list, June 12 to June 23, 1979.
‡On disabled list, May 4 to May 14, June 12 to June 23 and July 10, 1980 through remainder of season.

DAVID NOEL SHIPANOFF
(Dave)

Born December 13, 1959, at Edmonton, Alberta.
Height, 6.00. Weight, 175.
Throws and bats righthanded.

Led Southern League in saves with 18 and games finished in relief with 46 in 1983.
Led Carolina League in saves with 30 and games finished in relief with 56 in 1982.

Year Club	League	G.	IP.	W.	L.	Pct.	H.	R.	ER.	SO.	BB.	ERA.
1980—Medicine Hat.................	Pioneer	8	36	1	4	.200	49	37	31	19	23	7.75
1981—Florence	S. Atlantic	52	101	7	7	.500	78	40	30	101	44	2.67
1982—Kinston	Carolina	*63	92⅔	7	3	.700	57	22	20	105	46	1.94
1983—Knoxville	Southern	●61	69⅔	6	3	.667	53	32	26	73	51	3.36
1983—Syracuse	Int'national	8	11	0	1	.000	9	4	4	18	9	3.27

Signed as free agent by Toronto Blue Jays' organization, July 19, 1980.

ROBERT CHARLES SHIRLEY
(Bob)

Born June 25, 1954, at Oklahoma City, Okla.
Height, 5.11. Weight, 180.
Throws left and bats righthanded.
Attended University of Oklahoma, Norman, Okla.

Year Club	League	G.	IP.	W.	L.	Pct.	H.	R.	ER.	SO.	BB.	ERA.
1976—Amarillo.................	Texas	16	111	9	5	.643	113	55	41	90	39	3.32
1976—Hawaii	P. Coast	13	81	5	5	.500	91	62	47	47	24	5.22
1977—San Diego	National	39	214	12	18	.400	215	107	88	146	100	3.70
1978—San Diego	National	50	166	8	11	.421	164	75	68	102	61	3.69
1979—San Diego	National	49	205	8	16	.333	196	89	77	117	59	3.38
1980—San Diego†	National	59	137	11	12	.478	143	58	54	67	54	3.55
1981—St. Louis‡	National	28	79	6	4	.600	78	42	36	36	34	4.10
1982—Cincinnati§	National	41	152⅔	8	13	.381	138	74	61	89	73	3.60
1983—New York.................	American	25	108	5	8	.385	122	71	61	53	36	5.08
National League Totals................................		266	953⅔	53	74	.417	934	445	384	557	381	3.62
American League Totals..........................		25	108	5	8	.385	122	71	61	53	36	5.08
Major League Totals.............................		291	1061⅔	58	82	.414	1056	516	445	610	417	3.77

Selected by Los Angeles Dodgers' organization in 38th round of free-agent draft, June 6, 1972.
Selected by San Francisco Giants' organization in 5th round of free-agent draft, June 4, 1975.
Selected by San Diego Padres' organization in secondary phase of free-agent draft, January 7, 1976.
†Traded with Pitcher Rollie Fingers, Catcher-First Baseman Gene Tenace and a player to be named later to St. Louis Cardinals for Catchers Terry Kennedy and Steve Swisher, Pitchers John Littlefield, Al Olmsted, John Urrea and Kim Seaman and Infielder Mike Phillips, December 8, 1980; St. Louis organization acquired Catcher Bob Geren to complete deal, December 10, 1980.
‡Traded to Cincinnati Reds for Pitchers Jeff Lahti and Jose Brito, April 1, 1982.
§Granted free agency, November 10, 1982; signed by New York Yankees, December 10, 1982.

ERIC VAUGHN SHOW
Name rhymes with Chow.

Born May 19, 1956, at Riverside, Calif.
Height, 6.01. Weight, 185.
Throws and bats righthanded.
Attended University of California at Riverside, Riverside, Calif.

Led Texas League in hit batsmen with 10 in 1980.

Year Club	League	G.	IP.	W.	L.	Pct.	H.	R.	ER.	SO.	BB.	ERA.
1978—Walla Walla	Northwest	11	60	5	2	.714	47	28	19	43	20	2.85

Year	Club	League	G.	IP.	W.	L.	Pct.	H.	R.	ER.	SO.	BB.	ERA.
1979—Reno	California	28	169	13	9	.591	144	79	67	186	92	3.57
1980—Amarillo	Texas	26	166	12	6	.667	141	81	69	144	81	3.74
1981—Hawaii	P. Coast	34	85	7	3	.700	67	30	24	70	35	2.54
1981—San Diego	National	15	23	1	3	.250	17	9	8	22	9	3.13
1982—San Diego	National	47	150	10	6	.625	117	49	44	88	48	2.64
1983—San Diego	National	35	200⅔	15	12	.556	201	97	93	120	74	4.17
Major League Totals		97	373⅓	26	21	.553	335	155	145	230	131	3.49

Selected by Minnesota Twins' organization in 36th round of free-agent draft, June 5, 1974.
Selected by San Diego Padres' organization in 18th round of free-agent draft, June 6, 1978.

NELSON BERNARD SIMMONS III

Born June 27, 1963, at Washington, D. C.
Height, 6.01. Weight, 195.
Throws right and bats left and righthanded.

Led Florida State League in bases on balls received with 96 and intentional bases on balls received with 13 in 1982.

Year	Club	League	Pos.	G.	AB.	R.	H.	2B.	3B.	HR.	RBI.	B.A.	PO.	A.	E.	F.A.
1981—Bristol	Appal.	OF	69	★267	36	79	14	1	10	45	.296	62	7	8	.896
1982—Lakeland	Fla. St.	OF	133	491	68	144	24	8	9	61	.293	178	7	●12	.939
1982—Birmingham	South.	OF	8	30	2	6	0	0	0	4	.200	11	0	0	1.000
1983—Birmingham	South.	OF	118	404	57	110	17	1	11	64	.272	174	11	★14	.930

Selected by Detroit Tigers' organization in 2nd round of free-agent draft, June 8, 1981.

TED LYLE SIMMONS

Born August 9, 1949, at Highland Park, Mich.
Height, 6.00. Weight, 200.
Throws right and bats left and righthanded.
Attended Wayne State University, Detroit, Mich. and
University of Michigan, Ann Arbor, Mich.

Established major league record for most intentional bases on balls by switch-hitter, season, since 1955 (25), 1977.
Established National League records for most home runs by switch hitter, career (172); fewest errors by catcher, season, for leader in errors (15), 1975.
Tied National League record for most games, switch-hit home runs, season (1), April 17, 1975 and June 11, 1979; most games switch-hit home runs, league (2).
Switch-hit home runs in one game three times: April 17, 1975, June 11, 1979 and May 2, 1982.
Led National League in intentional bases on balls received with 19 in 1976 and 25 in 1977.
Led National League in grounding into double plays with 29 in 1973.
Led National League catchers in putouts with 842 in 1972 and 888 in 1973.
Led National League catchers in assists with 78 in 1972 and 74 in 1973.
Led National League catchers in total chances with 928 in 1972, 975 in 1973 and 880 in 1975.
Led National League in passed balls with 25 in 1973, 28 in 1975 and 14 in 1979.
Led California League catchers in putouts with 984 in 1968.
Tied for California League lead in being hit by pitch with 9 in 1968.
Named catcher on THE SPORTING NEWS National League All-Star Team, 1977 through 1979.
Named catcher on THE SPORTING NEWS National League Silver Slugger team, 1980.
Named California League Most Valuable Player, 1968.
Received reported $50,000 bonus to sign with St. Louis Cardinals, 1967.

Year	Club	League	Pos.	G.	AB.	R.	H.	2B.	3B.	HR.	RBI.	B.A.	PO.	A.	E.	F.A.
1967—Sarasota Cards	Gulf C.	C	6	20	5	7	1	1	2	8	.350	33	0	0	1.000
1967—Cedar Rapids	Midw.	OF-C	47	171	15	46	11	2	4	34	.269	119	8	3	.977
1968—Modesto	Calif.	★C-OF	136	493	86	163	30	2	28	★117	★.331	989	79	★16	.985
1968—St. Louis	Nat.	C	2	3	0	1	0	0	0	0	.333	3	1	0	1.000
1969—Tulsa	A. A.	C-3-O-1	129	499	80	158	33	4	16	88	.317	463	92	19	.967
1969—St. Louis†	Nat.	C	5	14	0	3	0	1	0	3	.214	22	0	1	.957
1970—Tulsa	A. A.	C	15	51	10	19	4	1	1	8	.373	99	7	0	1.000
1970—St. Louis	Nat.	C	82	284	29	69	8	2	3	24	.243	466	37	5	.990
1971—St. Louis‡	Nat.	C	133	510	64	155	32	4	7	77	.304	747	52	9	.989
1972—St. Louis	Nat.	C-1B	152	594	70	180	36	6	16	96	.303	967	93	13	.988
1973—St. Louis	Nat.	C-1B-OF	161	619	62	192	36	2	13	91	.310	932	78	14	.986
1974—St. Louis	Nat.	C-1B	152	599	66	163	33	6	20	103	.272	813	87	15	.984
1975—St. Louis	Nat.	★C-1B-OF	157	581	80	193	32	3	18	100	.332	818	64	★15	.983
1976—St. Louis	Nat.	C-1-O-3	150	546	60	159	35	3	5	75	.291	726	88	10	.988
1977—St. Louis	Nat.	C-OF	150	516	82	164	25	3	21	95	.318	683	75	10	.987
1978—St. Louis	Nat.	★C-OF	152	516	71	148	40	5	22	80	.287	703	★88	10	.988
1979—St. Louis§	Nat.	C	123	448	68	127	22	0	26	87	.283	606	69	10	.985
1980—St. Louis x	Nat.	C-OF	145	495	84	150	33	2	21	98	.303	528	71	10	.984
1981—Milwaukee	Amer.	C-1B	100	380	45	82	13	3	14	61	.216	333	41	8	.979
1982—Milwaukee	Amer.	C	137	539	73	145	29	0	23	97	.269	570	62	3	★.995
1983—Milwaukee y	Amer.	C	153	600	76	185	39	3	13	108	.308	395	41	11	.975
National League Totals		1564	5725	736	1704	332	37	172	929	.298	8014	803	122	.986
American League Totals		390	1519	194	412	81	6	50	266	.271	1298	144	22	.985
Major League Totals		1954	7244	930	2116	413	43	222	1195	.292	9312	947	144	.986

Selected by St. Louis Cardinals' organization in 1st round (10th player selected) of free-agent draft, June 6, 1967.
†On military list, December 12, 1969 through May 9, 1970.
‡On military list, June 19 to July 4, 1971.
§On disabled list, June 25 to July 24, 1979.
xTraded with Pitchers Rollie Fingers and Pete Vuckovich to Milwaukee Brewers for Pitchers Lary Sorensen and Dave LaPoint and Outfielders Sixto Lezcano and David Green, December 12, 1980.
yGranted free agency, November 7, 1983.

DIVISION SERIES RECORD

Year Club	League	Pos.	G.	AB.	R.	H.	2B.	3B.	HR.	RBI.	B.A.	PO.	A.	E.	F.A.
1981—Milwaukee............	Amer.	C	5	18	1	4	1	0	1	4	.222	23	2	1	.962

CHAMPIONSHIP SERIES RECORD

Year Club	League	Pos.	G.	AB.	R.	H.	2B.	3B.	HR.	RBI.	B.A.	PO.	A.	E.	F.A.
1982—Milwaukee............	Amer.	C	5	18	3	3	0	0	0	1	.167	36	3	0	1.000

WORLD SERIES RECORD

Tied World Series record for fewest putouts by catcher, game (1), October 15, 1982.

Year Club	League	Pos.	G.	AB.	R.	H.	2B.	3B.	HR.	RBI.	B.A.	PO.	A.	E.	F.A.
1982—Milwaukee............	Amer.	C	7	23	2	4	0	0	2	3	.174	28	2	1	.968

ALL-STAR GAME RECORD

Year League	Pos.	AB.	R.	H.	2B.	3B.	HR.	RBI.	B.A.	PO.	A.	E.	F.A.
1973—National	PH-C	1	0	0	0	0	0	0	.000	1	1	0	1.000
1977—National	C	3	0	0	0	0	0	0	.000	5	0	0	1.000
1978—National	C	3	0	1	0	0	0	0	.333	4	1	0	1.000
1981—American	PH	1	0	1	0	0	0	1	1.000	0	0	0	.000
1983—American	C	2	0	0	0	0	0	0	.000	4	0	0	1.000
All-Star Game Totals....................		10	0	2	0	0	0	1	.200	14	2	0	1.000

Member of National League All-Star Team for 1972 and 1974 games; did not play.
Named to National League All-Star Team for 1979 game; replaced due to injury.

JOE ALLEN SIMPSON

Born December 31, 1951, at Purcell, Okla.
Height, 6.03. Weight, 175.
Throws and bats lefthanded.
Attended University of Oklahoma, Norman, Okla.

Led Pacific Coast League in caught stealing with 20 in 1975 and 16 in 1977.

Year Club	League	Pos.	G.	AB.	R.	H.	2B.	3B.	HR.	RBI.	B.A.	PO.	A.	E.	F.A.
1973—Albuquerque........	P. C.	OF	15	54	10	12	0	0	0	6	.222	40	1	4	.911
1973—Bakersfield...........	Calif.	OF	61	227	37	69	4	1	1	24	.304	127	4	3	.978
1974—Waterbury............	East.	OF	117	406	59	121	18	6	1	30	.298	256	16	14	.951
1974—Albuquerque........	P. C.	OF	13	43	2	7	1	1	0	0	.163	29	2	0	1.000
1975—Albuquerque†.......	P. C.	OF	133	514	84	142	24	6	2	49	.276	289	8	5	.983
1975—Los Angeles	Nat.	OF	9	6	3	2	0	0	0	0	.333	5	0	0	1.000
1976—Albuquerque........	P. C.	OF-1B	108	419	77	131	19	7	4	60	.313	193	15	8	.961
1976—Los Angeles	Nat.	OF	23	30	2	4	1	0	0	0	.133	24	0	0	1.000
1977—Albuquerque........	P. C.	OF	112	436	80	152	24	11	2	74	.349	260	10	6	.978
1977—Los Angeles	Nat.	OF-1B	29	23	2	4	0	0	0	1	.174	24	2	1	.963
1978—Albuquerque‡.......	P. C.	●OF-1B	★140	528	110	163	24	10	5	73	.309	310	20	●12	.965
1978—Los Angeles‡	Nat.	OF	10	5	1	2	0	0	0	1	.400	8	0	0	1.000
1979—Seattle..................	Amer.	OF	120	265	29	75	11	0	0	27	.283	162	10	6	.966
1980—Seattle..................	Amer.	OF	129	365	42	91	15	3	3	34	.249	220	2	7	.932
1981—Seattle..................	Amer.	OF	91	288	32	64	11	3	2	30	.222	219	5	5	.978
1982—Seattle§................	Amer.	OF	105	296	39	76	14	4	2	23	.257	177	7	3	.984
1983—Kansas City..........	Amer.	1B-OF-P	91	119	16	20	2	2	0	8	.168	242	18	2	.992
National League Totals.............................			71	64	8	12	1	0	0	2	.188	61	2	1	.984
American League Totals...........................			536	1333	158	326	53	12	9	122	.245	1020	52	23	.979
Major League Totals.................................			607	1397	166	338	54	12	9	124	.242	1081	54	24	.979

Selected by Washington Senators' organization in 14th round of free-agent draft, June 4, 1970.
Selected by Los Angeles Dodgers' organization in 3rd round of free-agent draft, June 5, 1973.
†On disabled list, April 10 to April 20, 1975.
‡Sold to Seattle Mariners, April 2, 1979.
§Drafted by Kansas City Royals, December 6, 1982.

PITCHING RECORD

Year Club	League	G.	IP.	W.	L.	Pct.	H.	R.	ER.	SO.	BB.	ERA.
1983—Kansas City......................	American	2	3	0	0	.000	4	1	1	1	2	3.00

MATTHEW STEPHEN SINATRO
(Matt)

Born March 22, 1960, at West Hartford, Conn.
Height, 5.09. Weight, 174.
Throws and bats righthanded.

Led International League catchers in total chances with 710 in 1983.
Led Southern League catchers in double plays with 10 in 1980.
Tied for Western Carolinas League lead in caught stealing with 15 in 1979.

Year Club	League	Pos.	G.	AB.	R.	H.	2B.	3B.	HR.	RBI.	B.A.	PO.	A.	E.	F.A.
1978—Kingsport...............	Appal.	C	35	112	15	23	7	0	0	6	.205	198	26	2	.991
1979—Greenwood...........	W. Car.	C	120	385	54	97	16	4	7	57	.252	639	69	11	.985
1980—Savannah..............	South.	C	122	449	76	125	16	1	11	50	.278	514	70	15	.975
1981—Richmond.............	Int.	C	121	430	43	101	13	2	6	53	.235	738	78	12	.986
1981—Atlanta	Nat.	C	12	32	4	9	1	1	0	4	.281	56	10	0	1.000
1982—Atlanta	Nat.	C	37	81	10	11	2	0	1	4	.136	112	25	0	1.000

Year Club League	Pos.	G.	AB.	R.	H.	2B.	3B.	HR.	RBI.	B.A.	PO.	A.	E.	F.A.
1982—Richmond.............. Int.	C	72	246	39	62	7	1	8	29	.252	423	53	5	.990
1983—Richmond.............. Int.	C	110	365	36	77	11	1	4	41	.211	*642	60	8	.989
1983—Atlanta .... Nat.	C	7	12	0	2	0	0	0	2	.167	24	5	1	.967
Major League Totals....................................		56	125	14	22	3	1	1	10	.176	192	40	1	.996

Selected by Atlanta Braves' organization in 2nd round of free-agent draft, June 6, 1978.

KENNETH WAYNE SINGLETON
(Ken)

Born June 10, 1947, at New York, N. Y.
Height, 6.04. Weight, 212.
Throws right and bats left and righthanded.
Attended Hofstra University, Hempstead, N. Y.
Uncle of Glenn Rivers, rookie guard with Atlanta Hawks; nephew
of Harvey Singleton, former tackle with Toronto Argonauts.

Tied major league record for most years with no stolen bases, 150 or more games (4).
Tied National League record for most home runs, switch-hitting, one month, 9, July, 1973.
Led American League in grounding into double plays with 21 in 1981.
Led American League in game-winning RBIs with 19 in 1980.
Led American League in intentional bases on balls received with 16 in 1979 and 19 in 1983.
Led California League in sacrifice flies with 6 in 1968.
Led Florida State League in bases on balls received with 87 in 1967.
Named outfielder on THE SPORTING NEWS American League All-Star Team, 1979.

Year Club League	Pos.	G.	AB.	R.	H.	2B.	3B.	HR.	RBI.	B.A.	PO.	A.	E.	F.A.
1967—Winter Haven....... Fla. St.	OF-1B	102	278	49	77	17	1	4	41	.277	222	7	5	.979
1968—Raleigh-Durham...Carol.	1B-OF	26	74	21	19	3	0	3	12	.257	176	8	5	.974
1968—Visalia .... Calif.	OF-1B	80	263	61	83	5	0	11	35	.316	187	12	7	.966
1968—Jacksonville........... Int.	OF-1B	29	78	12	16	5	1	2	10	.205	34	0	2	.944
1969—Memphis............. Texas	OF-1B	115	366	65	113	16	6	10	65	.309	234	10	3	.988
1970—Tidewater.............. Int.	OF	64	219	48	85	16	1	17	46	.388	92	4	2	.980
1970—New York............ Nat.	OF	69	198	22	52	8	0	5	26	.263	90	1	3	.968
1971—New York†........... Nat.	OF	115	298	34	73	5	0	13	46	.245	143	5	4	.974
1972—Montreal.............. Nat.	OF	142	507	77	139	23	2	14	50	.274	236	9	7	.972
1973—Montreal.............. Nat.	OF	●162	560	100	169	26	2	23	103	.302	278	*20	5	.983
1974—Montreal‡............. Nat.	OF	148	511	68	141	20	2	9	74	.276	224	7	11	.955
1975—Baltimore .... Amer.	OF	155	586	88	176	37	4	15	55	.300	283	9	3	.990
1976—Baltimore .... Amer.	OF	154	544	62	151	25	2	13	70	.278	278	9	5	.983
1977—Baltimore .... Amer.	OF	152	536	90	176	24	0	24	99	.328	278	8	4	.986
1978—Baltimore .... Amer.	OF	149	502	67	147	21	2	20	81	.293	244	1	6	.976
1979—Baltimore .... Amer.	OF	159	570	93	168	29	1	35	111	.295	247	8	5	.981
1980—Baltimore .... Amer.	OF	156	583	85	177	28	3	24	104	.304	248	3	4	.984
1981—Baltimore .... Amer.	OF	103	363	48	101	16	1	13	49	.278	125	2	0	*1.000
1982—Baltimore .... Amer.	OF	156	561	71	141	27	2	14	77	.251	10	0	0	1.000
1983—Baltimore .... Amer.	DH	151	507	52	140	21	3	18	84	.276	0	0	0	.000
National League Totals............................		636	2074	301	574	82	6	64	299	.277	971	42	30	.971
American League Totals.........................		1335	4752	656	1377	228	18	176	730	.290	1713	40	27	.985
Major League Totals..............................		1971	6826	957	1951	310	24	240	1029	.286	2684	82	57	.980

Selected by New York Mets' organization in 1st round (third player selected) of free-agent draft, January, 1967.

†Traded with First Baseman Mike Jorgensen and Infielder Tim Foli To Montreal Expos for Outfielder Rusty Staub, April 6, 1972.

‡Traded with Pitcher Mike Torrez to Baltimore Orioles for Pitchers Dave McNally and Bill Kirkpatrick and Outfielder Rich Coggins, December 4, 1974.

CHAMPIONSHIP SERIES RECORD

Year Club League	Pos.	G.	AB.	R.	H.	2B.	3B.	HR.	RBI.	B.A.	PO.	A.	E.	F.A.
1979—Baltimore .... Amer.	OF	4	16	4	6	2	0	0	2	.375	5	1	0	1.000
1983—Baltimore .... Amer.	DH	4	12	0	3	2	0	0	1	.250	0	0	0	.000
Championship Series Totals		8	28	4	9	4	0	0	3	.321	5	1	0	1.000

WORLD SERIES RECORD

Year Club League	Pos.	G.	AB.	R.	H.	2B.	3B.	HR.	RBI.	B.A.	PO.	A.	E.	F.A.
1979—Baltimore .... Amer.	OF	7	28	1	10	1	0	0	2	.357	9	0	0	1.000
1983—Baltimore .... Amer.	PH	2	1	0	0	0	0	0	1	.000	0	0	0	.000
World Series Totals................................		9	29	1	10	1	0	0	3	.345	9	0	0	1.000

ALL-STAR GAME RECORD

Year League	Pos.	AB.	R.	H.	2B.	3B.	HR.	RBI.	B.A.	PO.	A.	E.	F.A.
1977—American.............................	OF	0	0	0	0	0	0	0	.000	0	0	0	.000
1979—American	PH	1	0	0	0	0	0	0	.000	0	0	0	.000
1981—American	OF	3	2	2	0	0	1	1	.667	0	0	0	.000
All-Star Game Totals		4	2	2	0	0	1	1	.500	0	0	0	.000

—DID YOU KNOW—

That the Chicago Cubs had more shutouts than complete games in 1983? Cub pitchers accumulated 10 shutouts, but hurled only nine complete games.

DOUGLAS RANDALL SISK
(Doug)

Born September 26, 1957, at Renton, Wash.
Height, 6.02. Weight, 210.
Throws and bats righthanded.
Attended Green River Community College, Auburn, Wash. and received bachelor of science degree
in criminal justice from Washington State University, Pullman, Wash.

Major League saves: 1982 (1), 1983 (11). Total—12.
Led Appalachian League pitchers in games started with 15 in 1980.

Year Club	League	G.	IP.	W.	L.	Pct.	H.	R.	ER.	SO.	BB.	ERA.
1980—Kingsport	Ap'lachian	15	*98	●8	5	.615	*91	46	29	41	45	2.66
1981—Lynchburg	Carolina	36	83	3	2	.600	78	35	30	61	32	3.25
1981—Jackson	Texas	14	25	3	0	1.000	23	11	10	15	12	3.60
1982—Jackson	Texas	44	138	11	8	.611	136	59	41	53	58	*2.67
1982—New York	National	8	8⅔	0	1	.000	5	1	1	4	4	1.04
1983—New York	National	67	104⅓	5	4	.556	88	38	26	33	59	2.24
Major League Totals		75	113	5	5	.500	93	39	27	37	63	2.15

Signed as free agent by New York Mets' organization, June 10, 1980.

JAMES SIWY

Name pronounced SEE-wee.

(Jim)

Born September 20, 1958, at Central Falls, R. I.
Height, 6.04. Weight, 200.
Throws and bats righthanded.
Attended Rhode Island College, Providence, R.I.

Tied for Pacific Coast League lead in hit batsmen with 10 in 1982.

Year Club	League	G.	IP.	W.	L.	Pct.	H.	R.	ER.	SO.	BB.	ERA.
1980—Sarasota White Sox†	Gulf Coast				(Did not play)							
1981—Appleton	Midwest	8	55	5	0	1.000	47	17	12	32	12	1.96
1981—Glens Falls	Eastern	16	110	11	4	.733	125	57	47	45	19	3.85
1982—Edmonton‡	P. Coast	26	171⅔	12	8	.600	184	84	77	79	58	4.04
1982—Chicago	American	2	7	0	0	.000	10	8	8	3	5	10.29
1983—Denver§	Am. Assoc.	21	51⅓	3	3	.500	60	41	35	36	25	6.14
Major League Totals		2	7	0	0	.000	10	8	8	3	5	10.29

Selected by Chicago White Sox' organization in 3rd round of free-agent draft, January 8, 1980.
†On restricted list, June 23, 1980; transferred to voluntary retired list, July 3, 1980 through January 12, 1981.
‡On disabled list, April 13 to April 23, 1982.
§On disabled list, June 22 to July 2 and July 19, 1983 through remainder of season.

JOEL PATRICK SKINNER

Born February 21, 1961, at San Diego, Calif.
Height, 6.04. Weight, 205.
Throws and bats righthanded.
Attended San Diego Mesa College, San Diego, Calif.
Son of Bob Skinner, outfielder-first baseman with Pittsburgh Pirates, Cincinnati Reds and St. Louis
Cardinals, 1954 through 1966; manager, Philadelphia Phillies, 1968 and 1969, manager,
San Diego Padres, 1977; coach, San Diego Padres, 1977; coach, California Angels, 1978;
and coach with Pittsburgh Pirates since 1979.

Tied for South Atlantic League lead in double plays by catchers with 7 in 1980.

Year Club	League	Pos.	G.	AB.	R.	H.	2B.	3B.	HR.	RBI.	B.A.	PO.	A.	E.	F.A.
1980—Shelby	S. Atl.	C	100	324	36	73	15	2	7	27	.225	536	63	18	.971
1981—Greenwood†‡	S. Atl.	C	117	428	48	114	25	2	11	63	.266	766	42	*22	.974
1982—Glens Falls	East.	C	120	422	49	107	11	6	7	65	.254	726	80	12	.985
1983—Denver	A. A.	C	108	361	55	94	15	5	12	50	.260	550	54	5	.992
1983—Chicago	Amer.	C	6	11	2	3	0	0	0	1	.273	20	4	1	.960
Major League Totals			6	11	2	3	0	0	0	1	.273	20	4	1	.960

Selected by Pittsburgh Pirates' organization in 36th round of free-agent draft, June 5, 1979.
†On disabled list, June 1 to June 13, 1981.
‡Selected by Chicago White Sox' organization in player compensation pool draft, February 2, 1982. (Chicago
received compensation for Philadelphia Phillies' signing of free agent Pitcher Ed Farmer, January 28, 1982.)

ROBERT JACOB SKUBE

Name pronounced Skoo-be.

(Bob)

Born October 8, 1957, at Northridge, Calif.
Height, 6.00. Weight, 180.
Throws and bats lefthanded.
Attended University of Southern California, Los Angeles, Calif.
Nephew of John Skube, minor league infielder, 1930.

Led California League in bases on balls received with 120 in 1980.
Led Pacific Coast League outfielders in double plays with 6 in 1982.

Year Club	League	Pos.	G.	AB.	R.	H.	2B.	3B.	HR.	RBI.	B.A.	PO.	A.	E.	F.A.
1979—Burlington	Midw.	OF-1B	54	194	26	57	14	1	9	45	.294	123	10	8	.943
1979—Stockton	Calif.	OF	1	5	1	1	0	0	0	0	.200	1	0	0	1.000
1980—Stockton	Calif.	OF-1B	135	453	91	132	26	7	19	81	.291	512	34	15	.973
1981—El Paso	Texas	OF	114	398	89	113	23	5	18	59	.284	170	19	9	.955
1982—Vancouver	P. C.	OF-1B	130	433	55	121	26	2	13	61	.279	262	17	13	.955
1982—Milwaukee	Amer.	OF	4	3	0	2	0	0	0	0	.667	0	0	0	.000
1983—Milwaukee	Amer.	OF-1B	12	25	2	5	1	1	0	9	.200	22	0	0	1.000
1983—Vancouver	P. C.	OF-1B	40	129	15	27	3	0	3	8	.209	104	7	1	.991
Major League Totals			16	28	2	7	1	1	0	9	.250	22	0	0	1.000

Selected by Atlanta Braves' organization in 5th round of free-agent draft, June 4, 1975.
Selected by St. Louis Cardinals' organization in 18th round of free-agent draft, June 6, 1978.
Selected by Milwaukee Brewers' organization in 13th round of free-agent draft, June 6, 1979.

JAMES MICHAEL SLATON
(Jim)

Born June 19, 1950, at Long Beach, Calif.
Height, 6.00. Weight, 185.
Throws and bats righthanded.
Attended Antelope Valley College, Lancaster, Calif.

Pitched 5-0 no-hit victory against Wichita, August 3, 1972.

Year Club	League	G.	IP.	W.	L.	Pct.	H.	R.	ER.	SO.	BB.	ERA.
1969—Billings	Pioneer	2	8	1	0	1.000	1	0	0	16	0	0.00
1969—Clinton	Midwest	13	82	6	3	.667	65	27	26	83	34	2.85
1970—Clinton†	Midwest	2	18	1	1	.500	9	4	3	15	5	1.50
1971—Evansville	Am. Assoc.	4	32	1	0	1.000	22	9	5	26	9	1.39
1971—Milwaukee	American	26	148	10	8	.556	140	67	62	63	71	3.77
1972—Evansville	Am. Assoc.	16	114	11	2	.846	97	39	37	68	37	2.92
1972—Milwaukee	American	9	44	1	6	.143	50	31	27	17	21	5.52
1973—Milwaukee	American	38	276	13	15	.464	266	127	114	134	99	3.72
1974—Milwaukee	American	40	250	13	16	.448	255	117	109	126	102	3.92
1975—Milwaukee	American	37	217	11	18	.379	238	129	109	119	90	4.52
1976—Milwaukee	American	38	293	14	15	.483	*287	•126	112	138	94	3.44
1977—Milwaukee‡	American	32	221	10	14	.417	223	104	88	104	77	3.58
1978—Detroit§	American	35	234	17	11	.607	235	117	107	92	85	4.12
1979—Milwaukee	American	32	213	15	9	.625	229	95	86	80	54	3.63
1980—Milwaukee x	American	3	16	1	1	.500	17	10	8	4	5	4.50
1981—Milwaukee	American	24	117	5	7	.417	120	60	57	47	50	4.38
1982—Milwaukee y	American	39	117⅔	10	6	.625	117	48	43	59	41	3.29
1983—Milwaukee z	American	46	112⅓	14	6	.700	112	57	54	38	56	4.33
Major League Totals		399	2259	134	132	.504	2289	1088	976	1021	845	3.89

Selected by Seattle Pilots' organization in 14th round of free-agent draft, June 5, 1969.
†On military list, May 8, 1970 through remainder of season.
‡Traded with Pitcher Rich Folkers to Detroit Tigers for Outfielder Ben Oglivie, December 9, 1977.
§Granted free agency, November 2, 1978; signed by Milwaukee Brewers, November 28, 1978.
xOn disabled list, May 25 to October 1, 1980.
yOn disabled list, April 1 to April 23, 1982.
zTraded to California Angels for Outfielder Bobby Clark, December 20, 1983.

DIVISION SERIES RECORD

Year Club	League	G.	IP.	W.	L.	Pct.	H.	R.	ER.	SO.	BB.	ERA.
1981—Milwaukee	American	4	6	0	0	.000	6	2	2	2	0	3.00

CHAMPIONSHIP SERIES RECORD

Year Club	League	G.	IP.	W.	L.	Pct.	H.	R.	ER.	SO.	BB.	ERA.
1982—Milwaukee	American	2	4⅔	0	0	.000	3	2	1	3	1	1.93

WORLD SERIES RECORD

Year Club	League	G.	IP.	W.	L.	Pct.	H.	R.	ER.	SO.	BB.	ERA.
1982—Milwaukee	American	2	2⅔	1	0	1.000	1	0	0	1	2	0.00

ALL-STAR GAME RECORD

Member of American League All-Star Team in 1977; did not play.

DONALD MARTIN SLAUGHT
(Don)

Born September 11, 1959, at Long Beach, Calif.
Height, 6.00. Weight, 185.
Throws and bats righthanded.

Year Club	League	Pos.	G.	AB.	R.	H.	2B.	3B.	HR.	RBI.	B.A.	PO.	A.	E.	F.A.
1980—Ft. Myers	Fla. St.	C	50	176	13	46	9	0	2	16	.261	175	34	4	.981
1981—Jacksonville	South.	C-1B	96	379	45	127	21	2	6	44	.335	482	61	9	.984
1981—Omaha†	A. A.	C	22	71	10	21	4	0	2	8	.296	91	7	3	.970
1982—Omaha‡	A. A.	C	53	206	29	55	10	1	4	16	.267	216	25	5	.980

Year	Club	League	Pos.	G.	AB.	R.	H.	2B.	3B.	HR.	RBI.	B.A.	PO.	A.	E.	F.A.
1982—Kansas City	Amer.		C	43	115	14	32	6	0	3	8	.278	156	7	1	.994
1983—Kansas City§	Amer.		C	83	276	21	86	13	4	0	28	.312	299	18	12	.964
Major League Totals				126	391	35	118	19	4	3	36	.302	455	25	13	.974

Selected by Milwaukee Brewers' organization in 19th round of free-agent draft, June 5, 1979.
Selected by Kansas City Royals' organization in 7th round of free-agent draft, June 3, 1980.
†On disabled list, August 16 to September 29, 1981.
‡On disabled list, April 21 to May 15, 1982.
§On supplemental disabled list, May 16 to June 1, 1983.

ROY FREDERICK SMALLEY III

Born October 25, 1952, at Los Angeles, Calif.
Height, 6.01. Weight, 182.
Throws right and bats left and righthanded.
Attended Los Angeles City Community College, Los Angeles, Calif., and
University of Southern California, Los Angeles, Calif.
Son of Roy Smalley, Jr., infielder with Chicago Cubs, Milwaukee Braves and
Philadelphia Phillies, 1948 through 1958; nephew of Gene Mauch, infielder with Brooklyn, Pittsburgh,
Chicago NL, Boston and St. Louis, 1944, 1945, 1947, 1948 through 1952, 1956 and 1957; manager with
Philadelphia, Montreal, Minnesota and California, 1960 through 1982; and currently
Director of Player Personnel with California Angels.

Tied major league record for most strikeouts, two consecutive games (8), August 28 and 29, 1976 (26 innings).
Established American League record for most assists by shortstop, season (572), 1979.
Switch-hit home runs in one game, September 5, 1982.
Led American League in sacrifice hits with 25 in 1976.
Led American League shortstops in double plays with 116 in 1977, with 121 in 1978 and with 144 in 1979.
Led American League shortstops in putouts with 296 in 1979.
Led American League shortstops in total chances with 792 in 1977, 839 in 1978 and 897 in 1979.
Named shortstop on THE SPORTING NEWS American League All-Star Team, 1979.
Received reported $100,000 bonus to sign with Texas Rangers, 1974.

Year	Club	League	Pos.	G.	AB.	R.	H.	2B.	3B.	HR.	RBI.	B.A.	PO.	A.	E.	F.A.
1974—Pittsfield	East.		SS	125	406	74	102	22	5	14	42	.251	146	376	*42	.926
1975—Spokane	P. C.		SS-2B	43	162	26	55	8	1	2	19	.340	88	151	10	.960
1975—Texas	Amer.		SS-2B-C	78	250	22	57	8	0	3	33	.228	108	232	20	.944
1976—Tex.†-Minn.	Amer.		SS-2B	144	513	61	133	18	3	3	44	.259	274	447	26	.965
1977—Minnesota	Amer.		SS	150	584	93	135	21	5	6	56	.231	255	*504	33	.958
1978—Minnesota	Amer.		SS	158	586	80	160	31	3	19	77	.273	*287	*527	25	.970
1979—Minnesota	Amer.		*SS-1B	●162	621	94	168	28	3	24	95	.271	305	*572	29	.968
1980—Minnesota	Amer.		SS-1B	133	486	64	135	24	1	12	63	.278	226	448	17	.990
1981—Minnesota	Amer.		SS-1B	56	167	24	44	7	1	7	22	.263	62	89	8	.950
1982—Minn.‡-N.Y.	Amer.		SS-3B-2B	146	499	57	127	15	2	20	67	.255	142	367	15	.971
1983—New York	Amer.		SS-3B-1B	130	451	70	124	24	1	18	62	.275	289	295	21	.965
Major League Totals				1157	4157	565	1083	176	19	112	519	.261	1948	3481	194	.965

Selected by Montreal Expos' organization in 35th round of free-agent draft, June 4, 1970.
Selected by Boston Red Sox' organization in secondary phase of free-agent draft, January 13, 1971.
Selected by St. Louis Cardinals' organization in secondary phase of free-agent draft, June 8, 1971.
Selected by Boston Red Sox' organization in secondary phase of free-agent draft, January 12, 1972.
Selected by Texas Rangers' organization in 1st round (first player selected) of free-agent draft, January 9, 1974.
†Traded with Pitchers Bill Singer and Jim Gideon, Infielder Mike Cubbage, and $250,000 cash to Minnesota Twins for Pitcher Bert Blyleven and Shortstop Danny Thompson, June 1, 1976.
‡Traded to New York Yankees for Pitchers Ron Davis and Paul Boris, Shortstop Greg Gagne and a reported $400,000, April 10, 1982.

ALL-STAR GAME RECORD

Year	League	Pos.	AB.	R.	H.	2B.	3B.	HR.	RBI.	B.A.	PO.	A.	E.	F.A.
1979—American		SS	3	0	0	0	0	0	0	.000	2	2	0	1.000

BRYN NELSON SMITH

Born August 11, 1955, at Marietta, Ga.
Height, 6.02. Weight, 200.
Throws and bats righthanded.
Attended Allan Hancock College, Santa Maria, Calif.

Tied for American Association lead in complete games with 9 in 1981.
Tied for Southern League lead in complete games with 16 in 1977 and 12 in 1980.
Named American Association Pitcher of the Year, 1981.

Year	Club	League	G.	IP.	W.	L.	Pct.	H.	R.	ER.	SO.	BB.	ERA.
1975—Miami	Florida St.		26	139	11	7	.611	117	48	33	93	59	2.14
1976—Miami	Florida St.		23	164	10	10	.500	140	72	51	119	62	2.80
1977—Charlotte†	Southern		27	*206	*15	11	.577	*195	78	63	103	57	2.75
1978—Denver	Am. Assoc.		11	54	0	6	.000	79	48	41	25	14	6.83
1978—Memphis‡	Southern		11	69	4	6	.400	53	28	19	48	31	2.48
1979—Memphis	Southern		27	184	11	10	.524	175	80	69	115	74	3.38
1980—Memphis	Southern		27	181	10	9	.526	179	75	56	110	54	2.78
1981—Denver	Am. Assoc.		29	*183	*15	5	*.750	166	80	62	127	42	3.05
1981—Montreal	National		7	13	1	0	1.000	14	4	4	9	3	2.77
1982—Wichita	Am. Assoc.		3	23⅔	2	0	1.000	21	5	5	15	2	1.90
1982—Montreal	National		47	79⅓	2	4	.333	81	43	37	50	23	4.20
1983—Montreal	National		49	155⅓	6	11	.353	142	51	43	101	43	2.49
Major League Totals			103	247⅔	9	15	.375	237	98	84	160	69	3.05

Selected by St. Louis Cardinals' organization in the 49th round of free-agent draft, June 5, 1973.
Signed as free agent by Baltimore Orioles' organization, December 18, 1974.
†Traded with Pitchers Rudy May and Randy Miller by Baltimore Orioles' organization to Montreal Expos' organization for Pitchers Don Stanhouse and Joe Kerrigan and Outfielder Gary Roenicke, December 7, 1977.
‡On disabled list, August 5 to August 17, 1978.

CHRISTOPHER WILLIAM SMITH
(Chris)

Born July 18, 1957, at Torrance, Calif.
Height, 6.00. Weight, 185.
Throws right and bats left and righthanded.
Received bachelor of science degree from University of Southern California, Los Angeles, Calif.

Year	Club	League	Pos.	G.	AB.	R.	H.	2B.	3B.	HR.	RBI.	B.A.	PO.	A.	E.	F.A.
1978—Tucson		P. C.	3B	19	62	5	16	4	0	0	8	.258	2	13	4	.789
1979—Tulsa†‡		Texas	3B-OF-1B	98	354	46	117	18	3	6	54	.331	26	28	6	.900
1980—Denver		A. A.	DH-PH	9	25	3	5	0	0	1	3	.200	0	0	0	.000
1980—Memphis		South.	3B-1B-OF	8	9	336	51	102	16	1	12	.304	160	86	15	.943
1981—Denver		A. A.	OF-3B	38	132	22	40	9	1	1	17	.303	18	6	2	.923
1981—Montreal		Nat.	2B	7	7	0	0	0	0	0	0	.000	0	1	0	1.000
1982—Wichita		A. A.	3B-OF-1B	115	445	79	145	27	9	14	84	.326	39	26	4	.942
1982—Montreal§		Nat.	PH	2	2	0	0	0	0	0	0	.000	0	0	0	.000
1983—Phoenix		P. C.	OF-1B	123	449	88	170	31	5	21	102	★.379	166	11	6	.967
1983—San Francisco x		Nat.	1B-OF-3B	22	67	13	22	6	1	1	11	.328	118	8	3	.977
Major League Totals				31	76	13	22	6	1	1	11	.289	118	9	3	.977

Selected by Baltimore Orioles' organization in 30th round of free-agent draft, June 4, 1975.
Selected by Texas Rangers' organization in 11th round of free-agent draft, June 6, 1978.
†On disabled list, May 10 to June 10, 1979.
‡Traded with Infielder-Outfielder LaRue Washington to Montreal Expos' organization for First Baseman-Outfielder Rusty Staub, March 31, 1980.
§Traded to San Francisco Giants for Outfielder Jim Wohlford, February 2, 1983.
xReleased, October 27, 1983; signed by Yakult Swallows of Japanese baseball.

DAVID STANLEY SMITH JR.
(Dave)

Born January 21, 1955, at San Francisco, Calif.
Height, 6.01. Weight, 195.
Throws and bats righthanded.
Attended San Diego State University, San Diego, Calif.

Major League saves: 1980 (10), 1981 (8), 1982 (11), 1983 (6). Total—35.

Year	Club	League	G.	IP.	W.	L.	Pct.	H.	R.	ER.	SO.	BB.	ERA.
1976—Covington		Ap'lachian	15	97	5	5	.500	80	40	29	71	28	2.69
1977—Cocoa		Florida St.	14	93	7	5	.583	97	40	32	81	31	3.10
1977—Columbus		Southern	9	54	3	5	.375	52	2	21	29	24	3.50
1978—Columbus		Southern	26	181	10	13	.435	170	89	70	114	88	3.48
1979—Charleston		Int'national	34	160	7	8	.467	159	80	65	90	44	3.66
1980—Houston		National	57	103	7	5	.583	90	24	22	85	32	1.92
1981—Houston		National	42	75	5	3	.625	54	26	23	52	23	2.76
1982—Houston†		National	49	63⅓	5	4	.556	69	30	27	28	31	3.84
1983—Houston		National	42	72⅔	3	1	.750	72	32	25	41	36	3.10
Major League Totals			190	314	20	13	.606	285	112	97	206	122	2.78

Selected by Houston Astros' organization in 8th round of free-agent draft, June 8, 1976.
†On disabled list, June 27 to July 18, 1982.

DIVISION SERIES RECORD

Year	Club	League	G.	IP.	W.	L.	Pct.	H.	R.	ER.	SO.	BB.	ERA.
1981—Houston		National	2	2⅓	0	0	.000	2	1	1	4	0	3.86

CHAMPIONSHIP SERIES RECORD

Year	Club	League	G.	IP.	W.	L.	Pct.	H.	R.	ER.	SO.	BB.	ERA.
1980—Houston		National	3	2⅓	1	0	1.000	4	1	1	4	2	3.86

DAVID WAYNE SMITH

Born August 30, 1957, at Tomball, Tex.
Height, 6.01. Weight, 190.
Throws and bats righthanded.
Attended Lamar University, Beaumont, Tex.

Year	Club	League	G.	IP.	W.	L.	Pct.	H.	R.	ER.	SO.	BB.	ERA.
1979—Grays Harbor		Northwest	14	70	3	5	.375	81	40	34	60	31	4.37
1980—Lynchburg		Carolina	29	113	8	7	.533	121	60	42	63	63	3.35
1981—Lynchburg		Carolina	28	61	5	2	.714	59	25	16	41	26	2.36
1981—Jackson†		Texas	24	56	4	4	.500	55	32	28	42	25	4.50
1982—Holyoke		Eastern	39	142⅔	4	9	.308	154	80	54	104	70	3.41
1983—Nashua		Eastern	24	36⅓	2	2	.500	32	9	8	30	15	1.98
1983—Edmonton		P. Coast	23	38⅓	6	3	.667	40	24	24	22	26	5.17

Selected by New York Mets' organization in 27th round of free-agent draft, June 5, 1979.
†Drafted by Salt Lake City (California Angels' organization), December 8, 1981.

JAMES LORNE SMITH
(Jimmy)

Born September 8, 1954, at Santa Monica, Calif.
Height, 6.03. Weight, 185.
Throws and bats righthanded.
Attended El Camino College, Torrance, Calif., and California State
University at Long Beach, Long Beach, Calif.

Led Pacific Coast League shortstops in fielding percentage with .980 in 1981.
Led International League shortstops in double plays with 66 in 1979.
Led Southern League shortstops in double plays with 111 in 1977.
Tied for Appalachian League lead in sacrifice flies with 8 in 1976.

Year	Club	League	Pos.	G.	AB.	R.	H.	2B.	3B.	HR.	RBI.	B.A.	PO.	A.	E.	F.A.
1976—Bluefield	Appal.		SS	•70	262	46	76	14	1	5	35	.290	*101	*206	14	*.956
1977—Charlotte	South.		SS	125	424	51	85	14	1	10	41	.200	216	*460	26	*.963
1978—Rochester†	Int.		SS	102	290	37	64	11	0	6	26	.221	147	353	25	*.952
1979—Rochester	Int.		SS	130	404	48	96	15	2	4	34	.238	*240	*358	26	.958
1980—Roch.‡§-Tide. x	Int.		SS-3B	89	290	23	71	17	1	5	34	.245	111	192	15	.953
1981—Portland	P. C.		SS-2B	129	386	53	97	16	5	10	51	.251	210	289	10	.980
1982—Pittsburgh y	Nat.		SS-2B-3B	42	42	5	10	2	1	0	4	.238	34	50	7	.923
1983—Denver z	A. A.		SS	94	319	55	93	17	4	7	45	.292	148	287	18	.960
Major League Totals				42	42	5	10	2	1	0	4	.238	34	50	7	.923

Selected by Baltimore Orioles' organization in 6th round of free-agent draft, June 8, 1976.
†On disabled list, May 4 to June 7, 1978.
‡On disabled list, April 16 to May 14, 1980.
§Loaned to Tidewater (New York Mets' organization), June 3, 1980; returned, September 3, 1980.
xSold to Portland (Pittsburgh Pirates' organization), April 5, 1981.
yLoaned to Denver (Chicago White Sox' organization), April 4, 1983; returned, September 21, 1983.
zGranted free agency, October 15, 1983; signed by Detroit Tigers, October 31, 1983.

KENNETH EARL SMITH
(Ken)

Born Feburary 12, 1958, at Youngstown, O.
Height, 6.01. Weight, 195.
Throws right and bats lefthanded.
Attended Youngstown State University, Youngstown, O.

Led International League batters in strikeouts with 106 in 1980.
Led Southern League in bases on balls received with 102 in 1979.
Led International League first basemen in putouts with 1,158, assists with 84 and double plays with 95 in 1980.

Year	Club	League	Pos.	G.	AB.	R.	H.	2B.	3B.	HR.	RBI.	B.A.	PO.	A.	E.	F.A.
1976—Brad. Braves	Gulf C.		OF-1B	32	94	24	24	3	1	1	12	.255	78	6	4	.955
1977—Greenwood†	W. Car.		OF-1B	67	212	38	64	7	0	1	25	.302	89	5	4	.959
1978—Savannah	South.		OF	138	462	55	110	19	5	2	40	.238	225	10	10	.959
1979—Savannah	South.		1B-OF	141	449	71	112	12	4	10	51	.249	1188	85	7	.995
1980—Richmond	Int.		1-O-2-3	132	418	61	103	17	4	12	53	.246	1167	86	15	.988
1981—Richmond	Int.		1B-OF	129	478	64	128	9	6	11	60	.268	1062	84	12	.990
1981—Atlanta	Nat.		1B	5	3	0	1	1	0	0	0	.333	6	1	0	1.000
1982—Atlanta	Nat.		1B-OF	48	41	6	12	1	0	0	3	.293	15	1	0	1.000
1982—Richmond	Int.		OF	43	129	24	34	3	0	8	25	.264	27	2	1	.967
1983—Atlanta	Nat.		1B	30	12	2	2	0	0	1	2	.167	27	6	0	1.000
1983—Richmond‡	Int.		1B-OF	52	174	36	49	8	2	4	31	.282	281	16	2	.993
Major League Totals				83	56	8	15	2	0	1	5	.268	48	8	0	1.000

Selected by Atlanta Braves' organization in 1st round (third player selected) of free-agent draft, June 8, 1976.
†On disabled list, April 27 to June 24, 1977.
‡Granted free agency, October 20, 1983.

LEE ARTHUR SMITH

Born December 4, 1957, at Jamestown, La.
Height, 6.05. Weight, 220.
Throws and bats righthanded.
Attended Northwestern State University, Natchitoches, La.

Major League saves: 1981 (1), 1982 (17), 1983 (29). Total—47.
Led National League in saves with 29 and games finished in relief with 56 in 1983.
Tied for American Association lead in wild pitches with 16 in 1980.
Named National League co-Fireman of the Year by THE SPORTING NEWS, 1983.

Year	Club	League	G.	IP.	W.	L.	Pct.	H.	R.	ER.	SO.	BB.	ERA.
1975—Bradenton Cubs	Gulf Coast	10	62	3	5	.375	35	23	16	35	*49	2.32
1976—Pompano Beach	Florida St.	26	101	4	8	.333	120	76	60	52	74	5.35
1977—Pompano Beach	Florida St.	26	130	10	4	.714	131	67	62	82	85	4.29
1978—Midland	Texas	30	155	8	10	.444	161	122	103	71	*128	5.98
1979—Midland	Texas	35	104	9	5	.643	122	65	57	46	85	4.93
1980—Wichita	Am. Assoc.	50	90	4	7	.364	70	49	37	63	56	3.70
1980—Chicago	National	18	22	2	0	1.000	21	9	7	17	14	2.86
1981—Chicago	National	40	67	3	6	.333	57	31	26	50	31	3.49
1982—Chicago	National	72	117	2	5	.286	105	38	35	99	37	2.69
1983—Chicago	National	66	103⅓	4	10	.286	70	23	19	91	41	1.65
Major League Totals		196	309⅓	11	21	.344	253	101	87	257	123	2.53

Selected by Chicago Cubs' organization in 2nd round of free-agent draft, June 4, 1975.

Year League	IP.	W.	L.	Pct.	H.	R.	ER.	SO.	BB.	ERA.
1983—National	1	0	0	.000	2	2	1	1	0	9.00

LEROY PURDY SMITH III
(Roy)

Born September 6, 1961, at Mt. Vernon, N.Y.
Height, 6.03. Weight, 205.
Throws and bats righthanded.
Attended Fordham University, Bronx, N.Y.

Tied for Carolina League lead in shutouts with 3 in 1980.
Named Carolina League Pitcher of the Year, 1980.

Year Club	League	G.	IP.	W.	L.	Pct.	H.	R.	ER.	SO.	BB.	ERA.
1979—Helena	Pioneer	5	36	5	0	1.000	21	16	10	42	16	2.50
1980—Peninsula	Carolina	27	163	*17	6	.739	101	54	47	134	63	2.60
1981—Reading	Eastern	27	161	11	8	.579	123	92	79	117	97	4.42
1982—Reading†	Eastern	26	166	10	8	.556	141	81	71	122	82	3.85
1983—Charleston	Int'national	27	155⅓	6	8	.429	166	101	89	95	75	5.16

Selected by Philadelphia Phillies' organization in 3rd round of free-agent draft, June 5, 1979.
†Traded with Pitcher Jerry Reed and Outfielder Wil Culmer to Cleveland Indians for Pitcher John Denny, September 12, 1982.

LONNIE SMITH

Born December 22, 1955, at Chicago, Ill.
Height, 5.09. Weight, 170.
Throws and bats righthanded.

Tied modern National League record for most stolen bases, game, (5), September 4, 1982.
Major League stolen bases: 1978 (4), 1979 (2), 1980 (33), 1981 (21), 1982 (68), 1983 (43). Total—171.
Led National League in being hit by pitch with 9 in 1982 and tied for lead with 9 in 1983.
Tied for National League lead in caught stealing with 26 in 1982.
Tied for National League lead in double plays by outfielders with 4 in 1983.
Led American Association in stolen bases with 66 and caught stealing with 19 in 1978.
Led Western Carolinas League in stolen bases with 56 and tied for lead in caught stealing with 14 in 1975.
Led American Association outfielders in double plays with 5 in 1978.
Named National League Rookie Player of the Year by THE SPORTING NEWS, 1980.
Named outfielder on THE SPORTING NEWS National League All-Star Team, 1982.

Year Club	League	Pos.	G.	AB.	R.	H.	2B.	3B.	HR.	RBI.	B.A.	PO.	A.	E.	F.A.
1974—Auburn	NYP	OF	61	210	48	60	10	4	5	27	.286	143	6	●9	.943
1975—Spartanburg	W. Car.	OF	131	465	*114	*150	23	4	7	40	.323	*317	9	11	.967
1976—Oklahoma City	A. A.	OF	134	483	*93	149	24	9	8	54	.308	200	4	*14	.936
1977—Oklahoma City	A. A.	OF	125	477	91	132	14	10	4	41	.277	231	8	*13	.948
1978—Oklahoma City†	A. A.	OF	125	480	103	151	20	5	7	43	.315	274	*21	*12	.961
1978—Philadelphia	Nat.	OF	17	4	6	0	0	0	0	0	.000	5	1	0	1.000
1979—Oklahoma City	A. A.	OF	110	451	*106	149	26	9	7	44	.330	268	13	*12	.959
1979—Philadelphia	Nat.	OF	17	30	4	5	2	0	0	3	.167	19	1	0	1.000
1980—Philadelphia	Nat.	OF	100	298	69	101	14	4	3	20	.339	121	2	4	.969
1981—Philadelphia‡	Nat.	OF	62	176	40	57	14	3	2	11	.324	91	10	3	.971
1982—St. Louis	Nat.	OF	156	592	*120	182	35	8	8	69	.307	303	●16	10	.970
1983—St. Louis§	Nat.	OF	130	492	83	158	31	5	8	45	.321	225	14	*15	.941
Major League Totals			482	1592	322	503	96	20	21	148	.316	764	44	32	.962

Selected by Philadelphia Phillies' organization in 1st round (third player selected) of free-agent draft, June 5, 1974.
†On disabled list, April 14 to April 25, 1978.
‡Traded with a player to be named later to Cleveland Indians for Catcher Bo Diaz, November 20, 1981; Traded by Cleveland to St. Louis Cardinals for Pitchers Lary Sorensen and Silvio Martinez, November 20, 1981. Cleveland organization acquired Pitcher Scott Munninghoff to complete first deal, December 9, 1981.
§On disabled list, June 11 to July 8, 1983.

DIVISION SERIES RECORD

Year Club	League	Pos.	G.	AB.	R.	H.	2B.	3B.	HR.	RBI.	B.A.	PO.	A.	E.	F.A.
1981—Philadelphia	Nat.	OF	5	19	1	5	1	0	0	0	.263	6	1	0	1.000

CHAMPIONSHIP SERIES RECORD

Year Club	League	Pos.	G.	AB.	R.	H.	2B.	3B.	HR.	RBI.	B.A.	PO.	A.	E.	F.A.
1980—Philadelphia	Nat.	PR-OF	3	5	2	3	0	0	0	0	.600	2	1	0	1.000
1982—St. Louis	Nat.	OF	3	11	1	3	0	0	0	1	.273	2	0	0	1.000
Championship Series Totals			6	16	3	6	0	0	0	1	.375	4	1	0	1.000

WORLD SERIES RECORD

Year Club	League	Pos.	G.	AB.	R.	H.	2B.	3B.	HR.	RBI.	B.A.	PO.	A.	E.	F.A.
1980—Philadelphia	Nat.	PR-O-DH	6	19	2	5	1	0	0	1	.263	4	1	0	1.000
1982—St. Louis	Nat.	OF-DH	7	28	6	9	4	1	0	1	.321	11	0	0	1.000
World Series Totals			13	47	8	14	5	1	0	2	.298	15	1	0	1.000

ALL-STAR GAME RECORD

Year League	Pos.	AB.	R.	H.	2B.	3B.	HR.	RBI.	B.A.	PO.	A.	E.	F.A.
1982—National	OF	0	0	0	0	0	0	0	.000	1	0	0	1.000

MARK CHRISTOPHER SMITH

Born November 23, 1955, at Arlington, Va.
Height, 6.02. Weight, 190.
Throws right and bats lefthanded.
Attended Ferrum College, Ferrum, Va., and
American University, Washington, D.C.

Led Appalachian League pitchers in complete games with 8 and tied for lead in games started with 14 and hit batsmen with 6 in 1977.

Year Club	League	G.	IP.	W.	L.	Pct.	H.	R.	ER.	SO.	BB.	ERA.
1977—Bluefield	Ap'lachian	14	98	7	5	.583	75	41	33	★89	53	3.03
1978—Miami	Florida St.	27	186	15	9	.625	177	89	★77	110	73	3.73
1978—Rochester	Int'national	3	15	0	3	.000	20	17	15	4	10	9.00
1979—Charlotte†						(Did not play)						
1980—Alexandria‡	Carolina	8	32	0	2	.000	37	25	22	25	20	6.19
1980—Charlotte§	Southern	3	15	1	1	.500	19	14	13	6	6	7.80
1981—Charlotte	Southern	25	163	8	6	.571	165	90	73	113	58	4.03
1982—Charlotte	Southern	26	100⅓	6	8	.429	101	70	62	72	60	5.56
1982—Rochester	Int'national	2	3⅔	0	0	.000	2	1	1	3	6	2.45
1983—Rochester x	Int'national	21	49	2	3	.400	50	31	29	35	46	5.33
1983—Tacoma	P. Coast	11	43⅓	2	2	.500	33	21	18	34	20	3.74
1983—Oakland	American	8	14⅔	1	0	1.000	24	11	11	10	6	6.75
Major League Totals		8	14⅔	1	0	1.000	24	11	11	10	6	6.75

Selected by Baltimore Orioles' organization in 9th round of free-agent draft, June 7, 1977.
†On disabled list, April 16, 1979 through remainder of season.
‡On disabled list, May 14 to June 21, 1980.
§On disabled list, August 3, 1980 through remainder of season.
xTraded to Tacoma (Oakland A's organization) for Pitcher Jerry King, July 6, 1983.

MICHAEL ANTHONY SMITH
(Mike)

Born February 23, 1961, at Jackson, Miss.
Height, 6.01. Weight, 195.
Throws right and bats right and lefthanded.
Attended Utica Junior College, Utica, Miss.

Led Florida State League in saves with 21 in 1982.

Year Club	League	G.	IP.	W.	L.	Pct.	H.	R.	ER.	SO.	BB.	ERA.
1981—Billings	Pion.	22	46	5	5	.500	39	21	7	52	19	1.37
1982—Tampa	Florida St.	48	80⅓	7	1	.875	55	17	11	80	42	1.23
1983—Waterbury†	Eastern	22	28⅔	2	5	.286	18	13	9	16	25	2.83

Signed as free agent by Cincinnati Reds' organization, May 11, 1981.
†On disabled list, June 28, 1983 through remainder of season.

OSBORNE EARL SMITH
(Ozzie)

Born December 26, 1954, at Mobile, Ala.
Height, 5.10. Weight, 150.
Throws right and bats left and righthanded.
Attended California Polytechnic State University, San Luis Obispo, Calif.

Established major league record for most assists by shortstop, season (621), 1980.
Tied major league record for most consecutive years leading league in assists, shortstop (4), 1979 through 1982.
Major League stolen bases: 1978 (40), 1979 (28), 1980 (57), 1981 (22), 1982 (25), 1983 (34). Total—206.
Led National League in sacrifice hits with 28 in 1978 and 23 in 1980.
Led National League shortstops in total chances with 933 in 1980, 658 in 1981 and 844 in 1983.
Led National League shortstops in double plays with 113 in 1980.
Led Northwest League in stolen bases with 30 in 1977.
Led Northwest League shortstops in double plays with 40 in 1977.
Named shortstop on THE SPORTING NEWS National League All-Star Team, 1982.
Named shortstop on THE SPORTING NEWS National League All-Star fielding team, 1980 through 1983.

Year Club	League	Pos.	G.	AB.	R.	H.	2B.	3B.	HR.	RBI.	B.A.	PO.	A.	E.	F.A.
1977—Walla Walla	N'west	SS	●68	★287	★69	87	10	2	1	35	.303	130	★254	23	★.943
1978—San Diego	Nat.	SS	159	590	69	152	17	6	1	46	.258	264	548	25	.970
1979—San Diego	Nat.	SS	156	587	77	124	18	6	0	27	.211	256	★555	20	.976
1980—San Diego	Nat.	SS	158	609	67	140	18	5	0	35	.230	★288	★621	24	.974
1981—San Diego†	Nat.	SS	●110	★450	53	100	11	2	0	21	.222	220	★422	16	★.976
1982—St. Louis	Nat.	SS	140	488	58	121	24	1	2	43	.248	279	★535	13	★.984
1983—St. Louis	Nat.	SS	159	552	69	134	30	6	3	50	.243	★304	519	21	.975
Major League Totals			882	3276	393	771	118	26	6	222	.235	1611	3200	119	.976

Selected by Detroit Tigers' organization in 7th round of free-agent draft, June 8, 1976.
Selected by San Diego Padres' organization in 4th round of free-agent draft, June 7, 1977.
†Traded to St. Louis Cardinals for Shortstop Garry Templeton, February 11, 1982.

CHAMPIONSHIP SERIES RECORD

Year Club	League	Pos.	G.	AB.	R.	H.	2B.	3B.	HR.	RBI.	B.A.	PO.	A.	E.	F.A.
1982—St. Louis	Nat.	SS	3	9	0	5	0	0	0	3	.556	4	11	0	1.000

Established World Series record for most putouts by shortstop, seven-game Series (22), 1982.

Year Club	League	Pos.	G.	AB.	R.	H.	2B.	3B.	HR.	RBI.	B.A.	PO.	A.	E.	F.A.
1982—St. Louis.................	Nat.	SS	7	24	3	5	0	0	0	1	.208	22	17	0	1.000

ALL-STAR GAME RECORD

Year League	Pos.	AB.	R.	H.	2B.	3B.	HR.	RBI.	B.A.	PO.	A.	E.	F.A.
1981—National..	SS	0	0	0	0	0	0	0	.000	1	0	0	1.000
1982—National..	PR-SS	0	0	0	0	0	0	0	.000	0	1	0	1.000
1983—National..	SS	2	1	1	0	0	0	0	.500	0	0	0	.000
All-Star Game Totals		2	1	1	0	0	0	0	.500	1	1	0	1.000

PATRICK KEITH SMITH
(Known by middle name.)

Born October 20, 1961, at Los Angeles, Calif.
Height, 6.01. Weight, 175.
Throws and bats righthanded.

Led New York-Pennsylvania League in sacrifice hits with 9 in 1980.

Year Club	League	Pos.	G.	AB.	R.	H.	2B.	3B.	HR.	RBI.	B.A.	PO.	A.	E.	F.A.
1979—Oneonta.................	NYP	SS	56	119	19	29	0	0	0	9	.244	65	115	21	.896
1980—Greensboro†.........	S. Atl.	SS	21	63	10	12	3	0	0	1	.190	23	47	5	.933
1980—Oneonta.................	NYP	SS	65	193	32	47	2	0	0	11	.244	*104	186	21	*.932
1981—Oneonta.................	NYP	SS	19	50	8	10	1	0	0	3	.200	30	52	7	.921
1981—Greensboro............	S. Atl.	SS-3B	33	60	14	12	0	0	0	4	.200	25	67	4	.958
1982—Ft. Lauderdale	Fla. St.	S-2-3-1	94	178	26	39	8	0	0	11	.219	130	184	13	.960
1982—Nashville..............	South.	SS	4	12	0	0	0	0	0	0	.000	4	13	1	.944
1983—Nashville..............	South.	SS-2B	141	426	78	110	8	4	8	38	.258	240	445	37	.949

Selected by New York Yankees' organization in 15th round of free-agent draft, June 5, 1979.
†On disabled list, June 5 to June 15, 1980.

RAYMOND EDWARD SMITH
(Ray)

Born September 18, 1955, at Glendale, Calif.
Height, 6.01. Weight, 188.
Throws and bats righthanded.
Attended Mira Costa College, Oceanside, Calif., and received bachelor of science degree
in recreation administration from University of Oregon, Eugene, Ore in 1976.

Year Club	League	Pos.	G.	AB.	R.	H.	2B.	3B.	HR.	RBI.	B.A.	PO.	A.	E.	F.A.
1977—Visalia	Calif.	SS	33	120	23	43	6	0	1	20	.358	54	101	19	.891
1977—Elizabethton	Appal.	C-1-3-S	63	234	50	71	13	1	7	42	.303	371	39	4	.990
1978—Orlando†	South.	C	72	216	26	58	10	0	2	31	.269	310	23	13	.962
1979—Toledo	Int.	C-3B	78	233	24	58	7	3	3	24	.249	358	28	11	.972
1980—Toledo	Int.	C	115	398	36	109	14	4	0	46	.274	461	64	7	.987
1981—Minnesota‡..........	Amer.	C	15	40	4	8	1	0	1	1	.200	65	3	0	1.000
1982—Toledo	Int.	C	94	305	25	83	13	2	6	43	.272	449	59	11	.979
1982—Minnesota............	Amer.	C	9	23	1	5	0	1	0	1	.217	44	2	0	1.000
1983—Minnesota............	Amer.	C	59	152	11	34	5	0	0	8	.224	272	27	5	.984
Major League Totals...................................			83	215	16	47	6	1	1	10	.219	381	32	5	.988

Signed as free agent by Minnesota Twins' organization, January 24, 1977.
†On disabled list, May 23 to June 3, 1978.
‡On disabled list, May 8, 1981 through remainder of season.

BILLY MIKE SMITHSON
(Known by middle name.)

Born January 21, 1955, at Centerville, Tenn.
Height, 6.08. Weight, 205.
Throws right and bats lefthanded.
Attended University of Tennessee, Knoxville, Tenn.

Tied for International League lead in intentional bases on balls issued with 13 in 1980.

Year Club	League	G.	IP.	W.	L.	Pct.	H.	R.	ER.	SO.	BB.	ERA.
1976—Winter Haven.............................	Florida St.	11	64	4	3	.571	63	27	22	29	20	3.09
1977—Winter Haven.............................	Florida St.	25	172	13	8	.619	170	56	53	92	41	2.77
1977—Bristol.......................................	Eastern	1	3	0	1	.000	8	7	7	1	0	21.00
1978—Bristol.......................................	Eastern	27	160	11	10	.524	178	92	81	86	76	4.56
1979—Bristol.......................................	Eastern	*48	132	8	12	.400	128	82	69	89	53	4.70
1980—Pawtucket.................................	Int'national	*50	99	5	9	.357	95	50	32	73	45	2.91
1981—Pawtucket†...............................	Int'national	34	91	2	4	.333	74	44	39	82	45	3.86
1982—Denver.......................................	Am. Assoc.	29	152⅔	11	7	.611	149	82	77	*144	47	4.54
1982—Texas...	American	8	46⅔	3	4	.429	51	26	26	24	13	5.01
1983—Texas‡.......................................	American	33	223⅓	10	14	.417	233	102	97	135	71	3.91
Major League Totals.............................		41	270	13	18	.419	284	128	123	159	84	4.10

Selected by Boston Red Sox' organization in 5th round of free-agent draft, June 8, 1976.
†Traded to Texas Rangers' organization for Pitcher John Henry Johnson, April 9, 1982.
‡Traded with Pitcher John Butcher and Catcher Sam Sorce to Minnesota Twins for Outfielder Gary Ward, December 7, 1983.

NATHANIEL SNELL
(Nat)

Born September 2, 1955, at Orangeburg, S.C.
Height, 6.04. Weight, 190.
Throws and bats righthanded.
Attended Tennessee State University, Nashville, Tenn.

Led Southern League in home runs allowed with 20 in 1978.

Year Club	League	G.	IP.	W.	L.	Pct.	H.	R.	ER.	SO.	BB.	ERA.
1977—Miami	Florida St.	16	106	7	7	.500	106	41	20	68	15	1.70
1978—Charlotte	Southern	28	193	7	13	.350	*193	91	78	97	44	3.64
1979—Charlotte	Southern	10	65	5	2	.714	65	30	27	42	29	3.74
1979—Rochester†‡	Int'national	12	76	4	7	.364	72	44	37	35	22	4.38
1980—Shreveport§	Texas	33	64	4	4	.500	77	38	32	44	18	4.50
1981—Charlotte	Southern	8	38	1	2	.333	32	14	11	19	10	2.61
1981—Rochester	Int'national	15	41	1	3	.250	33	14	12	20	7	2.63
1982—Rochester x	Int'national	37	83⅓	4	6	.400	83	40	34	31	26	3.67
1983—Charlotte	Southern	15	22⅔	1	0	1.000	15	0	0	7	6	0.00
1983—Rochester y	Int'national	39	70	6	2	.750	71	29	28	46	17	3.60

Selected by Baltimore Orioles' organization in 18th round of free-agent draft, June 6, 1972.
Selected by Atlanta Braves' organization in 22nd round of free-agent draft, June 4, 1975.
Signed as free agent by Baltimore Orioles' organization, September 5, 1976.
†On disabled list, July 17 to August 5, 1979.
‡Drafted by Phoenix (San Francisco Giants' organization), December 4, 1979.
§Released, March 27, 1981; signed by Charlotte (Baltimore Orioles' organization), May 26, 1981.
xOn disabled list, May 3 to June 9, 1982.
yGranted free agency, October 20, 1983.

MICHAEL WAYNE SODDERS
(Mike)

Born December 26, 1958, at Compton, Calif.
Height, 6.03. Weight, 200.
Throws and bats righthanded.
Attended Orange Coast College, Costa Mesa, Calif., and received degree in business
from Arizona State University, Tempe, Ariz.

Received reported $42,500 bonus to sign with Minnesota Twins, 1981.

Year Club	League	Pos.	G.	AB.	R.	H.	2B.	3B.	HR.	RBI.	B.A.	PO.	A.	E.	F.A.
1981—Wisconsin Rapids	Midw.	1B-3B	23	78	6	14	2	0	2	15	.179	59	7	3	.957
1982—Toledo	Int.	3B	37	122	17	26	6	0	2	7	.213	18	68	7	.925
1982—Orlando†	South.	3B-1B-OF	61	207	28	52	13	1	8	30	.251	43	138	9	.953
1983—Orlando‡	South.	1B-3B-OF	67	242	37	56	9	2	9	41	.231	412	57	5	.989
1983—Glens Falls	East.	3B-OF-1B	68	215	30	54	10	2	8	36	.251	80	118	9	.957

Selected by New York Mets' organization in 12th round of free-agent draft, January 9, 1979.
Selected by Minnesota Twins' organization in 1st round (11th player selected) of free-agent draft, June 8, 1981.
†On disabled list, July 8 to August 3, 1982.
‡Traded to Chicago White Sox' organization for Outfielder Rusty Kuntz, June 21, 1983.

JULIO CESAR SOLANO

Born January 8, 1960, at Agua Blanca, Dominican Republic.
Height, 6.01. Weight, 155.
Throws and bats righthanded.

Led South Atlantic League in hit batsmen with 11 and tied for lead in games started by pitchers with 27 and shutouts with 3 in 1982.

Year Club	League	G.	IP.	W.	L.	Pct.	H.	R.	ER.	SO.	BB.	ERA.
1980—Sarasota Astros-Orange	Gulf Coast	18	38	5	2	.714	31	16	11	29	23	2.61
1981—Sarasota Astros-Blue	Gulf Coast	17	74	4	4	.500	71	47	32	45	36	3.89
1982—Asheville	S. Atlantic	28	178	10	7	.588	165	89	70	163	116	3.54
1983—Houston	National	4	6	0	2	.000	5	5	4	3	4	6.00
1983—Tucson	P. Coast	29	161⅔	10	7	.588	183	104	89	123	71	4.95
Major League Totals		4	6	0	2	.000	5	5	4	3	4	6.00

Signed as free agent by Houston Astros' organization, November 21, 1979.

LARY ALAN SORENSEN

Born October 4, 1955, at Detroit, Mich.
Height, 6.02. Weight, 200.
Throws and bats righthanded.
Attending University of Michigan, Ann Arbor, Mich.

Tied for National League lead in balks with 5 in 1981.
Tied for Pacific Coast League lead in shutouts with 3 in 1977.
Tied for New York-Pennsylvania league lead in complete games with 7 and shutouts with 2 in 1976.

Year Club	League	G.	IP.	W.	L.	Pct.	H.	R.	ER.	SO.	BB.	ERA.
1976—Newark	NYP	13	75	6	2	.750	58	22	19	65	27	2.28
1976—Berkshire	Eastern	7	41	0	3	.000	44	19	15	25	16	3.29
1977—Spokane	P. Coast	12	72	5	5	.500	79	41	37	43	31	4.63
1977—Milwaukee	American	23	142	7	10	.412	147	72	69	57	36	4.37
1978—Milwaukee	American	37	281	18	12	.600	277	111	100	78	50	3.20

Year Club	League	G.	IP.	W.	L.	Pct.	H.	R.	ER.	SO.	BB.	ERA.
1979—Milwaukee	American	34	235	15	14	.517	250	113	104	63	42	3.98
1980—Milwaukee†	American	35	196	12	10	.545	242	91	80	54	45	3.67
1981—St. Louis‡	National	23	140	7	7	.500	149	59	51	52	26	3.28
1982—Cleveland	American	32	189⅓	10	15	.400	251	130	118	62	55	5.61
1983—Cleveland§	American	36	222⅔	12	11	.522	238	112	105	76	65	4.24
American League Totals		197	1266	74	72	.507	1405	629	576	390	293	4.09
National League Totals		23	140	7	7	.500	149	59	51	52	26	3.28
Major League Totals		220	1406	81	79	.506	1554	688	627	442	319	4.01

Selected by Milwaukee Brewers' organization in 8th round of free-agent draft, June 8, 1976.

†Traded with Outfielders Sixto Lezcano and David Green and Pitcher Dave LaPoint to St. Louis Cardinals for Pitchers Rollie Fingers and Pete Vuckovich and Catcher Ted Simmons, December 12, 1980.

‡Traded with Pitcher Silvio Martinez to Cleveland Indians for Outfielder Lonnie Smith, November 20, 1981.

§Granted free agency, November 7, 1983.

ALL-STAR GAME RECORD

Year League	IP.	W.	L.	Pct.	H.	R.	ER.	SO.	BB.	ERA.
1978—American	3	0	0	.000	1	0	0	0	0	0.00

ELIAS SOSA (MARTINEZ)

First name pronounced E-lee-us.

Born June 10, 1950, at La Vega, Dominican Republic.
Height, 6.02. Weight, 205.
Throws and bats righthanded.

Major League saves: 1972 (3), 1973 (18), 1974 (6), 1975 (2), 1976 (4), 1977 (1), 1978 (14), 1979 (18), 1980 (9), 1981 (3), 1982 (4), 1983 (1). Total—83.

Year Club	League	G.	IP.	W.	L.	Pct.	H.	R.	ER.	SO.	BB.	ERA.
1968—Salt Lake City	Pioneer	8	18	0	5	.000	33	32	16	15	14	8.00
1969—Decatur	Midwest	9	22	0	1	.000	27	13	11	24	17	4.50
1969—Great Falls	Pioneer	14	27	0	2	.000	22	21	18	38	22	6.00
1970—Amarillo	Texas	3	5	0	0	.000	3	2	1	2	4	1.80
1970—Fresno	California	21	102	6	8	.429	119	66	58	95	39	5.12
1971—Fresno	California	31	152	12	9	.571	140	68	56	124	48	3.32
1972—Phoenix	P. Coast	55	120	10	2	.833	123	40	39	107	44	2.93
1972—San Francisco	National	8	16	0	1	.000	10	4	4	10	12	2.25
1973—San Francisco	National	71	107	10	4	.714	95	42	39	70	41	3.28
1974—San Francisco†	National	68	101	9	7	.563	94	54	39	48	45	3.48
1975—St. Louis‡-Atlanta	National	57	90	2	5	.286	92	49	43	46	43	4.30
1976—Atlanta§-Los Angeles	National	45	69	6	8	.429	71	42	34	52	25	4.43
1977—Los Angeles x	National	44	64	2	2	.500	42	15	14	47	12	1.97
1978—Oakland y	American	68	109	8	2	.800	106	37	32	61	44	2.64
1979—Montreal	National	62	97	8	7	.533	77	24	21	59	37	1.95
1980—Montreal	National	67	94	9	6	.600	104	33	32	58	19	3.06
1981—Montreal z	National	32	39	1	2	.333	46	16	16	18	8	3.69
1982—Detroit a	American	38	61	3	3	.500	64	31	30	24	18	4.43
1983—San Diego b	National	41	72⅓	1	4	.200	72	41	35	45	30	4.35
National League Totals		495	749⅓	48	46	.511	703	320	277	453	272	3.33
American League Totals		106	170	11	5	.688	170	68	62	85	62	3.28
Major League Totals		601	919⅓	59	51	.536	873	388	339	538	334	3.32

Signed as free agent by San Francisco Giants' organization, March 4, 1968.

†Traded with Catcher Ken Rudolph to St. Louis Cardinals for Catcher Marc Hill, October 14, 1974.

‡Traded with Pitcher Ray Sadecki to Atlanta Braves for Pitcher Ron Reed and a player to be named later, May 28, 1975; St. Louis Cardinals acquired Outfielder Wayne Nordhagen to complete deal, June 2, 1975.

§Traded (via waivers) with Infielder Lee Lacy to Los Angeles Dodgers for Pitcher Mike Marshall, June 23, 1976.

xSold on waivers to Pittsburgh Pirates, January 31, 1978. Traded from Pirates with Outfielder Miguel Dilone and a player to be named later to Oakland A's for Catcher Manny Sanguillen, April 4, 1978; Oakland acquired Infielder Mike Edwards to complete deal, April 10, 1978.

yGranted free agency, November 2, 1978; signed by Montreal Expos, January 8, 1979.

zSold to Detroit Tigers, March 30, 1982.

aSold to San Diego Padres, October 7, 1982.

bGranted free agency, November 7, 1983.

DIVISION SERIES RECORD

Year Club	League	G.	IP.	W.	L.	Pct.	H.	R.	ER.	SO.	BB.	ERA.
1981—Montreal	National	2	3	0	0	.000	4	2	1	1	0	3.00

CHAMPIONSHIP SERIES RECORD

Year Club	League	G.	IP.	W.	L.	Pct.	H.	R.	ER.	SO.	BB.	ERA.
1977—Los Angeles	National	2	2⅔	0	1	.000	5	4	3	0	0	10.13
1981—Montreal	National	1	⅓	0	0	.000	1	0	0	0	1	0.00
Championship Series Totals		3	3	0	1	.000	6	4	3	0	1	9.00

WORLD SERIES RECORD

Year Club	League	G.	IP.	W.	L.	Pct.	H.	R.	ER.	SO.	BB.	ERA.
1977—Los Angeles	Nat.	2	2⅓	0	0	.000	3	3	3	1	1	11.57

MIGUEL OLEA SOSA

Born May 15, 1960, at La Ramona, Dominican Republic.
Height, 5.10. Weight, 165.
Throws and bats righthanded.
Led Carolina League shortstops in double plays with 83 in 1982.
Led South Atlantic League shortstops in double plays with 78 in 1980.

Year Club	League	Pos.	G.	AB.	R.	H.	2B.	3B.	HR.	RBI.	B.A.	PO.	A.	E.	F.A.
1979—Bradenton Brav...	Gulf C.	SS	44	171	25	48	8	2	5	26	.281	52	128	★22	.891
1980—Anderson	S. Atl.	SS	125	511	81	137	23	3	18	92	.268	186	★397	49	.922
1980—Durham	Carol.	SS	5	23	5	8	3	0	1	5	.348	15	15	3	.909
1981—Durham	Carol.	SS	118	479	63	132	22	4	17	70	.276	128	315	51	.897
1982—Durham	Carol.	SS	132	507	77	146	18	4	25	69	.288	185	★354	33	.942
1983—Savannah	South.	2B-SS	125	490	54	120	16	0	17	★93	.245	196	291	22	.957
1983—Richmond	Int.	2B	2	9	2	3	1	0	0	2	.333	5	8	0	1.000

Signed as free agent by Atlanta Braves' organization, December 8, 1978.

MARIO MELVIN SOTO

Born July 12, 1956, Bani, Dominican Republic.
Height, 6.00. Weight, 185.
Throws and bats righthanded.
Tied for National League lead in games started by pitchers with 25 and home runs allowed with 13 in 1981.
Led National League in complete games with 18 and home runs allowed with 28 in 1983.
Led Florida State League in balks with 6 in 1976.
Tied for American Association lead in balks with 6 in 1978.

Year Club	League	G.	IP.	W.	L.	Pct.	H.	R.	ER.	SO.	BB.	ERA.
1974—Billings†	Pioneer					(Did not play)						
1975—Eugene	Northwest	5	30	2	3	.400	33	21	14	11	18	4.20
1976—Tampa	Florida St.	26	★197	13	7	.650	142	54	41	★124	80	1.87
1977—Indianapolis	Am. Assoc.	18	123	11	5	.688	100	51	42	109	61	3.07
1977—Cincinnati	National	12	61	2	6	.250	60	38	36	44	26	5.31
1978—Indianapolis	Am. Assoc.	26	160	9	12	.429	129	102	89	121	95	5.01
1978—Cincinnati	National	5	18	1	0	1.000	13	5	5	13	13	2.50
1979—Indianapolis‡	Am. Assoc.	15	25	1	1	.500	20	11	11	38	18	3.96
1979—Cincinnati	National	25	37	3	2	.600	33	25	22	32	30	5.35
1980—Cincinnati	National	53	190	10	8	.556	126	72	65	182	84	3.08
1981—Cincinnati	National	25	175	12	9	.571	142	69	64	151	61	3.29
1982—Cincinnati	National	35	257⅔	14	13	.519	202	88	80	274	71	2.79
1983—Cincinnati	National	34	273⅔	17	13	.567	207	96	82	242	95	2.70
Major League Totals		189	1012⅓	59	51	.536	783	393	354	938	380	3.15

Signed as free agent by Cincinnati Reds' organization, December 3, 1973.
†On disabled list, July 1 to September 17, 1974.
‡On disabled list, April 13 to May 21, 1979.

CHAMPIONSHIP SERIES RECORD

Year Club	League	G.	IP.	W.	L.	Pct.	H.	R.	ER.	SO.	BB.	ERA.
1979—Cincinnati	National	1	2	0	0	.000	0	0	0	1	0	0.00

ALL-STAR GAME RECORD

Year League	IP.	W.	L.	Pct.	H.	R.	ER.	SO.	BB.	ERA.
1982—National	2	0	0	.000	3	0	0	4	0	0.00
1983—National	2	0	1	.000	2	2	0	2	2	0.00
All-Star Game Totals	4	0	1	.000	5	2	0	6	2	0.00

CHRIS EDWARD SPEIER

Name pronounced Spire.

Born June 28, 1950, at Alameda, Calif.
Height, 6.01. Weight, 175.
Throws and bats righthanded.
Attended University of Santa Barbara, Santa Barbara, Calif.
Hit for the cycle, July 20, 1978.
Led Texas League shortstops in putouts with 223 and assists with 325 in 1970.
Named shortstop on THE SPORTING NEWS National League All-Star Team, 1972.

Year Club	League	Pos.	G.	AB.	R.	H.	2B.	3B.	HR.	RBI.	B.A.	PO.	A.	E.	F.A.
1970—Amarillo	Texas	SS-3B-OF	129	460	44	130	20	5	6	66	.283	224	327	38	.935
1971—San Francisco	Nat.	SS	157	601	74	141	17	6	8	46	.235	239	517	●33	.953
1972—San Francisco	Nat.	SS	150	562	74	151	25	2	15	71	.269	243	★517	20	.974
1973—San Francisco	Nat.	●SS-2B	153	542	58	135	17	4	11	71	.249	255	471	●33	.957
1974—San Francisco	Nat.	SS-2B	141	501	55	125	19	5	9	53	.250	215	453	21	.970
1975—San Francisco	Nat.	★SS-3B	141	487	60	132	30	5	10	69	.271	247	421	12	★.982
1976—San Francisco	Nat.	S-2-3-1	145	495	51	112	18	4	3	40	.226	241	464	19	.974
1977—S.F.†-Mont.	Nat.	SS	145	548	59	128	31	6	5	38	.234	239	455	23	.968
1978—Montreal	Nat.	SS	150	501	47	126	18	3	5	51	.251	245	467	18	.975
1979—Montreal‡	Nat.	SS	113	344	31	78	13	1	7	26	.227	194	355	17	.970
1980—Montreal	Nat.	SS-3B	128	388	35	103	14	4	1	32	.265	187	397	21	.965
1981—Montreal§	Nat.	SS	96	307	33	69	10	2	2	25	.225	175	280	17	.964

Year Club League	Pos.	G.	AB.	R.	H.	2B.	3B.	HR.	RBI.	B.A.	PO.	A.	E.	F.A.
1982—Montreal .... Nat.	SS	156	530	41	136	26	4	7	60	.257	291	405	13	.982
1983—Montreal x .... Nat.	SS-3B-2B	88	261	31	67	12	2	2	22	.257	117	203	14	.958
Major League Totals....................		1763	6067	649	1503	250	48	85	604	.248	2888	5405	261	.969

Selected by Washington Senators' organization in 11th round of free-agent draft, June 7, 1968.
Selected by San Francisco Giants' organization in secondary phase of free-agent draft, January 17, 1970.
†Traded to Montreal Expos for Shortstop Tim Foli, April 27, 1977.
‡On supplemental disabled list, July 8 to July 27, 1979.
§Granted free agency, November 13, 1981; re-signed by Expos, January 12, 1982.
xOn supplemental disabled list, May 29 to June 13, 1983.

DIVISION SERIES RECORD

Year Club League	Pos.	G.	AB.	R.	H.	2B.	3B.	HR.	RBI.	B.A.	PO.	A.	E.	F.A.
1981—Montreal .... Nat.	SS	5	15	4	6	2	0	0	3	.400	16	15	0	1.000

CHAMPIONSHIP SERIES RECORD

Year Club League	Pos.	G.	AB.	R.	H.	2B.	3B.	HR.	RBI.	B.A.	PO.	A.	E.	F.A.
1971—San Francisco ...... Nat.	SS	4	14	4	5	1	0	1	1	.357	3	14	1	.944
1981—Montreal .... Nat.	SS	5	16	0	3	0	0	0	0	.188	15	16	2	.939
Championship Series Totals		9	30	4	8	1	0	1	1	.267	18	30	3	.941

ALL-STAR GAME RECORD

Year League	Pos.	AB.	R.	H.	2B.	3B.	HR.	RBI.	B.A.	PO.	A.	E.	F.A.
1972—National	SS	2	0	0	0	0	0	0	.000	1	5	0	1.000
1973—National	SS	2	0	0	0	0	0	0	.000	1	1	0	1.000
All-Star Game Totals		4	0	0	0	0	0	0	.000	2	6	0	1.000

Member of National League All-Star Team in 1974 game; did not play.

DANIEL RAY SPILLNER
(Dan)

Born November 27, 1951, at Casper, Wyo.
Height, 6.01. Weight, 190.
Throws and bats righthanded.
Attended Green River Community College, Auburn, Wash.

Major League saves: 1975 (1), 1977 (6), 1978 (3), 1979 (1), 1981 (7), 1982 (21), 1983 (8). Total—47.
Led Pacific Coast League in home runs allowed with 27 in 1973.
Led Texas League in home runs allowed with 21 in 1972.

Year Club	League	G.	IP.	W.	L.	Pct.	H.	R.	ER.	SO.	BB.	ERA.
1970—Tri-City	Northwest	7	29	1	1	.500	37	21	18	21	15	5.59
1971—Lodi	California	25	148	10	5	.667	177	102	87	96	55	5.29
1972—Alexandria	Texas	27	180	16	7	.696	156	75	68	*85	85	3.41
1973—Hawaii	P. Coast	32	188	10	11	.476	188	105	86	124	85	4.12
1974—Hawaii	P. Coast	7	54	4	2	.667	49	24	22	47	18	3.67
1974—San Diego	National	30	148	9	11	.450	153	78	66	95	70	4.01
1975—San Diego	National	37	167	5	13	.278	194	93	79	104	63	4.26
1976—San Diego†	National	32	107	2	11	.154	120	70	60	57	55	5.05
1977—Hawaii	P. Coast	3	16	1	1	.500	21	6	6	8	4	3.38
1977—San Diego	National	76	123	7	6	.538	130	61	51	74	60	3.73
1978—San Diego‡	National	17	26	1	0	1.000	32	15	13	16	7	4.50
1978—Cleveland	American	36	56	3	1	.750	54	26	23	48	21	3.70
1979—Cleveland	American	49	158	9	5	.643	153	82	81	97	64	4.61
1980—Cleveland§	American	34	194	16	11	.593	225	122	114	100	74	5.29
1981—Cleveland	American	32	97	4	4	.500	86	41	34	59	39	3.15
1982—Cleveland	American	65	133⅔	12	10	.545	117	44	37	90	45	2.49
1983—Cleveland	American	60	92⅓	2	9	.182	117	54	52	48	38	5.07
American League Totals..		276	731	46	40	.535	752	369	341	442	281	4.20
National League Totals..		192	571	24	41	.369	629	317	269	346	255	4.24
Major League Totals....................		468	1302	70	81	.464	1381	686	610	788	536	4.22

Selected by San Diego Padres' organization in 2nd round of free-agent draft, June 4, 1970.
†On disabled list, August 3, 1976 through remainder of season.
‡Traded to Cleveland Indians for Pitcher Dennis Kinney, June 14, 1978.
§Granted free agency, October 24, 1980; re-signed by Indians, December 8, 1980.

WILLIAM HARRY SPILMAN
(Known by middle name.)

Born July 18, 1954, at Albany, Ga.
Height, 6.01. Weight, 190.
Throws right and bats lefthanded.
Son of Harry Spilman, catcher in Los Angeles Dodgers' organization, 1952.

Led Eastern League in total bases with 277 and intentional bases on balls received with 19 in 1977.
Named Eastern League Player of the Year, 1977.

Year Club	League	Pos.	G.	AB.	R.	H.	2B.	3B.	HR.	RBI.	B.A.	PO.	A.	E.	F.A.
1974—Billings	Pion.	1B-3B	54	178	29	55	12	2	2	30	.309	92	8	3	.971
1975—Tampa	Fla. St.	1B	115	348	33	90	13	1	1	38	.259	946	56	●17	.983
1976—Tampa	Fla. St.	1B	118	361	50	90	12	5	6	35	.249	986	70	16	.985

Year Club	League	Pos.	G.	AB.	R.	H.	2B.	3B.	HR.	RBI.	B.A.	PO.	A.	E.	F.A.
1977—Three Rivers	East.	1B	133	493	●94	★184	★39	3	16	78	★.373	1095	78	7	.994
1978—Indianapolis	A. A.	3B-1B	133	488	95	144	26	4	13	79	.295	262	184	23	.951
1978—Cincinnati	Nat.	PH	4	4	1	1	0	0	0	0	.250	0	0	0	.000
1979—Indianapolis	A. A.	3B-1B	71	267	42	77	13	3	3	27	.288	154	92	8	.969
1979—Cincinnati	Nat.	1B-3B-OF	43	56	7	12	3	0	0	5	.214	64	11	0	1.000
1980—Cincinnati	Nat.	1-3-O-C	65	101	14	27	4	0	4	19	.267	132	15	2	.987
1981—Cinc.†-Hou.	Nat.	1B	51	58	9	14	1	0	0	4	.241	62	5	1	.985
1982—Tucson	P. C.	1B-3B	53	190	34	63	16	3	6	33	.332	307	13	3	.991
1982—Houston	Nat.	1B	38	61	7	17	2	0	3	11	.279	86	5	1	.989
1983—Houston	Nat.	1B-C	42	78	7	13	3	0	1	9	.167	138	8	0	1.000
Major League Totals			243	358	45	84	13	0	8	48	.235	482	44	4	.992

Signed as free agent by Cincinnati Reds' organization, June 25, 1974.
†Traded to Houston Astros for Second Baseman Rafael Landestoy, June 8, 1981.

DIVISION SERIES RECORD

Year Club	League	Pos.	G.	AB.	R.	H.	2B.	3B.	HR.	RBI.	B.A.	PO.	A.	E.	F.A.
1981—Houston	Nat.	PH	1	1	0	0	0	0	0	0	.000	0	0	0	.000

CHAMPIONSHIP SERIES RECORD

Year Club	League	Pos.	G.	AB.	R.	H.	2B.	3B.	HR.	RBI.	B.A.	PO.	A.	E.	F.A.
1979—Cincinnati	Nat.	PH	2	2	0	0	0	0	0	0	.000	0	0	0	.000

PAUL WILLIAM SPLITTORFF JR.
Name pronounced SPLIT-orf.

Born October 8, 1946, at Evansville, Ind.
Height, 6.03. Weight, 210.
Throws and bats lefthanded.
Received bachelor of science degree in business
administration from Morningside College, Sioux City, Ia.

Established American League record for most games started, none complete, season (28), 1982.
Led American Association in home runs allowed with 25 and tied for lead in complete games with 11 in 1969.
Led New York-Pennsylvania League in wild pitches with 17, home runs allowed with 11 and tied for lead in complete games with 11 and balks with 2 in 1968.

Year Club	League	G.	IP.	W.	L.	Pct.	H.	R.	ER.	SO.	BB.	ERA.
1968—Corning	NYP	16	●120	8	5	.615	★127	56	46	●136	47	3.45
1969—Omaha	Am. Assoc.	28	174	12	10	.545	201	101	88	101	63	4.55
1970—Omaha	Am. Assoc.	28	162	8	12	.400	192	87	69	91	55	3.83
1970—Kansas City	American	2	9	0	1	.000	16	9	7	10	5	7.00
1971—Omaha	Am. Assoc.	8	61	5	2	.714	51	16	10	51	10	1.48
1971—Kansas City	American	22	144	8	9	.471	129	49	43	80	35	2.69
1972—Kansas City	American	35	216	12	12	.500	189	81	75	140	67	3.13
1973—Kansas City	American	38	262	20	11	.645	279	135	116	110	78	3.98
1974—Kansas City	American	36	226	13	19	.406	252	122	103	90	75	4.10
1975—Kansas City	American	35	159	9	10	.474	156	75	56	76	56	3.17
1976—Kansas City†	American	26	159	11	8	.579	169	79	70	59	59	3.96
1977—Kansas City	American	37	229	16	6	★.727	243	104	94	99	83	3.69
1978—Kansas City	American	39	262	19	13	.594	244	113	99	76	60	3.40
1979—Kansas City	American	36	240	15	17	.469	248	137	113	77	77	4.24
1980—Kansas City	American	34	204	14	11	.560	236	101	94	53	43	4.15
1981—Kansas City	American	21	99	5	5	.500	111	48	48	48	23	4.36
1982—Kansas City‡	American	29	162	10	10	.500	166	83	77	74	57	4.28
1983—Kansas City	American	27	156	13	8	.619	159	77	63	61	52	3.63
Major League Totals		417	2527	165	140	.541	2597	1213	1058	1053	770	3.77

Selected by Kansas City Royals' organization in 22nd round of free-agent draft, June 7, 1968.
†On disabled list, July 28 to September 4, 1976.
‡Granted free agency, November 10, 1982; re-signed by Royals, December 29, 1982.

CHAMPIONSHIP SERIES RECORD

Year Club	League	G.	IP.	W.	L.	Pct.	H.	R.	ER.	SO.	BB.	ERA.
1976—Kansas City	American	2	9⅓	1	0	1.000	7	2	2	2	5	1.93
1977—Kansas City	American	2	15	1	0	1.000	14	4	4	4	3	2.40
1978—Kansas City	American	1	7⅓	0	0	.000	9	5	4	2	0	4.91
1980—Kansas City	American	1	5⅓	0	0	.000	5	1	1	3	2	1.69
Championship Series Totals		6	37	2	0	1.000	35	12	11	11	10	2.68

WORLD SERIES RECORD

Year Club	League	G.	IP.	W.	L.	Pct.	H.	R.	ER.	SO.	BB.	ERA.
1980—Kansas City	American	1	1⅔	0	0	.000	4	1	1	0	0	5.40

—DID YOU KNOW—

That lefthander Dave Righetti's no-hitter on July 4, 1983, was the first by a Yankee since Don Larsen's perfect game against Brooklyn in Game 5 of the 1956 World Series? Righetti was a 4-0 winner over the Boston Red Sox.

MICHAEL LYNN SQUIRES
(Mike)

Born March 5, 1952, at Kalamazoo, Mich.
Height, 5.11. Weight, 185.
Throws and bats lefthanded.
Attended Kalamazoo Valley Community College, Kalamazoo, Mich.
and Western Michigan University, Kalamazoo, Mich.
Son of Lynn Squires, scout with Chicago White Sox.

Led American Association first basemen in fielding percentage with .995 in 1978.
Tied for American Association lead in caught stealing with 13 in 1977.
Named first baseman on THE SPORTING NEWS American League All-Star fielding team, 1981.
Named Southern League Most Valuable Player, 1975.

Year Club	League	Pos.	G.	AB.	R.	H.	2B.	3B.	HR.	RBI.	B.A.	PO.	A.	E.	F.A.
1973—Appleton	Midw.	1B-OF-P	68	228	42	68	7	3	3	37	.298	479	44	4	.992
1974—Knoxville	South.	1B	136	481	74	138	23	5	6	69	.287	★1173	★80	5	★.996
1975—Knoxville	South.	1B	129	448	68	136	23	5	3	50	.304	1085	78	6	★.995
1975—Chicago	Amer.	1B	20	65	5	15	0	0	0	4	.231	155	12	2	.988
1976—Iowa	A. A.	★1B-P	124	336	37	85	18	1	2	40	.253	823	47	4	★.995
1977—Iowa	A. A.	1B-OF-P	126	415	67	134	29	4	1	45	.323	897	65	7	.993
1977—Chicago	Amer.	1B	3	3	0	0	0	0	0	0	.000	8	1	0	1.000
1978—Iowa	A. A.	1B-OF	115	449	70	140	24	3	5	48	.312	922	71	6	.994
1978—Chicago	Amer.	1B	46	150	25	42	9	2	0	19	.280	361	20	1	.997
1979—Chicago	Amer.	1B-OF	122	295	44	78	10	1	2	22	.264	744	60	4	.995
1980—Chicago	Amer.	1B-C	131	343	38	97	11	3	2	33	.283	905	68	5	.995
1981—Chicago	Amer.	1B-OF	92	294	35	78	9	0	0	25	.265	729	58	6	.992
1982—Chicago	Amer.	1B	116	195	33	52	9	3	1	21	.267	512	48	3	.995
1983—Chicago	Amer.	★1B-3B	143	153	21	34	4	1	1	11	.222	515	40	2	★.996
Major League Totals			673	1498	201	396	52	10	6	135	.264	3929	307	23	.995

Selected by Chicago White Sox' organization in 18th round of free-agent draft, June 5, 1973.

CHAMPIONSHIP SERIES RECORD

Year Club	League	Pos.	G.	AB.	R.	H.	2B.	3B.	HR.	RBI.	B.A.	PO.	A.	E.	F.A.
1983—Chicago	Amer.	1B-PH-PR	4	4	0	0	0	0	0	0	.000	6	0	0	1.000

PITCHING RECORD

Year Club	League	G.	IP.	W.	L.	Pct.	H.	R.	ER.	SO.	BB.	ERA.
1973—Appleton	Midwest	1	1/3	0	0	.000	0	0	0	1	1	0.00
1976—Iowa	Am. Assoc.	1	2	0	0	.000	5	4	4	1	1	18.00
1977—Iowa	Am. Assoc.	1	1	0	0	.000	1	0	0	1	0	0.00

ROBERT WILLIAM STANLEY
(Bob)

Born November 10, 1954, at Portland, Me.
Height, 6.04. Weight, 205.
Throws and bats righthanded.

Established American League record for most innings pitched by relief pitcher, season (168⅓), 1982.
Major League saves: 1977 (3), 1978 (10), 1979 (1), 1980 (14), 1982 (14), 1983 (33). Total—75.
Led American League in hit batsmen with 11 and tied for lead in games started by pitchers with 27 in 1976.
Led New York-Pennsylvania League pitchers in games started with 15 in 1974.
Tied for Florida State League lead in games started by pitchers with 26 in 1975.

Year Club	League	G.	IP.	W.	L.	Pct.	H.	R.	ER.	SO.	BB.	ERA.
1974—Elmira	NYP	15	86	6	6	.500	94	57	44	45	40	4.60
1975—Winter Haven	Florida St.	27	169	5	★17	.227	136	76	55	73	74	2.93
1976—Bristol†	Eastern	27	186	15	9	.625	176	76	55	78	83	2.66
1977—Boston	American	41	151	8	7	.533	176	74	67	44	43	3.99
1978—Boston	American	52	142	15	2	.882	142	50	41	38	34	2.60
1979—Boston	American	40	217	16	12	.571	250	110	96	56	44	3.98
1980—Boston	American	52	175	10	8	.556	186	75	66	71	52	3.39
1981—Boston	American	35	99	10	8	.556	110	46	42	28	38	3.82
1982—Boston	American	48	168⅓	12	7	.632	161	60	58	83	50	3.10
1983—Boston	American	64	145⅓	8	10	.444	145	56	46	65	38	2.85
Major League Totals		332	1097⅔	79	54	.594	1170	471	416	385	299	3.41

Selected by Los Angeles Dodgers' organization in 9th round of free-agent draft, June 5, 1973.
Selected by Boston Red Sox' organization in secondary phase of free-agent draft, January 9, 1974.
†On disabled list, June 19 to June 24, 1976.

ALL-STAR GAME RECORD

Year League	IP.	W.	L.	Pct.	H.	R.	ER.	SO.	BB.	ERA.
1979—American	2	0	0	.000	1	1	1	0	0	4.50
1983—American	2	0	0	.000	2	0	0	0	0	0.00
All-Star Game Totals	4	0	0	.000	3	1	1	0	0	2.25

—DID YOU KNOW—

That Red Sox Manager Ralph Houk, who won pennants in his first three years as a major league manager with the Yankees (1961-62-63), has not won a pennant since?

MICHAEL THOMAS STANTON
(Mike)

Born September 25, 1952, at St. Louis, Mo.
Height, 6.02. Weight, 200.
Throws and bats righthanded.
Attended Miami-Dade Community College (South), Miami, Fla.

Major league saves: 1975 (1), 1980 (5), 1981 (2), 1982 (7), 1983 (7). Total—22.
Tied for Southern League lead in games started by pitchers with 27 in 1974.

Year Club	League	G.	IP.	W.	L.	Pct.	H.	R.	ER.	SO.	BB.	ERA.
1973—Covington	Ap'lachian	7	51	2	3	.400	34	26	11	70	21	1.94
1973—Cedar Rapids	Midwest	7	53	3	2	.600	40	16	8	59	18	1.36
1974—Columbus	Southern	27	179	11	*15	.423	158	85	61	*146	*121	3.07
1975—Iowa	Am. Assoc.	18	107	5	11	.313	95	56	49	105	66	4.12
1975—Houston	National	7	17	0	2	.000	20	14	14	16	20	7.41
1975—Columbus	Southern	10	39	2	3	.400	31	13	10	41	19	2.31
1976—Memphis	Int'national	21	128	6	11	.353	135	88	69	101	67	4.85
1977—Charleston†‡	Int'national	20	116	8	7	.533	115	53	44	81	47	3.41
1978—Syracuse§	Int'national	31	143	6	12	.333	155	*110	87	116	105	5.48
1979—Maracaibo x	Inter-Amer.	5	30	3	2	.600	24	15	9	7	7	2.70
1979—Tacoma	P. Coast	8	45	3	3	.500	43	17	12	34	23	2.40
1980—Cleveland	American	51	86	1	3	.250	98	57	51	74	44	5.34
1981—Cleveland yza	American	24	43	3	3	.500	43	21	21	34	18	4.40
1982—Seattle	American	56	71⅓	2	4	.333	70	37	33	49	21	4.16
1983—Seattle	American	50	65	2	3	.400	65	26	24	47	28	3.32
National League Totals		7	17	0	2	.000	20	14	14	16	20	7.41
American League Totals		181	265⅓	8	13	.381	276	141	129	204	111	4.38
Major League Totals		188	282⅓	8	15	.348	296	155	143	220	131	4.56

Selected by Atlanta Braves' organization in 9th round of free-agent draft, June 8, 1971.
Selected by Kansas City Royals' organization in secondary phase of free-agent draft, January 12, 1972.
Selected by Texas Rangers' organization in secondary phase of free-agent draft, June 6, 1972.
Selected by Houston Astros' organization in secondary phase of free-agent draft, January 10, 1973.
†On disabled list, June 19 to July 4, 1977.
‡Sold to Toronto Blue Jays' organization, March 29, 1978.
§Sold to Maracaibo of Inter-American League, April 7, 1979.
xSigned as free agent by Cleveland Indians' organization after Inter-American League folded, July 18, 1979.
ySold to St. Louis Cardinals, December 7, 1981.
zSold to Cleveland Indians' organization, February 8, 1982.
aReleased, February 13, 1982; signed by Seattle Mariners, April 5, 1982.

DAVID LESLIE STAPLETON
(Dave)

Born January 16, 1954, at Fairhope, Ala.
Height, 6.01. Weight, 170.
Throws and bats righthanded.
Received bachelor of science degree in education from
University of South Alabama, Mobile, Ala.

Led International League in total bases with 249 in 1979.
Named International League co-Most Valuable Player, 1979.

Year Club	League	Pos.	G.	AB.	R.	H.	2B.	3B.	HR.	RBI.	B.A.	PO.	A.	E.	F.A.
1975—Winter Haven	Fla. St.	2B-SS-OF	56	199	23	48	8	1	1	14	.241	106	143	14	.947
1976—Winter Haven	Fla. St.	3-2-1-S-O	118	400	67	115	13	2	4	38	.288	164	248	17	.960
1977—Bristol	East.	2B-3B	86	304	52	93	21	4	8	28	.306	147	174	14	.958
1977—Pawtucket	Int.	3-1-2-S-O	25	74	9	18	5	0	1	9	.243	34	29	2	.969
1978—Pawtucket†	Int.	3-2-1-S	113	432	69	112	26	3	11	49	.259	155	224	21	.948
1979—Pawtucket	Int.	1-3-2-S-O	140	*553	*88	*169	*33	3	15	64	.306	651	231	9	.990
1980—Pawtucket	Int.	1-2-3-O	37	150	25	51	3	1	3	19	.340	239	53	8	.973
1980—Boston	Amer.	2-1-O-3	106	449	61	144	33	5	7	45	.321	269	338	12	.981
1981—Boston	Amer.	S-3-2-1	93	355	45	101	17	1	10	42	.285	260	204	17	.965
1982—Boston	Amer.	1-S-2-3-O	150	538	66	142	28	1	14	65	.264	1032	179	13	.989
1983—Boston	Amer.	1B-2B	151	542	54	134	31	1	10	66	.247	1249	105	10	.993
Major League Totals			500	1884	226	521	109	8	41	218	.277	2810	826	52	.986

Selected by Boston Red Sox' organization in 10th round of free-agent draft, June 4, 1975.
†On disabled list, April 10 to May 5, 1978.

DANIEL JOSEPH STAUB
(Rusty)
(Named by nurses in hospital of birth for his hair.)

Born April 1, 1944, at New Orleans, La.
Height, 6.02. Weight, 215.
Throws right and bats lefthanded.

Established major league records for most games, pinch-hitter, season (94), 1983; most at-bats pinch-hitter, season (81), 1983.
Tied major league records for most seasons, consecutive, leading league, grounded into double plays (2), 1976 and 1977; most consecutive hits during season by pinch-hitter (8), June 11 through June 26, first game, 1983.
Led American League in grounding into double plays with 23 in 1976 and 27 in 1977.

Tied for National League lead in double plays by outfielders with 5 in 1971, 5 in 1973 and 5 in 1974.
Led Carolina League first basemen in double plays with 123 in 1962.
Named designated hitter on THE SPORTING NEWS American League All-Star Team, 1978.
Named Carolina League Most Valuable Player, 1962.
Received reported $100,000 bonus to sign with Houston Astros, 1961.

Year	Club	League	Pos.	G.	AB.	R.	H.	2B.	3B.	HR.	RBI.	B.A.	PO.	A.	E.	F.A.
1962—Durham	Carol.	1B	●140	509	●115	149	20	4	23	93	.293	★1247	★76	★20	.985
1963—Houston	Nat.	1B-OF	150	513	43	115	17	4	6	45	.224	963	63	11	.989
1964—Houston	Nat.	1B-OF	89	292	26	63	10	2	8	35	.216	512	30	9	.984
1964—Oklahoma City	P. C.	OF-1B	71	226	55	71	13	1	20	45	.314	306	22	5	.985
1965—Houston	Nat.	OF-1B	131	410	43	105	20	1	14	63	.256	203	12	11	.951
1966—Houston	Nat.	OF-1B	153	554	60	155	28	3	13	81	.280	291	15	12	.962
1967—Houston†	Nat.	OF	149	546	71	182	★44	1	10	74	.333	269	10	11	.962
1968—Houston†	Nat.	1B-OF	161	591	54	172	37	1	6	72	.291	1336	94	13	.991
1969—Montreal	Nat.	OF	158	549	89	166	26	5	29	79	.302	265	★16	10	.966
1970—Montreal	Nat.	OF	160	569	98	156	23	7	30	94	.274	308	14	5	.985
1971—Montreal‡	Nat.	OF	★162	599	94	186	34	6	19	97	.311	290	★20	★18	.945
1972—New York§	Nat.	OF	66	239	32	70	11	0	9	38	.293	108	4	2	.982
1973—New York	Nat.	OF	152	585	77	163	36	1	15	76	.279	297	17	7	.978
1974—New York	Nat.	OF	151	561	65	145	22	2	19	78	.258	262	★19	5	.983
1975—New York x	Nat.	OF	155	574	93	162	30	4	19	105	.282	267	★15	4	.986
1976—Detroit	Amer.	OF	●161	589	73	176	28	3	15	96	.299	218	8	7	.970
1977—Detroit	Amer.	DH	158	623	84	173	34	3	22	101	.278	0	0	0	.000
1978—Detroit	Amer.	DH	162	642	75	175	30	1	24	121	.273	0	0	0	.000
1979—Detroit yz	Amer.	DH	68	246	32	58	12	1	9	40	.236	0	0	0	.000
1979—Montreal a	Nat.	1B-OF	38	86	9	23	3	0	3	14	.267	156	7	1	.994
1980—Texas bc	Amer.	1B-OF	109	340	42	102	23	2	9	55	.300	262	14	6	.979
1981—New York	Nat.	1B	70	161	9	51	9	0	5	21	.317	339	20	4	.989
1982—New York d	Nat.	OF-1B	112	219	11	53	9	0	3	27	.242	172	19	2	.990
1983—New York	Nat.	1B-OF	104	115	5	34	6	0	3	28	.296	40	5	2	.957
American League Totals			658	2440	306	684	127	10	79	413	.280	480	22	13	.975
National League Totals			2161	7163	879	2001	365	37	211	1027	.279	6078	380	127	.981
Major League Totals			2819	9603	1185	2685	492	47	290	1440	.280	6558	402	140	.980

Signed as free agent by Houston Astros' organization, September 11, 1961.
†Traded to Montreal Expos for First Baseman Donn Clendenon and Outfielder Jesus Alou, January 22, 1969. Clendenon refused to report to Houston; Pitchers John Billingham and Drannon (Skip) Guinn and cash sent to Houston to complete deal, April 8, 1969.
‡Traded to New York Mets for Outfielder Ken Singleton, First Baseman Mike Jorgensen and Infielder Tim Foli, April 6, 1972.
§On disabled list, July 21 to September 1, 1972.
xTraded with Pitcher Bill Laxton to Detroit Tigers for Pitcher Mickey Lolich and Outfielder Billy Baldwin, December 12, 1975.
yOn disqualified list, April 5 to May 1, 1979.
zSold to Montreal Expos, July 20, 1979.
aTraded to Texas Rangers for Second Baseman LaRue Washington and Third Baseman Chris Smith, March 31, 1980.
bOn supplemental disabled list, May 1 to June 5, 1980.
cGranted free agency, October 23, 1980; signed by New York Mets, December 16, 1980.
dPlayer-coach.

CHAMPIONSHIP SERIES RECORD

Established Championship Series records for most home runs, five-game Series (3), 1973; most home runs, two consecutive innings (2), October 8, 1973 (first and second innings).
Established National League Championship Series records for highest slugging average, five-game Series (.800), 1973; most runs batted in, five-game Series (5), 1973.

Year	Club	League	Pos.	G.	AB.	R.	H.	2B.	3B.	HR.	RBI.	B.A.	PO.	A.	E.	F.A.
1973—New York	Nat.	OF	4	15	4	3	0	0	3	5	.200	10	0	0	1.000

WORLD SERIES RECORD

Tied World Series record for most times reached first base safely, game (batting 1.000) (5), October 4, 1973.

Year	Club	League	Pos.	G.	AB.	R.	H.	2B.	3B.	HR.	RBI.	B.A.	PO.	A.	E.	F.A.
1973—New York	Nat.	OF-PH	7	26	1	11	2	0	1	6	.423	5	0	0	1.000

ALL-STAR GAME RECORD

Year	League	Pos.	AB.	R.	H.	2B.	3B.	HR.	RBI.	B.A.	PO.	A.	E.	F.A.
1967—National		PH	1	0	1	0	0	0	0	1.000	0	0	0	.000
1968—National		PH	1	0	0	0	0	0	0	.000	0	0	0	.000
1970—National		PH	1	0	0	0	0	0	0	.000	0	0	0	.000
1976—American		OF	2	0	2	0	0	0	0	1.000	1	0	0	1.000
All-Star Game Totals			5	0	3	0	0	0	0	.600	1	0	0	1.000

Member of National League All-Star Team for 1969 and 1971 games; did not play.

JOHN HARDIN STEARNS

Born August 21, 1951, at Denver, Colo.
Height, 6.00. Weight, 185.
Throws and bats righthanded.
Attended University of Colorado, Boulder, Colo.
Brother of Bill Stearns, catcher in New York Yankees' organization, 1971 through 1978.

Led International League catchers in assists with 61 in 1976.
Tied for Carolina League lead in double plays by catchers with 9 in 1974.
Selected by Buffalo Bills in 17th round of 1973 NFL draft.

Year Club	League	Pos.	G.	AB.	R.	H.	2B.	3B.	HR.	RBI.	B.A.	PO.	A.	E.	F.A.
1973—Reading	East.	C-O-3-1	67	166	28	40	7	4	3	24	.241	232	33	4	.985
1974—Rocky Mount........	Carol.	C-OF-1B	62	230	41	79	16	4	4	38	.343	400	62	13	.973
1974—Toledo	Int.	C-3B	77	278	34	74	9	2	3	28	.266	414	49	5	.989
1974—Philadelphia†	Nat.	C	1	2	0	1	0	0	0	0	.500	1	0	0	1.000
1975—New York.............	Nat.	C	59	169	25	32	5	1	3	10	.189	297	40	2	.994
1976—New York.............	Nat.	C	32	103	13	27	6	0	2	10	.262	200	20	3	.987
1976—Tidewater.............	Int.	C-3B	102	332	64	103	17	2	10	45	.310	416	100	14	.974
1977—New York.............	Nat.	C-1B	139	431	52	108	25	1	12	55	.251	772	79	19	.978
1978—New York.............	Nat.	C-3B	143	477	65	126	24	1	15	73	.264	711	84	12	.985
1979—New York.............	Nat.	C-1-3-O	155	538	58	131	29	2	9	66	.243	754	107	16	.982
1980—New York‡...........	Nat.	C-1B-3B	91	319	42	91	25	1	0	45	.285	552	61	8	.987
1981—New York.............	Nat.	C-1B-3B	80	273	25	74	12	1	1	24	.271	360	52	7	.983
1982—New York§..........	Nat.	C-3B	98	352	46	103	25	3	4	28	.293	384	74	10	.979
1983—New York x	Nat.	PR	4	0	2	0	0	0	0	0	.000	0	0	0	.000
Major League Totals....................			802	2664	328	693	151	10	46	311	.260	4031	517	77	.983

Selected by Oakland A's organization in 17th round of free-agent draft, June 5, 1969.
Selected by Philadelphia Phillies' organization in 1st round (second player selected) of free-agent draft, June 5, 1973.

†Traded with Outfielder Del Unser and Pitcher Mac Scarce to New York Mets for Pitcher Tug McGraw and Outfielders Don Hahn and Dave Schneck, December 3, 1974.

‡On supplemental disabled list, July 27, 1980; transferred to disabled list, August 20, 1980 through remainder of season.

§On supplemental disabled list, August 20 to September 6, 1982.

xOn supplemental disabled list, March 27 to April 12 and April 16, 1983, then transferred to disabled list, May 1, 1983, then transferred to emergency disabled list, June 13 to September 2, 1983.

ALL-STAR GAME RECORD

Year League	Pos.	AB.	R.	H.	2B.	3B.	HR.	RBI.	B.A.	PO.	A.	E.	F.A.
1977—National	C	0	0	0	0	0	0	0	.000	2	0	0	1.000
1980—National	C	1	0	0	0	0	0	0	.000	5	0	0	1.000
1982—National	C	0	0	0	0	0	0	0	.000	0	0	0	.000
All-Star Game Totals		1	0	0	0	0	0	0	.000	7	0	0	1.000

Member of National League All-Star Team for 1979 game; did not play.

JOHN ROBERT STEFERO

Born September 22, 1959, at Sumter, S.C.
Height, 5.08. Weight, 185.
Throws right and bats lefthanded.

Tied for Appalachian League lead in errors by third baseman with 18 in 1979.

Year Club	League	Pos.	G.	AB.	R.	H.	2B.	3B.	HR.	RBI.	B.A.	PO.	A.	E.	F.A.
1979—Bluefield.................	Appal.	3B-C	59	200	37	55	11	2	8	42	.275	58	95	19	.890
1980—Miami	Fla. St.	C	101	307	32	66	9	4	5	30	.215	352	63	*14	.967
1981—Hagerstown†	Carol.	C-3B-OF	111	338	69	97	16	2	25	82	.287	630	74	16	.978
1982—Charlotte...............	South.	C-OF-3B	115	357	45	82	9	2	17	60	.230	435	51	17	.966
1983—Charlotte...............	South.	C-OF	61	205	33	63	9	0	16	34	.307	261	40	12	.962
1983—Baltimore	Amer.	C	9	11	2	5	1	0	0	4	.455	20	3	2	.920
1983—Rochester	Int.	C	35	97	13	19	5	0	2	5	.196	153	26	4	.978
Major League Totals....................			9	11	2	5	1	0	0	4	.455	20	3	2	.920

Signed as free agent by Baltimore Orioles' organization, June 26, 1979.
†On disabled list, August 31 to September 11, 1981.

DAVID WILLIAM STEGMAN
(Dave)

Born January 30, 1954, at Inglewood, Calif.
Height, 5.11. Weight, 190.
Throws and bats righthanded.
Received bachelor of science degree in engineering and math from University of Arizona, Tucson, Ariz.

Led American Association in bases on balls received with 100 in 1983.

Year Club	League	Pos.	G.	AB.	R.	H.	2B.	3B.	HR.	RBI.	B.A.	PO.	A.	E.	F.A.
1976—Montgomery........	South.	OF	61	188	31	50	8	0	0	20	.266	105	2	3	.973
1977—Montgomery........	South.	OF	67	226	55	78	19	5	11	59	.345	132	6	1	.993
1977—Evansville	A. A.	OF	50	153	25	34	12	0	6	18	.222	99	4	6	.945
1978—Evansville	A. A.	*OF-C	●135	462	95	122	30	1	14	67	.264	299	8	3	*.990
1978—Detroit...................	Amer.	OF	8	14	3	4	2	0	1	3	.286	11	0	0	1.000
1979—Evansville	A. A.	OF	133	506	95	153	33	2	11	60	.302	*322	12	5	.985
1979—Detroit...................	Amer.	OF	12	31	6	6	0	0	3	5	.194	35	0	0	1.000
1980—Evansville	A. A.	OF	18	59	11	12	2	1	1	6	.203	37	1	1	.974
1980—Detroit††‡............	Amer.	OF	65	130	12	23	5	0	2	9	.177	82	1	1	.988
1981—Columbus..............	Int.	OF	90	227	42	66	15	1	6	24	.291	128	2	3	.977
1982—Columbus..............	Int.	OF-3B	115	383	71	104	18	2	10	53	.272	206	29	4	.983
1982—New York§...........	Amer.	PR	2	0	0	0	0	0	0	0	.000	0	0	0	.000

— 459 —

Year Club	League	Pos.	G.	AB.	R.	H.	2B.	3B.	HR.	RBI.	B.A.	PO.	A.	E.	F.A.
1983—Denver	A A.	OF	111	395	94	132	30	6	7	54	.334	231	11	3	.988
1983—Chicago	Amer.	OF	30	53	5	9	2	0	0	4	.170	31	1	0	1.000
Major League Totals....................................			117	228	26	42	9	0	6	21	.184	159	2	1	.994

Selected by Minnesota Twins' organization in 10th round of free-agent draft, June 6, 1972.
Selected by Boston Red Sox' organization in 9th round of free-agent draft, June 4, 1975.
Selected by Atlanta Braves' organization in secondary phase of free-agent draft, January 7, 1976.
Selected by Detroit Tigers' organization in secondary phase of free-agent draft, June 8, 1976.
†Traded to San Diego Padres for Pitcher Dennis Kinney, December 12, 1980.
‡Traded by San Diego to New York Yankees' organization, April 30, 1981, completing deal in which New York organization traded Pitcher Byron Ballard to San Diego organization for a player to be named later, April 6, 1981.
§Granted free agency, October 22, 1982; signed by Chicago White Sox' organization, January 26, 1983.

WILLIAM ALLEN STEIN
(Bill)

Born January 21, 1947, at Battle Creek, Mich.
Height, 5.10. Weight, 175.
Throws and bats righthanded.
Attended Brevard Junior College, Cocoa, Fla., and Southern Illinois
University, Carbondale, Ill.

Established American League record for most consecutive hits during season by pinch-hitter (7), April 14 through May 25, 1981.
Led American Association in total bases with 274 in 1974.

Year Club	League	Pos.	G.	AB.	R.	H.	2B.	3B.	HR.	RBI.	B.A.	PO.	A.	E.	F.A.
1969—Tulsa	A. A.	2B-3B-SS	62	183	24	54	11	5	1	20	.295	81	97	9	.952
1970—Arkansas................	Texas	2B-OF-SS	114	429	56	124	21	2	8	52	.289	179	198	17	.957
1971—Tulsa†	A. A.	O-3-2-P	103	389	50	106	22	4	8	67	.272	154	86	13	.949
1972—Tulsa	A. A.	O-2-3-1	103	360	49	100	26	4	5	36	.278	146	52	5	.975
1972—St. Louis................	Nat.	3B-OF	14	35	2	11	0	1	2	3	.314	5	4	0	1.000
1973—St. Louis................	Nat.	OF-1B-3B	32	55	4	12	2	0	0	2	.218	37	1	0	1.000
1973—Tulsa‡§................	A. A.	3B	21	81	12	23	2	1	0	8	.284	8	37	1	.978
1974—Iowa....................	A. A.	3B-OF	●135	543	★107	★178	32	8	16	74	.328	89	204	13	.958
1974—Chicago	Amer.	3B	13	43	5	12	1	0	0	5	.279	7	20	4	.871
1975—Chicago	Amer.	2B-3B-OF	76	226	23	61	7	1	3	21	.270	87	118	9	.958
1976—Chicago x.............	Amer.	2-3-1-S-O	117	392	32	105	15	2	4	36	.268	161	243	19	.955
1977—Seattle	Amer.	★3B-SS	151	556	53	144	26	5	13	67	.259	★146	255	15	.964
1978—Seattle	Amer.	3B	114	403	41	105	24	4	4	37	.261	72	244	24	.929
1979—Seattle y	Amer.	3B-2B-SS	88	250	28	62	9	2	7	27	.248	64	162	7	.970
1980—Seattle za	Amer.	3B-2B-1B	67	198	16	53	5	1	5	27	.268	119	115	4	.983
1981—Texas....................	Amer.	1-O-3-2-S	53	115	21	38	6	0	2	22	.330	166	26	2	.990
1982—Texas....................	Amer.	2-3-S-1-O	85	184	14	44	8	0	1	16	.239	72	122	6	.970
1983—Texas....................	Amer.	2B-1B-3B	78	232	21	72	15	1	2	33	.310	222	103	5	.985
American League Totals........................			842	2599	254	696	116	16	41	291	.268	1116	1408	95	.964
National League Totals............................			46	90	6	23	2	1	2	5	.256	42	5	0	1.000
Major League Totals....................................			888	2689	260	719	118	17	43	296	.267	1158	1413	95	.964

Selected by Baltimore Orioles' organization in 33rd round of free-agent draft, June 7, 1968.
Selected by St. Louis Cardinals' organization in 27th round of free-agent draft, June 5, 1969.
†On temporary inactive list, July 1 to July 12, 1971.
‡Traded to California Angels' organization for Infielder Jerry DaVanon, September 25, 1973.
§Sold by California Angels to Chicago White Sox, April 3, 1974; California acquired Pitcher Steve Blateric to complete deal, August 1, 1974.
xSelected by Seattle Mariners in American League expansion draft, November 5, 1976.
yOn supplemental disabled list, May 25 to June 15, 1979.
zOn supplemental disabled list, June 2, 1980; transferred to disabled list, June 12 to July 22, 1980.
aGranted free agency, October 22, 1980; signed by Texas Rangers, December 18, 1980.

PITCHING RECORD

Year Club	League	G.	IP.	W.	L.	Pct.	H.	R.	ER.	SO.	BB.	ERA.
1971—Tulsa	Am. Assoc.	1	6	0	0	.000	8	3	3	6	0	4.50

RICKY FRANCIS STEIRER
Name pronounced STY-rer.

Born August 27, 1956, at Baltimore, Md.
Height, 6.04. Weight, 200.
Throws and bats righthanded.

Tied for California League lead in games started by pitchers with 28 and complete games with 11 in 1979.

Year Club	League	G.	IP.	W.	L.	Pct.	H.	R.	ER.	SO.	BB.	ERA.
1977—Davenport	Midwest	15	101	6	5	.545	116	50	41	70	26	3.65
1978—Salinas.....................	California	27	122	6	7	.462	149	74	64	62	52	4.72
1979—Salinas.....................	California	29	193	11	13	.458	210	106	83	119	66	3.87
1980—El Paso.....................	Texas	29	148	5	11	.313	208	121	98	87	58	5.96
1981—Salt Lake City..............	P. Coast	28	116	5	7	.417	133	73	59	65	37	4.58
1982—Spokane.....................	P. Coast	30	92⅓	7	7	.500	92	41	36	66	30	3.51
1982—California..................	American	10	26⅓	1	0	1.000	25	14	11	14	11	3.76
1983—Edmonton....................	P. Coast	28	86⅔	7	7	.500	85	50	37	58	33	3.84
1983—California..................	American	19	61⅔	3	2	.600	77	40	33	25	18	4.82
Major League Totals.................		29	88	4	2	.667	102	54	44	39	29	4.50

Selected by California Angels' organization in 5th round of free-agent draft, June 7, 1977.

MICHAEL STEVEN STENHOUSE
(Mike)

Born May 29, 1958, at Pueblo, Colo.
Height, 6.01. Weight, 185.
Throws right and bats lefthanded.
Attended Harvard University, Cambridge, Mass.
Son of David Stenhouse, pitcher with Washington Senators, 1962 through 1964;
brother of David Stenhouse, Jr., catcher in Toronto Blue Jays' organization.

Led American Association in slugging percentage with .681 in 1983.
Led Florida State League in game-winning RBIs with 12 and bases on balls received with 123 in 1980.
Named American Association Most Valuable Player, 1983.

Year	Club	League	Pos.	G.	AB.	R.	H.	2B.	3B.	HR.	RBI.	B.A.	PO.	A.	E.	F.A.
1980—W. Palm Beach....	Fla. St.	1B-OF	133	439	77	120	17	7	13	71	.273	912	56	12	.988
1980—Memphis...............	South.	OF-1B	1	3	0	0	0	0	0	0	.000	2	0	0	1.000
1981—Memphis†.............	South.	OF-1B	118	397	64	108	25	7	14	72	.272	407	26	6	.986
1982—Wichita................	A. A.	OF	134	436	94	126	25	3	25	80	.289	243	6	6	.976
1982—Montreal...............	Nat.	PH	1	1	0	0	0	0	0	0	.000	0	0	0	.000
1983—Wichita................	A. A.	1B-OF	109	361	93	128	33	5	25	93	*.355	681	48	8	.989
1983—Montreal...............	Nat.	OF-1B	24	40	2	5	1	0	0	2	.125	37	2	0	1.000
Major League Totals...................................			25	41	2	5	1	0	0	2	.122	37	2	0	1.000

Selected by Oakland A's organizaton in 1st round (26th player selected) of free-agent draft, June 5, 1979.
Selected by Montreal Expos' organization in secondary phase of free-agent draft, January 8, 1980.
†On disabled list, April 9 to April 29, 1981.

PHILLIP RAYMOND STEPHENSON
(Phil)

Born September 19, 1960, at Guthrie, Okla.
Height, 6.01. Weight, 190.
Throws and bats lefthanded.
Attended Wichita State University, Wichita, Kan.

Led Eastern League in bases on balls received with 114 and tied for lead in sacrifice flies with 10 in 1983.

Year	Club	League	Pos.	G.	AB.	R.	H.	2B.	3B.	HR.	RBI.	B.A.	PO.	A.	E.	F.A.
1982—Modesto.................	Calif.	1B	64	212	39	60	14	2	5	26	.283	436	39	4	.992
1983—Albany...................	East.	●1B-OF	133	436	90	122	●30	3	19	77	.280	771	85	●14	.984

Selected by Montreal Expos' organization in 5th round of free-agent draft, June 8, 1981.
Selected by Oakland A's organization in 3rd round of free-agent draft, June 7, 1982.

JOHN PATRICK STEVENSON

Born September 4, 1959, at Victorville, Calif.
Height, 5.10. Weight, 165.
Throws and bats righthanded.
Attended University of Southern California, Los Angeles, Calif.;
Los Angeles Valley College, Van Nuys, Calif.,
and Pepperdine University, Malibu, Calif.
Son of John R. Stevenson, minor league infielder, 1956.

Year	Club	League	Pos.	G.	AB.	R.	H.	2B.	3B.	HR.	RBI.	B.A.	PO.	A.	E.	F.A.
1979—Walla·Walla..........	N'west	SS-3B	24	79	14	27	3	2	0	5	.342	41	76	8	.936
1979—Reno	Calif.	SS	46	180	41	45	6	3	2	15	.250	84	139	17	.929
1980—Reno	Calif.	SS	117	436	86	122	14	10	7	53	.280	218	*421	*41	.940
1981—Amarillo.................	Texas	SS	111	365	48	93	11	3	1	43	.255	152	360	*53	.906
1982—Amar.†-Shreve.‡ ..	Texas	SS	46	165	25	44	7	1	0	13	.267	82	108	17	.918
1983—Shreveport§..........	Texas	SS	104	398	63	127	26	2	4	37	.319	155	336	29	.944

Selected by San Diego Padres' organization in 1st round (13th player selected) of free-agent draft, January 9, 1979.
†Released, May 20, 1982; signed by Shreveport (San Francisco Giants' organization), June 1, 1982.
‡On disabled list, June 25, 1982 through remainder of season.
§On disabled list, April 8 to April 18 and July 7 to July 31, 1983.

DAVID KEITH STEWART
(Dave)

Born February 19, 1957, at Oakland, Calif.
Height, 6.02. Weight, 200.
Throws and bats righthanded.

Major League saves: 1981 (6), 1982 (1), 1983 (8). Total—15.
Led Pacific Coast League pitchers in games started with 29 in 1980.
Tied for Texas League lead in games started by pitchers with 28 in 1978.
Tied for Midwest League lead in complete games with 15, shutouts with 3 and balks with 3 in 1977.

Year	Club	League	G.	IP.	W.	L.	Pct.	H.	R.	ER.	SO.	BB.	ERA.
1975—Bellingham....................	Northwest	22	49	0	5	.000	59	46	30	37	49	5.51
1976—Danville.........................	Midwest	4	10	0	2	.000	17	20	18	10	16	16.20
1976—Bellingham....................	Northwest	24	50	1	1	.500	47	35	28	53	58	5.04
1977—Clinton	Midwest	24	176	*17	4	*.810	152	52	42	144	72	2.15
1977—Albuquerque.................	P. Coast	1	6	1	0	1.000	4	3	3	3	6	4.50
1978—San Antonio.................	Texas	28	*193	14	12	.538	181	99	79	130	97	3.68
1978—Los Angeles ....:..	National	1	2	0	0	.000	1	0	0	1	0	0.00
1979—Albuquerque.................	P. Coast	28	170	11	12	.478	198	112	99	105	81	5.24

Year Club	League	G.	IP.	W.	L.	Pct.	H.	R.	ER.	SO.	BB.	ERA.
1980—Albuquerque	P. Coast	31	★202	●15	10	.600	189	94	83	125	89	3.70
1981—Los Angeles	National	32	43	4	3	.571	40	13	12	29	14	2.51
1982—Los Angeles	National	45	146⅓	9	8	.529	137	72	62	80	49	3.81
1983—Los Angeles†	National	46	76	5	2	.714	67	28	25	54	33	2.96
1983—Texas	American	8	59	5	2	.714	50	15	14	24	17	2.14
National League Totals		124	267⅓	18	13	.581	245	113	99	164	96	3.33
American League Totals		8	59	5	2	.714	50	15	14	24	17	2.14
Major League Totals		132	326⅓	23	15	.605	295	128	113	188	113	3.12

Selected by Los Angeles Dodgers' organization in 16th round of free-agent draft, June 4, 1975.

†Traded with a player to be named later to Texas Rangers for Pitcher Rick Honeycutt, August 19, 1983; Texas acquired Pitcher Ricky Wright to complete deal, September 16, 1983.

DIVISION SERIES RECORD

Year Club	League	G.	IP.	W.	L.	Pct.	H.	R.	ER.	SO.	BB.	ERA.
1981—Los Angeles	National	2	⅔	0	2	.000	4	3	3	1	0	40.50

WORLD SERIES RECORD

Year Club	League	G.	IP.	W.	L.	Pct.	H.	R.	ER.	SO.	BB.	ERA.
1981—Los Angeles	National	2	1⅔	0	0	.000	1	0	0	1	2	0.00

SAMUEL LEE STEWART JR.
(Sammy)

Born October 28, 1954, at Asheville, N.C.
Height, 6.03. Weight, 208.
Throws and bats righthanded.
Attended Montreat-Anderson Junior College, Montreat, N.C.

Established major league record for most consecutive strikeouts, first major league game (7), September 1, 1978 (second game).

Pitched seven-inning, 1-0 no-hit victory against Winter Haven, July 20, 1976.

Major League saves: 1979 (1), 1980 (3), 1981 (4), 1982 (5), 1983 (7). Total—20.

Year Club	League	G.	IP.	W.	L.	Pct.	H.	R.	ER.	SO.	BB.	ERA.
1975—Bluefield	Ap'lachian	18	43	3	3	.500	62	44	29	29	26	6.07
1976—Miami	Florida St.	23	182	12	8	.600	147	65	49	79	★86	2.42
1977—Rochester	Int'national	10	54	0	5	.000	68	41	38	28	35	6.33
1977—Charlotte	Southern	16	117	9	6	.600	93	32	27	56	45	★2.08
1978—Rochester	Int'national	27	173	13	10	.565	168	90	73	111	93	3.80
1978—Baltimore	American	2	11	1	1	.500	10	5	4	11	3	3.27
1979—Baltimore	American	31	118	8	5	.615	96	47	46	71	71	3.51
1980—Baltimore	American	33	119	7	7	.500	103	51	47	78	60	3.55
1981—Baltimore	American	29	112	4	8	.333	89	33	29	57	57	2.33
1982—Baltimore†	American	38	139	10	9	.526	140	68	64	69	62	4.14
1982—Hagerstown	Carolina	2	8	0	0	.000	8	2	2	6	1	2.25
1983—Baltimore‡	American	58	144⅓	9	4	.692	138	60	58	95	67	3.62
Major League Totals		191	643⅓	39	34	.534	576	264	248	381	320	3.47

Selected by Kansas City Royals' organization in 28th round of free-agent draft, June 5, 1974.

Signed as free agent by Baltimore Orioles' organization, June 15, 1975.

†On disabled list, June 22 to July 15, 1982; included rehabilitation disability assignment to Hagerstown, July 7 to July 15, 1982.

‡Appeared in one game as a pinch-runner.

CHAMPIONSHIP SERIES RECORD

Year Club	League	G.	IP.	W.	L.	Pct.	H.	R.	ER.	SO.	BB.	ERA.
1983—Baltimore	American	2	4⅓	0	0	.000	2	0	0	2	1	0.00

WORLD SERIES RECORD

Year Club	League	G.	IP.	W.	L.	Pct.	H.	R.	ER.	SO.	BB.	ERA.
1979—Baltimore	American	1	2⅔	0	0	.000	4	0	0	0	1	0.00
1983—Baltimore	American	3	5	0	0	.000	2	0	0	6	2	0.00
World Series Totals		4	7⅔	0	0	.000	6	0	0	6	3	0.00

DAVID ANDREW STIEB

Name pronounced Steeb.

(Dave)

Born July 22, 1957, at Santa Ana, Calif.
Height, 6.01. Weight, 185.
Throws and bats righthanded.
Attended Santa Ana College, Santa Ana, Calif., and
Southern Illinois University, Carbondale, Ill.
Brother of Steve Stieb, catcher in Atlanta Braves' organization, 1979 through 1981.

Led American League in hit batsmen with 14 in 1983 and tied for lead with 11 in 1981.

Led American League in complete games with 19 and shutouts with 5 in 1982.

Named American League Pitcher of the Year by THE SPORTING NEWS, 1982.

Named righthanded pitcher on THE SPORTING NEWS American League All-Star Team, 1982.

Year Club	League	G.	IP.	W.	L.	Pct.	H.	R.	ER.	SO.	BB.	ERA.
1978—Dunedin	Florida St.	4	26	2	0	1.000	23	10	6	8	1	2.08
1979—Dunedin	Florida St.	8	51	5	0	1.000	54	30	24	38	28	4.24
1979—Syracuse	Int'national	7	51	5	2	.714	39	15	12	20	14	2.12
1979—Toronto	American	18	129	8	8	.500	139	70	62	52	48	4.33
1980—Toronto†	American	34	243	12	15	.444	232	108	100	108	83	3.70
1981—Toronto	American	25	184	11	10	.524	148	70	65	89	61	3.18
1982—Toronto	American	38	★288⅓	17	14	.548	★271	116	104	141	75	3.25
1983—Toronto	American	36	278	17	12	.586	223	105	94	187	93	3.04
Major League Totals		151	1122⅓	65	59	.524	1013	469	425	577	360	3.41

Selected by Toronto Blue Jays' organization in 5th round of free-agent draft, June 6, 1978.
†Appeared in one game as outfielder with no chances.

ALL-STAR GAME RECORD

Tied All-Star Game record for most wild pitches, inning and game (2), July 8, 1980 (seventh inning).

Year League	IP.	W.	L.	Pct.	H.	R.	ER.	SO.	BB.	ERA.
1980—American	1	0	0	.000	1	1	0	0	2	0.00
1981—American	1⅔	0	0	.000	1	0	0	1	1	0.00
1983—American	3	1	0	1.000	0	1	0	4	1	0.00
All-Star Game Totals	5⅔	1	0	1.000	2	2	0	5	4	0.00

RECORD AS OUTFIELDER

Year Club	League	Pos.	G.	AB.	R.	H.	2B.	3B.	HR.	RBI.	B.A.	PO.	A.	E.	F.A.
1978—Dunedin	Fla. St.	OF-P	35	99	10	19	3	0	1	9	.192	85	7	3	.968

ROBERT LYLE STODDARD
(Bob)

Born March 8, 1957, at Morgan Hill, Calif.
Height, 6.01. Weight, 190.
Throws and bats righthanded.
Attended Gavilan College, Gilroy, Calif., and
Fresno State University, Fresno, Calif.

Year Club	League	G.	IP.	W.	L.	Pct.	H.	R.	ER.	SO.	BB.	ERA.
1978—Stockton	California	10	51	1	6	.143	46	36	31	47	39	5.47
1979—Stockton	California	20	120	7	5	.583	78	45	40	104	58	3.00
1980—Spokane†	P. Coast	21	124	4	9	.308	147	84	68	84	53	4.94
1981—Spokane‡	P. Coast	19	121	10	4	.714	117	47	39	70	41	2.90
1981—Seattle	American	5	35	2	1	.667	35	10	10	22	9	2.57
1982—Salt Lake City	P. Coast	24	147	7	11	.389	158	91	85	86	65	5.20
1982—Seattle	American	9	67⅓	3	3	.500	48	22	18	24	18	2.41
1983—Seattle	American	35	175⅔	9	17	.346	182	95	86	87	58	4.41
Major League Totals		49	278	14	21	.400	265	127	114	133	85	3.69

Selected by Milwaukee Brewers' organization in 19th round of free-agent draft, June 4, 1975.
Selected by Atlanta Braves' organization in secondary phase of free-agent draft, January 7, 1976.
Selected by Oakland A's organization in secondary phase of free-agent draft, June 8, 1976.
Selected by Seattle Mariners' organization in 10th round of free-agent draft, June 6, 1978.
†On disabled list, April 10 to April 24 and May 14 to May 26, 1980.
‡On disabled list, April 15 to April 27, June 7 to June 19 and July 24 to August 9, 1981.

TIMOTHY PAUL STODDARD
(Tim)

Born January 24, 1953, at East Chicago, Ind.
Height, 6.07. Weight, 250.
Throws and bats righthanded.
Attended North Carolina State University, Raleigh, N. C.

Major League saves: 1979 (3), 1980 (26), 1981 (7), 1982 (12), 1983 (9). Total—57.
Tied for Southern League lead in wild pitches with 17 in 1977.

Year Club	League	G.	IP.	W.	L.	Pct.	H.	R.	ER.	SO.	BB.	ERA.
1975—Knoxville	Southern	31	66	3	4	.429	66	40	31	37	43	4.23
1975—Chicago	American	1	1	0	0	.000	2	1	1	0	0	9.00
1976—Knoxville	Southern	20	140	9	8	.529	147	55	45	62	60	2.89
1976—Iowa†	Am. Assoc.	12	29	0	2	.000	37	20	18	20	15	5.59
1977—Charlotte	Southern	36	174	10	7	.588	175	75	62	94	66	3.21
1978—Rochester‡	Int'national	45	76	7	3	.700	80	28	22	70	32	2.61
1978—Baltimore	American	8	18	0	1	.000	22	17	12	14	8	6.00
1979—Baltimore§	American	29	58	3	1	.750	44	12	11	47	19	1.71
1980—Baltimore	American	64	86	5	3	.625	72	27	24	64	38	2.51
1981—Baltimore	American	31	37	4	2	.667	38	16	16	32	18	3.89
1982—Baltimore xy	American	50	56	3	4	.429	53	26	25	42	29	4.02
1982—Rochester	Int'national	5	6	0	0	.000	2	1	1	6	2	1.50
1983—Baltimore z	American	47	57⅔	4	3	.571	65	39	39	50	29	6.09
Major League Totals		230	313⅔	19	14	.576	296	138	128	249	141	3.67

Selected by Texas Rangers' organization in 24th round of free-agent draft, June 5, 1974.
Selected by Chicago White Sox' organization in secondary phase of free-agent draft, January 9, 1975.
†Released, March 28, 1977; signed by Charlotte (Baltimore Orioles' organization), April 8, 1977.
‡On disabled list, June 15 to July 9, 1978.

§On disabled list, July 21 to September 1, 1979.
xOn disabled list, March 31 to May 5, 1982; included rehabilitation disability assignment to Rochester, April 27 to May 5, 1982.
yOn emergency disabled list, September 7, 1982 through remainder of season.
zTraded to Oakland A's for Third Baseman Wayne Gross, December 9, 1983.

WORLD SERIES RECORD

Year Club	League	G.	IP.	W.	L.	Pct.	H.	R.	ER.	SO.	BB.	ERA.
1979—Baltimore	American	4	5	1	0	1.000	6	3	3	3	1	5.40

JEFFERY GLEN STONE
(Jeff)

Born December 26, 1960, at Kennett, Mo.
Height, 6.00. Weight, 175.
Throws right and bats lefthanded.
Led Carolina League in stolen bases with 94 in 1982.
Led South Atlantic League in being hit by pitch with 15 and stolen bases with 123 in 1981.
Led South Atlantic League outfielders in total chances with 290 in 1981.
Named Eastern League Most Valuable Player, 1983.

Year Club	League	Pos.	G.	AB.	R.	H.	2B.	3B.	HR.	RBI.	B.A.	PO.	A.	E.	F.A.
1980—Central Oregon	N'west	OF	55	241	52	63	12	4	0	19	.261	116	4	4	.968
1981—Spartanburg..........	S. Atl.	OF	134	516	*108	143	13	9	3	53	.277	*264	11	15	.948
1982—Peninsula..............	Carol.	OF	*137	*559	110	166	18	*13	2	50	.297	●276	9	8	.973
1983—Reading†...............	East.	OF	125	492	*109	156	25	10	9	67	.317	226	6	9	.963
1983—Philadelphia	Nat.	OF	9	4	2	3	0	2	0	3	.750	0	0	0	.000
Major League Totals....................			9	4	2	3	0	2	0	3	.750	0	0	0	.000

Signed as free agent by Philadelphia Phillies' organization, August 26, 1979.
†On disabled list, May 11 to May 21, 1983.

DARRYL EUGENE STRAWBERRY

Born March 12, 1962, at Los Angeles, Calif.
Height, 6.05. Weight, 190.
Throws and bats lefthanded.
Brother of Michael Strawberry, outfielder in Los Angeles Dodgers' organization, 1980 and 1981.
Major League stolen bases: 1983 (19).
Led Texas League in slugging percentage with .602, bases on balls received with 100 and caught stealing with 22 in 1982.
Named National League Rookie Player of the Year by THE SPORTING NEWS, 1983.
Named National League Rookie of the Year by Baseball Writers' Association of America, 1983.
Named Texas League Most Valuable Player, 1982.
Received reported $200,000 bonus to sign with New York Mets, 1980.

Year Club	League	Pos.	G.	AB.	R.	H.	2B.	3B.	HR.	RBI.	B.A.	PO.	A.	E.	F.A.
1980—Kingsport..............	Appal.	OF	44	157	27	42	5	2	5	20	.268	55	4	3	.952
1981—Lynchburg............	Carol.	OF	123	420	84	107	22	6	3	78	.255	173	8	13	.933
1982—Jackson	Texas	OF	129	435	93	123	19	9	*34	97	.283	211	8	9	.961
1983—Tidewater.............	Int.	OF	16	57	12	19	4	1	3	13	.333	22	0	4	.846
1983—New York.............	Nat.	OF	122	420	63	108	15	7	26	74	.257	232	8	4	.984
Major League Totals...................			122	420	63	108	15	7	26	74	.257	232	8	4	.984

Selected by New York Mets' organization in 1st round (first player selected) of free-agent draft, June 3, 1980.

FRANKLIN LEE STUBBS

Born October 21, 1960, at Laurinburg, N.C.
Height, 6.02. Weight, 205.
Throws and bats lefthanded.
Attended Virginia Tech., Blacksburg, Va.

Year Club	League	Pos.	G.	AB.	R.	H.	2B.	3B.	HR.	RBI.	B.A.	PO.	A.	E.	F.A.
1982—Vero Beach†	Fla. St.	1B	16	54	6	11	1	1	3	5	.204	134	3	3	.979
1983—San Antonio..........	Texas	1B-OF	47	173	35	54	8	3	12	52	.312	425	23	5	.989
1983—Albuquerque	P. C.	OF-1B	76	267	49	74	16	3	16	58	.277	106	3	6	.948

Selected by Los Angeles Dodgers' organization in 1st round (19th player selected) of free-agent draft, June 7, 1982.
†On disabled list, July 5, 1982 through remainder of season.

JOHN ANTON STUPER

Born May 9, 1957, at Butler, Pa.
Height, 6.02. Weight, 200.
Throws and bats righthanded.
Attended Butler County Community College, Butler, Pa., Point Park College, Pittsburgh, Pa.,
and received bachelor of arts degree in English from LaRoche College, Pittsburgh, Pa., in 1980.
Tied for American Association lead in shutouts with 2 in 1982.

Year Club	League	G.	IP.	W.	L.	Pct.	H.	R.	ER.	SO.	BB.	ERA.
1978—Charleston†....................................	W. Carol.	13	76	4	8	.333	85	59	45	36	62	5.33
1979—St. Petersburg..............................	Florida St.	42	93	2	5	.286	84	38	28	62	54	2.71
1980—St. Petersburg..............................	Florida St.	24	39	1	4	.200	38	12	10	28	19	2.31
1980—Arkansas.....................................	Texas	25	88	7	2	.778	77	28	24	57	40	2.45
1981—Springfield.......................................	Am. Assoc.	28	161	6	14	.300	175	101	88	59	85	4.92

Year Club	League	G.	IP.	W.	L.	Pct.	H.	R.	ER.	SO.	BB.	ERA.
1982—Louisville	Am. Assoc.	8	61⅔	7	1	.875	49	11	10	42	16	1.46
1982—St. Louis	National	23	136⅔	9	7	.563	137	55	51	53	55	3.36
1983—St. Louis	National	40	198	12	11	.522	202	95	81	81	71	3.68
Major League Totals		63	334⅔	21	18	.538	339	150	132	134	126	3.55

Selected by Pittsburgh Pirates' organization in 18th round of free-agent draft, June 6, 1978.
†Traded to St. Louis Cardinals' organization for Infielder Tommy Sandt, January 25, 1979.

CHAMPIONSHIP SERIES RECORD

Year Club	League	G.	IP.	W.	L.	Pct.	H.	R.	ER.	SO.	BB.	ERA.
1982—St. Louis	National	1	6	0	0	.000	4	3	2	4	1	3.00

WORLD SERIES RECORD

Tied World Series records for most wild pitches, game (2), October 13, 1982; most wild pitches, Series (3), 1982.

Year Club	League	G.	IP.	W.	L.	Pct.	H.	R.	ER.	SO.	BB.	ERA.
1982—St. Louis	National	2	13	1	0	1.000	10	5	5	5	5	3.46

GUY PATRICK SULARZ

Name pronounced SOO-lars.

Born November 7, 1955, at Minneapolis, Minn.
Height, 5.11. Weight, 165.
Throws and bats righthanded.

Led Pacific Coast League in grounding into double plays with 20 in 1983.
Led Pacific Coast League third basemen in assists with 313 and tied for lead in double plays with 32 in 1981.
Led Pacific Coast League shortstops in putouts with 229, assists with 471, double plays with 131 and fielding percentage with .962 in 1978.

Year Club	League	Pos.	G.	AB.	R.	H.	2B.	3B.	HR.	RBI.	B.A.	PO.	A.	E.	F.A.
1974—Great Falls	Pion.	OF-P-3B	47	92	24	21	3	0	1	12	.228	33	6	1	.975
1975—Fresno†	Calif.	SS-2B-OF	92	293	46	83	16	2	1	28	.283	116	202	32	.877
1976—Fresno	Calif.	S-3-2-O	134	497	87	135	22	5	0	60	.272	138	269	38	.915
1977—Waterbury	East.	SS-2B	134	491	64	134	22	5	1	52	.273	201	413	33	.949
1978—Phoenix‡	P. C.	SS-3B	130	463	67	140	24	7	2	63	.302	230	477	31	.958
1979—Phoenix§	P. C.	3-2-S-O	144	521	79	153	23	4	2	68	.294	285	92	14	.964
1980—Phoenix x	P. C.	3B-S-2B	88	306	44	84	17	0	2	26	.275	129	234	13	.965
1980—San Francisco	Nat.	2B-3B	25	65	3	16	1	1	0	3	.246	50	79	3	.977
1981—Phoenix	P. C.	3B-1B-2B	132	515	86	167	17	8	2	56	.324	113	315	15	.966
1981—San Francisco	Nat.	2B-3B	10	20	0	4	0	0	2	2	.200	9	24	0	1.000
1982—San Francisco	Nat.	SS-3B-2B	63	101	15	23	3	0	1	7	.228	57	100	7	.957
1982—Phoenix	P. C.	3B-SS	9	39	8	17	0	1	1	7	.436	11	23	0	1.000
1983—Phoenix	P. C.	3B-SS-2B	134	484	76	153	23	7	5	58	.316	117	293	31	.930
1983—San Francisco	Nat.	SS-3B	10	20	3	2	0	0	0	0	.100	10	20	2	.938
Major League Totals			108	206	21	45	4	1	1	12	.218	126	223	12	.967

Selected by San Francisco Giants' organization in 10th round of free-agent draft, June 5, 1974.
†On disabled list, July 3 to July 20, 1975.
‡On disabled list, June 27 to July 7, 1978.
§Drafted by Minnesota Twins, December 3, 1979; returned, April 1, 1980.
xOn disabled list, May 4 to May 30, 1980.

PITCHING RECORD

Year Club	League	G.	IP.	W.	L.	Pct.	H.	R.	ER.	SO.	BB.	ERA.
1974—Great Falls	Pioneer	3	12	0	1	.000	8	4	4	9	5	3.00

MARC COOPER SULLIVAN

Born July 25, 1958, at Quincy, Mass.
Height, 6.04. Weight, 198.
Throws and bats righthanded.
Attended University of Florida, Gainesville, Fla.
Son of Haywood Sullivan, catcher with Boston Red Sox and Kansas City A's, 1955, 1957 and 1959 through 1963;
manager, Kansas City A's, 1965; Vice-President of Player Personnel, Boston Red Sox,
1966 through 1977; and Boston Red Sox Executive Vice-President,
General Manager and General Partner since 1978.

Led Eastern League catchers in double plays with 13 in 1982.
Led Carolina League catchers in putouts with 788 in 1981.

Year Club	League	Pos.	G.	AB.	R.	H.	2B.	3B.	HR.	RBI.	B.A.	PO.	A.	E.	F.A.
1979—Winter Haven	Fla. St.	C	31	92	8	19	2	1	0	10	.207	146	20	2	.988
1980—Winter Haven	Fla. St.	C-1B	94	293	32	66	8	3	4	30	.225	482	75	11	.981
1981—Winston-Salem	Carol.	*C-OF-1B	120	406	67	109	21	1	14	64	.268	792	*114	15	*.984
1982—Bristol	East.	*C-1B	117	369	31	75	8	2	1	33	.203	728	*89	13	.984
1982—Pawtucket	Int.	C	4	10	0	2	0	0	0	1	.200	19	4	1	.958
1982—Boston	Amer.	C	2	6	0	2	0	0	0	0	.333	9	2	0	1.000
1983—New Britain	East.	C-1B	73	231	30	53	15	1	7	43	.229	503	32	7	.987
1983—Pawtucket	Int.	C-1B	27	70	9	13	3	0	1	7	.186	107	14	2	.984
Major League Totals			2	6	0	2	0	0	0	0	.333	9	2	0	1.000

Selected by Boston Red Sox' organization in 2nd round of free-agent draft, June 5, 1979.

JOHN J. SUMMERS
(Champ)

Born June 15, 1948, at Bremerton, Wash.
Height, 6.02. Weight, 205.
Throws right and bats lefthanded.
Attended Nicholls State University, Thibodaux, La., and Southern Illinois University at
Edwardsville, Edwardsville, Ill.

Led American Association in total bases with 307 and tied for lead in being hit by pitch with 9 in 1978.
Named Minor League Player of the Year by THE SPORTING NEWS, 1978.
Named American Association Most Valuable Player, 1978.

Year Club	League	Pos.	G	AB	R	H	2B	3B	HR	RBI	B.A.	PO	A	E	F.A.
1971—C. Bay-N. Bend.....	N'west.	OF	65	222	36	56	8	5	3	34	.252	90	6	6	.941
1972—Burlington	Midw.	OF-1B	97	273	43	84	20	0	10	54	.308	210	13	9	.961
1973—Tucson...................	P. C.	OF-1B-3B	94	288	49	96	15	5	8	45	.333	97	4	3	.971
1974—Tucson...................	P. C.	OF	94	334	49	88	13	6	10	59	.263	139	4	3	.999
1974—Oakland..................	Amer.	OF	20	24	2	3	1	0	0	3	.125	6	0	0	1.000
1975—Tucson†..................	P. C.	OF	17	54	5	17	0	2	0	6	.315	21	0	0	1.000
1975—Chicago..................	Nat.	OF	76	91	14	21	5	1	1	16	.231	16	0	2	.889
1976—Chicago‡...............	Nat.	OF-1B-C	83	126	11	26	2	0	3	13	.206	95	5	1	.990
1977—Cincinnati..............	Nat.	OF-3B	59	76	11	13	4	0	3	6	.171	24	2	0	1.000
1978—Indianapolis	A. A.	OF-1B	132	462	98	*170	25	5	*34	*124	.368	261	8	9	.968
1978—Cincinnati.............	Nat.	OF	13	35	4	9	2	0	1	3	.257	14	0	1	.933
1979—Cincinnati§...........	Nat.	OF-1B	27	60	10	12	2	1	1	11	.200	56	6	2	.969
1979—Detroit...................	Amer.	OF-1B	90	246	47	77	12	1	20	51	.313	110	4	1	.991
1980—Detroit...................	Amer.	OF-1B	120	347	61	103	19	1	17	60	.297	60	1	3	.953
1981—Detroit xy...........	Amer.	OF	64	165	16	42	8	0	3	21	.255	26	1	1	.964
1982—San Francisco	Nat.	OF-1B	70	125	15	31	5	0	4	19	.248	46	3	4	.925
1983—San Francisco za .	Nat.	OF	29	22	3	3	0	0	0	3	.136	2	0	0	1.000
National League Totals............................			357	535	68	115	20	2	13	71	.215	253	16	10	.964
American League Totals			294	782	126	225	40	2	40	135	.288	202	6	5	.977
Major League Totals................................			651	1317	194	340	60	4	53	206	.258	455	22	15	.970

Signed as free agent by Oakland A's organization, June 12, 1971.
†Traded to Chicago Cubs, April 29, 1975, completing deal in which Chicago traded Pitcher Jim Todd to Oakland A's for a player to be named later, April 6, 1975.
‡Traded to Cincinnati Reds' organization for Outfielder Dave Schneck, February 16, 1977.
§Traded to Detroit Tigers for a player to be named later, May 25, 1979; Cincinnati acquired Pitcher Sheldon Burnside to complete deal, October 25, 1979.
xOn supplemental disabled list, August 17 to September 1, 1981.
yTraded to San Francisco Giants for Infielder Enos Cabell and cash, March 4, 1982.
zOn disabled list, June 27 to September 1, 1983.
aTraded to San Diego Padres for Infielder Joe Pittman and a player to be named later, December 5, 1983; San Francisco acquired outfielder Tommy Francis to complete deal, December 7, 1983.

JAMES HOWARD SUNDBERG
(Jim)

Born May 18, 1951, at Galesburg, Ill.
Height, 6.00. Weight, 196.
Throws and bats righthanded.
Attended University of Iowa, Iowa City, Iowa.

Tied major league records for most seasons leading league in assists by catcher (6); most assists by catcher, inning (3), September 3, 1976 (fifth inning); fewest errors by catcher, season (4), 1979.
Established American League record for highest fielding percentage by catcher, season (.995), 1979.
Tied American League record for most games, catcher, season (155), 1975.
Led American League in passed balls with 8 in 1981 and 16 in 1982.
Led American League catchers in total chances with 909 in 1975, 822 in 1976, 909 in 1977, 863 in 1978, 833 in 1979 and 936 in 1980.
Led American League catchers in double plays with 15 in 1974, 11 in 1976 and 15 in 1982.
Tied for American League lead in passed balls with 17 in 1980.
Tied for American League lead in double plays by catchers with 12 in 1977 and 14 in 1978.
Named catcher on THE SPORTING NEWS American League All-Star Team, 1978 and 1981.
Named catcher on THE SPORTING NEWS American League All-Star fielding team, 1976 through 1981.

Year Club	League	Pos.	G	AB	R	H	2B	3B	HR	RBI	B.A.	PO	A	E	F.A.
1973—Pittsfield	East.	C	91	242	39	72	14	0	5	40	.298	449	52	3	*.994
1974—Texas.....................	Amer.	C	132	368	45	91	13	3	3	36	.247	722	69	8	.990
1975—Texas.....................	Amer.	C	155	472	45	94	9	0	6	36	.199	*791	*101	17	.981
1976—Texas.....................	Amer.	C	140	448	33	102	24	2	3	34	.228	*719	*96	7	*.991
1977—Texas.....................	Amer.	C	149	453	61	132	20	3	6	65	.291	*801	*103	5	*.994
1978—Texas.....................	Amer.	C	149	518	54	144	23	6	6	58	.278	*769	*91	3	*.997
1979—Texas.....................	Amer.	C	150	495	50	136	23	4	5	64	.275	*754	75	4	*.995
1980—Texas.....................	Amer.	C	151	505	59	138	24	1	10	63	.273	*853	*76	7	.993
1981—Texas.....................	Amer.	*C-OF	102	339	42	94	17	2	3	28	.277	465	*52	2	*.996
1982—Texas.....................	Amer.	C-OF	139	470	37	118	22	5	10	47	.251	612	69	6	.991
1983—Texas†...................	Amer.	C	131	378	30	76	14	0	2	28	.201	618	56	5	.993
Major League Totals.................................			1398	4446	456	1125	189	26	54	459	.253	7104	788	64	.992

Selected by Oakland A's organization in 14th round of free-agent draft, June 5, 1969.
Selected by Texas Rangers' organization in 8th round of free-agent draft, June 6, 1972.
Selected by Texas Rangers' organization in secondary phase of free-agent draft, January 10, 1973.
†Traded to Milwaukee Brewers for Catcher Ned Yost and Pitcher Dan Scarpetta, December 8, 1983.

Year League	Pos.	AB.	R.	H.	2B.	3B.	HR.	RBI.	B.A.	PO.	A.	E.	F.A.
1978—American	C	0	0	0	0	0	0	0	.000	2	1	0	1.000

Member of American League All-Star Team in 1974 game; did not play.

RICHARD LEE SUTCLIFFE
(Rick)

Born June 21, 1956, at Independence, Mo.
Height, 6.06. Weight, 200.
Throws right and bats lefthanded.
Brother of Terry Sutcliffe, pitcher in Los Angeles Dodgers' organization, 1979 through 1981.

Led California League pitchers in games started with 28 in 1975.
Tied for Northwest League lead in shutouts with 2 in 1974.
Named National League Rookie Pitcher of the Year by THE SPORTING NEWS, 1979.
Named National League Rookie of the Year by Baseball Writers' Association of America, 1979.
Received reported $80,000 bonus to sign with Los Angeles Dodgers, 1974.

Year Club	League	G.	IP.	W.	L.	Pct.	H.	R.	ER.	SO.	BB.	ERA.
1974—Bellingham	Northwest	17	95	10	3	.769	79	42	35	69	48	3.32
1975—Bakersfield	California	28	193	8	★16	.333	★214	★115	★89	91	68	4.15
1976—Waterbury	Eastern	30	187	10	11	.476	★187	90	66	121	45	3.18
1976—Los Angeles	National	1	5	0	0	.000	2	0	0	3	1	0.00
1977—Albuquerque†	P. Coast	17	77	3	10	.231	96	67	55	48	63	6.43
1978—Albuquerque	P. Coast	30	184	13	6	.684	179	101	91	99	92	4.45
1978—Los Angeles	National	2	2	0	0	.000	2	0	0	0	1	0.00
1979—Los Angeles	National	39	242	17	10	.630	217	104	93	117	97	3.46
1980—Los Angeles	National	42	110	3	9	.250	122	73	68	59	55	5.56
1981—Los Angeles‡§	National	14	47	2	2	.500	41	24	21	16	20	4.02
1982—Cleveland	American	34	216	14	8	.636	174	81	71	142	98	★2.96
1983—Cleveland	American	36	243⅓	17	11	.607	251	131	116	160	102	4.29
National League Totals		98	406	22	21	.512	384	201	182	195	174	4.03
American League Totals		70	459⅓	31	19	.620	425	212	187	302	200	3.66
Major League Totals		168	865⅓	53	40	.570	809	413	369	497	374	3.84

Selected by Los Angeles Dodgers' organization in 1st round (21st player selected) of free-agent draft, June 5, 1974.
†On disabled list, May 3 to May 24, 1977.
‡On disabled list, August 14 to September 5, 1981.
§Traded with Second Baseman Jack Perconte to Cleveland Indians for Outfielder Jorge Orta, Catcher Jack Fimple and Pitcher Larry White, December 9, 1981.

ALL-STAR GAME RECORD
Member of American League All-Star Team in 1983; did not play.

HOWARD BRUCE SUTTER
Name pronounced SUIT-er.
(Known by middle name.)

Born January 8, 1953, at Lancaster, Pa.
Height, 6.02. Weight, 190.
Throws and bats righthanded.

Tied major league record for striking out side on 9 pitches, September 8, 1977 (ninth inning).
Established National League record for most saves, lifetime (215).
Tied National League records for most consecutive strikeouts by relief pitcher, game (6), September 8, 1977; most saves, season (37), 1979.
Major League saves: 1976 (10), 1977 (31), 1978 (27), 1979 (37), 1980 (28), 1981 (25), 1982 (36), 1983 (21). Total—215.
Led National League in saves with 37 in 1979, 28 in 1980, 25 in 1981 and 36 in 1982.
Tied for Texas League lead in saves with 13 in 1975.
Won National League Cy Young Memorial Award, 1979.
Named National League Fireman of the Year by THE SPORTING NEWS, 1979, 1981 and 1982.

Year Club	League	G.	IP.	W.	L.	Pct.	H.	R.	ER.	SO.	BB.	ERA.
1972—Bradenton Cubs	Gulf Coast	2	5	0	0	.000	3	0	0	4	0	0.00
1973—Quincy	Midwest	40	85	3	3	.500	94	52	39	76	27	4.13
1974—Key West†	Florida St.	18	40	1	5	.167	26	9	6	50	13	1.35
1974—Midland	Texas	8	25	1	2	.333	22	6	4	14	6	1.44
1975—Midland	Texas	41	67	5	7	.417	64	26	16	50	21	2.15
1976—Wichita	Am. Assoc.	7	12	2	1	.667	9	3	2	16	4	1.50
1976—Chicago	National	52	83	6	3	.667	63	27	25	73	26	2.71
1977—Chicago‡	National	62	107	7	3	.700	69	21	16	129	23	1.35
1978—Chicago	National	64	99	8	10	.444	82	44	35	106	34	3.18
1979—Chicago	National	62	101	6	6	.500	67	29	25	110	32	2.23
1980—Chicago§	National	60	102	5	8	.385	90	35	30	76	34	2.65
1981—St. Louis	National	48	82	3	5	.375	64	24	24	57	24	2.63
1982—St. Louis	National	70	102⅓	9	8	.529	88	38	33	61	34	2.90
1983—St. Louis	National	60	89⅓	9	10	.474	90	45	42	64	30	4.23
Major League Totals		478	765⅔	53	53	.500	613	263	230	676	237	2.70

Selected by Washington Senators' organization in 21st round of free-agent draft, June 4, 1970.
Signed as free agent by Chicago Cubs' organization, September 9, 1971.
†On disabled list, May 22 to July 28, 1974.
‡On disabled list, August 2 to August 23, 1977.

§Traded to St. Louis Cardinals for Third Baseman Ken Reitz, Outfielder-First Baseman Leon Durham and a player to be named later, December 9, 1980; Chicago Cubs acquired Third Baseman Tye Waller to complete deal, December 22, 1980.

CHAMPIONSHIP SERIES RECORD

Year Club	League	G.	IP.	W.	L.	Pct.	H.	R.	ER.	SO.	BB.	ERA.
1982—St. Louis	National	2	4⅓	1	0	1.000	0	0	0	1	0	0.00

WORLD SERIES RECORD

Year Club	League	G.	IP.	W.	L.	Pct.	H.	R.	ER.	SO.	BB.	ERA.
1982—St. Louis	National	4	7⅔	1	0	1.000	6	4	4	6	3	4.70

ALL-STAR GAME RECORD

Year League	IP.	W.	L.	Pct.	H.	R.	ER.	SO.	BB.	ERA.
1978—National	1⅔	1	0	1.000	0	0	0	2	0	0.00
1979—National	2	1	0	1.000	2	0	0	3	2	0.00
1980—National	2	0	0	.000	0	0	0	1	1	0.00
1981—National	1	0	0	.000	0	0	0	1	0	0.00
All-Star Game Totals	6⅔	2	0	1.000	2	0	0	7	3	0.00

Named to National League All-Star Team in 1977; replaced due to injury.

DONALD HOWARD SUTTON
(Don)

Born April 2, 1945, at Clio, Ala.
Height, 6.01. Weight, 190.
Throws and bats righthanded.
Attended Mississippi College, Clinton, Miss., and Whittier College, Whittier, Calif.

Established major league records for most consecutive games lost to one club, lifetime (13), 1966 through 1969, (vs. Chicago); most consecutive years with 100 or more strikeouts (18).
Tied major league record for most years with 100 or more strikeouts (18).
Tied National League record for most consecutive home runs allowed, inning (3), May 27, 1980 (third inning).
Tied modern National League record for most one-hit games, lifetime (5).
Led National League pitchers in games started with 40 in 1974.
Led National League in shutouts with 9 in 1972.
Tied for National League lead in balks with 3 in 1968.
Named National League Rookie Pitcher of the Year by THE SPORTING NEWS, 1966.
Named righthanded pitcher on THE SPORTING NEWS National League All-Star Team, 1976.
Named Texas League Player of the Year, 1965.

Year Club	League	G.	IP.	W.	L.	Pct.	H.	R.	ER.	SO.	BB.	ERA.
1965—Santa Barbara	California	10	84	8	1	.889	59	18	14	101	15	1.50
1965—Albuquerque	Texas	21	165	15	6	★.714	151	60	51	138	30	2.78
1966—Los Angeles	National	37	226	12	12	.500	192	82	75	209	52	2.99
1967—Los Angeles	National	37	233	11	15	.423	223	106	102	169	57	3.94
1968—Spokane	P. Coast	2	16	1	1	.500	11	2	2	19	5	1.13
1968—Los Angeles	National	35	208	11	15	.423	179	64	60	162	59	2.60
1969—Los Angeles	National	41	293	17	18	.486	269	123	113	217	91	3.47
1970—Los Angeles	National	38	260	15	13	.536	251	127	●118	201	78	4.08
1971—Los Angeles	National	38	265	17	12	.586	231	85	75	194	55	2.55
1972—Los Angeles	National	33	273	19	9	.679	186	78	63	207	63	2.08
1973—Los Angeles	National	33	256	18	10	.643	196	78	69	200	56	2.43
1974—Los Angeles	National	40	276	19	9	.679	241	111	99	179	80	3.23
1975—Los Angeles	National	35	254	16	13	.552	202	87	81	175	62	2.87
1976—Los Angeles	National	35	268	21	10	.677	231	98	91	161	82	3.06
1977—Los Angeles	National	33	240	14	8	.636	207	93	85	150	69	3.19
1978—Los Angeles	National	34	238	15	11	.577	228	109	94	154	54	3.55
1979—Los Angeles†	National	33	226	12	15	.444	201	109	96	146	61	3.82
1980—Los Angeles†	National	32	212	13	5	.722	163	56	52	128	47	★2.21
1981—Houston	National	23	159	11	9	.550	132	51	46	104	29	2.60
1982—Houston‡	National	27	195	13	8	.619	169	75	65	139	46	3.00
1982—Milwaukee	American	7	54⅔	4	1	.800	55	21	20	36	18	3.29
1983—Milwaukee	American	31	220⅓	8	13	.381	209	109	100	134	54	4.08
National League Totals		584	4082	254	192	.570	3501	1532	1384	2895	1041	3.05
American League Totals		38	275	12	14	.462	264	130	120	170	72	3.93
Major League Totals		622	4357	266	206	.564	3765	1662	1504	3065	1113	3.11

Signed as free agent by Los Angeles Dodgers' organization, September 11, 1964.
†Granted free agency, October 23, 1980; signed by Houston Astros, December 4, 1980.
‡Traded to Milwaukee Brewers for three players to be named later, August 30, 1982; Houston Astros acquired Pitchers Frank DiPino and Mike Madden and Outfielder Kevin Bass to complete deal, September 3, 1982.

CHAMPIONSHIP SERIES RECORD

Established Championship Series records for most consecutive scoreless innings, Series (15⅔), 1974; most innings pitched, four-game Series (17), 1974.
Tied Championship Series record for most games won, Series (2), 1974.
Established National League Championship Series record for most consecutive scoreless innings, total Series (15⅔).
Tied National League Championship Series records for most games won, total Series (3); most complete games, total Series (2); most strikeouts four-game Series (13), 1974.

Year Club	League	G.	IP.	W.	L.	Pct.	H.	R.	ER.	SO.	BB.	ERA.
1974—Los Angeles	National	2	17	2	0	1.000	7	1	1	13	2	0.53
1977—Los Angeles	National	1	9	1	0	1.000	9	1	1	4	0	1.00
1978—Los Angeles	National	1	5⅔	0	1	.000	7	7	4	0	2	6.35
1982—Milwaukee	American	1	7⅔	1	0	1.000	8	3	3	9	2	3.52
Championship Series Totals		5	39⅓	4	1	.800	31	12	9	26	6	2.06

WORLD SERIES RECORD

Tied World Series records for most consecutive home runs allowed, inning (2), October 16, 1977 (eighth inning); most runs allowed, six-game Series (10), 1978.

Year Club	League	G.	IP.	W.	L.	Pct.	H.	R.	ER.	SO.	BB.	ERA.
1974—Los Angeles	National	2	13	1	0	1.000	9	4	4	12	3	2.77
1977—Los Angeles	National	2	16	1	0	1.000	17	7	7	6	1	3.94
1978—Los Angeles	National	2	12	0	2	.000	17	10	10	8	4	7.50
1982—Milwaukee	American	2	10⅓	0	1	.000	12	11	9	5	1	7.84
World Series Totals		8	51⅓	2	3	.400	55	32	30	31	9	5.26

ALL-STAR GAME RECORD

Year League		IP.	W.	L.	Pct.	H.	R.	ER.	SO.	BB.	ERA.
1972—National		2	0	0	.000	1	0	0	2	0	0.00
1973—National		1	0	0	.000	0	0	0	0	0	0.00
1975—National		2	0	0	.000	3	0	0	1	0	0.00
1977—National		3	1	0	1.000	1	0	0	4	1	0.00
All-Star Game Totals		8	1	0	1.000	5	0	0	7	1	0.00

WILLIAM DAVID SWAGGERTY
(Bill)

Born December 5, 1956, at Sanford, Fla.
Height, 6.02. Weight, 190.
Throws and bats righthanded.
Attended St. John's River Community College, Palatka, Fla., and Stetson University, Deland, Fla.

Year Club	League	G.	IP.	W.	L.	Pct.	H.	R.	ER.	SO.	BB.	ERA.
1979—Bluefield	Appal.	17	68	5	3	.625	76	45	36	36	28	4.79
1980—Miami	Florida St.	19	43	3	1	.750	39	16	11	25	22	2.30
1980—Charlotte	Southern	26	51	3	6	.333	47	20	14	23	24	2.47
1981—Charlotte†	Southern	35	49	8	5	.615	35	15	11	26	19	2.02
1982—Rochester‡	Int'national	29	92	6	5	.545	111	63	55	27	59	5.38
1983—Rochester§	Int'national	25	118⅓	9	6	.600	136	67	61	25	37	4.64
1983—Baltimore	American	7	21⅔	1	1	.500	23	8	7	7	6	2.91
Major League Totals		7	21⅔	1	1	.500	23	8	7	7	6	2.91

Selected by Baltimore Orioles' organization in 25th round of free-agent draft, June 5, 1979.
†On disabled list, June 1 to June 24, 1981.
‡On disabled list, August 27, 1982 through remainder of season.
§On disabled list, April 12 to May 6, 1983.

CRAIG STEVEN SWAN

Born November 30, 1950, at Van Nuys, Calif.
Height, 6.03. Weight, 215.
Throws and bats righthanded.
Attended Arizona State University, Tempe, Ariz.

Led International League in complete games with 13 in 1975.
Tied for International League lead in shutouts with 4 in 1973.
Named International League Pitcher of the Year, 1975.

Year Club	League	G.	IP.	W.	L.	Pct.	H.	R.	ER.	SO.	BB.	ERA.
1972—Memphis	Texas	14	108	7	3	.700	102	28	27	81	26	2.25
1973—Tidewater†	Int'national	16	100	7	5	.583	88	30	26	79	25	2.34
1973—New York	National	3	8	0	1	.000	16	9	8	4	2	9.00
1974—Tidewater	Int'national	9	51	2	3	.400	53	29	27	31	17	4.76
1974—New York‡	National	7	30	1	3	.250	28	19	15	10	21	4.50
1975—Tidewater	Int'national	26	165	13	7	.650	136	48	44	111	38	2.40
1975—New York	National	6	31	1	3	.250	38	22	22	19	13	6.39
1976—New York	National	23	132	6	9	.400	129	64	52	89	44	3.55
1977—New York	National	26	147	9	10	.474	153	76	69	71	56	4.22
1978—New York	National	29	207	9	6	.600	164	62	56	125	58	★2.43
1979—New York	National	35	251	14	13	.519	241	102	92	145	57	3.30
1980—New York§x	National	27	126	5	9	.357	117	59	51	79	30	3.64
1981—New York y	National	5	14	0	2	.000	10	6	5	9	1	3.21
1982—New York	National	37	166⅓	11	7	.611	165	70	62	67	37	3.35
1983—New York	National	27	96⅓	2	8	.200	112	63	59	43	42	5.51
Major League Totals		225	1208⅔	58	71	.450	1173	552	530	491	661	361	3.66

Selected by St. Louis Cardinals' organization in 8th round of free-agent draft, June 7, 1968.
Selected by New York Mets' organization in 3rd round of free-agent draft, June 6, 1972.
†On disabled list, June 5 to June 25, 1973.
‡On disabled list, June 14 to July 22, 1974.
§On disabled list, July 16 to August 16, 1980.

RICHARD JOE SWEET
(Rick)

Born September 7, 1952, at Longview, Wash.
Height, 6.00. Weight, 187.
Throws right and bats right and lefthanded.
Attended Gonzaga University, Spokane, Wash.

Led Pacific Coast League catchers in double plays with 11 in 1977.
Led Texas League catchers in errors with 15 and double plays with 13 in 1976.
Led Northwest League catchers in fielding percentage with .982 in 1975.
Tied for Northwest League lead in total bases with 149 in 1975.

Year	Club	League	Pos.	G.	AB.	R.	H.	2B.	3B.	HR.	RBI.	B.A.	PO.	A.	E.	F.A.
1975—Walla Walla	N'west		C-1B	75	260	48	91	21	2	11	∗66	∗.350	471	53	11	.979
1976—Amarillo	Texas		C-1-3-O	117	412	63	116	22	5	4	67	.282	627	49	19	.973
1977—Hawaii	P. C.		C-1-2-3	128	452	87	146	35	4	11	67	.323	459	72	10	.982
1978—San Diego	Nat.		C	88	226	15	50	8	0	1	11	.221	337	33	6	.984
1979—Hawaii	P. C.		C-1B	135	452	59	116	17	4	5	52	.257	763	72	11	.987
1980—Hawaii†‡	P. C.		C-3B-1B	99	337	42	88	11	3	1	35	.261	376	100	16	.967
1981—Tidewater	Int.		C-3B-1B	128	462	58	128	30	1	4	55	.277	422	81	13	.975
1982—New York§	Nat.		PH	3	3	0	1	0	0	0	0	.333	0	0	0	.000
1982—Seattle	Amer.		C	88	258	29	66	6	1	4	24	.256	431	26	3	.993
1983—Seattle x	Amer.		C	93	249	18	55	9	0	1	22	.221	413	34	6	.987
National League Totals				91	229	15	51	8	0	1	11	.223	337	33	6	.984
American League Totals				181	507	47	121	15	1	5	46	.239	844	60	9	.990
Major League Totals				272	736	62	172	23	1	6	57	.234	1181	93	15	.988

Selected by Pittsburgh Pirates' organization in 31st round of free-agent draft, June 5, 1974.
Selected by San Diego Padres' organization in secondary phase of free-agent draft, January 9, 1975.
†On disabled list, July 12 to July 22, 1980.
‡Sold to Tidewater (New York Mets' organization), December 15, 1980.
§Sold to Seattle Mariners, May 21, 1982.
xOn supplemental disabled list, March 27 to April 15, 1983.

PATRICK SEAN TABLER
(Pat)

Born February 2, 1958, at Hamilton, O.
Height, 6.03. Weight, 185.
Throws and bats righthanded.

Led Southern League in game-winning RBIs with 13 in 1980.
Led American Association third basemen in total chances with 361 in 1982.
Tied for American Association lead in sacrifice flies with 9 in 1982.

Year	Club	League	Pos.	G.	AB.	R.	H.	2B.	3B.	HR.	RBI.	B.A.	PO.	A.	E.	F.A.
1976—Oneonta	NYP		3B-OF	65	238	27	55	3	0	1	20	.231	79	71	12	.926
1977—Ft. Lauderdale	Fla. St.		3B	110	391	35	93	7	1	1	36	.238	87	209	∗35	.894
1978—Ft. Lauderdale	Fla. St.		1B-3B-OF	138	455	56	124	9	5	5	70	.273	855	88	15	.984
1979—Ft. Lauderdale	Fla. St.		O-3-2-1	75	247	39	78	12	4	2	33	.316	102	41	11	.929
1979—West Haven	East.		2B-OF	56	190	33	57	15	3	6	36	.300	124	169	13	.958
1980—Nashville	South.		2B	136	479	82	142	38	8	16	83	.296	262	361	∗27	.958
1981—Columbus†	Int.		2B-3B	52	179	41	53	14	3	11	33	.296	66	116	14	.929
1981—Iowa	A. A.		2B	63	222	41	68	13	3	6	37	.306	110	141	4	.984
1981—Chicago	Nat.		2B	35	101	11	19	3	1	1	5	.188	70	93	3	.982
1982—Iowa	A. A.		∗3B-1B	129	441	89	151	32	∗11	17	105	.342	∗112	∗215	∗34	.906
1982—Chicago‡§	Nat.		3B	25	85	9	20	4	2	1	7	.235	23	33	3	.949
1983—Charleston	Int.		3B	4	14	2	3	0	1	0	2	.214	2	4	3	.667
1983—Cleveland	Amer.		OF-3B-2B	124	430	56	125	23	5	6	65	.291	197	55	11	.958
National League Totals				60	186	20	39	7	3	2	12	.210	93	126	6	.973
American League Totals				124	430	56	125	23	5	6	65	.291	197	55	11	.958
Major League Totals				184	616	76	164	30	8	8	77	.266	290	181	17	.965

Selected by New York Yankees' organization in 1st round (16th player selected) of free-agent draft, June 8, 1976.

†Acquired on waivers by Chicago Cubs for two players to be named later, August 19, 1981; New York Yankees acquired Pitcher Bill Caudill, April 1, 1982, and New York organization acquired Pitcher Jay Howell, August 2, 1982, to complete deal.

‡Traded with Pitchers Dick Tidrow and Randy Martz and Infielder Scott Fletcher to Chicago White Sox for Pitchers Steve Trout and Warren Brusstar, January 25, 1983.

§Traded to Cleveland Indians for Shortstop Jerry Dybzinski, April 1, 1983.

FRANK DARYL TANANA
Name rhymes with Banana.

Born July 3, 1953, at Detroit, Mich.
Height, 6.03. Weight, 195.
Throws and bats lefthanded.
Attended California State University at Fullerton, Calif.
Son of Frank Richard Tanana, minor league outfielder, 1952 through 1956.

Established American League record for most balks, season (8), 1978.
Tied American League record for most consecutive hits allowed, start of game (5), May 18, 1980.
Led American League in balks with 8 in 1978.
Led American League in shutouts with 7 in 1977.
Led Texas League in complete games with 15 in 1973.
Named American League Rookie Pitcher of the Year by THE SPORTING NEWS, 1974.
Named lefthanded pitcher on THE SPORTING NEWS American League All-Star Team, 1976 and 1977.
Named Texas League Pitcher of the Year, 1973.

Year Club	League	G.	IP.	W.	L.	Pct.	H.	R.	ER.	SO.	BB.	ERA.
1971—Idaho Falls†	Pioneer	....	....	....	....	....	....	....	....	....	....	....
1972—Quad Cities	Midwest	19	129	7	2	.778	111	48	40	134	57	2.79
1973—El Paso	Texas	26	*206	16	6	.727	170	72	62	*197	63	2.71
1973—Salt Lake City	P. Coast	2	14	1	0	1.000	11	5	4	15	2	2.57
1973—California	American	4	26	2	2	.500	20	11	9	22	8	3.12
1974—California	American	39	269	14	19	.424	262	104	93	180	77	3.11
1975—California	American	34	257	16	9	.640	211	80	75	*269	73	2.63
1976—California	American	34	288	19	10	.655	212	88	78	261	73	2.44
1977—California	American	31	241	15	9	.625	201	72	68	205	61	*2.54
1978—California	American	33	239	18	12	.600	239	108	97	137	60	3.65
1979—California‡	American	18	90	7	5	.583	93	44	39	46	25	3.90
1980—California§	American	32	204	11	12	.478	223	107	94	113	45	4.15
1981—Boston x	American	24	141	4	10	.286	142	70	63	78	43	4.02
1982—Texas	American	30	194⅓	7	●18	.280	199	102	91	87	55	4.21
1983—Texas	American	29	159⅓	7	9	.438	144	70	56	108	49	3.16
Major League Totals		308	2108⅔	120	115	.511	1946	856	763	1506	569	3.26

Selected by California Angels' organization in 1st round (13th player selected) of free-agent draft, June 8, 1971.
†Appeared in one game as pinch runner (did not pitch due to a sore arm).
‡On disabled list, July 9 to September 4, 1979.
§Traded with Pitcher Jim Dorsey and Outfielder Joe Rudi to Boston Red Sox for Outfielder Fred Lynn and Pitcher Steve Renko, January 23, 1981.
xGranted free agency, November 13, 1981; signed by Texas Rangers, January 6, 1982.

CHAMPIONSHIP SERIES RECORD

Year Club	League	G.	IP.	W.	L.	Pct.	H.	R.	ER.	SO.	BB.	ERA.
1979—California	American	1	5	0	0	.000	6	2	2	3	2	3.60

ALL-STAR GAME RECORD

Year League	IP.	W.	L.	Pct.	H.	R.	ER.	SO.	BB.	ERA.
1976—American	2	0	0	.000	3	3	3	0	1	6.00

Named to American League All-Star Team for the 1977 game; replaced due to injury.
Named to American League All-Star Team for 1978 game; did not play.

DANILO TARTABULL
(Dan)

Born October 30, 1962, at Cienfuegos, Cuba.
Height, 6.01. Weight, 185.
Throws and bats righthanded.
Son of Jose Tartabull, outfielder with Kansas City A's,
Boston Red Sox and Oakland A's, 1962 through 1970.

Led Florida State League third basemen in errors with 29 in 1981.
Named Florida State League Most Valuable Player, 1981.

Year Club	League	Pos.	G.	AB.	R.	H.	2B.	3B.	HR.	RBI.	B.A.	PO.	A.	E.	F.A.
1980—Billings	Pion.	3B-OF-2B	59	157	33	47	10	0	2	27	.299	34	54	14	.863
1981—Tampa	Fla. St.	3B-2B	127	422	86	131	*28	10	14	81	*.310	150	248	39	.911
1982—Waterbury†	East.	2B	126	409	64	93	17	3	17	63	.227	237	306	*32	.944
1983—Chattanooga	South.	2B	128	481	95	145	32	7	13	66	.301	252	405	23	.966

Selected by Cincinnati Reds' organization in 3rd round of free-agent draft, June 3, 1980.
†Selected by Seattle Mariners' organization in player compensation pool draft, January 20, 1983. (Seattle received compensation for Chicago White Sox' signing of free-agent Pitcher Floyd Bannister, December 13, 1982.)

ALEJANDRO ANTONIO TAVERAS (BETANCES)
Name pronounced Tuh-VAIR-us.
(Alex)

Born October 9, 1955, at Tamboril, Santiago, Dominican Republic.
Height, 5.09. Weight, 165.
Throws and bats righthanded.

Led American Association in sacrifice hits with 17 in 1975.
Led Midwest League in caught stealing with 14 in 1974.
Led Texas League shortstops in double plays with 80 in 1980.

Year Club	League	Pos.	G.	AB.	R.	H.	2B.	3B.	HR.	RBI.	B.A.	PO.	A.	E.	F.A.
1974—Cedar Rapids	Midw.	SS	110	383	64	109	13	3	1	32	.285	163	260	33	.928
1975—Iowa	A. A.	SS	135	489	58	125	15	4	0	36	.256	207	385	33	.947
1976—Memphis	Int.	SS	128	447	70	103	9	6	0	42	.230	211	367	30	.951
1976—Houston	Nat.	SS-2B	14	46	3	10	0	0	0	2	.217	26	44	3	.960
1977—Charleston	Int.	SS-2B	47	148	12	22	1	2	0	9	.149	76	139	11	.951
1977—Columbus†	South.	2B	49	167	27	36	5	1	1	9	.216	103	131	9	.936

Year	Club	League	Pos.	G.	AB.	R.	H.	2B.	3B.	HR.	RBI.	B.A.	PO.	A.	E.	F.A.
1978—San Antonio	Texas	SS	105	362	65	95	11	8	1	44	.262	172	275	27	.943
1978—Albuquerque	P. C.	SS	24	76	9	17	2	2	0	11	.224	38	61	8	.925
1979—Albuquerque	P. C.	SS	119	402	55	104	12	5	0	55	.259	199	305	23	.956
1980—San Antonio	Texas	SS	115	426	66	121	18	2	6	54	.284	★202	368	26	★.956
1981—Albuquerque‡	P. C.	SS-2B	13	30	6	13	1	0	0	5	.433	23	15	1	.974
1982—Albuquerque	P. C.	SS-2B-3B	24	67	14	18	4	0	0	7	.269	38	68	3	.972
1982—San Antonio	Texas	SS-2B	73	250	45	82	20	1	5	37	.328	107	212	16	.952
1982—Los Angeles	Nat.	3B-2B-SS	11	3	1	1	1	0	0	2	.333	3	10	0	1.000
1983—Los Angeles	Nat.	SS-2B-3B	10	4	0	0	0	0	0	0	.000	3	5	0	1.000
1983—Albuquerque	P. C.	2B-SS	110	361	71	116	25	4	8	74	.321	223	315	18	.968
Major League Totals			35	53	4	11	1	0	0	4	.208	32	59	3	.968

Signed as free agent by Houston Astros' organization, March 14, 1974.

†Traded with a player to be named later to Los Angeles Dodgers' organization for Outfielder Danny Walton, September 5, 1977; Los Angeles organization acquired Outfielder Bob Dethridge to complete deal, September 16, 1977.

‡On disabled list, June 10, 1981 through remainder of season.

DWIGHT BERNARD TAYLOR

Born March 24, 1960, at Los Angeles, Calif.
Height, 5.11. Weight, 170.
Throws and bats lefthanded.
Attended University of Arizona, Tucson, Ariz.

Led Eastern League in stolen bases with 95 in 1983.

Year	Club	League	Pos.	G.	AB.	R.	H.	2B.	3B.	HR.	RBI.	B.A.	PO.	A.	E.	F.A.
1981—Waterloo	Midw.	OF	49	153	25	33	4	0	0	13	.216	51	6	2	.966
1982—Waterloo	Midw.	OF	27	101	28	27	4	1	0	6	.267	49	3	1	.981
1982—Chattanooga	South.	OF	110	426	71	123	10	9	2	33	.289	256	9	14	.950
1983—Buffalo	East.	OF	131	451	95	136	13	4	8	38	.302	223	10	9	.963

Selected by Philadelphia Phillies' organization in 11th round of free-agent draft, June 6, 1978.

Selected by Cleveland Indians' organization in 7th round of free-agent draft, June 8, 1981.

KENTON CHARLES TEKULVE

Name pronounced Tuh-KULL-vee.

(Kent)

Born March 5, 1947, at Cincinnati, O.
Height, 6.04. Weight, 175.
Throws and bats righthanded.
Received bachelor of science degree in physical education
from Marietta College, Marietta, O.

Tied major league records for most intentional bases on balls allowed, season (23), 1982; most consecutive games won by relief pitcher, three consecutive games (3), May 6, 7, 9, 1980.

Major League saves: 1975 (5), 1976 (9), 1977 (7), 1978 (31), 1979 (31), 1980 (21), 1981 (3), 1982 (20), 1983 (18). Total—145.

Led National League in intentional bases on balls issued with 20 in 1979, 23 in 1982 and tied for lead with 16 in 1980.

Led National League in games finished in relief with 65 in 1978, 67 in 1979 and tied for lead with 56 in 1983.

Year	Club	League	G.	IP.	W.	L.	Pct.	H.	R.	ER.	SO.	BB.	ERA.
1969—Geneva	NYP	9	53	6	2	.750	40	15	10	60	22	1.70
1970—Salem	Carolina	41	79	4	6	.400	68	29	17	75	51	1.94
1971—Salem	Carolina	47	75	11	5	.688	77	36	29	62	31	3.48
1971—Waterbury	Eastern	2	3	0	0	.000	3	0	0	0	2	0.00
1972—Sherbrooke	Eastern	31	72	7	6	.538	61	24	21	54	22	2.63
1972—Charleston	Int'national	9	22	2	1	.667	22	10	10	9	10	4.09
1973—Sherbrooke	Eastern	★57	94	●12	4	★.750	70	24	16	89	35	1.53
1974—Charleston	Int'national	35	60	6	3	.667	50	20	15	38	21	2.25
1974—Pittsburgh	National	8	9	1	1	.500	12	6	6	6	5	6.00
1975—Charleston	Int'national	24	71	5	4	.556	47	23	14	46	19	1.77
1975—Pittsburgh	National	34	56	1	2	.333	43	20	14	28	23	2.25
1976—Pittsburgh	National	64	103	5	3	.625	91	30	28	68	25	2.45
1977—Pittsburgh	National	72	103	10	1	.909	89	41	35	59	33	3.06
1978—Pittsburgh	National	★91	135	8	7	.533	115	44	35	77	55	2.33
1979—Pittsburgh†	National	★94	134	10	8	.556	109	46	41	75	49	2.75
1980—Pittsburgh	National	78	93	8	12	.400	96	39	35	47	40	3.39
1981—Pittsburgh	National	45	65	5	5	.500	61	19	18	34	17	2.49
1982—Pittsburgh	National	★85	128⅔	12	8	.600	113	47	41	66	46	2.87
1983—Pittsburgh‡	National	76	99	7	5	.583	78	27	18	52	36	1.64
Major League Totals		647	925⅔	67	52	.563	807	319	271	512	329	2.63

Signed as free agent by Pittsburgh Pirates' organization, July 16, 1969.

†Appeared in one game as an outfielder with one putout.

‡Granted free agency, November 7, 1983; re-signed by Pirates, December 22, 1983.

CHAMPIONSHIP SERIES RECORD

Year	Club	League	G.	IP.	W.	L.	Pct.	H.	R.	ER.	SO.	BB.	ERA.
1975—Pittsburgh	National	2	1⅓	0	0	.000	3	1	1	2	1	6.75
1979—Pittsburgh	National	2	2⅔	0	0	.000	2	1	1	2	2	3.38
Championship Series Totals		4	4	0	0	.000	5	2	2	4	3	4.50

Established World Series record for most saves, seven-game Series (3), 1979.

Year	Club	League	G.	IP.	W.	L.	Pct.	H.	R.	ER.	SO.	BB.	ERA.
1979—Pittsburgh	National	5	9⅓	0	1	.000	4	3	3	10	3	2.89

ALL-STAR GAME RECORD

Member of National League All-Star Team in 1980; did not play.

THOMAS JOHN TELLMANN
(Tom)

Born March 29, 1954, at Warren, Pa.
Height, 6.04. Weight, 185.
Throws and bats righthanded.
Received bachelor of arts degree in physical education from
Grand Canyon College, Phoenix, Ariz.

Major League saves: 1980 (1), 1983 (8). Total—9.
Led Pacific Coast League in shutouts with 4 in 1980.
Led California League in saves with 12 and intentional bases on balls issued with 9 in 1977.

Year	Club	League	G.	IP.	W.	L.	Pct.	H.	R.	ER.	SO.	BB.	ERA.
1976—Walla Walla	Northwest	17	69	3	4	.429	56	37	25	46	33	3.26
1977—Reno	California	48	88	8	7	.533	92	50	33	82	32	3.38
1978—Amarillo	Texas	48	76	5	6	.455	74	29	22	48	25	2.61
1979—Hawaii	P. Coast	44	83	4	8	.333	98	37	27	51	40	2.93
1979—San Diego	National	1	3	0	0	.000	7	5	5	1	0	15.00
1980—Hawaii	P. Coast	24	170	13	5	.722	155	74	61	83	58	3.23
1980—San Diego	National	6	22	3	0	1.000	23	5	4	9	8	1.64
1981—Hawaii	P. Coast	25	176	12	11	.522	189	78	71	67	53	3.63
1982—Hawaii†	P. Coast	41	104	7	7	.500	113	56	44	55	36	3.81
1983—Milwaukee	American	44	99⅔	9	4	.692	95	34	31	48	35	2.80
National League Totals		7	25	3	0	1.000	30	10	9	10	8	3.24
American League Totals		44	99⅔	9	4	.692	95	34	31	48	35	2.80
Major League Totals		51	124⅔	12	4	.750	125	44	40	58	43	2.89

Selected by San Diego Padres' organization in 11th round of free-agent draft, June 8, 1976.
†Traded to Milwaukee Brewers' organization for Pitchers Weldon Swift and Tim Cook, October 15, 1982.

GARRY LEWIS TEMPLETON

Born March 24, 1956, at Lockey, Tex.
Height, 5.11. Weight, 190.
Throws right and bats left and righthanded.
Brother of Ken Templeton, outfielder in Oakland A's organization, 1972 through 1974; son of
Spiavia Templeton, former infielder in the Negro Leagues.

Tied major league records by collecting 100 or more hits righthanded and lefthanded, season, 1979; most consecutive seasons leading league, three-base hits (3), 1977 through 1979.
Tied modern major league record for most three-base hits by switch hitter, season, (19), 1979.
Major League stolen bases: 1976 (11), 1977 (28), 1978 (34), 1979 (26), 1980 (31), 1981 (8), 1982 (27), 1983 (16). Total—181.
Led National League shortstops in total chances with 848 in 1978 and 851 in 1979.
Led National League shortstops in double plays with 108 in 1978.
Tied for National League lead in caught stealing with 24 in 1977.
Tied for National League lead in double plays by shortstops with 102 in 1979.
Named shortstop on THE SPORTING NEWS National League All-Star Team, 1977, 1979 and 1980.
Named shortstop on THE SPORTING NEWS National League Silver Slugger team, 1980.
Received reported $40,000 bonus to sign with St. Louis Cardinals, 1974.

Year	Club	League	Pos.	G.	AB.	R.	H.	2B.	3B.	HR.	RBI.	B.A.	PO.	A.	E.	F.A.
1974—Sarasota Cards	Gulf C.	SS	18	71	11	19	1	0	3	10	.268	15	41	3	.949
1974—St. Petersburg	Fla. St.	SS	23	95	3	20	1	0	0	2	.211	42	64	7	.938
1975—St. Petersburg	Fla. St.	SS	82	349	50	92	7	8	1	32	.264	130	253	29	.930
1975—Arkansas	Texas	SS	42	177	36	71	9	4	2	20	.401	60	131	18	.914
1976—Tulsa	A. A.	★S-3-O	106	443	65	142	24	★15	6	38	.321	★178	319	34	.936
1976—St. Louis	Nat.	SS	53	213	32	62	8	2	1	17	.291	111	172	24	.922
1977—St. Louis	Nat.	SS	153	621	94	200	19	★18	8	79	.322	285	453	32	.958
1978—St. Louis	Nat.	SS	155	647	82	181	31	★13	2	47	.280	★285	523	★40	.953
1979—St. Louis	Nat.	SS	154	672	105	★211	32	★19	9	62	.314	★292	525	★34	.960
1980—St. Louis†‡	Nat.	SS	118	504	83	161	19	9	4	43	.319	223	451	★29	.959
1981—St. Louis§ x	Nat.	SS	80	333	47	96	16	8	1	33	.288	160	272	18	.960
1982—San Diego	Nat.	SS	141	563	76	139	25	8	6	64	.247	220	422	26	.961
1983—San Diego y	Nat.	SS	126	460	39	121	20	2	3	40	.263	219	355	24	.960
Major League Totals			980	4013	558	1171	170	79	34	385	.292	1795	3173	227	.956

Selected by St. Louis Cardinals' organization in 1st round (13th player selected) of free-agent draft, June 5, 1974.
†On disabled list, July 24 to August 14, 1980.
‡On supplemental disabled list, August 24 to September 8, 1980.
§On suspended list, August 26, 1981; transferred to supplemental disabled list, August 28 to September 14, 1981.
xTraded to San Diego Padres for Shortstop Ozzie Smith, February 11, 1982.
yOn supplemental disabled list, April 28 to May 17, 1983.

Year	League	Pos.	AB.	R.	H.	2B.	3B.	HR.	RBI.	B.A.	PO.	A.	E.	F.A.
1977—National		SS	1	1	1	1	0	0	0	1.000	1	2	1	.750

Named to National League All-Star Team for 1979 game; declined.

FURY GENE TENACE

Name pronounced TEN-nis.

(Known by middle name.)

Born October 10, 1946, at Russelton, Pa.
Height, 6.00. Weight, 195.
Throws and bats righthanded.

Established major league records for fewest singles, season, 150 or more games (58), 1974; fewest chances offered by first baseman, two consecutive games, 17 innings (5), August 31 and September 1, 1974.

Tied major league records for fewest chances accepted and fewest putouts, first baseman, game (0), September 1, 1974.

Tied American League record for most chances accepted by catcher, inning (4), May 24, 1975 (fifth inning).

Led National League in bases on balls received with 125 and being hit by pitch wiith 13 in 1977.

Led American League in bases on balls received with 110 in 1974.

Led National League catchers in fielding percentage with .998 in 1979.

Led Carolina League catchers in double plays with 13 in 1968 and Southern League catchers with 7 in 1969.

Year	Club	League	Pos.	G.	AB.	R.	H.	2B.	3B.	HR.	RBI.	B.A.	PO.	A.	E.	F.A.
1965—Shelby	W. Car.	OF	32	93	10	17	2	1	2	6	.183	22	2	1	.960
1966—Leesburg	Fla. St.	1-O-3-P	91	228	28	48	8	2	1	24	.211	310	23	12	.965
1967—Peninsula	Carol.	OF	3	7	0	0	0	0	0	1	.000	2	1	0	1.000
1967—Leesburg	Fla. St.	C-1B-P	106	354	47	94	12	2	6	44	.266	204	14	11	.952
1968—Peninsula	Carol.	C-O-3-1-P	132	435	78	123	20	3	21	71	.283	639	68	17	.977
1969—Birmingham	South.	C-OF-3B	89	276	56	88	20	4	20	74	.319	442	51	7	.986
1969—Oakland	Amer.	C	16	38	1	6	0	0	1	2	.158	61	6	0	1.000
1970—Iowa	A. A.	C-OF	93	319	54	90	24	1	16	63	.282	534	57	9	.985
1970—Oakland	Amer.	C	38	105	19	32	6	0	7	20	.305	180	18	2	.990
1971—Oakland	Amer.	C-OF	65	179	26	49	7	0	7	25	.274	300	20	2	.994
1972—Oakland	Amer.	C-O-1-3-2	82	227	22	51	5	3	5	32	.225	329	23	7	.981
1973—Oakland	Amer.	1B-C-2B	160	510	83	132	18	2	24	84	.259	1218	71	14	.989
1974—Oakland	Amer.	1B-C-2B	158	484	71	102	17	1	26	73	.211	1110	83	10	.992
1975—Oakland	Amer.	C-1B	158	498	83	127	17	0	29	87	.255	942	84	11	.989
1976—Oakland†‡	Amer.	1B-C	128	417	64	104	19	1	22	66	.249	840	56	8	.991
1977—San Diego	Nat.	C-1B-3B	147	437	66	102	24	4	15	61	.233	820	112	16	.983
1978—San Diego	Nat.	1B-C-3B	142	401	60	90	18	4	16	61	.224	944	79	8	.992
1979—San Diego§	Nat.	C-1B	151	463	61	122	16	4	20	67	.263	995	83	8	.993
1980—San Diego§	Nat.	C-1B	133	316	46	70	11	1	17	50	.222	540	56	11	.982
1981—St. Louis	Nat.	C-1B	58	129	26	30	7	0	5	22	.233	165	22	3	.984
1982—St. Louis xy	Nat.	C-1B	66	124	18	32	9	0	7	18	.258	188	24	1	.995
1983—Pittsburgh z	Nat.	1B-C-OF	53	62	7	11	5	0	0	6	.177	99	6	2	.981
American League Totals			805	2458	369	603	89	7	121	389	.245	4980	361	54	.990
National League Totals			750	1932	284	457	90	13	80	285	.237	3751	382	49	.988
Major League Totals			1555	4390	653	1060	179	20	201	674	.241	8731	743	103	.989

Selected by Kansas City A's organization in 11th round of free-agent draft, June 19, 1965.

†On disabled list, April 30 to May 27, 1976.

‡Granted free agency, November 1, 1976; signed by San Diego Padres, December 14, 1976.

§Traded with Pitchers Rollie Fingers and Bob Shirley and a player to be named later to St. Louis Cardinals for Catchers Terry Kennedy and Steve Swisher, Pitchers John Littlefield, Al Olmsted, Kim Seaman and John Urrea and Infielder Mike Phillips, December 8, 1980; St. Louis organization acquired Catcher Bob Geren to complete deal, December 10, 1980.

xOn disabled list, March 22 to April 12 and May 20 to June 14, 1982.

yGranted free agency, November 10, 1982; signed by Pittsburgh Pirates, December 1, 1982.

zOn supplemental disabled list, August 8 to September 1, 1983.

CHAMPIONSHIP SERIES RECORD

Tied American League Championship Series record for most positions played, total Series (3).

Year	Club	League	Pos.	G.	AB.	R.	H.	2B.	3B.	HR.	RBI.	B.A.	PO.	A.	E.	F.A.
1971—Oakland	Amer.	C	1	3	0	0	0	0	0	0	.000	8	0	0	1.000
1972—Oakland	Amer.	C-2B	5	17	1	1	0	0	0	1	.059	21	5	1	.963
1973—Oakland	Amer.	1B-C	5	17	3	4	1	0	0	0	.235	40	3	0	1.000
1974—Oakland	Amer.	1B	4	11	1	0	0	0	0	1	.000	35	2	0	1.000
1975—Oakland	Amer.	C-1B	3	9	0	0	0	0	0	0	.000	19	1	0	1.000
Championship Series Totals			18	57	5	5	1	0	0	2	.088	123	11	1	.993

WORLD SERIES RECORD

Established World Series record for slugging percentage, 7-game series, .913, 1972.

Tied World Series records for most home runs, seven-game Series (4), 1972; most bases on balls, seven-game Series (11), 1973; most double plays by first baseman, game (4), October 17, 1973.

First player to hit two home runs in first two World Series at bats, October 14, 1972.

Year	Club	League	Pos.	G.	AB.	R.	H.	2B.	3B.	HR.	RBI.	B.A.	PO.	A.	E.	F.A.
1972—Oakland	Amer.	C-1B	7	23	5	8	1	0	4	9	.348	48	5	1	.981
1973—Oakland	Amer.	1B-C	7	19	0	3	1	0	0	3	.158	57	2	2	.967
1974—Oakland	Amer.	1B	5	9	0	2	0	0	0	0	.222	20	1	0	1.000
1982—St. Louis	Nat.	DH-PH	5	6	0	0	0	0	0	0	.000	0	0	0	.000
World Series Totals			24	57	5	13	2	0	4	12	.228	125	8	3	.978

Year	League	Pos.	AB.	R.	H.	2B.	3B.	HR.	RBI.	B.A.	PO.	A.	E.	F.A.
1975—American		1B-C	3	1	0	0	0	0	0	.000	4	0	1	.800

PITCHING RECORD

Year	Club	League	G.	IP.	W.	L.	Pct.	H.	R.	ER.	SO.	BB.	ERA.
1966—Leesburg		Florida St.	3	17	0	1	.000	24	7	4	8	6	2.12
1967—Leesburg		Florida St.	4	8	0	0	.000	4	0	0	8	1	0.00
1968—Peninsula		Carolina	2	3	0	0	.000	4	1	1	0	1	3.00

CHARLES WALTER TERRELL

Name pronounced TEAR-el.

(Walt)

Born May 11, 1958, at Jeffersonville, Ind.
Height, 6.02. Weight, 205.
Throws right and bats lefthanded.
Received degree from Morehead State University, Morehead, Ky. in 1980.

Tied for International League lead in intentional bases on balls issued with 9 in 1982.
Named International League Pitcher of the Year, 1983.

Year	Club	League	G.	IP.	W.	L.	Pct.	H.	R.	ER.	SO.	BB.	ERA.
1980—Sarasota Rangers		Gulf Coast	7	38	3	2	.600	20	11	6	23	12	1.42
1980—Asheville		S. Atlantic	3	8	1	1	.500	11	9	6	5	8	6.75
1981—Tulsa†		Texas	27	174	●15	7	.682	158	74	60	123	63	3.10
1982—Tidewater‡		Int'national	21	138⅔	7	8	.467	130	69	61	74	72	3.96
1982—New York		National	3	21	0	3	.000	22	12	8	8	14	3.43
1983—Tidewater		Int'national	12	86⅔	10	1	*.909	76	34	30	58	44	3.12
1983—New York		National	21	133⅔	8	8	.500	123	57	53	59	55	3.57
Major League Totals			24	154⅔	8	11	.421	145	69	61	67	69	3.55

Selected by New York Mets' organization in 15th round of free-agent draft, June 5, 1979.
Selected by Texas Rangers' organization in 33rd round of free-agent draft, June 3, 1980.
†Traded with Pitcher Ron Darling to New York Mets' organization for Outfielder Lee Mazzilli, April 1, 1982.
‡On disabled list, July 19 to August 2, 1982.

MICKEY LEE TETTLETON

Born September 16, 1960, at Oklahoma City, Okla.
Height, 6.01. Weight, 190.
Throws right and bats left and righthanded.
Attended Oklahoma State University, Stillwater, Okla.

Year	Club	League	Pos.	G.	AB.	R.	H.	2B.	3B.	HR.	RBI.	B.A.	PO.	A.	E.	F.A.
1981—Modesto		Calif.	C-OF-1B	48	138	28	34	3	0	5	19	.246	235	31	14	.950
1982—Modesto†		Calif.	C-OF	88	253	44	63	18	0	8	37	.249	424	36	8	.983
1983—Modesto		Calif.	C-OF	124	378	55	92	18	2	7	62	.243	582	46	11	.983

Selected by Oakland A's organization in 5th round of free-agent draft, June 8, 1981.
†On disabled list, July 16 to August 13, 1982.

TIMOTHY SHAWN TEUFEL

Name pronounced TUFF-el.

(Tim)

Born July 7, 1958, at Greenwich, Conn.
Height, 6.00. Weight, 175.
Throws and bats righthanded.
Attended St. Petersburg Junior College, St. Petersburg, Fla.,
and Clemson University, Clemson, S. C.

Led International League second basemen in putouts with 304, assists with 394, total chances with 711 and double plays with 109 in 1983.
Named International League Player of the Year, 1983.

Year	Club	League	Pos.	G.	AB.	R.	H.	2B.	3B.	HR.	RBI.	B.A.	PO.	A.	E.	F.A.
1980—Orlando		South.	2B	86	287	38	76	15	3	11	47	.265	196	246	17	.963
1981—Orlando		South.	2B	128	416	69	103	21	5	17	60	.248	312	376	20	.972
1982—Orlando		South.	2B	100	340	52	96	12	4	9	56	.282	231	185	15	.965
1982—Toledo		Int.	2B	45	149	25	42	10	4	6	20	.282	99	139	3	.988
1983—Toledo		Int.	2B-SS	136	471	103	152	27	6	27	100	.323	306	401	14	.981
1983—Minnesota		Amer.	2B-SS	21	78	11	24	7	1	3	6	.308	47	58	1	.991
Major League Totals				21	78	11	24	7	1	3	6	.308	47	58	1	.991

Selected by Milwaukee Brewers' organization in 16th round of free-agent draft, June 6, 1978.
Selected by Chicago White Sox' organization in secondary phase of free-agent draft, June 5, 1979.
Selected by Minnesota Twins' organization in 2nd round of free-agent draft, June 3, 1980.

ROBERT A. TEWKSBURY

(Bob)

Born November 30, 1960, at Penacock, N. H.
Height, 6.04. Weight, 200.
Throws and bats righthanded.
Attended St. Leo College, St. Leo, Fla.

Led Florida State League in shutouts with 5 and tied for lead in complete games with 13 in 1982.

Year Club	League	G.	IP.	W.	L.	Pct.	H.	R.	ER.	SO.	BB.	ERA.
1981—Oneonta	NYP	14	85	7	3	.700	85	43	34	62	37	3.40
1982—Ft. Lauderdale	Florida St.	24	181⅓	*15	4	.789	146	46	38	92	47	*1.88
1983—Ft. Lauderdale†	Florida St.	2	16	2	0	1.000	6	1	0	5	1	0.00
1983—Nashville	Southern	7	51	5	1	.833	49	20	16	15	10	2.82

Selected by New York Yankees' organization in 19th round of free-agent draft, June 8, 1981.
†On disabled list, April 8 to June 7, 1983.

DERREL OSBON THOMAS

Born January 14, 1951, at Los Angeles, Calif.
Height, 6.00. Weight, 160.
Throws right and bats right and lefthanded.

Led American Association second basemen in putouts with 226 and fielding percentage with .979 in 1971.

Year Club	League	Pos.	G.	AB.	R.	H.	2B.	3B.	HR.	RBI.	B.A.	PO.	A.	E.	F.A.
1969—Cocoa	Fla. St.	SS	33	114	17	33	5	3	0	8	.289	57	75	22	.857
1969—Okla. City	A. A.	SS-OF	36	154	21	48	4	6	0	17	.312	50	64	11	.912
1970—Columbus	South.	SS-2B	38	156	24	38	5	4	4	12	.244	60	95	14	.917
1970—Okla. City	A. A.	SS-2B-OF	75	272	39	73	5	6	4	21	.268	126	156	20	.934
1971—Okla. City	A. A.	2B-SS	122	486	74	139	22	8	3	42	.286	257	325	15	.975
1971—Houston†	Nat.	2B	5	5	0	0	0	0	0	0	.000	3	2	0	1.000
1972—Hawaii	P. C.	OF-2B	6	27	2	4	2	0	0	3	.148	13	6	2	.905
1972—San Diego	Nat.	2B-SS-OF	130	500	48	115	15	5	5	36	.230	290	357	26	.961
1973—San Diego	Nat.	SS-2B	113	404	41	96	7	1	0	22	.238	211	324	37	.935
1974—San Diego‡	Nat.	2-3-O-S	141	523	48	129	24	6	3	41	.247	310	336	18	.973
1975—San Francisco	Nat.	2B-OF	144	540	99	149	21	9	6	48	.276	349	372	19	.974
1976—San Francisco§	Nat.	2-O-3-S	81	272	38	63	5	4	2	19	.232	163	215	15	.962
1977—San Francisco x	Nat.	O-2-S-3-1	148	506	75	135	13	10	8	44	.267	307	158	14	.971
1978—San Diego yz	Nat.	O-2-3-1	128	352	36	80	10	2	3	26	.227	328	168	12	.976
1979—Los Angeles	Nat.	O-3-2-S-1	141	406	47	104	15	4	5	44	.256	298	38	5	.985
1980—Los Angeles	Nat.	O-S-2-C-3	117	297	32	79	18	3	1	22	.266	203	175	14	.964
1981—Los Angeles	Nat.	2-S-O-3	80	218	25	54	4	0	4	24	.248	133	144	14	.952
1982—Los Angeles a	Nat.	O-2-3-S	66	98	13	26	2	1	0	2	.265	58	58	4	.967
1983—Los Angeles bc	Nat.	O-S-2-3	118	192	38	48	6	6	2	8	.250	134	51	5	.974
Major League Totals			1412	4313	540	1078	140	51	39	436	.250	2787	2398	183	.966

Selected by Houston Astros' organization in 1st round (first player selected) of free-agent draft, February 1, 1969.
†Traded with Pitchers Bill Greif and Mark Schaeffer to San Diego Padres for Pitcher Dave Roberts, December 3, 1971.
‡Traded to San Francisco Giants for Second Baseman Tito Fuentes and Pitcher Butch Metzger, December 6, 1974.
§On disabled list, July 12 to September 15, 1976.
xTraded to San Diego Padres for Catcher-Infielder Mike Ivie, February 28, 1978.
yOn supplemental disabled list, July 3 to July 22, 1978.
zGranted free agency, November 2, 1978; signed by Los Angeles Dodgers November 14, 1978.
aOn disabled list, June 25, 1982; transferred to emergency disabled list, July 28 to September 1, 1982.
bOn disabled list, May 3 to June 4, 1983.
cGranted free agency, November 7, 1983.

DIVISION SERIES RECORD

Year Club	League	Pos.	G.	AB.	R.	H.	2B.	3B.	HR.	RBI.	B.A.	PO.	A.	E.	F.A.
1981—Los Angeles	Nat.	OF	4	2	1	0	0	0	0	0	.000	0	0	0	.000

CHAMPIONSHIP SERIES RECORD

Year Club	League	Pos.	G.	AB.	R.	H.	2B.	3B.	HR.	RBI.	B.A.	PO.	A.	E.	F.A.
1981—Los Angeles	Nat.	PR-3-OF	2	1	2	1	0	0	0	0	1.000	1	0	0	1.000
1983—Los Angeles	Nat.	OF-PH	4	9	0	4	1	0	0	0	.444	7	0	0	1.000
Championship Series Totals			6	10	2	5	1	0	0	0	.500	8	0	0	1.000

WORLD SERIES RECORD

Tied World Series record for most positions played, Series (3), 1981 (shortstop, centerfield, third base).

Year Club	League	Pos.	G.	AB.	R.	H.	2B.	3B.	HR.	RBI.	B.A.	PO.	A.	E.	F.A.
1981—Los Angeles	Nat.	PH-S-O-3	5	7	2	0	0	0	0	1	.000	4	1	0	1.000

JAMES GORMAN THOMAS III

(Known by middle name.)

Born December 12, 1950, at Charleston, S. C.
Height, 6.03. Weight, 200.
Throws and bats righthanded.
Attended Baptist College, Charleston, S. C.

Tied major league records for most strikeouts, two consecutive games (8), July 27 and 28, 1975; most strikeouts, three consecutive games (10), July 27 through 29, 1975.
Tied American League records for most consecutive strikeouts (8), July 27 through 29, 1975; most strikeouts, season (175), 1979; most years with 400 or more putouts, outfielder (4).
Led American League batters in strikeouts with 175 in 1979, 170 in 1980 and tied for lead with 133 in 1978.
Led Pacific Coast League in total bases with 320 in 1977.
Led Pacific Coast League batters in strikeouts with 175 in 1974.
Led Texas League batters in strikeouts with 171 in 1972.
Led Midwest League batters in strikeouts with 170 in 1971.

Tied for Texas League lead in double plays by outfielders with 4 in 1972.
Named outfielder on THE SPORTING NEWS American League All-Star Team, 1982.

Year	Club	League	Pos.	G.	AB.	R.	H.	2B.	3B.	HR.	RBI.	B.A.	PO.	A.	E.	F.A.
1969—Billings		Pion.	SS-1B	41	142	23	42	10	3	4	28	.296	94	82	27	.867
1970—Clinton†		Midw.	SS-3B-2B	85	297	36	63	5	4	8	39	.212	105	186	28	.912
1971—Danville		Midw.	OF-3B	121	457	82	112	20	4	★31	83	.245	195	14	10	.954
1972—San Antonio		Texas	★OF-1B	135	465	70	112	22	2	★26	68	.241	★305	★24	6	★.982
1973—Evansville		A. A.	OF	46	146	26	31	6	0	8	18	.212	66	3	4	.945
1973—Milwaukee		Amer.	OF-3B	59	155	16	29	7	1	2	11	.187	87	1	4	.957
1974—Sacramento		P. C.	OF	138	474	117	141	15	1	51	122	.297	302	16	10	.970
1974—Milwaukee		Amer.	OF	17	46	10	12	4	0	2	11	.261	26	0	0	1.000
1975—Milwaukee		Amer.	OF	121	240	34	43	12	2	10	28	.179	215	5	9	.961
1976—Milwaukee		Amer.	OF-3B	99	227	27	45	9	2	8	36	.198	211	4	4	.982
1977—Spokane‡§		P. C.	OF	143	500	114	161	41	5	36	114	.322	325	13	7	★.980
1978—Milwaukee		Amer.	OF	137	452	70	111	24	1	32	86	.246	345	5	6	.983
1979—Milwaukee		Amer.	OF	156	557	97	136	29	0	★45	123	.244	435	4	4	.991
1980—Milwaukee		Amer.	OF	162	628	78	150	26	3	38	105	.239	455	6	7	.985
1981—Milwaukee		Amer.	OF	103	363	54	94	22	0	21	65	.259	221	8	5	.979
1982—Milwaukee		Amer.	OF	158	567	96	139	29	1	●39	112	.245	427	11	4	.991
1983—Milw. x-Clev. y		Amer.	OF	152	535	72	112	23	1	22	69	.209	439	7	7	.985
Major League Totals				1164	3770	554	871	185	11	219	646	.231	2861	51	50	.983

Selected by Seattle Pilots' organization in 1st round (21st player selected) of free-agent draft, June 5, 1969.

†On restricted list, March 4 to May 30, 1970.

‡Traded to Texas Rangers, October 25, 1977, completing deal in which Texas traded Outfielder-First Baseman Ed Kirkpatrick to Milwaukee Brewers for a player to be named later, August 20, 1977.

§Sold to Milwaukee Brewers, February 8, 1978.

xTraded with Pitchers Jamie Easterly and Ernie Camacho to Cleveland Indians for Outfielder Rick Manning and Pitcher Rick Waits, June 6, 1983.

yTraded with Second Baseman Jack Perconte to Seattle Mariners for Second Baseman Tony Bernazard, December 7, 1983.

DIVISION SERIES RECORD

Year	Club	League	Pos.	G.	AB.	R.	H.	2B.	3B.	HR.	RBI.	B.A.	PO.	A.	E.	F.A.
1981—Milwaukee		Amer.	OF	5	18	2	2	0	0	1	1	.111	12	0	0	1.000

CHAMPIONSHIP SERIES RECORD

Tied Championship Series record for hitting home run in first Series at-bat, October 5, 1982.

Year	Club	League	Pos.	G.	AB.	R.	H.	2B.	3B.	HR.	RBI.	B.A.	PO.	A.	E.	F.A.
1982—Milwaukee		Amer.	OF	5	16	1	1	0	0	1	3	.063	13	0	0	1.000

WORLD SERIES RECORD

Tied World Series record for most at-bats, inning (2), October 16, 1982 (seventh inning).

Year	Club	League	Pos.	G.	AB.	R.	H.	2B.	3B.	HR.	RBI.	B.A.	PO.	A.	E.	F.A.
1982—Milwaukee		Amer.	OF	7	26	0	3	0	0	0	3	.115	15	0	0	1.000

ALL-STAR GAME RECORD

Year	League	Pos.	AB.	R.	H.	2B.	3B.	HR.	RBI.	B.A.	PO.	A.	E.	F.A.
1981—American		PH	1	0	0	0	0	0	0	.000	0	0	0	.000

ROY JUSTIN THOMAS

Born June 22, 1953, at Quantico, Va.
Height, 6.05. Weight, 215.
Throws and bats righthanded.
Attended University of Tampa, Tampa, Fla., and De Anza College, Cupertino, Calif.

Pitched seven-inning, 2-0 no-hit victory against West Haven, August 20, 1974 (second game).
Led Pacific Coast League in wild pitches with 27 and tied for lead in hit batsmen with 10 in 1983.
Led American Association in wild pitches with 17 in 1976.
Led Eastern League in games started by pitchers with 27 in 1974.
Led Carolina League in shutouts with 6 in 1973.
Received reported $75,000 bonus to sign with Philadelphia Phillies, 1971.

Year	Club	League	G.	IP.	W.	L.	Pct.	H.	R.	ER.	SO.	BB.	ERA.
1971—Walla Walla		Northwest	7	12	0	3	.000	19	22	14	8	16	10.50
1972—Spartanburg		W. Carol.	24	152	11	7	.611	128	67	58	128	62	3.43
1973—Rocky Mount		Carolina	26	169	●15	8	.652	119	53	42	★193	72	★2.24
1973—Reading		Eastern	2	16	2	0	1.000	11	2	2	14	7	1.13
1974—Reading		Eastern	27	●191	14	11	.560	154	77	55	★168	89	2.59
1974—Toledo		Int'national	2	7	0	0	.000	5	3	1	5	2	1.29
1975—Toledo		Int'national	19	119	4	9	.308	112	63	53	95	49	4.01
1975—Reading†		Eastern	10	67	6	3	.667	50	22	19	53	29	2.55
1976—Iowa‡§		Am. Assoc.	27	168	6	11	.353	167	89	70	103	72	3.75
1977—Charleston		Int'national	44	168	11	6	.647	151	63	59	71	65	3.16
1977—Houston		National	4	6	0	0	.000	5	2	2	4	3	3.00
1978—Charleston x		Int'national	28	66	9	4	.692	63	28	23	40	30	3.14
1978—St. Louis		National	16	28	1	1	.500	21	14	12	16	16	3.86
1979—Springfield		Am. Assoc.	17	74	5	6	.455	79	55	48	85	31	5.84
1979—St. Louis		National	26	77	3	4	.429	66	29	25	44	24	2.92
1980—St. Louis		National	24	55	2	3	.400	59	32	29	22	25	4.75
1980—Springfield y		Am. Assoc.	19	37	5	1	.833	34	18	14	36	18	3.41

Year Club	League	G.	IP.	W.	L.	Pct.	H.	R.	ER.	SO.	BB.	ERA.
1981—Tacoma z	P. Coast	36	165	12	8	.600	137	61	56	111	49	3.05
1982—Salt Lake City	P. Coast	33	156⅔	8	9	.471	195	112	98	96	84	5.63
1983—Seattle	American	43	88⅔	3	1	.750	95	44	34	77	32	3.45
National League Totals		70	166	6	8	.429	151	77	68	86	68	3.69
American League Totals		43	88⅔	3	1	.750	95	44	34	77	32	3.45
Major League Totals		113	254⅔	9	9	.500	246	121	102	163	100	3.60

Selected by Philadelphia Phillies' organization in 1st round (sixth player selected) of free-agent draft, June 8, 1971.

†Traded with Pitcher Dick Ruthven and Infielder-Outfielder Alan Bannister by Philadelphia Phillies to Chicago White Sox for Pitcher Jim Kaat and Shortstop Mike Buskey, December 10, 1975.

‡Selected by Seattle Mariners in American League expansion draft, November 5, 1976.

§Traded to Houston Astros for Infielder Larry Milbourne, March 30, 1977.

xSold on waivers to St. Louis Cardinals, June 23, 1978.

yDrafted by Oakland A's, December 8, 1980.

zTraded to Seattle Mariners' organization for Outfielder Rusty McNealy and Pitcher Tim Hallgren, December 9, 1981.

JASON DOLPH THOMPSON

Born July 6, 1954, at Hollywood, Calif.
Height, 6.03. Weight, 210.
Throws and bats lefthanded.
Attended California State University at Northridge, Northridge, Calif.

Led American League first basemen in double plays with 153 in 1978.
Led American League first basemen in total chances with 1,712 in 1977.

Year Club	League	Pos.	G.	AB.	R.	H.	2B.	3B.	HR.	RBI.	B.A.	PO.	A.	E.	F.A.
1975—Montgomery	South.	1B	75	222	42	72	12	1	10	38	.324	633	47	10	.986
1976—Evansville	A. A.	1B	4	16	3	5	0	0	3	6	.313	29	7	0	1.000
1976—Detroit	Amer.	1B	123	412	45	90	12	1	17	54	.218	1157	88	8	.994
1977—Detroit	Amer.	1B	158	585	87	158	24	5	31	105	.270	★1599	97	16	.991
1978—Detroit	Amer.	1B	153	589	79	169	25	3	26	96	.287	1503	92	11	.993
1979—Detroit	Amer.	1B	145	492	58	121	16	1	20	79	.246	1176	91	8	.994
1980—Det.†-Calif.‡	Amer.	1B	138	438	69	126	19	0	21	90	.288	679	51	0	1.000
1981—Pittsburgh	Nat.	1B	86	223	36	54	13	0	15	42	.242	590	46	7	.989
1982—Pittsburgh	Nat.	1B	156	550	87	156	32	0	31	101	.284	1395	105	10	.993
1983—Pittsburgh	Nat.	1B	152	517	70	134	20	1	18	76	.259	1266	89	9	.993
American League Totals			717	2516	338	664	96	10	115	424	.264	6114	419	43	.993
National League Totals			394	1290	193	344	65	1	64	219	.267	3251	240	26	.993
Major League Totals			1111	3806	531	1008	161	11	179	643	.265	9365	659	69	.993

Selected by Los Angeles Dodgers' organization in 15th round of free-agent draft, June 6, 1972.

Selected by Detroit Tigers' organization in 4th round of free-agent draft, June 4, 1975.

†Traded to California Angels for Outfielder Al Cowens, May 27, 1980.

‡Traded to Pittsburgh Pirates for Catcher Ed Ott and Pitcher Mickey Mahler, April 1, 1981.

ALL-STAR GAME RECORD

Year League	Pos.	AB.	R.	H.	2B.	3B.	HR.	RBI.	B.A.	PO.	A.	E.	F.A.
1978—American	PH	1	0	0	0	0	0	0	.000	0	0	0	.000
1982—National	PH	1	0	0	0	0	0	0	.000	0	0	0	.000
All-Star Game Totals		2	0	0	0	0	0	0	.000	0	0	0	.000

Member of American League All-Star Team in 1977; did not play.

RICHARD NEIL THOMPSON
(Rick)

Born November 1, 1958, at New York, N.Y.
Height, 6.03. Weight, 215.
Throws and bats righthanded.
Attended Amherst College, Amherst, Mass.

Year Club	League	G.	IP.	W.	L.	Pct.	H.	R.	ER.	SO.	BB.	ERA.
1980—Batavia	NYP	7	12	2	0	1.000	12	3	1	16	6	0.75
1981—Waterloo	Midwest	28	122	5	6	.455	112	67	56	109	55	4.13
1982—Chattanooga	Southern	50	78	7	6	.538	69	39	35	55	36	4.04
1983—Buffalo	Eastern	43	78⅔	3	7	.300	67	33	25	61	46	2.86

Selected by Cleveland Indians' organization in 7th round of free-agent draft, June 3, 1980.

VERNON SCOT THOMPSON
(Known by middle name.)

Born December 7, 1955, at Grove City, Pa.
Height, 6.03. Weight, 175.
Throws and bats lefthanded.
Son of William K. Thompson, minor league first baseman-outfielder, 1953 through 1962;
brother of Joe Thompson, minor league first baseman, 1976.

Led American Association first basemen in fielding percentage with .994 in 1977.

Year Club	League	Pos.	G.	AB.	R.	H.	2B.	3B.	HR.	RBI.	B.A.	PO.	A.	E.	F.A.
1974—Bradenton Cubs	Gulf C.	OF-1B	47	169	22	43	6	3	1	19	.254	86	7	5	.948
1975—Key West	Fla. St.	OF-1B	123	424	40	95	6	3	3	41	.224	186	10	12	.942
1976—Midland	Texas	1B-OF	116	425	47	121	11	2	7	54	.285	766	50	12	.985

Year Club	League	Pos.	G.	AB.	R.	H.	2B.	3B.	HR.	RBI.	B.A.	PO.	A.	E.	F.A.
1977—Wichita	A. A.	1B-OF	124	446	77	136	24	5	11	54	.305	920	62	7	.993
1978—Wichita	A. A.	1B-OF	●135	*519	83	169	*33	7	10	64	.326	873	59	13	.986
1978—Chicago	Nat.	OF-1B	19	36	7	15	3	0	0	2	.417	14	1	0	1.000
1979—Chicago	Nat.	OF	128	346	36	100	13	5	2	29	.289	161	7	5	.971
1980—Chicago†	Nat.	OF-1B	102	226	26	48	10	1	2	13	.212	149	6	4	.975
1981—Chicago	Nat.	OF-1B	57	115	8	19	5	0	0	8	.209	56	1	2	.966
1981—Iowa	A. A.	OF	69	277	35	74	10	0	2	29	.267	177	3	6	.968
1982—Iowa	A. A.	1B-OF	29	93	17	32	6	0	2	11	.344	40	3	3	.935
1982—Chicago‡	Nat.	OF-1B	49	74	11	27	5	1	0	7	.365	39	3	0	1.000
1983—Chicago	Nat.	OF-1B	53	88	4	17	3	1	0	10	.193	29	0	0	1.000
1983—Iowa	A. A.	OF-1B	25	86	9	18	3	0	1	8	.209	56	2	0	1.000
Major League Totals			408	885	92	226	39	8	4	69	.255	448	18	11	.977

Selected by Chicago Cubs' organization in 1st round (seventh player selected) of free-agent draft, June 5, 1974.
†On supplemental disabled list, July 10, 1980; transferred to disabled list, July 10 to August 6, 1980.
‡On supplemental disabled list, June 18 to July 22, 1982.

RICHARD W. THON

(Dickie)

Born June 20, 1958, at South Bend, Ind.
Height, 5.11. Weight, 150.
Throws and bats righthanded.
Grandson of Fred Thon, minor league pitcher, 1940.

Tied National League record for fewest triples, season, for league leader in triples (10), 1982.
Major League stolen bases: 1980 (7), 1981 (6), 1982 (37), 1983 (34). Total—84.
Led National League in game-winning RBIs with 18 in 1983.
Named shortstop on THE SPORTING NEWS National League All-Star Team, 1983.
Named shortstop on THE SPORTING NEWS National League Silver Slugger team, 1983.

Year Club	League	Pos.	G.	AB.	R.	H.	2B.	3B.	HR.	RBI.	B.A.	PO.	A.	E.	F.A.
1976—Quad Cities	Midw.	SS	69	246	46	68	11	4	1	32	.276	96	193	32	.900
1977—Salinas	Calif.	SS	56	225	48	71	13	2	4	44	.316	95	162	13	.952
1977—Salt Lake City	P. C.	SS	77	274	47	79	9	3	8	43	.288	129	242	26	.935
1978—Salt Lake City	P. C.	2B-SS	130	439	67	113	17	3	1	47	.257	273	380	26	.962
1979—Salt Lake City	P. C.	SS-2B	38	162	25	47	3	1	2	21	.290	70	120	11	.945
1979—California	Amer.	2B-SS-3B	35	56	6	19	3	0	0	8	.339	38	46	8	.913
1980—Salt Lake City	P. C.	2B-SS	40	155	28	61	14	2	2	28	.394	81	107	12	.940
1980—California†	Amer.	S-2-3-1	80	267	32	68	12	2	0	15	.255	70	124	10	.951
1981—Houston	Nat.	2B-SS-3B	49	95	13	26	6	0	0	3	.274	53	63	6	.951
1982—Houston	Nat.	SS-3B-2B	136	496	73	137	31	*10	3	36	.276	183	412	17	.972
1983—Houston	Nat.	SS	154	619	81	177	28	9	20	79	.286	258	*533	28	.966
American League Totals			115	323	38	87	15	2	0	23	.269	108	170	18	.939
National League Totals			339	1210	167	340	65	19	23	118	.281	494	1008	51	.967
Major League Totals			454	1533	205	427	80	21	23	141	.279	602	1178	69	.963

Signed as free agent by California Angels' organization, November 23, 1975.
†Traded to Houston Astros for Pitcher Ken Forsch, April 1, 1981.

DIVISION SERIES RECORD

Year Club	League	Pos.	G.	AB.	R.	H.	2B.	3B.	HR.	RBI.	B.A.	PO.	A.	E.	F.A.
1981—Houston	Nat.	SS-PH	4	11	0	2	0	0	0	0	.182	5	10	1	.938

CHAMPIONSHIP SERIES RECORD

Year Club	League	Pos.	G.	AB.	R.	H.	2B.	3B.	HR.	RBI.	B.A.	PO.	A.	E.	F.A.
1979—California	Amer.	PR-SS	1	0	1	0	0	0	0	0	.000	0	0	0	.000

ALL-STAR GAME RECORD

Year League	Pos.	AB.	R.	H.	2B.	3B.	HR.	RBI.	B.A.	PO.	A.	E.	F.A.
1983—National	PH-SS	3	0	1	0	0	0	0	.333	0	2	0	1.000

ANDRE THORNTON

Born August 13, 1949, at Tuskegee, Ala.
Height, 6.02. Weight, 205.
Throws and bats righthanded.
Attended Cheyney State College, Cheyney, Pa.
Brother-in-law of Pat Kelly, outfielder with Minnesota, Kansas City, Chicago AL, Baltimore and Cleveland, 1967 through 1981.

Tied major league record for most assists, first baseman, inning (3), August 22, 1975 (5th inning).
Hit for the cycle, April 22, 1978.
Tied for American League lead in intentional bases on balls received with 18 in 1982.
Led Western Carolinas League first basemen in errors with 19 in 1969.
Led Northwest League first basemen in double plays with 35 in 1968.
Tied for Eastern League lead in caught stealing with 8 in 1971.
Named American League Comeback Player of the Year by THE SPORTING NEWS, 1982.

Year Club	League	Pos.	G.	AB.	R.	H.	2B.	3B.	HR.	RBI.	B.A.	PO.	A.	E.	F.A.
1967—Huron†	North.	3B-OF	19	55	3	10	1	2	1	3	.182	7	9	10	.615
1968—Eugene‡	N'west.	1B	56	185	27	46	9	2	5	31	.249	*427	*24	10	*.978
1969—Spartanburg§	W. Car.	1B-3B-OF	90	299	56	75	13	4	13	51	.251	701	45	20	.974

Year Club	League	Pos.	G.	AB.	R.	H.	2B.	3B.	HR.	RBI.	B.A.	PO.	A.	E.	F.A.
1970—Peninsula x	Carol.	1B	67	193	24	48	7	2	5	23	.249	499	30	5	.991
1971—Reading y	East.	1B	116	367	67	98	18	1	26	76	.267	1006	48	15	.986
1972—Eugene z	P. C.	1B-3B	46	141	22	45	8	2	6	29	.319	224	46	11	.961
1972—Richmond abc	Int.	1B-OF	49	159	30	42	5	0	14	36	.264	379	33	6	.986
1973—Richmond d	Int.	3B-1B-0F	16	49	8	10	2	0	4	8	.204	67	17	5	.944
1973—Wichita	A. A.	1B	40	135	34	39	2	0	17	45	.289	362	23	1	.997
1973—Chicago	Nat.	1B	17	35	3	7	3	0	0	2	.200	81	10	1	.989
1974—Chicago	Nat.	1B-3B	107	303	41	79	16	4	10	46	.261	760	70	7	.992
1975—Chicago e	Nat.	1B-3B	120	372	70	109	21	4	18	60	.293	984	77	13	.988
1976—Chi. f-Mont. gh	Nat.	1B-OF	96	268	28	52	11	2	11	38	.194	542	46	6	.990
1977—Cleveland	Amer.	1B	131	433	77	114	20	5	28	70	.263	1026	71	6	.995
1978—Cleveland	Amer.	1B	145	508	97	133	22	4	33	105	.262	1327	106	7	.995
1979—Cleveland	Amer.	1B	143	515	89	120	31	1	26	93	.233	1089	82	7	.994
1980—Cleveland i	Amer.					(Did not play)									
1981—Cleveland j	Amer.	1B	69	226	22	54	12	0	6	30	.239	67	5	1	.986
1982—Cleveland	Amer.	1B	161	589	90	161	26	1	32	116	.273	76	5	0	1.000
1983—Cleveland†	Amer.	1B	141	508	78	143	27	1	17	77	.281	201	21	2	.991
American League Totals			790	2779	453	725	138	12	142	491	.261	3786	290	23	.994
National League Totals			340	978	142	247	51	10	39	146	.252	2367	203	27	.990
Major League Totals			1130	3757	595	972	189	22	181	637	.259	6153	493	50	.993

Signed as free agent by Philadelphia Phillies' organization, August 6, 1967.

†On military list, December 29, 1967 through May 1, 1968.

‡On temporary inactive list, June 1 to July 2, 1968.

§On temporary inactive list, June 4 to June 24, 1969.

xOn temporary inactive list, June 11 to June 30, 1970.

yOn temporary inactive list, June 7 to June 26, 1971.

zTraded with Pitcher Joe Hoerner to Atlanta Braves for Pitchers Jim Nash and Gary Neibauer, June 15, 1972.

aOn temporary inactive list, June 28 to July 1, 1972.

bOn disabled list, July 5 to July 16, 1972.

cOn temporary inactive list, August 1 to August 4, 1972.

dTraded to Chicago Cubs for First Baseman Joe Pepitone, May 19, 1973.

eOn disabled list, April 1 to May 4, 1975.

fTraded to Montreal Expos for Pitcher Steve Renko and Outfielder-First Baseman Larry Biittner, May 17, 1976.

gOn disabled list, June 10 to July 1, 1976.

hTraded to Cleveland Indians for Pitcher Jackie Brown, December 10, 1976.

iOn disabled list, March 28 to June 9 and June 19 to October 13, 1980.

jOn supplemental disabled list, March 30 to April 17 and August 24 to September 8, 1981.

ALL-STAR GAME RECORD

Year League	Pos.	AB.	R.	H.	2B.	3B.	HR.	RBI.	B.A.	PO.	A.	E.	F.A.
1982—American	PH	1	0	0	0	0	0	0	.000	0	0	0	.000

MARK ANTHONY THURMOND

Born September 12, 1956, at Houston, Tex.
Height, 6.00. Weight, 190.
Throws and bats lefthanded.
Received bachelor of science degree in finance from
Texas A&M University, College Station, Tex. in 1979.

Tied for Texas League lead in games started by pitchers with 27 in 1981.

Year Club	League	G.	IP.	W.	L.	Pct.	H.	R.	ER.	SO.	BB.	ERA.
1979—Amarillo	Texas	17	62	3	5	.375	89	52	39	46	31	5.66
1980—Amarillo†	Texas	26	156	10	9	.526	164	80	67	125	61	3.87
1981—Amarillo	Texas	27	193	12	5	.706	202	86	70	128	56	3.26
1982—Hawaii	P. Coast	28	194⅓	12	10	.545	202	88	77	106	58	3.57
1983—Las Vegas	P. Coast	19	63	6	1	.857	63	28	23	38	24	3.29
1983—San Diego	National	21	115⅓	7	3	.700	104	40	34	49	33	2.65
Major League Totals		21	115⅓	7	3	.700	104	40	34	49	33	2.65

Selected by San Diego Padres' organization in 24th round of free-agent draft, June 6, 1978.

Selected by San Diego Padres' organization in 5th round of free-agent draft, June 5, 1979.

†On disabled list, July 5 to July 16, 1980.

JAY LINDSEY TIBBS

Born January 4, 1962, at Birmingham, Ala.
Height, 6.03. Weight, 185.
Throws and bats righthanded.

Year Club	League	G.	IP.	W.	L.	Pct.	H.	R.	ER.	SO.	BB.	ERA.
1980—Kingsport	Ap'lachian	12	76	3	7	.300	88	54	37	45	32	4.38
1981—Lynchburg	Carolina	15	72	2	7	.222	89	65	55	41	34	6.88
1981—Shelby	W. Carol.	13	89	4	8	.333	87	56	38	57	33	3.84
1982—Lynchburg†	Carolina	7	38⅓	2	4	.333	42	28	24	31	23	5.63
1982—Jackson	Texas	1	3⅓	0	0	.000	2	1	0	3	1	0.00
1983—Lynchburg‡	Carolina	28	203⅔	14	8	.636	172	94	66	170	96	2.92

Selected by New York Mets' organization in 2nd round of free-agent draft, June 3, 1980.

†On disabled list, July 21 to August 29, 1982.

‡Drafted by Philadelphia Phillies, December 5, 1983.

RICHARD WILLIAM TIDROW
(Dick)

Born May 14, 1947, at San Francisco, Calif.
Height, 6.04. Weight, 213.
Throws and bats righthanded.
Attended Chabot College, Hayward, Calif.

Major League saves: 1974 (1), 1975 (5), 1976 (10), 1977 (5), 1979 (6), 1980 (6), 1981 (9), 1982 (6), 1983 (7). Total—55.
Tied for National League lead in intentional bases on balls issued with 16 in 1980 and 15 in 1981.
Tied for American League lead in intentional bases on balls issued with 11 in 1977.
Led American Association in home runs allowed with 21 and tied for lead in hit batsmen with 8 in 1971.
Named American League Rookie Pitcher of the Year by THE SPORTING NEWS, 1972.

Year Club	League	G.	IP.	W.	L.	Pct.	H.	R.	ER.	SO.	BB.	ERA.
1967—Reno	California	7	19	0	1	.000	20	16	14	18	10	6.63
1967—Rock Hill	W. Carol.	4	16	0	1	.000	15	10	10	9	9	5.63
1968—Reno†	California	6	8	1	0	1.000	3	0	0	11	4	0.00
1969—Reno	California	25	187	15	6	.714	170	71	55	189	48	2.65
1970—Wichita	Am. Assoc.	18	83	3	4	.429	99	49	47	71	29	5.10
1970—Reno	California	6	35	2	2	.500	35	16	10	33	12	2.57
1971—Wichita	Am. Assoc.	20	124	8	6	.571	123	61	57	81	45	4.15
1971—Reno	California	7	38	4	0	1.000	38	16	14	29	11	3.32
1972—Cleveland	American	39	237	14	15	.483	200	83	73	123	70	2.77
1973—Cleveland	American	42	275	14	16	.467	289	150	135	138	95	4.42
1974—Cleveland‡-New York	American	37	210	12	12	.500	226	116	97	108	66	4.16
1975—New York§	American	37	69	6	3	.667	65	27	24	38	31	3.13
1976—New York	American	47	92	4	5	.444	80	29	27	65	24	2.64
1977—New York	American	49	151	11	4	.733	143	57	53	83	41	3.16
1978—New York	American	31	185	7	11	.389	191	87	79	73	53	3.84
1979—New York x	American	14	23	2	1	.667	38	20	20	7	4	7.83
1979—Chicago	National	63	103	11	5	.688	86	35	31	68	42	2.71
1980—Chicago	National	*84	116	6	5	.545	97	44	36	97	53	2.79
1981—Chicago y	National	51	75	3	10	.231	73	45	42	39	30	5.04
1982—Chicago z	National	65	103⅔	8	3	.727	106	45	39	62	29	3.39
1983—Chicago a	American	50	91⅔	2	4	.333	86	50	43	66	34	4.22
American League Totals		346	1333⅔	72	71	.503	1318	619	551	701	418	3.72
National League Totals		263	397⅔	28	23	.549	362	169	148	266	154	3.35
Major League Totals		609	1731⅓	100	94	.515	1680	788	699	967	572	3.63

Selected by Washington Senators' organization in 22nd round of free-agent draft, June, 1965.
Selected by San Francisco Giants' organization in secondary phase of free-agent draft, January 29, 1966.
Selected by Cincinnati Reds' organization in 3rd round of free-agent draft, June, 1966.
Selected by Cleveland Indians' organization in secondary phase of free-agent draft, January 28, 1967.
†On military list, January 7 to August 13, 1968.
‡Traded with First Baseman Chris Chambliss and Pitcher Cecil Upshaw to New York Yankees for Pitchers Fritz Peterson, Fred Beene, Steve Kline and Tom Buskey, April 26, 1974.
§On disabled list, March 29 to April 19 and August 19, 1975 through remainder of season.
xTraded to Chicago Cubs for Pitcher Ray Burris, May 23, 1979.
yGranted free agency, November 13, 1981; re-signed by Cubs, February 19, 1982.
zTraded with Pitcher Randy Martz and Infielders Scott Fletcher and Pat Tabler to Chicago White Sox for Pitchers Steve Trout and Warren Brusstar, January 25, 1983.
aReleased, October 31, 1983.

CHAMPIONSHIP SERIES RECORD

Year Club	League	G.	IP.	W.	L.	Pct.	H.	R.	ER.	SO.	BB.	ERA.
1976—New York	American	3	7⅓	1	0	1.000	6	4	3	0	4	3.68
1977—New York	American	2	7	0	0	.000	6	3	3	3	3	3.86
1978—New York	American	1	5⅔	0	0	.000	8	3	3	1	2	4.76
1983—Chicago	American	1	3	0	0	.000	1	1	1	3	3	3.00
Championship Series Totals		7	23	1	0	1.000	21	11	10	7	12	3.91

WORLD SERIES RECORD

Year Club	League	G.	IP.	W.	L.	Pct.	H.	R.	ER.	SO.	BB.	ERA.
1976—New York	American	2	2⅓	0	0	.000	5	2	2	1	1	7.71
1977—New York	American	2	2⅔	0	0	.000	5	2	2	1	0	4.91
1978—New York	American	2	4⅔	0	0	.000	4	1	1	5	0	1.93
World Series Totals		6	10⅔	0	0	.000	14	5	5	7	1	4.22

RONALD IRVIN TINGLEY
(Ron)

Born May 27, 1959, at Presque Isle, Maine.
Height, 6.02. Weight, 160.
Throws and bats righthanded.

Year Club	League	Pos.	G.	AB.	R.	H.	2B.	3B.	HR.	RBI.	B.A.	PO.	A.	E.	F.A.
1977—Walla Walla	N'west.	OF	21	33	8	5	0	0	1	3	.152	5	2	0	1.000
1978—Walla Walla	N'west.	OF-C	43	140	22	29	2	0	2	21	.207	149	16	8	.954
1979—Santa Clara	Calif.	C-OF	52	143	11	29	4	1	0	17	.203	258	42	8	.974
1979—Amarillo	Texas	C-OF	30	90	16	23	4	1	1	6	.256	133	17	4	.974
1980—Reno†	Calif.	C-OF	65	204	37	61	3	3	3	35	.299	333	46	10	.974
1981—Amarillo	Texas	C-1B-OF	116	379	72	109	9	*10	13	60	.288	607	47	11	.983
1982—Hawaii	P. C.	C	115	362	45	95	13	8	6	42	.262	540	77	12	.981

Year	Club	League	Pos.	G.	AB.	R.	H.	2B.	3B.	HR.	RBI.	B.A.	PO.	A.	E.	F.A.
1982—San Diego	Nat.		C	8	20	0	2	0	0	0	0	.100	40	4	2	.957
1983—Las Vegas	P. C.		C	92	294	44	83	15	6	10	48	.282	449	55	12	.977
Major League Totals				8	20	0	2	0	0	0	0	.100	40	4	2	.957

Selected by San Diego Padres' organization in 10th round of free-agent draft, June 7, 1977.
†On disabled list, April 10 to April 29, 1980.

PITCHING RECORD

Year	Club	League	G.	IP.	W.	L.	Pct.	H.	R.	ER.	SO.	BB.	ERA.
1979—Santa Clara	California		1	1	0	0	.000	4	5	1	2	2	9.00

DAVID VANCE TOBIK

Name pronounced TOE-bick.

(Dave)

Born March 2, 1953, at Euclid, O.
Height, 6.01. Weight, 195.
Throws and bats righthanded.
Received bachelor of business administration degree from Ohio University, Athens, O.

Major League saves: 1979 (3), 1981 (1), 1982 (9), 1983 (9). Total—22.

Year	Club	League	G.	IP.	W.	L.	Pct.	H.	R.	ER.	SO.	BB.	ERA.
1975—Lakeland	Florida St.	5	36	1	4	.200	29	14	10	22	19	2.50
1975—Montgomery	Southern	20	99	6	9	.400	7	57	48	62	44	4.36
1976—Lakeland	Florida St.	6	42	3	1	.750	28	11	5	29	15	1.07
1976—Montgomery†	Southern	18	63	4	5	.444	56	33	26	44	32	3.71
1977—Montgomery	Southern	27	48	4	4	.500	31	17	14	42	17	2.63
1977—Evansville	Am. Assoc.	13	19	4	1	.800	19	8	7	17	9	3.32
1978—Evansville	Am. Assoc.	33	79	5	4	.556	71	43	30	70	26	3.42
1978—Detroit	American	5	12	0	0	.000	2	5	5	11	3	3.75
1979—Evansville	Am. Assoc.	19	38	4	0	1.000	24	6	2	45	13	0.47
1979—Detroit	American	37	69	3	5	.375	59	34	33	48	25	4.30
1980—Evansville	Am. Assoc.	30	48	3	3	.500	35	22	21	49	26	3.94
1980—Detroit	American	17	61	1	0	1.000	61	27	27	34	21	3.98
1981—Detroit	American	27	60	2	2	.500	47	19	18	32	33	2.70
1982—Detroit‡	American	51	98⅔	4	9	.308	86	45	39	63	38	3.56
1983—Texas	American	27	44	2	1	.667	36	18	18	30	13	3.68
1983—Oklahoma City	Am. Assoc.	12	20⅓	3	0	1.000	13	8	8	14	10	3.54
Major League Totals		164	344⅔	12	17	.414	301	148	140	218	133	3.66

Selected by Montreal Expos' organization in 3rd round of free-agent draft, June 5, 1974.
Selected by Detroit Tigers' organization in secondary phase of free-agent draft, January 9, 1975.
†On disabled list, June 3 to June 24, 1976.
‡Traded to Texas Rangers for Outfielder Johnny Grubb, March 24, 1983.

FREDDIE LEE TOLIVER

Born February 3, 1961, at Natchez, Miss.
Height, 6.01. Weight, 170.
Throws and bats righthanded.

Year	Club	League	G.	IP.	W.	L.	Pct.	H.	R.	ER.	SO.	BB.	ERA.
1979—Oneonta	NYP	13	77	*10	2	.833	46	28	18	71	66	2.10
1980—Fort Lauderdale	Florida St.	3	8	0	2	.000	14	15	13	4	10	14.63
1980—Greensboro†	S. Atlantic	20	126	6	8	.429	98	60	40	96	89	2.86
1981—Greensboro‡§	S. Atlantic	17	80	5	3	.625	67	38	31	62	56	3.49
1982—Cedar Rapids	Midwest	23	115	6	7	.462	114	77	54	117	66	4.23
1982—Indianapolis	Am. Assoc.	4	20⅔	2	2	.500	20	10	9	19	13	3.92
1983—Indianapolis	Am. Assoc.	26	166⅔	8	10	.444	151	93	84	112	*110	4.54

Selected by New York Yankees' organization in 3rd round of free-agent draft, June 5, 1979.
†On disabled list, May 23 to June 6, 1980.
‡On disabled list, April 9 to May 27, 1981.
§Traded to Cincinnati Reds' organization, December 10, 1981, completing deal in which Cincinnati traded Outfielder Ken Griffey to New York Yankees for Pitcher Brian Ryder and a player to be named later, November 4, 1981.

JIMMY WAYNE TOLLESON

(Known by middle name.)

Born November 22, 1955, at Spartanburg, S. C.
Height, 5.09. Weight, 160.
Throws right and bats left and righthanded.
Attended Western Carolina University, Cullowhee, N. C.

Major League stolen bases: 1981 (2), 1982 (1), 1983 (33). Total—36.

Year	Club	League	Pos.	G.	AB.	R.	H.	2B.	3B.	HR.	RBI.	B.A.	PO.	A.	E.	F.A.
1978—Asheville	W. Car.		3B-SS	70	212	35	57	4	1	0	21	.269	85	175	20	.929
1979—Tulsa	Texas		SS	130	418	43	98	9	7	1	36	.234	179	413	*41	.935
1980—Tulsa	Texas		SS	131	452	69	124	19	7	1	30	.274	161	395	31	.947
1981—Wichita	A. A.		3-S-2-O	107	375	58	98	9	4	3	38	.261	96	259	15	.959
1981—Texas	Amer.		3B-SS	14	24	6	4	0	0	0	1	.167	5	8	0	1.000

Year	Club	League	Pos.	G.	AB.	R.	H.	2B.	3B.	HR.	RBI.	B.A.	PO.	A.	E.	F.A.
1982—Texas	Amer.		SS-3B-2B	38	70	6	8	1	0	0	2	.114	47	70	5	.959
1982—Denver	A. A.		SS	71	266	48	64	9	3	4	27	.241	97	195	6	.980
1983—Texas	Amer.		2B-SS	134	470	64	122	13	2	3	20	.260	268	372	17	.974
Major League Totals				186	564	76	134	14	2	3	23	.238	320	450	22	.972

Selected by Pittsburgh Pirates' organization in 12th round of free-agent draft, June 7, 1977.
Selected by Texas Rangers' organization in 8th round of free-agent draft, June 6, 1978.

TIMOTHY LEE TOLMAN
(Tim)

Born April 20, 1956, at Santa Monica, Calif.
Height, 6.00. Weight, 190.
Throws and bats righthanded.
Attended University of Southern California, Los Angeles, Calif.

Led Gulf Coast League in being hit by pitch with 5 in 1978.
Led Southern League first basemen in assists with 90 in 1980.
Led Florida State League first basemen in errors with 17 in 1979.

Year	Club	League	Pos.	G.	AB.	R.	H.	2B.	3B.	HR.	RBI.	B.A.	PO.	A.	E.	F.A.
1978—Sarasota Astros	Gulf C.		1B	39	122	25	42	5	6	0	23	*.344	292	21	4	.987
1978—Daytona Beach	Fla. St.		OF-1B	7	25	2	7	2	0	0	5	.280	24	2	0	1.000
1979—Daytona Beach	Fla. St.		1B-3B-OF	131	422	62	122	13	3	1	53	.289	688	93	26	.968
1980—Columbus	South.		1B-OF	139	481	67	142	37	4	7	73	.295	980	93	15	.986
1981—Tucson	P. C.		OF-1B	137	479	85	154	28	8	14	99	.322	735	49	10	.987
1981—Houston	Nat.		OF	4	8	0	1	0	0	0	0	.125	2	0	0	1.000
1982—Tucson	P. C.		OF-1B-3B	125	473	93	143	31	6	15	82	.302	525	46	15	.974
1982—Houston	Nat.		OF-1B	15	26	4	5	2	0	1	3	.192	17	1	0	1.000
1983—Houston	Nat.		1B-OF	43	56	4	11	4	0	2	10	.196	55	2	0	1.000
1983—Tucson	P. C.		1B-OF	7	24	4	9	2	0	1	6	.375	31	3	0	1.000
Major League Totals				62	90	8	17	6	0	3	13	.189	74	3	0	1.000

Selected by Houston Astros' organization in 12th round of free-agent draft, June 6, 1978.

DAVID ALLEN TOMLIN
(Dave)

Born June 22, 1949, at Maysville, Ky.
Height, 6.02. Weight, 185.
Throws and bats lefthanded.

Led Appalachian League pitchers in games started with 13 and tied for lead in complete games with 6 in 1967.

Year	Club	League	G.	IP.	W.	L.	Pct.	H.	R.	ER.	SO.	BB.	ERA.
1967—Wytheville	Ap'lachian	14	85	•7	6	.538	*93	55	41	47	43	4.34
1968—Tampa	Florida St.	37	56	6	3	.667	47	19	15	38	16	2.41
1969—Tampa	Florida St.	23	44	5	1	.833	34	18	14	25	22	2.86
1970—Asheville	Southern	25	139	6	10	.375	135	62	48	73	58	3.11
1971—Indianapolis	Am. Assoc.	41	61	7	4	.636	46	19	15	50	24	2.23
1972—Indianapolis	Am. Assoc.	36	90	5	6	.455	83	30	28	86	36	2.79
1972—Cincinnati	National	3	4	0	0	.000	7	4	4	2	1	9.00
1973—Indianapolis	Am. Assoc.	25	31	1	3	.250	29	15	12	26	11	3.52
1973—Cincinnati†	National	16	28	1	2	.333	24	15	15	20	15	4.82
1974—Hawaii	P. Coast	25	48	5	1	.833	33	10	9	48	20	1.69
1974—San Diego	National	47	58	2	0	1.000	59	29	28	29	30	4.34
1975—San Diego	National	67	83	4	2	.667	87	38	30	48	31	3.25
1976—San Diego	National	49	73	0	1	.000	62	24	23	43	20	2.84
1977—San Diego‡§	National	76	102	4	4	.500	98	38	34	55	32	3.00
1978—Cincinnati	National	57	62	9	1	.900	88	54	40	32	30	5.81
1979—Cincinnati	National	53	58	2	2	.500	59	29	17	30	18	2.64
1980—Cincinnati x	National	27	26	3	0	1.000	38	17	16	6	11	5.54
1981—Syracuse y	Int'national	38	57	2	3	.400	67	25	23	36	19	3.63
1982—Indianapolis z	Am. Assoc.	*64	91⅔	9	2	.818	96	39	36	67	30	3.53
1982—Montreal	National	1	2	0	0	.000	1	1	1	2	1	4.50
1983—Wichita a	Am. Assoc.	41	52⅓	4	1	.800	44	21	21	44	18	3.61
1983—Pittsburgh b	National	5	4	0	0	.000	6	4	3	5	1	6.75
Major League Totals		401	500	25	12	.676	529	253	211	272	190	3.80

Selected by Cincinnati Reds' organization in 29th round of free-agent draft, June 6, 1967.
†Traded with Outfielder Bobby Tolan to San Diego Padres for Pitcher Clay Kirby, November 9, 1973.
‡Traded with $125,000 to Texas Rangers for Pitcher Gaylord Perry, February 15, 1978.
§Sold to Cincinnati Reds, March 28, 1978.
xReleased, September 2, 1980; signed by Syracuse (Toronto Blue Jays' organization), February 26, 1981.
yReleased, April 8, 1982; signed by Indianapolis (Cincinnati Reds' organization), April 22, 1982.
zSold to Montreal Expos, September 8, 1982.
aSold to Pittsburgh Pirates, August 2, 1983.
bGranted free agency, November 7, 1983; invited to Pittsburgh Pirates' spring training.

CHAMPIONSHIP SERIES RECORD

Year	Club	League	G.	IP.	W.	L.	Pct.	H.	R.	ER.	SO.	BB.	ERA.
1973—Cincinnati	National	1	1⅔	0	0	.000	5	3	3	1	1	16.20
1979—Cincinnati	National	3	3	0	0	.000	3	1	0	3	2	0.00
Championship Series Totals		4	4⅔	0	0	.000	8	4	3	4	3	5.79

MICHAEL AUGUSTINE TORREZ
(Mike)

Born August 28, 1946, at Topeka, Kan.
Height, 6:05. Weight, 210.
Throws and bats righthanded.

Received reported $20,000 bonus to sign with St. Louis Cardinals, 1965.

Year	Club	League	G.	IP.	W.	L.	Pct.	H.	R.	ER.	SO.	BB.	ERA.
1965—Raleigh	Carolina	20	94	4	8	.333	92	66	50	81	75	4.79
1966—Rock Hill	W. Carol.	15	90	7	4	.636	63	35	25	85	37	2.50
1966—Arkansas	Texas	15	79	3	9	.250	73	44	23	65	42	2.62
1967—Tulsa	P. Coast	29	190	10	10	.500	152	82	70	155	★108	3.32
1967—St. Louis	National	3	6	0	1	.000	5	2	2	5	1	3.00
1968—St. Louis	National	5	19	2	1	.667	20	7	6	6	12	2.84
1968—Tulsa	P. Coast	16	86	8	2	.800	74	33	31	82	36	3.24
1969—St. Louis	National	24	108	10	4	.714	96	47	43	61	62	3.58
1970—St. Louis	National	30	179	8	10	.444	168	96	84	100	103	4.22
1971—Winnipeg	Int'national	18	75	2	4	.333	96	72	68	45	52	8.16
1971—St. Louis†-Montreal	National	10	39	1	2	.333	45	27	24	10	31	5.54
1972—Montreal	National	34	243	16	12	.571	215	97	90	112	103	3.33
1973—Montreal	National	35	208	9	12	.429	207	116	103	90	115	4.46
1974—Montreal‡	National	32	186	15	8	.652	184	90	74	92	84	3.58
1975—Baltimore§	American	36	271	20	9	★.690	238	103	92	119	★133	3.06
1976—Oakland	American	39	266	16	12	.571	231	93	74	115	87	2.50
1977—Oakland x-New York y	American	35	243	17	13	.567	235	113	105	102	86	3.89
1978—Boston	American	36	250	16	13	.552	272	122	110	120	99	3.96
1979—Boston	American	36	252	16	13	.552	254	★144	★126	125	★121	4.50
1980—Boston	American	36	207	9	16	.360	256	124	117	97	75	5.09
1981—Boston	American	22	127	10	3	.769	130	61	52	54	51	3.69
1982—Boston z	American	31	175⅔	9	9	.500	196	107	102	84	74	5.23
1983—New York	National	39	221⅓	10	★17	.370	227	120	★108	94	★113	4.37
American League Totals		271	1791⅔	113	88	.562	1712	867	778	816	726	3.91
National League Totals		212	1210⅓	71	67	.514	1167	602	534	570	624	3.97
Major League Totals		483	3002	184	155	.543	2879	1469	1312	1386	1350	3.93

Signed as free agent by St. Louis Cardinals' organization, September 10, 1964.

†Traded to Montreal Expos' organization for Pitcher Bob Reynolds, June 15, 1971.

‡Traded with Outfielder Ken Singleton to Baltimore Orioles for Outfielder Rich Coggins and Pitchers Dave McNally and Bill Kirkpatrick, December 4, 1974.

§Traded with Outfielder Don Baylor and Pitcher Paul Mitchell to Oakland Athletics for Outfielder Reggie Jackson and Pitchers Ken Holtzman and Bill Van Bommel, April 2, 1976.

xTraded to New York Yankees for Pitcher Dock Ellis, Infielder Marty Perez, and Outfielder Larry Murray, April 27, 1977.

yGranted free agency, October 31, 1977; signed by Boston Red Sox, November 23, 1977.

zTraded to New York Mets for a player to be named later, January 13, 1983; Boston Red Sox acquired Third Baseman Mike Davis to complete deal, February 15, 1983.

CHAMPIONSHIP SERIES RECORD

Year	Club	League	G.	IP.	W.	L.	Pct.	H.	R.	ER.	SO.	BB.	ERA.
1977—New York	American	2	11	0	1	.000	11	5	5	5	5	4.09

WORLD SERIES RECORD

Year	Club	League	G.	IP.	W.	L.	Pct.	H.	R.	ER.	SO.	BB.	ERA.
1977—New York	American	2	18	2	0	1.000	16	7	5	15	5	2.50

KELVIN CURTIS TORVE

Born January 10, 1960, at Rapid City, S.D.
Height, 6.03. Weight, 190.
Throws right and bats lefthanded.

Received bachelor of science degree in marketing from Oral Roberts University, Tulsa, Okla.

Led Texas League in intentional bases on balls received with 11 and tied for lead in sacrifice flies with 9 in 1982.

Year	Club	League	Pos.	G.	AB.	R.	H.	2B.	3B.	HR.	RBI.	B.A.	PO.	A.	E.	F.A.
1981—Clinton	Midw.	1B	57	211	27	55	10	0	1	27	.261	538	41	4	.993
1982—Shreveport	Texas	1B	127	449	66	137	29	7	15	84	.305	1040	★96	17	.985
1983—Phoenix	P. C.	1B	115	392	58	102	21	5	4	54	.260	730	53	10	.987

Selected by San Francisco Giants' organization in 2nd round of free-agent draft, June 8, 1981.

ALAN STUART TRAMMELL

Name pronounced TRAM-mull.

Born February 21, 1958, at Garden Grove, Calif.
Height, 6.00. Weight, 170.
Throws and bats righthanded.

Led American League in sacrifice hits with 16 in 1981 and 15 in 1983.
Named American League Comeback Player of the Year by THE SPORTING NEWS, 1983.
Named shortstop on THE SPORTING NEWS American League All-Star fielding team, 1980, 1981 and 1983.
Named Southern League Most Valuable Player, 1977.

Year—Club	League	Pos.	G.	AB.	R.	H.	2B.	3B.	HR.	RBI.	B.A.	PO.	A.	E.	F.A.
1976—Bristol	Appal.	SS	41	140	27	38	2	2	0	7	.271	59	131	12	.941
1976—Montgomery	South.	SS	21	56	4	10	0	0	0	2	.179	40	64	2	.981
1977—Montgomery	South.	SS	134	454	78	132	9	*19	3	50	.291	188	397	27	.956
1977—Detroit	Amer.	SS	19	43	6	8	0	0	0	0	.186	15	34	2	.961
1978—Detroit	Amer.	SS	139	448	49	120	14	6	2	34	.268	239	421	14	.979
1979—Detroit	Amer.	SS	142	460	68	127	11	4	6	50	.276	245	388	26	.961
1980—Detroit	Amer.	SS	146	560	107	168	21	5	9	65	.300	225	412	13	.980
1981—Detroit	Amer.	SS	105	392	52	101	15	3	2	31	.258	181	347	9	.983
1982—Detroit	Amer.	SS	157	489	66	126	34	3	9	57	.258	259	459	16	.978
1983—Detroit	Amer.	SS	142	505	83	161	31	2	14	66	.319	236	367	13	.979
Major League Totals			850	2897	431	811	126	23	42	303	.280	1400	2428	93	.976

Selected by Detroit Tigers' organization in 2nd round of free-agent draft, June 8, 1976.

ALL-STAR GAME RECORD

Year League	Pos.	AB.	R.	H.	2B.	3B.	HR.	RBI.	B.A.	PO.	A.	E.	F.A.
1980—American	SS	0	0	0	0	0	0	0	.000	0	0	0	.000

WILLIAM EDWARD TRAVERS
(Bill)

Born October 27, 1952, at Norwood, Mass.
Height, 6:04. Weight, 187.
Throws and bats lefthanded.

Pitched 16-1 no-hit victory against Quad Cities, May 30, 1971.
Tied for Pacific Coast League lead in shutouts with 3 in 1975.

Year—Club	League	G.	IP.	W.	L.	Pct.	H.	R.	ER.	SO.	BB.	ERA.
1970—Clinton	Midwest	10	48	1	6	.143	53	35	30	38	26	5.63
1971—Danville	Midwest	21	137	7	8	.467	126	63	46	98	33	3.02
1972—San Antonio	Texas	17	89	3	7	.300	87	37	29	77	26	2.93
1973—Evansville†	Am. Assoc.	2	3	0	0	.000	4	3	3	3	3	9.00
1974—Sacramento	P. Coast	5	23	2	3	.400	19	22	17	16	20	6.65
1974—Milwaukee	American	23	53	2	3	.400	59	29	29	31	30	4.92
1975—Sacramento	P. Coast	12	61	3	3	.500	55	24	20	46	31	2.95
1975—Milwaukee	American	28	136	6	11	.353	130	78	65	57	60	4.30
1976—Milwaukee	American	34	240	15	16	.484	211	92	75	120	95	2.81
1977—Milwaukee‡	American	19	122	4	12	.250	140	75	71	49	57	5.24
1978—Milwaukee§	American	28	176	12	11	.522	184	93	86	66	58	4.40
1979—Milwaukee	American	30	187	14	8	.636	196	89	81	74	45	3.90
1980—Milwaukee x	American	29	154	12	6	.667	147	76	67	62	47	3.92
1981—California y	American	4	10	0	1	.000	14	11	9	5	4	8.10
1981—Redwood	California	1	1	0	0	.000	1	1	0	0	0	0.00
1982—California z	American					(Did not play)						
1983—California a	American	10	42⅔	0	3	.000	58	32	28	24	19	5.91
1983—Edmonton b	P. Coast	3	18	1	0	1.000	18	13	11	8	8	5.50
Major League Totals		205	1120⅔	65	71	.478	1139	575	511	488	415	4.10

Selected by Milwaukee Brewers' organization in 6th round of free-agent draft, June 4, 1970.
†On disabled list, April 13 to May 16 and June 17 to September 4, 1973.
‡On disabled list, June 6 to July 15, 1977.
§On disabled list, March 22 to May 12, 1978.
xGranted free agency, October 22, 1980; signed by California Angels, January 26, 1981.
yOn disabled list, May 6, 1981 through remainder of season; included rehabilitation disability assignment to Redwood, August 10 to August 30, 1981.
zOn disabled list, April 5, 1982; transferred to emergency disabled list, April 26, 1982 through remainder of season.
aOn disabled list, March 30 to May 10, 1983; included rehabilitation disability assignment to Edmonton, April 21 to May 10, 1983.
bReleased, July 19, 1983.

ALL-STAR GAME RECORD

Member of American League All-Star Team in 1976; did not play.

ALEJANDRO TREVINO (CASTRO)
(Alex)

Born August 26, 1957, at Monterrey, Mexico.
Height, 5.10. Weight, 165.
Throws and bats righthanded.
Attended University of Nuevo Leon, Monterrey, Mexico.
Brother of Bobby Trevino, outfielder with California Angels, 1968; outfielder in Mexican League, 1970 through 1979; manager, Tabasco, 1977, Tampico, 1979, and Toluca, 1980.

Led Midwest League catchers in putouts with 847 and assists with 102 in 1977.
Led Carolina League in passed balls with 18 in 1976.

Year—Club	League	Pos.	G.	AB.	R.	H.	2B.	3B.	HR.	RBI.	B.A.	PO.	A.	E.	F.A.
1973—Victoria†	Mx. Cen.	C-OF	12	26	3	6	1	0	0	2	.231	26	5	1	.969
1974—Marion	Appal.	C-SS	12	16	0	1	0	0	0	1	.063	15	0	0	1.000
1975—Marion	Appal.	C-2B-OF	22	60	10	12	1	0	0	3	.200	96	8	6	.963
1976—Lynchburg	Carol.	C-3-2-S	94	284	17	57	11	2	0	31	.201	400	130	18	.967
1977—Wausau	Midw.	C-2-1-3	128	422	57	100	10	0	2	36	.237	865	110	15	.985
1978—Tidewater	Int.	C-3B	87	262	44	77	13	2	5	37	.294	303	68	11	.971

Year Club	League	Pos.	G.	AB.	R.	H.	2B.	3B.	HR.	RBI.	B.A.	PO.	A.	E.	F.A.
1978—New York	Nat.	C-3B	6	12	3	3	0	0	0	0	.250	12	4	0	1.000
1979—New York	Nat.	C-3B-2B	79	207	24	56	11	1	0	20	.271	229	71	9	.971
1980—New York	Nat.	C-3B-2B	106	355	26	91	11	2	0	37	.256	450	76	16	.970
1981—New York‡	Nat.	C-2-O-3	56	149	17	39	2	0	0	10	.262	215	25	9	.964
1982—Cincinnati	Nat.	*C-3B	120	355	24	89	10	3	1	33	.251	725	61	*17	.979
1983—Cincinnati	Nat.	C-3B-2B	74	167	14	36	8	1	1	13	.216	359	32	5	.987
Major League Totals			441	1245	108	314	42	7	2	113	.252	1990	269	56	.976

Signed as free agent by Victoria, May 16, 1974.

†Sold to New York Mets' organization, May 22, 1974.

‡Traded with Pitchers Jim Kern and Greg Harris to Cincinnati Reds for Outfielder George Foster, February 10, 1982.

JESUS MANUEL TRILLO (MARCANO)

Name pronounced TREE-yo.

(Manny)

Born December 25, 1950, at Caritito, Monagas, Venezuela.
Height, 6.01. Weight, 164.
Throws and bats righthanded.
Attended Colegio Libertador Bolivar, Maturin, Monagas, Venz.

Established major league records for most consecutive errorless games by second baseman, season (89), 1982; most consecutive errorless chances accepted by second baseman, season (479), 1982.
Led National League second basemen in double plays with 99 in 1978.
Led National League second basemen in total chances with 822 in 1977 and 878 in 1978.
Led Pacific Coast League second basemen in double plays with 113 in 1973.
Named second baseman on THE SPORTING NEWS National League All-Star Team, 1980 through 1982.
Named second baseman on THE SPORTING NEWS National League All-Star fielding team, 1979, 1981 and 1982.
Named second baseman on THE SPORTING NEWS National League Silver Slugger team, 1980 and 1981.

Year Club	League	Pos.	G.	AB.	R.	H.	2B.	3B.	HR.	RBI.	B.A.	PO.	A.	E.	F.A.
1968—Huron†	North.	SS-3B-C	35	92	8	24	2	1	0	4	.261	35	48	5	.943
1969—Spartanburg‡	W. Car.	3-C-S-2	83	275	41	77	18	0	1	26	.280	188	98	12	.960
1970—Birmingham	South.	3B-2B-SS	84	241	26	63	10	1	2	19	.261	101	130	14	.943
1971—Birmingham§	South.	3B-SS	107	371	37	104	18	1	5	44	.280	110	212	31	.912
1972—Iowa	A. A.	3B-2B-SS	133	509	67	153	27	6	9	53	.301	176	304	28	.945
1973—Tucson	P. C.	*2B-OF	135	519	76	162	25	7	8	78	.312	*304	*373	19	*.973
1973—Oakland	Amer.	2B	17	12	0	3	2	0	0	3	.250	15	17	2	.941
1974—Tucson	P. C.	2B	85	320	31	81	19	1	2	39	.253	198	256	12	.974
1974—Oakland x	Amer.	2B	21	33	3	5	0	0	0	2	.152	31	43	4	.949
1975—Chicago	Nat.	*2B-SS	154	545	55	135	12	2	7	70	.248	350	*509	*29	.967
1976—Chicago	Nat.	*2B-3B	158	582	42	139	24	3	4	59	.239	350	*527	17	.981
1977—Chicago	Nat.	2B	152	504	51	141	18	5	7	57	.280	330	*467	*25	.970
1978—Chicago y	Nat.	2B	152	552	53	144	17	5	4	55	.261	354	*505	19	.978
1979—Philadelphia z	Nat.	2B	118	431	40	112	22	1	6	42	.260	270	368	10	.985
1980—Philadelphia a	Nat.	2B	141	531	68	155	25	9	7	43	.292	*360	467	11	.987
1981—Philadelphia	Nat.	2B	94	349	37	100	14	3	6	36	.287	*245	286	7	.987
1982—Philadelphia b	Nat.	2B	149	549	52	149	24	1	0	39	.271	343	441	5	*.994
1983—Cleveland cd	Amer.	2B	88	320	33	87	13	1	1	29	.272	172	269	5	.989
1983—Montreal e	Nat.	2B	31	121	16	32	8	0	2	16	.264	57	86	3	.979
American League Totals			126	365	36	95	15	1	1	34	.260	218	329	11	.980
National League Totals			1149	4164	414	1107	164	29	43	417	.266	2659	3656	126	.980
Major League Totals			1275	4529	450	1202	179	30	44	451	.265	2877	3985	137	.980

Signed as free agent by Philadelphia Phillies' organization, January 26, 1968.

†On disabled list, August 16 to September 3, 1968.

‡Drafted by Birmingham (Oakland Athletics' organization), December 1, 1969.

§On disabled list, May 1 to May 20, 1971.

xTraded with Pitchers Darold Knowles and Bob Locker to Chicago Cubs for First Baseman-Outfielder Billy Williams, October 23, 1974.

yTraded with Outfielder Greg Gross and Catcher Dave Rader to Philadelphia Phillies for Outfielder Jerry Martin, Catcher Barry Foote, Second Baseman Ted Sizemore and Pitchers Derek Botelho and Henry Mack, February 23, 1979.

zOn disabled list, May 4 to June 16, 1979.

aOn supplemental disabled list, April 20 to May 7, 1980.

bTraded with Outfielder George Vukovich, Infielder Julio Franco, Pitcher Jay Baller and Catcher Gerry Willard to Cleveland Indians for Outfielder Von Hayes, December 9, 1982.

cOn supplemental disabled list, July 24 to August 8, 1983.

dTraded to Montreal Expos for outfielder Don Carter and cash, August 17, 1983.

eGranted free agency, November 7, 1983; signed by San Francisco Giants, December 22, 1983.

DIVISION SERIES RECORD

Year Club	League	Pos.	G.	AB.	R.	H.	2B.	3B.	HR.	RBI.	B.A.	PO.	A.	E.	F.A.
1981—Philadelphia	Nat.	2B	5	16	1	3	0	0	0	1	.188	15	10	0	1.000

CHAMPIONSHIP SERIES RECORD

Year Club	League	Pos.	G.	AB.	R.	H.	2B.	3B.	HR.	RBI.	B.A.	PO.	A.	E.	F.A.
1974—Oakland	Amer.	PR	1	0	1	0	0	0	0	0	.000	0	0	0	.000
1980—Philadelphia	Nat.	2B	5	21	1	8	2	1	0	4	.381	18	25	1	.977
Championship Series Totals			6	21	2	8	2	1	0	4	.381	18	25	1	.977

WORLD SERIES RECORD

Year Club League	Pos.	G.	AB.	R.	H.	2B.	3B.	HR.	RBI.	B.A.	PO.	A.	E.	F.A.
1980—Philadelphia .... Nat.	2B	6	23	4	5	2	0	0	2	.217	14	25	1	.975

ALL-STAR GAME RECORD

Year League	Pos.	AB.	R.	H.	2B.	3B.	HR.	RBI.	B.A.	PO.	A.	E.	F.A.
1977—National...............................	2B	1	0	0	0	0	0	0	.000	0	1	0	1.000
1981—National...............................	2B	2	0	0	0	0	0	0	.000	1	1	0	1.000
1982—National...............................	2B	2	0	1	0	0	0	0	.500	0	1	0	1.000
1983—American..........................	2B	3	1	1	0	0	0	0	.333	3	1	0	1.000
All-Star Game Totals		8	1	2	0	0	0	0	.250	4	4	0	1.000

STEVEN RUSSELL TROUT
(Steve)

Born July 30, 1957, at Detroit, Mich.
Height, 6.04. Weight, 195.
Throws and bats lefthanded.
Son of Dizzy Trout, pitcher with Detroit Tigers, Boston Red Sox and
Baltimore Orioles, 1939 through 1952 and 1957.

Led American League in hit batsmen with 9 in 1980.

Year Club	League	G.	IP.	W.	L.	Pct.	H.	R.	ER.	SO.	BB.	ERA.
1976—Sarasota White Sox......................	Gulf Coast	9	38	1	3	.250	28	18	11	35	29	2.61
1977—Appleton	Midwest	21	111	6	8	.429	113	66	50	101	66	4.05
1977—Iowa	Am. Assoc.	5	24	0	4	.000	27	16	15	14	11	5.63
1978—Knoxville	Southern	12	71	8	3	.727	46	16	13	48	33	1.65
1978—Iowa	Am. Assoc.	9	55	3	4	.429	57	36	32	38	22	5.24
1978—Chicago	American	4	22	3	0	1.000	19	10	10	11	11	4.09
1979—Iowa	Am. Assoc.	4	27	3	1	.750	24	10	9	12	19	3.00
1979—Chicago	American	34	155	11	8	.579	165	77	67	76	59	3.89
1980—Chicago	American	32	200	9	16	.360	229	102	82	89	49	3.69
1981—Chicago	American	20	125	8	7	.533	122	53	48	54	38	3.46
1982—Chicago†	American	25	120⅓	6	9	.400	130	76	57	62	50	4.26
1983—Chicago	National	34	180	10	14	.417	217	105	93	80	59	4.65
American League Totals...		115	622⅓	37	40	.481	665	318	264	292	207	3.82
National League Totals......................................		34	180	10	14	.417	217	105	93	80	59	4.65
Major League Totals....................................		149	802⅓	47	54	.465	882	423	357	372	266	4.00

Selected by Chicago White Sox' organization in 1st round (eighth player selected) of free-agent draft, June 8, 1976.
†Traded with Pitcher Warren Brusstar to Chicago Cubs for Pitchers Dick Tidrow and Randy Martz and Infielders Scott Fletcher and Pat Tabler, January 25, 1983.

JOHN THOMAS TUDOR

Born February 2, 1954, at Schenectady, N.Y.
Height, 6.00. Weight, 185.
Throws and bats lefthanded.
Attended North Shore Community College, Beverly, Mass. and received bachelor of science degree in
criminal justice from Georgia Southern College, Statesboro, Ga.

Pitched seven-inning, 2-0 no-hit victory against Reading, June 28, 1977.

Year Club	League	G.	IP.	W.	L.	Pct.	H.	R.	ER.	SO.	BB.	ERA.
1976—Winston-Salem	Carolina	25	82	5	2	.714	77	26	25	76	28	2.74
1977—Bristol..	Eastern	27	115	6	5	.545	113	57	45	78	35	3.52
1977—Pawtucket......................................	Int'national	4	4	1	1	.500	5	1	1	1	3	2.25
1978—Pawtucket......................................	Int'national	26	105	7	4	.636	100	46	36	83	56	3.09
1979—Pawtucket......................................	Int'national	25	163	10	11	.476	145	73	53	103	52	2.93
1979—Boston..	American	6	28	1	2	.333	39	23	20	11	9	6.43
1980—Pawtucket......................................	Int'national	12	74	4	5	.444	67	36	30	51	33	3.65
1980—Boston..	American	16	92	8	5	.615	81	35	31	45	31	3.03
1981—Boston..	American	18	79	4	3	.571	74	44	40	44	28	4.56
1982—Boston..	American	32	195⅔	13	10	.565	215	90	79	146	59	3.63
1983—Boston†..	American	34	242	13	12	.520	236	122	110	136	81	4.09
Major League Totals....................................		106	636⅔	39	32	.549	645	314	280	382	208	3.96

Selected by New York Mets' organization in 21st round of free-agent draft, June 4, 1975.
Selected by Boston Red Sox' organization in secondary phase of free-agent draft, January 7, 1976.
†Traded to Pittsburgh Pirates for Outfielder Mike Easler, December 6, 1983.

ROBERT MALCOLM TUFTS
(Bob)

Born November 2, 1955, at Medford, Mass.
Height, 6.05. Weight, 210.
Throws and bats lefthanded.
Received bachelor of arts degree in economics from Princeton University, Princeton, N.J. in 1977.
Brother of Bill Tufts, pitcher in Chicago Cubs' organization, 1975 and 1976.

Led American Association in games finished in relief with 46 in 1982.
Tied for Texas League lead in complete games with 12 in 1979.

Year Club	League	G.	IP.	W.	L.	Pct.	H.	R.	ER.	SO.	BB.	ERA.
1977—Great Falls	Pioneer	3	15	2	1	.667	20	13	12	7	6	7.20
1977—Cedar Rapids	Midwest	9	55	4	4	.500	59	32	20	28	19	3.27
1978—Waterbury	Eastern	21	143	13	5	.722	135	49	45	83	42	2.83
1978—Phoenix	P. Coast	8	48	3	2	.600	70	32	28	6	20	5.25
1979—Shreveport	Texas	26	176	★14	10	.583	175	60	48	75	69	2.45
1980—Phoenix	P. Coast	38	127	4	7	.364	166	103	92	54	63	6.52
1981—Phoenix	P. Coast	30	69	9	2	.818	59	22	13	38	29	1.70
1981—San Francisco†	National	11	15	0	0	.000	20	9	6	12	6	3.60
1982—Omaha	Am. Assoc.	59	95⅓	10	6	.625	74	28	17	52	30	1.60
1982—Kansas City	American	10	20	2	0	1.000	24	10	10	13	3	4.50
1983—Kansas City	American	6	6⅔	0	0	.000	16	8	6	3	5	8.10
1983—Omaha‡-Indianapolis§	Am. Assoc.	30	40⅔	2	3	.400	52	29	27	24	12	5.98
National League Totals		11	15	0	0	.000	20	9	6	12	6	3.60
American League Totals		16	26⅔	2	0	1.000	40	18	16	16	8	5.40
Major League Totals		27	41⅔	2	0	1.000	60	27	22	28	14	4.75

Selected by San Francisco Giants' organization in 12th round of free-agent draft, June 7, 1977.

†Traded with Pitcher Vida Blue to Kansas City Royals for Pitchers Atlee Hammaker, Craig Chamberlain and Renie Martin and a player to be named later, March 30, 1982; San Francisco Giants' organization acquired Second Baseman Brad Wellman to complete deal, April 19, 1982.

‡Traded to Cincinnati Reds for Pitcher Charlie Leibrandt, June 7, 1983.

§Granted free agency, October 20, 1983.

BYRON LEE TUNNELL

Name pronounced TUNN-ul.

(Known by middle name.)

Born October 30, 1960, at Tyler, Tex.
Height, 6.00. Weight, 180.
Throws and bats righthanded.
Attended Baylor University, Waco, Tex.

Year Club	League	G.	IP.	W.	L.	Pct.	H.	R.	ER.	SO.	BB.	ERA.
1981—Bradenton Pirates	Gulf Coast	1	4	0	0	.000	0	0	0	6	1	0.00
1981—Buffalo	Eastern	12	71	5	5	.500	76	38	35	45	37	4.44
1982—Portland	P. Coast	28	189⅔	12	9	.571	182	93	73	112	91	3.46
1982—Pittsburgh	National	5	18⅓	1	1	.500	17	8	8	4	5	3.93
1983—Pittsburgh	National	35	177⅔	11	6	.647	167	81	72	95	58	3.65
Major League Totals		40	196	12	7	.632	184	89	80	99	63	3.67

Selected by Pittsburgh Pirates' organization in 2nd round of free-agent draft, June 8, 1981.

JOHN WEBBER TURNER
(Jerry)

Born January 17, 1954, at Texarkana, Ark.
Height, 5.09. Weight, 180.
Throws and bats lefthanded.

Led Northwest League in caught stealing with 11 in 1973.

Year Club	League	Pos.	G.	AB.	R.	H.	2B.	3B.	HR.	RBI.	B.A.	PO.	A.	E.	F.A.
1972—Tri-City	N'west.	OF	66	199	44	75	7	3	6	47	★.377	69	★10	12	.868
1973—Alexandria†	Texas	OF	75	269	30	69	15	1	7	28	.257	103	6	8	.932
1974—Alexandria	Texas	OF	130	472	77	154	24	5	18	68	.326	247	13	★21	.925
1974—San Diego	Nat.	OF	17	48	4	14	1	0	0	2	.292	14	1	0	1.000
1975—Hawaii	P. C.	OF	142	535	88	★176	27	3	11	91	.329	195	9	★16	.927
1975—San Diego	Nat.	OF	11	22	1	6	0	0	0	0	.273	10	0	1	.909
1976—San Diego	Nat.	OF	105	281	41	75	16	5	5	37	.267	115	6	5	.960
1977—San Diego	Nat.	OF	118	289	43	71	16	1	10	48	.246	114	10	7	.947
1978—San Diego	Nat.	OF·	106	225	28	63	9	1	8	37	.280	91	5	3	.970
1979—San Diego	Nat.	OF	138	448	55	111	23	2	9	61	.248	197	7	9	.958
1980—San Diego‡	Nat.	OF	85	153	22	44	5	0	3	18	.288	44	2	0	1.000
1981—San Diego§	Nat.	OF	33	31	5	7	0	0	2	6	.226	5	0	1	.833
1981—Chicago x	Amer.	OF	10	12	1	2	0	0	0	2	.167	2	0	0	1.000
1982—Detroit y	Amer.	OF	85	210	21	52	3	0	8	27	.248	10	0	1	.909
1983—San Diego	Nat.	OF	25	23	1	3	0	0	0	0	.130	0	0	0	.000
1983—Las Vegas z-Port.	P. C.	OF	29	80	10	23	5	1	3	20	.288	2	0	0	1.000
National League Totals			638	1520	200	394	70	9	37	209	.259	590	31	26	.960
American League Totals			95	222	22	54	3	0	8	29	.243	12	0	1	.923
Major League Totals			733	1742	222	448	73	9	45	238	.257	602	31	27	.959

Selected by San Diego Padres' organization in 10th round of free-agent draft, June 6, 1972.

†On disabled list, July 22 to September 7, 1973.

‡On disabled list, August 15, 1980 through remainder of season.

§Sold to Chicago White Sox, September 9, 1981.

xGranted free agency, November 13, 1981; signed by Detroit Tigers, February 12, 1982.

yReleased, October 8, 1982; signed by San Diego Padres' organization. February 28, 1983.

zReleased, July 26, 1983; signed by Portland (Philadelphia Phillies' organization), August 11, 1983.

GERALD RAYMOND UJDUR

Named pronounced YOU-jer.

(Jerry)

Born March 5, 1957, at Duluth, Minn.
Height, 6.01. Weight, 195.
Throws and bats righthanded.
Attended University of Minnesota, Minneapolis, Minn.

Tied for American Association lead in shutouts with 3 in 1980.

Year Club	League	G.	IP.	W.	L.	Pct.	H.	R.	ER.	SO.	BB.	ERA.
1978—Lakeland	Florida St.	13	64	5	2	.714	54	22	17	23	20	2.39
1979—Montgomery†	Southern	19	37	2	5	.286	48	27	23	30	16	5.59
1980—Evansville	Am. Assoc.	29	115	9	4	.692	103	54	43	62	38	3.37
1980—Detroit	American	9	21	1	0	1.000	36	20	18	8	10	7.71
1981—Evansville	Am. Assoc.	25	163	7	10	.412	170	94	74	88	60	4.09
1981—Detroit	American	4	14	0	0	.000	19	12	10	5	5	6.43
1982—Evansville‡	Am. Assoc.	8	47⅓	2	4	.333	42	23	20	30	14	3.80
1982—Detroit	American	25	178	10	10	.500	150	76	73	86	69	3.69
1983—Detroit	American	11	34	0	4	.000	41	33	27	13	20	7.15
1983—Evansville	Am. Assoc.	18	106⅔	3	7	.300	122	87	74	46	59	6.24
Major League Totals		49	247	11	14	.440	246	141	128	112	104	4.66

Selected by Detroit Tigers' organization in 4th round of free-agent draft, June 6, 1978.
†On temporary inactive list, April 16 to July 9, 1979.
‡On disabled list, April 13 to April 24, 1982.

SCOTT MATTHEW ULLGER

Name pronounced ULL-jer.

Born June 10, 1956, at New York, N.Y.
Height, 6.03. Weight, 196.
Throws and bats righthanded.
Attended St. John's University, Jamaica, N.Y.

Tied for Southern League lead in sacrifice flies with 9 in 1981.

Year Club	League	Pos.	G.	AB.	R.	H.	2B.	3B.	HR.	RBI.	B.A.	PO.	A.	E.	F.A.
1977—Wisconsin Rapids	Midw.	3B	81	276	52	81	17	4	5	35	.293	54	101	13	.912
1978—Visalia	Calif.	3B-SS-2B	134	465	105	149	★36	2	20	108	.320	124	289	33	.926
1979—Orlando	South.	3B-SS-OF	126	412	66	111	21	4	8	50	.269	95	219	29	.915
1980—Orlando	South.	OF	135	460	55	121	25	0	8	51	.263	283	11	4	★.987
1981—Orlando	South.	OF-1B-3B	138	483	86	130	23	2	20	87	.269	268	27	6	.980
1982—Toledo	Int.	OF-3B-1B	115	352	77	102	16	4	14	60	.290	201	29	4	.983
1983—Minnesota	Amer.	1B-3B	35	79	8	15	4	0	0	5	.190	186	11	2	.990
Major League Totals			35	79	8	15	4	0	0	5	.190	186	11	2	.990

Selected by Minnesota Twins' organization in 18th round of free-agent draft, June 7, 1977.

PATRICK JOHN UNDERWOOD

(Pat)

Born February 9, 1957, at Kokomo, Ind.
Height, 6.00. Weight, 175.
Throws and bats lefthanded.
Brother of Tom Underwood, pitcher with Philadelphia, St. Louis, Toronto,
New York Yankees and Oakland, 1974 through 1983.

Tied for American Association lead in games started by pitchers with 26 in 1981.

Year Club	League	G.	IP.	W.	L.	Pct.	H.	R.	ER.	SO.	BB.	ERA.
1976—Lakeland	Florida St.	12	77	6	2	.750	63	26	19	45	32	2.22
1977—Montgomery	Southern	14	104	9	2	.818	82	46	39	64	37	3.38
1977—Evansville	Am. Assoc.	16	50	3	5	.375	57	39	29	37	22	5.22
1978—Evansville†	Am. Assoc.	20	104	5	5	.500	116	57	48	73	31	4.15
1979—Evansville	Am. Assoc.	7	48	2	3	.400	41	20	15	35	17	2.81
1979—Detroit	American	27	122	6	4	.600	126	64	62	83	29	4.57
1980—Detroit	American	49	113	3	6	.333	121	51	45	60	35	3.58
1981—Evansville	Am. Assoc.	26	165	9	8	.529	158	86	73	90	44	3.98
1982—Detroit	American	33	99	4	8	.333	108	66	52	43	22	4.73
1983—Evansville‡-Indianapolis§	Am. Assoc.	20	94⅔	7	4	.636	96	48	43	51	27	4.09
1983—Detroit	American	4	10⅓	0	0	.000	11	10	10	2	6	8.71
Major League Totals		113	344⅓	13	18	.419	366	191	169	188	92	4.42

Selected by Detroit Tigers' organization in 1st round (second player selected) of free-agent draft, June 8, 1976.
†On disabled list, June 30 to August 12, 1978.
‡Traded to Cincinnati Reds' organization for Third Baseman Wayne Krenchicki, June 30, 1983.
§Drafted by Texas Rangers, December 5, 1983.

THOMAS GERALD UNDERWOOD

(Tom)

Born December 22, 1953, at Kokomo, Ind.
Height, 5.11. Weight, 185.
Throws left and bats righthanded.
Brother of Pat Underwood, pitcher with Texas Rangers.

Named Western Carolinas League Most Valuable Pitcher, 1973.

Year Club	League	G	IP	W	L	Pct.	H	R	ER	SO	BB	ERA
1973—Spartanburg	W. Carol.	26	193	13	6	.684	137	66	45	*187	79	*2.10
1974—Reading	Eastern	23	165	14	5	●.737	134	65	46	157	69	2.51
1974—Toledo	Int'national	3	9	0	1	.000	8	4	4	11	4	4.00
1974—Philadelphia	National	7	13	1	0	1.000	15	8	7	8	5	4.85
1975—Philadelphia	National	35	219	14	13	.519	221	110	101	123	84	4.15
1976—Philadelphia	National	33	156	10	5	.667	154	63	61	94	63	3.52
1977—Phil.†-St.L.‡	National	33	133	9	11	.450	148	82	74	86	75	5.01
1978—Toronto	American	31	198	6	14	.300	201	105	90	139	87	4.09
1979—Toronto§	American	33	227	9	16	.360	213	113	93	127	95	3.69
1980—New York	American	38	187	13	9	.591	163	85	76	116	66	3.66
1981—New York x-Oakland	American	25	84	4	6	.400	69	38	34	75	38	3.64
1982—Oakland	American	56	153	10	6	.625	136	66	56	79	68	3.29
1983—Oakland y	American	51	142⅔	9	7	.563	156	69	65	62	50	4.04
National League Totals		108	521	34	29	.540	538	263	243	311	227	4.20
American League Totals		234	993⅔	51	58	.468	938	476	414	598	404	3.75
Major League Totals		342	1514⅔	85	87	.494	1476	739	657	909	631	3.90

Selected by Philadelphia Phillies' organization in 2nd round of free-agent draft, June 6, 1972.

†Traded with First Baseman Dane Iorg and Outfielder Rick Bosetti to St. Louis Cardinals for Pitcher Steve Waterbury and Outfielder Bake McBride, June 15, 1977.

‡Traded with Pitcher Victor Cruz to Toronto Blue Jays for Pitcher Pete Vuckovich and a player to be named later, December 6, 1977; St. Louis Cardinals' organization acquired Outfielder John Scott to complete deal, December 16, 1977.

§Traded with Catcher Rick Cerone and Outfielder Ted Wilborn to New York Yankees for First Baseman Chris Chambliss, Infielder Damaso Garcia and Pitcher Paul Mirabella, November 1, 1979.

xTraded with First Baseman Jim Spencer to Oakland A's for First Baseman Dave Revering, Outfielder Mike Patterson and Pitcher Chuck Dougherty, May 20, 1981.

yGranted free agency, November 7, 1983.

DIVISION SERIES RECORD

Year Club	League	G	IP	W	L	Pct.	H	R	ER	SO	BB	ERA
1981—Oakland	American	1	⅓	0	0	.000	0	0	0	1	0	0.00

CHAMPIONSHIP SERIES RECORD

Tied Championship Series record for most clubs, total Series (3).

Year Club	League	G	IP	W	L	Pct.	H	R	ER	SO	BB	ERA
1976—Philadelphia	National	1	⅓	0	0	.000	1	0	0	0	2	0.00
1980—New York	American	2	3	0	0	.000	3	2	0	3	0	0.00
1981—Oakland	American	2	1⅓	0	0	.000	4	2	2	0	2	13.50
Championship Series Totals		5	4⅔	0	0	.000	8	4	2	3	4	3.86

WILLIE CLAY UPSHAW

Born April 27, 1957, at Blanco, Tex.
Height, 6.00. Weight, 185.
Throws and bats lefthanded.
Cousin of Gene Upshaw, guard with Oakland Raiders, 1967 through 1981;
and currently executive director of NFL Players Association; and Marvin Upshaw,
lineman with Cleveland Browns, Kansas City Chiefs and St. Louis Cardinals, 1968 through 1976.

Led American League first basemen in total chances with 1,556 in 1982.

Year Club	League	Pos.	G	AB	R	H	2B	3B	HR	RBI	B.A.	PO	A	E	F.A.
1975—Oneonta	NYP	OF	29	91	8	8	1	0	0	4	.088	7	1	0	1.000
1976—Ft. Lauderdale	Fla. St.	OF	84	263	20	60	6	0	3	22	.228	22	0	0	1.000
1977—Ft. Lauderdale	Fla. St.	1B-OF	87	335	38	92	13	7	3	29	.275	358	31	14	.965
1977—West Haven†	East.	OF-1B	41	157	20	47	5	2	4	22	.299	40	0	4	.909
1978—Toronto	Amer.	OF-1B	95	224	26	53	8	2	1	17	.237	131	4	7	.951
1979—Syracuse	Int.	OF-1B	140	526	71	131	25	8	12	68	.249	544	24	14	.976
1980—Syracuse	Int.	OF-1B	100	358	55	91	13	7	9	52	.254	355	19	7	.982
1980—Toronto	Amer.	1B-OF	34	61	10	13	3	1	1	5	.213	51	7	1	.983
1981—Toronto	Amer.	1B-OF	61	111	15	19	3	1	4	10	.171	72	6	0	1.000
1982—Toronto	Amer.	1B	160	580	77	155	25	7	21	75	.267	*1438	101	*17	.989
1983—Toronto	Amer.	1B	160	579	99	177	26	7	27	104	.306	1294	117	*21	.985
Major League Totals			510	1555	227	417	65	18	54	211	.268	2986	235	46	.986

Selected by New York Yankees' organization in 5th round of free-agent draft, June 4, 1975.

†Drafted by Toronto Blue Jays, December 5, 1977.

MICHAEL LEWIS VAIL
(Mike)

Born November 10, 1951, at San Francisco, Calif.
Height, 6.00. Weight, 185.
Throws and bats righthanded.
Attended De Anza College, Cupertino, Calif.

Tied major league record for most strikeouts, doubleheader (7), September 26, 1975 (24 innings).

Tied modern National League record for most consecutive games, one or more hits, rookie season (23), August 22 through September 15, 1975.

Tied for California League lead in double plays by outfielders with 3 in 1973.

Named International League Most Valuable Player, 1975.

Year Club	League	Pos.	G.	AB.	R.	H.	2B.	3B.	HR.	RBI.	B.A.	PO.	A.	E.	F.A.
1971—Sarasota Cards.....	Gulf C.	3B-2B	35	95	6	24	4	1	0	17	.253	18	53	5	.934
1972—Modesto	Calif.	3B	42	136	15	32	5	0	4	17	.235	30	57	15	.853
1972—Cedar Rapids........	Midw.	3B-OF	61	202	19	49	7	1	7	37	.243	48	50	14	.875
1972—Arkansas..............	Texas	3B-OF	19	65	4	12	6	0	1	7	.185	23	14	1	.974
1973—Modesto	Calif.	★OF-3B	134	479	81	133	●31	9	15	80	.278	150	★23	12	.935
1974—Modesto	Calif.	OF	62	221	37	79	15	3	7	41	.357	113	2	6	.950
1974—Arkansas†.............	Texas	OF	73	261	31	82	7	4	8	35	.314	116	6	4	.968
1975—Tidewater..............	Int.	OF	115	409	53	140	23	★9	7	79	★.342	182	9	2	.990
1975—New York.............	Nat.	OF	38	162	17	49	8	1	3	17	.302	92	9	3	.971
1976—New York‡...........	Nat.	OF	53	143	8	31	5	1	0	9	.217	63	1	4	.941
1977—New York§...........	Nat.	OF	108	279	29	73	12	1	8	35	.262	159	5	6	.965
1978—Portland	P. C.	OF	14	56	10	22	2	0	4	19	.393	14	1	0	1.000
1978—Cleveland x	Amer.	OF	14	34	2	8	2	1	0	2	.235	18	0	0	1.000
1978—Chicago	Nat.	OF-3B	74	180	15	60	6	2	4	33	.333	50	1	1	.981
1979—Chicago	Nat.	OF-3B	87	179	28	60	8	2	7	35	.335	51	4	2	.965
1980—Chicago y	Nat.	OF	114	312	30	93	17	2	6	47	.298	126	5	5	.963
1981—Cincinnati z	Nat.	OF	31	31	1	5	0	0	0	3	.161	3	0	0	1.000
1982—Cincinnati a	Nat.	OF	78	189	9	48	10	1	4	29	.254	72	7	1	.988
1983—S.F. b-Mont.	Nat.	OF-1B-3B	52	79	6	19	3	0	2	7	.241	50	5	1	.982
National League Totals...........................			635	1554	143	438	69	10	34	215	.282	666	37	23	.968
American League Totals........................			14	34	2	8	2	1	0	2	.235	18	0	0	1.000
Major League Totals..................................			649	1588	145	446	71	11	34	217	.281	684	37	23	.969

Selected by Los Angeles Dodgers' organization in 10th round of free-agent draft, June 4, 1970.
Selected by St. Louis Cardinals' organization in secondary phase of free-agent draft, January 13, 1971.
†Traded with Infielder Jack Heidemann by St. Louis Cardinals to New York Mets for Infielder Teddy Martinez, December 11, 1974.
‡On disabled list, April 1 to June 15, 1976.
§Sold on waivers to Cleveland Indians, March 25, 1978.
xTraded to Chicago Cubs for Outfielder Joe Wallis, June 15, 1978.
yTraded to Cincinnati Reds for Outfielder Hector Cruz, December 12, 1980.
zGranted free agency, November 13, 1981; re-signed by Reds, November 27, 1981.
aTraded to San Francisco Giants for Pitcher Rich Gale, January 5, 1983.
bTraded to Montreal Expos for Infielder Wallace Johnson, May 25, 1983.

JULIO JULIAN VALDEZ

Born June 3, 1956, at Nizao de Peravia, Dominican Republic.
Height, 6.02. Weight, 150.
Throws right and bats left and righthanded.

Led International League in being hit by pitch with 10 in 1981.
Led Carolina League in sacrifice hits with 15 and being hit by pitch with 14 in 1977.
Led Carolina League shortstops in putouts with 237 and double plays with 76 in 1977.

Year Club	League	Pos.	G.	AB.	R.	H.	2B.	3B.	HR.	RBI.	B.A.	PO.	A.	E.	F.A.
1976—Winter Haven.......	Fla. St.	SS-3B	76	185	12	25	3	1	0	10	.135	78	142	20	.917
1977—Winston-Salem	Carol.	★SS-2B	132	451	66	112	19	4	8	47	.248	239	★368	★45	★.931
1978—Bristol.................	East.	SS	124	396	50	105	13	3	8	56	.265	★213	285	39	.927
1979—Pawtucket†	Int.	SS	103	370	43	82	12	6	5	31	.222	178	305	★34	.934
1980—Pawtucket	Int.	SS-1B-OF	101	279	22	61	10	3	4	27	.219	164	288	29	.940
1980—Boston...................	Amer.	SS	8	19	4	5	1	0	1	4	.263	17	26	3	.935
1981—Pawtucket	Int.	SS	112	384	45	99	7	4	6	27	.258	173	327	28	.947
1981—Boston...................	Amer.	SS	17	23	1	5	0	0	0	3	.217	12	30	2	.955
1982—Boston...................	Amer.	SS	28	20	3	5	1	0	0	1	.250	16	24	1	.976
1983—Boston‡.................	Amer.	2B-SS	12	25	3	3	0	0	0	0	.120	16	16	2	.941
1983—New Britain	East.	1-S-3-2	21	69	3	10	1	1	0	5	.145	91	36	1	.992
Major League Totals..................................			65	87	11	18	2	0	1	8	.207	61	96	8	.952

Signed as free agent by Boston Red Sox' organization, December 12, 1975.
†On disabled list, May 29 to July 2, 1979.
‡On restricted list, May 9 to July 1, 1983.

ELLIS CLARENCE VALENTINE

Born July 30, 1954, at Helena, Ark.
Height, 6.04. Weight, 218.
Throws and bats righthanded.

Led International League in total bases with 226 in 1975.
Led Eastern League outfielders in double plays with 5 in 1974.
Named outfielder on THE SPORTING NEWS National League All-Star fielding team, 1978.

Year Club	League	Pos.	G.	AB.	R.	H.	2B.	3B.	HR.	RBI.	B.A.	PO.	A.	E.	F.A.
1972—Cocoa Expos.........	Fl. E.C.	OF	53	177	24	47	8	0	1	18	.266	76	4	1	.988
1973—W. Palm Beach....	Fla. St.	OF	119	403	59	124	18	4	8	61	.308	169	11	5	.973
1974—Quebec City	East.	OF	130	426	46	112	11	7	5	50	.263	204	★20	10	.957
1975—Memphis...............	Int.	OF-1B	★139	494	★87	★151	●30	3	13	66	.306	266	12	6	.979
1975—Montreal...............	Nat.	OF	12	33	2	12	4	0	1	3	.364	12	1	2	.867
1976—Denver.................	A. A.	OF	57	204	31	63	9	1	7	32	.309	122	8	2	.985
1976—Montreal...............	Nat.	OF	94	305	36	85	15	2	7	39	.279	162	12	5	.972
1977—Montreal...............	Nat.	OF	127	508	63	149	28	2	25	76	.293	232	9	7	.972
1978—Montreal†.............	Nat.	OF	151	570	75	165	35	2	25	76	.289	296	●24	10	.970
1979—Montreal...............	Nat.	OF	146	548	73	151	29	3	21	82	.276	281	10	5	.983
1980—Montreal‡.............	Nat.	OF	86	311	40	98	22	2	13	67	.315	154	6	5	.970

Year Club League	Pos.	G.	AB.	R.	H.	2B.	3B.	HR.	RBI.	B.A.	PO.	A.	E.	F.A.
1981—Mont.§x-N.Y......... Nat.	OF	70	245	23	51	11	1	8	36	.208	115	8	4	.969
1982—New York y .... Nat.	OF	111	337	33	97	14	1	8	48	.288	159	10	3	.983
1983—California z........... Amer.	OF	86	271	30	65	10	2	13	43	.240	152	5	6	.963
1983—Edmonton.............. P. C.	OF	3	9	2	2	0	0	0	0	.222	3	0	0	1.000
National League Totals.............................		797	2857	345	808	158	13	108	427	.283	1411	80	41	.973
American League Totals...........................		86	271	30	65	10	2	13	43	.240	152	5	6	.963
Major League Totals....................................		883	3128	375	873	168	15	121	470	.279	1563	85	47	.972

Selected by Montreal Expos' organization in 2nd round of free-agent draft, June 6, 1972.

†On suspended list, September 20 to September 22, 1978.

‡On disabled list, May 31 to July 6, 1980.

§On supplemental disabled list, May 20 to June 5, 1981.

xTraded to New York Mets for Pitcher Jeff Reardon and Outfielder Dan Norman, May 29, 1981.

yGranted free agency, November 10, 1982; signed by California Angels, January 21, 1983.

zOn disabled list, March 30 to May 6, 1983; included rehabilitation disability assignment to Edmonton, May 2 to May 6, 1983.

ALL-STAR GAME RECORD

Year League	Pos.	AB.	R.	H.	2B.	3B.	HR.	RBI.	B.A.	PO.	A.	E.	F.A.
1977—National	OF	1	0	0	0	0	0	0	.000	0	0	0	.000

FERNANDO VALENZUELA (ANGUAMEA)

Name pronounced Val-en-ZWAY-luh.

Born November 1, 1960, at Navajoa, Sonora, Mexico.
Height, 5.11. Weight, 180.
Throws and bats lefthanded.

Tied modern major league record for most shutout games won or tied, rookie year (8), 1981.
Led National League in complete games with 11 and shutouts with 8 in 1981.
Tied for National League lead in games started by pitchers with 25 in 1981.
Led Mexican Center League in wild pitches with 13 in 1978.
Named Major League Player of the Year by The Sporting News, 1981.
Named National League Pitcher of the Year by The Sporting News, 1981.
Won National League Cy Young Memorial Award, 1981.
Named National League Rookie Pitcher of the Year by The Sporting News, 1981.
Named National League Rookie of the Year by Baseball Writers' Association of America, 1981.
Named lefthanded pitcher on The Sporting News National League All-Star Team, 1981.
Named pitcher on The Sporting News National League Silver Slugger team, 1981 and 1983.

Year Club	League	G.	IP.	W.	L.	Pct.	H.	R.	ER.	SO.	BB.	ERA.
1978—Guanajuato	Mex. Cent.	16	93	5	6	.455	88	46	23	*91	46	2.23
1979—Yucatan†	Mexican	26	181	10	12	.455	157	68	50	141	70	2.49
1979—Lodi	California	3	24	1	2	.333	21	10	3	18	3	1.13
1980—San Antonio....................................	Texas	27	174	13	9	.591	156	70	60	*162	70	3.10
1980—Los Angeles	National	10	18	2	0	1.000	8	2	0	16	5	0.00
1981—Los Angeles	National	25	*192	13	7	.650	140	55	53	*180	61	2.48
1982—Los Angeles‡	National	37	285	19	13	.594	247	105	91	199	83	2.87
1983—Los Angeles	National	35	257	15	10	.600	245	*122	107	189	99	3.75
Major League Totals....................................		107	752	49	30	.620	640	284	251	584	248	3.00

†Sold to Los Angeles Dodgers' organization, July 6, 1979.

‡Appeared in one game as outfielder with no chances.

DIVISION SERIES RECORD

Year Club	League	G.	IP.	W.	L.	Pct.	H.	R.	ER.	SO.	BB.	ERA.
1981—Los Angeles	National	2	17	1	0	1.000	10	2	2	10	3	1.06

CHAMPIONSHIP SERIES RECORD

Year Club	League	G.	IP.	W.	L.	Pct.	H.	R.	ER.	SO.	BB.	ERA.
1981—Los Angeles	National	2	14⅔	1	1	.500	10	4	4	10	5	2.45
1983—Los Angeles	National	1	8	1	0	1.000	7	1	1	5	4	1.13
Championship Series Totals		3	22⅔	2	1	.667	17	5	5	15	9	1.99

WORLD SERIES RECORD

Year Club	League	G.	IP.	W.	L.	Pct.	H.	R.	ER.	SO.	BB.	ERA.
1981—Los Angeles	National	1	9	1	0	1.000	9	4	4	6	7	4.00

ALL-STAR GAME RECORD

Year League		IP.	W.	L.	Pct.	H.	R.	ER.	SO.	BB.	ERA.
1981—National..		1	0	0	.000	2	0	0	0	0	0.00
1982—National..		⅔	0	0	.000	0	0	0	0	2	0.00
All-Star Game Totals		1⅔	0	0	.000	2	0	0	0	2	0.00

Member of National League All-Star Team in 1983; did not play.

EDWARD JOHN VANDE BERG

(Ed)

Born October 26, 1958, at Redlands, Calif.
Height, 6.01. Weight, 170.
Throws left and bats righthanded.
Attended San Bernardino Valley, San Bernardino, Calif. and Arizona State University, Tempe, Ariz.

Established major league record for most games by pitcher, rookie season (78), 1982.
Major League saves: 1982 (5), 1983 (5). Total—10.
Tied for Northwest League lead in games started by pitchers with 14 in 1980.
Named American League Rookie Pitcher of the Year by THE SPORTING NEWS, 1982.

Year Club	League	G.	IP.	W.	L.	Pct.	H.	R.	ER.	SO.	BB.	ERA.
1980—Bellingham	Northwest	14	101	9	0	*1.000	82	40	32	78	46	2.85
1981—Spokane	P. Coast	49	62	4	3	.571	62	33	26	49	29	3.77
1982—Seattle	American	*78	76	9	4	.692	54	21	20	60	32	2.37
1983—Seattle	American	68	64⅓	2	4	.333	59	32	24	49	22	3.36
Major League Totals		146	140⅓	11	8	.579	113	53	44	109	54	2.82

Selected by San Diego Padres' organization in 3rd round of free-agent draft, January 10, 1978.
Selected by St. Louis Cardinals' organization in secondary phase of free-agent draft, June 6, 1978.
Selected by Seattle Mariners' organization in 13th round of free-agent draft, June 3, 1980.

DAVID THOMAS VAN GORDER
(Dave)

Born March 27, 1957, at Los Angeles, Calif.
Height, 6.02. Weight, 205.
Throws and bats righthanded.
Attended University of Southern California, Los Angeles, Calif.

Led American Association catchers in putouts with 666, total chances with 736 and double plays with 14 in 1983.
Led American Association catchers in putouts with 705, total chances with 785, and fielding percentage with .991 in 1981.

Year Club	League	Pos.	G.	AB.	R.	H.	2B.	3B.	HR.	RBI.	B.A.	PO.	A.	E.	F.A.
1978—Nashville	South.	C	73	217	23	57	10	0	1	25	.263	396	38	5	.989
1979—Nashville	South.	C	137	461	58	131	27	1	6	64	.284	*726	*74	6	*.993
1980—Indianapolis†	A. A.	*C-1B	71	253	11	57	12	1	3	26	.225	442	45	4	*.992
1981—Indianapolis	A. A.	C-1B	123	432	50	108	21	0	15	66	.250	712	75	8	.990
1982—Indianapolis	A. A.	C	54	174	21	46	7	0	4	29	.264	260	36	3	.990
1982—Cincinnati	Nat.	C	51	137	4	25	3	1	0	7	.182	273	18	4	.986
1983—Indianapolis	A. A.	*C-OF	117	380	38	86	17	0	5	48	.226	673	68	3	*.996
Major League Totals			51	137	4	25	3	1	0	7	.182	273	18	4	.986

Selected by Philadelphia Phillies' organization in 9th round of free-agent draft, June 4, 1975.
Selected by Cincinnati Reds' organization in 2nd round of free-agent draft, June 6, 1978.
†On disabled list, July 10 to September 30, 1980.

ANDREW JAMES VAN SLYKE
(Andy)

Born December 21, 1960, at Utica, N.Y.
Height, 6.01. Weight, 190.
Throws right and bats lefthanded.

Major League stolen bases: 1983 (21).

Year Club	League	Pos.	G.	AB.	R.	H.	2B.	3B.	HR.	RBI.	B.A.	PO.	A.	E.	F.A.
1979—Johnson City†	Appal.					(Did not play)									
1980—Gastonia	S. Atl.	OF	126	426	62	115	15	4	8	59	.270	177	16	●16	.923
1981—St. Petersburg‡	Fla. St.	OF	94	282	42	62	11	3	1	25	.220	168	10	5	.973
1982—Arkansas	Texas	OF	123	416	83	116	13	*11	16	70	.279	266	17	7	.976
1983—Louisville	A. A.	3B-1B-OF	54	220	52	81	21	4	6	41	.368	201	78	16	.946
1983—St. Louis	Nat.	OF-3B-1B	101	309	51	81	15	5	8	38	.262	203	59	6	.978
Major League Totals			101	309	51	81	15	5	8	38	.262	203	59	6	.978

Selected by St. Louis Cardinals' organization in 1st round (sixth player selected) of free-agent draft, June 5, 1979.
†On disabled list, June 8, 1979 through remainder of season.
‡On disabled list, April 10 to May 14, 1981.

HEDIBERTO VARGAS (RODRIGUEZ)
(Hedi)

Born February 23, 1959, at Guanica, Puerto Rico.
Height, 6.04. Weight, 215.
Throws and bats righthanded.

Led Eastern League in total bases with 242 in 1980.
Led Eastern League first basemen in double plays with 115 in 1980.
Tied for Gulf Coast League lead in errors by first basemen with 8 in 1977.

Year Club	League	Pos.	G.	AB.	R.	H.	2B.	3B.	HR.	RBI.	B.A.	PO.	A.	E.	F.A.
1977—Brad. Pirates	Gulf C.	1B-OF	47	165	21	52	5	6	2	18	.315	300	14	9	.972
1978—Charleston	W. Car.	1B-OF	56	189	18	46	12	1	3	18	.243	109	6	7	.943
1978—Niagara Falls	NYP	1B-OF	57	205	35	47	11	1	4	23	.229	472	25	14	.973
1979—Shelby	W. Car.	1B-OF	126	440	76	124	23	5	*31	78	.282	868	49	11	.988
1980—Buffalo	East.	1B	133	509	78	138	28	2	24	87	.271	*1268	85	●15	.989
1981—Buffalo	East.	1B-OF	125	419	65	115	23	3	25	84	.274	688	44	5	.993
1982—Portland	P. C.	1B	124	440	87	137	27	2	28	80	.311	1016	64	13	.988
1982—Pittsburgh	Nat.	1B	8	8	1	3	1	0	0	3	.375	16	1	0	1.000
1983—Lynn†	East.	1B	20	71	13	22	5	0	2	13	.310	141	12	3	.981
1983—Hawaii	P. C.	1B-OF	53	204	30	71	19	0	12	46	.348	318	13	9	.974
Major League Totals			8	8	1	3	1	0	0	3	.375	16	1	0	1.000

Signed as free agent by Pittsburgh Pirates' organization, January 17, 1977.

†On Pittsburgh disabled list, April 4 to June 24, 1983; included rehabilitation disability assignment to Lynn, June 2 to June 21, 1983.

LEONEL RIVERA VARGAS
(Leo)

Born September 12, 1957, at San Pedro de Macoris, D. R.
Height, 6.01. Weight, 180.
Throws and bats righthanded.

Tied for South Atlantic League lead in sacrifice flies with 10 in 1979.

Year Club	League	Pos.	G.	AB.	R.	H.	2B.	3B.	HR.	RBI.	B.A.	PO.	A.	E.	F.A.
1977—Bradenton Brav...	Gulf C.	OF	52	200	26	57	6	3	1	20	.285	★101	8	2	.982
1978—Kingsport..............	Appal.	OF	68	262	38	76	18	●6	3	39	.290	141	3	★11	.929
1979—Greenwood........	W. Car.	OF	125	455	74	127	21	5	11	73	.279	188	6	8	.960
1980—Savannah†	South.	OF	106	370	48	94	14	3	12	61	.254	175	12	7	.964
1981—Savannah	South.	OF	140	499	73	132	20	2	32	76	.265	222	22	13	.949
1982—Richmond...........	Int.	OF	115	413	54	110	16	1	12	70	.266	161	10	10	.945
1983—Richmond‡...........	Int.	OF	112	408	69	118	19	1	19	75	.289	189	3	7	.965

Signed as free agent by Atlanta Braves' organization, November 1, 1976.

†On disabled list, April 27 to May 9 and July 1 to July 12, 1980.

‡On disabled list, May 7 to May 17, 1983.

OTONIEL VELEZ (FRANCESCHI)
(Otto)

Born November 29, 1950, at Ponce, Puerto Rico.
Height, 6.00. Weight, 195.
Throws and bats righthanded.

Tied American League records for most home runs, 10-inning game (3), May 4, 1980; most home runs, doubleheader, home run in each game (4), May 4, 1980.

Hit three home runs in a game, May 4, 1980 (10 innings, first game).

Led International League in bases on balls received with 130 in 1973 and 87 in 1975.

Named Appalachian League Player of the Year, 1970.

Year Club	League	Pos.	G.	AB.	R.	H.	2B.	3B.	HR.	RBI.	B.A.	PO.	A.	E.	F.A.
1970—Ft. Lauderdale†	Fla. St.	OF	20	54	7	9	0	1	0	4	.167	27	2	2	.935
1970—Johnson City	Appal.	3B-2B-OF	53	176	★49	65	10	4	7	●44	★.369	61	83	15	.906
1971—Kinston..................	Carol.	3B	113	384	82	119	21	4	16	73	.310	68	172	25	.906
1972—West Haven	East.	3B-OF-1B	122	409	64	102	17	1	13	68	.249	102	211	28	.918
1973—Syracuse	Int.	OF-3B	138	409	92	110	19	7	29	98	.269	177	11	10	.949
1973—New York.............	Amer.	OF	23	77	9	15	4	0	2	7	.195	45	2	2	.959
1974—Syracuse	Int.	1B-2B-3B	65	200	44	62	13	0	13	35	.310	474	39	13	.975
1974—New York.............	Amer.	1B-OF-3B	27	67	9	14	1	1	2	10	.209	140	8	3	.980
1975—Syracuse‡	Int.	3B-1B	81	244	56	61	18	2	10	35	.250	302	90	19	.954
1975—New York.............	Amer.	1B	6	8	0	2	0	0	1	1	.250	11	0	0	1.000
1976—New York§...........	Amer.	OF-1B-3B	49	94	11	25	6	0	2	10	.266	89	2	2	.978
1977—Toronto	Amer.	OF	120	360	50	92	19	3	16	62	.256	140	5	4	.973
1978—Toronto	Amer.	OF-1B	91	248	29	66	14	2	9	38	.266	161	12	3	.983
1979—Toronto	Amer.	OF-1B	99	274	45	79	21	0	15	48	.288	159	5	4	.976
1980—Toronto x..............	Amer.	1B	104	357	54	96	12	3	20	62	.269	36	3	1	.975
1981—Toronto	Amer.	1B	80	240	32	51	9	2	11	28	.213	9	0	0	1.000
1982—Toronto y.............	Amer.	DH	28	52	4	10	1	0	1	5	.192	0	0	0	.000
1982—Syracuse z	Int.	DH	7	19	1	3	1	0	0	0	.158	0	0	0	.000
1983—Charleston	Int.	1B	48	142	27	44	9	0	9	42	.310	1	1	0	1.000
1983—Cleveland..............	Amer.	DH	10	25	1	2	0	0	1	1	.080	0	0	0	.000
Major League Totals....................			637	1802	244	452	87	11	78	272	.251	790	37	19	.978

Signed as free agent by New York Yankees' organization, December 23, 1969.

†On disabled list, May 19 to June 6, 1970.

‡On disabled list, June 10 to August 2, 1975.

§Selected by Toronto Blue Jays in American League expansion draft, November 5, 1976.

xOn disabled list, August 29, 1980 through remainder of season.

yOn supplemental disabled list, June 4 to June 22 and June 25 to July 8, 1982.

zReleased, September 7, 1982; signed by Cleveland Indians' organization, February 7, 1983.

CHAMPIONSHIP SERIES RECORD

Year Club	League	Pos.	G.	AB.	R.	H.	2B.	3B.	HR.	RBI.	B.A.	PO.	A.	E.	F.A.
1976—New York..............	Amer.	PH	1	1	0	0	0	0	0	0	.000	0	0	0	.000

WORLD SERIES RECORD

Tied World Series record for most strikeouts by pinch-hitter, Series (3), 1976.

Year Club	League	Pos.	G.	AB.	R.	H.	2B.	3B.	HR.	RBI.	B.A.	PO.	A.	E.	F.A.
1976—New York..............	Amer.	PH	3	3	0	0	0	0	0	0	.000	0	0	0	.000

WILLIAM McKINLEY VENABLE JR.
(Max)

Born June 6, 1957, at Phoenix, Ariz.
Height, 5.10. Weight, 185.
Throws right and bats lefthanded.

Year Club	League	Pos.	G.	AB.	R.	H.	2B.	3B.	HR.	RBI.	B.A.	PO.	A.	E.	F.A.
1976—Bellingham†	N'west	OF	51	162	25	35	2	0	1	16	.216	58	4	8	.886
1977—Clinton	Midw.	OF-2B	125	425	72	115	19	4	9	63	.271	149	13	13	.926
1978—Lodi‡	Calif.	OF	●140	566	134	180	30	9	17	101	.318	220	8	8	.966
1979—San Francisco	Nat.	OF	55	85	12	14	1	1	0	3	.165	25	30	2	.914
1979—Shreveport	Texas	OF	18	69	11	16	1	2	0	3	.232	28	2	1	.968
1979—Phoenix	P. C.	OF	38	150	27	46	5	4	0	11	.307	96	4	3	.971
1980—Phoenix	P. C.	OF	78	312	52	89	10	10	5	40	.285	179	7	4	.979
1980—San Francisco	Nat.	OF	64	138	13	37	5	0	0	10	.268	61	0	0	1.000
1981—Phoenix§	P. C.	OF	104	428	81	122	24	10	8	48	.285	263	6	3	.989
1981—San Francisco	Nat.	OF	18	32	2	6	0	2	0	1	.188	12	0	0	1.000
1982—San Francisco x	Nat.	OF	71	125	17	28	2	1	1	7	.224	66	6	1	.986
1982—Phoenix	P. C.	OF	8	32	5	8	1	2	0	3	.250	16	0	0	1.000
1983—San Francisco	Nat.	OF	94	228	28	50	7	4	6	27	.219	141	5	1	.993
Major League Totals			302	608	72	135	15	8	7	48	.222	305	41	4	.989

Selected by Los Angeles Dodgers' organization in 3rd round of free-agent draft, June 8, 1976
†On disabled list, June 26 to July 10, 1976.
‡Drafted by San Francisco Giants, December 4, 1978.
§On disabled list, April 23 to May 16, 1981.
xOn supplemental disabled list, April 21, 1982; transferred to disabled list, May 8 to June 1, 1982; included rehabilitation disability assignment to Phoenix, May 22 to June 1, 1982.

THOMAS MARTIN VERYZER

Name pronounced Vuh-RISE-er.

(Tom)

Born February 11, 1953, at Islip, N.Y.
Height, 6.01. Weight, 185.
Throws and bats righthanded.
Brother of Jim Veryzer, outfielder in Detroit Tigers' organization, 1971 and 1972.
Tied for Southern League lead in sacrifice flies with 7 in 1972.
Named Appalachian League co-Player of the Year, 1971.

Year Club	League	Pos.	G.	AB.	R.	H.	2B.	3B.	HR.	RBI.	B.A.	PO.	A.	E.	F.A.
1971—Bristol	Appal.	SS	51	169	27	38	7	4	4	20	.225	68	137	19	*.915
1972—Montgomery†	South.	SS	111	381	36	84	20	4	8	49	.220	166	358	26	.953
1973—Toledo	Int.	SS	94	284	32	71	11	5	3	26	.250	155	239	28	.934
1973—Detroit	Amer.	SS	18	20	1	6	0	1	0	2	.300	6	12	3	.857
1974—Evansville‡	A. A.	SS	67	223	36	66	7	1	11	36	.296	109	207	15	.955
1974—Detroit	Amer.	SS	22	55	4	13	2	0	2	9	.236	18	33	4	.927
1975—Detroit	Amer.	SS	128	404	37	102	13	1	5	48	.252	215	358	24	.960
1976—Detroit§	Amer.	SS	97	354	31	83	8	2	1	25	.234	164	313	17	.966
1977—Detroit x	Amer.	SS	125	350	31	69	12	1	2	28	.197	185	377	18	.969
1978—Cleveland	Amer.	SS	130	421	48	114	18	4	1	32	.271	177	375	21	.963
1979—Cleveland	Amer.	SS	149	449	41	99	9	3	0	34	.220	238	446	18	.974
1980—Cleveland	Amer.	SS	109	358	28	97	12	0	2	28	.271	169	331	15	.971
1981—Cleveland y	Amer.	SS	75	221	13	54	4	0	0	14	.244	121	207	10	.970
1982—New York za	2B-SS	40	54	6	18	2	0	4	.333	40	44	7	.923
1983—Chicago	Nat.	SS-3B	59	88	5	18	3	0	1	3	.205	27	72	2	.980
American League Totals			853	2632	234	637	78	12	13	220	.242	1293	2452	130	.966
National League Totals			99	142	11	36	5	0	1	7	.254	67	116	9	.953
Major League Totals			952	2774	245	673	83	12	14	227	.243	1360	2568	139	.966

Selected by Detroit Tigers' organization in 1st round (11th player selected) of free-agent draft, June 8, 1971.
†On disabled list, April 11 to April 28, 1972.
‡On disabled list, June 5 to July 6, 1974.
§On disabled list, August 19 to October 4, 1976.
xTraded to Cleveland Indians for Outfielder Charlie Spikes, December 9, 1977.
yTraded to New York Mets for Pitcher Ray Searage, January 8, 1982.
zOn disabled list, June 2 to August 31, 1982.
aTraded to Chicago Cubs for Pitchers Bob Schilling and Craig Weissman, April 2, 1983.

FRANK JOHN VIOLA JR.

Name pronounced Vy-OH-luh.

Born April 19, 1960, at Hempstead, N.Y.
Height, 6.04. Weight, 200.
Throws and bats lefthanded.
Attended St. John's University, Jamaica, N.Y.

Year Club	League	G.	IP.	W.	L.	Pct.	H.	R.	ER.	SO.	BB.	ERA.
1981—Orlando	Southern	17	97	5	4	.556	112	47	37	50	33	3.43
1982—Toledo	Int'national	8	58	2	3	.400	61	27	25	34	18	3.88
1982—Minnesota	American	22	126	4	10	.286	152	77	73	84	38	5.21
1983—Minnesota	American	35	210	7	15	.318	*141	*128	127	92	5.49
Major League Totals		57	336	11	25	.306	394	218	201	211	130	5.38

Selected by Kansas City Royals' organization in 16th round of free-agent draft, June 6, 1978.
Selected by Minnesota Twins' organization in 2nd round of free-agent draft, June 8, 1981.

OSVALDO JOSE VIRGIL JR.
(Ozzie)

Born December 7, 1956, at Mayaguez, P. R.
Height, 6.01. Weight, 195.
Throws and bats righthanded.
Son of Ozzie Virgil, infielder-catcher with New York N.L., Detroit, Kansas City,
Baltimore, Pittsburgh and San Francisco, 1956 through 1958, 1960 through 1962, 1965,
1966 and 1969; coach, San Francisco Giants, 1970 through 1972, 1974 and 1975; scout, San Francisco Giants, 1973; coach,
Montreal Expos, 1976 through 1981; and coach with San Diego Padres since 1982.

Led Carolina League in total bases with 234 in 1978.
Named Carolina League Most Valuable Player, 1978.

Year Club	League	Pos.	G.	AB.	R.	H.	2B.	3B.	HR.	RBI.	B.A.	PO.	A.	E.	F.A.
1976—Auburn	NYP	C	39	113	10	16	1	2	1	10	.142	153	14	5	.971
1977—Spartanburg	W. Car.	C	107	365	53	103	21	1	14	54	.282	502	*68	18	.969
1978—Peninsula	Carol.	C	126	409	79	124	21	1	*29	*98	.303	581	45	8	.987
1979—Reading	East.	C	128	429	57	99	17	1	8	66	.231	532	64	12	.980
1980—Reading	East.	C-1B	135	456	92	123	15	2	28	*104	.270	592	62	16	.976
1980—Philadelphia	Nat.	C	1	5	1	1	1	0	0	0	.200	4	0	0	1.000
1981—Oklahoma City†	A. A.	C	83	275	41	63	11	2	11	44	.229	201	28	4	.983
1981—Philadelphia	Nat.	C	6	6	0	0	0	0	0	0	.000	2	0	0	1.000
1982—Philadelphia	Nat.	C	49	101	11	24	6	0	3	8	.238	173	14	7	.964
1983—Philadelphia	Nat.	C	55	140	11	30	7	0	6	23	.214	228	24	9	.966
Major League Totals			111	252	23	55	14	0	9	31	.218	407	38	16	.965

Selected by Philadelphia Phillies' organization in 6th round of free-agent draft, June 8, 1976.
†On disabled list, April 14 to April 27 and June 2 to June 29, 1981.

CHAMPIONSHIP SERIES RECORD

Year Club	League	Pos.	G.	AB.	R.	H.	2B.	3B.	HR.	RBI.	B.A.	PO.	A.	E.	F.A.
1983—Philadelphia	Nat.	PH	1	1	0	0	0	0	0	0	.000	0	0	0	.000

WORLD SERIES RECORD

Year Club	League	Pos.	G.	AB.	R.	H.	2B.	3B.	HR.	RBI.	B.A.	PO.	A.	E.	F.A.
1983—Philadelphia	Nat.	PH-C	3	2	0	1	0	0	0	1	.500	1	0	0	1.000

DAVID VON OHLEN

Born October 25, 1958, at Flushing, N.Y.
Height, 6.02. Weight, 200.
Throws and bats lefthanded.

Year Club	League	G.	IP.	W.	L.	Pct.	H.	R.	ER.	SO.	BB.	ERA.
1976—Marion	Ap'lachian	5	20	1	0	1.000	11	5	3	12	6	1.35
1976—Wausau	Midwest	9	31	1	4	.200	42	27	16	18	21	4.65
1977—Lynchburg	Carolina	37	65	6	3	.667	75	39	34	49	28	4.71
1978—Lynchburg	Carolina	34	72	6	7	.462	62	28	23	54	22	2.88
1979—Jackson	Texas	37	34	4	1	.800	28	11	7	26	10	1.85
1980—Tidewater	Int'national	45	87	5	4	.556	88	40	31	44	27	3.21
1981—Jackson	Texas	11	29	4	0	1.000	20	3	3	24	4	0.93
1981—Tidewater†	Int'national	10	25	0	4	.000	30	22	16	18	11	5.76
1982—Tidewater‡	Int'national	36	64⅓	4	1	.800	64	22	20	44	25	2.80
1983—Louisville	Am. Assoc.	12	15⅓	1	0	1.000	16	8	8	13	5	4.70
1983—St. Louis	National	46	68⅓	3	2	.600	71	27	25	21	25	3.29
Major League Totals		46	68⅓	3	2	.600	71	27	25	21	25	3.29

Selected by New York Mets' organization in 17th round of free-agent draft, June 8, 1976.
†On disabled list, July 19 to September 1, 1981.
‡Granted free agency, October 22, 1982; signed by St. Louis Cardinals, December, 1982.

PETER DENNIS VUCKOVICH
Name pronounced VOO-ko-vitch.
(Pete)

Born October 27, 1952, at Johnstown, Pa.
Height, 6.04. Weight, 220.
Throws and bats righthanded.
Attended Clarion State College, Clarion, Pa.

Won American League Cy Young Memorial Award, 1982.

Year Club	League	G.	IP.	W.	L.	Pct.	H.	R.	ER.	SO.	BB.	ERA.
1974—Appleton	Midwest	5	15	1	0	1.000	10	2	2	22	3	1.20
1974—Knoxville	Southern	13	47	2	5	.286	50	32	22	42	29	4.21
1975—Denver	Am. Assoc.	19	116	11	4	●.733	103	63	56	86	54	4.34
1975—Chicago	American	4	10	0	1	.000	17	15	15	5	7	13.50
1976—Chicago†	American	33	110	7	4	.636	122	59	57	62	60	4.66
1977—Toronto‡	American	53	148	7	7	.500	143	64	57	123	59	3.47
1978—St. Louis	National	45	198	12	12	.500	187	65	56	149	59	2.55
1979—St. Louis	National	34	233	15	10	.600	229	108	93	145	64	3.59
1980—St. Louis§	National	32	222	12	9	.571	203	96	84	132	68	3.41
1981—Milwaukee	American	24	150	●14	4	*.778	137	61	59	84	57	3.54

Year—Club	League	G.	IP.	W.	L.	Pct.	H.	R.	ER.	SO.	BB.	ERA.
1982—Milwaukee	American	30	223⅔	18	6	●.750	234	96	83	105	102	3.34
1983—Milwaukee x	American	3	14⅔	0	2	.000	15	9	8	10	10	4.91
American League Totals		147	656⅓	46	24	.657	668	304	279	389	295	3.83
National League Totals		111	653	39	31	.557	619	269	233	426	191	3.21
Major League Totals		258	1309⅓	85	55	.607	1287	573	512	815	486	3.52

Selected by Chicago White Sox' organization in 3rd round of free-agent draft, June 5, 1974.

†Selected by Toronto Blue Jays in American League expansion draft, November 5, 1976.

‡Traded with a player to be named later to St. Louis Cardinals for Pitchers Tom Underwood and Victor Cruz, December 6, 1977. St. Louis organization acquired Outfielder John Scott to complete deal, December 16, 1977.

§Traded with Pitcher Rollie Fingers and Catcher Ted Simmons to Milwaukee Brewers for Outfielders Sixto Lezcano and David Green and Pitchers Lary Sorensen and Dave LaPoint, December 12, 1980.

xOn disabled list, March 24, 1983, then transferred to emergency disabled list, July 13 to August 22, 1983.

DIVISION SERIES RECORD

Year—Club	League	G.	IP.	W.	L.	Pct.	H.	R.	ER.	SO.	BB.	ERA.
1981—Milwaukee	American	2	5⅓	1	0	1.000	2	1	0	4	3	0.00

CHAMPIONSHIP SERIES RECORD

Year—Club	League	G.	IP.	W.	L.	Pct.	H.	R.	ER.	SO.	BB.	ERA.
1982—Milwaukee	American	2	14⅓	0	1	.000	15	7	7	8	7	4.40

WORLD SERIES RECORD

Year—Club	League	G.	IP.	W.	L.	Pct.	H.	R.	ER.	SO.	BB.	ERA.
1982—Milwaukee	American	2	14	0	1	.000	16	9	7	4	5	4.50

GEORGE STEPHEN VUKOVICH

Name pronounced VOO-ko-vitch.

Born June 24, 1956, at Chicago, Ill.
Height, 6.00. Weight, 198.
Throws right and bats lefthanded.
Attended Southern Illinois University, Carbondale, Ill.

Led Eastern League in sacrifice flies with 14 in 1979.
Tied for Eastern League lead in double plays by outfielders with 3 in 1979.

Year—Club	League	Pos.	G.	AB.	R.	H.	2B.	3B.	HR.	RBI.	B.A.	PO.	A.	E.	F.A.
1977—Auburn	NYP	OF	1	2	0	1	0	0	0	0	.500	0	0	0	.000
1978—Peninsula	Carol.	OF-1B	135	453	★94	141	26	●9	10	69	.311	208	14	10	.957
1979—Reading	East.	OF	138	501	80	147	14	10	13	88	.293	238	13	8	.969
1980—Philadelphia	Nat.	OF	78	58	6	13	1	1	0	8	.224	14	0	1	.933
1981—Oklahoma City	A. A.	OF-1B	62	232	40	70	15	2	8	48	.302	99	8	1	.991
1981—Philadelphia	Nat.	OF	20	26	5	10	0	0	1	4	.385	10	0	0	1.000
1982—Philadelphia†	Nat.	OF	123	335	41	91	18	2	6	42	.272	168	4	4	.977
1983—Cleveland	Amer.	OF	124	312	31	77	13	2	3	44	.247	203	3	3	.986
National League Totals			221	419	52	114	19	3	7	54	.272	192	4	5	.975
American League Totals			124	312	31	77	13	2	3	44	.247	203	3	3	.986
Major League Totals			345	731	83	191	32	5	10	98	.261	395	7	8	.980

Selected by Philadelphia Phillies' organization in 4th round of free-agent draft, June 7, 1977.

†Traded with Second Baseman Manny Trillo, Infielder Julio Franco, Pitcher Jay Baller and Catcher Gerry Willard to Cleveland Indians for Outfielder Von Hayes, December 9, 1982.

DIVISION SERIES RECORD

Year—Club	League	Pos.	G.	AB.	R.	H.	2B.	3B.	HR.	RBI.	B.A.	PO.	A.	E.	F.A.
1981—Philadelphia	Nat.	PH-OF	5	9	1	4	0	0	1	2	.444	6	0	0	1.000

CHAMPIONSHIP SERIES RECORD

Year—Club	League	Pos.	G.	AB.	R.	H.	2B.	3B.	HR.	RBI.	B.A.	PO.	A.	E.	F.A.
1980—Philadelphia	Nat.	OF-PH	4	3	0	0	0	0	0	0	.000	0	0	0	.000

THOMAS DAVID WADDELL
(Tom)

Born September 17, 1958, at Dundee, Scotland.
Height, 6.01. Weight, 185.
Throws and bats righthanded.
Received degree from Manhattan College, Bronx, N.Y.

Year—Club	League	G.	IP.	W.	L.	Pct.	H.	R.	ER.	SO.	BB.	ERA.
1981—Bradenton Braves	Gulf Coast	2	10	0	1	.000	5	2	1	7	1	0.90
1981—Anderson	S. Atlantic	13	63	6	3	.667	57	24	20	51	12	2.86
1982—Anderson	S. Atlantic	4	9⅓	0	0	.000	9	5	5	13	6	4.82
1982—Durham	Carol.	42	74⅓	5	3	.625	44	20	12	102	26	1.45
1983—Savannah†	Southern	29	44⅓	8	2	.800	32	11	7	40	13	1.42
1983—Richmond‡	Int'national	13	24⅔	5	0	1.000	26	12	12	29	6	4.38

Signed as free agent by Atlanta Braves' organization, April 1, 1981.

†On disabled list, May 17 to May 31, 1983.

‡Drafted by Cleveland Indians, December 5, 1983.

MARK DUANE WAGNER

Born March 4, 1954, at Conneaut, O.
Height, 6.01. Weight, 175.
Throws and bats righthanded.

Year Club	League	Pos.	G.	AB.	R.	H.	2B.	3B.	HR.	RBI.	B.A.	PO.	A.	E.	F.A.
1972—Bristol	Appal.	2B-SS-3B	56	196	35	40	5	2	2	13	.204	106	142	19	.929
1973—Clinton	Midw.	SS	122	451	51	125	16	1	1	48	.277	169	★348	34	.938
1974—Lakeland†	Fla. St.	SS	23	77	12	21	1	1	0	10	.273	27	70	9	.915
1975—Clinton	Midw.	SS	119	436	52	111	11	4	1	50	.255	★175	339	31	★.943
1976—Evansville	A. A.	SS	107	304	32	79	9	5	1	22	.260	148	297	★36	.925
1976—Detroit	Amer.	SS	39	115	9	30	2	3	0	12	.261	60	135	11	.947
1977—Evansville	A. A.	SS	64	222	33	68	12	6	3	27	.306	97	189	13	.957
1977—Detroit	Amer.	SS-2B	22	48	4	7	0	1	1	3	.146	15	58	6	.924
1978—Detroit	Amer.	SS-2B	39	109	10	26	1	2	0	6	.239	57	81	5	.965
1979—Detroit	Amer.	SS-2B-3B	75	146	16	40	3	0	1	13	.274	88	146	8	.967
1980—Detroit‡§	Amer.	SS-3B-2B	45	72	5	17	1	0	0	3	.236	43	61	7	.937
1981—Texas	Amer.	SS-2B-3B	50	85	15	22	4	1	1	14	.259	54	87	5	.966
1982—Texas x	Amer.	SS	60	179	14	43	4	1	0	8	.240	77	197	13	.955
1983—Texas yz	Amer.	SS	2	2	0	0	0	0	0	0	.000	2	4	0	1.000
1983—Evansville a	A. A.	SS-3B	36	106	8	22	2	1	0	5	.208	66	79	8	.948
Major League Totals			332	756	73	185	15	8	3	59	.245	396	769	55	.955

Selected by Detroit Tigers' organization in 19th round of free-agent draft, June 6, 1972.
†On disabled list, May 10, 1974 through remainder of season.
‡On supplemental disabled list, May 28 to June 18, 1980.
§Traded to Texas Rangers for Pitcher Kevin Saucier, December 10, 1980.
xOn supplemental disabled list, July 20 to October 1, 1982.
yOn supplemental disabled list, April 2 to April 22, 1983.
zLoaned to Evansville (Detroit Tigers' organization), June 24, 1983; returned, September 2, 1983.
aGranted free agency, November 7, 1983.

MICHAEL RICHARD WAITS
(Rick)

Born May 15, 1952, at Atlanta, Ga.
Height, 6.03. Weight, 195.
Throws left and bats left and righthanded.
Attended Clayton Junior College and Atlanta Baptist College, Chamblee, Ga.

Tied for Eastern League lead in balks with 2 in 1971.

Year Club	League	G.	IP.	W.	L.	Pct.	H.	R.	ER.	SO.	BB.	ERA.
1970—Anderson	W. Carol.	9	42	2	3	.400	27	25	22	37	33	4.71
1971—Pittsfield	Eastern	25	139	5	9	.357	123	65	50	98	82	3.24
1972—Pittsfield	Eastern	25	116	8	8	.500	104	66	40	84	82	3.10
1973—Spokane	P. Coast	28	154	14	7	.667	153	96	67	99	103	3.92
1973—Texas	American	1	1	0	0	.000	1	1	1	0	1	9.00
1974—Spokane	P. Coast	26	153	12	6	.667	152	98	75	90	95	4.41
1975—Spokane†	P. Coast	11	67	5	4	.556	76	46	36	38	37	4.84
1975—Oklahoma City	Am. Assoc.	9	53	1	5	.167	55	29	26	31	27	4.42
1975—Cleveland	American	16	70	6	2	.750	57	25	23	34	25	2.96
1976—Cleveland‡	American	26	124	7	9	.438	143	60	55	65	54	3.99
1977—Cleveland	American	37	135	9	7	.563	132	67	60	62	64	4.00
1978—Cleveland	American	34	230	13	15	.464	206	97	82	97	86	3.21
1979—Cleveland	American	34	231	16	13	.552	230	123	114	91	91	4.44
1980—Cleveland	American	33	224	13	14	.481	231	118	111	109	82	4.46
1981—Cleveland§	American	22	126	8	10	.444	173	74	69	51	44	4.93
1982—Cleveland	American	25	115	2	13	.133	128	74	69	44	57	5.40
1983—Cleveland x-Milwaukee y	American	18	49⅔	0	3	.000	62	33	27	33	20	4.89
Major League Totals		246	1305⅔	74	86	.463	1363	672	611	586	524	4.21

Selected by Washington Senators' organization in 5th round of free-agent draft, June 4, 1970.
†Traded with Pitchers Jim Bibby and Jackie Brown and an estimated $100,000 to Cleveland Indians for Pitcher Gaylord Perry, June 12, 1975.
‡On disabled list, April 30 to May 29, 1976.
§Granted free agency, November 13, 1981; re-signed by Indians, January 15, 1982.
xTraded with Outfielder Rick Manning to Milwaukee Brewers for Outfielder Gorman Thomas and Pitchers Jamie Easterly and Ernie Camacho, June 6, 1983.
yOn disabled list, July 11 to September 1, 1983.

ROBERT VERNON WALK
(Bob)

Born November 26, 1956, at Van Nuys, Calif.
Height, 6.03. Weight, 200.
Throws and bats righthanded.
Attended College of the Canyons, Valencia, Calif.

Led International League in complete games with 11 and tied for lead in games started by pitchers with 28 and home runs allowed with 22 in 1983.
Led Carolina League in hit batsmen with 13 in 1978.

Year Club	League	G.	IP.	W.	L.	Pct.	H.	R.	ER.	SO.	BB.	ERA.
1977—Spartanburg	W. Carol.	15	99	6	9	.400	90	55	40	66	46	3.64
1977—Peninsula	Carolina	8	36	0	2	.000	44	31	17	23	20	4.25

Year Club	League	G.	IP.	W.	L.	Pct.	H.	R.	ER.	SO.	BB.	ERA.
1978—Peninsula	Carolina	26	187	13	8	.619	147	58	44	150	64	2.12
1979—Reading	Eastern	24	185	12	7	.632	156	62	46	*135	77	*2.24
1980—Oklahoma City	Am. Assoc.	8	49	5	1	.833	39	21	16	36	17	2.94
1980—Philadelphia†	National	27	152	11	7	.611	163	82	77	94	71	4.56
1981—Atlanta‡	National	12	43	1	4	.200	41	25	22	16	23	4.60
1981—Richmond	Int'national	4	22	2	1	.667	18	7	6	13	11	2.45
1982—Atlanta	National	32	164⅓	11	9	.550	179	101	89	84	59	4.87
1983—Richmond	Int'national	28	*185	11	12	.478	179	*119	*107	123	102	5.21
1983—Atlanta	National	1	3⅔	0	0	.000	7	3	3	4	2	7.36
Major League Totals		72	342	23	20	.535	390	211	191	198	155	5.03

Selected by California Angels' organization in 5th round of free-agent draft, January 9, 1975.
Selected by Philadelphia Phillies' organization in 5th round of free-agent draft, January 7, 1976.
Selected by Philadelphia Phillies' organization in secondary phase of free-agent draft, June 8, 1976.
†Traded to Atlanta Braves for Outfielder Gary Matthews, March 25, 1981.
‡On disabled list, May 26 to August 9, 1981.

CHAMPIONSHIP SERIES RECORD

Year Club	League	G.	IP.	W.	L.	Pct.	H.	R.	ER.	SO.	BB.	ERA.
1982—Atlanta	National	1	1	0	0	.000	3	1	1	1	1	9.00

WORLD SERIES RECORD

Year Club	League	G.	IP.	W.	L.	Pct.	H.	R.	ER.	SO.	BB.	ERA.
1980—Philadelphia	National	1	7	1	0	1.000	8	6	6	3	3	7.71

CLEOTHA WALKER
(Chico)

Born November 25, 1957, at Jackson, Miss.
Height, 5.09. Weight, 170.
Throws right and bats left and righthanded.

Led Eastern League in caught stealing with 16 in 1979.
Tied for International League lead in double plays by second basemen with 74 in 1980.

Year—Club	League	Pos.	G.	AB.	R.	H.	2B.	3B.	HR.	RBI.	B.A.	PO.	A.	E.	F.A.
1976—Elmira	NYP	2B	22	28	9	5	1	2	0	1	.179	9	18	3	.900
1977—Elmira	NYP	2B-SS	64	227	26	50	4	3	1	14	.220	122	196	15	.955
1978—Winter Haven	Fla. St.	SS-3B-2B	133	480	66	134	10	6	3	52	.279	172	380	42	.929
1979—Bristol†	East.	2B	123	498	75	132	19	*12	8	57	.265	252	357	23	.964
1980—Pawtucket	Int.	2B	139	536	59	146	18	7	8	52	.272	252	*394	*21	.969
1980—Boston	Amer.	2B	19	57	3	12	0	0	1	5	.211	15	31	2	.958
1981—Pawtucket	Int.	OF-2B-3B	138	535	50	148	21	5	17	68	.277	209	178	13	.968
1981—Boston	Amer.	2B	6	17	3	6	0	0	0	2	.353	4	10	0	1.000
1982—Pawtucket	Int.	O-2-3-S	133	494	71	124	22	2	15	66	.251	209	48	11	.959
1983—Pawtucket	Int.	3-O-S-2	125	442	78	119	18	1	18	56	.269	122	126	16	.939
1983—Boston	Amer.	OF	4	5	2	2	0	2	0	1	.400	4	1	0	1.000
Major League Totals			29	79	8	20	0	2	1	8	.253	23	42	2	.970

Selected by Boston Red Sox' organization in 22nd round of free-agent draft, June 8, 1976.
†On disabled list, August 22 to September 19, 1979.

DUANE ALLEN WALKER

Born March 13, 1957, at Pasadena, Tex.
Height, 6.00. Weight, 180.
Throws and bats lefthanded.
Attended San Jacinto College, Pasadena, Tex.

Year—Club	League	Pos.	G.	AB.	R.	H.	2B.	3B.	HR.	RBI.	B.A.	PO.	A.	E.	F.A.
1976—Tampa	Fla. St.	OF	29	91	9	19	1	0	0	3	.209	36	5	2	.953
1976—Eugene	N'west.	OF	46	172	41	49	11	5	10	24	.285	51	5	3	.949
1977—Tampa	Fla. St.	OF	122	466	67	116	13	7	2	37	.249	180	12	3	.985
1978—Nashville	South.	OF	103	288	38	69	15	3	2	31	.240	133	7	5	.966
1979—Nashville	South.	OF	143	545	97	165	28	*15	9	57	.303	237	9	12	.953
1980—Indianapolis	A. A.	OF	109	351	41	87	16	4	6	30	.248	169	14	9	.953
1981—Indianapolis	A. A.	OF	130	450	80	127	22	1	19	80	.282	213	3	6	.973
1982—Indianapolis	A. A.	OF	36	115	21	33	6	1	4	19	.287	68	3	2	.973
1982—Cincinnati	Nat.	OF	86	239	26	52	10	0	5	22	.218	110	7	1	.992
1983—Cincinnati	Nat.	OF	109	225	14	53	12	1	2	29	.236	104	4	5	.956
Major League Totals			195	464	40	105	22	1	7	51	.226	214	11	6	.974

Selected by San Francisco Giants' organization in 34th round of free-agent draft, June 4, 1975.
Selected by Cincinnati Reds' organization in secondary phase of free-agent draft, January 7, 1976.

GREGORY LEE WALKER
(Greg)

Born October 6, 1959, at Douglas, Ga.
Height, 6.03. Weight, 210.
Throws right and bats lefthanded.

Led Midwest League first basemen in double plays with 108 in 1980.

Year Club	League	Pos.	G.	AB.	R.	H.	2B.	3B.	HR.	RBI.	B.A.	PO.	A.	E.	F.A.
1977—Auburn†	NYP	1B	33	98	12	25	1	2	2	8	.255	5	0	0	1.000
1978—Spartanburg.........	W. Car.	1B-3B-C	100	341	51	71	16	2	11	47	.208	538	50	13	.978
1979—Peninsula‡...........	Carol.	1B	122	446	59	125	*27	4	10	61	.280	973	53	19	.982
1980—Appleton	Midw.	1B	135	464	88	130	20	3	21	*98	.280	*1298	*88	10	*.993
1981—Glens Falls	East.	1B	135	508	*117	*163	*33	2	22	86	.321	*1215	77	11	.992
1982—Edmonton§..........	P. C.	1B	35	117	18	41	8	0	3	12	.350	94	11	0	1.000
1982—Chicago	Amer.	DH	11	17	3	7	2	1	2	7	.412	0	0	0	.000
1983—Chicago	Amer.	1B	118	307	32	83	16	3	10	55	.270	426	19	7	.985
Major League Totals..................................			129	324	35	90	18	4	12	62	.278	426	19	7	.985

Selected by Philadelphia Phillies' organization in 20th round of free-agent draft, June 7, 1977.
†On disabled list, June 21 to September 30, 1977.
‡Drafted by Iowa (Chicago White Sox' organization), December 4, 1979.
§On disabled list, April 23 to July 27, 1982.

CHAMPIONSHIP SERIES RECORD

Year Club	League	Pos.	G.	AB.	R.	H.	2B.	3B.	HR.	RBI.	B.A.	PO.	A.	E.	F.A.
1983—Chicago	Amer.	PH-1B	2	3	0	1	0	0	0	0	.333	7	1	0	1.000

MICHAEL GLEN WALKER
(Known by middle name.)

Born January 31, 1958, at Los Angeles, Calif.
Height, 6.00. Weight, 195.
Throws and bats righthanded.
Attended Green River Community College, Auburn, Wash., and
Washington State University, Pullman, Wash.

Tied for Pacific Coast League lead in assists by outfielders with 18 in 1983.
Led Midwest League in total bases with 251, slugging percentage with .569 and game-winning RBIs with 13 in 1981.
Led Northwest League outfielders in double plays with 6 in 1980.

Year Club	League	Pos.	G.	AB.	R.	H.	2B.	3B.	HR.	RBI.	B.A.	PO.	A.	E.	F.A.
1980—Bellingham	N'west	OF-2B	70	285	49	86	20	2	15	65	.302	109	17	4	.969
1981—Wausau..................	Midw.	*OF-2B	119	441	80	125	21	0	*35	*111	.283	148	*14	3	.982
1982—Lynn........................	East.	OF	68	255	40	82	12	1	11	55	.322	43	1	0	1.000
1982—Salt Lake City.......	P. C.	OF	44	142	23	43	6	1	9	30	.303	52	2	5	.915
1983—Salt Lake City.......	P. C.	OF-3B	124	481	68	126	28	4	15	86	.262	184	31	14	.939

Selected by Seattle Mariners' organization in 11th round of free-agent draft, June 3, 1980.

TIMOTHY CHARLES WALLACH
(Tim)

Born September 14, 1957, at Huntington Park, Calif.
Height, 6.03. Weight, 220.
Throws and bats righthanded.
Attended Saddleback Junior College, Mission Viejo, Calif., and
California State University at Fullerton, Fullerton, Calif.

Tied major league record by hitting home run in first major league at-bat, September 6, 1980.
Led American Association in total bases with 295, game-winning RBIs with 16 and tied for lead in sacrifice flies with 9 in 1980.
Named College Player of the Year by THE SPORTING NEWS, 1979.
Received reported $90,000 bonus to sign with Montreal Expos, 1979.

Year Club	League	Pos.	G.	AB.	R.	H.	2B.	3B.	HR.	RBI.	B.A.	PO.	A.	E.	F.A.
1979—Memphis................	South.	1B-3B	75	257	50	84	16	4	18	51	.327	290	35	4	.988
1980—Denver	A. A.	3B-OF-1B	134	512	103	144	29	7	36	124	.281	222	147	21	.946
1980—Montreal	Nat.	OF-1B	5	11	1	2	0	0	1	2	.182	12	0	0	1.000
1981—Montreal	Nat.	OF-1B-3B	71	212	19	50	9	1	4	13	.236	207	31	1	.996
1982—Montreal	Nat.	*3-O-1	158	596	89	160	31	3	28	97	.268	*132	287	23	.948
1983—Montreal	Nat.	3B	156	581	54	156	33	3	19	70	.269	*151	265	19	.956
Major League Totals..................................			390	1400	163	368	73	7	52	182	.263	502	583	43	.962

Selected by California Angels' organization in 8th round of free-agent draft, June 6, 1978.
Selected by Montreal Expos' organization in 1st round (10th player selected) of free-agent draft, June 5, 1979.

DIVISION SERIES RECORD

Year Club	League	Pos.	G.	AB.	R.	H.	2B.	3B.	HR.	RBI.	B.A.	PO.	A.	E.	F.A.
1981—Montreal	Nat.	OF	4	4	1	1	1	0	0	0	.250	4	0	0	1.000

CHAMPIONSHIP SERIES RECORD

Year Club	League	Pos.	G.	AB.	R.	H.	2B.	3B.	HR.	RBI.	B.A.	PO.	A.	E.	F.A.
1981—Montreal	Nat.	PH	1	1	0	0	0	0	0	0	.000	0	0	0	.000

DENNIS MARTIN WALLING
(Denny)

Born April 17, 1954, at Neptune, N.J.
Height, 6.01. Weight, 185.
Throws right and bats lefthanded.
Attended Brookdale Community College, Lincroft, N.J., and
Clemson University, Clemson, S.C.
Brother of Gregory Walling, minor league outfielder, 1967.

Year Club	League	Pos.	G.	AB.	R.	H.	2B.	3B.	HR.	RBI.	B.A.	PO.	A.	E.	F.A.
1975—Oakland..................	Amer.	OF	6	8	0	1	1	0	0	2	.125	3	0	0	1.000
1976—Chattanooga	South.	OF	115	369	48	95	15	5	9	42	.257	241	8	2	*.992
1976—Oakland..................	Amer.	OF	3	11	1	3	0	0	0	0	.273	8	0	1	.889
1977—San Jose†‡............	P. C.	OF	3	10	1	3	0	0	0	4	.300	8	0	0	1.000
1977—Charleston.............	Int.	OF	29	89	17	31	4	1	4	14	.348	66	0	0	1.000
1977—Houston	Nat.	OF	6	21	1	6	0	1	0	6	.286	14	0	0	1.000
1978—Houston	Nat.	OF	120	247	30	62	11	3	3	36	.251	140	4	3	.980
1979—Houston	Nat.	OF	82	147	21	48	8	4	3	31	.327	65	2	1	.985
1980—Houston	Nat.	1B-OF	100	284	30	85	6	5	3	29	.299	525	31	6	.989
1981—Houston	Nat.	1B-OF	65	158	23	37	6	0	5	23	.234	226	9	2	.992
1982—Houston	Nat.	OF-1B	85	146	22	30	4	1	1	14	.205	167	11	1	.994
1983—Houston§	Nat.	1B-3B-OF	100	135	24	40	5	3	3	19	.296	134	29	6	.964
American League Totals..........................			9	19	1	4	1	0	0	2	.210	11	0	1	.917
National League Totals.............................			558	1138	151	308	40	17	18	158	.271	1271	86	19	.986
Major League Totals...........................			567	1157	152	312	41	17	18	160	.270	1282	86	20	.986

Selected by San Francisco Giants' organization in 8th round of free-agent draft, June 5, 1974.
Selected by Oakland A's organization in secondary phase of free-agent draft, June 4, 1975.
†On disabled list, April 18 to June 15, 1975.
‡Traded with cash to Houston Astros' organization for Outfielder Willie Crawford, June 15, 1977.
§Granted free agency, November 7, 1983; re-signed by Astros, December 20, 1983.

DIVISION SERIES RECORD

Year Club	League	Pos.	G.	AB.	R.	H.	2B.	3B.	HR.	RBI.	B.A.	PO.	A.	E.	F.A.
1981—Houston	Nat.	PH-1B	3	6	0	2	0	0	0	1	.333	6	1	1	.875

CHAMPIONSHIP SERIES RECORD

Year Club	League	Pos.	G.	AB.	R.	H.	2B.	3B.	HR.	RBI.	B.A.	PO.	A.	E.	F.A.
1980—Houston	Nat.	1-O-PH	3	9	2	1	0	0	0	2	.111	6	0	0	1.000

MICHAEL CHARLES WALTERS
(Mike)

Born October 18, 1957, at St. Louis, Mo.
Height, 6.05. Weight, 200.
Throws and bats righthanded.
Attended Chaffey Junior College, Alta Loma, Calif.

Year Club	League	G.	IP.	W.	L.	Pct.	H.	R.	ER.	SO.	BB.	ERA.
1977—Idaho Falls	Pioneer	7	36	2	1	.667	49	24	22	29	15	5.50
1977—Davenport	Midwest	6	39	2	2	.500	34	14	11	15	11	2.54
1978—Salinas†	California	15	102	7	3	.700	103	49	40	52	30	3.53
1979—Salinas‡	California	11	35	0	4	.000	47	34	33	17	23	8.49
1980—Redwood	California	9	49	2	2	.500	56	36	34	29	20	6.24
1980—El Paso	Texas	29	96	5	5	.500	116	59	46	46	33	4.31
1981—Salt Lake City	P. Coast	47	79	7	6	.538	83	32	25	52	23	2.85
1982—Spokane§	P. Coast	10	15	2	0	1.000	12	2	2	4	8	1.20
1982—Toledo	Int'national	41	66	4	4	.500	72	31	28	22	22	3.82
1983—Toledo	Int'national	27	46	3	0	1.000	37	10	10	29	17	1.96
1983—Minnesota.......................................	American	23	59	1	1	.500	52	31	27	21	20	4.12
Major League Totals................................		23	59	1	1	.500	52	31	27	21	20	4.12

Selected by Los Angeles Dodgers' organization in 18th round of free-agent draft, June 4, 1975.
Selected by Detroit Tigers' organization in secondary phase of free-agent draft, January 7, 1976.
Selected by Los Angeles Dodgers' organization in secondary phase of free-agent draft, June 8, 1976.
Selected by Minnesota Twins' organization in secondary phase of free-agent draft, January 11, 1977.
Selected by California Angels' organization in secondary phase of free-agent draft, June 7, 1977.
†On disabled list, July 10, 1978 through remainder of season.
‡On disabled list, April 12 to June 14, 1979.
§Traded with Outfielder Tom Brunansky and cash to Minnesota Twins for Pitcher Doug Corbett and Second Baseman Rob Wilfong, May 12, 1982.

GARY LAMELL WARD

Born December 6, 1953, at Los Angeles, Calif.
Height, 6.02. Weight, 207.
Throws and bats righthanded.

Hit for the cycle, September 18, 1980 (first game).
Led American League outfielders in double plays with 4 in 1981.
Led New York-Pennsylvania League first basemen in errors with 12 in 1973.
Tied for Midwest League lead in assists by outfielders with 18 in 1974.

Year Club	League	Pos.	G.	AB.	R.	H.	2B.	3B.	HR.	RBI.	B.A.	PO.	A.	E.	F.A.
1973—Geneva..................	NYP	1B-OF-3B	61	211	36	57	13	1	10	38	.270	336	20	14	.962
1974—Wis. Rapids	Midw.	OF-1B	126	*467	*104	122	12	5	26	78	.261	184	19	11	.949
1975—Orlando	South.	OF-C	124	438	45	117	18	5	8	71	.267	204	10	4	.982
1976—Orlando	South.	OF	132	475	50	119	17	2	9	65	.251	235	●16	●10	.962
1977—Tacoma.................	P. C.	OF-3B	125	413	62	97	15	8	8	43	.235	212	34	10	.961
1978—Toledo	Int.	*O-1-3	139	511	82	150	20	12	14	79	.294	260	6	*13	.953
1979—Toledo	Int.	OF	134	506	75	133	16	9	13	67	.263	323	12	●11	.968
1979—Minnesota.............	Amer.	DH-PH	10	14	2	4	0	0	0	1	.286	0	0	0	.000
1980—Toledo†	Int.	OF-1B	128	496	82	140	22	8	13	66	.282	269	14	8	.973

Year Club League	Pos.	G.	AB.	R.	H.	2B.	3B.	HR.	RBI.	B.A.	PO.	A.	E.	F.A.
1980—Minnesota.............. Amer.	OF	13	41	11	19	6	2	1	10	.463	14	0	0	1.000
1981—Minnesota.............. Amer.	OF	85	295	42	78	7	6	3	29	.264	185	8	5	.975
1982—Minnesota.............. Amer.	OF	152	570	85	165	33	7	28	91	.289	343	13	4	.989
1983—Minnesota‡.......... Amer.	OF	157	623	76	173	34	5	19	88	.278	374	*24	9	.978
Major League Totals...................................		417	1543	216	439	80	20	51	219	.285	916	45	18	.982

Signed as free agent by Minnesota Twins' organization, August 29, 1972.

†On disabled list, April 16 to April 26, 1980.

‡Traded to Texas Rangers for Pitchers Mike Smithson and John Butcher and Catcher Sam Sorce, December 7, 1983.

ALL-STAR GAME RECORD

Year League	Pos.	AB.	R.	H.	2B.	3B.	HR.	RBI.	B.A.	PO.	A.	E.	F.A.
1983—American	PH	1	0	0	0	0	0	0	.000	0	0	0	.000

ROY DUANE WARD

(Known by middle name.)

Born May 28, 1964, at Parkview, N.M.

Height, 6.04. Weight, 185.

Throws and bats righthanded.

Year Club League	G.	IP.	W.	L.	Pct.	H.	R.	ER.	SO.	BB.	ERA.
1982—Bradenton Braves........................ Gulf Coast	8	45⅔	2	3	.400	45	25	23	31	24	4.53
1982—Anderson .... S. Atlantic	5	23⅔	1	2	.333	24	16	14	18	15	5.32
1983—Durham.................................... Carolina	28	178⅓	11	13	.458	165	103	85	115	75	4.29

Selected by Atlanta Braves' organization in 1st round (ninth player selected) of free-agent draft, June 7, 1982.

MICHAEL BRUCE WARREN

(Mike)

Born March 26, 1961, at Inglewood, Calif.

Height, 6.01. Weight, 175.

Throws and bats righthanded.

Pitched 3-0 no-hit victory against Chicago White Sox, September 29, 1983.

Year Club League	G.	IP.	W.	L.	Pct.	H.	R.	ER.	SO.	BB.	ERA.
1979—Bristol................................. Ap'lachian	13	36	0	3	.000	32	27	16	43	40	4.00
1980—Bristol................................. Ap'lachian	12	68	2	7	.222	68	51	40	45	39	5.29
1980—Lakeland†.. Florida St.	13	52	3	6	.333	60	45	41	33	48	7.10
1981—Modesto‡.. California	22	123	9	6	.600	110	76	57	91	74	4.17
1982—Stockton§-Modesto .... California	28	195	*19	4	*.826	160	76	65	154	83	3.00
1983—Albany.. Eastern	10	72	6	2	.750	56	38	26	87	33	3.25
1983—Oakland............................... American	12	65⅔	5	3	.625	51	33	30	30	18	4.11
1983—Tacoma............................... P. Coast	11	79	6	3	.667	72	34	31	85	36	3.53
Major League Totals......................................	12	65⅔	5	3	.625	51	33	30	30	18	4.11

Selected by Detroit Tigers' organization in 12th round of free-agent draft, June 5, 1979.

†Released, April 2, 1981; signed by Modesto (Oakland A's organization), April 30, 1981.

‡Drafted by Vancouver (Milwaukee Brewers' organization) December 8, 1981.

§Traded with First Baseman John Evans to Oakland A's organization for Infielder Rob Picciolo, May 14, 1982.

CLAUDELL WASHINGTON

Born August 31, 1954, at Los Angeles, Calif.

Height, 6.00. Weight, 190.

Throws and bats lefthanded.

Brother of Don Washington, outfielder in Los Angeles Dodgers' and Oakland A's organizations, 1975 through 1977.

Hit three home runs in a game, July 14, 1979 and June 22, 1980.

Major league stolen bases: 1974 (6), 1975 (40), 1976 (37), 1977 (21), 1978 (5), 1979 (19), 1980 (21), 1981 (12), 1982 (33), 1983 (31). Total—225.

Led Midwest League in total bases with 218 in 1973.

Year Club League	Pos.	G.	AB.	R.	H.	2B.	3B.	HR.	RBI.	B.A.	PO.	A.	E.	F.A.
1972—C's Bay-N. Bend....N'west.	OF	33	111	13	31	3	2	2	15	.279	37	1	6	.864
1973—Burlington .... Midw.	OF	108	447	*92	144	25	5	13	81	.322	149	10	*15	.914
1974—Birmingham .... South.	OF	74	294	64	106	23	3	11	55	.361	116	5	13	.903
1974—Oakland.................. Amer.	OF	73	221	16	63	10	5	0	19	.285	63	2	1	.985
1975—Oakland.................. Amer.	OF	148	590	86	182	24	7	10	77	.308	305	8	7	.978
1976—Oakland†‡.............. Amer.	●OF	134	490	65	126	20	6	5	53	.257	276	10	●11	.963
1977—Texas§.................... Amer.	OF	129	521	63	148	31	2	12	68	.284	255	11	6	.978
1978—Tex. x-Chi. y .... Amer.	OF	98	356	34	90	16	5	6	33	.253	170	6	8	.957
1979—Chicago .... Amer.	OF	131	471	79	132	33	5	13	66	.280	256	7	7	.974
1980—Chicago z................ Amer.	OF	32	90	15	26	4	2	1	12	.289	41	1	3	.933
1980—New York a .... Nat.	OF	79	284	38	78	16	4	10	42	.275	123	12	3	.978
1981—Atlanta b............... Nat.	OF	85	320	37	93	22	3	5	37	.291	145	5	1	.993
1982—Atlanta .... Nat.	OF	150	563	94	150	24	6	16	80	.266	221	9	12	.950
1983—Atlanta .... Nat.	OF	134	496	75	138	24	8	9	44	.278	218	8	6	.974
American League Totals...........................		745	2739	358	767	138	32	47	328	.280	1366	45	43	.970
National League Totals.............................		448	1663	244	459	86	21	40	203	.276	707	34	22	.971
Major League Totals....................................		1193	4402	602	1226	224	*53	87	531	.279	2073	79	65	.971

Signed as free agent by Oakland A's organization, July 7, 1972.
†On disabled list, August 16 to September 1, 1976.
‡Traded to Texas Rangers for Pitcher Jim Umbarger, Infielder Rodney Scott and cash estimated at $100,000, March 26, 1977.
§On supplemental disabled list, May 27 to June 11, 1977.
xTraded with Outfielder Rusty Torres and cash to Chicago White Sox for Outfielder Bobby Bonds, May 16, 1978.
yOn supplemental disabled list, May 22 to June 16, 1978.
zTraded to New York Mets for Pitcher Jesse Anderson, June 7, 1980.
aGranted free agency, October 31, 1980; signed by Atlanta Braves, November 15, 1980.
bOn supplemental disabled list, June 5 to August 9, 1981.

CHAMPIONSHIP SERIES RECORD

Year	Club	League	Pos.	G.	AB.	R.	H.	2B.	3B.	HR.	RBI.	B.A.	PO.	A.	E.	F.A.
1974—Oakland	Amer.	OF-PH	4	11	1	3	1	0	0	0	.273	11	0	0	1.000
1975—Oakland	Amer.	OF-DH	3	12	1	3	1	0	0	1	.250	1	0	2	.333
1982—Atlanta	Nat.	OF	3	9	0	3	0	0	0	0	.333	5	1	0	1.000
Championship Series Totals			10	32	2	9	2	0	0	1	.281	17	1	2	.900

WORLD SERIES RECORD

Tied World Series record for most positions played, Series (3), 1974 (all three outfield positions).

Year	Club	League	Pos.	G.	AB.	R.	H.	2B.	3B.	HR.	RBI.	B.A.	PO.	A.	E.	F.A.
1974—Oakland	Amer.	OF-PH	5	7	1	4	0	0	0	0	.571	3	0	0	1.000

ALL-STAR GAME RECORD

Year	League	Pos.	AB.	R.	H.	2B.	3B.	HR.	RBI.	B.A.	PO.	A.	E.	F.A.
1975—American	PR-OF	1	0	1	0	0	0	0	1.000	1	0	0	1.000

RANDY LYNN WASHINGTON

Born August 17, 1963, at Stockton, Calif.
Height, 5.11. Weight, 190.
Throws and bats righthanded.

Year	Club	League	Pos.	G.	AB.	R.	H.	2B.	3B.	HR.	RBI.	B.A.	PO.	A.	E.	F.A.
1981—Batavia	NYP.	OF	66	226	41	74	11	*8	11	48	.327	107	6	8	.934
1982—Waterloo†	Midw.	OF	18	41	6	7	2	0	0	8	.171	20	1	4	.840
1982—Batavia	NYP.	OF	65	225	31	65	12	0	10	46	.289	89	5	5	.949
1983—Waterloo	Midw.	OF	127	413	66	120	24	3	19	89	.291	147	12	4	.975

Selected by Cleveland Indians' organization in 4th round of free-agent draft, June 8, 1981.
†On disabled list, April 9 to May 3, 1982.

RONALD WASHINGTON
(Ron)

Born April 29, 1952, at New Orleans, La.
Height, 5.11. Weight, 160.
Throws and bats righthanded.
Attended Manatee Junior College, Bradenton, Fla.

Year	Club	League	Pos.	G.	AB.	R.	H.	2B.	3B.	HR.	RBI.	B.A.	PO.	A.	E.	F.A.
1971—Sara. Royals†	Gulf C.	C	38	127	29	37	2	●6	1	23	.291	*213	23	3	*.987
1972—Waterloo	Midw.	C-OF-3B	76	241	37	55	3	1	1	30	.228	424	48	8	.983
1973—Waterloo	Midw.	SS	85	289	35	80	13	5	6	34	.277	130	198	29	.919
1974—San Jose‡	Calif.	2B-SS-C	109	425	49	104	16	3	2	41	.245	233	266	33	.938
1975—Jacksonville§	South.	2-3-S-1	96	267	22	61	7	1	0	20	.228	133	199	22	.938
1976—Waterbury x	East.	3B-2B	115	436	61	128	9	10	4	32	.294	170	249	26	.942
1977—San Antonio	Texas	SS	39	158	24	44	8	4	0	13	.278	78	92	12	.934
1977—Albuquerque	P. C.	SS	85	359	71	116	17	8	8	59	.323	204	250	*33	.932
1977—Los Angeles	Nat.	SS	10	19	4	7	0	0	0	1	.368	4	14	3	.857
1978—Albuquerque z	P. C.	3B	31	122	26	42	10	3	5	32	.344	23	58	8	.910
1979—Aguila	Mex.	3B	42	165	22	43	3	3	0	14	.261	35	96	10	.929
1979—Tidewater a	Int.	3B-SS	83	273	18	72	13	4	1	26	.264	77	157	13	.947
1980—Toledo	Int.	3B-2B-SS	114	407	62	117	●31	5	3	36	.287	131	268	30	.930
1981—Toledo	Int.	3B-OF-SS	138	*544	84	157	27	8	15	54	.289	130	287	26	.941
1981—Minnesota	Amer.	SS-OF	28	84	8	19	3	1	0	5	.226	64	80	8	.947
1982—Minnesota	Amer.	SS-2B-3B	119	451	48	122	17	6	5	39	.271	201	269	13	.973
1983—Minnesota	Amer.	SS-2B-3B	99	317	28	78	7	3	4	26	.246	140	246	16	.960
National League Totals			10	19	4	7	0	0	0	1	.368	4	14	3	.857
American League Totals			246	852	84	219	27	10	9	70	.257	405	595	37	.964
Major League Totals			256	871	88	226	27	10	9	71	.259	409	609	40	.962

Signed as free agent by Kansas City Royals' organization, July 17, 1970.
†On military list, September 30, 1971 through March 3, 1972.
‡On temporary inactive list, July 4 to July 25, 1974.
§On disabled list, June 19 to June 30, 1975.
xTraded to Los Angeles Dodgers' organization for Catcher Steve Patchin, November 2, 1976.
yOn temporary inactive list, April 12 to April 22, 1977.
zOn disabled list, May 12 to June 26 and July 17 to September 10, 1978.
aTraded to Minnesota Twins' organization for Infielder Wayne Caughey, March 26, 1980.

U. L. WASHINGTON

Born October 27, 1953, at Atoka, Okla.
Height, 5.11. Weight, 175.
Throws right and bats left and righthanded.
Attended Murray State College, Tishomingo, Okla.

Switch-hit home runs in one game, September 21, 1979.
Major League stolen bases: 1977 (1), 1978 (12), 1979 (10), 1980 (20), 1981 (10), 1982 (23), 1983 (40). Total—116.
Led American Association batters in strikeouts with 145 in 1975.
Led Appalachian League in sacrifice flies with 8 in 1973.
Led Appalachian League shortstops in double plays with 29 in 1973.

Year Club	League	Pos.	G.	AB.	R.	H.	2B.	3B.	HR.	RBI.	B.A.	PO.	A.	E.	F.A.
1973—Kingsport	Appal.	SS	68	244	47	69	14	4	5	51	.283	89	176	36	.880
1974—San Jose	Calif.	SS-2B	68	245	38	61	9	2	6	21	.249	81	201	34	.892
1974—Jacksonville	South.	SS	47	167	29	43	11	1	2	20	.257	71	172	17	.935
1975—Omaha	A. A.	SS	128	475	60	113	11	8	5	37	.238	195	367	★46	.924
1976—Omaha†	A. A.	SS	30	120	20	30	3	2	4	16	.250	48	102	15	.909
1977—Omaha	A. A.	★SS-2B	131	★514	82	131	13	10	2	37	.255	218	391	★48	.927
1977—Kansas City	Amer.	SS	10	20	0	4	1	1	0	1	.200	13	21	5	.872
1978—Kansas City	Amer.	SS-2B	69	129	10	34	2	1	0	9	.264	79	92	9	.950
1979—Kansas City	Amer.	SS-2B-3B	101	268	32	68	12	5	2	25	.254	174	243	18	.959
1980—Kansas City	Amer.	SS	153	549	79	150	16	11	6	53	.273	237	467	32	.957
1981—Kansas City	Amer.	SS	98	339	40	77	19	1	2	29	.227	135	297	12	.973
1982—Kansas City‡	Amer.	SS	119	437	64	125	19	3	10	60	.286	173	371	22	.961
1983—Kansas City	Amer.	SS	144	547	76	129	19	6	5	41	.236	201	448	★36	.947
Major League Totals			694	2289	301	587	88	28	25	218	.256	1012	1939	134	.957

Signed as free agent by Kansas City Royals' organization, August 4, 1972.
†On disabled list, May 21 to September 6, 1976.
‡On disabled list, May 3 to May 26, 1982.

DIVISION SERIES RECORD

Year Club	League	Pos.	G.	AB.	R.	H.	2B.	3B.	HR.	RBI.	B.A.	PO.	A.	E.	F.A.
1981—Kansas City	Amer.	SS	3	9	0	2	0	0	0	0	.222	7	11	1	.947

CHAMPIONSHIP SERIES RECORD

Year Club	League	Pos.	G.	AB.	R.	H.	2B.	3B.	HR.	RBI.	B.A.	PO.	A.	E.	F.A.
1980—Kansas City	Amer.	SS	3	11	1	4	1	0	0	1	.364	5	7	0	1.000

WORLD SERIES RECORD

Year Club	League	Pos.	G.	AB.	R.	H.	2B.	3B.	HR.	RBI.	B.A.	PO.	A.	E.	F.A.
1980—Kansas City	Amer.	SS	6	22	1	6	0	0	0	2	.273	8	20	1	.966

JOHN DAVID WATHAN

Born October 4, 1949, at Cedar Rapids, Ia.
Height, 6.02. Weight, 205.
Throws and bats righthanded.
Attended University of San Diego, San Diego, Calif., and
Mount Mercy College, Cedar Rapids, Ia.

Major League stolen bases: 1977 (2), 1978 (2), 1979 (2), 1980 (17), 1981 (11), 1982 (36), 1983 (28). Total—98.

Year Club	League	Pos.	G.	AB.	R.	H.	2B.	3B.	HR.	RBI.	B.A.	PO.	A.	E.	F.A.
1971—San Jose	Calif.	C-OF	64	215	37	56	11	2	1	29	.260	438	31	14	.971
1971—Waterloo	Midw.	C-OF-1B	43	147	31	41	4	4	3	21	.279	282	18	1	.997
1972—San Jose†	Calif.	C-1B-3B	48	148	25	40	8	0	4	15	.270	324	31	3	.992
1972—Omaha	A. A.	C	18	51	8	15	1	1	0	2	.294	94	5	1	.990
1972—Jacksonville	South.	C	16	54	6	17	3	1	0	3	.315	111	7	4	.967
1973—Jacksonville‡	South.	C-1B-3B	65	233	20	58	8	3	5	34	.249	294	28	4	.988
1974—Jacksonville	South.	1B-OF-C	120	428	63	105	14	2	7	47	.245	760	50	7	.991
1975—Omaha	A. A.	C-OF	104	360	42	109	14	4	8	46	.303	532	45	10	.983
1976—Omaha§	A. A.	C-OF	24	84	4	13	5	0	0	6	.155	128	14	4	.973
1976—Kansas City	Amer.	C-1B	27	42	5	12	1	0	0	5	.286	63	4	1	.985
1977—Kansas City	Amer.	C-1B	55	119	18	39	5	3	2	21	.328	156	9	2	.988
1978—Kansas City x	Amer.	1B-C	67	190	19	57	10	1	2	28	.300	385	28	2	.995
1979—Kansas City	Amer.	1B-OF-C	90	199	26	41	7	3	2	28	.206	336	24	3	.992
1980—Kansas City	Amer.	C-OF-1B	126	453	57	138	14	7	6	58	.305	472	33	8	.984
1981—Kansas City	Amer.	C-OF-1B	89	301	24	76	9	3	1	19	.252	316	28	7	.980
1982—Kansas City y	Amer.	C-1B	121	448	79	121	11	3	3	51	.270	482	40	10	.981
1983—Kansas City	Amer.	C-1B-OF	128	437	49	107	18	3	2	32	.245	615	58	9	.987
Major League Totals			703	2189	277	591	75	23	18	242	.270	2825	224	42	.986

Selected by Kansas City Royals' organization in 4th round of free-agent draft, January 13, 1971.
†On disabled list, May 5 to May 30, 1972.
‡On disabled list, May 25 to June 28, 1973.
§On disabled list, July 29 to September 1, 1976.
xOn supplemental disabled list, June 16, 1978; transferred to disabled list, June 29 to July 7, 1978.
yOn disabled list, July 6 to August 10, 1982.

DIVISION SERIES RECORD

Year Club	League	Pos.	G.	AB.	R.	H.	2B.	3B.	HR.	RBI.	B.A.	PO.	A.	E.	F.A.
1981—Kansas City	Amer.	C	3	10	1	3	0	0	0	0	.300	11	4	1	.938

Year Club	League	Pos.	G.	AB.	R.	H.	2B.	3B.	HR.	RBI.	B.A.	PO.	A.	E.	F.A.
1976—Kansas City..........	Amer.	C	1	0	0	0	0	0	0	0	.000	0	0	0	.000
1977—Kansas City..........	Amer.	C-1-D-PH	4	6	0	0	0	0	0	0	.000	19	0	0	1.000
1978—Kansas City..........	Amer.	1B	1	3	0	0	0	0	0	0	.000	7	0	0	1.000
1980—Kansas City..........	Amer.	OF-PH	3	6	1	0	0	0	0	0	.000	7	0	0	1.000
Championship Series Totals			9	15	1	0	0	0	0	0	.000	33	0	0	1.000

WORLD SERIES RECORD

Year Club	League	Pos.	G.	AB.	R.	H.	2B.	3B.	HR.	RBI.	B.A.	PO.	A.	E.	F.A.
1980—Kansas City..........	Amer.	PH-OF-C	3	7	1	2	0	0	0	1	.286	7	1	0	1.000

ROBERT JOSE WATSON
(Bob)

Born April 10, 1946, at Los Angeles, Calif.
Height, 6.02. Weight, 212.
Throws and bats righthanded.
Attended Los Angeles Harbor College, Wilmington, Calif.

Established major league record by hitting for the cycle in both leagues, June 24, 1977 and September 15, 1979.
Tied major league record for fewest times caught stealing, season, 150 or more games (0), 1977.
Hit for the cycle, June 24, 1977 and September 15, 1979.
Led Florida State League catchers in double plays with 14 in 1966.

Year Club	League	Pos.	G.	AB.	R.	H.	2B.	3B.	HR.	RBI.	B.A.	PO.	A.	E.	F.A.
1965—Salisbury...............	W. Car.	C	80	309	51	88	20	3	12	55	.285	476	25	15	.971
1966—Cocoa....................	Fla. St.	C-OF	105	348	56	105	21	8	10	55	.302	529	36	13	.978
1966—Houston.................	Nat.	PH	1	1	0	0	0	0	0	0	.000	0	0	0	.000
1967—Amarillo.................	Texas	*1B-OF	96	351	73	98	14	5	14	60	.279	778	41	*17	.980
1967—Oklahoma City.....	P. C.	OF-1B	41	148	18	39	4	2	5	15	.264	64	3	3	.957
1967—Houston.................	Nat.	1B	6	14	1	3	0	0	1	2	.214	21	2	1	.958
1968—Oklahoma City.....	P. C.	OF	20	76	14	30	7	2	5	16	.395	34	0	2	.944
1968—Houston†..............	Nat.	OF	45	140	13	32	7	0	2	8	.229	46	0	6	.885
1969—Savannah...............	South.	C-1B	26	96	19	25	4	0	4	10	.260	178	12	5	.974
1969—Oklahoma City.....	A. A.	C-1-O-2	61	223	41	91	14	4	7	48	.408	369	25	9	.978
1969—Houston.................	Nat.	OF-1B-C	20	40	3	11	3	0	3	3	.275	46	3	0	1.000
1970—Houston‡..............	Nat.	1B-C-OF	97	327	48	89	19	2	11	61	.272	707	40	6	.992
1971—Houston§..............	Nat.	OF-1B	129	468	49	135	17	3	9	67	.288	470	18	7	.986
1972—Houston.................	Nat.	OF-1B	147	548	74	171	27	4	16	86	.312	231	7	5	.979
1973—Houston.................	Nat.	OF-1B-C	158	573	97	179	24	3	16	94	.312	433	11	12	.974
1974—Houston.................	Nat.	OF-1B	150	524	69	156	19	4	11	67	.298	237	12	4	.984
1975—Houston.................	Nat.	1B-OF	132	485	67	157	27	1	18	85	.324	1089	70	8	.993
1976—Houston.................	Nat.	1B	157	585	76	183	31	3	16	102	.313	1395	96	15	.990
1977—Houston.................	Nat.	1B	151	554	77	160	38	6	22	110	.289	1331	*118	9	.994
1978—Houston.................	Nat.	1B	139	461	51	133	25	4	14	79	.289	974	95	9	.992
1979—Houston x..............	Nat.	1B	49	163	15	39	4	0	3	18	.239	371	33	3	.993
1979—Boston y	Amer.	1B	84	312	48	105	19	4	13	53	.337	547	47	7	.988
1980—New York.............	Amer.	1B	130	469	62	144	25	3	13	68	.307	851	63	9	.990
1981—New York z............	Amer.	1B	59	156	15	33	3	3	6	12	.212	367	25	1	.997
1982—New York a	Amer.	1B	7	17	3	4	3	0	0	3	.235	40	0	0	1.000
1982—Atlanta	Nat.	1B-OF	57	114	16	28	3	1	5	22	.246	208	8	0	1.000
1983—Atlanta	Nat.	1B	65	149	14	46	9	0	6	37	.309	280	19	5	.984
National League Totals............			1508	5146	670	1522	253	31	150	841	.296	7839	532	90	.989
American League Totals............			280	954	128	286	50	10	32	136	.300	1783	135	17	.991
Major League Totals.................			1783	6100	798	1808	303	41	182	977	.296	9622	667	107	.990

Signed as free agent by Houston Astros' organization, January 31, 1965.
†On disabled list August 3, 1968 through remainder of season.
‡On military list, August 8 to August 24, 1970.
§On military list, July 17 to August 2, 1971.
xTraded to Boston Red Sox for Pitcher Pete Ladd and a player to be named later, June 13, 1979; Houston Astros acquired Pitcher Bob Sprowl to complete deal, June 19, 1979.
yGranted free agency, November 1, 1979; signed by New York Yankees, November 8, 1979.
zOn supplemental disabled list, May 13 to June 5, 1981.
aTraded to Atlanta Braves for Pitcher Scott Patterson, April 23, 1982.

DIVISION SERIES RECORD

Year Club	League	Pos.	G.	AB.	R.	H.	2B.	3B.	HR.	RBI.	B.A.	PO.	A.	E.	F.A.
1981—New York.............	Amer.	1B	5	16	2	7	0	0	0	1	.438	36	3	1	.975

CHAMPIONSHIP SERIES RECORD

Tied Championship Series record for most two-base hits, three-game Series (3), 1980.
Established American League Championship Series record for most long hits, three-game Series (4), 1980.
Tied American League Championship Series record for highest slugging average, three-game Series (.917), 1980.

Year Club	League	Pos.	G.	AB.	R.	H.	2B.	3B.	HR.	RBI.	B.A.	PO.	A.	E.	F.A.
1980—New York.............	Amer.	1B	3	12	0	6	3	1	0	0	.500	28	5	1	.971
1981—New York.............	Amer.	1B	3	12	0	3	0	0	0	1	.250	17	0	0	1.000
Championship Series Totals			6	24	0	9	3	1	0	1	.375	45	5	1	.980

Tied World Series record for hitting home run in first Series at bat, October 20, 1981 (first inning).

Year	Club	League	Pos.	G.	AB.	R.	H.	2B.	3B.	HR.	RBI.	B.A.	PO.	A.	E.	F.A.
1981—New York		Amer.	1B	6	22	2	7	1	0	2	7	.318	51	0	0	1.000

ALL-STAR GAME RECORD

Year	League	Pos.	AB.	R.	H.	2B.	3B.	HR.	RBI.	B.A.	PO.	A.	E.	F.A.
1973—National		OF	0	0	0	0	0	0	0	.000	0	0	0	.000
1975—National		PH	1	0	0	0	0	0	0	.000	0	0	0	.000
All-Star Game Totals			1	0	0	0	0	0	0	.000	0	0	0	.000

JAMES FRANCIS WEAVER
(Jim)

Born October 10, 1959, at Kingston, N.Y.
Height, 6.03. Weight, 190.
Throws and bats lefthanded.
Attended Manatee Junior College, Bradenton, Fla., and
Florida State University, Tallahassee, Fla.

Led California League in intentional bases on balls received with 11 in 1982.
Tied for Southern League lead in double plays by outfielders with 4 in 1983.

Year	Club	League	Pos.	G.	AB.	R.	H.	2B.	3B.	HR.	RBI.	B.A.	PO.	A.	E.	F.A.
1980—Orlando		South.	OF	58	208	19	44	9	0	0	15	.212	121	3	3	.976
1981—Orlando		South.	OF	17	57	6	12	2	0	1	9	.211	21	1	2	.917
1981—Visalia		Calif.	OF	81	300	53	85	12	5	7	44	.283	110	7	4	.967
1982—Visalia		Calif.	OF	125	454	68	130	21	4	15	86	.286	261	6	9	.967
1983—Orlando		South.	OF	138	497	85	123	25	2	15	84	.247	259	20	9	.969

Selected by Montreal Expos' organization in 2nd round of free-agent draft, January 9, 1979.
Selected by Minnesota Twins' organization in 2nd round of free-agent draft, June 3, 1980.

MITCHELL DEAN WEBSTER
(Mitch)

Born May 16, 1959, at Larned, Kan.
Height, 6.01. Weight, 170.
Throws left and bats left and righthanded.

Led International League outfielders in double plays with 5 and total chances with 385 in 1982.

Year	Club	League	Pos.	G.	AB.	R.	H.	2B.	3B.	HR.	RBI.	B.A.	PO.	A.	E.	F.A.
1977—Lethbridge		Pion	OF	55	168	45	59	4	0	0	31	.351	81	3	8	.913
1978—Clinton		Midw.	OF	45	157	18	38	3	1	0	9	.242	92	6	7	.933
1978—Lethbridge		Pion.	OF	55	182	58	58	5	1	0	18	.319	77	3	0	*1.000
1979—Clinton†		Midw.	OF	123	473	95	*154	17	7	2	40	*.326	*272	10	10	.966
1980—Syracuse		Int.	OF	49	161	23	35	4	2	1	12	.217	112	3	5	.958
1980—Kinston		Carol.	OF	65	258	43	76	7	3	0	28	.295	129	8	5	.965
1981—Knoxville		South.	OF	140	554	89	163	26	6	1	42	.294	317	7	10	.970
1982—Syracuse		Int.	OF	137	513	95	144	21	7	13	68	.281	*367	16	2	*.995
1983—Syracuse		Int.	OF-1B	135	462	77	120	26	8	9	45	.260	266	16	10	.966
1983—Toronto		Amer.	OF	11	11	2	2	0	0	0	0	.182	5	0	0	1.000
Major League Totals				11	11	2	2	0	0	0	0	.182	5	0	0	1.000

Selected by Los Angeles Dodgers' organization in 23rd round of free-agent draft, June 7, 1977.
†Drafted by Syracuse (Toronto Blue Jays' organization), December 4, 1979.

WILLIAM EDWARD WEGMAN
(Bill)

Born December 19, 1962, at Cincinnati, O.
Height, 6.05. Weight, 200.
Throws and bats righthanded.

Led California League in balks with 5 and tied for lead in complete games with 15 and shutouts with 4 in 1983.

Year	Club	League	G.	IP.	W.	L.	Pct.	H.	R.	ER.	SO.	BB.	ERA.
1981—Butte		Pioneer	14	82	6	5	.545	94	51	38	47	44	4.17
1982—Beloit		Midwest	25	179⅔	12	6	.667	176	77	56	129	38	2.81
1983—Stockton		California	24	186⅔	*16	5	.762	149	33	27	135	45	*1.30

Selected by Milwaukee Brewers' organization in 5th round of free-agent draft, June 8, 1981.

ROBERT LYNN WELCH
(Bob)

Born November 3, 1956, at Detroit, Mich.
Height, 6.03. Weight, 190.
Throws and bats righthanded.
Attended Eastern Michigan University, Ypsilanti, Mich.

Year	Club	League	G.	IP.	W.	L.	Pct.	H.	R.	ER.	SO.	BB.	ERA.
1977—San Antonio		Texas	14	71	4	5	.444	94	44	35	56	17	4.44
1978—Albuquerque		P. Coast	11	69	5	1	.833	72	33	29	53	19	3.78
1978—Los Angeles		National	23	111	7	4	.636	92	28	25	66	26	2.03

Year Club	League	G.	IP.	W.	L.	Pct.	H.	R.	ER.	SO.	BB.	ERA.
1979—Los Angeles	National	25	81	5	6	.455	82	42	36	64	32	4.00
1980—Los Angeles	National	32	214	14	9	.609	190	85	78	141	79	3.28
1981—Los Angeles	National	23	141	9	5	.643	141	56	54	88	41	3.45
1982—Los Angeles†	National	36	235⅔	16	11	.593	199	94	88	176	81	3.36
1983—Los Angeles	National	31	204	15	12	.556	164	73	60	156	72	2.65
Major League Totals		170	986⅔	66	47	.584	868	378	341	691	331	3.11

Selected by Chicago Cubs' organization in 14th round of free-agent draft, June 5, 1974.
Selected by Los Angeles Dodgers' organization in 1st round (20th player selected) of free-agent draft, June 7, 1977.
†Appeared in one game as outfielder with no chances.

DIVISION SERIES RECORD

Year Club	League	G.	IP.	W.	L.	Pct.	H.	R.	ER.	SO.	BB.	ERA.
1981—Los Angeles	National	1	1	0	0	.000	0	0	0	1	1	0.00

CHAMPIONSHIP SERIES RECORD

Year Club	League	G.	IP.	W.	L.	Pct.	H.	R.	ER.	SO.	BB.	ERA.
1978—Los Angeles	National	1	4⅓	1	0	1.000	2	1	1	5	0	2.08
1981—Los Angeles	National	3	1⅔	0	0	.000	2	1	1	2	0	5.40
1983—Los Angeles	National	1	1⅓	0	1	.000	0	2	1	0	2	6.75
Championship Series Totals		5	7⅓	1	1	.500	4	4	3	7	2	3.68

WORLD SERIES RECORD

Year Club	League	G.	IP.	W.	L.	Pct.	H.	R.	ER.	SO.	BB.	ERA.
1978—Los Angeles	National	3	4⅓	0	1	.000	4	3	3	6	2	6.23
1981—Los Angeles	National	1	0	0	0	.000	3	2	2	0	1	....
World Series Totals		4	4⅓	0	1	.000	7	5	5	6	3	10.38

ALL-STAR GAME RECORD

Year League		IP.	W.	L.	Pct.	H.	R.	ER.	SO.	BB.	ERA.
1980—National		3	0	0	.000	5	2	2	4	1	6.00

DONALD RAY WELCHEL

Name pronounced WELL-chul.

(Don)

Born February 3, 1957, at Atlanta, Tex.
Height, 6.04. Weight, 205.
Throws and bats righthanded.
Attended Sam Houston State University, Huntsville, Tex.

Tied for Southern League lead in complete games with 12 in 1980.

Year Club	League	G.	IP.	W.	L.	Pct.	H.	R.	ER.	SO.	BB.	ERA.
1978—Bluefield	Ap'lachian	12	89	4	5	.444	78	30	24	57	25	2.43
1978—Miami	Florida St.	2	15	2	0	1.000	13	5	3	10	5	1.80
1979—Miami	Florida St.	14	95	5	6	.455	86	34	31	53	34	2.94
1979—Charlotte	Southern	13	86	5	4	.556	95	47	37	40	39	3.87
1980—Charlotte	Southern	28	202	9	12	.429	*210	86	65	56	47	2.90
1981—Rochester	Int'national	8	12	1	1	.500	9	5	3	7	4	2.25
1981—Charlotte	Southern	22	16	13	7	.650	161	76	52	90	63	2.91
1982—Rochester	Int'national	30	163	12	7	.632	180	91	84	82	82	4.64
1982—Baltimore	American	2	4⅓	1	0	1.000	6	6	4	3	2	8.31
1983—Baltimore	American	11	26⅔	0	2	.000	33	18	16	16	10	5.40
1983—Rochester	Int'national	18	110⅔	4	12	.250	128	65	57	61	46	4.64
Major League Totals		13	31	1	2	.333	39	24	20	19	12	5.81

Selected by Cincinnati Reds' organization in 10th round of free-agent draft, June 4, 1975.
Selected by Baltimore Orioles' organization in 7th round of free-agent draft, June 6, 1978.

BRAD EUGENE WELLMAN

Born August 17, 1959, at Lodi, Calif.
Height, 6.00. Weight, 165.
Throws and bats righthanded.

Year Club	League	Pos.	G.	AB.	R.	H.	2B.	3B.	HR.	RBI.	B.A.	PO.	A.	E.	F.A.
1979—Sarasota Royals	Gulf C.	SS	48	170	24	44	6	0	2	24	.259	79	159	20	.922
1980—Ft. Myers	Fla. St.	2B-SS	105	390	67	130	15	7	1	39	.333	175	301	27	.946
1981—Jacksonville	South	2B-SS	135	498	72	131	25	2	6	47	.263	286	368	25	.963
1982—Omaha†	A. A.	2B	6	24	5	7	3	0	1	3	.292	14	23	0	1.000
1982—Phoenix	P. C.	2B-3B	102	339	64	110	19	7	4	42	.324	201	257	14	.970
1982—San Francisco	Nat.	2B	6	4	1	1	0	0	0	0	.250	0	1	0	1.000
1983—Phoenix	P. C.	2B-SS	45	167	32	52	6	4	2	28	.311	79	123	4	.981
1983—San Francisco	Nat.	2B-SS	82	182	15	39	3	0	1	16	.214	94	167	9	.967
Major League Totals			88	186	16	40	3	0	1	16	.215	94	168	9	.967

Signed as free agent by Kansas City Royals' organization, August 27, 1978.
†Traded to San Francisco Giants' organization, April 19, 1982, completing deal in which San Francisco traded Pitchers Vida Blue and Bob Tufts to Kansas City Royals for Pitchers Atlee Hammaker, Craig Chamberlain and Renie Martin and a player to be named later, March 30, 1982.

CHRISTOPHER CHARLES WELSH
(Chris)

Born April 14, 1955, at Wilmington, Del.
Height, 6.02. Weight, 185.
Throws and bats lefthanded.
Received bachelor of arts degree in marketing from
University of South Florida, Tampa, Fla.

Led New York-Pennsylvania League in complete games with 12, shutouts with 4 and tied for lead in games started by pitchers with 14 in 1977.

Tied for Eastern League lead in wild pitches with 18 and balks with 2 in 1978.

Year Club	League	G.	IP.	W.	L.	Pct.	H.	R.	ER.	SO.	BB.	ERA.
1977—Oneonta	NYP	14	*112	8	5	.615	77	40	31	*125	54	2.49
1978—Ft. Lauderdale	Florida St.	2	15	1	1	.500	5	5	1	13	10	0.60
1978—West Haven	Eastern	24	164	11	9	.550	159	88	63	115	68	3.46
1979—Columbus	Int'national	36	114	8	4	.667	120	67	59	79	48	4.70
1980—Columbus†	Int'national	29	158	9	12	.429	134	78	48	84	68	2.73
1981—San Diego	National	22	124	6	7	.462	122	55	52	51	41	3.77
1982—San Diego‡	National	28	139⅓	8	8	.500	146	88	76	48	63	4.91
1983—San Diego§-Montreal	National	23	59	0	2	.000	59	35	29	22	20	4.42
1983—Wichita	Am. Assoc.	11	56⅔	3	6	.333	72	47	44	27	29	6.99
Major League Totals		73	322⅓	14	17	.452	327	178	157	121	124	4.38

Selected by New York Yankees' organization in 24th round of free-agent draft, June 8, 1976.
Selected by New York Yankees' organization in 21st round of free-agent draft, June 7, 1977.
†Traded with Outfielders Ruppert Jones and Joe Lefebvre and Pitcher Tim Lollar to San Diego Padres for Outfielder Jerry Mumphrey and Pitcher John Pacella, April 1, 1981.
‡On disabled list, March 23 to April 27, 1982.
§Sold to Montreal Expos, May 4, 1983.

DONALD PAUL WERNER
(Don)

Born March 8, 1953, at Appleton, Wis.
Height, 6.01. Weight, 180.
Throws and bats righthanded.

Led American Association catchers in double plays with 9 in 1979.

Year Club	League	Pos.	G.	AB.	R.	H.	2B.	3B.	HR.	RBI.	B.A.	PO.	A.	E.	F.A.
1971—Brad'ton Reds	Gulf C.	C-3B	10	21	7	7	1	1	0	5	.333	45	2	1	.979
1971—Tampa	Fla. St.	C	36	122	10	21	3	1	0	16	.172	186	22	1	.995
1972—Tampa	Fla. St.	C	116	377	42	97	8	1	1	31	.257	736	75	15	.982
1973—Three Rivers	East.	C-OF	110	284	31	57	9	1	5	34	.201	452	47	11	.978
1974—Tampa	Fla. St.	C	120	397	44	92	13	1	2	38	.232	580	71	3	*.995
1975—Indianapolis	A. A.	C	86	228	39	64	11	5	9	34	.281	423	51	7	*.985
1975—Cincinnati	Nat.	C	7	8	0	1	0	0	0	0	.125	10	2	1	.923
1976—Indianapolis	A. A.	C-1B	38	112	14	23	4	1	1	12	.205	208	28	6	.975
1976—Richmond	Int.	C-OF	49	151	19	40	1	1	2	21	.265	215	22	5	.979
1976—Cincinnati	Nat.	C	3	4	0	2	1	0	0	1	.500	7	2	0	1.000
1977—Indianapolis†	A. A.	C-1B	34	94	12	20	5	1	5	13	.213	182	23	4	.981
1977—Cincinnati	Nat.	C	10	23	3	4	0	0	2	4	.174	44	4	0	1.000
1978—Indianapolis	A. A.	C	40	125	14	30	6	1	3	22	.240	202	24	7	.970
1978—Cincinnati	Nat.	C	50	113	7	17	2	1	0	11	.150	214	21	3	.987
1979—Indianapolis	A. A.	C-1-O-3	99	260	35	66	18	3	7	36	.254	476	57	12	.978
1980—Cincinnati	Nat.	C	24	64	2	11	2	0	0	5	.172	119	6	5	.962
1980—Indianapolis‡	A. A.	C-1B-3B	65	219	32	60	10	2	6	35	.274	355	25	8	.979
1981—Wichita	A. A.	C-1B	83	246	23	67	13	1	4	26	.272	336	29	4	.989
1981—Texas	Amer.	DH	2	8	1	2	0	0	0	0	.250	0	0	0	.000
1982—Denver	A. A.	C	8	16	2	7	2	0	1	2	.438	41	4	1	.978
1982—Texas	Amer.	C	22	59	4	12	2	0	0	3	.203	91	5	2	.980
1983—Oklahoma City§x	A. A.	C-OF-3B	76	232	39	67	14	1	6	38	.289	241	20	6	.978
National League Totals			94	212	12	35	5	1	2	21	.165	390	35	9	.979
American League Totals			24	67	5	14	2	0	0	3	.209	91	5	2	.980
Major League Totals			118	279	17	49	7	1	2	24	.176	481	40	11	.979

Selected by Cincinnati Reds' organization in 5th round of free-agent draft, June 8, 1971.
†On disabled list, May 3 to July 27, 1977.
‡Traded to Texas Rangers' organization for Catcher Greg Mahlberg, December 16, 1980.
§On suspended list, April 15 to April 26, 1983.
xGranted free agency, October 20, 1983; signed by Kansas City Royals, December 9, 1983.

STEFAN MATTHEW WEVER

Name pronounced WE-ver.
Born April 22, 1958, at Marburg, West Germany.
Height, 6.08. Weight, 245.
Throws and bats righthanded.
Attended University of California at Santa Barbara, Santa
Barbara, Calif., and University of California, Berkeley, Calif.

Led Florida State League in balks with 7 in 1980.
Named Southern League Pitcher of the Year, 1982.

Year Club	League	G.	IP.	W.	L.	Pct.	H.	R.	ER.	SO.	BB.	ERA.
1979—Oneonta	NYP	10	66	6	3	.667	43	24	13	70	36	★1.77
1980—Ft. Lauderdale†	Florida St.	15	94	7	3	.700	70	44	38	67	54	3.64
1981—Ft. Lauderdale	Florida St.	12	81	7	3	.700	55	25	18	80	29	2.00
1981—Nashville‡	Southern	9	66	5	2	.714	54	22	15	39	30	2.05
1982—Nashville	Southern	29	214	●16	6	.727	176	75	66	★191	80	★2.78
1982—New York	American	1	2⅔	0	1	.000	6	9	8	2	3	27.00
1983—Columbus§	Int'national	7	23	1	4	.200	32	27	25	10	19	9.78
Major League Totals		1	2⅔	0	1	.000	6	9	8	2	3	27.00

Selected by New York Yankees' organization in 6th round of free-agent draft, June 5, 1979.
†On disabled list, June 14 to July 13, 1980.
‡On disabled list, July 2 to July 23, 1981.
§On disabled list, May 20, 1983 through remainder of season.

LOUIS RODMAN WHITAKER
(Lou)

Born May 12, 1957, at Brooklyn, N.Y.
Height, 5.11. Weight, 160.
Throws right and bats lefthanded.

Led American League second basemen in total chances with 811 and double plays with 120 in 1982.
Led Florida State League second basemen in double plays with 30 in 1976.
Named second baseman on THE SPORTING NEWS American League All-Star Team, 1983.
Named second baseman on THE SPORTING NEWS American League All-Star fielding team, 1983.
Named second baseman on THE SPORTING NEWS American League Silver Slugger team, 1983.
Named American League Rookie of the Year by Baseball Writers' Association of America, 1978.
Named Florida State League Most Valuable Player, 1976.

Year Club	League	Pos.	G.	AB.	R.	H.	2B.	3B.	HR.	RBI.	B.A.	PO.	A.	E.	F.A.
1975—Bristol	Appal.	3B-SS	42	114	17	27	6	1	1	17	.237	38	82	16	.882
1976—Lakeland	Fla. St.	3B	124	343	★70	129	12	5	1	62	.297	★99	★267	★30	★.924
1977—Montgomery†	South.	2B	107	396	★81	111	13	4	3	48	.280	208	285	15	.970
1977—Detroit	Amer.	2B	11	32	5	8	1	0	0	2	.250	17	18	0	1.000
1978—Detroit	Amer.	2B	139	484	71	138	12	7	3	58	.285	301	458	17	.978
1979—Detroit‡	Amer.	2B	127	423	75	121	14	8	3	42	.286	280	369	9	.986
1980—Detroit	Amer.	2B	145	477	68	111	19	1	1	45	.233	340	428	12	.985
1981—Detroit	Amer.	2B	109	335	48	88	14	4	5	36	.263	227	★354	9	.985
1982—Detroit	Amer.	2B	152	560	76	160	22	8	15	65	.286	331	★470	10	★.988
1983—Detroit	Amer.	2B	161	643	94	206	40	6	12	72	.320	299	447	13	.983
Major League Totals			844	2954	437	832	122	34	39	320	.282	1595	2544	70	.983

Selected by Detroit Tigers' organization in 5th round of free-agent draft, June 4, 1975.
†On disabled list, May 3 to May 14, 1977.
‡On supplemental disabled list, June 13 to June 28, 1979.

ALL-STAR GAME RECORD

Year League	Pos.	AB.	R.	H.	2B.	3B.	HR.	RBI.	B.A.	PO.	A.	E.	F.A.
1983—American	PH-2B	1	1	1	0	1	0	2	1.000	1	0	0	1.000

FRANK WHITE JR.

Born September 4, 1950, at Greenville, Miss.
Height, 5.11. Weight, 170.
Throws and bats righthanded.

Hit for the cycle, September 26, 1979 and August 3, 1982.
Led Gulf Coast League in stolen bases with 18 in 1971.
Led Gulf Coast League shortstops in double plays with 27 in 1971.
Named second baseman on THE SPORTING NEWS American League All-Star Team, 1978.
Named second baseman on THE SPORTING NEWS American League All-Star fielding team, 1977 through 1982.

Year Club	League	Pos.	G.	AB.	R.	H.	2B.	3B.	HR.	RBI.	B.A.	PO.	A.	E.	F.A.
1971—Sara. Royals	Gulf C.	SS	50	158	31	39	6	3	1	21	.247	70	★149	17	★.928
1972—San Jose	Calif.	SS	49	187	44	55	7	2	10	26	.294	77	138	14	.939
1972—Jacksonville	South.	SS	91	333	34	84	12	2	2	23	.252	124	306	31	.933
1973—Omaha	A. A.	2B-SS	86	348	49	92	19	2	4	32	.264	163	221	21	.948
1973—Kansas City	Amer.	SS-2B	51	139	20	31	6	1	0	5	.223	71	121	12	.941
1974—Kansas City	Amer.	2B-SS-3B	99	204	19	45	6	3	1	18	.221	119	189	12	.963
1975—Kansas City	Amer.	2-S-3-C	111	304	43	76	10	2	7	36	.250	182	275	12	.974
1976—Kansas City	Amer.	2B-SS	152	446	39	102	17	6	2	46	.229	296	479	23	.971
1977—Kansas City	Amer.	★2B-SS	152	474	59	116	21	5	5	20	.245	310	437	8	★.989
1978—Kansas City	Amer.	2B	143	461	66	127	24	6	7	50	.275	325	385	16	.978
1979—Kansas City†	Amer.	2B	127	467	73	124	26	4	10	48	.266	317	332	12	.982
1980—Kansas City	Amer.	2B	154	560	70	148	23	4	7	60	.264	395	448	10	.988
1981—Kansas City	Amer.	2B	94	364	35	91	17	1	9	38	.250	226	263	6	.988
1982—Kansas City	Amer.	2B	145	524	71	156	45	6	11	56	.298	★361	389	★17	.978
1983—Kansas City	Amer.	2B	146	549	52	143	35	6	11	77	.260	★390	442	8	★.990
Major League Totals			1374	4492	547	1159	230	44	70	484	.258	2992	3760	136	.980

Signed as free agent by Kansas City Royals' organization, July 2, 1970.
†On supplemental disabled list, May 9, 1979; transferred to disabled list, June 10 to June 11, 1979.

DIVISION SERIES RECORD

Year Club	League	Pos.	G.	AB.	R.	H.	2B.	3B.	HR.	RBI.	B.A.	PO.	A.	E.	F.A.
1981—Kansas City	Amer.	2B	3	11	1	2	0	0	0	0	.182	5	6	1	.917

CHAMPIONSHIP SERIES RECORD

Year Club	League	Pos.	G.	AB.	R.	H.	2B.	3B.	HR.	RBI.	B.A.	PO.	A.	E.	F.A.
1976—Kansas City..........	Amer.	2B-PR	4	8	2	1	0	0	0	0	.125	6	11	0	1.000
1977—Kansas City..........	Amer.	2B	5	18	1	5	1	0	0	2	.278	13	16	0	1.000
1978—Kansas City..........	Amer.	2B	4	13	1	3	0	0	0	2	.231	9	12	0	1.000
1980—Kansas City..........	Amer.	2B	3	11	3	6	1	0	1	3	.545	9	10	1	.950
Championship Series Totals			16	50	7	15	2	0	1	7	.300	37	49	1	.989

WORLD SERIES RECORD

Tied World Series records for fewest runs, Series (0), 1980; most at-bats, nine-inning game, no hits (5), October 18, 1980; Most unassisted double plays by second baseman, game (1), October 17, 1980.

Year Club	League	Pos.	G.	AB.	R.	H.	2B.	3B.	HR.	RBI.	B.A.	PO.	A.	E.	F.A.
1980—Kansas City..........	Amer.	2B	6	25	0	2	0	0	0	0	.080	13	21	2	.944

ALL-STAR GAME RECORD

Year League	Pos.	AB.	R.	H.	2B.	3B.	HR.	RBI.	B.A.	PO.	A.	E.	F.A.
1978—American	2B	1	0	0	0	0	0	0	.000	1	2	0	1.000
1979—American	2B	2	0	0	0	0	0	0	.000	2	2	0	1.000
1981—American	PR-2B	1	0	0	0	0	0	0	.000	1	0	0	1.000
1982—American	2B	1	0	0	0	0	0	0	.000	2	1	0	1.000
All-Star Game Totals		5	0	0	0	0	0	0	.000	6	5	0	1.000

JEROME CARDELL WHITE
(Jerry)

Born August 23, 1952, at Shirley, Mass.
Height, 5.11. Weight, 172.
Throws right and bats left and righthanded.
Attended City College of San Francisco, San Francisco, Calif.

Year Club	League	Pos.	G.	AB.	R.	H.	2B.	3B.	HR.	RBI.	B.A.	PO.	A.	E.	F.A.
1970—Bradenton Expos	Gulf C.	OF	55	201	32	58	10	2	1	16	.289	102	5	5	.955
1971—W. Palm Beach....	Fla. St.	OF	130	505	71	132	17	4	2	32	.261	222	4	●13	.946
1972—Quebec City†	East.	OF	26	56	4	13	1	0	0	2	.232	46	1	0	1.000
1972—W. Palm Beach....	Fla. St.	OF	27	96	13	28	1	1	1	13	.292	63	1	2	.970
1973—Peninsula‡	Int.	OF	112	360	50	99	10	6	1	30	.275	182	7	5	.974
1974—Quebec City..........	East.	OF	21	69	13	17	2	2	0	5	.246	35	2	1	.974
1974—Memphis..............	Int.	OF	77	175	28	45	6	2	3	17	.257	87	5	1	.989
1974—Montreal..............	Nat.	OF	9	10	0	4	1	1	0	2	.400	6	0	0	1.000
1975—Memphis..............	Int.	OF	98	354	44	105	16	5	10	45	.297	223	6	6	.974
1975—Montreal..............	Nat.	OF	39	97	14	29	4	1	2	7	.299	81	1	2	.976
1976—Montreal..............	Nat.	OF	114	278	32	68	11	1	2	21	.245	157	4	3	.982
1977—Denver	A. A.	OF-1B	123	463	92	145	32	9	14	57	.313	235	7	6	.976
1977—Montreal..............	Nat.	OF	16	21	4	4	0	0	1	1	.190	5	0	0	1.000
1978—Denver	A. A.	OF	27	100	22	29	4	0	5	19	.290	53	0	1	.981
1978—Chi.§-Mtl. x	Nat.	OF	77	146	24	39	6	0	1	10	.267	102	4	2	.981
1979—Montreal..............	Nat.	OF	88	138	30	41	7	1	3	18	.297	55	2	1	.983
1980—Montreal..............	Nat.	OF	110	214	22	56	9	3	7	23	.262	101	5	6	.946
1981—Montreal..............	Nat.	OF	59	119	11	26	5	1	3	11	.218	58	2	3	.952
1982—Montreal y............	Nat.	OF	69	115	13	28	6	1	2	13	.243	40	1	0	1.000
1983—Montreal z............	Nat.	OF	40	34	4	5	1	0	0	0	.147	13	0	0	1.000
1983—Wichita z..............	Int.	OF	32	101	18	25	7	2	1	8	.248	45	2	0	1.000
Major League Totals.....................................			621	1170	154	300	50	9	20	106	256	618	19	17	.974

Selected by Montreal Expos' organization in 14th round of free-agent draft, June 4, 1970.
†On temporary inactive list, April 22 to June 24, 1972.
‡On temporary inactive list, July 28 to August 14, 1973.
§Traded to Chicago Cubs, June 23, 1978, completing deal in which Chicago traded Pitcher Woodie Fryman to Montreal Expos for a player to be named later, June 9, 1978.
xTraded with Infielder-Outfielder Rodney Scott to Montreal Expos for Outfielder Sam Mejias, December 14, 1978.
yOn supplemental disabled list, June 30 to July 15, 1982.
zGranted free agency, November 7, 1983.

DIVISION SERIES RECORD

Year Club	League	Pos.	G.	AB.	R.	H.	2B.	3B.	HR.	RBI.	B.A.	PO.	A.	E.	F.A.
1981—Montreal	Nat.	OF	5	18	3	3	1	0	0	1	.167	11	0	0	1.000

CHAMPIONSHIP SERIES RECORD

Year Club	League	Pos.	G.	AB.	R.	H.	2B.	3B.	HR.	RBI.	B.A.	PO.	A.	E.	F.A.
1981—Montreal	Nat.	OF	5	16	2	5	1	0	1	3	.313	6	0	0	1.000

LARRY DAVID WHITE

Born September 25, 1958, at San Fernando, Calif.
Height, 6.04. Weight, 185.
Throws and bats righthanded.
Attended Los Angeles Pierce College, Woodland Hills, Calif., and
San Francisco State University, San Francisco, Calif.

Led Pacific Coast League in hit batsmen with 10 in 1983.
Led Southern League in balks with 5 in 1981.

Year—Club	League	G.	IP.	W.	L.	Pct.	H.	R.	ER.	SO.	BB.	ERA.
1979—Batavia	NYP	12	41	3	0	1.000	30	24	21	21	30	4.61
1979—Waterloo	Midwest	1	6	0	1	.000	4	4	1	8	2	1.50
1980—Waterloo	Midwest	26	179	15	7	.682	143	85	66	120	86	3.32
1981—Chattanooga†	Southern	27	172	10	12	.455	158	93	67	101	65	3.51
1982—Albuquerque	P. Coast	28	165	12	5	.706	168	93	81	114	81	4.42
1983—Albuquerque	P. Coast	29	184⅔	13	8	.619	201	96	77	135	93	3.75
1983—Los Angeles	National	4	7	0	0	.000	4	1	1	5	3	1.29
Major League Totals		4	7	0	0	.000	4	1	1	5	3	1.29

Selected by Oakland A's organization in 10th round of free-agent draft, January 10, 1978.
Selected by Cleveland Indians' organization in 31st round of free-agent draft, June 5, 1979.
†Traded with Outfielder Jorge Orta and Catcher Jack Fimple to Los Angeles Dodgers for Pitcher Rick Sutcliffe and Second Baseman Jack Perconte, December 9, 1981.

LEONARD JOSEPH WHITEHOUSE JR.
(Len)

Born September 10, 1957, at Burlington, Vt.
Height, 5.09. Weight, 175.
Throws and bats lefthanded.

Pitched seven-inning, 2-0 no-hit victory against Shreveport, June 22, 1979 (second game).

Year—Club	League	G.	IP.	W.	L.	Pct.	H.	R.	ER.	SO.	BB.	ERA.
1977—Asheville	W. Carol.	5	7	0	2	.000	15	15	7	3	6	9.00
1977—Sarasota Rangers	Gulf Coast	11	40	3	3	.500	45	30	20	27	21	4.50
1978—Asheville	W. Carol.	32	92	6	6	.500	89	60	44	79	57	4.30
1979—Tulsa	Texas	25	102	5	7	.417	126	75	64	79	45	5.65
1980—Tulsa	Texas	10	48	3	2	.600	52	35	29	38	22	5.44
1980—Charleston	Int'national	18	99	8	9	.471	110	62	47	64	37	4.27
1981—Wichita	Am. Assoc.	20	105	6	5	.545	106	51	45	59	39	3.86
1981—Texas	American	2	3	0	1	.000	8	7	6	2	2	18.00
1982—Denver†	Am. Assoc.	30	121⅓	4	8	.333	146	97	85	65	45	6.30
1983—Minnesota	American	60	73⅔	7	1	.875	70	34	34	44	44	4.15
Major League Totals		62	76⅔	7	2	.778	78	41	40	46	46	4.70

Signed as free agent by Texas Rangers' organization, December 25, 1976.
†Traded to Minnesota Twins for Pitcher John Pacella, November 1, 1982.

TERRY BERTLAND WHITFIELD

Born January 12, 1953, at Blythe, Calif.
Height, 6.01. Weight, 200.
Throws right and bats lefthanded.

Led International League batters in strikeouts with 129 in 1974.
Led Carolina League in total bases with 234 in 1973.
Led Appalachian League in total bases with 125 in 1971.
Tied for International League lead in double plays by outfielders with 3 in 1976.
Named Carolina League Player of the Year, 1973.
Named Appalachian League co-Player of the Year, 1971.

Year—Club	League	Pos.	G.	AB.	R.	H.	2B.	3B.	HR.	RBI.	B.A.	PO.	A.	E.	F.A.
1971—Johnson City	Appal.	OF	67	252	42	73	14	4	★10	★43	.290	104	6	●9	.924
1972—Ft. Lauderdale	Fla. St.	OF	49	153	21	25	3	5	1	15	.163	57	4	5	.924
1972—Oneonta	NYP	OF	●70	256	★65	70	6	●11	3	47	.273	120	7	3	.977
1973—Kinston	Carol.	OF	129	451	94	151	25	2	●18	81	★.335	197	9	11	.949
1974—Syracuse	Int.	OF	140	499	71	129	25	4	17	71	.259	★345	12	5	.986
1974—New York	Amer.	OF	2	5	0	1	0	0	0	0	.200	0	0	0	.000
1975—Syracuse	Int.	OF	111	390	47	106	24	4	11	69	.272	208	10	10	.956
1975—New York	Amer.	OF	28	81	9	22	1	1	0	7	.272	42	3	1	.978
1976—Syracuse	Int.	OF	●138	★525	81	152	25	6	16	89	.290	208	13	15	.936
1976—New York†	Amer.	OF	1	0	0	0	0	0	0	0	.000	0	0	0	.000
1977—San Francisco	Nat.	OF	114	326	41	93	21	3	7	36	.285	167	4	5	.972
1978—San Francisco	Nat.	OF	149	488	70	141	20	2	10	32	.289	249	7	3	.988
1979—San Francisco	Nat.	OF	133	394	52	113	20	4	5	44	.287	167	10	8	.957
1980—San Francisco‡	Nat.	OF	118	321	38	95	16	2	4	26	.296	140	11	2	.987
1981—Seibu	Pacific	OF	123	469	....	148	....	....	22	100	.316	Figures unavailable			
1982—Seibu	Pacific	OF	122	453	....	123	....	....	25	71	.272	Figures unavailable			
1983—Seibu	Pacific	OF	129	485	....	135	....	....	38	109	.278	Figures unavailable			
American League Totals			31	86	9	23	1	1	0	7	.267	42	3	1	.978
National League Totals			514	1529	201	442	77	11	26	138	.289	723	32	18	.977
Major League Totals			545	1615	210	465	78	12	26	145	.288	765	35	19	.977

Selected by New York Yankees' organization in 21st round of free-agent draft, June 8, 1971.
†Traded to San Francisco Giants for Second Baseman Marty Perez, March 14, 1977.
‡Sold to Seibu Lions of Japanese baseball, March 4, 1981.

EDDIE LEE WHITSON
(Ed)

Born May 19, 1955, at Johnson City, Tenn.
Height, 6.03. Weight, 200.
Throws and bats righthanded.

Led Carolina League in complete games with 16 in 1976.
Led Western Carolinas League in hit batsmen with 15 in 1975.

Year	Club	League	G.	IP.	W.	L.	Pct.	H.	R.	ER.	SO.	BB.	ERA.
1974—Bradenton Pirates	Gulf Coast	8	44	1	4	.200	45	28	21	25	15	4.30
1975—Charleston	W. Carol.	24	142	8	★15	.348	140	★96	★80	120	99	5.07
1976—Salem	Carolina	26	★203	●15	9	.625	168	75	57	★186	65	2.53
1977—Columbus	Int'national	26	175	8	13	.381	175	74	65	120	68	3.34
1977—Pittsburgh	National	5	16	1	0	1.000	11	6	6	10	9	3.38
1978—Columbus	Int'national	7	51	2	2	.500	56	25	21	55	10	3.71
1978—Pittsburgh	National	43	74	5	6	.455	66	31	27	64	37	3.28
1979—Pittsburgh†-San Francisco	National	37	158	7	11	.389	151	83	72	93	75	4.10
1980—San Francisco	National	34	212	11	13	.458	222	88	73	90	56	3.10
1981—San Francisco‡	National	22	123	6	9	.400	130	61	55	65	47	4.02
1982—Cleveland§	American	40	107⅔	4	2	.667	91	43	39	61	58	3.26
1983—San Diego x	National	31	144⅓	5	7	.417	143	73	69	81	50	4.30
1983—Las Vegas	P. Coast	3	12	1	0	1.000	15	9	9	11	5	6.75
National League Totals		172	727⅓	35	46	.432	723	342	302	403	274	3.74
American League Totals		40	107⅔	4	2	.667	91	43	39	61	58	3.26
Major League Totals		212	835	39	48	.448	814	385	341	464	332	3.68

Selected by Pittsburgh Pirates' organization in 6th round of free-agent draft, June 5, 1974.
†Traded with Pitchers Fred Breining and Al Holland to San Francisco Giants for Infielders Bill Madlock and Lenny Randle and Pitcher Dave Roberts, June 28, 1979.
‡Traded to Cleveland Indians for Second Baseman Duane Kuiper, November 16, 1981.
§Traded to San Diego Padres for Pitcher Juan Eichelberger and First Baseman-Outfielder Broderick Perkins, November 18, 1982.
xOn disabled list, April 18 to May 28, 1983; included rehabilitation disability assignment to Las Vegas, May 10 to May 28, 1983.

ALL-STAR GAME RECORD

Member of National League All-Star Team in 1980; did not play.

LEO ERNEST WHITT
(Ernie)

Born June 13, 1952, Detroit, Mich.
Height, 6.02. Weight, 200.
Throws right and bats lefthanded.
Attended Macomb County Community College, Warren, Mich.

Led International League in passed balls with 16 in 1978.
Led Eastern League catchers in fielding percentage with .992 in 1974.
Tied for Carolina League lead in double plays by catchers with 7 in 1973.

Year	Club	League	Pos.	G.	AB.	R.	H.	2B.	3B.	HR.	RBI.	B.A.	PO.	A.	E.	F.A.
1972—Williamsport	NYP	1B	1	4	1	2	1	0	0	0	.500	8	1	0	1.000
1972—Winter Haven	Fla. St.	C-1B-OF	31	82	3	15	1	1	0	7	.183	151	14	5	.971
1973—Winston-Salem	Carol.	C-OF-1B	130	424	63	123	23	3	1	50	.290	686	70	15	.980
1974—Bristol	East.	C-OF-1B	111	385	55	96	10	1	9	56	.249	557	50	6	.990
1975—Bristol†	East.	C-OF	82	252	29	64	9	1	2	19	.254	357	36	7	.982
1976—Bristol	East.	C	26	87	12	19	2	3	1	10	.218	127	25	1	.993
1976—Rhode Island	Int.	C-1-O-3	90	304	33	81	16	2	7	42	.266	487	59	9	.984
1976—Boston‡	Amer.	C	8	18	4	4	2	0	1	3	.222	24	0	0	1.000
1977—Charleston	Int.	C-3B	29	94	12	24	6	0	0	7	.255	129	28	7	.957
1977—Toronto§	Amer.	C	23	41	4	7	3	0	0	6	.171	62	4	0	1.000
1978—Syracuse	Int.	C-1B-OF	121	399	50	98	16	3	12	53	.246	673	79	7	.991
1978—Toronto	Amer.	C	2	4	0	0	0	0	0	0	.000	7	1	0	1.000
1979—Syracuse	Int.	★C-OF-3B	114	382	32	95	18	4	7	43	.249	494	69	3	★.995
1980—Toronto	Amer.	C	106	295	23	70	12	2	6	34	.237	436	56	7	.986
1981—Toronto	Amer.	C	74	195	16	46	9	0	1	16	.236	297	46	3	.991
1982—Toronto	Amer.	C	105	284	28	74	14	2	11	42	.261	406	30	8	.982
1983—Toronto	Amer.	C	123	344	53	88	15	2	17	56	.256	554	50	5	.992
Major League Totals			441	1181	128	289	55	6	36	157	.245	1786	187	23	.988

Selected by Boston Red Sox' organization in 15th round of free-agent draft, June 6, 1972.
†On disabled list, April 11 to June 13, 1975.
‡Selected by Toronto Blue Jays in American League expansion draft, November 5, 1976.
§On supplemental disabled list, August 17 to September 27, 1977.

THOMAS ROBERT WIEGHAUS
Name pronounced WIG-house.

(Tom)

Born February 1, 1957, at Chicago Heights, Ill.
Height, 6.00. Weight, 195.
Throws and bats righthanded.
Attended Illinois State University, Normal, Ill.

Led American Association catchers in total chances with 675 in 1982.
Led Florida State League catchers in double plays with 10 in 1979.
Tied for New York-Pennsylvania League lead in double plays by catchers with 7 in 1978.

Year Club	League	Pos.	G.	AB.	R.	H.	2B.	3B.	HR.	RBI.	B.A.	PO.	A.	E.	F.A.
1978—Jamestown...........	NYP	C	63	202	28	49	10	2	0	19	.243	*438	*54	8	.984
1979—W. Palm Beach....	Fla. St.	C	121	382	41	83	15	0	2	35	.217	*742	95	11	*.987
1980—Memphis................	South.	C	120	371	44	101	13	1	4	44	.272	*678	*82	9	.988
1981—Denver ...,..........	A. A.	C	124	345	48	83	13	1	4	50	.241	621	*87	11	.985
1981—Montreal................	Nat.	C	1	1	0	0	0	0	0	0	.000	5	0	0	1.000
1982—Wich.†-Okla. City.	A. A.	C	111	390	48	114	17	2	7	49	.292	*605	64	6	.991
1983—Wichita..................	A. A.	C-P	82	260	28	63	9	0	3	28	.242	419	42	2	.996
1983—Montreal................	Nat.	C	1	0	0	0	0	0	0	0	.000	1	0	0	1.000
Major League Totals..................................			2	1	0	0	0	0	0	0	.000	6	0	0	1.000

Selected by Oakland A's organization in 10th round of free-agent draft, June 4, 1975.
Selected by Montreal Expos' organization in 10th round of free-agent draft, June 6, 1978.
†Loaned to Oklahoma City (Philadelphia Phillies' organization), April 21, 1982; returned, May 21, 1982.

PITCHING RECORD

Year Club	League	G.	IP.	W.	L.	Pct.	H.	R.	ER.	SO.	BB.	ERA.
1983—Wichita..	Am. Assoc.	1	1	0	0	.000	1	0	0	0	0	0.00

ALAN ANTHONY WIGGINS

Born February 17, 1958, at Los Angeles, Calif.
Height, 6.02. Weight, 160.
Throws right and bats left and righthanded.
Attended Pasadena City College, Pasadena, Calif.

Major League stolen bases: 1981 (2), 1982 (33), 1983 (66). Total—101.
Led California League in stolen bases with 120 in 1980.
Tied for Pioneer League lead in sacrifice hits with 5 in 1977.

Year Club	League	Pos.	G.	AB.	R.	H.	2B.	3B.	HR.	RBI.	B.A.	PO.	A.	E.	F.A.
1977—Idaho Falls...........	Pion.	2B	63	225	64	61	3	1	1	23	.271	137	163	28	.915
1978—Quad Cities†‡........	Midw.	2B	49	169	30	34	3	0	1	12	.201	96	130	12	.950
1979—Clinton...................	Midw.	S-O-1-2-3	95	296	57	76	3	1	0	27	.257	196	198	32	.925
1980—Lodi§.....................	Calif.	O-2-1-S	135	513	108	148	10	5	0	35	.288	365	76	23	.950
1981—Hawaii...................	P. C.	OF-2B	133	513	97	155	17	8	0	33	.302	234	26	7	.974
1981—San Diego	Nat.	OF	15	14	4	5	0	0	0	0	.357	6	0	2	.750
1982—Hawaii..................	P. C.	OF	19	77	14	24	2	4	1	4	.312	33	4	0	1.000
1982—San Diego x...........	Nat.	OF-2B	72	254	40	65	3	3	1	15	.256	140	8	5	.967
1983—San Diego	Nat.	OF-1B	144	503	83	139	20	2	0	22	.276	572	35	8	.987
Major League Totals..................................			231	771	127	209	23	5	1	37	.271	718	43	15	.981

Selected by California Angels' organization in 1st round (seventh player selected) of free-agent draft, January 11, 1977.
†On suspended list, June 8 to June 10, 1978.
‡Released, June 10, 1978; signed by Los Angeles Dodgers' organization, January 26, 1979.
§Drafted by San Diego Padres, December 8, 1980.
xOn supplemental disabled list, July 21, 1982, then transferred to disabled list, August 6, 1982, then transferred to suspended list, August 20 to September 19, 1982.

THADDEAUS IGLEHART WILBORN
(Ted)

Born December 16, 1958, at Waco, Tex.
Height, 6.00. Weight, 170.
Throws right and bats right and lefthanded.

Led New York-Pennsylvania League in stolen bases with 57 and caught stealing with 9 in 1978.
Led New York-Pennsylvania League outfielders in double plays with 3 in 1978.

Year Club	League	Pos.	G.	AB.	R.	H.	2B.	3B.	HR.	RBI.	B.A.	PO.	A.	E.	F.A.
1976—Oneonta.................	NYP	OF	28	85	8	16	3	0	0	4	.188	48	3	2	.962
1977—Ft. Lauderdale	Fla. St.	OF	84	223	39	48	8	2	0	10	.215	168	7	3	.983
1978—Ft. Lauderdale	Fla. St.	OF	41	70	10	13	1	0	0	3	.186	41	2	3	.935
1978—Oneonta†..............	NYP	OF	65	220	63	68	5	2	5	29	.309	*138	6	*4	.973
1979—Toronto	Amer.	OF	22	12	3	0	0	0	0	0	.000	7	0	1	.875
1979—Syracuse‡	Int.	OF	61	227	28	56	5	1	1	10	.247	168	8	0	1.000
1980—Nashville§.............	South.	OF	121	455	70	123	15	*14	6	63	.270	210	7	7	.969
1980—New York	Amer.	OF	8	8	2	2	0	0	0	1	.250	6	1	0	1.000
1981—Nashville x	South.	OF-2B	140	553	*106	163	21	12	9	85	.295	232	60	14	.954
1982—Phoenix.................	P. C.	OF-2B	132	501	69	129	20	12	2	58	.257	290	13	10	.968
1983—Phoenix.................	P. C.	OF-2B	125	417	60	120	9	8	7	64	.288	221	78	14	.955
Major League Totals..................................			30	20	5	2	0	0	0	1	.100	13	1	1	.933

Selected by New York Yankees' organization in 4th round of free-agent draft, June 8, 1976.
†Drafted by Toronto Blue Jays, December 4, 1978.
‡Traded with Catcher Rick Cerone and Pitcher Tom Underwood to New York Yankees for First Baseman Chris Chambliss, Infielder Damaso Garcia and Pitcher Paul Mirabella, November 1, 1979.
§On disabled list, April 11 to April 21, 1980.
xTraded with Pitcher Andy McGaffigan to San Francisco Giants' organization for Pitcher Doyle Alexander, March 30, 1982.

MILTON EDWARD WILCOX
(Milt)

Born April 20, 1950, at Honolulu, Hawaii.
Height, 6.02. Weight, 215.
Throws and bats righthanded.

Pitched seven-inning, 2-0 no-hit victory against Evansville, July 4, 1970.
Led American Association in shutouts with 5 in 1970 and tied for lead with 3 in 1971.
Named American Association Pitcher of the Year, 1970.

Year	Club	League	G.	IP.	W.	L.	Pct.	H.	R.	ER.	SO.	BB.	ERA.
1968—Tampa	Florida St.	8	47	3	3	.500	28	11	7	48	18	1.34
1968—Sarasota Reds	Gulf Coast	6	33	3	2	.600	24	10	4	33	11	1.09
1969—Tampa†‡	Florida St.	15	46	4	1	.800	53	30	28	38	29	5.48
1970—Indianapolis	Am. Assoc.	28	168	12	10	.545	144	58	53	110	53	2.84
1970—Cincinnati	National	5	22	3	1	.750	19	6	6	13	7	2.45
1971—Indianapolis	Am. Assoc.	16	102	8	5	.615	84	29	25	62	22	2.20
1971—Cincinnati§	National	18	43	2	2	.500	43	22	16	21	17	3.35
1972—Cleveland	American	32	156	7	14	.333	145	67	59	90	72	3.40
1973—Cleveland xy	American	26	134	8	10	.444	143	90	87	82	68	5.84
1974—Cleveland za	American	41	71	2	2	.500	74	42	37	33	24	4.69
1975—Wichita	Am. Assoc.	8	48	4	3	.571	56	31	23	18	15	4.31
1975—Chicago	National	25	38	0	1	.000	50	27	24	21	17	5.68
1976—Wichita b-Evansville	Am. Assoc.	27	130	6	7	.462	141	72	55	94	63	3.81
1977—Evansville	Am. Assoc.	14	107	9	4	.692	89	38	29	69	40	2.44
1977—Detroit	American	20	106	6	2	.750	96	46	43	82	37	3.65
1978—Detroit	American	29	215	13	12	.520	208	94	90	132	68	3.77
1979—Detroit	American	33	196	12	10	.545	201	105	95	109	73	4.36
1980—Detroit	American	32	199	13	11	.542	201	112	99	97	68	4.48
1981—Detroit	American	24	166	12	9	.571	152	61	56	79	52	3.04
1982—Detroit c	American	29	193⅔	12	10	.545	187	91	78	112	85	3.62
1983—Detroit d	American	26	186	11	10	.524	164	89	82	101	74	3.97
1983—Evansville e	Am. Assoc.	2	8	0	1	.000	8	5	3	5	6	3.38
National League Totals		48	103	5	4	.556	112	55	46	55	41	4.02
American League Totals		292	1622⅔	96	90	.516	1571	797	726	917	621	4.03
Major League Totals		340	1725⅔	101	94	.518	1683	852	772	972	662	4.03

Selected by Cincinnati Reds' organization in 2nd round of free-agent draft, June 7, 1968.
†On military list, April 16 to May 9, 1969.
‡On temporary inactive list, June 11 to July 1, 1969.
§Traded to Cleveland Indians for Outfielder Ted Uhlaender, December 6, 1971.
xOn military list, June 16 to June 30, 1973.
yOn disabled list, July 24 to August 15, 1973.
zOn military list, July 20 to August 4, 1974.
aTraded to Chicago Cubs for Pitcher Dave LaRoche and Outfielder Brock Davis, February 28, 1975.
bSold to Detroit Tigers, June 10, 1976.
cOn disabled list, July 19 to August 9, 1982.
dOn disabled list, August 1 to September 1, 1983; included rehabilitation disability assignment to Evansville, August 12 to September 1, 1983.
eGranted free agency, November 7, 1983; re-signed by Tigers, December 29, 1983.

CHAMPIONSHIP SERIES RECORD

Year	Club	League	G.	IP.	W.	L.	Pct.	H.	R.	ER.	SO.	BB.	ERA.
1970—Cincinnati	National	1	3	1	0	1.000	1	0	0	5	2	0.00

WORLD SERIES RECORD

Year	Club	League	G.	IP.	W.	L.	Pct.	H.	R.	ER.	SO.	BB.	ERA.
1970—Cincinnati	National	2	2	0	1	.000	3	2	2	2	0	9.00

ROBERT DONALD WILFONG
(Rob)

Born September 1, 1953, at Pasadena, Calif.
Height, 6.01. Weight, 185.
Throws right and bats lefthanded.
Attended Mount San Antonio Junior College, Walnut, Calif.
Brother of James Wilfong, outfielder in Detroit Tigers' organization, 1978.

Established American League record for highest fielding percentage by second baseman, season, 100 or more games (.99481), 1980.
Led American League in sacrifice hits with 25 in 1979.
Led American League second basemen in fielding percentage with .995 in 1980.

Year	Club	League	Pos.	G.	AB.	R.	H.	2B.	3B.	HR.	RBI.	B.A.	PO.	A.	E.	F.A.
1972—Charlotte†	W. Car.	2B	102	363	64	107	18	2	2	35	.295	212	224	16	.965
1973—Lynchburg	Carol.	2B	131	520	94	143	13	9	7	37	.275	★323	326	18	.973
1974—Orlando	South.	2B	109	403	58	99	7	4	3	23	.246	249	303	8	★.986
1975—Orlando	South.	2B	125	403	54	99	14	1	4	37	.246	274	347	16	.975
1976—Tacoma	P. C.	2B	69	220	41	67	8	3	3	16	.305	163	191	6	.983
1977—Tacoma	P. C.	2B	34	123	26	40	8	1	2	17	.325	83	101	8	.958
1977—Minnesota	Amer.	2B	73	171	22	42	1	1	1	13	.246	114	164	12	.959
1978—Minnesota‡	Amer.	2B	92	199	23	53	8	0	1	11	.266	152	196	5	.986
1979—Minnesota	Amer.	2B-OF	140	419	71	131	22	6	9	59	.313	287	379	14	.979

Year	Club	League	Pos.	G.	AB.	R.	H.	2B.	3B.	HR.	RBI.	B.A.	PO.	A.	E.	F.A.
1980—Minnesota	Amer.	2B-OF	131	416	55	103	16	5	8	45	.248	245	338	4	.993
1981—Minnesota	Amer.	2B	93	305	32	75	11	3	3	19	.246	183	268	9	.980
1982—Minn.§-Calif.	Amer.	2-3-O-S	80	183	24	38	5	2	1	16	.208	69	155	5	.978
1983—California	Amer.	2B-3B-SS	65	177	17	45	7	1	2	17	.254	107	144	2	.992
Major League Totals			674	1870	244	487	70	18	25	180	.260	1157	1644	51	.982

Selected by Minnesota Twins' organization in 13th round of free-agent draft, June 8, 1971.
†On disabled list, May 22 to June 2, 1972.
‡On supplemental disabled list, March 22 to April 7, 1978.
§Traded with Pitcher Doug Corbett to California Angels for Outfielder Tom Brunansky, Pitcher Mike Walters and cash, May 12, 1982.

CHAMPIONSHIP SERIES RECORD

Year	Club	League	Pos.	G.	AB.	R.	H.	2B.	3B.	HR.	RBI.	B.A.	PO.	A.	E.	F.A.
1982—California	Amer.	PH-PR	2	1	0	0	0	0	0	0	.000	0	0	0	.000

CURTIS VERNON WILKERSON
(Curt)

Born April 26, 1961, at Petersburg, Va.
Height, 5.09. Weight, 160.
Throws right and bats left and righthanded.

Tied for Texas League lead in sacrifice hits with 11 in 1982.

Year	Club	League	Pos.	G.	AB.	R.	H.	2B.	3B.	HR.	RBI.	B.A.	PO.	A.	E.	F.A.
1980—Sarasota Rangers	Gulf C.	SS-2B	37	105	15	20	2	0	0	8	.190	38	86	17	.879
1981—Asheville	S. Atl.	SS-2B	106	333	45	68	7	3	0	19	.204	188	372	28	.952
1982—Burlington	Midw.	SS-2B	56	198	18	50	6	0	0	13	.253	78	159	16	.937
1982—Tulsa	Texas	SS	72	266	32	71	6	3	2	14	.267	102	225	18	.948
1983—Oklahoma City†	A. A.	SS	89	343	51	107	19	4	3	31	.312	135	272	19	.955
1983—Texas	Amer.	SS-2B-3B	16	35	7	6	0	1	0	1	.171	18	31	1	.980
Major League Totals			16	35	7	6	0	1	0	1	.171	18	31	1	.980

Selected by Texas Rangers' organization in 4th round of free-agent draft, June 3, 1980.
†On disabled list, May 19 to June 21, 1983.

GERALD DUANE WILLARD JR.
(Jerry)

Born March 14, 1960, at Oxnard, Calif.
Height, 6.02. Weight, 200.
Throws right and bats lefthanded.
Attended Oxnard College, Oxnard, Calif.

Led International League catchers in assists with 78 in 1983.

Year	Club	League	Pos.	G.	AB.	R.	H.	2B.	3B.	HR.	RBI.	B.A.	PO.	A.	E.	F.A.
1980—Central Oregon	N'west	C	65	231	53	85	21	1	5	59	.368	283	37	★18	.947
1981—Peninsula	Carol.	C	107	334	43	87	17	1	12	60	.260	319	28	3	.991
1982—Reading	East.	C	81	281	43	82	10	1	12	51	.292	534	64	13	.979
1982—Oklahoma City†	A. A.	C	36	95	13	22	5	0	2	14	.232	169	35	8	.962
1983—Charleston	Int.	C-3B-OF	127	396	61	119	22	2	19	77	.301	613	79	12	.983

Signed as free agent by Philadelphia Phillies' organization, December 20, 1979.
†Traded with Second Baseman Manny Trillo, Infielder Julio Franco, Outfielder George Vukovich and Pitcher Jay Baller to Cleveland Indians for Outfielder Von Hayes, December 9, 1982.

ALBERTO WILLIAMS (DeSOUZA)
(Al)

Born May 7, 1954, at Maiguetio, Venezuela
Height, 6.04. Weight, 190.
Throws and bats righthanded.

Year	Club	League	G.	IP.	W.	L.	Pct.	H.	R.	ER.	SO.	BB.	ERA.
1975—Charleston	W. Carol.	29	148	4	12	.250	148	94	63	115	65	3.83
1976—Charleston†	W. Carol.	26	46	4	1	.800	39	25	24	49	22	4.70
1979—Panama-Caracas‡	Int.-Amer.	17	76	1	7	.125	79	40	32	★52	27	3.79
1980—Toledo	Int'national	15	107	9	3	.750	85	34	25	59	32	2.10
1980—Minnesota	American	18	77	6	2	.750	73	33	30	35	30	3.51
1981—Minnesota	American	23	150	6	10	.375	160	72	68	76	52	4.08
1982—Minnesota	American	26	153⅔	9	7	.563	166	74	72	61	55	4.22
1982—Toledo	Int'national	3	21	3	0	1.000	13	5	5	14	7	2.14
1983—Minnesota	American	36	193⅓	11	14	.440	196	105	89	68	68	4.14
Major League Totals		103	574	32	33	.492	595	284	259	240	205	4.06

Signed as free agent by Pittsburgh Pirates' organization, February 20, 1975.
†Released, July 2, 1976; signed by Panama of Inter-American League, April 11, 1979.
‡Declared free agent when Inter-American League folded, June 30, 1979; signed by Minnesota Twins' organization, January 6, 1980.

BRUCE ALLEN WILLIAMS

Born December 28, 1962, at Orange, Calif.
Height, 6.01. Weight, 220.
Throws and bats righthanded.

Year Club	League	G.	IP.	W.	L.	Pct.	H.	R.	ER.	SO.	BB.	ERA.
1981—Butte	Pioneer	13	27	1	1	.500	30	48	36	31	51	12.00
1982—Pikeville	Pioneer	11	60	3	5	.375	48	43	28	61	63	4.20
1983—Beloit	Midwest	41	74⅔	9	5	.643	33	44	38	101	100	4.58

Selected by Milwaukee Brewers' organization in 4th round of free-agent draft, June 8, 1981.

DALLAS McKINLEY WILLIAMS JR.

Born February 28, 1958, at Brooklyn, N. Y.
Height, 5.11. Weight, 165.
Throws and bats lefthanded.

Led American Association in caught stealing with 15 in 1982.
Led International League in stolen bases with 51 and caught stealing with 18 in 1981.
Led Florida State League in caught stealing with 21 in 1977.
Led Florida State League outfielders in double plays with 5 in 1977.
Tied for American Association lead in double plays by outfielders with 5 in 1982.

Year Club	League	Pos.	G.	AB.	R.	H.	2B.	3B.	HR.	RBI.	B.A.	PO.	A.	E.	F.A.
1976—Bluefield	Appal.	OF	69	256	26	69	8	1	3	30	.270	★161	★11	7	.961
1977—Miami	Fla. St.	OF	125	464	56	126	17	4	2	50	.272	295	10	★16	.950
1978—Charlotte	South.	OF	139	★549	52	145	17	4	2	35	.264	315	18	10	.971
1979—Charlotte	South.	OF	133	519	68	144	25	2	12	52	.277	319	16	10	.971
1980—Rochester	Int.	OF	137	529	63	143	21	2	11	54	.270	330	11	5	.986
1981—Rochester†	Int.	OF	127	523	69	148	17	3	9	48	.283	239	11	11	.958
1981—Baltimore‡	Amer.	OF	2	2	0	1	0	0	0	0	.500	1	0	0	1.000
1982—Indianapolis	A. A.	OF	132	★514	75	154	26	8	7	74	.300	300	12	4	.987
1983—Indianapolis	A. A.	OF	132	512	75	★168	30	8	11	75	.328	264	★16	★13	.956
1983—Cincinnati	Nat.	OF	18	36	2	2	0	0	0	1	.056	18	0	0	1.000
American League Totals			2	2	0	1	0	0	0	0	.500	1	0	0	1.000
National League Totals			18	36	2	2	0	0	0	1	.056	18	0	0	1.000
Major League Totals			20	38	2	3	0	0	0	1	.079	19	0	0	1.000

Selected by Baltimore Orioles' organization in 1st round (20th player selected) of free-agent draft, June 8, 1976.
†On disabled list, May 24 to June 3, 1981.
‡Traded with Pitcher Brooks Carey to Cincinnati Reds' organization for Catcher Joe Nolan, March 26, 1982.

FRANK LEE WILLIAMS

Born February 13, 1958, at Seattle, Wash.
Height, 6.01. Weight, 180.
Throws and bats righthanded.
Attended Shoreline Community College, Seattle, Wash.,
and Lewis-Clark State College, Lewiston, Ida.

Led California League in hit batsmen with 18 in 1980 and 13 in 1981.
Led Pioneer League in hit batsmen with 9 in 1979.
Tied for Texas League lead in hit batsmen with 13 in 1982.
Tied for California League lead in complete games with 14 in 1981.

Year Club	League	G.	IP.	W.	L.	Pct.	H.	R.	ER.	SO.	BB.	ERA.
1979—Great Falls	Pioneer	13	91	6	●7	.462	85	53	34	81	53	3.36
1980—Fresno	California	21	114	12	3	.800	105	53	42	80	70	3.32
1981—Fresno	California	27	187	14	9	.609	170	81	70	170	85	3.37
1982—Shreveport	Texas	27	169⅔	11	9	.550	143	96	74	145	99	3.93
1983—Shreveport	Texas	21	42	7	2	.778	22	14	8	54	25	1.71
1983—Phoenix	P. Coast	25	47⅔	5	3	.625	45	22	19	37	24	3.59

Selected by San Francisco Giants' organization in 11th round of free-agent draft, June 5, 1979.

MATTHEW EVAN WILLIAMS
(Matt)

Born July 25, 1959, at Houston, Tex.
Height, 6.02. Weight, 195.
Throws and bats righthanded.
Received bachelor of arts degree in managerial studies
from Rice University, Houston, Tex.

Led Southern League in wild pitches with 31 in 1982.

Year Club	League	G.	IP.	W.	L.	Pct.	H.	R.	ER.	SO.	BB.	ERA.
1981—Florence	S. Atlantic	15	91	7	4	.636	81	33	22	76	27	2.18
1982—Knoxville	Southern	28	193⅓	11	13	.458	173	106	92	157	107	4.28
1983—Syracuse	Int'national	20	139⅔	7	8	.467	100	60	55	110	64	3.54
1983—Toronto	American	4	8	1	1	.500	13	13	13	5	7	14.63
Major League Totals		4	8	1	1	.500	13	13	13	5	7	14.63

Selected by Milwaukee Brewers' organization in 4th round of free-agent draft, June 3, 1980.
Selected by Toronto Blue Jays' organization in 1st round (fifth player selected) of free-agent draft, June 8, 1981.

REGINALD DEWAYNE WILLIAMS
(Reggie)

Born August 29, 1960, at Memphis, Tenn.
Height, 5.11. Weight, 185.
Throws and bats righthanded.
Received bachelor of science degree in business
from Southern University, New Orleans, La.

Year Club League	Pos.	G.	AB.	R.	H.	2B.	3B.	HR.	RBI.	B.A.	PO.	A.	E.	F.A.
1982—Lethbridge .... Pion.	OF	67	253	40	76	8	2	3	33	.300	★141	12	7	.956
1983—Vero Beach† .... Fla. St.	OF	81	293	53	83	11	3	4	32	.283	142	3	8	.948

Selected by St. Louis Cardinals' organization in 6th round of free-agent draft, June 8, 1981.
Selected by Los Angeles Dodgers' organization in 13th round of free-agent draft, June 7, 1982.
†On disabled list, June 22 to August 11, 1983.

FRANK LEE WILLS JR.

Born October 26, 1958, at New Orleans, La.
Height, 6.02. Weight, 200.
Throws and bats righthanded.
Attended Tulane University, New Orleans, La.

Tied for Southern League lead in wild pitches with 15 in 1981.

Year Club League	G.	IP.	W.	L.	Pct.	H.	R.	ER.	SO.	BB.	ERA.
1980—Sarasota Royals-Blue .... Gulf Coast	4	23	2	0	1.000	18	7	5	20	8	1.96
1980—Charleston .... S. Atlantic	9	57	2	5	.286	59	33	23	48	32	3.63
1981—Jacksonville .... Southern	27	192	9	14	.391	199	104	85	174	91	3.98
1982—Omaha .... Am. Assoc.	41	107⅓	7	10	.412	110	71	62	77	★81	5.20
1983—Jacksonville .... Southern	8	54⅓	5	2	.714	44	19	15	40	23	2.48
1983—Omaha .... Am. Assoc.	16	95	4	11	.267	96	56	50	65	45	4.74
1983—Kansas City .... American	6	34⅔	2	1	.667	35	17	16	23	15	4.15
Major League Totals.................................	6	34⅔	2	1	.667	35	17	16	23	15	4.15

Selected by Kansas City Royals' organization in 1st round (16th player selected) of free-agent draft, June 3, 1980.

GLENN DWIGHT WILSON

Born December 22, 1958, at Baytown, Tex.
Height, 6.01. Weight, 195.
Throws and bats righthanded.
Attended Sam Houston State University, Huntsville, Tex.

Received reported $60,000 bonus to sign with Detroit Tigers, 1980.

Year Club League	Pos.	G.	AB.	R.	H.	2B.	3B.	HR.	RBI.	B.A.	PO.	A.	E.	F.A.
1980—Montgomery .... South.	3B	77	284	36	75	16	2	7	31	.264	56	189	★33	.881
1981—Birmingham .... South.	OF	124	496	77	152	24	6	18	82	.306	292	18	5	.984
1981—Evansville .... A. A.	OF-1B	10	37	5	9	2	0	2	7	.243	16	2	0	1.000
1982—Detroit.................. Amer.	OF	84	322	39	94	15	1	12	34	.292	376	4	5	.987
1982—Evansville† .... A. A.	OF	42	165	24	46	7	2	10	33	.279	96	6	3	.971
1983—Detroit.................. Amer.	OF	144	503	55	135	25	6	11	65	.268	225	12	3	.988
Major League Totals.................................		228	825	94	229	40	7	23	99	.278	601	16	8	.987

Selected by Detroit Tigers' organization in 1st round (18th player selected) of free-agent draft, June 3, 1980.
†On disabled list, May 27 to June 9 and June 17 to June 27, 1982.

JAMES GEORGE WILSON
(Jim)

Born December 29, 1960, at Corvallis, Ore.
Height, 6.03. Weight, 230.
Throws and bats righthanded.
Attended Oregon State University, Corvallis, Ore.

Led Eastern League in being hit by pitch with 10 and tied for lead in grounding into double plays with 18 in 1983.

Year Club League	Pos.	G.	AB.	R.	H.	2B.	3B.	HR.	RBI.	B.A.	PO.	A.	E.	F.A.
1982—Chattanooga .... South.	1B	11	40	3	7	1	0	0	5	.175	29	1	1	.968
1982—Waterloo .... Midw.	3B-OF-1B	55	204	40	73	17	1	14	48	.358	17	32	8	.860
1983—Buffalo .... East.	1B	136	496	84	144	25	0	26	★105	.290	701	57	13	.983

Selected by Cleveland Indians' organization in 2nd round of free-agent draft, June 7, 1982.

MICHAEL WILSON
(Mike or Tack)

Born May 16, 1956, at Shreveport, La.
Height, 5.10. Weight, 192.
Throws and bats righthanded.
Attended Laney College, Oakland, Calif.

Led Texas League in stolen bases with 56 and caught stealing with 24 in 1979.
Led California League in caught stealing with 25 and tied for lead in being hit by pitch with 11 in 1978.
Led Northwest League in stolen bases with 36 and tied for lead in caught stealing with 10 in 1976.
Led Texas League outfielders in double plays with 8 in 1979.

Year Club	League	Pos.	G.	AB.	R.	H.	2B.	3B.	HR.	RBI.	B.A.	PO.	A.	E.	F.A.
1976—Danville	Midw.	PH	2	2	1	1	0	0	0	0	.500	0	0	0	.000
1976—Bellingham	N'west.	2-S-O-3	66	225	47	74	7	*8	0	20	.329	123	137	17	.939
1977—Clinton†	Midw.	OF	44	148	46	40	5	5	1	14	.270	93	3	3	.970
1977—Greys Harbor‡§..	N'west.	2B-OF	40	144	29	48	9	2	3	17	.333	110	126	15	.940
1978—Visalia	Calif.	OF	134	525	126	183	24	4	5	79	.349	348	11	15	.960
1979—San Antonio	Texas	OF	130	492	105	155	27	7	6	42	.315	243	9	7	.973
1980—Albuquerque	P. C.	OF-2B	131	478	*110	139	19	8	2	47	.291	228	8	3	.987
1981—Albuquerque	P. C.	OF-2B	96	330	68	104	15	10	2	64	.315	81	5	2	.977
1982—Albuquerque x.....	P. C.	OF-2B	99	368	77	139	25	6	2	56	.378	61	11	3	.960
1983—Minnesota	Amer.	OF	5	4	4	1	1	0	0	1	.250	1	0	0	1.000
1983—Toledo	Int.	OF	109	416	71	135	20	3	3	33	.325	191	10	6	.971
Major League Totals...................			5	4	4	1	1	0	0	1	.250	1	0	0	1.000

Signed as free agent by Los Angeles Dodgers' organization, December 11, 1975.
†Loaned to Greys Harbor (Co-op), June 16, 1977; returned, August 28, 1977.
‡On disabled list, August 6 to August 28, 1977.
§Loaned to Visalia (Minnesota Twins' organization), April 4, 1978; returned, September 10, 1978.
xTraded to Minnesota Twins for Shortstop Ivan Mesa, March 29, 1983.

WILLIAM HAYWARD WILSON
(Mookie)

Born February 9, 1956, at Bamberg, S. C.
Height, 5.10. Weight, 170.
Throws right and bats right and lefthanded.
Attended Spartanburg Methodist College, Spartanburg, S. C.,
and University of South Carolina, Columbia, S. C.

Major League stolen bases: 1980 (7), 1981 (24), 1982 (58), 1983 (54). Total—143.

Year Club	League	Pos.	G.	AB.	R.	H.	2B.	3B.	HR.	RBI.	B.A.	PO.	A.	E.	F.A.
1977—Wausau..................	Midw.	OF	68	245	50	71	10	2	6	32	.290	150	8	9	.946
1978—Jackson	Texas	OF	132	497	72	145	13	*15	7	72	.292	282	10	7	.977
1979—Tidewater.............	Int.	OF	*141	529	84	141	22	10	5	36	.267	317	11	7	.979
1980—Tidewater.............	Int.	OF	132	515	*92	*152	11	*14	4	44	.295	*350	11	7	.981
1980—New York.............	Nat.	OF	27	105	16	26	5	3	0	4	.248	72	1	2	.973
1981—New York.............	Nat.	OF	92	328	49	89	8	8	3	14	.271	226	3	4	.983
1982—New York.............	Nat.	OF	159	639	90	178	25	9	5	55	.279	415	12	5	.988
1983—New York.............	Nat.	OF	152	*638	91	176	25	6	7	51	.276	422	5	7	.984
Major League Totals.....................			430	1710	246	469	63	26	15	124	.274	1135	21	18	.985

Selected by Los Angeles Dodgers' organization in 4th round of free-agent draft, January 7, 1976.
Selected by New York Mets' organization in 2nd round of free-agent draft, June 7, 1977.

WILLIE JAMES WILSON

Born July 9, 1955, at Montgomery, Ala.
Height, 6.03. Weight, 187.
Throws right and bats left and righthanded.

Established major league records for most at-bats season (705), 1980; most at-bats by switch-hitter, season (705), 1980; highest stolen base percentage, lifetime, 300 or more attempts (.842).
Tied major league records by collecting 100 or more hits righthanded and lefthanded, season, 1980; for most hits by switch-hitter, season (230), 1980.
Established American League records for fewest times, grounded into double play, season (1), 1979; most one-base hits by switch-hitter, season (184), 1980.
Tied American League records for most three-base hits by switch-hitter, season (15), 1980, 1982; most consecutive stolen bases without caught stealing (32); fewest times caught stealing, season, 50 or more stolen bases (8), 1983.
Major League stolen bases: 1976 (2), 1977 (6), 1978 (46), 1979 (83), 1980 (79), 1981 (34), 1982 (37), 1983 (59). Total—346.
Switch-hit home runs in one game, June 15, 1979.
Led American League in stolen bases with 83 in 1979.
Led Gulf Coast League in stolen bases with 24 in 1974, Midwest League with 76 in 1975 and American Association with 74 in 1977.
Led Midwest League in being hit by pitch with 13 in 1975.
Named outfielder on THE SPORTING NEWS American League All-Star fielding team, 1980.
Named outfielder on THE SPORTING NEWS American League Silver Slugger team, 1980 and 1982.
Named Midwest League Most Valuable Player, 1975.
Received reported $90,000 bonus to sign with Kansas City Royals, 1974.

Year Club	League	Pos.	G.	AB.	R.	H.	2B.	3B.	HR.	RBI.	B.A.	PO.	A.	E.	F.A.
1974—Sarasota Royals....Gulf C.		OF	47	155	30	39	3	5	1	14	.252	92	8	4	.962
1975—Waterloo...............	Midw.	OF	127	486	92	*132	18	4	8	73	.272	249	●17	*17	.940
1976—Jacksonville..........	South.	OF	107	388	54	98	13	6	1	35	.253	273	5	8	.972
1976—Kansas City..........	Amer.	OF	12	6	0	1	0	0	0	0	.167	6	1	1	.875
1977—Omaha..................	A. A.	OF	132	495	67	139	10	6	4	47	.281	*278	7	11	.963
1977—Kansas City..........	Amer.	OF	13	34	10	11	2	0	0	1	.324	24	0	1	.960
1978—Kansas City..........	Amer.	OF	127	198	43	43	8	2	0	16	.217	171	6	4	.978
1979—Kansas City..........	Amer.	OF	154	588	113	185	18	13	6	49	.315	384	12	6	.985
1980—Kansas City..........	Amer.	OF	161	*705	*133	*230	28	●15	3	49	.326	482	9	6	.988
1981—Kansas City..........	Amer.	OF	102	439	54	133	10	7	1	32	.303	299	*14	4	.987
1982—Kansas City..........	Amer.	OF	136	585	87	194	19	*15	3	46	.332	215	8	3	.987
1983—Kansas City††‡......	Amer.	OF	137	576	90	159	22	8	2	33	.276	354	3	9	.975
Major League Totals...................			842	3131	530	956	107	62	15	226	.305	1935	53	34	.983

Selected by Kansas City Royals' organization in 1st round (18th player selected) of free-agent draft, June 5, 1974.
†On supplemental disabled list, August 21 to September 6, 1983.
‡On suspended list, December 15, 1983.

DIVISION SERIES RECORD

Year Club	League	Pos.	G.	AB.	R.	H.	2B.	3B.	HR.	RBI.	B.A.	PO.	A.	E.	F.A.
1981—Kansas City.......... Amer.		OF	3	13	0	4	0	0	0	1	.308	6	0	0	1.000

CHAMPIONSHIP SERIES RECORD

Year Club	League	Pos.	G.	AB.	R.	H.	2B.	3B.	HR.	RBI.	B.A.	PO.	A.	E.	F.A.
1978—Kansas City.......... Amer.		PR-OF	3	4	0	1	0	0	0	0	.250	2	0	0	1.000
1980—Kansas City.......... Amer.		OF	3	13	2	4	2	1	0	4	.308	6	1	0	1.000
Championship Series Totals			6	17	2	5	2	1	0	4	.294	8	1	0	1.000

WORLD SERIES RECORD

Established World Series record for most strikeouts, six-game and any length Series (12), 1980.
Tied World Series record for most at bats, inning (2), October 18, 1980 (first inning).

Year Club	League	Pos.	G.	AB.	R.	H.	2B.	3B.	HR.	RBI.	B.A.	PO.	A.	E.	F.A.
1980—Kansas City.......... Amer.		OF	6	26	3	4	1	0	0	0	.154	15	1	0	1.000

ALL-STAR GAME RECORD

Year League	Pos.	AB.	R.	H.	2B.	3B.	HR.	RBI.	B.A.	PO.	A.	E.	F.A.
1982—American	OF	2	0	0	0	0	0	0	.000	1	0	0	1.000
1983—American	OF	1	0	1	1	0	0	1	1.000	2	0	0	1.000
All-Star Game Totals		3	0	1	1	0	0	1	.333	3	0	0	1.000

DAVID MARK WINFIELD
(Dave)

Born October 3, 1951, at St. Paul, Minn.
Height, 6.06. Weight, 220.
Throws and bats righthanded.
Attended University of Minnesota, Minneapolis, Minn.

Major League stolen bases: 1974 (9), 1975 (23), 1976 (26), 1977 (16), 1978 (21), 1979 (15), 1980 (23), 1981 (11), 1982 (5) 1983 (15). Total—164.
Led National League in total bases with 333 and intentional bases on balls received with 24 in 1979.
Named outfielder on THE SPORTING NEWS American League All-Star Team, 1982 and 1983.
Named outfielder on THE SPORTING NEWS National League All-Star Team, 1979.
Named outfielder on THE SPORTING NEWS American League All-Star fielding team, 1982 and 1983.
Named outfielder on THE SPORTING NEWS National League All-Star fielding team, 1979 and 1980.
Named outfielder on THE SPORTING NEWS American League Silver Slugger team, 1981 through 1983.
Received reported $100,000 bonus to sign with San Diego Padres, 1973.
Selected by Atlanta Hawks in 5th round of 1973 NBA draft.
Selected by Utah Stars in 6th round of 1973 ABA draft.
Selected by Minnesota Vikings in 17th round of 1973 NFL draft.

Year Club	League	Pos.	G.	AB.	R.	H.	2B.	3B.	HR.	RBI.	B.A.	PO.	A.	E.	F.A.
1973—San Diego .... Nat.		OF-1B	56	141	9	39	4	1	3	12	.277	65	1	3	.957
1974—San Diego .... Nat.		OF	145	498	57	132	18	4	20	75	.265	276	11	●12	.960
1975—San Diego .... Nat.		OF	143	509	74	136	20	2	15	76	.267	302	9	9	.972
1976—San Diego .... Nat.		OF	137	492	81	139	26	4	13	69	.283	304	★15	6	.982
1977—San Diego .... Nat.		OF	157	615	104	169	29	7	25	92	.275	368	15	11	.972
1978—San Diego .... Nat.		OF-1B	158	587	88	181	30	5	24	97	.308	328	8	7	.980
1979—San Diego .... Nat.		OF	159	597	97	184	27	10	34	★118	.308	344	14	5	.986
1980—San Diego† .... Nat.		OF	162	558	89	154	25	6	20	87	.276	273	20	4	.987
1981—New York............. Amer.		OF	105	388	52	114	25	1	13	68	.294	196	1	3	.985
1982—New York‡........... Amer.		OF	140	539	84	151	24	8	37	106	.280	279	★17	8	.974
1983—New York............. Amer.		OF	152	598	99	169	26	8	32	116	.283	313	5	7	.978
National League Totals............................		1117	3997	599	1134	179	39	154	626	.284	2260	93	57	.976
American League Totals..........................		397	1525	235	434	75	17	82	290	.285	788	23	18	.978
Major League Totals..................................		1514	5522	834	1568	254	56	236	916	.284	3048	116	75	.977

Selected by Baltimore Orioles' organization in 40th round of free-agent draft, June 5, 1969.
Selected by San Diego Padres' organization in 1st round (fourth player selected) of free-agent draft, June 5, 1973.
†Granted free agency, October 22, 1980; signed by New York Yankees, December 15, 1980.
‡On supplemental disabled list, May 20 to June 4, 1982.

DIVISION SERIES RECORD

Year Club	League	Pos.	G.	AB.	R.	H.	2B.	3B.	HR.	RBI.	B.A.	PO.	A.	E.	F.A.
1981—New York............. Amer.		OF	5	20	2	7	3	0	0	0	.350	10	1	0	1.000

CHAMPIONSHIP SERIES RECORD

Year Club	League	Pos.	G.	AB.	R.	H.	2B.	3B.	HR.	RBI.	B.A.	PO.	A.	E.	F.A.
1981—New York............. Amer.		OF	3	13	2	2	1	0	0	2	.154	6	0	0	1.000

WORLD SERIES RECORD

Tied World Series record for fewest runs, Series (0), 1981.

Year Club	League	Pos.	G.	AB.	R.	H.	2B.	3B.	HR.	RBI.	B.A.	PO.	A.	E.	F.A.
1981—New York............. Amer.		OF	6	22	0	1	0	0	0	1	.045	13	1	0	1.000

Tied All-Star Game record for most at bats, game (5), July 17, 1979.

Year	League	Pos.	AB.	R.	H.	2B.	3B.	HR.	RBI.	B.A.	PO.	A.	E.	F.A.
1977—National		OF	2	0	2	1	0	0	2	1.000	1	0	0	1.000
1978—National		OF	2	1	1	0	0	0	0	.500	1	0	0	1.000
1979—National		OF	5	1	1	1	0	0	1	.200	3	0	0	1.000
1980—National		OF	2	0	0	0	0	0	1	.000	2	0	0	1.000
1981—American		OF	4	0	0	0	0	0	0	.000	0	1	0	1.000
1982—American		OF	2	0	1	0	0	0	0	.500	0	0	0	.000
1983—American		OF	3	2	3	1	0	0	1	1.000	3	0	0	1.000
All-Star Game Totals			20	4	8	3	0	0	5	.400	10	1	0	1.000

JAMES FRANCIS WINN
(Jim)

Born September 23, 1959, at Stockton, Calif.
Height, 6.03. Weight, 190.
Throws and bats righthanded.
Attended John Brown University, Siloam Springs, Ark.

Year	Club	League	G.	IP.	W.	L.	Pct.	H.	R.	ER.	SO.	BB.	ERA.
1981—Bradenton Pirates	Gulf Coast	1	4	0	0	.000	1	0	0	6	0	0.00
1981—Buffalo	Eastern	12	65	2	5	.286	60	40	33	44	23	4.57
1982—Buffalo†	Eastern	3	6⅔	0	2	.000	6	7	4	7	5	5.40
1982—Alexandria	Carolina	7	28	1	2	.333	31	17	12	20	11	3.86
1983—Pittsburgh	National	7	11	0	0	.000	12	9	9	3	6	7.36
1983—Hawaii	P. Coast	31	38⅔	0	1	.000	49	23	17	22	22	3.96
Major League Totals		7	11	0	0	.000	12	9	9	3	6	7.36

Selected by Pittsburgh Pirates' organization in 1st round (14th player selected) of free-agent draft, June 8, 1981.
†On disabled list, April 12 to May 24 and June 8 to July 16, 1982.

HERMAN S. WINNINGHAM

Born December 1, 1961, at Orangeburg, S.C.
Height, 6.00. Weight, 165.
Throws right and bats lefthanded.
Attended DeKalb Community College South, Decatur, Ga.

Year	Club	League	Pos.	G.	AB.	R.	H.	2B.	3B.	HR.	RBI.	B.A.	PO.	A.	E.	F.A.
1981—Kingsport	Appal.	OF	58	204	44	52	7	4	2	14	.255	128	3	2	*.985
1982—Lynchburg	Carol.	OF	120	430	65	127	20	5	6	61	.295	235	6	5	.980
1983—Jackson	Texas	OF	78	288	54	102	13	6	4	41	.354	157	5	6	.964
1983—Tidewater	Int.	OF	29	113	18	30	5	2	1	11	.265	70	1	3	.959

Selected by Pittsburgh Pirates' organization in 38th round of free-agent draft, June 5, 1979.
Selected by Milwaukee Brewers' organization in secondary phase of free-agent draft, January 8, 1980.
Selected by Montreal Expos' organization in secondary phase of free-agent draft, June 3, 1980.
Selected by New York Mets' organization in secondary phase of free-agent draft, January 13, 1981.

MATTHEW LIITTLETON WINTERS
(Matt)

Born March 18, 1960, at Buffalo, N.Y.
Height, 6.03. Weight, 200.
Throws right and bats lefthanded.
Led South Atlantic League in bases on balls received with 118 in 1982.
Led South Atlantic League in game-winning RBIs with 12 in 1980 and tied for lead with 12 in 1982.
Named South Atlantic League Most Valuable Player, 1982.

Year	Club	League	Pos.	G.	AB.	R.	H.	2B.	3B.	HR.	RBI.	B.A.	PO.	A.	E.	F.A.
1978—Oneonta	NYP	OF	60	203	38	53	7	*11	2	36	.261	79	6	4	.955
1979—Ft. Lauderdale	Fla. St.	OF	34	89	8	14	2	1	1	10	.157	28	1	2	.935
1979—Oneonta	NYP	OF-1B	62	188	40	53	6	2	●10	38	.282	79	2	4	.953
1980—Greensboro	S. Atl.	OF-1B	112	363	72	116	15	2	20	92	.320	165	10	7	.962
1981—Greensboro	S. Atl.	OF-1B	!25	404	85	121	23	2	16	76	.300	109	10	5	.960
1982—Greensboro	S. Atl.	OF-1B	104	326	76	106	20	2	20	93	.325	163	3	3	.982
1982—Nashville	South.	OF	29	99	22	30	5	2	4	17	.303	40	3	0	1.000
1983—Columbus	Int.	OF	133	431	89	126	24	3	29	99	.292	150	2	2	.987

Selected by New York Yankees' organization in 1st round (24th player selected) of free-agent draft, June 6, 1978.

MICHAEL ATWATER WITT
(Mike)

Born July 20, 1960, at Fullerton, Calif.
Height, 6.07. Weight, 185.
Throws and bats righthanded.
Attending Cypress Junior College, Cypress, Calif.
Tied for American League lead in hit batsmen with 11 in 1981.

Year	Club	League	G.	IP.	W.	L.	Pct.	H.	R.	ER.	SO.	BB.	ERA.
1978—Idaho Falls	Pioneer	13	86	7	1	.875	88	45	34	79	26	3.56
1979—Salinas	California	30	141	8	10	.444	156	96	80	94	70	5.11

Year Club	League	G.	IP.	W.	L.	Pct.	H.	R.	ER.	SO.	BB.	ERA.
1980—Salinas	California	13	90	7	3	.700	85	30	21	76	35	2.10
1980—El Paso	Texas	12	70	5	5	.500	72	53	45	64	39	5.79
1981—California	American	22	129	8	9	.471	123	60	47	75	47	3.28
1982—California	American	33	179⅔	8	6	.571	177	77	70	85	47	3.51
1983—California	American	43	154	7	14	.333	173	90	84	77	75	4.91
Major League Totals		98	462⅔	23	29	.442	473	227	201	237	169	3.91

Selected by California Angels' organization in 4th round of free-agent draft, June 6, 1978.

CHAMPIONSHIP SERIES RECORD

Year Club	League	G.	IP.	W.	L.	Pct.	H.	R.	ER.	SO.	BB.	ERA.
1982—California	American	1	3	0	0	.000	2	2	2	3	2	6.00

JOHNNY BILTON WOCKENFUSS

Name pronounced WAHK-en-fuss.

(John)

Born February 27, 1949, at Welch, W. Va.
Height, 6.00. Weight, 180.
Throws and bats righthanded.

Tied major league record for most unassisted double plays by catcher, game (1), June 21, 1975.
Led American Association in passed balls with 10 in 1974.
Led Eastern League catchers in putouts with 770 and tied for lead in passed balls with 24 in 1972.
Led Eastern League outfielders in fielding percentage with .987 in 1970.

Year Club	League	Pos.	G.	AB.	R.	H.	2B.	3B.	HR.	RBI.	B.A.	PO.	A.	E.	F.A.
1967—Geneva	NYP	OF	3	7	0	1	0	0	0	1	.143	0	0	1	.000
1968—Geneva	NYP	OF-3B	39	132	13	26	1	1	4	17	.197	50	5	7	.887
1969—Burlington	Carol.	OF	62	197	23	33	7	1	4	15	.168	110	4	4	.966
1969—Shelby	W. Car.	OF	39	157	26	51	12	0	7	29	.325	77	7	4	.955
1970—Pittsfield	East.	OF-3B-2B	123	429	65	106	11	6	15	44	.247	219	11	4	.983
1971—Pittsfield	East.	OF-C	103	331	37	77	11	1	9	41	.233	182	5	3	.984
1972—Pittsfield	East.	*C-OF	125	410	57	118	20	2	9	60	.288	772	*68	7	*.992
1973—Spokane†	P. C.	C-OF	20	54	6	11	2	0	1	6	.204	64	4	3	.953
1973—Tulsa‡	A. A.	C-OF	60	184	22	49	12	1	2	22	.266	298	32	5	.985
1974—Evansville	A. A.	C	84	233	40	64	11	2	10	43	.275	412	41	10	.978
1974—Detroit	Amer.	C	13	29	1	4	1	0	0	2	.138	45	10	4	.932
1975—Evansville	A. A.	C-OF	43	142	20	41	11	0	6	28	.289	174	26	3	.985
1975—Detroit	Amer.	C	35	118	15	27	6	3	4	13	.229	195	23	4	.982
1976—Detroit	Amer.	C	60	144	18	32	7	2	3	10	.222	221	19	15	.941
1977—Detroit	Amer.	C-OF	53	164	26	45	8	1	9	25	.274	181	20	3	.985
1978—Detroit	Amer.	OF	71	187	23	53	5	0	7	22	.283	89	2	2	.978
1979—Detroit	Amer.	1B-C-OF	87	231	27	61	9	1	15	46	.264	318	26	3	.991
1980—Detroit	Amer.	1B-OF-C	126	372	56	102	13	2	16	65	.274	575	47	11	.983
1981—Detroit	Amer.	1B-C-OF	70	172	20	37	4	0	9	25	.215	197	6	3	.985
1982—Detroit	Amer.	C-1-O-3	70	193	28	58	9	0	8	32	.301	228	14	2	.992
1983—Detroit	Amer.	C-1-3-O	92	245	32	66	8	1	9	44	.269	225	21	2	.992
Major League Totals			677	1855	246	485	70	10	80	284	.261	2274	188	51	.980

Selected by Washington Senators' organization in 42nd round of free-agent draft, June 6, 1967.
†Traded with Pitcher Mike Nagy to St. Louis Cardinals for Pitcher Jim Bibby, June 6, 1973.
‡Traded to Detroit Tigers for Infielder Larry Elliott, December 3, 1973.

JAMES EUGENE WOHLFORD

(Jim)

Born February 28, 1951, at Visalia, Calif.
Height, 5.11. Weight, 175.
Throws and bats righthanded.
Attended College of the Sequoias, Visalia, Calif.

Led Pioneer League in stolen bases with 32 in 1970.
Led American Association second basemen in errors with 27 in 1972.
Led Pioneer League shortstops in errors with 33 in 1970.

Year Club	League	Pos.	G.	AB.	R.	H.	2B.	3B.	HR.	RBI.	B.A.	PO.	A.	E.	F.A.
1970—Billings	Pion.	SS-2B-3B	62	221	42	68	7	2	3	37	.308	72	158	36	.865
1971—San Jose	Calif.	2B-SS	120	491	82	149	27	6	11	41	.303	193	327	30	.945
1972—Omaha	A. A.	2B-3B-OF	132	475	75	138	13	10	7	47	.291	247	292	32	.944
1972—Kansas City	Amer.	2B	15	25	3	6	1	0	0	0	.240	7	12	1	.950
1973—Omaha	A. A.	OF	65	246	30	76	9	4	3	30	.309	91	5	2	.980
1973—Kansas City	Amer.	OF	45	109	21	29	1	3	2	10	.266	31	2	0	1.000
1974—Kansas City	Amer.	OF	143	501	55	136	16	7	2	44	.271	273	7	5	.982
1975—Kansas City	Amer.	OF	116	353	45	90	10	5	0	30	.255	175	9	9	.953
1976—Kansas City†	Amer.	OF-2B	107	293	47	73	10	2	1	24	.249	190	8	5	.975
1977—Milwaukee	Amer.	OF-2B	129	391	41	97	16	3	2	36	.248	246	7	5	.981
1978—Milwaukee	Amer.	OF	46	118	16	35	7	2	1	19	.297	52	2	1	.982
1979—Milwaukee‡	Amer.	OF	63	175	19	46	13	1	1	17	.263	126	0	4	.969
1980—San Francisco	Nat.	OF-3B	91	193	17	54	6	4	1	24	.280	89	3	2	.979
1981—San Francisco	Nat.	OF	50	68	4	11	3	0	1	7	.162	3	1	0	1.000

Year Club League	Pos.	G.	AB.	R.	H.	2B.	3B.	HR.	RBI.	B.A.	PO.	A.	E.	F.A.
1982—San Francisco§ .... Nat.	OF	97	250	37	64	12	1	2	25	.256	122	4	1	.992
1983—Montreal .... Nat.	OF	83	141	7	39	8	0	1	14	.277	80	2	1	.988
American League Totals		664	1965	247	512	74	23	9	190	.261	1100	47	30	.975
National League Totals		321	652	65	168	29	5	5	70	.258	294	10	4	.987
Major League Totals		985	2617	312	680	103	28	14	260	.260	1394	57	34	.977

Selected by California Angels' organization in 11th round of free-agent draft, June 5, 1969.
Selected by Kansas City Royals' organization in secondary phase of free-agent draft, January 17, 1970.
†Traded with Infielder Jamie Quirk and a player to be named later to Milwaukee Brewers for Pitcher Jim Colborn and Catcher Darrell Porter, December 6, 1976; Milwaukee acquired Pitcher Bob McClure to complete deal, March 15, 1977.
‡Granted free agency, November 1, 1979; signed by San Francisco Giants, November 28, 1979.
§Traded to Montreal Expos for Infielder Chris Smith, February 2, 1983.

CHAMPIONSHIP SERIES RECORD

Year Club League	Pos.	G.	AB.	R.	H.	2B.	3B.	HR.	RBI.	B.A.	PO.	A.	E.	F.A.
1976—Kansas City .... Amer.	OF-PH	5	11	3	2	0	0	0	0	.182	7	0	0	1.000

EDWARD DAVID WOJNA

Name pronounced WAHJ-na.

(Ed)

Born August 20, 1960, at Bridgeport, Conn.
Height, 6.01. Weight, 195.
Throws and bats righthanded.
Attended Indian River Community College, Ft. Pierce, Fla.

Led Eastern League in hit batsmen with 9 in 1983.

Year Club League	G.	IP.	W.	L.	Pct.	H.	R.	ER.	SO.	BB.	ERA.
1981—Spartanburg .... S. Atlantic	27	178	11	13	.458	181	●107	●82	130	69	4.15
1982—Peninsula .... Carolina	27	176⅔	12	8	.600	156	79	57	116	49	2.90
1983—Reading† .... Eastern	28	161⅔	13	7	.650	147	80	66	83	78	3.67

Selected by Baltimore Orioles' organization in 6th round of free-agent draft, January 8, 1980.
Selected by Philadelphia Phillies' organization in secondary phase of free-agent draft, June 3, 1980.
†Traded with Pitchers Marty Decker, Darren Burroughs and Lance McCullers to San Diego Padres, September 20, 1983, as partial completion of deal in which San Diego traded Outfielder Sixto Lezcano and a player to be named later to Philadelphia Phillies for four players to be named later, August 31, 1983; Philadelphia organization acquired Pitcher Steve Fireovid to complete deal, October 11, 1983.

GARY LEE WOODS

Born July 20, 1954, at Santa Barbara, Calif.
Height, 6.02. Weight, 190.
Throws and bats righthanded.
Attended Santa Barbara City Junior College, Santa Barbara, Calif.

Led Pacific Coast League outfielders in putouts with 354 in 1976.

Year Club League	Pos.	G.	AB.	R.	H.	2B.	3B.	HR.	RBI.	B.A.	PO.	A.	E.	F.A.
1973—Lewiston .... N'west.	OF	63	220	23	45	7	3	2	15	.205	87	2	7	.927
1974—Burlington .... Midw.	OF	117	405	68	115	★30	3	11	59	.284	228	4	8	.967
1975—Birmingham .... South.	OF	134	484	76	126	15	6	1	43	.260	★366	★20	7	.982
1976—Tucson .... P. C.	OF-3B	137	526	79	162	22	6	8	67	.308	355	14	13	.966
1976—Oakland† .... Amer.	OF	6	8	0	1	0	0	0	0	.125	7	0	0	1.000
1977—Toronto .... Amer.	OF	60	227	21	49	9	1	0	17	.216	154	4	1	.994
1977—Toledo .... Int.	OF	89	313	46	85	17	4	4	33	.272	231	5	6	.975
1978—Syracuse .... Int.	OF	133	504	74	136	★33	6	13	45	.270	★316	8	11	.967
1978—Toronto‡ .... Amer.	OF	8	19	1	3	1	0	0	0	.158	12	0	0	1.000
1979—Charleston§ .... Int.	OF	97	338	46	20	25	1	6	49	.266	253	7	9	.967
1980—Tucson .... P. C.	OF	140	517	102	162	★42	6	8	86	.313	264	13	5	.982
1980—Houston .... Nat.	OF	19	53	8	20	5	0	2	15	.377	19	1	0	1.000
1981—Houston x .... Nat.	OF	54	110	10	23	4	1	0	12	.209	61	1	1	.984
1982—Chicago .... Nat.	OF	117	245	28	66	15	1	4	30	.269	161	6	0	1.000
1983—Chicago y .... Nat.	OF-2B	93	190	25	46	9	0	4	22	.242	97	4	3	.971
American League Totals		74	254	22	53	10	1	0	17	.209	173	4	1	.994
National League Totals		283	598	71	155	33	2	10	79	.259	338	12	4	.989
Major League Totals		357	852	93	208	43	3	10	96	.244	511	16	5	.991

Signed as free agent by Oakland A's organization, May 12, 1973.
†Selected by Toronto Blue Jays in American League expansion draft, November 5, 1976.
‡Traded to Houston Astros for Outfielder Don Pisker, December 5, 1978.
§On disabled list, July 14 to August 13, 1979.
xTraded to Chicago Cubs' organization for Outfielder Jim Tracy, December 9, 1981.
yOn supplemental disabled list, July 15 to July 30, 1983.

DIVISION SERIES RECORD

Year Club League	Pos.	G.	AB.	R.	H.	2B.	3B.	HR.	RBI.	B.A.	PO.	A.	E.	F.A.
1981—Houston .... Nat.	PH	2	2	0	0	0	0	0	0	.000	0	0	0	.000

CHAMPIONSHIP SERIES RECORD

Year Club League	Pos.	G.	AB.	R.	H.	2B.	3B.	HR.	RBI.	B.A.	PO.	A.	E.	F.A.
1980—Houston .... Nat.	OF-PH	4	8	0	2	0	0	0	1	.250	1	0	0	1.000

ROBERT JOHN WOODWARD
(Rob)

Born September 28, 1962, at Hanover, N.H.
Height, 6.02. Weight, 185.
Throws and bats righthanded.
Tied for Carolina League lead in games started by pitchers with 29 in 1983.

Year Club	League	G.	IP.	W.	L.	Pct.	H.	R.	ER.	SO.	BB.	ERA.
1981—Elmira	NYP	12	77	4	3	.571	77	38	29	47	23	3.39
1982—Winter Haven	Florida St.	27	126⅔	7	9	.438	140	85	72	50	62	5.12
1983—Winston-Salem	Carolina	30	197⅔	13	11	.542	177	103	91	157	100	4.14

Selected by Boston Red Sox' organization in 3rd round of free-agent draft, June 8, 1981.

TODD ROLAND WORRELL

Name pronounced Worr-ELL.

Born September 28, 1959, at Arcadia, Calif.
Height, 6.05. Weight, 215.
Throws and bats righthanded.
Received bachelor of science degree in Christian education from
Biola College, La Mirada, Calif.

Year Club	League	G.	IP.	W.	L.	Pct.	H.	R.	ER.	SO.	BB.	ERA.
1982—Erie	NYP	9	51⅔	4	1	.800	52	23	19	57	15	3.31
1983—Louisville	Am. Assoc.	15	79⅔	4	2	.667	76	49	42	46	42	4.74
1983—Arkansas	Texas	10	70⅓	5	2	.714	57	33	24	74	37	3.07

Selected by St. Louis Cardinals' organization in 1st round (21st player selected) of free-agent draft, June 7, 1982.

RICHARD COOPER WORTHAM
(Rich)

Born October 22, 1953, at Odessa, Tex.
Height, 6.00. Weight, 185.
Throws left and bats righthanded.
Attended University of Texas, Austin, Tex.
Tied for American Association lead in wild pitches with 11 in 1981.

Year Club	League	G.	IP.	W.	L.	Pct.	H.	R.	ER.	SO.	BB.	ERA.
1976—Knoxville	Southern	11	68	4	2	.667	58	33	32	56	38	4.24
1977—Iowa	Am. Assoc.	9	31	1	3	.250	54	39	30	22	20	8.71
1977—Knoxville	Southern	22	114	9	7	.563	116	62	32	80	45	2.53
1978—Iowa	Am. Assoc.	22	138	5	8	.385	136	75	61	73	54	3.98
1978—Chicago	American	8	59	3	2	.600	59	24	20	25	23	3.05
1979—Chicago	American	34	204	14	14	.500	195	126	111	119	100	4.90
1980—Chicago†	American	41	92	4	7	.364	102	73	61	58	58	5.97
1981—Denver	Am. Assoc.	16	77	6	6	.500	57	48	41	33	71	4.79
1981—Memphis‡	Southern	5	18	1	0	1.000	15	17	16	8	28	8.00
1982—Reading§	Eastern	24	36⅔	0	5	.000	47	51	47	27	58	11.54
1983—Albany x	Eastern	4	11	0	3	.000	11	15	14	6	16	11.45
1983—Modesto	California	14	44	2	3	.400	45	41	33	44	42	6.75
1983—Oakland	American	1	0	0	0	.000	3	1	1	0	1	....
Major League Totals		84	355	21	23	.477	359	224	193	189	182	4.89

Selected by Texas Rangers' organization in 5th round of free-agent draft, June 6, 1972.
Selected by New York Mets' organization in 14th round of free-agent draft, June 4, 1975.
Selected by Chicago White Sox' organization in secondary phase of free-agent draft, January 7, 1976.
†Traded to Montreal Expos for Second Baseman Tony Bernazard, December 12, 1980.
‡Released, April 1, 1982; signed by Reading (Philadelphia Phillies' organization), May 14, 1982.
§Released, January 7, 1983; signed by Tacoma (Oakland A's organization), January 25, 1983.
xOn temporary inactive list, May 17 to June 15, 1983.

RONALD ALLAN WOTUS
(Ron)

Born March 3, 1961, at Colchester, Conn.
Height, 6.01. Weight, 165.
Throws and bats righthanded.

Year Club	League	Pos.	G.	AB.	R.	H.	2B.	3B.	HR.	RBI.	B.A.	PO.	A.	E.	F.A.
1979—Bradenton Pir.	Gulf C.	SS-1B-3B	40	147	16	40	6	2	1	14	.272	148	93	8	.968
1979—Salem	Carol.	3B-1B	8	26	4	8	0	0	0	2	.308	17	22	2	.951
1980—Shelby†	S. Atl.	SS-3B	45	158	19	36	7	1	0	19	.228	61	105	8	.954
1981—Hagers.-Alex.	Carol.	S-3-2-1	134	487	72	138	20	4	4	63	.283	178	306	27	.947
1982—Buffalo	East.	2-O-S-1-3	86	321	50	96	13	4	8	39	.299	171	174	17	.953
1982—Portland	P. C.	2B-SS	42	145	27	42	6	5	3	23	.290	65	88	4	.975
1983—Hawaii	P. C.	2B-SS-1B	125	465	94	140	28	6	10	62	.301	286	324	19	.970
1983—Pittsburgh	Nat.	SS-2B	5	3	0	0	0	0	0	0	.000	2	2	0	1.000
Major League Totals			5	3	0	0	0	0	0	0	.000	2	2	0	1.000

Selected by Pittsburgh Pirates' organization in 16th round of free-agent draft, June 5, 1979.
†On disabled list, June 28, 1980 through remainder of season.

GEORGE DEWITT WRIGHT

Born December 22, 1958, at Oklahoma City, Okla.
Height, 5.11. Weight, 185.
Throws right and bats right and lefthanded.

Led Western Carolinas League outfielders in double plays with 6 in 1979.
Tied for Texas League lead in double plays by outfielders with 4 in 1980.

Year—Club	League	Pos.	G.	AB.	R.	H.	2B.	3B.	HR.	RBI.	B.A.	PO.	A.	E.	F.A.
1977—Sarasota Rangers	Gulf C.	OF	31	87	11	16	0	2	0	8	.184	44	4	1	.980
1978—Asheville	W. Car.	OF	110	335	66	83	16	1	1	27	.248	203	15	7	.969
1979—Asheville	W. Car.	OF	115	379	53	97	17	4	4	40	.256	★245	★22	7	.974
1980—Tulsa	Texas	OF	●136	458	60	126	22	5	5	65	.275	★319	22	11	.969
1981—Tulsa	Texas	OF	●133	489	58	127	29	8	11	58	.260	286	8	7	.977
1982—Texas	Amer.	OF	150	557	69	147	20	5	11	50	.264	398	14	8	.981
1983—Texas	Amer.	OF	●162	634	79	175	28	6	18	80	.276	460	6	7	.985
Major League Totals			312	1191	148	322	48	11	29	130	.270	858	20	15	.983

Selected by Texas Rangers' organization in 4th round of free-agent draft, June 7, 1977.

JAMES RICHARD WRIGHT
(Ricky)

Born November 22, 1958, at Paris, Texas.
Height, 6.03. Weight, 175.
Throws and bats lefthanded.
Attended Paris Junior College, Paris, Texas,
and University of Texas, Austin, Texas.

Pitched 4-2 no-hit victory against Portland, May 4, 1983.
Led Texas League in wild pitches with 17 and tied for lead in balks with 4 in 1980.

Year—Club	League	G.	IP.	W.	L.	Pct.	H.	R.	ER.	SO.	BB.	ERA.
1980—San Antonio†	Texas	23	152	8	10	.444	144	85	71	127	85	4.20
1981—Albuquerque	P. Coast	27	155	14	6	.700	141	81	73	112	90	4.24
1982—Albuquerque‡	P. Coast	15	60⅓	4	3	.571	63	45	38	57	36	5.67
1982—Los Angeles	National	14	32⅔	2	1	.667	28	12	11	24	20	3.03
1983—Albuquerque	P. Coast	33	83⅓	7	6	.538	75	60	45	68	58	4.86
1983—Los Angeles§	National	6	6⅓	0	0	.000	5	2	2	5	2	2.84
1983—Texas	American	1	2	0	0	.000	0	0	0	0	2	0.00
National League Totals		20	39	2	1	.667	33	14	13	29	22	3.00
American League Totals		1	2	0	0	.000	0	0	0	0	2	0.00
Major League Totals		21	41	2	1	.667	33	14	13	31	23	2.85

Selected by St. Louis Cardinals' organization in 2nd round of free-agent draft, June 7, 1977.
Selected by Los Angeles Dodgers' organization in secondary phase of free-agent draft, January 8, 1980.
†On temporary inactive list, July 26 to August 14, 1980.
‡On disabled list, April 5 to May 10, 1982.
§Traded to Texas Rangers, September 16, 1983, completing deal in which Los Angeles Dodgers traded Pitcher Dave Stewart and a player to be named later to Texas for Pitcher Rick Honeycutt, August 19, 1983.

HAROLD DELANO WYNEGAR JR.

Name pronounced WY-nuh-ger.

(Butch)

Born March 14, 1956, at York, Pa.
Height, 6.00. Weight, 194.
Throws right and bats left and righthanded.

Led American League catchers in double plays with 13 in 1980.
Led California League in bases on balls received with 142 in 1975.
Led Appalachian League catchers in double plays with 9 in 1974.
Named American League Rookie Player of the Year by THE SPORTING NEWS, 1976.

Year—Club	League	Pos.	G.	AB.	R.	H.	2B.	3B.	HR.	RBI.	B.A.	PO.	A.	E.	F.A.
1974—Elizabethton	Appal.	C	60	191	32	66	10	0	8	51	★.346	344	39	5	★.987
1975—Reno	Calif.	C	●139	468	106	147	18	6	19	★112	.314	★734	★99	9	★.989
1976—Minnesota	Amer.	C	149	534	58	139	21	2	10	69	.260	650	78	★16	.978
1977—Minnesota	Amer.	C-3B	144	532	76	139	22	3	10	79	.261	676	84	5	.993
1978—Minnesota	Amer.	C-3B	135	454	36	104	22	1	4	45	.229	582	70	8	.988
1979—Minnesota	Amer.	C	149	504	74	136	20	0	7	57	.270	653	65	6	.992
1980—Minnesota	Amer.	C	146	486	61	124	18	3	5	57	.255	670	72	9	.988
1981—Minnesota†‡	Amer.	C	47	150	11	37	5	0	0	10	.247	162	24	1	.995
1982—Minn.§-N.Y. x	Amer.	C	87	277	36	74	12	1	4	28	.267	523	26	5	.991
1983—New York y	Amer.	C	94	301	40	89	18	2	6	42	.296	480	29	8	.985
Major League Totals			1051	3238	392	842	138	12	46	387	.260	4396	448	58	.988

Selected by Minnesota Twins' organization in 2nd round of free-agent draft, June 5, 1974.
†On disabled list, April 6 to May 16, 1981.
‡On supplemental disabled list, August 26 to September 11, 1981.
§Traded with Pitcher Roger Erickson to New York Yankees for Infielder Larry Milbourne and Pitchers John Pacella and Pete Filson, May 12, 1982.
xOn supplemental disabled list, July 25, 1982, then transferred to disabled list, August 16 to September 1, 1982.
yOn supplemental disabled list, May 12 to May 27, 1983.

ALL-STAR GAME RECORD

Year League	Pos.	AB.	R.	H.	2B.	3B.	HR.	RBI.	B.A.	PO.	A.	E.	F.A.
1976—American	PH	0	0	0	0	0	0	0	.000	0	0	0	.000
1977—American	C	2	1	1	0	0	0	0	.500	3	0	0	1.000
All-Star Game Totals		2	1	1	0	0	0	0	.500	3	0	0	1.000

MARVELL WYNNE

Name pronounced Win.

Born December 17, 1959, at Chicago, Ill.
Height, 5.11. Weight, 176.
Throws and bats lefthanded.

Led South Atlantic League in total bases with 256 in 1980.
Led South Atlantic League outfielders in assists with 17 in 1980.
Tied for International League lead in game-winning RBIs with 14 in 1982.
Tied for Gulf Coast League lead in being hit by pitch with 5 in 1979.

Year Club	League	Pos.	G.	AB.	R.	H.	2B.	3B.	HR.	RBI.	B.A.	PO.	A.	E.	F.A.
1979—Sarasota Royals	Gulf C.	OF	50	190	21	54	6	4	4	28	.284	108	9	4	.967
1980—Charleston†	S. Atl.	OF-2B-3B	137	★547	106	152	20	★15	18	98	.278	281	19	13	.958
1981—Jackson	Texas	OF	127	497	69	142	29	2	4	50	.286	267	21	6	.980
1982—Tidewater	Int.	OF	130	512	76	118	15	7	10	65	.230	283	13	12	.961
1983—Tidewater‡	Int.	OF	51	175	32	50	13	1	3	29	.286	114	5	2	.983
1983—Pittsburgh	Nat.	OF	103	366	66	89	16	2	7	26	.243	223	3	4	.983
Major League Totals			103	366	66	89	16	2	7	26	.243	223	3	4	.983

Signed as free agent by Kansas City Royals' organization, September 3, 1978.
†Traded with Pitcher John Skinner to New York Mets' organization for Pitcher Juan Berenguer, March 31, 1981.
‡Traded with Pitcher Steve Senteney to Pittsburgh Pirates for Catcher Junior Ortiz and Pitcher Arthur Ray, June 14, 1983.

CARL MICHAEL YASTRZEMSKI

Name pronounced Yah-STREM-skee.

Born August 22, 1939, at Southampton, N. Y.
Height, 5.11. Weight, 185.
Throws right and bats lefthanded.
Attended University of Notre Dame, Notre Dame, Ind., and received bachelor of science degree
in business administration from Merrimack College, North Andover, Mass.

Established major league records for most games, lifetime (3,308); lowest batting average, season, leader in batting (.301), 1968; most years leading league in assists by outfielders (7) 1977; most times grounded into double play by lefthanded batter, season (30), 1964.

Tied major league records for most seasons, 100 or more games (22); most seasons, one club (23), most consecutive seasons, one club (23); fewest triples, season, 150 or more games (0), 1970; fewest double plays by outfielder, season, for leader in double plays (4), 1971; most home runs, two consecutive games (5), May 19 and 20, 1976; highest fielding percentage by outfielder, season, 100 or more games (1.000), 1977.

Established American League records for most at-bats, lifetime (11,988); most plate appearances, lifetime (13,990); most intentional bases on balls, lifetime (190); most consecutive seasons, 100 or more games (20); most times grounded into double play, lifetime (311).

Won American League Triple Crown, 1967.
Hit three home runs in a game, May 19, 1976.
Hit for the cycle, May 14, 1965.
Led American League in sacrifice flies with 9 in 1972.
Led American League in total bases with 360 in 1967 and 335 in 1970.
Led American League in slugging percentage with .536 in 1965, .622 in 1967 and .592 in 1970.
Led American League in bases on balls received with 95 in 1963 and 119 in 1968.
Led American League in grounding into double plays with 27 in 1962 and 30 in 1964.
Led American League outfielders in assists with 17 in 1969, 16 in 1977 and tied for lead with 19 in 1964.
Tied for American League lead in sacrifice flies with 11 in 1977.
Tied for American League lead in double plays by outfielders with 4 in 1971.
Named Major League Player of the Year by THE SPORTING NEWS, 1967.
Named American League Player of the Year by THE SPORTING NEWS, 1967.
Named American League Most Valuable Player by Baseball Writers' Association of America, 1967.
Named outfielder on THE SPORTING NEWS American League All-Star Team, 1963, 1965 and 1967.
Named outfielder on THE SPORTING NEWS American League All-Star fielding team, 1963, 1965, 1967 through 1969, 1971 and 1977.
Named Carolina League Most Valuable Player, 1959.
Received reported $100,000 bonus to sign with Boston Red Sox, 1958.

Year Club	League	Pos.	G.	AB.	R.	H.	2B.	3B.	HR.	RBI.	B.A.	PO.	A.	E.	F.A.
1959—Raleigh	Carol.	★2B-SS	120	451	87	★170	★34	6	15	100	★.377	★255	284	★45	★.923
1960—Minneapolis	A. A.	OF	148	570	84	★193	36	8	7	69	.339	243	18	5	.981
1961—Boston	Amer.	OF	148	583	71	155	31	6	11	80	.266	248	12	10	.963
1962—Boston	Amer.	OF	160	646	99	191	43	6	19	94	.296	329	★15	★11	.969
1963—Boston	Amer.	OF	151	570	91	★183	★40	3	14	68	★.321	283	★18	6	.980
1964—Boston	Amer.	OF-3B	151	567	77	164	29	9	15	67	.289	372	24	11	.973
1965—Boston	Amer.	OF	133	494	78	154	●45	3	20	72	.312	222	11	3	.987
1966—Boston	Amer.	OF	160	594	81	165	★39	2	16	80	.278	310	★15	5	.985
1967—Boston	Amer.	OF	161	579	★112	★189	31	4	●44	★121	★.326	297	13	7	.978
1968—Boston	Amer.	OF-1B	157	539	90	162	32	2	23	74	★.301	315	13	3	.991
1969—Boston	Amer.	OF-1B	●162	603	96	154	28	2	40	111	.255	427	38	6	.987
1970—Boston	Amer.	1B-OF	161	566	★125	186	29	0	40	102	.329	816	64	14	.984

Year Club	League	Pos.	G.	AB.	R.	H.	2B.	3B.	HR.	RBI.	B.A.	PO.	A.	E.	F.A.
1971—Boston	Amer.	OF	148	508	75	129	21	2	15	70	.254	281	*16	2	.993
1972—Boston†	Amer.	OF-1B	125	455	70	120	18	2	12	68	.264	498	43	8	.985
1973—Boston	Amer.	1B-3B-OF	152	540	82	160	25	4	19	95	.296	979	119	18	.984
1974—Boston	Amer.	1B-OF	148	515	*93	155	25	2	15	79	.301	806	46	6	.993
1975—Boston	Amer.	1B-OF	149	543	91	146	30	1	14	60	.269	1217	88	5	.996
1976—Boston	Amer.	1B-OF	155	546	71	146	23	2	21	102	.267	922	55	4	.996
1977—Boston	Amer.	*OF-1B	150	558	99	165	27	3	28	102	.296	344	22	0	*1.000
1978—Boston	Amer.	OF-1B	144	523	70	145	21	2	17	81	.277	523	49	5	.991
1979—Boston	Amer.	1B-OF	147	518	69	140	28	1	21	87	.270	529	56	4	.993
1980—Boston	Amer.	OF-1B	105	364	49	100	21	1	15	50	.275	225	13	4	.983
1981—Boston	Amer.	1B	91	338	36	83	14	1	7	53	.246	353	34	3	.992
1982—Boston‡...............	Amer.	1B-OF	131	459	53	126	22	1	16	72	.275	119	10	0	1.000
1983—Boston‡...............	Amer.	1B-OF	119	380	38	101	24	0	10	56	.266	22	1	0	1.000
Major League Totals...................			3308	11988	1816	3419	646	59	452	1844	.285	10437	775	135	.988

Signed as free agent by Boston Red Sox' organization, November 29, 1958.
†On supplemental disabled list, May 10 to June 9, 1972.
‡On voluntarily retired list, October 25, 1983.

CHAMPIONSHIP SERIES RECORD

Year Club	League	Pos.	G.	AB.	R.	H.	2B.	3B.	HR.	RBI.	B.A.	PO.	A.	E.	F.A.
1975—Boston	Amer.	OF	3	11	4	5	1	0	1	2	.455	7	2	0	1.000

WORLD SERIES RECORD

Year Club	League	Pos.	G.	AB.	R.	H.	2B.	3B.	HR.	RBI.	B.A.	PO.	A.	E.	F.A.
1967—Boston	Amer.	OF	7	25	4	10	2	0	3	5	.400	16	2	0	1.000
1975—Boston‡.................	Amer.	OF-1B	7	29	7	9	0	0	0	4	.310	35	1	0	1.000
World Series Totals....................			14	54	11	19	2	0	3	9	.352	51	3	0	1.000

ALL-STAR GAME RECORD

Tied All-Star Game records for most hits, game (4), July 14, 1970; most one-base hits, game (3), July 14, 1970; most home runs by pinch-hitter, game (1), July 15, 1975.

Year League	Pos.	AB.	R.	H.	2B.	3B.	HR.	RBI.	B.A.	PO.	A.	E.	F.A.
1963—American.............................	OF	2	0	0	0	0	0	0	.000	1	0	0	1.000
1967—American.............................	OF	4	0	3	1	0	0	0	.750	2	0	0	1.000
1968—American.............................	OF	4	0	0	0	0	0	0	.000	0	0	0	.000
1969—American.............................	OF	1	0	0	0	0	0	0	.000	1	0.	0	1.000
1970—American.............................	OF-1B	6	1	4	1	0	0·	1	.667	8	0	0	1.000
1971—American.............................	OF	3	0	0	0	0	0	0	.000	0	0	0	.000
1972—American.............................	OF	3	0	0	0	0	0	0	.000	3	0	0	1.000
1974—American.............................	1B	1	0	0	0	0	0	0	.000	5	0	0	1.000
1975—American.............................	PH	1	1	1	0	0	1	3	1.000	0	0	0	.000
1976—American.............................	OF	2	0	0	0	0	0	0	.000	0	0	0	.000
1977—American.............................	OF	2	0	0	0	0	0	0	.000	0	0	0	.000
1979—American.............................	1B	3	0	2	0	0	0	1	.667	5	1	0	1.000
1982—American.............................	PH	1	0	0	0	0	0	0	.000	0	0	0	.000
1983—American.............................	PH	1	0	0	0	0	0	0	.000	0	0	0	.000
All-Star Game Totals........................		34	2	10	2	0	1	5	.294	25	1	0	1.000

Member of American League All-Star Team in 1966; did not play.
Named to American League All-Star Teams for 1965, 1973 and 1978 games; replaced due to injury.

STEPHEN WAYNE YEAGER

Name pronounced YAY-gur.

(Steve)

Born November 24, 1948, at Huntington, W. Va.
Height, 6.00. Weight, 200.
Throws and bats righthanded.
Nephew of retired Air Force Brigadier General Chuck Yeager, first man to break sound barrier.

Tied major league record for most putouts, extra-inning game, catcher (22), August 8, 1972 (19 innings).
Established National League record for most chances accepted, extra-inning game, catcher (24), August 8, 1972 (19 innings).

Year Club	League	Pos.	G.	AB.	R.	H.	2B.	3B.	HR.	RBI.	B.A.	PO.	A.	E.	F.A.
1967—Ogden	Pion.	C	1	0	0	0	0	0	0	0	.000	0	0	0	.000
1967—Dubuque	Midw.	C-1B	14	35	0	6	0	0	0	2	.171	67	3	3	.959
1968—Daytona Beach	Fla. St.	C	59	144	17	22	3	1	1	6	.153	314	23	9	.974
1969—Bakersfield...........	Calif.	C	22	65	8	10	1	0	0	2	.154	145	26	4	.977
1969—Albuquerque	Texas	PH	1	1	0	0	0	0	0	0	.000	0	0	0	.000
1970—Albuquerque	Texas	C-OF-3B	55	151	23	42	5	1	3	24	.278	224	29	5	.981
1971—Albuquerque	Texas	C	107	339	49	93	16	5	8	53	.274	678	84	*14	.982
1972—Albuquerque	P. C.	C	82	257	46	72	6	6	13	45	.280	494	26	9	.983
1972—Los Angeles	Nat.	C	35	106	18	29	0	1	4	15	.274	220	19	4	.984
1973—Los Angeles	Nat.	C	54	134	18	34	5	0	2	10	.254	230	24	5	.981
1974—Los Angeles	Nat.	C	94	316	41	84	16	1	12	41	.266	552	58	5	.992
1975—Los Angeles	Nat.	C	135	452	34	103	16	1	12	54	.228	*806	62	7	.992
1976—Los Angeles	Nat.	C	117	359	42	77	11	3	11	35	.214	522	*77	9	.985
1977—Los Angeles	Nat.	C	125	387	53	99	21	2	16	55	.256	690	89	*18	.977
1978—Los Angeles†	Nat.	C	94	228	19	44	7	0	4	23	.193	373	55	5	.988
1979—Los Angeles	Nat.	C	105	310	33	67	9	2	13	41	.216	513	56	9	.984

Year Club	League	Pos.	G.	AB.	R.	H.	2B.	3B.	HR.	RBI.	B.A.	PO.	A.	E.	F.A.
1980—Los Angeles	Nat.	C	96	227	20	48	8	0	2	20	.211	382	36	7	.984
1981—Los Angeles	Nat.	C	42	86	5	18	2	0	3	7	.209	142	13	1	.994
1982—Los Angeles‡	Nat.	C	82	196	13	48	5	2	2	18	.245	338	42	4	.990
1983—Los Angeles§.........	Nat.	C	113	335	31	68	8	3	15	41	.203	579	63	10	.985
Major League Totals...................			1092	3136	327	719	108	15	96	360	.229	5347	594	84	.986

Selected by Los Angeles Dodgers' organization in 4th round of free-agent draft, June 6, 1967.
†On supplemental disabled list, August 8 to August 25, 1978.
‡On disabled list, July 12 to August 9, 1982.
§On disabled list, August 1 to August 23, 1983.

DIVISION SERIES RECORD

Year Club	League	Pos.	G.	AB.	R.	H.	2B.	3B.	HR.	RBI.	B.A.	PO.	A.	E.	F.A.
1981—Los Angeles	Nat.	PH-C	2	5	1	2	1	0	0	0	.400	6	0	0	1.000

CHAMPIONSHIP SERIES RECORD

Year Club	League	Pos.	G.	AB.	R.	H.	2B.	3B.	HR.	RBI.	B.A.	PO.	A.	E.	F.A.
1974—Los Angeles	Nat.	C	3	9	1	0	0	0	0	0	.000	14	1	0	1.000
1977—Los Angeles	Nat.	C	4	13	1	3	0	0	0	2	.231	22	1	0	1.000
1978—Los Angeles	Nat.	C	4	13	2	3	0	0	1	2	.231	21	2	0	1.000
1981—Los Angeles	Nat.	PH-C	1	2	1	1	0	0	0	0	.500	2	0	0	1.000
1983—Los Angeles	Nat.	C	2	6	0	1	1	0	0	0	.167	7	1	0	1.000
Championship Series Totals			14	43	5	8	1	0	1	4	.186	66	5	0	1.000

WORLD SERIES RECORD

Tied World Series record for most at-bats, inning (2), October 28, 1981 (sixth inning).

Year Club	League	Pos.	G.	AB.	R.	H.	2B.	3B.	HR.	RBI.	B.A.	PO.	A.	E.	F.A.
1974—Los Angeles	Nat.	C	4	11	0	4	1	0	0	1	.364	32	4	1	.973
1977—Los Angeles	Nat.	C	6	19	2	6	1	0	2	5	.316	32	6	0	1.000
1978—Los Angeles	Nat.	C	5	13	2	3	1	0	0	0	.231	23	2	0	1.000
1981—Los Angeles	Nat.	PH-C	6	14	2	4	1	0	2	4	.286	20	0	0	1.000
World Series Totals.....................................			21	57	6	17	4	0	4	10	.298	107	12	1	.992

RICHARD MARTIN YETT

Born October 6, 1962, at Pomona, Calif.
Height, 6.01. Weight, 190.
Throws and bats righthanded.

Year Club	League	G.	IP.	W.	L.	Pct.	H.	R.	ER.	SO.	BB.	ERA.
1980—Elizabethton	Ap'lachian	10	52	3	4	.429	46	30	25	35	19	4.33
1981—Wisconsin Rapids..........................	Midwest	25	164	12	6	.667	147	87	67	121	77	3.68
1982—Visalia	California	27	196⅔	16	9	.640	183	98	80	121	97	3.66
1983—Orlando†	Southern	24	162	8	10	.444	153	82	68	93	78	3.78

Selected by Minnesota Twins' organization in 26th round of free-agent draft, June 3, 1980.
†On disabled list, April 8 to April 25, 1983.

DAVID LOUIS YOBS

Name pronounced Yabs.

(Dave)

Born January 17, 1959, at Encino, Calif.
Height, 6.00. Weight, 190.
Throws and bats lefthanded.
Attended Los Angeles Valley College, Van Nuys, Calif.,
and Oral Roberts University, Tulsa, Okla.

Year Club	League	Pos.	G.	AB.	R.	H.	2B.	3B.	HR.	RBI.	B.A.	PO.	A.	E.	F.A.
1981—Appleton	Midw.	OF-1B	65	221	30	67	15	6	2	23	.303	81	5	5	.945
1982—Glens Falls†	East.	OF	119	441	72	131	26	1	25	93	.297	158	6	5	.970
1983—Denver	A. A.	OF	60	219	28	55	12	0	6	20	.251	50	4	4	.931
1983—Glens Falls............	East.	OF	54	184	31	58	16	0	8	28	.315	81	3	2	.977

Selected by California Angels' organization in 10th round of free-agent draft, January 10, 1978.
Selected by New York Yankees' organization in 8th round of free-agent draft, June 3, 1980.
Selected by Chicago White Sox' organization in 14th round of free-agent draft, June 8, 1981.
†On disabled list, July 29 to August 12, 1982.

EDGAR FREDERICK YOST

(Ned)

Born August 19, 1955, at Eureka, Calif.
Height, 6.01. Weight, 185.
Throws and bats righthanded.
Attended Chabot Junior College, Hayward, Calif.

Led Texas League in passed balls with 16 in 1976.

Year Club	League	Pos.	G.	AB.	R.	H.	2B.	3B.	HR.	RBI.	B.A.	PO.	A.	E.	F.A.
1974—Batavia..................	NYP	C	44	123	14	31	2	2	2	11	.252	199	21	∗11	.952
1975—Wausau	Midwest	C	79	265	26	51	7	0	6	27	.192	450	42	●19	.963
1976—Jackson.................	Texas	C	83	266	25	53	5	0	3	25	.199	390	42	7	.984

Year	Club	League	Pos.	G.	AB.	R.	H.	2B.	3B.	HR.	RBI.	B.A.	PO.	A.	E.	F.A.
1977—Jackson		Texas	C	30	94	7	29	9	0	1	8	.309	145	21	4	.976
1977—Tidewater†		Int.	C	60	165	27	48	8	1	12	31	.291	171	29	3	.985
1978—Spokane‡		P. C.	C	89	267	38	70	16	1	7	42	.262	367	49	15	.965
1979—Vancouver		P. C.	C	130	419	43	110	12	2	3	53	.263	604	64	10	.985
1980—Vancouver		P. C.	C-1B	80	259	32	80	20	4	2	41	.309	312	34	8	.977
1980—Milwaukee		Amer.	C	15	31	0	5	0	0	0	0	.161	41	5	0	1.000
1981—Milwaukee		Amer.	C	18	27	4	6	0	0	3	3	.222	37	6	2	.956
1982—Milwaukee		Amer.	C	40	98	13	27	6	3	1	8	.276	121	6	3	.977
1983—Milwaukee§x		Amer.	C	61	196	21	44	5	1	6	28	.224	252	16	8	.971
Major League Totals				134	352	38	82	11	4	10	39	.233	451	33	13	.974

Signed as free agent by New York Mets' organization, June 11, 1974.
†Drafted by Milwaukee Brewers, December 5, 1977.
‡On disabled list, July 10 to July 28, 1978.
§On supplemental disabled list, July 11, 1983, then transferred to disabled list, August 5 to August 15, 1983.
xTraded with Pitcher Dan Scarpetta to Texas Rangers for Catcher Jim Sundberg, December 8, 1983.

WORLD SERIES RECORD

Year	Club	League	Pos.	G.	AB.	R.	H.	2B.	3B.	HR.	RBI.	B.A.	PO.	A.	E.	F.A.
1982—Milwaukee		Amer.	C	1	0	0	0	0	0	0	0	.000	1	0	0	1.000

CURTIS ALLEN YOUNG
(Curt)

Born April 16, 1960, at Saginaw, Mich.
Height, 6.01. Weight, 180.
Throws left and bats righthanded.
Attended Central Michigan University, Mt. Pleasant, Mich.

Led California League pitchers in games started with 28 in 1982.

Year	Club	League	G.	IP.	W.	L.	Pct.	H.	R.	ER.	SO.	BB.	ERA.
1981—Medford		Northwest	8	53	2	2	.500	45	27	25	49	32	4.25
1981—Modesto		California	5	31	2	1	.667	28	15	12	22	16	3.48
1982—Modesto		California	28	205	15	8	.652	189	90	79	162	81	3.47
1983—Tacoma		P. Coast	27	158⅔	12	9	.571	175	94	89	109	52	5.05
1983—Oakland		American.	8	9	0	1	.000	17	17	16	5	5	16.00
Major League Totals			8	9	0	1	.000	17	17	16	5	5	16.00

Selected by Oakland A's organization in 4th round of free-agent draft, June 8, 1981.

JOHN ANTHONY YOUNG

Born December 14, 1960, at Meridian, Miss.
Height, 6.02. Weight, 175.
Throws left and bats righthanded.
Attended Black Hawk College, Moline, Ill., and
Bradley University, Peoria, Ill.

Year	Club	League	G.	IP.	W.	L.	Pct.	H.	R.	ER.	SO.	BB.	ERA.
1982—Erie		NYP	9	34	4	3	.571	35	20	18	41	21	4.76
1983—Springfield		Midwest	23	133⅓	15	4	.789	87	56	40	162	∗104	2.70

Selected by St. Louis Cardinals' organization in 3rd round of free-agent draft, June 7, 1982.

MATTHEW JOHN YOUNG
(Matt)

Born August 9, 1958, at Pasadena, Calif.
Height, 6.03. Weight, 200.
Throws and bats lefthanded.
Attended Pasadena City College, Pasadena, Calif., and
University of California at Los Angeles, Los Angeles, Calif.

Year	Club	League	G.	IP.	W.	L.	Pct.	H.	R.	ER.	SO.	BB.	ERA.
1980—Bellingham		Northwest	12	73	4	5	.444	73	46	40	53	62	4.93
1981—Lynn		Eastern	14	81	3	9	.250	80	47	36	57	38	4.00
1982—Salt Lake City		P. Coast	29	176	12	10	.545	192	113	91	118	75	4.65
1983—Seattle		American	33	203⅔	11	15	.423	178	86	74	130	79	3.27
Major League Totals			33	203⅔	11	15	.423	178	86	74	130	79	3.27

Selected by Boston Red Sox' organization in 2nd round of free-agent draft, January 10, 1978.
Selected by Seattle Mariners' organization in 2nd round of free-agent draft, June 3, 1980.

ALL-STAR GAME RECORD

Year	League	IP.	W.	L.	Pct.	H.	R.	ER.	SO.	BB.	ERA.
1983—American		1	0	0	.000	0	0	0	1	0	0.00

MICHAEL DARREN YOUNG
(Mike)

Born March 20, 1960, at Hayward, Calif.
Height, 6.02. Weight, 195.
Throws right and bats left and righthanded.
Attended Chabot College, Hayward, Calif.

Led International League batters in strikeouts with 140 in 1982.
Tied for Florida State League lead in double plays by outfielders with 4 in 1980.

Year	Club	League	Pos.	G.	AB.	R.	H.	2B.	3B.	HR.	RBI.	B.A.	PO.	A.	E.	F.A.
1980—Miami	Fla. St.	OF	115	393	72	105	13	8	5	52	.267	212	*17	7	.970
1981—Miami	Fla. St.	OF	63	235	32	81	19	6	3	34	.345	135	7	1	.993
1981—Charlotte	South.	OF	75	275	58	88	16	3	12	45	.320	190	5	5	.975
1981—Rochester	Int.	OF	1	3	0	1	0	0	0	0	.000	1	0	0	1.000
1982—Rochester	Int.	OF	137	502	86	133	22	11	16	62	.265	291	7	11	.964
1982—Baltimore	Amer.	OF	6	2	2	0	0	0	0	0	.000	1	0	0	1.000
1983—Rochester	Int.	OF	102	373	62	106	14	8	14	66	.284	198	4	6	.971
1983—Baltimore	Amer.	OF	25	36	5	6	2	1	0	2	.167	25	1	2	.929
Major League Totals				31	38	7	6	2	1	0	2	.158	26	1	2	.931

Selected by Cleveland Indians' organization in 7th round of free-agent draft, June 6, 1978.
Selected by Baltimore Orioles' organization in secondary phase of free-agent draft, January 8, 1980.

JOEL RANDOLPH YOUNGBLOOD III

Born August 28, 1951, at Houston, Tex.
Height, 5.11. Weight, 175.
Throws and bats righthanded.

Established major league record for most clubs, one or more hits for, one day (2), August 4, 1982.
Tied major league record for most clubs played, one day (2), August 4, 1982.
Led National League outfielders in double plays with 6 in 1980.
Led Northern League second basemen in errors with 19 in 1970.
Tied for Northern League lead in being hit by pitch with 5 in 1970.

Year	Club	League	Pos.	G.	AB.	R.	H.	2B.	3B.	HR.	RBI.	B.A.	PO.	A.	E.	F.A.
1970—Tampa	Fla. St.	SS	17	54	7	12	0	0	0	3	.222	22	40	9	.873
1970—Sioux Falls	North.	2B-3B-SS	65	236	27	53	11	1	0	17	.225	110	134	26	.904
1971—Tampa	Fla. St.	3B-SS-OF	136	443	75	113	25	4	5	44	.255	159	207	26	.934
1972—Three Rivers	East.	OF-3B	104	366	57	106	15	5	12	60	.290	118	80	30	.868
1973—Indianapolis	A. A.	OF-SS-3B	124	451	88	143	24	9	11	50	.317	136	112	28	.899
1974—Indianapolis†	A. A.	OF	103	316	55	90	17	4	13	49	.285	115	6	4	.968
1975—Indianapolis	A. A.	OF-2B	123	418	65	110	21	●9	6	51	.263	201	13	7	.968
1976—Cincinnati‡	Nat.	1-O-C-2	55	57	8	11	1	1	0	1	.193	15	3	1	.947
1977—St.L.§-N.Y.	Nat.	2B-OF-3B	95	209	17	51	13	1	0	12	.244	107	94	8	.962
1978—New York	Nat.	O-2-3-S	113	266	40	67	12	8	7	30	.252	160	96	13	.952
1979—New York	Nat.	OF-3B-2B	158	590	90	162	37	5	16	60	.275	337	57	9	.978
1980—New York	Nat.	OF-3B-2B	146	514	58	142	26	2	8	69	.276	318	65	13	.967
1981—New York x	Nat.	OF	43	143	16	50	10	2	4	25	.350	70	6	3	.962
1982—N.Y. y-Mont. z	Nat.	O-2-S-3	120	292	37	70	14	0	3	29	.240	149	23	7	.961
1983—San Francisco	Nat.	2B-3B-OF	124	373	59	109	20	3	17	53	.292	147	182	19	.945
Major League Totals				854	2444	325	662	133	22	55	279	.271	1303	526	73	.962

Selected by Cincinnati Reds' organization in 2nd round of free-agent draft, January 17, 1970.
†On disabled list, June 7 to June 19, 1974.
‡Traded to St. Louis Cardinals for Pitcher Bill Caudill, March 28, 1977.
§Traded to New York Mets for Shortstop Mike Phillips, June 15, 1977.
xOn supplemental disabled list, June 6 to August 1 and August 15 to September 15, 1981.
yTraded to Montreal Expos for a player to be named later, August 4, 1982; New York Mets' organization acquired Pitcher Tom Gorman to complete deal, August 14, 1982.
zGranted free agency, November 10, 1982; signed by San Francisco Giants, February 7, 1983.

ALL-STAR GAME RECORD

Year	League	Pos.	AB.	R.	H.	2B.	3B.	HR.	RBI.	B.A.	PO.	A.	E.	F.A.
1981—National		PH	1	0	0	0	0	0	0	.000	0	0	0	.000

ROBIN R. YOUNT

Born September 16, 1955, at Danville, Ill.
Height, 6.00. Weight, 170.
Throws and bats righthanded.
Brother of Larry Yount, pitcher with Houston Astros, 1971.

Led American League in total bases with 367 and slugging percentage with .578 in 1982.
Led American League shortstops in double plays with 104 and total chances with 831 in 1976.
Named Major League Player of the Year by The Sporting News, 1982.
Named American League Player of the Year by The Sporting News, 1982.
Named American League Most Valuable Player by Baseball Writers' Association of America, 1982.
Named shortstop on The Sporting News American League All-Star Team, 1978, 1980 and 1982.
Named shortstop on The Sporting News American League All-Star fielding team, 1982.
Named shortstop on The Sporting News American League Silver Slugger team, 1980 and 1982.

Year	Club	League	Pos.	G.	AB.	R.	H.	2B.	3B.	HR.	RBI.	B.A.	PO.	A.	E.	F.A.
1973—Newark	NYP	SS	64	242	29	69	15	3	3	25	.285	43	85	18	.877
1974—Milwaukee	Amer.	SS	107	344	48	86	14	5	3	26	.250	148	327	19	.962
1975—Milwaukee	Amer.	SS	147	558	67	149	28	2	8	52	.267	273	402	*44	.939
1976—Milwaukee	Amer.	●SS-OF	●161	638	59	161	19	3	2	54	.252	●290	510	31	.963
1977—Milwaukee	Amer.	SS	154	605	66	174	34	4	4	49	.288	256	449	29	.964
1978—Milwaukee†	Amer.	SS	127	502	66	147	23	9	9	71	.293	246	453	30	.959
1979—Milwaukee	Amer.	SS	149	577	72	154	26	5	8	51	.267	267	517	25	.969
1980—Milwaukee	Amer.	SS	143	611	121	179	*49	10	23	87	.293	239	455	28	.961
1981—Milwaukee	Amer.	SS	96	377	50	103	15	5	10	49	.273	161	370	8	*.985

Year Club	League	Pos.	G.	AB.	R.	H.	2B.	3B.	HR.	RBI.	B.A.	PO.	A.	E.	F.A.
1982—Milwaukee............	Amer.	SS	156	635	129	*210	●46	12	29	114	.331	253	*489	24	.969
1983—Milwaukee............	Amer.	SS	149	578	102	178	42	*10	17	80	.308	256	420	19	.973
Major League Totals....................................			1389	5425	780	1541	296	65	113	633	.284	2389	4392	254	.964

Selected by Milwaukee Brewers' organization in 1st round (third player selected) of free-agent draft, June 5, 1973.
†On supplemental disabled list, March 28 to May 3, 1978.

DIVISION SERIES RECORD

Year Club	League	Pos.	G.	AB.	R.	H.	2B.	3B.	HR.	RBI.	B.A.	PO.	A.	E.	F.A.
1981—Milwaukee............	Amer.	SS	5	19	4	6	0	1	0	1	.316	6	16	1	.957

CHAMPIONSHIP SERIES RECORD

Year Club	League	Pos.	G.	AB.	R.	H.	2B.	3B.	HR.	RBI.	B.A.	PO.	A.	E.	F.A.
1982—Milwaukee............	Amer.	SS	5	16	1	4	0	0	0	0	.250	11	12	1	.958

WORLD SERIES RECORD

Established World Series record for most games, Series, four or more hits (2), 1982.
Tied World Series record for most at-bats, nine-inning game, (6), October 12, 1982.

Year Club	League	Pos.	G.	AB.	R.	H.	2B.	3B.	HR.	RBI.	B.A.	PO.	A.	E.	F.A.
1982—Milwaukee............	Amer.	SS	7	29	6	12	3	0	1	6	.414	20	19	3	.929

ALL-STAR GAME RECORD

Year League	Pos.	AB.	R.	H.	2B.	3B.	HR.	RBI.	B.A.	PO.	A.	E.	F.A.
1980—American	SS	2	0	0	0	0	0	0	.000	3	2	0	1.000
1982—American	SS	3	0	0	0	0	0	0	.000	0	2	0	1.000
1983—American	SS	2	1	0	0	0	0	1	.000	0	1	0	1.000
All-Star Game Totals		7	1	0	0	0	0	1	.000	3	5	0	1.000

VINCENT CHARLES YUHAS
(Vinnie)

Born May 23, 1961, at New Brunswick, N.J.
Height, 6.01. Weight, 195.
Throws and bats righthanded.
Brother of Mike Yuhas, pitcher in Montreal Expos' organization, 1977.

Year Club	League	G.	IP.	W.	L.	Pct.	H.	R.	ER.	SO.	BB.	ERA.
1979—Sarasota Royals-Gold	Gulf Coast	12	53	5	1	.833	45	24	17	33	26	2.89
1980—Charleston	S. Atlantic	24	139	7	9	.438	169	82	67	73	39	4.34
1981—Ft. Myers	Florida St.	24	130	8	7	.533	152	75	60	97	38	4.15
1982—Jacksonville	Southern	14	105	7	5	.583	90	40	25	94	30	2.14
1982—Omaha†	Am. Assoc.	13	68⅓	4	2	.667	75	38	34	50	37	4.48
1983—Omaha†	Am. Assoc.	19	102⅔	7	7	.500	112	61	53	65	45	4.65

Selected by Kansas City Royals' organization in 24th round of free-agent draft, June 5, 1979.
†On disabled list, June 22 to July 23, 1983.

PATRICK PAUL ZACHRY
(Pat)

Born April 24, 1952, at Richmond, Tex.
Height, 6.05. Weight, 175.
Throws and bats righthanded.

Tied for National League lead in home runs allowed with 13 in 1981.
Led Eastern League in intentional bases on balls issued with 15 in 1973.
Named National League co-Rookie of the Year by Baseball Writers' Association of America, 1976.

Year Club	League	G.	IP.	W.	L.	Pct.	H.	R.	ER.	SO.	BB.	ERA.
1970—Bradenton Reds...........................	Gulf Coast	9	54	1	4	.200	53	29	15	55	24	2.50
1970—Sioux Falls.....................................	Northern	3	21	2	1	.677	20	9	8	19	5	3.43
1971—Tampa†	Florida St.	22	143	12	4	.750	125	58	.51	115	72	3.21
1972—Three Rivers	Eastern	25	133	7	7	.500	110	55	39	102	79	2.64
1973—Three Rivers	Eastern	42	178	●12	12	.500	158	81	65	130	*127	3.29
1974—Indianapolis	Am. Assoc.	33	151	10	7	.588	129	69	59	98	71	3.52
1975—Indianapolis	Am. Assoc.	27	159	10	7	.588	120	52	43	100	70	*2.44
1976—Cincinnati	National	38	204	14	7	.667	170	70	62	143	83	2.74
1977—Cincinnati‡-New York	National	31	195	10	13	.435	207	104	92	99	77	4.25
1978—New York§	National	21	138	10	6	.625	120	57	51	78	60	3.33
1979—New York x	National	7	43	5	1	.833	44	19	17	17	21	3.56
1980—New York y	National	28	165	6	10	.375	145	65	55	88	58	3.00
1981—New York ●	National	24	139	7	●14	.333	151	78	64	76	56	4.14
1982—New York z	National	36	137⅔	6	9	.400	149	69	62	69	57	4.05
1983—Los Angeles	National	40	61⅓	6	1	.857	63	22	17	36	21	2.49
Major League Totals..............................		225	1083	64	61	.512	1049	484	420	606	433	3.49

Selected by Cincinnati Reds' organization in 19th round of free-agent draft, June 4, 1970.
†Appeared in one game as a second baseman with two assists.
‡Traded with Infielder Doug Flynn and Outfielders Dan Norman and Steve Henderson to New York Mets for Pitcher Tom Seaver, June 15, 1977.
§On disabled list, August 1 to September 7, 1978.
xOn disabled list, April 24 to May 23 and June 10 to September 27, 1979.

yOn disabled list, April 27 to May 3, 1980.
zTraded to Los Angeles Dodgers for Outfielder Jorge Orta, December 28, 1982.

CHAMPIONSHIP SERIES RECORD

Year Club	League	G.	IP.	W.	L.	Pct.	H.	R.	ER.	SO.	BB.	ERA.
1976—Cincinnati	National	1	5	1	0	1.000	6	2	2	3	3	3.60
1983—Los Angeles	National	2	4	0	0	.000	4	1	1	2	2	2.25
Championship Series Totals		3	9	1	0	1.000	10	3	3	5	5	3.00

WORLD SERIES RECORD

Year Club	League	G.	IP.	W.	L.	Pct.	H.	R.	ER.	SO.	BB.	ERA.
1976—Cincinnati	National	1	6⅔	1	0	1.000	6	2	2	6	5	2.70

ALL-STAR GAME RECORD

Member of National League All-Star Team for 1978 game; did not play.

GEOFFREY CLAYTON ZAHN
(Geoff)

Born December 19, 1946, at Baltimore, Md.
Height, 6.01. Weight, 185.
Throws and bats lefthanded.
Received bachelor of science degree in education from
University of Michigan, Ann Arbor, Mich., in 1968.

Pitched 1-0 no-hit loss against St. Petersburg, June 30, 1968.
Tied for American League lead in home runs allowed with 18 in 1981.
Led Texas League in hit batsmen with 9 in 1971.
Named lefthanded pitcher on THE SPORTING NEWS American League All-Star Team, 1982.

Year Club	League	G.	IP.	W.	L.	Pct.	H.	R.	ER.	SO.	BB.	ERA.
1968—Daytona Beach†	Florida St.	21	138	8	9	.471	97	44	32	108	38	2.09
1969—Albuquerque‡§	Texas	15	98	9	3	.750	103	42	38	44	29	3.49
1970—Spokane x	P. Coast	27	53	1	1	.500	67	41	32	22	32	5.43
1971—Albuquerque y	Texas	29	164	8	12	.400	155	77	39	126	50	2.14
1972—El Paso	Texas	9	73	7	2	.778	54	21	15	77	17	1.85
1972—Albuquerque	P. Coast	18	109	10	1	.909	126	66	57	80	30	4.71
1973—Albuquerque z	P. Coast	25	177	13	8	.619	185	81	60	103	66	3.05
1973—Los Angeles	National	6	13	1	0	1.000	5	2	2	9	2	1.38
1974—Los Angeles	National	21	80	3	5	.375	78	28	18	33	16	2.03
1975—Los Angeles a-Chicago b	National	18	66	2	8	.200	69	40	34	22	31	4.64
1976—Wichita	Am. Assoc.	21	137	8	8	.500	142	81	65	66	61	4.27
1976—Chicago c	National	3	8	0	1	.000	16	10	10	4	2	11.25
1977—Minnesota	American	34	198	12	14	.462	234	116	103	88	66	4.68
1978—Minnesota	American	35	252	14	14	.500	260	101	85	106	81	3.04
1979—Minnesota d	American	26	169	13	7	.650	181	74	67	58	41	3.57
1980—Minnesota e	American	38	233	14	18	.438	273	138	114	96	66	4.40
1981—California	American	25	161	10	11	.476	181	⋆93	⋆79	52	43	4.42
1982—California	American	34	229⅓	18	8	.692	225	100	95	81	65	3.73
1983—California f	American	29	203	9	11	.450	212	90	75	81	51	3.33
American League Totals		221	1445⅓	90	83	.520	1566	712	618	562	413	3.85
National League Totals		48	167	6	14	.300	168	80	64	68	51	3.45
Major League Totals		269	1612⅓	96	97	.497	1734	792	682	630	464	3.81

Selected by Chicago White Sox' organization in 28th round of free-agent draft, June, 1966.
Selected by Boston Red Sox' organization in secondary phase of free-agent draft, January 28, 1967.
Selected by Detroit Tigers' organization in secondary phase of free-agent draft, June 7, 1967.
Selected by Los Angeles Dodgers' organization in secondary phase of free-agent draft, January 27, 1968.
†On restricted list, April 11 to May 2, 1968.
‡On temporary inactive list, April 22 to June 16, 1969.
§On disabled list, June 16 to July 7, 1969.
xAppeared as a first baseman with no chances.
yAppeared as an outfielder with no chances.
zOn disabled list, June 18 to June 30, 1973.
aTraded with Pitcher Eddie Solomon to Chicago Cubs for Pitcher Burt Hooton, May 2, 1975.
bOn disabled list, July 21 to September 2, 1975.
cReleased, January 17, 1977; signed by Minnesota Twins, March 18, 1977.
dOn disabled list, May 2 to June 2, 1979.
eGranted free agency, October 23, 1980; signed by California Angels, December 2, 1980.
fOn disabled list, June 10 to July 11, 1983.

CHAMPIONSHIP SERIES RECORD

Year Club	League	G.	IP.	W.	L.	Pct.	H.	R.	ER.	SO.	BB.	ERA.
1982—California	American	1	3⅔	0	1	.000	4	3	3	2	1	7.36

LLOYD JEFFREY ZASKE

Name pronounced ZASS-kee.

(Jeff)

Born October 6, 1960, at Seattle, Wash.
Height, 6.05. Weight, 180.
Throws and bats righthanded.

Led Eastern League in saves with 24 and games finished in relief with 44 in 1983.

Year Club	League	G.	IP.	W.	L.	Pct.	H.	R.	ER.	SO.	BB.	ERA.
1979—Shelby	W. Carol.	25	100	5	10	.333	91	80	58	88	96	5.22
1980—Salem	Carolina	26	132	8	10	.444	101	68	62	103	*116	4.23
1981—Buffalo	Eastern	4	10	0	1	.000	10	6	4	4	8	3.60
1981—Alexandria	Carolina	21	110	5	9	.357	105	64	54	75	72	4.42
1982—Alexandria	Carolina	48	74⅔	7	4	.636	63	30	24	84	29	2.89
1983—Lynn	Eastern	48	70⅓	5	3	.625	54	20	17	72	38	2.18
1983—Hawaii	P. Coast	6	6	1	0	1.000	6	4	4	4	6	6.00

Selected by Pittsburgh Pirates' organization in 27th round of free-agent draft, June 6, 1978.

RICHARD WALTER ZISK
(Richie)

Born February 6, 1949, at Brooklyn, N. Y.
Height, 6.01. Weight, 205.
Throws and bats righthanded.
Attended Seton Hall University, South Orange, N. J.
Brother of John Zisk, third baseman-outfielder in Philadelphia Phillies' organization, 1973 and 1974.

Tied major league record for fewest times caught stealing, season, 150 or more games (0), 1976.
Hit for the cycle, June 9, 1974.
Led American League outfielders in double plays with 6 in 1979.
Led International League in total bases with 252 in 1972.
Named American League Comeback Player of the Year by THE SPORTING NEWS, 1981.
Named designated hitter on THE SPORTING NEWS American League All-Star Team, 1981.
Named outfielder on THE SPORTING NEWS National League All-Star Team, 1974.
Named Appalachian League Player of the Year, 1967.

Year Club	League	Pos.	G.	AB.	R.	H.	2B.	3B.	HR.	RBI.	B.A.	PO.	A.	E.	F.A.
1967—Salem	Appal.	OF-1B	56	189	41	58	9	2	*16	51	.307	97	6	9	.920
1968—Gastonia	W. Car.	OF	53	185	32	52	8	1	13	41	.281	78	7	5	.944
1969—Salem†	Carol.	OF	78	265	43	84	12	5	11	45	.317	157	7	2	.988
1970—Waterbury	East.	OF	125	450	83	133	17	6	*34	88	.296	175	10	8	.959
1971—Charleston	Int.	OF	135	424	90	123	15	1	29	*109	.290	214	6	8	.965
1971—Pittsburgh	Nat.	OF	7	15	2	3	1	0	1	2	.200	7	0	0	1.000
1972—Charleston	Int.	OF	122	441	83	136	30	4	*26	86	.308	220	16	1	.996
1972—Pittsburgh	Nat.	OF	17	37	4	7	3	0	0	4	.189	14	1	1	.938
1973—Pittsburgh	Nat.	OF	103	333	44	108	23	7	10	54	.324	139	12	2	.987
1974—Pittsburgh	Nat.	OF	149	536	75	168	30	3	17	100	.313	312	9	5	.985
1975—Pittsburgh	Nat.	OF	147	504	69	146	27	3	20	75	.290	264	7	7	.975
1976—Pittsburgh‡	Nat.	OF	155	581	91	168	35	2	21	89	.289	300	11	4	.987
1977—Chicago§	Amer.	OF	141	531	78	154	17	6	30	101	.290	210	9	4	.982
1978—Texas x	Amer.	OF	140	511	68	134	19	1	22	85	.262	155	6	2	.988
1979—Texas	Amer.	OF	144	503	69	132	21	1	18	64	.262	234	10	7	.972
1980—Texas y	Amer.	OF	135	448	48	130	17	1	19	77	.290	45	3	1	.980
1981—Seattle	Amer.	DH	94	357	42	111	12	1	16	43	.311	0	0	0	.000
1982—Seattle	Amer.	DH	131	503	61	148	28	1	21	62	.292	0	0	0	.000
1983—Seattle z	Amer.	DH	90	285	30	69	12	0	12	36	.242	0	0	0	.000
American League Totals			875	3138	396	877	126	11	138	468	.279	644	28	14	.980
National League Totals			578	2006	285	600	119	15	69	324	.299	1036	40	19	.983
Major League Totals			1453	5144	681	1477	245	26	207	792	.287	1680	68	33	.981

Selected by Pittsburgh Pirates' organization in 3rd round of free-agent draft, June 6, 1967.
†On restricted list, April 2 to June 7, 1969.
‡Traded with Pitcher Silvio Martinez to Chicago White Sox for Pitchers Terry Forster and Rich Gossage, December 10, 1976.
§Granted free agency, November 2, 1977; signed by Texas Rangers, November 9, 1977.
xOn supplemental disabled list, July 21 to August 5, 1978.
yTraded with Pitchers Brian Allard, Ken Clay, Steve Finch and Jerry Don Gleaton and Shortstop Rick Auerbach to Seattle Mariners for Catcher Larry Cox, Pitcher Rick Honeycutt, Shortstop Mario Mendoza and Outfielders Willie Horton and Leon Roberts, December 12, 1980.
zOn supplemental disabled list, May 1 to May 21, 1983.

CHAMPIONSHIP SERIES RECORD

Year Club	League	Pos.	G.	AB.	R.	H.	2B.	3B.	HR.	RBI.	B.A.	PO.	A.	E.	F.A.
1974—Pittsburgh	Nat.	OF-PH	3	10	1	3	0	0	0	0	.300	2	0	0	1.000
1975—Pittsburgh	Nat.	OF	3	10	0	5	1	0	0	0	.500	8	0	0	1.000
Championship Series Totals			6	20	1	8	1	0	0	0	.400	10	0	0	1.000

ALL-STAR GAME RECORD

Year League	Pos.	AB.	R.	H.	2B.	3B.	HR.	RBI.	B.A.	PO.	A.	E.	F.A.
1977—American	OF	3	0	2	1	0	0	2	.667	0	0	0	.000
1978—American	OF	2	0	1	0	0	0	0	.500	0	0	0	.000
All-Star Game Totals		5	0	3	1	0	0	2	.600	0	0	0	.000

—DID YOU KNOW—

That after the Phillies' Steve Carlton notched his 300th career victory on September 23 against St. Louis, he suffered his 200th defeat in his next appearance on September 27 against the Cubs?

PAUL ZUVELLA

Name pronounced Zoo-VELL-a.
Born October 31, 1958, at San Mateo, Calif.
Height, 6.00. Weight, 170.
Throws and bats righthanded.
Received bachelor of arts degree in communications
from Stanford University, Stanford, Calif.
Led Southern League shortstops in total chances with 661 in 1981.

Year	Club	League	Pos.	G.	AB.	R.	H.	2B.	3B.	HR.	RBI.	B.A.	PO.	A.	E.	F.A.
1980—Bradenton Brav...	Gulf C.	SS	2	8	0	1	0	0	0	1	.125	4	9	1	.929
1980—Durham†	Carol.	SS	48	149	21	47	7	0	2	19	.315	58	140	12	.943
1981—Savannah	South.	SS	138	485	61	145	17	2	11	68	.299	220	★406	35	.947
1982—Richmond	Int.	SS	133	455	63	128	15	2	9	54	.281	245	335	22	.963
1982—Atlanta	Nat.	SS	2	1	0	0	0	0	0	0	.000	0	4	1	.800
1983—Richmond	Int.	SS	117	415	53	119	13	2	6	64	.287	169	324	18	.965
1983—Atlanta	Nat.	SS	3	5	0	0	0	0	0	0	.000	1	2	1	.750
Major League Totals				5	6	0	0	0	0	0	0	.000	1	6	2	.778

Selected by Milwaukee Brewers' organization in 11th round of free-agent draft, June 5, 1979.
Selected by Atlanta Braves' organization in 15th round of free-agent draft, June 3, 1980.
†On disabled list, August 27, 1980 through remainder of season.

PLAYER MOVES

The following player deals involve players in the Register with the transactions occurring after January 4, 1984 and including January 12.

CRUZ, JULIO: Re-signed by Chicago White Sox, January 8, 1984.

GOSSAGE, RICH: Signed by San Diego Padres, January 6, 1984.

HEBNER, RICHIE: Signed by Chicago Cubs, January 5, 1984.

LAMP, DENNIS: Signed by Toronto Blue Jays, January 10, 1984.

MALER, JIM: Traded to New York Mets for Pitcher John Semprini, January 11, 1984.

NIEKRO, PHIL: Signed by New York Yankees, January 6, 1984.

WHITFIELD, TERRY: Signed by Los Angeles Dodgers, January 12, 1984.

Major League Managers

JOSEPH SALVATORE ALTOBELLI
(Joe)
Baltimore Orioles

Born May 26, 1932, at Detroit, Mich.
Height, 6.00. Weight, 180.
Threw and batted lefthanded.

Led American Association first basemen in double plays with 146 in 1954, 126 in 1955 and 160 in 1962.
Led International League first basemen in double plays with 143 in 1960.

Year—Club	League	Pos.	G.	AB.	R.	H.	2B.	3B.	HR.	RBI.	B.A.	PO.	A.	E.	F.A.
1951—Daytona Beach....	Fla. St.	1B	●140	598	118	204	★40	19	8	101	.341	★1259	★90	★45	.967
1952—Reading.................	East.	1B	128	436	49	118	9	7	2	37	.271	1036	63	★20	.982
1953—Reading.................	East.	1B	148	528	76	155	28	9	4	65	.294	1092	★83	19	.984
1954—Indianapolis..........	A. A.	1B	149	551	73	158	31	10	6	79	.287	1120	84	12	.990
1955—Indianapolis..........	A. A.	1B	98	395	58	107	24	1	7	53	.271	322	61	14	.984
1955—Cleveland..............	Amer.	1B	42	75	8	15	3	0	2	5	.200	224	11	2	.992
1956—Indianapolis..........	A. A.	1B	145	528	69	134	18	10	19	81	.254	1181	100	15	.988
1957—Cleveland..............	Amer.	1B-OF	83	87	9	18	3	2	0	9	.207	158	9	1	.994
1957—Columbus..............	Int.	1B	22	77	16	18	5	1	2	10	.234	176	20	3	.985
1958—Indianapolis†........	A. A.	★1B-OF	133	463	60	133	24	4	12	74	.287	1012	83	14	★.987
1959—Toronto‡	Int.	1B	148	518	71	131	17	6	17	61	.253	1244	87	13	.990
1960—Montreal	Int.	1B	154	552	79	141	25	5	★31	★105	.255	★1401	101	14	.991
1961—Syracuse	Int.	1B-OF	96	351	50	90	11	4	10	47	.256	396	31	13	.968
1961—Minnesota§...........	Amer.	OF-1B	41	95	10	21	2	1	3	14	.221	54	1	2	.965
1962—Omaha	A. A.	1B	141	502	81	136	23	7	13	67	.271	★1247	★89	12	.991
1963—Rochester x	Int.	1B-OF	97	315	45	77	13	0	15	44	.244	361	31	4	.990
1964—Rochester	Int.	1B	122	345	35	86	11	1	11	52	.249	680	51	3	.996
1965—Rochester y	Int.	1B	117	393	51	116	11	3	20	59	.295	884	74	15	.985
1966—Rochester y	Int.	OF	25	60	5	14	5	0	1	5	.233	24	1	0	1.000
1967—Elmira	Int.	1B	3	7	0	1	0	0	0	2	.143	17	2	0	1.000
1970—Dal.-Ft. Worth	Tex.	1B-P	11	11	1	4	0	0	0	3	.364	17	1	2	.917
Major League Totals................................			166	257	27	54	8	3	5	28	.210	436	21	5	.989

†Sold by Cleveland Indians' organization to Toronto (International) for a reported $20,000, January 13, 1959.
‡Traded to Los Angeles Dodgers' organization for Third Baseman Clyde Parris, April 1, 1960.
§Released outright by Minnesota Twins' organization to Los Angeles Dodgers' organization, October 12, 1961.
xOn disabled list, May 13 to May 29 and July 19 to August 14, 1963.
yPlayer-coach.

RECORD AS PITCHER

Year—Club	League	G.	IP.	W.	L.	Pct.	H.	R.	ER.	SO.	BB.	ERA.
1970—Dallas-Ft. Worth	Texas	2	4	0	0	.000	5	8	6	1	3	13.50

RECORD AS MANAGER

Named Minor League Manager of the Year by The Sporting News, 1974.
Named International League Manager of the Year, 1971, 1976 and 1980.
Named Appalachian League Manager of the Year, 1967.

Year—Club	League	Position	W.	L.	Year—Club	League	Position	W.	L.
1966—Bluefield.................	Appal.	Third	38	33	1976—Rochester	Int.	xFirst	88	50
1967—Bluefield.................	Appal.	First	42	25	1977—San Francisco	Nat.	Fourth(W)	75	87
1968—Stockton.................	Calif.	Seventh	29	41	1978—San Francisco	Nat.	Third(W)	89	73
(Second Half)		Second	38	32	1979—San Francisco y.....	Nat.	Fourth(W)	61	79
1969—Dallas-Ft. Worth	Texas	Second(W)	75	58	1980—Columbus................	Int.	zFirst	83	57
1970—Dallas-Ft. Worth	Texas	Third(W)	63	73	1983—Baltimore	Amer.	First(E)	98	64
1971—Rochester	Int.	†First	86	54	National League Totals................			225	239
1972—Rochester	Int.	Fourth	76	68	American League Totals...............			98	64
1973—Rochester	Int.	‡First(A)	79	67	Major League Totals.......................			323	303
1974—Rochester	Int.	§First(N)	88	56					
1975—Rochester	Int.	Second	85	56					

	CHAMPIONSHIP SERIES RECORD					WORLD SERIES RECORD			
Year—Club	League		W.	L.	Year—Club	League		W.	L.
1983—Baltimore	American		3	1	1983—Baltimore	American		4	1

†Won playoffs by defeating Syracuse, three games to one and Tidewater, three games to two; won Junior World Series against Denver (American Association), four games to three.
‡Lost championship playoff to Charleston, three games to none.
§Won Governor's Cup by defeating Syracuse, four games to three, won League Championship by defeating Memphis, four games to two.
xLost semifinal playoff series to Richmond, three games to one.
yReplaced by Dave Bristol, September 5, 1979.
zWon playoffs from Richmond, three games to two; won championship series from Toledo, four games to one.
Coach, New York Yankees, 1981 and 1982.
Coach, American League All-Star Team, 1983.

GEORGE LEE ANDERSON
(Sparky)
Detroit Tigers

Born February 22, 1934, at Bridgewater, S. D.
Height, 5.09. Weight, 168.
Threw and batted righthanded.

Led Western League in sacrifice hits with 20 in 1954 and International League with 15 in 1960.
Led Texas League second basemen in double plays with 117 in 1955, Pacific Coast League with 135 in 1957 and International League with 104 in 1958 and 89 in 1960.
Led California League shortstops in double plays with 83 in 1953.
Tied for Texas League lead in sacrifice hits with 22 in 1955 and International League lead with 15 in 1960.

Year	Club	League	Pos.	G.	AB.	R.	H.	2B.	3B.	HR.	RBI.	B.A.	PO.	A.	E.	F.A.
1953—Santa Barbara	Calif.		SS	●141	★598	98	157	21	4	5	55	.263	★277	395	32	.955
1954—Pueblo	West.		2B	147	497	72	147	13	5	0	62	.296	★397	432	20	●.976
1955—Fort Worth	Texas		2B	158	594	86	158	24	1	0	42	.266	★456	★469	18	★.981
1956—Montreal	Int.		2B	140	453	65	135	17	5	0	47	.298	372	391	15	.981
1957—Los Angeles	P. C.		★●2B-SS	●168	619	74	161	15	0	2	35	.260	★524	★488	●15	★.985
1958—Montreal†	Int.		2B	●155	580	78	156	35	5	2	56	.269	★387	★464	10	★.983
1959—Philadelphia	Nat.		2B	152	477	42	104	9	3	0	34	.218	343	403	12	.984
1960—Toronto	Int.		2B	148	543	67	123	11	5	5	21	.227	319	★416	12	.984
1961—Toronto	Int.		2B	97	275	30	66	17	0	0	22	.240	189	203	6	.985
1962—Toronto	Int.		2B	124	432	56	111	18	2	2	38	.257	282	327	8	★.987
1963—Toronto	Int.		2B	116	358	56	89	12	5	3	25	.249	226	256	6	★.988
Major League Totals				152	477	42	104	9	3	0	34	.218	343	403	12	.984

†Recalled by Los Angeles Dodgers; traded to Philadelphia Phillies for Pitchers Jim Golden and Gene Snyder and Outfielder Eldon (Rip) Repulski, December 23, 1958.

RECORD AS MANAGER

Year	Club	League	Position	W.	L.
1964—Toronto	Int.		Fifth	80	72
1965—Rock Hill	W. Carol.		Eighth	24	40
(Second Half)			†First	35	23
1966—St. Petersburg	Fla. St.		Second	42	24
(Second Half)			‡First	49	21
1967—Modesto	Calif.		§Second	38	32
(Second Half)			xFirst	41	29

Year	Club	League	Position	W.	L.
1968—Asheville	South.		First	86	54
1970—Cincinnati	Nat.		First(W)	102	60
1971—Cincinnati	Nat.		yFourth(W)	79	83
1972—Cincinnati	Nat.		First(W)	95	59
1973—Cincinnati	Nat.		First(W)	99	63

Year	Club	League	Position	W.	L.
1974—Cincinnati	Nat.		Second(W)	98	64
1975—Cincinnati	Nat.		First(W)	108	54
1976—Cincinnati	Nat.		First(W)	102	60
1977—Cincinnati	Nat.		Second(W)	88	74
1978—Cincinnati	Nat.		Second(W)	92	69
1979—Detroit z	Amer.		Fifth(E)	56	50
1980—Detroit	Amer.		Fifth(E)	84	78
1981—Detroit a	Amer.			60	49
1982—Detroit	Amer.		Fourth(E)	83	79
1983—Detroit	Amer.		Second(E)	92	70
American League Totals				375	326
National League Totals				1238	912
Major League Totals				1238	912

†Won playoff against Salisbury (First Half winner), two games to none.
‡Lost playoff against Leesburg (First Half winner), three games to two.
§Tied for position with Santa Barbara.
xLost playoff against San Jose (First Half winner), two games to none.
yTied for position with Houston Astros.
zReplaced Les Moss (and interim manager Dick Tracewski) with club in fifth place (record of 29-26), June 14, 1979.
aFirst Half. . . . Fourth (E) (record of 31-26); Second Half. . . . Third (E) (record of 29-23).
Coach, San Diego Padres, 1969.
Manager, National League All-Star Team, 1971, 1973, 1976 and 1977.
Coach, National League All-Star Team, 1974.
Coach, American League All-Star Team, 1982.

CHAMPIONSHIP SERIES RECORD

Year	Club	League	W.	L.
1970—Cincinnati	National		3	0
1972—Cincinnati	National		3	2
1973—Cincinnati	National		2	3
1975—Cincinnati	National		3	0
1976—Cincinnati	National		3	0

WORLD SERIES RECORD

Year	Club	League	W.	L.
1970—Cincinnati	National		1	4
1972—Cincinnati	National		3	4
1975—Cincinnati	National		4	3
1976—Cincinnati	National		4	0

LAWRENCE PETER BERRA SR.
(Yogi)

(Named by boyhood pals on The Hill, the heavily-populated Italian
section of St. Louis. A Yogi was considered an odd character—
later in life the term grew to one of affection.)

New York Yankees

Born May 12, 1925, at St. Louis, Mo.
Height, 5.08. Weight, 191.
Threw right and batted lefthanded.
Father of Larry Berra, Jr., catcher in New York Mets' organization, 1971 and 1972; Tim Berra,
former wide receiver with New York Giants and Baltimore Colts; and Dale Berra,
third baseman with Pittsburgh Pirates.

Established major league records for most years leading league in games as catcher (8); most consecutive errorless games, catcher (148) and most consecutive chances accepted, no errors (950), July 28, 1957 (second game), through May 10, 1959 (second game).

Tied major league records for most years leading league in double plays, catcher (6); most unassisted double plays by catcher, lifetime (2); most years leading league in chances accepted by catcher (8).

Established American League record for most home runs by catcher, lifetime (313).

Led American League catchers in double plays with 18 in 1949, 16 in 1950, 25 in 1951, 10 in 1952, 14 in 1954 and 15 in 1956.

Led American League in passed balls with 7 in 1950.

Named American League Most Valuable Player, 1951, 1954 and 1955.

Named catcher on THE SPORTING NEWS Major League All-Star Teams, 1950, 1952, 1954 and 1956.

Elected to Hall of Fame, 1972.

Year Club League	Pos.	G.	AB.	R.	H.	2B.	3B.	HR.	RBI.	B.A.	PO.	A.	E.	F.A.
1943—Norfolk.................. Pied.	C	111	376	52	95	17	8	7	56	.253	*480	75	*16	.972
1944-45—Kansas City...... A. A.						(In Military Service)								
1946—Newark................. Int.	C-OF	77	277	41	87	14	1	15	59	.314	344	45	11	.973
1946—New York.............. Amer.	C	7	22	3	8	1	0	2	4	.364	28	6	0	1.000
1947—New York.............. Amer.	C-OF	83	293	41	82	15	3	11	54	.280	307	18	9	.973
1948—New York.............. Amer.	C-OF	125	469	70	143	24	10	14	98	.305	390	40	9	.979
1949—New York.............. Amer.	C	116	415	59	115	20	2	20	91	.277	544	60	7	.989
1950—New York.............. Amer.	C	151	597	116	192	30	6	28	124	.322	*777	●64	13	.985
1951—New York.............. Amer.	C	141	547	92	161	19	4	27	88	.294	*693	*82	●13	.984
1952—New York.............. Amer.	C	142	534	97	146	17	1	30	98	.273	*700	*73	6	.992
1953—New York.............. Amer.	C	137	503	80	149	23	5	27	108	.296	566	64	9	.986
1954—New York.............. Amer.	*C-3B	151	584	88	179	28	6	22	125	.307	*718	64	8	.990
1955—New York.............. Amer.	C	147	541	84	147	20	3	27	108	.272	*721	54	*13	.984
1956—New York.............. Amer.	*C-OF	140	521	93	155	29	2	30	105	.298	*733	57	*11	.986
1957—New York.............. Amer.	*C-OF	134	482	74	121	14	2	24	82	.251	*707	61	4	*.995
1958—New York.............. Amer.	*C-OF-1	122	433	60	115	17	3	22	90	.266	558	44	2	*.997
1959—New York.............. Amer.	*C-OF	131	472	64	134	25	1	19	69	.284	*706	62	4	*.995
1960—New York.............. Amer.	C-OF	120	359	46	99	14	1	15	62	.276	312	24	5	.985
1961—New York.............. Amer.	OF-C	119	395	62	107	11	0	22	61	.271	237	15	2	.992
1962—New York.............. Amer.	C-OF	86	232	25	52	8	0	10	35	.224	238	17	6	.977
1963—New York†............ Amer.	C	64	147	20	43	6	0	8	28	.293	244	13	3	.988
1964—New York‡............ Amer.					(Did not play—served as manager.)									
1965—New York.............. Nat.	C	4	9	1	2	0	0	0	0	.222	15	1	1	.941
American League Totals...........		2116	7546	1174	2148	321	49	358	1430	.285	9179	818	124	.988
National League Totals.............		4	9	1	2	0	0	0	0	.222	15	1	1	.941
Major League Totals.................		2120	7555	1175	2150	321	49	358	1430	.285	9194	819	125	.988

†Player-coach.

‡Released, October 16, 1964; signed as coach with New York Mets, November 17, 1964.

WORLD SERIES RECORD

Established World Series records for most Series played (14); most Series played, one club (14); most games (75); most games one club (75); most times on winning team (10); most at bats, total Series (259); most hits, total Series (71); most hits, total Series, one club (71); most one-base hits, total Series (49); most Series, one or more runs batted in (11); most Series, one or more runs (12); most Series, one or more bases on balls (13); most Series played by catcher (12); most games caught, total Series (63); most consecutive errorless games by catcher (30); most putouts by catcher, total Series (421); most assists by catcher, total Series (36); most chances accepted by catcher, total Series (457).

Tied World Series records for most consecutive Series played (5), 1949 through 1953; most Series, one or more hits (12); most Series, one or more home runs (9); most times hit by pitch, total Series (3); most double plays by catcher, total Series (6); most two-base hits, total Series (10); one or more hits, each game of seven-game Series, 1955; most positions played, Series (3), 1960 (left field, right field and catcher); most home runs as pinch-hitter, game (1), October 2, 1947 (first player to hit pinch-hit home run); most times hit by pitch, game (2), October 2, 1953; most home runs with bases filled, game (1), October 5, 1956; most runs batted in, inning (4), October 5, 1956; fewest putouts by catcher, game (1), October 3, 1952 and October 10, 1956.

Year Club League	Pos.	G.	AB.	R.	H.	2B.	3B.	HR.	RBI.	B.A.	PO.	A.	E.	F.A.
1947—New York.............. Amer.	C-OF	6	19	2	3	0	0	1	2	.158	21	2	2	.920
1949—New York.............. Amer.	C	4	16	2	1	0	0	0	1	.063	37	3	0	1.000
1950—New York.............. Amer.	C	4	15	2	3	0	0	1	2	.200	30	1	0	1.000
1951—New York.............. Amer.	C	6	23	4	6	1	0	0	0	.261	27	3	1	.968
1952—New York.............. Amer.	C	7	28	2	6	1	0	2	3	.214	59	7	1	.985
1953—New York.............. Amer.	C	6	21	3	9	1	0	1	4	.429	36	3	0	1.000
1955—New York.............. Amer.	C	7	24	5	10	1	0	1	2	.417	40	4	0	1.000
1956—New York.............. Amer.	C	7	25	5	9	2	0	3	10	.360	50	3	0	1.000
1957—New York.............. Amer.	C	7	25	5	8	1	0	1	2	.320	44	2	1	.979
1958—New York.............. Amer.	C	7	27	3	6	3	0	0	2	.222	60	6	0	1.000
1960—New York.............. Amer.	C-OF-PH	7	22	6	7	0	0	1	8	.318	18	1	0	1.000
1961—New York.............. Amer.	OF	4	11	2	3	0	0	1	3	.273	11	0	1	.917
1962—New York.............. Amer.	C	2	2	0	0	0	0	0	0	.000	6	1	0	1.000
1963—New York.............. Amer.	PH	1	1	0	0	0	0	0	0	.000	0	0	0	.000
World Series Totals.....................		75	259	41	71	10	0	12	39	.274	439	36	6	.988

ALL-STAR GAME RECORD

Established All-Star Game records for most games played by catcher (14); most putouts by catcher, total games (61); most assists by catcher, total games (7); most chances accepted by catcher, total games (68).

Tied All-Star Game records for most putouts by catcher, game (10), July 10, 1956; most chances accepted by catcher, game (11), July 10, 1956.

Year League	Pos.	AB.	R.	H.	2B.	3B.	HR.	RBI.	B.A.	PO.	A.	E.	F.A.
1949—American	C	3	0	0	0	0	0	0	.000	2	1	0	1.000
1950—American	C	2	0	0	0	0	0	0	.000	2	0	0	1.000

Year League	Pos.	AB.	R.	H.	2B.	3B.	HR.	RBI.	B.A.	PO.	A.	E.	F.A.
1951—American	C	4	1	1	0	0	0	0	.250	4	2	1	.857
1952—American	C	2	0	0	0	0	0	0	.000	6	0	0	1.000
1953—American	C	4	0	0	0	0	0	0	.000	4	0	0	1.000
1954—American	C	4	2	2	0	0	0	0	.500	5	0	0	1.000
1955—American	C	6	1	1	0	0	0	0	.167	8	2	0	1.000
1956—American	C	2	0	2	0	0	0	0	1.000	10	1	0	1.000
1957—American	C	3	0	1	0	0	0	1	.333	6	0	0	1.000
1958—American	C	2	0	0	0	0	0	0	.000	3	0	0	1.000
1959—American (second game)	C	3	1	1	0	0	1	2	.333	2	0	0	1.000
1960—American (both games)	C	4	0	0	0	0	0	0	.000	9	1	0	1.000
1961—American (first game)	C	1	0	0	0	0	0	0	.000	0	0	0	.000
1962—American (second game)	PH	1	0	0	0	0	0	0	.000	0	0	0	.000
All-Star Game Totals		41	5	8	0	0	1	3	.195	61	7	1	.986

Member of American League All-Star Team in 1948, 1959 (first game) and 1961 (second game); did not play.

RECORD AS MANAGER

One of three managers to represent both leagues as manager in World Series, New York (American), 1964 and New York (National), 1973.

Year Club	League	Position	W.	L.
1964—New York	Amer.	First	99	63
1972—New York	Nat.	Third(E)	83	73
1973—New York	Nat.	First(E)	82	79
1974—New York	Nat.	Fifth(E)	71	91
1975—New York†	Nat.	Third (E)	56	53
American League Totals			99	63
National League Totals			292	296
Major League Totals			391	359

†Replaced by Roy McMillan, August 5.
Coach, New York Mets, 1965 through 1971; New York Yankees, 1976 through 1983.
Manager, National League All-Star Team, 1974.

CHAMPIONSHIP SERIES RECORD					WORLD SERIES RECORD				
Year Club	League		W.	L.	Year Club	League		W.	L.
1973—New York	National		3	2	1964—New York	American		3	4
					1973—New York	National		3	4

STEPHEN BOROS JR.

Name pronounced Boris.

(Steve)

Oakland A's

Born September 3, 1936, at Flint, Mich.
Height, 6.00. Weight, 185.
Threw and batted righthanded.
Received bachelor of arts degree in literature at University of Michigan, Ann Arbor, Mich.

Tied American League record for most errors by a third baseman, nine-inning game (4), August 23, 1962.
Hit three home runs in a game, August 6, 1962.
Led American Association in total bases with 329 in 1960.
Led Southern Association in stolen bases with 23 in 1959.
Named American Association Most Valuable Player, 1960.
Received reported $25,000 bonus to sign with Detroit Tigers, 1957.

Year Club	League	Pos.	G.	AB.	R.	H.	2B.	3B.	HR.	RBI.	B.A.	PO.	A.	E.	F.A.
1957—Detroit	Amer.	3B-SS	24	41	4	6	1	0	0	2	.146	8	27	3	.921
1958—Birmingham	South.	INF	44	138	24	36	3	2	6	17	.261	81	68	11	.931
1958—Charleston	A. A.	2B-3B	6	13	1	1	0	0	0	0	.077	7	8	1	.938
1958—Augusta	Sally	INF	77	269	53	69	7	2	14	36	.257	72	157	25	.902
1958—Detroit	Amer.	2B	6	2	0	0	0	0	0	0	.000	2	0	0	1.000
1959—Birmingham	South.	OF-3B-2B	147	522	89	159	24	7	16	85	.305	171	154	15	.956
1960—Denver	A. A.	3B	151	571	★128	181	42	8	30	●119	.317	110	●275	★31	.925
1961—Detroit†	Amer.	3B	116	396	51	107	18	2	5	62	.270	115	192	15	.953
1962—Detroit‡	Amer.	3B-2B	116	356	46	81	14	1	16	47	.228	118	163	21	.930
1963—Chicago§	Nat.	1B-OF	41	90	9	19	5	1	3	7	.211	126	7	4	.971
1964—San Diego	P. C.	3B	26	100	18	30	8	0	3	15	.300	13	39	1	.981
1964—Cincinnati	Nat.	3B	117	370	31	95	12	3	2	31	.257	95	204	12	.961
1965—Cincinnati	Nat.	3B	2	0	0	0	0	0	0	0	.000	0	1	0	1.000
1965—San Diego	P. C.	3B-SS-OF	117	420	73	113	28	6	12	30	.269	108	217	12	.964
1966—Buffalo	Int.	SS-3B-OF	106	330	51	92	16	1	13	40	.279	113	113	20	.919
1967—Buffalo x	Int.	2B-3B-OF	107	290	29	55	5	0	10	23	.190	155	182	17	.952
1968—Ind.-Van. y	P. C.	3B-2B-1B	100	320	24	85	15	0	1	32	.266	78	149	10	.958
1969—Omaha z	A. A.	3-1-2-O	103	309	56	84	13	5	4	53	.272	113	110	6	.974
American League Totals			262	795	101	194	33	3	21	111	.244	243	382	39	.941
National League Totals			160	460	40	114	17	4	5	38	.248	221	212	16	.964
Major League Totals			422	1255	141	308	50	7	26	149	.245	464	594	55	.951

†On disabled list, July 24 to September 1, 1961.
‡Traded to Chicago Cubs for Pitcher Bob Anderson, November 28, 1962.
§Sold to San Diego (Cincinnati Reds' organization), December 13, 1963.

yReleased, April 9, 1969; signed by Omaha (Kansas City Royals' organization), April 16, 1969.
zReleased, October 20, 1969.

RECORD AS MANAGER

Year Club	League	Position	W.	L.	Year Club	League	Position	W.	L.
1970—Waterloo	Midw.	Tenth	25	37	1973—San Jose	Calif.	†Third	36	34
(Second Half)		Tenth	24	36	(Second Half)		Second	39	31
1971—Waterloo	Midw.	Fifth(N)	20	37	1974—San Jose	Calif.	†Fourth	36	34
(Second Half)		†Second(N)	35	27	(Second Half)		‡First	45	25
1972—Waterloo	Midw.	Second(N)	37	26	1980—Calgary	Pion.	Third(N)	23	46
(Second Half)		Second(N)	35	27	1983—Oakland	Amer.	Fourth(W)	74	88
					Major League Totals			74	88

†Tied for position.
‡Lost playoff to Fresno (First Half winner), three games to two.
Coach, Kansas City Royals, 1975 through 1979; coach, Montreal Expos, 1981 and 1982.

PATRICK CORRALES

Name pronounced Corr-AL-ees.

(Pat)

Cleveland Indians

Born March 20, 1941, at Los Angeles, Calif.
Height, 6.00. Weight, 195.
Threw and batted righthanded.
Attended Fresno City College, Fresno, Calif.

Tied major league record for most times awarded first base on catcher's interference, game (2), September 29, 1965.
Led Florida State League catchers in double plays with 18 in 1960 and tied for Sally League lead with 10 in 1963.

Year Club	League	Pos.	G.	AB.	R.	H.	2B.	3B.	HR.	RBI.	B.A.	PO.	A.	E.	F.A.
1959—Bakersfield	Calif.	C	5	5	0	0	0	0	0	0	.000	4	2	1	.857
1959—Johnson City	Appal.	C	23	74	10	18	4	0	2	13	.243	124	5	3	.977
1960—Tampa	Fla. St.	C	128	386	73	95	18	5	1	60	.246	★1011	83	23	★.979
1961—Des Moines	I.I.I.	C	104	333	33	103	18	0	3	36	.309	707	42	★19	.975
1962—Dallas-Ft. W.	A. A.	C	42	121	10	27	6	1	2	14	.223	180	16	3	.985
1962—Williamsport	East.	C-OF	42	136	9	26	1	0	1	10	.191	237	24	7	.974
1963—Chattanooga	Sally	C	127	415	42	108	15	1	3	51	.260	715	59	17	.979
1964—Arkansas	P. C.	C	101	335	36	102	19	1	9	48	.304	682	51	7	.991
1964—Philadelphia	Nat.	PH	2	1	1	0	0	0	0	0	.000	0	0	0	.000
1965—Philadelphia†	Nat.	C	63	174	16	39	8	1	2	15	.224	358	24	7	.982
1965—Arkansas	P. C.	C	28	85	6	16	4	0	0	4	.188	181	14	2	.990
1966—St. Louis	Nat.	C	28	72	5	13	2	0	0	3	.181	133	23	4	.975
1967—Tulsa‡	P. C.	C-1B	130	435	55	119	18	1	10	54	.274	714	69	8	.990
1968—Indianapolis	P. C.	C-1B	77	242	26	66	11	3	6	34	.273	461	42	5	.990
1968—Cincinnati	Nat.	C	20	56	3	15	4	0	0	6	.268	101	8	1	.991
1969—Cincinnati	Nat.	C	29	72	10	19	5	0	1	5	.264	133	7	2	.986
1970—Cincinnati	Nat.	C	43	106	9	25	5	1	1	10	.236	167	11	3	.983
1971—Cincinnati	Nat.	C	40	94	6	17	2	0	0	6	.181	145	4	3	.980
1972—Indianapolis	A. A.	C	30	98	9	31	4	0	1	12	.316	193	10	0	1.000
1972—Cinn.§-S. Diego	Nat.	C	46	120	6	23	0	0	0	6	.192	251	23	2	.993
1973—San Diego	Nat.	C	29	72	7	15	2	1	0	3	.208	130	6	2	.986
1974—Hawaii x	P. C.	C	53	169	21	42	6	0	5	24	.249	324	17	3	.991
1975—Alexandria	Texas	C-1B	1	0	0	0	0	0	0	0	.000	4	0	0	1.000
Major League Totals			300	767	63	166	28	3	4	54	.216	1418	106	24	.984

†Traded with Pitcher Art Mahaffey and Outfielder Alex Johnson to St. Louis Cardinals for First Baseman Bill White, Shortstop Dick Groat and Catcher Bob Uecker, October 27, 1965.
‡Recalled by St. Louis Cardinals; traded to Cincinnati Reds' organization with Infielder Jim Williams for Catcher John Edwards, February 8, 1968.
§Traded to San Diego Padres for Catcher Bob Barton, June 11, 1972.
xReleased, September 27, 1974.

WORLD SERIES RECORD

Year Club	League	Pos.	G.	AB.	R.	H.	2B.	3B.	HR.	RBI.	B.A.	PO.	A.	E.	F.A.
1970—Cincinnati	Nat.	PH	1	1	0	0	0	0	0	0	.000	0	0	0	.000

RECORD AS MANAGER

Year Club	League	Position	W.	L.
1975—Alexandria	Texas	Fourth(E)	58	72
1978—Texas†	Amer.	‡Second(W)	1	0
1979—Texas	Amer.	Third (W)	83	79
1982—Philadelphia	Nat.	Second(E)	89	73
1983—Philadelphia§	Nat.	First(E)	43	42
1983—Cleveland x	Amer.	Seventh(E)	30	32
American League Totals			114	111
National League Totals			132	115
Major League Totals			246	226

†Replaced Billy Hunter with club tied for second place (record of 86-75), October 1, 1978.
‡Tied for position with California Angels.
§Replaced by Paul Owens, July 18, 1983.
xReplaced Mike Ferraro with club in seventh place (record of 40-60), July 31, 1983.
Coach, Texas Rangers, part of 1975 through September 30, 1978.
Coach, American League All-Star Team, 1979.
Coach, National League All-Star Team, 1983.

ROBERT JOE COX
(Bobby)
Toronto Blue Jays

Born May 21, 1941, at Tulsa, Okla.
Height, 6.00. Weight, 185.
Threw and batted righthanded.
Attended Reedley Junior College, Reedley, Calif.

Led Alabama-Florida League shortstops in double plays with 71 in 1961.
Received reported $40,000 bonus to sign with Los Angeles Dodgers, 1959.

Year	Club	League	Pos.	G.	AB.	R.	H.	2B.	3B.	HR.	RBI.	B.A.	PO.	A.	E.	F.A.
1960—Reno	Calif.		2B	125	440	99	112	20	5	13	75	.255	282	*385	*39	.945
1961—Salem	N'west		2B	14	44	3	9	2	0	0	2	.205	25	25	2	.962
1961—Panama City	Ala.-Fl.		2B	92	335	66	102	27	4	17	73	.304	220	247	8	*.983
1962—Salem	N'west		3B-2B	*141	514	83	143	26	7	16	82	.278	174	296	28	.944
1963—Albuquerque	Texas		3B	17	53	5	15	2	0	2	5	.283	8	27	1	.972
1963—Great Falls	Pion.		3B	109	407	103	137	*31	4	19	85	.337	82	211	21	*.933
1964—Albuquerque	Texas		2B	138	523	98	152	29	13	16	91	.291	*322	*415	*28	.963
1965—Salt Lake City	P. C.		*3B-2B	136	473	58	125	32	1	12	55	.264	133	337	22	*.955
1966—Tacoma	P. C.		3B-2B	10	34	2	4	1	0	0	4	.118	23	15	0	1.000
1966—Austin	Texas		2B-3B	92	339	35	77	11	1	7	30	.227	140	216	12	.967
1967—Richmond†	Int.		3B-1B	99	350	52	104	17	4	14	51	.297	84	136	8	.965
1968—New York	Amer.		3B	135	437	33	100	15	1	7	41	.229	98	279	17	.957
1969—New York	Amer.		3B-2B	85	191	17	41	7	1	2	17	.215	50	147	11	.947
1970—Syracuse‡	Int.		3B-SS-2B	90	251	34	55	15	0	9	30	.219	86	163	13	.950
1971—Ft. Lauderdale§	Fla. St.		2B	4	9	1	1	0	0	0	0	.111	3	3	0	1.000
Major League Totals				220	628	50	141	22	2	9	58	.224	148	426	28	.953

†Recalled by Atlanta Braves; traded to New York Yankees for Catcher Bob Tillman and Pitcher Dale Roberts (latter transferred to Richmond), December 7, 1967.
‡On disabled list, May 28 through June 18, 1970.
§Player-manager.

PITCHING RECORD

Year	Club	League	G.	IP.	W.	L.	Pct.	H.	R.	ER.	SO.	BB.	ERA.
1971—Ft. Lauderdale	Florida St.	3	10	1	0	1.000	15	9	6	4	5	5.40

RECORD AS MANAGER

Year	Club	League	Position	W.	L.	Year	Club	League	Position	W.	L.
1971—Ft. Lauderdale	Fla. St.	Fourth(E)	71	70	1980—Atlanta	Nat.	Fourth(W)	81	80
1972—West Haven	†East.	First (A.)	84	56	1981—Atlanta§	Nat.		50	56
1973—Syracuse	Int.	Third(Am.)	76	70	1982—Toronto	Amer.	xSixth(E)	78	84
1974—Syracuse	Int.	Second(N)	74	70	1983—Toronto	Amer.	Fourth(E)	89	73
1975—Syracuse	Int.	Third	72	64	National League Totals			266	323
1976—Syracuse	‡Int.	Second	82	57	American League Totals			167	157
1978—Atlanta	Nat.	Sixth(W)	69	93	Major League Totals			433	480
1979—Atlanta	Nat.	Sixth(W)	66	94					

†Defeated Three Rivers in playoff, three games to none.
‡Won playoffs by defeating Memphis, three games to none; and Richmond (finals), three games to one.
§First Half.... Fourth (W) (record of 25-29); Second Half.... Fifth (W) (record of 25-27).
xTied for position with Cleveland Indians.
Coach, New York Yankees, 1977.

DELMAR WESLEY CRANDALL
(Del)
Seattle Mariners

Born March 5, 1930, at Ontario, Calif.
Height, 6.01. Weight, 202.
Threw and batted righthanded.

Tied major league record for most years leading league, catcher in assists (6), 1960.
Led National League catchers in double plays, 1953 through 1959, and led in passed balls, 1960.
Received Gold Glove award as outstanding National League fielding catcher, 1958 through 1960 and 1962.
Named catcher on THE SPORTING NEWS All-Star Major League Team, 1958 through 1960.
Named catcher on THE SPORTING NEWS All-Star National League Team, 1962.

Year	Club	League	Pos.	G.	AB.	R.	H.	2B.	3B.	HR.	RBI.	B.A.	PO.	A.	E.	F.A.
1948—Leavenworth	W. A.		C	123	425	81	129	27	4	15	84	.304	575	71	16	.976
1948—Milwaukee	A. A.		C	5	12	1	1	0	0	0	0	.083	17	1	0	1.000
1949—Evansville	I. I. I.		C	38	154	26	54	13	3	8	36	.351	250	29	3	.989
1949—Boston	Nat.		C	67	228	21	60	10	1	4	34	.263	287	39	6	.982
1950—Boston	Nat.		C-1B	79	255	21	56	11	0	4	37	.220	319	41	12	.968

Year Club League	Pos.	G.	AB.	R.	H.	2B.	3B.	HR.	RBI.	B.A.	PO.	A.	E.	F.A.
1951-52—Boston............... Nat.					(In Military Service)									
1953—Milwaukee............. Nat.	C	116	382	55	104	13	1	15	51	.272	556	*62	9	.986
1954—Milwaukee............. Nat.	C	138	463	60	112	18	2	21	64	.242	*665	*79	8	.989
1955—Milwaukee............. Nat.	C	133	440	61	104	15	2	26	62	.236	611	67	*10	.985
1956—Milwaukee............. Nat.	C	112	311	37	74	14	2	16	48	.238	448	44	2	*.996
1957—Milwaukee............. Nat.	*C-O-1B	118	383	45	97	11	2	15	46	.253	429	*60	7	.986
1958—Milwaukee............. Nat.	C	131	427	50	116	23	1	18	63	.272	*659	*64	7	*.990
1959—Milwaukee............. Nat.	C	150	518	65	133	19	2	21	72	.257	783	*71	5	*.994
1960—Milwaukee............. Nat.	C	142	537	81	158	14	1	19	77	.294	*764	*70	10	.988
1961—Milwaukee†.......... Nat.	C	15	30	3	6	3	0	0	1	.200	17	3	0	1.000
1962—Milwaukee‡.......... Nat.	*C-1B	107	350	35	104	12	3	8	45	.297	488	55	3	*.995
1963—Milwaukee‡.......... Nat.	C-1B	86	259	18	52	4	0	3	28	.201	459	43	4	.992
1964—San Francisco§ .... Nat.	C	69	195	12	45	8	1	3	11	.231	402	30	3	.993
1965—Pittsburgh x......... Nat.	C	60	140	11	30	2	0	2	10	.214	248	23	1	996
1966—Cleveland yz......... Amer.	C	50	108	10	25	2	0	4	8	.231	304	15	3	.991
1969—Albuquerque a...... Texas	....	1	2	0	1	0	0	0	0	.500	....	....	....	....
1970—Albuquerque a...... Texas	P-3B	2	4	0	0	0	0	0	0	.000	0	0	0	.000
National League Totals............................		1523	4918	575	1251	177	18	175	649	.254	7145	751	87	.989
American League Totals..........................		50	108	10	25	2	0	4	8	.231	304	15	3	.991
Major League Totals.................................		1573	5026	585	1276	179	18	179	657	.254	7449	766	90	.989

†On disabled list most of season due to arm trouble.
‡Traded to San Francisco Giants with Pitchers Bob Hendley and Bob Shaw for Pitcher Billy Hoeft, Catcher Ed Bailey, Infielder Ernie Bowman and Outfielder Felipe Alou. All players but Bowman changed clubs December 3, 1963—he being promised added player in deal and transferred January 8, 1964.
§Traded to Pittsburgh Pirates for Pitcher Bob Priddy and Outfielder-First Baseman Bob Burda, February 11, 1965; Burda was transferred from Columbus roster to Giants' Tacoma farm club.
xReleased by Pittsburgh Pirates and signed by Cleveland Indians, November 30, 1965.
yOn disabled list, June 4 through June 24, 1966.
zReleased, October 14, 1966.
aPlayer-manager.

WORLD SERIES RECORD

Tied World Series record for most double plays started by catcher in seven-game Series (2), 1957.

Year Club League	Pos.	G.	AB.	R.	H.	2B.	3B.	HR.	RBI.	B.A.	PO.	A.	E.	F.A.
1957—Milwaukee............. Nat.	C	6	19	1	4	0	0	1	1	.211	21	4	0	1.000
1958—Milwaukee............. Nat.	C	7	25	4	6	0	0	1	3	.240	43	5	0	1.000
World Series Totals.....................		13	44	5	10	0	0	2	4	.227	64	9	0	1.000

ALL-STAR GAME RECORD

Year League	Pos.	AB.	R.	H.	2B.	3B.	HR.	RBI.	B.A.	PO.	A.	E.	F.A.
1955—National......................	C	1	0	0	0	0	0	0	.000	1	0	0	1.000
1958—National......................	C	4	0	0	0	0	0	0	.000	5	0	0	1.000
1959—National (both games)................	C	5	1	2	0	0	0	1	.400	17	1	0	1.000
1960—National (both games)................	C	5	1	2	0	0	1	1	.400	7	0	0	1.000
1962—National (both games)................	C	5	0	0	0	0	0	0	.000	8	0	0	1.000
All-Star Game Totals		20	2	4	0	0	1	2	.200	38	1	0	1.000

PITCHING RECORD

Year Club	League	G.	IP.	W.	L.	Pct.	H.	R.	ER.	SO.	BB.	ERA.
1970—Albuquerque.................... Texas		2	3	1	0	1.000	2	0	0	2	2	0.00

RECORD AS MANAGER

Year Club League	Position	W.	L.	Year Club League	Position	W.	L.
1969—Albuquerque.......... Texas	Fourth(W)	67	69	1979—Albuquerque.......... P. Coast	First(S)	41	32
1970—Albuquerque†........ Texas	First(W)	83	52	(Second Half)	z Second(S)	45	30
1971—Evansville .... A. A.	Fourth(E)	60	78	1980—Albuquerque.......... P. Coast	Second(S)	39	33
1972—Evansville .... A. A.	Second(E)	21	17	(Second Half)	a First(S)	46	29
1972—Milwaukee‡........... Amer.	Sixth(E)	54	70	1981—Albuquerque.......... P. Coast	First(S)	46	22
1973—Milwaukee............. Amer.	Fifth(E)	74	88	(Second Half)	b First(S)	48	16
1974—Milwaukee............. Amer.	Fifth(E)	76	86	1982—Albuquerque.......... P. Coast	First(S)	46	25
1975—Milwaukee§............ Amer.	Fifth(E)	67	94	(Second Half)	c Second(S)	39	33
1976—Salinas .... Calif.	x First	48	23	1983—Albuquerque.......... P. Coast	Second(S)	41	30
(Second Half)	Second	43	26	1983—Seattle d.................. Amer.	Seventh(W)	34	55
1978—Albuquerque y........ P. Coast	First(E)	78	62	Major League Totals..		305	393

†Won playoff against Memphis, three games to one.
‡Replaced Dave Bristol, May 30, 1972.
§Replaced by interim Manager Harvey Kuenn, September 28, 1975.
xLost playoff to Reno, three games to one.
yWon semifinals against Salt Lake City, three games to none; ruled co-champion with Tacoma.
zLost playoff against Salt Lake City, two games to none.
aWon playoffs defeating Tucson, two games to none; and Hawaii, three games to two.
bWon playoffs defeating Tacoma, three games to one.
cWon playoffs defeating Salt Lake City, two games to none; and Spokane, four games to two.
dReplaced Rene Lachemann with club in seventh place (record of 26-47), May 25, 1983.
Coach, California Angels, 1977.

JAMES GOTTFRIED FREY
(Jim)
Chicago Cubs

Born May 26, 1931, at Cleveland, O.
Height, 5.09. Weight, 170.
Threw and batted lefthanded.
Attended Ohio State University, Columbus, O.

Led Texas League in total bases with 294 and tied for lead in stolen bases with 21 in 1957.
Named Most Valuable Player in Texas League, 1957.

Year	Club	League	Pos.	G.	AB.	R.	H.	2B.	3B.	HR.	RBI.	B.A.	PO.	A.	E.	F.A.
1950—Evansville	I. I. I.						(appeared in less than 10 games; no record available)									
1950—Paducah	M.O.V.	OF	106	412	73	134	21	11	1	58	.325	180	17	6	.970
1951—Evansville	I.I.I.	OF	119	447	69	145	24	9	1	58	.324	197	18	10	.956
1952—Hartford	East.	OF	20	80	12	21	8	0	0	7	.263	23	2	0	1.000
1952—Evansville	I.I.I.	OF	90	307	66	103	25	3	2	54	.336	145	15	6	.964
1953—Jacksonville	So. Atl.	OF	117	429	64	136	25	4	2	37	.317	241	18	2	★.992
1954—Jacksonville	So. Atl.	OF	139	529	89	167	★40	4	11	65	.316	314	18	5	.985
1955—Toledo	A. A.	OF	142	486	88	137	36	0	4	54	.282	209	17	11	.954
1956—Atlanta	S. A.	OF	25	87	14	22	4	0	1	11	.253	39	5	2	.957
1956—Austin†-Ft. W.‡	Texas	OF	126	447	63	125	20	2	6	39	.280	224	7	10	.959
1957—Tulsa§	Texas	OF	★155	589	★102	★198	★50	★11	8	74	★.336	310	16	12	.964
1958—Omaha	A. A.	OF	117	420	63	119	19	7	4	45	.283	211	8	6	.973
1959—Rochester	Int.	OF	114	338	56	100	17	2	11	42	.296	157	7	4	.976
1960—Rochester x	Int.	OF	125	441	78	140	21	4	16	66	★.317	199	12	8	.963
1961—Buffalo	Int.	OF	115	354	49	93	17	1	10	47	.263	180	8	4	.979
1962—Buffalo y	Int.	OF	134	448	67	121	18	1	16	59	.270	196	17	5	.977
1963—Col.z-Atl.ab	Int.	OF	62	108	11	28	3	0	2	12	.259	29	2	3	.912

†Traded by Milwaukee Braves' organization to Brooklyn Dodgers' organization for Outfielder Ray Shearer, July 4, 1956.
‡Sold by Brooklyn Dodgers' organization to Tulsa, April 12, 1957.
§Sold to St. Louis Cardinals' organization, July 31, 1957, to be announced after the season was over.
xReleased by St. Louis Cardinals' organization to Buffalo, October 5, 1960.
yReleased to Pittsburgh Pirates' organization, December 3, 1962.
zReleased, May 7, 1963; signed as free agent by St. Louis Cardinals' organization, May 18, 1963.
aOn disabled list, July 8 to July 29, 1963.
bReleased, October 15, 1963.

PITCHING RECORD

Year	Club	League	G.	IP.	W.	L.	Pct.	H.	R.	ER.	SO.	BB.	ERA.
1956—Austin	Texas	1	....	0	0	.000	....	....	....	....	....	....
1957—Tulsa	Texas	4	....	0	0	.000	....	....	....	....	....	....
1960—Rochester	Int'national	1	....	0	0	.000	....	....	....	....	....	....
1961—Buffalo	Int'national	2	....	0	0	.000	....	....	....	....	....	....

RECORD AS MANAGER

Year	Club	League	Position	W.	L.
1964—Bluefield	Appal.	Fourth	27	44
1965—Bluefield	Appal.	Fifth	31	38
1980—Kansas City	Amer.	First(W)	97	65
1981—Kansas City†‡	Amer.		30	40
Major League Totals			127	105

CHAMPIONSHIP SERIES RECORD

Year	Club	League	W.	L.
1980—Kansas City	American	3	0

WORLD SERIES RECORD

Year	Club	League	W.	L.
1980—Kansas City	American	2	4

†Replaced by Dick Howser, August 31, 1981.
‡First Half....Fifth(W) (record of 20-30); Second Half....Third(W) (record of 10-10).
Scout, Baltimore Orioles, 1966 through 1969; coach, Baltimore Orioles, 1970 through 1979; coach, New York Mets, 1982 and 1983.
Manager, American League All-Star Team, 1981.
Coach, American League All-Star Team, 1980.

WILLIAM FREDERICK GARDNER
(Billy)
Minnesota Twins

Born July 19, 1927, at New London, Conn.
Height, 6.00. Weight, 180.
Threw and batted righthanded.

Established major league record for fewest assists by second baseman, season, 150 or more games (350), 1958.
Tied American League record for most putouts by second baseman, extra-inning game (12), May 21, 1957 (16 innings).
Led American League second basemen in double plays in 1959.

Year	Club	League	Pos.	G.	AB.	R.	H.	2B.	3B.	HR.	RBI.	B.A.	PO.	A.	E.	F.A.
1945—Bristol	Appal.	3B	74	304	67	100	16	6	5	56	.329	★107	★132	11	★.956
1945—Jersey City	Int.	3B-OF	49	172	16	47	4	2	1	20	.273	55	75	8	.942
1946—Jersey City	Int.					(In Military Service)										
1947—Jacksonville	Sally	3B-SS	110	423	55	111	18	5	1	41	.262	129	191	32	.909
1948—Jacksonville	Sally	3B	●154	548	66	140	26	4	3	66	.255	★150	262	★36	.920
1949—Minneapolis	A. A.	3B	17	28	7	5	0	0	2	6	.179	5	16	4	.840

Year	Club	League	Pos.	G.	AB.	R.	H.	2B.	3B.	HR.	RBI.	B.A.	PO.	A.	E.	F.A.
1949—Jersey City	Int.		3B	17	45	6	11	1	0	0	1	.244	18	25	4	.915
1950—Sioux City	West.		3B	154	581	96	176	32	7	22	118	.303	★159	★335	★48	.911
1951—Ottawa	Int.		3B	150	555	56	128	19	6	3	37	.231	●182	279	★36	.928
1952—Minneapolis	A. A.		INF-OF	93	224	29	58	15	1	1	15	.259	109	165	23	.923
1953—Nashville	South.		★SS-3B	153	591	88	182	●42	5	10	71	.308	255	444	★42	.943
1954—New York	Nat.		INF	62	108	10	23	5	0	1	7	.213	42	82	2	.984
1955—New York	Nat.		INF	59	187	26	38	10	1	3	17	.203	76	139	13	.943
1955—Minneapolis†	A. A.		INF	73	290	55	90	15	1	17	48	.310	161	210	17	.956
1956—Baltimore	Amer.		INF	144	515	53	119	16	2	11	50	.231	301	386	18	.974
1957—Baltimore	Amer.		★2B-SS	154	★644	79	169	★36	3	6	55	.262	406	450	12	★.986
1958—Baltimore	Amer.		2B-SS	151	560	32	126	28	2	3	33	.225	354	356	11	.985
1959—Baltimore‡	Amer.		★2-S-3	140	401	34	87	13	2	6	27	.217	334	393	★18	.976
1960—Washington	Amer.		★2B-SS	145	592	71	152	26	5	9	56	.257	360	418	★21	.974
1961—Minn.§-N.Y.	Amer.		2B-3B	86	253	24	57	14	0	2	13	.225	121	160	11	.962
1962—N.Y.x-Boston	Amer.		INF	57	200	23	54	9	2	0	12	.270	80	125	10	.953
1963—Boston y	Amer.		2B-3B	36	84	4	16	2	1	0	1	.190	37	59	1	.990
1964—Seattle z	P. C.		2B	101	308	23	69	8	4	1	28	.224	173	226	11	.973
1967—Pittsfield a	East.		3B	2	2	0	0	0	0	0	0	.000	1	0	0	1.000
1969—Pittsfield a	East.		2B	2	3	1	1	0	0	0	0	.333	3	2	0	1.000
1971—Pawtucket a	East.		PH	1	1	0	0	0	0	0	0	.000	0	0	0	.000
American League Totals				913	3249	320	780	144	17	37	247	.240	1993	2347	102	.997
National League Totals				121	295	36	61	15	1	4	24	.207	118	221	15	.958
Major League Totals				1034	3544	356	841	159	18	41	271	.237	2111	2568	117	.976

†Started 1956 season with New York Giants; sold to Baltimore Orioles for reported $20,000, April 21, 1956.
‡Traded to Washington Senators for Catcher Clint Courtney and Infielder Ron Samford, April, 1960.
§Traded to New York Yankees for Pitcher Danny McDevitt, June 14, 1961.
xTraded to Boston Red Sox for cash and transfer of Outfielder Tom Umphlett from Seattle, Pacific Coast League, to Richmond, International League, June 21, 1962.
yReleased by Boston Red Sox, October 2, 1963.
zPlayer-coach.
aPlayer-manager.

WORLD SERIES RECORD

Year	Club	League	Pos.	G.	AB.	R.	H.	2B.	3B.	HR.	RBI.	B.A.	PO.	A.	E.	F.A.
1961—New York	Amer.		PH	1	1	0	0	0	0	0	0	.000	0	0	0	.000

RECORD AS MANAGER

Named American Association Manager of the Year, 1980.
Named Southern League Manager of the Year, 1973.
Named Eastern League Manager of the Year, 1968.

Year	Club	League	Position	W.	L.	Year	Club	League	Position	W.	L.
1967—Pittsfield	East.	Second(E)	75	62		1976—Omaha	A. A.	xFirst(E)	78	58
1968—Pittsfield	East.	†First	84	55		1979—Memphis	South.	yzFirst(W)	36	34
1969—Pittsfield	East.	Fourth	68	72		(Second Half)		Second(W)	46	28
1970—Louisville	Int.	Sixth	69	71		1980—Denver	A. A.	aFirst(W)	92	44
1971—Pawtucket	East.	Third(Am.)	63	76		1981—Minnesota bc	Amer.		30	43
1972—Jacksonville	South.	Fourth(E)	64	75		1982—Minnesota	Amer.	Seventh(W)	60	102
1973—Jacksonville	South.	‡First(E)	76	60		1983—Minnesota	Amer.	dFifth	70	92
1974—Jacksonville	South.	§First(E)	78	60		Major League Totals			160	237
1975—Omaha	A. A.	Third(E)	67	69						

†Lost playoff to Reading, three games to one.
‡Lost playoff to Montgomery, three games to one.
§Lost playoff to Knoxville, three games to two.
xLost playoff to Denver, four games to one.
yTied for position and won one-game first-half playoff from Montgomery.
zLost playoff to Nashville, two games to one.
aLost championship playoffs to Springfield, four games to one.
bFirst Half. . . . Seventh(W) (record of 6-14); Second Half. . . . Fourth(W) (record of 24-29).
cReplaced John Goryl with club in sixth place (record of 11-25), May 22, 1981.
dTied for position with California Angels.
Coach, Boston Red Sox' organization, October 1964 through 1966; coach, Montreal Expos, 1977 and 1978; coach, Minnesota Twins, December 5, 1980 through June 21, 1981.
Coach, American League All-Star Team, 1983.

DORREL NORMAN ELVERT HERZOG
(Relly and Whitey)

(Named "Relly" by mother from his first name; "Whitey" by Bill Speith, McAlester sportscaster, because of light hair.)

St. Louis Cardinals

Born November 9, 1931, at New Athens, Ill.
Height, 5.11½. Weight, 187.
Threw and batted lefthanded.

Year	Club	League	Pos.	G.	AB.	R.	H.	2B.	3B.	HR.	RBI.	B.A.	PO.	A.	E.	F.A.
1949—McAlester	Soo. St.		OF	96	398	53	111	19	7	0	31	.279	222	14	0	★1.000
1950—McAlester	Soo. St.		OF	132	467	107	164	36	10	4	85	.351	272	15	7	★.976
1951—Norfolk	Pied.		OF	5	17	5	1	0	0	0	2	.059	13	0	1	.926

Year—Club	League	Pos.	G.	AB.	R.	H.	2B.	3B.	HR.	RBI.	B.A.	PO.	A.	E.	F.A.
1951—Joplin	W. A.	OF-1B	113	418	99	119	14	8	7	48	.285	454	19	9	.981
1952—Beaumont	Texas	OF	35	121	11	24	4	1	0	9	.198	83	3	5	.945
1952—Quincy	I. I. I.	OF	68	225	53	65	9	6	7	44	.289	131	9	5	.966
1952—Kansas City	A. A.	OF-1B	14	27	5	8	1	0	1	5	.296	21	1	1	.957
1953-54—						(In Military Service.)									
1955—Denver†	A. A.	OF-1B	149	515	101	149	24	7	21	98	.289	324	10	4	.988
1956—Washington	Amer.	OF-1B	117	421	49	103	13	7	4	35	.245	274	10	7	.976
1957—Washington	Amer.	OF	36	78	7	13	3	0	0	4	.167	53	0	1	.981
1957—Miami	Int.	OF	77	257	48	70	14	5	2	25	.272	114	5	4	.967
1958—Wash.‡-K.C.	Amer.	OF-1B	96	101	11	23	1	2	0	9	.228	146	6	3	.981
1959—Kansas City	Amer.	OF-1B	38	123	25	36	7	1	1	9	.293	87	2	3	.967
1960—Kansas City§	Amer.	OF-1B	83	252	43	67	10	2	8	38	.266	137	6	4	.973
1961—Baltimore	Amer.	OF	113	323	39	94	11	6	5	35	.291	143	2	0	1.000
1962—Baltimore x	Amer.	OF	99	263	34	70	13	1	7	35	.266	132	4	3	.978
1963—Detroit	Amer.	1B-OF	52	53	5	8	2	1	0	7	.151	44	1	1	.978
Major League Totals			634	1614	213	414	60	20	25	172	.257	1016	31	22	.979

†Traded to Washington Senators with Pitcher Bob Wiesler, Catcher Lou Berberet, Second Baseman Herb Plews and Outfielder Dick Tettelbach for pitcher Maury McDermott and Shortstop Bob Kline (assigned to the Yankees' American Association farm club—Denver). Other players in deal assigned February 8, 1956; Herzog, April 2, 1956.

‡Sold to Kansas City Athletics, May 14, 1958.

§Traded to Baltimore Orioles with Outfielder Russ Snyder and a player to be named at later date, for Pitcher Jim Archer, Catcher Clint Courtney, First Baseman Bob Boyd, Infielder Wayne Causey and Outfielder Al Pilarcik, January 24, 1961; Courtney returned to the Orioles, April 15, 1961, to complete deal.

xTraded to Detroit Tigers with Catcher Gus Triandos for Catcher Dick Brown, November 26, 1962.

RECORD AS MANAGER

Named Man of the Year by THE SPORTING NEWS, 1982.
Named Major League Manager of the Year by THE SPORTING NEWS, 1982.

Year—Club	League	Position	W.	L.	Year—Club	League	Position	W.	L.
1973—Texas†	Amer.	Sixth(W)	47	91	1981—St. Louis z	Nat.		59	43
1974—California‡	Amer.	Sixth(W)	2	2	1982—St. Louis	Nat.	First(E)	92	70
1975—Kansas City§	Amer.	Second(W)	41	25	1983—St. Louis	Nat.	Fourth(E)	79	83
1976—Kansas City	Amer.	First(W)	90	72	National League Totals			268	231
1977—Kansas City	Amer.	First(W)	102	60	American League Totals			459	397
1978—Kansas City	Amer.	First(W)	92	70	Major League Totals			727	628
1979—Kansas City	Amer.	Second(W)	85	77					
1980—St. Louis xy	Nat.	Fourth(E)	38	35					

†Replaced by Billy Martin, September 8, 1973 (Del Wilber served as interim manager, September 7).

‡Served as interim manager, June 27 to June 30, 1974 after Dick Williams replaced Bobby Winkles, June 26.

§Replaced Jack McKeon with club in second place (record of 50-46), July 24, 1975.

xReplaced Ken Boyer (and interim manager Jack Krol) with club in sixth place (record of 18-33), June 9, 1980.

yNamed General Manager, August 28, 1980, with Red Schoendienst serving as manager remainder of season.

zFirst Half. . . . Second(E) (record of 30-20); Second Half. . . . Second(E) (record of 29-23).

Scout, Kansas City Athletics, 1964.; coach, Kansas City Athletics, 1965; New York Mets, 1966; California Angels, 1974 and part of 1975.

Director of Player Development, New York Mets, 1967 through 1972.

Manager, National League All-Star Team, 1983.

Coach, American League All-Star Team, 1973, 1974 and 1978.

CHAMPIONSHIP SERIES RECORD

Year—Club	League	W.	L.
1976—Kansas City	American	2	3
1977—Kansas City	American	2	3
1978—Kansas City	American	1	3
1982—St. Louis	National	3	0

WORLD SERIES RECORD

Year—Club	League	W.	L.
1982—St. Louis	National	4	3

RALPH GEORGE HOUK
Boston Red Sox

Born August 9, 1919, at Lawrence, Kan.
Height, 5.11. Weight, 198.
Threw and batted righthanded.

Year—Club	League	Pos.	G.	AB.	R.	H.	2B.	3B.	HR.	RBI.	B.A.	PO.	A.	E.	F.A.
1939—Neosho	Ak. Mo.	C	119	427	69	122	15	6	1	56	.286	634	★79	13	★.982
1940—Joplin	W. A.	C	110	364	53	114	18	7	0	63	.313	517	78	10	★.983
1941—Binghamton	East.	C	5	9	3	3	0	0	0	0	.333	9	1	1	.909
1941—Augusta	Sally	C	97	340	37	92	11	5	1	48	.271	542	62	12	.981
1942-45—Bing'ton	East.					(In Military Service)									
1946—Kansas City	A. A.	C	8	23	5	8	2	0	1	1	.348	28	5	0	1.000
1946—Beaumont	Texas	C-OF	87	279	38	82	20	2	0	40	.294	297	45	9	.974
1947—New York	Amer.	C	41	92	7	25	3	1	0	12	.272	138	13	2	.987
1948—Kansas City	A. A.	★C-3B	103	364	54	110	24	5	1	49	.302	464	★72	7	.987
1948—New York	Amer.	C	14	29	3	8	2	0	0	3	.276	41	5	0	1.000
1949—New York	Amer.	C	5	7	0	4	0	0	0	1	.571	8	0	1	.889
1949—Kansas City	A. A.	C	95	313	47	86	18	1	0	36	.275	398	48	7	.985
1950—New York	Amer.	C	10	9	0	1	1	0	0	1	.111	12	1	1	.929
1951—New York	Amer.	C	3	5	0	1	0	0	0	2	.200	2	1	0	1.000
1952—New York	Amer.	C	9	6	0	2	0	0	0	0	.333	10	1	1	.917

Year—Club	League	Pos.	G.	AB.	R.	H.	2B.	3B.	HR.	RBI.	B.A.	PO.	A.	E.	F.A.
1953—New York	Amer.	C	8	9	2	2	0	0	0	1	.222	10	0	0	1.000
1954—New York	Amer.	PH	1	1	0	0	0	0	0	0	.000	0	0	0	.000
1955—Denver	A. A.	C	15	26	1	4	3	0	0	4	.154	33	1	3	.919
1956—Denver	A. A.	C	1	4	0	0	0	0	0	0	.000	7	1	0	1.000
Major League Totals			91	158	12	43	6	1	0	20	.272	221	21	5	.980

WORLD SERIES RECORD

Year—Club	League	Pos.	G.	AB.	R.	H.	2B.	3B.	HR.	RBI.	B.A.	PO.	A.	E.	F.A.
1947—New York	Amer.	PH	1	1	0	1	0	0	0	0	1.000	0	0	0	.000
1952—New York	Amer.	PH	1	1	0	0	0	0	0	0	.000	0	0	0	.000
World Series Totals			2	2	0	1	0	0	0	0	.500	0	0	0	.000

RECORD AS MANAGER

Named Major League Manager of the Year by THE SPORTING NEWS, 1961.

Year—Club	League	Position	W.	L.	Year—Club	League	Position	W.	L.
1955—Denver	A. A.	†Third	83	71	1972—New York	Amer.	Fourth(E)	79	76
1956—Denver	A. A.	Second	87	67	1973—New York	Amer.	Fourth(E)	80	82
1957—Denver	A. A.	‡Second	90	64	1974—Detroit	Amer.	Sixth(E)	72	90
1961—New York	Amer.	First	109	53	1975—Detroit	Amer.	Sixth(E)	57	102
1962—New York	Amer.	First	96	66	1976—Detroit	Amer.	Fifth(E)	74	87
1963—New York§	Amer.	First	104	57	1977—Detroit	Amer.	Fourth(E)	74	88
1966—New York	Amer.	Tenth	66	73	1978—Detroit	Amer.	Fifth(E)	86	76
1967—New York	Amer.	Ninth	72	90	1981—Boston x	Amer.		59	49
1968—New York	Amer.	Fifth	83	79	1982—Boston	Amer.	Third(E)	89	73
1969—New York	Amer.	Fifth(E)	80	81	1983—Boston	Amer.	Sixth(E)	78	84
1970—New York	Amer.	Second(E)	93	69	Major League Totals			1533	1455
1971—New York	Amer.	Fourth(E)	82	80					

†Tied for position.

‡Won playoffs by defeating Minneapolis, four games to none and St. Paul, four games to two; won Junior World Series against Buffalo (International League), four games to one.

§Replaced Johnny Keane with club in tenth place (record of 4-16), May 7, 1966.

xFirst Half.... Fifth (E) (record of 30-26); Second Half.... Second (E) (record of 29-23).

Coach, New York Yankees, part of 1953 and 1954 seasons and 1958 through 1960; vice-president-general manager, New York Yankees, 1964 through May 6, 1966.

Manager, American League All-Star Team, 1962 and 1963.

Coach, American League All-Star Team, 1970.

WORLD SERIES RECORD

Year—Club	League	W.	L.
1961—New York	American	4	1
1962—New York	American	4	3
1963—New York	American	0	4

RICHARD DALTON HOWSER
(Dick)
Kansas City Royals

Born May 14, 1937, at Miami, Fla.
Height, 5.09. Weight, 155.
Threw and batted righthanded.
Received bachelor of science degree in education from
Florida State University, Tallahassee, Fla.

Tied American League record for most games played by shortstop, season (162), 1964.
Tied for American League lead in sacrifice hits with 6 in 1964.
Led Three-I League in stolen bases with 31 in 1959.
Named American League Rookie of the Year by THE SPORTING NEWS, 1961.
Received reported $21,000 bonus to sign with Kansas City Athletics, 1958.

Year—Club	League	Pos.	G.	AB.	R.	H.	2B.	3B.	HR.	RBI.	B.A.	PO.	A.	E.	F.A.
1958—Winona	I.I.I.	SS	83	333	80	96	16	1	6	30	.288	152	233	28	.932
1959—Sioux City	I.I.I.	2B-SS	111	392	●107	109	17	5	4	39	.278	240	289	33	.941
1960—Sioux City	I.I.I.	SS	44	149	59	52	15	1	5	21	.349	63	130	20	.906
1960—Shreveport	South.	SS	88	331	78	112	20	6	4	38	.338	189	270	31	.937
1961—Kansas City	Amer.	SS	158	611	108	171	29	6	3	45	.280	*299	427	*38	.950
1962—Kansas City†	Amer.	SS	83	286	53	68	8	3	6	34	.238	138	191	13	.962
1963—K.C.‡-Cleve.	Amer.	SS	64	203	29	48	5	0	1	11	.236	101	113	11	.951
1964—Cleveland	Amer.	SS	162	637	101	163	23	4	3	52	.256	291	463	20	.974
1965—Cleveland	Amer.	SS-2B	107	307	47	72	8	2	1	6	.235	144	211	7	.981
1966—Cleveland§	Amer.	SS-2B	67	140	18	32	9	1	2	4	.229	53	95	5	.967
1967—New York x	Amer.	2B-3B-SS	63	149	18	40	6	0	0	10	.268	64	76	3	.979
1968—New York	Amer.	2B-3B-SS	85	150	24	23	2	1	0	3	.153	61	106	3	.982
Major League Totals			789	2483	398	617	90	17	16	165	.248	1151	1682	100	.966

†On disabled list, June 26 to August 10, 1962.

‡Traded to Cleveland Indians with Catcher Jose Azcue for Catcher Howard Edwards and reported $100,000, May 25, 1963.

§Traded to New York Yankees for Pitcher Gil Downs and cash, December 20, 1966.

xOn disabled list, July 17 to September 1, 1967.

ALL-STAR GAME RECORD

Year League	Pos.	AB.	R.	H.	2B.	3B.	HR.	RBI.	B.A.	PO.	A.	E.	F.A.
1961—American (first game)	3B	1	0	0	0	0	0	0	.000	0	1	0	1.000

Member of American League All-Star Team in 1961 (second game); did not play.

RECORD AS MANAGER

Year Club	League	Position	W.	L.
1980—New York	Amer.	First(E)	103	59
1981—Kansas City†‡	Amer.		20	13
1982—Kansas City	Amer.	Second(W)	90	72
1983—Kansas City	Amer.	Second(W)	79	83
Major League Totals			292	227

†Replaced Jim Frey with club in third place during second half (record of 10-10), August 31, 1981.
‡Second Half. . . . First(W) (record of 20-13).
Coach, New York Yankees, 1969 through 1978, scout, New York Yankees, November 21, 1980 through August 30, 1981.
Baseball coach at Florida State University, 1979. Record: 43 wins, 17 losses, 1 tie.
Coach, American League All-Star Team, 1982.

DIVISION SERIES RECORD

Year Club	League	W.	L.
1981—Kansas City	American	0	3

CHAMPIONSHIP SERIES RECORD

Year Club	League	W.	L.
1980—New York	American	0	3

DAVID ALLEN JOHNSON
(Dave)
New York Mets

Born January 30, 1943, at Orlando, Fla.
Height, 6.01. Weight, 182.
Threw and batted righthanded.
Attended Texas A&M University, College Station, Tex., received bachelor of
science degree in mathematics from Trinity University, San Antonio, Tex.,
and attended Johns Hopkins University, Baltimore, Md.

Established major league record for most home runs by second baseman, season, (43), 1973.
Tied major league records for fewest triples, season (150 or more games), (0), 1973; most home runs, bases filled, season, pinch-hitter (2), 1978.
Tied for American League lead in sacrifice flies with 8 in 1967.
Led National League second basemen in total chances with 877 and tied for lead in double plays with 106 in 1973.
Led American League second basemen in double plays with 103 in 1971.
Led California League shortstops in double plays with 63 in 1962.
Named National League Comeback Player of the Year by THE SPORTING NEWS, 1973.
Named second baseman on THE SPORTING NEWS National League All-Star Team, 1973.
Named second baseman on THE SPORTING NEWS American League All-Star Team, 1970.
Named second baseman on THE SPORTING NEWS American League All-Star fielding team, 1969 through 1971.

Year Club	League	Pos.	G.	AB.	R.	H.	2B.	3B.	HR.	RBI.	B.A.	PO.	A.	E.	F.A.
1962—Stockton	Calif.	SS	97	343	58	106	18	●12	10	63	.309	135	307	40	★.917
1963—Elmira	East.	SS-2B	63	233	47	76	11	6	13	42	.326	115	155	12	.957
1963—Rochester	Int.	2B-OF	63	211	31	52	9	3	6	22	.246	141	138	11	.962
1964—Rochester	Int.	2B-SS	●155	590	87	156	29	14	19	73	.264	326	445	39	.952
1965—Baltimore	Amer.	3B-2B-SS	20	47	5	8	3	0	0	1	.170	11	37	3	.941
1965—Rochester	Int.	SS	52	193	29	58	9	3	4	22	.301	96	161	10	.963
1966—Baltimore	Amer.	★2B-SS	131	501	47	129	20	3	7	56	.257	294	357	★20	.970
1967—Baltimore	Amer.	2B-3B	148	510	62	126	30	3	10	64	.247	344	351	14	.980
1968—Baltimore	Amer.	2B-SS	145	504	50	122	24	4	9	56	.242	294	370	15	.978
1969—Baltimore	Amer.	2B-SS	142	511	52	143	34	1	7	57	.280	358	370	12	.984
1970—Baltimore	Amer.	●2B-SS	149	530	68	149	27	1	10	53	.281	●382	391	8	.990
1971—Baltimore	Amer.	2B	142	510	67	144	26	1	18	72	.282	361	367	12	.984
1972—Baltimore†	Amer.	2B	118	376	31	83	22	3	5	32	.221	286	307	6	★.990
1973—Atlanta	Nat.	2B	157	559	84	151	25	0	43	99	.270	383	464	★30	.966
1974—Atlanta	Nat.	1B-2B	136	454	56	114	18	0	15	62	.251	789	231	11	.989
1975—Atlanta‡	Nat.	PH	1	1	0	1	1	0	0	1	1.000	0	0	0	.000
1975—Yomiuri	Central	3B-SS	91	289	29	57	7	0	13	38	.197	85	157	11	.957
1976—Yomiuri§	Central	2B-3B-1B	108	371	48	102	16	2	26	74	.275	226	28	11	.979
1977—Philadelphia x	Nat.	1B-2B-3B	78	156	23	50	9	1	8	36	.321	299	31	0	1.000
1978—Phil. y-Chi. z	Nat.	3B-2B-1B	68	138	19	32	3	1	4	20	.232	61	63	11	.919
1979—Miami	Int.-Am.	1B	10	25	7	6	2	0	1	2	.240	Figures Unavailable			
American League Totals			995	3489	382	904	186	16	66	391	.259	2330	2550	90	.982
National League Totals			440	1308	182	348	56	2	70	218	.266	1532	789	52	.978
Major League Totals			1435	4797	564	1252	242	18	136	609	.261	3862	3339	142	.981

†Traded with Pitchers Pat Dobson and Roric Harrison and Catcher Johnny Oates to Atlanta Braves for Catcher Earl Williams and Infielder Taylor Duncan, November 30, 1972.
‡Released, April 11, 1975; signed by Yomiuri Giants of Japanese baseball.
§Released, January 21, 1977; signed as free agent with Philadelphia Phillies, February 3, 1977.
xOn supplemental disabled list, June 15 to July 1, 1977.
yTraded to Chicago Cubs for Pitcher Larry Anderson, August 6, 1978.
zReleased, October 17, 1978.

CHAMPIONSHIP SERIES RECORD

Tied American League Championship Series record for most home runs, three-game Series (2), 1970.

Year Club	League	Pos.	G.	AB.	R.	H.	2B.	3B.	HR.	RBI.	B.A.	PO.	A.	E.	F.A.
1969—Baltimore	Amer.	2B	3	13	2	3	0	0	0	0	.231	5	11	0	1.000
1970—Baltimore	Amer.	2B	3	11	4	4	0	0	2	4	.364	11	4	0	1.000
1971—Baltimore	Amer.	2B	3	10	2	3	2	0	0	0	.300	5	6	1	.917
1977—Philadelphia	Nat.	1B	1	4	0	1	0	0	0	2	.250	8	0	0	1.000
Championship Series Totals			10	38	8	11	2	0	2	6	.289	29	21	1	.980

WORLD SERIES RECORD

Established World Series record for highest fielding average by second baseman, four-game Series (1.000 with 24 chances), 1966.

Year Club	League	Pos.	G.	AB.	R.	H.	2B.	3B.	HR.	RBI.	B.A.	PO.	A.	E.	F.A.
1966—Baltimore	Amer.	2B	4	14	1	4	1	0	0	1	.286	12	12	0	1.000
1969—Baltimore	Amer.	2B	5	16	1	1	0	0	0	0	.063	8	15	0	1.000
1970—Baltimore	Amer.	2B	5	16	2	5	2	0	0	2	.313	15	9	0	1.000
1971—Baltimore	Amer.	2B	7	27	1	4	0	0	0	3	.148	18	12	0	1.000
World Series Totals			21	73	5	14	3	0	0	6	.192	53	48	0	1.000

ALL-STAR GAME RECORD

Year League	Pos.	AB.	R.	H.	2B.	3B.	HR.	RBI.	B.A.	PO.	A.	E.	F.A.
1968—American	2B	1	0	0	0	0	0	0	.000	1	1	0	1.000
1970—American	2B	5	0	1	0	0	0	0	.200	5	1	0	1.000
1973—National	2B	1	0	0	0	0	0	0	.000	1	1	0	1.000
All-Star Game Totals		7	0	1	0	0	0	0	.143	7	3	0	1.000

Named to American League All-Star Team for 1969 game; replaced due to injury.

RECORD AS MANAGER

Year Club	League	Position	W.	L.
1979—Miami	Inter-Amer.	First	43	17
(Second Half)		First	8	4
1981—Jackson	Texas	†First(E)	39	27
(Second Half)		Third(E)	29	39
1983—Tidewater	Int.	‡Fourth	71	68

†Defeated Tulsa, two games to one, and San Antonio (finals), three games to none, for championship.
‡Defeated Columbus, three games to two, and Richmond (finals), three games to one, for championship.
Instructor, New York Mets' organization, 1982.

RENE GEORGE LACHEMANN

Name pronounced LATCH-man.

Milwaukee Brewers

Born May 4, 1945, at Los Angeles, Calif.
Height, 6.00. Weight, 195.
Threw and batted righthanded.
Attended University of Southern California, Los Angeles, Calif.
Brother of Marcel Lachemann, pitcher with Oakland A's, 1969 through 1971; and
Bill Lachemann, catcher with Los Angeles Dodgers' organization, 1955 through 1963;
and currently manager in San Francisco Giants' organization.

Led Midwest League catchers in double plays with 14 in 1964 and Pacific Coast League with 13 in 1967.

Year Club	League	Pos.	G.	AB.	R.	H.	2B.	3B.	HR.	RBI.	B.A.	PO.	A.	E.	F.A.
1964—Burlington	Midw.	C	99	335	52	94	14	1	∗24	82	.281	743	55	10	.988
1964—Birmingham	South.	C	3	6	1	4	1	0	0	1	.667	7	1	0	1.000
1965—Kansas City	Amer.	C	92	216	20	49	7	1	9	29	.227	361	27	8	.980
1966—Mobile†	South.	∙ C	119	434	48	111	17	1	15	65	.256	819	48	13	.985
1966—Kansas City	Amer.	C	7	5	0	1	1	0	0	0	.200	10	1	0	1.000
1967—Vancouver	P. C.	C	123	410	26	91	16	0	6	53	.222	∗811	68	10	.989
1968—Oakland	Amer.	C	19	60	3	9	1	0	0	4	.150	82	5	3	.967
1968—Vancouver	P. C.	C-1B	63	193	14	48	7	0	4	14	.249	351	22	7	.982
1969—Iowa	A. A.	1B-C	107	415	47	106	18	1	20	66	.255	782	62	10	.988
1970—Iowa	A. A.	1-3-2-C	61	171	25	44	10	0	5	20	.257	365	29	7	.983
1971—Iowa	A. A.	1-3-C-2	92	314	42	76	16	1	17	48	.242	542	65	10	.984
1972—Iowa	A. A.	1-C-O-3	95	236	25	51	6	0	11	37	.216	347	18	6	.984
Major League Totals			118	281	23	59	9	1	9	33	.210	453	33	11	.978

Signed as free agent by Kansas City A's organization, September 18, 1963.
†On disabled list, July 19 to July 29, 1966.

RECORD AS MANAGER

Named Southern League Manager of the Year, 1976.

Year Club	League	Position	W.	L.	Year Club	League	Position	W.	L.
1973—Burlington	Midw.	Fifth(S)	24	23	1979—Spokane	P. C.	Second(N)	39	32
(Second Half)		Third(S)	30	32	(Second Half)		Fifth(N)	29	47
1974—Burlington	Midw.	Second(S)	29	28	1980—Spokane	P. C.	Fifth(N)	24	41
(Second Half)		Second(S)	32	31	(Second Half)		Second(N)	36	39
1975—Modesto	Calif.	Sixth	33	37	1981—Spokane	P. C.	Second(N)	11	9
(Second Half)		Fifth	35	35	1981—Seattle‡§	Amer.		38	47
1976—Chattanooga†	South.	First(W)	34	30	1982—Seattle	Amer.	Fourth(W)	76	86
(Second Half)		Second(W)	36	38	1983—Seattle x	Amer.	Seventh(W)	26	47
1977—San Jose	P. C.	Fourth	64	80	Major League Totals			140	180
1978—San Jose	P. C.	Fifth	53	87					

†Lost one-game playoff to Montgomery for West Division Championship.
‡First Half. . . . Sixth(W) (record of 15-18); Second Half. . . . Fifth(W) (record of 23-29).
§Replaced Maury Wills with club in seventh place (record of 6-18), May 6, 1981.
xReplaced by Del Crandall, June 25, 1983.

ANTHONY LaRUSSA JR.
(Tony)
Chicago White Sox

Born October 4, 1944, at Tampa, Fla.
Height, 6.00. Weight, 185.
Threw and batted righthanded.
Attended University of Tampa, Tampa, Fla., and received degree in industrial management from
University of Southern Florida, Tampa, Fla.; and received law degree from
Florida State University, Tallahassee, Fla. in 1980.

Led International League in being hit by pitch with 11 in 1972.

Year—Club	League	Pos.	G.	AB.	R.	H.	2B.	3B.	HR.	RBI.	B.A.	PO.	A.	E.	F.A.
1962—Daytona Beach	Fla. St.	SS	64	225	37	58	7	0	1	32	.258	135	173	38	.890
1962—Binghamton	East.	SS-2B	12	43	3	8	0	0	0	4	.186	20	27	8	.855
1963—Kansas City	Amer.	SS-2B	34	44	4	11	1	1	0	1	.250	29	25	2	.964
1964—Lewiston†	N'west	2B-SS	90	329	50	77	22	1	1	25	.234	188	218	18	.958
1965—Birmingham‡	South.	2B	75	259	24	50	11	2	1	18	.193	202	161	21	.945
1966—Modesto	Calif.	2B	81	316	67	92	20	1	7	54	.291	201	212	20	.954
1966—Mobile	South.	2B	51	170	20	50	9	4	4	26	.294	117	133	10	.962
1967—Birmingham§	South.	2B	41	139	12	32	6	1	5	22	.230	88	120	5	.977
1968—Oakland	Amer.	PH	5	3	0	1	0	0	0	0	.333	0	0	0	.000
1968—Vancouver	P. C.	2B	122	455	55	109	16	8	5	29	.240	249	321	14	★.976
1969—Iowa	A. A.	2B	67	235	37	72	11	1	4	27	.306	177	222	15	.964
1969—Oakland	Amer.	PH	8	8	0	0	0	0	0	0	.000	0	0	0	.000
1970—Iowa	A. A.	2B	22	88	13	22	5	0	2	5	.250	52	59	3	.974
1970—Oakland	Amer.	2B	52	106	6	21	4	1	0	6	.198	67	89	5	.969
1971—Iowa	A. A.	2-3-S-O	28	107	21	31	5	1	2	11	.290	70	85	2	.987
1971—Oakland x	Amer.	2B-SS-3B	23	8	3	0	0	0	0	0	.000	8	7	2	.882
1971—Atlanta	Nat.	2B	9	7	1	2	0	0	0	0	.286	8	6	1	.933
1972—Richmond y	Int.	2B	122	389	68	120	13	2	10	42	.308	305	289	20	.967
1973—Wichita	A. A.	2B-1B-3B	106	392	82	123	16	0	5	75	.314	423	213	26	.961
1973—Chicago z	Nat.	PR	1	0	1	0	0	0	0	0	.000	0	0	0	.000
1974—Charleston a	Int.	2B	139	457	50	119	17	1	8	35	.260	262	★378	17	.974
1975—Denver	A. A.	3-O-S-2	118	354	87	99	23	2	7	46	.280	95	91	10	.949
1976—Iowa bc	A. A.	INF-O-P	107	332	53	86	11	0	4	34	.259	132	160	22	.930
1977—New Orleans de	A. A.	2B-3B	50	128	17	24	2	2	3	6	.188	66	87	7	.956
American League Totals			122	169	13	33	5	2	0	7	.195	104	121	9	.962
National League Totals			10	7	2	2	0	0	0	0	.286	8	6	1	.933
Major League Totals			132	176	15	35	5	2	0	7	.199	112	127	10	.960

†On disabled list, May 9 to September 8, 1964.
‡On disabled list, June 3 to July 15, 1965.
§On disabled list, April 12 to May 6 and July 3 to September 5, 1967.
xSold to Atlanta Braves, August 14, 1971.
yTraded to Chicago Cubs for Pitcher Tom Phoebus, October 20, 1972.
zSold to Pittsburgh Pirates' organization.
aReleased, April 4, 1975; signed by Chicago White Sox' organization, April 7, 1975.
bOn disabled list, August 8 to August 18, 1976.
cSold to St. Louis Cardinals' organization, December 13, 1976.
dNamed coach, June 20, 1977.
eReleased, September 29, 1977.

PITCHING RECORD

Year—Club	League	G.	IP.	W.	L.	Pct.	H.	R.	ER.	SO.	BB.	ERA.
1976—Iowa	Am. Assoc.	3	3	0	0	.000	3	1	1	0	0	3.00

RECORD AS MANAGER

Named Major League Manager of the Year by THE SPORTING NEWS, 1983.

Year—Club	League	Position	W.	L.	Year—Club	League	Position	W.	L.
1978—Knoxville	South.	First(W)	49	21	1981—Chicago x	Amer.		54	52
(Second Half)†		Third(W)	4	4	1982—Chicago	Amer.	Third(W)	87	75
1979—Iowa‡	A. A.	Second(E)	54	52	1983—Chicago	Amer.	First(W)	99	63
1979—Chicago§	Amer.	Fifth(W)	27	27	Major League Totals			337	307
1980—Chicago	Amer.	Fifth(W)	70	90					

†Replaced by Joe Jones, July 3, 1978.
‡Replaced by Joe Sparks, August 3, 1979.
§Replaced Don Kessinger with club in fifth place (record of 46-60), August 3, 1979.
xFirst Half. . . . Third (W) (record 31-22); Second Half. . . . Sixth (W) (record of 23-30).
Coach, Chicago White Sox, July 3 through remainder of 1978 season.

CHAMPIONSHIP SERIES RECORD

Year—Club	League	W.	L.
1983—Chicago	American	1	3

THOMAS CHARLES LASORDA
Name pronounced Luh-SORR-duh.

(Tom)
Los Angeles Dodgers

Born September 22, 1927, at Norristown, Pa.
Height, 5.09. Weight, 195.
Threw and batted lefthanded.

Tied National League record by making three wild pitches in an inning, first inning, May 5, 1955.
Led International League in complete games with 16 and tied for lead in shutouts with 5 in 1958.
Led Canadian-American League in wild pitches with 20 in 1948 and led International League with 14 in 1953.
Named International League Pitcher of the Year, 1958.

Year Club	League	G.	IP.	W.	L.	Pct.	H.	R.	ER.	SO.	BB.	ERA.
1945—Concord	N. C. St.	27	121	3	12	.200	115	84	55	91	100	4.09
1946-47—†	E. Shore					(In Military Service)						
1948—Schenectady‡§	Can.-Am.	32	192	9	12	.429	180	122	99	195	153	4.64
1949—Greenville	Sally	45	178	7	7	.500	141	81	58	151	138	2.93
1950—Montreal	Int'national	31	146	9	4	.692	136	73	60	85	82	3.70
1951—Montreal	Int'national	31	165	12	8	.600	145	75	64	80	87	3.49
1952—Montreal	Int'national	33	182	14	5	.737	156	90	74	77	93	3.66
1953—Montreal	Int'national	36	208	17	8	.680	171	77	65	122	94	2.81
1954—Montreal	Int'national	23	154	14	5	.737	142	66	60	75	79	3.51
1954—Brooklyn	National	4	9	0	0	.000	8	5	5	5	5	5.00
1955—Brooklyn	National	4	4	0	0	.000	5	6	6	4	6	13.50
1955—Montreal x	Int'national	22	143	9	8	.529	125	58	52	92	62	3.27
1956—Kansas City y	American	18	45	0	4	.000	40	38	31	28	45	6.20
1956—Denver	Am. Assoc.	16	83	3	4	.429	94	54	46	54	34	4.99
1957—Denver z	Am. Assoc.	6	17	0	2	.000	29	25	23	8	6	12.18
1957—Los Angeles	P. Coast	29	132	7	10	.412	134	73	57	72	59	3.90
1958—Montreal	Int'national	34	★230	★18	6	.750	191	77	64	126	76	2.50
1959—Montreal	Int'national	29	188	12	8	.600	192	93	80	64	77	3.83
1960—Montreal a	Int'national	12	45	2	5	.286	79	48	41	17	24	8.20
American League Totals		18	45	0	4	.000	40	38	31	28	45	6.20
National League Totals		8	13	0	0	.000	13	11	11	9	11	7.62
Major League Totals		26	58	0	4	.000	53	49	42	37	56	6.52

†On National Defense list, May 14, 1946 through February 2, 1948.
‡On disabled list, July 9 to July 19, 1948.
§Drafted by Nashua (Brooklyn Dodgers' organization) from Philadelphia Phillies' organization, November 24, 1948.
xSold by Brooklyn Dodgers' organization to Kansas City Athletics for an estimated $35,000, March 2, 1956.
yTraded to New York Yankees for Pitcher Wally Burnette and cash, July 11, 1956.
zSold by New York Yankees' organization to Brooklyn Dodgers' organization, May 26, 1957.
aReleased, July 9, 1960.

RECORD AS MANAGER

Named Minor League Manager of the Year by THE SPORTING NEWS, 1970.
Named Pacific Coast League co-Manager of the Year, 1970.
Named Pioneer League Manager of the Year, 1967.

Year Club	League	Position	W.	L.	Year Club	League	Position	W.	L.
1966—Ogden	Pion.	First	39	27	1977—Los Angeles	Nat.	First(W)	98	64
1967—Ogden	Pion.	First	41	25	1978—Los Angeles	Nat.	First(W)	95	67
1968—Ogden	Pion.	First	39	25	1979—Los Angeles	Nat.	Third(W)	79	83
1969—Spokane	P. C.	Second(N)	71	73	1980—Los Angeles	Nat.	Second(W)	92	71
1970—Spokane	P. C.	†First(N)	94	52	1981—Los Angeles x	Nat.		63	47
1971—Spokane	P. C.	Third(N)	69	76	1982—Los Angeles	Nat.	Second(W)	88	74
1972—Albuquerque	P. C.	‡First(E)	92	56	1983—Los Angeles	Nat.	First(W)	91	71
1976—Los Angeles§	Nat.	Second(W)	2	2	Major League Totals			608	479

†Won championship playoff against Hawaii, four games to none.
‡Won championship playoff against Eugene, three games to one.
§Replaced retiring Walter Alston with club in second place (record of 90-68), September 29, 1976.
xFirst Half.... First(W) (record of 36-21); Second Half.... Fourth(W) (record of 27-26).
Scout, Los Angeles Dodgers, 1961 through 1965; manager Los Angeles farm team in Arizona Instructional League, 1969; coach, Los Angeles Dodgers, 1973 through 1976.
Manager, National League All-Star Team, 1978, 1979 and 1982.
Coach, National League All-Star Team, 1977 and 1983.

DIVISION SERIES RECORD

Year Club	League	W.	L.
1981—Los Angeles	National	3	2

CHAMPIONSHIP SERIES RECORD

Year Club	League	W.	L.
1977—Los Angeles	National	3	1
1978—Los Angeles	National	3	1
1981—Los Angeles	National	3	2
1983—Los Angeles	National	1	3

WORLD SERIES RECORD

Year Club	League	W.	L.
1977—Los Angeles	National	2	4
1978—Los Angeles	National	2	4
1981—Los Angeles	National	4	2

ROBERT PERRY LILLIS
(Bob)
Houston Astros

Born June 2, 1930, at Altadena, Calif.
Height, 5.11. Weight, 168.
Threw and batted righthanded.
Attended University of Southern California, Los Angeles, Calif.

Year Club	League	Pos.	G.	AB.	R.	H.	2B.	3B.	HR.	RBI.	B.A.	PO.	A.	E.	F.A.
1951—Pueblo	West.	SS	37	141	17	34	6	3	0	13	.241	80	104	12	.939
1951—Newport News	Pied.	SS	39	136	16	28	1	3	0	12	.206	59	110	10	.944
1952—Elmira	East.	SS	76	310	35	63	15	1	0	18	.203	147	221	18	.953
1953—Newport News	Pied.	SS	129	523	★102	152	25	6	3	60	.291	★311	★443	★40	.950
1954-55—Mobile	South.					(In Military Service)									
1956—St. Paul	A. A.	SS	144	★590	96	157	33	2	18	65	.266	★304	395	27	★.963
1957—St. Paul	A. A.	SS	★154	★598	72	155	26	5	2	49	.259	★323	477	30	●.964
1958—St. Paul	A. A.	SS	67	272	42	74	10	6	3	17	.272	136	193	17	.951
1958—Los Angeles	Nat.	SS	20	69	10	27	3	1	1	5	.391	29	52	3	.964
1959—Los Angeles	Nat.	SS	30	48	7	11	2	0	0	2	.229	27	52	7	.919
1959—Spokane	P. C.	SS	103	406	50	116	17	6	3	27	.286	206	352	17	★.970
1960—Los Angeles	Nat.	SS-3B-2B	48	60	6	16	4	0	0	6	.267	40	52	1	.989
1961—L.A.†-St.L.‡	Nat.	SS-2B-3B	105	239	24	51	4	0	0	22	.213	123	201	19	.945
1962—Houston	Nat.	SS-2B-3B	129	457	38	114	12	4	1	30	.249	223	378	15	.976
1963—Houston	Nat.	SS-2B-3B	147	469	31	93	13	1	1	19	.198	249	375	26	.960
1964—Houston	Nat.	2B-SS-3B	109	332	31	89	11	2	0	17	.268	169	236	10	.976
1965—Houston	Nat.	SS-3B-2B	124	408	34	90	12	1	0	20	.221	206	304	16	.970
1966—Houston	Nat.	2B-SS-3B	68	164	14	38	6	0	0	11	.232	99	109	10	.954
1967—Houston	Nat.	SS-2B-3B	37	82	3	20	1	0	0	5	.244	27	66	7	.930
Major League Totals			817	2328	198	549	68	9	3	137	.236	1192	1825	114	.964

†Traded to St. Louis Cardinals with Outfielder Carl Warwick for Infielder Daryl Spencer, May 30, 1961.
‡Selected by Houston Colts in National League expansion draft, October 10, 1961.

RECORD AS MANAGER

Year Club	League	Position	W.	L.
1982—Houston†	Nat.	Fifth(W)	28	23
1983—Houston	Nat.	Third(W)	85	77
Major League Totals			113	100

†Replaced Bill Virdon with club in fifth place (record of 49-62), August 10, 1982.
Scout, Houston Astros, 1968 through 1970; Director of Minor League Instruction, Houston Astros, 1972; coach, Houston Astros, part of 1967 and 1973 through August 10, 1982.

JOHN FRANCIS McNAMARA
California Angels

Born June 4, 1932, at Sacramento, Calif.
Height, 5.10. Weight, 175.
Threw and batted righthanded.
Attended Sacramento State College, Sacramento, Calif.

Led Northwest League in sacrifice hits with 18 in 1959.
Led Northwest League catchers in double plays with 15 in 1958, 10 in 1959 and 14 in 1962.

Year Club	League	Pos.	G.	AB.	R.	H.	2B.	3B.	HR.	RBI.	B.A.	PO.	A.	E.	F.A.
1951—Fresno	Calif.	C	60	182	20	38	2	0	0	12	.209	284	46	11	.968
1952—Houston	Texas	....	6	13	0	1	0	0	0	0	.077	....	....	....	....
1952—Lynchburg	Pied.	C	102	303	25	54	8	0	0	19	.178	489	57	8	★.986
1953—Winston-Salem	Carol.					(In Military Service)									
1954—Omaha†	West.					(In Military Service)									
1955—Lewiston	N'west	C	129	427	49	102	24	4	1	54	.239	544	★93	●15	.977
1956—Sacramento	P. C.	C	76	181	22	31	5	1	1	18	.171	256	25	0	1.000
1956—Albuquerque	West.	C	29	83	11	23	2	2	1	9	.277	191	23	1	.995
1957—Tulsa	Texas	C	19	47	5	7	2	0	0	5	.149	92	9	2	.981
1957—Amarillo	West.	C	43	93	17	26	8	0	0	21	.280	177	13	3	.984
1958—Lewiston	N'west	C	133	439	62	117	20	2	2	63	.276	★892	★76	9	★.991
1959—Lewiston	N'west	C	141	491	74	122	25	4	1	44	.248	714	★84	8	.990
1960—Lewiston	N'west	C	120	387	62	98	19	2	0	42	.253	★726	48	7	★.991
1961—Lewiston	N'west	C	77	204	28	54	6	0	0	27	.265	368	37	4	.990
1962—Lewiston	N'west	C	93	281	41	77	11	2	1	33	.274	670	74	8	★.989
1963—Binghamton	East.	C	69	199	19	45	10	1	0	24	.226	483	34	2	.996
1964—Dallas	P. C.	C-3B	13	13	1	6	0	0	0	1	.194	58	7	0	1.000
1965—Birmingham	South.					(Did Not Play)									
1966—Mobile	South.	C	8	17	3	4	0	0	0	0	.235	44	1	0	1.000
1967—Birmingham	South.	C	2	6	1	0	0	0	0	1	.000	10	1	0	1.000

†Released by St. Louis Cardinals' organization, April 16, 1955.

PITCHING RECORD

Year Club	League	G.	IP.	W.	L.	Pct.	H.	R.	ER.	SO.	BB.	ERA.
1960—Lewiston	Northwest	5	....	0	0	.000	....	....	....	....	....	....
1961—Lewiston	Northwest	4	....	0	0	.000	....	....	...	....	....	....
1962—Lewiston	Northwest	4	9	0	0	.000	13	6	6	3	2	6.00
1963—Binghamton	Eastern	1	1	0	0	.000	0	0	0	0	0	0.00

RECORD AS MANAGER

Year	Club	League	Position	W.	L.	Year	Club	League	Position	W.	L.
1959—Lewiston	N'west	Second	36	34		1970—Oakland	Amer.	Second(W)	89	73
(Second Half)		Third	39	32		1974—San Diego	Nat.	Sixth(W)	60	102
1960—Lewiston	N'west	Third	38	29		1975—San Diego	Nat.	Fourth(W)	71	91
(Second Half)		Third	40	34		1976—San Diego	Nat.	Fifth(W)	73	89
1961—Lewiston	N'west	†First	41	25		1977—San Diego§	Nat.	Fifth(W)	20	28
(Second Half)		Second	43	31		1979—Cincinnati	Nat.	First(W)	90	71
1962—Lewiston	N'west	Fifth	31	38		1980—Cincinnati	Nat.	Third(W)	89	73
(Second Half)		Fourth	35	37		1981—Cincinnati x	Nat.		66	42
1963—Binghamton	East.	Fourth	65	75		1982—Cincinnati y	Nat.	Sixth(W)	34	58
1964—Dallas	P. C.	Sixth(E)	53	104		1983—California	Amer.	zFifth	70	92
1965—Birmingham	South.	Eighth	54	85		American League Totals			167	170
1966—Mobile	South.	First	88	52		National League Totals			503	554
1967—Birmingham	South.	First	84	55		Major League Totals			670	724
1969—Oakland‡	Amer.	Second(W)	8	5						

†Won playoff by defeating Yakima (Second Half winner), four games to one.
‡Replaced Hank Bauer with club in second place (record of 80-69), September 19, 1969.
§Replaced by Alvin Dark, May 30, 1977 (Bob Skinner served as interim manager, May 29).
xFirst Half....Second (W) (record of 35-21); Second Half....Second (W) (record of 31-21).
yReplaced by Russ Nixon, July 21, 1982.
zTied for position with Minnesota Twins.
Coach, Oakland Athletics, 1968 and 1969; San Francisco Giants, 1971 through 1973; California Angels, 1978.
Coach, National League All-Star Team, 1976, 1980 and 1982.

CHAMPIONSHIP SERIES RECORD

Year	Club	League	W.	L.
1979—Cincinnati	National		0	3

PAUL FRANCIS OWENS
Philadelphia Phillies

Born February 7, 1926, at Salamanca, N.Y.
Height, 6.03. Weight, 185.
Threw and batted righthanded.
Received bachelor of science degree in physical education from
St. Bonaventure University, St. Bonaventure, N.Y. in 1951.

Year	Club	League	Pos.	G.	AB.	R.	H.	2B.	3B.	HR.	RBI.	B.A.	PO.	A.	E.	F.A.
1951—Olean	Pony	1B	111	459	129	187	32	9	17	101	*.407	804	37	27	.969
1952—Winston-Salem	Carol.	1B-3B	136	535	98	181	34	7	11	105	.338	1024	117	26	.978
1953-54†			(Out of Organized Baseball)													
1955—Olean‡	Pa.-O.-NY	1B-2B	126	457	105	177	30	6	9	86	.387	916	70	22	.978
1956—Olean‡	Pa.-O.-NY	1B-OF	114	399	87	147	34	3	9	76	*.368	601	50	9	.986
1957—Olean‡§	NYP	1B	107	369	90	150	30	2	13	88	*.407	883	66	17	.982
1958—Bakersfield	Calif.	1B	31	98	11	25	2	4	0	14	.255	229	17	4	.984

†On voluntarily retired list, April 28, 1953 through March 7, 1955.
‡Player-manager.
§On temporary inactive list, July 18 to July 28, 1957.

RECORD AS MANAGER

Year	Club	League	Position	W.	L.	Year	Club	League	Position	W.	L.
1955—Olean	Pa.-Ont.-NY	Eighth	46	80		1959—Bakersfield§	Calif.	xFirst	42	29
1956—Olean	Pa.-Ont.-NY	†Third	65	58		(Second Half)		Fourth	28	42
1957—Olean	NYP	Fifth	52	65		1972—Philadelphia y	Nat.	Sixth(E)	33	47
1958—Bakersfield	Calif.	Third	39	33		1983—Philadelphia z	Nat.	First(E)	47	30
(Second Half)		‡First	45	22		Major League Totals			80	77

†Defeated Corning, two games to one, and lost to Wellsville (finals), three games to two.
‡Lost to Visalia in semifinals, two games to one.
§Had one hit in three at-bats.
xLost to Modesto, four games to one.
yReplaced Frank Lucchesi with club in fifth place (record of 26-50), July 10, 1972.
zReplaced Pat Corrales with club in first place (record of 43-42), July 18, 1983.
Scout, Philadelphia Phillies, 1960 through May 22, 1965; Director, Scouting and Minor Leagues, Philadelphia Phillies, May 22, 1965 through June 3, 1972; General Manager, Philadelphia Phillies, June 3, 1972 to present.

CHAMPIONSHIP SERIES RECORD

Year	Club	League	W.	L.
1983—Philadelphia	National		3	1

WORLD SERIES RECORD

Year	Club	League	W.	L.
1983—Philadelphia	National		1	4

—DID YOU KNOW—

That Phillies Manager Paul Owens twice batted above .400 as a minor league player? Owens, as a 27-year-old first baseman, hit a league-leading .407 for Olean of the Class D Pony League in 1951 and matched that figure in 1957 when, serving as Olean's playing manager, he won another batting championship.

DOUGLAS LEE RADER
(Doug)
Texas Rangers

Born July 30, 1944, at Chicago, Ill.
Height, 6.03. Weight, 210.
Throws and bats righthanded.
Attended Illinois Wesleyan University, Bloomington, Ill.

Led National League third basemen in total chances with 479 and tied for lead in double plays with 31 in 1972.
Led National League third basemen in putouts with 147 and double plays with 39 in 1970.
Named third baseman on THE SPORTING NEWS National League All-Star fielding team, 1970 through 1973.
Received reported $25,000 bonus to sign with Houston Astros, 1964.

Year	Club	League	Pos.	G.	AB.	R.	H.	2B.	3B.	HR.	RBI.	B.A.	PO.	A.	E.	F.A.
1965—Durham	Carol.	3B-OF	112	330	44	69	14	1	14	38	.209	111	185	21	.934
1966—Amarillo	Texas	3B	138	527	85	*153	21	12	16	74	.290	102	240	27	.927
1967—Oklahoma City	P. C.	3B	75	273	40	80	23	5	9	44	.293	47	110	12	.929
1967—Houston	Nat.	1B-3B	47	162	24	54	10	4	2	26	.333	270	33	8	.974
1968—Houston	Nat.	3B-1B	98	333	42	89	16	4	6	43	.267	130	171	22	.932
1969—Houston	Nat.	3B-1B	155	569	62	140	25	3	11	83	.246	140	307	26	.945
1970—Houston	Nat.	*3B-1B	156	576	90	145	25	3	25	87	.252	149	*357	18	*.966
1971—Houston	Nat.	3B	135	484	51	118	21	4	12	56	.244	93	275	●21	.946
1972—Houston	Nat.	3B	152	533	70	131	24	7	22	90	.237	119	*340	20	.958
1973—Houston	Nat.	3B	154	574	79	146	26	0	21	89	.254	*134	296	*25	.945
1974—Houston	Nat.	3B	152	533	61	137	27	3	17	78	.257	128	347	17	.965
1975—Houston†	Nat.	*3B-SS	129	448	41	100	23	2	12	48	.223	114	259	11	*.971
1976—San Diego	Nat.	3B	139	471	45	121	22	4	9	55	.257	109	318	20	.955
1977—San Diego‡	Nat.	3B	52	170	19	46	8	3	5	27	.271	43	104	6	.961
1977—Toronto§	Amer.	3B-1B-OF	96	313	47	75	18	2	13	40	.240	97	106	7	.967
National League Totals			1369	4873	584	1227	227	37	142	682	.252	1429	2807	194	.956
American League Totals			96	313	47	75	18	2	13	40	.240	97	106	7	.967
Major League Totals			1465	5186	631	1302	245	39	155	722	.251	1526	2913	201	.957

Signed as free agent by Houston Colt .45s' organization, September 13, 1964.
†Traded to San Diego Padres for Pitchers Joe McIntosh and Larry Hardy, December 11, 1975.
‡Sold to Toronto Blue Jays, June 8, 1977.
§Released, March 18, 1978.

RECORD AS MANAGER

Year	Club	League	Position	W.	L.
1980—Hawaii	P. C.		First(N)	40	25
	(Second Half)		Third(N)	36	40
1981—Hawaii	P. C.		First(N)	35	31
	(Second Half)		Third(N)	37	34
1982—Hawaii	P. C.		Second(S)	36	35
	(Second Half)		Third(S)	37	36
1983—Texas	Amer.		Third(W)	77	85
Major League Totals				77	85

Coach, San Diego Padres, 1979.

VERNON FRED RAPP
(Vern)
Cincinnati Reds

Born May 11, 1928, at St. Louis, Mo.
Height, 6.00. Weight, 195.
Threw and batted righthanded.

Year	Club	League	Pos.	G.	AB.	R.	H.	2B.	3B.	HR.	RBI.	B.A.	PO.	A.	E.	F.A.
1946—Marion	Ohio St.	C-OF	115	375	86	118	16	8	14	89	.315	452	73	30	.946
1947—St. Joseph	W. A.	C	101	365	59	103	21	9	6	81	.282	532	76	15	.976
1948—Omaha	West.	C	56	186	30	61	12	1	9	31	.328	298	40	15	.958
1948—Columbus	A. A.	C	7	19	6	7	0	0	1	3	.368	....	....	....	......
1949—Columbus	A. A.	C	77	249	30	64	14	5	6	29	.257	313	40	14	.962
1950—Houston	Texas	C	72	186	19	35	5	4	4	21	.188	217	25	8	.968
1951-52—Columbus	A. A.				(In Military Service)											
1953—Rochester†	Int.	C	97	282	35	71	15	9	1	30	.252	290	33	6	.982
1954—Kansas City‡	A. A.	C	28	66	9	17	3	0	1	9	.258	128	10	0	1.000
1955—Charleston§x	A. A.	C	70	192	17	46	5	1	7	19	.240	171	26	6	.970
1956—Minneapolis y	A. A.	C	85	205	28	62	8	2	11	32	.302	263	26	9	.970
1957—Louisville z	A. A.	C	77	246	58	13	1	4	4	31	.236	514	42	7	.988
1958—Denver a	A. A.	1B-C	93	274	48	78	12	2	14	55	.285	436	39	10	.979
1959—Denver a	A. A.	C	89	212	18	53	10	3	4	31	.250	194	30	4	.982
1960—Denver ab	A. A.	C	36	99	9	14	4	0	2	12	.141	146	12	2	.988
1961—Modesto§	Calif.	PH	3	1	0	1	0	0	0	0	1.000	....	....	....	......
1966—Little Rock§	Texas	PH	1	1	0	1	0	0	0	0	1.000	....	....	....	......
1976—Denver§	A. A.	C	1	1	0	1	0	0	0	1	1.000	0	0	0	.000

†Loaned by St. Louis Cardinals' organization to New York Yankees' organization, May 24, 1954.
‡Returned by Yankees' organization to Cardinals' organization, July 26, 1954. On disabled list, August 12 to September 30, 1954. Released by St. Louis Cardinals' organization, September 30, 1954; signed as free agent by Charleston, December 11, 1954.

§Player-manager.
xReleased, December 14, 1955; signed as free agent by New York Giants' organization, January 10, 1956.
yReleased by New York Giants' organization to Louisville, January 12, 1957.
zReleased to Denver (N.Y. Yankees' organization), April 2, 1958.
aPlayer-coach.
bReleased to Detroit Tigers' organization, October 12, 1960.

PITCHING RECORD

Year Club	League	G.	IP.	W.	L.	Pct.	H.	R.	ER.	SO.	BB.	ERA.
1959—Denver†	Am. Assoc.	5	...	0	0	.000	...	...	...	...	...	......
1961—Modesto‡	California	2	...	0	0	.000	...	...	...	...	...	......
1966—Arkansas‡	Texas	1	2	0	0	.000	0	0	0	2	0	0.00

†Player-coach.
‡Player-manager.

RECORD AS MANAGER

Named Minor League Manager of the Year by THE SPORTING NEWS, 1976.

Year Club	League	Position	W.	L.	Year Club	League	Position	W.	L.
1955—Charleston†	A. A.	Eighth	19	40	1971—Indianapolis	A. A.	zFirst(E)	84	55
1961—Modesto	Calif.	Fourth	30	39	1972—Indianapolis	A. A.	Fourth(E)	61	79
(Second Half)		Sixth	27	43	1973—Indianapolis	A. A.	Second(E)	74	62
1962—Greensboro‡	Carol.	Fifth	65	75	1974—Indianapolis	A. A.	aFirst(E)	78	57
1965—Tulsa	Texas	§First(E)	81	60	1975—Indianapolis	A. A.	Second(E)	71	64
1966—Arkansas	Texas	xFirst	81	59	1976—Denver	A. A.	bFirst	86	50
1967—Arkansas	Texas	Fifth	63	77	1977—St. Louis	Nat.	Third(E)	83	79
1968—Arkansas	Texas	yFirst(E)	82	58	1978—St. Louis c	Nat.	Sixth(E)	6	10
1969—Indianapolis	A. A.	Third	74	66					
1970—Indianapolis	A. A.	Third(E)	71	69	Major League Totals			89	89

†Replaced Danny Murtaugh, July 16, 1955.
‡Replaced by Steven Souchock, August 11, 1962.
§Lost playoff to Albuquerque, three games to one.
xLost playoff to Austin, two games to one.
yLost playoff to El Paso, three games to one.
zLost playoff to Denver, four games to three.
aLost playoff to Tulsa, four games to three.
bWon playoff by defeating Omaha, four games to two.
cReplaced by interim manager Jack Krol, April 25, 1978.
Coach, Montreal Expos, 1979 through 1983.

FRANK ROBINSON
San Francisco Giants

Born August 31, 1935, at Beaumont, Tex.
Height, 6.01. Weight, 194.
Threw and batted righthanded.
Attended Xavier University, Cincinnati, O.

Established major league record for most consecutive seasons leading league, intentional bases on balls (4), 1961 through 1964 (tied in 1962).
Established modern major league record for most times hit by pitch, rookie season (20), 1956.
Tied major league records for most home runs, bases filled, game (2), June 26, 1970; most home runs, bases filled, two successive at bats (2), June 26, 1970; most runs batted in, two successive innings (8), June 26, 1970 (fifth and sixth innings); fewest putouts, first baseman, game (0), July 1, 1971; most home runs, rookie season (38), 1956; most years leading league, intentional bases on balls, since 1955 (4).
Hit three home runs in a game, August 22, 1959.
Hit for the cycle, May 2, 1959.
Won American League Triple Crown, 1966.
Led National League in slugging percentage with .595 in 1960, .611 in 1961 and .624 in 1962.
Led American League in total bases with 367 and in slugging percentage with .637 in 1966.
Led American League in being hit by pitch with 13 in 1969.
Led National League in being hit by pitch with 20 in 1956, 8 in 1959, 9 in 1960, 11 in 1962, 14 in 1963 and 18 in 1965.
Led National League in intentional bases on balls received with 23 in 1961, 20 in 1963, 20 in 1964 and tied for lead with 16 in 1962.
Led National League in sacrifice flies with 10 in 1961.
Led National League first basemen in double plays with 111 in 1959.
Tied for American League lead in sacrifice flies with 7 in 1966.
Named Major League Player of the Year by THE SPORTING NEWS, 1966.
Named American League Player of the Year by THE SPORTING NEWS, 1966.
Named American League Most Valuable Player by Baseball Writers' Association of America, 1966.
Named National League Player of the Year by THE SPORTING NEWS, 1961.
Named National League Most Valuable Player by Baseball Writers' Association of America, 1961.
Named National League Rookie of the Year by THE SPORTING NEWS, 1956.
Named National League Rookie of the Year by Baseball Writers' Association of America, 1956.
Named outfielder on THE SPORTING NEWS American League All-Star Team, 1966 and 1967.
Named outfielder on THE SPORTING NEWS National League All-Star Team, 1961 and 1962.
Named outfielder on THE SPORTING NEWS National League All-Star fielding team, 1958.
Elected to Hall of Fame, 1982.

Year	Club	League	Pos.	G.	AB.	R.	H.	2B.	3B.	HR.	RBI.	B.A.	PO.	A.	E.	F.A.
1953—Ogden	Pion.	OF-3B-1B	72	270	70	94	20	6	17	83	.348	105	28	18	.881
1954—Tulsa	Texas	2B-3B	8	30	4	8	0	0	0	1	.267	17	15	1	.970
1954—Columbia	Sally	OF-3B-2B	132	491	*112	165	32	9	25	110	.336	258	63	18	.947
1955—Columbia	Sally	OF-1B	80	243	50	64	15	7	12	52	.263	203	3	4	.981
1956—Cincinnati	Nat.	OF	152	572	*122	166	27	6	38	83	.290	323	5	8	.976
1957—Cincinnati	Nat.	OF-1B	150	611	97	197	29	5	29	75	.322	487	36	6	.989
1958—Cincinnati	Nat.	OF-3B	148	554	90	149	25	6	31	83	.269	314	24	6	.983
1959—Cincinnati	Nat.	1B-OF	146	540	106	168	31	4	36	125	.311	1049	78	18	.984
1960—Cincinnati	Nat.	1B-OF-3B	139	464	86	138	33	6	31	83	.297	775	62	10	.988
1961—Cincinnati	Nat.	OF-3B	153	545	117	176	32	7	37	124	.323	284	15	3	.990
1962—Cincinnati	Nat.	OF	162	609	*134	208	*51	2	39	136	.342	315	10	2	.994
1963—Cincinnati	Nat.	OF-1B	140	482	79	125	19	3	21	91	.259	238	13	4	.984
1964—Cincinnati	Nat.	OF	156	568	103	174	38	6	29	96	.306	279	7	4	.986
1965—Cincinnati†	Nat.	OF	156	582	109	172	33	5	33	113	.296	282	5	3	.990
1966—Baltimore	Amer.	OF-1B	155	576	*122	182	34	2	*49	*122	*.316	282	6	5	.983
1967—Baltimore	Amer.	OF-1B	129	479	83	149	23	7	30	94	.311	207	8	2	.991
1968—Baltimore	Amer.	OF-1B	130	421	69	113	27	1	15	52	.268	193	5	7	.966
1969—Baltimore	Amer.	OF-1B	148	539	111	166	19	5	32	100	.308	367	19	5	.987
1970—Baltimore	Amer.	OF-1B	132	471	88	144	24	1	25	78	.306	262	11	4	.986
1971—Baltimore‡	Amer.	OF-1B	133	455	82	128	16	2	28	99	.281	449	20	11	.977
1972—Los Angeles§	Nat.	OF	103	342	41	86	6	1	19	59	.251	168	6	6	.967
1973—California	Amer.	OF	147	534	85	142	29	0	30	97	.266	38	3	1	.976
1974—Calif. x-Cleve.	Amer.	1B-OF	144	477	81	117	27	3	22	68	.245	23	0	1	.958
1975—Cleveland yz	Amer.	DH-PH	49	118	19	28	5	0	9	24	.237	0	0	0	.000
1976—Cleveland yab	Amer.	1B-OF	36	67	5	15	0	0	3	10	.224	11	0	0	1.000
National League Totals			1605	5869	1084	1759	324	51	343	1068	.300	4514	261	70	.986
American League Totals			1203	4137	745	1184	204	21	243	744	.286	1832	72	36	.981
Major League Totals			2808	10006	1829	2943	528	72	586	1812	.294	6346	333	106	.984

†Traded to Baltimore Orioles for Outfielder Dick Simpson and Pitchers Milt Pappas and Jack Baldschun, December 9, 1965.

‡Traded with Pitcher Pete Richert to Los Angeles Dodgers for Pitchers Doyle Alexander and Bob O'Brien, Catcher Sergio Robles and First Baseman-Outfielder Royle Stillman, December 2, 1971.

§Traded with Infielders Billy Grabarkewitz and Bob Valentine and Pitchers Bill Singer and Mike Strahler to California Angels for Third Baseman Ken McMullen and Pitcher Andy Messersmith, November 28, 1972.

xReleased on waivers to Cleveland Indians, September 12, 1974; Indians assigned Outfielder Rusty Torres and Catcher Ken Suarez to Angels, December 4, 1974, to complete deal.

yPlayer-manager.

zOn supplemental disabled list, July 4 to July 23, 1975.

aOn supplemental disabled list, April 4, 1976; transferred to disabled list, April 14 to April 26, 1976.

bReleased October 5, 1976.

CHAMPIONSHIP SERIES RECORD

Tied Championship Series records for hitting home run in first Championship Series at bat, October 4, 1969; most at bats, inning (2), October 3, 1970 (fourth inning).

Year	Club	League	Pos.	G.	AB.	R.	H.	2B.	3B.	HR.	RBI.	B.A.	PO.	A.	E.	F.A.
1969—Baltimore	Amer.	OF	3	12	1	4	2	0	1	2	.333	2	0	1	.667
1970—Baltimore	Amer.	OF	3	10	3	2	0	0	1	2	.200	2	0	0	1.000
1971—Baltimore	Amer.	OF	3	12	2	1	1	0	0	1	.083	7	0	0	1.000
Championship Series Totals			9	34	6	7	3	0	2	5	.206	11	0	1	.917

WORLD SERIES RECORD

Tied World Series record for most times hit by pitcher, game (2), October 8, 1961; most times hit by pitch, total Series (3); most times home run won 1-0 game (1), October 9, 1966; most putouts and chances accepted game by right fielder (7), October 14, 1969.

Year	Club	League	Pos.	G.	AB.	R.	H.	2B.	3B.	HR.	RBI.	B.A.	PO.	A.	E.	F.A.
1961—Cincinnati	Nat.	OF	5	15	3	3	2	0	1	4	.200	5	0	0	1.000
1966—Baltimore	Amer.	OF	4	14	4	4	0	1	2	3	.286	6	0	0	1.000
1969—Baltimore	Amer.	OF	5	16	2	3	0	0	1	1	.188	13	0	0	1.000
1970—Baltimore	Amer.	OF	5	22	5	6	0	0	2	4	.273	7	0	0	1.000
1971—Baltimore	Amer.	OF	7	25	5	7	0	0	2	2	.280	12	0	0	1.000
World Series Totals			26	92	19	23	2	1	8	14	.250	43	0	0	1.000

ALL-STAR GAME RECORD

Year	League	Pos.	AB.	R.	H.	2B.	3B.	HR.	RBI.	B.A.	PO.	A.	E.	F.A.
1956—National		OF	2	0	0	0	0	0	0	.000	1	0	0	1.000
1957—National		OF	2	0	1	0	0	0	0	.500	5	0	0	1.000
1959—National (second game)		1B	3	1	3	0	0	1	1	1.000	3	0	1	.750
1961—National (first game)		OF	1	0	1	0	0	0	0	1.000	2	0	0	1.000
1962—National (second game)		OF	3	0	0	0	0	0	0	.000	1	0	0	1.000
1965—National		PH	1	0	0	0	0	0	0	.000	0	0	0	.000
1966—American		OF	4	0	0	0	0	0	0	.000	2	0	0	1.000
1969—American		OF	2	0	0	0	0	0	0	.000	0	0	0	.000
1970—American		OF	3	0	0	0	0	0	0	.000	1	0	0	1.000
1971—American		OF	2	1	1	0	0	1	2	.500	2	0	0	1.000
1974—American		PH	1	0	0	0	0	0	0	.000	0	0	0	.000
All-Star Game Totals			24	2	6	0	0	2	3	.250	17	0	1	.944

Member of National League All-Star Team in 1959 (first game) and 1961 (second game); did not play.
Named to American League Team for 1967 game; replaced due to injury.

RECORD AS MANAGER

Year Club	League	Position	W.	L.				
1975—Cleveland	Amer.	Fourth(E)	79	80	1982—San Francisco .... Nat.	Third(W)	87	75
1976—Cleveland	Amer.	Fourth(E)	81	78	1983—San Francisco .... Nat.	Fifth(W)	79	83
1977—Cleveland†	Amer.	Sixth(E)	26	31	National League Totals		222	213
1978—Rochester‡	Int.	Sixth	58	64	American League Totals		186	189
1981—San Francisco§	Nat.		56	55	Major League Totals		408	402

†Replaced by Jeff Torborg, June 19, 1977.
‡Replaced interim manager Al Widmar (replacing Ken Boyer), May 8, 1978.
§First Half . . . Fifth (W) (record of 27-32); Second Half . . . Third (W) (record of 29-23).
Coach, California Angels, July 11 through remainder of 1977 season; Coach, Baltimore Orioles, beginning of 1978 season through May 8, 1978, 1979 and 1980.
Coach, American League All-Star Team, 1980.

CHARLES WILLIAM TANNER JR.
(Chuck)
Pittsburgh Pirates

Born July 4, 1929, at New Castle, Pa.
Height, 6.00. Weight, 185.
Threw and batted lefthanded.
Father of Mark Tanner, minor league pitcher, 1972 through 1975;
and Bruce Tanner, pitcher in Chicago White Sox' organization.

Tied major league record by hitting home run in first time at bat in major leagues, eighth inning, April 12, 1955.

Year Club	League	Pos.	G.	AB.	R.	H.	2B.	3B.	HR.	RBI.	B.A.	PO.	A.	E.	F.A.
1946—Evansville	I.I.I.	OF	2	1	0	0	0	0	0	0	.000	0	0	1	.000
1946—Owensboro	Kitty	OF	23	80	15	20	3	1	0	7	.250	50	3	4	.930
1947—Owensboro	Kitty	OF	25	104	32	35	9	3	0	20	.337	47	3	2	.962
1947—Eau Claire	North.	OF	40	151	29	49	6	3	7	27	.325	76	3	9	.898
1948—Eau Claire	North.	OF	67	263	60	95	22	5	7	52	.361	89	4	9	.912
1948—Pawtucket	N. Eng.	OF	46	171	26	47	1	6	2	20	.275	60	6	5	.930
1949—Denver	West.	OF	124	467	92	146	32	5	5	53	.313	206	13	12	.948
1950—Denver	West.	OF	154	619	111	*195	34	9	7	86	.315	248	16	14	.950
1951—Atlanta	South.	OF	134	506	84	161	28	6	4	44	.318	286	6	4	.986
1952—Milwaukee	A. A.	OF	11	27	2	4	1	1	0	4	.148	11	1	0	1.000
1952—Atlanta	South.	OF	117	440	64	152	18	11	2	65	.345	212	9	6	.974
1953—Toledo	A. A.	OF	17	52	5	10	3	0	2	5	.192	29	2	0	1.000
1953—Atlanta	South.	OF	126	465	71	148	29	11	6	57	.318	220	8	3	.987
1954—Atlanta	South.	OF	●155	594	109	192	35	12	20	101	.323	290	21	7	.978
1955—Milwaukee	Nat.	OF	97	243	27	60	9	3	6	27	.247	101	4	2	.981
1956—Milwaukee	Nat.	OF	60	63	6	15	2	0	1	4	.238	4	0	1	.800
1957—Mil.†-Chi.	Nat.	OF	117	387	47	108	19	2	9	48	.279	191	5	2	.990
1958—Chicago‡	Nat.	OF	73	103	10	27	6	0	4	17	.262	21	0	1	.955
1959—Minneapolis§	A. A.	OF	152	549	79	175	*41	10	12	78	.319	194	5	4	.980
1959—Cleveland	Amer.	OF	14	48	6	12	2	0	1	5	.250	18	0	0	1.000
1960—Cleveland	Amer.	OF	21	25	2	7	1	0	0	4	.280	5	0	0	1.000
1960—Toronto	Int.	OF	28	92	13	27	5	2	4	14	.293	40	1	0	1.000
1961—Toronto x	Int.	OF	70	218	19	49	5	3	6	22	.225	84	7	3	.968
1961—Dallas-Ft. Worth	A. A.	OF	48	170	28	51	12	5	1	18	.300	74	5	5	.940
1961—Los Angeles	Amer.	OF	7	8	0	1	0	0	0	0	.125	0	0	0	.000
1962—Los Angeles	Amer.	OF	7	8	0	1	0	0	0	0	.125	0	0	0	.000
1962—Dallas-Ft. Worth	A. A.	OF	114	359	43	113	28	2	5	41	.315	181	16	8	.961
1968—El Paso	Texas	PH	1	1	0	0	0	0	0	0	.000	0	0	0	.000
American League Totals			49	89	8	21	3	0	1	9	.236	23	0	0	1.000
National League Totals			347	796	90	210	36	5	20	96	.264	317	9	6	.982
Major League Totals			396	885	98	231	39	5	21	105	.261	340	9	6	.983

†Sold on waivers to Chicago Cubs, June 8, 1957.
‡Traded to Boston Red Sox for Pitcher Robert W. Smith, March 9, 1959.
§Purchased from Boston Red Sox by Cleveland Indians, September 9, 1959.
xSold by Cleveland Indians to Los Angeles Angels, September 8, 1961.

RECORD AS MANAGER

Named Major League Manager of the Year by THE SPORTING NEWS 1972.
Named Pacific Coast League co-Manager of the Year, 1970.

Year Club	League	Position	W.	L.	Year Club	League	Position	W.	L.
1963—Quad Cities	Midw.	Fourth	29	32	1974—Chicago	Amer.	Fourth(W)	80	80
(Second Half)		Second	37	25	1975—Chicago	Amer.	Fifth(W)	75	86
1964—Quad Cities	Midw.	Eighth	24	31	1976—Oakland x	Amer.	Second(W)	87	74
(Second Half)		Second	38	25	1977—Pittsburgh	Nat.	Second(E)	96	66
1965—El Paso	Texas	Third(W)	53	87	1978—Pittsburgh	Nat.	Second(E)	88	73
1966—El Paso	Texas	Fifth	62	78	1979—Pittsburgh	Nat.	First(E)	98	64
1967—Seattle	P. C.	Fifth(W)	69	79	1980—Pittsburgh	Nat.	Third(E)	83	79
1968—El Paso	Texas	†First(W)	77	60	1981—Pittsburgh y	Nat.		46	56
1969—Hawaii	P. C.	Third(S)	74	72	1982—Pittsburgh	Nat.	Fourth(E)	84	78
1970—Hawaii	P. C.	‡First(S)	98	48	1983—Pittsburgh	Nat.	Second(E)	84	78
1970—Chicago§	Amer.	Sixth(W)	3	13	National League Totals			579	494
1971—Chicago	Amer.	Third(W)	79	83	American League Totals			488	488
1972—Chicago	Amer.	Second(W)	87	67	Major League Totals			1067	982
1973—Chicago	Amer.	Fifth(W)	77	83					

†Won playoff by defeating Arkansas, three games to one.
‡Lost playoff to Spokane, four games to none.
§Replaced Don Gutteridge (and interim manager Billy Adair) with club in sixth place (record of 53-93), September 14, 1970.
xTraded to Pittsburgh Pirates for Catcher Manny Sanguillen and $100,000 cash, November 5, 1976.
yFirst Half. . . . Fourth(E) (record of 25-23); Second Half. . . . Sixth(E) (record of 21-33).
Manager, National League All-Star Team, 1980.
Coach, American League All-Star Team, 1973.
Coach, National League All-Star Team, 1978 and 1982.

<table>
<tr><th colspan="6">CHAMPIONSHIP SERIES RECORD</th><th colspan="6">WORLD SERIES RECORD</th></tr>
<tr><td>Year</td><td>Club</td><td>League</td><td>W.</td><td>L.</td><td></td><td>Year</td><td>Club</td><td>League</td><td>W.</td><td>L.</td></tr>
<tr><td>1979—Pittsburgh</td><td></td><td>National</td><td>3</td><td>0</td><td></td><td>1979—Pittsburgh</td><td></td><td>National</td><td>4</td><td>3</td></tr>
</table>

JOSEPH PAUL TORRE
(Joe)
Atlanta Braves

Born July 18, 1940, at Brooklyn, N. Y.
Height, 6.01. Weight, 210.
Threw and batted righthanded.
Brother of Frank Torre, first baseman with Milwaukee Braves and
Philadelphia Phillies, 1956 through 1960, 1962 and 1963.

Tied major league record for most consecutive times grounded into double play (4), July 21, 1975.
Hit for the cycle, June 27, 1973.
Led National League in total bases with 352 in 1971.
Led National League in grounding into double plays with 26 in 1964, 22 in 1965, 22 in 1967 and 21 in 1968.
Led National League first basemen in assists with 102 and double plays with 144 in 1974.
Led National League catchers in double plays with 12 in 1967.
Led National League catchers in fielding percentage with .995 in 1964 and .996 in 1968.
Named Major League Player of the Year by THE SPORTING NEWS, 1971.
Named National League Player of the Year by THE SPORTING NEWS, 1971.
Named National League Most Valuable Player by Baseball Writers' Association of America, 1971.
Named third baseman on THE SPORTING NEWS National League All-Star Team, 1971.
Named catcher on THE SPORTING NEWS National League All-Star Team, 1964 through 1966.
Named catcher on THE SPORTING NEWS National League All-Star fielding team, 1965.

Year	Club	League	Pos.	G.	AB.	R.	H.	2B.	3B.	HR.	RBI.	B.A.	PO.	A.	E.	F.A.
1960—Eau Claire	North.		C	117	369	63	127	23	3	16	74	★.344	636	64	9	.987
1960—Milwaukee	Nat.		PH	2	2	0	1	0	0	0	0	.500	0	0	0	.000
1961—Louisville	A. A.		C	27	111	18	38	8	2	3	24	.342	185	14	2	.990
1961—Milwaukee	Nat.		C	113	406	40	113	21	4	10	42	.278	494	50	10	.982
1962—Milwaukee	Nat.		C	80	220	23	62	8	1	5	26	.282	325	39	5	.986
1963—Milwaukee	Nat.		C-1B-OF	142	501	57	147	19	4	14	71	.293	919	76	6	.994
1964—Milwaukee	Nat.		C-1B	154	601	87	193	36	5	20	109	.321	1081	94	7	.994
1965—Milwaukee	Nat.		C-1B	148	523	68	152	21	1	27	80	.291	1022	73	8	.993
1966—Atlanta	Nat.		C-1B	148	546	83	172	20	3	36	101	.315	874	87	12	.988
1967—Atlanta	Nat.		C-1B	135	477	67	132	18	1	20	68	.277	881	88	8	.991
1968—Atlanta†	Nat.		C-1B	115	424	45	115	11	2	10	55	.271	733	48	2	.997
1969—St. Louis	Nat.		1B-C	159	602	72	174	29	6	18	101	.289	1360	91	7	.995
1970—St. Louis	Nat.		C-3B-1B	●161	624	89	203	27	9	21	100	.325	651	162	13	.984
1971—St. Louis	Nat.		3B	161	634	97	★230	34	8	24	★137	★.363	★136	271	●21	.951
1972—St. Louis	Nat.		3B-1B	149	544	71	157	26	6	11	81	.289	336	198	15	.973
1973—St. Louis	Nat.		1B-3B	141	519	67	149	17	2	13	69	.287	881	128	12	.988
1974—St. Louis‡	Nat.		1B-3B	147	529	59	149	28	1	11	70	.282	1173	121	14	.989
1975—New York	Nat.		3B-1B	114	361	33	89	16	3	6	35	.247	172	157	15	.956
1976—New York	Nat.		1B-3B	114	310	36	95	10	3	5	31	.306	593	52	7	.989
1977—New York§	Nat.		1B-3B	26	51	2	9	3	0	1	9	.176	83	3	1	.989
Major League Totals				2209	7874	996	2342	344	59	252	1185	.297	11618	1731	163	.988

†Traded to St. Louis Cardinals for First Baseman Orlando Cepeda, March 17, 1969.
‡Traded to New York Mets for Pitchers Tommy Moore and Ray Sadecki, October 13, 1974.
§Player-manager, beginning May 31, until released as player, June 18, 1977.

ALL-STAR GAME RECORD

Year	League	Pos.	AB.	R.	H.	2B.	3B.	HR.	RBI.	B.A.	PO.	A.	E.	F.A.
1964—National		C	2	0	0	0	0	0	0	.000	5	0	0	1.000
1965—National		C	4	1	1	0	0	1	2	.250	5	1	0	1.000
1966—National		C	3	0	0	0	0	0	0	.000	5	0	0	1.000
1967—National		C	2	0	0	0	0	0	0	.000	4	1	0	1.000
1970—National		PH	1	0	0	0	0	0	0	.000	0	0	0	.000
1971—National		3B	3	0	0	0	0	0	0	.000	1	0	0	1.000
1972—National		3B	3	0	1	0	0	0	0	.333	1	2	0	1.000
1973—National		1B-3B	3	0	0	0	0	0	0	.000	5	0	0	1.000
All-Star Game Totals			21	1	2	0	0	1	2	.095	26	4	0	1.000

Member of National League All-Star Team for the 1963 game; did not play.

Year	Club	League	Position	W.	L.
1977—New York†	Nat.	Sixth(E)	49	68
1978—New York	Nat.	Sixth(E)	66	96
1979—New York	Nat.	Sixth(E)	63	99
1980—New York	Nat.	Fifth(E)	67	95
1981—New York‡	Nat.		41	62
1982—Atlanta	Nat.	First(W)	89	73
1983—Atlanta	Nat.	Second(W)	88	74
Major League Totals				463	567

†Replaced Joe Frazier with club in sixth place (record of 15-30), May 31, 1977.
‡First Half . . . . Fifth (E) (record of 17-34); Second Half . . . . Fourth (E) (record of 24-28).
Coach, National League All-Star Team, 1983.

CHAMPIONSHIP SERIES RECORD

Year	Club	League	W.	L.
1982—Atlanta	National	0	3

WILLIAM CHARLES VIRDON
(Bill)
Montreal Expos
Born June 9, 1931, at Royal Oak Township, Mich.
Height, 6.00. Weight, 185.
Threw right and batted lefthanded.
Attended Drury College, Springfield, Mo.

Tied major league record for most assists by an outfielder, inning (2), second inning, second game, August 10, 1958; tied National League record for fewest triples, season, for leader in triples, (10), in 1962.
Led National League outfielders in double plays with 5 in 1959.
Named National League Rookie of the Year by THE SPORTING NEWS, 1955.
Named National League Rookie of the Year by Baseball Writers' Association of America, 1955.
Named outfielder on THE SPORTING NEWS National League All-Star fielding team, 1962.

Year	Club	League	Pos.	G.	AB.	R.	H.	2B.	3B.	HR.	RBI.	B.A.	PO.	A.	E.	F.A.
1950—Independence	K-O-M	OF	119	★501	82	134	29	10	6	76	.267	215	★20	12	.951
1950—Kansas City	A. A.	OF	14	41	3	14	3	0	0	3	.341	13	1	1	.933
1951—Norfolk	Pied.	OF	118	486	91	139	20	4	6	48	.286	297	19	10	.969
1952—Binghamton	East.	OF	122	467	57	122	13	9	2	46	.261	300	●18	11	.967
1953—Kansas City	A. A.	OF	95	330	51	77	13	4	6	25	.233	174	8	7	.963
1953—Birmingham†	South.	OF	42	164	27	52	7	2	3	14	.317	96	7	4	.963
1954—Rochester	Int.	OF	139	505	85	168	28	11	22	98	★.333	361	6	14	.963
1955—St. Louis	Nat.	OF	144	534	58	150	18	6	17	68	.281	339	7	12	.966
1956—St. L.‡-Pitts.	Nat.	OF	●157	580	77	185	23	10	10	46	.319	387	12	5	.988
1957—Pittsburgh	Nat.	OF	144	561	59	141	28	11	8	50	.251	403	13	6	.986
1958—Pittsburgh	Nat.	OF	144	604	75	161	24	11	9	46	.267	401	11	3	.993
1959—Pittsburgh	Nat.	OF	144	519	67	132	24	2	8	41	.254	404	16	9	.979
1960—Pittsburgh	Nat.	OF	120	409	60	108	16	9	8	40	.264	272	10	5	.983
1961—Pittsburgh	Nat.	OF	146	599	81	156	22	8	9	58	.260	384	6	6	.985
1962—Pittsburgh	Nat.	OF	156	663	82	164	27	●10	6	47	.247	360	11	9	.976
1963—Pittsburgh	Nat.	OF	142	554	58	149	22	6	8	53	.269	323	6	4	.988
1964—Pittsburgh	Nat.	OF	145	473	59	115	11	3	3	27	.243	243	5	6	.976
1965—Pittsburgh	Nat.	OF	135	481	58	134	22	5	4	24	.279	260	3	8	.970
1966—Williamsport	East.	OF	5	7	0	0	0	0	0	0	.000	1	0	0	1.000
1967—							(Did Not Play)									
1968—Pittsburgh	Nat.	OF	6	3	1	1	0	0	1	2	.333	1	0	0	1.000
Major League Totals				1583	5980	735	1596	237	81	91	502	.267	3777	100	73	.981

†Traded to St. Louis Cardinals by New York Yankees with Pitcher Mel Wright and Outfielder Emil Tellinger for Outfielder Enos (Country) Slaughter, April 11, 1954.
‡Traded to Pittsburgh Pirates for Pitcher Dick Littlefield and Outfielder Bobby Del Greco, May 17, 1956.

WORLD SERIES RECORD

Year	Club	League	Pos.	G.	AB.	R.	H.	2B.	3B.	HR.	RBI.	B.A.	PO.	A.	E.	F.A.
1960—Pittsburgh	Nat.	OF	7	29	2	7	3	0	0	5	.241	18	0	1	.947

RECORD AS MANAGER

Named Major League Manager of the Year by THE SPORTING NEWS, 1974 and 1980.
Tied major league record for most clubs managed, season, 2, in 1975.

Year	Club	League	Position	W.	L.	Year	Club	League	Position	W.	L.
1966—Williamsport	East	Fourth	68	72	1979—Houston	Nat.	Second(W)	89	73
1967—Jacksonville	Int.	Fifth	66	73	1980—Houston	Nat.	First(W)	93	70
1972—Pittsburgh	Nat.	First(E)	96	59	1981—Houston x	Nat.		61	49
1973—Pittsburgh†	Nat.	Third(E)	67	69	1982—Houston y	Nat.	Fifth(W)	49	62
1974—New York	Amer.	Second(E)	89	73	1983—Montreal	Nat.	Third(E)	82	80
1975—New York‡	Amer.	Third(E)	53	51	National League Totals				789	730
1975—Houston§	Nat.	Sixth(W)	17	17	American League Totals				142	124
1976—Houston	Nat.	Third(W)	80	82	Major League Totals				931	854
1977—Houston	Nat.	Third(W)	81	81						
1978—Houston	Nat.	Fifth(W)	74	88						

†Replaced by Danny Murtaugh, September 7, 1973.

‡Replaced by Billy Martin, August 1, 1975.
§Replaced Preston Gomez, August 19 with club in sixth place (record of 47-80), August 19, 1975.
xFirst Half. . . . Third(W) (record of 28-29); Second Half. . . . First(W) (record of 33-20).
yReplaced by Bob Lillis, August 10, 1982.
Coach, Pittsburgh Pirates, 1968 through 1971.
Coach, National League All-Star Team, 1973, 1980 and 1981.

	DIVISION SERIES RECORD					CHAMPIONSHIP SERIES RECORD			
Year	Club	League	W.	L.	Year	Club	League	W.	L.
1981—Houston	National		2	3	1972—Pittsburgh	National		2	3
					1980—Houston	National		2	3

RICHARD HIRSHFELD WILLIAMS
(Dick)
San Diego Padres

Born May 7, 1929, at St. Louis, Mo.
Height, 6.00. Weight, 190.
Threw and batted righthanded.
Attended Pasadena City College, Pasadena, Calif.
Father of Ricky Williams, pitcher in Montreal Expos' organization, 1977 through 1980.

Year	Club	League	Pos.	G.	AB.	R.	H.	2B.	3B.	HR.	RBI.	B.A.	PO.	A.	E.	F.A.
1947—Santa Barbara	Calif.	OF-3B	79	313	47	77	20	2	4	50	.246	165	36	5	.976
1948—Santa Barbara	Calif.	OF	97	385	82	129	29	2	16	90	.335	245	19	9	.967
1948—Fort Worth	Texas	OF-3B	41	140	16	29	1	0	4	16	.207	60	2	1	.984
1949—Fort Worth	Texas	★O-2-3	154	562	109	174	30	6	23	114	.310	★446	18	8	.983
1950—Fort Worth	Texas	OF	144	510	69	153	30	1	11	72	.300	401	20	6	.986
1951—Brooklyn†	Nat.	OF	23	60	5	12	3	1	1	5	.200	21	1	0	1.000
1952—Brooklyn	Nat.	OF-1B-3B	36	68	13	21	4	1	0	11	.309	51	3	0	1.000
1953—Brooklyn	Nat.	OF	30	55	4	12	2	0	2	5	.218	24	0	2	.923
1953—Montreal	Int.	OF	66	230	28	64	12	1	2	33	.278	111	3	2	.983
1954—Brooklyn	Nat.	OF	16	34	5	5	0	0	1	2	.147	12	0	0	1.000
1954—St. Paul	A. A.	OF-1B	49	162	23	40	8	0	6	18	.247	212	15	3	.987
1955—Fort Worth	Texas	OF-1B	153	596	82	189	29	4	24	91	.317	580	22	7	.989
1956—Brooklyn	Nat.	PH	7	7	0	2	0	0	0	0	.286	0	0	0	.000
1956—Montreal‡	Int.	1B	13	50	3	13	3	0	0	6	.260	106	17	4	.969
1956—Baltimore	Amer.	O-1-2-3	87	353	45	101	18	4	11	37	.286	249	17	4	.985
1957—Balt.§-Cleve.x	Amer.	OF-3B-1B	114	372	49	97	17	2	7	34	.261	244	72	8	.975
1958—Baltimore y	Amer.	O-3-1-2	128	409	36	113	17	0	4	32	.276	359	61	8	.981
1959—Kansas City	Amer.	3-1-O-2	130	488	72	130	33	1	16	75	.266	349	181	13	.976
1960—Kansas City z	Amer.	3B-1B-OF	127	420	47	121	31	0	12	65	.288	376	131	11	.979
1961—Baltimore	Amer.	OF-1B-3B	103	310	37	64	15	2	8	24	.206	209	16	3	.987
1962—Baltimore a b	Amer.	OF-1B-3B	82	178	20	44	7	1	1	18	.247	180	13	0	1.000
1963—Boston	Amer.	3B-1B-OF	79	136	15	35	8	0	2	12	.257	64	28	1	.989
1964—Boston	Amer.	1B-3B-OF	61	69	10	11	2	0	5	11	.159	50	21	1	.986
American League Totals			911	2735	331	716	148	10	66	308	.262	2080	540	49	.982
National League Totals			112	224	27	52	9	2	4	23	.232	108	4	2	.982
Major League Totals			1023	2959	358	768	157	12	70	331	.260	2188	544	51	.982

†On National Defense Service List, February 7 to May 29, 1951.
‡Recalled by Brooklyn Dodgers and sold to Baltimore Orioles, June 25, 1956.
§Traded to Cleveland Indians for Outfielder Jim Busby, June 13, 1957.
xTraded with Pitcher Bud Daley and Outfielder Gene Woodling to Baltimore Orioles for Pitcher Don Ferrarese and Outfielder Larry Doby, April 1, 1958.
yTraded to Kansas City Athletics for Shortstop Chico Carrasquel, October 2, 1958.
zTraded with Pitcher Dick Hall to Baltimore Orioles for Pitcher Jerry Walker and Outfielder Chuck Essegian, April 13, 1961.
aSold to Houston Colts, October 12, 1962.
bTraded by Houston Colts to Boston Red Sox for Outfielder Carroll Hardy, December 10, 1962.

WORLD SERIES RECORD

Year	Club	League	Pos.	G.	AB.	R.	H.	2B.	3B.	HR.	RBI.	B.A.	PO.	A.	E.	F.A.
1953—Brooklyn	Nat.	PH	3	2	0	1	0	0	0	0	.500	0	0	0	.000

RECORD AS MANAGER

Named Major League Manager of the Year by THE SPORTING NEWS, 1967.

Year	Club	League	Position	W.	L.	Year	Club	League	Position	W.	L.
1965—Toronto	Int.	†Third	81	64	1977—Montreal	Nat.	Fifth(E)	75	87		
1966—Toronto	Int.	‡Second	82	65	1978—Montreal	Nat.	Fourth(E)	76	86		
1967—Boston	Amer.	First	92	70	1979—Montreal	Nat.	Second(E)	95	65		
1968—Boston	Amer.	Fourth	86	76	1980—Montreal	Nat.	Second(E)	90	72		
1969—Boston§	Amer.	Third(E)	82	71	1981—Montreal ab	Nat.		44	37		
1971—Oakland	Amer.	First(W)	101	60	1982—San Diego	Nat.	Fourth(W)	81	81		
1972—Oakland	Amer.	First(W)	93	62	1983—San Diego	Nat.	Fourth(W)	81	81		
1973—Oakland x	Amer.	First(W)	94	68	National League Totals				542	509	
1974—California y	Amer.	Sixth(W)	36	48	American League Totals				695	601	
1975—California	Amer.	Sixth(W)	72	89	Major League Totals				1237	1110	
1976—California z	Amer.	Fourth(W)	39	57							

†Won playoffs by defeating Atlanta, four games to none and Columbus, four games to one.

‡Tied for position during regular season. Won playoffs by defeating Columbus, three games to two and Richmond, four games to one.

§Replaced by interim manager Eddie Popowski, September 23, 1969.

xQuit as manager of the Oakland Athletics following 1973 World Series. Signed contract to manage New York Yankees but American League President Joe Cronin ruled that Williams must honor the two years remaining on his Oakland contract.

yReplaced Bobby Winkles (and interim manager Whitey Herzog) with club in sixth place (record of 32-46), July 1, 1974.

zReplaced by Norm Sherry, July 23, 1976.

aFirst Half . . . . Third (E) (record of 30-25); Second Half . . . . Second (E) (record of 14-12).

bReplaced by Jim Fanning, September 8, 1981.

Coach, Montreal Expos, 1970.

Manager, American League All-Star Team, 1968, 1973 and 1974.

Coach, American League All-Star Team, 1972.

Coach, National League All-Star Team, 1981.

CHAMPIONSHIP SERIES RECORD					WORLD SERIES RECORD				
Year	Club	League	W.	L.	Year	Club	League	W.	L.
1971—Oakland	....	American	0	3	1967—Boston	....	American	3	4
1972—Oakland	....	American	3	2	1972—Oakland	....	American	4	3
1973—Oakland	....	American	3	2	1973—Oakland	....	American	4	3

NOTES

NOTES